The Oxford Companion to Twentieth-Century Literature in English

The Oxford Companion to Twentieth-Century Literature in English

EDITED BY

JENNY STRINGER

WITH AN INTRODUCTION BY

JOHN SUTHERLAND

Oxford New York

OXFORD UNIVERSITY PRESS

1996

Oxford University Press, Walton Street, Oxford OX2 6DP

Oxford New York
Athens Auckland Bangkok Bogata Bombay
Buenos Aires Calcutta Cape Town Dar es Salaam
Delhi Florence Hong Kong Istanbul Karachi
Kuala Lumpur Madras Madrid Melbourne
Mexico City Nairobi Paris Singapore
Taipei Tokyo Toronto
and associated companies in
Berlin Ibadan

Oxford is a trade mark of Oxford University Press

Published in the United States
by Oxford University Press Inc., New York

British Library Cataloguing in Publication Data
Data available

Library of Congress Cataloging in Publication Data
Data available

ISBN 0–19–212271–1

1 3 5 7 9 10 8 6 4 2

Typeset by Hope Services (Abingdon) Ltd.
Printed in Great Britain
on acid-free paper by
The Bath Press,
Bath, Somerset

CONTENTS

Editor's Foreword vii

Advisers and Contributors x

Introduction by John Sutherland xi

A–Z Entries 1

Appendix: Literary Prizes 747

EDITOR'S FOREWORD

THE aim of this book is to present an overview of literature in English from 1900 to the present day in a single volume. Representing as it does all geographical areas of the Anglophone world and a wide range of writing, *The Oxford Companion to Twentieth-Century Literature in English* is intended to be read for pleasure as well as being a useful source of information to students and teachers of literature. Its scope extends from the United Kingdom, Ireland, and America, to Australia, Canada, New Zealand, Asia, Africa, and the Caribbean.

Writers form the main component of this book; novelists, dramatists, and poets are the key figures. But in presenting literature in its broadest sense, and recognizing its flexible boundaries, we have also included, on a more selective basis, biographers, travel writers, critics, scholars, historians, and journalists. In adopting this inclusive approach we have extended the coverage to some major philosophers, economists, and sociologists in acknowledgement of their significant contributions to twentieth-century thought and ideology. The other component consists of about 650 essays on related subjects, from important individual works to genres, critical concepts, periodicals, literary groups, and movements. A network of cross-references allows the reader to range over vast territories of the century's literature in English, to observe the interactions between writers and subjects, and be guided to much supplementary information.

In producing a reference book of such diversity the most daunting task for an editor, and ultimately the most contentious, is deciding who and what to include. My starting point was a list of major writers whose reputations have secured them a place in any reference book of twentieth-century writing in English, a fairly effortless task performed in buoyant anticipation. The fun began when this master list generated a series of sub-lists which themselves produced further offshoots. Faced with such flourishing literary activity, and the limitations of space, I established some ground rules. In attempting to present a balanced and comprehensive account of a broad range of literary forms and a multi-national group of authors, literary merit was not the only consideration; national or ethnic identity and a fair representation of the various periods of the twentieth century also played an important part. To qualify for inclusion each author must have lived beyond 1900, published at least three books, and achieved a significant degree of international or national recognition. There are exceptions: in some instances a writer included may have produced one or two widely acclaimed books or may significantly represent a literary culture in its formative phases. We have taken risks with some younger writers who have shown exceptional promise at the beginning of their literary careers. In the case of authors who were born in the nineteenth century but lived beyond 1900, only those who published significant works in the twentieth century have been included. Henry James, Bernard Shaw, and H. G. Wells fall into this category, as does Thomas Hardy who was a nineteenth-century novelist and a twentieth-century poet, but Algernon Swinburne, Rider Haggard, and Mark

Twain do not. Samuel Butler (d. 1902) is in, and so is his *Erewhon Revisited* (1901), but like other nineteenth-century novels—including all of Thomas Hardy's—*Erewhon* (1872) is out. There is no children's literature nor is there literature in translation except where the author has been the translator of his or her own works.

Over the century, and even during the five years of compiling this book, fashions have shifted, new writers have emerged, others have published ever more important works or changed direction, some have faded into obscurity or died. These and many other factors have meant that entries were continually being updated and reassessed. In trying to keep up to date we have kept a watchful eye on recent publications but many more will have appeared by the time this *Companion* is in the bookshops.

The author entries are composed of brief biographical details, descriptions of selected works, typical characteristics, literary achievements, and general critical comments; adverse criticism has been eschewed in favour of a broad consensus of literary taste. We have also tried to place writers in the context of time and place. Further reading is suggested in the case of more important authors. The length of the entries varies and ought not to be seen as a measure of a writer's importance. There are many factors which determine the length of an entry: prolific writers do not lend themselves easily to brief summary, regardless of their celebrity or lack of it; some writers have more noteworthy biographies or literary connections while others need more space because their literary achievements are particularly diverse or complex; neglected or emerging writers require fuller description because their lives and works may hitherto be unrecorded.

In taking stock of some of the dilemmas faced by an editor whose brief is 'twentieth-century literature in English', and in outlining the principles involved, I also acknowledge the impossibility of producing a reference book to suit everyone's taste. Some will be disappointed by omissions or irritated by errors, but I hope that most readers will find enjoyment in the *Companion*'s rich diversity and geographical scope. I have sought much assistance from advisers and contributors. During the preparation of this book, their enduring enthusiasm for the project has been the source of sustenance for my sometimes flagging devotion. The *Companion* is essentially a collaborative work, a series of mini-biographies and essays combining the imaginative insights and scholarship of a dedicated group of co-authors. Other than giving brief guidelines, I have not attempted to adopt a rigid format for the entries gathered here. The different perceptions and modes of writing, from the sternly scholarly to the lightly whimsical, reflect the multifarious nature of the ground that has been covered.

My thanks therefore go first to all the contributors and advisers for their Herculean efforts and for guiding me through many a labyrinthine path. My special thanks to John Sutherland who has been a leading light and has written a magnificent Introduction. I am particularly grateful to Lynn Knight, Aamer Hussein, Douglas Houston, and Henry Claridge who so willingly helped me with some frantic updating through a long hot summer. I have had much support from the OUP. My thanks go especially to Kim Scott Walwyn who encouraged me to take on the project and gave me much guidance in the early phases, and to Frances Whistler who kept the show on the road with firmness and good humour. I have shared a joke or two with Margaret Aherne, the copy-editor, whose meticulous eye for detail has saved me from much embarrassment. I also thank Judith Landry who has helped in ways too numerous to mention. I am eternally grateful to my sons and daughter, Antony, Benedict, Nicholas, and Polly, who have saved me from many a scrape and applied themselves to anything from counting words to computer failure. I am greatly indebted to Margaret Drabble. It was during my five-year apprenticeship on *The Oxford Companion to English Literature* that the idea of a twentieth-century volume was first conceived. She has made herself available for consultation throughout the course of editing this work and was its main source of inspiration.

JENNY STRINGER
London, 1996

ADVISERS AND CONTRIBUTORS

Advisers

T. J. Binyon
Margaret Busby
Henry Claridge
John Clute
Margaret Drabble
Emory Elliott
Stephen Fender
Maggie Gee
Michael Holroyd
Douglas Houston
Aamer Hussein
Lionel Kelly
Lynn Knight
Hermione Lee
Murray Milgate
Benedict Nightingale
Peter Quartermaine
Mario Relich
Galen Strawson
John Sutherland
John Thieme
Michael Wood

Contributors

Bronte Adams
Walter Allen
José Miguel Amaya
Kathlyn Barros Escandón
Ian A. Bell
Paul Binding
T. J. Binyon
Frank Birbalsingh
Wendy Brandmark
Margaret Busby
Laura Holliday Butcher
Henry Claridge
John Clute
Clare Colvin
Judy Cooke
Maria Couto
Wei Ming Dariotis
Michael Diviney
Theresa Dolan
Margaret Drabble
Lindsay Duguid
Ira Elliott
Matthew Elliot
Steve Ellis
Isobel English
Anthony Fothergill
Gill Frith
Eileen Chai-Ching Fung
Harriet Goodman
Prabhu Guptara
Robert Hampson
John Harris
Deborah Hatheway
Michael Heumann
Alan Hollinghurst
Douglas Houston
Aamer Hussein
Cornelius Kavanagh
Lionel Kelly
Lynn Knight
Christina Koning
Harry Lansdowne
R. H. Lass
Martin Latham
A. Robert Lee
Hermione Lee
Ffrangcon Lewis
Shirley Geok-lin Lim
Kimberly Dawn Lutz
Christine MacLeod
Deborah Madsen
Clive Meachen
Marilyn M. Mehaffy
Rod Mengham
Peter Middleton
Murray Milgate
Framji Minwalla
Bart Moore-Gilbert
Jill Neville
Benedict Nightingale
Kenneth Notz
Sean O'Brien
Kimberly Orijan
Sharon Ouditt
Patrick Parrinder
Mary Paul
David Porter
Alexandra Pringle
Peter Quartermaine
Gay Raines
Mario Relich
Chris Ruiz-Velasco
Rick Rylance
Roger Sabin
Patrick B. Sharp
Carlton Smith
Jules Smith
Judith P. Stelboum
Randall Stevenson
Jenny Stringer
John Sutherland
Trudi Tate
Olga Taxidou
Alan Taylor
Anna-Marie Taylor
Blythe Tellesfen
John Thieme
Philippa Toomey
Clifford E. Trafzer
Marina Warner
Kate Carnell Watt
Nigel Wheale
W. V. Whitehead
Angela Noelle Williams
Tom Winnifrith
Michael Wood
Tim Woods

INTRODUCTION

BY JOHN SUTHERLAND

THERE used to be in post-war British music hall a performer called Lesley Welch. 'The Memory Man', as Welch was professionally known, would call for questions from the theatre or radio audience on any aspect of sport—such things as what horse came third in the Derby in 1938, or how many runs Denis Compton scored for Middlesex in June 1948. Welch (an honest performer, to all appearances, unlike the corrupted contestants on the contemporary American quiz show, 'Twenty-one') would invariably answer correctly. The reaction of the audience was that of Goldsmith's gazing rustics:

> And still they gazed, and still the wonder grew
> That one small head could carry all he knew

The basic assumption in Welch's routine was that in the 1950s one person, one brain, albeit an unusually capacious organ, could even at this late date contain every memorable fact about British sport. Much the same confidence underlay the launch of the Oxford University Press 'Companions' to literature in the early 1930s. In essence the series was a cool Oxonian response to the alarming massification of the literary object over the previous hundred years. All through the nineteenth century the store of literature had increased inexorably. In the 1760s, there were a hundred new novels annually; by 1900 it was two thousand. So too with poetry, plays, and all the peripherals of the writing and publishing professions. Unlike cabbages, books do not disappear with consumption but accrete as part of the literary record (as backlist, library holdings, or reprints). There were any number of historical factors making for what an appalled Henry James called, in 1900, 'monstrous multiplications'. To enumerate just a few: the lifting of the 'taxes on knowledge' in the first half of the nineteenth century; the innovation of steam presses which turned out books and newspapers on an industrial scale and steamships which joined the two vast Anglophone markets; stereotyping, which permitted mass reprintings of popular books; the 1870s British universal education acts which propelled the lower classes into literacy; the invention of the book club in early twentieth-century America. Every book trade advance meant more books. More books meant more 'Literature' (using the definitions of the Dewey Decimal System, 'Literature' generally comprises between ten and twenty per cent of total book production).

A number of systems were developed to control the exploding mass of literature during the second half of the nineteenth century and the early part of the twentieth century. Typically these systems served to reduce the unmanageable bulk of literature to a commodity that could be handled by a single, moderately industrious, 'well-read', person. Sir John Lubbock's '100 Best Books' in 1891, for instance (initially issued as a supplement to the *Contemporary Review*), triggered off a mania for such handy listings. In a few years this selective mania had evolved into popular 'libraries' such as OUP's 'World's Classics', and Dent's 'Everyman'. Dent's series carried on its flyleaf a talismanic motto, indicating its mission to help the reader through the jungle of modern literature 'Everyman, I will go with thee, and be thy guide'. In poetry, *The Oxford Book of English Verse* (1900) imposed a similar order on poetry and performed a similar blind-man's dog service for the lay-reader.

These 'select' libraries and authoritative anthologies reduced the exploding mass of English literature to 'classic' dimensions—that is, the fixed quantum of texts that make up Greek and Latin literature. (The Packard Research Center's databased archive of all classical literature comes in at around fifty megabytes of computer storage space: it will still be fifty megabytes in a thousand years' time, presumably.) It was from the same desire to impose humane intellectual order on the chaotic literary abundance of modern times that the first *Oxford Companion to English Literature*, by Sir Paul Harvey, emerged in 1932. Like Arthur Quiller-Couch (the compiler of the first *Oxford Book of English Verse*) Harvey was in the tradition of Oxford amateurs—unlike the scientific I. A. Richards and rigorous F. R. Leavis, literary critics who were, in the 1930s, coming into their own at Cambridge University. 'This volume,' Harvey began his Introduction by asserting, 'will serve its purpose if it proves a useful companion to ordinary, everyday readers of English literature'. In that modest goal, Harvey probably had himself in mind. Born in 1869, the young Harvey had progressed from Rugby to New College Oxford, where he graduated first class, Lit. Hum. A product of the new School of English at the University, he went into the Civil Service. He was knighted for his professional achievements in 1911. At the time of his retirement Sir Paul had risen to the rank of Financial Advisor to the colonies. In his sixties, he published *The Oxford Companion to English Literature* (1932) and *The Oxford Companion to Classical Literature* (1937). He died in 1948, still at work on *The Oxford Companion to French Literature* (eventually finished by another hand, in 1959). *OCEL*, for which he remains best known to posterity, was the work of his leisure hours.

What Harvey's *Companion* presents is the anatomy of a well-stored, first-class mind with an essentially amateur literary expertise. The *Companion* offers a miscellaneous web of information, all of which coexisted, one assumes, in Sir Paul's own brain. The contents make up a *pot pourri* of author biographies (including many foreign authors—Harvey was not severe about definitions), plot summaries (including operas), historical highlights (Waterloo, Bannockburn), profiles of kings, queens, great world-historical figures, and famous criminals, glosses on classical names, allusions, and tags, explanations of such obscure terms as 'carpet-bagger', 'Carfax', 'Capitol', and 'Caput Mortuum'. The *Companion* must, one imagines, have been invaluable to *Times* crossword compilers. Harvey included a sizeable slab of American works and authors, on the chauvinistic grounds that American literature was substantially English literature written in America. The whole structure rested on two mighty foundations—Shakespeare and Walter Scott. As in the *OED* (in which Scott and Shakespeare were the two most cited sources) these two great national laureates were the copestones and their works the touchstones of the national literature.

OCEL represented an urbane, one-volume Virgilian companion to the cultural ensemble denoted by the term 'English Literature'. If one wanted a single adjective to describe the principles on which it was constructed, it would be 'amateur' or (to use cricket's term) 'gentlemanly'. Cambridge took, as usual, a more scientific line, with its massive, committee-written *Cambridge History of English Literature* (1917, repr. 1933). This 15-volume production made up an encyclopaedia on the subject. It was prepared by a team of professional academics. The resulting compilation was bland, uniform, apparatus-laden, exact, and—by comparison with Harvey's *Companion*—not exactly companionable.

OCEL was an immediate success, going through two impressions in 1932. The twenty-first impression (called, with various updating revisions, the 'Fourth Edition') was published in 1967. It was substantially what had been in print for the last 35 years. In the 1970s, OUP decided that a major overhaul was in order. But exactly what form the necessary reorganization should take posed dilemmas. Who should be chosen as possessing the representatively 'well-stored' mind of the late twentieth century? Or should the original, single-mind, 'Companionate', concept be dropped altogether in favour of a committee, or a task-force of anonymous professional compilers and contributors? How had the elements of indispensable literary knowledge changed over the previous half-century with the growth and spread of higher education, and how should these changes be accommodated? Was what Harvey had called 'completeness within a modest compass' still a feasible goal?

In the event, the Delegates of the Press chose shrewdly. They selected Margaret Drabble as editor in chief. One of the country's admired novelists, Drabble had a first-class degree in literature from Cambridge, but had never been a professional academic. If Harvey was the archetypal 'ordinary, everyday reader' with a first-class mind, Drabble was the intellectual of the 1970s. She was formidably well-read, a role-model for younger women writers, and politically *engagée*.

Drabble was assisted in her task (which was to take her five years) by Jenny Stringer, a free-lance writer. Astutely, the editor retained a large core of Harvey's more substantial entries. New entries were commissioned from a corps of 76 sub-contracted contributors (most of them academics). Entries were brought up to date, but not up to the minute (the initial cut-off date for author-entries of 1939—Drabble's own year of birth was relaxed in the 1995 edition which had 59 new entries on contemporary authors). Drabble deferred to 'increasing specialization and professionalism of English studies' by making the revised *Companion* friendlier to the bright 'A' level student and undergraduate user in the country's sixty or so English departments. The selection was 'in some respects narrower', as Drabble noted in her Introduction. The quirkier elements of Harvey's *Companion* were dropped: 'dollars and pieces of eight have gone, the Cinque Ports have gone, and so has the Doge of Venice', Drabble recorded—rather ruefully. The white, middle-class, Oxonian masculinist tone of the original enterprise was diluted, but not entirely removed. The Walter Scott entries were left intact as an affectionate monument to Harvey's founding vision. The double-column, unillustrated, reassuringly antique format was retained. On the shelf, stripped of its dustjacket, the 'Fifth Edition' looked very much like its venerable predecessor—only newer and less faded.

The Drabble Fifth Edition of *OCEL* (which was priced enticingly low for the 1984 buyer at £15.00) went on to sell phenomenally well, penetrating well beyond the traditional reference-library market. It was, manifestly, a popular gift at Christmas time. In terms of sales, the Fifth Edition was probably the most successful venture of its kind in academic publishing in the 1980s. It certainly outsold glitzier, heavily illustrated, more consciously modish rivals. And it is worth pondering why *OCEL5* was so much to the taste of the general reading public in the 1980s and 1990s. Obviously a portmanteau container with everything worth knowing about English literature (carrying Oxford University's seal of approval) had a perennial appeal for any self-improving person. But what principally attracted customers, and satisfied users, was the core of humane knowledge which the editor retained while at the same time broadening and 'academicizing' the perspective of the project. *OCEL5* not only reduced English literature to manageable proportions—so that one could 'see it whole'—the new *Companion* communicated a confident sense of the enduring value of English literature at the end of the century. In this respect, it was as much a book to browse in as a source to refer to for ready information.

The Oxford Companion to Twentieth-Century Literature in English descends lineally from *OCEL5*, both in conception and in the person of its editor, Jenny Stringer. The task proposed by this latest venture is formidable. 'Twentieth-Century Literature in English' is a fast-moving target. The coverage comes up to the moment, giving a snapshot of contemporary literature as it is currently evolving, yet at the same time going back to the modernist, turn-of-the-twentieth-century roots in which the various national traditions are grounded. At the forward edge—where it is still 'living'—literature is accumulating, and its definition changing, day by day. The nearer one is in time to the literary object, the harder it is to be sure of status. Most of us rely on history to make our most important literary critical judgements. Who to put in? who not to put in? becomes a fiendishly tricky question with currently-active authors. The name recognition factor is palpably lower, imposing a harder burden on the compiler to justify inclusion. Living authors means authors in flux, a factor which has necessitated the renovation of entries almost as soon as they are written. Most drastically authors (such as Angela Carter or Graham Greene) have died in the interval between writing them up and publishing. A writer such as Wole Soyinka goes into exile, and the whole judgement on his literary achievement needs to be revised in the light of that event.

Most of all it is the sheer quantity of 'Twentieth-Century Literature in English' that is daunting to any would-be selector and compiler. In bulk it surpasses any other standard category one can think of, comprising as it does all genres, and some two dozen national literatures—including the world's largest. Year for year, the twentieth century has seen more literary production than in any previous period. It would not be perverse to propose a companion to any one decade. Raymond Williams once pointed out that a lifetime would be insufficient to cover the literary production of a single year in modern times. Accompanying these deterring enlargements is the new definition 'Literature in English'—a much more complex formulation, it turns out, than 'English Literature'. English is one of the major world languages (the others being Russian, Chinese, Spanish, and French) and, in terms of the literature that passes through it, English is probably the most heterogeneous and dialect-rich. Within the general category 'Literature in English', space has been allocated equitably to three main territories. Some thirty per cent of the author entries cover American writing, thirty per cent cover British writing, the remaining percentage goes to writing from other areas of the Anglophone world. As will be clear, this *Companion*—like the recently published *Oxford Companion to Literature in French* (ed. Peter France, 1995)—disavows the idea of literature as an intrinsically national possession ('English Literature', 'American Literature', 'French Literature'). A logical, although logistically inconvenient, next step would have been to include the huge corpus of literary work translated into English from other languages. It would not be far-fetched, for example, to argue that the most historically potent writer of fiction in English in the 1970s was Alexander Solzhenitsyn, who never penned an English word in his life. A similar argument could be made for Jean Genet and Frantz Fanon in the 1960s. This is, however, the province of a volume already in preparation at OUP. Embedded in the (already overpacked) title, 'The Oxford Companion to Twentieth-Century Literature in English', is the qualification, 'Literature *Originally* in English'.

Internationalization and a more scrupulous attention to region enlarges the scale of the project, as does the recruitment of women in large numbers into literary activity, particularly following liberationist initiatives in the 1960s. The sex ratio in the twentieth-century *Companion* is three to one. A spot check of the two previous *Companions* suggests a ratio of between five and seven to one. The simplest, if most arduous, solution to the size problems confronting Stringer when she began work on the *Companion* would have been to embark on a total listing such as is given by the all-inclusive *Contemporary Authors* (1962), a serial compilation which by 1995 had attained 200 volumes and 100,000 authorial profiles. *Contemporary Authors* is invaluable to the researcher in the modern field, but it gives little more 'guidance' than a telephone directory. Authors of all kinds of book are eligible, whether of auto-repair manuals or L-A-N-G-U-A-G-E poetry. Stringer, by contrast, has retained the hereditary *Companion* category, 'Literature', and the discriminatory duties the term imposes. *The Oxford Companion to Twentieth-Century Literature in English* is not an open-ended directory, nor a database, but a guide. As such, what it keeps out of the picture is as formative as what it includes. While aiming for maximal comprehensiveness and meaningful levels of literary significance, Stringer and her contributors have kept the compilation within the dimensions of manageability represented by the single volume—a volume no larger in physical size and wordage than its sibling *Companions*. A cost is paid in the *Companion*'s internal architecture. Stringer, unlike the compilers of *OCEL* and *OCEL5*, cannot afford the luxury of wordy digression or flights of personality. The bulk of entries in the twentieth-century *Companion*—some 2,400 out of about 3,000—are authorial (this proportion, incidentally, represents a shift from earlier *Companions*). The remaining entries cover genres ('Beat Poetry', 'Detective Fiction'), groups and movements, critical concepts, periodicals, and supremely important single works; in addition there are some 400 cross-references. The apportionment of space within entries descends from a pantheon of writers (D. H. Lawrence, Henry James, Thomas Hardy, T. S. Eliot, Virginia Woolf, Bernard Shaw) who rate over 1,000 words. This nucleus of twentieth-century immortals selects itself. Ranked beneath them are a first and second division whose inclusions may be more contentious. The average length of the entries is around 270 words. The ratio between longest and shortest contrasts with the occasional extreme brevity and lavish length of different entries in earlier *Companions*.

In its author entries *The Oxford Companion to Twentieth-Century Literature in English* offers bio-bibliographical information to a high degree of specification, and throughout the book the network of cross-references maps out a range of linked areas within the *Companion*'s total coverage. As well as immediately providing information for the general reader, the book will connect with a body of increasingly computerized assemblies of literary knowledge. For many readers it will serve as the starting-point for further extended searches in the electronic environment. In this respect, the *Companion* is a resource which will, as they become familiar with it, generate its own corps of advanced users. Those browsing through it for the first time will find its subject matter ('Literature') presented not as an inert canonical set of books, classical authors, and facts 'which every civilized person should know' (as in E. D. Hirsch's *Cultural Literacy*) but as an *activity* with which readers, on their part, can interact.

What salient facts does this *Companion*, considered in its totality, convey about literature in English in the twentieth century? Principally, one perceives that creative writing has moved out in all directions at once, confounding easy generalizations. It would be safe to assert, for instance, that viewed from one angle, literature in English is—in its various manifestations—more nationalistic (more American, more Scottish, more Australian) than ever before. No minority but now has its literary voice and literary platform. But, equally, one may assert that literature in English is more supranational (or indifferent to nationality) in its pretensions than it has ever been. Feminist writing, to take an obvious example, is typically writing without frontiers, in which women talk to women irrespective of place, class, historical period, or national origin. If one compares a novelist like Toni Morrison (winner of the Nobel Prize for Literature in 1993) with Rudyard Kipling (winner in 1907) it is clear that the African-American novelist (who refers to herself as 'a Third-world woman in America') is an artist who spans the first and third worlds in ways in which Kipling (whose east could never meet his west) does not. *Beloved*—a novel which is almost as popular in Britain as it is in America—is dedicated not to Morrison's millions of readers across the English-speaking world, but to the 'sixty million and more' of expatriated Africans whose native language, with everything else, was taken away from them. It is evident that contemporary writers with a specifically gay affiliation (such as Adam Mars Jones, Paul Monette, Larry Kramer) similarly speak across national frontiers (sometimes more readily, one suspects, than they speak across gender boundaries). A genre such as science fiction is as international as its annual World Conventions, and it is often difficult for readers to identify a practitioner's national origin without guidance. One of the most interesting categories of writer represented in this *Companion* are those who have written in the fractional spaces between nationalities and ethnicities: Amy Tan and Hanif Kureishi come to mind as novelists whose fiction fruitfully locates itself in the second-generation immigrant's dual consciousness of where the parents came from and where the children are. Is Kureishi to be considered a British or a

Pakistani literary possession?—both. Is *The Joy Luck Club* a novel of Chinese or American experience?—both. One of the literary-sociological deductions one draws from the *Companion* is that in this century there has been significantly more trans-national movement and transplantation of writing across traditional boundaries. Sylvia Plath, to take a high-profile example, began her published writing career as a minor American novelist; she died as Britain's most admired woman poet. It requires delicate dissective powers to determine where the 'New Zealander' in Katherine Mansfield ends, and the 'Londoner' begins.

At a lower level of literary aspiration, bestsellers have become notably supranational during the course of the century. Frederick Forsyth, English by origin, lives in Ireland for tax reasons and sells most of his books in America. Arthur Hailey was born in England, took Canadian citizenship, lived for the later part of his career in the Bahamas, and directed the blockbusters of his writing maturity primarily at American readers. If one looks at the *New York Times* or London *Sunday Times* bestseller lists in any week, one sees an extraordinary degree of national interpenetration—mainly between Britain and America, but often taking in writers of other origins as well (Boris Pasternak and Vladimir Nabokov competed between them for top place in the bestseller lists in 1958). John Grisham fills the shopwindow of Hatchard's in Piccadilly and Frederick Forsyth proudly dominates the dumpbins in Barnes and Noble's establishments in New York. In this respect, popular fiction like popular music has accommodated to the vastness of the world market. This tendency towards the globalization of culture is accepted as something natural by younger readers of literature. (Some of them may resent the absence from the *Companion* of such contemporary troubadours as Ice Cube, Patti Smith, and Michael Stipe—'poets' whose constituency is as world-wide as MTV.) Inevitably the internationalization of literature will be accelerated by the Internet—a system based, momentously, on English as its lingua franca. It is only a matter of time before 'Literature in English' adapts to the net as a delivery system (before this can be fully achieved, however, intractable copyright problems must be solved by a legal code which finds it harder to adapt to the global electronic environment than does creative writing).

The global, supranational, market for literature often moves in mysterious ways. W. H. Auden became a super-selling and more world-famous writer than he had ever been in his lifetime, in 1994. The reason was the unexpected box-office success in America of *Four Weddings and a Funeral*, a low-budget British film. It features (in its 'funeral' segment) a public reading of one of Auden's poems, 'Stop all the clocks, cut off the telephone' (1936). This sparked off a voracious demand for reprints of Auden's poetry—featuring the 'hit' poem—among an audience which is traditionally impervious to the mandarin charms of modern verse. One can see such phenomena as reassuring, or obscurely terrifying.

One of the more illuminating paradoxes in twentieth-century literature is that some of its most important practitioners have exploited the nationalist and the supranational dimensions of their work simultaneously. Thomas Keneally, for instance, is in one of his many parts the most chauvinistically Australian of writers. In the 1990s, much of Keneally's extra-literary energy has been devoted to ridding his country of the last vestiges of colonial rule (in the form of Commonwealth membership and loyalty to the British monarch). Some of Keneally's work—such as the study of aboriginal *mentalité*, *The Chant of Jimmie Blacksmith* (1972), or his bicentennial historical novel *The Playmaker* (1987)—might be thought parochial in terms of a global market which has not traditionally shown much fascination with things Australian. Yet with his novel *Schindler's Ark* (which won the Booker Prize in 1982), adapted by Steven Spielberg in the film *Schindler's List*, Keneally enjoyed a lease of vast international popularity. Paradoxically, this laureate of the outback became the author most effectively to contradict Theodor Adorno's grim axiom that writing literature after Auschwitz is an impossibility.

One of the major trends which has conditioned the evolution of twentieth-century literature is decensorship. Many of the writers profiled in this *Companion* have been, in their time, prohibited: James Joyce, Henry Miller, D. H. Lawrence are famous (once notorious) instances. For 'Literature in English', the modern period is one of ever-expanding freedom of expression. Some of the thresholds are dramatic. The post-1959 novels of Norman Mailer would have been unpublishable before that date (when the *Lady Chatterley's Lover* trial was successfully concluded in America). A British bookseller before 1960 would have been looking at a long jail-sentence for selling the novels Martin Amis has been producing for the last twenty years. There are, however, exceptions which test this rule. While censorship generally has receded, intransigent pockets have remained in places like South Africa before the 1990s. Paradoxically, these nests of cultural oppression have generated (as in censored Russian literature of the nineteenth century) harvests of rich literary creativity. Writers of indubitable world-class status, such as Nadine Gordimer, Athol Fugard, J. M. Coetzee, did not merely survive, but flourished under Apartheid regimes rabidly inimical to their literary activity.

Having made these points about the general internationalization and liberation of literature (both of which are heartening from a liberal point of view) one must enter a caveat. The more cost-expensive forms of literature (notably the novel) have inexorably gravitated to the most developed publishing industries in the western world—those of America and of Britain. Thus, for instance, two of the most eminent of sub-continental Indian writers of fiction—Salman Rushdie and Vikram Seth—frequently launch their work in London and in New York, with 'conglomerated' and multi-national publishing houses (although Seth insisted that *A Suitable Boy* be simultaneously launched in India). Unusually, Peter Carey, the Booker-prize winning Australian novelist (with *Oscar and Lucinda*, 1988) has maintained a relationship, after his overseas triumphs, with the University of Queensland Press which published his early short stories. But such fidelity is rare. Most successful writers, and most would-be successful writers of fiction, have to follow the money. The money is US dollars and pounds sterling. This sense that one's 'market' is so far from one's literary roots can throw up artistic dilemmas. The West Indian novel is one of the glories of post-war writing in English; yet there is no domestic book trade, nor a regional reading public sufficient to support the extraordinarily gifted writers in English that the Caribbean has produced. They must publish (and be largely read) in the UK, and to a lesser extent on the eastern seaboard of the US. The need to reside where their income is primarily earned has clearly had a formative effect on the careers of writers such as V. S. Naipaul and Wilson Harris.

While readers pay great attention to the author's name on a book's title-page, they typically fail to register the imprint that accompanies it. The oversight is significant. If, for instance, one contemplates Booker Prize shortlisted candidates and winners over the years (see Appendix for Booker Prize winners) they would seem, to judge by origins, to be admirably diverse—to the point of postcolonial correctness. Novelists of Australian, New Zealand, Canadian, Indian, Nigerian, and Japanese extraction can be found. So multi-cultural have the winners been that home-grown writers have grumbled about level playing-fields. But it is a main desideratum of the awarders of the Prize that the work shall first have been published in the United Kingdom—that it shall be, in other words, the assigned property of the British publishing industry. However diverse the natal origins and cultural affiliations of Booker novelists, their publishers (co-owners of the work) are invariably London-based. So too with prestigious annual prizes awarded by, for instance, the *Los Angeles Times* in five main categories of literary activity. The judges have been assiduous in noticing Chicano and Asian-American writers who cater to large constituencies in southern California. But such writers will typically have been brought to their readers by an American book trade which is, at its executive level, as white-Anglo-male as any other corridor of high power in the United States.

The Royal Commission which in 1975 looked into the Canadian publishing industry noted the extraordinary paucity of indigenous novels published in the country, in either of the two principal languages. 'Canadian' novelists like Mordecai Richler were based in London, other prominent Canadian novelists like Leonard Cohen (the balladeer, but also author of *Beautiful Losers*) marketed their fiction principally in the United States, and catered mainly for a US readership. Despite subsequent attempts to redress this situation by aggressive programmes of subsidy and protective legislation, Canada has not succeeded in repatriating its literature.

In creative writing, as in other spheres of late-twentieth-century life, the multinational, New York- and London-based company is old empire writ new. Post-colonial much recent writing may be: post-colonial the publishing industry is not. In 1947, in an agreement on 'world rights' which was as momentous for literature in English as was the Yalta meeting for post-war international relations, the British and American publishing industries agreed to carve the English speaking world into two huge sectors. America would have its own territory (i.e. only American publishers could supply it), the UK would have its 'traditional market' (i.e. the former empire and Commonwealth), Canada would be an open territory. This 'paper curtain' (unlike its iron equivalent) is still effectively in place. For many writers it means that—unless 'overseas rights' can be sold—they may be kept out of large sectors of the English-speaking world. One can argue, of course, that this rational arrangement is for everyone's good. But it does not conduce to the freedom of writers.

So too with decensorhip and the unfettered 'liberation' which it seems to denote. In one sense writers are freer to express themselves as the twentieth century comes to an end than they have ever been. The obscenity, blasphemy, and libel laws which traditionally have been used to oppress literature are much relaxed and in some cases they have become dead letters. But if expression is freer, literature as a 'commodity' is more jealously owned and monopolistically protected than it has ever been. As laws affecting censorship have been rolled back over the last hundred years, those affecting copyright have been progressively tightened, refined, and expanded. It is safe to predict that one main group of users of this *Companion* will be publishers and their legal advisers, checking—by reference to crucial dates—when authors and their works come into public domain. That threshold in Britain has, from 1995, been extended from fifty to seventy years after death. It is very likely that the rest of the English-speaking world will follow suit. The postponement of public domain inhibits the free circulation of literature in its cheapest reprint forms—something on which the general health of culture depends.

Poetry, which can be produced and distributed with little capital expenditure, and which is of negligible significance commercially, has managed better than fiction to retain its local, regional, and coterie flavours. The Liverpool poets, the Brixton Afro-Caribbean poets, and the still active Beats round Lawrence Ferlinghetti's City Lights Bookshop in San Francisco all testify to the vigour of poetry at the grassroots, and its ability to thrive at that level. If one is curious about the regional and local recesses of twentieth-century literature, poetry is the place to look. This *Companion* is particularly attentive to the many groups, collectives, and workshops which have generated poetry and kept its flame alight in the last one hundred years.

One surprising feature in the survey of material contained in the twentieth-century *Companion* is that, although there is a long list of new names, there seem to be relatively few new forms of literature. Novelists, poets, dramatists, journalists, essayists (including literary critics and reviewers), and biographers predominate. There are innovative entries in the fields of television drama (David Mercer, Dennis Potter). But even these can be seen as sub-divisions of traditionally-staged drama. There are new narrative genres ('campus novels', 'cyberpunk', 'the New Journalism'), but nothing as dramatic as the rise of the novel as a major literary form in the eighteenth century. It is hard to find a central field of literary activity not represented in Harvey's *Companion*. It would seem to be as difficult to invent a new literary genre as it is to invent a new vice.

In his 1899 survey of English letters, *The Pen and the Book*, Walter Besant estimated that at the end of the nineteenth century there were some 1,200 professional writers in England, of whom around 200 were wholly self-supporting by their pens. One to six would seem to be a fair estimate of the ratio in the twentieth-century *Companion*. It is still the case that 'Literature' (as opposed to 'Popular Literature') is a penurious calling. One of the startling revelations in Margaret Drabble's 1995 life of Angus Wilson is that in his most remunerative year, this preeminent novelist earned less than £12,000. In *his* best year, Stephen King earned $5 million in publishers' advances. Not all literary genres yield even a subsistence wage. Probably no more than a score of the poets profiled in this *Companion* have managed to wrest a decent living from poetry alone. It is only at its less creative margins (in journalism, for example) that secure salaries, paid holidays, and pensions are to be had. The huge proliferation of names in this *Companion* should not mislead anyone into thinking that for the average practitioner the literary vocation is much better rewarded than it was in Dr Johnson's time. There are merely more Richard Savages.

One of the ways in which American writers (particularly poets) have sought to keep body and soul together in the later twentieth century is by attaching themselves to colleges as 'writers in residence'. This relates to an overwhelming feature of modern 'Literature in English'—the ubiquitous influence of the academy. Institutions of higher learning have had a formative effect on twentieth-century creative writing in three direct ways. As with writers in residence, they have been patrons, absorbing many of the functions of the church in earlier centuries. A more subtle form of patronage—or institutional favour—is represented by a university's taking over the care of a living writer's literary remains. A writer's stock is similarly raised when his or her work is approved for doctoral work. The two most popular subjects for Ph.D. dissertations in the early 1990s were, one is told, the poet John Ashbery and Samuel Beckett. The sales represented by academic attention of this kind are probably nugatory. But to be set for advanced study guarantees what matters more to ambitious writers—critical reputation and a place in literary posterity.

More pervasively, academic criticism (through scholarly publication, or the taking over of reviews in opinion-forming organs) has made the practising writer acutely aware of 'tradition', fostering a symptomatic self-reflexivity and an epidemic 'anxiety of influence' (as Harold Bloom has called it). In the twentieth century, writers are more conscious of other writers. Colleges and universities, as they have expanded (particularly after the 1950s in America, and the 1960s in Britain), have brought into existence a large, sophisticated readership—an audience, that is, grounded in literary history and trained in literary criticism. This has fed back into a palpable enrichment of what was disdained, half a century earlier, as the 'middlebrow' public. This *Companion* recognizes the cultural power of the academy in the twentieth century by the inclusion of influential literary critics (Edward Said, for instance) and entries on such institutions as the MLA.

How then should *The Oxford Companion to Twentieth-Century Literature in English* be used? Self-evidently the volume will be invaluable for the practical educational tasks of curriculum formation and anthology-making. Students will find it a ready source of literary reference. It will be an attractive repository of fact for those who wish to discover new things and for those who wish to check what they already know—or think they know. Not least, the *Companion* may be browsed in for that peculiar pleasure which is to be had from the contemplation of order imposed on an unimaginably complex and diverse field of human activity.

A

Aaron's Rod, a novel by D. H. *Lawrence, published in 1922. Aaron Sisson, a checkweighman in a Nottinghamshire colliery, and amateur piccolo player, suddenly leaves his wife and children on Christmas Eve immediately after the First World War. He goes to London, where he joins the Covent Garden orchestra and becomes involved with a smart set of bohemian people, led by Jim Bricknell, a man obsessed with the importance of filling himself with food and love. Aaron encounters the writer Rawdon Lilly and his Norwegian wife, Tanny. When Aaron becomes ill in body and soul, Lilly nurses him and the two become intimate friends. Though they quarrel, particularly over the war, Lilly exercises a powerful influence over Aaron; after an emotional visit to his abandoned wife in the Midlands, Aaron follows Lilly to Italy. There, an unfulfilling affair with an American-born marchesa, and the shattering of his flute in an anarchist bomb attack, lead Aaron to despair. Lilly urges him to yield to the 'deep power-soul' and unfold his own destiny. Loosely episodic in form, the novel contains some of Lawrence's most passionate writing about the First World War and reveals the sense of release that Italy provided him. The title of the book refers to the biblical Aaron, the brother of Moses and founder of the priesthood, whose blossoming Rod is a symbol of miraculous authority.

ABBENSETTS, Michael (1938–), Guyanese playwright, born in British Guyana, educated there and in Quebec and Montreal. His plays offer a view of black immigrant life in Britain and present difficult situations within a broad tradition of comedy. The humour arises primarily from incongruity, though there are fine instances of verbal felicity and wit. He established his reputation with his play *Sweet Talk* in 1973, and in 1974 became dramatist-in-residence at the Royal Court Theatre, London. His other stage plays include *Alterations* (1978), *Samba* (1980), *In the Mood* (1981), *Outlaw* (1983), and *El Dorado* (1984). Among his many radio plays are *Home Again* (1975), *The Sunny Side of the Street* (1977), *Brothers of the Sword* (1978), *The Fast Lane* (1980), and *The Dark Horse* (1981), but he has reached his widest audience with his television plays, such as *The Museum Attendant* (1973), *Inner City Blues* (1975), *Crime and Passion* (1976), *Black Christmas* (1977), *Roadrunner* (1977), *Empire Road* (1977; a series), and *Easy Money* (1982).

Abbey Theatre, The, the home of the Irish National Theatre Society, named after Abbey Street in Dublin, where its permanent theatre was established in 1904. Following discussions between W. B. *Yeats, Lady Augusta *Gregory, and Edward *Martyn, the Irish Literary Theatre was founded and staged its first productions of Yeats's *The Countess Cathleen* and Martyn's *The Heather Field* in 1899. In 1901 Yeats's disagreements with Martyn led him to join with the actors Frank and William Fay to form the Irish National Dramatic Society, which produced his **Cathleen Ni Houlihan* and *The Pot of Broth* in 1902. The Irish Literary Theatre and the Irish National Dramatic Society subsequently amalgamated to become the Irish National Theatre Society, which staged J. M. Synge's **Riders to the Sea* in 1904. In that year Miss Annie F. Horniman provided the company with funding to purchase and equip the theatre in Abbey Street. On its opening night in 1904, the Abbey Theatre presented Yeats's *On Baile's Strand*, *Cathleen Ni Houlihan*, and Lady Gregory's *Spreading the News*. Tensions between those who supported the theatre as a platform for political nationalism and those for whom it was primarily an artistic forum were brought to a head when Synge's *The *Playboy of the Western World* was produced in 1907. Miss Horniman withdrew her patronage in 1910 when Yeats defied her request to close the theatre for the funeral of Edward VII. George Bernard *Shaw and Padraic *Colum were among the dramatists who consolidated the reputation of the Abbey company, which won acclaim on its early tours of England for the restrained naturalism of its acting style. Sean O'Casey's *The *Shadow of a Gunman*, **Juno and the Paycock*, and *The *Plough and the Stars* were the most successful productions of the 1920s. In 1925 the Irish Government began its subsidy of the Abbey, making it the first theatre in the English-speaking world to receive state support. In 1951 the buildings were destroyed by fire and the company was based in Dublin's Queen's Theatre until 1966, when a new Abbey Theatre was opened on the original site.

ABERCROMBIE, Lascelles (1881–1938), British poet, dramatist, and critic, born in Ashton-under-Mersey, Cheshire, educated at Victoria University, Manchester. Having distinguished himself as a literary journalist, he lectured at the universities of Liverpool and Leeds before becoming Goldsmiths' Reader in English at New College, Oxford. With Wilfrid *Gibson and Walter *de la Mare, he was a recipient of the posthumous royalties produced by Rupert *Brooke's works. *Interludes and Poems* (1908) was his first collection of verse; numerous succeeding volumes include *Emblems of Love* (1912) and the posthumous *Lyrics and Unfinished Poems* (1940). A collected edition of his poetry appeared in 1930. Although capable of a straightforwardly individual tone and of imaginatively powerful metaphorical effects, he remained stylistically constrained by the conventions of Victorian verse. A leading contributor to Edward Marsh's **Georgian Poetry* anthologies, his criticism tended to espouse the qualities associated with Georgian poetry. Much of his most original poetry is contained in his verse-dramas, for which he was held in high regard; his works in the genre include *The End of the World* (1915) and *The Sale of St Thomas* (1931). Among his critical works are *Thomas Hardy* (1912), *The Idea of Great Poetry* (1925), and *Principles of Literary Criticism* (1932).

ABISH, Walter (1931–), American novelist and short-story writer, born in Vienna; he grew up in China and Israel before settling in the USA. He has worked as a lecturer and teacher in a variety of American colleges and universities since 1975. His work is characterized by an experimentalism and a sense of philosophical enquiry which have led to some claims that he can in some way be separated from the sources and strengths of American writing. His early collection of poems, *Duel Site* (1970), was followed by several works of fiction including the novels *The Alphabetical Africa* (1974), *In the Future Perfect* (1975), *How German Is It?* (1979), *Ninety-Nine: The New Meaning* (1990), and *Eclipse Fever* (1993). In each work different techniques are employed to investigate the connections and spaces between reality and language, and to develop insights into both American and non-American cultures from his double position of insider and outsider. His works have also been published widely in anthologies, and in magazines such as the **Partisan Review*, **Transatlantic Review*, *New York Arts Journal*, and **Paris Review*. A collection of fiction entitled *Destiny: Tomorrow's Truth* appeared in 1992.

ABRAHAMS, Peter (1919–), South African novelist and journalist, born in Vredetorp, Johannesburg, and largely self-taught. His first work, a collection of short stories, *Dark Testament* (1942), appeared after he settled in London in 1941. Several novels about life in South Africa's ghettoes followed, including *Song of the City* (1945), *Mine Boy* (1946), and *The Path of Thunder* (1948). Though mainly in a naturalistic style, narrative techniques derived from African oral traditions also inform these novels. The pieces collected in *Return to Goli* (1953) describe his visit to South Africa; they originally appeared in the *Observer* to which Abrahams contributed regularly. *Tell Freedom*, his autobiography, appeared in 1954. In 1957 he moved to Jamaica, where he became editor of the *West Indian Economist*. Later novels go beyond the purely South African context, and are noted for their acute political perceptiveness. These include *Wild Conquest* (1950), a historical novel about tensions among the Barolong, Boers, and Matabele; *A Wreath for Udomo* (1956), which prophetically highlighted some of the problems facing post-independence African states, and focuses on the tragic dilemmas of a charismatic ruler, said to be modelled on Nkrumah of Ghana; *This Island Now* (1966), set in the Caribbean, and further exploring the hard choices of a post-independence leader; and *The View from Coyaba* (1985), a historical novel about the struggles for liberation among African slaves and their descendants. See Kolawole Ongungbesan, *The Writing of Peter Abrahams* (1979).

Absalom, Absalom!, a novel by William *Faulkner, published in 1936. The story, which centres on the rise and fall of Thomas Sutpen, begins in 1833 when Sutpen arrives in Jefferson, Mississippi, having left his home state of West Virginia and settled in Haiti where he married a planter's daughter, Eulalia Bon. By Eulalia he had a son, Charles Bon, but on his discovering Eulalia's black ancestry both she and the son were abandoned. Sutpen begins to establish himself in Jefferson, acquires an estate, builds a mansion (designed by a French architect), marries the daughter of a respectable Southern family, by whom he has two children, Judith and Henry, and is made a Colonel in Jefferson's regiment during the Civil War. He returns from the war to find his plantation in ruins and to discover that Charles Bon has been murdered by his half-brother, Henry, who has sought to prevent the miscegenation that would ensue were Charles to marry Judith, as had been his intention. Henry disappears and Sutpen, who still seeks an heir, seduces Milly Jones, the granddaughter of Wash Jones, a squatter on his land. Milly bears him a daughter, but not a son, and when Sutpen disowns both Milly and his illegitimate daughter Wash Jones murders him. Sutpen's estate is left to Clytie (Clytemnestra), his daughter by a mulatto slave, and it is she who, at the end of the novel, sets fire to Sutpen's house, killing both herself and Sutpen's son Henry and thus bringing the tragedy to its end; all that remains of the Sutpen dynasty is Jim Bond, an idiot, Sutpen's only living descendant, howling in the ashes of the burned house.

The story is possibly the most melodramatic in all of Faulkner's fiction but the interest of the novel lies very much in the intricate manner in which it is told. It is constructed through the accounts of three narrators: Miss Rosa Coldfield, Sutpen's sister-in-law, tells the story to Quentin Compson, a character from an earlier Faulkner novel, *The *Sound and the Fury* (1929), before his departure for Harvard University; Rosa's story is supplemented by information provided by Quentin's father, Jason Compson III; and Quentin, in turn, tells the story to Shrevelin McCannon, his Canadian room-mate at Harvard. There is no reliable narrator and the reader has to piece the narrative together from incomplete and subjective accounts of Sutpen's rise and fall. The novel has been considered the most 'Conradian' of Faulkner's major works, the resemblances in fictional technique to *Conrad's novel **Chance* (1914) being particularly striking. See

Faulkner's 'Absalom, Absalom!': A Critical Casebook (1984), edited by Elizabeth Muhlenfeld.

ABSE, Dannie (1923–), British poet, born of a Welsh-Jewish family in Cardiff, where he attended the Welsh National School of Medicine before studying in London at King's College and Westminster Hospital. He qualified as a doctor in 1950. *After Every Green Thing* (1948) was the first of his principal collections of poetry, which also include *Tenants of the House* (1957), *Funland and Other Poems* (1973), *Ask the Bloody Horse* (1986), *Remembrance of Crimes Past* (1990), and *On the Evening Road* (1994). His poetry's accessibly discursive tone accommodates a wide range of emotional and imaginative intensities; compassion and a wryly anecdotal humour combine to unusual and sometimes highly disquieting effect in the best of his work. *White Coat, Purple Coat: Collected Poems 1948–1988* appeared in 1989, His novels include *Ash on a Young Man's Sleeve* (1954) and *O. Jones, O. Jones* (1970), both of which draw on his experiences as a student. He has also published several autobiographical works including *A Poet in the Family* (1974), *A Strong Dose of Myself* (1983), *There was a Young Man from Cardiff* (1991), and *Intermittent Journals* (1994). The best-known of his numerous plays are collected in *The View from Row C* (1990). Among his other writings is *Medicine on Trial* (1968), an evaluation of modern medical practices.

Absurd, Theatre of the, was a term pioneered by the British critic Martin Esslin and used to characterize the work of certain key playwrights in the 1950s and 1960s. Though its roots may be traced back as far as Jarry's *Ubu Roi* in 1896, and perhaps to Strindberg's expressionist work, its more immediate inspiration was Camus's essay *The Myth of Sisyphus*, published during the Second World War, in 1942. This disseminated the idea, soon given greater credibility by Hiroshima and the discovery of the scope of the Holocaust, that man was a stranger in an irrational universe, deprived of 'illusions and light', bereft of purpose, and hence subject to a metaphysical and moral anguish, or 'feeling of Absurdity'. The key attempt to give dramatic definition to this state of mind was Beckett's **Waiting for Godot*, in which two exemplary derelicts wait helplessly for a salvation that seems highly unlikely ever to materialize; but important contributions, usually emphasizing the irrationality of the world and the illogic of human behaviour, and often harshly comic in tone, also came from Ionesco, Adamov, Vian, Arrabal, and other dramatists, as well as Beckett himself in subsequent years. Attempts were made to claim the lightweight N. F. *Simpson and the weightier Harold *Pinter of *The Birthday Party* and *The Dumb Waiter* for the Theatre of the Absurd; but it was always more a European than a British phenomenon.

Absurd Person Singular, a play by Alan *Ayckbourn, first performed in 1972; it well exemplifies its author's technical adventurousness and the moral seriousness he brings to comedy. Each of the three acts is set in a different kitchen on a consecutive Christmas Eve, and each charts the changing circumstances of three couples: the lower middle-class Sidney Hopcroft, who moves from insecurity to assurance with his growing business success, and his wife Jane; the adulterous architect Geoffrey, whose reputation collapses along with one of his buildings, and Eva, who is transformed by his failure from an anguished neurotic to the dominant figure in their marriage; and Ronald, the manager of the local bank, and Marion, whose upper middle-class arrogance is subverted by worsening alcoholism. The play ends with a graphic reminder of the social mobility that has been its main theme, a frantic party in which the educated professionals literally dance to the *nouveau riche* Sidney's tune; but the most critically admired act is the second, which somehow succeeds in finding a not unsympathetic humour in Eva's attempts to poison, hang, gas, knife, and defenestrate herself.

ACHEBE, (Albert) Chinua(lumogu) (1930–), Nigerian novelist, poet, and critic, born in Ogidi, Eastern Nigeria, educated at the University College of Ibadan. Before the Nigerian Civil War (1967–70), Achebe worked as a broadcaster. Among other academic appointments, he was Professor of English at the University of Massachusetts, and Emeritus Professor of Literature at the University of Nigeria (Nsukka). His first novel, *Things Fall Apart* (1958), is one of the most famous African novels in English, and has been translated into many languages. It imaginatively recreates traditional life in Igbo villages before the onset of modernity, and focuses on the headstrong Okonkwo who opposes, with tragic consequences, both converted Christians and British colonial interference. As in much of Achebe's work, the novel subtly interweaves traditional story-telling and modern narrative. Moving from tragedy to satiric irony, *No Longer at Ease* (1960) follows the fate of Okonkwo's grandson, Obi, who obtains a loan from his village to be educated in England. The novel examines the pressures leading to white-collar corruption in Nigeria. *Arrow of God* (1964), set in the 1920s, focuses on Ezeulu, the chief priest of an Igbo village, and his conflict with his Western-educated son, who has become a Christian convert. These three novels were published as *The African Trilogy* in 1988. *A Man of the People* (1966), a bitter satire about a demagogic politician, was so prophetic about the imminence of domestic military intervention in an independent Nigeria that only two days after its first publication the country suffered its first military coup. As a literary and cultural critic, Achebe has consistently argued that the African novel must deal with social realities, and avoid a spurious universality, as advocated by 'colonialist critics'. In 1969 Achebe undertook an American speaking tour, together with Gabriel *Okara and Cyprian *Ekwensi, on behalf of the Biafran cause. *Beware Soul Brother* (1971, revised 1972; US title *Christmas in Biafra and Other Poems*, 1973), a collection of poems, and *Girls at War and Other Stories* (1972) reflect his reactions to the Nigerian Civil War. His essays are collected in

Morning Yet on Creation Day (1975) and *Hopes and Impediments* (1988). Two of his most controversial essays are 'The Novelist as Teacher' and 'An Image of Africa: Racism in Conrad's *Heart of Darkness*'. Achebe has also written collections of short stories including *The Sacrificial Egg* (1962), as well as children's books. His novel *Anthills of the Savannah* (1987) is a coruscating portrayal of power corrupting a ruling clique, most of whose members had been at school together. Internal rivalries, a collective inability to control, and the paranoid tendencies of a Sandhurst-trained military ruler lead to soul-searching on the part, particularly, of Ikem Osidi, poet and newspaper editor, and Chris Oriko, Commissioner for Education, both helped by the emancipated Beatrice Okoh. Achebe is the editor of *The Heinemann Book of Contemporary African Short Stories* (1992). See C. L. Innes, *Chinua Achebe* (1990).

ACKER, Kathy (1947–), American dramatist, novelist, and poet, born in New York, educated at the Universities of Brandeis and California. In her narratives, documentary accounts of historical events are juxtaposed with grim imaginings on the modern world. Classic texts are often used to pass comment on literary tradition, and to provide a disquieting context for her bleak visions of late twentieth-century Western society. *Blood and Guts in High School* (1978), an account of young Janey Smith's trials and tribulations, incorporates dream maps, Persian poems, gritty realism, and fantastical encounters with Jean Genet and President Carter. In *Don Quixote* (1986) she uses Cervantes together with pastiches of Wedekind and de Sade amongst others, to provide a picaresque structure for a female Quixote's wanderings around the impoverished social and political landscape of post-war America. From her early writings under the pseudonym of 'The Black Tarantula' onwards, graphic descriptions of the sex act have been prominent in her work, reflecting Acker's former employment as a stripper and in porn films. Early short stories are collected in *The Adult Life of Toulouse Lautrec* (1975) and *Kathy Goes to Haiti* (1978). Later works include *Empire of the Senseless* (1988), a female version of Genet's novel *Journal du Voleur*, and *In Memoriam to Identity* (1990), a fictional account of the relationship between Rimbaud and Verlaine. Acker has also written poetry, plays, art criticism, screenplays including *Variety* (1985), and an opera libretto, *The Birth of the Poet* (1985). Variously described as 'post-punk porn', 'post-modernist', and 'feminist counter-culture', her work has been compared with that of writers such as W. S. *Burroughs and Jean Genet.

ACKERLEY, J(oseph) R(andolph) (1896–1967), British novelist, memoirist, and belletrist, born in London, educated at Cambridge University. As literary editor of *The *Listener* (1935–59), he commissioned work from writers such as E. M. *Forster and Christopher *Isherwood. *Hindoo Holiday* (1932) describes his experiences as private secretary to an Indian Maharajah. Ackerley shows a determination to accept vagaries of human behaviour, a refusal to judge by conventional standards. His apparently light style conceals sharpness of insight. *My Dog Tulip* (1956) and the successful novel *We Think the World of You* (1960) are born of his intense love for his Alsatian bitch, Queenie; the novel also conveys delicately but surely homosexual entanglement, even if the terms in which it does so belong to an era of proscription. The memoir *My Father and Myself* (1968) tells of Ackerley's discovery of his father's extraordinary double life (he had another family which he concealed from Ackerley's mother). It also delineates in a remarkably candid manner Ackerley's own homosexual life.

ACKLAND, Rodney (1908–90), British dramatist, born in Westcliffe-on-Sea, educated at Balham Grammar School and the Central School of Speech Training and Dramatic Art. He worked as an actor while developing his craft as a playwright. His work includes adaptations, notably of Hugh Walpole's *The Old Ladies* (1935) and Dostoevsky's *Crime and Punishment* (1947), as well as *Strange Orchestra* (1931), *Birthday* (1934), *Before the Party* (1949), *A Dead Secret* (1957), and other original pieces. His best-known and most frequently revived play, remains *The Dark River* (1938), which primarily involves the contrasting reactions of a cross-section of people—some frivolous and nostalgically concerned with the past, others rather more responsibly concerned with the present and the future—to the Spanish Civil War and the dangers posed by fascism. Because of its careful portraiture of individuals cut off in the English countryside, along with its sense that traditional ways of life are threatened and perhaps doomed, it has been compared, albeit generously, with the work of Chekhov. Ackland also wrote numerous film scripts, collaborating with Terence *Rattigan on *Uncensored* and *Bond Street*, and published an autobiography, *The Celluloid Mistress* (1954).

ACKROYD, Peter (1949–), British novelist, poet, biographer, and literary critic, born in London, educated at Clare College, Cambridge, and Yale. London is a touchstone as much as a setting for many of his works. With *Notes for a New Culture: An Essay on Modernism* (1976), Ackroyd announced his impatience with contemporary English culture and the tradition of realistic fiction. He launched into literary fiction with *The Great Fire of London* (1982), in which a film director attempts to recreate *Little Dorrit* in the abandoned wing of a modern prison. *The Last Testament of Oscar Wilde* (1983; Somerset Maugham Award), a fictional memoir told in Wilde's own extravagant voice, is a brilliant parody. **Hawksmoor* (1985; Whitbread Prize) is an astonishing feat of erudite invention. *Chatterton* (1987) features a young would-be poet and an eccentric older novelist persuaded that Thomas Chatterton may have faked his own suicide in 1770 to live on as a great plagiarist. Contributions in Chatterton's 'own' voice offer an alternative theory, while further chapters depict Henry Wallis, halfway between Chatterton's time and our own, painting his famous

'Death of Chatterton' with George Meredith as his model. *First Light* (1989) again displayed Ackroyd's gift for evoking the magic of other arts, in this case both archaeology and astronomy. *English Music* (1992), narrated by Timothy Harcombe, the son of a spiritualist healer practising in London during the 1920s, moves back and forth in time, portraying significant moments in English history through a series of visionary sequences. The past is similarly invoked in *The House of Doctor Dee* (1993) when its narrator, Matthew Palmer, inherits a house in Clerkenwell, formerly inhabited by the Elizabethan magus, John Dee, and is drawn into bizarre negotiations with his dead father. *Dan Leno and the Limehouse Golem* (1994), set in Victorian London, is inscribed with the author's characteristic blend of Dickensian pastiche and contemporary knowingness, and concerns a series of gruesome East End murders, thought to have been committed by a monster from Jewish folklore—the 'Golem' of the title. Amongst those also suspected of the murders, which foreshadow those of Jack the Ripper, are figures as diverse as Karl Marx, George Gissing, and the music hall comedian, Dan Leno. In this, as in his earlier work, Ackroyd mixes fact and fiction, past and present, with apparent indifference to verisimilitude; the result, as ever, is surprisingly plausible. His works of non-fiction include collections of poetry, notably *The Diversions of Purley* (1987), and *Dressing Up* (1979), a study of transvestism and drag. Ackroyd has received wide critical acclaim for his biographies of Ezra *Pound (1981), Charles Dickens (1990) and Blake (1995). His *T. S. Eliot* (1984; Whitbread Prize) greatly contributed to the understanding and desanctification of that monumental figure.

ACOSTA, Oscar (Zeta) (1935–74?), Chicano writer, born in El Paso, Texas. Acosta was a controversial figure whose narratives focused on ethnicity and the cultural history of the Chicano people. Also a lawyer, he was lead attorney for the defence of some of the Chicano movement members whose exploits are detailed in his work. He was a friend of Hunter S. *Thompson and provided the basis for the presentation of his 'sidekick' Dr Gonzo, the attorney, in *Fear and Loathing in Las Vegas* (1972). *The Autobiography of a Brown Buffalo* (1972), his best-known work, is a fictional autobiography describing his transformation from an alienated Chicano poverty lawyer into a major figure in the Chicano movement in Los Angeles; *The Revolt of the Cockroach People* (1973) follows his exploits as he activates the Chicano, and continues to develop his cultural identity. Acosta disappeared in May 1974, when writing a journalistic piece on cocaine smuggling from Mexico into the USA. He was last heard from when he placed a telephone call from Mazatlan, Sinaloa, to his son, Marco. See LATINO/LATINA LITERATURE IN ENGLISH.

ACTON, Sir Harold (Mario Mitchell) (1904–94), British art historian, poet, and aesthete, born in Florence, educated at Eton and Christ Church, Oxford. His early volume of poems *Aquarium* (1923), which appeared while he was at Oxford, was followed by further volumes including *This Chaos* (1930). Acton travelled widely from 1932, in America, Europe, and China. His fascination with China led to the publication of several books on its theatre, culture, and poetry and his novel *Peonies and Ponies* (1941), set in China. Other works include *Prince Isidore* (1950), a fantasy; *Tit for Tat and other Tales* (1972); *The Last Medici* (1932) and *The Bourbons of Naples* (1956), both historical studies. Shortly after service in the RAF during the Second World War Acton began writing the work for which he is best known, *Memoirs of an Aesthete* (1948), his first volume of autobiography which vividly records the first 35 years of his life; *More Memoirs* appeared in 1970. Acton spent most of his life in his family home, 'La Pietra', in the hilly outskirts of Florence. Evelyn *Waugh's character Anthony Blanche (in *Brideshead Revisited*) is thought to be based on Acton.

Ada or Ardor: A Family Chronicle, a novel by Vladimir *Nabokov, published in 1969. Nabokov's longest and perhaps most ambitious novel, *Ada* is, in part, his homage to the nineteenth-century Russian novel, notably Tolstoy's *Anna Karenina* which it most obviously, and parodically, echoes. Though it has an ostensibly historical setting, the novel marks the beginning of Nabokov's 'flirtation' with the resources of *science fiction: the Antiterra of *Ada* is an 'alternative world' that re-imagines pre-revolutionary Russia without invoking precise historical analogies. *Ada* has been seen as Nabokov's **Finnegans Wake* for its multicultural, multilingual allusiveness. Brian Boyd has written a full-length study, *Nabokov's 'Ada': The Place of Consciousness* (1985).

Adam International Review, a literary quarterly published in London since 1941. (*Adam* is an acronym for 'Arts, Drama, Architecture, Music'.) The editor, Miron Grindea (1909–   ), originally from Romania, settled in England in September 1939. Grindea conceived of his journal as a showcase for the best British and European writing, with occasional forays into the literature of other continents. Its contributors, writing both in English and in French, included Anthony *Powell, Max *Beerbohm, W. H. *Auden, H. G. *Wells, Thomas Mann, André Gide, and François Mauriac, sometimes featuring drawings by artists like Picasso and Chagall. Early numbers featured T. S. *Eliot's 'Reflections on the Unity of European Culture' (1946) and 'The Aims of Poetic Drama' (1949), as well as Winston *Churchill on Bernard *Shaw. Others included issues on Proust (with valuable contributions by his biographer, George *Painter), Balzac, Tolstoy, Strindberg, Dylan *Thomas, Evelyn *Waugh, Graham *Greene, and Joyce *Cary. The 300th issue (1965), published in book form as *Adam 300* (1966), contained two hitherto unknown short stories by Chekhov, forty-six letters by Katherine *Mansfield, an unpublished essay by James *Joyce on Defoe, and sketches by Modigliani. *The London Library* (1978) was another issue published in book form. *Adam* is also distinguished by Grindea's lengthy and often provocative editorials. With Stephen *Spender, Benjamin Britten, and Henry Moore he founded, in 1943, the International Arts Guild.

ADAMS, Andy (1859–1935), American novelist, born in Whitley County, Indiana. Adams gained his knowledge of the world 'from the hurricane deck of a Texas horse'; his deep familiarity with the world of the cowboy and cattleman made him one of the few writers of cowboy fiction to have achieved real literary merit. He became a cowboy in Texas, then settled in Colorado from where he wrote *The Log of a Cowboy* (1903), an account of the cowboy's life structured around a cattle drive from the Rio Grande to Montana; it is narrated by the cowhand Tom Quirk, who reappears in *The Matchmaker* (1904) and in *The Outlet* (1905), a more complex work giving detailed depictions of the socio-political dimensions of the cattle drive. *Cattle Brands* (1906) is a collection of stories about frontier life in the late nineteenth century; *Reed Anthony, Cowman: An Autobiography* (1907) is the story of a Confederate army veteran who becomes an influential Texas cattle rancher.

ADAMS, Douglas (Noel) (1952–), British novelist and scriptwriter, born in Cambridge, educated at St John's College, Cambridge. He is best known for *The Hitch-Hiker's Guide to the Galaxy* (1979) and its sequels, *The Restaurant at the End of the Universe* (1980), *Life, the Universe, and Everything* (1982), *So Long, and Thanks for All the Fish* (1984), and *Mostly Harmless* (1992), all of which originated in a 1978 BBC radio series later transferred to television. In these novels, two characters (the human Arthur Dent, and the humanoid alien Ford Prefect, author of the actual *Guide*) travel through space after Earth has been demolished to make way for an interstellar bypass. Their adventures hitch-hiking across the galaxy are picaresque, involving a series of bizarre encounters with alien life-forms, including a super-intelligent species of white mice intent on discovering, with the aid of the vast, organic computer which is the Earth, the meaning of 'life, the universe and everything'. Written in a comic idiom, their adventures parody *science fiction conventions, while subtly extolling the allures of *space opera. A later series of metaphysical detective novels includes *Dirk Gently's Holistic Detective Agency* (1987) and *The Long Dark Tea-Time of the Soul* (1988).

ADAMS, Henry (Brooks) (1838–1918), American historian and man of letters, born in Boston, educated at Harvard. Adams was the grandson of President John Quincy Adams and the great-grandson of President John Adams, and the son of Charles Francis Adams, an ambassador to Britain. He served as his father's secretary in London during the American Civil War. His first published work, on Captain John Smith, appeared in 1867, after which he abandoned any aspirations to political office, and became a writer and teacher of history at Harvard University. Until 1877, he also edited *The *North American Review* and during this period married Marian Hooper, whose later suicide was to throw him into a profound depression. His first major work was the *Life of Albert Gallatin* (1879), a biography in which judicious quotation is interspersed with interpretative commentary. A short stay in Washington produced the novels *Democracy* (1880), a satirical study of Washington politics and which later served as the model for Joan *Didion's novel of the same title, and *Esther* (1884), an astringent portrait of New York society life whose theme is the conflict of science and religion. Other historical works include *John Randolph* (1882) and the monumental *History of the United States During the Administrations of Thomas Jefferson and James Madison* (1889–1891; 9 volumes), which explored the dilemmas of attempting to maintain egalitarian government in a political world whose motivation was to consolidate power. After two visits to Europe, he returned again to Washington where the effects of the contrasting images of the huge dynamo at the 1900 Paris Exposition and the medieval iconography of the Virgin Mary came together to give shape to his historical thought thereafter. In **Mont-Saint-Michel and Chartres* (1904) and *The *Education of Henry Adams* (1907), this was expressed as a contrast between the unity of thirteenth-century ideas as opposed to the dynamism of modern thinking. His application of theories culled from thermodynamics and the dissipation of energy to the study of human history produced some remarkable insights into the nature of historical progress, not least of which is the belief in entropic tendencies in physics and human matters, which undermines the idea of inevitable progress. This notion is continued in *A Letter to American Teachers of History* (1910), where Adams makes an ambitious attempt to generalize history in terms of the laws of contemporary science in a series of speculative essays (e.g. 'The Rule of Phase Applied to History').

ADAMS, Richard (1920–), British novelist, born in Berkshire, educated at Oxford University. His hugely popular first novel, *Watership Down* (1972), a fantasy about a community of rabbits, was enjoyed by both adults and children, and established his curious gift of understanding animals, which are at the centre also of his well-known novels *Shardik* (1974) and *Plague Dogs* (1977). Adams employed a variety of human protagonists in *The Girl in a Swing* (1980), a supernatural thriller, and in *Maia* (1984), an epic fantasy of love and war. *Traveller* (1988) is an unusual account of the American Civil War seen through the eyes of Traveller, General E. Lee's horse, and told by Traveller to Tom, a domestic cat in his stables. Adams has confessed to being more interested in telling a good story than in writing 'great literature', and he has found the literary establishment reciprocating with consistent critical disdain. *The Day Gone By* (1990) is an autobiography.

ADAMSON, Robert (1944–), Australian poet, born in Sydney. As a youth he spent some time in reform schools and in prison. Subsequently he became involved in the development of the 'New Australian Poetry' movement of the 1960s and 1970s becoming editor, in 1970, of the magazine *New Poetry* which was a platform for the movement's predominantly modernist and experimental outlook. His first collection, *Canticles on the Skin* (1970), is largely based on his adolescent experiences. *The Rumour* (1971), whose long title poem is an exploration of the poetic imagination, is experimental in form and was a significant contribution to the new romanticism evolving at that time. The poems in *Swamp Riddles* (1974) display a powerful response to the natural world and the scenery of the Hawkesbury River area where he lives. In *Cross the Border* (1977) the influence of Mallarmé and Arthurian legend is evident. *Where I Come From* (1979) contains poems based on recollections of his early life. Later collections include *The Law at Heart's Desire* (1983), *The Clean Dark* (1989), *Selected Poems 1970–1989* (1990), and *Waving to Hart Crane* (1994). His experimental novel *Zimmer's Essay* (1974; with Bruce Handford) is based on his prison experiences; *Words of the State* (1992), an autobiographical novella, consists of prose passages, poems, and photographs that evoke his childhood and early life.

Adaptation. There is a sense in which every literary work involves some degree of adaptation. From the classical Greek tragedies, which adapted myths, to their Renaissance equivalents, through to the modernist experimentations of the twentieth century, adaptation seems to be a structural literary device. The Roman writers Terence, Plautus, and Seneca adapted the works of the classical Greek playwrights (mainly Euripides). In turn, they provided much of the source material for the plays of Ben Jonson and William Shakespeare. Each case of adaptation involves a complex set of relationships with the original text, ranging from interpretation and modernization to appropriation and critique. The latter is more dominant in the twentieth century, particularly with the rise of *Modernism during its first few decades. Classical texts were adapted as part of Modernism's critique of the European cultural tradition, notably James *Joyce's *Ulysses*, or in an attempt to make a statement about contemporary reality, such as Jean Anouilh's *Antigone*. The relationship between the source text and the adaptation is more complex when it involves a change of genre: this could be from book to opera or, more recently, from book to film. Nineteenth-century novels, in particular, seem to provide good source material for adaptations. Indeed, some scholars believe that the twentieth-century film presents the legacy of the nineteenth-century novel. The rise of cinematic adaptations has given rise to considerable theory in the area.

Adaptation seems to share some of the qualities of the term 'intertextuality' as it was coined by the theorists Mikhail Bakhtin and Julia Kristeva. According to them, intertextuality refers to the way in which a text establishes relationships with other texts, literary or not, diachronic or contemporary, in such a way that it positions itself historically and culturally. In this sense, adaptation can comprise one aspect of the intertextual relationships that a text establishes. In the context of post-modernity where originality and the 'new' are no longer desirable attributes, adaptation acquires new qualities. A play like Heiner Müller's *Quartet* (1982) no longer presents itself as an adaptation although it is based on the eighteenth-century French novel *Dangerous Liaisons* by Le Clos. The same source is adapted by Christopher *Hampton into a play of the same title and then transfers to the cinema. Müller's text does not reveal its sources and, in doing so, claims originality for what is essentially an adaptation. In a characteristically post-modern fashion the reworking of a text becomes such an integral part of its composition that it no longer needs to acknowledge its source. In a way this is formally accepting that any mode of writing involves a degree of adaptation, so much so that this need no longer be stated. See also POST-MODERNISM.

ADCOCK, (Kareen) Fleur (1934–), New Zealand poet, born in Papakura, New Zealand; much of her childhood was spent in Britain. Having returned to New Zealand in 1947, she was educated at the Victoria University of Wellington, where she obtained an MA in Classics. After a period lecturing at the University of Otago, Dunedin, she worked as a librarian at the Turnbull Library in Wellington and then at the Foreign and Commonwealth Office in London after emigrating to Britain in 1963. In 1979 she became a freelance writer. *The Eye of the Hurricane* (1964), her first volume of poetry, was published in New Zealand. Her numerous subsequent collections include *High Tide in the Garden* (1971), *The Inner Harbour* (1979), *The Incident Book* (1986), and *Time-Zones* (1991). A *Selected Poems* was published in 1983. Her earlier verse centred on themes arising from personal relationships and domestic perceptions, which were often treated with unsettling candour. Since the mid-1970s she has displayed an increasing interest in the possibilities of transposing her experience into fictive narratives; 'The Ex-Queen among the Astronomers' is a memorable example of her success in this mode, its opulent imagery woven into stanzas indicating her considerable skills in versification. A similar level of accomplishment is evident in *The Virgin and the Nightingale* (1983), her elegant and often wittily erotic versions of medieval Latin poetry. Her other publications include *Orient Express* (1989), which contains her translations from the work of the Romanian poet Grete Tartler. Adcock has edited various works, which include *The Faber Book of Twentieth Century Women's Poetry* (1987) and the *Oxford Book of Contemporary New Zealand Poetry* (1983).

ADE, George (1866–1944), American humourist, journalist, librettist, and dramatist, born in Kentland, Indiana. Ade was a master of the contemporary vernacular language, especially the slang of the youth of his time; his *Fables in Slang* (1899) were seen as informed examples of the language of the common American. His first play, *The Night of the Fourth* (1901), was a failure but he achieved success with the libretto for *The Sultan of Sulu* (1902), and his libretto for *Peggy from Paris* (1903) confirmed his acceptance in the popular theatre. Success continued with the comedies *The County Chairman* (1903) and *The College Widow* (1904), which was made into the highly successful musical comedy *Leave It to Jane* (1917), with music by Jerome Kern and lyrics by P. G. *Wodehouse. Ade had further success with genial satires on student life, notably *Just Out of College* (1905) and *Father and the Boys* (1908), and with his librettos for the *Fair Co-ed* (1909) and *The Old Town* (1910).

Adelphi, The, a literary periodical founded in 1923 by John Middleton *Murry, who edited it until 1930 and remained influential in determining its character until 1948. Murry's intentions centred on providing a platform for the ideas of D. H. *Lawrence, who contributed nineteen pieces, and himself; he also saw the magazine as a medium for the posthumous publication of the work of Katherine *Mansfield, his wife, who died in the year of its formation. By 1925 financial difficulties became apparent and after a successful appeal for readers' support it was reconstituted as *The New Adelphi* in 1927. Contributors under Murry's editorship included Robert *Graves, Edmund *Blunden, Edwin *Muir, and W. B. *Yeats. Lawrence, who had belittled Murry's efforts, was not featured in *The New Adelphi*, although the last issue Murry edited was devoted to commemorating Lawrence's achievement following his death in 1930. In that year the magazine was taken over by Max Plowman and Richard Rees and reverted to the title *The Adelphi*. Dorothy *Richardson, Herbert *Read, George *Saintsbury, and William *Plomer were among its essayists and reviewers, and poetry by W. H. *Auden, A. S. J. *Tessimond, C. *Day Lewis, and Michael *Roberts was published. During the 1930s contributions from Edmund *Wilson, Theodore *Roethke, James *Thurber, and others added an American dimension. It continued to publish work by emerging authors until it ceased appearing in 1955; Vernon *Scannell, Donald *Davie, Denton *Welch, James *Kirkup, and Charles *Causley are among the writers whose reputations *The Adelphi* helped to establish in its later years.

Admirable Crichton, The, a play by James *Barrie, first performed in 1902. A prominent peer, Lord Loam, his daughters, and others are shipwrecked on a desert island, where English social divisions quickly prove themselves irrelevant. The butler, Crichton, takes command, Loam becomes a 'jolly-looking labouring man', and others find the level their abilities decree. But just as Loam's eldest daughter, Lady Mary, has gratefully accepted Crichton's proposal of marriage, rescuers appear to take the group back home, where the traditional relationships reassert themselves. 'You are the best man among us', Lady Mary tells Crichton. 'On an island, my lady perhaps; but in England, no', he replies, provoking the riposte, 'then there is something wrong with England'. Barrie's view, too, would seem to be that status and talent are often at odds in class-bound Britain; and, though the tone of the play is gentle and humorous, it may be seen as an example of the socially aware drama which, thanks to the efforts of *Shaw, *Granville-Barker, *Galsworthy, and others, was to become increasingly evident in the Edwardian period.

ADNAN, Etel (1925–), poet and writer, born in Beirut to a Muslim Arab father and a Greek mother, educated at the Sorbonne in Paris, and at Berkeley and Harvard in the USA. Though much of her early work was in French, Adnan has, since the early 1980s, written exclusively in English in a variety of genres. Her poetry, collected in volumes such as *The Indian Never Had a Horse* (1982), *The Arab Apocalypse* (1989), and *The Spring Flowers Own and the Manifestation of the Voyage* (1990), covers a range of themes from the natural world to current affairs, but is always marked by autobiographical motifs: expatriation, the Lebanese civil war, the love of women, loss of language, and the confusion of today's world with its shifting boundaries. Two works of prose, the narrative *Paris, When It's Naked* (1993) and *Of Cities and Women (Letters to Fawwaz)* (1993), complement each other and the author's poetry, looking at the century's end with unjaundiced but optimistic eyes. Adnan's acclaimed novel of one woman's fatal struggles with the Lebanese war, *Sitt Marie Rose* (1978), was translated into English in 1982, and is widely considered a feminist classic.

Adrian Mole, see TOWNSEND, SUE.

Adventures of Augie March, The, a novel by Saul *Bellow, published in 1953. A retrospectively narrated autobiography, this picaresque novel charts the life of Augie March, a Chicago Jew, through early childhood to his post-war maturity as a black marketeer in Europe. The opening line, 'I am an American, Chicago born—Chicago, that somber city—and go at things as I have taught myself, free-style, and will make the record in my own way . . .', establishes the novel as a quest for identity. Along the way, Augie March experiences grief, loss, and betrayal, as he outgrows his family (although he remains strongly attached to his mother, Grandma Lausch, and his retarded brother George), the Depression, and Chicago. He goes through a variety of jobs and adventures, from being a 'man at arms' for the crooked businessman William Einhorn then the salesman protégé of Mrs Renling, before meeting the 'upper-class' Thea Fenchel. Escaping this net of wealth for a time, he gets involved in crime with Joe Gorman, and then steals books in order to attend the University of Chicago. After a series of affairs, Augie meets Thea again and they pass through exploits in Mexico, before Augie finally ends up in Europe married to an actress. Moving through different milieux, the novel has a broad linguistic scope, ranging from the language of the Jewish immigrants to the intercourse of University of Chicago intellectuals. Augie's search for his personal integrity is constantly tested through various symbolic encounters, and the novel's conclusion appears to be merely a temporary resolution of stability.

'AE', see RUSSELL, GEORGE WILLIAM.

Aerodrome, see WARNER, REX.

African Farm, The Story of an, see SCHREINER, OLIVE.

AGARD, John (1949–), Guyanese poet, born in British Guiana; he came to England in 1977, where he has worked as a Touring Lecturer for the Commonwealth Institute in London. His poems, often expressed in vernacular and dialect, are written primarily for performance. He is at his best when amusingly satirical. Poems like 'Listen Mr Oxford Don' and 'English Girl Eats Her First Mango', for instance, challenge preconceptions about Caribbean culture. *Mangoes & Bullets* (1985) includes new poems as well as those from such earlier collections as *Shoot Me with Flowers* (1973), *Man to Pan* (1982), *Limbo Dancer in Dark Glasses* (1983), and *Palm Tree King* (1983). Later books include *Lovelines for a Goat-Born Lady* (1990) and numerous books for children, including *Laughter Is an Egg* (1990) and *Grandfather's Old Bruk-a-Down Car* (1994). He is also the editor of *Life Doesn't Frighten Me at All* (1989). See also DUB POETRY.

AGATE, James (1877–1947), British dramatic critic, born in Pendleton, Lancashire, the son of a cotton manufacturer's agent, and educated at Manchester Grammar School. He went into his father's business, and was still working there when, in 1907, he joined the *Manchester Guardian*'s team of reviewers. His first book of essays on the theatre, *Buzz, Buzz!*, was published in 1918, while he was serving as a captain in the Army Service Corps. After the war, he became theatre critic of the *Saturday Review*, moving to *The Sunday Times* in the same capacity in 1923, and remaining there until his death. He was dramatic critic for the BBC from 1925 to 1932; he also wrote novels, and from 1935 onward published his diaries annually under the title of *Ego*. Like Hazlitt, his model, he was most acute when it came to writing about the performers of his day and comparing them to the great actors and actresses of the past; but he also responded enthusiastically to *O'Casey and to Chekhov, whose still unfamiliar *Cherry Orchard* he described in 1925 as 'one of the great plays of the world'.

Age of Anxiety, The, a long poem by W. H. *Auden, published in 1947. Almost entirely in alliterative verse, its six parts are set in wartime New York. Malin, Quant, Emble, and Rosetta, the protagonists, respectively represent thought, intuition, sensation, and feeling, the Jungian psychic faculties, which Auden designates explicitly in *For the Time Being* (1944). As an allegory of the reintegration of the fragmented self, the narrative brings the four, each of whom is drinking alone at the start, into close community. After their philosophical discourse on the human condition in the 'The Seven Ages', the second section, they undertake the revelatory dream-journey of 'The Seven Stages'; this substantial passage forms Auden's most concentrated use of topographical imagery in its elaborately structured landscapes, which sustain symbolic correspondences with the human body. Sections four and five, 'The Dirge' and 'The Masque', unite the four in Rosetta's flat, where the euphoric mood established yields to disillusioned confrontations with reality after they have disbanded. The unconditional acceptance of the Christian existential imperatives in Malin's final speech in 'The Epilogue' provisionally concludes the religious, ethical, and epistemological questings that dominate Auden's poetry of the early 1940s. The theologian Paul Tillich valued the poem highly as a reflection of the spiritual and psychological conditions of its time; Marianne *Moore noted its 'mechanics of consummate virtuosity', indicating the fluency and ingenuity with which its complex patterns of significance imaginatively cohere.

Age of Innocence, The, a novel by Edith *Wharton, published in 1920. It won the first Pulitzer Prize to be awarded to a woman and was dramatized in 1928 by Margaret Ayer Barnes. The young lawyer Newland Archer is about to announce his engagement to May Welland, a beautiful girl from a high society New York family of the 1870s. Although he loves her, he perceives her innocence as artificial. Before their marriage, Countess Ellen Olenska, May's cousin, arrives from Europe after a failed marriage to a debauched Polish count. Owing to social taboo, Ellen has not divorced him, and is shunned by her friends. However, May encourages Newland's support of Ellen, and through his friendship with her he discovers that she possesses the qualities that he sought but did not find in May. Despite his love for Ellen, Newland is forced into a convention-bound marriage to May. Upon learning of May's pregnancy, Ellen returns to Europe. After May's death, Newland visits Paris with his son, Dallas, but whilst now free to marry Ellen, prefers to retain her 'as the composite vision of all that he had missed'.

AGEE, James (1909–55), American novelist, poet, film critic, and screenwriter, born in Knoxville, Tennessee, educated at Harvard. His early collection *Permit Me Voyage* (1934) was the only volume of poems to be published in his lifetime. In conjunction with the photographer Walker Evans, he produced *Let Us Now Praise Famous Men* (1941), a moving account of the plight of Southern sharecroppers during the Depression, which departed from the usual objective reporting for a more subjective, impressionistic style. His best-known fictional works are *The Morning Watch* (1951), dealing with religious piety in a boys' school in Tennessee; and the semi-autobiographical *A *Death in the Family* (1957; Pulitzer Prize). He was a journalist for *Fortune* and *Time*, 1932–48, and a film reviewer and critic for *Nation* and other journals; collections of his writings on film were later published as *Agee on Film* (1958) and *Agee on Film II* (1960). After 1948 he worked mostly as a screenwriter and produced the screenplays for *The Quiet One* (1949), John Huston's *The African Queen* (1951), *The Bride Comes to Yellow Sky* (1953), and Charles Laughton's *The Night of the Hunter* (1955), amongst others. His early friendship with an Episcopalian minister, Father Flye, is recorded in *Letters from James Agee to Father Flye* (1962). *The Collected Poems of James Agee*, edited by Robert Fitzgerald, appeared in 1968.

Agenda, a quarterly journal devoted to poetry and criticism, founded in 1959 by William Cookson. Ezra *Pound, with whom Cookson had corresponded since 1955, was the *éminence grise* behind the magazine and its stated policy of 'communication between isolated outposts' of poetic activity; its interest in foreign poetry was also made clear and early editions featured translations of work by poets from various parts of Europe and elsewhere. Cookson's belief that 'our poetry is to be revitalized . . . by a study of modern American poetry' was reflected in the attention given to American verse; Pound, W. C. *Williams, Louis *Zukofsky, Robert *Lowell, and Theodore *Roethke are among the American poets whose work has been featured and to whom the magazine has devoted special issues. British authors in whom particular interest has been taken include Basil *Bunting, David *Jones, Hugh *MacDiarmid, and Geoffrey *Hill. Special issues have also been produced on particular aspects of poetic technique, notably the 'Rhythm Issue' for Autumn/Winter 1972/3; this took the form of a symposium with W. H. *Auden, Donald *Davie, Thom *Gunn, George *MacBeth, and Charles *Tomlinson among the participants. In 1971 Peter *Dale became Cookson's associate editor; their occasional divergences of opinion have added vigour and balance to the journal, which remains one of the foremost in its field.

Agrarians, The, a name given to specific Southern US poets and writers who espoused an ideology that championed regionalism and an agrarian economy for the South in the late 1920s and early 1930s. This group published *The Fugitive* (1922–5), a bi-monthly magazine based in Nashville, Tennessee, which combined poetry and criticism attacking the 'high-caste Brahmins of the Old South', in the phrase of the editorial. Perceiving themselves to have been invaded by Northern capitalist monopolies, their critique was aimed at what they took to be the cultural provincialism and fast-growing materialism of the region. Most of the contributors were associated with Vanderbilt University, among them Donald *Davidson, Cleanth *Brooks, Andrew *Lytle, Merrill *Moore, John Crowe *Ransom, Laura *Riding, Allen *Tate, and Robert Penn *Warren, and what came to be known as the 'Southern Literary Renaissance' sprang from the work centred on this group. The magazine was also a mouthpiece for the ideology, theory, and techniques of *New Criticism, a form of critical analysis which focused on the elements of the isolated literary work as they illuminate the whole. It characterized itself as upholding, in the poetic and aesthetic realm, the sensuous integrity of human experience which was being demolished by the activities of scientific rationalism.

AI, pseudonym of Florence ANTHONY (1947–), American poet, born in Tucson, Arizona, of mixed Japanese, Choctaw, African-American, and Irish ancestry, raised in Las Vegas and San Francisco, and educated at the University of Arizona where she immersed herself in Buddhism. Her eclectic and peaceable upbringing makes a striking contrast to the world of her first collection of poems, *Cruelty* (1973), soliloquies which speak from, and to, sexual violence, abortion, hanging, the conflicting energies of lust, suicide, and child-beating. AI's style of poetic utterance has rarely been other than tough-edged. In *Killing Floor* (1979), the poem 'The Kid' assumes the voice of a boy-murderer who methodically and pathologically destroys his entire family only to emerge sweet-faced and apparently undisturbed. *Sin* (1986) attempts a yet more complex series of personae—ruminations, for the most part, of men of power, from the Kennedy brothers to Joe McCarthy to Robert Oppenheimer, although in 'The Good Shepherd: Atlanta 1981' the speaker, chillingly, is the anonymous mass-murderer of Atlanta's black youth. *Fate: New Poems* (1991) offers a gallery of characters, notably General George Custer, Mary Jo Kopechne, Elvis Presley, Lenny Bruce, and Lyndon Johnson.

AICKMAN, Robert (1914–81), British writer, born and educated in London. He played an important part in the founding of the Inland Waterways Association after the Second World War. From the publication of *We Are for the Dark* (1951; with Elizabeth Jane *Howard), he became increasingly recognized as a fine exponent of the ghost story. On his title pages, Aickman described his work as 'strange stories'. His collections include *Dark Entries* (1964), *Powers of Darkness* (1966), *Sub Rosa* (1968), *Cold Hand in Mine* (1976), *Tales of Love and Death* (1977), *Intrusions* (1980), *Night Voices* (1985), and *The Wine-Dark Sea* (1988). In his subtle autobiography, *The Attempted Rescue* (1966), Aickman alluded to the coercions of class and family and how they had affected his life. These themes appear frequently in his fiction; from 'The Trains' (1951) and 'Ringing the Changes' (1955) to 'Pages from a Young Girl's Journal' (1973) and 'The Stains' (1980), Aickman consistently represented an invasive 'strangeness' of the world as an analogue of the psychic distress of modern man.

AIDOO, Ama Ata (formerly Christina Ama Aidee) (1942–), Ghanaian playwright, novelist, poet, and short-story writer, born in Ghana, educated at the University of Ghana in Legon, and Stanford University. She has taught at various African universities. Her plays are much concerned with the position of women in African society, and with constructively firm criticism of Ghanaian society. Formally, her work is greatly inspired by oral sources and story-telling traditions. Published plays include *The Dilemma of a Ghost* (1965), about the problems faced by a black American girl who marries into a Ghanaian family, and *Anowa* (1969), a play which reworks an old Ghanaian legend. Other works include *No Sweetness Here* (1971), a collection of short stories; *Out Sister Killjoy* (1977), a novel about a Ghanaian student's critical reactions to European society, and her subsequent reassessment of African society when she returns from her studies in West Germany and London; and *Changes* (1991), a love story. She has also published two collections of poems, *Someone Talking to Sometime* (1985) and *An Angry Letter in January* (1992), which explore her cultural and political concerns for the present state of Africa.

AIKEN, Conrad (Potter) (1889–1973), American poet and critic, born at Savannah, Georgia, educated at Harvard, where he began a long friendship with T. S. *Eliot. During the 1920s he supplied 'Letters from America' for the **London Mercury* and the **Athenaeum*. The narrative poems of *Earth Triumphant* (1914), which reflect the influence of John *Masefield, began his prolific career as a poet; succeeding collections include *The Jig Forslin: A Symphony* (1916), initiating his interest in psychological parable; *The Charnel Rose, Senlin* (1918), a fictionalized verse-autobiography; and *The House of Dust* (1920), a symbolic treatment of the individual's quest for identity in the city, a theme to which he returned in *Brownstone Eclogues* (1944). *John Deth* (1930) revealed the explicitly metaphysical dimensions of his imagination which were most fully realized in the powerful symbolic landscapes of *Preludes for Memnon* (1931) and the dramatic spiritual allegory of *The Coming Forth by Day of Osiris Jones* (1931). Among his later collections of poetry, which expressed his idiosyncratic existential philosophy, were *Skylight One* (1949) and *Letter from Li Po* (1955). Although Aiken was closely associated with the development of poetic *Modernism, his experimental tendencies co-existed with a firm allegiance to the rhetorical effects of Romanticism. His *Collected Poems* of 1953 was revised in 1973. His work as a novelist shares his poetry's preoccupations with psychological and spiritual dimensions of experience. He described *Blue Voyage* (1927) and *The Great Circle* (1933) as 'profoundly autobiographical' in their respective accounts of a writer taking stock of his achievement in mid-career. The leitmotif of journeying as an allegory of psychic development is strongly present in *A Heart for the Gods of Mexico* (1939) and *Conversation, or Pilgrim's Progress* (1940). *Scepticisms* (1919), a collection of his early literary journalism, displays the confidence of judgement and directness of tone that remained characteristic of his criticism. His influential commentaries on the work of a wide range of poets were collected as *A Reviewer's ABC* (1966). The autobiographical *Ushant* (1952, revised edition 1972) is often regarded as the finest of his prose works. A biography by Edward Butscher was published in 1988.

AIKEN, Joan (Delano) (1924–), British writer, the daughter of Conrad *Aiken, born in Rye, Sussex. She is best known for her highly imaginative stories for young children in *All You've Ever Wanted* (1953) and many subsequent volumes. Her sharp sense of fantasy made her tales remarkably unpredictable. Among her novels for older children were *The Wolves of Willoughby Chase* (1962) and its sequels, set in an alternative eighteenth-century England; notable among these was the novel *Is* (1992), which advanced the series to a darkly imagined nineteenth century. Works such as her novels *Midnight is a Place* (1974) and *The Shadow Guests* (1980), and the stories collected in *A Small Pinch of Weather* (1969) and *A Bundle of Nerves* (1976) are also darker in tone. These bear a close resemblance to the occasionally savage adult tales in *The Windscreen Weepers* (1969). Aiken published a series of detective novels in the 1960s, including *Trouble with Product X* (1966) and *Hate Begins at Home* (1967). Historical novels such as *The Lightning Tree* (1980) and *Mansfield Revisited* (1984), which is a continuation of the Jane Austen novel, tended towards black comedy. *The Haunting of Lamb House* (1991), set in Rye, is a ghost story.

ALBEE, Edward (Franklin) (1928–), American playwright, born in Washington, DC, and adopted by a millionaire theatre owner. He had an unhappy childhood, attending expensive private schools and later working at unskilled jobs before becoming established as a writer in his early thirties. Thornton *Wilder encouraged him to write seriously, and he became one of the dominant group in the American theatre in the early 1960s, with Richardson, *Gelber, and *Kopit. All were influenced by European drama in general and by the Theatre of the *Absurd in particular, and *The *Zoo Story* (1959) and *The Death of Bessie Smith* (1960) were first performed in Berlin. These plays, and *The Sandbox* (1960), *Fam and Yam* (1960), and *The American Dream* (1961), represent a concerted onslaught on the corrosive effects of American materialism. His first full-length play, **Who's Afraid of Virginia Woolf?* (1962), made his reputation as a major playwright and continued the attack on middle-class values. *Tiny Alice* (1964) explores both the human and divine realms, being simultaneously a metaphysical and a conventional murder mystery. *A Delicate Balance* (1966; Pulitzer Prize), is an interaction between two couples who end up in despair, incapable of distinguishing between society and self. *Box and Quotations from Chairman Mao Tse Tung: Two Inter-Related Plays* (1968) adopts a more experimental form, in which Albee explores the relationship between art and suffering. In *All Over* (1971), the dying of an upper middle-class man off-stage brings together his family, friends, and mistress in a discussion of his life; by the end, they have all retreated to their own discontented states of self-absorption. In *Seascape* (1975; Pulitzer Prize), a married couple encounter a humanoid from a past evolutionary era. Plays such as *Listening* (1976),

Counting the Ways (1977), *The Lady from Dubuque* (1978), and *The Man Who Had Three Arms* (1983), were less successful. With *Three Tall Women* (1991; Pulitzer Prize), Albee displayed his former energy in a powerful examination of old age and change. He has also adapted for the stage other writers' works, including Herman Melville's 'Bartleby' as an opera (1961), Carson *McCullers' *The Ballad of the Sad Café* (1963), and Truman *Capote's *Breakfast at Tiffany's* (1966). His intention as a dramatist has always been 'to offend—as well as to entertain and amuse'.

ALDINGTON, Richard (Edward Godfree) (1892–1962), British poet, novelist, and biographer, born in Hampshire, educated at University College, London. An early exponent of *Imagism, he met Hilda *Doolittle, whom he married in 1913, through his friendship with Ezra *Pound. He became assistant editor of *The *Egoist* in 1914. His experiences on the Western Front in the First World War engendered the deep embitterment which informs much of his later work. *Images 1910–1915* (1915), his first collection of poetry, was followed by numerous volumes which include *Images of War* (1919), *A Fool i' the Forest* (1925), and *The Crystal World* (1937); a *Complete Poems* was published in 1948. He became widely known as a novelist with the quasi-autobiographical *Death of a Hero* (1929, abridged; Paris, 1930, unexpurgated), which follows the fortunes of its principal protagonist from his youth and unorthodox marriage to death in action in 1918. Among his other novels is *Stepping Heavenward* (1931), substantially a caricature of T. S. *Eliot, who found it deeply offensive. During the Second World War, Aldington settled in the USA and began producing a series of biographies which include *Wellington* (1946); *Portrait of a Genius, But . . .* (1950), his disparaging treatment of D. H. *Lawrence; and *Lawrence of Arabia: A Biographical Enquiry* (1955), which attacked its subject as an 'impudent mythomaniac'. *Life for Life's Sake* (1941) is his autobiography. *Richard Aldington: A Biography* by Charles Doyle was published in 1989.

ALDISS, Brian (Wilson) (1925–), British writer, born in East Dereham, Norfolk, educated at Framlingham College and East Buckland College. He served in the Royal Signals during 1943–7, an experience which generated more than one book. He is best known for his *science fiction works and his involvement in science fiction as a literary genre. His early publications include the fine stories collected in *Space, Time, and Nathaniel: Presciences* (1957); the novel *Non-Stop* (1958), set in the closed world of a slower-than-light starship; and *Hothouse* (1962), a set of linked tales set in the tropical fecundity of a dying Earth—fecundity and death recur in much of his work. Aldiss published essays and reviews from the 1950s and became an unofficial spokesman in the world of letters for the science fiction genre. He eloquently demonstrated its potential and its accomplishments in many anthologies, in collections of essays, such as *This World and Nearer Ones* (1979) and *The Pale Shadow of Science* (1985), and in *Billion Year Spree* (1973), much expanded (with David Wingrove) as *Trillion Year Spree* (1986), a perceptive history of the genre. In this book, and in the novel *Frankenstein Unbound* (1973), he argued that science fiction properly began with Mary Shelley's *Frankenstein* (1819), at the point where Romance met the scientific / industrial revolution. Intense, bleak novels of the early 1960s, such as *The Dark Light Years* (1964), *Greybeard* (1964), and *Earthworks* (1965), were succeeded by a trio of formal and linguistic experiments in *An Age* (1967), *Report on Probability A* (1968), and *Barefoot in the Head* (1969), which consciously applied Joycean experimentation in its depiction of a drug-fuelled war. *The Malacia Tapestry* (1976) parodies the aristocratic, entropy-choked cityscapes of the far future; *Moreau's Other Island* (1980) develops the theme of H. G. *Wells's *The Island of Doctor Moreau* (1896); and in the Helliconia trilogy (*Helliconia Spring*, 1982; *Helliconia Summer*, 1983; *Helliconia Winter*, 1985) he constructed a world on an enormous scale transforming it into a forum for the dramatic representation of humans rooted in time, circumstance, entropy, and death. Among his many collections of stories are *The Canopy of Time* (1959), *The Airs of Earth* (1963), *The Saliva Tree* (1966), *The Moment of Eclipse* (1970), *Last Orders* (1977), *Seasons in Flight* (1984), and *A Tupolev Too Far* (1993); and the two omnibus collections *Man in His Time* (1988) and *A Romance of the Equator* (1989). Non-generic novels include *The Hand-Reared Boy* (1970), *Life in the West* (1980), and *Somewhere East of Life* (1994). *Bury My Heart at W H Smith's* (1990) is a literary memoir.

ALEXENDER, Meena (1951–), Indian poet and writer, born in Allahabad to a Christian family from Kerala, educated at Khartoum University and the University of Nottingham; she subsequently became resident in the USA. After she published several volumes of poetry in India, including *The Bird's Bright Wing* (1976), *I Root My Name* (1977), and *Stone Roots* (1980), she produced *The House of a Thousand Doors* (1989), a volume composed of poems and prose examining the recesses of the author's personal and historical memory, as well as her experiences of travel and migration. The volume of memoirs *Fault Lines* (1992) tells, in lyrical prose that combines the meditative with the analytical, the stories that underlie the poems. *Nampalli Road* (1991) is a novel of social and feminist concerns, including police brutality and rape, set in the Indian city of Hyderabad. *River and Bridge* (1993) is a collection of recent poems, some of an overtly political nature.

Alexandria Quartet, The, see DURRELL, LAWRENCE.

ALGREN, Nelson (1909–81), American novelist, journalist, and short-story writer, born Nelson Ahlgren Abraham in Detroit, Michigan, of a Swedish immigrant family; educated at the University of Illinois, Urbana. Though not a native of Chicago, Algren's writings are associated with that city in a way which invites comparison with the work of Theodore *Dreiser and Saul *Bellow. Algren followed various occupations before assuming editorship of the Illinois Writers' Project for the Works Progress Administration between 1936 and 1940. His first novel, *Somebody in Boots* (1935), placed him firmly in the short-lived American tradition of 'proletarian realism' in its fictionalized account of Algren's own experiences of life as a hobo and itinerant worker; the novel was sympathetically received by left-wing critics eager to praise the tough naturalism of young 'Depression era' writers. *Never Come Morning* (1942) is a violent tale of rape and murder with a doomed Polish boxer as its hero. In its depiction of gang life among the poorer white immigrants of Chicago the novel caused much offence, notably to the Polish Roman Catholic Union which successfully campaigned for the novel to be banned from the Chicago Public Library. It was followed by an important collection of short stories, *The Neon Wilderness* (1946), and the impressive *The Man with the Golden Arm* (1949), which earned Algren the distinction of being the first American writer to receive the National Book Award. The novel had sociological as well as literary importance in its sympathetic and powerfully persuasive depiction of the life of a drug addict; it brought Algren international fame, in part through its screen adaptation (with Frank Sinatra in the lead role). Algren's last novel, *A Walk on the Wild Side* (1956), is an unsuccessful attempt to rework materials and themes from *Somebody in Boots*, but it was his own favourite work and he spoke of it as 'an American fantasy—a poem written to an American beat as truly as *Huckleberry Finn* . . .', and some critics claim that its influence is felt in 1960s films such as *Easy Rider* and *Midnight Cowboy*. A critical biography, *Nelson Algren*, by Martha Heasley Cox and Wayne Chatterton, appeared in 1975.

ALI, Ahmed (1910–94), Pakistani novelist, critic, and poet, born in Delhi, educated at the Universities of Aligarh and Lucknow. Ali was for some years, after his move to Pakistan upon the Partition of India, a diplomat; he served, among other postings, in China. He began his literary career as a short-story writer in his native Urdu in the 1930s; he was associated with the Progressive Writers Association, which brought Marxist and Freudian ideology and a *modernist aesthetic to Indian fiction. Some of his fiction is collected and translated (by himself and his son) in *The Prison-House* (1985), which displays his ability to move from social realism to Kafkaesque political parable. Ali is best known outside Pakistan as the author of the influential novel *Twilight in Delhi* (1940), which deals with the decline of Northern India's Muslim élite at the turn of the century through the eyes of one family and its intimates. His second novel, *Ocean of Night* (1964), the poetic romance of a courtesan with an aristocrat, evokes the Persian and Urdu mystic poetry Ali loved. He also published a volume of poems, *Purple Gold Mountain* (1960), and has edited or translated several anthologies of Urdu literature including *The Golden Tradition* (1973), *Selected Pakistani Stories* (1988), and a translation of the Koran from Arabic (1984).

ALI, Tariq (1943–), Pakistani writer, born in Lahore, educated in Pakistan and at Oxford University. He first gained a reputation as a Marxist journalist and political activist (he was involved with the Vietnam Solidarity campaign), and later worked as a documentary film-maker and television producer. His Marxist orientation is reflected in his first published works, including *Pakistan: People's Power or Military Rule* (1970) and *Can Pakistan Survive?* (1983). Ali turned to creative writing late in his career, with *Partition* (1987), a screenplay adapted from an Urdu short story, which was followed by *Iranian Nights* (1989), a play written with Howard *Brenton, based on the *Rushdie affair. His first novel, *Redemption* (1990), is a satirical comment on the vagaries of the far left in Britain and the consequences upon intellectuals of the fall of Eastern European communism. His next, *The Shadow of the Pomegranate* (1992), set in 1500 in Southern Spain and written to coincide with the commemoration of 1492, is an entertaining account of the fortunes of one Muslim family in the aftermath of the fall of Granada and the rise of Christian fundamentalism in Spain.

Alice B. Toklas, see AUTOBIOGRAPHY OF ALICE B. TOKLAS, THE.

ALLEN, (William) Hervey (1889–1949), American historical novelist, poet, and biographer, born in Pittsburgh, Pennsylvania, educated at the University of Pittsburgh, the United States Naval Academy, and Harvard. His experiences on active service during the First World War inform a number of the poems in *Wampum and Old Gold* (1921), his first book, and are recorded in detail in the autobiographical *Towards the Flame* (1926). With *Israfel: The Life and Times of Edgar Allan Poe* (1926) he established his reputation. His poetry, essentially of an ornately late Romantic character, appeared in numerous further collections including *Earth Moods* (1925) and *New Legends* (1929). *Anthony Adverse* (1933), a novel of some 1,200 pages recording the adventures of its eponymous protagonist during the Napoleonic era, proved enormously successful throughout the 1930s. *Action at Aquila* (1938) took the American Civil War for its setting and anticipated the major engagement with American history he proposed in a five-part treatment of pre-revolutionary Pennsylvania and New York entitled 'The Disinherited'; Allen died before completing the work, three sections of which, *The Forest and The Fort* (1943), *Bedford Village* (1944), and *Toward the Morning* (1948), were posthumously collected as *The City in the Dawn* in 1950.

ALLEN, Paula Gunn (1939–), American writer of mixed Laguna / Sioux and Lebanese descent, born in New Mexico, educated at the Universities of Oregon and New Mexico. She is the cousin of Leslie Marmon *Silko. Allen held a number of academic posts before joining the Native American Studies programme at the University of California at Berkeley. Her writing is inseparable from her political activism as a feminist, pacifist, and environmentalist. As editor of *Studies in*

American Indian Literature: Critical Essays and Course Designs (1983) she has done much to popularize the teaching of Native American literature. Allen sees feminism as synonymous with tribal heritage, an identification explored in her study *The Sacred Hoop: Recovering the Feminine in American Indian Traditions* (1986) and given imaginative treatment in her novel *The Woman Who Owned the Shadows* (1983) in which traditional legends, images, and motifs are used to describe the struggle for survival of a woman of mixed blood; *Grandmothers of the Light* (1992) presents Indian tribal myths. In her writing Allen explores the values of a woman-centred culture which were lost to Native American women with the white invasion of North America. In volumes of poetry such as *Shadow Country* (1982) and *Skins and Bones: Poems 1979–87* (1988), she draws upon female traditions which celebrate continuance in contrast with male traditions of war and death. See also NATIVE AMERICAN LITERATURE.

ALLEN, Walter (Ernest) (1911–95), English novelist and critic, born in Birmingham, educated at Birmingham University. Among his many academic appointments he was Professor and Chairman of English Studies, New University of Ulster, Coleraine (1967–73). In the 1930s he wrote three realistic novels about English working-class life, *Innocence is Drowned* (1938), *Blind Man's Ditch* (1939), and *Living Space* (1940), all set in Birmingham, and reflecting the political and social tensions of the time. His finest novel is generally considered to be *All in a Lifetime* (1959; US title *Threescore and Ten*); through its narrator, an old man in his middle seventies, social change and the rise of the Labour Party are vividly described. Widely known as a critic and literary historian of the novel, his critical works include *The English Novel* (1954) and *The Short Story in English* (1981); and studies of *Arnold Bennett* (1948), *Joyce Cary* (1953), and *George Eliot* (1964), among others. *As I Walked Down New Grub Street: Memories of a Writing Life* (1981) is an autobiography.

ALLINGHAM, Margery (1904–66), British detective story writer, born in London, educated at the Perse School for Girls, Cambridge. With *The Crime at Black Dudley* (1929) she began a series of nearly twenty novels and a number of short stories in which the detective is the languid, blond, and aristocratic Albert Campion, reputedly related to the royal family, a character very similar to Dorothy *Sayers's Lord Peter Wimsey. Allingham writes with great verve and energy; she delights in creating odd, *outré* settings and peopling them with eccentric, but never unbelievable, characters, though she occasionally lapses into melodrama. Outstanding are *Dancers in Mourning* (1937) and *The Fashion in Shrouds* (1938), though the more serious *Tiger in the Smoke* (1952), the story of a hunt for a vicious yet not wholly unsympathetic murderer, is probably her masterpiece. After her death her husband, Philip Youngman Carter, completed an unfinished Campion novel and later added two more to the series.

All My Sons, a play by Arthur *Miller, published in 1947. An Ibsen-like drama of moral evasion and confrontation, it concerns the Keller family, the head of which, Joe Keller, a self-made businessman, has been acquitted of the charge of connivance in the sale of defective cylinder heads to the US Air Force during the Second World War, a crime for which his neighbour and employee, Steve Deever, has been imprisoned. One of Joe's two sons, Larry, has been reported missing and, despite the fact that three years have gone by and the war is over, his mother refuses to believe that he is dead and tries to block the engagement of his brother, the easy-going Chris, to Larry's girlfriend, Annie. It emerges during the course of the play that Joe knew that the cylinder heads were cracked and that he was in fact as culpable—and as responsible for the ensuing deaths of US airmen—as Deever; it is eventually revealed that Larry knew this too, and, far from being killed in action, had committed suicide out of shame. Despite its occasional moments of near melodrama, the play is a powerful work and offers a convincing portrayal of the contradictions of American middle-class life.

ALLOTT, Kenneth (1912–73), British poet, born in Glamorganshire; he grew up in Cumberland and was educated at the University of Durham and St Edmund Hall, Oxford. He became a leading contributor of poetry to **New Verse*, of which he was assistant editor from 1936 to 1939. In 1946 he began lecturing at the University of Liverpool, where he was A. C. *Bradley Professor of Modern English Literature (1964–73). His reputation as a poet rests on *Poems* (1938) and *The Ventriloquist's Doll* (1943), after which he published no further collections. His highly accomplished verse is often intensely atmospheric in its elegiac concern with impending historical catastrophe. Elsewhere the clarity and precision of his imagery, which sometimes suggests a muted surrealism, are used to bitterly satirical effect. *Collected Poems* (1975) contains his two collections together with a number of poems written between 1943 and 1957. His other works include *The Rhubarb Tree* (1938), an ingenious comic novel written with Stephen Tait, with whom he also wrote a dramatic adaptation of E. M. *Forster's *A Room with a View* (1951), and the critical and biographical study *Jules Verne* (1940). He edited, amongst other works, *The Poems of Matthew Arnold* (1965), the standard edition of Arnold's verse, and *The Penguin Book of Contemporary Verse* (1950).

All the King's Men, see WARREN, ROBERT PENN.

ALTHER, Lisa (1944–), American novelist, born in Tennessee, educated at Wellesley College. Alther achieved popular success with her first novel, *Kinflicks* (1976); based on the events of her life after leaving her native Tennessee to move north, the novel explores the nature of the relationship between mother and daughter. Called back home by the imminent death of her mother, the heroine considers all those influences which have shaped and determined her family relationships. Similar concerns are reflected in *Original Sin* (1981), in which a group of characters who have left Tennessee for the North are recalled for a funeral; through the collective recollections of their experiences, Alther presents a satirical view of authoritative social institutions. *Other Women* (1984) explores further the possibilities represented by lesbian relationships, a theme introduced in *Kinflicks* and further examined in *Five Minutes in Heaven* (1995) which also deals with mourning and loss. Alther's vision of personal and political relations is generally pessimistic though she combines this dark view with a powerful strain of black humour, particularly in her use of the grotesque.

ALUKO, T(imothy) M(ofolorunse) (1918–), Nigerian novelist, born in Ilesha, Western Nigeria, educated at Government College (Ibadan), Lagos University, and the University of London. He was director of public works for Nigeria's Western Region, and in 1966 became senior lecturer in engineering at Lagos University. His most accomplished novel, *One Man, One Matchet* (1964), set in pre-independence Nigeria, depicts with comic verve political conflicts between traditionalists and modernizers in a coca-growing village. His first novel, *One Man, One Wife* (1959), was equally shrewd in its depiction of village politics, pitting Christians against the authority of traditional chiefs. Other novels include *Kinsman and Foreman* (1966), about a civil servant's struggles to resist the demands of his relations; *Chief the Honourable Minister* (1970), which deals with the problems of government at the top; *His Worshipped Majesty* (1972), which focuses on the loss of political power by traditional chiefs; and *Wrong Ones in the Dock* (1982), which denounces certain aspects of the Nigerian legal system. Despite his exposure of political chicanery, Aluko, unlike many other prominent African novelists, such as Chinua *Achebe and *Ngugi wa Thiong'o, appears to be a champion of the post-independence élites in government and civil service.

ALVAREZ, Al(fred) (1929–), British critic, poet, and novelist, born in London, educated at Corpus Christi College, Oxford. In addition to his work as a freelance writer, he has held numerous visiting posts at American universities. *The Shaping Spirit* (1958), a discussion of modern English and American poetry, was the first of his critical works. Subsequent studies include *The School of Donne* (1961) and *The Savage God* (1971), which contained his controversial treatment of the suicide of Sylvia *Plath; *Beyond All This Fiddle* (1968) is a collection of his essays. He edited the widely read anthology *The *New Poetry* (1962) and *The Faber Book of Modern European Poetry* (1992). His poetry collections include *The End of It* (1958), *Apparition* (1971), and *Autumn to Autumn and Selected Poems 1953–1976* (1978). His concentrated verse forms are vehicles for poetry of unusual emotional intensity. *Hunt* (1978), notable for the rapidity of its witty dialogue, and *Day of Atonement* (1991), an urgent evocation of London's underworld, are among his novels. Alvarez's other works include *The Biggest Game in Town* (1983), which draws on his enthusiasm for poker; *Feeding the Rat* (1988), a biography of the British mountaineer Mo Anthoine; and *Night* (1995), an exploration of night life, night language, sleep, and dreams.

ALVAREZ, Julia (1950–), American Latina novelist; born in New York, she spent her early years in the Dominican Republic. Alvarez later became a professor of English at Middlebury College, Vermont. Her first novel, *How the Garcia Girls Lost Their Accent* (1991), written in reverse chronological order, recounts the events surrounding the immigration of the fictional Garcia family to the US. Much like Alvarez and her own sisters, the Garcia girls, Yolanda (who acts as Alvarez's alter ego), Carla, Sandi, and Sofia struggle to adapt to their new life and begin the often emotional and challenging process of assimilation into American culture. Her second novel, *In the Time of Butterflies* (1994), is based on the actual lives and tragic deaths of three beautiful convent-educated sisters in the Dominican Republic who are known as Las Mariposas ('The Butterflies'); Alvarez characterizes the voices of the sisters as they describe the everyday horrors of life following their decision to oppose the dictatorship of General Trujillo. Alvarez has been praised for her construction of character and for her use of English to convey the sounds of Spanish. She is also the author of several collections of poetry, most notably *Homecoming* (1984). See LATINO / LATINA LITERATURE IN ENGLISH.

AMADI, Elechi (1934–), Nigerian novelist and teacher, born in Aluu, near Port Harcourt in Eastern Nigeria, educated at University College, Ibadan. After being employed as a surveyor for several years during 1953–60, he became a teacher, and has since held several Government and academic posts in Nigeria. Amadi served in the Nigerian Federal Army (1963–6 and 1968–9). During the Nigerian Civil War (1967–70) he was imprisoned twice by the Biafran government, but on his second release he rejoined the Federal forces. His experiences of the war are detailed in *Sunset in Biafra* (1973), one of the most powerful memoirs to emerge from that conflict. His first novel, *The Concubine* (1966), set in a riverine Delta community, concerns a young woman who brings misfortune to her male admirers; it gives an authentic depiction of traditional village life and also encompasses the supernatural within a convincingly realistic framework. *The Great Ponds* (1969) has similar qualities, focusing on a feud between two groups of pre-colonial villagers over control of a pond which is of immense importance to their livelihood and way of life. *The Slave* (1978) deals with an attempt by a social outcast, and 'osu', or slave of the god Amadioha, to return to his ancestral village; *Estrangement* (1986), set in the aftermath of the Nigerian Civil War, describes the psychological effects of the conflict on some of its survivors. Amadi's dramatic works include the two plays published in *Peppersoup and The Road to Ibadan* (1977) and *Dancer of Johannesburg* (1979).

Ambassadors, The, a novel by Henry *James, published in 1903. When Chad Newsome does not return from Paris to take up his family responsibilities, his mother sends as an 'ambassador' the intelligent and conscientious American editor Lambert Strether. In Paris, he gradually learns the reasons for Chad's desire to remain in the Old World culture, with its fascinations and satisfactions in the shape of the Mme de Vionet. Succumbing to the lifestyle, Strether abandons his mission, and another group of 'ambassadors' are sent to Europe after him and Chad, namely Mrs Newsome's sister, Mrs Pocock, her husband Jim, and Jim's inexperienced sister Mamie. The situation gradually becomes humorous as these people fail to understand how Strether and Chad have been changed. Chad determines to remain in Paris, whilst Strether is persuaded to return to the USA, even though this means the cessation of his attachment to Maria Gostrey, an expatriate who has accompanied his cultural education. The novel deals with James's abiding interest in the cultural differences between Europe and America, and the circles within circles of social and cultural groupings.

Ambit, a magazine founded in 1959 by Martin Bax in an attempt to invigorate British poetry, which he saw as having taken on an apathetic character; since then it has appeared as a quarterly, publishing stories, graphics, critical articles, and reviews. The lively tone of Bax's initial editorials anticipated the flamboyantly irreverent and anarchically experimental character *Ambit* rapidly assumed; the erotic and sometimes scatological tendency of some of the writing and illustrations it carried in the early 1970s caused Roy *Fuller to protest that its Arts Council subsidy should be withdrawn on the grounds that it was 'often pornographic, occasionally obscene'. Alan *Brownjohn, Peter *Porter, Edwin *Brock, Tony *Connor, and Peter *Redgrove contributed poetry in its early years and remained associated with the magazine through the following decades. *Ambit*'s innovative ethos became pronounced in the 1960s when emphatically unconventional work by George *MacBeth, Ivor *Cutler, Eduardo Paolozzi, and others appeared frequently; *concrete poetry and collages combining graphic and textual elements were also regularly featured. The authors whose prose fiction has been published in the journal include Christopher *Middleton, J. G. *Ballard, and William *Burroughs. Gavin *Ewart, Herbert *Lomas, and Vernon *Scannell are among the critics who have maintained *Ambit*'s high standards of reviewing. The magazine is among the most valuable and stimulating to have appeared in Britain since the 1930s.

AMBLER, Eric (1909–), British thriller writer, born in London; he studied engineering at London University, and later worked in advertising. Ambler served in the Royal Artillery during the Second World War, rising to the rank of lieutenant-colonel and becoming assistant director of Army Kinematography; later he produced films for the J. Arthur Rank Organisation and wrote numerous screenplays, his adaptation of Nicholas *Monsarrat's *The Cruel Sea* (1953) being nominated for an Academy Award. Ambler's early thrillers—*The Dark Frontier* (1936) is the first—are usually set in Central Europe or the Levant, and are written, as a conscious reaction against *Buchan and *Sapper, from a left-wing political point of view, illustrated, for example, by the sympathetic portrait of Zaleshoff, a Soviet agent, who appears in *Uncommon Danger* (1937; US title *Background to Danger*) and *Cause for Alarm* (1938). The best of the pre-war novels are *Epitaph for a Spy* (1938) and *The Mask of Dimitrios* (1939; US title *A Coffin for Dimitrios*). Ambler's post-war work is less homogeneous: he has experimented in a number of directions, mingling comedy with suspense, for example, in *The Light of Day* (1962; also published in the USA as *Topkapi*) and *Dirty Story* (1967). The best of the later novels is perhaps *Doctor Frigo* (1974), set in the French Antilles, but *The Night-Comers* (1956; US title *State of Siege*), *The Intercom Conspiracy* (1969), *Send No More Roses* (1977; US title *The Siege of the Villa Lipp*), and *The Care of Time* (1981) are also worthy of mention. An autobiography, *Here Lies Eric Ambler*, appeared in 1985.

American Dream, An, see MAILER, NORMAN.

American Mercury, The, a monthly magazine founded in 1924 with H. L. *Mencken and George Jean *Nathan as editors. Urbanely scathing commentary on the social and cultural follies of contemporary America was Mencken's speciality, the prohibition of alcohol being a recurrent object of his scorn. Nathan directed the magazine's interest towards drama; the entire text of Eugene *O'Neill's *All God's Chillun Got Wings* appeared in the second issue. Although Nathan resigned as co-editor in 1925, he continued to contribute drama criticism until 1930. Literature in general was well represented, Sinclair *Lewis, Theodore *Dreiser, Vachel *Lindsay, Edgar Lee *Masters, Carl *Sandburg, and Sherwood *Anderson being among the writers featured. Hostility was displayed towards authors and movements viewed as pretentious. The first issue contained Ernest Boyd's satirical article 'Aesthete, Model 1924'; Allen *Tate, Malcolm *Cowley, William Carlos *Williams, Hart *Crane, and others responded by publishing a single edition of *Aesthete, 1925*, in which much wit was exercised at the expense of Mencken and his colleagues. American history, literary biography, and aspects of American linguistic usage were subjects of regular articles. Mencken's editorship ended in 1933, when the magazine came under the control of L. E. Spivak. Domestic and international politics became the predominant concerns during its eventual decline to an unimportant right-wing journal. It ceased publication in 1975.

American Tragedy, An, a novel by Theodore *Dreiser, published in 1925. The plot draws on the 1906 New York murder trial of Chester Gillette. Clyde Griffiths, son of poor street missionaries in Kansas

City, yearns for wealth and social status and finds work as a bellhop in a luxury hotel, where he shares the fast life of his fellow workers. But, after a joyriding accident in which a little girl is killed, Clyde flees to Chicago where he meets Samuel Griffiths, his uncle, who employs him in his collar factory in Lycurgus, New York State. Clyde's job is menial and he becomes acutely aware of the wealth his cousins enjoy. He meets and seduces Roberta Alden, a working-class girl, but simultaneously falls in love with Sondra Finchley, a wealthy socialite; by the time Sondra becomes interested in Clyde, he has discovered that Roberta is pregnant. He decides to lure Roberta to an out-of-season lake resort and murder her by faking a boating accident. Clyde loses his nerve at the crucial moment, but Roberta does drown accidentally and Clyde swims to safety. However, he bungles his attempts to cover his tracks and is arrested. Orville W. Mason, a talented district attorney, becomes obsessed with convicting Clyde, and builds up an unanswerable case. Mason's honest thoroughness, coupled with the inept lies of the defence lawyers, prevent the truth from being revealed, and Clyde is convicted, condemned, and executed. See also PROLETARIAN LITERATURE IN THE USA.

AMIS, Sir Kingsley (1922–95), British novelist and poet, born in South London, educated at the City of London School and St John's College, Oxford. He was the father of Martin *Amis. Between 1949 and 1963 he taught at the University College of Swansea, Princeton University, and Peterhouse, Cambridge. Amis won immediate fame with his first novel, **Lucky Jim* (1954); in its portrayal of the *'Angry Young Man', Jim Dixon, a lecturer in a provincial university, the novel displayed an irreverence towards the establishment and a satirical humour which were to characterize his work as a whole. *That Uncertain Feeling* (1955), also with a university setting, confirmed Amis as an iconoclast whose dislike of all forms of dogma allied him as much with satirists on the Left as on the Right. Other novels of the period include *I Like It Here* (1958), set in Portugal; *Take a Girl Like You* (1960), which dealt with the relationship between Jenny Bunn, one of his more sympathetic female characters, and her philandering suitor Patrick Standish, to which he wrote a sequel (*Difficulties with Girls*, 1988); *One Fat Englishman* (1963), about an English academic on sabbatical in America; and *I Want It Now* (1968), which satirizes the heartless amorality of the 1960s, a theme also explored in *Girl, 20* (1971) which deals with a middle-aged man's infatuation with a much younger woman.

Throughout his career, Amis interspersed his comic novels of manners with exercises in a wide variety of fictional genres. *The Anti-Death League* (1966) incorporated metaphysical speculation about the existence of God into a conventional spy story; *The Green Man* (1969) is a ghost story; *The Riverside Villas Murder* (1973) a murder mystery; *Russian Hide and Seek* (1980) an offbeat thriller about the Cold War. Perhaps his most ambitious experiment is *The Alteration* (1976), a dystopian fantasy describing Europe as it might have been if the Reformation had not taken place. Other works of fiction include the blackly comic *Ending Up* (1974), which casts a cold eye on the indignities of ageing and death; *Jake's Thing* (1978), which treats the central character's impotence as a subject for farce; and *Stanley and the Women* (1984), which displays a certain ambivalence towards its hero's misogynistic attitudes. Altogether darker in mood than his earlier work is *The Old Devils* (1986; Booker Prize); set in an imaginary town in South Wales, the novel concerns the relationships between a group of friends who have known each other since their college days in the 1950s, and casts a sardonic eye on a whole range of topics: the problems of ageing, the Welsh character, artistic integrity, alcoholism, and death. *The Folks That Live on the Hill* (1990), set in London, exhibits the hostility towards aspects of life—in particular, changes in sexual mores—and the preoccupation with the decline of Britain which is characteristic of his later novels. The pessimistic and reactionary tone of the work is alleviated, as in most of his novels, by the brilliance of his comic invective. In *The Russian Girl* (1992) Amis returns to the theme of artistic integrity which is contrasted with personal sincerity in its portrayal of the relationship between Richard Vaisey, a married lecturer, and Anna Danilova, the beautiful Russian girl with whom he falls in love. Other less attractive motifs, such as the author's tendency to portray women as selfish and manipulative, also recur. *You Can't Do Both* (1994) attempts to show, in its account of its central character's progression from childhood to disillusioned adulthood, the way that people are shaped by their upbringing. *The Biographer's Moustache* (1995) is a comic work about a snobbish mediocre novelist, and his pretentious chums, who becomes the subject of a biography by a second-rate journalist with a moustache.

Although renowned for his fiction, which also includes several volumes of short stories (including *Mrs Barrett's Secret*, 1993, and *Collected Short Stories*, 1980), Amis was also a poet of considerable repute. His early collections, *Bright November* (1947) and *A Frame of Mind* (1953), indicated his skill in the manipulation of traditional forms and established the dry individuality of tone characteristic of *A Case of Samples* (1956). The latter collection appeared in the same year as Robert Conquest's **New Lines* anthology, in which Amis was represented; the combination of colloquial directness and a scrupulously sceptical intelligence in much of his work of the time identified him firmly as a poet of the *Movement. Later volumes include *A Look Around the Estate* (1967) and *Collected Poems: 1944–1979* (1980); he also edited *The New Oxford Book of Light Verse* (1978) and *The Amis Anthology: A Personal Choice of English Verse* (1988). Amongst other non-fiction works are a study of Rudyard *Kipling (1975), *New Maps of Hell: A Survey of Science Fiction* (1960); *The James Bond Dossier* (1965); and *The Golden Age of Science Fiction* (1981). His *Memoirs* (1991), a collection of autobiographical essays, are notable for their frankness concerning the author's friends and enemies. Amis was formerly married to Elizabeth Jane *Howard. He was awarded the CBE in 1981 and was knighted in 1990.

AMIS, Martin (1949–), English novelist, born in Oxford, the son of Kingsley *Amis, educated at Exeter College, Oxford. Amis began his literary career with *The Rachel Papers* (1973; Somerset Maugham Award, 1974), a scabrously funny account of a young man's sentimental education, narrated in the first person by its precociously articulate 19-year-old hero, Charles Highway. *Dead Babies* (1975) is a surreal black comedy set in a country rectory inhabited by louche, aristocratic Quentin Villiers, his wife Celia, and an assortment of freaks, sybarites, and psychopaths. Amis explored ideas about the nature of identity in his equally disturbing *Success* (1978) and in his later fiction which abounds with doubles, schizophrenics, and mirror images. *Other People* (1981), narrated in the third person, concerns Mary Lamb, an amnesiac wandering the streets of London in search of her lover who may be her killer. The novel contains many passages of fine descriptive writing whose imagery is reminiscent of the *Martian poets. *Money* (1984), set in 1981, concerns the materialistic greed of the period and the disintegration of post-war egalitarianism. Its obese and lascivious hero, John Self, is a film producer entailed in tying up the financial backing for his first major film. Moving between London and New York, the novel chronicles the stages of Self's quest for wealth and sexual gratification and describes his encounters with a variety of grotesques. Despite its overt preoccupation with various forms of exchange, the novel's central theme is the nature of identity. A looming but unspecified catastrophe underlies *London Fields* (1989); set in 1999, it concerns a beautiful *femme fatale*, Nicola Six, whose quest for annihilation unfolds in a background of seedy urban wasteland. Despite its overt concern for the destruction of the planet, the novel is as blackly comic and as stylistically exuberant as much of his work. The more experimental *Time's Arrow* (1991) represents a departure from Amis's previous work; borrowing a narrative conceit from an episode in K. Vonnegut's **Slaughterhouse-Five*, Amis envisages a world where time runs backwards and in which everything, morality included, is turned on its head. This and the fact that the novel's protagonist, first encountered in old age and later seen in earlier incarnations, is a former Nazi officer overseeing the medical experiments on concentration camp prisoners at Auschwitz, provoked controversy when the novel first appeared. *The Information* (1995) was similarly controversial, not so much for its subject, but for the substantial advance (of about £500,000) negotiated by the author's American agent. The novel deals with familiar themes of literary jealousy, the conflict between creative integrity and worldly success, and the breakdown of urban society; with *Money* and *London Fields*, *The Information* completes Amis's 'London' trilogy. Stylistically, Amis remains one of the most inventive of his contemporaries; at its best, his writing displays a sharpness of focus and a linguistic concentration which, while undoubtedly highly mannered, offers diverse pleasures to the reader. This, combined with the appealing cynicism of his observations, has made him one of the most widely admired and imitated writers of his generation. A collection of essays on American themes, *The Moronic Inferno* (1986), includes interviews with writers he admires, such as S. *Bellow and J. *Updike. Other writers for whom he has expressed admiration and whose influence can be discerned in his work include V. *Nabokov, J. G. *Ballard, and J. Borges. He has also published a collection of short stories, *Einstein's Monsters* (1987), which deal with the nuclear threat, and a collection of journalistic pieces and literary criticism, *Visiting Mrs Nabokov* (1993).

AMMONS, A(rchie) R(andolph) (1926–), American poet, born in Whiteville, North Carolina, educated at the University of California at Berkeley. After twelve years as an executive with a glass manufacturing company, in 1964 he began his academic career at Cornell University, where he became Goldwin Smith Professor of English in 1973. The examples of Ezra *Pound and William Carlos *Williams informed the ambitiously inclusive thematic and descriptive scope of his first book of verse, *Ommateum, with Doxology* (1955). *Expressions at Sea Level* (1964) and *Corson's Inlet* (1965) gained him wide recognition and established the disciplined informality of tone and finely cadenced exploratory verse forms characteristic of his work. The title poem of the latter volume is among his best-known works, richly demonstrating the meditative interactions between natural phenomena and the individual consciousness which are central to much of his poetry. The highly discursive verse-journal *Tape for the Turn of the Year* (1965) emphasized his interest in experimentation, its sinuously extended form determined by the decision to compose the poem on a narrow roll of adding-machine paper. Ammons has continued to divide his achievement between long, thematically mobile sequences and shorter lyric treatments in his numerous subsequent books, which include *Sphere: The Form of Motion* (1974), *Six-Piece Suite* (1979), *Selected Longer Poems* (1980), *Lake Effect Country* (1983), *Sumerian Vistas* (1987), *Really Short Poems* (1991), and *Garbage* (1994); *Selected Poems* (1986) is a representative edition of his verse.

ANAND, Mulk Raj (1905–), Indian novelist, born in Peshawar, educated at the Universities of Lahore, London, and Cambridge. Deeply influenced by his years in England, where he was exposed to the aesthetic of the *Bloomsbury set and E. M. *Forster and to the evolving theories of the left, Anand published his first and best-known novel, *Untouchable*, in 1935. The novel, which was dramatized in 1989, centres on the tribulations and aspirations of a young street-cleaner, whose political consciousness is awakened by Gandhi's call for social equality in an independent India. Anand's novels and short stories, including *Coolie* (1936), *Two Leaves and a Bud* (1937), *Across the Black Water* (1940), and *The Sword and the Sickle* (1942) attempt to cross the formal boundaries of the traditional European novel in search of a hybrid genre that combines the intonations of Indian languages and the vitality of indigenous folk-narratives with the techniques of contemporary literary practice. Among subsequent works are *The Big Heart* (1945), *The Private Life of an Indian Prince* (1953), and *The Old Woman and the Cow* (1960; reprinted as *Gauri*, 1976); and four volumes of a projected autobiographical *roman-fleuve*: *Seven Summers* (1951); *Morning Face* (1968); *Confessions of a Lover* (1976); and *The Bubble* (1984), in which Anand breaks away from the restrained narrative methods of his earlier works, combining letters, diary entries, and excerpts from the hero's novel-in-process to polyphonic effect. Anand remains an ardent spokesman for human rights, and is venerated as India's leading man of English letters.

ANAYA, Rudolfo A(lfonso) (1937–), Chicano novelist, poet, dramatist, and writer, born in New Mexico, educated at the University of New Mexico of which he became Professor of English in 1988. He is best known for the trilogy *Bless Me, Ultima* (1972), *Heart of Aztlán* (1976), and *Tortuga* (1979). Anaya's narrative technique weaves together the historical with the mythical, the imaginative or fantastic, and the ritual aspects of Chicano life to explore the conflict between ethnic and Anglo-American cultures. Whether dealing with life in rural New Mexico or in the urban ghettos of modern America, Anaya's enduring concern is with the richness of Chicano culture and the possibilities that are available for Chicano cultural identity. This concern with racial identity and the conflicts involved in the cross-cultural environment of modern America pervades Anaya's work, including the poetry collection *The Adventures of Juan Chicaspatas* (1985), *The Silence of the Llano: Short Stories* (1982), the novel *Lord of the Dawn: The Legend of Quetzalcoatl* (1987), the travel narrative *A Chicano in China* (1986), and the play *The Season of la Llorona* (1979). Anaya has edited the anthologies *Cuentos/Tales of the Hispanic Southwest* (1980) and *Cuentos Chicanos: A Short Story Anthology* (1984), *Voces/An Anthology of Nuevo Mexicano Writers* (1987), and, with Francisco Lomeli, *Aztlan: Essays on the Chicano Homeland* (1989). See LATINO/LATINA LITERATURE IN ENGLISH.

ANDERSON, Barbara (1926–), New Zealand novelist, educated at the Universities of Dunedin and Wellington. She came late to a writing career, beginning with radio plays. Her first book was a collection of short stories, *I Think We Should Go to the Jungle* (1989), praised for its perception of love and grief in everyday life, which earned Anderson comparisons with Raymond *Carver and Flaubert. Her first novel, *Girls High* (1990), set in a school, was less successful, but *Portrait of the Artist's Wife* (1992) confirmed her abilities as a novelist. *All the Nice Girls* (1993), widely considered her finest novel, is a tale of adulterous passion, set in New Zealand in 1962, and containing the characteristic Anderson combination of wit, buoyant prose, and emotional insight.

ANDERSON, Jessica (1925–), Australian novelist and short-story writer, born in Brisbane. She spent several years in England but has lived mainly in Sydney where her first novel, *An Ordinary Lunacy* (1963), is set. *The Last Man's Head* (1970) is an unusual crime novel delivered in her characteristically laconic and ironic style. Her novels display her gift for psychological observation and social commentary. *The Commandant* (1975), a historical novel, concerns the life of Captain Patrick Logan, the commandant of the Moreton Bay penal settlement, but is written from a feminist angle. *Tirra Lirra by the River* (1978) focuses on an elderly woman who returns to her childhood home in Queensland after a long absence spent in Sydney and London. *The Impersonators* (1980; US title *The Only Daughter*) deals with the experiences of an Australian family. *Taking Shelter* (1990) is more experimental in its presentation of the central character's dreams and reflections. *One of the Wattle Birds* (1994) examines deception and the power of the past, through a woman who is haunted by questions about her mother. *Stories from the Warm Zone and Sydney Stories* appeared in 1987.

ANDERSON, Maxwell (1888–1959), American playwright, born in Atlantic, Pennsylvania, brought up in North Dakota, educated at Stanford University. In 1918 he moved to New York where he worked on various journals and helped found *Measure*, a magazine of verse. His own collection of poems, *You Who Have Dreams*, appeared in 1925. His first play, the verse tragedy *White Desert* (1923), was drawn from childhood memories and told the story of damaged lives in North Dakota. Thereafter, he frequently co-operated with either Laurence Stallings, the drama critic of the *World*, or Harold Hickerson, to produce a series of dramas based on social issues in the USA. These included the immensely successful war play *What Price Glory?* (1924); a prose comedy about marriage, *Saturday's Children* (1927); *Gods of the Lightning* (1928), and *Winterset* (1935), both based on the Sacco and Vanzetti case. As well as serious works he demonstrated his skills for comedy in such works as *Both Your Houses* (1933; Pulitzer Prize), a witty satire about political corruption; *High Tor* (1936) and *The Star Wagon* (1937), both comic satires about materialism; and the musical comedy *Knickerbocker Holiday* (1938), a collaboration with Kurt Weill. Anderson specialized in verse-drama, using history to illuminate contemporary issues in *Elizabeth the Queen* (1930), about a love affair between Elizabeth I and Lord Essex; and in *Night Over Taos* (1932), *Mary of Scotland* (1933), *Valley Forge* (1934), and *The Masque of Kings* (1937). He was instrumental in establishing the Playwright's Company in 1938. During the Second World War he wrote both anti-fascist plays and accounts of the lives of ordinary soldiers, with *Key Largo* (1939), about an

American fighting in the Spanish Civil War, *Candle in the Wind* (1941), *The Eve of St Mark* (1942), and *Storm Operation* (1944). He continued to work in a variety of forms and subjects, producing such works as *Joan of Lorraine* (1946), about Joan of Arc; *Anne of a Thousand Days* (1948), a stylized treatment of Anne Boleyn; and the dramatization of Alan Paton's **Cry, the Beloved Country*, entitled *Lost in the Stars* (1948). Other works include *Off Broadway* (1947), a collection of essays on playwriting; *Barefoot in Athens* (1951), about Socrates; and *The Bad Seed* (1954), an adaptation of a novel by William March about an evil child.

ANDERSON, Poul (William) (1926–), American writer of *science fiction and fantasy, born in Bristol, Pennsylvania, educated at the University of Minnesota. A Nordic melancholy runs through much of his fantasy including his best-known works, *Brain Wave* (1954) and *Tau Zero* (1970), but *The High Crusade* (1960) is one of the few humorous science fiction novels of quality. Though the physical range of his science fiction is wide, including several long series set in complex universes, its protagonists share a wry pessimism about any ultimate victory; and his most famous character, Dominic Flandry, serves in defence of a doomed Terran empire. The sequence beginning with *Harvest of Stars* (1993) models a myth of the near future. His shorter work, much of it eloquently based on technological speculations, has been collected in many volumes, notably *The Earth Book of Stormgate* (1978), *The Night Face* (1979), and *The Long Night* (1983).

ANDERSON, Robert W(oodruff) (1917–), American playwright, born in New York City, educated at Harvard. His first play, *Come Marching Home* (1945), is a study in the political idealism of an ex-serviceman whose aspirations conflict with the complacency of the community in which he seeks political election. He is best known for *Tea and Sympathy* (1953; directed by Elia Kazan), which had a broadway run of 712 performances. Set in a New England boys' school, the play deals with a teenager whose shyness and sensitivity set him apart from his peers; suspected of homosexuality, his masculinity is persistently challenged by the headmaster and his own father. The play is notable for its final act in which the headmaster's wife, played by Deborah Kerr, offers herself to the boy to reassure him. Anderson subsequently enjoyed success on Broadway with *You Know I Can't Hear You When the Water's Running* (1967). His other plays include *Love Revisited* (1951), *All Summer Long* (1953), *Silent Night, Lonely Night* (1959), *The Days Between* (1965), *I Never Sang for My Father* (1968), and *Free and Clear* (1983). Anderson has enjoyed respect for his technical skill and his treatment of sex and marriage, but his plays lack the psychological subtlety of contemporaries such as Arthur *Miller, Tennessee *Williams or Edward *Albee.

ANDERSON, Sherwood (1876–1941), American noveliyst and short-story writer, born in Camden, Ohio, into an itinerant poor white family. He served in the Spanish-American War and held a succession of jobs before abandoning his wife and family to move to Chicago in 1912 to become a full-time writer with the encouragement of Carl *Sandburg, Theodore *Dreiser, and Floyd *Dell he published his first novels, *Windy McPherson's Son* (1916) and *Marching Men* (1917), both concerned with the claustrophobia of small town life. It was the appearance of **Winesburg, Ohio* (1919) which first brought him widespread attention, establishing him as a leading figure in the Chicago literary renaissance. The evocation of small town life and distrust of mechanization were to set the tone for much of what followed. Among the later fictional works were **Poor White* (1920), a novel concerning the effects of the invasion of rural life by modern machinery; *Dark Laughter* (1925), whose style is markedly influenced by Gertrude *Stein in its placing value on the 'primitive' over the 'civilized'; and *Beyond Desire* (1932), a novel dealing with the Southern textile mill labour struggles. He also wrote poetry and volumes of social philosophy, of which *Perhaps Women* (1931) is of particular contemporary interest. His short stories, collected in volumes such as *The Triumph of the Egg* (1921), *Horses and Men* (1923), and *Death in the Woods* (1933) were popular at the time. His autobiographical writings include *Tar: A Midwest Childhood* (1925) and *The Story Teller's Story* (1924), the *Memoirs* (1942), and *Letters* (1953). He exerted considerable influence over such writers as *Hemingway and *Faulkner, both of whom owe their first publications to his efforts. His reputation waned in the 1930s and he died in virtual obscurity while travelling in Central America, but his reputation revived in later years.

ANDREWS, Bruce (1948–), American poet, born in Chicago, educated at Harvard. He settled in New York in 1975, where he became a professor of politics at Fordham. He was editor of *L-A-N-G-U-A-G-E* with Charles *Bernstein (1979–81). He is a performance artist and poet whose texts are some of the most radical of the Language school (see LANGUAGE POETRY); his poetry tries 'to cast doubt on each and every "natural" construction of language'. Small linguistic units, idioms, phrases, and single words, taken from different, sometimes mutually exclusive registers, especially discourses which are socially sensitive and resonant to contemporary ears, enable the poetry to 'suggest a *social* undecidability'. *I Don't Have Any Paper So Shut Up (or, Social Romanticism)* (1990) comes as close as any American poet to fulfilling Whitman's aim of allowing the 'forbidden voices, voices of sexes and lusts' to speak, a vast cacophony of urban self-presentational idioms, even when these are in violent opposition to one another. Other works include *Getting Ready to Have Been Frightened* (1978/1988), *Love Songs* (1982), *Give Em Enough Rope* (1987), *Tizzy Boost* (1993), and *Moebius* (1993). His influential essays have appeared in *The L-A-N-G-U-A-G-E Book* (1984) and *The Politics of Poetic Form* (1990).

ANGELOU, Maya (Marguerite Annie Johnson) (1928–), African-American autobiographical writer and poet, born in St Louis, Missouri, educated at Mission High School, San Francisco. She was largely brought up in Stamps, Arkansas by her paternal grandmother and in 1940 she rejoined her mother in San Francisco. In the 1950s she moved to New York, where she joined the Harlem Writers' Guild, performed in off-Broadway productions, and sang in night-clubs. Later she became an administrator at the University of Ghana, and editor of *African Review*. More recently she has been Reynolds Professor of American Studies at Wake Forest University in North Carolina. Best known for her five autobiographical books, the first and best-known volume, **I Know Why the Caged Bird Sings* (1970), powerfully describes her childhood in the American South of the 1930s. *Gather Together in My Name* (1974) continues her story as an unmarried mother in post-war America. *Singin' and Swingin' and Gettin' Merry Like Christmas* (1976) highlights her activities in music, theatre, and dance. *The Heart of a Woman* (1981) focuses on her political activities, particularly with Martin Luther King and Malcolm X, and her short-lived marriage to Vusumzi Make, an exiled South African political activist. The final volume, *All God's Children Need Travelling Shoes* (1986), describes her sojourn in Africa. Angelou is also well known as a reciter of her own verse. Her collections include *Just Give Me a Cool Drink of Water 'Fore I Diiie* (1971), *Oh Pray My Wings Are Gonna Fit Me Well* (1975), and *Now Sheba Sings the Song* (1987). She also wrote plays, including *The Last of These* (1966) and *Ajax* (1974), adapted from Sophocles, as well as the screenplays of *Georgia, Georgia* (1972) and *All Day Long* (1974). *The Inheritors* (1976) is one of her many documentaries about African-Americans written for television. Her press and television interviews have been collected in *Conversations with Maya Angelou* (1989), edited by Jeffrey M. Elliot. See Dolly A. McPherson, *Order out of Chaos: The Autobiographical Works of Maya Angelou* (1991).

Anglo-Saxon Attitudes, a novel by Angus *Wilson, published in 1956. The novel concerns the excavation of a tomb in Suffolk, of the seventh-century Bishop Eorpwald, which has had a profound effect on Anglo-Saxon scholarship. Its central figure is Gerald Middleton, Professor Emeritus of Early Medieval History, who considers the discoveries to be fake, but for his own reasons has concealed this belief from the public. In late middle age he decides that this evasiveness must cease and embarks on a search for the truth, knowing that this will entail a scandal. The story is clearly based on the Piltdown affair and symbolizes the falsehood inherent in the British people's concept of themselves. Situations and people—including Middleton's wife, the idealistic and perverse Ingeborg, and her much-loved son Johnnie—are presented with brilliance and irony, which does not preclude the pathetic or the serious. With its large cast of characters and its complex plot, which serves both to introduce a wide variety of social milieux and to act as a metaphor for the book's concerns, the novel invites comparison with its Victorian counterparts, above all Dickens.

Anglo-Welsh Poetry; although Welsh poets have written work of note in English since the seventeenth century, the term 'Anglo-Welsh poetry' was not in general use until the late 1930s, when it was given currency by Keidrych Rhys's *Wales*, established in 1937, and *The Welsh Review*, edited by Gwyn Jones from its inception in 1939. Among the poets whose work they published were Idris *Davies, Hugh Menai, Glyn Jones, Alun *Lewis, Dylan *Thomas, and Vernon *Watkins. R. S. *Thomas, Raymond *Garlick, and Anthony *Conran were the principal Welsh poets writing in English throughout the 1950s, for whom *The Anglo-Welsh Review*, begun as *Dock Leaves* in 1949, provided a forum. The resurgence of Welsh nationalism during the 1960s gave rise to a period of heightened poetic activity marked by the founding in 1965 of *Poetry Wales* by Meic Stephens; Gillian *Clarke, Tony *Curtis, Robert *Minhinnick, Leslie *Norris, John *Ormond, and John *Tripp are among the poets who have been associated with the journal, which continues to appear. In 1980 Poetry Wales Press was formed and has produced many editions of poetry by Anglo-Welsh authors, latterly under the Seren Books imprint. *The Cost of Strangeness* (1982) by Anthony Conran is a critical survey of Anglo-Welsh poetry, anthologies of which include *The Oxford Book of Welsh Verse in English* (edited by Gwyn Jones, 1977) and *The Bright Field* (edited by Meic Stephens, 1991).

Angry Penguins, an Australian quarterly (1940–6), first edited by Max Harris (later joined by John Reed). It contained poetry and reviews of literature, jazz, film, and sociology as well as art reproduction, from painters such as Sydney Nolan and Arthur Boyd. Where poetry was concerned, the editorial rejection of existing national socialist canons, in favour of the influence of European modernism, was too brash for some tastes, and laid the journal open to the Ern Malley hoax, which effectively killed it. Two poets, James *McAuley and Harold Stewart, who professed themselves anxious about the gradual decay of meaning and skill in contemporary verse, concocted sixteen poems from a mass of printed material, drawn from a swamp drainage report, a dictionary, Shakespeare, and other miscellaneous reading matter, and submitted it to *Angry Penguins* as the work of a recently dead, unknown insurance salesman. Believing it to be a work of originality, the autumn 1944 number became a special issue 'To commemorate the Australian Poet, Ern Malley'. The hoax constituted a triumph for the anti-modernists which resounded internationally, and set back the influence of modernism in Australia for some time.

Angry Young Men, a term that, starting in the mid-1950s, was loosely applied to some of the younger, more alienated and abrasive British dramatists and novelists of the period, among them Alan *Sillitoe, John *Braine, John *Wain, and especially John

*Osborne. Though the expression is sometimes said to derive from the title of a work by the Irish writer Leslie Paul, *Angry Young Man* (1951), its probable inception was an offhand remark by George Fearon, the press officer at the Royal Court when **Look Back in Anger* was first staged there in 1956. According to its author, Osborne himself, in his memoirs *Almost a Gentleman*, Fearon 'looked at me cheerfully as if he were Albert Pierrepoint [the state executioner] guessing my weight: "I suppose you're really an Angry Young Man".' The same catch-phrase, repeated to journalists, became 'a boon to headline-writers ever after'.

Animal Farm, a novel by George *Orwell, published in 1945. Orwell's most famous and widely read work, *Animal Farm* is a political fable that partly recounts, in an allegorical mode, the aftermath of the Russian revolution, and partly illustrates a belief in the universal tendency of power to corrupt. The major characters are all animals, who have overthrown their human masters to establish a collective farm run on egalitarian lines. Before long, a hierarchical power structure re-emerges, with the pigs forming a ruling élite. Their progressive detachment from the rest of the animals has the same alienating effect as the Bolshevik Party's leading role in post-revolutionary Russia. The pigs themselves divide into two factions, led by a Stalin-like Napoleon on one side, and a Trotsky-like Snowball on the other. The heroic sufferings of the Soviet peoples are reflected in the dedication of Boxer the carthorse, who is killed by his Stakhanovite workload, while the idiocies of political orthodoxy are satirized in the behaviour of the sheep with their repeatedly bleated slogan 'Four legs good, two legs bad'. By the end of the story, the pigs' regime has become more savage than the one it replaced, and the final betrayal of the revolution is expressed in the bewilderment of the starved and exhausted 'lower' animals: 'The creatures outside looked from pig to man, and from man to pig, and from pig to man again: but already it was impossible to say which was which.' The most effective writing in the book deals with the attempts of those in power constantly to rewrite history, to redefine what is true and what is false, and to revise the first principles of their political programme. The most memorable example of this tendency in *Animal Farm* is the pigs' reformulation of their original 'commandment', 'ALL ANIMALS ARE EQUAL', to read 'ALL ANIMALS ARE EQUAL/BUT SOME ANIMALS ARE MORE EQUAL THAN OTHERS'. The most controversial aspect of the writing is its tendency to simplify complex historical situations. Partly for this reason, it has been thought a text suitable for children, although Orwell was surprised to discover this, and when it was published went out to remove copies from the children's section in bookshops and place them on more appropriate shelves.

Anna of the Five Towns, a novel by Arnold *Bennett, published in 1902; in it he names and recreates the region portrayed in his best work. It is, in his own words, 'a study in parental tyranny' in its description of the struggles of young Anna Tellwright to resist her rich, miserly father, Ephraim. She boldly burns a bill of exchange to prevent the prosecution of defaulting tenant Willy Price, son of embezzler and suicide Titus Price, but the force of place and custom is too strong for her, and in the end she marries the respectable Henry Mynors. The novel's strength lies not in plot but in the detailed description of Sunday school meetings, financial obsessions, rent collecting, and provincial houses and furniture; and in its one passage of escape, when Anna takes a holiday on the Isle of Man.

Anne of Green Gables, see MONTGOMERY, L. M..

Ann Veronica, a novel by H. G.*Wells, published in 1909. In this novel of suburban rebellion Ann Veronica Stanley, a 21-year-old science student, refuses to accept her father's authority, leaves home, and looks unsuccessfully for work in London. She becomes indebted to Ramage, a businessman who tries to take advantage of her innocence, and falls in love with Capes, a married biology instructor. Meanwhile, her female mentor Miss Miniver introduces her to the suffragette movement. She takes part in an attempt to storm the House of Commons, and is arrested and imprisoned. Once released, she declares her love for Capes and frees herself from her other financial and emotional entanglements. Wells claimed to have been the first popular novelist to portray a sexually aggressive heroine who 'fell in love, and showed it', instead of waiting for the man to make the first moves. Certainly the book caused intense controversy, partly fuelled by the air of scandal surrounding its author at the time of publication. The *Spectator* denounced it as a 'poisonous book' undermining the institution of the family. *Ann Veronica* played a part in the history of women's liberation, despite Wells's hostile caricatures of the suffragette leaders, whose aims he regarded as too narrow. Later feminists have looked somewhat quizzically at what the American critic Freda Kirchwey called Wells's 'Patented Feminism—Very Perishable'; but Ann Veronica's unaffected bluntness and her defiant rejection of the conventional forms of male domination and male posturing make this one of the most vibrant of propaganda novels.

Another Country, a novel by James *Baldwin, published in 1962. Considered by many critics to be Baldwin's finest mature work of fiction, the novel examines, from a variety of perspectives, the lives, destinies, and sensibilities of a group of characters linked by their love for the singer, Rufus. The tragic Rufus dominates the first few chapters, allowing Baldwin to comment on the effect of heritage and history—in Rufus's case, African-American—on the individual psyche. Rufus's unhappy love affair with a white Southern woman mirrors the racial tensions in society at large. His suicide forms the turning point of the novel, since it forces the other characters, women and men, hetero- and homosexual, black and white, to confront their conflicts and desires in search of release from the adversity of their mental and social circumstances. Among these characters are Rufus's sister Ida, her (white) lover Vivaldo, the writer Richard and his wife Cass, and the actor Eric. Baldwin's comprehension of emotions and their social production, the evocative power of his prose, and, above all, his portrayal of Eric—who unintentionally dominates the novel and, in his honest and positive acceptance of his homosexuality, serves as a catalyst for the conflicts of its other characters—combine to make it one of his most important and accessible works, with a relevance beyond the span of its time.

Another Time, a collection of poetry by W. H. *Auden, published in 1940, his first after his move to New York in January 1939. In addition to work produced in England subsequent to **Look, Stranger!* (1936), the volume contained numerous well-known poems written after his arrival in the USA, among them 'In Memory of W. B. Yeats', 'In Memory of Sigmund Freud', 'The Prophets', and 'The Unknown Citizen'. The tonal, emotional, and imaginative range of the collection is considerable, reflecting the extensive revisions in Auden's thinking that took place in the late 1930s: the chilling ballads of 1937 ('As I Walked out One Morning', 'Miss Gee', among others), products of the failure of his political optimism, contrast radically with the warmly affirmative tone of the philosophical love poems, including 'Warm and Still Are the Lucky Miles', 'Heavy Date', and 'Law Like Love', written in 1939; the Christian existentialist position he had adopted after arriving in the USA is apparent in the clarity and confidence of statement exemplified by 'The Hidden Law' and 'Another Time'. The technical compass of the book is also remarkable; the new degree of freedom and flexibility evident in the poised conversational manner typified by 'Like a Vocation' (May 1939) co-exists with the virtuosity in the use of strict rhyming forms that is most apparent in 'The Riddle' (June 1939). The presence of 'Spain, 1937' and 'September 1, 1939', two celebrated poems Auden later discarded, adds to the extraordinary scope and richness of the book, which constitutes the most significantly transitional volume of Auden's career.

ANSTEY, F., pseudonym of Thomas Anstey GUTHRIE (1856–1934), British writer, born in London, educated at Trinity Hall, Cambridge, and trained for the Bar. A prolific author of novels of humour and fantasy, he is best known for his first book, *Vice Versa* (1882), which was filmed by Peter Ustinov and televised; subtitled 'A Lesson to Fathers', the novel concerns a father, Mr Bultitude, who adopts the age and persona of his son (and vice versa) and suffers comically the tortures of a child at boarding school. From 1887 Anstey was associated with *Punch*, in which most of his comic sketches first appeared; these were subsequently collected in volumes such as *Voces Populi* (1890) and *Mr Punch's Pocket Ibsen* (1893). His stories and novels of *fantasy and *science fiction, including *The Tinted Venus* (1885), *A Fallen Idol* (1886), *Tourmanlin's Time Cheques* (1891), *The Brass Bottle* (1900), and *In Brief Authority* (1915), in which Anstey amusingly undercut the assumptions of his world, still give pleasure. The stories in *The Black Poodle* (1884) and *The Talking Horse* (1892) are similarly humorous. His autobiography, *A Long Retrospect*, appeared in 1936.

Antaeus, a literary periodical begun in Tangier in 1969 by Paul *Bowles in association with the publisher Drue Heinz and Daniel Halpern, who has remained its principal editor. The first issue, published in 1970, was followed by a further sixty prior to the appearance of the substantial and attractively produced *Antaeus: Jubilee Edition* in 1990. Among the authors of prose fiction whose work has been featured are Edna *O'Brien, Italo Calvino, Raymond *Carver, John *Fowles, V. S. *Naipaul, and William *Trevor; the poets contributing to the magazine have included W. H. *Auden, Joseph *Brodsky, Czeslaw Milosz, John *Ashbery, Seamus *Heaney, Yanis Ritsos, James *Merrill, and Derek *Walcott. Numerous special issues have concentrated on such topics as autobiography, letters, diaries, and nature writing. During its first two decades *Antaeus* established itself alongside the **Paris Review* as a leading forum for international writing in English and the publication of important work in translation.

Anthills of the Savannah, see ACHEBE, CHINUA.

Anthologies; many anthologies of poetry defining the aesthetic or ideological standpoints of successive schools or movements have appeared in the twentieth century. **Georgian Poetry* (1912–22) disseminated new work by young poets with the intention of revitalizing verse at a time when late Victorian reputations remained predominant. The Georgians, however, were identified with a moribund literary tradition by the Imagists (see IMAGISM), whose first anthology in 1914 formally inaugurated poetic *Modernism. Antagonism towards the Georgians was also expressed by the *Sitwells in annual editions of *Wheels* (1916–21), while Sir J. C. *Squire's *Selections from Modern Poets* (1921–34) defended the conservative position. Subsequent anthologies with an emphasis on innovation include Louis *Zukofsky's *An 'Objectivists' Anthology* (1932; see OBJECTIVIST POETRY) and Ezra *Pound's *Active Anthology* (1933). Michael *Roberts's *New Signatures* (1932) and *New Country* (1933) announced the political orientation of poetry in the 1930s and featured work by most of the decade's best-known British poets. Roberts also edited *The *Faber Book of Modern Verse* (1936), which introduced many of the century's most notable poets to a general readership. J. F. *Hendry's *The New Apocalypse* (1939) named a movement which repudiated the rationalism they saw as dominating the poetry of the day; two further anthologies maintained their ascendancy throughout the 1940s. Reaction against the extravagant romanticism of the *New Apocalypse was signalled by Robert

Conquest's *New Lines* (1956), arguably the last of the pervasively influential anthologies, from which the *Movement emerged as a new poetic orthodoxy. Al Alvarez's *The *New Poetry* (1962, revised 1966), which contested the claims of *New Lines*, and *A Group Anthology* (1963), edited by Philip *Hobsbaum and Edward *Lucie-Smith, both featured numerous noteworthy members of the *Group. The pluralism which increasingly characterized poetry in English from the 1960s diminished the anthology's former importance as a means of asserting the centrality of particular movements. Blake *Morrison and Andrew *Motion, editors of *The Penguin Book of Contemporary British Poetry* (1982), discreetly promoted *Martian poetry; *A Various Art* (1987), edited by Andrew Crozier and Tim Longville, strongly espoused the work of seventeen poets chiefly associated with the British *small presses. There have also been many collections representing the poetry of regions and countries whose literatures are substantially in English, the following being notable among them: *Modern Scottish Poetry* (1986), edited by Maurice Lindsay; *The Bright Field: An Anthology of Contemporary Poetry from Wales* (1991), edited by Meic Stephens; *The Faber Book of Contemporary Irish Poetry* (1986), edited by Paul *Muldoon; *The Heinemann Book of African Poetry in English* (1990), edited by Adewale *Maja-Pearce; *The Faber Book of Contemporary American Poetry* (1985), edited by Helen Vendler; *The Penguin Book of Caribbean Verse in English* (1986), edited by Paula Burnett; and *The Golden Apples of the Sun: Twentieth Century Australian Poetry* (1980), edited by Chris *Wallace-Crabbe. The impact of feminism and revised attitudes to homosexuality during the 1980s were reflected in numerous anthologies, including *The Bloodaxe Book of Contemporary Women Poets* (1985), edited by Jeni *Couzyn, and *Naming the Waves: Contemporary Lesbian Poetry* (1988), edited by Christian McEwen. Anthologies have been devoted to an extraordinary range of subjects and themes, love and war having been given recurrent attention; *The Penguin Book of Love Poetry* (1974) and *The Oxford Book of War Poetry* (1984), both edited by Jon *Stallworthy, are well-known examples.

ANTHONY, Evelyn (1928–), British novelist, born in London; she became a full-time writer in 1949. Among her early historical novels are *Imperial Highness* (1953), on the life of Catherine the Great; the treatments of British monarchs in *Victoria* (1959) and *Elizabeth* (1960); and *Clandara* (1963), which marked her work's departure from its firm grounding in historical fact. *Assassin* (1970), the first of her numerous thrillers in modern settings, was followed by *The Poellenberg Inheritance* (1972), *The Occupying Power* (1973), and *The Grave of Truth* (1979), each drawing on events in the Second World War. Her other publications include *The Tamarind Seed* (1971), which was made into a successful film, and *No Enemy but Time* (1987), centring on political tensions in Northern Ireland.

ANTHONY, Michael (1932–), Trinidadian novelist, short-story writer, and journalist, born in Mayaro, Trinidad. In 1954 he migrated to England where he later worked as a journalist for Reuters in London. During 1967–70 he and his family lived in Rio de Janeiro, Brazil, where he worked as a diplomat, returning to Trinidad in 1970. His novels are very much about the day-to-day concerns of ordinary people, being particularly notable for their focus on childhood, and the child's viewpoint. Two of the best are semi-autobiographical: *The Year in San Fernando* (1965), which plunges into the emotionally insecure world of a 12-year-old boy who works as a servant in the home of an occasionally cruel and thoughtless wealthy family; and *Green Days by the River* (1967), about a boy who misses his father whom, like Anthony himself, he lost at an early age. Other novels include *The Games Were Coming* (1963), *Streets of Conflict* (1976), and *All That Glitters* (1981). His collections of short stories include *Cricket on the Road* (1973) and *The Chieftain's Carnival and Other Stories* (1993). *King of the Masquerade* (1979) is a children's novel. Journalistic works include *Profile of Trinidad* (1975) and *Bright Road to El Dorado* (1982). *The Golden Quest: The Four Voyages of Christopher Columbus* (1992) is a historical study.

Antic Hay, a novel by A. *Huxley, published in 1923. Regarded at the time as an 'immoral' book as much for its intellectual irreverence as for its open depiction of sexual affairs, drug-taking, jazz clubs, and birth control, the novel made Huxley a hero to the younger generation of 1920s readers. The febrile atmosphere of the novel, set amongst post-war London's fashionable artistic bohemia, is indebted to *The *Waste Land*'s diagnosis of spiritual emptiness, in an era of dislocated social values and modernism in the arts. But there are also several comic, even farcical, episodes involving the main protagonist, Theodore Gumbril Jr; especially the Patent Small-Clothes (inflatable underwear) with which he hopes to make a fortune, and his adventures disguised as 'Toto', the Rabelaisian Complete Man. Huxley's satirical wit fixes upon outmoded Edwardian ideals, but also on the excesses of modern artists and scientists. The novel ends appropriately in futility: Gumbril and the Vamp Myra Viveash (resembling Nancy Cunard) taxi back and forth across London in a vain search for drinking companions, disillusioned by sensation-seeking and each other.

ANTIN, David (1932–), American performance poet, born in Brooklyn, New York, educated at New York University. Antin was already the author of several books of poetry, including one of the finest contemporary elegies, 'Definitions for Mendy', when he began experimenting with talks as the basis for making poems. Since 'Talking at Pomona' (*Talking*, 1972), he has not published conventional poems; instead he gives improvised talks for public audiences, and then uses tapes to create a revised version for publication. These performances enable him to make relations between speech and writing, writer and audience, composition and text, highly visible: 'I've never liked the idea of going into a closet to address myself over a typewriter   what kind of talking is that?' Talk interests him because 'a new thing manifests itself in talking before it manifests itself anywhere else', and even 'the self   itself   is emergent in discourse' (his texts have no punctuation, and phrases are grouped together to indicate pauses for thought and breath). Like many of his contemporary New American Poets, he uses autobiography, without confessionalism, as the material for investigating the nature of the self. Antin became Professor of Art at the University of California, San Diego, and questions of aesthetics drawn from his wide knowledge of art history, linguistics, ethnography, and literature are prominent in the talks. His main collections include *talking at the boundaries* (1976), *tuning* (1984), and *Selected Poems 1963–1973* (1991).

ANZALDÚA, Gloria (1942–), Chicana writer and poet, born in Hargill, Texas, educated at Pan American University, the University of Texas at Austin, and the University of California at Santa Cruz. Her approach to Chicana lesbian feminist studies was met with resistance at the academic institutions she attended in the 1980s. She and Cherrie *Moraga co-edited a breakthrough anthology of writings by feminists of colour entitled *This Bridge Called My Back: Radical Writings by Women of Color* (1981) which generated a great deal of interest in Third World feminism. In her major work, *Borderlands/La Frontera* (1987), a highly autobiographical text, Anzaldúa mixes literary genres and freely uses both Spanish and English to convey a sense of her Chicana identity and the Chicano people's cultural *mestizaje*, or blending. The book was highly acclaimed and within two years became widely taught at academic institutions across the USA. *Making Face, Making Soul/Haciendo Caras: Creative and Critical Perspectives by Women of Color* (1990) displays her continuing interest in a wide variety of feminist issues and her commitment to furthering the publication of works by women of colour. See LATINO/LATINA LITERATURE IN ENGLISH.

Apes of God, The, a novel by Wyndham *Lewis, published in 1930. The novel, a satirical *roman-à-clef*, established Lewis's reputation as the scourge of literary London and 'Enemy' of such circles as the *Bloomsbury Group and the *Sitwell coterie, whom he regarded as dilettantes and poseurs. Descriptions of Osbert and Edith Sitwell (Lord Osmund and Lady Harriet Finnian Shaw), Stephen *Spender (Dan Boleyn), and such literary luminaries as V. *Woolf, T. S. *Eliot, James *Joyce, Vanessa and Clive *Bell, Lytton *Strachey, Roy *Campbell, and Edwin *Muir, are portrayed with the savage humour and the eye for graphic detail with which Lewis has become identified. The work, which demonstrates Lewis's theory of the 'external' nature of satire at its most extreme, consists of a series of loosely connected set pieces; the plot, such as it is, follows the meanderings of the imbecilic and beautiful young poet, Dan Boleyn, from one encounter with fashionable literary London to the next, culminating in the satirical *Walpurgisnacht* of the final chapter, 'Lord Osmund's Lenten Party'. Dan's mentor, the sinister Horace Zagreus (whose liking for practical jokes owes something to Virginia Woolf's eccentric friend, Horace de Vere Cole), guides him from Bloomsbury tea-party to lesbian artist's studio to literary luncheon. Lewis himself appears only *in absentia*, as the much reviled writer, Pierpoint—named after the celebrated executioner—whose Nietzschean ideas on the role of the artist in society echo those expounded in Lewis's polemical work, *The Art of Being Ruled*. Despite the work's virtuosity and inventiveness, many readers have found the static, discursive nature of the narrative unrewarding.

Apocalyptic Literature, a term derived from a Greek verb meaning 'to uncover' or 'to disclose' a revelation, hence the title of the last book of the New Testament. The term refers to the end of the present world and the coming of the messiah's kingdom. There is a long tradition of Jewish and Christian apocalyptic writing, but the modern use of the term tends to focus on esoteric or secular endings, particularly those which come about by violence. Thus, *Yeats's poem 'The Second Coming' alludes to the turbulence associated with the end of a 2,000-year cycle, and much of the fiction of J. G. *Ballard can be described as apocalyptic, since it evokes a world threatened or already overwhelmed by nuclear devastation. There has been a strongly apocalyptic vein in *science fiction since the 1960s. F. *Kermode's *The Sense of an Ending* (1967), a chapter of which is called 'The Modern Apocalypse', discusses the implications for fictional narrative of linear views of history and of the images a culture finds for its always approaching end.

Apostles, The, a society founded for discussion and debate at Cambridge University in 1820 under the title 'the Cambridge Conversazione Society'. Because they were twelve in number and tended towards evangelical Christianity, the founding members became known as 'the Apostles'. In the course of the nineteenth century, the society developed into a forum for radical nonconformity and intellectual speculation. Under the presiding influence of G. E. *Moore, the society entered its most celebrated era in the early years of the twentieth century, when its membership included Rupert *Brooke, E. M. *Forster, Roger *Fry, J. M. *Keynes, Bertrand *Russell, Lytton *Strachey, and Leonard *Woolf. Ludwig *Wittgenstein was briefly an active member in 1912. The society was associated with the recruitment of Soviet agents during the 1930s, when Anthony Blunt and Guy Burgess were influential members. Lord Annan, Eric *Hobsbawm, Jonathan Miller, Karl *Miller, and Lord Rothschild are among the more recent distinguished Apostles. Membership of the society is by invitation and its procedures are traditionally cloaked in secrecy. Since the early 1970s women have been admitted. *The Cambridge Apostles* by Richard Deacon appeared in 1985.

Apple Cart, The, a play by G. B. *Shaw, first performed in Polish in Warsaw in June 1929 and in English at the Malvern Festival two months later. Set in the future, it mainly involves conflict between the astute and effective King Magnus and an inept and quarrelsome Cabinet ('like an overcrowded third-class railway carriage') in a Britain where the most powerful institution is a capitalist conglomerate, Breakages Limited, which suppresses every invention that would challenge its programme of planned obsolescence. Magnus argues that he stands above 'the tyranny of popular ignorance' and for 'the great abstractions, for conscience and virtue; for the eternal against the expedient; for the evolutionary appetite against the day's gluttony; for intellectual integrity, for humanity, for the rescue of industry from commercialism and of science from professionalism'. Nevertheless, the Prime Minister, Proteus, presses his ultimatum: if the king will not stop interfering in public affairs, the government will resign. After an interlude with his mistress Orinthia, who unsuccessfully urges him to renounce politics for a 'noble and beautiful life' with her, Magnus tells the Cabinet he will abdicate and run for Parliament, a prospect that frightens Proteus into withdrawing his ultimatum. The country may stutter on; but, in Shaw's anti-democratic view, only an individual with the capacity and courage of Magnus can stand up either to Breakages Limited or to an expansionist USA, which is threatening to annex Britain under the guise of rejoining the Empire.

Arcadia, a play by Tom *Stoppard, first performed and published in 1993. The action of this intricately plotted piece occurs in a mansion called Sidley Park in both the early nineteenth and late twentieth centuries, which allows the same room, often identically furnished, to be used for both periods. Half of the action concerns the Coverly family, in particular the adolescent Thomasina, an embryonic mathematical genius who stumbles on a Second Law of Thermodynamics, among other things. The other half is mainly concerned with the efforts of an academic, Bernard Nightingale, to prove that Byron not only visited the estate but was forced to flee Britain after killing a minor poet in a duel there. His thesis proves to be false, but its unravelling gives the piece much of its tension and, emphasizing as it does the unreliability of probability and the elusiveness of truth, some of its meaning. The overall theme, as befits a play occurring both during the Romantic period and at a time still assessing the implications of Chaos Theory, may be summed up as the breakdown of order: in physics and mathematics, in writing, in sexual mores, and, since Sidley Park is being replanned according to neo-Gothic principles, even in landscape gardening. The premature death of Thomasina, and the shattering effect she and her thinking have on her tutor Septimus, add a strongly emotional dimension to what is always a witty and intelligent comedy of ideas.

ARCHER, William (1856–1924), British translator and dramatic critic, born in Scotland, educated in Edinburgh; he served as a critic for *The World*, *Tribune*, and the *Manchester Guardian*, among other publications. However, his most important contribution to literature and the theatre was to introduce Ibsen to Britain and crusade for the acceptance of his drama. This task began in 1880, when his abridged version of *The Pillars of Society* was produced in London under the title of *Quicksands*, and culminated in the publication of his translation of Ibsen's works in twelve volumes, starting in 1906. Archer also wrote and edited numerous books on drama and the theatre, and had one play performed, a melodrama entitled *The Green Goddess* (1920).

Archetype, a term used to describe an original model, symbol, or theme, which recurs in literature, myths, ritual, fairy-tales, etc. Jung introduced the term into psychology to mean 'a pervasive idea, image or symbol that forms part of the collective unconscious' (*OED*, 1972 Supplement). It also finds its way into literature via the anthropological work of J. G. *Frazer (*The Golden Bough*, 12 volumes, 1890–1915) and Jessie Weston (*From Ritual to Romance*, 1920), who greatly influenced a number of *Modernist writers. Literary criticism with a Jungian slant has devoted itself to detecting archetypal figures such as those of the Divine Child, the Earth Mother, and the Enchanted Prince. Anthropological criticism interests itself in recurring cross-cultural patterns and stories, like rituals of fertility and tales of dying and reborn gods. Critical works reflecting these approaches are Maud Bodkin's *Archetypal Patterns in Poetry* (1934) and Northrop *Frye's *Anatomy of Criticism* (1957).

ARDEN, John (1930–), British playwright, born in Barnsley, Yorkshire, educated at Cambridge University and the Edinburgh College of Art; he briefly practised as an architect. His principal plays are *Live Like Pigs* (1958), about conflict between the 'deserving' and 'undeserving' classes on a housing estate; **Serjeant Musgrave's Dance* (1959); *The Happy Haven* (1960), in which a group of old people rebel against their patronizing doctor; *The Workhouse Donkey* (1963), about a puritan police chief attempting to bring order to a corrupt Yorkshire town; **Armstrong's Last Goodnight* (1964), which some critics view as Arden's best play; *Left-Handed Liberty* (1965), his portrait of King John and what he regards as the failure of Magna Carta; and the sprawling Arthurian epic *Island of the Mighty* (1972), written in conjunction with his wife, Margaretta D'Arcy. *The Hero Rises Up* (1968), about Nelson and Lady Hamilton, *The Ballygombeen Bequest* (1972), about Irish absentee landlordism, and other works are the fruit of the same collaboration. The theme of Arden's earlier work is the difficulty of coercing, constraining, or otherwise controlling the unruly human animal; at best it combines exuberance and colour with intellectual complexity and a refusal to countenance rigid moral absolutes. In the 1970s, however, Arden revised his dramatic beliefs, a process discernible in two radio plays, the autobiographical *The Bagman* (1970) and *Pearl* (1978), about a dramatist trying to forge links between anti-royalist factions in the seventeenth century. What he regarded as widespread social injustice decided him to write committed, polemic plays rather than the intellectually balanced ones for which he had become highly regarded. His first novel, *Silence Among the Weapons* (1982), was followed by several others, including *Jack Juggler and the Emperor's Whore* (1995).

Ariel, Sylvia *Plath's best-known collection of poetry, published posthumously in 1965. Although her preceding volume, *The Colossus* (1960), was accorded a favourable reception, the magnitude of her poetic talent was not apparent until *Ariel* appeared. Its forty poems, mostly in precisely cadenced stanzaic free verse, display remarkable technical assurance; an abundance of acutely vivid visual and tactile imagery gives substance to the directness of statement which forms the basis of much of the poetry. 'Lady Lazarus', strongly informed by her history of attempted suicide, and 'Daddy', a poem alluding to her father's death and her troubled marriage, are notable among the highly dramatic treatments of personal experience which led critics to classify *Ariel* as *confessional poetry. Psychological alienation is powerfully expressed by the estranging accumulations of imagery in 'Tulips' and 'Berck-Plage', two of the collection's most deeply disquieting poems. The feminist critique of social conformity implied at many points is clearest in the blackly humorous commentary on marriage in 'The Applicant'. Elsewhere, Plath writes with brilliant unconventionality of her responses to landscape, as in 'The Moon and the Yew Tree' and 'Letter in November', the latter approaching the purity of lyrical affirmation evident in 'Morning Song' and 'Balloons', poems deriving from her experience of motherhood. Unremitting imaginative energy confers a compelling unity on the collection's varied contents, making it one of the most memorable volumes of poetry to appear in the post-war era.

ARLEN, Michael, originally Dikran Kouyoumdjian (1895–1956), British novelist, the son of an Armenian merchant; he was born in Roustchouk, Bulgaria, but grew up in Britain from 1901 onward, and was educated at Malvern College and Edinburgh University. Having begun publishing his fiction as 'Michael Arlen' he assumed that name when he took British nationality in 1922. Edmund *Goose recommended the publication of *The London Venture* (1920), his first novel. His reputation as a leading novelist of the day was firmly established with *The Green Hat* (1924), one of the best-selling books of the 1920s; vividly descriptive and wittily mannered, its narrative of affluent hedonism, sexual liberation, and bitter disillusionment appealed strongly to the post-war *Zeitgeist*. The book's Mayfair setting and sophisticated social milieu were staple ingredients of his most characteristic work, which also includes the short stories of *These Charming People* (1923) and *May Fair* (1925) and the novels *Lily Christine* (1929), *Men Dislike Women* (1931), *Hell! Said The Duchess* (1934), and *Flying Dutchman* (1939). In the course of the 1930s his popularity declined. He lived on the Cote d'Azur from 1928 to 1939. Following his service with the Civil Defence during the Second World War he moved to the USA in 1945 where he worked as a writer of screenplays.

ARMAH, Ayi Kwei (1938–), Ghanaian novelist and journalist, born in Takoradi, educated at the University of Ghana at Legon, and at Harvard. He worked as a scriptwriter and teacher in Ghana, and was editor and translator for *Jeune Afrique* in Paris. His first novel, *The Beautyful Ones Are not yet Born* (1968), was a bleak, vitriolic attack on widespread corruption in Ghanaian life as he saw it, its title borrowed from a slogan on a 'mammy' wagon, or lorry like the type often used for electioneering purposes. Its fiercely scatological imagery appears to reflect the author's own Swiftian disgust at the broken promises of post-independence politicians. *Fragments* (1970) and *Why Are We so Blest?* (1972) are equally disillusioned, but less vitriolic. *Two Thousand Seasons* (1973) and *The Healers* (1978) display a more expansive historical vision, though still uncompromising in moral stance; the former deals with the depredations of Islam and Christianity against traditional African culture, with *griot* storytellers at the forefront of resistance, and the latter examines the consequences of the British invasion of Asante. See Robert Fraser, *The Novels of Ayi Kwei Armah* (1980).

Armies of the Night: History as a Novel, the Novel as History, The, a novel by Norman *Mailer, published in 1968. The novel is Mailer's on-the-spot report of the huge 1967 march on the Pentagon proclaiming against the Vietnam War, which plays off political protest against private satire and comedy. In exploring the relation of fiction to history, he employs a mode of fictionalized journalism known as the *'new journalism'. The novel has a strictly defined sense of place and time, and the effects which register on the participant-protagonist occur within the given historical facts. The occasional use of other names for the narrator suggests a variety of behaviour—the Ruminant, the Beast, the Existentialist, the Historian, the Novelist, the General, the Protagonist. This improvisation of identities is partly a stylistic device for variety, and partly Mailer's accommodation to the pluralism of American society. The power of the book lies in his analytical writing—his observations of the behaviour of the soldiers, the demonstrators, and his own. The book won a Pulitzer Prize in 1969.

ARMITAGE, Simon (1963–), British poet, born in Huddersfield, West Yorkshire, educated at Portsmouth Polytechnic and the University of Manchester. In 1981 he commenced work as a probation officer in Oldham. Following the appearance of several pamphlet editions of his verse, *Zoom!*, his first substantial collection of poetry, appeared to widespread acclaim in 1989. *Kid* (1992) and *Book of Matches*

(1993), his principal subsequent volumes, established him as one of the most highly regarded poets of the day. The graphically documented engagement with a wide range of social and cultural issues that pervades Armitage's writing repeatedly reflects his experiences as a probation officer. His highly inventive verse is noted for combining remarkably deft technical accomplishment with a wittily robust conversational manner. His other publications include *Xanadu* (1992), which formed the basis for a broadcast in the BBC's 'Words on Film' television series.

Armstrong's Last Goodnight, a play by John *Arden, first performed in 1964. Set in the Scotland of the early sixteenth century and subtitled 'an exercise in diplomacy', it mainly concerns the conflict between Sir David Lindsay of the Mount, James V's tutor and chief herald, and Johnny Armstrong of Gilnockie. The former, 'ane very subtle practiser', undertakes to tame the latter, a wild freebooter whose cross-border raids are imperilling a precarious peace between the English and the Scots. Lindsay persuades the king to make Armstrong his warden and lieutenant, and copes as resourcefully as he can with the enmity his policies cause at court and elsewhere; but he reckons without the waywardness and destructiveness of Armstrong himself. As his secretary tells him, after being fatally stabbed by the fanatical evangelist whom Armstrong has installed in his castle, he 'can never accept the gravity of ane other man's violence'. The play ends with Lindsay not merely renouncing his determination to bring Armstrong 'intil the king's peace and order', but luring him to his death with a false promise of safe conduct. As often in Arden's work, reason proves insufficient when confronted with human complexity and human perversity.

ARNOW, Harriette (1908–86), American novelist, born in Wayne County, Kentucky, educated at the University of Louisville. Her writing career began with the publication of *The Mountain Path* (1936), followed by *The Hunter's Horn* (1949), the second volume of what was to be known as the Kentucky Trilogy. *The Dollmaker* (1954), the trilogy's final volume, remains her most celebrated work, and is widely considered a minor American classic; it tells the story of Gertie Nevels, who, when displaced from her rural home by her husband's migration to work in an urban factory, discovers a talent for whittling figures from wood. Compelled to create a masterwork—which may be an image either of Jesus or of Judas—Gertie nevertheless subjugates her natural gift in the cause of financial survival, producing, instead, cheap dolls for the mass market. Filmed for television in 1982 with Jane Fonda in the title role, the novel raises questions of feminism, creativity, and survival never quite equalled in Arnow's other works, which include the novels *The Weedkiller's Daughter* (1970) and *The Kentucky Trace: A Novel of the American Revolution* (1974).

Artist of the Floating World, An, see ISHIGURO, KAZUO.

Ascent of F6, The, the second and most successful of the dramatic works by W. H. *Auden and Christopher *Isherwood, published in 1936, the others being *The Dog Beneath the Skin* (1935) and *On the Frontier* (1938); all combine verse and prose. It was first produced in 1937 by the *Group Theatre, with music by Benjamin Britten. The narrative is based on Britain's imperialist interest in the conquest of F6, a mountain on the border between British Sudoland and Ostnian Sudoland; the natives of both parts of Sudoland hold F6 in superstitious awe, and will give their allegiance to the first colonial power to mount a successful expedition to the summit. Michael Ransom, the play's hero and a climber of great repute, is asked to undertake the ascent, but refuses until his mother prevails upon him. In the course of the climb all his party are killed; Ransom completes the climb to be confronted by a veiled figure on the summit, who is revealed to be his mother at the moment of his death. The work's satire on political and economic power centres on a group of stock figures who include Lord Stagmantle, a press peer, and General Dellaby-Couch, former military governor of Sudoland; Mr and Mrs A feature throughout as representatives of the general population in touch with events through the medium of the radio. Ransom's psychology is, however, a source of deeper interest in terms of the play's study of the oedipal dynamics of his heroism; it is the last of Auden's works to be dominated by the figure of the leader and, in Edward *Mendelson's interpretation, forms a renunciation of the culturally redemptive terms in which he had formerly conceived of his role as a poet.

ASH, John (1948–), British poet, born in Manchester, educated at the University of Birmingham. He was a teacher and research assistant from 1969 to 1975, and subsequently a lecturer and freelance writer, becoming domiciled in New York in 1985. Initially, his poetry took as its principal models the work of the French Symbolistes, with his responses to the American examples of Wallace *Stevens, John *Ashbery, and others proving formative in his writing's later development. His collections of poetry include *Casino* (1978), *The Bed and Other Poems* (1981), *The Goodbyes* (1982), *The Branching Stairs* (1984), *Disbelief* (1987), and *The Burnt Pages* (1991). An exuberance of aesthetic gesture in a context of wittily rendered urban realism is characteristic of the innovative and attractive quality of much of his poetry. He has also published, with Louis Turner, a work on tourism entitled *The Golden Hordes* (1976).

ASHBERY, John (Lawrence) (1927–), American poet, born in Rochester, New York, educated at Harvard and Columbia Universities. After working as a publisher's copywriter in New York, from 1960 to 1965 he lived in Paris. He wrote art criticism for various periodicals, including *Art News*, of which he became editor upon returning to New York. From 1974 to 1990 he was Professor of English at Brooklyn College, New York. His early collections of verse include *Turandot and Other Poems* (1953), *Some Trees* (1956), for which W. H. *Auden supplied a foreword, *The Tennis Court Oath* (1962), and *The Double Dream of Spring* (1970). With Kenneth *Koch, Frank *O'Hara, and James *Schuyler, Ashbery was a leading member of the *New York School of Poets in the late 1950s; his poetry of the period exemplifies the movement's characteristic use of compelling visual imagery as the active principle in their work. **Self-Portrait in a Convex Mirror* (1975) made him widely accepted as a poet of importance and initiated the preoccupation with long, thematically mobile poems which continued with *Houseboat Days* (1977), *As We Know* (1981), and *A Wave* (1984). Although Ashbery's work has been adversely criticized for its apparent evasions of paraphrasable meaning, its meditative qualities, sharply defined images, and communication of mood relate it to the lyrical and elegiac traditions of poetry. The flux of images and sensations suggested by many of his poems has been identified as an influence in the emergence of *Language Poetry. *Selected Poems* (1985, revised edition 1987) was followed by *April Galleons* (1987), *The Ice Storm* (1987), *Flow Chart* (1991), *Hotel Lautreamont* (1992), and *And the Stars were Shining* (1994). Ashbery's art criticism is chiefly collected in *Reported Sightings: Art Chronicles 1957–1987* (edited by David Bergmann, 1989). His works for the stage, *The Heroes*, *The Compromise*, and *The Philosopher*, were published as *Three Plays* in 1978. *A Nest of Ninnies* (1969), a satirical novel parodying American suburban values, was written in collaboration with James Schuyler.

ASHBY, Cliff (1919–), British poet and novelist, born in Norfolk; he left school at the age of 14 to work as a window-dresser in Leeds. He was subsequently employed in a variety of agricultural and clerical capacities in Yorkshire and London. *In the Vulgar Tongue* (1968), his first collection of poetry, was followed by *The Dogs of Dewsbury* (1976) and *Lies and Dreams* (1980). Much of Ashby's poetry presents versions of his autobiographical and observational experience of the Leeds area with a compelling unsentimentality and documentary vividness. A dourly humorous disenchantment contributes to the remarkable levelness of tone common to harrowingly personal poems and scathing reflections on the spiritual bankruptcy of modern existence. *Plain Song: Collected Poems* appeared in 1985. His uncompromising concern with the quality of life is also evident in his two novels, *The Old Old Story* and *How and Why*, both of which appeared in 1969.

ASHDOWN, Clifford, see FREEMAN, R. AUSTIN.

ASHFORD, Daisy (1881–1972), British child author, born in Petersham, Surrey. She is primarily known for *The Young Visiters*, the short society novel which she wrote at the age of nine. The notebook containing the novel was rediscovered by her in adult life and sent by a friend to Frank *Swinnerton. Published in 1919 by Chatto and Windus, with its original misspellings and an arch introduction by J. M. *Barrie, it was an immediate bestseller. Its child's view of high society (dukes and earls having 'levies' in 'Crystall Pallace') and its heavily romantic plot make it an engaging and enduring popular work. It appeared in an illustrated edition with pictures by Ralph Steadman in the 1960s and was turned into a play in 1920, and into a musical in 1968. In 1965 *Love and Marriage*, which contained two stories by her and one by her sister Angela, also had some success.

ASHTON-WARNER, Sylvia (1908–84), New Zealand novelist and educationalist, born in Stratford, a small town in the farming area of Taranki, educated at Teachers' College in Auckland. An educational innovator who taught predominantly Maori children in small rural communities, such as Hawkes and Bay of Plenty, Ashton-Warner utilized her personal theory of a 'key vocabulary' as a means of releasing the creative energies of her students. Her attempt was to prize creative individuality amongst the most underprivileged, whom other teachers and educational administrators often neglected. She told the story of these endeavours in her first novel, *Spinster* (1958), and went on to produce a number of novels including *Incense to Idols* (1960), *Bell Call* (1964), *Greenstone* (1966), and *Three* (1971), all of which reflect the author's response to education, communication, and the restraints imposed by modern society. Her teaching experiences are recalled in *Teacher* (1963), *Myself* (1967), and *Spearpoint: 'Teacher' in America* (1972). An autobiography, *I Passed this Way*, was published in 1979. The story of her struggle to be taken seriously as both novelist and educator are documented in Lynley Hood's biography *Sylvia!* (1988).

Asian-American Literature is usually centred on the identities of Americans of Asian descent in the context of their immigration histories beginning in 1850 with immigrants from China. Japanese immigrants began to arrive in 1885, followed in the early 1900s by immigrants from South Korea, South Asia, and the Philippines. These periods of immigration occurred in response to shortages of labour in the USA and ended with legislative exclusion. In essays and in the stories collected in *Mrs Spring Fragrance* (1912), Sui Sin Far (Edith Maud Eaton, 1865–1914), the daughter of a British father and a Chinese mother, vividly describes the struggles of immigrant Chinese at a time when US exclusion, alien land, and miscegenation laws made them unwelcome. Carlos Bulosan's *America Is in the Heart* (1946) is another such classical representation, following Carlos, a Filipino immigrant, as he and other migrant workers struggle for social justice and acceptance during a time of nativist American hostility to Asian immigration.

Different immigration histories of national-origin communities give rise to writings reflective of cross-generational concerns and styles. Chinese-language poems written by immigrant Chinese on the walls of the Angel Island detention barracks (*Island: Poetry and History of Chinese Immigrants on Angel Island 1910–1940*, ed. Him Mark Lai and others, 1980), as well as *Issei* (first-generation Japanese-American) *tankas*, have been translated, and added to the archival 'canon' of Asian-American literature. Such heterogeneous representations help to overturn stereotypes of 'inscrutable' Asian-Americans. Three early Asian-American anthologies, *Asian-American Authors* (ed. Kai-yu Hsu and others, 1972), *Asian-American Heritage* (ed. David Hsin-Fu Wang, 1974), and *Aiiieeeee!* (1975), suggested that the 'melting pot' paradigm was inadequate to an understanding of Asian-American cultural identity. Influenced by the 1960s black civil rights movement, the editors of *Aiiieeeee!*, who later published plays (Frank *Chin, *The Chickencoop Chinaman*, 1981), novels (Shawn Wong, *Homebase*, 1979), short stories (Jeffery Paul Chan), and poetry (Lawson Inada, *Legends from Camp*, 1993), went further in adopting a cultural nationalist stance.

Drawn from different national-origin communities, memoirs were the favoured genre with immigrant and first-generation writers. Younghill Kang's *The Grass Roof* (1931), Pardee Lowe's *Father and Glorious Descendant* (1949), and Jade Snow Wong's *Fifth Chinese Daughter* (1950) satisfied an American audience's curiosity about the strangers in their midst. Japanese-American internment history has been a major source for memoirs, poetry, and other literary works (Monica Sone's *Nisei Daughter*, 1956; Jeanne Wakatsuki Houston and James D. Houston's *Farewell to Manzanar*, 1973; and Mitsuye Yamada's poems in *Desert Run*, 1988). Chinese- and Japanese-Americans began publishing imaginative literature in the 1950s (Diana Chang's *The Frontiers of Love* received critical notice in 1956), but South Asian, Vietnamese, Hmong, and other newer Asian-American groups have also begun actively publishing in multiple genres. Wendy Law-Yone's *The Coffin Tree* (1983) narrates a Burmese-American initiation into the USA; Li-Young Lee, an Indonesian Chinese-American, has published poetry (*Rose*, 1986) and a memoir (*The Winged Seed*, 1994), as has Malaysian-American Shirley Geok-lin *Lim (*Among the White Moon Faces*, 1996).

After the awards garnered by Maxine Hong *Kingston's memoirs, *The Woman Warrior* (1976), much Asian-American writing has received critical acclaim; among these are the plays of David Henry *Hwang (*FOB and Other Plays*, 1990) and Cathy *Song (*Picture Bride*, 1983); the poetry of Garrett Hongo (*The River of Heaven*, 1988), Amy *Tan (*The Joy Luck Club*, 1989), Bharati *Mukherjee (*Jasmine*, 1989), and Gish Jen (*Typical American*, 1991); the novels of Faye Ng (*Bone*, 1993), Hisaye Yamamoto (*Seventeen Syllables*, 1988), and David Wong Louie (*Pangs of Love*, 1992); and Wakako Yamauchi's stories (*Songs My Mother Taught Me*, 1994).

In works that treat Asian-American women's struggles against Asian and American patriarchal attitudes, race analysis operates simultaneously with gender analysis. Maxine Hong Kingston's *The Woman Warrior* is a complex series of narratives growing up in an asymmetrically gendered community. The anthologies *The Forbidden Stitch* (ed. Shirley Geok-lin Lim and others, 1989), *Making Waves* (ed. Asian Women United of California, 1989), *Home to Stay* (ed. Sylvia Watanabe and others, 1990), *Our Feet Walk the Sky* (ed. The Women of South Asian Descent Collective, 1993), and others contain writing protesting female subordination and male privilege.

Many Asian-American works still centre on heterosexual characters and focus on identity questions and ethnic community conflicts, among them widely taught works like Toshio Mori's *Yokohama, California* (1949), John Okada's *No-No Boy* (1957), Louis Chu's *Eat a Bowl of Tea* (1961), Bienvenido Santos's *Scent of Apples* (1979), Kingston's *China Men* (1980), and Kim Ronyoung's *Clay Walls* (1987). Many of these fictions are also regionally identified: for example, Okada's, Mori's, Kingston's, and Kim's narratives are set in ethnic-specific enclaves on the US West Coast, and Chu's novel in New York's Chinatown. Works written out of Hawaii, such as Milton Murayama's novel *All I Asking for Is My Body* (1975) and Lois-Ann Yamanaka's poems in *Saturday Night at the Pahala Theatre* (1993), expressing a strong island identity, exploit English registers and dialect resources.

Younger contemporary writers, like novelist Cynthia Kadohata (*In the Valley of the Heart*, 1993) and playwright Philip K. Gotanda (*Yankee Dawg You Die*, 1991), following on Kingston's *tour-de-force* novel *Tripmaster Monkey* (1989), experiment with post-modernist techniques of parody, irony, pastiche, and *bricolage*, challenge the interlocking categories of 'race', class, and gender, and include sexual identity as central to the themes of identity. Using similar techniques, Jessica Hagedorn's *Dogeaters* (1990), set in the Philippines, is a critique of US colonialism and the Marcos military regime, while celebrating Filipino cultural hybridity. Chang-Rae Lee's *Native Speaker* (1995) uses the devices of a thriller to depict the lives of Koreans in New York; the leading themes of the novel are language and identity. Many anthologies offer a range of poetry (*Breaking Silence*, ed. Joseph Bruchac, 1983; *The Open Boat*, ed. Garrett Hongo, 1993), fiction (*Charlie Chan Is Dead*, ed. Jessica Hagedorn, 1993), and drama (*Between Worlds*, ed. Misha Berson, 1990; *The Politics of Life*, ed. Velina Hasu Houston, 1993; *Unbroken Thread*, ed. Roberta Uno, 1993), and testify to the diversity of styles, genres, and voices underlining the vitality of Asian-American writing.

As I Lay Dying, a novel by William *Faulkner, published in 1930. Faulkner's fifth novel, and one of his greatest, it tells the story of Addie Bundren and the ordeals of her husband and children, after her death, as they transport her body in its coffin to the family plot in Jefferson, Mississippi for burial. In the course of their almost epic journey her husband, Anse, her children, Cash, Darl, Dewey Dell, Jewel, and Vardaman, and several neighbours and family friends all reveal their relationship with Addie. We learn that Jewel is her illegitimate son by the Reverend Whitfield, that her daughter Dewey Dell is pregnant and is seeking an abortion, and that Anse is looking for a new wife. Their journey is beset with various mishaps: in trying to cross a flooded river Cash's leg is broken (it is 'repaired' by being set in concrete) and the coffin breaks free and is rescued by Jewel; at another point they stop at a farm barn where Darl, struck by the absurdity of their ordeal, sets fire to the barn in the hope that this will cremate his mother's body, and, again, it is Jewel who saves it from the conflagration. Faulkner, who had a particular affection for *As I Lay Dying*, said that his intention was to subject his fictional family 'to the two greatest catastrophes which man can suffer—flood and fire', though critics have sometimes been more preoccupied by the narrative method he employs: the novel is told in a series of fifty-nine short interior monologues, most of them written in the present tense, which are shared among fifteen different narrators (there is no authorial point of view), including Addie herself, who speaks to us as if from 'beyond'. As a consequence, the reader is prevented from identifying with any one narrator, though Darl with nineteen sections is the most frequently used voice. The novel is notable for its fluctuations in mood and tone from the comic to the tragic. Of all Faulkner's early novels, *As I Lay Dying* most strikingly reveals his prodigious gift for a kind of grotesque comedy. See *Faulkner's 'As I Lay Dying'* (1973) by André Bleikasten.

ASIMOV, Isaac (1920–92), American author, born in Petrovichi, Russia; he grew up in New York, where he was educated at Columbia University. In 1949 he began his academic career at Boston University Medical School, where he later became Professor of Biochemistry. Throughout the 1940s his *science fiction stories appeared in American magazines. The 'Three Laws of Robotics', forbidding robots to harm human beings, which had wide influence over the fictional presentation of robots, were proposed in his celebrated story 'Nightfall', published in 1941. Much of his writing of the period was assembled into *Foundation* (1951), *Foundation and Empire* (1952), and *Second Foundation* (1953), a narrative of the decline and renewal of a civilization in the distant future. Also among the most notable of his earlier science fiction publications are the short stories of *I, Robot* (1950) and *The Rest of the Robots* (1964) and the novels *The Caves of Steel* (1954) and *The Naked Sun* (1957). Basing his lucidly written fiction in highly informed scientific speculation, Asimov was strongly instrumental in establishing the concept of variable futures as an essential of much science fiction writing. After producing comparatively little science fiction from about 1960 onward, he extended the imaginative ambit of his earlier work in numerous novels, among them *Foundation's Edge* (1982), *The Robots of Dawn* (1983), *Prelude to Foundation* (1988), and *Forward the Foundation* (1993). *The Complete Stories* appeared in two volumes in 1990 and 1992. The extraordinarily prolific Asimov published almost 500 works including science fiction, scientific works, histories, and writing in other genres. *Magic* (1996; stories and essays) appeared posthumously. *In Memory Yet Green* (1979) and *In Joy Still Felt* (1980) are autobiographies. See UTOPIA AND ANTI-UTOPIA.

As I Walked Out One Midsummer Morning, see LEE, LAURIE.

Assistant, The, a novel by Bernard *Malamud, published in 1957. A naturalistic novel, it focuses upon a Jewish grocer, Morris Bober, whose attempts to eke out a decent living in a small shop in New York are constantly running into failure. The Gentile Italian small-time thief Frankie Alpine holds up the shop and then, stricken with guilt, returns to act as Bober's assistant. After a period of despising Bober's patient suffering, Frankie slowly adopts the grocer's role when Bober dies of pneumonia. Frankie falls in love with Bober's daughter, Helen, who is initially repulsed by him, and after a brief relationship, they part. Frankie appears to become a substitute for Bober's role as he undergoes a purification through pain and suffering. The novel describes a man who searches for expiation for his crimes, but actually only compounds his guilt. This sharpens Malamud's general focus on the definition of the Jew as a suffering human with a good heart. The novel also explores the collision between emotional bonds and cultural barriers in its representation of the tensions and ambiguous connections between the Jews and Gentiles in New York.

ASTLEY, Thea (1925–), Australian novelist and short-story writer, born in Brisbane, educated at the University of Queensland. She worked as a schoolteacher in Queensland and in New South Wales, then taught at Sydney's Macquarie University (1968–80). Her fiction shrewdly examines the vanities of social existence through a complex tension between perceptive and insensitive characters, and always with a wry humour and alertness to detail. Portraits of bigotry and destructive ill-will in small-town northern Queensland life are sobering in, for example, the novels *A Descant for Gossips* (1960) and *A Kindness Cup* (1974). In *The Well-Dressed Explorer* (1962) and *The Acolyte* (1972) she drew more generally on the all-consuming selfishness of the central characters. *An Item from the Late News* (1982), set in a dilapidated mining town, employed reference to myths ancient and modern in demonstrating Astley's talent for exploring situations in which individuals seek to preserve their identity in the face of collapsing social and religious values; *Beachmasters* (1985) charted the legacy of American presence in the Pacific during the Second World War. *Hunting the Wild Pineapple* (1979) is a collection of short stories; *It's Raining in Mango: Pictures from a Family Album* (1987) is a series of interlinked stories placing one family's development in the context of North Queensland's own. *Reaching Tin River* (1989), a new departure in her work, concentrating on the heroine's personal search for a mother, a father, and for herself, was followed by *The Slow Natives* (1990). The two novellas that form *Vanishing*

Points (1992) are also linked by characters and theme; *Coda* (1994), a satirical view of old age, is a recent novel. The recipient of numerous awards, Astley was made a creative fellow of the Australia Council in 1993.

Athenaeum, The, a periodical devoted to literature, art, and science founded in 1828 by J. S. Buckingham, who was succeeded as editor in 1830 by Charles Dilke, under whose direction it became the best-selling weekly magazine of its kind. Charles Lamb, W. S. Landor, Thomas Carlyle, Robert Browning, and Walter Pater were among the contributors who established its reputation for the quality of its critical commentaries on literature, drama, painting, and music. The *Athenaeum*'s most memorable period in the twentieth century was under John Middleton *Murry's editorship between 1919 and 1921, when T. S. *Eliot contributed some thirty-five items; work by Edith *Sitwell, Robert *Graves, Wilfred *Owen, Edmund *Blunden, and Aldous *Huxley was also published. In 1921 it merged with the *Nation* and continued for ten years as the *Nation and Athenaeum*; from 1923 it became a mouthpiece for liberal political opinion under the control of a group led by J. M. *Keynes. Leonard *Woolf was editor of its literary pages, which published writing by Virginia *Woolf, Lytton *Strachey, Gilbert Murray, and Maxim Gorky. In 1931 a further merger with the **New Statesman* effectively marked the end of the *Athenaeum*. L. A. Marchand's study *The Athenaeum* appeared in 1941.

ATHERTON, Gertrude (Franklin, née Horn) (1857–1948), American novelist, born in San Francisco, educated in private schools in California and Kentucky. Atherton's reputation has grown increasingly, due to the critical preoccupation with American women's writing, and a renewed interest in the literature of the Far West. Her first work of fiction, *What Dreams May Come*, appeared in 1888 but her best work dates from the turn of the century. *The Californians* (1898) deals intelligently with the conflict of Anglo-Saxon and Hispanic culture; she also wrote what have been called 'society novels', among which are *Julia France and Her Times* (1912) and *Black Oxen* (1923). She was both prolific and successful, and in addition to works of fiction wrote *California: An Intimate History* (1914, 1927), three volumes of essays, and a volume of autobiography, *Adventures of a Novelist* (1932). She was elected a Chevalier of the Legion d'Honneur in 1925 and was president of the American National Academy of Literature in 1934. *Atherton* (1979) by Charlotte S. McClure is a critical study.

At Swim-Two-Birds, Flann *O'Brien's first novel, published in 1939. Graham *Greene, then a publisher's reader, recommended its acceptance, noting O'Brien's attempt 'to present, simultaneously, as it were, all the literary traditions of Ireland'. The book is strongly informed by the author's familiarity with Gaelic literature; *The Madness of Sweeney*, a long Middle Irish poem whose hero is cursed with peripatetic derangement, forms a basis for one of the principal dimensions of fantasy. Pastiches of numerous modern and traditional genres are central to O'Brien's methods. The experimental character of *At Swim-Two-Birds* shows the influence of James *Joyce, who eventually acclaimed the novel, while its fantastic aspects recall James *Stephens's writing. It is considered a work of *post-modernism *avant la lettre* for the textual reflexiveness and explication of the processes of fiction inherent in its stratified narrative: the first-person narrator is a Dublin student writing a novel in which an author named Trellis is working on a book using his technique of 'aestho-autogamy'; by this means Trellis's characters come to life and one begins his own novel in which Trellis is entrapped as a fictional creation. This ingeniously complex plot is handled with great dexterity and provides the means by which *At Swim-Two-Birds* achieves its enormous diversity and great range of tones. Dylan *Thomas stated in a review that the book 'establishes Mr O'Brien in the forefront of contemporary writing'; it did not, however, command a wide readership until its re-appearance in 1960.

ATWOOD, Margaret (1939–), Canadian novelist, poet, and critic, born in Ottawa, educated at the University of Toronto, and at Radcliffe College. After an early collection of poems, *Double Persephone* (1961), the highly acclaimed collection *The Circle Game* (1966) established Atwood as one of her generation's foremost Canadian poets, matched by a reputation as an outspoken feminist critic. Her first novel, *The Edible Woman* (1969), adopts the mode of social satire, refracted through the lens of feminism, in a tale of suppressed creativity, marital ennui, and eating disorders. Several volumes of poetry and prose followed throughout the 1970s, notably *The Journals of Susanna Moody* (1970), which foreshadowed the sombre, reflective mood and the obsession with Canada's landscape and heritage that fuels her controversial and seminal study of similar themes in Canadian literature, *Survival* (1972). Her second novel, **Surfacing* (1972), locates this distinctive Canadian preoccupation in a unique and distinguished feminist fable. *Lady Oracle* (1976) is a diverting comic look at the self-fictions of romantic writers. Her fourth novel, *Life Before Man* (1979), established her as a major novelist with a wide canvas and an ability to organize plot and structure within the conventions of a domestic and social realism rewritten to accommodate her feminist critique. Though political, philosophical, and aesthetic ideas are relegated to the subterrain of the novel's predominantly social and psychological discourse, Atwood's subtle introduction of the impingement of remote Third World realities on the cushioned liberal Canadian consciousness reflects a crucial development in her *œuvre*. 'This above all: to refuse to be a victim', Atwood had written in *Surfacing*; this early credo effectively surfaces in the collection of poetry *True*

Stories (1981), bearing witness to unspeakable acts of torture, brutality, racism, and despair, and in the bold, incisive novel *Bodily Harm* (1982), set in the Caribbean, which conflates feminist metaphors of body, gender, and sexuality with a powerful portrayal of the domination and manipulation of the Third World by the First. The powerful *The *Handmaid's Tale* (1986), and the quieter and more intimate **Cat's Eye* (1989), place Atwood among the finest contemporary writers in the English language. Among her other works are two collections of short stories, *Dancing Girls* (1977) and *Bluebeard's Egg* (1983); and a genre-defying collection of short poetic prose texts, *Murder in the Dark* (1984). A selection of occasional critical prose, *Second Words* (1982), provides a useful commentary on the author's aesthetic, her influences and working method, and her evolving political perspectives. *Poems 1976–1986* appeared in 1992, as did *Good Bones*, a collection of prose fragments dealing with myth, memory, and imagination. The massive, multivocal, and controversial *The Robber Bridegroom* (1993) continued Atwood's wry and painful examination, commenced with *Cat's Eye*, of post-feminist gender politics; here, the life, disappearances and death of the seemingly malignant, destructive, and evil Zenia serve as the catalyst for three women's ultimate recognition of themselves.

AUDEN, W(ystan) H(ugh) (1907–73), British poet, born in York, educated at Christ Church, Oxford. In 1928 an edition of twenty of his poems was hand-printed by Stephen *Spender, who, with Louis *MacNeice and C. *Day Lewis, was among his acquaintances as a student. The great stylistic originality of the collection owed much to his success in assimilating aspects of poetic *Modernism while retaining affinities with more traditional modes. He also completed the experimental verse-drama 'Paid on Both Sides: A Charade' in 1928; T. S. *Eliot accepted it for the **Criterion* and, as a director of *Faber and Faber, undertook publication of *Poems* (1930, revised edition 1932). The volume included '1929', 'Consider', and other poems indicative of the political and psychological radicalism which Auden absorbed while living in Berlin in 1928 and 1929. *The *Orators* (1932) sustained the Modernist experimentation of 'Paid on Both Sides'; the work's theme of political extremism links it to numerous approximately contemporaneous poems included in **Look, Stranger!* (1936). The urgency with which he addressed the contemporary sense of imminent cultural crisis rapidly identified him as the leader of a group of poets noted for their work's commitment to socialism and the use of urban and industrial imagery (see PYLON SCHOOL). His political stance is also apparent from the Brechtian verse-dramas (see EXPRESSIONISM) he wrote for the *Group Theatre: following *The Dance of Death* (1933), a burlesque phantasmagoria denouncing bourgeois values, *The Dog Beneath the Skin* (1935), *The *Ascent of F6* (1936), and *On the Frontier* (1938) were written in collaboration with Christopher *Isherwood. Having worked as a schoolteacher in Helensburgh and Colwall from 1929, in 1935 Auden moved to London and worked briefly with the GPO Film Unit. A trip to Iceland with MacNeice in 1936 produced *Letters from Iceland* (1937), a miscellany of verse and prose by both authors; while often highly entertaining, the book conveys a profound spiritual disquiet which becomes more distinct in Auden's work over the next two years. He went to Spain in 1937 to broadcast propaganda for the Republican cause; 'Spain 1937' was written upon his return. In 1938 he sailed for China with Isherwood to gather materials for a book on the Sino-Japanese war. *Journey to a War* (1939) resulted, Auden's most significant contribution being the sequence later collected as 'Sonnets from China'; the twenty-one poems indicate the increasingly philosophical and metaphysical tendency of his thought, which culminated in his return to the Church in 1939. In that year he emigrated to the USA and met Chester Kallman, who became his lover and remained his companion for the rest of his life. The poetry of **Another Time* (1940) demonstrated the increased imaginative scope to which he gained access in America. He became a US citizen in 1946.

The investigation of the historical and philosophical contexts of the Second World War in *The Double Man* (1941), published in Britain as *New Year Letter* (1941), marked the start of a series of long poems forming an ambitious exposition of his ethical, artistic, and religious beliefs. The title poem of *For the Time Being* (1944) combines a treatment of the Nativity with a stringent critique of modern cultural materialism; the volume also contained 'The Sea and the Mirror', his 'Commentary on Shakespeare's *The Tempest*', which includes some of his most opulently lyrical verse. *The *Age of Anxiety* (1948), the last of the long poems, forms a dramatic summation of the series. Having produced a libretto in 1941 for Benjamin Britten's *Paul Bunyan* (1976), in 1947 Auden began the first of numerous collaborations with Kallman when commissioned by Igor Stravinsky to write a libretto for *The Rake's Progress* (1951); their other operatic works include a translation of *The Magic Flute* (1956) and the libretto for Hans Werner Henze's *Elegy for Young Lovers* (1961). *Nones* (1951) contained 'In Praise of Limestone' and other poems drawing local imagery from the Italian island of Ischia, where Auden spent his summers between 1948 and 1957. The volume established the extraordinary technical, tonal, and thematic range of his later poetry. Subsequent volumes include *The *Shield of Achilles* (1955), *Homage to Clio* (1960), *City without Walls* (1969), and *Epistle to a Godson* (1972). Central to much of the work they contain is a concern to define the terms of a just and humane civilization; among the topics recurrently raised are the interrelations of man and nature, modern history, linguistics, religion, and various branches of science. In 1956 Auden became Oxford Professor of Poetry and in the following year bought the house in Kirschstetten, Austria, which is celebrated in *About the House* of 1965. He continued to spend part of each year in New York until 1972, when a cottage in the grounds of Christ Church, Oxford, became his alternative residence. His principal writings as a critic are *The Enchafed Flood* (1950), essays on the psychology and symbolism of Romantic literature; *The Dyer's Hand* (1962), a substantial collection of essays stating his conceptions of poetry and art in general; and *Secondary Worlds* (1968), a consideration of relations between artistic creation and the primary world of common experience. Edward *Mendelson is the editor of *Collected Poems* (1976) and *The English Auden* (1977), a comprehensive collection of his work up to 1939. Humphrey *Carpenter's *W. H. Auden* appeared in 1981. See also *The Hidden Law: The Poetry of W. H. Auden* (1993) by Anthony *Hecht, and *Libretti and Other Dramatic Writings by W. H. Auden, 1939–1973* (1993).

Augie March, see ADVENTURES OF AUGIE MARCH, THE.

AUSTER, Paul (1947–), American novelist, born in Newark, New Jersey, educated at Columbia University. His *The New York Trilogy* (1987) was widely praised for its *post-modernist deconstruction of fictional modes—in particular, that of the detective story—and for its lyrical and allusive style. The first novel in the series, *City of Glass* (1985), uses the detective story form to explore themes of identity and the relationship between words and meaning. The protagonist is a writer, Daniel Quinn, who, through a case of mistaken identity, becomes involved in a search for a missing person, who may or may not be about to commit a murder. *Ghosts* (1986) is a Borgesian fable involving two private eyes, each hired, unknown to himself, to watch the other. The final part of the trilogy, *The Locked Room* (1987), involves another writer-as-private-eye engaged by the wife of his best friend to track down her missing husband. New York, or a version of it, is also the background for the apocalyptic fantasy *In the Country of Last Things* (1987), in which the narrator, Anna Blume, searches for her lost brother in an urban landscape which disintegrates around her. *Moon Palace* (1989) is another fusion of modernist experimentalism with American myth, in which the narrator, Marco Stanley Fogg, searches for the truth about his own past. *The Music of Chance* (1990) broke free of the urban setting with a peripatetic novel in which the protagonist, a professional card-player, spends his life travelling across America. *Leviathan* (1992), another experimental work, was followed by *Mr Vertigo* (1994), which is set in the 1920s and concerns the significantly named Walter Rawley, a boy from a small Midwestern town, who joins a travelling fair and learns to fly. In this, as in his previous fictions, Auster blends *magic realism with actuality, never allowing the reader to forget that his main subject is the process of writing itself. Among his other works, which include translations from the French and several volumes of poems, are *The Invention of Solitude* (1982), a meditation on death focusing around the writer's memories of his late father and his relationship with his young son, and *Ground Work* (1990), a collection of poems and essays, which deals with many of the themes considered in his fiction.

AUSTIN, J(ohn) L(angshaw) (1911–60), British philosopher, born in Lancaster, educated at Balliol College, Oxford; he was White's Professor of Moral Philosophy at Oxford from 1952 until his death. A writer and lecturer of uncommon wit and style, Austin's characteristic approach involved applying the rigour of classical textual scholarship to 'ordinary language'. During his lifetime, his work was mostly disseminated through a few learned papers (notably 'Other Minds' and 'A Plea for Excuses') and through his teaching. In *Sense and Sensibilia* (1962), Austin argued with great cogency against the fashionable 'sense-data' theory associated with A. J. *Ayer and the logical positivists. In examining how we talk about the world rather than whether or not we perceive it, Austin moved philosophy much closer to linguistics, and in his most widely read book, *How To Do Things with Words* (1962), he offered a series of important distinctions to be found within conventional usage. For Austin, as for John *Searle, language could be functional or performative as well as descriptive (or 'constative'). The performative utterance is an 'illocutionary' act, whereas the constative utterance is a 'locutionary' act. In developing these fine distinctions, Austin displayed the sensitivity of a subtle literary critic, and undermined the assumptions of much contemporary British philosophy. His stimulating essays appeared in *Collected Papers* (1961).

AUSTIN, Mary (Hunter) (1868–1934), American novelist, born in Carlinville, Illinois, educated at Blackborn College. In 1888 she moved to California to live on the fringes of the Mojave Desert, where she remained for over twenty years. *The Land of Little Rain* (1903) and *The Flock* (1906) vividly celebrate the region's landscape and indigenous culture, which pervade the historical novel *Isidro* (1905) and the short stories of *The Basket Woman* (1904) and *Lost Borders* (1909). From 1910 to 1923 she moved between Carmel, California, and New York; her political involvements of the period are reflected in the novel *No. 26 Jayne Street* (1920). She subsequently lived in Santa Fe, New Mexico, producing studies of Native American culture in the Southwestern deserts which include *The American Rhythm* (1923), a treatise on Native American poetry, and *Children Sing in the Far West* (1928), an anthology of songs and children's rhymes; *The Arrow Maker* (1911), her principal play, concerns a female Native American shaman. Her other novels include *Santa Lucia* (1908), *A Woman of Genius* (1912), and *The Ford* (1917). The mystical sensibility that becomes predominant in later works unites memorably with her love of the desert landscape in *Starry Adventure* (1931), her last novel. Among her numerous other publications are *The Green Bough* (1914) and *Small Town Man* (1925), novels propounding radical views of Christ, and her highly regarded autobiography *Earth Horizon* (1932). *I-Mary* (1983) is a biography by Augusta Fink.

Australian Literary Studies, a biennial journal originally conceived in 1963 by James *McAuley (then Reader in Poetry at the University of Tasmania) as a forum for specifically scholarly writing on Australian literature. The founding editor was L. T. Hergenhan with whom *ALS* moved from the University of Tasmania to the University of Queensland in 1975. Widely acknowledged work on the history of Australian literature has been accompanied by careful attention to current writing with essays on living authors in each issue. 'Notes and Documents', recording small, preliminary items of research, and a number of reviews, are regular features. The journal makes a major contribution to sustaining scholarship with an annual bibliography of Australian literary studies, primarily based upon the records of the Fryer Memorial Library, in the University of Queensland.

Autobiography of Alice B. Toklas, The, an autobiography by Gertrude *Stein, published in 1933. The autobiography, written as though the author were her private secretary, Alice B. Toklas (also her lifelong companion and lover), is important not so much for what it tells us about Gertrude Stein's life as for its evocation of American expatriate life in Paris and its occasionally philosophical commentary on twentieth-century culture. Unlike some of Stein's experimental prose writings, such as *Tender Buttons* (1914) and *The Making of Americans* (1925), *The Autobiography of Alice B. Toklas* is written in a relatively simple and direct manner and was very popular during her lifetime, although its treatment of certain figures provoked an attack from other Parisian writers and artists in *Testimony Against Gertrude Stein* (1935). A 'sequel', *Everybody's Autobiography*, was published in 1937. Ernest *Hemingway, who knew Stein in Paris and helped her type the manuscript of *The Making of Americans,* writes somewhat dismissively of her in *A Moveable Feast* (1964).

AVISON, Margaret (Kirkland) (1918–), Canadian poet, born in Galt, Ontario, educated at the University of Toronto, where she began working in administrative capacities in 1945. In 1968 she joined the staff of an evangelical mission in Toronto. *Winter Sun* (1960), her first volume of poetry, was widely acclaimed for the assured suppleness with which she sustained imaginative interactions of factual detail and abstract meditation. The bleakness of post-war modernity was conveyed by the tone and imagery of numerous lyrical explorations of psychological and existential uncertainties. A less complex, though sometimes intimidatingly minimal idiom was apparent in *The Dumbfounding* (1966), the title poem of which affirmed her exalted acceptance of the Christian faith. *Sunblue* (1978) consolidated the devotional tendency of her verse. Much of her work is characterized by the vivid economy and clarity of its imagery, a resource she has termed the 'optic heart' of her poetry. *Selected Poems* appeared in 1991. Her other works include the prose study *History of Toronto* (1951) and the translations of modern Hungarian poetry in *The Plough and the Pen* (with Ilona Duczynska and Karl Polanyi, 1963).

AWOONOR, Kofi, formerly known as George Awoonor WILLIAMS (1935–), Ghanaian poet and novelist, born at Wheta in the Volta Region, educated at the University of Ghana. Before moving to London in 1967, he was Director of the Ghana Film Corporation. He taught both at the University of London, and at the Stony Brook campus of New York State University, where he became Chairman of Comparative Literature. On release from prison for an alleged connection with an attempted coup, he became Professor of English at Cape Coast in 1976. His literary reputation rests chiefly on the poems in *Rediscovery* (1964) and *Night of My Blood* (1971), both of which adapt techniques from poetry by Ewe dirge singers to explore the modern African psyche. His translations of Ewe poetry, much of it sombre and tragic in tone, appear in *Guardians of the Sacred Word* (1974). Richly imagistic in texture, and politically allegorical, his novel *This Earth, My Brother: An Allegorical Tale of Africa* (1970) focuses on the search for meaning by a lawyer on the brink of a nervous breakdown. Other poetry collections include *Ride Me, Memory* (1973) and *The House by the Sea* (1978). *The Breast of the Earth* (1975), a major work of criticism, surveys the history, culture, and literature of Africa south of the Sahara.

AYCKBOURN, Alan (1939–), British playwright, born in London, the son of a musician and (his mother having remarried) stepson of a bank manager. He spent his formative years 'plumb centre of where I write about now', in company flats in small towns in south-east England. After working as an actor, he had four plays produced at the Theatre-in-the-Round in Scarborough, where he became artistic director in 1971 and where he presents the premières of almost all his new work. His first substantial success, the farce *Relatively Speaking* (1967), has been followed by transfers to London almost every year. Among the plays which have made him the most commercially successful contemporary British dramatist, as well as one of the most critically respected, are: *Time and Time Again* (1971), about a young man misused by women and by his insensitive brother-in-law; **Absurd Person Singular* (1972), which involves social mobility and personal change, and is set in three kitchens on three consecutive Christmas Eves; *The Norman Conquests* (1973), three self-sufficient plays showing the events of a fraught family weekend from the stance of different rooms in the same house; *Absent Friends* (1974), a comedy about the impact of a recently bereaved young man on unhappily married friends; *Bedroom Farce* (1975), another play about marital pains and confusions; *Just Between Ourselves* (1976), about a woman reduced to catatonic insensibility by her husband and envious mother-in-law; *Joking Apart* (1978), about the ability of the happy and successful to damage those around them; *Sisterly Feelings* (1979), a comedy about sibling rivalry, and also a play of chance and permutations, since the cast is required to play alternate scenes, depending on the fall of a coin tossed at the beginning; *Way Upstream* (1981), about events on a cabin cruiser hijacked by a modern pirate in the Norfolk Broads; *A Chorus of Disapproval* (1984), about the destruction unwittingly wreaked by a newcomer to an amateur operatic society; *Woman in Mind* (1985), another tale of a woman who retreats into hallucination and fantasy rather than face her unpleasant family; *A Small Family Business* (1987), about a respectable company which turns for profit to the drug trade; *Man of the Moment* (1988), a critique of media people who have made a bank robber a celebrity while relegating to obscurity the hero who disarmed him; *The Revengers Comedies* (1989), a picture of emotional destruction, distantly indebted to the Jacobeans, large enough to need two linked plays; *Wildest Dreams* (1991), about a group of suburbanites who escape from their drab existences by playing the fantasy-game Dungeons and Dragons; *Time of My Life* (1991), involving the disillusioning events that follow, and the ironically hopeful ones that precede, a cataclysmic family celebration; *Communicating Doors* (1994), a comedy-thriller which starts in the war-torn London of 2014 and concerns a prostitute who travels back through time in hopes of preventing a series of murders, including her own; and *A Word from Our Sponsor* (1995), another futuristic piece, this time centring on the havoc wreaked by a devil who agrees to finance and direct a nativity play.

As this description should show, Ayckbourn's work is notable for an adventurousness unusual in a popular playwright, and extending to both form and content. He enjoys setting himself tricky stylistic tasks, as in *How the Other Half Loves* (1969), where two living rooms co-exist on a single set, so that characters have only to swivel their chairs to participate in consecutive dinner parties. More importantly, his artistic aspiration is to 'write a completely serious play that makes people laugh all the time'. Accordingly, his comedies tend to be pessimistic in tone, and to treat harsh and even sombre subjects, among them domestic strife, conscious and unconscious cruelty, madness, and death, usually in a suburban middle-class setting. A good example of his methods would be the second act of *Absurd Person Singular*, in which a distraught wife, sick of her husband's adulteries, attempts to poison, gas, knife, electrocute, drown, and defenestrate herself, only to have each action amiably misinterpreted by helpful friends. Though Ayckbourn's later work has taken on a greater social and political edge, it is personal trouble and disaster which have characterized his most effective writing.

AYER, A(lfred) J(ules) (1910–89), English philosopher, born in London, educated at Eton and at Christ Church, Oxford; he also spent some time at the University of Vienna. He lectured at Oxford from 1933, became Grote Professor of the Philosophy of Mind and Logic at University College, London, in 1946, and Wykeham Professor of Logic at Oxford in 1959. His highly influential first book, *Language, Truth and Logic* (1936), offered a synthesis of the logical positivist ideas of the Vienna Circle and more traditional British linguistic analysis. Combining the sceptical intelligence of his tutor Gilbert *Ryle with the logical austerity of Rudolf *Carnap, Ayer zestfully demolished the notion that philosophy was engaged in identifying and disseminating arcane metaphysical truths about some transcendent reality, and so helped to set the terms of reference for the academic study of philosophy in Britain for the next fifty years. In debate with critics such as J. L. *Austin, much of Ayer's subsequent work sought to reconstruct the possibilities of rigorously empirical knowledge. Ayer maintained his forceful presence in British academic life in works such as *The Foundations of Empirical Knowledge* (1940), *Thinking and Meaning* (1947), *The Problem of Knowledge* (1956), and *The Concept of a Person* (1964). In later years Ayer turned to *belles-lettres* with two frank volumes of autobiography and brief studies of Voltaire, Thomas Paine, Hume, and *Wittgenstein.

AYRES, Pam (1947–), British poet, born in Stanford-in-the-Vale, Oxfordshire; upon leaving school at 15, she entered the Civil Service and afterwards served in the Women's Royal Air Force for four years, where she discovered her talent to amuse. After readings of her light verse on Radio Oxford and an appearance on the television programme *Opportunity Knocks* in 1975, she rapidly became highly popular for her wryly self-effacing style. *Some of Me Poetry* appeared in 1976, followed by *Some More of Me Poetry* (1976) and *Thoughts of a Late-Night Knitter* (1978), which together made up *All Pam's Poems* (1978), illustrated by Roy Garnham Elmore. Further volumes include *The Ballad of Bill Spinks' Bedstead* (1981) and *The Works* (1992; selected poems). Among her numerous children's books are *Bertha and the Racing Pigeon* (1979) and *The Crater* (1992). The remarkable popularity of her broadcast poetry and the considerable degree of celebrity thus generated resulted in sales of over two million copies of her books by 1981. Ballad idioms and other comic or burlesque forms are used with facility for her often humorously narrative poetry, which sometimes accommodates a compassionate perception of social events or the circumstances of birds and animals.

B

Babbitt, a novel by Sinclair *Lewis, published in 1922. The novel created a major controversy with its uncompromising assault on American virtue. The stereotypical, moral, small-town American businessman George Babbitt epitomizes the ethos of the Midwestern city Zenith. The first seven chapters retain Lewis's original idea to follow Babbitt through the events of one day. Subsequent chapters present set pieces which provide a sociology of middle-class American life, dealing with such topics as politics, leisure, club life, trade association conventions, conventional religion, labour relations, marriage and the family, the barbershop, and the speakeasy. There is little plot to unite these fragmentary interests, apart from Babbitt who moves through these chapters in the course of his rising discontent with the mores of his world. Various separate narratives include Babbitt's friendship with Paul Riesling, the one-time artist who is imprisoned after he shoots his wife; Babbitt's attempt to find sympathy in a liaison with Tanis Judique and 'the Bunch'; and Babbitt's final involvement with liberalism, and the Good Citizen League. The novel depicts an individual trapped in a stifling environment, who struggles for something better, but ultimately fails, and sinks back into compromising conformity. The final suggestion is that the humanist values of love and friendship are the only answers to Babbitt's problems.

BABBITT, Irving (1865–1933), American critic, born in Dayton, Ohio, educated at Harvard, where he held a professorship from 1912 until his death. The vigorous defence of the humanities in *Literature and the American College* (1908), his first major work, proved controversial for its harsh critique of the ethos of scientific progress which prevailed in American universities. The breadth of his cultural interests was passed on to his students through his courses in comparative literature, which ranged through classical, European, and Oriental materials. His emphasis on the ethical dimensions of literary studies was central to the emergence of the *New Humanism. Babbitt's philosophy was largely based on his view of Romanticism as a cultural aberration, responsible for the 'moral impressionism' of modern materialism with its worship of 'the quantitive life'; *The New Laokoon* (1910) argued that the arts had been reduced to a condition of moral anarchy by Romanticism, upon which a scathingly lucid attack was mounted in *Rousseau and Romanticism* (1919). T. S. *Eliot, who undertook postgraduate study with Babbitt in 1909, was deeply impressed by his ideas; the two exchanged letters until Babbitt's death. His other works include *Masters of Modern French Criticism* (1912), in which his conception of the cultural interactions of the past and the present foreshadow Eliot's 'Tradition and the Individual Talent'; and *Democracy and Leadership* (1924), an expression of his belief in a firmly regulated socio-cultural order. *Spanish Character* (1940) is a selection of his essays edited by F. Manchester and O. Shepard, the editors of *Irving Babbitt: Man and Teacher* (1941), a collection of memoirs and tributes.

Back to Methuselah, a play by G. B. *Shaw, first performed in 1922; it is its author's most complete dramatization of his theory of 'creative evolution'. Subtitled 'a metabiological pentateuch', it opens in the Garden of Eden, where Eve is confronted with a serpent who teaches her the facts of life and death and shares its evolutionary hopes: 'You imagine what you desire, you will what you imagine, and at last you create what you will.' After an episode involving Cain, pioneer of destruction and fake heroism, the action shifts to 1920. Lubin and Burge, parodies of Asquith and Lloyd George, come to discover whether there is party advantage in the new 'gospel' of Franklyn and Conrad Barnabas, brothers who believe that 'life is too short for man to take it seriously', that disasters such as the First World War will be avoided only if man learns wisdom by going 'back to Methuselah', and that creative evolution will be 'the religion of the 20th century', leading eventually to 'omnipotence and omniscience'. Then it is AD 2170, and 'the thing happens': the Barnabases' local vicar reappears as an archbishop who, like their parlourmaid, has lived nearly 300 years. The next section of the play occurs in AD 3000 and is set in an Ireland which, like the rest of Britain, is occupied by 'long-livers' who are currently considering whether to exterminate more ordinary beings. In their enlightenment, they treat with derision those representatives of the British Commonwealth, among them the Prime Minister and his conventionally minded father-in-law, who come from its headquarters in Baghdad to seek advice on the petty electoral matters that still absorb them. The play then leaps forward 'as far as thought can reach', to the year 31,920, when humans emerge as fully grown adolescents from eggs, absorb themselves for four years with love, the arts, and other supposed frivolities, and then develop into 'ancients', sexless, ascetic creatures who spend the rest of their very long lives in contemplation and wish only to escape from their bodies. Finally, the creator, Lilith, prophesies another stage in evolution, with life becoming pure intelligence and energy, 'a vortex freed from matter'. The play, though obviously difficult to take seriously on a literal level, contains plenty of lively observation, and remains of interest for the light it sheds both on Shaw's growing disenchantment with democratic politics and on his Manichaean mistrust of sense, feeling, and human relationships.

BAGNOLD, Enid (Algerine) (1889–1981), British novelist and playwright, born in Rochester; she spent her childhood in Jamaica, and was educated at Prior Field, Godalming, a progressive English boarding school. She became a student of Walter Sickert and later worked as a journalist for Frank *Harris with whom she had an affair. *A Diary Without Dates* (1917), recording her experiences as an ambulance driver during the First World War, formed the background of her first novel, *The Happy Foreigner* (1920). In 1920 she married Sir Roderick Jones, Chairman of Reuters, and established an artistic salon which included Gaudier Brzeska, H. G. *Wells, Vita *Sackville-West, and Rudyard *Kipling. Her children's book *National Velvet* (1935) became a classic after it was filmed in 1944 with Elizabeth Taylor playing the role of the girl who wins the Grand National on a horse that she won in a raffle. Other novels include *The Squire* (1928), about a stoic mother awaiting the birth of her fifth child while her husband is abroad; *Serena Blandish* (1924), which was adapted for the stage by S. N. *Behrman; and *The Loved and Envied* (1951), whose central character is based on Lady Diana Cooper. Her dramatic works include *Lottie Dundass* (1943), *Poor Judas* (1951), and *The Chinese Prime Minister* (1964); but none scored the success of *The Chalk Garden* (1955), about a mysterious governess with a criminal past who rescues a troubled girl from a sterile life with her eccentric grandmother. This was described by Kenneth *Tynan as perhaps 'the finest artificial comedy to have flowed from an English . . . pen since the death of Congreve'. Her autobiography appeared in 1964 and in 1976.

BAIL, Murray (1941–), Australian novelist, born in Adelaide. He lived in Britain, Europe, and India for several years and was a contributor to the **Times Literary Supplement* amongst other literary journals. The stories collected in *Contemporary Portraits and Other Stories* (1975), republished as *The Drover's Wife and Other Stories* (1986), were experimental in style and satirical in theme; the title story of the latter volume is a parody of Henry *Lawson's nationalist realist story 'The Drover's Wife'. Bail's first novel, *Homesickness* (1980), is a surreal and blackly comic examination of a group of Australians on a package tour to Europe. *Holden's Performance* (1987), again an idiosyncratic combination of slapstick and social commentary, charts the hero's rise in Australian society, through a mixture of luck and bizarre coincidence, to the eminent position of bodyguard to the Prime Minister. He has published a writer's notebook, *Longhand* (1989), and edited *The Faber Book of Contemporary Australian Short Stories* (1988).

BAILEY, H(enry) C(hristopher) (1878–1961), British writer of *detective fiction, born in London, educated at Corpus Christi College, Oxford. He was drama critic, war correspondent, and leader writer for the London *Daily Telegraph* from 1901 to 1946. Between the two world wars he published a large number of detective short stories and novels, which enjoyed great popularity in their day, but which have since been largely forgotten. His best-known detective is the indolent gourmet Dr Reggie Fortune, who appears chiefly in short stories—*Call Mr Fortune* (1920) is the first collection—of which the earlier are to be preferred, but is also the central character in several novels: *The Bishop's Crime* (1940) is perhaps the best. Bailey's novels about Joshua Clunk, a crooked solicitor, are less successful (*Garstons*, 1930).

BAILEY, Hilary (1936–), British novelist, short-story writer, and critic, born in Kent, educated at Newnham College, Cambridge. Her short stories have been published in magazines ranging from *Science Fantasy* to **Bananas*, and she edited **New Worlds* from 1973 to 1975. Her first novel, *Polly Put the Kettle On* (1975), was a lively portrait of the 1960s; a sequel, *As Time Goes By* (1988), brings its characters into the 1980s. Amongst other novels are *Mrs Mulvaney* (1975), set in the 1970s; *All the Days of My Life* (1984), a family saga focusing on Molly Flanders; and *Hennie Richards* (1985), whose protagonist is an international female smuggler. Her formidable story-telling ability is combined with a technique in which contemporary historical events, such as the downfall of the Kray brothers and the bombing campaigns of the Angry Brigade, are incorporated into the narrative. *The Cry from Street to Street* (1992), a fictionalized documentary account by an ex-prostitute, is set in the London of Jack the Ripper; *Cassandra: Princess of Troy* (1993) retells the myth of the Trojan War, while in *The Strange Adventures of Charlotte Holmes* (1994) Bailey returns to Victorian crime in a novel that challenges the status of her heroine's brother, the famous detective Sherlock Holmes. Subsequent novels include *Frankenstein's Bride* (1995). Her non-fiction work includes her biography of Vera *Brittain of 1987.

BAILEY, Paul (born Peter Harry) (1937–), British novelist and critic, born in London, and trained as an actor. He earned critical recognition for his first novel, *At the Jerusalem* (1967), a poignant and lively study of old people in a private institution. *Trespasses* (1970) followed, in which Bailey explores the disintegration of the persona under the pressures exerted by social conventions. Formally, *Trespasses* is mimetic of the fractured condition that is its theme, consisting of fragments which eventually coalesce. *A Distant Likeness* (1973) continues this fictive method in its presentation of a criminal sleuth haunted by the horrors and pathos of the cases he deals with. In *Peter Smart's Con-*

fessions (1977) there is a greater autobiographical element with the protagonist sharing his experience of the theatre; it is both bold and sensitive about homosexuality. *Old Soldiers* (1980) gives the subject of the split personality a more fully realized social context. *Gabriel's Lament* (1986) is a large-scale novel, narrated in both the first and the third person, and presents the central character's coming to terms with tragic truth. *Sugar Cane* (1993) is narrated by a female doctor in a genito-urinary clinic who develops a special interest in a young black patient; the narrative uncovers a background of young rent-boys and the shocking realities of AIDS. Bailey's work is often described as Dickensian, but this is to miss the essentially *post-modernist nature of his art, his literary absorption in twentieth-century writers such as I. B. *Singer, Flannery *O'Connor, and the Italian Giorgio Bassani, all of whom he admired for their ability to set characters in cultures under threat. A lively humour pervades his autobiography, *An Immaculate Mistake* (1990), not least where his own honestly presented sexuality is concerned. Bailey is also the editor of *The Oxford Book of London* (1991).

BAINBRIDGE, Beryl (1934–), British novelist, born in Liverpool and educated at the Merchant Taylor's School. She began her career as an actress in a Liverpool repertory company. Her first novel, *A Weekend With Claude* (1967), written in her distinctive laconic style, is a blackly comic account of a weekend in the country which ends with the accidental shooting of one of the protagonists. Her other novels include *Another Part of the Wood* (1968); *Harriet Said* (1972), in which the sexual experiment conducted by two schoolgirls goes disastrously wrong; *The Dressmaker* (1973), a novel set in wartime Liverpool concerning the relationships between a dejected 17-year-old girl and her two aunts; *The Bottle Factory Outing* (1974), which describes the macabre and comic events surrounding a small firm's annual outing; *Sweet William* (1975), about a compulsive philanderer; *Young Adolf* (1978), a comic exploration of a visit to Liverpool made by the 16-year-old Hitler during the 1900s; and *Winter Garden* (1980). A recurring theme in her work is the bizarre or unpredictable nature of real life; the most banal events are given a surreal edge and there is a pervasive sense, in her comic descriptions, of the absurdity underlying human behaviour. This is most clearly seen in her use of dialogue, which appears at first to mimic the vocabulary and cadences of real speech, but which in fact is as far from naturalism as her plots, many of which hinge on fantastic or macabre circumstances. Murder and accidental death often feature as the catalyst in an otherwise innocuous series of events. *Injury Time* (1977; Whitbread Award, 1978), for example, begins with a dinner party and ends with kidnapping and violence; *Watson's Apology* (1984) investigates the circumstances surrounding a Victorian schoolmaster's murder of his wife; and *An Awfully Big Adventure* (1989) deals with adultery, homosexuality, incest, and suicide, as perceived by its 16-year-old narrator, Stella, an ASM in a Liverpool repertory company. Infatuated with Meredith, the theatre manager, who is having an affair with another man, Stella allows herself to be drawn into a relationship with an ageing actor, O'Hara, for whom the affair has terrible consequences. In this, as in much of Bainbridge's fiction, events are seen from the point of view of a naïve, but not necessarily innocent, protagonist, a technique which gives the narrative an ironic dimension characteristic of her work as a whole.

BAKER, George Pierce (1866–1935), American drama teacher, born in Providence, Rhode Island, educated at Harvard. Baker later became one of Harvard's most inspirational drama teachers. His play-writing course, 'English 47', and the '47 Workshop' which sprang from it, had an incalculable effect upon the development of the American commercial theatre in the 1920s and 1930s; his pupils included Philip *Barry, S. N. *Behrman, Eugene *O'Neill, Edward Sheldon, John *Dos Passos, and Thomas *Wolfe. Baker's skill lay in his capacity to nurture all the arts of the theatre through creating the conditions in which apprentice writers could make their individual experiments under his wisely practical tutelage. He moved to Yale in 1925 where he directed the University Theatre at Yale. Baker's publications include *The Development of Shakespeare as a Dramatist* (1907), *Some Unpublished Correspondence of David Garrick* (1907), *Dramatic Technique* (1919), and *Modern American Plays* (1920).

BAKER, Houston A(lfred, Jr) (1943–), African-American critic, born in Louisville, Kentucky, educated at Howard University and UCLA; amongst other academic posts, he was appointed Professor of English at the University of Virginia. His considerable scholarly output has long established him as a major African-American literary authority and critic. The best known of his studies include *Long Black Song: Essays in Black American Literature and Culture* (1972), an analysis of black vernacularism and folklore from Frederick Douglass to Richard *Wright; *Singers of Daybreak: Studies in Black American Literature* (1974), linked essays on the imaginative achievement of Paul *Dunbar, Jean *Toomer, Ralph *Ellison, and George Cain; *The Journey Back: Issues in Black Literature and Criticism* (1980), a consideration of African-American 'textuality'; *Blues, Ideology, and Afro-American Literature* (1984), an overview of the poetics of America's black writing—blues, but also language, voice, and phrasing; *Modernism and The Harlem Renaissance* (1987), a reassessment of the creative variety and achievements of the 1920s black efflorescence signalled in Alain *Locke's manifesto-anthology, *The *New Negro*; and *Workings of the Spirit* (1991), a chronicle, in Alice *Walker's term, of the 'womanist' expressivity of black women from Harriet Jacobs/Linda Brent through Zora Neale *Hurston to Toni *Morrison. Baker is also a published poet, notably in *No Matter Where You Travel, You Still Be Black* (1979) and *Blues Journey, Home* (1985), as well as a frequent editor and anthologist, and a contributor to eminent academic journals.

BAKER, Nicholson (1957–), American novelist, born in New York, educated at Haverford College, Pennsylvania. His first novel, *The Mezzanine* (1989), is a comic odyssey compressing a wide variety of reflections on life, death, consumer society, and literature into the space of a single lunch-hour as described by Howie, its eccentric hero. In *Room Temperature* (1990) the narrator, Mike, muses about his marriage and other related topics, while giving a bottle to his baby daughter. These two short works display a playful erudition and love of digression which is reminiscent of Flann *O'Brien and James *Joyce. *U and I* (1991), an idiosyncratic essay on the author's obsession with the life and works of J. *Updike, was widely regarded as a comic *tour de force*. *Vox* (1992) simply consists of a conversation between a man and a woman, strangers to one another, who have called a telephone sex line in search of salacious conversation, and end up with more than either has bargained for. *The Fermata* (1994) extended this preoccupation with bizarre sexual encounters in its depiction of Arno Strine, a middle-aged man with the power to arrest time, who uses this unusual skill to further his own onanistic desires. These latter two novels show sex as essentially comic, and contain passages which parody the excesses of pornographic writing without conveying the slightest eroticism. *The Size of Thoughts* (1996) is a collection of essays.

BALCHIN, Nigel (1908–70), British novelist and scientist, born in Wiltshire, educated at Cambridge University. Under the pseudonym Mark Spade he contributed humorous articles to *Punch* which were collected in *How To Run a Bassoon Factory* (1934). Balchin began to establish himself as a writer of sharp realistic novels with *Lightbody on Liberty* (1936). During the Second World War he served as Deputy Scientific Advisor to the Army Council; the war provided the setting of much of his finest work including the highly successful novel *The Small Back Room* (1943). Professional and moral questions faced by scientists are expressed in works such as *Darkness Falls from the Air* (1940) and *Mine Own Executioner* (1945). *Lord, I Was Afraid* (1947) was ambitious and experimental and perhaps the best of his later novels.

BALDWIN, James (Arthur) (1924–87), American novelist, dramatist, and social critic, born in New York City, where he was educated. He was on the National Advisory Board of CORE (Congress on Racial Equality). From 1948 onwards he divided his time between New York and France. His first novel, **Go Tell It on the Mountain* (1953), inspired by his own childhood, is a modern classic of Black American literature. His second, the skilfully structured and economically narrated **Giovanni's Room* (1956), is the confessional monologue of a white American and probably the first novel to deal so openly with tragic homosexual love. It is, almost exclusively in Baldwin's work, unconnected with issues of race or interracial sexual and social relationships, unlike his most impressive novel, **Another Country* (1962), which conflates and adds to the psychological and political concerns of his earlier works. His poignant short stories are collected in *Going to Meet the Man* (1965).

Baldwin's early fictions represent his finest imaginative work and alone would ensure him a place in American literary history. However, later novels only repeat in flashes the evident creative genius of his youth; although they are lyrical and compelling, they are held by some critics to be flawed, because of their strongly polemical content and somewhat repetitive nature. These include *Tell Me How Long the Train's Been Gone* (1968) and *If Beale Street Could Talk* (1974), the tragic love story of a black prisoner. *Just Above My Head* (1979), about the blighted destiny of a gospel singer, has much of the strength of Baldwin's earlier fictions, but by then he had been displaced by a younger generation of writers black and white, and was largely identified with his frequently fiercely polemical writings on race, politics, and sexuality. These provocative and highly influential essays earned him a lasting reputation as one of America's greatest essayists of the twentieth century; they are collected in several volumes including *Notes of a Native Son* (1955), which contains a seminal essay on Richard *Wright; *Nobody Knows My Name* (1961); *The Fire Next Time* (1963); and *No Name in the Street* (1972). *The Devil Finds Work* (1976) is an incisive essay on American movies. *The Evidence of Things Not Seen* (1985) is a grim meditation on the racially motivated series of child murders in Atlanta, Georgia, in 1979. These works are collected, with additional material, in *The Price of a Ticket: Collected Non-Fiction 1948–1985* (1985). *A Rap on Race* (1971) and *A Dialogue* (1973) contain, respectively, conversations with anthropologist Margaret Mead and writer Nikki *Giovanni. At his imaginative peak, Baldwin also wrote two successful plays: *Amen Corner* (1958, performed 1965), praised by Caryl *Phillips as his finest, in both secular and religious terms; and *Blues for Mr. Charlie* (1964), distantly based upon the case of Emmett Till who, after he was acquitted of it, confessed to a racist murder. Baldwin was also the author of *One Day When I Was Lost* (1972), a play about Malcolm X, and of *Jimmy's Blues: Selected Poems* (1983). Biographies are *Talking at the Gates: A Life of James Baldwin*, by James Campbell (1991), and *James Baldwin: A Biography*, by David Leeming (1994). See also ETHNICITY.

Balkan Trilogy, The, a trilogy of novels by O. *Manning, consisting of *The Great Fortune* (1960), *The Spoilt City* (1962), and *Friends and Heroes* (1965), published in one volume in 1987 (see also LEVANT TRILOGY, THE).

The Great Fortune opens with the arrival in Bucharest of Guy Pringle, a young British Council lecturer, and his wife, Harriet, whom he has just married. Set in 1939, with Europe on the point of war, the Bucharest expatriate society is split into rival factions. Some, like the incorrigible reprobate Prince

Yakimov, a Russian *émigré* down on his luck, pledge allegiance to neither faction. Guy, whose Marxist idealism co-exists with a certain naïvety about the political in-fighting at the British Council, allows his position to be undermined by unscrupulous colleagues. He displays a similar lack of insight in his relations with Sophie Oresanu, a seductive Romanian girl whose spiteful behaviour towards Harriet contributes towards the latter's misgivings about her marriage. The book ends with the news that France has fallen to the Nazis.

The Spoilt City opens with Bucharest in turmoil; the British contingent, anticipating the Nazi invasion, are making plans to escape. Guy and Harriet offer shelter to Sasha Drucker, a Jewish boy from a wealthy family, whose father has been imprisoned, but their plans to save him are sabotaged by Yakimov, who betrays him to the Germans in order to gain personal advantage. The situation becomes increasingly dangerous and Guy persuades Harriet to leave for Athens, where he promises to follow her in due course.

Friends and Heroes is set in Athens and concerns the Pringles' attempts to establish some kind of security in the midst of the deteriorating international situation. Guy's plans to find work are repeatedly thwarted by his colleagues, including the rascally Dubedat and Lush and the overbearing Lord Pinkrose, and he is reduced to organizing an RAF concert party, which he does with enthusiasm, much to Harriet's chagrin. Harriet becomes involved with Charles Warden, a young British officer stationed in the city, but stops short of having an affair with him when it becomes clear that he is in love with her. As the novel closes, the political situation is once more dangerously unstable: the Germans have entered Greece; Yakimov, who has followed the British contingent to Athens, is killed by a sniper's bullet; and the Pringles, together with most of their British Council associates, secure a passage to Alexandria.

BALLARD, J(ames) G(raham) (1930–), British writer, born in Shanghai, educated at King's College, Cambridge. During the Second World War he was interned by the Japanese and this traumatic experience of his early years has influenced much of his fiction; he made direct use of the material only in his autobiographical novel, *Empire of the Sun* (1984; later filmed by S. Spielberg), the success of which widened the high reputation he had gained as an author of apocalyptic *science fiction (see also APOCALYPTIC LITERATURE). He returned to Britain in 1946 and trained as a doctor at Cambridge (without taking a degree). By 1956 he had begun a long association with **New Worlds* magazine and was publishing his experimental short stories; the best of these appeared in *The Voices of Time* (1962), *Billenium* (1962), *The Four-Dimensional Nightmare* (1963), *The Terminal Beach* (1964), and *Vermilion Sands* (1971). The abandoned concrete landscapes, the transfixed passivity of their protagonists, the sense of impending doom, the stark and vivid prose, all made Ballard's work unmistakable. He was widely imitated by writers impressed by the hypnotic veracity of his despair. In his early novels, *The Drowned World* (1962), *The Drought* (1965), and *The Crystal World* (1966), a different apocalypse ravages and transfigures the world. Only in *The Wind from Nowhere* (1962) does a protagonist engage in a fight against disaster in traditional science-fiction manner. Later volumes see the protagonist (usually male) approaching the apocalypse as a mystical consummation. After *The Atrocity Exhibition* (1970), an experimental work, there appeared *Crash* (1973), *Concrete Island* (1974), and *High Rise* (1975), which contain his finest and most violent explorations of what J. B. *Priestley described as 'inner space', a term now indelibly associated with Ballard's work in which he has expressed the conviction that the most fearful science-fictional landscapes lie within the human heart. Later works include *Hello America* (1981); *The Day of Creation* (1987); *Running Wild* (1988), which anatomized the Britain of today; *Rushing to Paradise* (1994); the stories collected in *War Fever* (1990), which focused on public issues of the 1990s; and a collection of reviews and essays, *A User's Guide to the Millenium* (1995).

BAMBARA, Toni Cade (1931–), African-American short-story writer, novelist, and scriptwriter, born in New York, where she was educated at City University. During the early 1960s, when she emerged as a noted civil rights activist, she worked in a New York community centre. After teaching at City University, she became an assistant professor at Rutgers University in 1969. Her writing is closely aligned with her political convictions, which she has summarized as 'Pan-Africanist-socialist-feminist'. *Gorilla, My Love* (1972) and *The Sea Birds Are Still Alive* (1977) are collections of her short stories, which are distinguished by the acuteness of their socio-cultural observations and their energetically colloquial idioms. *The Salt Eaters*, her novel of 1980, reflects the profound changes of mood in the USA after the Vietnam War. Her work as a scriptwriter includes the screenplay for the film of Toni *Morrison's novel *Tar Baby* (1981). She is the editor of the widely read anthologies *The Black Woman* (1970) and *Tales and Stories for Black Folks* (1971).

Banana Bottom, a novel by C. *McKay, published in 1933. Set in Jamaica, its theme is cultural dualism, the clash between European and indigenous black values. The central character is Bita Plant, from the village of Banana Bottom, who is raped at the age of 12 by an idiot youth. The Craigs, a white missionary couple, adopt Bita as their protégée and send her to be educated in England. After years abroad, Bita returns to the island as a piano-playing paragon to assist her benefactors. However, she becomes restless at the Mission. Falling under the spell of an unlearned dandy named Hopping Dick, she rebels against the Calvinist domination of her guardians. An attempt to arrange a respectable marriage between Bita and a young divinity student is brought to an abrupt halt when the prospective bridegroom is caught in an act of bestiality. Rediscovering Banana Bottom, Bita is at home among its unaffected pleasures and personalities, which her sophisticated education should have taught her to dismiss as vulgar amusements and bad company. One link with the cultivated life is in her friendship with Squire Gensir, an elderly Englishman who lives simply among the villagers, collecting and celebrating their folk culture. Eventually marrying Jubban, a stalwart peasant, she finds no contradiction in linking her destiny with his: 'Her music, her reading, her thinking were the flowers of her intelligence and he the root in the earth upon which she was grafted, both nourished by the same soil.'

Bananas, a literary journal founded in 1975 by Emma *Tennant, who intended it as a means of publishing a broad range of imaginative writing. It was originally subtitled 'the literary newspaper', appearing in folio with a striking red and black cover design and featuring short stories, poems, articles, reviews, and illustrations. Contributors to early issues included Angela *Carter, Tom *Disch, J. G. *Ballard, William *Burroughs, Lorna Sage, and Ruth *Fainlight. In 1978 the ownership and editorship of *Bananas* passed to Abigail Mozley, under whose direction it assumed magazine format and promoted regional (see REGIONAL POETRY) writing through the appointment of editorial correspondents in various parts of Britain. Andrew *Motion, Peter *Didsbury, Helen *Dunmore, and William *Scammell were among the poets whose work appeared in the journal in the early stages of their careers. Special issues were produced on Russian, French, German, Spanish, and South American writing. *Bananas* ceased publication after its twenty-fourth issue in January 1981.

BANKS, Iain M(enzies) (1954–), Scottish writer, born in Fife, educated at Stirling University. He lived in London and Kent from 1979 to 1988, then moved to Edinburgh. He is best known for his first novel, *The Wasp Factory* (1984), in which the mental games of an isolated adolescent become part of reality, and for *The Bridge* (1986), in which a comatose patient is compelled to discover the significance of the great bridge which controls his dreams, and which seems to embody the structure of his entire life. Other novels of similar imaginative impact are *Walking on Glass* (1985), *Espedair Street* (1987), *Canal Dreams* (1989), and *The Crow Road* (1992). More humorous in vein is *Whit* (1995), about a teenager's involvement with a religious cult. His *science fiction novels *Consider Phlebas* (1987), *The Player of Games* (1988), *The State of the Art* (1989), and *The Use of Weapons* (1990) form 'The Culture', a series of expansive adventures within a galaxy-spanning Culture founded on a vision of post-capitalist plenitude, while *Against a Dark Background* (1993) explores his heroine's conflict with a sinister cult seeking to control the universe. *Feersum Endjinn* (1994) depicts the savage war between a royal line and a technocratic faction on a poisoned planet. An imaginative large-scale narrative, it demonstrates Banks's powerful use of technological fantasy.

BANKS, Russell (1940–), American novelist, born in Newton, Massachusetts, educated at Colgate University, Hamilton, New York, and the University of Carolina, Chapel Hill. His first novel, *Family Life* (1974), is a satirical fable set in an imaginary kingdom. Other novels, though they may be set in the past, follow a post-modernist trajectory. These include *Hamilton Stark* (1978); *The Book of Jamaica* (1980), in which an academic researches the history of the Maroons of that country, and is ambivalently accepted by them; and *The Relation of My Imprisonment* (1983), a story of religious heresy and puritan dissent. His most celebrated novel, *Continental Drift* (1985), tells of the linked destinies of the blue-collar family man Bob, and Vanise, a destitute Haitian refugee and mother. Banks's rich prose and strong narrative drive are evident in the novels *Affliction* (1989) and *The Sweet Hereafter* (1991), in which he continues what has been described as his 'shattering dissection of contemporary American life'. *Rule of the Bone* (1995) concerns Bone, a homeless boy who has drifted into petty crime, whose life is changed by his encounter with the Rastafarian I-Man, with whom he embarks on an adventurous journey which culminates in Jamaica. His short-story collections include *Searching for Survivors* (1975) and *Success Stories* (1986).

BANVILLE, John (1945–), Irish novelist, born in Wexford, Ireland, educated at the Christian Brothers School and St Peter's College, Wexford. In 1970 he published *Long Lankin*, a collection of short stories which, like Joyce's **Dubliners*, examined Irish life from the perspective of several characters, dealing with different stages in their lives from childhood to adulthood; a novella, 'The Possessed', was also included. *Nightspawn* (1971) was a sequel to the novella, exploring the relationship between truth and fiction through the consciousness of its writer-hero, Ben White. *Birchwood* (1973) developed some of the earlier work's themes; its narrator, Gabriel Godwin, is an Irish writer engaged on a Proustian quest for 'time misplaced'. The relationship between creation and reality is explored in many of Banville's novels. Using historical figures, in *Doctor Copernicus* (1976; James Tait Black Memorial Prize), *Kepler* (1981), and *The Newton Letter* (1982), Banville explored the idea of science as an art form and of scientists as 'the makers . . . of supreme fictions'. More sombre and set in the present is *Mefisto* (1986), which, as the title implies, is Banville's reworking of the classic Dr Faustus theme; the novel focuses on the mathematically gifted Gabriel Swan, who seeks a numerical solution to his quest for order and meaning in life. *The Book of Evidence* (1989) is a haunting anatomy of a murder, seen from the point of view of the murderer, Montgomery, who abducts and kills a young woman during an incompetently executed art theft and is then tormented by the horror of his act. In the sequel, *Ghosts* (1993), which contains parallels with *The*

Tempest, Banville's murderer, who has retreated to an Arcadian island to study a painter resembling Watteau, is disturbed and returned to the 'human world' of despair by castaways, one of whom recalls the past he is striving to exorcise. *Athena* (1995) sees the murderer (renamed Morrow) hired to authenticate a group of paintings, and seduced by 'A' (Athena) into an atavistic relationship which beckons his descent into a further personal hell and Banville's continuing excavation of truth and fraud, art and the imagination. The novel completes a trilogy of loss, guilt, and hauntings, praised for the wit and originality of its diction. John Banville became literary editor of the *Irish Times* in 1989.

BARAKA, (Imamu) Amiri (originally LeRoi Jones) (1934–), African-American playwright and social activist, born in Newark, New Jersey, educated at Howard and Columbia Universities. Baraka exerted a profound influence on the development and direction of black writing and culture. His first published work was the long sardonic poem *Preface to a Twenty Volume Suicide Note* (1961) with its vivid imagery and infusion of black culture and reference. This was followed by *The Dead Lecturer* (1964) with its call for black political commitment. Associated with the *Beat poets like Allen *Ginsberg and with the poets of the *New York School such as Frank *O'Hara, he explored new metrics and ways of notation on the page. He turned for models to the '*Projective Verse' of Charles *Olson and to the other rhythms he knew from black music like the blues. In 1958 he established the *little magazines *Yugen* and *Floating Bear*, and Totem Press, printing work by such writers as Allen Ginsberg, Charles Olson, Gary *Snyder, and Frank O'Hara. His predominant focus was on the divided self, whose pain emerges from being a black intellectual in a white world. Feeling the pressures of racism, he became increasingly outspoken and separate from the white literary circles in which he had been a significant participant. After the acclaimed play **Dutchman* (1964), a stylized treatment of inter-racial hostility, there followed a series of influential plays in the 1960s, *The Slave* (1964), *The Baptism* and *The Toilet* (both 1967), and *Four Black Revolutionary Plays* (1969), where he turned to explore the violent basis of relationships between whites and blacks, with the employment of extremely harsh images and stage techniques. He was a founder of the Black Arts Repertory Theatre in Harlem in 1965, which became the model for further black theatres throughout the country. During the 1960s he moved towards the black nationalism of the Nation of Islam, converting to Islam in 1968, changing his name to Imamu (later Amiri) Baraka. His poetry in *Black Art* (1966) and *Black Magic: Poems 1961–1967* (1969) continued to demand a black art and culture; whilst in his prose, the autobiographical novel *The System of Dante's Hell* (1965), *Home: Social Essays* (1966), the collection of short stories *Tales* (1967), and *Raise, Race, Rays, Raze* (1972), he analysed and commented upon the issues of race in American culture. In the 1970s he moved closer to the politics of Marxist-Leninism, producing Marxist poetry collections such as *Hard Facts* (1975) and the Marxist essays *Daggers and Javelins* (1984). He has continued to write poetry, publishing *In the Tradition: For Black Arthur Blythe* (1980) and *Reggae or Not! Poems* (1982), and embarked on an epic poem entitled *Why's/Wise*. Collections of his poetry and prose appeared in 1979, and *The Autobiography of LeRoi Jones/Amiri Baraka* was published in 1984. In addition, Baraka has written two influential accounts of black music, analysing its development from slave songs to the avant-garde jazz of Ornette Coleman and John Coltrane in *Blues People: Negro Music in White America* (1963) and *Black Music* (1968). Recent work includes *Shy's Wise, Y's: The Griot's Tale* (1994).

BARBELLION, W(ilhelm) N(ero) P(ilate), pseudonym of Bruce Frederick CUMMINGS (1889–1919), British diarist, born in Barnstaple, Devon. As a boy he conceived a keen interest in natural phenomena and achieved a high degree of self-education in biology. In 1912 he became an official of the Natural History Museum in London. He published work in the *Proceedings* of the Zoological Society and the *Journal of Botany*, and supplied other periodicals with more general articles. He resigned from his post in 1917 due to the onset of disseminated sclerosis. The voluminous diaries he had kept since 1903 provided material for the writing to which he subsequently devoted himself; *The Journal of a Disappointed Man* (1919), for which H. G. *Wells wrote an introduction, appeared under the 'Barbellion' pseudonym shortly before his death, rapidly gaining him a reputation as a major diarist. The work's intensely personal introspection combined to highly original effect with a nervously energetic style and an attitude of scientific detachment towards the self. A. J. and H. R. Cummings edited the *Journal*'s sequels, *Enjoying Life and Other Literary Remains* (1919) and *A Last Diary* (1920). R. H. Hellyar's *W. N. P. Barbellion* was published in 1926.

BARDWELL, Leland (1928–), Irish novelist and poet, born in India, where her father was working on the Madras Southern and Midland Railways; she grew up in Leixlip, Co. Kildare and was educated in Co. Kildare. She taught in Scotland, then lived in Paris and London before settling in Co. Monaghan. Among Bardwell's collections of poems are *The Mad Cyclist* (1970), *The Fly and the Bed Bug* (1984), and *Dostoevsky's Grave: Selected Poems* (1991). Her novels include *Girl on a Bicycle* (1977), described by Anthony *Burgess as 'a period gem', and *There We Have Been* (1989). The Attic Press in Dublin, which is strongly associated with women's writing, published a collection of her short stories, *Different Kinds of Love* (1987). She has also written for the theatre, television, and radio, for which she scripted a play based on the life of Edith Piaf. Bardwell's work has tended to concentrate upon the socio-political differences between Catholics and Protestants in Southern Ireland.

BARFOOT, Joan (1946–), Canadian novelist, born in Owen Sound, Ontario, educated at the University of Western Ontario. After graduating she began working as a journalist and joined the London, Ontario, *Free Press* in 1976. *Abra* (1978, UK title *Gaining Ground*, 1980), the first of Barfoot's radical feminist novels, deals with a young woman who leaves her husband and child to live in the Canadian wilderness. In *Dancing in the Dark* (1982; filmed in 1986) a criminally insane woman recounts her reasons for killing her unfaithful husband and searches for psychological freedom within the confines of her prison. *Duet for Three* (1985) and *Family News* (1989) analyse relations between mothers and daughters in terms of the quest for self-knowledge as the basis for authentic identity. Tensions between fantasy and reality reach a compelling intensity in *Plain Jane* (1992), in which a withdrawn female librarian begins corresponding with a convicted male criminal. *Charlotte and Claudia Keeping in Touch* (1992) is lighter in tone and deals affirmatively with a long-standing friendship between two women.

BARING, Maurice (1874–1945), British writer, born in London, educated at Trinity College, Cambridge. After the crash of his family's bank (Baring's Bank) in 1890 he worked as a diplomat in Europe, forming a close association with Russia, where he went to live in 1904, reporting on the Russo-Japanese war. He is credited with having discovered Chekhov's work in Moscow and introducing it to the West. His nonfiction works include *Landscapes in Russian Literature* (1910), *An Outline of Russian Literature* (1914), and *The Oxford Book of Russian Verse* (1924). Among his many novels are *C* (1924), *Cat's Cradle* (1925), *Daphne Adeane* (1926), and *The Coat without Seam* (1929). His conversion to Roman Catholicism was a turning point in his life, and with Hilaire *Belloc and G. K. *Chesterton he was regarded as a 'Catholic' writer; his two historical novels, *Robert Peckham* (1930) and *In My End Is My Beginning* (1931, on Mary, Queen of Scots), are on Catholic subjects. His wit is apparent in his autobiography *The Puppet Show of Memory* (1922), and in *Dead Letters* (1910) and *Lost Diaries* (1913) which gather imaginary communications from historical and literary characters. *Have You Anything To Declare?* (1937) was a personal anthology.

BARKER, A(udrey), L(illian) (1918–), British short-story writer and novelist, born in Kent. Her first highly praised collection of stories, *The Innocents* (1948), was followed by a novel, *Apology for a Hero* (1950). Further collections of stories confirmed her reputation as a leading practitioner of her craft; she also continued to experiment with form. *The Middling* (1967) and *A Heavy Feather* (1978) are fragmented narratives loosely linked by theme and perspective; *A Source of Embarrassment* (1974) is a tightly woven domestic satire; *John Brown's Body* (1969) is a taut *tour de force* of psychological unease. Praised by contemporaries such as Francis *King and Rebecca *West, Barker's novels and stories of the 1970s and 1980s present her distinctive tragi-comic vision with an increasing craftsmanship and economy of style, culminating in one of her finest novels, *The Gooseboy* (1987). The bitter levity of her vision is again displayed in *The Woman Who Talked to Herself* (1989); the book's subtitle, 'An Articulated Novel', fittingly sums up Barker's eclectic attitude to fictional form. *Zeph* (1992), an unconventional rites-of-passage novel, is the comic monologue of a young woman who, without any natural talent, determines to be a writer. *Any Excuse for a Party* (1991) is a retrospective collection of Barker's best short fiction, and *Elements of Doubt* (1992) collects her ghost stories.

BARKER, George (Granville) (1913–91), British poet, born in Loughton, Essex, educated at the Regent Street Polytechnic. From 1930 onward he lived mainly as a freelance writer and held visiting professorships at universities in America, Japan, and elsewhere. Following the appearance of *Thirty Preliminary Poems* in 1933, he gained considerable critical attention in 1935 with *Poems* and *Janus*, the latter consisting of two prose pieces entitled 'The Documents of Death' and 'The Bacchants'. T. S. *Eliot, Barker's publisher at *Faber and Faber, arranged a modest income for him, and W. B. *Yeats conferred on him the distinction of being the youngest contributor to his *Oxford Book of Modern Verse* (1936). Throughout the 1930s his poetry maintained a high level of rhetorical and emotional energy, partaking of surrealism's imaginative licence while remaining fundamentally conventional in form. *Calamiterror* (1937) typifies his fondness for long sequences amalgamating numerous themes in its cumulative responses to the Spanish Civil War, visionary experiences, and socio-cultural conditions in general. With Dylan *Thomas, he was the chief progenitor of the extravagant manner identified with the poets of the *New Apocalypse. The essentially metaphysical character of his poetry became more consistently apparent during the 1940s in a succession of volumes which include *Lament and Triumph* (1940) and *Sacred and Secular Elegies* (1943). Faith and doubt remain dominant elements beneath the irreverent surfaces of *The True Confession of George Barker* (1950; revised and enlarged 1965), which reviews the habitual preoccupations of his writing, among them guilt, sexuality, and death. His later collections of verse, which include *The Golden Chains* (1968), *Poems of Places and People* (1971), and *Anno Domino* (1983), exhibit a mood of elegiac contemplation and are more conversationally relaxed in tone than hitherto. A *Collected Poems*, edited by Robert Fraser, was produced in 1987. Among his other writings is the complexly symbolic novel *The Dead Seagull* (1950).

BARKER, Howard (1946–), British dramatist, born in London, educated at Sussex University. His first substantial works were *Claw* (1975), about a petty criminal exploited and finally eliminated by a corrupt establishment, and *Stripwell* (1975), in which it is the representative of authority, a self-doubting judge, who ends up killed, this time by a vengeful sociopath. These plays, which can be compared with those of

Howard *Brenton and David *Hare, have been followed by others equally combative in their social criticism but more darkly comic in tone and increasingly exotic in their language and form. Some, notably *That Good between Us* (1977) and *The Hang of the Gaol* (1978), offer somewhat nightmarish visions of political oppression in a Britain of the near future. Other plays include *Fair Slaughter* (1977); *The Loud Boy's Life* (1980); *No End of Blame* (1981), about the growing despair of a radical cartoonist; *Victory* (1983), about corruption and persecution after the restoration of Charles II; *The Power of the Dog* (1984); *The Castle* (1985); *Seven Lears* (1989); *The Europeans* (1993); and *Hated Nightfall* (1994). Barker's *Scenes from an Execution*, which involves the repression of a heterodox woman painter in imperial Venice, and raises questions about censorship and artistic freedom, was broadcast on radio in 1984 and staged in 1990. He has also written for television, and made a modern stage adaptation of Middleton's *Women Beware Women* (1986).

BARKER, Pat (1943–), British novelist, born in Thornaby-on-Tees, educated at the London School of Economics. Barker's early novels focused on the grim lives of working-class people in the north of England. Her first novel, *Union Street* (1982), was more a collection of linked stories about the lives of seven women on a working-class street in a northern English city. Though often shocking in its depiction of violence, poverty, and hopelessness, it also celebrates the courage and wit of women who hold their families and communities together. *Century's Daughter* (1986) chronicles the life of an elderly woman, born into a large impoverished family, who now lives in a decaying house due for demolition by the Council. Like most of Barker's work, it has a strong historical perspective; she links not only the woman's past and present, but the poverty of the early part of the century with the recession and unemployment in Britain in the 1980s. Her other novels of this period include *Blow Your House Down* (1984) and *The Man Who Wasn't There* (1989). Barker changed direction radically with an acclaimed trilogy of novels that deal with the effects of the First World War: *Regeneration* (1991), in which the torments of war are articulated in a therapeutic talking relationship between doctor and patient, *The Eye in the Door* (1993), in which the homosexuality of acclaimed public figures becomes the occasion for a witch-hunt, and *The Ghost Road* (1995; Booker Prize), a powerful treatment of the relativity of cultural and sexual values. All three novels are densely laden with the issues of the time: psychiatry and psychoanalysis, shell-shock, creative responses to war, and political intrigues in a rapidly changing age.

BARLEY, Nigel (1947–), British writer on anthropology and travel; after gaining a doctorate in anthropology at Oxford, Barley taught at London University until 1978, when he left for two years in Cameroon. His researches provided a basis for *The Innocent Anthropologist* (1983), which was acclaimed for the accessibility and humour of its evocation of life among the Dowayo people. The book's witty critique of conventional anthropology is sustained in *A Plague of Caterpillars* (1986) and *Not a Hazardous Sport* (1988), which reflect Barley's experiences as a fieldworker and traveller in Indonesia. His other publications include *Native Land* (1990), on the rituals of English life; *The Coast* (1990), a humorous novel set in Nigeria; *The Duke of Puddle Dock* (1991), a work of travel and biography tracing the career of Sir Stamford Raffles; and *Smashing Pots* (1994), about African earthenware.

BARNES, Djuna (1892–1982), American novelist, poet, short-story writer, and playwright, born in Cornwall-on-Hudson, New York, educated at the Pratt Institute, Brooklyn and the Arts Student League, New York. She worked as a journalist and also published some stories in *The *Dial* and *Vanity Fair*. Her first collection of poems and stories appeared in *The Book of Repulsive Women* (1915), which satirized the stereotypes of female sexuality. Her first play, *Three from the Earth* (1919), was followed by *Kurzy of the Sea* (1919), *An Irish Triangle* (1919), *To the Dogs* (1923), *The Dove* (1923), and *She Tells Her Daughters* (1923). In 1920 she left for Paris where she lived for twelve years, during which time she enjoyed a high reputation as a writer and moved in the artistic circles of Mina *Loy and Gertrude *Stein. Her work of this period includes *A Book* (1923), later reissued in an extended version entitled *A Night among the Horses* (1929); *Ryder* (1928), a bestseller which exposed the sufferings of women under patriarchy in a brilliant stylistic parody; and *Ladies' Almanack* (1928), which celebrated female sexuality and mocked eighteenth-century language. She achieved fame with the publication of *Nightwood* (1936), edited and introduced by T. S. *Eliot. A novel about complex and difficult relationships set in homosexual Paris in the 1920s, she again explores women's position within patriarchy. After settling in Greenwich Village in 1937, a long period of virtual silence followed, broken in 1958 by the publication of the blank-verse play *The Antiphon*, in which a mother and daughter act out their tense relationship in the family. *Spillway* (1962), a collection of stories, was followed by two essays based on Paris in the 1920s in *Vagaries Malicieux* (1975). Early and previously uncollected work appeared in *Smoke and Other Early Stories* (1982), and later, in Alyce Barry's edition *I Could never Be Lonely without a Husband: Interviews by Djuna Barnes* (1985).

BARNES, Julian (Patrick) (1946–), British novelist, born in Leicester, educated at Oxford University. In his first novel, *Metroland* (1980; Somerset Maugham Award, 1981), his precocious hero, Christopher Lloyd, recounts the events of his suburban childhood, his student days in Paris in 1968, and his eventual return, with wife and baby, to the peaceful suburban landscapes of 'Metroland'. *Before She Met Me* (1982), a study of murderous obsession and marital claustrophobia, was followed by the novel with which Barnes consolidated his reputation as one of the more innovative and witty of the younger generation of writers.

Flaubert's Parrot (1984), which was awarded the Prix Medicis in France, is narrated by Geoffrey Braithwaite, a retired doctor and widowed cuckold, who attempts to come to terms with the bitterness of his memories by pursuing his obsession for the writings of Flaubert, whilst on a touring holiday in France. Amalgamating scholarly allusion, tourist guide, exam questions on *Madame Bovary*, and eccentric biographical facts about the life of the great French novelist, the book displays Barnes's prevailing interest in the relationship between life and art. *Staring at the Sun* (1986), a more conventional narrative, follows its female protagonist from her girlhood in wartime Britain, through her unsuccessful marriage to great old age, in a future society of 2020. *A History of the World in 10½ Chapters* (1989) shows the writer at his most playful and experimental in his treatment of a number of related themes: the nature of art, religion, love, and death. The work takes the form of a series of ingeniously linked stories, whose central image is that of the Ark. The first of these, for example, is narrated by a woodworm 'stowaway' on Noah's Ark during the Great Flood; another memorably describes the painting of Géricault's masterpiece 'The Raft of the Medusa'; a third is about an American astronaut who becomes involved in a search for the 'true' Ark. *Talking It Over* (1991), although perhaps less unconventional in form, picks up where the earlier work left off, with a meditation on the vicissitudes of love. *The Porcupine* (1992) is set in an unnamed Eastern European country and concerns the trial of its former dictator following the overthrow of the communist regime over which he presided for many years. As crisply written and ironic as his previous work, it displays yet another side to Barnes's apparently effortless versatility. *Cross Channel* (1996) is a collection of short stories set in France. Unlike many of his contemporaries, the author has shown himself to be at ease in a number of different literary forms, ranging from the essay to the comedy of manners, from *Letters from London* (1995), his contributions on topical themes to the *New Yorker*, to the detective novels written under the pseudonym 'Dan Kavanagh'. Barnes has also worked as literary editor and television critic for the *New Statesman*, *The Sunday Times* and the *Observer*.

BARNES, Peter (1931–), British dramatist, born in London, educated at Stroud Grammar School. He was a film critic, a film story editor, and a screenwriter before he turned his attention to the theatre. His first successful work was *The Ruling Class* (1968), a 'baroque comedy' satirizing a supposedly decadent and moribund British aristocracy in scathing terms. It was followed by other plays ambitious in terms of both style and content, several of them dealing sceptically and sardonically with political and religious subjects, many of them consciously indebted to the Jacobeans, particularly Ben Jonson, and most of them set in relatively remote periods and distant places. These include a double bill (1969) comprising *Leonardo's Last Supper*, a gothic comedy about the Renaissance painter, and *Noonday Demons*, about two wrangling fourth-century holy men; *The Bewitched* (1974), about the last of the Spanish Habsburgs and the era of the *auto-da-fé*; *Laughter* (1978), two linked plays, one about Ivan the Terrible, the other about Auschwitz, each attempting to explore the nature and limits of humour; *Red Noses* (1985), about a troupe of clowns wandering through mainland Europe during the Black Death; and *Sunsets and Glories* (1990), about the thirteenth-century hermit who became Pope Celestine V. Among his many adaptations are Wedekind's *Lulu* plays, and Jonson's *The Devil Is an Ass* and *Bartholomew Fair*. He has also written for television, in 1992 celebrating the 500th anniversary of the discovery of America with a characteristically harsh and cynical play, *Goodbye Columbus*.

BARNETT, Correlli (Douglas) (1927–), British military historian, born at Norbury in Surrey, educated at Exeter College, Oxford. In 1977 he became Keeper of the Churchill Archives Centre at Cambridge University. *The Desert Generals* (1960), a controversial study of the North African Campaign, established Barnett's reputation as a military historian; his subsequent works, which are noted for their concentration and lucidity, include *The Swordbearers* (1963), on the commanders of the First World War; *Britain and Her Army* (1970), a review of interactions between the army and society in Britain from the Tudor era onward; *The Great War* (1979); and *Engage the Enemy more Closely* (1991), a survey of the Royal Navy in the Second World War. Barnett's 'Pride and the Fall' series, an analysis of Britain's industrial and political decline since the late nineteenth century, includes *The Collapse of British Power* (1972), *The Audit of War* (1986), and *The Lost Victory: British Dreams, British Realities, 1945–50* (1995).

Barren Ground, a novel by Ellen *Glasgow, published in 1925. Its central figure, Dorinda Oakley, is the daughter of a poor farmer in Virginia of Scottish-Irish stock. She goes to work in Nathan Pedlar's store and falls in love with Jason Greylock, the feckless son of the village doctor; the day before their wedding Jason is obliged to marry an earlier fiancée. Distressed, Dorinda leaves for New York where she is employed as a children's nurse by Dr Faraday, who had come to her aid after a road accident. At her father's death Dorinda returns home to find the family farm run down and overgrown with broomsedge. Both her mother, now an invalid, and her idle brother Rufus are unable to manage the farm and Dorinda sets about restoring it. Later she marries Nathan Pedlar, as much out of compassion as of love, and after Nathan's death, looks after her first love, Jason, now an alcoholic, until his death. In order for the 'barren ground' to yield the desired crops the land has to be worked with taxing energy, the non-productive indigenous growths of the area being broomsedge, pine, and life-everlasting. Each of these plants gives its name to a section of the novel: broomsedge stands for the sexual impulse; pine for the brooding presence of sickness and death; and life-everlasting for that nameless force which enables people like Dorinda to persevere through all adversities until death.

BARRIE, Sir J(ames) M(atthew) (1860–1937), British writer, born in Kirriemuir, Scotland, the son of a weaver, educated at Edinburgh University. He turned first to journalism with the *Nottinghamshire Journal*, a period reflected in *When a Man's Single* (1888). After producing several sentimental *Kailyard sketches and stories about Thrums (a fictional version of Kirriemuir), such as *Auld Licht Idylls* (1888), *A Window in Thrums* (1889), and *The Little Minister* (1891), Barrie made the stage his career. His principal plays were *The *Admirable Crichton* (1902); the perennial children's favourite, *Peter Pan* (1904); *Alice Sit-By-the-Fire* (1905), an amusing parody of the society plays made fashionable by *Pinero and others; **What Every Woman Knows* (1908); the interesting *Dear Brutus* (1917), in which a magician gives his guests a glimpse of the alternative lives they might have led, showing that their disappointments come more from inner inadequacy than external chance; *Mary Rose* (1920), about a young wife and mother stolen by fairies; and the Biblical drama *The Boy David* (1936). From the first Barrie faced accusations of sentimentality, partly because of his whimsical imagination, his fondness for magic islands and enchanted forests, and partly because of the number of amiable and charming characters he introduced into his work. In particular, he tended to idealize childhood and maternal devotion. But, as Max *Beerbohm wrote, his 'excesses in the sweetly sad' must be measured against 'his humour, his curious inventiveness, his sure sense for dramatic effect'. As a Scot, he took a special delight in gently mocking what he saw as the frivolity of the English, especially the upper-class English: *The Admirable Crichton* and *Little Mary* (1903) both have such satiric edge. And if he refused seriously to confront pain or evil, his work is often marked by a distinctive melancholy, usually associated with an unwilling or unacknowledged awareness that innocence cannot indefinitely survive contact with reality.

BARRY, Philip (Jerome Quinn) (1896–1949), American dramatist, born in Rochester, New York, educated at Yale. Barry was a frail child whose early years of invalidism turned him into an avid reader, who developed a reputation for precocious wit. At Yale he won the Yale dramatic society prize for his first play, *Autonomy*. He enrolled in George Pierce *Baker's famous '47 Workshop' at Harvard, a workshop drama school for aspiring playwrights later attended by Eugene *O'Neill. His next play, *The Jilts*, later renamed *You and I* (1923), was the first of his many Broadway successes in which the eternal conflict between the claims of art and mammon is enlivened by Barry's witty epigrammatic style. Thereafter Barry's career as a dramatist was marked by the high success of his comedies of marital and sexual difficulties, and the relative failure of his work when it reflected a dimension of experiential despair which often drew him to fantasy. His other plays include *Paris Bound* (1927), *Holiday* (1928), *Hotel Universe* (1930), *Tomorrow and Tomorrow* (1931), and *The Animal Kingdom* (1932). Perhaps his greatest success was *The Philadelphia Story* (1939), which was later made into a film starring Katherine Hepburn, Cary Grant, and James Stewart.

BARRY, Sebastian (1955–), Irish poet, novelist, and dramatist, born in Dublin, educated at Trinity College, Dublin. He lived in Europe, America, and England before returning to Ireland. Barry's poetry collections include *The Water-Colourist* (1983), and in 1986 he edited *The Inherited Boundaries*, an anthology of 'younger' poets from the Republic. His plays include *Boss Grady's Boys*, which was produced at the *Abbey Theatre in 1988 and published in *Prayers of Sherkin; Boss Grady's Boys: Two Plays* (1991). His novel *The Engine of Owl-Light* (1987) is a poetically intense and experimental work set in America. Barry's fiction is similar to that of some contemporary Irish writers, such as Neil *Jordan and Aidan *Mathews, in looking away from traditionally insular concerns towards more personal, 'foreign' influences.

BARSTOW, Stan(ley) (1928–), English novelist, born in Horbury, Yorkshire into a mining family, and educated at Ossett Grammar School. From 1944 to 1962 he worked as a draughtsman and sales executive in the engineering industry; he graduated with an MA from the Open University in 1982. Barstow's emergence as a writer in 1960 coincided with that of John *Braine, Alan *Sillitoe, and other *'angry young men'. His first novel, *A *Kind of Loving* (1960), a candid and moving story of contemporary pressures on love and marriage, was an immediate success and was followed by a celebrated film version in 1962. Having helped to put the north of England and the working-class hero on the literary map, Barstow continued to search for the universal within a canvas of northern provincial life. Set in the same fictitious town of Cressley were two sequels to his first novel, *The Watchers on the Shore* (1966) and *The Right True End* (1976), which follow its hero, Vic Brown, through the break-up of his unfortunate marriage and into a more fulfilling and loving relationship; the trilogy was published as *A Kind of Loving: The Vic Brown Trilogy* in 1981 and adapted for television in the same year. After *Ask Me Tomorrow* (1962), an introspective work about a writer, appeared *Joby* (1964), written from the point of view of an 11-year-old boy whose own problems are matched by the impending crisis of the Second World War. Realistic settings and a continuing concern with marriage and loneliness characterize *A Raging Calm* (1968; adapted for television, 1974), and *A Brother's Tale* (1980). The Yorkshire town of 'Daker' during the Second World War is the setting for Barstow's trilogy comprising *Just You Wait and See* (1986), *Give Us This Day* (1989), and *Next of Kin* (1991); focusing on the Palmer family it vividly evokes the atmosphere of a small town plunged into war. In his short stories, volumes of which include *The Desperadoes and Other*

Stories (1961), *A Season with Eros* (1971), and *The Glad Eye and Other Stories* (1984), Barstow shows a realistic appreciation of contemporary concerns.

BARTH, John (1930–), American novelist and short-story writer, born in Cambridge, Maryland, educated at Julliard School of Music, New York City, where he studied orchestration, but he turned towards an academic career in literature after completing a Master's degree at Johns Hopkins University. From 1953 until 1965 he taught in the Department of English at Pennsylvania State University and he was a Professor of English at the State University of New York at Buffalo between 1965 and 1973; in 1973 he became Centennial Professor of English and Creative Writing at Johns Hopkins. His first two novels, *The Floating Opera* (1956; revised edition 1967) and *The End of the Road* (1958; revised edition 1967) are realistic in their fictional techniques but also show the preoccupation with abstract, metaphysical problems and his gift for comedy that characterize the later fiction on which his reputation largely rests. His third novel, *The* **Sot-Weed Factor* (1960), perhaps his greatest, is an exuberant, immensely inventive, pastiche of late seventeenth-century English prose that centres around the progress of the poet Ebenezer Cooke in the New World. This was followed by **Giles Goat-Boy; or, The Revised New Syllabus* (1966), an equally ambitious novel in which the world is fictionally re-imagined as a giant university divided into 'East' and 'West' campuses, each controlled by giant computers. His later writings include two volumes of short stories, *Lost in the Funhouse* (1968) (see METAFICTION) and *Chimera* (1972), and the novels, *Letters* (1979), an epistolary novel notable for its *post-modernist use of the author as one of the characters; *Sabbatical: A Romance* (1982); *The Tidewater Tales: A Novel* (1987); and *Last Voyage of Somebody the Sailor* (1991). In addition, he has published two volumes of non-fictional prose, *The Literature of Exhaustion, and the Literature of Replenishment* (1982) and *The Friday Book: Essays and Other Non-Fiction* (1984). He has been the recipient of grants from the Rockefeller Foundation and the American Academy, and he won the National Book Award in 1973. See *Passionate Virtuosity: The Fiction of Barth* (1983), by Charles B. Harris.

BARTHELME, Donald (1931–89), American short-story writer and novelist, born in Philadelphia; he was brought up in Texas, and later moved to New York. Variously described as an 'anti-novelist' and a 'poet of order gone', Barthelme will be remembered for pushing the short story to its furthest experimental limits, and for the poetic and unvarnished beauty of his prose style. He was a member of a generation of writers such as *Coover, *John Hawkes, *Gaddis, *Gass, *Pynchon, *Barth, and *Vonnegut, all of them loosely united in their foregrounding of language and form, the vague irrealism of their work, and their preference of pattern over plot and voice over character. Barthelme resisted identification with the minimalist trend but acknowledged the similarity of his work, in its formal aspects, to a distinctive school of twentieth-century writing remarkable above all for its range and diversity. His first experiment in non-linear narrative was the volume of short texts *Come Back, Dr Caligari* (1964), followed by *Unspeakable Practices, Unnatural Acts* (1968). His reputation was securely established with the short novel *Snow White* (1967), a contemporary parodic reworking of the Disney film. Other volumes include *City Life* (1970), *Sadness* (1972), and *Guilty Pleasures* (1974). Barthelme's thematic concern was with twentieth-century dislocation in all its aspects; he used a wide variety of textual strategies ranging from satire and parody to collage and an approximation of prose poetry. Critics saw in his later volumes of fiction an increasing mastery of language and a fascination with its limits: these include the novel *The Dead Father* (1975); *Amateurs* (1976), a collection of fables; and *Great Days* (1979), composed almost entirely of dialogue. His stories are collected in *Forty Stories* (1988) and *Sixty Stories* (1989). A posthumous novel, *The King* (1990), a reworking of Arthurian legends, was hailed by Salman *Rushdie for its visionary qualities and its relevance in the time of the Gulf War.

BATES, H(erbert) E(rnest) (1905–74), British novelist and short-story writer, born in Northamptonshire. His first novel, *The Two Sisters* (1926), was followed by a stream of novels and short stories as well as plays, essays, gardening books, children's books, and several volumes of autobiography. He was at his best with the short story and acknowledged Guy de Maupassant as his major influence. Early novels such as *The Fallow Land* (1932) and *The Poacher* (1935) were mainly on rural themes, and his vivid descriptions of country landscapes, seasons, and country folk characterizes much of his work. During the Second World War he served as a Squadron Leader in the RAF, and published several volumes of war tales under the pseudonym 'Flying Officer X' as well as the highly popular novels *Fair Stood the Wind for France* (1944) and *The Cruise of 'The Breadwinner'* (1946); this period and his later wartime experiences in Burma and India, described in novels such as *The Purple Plain* (1947) and *The Jacaranda Tree* (1949), saw a broadening of background, a deepening of psychological insights, and a developing sombre and compassionate tone. Other novels include *Love for Lydia* (1952), *The Darling Buds of May* (1958), and *The Triple Echo* (1970). His many volumes of stories include *The Woman Who Had Imagination* (1934), *The Flying Goat* (1939), *The Daffodil Sky* (1955), and the posthumously published *The Yellow Meads of Asphodel* (1976).

BATESON, F(rederick) (Noel) W(ilse) (1901–78), British critic and editor, the son of a cotton broker, born at Styal in Cheshire, educated at Trinity College, Oxford, and Harvard. His early publications include *English Comic Drama, 1700–1750* (1929). As an editor with Cambridge University Press from 1929 to 1940, he was responsible for preparing the *Cambridge Bibliography of English Literature* (1940). After a period as an agricultural administrator during the Second World War, he lectured at Oxford University from 1946 to 1969. In 1951 he founded *Essays in Criticism*, which succeeded **Scrutiny* as the pre-eminent scholarly journal in its field after the latter's demise in 1953; he continued to edit the periodical until 1974. Among his principal critical works, which emphasize the need to evaluate literature with reference to its historical contexts, are *English Poetry and the English Language* (1934), *Wordsworth: A Re-interpretation* (1954), and *The Language of Literature* (1971). Other publications under his editorship include *The Works of Congreve* (1930) and Matthew Arnold's *Essays on English Literature* (1965).

BAUGHAN, Blanche (1870–1958), New Zealand poet, born in England; despite parental opposition she attended London University. She then became involved with women's suffrage and worked amongst the poor in London's East End before settling in New Zealand in 1900. Her first works, *Verses* (1898) and *Reuben and Other Poems* (1903), were published in England but subsequent works in New Zealand, the first of which, *Shingle-Short and Other Verses* (1908), is a long verse monologue written in New Zealand idiom. She is particularly noted for her concern for ordinary lives amidst the exotic landscape, and her much anthologized 'Bush Section' is valued for the energy and verve of its long Whitmanesque lines which vividly describe the deforested landscape. *Brown Bread from a Colonial Oven* (1912) is a series of vivid prose portraits of colonial life, while *Poems from the Port Hills, Christchurch* (1923) captures life as it was in the early days of settlement. Baughan subsequently concentrated on travel writing and her work as a prison reformer.

BAWDEN, Nina (Mary) (née Mabey) (1925–), British novelist, born in London, educated at Somerville College, Oxford. Bawden has published many books for both adults and children. The cross-fertilization between her adult and her children's works is unusually marked. She reworked her adult novel *Evil by the Sea* (1957), publishing a version for children in 1976, and many of her concerns—difficult children, neglected childhoods, the gap between generations—are common to both kinds of writing. She excels at portraits of modern middle-class family life in contemporary London, but frequently returns to the past as a repository of secrets and hidden influences. Two of her most powerful children's books, *Carrie's War* (1973) and *The Peppermint Pig* (1975), are set in the recent past and deal with children in exile from their homes; the former evokes her experiences as an evacuee during the Second World War, a formative period on which she drew in her adult novel *Circles of Deceit* (1987) and in a short book for children, *Keeping Henry* (1988). Many of her adult novels, notably *Anna Apparent* (1972), *Afternoon of a Good Woman* (1976), *Walking Naked* (1981), and *The Ice House* (1983) deal with the exposure of a suffering self beneath the prosperous surface. The painful feelings of women in her adult novels have a parallel in the anxieties children suffer at the hands of untrustworthy adults in her children's books. *Family Money* (1991), an ironic tale of families, ageing, and inheritance, harnesses the tempo of a thriller to an examination of the manners and morals of an acquisitive society. *In My Own Time: Almost an Autobiography* (1994) recalls the 'myths, half-truths, fancies and deceits that make up family history' and gives a moving portrait of her oldest son, who was a schizophrenic. Bawden received the CBE in 1995.

BAXTER, James K(eir) (1926–72), New Zealand poet, born in Dunedin, educated at Quaker schools in England and New Zealand. A major spiritual and literary figure, he blended a passionate concern for everyday New Zealand life with a dedication to basic Christian principles and myths. With the collections *Beyond the Palisade* (1944) and *Blow, Wind of Fruitfulness* (1948), Baxter became the leading poet of his generation in New Zealand. In 1957 Baxter's often stormy life underwent a major change when he became both teetotal and a Catholic; *In Fires of No Return* (1958) reflects this period. *Pig Island Letters* (1966) demonstrated new assurance and a range of poetic voice which encompassed the extremes of his own experience, from drink and sleeping rough to religious meditation and the torments of the flesh. *Aspects of Poetry in New Zealand* (1967) gave insights into his critical outlook. He reaffirmed his stature with *The Rock Woman* (1969), a selection of poems. Baxter was increasingly devoted to an idiosyncratic kind of community work, often amongst young Maori people, and from 1970 he established a commune for 'hippy drop-outs' alongside a Maori Catholic community on the Wanganui River; *Jerusalem Sonnets* (1970) and *Jerusalem Daybook* (1971) reflect this period. Two volumes of plays were published in 1971, and Baxter was correcting proofs of *Autumn Testament* (1972) when he died. The posthumous *Unpublished Poems 1945–1972* (1976) further enhanced Baxter's standing. *James K. Baxter as Critic* (1978), edited by Frank McKay, revealed influences as diverse as *Hardy, *Yeats, *MacNeice, *Durrell, and *Lowell. *Collected Poems* (1980; corrected 1981) was edited by J. E. Weir, and *Collected Plays* (1982) was edited by Howard McNaughton. Studies are *James K. Baxter* by Mike *Doyle (1976) and *The Life of James K. Baxter* by Frank McKay (1990).

BAYNTON, Barbara (1857–1929), Australian author, born in New South Wales. Her early life was turbulent; having been deserted by her first husband in 1887, she moved to Sydney and in 1890 married Thomas Baynton, a retired surgeon with literary interests. In 1896 she began publishing stories, first in the **Bulletin*. After her first visit to London in 1902, and Baynton's death in 1904, she spent more frequent periods in England and for a short time, from 1921, she was married to Lord Headley. Her first collection, *Bush Studies* (1902), depicts the grim exigencies of bush life in the early years of the century, in a starkly realist tone. Many of the protagonists are women, frequently harshly treated by their menfolk, who become the victims of cruel circumstance. In one story, 'The Chosen Vessel', a women left alone in a remote bush hut is raped and murdered by a passing swagman; in 'Billy Skywonkie', a young woman of mixed race journeys to a bush station in search of work, only to be rejected on the grounds of her colour. A new edition of the book, *Cobbers* (1917), contained additional stories. *Human Toll* (1907) is a novel. Her work has been brought back into focus by *feminist criticism.

Beacon, The, a literary magazine edited by Albert *Gomes in Trinidad between 1931 and 1933. It totalled twenty-eight issues, and was revived for one further issue in November 1939. Rather more politically focused than its immediate predecessor, **Trinidad*, the magazine served, as its editor put it, to debunk 'bourgeois morality, obscurantist religion and primitive capitalism'. *The Beacon* therefore aroused bitter opposition, particularly from the colonial authorities and the Catholic Church. Its contributors included such politically radical West Indian writers as the novelists Alfred *Mendes and Ralph *De Bossière, and the historian C. L. R. *James. *The Beacon*'s greatest achievement was to encourage West Indian writers to examine their own societies, and to discard Eurocentric preconceptions and literary conventions. See Reinhard W. Sander and Peter K. Ayers (eds.), *From Trinidad: An Anthology of Early West Indian Writing* (1978).

BEAR, Greg(ory) (Dale) (1951–), American *science fiction writer, born in San Diego, California, educated at San Diego State University. His first works were *space operas such as *Hegira* (1979) and *Strength of Stones* (1981). His more substantial later works include *Blood Music* (1985), which deals with the consequences of biological experiment; *Eon* (1985) and its sequels *Eternity* (1988) and *Legacy* (1995), which describe the aftermath of nuclear war; *The Forge of God* (1987), which again deals with catastrophe; and *Queen of Angels* (1990), which predicts a high-tech, ecologically sound twenty-first century, and was followed by a sequel, *Moving Mars* (1993).

Beat Generation, The, a term applied to a group of writers who established a rebellion against society and came to prominence about 1956, centred in San Francisco and New York City. Whilst their activities overlapped with the development of the *San Francisco Renaissance, and with the influences and developments of figures like Charles *Olson and Robert *Creeley of the *Black Mountain School, their inception came about in New York City in the late 1940s, when Allen *Ginsberg, William *Burroughs, Jack *Kerouac, and others met in bars and cafeterias around Columbia University. Writing in the 1958 *Esquire* magazine, Jack Kerouac summarized the philosophy of the Beats: '... a generation of crazy illuminated hipsters suddenly rising and roaming America, serious, curious, bumming and hitchhiking everywhere, ragged beatific, beautiful in an ugly graceful new way—a vision gleaned from the way we had heard the word *beat*, meaning down and out but full of intense conviction.' Manifesting a weariness of corruption and a thoroughgoing critique of the crass commercialism of modern society, such writers as Kerouac, Ginsberg, Burroughs, Gregory *Corso, Lawrence *Ferlinghetti, and John Clellon *Holmes expressed themselves in a 'hip' vocabulary, combined with phrases and experiences from their dealings with Buddhism and Oriental philosophies, and their significant association with the jazz music and rhythms of people like Charlie Parker, Dizzy Gillespie, Miles Davis, and Thelonious Monk. The 'anti-establishment Beat bum' included other such figures as Carl Solomon, Michael *McClure, Philip *Whalen, Gary *Snyder, and Philip Lamantia. Like many movements, they were largely the projection of the media, albeit aided and abetted by its participants. One of the pervasive fictions surrounding the Beat writers was their cult of energy, their tendency to exalt the present over the past, action over reflection, movement over stasis. Yet many of the Beat works also show an anxiety about attaining such a position, revealing a solitude and vulnerability despite the competing and contradictory demands of participation and communalism. These positions are evident in various works which have come to be regarded as seminal within the Beat movement, such as Jack Kerouac's **On The Road* (1957), a narrative about the experiences encountered on a road journey across the USA; Allen Ginsberg's **Howl* (1956), an angry and vituperative critique of contemporary social values and mores; and Michael McClure's *Ghost Tantras* (1964), a formulation of poetry as beast language. There are various books about the Beats, but significant among them are Michael McClure's *Scratching the Beat Surface* (1982), and Arthur Knight and Kit Knight (eds.), *The Beat Vision* (1987).

Beatles, The, a popular music group from Liverpool consisting of George Harrison (1943–), John Lennon (1940–80), Paul McCartney (1942–), and Ringo Starr (1940–), which enjoyed enormous international acclaim from 1963 until it disbanded in 1970. Lennon and McCartney composed most of the group's repertoire, showing increasingly innovative melodic and lyrical abilities as their careers progressed. In 1965 each of the members was awarded the MBE. Their work took on a markedly experimental character in the *Revolver* album of 1966. *Sergeant Pepper's Lonely Hearts Club Band* (1967) set new artistic standards for popular music, drawing favourable responses from serious cultural commentators for the poetic and compositional achievements it represented. Lennon, whose idiosyncratic literary talent is evident in his books *In His Own Write* (1964) and *A Spaniard in the Works* (1965), was murdered in New York in 1980. Harrison, McCartney, and Starr have remained individually successful as entertainers since The Beatles broke up. *Shout!* (1981) by Philip Norman is the best of numerous histories of the group.

BEATTIE, Ann (1947–), American novelist and short-story writer, born in Washington, DC, educated at the American University and the University of Connecticut; she has taught at Harvard and the University of Virginia. Beattie is known for her precise observations of suburban, middle-class life. Her early work in the collection of stories *Distortions* (1976) and the novel *Chilly Scenes of Winter* (1976) documents the fate of the idealism of the 1960s as 'the Woodstock generation' settles into comfortable middle-class middle age. Her novel *Falling in Place* (1980) is similarly concerned with the emotional disjunctures involved in being a contemporary urban American citizen and chronicles, largely through the eyes of the children, the breakdown of a conventional American marriage. *Love Always* (1985) combines a realistic attention to descriptive and thematic details with a satirical strain of black humour in its account of the world of contemporary media. Beattie's stories, which appear frequently in the *New Yorker*, have been collected in *Secrets and Surprises* (1979), *The Burning House* (1982), and *Where You'll Find Me* (1986); *Picturing Will* (1990) is a later novel.

BEAUMAN, Sally, see ROMANTIC FICTION.

BEAVER, Bruce (1928–), Australian poet, born in Manly, New South Wales. He led a peripatetic early life, including four years spent in New Zealand. As a young man he had suffered from manic depression and his early collections of poetry, *Under the Bridge* (1961), *Seawall and Shoreline* (1964), and *Open at Random* (1967), reflect his inner turmoil. *Letters to Live Poets* (1969), his major work, was written at great speed at a time when he thought he would lose his mind completely; the 'Letters' are confessional in tone and his reflections upon childhood and manhood, fears and obsessions, are effectively set against striking images of landscapes. *Lauds and Plaints* (1974), a sequence of poems celebrating the human spirit, combines a new optimism with effective experiments in form. *Odes and Days* (1975) includes poems addressed to Beethoven, Mahler, Holderlin, and Rilke. Other volumes include *Death's Directives* (1978), *As It Was* (1979), a prose poem, *Charmed Lives* (1988), and *Anima and Other Poems* (1994). He has also published several novels. *New and Selected Poetry 1960–1990* appeared in 1991. As an editor of *Poetry Australia* he contributed to the development of the 'New Australian Poetry' in the 1960s and 1970s.

BEAVERBROOK, William Maxwell ('Max') Aitken, 1st Baron (1879–1964), newspaper proprietor. Having made a fortune in his native Canada, he came to England in 1910 and began a career in politics, rising to the position of Lord Privy Seal in Churchill's wartime Cabinet in 1943. Raised to the peerage in 1916 Beaverbrook became the most powerful figure in popular journalism, acquiring the *Daily Express*, the *Evening Standard*, and the *Sunday Express* during the course of his energetic career. A champion of the British Empire, he used his papers to crusade for his own, often controversial, political causes. He wrote several books on politics and the First World War, including *The Decline and Fall of Lloyd George* (1963). Lord Ottercove, in the novels of *Gerhardie, is modelled on Beaverbrook.

BECKETT, Samuel (Barclay) (1906–89), Irish playwright, born at Foxrock, near Dublin, the son of a quantity surveyor, and brought up as a Protestant. He was educated at Portora Royal School, Co. Fermanagh, and at Trinity College, Dublin, where he took a degree in modern languages. After nine months spent teaching French in Belfast, he became *lecteur d'anglais* at the Ecole Normale Superieure in Paris, where he formed a strong friendship with James *Joyce and where, after several unsettled years, he was to settle. His first published work, an essay on Joyce, and his first story, 'Assumption', both appeared in 1929. He went on to write literary journalism, translate, bring out a study of Proust in 1931, and produce his own poetry and fiction, publishing a collection of stories, *More Pricks Than Kicks*, in 1934. A volume of verse, *Echoes Bones and Other Precipitates* (1935), was followed in 1938 by *Murphy*, which made no public impact but launched him as a novelist. *Waft* was his next work in this genre, written in 1943 while he was a member of the French resistance and in hiding from the Nazis, but not published until 1953. By that time the trilogy of novels *Molloy* (1951), *Malone Dies* (1951), and *The Unnameable* (1953) had appeared in Paris, all originally written in French, all soliloquies paying a kind of anti-tribute to a grim, confusing, bleakly funny world. In terms of both style and feeling—most neatly summed up in the epigrammatic 'You must go on, I can't go on, I'll go on'—they have much in common with the plays that, with occasional exceptions, preoccupied Beckett for the rest of his writing life. **Waiting for Godot*, originally performed in French as *En Attendant Godot* in Paris in 1953, established him as a dramatist of originality and importance. There followed many other contributions to what came to be known as the Theatre of the *Absurd. The earlier of these include **Endgame* (1957); **Krapp's Last Tape* (1958), in which a cynical and decrepit old man listens to the recorded voice of his younger, more hopeful self; **Happy Days* (1961), in which a very ordinary middle-aged woman chatters cheerfully, seemingly oblivious of the fact that she is buried in a pile of sand, first up to her waist, then to her neck; and *Play* (1964), a triangle-drama in which husband, wife, and lover, trapped in funeral urns, endlessly re-enact their drab and sordid encounters. The plays of this period imply that man has been abandoned, for reasons unknown, in a world apparently designed to frustrate, disappoint, and hurt him; they show people pluckily enduring while suggesting that wisdom would be to submit resignedly to 'the void'; they find strikingly fresh theatrical forms for their author's bleak ruminations on the vanity of human wishes.

Beckett's attitudes changed little in his later plays, but their expression became more concise and concentrated. In *Not I (1972) the audience sees only a spotlit mouth, which incoherently babbles out its owner's sorry life-story; in *That Time* (1976) an aged tramp's face listens to his own voice, free-associating his particular history; in *Footfalls* (1976) a ghostly woman trudges obsessively to and fro, 'revolving it all'; in *Rockaby* (1981) a much older woman sits in a rocking-chair, fatalistically preparing herself for oblivion; in *Catastrophe* (1982), dedicated to the dissident playwright Vaclav Havel and one of the few Beckett works with any political edge, a shivering prisoner is readied for public humiliation by an arrogant apparatchik. The plays of this period can be difficult, but their verbal beauty and visual daring are remarkable. Beckett also wrote for television (*Eh Joe, Ghost Trio, . . . but the clouds . . ., Quad*) and for radio (*All That Fall, Embers, Rough for Radio I, Rough for Radio II, Words and Music, Cascando*), and a silent movie which featured Buster Keaton, *Film*. He was awarded the Nobel Prize in 1969. Deirdre Bair's *Samuel Beckett: An Autobiography*, written without the author's permission, was published in 1978. Among the many critical studies of his work are Enoch Brater's *Beyond Minimalism* (1987) and *Why Beckett* (1989), and Beryl and John Fletcher's *A Student's Guide to the Plays of Samuel Beckett* (1985).

BEDFORD, Sybille (1911–), British novelist and essayist, born in Charlottenburg, Germany; she has used her cosmopolitan background to explore the complexities of European heritage and experience. Her first novel, *A Legacy* (1956), depicts a German aristocratic family whose way of life is undermined by the Prussian hegemony, which values efficiency and military might over gentler, more civilized values. In *A Favourite of the Gods* (1963) and *A Compass Error* (1968) she deals with a mother and daughter, Constanza and Flavia, and their life in Italy, France, and England between the wars. Constanza, the daughter of a rich American woman and an Italian prince, marries an English politician but later goes to live with a lover in the South of France, at a time when the region was beginning to attract the fashionable and the artistic. Flavia, whose story dominates the second novel, is sexually attracted to women not men; her predicament is drawn with great richness of detail. Bedford's lucid style, as much French as it is English, has contributed to the success of her other books, which include a two-volume life of Aldous *Huxley (1973 and 1974); an idiosyncratic and vivid travelogue of Mexico, *The Sudden View* (1953; reissued as *A Visit to Don Otavio*, 1960); *The Best We Can Do: The Trial of Dr John Bodkin Adams* (1958); *The Faces of Justice* (1961); and a collection of essays, *As It Was* (1990), which contains a remarkable account of the trial in Frankfurt of twenty-two former staff of Auschwitz concentration camp. *Jigsaw* (1989) is a memoir written as fiction, about Bedford's eccentric and artistic family.

BEER, Patricia (1924–), British poet, born in Exmouth, Devon, educated at the University of Exeter and St Hilda's College, Oxford; her father was a railway clerk and her mother a member of the Plymouth Brethren. *Mrs Beer's House* (1968) is a memorably vivid account of her early years and family background. She taught at various universities in Italy and at Goldsmiths' College, London. Her first collection of poetry was *Loss of the Magyar* (1959); further volumes include *Just Like the Resurrection* (1967), *The Estuary* (1971), *The Lie of the Land* (1983), *Collected Poems* (1988), and *Friend of Heraclitus* (1993). Her poetry ranges widely through personal, anecdotal, and historical subject matter, and frequently centres on the theme of mortality. The West Country is a distinct presence in her collections, contributing local detail and elements of legend and folklore to numerous poems. In her best work, a wry wit and a sometimes disturbing imagination combine with a highly developed descriptive talent to produce poems at once entertaining and latently serious. Her historical novel *Moon's Ottery* (1978) is set in Elizabethan Devon. Her critical works include *An Introduction to the Metaphysical Poets* (1972) and *Reader, I Married Him* (1974), which anticipated the burgeoning of *feminist criticism. Among her dramatic writings is *Pride, Prejudice, and the Woman Question* (1975), a play for radio.

BEERBOHM, (Sir Henry) Max(imilian) (1872–1956), British essayist and critic, born in London, educated at Merton College, Oxford. From 1892 he was publishing caricatures (signed 'Max') in the *Strand* and other periodicals, satirizing literary and political figures in his characteristic urbane and ironic tone; in 1894 the first of his essays, 'A Defence of Cosmetics', appeared in *The Yellow Book*. As half-brother to the actor-manager Herbert Beerbohm Tree he had already moved in theatrical circles when he succeeded G. B. *Shaw in 1898 as dramatic critic of the *Saturday Review*; his drama criticism was later collected in *Around Theatres* (1953) and *More Theatres* (1968). He also published *The Happy Hypocrite: A Fairy Tale for Tired Men* (1897) and collections of essays in *The Works of Max Beerbohm* (1896), *More* (1899), *Yet Again* (1909), *And Even Now* (1920), and *A Variety of Things* (1928). His cartoons, published as *Caricatures of Twenty-Five Gentlemen* (1896), *The Poets' Corner* (1904), *A Book of Caricatures* (1907), *Fifty Caricatures* (1913), and *Rosetti and His Circle* (1922), have a wicked eye for the absurdities of writers such as *Yeats, Wilde, or *Wells, without mocking their talents; like *A Christmas Garland* (1912), a brilliant collection of parodies of Wells, Henry *James, *Conrad, and others, they can be seen as an astute and unconventional form of literary criticism. *Zuleika Dobson* (1911), his best-known work, is a fantasy set at Oxford University which captured the atmosphere of the 1890s. *Seven Men* (1919) is a collection of short stories. The First World War drew a biting satire from Beerbohm (*A Survey*, 1921), and in the Second World War he began the radio broadcasts collected in *Mainly on the Air* (1957). A collection of his work was published in 1970 by The Bodley Head. He was knighted in 1939. Lord David *Cecil's *Max: A Biography* (1964) is an affectionate portrait.

Beginning of Spring, The, see FITZGERALD, PENELOPE.

BEHAN, Brendan (1923–64), Irish playwright, born in Dublin, son of a housepainter with strong republican sympathies. Behan, too, joined the IRA and was arrested and incarcerated after an unsuccessful bombing mission to Liverpool, a period he described in his entertaining memoir *Borstal Boy* (1958). His best-known plays are *The Hostage* (1958) and *The *Quare Fellow* (1959); both combine ebullient, anarchic humour with an undeniable seriousness of purpose. *The Hostage* concerns an English soldier held in a Dublin brothel; it shows Behan's own political disillusion, mocking and deglamorizing patriotic pretence in the tradition of Synge's **Playboy of the Western World* and O'Casey's *The *Plough and the Stars*. *The Quare Fellow*, set in a prison in the hours before a hanging, mounts a robust case against capital punishment, and left the critic Kenneth *Tynan feeling 'overwhelmed, and thanking the powers that be' for Sydney Silverman, the leading abolitionist of the day.

BEHRMAN, S(amuel) N(athaniel) (1893–1973), American dramatist, born in Worcester, Massachusetts, educated at Clark, Harvard, and Columbia Universities. He enrolled in George Pierce *Baker's '47 Workshop' at Harvard, and went on to graduate work at Columbia University under Brander Matthews and St John Ervine. Of Behrman's twenty-six plays, several were co-authored, and some were adaptations, such as his version of Jean Giradoux's *Amphitryon 38* (1937) and of Marcel Achard's *Auprès de Ma Blonde* as *I Know My Love* (1949), both written for America's foremost acting duo, the Lunts. His first success was with *The Second Man* (1927), a comedy about a novelist torn between two women; this motif of a central protagonist faced by mutually exclusive choices—in social and sexual relations, and in vocation—is common in his work. His best plays are *Biography* (1932), about the emotional conflicts which polarize the life of a successful woman portrait painter, and the semi-autobiographical *No Time for Comedy* (1939), in which a writer of popular comedies yearns to write serious plays. Behrman's resolute yet stylish dialogue was perfectly suited to the sophisticated social world represented in his plays.

BELASCO, David (1859–1931), American dramatist, born in San Francisco. Belasco wrote his first play at the age of 12 and worked in the theatre from the age of 14. Though he spent his apprentice years in San Francisco as an actor, producer, stage manager, and eventually theatre manager, his name is indelibly linked with the history of the theatre in New York from the mid-1880s to the early 1920s. He also had a talent for discovering gifted actors and actresses. In costumes, sets, and props, Belasco was obsessed with the demands of visual realism which led him to extraordinary feats of setting, and he pioneered the use of special lighting effects to strengthen the emotional appeal of a scene. He established his reputation as a playwright with an American Civil War drama, *The Heart of Maryland* (1895). His stage adaptation of John Luther Long's short story *Madame Butterfly* (1900), and his play about the 1849 California Gold Rush *The Girl of the Golden West* (1905), were made into operas by Puccini, which have become part of the standard repertoire.

BELBEN, Rosalind (1941–), British novelist, born in Dorset, the daughter of a naval officer. She is one of a handful of women novelists engaged in experimenting with fictional form in the European tradition. The author of several novels including *The Limit* (1974), Belben received the recognition she deserves only with the publication of *Is Beauty Good* (1989) and the reappearance of an earlier work, *Dreaming of Dead People* (1979). The former, which defies categorization, is a series of texts, prose poems, or meditations on the loss of the natural world. No one narrative voice unifies the work; rather, Belben uses polyphony to fine effect in her depiction of a decaying but recognizable world. Comparisons with Beckett are both appropriate and marginal; though the wit, irony, and bitter poetry of Belben's authorial voice does bear some resemblance to his, her vision is ultimately life-affirming. *Dreaming of Dead People* is a self-mocking confessional novel somewhat in the mode of Eva *Figes; alternately wry and poetic, structured around a core of fable (Robin Hood), the novel has a ribald, earthy attitude to sex and loneliness sometimes lacking in the works of Belben's fellow experimentalists, and is not dissimilar to the work of the mature Edna *O'Brien. *Choosing Spectacles* (1995) is more conventional in both style and structure than Belben's recent fictions, and yet characteristic of its author. Its central figure, a disaffected Eastern European, learns from his encounter with Europe, the Middle East, and Israel that politics and life yield no simple solutions.

BELL, (Arthur) Clive (Howard) (1881–1964), British art and literary critic, born at East Shefford, Bedfordshire, educated at Cambridge University. A central figure of the *Bloomsbury Group, he married Vanessa Stephen, elder sister to V. *Woolf, in 1907. At Cambridge, Bell became influenced by the moral philosophy of G. E. *Moore with its emphasis on the importance of the enjoyment of conversation and beautiful objects, which Moore considered to be 'the rational ultimate end of social progress'. Bell's concept of 'Significant Form'—in which the form, rather than the subject, of a work of art was the origin of a specific aesthetic emotion—was explored in *Art* (1914); this theory was influenced by Roger *Fry who, with Bell, stimulated public interest in the Post-Impressionists. Bell's other works include *Poems* (1921), *Since Cezanne* (1922), *Civilization* (1928), and *Proust* (1929). His memoirs, *Old Friends: Personal Recollections* (1956), contain interesting portraits of members of the Bloomsbury Group.

BELL, Gertrude (Margaret Lowthian) (1868–1926), British writer on travel and archaeology, born in Washington, County Durham, educated at Lady

Margaret Hall, Oxford; she subsequently acquired Persian and Arabic in the course of her extensive travels. In 1905 she began some ten years' work as an archaeologist. *The Desert and the Sown* (1907) formed an account of her first major expedition, which took her from Jerusalem to Konya in Turkey. She sustained a long friendship with T. E. *Lawrence after meeting him at the Carchemish excavations in 1911. *The Thousand and One Churches* (1909) and *The Palace and Mosque at Ukhaidir* (1914) are her most notable archaeological works. Recruited as an intelligence officer in 1915, she conducted liaison work throughout the Middle East and was posted in 1917 to Baghdad, where she founded Iraq's National Museum in 1923 and was chiefly resident until her death. Her other works include the translations of *Poems from the Divan of Hafiz* (1897) and the travel writings of *Safar Nameh: Persian Pictures* (1894) and *Amurath to Amurath* (1911). Her *Letters* (1927) were edited by Florence Bell. Susan Goodman's biography of Bell appeared in 1985.

BELL, Madison Smartt (1957–), American novelist and short-story writer, born on a farm in Nashville, Tennessee, educated at Princeton and Hollins College. He became a director of 185 Corporation, an artists' co-operative, and a teacher of creative writing. A European existentialism pervades his work, though it focuses largely on quintessentially American locales and often employs popular genres such as the thriller. His style is disaffected and laconic, reflective of a generation which has lost contact with old beliefs and which sustains itself through a kind of desperate mobility. His books include *The Washington Square Ensemble* (1983), *Straight Cut* (1986), *Zero db* (1987), *Barking Man* (1990), *Save Me, Joe Louis* (1993), and the ambitious *All Souls' Rising* (1996) about the 1802 uprising in Haiti.

BELL, Martin (1918–78), British poet, born in Southampton, where he was educated at the University. By profession he was a schoolteacher, and, latterly, an opera critic and lecturer. In 1964 he received the first of the Arts Council's Poetry Bursaries, and was Gregory Fellow of Poetry at Leeds University from 1967 to 1969. Bell's publishing history is unusual in that his *Collected Poems: 1937–66* (1967) was the only independent collection he published in his lifetime; his experiences on active service during the Second World War had a disruptive effect on his development as a poet, with the result that he did not resume the serious practice of poetry until the mid-1950s. In 1962 his work appeared with poetry by George *Barker and Charles *Causley in *Penguin Modern Poets: 3*. Thematically and stylistically wide-ranging, Bell's writing recurrently draws upon his experiences as a soldier and a schoolteacher, which provide material for the wittily irreverent satires of patriotism and social convention in numerous poems. His ironically modulated tone often recalls the dandyism of Laforgue and other nineteenth-century French poets whose works he translated extensively. A senior member of the *Group, his energetic and imaginative style was a major influence on the work of several other members; he is referred to in Peter *Porter's introduction to *Martin Bell: Complete Poems* (1988) as 'father and tone-setter of Group discussions'.

Bell, The, a literary and socio-cultural periodical founded in 1940 by Sean *O'Faolain. Elizabeth *Bowen, Flann *O'Brien, Patrick *Kavanagh, Frank *O'Connor, and Jack B. *Yeats were among the contributors to the first issue. In the course of its fourteen-year career, the *Bell* was variously subtitled 'A Survey of Irish Life', 'A Magazine of Creative Fiction', and 'A Magazine of Ireland Today'; its concern with social and political matters gave rise to incisive commentaries on such topics as state censorship in Ireland, on which G. B. *Shaw wrote in an issue of 1945, the restrictive influence of the Church, and reactionary tendencies in Irish literature. In 1946 Peadar *O'Donnell succeeded O'Faolain as editor, although the latter remained closely involved with the journal; under O'Donnell's direction the *Bell*'s socialist character became more pronounced and its critiques of Irish affairs more aggressive. W. R. *Rodgers and Louis *MacNeice were among the authors whose work sustained the magazine's connection with cultural activities in Ulster, in addition to which it repeatedly featured writing from various parts of Europe. The young Irish authors of the 1940s and 1950s whose reputations the *Bell* was important in fostering include Anthony *Cronin, John *Montague, Thomas *Kinsella, Brendan *Behan, and Conor Cruise *O'Brien. Having undergone financial difficulties which resulted in its temporary closure between 1948 and 1950, it finally ceased appearing in 1954. With the **Dublin Magazine*, the *Bell* is accounted the most important literary and intellectual journal of Ireland in the twentieth century.

Bell Jar, The, a novel by Sylvia *Plath, published under the pseudonym 'Victoria Lucas' in 1963. Its vivid, sometimes disturbingly evocative, imagery links it with her poetry. The title is supplied by the recurrent metaphor of 'the bell jar' as an enclosing barrier between the central protagonist, Esther Greenwood, and the possibility of valid relations with others. The narrative corresponds to the author's experiences in 1953, when she was a student guest editor of the magazine *Mademoiselle*; Esther undergoes growing emotional and intellectual conflicts following her move from university into the sophisticated environment of the New York fashion journal to which she has been appointed temporarily. Her ultimate rejection of the values represented by the magazine is enacted when she throws her expensive clothes out across the city from the top of a building; the incident also marks the advent of an acute phase of psychological instability, which culminates in attempted suicide. The concluding chapters chart a process of gradual recovery during Esther's hospitalization. Principal factors in her social alienation are her renunciation of the conventional attitudes to femininity chiefly articulated through Mrs Willard, the mother of her former boyfriend, and her sense that the artistic freedom she desires is repeatedly threatened with betrayal. Plath's story of late adolescent breakdown was compared by numerous critics to Salinger's *The *Catcher in the Rye*, a book with which *The Bell Jar* has in common its humorously cynical tone.

BELLOC, (Joseph) Hilaire (Pierre) (1870–1953), British writer, born in France to a French father and an English mother; he was educated at Balliol College, Oxford. Belloc took up journalism, contributing articles to *The Speaker*, a political and literary journal, sometimes in collaboration with *Chesterton, and soon earned a reputation as a writer of great versatility in both prose and poetry. His verses for children, which included *The Bad Child's Book of Beasts* (1896), *More Beasts for Worse Children* (1896), and *Cautionary Tales for Children* (1907), became justly famous. More serious lyrics were contained in *Verses and Sonnets* (1896, later withdrawn), *Sonnets and Verses* (1923), and *Complete Verse* (edited by W. N. Roughead, 1954). From 1906 to 1909 he was literary editor of the *Morning Post* during which period he was also Liberal MP for Salford; he disliked party politics, however, and attacked the values of contemporary society, often with his friend Chesterton, in *Pongo and the Bull* (1910), *The Servile State* (1912), and his paper *The Eye-Witness* (1911). Like Chesterton he was a staunch Catholic, arguing that cause in *Europe and Faith* (1920). As a historian, he wrote *The French Revolution* (1911), a succession of biographies of its principal historical figures, as well as lives of *Charles I* (1933) and *Cromwell* (1934); all are better known for their vitality than their impartiality. His travel books include *The Cruise of the Nona* (1925); *The Path to Rome* (1902), an account of a pilgrimage on foot from the Moselle Valley to the Vatican, for which Belloc provided his own illustrations; *Paris* (1900), *Sussex* (1906), and *The Pyrenees* (1909). His novels, some of which were illustrated by Chesterton, included *Mr Clutterbuck's Election* (1908), *The Girondin* (1911), *The Green Overcoat* (1912), and *Belinda* (1928), an original and touching love story. A biography by A. N. Wilson was published in 1984.

BELLOC-LOWNDES, Marie (1867–1947), British novelist and autobiographer, born in London, brought up mainly in France. The older sister of H. *Belloc, she wrote several volumes of memoirs, including *I, too, Have Lived in Arcadia* (1941), *Where Love and Friendship Dwelt* (1943), and *The Merry Wives of Westminster* (1946). She worked as a journalist for W. T. Stead and for Oscar Wilde; and of her many novels *The Lodger* (1913), based on the case of Jack the Ripper, is considered a minor classic. *The Diaries and Letters of Marie Belloc-Lowndes 1911–1947*, edited by her daughter Susan (1971), gives a picture of her life as a member of literary and fashionable society in the early years of the century.

BELLOW, Saul (1915–), American novelist, born in Lachine, Quebec, to Russian emigrant parents; he grew up in a Jewish ghetto in Montreal before moving to Chicago when he was nine. He was educated at the universities of Chicago, Northwestern, and Wisconsin. He has since taught English at a number of colleges, and served in the Merchant Marines during the Second World War. Since 1944 he has been a leading exponent of realism and an articulate voice of humanism in the USA, with his comic and tragic explorations of the modern predicament. His first novel, *Dangling Man* (1944), prepared many of the recurrent themes of his work, with its detailed study of a man suspended between civilian and military life. This study of isolation and philosophical investigation recurs in later novels, including *The Victim* (1947), in which Asa Leventhal finds himself locked in a system of anti-Semitic victimization and torment with Kirby Allbee. *The *Adventures of Augie March* (1953) brought him his first major success, with a tale of a Chicago boy battling through a life of difficulty and antagonism. After *Seize the Day* (1956), which clearly sets out Bellow's humanist aim to reinstitute the self against its annihilation, came **Henderson the Rain King* (1959). This novel provides one of the characteristic sentences from Bellow's work, that 'there are displaced persons everywhere', a notion upon which his writing works a series of variations. Set in a Jewish milieu, **Herzog* (1964) presents the dilemmas and crises which assail a middle-aged intellectual as he adjusts to cultural assimilation into Western Christian life. A series of plays, *The Last Analysis* (1965) and *Out from Under*, *A Wen*, and *Orange Soufflé*, collected in *Under the Weather* (1966), was followed by *Mosby's Memoirs and Other Stories* (1968). *Mr Sammler's Planet* (1970) criticizes the weaknesses of modern society through the eyes of a concentration camp survivor as he undergoes the trials of living in contemporary New York. **Humboldt's Gift* (1975; Pulitzer Prize) was followed by *To Jerusalem and Back: A Personal Account* (1976), a travelogue. *The Dean's December* (1982) offers a sour vision of the contemporary USA and Eastern Europe, as both encroach upon the central character of the novel. In this novel there is a strongly apocalyptic note, as Bellow became more convinced that the USA was being overhauled by forces which threatened the sanctity of the individual. In more recent years, this pessimism has led him to espouse increasingly conservative views. At the same time the tension between religious and secular concerns which has echoed through the novels seems now to fall on the side of examining human reason as though it were strictly limited in its efficacy. His prose style has moved towards a richness which belies his early comment that he wished his work to be viewed simply as entertainment. *Him with His Foot in His Mouth and Other Stories* (1984) was followed by *More Die of Heart Break* (1987), about a marriage between two apparently incompatible people, and *The Bellarosa Connection* (1989), a novel about a Jewish immigrant into the USA, while *Something To Remember Me By* (1991) collects three stories. He was awarded the Nobel Prize for Literature in 1976.

Beloved, a novel by Toni *Morrison, published in 1987 and winner of the Pulitzer Prize. The novel is loosely based on a true story and begins in 1873 Ohio where Sethe, an escaped slave, is living an isolated existence at 124 Bluestone Road with her daughter Denver and a poltergeist; her two sons, Howard and Buglar, had fled when they were only thirteen years old, and their grandmother Baby Suggs had died soon afterwards. The narrative moves from present to past with the painful 'rememories' of the characters: their horrific experiences as slaves at Sweet Home where Sethe had 'married' Halle Suggs; Halle's inexplicable disappearance; Sethe's dramatic escape during which she gave birth to her fourth child; her reunion with Baby Suggs at Bluestone Road; and Sethe's attempt to murder her children when threatened with recapture after only twenty-eight days of freedom. Three children were saved but 'crawling baby' ('Beloved') died after Sethe had cut her throat. This act brought an end to the 'twenty-eight days of having women friends, a mother-in-law, and all her children together'. For years they have tolerated the poltergeist in a state of numbed despair but '124 was spiteful. Full of a baby's venom'. With the arrival of Paul D, one of the former Sweet Home slaves, their loneliness is interrupted. He becomes Sethe's lover and banishes the poltergeist, but after a day at the carnival they return to find a young girl waiting by the gate; she is none other than the physical manifestation of Beloved. Denver at first enjoys her companionship but Beloved's increasing demands for her mother's affection create tensions, especially between Sethe and Paul D who has also succumbed to Beloved's sexual desires. He leaves and the situation deteriorates. The neighbourhood is alerted by rumours of impending danger at 124 and a group of black women gather round the house in a ritual that exorcises the ghost. In prose of great lyricism Morrison skilfully uses supernatural elements to explore the lost history of African-American slaves and the impact on them of the barbaric practices of the institutionalized slave system. Morrison gives her protagonists a fairly happy ending, celebrating resilience and survival; but the effects of systematic cruelty and destruction upon an entire community are left unresolved.

BENCHLEY, Robert (Charles) (1889–1945), American essayist, playwright, and reviewer, born in Worcester, Massachusetts, educated at Harvard. Benchley rose to a prominent position in the New York literary world by the end of the First World War; he was drama critic then managing editor of *Vanity Fair*, and a regular contributor to many New York journals including the **New Yorker*, of which he was a founder member and drama critic. With Dorothy *Parker, Robert E. Sheridan, and others he established the influential Algonquin Hotel Round Table in 1920, which acted as a focal point for that group of brilliant young humorists which was to dominate the pages of the *New Yorker* for the next two decades. His essays and sketches first appeared in *Of All Things!* (1921), which was followed by another twelve collections in addition to several selections of his best writings, notably *Inside Benchley* (1942). He was also a minor actor and appeared in many films between 1928 and 1945. As an urbane and sophisticated humorist his influence has been acknowledged by E. B. *White and James *Thurber. *Benchley: A Biography*, by his brother, Nathaniel Benchley, appeared in 1955.

Bend in the River, A, a novel by V. S. *Naipaul, published in 1979. It is narrated by Salim, an East African of Indian provenance, who, in the aftermath of the disruptions and racial conflicts that result from the politics of African independence, migrates inland to rebuild his career in an unnamed country that resembles Zaire. Here, embodied in a vividly portrayed group of characters both African and Asian, he encounters the new attitudes engendered by colonialism; among these characters are his childhood servant Metty, the sorceress Zabeth and her son Ferdinand (Salim's would-be protégé), the Indian couple Mahesh and Shoba, and the cynical merchant Nazruddin. Salim's transient stability is shaken by the changes in a society caught between the old and the new. He is eventually engulfed in the vortex of prevalent rage and despair, with unfortunate consequences. The perspective of a narrator of Indian origin—simultaneously insider and outsider—serves to illustrate Naipaul's views of post-colonial Africa, allowing him to express contentious opinions in the voice of an onlooker distanced by status and culture from the society he describes. The strength of the novel's fictional elements—description, dialogue, and characterization—ultimately prevail over its powerfully documentary and topical content.

BENÉT, Stephen Vincent (1898–1943), American poet, born at Bethlehem, Pennsylvania, educated at Yale. As an undergraduate he published two collections of verse, *Five Men and Pompey* (1915) and *Young Adventure* (1918). His first novel, *The Beginning of Wisdom* (1921), draws heavily on his experiences of university. Subsequent novels include *Jean Huguenot* (1923) and *Spanish Bayonet* (1926). As a writer of prose his accomplishment was more evident in his short stories; among his collections are *Tales Before Midnight* (1939) and *Thirteen O'Clock* (1937), the latter containing the well-known 'The Devil and Daniel Webster'. *John Brown's Body* (1928; Pulitzer Prize) gained him a considerable reputation as a poet. Its compelling use of traditional modes and its imaginative engagement with American history set the pattern for much of his later work, notably *Ballads and Poems* (1931) and *Western Star* (1943; Pulitzer Prize), the first part of an unfinished epic poem on the Western migrations of the nineteenth century. The rhetorical free verse of *The Burning City* (1937) included 'Litany for Dictatorships', his powerful denunciation of European fascism; his impassioned espousal of the democratic spirit continued in *Nightmare at Noon* (1940), the title poem warning America against indifference in the face of events in Europe. *Selected Works* appeared in two volumes in 1942. His *Selected Letters* (1960) was edited by C. A. Fenton, whose biography of Benét was published in 1958.

BENÉT, William Rose (1886–1950), American poet and literary journalist, born in Fort Hamilton, New York, educated at Yale. The elder brother of the poet Stephen Vincent *Benét and the third husband of the novelist and poet Elinor *Wylie, Benét was associate editor of the *Literary Review* of the New York *Evening Post* and in 1924 he co-founded, with Christopher Morley, the influential *Saturday Review of Literature*. He compiled over fifteen anthologies of prose and poetry including the *The Reader's Encyclopaedia* (1948). His early verse, such as that collected in *Merchants from Cathay* (1913), or *The Falconer of God and Other Poems* (1914), is marked by strong rhythms and somewhat naïve democratic sentiment, while his later poems show the influence of free verse and modernist experimentation with monologue and dialogue in a manner that invites comparison with Robert *Frost. Among other works are *The Dust which Is God* (1941; Pulitzer Prize), an autobiographical verse narrative; *The First Person Singular* (1922), a novel; and *Day's End* (1939), a play. His public appointments included the secretaryship of the National Institute of Arts and Letters. Stanley Olson's *Elinor Wylie, A Life Apart: A Biography* (1979) contains some discussion of Benét's life and works.

BENNETT, Alan (1934–), British dramatist, born in Yorkshire, educated at Exeter College, Oxford. He first came to prominence as one of the authors and performers of the anti-establishment revue *Beyond the Fringe* (1960). There is also a satiric thrust to some of his own plays, notably *Forty Years On* (1968), set in the assembly hall of Albion House, a public school, in which scenes involving the headmaster and his colleagues are intercut with extracts from the school play, itself a series of witty skits on the cultural and political history of establishment England in the twentieth century. This treats subjects ranging from Virginia *Woolf, T. E. *Lawrence, and James *Baldwin to the British nanny with a gentle mockery and a rueful nostalgia, a mix characteristic of his work in general. His subsequent plays, though always marked by wry, sophisticated humour, have been more serious in intent and often more melancholy in tone. They include *Getting On* (1971), about a disillusioned Member of Parliament; *Habeas Corpus* (1973), about contemporary sexual mores; *The Old Country* (1977), about a British traitor living in Soviet Russia; *Enjoy* (1980), about the decline of both northern England and the family; and *Kafka's Dick* (1986), in which the Czech writer visits contemporary Britain. A play of broader scope is *The Madness of George III* (1991), about the personal and political ramifications of 'Farmer George's' affliction with porphyria. Bennett has also written screenplays for the films *A Private Function* and *Prick Up Your Ears*, and many dramatic pieces for television: among them *An Englishman Abroad*, a portrait of the spy Guy Burgess in Moscow, and *Talking Heads* (1989), a series of monologues which demonstrates another of his qualities, a humane yet humorous understanding of lonely, sad lives. His adaptation of Kenneth Grahame's *A Wind in the Willows* scored a major success at the National Theatre in 1990. *Writing Home*, a collection of his essays, personal observations and recollections, and introductions to his plays, appeared in 1995.

BENNETT, (Enoch) Arnold (1867–1931), British novelist, born in Hanley, Staffordshire, the eldest son of a self-educated and self-made solicitor who had struggled up to professional status from a family of potters and shopkeepers. Bennett was also destined for the law but he continued (uncharacteristically) to fail his legal examinations, rebelled against his dominating father, and escaped to London, where, after working briefly as a solicitor's clerk, he began to earn his living as a journalist and writer. In 1893 he became assistant editor and then editor of the periodical *Woman*, to which he contributed under various pseudonyms. His first serious short story, 'A Letter Home', was published in 1895 in *The Yellow Book*, and in 1898 appeared his first, somewhat gloomy, realistic novel, *A Man from the North*, about aspiring writer Richard Larch. He also began to write sensational fiction; *The Grand Babylon Hotel* (1902) was the first of many works to bear witness to Bennett's love of the fantasy world of luxury hotels (particularly the Savoy) and his penchant for writing about millionaires, chefs, and smart modern women. After his father's death in 1902 he published **Anna of the Five Towns* and moved to Paris, where in 1907 he married Marguerite Soulie. He taught himself French, greatly admired the French realists, and became a lifelong Francophile: many of his works show an interesting cross-fertilization of French and home-grown realism. *The Grim Smile of the Five Towns* (short stories, 1907) was followed by one of the best of his lighter works, *Buried Alive* (1908), about a famous painter who chooses to change places with his dead valet and 'disappear'; his masterpieces *The *Old Wives' Tale* (1908) and *The *Clayhanger Trilogy* (*Clayhanger*, 1910; *Hilda Lessways*, 1911; *These Twain*, 1916; and a sequel, *The Roll Call*, 1918), both based largely in the 'Five Towns' or Potteries; and *The Card* (1911), the highly successful account of the warm-hearted opportunist adventurer, Denry Machin. In 1912 Bennett moved back to England, where he settled permanently and continued to produce much fiction of varying quality, including the short stories in *The Matador of the Five Towns* (1912), and the novels *The Regent* (1913), which features the Card as a theatrical impresario; *The Pretty Lady* (1918), about a gold-hearted courtesan; *Mr Prohack* (1922), a fantasy of sudden riches; **Riceyman Steps* (1923), written after his separation from his wife and meeting with actress Dorothy Cheston, thenceforward his lifelong companion; *Lord Raingo* (1926), set in political circles, with which he had become familiar through his wartime friendship with *Beaverbrook; and *Imperial Palace* (1930), his last long novel of hotel life. Throughout his career Bennett was passionately interested in the theatre, where he had several successes, notably *Milestones* (1912), a family drama written in collaboration with E. Knoblock, and *The Great Adventure* (1913), a dramatization of *Buried Alive*. He also wrote a great deal of popular journalism, showing a populist gift for conveying information and enthusiasm in such volumes as *Literary Taste: How To Form It* (1909) and *How To Live on 24 Hours a Day* (1912). At different periods he wrote regularly on varying topics for the *New Age*, the *Daily News*, and the *New Statesman*, and from 1926 until his death contributed a weekly article on books to the *Evening Standard*. From 1896 he kept a *Journal*, consciously modelled on that of the Goncourt brothers, which was published in 1932–3, edited by Newman Flower; it gives a vivid portrait of his life and times and his rise through discipline and obsessional hard work to the position of one of the most influential and best-paid authors of the age. He died at his flat at Chiltern Court, Baker Street, after contracting typhoid in Paris. His letters, edited by James Hepburn, were published in three volumes (1966–70), and there is a biography by Margaret Drabble (1974). Bennett's reputation suffered in his later years from attacks by a younger generation of writers, notably Virginia *Woolf who used him as an example of the realist-materialist pre-modernist school in, for example, her essay 'Mr Bennett and Mrs Brown' (1923). His work never recovered the wide popularity it enjoyed during his lifetime, and although many of his works are still much enjoyed and admired, he has, like his friends and contemporaries H. G. *Wells and John *Galsworthy, received little academic attention.

BENNETT, Louise (1919–), Jamaican poet, born in Kingston, Jamaica, educated in Jamaica and at the Royal Academy of Dramatic Art in London. She worked briefly for the BBC. When she first composed verses in 'patois' or Jamaican dialect in the 1930s and 1940s, Bennett used the language of the common people which was regarded as uneducated. But her early books such as *(Jamaica) Dialect Verses* (1942), *Jamaican Humour in Dialect* (1943), and *Anancy Poems in Dialect* (1944) indicate a passionate interest in using local speech to dramatize or comment on scenes, personalities, or issues drawn from ordinary life in Jamaica. Later, she gave readings and performances of her work which helped to establish her as both a poet and an authority on Jamaican folklore. Bennett's contribution to Caribbean literature is seminal in that her work introduced 'Creole' or 'Nation Language' to a wider public. Her later books, *Jamaican Labrish* (1966) and *Selected Poems* (1982), confirm her primary achievement: the transformation into literature of subjects and techniques normally considered appropriate only in oral art or folklore. She has received many awards including the Order of Jamaica (1974).

BENSLEY, Connie (1929–), British poet, born in south-west London. She has worked as a secretary, a medical copywriter, and in a bookshop. Having married and raised a family she began writing poems for publication in 1976; within twelve months her work had begun appearing in leading literary journals. Her first collection, *Progress Report* (1981), was followed by further volumes, including *Moving In* (1984), *Central Reservations: New and Selected Poems* (1990), and *Choosing to Be a Swan* (1994). Bensley's writing is characterized by an incisive clarity and appealing wit. She frequently bases poems on her views of social and personal behaviour, producing work that combines a telling economy of observation with a compassionately understated sense of the satirical. She has also written a number of plays for television and radio.

BENSON, A(rthur) C(hristopher) (1862–1925), British writer, brother of E. F. and R. H. *Benson, born at Wellington College, Berkshire, of which his father, E. W. Benson (1829–96), who later became Archbishop of Canterbury, was the first headmaster; he was educated at King's College, Cambridge. In 1904 he was elected a fellow of Magdalene College, of which he became Master in 1915. Among his early works in a prolific career are his *Life* of his father (1899); *Fasti Etonenses* (1899), a history of Eton; and the stories collected in *The Hill of Trouble* (1903) and *The Isles of Sunset* (1905). He produced numerous critical biographies, including those of *Rosetti* (1904), *Fitzgerald* (1905), and *Ruskin* (1911), and a succession of collections of essays, among which are *From a College Window* (1906) and *Escape* (1915). With the Second Viscount Esher, he edited three volumes of *Selections from the Correspondence of Queen Victoria* (1907), with whom he had been acquainted. He also enjoyed a considerable reputation as a poet and remains best known for 'Land of Hope and Glory', originally published with Elgar's music in 1902 as *Coronation Ode* for the coronation of King Edward VII; *The Poems of A. C. Benson* appeared in 1909. Between 1897 and 1925 he compiled a diary covering some 180 manuscript volumes, selections from which were published under Percy *Lubbock's editorship in 1926. Due to the acutely personal nature of the material, the diaries were not available for inspection until 1975, when David Newsome gained access to them for his biographical study entitled *On the Edge of Paradise* (1980); Newsome also edited *Edwardian Excursions* (1981), which contains further selections from the diaries.

BENSON, E(dward) F(rederic) (1867–1940), British novelist, brother of A. C. and R. H. *Benson, born at Wellington College, Berkshire, educated at King's College, Cambridge and the British School of Archaeology in Athens. His successful first novel, *Dodo* (1893), was followed by a stream of novels, biographies, and reminiscences. He is most famous for the series of comic novels he published during the 1920s and 1930s, the 'Mapp and Lucia' books, which satirize provincial life in the small coastal town of Tilling (Rye) and which contain, in the characters of Lucia, *grande dame* of Tilling, and her rival, Miss Mapp, two of the most endearing comic types in British fiction.

The novels include *Queen Lucia* (1920), *Miss Mapp* (1922), *Lucia in London* (1927), *Mapp and Lucia* (1931), *Lucia's Progress* (1935), and *Trouble for Lucia* (1937). In 1918 Benson moved to Rye, living at Lamb House, formerly the home of H. *James, and was elected mayor of the town in 1934 (an experience amusingly reflected in his Mapp and Lucia stories). His other fiction includes several volumes of ghost stories, such as *The Room in the Tower* (1912) and *Visible and Invisible* (1923), as well as novels such as the tragi-comic *Mrs Ames* (1912) and *Paying Guests* (1929). *As We Were* (1930) and *Final Edition* (1940) are autobiographies. He was awarded the OBE and made an Honorary Fellow of Magdalen College, Oxford. A biography by Brian *Masters appeared in 1991.

BENSON, Peter (1956–), British novelist, born in Broadstairs, Kent. He was living in Dorset, where he worked as a basketmaker, when his first novel, *The Levels* (1987), was published. The novel is a subtle adolescent romance set in the Dorset countryside, with rich resonances of folklore and myth. His interest in archetypal structure and his keen novelistic intelligence are displayed in *A Lesser Dependency* (1988), a more controversial work. In its challenging theme and its fragmented structure, this novel represents a radical departure from the formal simplicity of his first novel. *The Other Occupant* (1989) is the terse account of a young man's deep emotional involvement with an elderly woman dying of cancer, which returns to the more conventional first-person narration and the rural setting of *The Levels* with the larger themes of death, rural bigotry, and violence. *Odo's Hanging* (1993), in characteristically simple, image-laden language, tells of the making of the Bayeux tapestry in the voice of a deaf-mute. *Riptide* (1994) interweaves images of surfing and turbulent sexuality in a story of a boy's encounter with, and ultimate loss of, his lost mother.

BENSON, R(obert) H(ugh), The Very Reverend (1871–1914), British writer, younger brother of A. C. and E. F. *Benson, son of E. W. Benson, Archbishop of Canterbury. Ordained in the Anglican Church, he became a Roman Catholic in 1903 and rose to high office in the priesthood. Like his brothers he was a prolific writer, producing many novels, some of which were apocalyptic (*The Lord of the World*, 1907), some historical (*Come Rack! Come Rope!*, 1912), and some concerned with contemporary moral dilemmas, featuring virtuous Roman Catholics, as in *The Sentimentalists* (1906), about saving a nearly lost soul, and *The Average Man* (1913). He also wrote books on religion, and was briefly a friend and collaborator of F. W. *Rolfe.

BENTLEY, Edmund Clerihew (1875–1956), British journalist and writer of *detective fiction and light verse, born in London, educated at Merton College, Oxford. He was called to the Bar in 1902 but subsequently became a journalist on the *Daily News* and on the *Daily Telegraph*, where he was leader writer from 1912 to 1934. In *Biography for Beginners* (1905), illustrated by his lifelong friend G. K. *Chesterton, he invented the epigrammatic verse form called 'clerihew' after his second name. His detective story *Trent's Last Case* (1913, US title *The Woman in Black*) has been immensely popular since its publication and has been made into three films, in the last of which (1953) Orson Welles played the financier Sigsbee Manderson, the murder victim. Intended, in the author's words, as 'an exposure of detective stories', it in fact proved influential in the later development of the genre; its hero, Philip Trent, a witty, occasionally facetious young artist, whose speech is full of literary quotations, is the first in a long line of similar fictional detectives, including, for example, Dorothy *Sayers's Lord Peter Wimsey. *Trent's Own Case* (1936, written in collaboration with H. Warner Allen) and *Trent Intervenes* (1938), a collection of short stories, are less successful. Other works include a thriller, *Elephant's Work: An Enigma* (1950; US title *The Chill*) and an autobiography, *Those Days* (1940).

BENTLEY, Phyllis (1894–1977), British novelist, born in Halifax, West Yorkshire, educated at Cheltenham Ladies' College and the University of London. She wrote nearly thirty books, including nineteen novels, many of them set in the West Riding of Yorkshire, including *Environment* (1922), her first novel, and *Carr* (1929). Success first came with *Inheritance* (1932), which began a saga about the Oldroyd family of mill owners covering several decades beginning with the Industrial Revolution; the last in the series was *A Man of His Time* (1966). *A Modern Tragedy* (1934) reflects the Depression of the 1930s; and *Manhold* (1941) moves back to the eighteenth century. Later works include the novel *Sheep May Safely Graze* (1972), and a collection of *Tales of West Riding* (1974). She also wrote extensively about the Brontë family, in such works as *The Brontës* (1947), *The Young Brontës* (1960), and *The Brontës and Their World* (1969), and edited the Heather edition of their works. Her autobiography, *O Dreams, O Destinations*, appeared in 1962.

BERENSON, Bernard (1865–1959), American art historian, born near Vilnius in Lithuania; from 1875 onward he grew up in Boston, Massachusetts, and was educated at Harvard. As a student he was influenced in the eventual formulation of his theories concerning the tactile and spatial values of art by William *James's emphasis on the primarily subjective nature of aesthetic experience. In 1887 he left America, travelling widely in Europe before settling near Florence in 1900 at I Tatti, the villa he later bequeathed to Harvard. Throughout the 1890s he acquired an unrivalled knowledge of Italian painting; his four monographs on Renaissance art, *The Venetian Painters* (1894), *The Florentine Painters* (1896), *The Central Italian Painters* (1897), and *The North Italian Painters* (1907), collected as *Italian Painters of the Renaissance* (1930), were held in such regard that they were referred to as 'the Four Gospels'. He became very wealthy by availing art dealers of his skill in the attribution of paintings, and from 1906 to 1939 was in close association with Lord Duveen, the leading international dealer of the day. His other studies of Italian painting include *Venetian Paintings in America* (1916) and *Sienese Paintings* (1918); *Italian Pictures of the Renaissance* (1932) lists the locations of paintings by the principal artists. Latterly, he wrote numerous works of a more general nature, among which are *Aesthetics and History in the Visual Arts* (1948), the clearest statement of his belief in the 'life enhancement' afforded by art, and *Seeing and Knowing* (1954). His tastes in painting did not extend to twentieth-century art, much of which he despised, although he greatly admired Cezanne. *Sketch for a Self-Portrait* (1949), *Rumor and Reflection* (1952), his wartime journal, and *Passionate Sightseer* (1960) are autobiographical works rich in critical and philosophical commentary; *Sunset and Twilight* (edited by N. Mariano, 1963) contains selections from his diaries from 1947 to 1958. Meryle Secrest's *Being Bernard Berenson* (1979) is the fullest of several biographies.

BERESFORD, J(ohn) D(avys) (1873–1947), British novelist, born in Castor, Northamptonshire, educated at Oundle School. After many years working as a draughtsman in an architect's office he turned to fiction. He received high praise from the critics with his first novel, *Jacob Stahl* (1911), the first volume of a trilogy which also included *A Candidate for Truth* (1912) and *The Invisible Event* (1915). He continued to produce many more realistic and traditional novels including several *science fiction works, such as *The Hampdenshire Wonder* (1911), *Goslings* (1913), and *The Camberwell Miracle* (1933), which presented a dark view of the consequences of change in the manner of H. G. *Wells.

BERGER, John (Peter) (1926–), British novelist, artist, and art critic, born in Stoke Newington, London, educated at London's Central School of Art and Chelsea School of Art. Among his influential works as an art critic are *Permanent Red: Essays in Seeing* (1960), *The Success and Failure of Picasso* (1965), *Art and Revolution: Ernst Neizvestny and the Role of the Artist in the U.S.S.R* (1969), *The Moment of Cubism and Other Essays* (1969), and *Ways of Seeing* (1972), based on a BBC television series and celebrated for its iconoclasm about traditional notions of art. Open-ended rather than dogmatic, his art criticism is very much concerned with the pressures of social context and class relations on artistic form. Notably European in outlook, his novels include *A Painter of Our Time* (1958), about an artist affected by the Hungarian Revolution of 1956; *The Foot of Clive* (1962); *Corker's Freedom* (1964); and G (1972; Booker Prize), a highly experimental novel about a Don Juan in pre-First World War Trieste. His collaborations with photographer Jean Mohr include *A Fortunate Man: The Story of a Country Doctor* (1967), *A Seventh Man: Migrant Workers in Europe* (1975), and *Another Way of Telling* (1982), on the aesthetics of photography. His screenplays in collaboration with Swiss film director Alain Tanner consist of *La Salamandre* (1971), *Le Milieu du Monde* (1974), and *Jonas* (1976). Berger's years living and working in a small peasant community in the French Alps resulted in his fictional trilogy *Into Their Labours* (1992) which consists of *Pig Earth* (1979), *Once in Europa* (1987), which he described as 'a collection of love stories set against the disappearance of "modernisation" of such village life', and *Lilac and Flag* (1990). In his novel *To The Wedding* (1995) a family travels from different parts of Europe to converge at a wedding. Essays on art, aesthetics, and politics are collected in *Keeping a Rendezvous* (1992).

BERGER, Thomas (1924–), American novelist, born in Cincinnati, Ohio, educated at the University of Cincinnati and Columbia University. His first novel, *Crazy in Berlin* (1958), introduced the figure of Carlos Reinhart, who reappears in *Reinhart in Love* (1961), *Vital Parts* (1970), and *Reinhart's Women* (1982). Reinhart moves through the world encapsulated in the bubble of the American dream, an innocent and honest man continually assaulted by a selfish society. Berger's ironies form an extended critique not only of the contemporary world but also of its historical antecedents; as *Little Big Man* (1964) makes clear, the sustaining myth of the American West is actually founded on a series of lies and half-truths. Berger presents Custer as a vain psychotic, and the settling of the frontier is seen as an act of genocide which exterminated virtually every trace of a noble, democratic race. Berger's Indians practise a kind of sexual and religious tolerance which is entirely at variance with the hypocritical puritanism of their white conquerors. The book's central figure is an utterly marginalized man, unable to integrate himself fully into the Indian way of life and unwilling to associate himself with its destroyers. He nevertheless remains the voice of conscience; his distance from America reflects Berger's own detachment from his native land. Yet, despite his reputation as a black humorist, Berger remains committed to American ideals.

BERGONZI, Bernard (1929–), British critic, born in London; he left school at 15 to work as a clerk. He was subsequently educated at Newbattle Abbey College, Dalkeith, and Wadham College, Oxford. In 1971 he became Professor of English at the University of Warwick. *The Early H. G. Wells* (1961) was the first of his numerous works of criticism, which also include *Heroes' Twilight* (1965), a study of the literature of the First World War; *T. S. Eliot* (1972); *Reading the Thirties: Texts and Contexts* (1978); *The Myth of Modernism and Twentieth Century Literature* (1986); *Exploding English* (1990), his sometimes provocative analysis of the present state of English studies; and *Wartime and Aftermath: English Literature and Its Background, 1939–1960* (1993). He has published two collections of poetry, *Descartes and the Animals* (1954) and *Years* (1979), which display an attractive combination of concentration and accessibility and frequently make use of a shrewdly understated wit. His novel *The Roman Persuasion* (1981) draws on his extensive knowledge of the 1930s to evoke the ambivalent reactions of an English Catholic family to the Spanish Civil War.

BERKELEY, Anthony, pseudonym of Anthony Berkeley COX (1893–1971), British crime writer, born in Watford, educated at University College, London. He contributed to *Punch*, and under his own name published several comic novels (e.g. *Brenda Entertains*, 1925); as Francis Iles he reviewed crime and other fiction for the *Daily Telegraph* and later the *Sunday Times* and *Manchester Guardian*. *The Layton Court Mystery* (1925) was the first of a series of bright and amusing detective stories written under the name of Berkeley, most of which have the amateur detective Roger Sheringham as their central figure. Others include *The Wychford Poisoning Case* (1926), *The Silk Stocking Murders* (1928), *The Piccadilly Murder* (1929), *Jumping Jenny* (1933; US title *Dead Mrs Stratton*), and *The Poisoned Chocolates Case* (1929), originally a short story, which is undoubtedly the best. Very different from these are the three powerful and realistic psychological studies of crime and murder published under the name of Francis Iles—*Malice Aforethought* (1931), *Before the Fact* (1932), and *As for the Woman* (1939), which have little or no detective element. He was the founder, in 1928, of the Detection Club and became its first honorary secretary.

BERKOFF, Steven (1937–), British dramatist, born in London, educated at Hackney Downs Grammar School; he studied mime at the École Jacques Le Coq, Paris, finished his training for the stage at the Webber-Douglas Academy in London, and has since frequently appeared in adaptations and original plays written by himself. His work has always been notable for the opportunities it offers actors for bravura physical invention. It has also been marked by verbal daring, often comprising parodic poetic effects, and by a fierce anti-establishment thrust. His dramatic versions of other people's writings include Kafka's *The Penal Colony* (1968), *Metamorphosis* (1969), and *The Trial* (1971); Aeschylus's *Agamemnon* (1973); Poe's *Fall of the House of Usher* (1974); and Wilde's *Salome* (1989). His own plays include exotic portraits of contemporary London, *East* (1975) and *West* (1983); *Greek* (1979), a raucous satire of the Oedipus story; *Decadence* (1981), a bitter and scathing portrait of English social divisions as represented by an arrogant, gourmandizing upper-class lout and the working-class man he effortlessly intimidates; and *Kvetch* (1986), which switches from dialogue to aside in what becomes a feverish exposure of the fears, frustrations, and tensions beneath the surface of conventional lower middle-class life; *One Man* (1993), a trio of solo plays including one which memorably permitted Berkoff to embody both a yobbish East Ender and his dog; and *Brighton Beach Scumbags* (1994), about the doleful joys of a group of friends at a seaside resort.

BERLIN, Sir Isaiah (1909–), British moral and political philosopher and historian of ideas, born at Riga in Latvia, the son of a timber merchant, educated at St Paul's School and Corpus Christi College, Oxford, gaining his MA in 1935. Throughout his career he has lectured at Oxford, and was President of Wolfson College from 1966 to 1975. He has also held numerous visiting professorships in the USA and was President of the British Academy between 1974 and 1978. The critique of determinist philosophies of history in *Historical Inevitability* (1954) has remained central to his work; Berlin emphasizes the ultimate incompatibility of historical determinism with the free will of the individual. The essentially plural nature of morality was the principal theme of his seminal *Two Concepts of Liberty* (1959), which was collected with *Historical Inevitability* and two other works under the title *Four Essays on Liberty* (1969); the book confirmed his reputation as one of the leading liberal intellectuals of the twentieth century. His other publications include *Essays on J. L. Austin* (1973), *Vico and Herder: Two Studies in the History of Ideas* (1976), and *The Magus of the North: J. G. Hamana and the Origins of Modern Irrationalism* (1993). *Russian Thinkers* (1978), *Concepts and Categories* (1978), *Against the Current* (1979), *Personal Impressions* (1980), and *The Crooked Timber of Humanity* (1990) are collections of his essays edited by Henry Hardy. Berlin has also produced translations from the Russian, among which are versions of Turgenev's *First Love* (1950) and *A Month in the Country* (1981). *Isaiah Berlin: A Celebration*, edited by Edna and Avishai Margalit, appeared in 1991.

BERNSTEIN, Charles (1950–), American poet, born in New York, educated at Harvard; he became David Gray Professor of Poetry at the State University of New York at Buffalo, successor to Robert *Creeley. Editor of *L-A-N-G-U-A-G-E* with Bruce *Andrews, editor of *The Politics of Poetic Form* (1990), author of two collections of essays *Content's Dream* (1986) and *A Poetics* (1992), he has done as much as anyone to publicize and theorize *Language Poetry in which 'the text calls upon the reader to be actively involved in the process of constituting its meaning'. Hence his joke about romanticism in poetry: 'Poetry is like a swoon, with this difference: | it brings you to your senses' ('The Klupzy Girl'). This conviction of the power of radical formal experimentation to challenge the 'incredible amount of illusory materiality' in contemporary culture results in a witty, sometimes comic or satiric collaging of different discourses ranging from personal statements, official jargon, science, and traditional poetic language. He writes mostly shorter poems, collected in books such as *Controlling Interests* (1980), *Resistance* (1983), *The Sophist* (1987), *The Absent Father in Dumbo* (1990), and *Dark City* (1994); an edited collection, *Live at the Ear*, appeared in 1994. His poems are capable of a bravura lyricism, elegant musical phrasing, and complex puns in an impressive range of styles.

BERRIGAN, Ted (1934–83), American poet, born Providence, Rhode Island; he spent three years in the United States army before studying at the University of Tulsa, and from there he moved to New York City in 1960. It was through his residence in the city and his founding, and editing, of *'C' Magazine* that he became associated with the *New York School of Poets; like many of the poets, notably John *Ashbery and Frank *O'Hara, Berrigan's work evinces a preoccupation with effects drawn from the influences of surrealism, abstract expressionist painting, and serial music. His first volume of verse was *Sonnets* (1964) and subsequent volumes include *Bean Spasms* (1967; co-authored with Ron Padgett), *Many Happy Returns to Dick Gallup* (1967), *In the Early Morning Rain* (1970), and *So Going Around Cities: New and Selected Poems, 1958-1979* (1980). Berrigan held teaching positions at the University of Iowa and the University of Essex.

BERRY, James (1924–), British poet, born in Boston, Jamaica; he arrived in London in 1948. After years of working as a telegraphist (1951–77), he became a full-time writer. He conducts writing workshops at comprehensive schools and has taken an active interest in multicultural education. Rooted in Jamaican proverbs and folklore, and imbued with avuncular wisdom, many of his poems are in Creole dialect, or Nation Language, as he calls it, following Edward Kamau *Brathwaite. His collections include *Fractured Circles* (1979), *Lucy's Letter and Loving* (1982), *Chain of Days* (1985), and *Hot Earth, Cold Earth* (1995). 'Fantasy of an African Boy' won the British National Poetry Competition in 1981. He has published several books for children, including *Anancy-Spiderman* (1989) and *The Future-Telling Lady* (1991), collections of short stories. He has also edited pioneering anthologies of poems by black British writers including *Bluefoot Traveller* (1976), *Dance to a Different Drum* (1983, a Brixton Festival anthology), and *News for Babylon* (1984). He was awarded an OBE in 1990. See also JAZZ POETRY and DUB POETRY.

BERRY, Wendell (Erdman) (1934–), American poet, novelist, and essayist, born in Henry County, Kentucky, educated at the University of Kentucky, where he became Distinguished Professor of English in 1971. The intensity of his writing's involvement with the human and natural characters of his native locality has gained him recognition as one of the leading regional writers of the twentieth century. *Nathan Coulter* (1960), *A Place on Earth* (1967), *The Memory of Old Jack* (1974), and *Remembering* (1988) form a series of novels chronicling social and economic change in a Kentucky tobacco-farming community from the late 1930s onward. *A Continuous Harmony* (1972), *The Gift of Good Land* (1981), *What Are People for?* (1990), and *Sex, Economy, Freedom and Community* (1993) are among the numerous collections of essays in which his experiences as a farmer and his wide erudition combine in discussing the cultural and economic bases of viable forms of community; he is widely regarded as a leading authority on ecologically sustainable agriculture. The critique of modern materialism that is a recurrent theme in his prose also informs his poetry, collections of which include *The Broken Ground* (1966), *The Country of Marriage* (1974), *The Wheel* (1982), and *Sabbaths* (1987). His verse displays a high degree of accomplishment in both traditional forms and eloquently direct free verse. *Collected Poems 1957–1982* appeared in 1985. Among his other publications is *The Wild Birds* (1986), a collection of short stories.

BERRYMAN, John (1914–72), American poet, born John Smith in McAlester, Oklahoma; his father committed suicide in 1926 and he subsequently adopted his stepfather's name. He was educated at Columbia University, New York, and at Clare College, Cambridge. From 1939 onwards he was a lecturer and latterly a professor at various American universities, notably the University of Minnesota. His poems began appearing in periodicals in 1935 and attracted favourable critical responses when a selection was featured in *Five Young American Poets* (1940). *Poems* (1942) and *The Dispossessed* (1948) established him as one of the leading American poets of the generation that included Robert *Lowell, Delmore *Schwartz, and Randall *Jarrell. Berryman described his earlier verse as Anglo-American 'period style', considering it to rely broadly upon the examples of *Yeats and *Auden; his great accomplishment and individuality of voice were, however, clear in poems like 'The Moon and the Night and the Men' and 'Canto Amore'. *Homage to Mistress Bradstreet* (1956) gained him wider recognition, drawing comparisons with *The *Waste Land* from Frank *Kermode and Edmund *Wilson for the force and originality of the complex interactions between its personal, historical, and cultural dimensions. *Berryman's Sonnets* (1967) confirmed his ability to combine a highly developed command of traditional forms with the emotional and intellectual urgency conveyed by the range and individuality of his tones. The breadth of reference, technical adaptability, and psychological intensities of his poetry culminated in *77 Dream Songs* (1964) and *His Toy, His Dream, His Rest: 308 Dream Songs* (1968), which appeared in a collected edition as *The *Dream Songs* in 1969. In *Love and Fame* (1971) the religious elements intermittently present in earlier work achieve consolidated expression in the conversationally discursive 'Eleven Addresses to the Lord'. A *Collected Poems*, edited by Charles Thornbury, was produced in 1990. For many years Berryman's compulsive and erratic behaviour resulted in recurrent admissions to psychiatric hospitals; he killed himself by jumping from a bridge in Minneapolis in 1972. The energetic development of his poetry provides a notable instance of success in following *Empson's injunction to 'learn a style from despair'. Among his other works are the biography *Stephen Crane* (1951), a collection of essays entitled *The Freedom of the Poet* (1976), and the autobiographical novel *Recovery* (1973). *The Life of John Berryman* by John Haffenden was published in 1982. See also CONFESSIONAL POETRY.

BESTER, Alfred (1913–87), American writer of *science fiction, born in New York, educated at the University of Pennsylvania. He is best known for his short stories of the 1950s and for his novels *The Demolished Man* (1953), which combined science fiction and the thriller in its depiction of a murderer who attempts to outwit the police in a society of the future, and *Tiger! Tiger!* (1956), which transposed the plot of A. Dumas's *The Count of Monte Cristo* (1844) into a 25th-century world of predatory corporations, space travel, and exorbitant passions. Bester's work influenced the new writers in the genre of the 1960s including S. R. *Delany, T. M. *Disch, and R. *Zelazny. His later novels include *The Computer Connection* (1975).

Bestsellers (and 'Bestsellerism') are particularly associated with the twentieth-century American book trade. The practice of systematically identifying certain books as noteworthy for the speed and volume of their sales began with the American monthly magazine *The Bookman*, and its editor, Harry Thurston Peck, in 1895. The magazine was the first to list a selection of new titles, 'in order of demand'. In the 1890s, the fiction bestseller lists of *The Bookman* were dominated by British titles. The earliest recorded use of the noun 'bestseller' is 1902. In 1912 the American trade magazine *Publisher's Weekly* began issuing a bestseller list, which has been authoritative in America ever since. A year later the magazine began dividing bestsellers into fiction and non-fiction (although the term 'bestseller' automatically evokes a certain kind of novel), and since 1913 further subdivisions have emerged.

Examining *Publisher's Weekly* records in 1945, Alice Payne Hackett determined that the all-time bestseller was Charles Monroe Sheldon's crude Christian epic *In His Steps* (1895) with cumulative sales over sixty years of over eight million. *Gone with the Wind* (1936) had clocked up three and a half million in nine years (these figures disregarded Book Club sales). Undertaking a similar exercise in 1965, Hackett calculated that Grace Metalious's steamy saga of sex in a New England suburb, *Peyton Place* (1956), had sold almost ten million in less than ten years. Lawrence's newly publishable (since 1959) **Lady Chatterley's Lover* had achieved sales of 6.3 million, and Harold Robbins's fictionalized, and sensationalized, account of the life and loves of Howard Hughes, *The Carpetbaggers* (1960), came in at 5.5 million. In 1975 Hackett discovered that with the paperback 'revolution' of the late 1960s, a further exponential growth had occurred. There were now novels like Mario Puzo's *The Godfather* (1969), Peter Blatty's *The Exorcist* (1971), and Erich Segal's *Love Story* (1970) which sold ten million or more in five years. In the 1980s and 1990s, despite competition from other media, sales of bestselling novels continued to rocket—in both hardback and paperback. In the 1980s, Stephen *King's novels were routinely brought out in first print runs of a million in the expensive form, and many millions in cheap form.

Over the decades, bestseller lists have also begun to emerge in regional newspapers and in Sunday supplements (for example, the *Los Angeles Times*, the *Washington Post*, and the *Chicago Tribune*). But nationally, the *Publisher's Weekly* and *New York Times* lists dominate. In Britain (and Europe generally) there was considerable resistance to bestseller lists which, it was felt, distorted customers' buying habits, creating a 'stampede' mentality and inhibiting the range of bookshops' stock. The first reliable lists were introduced in England by *The Bookseller* and *The Sunday Times* in the mid-1970s. They are now an established feature of the British book trade, which has in other ways accommodated to American high-pressure salesmanship (notably in the practice of discounting the sales price of books which figure on the lists).

'Literature' has an uneasy relationship with bestsellerism. In Britain, particularly, the machinery involved has been seen as culturally pernicious (this view was put forward very influentially by Q. D. Leavis in *Fiction and the Reading Public*, 1932). None the less, a number of British writers (notably Graham *Greene, with his 'entertainments') achieved bestseller status. In America the literary quality of supersellers tended to be low, and their content bland, during the inter-war years. An exception was John Steinbeck's angry muck-racking *The *Grapes of Wrath*, which was the top novel in America in 1939. A significant breakthrough occurred in 1958, when Boris Pasternak's *Dr Zhivago* made number 1, and Vladimir Nabokov's **Lolita* number 2 on the American list. Thereafter it was unusual for 'quality' bestsellers to be absent. Some, like Philip Roth's **Portnoy's Complaint* (number 2 in 1963), or any of Norman *Mailer's early novels, were sexually 'frank', exploiting the freedom achieved by the acquittal of *Lady Chatterley* in 1959 (1960 in the UK). But also the elevated level of bestsellers would seem to reflect the huge investments in education undertaken by the USA and Britain after the Second World War. At times, the lists seem to reflect two publics: in 1973, for instance, the top-selling novel was Jacqueline Susann's *Once Is not Enough*, and the third title, Kurt *Vonnegut's *Breakfast of Champions*. In Britain in the 1990s, although sales are proportionately much lower than in America, novelists like Martin *Amis, Julian *Barnes, Vikram *Seth, Salman *Rushdie, and A. S. *Byatt have topped the bestseller lists.

Various definitions of what a 'bestseller' is have been attempted. Frank Luther Mott's calculus ('a total sale equal to one per cent of the current population of the continental United States in the decade in which it was published') is statistically neat, but comes up with some odd results, since it minimizes rate of sale. Bestsellers are books of the year (sometimes of the month, or week), not the decade. The best working definition of a bestseller is a work which appears in the bestseller lists. Historical surveys of twentieth-century bestsellers can be found in F. L. Mott's *Golden Multitudes: The Story of Best Sellers in the United States* (1947); Alice Payne Hackett's regular updates to her initial *Fifty Years of Best Sellers, 1895–1945* (1945); and *Bowker's Annual of Library and Book Trade Information* which summarizes the year's bestsellers in America. There is nothing equivalent in the UK, although Alex Hamilton in the *Guardian* newspaper and the London *Evening Standard* Diary column attempt an annual round-up of the year's bestsellers.

BETHELL, (Mary) Ursula (pseudonym, Evelyn Hayes) (1874–1945), New Zealand poet, born in Rangiora near Christchurch, educated at schools in Oxford and Geneva. From 1890 until 1908 Bethell worked with the poor and underprivileged as a member of an Anglican community in London and returned to New Zealand after the First World War. At the age of about 50 she began writing. Her poetry is characterized by a plainness and spareness (as well as freshness of image) which distinguishes it from the more ornamented verse the country had previously produced. *From a Garden in the Antipodes* (1929) was originally composed as letters to a friend, and, as in Bethell's other collections, *Time and Place* (1936) and *Day and Night: Poems 1924–1935* (1939), the domestic focus is combined with religious belief and a broad range of general and classical reference. Her work has also been seen as part of the construction of a national identity. In her lifetime all collections were published under a pseudonym, but Bethell herself was a considerable literary figure in the Christchurch of the day and mentor to the younger Caxton group, notably Denis *Glover and Allen *Curnow. Her posthumously published *Collected Poems* (1950) was republished in 1985 with an introduction by Vincent *O'Sullivan.

BETJEMAN, Sir John (1906–84), British poet, born in Highgate, London; his childhood and youth are described in detail in his blank-verse autobiography **Summoned by Bells* (1960). He was educated at Highgate Junior School, where T. S. *Eliot was among his teachers, at Marlborough College, and at Magdalen College, Oxford, where he became well acquainted with W. H. *Auden and Maurice *Bowra; he impressed the latter with his 'extraordinary originality' as a wittily accomplished poet and independently minded aesthete and bon viveur. Having left Oxford without a degree, he was briefly engaged as a schoolmaster, before he began writing for the *Architectural Review* in 1931. *Mount Zion*, his first collection of poetry, appeared in 1932, and was followed by numerous volumes, among which are *Continual Dew* (1937), *New Bats in Old Belfries* (1945), *A Few Late Chrysanthemums* (1954), and *A Nip in the Air* (1974). Betjeman was a widely popular poet by the time his *Collected Poems* appeared in 1958; the book was remarkably successful, running to ten impressions by 1960, before the appearance of an enlarged second edition in 1962. Although largely discounted by successive generations of academic critics, his poetry displays a technical virtuosity and an emotional, intellectual, and imaginative cohesion which argue for his stature as a major talent. Philip *Larkin was among the most fervent of his admirers, noting the generous range of his work and the attractive eccentricity of his 'heterogeneous world of farce and fury, where sports girls and old nuns jostle with town clerks and impoverished Irish Peers'. From the early 1930s onward he produced books on architecture and topography, which include *Ghastly Good Taste* (1933), *Vintage London* (1942), and *Cornwall* (1965). In 1972 he succeeded C. *Day Lewis as Poet Laureate. *Young Betjeman* (1988) is the first part of Bevis Hillier's authorized biography. See also TOPOGRAPHICAL POETRY.

Between the Acts, V. *Woolf's last novel, published posthumously in 1941. Unrevised, it is constructed in short scenes of dialogue, dramatic speech, and fragmentary descriptions with recurring motifs. It expresses Woolf's interest at this time in an English history made up of a community of obscure, ordinary lives, in the possibility of anonymity of the author, in the relation between groups and individuals (she was reading Freud), and in the decay of traditional language into 'orts, scraps and fragments'. The setting is an English manor house, Pointz Hall, on a single summer day in war-time. The Oliver family, who have lived in the house for 120 years, consists of the older generation, Bartholomew Oliver and his sister Lucy Swithin (whose arguments over rational fact versus mystical faith rather resemble those of the Ramsays in **To the Lighthouse*), Isa and Giles Oliver, and their small son. Theirs is a difficult marriage: Isa writes poetry secretly and fantasizes about a neighbouring farmer; Giles is hostile and aggressive. Two uninvited lunch guests, the crude Mrs Manresa and the awkward homosexual William Dodge, increase the tension. In the afternoon the village pageant is put on by Miss La Trobe, the novel's artist figure, lonely, eccentric, lesbian, who uses every means she has—pastiche, tableaux, music, repetition, a megaphone, silence, nature itself—to attempt to make an unresponsive audience understand English history and see themselves in the broken mirrors she holds up to them. She feels she has failed, though Mrs Swithin seems to understand her. The day ends as Giles and Isa resume, as in a play, the marital pattern of fighting and love.

Beyond the Horizon, a three-act tragedy by Eugene *O'Neill, first produced in 1920 when it won a Pulitzer Prize. Often regarded as the play which marks the onset of serious modern American drama, *Beyond the Horizon* is an exploration of the bondage of family life which constrains the ambitions of its central characters. In addition, it offers an early version of a characteristic figure of O'Neill's theatre, the would-be poet whose circumstances confine him to a place and mode of life which frustrates his idealism. The brothers Robert and Andrew Mayo, studies in contrasting types who are bonded by a deep sibling love, grow up on their parents' New England farm: Robert, the dreamer, signs on his uncle's ship seeking to fulfil his dreams of romantic otherness through exploration of the world beyond his immediate horizons, intending Andrew to take over the farm. However, they are both in love with the same woman, Ruth Atkins; just before Robert is to leave, Ruth persuades him to marry her and stay behind, and Andrew sails in his place. The impractical Robert brings the farm to ruin, and his marriage becomes a lifeless ritual, briefly propped up by the birth of a daughter, Mary, who dies in early childhood. Andrew, whose experiences at sea have made him tough and unemotional, finally returns when Robert is dying of consumption. Urged by Robert to marry Ruth and save the farm, Andrew turns on Ruth in a frenzy of bitter repudiation for her failure with Robert. The immediate source of *Beyond the Horizon* was a play by the Irish writer T. C. *Murray, *Birthright*; in the depiction of Robert and Ruth's marital disharmony, O'Neill also drew on his knowledge of Strindberg's plays. This play provides an early example of the dramatic arena of familial conflict that he would eventually make his own in the history of modern American theatre.

BHATTACHARYA, Bhabani (1910–88), Indian novelist, born in Bhagalpur, educated in Patna and in London. He is strongly influenced by Rabindranath *Tagore and Mahatma Gandhi. Social realism, with a social purpose, marks Bhattacharya's work, showing its affinity with the work of Mulk Raj *Anand. *So Many Hungers* (1947) deals with exploitation and greed set against the background of the Independence movement and the Bengal famine of the early 1940s. The 'hungers' of the title are seen through the eyes of Kajoli, a destitute village girl. In *He Who Rides a Tiger* (1952), a poor blacksmith, Kalo, is jailed for stealing a bunch of bananas and vows revenge on society. Posing as a holy brahmin who has had a miraculous vision, Kalo thrives on the fraud until he discovers that he cannot dismount the 'tiger', which he has created, without ruining himself. Other works of fiction include the novels *Music for Mohini* (1952), *A Goddess Named Gold* (1960), and *A Dream in Hawaii* (1978), and the short stories in *Steel Hawk* (1968).

BIDART, Frank (1939–), American poet, born in Bakersfield, California, educated at the University of California at Riverside and at Harvard University. Bidart studied under Robert *Lowell at Harvard and is generally discussed as one of that younger generation of 'post-confessional' poets which acknowledges Lowell as a major influence whilst at the same time seeking to extend and develop the confessional lyric medium he bequeathed. Bidart's verse is notable for its attempt to dramatize ordinary speech, and individual poems often take the form of dramatic monologues in a manner that resembles the similar use of this medium in the poetry of Robert Browning and Robert Frost. His volumes of verse include *Golden State* (1973), *The Book of the Body* (1977), *The Sacrifice* (1983), and *In the Western Night: Collected Poems, 1965–1990* (1990). Bidart became a Professor of English at Wellesley College and has also taught at Brandeis University and the University of California at Berkeley.

BIDGOOD, Ruth (1922–), Anglo-Welsh poet, born in Seven Sisters, near Neath, Glamorgan; after reading English at Oxford, she served in the Women's Royal Naval Service and subsequently worked for *Chambers Encyclopaedia* in London. *The Given Time* (1962), her first collection of poetry, was followed by *Not Without Homage* (1975), *The Print of Miracle* (1978), *Kindred* (1986), *Lighting Candles* (1982), and *Selected Poems* (1992). Her poetry displays a recurrent concern with her surroundings in Abergwesyn, Breconshire, where she has lived since 1960. In much of her work, imaginative and emotional content is deftly interfused into treatments of topographical, social, or historical aspects of the locality.

BIERCE, Ambrose (Gwinett) (1842–1914?), American journalist, born in Horse Cave Creek, Ohio. He fought in the Civil War, and after extensive travels in America, moved to San Francisco and became a columnist for numerous magazines and newspapers. He travelled to England in 1872, where he wrote under the pseudonym 'Dod Grile', and published three compilations of his witty sketches: *Nuggets and Dust Panned out in California* (1873), *The Fiend's Delight* (1873), and *Cobwebs from an Empty Skull* (1874). On his return to San Francisco in 1877 he wrote for Hearst's *Examiner*, becoming the most provocative writing force on the West Coast, his frequent vitriol earning him the nickname 'Bitter Bierce'. His *Tales of Soldiers and Civilians* (1891; retitled *In the Midst of Life*, 1892), widely acclaimed for such short stories of the American Civil War as 'Chickamauga' and 'An Occurrence at Owl Creek Bridge', and his further collection *Can Such Things Be?* (1893), established him as a writer of sardonic humour, aptly contrasting images of horror and beauty, and a master of the unexpected ending. His subsequent works included the *The Monk and the Hangman's Daughter* (1892), a medieval romance; *Fantastic Fables* (1899); *Shapes of Clay* (1903), satiric verse; and *Collected Works* (12 volumes; 1909–12). *The Cynic's Word Book* (1906), later retitled *The Devil's Dictionary* (1911), is a compendium of cynical and witty definitions attacking politicians, materialistic values, and bourgeois life. *The Enlarged Devil's Dictionary*, edited by E. J. Hopkin, appeared in 1967. In 1913 Bierce travelled into revolutionary Mexico, where he mysteriously vanished.

Big Sleep, The, a novel by Raymond *Chandler, published in 1939. *The Big Sleep* is the first of Chandler's series of detective novels which feature Philip Marlowe as their hero and, many would argue, the greatest. The complex plot, however, has perplexed many readers and after the novel was adapted for the cinema in 1946 the director, Howard Hawks, is reputed to have said that 'neither the author, the writer, nor myself knew who had killed whom'. (The screenplay was written by William *Faulkner.) Chandler's prose, which owes much to the influence of Ernest *Hemingway, is strikingly effective here in giving a surreal sense to the city of Los Angeles where the action takes place.

BILLINGTON, Rachel (1942–), British novelist, born in Oxford, educated at London University. She is the daughter of Francis Pakenham, the 7th Earl of Longford, and Elizabeth, Countess of *Longford, and the sister of Antonia *Fraser. Her protagonists are almost invariably drawn from the gentry. Her first two novels, *All Things Nice* (1969) and *The Big Dipper* (1970), are comedies of manners, but beneath the caustic wit, there is a more sombre, even violent, tendency which is apparent in *Lilacs Out of the Dead Land* (1971) and developed in successive works. Obsessive passion is the predominant theme in *Cock Robin* (1972), *Beautiful* (1974), and *A Painted Devil* (1975), all of which demonstrate her elegant prose style and her skilful use of dialogue. *A Woman's Age* (1979), more epic in scale, centres on the life of its female protagonist from a difficult past to a promising political career. *Occasion of Sin* (1982) is Billington's reworking of Tolstoy's *Anna Karenina*. In *Loving Attitudes* (1988), she explored the relationship between a middle-aged woman and the daughter she had given up for adoption over twenty years before. *Bodily Harm* (1992), a psychologically acute, discomforting love story, is alternately narrated by an aggressor and his victim, each damaged by childhood events. As well as novels, which also include *The Garish Day* (1985), *Theo and Matilda* (1990), *The Family Year* (1992), and *Magic and Fate* (1996), Billington has also written children's books, plays for television, and *The Great Umbilical* (1994), concerning the relationship between mothers and daughters.

Bim, a Caribbean literary magazine which first appeared in December 1942, published by the Young Men's Progressive Club, under the founding editorship of the late Barbadian writer Frank Collymore; among subsequent editors have been A. N. Forde, Edward Kamau *Brathwaite, John Wickham, and E. L. Cozier. Together with the Guyanese journal *Kyk-Over-Al* (1945–61) it exerted a great influence over the development of Caribbean literature. Produced twice yearly in Barbados, *Bim* was the most important literary outlet in the Caribbean during the formative years of West Indian literature. George *Lamming wrote in an introduction to the June 1955 issue: 'There are not many West Indian writers today who did not use *Bim* as a kind of platform, the surest, if not the only avenue, by which they might reach a literate and sensitive reading public, and almost all of the West Indians who are now writers in a more professional sense and whose work has compelled the attention of readers and writers in other countries, were introduced, so to speak, by *Bim*.' The younger Caribbean journal **Savacou* produced a special issue (7/8, 1973) as a 70th-birthday tribute to Collymore, including reprints from back issues of *Bim* as well as new writing by its contributors.

BINCHY, Maeve (1940–), Irish romantic novelist and short-story writer, born in Dublin, educated at University College, Dublin; she became a columnist for the *Irish Times* in 1968. She published three collections of short stories before her first and best-known novel, *Light a Penny Candle*, appeared in 1982. The story of Elizabeth, a girl evacuated from London to a small Irish village in the Second World War, and her lifelong friend, Aisling, it has an emotional power that owes much to contrasts between village and city. Similar contrasts are evident in Binchy's subsequent novels, including *Echoes* (1985), *Firefly Summer* (1987), *Silver Wedding* (1988), and *Circle of Friends* (1990). *The Copper Beech* (1992) interweaves the lives of individuals with the life of a community, while in *The Glass Lake* (1994) a woman leaves her husband and children and disappears to England, in order to escape the religious and cultural oppression of 1950s' Ireland.

BINYON, (Robert) Laurence (1869–1943), British poet and art historian, born in Lancaster, educated at Trinity College, Oxford. He worked throughout his career at the British Museum, where he became Keeper of the Department of Oriental Prints and Books. The best-known of his numerous works as an art historian is *Painting in the Far East* (1908). As a poet, he is inevitably remembered for his 'For the Fallen' ('They shall not grow old, as we that are left grow old . . .'), which was collected in *The Winnowing Fan: Poems on the Great War* (1914). He went to the Western Front in 1916 as a Red Cross orderly and produced a further collection of poems directly concerned with the war, *The Cause* (1918). The authoritative public tone he achieved in response to the Great War was sustained in later collections, among them the long ode *The Idols* (1928), *The North Star* (1941), and *The Burning of the Leaves* (1944), his widely acclaimed meditation on the Second World War. A *Collected Poems* in two volumes appeared in 1931. He wrote a number of verse-dramas, which include *Attila* (1907) and *Arthur* (1923), the latter with music by Elgar. The refinement and lucidity of his style are well displayed in his *terza rima* translation of Dante's *Divina Commedia* (1933, 1938, 1943). His other works include the critical studies *English Poetry and Its Relation to Painting and the Other Arts* (1919) and *Landscape in English Art and Poetry* (1931).

Biography; modern biography begins with James Boswell's comprehensive attention to his subject's character and habits in *The Life of Samuel Johnson* (1791), which bears out his preface's claim that 'I profess to write not his panegyrick, . . . but his life'. Throughout the Victorian era, however, biography was largely given over to memorializing the great and good as examples of the link between virtue and achievement, an ethos culminating in the foundation of the *Dictionary of National Biography* in 1882. Reaction against the conventions of nineteenth-century biography came in the form of Lytton *Strachey's iconoclastic accounts of Matthew Arnold, Florence Nightingale, Cardinal Manning, and General Gordon in *Eminent Victorians* (1918). He also produced a wittily irreverent life of Queen Victoria (1921) and the melodramatic *Elizabeth and Essex* (1928), the latter initiating the Freudian mode of biography in its attention to psychological dimensions of experience. Strachey's selective procedures, his energetic, if occasionally erratic, spirit of free enquiry, and his careful narrative constructions provided a working example for many succeeding writers. Among the books which sustained the development of biography from the late 1920s are *The Stricken Deer* (1929), David *Cecil's imaginative life of William Cowper, and Peter *Quennell's *Four Portraits* (1945), dealing with Boswell, Edward Gibbon, Laurence Sterne, and John Wilkes. The succession of popular biographical studies published by Hesketh *Pearson from 1930 onward indicates the increasing interest of a general readership in biography. Richard Aldington's *Portrait of a Genius, But . . .* (1950), his treatment of D. H. *Lawrence, and the especially vitriolic *Lawrence of Arabia: A Biographical Enquiry* (1955) both exemplify the frequent tendency of post-war biographies to shock venerators of their subjects. *The Untried Years*, the first part of Leon *Edel's five-volume *Henry James* (1953–72), and Erik *Erikson's *Young Man Luther* (1958) established the value of a directly psychoanalytical approach; the markedly clinical nature of Erikson's work is reflected in his designation of it as 'psychobiography'. Freudian theory was evident in the procedures of many biographers throughout the 1950s and 1960s, the Oedipus complex often constituting a central device; latterly, the approach has been discredited for its reductive questing after conclusive explanations for the courses of lives and works.

The ascendancy of biography as a literary form in more recent decades may be dated from Richard *Ellmann's *James Joyce* (1959) and George *Painter's *Marcel Proust* (two volumes, 1959, 1965). These extended studies combined strong narrative development and penetrating critical intelligence with assiduous detailing of their subjects' lives and socio-cultural situations; they set the pattern for numerous distinguished works, among which are the following: Michael *Holroyd's life of Lytton Strachey (two volumes, 1967–8); Robert *Gittings's *John Keats* (1968); Jon *Stallworthy's *Wilfred Owen* (1974); Anne *Thwaite's *Edmund Gosse* (1984); Maynard Mack's *Alexander Pope* (1985); Humphrey *Carpenter's *A Serious Character* (1988), the fullest available life of Ezra *Pound. The steady chronological progression, naturalistic procedures, and crowded casts of protagonists of such books suggest that biography's present marked popularity may result from its surrogacy for the traditional long novel at a time when prose fiction frequently aspires to innovation.

Experimental strategies have been repeatedly employed in the writing of lives. The compendious *Dickens* (1990) by Peter *Ackroyd succeeds in fusing scholarship of the order that won acclaim for his *T. S. Eliot* (1984) with audacious imaginative departures. Written in the authorial first person, A. J. A. *Symons's *The Quest for Corvo: An Experiment in Biography* (1934) is dramatically effective in emphasizing the investigative nature of biographical research. In a similar vein, Richard *Holmes's *Footsteps* (1985) alternates between biography and autobiography in its account of the travels through Europe which preceded his writing of *Shelley: The Pursuit* (1974). Ian *Hamilton's *In Search of J. D. Salinger* (1988) also draws on its author's subjective experiences in its description of the protracted legal conflicts with his reclusive subject; the book finally appeared after litigation led to the withdrawal of two previous versions.

Numerous critics view biography as the primary mechanism of the cult of literary personality, fostering interest in authors' lives at the expense of attention to their works. Apologists for the genre maintain that it represents the tradition of descriptive criticism in an age dominated by modes of literary theory which are often considered aridly abstract; through the identification of connections between the life and the works, texts are firmly related to the social and cultural conditions prevailing at the time of composition and their implications for the present may be more clearly discerned. In an age of ethical and aesthetic pluralism, the remarkably wide readership for scholarly biographies is a welcome index of the continuity of a common literary culture. Informative discussions of the subject are contained in Robert Gittings's *The Nature of Biography* (1978); *The Biographer's Art*, edited by Jeffrey Meyers (1989); and *The Troubled Face of Biography*, edited by Eric Homberger and John Charmley (1988).

BIRMINGHAM, George A., pseudonym of James Owen HANNAY (1865–1950), Anglo-Irish novelist and Church of Ireland clergyman, born in Belfast, educated at Trinity College, Dublin, and ordained in 1889. He was rector of Westport, County Mayo, from 1892 to 1913. In such early novels as *The Seething Pot* (1905), *Hyacinth* (1906), and *The Bad Times* (1908), he explored Irish political issues from a moderate nationalist standpoint. He is best known for his light-hearted popular novels, many of which focus on the red-haired curate, the reverend J. J. Meldon, and are comic portraits of Irish life and manners. They include *Spanish Gold* (1908), *The Lighter Side of Irish Life* (1911), and *Send for Dr. O'Grady* (1923). *The Red Hand of Ulster* (1912) satirized Unionist militancy, and proved to be all too prophetic. His comedy *General John Regan* (1913), a gentle dig at nationalism, sparked a riot, and a subsequent boycott of his writings. His other works include *A Padre in France* (1918), recording his experiences as an army chaplain during the First World War; *An Irishman Looks at His World* (1919); *A Public Scandal and Other Stories* (1922); *A Wayfarer in Hungary* (1925); and *Pleasant Places* (1934), his autobiography. He particularly valued his works of ecclesiastical history, *The Spirit and Origin of Christian Monasticism* (1903) and *The Wisdom of the Desert* (1904).

BIRNEY, (Alfred) Earle (1904–95), Canadian poet and novelist, born in Calgary and brought up on farms in Alberta and British Columbia; he was educated at the universities of British Columbia, Toronto, and California (Berkeley). Birney was a prominent Trotskyite in the 1930s, an experience about which he wrote in his novel *Down the Long Table* (1955). From 1946 until his retirement in 1965 he was Professor of Medieval Literature at the University of British Columbia. One of Canada's most important poets, Birney has written in a wide variety of styles and about a vast range of subjects, Canadian and international. His early verse was influenced by *Auden and demonstrates a belief in the power of art as an agent for social change. This phase of his writing made extensive use of myth and was strongly influenced by his scholarly interests in early English culture. Subsequently he moved on to write free verse, *concrete poetry, and work in which North American oral idioms are more prominent. His volumes of poetry include *David* (1942), *Strait of Anian* (1948), *Ice Cod Bell and Stone* (1962), and *Near False Creek Mouth* (1964). Birney continued to write poetry after his retirement, and his *Collected Poems* appeared in 1975. His most important work in other genres includes the comic picaresque novel *Turvey* (1949) and the verse-drama *The Damnation of Vancouver* (original title: *Trial of a City*, 1952), which considers whether modern civilization should be destroyed.

Birthday Party, The, a play by Harold *Pinter, performed in 1958 and published in 1959. Pinter's first full-length play, a critical and box office failure when first produced, it involves the mental destruction of a young pianist living obscurely in a seaside town. It is never clear what Stanley Webber has done to attract the malignant attentions of Goldberg and McCann; but these two sinister intruders come to stay in the boarding house where he rooms, throw a bewildering number of improbable accusations at him, and then break his spirit at a birthday party they organize for him. The next day they take him, transformed into a zombie in a business suit, to some unspecified destination. The play, though more surreal and less naturalistic than the plays Pinter was to write in the 1960s, is still characteristic in its combination of ordinary, idiomatic language and an atmosphere of mystery and menace. It has been subjected to various interpretations, for instance as a metaphorical portrayal of the trauma of growing up and joining the adult world, but it is probably best regarded as an evocation of insecurity and dread, the more unsettling for being unspecific.

BISHOP, Elizabeth (1911–79), American poet, born in Worcester, Massachusetts, educated at Vassar College, New York; she was brought up from early infancy by her grandparents after her father died and her mother became chronically ill. She spent her first six years in Great Village, Nova Scotia, which is vividly recalled in her short story 'Primer Class', then returned to Worcester. The poetry she wrote as a student includes 'The Flood' and 'Some Dreams They Forgot', works in which her characteristic combination of an almost casual tone and idiosyncratic meticulousness of form is already apparent. In 1934 she began her lasting friendship with Marianne *Moore, with whose poetry her own has in common its purposive and precise richness of concrete imagery and its qualities of deft moral implication; 'Efforts of Affection', a memoir of Moore, is included in her *Collected Prose* of 1984. *North & South* (1946), her first collection of verse, was widely acclaimed. The poems were reprinted with eighteen additional pieces, including 'At the Fishhouses', one of her best-known works, as *Poems: North & South/A Cold Spring* in 1955. She held the post of Poetry Consultant at the Library of Congress in 1949–50 and was resident in Brazil between 1951 and 1966. *Questions of Travel* (1965) contains poetry vividly informed by her experiences of South America. Brazilian folklore and the exotic fecundity of her natural surroundings are adapted to disquietingly intense effect in 'The Riverman'. Her ability to embody a sense of mystery in sharply delineated imagery is equally evident in 'The Man-Moth', 'A Letter To N. Y.', and other poems. 'Visits to St Elizabeth's', a memorable account of her meetings with Ezra *Pound during his post-war confinement, also appears in the volume of 1965. *Geography III* (1976), her last collection of poetry, featured work of new emotional directness and meditative eloquence. *Complete Poems, 1927–1979* was published in 1984.

BISHOP, John Peale (1892–1944), American poet, born in West Virginia, educated at Princeton. As a student he began lasting friendships with Edmund *Wilson, his collaborator on *The Undertaker's Garland* (1922), a humorous miscellany of verse and prose about death, and F. Scott *Fitzgerald, who is said to have taken Bishop as the model for Tim D'Invilliers in *This Side of Paradise* (1920). Although many of his contemporaries admired the lyrical concentration and classical precision of his verse, he published only three principal collections, *Green Fruit* (1917), *Now with His Love* (1933), and *Minute Particulars* (1936). The last contains much of his best work, written after he took up residence at Cape Cod, Massachusetts, in 1934 upon returning from France where he had lived since the early 1920s; 'A Subject of Sea-Change' is perhaps his finest poem, its compelling philosophical eloquence sustained with maritime imagery of rich particularity. His Virginia background is reflected in much of his writing, which is deeply informed by his elegiac sense of the passing of the patrician culture of the pre-Civil War era; the short stories of *Many Thousands Gone* (1931) are predominantly given Virginian settings. He also produced the highly regarded novel *Act of Darkness* (1935) and made valuable contributions to the **Kenyon Review* and other leading critical journals. Edmund Wilson edited his *Collected Essays* (1948); *Collected Poems* (1948) was edited by Allen *Tate, whose correspondence with Bishop was published under the title *The Republic of Letters* (1981, edited by T. D. Young). Elizabeth Spindler's *John Peale Bishop: A Biography* appeared in 1980.

BISSETT, Bill (1939–), Canadian poet, born in Halifax, Nova Scotia, educated at Dalhousie University and the University of British Columbia. In addition to his activities as a writer and publisher, chiefly with the Blewointmentpress, Vancouver, from 1963 to 1983, Bissett has worked in a wide variety of occupations. His idiosyncratically experimental poetry, which has appeared in some sixty books since *Th jinx ship nd othr trips* (1966), is characterized by phonetic spellings, lower case typography, and a tenacious philosophical and political radicalism. His better-known publications include *nobody owns the earth* (1971), *MEDICINE my mouths on fire* (1974), *Plutonium Missing* (1978), *canada gees mate for life* (1985), and *hard 2 beleev* (1990). His deliberately restricted vocabulary confers an emphatic primitivism on the monosyllabic nouns and verbs that dominate his work. *Selected Poems: Beyond Even Faithful Legends* appeared in 1980.

BISSOONDATH, Neil (1955–), Trinidadian novelist and short-story writer, born in Arima, Trinidad, the nephew of V. S. *Naipaul; in 1973 he emigrated to Canada, and was educated at York University, Toronto. The bleakly compassionate treatments of the lives of immigrants to Canada in *Digging Up the Mountains* (1985), his first collection of stories, initiated the concern with exile and cultural displacement which pervades his work. *A Casual Brutality* (1988), his first novel, deals with the tragic consequences of a doctor's return to his native Caribbean, where violent political upheaval dispossesses him of any sense of belonging. A further collection of stories, *On the Eve of Uncertain Tomorrows* (1990), recurrently portrays the vulnerability to exploitation and injustice which immigrants from different cultural backgrounds have in common in Canadian cities. *The Innocence of Age* (1992), Bissoondath's second novel, has a white Canadian as its chief protagonist, whose alienation from an increasingly materialistic and violent Toronto forms the basis of his identification with members of the immigrant population.

BLACKBURN, Paul (1926–71), American poet, born in St Albans, Vermont, educated at New York University and the University of Wisconsin. He was poetry editor of the **Nation* in 1962 and subsequently held various appointments as a writer-in-residence before becoming a lecturer at the City College of New York in 1968. His earlier collections of verse include *The Dissolving Fabric* (1955), *Brooklyn-Manhattan Transit* (1960), and *The Nets* (1961). Blackburn's open poetic forms and experimentally dispersed typographical effects indicated his affinities with the group of poets associated with *Black Mountain College, in whose *Black Mountain Review* his work appeared. *The Cities* (1967) gained him a wider readership through its skilfully precise evocations of the numinous aspects of everyday phenomena. His ability to imbue a sometimes disturbing directness of manner with unobtrusive suggestions of traditional lyric modes is among the most impressive qualities of his poetry. Among his numerous further publications are *In, On, or About the Premises* (1968), *Halfway Down the Coast* (1975), and *The Journals* (1975), a record in poetry and prose of his last years. *Collected Poems* (1985) is edited by E. Jarolim. His works as a translator include *Proensa* (1953), his highly regarded versions of Provençal lyrics, and *Hunk of Skin* (1968), his translations of poems by Pablo Picasso.

BLACKBURN, Thomas (Eliel Fenwick) (1916–77), British poet, born in Hensingham, Cumberland, educated at Cambridge and Durham Universities. He was a lecturer at the University of Leeds from 1964 to 1966. His first collection of poetry, *The Outer Darkness* (1951), was followed by numerous others, including *The Next Word* (1958), *A Smell of Burning* (1961), *The Fourth Man* (1971), *Bread for the Winter Birds* (1980), and *The Adjacent Kingdom: Collected Last Poems* (1988; edited by Jean MacVean). His early poetry, while richly musical and thematically original, is sometimes conspicuously influenced by *Yeats. A plainer and more flexible voice emerged during the 1960s when he began producing poetry of urgency and poise in response to his religious and psychological preoccupations. His work received generous attention in *Rule and Energy* (1963), John Press's important survey of post-war British poetry. Among his prose works are *A Clip of Steel* (1969), an autobiography recounting his devastatingly traumatic childhood experiences; *The Feast of the Wolf* (1971), a novel; and *The Price of an Eye* (1974), his critical work on modern poetry.

Black Dogs, see MCEWAN, IAN.

BLACK ELK (1863–1950), Native American, a Lakota of the Oglala band of Sioux Indians. Cousin to Crazy Horse, he was a *wichasha wakon*—a holy man or priest—visited by a series of visions which gave him confirmation of his adopted role. In August 1930 the American poet John G. *Neihardt, known also as Flaming Rainbow, visited Black Elk and, using Black Elk's son Ben as an interpreter, conducted a series of talks with him. The results were published as *Black Elk Speaks* (1932), which has since become the most famous of all Native American narratives. Black Elk lived through Custer's defeat at the battle of the Little Big Horn, witnessed the Ghost Dance religion, and survived the massacre of his people at Wounded Knee. He toured Italy, France, and England with Buffalo Bill, even dancing in front of Queen Victoria. More than an autobiography or a history of the Sioux, *Black Elk Speaks* is also a book of instruction: Black Elk's primary aim was to 'save his Great Vision for men'. Neihardt conveys Black Elk's sense of the Great Being who is 'older than all need, older than all pain and prayer'. In 1947 Joseph Epes Brown also visited Black Elk; the result was *The Sacred Pipe* (1953), in which Black Elk concentrated on 'the Seven Rites of the Oglala Sioux'. The book contains a detailed and moving account of the religious practices of the Sioux Indians. In 1973 Neihardt released a three-record set of readings and reminiscences of Black Elk and other Indians, his voice registering beautifully the passion and humanity of their understanding of the world. See also NATIVE AMERICAN WRITING.

Black Mask, American *pulp magazine, specializing in *hardboiled detective fiction. Originally founded (and later repudiated) by H. L. *Mencken in 1920, *Black Mask* was at its peak under the editorship of Captain Joseph T. Shaw from 1920 to 1936. Between eye-catchingly lurid covers, the magazine offered unadorned, briskly told violent stories, introducing the highly influential character of the world-weary private eye, the 'hardboiled dick'. The first of these was 'Race Williams', invented by the prolific Carroll John Daly (1889–1958), but more importantly, Shaw encouraged a team of writers, including more prominent figures like Erle Stanley *Gardner, the creator of the 'Perry Mason' courtroom books, and so helped establish a tough and frank indigenous American style of crime writing, in opposition to the cosier British traditions. Although there were a number of magazines of this kind, like *Dime Mystery* and *Spicy Detective*, now long forgotten, *Black Mask* is best remembered as the journal which published the first story by Raymond *Chandler—'Blackmailers Don't Shoot' (1933)—and which introduced the remarkable talent of Dashiell *Hammett, whose 'Continental Op' stories appeared regularly in the early 1930s. Although Shaw had no pretensions to literary esteem, his firm editorship helped disseminate a lean, fast-moving prose style and set influential terms of reference for more serious later writers.

Black Mountain Writers, a group of American poets and writers, who were associated with Black Mountain College in Asheville, North Carolina. Black Mountain College was established in 1933, largely funded by John Andrew Rice, as an experiment in communitarian, liberal arts education, but its fame as a centre of vibrant experimentation in the arts was largely made in the early 1950s. The philosopher John *Dewey became a member of the college's advisory board, in its early years, but under the directorship of the painter Josef Albers in the 1940s the role of the college in the artistic life of America became more influential. As a consequence of Albers's leadership the college attracted the painters Willem de Koonig, Robert Motherwell, and Robert Rauschenberg; the musicians John Cage, Lou Harrison, and Heinrich Jalowetz; the choreographer Merce Cunningham; and the poets Robert *Creeley, Robert *Duncan, Charles *Olson, and John Weiners. Olson was closely allied to the College from 1948 until as Rector he closed it down in 1956. During Olson's rectorship, Robert Duncan and Robert Creeley taught at the College, whilst such writers as Ed *Dorn, Robert *Kelly, Joel Oppenheimer, and Gilbert *Sorrentino were among the students. Their poetry was published in *The Black Mountain Review* (1954–7), edited by Creeley, which became a focus for avant-garde writing; it also featured such writers as Tom Field, Michael Rumaker, Fielding *Dawson, Jack *Kerouac, Kenneth *Rexroth, William Carlos *Williams, Denise *Levertov, Paul *Blackburn, and Larry Eigner, some of them also associated with the *Beats and the *San Francisco Renaissance. They were generally indebted to the 'open' forms begun by Ezra *Pound and continued by William Carlos Williams and *Zukovfsky. The Black Mountain group proposed a physiology of consciousness as the basis for a formal revolution, as outlined in Olson's influential essay *'Projective Verse' (1950). Olsen proclaimed the necessity of avoiding 'the lyrical interference of the individual as ego' and, in seeking to redefine the structures of literacy itself, he advocated the necessity of manipulating syntax, typography, and logical structures. In his essay 'Human Universe' (1965), Olson described poetic activity not as referential or mimetic, but reality itself. The 'open' poetics urged a repositioning of the self, as a participating rather than dominating figure in larger, unknown forces. Much of this thought was developed in Olson's correspondence with Cid *Corman, the editor of the magazine *Origin*, and can be seen in Olson's *Letters for Origin* (1969). With the publication of Donald Allen's influential anthology *The New American Poetry* (1960), the Black Mountain writers became recognized as a force in contemporary poetry which proposed an alternative *Modernism to that constructed by T. S. *Eliot and the *New Criticism.

BLACKMUR, R(ichard) P(almer) (1904–65), American critic and poet, born in Springfield, Massachusetts. Self-taught, at first a freelance essayist and man of letters, he later became a much-admired professor at Princeton University. He is often associated with the *New Criticism, but too eccentric to be easily assimilated to any movement. He published three volumes of verse—*From Jordan's Delight* (1937), *The Second World* (1942), and *The Good European* (1947)—initially much influenced by *Yeats but later developing a more personal, less secondary voice. The poetry is tense, carefully wrought, allusive, intelligent but sometimes rather cramped. Blackmur's prose is fluid, complex, and occasionally arcane, a perfect vehicle for the difficult, oblique insights he specialized in. Thought by T. S. *Eliot and others to be the best close reader modern poetry had found, he demanded form in art, was fiercely opposed to what he saw as the fallacy of immediate expression, but understood that form itself needed to be various and could look formless to conventional eyes. He concentrated on contemporary poetry in his early critical works—Wallace *Stevens, Marianne *Moore, Eliot, Ezra *Pound—but later became interested in the European novel and in large questions of culture. The modern world, he thought, had developed 'techniques of trouble' in art and science, but had not learned how to deal with the trouble it found; so that the *anni mirabiles* of *Modernism (*Anni Mirabiles* was the title of a series of lectures Blackmur gave at the Library of Congress in 1956) were not only triumphant and dramatic years but prophetic ones, announcing a difficult, possibly unmanageable period we have scarcely begun to know. Blackmur was a great believer in the dignity and authority of failure—earned failure, that is, the sort that comes harder than success. Throughout his career he was much interested in Henry *James and Henry *Adams, whom he regarded as opposite and complementary poles of the American imagination. His chief critical works are *The Double Agent* (1935), *The Expense of Greatness* (1940), *Language as Gesture* (1951), *The Lion and the Honeycomb* (1955), and *Eleven*

Essays in the European Novel (1964). See also POST-MODERNISM.

BLACKWOOD, Algernon (Henry) (1869–1951), British writer of ghost stories and novels, born in Kent, educated at Edinburgh University. He travelled widely and worked as a journalist in New York—a period reflected in *Episodes before Thirty* (1923). He gained considerable success with his first collections, *The Empty House* (1906) and *The Listener* (1907), and was encouraged by H. *Belloc. His interest in the occult and his expressive pantheism generated a series of highly original nature tales, whose ghostly protagonists were manifestations of natural forces. He wrote more than thirty books which include *Pan's Garden* (1910), *The Lost Valley* (1910), *Incredible Adventures* (1914), *Day and Night Stories* (1917), *Strange Stories* (1929), and *Tales of the Uncanny and Supernatural* (1949).

BLACKWOOD, Caroline, born Caroline Hamilton-Temple-Blackwood (1931–96), British novelist and essayist, daughter of the Marquess of Dufferin and Ava, born in Ireland where she grew up on her family's estates in Clandeboye, Co. Down; she was educated mainly in England. She married the painter Lucien Freud; after her divorce, she married the musician Israel Citkovitz, and later, the poet Robert *Lowell who wrote about their relationship in *The Dolphin* (1973). Her first novel, *The Stepdaughter* (1976), set in Manhattan, reworks the epistolary form to present the monologue of an abandoned, embittered woman trapped in her own guilt and yet unable to escape its prison. The novel displayed Blackwood's emphasis on inevitability and determinism, and her ability to weave the strands of religious and philosophical discourse. *Great-Granny Blackwood* (1977), which reconstructs the lives and fortunes of an aristocratic family through the lives of its women, is rich with surrealistic set-pieces and is blackly humorous. *The Fate of Mary Rose* (1981) demonstrated an increasing maturity of craftsmanship; narrated by a cold historian, the novel's central metaphor of the rape and murder of a little girl illustrates in chilling detail the selfishness of emotional relationships as the narrator's family, and his extramarital attachment, dissolve under the pressures of fear and uncertainty. *Corrigan* (1984) concerns a widow's involvement with the ambivalent figure of Corrigan—saviour or con-man—and reflected Blackwood's fascination with the relativity of truth. Her non-fiction works include *On the Perimeter* (1984), an account of the women at the Greenham Common peace camp, and *In the Pink* (1987), a long essay on hunting.

BLAIR, Eric Arthur, see ORWELL, GEORGE.

BLAISE, Clark (1940–), Canadian novelist and short-story writer, born in Fargo, North Dakota, educated at Denison University and the University of Iowa. Since 1964, when he began lecturing at the University of Wisconsin, Blaise has held a succession of posts at universities throughout North America. He became a Canadian citizen in 1973. The autobiographical dimension in much of his highly regarded fiction is integral to his treatments of the impermanence and relativity of personal identity. His novels, *Lunar Attractions* (1979) and *Lusts* (1983), respectively form a moving account of confused adolescence and an obsessive rehearsal of the significances of a wife's suicide. His short-stories in *A North American Education* (1973), *Tribal Justice* (1974), and *Resident Alien* (1986) are widely considered to represent his central achievement. *I Had A Father: A Post-Modern Autobiography* appeared in 1993. With his wife Bharati *Mukerjee, Blaise is the co-author of *Days and Nights in Calcutta* (1977), a journal of their year in India, and *The Sorrow and the Terror: the Haunting Legacy of the Air India Tragedy* (1987).

BLAKE, Nicholas, see DAY LEWIS, C.

Blast, a magazine, subtitled 'the Review of the Great English Vortex', founded in London in 1914 by Wyndham *Lewis. The first issue generated much publicity and controversy; only one further edition was published, the 'War Number' of July 1915, which, with the exception of T. S. *Eliot's 'Preludes' and 'Rhapsody on a Windy Night', contains less work of interest than its predecessor. Ezra *Pound, the magazine's co-editor, the sculptor Henri Gaudier-Brzeska, and the painter Edward Wadsworth were Lewis's chief collaborators. Together they formed the core of the *Vorticist movement in art and literature, which violently rejected the aesthetic values of the nineteenth century; Pound described 'the Vortex' as a 'radiant node or cluster . . . from which, and through which, and into which, ideas are constantly rushing', drawing on astronomical theories of the spiral as the fundamental form of cosmic energy to express the Vorticists' search for a new dynamism in their art. Jacob Epstein, William Roberts, and Christopher Nevison were also closely associated with Vorticism in sculpture and painting. The movement's most characteristic literary manifestation is Lewis's futuristic play 'Enemy of the Stars', which appeared in the first issue of *Blast*; it also contained a number of poems and a 'Vortex' by Pound, Ford Madox *Ford's 'The Saddest Story', which eventually formed part of his *The Good Soldier* (1915), Rebecca *West's story 'Indissoluble Matrimony', and a series of photographic illustrations of works by Vorticist artists. The magazine's most remarkable feature was its lengthy introductory section of provocative manifestos and typographically experimental lists under the reiterated headings 'BLAST', 'CURSE', and 'BLESS'; the many targets of its excecrations included 'The BRITANNIC AESTHETE / cream of the snobbish earth' and 'the years 1837 to 1900'; among the blessed were 'the vast planetary abstraction of the OCEAN' and 'the HAIRDRESSER for correcting the grotesque anachronisms of our physique'. Further radical attacks on the cultural status quo were made in Lewis's extensive 'Vorteces and Notes'. *Blast* and Vorticism, which, although defunct as a movement by 1916, have seminal importance in British *Modernism, are considered at length in Timothy Materer's *Vortex: Pound, Eliot, and Lewis* (1979). See also FUTURISM.

BLEASDALE, Alan (1946–), British playwright, born in Liverpool, educated at Padgate Teacher Training College and Liverpool Polytechnic. He worked as a teacher before writing a series of plays, many of them combining humour with dramatic punch, for theatres in his native city, Liverpool. Two of these, *Having a Ball* (1981), a farcical comedy involving a series of confusions in a vasectomy clinic, and *Are You Lonesome Tonight?* (1985), a musical about Elvis Presley, transferred to London. Other stage plays include *Fat Harold and the Last Twenty Six* (1975), about corruption in the Liverpool docks; *The Party's Over* (1975), about a probation hostel for young women; *No More Sitting on the Old School Bench* (1977), about staff conflict in a multi-racial comprehensive school; and the socially conscious farce *On the Ledge* (1993), in which petty thieves, a villainous property developer, and other exemplary characters pursue each other round the top of a Liverpool tower block while rioters create havoc below. Bleasdale is, however, best known for his television work, notably two powerful and topical series, *The Boys from the Blackstuff* (1982), about unemployed men in Liverpool, and *GBH* (1991), about left-wing politics and corruption in an unnamed northern city.

BLISH, James (1921–75), American *science fiction writer and critic, born in East Orange, New Jersey, educated at Rutgers and Columbia Universities; he lived in England in later years. Among his best-known works are *A Case of Conscience* (1958), a dramatized debate about the theological status of an alien race; *Cities in Flight* (1970), a collection of four earlier works in which Earth cities like New York literally take off and orbit the planet; *The Seedling Stars* (1957), a collection of short stories; *Doctor Mirabilis* (1964), a fictional study of Roger Bacon; and *Black Easter; Or, Faust Aleph-Null* (1968), a discussion on the death of God. Blish's criticism was collected in *The Issue at Hand* (1964), *More Issues at Hand* (1970), and *The Tale that Wags the Dog* (1988). See also SPACE OPERA.

BLIXEN, Karen (Christentze), née Dinesen (1885–1962), Danish writer, born in Rungsted, Denmark; she studied at the Royal Academy of Fine Arts in Copenhagen. Her works in English were written mainly under the name Isak Dinesen. In 1914 she married her cousin, Baron Blor-Blixen Finecke, and together they set up a coffee plantation in Kenya. The marriage was dissolved in 1921, but she stayed on in Kenya until 1931, and then returned to live in her Danish family estate, Rungstedlung. It was in Kenya that she wrote her most famous work, *Seven Gothic Tales* (1934); the great artistry of these stories belies her claim that 'I began to write there to amuse myself in the rainy season'. Focusing on extreme mental states and often grotesque characters, the tales quarry a mine of supernatural lore. Other collections of stories, which appear also in Danish versions, include *Winter's Tales* (1942), *Last Tales* (1957), *Anecdotes of Destiny* (1958), and *Ehrengard* (1963). Her great love of East African wildlife and landscape, together with nostalgia for colonial life, are reflected in her highly popular memoir, *Out of Africa* (1937), later made into an award-winning film. She returned to similar themes in *Shadows on the Grass* (1961). The posthumous *Letters from Africa: 1914–1931* (1981; edited by Frans Lasson; translated from the Danish by Ann Born) paints a less idealized picture of life on the coffee farm. Her critical writings are collected in *Essays* (1965) and *Daguerreotypes and Other Essays* (1979). See Judith Thurman, *Isak Dinesen: The Life of Karen Blixen* (1982).

Bloody Chamber, The, a collection of stories by Angela *Carter, published in 1979. The stories are united by their common origin in the world of European folklore and fable, refracted through the lens of contemporary critical and psychoanalytical theories; the influence of Freud, Propp, and *Barthes may be discerned. Carter's lavish prose style also displays her affection for the gothic, and the influence of such masters of the modern tale as Borges, Isak Dinesen (Karen *Blixen), and Christina *Stead, first revealed in her experimental collection *Fireworks* (1974). The stories here are mostly interpretations of the fairytales of Charles Perrault and the Brothers Grimm. Traditional children's stories such as Beauty and the Beast, Bluebeard, and Little Red Riding Hood are reworked to explore their repressed content: the violence and fear connected with the erotic, sexuality, and the unconscious, represented by metamorphoses and the figures of werewolves, weretigers, and other fantastic creatures. The legend of the vampire also appears, in female form. Carter's poetic prose, and her obvious joy in story-telling, make of the stories adult renderings of familiar fables, somewhat lighter than the radical critiques (virtually *metafiction) contained in her later, related collection *Black Venus* (1985). Its influence can be discerned in the writings of Marina *Warner, Jeanette *Winterson, and Sara *Maitland. A film, *The Company of Wolves*, was inspired by some of its tales.

BLOOM, Harold (1930–), American critic, born in New York, educated at Cornell and Yale universities. Among other academic posts he was Professor of English at Yale (1965–74). He is known for his early work on the English Romantic poets (*Shelley's Mythmaking*, 1959; *The Visionary Company*, 1962) and for his theory of 'strong' reading, expressed in a series of books beginning with *The Anxiety of Influence* (1973). In Bloom's view the history of poetry is the history of a sequence of Oedipal struggles, sons against fathers. The son chooses his poetic progenitor, as Wordsworth chose Milton, for example, but must then submit to, work through, and throw off the father's influence. The battle is stylistic rather than psychological, however, a matter of voice and language rather than personal aggression or uncertainty. Bloom offers a detailed graph of possible relations between poets, complete with technical terms and copious quotation, brilliantly interpreted, illustrating the stages of the struggle. A 'strong' reading may be academically reckless, but it will be a reading the poet needs, and even deviant, will still be responsive to real powers in the original, fathering work. At times too eager for clues—Wordsworth's 'blind man' in 'Tintern Abbey' can only be Milton—Bloom's writing is mostly agile and subtle, seeking multiple connections rather than reductions. It displays a passion for poetry and considerable wit, as when an earlier poet is said to be 'influenced' by a later one, because the sound of the later voice has become unmistakable: thus we might hear Eliot in Tennyson rather than the other way round. Bloom is also interested in Gnosticism and the cabbala, and has written a haunting fantasy novel, *The Flight to Lucifer* (1979), set on another world, where mystical questions are forms of high adventure. In *Ruin the Sacred Truths* (1989) and *The Western Canon* (1994), themes of cultural history and textual criticism are further explored.

BLOOMFIELD, Leonard (1887–1949), American linguist, born in Chicago, educated at Harvard, the University of Wisconsin, and the University of Chicago, where he became Professor of Germanic Philology in 1927. From 1940 until his death he was Professor of Linguistics at Yale. *An Introduction to Linguistics* (1914) based its theory of language on the mentalist psychology of Wilhelm Wundt (1832–1920), presenting an orthodox survey of speech and syntax viewed as functions of subjective psychological processes. While at Ohio State University, where he held a professorship from 1921 to 1927, Bloomfield was influenced by the behaviourist psychology of Albert Paul Weiss (1879–1931), which provided a model for the empirical approach of *Language* (1933). The work effectively established linguistics as an autonomous science: although indebted to Weiss's methods, Bloomfield's emphasis on *Language*'s freedom from any programmatic dependence on psychological theory had axiomatic significance for his later work and that of his followers. His attention to the internal structures of individual languages as the basis for his analytical procedures was central to developments in structural linguistics; in *Outline Guide for the Study of Foreign Languages* (1942) and other works he successfully extended his principles to the field of applied linguistics. In the course of the 1950s his work was supplanted by that of Noam *Chomsky, who retained Bloomfield's analytical systems while rejecting his behaviourist assumptions. Charles Hockett's edition of *A Leonard Bloomfield Anthology* (1970) indicates the scope of Bloomfield's interests in Indo-European, Malayo-Polynesian, and Native American languages.

Bloomsbury Group: a loosely knit group of friends, who began to meet in or around 1905, initially at 46 Gordon Square in Bloomsbury, the home of the children of Leslie Stephen (Virginia *Woolf, Vanessa Bell, and Adrian and Thoby Stephen). In 1899 Thoby Stephen, Clive *Bell, Lytton *Strachey, Saxon Sydney Turner, and Leonard *Woolf had all entered Trinity College, Cambridge. As members of the *Apostles (except for Stephen and Bell), they were dedicated to 'love, the creation and enjoyment of aesthetic experience and the pursuit of knowledge' (G. E. *Moore). In 1905 Thoby Stephen began to institute 'Thursday Evenings', when the friends (joined by Desmond *MacCarthy and, in 1910, Roger *Fry) would meet with Vanessa and Virginia, the Stephen sisters.

The mood was one of conscious revolt against the aesthetic, social, and sexual restrictions of Victorian England, and is probably best characterized by Strachey's iconoclastic *Eminent Victorians* (1918). They attacked the lack of imagination and the hypocrisy of the English monied classes and took great pleasure in offending the British philistine. They were writers, publishers, artists, economists: the genteel wing of the avant-garde of the time, who not only staged subversive events—ranging in seriousness from the Dreadnought Hoax to the First Post-Impressionist Exhibition (both 1910)—but who also actively encouraged new talent through, for example, the *Hogarth Press.

Their mood of exclusivism and class consciousness, however, was deeply alienating to some. D. H. *Lawrence had no time for them, Wyndham *Lewis hated the effeminacy of the culture, F. R. *Leavis thought them pretentious and shallow. The extent to which they shared an aesthetic creed is debatable: the group expanded during and after the First World War as younger members such as David *Garnett, Francis Birrell, and Dora Carrington became involved. A vast number of biographies, autobiographies, memoirs, and letters have been produced. Quentin Bell's book *Bloomsbury* (1968) offers an insider's account of the group. Michael *Holroyd's two-volume biography of Lytton Strachey (1968) sought to reassess the influence of Bloomsbury, after the reputation of the group had declined in the 1940s and 1950s.

Bluest Eye, The, a novel by Toni *Morrison, published in 1970. The voices of Claudia, a young black girl, and an omniscient narrator describe a year in the grim life of Pecola Breedlove, a black girl from Ohio. Pecola is maddened by the disparity between her life and the images of beauty and sophistication disseminated by the hegemonic white culture. In her search for a more acceptable face, she finds this in the blue eyes of Claudia's doll. Rejected by her mother and abused by her father, Pecola meets Soaphead Church, a local seer, and begs him for blue eyes which he grants after a staged miracle. Finally blue-eyed, we are left with a fragmented Pecola living in a world of fantasy. On a larger scale the novel depicts the destruction of a black family by the forces of white, racist society. Many scenes in the novel are powerful and disturbing (Pecola's incestuous relationship with her father, for example) but Morrison's prose is never melodramatic or sentimental, and like many of her early novels the strength of *The Bluest Eye* lies in its treatment of family secrets.

BLUNDEN, Edmund (Charles) (1896–1974), British poet, born in London; he grew up in Yalding, Kent, and was educated at Queen's College, Oxford. Of the many poems he wrote during active service on the Western Front from 1915 to 1919, a number are among the best examples of the poetry of the First World War (see WAR POETRY). His experiences as a soldier strongly informed his later writing, achieving their fullest expression in the autobiographical prose of *Undertones of War* (1928), which also contains thirty-two of his most memorable war poems; as a record of the radical shifts in personal and cultural orientation effected by the conflict, the work is equalled only by Graves's **Goodbye to All That* (1929). In 1920 Blunden became Middleton *Murry's assistant editor on *The *Athenaeum*. Throughout the 1930s he taught at Merton College, Oxford, and subsequently joined the staff of the **Times Literary Supplement*. He was Professor of English at the University of Hong Kong from 1953 to 1964 and was elected Professor of Poetry at Oxford in 1966, retiring after eighteen months through ill health. Following early collections of his poetry in 1914 and 1916, Blunden's reputation was established with *The Waggoner* (1920); *The Shepherd* (1922) and *English Poems* (1925) are among the best-known of many succeeding volumes. *Collected Poems* (1930) and *Poems: 1930–1940* (1940) remain the principal editions of his work. The most substantial representation of his later writing is *A Hong Kong House: Poems 1951–1961* (1962). Critical disparagement of the *Georgian poets, among whom Blunden was numbered, has tended to diminish his standing; but while a great deal of his verse is devoted to nature and landscape, often in the Kent countryside, its intricate musicality, precise imagery, and imaginative power distinguish it entirely from mediocre Georgian poetry. As a scholar and editor, his editions of the poetry of John Clare (1920) and Ivor *Gurney (1954) rescued their work from obscurity. He also produced numerous books of criticism and literary biography, among which are the collection of essays entitled *Votive Tablets* (1931), *Leigh Hunt* (1930), and *Charles Lamb* (1954). See *Edmund Blunden* (1990) by Barry Webb.

BLUNT, Wilfred Scawen (1840–1922), British poet and campaigner against imperialism; born into a family of wealthy Sussex landowners, he entered the diplomatic service at the age of 18. He was posted to various European capitals, including Paris, where he sustained an affair with 'Skittles', a well-known *demi-mondaine*, from which much of his subsequent love poetry derived. In 1869 he married Annabella King-Noel, the granddaughter of Byron, and resigned from his career as a diplomat. His first collection of verse was *Sonnets and Songs*, published under the pseudonym 'Proteus' in 1875, which later appeared in several revised editions. Numerous volumes followed, including *Esther* (1892) and *Griselda*, his verse-novel of 1893. Love lyrics, often of a candour unusual in the late Victorian era, remained a dominant aspect of his poetry, which also dwelt on the Sussex countryside and incorporated translations from the work of Arabian poets. His collected *Love Poems* appeared in 1902; two volumes of *The Poetical Works of Wilfred Scawen Blunt* were published in 1914. In 1875 he began his extensive travels in the Middle East, conceiving the strong antipathy to British imperialism which led him to work for political independence for Egypt, Arabia, India, and Ireland. His political publications include *In Vinculis* (1889), a poem written after he was imprisoned for a speech espousing Irish nationalism, and the prose treatises *Secret History of the English Occupation of Egypt* (1907) and *The Land War in Ireland* (1912). He numbered many leading figures in literature and politics among his admirers in his later years, including George Bernard *Shaw, who expressed his approval of Blunt's opinions in the preface to *John Bull's Other Island* (1904). His *Diaries* were published in two volumes in 1919 and 1920. Elizabeth Longford's biography *A Pilgrimage of Passion* appeared in 1979.

BLY, Robert (Elwood) (1926–), American poet, born in Madison, Minnesota, educated at Harvard and the University of Iowa. In 1958 he founded *The Fifties*, a important literary magazine of the period, in conjunction with the Fifties Press. He is also well known as a prolific translator of poetry. His first collection of poetry, *Silence in the Snowy Fields* (1962), derived much of its imagery from his native surroundings in rural Minnesota. During the late 1960s he organized and participated in many poetry readings mounted as a form of protest against the Vietnam War (see VIETNAM WRITING); *The Light around the Body* (1967) and *The Teeth Mother Naked at Last* (1970) project harsh critiques of modern American culture in poems notable for their disquieting successions of imagery and compelling free-verse rhythms. *Point Reyes Poems* (1974), *The Man in the Black Coat Turns* (1981), and *Loving a Woman in Two Worlds* (1985) are among the numerous subsequent collections of his verse, in which a development towards a poised contemplative mode is apparent. His prose poems appeared in *This Body Is Made of Camphor and Gopherwood* (1977) and in a collected edition, *What Have I Ever Lost by Dying* (1992). *A Love of Minute Particulars* (1985) is a British selected edition of his work since 1968. Notable among his other publications is *Iron John* (1990), an imaginative treatment of the psychology of the male in modern culture, which attracted widespread attention in the USA and elsewhere.

BLYTHE, Ronald (George) (1922–), British author, born in Suffolk; he began by writing fiction and short stories, many of them based on gossip and ghost stories from his native county. *The Stories of Ronald Blythe* (1985) includes work published from 1957. With *The Age of Illusion* (1963), a study of England between the wars, he moved to highly literate sociological reflection. He is perhaps best known for his eloquent attention to the particular in two collections of tape-recorded interviews from a typical Suffolk village. *Akenfield: Portrait of an English Village* (1969) opens with an evocative description of the place and the changes it has seen, then lets the people speak, from the ageing farm-worker to the gravedigger. *The View in Winter: Reflections on Old Age* (1979) uses the same method to provide a picture of old age and the taboos with which it is surrounded. *Divine Landscape* (1986, with photographer Edwin Smith) is an illustrated treatment of landscapes with literary associations. Blythe has also published essays and criticism, and has edited a number of anthologies, including *Each Returning Day* (1989), extracts from diaries, and *Private Words: Letters and Diaries from the Second World War* (1991).

BOGAN, Louise (1897–1970), American poet, born at Livermore Falls, Maine, educated at Boston University. From 1931 to 1968 she was poetry critic for the *New Yorker*, exercising considerable influence through her concisely articulate reviews. She became Poetry Consultant to the Library of Congress in 1945. *Body of This Death*, her first volume of poetry, appeared in 1923. Her other principal collections are *Dark Summer* (1929), *The Sleeping Fury* (1937), in which the erotic impulse behind much of her poetry is most clearly sensed, *Poems and New Poems* (1941), and *The Blue Estuaries* (1968). Like Allen *Tate, Yvor *Winters, and others of her generation, she established a productive interaction between her highly accomplished use of traditional forms and poetic *Modernism's emphasis on the essential functions of imagery. Her best work is characterized by the poise and economy with which its refined lyrical intensities are sustained. *Collected Poems, 1923–1953* was published in 1954. Her criticism, chiefly drawn from her writing for the *New Yorker*, is represented by *Achievement in American Poetry, 1900–1950* (1951), *Selected Criticism* (1955), and *A Poet's Alphabet* (1970). Bogan's autobiography *Journey around My Room* (1981) was edited by Ruth Limmer, who was also the editor of *What the Woman Lived* (1973), a collection of her letters. *Louise Bogan: A Portrait* by Elizabeth Frank appeared in 1985.

BOLAND, Eavan (Aisling) (1944–), Irish poet, born in Dublin, educated at Trinity College, Dublin. One of the foremost women poets in Ireland, her collections of poems include *New Territory* (1967), *The War Horse* (1975), *In Her Own Image* (1980), *Night Feed* (1982), *The Journey* (1987), *Outside History* (1990), and *In a Time of Violence* (1994). Her *Selected Poems* (1989) demonstrated the range of interests and tonalities in her work, which accommodates traditional Irish themes, incisive commentaries on contemporary subjects, and intimately personal poems of relationships and womanhood. Boland's prose works include the critical study *A Kind of Scar: The Woman Poet in the National Tradition* (1989), and the autobiographical *Object Lessons* (1995).

BOLD, Alan (Norman) (1943–), Scottish poet and critic, born in Edinburgh, where he was educated at the University. After working on the editorial staff of the *Times Educational Supplement*, he became a freelance writer in 1967. *Society Inebrious* (1965), his first collection of poetry, was followed by numerous further volumes, which include *To Find the New* (1967), *A Perpetual Motion Machine* (1969), *This Fine Day* (1979), *In This Corner* (1983), and *Homage to MacDiarmid* (1985). The politically declamatory qualities of Bold's early verse modulate as his work progresses into the clarity and directness with which he addresses a wide range of social, cultural, and personal themes. He has also produced collections in Scots dialect, among which is the buoyantly humorous *Summoned by Knox* (1984). Bold's numerous critical studies include *George Mackay Brown* (1978), and his highly acclaimed biography, *MacDiarmid: The Terrible Crystal*; *An Open Book* (1990) is a volume of critical essays. Among the many anthologies he has edited are *Making Love: The Picador Book of Erotic Verse* (1978) and *The Penguin Book of Socialist Verse* (1970). A novel, *East Is West*, appeared in 1991.

BOLGER, Dermot (1959–), Irish novelist, playwright, poet, and publisher, born in Finglas, north Dublin, educated at Beneavin College, Finglas. As editor of The Raven Arts Press in Dublin, Bolger was responsible for the production of an important anthology of contemporary poetry written in the Irish language, *The Bright Wave/An Tonn Gheal* (1986). He is committed to the publication of work which reinterprets the history of modern Ireland by unveiling the failure of its political ideals and the lies of its 'economic miracle', a commitment reflected in his own writing. His metaphors are frequently derived from the details of local history and the origin of *logainmeacha* (place-names), such as the hidden 'crystal stream' of Finglas in his novel *The Woman's Daughter* (1987; revised 1991). Bolger's poetry, collections of which include *Never A Dull Moment* (1978), *The Habit of Flesh* (1980), *Finglas Lillies* (1981), *No Waiting America* (1982) and *Internal Exiles* (1985), is thematically significant in revealing the genesis of his concern, in his fiction and drama, with deprived urban Dublin, emigration, and the tragedy of Ireland's 'internal exiles'. His novels *Night Shift* (1985) and *The Woman's Daughter* invert the traditional view of the Irish as exiles by portraying the plight of people living in Ireland, who have been politically and economically excluded from their own country. *The Journey Home* (1990), a thriller, also incorporates an attack on political corruption, a prediction of the implications of Ireland's membership of the European Community, and a portrayal of exile as a smokescreen which has served successive Irish Governments in distracting attention from the problems at 'Home'. *Emily's Shoes* (1992) is an intensely introspective narrative of a young Irish shoe-fetishist searching for identity in a sordid Dublin environment; the novel was praised for the spare clarity of its prose and brilliant eye for detail. In *Second Life* (1994), a conflation of ghost story and detective fiction, the protagonist, adopted as a child, loses his identity after a car crash and goes in search of himself and his background through layers of personal and ancestral memory. Bolger's first play, *The*

Lament for Arthur Cleary (1989), transposes an old story of injustice and murder from its original setting of Ireland during the Penal Laws, to contemporary Dublin. The play is characteristic of Bolger's use of the past and the present to create palimpsests of meaning and was included, together with *The Tramway End* (1990), *The Holy Ground* (1991) and *One Last White Horse* (1991) in *A Dublin Quartet* (1992). Bolger edited *The Picador Book of Irish Contemporary Fiction* (1993).

BOLT, Robert (Oxton) (1924–95), British dramatist, born and educated in Manchester, the son of a shopkeeper. He was working as a schoolmaster when his *Flowering Cherry* was performed in London in 1957. That play, about a salesman who impotently dreams of escape to the country, was followed by *The Tiger and the Horse* (1960), which reflected Bolt's own involvement in anti-nuclear politics. *Vivat, Vivat Regina* (1970) and *State of Revolution* (1977), respectively involving Elizabeth's destruction of Mary, Queen of Scots and the compromises forced on the Bolsheviks after their seizure of power, both achieved modest success; but Bolt's most enduring play has proved to be his study of Thomas More, *A Man for All Seasons* (1960). This shows More's at first affectionate relationship with Henry VIII, his resignation as Chancellor and 'eloquent silence' after the King's divorce, remarriage, and rejection of the 'Bishop of Rome', his refusal to deny the spiritual authority of the pope, his imprisonment, trial, conviction, and execution. Telling all this in a somewhat Brechtian style, with a character called the 'Common Man' as occasional narrator and commentator, Bolt substantially fulfils his declared aim as a dramatist, which is to combine thoughtfulness with theatricality, a degree of moral subtlety with an audience's 'straightforward, childlike, primitive desire to know'. He has also written several important screenplays, notably for *Lawrence of Arabia* and *Dr Zhivago*, as well as for the film of his own *A Man for All Seasons*.

BOND, (Thomas) Edward (1934–), British dramatist, born in north London, the son of a labourer, and educated at a secondary modern school. After National Service in the army and a series of dead-end jobs, he wrote *The Pope's Wedding*, a portrait of a frustrated, inarticulate, and finally murderous country labourer; it was given a Sunday-night performance at the Royal Court Theatre in 1962. His next play, *Saved*, another tale of alienation and violence, this time among the urban young, caused great controversy on its first production in 1966. It was banned by the censor, presented under club conditions by the Royal Court, and attacked by many critics, mainly because of a scene in which hooligans stoned to death a baby in its pram. Other provocative plays followed, prime among them *Narrow Road to the Deep North* (1968), about local tyranny and British imperialism in nineteenth-century Japan; *Early Morning* (1968), a surreal comedy set in Victorian high places, and including a love affair between the Queen and Florence Nightingale; *Lear* (1971) a rewriting of Shakespeare's tragedy from a modern socialist stance; *The Sea* (1973), a black comedy set in a coastal community ruled by an imperious lady-of-the-manor; *Bingo* (1973), a contentiously conceived play about the last days of Shakespeare; *The Fool* (1975), which follows the poet John Clare into the madhouse and which, in Bond's view, illustrates the fate of the principled artist in an unjust society; *The Woman* (1978), about the aftermath of the Trojan War; *The Bundle* (1978), a tale of oppression and resistance, again set in nineteenth-century Japan; *The Worlds* (1979), an apologia for working-class terrorism, this time set in contemporary Britain; *Restoration* (1981), a dark comedy about corruption in the seventeenth century; *The War Plays* (1986), about power politics, militarism, and the likely effect of the H-bomb; and *Jackets* (1990), another highly sceptical look at the army and its pretensions. Bond's work, at first obliquely, then more directly, and recently bluntly and crudely, has continued to offer fierce indictments of a capitalist system and a ruling class he believes to be unalterably corrupt and corrupting. Indeed, he has come to believe that almost any means of overturning what he sees as institutionalized injustice must itself be just. Accordingly, he has described himself as a revolutionary socialist and his drama as 'rational theatre', dividing it into 'question plays' and 'answer plays'. His earlier, more questioning efforts were notable for the violent effects with which he illustrated his anti-establishment thinking; his later ones have tended to be less horrific, but also less vital and more doctrinaire. In each case, he has often set the action in relatively remote times and places, thus creating vivid and unusual effects, but not always making his work more credible as a comment on the contemporary world. At his best, however, he combines incisiveness of characterization, lucidity of dialogue, a powerful immediacy of event, and imaginative size and scope. Bond is also a notable essayist, and has written prefaces to several of his plays which explore the implications of his socialist views with an articulacy and passion which can become dogmatic.

Bonfire of the Vanities, The, see WOLFE, TOM.

BONTEMPS, Arna (1902–73), American poet, short-story writer, and novelist, born in Alexandria, Louisiana, educated at Pacific Union College, California and at the University of Chicago. He moved to the Harlem district of New York at the beginning of the *Harlem Renaissance, where he became well known as a poet. Most of his poems were published in the 1920s for periodicals such as *The Crisis* and were collected in *Personals* (1963). Though terse in a modernist manner, his poems also echo cadences from traditional African-American Christianity. In the early 1930s, during the Depression, he lived in Alabama, which inspired his grim short stories, *The Old South: A Summer Tragedy and Other Stories of the Thirties* (1973). He later became university librarian at Fisk University (1943–66), subsequently joining the faculty of the University of Illinois, Chicago Circle. His best-known novel, *Black Thunder* (1935), deals vividly with Virginia slave revolts in 1800. Other works of fiction include *God Sends Sunday* (1931) and *Drums at Dusk* (1939). With Langston *Hughes, he edited *The Poetry of the Negro 1764–1949* (1949) and *The Book of Negro Folklore* (1959). He also edited *Great Slave Narratives* (1969) and *The Harlem Renaissance Remembered* (1972). (See also NEW NEGRO.)

BOSMAN, Herman Charles (1905–51), South African short-story writer and journalist, born at Kuils River, Cape Province. Though of Afrikaner background, he acquired an English education in Johannesburg. *Cold Stone Jug* (1949) is a sardonic account, bristling with humour and irony, of his four and a half years in prison for fatally shooting his stepbrother during a quarrel. His short stories, which were much admired by Roy *Campbell, describe the rigours of rural Afrikaner life, often with broad humour resembling that of American frontier writers such as Mark Twain. Collections of his short stories, which have increasingly enhanced his reputation, include *Mafeking Road* (1947), *Unto Dust* (1963), *Jurie Steyn's Post Office* (1971), and *A Bekkersdal Marathon* (1971). His two novels are *Jacaranda in the Night* (1947) and *Willemsdorp* (1977). Other publications include *A Cask of Jerepigo* (1957), which contains essays and sketches, and his *Collected Works* (1981), in two volumes.

Botteghe Oscure, an international literary review, the title of which means 'dark shops', founded in Rome in 1949 by Princess Marguerite Caetani (1880–1963), who edited it until its closure in 1960. Caetani had been editor of *Commerce* between 1924 and 1932 in Paris, publishing work by many of the leading writers of the day, including James *Joyce, Federico Garcia Lorca, Franz Kafka, Virginia *Woolf, and Rainer Maria Rilke. *Botteghe Oscure*, which ran for twenty-five issues of up to 500 pages, featured writing in English, French, German, Italian, and Spanish and was distributed in Britain, the USA, Holland, Germany, Australia, and Japan; the contributions in English, which made up over half the total volume of work, tended to be predominantly by poets, who included W. H. *Auden, Wallace *Stevens, Dylan *Thomas, Hugh *MacDiarmid, Thom *Gunn, Louis *MacNeice, Robert *Lowell, and Marianne *Moore. Among the eminent Europeans whose writing appeared were Octavio Paz, Günter Grass, Carlos Fuentes, Italo Calvino, Albert Camus, Alberto Moravia, and Andre Malraux. The periodical published work by many authors at early stages of their careers and constituted a uniquely catholic international forum for creative writing during the post-war years; it was dedicated, as Archibald *MacLeish wrote in his introduction to the index published in 1964, 'to the proposition that literature exists in a wider and more integral world than politics'.

BOTTOMLEY, Gordon (1874–1948), British poet and verse-dramatist, born in Keighley, Yorkshire, educated at Keighley Grammar School. In 1892 he was forced by illness to abandon his intended career in banking and concentrated instead on writing. *The Mickle Drede* (1896), the first of his collections of verse, displays the interest in Celtic and supernatural themes that is an abiding feature of his work. He produced four further volumes of poetry, *Poems at White-Nights* (1899), *The Gate of Smaragdus* (1904), and two series of *Chambers of Imagery* (1907, 1912), earning high regard for his technical skill and his powerfully imaginative creation of mood. He subsequently concentrated on verse-drama and wrote a long succession of thematically ambitious plays; *The Riding to Lithend* (1909), based on Norse legend, was followed by *King Lear's Wife* (1915), the first of his 'prologues to Shakespeare', which was acclaimed as a masterpiece when performed in London in 1916. *Gruach* (1921), a treatment of the early life of Lady Macbeth, was produced by the Scottish National Theatre in 1923. He referred to his later verse-dramas as plays 'for a theatre unborn' and worked in a minimalist vein deriving from Noh theatre and W. B. *Yeats's more experimental dramatic writings. *Lyric Plays* and *Choric Plays* appeared in 1932 and 1939 respectively. *A Stage for Poetry* (1948) outlines his conceptions of verse-drama. C. C. Abbott's edition of *Poems and Plays* was published in 1953.

BOURJAILY, Vance (1922–), American novelist, born in Cleveland, Ohio, educated at Bowdoin College, Maine. His first novel, *The End of My Life* (1947), the story of four young American volunteers in the British Army ambulance corps during the Second World War, established him as a distinctive voice amongst a younger generation of American novelists who began their literary careers in the late 1940s. Of his later novels, *The Violated* (1958) is perhaps his most ambitious and sustained his early promise. His other novels include *The Hound of Earth* (1954), which concerns a scientist who deserts his job and family after the dropping of the atomic bomb on Hiroshima; *Confessions of a Spent Youth* (1960), a salacious semi-autobiographical work; *Brill Among the Ruins* (1970); *Now Playing at Canterbury* (1976), a Chaucerian pastiche set in the America of the 1960s and early 1970s; *A Game Men Play* (1980); *The Great Fake Book* (1986); and *Old Soldier* (1990). *The Unnatural Enemy* (1963), *Country Matters* (1973), and *Fishing by Mail* (1993) are non-fictional works about country life, the first notable for its treatment of the ethics of hunting. Bourjaily served with the American Field Service during the Second World War and from 1958 until 1980 was a professor in the *Iowa Writers' Workshop.

BOURNE, Randolph (1886–1918), American literary and social critic, born in Bloomfield, New Jersey, educated at Princeton and Columbia Universities. Born with a severe facial disfigurement, as a child he suffered tuberculosis of the spine which retarded his growth. A leading radical intellectual of his generation, at Columbia Bourne was influenced by the historian Charles Beard, the anthropologist Franz Boas, and John *Dewey. His essays appeared in *Atlantic Monthly* and the *Columbia Monthly* and were collected in *Youth and Life* (1913). In 1913 he travelled and studied in Europe. As a contributing editor to the **New Republic* he observed the progressive school system in Gary, Indiana and published his observations in his first substantial work of educational theory, *The Gary Schools* (1916). Bourne's opposition to American involvement in the First World War prompted some of his most trenchant political and social criticism, notably his series of essays published in *The *Seven Arts* in 1917; his position caused a rift with his intellectual mentors, especially John Dewey whose philosophy he had called 'our American religion', and drew criticism from Van Wyck *Brooks and Walter *Lippmann. Later essays in *The Menorah Journal*, the *New Republic*, and *The Yale Review* explored the idea of a heterogeneous culture in the USA and questioned the desirability of the 'melting pot'. Bourne left unfinished an important essay in political theory, 'The State'. *The Radical Will* (1977) is an anthology of his writings; *Forgotten Prophet: The Life of Randolph Bourne* (1984) by Bruce Clayton is a biography.

BOWEN, Elizabeth (Dorothea Cole) (1899–1973), Anglo-Irish novelist, short-story writer, and essayist, born in Dublin. An only child, she grew up in Protestant, Georgian Dublin and at the family home in County Cork, which she described in *Bowen's Court* (1942). At 13, after her father's breakdown and her mother's death, she was taken to Kent, but divided her adult life between Ireland and England. Her first collection of stories, *Encounters*, appeared in 1923; in the same year she married the educationalist and BBC administrator Alan Cameron. They lived in Northampton, Oxford, and, from 1935, Clarence Terrace, Regents Park, which was bombed in 1944. Her novels are *The Hotel* (1927); *The Last September* (1929), her own favourite, set in Ireland in the Troubles; *Friends and Relations* (1931); *To the North* (1932), a story of sexual betrayal set in London; *The House in Paris* (1935), of a memorable day spent by two children, Henrietta and Leopold, in Mme Fisher's Gothic house, intercut with the passionate story of Leopold's parents; *The *Death of the Heart* (1938); *The *Heat of the Day* (1949); *A World of Love* (1955), a romantic Irish ghost story; *The Little Girls* (1964); and *Eva Trout* (1969). Of her many short stories, the best deal with the supernatural ('Foothold', 'The Cat Jumps'), English betrayal and deracination ('The Disinherited', 'Ivy Gripped the Steps'), Anglo-Irish relations ('Her Table Spread', 'Sunday Afternoon'), children ('The Tommy Crans', 'Tears, Idle Tears'), and above all the atmosphere of wartime London ('Mysterious Kor', 'The Demon Lover', 'The Happy Autumn Fields'). Angus *Wilson, in his Introduction to her *Collected Stories* (1980), called her one of the great writers of the Blitz. After Cameron's death in 1959 and the sale of Bowen's Court, she lived mainly in Oxford, America, where she taught, and Hythe. Bowen's subjects are the loss of innocence and the conflict between what she calls the 'lunatic giant' in all of us—our childish, unsocialized, extremist egos—and the knowing, compromised grown-up world. From her Anglo-Irish background she derives a mixture of edgy alienation and a respect for classical impersonality and good form. Her characters are reckless, romantic sensationalists—orphans, spies, criminals, adulterers—and there is violence and danger in her books. Her style is mannered, elegant, and witty. Henry *James, Proust, and Flaubert are strong influences, as is the gothic atmosphere of Sheridan Le Fanu. Above all, she evokes a spiritual condition through a landscape—the 'Bowen terrain'—whether it is the 'Big House' in Ireland, out-of-season resorts, London flats and houses, or claustrophobic suburban villas. Bowen has been more read in America and Ireland than in Britain, but she can be compared to other writers published between the 1920s and 1960s, some of them her friends (Henry *Green, Ivy *Compton-Burnett, L. P. *Hartley, Rosamond *Lehmann) whose value is now being reassessed. See V. Glendinning, *Elizabeth Bowen: Portrait of a Writer* (1977); H. Lee, *Elizabeth Bowen: An Estimation* (1981), and (ed.) *The Mulberry Tree: Writings of Elizabeth Bowen* (1986); P. Craig, *Elizabeth Bowen* (1986).

BOWEN, Marjorie, pseudonym of Gabrielle Margaret Vere CAMPBELL (1886–1952), British writer of historical novels which were also published under the names George R. Preed, Margaret Campbell, and Joseph Shearing. She was born on Hayling Island, Hampshire, and became a Fellow of the Royal Society of Literature and of the Royal Historical Society. Her first novel, *The Viper of Milan* (1906), about the Visconti family, was acknowledged as an influence by G. *Greene (who referred to the book in *Travels with My Aunt* and who also spoke warmly of Bowen's work in his 1951 essay 'The Lost Childhood'). This was followed by over seventy novels on historical themes, including *The Carnival of Florence* (1915), as well as biographical studies of Mary Wollstonecraft (1937), Maurice de Saxe (1938), and John Knox (1941).

BOWERING, George (1935–), Canadian poet, fiction writer, and critic, born in the Okanagan Valley region of British Columbia, where he grew up; he was educated at the University of British Columbia. Bowering's early poetry, which includes the volumes *Points on the Grid* (1964), *The Man in Yellow Boots* (1965), *Rocky Mountain Foot* (1968), and *The Gangs of Kosmos* (1969), was strongly influenced by the *Black Mountain Poets—Robert *Creeley was his thesis adviser in Vancouver. He was a founding editor of the avant-garde Vancouver poetry magazine *TISH*. Subsequently Bowering has worked in several Canadian universities. Around 1970 he began to produce book-length 'long poems'; his work in this vein includes *George Vancouver* (1970) and *Autobiology* (1972). A prolific writer, he has published more than forty books. His fictional work includes *Mirror on the Floor* (1967); *A Short Sad Book* (1977); *Burning Water* (1980), a deconstructed novelistic account of George Vancouver's quest for the Northwest Passage; *A Place to Die* (1983); and *Taking the Field: The Best of Baseball Fiction* (1990) which Bowering edited. Among his other volumes of verse are *In the Flesh* (1974), *Another Mount* (1979), *West Window: Selected Poetry* (1982), and *Urban Snow* (1992). Later work includes a meditation on Rilke's *Duino Elegies*, entitled *Kerrisdale Elegies* (1984), *Caprice* (1987), *Harry's Fragments* (1990), and *Rain Barrel* (1994). His critical writing includes *Al Purdy* (1970), *A Way with Words* (1982), and *Imaginary Hand* (1988).

BOWLES, Jane (1917–73), American writer, born in New York of a German Jewish father and a Hungarian mother. Educated privately, she travelled in Europe and moved in artistic and literary circles, meeting Celine, E. E. *Cummings, Klaus Mann, and Paul *Bowles whom she married in 1938. After extensive travels the couple became the centre of an expatriate literary group including Allen *Ginsberg, William *Burroughs, Alan *Sillitoe, and Ruth *Fainlight.

Bowles has been highly praised by contemporaries—such as Tennessee *Williams, Truman *Capote (who referred to her as a 'modern legend'), and John *Ashbery—for the irony and surrealism with which she describes the bisexual, nihilistic ambience of her fictions. Although it is held that her career was curtailed by the cerebral haemorrhage she suffered in 1957, she had never been prolific. Her reputation rested on her single novel *Two Serious Ladies* (1943); with echoes of Kafka and *Compton-Burnett, it tells the story of Miss Goering, whose ideal of sainthood dissolves into sexual servitude to dubious characters, and Mrs Copperfield, who abandons a respectable marriage in pursuit of a native Panamian prostitute. It contributed to the revival of a modern gothic sensibility. A play, *The Summer House*, appeared in 1954. Bowles's early physical decline, the interest in forgotten women writers, and the bizarre stories circulated about her life, have perhaps contributed to her cult literary status. Her stories were collected in *Plain Pleasures* (1966), which includes such notable fictions as 'Camp Cataract' (1949) and 'A Stick of Green Candy' (1957). The title story is indicative of Bowles's technique and vision: a lonely widow meets an equally lonely man, but their mutual gestures of communication end in drunken misunderstanding, sexual confusion and the threat of cruel estrangement.

The Collected Works (1966) combines the stories with the play; unpublished and early works such as the puppet play *A Quarrelling Pair* continue to surface in extended posthumous volumes of her *œuvre* such as *Feminine Wiles* (1976) and *Everything is Nice* (1989). There is a biography by Millicent Dillon, *A Little Original Sin* (1981).

BOWLES, Paul (1910–86), American novelist, 'translator', poet, and short-story writer, born in New York, educated at the University of Virginia. A composer long before he became a writer, Bowles studied under Aaron Copland and produced three operas, four ballets, and numerous other musical compositions. He turned to literature in mid-life, publishing his first novel, *The Sheltering Sky*, in 1949. As a writer who has stressed the spiritual impoverishment of the West and the sustenance to be gained from encounters with the primitive, both social and psychological, and whose work deals with various forms of deviant sexuality, he has something of a cult reputation. His earlier novels are fairly conventional and demonstrate his passionate love of Arab culture—from 1952 onwards he lived in Tangier. Most of his later works are termed 'translations' and present themselves as transcriptions, supposedly edited from tape recordings, of the words of a young Moroccan servant, Mohammed Mrabet, with whom Bowles had a close relationship. These include *Love with a Few Hairs* (1967), *M'Hashish* (1969), *The Boy Who Set the Fire* (1974), and *The Beach Café and The Voice* (1976). Among his other writings are the novels *Let It Come Down* (1952), *The Spider's House* (1955), and *Up Above the World* (1966); the short stories *Pages from Cold Point* (1968); a collection of poems, *Scenes* (1968); and an autobiography, *Without Stopping* (1972). A biography, *An Invisible Spectator*, by Christopher Sawyer Laucanno, appeared in 1989.

BOWRA, Sir (Cecil) Maurice (1898–1971), British scholar and critic, born in Kiukiang, China, the son of a British customs commissioner, educated at New College, Oxford. In 1922 he became a fellow of Wadham College, where he remained in residence until his death. As warden of the college from 1938 to 1970, he was celebrated for his hospitality and unconventional good humour; John *Betjeman recalls him with affection in **Summoned by Bells* (1960). His earlier works, which include *Tradition and Design in The Iliad* (1930) and *Early Greek Elegists* (1938), established his considerable reputation as an expositor of classical literature. *The Heritage of Symbolism* (1943) was the first of his numerous books on nineteenth- and twentieth-century European and English poetry; among his subsequent studies, notable for their breadth of reference and interpretative skill, are *The Creative Experiment* (1949), on European poetry since 1912, *Poetry and Politics, 1900–1960* (1966), and the collected essays of *In General and Particular* (1964). His later works as a Hellenist include *Problems in Greek Poetry* (1953) and a translation of *The Odes of Pindar* (1969). He was Oxford Professor of Poetry from 1946 to 1951. *Memories, 1898–1939* (1966) is his autobiography.

BOYD, John (1912–), Northern Irish playwright, born in working-class East Belfast, educated at Queen's University, Belfast and Trinity College, Dublin. Boyd refers to himself as 'an Irish playwright with a Protestant background'. The first volume of his autobiography, *Out of My Class* (1985), recalls a childhood filled with the mythology of sectarian rivalry and hatred. He has said that 'the sectarian divide that poisons the air of the community I write about is a smokescreen, a camouflage to obscure the social problems'. Boyd taught at schools in Newry, Lisburn, and Belfast before working as a producer for BBC Northern Ireland, a career which he recounts in *The Middle of My Journey* (1990). He was the editor of the literary journal *Lagan* in 1942–6; he became literary adviser to the Lyric Theatre, Belfast (see ULSTER

LITERARY THEATRE), and edited its publication, *Threshold*, from 1971. Boyd's first play, *The Blood of Colonel Lamb*, written in 1967, was considered too controversial for the North in its attack on Protestant extremism; it was revised as *The Assassin* (1969) and successfully staged at the Dublin Theatre Festival. His next play, *The Flats* (1971), with a set that expresses the claustrophobic bleakness of Belfast, presents the tragedy of a Catholic family's struggle to survive a single day of 'the Troubles'. Boyd represents an entire community under siege while establishing a difference between the universal needs of an individual and the blind particularity of collective violence. *The Farm* (1972), *Guests* (1974), *The Street* (1977), and *Facing North* (1981) further examine these themes. Boyd has been noted for his ability to reproduce the speech of working-class Belfast which, as a common language, is used tragically to express factional hatred. He is widely regarded as Northern Ireland's most important playwright.

BOYD, Martin (1893–1972), Australian novelist, born in Lucerne, Switzerland, educated in Melbourne. He came from a distinguished Victorian family of artists and architects. He enlisted in England with the Royal Flying Corps for service during the First World War. Spiritual restlessness and cultural enquiry inform his writings and his life; both reflect allegiance to, and interest in, traditions drawn as much from Europe as from Australia, and especially a complex individual response to a shared past. *The Montforts* (1928) was of great historical sweep, tracing the story of his mother's family in Victoria from 1850 to 1914. In *Lucinda Brayford* (1946) Boyd pursued his enduring concern with the differing standards of personal fulfilment and material well-being. The 'Langton tetralogy' (*The Cardboard Crown*, 1952; *A Difficult Young Man*, 1955; *Outbreak of Love*, 1957; and *When Blackbirds Sing*, 1962) explores the history of the Langton family through almost a century, largely through the eyes of family elder Guy Langton, and offers a unique portrait of Australian and British life of the period. *A Single Flame* (1939) and *Day of My Delight* (1965) were autobiographical, illuminating the concern for purpose and structure which informs all Boyd's fiction.

BOYD, William (1952–), British novelist, born in Accra, Ghana, educated at the universities of Nice and Glasgow, and at Jesus College, Oxford. He was a lecturer in English at St Hilda's College, Oxford (1975–80) and a television critic for the *New Statesman* (1981–3). *On the Yankee Station* (1981; revised edition 1988), a collection of stories, was followed by *A Good Man in Africa* (1981; Whitbread Prize), a comic novel set in an imaginary African country, and *An Ice-Cream War* (1982) which describes the fiasco on the Eastern African Front during the First World War. In 1983 Boyd was among the writers elected by the Book Marketing Council as a Best Young British Novelist. His next book, *Stars and Bars* (1984), a wryly humorous look at America from an English perspective, consolidated his reputation as a comic writer. Boyd expanded his range considerably with *The New Confessions* (1987), an ambitious novel dealing with themes of Art and Illusion and spanning the first seventy years of the twentieth century: from Edinburgh in the 1900s to the Western Front in 1918; from Berlin during the Weimar Republic to Hollywood in the McCarthyite era. Its central character, John James Todd, is a filmmaker obsessed with the creation of a single masterwork based on Rousseau's *Confessions*. The protagonist of *Brazzaville Beach* (1990) is a young scientist, Hope Clearwater, who is studying behaviour patterns in primates in Central Africa. The first-person narrative moves between the present—Hope's struggle to achieve recognition for her scientific discoveries in the face of opposition from senior colleagues—and passages set in the recent past, which deal with her disastrous marriage to a brilliant but unstable mathematician. *The Blue Afternoon* (1993), set in Los Angeles during the 1930s, concerned a young woman's relationship with an enigmatic stranger claiming to be her father, with whom she undertakes a journey into the past. The novel was acclaimed for its atmospheric recreation of time and place, as well as for its insights into the mind of its female protagonist—the second time Boyd had attempted to write from a woman's point of view. It was followed by a collection of short stories, *The Destiny of Natalie 'X' and Other Stories* (1995) which, like several of his novels, deals with unsatisfactory love affairs played out against a variety of different European backgrounds. After the farcical comedy of his early novels, which were strongly reminiscent of the satirical writings of E. *Waugh, Boyd has established himself as a writer of lyrical, elegiac fictions, often set in the past, which deal with aspects of memory through a series of linked and overlapping narratives.

BOYLAN, Clare (1948–), Irish novelist, short-story writer, and journalist, born in Dublin. Her first novel, *Holy Pictures* (1983), is a powerfully evocative, tragicomic child's-eye view of Dublin life in the 1920s. This was followed by *Last Resorts* (1984), a novel describing the erotic adventures of Harriet, mother of three teenage children, on a Greek holiday island; and *Black Baby* (1988), a comic novel about a child sold to a woman by nuns. *Home Rule* (1992), a prequel to *Holy Pictures*, observes the Devlin family's turn-of-the-century battles against poverty, its humour leavened by a wry lament for the plight of Irish wives. Boylan's prose is fresh, poetic, and colourful, rich in apt and startling similes; she has a particular gift for recalling the vivid impressions, physical sensations, and misunderstandings of childhood, coupled with a reckless panache when describing adult affairs and amorous misadventures. Her volumes of short stories include *A Nail on the Head* (1983), *Concerning Virgins* (1989), and *That Bad Woman* (1995). She contributed an autobiographical sketch of her middle-class Dublin childhood to *A Portrait of the Artist as a Young Girl* (1986, ed. John Quinn). Boylan is the editor of *The Agony and the Ego:*

The Art and Strategy of Fiction Writing (1993), and of *The Literary Companion to Cats* (1995).

BOYLE, Kay (1902–), American writer, born in Minnesota, educated at the Cincinnati Conservatory of Music and the Ohio Mechanics Institute. She moved with her first husband to France, and lived in Europe for twenty years. Much of her fiction draws on autobiographical sources; a memoir, *Being Geniuses Together* (1938), co-authored with Robert *McAlmon, movingly chronicles her experiences in Paris and elsewhere.

Boyle's deserved reputation as an innovative *Modernist novelist rests on the relatively recent recognition of at least three of her works as feminist classics. She has herself criticized these works for being overly sympathetic to their autobiographical American heroine's perspective; but her intense and controlled use of lyrical imagery, combined with its personal tone, contributes greatly to the charm of *Plagued by the Nightingale* (1930), her first novel. The American Bridget, living in the conservative bosom of her French husband's wealthy family, is forced to choose between her sensual desires and her loyalty to her husband. In *Year Before Last* (1932), Boyle tells the story of the relationship of her American fictional alter ego, renamed Hannah, with the idealistic editor and writer Martin, who is dying of tuberculosis. It is probably the finest of her novels, deriving its conviction from personal grief. *My Next Bride* (1934), darker and more bitter, draws on another true encounter, and reveals Boyle's increasing ability to transform her autobiographical heroine into a convincing fictional character. Later novels, generated by the Second World War, including *Avalanche* (1944), *Primer for Combat* (1942), and *A Frenchman Must Die* (1946), were less successful. However, in the autumnal *Underground Woman* (1975), the story of a woman jailed for her involvement in anti-war protests during the Vietnam War and confronted with her daughter's vagrant lifestyle, Boyle again displays her considerable strengths as a novelist. These are underwritten by her exemplary and vocal concern for political and social justice and Civil Rights which is also evident in a collection of essays, *Words That Must Somehow Be Said* (1985).

Boyle began her literary career as a short-story writer with the collection *Wedding Day* (1929); she has since displayed consistent proficiency in the form. The best stories from her collections, which include *The White Horses of Vienna* (1936), the war-inspired *The Smoking Mountain* (1951), and *Nothing Ever Breaks Except the Heart* (1966), are arranged thematically and chronologically in *Fifty Stories* (1980). She is also the author of several volumes of poetry, including *A Statement* (1932), *Collected Poems* (1962), and *This Is Not a Letter* (1985).

BOYLE, Patrick (1905–82), Northern Irish short-story writer and novelist, born in Co. Antrim, educated at Coleraine Academical Institution. He worked with Ulster Bank for 45 years and retired as manager of their Wexford branch. Boyle began writing late in life and achieved recognition by winning *The Irish Times* Short Story Competition in 1965. He confirmed his reputation with a collection of stories, *At Night All Cats Are Grey* (1966), and a novel, *Like Any Other Man* (1966), which satirizes the stagnant life of a country town through its portrayal of a drunken, philandering, and ultimately doomed, bank manager. Boyle's short stories are more sympathetic and it is in this genre that his talent is most evident. His three collections, *At Night All Cats Are Grey*, *All Looks Yellow to the Jaundiced Eye* (1969), and *A View from Calvary* (1976), contain stories which rank with those of Frank *O'Connor and Sean *O'Faolain.

BOYLE, T(homas) Coraghessan (1948–), American novelist, born in Peekshill, New York, the grandson of Irish immigrants. He was educated at the State University of New York and the University of Iowa, where his teachers at the *Iowa Writers' Workshop included J. *Cheever and J. *Irving. A collection of short stories, *Descent of Man* (1979), was followed by a novel, *Water Music* (1981), which is set in 1795 and interweaves scenes of London low-life with an account of the adventures of the explorer Mungo Park in the Sahara. Other works include *Budding Prospects* (1984), about a professional marijuana grower; *Greasy Lake and Other Stories* (1985), based on the author's troubled childhood; *East is East* (1990), about a Japanese man's encounter with American culture; *The Road to Wellville* (1993), set in turn-of-the-century Michigan, and focusing on the inventor of the cornflake, John Harvey Kellogg; *Without a Hero* (1995), a collection of short stories dealing with millennial anxieties; and *The Tortilla Curtain* (1995), a seriocomic view of middle-class values in contemporary California. His style blends surrealism with anarchic humour and displays a relish for the more bizarre episodes of history; he has acknowledged the influence of D. *Barthelme, J. *Barth, and T. *Pynchon.

Boy's Own Story, A, a novel by Edmund *White, published in 1982. This deceptively simple story, with marked autobiographical overtones, of a young boy's journey to sexual and intellectual self-awareness, reworks the conventional American *bildungsroman* (and its European prototype) to include an exclusively homosexual perspective and sensibility that entirely avoids shame, guilt, and self-hatred. Elegantly—and at times extravagantly—written and meticulously crafted, it is distinguished by its fine powers of observation, its evocation of life in small town America, and its careful balance of anecdote and introspection. Its apparent disregard for conventions of plot and narrative drive may be interpreted as an artful device that convinces the reader of the reality of the experience the writer depicts, encouraging identification and thus rendering universal a theme that had been previously treated (as in James Baldwin's **Giovanni's Room*) as an occasion for self-torment. Thus it can be said that White, in this novel and its sequel *The Beautiful Room is Empty*, has retrieved 'gay fiction' from the margins to which it was hitherto relegated and located it as a thriving trend in contemporary American literature; not without irony, since the joy with which he wrote has been replaced by a deep awareness of the impact of Aids on all depictions of contemporary sexuality.

BRACKENBURY, Alison (1953–), British poet, born in Gainsborough, Lincolnshire, educated at St Hugh's College, Oxford. *Dreams of Power* (1981), her first substantial collection of verse, contained an impressive sequence in the voice of a woman at the court of Elizabeth I. *Breaking Ground* (1984), its long title poem structured around events in the life of John Clare, was followed by *Christmas Roses* (1988), which contained numerous lyric poems of remarkable refinement and concentration, and *Selected Poems* (1991). The emotional and imaginative sensitivity apparent in many of her poems is given substance and clarity by precisely observed natural and domestic imagery. In the title poem of *1829* (1995), Mozart's widow reflects upon her past.

BRADBROOK, Muriel (Clara) (1909–93), British scholar and critic, born in Wallasey, Cheshire, educated at Girton College, Cambridge, where she taught throughout her career; in 1968 she became Mistress of the college, of which she produced a history entitled *That Infidel Place* (1969) to mark its centenary in 1969. She was best known for her contributions to Elizabethan and Shakespearian studies, which are highly regarded for her detailed knowledge of the social and cultural contexts of the period. *Themes and Conventions of Elizabethan Tragedy* (1934), *Shakespeare and Elizabethan Poetry* (1951), *The Growth and Structure of Elizabethan Comedy* (1955), *The Rise of the Common Player* (1962), *Shakespeare the Craftsman* (1969), and *The Living Monument* (1976) are the six volumes of her *History of Elizabethan Drama*, which were published together in 1979. Among her other publications are *The School of Night* (1936), a study of Elizabethan intellectual heterodoxy; *Ibsen the Norwegian* (1946); and *Malcolm Lowry: His Art and Early Life* (1974). The *Collected Papers of Muriel Bradbrook*, covering a wide variety of topics, appeared in four volumes between 1982 and 1989.

BRADBURY, Malcolm (Stanley) (1932–), British novelist and critic, born in Sheffield, educated at the universities of Leicester, London, Indiana, and Manchester. From 1970 until 1995 he was Professor of American Studies at the University of East Anglia. His first novel, *Eating People Is Wrong* (1959), with its university setting and cast of eccentric characters, usually academics, established the pattern which his later books were to follow, such as *Stepping Westward* (1965; stories), set on an American campus, and the novel *Who Do You Think You Are?* (1976; see CAMPUS NOVEL). Bradbury won wide recognition with *The History Man* (1975; adapted by Bradbury for television), a hilarious satire, set in 1972, of the fashionable left-wing pretensions of a group of academics at a new 'plate-glass' university; among its characters is the memorably repellent figure of Dr Howard Kirk, Marxist historian and champion of the Permissive Society. *Rates of Exchange* (1983) explores forms of cultural, linguistic, and sexual exchange through the medium of its central character, Dr Angus Petworth, a Professor of Linguistics on a British Council exchange in the imaginary East European city of Slaka. *Cuts* (1987) deals with the decline of the Welfare State and the cuts in higher education which were felt throughout the 1980s, and beyond, in British universities. Despite its sombre subject, the tone of the work is essentially comic, and incorporates images of cutting and splicing associated with the cinematic industry into which the hero, a failed academic, has been conscripted as a writer of screenplays. *Doctor Criminale* (1992) deals with themes with which the author has become increasingly concerned in recent years—the nature of modern history, and what it is to be a member of the ever-changing European community. Bradbury's narrator, Francis Jay, is a journalist in pursuit of the eponymous and elusive Criminale—an eminent philosopher with a dubious past—who tracks his quarry across eight different countries and through a number of international conferences, before eventually running him to ground. Like many of his earlier works, the novel is principally a vehicle for ideas, whose humour is derived from its parodies of academic jargon—particularly that of semiotics—rather than from the more conventional novelistic attributes such as plot and character writing. Other works of fiction include *Unsent Letters* (1988), a collection of humorous letters to imaginary correspondents, and *The After Dinner Game* (1982), a collection of plays for television.

As a critic, Bradbury's specialization is British and American fiction of the twentieth century, with particular reference to the social and philosophical implications of *Modernism. Among his critical works are *What Is a Novel?* (1969), *The Social Contexts of Modern English Literature* (1971), *Saul Bellow* (1982), *The Modern World* (1989), and *The Modern British Novel* (1993). *Possibilities* (1972), *No, Not Bloomsbury* (1988), and *Dangerous Pilgrimages* (1994) are collections of essays. In considering the functions and values of literature in an era in which the assumptions of liberal humanism are challenged, he has mediated between the traditions of critical discourse and recent innovations in literary theory; his misgivings regarding the extremes of *post-structuralist practices give rise to his humorous account of a self-deconstructing critic in the fictional *My Strange Quest for Mensonge* (1988). He has also edited *Class Work* (1995), an anthology of short fiction produced on the creative writing course he ran at East Anglia.

BRADBURY, Ray (Douglas) (1920–), American novelist and short-story writer, born in Waukegan, Illinois, educated at Los Angeles High School. Among his best-known collections of interlinked stories are *The Martian Chronicles* (1950; UK title *The Silver Locusts*,

1951) containing 'The Fire Balloons', set on Mars, concerning missionary priests and ethereal aliens; and *The Illustrated Man* (1951), in which a mythical circus man's tattoos come eerily to life as fantastic tales. *The Golden Apples of the Sun* (1953), the title of which alludes to *Yeats's 'The Song of Wandering Aengus', contains stories mainly set in the future, several of them dealing with wanderers, such as the title story about the captain of a spaceship whose task is to skim the surface of the sun. His many other collections include *Dark Carnival* (1947), *The October Country* (1955), *A Medicine for Melancholy* (1959; UK title *The Day It Rained Forever*), *The Machineries of Joy* (1966), *I Sing the Body Electric!* (1969), *The Last Circus and the Electrocution* (1980), *A Memory of Murder* (1984), *The Townbee Convector* (1988), and *The Smile* (1991). His most renowned novel, *Fahrenheit 451* (1953), filmed by François Truffaut in 1966, is a moral fable set in a nightmarish near future dystopia; the title refers to the temperature 'at which book-paper catches fire and burns', and the main task of the firemen is to seek out books and burn them. The fireman hero, Montag, gradually discovers the evil inherent in this dream-like totalitarian system, and after betrayal by his wife and colleagues, joins a group of people dedicated to the task of memorizing all the great books for future posterity. Other novels include the horror-fantasy *Something Wicked This Way Comes* (1963; filmed in 1983); *Death Is a Lonely Business* (1985), a *hardboiled murder mystery; and *A Graveyard for Lunatics* (1990), set in the Hollywood of the 1950s. Bradbury has also written plays, published in *The Wonderful Ice Cream Suit* (1972), and film scripts, including *It Came from Outer Space* (1952), *Moby Dick* (1954), and *The Picasso Summer* (1968); *On Stage: A Chrestomathy of His Plays* (1991) is a selection of his work. Dandelion Crater, on the surface of the moon, was so named by Apollo astronauts in honour of *Dandelion Wine* (1957), in which interlinked stories spring from the imagination of a young boy during the summer of 1928. Bradbury was commended by Brian* Aldiss as 'the Hans Christian Andersen of the jet age'; his combination of humour and visionary intensity often reflects a nostalgia for childhood, and American small-town life. He has also published *Green Shadows, White Whale* (1992), an account of his experiences in the early 1950s when he worked in Ireland as scriptwriter on John Huston's film *Moby Dick*; and the essays *Yestermorrow: Obvious Answers to Impossible Futures* (1991) and *Journey to far Metaphor* (1994).

BRADLEY, A(ndrew) C(ecil) (1851–1935), British critic, born in Cheltenham, the brother of F. H. *Bradley; he was educated at Balliol College, Oxford, where he lectured from 1876 to 1882, when he accepted a professorship at Liverpool University. In 1901 he became Oxford Professor of Poetry, producing his most notable work during the five years of the appointment. The essays of *Shakespearean Tragedy* (1904) established him as the leading Shakespearian critic of his day and offer what L. C. *Knights termed 'the most illustrious example' of the 'discussion of Shakespeare's tragedies in terms of the characters of which they are composed'; Knights and others associated with **Scrutiny* dismissed his methods as sentimentally speculative. His *Oxford Lectures on Poetry* (1909) were dominated by further examples of his work on Shakespeare, which remains notable for his magisterial style and the acuteness of many of his insights. Other publications by Bradley include *Miscellany* (1929), a collection of essays; and *Ideals of Religion* (1940), which originated in his work as Gifford Lecturer at the University of Glasgow in 1907 and 1908.

BRADLEY, F(rancis) H(erbert) (1846–1924), British philosopher, born at Clapham, the brother of A. C. *Bradley; he was educated at University College, Oxford. In 1870 he was elected a fellow of Merton College, Oxford, where he remained in somewhat reclusive residence until his death. With T. H. Green (1836–82), he was Oxford's leading proponent of Hegelian thought, which forms the basis for his *Ethical Studies* (1876) and *The Principles of Logic* (1883); the works were in part repudiations of the utilitarianism of J. S. Mill (1806–73) and demonstrated Bradley's 'polemical irony and his obvious zest in using it', to quote from T. S. *Eliot's 1927 review of a reissue of *Ethical Studies*. Eliot, who produced a doctoral thesis on Bradley's philosophy in 1916, was deeply impressed by his ability to combine a high degree of metaphysical scepticism with a belief in the ultimate unity of all phenomena. His work on metaphysics is principally contained in *Appearance and Reality* (1893) and *Essays on Truth and Reality* (1914). R. Wollheim's *F. H. Bradley* was published in 1959.

BRADLEY, Henry (1845–1923), British lexicographer, born in Manchester; following an elementary education he became a clerk in a Sheffield cutlery business, where he remained for twenty years, achieving a remarkable knowledge of numerous European and classical languages in his spare time. In 1884 he moved to London. His abilities as a philologist came to notice through his extended review in the *Academy* of the first part of the *New English Dictionary* (1884), later known as the *Oxford English Dictionary*. He began contributing articles to the Dictionary and in 1888 was appointed assistant editor; he succeeded James *Murray as senior editor in 1915. From 1896 onward he lived in Oxford, becoming a fellow of Exeter College in 1896. The best-known of his works of independent authorship is the widely read *The Making of English* (1904); his many articles, which include 'English Place Names', a seminal study in toponymy, were published as *The Collected Papers of Henry Bradley* in 1928. Among his other works is his edition of Caxton's *Dialogues in French and English* (1900).

BRAGG, Melvyn (1939–), British novelist, journalist, and playwright, born in Cumbria, educated at Wadham College, Oxford. A sense of place is crucial to his fiction which is for the most part set in Cumbria and celebrates its dialect and landscape. Many of his novels describe the interaction between social expectation and the psychological and emotional development of individual men and women. They include *For Want of a Nail* (1965), and his 'Cumbrian Trilogy', *The Hired Man* (1969), *A Place in England* (1971), and *Kingdom Come* (1980), which emphasizes the physical hardships endured by agricultural labourers in the early years of the century and suggests that later generations of the Tallentire family (the main protagonists) find it difficult to engage with the contemporary world with the same vigour as their forebears. As well as his work as a screenwriter for film and television, which includes the successful 1984 adaptation of his novel *The Hired Man* for the stage, Bragg has a considerable reputation as a producer and presenter of arts programmes on television; he draws on this milieu in *Love and Glory* (1983), depicting the struggle between two ambitious men, an actor and a television producer. *The Maid of Buttermere* (1987) returns to a pastoral setting and fictionalizes the story of a nineteenth-century con man who bigamously marries an innkeeper's daughter. Later works include *A Time To Dance* (1990), *Crystal Rooms* (1992), and *Credo* (1996). *The Seventh Seal* (1993) is a critical appreciation of Bergman's film, and includes an account of Bragg's meeting with Bergman.

BRAINE, John (Gerard) (1922–86), British novelist, born in Bradford, Yorkshire, educated at St Bede's Grammar School, Bradford; he was prominent among the *'Angry Young Men' of northern English fiction. Braine had worked as a librarian in the north of England. He began writing **Room at the Top* (1957) while recovering from TB in a sanatorium. Its realistic portrayal of life in a dour provincial town, and its story of the cynical Joe Lampton making his way to the top, set the agenda for a whole genre of contemporary writing; the novel was made into a film in 1959. His second novel, *The Vodi* (1959), was a supernatural tale concerning a TB patient plagued by judgemental aliens. He returned to the characters and setting of his first book in *Life at the Top* (1962); Joe Lampton has married the boss's daughter but becomes disenchanted with the bourgeois world he had pursued with such unscrupulousness. Braine subsequently moved to the south of England and abandoned his angry left-wing political position. His finest novel of this period is *The Jealous God* (1964), a hard-edged story of a Catholic schoolmaster caught between the repellent forces of marriage and the priesthood in a community which recognizes no other vocations. Braine's later works include *The Crying Game* (1968); *Stay with Me till Morning* (1970), which was televised; *The Pious Agent* (1975), a thriller; *One and Last Love* (1981); and the autobiographical novel *These Golden Days* (1985). *Man at the Top* was a television series based on his early novels. A prolific literary journalist, Braine published a study of J. B. Priestley in 1979.

BRAITHWAITE, E(dward) R(icardo) (1912–), Guyanese autobiographical writer, diplomat, and teacher, born in Georgetown, British Guiana, educated at City College, New York and the Universities of Cambridge and London. His varied career included service with the RAF in the Second World War, and as Permanent Representative of Guyana at the United Nations. *To Sir, With Love* (1959), about his experiences as a teacher in London, was an international bestseller. Other novels include *Paid Servant* (1962), about his experiences as a social worker; *Choice of Straws* (1965), which tackles racism among the white working class; and *Reluctant Neighbours* (1972). His visit to Africa is recorded in the trenchant *A Kind of Homecoming* (1962), and to South Africa in *Honorary White* (1975), perhaps his best book. It chronicles his almost farcical encounters with the white authorities, who suspended the rigours of apartheid in recognition of his 'celebrity' status.

BRAITHWAITE, William Stanley (Beaumont) (1878–1962), American poet and editor, born in Boston of West Indian parents; he attended Boston Latin School. He began his long career as literary editor with the *Boston Evening Transcript* in 1905. *Lyrics of Life and Love* (1904), his first collection of poetry, was followed by *The House of Falling Leaves* (1908) and *Selected Poems* (1948). His verse is characterized by the meditative romanticism of its themes and its accomplished use of the sonnet and other traditional forms. As an editor he was hospitable to more innovative work and contributed valuably to the development of American poetry in the earlier decades of the century. The most notable of the many anthologies of verse he produced are the seventeen annual issues of the *Anthology of Magazine Verse and Yearbook of American Poetry* (1913–29), in which he promoted the work of Countee *Cullen and others associated with the *Harlem Renaissance. His other publications include the novel *Going over Tindal* (1924), the short stories of *Frost on the Green Tree* (1928), and *The Bewitched Parsonage* (1950), a study of the Brontës. He became Professor of Creative Literature at the University of Atlanta in 1935. *The House under Arcturus* (1941) is his autobiography.

BRAMAH, Ernest, pseudonym of Ernest Bramah SMITH (1868–1942), British writer, born near Manchester; he was a farmer for some years, the experience providing material for his first book, *English Farming and why I Turned It Up* (1894). He was also a provincial journalist, and secretary to Jerome K. *Jerome before becoming a writer. His best-known works, praised by *Belloc and *Chesterton, are the short stories relating the activities of Kai Lung, an itinerant Chinese story-teller, written in a superbly polished, ludicrously exaggerated imitation of conventional Chinese modes of address and narration (*The Wallet of Kai Lung*, 1900, and other collections). His detective short stories are not only excellent as detection, but also interesting in that their hero, Max Carrados, is one of the few blind detectives in fiction. There are several collections, of which *Max Carrados* (1914) is the first. In the introduction to *The Eyes of Max Carrados* (1923), Bramah defends himself against the accusation that he has exaggerated his detective's abilities, citing instances of the power of the blind to develop their other senses.

BRAND, Dionne (1953–), Trinidadian poet and short-story writer, born in Guayaguayare, Trinidad, where she was educated at Naporima Girls' School. In 1970 she moved to Canada and graduated from the University of Toronto in 1975. With the exception of a period as a communications co-ordinator in Grenada which ended with the USA's invasion of the island in 1983, she has continued to live in Toronto, where she is widely active in community work. Her collections of poetry include *'Fore Day Morning* (1978), *Primitive Offensive* (1982), *Chronicles of the Hostile Sun* (1984), and *No Language Is Neutral* (1990). Her verse, characterized by thematic interactions between history and the present and by precisely observed imagery, uses her personal experience to chart the emotional and cultural tensions generated by immigration. *Sans Souci and Other Tales* (1988) is a collection of her short stories, which are set in both Canada and the Caribbean. *No Burden To Carry* (1992) is a non-fiction work documenting the lives of black women in Canada.

BRASCH, Charles (1909–73), New Zealand poet, born in Dunedin, educated at Oxford University. He travelled widely in Europe, Africa, and America before finally settling in New Zealand after the Second World War. Together with fellow poet Denis *Glover, Brasch was the founding editor of the major New Zealand literary journal **Landfall* in 1947; he continued his editorship until his retirement in 1966. *Landfall Country* (1962), edited by Brasch, is a selection from the journal's distinguished contributors. Brasch's early collections of poems, *The Land and Its People* (1939) and *Home Ground* (1943), were mythopoeic in tone while in later works, such as *The Estate* (1957) and *Ambulando* (1964), a more elegiac tendency exists. These collections were respected at the time for their sincerity, their poised concern for landscape, and their personal/national attitudes (notably in the moving and restrained poem 'The Islands (ii)'). *Collected Poems* (1984) allowed a proper appreciation of his achievement. Both Vincent *O'Sullivan and Ian *Wedde have made significant assessments of Brasch's work. His autobiography, *Indirections*, appeared in 1980.

BRATHWAITE, Edward Kamau (1930–), Barbadian poet, born in Bridgetown, Barbados, educated at Pembroke College, Oxford, and the University of Sussex. After working as an Education Officer in Ghana, in 1962 he began teaching at the University of the West Indies, where he became Professor of Social and Cultural History in 1982. His poetry and his writings as a historian display a common concern with the cultural heritage of the Caribbean and American descendants of Africans dispersed into slavery from the seventeenth century onward. *The Arrivants: A New World Trilogy* (1973), consisting of *Rights of Passage* (1967), *Masks* (1968), and *Islands* (1969), uses an autobiographical framework to trace global patterns in the historical and contemporary conditions of the African peoples. A further trilogy comprising *Mother Poem* (1977), *Sun Poem* (1982), and *X-Self* (1987) sustains his investigation of personal and cultural identity, encompassing interpretations of economic, political, and religious developments since the Roman Empire in its increasingly expansive movement towards an affirmative vision of growth and change. Vivid imagery, an energetic variety of tonal and rhythmical effects, and inventively experimental forms are among the characteristics of his verse, which addresses its complex spectrum of themes with compelling directness. His other volumes of poems include *Other Exiles* (1975), *Third World Poems* (1983), and *Middle Passages* (1992). Notable among his works as a cultural historian are *Folk Culture of the Slaves in Jamaica* (1970), *Caribbean Man in Time and Space* (1974), and *History of the Voice: The Development of Nation Language in Anglophone Caribbean Poetry* (1984).

BRAUTIGAN, Richard (1935–84), American novelist, short-story writer, and poet, born in Tacoma, Washington. Brautigan came to prominence in the 1960s as a leading exponent of a new society. He lived in San Francisco for many years before moving to Montana at the end of the 1970s. Influenced by the *San Francisco Renaissance and the *Beat writers, he is often remembered as one of the voices of hippy life. He wrote a wide range of early poetry including *The Return of the Rivers* (*c.*1957), *The Galilee Hitch-Hiker* (1958), *Lay the Marble Tea* (1959), and *The Octopus Frontier* (1960). His first novel, *A Confederate General from Big Sur* (1964), was followed by the huge success of *Trout Fishing in America* (1967), which describes a nostalgic search for the perfect fishing spot, taking one on a quest through a variety of landscapes including San Francisco city parks, Oregon forests, Idaho campingsites, and a Filipino laundry; the failure to reach the goal indicates the degenerate cultural environment of the USA. *Watermelon Sugar* (1968) portrays life in a commune that has defined its way of life in contradistinction to the social structures of the outside world. His other novels include *The Abortion: An Historical Romance* (1971), *The Hawkline Monster: A Gothic Western* (1974), *Willard and His Bowling Trophies: A Perverse Mystery* (1974), *Sombrero Fallout: A Japanese Novel* (1976), *Dreaming of Babylon: A Private Eye Novel, 1942* (1977), and *The Tokyo–Montana Express* (1980). *Revenge of the Lawn: Stories 1962–1970* appeared in 1971. Frequently anarchically whimsical in their structures and statements, the novels are marked with understatement and a 'throwaway' tone, as they explode the pretensions of middle America. He continued writing poetry about unrestrained sexuality and personal encounters; collections include *All Watched over by Machines of Loving Grace* (1967), *The Pill versus the Springhill Mine Disaster* (1968), *Please Plant This Book* (1968, a combination of poems and seed packets), *Rommel Drives on deep into Egypt* (1970), *Loading Mercury with a Pitchfork* (1976), and *June 30th, June 30th*

(1978). The early formal playfulness and humour began to give way to an increasingly dark view of American culture as the 1970s progressed, with his final book, *So the Wind Won't Blow It Away* (1982), appearing shortly before his suicide.

Brave New World, a novel by A. *Huxley, published in 1932. An anti-utopian satire, originally conceived as a parody of H. G. *Wells's *Men like Gods* (1927), it describes a scientifically determined future where history and the family have been abolished, and Henry Ford is the deity. Reproduction takes place in bottles by 'Bokanovsky's Process'; humans are graded from Alphas to Epsilons, subjected to neo-Pavlovian conditioning, and take their places in a utilitarian World State manipulated by Controllers. The plot hinges on a discontented Alpha Plus, 'Bernard Marx', who journeys to a New Mexican reservation and brings back a Natural Man reared on 'forbidden' books. The Shakespeare-spouting 'John Savage' is at first intrigued, then increasingly disgusted by the New World's sterile hedonism—sex without consequences, the ubiquitous use of 'soma', an all-purpose pleasure drug—and lack of individual freedom; his debate with 'Mustapha Mond' is used to dramatize Huxley's own ethical scepticism about purely technological progress. Located in the 'seventh century of Our Ford', *Brave New World* deals with contemporary political and scientific ideas (reflected in characters' names like 'Lenina', 'Benito Hoover') and the then-competing world systems, communism and capitalism. The novel remains popular, partly due to its prophetic elements. Some aspects, such as state slogans 'COMMUNITY, IDENTITY, STABILITY' and mental conditioning, anticipated Orwell's **Nineteen Eighty-Four*, but Huxley's focus was on 'the advancement of science as it affects human individuals', not the nature of totalitarianism. See UTOPIA AND ANTI-UTOPIA.

Brazzaville Beach, see BOYD, WILLIAM.

Breakfast at Tiffany's, see CAPOTE, TRUMAN.

BREEZE, Jean 'Binta' (1956–), Jamaican poet, born in Pattyhill, a village in north-east Jamaica. After working as a teacher, in 1978 she entered the Jamaican School of Drama, where she adopted the African name 'Binta', meaning 'close to the heart'. She subsequently emerged as Jamaica's first female exponent of *'dub' poetry, a mode of reading of verse to the rhythms of reggae music. *Answers* (1983), *Riddym Ravings and Other Poems* (1988), and *Spring Cleaning* (1992) are her principal collections of verse. She is noted for her energetic performances of poems, making imaginative use of Jamaican dialect in dramatic monologue forms. The most readily available recordings of her readings are featured on the widely distributed *Word Soun' 'Ave Power, Reggae Power* (1985). Her work is also rich in the distinctively understated lyricism and compassion of many poems deriving from her observations of everyday experience. Among her works as a dramatist is the screenplay for the film *Hallelujah Anyhow* (1990).

BRENAN, Gerald (Edward Fitzgerald) (1894–1987), British writer on Spain and Spanish culture, born in Malta, educated at Radley College. Following distinguished service in the First World War, he travelled to Spain in 1919 with the intention of becoming a writer; *South from Granada* (1957) is his retrospective account of this period. With the exception of an interlude in London during which he wrote and published fiction under the pseudonym 'George Beaton', he spent most of his life from the early 1930s onward in Malaga. *The Spanish Labyrinth* (1943) formed a penetrating survey of the cultural and historical contexts of the Spanish Civil War. *The Face of Spain* (1950), a richly digressive and humanely perceptive view of conditions under General Franco, confirmed his reputation as the most authoritative British writer on modern Spain. His other works include *The Literature of the Spanish People* (1953), a critical history, and the autobiographies *A Life of One's Own* (1962) and *Personal Record* (1974). There is a biography, *Gerald Brenan: The Interior Castle* (1992), by Jonathan Gathorne-Hardy.

BRENNAN, C(hristopher) J(ohn) (1870–1932), Australian poet and critic, born in Sydney, educated at the Universities of Sydney and Berlin. The strong influence in his work of the French Symbolist poets and European literature of the nineteenth century was seen as a departure from the nationalist-radical verse prevalent in Australia at that time and may have resulted in the mixed reception of his two early collections of 1897. His major work, *Poems (1913)* (1914), incorporated material from his earlier work, much of it influenced by Mallarmé and by his experiences in Berlin; it draws on myths of fall and redemption, and explores the nature of love and fulfilment and man's essential dualism. In 1920 Brennan was appointed Associate Professor of German and Comparative Literature at the University of Sydney but his somewhat controversial character, and scandal surrounding his private life, increased his isolation in later years. *A Chant of Doom and Other Verses* (1918) denounced Germany's role in the First World War. *The Burden of Tyre: Fifteen Poems by C. J. Brennan* (1953; edited by Harry F. Chaplin), early poems attacking Britain's involvement in the Boer War, and *The Prose of Christopher Brennan* (1962; edited by A. R. Chisholm and J. J. Quinn), a critical work, appeared posthumously.

BRENTON, Howard (1942–), British dramatist, born in Portsmouth, the son of a policeman, educated at Cambridge University. After working as a stage manager at various repertory companies, he joined Portable Theatre, one of whose founders was David *Hare, with whom he was eventually to write a play about municipal corruption, *Brassneck* (1973), and *Pravda* (1986), a Jonsonian comedy about British journalism and a predatory press baron. The plays which first brought him to notice in his own right, however, were two surreal one-act works, *Christie Dances* (1969) and *Hitler Dances* (1972). Then came numerous plays more openly and naturalistically dealing with Britain and British politics from a radical stance: *Magnificence*

(1973), about a squatter who becomes a terrorist after a bailiff's violence causes his wife to miscarry; *The Churchill Play* (1973), set in the near future, inside a prison camp for British dissidents; *Weapons of Happiness* (1976), about the unsuccessful occupation of a factory; a lively picture of Derby Day, *Epsom Downs* (1977); and *The Romans in Britain*, which caused great controversy when the National Theatre staged it in 1980, though less because of the parallels it drew between Caesar's invasion of Britain and the British army's presence in Ulster than because of one particular scene, involving the homosexual rape of a druid. *Moscow Gold* (1990), a theatrical tribute to President Gorbachev written in collaboration with Tariq *Ali, was followed by another play derived from the recent upheavals in the former Soviet bloc, this time written by Brenton alone: *Berlin Bertie* (1992), in which an East German secret policeman and a woman whose husband has been exposed as a Stasi agent meet again in a run-down section of London. As with Hare, Brenton's plays tend towards the epic, and often move between locations in sudden, cinematic jumps. He published *Hot Irons*, a collection of essays and extracts from his diaries, in 1995.

Brewster Place, see WOMEN OF BREWSTER PLACE, THE.

BREYTENBACH, Breyten (1939–), South African poet, novelist, and painter, born in Bonnievale, Cape Province. In 1961 he settled in Paris, where he married Yolande Ngo Thi Hoong Lien, whose father was finance minister in the government of Ngo Dinh Diem of South Vietnam. Breytenbach's work as a visual artist and his writing, which began with books of poems in Afrikaans, are much informed by the pain of exile, and acute awareness of world-wide political turbulence. In the early 1970s he visited South Africa on several occasions where his opposition to the apartheid regime was made blatantly clear; his first such visit is described in the ironically titled *A Season in Paradise* (1973). In 1975 he was arrested and sentenced to nine years in prison under the Terrorism Act. He was finally released in 1981 following representations from the French president François Mitterrand. His prison poems, sombre with apocalyptic dread, are generally considered his finest; a selection, together with prose pieces, has been translated and published as *In Africa even the Flies Are Happy* (1978). Other works include *Sinking Ship Blues* (1977), translated from Afrikaans, *And Death White as Words* (1978), *Mouroir: Mirrornotes of a Novel* (1984), *All One Horse: Fictions and Images* (1990, short stories), and *Painting in the Eye* (1993). His chief works in English are *The True Confessions of an Albino Terrorist* (1984), an agonized memoir of his incarceration; and a novel, *Memory of Snow and Dust* (1989), allusive and complex in its imagery, which examines the conflicts within Breytenbach's own psyche between spiritual yearning and the need to be politically effective. *Return to Paradise* (1993) records his disillusioned journey through post-apartheid South Africa in 1991.

Brideshead Revisited, a novel by Evelyn *Waugh, published in 1945. The novel, which takes the form of an extended flashback, is narrated by Charles Ryder, an army officer billeted at the eponymous country house, owned by an aristocratic Roman Catholic family headed by Lord and Lady Marchmain. Charles had visited Brideshead with Sebastian Flyte, the Marchmains' younger son, when both were Oxford undergraduates. In the course of the narrative Ryder conveys his fascination with the family, all of whom are eccentric or unhappy in some way: the gifted but unstable Sebastian has alcoholic tendencies; Lady Marchmain is unhappily married but refuses to divorce her husband, who lives in Venice with his mistress; the heir, Lord Brideshead, is as fanatically devout as his mother, and even the sisters, Julia and Cordelia, seem ill at ease with their role. Interspersed with passages describing the somewhat fraught family gatherings at Brideshead are those evoking the hedonism of Oxford between the wars; amongst the minor characters is the decadent aesthete Anthony Blanch (based on Brian Howard, one of Waugh's Oxford contemporaries). Events such as the General Strike of 1926 are described in passing, but do not really impinge on the plot, which remains principally concerned with the vicissitudes of the Flyte siblings: Sebastian, now a confirmed alcoholic, goes to live in North Africa, where his condition deteriorates rapidly; Julia, unhappily married, admits her love for Charles, also married, and the two plan to divorce their respective spouses, but are prevented from doing so by Julia's religious convictions. The final scenes are dominated by Julia's struggle with her conscience and her eventual decision to relinquish Charles, most of which takes place as her father, Lord Marchmain, is dying. The closing pages, which form an Epilogue, return to the opening wartime setting; the work ends, despite the narrator's nostalgic sadness for all that he has lost, on a note of cautious optimism. The novel was adapted for television in 1980.

Bridge, The, Hart *Crane's long poem setting out his 'Myth of America', published in 1930. The lyrical realism of the poem, 'To Brooklyn Bridge', identifies the bridge as symbol of the sequence's imaginative development. The eight succeeding sections form an impressionistic survey of the human and natural characters of America. Columbus's dramatic monologue in 'Ave Maria', the first part, recognizes the divine purpose for the country as 'one shore beyond desire'. The second part, 'Powhatan's Daughter', vividly evokes human activity and potential in the passage entitled 'The River', which opens with an experimental collage of advertising slogans. Pocahontas emerges through an abundance of sensually precise natural imagery as a feminine embodiment of the land itself and its indigenous culture. 'Cape Hatteras', the fourth section, uses its address to Walt Whitman as a basis for a lyrically compelling celebration of the spirit of progress. The sixth section, 'Quaker Hill', forms a critique of the materialist constraints on America's utopian potential, which has its antithesis in the view of urban degradation in 'The Tunnel', the penultimate section. 'Atlantis', the conclusion, returns to the opening's view of the bridge, its 'one arc synoptic of all tides' the symbol and reality around which the final exalted affirmation accumulates. Crane intended the poem, his 'symbol of our constructive future', as a corrective to the pessimism of T. S. Eliot's *The *Waste Land*; its expansive vision is sustained by a vibrant technical versatility and the remarkable geographical and thematic mobility with which it charts the actuality and ideal of America.

Bridge of San Luis Rey, The, a novel by Thornton *Wilder, published in 1927 (Pulitzer Prize). A historical romance, set in eighteenth-century Spanish colonial Peru, it examines the lives and deaths of the five travellers who are killed when the eponymous bridge collapses. Father Juniper, a Franciscan priest, believes that the deaths are part of God's grand design, and he sets out to prove this by scientific demonstration. The results of his investigations over six years are collected in a book which is deemed heretical. Brother Juniper is burned at the stake with his book, but a copy survives. The characters in the novel are the eccentric Marquesa de Montemayor; her unhappy companion, the Indian girl Pepita; Uncle Pio, the former teacher of the famous actress, La Perichole; his ward, Jaime, La Perichole's illegitimate son; and Esteban, who is deeply devoted to his dead twin brother, Manuel, La Perichole's lover. Apart from detailing the lives of these five characters, the novel is partly a theological-philosophical reflection on fate and providence, and this sense of chance brings all the characters to the bridge at the same time, representing life as unified, albeit mysteriously.

BRIDGES, Robert (Seymour) (1844–1930), British poet, critic, and editor, born in Walmer, Kent, educated at Eton and Corpus Christi College, Oxford. After studying at St Bartholomew's Hospital, he became a consulting physician at Great Ormond Street Children's Hospital. In 1881 he ceased medical practice in order to concentrate on his literary activities. His first collection of verse, *Poems* (1873), was followed by many volumes, including the sonnet sequence *The Growth of Love* (1876), the long poems *Prometheus the Firegiver* (1883) and *Eros and Psyche* (1885), and *The Humours of the Court* (1890). His *Poetical Works* appeared in six volumes between 1898 and 1905, with the publication in 1912 of a very popular single-volume edition. He was among the founders of the Society for Pure English in 1913, the year in which he succeeded Alfred Austin as Poet Laureate. Among his later volumes of poetry are *October and Other Poems* (1920), which contained a number of poems on the Great War, and *New Verse* (1925). *Testament of Beauty* was published to widespread acclaim in 1929; its four books form a lyrical and meditative exposition of his theistic rationalism, which derived from the philosophy of *Santayana. Bridges regarded the work as the summation of his career as a poet. Its long verse lines are the result of his interest in combining the properties of quantitive classical metres and the stress patterns of English prosody. He edited numerous anthologies of prose and poetry, and produced the first edition of Gerard Manley Hopkins's *Poems* in 1918; Hopkins's friendship and correspondence with Bridges since their meeting at Oxford are dealt with in Jean-Georges Ritz's *Robert Bridges and Gerard Manley Hopkins, 1863–1889: A Literary Friendship* (1960). The best-known of Bridges's many works as a critic are his monographs *Milton's Prosody* (1893) and *John Keats* (1895). He was keenly interested in the musical settings of words, collaborating on four occasions with the musician Hubert Parry and editing several editions of the *Yattendon Hymnal*. There is a biography by Edward *Thompson (1944); *Selected Letters of Robert Bridges*, edited by Donald E. Sandford, was published in two volumes in 1984.

BRIDIE, James, pseudonym of Osborne Henry MAVOR (1888–1951), Scottish playwright, born in Glasgow, the son of an engineer, educated at Glasgow University. Bridie became a prominent physician and did not begin seriously to write for the theatre until he was 40, when *The Sunlight Sonata* was performed in his home city of Glasgow. Thereafter he became enormously prolific; by his death he had completed forty-two plays, and was regarded as Scotland's leading dramatist. He saw the purpose of his quirky, genial drama as primarily to entertain, but secondarily and importantly to leave his audience, not with any firm conclusions, but 'whirling with speculations', often about metaphysical matters. Accordingly, he turned to biblical themes in several colloquial plays: most successfully in *Tobias and the Angel* (1930), in which the protagonist, accompanied by Raphael, is transformed by his adventures from an unassuming 'little worm' into a young man of genuine courage and spirit; but also in the lively *Jonah and the Whale* (1932) and *Susannah and the Elders* (1937). Other work with religious implications includes *A Sleeping Clergyman* (1933), in which a cleric symbolizing God snoozes while an exemplary family works out its and the world's destiny; *Mr Bolfry* (1943), in which a Calvinist minister is visited by an intellectually plausible devil; and the dramatic biography *John Knox* (1947). Other plays, notably *The Anatomist* (1930), about anti-scientific prejudice at the time of Burke and Hare; the thriller *Dr Angelus* (1947); *Daphne Laureola* (1949), a portrait of loneliness; and the unwontedly dark morality *The Baikie Charivari* (1950), serve to emphasize Bridie's abiding intellectual curiosity and diversity of interest. Among his other public activities, he helped establish the Glasgow Citizen's Theatre in 1943 and founded the first College of Drama in Scotland in 1950.

BRIERLEY, Walter (1900–72), English novelist, born in Waingroves, Derbyshire, of a mining family. Brierley became a miner himself and after attending Workers' Educational Association classes he won a miners' union scholarship to Nottingham University; however, unable to adjust to academic life, he returned to the pit. He sent an early manuscript to John *Hampson, who passed it to Walter *Allen; it aroused both writers' attention for its portrayal of a coal miner humiliated by the means test, and Brierley was encouraged to write what was to be his best-known novel, *Means Test Man* (1935). The novel remains a study of the effects of unemployment on a sensitive mind, and a cry of pain and outrage at the indignity of no longer having status or function in the community. Far from being a proletariate, the novel today appears more middle-class in tone. Brierley subsequently wrote the less distinguished *Sandwich Man* (1937), *Dalby Green* (1938), and *Danny* (1940), and became an education welfare officer in Derby until his retirement in 1965.

Briggflatts, a poem by Basil *Bunting, published in 1966, and widely regarded as the last major work of poetic *Modernism. Prior to its composition in 1965, Bunting had written little since returning to Britain from Persia in 1952; the growth of interest in his poetry initiated by Tom *Pickard stimulated Bunting to produce *Briggflatts*. Having accumulated over 10,000 lines, he concentrated his material into the 700 lines of text constituting the published work; into its five sections the poem compresses fifty years of autobiographical experience vividly inlaid with observational detail, mostly drawn from Bunting's natural surroundings in Northumbria. The elegiac retrospection, both personal and historical, and stoical anticipation of death that are thematically central often fuse inextricably with the lyric and celebratory modes affirming the poem's sustaining sense of locality. The emphatically Northumbrian character of *Briggflatts* makes it a manifestation *par excellence* of *regional poetry. The poem's strongly alliterative language and purposive allusions to Norse and Celtic cultures unequivocally align it with northern poetic traditions. Bunting claimed its structure was determined upon the model of Scarlatti's compositional procedures before any of the text was written; he insisted that the verbal music of *Briggflatts* took primacy over any considerations of meaning, thus drawing attention to the rich orchestration of consonantal and assonantal correspondences maintained with great skill throughout the poem.

BRIGGS, Asa (1921–), English historian, born in Keighley, Yorkshire, educated at Keighley Grammar School, Sidney Sussex College, Cambridge, and the University of London. Amongst other academic posts he was Provost of Worcester College, Oxford during 1976–91, and Chancellor of the Open University 1978–1994. A pioneer in the historical study of Victorian cities, Briggs stresses the important role of literature in illuminating the Victorian world. Among his major works are *History of Birmingham: 1865–1938* (1952), *Victorian People* (1954), *The Age of Improvement: 1783–1867* (1959), *Victorian Cities* (1963), *William Cobbett* (1967), *Marx in London* (1982), *A Social History of England* (1983), *Victorian Things* (1988), and *Channel Islands: Occupation and Liberation* (1995). He also wrote a five-volume *History of Broadcasting in the United Kingdom* (1961–95) and edited, with John Saville, *Essays in Labour History* (3 volumes; 1960–77). His *Collected Essays* (1985–91) were published in three volumes. He was created a life peer in 1976.

BRIGHOUSE, Harold (1882–1958), British playwright; he was the son of a Manchester businessman, and became the best-known exponent of the realistic drama associated with the repertory seasons at the city's Gaiety Theatre. He wrote *The Northerners* (1914), *Zack* (1920), and nearly twenty other plays, the best of them notable for the entertaining characterization of often oppressive and domineering Lancashire people; but, as he himself admitted in his autobiography, his reputation came overwhelmingly to depend on one only, **Hobson's Choice* (1915).

Brighter Sun, A, S. *Selvon's first novel, published in 1952, in which the author deals with race relations in Trinidad, particularly the integration of the descendants of East Indian indentured workers with the island's people of African descent. Tiger, the reflective Indian peasant hero, is the son of an agricultural labourer who, fresh from an arranged Hindu marriage, leaves his family in the sugar-cane belt to settle in a suburban village closer to the city. The novel traces his development into manhood, fatherhood, and expanded consciousness after he moves with his young wife Urmilla from a closed community to a multi-racial one, where their neighbours are the black couple Joe and Rita. The interaction between the couples, in the course of which, alongside domestic responsibilities, Tiger acquires a view of responsible citizenship, seems to presage a bright future for a new society freed from the racially isolated past. Selvon's flexible use of dialect reflects the inner experience of his central character, and it is in this novel that dialect first becomes the language of consciousness in West Indian fiction. A sequel, *Turn Again Tiger*, was published in 1958.

Brighton Rock, a novel by Graham *Greene, published in 1938. Set among Brighton racecourse razor gangs, it is in part a detective story, showing the murder of Hale by the 17-year-old Pinkie and his gang; Pinkie's courtship of Rose, whom he marries to prevent her giving evidence against him; and his pursuit by Ida Arnold, strangely determined, after a brief meeting with Hale, to give up her life of pleasure until she convicts his killers. *Brighton Rock* shares in this way the seedy urban background of Greene's 1930s 'entertainments', and their interest in shady or actually criminal activities, but it is also the first of his novels to reveal the Catholic faith to which he was converted in 1926. As Greene remarks, this new direction first appears in the course of the novel itself: after the first fifty pages, the detective story partly gives way to explicit investigation of religion and morality—to contrasts of Ida's complacent conviction of the nature of right and wrong with Rose and Pinkie's more profound awareness of good and evil. They are shown, as Catholics, to inhabit a moral universe larger and more mysterious than anything available to Ida's kind; one in which even Pinkie's dedication to evil, even his eventual suicide, may not place him beyond 'the appalling strangeness of the mercy of God'. Religious questions of this kind are more fully integrated into Greene's later writing, shaping the successful phase which follows from *Brighton Rock* and includes *The *Power and the Glory* (1940), *The *Heart of the Matter* (1948), and *The *End of the Affair* (1951).

BRINK, André (Philippus) (1935–), South African novelist and playwright, born in Vrede, educated at the University of Potchefstroom and at the Sorbonne. The extension of his cultural and political horizons as a student in Paris led Brink to declare: 'I was born on a bench in the Luxembourg Gardens in Paris, in the early spring of 1960.' While his many plays are in Afrikaans, his novels are generally written and published in both Afrikaans and English, with the English versions translated by himself. They have encountered trouble with the censor in South Africa for their open attacks on apartheid. His seventh novel, *Looking on Darkness* (1974; in Afrikaans, *Kennis van die aand*, 1973) was also the first book in Afrikaans to be banned. His translation of his fourth Afrikaans novel, *File on a Diplomat* (1967), was later published as *The Ambassador* (1985). Criticism of sensationalism should be qualified by the fact that Brink himself views Afrikaner society as being in a state of apocalyptic danger, a fear which he courageously confronts in his own novels. Two of his most effective novels are the powerful *A Chain of Voices* (1982), its multiple narratives dealing with a historical slave rebellion on an Afrikaner farm in the Cape in 1825, and *States of Emergency* (1988), its background being the 'deranged year' of 1985, when rebellion flared throughout South Africa, and a state of emergency was declared. Other novels which explore the Afrikaner psyche include *Rumours of Rain* (1978); *A Dry White Season* (1979); *The Wall of the Plague* (1984); *An Act of Terror* (1991), a thriller exploring an attempted assassination of the South African president; *The First Life of Adamastor* (1993), which makes use of Camões' myth of demonic love and suffering and Khoi myths of creation to allegorize the roots of racial schism in South Africa; *On the Contrary* (1993), in which Brink makes use of Quixotic legends and eighteenth-century South African conflict in his examination of Afrikaner consciousness; *Imaginings of Sand* (1996) looks at South Africa's past and anticipates its future following the 1994 elections. With J. M. *Coetzee he edited an anthology of contemporary South African writing, *A Land Apart* (1986). Essays are collected in *Mapmakers: Writing in a State of Siege* (1983).

BRITTAIN, Vera (Mary) (1893–1970), British author, pacifist, and feminist, born in Newcastle-under-Lyme, Staffordshire. Her education at Somerville College, Oxford, was interrupted from 1915 to 1918 by service in London, France, and Malta as a nurse with the Volunteer Aid Detachment; her *Verses of a V.A.D.* (1918) reflect the vigorous pacifism with which she responded to her experiences of warfare. *The Dark Tide* (1923), the first of her five novels, all of which contain a strong autobiographical element, provoked controversy through its depiction of conditions in Oxford's women's colleges. She remains best known for *Testament of Youth* (1933), her account of her life up to 1925; Brittain intended the work, which is memorable for its movingly idealistic portrayals of 'the stark agonies of my generation' during the First World War, as a counterpart from a woman's viewpoint to the numerous memoirs of the war by male authors. The book gained her an international reputation as a spokeswoman for pacifism, and over the next three decades she lectured widely in Europe, Asia, and America; her other works as a pacifist include *Seeds of Chaos* (1944), which drew sharp criticism for its condemnation of the British and American bombing campaigns during the Second World War, and the historical study *The Rebel Passion* (1964). Among her numerous significant contributions to modern feminist literature are *Lady into Woman: A History of Women from Victoria to Elizabeth II* (1953), and *Testament of Friendship* (1940), a remarkable commemoration of her relationship with Winifred *Holtby. *Testament of Experience* (1957) continues her autobiography up to the year 1950 and forms a richly detailed record of social and historical developments of the period. A. G. Bishop edited three volumes of Brittain's diaries (1981, 1986, 1989); *Testament of a Peace Lover* (edited by A. Eden-Green) is a collection of her letters.

BROAD, C(harlie) D(unbar) (1887–1971), British philosopher, born at Harlesden, Middlesex, the son of a wine merchant, educated at Dulwich College and at Trinity College, Cambridge. He began his academic career as a lecturer at the University of St Andrews. After holding a professorship in philosophy at Bristol from 1920 to 1922, he became a fellow and lecturer of Trinity College. He remained at Cambridge, where he was Knightsbridge Professor of Moral Philosophy between 1933 and 1953, until his death. He knew Bertrand *Russell as a student and shared his belief in the primacy of scientific reasoning over common sense, a conviction reflected in *Perception, Physics, and Reality* (1914), Broad's first major work. His reputation rests on his lucid investigations of a remarkable range of philosophical problems and his analytical expositions of the insights of other thinkers; his writing more than justifies his modest claim in *Scientific Thought* (1923) to possessing 'the . . . power of stating things clearly and not superficially'. His controversial interest in psychic phenomena emerged in the course of his examination of the relations between mind and matter in *The Mind and Its Place in Nature* (1925); his writings on parapsychology are chiefly collected in *Religion, Philosophy, and Psychical Research* (1953) and *Lectures on Psychical Research* (1962). The fullest statement of Broad's philosophical position is given in his

Examination of McTaggart's Philosophy (two volumes, 1933–8), which is considered his most important work. *The Philosophy of C. D. Broad* (edited by P. A. Schilpp, 1959) contains Broad's idiosyncratically revealing 'Autobiography' and 'Reply to Critics' in addition to essays by twenty-one contributors. His *Critical Essays in Moral Philosophy* (1971) is edited by D. R. Cheney.

BROCK, Edwin (1927–), British poet, born in London; following a grammar school education he worked as a police constable and an advertising copywriter until 1972, when he became a freelance writer. He became poetry editor of **Ambit* in 1960. His earlier collections of poetry include *An Attempt at Exorcism* (1959), *A Family Affair* (1960), and *With Love from Judas* (1963), which contain numerous disquietingly intense treatments of domestic experience. *A Cold Day at the Zoo* (1970), *The Blocked Heart* (1975), and *The River and the Train* (1979) are among his subsequent volumes; *Song of the Battery Hen* (1977) and *Five Ways To Kill a Man* (1990) are selected editions, the latter containing much previously uncollected verse. His later work typically unites a disciplined freedom of form with an incisive straightforwardness to explore a wide range of social and personal concerns. His other works include the autobiographical verse and prose of *Here Now, Always* (1977) and the novel *The Little White God* (1962). He has also written plays for radio and television.

BRODBER, Erna (1940–), Jamaican novelist and sociologist, born in the village of Woodside, Jamaica; she was educated at the University of the West Indies, where she joined the staff of the Institute of Social and Economic Research in 1975. Her early works as a sociologist include *Abandonment of Children in Jamaica* (1974) and *A Study of Yards in the City of Kingston* (1975). Her first novel, *Jane and Louisa Will Come Home Soon* (1980), which originated in her work on abnormal psychology, is strongly informed by the themes of displacement and alienation; stylistically, it combines strong elements of Jamaica's oral tradition with fluent use of *stream of consciousness techniques. *Myal* (1988), more conventional in form, is a highly imaginative exploration of the tensions between the rationalism of modern culture and the persistence of a powerful cultural heritage. Another novel, *Louisiana*, appeared in 1994. Her other works include *Perceptions of Caribbean Women: Towards a Documentation of Stereotypes* (1982).

BRODKEY, Harold (1930–96), American novelist and short-story writer, born in Alton, Illinois, educated at Harvard. He was Associate Professor of English at Cornell University and also taught at the City University of New York. Until the publication of his novel *The Runaway Soul* (1991), Brodkey's reputation was based mainly on a handful of short stories, most of them published in *The New Yorker* and *Esquire*. His first collection, *First Love and Other Sorrows* (1957), was greeted with almost universal acclaim. His reputation was then sustained by the promise of a novel, initially entitled *A Party of Animals*; for years, despite constant announcements of its imminent publication, the novel failed to appear and Brodkey became the subject of intense speculation. *The Runaway Soul* (1991) is a remarkable novel, whose evocation of the world of childhood and adolescence belongs to a mainstream American tradition. The exhaustive detail and exuberant linguistic playfulness is reminiscent of both Walt Whitman and Jack *Kerouac; like them, he tried to find a new language to convey the intelligence of the body and of the world of dreaming which accompanies it. *Profane Friendship* (1994), a study of sexual obsession and inversion, was written in a plainer style, though not as plain as his dignified and harrowing memoir 'My Life, My Wife and Aids' (1994); Broadkey died of an AIDS-related illness. His other publications include two volumes of short stories, *Women and Angels* (1985) and *Stories in an Almost Classical Mode* (1988; UK title, *The Abundant Dreamer*, 1989); and *A Poem about Testimony and Argument* (1986).

BRODSKY, Joseph (Alexandrovich) (1940–96), Russian poet, born in Leningrad; he left school at the age of 15. Some of his poetry appeared in *samizdat* magazines before his arrest in 1964 for 'social parasitism'. Sentenced to five years' servitude in the Arkhangelsk region of northern Russia, he was released after eighteen months following appeals on his behalf by Dmitri Shostakovich, Anna Akhmatova, and others who affirmed the value of his verse. The Russian texts of his *Stikhotvoreniia i poemy* ('longer and shorter poems') were published in America in 1965. Under the dispensation permitting the emigration of Soviet Jews to Israel, he left the USSR in 1972 and was later refused permission to return. He settled in America, holding various posts as poet-in-residence before becoming Professor of Literature at Mount Holyoke College, Massachusetts, in 1981. The first significant appearance of his work in translation was *Elegy for John Donne and Other Poems* (1967); subsequent publications include *Selected Poems* (1973), *A Part of Speech* (1980), *To Urania: Selected Poems 1965–1985* (1988), and *So Forth* (1995). The expansive lyrical and elegiac qualities of his verse survive impressively in translation; Anthony *Hecht, Derek *Walcott, and Richard *Wilbur are among the translators with whom he worked. Much of his poetry is on an ambitious scale, pursuing his preoccupations with human suffering and redemptive possibilities; his informally factual mode takes on a power of mythical suggestion through his remarkably imaginative use of precisely observed local detail. In 1987 he was awarded the Nobel Prize for Literature. Among his other works are the play *Marbles* (1989), an allegorical treatment of the limits of politically determined existence; *Less than One* (1986), a collection of his essays; and *Watermark* (1992), a travel book about Venice.

BROMFIELD, Louis (1896–1956), American novelist, born in Mansfield, Ohio; he studied at Columbia University before serving in the First World War. His sequence of four novels, *The Green Bay Tree* (1924), *Possession* (1925), *Early Autumn* (1926; Pulitzer Prize), and *A Good Woman* (1927), which centred on a New England farming family, effectively illustrated Bromfield's egalitarian philosophy with its emphasis on the virtues of agrarian democracy and individual initiative. With *The Strange Case of Annie Spragg* (1928) and *Twenty-Four Hours* (1930), Bromfield displayed a technical proficiency in the construction of linked narratives converging on a single event. However, critics frequently dismissed his intelligent, perceptive fictions as outmoded. Bromfield's visit to India in 1932 resulted in *The Rains Came* (1937), a powerful novel which displayed his narrative drive, evocative descriptive prose, an unashamed romantic idealism, and a concern with social progress. Bromfield's Indian fictions, which included *Night in Bombay* (1940), present a fascinating portrayal of a time and a nation prepared for radical change. His other novels include *Mrs Parkington* (1943), a portrait of a typical Bromfield heroine, a powerful and innovative woman; *Colorado* (1947), a spoof of the *Western genre; and *The Wild Country* (1948), a haunting study of adolescent sexuality set in Ohio farming country. *Pleasant Valley* (1945) and *Malabar Farm* (1948) are non-fiction works based on his experiences as a farmer in Ohio from 1939.

BROOKE, Jocelyn (1908–66), British novelist, born at Sandgate, Kent, educated at Worcester College, Oxford. He worked in the book and the wine trades, and served in the Royal Army Medical Corps during the Second World War. Brooke's novels explore the public school world, with its post-educational bastions, the army, the Foreign Office, the artistic professions, and homosexuality. *The Military Orchid* (1948), a fictionalized memoir, confirmed him as an accute observer of the natural world; it became the first part of 'The Orchid' trilogy with *A Mine of Serpents* (1949) and *The Goose Cathedral* (1950). *Private View* (1955), a semi-memoir, is composed of four portraits including the memorable 'Gerald Brockhurst', public school athlete. More orthodox fiction includes *The Scapegoat* (1948), which focuses on sado-masochism; *The Image of a Drawn Sword* (1950), a Kafkaesque quasi-fantasy of the army; *The Passing of a Hero* (1953); and *Conventional Weapons* (1961). Brooke also wrote a study of the British orchid, critical appreciations of Elizabeth *Bowen and John *Betjeman, and edited the works of Denton *Welch. His reputation sank after his death but revived during the early 1980s under the championship of Anthony *Powell.

BROOKE, Rupert (Chawner) (1887–1915), British poet, born in Rugby, educated at King's College, Cambridge, where he was president of the *Fabian Society and became a fellow in 1913. In 1911 and 1912 he lived in Germany, where he wrote a melodrama entitled *Lithuania* (1915) and numerous poems, of which 'The Old Vicarage, Grantchester' is the best-known. His first collection, *Poems*, appeared in 1911. He subsequently assisted Edward *Marsh in planning the **Georgian Poetry* series (1912–22), the first of which did much to advance his reputation. Brooke's circle of acquaintances widened to include most of the influential writers of the day; referred to by W. B. *Yeats as 'the most beautiful man in England', his eminence among the pre-war *jeunesse dorée* contributed to his enormous posthumous fame. In 1913 he visited the USA, Canada, and the Pacific Islands while convalescing from a nervous disorder and produced a series of articles for the *Westminster Gazette*; some were later published, with a preface by Henry *James, as *Letters from America* (1916). The trip also resulted in some of his best poems, collected in *1914 and Other Poems* (1915) under the section heading 'The South Seas'. After his return in 1914 he volunteered for active service and received a commission with the Royal Naval Division. On a brief expedition to Antwerp he witnessed scenes of misery which strengthened his zeal for the British cause, and shortly afterwards produced the five sonnets forming the title sequence of *1914*. These were published in *New Numbers* early in 1915. The following Easter Sunday 'The Soldier' ('If I should die, think only this of me . . .') was read from the pulpit by the Dean of St Paul's; a report including the sonnet's text in *The Times* elevated Brooke to the embodiment of self-sacrificing idealism. By the time news of this reached him he had fallen ill on his way to the Dardanelles; he died on 23 April of septicaemia aboard a French hospital ship. The *Poetical Works* (1946) was edited by Sir Geoffrey *Keynes. His monumental reputation declined with the waning popularity of Georgian Poetry in the 1920s. Among poets engaged in the war, the reaction against his work came swiftly; Charles Hamilton *Sorley was among the first dissenters, remarking in 1915 on the falseness of Brooke's 'sentimental attitude'. Biographies include those by Christopher *Hassall (1964) and John *Lehmann (1980).

BROOKE-ROSE, Christine (1926–), British novelist and critic, born in Brussels; she grew up in Switzerland and later attended Somerville College, Oxford. In 1975 she became a professor of American literature at the University of Paris VII. Though her fiction began to appear in the late 1950s, Brooke-Rose's early novels were much influenced by *Murdoch. An illness in the 1960s and her readings in the *nouveau roman* radically changed her style. *Out* (1964), *Such* (1966), *Between* (1968), and *Thru* (1975), published in one volume as *The Christine Brooke-Rose Omnibus* (1986), display a gamut of *post-modernist influences, ranging from the detached objectivity of Robbe-Grillet in the early work to the linguistic play associated with *post-structuralism in the later novels. In her more recent novels *Amalgammemnon* (1984), *Xorandor* (1986), and *Verbivore* (1989), Brooke-Rose puts into fictional practice the theories of deconstruction associated with Derrida, while revealing an obsessive concern with modern technology. *Textermination* (1991), a characteristically playful construction of puns and literary references, was followed by the autobiographical *Remake* (1996), which uses material from the seventy years of its author's life to compose an experimental third-person novel. She has also published the essays *Stories, Theories and Things* (1991), which examine the nature and determination of the canon.

BROOKNER, Anita (1928–), English novelist and art historian, born in London, educated at King's College, University of London, and the Courtauld Institute. Brookner has held several distinguished academic posts (Slade Professor, University of Cambridge, 1967–8; Reader at the Courtauld Institute, 1977–8; Fellow of New Hall, Cambridge) and has published books on eighteenth-century painting (*Watteau*, 1968; *The Genius of the Future: Studies in French Art Criticism*, 1971; *Greuze*, 1972; *Jacques-Louis David*, 1981). Beginning with *A Start in Life* (1981), she has produced a novel almost every year, including *Providence* (1982), *Look at Me* (1983), *Hotel du Lac* (1984; Booker Prize), *Family and Friends* (1985), *A Misalliance* (1986), *A Friend from England* (1987), *Latecomers* (1988), *Lewis Percy* (1989), *Brief Lives* (1990), *A Closed Eye* (1991), *Fraud* (1992), *A Private View* (1994), *Incidents in the Rue Laugier* (1995), and *Altered States* (1996). The Brookner heroine has become a recognized type. She is solitary, and feels 'a stranger to the rest of the world'. (This alienation may take clinical form, such as fear of water or agoraphobia.) She is in love with a romantic (and somewhat unfocused) male character who rejects, ignores, or betrays her; in *Hotel du Lac*, Edith Hope, a writer of escapist romances, has been in love with a married art auctioneer and, like many of Brookner's heroines, has cultivated a 'meek and complaisant' personality. When she rejects the chance of marrying a dull companionable man, she is banished by her friends to a Swiss hotel, where she broods on her past, and finally comes to believe in her own romances. A Brookner heroine may also be recently orphaned (Frances in *Look At Me*) or have sacrificed her life to the demands of self-centred European parents (Ruth in *A Start in Life*, Mimi in *Family and Friends*). She is often drawn to a 'misalliance' with couples or families living cosy, greedy lives of domestic bliss or sensual excess. In Brookner's fiction, the tortoise loses and the hare wins. To combat the pain of defeat the heroine cultivates a meticulous, even dandyish, self-presentation (Blanche in *A Misalliance*, Rachel in *A Friend from England*), which matches the author's dry, witty narrative. The Brookner heroine is usually highly cultured and the novels are often dominated by a cultural reference, such as the Giorgione painting in *A Friend from England*. Some heroines are more likeable than others (Rachel in *A Friend from England* is a horrifying character; Frances in *Look at Me* is painfully sympathetic). In *Lewis Percy*, the Brookner heroine is a man, a timid Francophile offered one chance of happiness. Though her cool narrative manner is French in style, the emotions are in a tradition of English women writers from Charlotte Brontë to Elizabeth *Bowen and Rosamond *Lehmann, and she is also a great admirer of Edith *Wharton. This, and her reasoned wariness of feminism, gives her writing an old-fashioned air, and has led to accusations of conservatism, sentimentality, and élitism. She is also criticized for lack of dialogue, though this is countered by her close attention to details, her clear eye for human behaviour, and her strong evocation of emotional mood. Within its limited parameters her fiction is powerfully obsessional, disturbing, and severe.

BROOKS, Cleanth (1906–90), American literary critic, born in Murray, Kentucky, educated at Vanderbilt, Tulane, and Oxford Universities. A key figure in the development of the *New Criticism, he was taught by John Crowe *Ransom at Vanderbilt University where he was befriended by Allen *Tate and Robert Penn *Warren, and loosely associated with the Fugitive (*Agrarian) group. He became professor at Louisiana State University and, with Robert Penn Warren, established *The Southern Review* which championed the New Criticism and fought, successfully, against what was left of the old, *belles-lettristic*, historical criticism. His *Modern Poetry and the Tradition* (1939) was influential both in its application of New Critical methods of close reading and in its argument that modern poetry (notably that of *Eliot, *Yeats, and *Auden) is anchored in the tradition of seventeenth-century metaphysical poetry. Among his other publications are *Understanding Poetry: An Anthology for College Students* (1938; with Robert Penn Warren; revised edition 1950); *The Well-Wrought Urn: Studies in the Structure of Poetry* (1947), which included two important statements of the philosophy of the New Criticism, 'The Language of Paradox' and 'The Heresy of Paraphrase'; *Literary Criticism: A Short History* (1957; with William K. Wimsatt); *The Hidden God: Studies in Hemingway, Faulkner, Yeats, Eliot, and Warren* (1963); and *William Faulkner: The Yoknapatawpha Country* (1963). Brooks was Gray Professor of Rhetoric at Yale (1947–90) and Cultural Attaché at the American Embassy in London (1964–6). See *The Possibilities of Order: Cleanth Brooks and His Work* (1976; edited by Lewis P. Simpson).

BROOKS, Gwendolyn (1917–), American poet, born in Topeka, Kansas. She grew up in Chicago, where she was educated at Wilson Junior College; the city, where she has spent most of her life, and its black community are central to most of her work. She has held visiting posts at various American universities and was Consultant in Poetry at the Library of Congress in 1985 and 1986. *A Street in Bronzeville* (1945) was her first collection of verse; other early publications include *Annie Allen* (1949), for which she became the first black American to receive a Pulitzer Prize for poetry, and *The Bean Eaters* (1960). Such work brings a lucidly objective social-realism and poised technical accomplishment to its fundamentally humane treatments of a wide spectrum of urban experiences. Following her participation at a black writers' conference in 1967, her poetry took on a new freedom of form and assumed a tone of unequivocal political engagement on behalf of African-Americans; among her later collections are *In the Mecca* (1968), *Aurora* (1972), *The Near-Johannesburg Boy* (1986), and *Gottschalk and the Grande Tarantelle* (1988). Brooks is also the author of the novel *Maud Martha* (1953), which deals with a young black woman's struggle against racial discrimination, and the impressionistic autobiography of *Report from Part One* (1972). Representative editions of her work are *Selected Poems* (1963) and the miscellany entitled *The World of Gwendolyn Brooks* (1971). G. E. Kent's *A Life of Gwendolyn Brooks* appeared in 1990.

BROOKS, Van Wyck (1886–1963), American critic, born in Plainfield, New Jersey, educated at Harvard. From 1907 to 1909 he lived in London, where he wrote *The Wine of the Puritans* (1908); its thesis that the Puritan ethos led to the aesthetic impoverishment of American literary culture was sustained in *The Malady of the Ideal* (1913). *America's Coming of Age* (1915) outlined his conception of an American literature liberated from dependence on European models. In 1916 he became associate editor of *The *Seven Arts*, energetically promoting the cultural regeneration of America. *The Ordeal of Mark Twain* (1920) and *The Pilgrimage of Henry James* (1925) are among the earliest works to apply psychoanalytical principles to literary criticism; in the case of Twain, Brooks concluded that his native genius had been diminished by the pressures of the American socio-cultural context, which had forced James to opt for exile and a deforming over-refinement. Following a severe breakdown in 1925, his writing ceased to be adversely critical of the nineteenth-century traditions of American literature. His major work from the early 1930s onward was the descriptive survey of American writing in the numerous volumes of his *Makers and Finders* series; these include *The Flowering of New England, 1815–1865* (1936; Pulitzer Prize), *New England: Indian Summer, 1865–1915* (1940), *The Times of Melville and Whitman* (1947), and *The Confident Years, 1885–1915* (1952). His antagonism to *Modernism, and to T. S. *Eliot in particular, is evident in *On Literature Today* (1941) and *The Writer in America* (1953). Among his many other publications are *The Dreaming of Arcadia: American Writers and Artists in Italy, 1760–1915* (1958) and *Fenollosa and His Circle* (1962). His autobiographical writings were posthumously collected as *An Autobiography* (1965). James Hoopes's *Van Wyck Brooks: In Search of American Culture* appeared in 1977.

BROPHY, Brigid (Antonia Susan) (1929–95), British novelist, biographer, and critic, born in London, educated at St Hugh's College, Oxford. A classicist, atheist, and humanist, she campaigned tirelessly for animals' and authors' rights. In 1972 (with Maureen *Duffy, Lettice *Cooper, and Francis *King) she was a founder member of the Writers' Action Group which secured Public Lending Rights (1979); she also held offices at the Writers' Guild, the Society of Authors, and the Authors' Lending and Copyright Society, and was a president of the National Anti-Vivisection Society. Her first novel, *Hackenfeller's Ape* (1953), explores the relationship between an ape in London Zoo and a professor who observes its mating habits. Other novels include *The King of a Rainy Country* (1956); *Flesh* (1962); *The Finishing Touch* (1963), which features a headmistress based on Anthony Blunt; *The Snow Ball* (1964), a notable baroque comedy of manners that draws upon Mozart's opera *Don Giovanni*; and *In Transit* (1969), an experimental examination of gender and personality. *Palace without Chairs* (1978), a mature Shavian allegory about democracy, appeared a year before she was struck down by multiple sclerosis. Brophy's other works include *The Crown Princess and Other Stories* (1953); a play, *The Burglar* (perf. 1967); *Mozart the Dramatist: A New View of Mozart, His Opera and His Age* (1964); and *Prancing Novelist: A Defence of Fiction in the Form of a Critical Biography in Praise of Ronald Firbank* (1973), a lengthy defence of the author with whom her own work was also compared. *Fifty Works of English Literature We Could Do Without* (1967), co-authored by her husband Sir Michael Levey and Charles Osborne, proved controversial on its publication; *Baroque 'n' Roll* (1987), which features a courageous account of the disease that foreshortened her career, and *Reads* (1989) are among her collections of essays. Brophy was a Fellow of the Royal Society of Literature; her writing was characterized by erudition, wit, and incisiveness.

BROSTER, D(orothy) K(athleen) (1878–1950), British novelist, born near Liverpool, educated at St Hilda's College, Oxford. During the First World War she was a volunteer at a hospital in France and subsequently became the secretary to a professor at Oxford. Her first novel, *Chantemerle*, appeared in 1911. She is best known for her compelling chronicle of the Jacobite Rebellion of 1745 in *The Flight of the Heron* (1925), *The Gleam in the North* (1927), and *The Dark Mile* (1929), which were collected as *The Jacobite Trilogy* in 1984; the books are highly regarded for the historical accuracy with which they present the Highland communities of the eighteenth century. Her other novels include *Almond, Wild Almond* (1933) and *The Captain's Lady* (1947).

Brother Man, the second of R. *Mais's three novels, published in 1954; it features the Kingston shanty town that was also the setting for Mais's earlier *The Hills Were Joyful Together*. The book's eponymous protagonist is a shoemaker and an adherent of the Rastafarian religious movement that began in Jamaica in the early 1930s, a response by a minority of the underprivileged black community to the hopelessness of their situation but for its first three decades seen as a threat by the majority. Brother Man—whose actual name is John Power—and his Christ-like progress is the focus of the story; with his growing reputation as healer and holy man he seems to embody the roles of both John the Baptist and Jesus for the urban proletariat among whom he lives. But the people of Orange Lane as a group express clearly the author's socio-political commitment. There are three central pairs of characters: Brother Man and Minette, a young woman who is physically attracted to him but whom he apparently thinks of only as a daughter; Girlie and Papacita, who passes counterfeit coins and whose moral degeneracy contrasts with Brother Man's spiritual purity; and the sisters Jesmina and the disturbed Cordelia, who represents a force for evil. Papacita desires Minette and vows to find a way to separate her from Brother Man. The discrediting of Brother Man begins when counterfeit coins are found planted in his house; eventually, general feelings of betrayal make people turn against him. Attacked by a mob, he is stoned unconscious. Three days later, in a symbolic resurrection, he regains consciousness, to learn that neighbours have been enquiring after him, and his faith in brotherhood appears to be confirmed. The structure of the novel is complex and original, likened by E. K. *Brathwaite to that of jazz, broken into five episodic chapters each introduced by a 'Chorus of People in the Lane' interpreting the action, establishing the mood, and preparing the reader for what is to happen. The language effectively alternates between Standard English and Jamaican patois, with biblical echoes in Brother Man's simple and direct expression.

BROUMAS, Olga (1949–), American poet, born in Syros, Greece, educated at the Universities of Pennsylvania and Oregon. Her collection *Beginning with O* (1977) won the Yale University Younger Poets Award and received praise from Stanley *Kunitz for its 'explicit sexuality and Sapphic orientation'. The poems in *Sole Sauvage* (1979) and *Pastoral Jazz* (1983) focus on images and language reflecting experience from a woman's viewpoint. Two translations of poetry by the Greek Nobel Laureate, Odysseas Elytis, *What I Love* (1986) and *The Little Mariner* (1988), illustrate the influence and recurring use of ancient Greek poetic forms in her poetry. In *Perpetua* (1989) the poems have a narrative structure, contemplating the poet's relationships with family, friends, and lovers. Broumas collaborated with Jane Miller in *Black Holes, Black Stockings* (1985), and with T. Begley in *Sappho's Gymnasium* (1994) which shows the influence of Sappho and Elytis. Broumas is intent on delineating a specifically lesbian language which encompasses the physical and emotional intensities of love and desire between women.

BROWN, Christy (1932–81), Irish novelist and poet, born in Dublin, the son of a bricklayer and one of twenty-three children. A victim of cerebral palsy, he was able to write only with the aid of his left foot, which he used to operate a specially adapted typewriter. *My Left Foot* (1954), an autobiography describing his fight to overcome his disability, was later made into an award-winning film; it was followed by an autobiographical novel, *Down All the Days* (1970), which is set, like much of his work, in Dublin. His second novel, *A Shadow on Summer* (1974), follows its protagonist, a crippled writer, Riley McCombe, to America, where he becomes involved with a beautiful photographer. *Wild Grow the Lilies* (1976) described the peregrinations around Dublin of an Irish journalist in search of a story. *A Promising Career*, a novel set in London and concerning a young couple caught up in the corrupt world of the recording industry, and *Collected Poems*, were published posthumously in 1982.

BROWN, E(dward) K(illoran) (1905–51), Canadian critic, born in Toronto, educated at the universities of Toronto and Paris; he subsequently taught in Toronto and at Cornell and Chicago Universities. Brown wrote on a wide range of subjects and authors, including Matthew Arnold and Willa *Cather, but his most important critical and editorial work was concerned with Canadian literature at a time when the subject was still in its infancy. His best-known book, *On Canadian Poetry* (1943), which incorporates some of his earlier influential essays, attempted to chart the struggle of the Canadian poet against what Brown saw as an essentially philistine society, and to identify the distinctive qualities of the Canadian literary tradition. He also wrote studies of the work of two of the 'Confederation Poets', Archibald Lampman and Duncan Campbell *Scott, whom he regarded as particularly important in the evolution of Canadian poetry.

BROWN, George Douglas (1869–1902), Scottish novelist, born in Ayrshire, the illegitimate son of a farmer, and brought up in difficult circumstances. He was educated at Glasgow University and Balliol College, Oxford. Moving to London to pursue a writing career, he began writing fiction for magazines and published pseudonymously a historical romance, *Love and a Sword* (1899). His single masterpiece, *The House with the Green Shutters* (1901), is set in the Lowlands town of Barbie, depicted as a nest of spite and petty intrigue. The central character is Gourlay, a trade magnate who has succeeded through canniness and 'brute force of character' in the carrying business. He is tyrannical in his dealings with his feckless wife, on whose dowry he built his business, and with his weak son and his self-effacing daughter; all are crushed by the monstrous strength of his domination. The 'passion of his life' is his house which he sees as a symbol of triumph over the village. Uncompromising in his rendering of cruelty and misery, Brown describes the rise and the fall of the House of Gourlay, its destruction from within and without, and the disgrace brought about by his son who, unable to meet his father's expectations, surrenders to drink. The novel was praised for its departure from the *'Kailyard' school of sentimental novels portraying Scottish provincial life. Among others, it was admired by F. R. *Leavis and J. B. *Priestley, and has influenced writers such as Lewis Grassic *Gibbon. Brown died of pneumonia leaving behind the drafts for two novels, *The Novelist* and *The Incompatibles*.

BROWN, George Mackay (1921–96), British poet and novelist, born in Stromness, Orkney, educated at Stromness Academy and Newbattle Abbey College, Dalkeith, where Edwin *Muir, warden of the college, encouraged him as a poet. He later gained an MA at the University of Edinburgh. *Loaves and Fishes* (1959), his first substantial collection of verse, was followed by numerous volumes, including *The Year of the Whale* (1965), *Winterfold* (1976), and *The Wreck of the Archangel* (1989). The landscapes, history, and communities of Orkney are imaginatively transposed in his verse and prose into the archives of 'Hamnavoe', as his native islands are known in his work. *Fishermen with Ploughs* (1971), a poetic sequence surveying developments from the time of the Vikings to the modern age, is his most concentrated historical treatment of the locality. At the centre of his work is a visionary sense of the sacrosanctity of ancient patterns of life and their interaction with unspoilt natural surroundings. Stylistically, his poetry is notable for the extreme refinement and clarity of its diction and rhythms, a characteristic apparent in forms ranging from highly disciplined free verse to robust ballad stanzas. *Selected Poems 1954–1983* appeared in 1991. *A Calendar of Love* (1967) was the first of his several collections of short stories, which also include the highly acclaimed *A Time To Keep* (1969), *The Sun's Net* (1976), and *Winter Tales* (1996). His work in prose forms an extension of the narrative impulse which is often apparent in his poetry; many of his stories evoke an ideal of community in a richly fluent style of great strength and simplicity. **Greenvoe* (1972) is the best known of his novels, others being *Magnus* (1973), centring on the martyrdom of St Magnus, *Vinland* (1992), which richly evokes the Viking era, and *Beside the Ocean of Time* (1994). Among Brown's several collections of essays are *Letters from Hamnavoe* (1975) and *Under Brinkie's Brae* (1979), which contains selections from his journalism. His published work as a dramatist includes *Three Plays* (1984), which collects *The Loom of Light*, *The Voyage of St Brandon*, and *The Well*.

BROWN, Rita Mae (1944–), American novelist and poet born in Hanover, Pennsylvania, educated at the University of Florida, New York University, and the New York School of Visual Arts. Brown's works are deeply influenced by her commitment to the feminist and Gay Liberation movements. She is best known as the author of *Rubyfruit Jungle*, a sparklingly funny account of one woman's intellectual and sexual odyssey which, because of its erotic lesbian content, was rejected by several publishers before finally appearing in 1973. *A Plain Brown Rapper* (1976) sets out Brown's view of the women's movement in its first decade and reveals her abiding sympathy with women on the edge of society, including women of colour, lesbians, and working-class women. These sympathies inform her poetry, published in such politically charged volumes as *The Hand that Cradles the Rock* (1971), *Songs to a Handsome Woman* (1973), and *Poems* (1987). Novels like *Six of One* (1978) characteristically chronicle relationships between women. *Southern Discomfort* (1982), set in the context of a racially segregated community, tells of a love affair between a black adolescent and an older white woman. *Sudden Death* (1983) draws on Brown's own relationship with tennis champion Martina Navratilova to reveal the corrupt world of international tennis. Later novels include *High Hearts* (1986) a historical work, centred on the fortunes of a Southern woman fighting incognito with the Confederate army, and *Bingo* (1988).

BROWN, Sterling A(llen) (1901–89), African-American poet and critic, born in Washington, DC, educated at Williams College, Massachusetts and at Harvard. In 1929 he became Professor of English at Howard University. Regarded as one of the fathers of modern African-American literature, his contribution as writer, teacher, editor, and reviewer spanned half a century from the *Harlem Renaissance to the era of Black Power. His first book, *Southern Road* (1932), is a rich collection of folk 'portraitures'. Like Langston *Hughes, Brown drew on the traditional idioms of work song, ballad, spiritual, and blues, believing that to reinterpret and affirm black folk experience was 'one of the most important tasks for Negro poetry'. His commitment to this task informed a wide range of other literary and critical activities, including editorial work for the *Federal Writers' Project (1936–9), influential cultural surveys (*The Negro in American Fiction* and *Negro Poetry and Drama*, both 1937), and a landmark anthology, *The Negro Caravan* (1941). A further volume of his own poetry is *The Last Ride of Wild Bill* (1975); the early *No Hiding Place*, rejected by publishers in the 1930s on political grounds, finally appeared in *Collected Poems* (1980).

BROWN, Stewart (1951–), British poet and editor, born in Southampton, educated at Sussex University and University College, Aberystwyth. After teaching at schools and colleges in Britain, Jamaica, and Nigeria, he became a lecturer at the Centre for West African Studies in the University of Birmingham in 1988. Brown published numerous pamphlets before the appearance of *Zinder* (1986), his first substantial collection of poetry; the title poem, an incisive critique of post-colonial French North Africa, displays his characteristic ability to write from the intersection of personal experience and broad socio-cultural concerns. *Lugard's Bridge* (1989) frequently employs a fiercely sardonic wit in communicating his highly informed view of the shabby legacy of imperialism in Nigeria. The collection, which was widely acclaimed, also features disarmingly direct poems of familial affection and some radically experimental writing. Brown's extensive work as an editor includes the anthologies *Caribbean Poetry Now* (1984) and *Writers from Africa* (1989); *The Art of Derek Walcott* (1991), a collection of essays; and *The Art of E. K. Brathwaite* (1994).

Brown Girl, Brownstones, a novel by Paule *Marshall, published in 1959. This compassionate and richly layered novel relates the story of Selina Boyce, the daughter of Barbadian immigrants, and through her perspective, the story of her parents, Silla and Deighton. A gallery of minor portraits provides a panoramic view of black life in Brooklyn. Brought up by her hard-working, austere, and resilient mother,

Selina yearns for freedom, always aware of its negative aspects as embodied by her feckless, doomed father. Her love for her mother is underwritten by the double legacy of guilt and sacrifice she must bear, and the Caribbean roots she longs to recover. The novel works on several levels: as a feminist *bildungsroman*; as a study of the Caribbean immigrant experience in the context of the wider black American community; and as a loving tribute to the strength, resilience, and humour of Caribbean women.

Browning Version, The, a one-act play by Terence *Rattigan, first performed in 1948. It involves Arthur Crocker-Harris, once a brilliant classical scholar, now 'the Himmler of the Lower Fifth', a schoolmaster said to be 'shrivelled up inside like a nut'. He is forced to leave the school where he has long taught, denied a pension, and even asked to cede pride of place at Prize Day to a younger, more popular man. When a pupil gives him Robert Browning's version of Aeschylus's *Agamemnon*, he uncharacteristically breaks down, only to be told by his bitter and vindictive wife that the boy's present is self-serving. Her lover, another master, is horrified by the cruelty and injustice of this, and confesses the affair to Crocker-Harris, who replies that he has known about it all along. At the end he finds the strength to confront his humiliation and pain, and announces that he will exercise the privilege his seniority gives him at Prize Day. The play is generally felt to be one of Rattigan's most successful studies of loneliness and emotional failure.

BROWNJOHN, Alan (Charles) (1931–), British poet, born in Catford, South London, educated at Merton College, Oxford. After working as a schoolteacher from 1957 to 1965, he was a senior lecturer at Battersea College of Education until 1979, when he became a freelance writer. He was chairman of the Poetry Society from 1982 to 1988. He is one of the foremost poets to have been associated with the *Group. His first substantial publication as a poet was *The Railings* (1961); succeeding volumes have included *Sandgrains on a Tray* (1969), *A Song of Good Life* (1975), *A Night in the Gazebo* (1980), *Collected Poems 1952–1986* (1988), *The Observation Car* (1990), and *In the Cruel Arcade* (1994). On the cover-notes to *The Railings*, Brownjohn identified the principal concerns of his poetry as 'love, politics, culture, time', themes which have remained central throughout his work. The socialist beliefs informing much of his verse are inseparable from the individuality and humanity with which he conducts his investigations of the quality of life. Contemplative, documentary, and satirical modes are characteristic of his writing, which is noted for its technical scrupulousness, intelligence, and understated wit. The best-known of his numerous books for children is *Brownjohn's Beasts* (1970). His first novel, *The Way You Tell Them*, subtitled 'a yarn of the nineties', appeared in 1990. Among his other publications is a version of Goethe's *Torquato Tasso* (1985) and the critical study *Philip Larkin* (1975).

BRUNNER, John (Kilian) (1934–), British *science fiction writer, born in Oxfordshire. From *Galactic Storm* (1952) onward he was a prolific producer of *space operas, among the best of which are *The Atlantic Abomination* (1960), *The Day of the Star Cities* (1965), and *The Long Result* (1965). At the same time, novels such as *The Brink* (1959), *The Whole Man* (1964), and *Squares of the City* (1965) were more ambitious. Four subsequent novels remain his main accomplishment: *Stand on Zanzibar* (1968) dealt with overpopulation in the near future; *The Jagged Orbit* (1969) encompassed racial politics; *The Sheep Look Up* (1972) focused on pollution; and *The Shockwave Rider* (1975) addressed the information revolution. Varyingly experimental in form, argumentative, and urgent, these four dystopias utilized science fiction conventions to address current dilemmas. Later work includes *The Great Steamboat Race* (1983), which affectionately recreated life on the Mississippi.

BRUTUS, Dennis (1924–), South African poet, teacher, and political activist, born in Salisbury, Rhodesia, educated at Fort Hare University College, and the University of Witwatersrand, where his studies were cut short by arrest in 1963 for activities against racialism in South African sport. He was frequently in prison or under house arrest for the next few years and finally left South Africa in 1966. He has served as Director of the World Campaign for the Release of South African prisoners, and President of the South African Non-Racial Open Competition for Olympic Sports, in which capacity he was largely responsible for the exclusion of South Africa from the Olympic Games. His first collection, *Sirens, Knuckles, Boots* (1963), published in Nigeria, when Brutus was in prison, is charged with erotic tension and political protest. Brutus characterizes himself as a quixotic troubadour in perhaps his best-known poem, an untitled Petrarcan sonnet, the emphasis being on his sense of danger, both personal and political. *Letters to Martha* (1968) is addressed to his sister-in-law, and so titled because as a banned writer in South Africa his poems could only be published as 'letters' from prison. Brutus's visits to Algeria and China resulted in *Poems from Algiers* and *China Poems*, both published in 1970. *A Simple Lust* (1973) collects poems from previous volumes, and others previously unpublished. Later collections include *Strains* (1975) and *Stubborn Hope* (1978).

BRYDEN, Bill (William Campbell Rough) (1942–), British playwright and director, born in Greenock, Renfrewshire, where he was educated at the High School; he worked with Scottish Television before becoming assistant director at the Belgrade Theatre, Coventry, in 1965. After periods at the Royal Court Theatre, London, and the Lyceum Theatre, Edinburgh, he joined the Royal National Theatre as associate director in 1975. From 1984 to 1993 he was Head of Drama for BBC Scotland. Bryden's best-known plays are *Willie Rough* (1972), a dramatization of the political fervour on Clydeside during the First World

War, and *Benny Lynch: Scenes from a Short Life* (1974), which deals with the career of the Scottish World Flyweight Boxing Champion. His other plays include *Old Movies* (1976), and *Civilians* (1980). His screenplay for *The Long Riders* (1980) was acclaimed for bringing new vitality to the *Western idiom. *Ill Fares the Land* (1982) and *The Holy City* (1985) are among the films he has written and directed.

BRYHER, pseudonym of Annie Winifred ELLERMAN (1894–1983), British novelist and philanthropist; born in Kent, she grew up in London. She was patron of many *Modernist writers, including Dorothy *Richardson, Djuna *Barnes, Edith *Sitwell, and Hilda *Doolittle (H.D) with whom she had a close relationship from 1918. In 1921, Bryher, a lesbian, entered a marriage of convenience with Robert *McAlmon and funded his Contact Editions. Two autobiographical novels, *Development* (1920) and *Two Selves* (1923), explore her artistic development and sexual identity. In 1927 she divorced McAlmon and married Kenneth Macpherson, with whom she founded *Close Up* (1927–33), the 'first journal of film criticism as art'; contributors included H.D., Gertrude *Stein, and Dorothy Richardson. She is best known for her historical novels, which include *The Fourteenth of October* (1952), *The Players' Boy* (1953), and *The Coin of Carthage* (1963). Other books include *Amy Lowell: A Critical Appreciation* (1918), *Film Problems of Soviet Russia* (1929), and *Beowulf* (1956), as well as memoirs, two volumes of poetry, and travel writings.

BUCHAN, John, 1st Baron Tweedsmuir (1875–1940), Scottish writer, diplomat, and politician, born in Perth, the eldest son of a minister in the Free Church of Scotland; he was educated at Glasgow University and Brasenose College, Oxford, where he was President of the Union, took a first in Greats, won the Stanhope history and the Newdigate poetry prizes, published a novel (*Sir Quixote of the Moors*, 1895) and a volume of essays (*Scholar Gypsy*, 1896), and contributed to *The Yellow Book*. Later he read for the Bar, and from 1901 to 1903 was in South Africa on the staff of Lord Milner, the High Commissioner. On his return he began a long association with Nelson's, the Scottish publishers, was a lieutenant-colonel in the Intelligence Corps during the First World War, and then Director of Intelligence in Beaverbrook's new Ministry of Information. He sat in the House of Commons as Member for the Scottish Universities during the 1920s, and was Governor-General of Canada (1935–40). His works are voluminous: the non-fiction includes lives of Montrose (1913, revised 1928), Scott (1932), Cromwell (1934), and Augustus (1937), and a four-volume history of the First World War. He is best remembered, however, for his adventure stories, which he termed 'shockers', most of which feature a recurring group of interconnected heroes (Richard Hannay, Sandy Arbuthnot, Peter Pienaar, Edward Leithen, etc.); the first, which introduces Hannay, is *The Thirty-Nine Steps* (1915; filmed by Alfred Hitchcock, 1935), written while convalescing at Broadstairs. Others include *Prester John* (1910; US title *The Great Diamond Pipe*), *Greenmantle* (1916), *The Three Hostages* (1924), *John Macnab* (1925), and *Sick Heart River* (1941; US title *Mountain Meadow*). Buchan himself, however, preferred his historical novels: they include *The Path of the King* (1921), *Midwinter* (1923), and *The Blanket of the Dark* (1931); *Witch Wood* (1927), set in his native Tweeddale in the seventeenth century, is probably the best. There is an autobiography, *Memory Hold-the-Door* (1940; US title *Pilgrim's War: An Essay in Recollection*) and a life by Janet Adam Smith (1965). See D. Daniell, *The Interpreter's House: A Critical Assessment of John Buchan* (1975).

BUCK, Pearl S(ydenstricker) (1892–1973), American novelist, born in West Virginia. She lived in China until her early middle age which gave her a unique, double perspective which was reflected in her most famous works of fiction. Her first novel, *East Wind: West Wind* (1930), was followed by *The Good Earth* (1931; Pulitzer Prize), the first volume of the saga of a Chinese family, written in the poetic rhythms and lyrical prose of the Bible; *Sons* (1932) and *A House Divided* (1935) completed the trilogy. *The Mother* (1934) and *Dragon Seed* (1942) are considered to be the works for which she will be remembered. Buck was awarded the Nobel Prize in 1938. Much of her most passionate work, including *Imperial Woman* (1954; a study in fiction of the Empress Tzu Hsi), *Letter from Peking* (1957), and *The Three Daughters of Madame Lian* (1969), continued to be set in China but for the vast majority of her readers her message was universal. Buck successfully employed an American setting in such popular classics as *Portrait of a Marriage* (1945), *Voices in the House* (1953), *The Time is Noon* (1967; a deeply autobiographical work), and *The Goddess Abides* (1972). Buck was famous for her humanitarian commitment to improved East–West relations and the cause of children of mixed race and war orphans.

BUCKLER, Ernest (1908–84), Canadian novelist, born in Dalhousie West, Nova Scotia, educated at Dalhousie University and the University of Toronto. His most famous work is his best-selling first novel, *The Mountain and the Valley* (1952), a seminal contribution to the literature of Maritime Canada. Told mainly in flashback, it is a *Kunstlerroman* which focuses on the figure of an unfulfilled artist and his romantic desire for a life beyond the farming community in which he grows up. *Ox Bells and Fireflies* (1968) is an imaginative memoir of Buckler's childhood, which celebrates a bygone rural era in a finely wrought style that links physical experiences and subjective speculation very effectively. Buckler also published a second novel, *The Cruelest Month* (1963); *The Rebellion of Young David* (1975), a collection of short stories; and *Whirligig* (1977), a book of humorous essays and poems.

BUCKLEY, Vincent (1925–89), Australian poet and critic, born in Romsey, Victoria, educated at Melbourne and Cambridge Universities. He is a poet and critic of considerable influence in Australia, not least in his strong sense of Irish ancestry and his involvement with the Catholic Church in Australia. Buckley's poetry engages an impressive range of concerns, from love to politics, horse-racing to history. Both of his first volumes, *The World's Flesh* (1954) and *Masters in Israel* (1961), explored the varying manifestations of love, human and divine, and the human embodiment of their relations; other collections are *Arcady and Other Places* (1966), *The Golden Builders and Other Poems* (1976), *Late Winter Child* (1979), and *Selected Poems* (1981). As a critic Buckley was instrumental in broadening the canon to include less 'traditional' Australian concerns: important collections are *Essays in Poetry: Mainly Australian* (1957), *Poetry and Morality* (1959), and *Poetry and the Sacred* (1968). The autobiography *Cutting Green Hay: Friendships, Movements and Cultural Conflicts in Australia's Great Decades* (1983) traced cultural post-war movements in Australia and Buckley's friendship with writers such as A. C. *Hope and James *McAuley. *Memory Ireland: Insights into the Contemporary Irish Condition* (1985) bore powerful witness to Buckley's increasing identification with the past and present of the country where he spent much time in later years, both in person and in the imagination. Posthumously published were *Last Poems* (1991) and *The Faber Book of Modern Australian Verse* (1991), with a thirty-page preface surveying Australian poetry from 1920 to 1980.

Buddha of Suburbia, The, see KUREISHI, HANIF.

BUKOWSKI, (Henry) Charles (1920–94), American poet, novelist, and short-story writer, born in Andernach, Germany, to a German mother and an American soldier; he was brought to Los Angeles as a small child. After attending Los Angeles City College he worked intermittently at a variety of unskilled jobs, most durably as a postman. He published stories in the mid-1940s, but his authentic writing career stemmed from a decade later when his poems, vigorously anti-academic and carrying an air of exclusion and embattlement, began appearing in *little magazines throughout the USA. Though clearly sharing certain concerns with the contemporaneous *Beat movement, his individualist ethos precluded formative contacts even with such loose literary groupings. Jon Edgar Webb's eclectic magazine *The Outsider* championed Bukowski's writing. His early chapbooks were followed by the full-length collections *It Catches My Heart in Its Hands* (1963) and *Crucifix in a Deathhand* (1965). Since becoming a full-time author in 1970, Bukowski's prolific output achieved an international readership. Among the most admired of his numerous volumes are *The Days Run Away like Wild Horses over the Hills* (1969); *Notes of a Dirty Old Man* (1973), a selection of his often scabrously funny underground newspaper columns; and *Burning in Water, Drowning in Flame* (1974), selected poems. Notable among his novels are *Post Office* (1971) and *Ham on Rye* (1982), the latter depicting his unruly adolescence during the Depression and thus a late addition to the Beat canon of revolt against Middle American values. Echoing Whitman, Bukowski's persona was disorderly, fleshy, and sensual, the predominant use of a first-person narrator seeking to create an impression of autobiographical immediacy and conversational spontaneity. His declared aim was to 'humanize' poetry, lowering the rhetorical tone by structurally simple language flavoured with slang and swear words, asides to the reader, and other humorous interjections. In his later years Bukowski's verse increasingly favoured the narrative mode, usually employing short lines replete with hardbitten or wise-cracking dialogue. Stories and poems in *Septuagenarian Stew* (1990) reflect his characteristic subject matters: painful relations with women and a brutal father; survival as a bum and self-taught writer in low-rent Los Angeles; gambling, sex, and drink; contemplation of death and ageing; defiant insistence on freedom and continued creation. At the time of his death Bukowski was the most widely read contemporary American author in translation. His final books were *The Last Night of the Earth Poems* (1992), *Run with the Hunted: A Charles Bukowski Reader* (1993), and *Screams from the Balcony: Selected Letters* (1993). *Pulp*, a spoof detective novel, appeared posthumously in 1994. *Hank: The Life of Charles Bukowski*, by Neeli Cherkovski, appeared in 1991; *Against the American Dream: Essays on Charles Bukowski*, by Russell Harrison, was published in 1994.

Bulletin, an Australian journal, founded in 1880 by J. F. Archibald and John Haynes. In 1961 it was sold to Consolidated Press and became more of a newspaper, although literature was reintroduced in a quarterly supplement in 1980, edited by Geoffrey Dutton. In its early stages the *Bulletin* contained a mixture of humour, illustrations, cartoons, political comment, and sports news. The new element in *Bulletin* was the invitation for the readership to contribute. As a result material from a bush readership began to appear; underlying the humour, which was a dominant note in the early years, was a sense of the grimness of bush life, accompanied by a radical hostility to harshness and repression in the social system. Paradoxically, a separate Red Page was created as a forum for writers, and over a period of seventy years the journal published works from the most famous in Australian letters. The editorial requirement of 'brevity, originality, realism and dramatic force' elicited the greatest of Australian short stories, and it was in the pages of the *Bulletin* that Australian literature's first major argument, between the realism of Henry *Lawson and the romanticism of Banjo *Paterson, was rehearsed in detail.

BULLINS, Ed (1935–), American playwright, born in Philadelphia, educated at Los Angeles City College and San Francisco State College. He was associate director of New Lafayette Theatre, New York (1967–73), editor of *Black Theatre* magazine (1969–74), and became producing director of Surviving Theatre, New York, from 1974. His plays are explorations of the constraints of ghetto life, and strategies of liberation, among African-Americans. One of his best plays, *The Duplex: A Love Fable in Four Movements* (prod. New York, 1970, pub. 1971), focuses on a young man, Steven Benson, who struggles to forge his own identity and liberate his energies, though threatened by the temptations of sexual and alcoholic oblivion. *The Wine Time* (prod. New York, 1968, pub. 1969) is the first of a projected twenty-play cycle about African-Americans entitled *20th. Century Cycle*. Omnibus editions of his many plays include *Five Plays* (1969), *Four Dynamite Plays* (1971), and *The Theme is Blackness* (1973). The latter contains the title play (prod. San Francisco, 1966); *Dialect Determinism* (prod. San Francisco, 1965), which argues against dogmatic militancy; and a few others, including very short but highly ingenious 'black revolutionary' commercials. Other books include *The Hungered One* (1971; short stories), *To Raise the Dead and Foretell the Future* (1971; verse), and *The Reluctant Rapist* (1973; a novel). Bullins was awarded the New York Drama Critics Circle award in 1975 and 1977.

BULLOCK, Alan (Louis Charles) (1914–), British historian, born in Bradford, educated at Wadham College, Oxford. He began his academic career at Oxford as a fellow of New College in 1945. He was instrumental in the formation of St Catherine's College, of which he became Founding Master in 1960. From 1967 to 1973 he was Vice-Chancellor of Oxford University. *Hitler: A Study in Tyranny* (1952) gained him an international reputation and has remained highly valued as an account of Hitler's career. The first two volumes of his *The Life and Times of Ernest Bevin* appeared in 1960 and 1967 respectively; to complete the third, *Ernest Bevin, Foreign Secretary* (1983), Bullock was obliged to wait until restrictions on the availability of many critical documents were removed. The work is regarded as a major contribution to twentieth-century British and international political history. Notable among his other publications are *The Humanist Tradition in the West* (1985) and *Hitler and Stalin: Parallel Lives* (1991). He was created Baron Bullock in 1976.

BULLOCK, Shan (1865–1935), Northern Irish novelist, born in Crom, Co. Fermanagh, educated at Farra School, Co. Westmeath; he was the son of a prosperous Protestant farmer and a bailiff to a large Fermanagh estate. He grew up with first-hand experience of the effects of economic and sectarian division in rural Ulster, an experience he reflected in most of his novels, including *By Thrasna River: The Story of a Townland* (1895), *The Squireen* (1903), and *The Loughsiders* (1924). After leaving school, Bullock went to London and spent the rest of his life working for the civil service. He recorded aspects of what he saw as a numbing and emasculating existence in his novel *Robert Thorne: The Story of a London Clerk* (1907). Bullock's novels are conspicuously autobiographical, and just as Robert Thorne longs to return to Ulster, his creator consistently wrote about the land and the farmers of his native Fermanagh. An exception is *Thomas Andrews, Shipbuilder* (1912), his novel concerning the building of the *Titanic* in the Belfast shipyards. Benedict *Kiely has noted that Bullock was the last Irish writer to witness a rural community whose life revolved around 'the Big House', a privilege which Bullock exploits valuably in his autobiography, *After Sixty Years* (1931).

BUNTING, Basil (1900–85), British poet, born at Scotswood, Northumberland, educated at Quaker schools in Yorkshire and Berkshire and at the London School of Economics. He became Ford Madox *Ford's assistant on the **Transatlantic Review* in Paris in 1923 and was subsequently a journalist in London. In 1929 he joined Ezra *Pound, whom he had known in Paris, at Rapollo in Italy, remaining there until 1933. Bunting's first volume of poetry, *Redimiculum Matteïarum*, was published in Milan in 1930. W. B. *Yeats referred to him as one of Pound's 'more savage disciples'; the compression of language, sense of the autonomy of poetic form, and the allusive habits of his verse indicate the debt to Pound he acknowledges in his introduction to his *Collected Poems* (1968; revised 1978 and 1990). After interludes in the Canary Islands and Britain, during the Second World War he was an interpreter with the RAF in Persia, where he remained as vice-consul at Isfahan until 1952. *The Spoils* (1965) reflects his wartime experiences. His interest in Persian literature led him to incorporate elements from the Persian epic *Shah-nama* (lit. 'Book of Kings') into the central section of **Briggflatts* (1966), the poem which made him well-known in Britain. *Poems* (1950) had been well received in the USA; on his return to Britain in 1952 he was, however, effectively unheard of and worked until 1966 on Newcastle's *Evening Chronicle*. Tom *Pickard stimulated British interest in Bunting's work, arranging for publication of *The Spoils* in 1965; *Loquitur* (1965), a collection of early poems, and *First Book of Odes* (1966) followed, preparing for the rapid establishment of his considerable reputation with *Briggflatts* and *Collected Poems*. Donald *Davie's *Under Briggflatts* (1989) argues for Bunting's central importance to British poetry of the previous thirty years as a master of the modernist idiom who remained rooted in the cultural and syntactical traditions of English verse. His other works include *Version of Horace* (1972) and *Uncollected Poems* (edited by Richard Caddell, 1991). See OBJECTIVIST POETRY.

BURCHFIELD, Robert (William) (1923–), New Zealand lexicographer, born in Wanganui, near Wellington, New Zealand, educated at Victoria University College, Wellington, and at Magdalen College, Oxford. After lecturing at Magdalen and Christ Church Colleges, he was appointed to the editorship of the new *Supplement to the Oxford English Dictionary* in 1957. From 1971 to 1984 he was the Chief Editor of Oxford English Dictionaries. The four volumes of the *Supplement* appeared in 1972, 1976, 1982, and 1986. He subsequently devoted himself to his work as senior research fellow at St Peter's

College. His other works as a lexicographer, grammarian, and philologist include *The Spoken Language as an Art Form* (1981), *The English Language* (1985), and *Studies in Lexicography* (1987). Although he considers English to be 'at an uneasy stage of its development', he retains a fundamentally optimistic view of the language's capacity to retain its richness and flexibility throughout increasingly rapid processes of expansion and change. *Unlocking the English Language* (1989) contains his T. S. Eliot Memorial Lectures delivered in 1988, together with eight additional essays. *Points of View: Aspects of Present Day English* (1992) discusses varieties of contemporary spoken English.

BURGESS, Anthony, pseudonym of John Anthony Burgess WILSON (1917–93), British novelist, composer, and critic, born in Manchester into a Catholic family, educated at the University of Manchester. An accomplished musician, Burgess maintained his interest in music throughout his varied career, composing orchestral works as well as those in more popular forms, including a musical version of Joyce's **Ulysses* (*Blooms of Dublin*, performed in 1982). After serving with the Royal Army Medical Corps in the Second World War, he was a teacher for some years. During 1954–60 he served in the Colonial Service as an education officer in Malaya and Borneo, an experience in the Far East which formed the background for his first three published novels, *Time for a Tiger* (1956), *The Enemy in the Blanket* (1958), and *Beds in the East* (1959), published together as *The Malayan Trilogy* (1964). After a mistaken medical diagnosis, giving him only one year to live, he wrote five novels in quick succession, including *The Right to an Answer* (1960), *The Doctor is Sick* (1960), *The Worm and the Ring* (1961), and *Devil of a State* (1961), in order to provide an estate for his wife. His best-known novel, *A *Clockwork Orange* (1962; filmed by Stanley Kubrick, 1971), demonstrated his linguistic virtuosity in its dystopian vision of an authoritarian near-future Britain. It was followed by many others, displaying a variety of different fictional modes, including *The Wanting Seed* (1962), a work of *science fiction; *Honey for the Bears* (1963), a satire about the Cold War; *Nothing like the Sun* (1964), a speculation on the identity of Shakespeare's Dark Lady; *Tremor of Intent* (1966), an elaborate thriller; *MF* (1971), about a young man's pilgrimage to the shrine of a celebrated poet; *The Napoleon Symphony* (1974), about Beethoven; and *ABBA ABBA* (1977), about the last days of John Keats. Later novels include **Earthly Powers* (1980), *The Kingdom of the Wicked* (1985), dealing with the early years of Christianity, and *Any Old Iron* (1989), about a twentieth-century quest for King Arthur's sword Excalibur. Burgess's last novel, *A Dead Man in Deptford* (1993), a rich evocation of Elizabethan London centring on the life and times of Christopher Marlowe, was considered by some critics to be his best. Among his most popular works are his comic novels tracing the adventures of the irascible middle-aged poet Mr Enderby, including *Inside Mr Enderby* (1963), *Enderby Outside* (1968), *The Clockwork Testament* (1974), and *Enderby's Dark Lady* (1984), which show the influence of James *Joyce and are considered by his peer, Gore *Vidal, to be even finer than the comedies of *Waugh. His critical works include studies of Shakespeare (1970), Joyce (*Here Comes Everybody*, 1965; *Joysprick*, 1973), D. H. *Lawrence (1985), and *Mozart and the Wolf Gang* (1991), an irreverent portrait of Mozart. He also published collections of essays, including *Urgent Copy* (1968), which contains writings on Waugh, *Shaw, Joyce, *Beckett, and *Greene; *Homage to QWERTYUIOP* (1986), a collection of his reviews; *Ninety-Nine Novels* (1984), a study of post-war fiction in Britain; an autobiography published in two parts as *Little Wilson and Big God* (1987) and *You've Had Your Time* (1990); an authoritative, idiosyncratic treatment of the nature of language, *A Mouthful of Air* (1992); and the posthumously published novel in verse, *Byrne* (1995). A prodigious intellect and polymath, with a cosmopolitan grasp of culture, Burgess contributed much to the world of letters.

BURKE, Kenneth (Duva) (1897–93), American critic, born in Pittsburgh, Pennsylvania, educated at Ohio State and Columbia Universities. Having established a reputation with his exotic short stories in *The White Oxen* (1924), during the late 1920s he gained wide notice for the critical articles containing his innovative theories of literary form which appeared in the **Dial* and elsewhere. He subsequently held numerous posts as a lecturer, notably at Bennington College, where he taught literary theory from 1943 to 1961. *Counter-Statement* (1931) and *Permanence and Change: An Anatomy of Purpose* (1935) won acclaim for the remarkable scope of his philosophical explications of the socio-cultural significance of artistic creation. *Attitudes towards History* (two volumes, 1937), an ambitious psychological and ethical evaluation of historical developments, was followed by *The Philosophy of Literary Form* (1941), *A Grammar of Motives* (1945), and *A Rhetoric of Motives* (1950); in these works Burke's proposition that 'man is a symbol-using animal' forms a basis for linguistic, philosophical, and psychological analyses of the interactions between literature, language, belief, and action. His later publications include *The Rhetoric of Religion* (1961), the collected essays of *Language as Symbolic Form* (1966), *Dramatism and Development* (1972), and *On Symbols and Society* (edited by J. R. Gusfield, 1989), a selection from Burke's more sociologically oriented writings. *Collected Poems* (1968) includes many of Burke's 'flowerishes', provocatively aphoristic pieces presented in extravagantly inventive calligraphic forms. In his poetry the energetic idiosyncrasy characterizing his other works is unbridled. Among his other books are *Towards a Better Life* (1932), a 'series of declamations or epistles' in fictional forms, and the collected short stories of *The Complete White Oxen* (1968).

BURNS, Alan (1929–), British novelist, born in London. He trained as a barrister before turning to writing, and later taught creative writing at the University of Minnesota. His works are experimental in form and bleak in outlook, depicting a sterile society on the brink of chaos. His first novel, *Europe after the Rain* (1965), whose title is taken from Max Ernst, exhibits a dual fascination with European *Modernism and American culture. It was followed by *Celebrations* (1965); *Babel* (1970), whose aphoristic nature reflects the fragmentation of the world which is being described; *Dreamerika!* (1972); *The Day Daddy Died* (1981); and *Revolutions of the Night* (1986), whose title is also taken from Ernst. Burns was a friend of the writers B. S. *Johnson and Ann *Quin and, although all three would have disclaimed being part of a literary movement, there are similarities of theme and preoccupation in their work.

BURNS, John Horne (1916–53), American novelist, born in Andover, Massachusetts, educated at Harvard. Burns's reputation has grown considerably since his death at the age of 36 and his first novel, *The Gallery* (1947), is now recognized as one of the great American novels of the Second World War. After service in military intelligence in the US Army in North Africa and Italy, Burns returned to the USA but subsequently took up residence in Italy. *The Gallery* reconstructs life around the Galleria Umberto in Allied occupied Naples at the end of the war through a series of what Burns calls 'portraits'. The novel is episodic and fragmentary in a manner that echoes that of John *Dos Passos, but the confrontation between American and Italian experience, both cultural and moral, evinces striking affinities with the treatment of the 'international theme' in the fiction of Henry *James. His later novels are *Lucifer with a Book* (1949), a largely satirical account of an American private school, and *A Cry of Children* (1952), a love story.

BURROUGHS, Edgar Rice (1875–1950), American writer of romantic *science fiction and *fantasy adventure novels, born in Chicago, educated at Phillips Academy, Andover and Michigan Military Academy. He is best known for his tales of Tarzan, who appeared in twenty-one novels from *Tarzan of the Apes* (1914) to *Tarzan and the Madman* (1964). The figure of Tarzan became familiar through film, radio, comic-book, and television incarnations. Several of Burroughs's science fiction novels are set on Mars and Venus, and include *A Princess of Mars* (1917) and its sequels. His rich imagination influenced later writers such as R. *Bradbury and M. *Moorcock.

BURROUGHS, William S(eward) (1914–), American novelist, born in St Louis, educated at Harvard. Burroughs served as the basis for the character of Old Bull in Kerouac's **On The Road*. Despite having close relations with the Columbia circle who formed the early core of the *Beat Generation, he later disclaimed any real affinity with this aesthetic movement, seeing his work as standing in a more 'European' line of experimentalism. He presents a life of aimless drifting, working as a journalist, private detective, and bartender from 1936 to 1944, when he became addicted to morphine. He moved to Mexico City in 1949, and in 1951 tragically shot his wife in a shooting accident, a matter dealt with indirectly in *Queer* (1986), a homosexual romance written just after the events in Mexico City. Several years of travel in South America and Morocco followed, where his first novel, *Junkie* (1953), was completed under the pseudonym of William Lee. In a painfully realistic portrayal of the life of an addict, *Junkie* tells the story of drug addicts' involvement with the underworld. It was in this work that Burroughs made the notorious statement that addiction was 'a biological need like water' and then proceeded to analyse the whole of human society from the perspective of this insight. The themes of addiction and totalitarianism continued to dominate his work even after his own withdrawal from heroin addiction in the late 1950s. From the masses of notes written whilst living in Tangier in 1953–8 came the notorious *The *Naked Lunch* (1959). Several other novels derive from the Tangier notes, all of which explore the techniques of *The Naked Lunch*, by introducing the 'cut-up' and 'fold-in' methods of collage writing. *The Naked Lunch*, *The Soft Machine* (1961), whose writing refers to the human brain, *The Ticket that Exploded* (1962), and *Nova Express* (1964) form a tetralogy which explores the activities of the Nova Mob in a science fiction world in which the addictions are found to be the work of the Mob. Other works produced at this time include *The Exterminator* (1960); *Minutes To Go: Poems* (1960, written with Sinclair Beiles and Gregory *Corso); *Dead Fingers Talk* (1963), a compilation of previous novels; and *The Yage Letters* (1963), with Allen *Ginsberg. The 1970s saw the publication of *Speed* (1970); *The Wild Boys: A Book of the Dead* (1971), about a group of homosexual hashish smokers who travel through time and space beyond social control; and *Port of Saints* (1973). There was a later resurgence in his writing, with the trilogy *Cities of the Red Night* (1981), in which characters from *The Wild Boys* return; *The Place of Dead Roads* (1983), set in the 1890s and featuring Will Seward Hall, an author of Westerns; and *The Western Lands* (1985). In 1990 he recorded his first record and published *Ghost of a Chance*, a novella in the territory of *Cities of the Red Night*. *My Education: A Book of Dreams* (1995) pays homage to Burroughs' Mentor Brion Gysin and others. *The Letters of William S. Burroughs 1945–1959*, edited by Oliver Harris, appeared in 1993. A biography, *Literary Outlaw: The Life and Times of William S. Burroughs* (1988), was written by Ted Morgan. The best critical introduction to his work remains *William Burroughs: The Algebra of Need* (1970) by Eric Mottram. Maintaining a huge cult following, Burroughs has exercised a considerable influence as an avant-garde theorist and forerunner of counter-cultures in rock music, film, and writing.

BURTON, Miles, see RHODE, JOHN.

BUTLER, (Frederick) Guy (1918–), South African poet and playwright, born in Cradock, Cape Province, educated at Rhodes University and

Brasenose College, Oxford. He was Professor of English at Rhodes University, Grahamstown (1950–78). Versatile in technique, and just as open to African as to European influences, Butler is equally proficient in lyric, meditative, and narrative modes of poetry. His powerfully moving elegy 'In Memoriam, J. A. R., Drowned, East London' has much in common with traditional African dirges. Volumes of poetry include *Stranger to Europe* (1952; enlarged edition 1960), *South of the Zambezi* (1966), *On First Seeing Florence* (1968), *Selected Poems* (1972), and *Songs and Ballads* (1978). Plays include *Take Root and Die* (1970), which was produced in Grahamstown in 1966, and *Cape Charade* (1968). Butler has also written two volumes of autobiography, *Karoo Morning* (1978) and *Bursting World* (1983). Together with Christopher Mann, he also edited *A New Book of South African Verse in English* (1979).

BUTLER, Marilyn (Speers) (1937–), British scholar and critic, born in Kingston-upon-Thames, London, educated at St Hilda's College, Oxford. In 1986 she became King Edward VII Professor of English Literature at Cambridge University. Her reputation as a specialist in the literature of the late eighteenth and early nineteenth centuries was established with *Maria Edgeworth* (1972), the fullest available biography of that author; *Jane Austen and the War of Ideas* (1975), *Peacock Displayed* (1979), and *Romantics, Rebels, and Reactionaries* (1981) are notable for their detailed examination of the social, cultural, and political climates of the period. Throughout much of the 1980s she was occupied with Janet Todd in editing the seven volumes of *The Works of Mary Wollstonecraft* (1989); Butler's other works of editorship include *Burke, Paine, Godwin, and the Revolution Controversy* (1984), an anthology of political writings, and a new edition of Mary Shelley's *Frankenstein* (1994), based on the original 1818 text.

BUTLER, Octavia (1947–), American *science fiction writer, born in Los Angeles, educated at Pasadena City College and California State University at Los Angeles. She received Hugo Awards for her short story 'Speech Sounds' and her novelette 'Bloodchild' in 1984 and 1985. Butler's novels incorporate African mythology, urban realism, and spiritual exegeses into tales of aliens, genetic mutation, and telepathy. Her heroes are strong and intelligent African and African-American females and her characters frequently strive to break away from the hierarchical restrictions of their lives towards a better world of intelligence and tolerance. Among her novels are the 'Patternist' series, including *Patternmaster* (1976), *Mind of My Mind* (1977), and *Wild Seed* (1980), which concern a community of telepaths and the roles played by genetics, gender, and race in the sustainment of this system; the 'Xenogenesis' series, including *Dawn* (1987), *Adulthood Rites* (1988), and *Imago* (1989), which details the consequences of crossbreeding between an alien race and the few human beings left alive following a nuclear holocaust; and *Parable of the Sower* (1993), which presents a twenty-first century world in the midst of disintegration, and a young African-American woman's search for a place where she and a community of believers might create a new society. See UTOPIA AND ANTI-UTOPIA.

BUTLER, Robert Olen (1945–), American novelist and short-story writer, born in Granite City, Illinois, educated at Northwestern University and the University of Iowa. Butler spent 1971 in Vietnam as a Vietnamese linguist while working for the US army military intelligence. His first novel, *The Alleys of Eden* (1981), introduced his three main themes of sexual obsession, cultural displacement, and the problematic legacy of Vietnam, the latter being a touchstone for many of his subsequent books. *A Good Scent from a Strange Mountain* (1992; Pulitzer Prize, 1993) is an interconnected series of stories concentrating on the attempt by Southern Vietnamese expatriates to integrate themselves into American culture; exquisitely written and moving, the book adds a vital and usually ignored dimension to American Vietnam fiction. Although the relative paucity of references to North Vietnam is noticeable, it is evident that Butler was uniquely qualified to look beyond the boundaries of his own culture. In its concentration on the details of sexual obsession, *They Whisper* (1994) expands on the ground covered by his first novel and offers a prose style even more intimate with the fevered imaginings implicit in its choice of subject matter. Butler became a professor at McNeese State University in Louisiana.

BUTLER, Samuel (1835–1902), British novelist, satirist, and speculative writer, born at Langar, Nottinghamshire, educated at St John's College, Cambridge. Renouncing the ecclesiastical traditions of his family, he went to New Zealand in 1859. His letters to his parents, which provide a vivid record of life on a sheep-station, were published by his father in 1863 as *A First Year in Canterbury Settlement*. His articles for the New Zealand press included 'Darwin among the Machines', out of which *Erewhon* (1872) later developed. Having returned to Britain in 1864, he settled in London and devoted himself to painting; however, discouraged by lack of success, he renewed his activity as a writer. *The Fair Haven* (1873), a drily ironic review of rationalist objections to the miraculous elements in Christianity, was announced as the work of 'the late John Pickard Owen'. *Life and Habit* (1878), *Luck or Cunning?* (1886), and other works sustain his critique of Darwin's theory of natural selection, which, he argued, failed to account for the functions of memory and volition in the processes of evolution. Among his other publications are *The Authoress of The Odyssey* (1897), purporting to prove that a young woman wrote the work, and *Shakespeare's Sonnets Reconsidered* (1899), which claims that the poems relate to a liaison with a young man of low character. Frequent travels in northern Italy gave rise to his writings on topography and art in *Alps and Sanctuaries of Piedmont and the Canton Ticino* (1881) and *Ex Voto* (1888). **Erewhon Revisited* was published in 1901 with the assistance of George Bernard *Shaw, on whom Butler's ideas made a deep impression. His hostility towards Victorian religious, social, and familial conventions found its strongest expression in *The *Way of All Flesh* (1903). His close friend Henry Festing Jones arranged the publication of *Seven Sonnets and a Psalm of Montreal* (1904) and, with A. T. Bartholomew, edited the twenty volumes of Butler's *Works* (1923–6). Butler may be accounted the principal progenitor of the widespread reaction against Victorian values among British authors in the first decades of the twentieth century. The first volume of Hans Peter Breur's complete edition of the *Note-Books*, which reveal the extraordinary scope of his interests, appeared in 1984. Peter Raby's *Samuel Butler* appeared in 1991.

BUZO, Alexander (John) (1944–), Australian dramatist, born in Sydney, educated at the University of New South Wales. *Three Plays* (1973) contains *Norm and Ahmed* (1969), *Rooted* (1969), and *the Roy Murphy Show* (1971), the best-known of his earlier Absurdist treatments of alienating conflicts between the individual and society. The Brechtian historical play *Macquarie* (1971) marks the closer approach to naturalistic realism which is sustained without the sacrifice of experimentation in *Tom* (1972), *Coralie Landsdowne Says No* (1974), and *Martello Towers* (1976); these, with Buzo's other plays of the 1970s, dramatize critical examinations of social and cultural values in contemporary Australia. *Big River* (1980) and *The Marginal Farm* (1981), published together in 1985, centre on the quest for personal viability in a period of accelerating change in Australia. His other plays include *Batman's Beach-head* (1973) and *Shellcove Road* (1989). Among Buzo's other publications are the humorous novels *The Search for Harry Allway* (1985) and *Prue Flies North* (1991), and *Tautology* (1981), a study of Australian English.

BYATT, A(ntonia) S(usan) (1936–), British novelist and critic, born in Sheffield, educated at The Mount School, York and Newnham College, Cambridge. Among several academic posts she has been a lecturer at University College, London; she has also travelled widely as a lecturer for the British Council. Her first novel, *Shadow of a Sun* (1964), describing young Anna Severell's division in loyalties between her novelist father and one of his admiring critics, already showed an intense understanding of the creative processes. *The Game* (1967) is a powerful study of the relationship of two sisters who in childhood shared an imaginative game, based on Arthurian legend, which has conditioned their subsequent lives. Byatt's ambitious novel sequence about a family in the north of England concerns the Potters, whose emotional and mental lives not only reflect important cultural tensions in English society but can be regarded as metaphors for abiding human conflicts. The first volume, *The Virgin in the Garden* (1978), set in North Yorkshire, mainly takes place in the symbolically significant year of 1953 (the year of the Coronation of Elizabeth II) and focuses on the three children of the English master, Bill Potter. *Still Life* (1986) continues the development of the Potters and their associates; this time a drama about Van Gogh is in progress. *Sugar and Other Stories* (1987) contains 'The July Ghost', a moving account of a woman's difficulty in coming to terms with her loved son's early death; 'On the Day that E. M. Forster Died', with its meditation on the nature of fiction in society; and 'Sugar', in which the author reflects on her childhood and her father's death. *Possession* (1990; Booker Prize) is a large-scale but intricately worked 'romance' in which contemporary researchers uncover a hitherto unknown emotional relationship between two Victorian poets, Randolph Henry Ash (based on Browning) and Christabel LaMotte (based on Christina Rossetti); the author is as concerned with the lives of her twentieth-century characters as with the great Victorians themselves, whose poetry she gives us in passages of sustained intensity too considerable to be called 'pastiche'. She is also the author of *Degrees of Freedom* (1965), a study of the fiction of Iris *Murdoch, a major influence on Byatt, and of *Wordsworth and Coleridge in Their Time* (1970). In *Passions of the Mind: Selected Writings* (1991), Byatt pursues some of the ideas underpinning her own fiction, the work of the great Victorians and of several twentieth-century women writers. The pair of novellas *Angels and Insects* (1993) reflect her continuing interest in nineteenth-century themes. In *The Matisse Stories* (1993), Byatt evokes the colour and light for which the painter is famed. *The Djinn in the Nightingale's Eye* (1994) is a collection of fairy tales that play on the conventions of the genre. With Alan *Hollinghurst, Byatt co-edited *New Writing 4* (1995), an anthology of prose and verse presenting 'a multi-faceted picture of modern Britain', and with Ignes Sodre she is the co-author of *Imagining Characters: Conversations on Women Writers* (1995). Byatt was awarded the CBE in 1990. She is the sister of the novelist Margaret *Drabble.

By Grand Central Station I Sat down and Wept, a novel by Elizabeth *Smart, first published in 1945, but hardly noticed until it was reissued in 1966 (in paperback) when it was hailed by the critic Brigid *Brophy as one of the half dozen masterpieces of poetic prose in the world. It is the story of a *coup de foudre* between the narrator and a married man (based on the poet George *Barker). With its flashing metaphors, hypnotic cadences, and liturgical rhythm the form and theme unite in emotional intensity. More an extended prose poem than a novel, it has been criticized for its lyrical excess. In one of the most striking sections Smart contrasts the 'Song of Songs' from the Old Testament with day-to-day frustrations as the lovers attempt to cross state borders in the 1930s to find a place where adultery is not an illegal act. This hymn to sexual love is Elizabeth Smart's most memorable work.

BYRON, Robert (1905–41), British travel writer, born in Wembley, London, educated at Merton College, Oxford, where he cultivated the independent aesthetic values central to his writings. In his final undergraduate year he made the journey to Greece recorded in *Europe in the Looking-Glass* (1926), its buoyant tone anticipating the energetic style of later works. *The Station* (1928), dealing with the monasteries of Mount Athos, and *The Byzantine Achievement* (1929) advance his belief that classical Greek culture found its most mature realization in Byzantine art and architecture. During the early 1930s he travelled widely in India, Persia, Tibet, Russia, and elsewhere. He was drowned while making his way to Meshed as a newspaper correspondent after the ship on which he was travelling was torpedoed. *The Road to Oxiana* (1937), his most celebrated work, investigates the origins of Islamic architecture in the course of a journey from Italy to India; the book, which retains the vivid immediacy of the journals from which it was prepared, combines erudition and entertainment in a manner that influenced numerous succeeding travel writers. Byron's other publications include *An Essay on India* (1931) and *First Russia, then Tibet* (1933). His sister Lucy Butler edited his *Letters Home* (1991).

C

CABELL, James Branch (1879–1958), American novelist, born in Richmond, Virginia, educated at the College of William and Mary, Williamsburg, Virginia. Cabell enjoyed considerable critical and commercial success in the 1920s, largely as a result of the suppression by the Comstock Society of his seventh novel, **Jurgen: A Comedy of Justice* (1919). Between 1898 and 1902 he worked for various newspapers before beginning ten years of genealogical research in America and Europe. During these years he published his first novel, *The Eagle's Shadow* (1904), three volumes of short stories, and, in 1909, a second novel, *The Cords of Vanity*. With *The Cream of the Jest: A Comedy of Evasions* (1917, revised edition 1923) Cabell came to the attention of the influential critic Burton Rascoe and within a few years he numbered Joseph *Hergesheimer, Sinclair *Lewis, H. L. *Mencken, and Carl *Van Vechten among his many admirers. Both *Jurgen* and *The Cream of the Jest* belong to the 'Poictesme cycle', a series of eighteen linked works dealing with the idealized, mythical country of Poictesme, and centred on Dom Manuel, the founder of Poictesme, whose offspring people Cabell's novels. These works are notable for the fertility of Cabell's imagination and the floridity of his prose. Cabell set his face against both the realist and modernist tendencies in post-First World War American fiction, and consequently became an increasingly marginal figure, critics seeing little beyond whimsy and escapism in his fiction. His other works include the play *The Jewel Merchants* (1921), three volumes of verse, various volumes of short stories, essays, and recollections, and *Joseph Hergesheimer* (1920), a study of a close friend. Studies of his works include Edmund Wilson's 'The James Branch Cabell Case Reopened' (*The New Yorker*, 21 April 1956), and *James Branch Cabell* (1962) by Joe Lee Davis.

CABRERA INFANTE, G(uillermo) (1929–), Cuban novelist, born in Gibara, Oriente Province, educated at the School of Journalism in Cuba, the son of the founders of the Cuban Communist Party. Among other posts, he was director of the Cuban Film Institute and cultural attaché at the Cuban Embassy in Brussels, before leaving Cuba in 1965 and becoming a British subject. *Holy Smoke* (1985), a wittily surreal account of cigars, combines the historical, social, and economic paradoxes of the New World with excursions into Hollywood films; the book is characteristically mined with puns. His novels translated from Spanish include *Three Trapped Tigers* (1971) and *Infante's Inferno* (1984). Works translated by the author, with others, include *View of Dawn in the Tropics* (1988; translated with S. J. Levine), an impressionistic modern history of Cuba; *A Twentieth-Century Job* (1991; translated with Kenneth Hall), a collection of his early film criticism; *Writes of Passage* (1993; translated with J. Brookesmith and P. Boyars), containing short stories; and *Mea Cuba* (1994; translated with Kenneth Hall), a collection of strongly anti-Castro writings-in-exile from 1968 to 1993, and other pieces. Among his screenplays, written in English, are the Hollywood films *Vanishing Points* (1969) and *The Lost City* (1990).

CAGE, John (1912–92), American composer, author, and printmaker, born in Los Angeles; he studied music and composition under Arnold Schoenberg, and at the New School for Social Research, with Adolph Weiss. Cage also travelled and studied a variety of disciplines, including architecture, Dadaism, oriental philosophy, and noise music with Edgard Varèse. In 1944–6, he was the musical director for the Merce Cunningham Dance School in New York. He later collaborated with Merce Cunningham and the painter Robert Rauschenberg on the first famous 'happening' entitled 'Theater Piece', organized at the *Black Mountain College in 1952. Cage has always been a controversial avant-garde composer and a major figure in American music. Central to his musical aesthetics is the exploration of the relations between chance operations and abstract structural principles, but perhaps his most significant impact on writing experiments was his sense that language is, in itself, sound. His first significant book was *Silence: Lectures and Writing* (1961), which demonstrated a variety of experimental ideas and lectures on writing, music, ballet, Varèse, Satie, and Rauschenberg. After *A Year From Monday: New Lectures and Writings* (1967), he published *M: Writings '67–'72* (1973), which embraced essays and verbal games organized by a variety of abstract principles on such subjects as Dadaism and fungi. There followed *Empty Words* (1973), described as 'text-sound poetry', which worked in four movements of the gradual decomposition of words and sounds, slowly inviting the audience to recompose their own sounds. Sound for Cage always remained primarily social, and his experiments with language and sound have been hugely influential on writers of the Black Mountain School and *'Language Poets'. Other books and collected essays include *X: Writings '79–'82* (1983), *I–IV* (1990), *First: Sixth* (1990), and *Aerial Six-Seven: Art Is Either a Complaint or Do Something Else* (1991). He also published several collaborative works which include the *Poet's Encyclopaedia* (1980) with Charles *Bukowski, John *Ashbery, and Robert *Creeley, *The Guests Go in to Supper* (1986) with Robert Ashley and Yoko Ono, and *Mud Book: How To Make Pies and Cakes* (1986) with Lois Long.

CAHAN, Abraham (1860–1951), American novelist and journalist, born in Podberezy, Lithuania, educated at Vilna Teachers Institute and law school in New York City. Cahan emigrated to the USA in 1882 and became an important figure in the Yiddish-speaking community of the Lower East Side of New York. He co-edited *Neie Zeit*, a Yiddish socialist newspaper, and from 1891 to 1894 was editor of the *Arbiter Zeitung*, a radical weekly which offered imaginative literature about immigrant life and promoted the socialist cause in the USA. Cahan's first novel, *Yekl: A Tale of the New York Ghetto* (1896) concerned the Americanization of the Jewish immigrant, a theme he continued in *The Imported Bridegroom and Other Stories of the New York Ghetto* (1898). Encouraged by the novelist William Dean *Howells, Cahan's most important work of fiction, *The Rise of David Levinsky* (1917), is influenced by Howells's *The Rise of Silas Lapham* (1885); the novel charts the rise of its eponymous hero from his squalid origins to a position of great economic and social power in the New York clothing industry. In 1897 Cahan helped to establish the *Jewish Daily Forward* and used it, during the 1920s, to promote his socialist views, notably his support of the Bolshevik regime in the Soviet Union, but his views changed by the 1930s when the newspaper became an organ of New Deal liberalism. *Bleter fun Mein Leben* (1926–31; five volumes) is an autobiography in Yiddish; *The Education of Abraham Cahan* (1969) is an English translation of the first two volumes. *From the Ghetto* (1977) by Jules Chametzky is an authoritative study of the fiction.

CAIN, James M(allahan) (1892–1977), American novelist aligned to the *'hardboiled' school of crime writers, born in Annapolis, Maryland, and educated at Washington College, Maryland. His first novel, *The Postman Always Rings Twice* (1934), helped establish the darker and more explicit style of crime writing; written as an unmediated first-person confession, it dramatizes the obsessions that sexual attraction and money create in weak characters. In both *The Postman Always Rings Twice* and *Double Indemnity* (1936), each successfully filmed, duplicitous women destroy the lives of flawed males who are driven to acts of extreme violence and passion. In these books, and in the social realism of *Mildred Pierce* (1941), Cain persistently returns to the gap between the lives people yearn for and the more straitened circumstances in which they live in the context of the Depression. Cain was a prolific writer, but most of his novels rework the basic theme and plot of his first novel with the result that his later fiction, including *The Butterfly* (1947), *Galatea* (1953), *The Magician's Wife* (1965), and *Rainbow's End* (1975), is now little read.

Cakes and Ale, a novel by W. Somerset *Maugham, published in 1930. Subtitled *The Skeleton in the Cupboard*, Maugham's novel raised contemporary ire for its satirical portraits. Hugh Walpole detected a cruel caricature of himself in the character of the meretricious author, Alroy Kear, and the superficially respectable Grand Old Man of English Letters, Edward Driffield, was commonly assumed to represent Thomas Hardy. The novel is written from the point of view of a middle-aged playwright, Willie Ashenden, who has been asked by Driffield's widow to supply his early memories of the author for inclusion in a sanitized biography. The narrative switches between the older Ashenden's cynical and witty musings on the London literary scene, and memories of his early life in Blackstable, a Kentish town where he originally encountered Driffield and his first wife Rosie Gann. The novel centres on the attractive, paradoxical character of Rosie, an earthy enchantress whose devil-may-care approach to life and love earn her the adoration of many and the censure of the class-ridden, misanthropic society of Blackstable. Maugham's satire on the widespread hypocrisy, which spreads from kitchen maids to celebrated hostesses, is combined with the restrained lyricism of Ashenden's romantic encounters with Rosie.

CALDWELL, Erskine (Preston) (1903–87), American novelist, born in White Oak, Georgia, the son of a Presbyterian minister, educated at the University of Virginia. His first major success was *Tobacco Road* (1932), dramatized by Jack Kirkland, about the Lesters, poor white farmers struggling to eke out an existence in the Deep South. This was followed by *God's Little Acre* (1933), a tale of sexual jealousy and intrigue in the Walden family in Georgia. Both novels are characterized by a heady mixture of social outrage and bawdy humour combined with an incisive sense of the qualities of folk culture. Regional life, and racial and social relations in the Deep South, characterize much of his fiction, such as *Journeyman* (1935), a sensational novel attempting to uncover certain religious exoticisms in the South; *Trouble in July* (1940); *Tragic Ground* (1944); *House in the Uplands* (1946); *The Sure Hand of God* (1947); *This Very Earth* (1948); *A Place Called Estherville* (1949); *A Lamp for Nightfall* (1952), set in Maine and dealing with old customs threatened by outlanders; *Gretta* (1955), the depiction of a nymphomaniac; *Jenny By Nature* (1961); *Summertime Island* (1968), a didactic romance narrated by a 16-year-old boy who comes of age on a fishing holiday; *The Weather Shelter* (1969); and *Annette* (1973). He has also written several collections of short stories, considered by many critics to include his finest writing: *We Are the Living* (1933); *Kneel to the Rising Sun* (1935); *Southways* (1938); *Jackpot* (1940); *American Earth* (1941); *Georgia Boy* (1943); *The Courting of Susie Brown* (1952); *Gulf Coast Stories* (1956); and *When You Think of Me* (1959). Despite his enormous productivity and popularity, his work has been less well received by critics after their initial enthusiasm in the 1930s. As well as fiction, he produced a number of short documentary and non-fictional works such as *Some American People* (1935), portraits of American life; *All Out on the Road to Smolensk* (1942), reminiscences about his war experiences; an autobiography in *Call It Experience* (1951); *Around About America* (1964), about travels around the USA; and *Afternoons in Mid-America* (1976). He collaborated with the photographer Margaret Bourke-White on *You Have Seen Their Faces* (1937), a photo-documentary on Southern sharecroppers during the Depression, *North of the Danube* (1939) about Czechoslovakia, and *Say! Is This the USA?* (1941).

Calendar of Modern Letters, The, a journal of criticism, poetry, and fiction founded in 1925 by Edgell *Rickword, Douglas Garman, and Bertram Higgins as a forum for critical discourse of a standard they felt the **Criterion* had initiated but failed to maintain. Poetry by Roy *Campbell, Siegfried *Sassoon, Robert *Graves, and Laura *Riding was published and Llewellyn *Powys and William *Plomer were among the contributors of short stories. The *Calendar* was noted for its consistent attention to European literature, articles on Rimbaud, Baudelaire, and Chekhov serving to increase British awareness of their work; its international contributors included Hart *Crane, Robert *Frost, and Luigi Pirandello. A Coleridgean insistence on the combination of emotion and intellect in good writing characterized the journal's consensus of critical opinion. E. M. *Forster, D. H. *Lawrence, Desmond *MacCarthy, J. C. *Ransom, and Aldous *Huxley were among the critics and essayists whose work sustained the clear, objective, and intellectually rigorous tone of the *Calendar*'s essays and reviews. The magazine ceased appearing in 1927, its circulation having fallen from a level of above 7,000 copies in its first year to around 1,000 by the tenth of its twelve issues. It was reissued in 1966 with an introduction by Malcolm *Bradbury, who spoke of its 'higher skill in exegesis than had been commonly found . . . in any critical paper'. Two volumes of essays from its 'Scrutinies' section were published under Rickword's editorship in 1928 and 1931; F. R. *Leavis, for whom the *Calendar* was an example in the establishment of **Scrutiny*, edited a further selection under the title *Towards Standards of Criticism* in 1933.

CALISHER, Hortense (1911–), American novelist and short-story writer, born in New York, educated at Hunter College. Calisher is widely held to be a more skilful writer of short fiction than of novels, but she has continued to experiment with both genres. Her short stories, collected in *In the Absence of Angels* (1953), *Collected Stories* (1975), *Saratoga, Hot* (1985), and other volumes, show a talent for the humorously absurd and present a gallery of stock characters which increase their appeal. Her first novel, *False Entry* (1962), the chronicle of a man's life from childhood to maturity, which ranges from England to the American South and New York City, was praised for its robust narrative and its elegantly lyrical prose; the sequel, *The New Yorkers* (1969), which rivals the earlier volume in style and length, is perhaps her best-known novel. Though Calisher's scenes of provincial life, drawing on her family background, and her New York portraits have earned her the highest praise, she has resolutely refused to be categorized and continues to seek for new, and often surrealistic, subject matter. *Journal from Ellipsia* (1965) and *Mysteries of Motion* (1983) are set in outer space; *Queenie* (1971) is a satire of contemporary sexual mores; *Standard Dreaming* (1972) figures a surgeon speculating on the uncertain future of mankind; and *The Bobby Soxer* (1986) is a tale of provincial life in the 1950s. *Herself* (1972) and *Kissing Cousins* (1988) are autobiographical works.

CALLAGHAN, Morley (1903–90), Canadian novelist, born in Toronto, educated at Toronto University and Osgoode Law School. In 1923, Callaghan met Ernest *Hemingway to whom he showed his *Three Stories and Ten Poems* (1923); Hemingway encouraged Callaghan to write, and took some of his work back to Paris with him. The day after his marriage in April 1929 Callaghan left for Paris. *That Summer in Paris* (1963) is an introduction to this period of his life and work; he met James *Joyce, Ford Madox *Ford, Sinclair *Lewis, and others, and had the rare experience of knocking down Ernest Hemingway in a boxing bout refereed by Scott *Fitzgerald. After his return from Paris Callaghan spent time in New York, where he knew writers such as Sherwood *Anderson, William *Saroyan, and William Carlos *Williams. Early fiction works were *Strange Fugitive* (1928), whose setting during Toronto's Prohibition period sharpened the focus on an individual unable to adjust to society; *It's Never Over* (1930); *A Broken Journey* (1932); *Such Is My Beloved* (1934); and *More Joy in Heaven* (1937). The poet F. R. *Scott said at the presentation to Callaghan of the Lorne Pierce Medal for Canadian Literature in 1960 that 'with the appearance of *Strange Fugitive* in 1928, Canadian fiction could no longer be regarded as a pale extension of the English tradition'. After 1933, Callaghan abandoned stress upon physical action, espousing an overtly Christian humanism which was to inform his subsequent writings. These include *The Loved and the Lost* (1951), *The Many Colored Coat* (1960), and *A Fine and Private Place* (1975). Later publications are the novel *Our Lady of the Snows* (1985) and *The Lost and Found Stories of Morley Callaghan* (1985); *A Time for Judas* (1983) was an extraordinary reworking of the Passion and Resurrection of Christ. In 1982 Callaghan was made a Companion of the Order of Canada.

Call It Sleep, see ROTH, HENRY.

Call of the Wild, The, a novel by Jack *London, published in 1903. The novel deals with the values of reciprocal love and fair play, and the qualities of hardiness and courage in adversity. Buck, the offspring of a St Bernard and a Scotch shepherd dog, lives on a comfortable home on a California estate. He is stolen and shipped to the Yukon, where he is trained as a sledge-dog and put into brutal service before winning the leadership of the dog-team. He learns the law of the fang and how to survive in the Arctic wilds, rejecting the old Californian morality of respect for others. An atavistic streak of savagery stirs in Buck, as he responds to the conditions in which he lives and works. Buck is rescued from near death and cared for by John Thornton, and a strong bond builds up between them. Buck gives his entire allegiance to Thornton, saving his life on a number of occasions. When Thornton is murdered by Indians, Buck goes on the rampage in the camp, killing several of them in revenge. He then flees into the wild, where he abandons human civilization and becomes the leader of a wolf pack. The novel finishes on a note of triumph and a celebration of the American values of freedom and innocence, where Buck 'sings a song of a younger world'.

CAMERON, (Mark) James (Walter) (1911–85), British journalist and travel writer, born in London; after attending various schools in France and England, he began his career as a journalist in 1930. From 1945 onward he worked as a foreign correspondent, becoming well known for the compassionately outspoken liberalism of his work, which included reports from the Korean War, conflicts in Africa, and Maoist China. He was the first Western journalist to enter Hanoi during the Vietnam War; his widely circulated film entitled *Western Eyewitness* (1965) and the book *Witness* (1966) were both controversially supportive of the North Vietnamese. His publications also include *Touch of the Sun* (1950), on his travels between 1946 and 1950; *1914* (1959), his study of British life at the outbreak of the First World War; and *Indian Summer* (1974), an expansive treatment of modern and historical aspects of India, which he visited frequently. *What a Way To Run the Tribe* (1968) and *Cameron in the Guardian* (1985) are collections of his newspaper articles.

CAMERON, (John) Norman (1905–53), British poet and translator, born in India, the son of a Scottish clergyman, educated at Oriel College, Oxford. After a posting in Nigeria with the Colonial Service, he spent some time in Majorca with Robert *Graves, whom he had met at Oxford, before working as an advertising copywriter in London from 1933 to 1939. Throughout the war he produced propaganda from British Forces' bases in North Africa, Italy, and Austria. From 1947 onwards he worked as a translator. *The Winter House* (1935), his first collection of poetry, was followed only by *Forgive Me, Sire* (1950) during his lifetime, although he was well known in literary circles through his frequent publications in **New Verse*, **Horizon*, and elsewhere. His carefully crafted poems often take the form of concentrated and fluently developed extended metaphors: his close friend Dylan *Thomas remarked 'A poem by Cameron *needs* no more than one image; it moves around one idea, from one logical point to another, making a full circle . . .' His translations include *Selected Verse Poems of Arthur Rimbaud* (1942) and his versions of Villon in *Poems* (1952). Among the numerous prose works he translated are Adolf Hitler's *Table Talk: 1941–1944* (with R. H. Stevens, 1953) and Balzac's *Cousin Pons* (1950). The fullest edition of his poetry is *Collected Poems and Selected Translations* (1990), edited by Warren Hope and Jonathan Barker.

CAMPBELL, Alistair Te Ariki (1925–), New Zealand poet, born in the Cook Islands in the Pacific, the son of a New Zealand trader and a Cook Island Maori, educated at Otago and Victoria Universities. At the age of seven, after the death of his parents, he was sent to Dunedin, in Otago, New Zealand, where he was raised in a less privileged environment, spending some years in an orphanage. His early poems, on themes of grieving and loss and marked by their intense use of natural imagery, were published in *Mine Eyes Dazzle* (1950), *Sanctuary of Spirits* (1964), *Wild Honey* (1964), and *Blue Rain* (1967). Campbell was married in the 1950s to the poet Fleur *Adcock and latterly to the poet Meg Campbell. Since the late 1970s, his poetry has been increasingly influenced by his reuniting with his Cook Island relatives. The landscape of *The Dark Lord of Savaiki* (1980) is of Tongareva—the landcrabs, mangoes, sandsharks, and coral of a Pacific island, and these poems are also marked by an increasing use of Polynesian references and language. *Collected Poems* (1981) was followed by *Soul Traps* (1985) and *Stone Rain: The Polynesian Strain* (1992). Campbell has also written radio plays and published an autobiography, *Island to Island* (1984). His novels include *The Frigate Bird* (1989) and *Sidewinder* (1991), which draw on his sense of mixed cultural loyalties and roots as Polynesian and New Zealander; and *Tia* (1993).

CAMPBELL, David (1915–79), Australian poet, born in New South Wales, educated at Cambridge University. Campbell's first volume of poems, *Speak With the Sun* (1949), with its ballads portraying the characters and landscape of the Australian outback, and his highly acclaimed war poem 'Men in Green', established his early reputation as a distinctly Australian poet. *The Miracle of Mullion Hill* (1956) develops these themes but includes several meditative lyrics. *Poems* (1962) reflects more universal interests and includes a sequence of pastoral lyrics. In *The Branch of Dodona and Other Poems, 1969–1970* (1970) he reworks the Jason and Medea legend in an acerbic commentary on contemporary life; *Devil's Rock and Other Poems, 1970–1972* (1974) captures aspects of Aboriginal culture and includes memories of Kenneth *Slessor and Douglas *Stewart. *Deaths and Pretty Cousins* (1975) was followed by *Words with a Black Orpington* (1978) in which his technique becomes more experimental. Posthumous collections include *The Man in the Honeysuckle* (1979) and *Collected Poems* (1988). He was poetry editor of the *Australian*; edited a number of anthologies including *Modern Australian Poetry* (1970); and translated, with

Rosemary *Dobson, several volumes of Russian verse. His short stories, many of which drew on his childhood experiences of life on a sheep station, appeared in *Evening Under Lamplight* (1959) and *Flame and Shadow* (1976).

CAMPBELL, Joseph (1879–1944), Irish poet, born in Belfast; he became a participant in the *Irish Revival after Padraic *Colum introduced him to Dublin literary circles in 1902. In 1906 he became a teacher in London, where he was secretary of the Irish Literary Society. Interned as a Republican during the upheavals leading to Ireland's independence, he went to New York upon his release, where he formed the School of Irish Studies in 1925 and began *The Irish Review* in 1934. He returned to Ireland in 1939. A great deal of Campbell's poetry has its origins in Gaelic culture. His first major achievement was to supply lyrics for Herbert Hughes's settings of *Songs of Uladh* in 1904, some of which have since passed into the Irish folk tradition. *The Garden of Bees* (1905), his first collection of poetry, was followed by *The Rushlight* (1906), *The Gilly of Christ* (1907), and *The Mountain Singer* (1909), each of which displays his elegant simplicity of style. A number of his finest poems appear in *Earth of Cualann* (1917), which Austin *Clarke, editor of Campbell's *Collected Poems* (1963), believed to contain the first use of free verse by an Irish writer. Campbell also wrote several plays, including *Judgement*, which was produced at the *Abbey Theatre in 1912. A critical biography, *Joseph Campbell: Poet and Nationalist*, by A. A. Kelly and Norah Saunders, appeared in 1988.

CAMPBELL, (Ignatius) Roy(ston Dunnachie) (1901–57), South African poet, born in Durban, South Africa; he fought in the First World War, having succeeded in joining the South African infantry at the age of 15, and arrived in England in 1918. In 1924 his reputation as a poet was established by *The Flaming Terrapin*; the work, in 1,400 rhymed lines, allegorically celebrates the principle of vitality, emblematized by the terrapin, and is characterized by the abundant energy of its natural imagery. In 1926 Campbell returned to South Africa, and founded the satirical magazine *Voorslag* (lit. 'Whiplash') with William *Plomer. *The Wayzgoose*, his poem attacking the South African intelligentsia, appeared in 1928. During the early 1930s he lived in Provence and engaged in bullfighting. *Adamastor* (1930), containing some of his best South African poems, was followed by *The Georgiad* (1931), a humorously offensive diatribe in verse against the *Bloomsbury Group. The poetry of *Flowering Reeds* (1933) was marked by a more contemplative tenor. Having become a Roman Catholic in 1935, his enthusiasm for religious ritual was indicated in the verse of *Mithraic Emblems* (1936). He fought for General Franco in the Spanish Civil War and espoused fascist values in the long poem *Flowering Rifle* (1939). He was, however, fully prepared to serve against Hitler with the King's African Rifles until invalided out in 1944. A *Collected Poems* was published in three volumes in 1949, 1957, and 1960, the third of which is devoted to his distinguished translations, principally of French and Spanish poetry. He died in a motor accident in Portugal. He published two volumes of autobiography, *Broken Record* (1934) and *Light on a Dark Horse* (1951), which tend to project a romanticized view of himself as a man of action. Peter Alexander's biography of Campbell appeared in 1952.

Campus Novel, a term describing a particular genre of novels, usually comic or satirical, which have a university setting and academics as principal characters. An early example was Kingsley Amis's **Lucky Jim* (1954), which is set at a Midlands red-brick university and features the comic escapades of a junior lecturer; other notable examples include Malcolm *Bradbury's *Eating People Is Wrong* (1959), about life at a provincial university, and *The History Man* (1975), a satirical novel set at a new 'plate-glass' university, which concerns the rise of an unscrupulous Professor of History. Bradbury's subsequent works, such as *Rates of Exchange* (1983), also feature academics as heroes but depart from the narrow university setting. David *Lodge—also, like Bradbury, a Professor of English—has written several novels which fall into the category: *Changing Places* (1975), subtitled 'A Tale of Two Campuses', wittily contrasts the straitened circumstances of British academics at a provincial university with the more glamorous and affluent lifestyle of their American counterparts. A sequel, *Small World* (1984), considers the peripatetic existence of academics on the literary conference circuit. Other recent additions to the genre include Howard *Jacobson's *Coming from Behind* (1983), a scabrously funny account of the tribulations of a young Jewish academic at a Northern polytechnic, which pays ironic homage to both Bradbury and Lodge. American campus novels include Mary *McCarthy's *The Groves of Academe* (1952); John Barth's **Giles Goat-Boy* (1966), a surreal work (subtitled 'The Revised New Syllabus') in which one of the main characters is a super-intelligent computer; and Alison *Lurie's *The War Between the Tates* (1974), which concerns the adulterous liaisons and political intrigues of a group of academics on a New England campus. A Canadian variation on the genre is offered by Robertson *Davies's *The Rebel Angels* (1982).

Canadian Forum, a monthly journal of political commentary and literature begun in 1920 by students and staff at the University of Toronto; it is the longest established periodical of its kind in Canada. It began as the successor to *The Rebel*, a *little magazine based at the University of Toronto, with which Barker Fairley, *Canadian Forum*'s first literary editor, and other founding members of the editorial board had been involved. Although enthusiastically concerned with conceptions of an independent national culture, the magazine remained in critical detachment from the indiscriminate endorsement of identifiably Canadian writing which its editors associated particularly with the *Canadian Bookman*. Poetry by Dorothy *Livesay, E. J. *Pratt, A. J. M. *Smith, and many others was regularly featured. Writers of note who were supported early in their careers by *Canadian Forum* include Earle *Birney, Margaret *Avison, Raymond *Souster, A. M. *Klein, and Margaret *Atwood. The magazine's continuing belief in the social functions of literature has been central to the integration of its literary and political dimensions. J. Francis White became the first full-time editor in 1927, since when Northrop *Frye, Milton Wilson, Abraham Rotstein, and John Hutcheson have been among his successors. J. L. Granatstein and Peter Stevens edited the anthology *Forum: Canadian Life and Letters, 1920–1970* (1972).

Canadian Literature, the first periodical to be devoted exclusively to critical consideration of writing produced in Canada. It has appeared quarterly since its establishment in 1959 by George Woodcock at the University of British Columbia, Vancouver. Woodcock was succeeded in 1977 by W. H. New. The journal's inception marked the growing confidence in the value of indigenous writing which was intrinsic to the strengthening belief in an independent cultural identity felt in Canada from the late 1950s onward. Woodcock's desire to avoid the subordination of critical objectivity to nationalist evaluations of literature has been fulfilled in the magazine's rigorous and eclectic ethos, which is equally free of doctrinaire adherence to any body of literary theory. Although criticism of literature in English has always been its first concern, *Canadian Literature* also publishes poetry and occasional samples of contemporary fiction, and regularly features commentary in French. Numerous anthologies of articles and essays from its pages have appeared, including Woodcock's editions of *The Sixties: Canadian Writers and Writing of the Decade* (1969) and *Poets and Critics: Essays from 'Canadian Literature', 1966–1974* (1974).

CANFIELD FISHER, Dorothy (1878–1958), American novelist born in Lawrence, Kansas, educated at the University of Nebraska (where she formed an enduring friendship with Willa *Cather), Ohio State University, and Columbia University. From 1907 onward she lived in Arlington, Vermont, drawing on its middle-class social milieu in most of her fiction. Her earlier novels, published under her maiden name of Dorothy Canfield, include *Gunhild* (1907), contrasting Norwegian and American values; *The Squirrel-Cage* (1912), the first of her treatments of marriage; and *The Bent Twig* (1915), dealing with tensions between a student and her idealistic parents. While the morality of her fiction is predictably conventional, her work is capable of considerable candour and intensity. Notable among her other novels are *The Brimming Cup* (1921), in which a woman is torn between her family and love for another man; *Her Son's Wife* (1926), centring on antipathies between a mother and daughter-in-law; and *The Deepening Stream* (1930), a partly autobiographical narrative of the growth of a woman's character. *Hillsboro People* (1915), *The Real Motive* (1916), and *Raw Material* (1923) are collections of short stories. *Vermont Tradition* (1953), a celebration of the history and culture of the region, is the best known of her non-fiction works, which also deal with educational methods and motherhood. There is a biography (1982) by Ida H. Washington.

CANIN, Ethan (1961–   ), American novelist, born in Ann Arbor, Michigan, educated at Harvard, where he studied medicine. His first collection of short stories, *Emperor of the Air* (1988), was followed by *Blue River* (1991), a novel about the lifelong rivalry between two brothers—one a successful ophthalmic surgeon, the other a hopeless drifter, and by *The Palace Thief* (1994), a collection of four thematically linked novellas, each focusing on a moment of 'uproar and disorder' in the life of its protagonist. His style, which is spare and lucid, with occasional flashes of lyricism, has been compared to *Updike's; he is similarly concerned with the epiphanies which occur in ordinary lives, specifically those of suburban America.

CANTOR, Jay (1948–   ), American novelist and essayist, born in New York City, educated at Harvard University and the University of California, Santa Cruz. He became a professor of literature at Tufts University. In his meticulously researched *The Death of Che Guevara* (1983), Cantor blends history and fiction to explore the intricacies of the man behind the legendary guerrilla fighter. *Krazy Kat* (1987), his second novel, is built on the character from George Herriman's comic strip of that name; the cartoon characters are subjected to various realities of modern life such as atomic weaponry and psychoanalysis in Cantor's version. A book of essays, *The Space Between: Literature and Politics* (1981), uses fictional and historical figures as well as personal reminiscences to analyse the present time. A later collection of essays is *Giving Birth to One's Own Mother* (1991).

Cantos, The, Ezra *Pound's compendious *magnum opus*, published in numerous sections between *A Draft of XVI Cantos* (1925) and *Drafts and Fragments of Cantos CX to CXVII* (1970); the fullest available text is *The Cantos* (1987). Having become dissatisfied with the essentially miniaturist idiom of *Imagism after about 1915, Pound sought to discover a form capable of accommodating the wide range of tones, thematic interests, and styles of verse which he had developed since around 1908. Three provisional sections appeared in *Poetry*, Chicago, in 1917, although it was not until his move to Paris in 1920 that he began his fifty years of sustained effort on *The Cantos*. The aesthetics of the *Vorticists, stressing the need for spatial integrity in artistic creation, and the impression made upon him by the architectonics of T. S. Eliot's *The *Waste Land* were of importance in determining the diversity and interrelatedness of the poems' constituent elements. Greek, Chinese, American, English, Italian, and African texts are among the materials invoked in Pound's projection of his, and Western civilization's, cultural frame of reference. Stylistically the work's range is enormous, extending from lyric modes of great refinement and delicacy to passages in the roughest American vernacular. The recurrence of literary, historical, legal, and mythological themes interwoven with autobiographical reflections unifies the shifting textures of the many sections, which can nevertheless succeed in being simultaneously baffling and compelling to the reader. W. Cookson's *A Guide to the Cantos of Ezra Pound* (1985) is among the most straightforward of the many commentaries on the work, which continues to generate controversy over its meanings and value.

CANTWELL, Robert (1908–78), American novelist, biographer, and editor, born in Little Falls (Vader), Washington, educated at the University of Washington. Cantwell is chiefly associated with the group of proletarian realists (see PROLETARIAN LITERATURE IN THE USA) who emerged in the USA in the early 1930s. Cantwell worked at an assortment of jobs, including coastguard and factory operator in a lumber mill, before moving to New York to begin a career in journalism. His first novel, *Laugh and Lie Down* (1931), draws on his experiences of mill work, and marked the beginnings of his literary conversion to the left. A more considerable work, *The Land of Plenty* (1935), again draws on Cantwell's industrial experience, here in the context of a labour–management dispute which turns into a strike. Cantwell also contributed regularly to the **New Republic* and *The *Nation* and in 1935 became an associate editor at *Time* magazine, a position he held until 1945 when he took over as literary editor at *Newsweek*. Other works include the biographies *Nathaniel Hawthorne: The American Years* (1948) and *Alexander Wilson* (1961); and *The Hidden Northwest* (1972), a historical study.

CAPOTE, Truman (1924–84), American writer, born in New Orleans, Louisiana. He left school at 15, by which time he had already been writing short stories for over a year. His earlier works defied many of the social conventions of the deeply conservative post-war years by their sympathetic portrayal of characters normally deemed immoral or amoral. Among his works of fiction are *Other Voices, Other Rooms* (1948), which discussed homosexuality; *A Tree of Night and Other Stories* (1949); *The Glass Harp* (1951; dramatized 1952), about people freeing themselves from social demands by living in a tree house; and *Breakfast at Tiffany's* (1958), a novella centred on the free-spirited Holly Golightly. His plays include *House of Flowers* (1954), a musical set in a Caribbean brothel; *The Thanksgiving Visitor* (1968); and *Trilogy; An Experiment in Multimedia* (1969). His travel writing appears in *Local Color* (1950) and *The Muses Are Heard* (1956), his account of a tour through Russia with the cast of *Porgy and Bess*. In 1966 he produced a collection of short stories, *A Christmas Memory*, and also achieved widespread notoriety with the publication of *In Cold Blood*, an early example of 'faction' (see NEW JOURNALISM) concerned with an infamous multiple murderer. He also enhanced his reputation with a procession of acerbic journalism and shorter prose pieces, some of which appeared in the collections *Then It All Came Down* (1976) and *Music for Chameleons* (1980). A large project provisionally called *Unanswered Prayers* was left unfinished at his unexpected death.

CARD, Orson Scott (1951–), American writer of *science fiction novels and stories, born in Richland, Washington, educated at Brigham Young University and the University of Utah. As a Mormon, his work could be interpreted as a form of advocacy; but the harsh dispassion of his best novels avert any sense of doctrine. Only in *A Woman of Destiny* (1984; later much expanded as *Saints*) and *The Folk of the Fringe* (1988) does he deal directly with the oddly compelling contours of his faith as a religion conditioned by American history. His science fiction, most notably *Ender's Game* (1985), *Speaker for the Dead* (1986), and *Xenocide* (1991), consists of grandiose tales of the rite of passage from childhood to ruler of the race. Beginning with *Seventh Son* (1987), Card has also written a series of fantasies about an alternative America.

Caretaker, The, a play by Harold *Pinter, performed and published in 1960. The drama that first brought Pinter substantial recognition and success involves the subtly shifting relationships of three characters. A former mental patient, Aston, rescues the tramp Davies from a brawl and brings him back to the junk-filled London attic which he inhabits, but which is actually owned by his brother Mick, a jobbing builder. As the play proceeds, the paranoid, shiftless Davies switches his allegiance from his benefactor, Aston, to the stronger Mick, who purports to be offering him a job as a caretaker and work as a painter and decorator. The latter's motives, as often in Pinter, are somewhat inscrutable; but it would seem that he outwits the tramp by luring him into making both false claims for himself and insulting remarks about Aston. By the end, both brothers have rejected Davies, and he is left with nothing but the forlorn hope of one day getting to Sidcup, a place where he improbably expects to find the solution to all his problems. The play's complexities are not easily summarized, but it has been well described by John *Arden as concerning 'the unexpected strength of family ties against an intruder'. It is notable for its charged atmosphere, for clipped, plain dialogue that says little but implies much, as well as for its richly humorous yet sympathetic characterization of the tramp Davies.

CAREW, Jan (Rynveld) (1925–), Guyanese novelist and poet, born in Agricola, British Guiana (now Guyana), educated at universities in America, Czechoslovakia, and France. He has lived and taught in Ghana, Jamaica, Canada, and more recently in Chicago, and was made Professor of African-American Studies at Northwestern University. His early novels, *Black Midas* (1958; US title *A Touch of Midas*, 1958) and *The Wild Coast* (1958), are notable for their vivid, resonant descriptions of the Guyanese landscape. Other novels include *The Last Barbarian* (1960), set in Harlem, and *Moscow Is Not My Mecca* (1964; published as *A Green Winter*, 1965), set in Soviet Russia. Poetry collections include *Streets of Eternity* (1952) and *Sea Drums in My Blood* (1980). *Sons of the Flying Wing* (1970), *Children of the Sun* (1976), and *Computer Killer* (1985) are among his many children's books. He has also published a collection of essays, *Fulcrums of Change* (1987); the historical studies *Grenada: The Hour Will Strike Again* (1985) and *Rape of Paradise: Columbus and the Origins of Western Racism* (1994); and a biographical study of Malcolm X, *Ghosts in Our Blood: With Malcolm X in Africa, England and the Caribbean* (1994).

CAREY, Peter (1943–), Australian novelist and short-story writer, born in Victoria, educated at Monash University, where he studied science. After working for advertising agencies in Melbourne and London he later established his own advertising agency in Sydney. His first two publications were short stories collected in *The Fat Man in History* (1974) and *War Crimes* (1979); grotesquely funny, set in frightening, futuristic worlds, they provide a scathing critique of contemporary values, and yet register compassion for the ungainly beings they feature. His first novel, *Bliss* (1981), displays a similar predilection for the bizarre in its account of the life of Harry Joy, an advertising man who dies three times and passes through hell, purgatory, and heaven; in this, as in his short fiction, Carey's writing provides a wryly inventive perspective on a modern world obsessed with materialism and with competitive values, offering surreal alternatives in which the reader is disturbingly deprived of traditional referents. His *magic realist novel *Illywhacker* (1985), narrated by a 139-year-old man, also showed his interest in 'extending reality'. *Oscar and Lucinda* (1988; Booker Prize) combined skilful pastiche of nineteenth-century novels such as Edmund Gosse's *Father and Son* with magic realist quest; Oscar Hopkins, a young Anglican clergyman, becomes obsessed with the idea of building a glass church in the Australian outback and enlists the aid of Lucinda Leplastrier, an eccentric heiress he meets on a ship bound for New South Wales. *The Tax Inspector* (1991) is a surreal black comedy about three generations of an Australian family: the central character, Benny Catchprice, loses his job in the family motor business on the day that the Tax Inspector, Maria Takis, who is eight months pregnant, arrives to begin her audit of the firm; other characters in the cast include an ageing matriarch, Granny Catchprice, and a child who wants to become an angel. In *The Unusual Life of Tristan Smith* (1994), Carey creates imaginary countries, folklore, and languages in a dazzling adventure that parodies colonial politics and is inhabited by the world of the theatre. His *Collected Short Stories* were published in 1995.

CARNAP, Rudolf (1891–1970), philosopher, born at Ronsdorf in Germany, educated at the universities of Freiburg and Jena. After military service in the First World War he was active within the Vienna Circle and lectured at the University of Vienna from 1926 to 1930, gaining recognition as a leading exponent of logical positivism. His first major work, *Der Logische Aufbau der Welt* ('The Logical Structure of the World'), appeared in 1928; the book's insistence on the need to establish direct relations between theoretical statements and areas of immediate experience formed the basis of his doctrine of 'physicalism'. In 1930 he founded the journal *Erkenntnis* with Hans Reichenbach, which developed into the principal platform for logical positivism. His profound investigations of abstract logic were extended into linguistic and mathematical territories in *Logische Syntax der Sprache* ('The Logical Syntax of Language') (1934). He held a professorship at the German University of Prague, where he was sought out by W. V. O. *Quine, until 1935, when he went to the USA to escape the intellectual constraints of Nazism. In 1941 he became a naturalized US citizen. He was Professor of Philosophy at Chicago from 1935 to 1952 and at the University of California, Los Angeles, from 1954 to 1961. From around 1940 onwards he was preoccupied with questions of probability and induction, producing *Logical Foundations of Probability*, widely regarded as a work of great importance, in 1950. Carnap's flexibility in modifying his somewhat rigid earlier views accorded with the fundamentally humane orientation of his thought, which was characteristically expressed with exemplary clarity and precision. His other works include *Formalization of Logic* (1943) and *Scheinprobleme in der Philosophy* ('Pseudo-Problems in Philosophy') (1960).

CARPENTER, Edward (1844–1929), British writer on social reform, born in Brighton, educated at Trinity Hall, Cambridge. In 1869 he was ordained in the Church of England but relinquished holy orders in 1872 and moved to Leeds to lecture with the University Extension movement. He met Walt Whitman, whom he revered, on trips to America in 1877 and 1884, recording his experiences in *Days with Walt Whitman* (1906). Carpenter employed Whitman's expansive idiom in *Towards Democracy*, a long poem on his vision of social and spiritual progress, which was repeatedly enlarged after its original publication in 1883. His writings on sexuality, religion, aesthetics, and a range of political topics won him international renown as a progressive thinker. Among the more notable of his many publications are *England's Ideal* (1885), an exposition of his socialist principles; *Civilization, its Cause and its Cure* (1889); *The Drama of Love and Death* (1912), an exposition of his beliefs in evolutionary meliorism; and the autobiographical *My Days and Dreams* (1916). *Homogenic Love and its Place in a Free Society* (1894), *The Intermediate Sex* (1908), and other works bear directly and unapologetically upon his homosexuality. Chushici Tsuzuki's *Edward Carpenter: Prophet of Human Fellowship* appeared in 1980.

CARPENTER, Humphrey (William Bouverie) (1946–), British biographer, born in Oxford, educated at Keble College, Oxford. He was a radio producer from 1968 to 1974, when he became a freelance writer and broadcaster. *J. R. R. Tolkien* (1977) was the first of his numerous biographies of literary figures; with Christopher Tolkien, he edited the *Letters of J. R. R. Tolkien* (1981). *The Inklings* (1977) deals with *Tolkien, Charles *Williams, C. S. *Lewis, and their circle at Oxford. His reputation as a biographer was fully established with *W. H. Auden* (1981), which displays the narrative fluency and thoroughness characteristic of his work. His subsequent publications include *Geniuses Together* (1987), a treatment of 'the *Lost Generation' of American writers in Paris during the 1920s; *A Serious Character* (1988), a biography of Ezra *Pound; *The Brideshead Generation* (1989), his lucidly organized study of Evelyn *Waugh and his contemporaries; and *Benjamin Britten* (1992). With his wife, Mari Prichard, Carpenter edited *The Oxford Companion to Children's Literature* (1984); notable among his numerous works for children is the series of 'Mr Majeika' books.

CARR, E(dward) H(allett) (1892–1982), British historian, born at Highgate, London, educated at Trinity College, Cambridge. From 1916 to 1936 he worked at the Foreign Office, where he rose to the rank of First Secretary. His wide diplomatic experience subsequently gained him a succession of academic posts. Throughout much of the Second World War he was assistant editor of *The Times*. During his years with the British Legation at Riga in the 1920s, Carr developed a deep interest in Russian culture and subsequently produced a series of biographical studies which include *Dostoevsky* (1931), *Karl Marx* (1934), and *Michael Bakunin* (1937). Among his earlier works as an authority on international affairs are *The Twenty Years' Crisis: 1919–1939* (1939), *Conditions of Peace* (1942), and *The Soviet Impact on the Western World* (1946), which demonstrate his belief in the need for co-operation with the USSR. *A History of Soviet Russia*, Carr's *magnum opus* on the emergence of the Soviet state from 1917 and 1929, appeared in fourteen volumes between 1950 and 1978. A controversial view of history as a dynamic progression based on shifting structures of power informs all his works, which also include *The New Society* (1951), *Twilight of the Comintern, 1930–1935* (1983), and the lectures and essays of *What Is History?* (1961) and *From Napoleon to Stalin* (1980).

CARR, Emily (1871–1945), Canadian painter and prose writer, born in Victoria, British Columbia. Canada's best-known woman artist, Carr studied painting in San Francisco, England, and Paris, but achieved widespread recognition only in her fifties. Her art is characterized by a passionate commitment to Native Canadian themes. She turned to writing when failing health forced her to curtail her work as a painter and potter. Her first book, *Klee Wyck* (1942), takes its title from the name (meaning 'Laughing One') given to her by her Nootka Indian friends; it is a collection of short stories which, like much of her art, celebrates the culture of the Native people of Canada's West Coast. Her other literary work offers vivid insights into later Victorian and early twentieth-century life on Vancouver Island; for example, *The Book of Small* (1942), and *The House of All Sorts* (1944), which describes Carr's experiences running a boarding house in Victoria, one of many ways in which she financed her career as a painter. *Growing Pains* (1946) is the first of a number of posthumously published and autobiographical works.

CARR, J(ames Joseph) L(loyd) (1912–), English novelist, born in Carlton Miniott, Yorkshire, educated at Castleford Secondary School, Yorkshire. Carr was a schoolteacher for many years, and served as an Intelligence Officer in the Royal Air Force during the Second World War. His first published novel, *A Day in Summer* (1963), a characteristic pot-pourri of convention and fancy, was followed by *A Season in Sinji* (1968), *The Harpole Report* (1972), and *How Steeple Sinderby Wanderers Won the F.A. Cup* (1975). Carr's best-known novel, *A Month in the Country* (1980), is the story of Birkin, a shell-shocked survivor of the First World War, who arrives at a north-country village with the task of uncovering a medieval wall-painting in the village church. As the work progresses and summer succumbs to autumn, Birkin becomes absorbed in the rhythms of village life and the lives of its characters. Among the several plot layers, involving the past and present, is the unravelling of a local family legend involving the unburying, by a young archaeologist, of a fourteenth-century ancestor buried in the church grounds which is the climax of the book. In *The Ballad of Pollock's Crossing* (1985) Carr gives full expression to his gift of comic fantasy, removing in 1929 a young Bradford schoolteacher to the American Midwest where he rearranges the syllabus, offering his class the Indian view of the Sioux's defeat at Wounded Knee instead of the obligatory Hiawatha exposition. Latterly, Carr founded his own press, publishing from a back bedroom curious dictionaries and maps.

CARR, John Dickson (1906–77), American *detective novelist who lived from 1932 to 1948 in England, where the majority of his books are set. His novels, which appeared under his own name and under that of Carter Dickson, are complicated puzzles, often highly ingenious variants of the locked-room mystery: a lecture on this subject is included in *The Hollow Man* (1935). In their method they can be compared with the stories of S. S. *Van Dine and Ellery *Queen, but have far more life and energy, while the detection is often leavened by a romantic sub-plot. The detective in Carr's own early stories is the French *juge d'instruction* Henri Bencolin (*It Walks by Night*, 1930), but he is soon replaced (*Hag's Nook*, 1933) by the stout and eccentric lexicographer Dr Gideon Fell, who appears in most of the author's novels and is obviously modelled on G. K. *Chesterton. The detective in the novels by Carter Dickson—the first is *The Plague Court Murders* (1934)—is the equally eccentric Sir Henry Merrivale, who later acquires Churchillian characteristics. Carr also wrote a number of historical romances with a detective element, such as *The Devil in Velvet* (1951), his most popular book, which is set in the London of Charles II, and the official biography of Sir Arthur Conan *Doyle.

CARRINGTON, Leonora (1917–), British novelist, short-story writer, and artist, born in Lancashire, educated in various Catholic convents. As a debutante in 1934, she was presented at court to George V (the inspiration of her 1936 story, *The Debutante*). While at art school at the Amedee Ozenfant Academy in London, she discovered Surrealism through the work of Herbert *Read; shortly afterwards she met Max Ernst, with whom she went to live in France, where she wrote many of the short fictions later collected in *The House of Fear* and *The Seventh Horse* (both 1988), macabre and comic tales showing the influence of the English nursery rhyme school. In 1940, during the fall of France, Carrington suffered a breakdown, which she later recounted in *Down Below* (1972), a frighteningly detailed memoir of a season in hell which has become a classic of surrealist literature. She later moved to Mexico City where her painting took precedence over her writing. She also wrote two novels: the alchemical fantasy *The Stone Door* (1966), and *The Hearing Trumpet* (1976), an off-beat comedy about old age and religious questing, both of which were first published in French translation.

CARROLL, Paul Vincent (1900–68), Irish dramatist, born in Blackrock, Co. Louth, educated at St Patrick's College, Dublin. He emigrated to Scotland in 1921 and taught in Glasgow until his first theatrical success in 1937. Carroll was one of a number of playwrights, including Lennox *Robinson, who contributed significantly to the prevalence of Realism at the *Abbey Theatre in the 1930s and 1940s. *Things that Are Caesar's* (1932), produced at the Abbey, is an early example of the profound influence of Ibsen on Carroll's dramas, an influence which later became a handicap; the play succeeds in universalizing an Irish tale of arranged marriage, entrapment, and the conflict between worldliness and spiritual aspiration. Carroll's first outstanding play, *Shadow and Substance* (1937), continues his didactic use of local settings and characters. The play achieves a balance between its portrayal of insular rural life and the grand theme of intellectual pride, as well as establishing Carroll's unique ability to characterize the Irish priest. His other plays include *The White Steed* and *The Coggerers*, both staged in 1939, and *The Devil Came from Dublin* (1952).

CARSON, Ciaran (1948–), Northern Irish poet, born in Belfast, where he was educated at Queen's University. After working as a schoolteacher and subsequently as a civil servant, he became Traditional Arts Officer of the Arts Council of Northern Ireland in 1975. *The New Estate* (1976), his first collection of verse, contained a wide range of poems on historical, social, and personal themes which frequently anticipated the urgent engagement with contemporary conditions in Ulster characteristic of his later writing. An expanded edition of the book which appeared in 1987 indicated the emergence of a strong narrative element in his work, a factor of considerable importance to the powerful originality of *The Irish For No* (1988). The book's impact is partly produced by the thoroughness of its evocation of Belfast, which provides the contexts for what Fintan O'Toole described as Carson's 'rare and terrifying ability to encapsulate history in an anecdote'. *Belfast Confetti* (1990) and *First Language* (1993) expand the imaginative compass of his work and display the increasing flexibility of his idiosyncratic verse forms. His other writings include *The Pocket Guide to Irish Traditional Music* (1986).

CARTER, Angela (1940–92), British novelist and short-story writer, born in Eastbourne, Sussex, educated at Bristol University. Although *magical realism may have been the inspiration for some of Carter's early novels, which include *Shadow Dance* (1966), *The Magic Toyshop* (1967), and *Love* (1971), from the beginning she showed a much wider cultural and historical awareness of the polyglot aesthetic tradition within which she was working. She drew upon sources such as Kleist, the French *conte cruel*, Dinesen (Karen *Blixen), *Stead, and Japanese tales, as is evident in *Fireworks* (1974), her first and pioneering collection of short fiction. The short story was successful as a vehicle for Carter's unusual talent, which combined erudition and transformative imagination. The brothers Grimm are the inspiration for *The *Bloody Chamber* (1979), probably her finest work, which recasts their traditional tales of metamorphosis in moulds that draw undogmatically on feminism and Freud; she adapted some of these stories for Neil *Jordan's film version entitled *The Company of Wolves* (1984). Carter's project of deconstructive interpretation and retelling continues in *Black Venus* (1985), drawing this time on histories, legends and literary fictions. Some of her earlier novels, such as *Heroes and Villains* (1969), *The Infernal Desire Machines of Doctor Hoffman* (1972), and *The Passion of New Eve* (1977), take place in *science fiction landscapes; but Carter successfully made the transition from fantastic to more accessible and pleasurable novels with her works set in worlds where reality and artifice intermingle. *Nights at the Circus* (1984), a love story set in the theatrical world of *fin-de-siècle* London, presents the quintessential Carter heroine, the trapeze artiste Fevvers who was born with wings. The comic **Wise Children* (1991), another theatrical novel, is Carter's tribute to Shakespearian comedies and displays a mellowing vision, more rooted in mundanity. Carter was a fine and varied critic, as her long feminist essay *The Sadeian Woman: An Exercise in Cultural History* (1979), and the reviews and occasional writings collected in *Nothing Sacred* (1982) and *Expletives Deleted* (1992), reveal.

Carter's early death left critics divided as to whether she was a major or a very original minor writer: nevertheless, her influence is evident in the work of celebrated contemporaries such as Michèle *Roberts, Marina *Warner, and Jeanette *Winterson among others. Along with *Rushdie, she is also to be credited with forcing British fiction away from its increasingly parochial concern with domestic or social realism by her insistence on textual diversity and the joy of passionate and eclectic reading. Her fascination with the macabre and erotic aspects of folklore and myth is evident in *The Virago Book of Fairy Tales* (1991) which she edited. Stories uncollected at Carter's death appear in the American *Ghosts and Old World Wonders* (1993); *Burning Your Boats: Collected Short Stories* appeared in 1995 with an introduction by Salman Rushdie. See *Flesh and the Mirror: Essays on the Art of Angela Carter* (1994), edited by Lorna Sage.

CARTER, Martin (Wylde) (1927–), Guyanese poet and politician, born in Georgetown, British Guiana (now Guyana), educated at Queen's College in Georgetown. He wrote and published poems privately in the 1950s, including *To a Dead Slave* (1951) and *The Kind Eagle* (1952), but it was a spell of three months in detention for his anti-colonial political activities which led to *Poems of Resistance* (1954), the collection which established his reputation as a major political poet. After independence, Carter became Minister of Public Information and Broadcasting, and represented Guyana at the United Nations. Stark, militant rhetoric dominates many of his poems, but others are characterized by compassion, and startling imagery. Many of his best, such as 'I Come from the Nigger Yard', fuse the political and the confessional. In 'For Milton Williams', a poem in *Poems of Succession* (1977), which also contains work from earlier collections, Carter, however, rejects any cosy nostalgia about his youthful political activism. His other volumes include *Poems of Shape and Motion* (1955), *Conversations* (1955), *Jail Me Quickly* (1963), and *Poems of Affinity: 1978–80* (1980).

CARTLAND, Barbara, see ROMANTIC FICTION.

CARTWRIGHT, Justin (1933–), British novelist, born in South Africa, educated at Trinity College, Oxford; he worked as a maker of documentary films and commercials before becoming a full-time writer. Cartwright's early novels *The Revenge* (1978) and *The Horse of Darius* (1980) are skilfully plotted thrillers about assassination attempts against powerful political figures. He first received considered acclaim for *Interior* (1989), a compelling serio-comic narrative set in South and West Africa which centres on the main protagonist's hazardous search for his missing father. Also set chiefly in Africa, *Masai Dreaming* (1993) sustains thematic tension between the rumoured barbarism of that continent and the stark barbarism of Nazi Germany. The vividly documentary satire of London as a zone of polarized social conditions in *Look At It This Way* (1990) anticipates the centrality of the city to *In Every Face I Meet* (1995), Cartwright's most highly regarded novel; the events of the novel take place mainly on one day in 1990, when Nelson Mandela's imminent freedom begins to re-vitalize the impotent idealism of an investment banker before events embroil him in murder charges.

CARVER, Raymond (1938–88), American short-story writer and poet, born in Oregon, educated at Chico State College and Humboldt State College; he also attended the *Iowa Writers' Workshop. His first volume of stories, *Put Yourself in My Shoes* (1974), was followed by *Will You Please Be Quiet, Please?* (1976), *Furious Seasons* (1977), and *What We Talk about when We Talk about Love* (1981). Carver wrote mostly about the domestic lives of the working class, drawing on his own background and experiences. His characters are travelling salesmen, waitresses, and office workers; his preferred themes are failed or broken marriages, chronic drunkenness (Carver was himself an alcoholic), repressed violence, and the failure of attempts to communicate. His stories, often presented as monologues, are remarkable for their stylistic economy; detail, though photographic, is spare and description reduced to essentials. Carver's work reflects the influence of *Hemingway in its simplicity and compression. He has been compared to Chekhov, described as a minimalist, and placed by perceptive critics in the wider category of American Realism with its undertow of sensationalism and violence. The stories of *Cathedral* (1983) display a new mellowness; the controlled use of the epiphanies absent from his earlier fictions emphasizes his belief in the ultimate triumph of good over evil. *Fires* (1983) is a miscellany of prose and verse. *Where I'm Calling from* (1988) gathers thirty stories from Carver's previous collections, and seven hitherto unpublished stories; the latter stories were also published as a separate volume, *Elephant* (1988). The impact of Carver's short career on the American literary scene can be gauged from the evident influence of his style on a new generation of American writers, including his own wife, Tess Gallagher, to whom some of his works are dedicated.

CARY, (Arthur) Joyce (Lunel) (1888–1957), British novelist, born in Londonderry, educated at Clifton College and Trinity College, Oxford. Much of his childhood was spent in Ireland, in Donegal, which provides the setting of *The House of Children* (1941). Cary studied art in Edinburgh, served in the Balkan War of 1912–13, and in 1913 joined the Nigerian political service, where he remained, except for an interval with the Nigerian regiment during the Cameroons campaign of 1915–16, until 1920, when he resigned through ill health. His first novel, *Aissa Saved* (1932), set in Nigeria, is an objective picture of conditions there, ironically doubting the white man's success in improving the morals of the indigenous population. *An American Visitor* (1933), likewise located in Nigeria, combines political parable with an inter-racial love affair; it was followed by *The African Witch* (1936) and *Castle Corner* (1938). His best-known novel, *Mister Johnson* (1939), is a classic of colonial literature, and reflects Cary's own experiences in the Nigerian Administration. Focusing on the eponymous hero, a Nigerian clerk, the novel portrays a bygone colonial life and a remarkable insight into the mind of the

African. His next two novels, *Charley Is My Darling* (1940) and *A House of Children* (1941), are centred on children. Cary's reputation rests on his blackly comic trilogy, *Herself Surprised* (1941), *To Be a Pilgrim* (1942), and *The Horse's Mouth* (1944; filmed 1959), described by Cary as a 'Triptych' and published together as *First Trilogy* (1958). Narrated in the first person, the trilogy is unified by the interrelated stories of the three main characters, all representing different backgrounds and offering different perspectives on art, morality, religion, and on each other's character: Sara Monday, 'a simple country girl in service', representing sensual domesticity but whose religious beliefs, having been inspired by the works of Charlotte M. Yonge, have given her 'strength in adversity'; Tom Wilcher, a lawyer with a strong sense of duty who tries to preserve his family fortune; and Gulley Jimson, the scurrilous and egocentric artist influenced by Blake and Stanley Spencer, whose perception of creativity and the artist's role is the main focus of the trilogy. The chief work of Cary's later years was a political trilogy, *Prisoner of Grace* (1952), *Except the Lord* (1953), and *Not Honour More* (1955). Using the same device he employed in the earlier trilogy, he casts an identical set of characters into differently angled first-person narratives. Other works include *Power in Man* (1939) and *The Process of Real Freedom* (1943), philosophical apologias of his liberal beliefs; *The Case for African Freedom* (1941); and *The Drunken Sailor* (1947), an allegorical poem.

CASEY, John (1939–), American novelist, short-story writer, and critic, born in Worcester, Massachusetts, educated at Harvard University and the University of Iowa. Casey moved to Charlottesville, Virginia in 1972 and became a teacher at the University of Virginia. His first novel, *An American Romance* (1977), was a critical success, but it was his second novel, *Spartina* (1989), the story of Dick Pierce, an embittered Rhode Island fisherman, that established his literary reputation. In *Spartina*, as in his earlier fiction, Casey's depiction of his hero is both realistic and human. He uses Dick's internal voice to convey the inner struggles that accompany his exterior predicaments: his struggle to attain the money to finish his boat, his involvement with a drug-runner, and his extra-marital affair, among others.

CASSIDY, John (1928–), British poet, born in Lancashire; he served with the East African Army before studying at the University of Manchester. From 1954 to 1976 he taught English at Leigh Grammar School, Leigh, Lancashire, and became a lecturer in literature and creative arts at Leigh College in 1976. After his work's inclusion in Faber's *Poetry Introduction: 3* (1975), he published several collections including *An Attitude of Mind* (1978), *Night Cries* (1982), and *Walking on Frogs* (1989). In numerous poems, Cassidy's treatments of wild creatures become vehicles for his recurrent sense of the tensions between urban and rural modes of existence. More frequently, however, his work is concerned with the social and personal implications of experience; he has produced many compassionate but penetratingly observed studies of individuals in whose circumstances or actions he imaginatively locates broader human significances.

Catcher in the Rye, The, a novel by J. D. *Salinger, published in 1951. The novel is narrated in lively vernacular by the 16-year-old Holden Caulfield, agile-minded, maverick, imaginative, and a boarder at an expensive prep school, Pencey. We see him leaving the school he disliked and going to New York City, where, dreading a confrontation with his parents (very distant figures throughout the novel) he checks into a cheap hotel. Here he accepts the elevator operator's offer of a whore for the night. Holden is, as he tells us, a virgin; indeed, it later transpires that for him virginity is a 'good', a revulsion against sex being an important constituent of his vision of life. He cannot perform with the whore, and her pimp demands more money and assaults Holden. The next day he makes unsatisfactory encounters with an old girlfriend and with his adored younger sister Phoebe, and spends the night at the home of one of the few adults for whom he has any regard; the man makes furtive homosexual advances to him. Holden decides to run away West, but realization of his love for Phoebe stays him, and he suffers a kind of breakdown of which writing this novel is a therapy. The character of Holden fills and animates the entire novel, to such a degree that it is not surprising he became widely adopted as a role-model for so many readers. While it is possible to find inconsistencies in Holden's viewpoint, it is impossible to deny both the reality and the power of Holden himself and the literary virtuosity and integrity with which he is presented. This unusually affecting novel has become a testament and an inspiration for generations of readers all over the world. Certain of its phrases and epiphanies have passed already into Western folklore.

Catch-22, a novel by Joseph *Heller, published in 1961. Heller's first and finest novel, it is generally regarded as one of the greatest comic works of post-war American fiction. It is equally often seen as a powerful expression of anti-war sentiment, but its concerns, as many critics have noted, are as much with the relationship of the individual to society as they are with the nature of war and patriotism. Much of the novel is set in an American airforce base on an imaginary Mediterranean island and is structured around a bomber squadron's missions during the Italian campaign of 1943–4; this, however, is essentially a background against which Heller creates a remarkable gallery of comic characters, most of them satirizing some salient aspect of American life: business enterprise, capitalism, the civil and military bureaucracy, the patriotic spirit among them. The famous philosophical 'catch' of the title, a paradox, is explained by one of the novel's characters, Doc Daneeka: 'Anyone who wants to get out of combat duty isn't really crazy'; and the novel's hero, Yossarian, spends much of his time trying to escape the remorseless grip in which 'catch-22' holds him.

CATHER, Willa (1876–1947), American novelist, born in Virginia where she lived until she was nine; her family then moved to Nebraska, to the prairie country pioneered by Central European and Scandinavian emigrants, individuals at once dour and passionately nostalgic, who were to inspire her most famous novels. She was educated at the University of Nebraska, where she studied classical literature (also an influence on her work, with its emphasis on the pastoral). After a period of teaching and journalism, during which she published her first volume of poems, *April Twilights* (1903), and a book of short stories, *The Troll Garden* (1905), she worked in New York on the staff of the famous 'muck-raking' periodical, *McClure's Magazine*, from 1906 to 1912, eventually becoming editor. Her first novel, *Alexander's Bridge* (1912), was followed by her first characteristic work, **O Pioneers!* (1913), whose title was taken from Walt Whitman and which concerns a Swedish immigrant family struggling to establish itself on the Nebraskan prairies; *The Song of the Lark* (1915), a study of the professional dedication of an opera singer, Thea Kronberg, who clearly stands for all artists; and **My Antonia* (1918), a pastoral of life on the prairies and perhaps her most consistently popular work. Then came *One of Ours* (1922), which won her many readers, but also made her enemies. Its hero is a young man who escapes from a stultifying existence on a Nebraska farm into the war in France. His eventual redemption through suffering and death was—understandably—attacked by *Hemingway, *Fitzgerald, and others, who felt that Cather was not writing from experience and was preaching a dubious moral. *A *Lost Lady* (1923) is a delicately wrought study of elegant, warm-hearted Marion Forrester, who emerges as less innocent than she at first seems; it was followed by *My Mortal Enemy* (1926), which deals with the runaway marriage of a selfish and wilful woman, Myra Henshawe, and by *The *Professor's House* (1925), perhaps her finest novel, which depicts the falling out of love with life of Professor St Peters, a distinguished academic and authority on Spanish New Mexico. **Death Comes for the Archbishop* (1927), a historical novel set in New Mexico, concerns the life and work of two French Catholic priests and expresses the author's admiration for the Catholic Church. Cather herself never converted to Catholicism, although she was attracted by the moral values embodied in it, which she saw as providing an alternative to the corruption of American society. Other novels include *Shadows on the Rock* (1931), set in seventeenth-century Quebec, which continued the Catholic theme; *Lucy Gayheart* (1935), about a Midwestern girl torn between the values of her home town and those of the artistic world; and *Sapphira and the Slave Girl* (1940), a study of jealousy and possessiveness, set in her native Virginia. As Hermione Lee's critical biography, *Willa Cather: A Life Saved Up* (1989) makes clear, Cather's most significant achievement is to have annexed for women and for America the pastoral form, previously the preserve of European, male writers, and in doing so, to have created works of rich and universal resonance.

Cathleen Ni Houlihan, a play by W. B. *Yeats, published in 1902, the year of its production at St Theresa's Hall by the Irish Literary Theatre in which Maud Gonne played the title role. It was enormously successful and must be considered Yeats's only truly popular work for the theatre. By comparison with his other dramas *Cathleen Ni Houlihan*, which is written mainly in prose, has a highly effective straightforwardness as a patriotic allegory. The aged and distressed figure of Cathleen Ni Houlihan symbolizes Ireland in the tradition of the country's personification in folklore as the Shan Van Vocht, or 'Poor Old Woman'; Cathleen's four fields, representing the four provinces of Ireland, have been seized by strangers and she appears at the house of Michael Gillane to seek assistance. Gillane is preparing for his marriage; Cathleen, who is presented as a powerfully mysterious figure, prevails upon him; he chooses self-sacrifice in Cathleen's cause rather than personal good fortune, moved by the assurance that those who help her 'shall be remembered forever'. Gonne's passionate performance, concluding with the old woman's transformation into a regal young beauty, emphasized the nationalist import of the play, which intensified the commitment to Irish independence of some of its audience. In the late poem 'The Man and the Echo' Yeats asks uneasily, with reference to the events of 1916, 'Did that play of mine send out | Certain men the English shot?'

Cat on a Hot Tin Roof, a play by Tennessee *Williams, published in 1955 and revised in 1974, when it was awarded the Pulitzer Prize. The play became notorious for its treatment of homosexuality, which is never directly presented, but is depicted in a way that took contemporary audiences by surprise. Set in the Deep South, in the Mississippi Delta, the drama has as its pivot the sixty-fifth birthday celebrations of the patriarch Big Daddy, who, unknown to himself, is dying of cancer. His elder son and daughter-in-law, parents of a large and growing family, display an avaricious desire to get their hands on the estate. His other daughter-in-law, Maggie, is determined this should not happen; her husband, Brick, a handsome ex-athlete who has taken to drink, is Big Daddy's favourite, even though the relationship is under strain. The reasons for this emerge as the drama progresses, and the father confronts the son with allegations about the nature of his relationship with Skipper, a former friend and fellow sportsman whose death appears to have been brought about by his unrequited love for Brick. Apparently appalled by this aspersion, Brick protests his innocence, claiming that the suggestion that the relationship was of a homosexual nature had been put about by Maggie, and that Skipper's death had been caused by his feelings of humiliation at the cruel rumour. He then turns the tables on his father, who has demanded to know the truth at all costs, by revealing to him the truth about his imminent death. Williams's exploration of the underlying theme of homosexuality, restrained as it is, prevented the play from being performed in Britain and elsewhere for many years. When it was eventually revived, Williams worked with the director Elia Kazan, who had also directed the original Broadway performance with Burl Ives as Big Daddy. Kazan suggested making some changes to the last act in order to show the essentially sympathetic character of Maggie and it is this version which is usually played, although some critics prefer the original, starker version.

Cat's Eye, a novel by Margaret *Atwood, published in 1989. Told from the perspective of a painter, Elaine Risley, this reflective yet profoundly critical novel works on several levels: as a sensitive exploration of women's relationships with other women, with their families, and with men; as an examination of the changing mores of feminism, and of the post-feminist ideology of the 1980s; as an account of the development of a woman artist, and the transformation of lived experience into art; and as a portrait of the changing panorama of four decades of Canadian life, both social and artistic. A retrospective exhibition of her work provides Elaine with the opportunity to examine the events that inspired her creations. The poetic introspection of her early memories, with its haunting description of her relationship with her brother, is marred by her recollection of her bond with Cordelia, alternately friend and adversary, which serves as a metaphor for the illusions and betrayals she encounters in her life. The sections set in the present allow Atwood's satirical vision full scope, as she portrays the attitude of the present generation of feminist critics to their erstwhile icons. Looking back at her past from the perspective of a relatively complacent middle age, Elaine revises her own attitudes and those of successive feminist generations to allow a wide margin for the privileges of domesticity, introspection, and contented relationships.

CAUDWELL, Christopher, pseudonym of Christopher St John SPRIGG (1907–37), British critic, born in Putney; at the age of 15 he became a reporter on the *Yorkshire Observer*. Having become interested in aviation, he moved to London as a writer on aeronautics, producing numerous books, which include *The Airship* (1931) and *Let's Learn To Fly* (1937). These and his detective stories, among which are *Fatality in Fleet Street* (1933) and *The Perfect Alibi* (1934), were published under his original name. In 1935 he joined the Communist Party, adopting his pseudonym and moving to London's East End to renounce his bourgeois identity. He contributed criticism and polemical pieces to **Left Review*, urging writers to political activity. In 1936 he joined the International Brigade, and was killed in Spain in the following year. The first British Marxist critic (see MARXIST LITERARY CRITICISM) of note, he outlined his theory of poetry as a product of man's struggle with his environment in *Illusion and Reality* (1937), which quickly established his posthumous reputation. His other works of criticism include *Studies in a Dying Culture* (1938), in which G. B. *Shaw, T. E. *Lawrence, and Sigmund Freud are among his subjects, and *Further Studies in a Dying Culture* (1949; edited by Edgell *Rickword). His poetry was featured in **New Verse*. *Collected Poems*, edited by Alan Young, was published in 1986. While pieces like 'Heil Baldwin' are bluntly effective as political satire, elsewhere his verse emanates a powerful imaginative disquiet exemplified by the frequently anthologized 'The Progress of Poetry'.

CAUSLEY, Charles (1917–), British poet, born at Launceston, Cornwall, educated at Launceston College and Peterborough Training College. Between 1940 and 1946 he served in the Royal Navy, an experience informing many of his earlier poems, and was a teacher in Cornwall until he became a freelance writer in 1976. Among his numerous collections of poetry are *Farewell Aggie Weston* (1951), *Union Street* (1958), *Johnny Alleluia* (1961), **Secret Destinations* (1984), *A Field of Vision* (1988), and *Collected Poems* (1992). Much of Causley's work is notable for its fluent adaptations of ballad forms and other traditional modes of verse. He creates an accessible poetry of common experience in which there frequently exists a latent irony between the archaism of form and the unsettling modernity of content. 'At the British War Cemetery, Bayeux' and 'Song of the Dying Gunner' are two well-known examples of his ability to combine conventional rhythms with sharp authenticity of detail and stringency of tone and feeling. His later verse has been acclaimed for its development of verse forms of greater substance and complexity than he had generally employed hitherto. Causley is among the most highly regarded of contemporary authors of verse for children, volumes of which include *Figgie Hobbin* (1970), *The Young Man of Cury* (1991), and *All Day Saturday* (1994). His plays include *How Pleasant To Know Mr Lear* (1948), and a collection of short stories entitled *Hands To Dance* (1951). See also TOPOGRAPHICAL POETRY.

CAUTE, (John) David (1936–), British novelist and historian, born in Alexandria, Egypt, educated at Wadham College, Oxford. A fellow of All Souls until 1965, he has subsequently held numerous visiting professorships in Britain and the USA. A radical Marxist view of Western civilization and its relations with the Third World informs a number of novels, including *At Fever Pitch* (1959), set during Ghana's emergence into nationhood, *The K-Factor* (1983), and *News from Nowhere* (1986), both of which reflect the turmoil preceding the establishment of Zimbabwe. Recognized as an intellectually stimulating writer, Caute has been censured for the dominance of political analysis in his fiction. Among his other novels are *The Occupation* (1971), concerning an academic's quest for self-knowledge; *The Women's Hour* (1991), a comedy of gender politics in a university context; and *Dr Orwell and Mr Blair* (1994). His other publications include the historical works *Communism and the French Intellectuals, 1914–1960* (1964) and *The Fellow Travellers* (1973), on the visits to Russia made by numerous leading twentieth-century European writers; and the biography *Joseph Losey: A Revenge on Life* (1994).

CECIL, Lord (Edward Christian) David (Gascoyne) (1902–86), British biographer and critic, the youngest son of James Gascoyne-Cecil, the fourth Marquess of Salisbury; he was educated at Christ Church, Oxford. In 1924 he became a fellow of Wadham College, Oxford, and was Goldsmith's Professor of English Literature at Oxford from 1948 to 1970. His study of Cowper, *The Stricken Deer* (1929), gained him wide notice as a scholarly biographer. His subsequent biographical studies include *The Young Melbourne* (1939), *Lord M.; Or the Later Life of Lord Melbourne* (1954), *Max: Sir Max Beerbohm* (1964), and *Visionary and Dreamer* (1969), his treatment of Samuel Palmer and Edward Burne-Jones. Among the numerous works in which Cecil combined biographical elements with critical analysis are *Early Victorian Novelists* (1934), *Two Quiet Lives* (1948), which deals with Thomas Gray and Dorothy Osborne, and *A Portrait of Jane Austen* (1978). The eloquent descriptive impressionism of much of his writing is firmly in the tradition of nineteenth-century *belles-lettres*, a tendency which resulted in the disparagement of his work by F. R. *Leavis and others associated with **Scrutiny*. *A Portrait by His Friends* (edited by Hannah Cranborne, 1990) is a collection of memoirs of Cecil.

Celtic Twilight, The. (i) A term which is applied, sometimes mildly disparagingly, to the literary and cultural resurgence otherwise referred to as the *Irish Revival. Its suggestions of romantically mystical fusions of myth, legend, and superstition indicate that it is restricted in its appropriateness to the period 1889–1900; during these years, the literature of the Irish Revival was to a large extent dominated by such preoccupations in its elegiac and nostalgic involvement with the lost indigenous culture and history of Ireland. From around 1900 onward the Revival was characterized by increasingly provocative and naturalistic writing, notably in the developments of Irish drama at the *Abbey Theatre. (ii) The phrase originated with W. B. *Yeats's collection of folk-tales and personal reminiscences entitled *The Celtic Twilight* and is evocative of the melancholy Gaelic Pre-Raphaelitism of much of his earlier verse. First published in 1893, the book contained material derived from Yeats's recollections of his early years in Sligo, when he had listened to the stories told by some of the area's inhabitants; a second edition appeared in 1902, featuring additional tales and legends from the Galway region. Yeats had previously produced two collections in a similar vein, *Fairy and Folk Tales of the Irish Peasantry* (1888) and *Irish Fairy Tales* (1892); these were substantially drawn from existing literary sources and *The Celtic Twilight* is of greater interest than either for its autobiographical element.

Cement Garden, The, see MCEWAN, IAN.

CHAMBERS, Sir E(dmund) K(erchever) (1866–1954), British historian of the English stage, born at West Ilsley, Berkshire, educated at Corpus Christi College, Oxford, where he produced an edition of Shakespeare's *Richard II* (1891). From 1892 until his retirement he held a succession of posts in the Civil Service, rising to become a Second Secretary. His reputation as a scholar was established with *The Mediaeval Stage* (2 volumes, 1903), a study of the dramatic tradition out of which the work of Shakespeare and his contemporaries arose. *The Elizabethan Stage* (4 volumes, 1923) displays his characteristic concern to present the history of English drama with detailed reference to its social and economic contexts. Among his numerous other publications are *William Shakespeare: A Study of the Facts and Problems* (2 volumes, 1930); *Arthur and Britain* (1927), a survey of the variant Arthurian legends; and the critical biographies *Samuel Taylor Coleridge* (1938) and *Matthew Arnold* (1947). His edition of the *Oxford Book of Sixteenth Century Verse* appeared in 1932. He was the first president of the Malone Society from 1906 to 1936.

CHAMBERS, R(aymond) W(ilson) (1874–1942), British philologist and literary historian, born at Staxton in East Yorkshire, educated at University College London (UCL). In 1900 he became a fellow of UCL, where he succeeded W. P. *Ker as Quain Professor in 1922. *Widsith: A Study in Old English Heroic Legend* (1912), an edition of *Beowulf* (1914), and *Beowulf: An Introduction* (1921) were among the works that established him as one of the twentieth century's foremost scholars of Old English literature. After the appearance of *England Before the Norman Conquest* (1926) the range of his activities broadened to extend from early Germanic literature to Shakespeare and Milton; the scope of his interests is reflected in *Man's Unconquerable Mind* (1939), a collection of essays on authors from Bede to A. E. *Housman, whom he had known well at UCL. His best-known work outside the specialized fields of his contributions to philology is *Thomas More* (1935), a study of More's literary and historical importance, which drew commendation from the Vatican.

Chance, a novel by Joseph *Conrad, published in 1913, serialized in the *New York Herald*, 1912. It was Conrad's first novel to achieve popular success and marked the return of Marlow as narrator. It is divided into two parts, 'The Damsel' and 'The Knight'. Part I recounts the early life of Flora de Barral, the traumatic incident in which Flora's sense of her own worth is destroyed by her governess, and shows how Flora's insecurity is reinforced by subsequent events. Marlow investigates the disappearance of Mrs Fyne's brother, Captain Anthony, which is solved by Flora's account of her relations with him. Part II recounts the complex relations of Captain Anthony, Flora, and her father on board the '*Ferndale*', the 'psychological cabin mystery of discomfort'. Flora is one of the 'damaged women' who are of central importance in Conrad's late fiction. The study of her character and career is framed, on the one hand, by the feminism of Mrs Fyne and, on the other, by the frequently misogynistic commentary of Marlow. It is complemented by the exploration, in Part II, of Captain Anthony's conception of masculinity and its relation to the code of chivalry he has inherited from his father.

CHANDLER, Raymond (1888–1959), American crime writer, born in Chicago, but brought up from the age of seven in England, where he was educated at Dulwich College. He returned to America in 1912 and, after serving in the Canadian Army and the Royal Air Force during the First World War, settled in California and became an executive for an oil company. Sacked for drunkenness in 1932, he wrote detective stories for *pulp magazines, including **Black Mask*, gradually developing the figure of the detective narrator who emerged as Philip Marlowe in his first novel, *The *Big Sleep* (1939; filmed by Howard Hawks with Humphrey Bogart as Marlowe, 1946). This was followed by his highly acclaimed *Farewell, My Lovely* (1940), *The High Window* (1942), *The Lady in the Lake* (1943), *The Little Sister* (1949; republished in the USA as *Marlowe*), *The Long Goodbye* (1953), and *Playback* (1958). He was also employed as a screenwriter in Hollywood, working on the screenplays for Billy Wilder's *Double Indemnity* (1944; from the novel by James M. *Cain) and Alfred Hitchcock's *Strangers on a Train* (1951; from the novel by Patricia *Highsmith). Greatly influenced by Dashiell *Hammett, whom he much admired, he strove to take the detective novel further than had his predecessor, to give it an extra dimension and turn it into literature; in the process he romanticized Hammett's hero, who became a kind of modern knight errant: 'Down these mean streets a man must go who is not himself mean, who is neither tarnished nor afraid', he wrote in the essay 'The Simple Art of Murder' (1944). His influence on later writers of private eye novels has been immense, though his works have been perhaps critically more valued in Britain than in America: in an appreciation (*Harper's*, 1948) *Auden spoke for many when he wrote that Chandler's novels were 'serious studies of a criminal milieu, the Great Wrong Place, and his powerful but extremely depressing books should be read and judged, not as escape literature, but as works of art'. There is a life by Frank MacShane (1976); see also Miriam Gross (ed.), *The World of Raymond Chandler* (1977) and Jerry Speir, *Raymond Chandler* (1981). (See DETECTIVE FICTION.)

CHAPLIN, Sid (1916–86), British novelist and short-story writer, born in Shildon, County Durham. After leaving school at the age of 14, he worked as a miner. Later, he won a scholarship to Fircroft College for Working Men, where he started writing, and became a specialist writer for the National Coal Board. An influence on writers like Alan *Sillitoe and Stan *Barstow, his novels offer a realistic evocation of life among Tyneside mining families, and reflect a vanishing British working-class culture. Among his best novels are *The Day of the Sardine* (1961), in which the protagonist, the moody Arthur Haggerston, anticipates a typical John *Braine hero but with more cynicism about his own aspirations to an affluent way of life; and *The Watchers and the Watched* (1962). His other novels include *My Fate Cries Out* (1949), *The Thin Seam* (1950), *The Big Room* (1960), *Sam in the Morning* (1965), and *The Mines of Alabaster* (1971). Among his collections of short stories are *The Leaping Lad* (1946) and *In Blackberry Time* (1987).

CHARLES, Faustin (1944–), Trinidadian poet and novelist, born in Trinidad, educated at the Universities of Kent and London. His poems are distinctively Caribbean in tone, and his 'animal' poems are reminiscent of Ted *Hughes in their forcefulness. Poetry collections include *The Expatriate* (1969), *Crab Track* (1973), and *Days and Nights in the Magic Forest* (1986). The game of cricket features prominently in some of his poems, and also in his children's book, *Anancy's Day of Cricket* (1986). Wilson *Harris appears to have inspired his novels which, like his poems, are dense with archetypal imagery; these include *Signposts of the Jumbie* (1981) and *The Black Magic Man of Brixton* (1985). *Tales from the West Indies* (1985) is a collection of short stories.

CHARTERIS, Leslie (1907–93), American writer, born as Leslie Charles Bowyer Lin in Singapore and educated in England; he lived in the USA from 1935, working as a scriptwriter in Hollywood and becoming a US citizen in 1946. He was the author of a long series of novels and short stories, beginning with *Meet the Tiger* (1928), in which the hero is the immaculately dressed English young man about town Simon Templar, known as the Saint, a modern-day Robin Hood who rights injustice and succours the oppressed while evading the police. Later novels are often set in the USA, including *The Saint in Miami* (1940). A number of films, in most of which George Sanders took the leading role, several television and a radio series have depicted Templar's adventures.

Charwoman's Daughter, see STEPHENS, JAMES.

CHARYN, Jerome (1937–), American novelist, born and educated in New York, where he has set at least fifteen of his mythic, nightmarish novels, from *Once Upon a Drosky* (1964) to *War Cries Over Avenue C* (1985). In *Panna Maria* (1982) Manhattan is reminiscent of the archaic Poland of Isaac Bashevis *Singer. *Pinocchio's Nose* (1983) deals with the same material in science fiction form. A sequence of linked detective novels, also set in New York, has been collected as *The Isaac Quartet* (1984), and *Metropolis* (1986) is a non-fiction analysis of the city. Other novels include *American Scrapbook* (1969), about the incarceration of Japanese-Americans in the Second World War; *The Tar Baby* (1973), a surreal parody of the groves-of-academe novel; *The Franklin Scare* (1977), an evocation of F. D. Roosevelt; and *Darlin' Bill* (1980), a fantasia on the imaginary West of Wild Bill Hickok.

CHATWIN, Bruce (1940–89), British novelist and travel writer, born in Sheffield, educated at Marlborough and at Edinburgh University, where he gained a degree in anthropology, a lifelong interest. His first book, *In Patagonia* (1978), a collection of travel writing, was followed by *The Viceroy of Ouidah* (1980), a fictional account of the life of a Brazilian adventurer, Francisco Manoel da Silva, set in Africa in the early 1800s. *On the Black Hill* (1982) described the relationship between Lewis and Benjamin Jones, twin brothers, living on a remote Welsh hill farm at the turn of the century. The novel was admired for the poetic intensity with which the author conveyed the details of his characters' isolated existence, and the strength of feeling between them. The widely praised *The Songlines* (1987), an idiosyncratic mixture of fiction, anthropological study, and travelogue, chronicled the writer's travels in the Australian desert following the 'songlines' or ancestral paths of the Aboriginal people. These paths form a network across the landscape, acting both as invisible frontiers and as the repositories of ancient Aboriginal myths of creation. *Utz* (1989) displayed another aspect of the writer's remarkable versatility. Set in post-war Prague, the novel meticulously describes the fanatical love of a collector of Meissen porcelain for the delicate pieces he has amassed over the years, and for which he has sacrificed everything, even his own freedom. The posthumously published *Photographs and Notebooks* (ed. David King and Francis Wyndham, 1993) were compiled from photographs and notes from Chatwin's travels in Mauritania, Niger, Mali, Dahomey, and Afghanistan.

CHAUDHURI, Amit (1962–), Indian writer, born in Bombay and brought up in Calcutta; he studied at University College, London, and Balliol College, Oxford, and was made Creative Arts Fellow at Wolfenden College, Oxford. His first work of fiction, *A Strange and Sublime Address* (1991), consists of a novella and some stories; the former describes, in elegant, evocative prose, the holidays of a young boy from Bombay with his family in Calcutta. Stronger on atmosphere than on narrative, the novel won the Betty Trask award that year, and the Commonwealth Writers Prize for best first book the following year. His second novel, *Afternoon Raag* (1993), which blurs the boundaries between essay, memoir, and fiction, is similarly brief, lyrical, and evocative; the central metaphor of Indian music runs through a young Indian student's account of life in England and his musings on the nature of foreignness and belonging.

CHAUDHURI, Nirad C(handra) (1897–), Indian historian, born in Kishorganj, Bengal, educated at the University of Calcutta; he worked as a clerk and as a secretary to the Nationalist leader Subhas Chandra Bose before becoming a freelance writer in 1952. In 1970 he settled in Oxford. In addition to offering an account of his early life, his *The Autobiography of an Unknown Indian* (1951) constituted an idiosyncratic and penetrating survey of India's political development in the years up to 1921. Equally a combination of autobiography and modern history, *Thy Hand, Great Anarch!* (1987) covers the years 1921 to 1952. *The Continent of Circe* (1965) analyses India's social and cultural situation. His biographies *Clive of India* (1974) and *Scholar Extraordinary* (1974), a study of Friedrich Max Müller (1823–1900), sustain the theme of relations between Britain and India which runs through much of his writing. His other works include *A Passage to England* (1959), on his first visit to Britain under the sponsorship of the BBC in 1955.

CHAVEZ, Denise (1948–), Hispanic dramatist, born in Las Cruces, New Mexico, educated at New Mexico State University, Trinity University in San Antonio, and the University of New Mexico. Her allegiance to the Southwest and the Latina experience has shaped her fiction and drama. While she grew up valuing education, Chavez was also critical, from an early age, of the institutions which can marginalize women and minorities. Chavez is a self-avowed 'performance writer'; her first play, *Noviates*, was produced in 1971, and she has received critical acclaim. Her collection of plays *Shattering the Myth: Plays by Hispanic Women* (1992) attempts to bring critical attention to the often ignored contemporary Latina drama. She is celebrated for her lyrical blending of poetry and prose as well as her exploration of feminine consciousness. Her aesthetic is shaped by a contemporary concern for language games, politics, and the human psyche. Much of her work reads as extended monologue. Her numerous works include the collections *Life Is a Two-Way Street* (1980), *The Last of the Menu Girls* (1986), and *Face of an Angel* (1990).

CHEEVER, John (1912–82), American novelist and short-story writer, born in Quincy, Massachusetts, educated at Thayer Academy, his expulsion from which became the subject of his earliest works. As well as producing a rich stream of books, he also taught creative writing at several colleges including Boston University. Cheever's short stories satirized New England suburban life with a sharply observant eye. These appeared in several volumes, including *The Way Some People Live: A Book of Stories* (1943), *The Enormous Radio and Other Stories* (1943), *The Housebreaker of Shady Hill and Other Stories* (1958), *Some People, Places and Things That Will Not Appear in My Next Novel* (1961), *The Brigadier and the Golf Widow* (1964), and *The World of Apples* (1973). This manner also shaped the two-novel sequence *The Wapshot Chronicle* (1957) and *The Wapshot Scandal* (1964), which tells of the decline of a once wealthy family in a small New England town. Through the narration of the adventures of two itinerant sons as they seek employment, the novels explore the conspicuous wealth and brashness of American life. In a similar social context, *Bullet Park* (1969) tells of the struggle between two men, Hammer and Nailes, in an environment of wealth and envy. The uncharacteristic *Falconer* (1977) is the taut tale of the ex-academic Farragut's prison life as he attempts to assemble some meaning in his existence. Cheever's other fiction works include *Oh, What a Paradise It Seems* (1982), a novel; and *The Stories of John Cheever* (1978), which was acclaimed by both critics and public, winning a Pulitzer Prize and several other awards. Although a minor scandal accompanied the posthumous publication of his letters and journals, his reputation as an important figure should remain unscathed.

CHESNUTT, Charles W(addell) (1858–1932), African-American short-story writer and novelist, born in Cleveland, Ohio. He passed the Ohio Bar examination in 1887, but subsequently worked mainly as a legal stenographer. Highly praised by William Dean Howells, Chesnutt's stories combine literary sophistication with a deep immersion in the culture and folklore of blacks in the American South. They appeared in the *Atlantic Monthly*, and were collected in *The Conjure Woman* (1899) and *The Wife of His Youth and Other Stories of the Color Line* (1899). His novels, though less widely read now, but equally successful as the stories in his own day, include *The House Behind the Cedars* (1900), *The Marrow of Tradition* (1901), and *The Colonel's Dream* (1905).

CHESTERTON, G(ilbert) K(eith) (1874–1936), English novelist, essayist, poet, and journalist, born on Campden Hill, London, educated at St Paul's School, London, and the Slade School of Art. An outspoken and controversial journalist, Chesterton wrote for the *Daily News*, *The Bookman*, and the *Illustrated London News*, contributed to *Eye Witness*, and was editor of *New Witness* (1916–23) and *G. K.'s Weekly* (1925–36). His friend, Hilaire *Belloc, several of whose books Chesterton illustrated, greatly influenced his political and religious thinking; jointly nicknamed 'the Chesterbelloc' by *Shaw, both writers expressed their pro-Boer anti-Imperialist stance in *The Speaker*. Chesterton was fervently anti-capitalist, opposed to technological advance, and became president of the Distribution League advocating a fair distribution of the nation's land. His first novel, *The Napoleon of Notting Hill* (1904), is a romance set in a future where London boroughs become warring city-states. *The Man Who Was Thursday* (1908), aptly subtitled 'A Nightmare', deals with a conspiracy by anarchists, each named after one day of the week. Other novels, all with elements of fantasy, include *The Ball and the Cross* (1910), *Manalive* (1912), *The Flying Inn* (1914), and *The Return of Don Quixote* (1927). Chesterton wrote many volumes of short stories, the most popular of which are the Father Brown stories, featuring the humble East Anglian Roman Catholic priest as master detective. The first collection, *The Innocence of Father Brown* (1911), was followed by *The Wisdom of Father Brown* (1914), *The Incredulity of Father Brown* (1926), *The Secret of Father Brown* (1927), and *The Scandal of Father Brown* (1935). The best stories, such as 'The Absence of Mr Glass', 'The Chief Mourner of Marne', 'The Insoluble Problem', 'The Mirror of the Magistrate', 'The Queer Feet', 'The Sins of Prince Saradine', and 'The Worst Crime in the World', are brilliantly and poetically written, with the plot often turning on an ingenious, original paradox. Read closely, the stories reveal themselves not so much as detective stories but as parables, in which moral theology is presented as detection. Chesterton became the first President of the Detection Club on its foundation by Anthony *Berkeley in 1928. As a critic, his literary judgements were invariably interwoven with his moral views. His critical works include *The Victorian Age in Literature* (1913); literary studies of *Robert Browning* (1903), *Heretics* (1905), *Charles Dickens* (1906), *Orthodoxy* (1909), *George Bernard Shaw* (1910), *William Blake* (1910), *Robert Louis Stevenson* (1927), and *Chaucer* (1932); and biographies of *St. Francis of Assisi* (1923), *William Cobbett* (1925), and *St. Thomas Aquinas* (1933). Chesterton became a Roman Catholic in 1922; he set out his religious views in *The Everlasting Man* (1925). He wrote collections of essays, plays, *A Short History of England* (1917), several volumes of verse, often celebrating the Englishness of England, including *Greybeards at Play* (1900), *The Wild Knight* (1900), *The Ballad of the White Horse* (1911), and *Collected Poems* (1927; revised 1933), and an *Autobiography* (1936). See *The Bodley Head G. K. Chesterton* (1984), edited by P. J. *Kavanagh; *Gilbert Keith Chesterton* (1944), by Maisie Ward; and *G. K. Chesterton: A Half Century of Views* (1987), edited by D. J. Conlon.

Chicago Critics, a group of critics and scholars at the University of Chicago who pursued what they thought of as an authentic *Formalism, a return to Aristotle and the formal principles of art. Their leading spokesman was R. S. Crane (1886–1967), who saw criticism not as a discipline but as an assembly of 'frameworks' or 'languages' for approaching literature. The urgent questions to be asked concerned what one 'thinks *with*' rather than 'thinks *about*'. There are resemblances between the Chicago critics and the Russian Formalists, but the Chicago School was more purist, and would have thought Shklovsky's conception of an art that helps us recover the 'sensation of life' was sentimental, mere moralizing criticism in a new disguise. The work of this school is perhaps best exemplified in *Critics and Criticism* (1952), a collection of essays edited by Crane.

Childermass, The, a novel by W. *Lewis, published in 1928. The novel, the first part of Lewis's unfinished tetralogy *The Human Age*, is his most idiosyncratic—even eccentric—work. Part surrealist fantasy, part polemic, it opens with a magnificent topographical description of the plains of Dis, or Hell, where Lewis's protagonists, Pullman and Sattersthwaite, find themselves at the beginning of their comic odyssey into the Afterlife. In the course of their journey towards the Magnetic City (Purgatory), they pass through a number of different 'time-zones', in which their surroundings are alternately static or fluid, and undergo various changes of age, sex, and persona. The work satirizes, amongst other things, Einstein's Theory of Relativity and Bergson's theories of time, as well as the 'stream of consciousness' method of Gertrude *Stein and James *Joyce. It also offers an indictment of the mass political movements of communism and fascism, which Lewis regarded as equally pernicious.

CHILDERS, (Robert) Erskine (1870–1922), British novelist, born in London, educated at Haileybury, and at Trinity College, Oxford. He fought in the Boer War and served in the Royal Naval Air Service during the First World War. In peacetime he was a clerk in the House of Commons (1895–1910). From 1910 he agitated for Home Rule in Ireland and used his own yacht, the *Asgard*, to supply German arms to the Irish volunteers in 1914. Elected to the Dáil Éireann in 1921, he was Principal Secretary to the delegation for the Irish–UK treaty. After the establishment of the Irish Free State, Childers joined the IRA, becoming Director of Publicity. He was court-martialled and executed in 1922. In *The Riddle of the Sands* (1903), his only work of fiction, two amateurs attempt to foil a German plan to mass a fleet of boats and barges in the Baltic for an invasion attempt on Britain. The novel is narrated by the socially adept Carruthers of the Foreign Office who joins Davies aboard the *Dulcibella*, a converted lifeboat cruising among the Frisian Islands. Together they ply the shallow channels between the sands off the coasts of Germany and Holland in pursuit of Dollmann, a former officer in the Royal Navy, now employed by the Germans. The chase builds up as the two amateurs gradually expose the Germans' plans. Though the book was a sensational bestseller, Childers's aim, and achievement, was to draw attention to the menace of an enemy yet to be acknowledged.

CHILDRESS, Alice (1920–), African-American playwright and novelist; born in Charleston, South Carolina, she grew up in Harlem, New York. She became an actress in the late 1930s and was director of the American Negro Theater School from 1941 to 1952. Among the best-known of her many plays are *Trouble in Mind* (1955), an inventive exploration of the theme of racial stereotyping, and *Wedding Band* (1961), centring on an inter-racial erotic relationship in the Southern states. In both her dramatic writings and her prose fiction she is noted for the uncompromising candour with which she treats controversial issues. Her novels include *A Hero ain't Nothing but a Sandwich* (1973), a harshly objective narrative of juvenile drug addiction, and *A Short Walk* (1979), which chronicles the life of a black woman in the early decades of the twentieth century. Among her other works is *Like One of the Family: Conversations from a Domestic's Life* (1956), a collection of wryly satirical monologues in the voice of 'Mildred', a black housemaid.

CHILDRESS, Mark (1957–), American novelist, born in Monroeville, Alabama, educated at the University of Alabama. His first novel, *A World Made of Fire* (1985), gained considerable attention for its sensitive evocation of rural Alabama in the first two decades of the twentieth century, and focuses on Stella, a young woman coming to terms with the death of her 'poor white' mother in a fire. *V for Victor* (1989) tells of an adolescent who unwittingly becomes involved with German spies during the Second World War. His third novel, *Tender* (1990), is epic in scope and concerns the origins and early career of a rock and roll star who bears more than a passing resemblance to Elvis Presley. The Civil Rights Movement and other liberating developments of the 1960s form the basis of *Crazy in Alabama* (1993). He has also published childrens' fiction.

CHIN, Frank (1940–), Asian-American novelist and playwright, born in Berkeley, California, educated at the University of California, Berkeley, the State University of Iowa, and the University of California, Santa Barbara. Chin, who was the first Chinese-American brakeman on the Southern Pacific Railroad, later became the first contemporary Chinese-American playwright to have his work staged in New York at the American Place Theatre: *The Chickencoop Chinaman* was performed in 1972, as was *The Year of the Dragon* (televised on PBS in 1975). He was a founding member of the East West Players, the longest-running Asian-American theatre company in the nation. For his work as co-editor of *Aiiieeeee! An Anthology of Asian American Writers*, a seminal anthology published in 1975 by Howard University Press, and for his recovery of 'lost' Asian-American authors such as Toshio Mori and John Okada, he is often considered the grandfather of *Asian-American literature. His own more recent work includes a collection of short fiction, *The Chinaman Pacific and Frisco RR Co* (1988), which includes excerpts from his unpublished novel, 'A Chinese Lady Dies'; the *Big Aiiieeeee! An Anthology of Chinese and Japanese American Literature* (1991); and the novels *Donald Duk* (1991), a *Bildungsroman* set in San Francisco's Chinatown, and *Gunga Din Highway* (1994).

CHINODYA, Shimmer (1957–), Zimbabwean novelist, born in Gweru, educated at the University of Zimbabwe and at the University of Iowa. He became editor-in-chief of the Curriculum Development Unit at the Zimbabwean Ministry of Education. Under the name 'B. S. Chiraska' he is the author of a number of educational textbooks and stories for children. *Dew in the Morning* (1982), his first novel, projects an affirmative view of post-Independence Zimbabwe through the understated lyricism with which it treats the human and natural aspects of its rural setting. The psychologically acute *Farai's Girls* (1984) investigates the nature of human relations through the chief protagonist's liaisons with a succession of girlfriends. In *Harvest of Thorns* (1989), the passage from adolescence to adulthood is dramatically projected in the narrative of growth to maturity against the background of the Zimbabwean War of Liberation. Chinodya is represented as a poet in T. O. McLoughlin's edition of *New Writing in Rhodesia* (1976).

CHINWEIZU (1943–), Nigerian poet and critic, born in Eluama Isuikwuato, in Imo State, Eastern Nigeria, educated at Government College, Afikpo, Massachusetts Institute of Technology, and the State University of New York at Buffalo. In the late 1970s, he taught Afro-American Studies at San Jose University,

California. Chinweizu's statement that the 'great unfinished business of African decolonization and development is my theme' is central to his poetry and criticism. *Energy Crisis and Other Poems* (1978) and *Invocations and Admonitions* (1986) are among his collections of poems, which engage a range of moral and political themes with reference to the whole of Africa. His verse reflects the rich oral traditions of African writing espoused in *Toward the Decolonization of African Literature* (with O. Jemie and I. Madubuike; two volumes, 1980, 1981), his best-known critical work. Chinweizu's other publications include *The West and the Rest of Us* (1975), a passionately polemical critique of economic and cultural exploitation in the Third World, and the satirical writings collected in *The Footrace* (1981).

CHIPASULA, Frank M(kalawile) (1949–), Malawian poet, born in Luanshya, Zambia; he was educated at the Universities of Zambia and Malawi and became a citizen of Malawi. After working as a freelance broadcaster with the Malawi Broadcasting Corporation and as an editor with the National Education Company of Zambia, he came under threat from the Malawian authorities as a political dissenter and entered voluntary exile in America in 1978. He gained higher degrees at Brown University and Yale and became an Associate Professor of Black Literature at the University of Nebraska. His earlier work is contained in *Visions and Reflections* (1972) and *O Earth Wait for Me* (1980), both published in Zambia. The long poem *Nightwatcher, Nightsong* (1986), the first of his books to be published in America, was followed in 1991 by the substantial collection *Whispers in the Wings*. Chipasula's poetry is characterized by the passionate conviction and power of its testimony to conditions of tyranny and injustice in Malawi. His verse draws equally on the folk idioms of Malawi and Zambia and the ironic sophistication of modern Western traditions. He is the editor of the anthologies *A Decade of Poetry* (1980) and *When My Brothers Come Home: Poems from Central and Southern Africa* (1985).

CHOMSKY, Noam (1928–), American critic and linguist, born in Philadelphia, educated at the University of Pennsylvania. He has held many academic posts in America and Britain, and in 1976 he became Professor of Linguistics at the Massachusetts Institute of Technology. For Chomsky the approaches to language of both traditionalists and structuralists were flawed or short-sighted. He saw the learning mind as neither a genetic reservoir nor a *tabula rasa* but the locus of a set of innate possibilities or capacities; above all, the ability to build entirely new sentences rather than (however elaborately) copy old ones. Chomsky spoke of the 'deep structures' of language, and of the relevance of a 'generative grammar', that is, of a set of rules which would permit the generation of coherent and intelligible sentences in a given language. 'Obviously', he wrote in *Aspects of the Theory of Syntax* (1965), 'every speaker of a language has mastered and internalized a generative grammar that expresses his knowledge of the language. This is not to say he is aware of the rules . . . or that his statements about his intuitive knowledge of the language are necessarily accurate . . . Thus a generative grammar attempts to specify what the speaker actually knows, not what he may report about his knowledge.' Chomsky's other major works are *Syntactic Structures* (1957) and *Cartesian Linguistics* (1966). His concept of 'linguistic competence'—what a native speaker of a language may reasonably be expected to be able to say and understand—has been adapted by *Reader-response theory, where the idea of an analogous 'literary competence' is often invoked. Chomsky is a radical critic of his country's foreign policies and was an important opponent of the US involvement in Vietnam. Among his best polemical works are *American Power and the New Mandarins* (1969), *Deterring Democracy* (1991), *Year 501: The Conquest Continues* (1993), *Rethinking Camelot: JFK, the Vietnam War and U.S. Political Culture* (1993), and *World Orders, Old and New* (1994). He has continued eloquently and indefatigably to campaign for the rights of repressed minorities in the Middle East and elsewhere.

CHRISTIE, Dame Agatha (Mary Clarissa), née Miller (1890–1976), British *detective fiction writer, born in Torquay, Devon; she studied singing and piano in Paris, and in 1914 married Archibald Christie, an officer in the Royal Flying Corps. As a hospital dispenser during the First World War she acquired a knowledge of poisons which she later put to good use in her detective stories. In 1926 an attack of amnesia, brought on by the death of her mother and the impending break-up of her marriage, led to a much-publicized disappearance, which ended when she was discovered in a hotel in Harrogate. She was divorced in 1928 and in 1930 married the archaeologist Max Mallowan, whom she accompanied on excavations in Syria and Iraq. In *The Mysterious Affair at Styles* (1920), the first of her detective novels, she introduced Hercule Poirot, the Belgian detective who reappeared in many of her sixty-six novels. Of the Poirot stories, the best are perhaps *The Murder of Roger Ackroyd* (1926), *Lord Edgware Dies* (1933; US title *Thirteen at Dinner*), *Murder on the Orient Express* (1934; US title *Murder in the Calais Coach*), *The A.B.C. Murders* (1936; US title *The Alphabet Murders*), *Cards on the Table* (1936), *One, Two, Buckle My Shoe* (1940; US title *The Patriotic Murders*, also published in the USA as *An Overdose of Death*), *Evil under the Sun* (1941), and *The Hollow* (1946; US title *Murder after Hours*). In *The Murder at the Vicarage* (1930), however, she introduced another detective, Miss Marple, an elderly spinster; the novels in which she appears are in some ways to be preferred to the Poirot stories. The best include *The Body in the Library* (1942), *The Moving Finger* (1942), *A Murder Is Announced* (1950), *They Do It with Mirrors* (1952; US title *Murder with Mirrors*), *4.50 from Paddington* (1957; US title *What Mrs McGillicuddy Saw!*; also published in the USA as *Murder She Said*). Other novels, featuring neither Poirot nor Miss Marple, are *Ten Little Niggers*

(1939; US title *And Then There Were None*; also published in the USA as *Ten Little Indians*), *The Pale Horse* (1961), and *Endless Night* (1967). She also published a large number of detective short stories, two volumes of verse, six romantic novels under the pseudonym Mary Westmacott, two self-portraits (*Come Tell Me How You Live*, 1946; *An Autobiography*, 1977), and some fifteen plays, adapted from her novels and short stories, including *The Mousetrap* (from the novelette *Three Blind Mice*, 1948), which has run continuously in London since 1952. Her enormous international success is perhaps due to her ingenuity in contriving plots and misdirecting the reader. Her style is undistinguished, though brisk, and her characterization is adequate for the demands of the genre. There is a biography by Janet Morgan (1984); see also R. Barnard, *A Talent to Deceive* (1980), P. D. Maida and N. B. Spornick, *Murder She Wrote* (1982), and C. Osborne, *The Life and Crimes of Agatha Christie* (1982).

CHRISTOPHER, John, pseudonym of Christopher Samuel YOUD (1922–), British writer, born in Lancashire, who also published novels under his own name, and as Peter Graaf and Hilary Ford. As Christopher, he became familiar to a large readership as the successor to J. *Wyndham in the field of *science fiction, and in novels such as *The Death of Grass* (1956) and *The World in Winter* (1962) he streamlined the 'cozy catastrophe' tale created by his mentor. This form of disaster narrative depicts an England threatened by catastrophe, and a family escaping into the countryside in search of new rural roots. Subsequently, he specialized in science fiction for adolescents, notably the tales collected in *The Tripods Trilogy* (1980), *The Sword of the Spirits Trilogy* (1980), and *A Dusk of Demons* (1993).

Chrysalids, The, see WYNDHAM, JOHN.

CHURCH, Richard Thomas (1893–1972), British poet and novelist, born in London, educated at Dulwich Hamlet School. He was a civil servant from 1909 to 1933, when he became a publisher's reader. *The Flood of Life*, his first collection of verse, appeared in 1917; some seventeen further volumes included *The Dream* (1922), *News From the Mountain* (1932), and *The Burning Bush* (1967). Church's poetry reflects his belief in the poet's duty to frame accessible affirmations of permanent human values. Meditation, emotion, and observation combine to Wordsworthian effect in his best work. With the exception of the free verse of *Mood Without Measure* (1928), he almost invariably used traditional verse forms. His career as a novelist began with *Oliver's Daughter* in 1930; notable among his numerous other novels are *The Porch* (1937) and *The Dangerous Years* (1956). The lyrically descriptive qualities of his verse are present in his fiction, which he regarded as continuous with his activities as a poet. Among his other works are three volumes of autobiography, *Over the Bridge* (1955), *The Golden Sovereign* (1957), and *The Voyage Home* (1964); the biography *Mary Shelley* (1928); and the critical study *The Growth of the English Novel* (1966).

CHURCHILL, Caryl (1938–), British playwright, born in London, educated in Canada and at Oxford University. She first attracted critical notice with *Owners* (1972), a sardonic comedy about the effects of property and profiteering on personal relationships. This was followed by *Objections to Sex and Violence* (1975), an exploration of the subjects of the title; *Light Shining in Buckinghamshire* (1975), about radical politics in the Cromwellian era; *Vinegar Tom* (1976), about the witchhunts and misogyny of the same era; and *Cloud Nine* (1979), a serio-comedy which moves from the colonies in Victorian times to contemporary London, and requires some of its actors to embody more than one gender as well as more than one character, by way of debating the uncertainties and confusions of sexuality. The impressive *Top Girls* (1982) opens with a surreal dinner party, hosted by the high-achieving managing director of a secretarial agency, Marlene, whose guests include exemplary women from history and legend, but in the realistic second half some harsh suggestions are made about the nature of women's 'liberation', Thatcherism, and the 'enterprise culture' of the 1980s. There followed *Fen* (1983), a portrait of a troubled rural community in East Anglia, and researched by the author in conjunction with the Joint Stock Company, which presented it; *Serious Money* (1987), a Jonsonian comedy of humours about financial practice and malpractice in the City of London; *Mad Forest* (1990), the result of field trips to Romania with drama students, and about that country before, during, and after the uprising against Ceausescu; and *The Skriker* (1994), a highly visual piece in which creatures from fairytales and folklore invade the lives of two working-class girls. Caryl Churchill is a socialist and a feminist, but her best plays are notable for their intelligent and open-minded exploration of social, political, and moral issues, as well as for their stylistic inventiveness.

CHURCHILL, Winston (1871–1947), American novelist, born in St Louis, Missouri, educated at the US Naval Academy, Annapolis, Maryland. Churchill's first novel, *The Celebrity: An Episode* (1898), was a satire on New York politics and journalism. *Richard Carvel* (1899), set during the American Revolution, brought Churchill fame and established his *métier* for romantic fiction with a historical setting in the American past. *The Crisis* (1901) concerns St Louis at the time of the Civil War, while *The Crossing* (1904) has affinities with the 'Leatherstocking' novels of James Fenimore Cooper with its background of the American frontier towards the close of the eighteenth century. *Coniston* (1906), *Mr. Crewe's Career* (1908), and *A Far Country* (1915) are explorations of the political and economic climate of pre-war America. Churchill, a friend of President Theodore Roosevelt, was the Progressive Party candidate for the governorship of New Hampshire in 1912. His late works, notably *The Uncharted Way* (1940), are mainly essays in Christian doctrine.

Novelist to a Generation: The Life and Thought of Winston Churchill (1976) is a study by Robert W. Schneider.

CHURCHILL, Sir Winston (Leonard) Spencer (1874–1965), British statesman and historian, born in Blenheim Palace, educated at Harrow and Sandhurst. While on military service in Cuba, India, and Africa from 1895 to 1899, he acted as war correspondent for various periodicals. Among his early publications are the campaign histories *The Story of the Malakand Field Force* (1898) and *The River War* (1899). His only novel, *Savrola*, a politically acute tale of revolution, appeared in 1900, the year he entered parliament as MP for Oldham. In 1955 he retired from an illustrious and often controversial political career after a second term as Prime Minister. His inspiring leadership, which drew on his remarkable powers of oratory, throughout the Second World War established him in the general regard as the greatest statesman of his age; *War Speeches 1940–1945* was published in 1946. The magisterial *The Second World War* (6 volumes, 1948–54) is the most valued of his histories, which also include *The World Crisis* (4 volumes, 1923–9), a study of the First World War, and *A History of the English-Speaking Peoples* (4 volumes, 1956–8), a survey of Britain and its influence from pre-history to the modern era. In 1953 he was awarded a Nobel Prize. Among Churchill's other works are the autobiographical *My Early Life* (1930), the biography of his celebrated forebear *Marlborough* (4 volumes, 1933–8), and *Great Contemporaries* (1937), which contains perceptive portraits of T. E. *Lawrence and others Churchill admired. Thirty-four volumes of his *Collected Works* appeared between 1973 and 1976. His son Randolph Churchill (1911–68) wrote the first two volumes (1966, 1967) of an official biography; a further six volumes (1971–88) were produced by Martin *Gilbert.

Cider with Rosie, see LEE, LAURIE.

CISNEROS, Sandra (1945–), American poet and novelist of Mexican-American extraction, born in Chicago, educated at the *Iowa Writers' Workshop. Her novel *The House on Mango Street* (1983) draws heavily upon childhood memories and an unadorned childlike idiom in its depiction of life in the Chicano community. Issues of racial and sexual oppression, poverty, and violence are explored in a number of interconnected vignettes which together form a modified autobiographical structure. *Woman Hollering Creek and Other Stories* (1991) continues the exploration of ethnic identity within the patriarchal context of Chicano culture. *Bad Boys* (1980) and *My Wicked Wicked Ways* (1987) are volumes of poems. See LATINO/LATINA LITERATURE IN ENGLISH.

CLAMPITT, Amy (1920–94), American poet, born into a Quaker family at New Providence, Iowa; she was educated at Grinnell College, and spent much of her working life in New York publishing. Her writing has been a case of spectacular late development: *Multitudes, Multitudes* appeared in 1974, and she was awarded a Guggenheim Fellowship in 1982. Clampitt's breakthrough came with *The Kingfisher* (1983), which won extravagant praise for its striking descriptions of natural phenomena ('Sea Mouse', 'Lindenbloom', 'The Sun Underfoot Amongst the Sundews'), its sumptuously literary language bringing comparisons with Hopkins, Dylan *Thomas, and Marianne *Moore. Her poems often involve journeys, classical myth, images of femaleness (as in 'A Procession at Candlemas'), and a sense of the natural world as numinous. *What the Light Was Like* (1985) exemplifies Clampitt's attachment to English and American landscape, and Romantic poets such as Keats. *Archaic Figure* (1987) favours a generally simpler, less cluttered diction to portray travels in Greece and Venice, and the lives of women writers. *Westward* (1991) concerns migrations: of peoples and lifestyles, plants and birds, across America.

CLARK, Brian (1932–), British playwright, born in Bournemouth, educated at the Central School of Speech and Drama and at Nottingham University; he became a teacher and, from 1968 to 1972, a staff tutor in drama at the University of Hull. His stage plays have attempted to give a human dimension to large social and political issues. They include *Can You Hear Me at the Back?* (1979), in which a middle-aged architect reassesses a life that has become both personally and professionally unfulfilling—he is in a sterile marriage, and has been responsible for the development of a drab and ugly 'new town'; and *The Petition* (1986), about the wife of a reactionary old general who, after fifty years of marriage, becomes involved in the campaign against nuclear weapons. But Clark remains best known for *Whose Life Is It, Anyway?* (1978), which involves a paralysed car crash victim's attempts to defy those officiously keeping him alive and becomes a powerful, yet often humorous, argument for euthanasia. That piece was adapted for the theatre from television, a medium for which Clark has written many 'one-off' plays and the serial *Telford's Change*.

CLARK, Kenneth (Mackenzie), Lord (1903–83), British art historian and critic, educated at Winchester and at Trinity College, Oxford. The influence of both Ruskin and *Berenson is evident in his first work, *The Gothic Revival* (1928). Of his many public appointments he was director of the National Gallery (1934–45), Slade Professor of Fine Art at Oxford (1946–50), and Chairman of the Arts Council (1953–60). In 1953 he published his greatest work *The Nude: A Study of Ideal Art*. His television series *Civilization*, published as a book in 1969, gained him a wide audience and a peerage; it argued that truly civilized art both expresses its times and transcends them. Other works include *Leonardo da Vinci* (1939), *Florentine Painting* (1945), *Landscape into Art* (1949), and two volumes of autobiography, *Another Part of the Wood* (1974) and *The Other Half* (1977).

CLARK BEKEDEREMO, J(ohn) P(epper) (1935–), Nigerian dramatist, poet, and critic, born in

Kiagbodo, Ijaw country, Niger Delta, educated at the University of Ibadan. Clark travelled to the USA as Parvin Fellow at Princeton in 1962; his view of America, in his hard-hitting, splenetic *America, Their America* (1964), caused considerable controversy. The poetry contained in *Poems* (1962) and *A Reed in the Tide* (1965) combines African and European techniques to unusual effect. *Casualties: Poems 1966–68* (1970) contains mainly poems which mourn the human losses suffered as a result of the Nigerian Civil War (1967–70). Poems from all three collections have been published in *A Decade of Tongues: Selected Poems 1958–68* (1981). Further collections include *State of the Union* (1985) and *Mandela and Other Poems* (1988). Drawing from Ijaw mythology and ritual, Clark's plays are more directly committed to African cultural values than his poetry. Those values imply a cosmos similar to Greek tragedy in his best-known play, *Song of a Goat* (1961, perf. 1962), written in a jagged blank verse. *Song of a Goat, The Masquerade*, and *The Raft*, all set in the Niger Delta, were collected in *Three Plays* (1964). Clark's research into Ijaw traditional myths and legends at Ibadan's Institute of African Studies has resulted in his scholarly edition and translation of *The Ozidi Saga* (1978) which has inspired both a play, *Ozidi* (1966), and a film, *The Ozidi of Atazi* (1969). The play, like the saga, focuses on Ozidi, a posthumous son born and raised to avenge his father's murder, and tragically killed in war by his own comrades. The film, directed by Frank Speed in close collaboration with Clark, records highlights of a seven-day festival in which villagers from the Niger Delta re-enact Ozidi's fate. *The Boat, The Return Home*, and *Full Circle*, each performed in 1981, are published in *The Bikoroa Plays* (1985). His *Collected Plays* appeared in 1992. Clark's series of essays on African poetry have been collected in *The Example of Shakespeare* (1970).

CLARKE, Arthur C(harles) (1917–), British writer, born in Somerset, educated at King's College, London. He is the only contemporary British author to dominate the entire field of *science fiction. He was noted for the originality and clarity of his non-fiction, much of it promulgating the lure and necessity of space travel, and as early as 1945 originated in an article the concept of the geosynchronous communication satellite. In his visions of the future he embodied a sense of the wisdom of technological progress. From 1946, with the publication of 'Rescue Party' in the American *Astounding*, Clarke's reputation became established, but it was with his fifth novel, *Childhood's End* (1953), that his true voice became heard; in this meditation on man's evolutionary destiny, a remoteness is combined with the urgent narrative techniques of the American *pulp tradition. Its hypnotic effect can also be seen in other novels, such as *The City and the Stars* (1956), *The Deep Range* (1957), *Rendezvous with Rama* (1973), and *The Fountains of Paradise* (1979). His shorter fiction appeared in several collections including *Expedition to Earth* (1953), *Reach for Tomorrow* (1956), *Tales from the White Hart* (1957), *The Other Side of the Sky* (1958), and *The Nine Billion Names of God* (1967). Clarke achieved wide recognition when his early short story was adapted by Stanley Kubrick into the film *2001: A Space Odyssey* (1968). See also UTOPIA AND ANTI-UTOPIA.

CLARKE, Austin (1896–1974), Irish poet and dramatist, born in Dublin, educated at University College, Dublin, where he became an English Assistant in 1917. His first volume of verse, a reworking of the legend of Diarmid and Grainne entitled *The Vengeance of Fionn*, appeared in 1917. Succeeding volumes included *The Sword of the West* (1921) and *Pilgrimage* (1929); these works made use of Irish myth and history from the medieval era, a period largely overlooked by *Yeats and his followers. He lived in England as a literary journalist from 1921 to 1937, when he returned to Dublin, devoting himself until the early 1950s to his interest in verse-drama. *The Plot Succeeds* (1950), which characteristically incorporates comic elements, is recognized as the best of his many plays. *Collected Plays* appeared in 1963. The historical dimension dominant in his earlier poetry was supplanted by more immediate personal and cultural concerns in *Night and Morning* of 1938. Absorbed in theatrical activities, he produced no further collections until *Ancient Lights* of 1955, which initiated his work's satirical engagement with aspects of modern Irish life. Thereafter he wrote and published poetry prolifically until his death. *Flight to Africa* (1963) contains a number of his finest poems; *The Horse Eaters* (1960) and *A Sermon on Swift* (1968) are among his other distinguished late collections. His poetry is noted for its metrical and musical intricacies, which draw on the traditions of Gaelic verse, and the sensual precision of its imagery. He also wrote three novels, *The Bright Temptation* (1932), *The Singing Men at Cashel* (1936), and *The Sun Dances at Easter* (1952), each of which was banned by the Irish authorities, and two volumes of autobiography, *Twice Round the Black Church* (1962) and *A Penny in the Clouds* (1968). His *Collected Poems* appeared in 1974. Susan Halpern's *Austin Clarke: His Life and Works* was published in 1974.

CLARKE, Austin C(hesterfield) (1934–), Barbados-born novelist, journalist, and broadcaster; he went to Canada in 1955 and studied at the University of Toronto. He has worked for the Canadian Broadcasting Corporation, served as cultural attaché at the Barbados Embassy in Washington, and taught at several universities including Yale. His first two novels, *Survivors of the Crossing* (1964) and *Amongst Thistles and Thorns* (1965), depict the impoverished conditions and deprivation of most people in Barbados. There followed three novels, *The Meeting Point* (1967), *Storm of Fortune* (1973), and *The Bigger Light* (1975), which provide the most complete fictional portrait that exists of black Caribbean immigrants in Canada. Collections of stories such as *When He Was Free and Young and Used To Wear Silks* (1971), *When Women Rule* (1985), and *Nine Men Who Laughed* (1985), extended this portrait and helped to establish Clarke's reputation as Canada's best-known black author. Later stories include *In This City* (1992). While his fiction exposes the discrimination and hardships faced by West Indian immigrants in Canada, it also reveals much good-humoured resilience. At the same time, Clarke shows little sympathy for the mechanistic habits of the dominant, urban culture in Canada. His novel *The Prime Minister* (1977) achieved some notoriety for its portrait of political corruption in Barbados, where it was banned. *Proud Empires* (1986), a comic novel about politics in 1950s Barbados, vividly evokes the sociocultural aspirations of the people. Thus his fiction combines both serious analysis and rollicking humour which is evident particularly in the pungent wit and vigorous speech of his characters. Clarke has received many awards, including the Casa de Las Americas prize (1980).

CLARKE, Gillian (1937–), British poet, born in Cardiff, educated at University College, Cardiff. She became a news researcher with the BBC in 1958, lectured at Gwent College of Art and Design (1975–84), and has worked extensively as a teacher of creative writing. From 1976 to 1984 she edited the *Anglo-Welsh Review*. Although her first two collections of poetry, *Snow on the Mountain* (1972) and *The Sundial* (1978), were favourably received, it was not until the appearance of *Letter from a Far Country* in 1982 that her work was widely acclaimed. *Selected Poems* (1985) and *Letting in the Rumour* (1989) confirmed her standing as one of the most important of contemporary British women poets. Many early poems displayed her ability to imbue firmly particularized incidents with lyrical and visionary significances. Among her most impressive work are the long sequences 'Letter from a Far Country' and 'Cofiant', exploratory meditations in which local and personal experience fuses with historical and cultural themes drawn from her family's past. The disciplined flexibility of structure in her verse continues to display a high level of accomplishment in *The King of Britain's Daughter* (1993).

CLAVELL, James (1924–94), British writer, film director, and producer, born in Australia, educated at the University of Birmingham. Captured by the Japanese during the Second World War, he spent three years in Changi, the infamous Japanese prisoner-of-war camp in Singapore; this formed the background to his first best-selling novel *King Rat* (1962), which was also filmed. Despite his experience, he has remained fascinated by the East, and his gift for an exciting story, impressively researched, has produced *Tai Pan* (1966); *Shogun* (1976, which was both filmed and made the subject of a TV series), an enormous novel on the impact of the West on seventeenth-century Japan; *Noble House* (1981); *Whirlwind* (1986); and *Gai-jin* (1993).

Clayhanger Trilogy, a series of three novels by Arnold *Bennett. *Clayhanger* (1910), set in the Five Towns (the 'Potteries' in Staffordshire), tells the story of the boyhood and young manhood of Edwin Clayhanger, son of the autocratic and strong-willed printer Darius Clayhanger who is determined that Edwin shall follow him into the printing works rather than pursue his own bent as an architect. The novel opens as Edwin leaves school at the age of 16, and describes his abortive rebellions and eventual acceptance of his fate, as he takes over the business on his father's death. The provincial Methodist background, Darius's penniless childhood and his rescue from the workhouse, and the growing prosperity and cultural aspirations of the family are described in sharply observed cumulative detail. The novel provides a wealth of accurate documentation about the manners and industry of the region; its characters include the handsome and domineering Auntie Hamps, Big James the printer, and various members of the socially superior Orgreaves family. *Hilda Lessways* (1911) describes the efforts of independent fatherless Hilda to make a career for herself as a journalist; her impulsive (and, as it turns out, bigamous) marriage to the romantically shady lawyer George Cannon; their life together as proprietors of 'Cannon's Boarding House' in Brighton; his exposure and flight; and her renewed interest in her former admirer Edwin Clayhanger. *These Twain* (1916) covers the ups and downs of the lively and often tempestuous marriage of Edwin and Hilda (who now has a son from her first liaison); her semi-accidental sighting of Cannon in Dartmoor prison; and the death of Auntie Hamps. *The Roll Call* (1918), a less successful sequel, follows the career of Hilda's son George as a London architect, and ends as he enlists in the army.

CLEMO, Jack (Reginald John) (1916–94), British poet, born near St Austell; he received elementary education at Trethosa village school. During childhood he suffered attacks of blindness, and became deaf prior to the complete loss of his sight in 1955. He began writing in his teens out of what he described as the 'instinctive effort to come to terms with abnormal circumstances'. His novel *Wilding Graft* was published to critical acclaim in 1948. *The Clay Verge* (1951), his first collection of poetry, was followed by numerous further volumes, which include *The Map of Clay* (1961), *Cactus on Carmel* (1967), *The Echoing Tip* (1971), and *A Different Drummer* (1986), *Selected Poems* (1988), *Approach to Murano* (1993), and *The Cured Arno* (1995). Much of his strongly crafted and austere poetry is of an idiosyncratically religious character, affirming the visionary qualities he located in the bare landscapes around the Cornish clay workings. He also repeatedly dealt with the theme of the compatibility of Christianity and eroticism. *The Invading Gospel* (1958) revealed his theological conceptions. He published two autobiographical works, *Confession of a Rebel* (1949) and *The Marriage of a Rebel* (1980). A further novel, *The Shadowed Bed*, originally drafted in 1938, appeared in 1986.

Clergyman's Daughter, A, a novel by George *Orwell, published in 1935. Orwell's first novel has an erratic story-line that is not entirely justified by the wanderings of its heroine Dorothy Hare, the clergyman's daughter of the title; after an attack of amnesia, she is plunged into the miseries of unemployment and vagrancy. The contrast between the setting of her restricted, church-going life and the harshness of the pauper's environment is thoroughly Orwellian; the self-conscious modishness of the more experimental passages of writing is much less so. Orwell is really engaged in two projects, seizing the opportunity for social critique in the course of analysing the nature of his spinster heroine's sexual repressions. In the end, the 'condition of England' elements seem irrelevant to the personal development of a character whose facile rehabilitation does not resolve the psychological tensions built up around powerful feelings of disgust and repugnance at the idea of physical contact. Orwell is not fully in control of his design, despite the evocativeness of his descriptions of life among hop-pickers in Kent, the desolation in his portrait of down-and-outs in Trafalgar Square, and the trenchancy of his account of the Dickensian private school, all reflecting aspects of his own experience.

CLIFF, Michelle (1946–), Jamaican novelist, poet, short-story writer, and editor, born in Kingston, Jamaica, educated at Wagner College and at the Warburg Institute, London University. She began writing after becoming involved in the women's movement in the 1970s and has become internationally known through essays, articles, lectures, and workshops on racism and feminism. Race, gender, and power are recurring themes in Cliff's writing. The main protagonist of her novels, *Abeng* (1984) and *No Telephone to Heaven* (1987), is Clare Savage, a light-skinned Jamaican who first comes to realize the relationship between colour and status, and then becomes a revolutionary. Cliff has also written autobiographical works, poetry, and prose poems, including *Claiming an Identity They Taught Me To Despise* (1980) and *The Land of Look Behind: Prose and Poetry* (1985). More recent fiction includes a collection of short stories, *Bodies of Water* (1990), and *Free Enterprise* (1993), a novel.

Clockwork Orange, A, a novel by Anthony *Burgess, published in 1962. The narrative is by 15-year-old hooligan Alex, using a teenage slang, 'Nadsat', invented by Burgess; it is set in an anarchic urban culture of the near future. Alex has a passion for music and hi-fi, and is a drug user. He and his friends embark on orgies of violence and destruction, in one of which a woman dies. In prison Alex is selected as guinea-pig for a form of aversion therapy devised by a social reformer. Considered a successful subject, he is released early. At home he discovers that his music and drugs have been confiscated by the authorities and a stranger is boarding in his room. Listening to Mozart in a record shop he finds that the therapy has destroyed his love of music. He is recognized and attacked by his former victims, who include a writer whom his gang crippled and whose wife they raped. In hospital Alex realizes he is now the centre of a political scandal over the therapy he has been given. The novel ends with Alex the helpless tool of government propaganda, but, enjoying Beethoven's Ninth Symphony and accompanying images of violence, ambiguously declaring himself 'cured'. The title is taken from a manuscript by the writer Alex's gang assaulted, which rejects the option of treating people like machines. The novel is about moral choice, most explicitly proposed by the repeated 'What's it going to be then?' at the head of each of its three sections.

CLOETE, Stuart (1897–1976), South African novelist and short-story writer, born in Paris, and educated in England. He served in the First World War, and remained in the British Army until 1925, subsequently taking up farming in South Africa. A prolific writer, he is best known for his trilogy of realistic historical novels about the Afrikaners: *Turning Wheels* (1937), which was banned in South Africa; *Watch for the Dawn* (1939), about the Great Trek; and *Rags of Glory* (1963), about their defeat in the Anglo-Boer War (1899–1902). Many of his novels, such as *The Soldier's Peach* (1959) and *The Looking Glass* (1963), are adventure stories set in bush or veld, and have been compared with the works of Rider *Haggard. *Mamba* (1955) and *Gazella* (1958) are set in the Congo and Mozambique respectively. In *The Thousand and One Nights of Jean Macaque* (1965) the eponymous hero is an old man nostalgically looking back on his past as a young rake in *fin de siècle* Paris. Other novels include *The Curve and the Tusk* (1953), on elephants and their poachers, and *The Abductors* (1970), which deals with the white slave traffic. *The Silver Trumpet and Other African Stories* (1961) contains some of his finest short stories. *A Victorian Son* (1971) and *The Gambler* (1973) are autobiographies.

COBBING, Bob (1920–), British poet, born in Enfield, Middlesex, educated at Enfield Grammar School and Bognor Training College. After working as a teacher and bookshop manager, he became a freelance writer and performer of his work in 1967. He has also edited several magazines, notably *Kroklok*, and publishes editions of experimental poetry under the Writers' Forum imprint. Although some of his early poems followed conventional procedures, Cobbing is best known for his dedicated pursuit of the possibilities of *concrete poetry and sound poetry. *Sound Poems: An ABC in Sound* (1965), his first substantial publication, was followed by some ninety titles; among the volumes of his collected works which have appeared since 1977 are *A Peal in Air* (1978), *Vowels and Consequences* (1985), and *Improvisation Is a Dirty Word: Collected Poems 12* (1990). The distinctions between textual and graphic art are obviated in Cobbing's writing, words and letters forming the material for highly ingenious visual arrangements. He regards his poems in their printed forms as scores for performance and has participated in most of the International Sound Poetry Festivals in Europe and America in recent decades. See also UNDERGROUND POETRY.

Cocktail Party, The, a verse-play by T. S. *Eliot, first produced in 1949 and published in 1950. Beginning and ending at a London cocktail party, the play traces the spiritual fortunes of Edward and Lavinia Chamberlayne and the former's mistress, Celia Coplestone. Central to the thematic development is the presence of the uninvited guest who is later revealed to be the eminent psychiatrist Sir Henry Harcourt-Reilly; the figure and his role in regenerating the Chamberlaynes' moribund marriage are obliquely modelled on Heracles in the *Alcestis* of Euripides. Sir Henry is the foremost of 'the Guardians', whose vaguely defined but benevolent functions are integral to the implicit theology of redemption around which the play is structured; through the agency of the Guardians, who provide the machinery of the plot, the principal characters are all led to greater self-knowledge and an increased awareness of the interdependence of individuals. The play ends with the Chamberlaynes awaiting their guests for another cocktail party, which promises to be a happier occasion. *The Cocktail Party* is notable for its apparently secular character, beneath the surface of which its moral and religious dimensions are unobtrusively adumbrated. While its verse is highly effective in suggesting the patterns and rhythms of speech, the play has less of the metaphoric life to be found in *The *Family Reunion*, his earlier play, which led to Eliot's admission that it was 'perhaps an open question whether there is any poetry in the play at all'.

COETZEE, J(ohn) M(ichael) (1940–), South African novelist, born in Cape Town, and educated at the Universities of Cape Town and Texas. *Dusklands* (1974) consists of two novellas ('The Vietnam Project' and 'The Narrative of Jacobus Coetzee'); madness and hunger for power on the part of both protagonists, one a technocrat obsessed by the Vietnam war, and the other a Boer patriarch on the verge of paranoia, are at the heart of both. His next three novels may be described as Kafkaesque parables of a South African society in danger of disintegration. Unlike his compatriot André *Brink, Coetzee's austere novels explore the Afrikaner psyche in a more oblique, stylistically more innovative, though equally apocalyptic manner. *In the Heart of the Country* (1977) depicts a young woman in an isolated farmstead who slides into anarchic violence and madness; it was made into a distinguished film, *Dust* (1985), with Jane Birkin, directed by Marion Hansel. *Waiting for the Barbarians* (1980; James Tait Black Memorial Prize), set in a desolate, mythical country, is narrated by a magistrate who faces crucial decisions when the inquisitorial Colonel Joll warns him against a 'barbarian' invasion. The implacably bleak allegory *Life and Times of Michael K* (1983; Booker Prize) has as its protagonist an ugly and slow-witted gardener in a Cape Town park; caught up in civil war, he desperately tries to find safety for himself and his mother. *Foe* (1986) is a retelling of Defoe's *Robinson Crusoe* in a contemporary context. Set in Cape Town, *Age of Iron* (1990) focuses on a mother, a retired classics teacher, writing to her daughter, who is dying of cancer. Her observations are those of an anxious white liberal. *The Master of Petersburg* (1994) is a novel based on the later life of Dostoevsky. Coetzee's non-fiction works include *White Writing* (1988), a selection of the novelist's essays on 'the Culture of Letters in South Africa', and *Doubling the Point: Essays and Interviews* (1992).

COGSWELL, Fred (1917–), Canadian poet, born in East Centreville, New Brunswick, and educated at the Universities of New Brunswick and Edinburgh. He subsequently followed an academic career at the University of New Brunswick, where he edited the influential magazine *Fiddlehead* and founded Fiddlehead Books, both of which made enormous contributions to the development of Canadian Maritime writing. His first collection of poetry, *The Stunted Strong*, appeared in 1954. It was followed by *Descent from Eden* (1959), *Star-People* (1968), *House without a Door* (1973), and *A Long Apprenticeship: Collected Poetry* (1980). More recent works include *Meditations: Fifty Sestinas* (1987), *An Edge to Life* (1987), *The Black and White Tapestry* (1989), *Watching an Eagle* (1991), and *In Praise of Old Music* (1992). His best work is concerned with chronicling the lives of ordinary Maritime Province people in a pithy, ironic style and, like the work of Alden *Nowlan, a writer whom he helped by introducing him to other poetry and poets, his verse has been compared with that of Edward Arlington Robinson. His accounts of ordinary lives are distinctly unpastoral lyrical ballads. While much of his poetry is written in traditional metrical forms, he also essayed a variety of modernist techniques. All his work, as creative writer and editor, is informed by a humane and eclectic stance. As a translator, he played an important part in helping to introduce Quebec poets to English-Canadian audiences.

COHEN, Leonard (1934–), Canadian poet, novelist, and composer-singer, born in Montreal, educated at McGill University under Louis *Dudek, who published his first volume of verse, *Let Us Compare Mythologies* (1956). Cohen achieved international fame in the 1960s and early 1970s with his bitter-sweet ironic songs and subsequently put his career as an entertainer before his writing. The evocative imagery and concern with contemporary mythologies in his songs and verse have led to his sometimes being viewed as a Canadian Bob *Dylan. His volumes of verse include *The Spice-Box of Earth* (1961), *Flowers for Hitler* (1964), *The Energy of Slaves* (1972), *Death of a Lady's Man* (1978), *Book of Mercy* (1984), and *Stranger Music: Selected Poems and Songs* (1993). His most important work as a writer is *Beautiful Losers* (1966), a fragmentary, early *post-modernist novel which Margaret *Atwood has seen as a quintessential expression of the Canadian victim mentality. Cohen's earlier novel, *The Favourite Game* (1963), based on his own experience, is a more conventional work about the son of wealthy Jewish parents who leaves for New York. His record albums include *Songs of Leonard*

Cohen (1967), *Songs of Love and Hate* (1971), *Death of a Lady's Man* (1977), *Various Positions* (1984), *I'm Your Man* (1988), and *The Future* (1992).

COHEN, Matt (1942–), Canadian novelist and short-story writer, born in Kingston, Ontario, educated at the University of Toronto and McMaster University. The fragmented, dreamlike narratives of his early novels, *Korsoniloff* (1969) and *Johnny Crackle Sings* (1971), initiated his abiding concern with the nature of personal identity in their depictions of crisis and breakdown. A more conventional manner is apparent in *The Disinherited* (1974), the first of a cycle of four novels set in Salem, Ontario, through which Cohen conducts an epic revaluation of rural Ontario's idyllic significance; 'The Salem Novels', which employ a remarkable range of narrative modes, continue with *The Colours of War* (1978), *The Sweet Second Summer of Kitty Malone* (1979), and *Flowers of Darkness* (1981). His other novels include *Wooden Hunters* (1975), *The Spanish Doctor* (1984), and *Emotional Arithmetic* (1990). Cohen's collections of short stories include *The Expatriate* (1982), *Café Le Dog* (1983) and *Freud: the Paris Notebooks* (1991). His poetry is collected in *Peach Melba* (1974) and *In Search of Leonardo* (1986).

Cold Comfort Farm, a novel by S. *Gibbons, published in 1932, a humorous parody of contemporary dialect novels of rural life, such as the lurid *Precious Bane* (1924) by Mary *Webb, as well as of Lawrence's philosophies and of Hardyesque pessimism. The cheerful heroine, 'Flora Poste', visits her Starkadder cousins (Judith, Amos, Seth, Ezra, Urk, and Caraway) in a dismal Sussex farmhouse under the tyranny of Aunt Ada Doom, 'the Dominant Grandmother theme'. Guided by The Higher Common Sense, Flora determines to disperse the atmosphere of fatalism and earthy sexuality: 'Nature is all very well in her place, but she must not be allowed to make things untidy.' The amorous inclinations of 'Mr Mybug', a bookish type seeking to prove that Branwell Brontë wrote *Wuthering Heights*, are dealt with by marriage to the local spinster Rennett. Though the comic contrast between the rural idiocy of the Starkadders and the swish county set that Flora moves amongst now seems rather dated, *Cold Comfort Farm* has become a minor classic of English literary humour. The 'finer passages' are indicated by asterisks for 'those who are not always sure whether a sentence is literature or whether it is sheer flapdoodle'.

COLE, G(eorge) D(ouglas) H(oward) (1889–1959), British socialist and dissenting economist, born in Cambridge, educated at St Paul's School and at Balliol College, Oxford; he became Reader in Economics in that university after the First World War and Professor of Social and Political Theory after the Second. Cole's contribution to the socialist movement in the first half of the twentieth century is rivalled only by that of the *Webbs (his adversaries within the *Fabian Society). He reaffirmed the guild socialist platform in *The World of Labour* (1913) and *Self Government in Industry* (1917). In the inter-war years he was influential in promoting Keynesian ideas in British labour circles. Already an opponent of unregulated capitalism, Cole regarded J. M. *Keynes's *General Theory* (1936) not only as a theoretical *tour de force*, but also as a legitimation of some of his own economic opinions. Surpassing Keynesianism, however, Cole advocated economic planning in a non-bureaucratic socialist democracy. He published more than 100 books, wrote numerous articles, biographical sketches, comments, and reviews. Other notable works are his *Life of Robert Owen* (1925), *A History of Socialist Thought* (1953–8), and *The Common People* (1938, with Raymond Postgate). He also wrote detective fiction in collaboration with his wife, Margaret (sister of Raymond Postgate), who wrote a biography of Cole.

COLEGATE, Isabel (1931–), British novelist, born in London; she left school at the age of 16. Her first novel, *The Blackmailer* (1958), dealt with the decline of the English aristocracy and the disintegration of class structures in the aftermath of the First World War, a theme to which she was to return in subsequent works, including *A Man of Power* (1960) and *The Great Occasion* (1962). Similarly, her trilogy of novels, *Orlando King* (1968), *Orlando at the Brazen Threshold* (1971), and *Agatha* (1973), are concerned with the nature of social change. *Statues in a Garden* (1964), a characteristically short and elegantly written work, portrays a group of aristocrats on the eve of the Great War, describing their effete and somewhat decadent lives with ironic humour. *The Shooting Party* (1981), which was also filmed, is set in 1913 and focuses on the aristocratic guests at a weekend shooting party in a large country house; its mood is underlined by one character's remark that 'an age, perhaps a civilization, is coming to an end'. *Deceits of Time* (1988) has a contemporary setting but deals as much with the past as Colegate's earlier work; its central character, Catherine Hillery, a biographer, is commissioned to write the biography of a well-known politician and former First World War hero, and discovers that the truth about his past is more complex than she had imagined. Colegate's later novels include *The Summer of the Royal Visit* (1991), narrated by a retired schoolmaster and amateur historian, who describes the events surrounding a proposed visit to his city by Queen Victoria, and *Winter Journey* (1995).

COLLIER, John (1901–80), British short-story writer and novelist, born in London, educated privately. After a period as poetry editor for **Time and Tide*, from the mid-1930s he spent much time in America and wrote several Hollywood screenplays. The bizarrely imaginative nature of his best-known work is exemplified by his first novel *His Monkey Wife* (1930), which deals with the marriage between an expatriate schoolteacher and a chimpanzee. His sardonic and often disquietingly macabre short stories were collected in *Presenting Moonshine* (1941), *The Touch of Nutmeg* (1943), *Fancies and Goodnights* (1951), *Pictures in the Fire* (1958), and *The John Collier Reader* (1972), with an introduction by A. *Burgess. *Tom's A-Cold* (1933) concerns a young leader of a rural settlement in an England many years after a holocaust has destroyed civilization. His later publications include *Milton's Paradise Lost; Screenplay for a Cinema of the Mind* (1973).

COLLINGWOOD, R(obin) G(eorge) (1889–1943), British philosopher, the son of John Ruskin's secretary; he was born in Lancashire, and educated at University College, Oxford, becoming a fellow of Pembroke College in 1912. After serving in the Intelligence Department of the Admiralty during the First World War, he lectured in philosophy at Oxford, where he became Wayneflete Professor of Metaphysical Philosophy in 1935. His earlier writings, notably *Religion and Philosophy* (1916) and *Speculum Mentis* (1924), constituted extensions of the tradition of philosophical idealism, which he defended formidably in *An Essay on Philosophical Method* (1933), often regarded as his most important work. The book's integrated view of philosophy and history was sustained in his *Essay on Metaphysics* (1940), in which he argued that the study of history subsumed that of philosophy; this was consistent with his increasing historical relativism, which led him to maintain that the task of metaphysics was to define the 'absolute presuppositions' governing culture and religion at particular historical periods. His other works include *The Principles of Art* (1938) and *The Idea of History* (1946). Collingwood was also an eminent authority on the archaeology of Britain under the Roman occupation; his *Roman Britain* (1937) formed the third volume of *An Economic Survey of Ancient Rome* (edited by Tenney Frank, 5 volumes, 1933–40); he was co-author with J. N. L. Myres of *Roman Britain and the English Settlements* (1936), the first volume of *The Oxford History of England* (edited by G. N. Clark, 15 volumes, 1934–65). His *An Autobiography* (1939) is remarkable for its almost complete avoidance of circumstantial matter, bearing out his claim that 'The autobiography of a man whose business is thinking should be the story of his thought.'

COLLINS, Barry (1941–), British dramatist, born in Halifax, educated at Queen's College, Oxford; he has worked as a teacher and journalist. His first play, *And Was Jerusalem Builded Here*, which involved militant Luddites protesting against the mechanization of the weaving industry in the Yorkshire of 1812, was performed in 1972; subsequent work includes a children's play, *Beauty and the Beast* (1973); *The Strongest Man in the World* (1978), about a Soviet miner crippled and turned rebellious by the drugs that have made him an Olympic weightlifting champion; *Toads* (1979); and several television plays. His best-known, most challenging, and most moving drama, however, remains *Judgement* (1974), about cannibalism in the Second World War. It is a two-and-a-half-hour monologue narrated by a Russian officer who, trapped for sixty days without food or water in a cellar, agreed with his comrades to draw lots by way of deciding who should devour whom, and somehow managed to survive his ordeal with a decency, a dignity, and a sense of camaraderie that the Soviet authorities found impossible to accept.

COLLINS, Jackie, see ROMANTIC FICTION.

COLLINS, Merle (*c.*1955–), Grenadian poet and novelist, born in Aruba. She was a teacher and Research Officer in Latin American Affairs (1979–83). After the US invasion of Grenada she moved to Britain, where she became a member of a performance group, 'African Dawn', and a notable performance poet, much committed to revolution, and to women's liberation, in Grenada and elsewhere. Many of the poems in *Because the Dawn Breaks* (1985) employ Creole dialect to great effect; a second volume of poems, *Rotten Pomerack*, appeared in 1992. Her novel *Angel* (1987), with much of its dialogue in Creole, chronicles three generations of Grenadian women in their struggles against colonialism and post-colonial dictatorship. The eponymous heroine is a headstrong, university-educated, and disillusioned young woman determined to bring about changes in Grenada which, she learns, can be obtained only by solidarity. Angel's relationship with her more conservative and conformist mother, Doodsie, gives the novel a welcome dimension of personal and family conflict beyond the merely political. *Rain Darling* (1990), a collection of short stories, continues her themes on Grenadians. In her novel *The Colour of Forgetting* (1995), her most imaginative, lyrical, and impassioned work, Collins pays tribute to the Caribbean; set in two imaginary islands, the novel recounts the story of several generations of an ordinary family. Collins has also edited *Watchers and Seekers: Creative Writing by Black Women in Britain* (1987).

COLLIS, John Stewart (1900–84), Irish biographer and writer on natural history, born in Dublin, educated at Balliol College, Oxford. His early published works, which brought him little success, include the novel *The Sounding Cataract* (1936). During the Second World War he worked as a farm labourer in the south of England, subsequently establishing his reputation as a writer with *While Following the Plough* (1946) and *Down to Earth* (1947); richly combining philosophical reflection with a minutely detailed account of traditional agricultural work, they were issued together under the title *The Worm Forgives the Plough* in 1973. The books' visionary expressions of the interdependence of the human and natural orders, which also characterize *The Triumph of the Tree* (1950), *The Moving Waters* (1955), and the autobiographical *Bound upon a Course* (1971), gained Collis eventual acclaim as a precursor of the ecological movement. Among his numerous biographies are *An Artist of Life* (1959), his study of Havelock *Ellis; *The Carlyles* (1973); and *Christopher Columbus* (1976).

Color Purple, The, see WALKER, ALICE.

COLUM, Padraic (1881–1972), Irish dramatist and poet, born in Longford, Ireland; he was educated at

Glasthule National School, Dublin, and began his working life as a clerk. He achieved prominence through the success of his plays *The Land* (1905) and *The Fiddler's House* (1907) at the *Abbey Theatre. *Thomas Muskerry* (1910) proved controversial for its sombrely realistic treatment of conditions in rural Ireland. In 1914 he emigrated to New York, lecturing at Columbia University in comparative literature and publishing many adaptations of Irish, Welsh, and Scandinavian legends for children. During the early 1930s he lived in Paris, becoming well acquainted with James *Joyce; with his wife, Mary Colum, he wrote the memoir *Our Friend James Joyce* (1958). *Wild Earth* (1907), his first collection of poetry, was followed by many volumes including *Creatures* (1927), *Flower Pieces* (1938), and *Images of Departure* (1968). *Poems*, a collected edition, appeared in 1953. His poetry is memorable for the refined lyricism and simplicity with which it celebrates and records aspects of rural Ireland. A prolific author, he also wrote novels, notably *The Flying Swans* (1957), and a biography of Arthur Griffith entitled *Ourselves Alone* (1959). A critical biography by Z. R. Bowen was published in 1970.

Comedians, a play by Trevor *Griffiths, performed in 1975 and published in 1976. It involves six working-class men, studying to become professional comedians with Eddie Waters, who believes that a good joke, far from exploiting prejudice or perpetuating racial or sexual stereotypes, truthfully illuminates the things that worry or frighten people. However, they are asked to audition for a London agent, Bert Challenor, who is 'not looking for philosophers but for someone who sees what the people want and gives it to them'. Some of the apprentice comedians try to remain true to their teacher's principles and are rejected; some renounce those principles and are accepted; and one, Gethin Price, ignores both Waters's ideas and Challenor's wishes. Dressed as a blend of the Soviet clown Grock and a football hooligan, and facing two dummies in evening dress, he uses his act for a ferocious display of class aggression. The play is an attempt partly to define the nature of humour, but mainly to use humour as a metaphor for people's behaviour in capitalist society, dividing its characters into opportunists, liberal humanists, and one lonely revolutionary.

Comics. The term refers to at least three different kinds of graphic and other work: drawings of jokes and serial adventures in certain newspapers (largely, initially American ones); certain (now mostly defunct) British magazines for children, offering stories, jokes, puzzles, and competitions; and (again largely American) colourful magazines depicting the exploits of superheroes and other creatures of fantasy. The first kind of comic—the comic strip—ranges from simple gags to mild pornography, and from Charles Schultz's 'Peanuts' to Peter O'Donell's 'Modesty Blaise', and includes satirical work like Garry Trudeau's 'Doonesbury', Steve Bell's running commentary on the ineptitudes of British political life, and Posy Simmonds' amusing but remorseless exposure of many layers of English pretension. The second kind of comic, represented by the continuing publication of *The Beano* and *The Dandy*, is fast becoming a historical footnote, but remains a part of the literary formation of many people, the place they first read printed fiction and gained their early experience of getting or not getting a graphic joke. The third kind of comic not only continues to sell ever more widely, but has begotten interesting progeny: the *graphic novel, often brilliantly drawn, where Batman, for instance, acquires a dark and near psychotic history, and where large contemporary issues of politics and philosophy are addressed through the sheer extravagance and anarchy of myth; and the comic-based film, like *Superman* or *Dick Tracy* or *Batman*, where the very colours of the comics, and their highly stylized worlds, lead us into zones of fantasy which more conventionally photographed films cannot reach. Not all of the heroes of contemporary comics are as amiable or typically virtuous as Captain Marvel and Captain America; but then the violent Judge Dredd and other avengers look like parodies of their forebears, the vigilante-fascists we hope we really do not need—or need only in the lurid dreams displayed and (we hope) exorcised by our comics.

Coming Up for Air, a novel by George *Orwell, published in 1939. *Coming Up for Air* is Orwell's most convincing novel of contemporary British life, although like several books written by members of Orwell's generation on the brink of the Second World War, it is also charged with memories of an Edwardian childhood. The poignancy of its flights of nostalgia, which circle round the rural landscapes of the Thames valley, is sharpened by premonitions of the coming war, and in particular of aerial bombardment. The reveries of its protagonist, George Bowling, are constantly interrupted by authorial regrets for a vanishing community: 'Is it gone for ever? I'm not certain. But I tell you it was a good world to live in. I belong to it. So do you.' Bowling is an overweight insurance salesman trapped in a life of suburban uniformity, and married to a wife whose only motivations are negative and financial: 'We can't afford it'; 'I don't know where the money's to come from'. The book was published by Gollancz, despite Orwell's inclusion of a chapter satirizing Gollancz's *Left Book Club. Orwell's criticisms of political faddism, of urbanization, and of technological progress are Blimpish on occasion, but the novel successfully catches a mood of reassessment, during a phase when the British were asking themselves what it was they thought they would be fighting for.

Common Reader, The (1925) and *The Common Reader: Second Series* (1932) were V. *Woolf's two collections of essays published in her lifetime, which she selected, revised, added to, and ordered from her enormous output of reviewing (mostly, anonymously, for the *Times Literary Supplement*). The title phrase is taken from Dr Johnson. The essays are written from the point of view of a highly cultured, widely read, largely self-educated 'outsider' to the educational establishment, asking, with energy, curiosity, intuition, and wit, of a great range of literature from Greeks and Elizabethans to contemporary fiction, 'how should one read a book?' *The Common Reader* has twenty-five essays, including 'On Not Knowing Greek', 'Defoe', 'Jane Austen', 'Modern Fiction', 'George Eliot', 'The Russian Point of View', '*Jane Eyre* and *Wuthering Heights*', and 'How It Strikes a Contemporary'. *The Common Reader: Second Series* has twenty-six essays, including '*Robinson Crusoe*', 'Mary Wollstonecraft', 'De Quincey's *Autobiography*', 'Dorothy Wordsworth', and 'How Should One Read a Book?'

COMPTON-BURNETT, Dame Ivy (1884–1969), British novelist, born in Pinner, Middlesex, one of the twelve children of a leading homoeopathic physician, James Compton-Burnett, and his second wife. She spent her childhood in Hove and continued to live there until she was 27, except for a period as a student of Classics at Royal Holloway College. Her early life was overshadowed by tragedy: her brother Guy died of pneumonia; another favourite brother, Noel, was killed during the First World War, and her two youngest sisters committed suicide. Her first novel, *Dolores* (1911), which was influenced by her admiration for George Eliot, but which she later repudiated, is untypical; only with the publication of *Pastors and Masters* (1925) did she begin to establish her distinctive style. The novel and its successors, which include *Brothers and Sisters* (1929), *Men and Wives* (1931), *More Women Than Men* (1933), *A House and Its Head* (1935), *Daughters and Sons* (1937), *A Family and a Fortune* (1939), *Parents and Children* (1941), *Elders and Betters* (1944) and many others, are variations on themes to do with power and the abuse of power, of which she herself wrote that 'nothing is so corrupting'. Each of the nineteen works she produced between 1925 and 1957 is set during the last twenty years of the nineteenth century; each has a domestic setting–frequently a Victorian country rectory inhabited by a large and inevitably unhappy family tyrannized by a cruel patriarch (or, on occasion, a matriarch); each displays the writer's mordantly ironic view of human relationships, in particular those between siblings and between parent and child. There is little physical description in her novels, in which most of the action and interplay of relationships is conveyed in the form of dialogue; tragic and often violent events are presented in a highly stylized and elliptical form and there is a vein of black comedy running throughout, which alleviates the cruelty of her scenarios. In this respect, and in its satirical mockery of late Victorian pieties, her work has much in common with that of Samuel *Butler, whose work was an influence, and with that of Evelyn *Waugh. She was hailed, by Raymond Mortimer and others, as a literary post-impressionist, whose work, eschewing conventional realism in favour of a concentrated, artificial, and idiosyncratic style, appeared startlingly modern in its preoccupations. Her later work became increasingly spare and condensed, although it is instantly recognizable for its ironic, almost aphoristic style and its extensive use of dialogue. Post-war works include: *Manservant and Maidservant* (1947), *Two Worlds and Their Ways* (1949), *Mother and Son* (1955), and *A Heritage and Its History* (1961). There is a definitive biography by Hilary *Spurling: *Ivy When Young: The Early Life of I. Compton-Burnett 1884–1919* (1974) and *Secrets of a Woman's Heart: The Later Life of I Compton-Burnett 1920–1969* (1984), which considers, amongst other aspects of her personal life, the importance of her friendship with Margaret Jourdain, with whom she lived for many years until the latter's death in 1951. She was made a Dame in 1967 and a Companion of Honour in 1968.

COMYNS, Barbara (1909–92), British novelist, born in Bidford-on-Avon, Warwickshire, educated at art schools in Stratford-on-Avon and London. Her unusual childhood, peopled by numerous sisters and governesses, a deaf mother, and an authoritarian father, was the subject of her first novel, *Sisters by a River* (1947), and is also the framework of two subsequent novels, *Who Was Changed and Who Was Dead* (1954) and *The Skin Chairs* (1962). Her later experiences of bohemian art-school life and her first marriage to an artist became the subject of her two most engaging novels, *Our Spoons Came from Woolworths* (1950) and *A Touch of Mistletoe* (1967). Her second marriage and life in Spain are depicted in *Out of the Red into the Blue* (1960). Her reputation largely rested on *The Vet's Daughter* (1959), which was acclaimed by Graham *Greene and turned into a musical, *The Clapham Wonder*, until her work was reprinted in the 1980s. Since then, she published *The Juniper Tree* (1985); an earlier unpublished work, *Mr Fox* (1987); and *The House of Dolls* (1989) which, in Comyns's characteristically *faux-naif* style, both wickedly amusing and plaintive, tells of four middle-aged ladies who become amateur prostitutes. Despite the childlike voices of her narrators, her piercing original view of family life and peculiar, often surreal, humour allied her work with that of Ivy *Compton-Burnett.

Concrete Poetry, the term describing poems in which the semantic values of the words composing them are complemented, and sometimes subsumed, by the graphic designs in which they are arranged on the page. Antecedents for writing of this kind include the 'pattern poems' of George Herbert, 'Easter Wings' being the best known, and aspects of Apollinaire's *Calligrammes* (1918), notably 'Il pleut', in which the words form vertical lines in mimesis of rain falling; practitioners of concrete poetry also acknowledge the influence of the collage techniques of Cubism and the linguistic experiments of Kurt Schwitters and others. Concrete poetry is, however, distinctly a phenomenon of the late 1950s and the 1960s. The international concrete poetry movement which flourished in Britain, Europe, and North and South America was inaugurated at the National Exhibition of Concrete

Art at São Paulo, Brazil, in 1956. The Brazilian poets' 'Pilot-Plan For Concrete Poetry' (1958) emphasizes the spatial nature of the genre in stating that 'concrete poetry begins by being aware of graphic space as a structural agent'; the reader's apprehension of a concrete poem is immediate in terms of its visual design, while the meanings of the words thus arranged are assimilated in the usual sequential manner. The leading practitioners of concrete poetry include Ian Hamilton *Finlay, Eugen Gomringer, Bob *Cobbing, Edwin *Morgan, and Sylvester Houedard. The last named is among those who have produced extreme manifestations of the mode; the extraordinary intricacy and elaborateness of the shapes into which letters and words are formed in his 'typestracts' provides the most interesting example of concrete poetry in which the graphic aspects are ascendant over semantic functions. Cobbing and Finlay are respectively noted as exponents of the allied forms of sound poetry and kinetic poetry. *An Anthology of Concrete Poetry* (1967) was edited by Emmett Williams.

CONDON, Richard (Thomas) (1915–96), American writer of *science fiction, born in New York City. He worked as a publicist in the film industry from 1936 to 1957. His extravagant fantasies on the American Dream varied in form from the spy thriller to political satire and science fiction. His vision was both comic and dark. In his best-known novel, *The Manchurian Candidate* (1959), a demagogic American senator, resembling Joseph McCarthy, is revealed as the agent of a Russian conspiracy against the government. Condon's satirical analysis of power and politics continued with *Mile High* (1969), in which Prohibition is created by the Mafia to protect their business interests; *The Vertical Smile* (1971); *Winter Kills* (1974), in which the ultimate killer of a Kennedy-like president is his own father; and *Death of a Politician* (1978), a savage destruction of a corrupt politician very similar to Richard Nixon. *An Infinity of Mirrors* (1964) explored the nightmare of Nazi Germany; *Any God Will Do* (1966) was a virtuoso depiction of insanity; *The Ecstacy Business* (1967) demolished Hollywood; and the Prizzi trilogy—*Prizzi's Honor* (1982), *Prizzi's Family* (1986), and *Prizzi's Glory* (1988)—mocked the American obsession with organized crime. *Emperor of America* (1990) and *The Final Addiction* (1991) are among his later novels.

Cone-Gatherers, The, the best-known of Robin *Jenkins's early novels, published in 1955. The narrative is set in Scotland during the Second World War and draws on Jenkins's experience of forestry work at this time, when he was a conscientious objector to military service. The 'cone-gatherers' of the title are the brothers Calum and Neil, who are collecting pine-cones on the estate of Lady Runcie-Campbell to provide seeds for a new forest. Calum, a simple hunchback with a visionary love of nature, possesses an innocence and gentleness which make him the object of the irrational hatred of Duror, the estate's gamekeeper and the novel's central figure, who resents the brothers' intrusion into his domain; Duror's progressive psychological deterioration culminates in his gratuitous murder of Calum, following which he kills himself. In emblematizing the tensions between good and evil in the human psyche, the novel forms the earliest mature demonstration of this central thematic preoccupation in much of Jenkins's work. His concern with the extent to which social conditioning affects personality and behaviour is also evident in the characterizations; a spectrum of attitudes and assumptions is established, which range from Lady Runcie-Campbell's ineffectually religious notions of patrician responsibility to the degraded narrow-mindedness displayed by some of the minor working-class figures.

Confederacy of Dunces, A, see TOOLE, JOHN KENNEDY.

Confessional Poetry, written principally by Americans during the 1960s, is characterized by great candour in the treatment of intimately autobiographical experiences and attitudes. The term was adopted by critics rather than by the poets to whose work it applied. The traditions of confessional literature extend back to St Augustine, and Donne, Hopkins, and others produced poetry notable for its revealingly personal content; confessional poetry is most specifically of the twentieth century in its affinities with psychoanalysis as a means of confronting painful or otherwise difficult emotional and mental states. The designation was first applied to Robert *Lowell's *Life Studies* (1959) because of the directness with which he wrote of his marital troubles, psychiatric difficulties, and often deeply ambivalent feelings towards his family. Lowell, however, stated his indebtedness in adopting such a forthright idiom to W. D. *Snodgrass, who had once been his student; Snodgrass's *Heart's Needle* (1960) used conventionally accomplished verse to present anguished accounts of his divorce and separation from his daughter. Anne *Sexton's *To Bedlam and Part of the Way Back* (1960) consolidated the impression of a confessional movement through the harrowing immediacy with which she described her depressive illness. John *Berryman's *77 Dream Songs* (1964) and Sylvia *Plath's *Ariel* (1965) also contain notable examples of the mode in numerous poems exposing their authors in states of affective disorder. Adrienne *Rich and Anthony *Hecht are among the other writers to have been labelled 'confessional' during the 1960s. Most of the poetry thus described exhibits a high degree of formal control. Although adversely criticized for its emphasis on pathological conditions and a narcissistic preoccupation with selfhood, confessional poetry led to an increased frankness in the more personal work of many American and British poets.

Confessions of Nat Turner, The, a novel by William *Styron, published in 1967. Set like much of his writing in the American South—in Southside Virginia, near Styron's own birthplace—the novel draws its inspiration from a historical incident, the slave insurrection that took place in 1831. The author attempts to examine the racism of his society by adopting the perspective of the black slave leader Nat Turner. Rather than the language of a plantation slave, Styron attributes to his protagonist the vocabulary of an intellectual capable of analysing and assessing his own situation and that of his people. Though the novel was praised for its historical accuracy and for raising the complex questions of racism, slavery, and the use of justified violence, it fell foul of the black separatist movement gaining strength at the time of its reception, and Styron has been criticized for his appropriation of a black sensibility and his superimposition of white cultural norms on black consciousness.

CONNELL, Evan (Shelby Jr) (1924–), American novelist and short-story writer, born in Kansas City, educated at Dartmouth College, University of Kansas, Stanford University, and Columbia University. Connell's early writings were in the short story form; his first collection, *The Anatomy Lesson and Other Stories* (1957), with its ironic satires of the provinciality and cultural aridity of Midwestern life, and *At the Crossroads* (1965), demonstrate his mastery of the contemporary short story. *St Augustine's Pigeon: The Selected Stories* (1980) includes sixteen stories dating from the 1950s. Connell's novels include *Mrs Bridge* (1959) and its 'companion piece', *Mr Bridge* (1969), both trenchant and ironic explorations of suburban life in the USA; *The Patriot* (1960) recounts the experiences of an American Air Force officer in the Second World War (Connell served as a naval aviator during 1943–5); and *Diary of a Rapist* (1966), which narrates an almost existential retreat into the self and is frequently disturbing for its insights into sexual violence. Connell's first published verse was the long single poem, *Notes From a Bottle Found on the Beach at Carmel* (1963), though his second collection, *Points for a Compass Rose* (1973), is more representative of his strengths as a poet. Other notable works are *The Connoisseur* (1974), *Double Honeymoon* (1976), and *The Alchymist's Journal* (1991); *A Long Desire* (1979) and *The White Lantern* (1980) are collections of essays.

CONNELLY, Marc(us Cook) (1890–1981), American dramatist, born in McKeesport, Pennsylvania. Connelly worked as a journalist before turning to the theatre. In collaboration with George S. *Kaufman in the early 1920s, he produced a series of comedies with a mocking satirical edge such as *Dulcy* (1921), and *Merton of the Movies* (1922), a satire on Hollywood in which a simple-minded grocery clerk becomes a star. Connelly's major work is *The Green Pastures* (1930; Pulitzer Prize), a version of Roark Bradford's stories of the Afro-American conception of Old Testament history, which dramatizes episodes from the Creation to the Crucifixion enacted in a series of tableaux in a small Southern black church.

CONNINGTON, J. J., pseudonym of Alfred Walter STEWART (1880–1947), Scottish academic and *detective fiction writer, born in Glasgow, educated at the universities of Glasgow, Marburg, and London. He was Professor of Chemistry from 1919 to 1944 at Queen's University, Belfast, and author of a number of respected treatises on chemistry. As Connington, he wrote over twenty solid and entertaining detective stories, beginning with *Death at Swaythling Court* (1926), in which the investigation is usually carried out either by Superintendent Ross (*The Eye in the Museum*, 1929; *The Two Tickets Puzzle*, 1930) or, more often, by Chief Constable Sir Clinton Driffield (*Murder in the Maze*, 1927; *The Sweepstake Murders*, 1931). As Connington he also published an unusual science fiction novel, *Nordenholt's Millions* (1923).

CONNOLLY, Cyril (Vernon) (1903–74), British essayist, editor, and critic, born in Coventry, educated at Balliol College, Oxford. After a period as secretary to Logan Pearsall *Smith, he began his career as a literary journalist and editor. He remains best known for his editorship of **Horizon*. *The Rock Pool* (1936), his first substantial publication, is an entertainingly insubstantial novel about a young Englishman in an artists' colony in the South of France; his unfinished novel entitled *Shade Those Laurels* (1990) was completed by Peter *Levi. *Enemies of Promise* (1938) contained a series of essays on the hazards placed in the way of literary talent, and the highly regarded autobiographical fragment 'A Georgian Boyhood'. His numerous further collections of essays and articles include *The Condemned Playground* (1945), *Ideas and Places* (1953), and *The Evening Colonnade* (1973). Among his other publications is *The Unquiet Grave: A Word Cycle*, an idiosyncratic assemblage of aphorisms published in 1944 under the pseudonym 'Palinurus'. David Pryce-Jones edited his journal and published it with a biographical study in *Connolly: Journal and Memoir* (1983).

CONNOR, Tony (John Anthony) (1930–), British poet, born in Manchester; after leaving school at 14, he worked as a textile designer between 1944 and 1960. In 1971 he became Professor of English at Wesleyan University, Connecticut. His first collection of poetry, *With Love Somehow* (1962), was followed by numerous others, including *Lodgers* (1965), *In the Happy Valley* (1971), *The Memoirs of Uncle Harry* (1974), and *New and Selected Poems* (1982), establishing him as one of the foremost poets in the domestic and regional modes ascendant in British writing during the 1960s and 1970s. His work is noted for the structural integrity and unsentimental realism with which he presents personal, anecdotal, and observational subjects. A further collection, *Spirits of Place* (1986), greatly extends the geographical ambit of his poetry, drawing heavily on Connor's experiences of India in addition to the English and American locales reflected in his previous work; *Metamorphic Adventures* (1995) is among his most recent volumes of verse. He has also produced translations and written numerous television plays.

CONQUEST, (George) Robert (Acworth) (1917–), British poet and historian, born in Great Malvern,

Worcester, educated at Magdalen College, Oxford. After active service in the Second World War, he held a series of diplomatic postings until 1956, when he began lecturing at the London School of Economics. Since 1959 he has lived mainly in America as a senior research fellow at various universities and institutions. He is recognized as one of the world's leading specialists in Soviet affairs and modern Russian history. His *Poems* appeared in 1955; *Between Mars and Venus* (1962), *Arias from a Love Opera* (1969), and *Forays* (1979) are among his subsequent collections. *New and Collected Poems* was published in 1988. He edited the two volumes of *New Lines* anthologies (1956, 1963), the first of which was the principal platform of The *Movement; Conquest's definition of their aims as 'a negative determination to avoid bad principles' applies to the precision of form and argument with which his own poems develop their fusions of thought and feeling. Numerous poems display the interest in science fiction evident in his novel *A World of Difference* (1955). With Kingsley *Amis, Conquest was co-editor of the science fiction anthology *Spectrum* (1961–5) and co-author of the humorous novel *The Egyptologists* (1965). His many publications on the USSR include *The Great Terror* (1973) and *The Harvest of Sorrow* (1986), which examine the effects of Stalin's policies in the 1930s. His translation of Alexander Solzhenitsyn's *Prussian Nights* appeared in 1973.

CONRAD, Joseph (Józef Teodor Konrad Nalecz Korzeniowski) (1857–1924), novelist and short-story writer, born at Berdyczów, in the Russian-annexed Polish Ukraine, into a family of land-owning Polish *szlachta* gentry. His father, Apollo Korzeniowski, a poet and translator of Shakespeare, Dickens, and Hugo, was a national political figure, active in the nationalist insurrectionary movements which had flowered since the 1795 partition and colonizing of Poland by Russia, Prussia, and Austria. Conrad's early upbringing was thus within a fervently patriotic household where an ethos of cosmopolitan cultural enlightenment, aristocratic duty and honour, and political revolution were in heady and paradoxical mix. In 1862, as punishment for Apollo's insurrectionary activism, the family was sent into exile in Vologda, in northern Russia. The later great themes of Conrad's writing—loyalty and betrayal, isolation and exile, duty and freedom—thus find their sources early in his life experience. His mother, Ewa, died in exile when Conrad was seven, followed in 1869 by Apollo soon after their return to Poland. The orphaned Conrad was brought up by his uncle, Tadeusz Bobrowski, who remained an abiding influence for another twenty-five years. The cautious Bobrowski did not manage to dissuade Conrad from his romantic ambition to go to sea, however, and in 1874 Conrad left for Marseilles and the start of some twenty years as a professional sailor.

Four years in Marseilles introduced him to a rich variety of cosmopolitan social and professional contacts, cultural and amorous excitements, gambling, gun-running, and a failed suicide attempt (1878). These Mediterranean experiences, together with ocean voyages in 1875 and 1876 on sailing-ships, first as passenger, then as crew, to the West Indies and possibly South America (Venezuela), provided Conrad with early material he was to exploit if not mythologize in his late novels *The Arrow of Gold* (1919) and *The Rover* (1923), as well as in his autobiographical essays *The Mirror of the Sea* (1906) and *A Personal Record* (1912). In 1878 he joined the British Merchant Navy, learning English in order to take successive mariner examinations—first mate in 1884, master in 1886, the same year he became a naturalized British subject. Conrad's British 'sea years', first plying the east coast of England, with later repeated ocean runs to India, the Far East, and Australia (when he met lifelong friend John *Galsworthy), provided him with the adventures, locations, characters, and above all the profound human experiences of endurance and fear, isolation and solidarity, idealism and disillusion, civility and barbarism, which his later literary works treat. **Heart of Darkness* (1902), based on his traumatic Congo journey in 1890 (and recorded in his 'Congo Diary', posthumously pub. 1978), is the most obvious and eloquent example of this treatment. Although Conrad started writing *Almayer's Folly*, his first novel, in 1889, it was not until 1894 that his career at sea in effect came to an end.

Not for another twenty years, however, with the publication of **Chance*, did Conrad earn a stable income from his writing, his financial stress relieved only by constant fiscal and moral support especially from his literary agent J. B. Pinker and from Edward *Garnett (who accepted *Almayer's Folly*, 1895, for publication with T. Fisher Unwin). In 1896 he married Jessie George, by whom he was to have two sons, Boris and John. Living mainly in Kent, he maintained strong and abiding friendships with some of the most influential literary figures of the age: Galsworthy, Garnett, aristocrat and socialist R. *Cunninghame Graham, and Kent neighbours Ford Madox Hueffer (*Ford), H. G. *Wells, Henry *James, and Stephen Crane, as well as Arthur *Symons and (later) Bertrand *Russell and André Gide. Both *Almayer's Folly* and *An Outcast of the Islands* (1896) received largely positive critical response, which complimented the unknown Conrad through flattering comparison with *Kipling and Stevenson. Both works share the exotic setting of the Malay Archipelago, and despite some heavy literary obviousness, they embody thematic and narrative concerns which anticipate his major works: elliptical narratives; subtle interweaving of the political, anthropological, and the personal; gender and racial stereotypes offered but also challenged. Some of these elements are also found in his first (uneven) volume of short stories, *Tales of Unrest* (1898), containing 'Karain', 'The Idiots', 'An Outpost of Progress' (a prototype for *Heart of Darkness*), 'The Return', and 'The Lagoon'.

Nigger of the 'Narcissus' (1897) marks the beginning of Conrad's 'major phase'. Its symbolic resonance beneath a realistic narrative, its story of nature's violence and human anxiety and of a ship as community threatened by mutiny, all contribute to its quintessential Conradian power. Its famous 'Preface', with Conrad's emphasis on the craft of Art and his almost programmatic 'impressionist' claim that 'my task is, by the power of the written word, to make you *see*', has itself become a central document of *Modernist aesthetics. **Lord Jim* (1900), *Heart of Darkness*, and *'Youth' (which appeared together with 'The *End of the Tether', 1902) develop a Conradian character-narrator, Marlow, who performs a crucial function in Conrad's work and who reappears much later in *Chance* (1913). A sea captain, intelligent, humane, and sceptical, Marlow represents a Victorian liberal outlook and source of moral perspective, who nevertheless should not be identified or confused with Conrad's own position. With Conrad's increasingly sophisticated narrative complexity and modernist ambivalences, Marlow as hero/problem typifies Conrad's inventiveness. While still drawing on his maritime experiences for some of his stories, his major novels are marked by experiments with narrative technique and disrupted chronological sequence, complex modes of ironic narrative distance, an increasing mastery over literary English (his third language), and an engagement with elemental thematic preoccupations—the temptations of illusion, the contradictions of freedom, and the vulnerability of all-too-human virtues like trust, love, and idealism. Briefly collaborating with Ford on *The Inheritors* (1901), a mix of science fiction and topical political allegory, and *Romance* (1903), a historical adventure narrative, Conrad continued independently with the writing of **Typhoon and Other Stories* ('Typhoon', 'Amy Foster', 'Falk', 'Tomorrow'; 1903), which was followed by arguably his most challenging, most complex historical political narrative, **Nostromo* (1904), set in an unstable South American state in the ambiguous throes of revolution. *The *Secret Agent* (1907) takes as its starting point the anarchist activities of 1890s' London, including the 1894 bomb attack on the Greenwich Observatory. Some of its preoccupations are mirrored in **Under Western Eyes* (1911). Conrad's completion of *Under Western Eyes* left him in a state of nervous breakdown, according to Jessie 'holding converse with his characters'. Extreme stress accompanied most of his writing for, as Cunninghame Graham said, Conrad 'almost needed a Caesarian operation of the soul before he was delivered of his masterpieces'. Whilst the years of his greatest novels also saw the publication of collections of short stories, *A Set of Six* (1908), *'Twixt Land and Sea* (which included 'The *Secret Sharer', 1912), and *Within the Tides* (1915), it was *Chance* (1913) which brought Conrad popular recognition and a bestseller for the first time in his career, thanks particularly to his American readership. **Victory* (1915), growing popularity, and plans for a collected edition end his major phase.

*The *Shadow-Line* (1917) alone is critically regarded as a major work of his final years. Despite public adulation in Britain and America, the offer (declined) of a knighthood, and the lucrative sale of film rights, his last years saw him perhaps in relative creative decline. Two attempts at playwriting, *Laughing Anne* (1920) and a dramatized *The Secret Agent* (1922), and late novels *The Arrow of Gold* (1919), *The Rescue* (1920, started in 1900), *The Rover* (1923), and the unfinished, posthumously published *Suspense* (1925) and *Tales of Hearsay* (1925) failed to command serious critical endorsement. *Notes on Life and Letters* (1921) and *Last Essays* (1926) contain late autobiographical and occasional pieces.

At his death Conrad was established as one of the leading early generation of Modernists, along with Henry James and Ford. Partly overshadowed in the 1930s by the younger generation of *Lawrence, *Joyce, *Woolf, and the 'Auden generation', Conrad's critical reputation was reasserted with F. R. *Leavis's essay in **Scrutiny* (1941), reprinted in the widely influential *The Great Tradition* (1948), which commended his 'moral Realism' and pronounced Conrad 'among the very greatest novelists in the language'. More recent criticism has moved away from mythic, psychological, and moral readings to stress narratological/linguistic, post-colonial, and gender approaches to his work. See J. Baines, *Joseph Conrad: A Critical Biography* (1960), F. R. Karl, *Joseph Conrad: The Three Lives* (1979), and Z. Najder, *Joseph Conrad: A Chronicle* (1983). Four (of eight) volumes of his *Collected Letters*, edited by F. Karl and L. Davies, have been published.

CONRAN, Anthony (1931–), British poet and translator, born in Kharghpur, India, educated at the University College of North Wales, Bangor, where he became Research Fellow and Tutor in English in 1957. His work as a poet and translator has involved him closely with the poetic literature of the Welsh language and of the Welsh metrical and assonantal traditions. His first collection of poetry, *Formal Poems* (1961), was followed by numerous others, among them *Spirit Level* (1974), *Life Fund* (1979), *Blodeuwedd and Other Poems* (1988), *Poems 1951–1967* (1974), and *Castles* (1993). Much of his verse reflects the communal functions of Welsh poetry in its celebratory or elegiac treatments of events within a localized culture. His best-known collection of translations is *The Penguin Book of Welsh Verse* (1967), which was highly acclaimed for its combination of accuracy and musicality. His other translations include *Eighteen Poems of Dante Alighieri* (1975). *The Cost of Strangeness* (1982) is a critical study of *Anglo-Welsh poetry.

CONRAN, Shirley, see ROMANTIC FICTION.

CONROY, Frank (1936–), American novelist and writer, educated at Haverford College. He has contributed to periodicals and magazines such as the **New Yorker*, the *Chicago Tribune*, and *Harper's*. His principal acclaim came for his autobiographical novel *Stop-Time* (1967), a memoir of boyhood and adolescence. Written in unpretentious prose, the novel begins with a lesson in brutality at a progressive boarding school, moves to a self-help settlement in Florida, then to a Connecticut mental home, and finally to New York City, where Conroy takes on a variety of jobs. Then, after his parents fall apart, he runs away to begin a new set of adventures. With a mixture of humour and irony, the book is a reflection on history and national geography. He has more recently edited *The Iowa Award: The Best Stories from 20 Years* (1992) and published the novel *Body and Soul* (1993).

CONROY, Jack (John) (Wesley) (1899–1980), American novelist and editor, born in Moberly, Missouri. Conroy lost his father and brother in a mining disaster and spent some years as a migratory worker. These circumstances inform his best-known novel, *The Disinherited* (1933), written with the encouragement of H. L. *Mencken. The book fictionalizes Conroy's own boyhood in a company-owned town, his itinerant labouring life, and experience of strikes and corruption, and ends with the protagonist's resolve to become active in the class struggle. Hailed at the time as a genuinely *proletarian novel, it now seems less ideological, with the vicissitudes of working-class characters balanced by its pastoral portrait of young love and small-town life. The novel remains an important example of the social literature produced by the Great Depression. Conroy's activities as an editor of *little magazines began with *The Rebel Poet*, but his major project was the Midwest-based *The Anvil*, which ran between 1933 and 1937 and became an exemplary model of literary and political commitment, printing work by Maxim Gorky, Nelson *Algren, and Langston *Hughes, among others. Conroy went on to be literary editor of two Chicago newspapers and the author of books for children. His last significant publication involved his editing *Writers In Revolt: The Anvil Anthology* (1973; with Curt Johnson).

Conservationist, The, see GORDIMER, NADINE.

CONSTANTINE, David (1944–), British poet, born in Salford, educated at Manchester Grammar School and at Wadham College, Oxford. He lectured at Durham University until 1981, when he became a fellow of Queen's College, Oxford. He became literary editor of *Argo* magazine. *A Brightness to Cast Shadows* (1981), his first collection of poetry, was followed by *Watching for Dolphins* (1983) and *Madder* (1987); *Selected Poems* appeared in 1991. Much of Constantine's work draws its strengths from his imaginative engagement with the mythical and religious dimensions of personal experience. Such characteristics co-exist with a strongly observed element of social realism and imagery of marked sensory vividness. His technical accomplishment covers a wide range of forms, extending from fluent use of traditional modes to the rhythmically cadenced lines in which he achieves his most individual effects. His other works include the novel *Davies* (1985), the critical study *Early Greek Travellers and the Hellenic Ideal* (1984), the biography *Hölderlin* (1988), and a long poem about the nineteenth-century German, *Caspar Hauser* (1994). He is also highly regarded as a translator for his *Selected Poems of Hölderlin* (1990).

Contemporary Review, The, a periodical founded in 1866 as the organ of the Metaphysical Society. Matthew Arnold, Walter Pater, William Ruskin, and Thomas Huxley were among the contributors who established its high reputation for the quality of its articles on literary, socio-cultural, and scientific topics. Sir Percy Bunting was its editor from 1882 to 1910. Around the turn of the century work by Rudyard *Kipling, W. B. *Yeats, and H. G. *Wells was featured and a continuing interest in European literature was initiated with essays on Ibsen and Tolstoy. In 1911 Bunting was succeeded as editor by George Peabody Gooch, who pursued his intention of making the *Review* the leading monthly on foreign affairs; Leonard *Woolf headed the foreign affairs section in 1922 and 1923, after which it was run by George Glasgow until 1954. The journal's authoritative commentaries on political and social matters were conducted from a position described by Gooch as 'just a little to the left of the centre'. During the 1930s the *Review* was also noted for its distinguished treatments of literature, science, and history by contributors who included Frederick Boas, Gilbert Murray, Julian *Huxley, and Arnold *Toynbee. In 1955 it absorbed the *Fortnightly Review*. Prior to his retirement in 1960, Gooch began including poetry as a regular aspect of the magazine; under Rosalind Wade's editorship, which commenced in 1970, short stories as well as poetry became a staple feature of the *Review*, in addition to which it has devoted considerable attention to the theatre.

COOK, David (1940–), British actor, novelist, and television playwright, born in Preston, Lancashire, educated at the Royal Academy of Dramatic Art. His first novel, *Albert's Memorial* (1972), introduces us to the widowed Mary and the homosexual Paul, both bereaved and marginal tragi-comic figures, the first of his gallery of portraits of eccentric and often vagrant characters, all of whom are seen with insight, wit, and sympathy. This was followed by *Happy Endings* (1974), the story of a disturbed 12-year-old boy accused of 'interfering' with a 5-year-old girl; *Walter* (1978), his best-known work, which describes the boyhood and youth of a mentally handicapped man, and its sequel, *Walter's Doves* (1979), in which Walter takes to the road with his friend June; *Sunrising* (1984), a historical novel set against the violent background of agricultural riots in the 1830s; *Missing Persons* (1986); *Crying Out Loud* (1988); and *Second Best* (1991), about a single male's attempt to adopt a 10-year-old boy, which was filmed with Anthony Hopkins in 1992. Cook's works show a particular feeling for the disadvantaged, both young and elderly, and a professional knowledge of the world of welfare and social service. He has also written educational programmes for slow learners.

COOKSON, Catherine (Anne) (1906–), British regional novelist, born in Tyne Dock, Jarrow. She is a popular and prolific writer, most of whose works are set in her native Tyneside. She was the illegitimate daughter of Kate McMullen, a domestic servant whom she believed was her sister, and whose story she tells in her interesting autobiography *Our Kate* (1969); Cookson herself went into service after leaving school at the age of 14. *Catherine Cookson Country* (1986) is another autobiographical work. Her writing career began after she moved south and joined the Hastings Writers' Circle in the 1940s. Many of her works feature a realistic working-class background with lively, unsentimental, earthy characters, and her heroines are strong, hardworking, and resourceful. She created the character of 'Mary Ann', who was to feature in a long series, beginning with *The Lord and Mary Ann* (1956). With *The Round Tower* (1968) Cookson received the Winifred Hotby Award for the best regional novel. Subsequent series were centred on the Mallen family (*The Mallen Streak*, 1973; *The Mallen Girl*, 1974; *The Mallen Letter*, 1974), and on Tilly Trotter (including *Tilly Trotter*, 1980; *Tilly Trotter Wed*, 1981; *Tilly Trotter Widowed*, 1982). More recent publications include *The Obsession* (1995), a more unusual novel dealing with a woman's need to protect her inheritance, and *Plainer Still* (1995), a memoir. See also ROMANTIC FICTION.

COOLIDGE, Clark (1939–), American poet, born in Providence, Rhode Island. Though associated with the *Language Poets, his work predates the movement and despite close contact with many of them he remains distinct from any movement, literary or political. His primary literary influences are Rilke, *Beckett, and *Kerouac, but jazz, geology, and painting (he wrote a collaborative work with the painter Philip Guston: *Baffling Means*, 1991) also play a large part. This poetic purist shares with many avant-garde artists of the 1950s and 1960s the belief that art is discovery, and so creates an exploratory 'improvisational momentum' in its composition which aims to 'tell the story that has never been thought before' in a writing which is itself the primary focus, rather than its subject matter. He is a consummate verbal musician, whose enormously inventive combinations of words, images, and objects not only explore the workings of language but suggest new forms of experience. *At Egypt* (1988) is a dense, vital work which observes both tourist and country with great wit and variety, constantly questioning itself as it takes on surprisingly Romantic themes such as the relations between mortality and representation. Other works include *Space* (1970), *Polaroid* (1975), *Quartz Hearts* (1978), *Mine: The One that Enters the Stories* (1982), *The Crystal Text* (1986), and *Odes of Roba* (1991).

COOPER, Giles (Stannus) (1918–66), British playwright, born in Carrickmines, County Dublin, educated at Lancing College. He was an actor and television script-editor until 1955, when he became a full-time playwright for stage, television, and radio. His works for the stage include *Everything in the Garden* (1962) and *The Spies Are Singing* (1966). *The Other Man* (1964), his best-known work for television, offered a disquieting alternative version of relations between Britain and Germany during the Nazi era; it was also adapted as a novel (1964). The finest of his many plays are his works for radio, which freed him from the constraints of naturalistic realism and permitted an imaginative engagement with Britain's post-war malaise which formed the thematic centre of much of his work. *Mathry Beacon* (1956) and *Unman, Wittering, and Zigo* (1958) are generally considered his masterpieces for radio. He was killed in a fall from a train in Surrey in 1966. The Giles Cooper Award instituted in 1978 is Britain's most coveted prize for radio drama.

COOPER, Lettice (Ulpha) (1897–1994), British novelist, born in Eccles, Lancashire, educated at Lady Margaret Hall, Oxford. Her first novel, *The Lighted Room* (1925), was one of ten written while she was in Yorkshire. The last of these, *National Provincial* (1938), led to an invitation to work in London, on the staff of **Time and Tide*, as editorial assistant and drama critic. During the Second World War, she was public relations officer for the Ministry of Food in London. The 1947 publication of *Black Bethlehem* and her biography of Robert Louis Stevenson marked Cooper's return to writing. From the outset, Cooper's project was to explore the 'truth of the human situation'. Her deliberate use of traditional form, domestic situations, and uneventful lives in her fiction places her in the mainstream of English writing by women from George Eliot onwards. Much of her fiction is set in her native Yorkshire, but her frequent visits to Italy, for which she had a deep and evident affection, are reflected by her use of its landscapes and interiors in many of her works, notably the ambitious and successful *Fenny* (1953). A lifelong socialist, Cooper studied the world she knew intimately with compassion and insight; she had a particular understanding of the workings of institutions, which is revealed in such works as *Three Lives* (1957), set in an adult education college, and the earlier *We Have Come to a Country* (1935), the action of which unfolds in an occupational centre for unemployed men. The last of her twenty novels, *Unusual Behaviour*, appeared in 1986, and the revival in 1987 of three earlier novels (*The New House*, 1936; *National Provincial*, and *Fenny*) brought Cooper's fiction to a new audience in her ninetieth year. She also wrote numerous children's books. She was Vice-Chairman (1975–8), then President of the English Pen Club (1979–81). Cooper was awarded an OBE in 1978.

COOPER, William, pseudonym of Harry Summerfield HOFF (1910–), English novelist, born in Crewe, Cheshire, educated at Christ's College, Cambridge. He was a physics teacher, served in the Royal Air Force during the Second World War, and worked for the Civil Service Commission and the Atomic Energy Authority. As H. S. Hoff he had written four novels before he became recognized with his fifth,

Scenes from Provincial Life (1950), by 'William Cooper', which considerably influenced younger novelists of the 1950s, including Kingsley *Amis, John *Braine, and Stan *Barstow. Sardonically comic and artfully realistic, it is narrated by a young lower-middle-class schoolteacher, Joe Lunn; much of the comedy revolves around the anti-hero's attempts to keep his girlfriend, Myrtle, happy while also avoiding marriage. *Scenes from Metropolitan Life* (1982), about Joe Lunn's Civil Service days, was written in 1951 but suppressed for many years under threat of libel; *Scenes from Married Life* (1961), which completes the trilogy, was followed by *Scenes from Later Life* (1983). Other novels include *Young People* (1958), about students at a provincial university in the 1930s; *Memoirs of a New Man* (1966), about a scientist; and *Immortality at Any Price* (1991), about an Oxford academic and biographer. Cooper's novels are important not just for their literary merit but also for their contribution to the 'new realism' school of British fiction. He also wrote *C. P. Snow* (1959; revised edition 1971) and *From Early Life* (1990), an autobiographical memoir.

COOVER, Robert (1932–), American novelist and short-story writer, born in Charles City, Iowa, educated at the universities of Southern Illinois, Indiana, and Chicago. Coover's novels turn away from traditional 'realist' forms, demonstrating a post-modern sense of 'reality' and history as 'made up', fabricated, or fictions (see NEW JOURNALISM). His first novel, *The Origin of the Brunists* (1966), was a study of the influence of charismatic religion on small-town America, and concerns the establishment of a religious cult by the survivor of a mining disaster. *The Universal Baseball Association, Inc., J. Henry Waugh, Prop.* (1968) is an allegorical novel which uses baseball as its principal metaphor to satirize American religious beliefs, and *Pricksongs and Descants* (1969) shows a developing interest in the overlapping boundaries between art and reality. This later developed into a technique which produced the startling *The Public Burning* (1976), in which the trial and judicial murder of the Rosenbergs overlaps with fantasy to produce a vigorous indictment of the McCarthy years. His other, later works *Whatever Happened to Gloomy Gus of the Chicago Bears?* (1977), in which he returned to his attack on Richard Nixon, *Spanking the Maid* (1981), a story about a sado-masochistic, obsessive relationship between a man and his maid, *Gerald's Party* (1986), *A Night at the Movies* (1987), and *Pinnochio in Venice* (1991) continued his characteristic self-reflexive preoccupation with the materiality of writing. His short story collections include *Hair o' the Chine* (1979), *After Lazarus: A Filmscript* (1980), *Charlie in the House of Rue* (1980), and *The Convention* (1982). He has also written several plays collected in *A Theological Position* (1972), and *In Bed One Night and Other Brief Encounters* (1983), which are nine satirical exercises in modernist writing.

COPE, Wendy (1945–), British poet, born in Erith, Kent, educated at St Hilda's College, Oxford. She became a schoolteacher in London. Her early publications include *Across the City* (1980) and *Hope and the 42 . . .* (1984). Her *Making Cocoa for Kingsley Amis* (1986) enjoyed considerable success; the book is most notable for its many parodies of the works of well-known poets, including T. S. *Eliot, Ted *Hughes, Craig *Raine, and Seamus *Heaney. In these, the highly developed technical facility and wit Cope possesses are masterfully combined with her sensitivity to the styles of her subjects, producing results that have earned her comparisons with Max *Beerbohm. Her subsequent publications include *Men and Their Boring Arguments* (1988) and *Serious Concerns* (1992), which features more reflective poetry on a wide range of topics. Cope also edited *Is That the New Moon?* (1989, illustrated by Christine Roche), an anthology of works by modern women poets. *Twiddling Your Thumbs* (1988) is a work for children illustrated by Christine Roche.

COPPARD, A(lfred) E(dgar) (1878–1957), British short-story writer and poet, born in Folkestone; ill-health curtailed his education at Lewes Road School, Brighton, when he was nine. After working in a variety of commercial capacities, he became a full-time writer in 1919, publishing his first book of stories, *Adam and Eve and Pinch Me*, in 1921. His many collections include *Fishmonger's Fiddle* (1925), *Silver Circus* (1928), *Crotty Shinkwin* (1932), *You Never Know, Do You?* (1939), and *Fearful Pleasures* (1946). Coppard viewed his work as extending the traditions of the ballad and folk-tale; masterful handling of rural dialogue characterizes much of his writing. His stories, which often display a compassionate concern with the lot of the misfit, combine transparent stylistic simplicity with profound imaginative analyses of human behaviour. *Hips and Haws* (1922), *Yokohama Garland* (1926), and *Cherry Ripe* (1935) are among the numerous volumes of his poetry, which is notable for the fluency and imagistic vividness of its free-verse forms and recurrently evokes the Elizabethan and Caroline periods. His other works include *It's Me, O Lord* (1957), the first volume of an unfinished autobiography.

CORBETT, Jim (James Edward) (1875–1955), British author and conservationist, born in Naini Tal, Kumaon, India, where he was educated at St Joseph's College. Apart from a period as a railway inspector and service in France during the First World War, Corbett spent most of his life as a farmer in Kumaon. He retained a deep commitment to the welfare of the local people, on whose behalf he stalked and killed a succession of man-eating tigers and leopards. He recorded these episodes along with wide-ranging accounts of his experiences of the wilds in *The Man-Eaters of Kumaon* (1946), *The Man-Eating Leopard of Rudraprayag* (1948), and *The Temple Tiger and More Man-Eaters of Kumaon* (1954). In 1935 he established the first game sanctuary in India at Garhwal, which became Corbett National Park in 1957. His other works include the substantially autobiographical *My India* (1952) and *Jungle Lore* (1953). *Carpet Sahib* (1986) is Martin Booth's biography of Corbett.

CORKERY, Daniel (1878–1964), Irish critic, dramatist, and short-story writer, born in Cork, educated at St Patrick's College, Dublin. In 1908 he founded, together with other nationalists, the Cork Dramatic Society, which produced plays in both Irish and English. Corkery's published plays include *The Labour Leader* (1920), *The Yellow Bittern and Other Plays* (1920), and *Resurrection* (1924). His collections of short stories, generally considered his best work, include *A Munster Twilight* (1916), *The Hounds of Banba* (1920), *The Stormy Hills* (1929), and *Earth out of Earth* (1939). As a short-story writer, he had a considerable influence on his younger contemporaries, Frank *O'Connor and Sean *O'Faolain. However, critical works like *The Hidden Ireland* (1925), on the Gaelic work of the Munster poets in the eighteenth-century, when ancient Irish culture was in the process of being ruthlessly suppressed, and *Synge and Anglo-Irish Literature* (1931), made the greatest impact in his own lifetime and opened up new areas of Irish literary history. He also wrote *The Threshold of Quiet* (1917), a novel, and *The Fortunes of the Irish Language* (1954). Corkery was appointed Senator by De Valera in 1951.

CORMAN, Cid (Sidney) (1924–), American editor and poet, born in Boston, Massachusetts, educated at Tufts College, the University of Michigan, the University of North Carolina, and, as a Fulbright Fellow, the Sorbonne. From 1949 to 1951 he presented a series of broadcasts entitled 'This is Poetry' for a Boston radio station, which featured readings by leading younger American poets and initiated contact with a number of the contributors to *Origin*, the seminal magazine of poetry Corman founded in 1951; Robert *Creeley, Charles *Olson, Paul *Blackburn, and other poets subsequently central to the poetic activities associated with *Black Mountain College were among those whose work appeared regularly. *The Gist of 'Origin'* (1975), edited by Corman, contains a wide selection of material from the periodical. In 1956 he established the Origin publishing imprint, one of the most enduring and valuable of the *small presses; from 1958 to 1979 the press was principally based in Kyoto, Japan, where he worked as a lecturer. The growing concentration and selective particularity of his own poetry during these years derived in part from his intimacy with Japanese literature, of which he has produced numerous translations, including *Cool Melon* (1959), versions of Basho, and *Peerless Mirror: Twenty Tanka from the Manyoshu* (1981). Corman's verse is firmly located in the modern American tradition stemming from the achievements of William Carlos *Williams and Ezra *Pound. The more discursively conversational lyricism of his earlier work was superseded by the fluently direct and atmospherically evocative brevity of the poems in *Sun Rock Man* (1962). His many subsequent collections, some of which exemplify the possibilities of an extreme poetic minimalism, include *Aegis: Selected Poems 1970–1980* (1984), and *In Particular: Poems New and Selected* (1986). *Where Were We Now?* (1991) is a collection of Corman's essays.

CORNFORD, Frances (1886–1960), British poet, the granddaughter of Charles Darwin; she was born in Cambridge, where her parents were both lecturers. In 1909 she married F. M. Cornford, one of Cambridge's leading classicists and later the University's Professor of Ancient Philosophy. John *Cornford was their son. She was encouraged in her early writing by Rupert *Brooke during his time studying at Cambridge and published *Poems*, her first volume, in 1910. Subsequent collections of her verse include *Spring Morning* (1915), *Autumn Midnight* (1923), *Mountains and Molehills* (1935), and *On a Calm Shore* (1960). Her *Collected Poems* appeared in 1954, and in 1959 she received the Queen's Gold Medal for Poetry. While some of her work displays the insipidity of the lesser poetry of the *Georgians, with whom she was associated, she frequently combines a disarming simplicity with incisive and unsettling commentaries on experience. A number of her poems achieve the hauntingly memorable quality that has resulted in the inclusion of 'To a Fat Lady Seen from a Train' and 'All Souls' Night' in numerous anthologies. She also translated French and Russian poetry, collaborating with Stephen *Spender to produce an English version of Paul Éluard's *Le Dur Désir de Durer* (1950).

CORNFORD, (Rupert) John (1915–36), British poet, born in Cambridgeshire, the son of Frances *Cornford and the eminent Cambridge classicist Professor F. M. Cornford; he was educated at the London School of Economics and at Trinity College, Cambridge, where he took a first in History. An active member of the Communist Party, he contributed the essay 'What Communism Stands For' to *Christianity and the Social Revolution* (1935, edited by John Lewis and others). In 1936 he travelled to Spain to join the International Brigade and was made leader of its English contingent. He was killed outside Lopera on the day after his twenty-first birthday. He began writing poetry at an early age in emulation of his mother, whose traditional style he dismissed when he encountered the work of T. S. *Eliot and W. H. *Auden. His poems attracted favourable notice when they appeared in **New Writing*. His finest work is contained in 'Poems from Spain, 1936', which frequently display a poised acuteness of concentration in the face of battle similar to that found in the writing of Keith *Douglas. *John Cornford: A Memoir* (1938), edited by Pat Sloan, collects many of his poems and some political essays, which show a concern with defining the nature of ideological commitment. *Understand the Weapon, Understand the Wound* (edited by J. Galassi, 1986) is an edition of his poetry, essays, and letters. *Journey to the Frontier: Julian Bell and John Cornford* (1986) is a 'dual biography' by William Abrahams and Peter Stansky.

Cornhill Magazine, The, founded in 1860 by George Murray Smith; it quickly achieved huge sales through its policy of offering the serialization of two novels in each issue. William Makepeace Thackeray, who edited it from 1860 to 1862, Anthony Trollope, George

Eliot, and Wilkie Collins were eminent among the contributors in its early years. Henry *James and Thomas *Hardy supplied novels serialized during the 1870s, when the magazine was edited by Leslie Stephen. Literary standards declined when his editorship ended in 1882, but rose again under Reginald John Smith, the editor between 1898 and 1916; during this period poems and prose pieces by Hardy were published and Sir Arthur *Quiller-Couch, Virginia *Woolf, Julian *Huxley, and Edmund *Gosse were among the contributors of essays and criticism. Work by Ford Madox Hueffer (later *Ford), Katherine *Tynan, and Robert *Bridges also appeared. After the First World War the *Cornhill* had a high reputation for its essays on literary history, biography, and criticism, though it became somewhat inert under the editorship of Lord Gorell in the 1930s and closed in 1939. In 1944 it re-emerged as a quarterly, edited by Peter *Quennell, who published verse and prose by a wide range of authors including John *Betjeman, Max *Beerbohm, Truman *Capote, Andre Gide, Evelyn *Waugh, and Somerset *Maugham. During the magazine's last decades it carried important work by Philip *Larkin, Robert *Graves, Frank *O'Connor, John *Fowles, Laurie *Lee, Joyce *Cary, and others; from 1955 onward, however, the continuing fall in its circulation proved irreversible and it ceased publication in 1975.

CORNWELL, Bernard, pseudonym of Bernard WIGGINS (1944–), British writer of historical novels, born in London. After studying at London University, he worked as a television producer for a number of years. His novels include *Sharpe's Eagle* (1981), which narrated the exploits of Richard Sharpe in Wellington's Army, as he fights his way up through the ranks; he continued his adventures in many subsequent novels, including *Sharpe's Waterloo* (1990) and *Sharpe's Battle* (1995), about the Peninsular War. The novels are carefully researched, the author having explored all the battlefields he writes about, but they should be taken as exciting narratives rather than military history. Other novels include *Redcoat* (1987), about Philadelphia in 1777; *Stormchild* (1991), an eco-political thriller; and a sequence of novels, *Rebel* (1993), *Copperhead* (1994), and *Battle Flag* (1995), about Nathaniel Starbuck, a heroic Yankee fighting on the wrong side in the American Civil War.

CORSO, Gregory (Nunzio) (1930–), American poet, born in New York; he was irregularly educated and sentenced to three years' imprisonment for attempted robbery at the age of 17. He subsequently worked as a labourer, a reporter, and a merchant seaman while pursuing his self-education. *The Vestal Lady on Brattle* (1955), his first collection of verse, was published in Cambridge, Massachusetts, where *In This Hung-Up Age*, the first of his several short plays, was produced in 1955. His meeting with Allen *Ginsberg and Jack *Kerouac in 1956 led to the establishment of his reputation as a poet of the *San Francisco Renaissance; his collections of the period include *Gasoline* (1958), *Bomb* (1958), and *The Happy Birthday of Death* (1960), which display the humour, politically directed moral outrage, and mystical rapture that are essential features of his writing. Since the early 1960s he has lived alternately in America and Europe and has held a number of posts at American universities. Among his many later publications, which sustain his characteristic richness of invention and vatic manner, are *Long Live Man* (1962), *Elegiac Feelings American* (1970), *Earth Egg* (1974), and *Wings, Wands, Windows* (1982); *Mindfield: New and Selected Poems* appeared in 1989. His other works include the novel *The American Express* (1961), a high-spirited adaptation of autobiographical material.

CORTEZ, Jayne (1936–), African-American jazz poet, born in Arizona. She has performed her poetry throughout the USA, Africa, Europe, and Latin America, and has made videos and recordings of her work, such as *Celebrations and Solitudes* (1975), *Unsubmissive Blues* (1980), *There It Is* (1982), *Maintain Control* (1987), and *Everywhere Drums* (1990). Characteristically political and topical, her poems are most effective when heard but also have impressive visual movement and musicality on the page and have been widely anthologized and translated. Her books include *Festivals and Funerals* (1971), *Scarifications* (1973), *Coagulations: New and Selected Poems* (1984), and *Poetic Magnetic* (1991).

CORVO, Baron, see ROLFE, F. W.

COTTON, John (1925–), British poet, born in London, educated at the University of London. He began his career as a schoolteacher in 1947 and was headmaster of Highfield Comprehensive School, Hemel Hempstead, from 1963 to 1985. With Ted *Walker, he founded the magazine *Priapus* in 1962, and was editor of the journal of the Private Libraries Association from 1969 to 1979. *Old Movies and Other Poems* (1971) was his first substantial collection of verse. His numerous subsequent volumes include *Kilroy Was Here: Poems 1970–74* (1975), *Day Book* (1983), and *Oh Those Happy Feet!* (1986); *Here's Looking at You Kid: New and Selected Poems* appeared in 1990. Travel and natural observation are among the themes of his poetry, which also deals recurrently with various aspects of the cinema, a subject he engages with an attractive combination of wit and nostalgia. His other publications include the critical survey *British Poetry since 1965* (1973).

Countess Cathleen, The, see YEATS, W. B.

Country Girls Trilogy, The, see O'BRIEN, EDNA.

Couples, see UPDIKE, JOHN.

COUZYN, Jeni (1942–), Canadian poet, born in South Africa, educated at the University of Natal. In 1966 she emigrated to Britain and established herself as a freelance writer. She became a Canadian citizen in 1975 and was appointed writer-in-residence at the University of Victoria, British Columbia, in 1976.

Flying, her first collection of poetry, was published in 1970; subsequent volumes include *Christmas in Africa* (1975), *A Time to be Born* (1981), *Life by Drowning: Selected Poems* (1985), and *That's It* (1993). Couzyn's poetry repeatedly engages the social, political, and imaginative implications of womanhood. Her desire for a poetry of broad social accessibility and her conception of the art as pre-eminently oral are reflected in the clarity and immediacy of much of her writing. Many of her most richly textured poems deal with her childhood in Africa. As an editor, she has produced two widely read anthologies of writing by women poets, *The Bloodaxe Book of Contemporary Women Poets* (1985) and *Singing Down the Bones* (1989).

COWARD, Sir Noël (Pierce) (1899–1973), British actor, dramatist, and composer, born in Teddington, Middlesex, the son of a piano salesman, and brought up in genteel poverty in the London suburbs. He went on the stage as a boy, and began to write prolifically as a young man, achieving fame and notoriety with *The *Vortex* (1924), in which he himself appeared as a drug addict tormented by his mother's adulteries. His long career as a dramatist produced other seriously intended plays, including the sentimental *This Happy Breed* (1942), about a lower-middle-class family between the wars; *Peace in Our Time* (1948), a speculative picture of Britain under Nazi occupation; and *Song at Twilight* (1966), a portrait and to some extent a self-portrait of a homosexual writer in old age. He also wrote musicals, notably *Bitter Sweet* (1929) and the patriotic pageant *Cavalcade* (1931). But he is best remembered for a series of comedies which fell into critical disrepute in the late 1950s, with the coming of a more socially conscious drama, but have since become widely lauded for their lively and idiosyncratic humour. Chief among these are the precocious *The Young Idea* (1921), about two adolescents who reconcile their divorced parents by separating the father from his disagreeable second wife and from 'county' society; *Fallen Angels* (1925), about two women waiting for the same glamorous Frenchman; **Hay Fever* (1925); **Private Lives* (1930); *Design for Living* (1933), about the creation of a successful *ménage à trois*, and a key play for those wishing to explore the subject of Coward's morality; *Blithe Spirit* (1941), about a mischievous ghost's attempts to steal her former husband from his second wife; and *Present Laughter* (1942), a portrait of a temperamental comedian. All these plays implicitly promote a hedonistic philosophy, in which sympathy goes to the sophisticated, carefree, witty, stylish, and defiantly and sometimes wickedly unconventional, while antipathy is reserved for the dull, staid, orthodox, and moralizing. The wit and panache with which Coward conveys such views primarily explains his improved standing in the stock-market of taste and the frequency with which his work is revived, not just in the West End of London, but by the National and other repertory theatres.

COWLEY, Malcolm (1898–1989), American historian, translator, critic, writer, and editor, born in Belsano, Pennsylvania, educated at Harvard. After some time in Europe, where he became associated with *Hemingway, *Scott Fitzgerald, and *Dos Passos (see LOST GENERATION), Cowley became an editor with the **New Republic*. Associated with the literary and political left in the 1930s, he helped organize the first League of American Writers Congress in 1935, and was a central figure in the heated debate over the relationship of politics and aesthetics. In 1934 he published *Exile's Return*, an autobiographical literary history of the 1920s. He then became an editor and literary adviser, and a prominent champion of such writers as *Faulkner, *Cheever, and *Kerouac. As a critic he was hailed for his treatment of Faulkner's writing. His later writings concentrated on literary history in *The Literary Situation* (1954) and *Think Back on Us: A Contemporary Chronicle of the 1930s* (1969); *Black Cargoes* (1954) is a history of the black slave trade. His poetry appeared in *Blue Juanita* (1929) and *The Dry Season* (1941). Cowley also translated such writers as Valéry and Gide and produced two volumes of memoirs, entitled *And I Worked at the Writer's Trade* (1978) and *The Dream of the Golden Mountains* (1980). See also PROLETARIAN LITERATURE IN THE USA.

COWPER, Richard, pseudonym of Colin Middleton MURRY (1926–), British writer, born in Bridport, Dorset, the son of J. M. *Murry, educated at Brasenose College, Oxford. As Colin Middleton Murry he wrote *One Hand Clapping* (1975) and *Shadows on the Grass* (1977), which were vivid memoirs of his famous family. As Colin Murry, he published several novels, including *The Golden Valley* (1958) and *A Path to the Sea* (1961). Cowper became known for his elegiac *science fiction portraits of a fragile England threatened by transcendental change; among these are *Breakthrough* (1967), *Time out of Mind* (1973), and *The Twilight of Briareus* (1974), which is perhaps his best novel. *The Road to Corlay* (1978) and its sequels, set in a similar landscape, concern a new Church which soon becomes doctrinaire. Cowper's elegant stories have been collected in *The Custodians* (1976), *The Web of the Magi* (1980), and *The Tithonian Factor* (1984).

COX, Anthony Berkeley, see BERKELEY, ANTHONY.

COZZENS, James Gould (1903–78), American novelist, born in Chicago, educated at Harvard University where he completed *Confusion* (1924), his first novel. Other early novels include *The Son of Perdition* (1929) and *S.S. San Pedro: A Tale of the Sea* (1931), set in Cuba and the US merchant navy, respectively. Cozzens's fiction is more generally concerned with the precise delineation of social manners and mores and the place of institutions in the affairs of mankind. *Men and Brethren* (1936) concerns the dilemma that confronts an Episcopalian minister who tries to assist another minister expelled from the church for homosexuality. *The Just and the Unjust* (1942) is a murder story, which centres on the role of the legal system in the defence of an ordered society against the forces of anarchy, while *Guard of Honour* (1948; Pulitzer Prize), set in the

Second World War at an airforce base in Florida, explores the related themes of command, duty, and responsibility within a military hierarchy. Cozzens won critical acclaim with *By Love Possessed* (1957); reviewers such as J. B. *Priestley and Angus *Wilson considered it one of the finest post-war American novels. Its theme is the operation of love, in all its various guises, over forty-eight hours of the life of a small American town. As so often in Cozzens's work, the conflict is between a puritanically stern moral education and the forces of change and modernity. His last novel is *Morning Noon and Night* (1968). *Children and Others* (1964) and *A Flower in Her Hair* (1974) are collections of short stories. In an age of experimentation, Cozzens's preoccupation with custom, law, and tradition earned him the opprobrium of many critics who associated his position with the conservatism and complacency of the Eisenhower era. It is only in more recent years that serious scrutiny of his work has emerged. *Just Representations: A Cozzens Reader* (1978; edited by Matthew J. Bruccoli) is an anthology of his writings, while the strongest case for his importance as a novelist is put by D. E. S. Maxwell in *Cozzens* (1964).

CRACE, Jim (James) (1946–), British novelist and short-story writer, born in Hertfordshire, educated at Birmingham College of Commerce and at London University. He worked for some time in educational television in the Sudan, and settled in Birmingham. His first full-length work was *Continent* (1986; Whitbread Prize), a collection of seven loosely connected but thematically interlinked stories from fictitious regions of an imaginary Third World, which blend folklore, anthropology, fable, and parable in a contemporary meditation on the people and cultures of developing countries and their relation to the developed world. *The Gift of Stones* (1988), set in the Stone Age at the dawn of the Bronze Age, and seen through the eyes of the one-armed 'story-teller' narrator and his adopted daughter, shows the plight of the simple tribe of 'stoneys' whose skill and expertise in fashioning flint is threatened by new technology. The prose is spare and lyrical, and the element of parable is subtly absorbed into the human narrative. *Arcadia* (1992) is a futuristic fable about the condition of cities in the late twentieth century, while *Signals of Distress* (1994) is a naturalistic exploration of the events that occur in a West Country town in the 1830s, when a ship runs aground.

CRAIGIE, Sir William Alexander (1867–1957), British lexicographer, born in Dundee, educated at the University of St Andrews. In 1897 he was invited to join the staff of the *New English Dictionary* (1928), as the *Oxford English Dictionary* was originally known. He remained engaged on the dictionary, of which he became a co-editor with James A. H. *Murray and Henry *Bradley in 1901, until 1933, when the first *Supplement* was published. He was responsible for 'N', 'Q', 'R', 'U', 'V', 'Si–Sq', and 'Wo–Wy', a contribution amounting to around one-fifth of the main work and one-third of the *Supplement*. Upon the dictionary's completion in 1928 he was knighted. He was Professor of English at the University of Chicago from 1925 to 1936 and co-edited the *Dictionary of American English* (1919–55). His other publications include *Specimens of Icelandic Rimur* (3 volumes, 1952), a comprehensive survey of the literature of Iceland, where he was held in high regard. His *Dictionary of the Older Scottish Tongue* remained unfinished at his death.

CRANE, (Harold) Hart (1899–1932), American poet, born in Garrettsville, Ohio, he grew up and was educated in Cleveland. In 1916 he established contacts with the literary circles associated with the **Little Review* and *The *Seven Arts*; the international *Modernism of the former and the latter's more conservative and nationalist aesthetics both affected his development as a poet—in much of his best work an experimental ethos and an emphatic urban realism combine with magisterial effects achieved through his virtuosity in the use of traditional forms. Throughout the early 1920s he lived in New York, working in various capacities while gaining increasing notice as a poet through his contributions to leading literary journals. *White Buildings*, his first collection of poetry, appeared to critical acclaim in 1926. Among the well-known works it contains are 'For the Marriage of Faustus and Helen', in which Crane's transcendentally lyrical view of his New York surroundings first achieves full expression, and the six poems of 'Voyages', an erotic and mystical meditation sustained by imagery of the sea. Encouraged by the success of *White Buildings*, Crane devoted himself to the completion of *The *Bridge* (1930), which is widely regarded as one of the major long poems of the twentieth century. The book was, however, disappointingly received by reviewers who failed to discern its underlying unity in terms of what Crane termed 'the *rationale* of metaphor'. In 1931 he travelled to Mexico to produce an epic poem based on the history of Montezuma; lack of progress on the work, together with accumulating personal difficulties, among them his increasingly heavy drinking and confusion regarding his sexuality, gave rise to the acute depression in which he jumped to his death from the boat on which he was returning to New York in April 1932. *Complete Poems* (1966) was edited by Brom Weber, who also edited Crane's *Letters* (1952). *Voyager*, John Unterecker's biography of Crane, appeared in 1969.

CREASEY, John (1908–73), British crime writer, undoubtedly the most prolific of all, who, from 1932 until his death, wrote over 560 novels under more than twenty pseudonyms. Best known are the Roger West and Richard Rollison ('the Toff') stories, written under his own name (*Inspector West Takes Charge*, 1942; *Introducing the Toff*, 1938) and the J. J. Marric police procedural novels in which the chief character is Commander George Gideon of Scotland Yard. The latter—*Gideon's Day* (1955) is the first—are to be preferred to the rest of his work. Under other pseudonyms he wrote romantic novels, Westerns, and juvenile fiction.

CREELEY, Robert (White) (1926–), American poet, born in Arlington, Massachusetts, educated at Harvard University, *Black Mountain College, and the University of New Mexico. He edited the *Black Mountain Review* from 1954 to 1957 and assisted Charles *Olson in developing his theories of *Projective Verse; *Charles Olson and Robert Creeley: The Complete Correspondence* (eight volumes, 1980–7) was edited by George F. Butterick. From the early 1960s he held a succession of posts at the University of New Mexico and the State University of New York, where he became Professor of Poetry and Humanities in 1989. Poems from numerous early collections, including *Le Fou* (1952) and *The Whip* (1957), were published to widespread critical acclaim as *For Love: Poems 1950–1960* (1962); much of the verse forms terse and fluently exploratory treatments of emotional and perceptual experience. Notable among his many succeeding volumes of the 1960s are *Words* (1967), *Numbers* (1968), and *Pieces* (1968), which display an intensifying concern with linguistic fidelity to the processes of consciousness. In the course of the 1970s his verse became increasingly concerned with memory and its interactions with immediate experience; the understated elegiac quality sensed in *Hello: A Journal* (1978) is more fully present in *Later* (1980), in which perspectives on the past intensify an awareness of transience and ageing. *Mirrors* (1984), *Memory Gardens* (1987), *Windows* (1990), and *Echoes* (1995), his principal subsequent collections, contain work of remarkable scope: a moving emotional directness coexists with the refined minimalism of his earlier manner, while many poems exhibit a rich particularity and the laconic good humour that has always been present in his work. *Collected Poems* appeared in 1982 and *Selected Poems, 1945–1990* in 1991. Among his other publications are *The Island* (1963), an autobiographical novel; the short stories of *The Gold Diggers* (1954, enlarged 1965) and *Mister Blue* (1964); and *Autobiography* (1990). *Collected Essays* (1989) forms a valuable chronicle of poetic developments in the post-war years.

CREWS, Harry (Eugene) (1935–), American novelist and short-story writer, born in Bacon County, Georgia; he served in the US Marine Corps (1953–6) then graduated from the University of Florida in 1960 where he taught and became professor of English in 1974. His early life was marked by poverty, extreme violence, the separation of his parents, and the premature death of his father. The horror of his background, as well as its particular wonders, is described in *A Childhood: The Biography of a Place* (1978) which records the extraordinary delineaments of a usually unremarked existence. His novels include *The Gospel Singer* (1968), *Naked in Garden Hills* (1969), *Car* (1972), *The Gypsy's Curse* (1974), *A Feast of Snakes* (1976), *All We Need of Hell* (1987), *The Knockout Artist* (1988), and *Scar Lover* (1992); *Classic Crews* (1993), which includes *A Childhood*, is an ideal introduction to his work. He is a satirist of biting wit, whose novels feature grotesques and misfits, frequently in bizarre situations and settings, who search for meaning and belief in a materialistic world of violence and sex. The relationship between disfigurement and identity is a central preoccupation of his writing which offers a stark contrast to the idea of perfectability which pervades much of American culture. Though his work tends to drift towards symbolism as it moves further away from his past, it nevertheless retains a unique vision and a distinctive style.

CRICK, Bernard (Rowland) (1929–), British political theorist and biographer, born in London, educated at the University of London, where, after holding a succession of academic posts in Britain and America, he became Professor of Politics at Birkbeck College in 1971. His numerous influential works include *In Defence of Politics* (1962); *Political Theory and Practice* (1969); *Crime, Rape, and Gin* (1974), a study of contemporary attitudes to violence, pornography, and addiction; the essays of *Political Thoughts and Polemics* (1990); and *20/20 Visions: The Future of Christianity in Britain* (1992). He remains best known for *George Orwell: A Life* (1980), the first authoritative biographical treatment of its subject, which was widely acclaimed for its sustained levelness of tone and unusually thorough research.

CRISPIN, Edmund, pseudonym of Robert Bruce MONTGOMERY (1921–78), British composer of choral and orchestral works, songs, and film music, who under this name wrote nine *detective novels and a number of short stories, beginning with *The Case of the Gilded Fly* (1944), written when he was an undergraduate at St John's College, Oxford. In all of the novels and most of the stories the detective is Gervase Fen, Professor of English at Oxford, a character reputedly modelled on a tutor at Crispin's own college. Crispin is one of the most amusing and witty English detective novelists, and at his best—in *The Moving Toyshop* (1946), which makes admirable use of an Oxford setting, *Love Lies Bleeding* (1948), or *The Long Divorce* (1951; alternative US title *A Noose for Her*)—combines these qualities with a solid plot and genuine detection. His last novel, *Glimpses of the Moon* (1977), is, however, a disappointment.

Criterion, The, a periodical founded with the financial support of Lady Rothermere in 1922 by T. S. *Eliot, who remained its editor until the final issue in 1939. Eliot's first wife Vivien supplied the title. *The *Waste Land* was published in the first issue. The magazine was taken over by the publishers Faber and Gwyer (later *Faber and Faber) after Eliot joined the firm in 1925. It rapidly gained an unrivalled reputation for literary quality, featuring work by most of the leading writers of the 1920s and encouraging the broad acceptance of *Modernism; Ezra *Pound, Virginia *Woolf, F. S. *Flint, W. B. *Yeats, Herbert *Read, E. M. *Forster, and I. A. *Richards were among its early contributors. It also regularly featured writing by a range of eminent European authors. In 1924 Eliot began his editorial commentaries, which tended to reflect his increasingly extreme conservative position on sociocultural matters and his sense of communism's threat to the European tradition. Nevertheless, the *Criterion* remained open to conflicting shades of opinion and printed work by W. H. *Auden, Stephen *Spender, Louis *MacNeice, Hugh *MacDiarmid, and others known for their socialist sympathies during the early 1930s. A collected edition of its seventy-one issues appeared in 1967, with a preface by Eliot expressing his satisfaction with its overall achievement.

Critical Quarterly, The, a literary periodical founded in 1959 by C. B. Cox and A. E. Dyson to provide a widely accessible forum for contemporary poetry and criticism. The poetic and critical tenets of the *Movement were reflected in its editorial policy, and Donald *Davie and Philip *Larkin were eminent among early contributors of poems and reviews. Other poets whose work appeared in its pages in the 1960s included Ted *Hughes, Seamus *Heaney, Charles *Tomlinson, R. S. *Thomas, and Sylvia *Plath; Raymond *Williams, Bernard *Bergonzi, John *Wain, and Malcolm *Bradbury supplied critical commentaries. The magazine was among the primary channels for the establishment of poetic reputations in its earlier years. The twice-yearly publication of a supplementary *Critical Survey* between 1960 and 1973 had considerable influence in addressing matters relating to secondary education. After a period of editorial hostility towards the innovative ethos prevalent in much of the poetry of the late 1960s, the magazine revived its interest in a broad variety of contemporary writing; a flexible policy has prevailed since the formation of an editorial board in 1978. Prose fiction has latterly become a regular feature; Tony *Harrison, Tom *Raworth, U. A. *Fanthorpe, and James *Fenton are among the poets who have contributed work to more recent issues.

Crock of Gold, The, see STEPHENS, JAMES.

CROFTS, Freeman Wills (1879–1957), British *detective novelist, born in Dublin; he worked for a Northern Irish railway company as an engineer until 1929. His first book, *The Cask* (1920), is perhaps his masterpiece, but his best-known character is Inspector Joseph French, who appears in all his novels from *Inspector French's Greatest Case* (1925) onwards. Middle-aged and avuncular, French achieves his results through dogged persistence, rather than brilliant feats of deduction, and became the model for a number of similar fictional policemen. Though the writing is pedestrian, Crofts's plots are complex and solid—Raymond *Chandler called him 'the soundest builder of them all'—and often turn on the cunning manipulation of a railway timetable, as in *Sir John Magill's Last Journey* (1930). Also to be recommended are *The Sea Mystery* (1928), *Death on the Way* (1932; US title *Double Death*), and *The Loss of the 'Jane Vosper'* (1936).

Crome Yellow, a novel by A. *Huxley, published in 1921. First establishing Huxley's reputation for witty dialogue and cynically funny observation, it has usually been read as a *roman-à-clef*, satirizing Ottoline *Morrell's circle at Garsington. Lady Ottoline is caricatured as 'Priscilla Wimbush', devotee of astrology and Inspirational writings such as her guest Mr Barbecue-Smith's *Pipe-Lines to the Infinite*. 'Scogan', a voluble and libidinous rationalist, is based on Bertrand *Russell and H. G. *Wells, and the temperamental painter 'Gombauld' on Mark Gertler; 'Mary' is perhaps Dora Carrington, while the deaf, continually sketching 'Jenny' suggests Dorothy Brett. Huxley himself appears as the poet 'Denis Stone', split between thought and action, ineffectual in his amorous designs upon 'Anne Wimbush'. Though light-hearted, *Crome Yellow* does contain certain embryonic Huxleyan concerns: human isolation and egotism, the search for love, and a balanced philosophy of life. In particular, Scogan's urging of 'scientific openness' and the Rational State looks forward to **Brave New World*.

CRONIN, Anthony (1926–), Irish poet, novelist, and critic, born in Enniscorthy, County Wexford, educated at University College, Dublin. In 1951 he became associate editor of *The *Bell*. His reminiscences of the city during the early 1950s are contained in *Dead as Doornails* (1976), which provides detailed portraits of Flann *O'Brien, Patrick *Kavanagh, and Brendan *Behan. His numerous collections of poetry include *Poems* (1957), *Collected Poems: 1950–1973* (1973), *R.M.S. Titanic* (1981), *The End of the Modern World* (1989), and *Relationships* (1994). Cronin's poetry is remarkable for the tone of relaxed urbanity with which it ranges widely through his philosophical and political preoccupations. Many of his poems form strenuously anti-romantic treatments of social and ideological aspects of modern Irish life. His novels, *The Life of Riley* (1964) and *Identity Papers* (1979), are often highly amusing in the unfoldings of their intricate narratives. His critical writings include *A Question of Modernity* (1966) and *Heritage Now* (1982), a survey of Irish literature in the English language. Among his other works is the biography of Flann O'Brien, *No Laughing Matter* (1989). In 1980 he was appointed Cultural and Artistic Adviser to the Irish Prime Minister.

CRONIN, A(rchibald) J(oseph) (1896–1981), Scottish novelist, born into an Irish-Scottish Catholic family in Cardross, Dumbartonshire, and educated at the University of Glasgow, where he studied medicine. He served in the First World War as a surgeon sub-lieutenant with the Royal Naval Volunteer Reserve; he then practised as a GP in Glasgow and London, and as a medical inspector of mines in South Wales. His first novel, *Hatter's Castle* (1931), set in a small Scottish town, combines a doomed love story with an account of the rise and fall of James Brodie, a hatter of overweening social ambition. The novel was hugely successful and established Cronin as a popular realist writer. Having given up medicine, Cronin produced a stream of bestsellers displaying the same narrative skill and humane spirit. The best known of these is

The Citadel (1937), a moral tale of a young physician's struggles to retain his integrity against the attraction of world success. Other notable works are *The Stars Look Down* (1941) and *The Keys of the Kingdom* (1942). His later work tended to the sentimental, perhaps because his tax-exile in Switzerland distanced him from the Scottish people and landscape which were his best inspiration. Many of his novels were successfully filmed, and the long-running television series *Dr Finlay's Casebook* was based on his characters.

CROSS, Amanda, pseudonym of Carolyn G(old) HEILBRUN (1926–), American academic and *detective story writer, educated at Wellesley College and Columbia University, and from 1972 Professor of English at Columbia; she is the author of critical studies on English literature and a number of detective stories, usually set in academic surroundings and written from a feminist point of view, in which Kate Fansler, Professor of English at an unnamed university in New York, brings the methods of literary criticism to bear on the crimes. *In the Last Analysis* (1964) is the first and perhaps the best; other titles include *The James Joyce Murder* (1967), *The Theban Mysteries* (1971), *Death in a Tenured Position* (1981; UK title *A Death in the Faculty*), and *A Trap for Fools* (1989).

CROSSLEY-HOLLAND, Kevin (John William) (1941–), British poet and translator, born in Mursley, Buckinghamshire, educated at St Edmund Hall, Oxford. He became Editorial Director at Victor Gollancz in 1972 and has held various academic posts. His first full collection, *The Rain Giver* (1972), was followed by several other volumes including *The Dream-House* (1976), *Waterslain* (1986), *The Painting Room* (1988), and *New and Selected Poems, 1965–1990* (1991). As a poet, Crossley-Holland is recurrently concerned with locating his personal experience within the historical and topographical landscapes of his work. The principal locus of his later poetry is East Anglia, which is most memorably evoked in *Waterslain*. In many of his finest poems idiosyncratic rhythms interact with rich patterns of assonance and alliteration to unusually musical effect. Among his highly regarded translations of Old English poetry are *Beowulf* (1968) and *The Exeter Riddle Book* (1979). *Havelok the Dane* (1965) and *The Labours of Herakles* (1993) are among his many works for children and juveniles. His other writings include *The Norse Myths: A Retelling* (1980). He has also edited numerous anthologies of stories and poetry.

CROTHERS, Rachel (1878–1958), American dramatist, born in Bloomington, Illinois, educated at the Stanhope-Wheatcroft School of Acting. Crothers's early career in the theatre was as an actress; she directed all her own works and abandoned acting when *Nora* (1903), her first play, was produced. She wrote eighteen plays including *The Three of Us* (1906), her first major success, *A Little Journey* (1918), *He and She* (1920), *Nice People* (1921), *Let Us Be Gay* (1929), *As Husbands Go* (1931), *When Ladies Meet* (1932), and *Susan and God* (1937). Crothers's subject was women and the constraints of their social condition, particularly in relation to marriage and the prevailing sexual mores in the early twentieth century. She explored these subjects with a steadfast humour and a consummate stagecraft, especially in her shift from melodramatic comedies to the 'discussion' plays such as *A Man's World* (1910) and *He and She*.

Crow, a sequence of some sixty poems by Ted *Hughes, published in 1970, which features the figure of Crow as the central protagonist. The actuality of the bird as a feeder on carrion and its sinister associations in legend inform Hughes's characterization of Crow as a mythical embodiment of the instinct of survival; the book's gnostic vision of 'the horror of Creation' postulates a metaphysical context in which God despairs, man suffers, and Crow alone enjoys the minimal triumph of 'Flying the black flag of himself'; the bird is both the victim and witness of numerous episodes of extreme violence on cosmic and historical levels from which he emerges unscathed and indomitable. The violence of incident in many of the narratives and parables which make up the collection is matched by the reductively and forcefully functional syntax and diction Hughes adopts; the impact of the recurrent black humour and scatological references is increased by the harshly colloquial usages frequently employed. These qualities reflect Hughes's conscious effort in *Crow* to achieve a mode free of what he described as 'the terrible, suffocating, maternal octopus of ancient English poetic tradition'; the result is a work of great imaginative scope constituting an original myth of 'the war between vitality and death', as Hughes termed the central concern of his poetry in 1971. Hughes subsequently extended the Crow sequence in the limited editions *A Few Crows* (1970), *Crow Wakes* (1971), and *Eat Crow* (1971); a revised edition of *Crow* with illustrations by Leonard Baskin, the American artist who partly inspired Hughes to produce the sequence, appeared in 1973.

CROW DOG, see NATIVE AMERICAN LITERATURE.

CROWLEY, John (1942–), American novelist, born in Presque Isle, Maine, educated at Indiana University. His work has developed from its roots in *science fiction through *fantasy to *magic realism. His first novel, *The Deep* (1975), replays the Wars of the Roses on an artificial planet in the depths of space; *Engine Summer* (1979) depicts a disintegrated rural America. Crowley's most accomplished work, *Little, Big* (1981), a fantasy set in America, is the chronicle of a family's involvement with the supernatural. *Aegypt* (1987) is an erudite fantasy on an alternative history of the world; set in rural America, it follows its protagonist, Pierce Moffat, on a quest for hermetic knowledge. *Love and Sleep* (1994) is the second volume in the projected sequence. Crowley's short stories are collected in *Novelty* (1989).

Crucible, The, a play by Arthur *Miller, first directed by Jed Harris at the Martin Beck Theatre on 22 January 1953, when it ran for 197 performances. John and Elizabeth Proctor employ Abigail Williams, the promiscuous niece of the Reverend Samuel Parris. Elizabeth dismisses the girl. In revenge, Abigail accuses Elizabeth of witchcraft, a volatile charge in the political/religious atmosphere of late seventeenth-century New England. John Proctor defends his wife at her trial, but admits to adultery with Abigail. Compelled by a brief ambition to save his own neck, he signs a confession of Elizabeth's guilt, but then recants, and is sentenced to death. Miller's skill in this play was to use the notorious seventeenth-century Salem witch trials as a historical parallel to the contemporary witch hunts of the McCarthy era, in which the House Un-American Activities Committee pursued all those in public and artistic life tainted with known or implied political unorthodoxy. The difficulty faced by Miller was in the invention of vocabulary and speech rhythms which were at once authentically seventeenth-century, and yet accessible to modern audiences. Miller disliked the French film adaptation, *Les Sorcières de Salem* (1955), with a screenplay by Jean-Paul Sartre, starring Yves Montand and Simone Signoret, because it 'imposed a simplistic class analysis on the play', making it 'Marxist in the worst sense'. Two notable productions in London were those by George Devine at the Royal Court Theatre in 1956, and by Laurence Olivier at the Old Vic in 1965.

Cry, the Beloved Country, A. *Paton's best-known and most successful novel—subtitled 'A story of comfort in desolation'—published in 1948. Its first two parts each begins with the identical lyrical sentences that are characteristic of Paton's emotional prose: 'There is a lovely road that runs from Ixopo into the hills . . .' In the first section, a humble old African priest, Stephen Kumalo, sets out from his home in Natal for Johannesburg—'All roads lead to Johannesburg'—to search for his sister Gertrude and his son Absalom, from whom he has not heard for some time. He discovers that his sister has turned to prostitution and his son, having fallen into bad company, faces the death sentence for murder. Absalom's victim, ironically, is a 'good' white man, Arthur Jarvis, who was dedicated to helping the African people and working to change the apartheid system. The second part of the novel focus on Jarvis's father, a landowner in the priest's own village, who reads through his son's papers in an attempt to understand his liberal ideas. Absalom at his trial admits that he killed out of fear, and is condemned to hang. Kumalo returns to Natal with Gertrude's son and Absalom's pregnant wife. In the last section of the novel, each father separately coming to terms with his personal loss, there is a reconciliation between Jarvis senior and Kumalo, and in Jarvis's determination to help the poor black community Paton advances the optimistic view that 'fear could not be cast out, but by love', seeing tolerance and Christian charity as the solution to South Africa's racial situation.

Crying of Lot 49, The, a novel by Thomas *Pynchon, published in 1966. The plot is essentially a fictional tool of convenience whereby Pynchon can explore what he takes to be the problematic, if not frequently conspiratorial, nature of reality. Oedipa Maas discovers she has been made the executrix of the estate of Pierce Inverarity, a former lover. This sets her off on an increasingly bizarre and sinister trail of detection during which she discovers what she believes to be a secret communication system dating from the sixteenth century, whose symbol is the Tristero (a muted posthorn). She believes that the bidder for Inverarity's stamp collection at an auction will solve the enigma of the Tristero, but the novel ends as she awaits the crying out of the relevant lot 49. Like many of the major works of American *post-modernism, the novel is a work of *metafiction, interrogating the nature of its own fictional universe as much as that of the ostensibly 'real' world through which Oedipa passes. His second, and shortest novel, *The Crying of Lot 49* contains much of his most inventive writing, notably in its hilarious parody of a Jacobean tragedy, but Pynchon himself is known to have a low opinion of it.

CULLEN, Countee (1903–46), American poet, born in Louisville, Kentucky; he grew up in Harlem, New York and was educated at New York University and Harvard, where his poetry was praised by Irving *Babbitt. *Color* (1925) gained him widespread acclaim. His subsequent volumes include *Copper Sun* (1927) and *The Black Christ* (1929). His poetry made fluent use of the traditional modes of English verse to articulate his impassioned concern with the experience of black Americans. A leading figure in the *Harlem Renaissance, he edited *Caroling Dusk* (1927), an anthology of poems by writers associated with the movement. During the 1930s he concentrated on his work as a playwright, which culminated in the successful Broadway production of the musical *St Louis Woman* (with Arna *Bontemps, 1946). *On These I Stand* (1947) contained previously uncollected poetry with a selection from his earlier volumes. His other works include a translation of Euripides' *Medea* (1935) and the novel *One Way to Heaven* (1932), which deals with moral and social divisions within the Harlem community. *My Soul's High Song* (edited by G. L. Early, 1991) collects his verse along with a variety of essays, travel writings, and autobiographical fragments. Alan R. Suchard's *Countee Cullen* appeared in 1984. See also ETHNICITY.

Cultural Materialism is a term which has, from the 1980s, become something of a catch-all, implying an interdisciplinary theoretical orientation which approaches 'cultural texts' (by no means exclusively literary ones) as materially produced by political and social forces, institutions of patronage, and ideological 'discourses' (educational, legal, religious, etc.) specific to their historical moment. Ostensibly coining it (despite earlier claims within the field of anthropology by Harris, *The Rise of Anthropological Theory*, 1965), Dollimore and Sinfield (*Political Shakespeare*, 1985) define the term as combining insights offered through

Marxist, feminist, and *post-structural critiques of traditional assumptions about cultural texts. Its self-declared task is to analyse them as embodying the complex cultural contradictions of the moment of their production, but unlike its American cousin, *New Historicism, cultural materialism lays claim to a theoretical method which escapes the limitations of *Formalism and holds a radical political commitment to expose traditional categories of critical thinking and hierarchy. The sophisticated Marxist theories of Walter Benjamin and Raymond *Williams are crucial influences. See also MARXIST LITERARY CRITICISM.

CUMMINGS, E(dward) E(stlin) (1894–1962), American poet and graphic artist, born in Cambridge, Massachusetts, educated at Harvard. In 1917 he volunteered for service in France with the Norton-Harjes Ambulance Corps. A censor's confusion over remarks in his letters led to his imprisonment for three months on suspicion of treasonable activity. The interlude formed the basis of his widely acclaimed first book, *The Enormous Room* (1922), which set the tone for most of his work in its iconoclastic testimony to radical individualism. *Tulips and Chimneys* (1923) was the first of his collections of verse. The **Dial* awarded him its annual poetry prize in 1925, the year in which the publication of *XLI Poems* and *&* enhanced his already considerable reputation. His idiosyncratic poetic forms advanced the *free-verse modes given currency by *Imagism to new levels of typographical ingenuity. Sophisticated punning, evocative verbal coinages, and the audacious use of vernacular idioms are also characteristic of his poetry. His ethos of individuality formed the basis for many satires against the collective mentality of political authorities; notable examples include 'Thanksgiving' and 'Kumrads die because they're told', respectively directed at the governments of the USA and USSR. The erotic candour in many of his poems made him a figure of controversy, although his deftness obviated any recourse to the vocabulary traditionally identifying literature as pornographic. His subsequent collections include *VV (ViVa)* (1931), *No Thanks* (1935), *1 × 1* (1944), and *95 Poems* (1958). He exhibited widely as a graphic artist and published *CIOPW* in 1931, the letters of the title respectively representing his chosen media of charcoal, ink, oils, pencil, and watercolour. *HIM* (1927) and *Santa Claus* (1946), which anticipate the drama of the absurd in their estranging comic and symbolic strategies, are his principal works for theatre. *Complete Poems: 1910–1962* was published in 1980. *Dreams in the Mirror* (1980) is a biography of Cummings by R. S. Kennedy.

CUNNINGHAM, J(ames) V(incent) (1911–95), American poet, born in Cumberland, Maryland, educated at Stanford University. His books include *The Helmsman* (1942), *The Judge Is Fury* (1947), *Doctor Drink* (1950), *Trivial, Vulgar & Exalted: Epigrams* (1957), *The Exclusions of a Rhyme: Poems and Epigrams* (1960), *To What Strangers, What Welcome: A Sequence of Short Poems* (1964), and *Some Salt: Poems and Epigrams* (1967). *The Collected Poems and Epigrams* appeared in 1971 and *Collected Essays* in 1976. Cunningham is an austere poet with a passion for exact statement in tightly controlled forms, whose ideal poetic models were those of Roman satire and the conceits of the most formal sixteenth- and seventeenth-century poetry. He stood against the self-expressive rhetoric and emotionalism of much of the most fashionable poetry of his times, including Romanticism, its post-Romantic modernist orthodoxy, as in the work of T. S. *Eliot and Wallace *Stevens, the open forms of those who wrote in the Poundian tradition, and the confessionalism much in vogue in the 1950s and 1960s. His chosen form is the classical epigram, his elected idiom the satiric and self-parodic, which allows for the play of wit and irony in his commentary on the absurdity of human life. He is the subject of a critical study by his mentor Yvor *Winters.

CUNNINGHAME GRAHAM, R(obert) B(ontine) (1852–1936), Scottish author, born in London, educated at Harrow. Much of his writing is deeply informed by his experiences of the various South American countries in which he lived from 1870 to 1881. His numerous biographies of South American figures include *Hernando de Soto* (1903) and *Pedro de Valdivia* (1926). In 1886 he became Member of Parliament for North-West Lanark, which he represented until 1892. He was active in the emergence of British socialism and was the first president of the Scottish National Party upon its foundation in 1928. His literary reputation was established with *Mogreb-el-Acksa* (1898), an account of a journey to the Moroccan city of Tarudant, which impressed his friends Joseph *Conrad and G. B. *Shaw. Among his other works as a travel writer are *A Vanished Arcadia* (1901), a description of the decayed Jesuit settlement in Paraguay, and *Cartagena and the Banks of the Sinú* (1920), on his explorations in Colombia. His volumes of short stories and essays include *The Ipané* (1899), *Success* (1902), *Brought Forward* (1916), and *Mirages* (1936). Biographical studies include A. F. Tschifelly's *Don Roberto* (1937).

CURNOW, Allen (1911–), New Zealand poet and critic, born in Timaru, educated at the universities of Canterbury and Auckland. He worked in journalism in New Zealand, London, and the USA before taking up academic posts at Auckland University. *Not in Narrow Seas* (1939) was a poem sequence with prose 'commentary' treading a mythopoeic line on New Zealand history and poetry; *Island & Time* (1941) included the fine long poem 'The Unhistoric Story' which was to prove a lasting landmark in poetic debate. Curnow's editing of the influential, and controversial, *Book of New Zealand Verse 1923–1945* (1945), which contained a powerfully argued 35-page Introduction, further developed his ideas of poetry, place, and history at a crucial moment in his nation's consciousness. Committed to the belief that poetry must reflect the specific issues of a time and place for New Zealand, he also held that 'Local reference ought never to decide our estimate of a poem's worth'. Also controversial was his edition of *The Penguin Book of New Zealand Verse* (1960); his introductions to these anthologies are central documents for discussion of New Zealand poetry. Other collections include *At Dead Low Water* (1949), *Poems 1949–1957* (1957), *A Small Room with Large Windows* (1962), *Trees, Effigies and Moving Objects* (1972), *An Abominable Temper* (1973), and *Collected Poems 1922–1973* (1974). *An Incorrigible Music* (1979) is a sequence of poems exploring the extremes of human violence, while *You Will Know When You Get There: Poems 1979–81* (1982) explored themes relating mostly to old age and mortality. *Selected Poems* (1982) confirmed the strong sense of sequential development in Curnow's poetic concerns; his strength as a poet is in his enduring engagement with the issues of time, history, and mutability. Later collections include *Continuum, New and Later Poems 1972–1988* (1988), and *Selected Poems 1940–1989* (1990). *Look Back Harder: Critical Writings 1935–1984* (1987) testifies to Curnow's formidable range of interests and to his unflagging energies.

CURTIS, Tony (1946–), British poet, born in Carmarthen, Dyfed, educated at University College, Swansea. After a period as a schoolteacher, he lectured at Glamorgan College of Education, Barry, and became a senior lecturer in English at the Polytechnic of Wales, Pontypridd, in 1979. His collections of verse include *Album* (1974), *Preparations* (1980), *Letting Go* (1983), *Selected Poems, 1970–1985* (1986), *The Last Candles* (1989), *Taken for Pearls* (1993), and *War Voices* (1995). The domestic and local modes which prevailed in his earlier poetry have been increasingly supplemented by poems responding to broader social concerns. His later writing is also marked by ambitious use of dramatic monologues to enact events geographically and historically remote from the contemporary Welsh context which forms a basis for much of his best work. His other publications include the critical monograph *Dannie Abse* (1985). Among his works as an editor is the anthology *The Poetry of Snowdonia* (1989).

Custom of the Country, The, a novel by Edith *Wharton, published in 1913. Set in the early twentieth century, the narrative recounts the successive marriages of the beautiful and ruthlessly avaricious Undine Spragg: to Ralph Marvell, the gentle yet vulnerable representative of the older New York; to the Marquis Raymond de Chelles of the old French aristocracy, with houses in Burgundy and the Faubourg St Germain; and to the immensely wealthy Elmer Moffatt, formerly of Apex City, Kansas, a robust member of the new American social breed who had been Undine's first husband in a short-lived secret marriage before becoming her fourth and last husband. Wharton constructs a subtle narrative of contrasts and similarities between a variety of customs and countries, of social structures and social types. Ralph Marvell's old-fashioned New York is contrasted with that of the invader and conqueror Peter van Degen, a gross millionaire playboy, who takes Undine as his mistress for two months. These in turn are contrasted with the fashionable Paris milieu, and the life of the French aristocracy. The novel is a fierce indictment of the mindless materialism Wharton sees infecting American life at the turn of the twentieth century.

CUTLER, Ivor (1923–), British humourist and poet; Cutler grew up in Glasgow, where he was educated at Shawlands Academy. He has been a freelance writer and performer of his work since the late 1950s. *Gruts* (1962) contained short stories and songs which had provoked controversy when they were previously broadcast on BBC radio; the stories, which established Cutler as an eccentric literary talent, are characteristically brief and constitute mutedly surreal and obliquely disturbing commentaries on human behaviour. *Cock-a-Doodle Don't* (1966) and *Life in a Scottish Sitting Room, Vol. 2* (1984) are further collections of his stories. Among his numerous collections of poetry are *Many Flies Have Feathers* (1973) and the prose poems of *A Nice Wee Present from Scotland* (1988). His poems, laconic but gently insistent, display his bizarre conceptions with a disquieting air of ordinariness. He is also well-known as an author of books for children. Recent humorous prose works include *Glasgow Dreamer* (1990), *Befriend and Bacterium* (1992), and *A Stuggy Pren* (1994).

Cyberpunk: a *science fiction term, used to define a loose movement of 1980s writers whose works anticipated the effects of the high-tech computerized world to come. The term was taken by editor Gardner Dozois from the title of a short story by Bruce Bethke and applied by him primarily to novels by William *Gibson and Bruce *Sterling to designate work which embraced the new cybernetic world-environment, while simultaneously debunking the long-held cultural assumption in American popular literature that heroic inventiveness would win the day. The central text espousing this vision is Gibson's *Neuromancer* (1984), a novel whose hero is a 'cyberspace cowboy' (an information thief) who electronically penetrates a world-encompassing computer net in search of data he can steal. His experiences inside the 'virtual reality' of the network and his punkish indifference to politics, power, or ethical issues signals an equally relevant message offered by cyberpunk writers: that the heroic autonomy of 'Western Man' counts for little now that he has become symbiotic with a world-system driven by data. Cyberpunk writers tend to use imagery and plot-lines abstracted from the doom-laden *films noirs* of the 1940s. Gibson and other cyberpunk writers such as K. W. Jeter, Rudy Rucker, Lewis Shiner, John Shirley, and Walter Jon Williams have set out to demonstrate the possibilities of a new high-tech world rather than scientific extrapolation for its own sake. The movement became a marketing term by about 1987, and derivative texts continue to be published, especially in the USA, but none of its originators any longer admit to the label.

D

DABYDEEN, Cyril (1945–), Canadian poet, born in Berbice, Guyana; he emigrated to Canada in 1970 and studied at Queen's University, Kingston, Ontario. Formerly a schoolteacher in Guyana, he taught at Algonquin College, Ottawa, from 1975 to 1981. In 1986 he became a teacher of creative writing at the University of Ottawa, taking up Canadian citizenship in 1976; he was appointed Poet Laureate of Ottawa in 1985. His poetry and fiction display a recurrent concern with the tensions of displacement and adjustment in relation to the experience of immigration. Collections of his verse include *Poems in Recession* (1972), *Heart's Frame* (1979), *Islands Lovelier than a Vision* (1986), and *Coastlands: New and Selected Poems* (1989). His vivid and inventive poetry draws equally upon his experiences of Canada and Guyana. His prose works include the short stories of *Still Close to the Island* (1980) and *Jogging in Havana* (1992), and the satirical novel *The Wizard Swami* (1989).

DABYDEEN, David (1956–), Guyanese poet, novelist, and art historian, born in Guyana, educated at Cambridge and London Universities. He has held a number of academic appointments in America. His first book, *Slave Song* (1984; Commonwealth Prize for Poetry), contains harshly 'anti-pastoral' monologues in Creole dialect recreating the brutally restricted and anguished lives of sugar plantation workers. The poetry in *Coolie Odyssey* (1988) is more reflective and directly personal though still firmly based on the East Indian experience, and the destructive legacy of colonialism, both in Britain and in Guyana. *Turner: New and Selected Poems* appeared in 1994. His first novel, *The Intended* (1990), is partly a critique of Joseph Conrad's **Heart of Darkness*; *Disappearance* (1993) explores the disillusionment of a Guyanese man whose notions of 'civilization' and 'antiquity' are contradicted by his encounter with a decaying, post-imperial Britain. Other works include *Hogarth's Blacks: Images of Blacks in Eighteenth-Century English Art* (1985), and *Hogarth, Walpole and Commercial Britain* (1987). With Nana Wilson-Tagoe he co-authored *A Reader's Guide to West Indian and Black British Literature* (1988).

Dada, an anarchic internationalist movement in art and literature which originated in Zurich in 1916, where the Cabaret Voltaire, a café opened by Hugo Ball, a German theatrical producer, provided a focus for exhibitions, readings, and other more experimental forms of creative activity. Dada, a French word for 'hobby-horse' chosen on impulse from a dictionary by Ball, formed a conscious reaction by various expatriate artists to the apparent futility of the First World War and the cultural failure it implied. The Zurich group included the Romanian poets Marcel Janco and Tristan Tzara, the movement's eventual leader, and the painters Hans Richter, Max Ernst, and Jean Arp. Initially sympathetic to Futurism and Cubism, as their belief in nihilism and disorder evolved, the Dadaists repudiated these movements as excessively programmatic; Tzara spoke of Dada's 'great task of destruction and negation' and Richter defined its sole principle as 'to outrage public opinion'. Although not named as such, characteristically Dadaist work was also produced in New York around 1916 by the photographer Man Ray, the sculptor Marcel Duchamp, and the painter Francis Picabia; with Dadaists from Berlin, Hanover, Barcelona, and other parts of Europe to which the movement had spread, they arrived in Paris in 1919–20. German Dada's early expiry resulted from the increasingly political motivation of its exponents, among whom were the writer Richard Huelsenbeck, the painter George Grosz, and the celebrated photo-montagist John Heartfield. Tzara quickly assumed a dominant position in the Paris group, who also included the French writers André Breton, Louis Aragon, and Paul Eluard. The movement climaxed in a series of energetically chaotic 'manifestations' in Paris in 1920 and 1921, after which rivalry developed between Breton, who advocated political purpose, and the resolutely nihilistic Tzara. From 1922 onward, Breton and his associates gradually transmuted Dada into *Surrealism.

D'AGUIAR, Fred(erick) (1960–), British poet and novelist, born in London of Guyanese parents. He spent his early years in Guyana, and returned to London in 1972 where he trained as a psychiatric nurse; he also read English and Caribbean Studies at the University of Kent. D'Aguiar's poems are notable for their humane yet unsentimental humour, and mastery of the Creole dialect. *Mama Dot* (1985) and *Airy Hall* (1989) contain poems ranging widely in subject, including those which vividly recall his childhood, and family relations. Based on his own grandmother, 'Mama Dot' is an archetypal figure of ageless, matriarchal wisdom. A more recent collection is *British Subjects* (1993). His play *A Jamaican Airman Foresees His Death* was staged at the Royal Court Theatre, London, in 1991; inspired by *Yeats, it celebrates the

West Indian contribution to the British Second World War effort. *The Longest Memory* (1994), his first novel, uses a series of dramatic monologues to create a compound picture of the culture of slavery on a Virginia plantation *circa* 1800. *Dear Future* (1996) confirmed D'Aguiar as a novelist of strength and originality.

DAHLBERG, Edward (1900–77), American novelist and essayist, born in Boston, Massachusetts; he left a Jewish orphanage to drift around the USA and Europe. He graduated from Columbia University in 1925. *Bottom Dogs* (1929), a novel dealing with his orphan years in Kansas City and Cleveland, was written as an expatriate and first appeared in London, with an introduction by D. H. *Lawrence. Dahlberg was on the literary left in the 1930s, writing for magazines such as *New Masses*, and producing *Those Who Perish* (1934), a specifically anti-Nazi novel. His early works were in a vernacular, social realist vein, but he developed a richly allusive prose full of classical and biblical references, seasoned with a recondite vocabulary. *Do These Bones Live* (1941) is his major work of polemical literary criticism and marks the change in style. A mentor to Charles *Olson, with whom he eventually quarrelled, Dahlberg seized upon America as a mythic subject. The essays in *The Flea of Sodom* (1950) and *The Sorrows of Priapus* (1957) are often bitterly critical of modern culture and remarkable for their moral astringency and preoccupation with myth. He returned to more conventional narrative in the 1960s, and his critical reputation began to be rewarded. Among other works, Dahlberg has written a literary autobiography, *Because I Was Flesh* (1964); *An Edward Dahlberg Reader* (1967); and *Epitaphs For Our Times* (1967), a volume of selected letters. In 1968 he was elected to the National Institute of Arts and Letters. Disputatious and rootless, Dahlberg's 'true parable lay in his own personal confessions of a Jew in America' (Paul Christensen).

DAICHES, David (1912–), British critic, born in Sunderland; he grew up in Edinburgh, where he was educated at the University. After gaining his D.Phil. at Oxford in 1939, he held professorships at the University of Chicago and Cornell University. Having returned to Britain in 1951, he lectured at Cambridge before becoming Professor of English at the University of Sussex in 1961. A critic of unusual range, his works, which evaluate literature with reference to its broader social and cultural contexts, include *Literature and Society* (1938), *Virginia Woolf* (1942), *Robert Burns* (1950, revised edition 1966), *Willa Cather* (1951), and *George Eliot: Middlemarch* (1962). Notable among his historical and biographical studies is *The Last Stuart: The Life and Times of Bonnie Prince Charlie* (1973). He has also produced a highly regarded body of autobiographical writing in *Two Worlds: An Edinburgh Jewish Childhood* (1957), *A Third World* (1971), and *Was* (1975). Since the late 1960s he has published books on a wide variety of topics, which include *Scotch Whisky: Its Past and Present* (1969), *Scotland and the Union* (1977), and *God and the Poets* (1984).

DALE, Peter (1938–), British poet, born in Addlestone, Surrey, educated at St Peter's College, Oxford. A schoolteacher by profession, he was appointed Head of English at Hinchley Wood School, Surrey, in 1972. In 1971 he became co-editor of **Agenda* magazine. His reputation was firmly established with *The Storms* (1968), his first substantial collection of verse, which earned him an Arts Council bursary in 1969. *Mortal Fire* (1970) contains his best-known work. Further collections of his verse include the sonnet sequence entitled *One Another* (1978), *Too Much of Water* (1983), and *Earth Light* (1991). Dale's work is strongest when the emotional immediacy of his subject matter compels him to an impressive plainness of form and diction. His technical range is broad, encompassing concise imagistic treatments, accomplished use of traditional forms, and discursive *vers libre*. Since the appearance of *The Legacy and Other Poems* (1971), translations in strict ballade stanzas of works by Villon, Dale has been increasingly highly valued as a translator. Among his numerous other volumes of translations are *Narrow Straits: Poems from the French* (1985).

D'ALPUGET, Blanche (1944–), Australian writer, born in Sydney, the daughter of Lou d'Alpuget, a well-known Sydney journalist; she herself worked as a journalist, and lived in Malaysia and Indonesia for a number of years. Her first novel, *Monkeys in the Dark* (1980), about a young Australian journalist's involvement with an Indonesian activist in the aftermath of the 1965 coup in Jakarta, has affiliations with Christopher *Koch's *The Year of Living Dangerously* (1978) in its exploration of Australia's relationship with the Far East. It was followed by the highly successful and award-winning *Turtle Beach* (1981), whose central character is also a journalist, which continued this broad focus in its examination of the traumatic connections between Vietnamese refugees in Malaysia and the Australian officials involved in their resettlement. *Winter in Jerusalem* (1986) describes a young woman's search for a deeper understanding of the city of her birth and her attempts to write a successful screenplay. *White Eye* (1994) is a murder mystery. Non-fiction works include a biography of Sir Richard Kirby (1977) and an acclaimed study of Australia's then Prime Minister, *Robert J. Hawke* (1982).

Dance to the Music of Time, A, a novel in twelve volumes by Anthony *Powell, published in 1951–75. Beginning with *A Question of Upbringing* (1951), ending with *Hearing Secret Harmonies* (1975), and borrowing its title and pervasive metaphor from Nicolas Poussin's painting in the Wallace Collection, London, the sequence is widely regarded as one of the main achievements in twentieth-century English fiction and Powell's finest work. Written in a typically rococo style, and calling frequently on chance and coincidence to effect connections, it is in essence the story of the first three-quarters of the century seen mainly from the vantage point of the upper classes and the bohemian *demi-monde*. Its narrator is the self-effacing Nicholas Jenkins, whose story begins at an English public school. Here we meet many characters who either reappear as time and novels pass, or who fade out altogether. Jenkins's generation grows up in the aftermath of the First World War and matures as Nazism rises and the Second World War begins to rage. Powell is rightly renowned for his ability to draw memorable comic characters and depict absurd situations, but this does not diminish the overlying seriousness of the work. His method is exemplified particularly by Widmerpool, the butt of school pranks who, though often seen as ridiculous by his peers, is a dogged achiever and a dark and damaged man. Among many unforgettable characters, some are relatives of Jenkins, like his Uncle Giles, the eccentric black sheep of the family; others, including X. Trapnel, a writer, Mr Deacon the artist, and the literary hustlers Quiggin and Members, are drawn from the creative fraternity to which the author belonged in youth and middle age. Powell's dance, though apparently improvised and haphazard, is strictly formal and rigidly structured. The novels are grouped in threes and symbolize the four seasons. *A Question of Upbringing* (1951), *A Buyer's Market* (1952), and *The Acceptance World* (1955) represent spring and, consequently, school, university, and the narrator's first adventures and misadventures in sex. The second trilogy, comprising *At Lady Molly's* (1957), *Casanova's Chinese Restaurant* (1960), and *The Kindly Ones* (1962), is symbolically summer, in which work and marriage dominate. The war years mark autumn and figure largely in *The Valley of Bones* (1964), *The Soldier's Art* (1966), and *The Military Philosophers* (1968). The final trilogy—*Books Do Furnish a Room* (1971), *Temporary Kings* (1973), and *Hearing Secret Harmonies* (1975)—moves to the dismal aftermath of war, in which Jenkins, now a writer in his sixties, recalls acquaintances either dead or lost with the passage of years. Winter closes as it opened the sequence with Jenkins reflecting that 'Even the formal measure of the Seasons seemed suspended in the wintry silence.'

Dancing at Lughnasa, a play by Brian *Friel, performed and published in 1990. This semi-autobiographical piece, set in 1936 in a decaying country house outside the fictional Irish village of Ballybeg, is narrated from some unspecified time in the future by Michael, the illegitimate son of Chris Mundy; and it involves her, her priest brother Jack, and her four sisters, Kate, Maggie, Rose, and Agnes. The principal events are visits by Michael's feckless Welsh father, the brief disappearance and probable seduction of the mentally backward Rose, and the gradual revelation that Jack, who has recently returned from a mission in Africa, has abandoned Catholicism for shamanism. One subject is the disintegration of home and family, soon to culminate in Rose's and Agnes's disastrous escape to England. Another is the paganism lurking below the shabby-genteel Christian surface and represented by the dancing that recurs during the play.

DANE, Clemence, pseudonym of Winifred ASHTON (1888–1965), British playwright and novelist, born in Blackheath, London. She studied art at the Slade School of Art and in Dresden, later becoming an actress. She achieved recognition with her first novels, *Regiment of Women* (1917) and *Legend* (1919), before turning to drama. Her later novels include *Broome Stages* (1931), a romantic presentation of theatrical life which establishes analogues between a family of actors and the Plantagenets. The first and most enduring of her many plays, *A Bill of Divorcement* (1921), concerns a woman who divorces on the grounds of her husband's insanity so that she can remarry. Other plays include *Will Shakespeare* (1921), *Granite* (1926), *Wild Decembers* (1933), about the Brontës, and a dramatized version of Max *Beerbohm's *The Happy Hypocrite*. In many of her works she was preoccupied by a romantic sense of England. Her pseudonym is derived from the church of St Clements Dane, London.

DARK, Eleanor (1901–85), Australian novelist, born in Sydney. She began contributing stories to the **Bulletin* and other journals from 1921. Her first novel, *Slow Dawning* (1932), like many of her works, was set in a small country town. *Prelude to Christopher* (1933), a more ambitious novel, displays a prevailing concern with the nature of time. *Return to Coolami* (1935) explores the inner worlds of four people during a long car journey through New South Wales. In *Sun Across the Sky* (1937) and *Waterway* (1938) the action takes place in a single day and centres on the interrelationship of the characters, some of whom appear in both novels. *The Little Company* (1945) centres on Gilbert Massey, a radical Sydney-based writer-publisher. Themes of pacifism, feminism, politics, and religion, and an intense psychological focus, characterize her works. The historical trilogy, *The Timeless Land* (1941), *Storm of Time* (1948), and *No Barrier* (1953), traces the development of European settlement in Australia from 1788 to 1813. Published in one volume as *The Timeless Land* in 1963, the trilogy is widely regarded as a landmark in Australian national literature for its realistic yet imaginative portrayal of an emergent society.

Dark as the Grave Wherein My Friend Is Laid, a novel by Malcolm *Lowry, published posthumously in 1968. Its title is taken from Abraham Cowley's elegy 'On the Death of Mr William Harvey'. The novel, which is largely autobiographical, and almost confessional in tone, concerns Sigbjorn Wilderness, a middle-aged writer with a serious drink problem who, accompanied by his wife, Primrose, journeys from his home in Canada to Mexico, on a kind of pilgrimage of self-discovery that is also a descent into hell. In theme and content, the book has many similarities with Lowry's greatest work, **Under the Volcano* (1947), although, unlike the earlier novel, it ends on a note of reconciliation and relative optimism, as Sigbjorn conquers the devils of his past and looks forward to a new life.

Darkness at Noon, a novel by Arthur *Koestler, published in 1940, translated from German, which George *Orwell regarded as a valuable 'interpretation of the Moscow "confessions" by someone with an inner knowledge of totalitarian methods'. The novel concerns Stalin's regime and his purge of the Soviet Communist Party during the late 1930s. Koestler, however, wrote it as a parable set in an anonymous state ruled by 'No. 1', believing that its central theme of the conflict between political expediency and individual morality was applicable to any revolutionary dictatorship, including Franco's Spain and Hitler's Germany. The novel begins with the arrest and imprisonment of the main character, Rubashov, who appears initially to be an innocent man accused of fabricated crimes. However, he undergoes successive interrogations by his former 'Party' subordinates Ivanov and Gletkin, which become dialogues in which Rubashov discovers that he is guilty of the sins of his persecutors. His confession and eventual execution are the logical consequences of his having believed in the revolution and its power to determine history: an objective process in which he, as an individual, is but 'a multitude of one million divided by one million'.

Darkness Visible, see GOLDING, WILLIAM.

DARYUSH, Elizabeth (1887–1977), British poet, the daughter of Robert *Bridges; she was born in London and educated privately. After her marriage in 1923 she travelled with her husband to Persia, his native country, and returned to England in 1927. Her first collection of poetry, *Charitessi* (1911), was followed by two other early volumes, *Verses* (1916) and *Sonnets from Hafez* (1921). She subsequently disclaimed these, however, considering her achievement as a poet to consist of a series of volumes from *Verses* (1930) to *Verses: Sixth Book* (1938). A *Selected Poems* with an introduction by Yvor *Winters was published in America in 1948, with a revised and enlarged British selected edition appearing in 1972. Daryush's interest in metrical experiment, also a feature of her father's poetry, resulted in her frequent use of syllabic metres, which she developed, generally in combination with rhyme, to a high degree of lyrical refinement. Her poetry is notable for the austerity and decorousness of its recurrent philosophical reflections on transience and for its idiosyncratic use of archaic diction. Donald *Davie edited her *Collected Poems* (1976), arguing in his introductory essay for wider recognition of her achievement as a contemplative and innovative poet.

DAS, Kamala (1934–), Indian writer, born in Malabar, India. Her autobiographical *My Story* (India, 1976; UK, 1978) is a highly introspective and subjective account of the creation and development of a woman poet. It is interspersed with some of Das's best verse. Famous, even notorious, for her poetic articulation of female sexuality and illicit passions, Das is actually a skilled chronicler of everyday experience, both emotive and perceptive. Her word-paintings of urban life are illuminated with images of the flux and change she perceives in India's streets. Das's collections of poetry include *Summer in Calcutta* (1965), *The Descendents* (1967), *The Old Playhouse* (1973), and *Tonight, This Savage Rite* (with Pritish Nandy, 1979). She has also experimented—albeit less successfully—with fiction in English (she is well known as a prose writer in her native Malayalam); a novel, *Alphabet of Lust* (1977), and a collection of short stories, *A Doll for the Child Prostitute* (1977), explore the hidden world of Indian sexuality.

DAVENPORT, Guy (Mattison) (1927–), American short-story writer, critic, poet, and translator, born in Anderson, South Carolina, educated at Duke University, Merton College, Oxford, and Harvard. He became Professor of English at the University of Kentucky in 1963. Among his earlier publications is *Motive and Method in the Cantos of Ezra Pound* (1954), the first of a series of works on that author. The scope of his criticism is demonstrated in the essays collected in *Geography of the Imagination* (1981) and *Every Force Evolves a Form* (1987), which range between remote classical antiquity and the culture of the present day. Davenport's eclectically authoritative erudition is also reflected in his short stories, which are noted for their mannered originality of style and audaciously inventive narratives: collections include *Tatlin!* (1974), *Da Vinci's Bicycle* (1979), *The Jules Verne Steam Balloon* (1987), and *The Drummer of the Eleventh North Devonshire Fusiliers* (1990). *Thasos and Ohio: Poems and Translations, 1950–1980* (1986) includes his versions of poetry by ancient Greek and modern European authors, among them Sappho, Anakreon, Rilke, and Cocteau, together with his own lucidly particular and metrically accomplished verse. Davenport is also an accomplished graphic artist and has worked as an illustrator of numerous books, including Hugh *Kenner's *The Stoic Comedians* (1964) and Ronald Johnson's *The Spirit Walks, the Rocks Will Talk* (1969).

DAVIDSON, Donald (Herbert) (1917–), American philosopher, born in Springfield, Massachusetts, educated at Harvard University. He has held professorships at Princeton, Rockefeller University, New York, the University of Chicago, and the University of California, Berkeley. He has also been a visiting professor at various universities throughout the world. Since the late 1960s he has exerted wide influence in analytical philosophy, particularly in respect of his concept of 'anomalous monism'; its application permits recognition of the indissoluble relation between mental events and physical reality while acknowledging that the former are not unconditionally governed by the laws of nature. His interrelated work on philosophies of language and mind issued in a theory of meaning which enabled him to suggest the common limitations of diverse conceptual systems. His reputation rests on a comparatively slender body of published work, principally *Words and Objections* (1969); his essays on the work of W. V. O. *Quine, *Essays on Action and Events* (1980); and *Inquiries into*

Truth and Interpretation (1984), his principal contribution to the philosophy of language. *Plato's Philebus* (1990) offers concepts on the philosophy of pleasure. Among the numerous works he has edited is *The Logic of Grammar* (1975). *Essays on Davidson*, edited by B. Vermazen and M. B. Hintikka, was published in 1985.

DAVIE, Donald (Alfred) (1922–95), British poet and critic, born in Barnsley, educated at St Catherine's College, Cambridge, where he absorbed the influence of F. R. *Leavis, upon whom he reflected in his volume of memoirs *These the Companions* (1982). After holding a succession of academic posts in Britain and Ireland, he was appointed to a professorship at Stanford University, California, in 1968 and became Professor of Humanities at Vanderbilt University, Nashville, Tennessee, in 1978. Davie's first work of note was the influential *Purity of Diction in English Verse* (1952); his arguments for a poetry of rigour and precision accorded with the practices of the *Movement, in which he achieved prominence with *Brides of Reason* (1955) and *A Winter Talent* (1957). The volumes are characterized by the accomplished use of rhyming forms in conventional metres to present neutrally toned statements on social, cultural, and personal themes. Subsequent collections include his version of Adam Mickiewicz's *Pan Tadeusz* in *The Forests of Lithuania* (1959); *Essex Poems* (1969); *In the Stopping Train* (1980); *To Scorch or Freeze* (1989); and *Collected Poems* (1990). From the early 1970s onward his verse became increasingly flexible; *The Shires* (1974), a series of descriptive meditations on English landscapes and regions, uses a remarkable range of forms, some conspicuously informal and relaxed. He was among the most highly regarded literary critics of the post-war era, much of his work being notable for its stimulating and provocative mediations between the claims of *Modernism and traditional poetic values. His numerous critical publications include *Ezra Pound: Poet as Sculptor* (1964), *Thomas Hardy and British Poetry* (1973), *Studies in Ezra Pound* (1991), and *The Eighteenth Century Hymn in England* (1993). *The Poet in the Imaginary Museum* (1977), *Under Briggflatts* (1989), and *Old Masters: Essays and Reflections on English and American Literature* (1992) are collections of essays.

DAVIES, Idris (1905–53), British poet, born in Rhymney, Monmouthshire. At the age of 14 he became a coal miner. When the mine in which he worked was closed after the General Strike of 1926, he studied at Loughborough College and the University of Nottingham, and subsequently worked as a teacher in London and Rhymney. *Gwalia Deserta* (1938), his first volume of poetry, contained thirty-six poems thematically unified by their often deeply elegiac concern with South Wales in the 1920s and 1930s. *The Angry Summer* (1943), his best-known work, consists of fifty poems in rhythmically supple free verse and ballad stanzas; the work presents a richly detailed account of the General Strike and its effects on Davies's native mining valleys, disarming humour and bitter irony tempering its often impassioned social concern. T. S. *Eliot wrote of these books that 'they are the best poetic document I know about a particular epoch in a particular place'. *Tonypandy and Other Poems* (1945) is a collection of more occasional verse. *Collected Poems* (1972) is edited by Islwyn Jenkins, whose *Idris Davies* appeared in 1972.

DAVIES, Robertson (1913–95), Canadian novelist and dramatist, born in Thamesville, Ontario, educated at Queen's University and at Balliol College, Oxford. Davies worked as an actor in England before returning to Canada, where he became a distinguished academic and editor of *The Peterborough Examiner* to which he contributed a weekly column under the pseudonym 'Samuel Marchbanks'. This writing is collected in *The Diary of Samuel Marchbanks* (1947), *The Table Talk of Samuel Marchbanks* (1949), and *Marchbanks' Almanack* (1967). His plays include *A Jig for the Gypsy* (1954) and *Hunting Stuart and Other Plays* (1972). It was, however, as a novelist that Davies was best known. Beginning with 'The Salterton Trilogy'—*Tempest-Tost* (1951), *Leaven of Malice* (1954), and *A Mixture of Frailties* (1958)—he published three novel sequences. The finest of these is 'The Deptford Trilogy' (*Fifth Business*, 1970; *The Manticore*, 1972; and *World of Wonders*, 1975), each part of which is written in a confessional first-person mode, which in some way reflects the characters' common origins in the small Ontario town after which the trilogy is named; the trilogy is also a cosmopolitan work with a broad mythic framework and incorporates much specialist knowledge on such subjects as hagiography, Jungian psychology, and carnival shows. *The Rebel Angels* (1981), *What's Bred in the Bone* (1985), and *The Lyre of Orpheus* (1988) form 'The Cornish Trilogy'. *Murther and Walking Spirits* (1991) explores ancestry and the derivation of individual identity via an inventive plot narrated by the deceased entertainments officer of a local newspaper who has been murdered by a film critic. Widely acclaimed for its scope, style, and narrative organization, *The Cunning Man* (1995) presents an overview of contemporary culture through three characters who thematically represent science, art/literature, and religion. He also published *The Stage Is All the World: The Theatrical Designs of Tanya Moiseiwitsch* (1994).

DAVIES, W(illiam) H(enry) (1871–1940), British poet, born in Newport, Monmouthshire. He was apprenticed to a picture-framer after elementary education, but became a vagrant and subsequently took part in the Klondike gold-rush, losing a leg while attempting to steal a ride on a train. He settled in London, living with great frugality on a small allowance from his grandmother. In 1905 he produced, at his own expense, a volume of poems entitled *The Soul's Destroyer*, and solicited sales by sending copies to eminent writers whose addresses he culled from *Who's Who*. George Bernard *Shaw responded generously, arranging reviews of the book in the literary press. Edward *Thomas offered him accommodation in his cottage near Sevenoaks and assisted with final revisions to the text of his *The Autobiography of a Super-Tramp*, which appeared with a preface by Shaw to widespread success in 1908. *Nature Poems and Others*, also published in 1908, was followed by numerous further collections of verse, which include *Farewell to Poesy* (1909) and *Songs of Joy* (1911). He was a contributor to each of the five **Georgian Poetry* (1912–22) anthologies. Much of his work takes the form of sensitive responses to natural phenomena in verse of moving simplicity and fluent technical assurance. Numerous poems display an acutely observed social concern, which can achieve macabre effectiveness as in 'The Rat' and 'The Inquest'. *Beggars* (1909), *The True Traveller* (1912), and *A Poet's Pilgrimage* (1918), further prose accounts of his experiences, are superior in style and structure to the novels *A Weak Woman* (1911) and *The Dancing Heart* (1927). His final work of autobiography was the posthumously published *Young Emma* (1980), which recounts his unorthodox courtship of the young woman he married in 1923. *Complete Poems* appeared in 1963, with an introduction by Osbert *Sitwell.

DAVIN, Dan(iel) (1913–90), New Zealand novelist and short-story writer, born in Invercargill, New Zealand, educated at Otago University and at Balliol College, Oxford. After war service he joined the Oxford University Press and produced the *Introduction to English Literature* (1947) with John *Mulgan. His novel *Cliffs of Fall* (1945) evoked memories of youth in New Zealand with a sense of isolation and conflict that is often present in Davin's work; *For the Rest of Our lives* (1947) directed wartime experiences in Africa to wider issues of meditative disenchantment which characterize much of Davin's work; *Roads from Home* (1949) was a fine working of personal experience. Davin edited *New Zealand Short Stories* and *Katherine Mansfield's Short Stories* in 1953, and his own interests and work in some ways echo those of *Mansfield. In his stories, a finely wrought realism is undercut by a profound scepticism towards earthly pleasures, a scepticism which itself derives from a sharp awareness of mortality. Davin's lasting interest in the handling of war in fiction reflects this balance of interests. His story collections include *Breathing Spaces* (1975) and *The Salamander and the Fire: Collected War Stories* (1986). He edited *Short Stories from the Second World War* in 1982.

DAVIOT, Gordon, TEY, JOSEPHINE.

DAVIS, Angela (Yvonne) (1944–), African-American essayist and political activist, born in Birmingham, Alabama, educated at Brandeis University, Goethe University, Frankfurt, and the University of California, San Diego. In 1969 she was appointed an assistant professor of philosophy at the University of California, Los Angeles. A leading figure in the Black Power movement of the late 1960s, she lost her academic post because of her alleged involvement in an attempt to free three prisoners from San Quentin prison. During her sixteen months in jail, she produced the essays and letters collected in *If They Come for Me in the Morning* (with Ruchel Magee and others, 1971). Her trial, which became a *cause célèbre*, resulted in her acquittal, following which she published *Lectures on Liberation* (1972). Her other writings, which reflect her Marxist and feminist beliefs, include *Women, Race and Class* (1981) and *Women, Culture and Politics* (1984). *Angela Davis: An Autobiography* appeared in 1974.

DAVIS, Dick (1945–), British poet, born in Portsmouth, educated at King's College, Cambridge, and the University of Manchester. He held a succession of teaching posts in Greece, Italy, Iran, and elsewhere from 1967 to 1988, when he became Assistant Professor of Persian at Ohio State University. His poetry was first collected with work by Clive *Wilmer and Robert *Wells in *Shade Mariners* (1970). *In the Distance* (1975) was his first independent collection; subsequent volumes include *Seeing the World* (1980) and *The Covenant* (1984). Davis has been highly acclaimed for the fluency with which he expresses his personal and cultural preoccupations in strict traditional forms. Much of his work displays an epigrammatic brevity and wit and is rich in precisely observed detail. *Devices and Desires: New and Selected Poems 1967–1987* appeared in 1989. His other publications include *Wisdom and Wilderness* (1983), a critical study of the work of Yvor *Winters. He is also highly regarded for his translations, which include a version of Farrad Attar's twelfth-century Persian religious allegory *The Conference of the Birds* (with Afkham Darbandi, 1984).

DAVIS, Jack (Leonard) (1917–), Australian poet and dramatist; the son of part-Aboriginal parents, he belongs to the Aboriginal Bibbulmun tribe of Western Australia. He worked for many years on cattle stations in the north of the state, a bitter experience which led him to return to Perth as a champion of the Aboriginal cause. He later became manager of the Perth Aboriginal Centre in 1967, director of the Aboriginal Advancement Council in the state in 1969, and joint editor of the Aboriginal magazine *Identity* from 1973 to 1979; in the latter capacity he encouraged the writing of Archie *Weller. *The First-Born and Other Poems* (1970) established Davis's poetic talent and commitment to the cause of Aboriginal rights, and a second volume, *Jagardoo: Poems from Aboriginal Australia*, appeared in 1978; both volumes reflect Davis's alertness both to Aboriginal heritage and to the issues of contemporary society. Further collections are *John Pat and Other Poems* (1988) and *A Black Life* (1992). A vivid and moving realism accounts for his success in the theatre: the problems Aboriginal people confront in Australian cities today were addressed in *The Dreamers* (1973), a one-act play which was revised and developed in 1982. *Kullark* (1979) was his sobering contribution to Western Australia's 150th anniversary; it presented case histories of the treatment of Aboriginal people and argued powerfully for a change in basic attitudes. The plays *No Sugar* (1985) and *Barungin: Smell the Wind* (1989) continued Davis's determination to keep Aboriginal history at the centre of contemporary Australian debate, as did *In Our Town* (1992), which deals with the racist response to a romance between an Aboriginal hero of the Second World War and a white woman. *A Boy's Life*, an autobiography of his childhood in the 1920s and 1930s, was published in 1991. He is the editor of *Paperback* (1990), an anthology of Black Australian writing.

DAWE, (Donald) Bruce (1930–), Australian poet, born in Geelong, Victoria; he left school at 16 and worked at many jobs prior to attending the universities of Melbourne and Queensland. Dawe's talent in articulating large issues through everyday concerns is clear from his first poetry volumes *No Fixed Address* (1962) and *A Need of Similar Name* (1965). A Roman Catholic poet, his concerns are non-sectarian; Dawe has written of his desire to speak for 'the lost people in our midst for whom no one speaks, and who cannot speak for themselves'. In volumes such as *Beyond the Subdivisions* (1969) and *Condolences of the Season* (1971) Dawe employs a vernacular voice at once laconic and expressive, the human (or perhaps Australian) instinct for wry understatement being used to capture the tenuousness of human achievement against the inexpressible finality of mortality. *Sometimes Gladness: Collected Poems 1954–1978* (1978; new edition 1983, with poems to 1982; new edition 1993, with poems to 1992) demonstrated the breadth of his achievements, not least the pervasive humour of what might seem pessimistic themes. Dawe finely exploits nuances of Australian language and speech to express perceptions of the transubstantiality of the ordinary in terms familiar yet complex. Other publications include *Towards Sunrise: Poems 1979–1985* (1986) and *This Side of Silence: Poems 1987–1990* (1990); and a collection of short stories, *Over Here, Harv!* (1983). See Ken Goodwin's *Adjacent Worlds: A Literary Life of Bruce Dawe* (1988) and *Bruce Dawe: Essays and Opinions* (1990).

DAWSON, Fielding (1930–), American novelist, short-story writer, and painter, born in New York City; he grew up in Kirkwood, Missouri and was educated at *Black Mountain College from 1949 to 1953. *The Black Mountain Book* (1970; revised and expanded, 1991) remains the most valuable memoir of the college during its *Olson era and the experience clearly set the agenda for Dawson's future development as a writer. A master of the kind of kinetic writing promulgated by and the *Beats, Dawson is also a Jungian who pays great attention to the material presented in his dreams. This gives his work a steady but flexible centre and helps to explain much of the intellectual and emotional engagement in his writing. He is a prolific writer whose novels include *Open Road* (1970), *The Mandalay Dream* (1971), *A Great Day For a Ballgame* (1973), and the *Penny Lane* series (1977–81). His collections of stories include *Krazy Kat/The Unveiling* (1969), *The Dream/Thunder Road* (1972), *The Sun Rises Into the Sky* (1973), and *The Man Who Changed Overnight* (1976). *The Orange in the Orange* (1994) comprises a novella and two stories which, like many of his other books, are closely interrelated. Like *Kerouac, he is deeply sensitive to the world of the child and, again like Kerouac, recognizes the degree to which that world persists into the world of the adult.

DAWSON, Jennifer (1929–), British novelist, born in South London. Her experiences as a social worker in a mental hospital in the late 1950s provided the background to much of her fiction, most notably in her first extraordinary Kafkaesque novel, *The Ha-Ha* (1961). Like Sylvia Plath's *The *Bell Jar*, it chronicles with harrowing precision a young woman's struggle with mental illness. Many of her novels explore the extremes, and the mundanities, of madness while offering passionate, often savage, indictments of a callous society. Dawson's further novels include *Fowler's Snare* (1963), *The Cold Country* (1965), *Strawberry Boy* (1976), *A Field of Scarlet Poppies* (1979), and a volume of short stories, *Hospital Wedding* (1978). A ten-year silence was broken with the publication of *The Upstairs People* (1988), an accomplished atmospheric exploration of family life in the 1930s, interwoven with her customary themes of madness. This was followed in 1989 by a sharp, satirical look at Oxford life, *Judasland*.

DAY, Clarence (Shepard) (1874–1935), American essayist and humorist, born in New York City, educated at Yale University. Day served in the US navy during the Spanish-American War (1898). He settled in New York and sought to establish himself as a writer and illustrator. *This Simian World* (1920), his satirical reflections on man's origins coupled with his fantastic speculations about man's alternative origins, and illustrated with his own drawings, brought him to the attention of the fledgling **New Yorker* magazine, to which he subsequently became a regular contributor. He remains best known for his autobiographical writings: *God and My Father* (1932) is a portrait of his Victorian New York childhood, and the second volume, *Life with Father* (1935), was successfully adapted for the stage in 1940; *Life with Mother* (1937) and *Father and I* (1940) appeared posthumously. Other works include *The Crow's Nest* (1921; enlarged and retitled *After All*, 1936), *Thoughts Without Words* (1928), *In the Green Mountain Country* (1934), and *Scenes from the Mesozoic and Other Drawings* (1935). His prose is notable for its precise, terse, yet eloquent satire.

DAY LEWIS, C. (Cecil Day-Lewis) (1904–72), British poet and, as 'Nicholas Blake', writer of detective fiction, born in Ballintogher, near Sligo, educated at Sherborne School and Wadham College, Oxford. The son of a clergyman, Day Lewis lived in England from 1905; in 1908 his mother died and he was looked after by the aunt to whom he paid moving tribute in the late poem 'My Mother's Sister'. At Oxford his literary associates included Stephen *Spender and W. H. *Auden, with whom he produced the 1927 edition of *Oxford Poetry*. Following two early volumes, *Transitional Poem* (1929) and *From Feathers to Iron* (1931), he published *The Magnetic Mountain* (1933), which frequently echoes Auden's style and diction and casts him in a heroic light in 'Look west, Wystan, lone flyers . . .' The volume established him as the most outspoken example of the poet as an instrument of revolutionary socialism; he outlined his views in *Revolution in Writing* (1935). He was a member of the Communist Party from 1935 to 1938 and with Auden, Spender, and *MacNeice, contributed to various left-wing journals. He also edited *The Mind in Chains* (1937), a collection of ideological essays, and *The Echoing Green* (1937), the first of his several anthologies of poetry. After the mid-1930s the socialist emphasis in his poetry gradually diminished; in 1937 Geoffrey *Grigson disparaged his incipient conservatism in becoming a member of the Book Society Committee, and by 1946, when he was appointed Clark Lecturer at Cambridge, he was firmly identified with the literary establishment. From 1951 to 1956 he was Oxford Professor of Poetry, and he succeeded *Masefield as Poet Laureate in 1968.

Although political elements are present in *Overtures to Death* (1938), the poetry has lost the hectoring urgency that was evident in earlier work. The astringent lyricism apparent in *Poems in Wartime* (1940) owes something to *Hardy's example; numerous subsequent collections include *An Italian Visit* (1953), *Pegasus and Other Poems* (1957), and *The Whispering Roots* (1970). A *Collected Poems* (1954) was supplemented by Ian Parsons's edition of *Poems of C. Day Lewis, 1925–1972* (1977); *Collected Poems of C. Day Lewis*, ed. Jill Balcon, was published in 1982 and *The Complete Poems* in 1992. His later poetry ranges through a variety of modes and levels of emotional and imaginative intensity: while some have praised his classical and allegorical manner, of which 'Pegasus' is a notable example, others have found it dryly formal; similarly, the refined rural lyricism of many poems is both admired and disregarded as inconsequentially *Georgian. Among the finest of his poems are those which form moving affirmations of deep personal affection. *The Friendly Tree* (1936) was the first of several autobiographical novels, and *The Buried Day* (1960) is a volume of autobiography. As 'Nicholas Blake' he published twenty well-constructed and entertaining detective stories between 1935 and 1968, in the majority of which the amateur detective is the Audenesque Nigel Strangeways, who takes his name from the Manchester prison and in his conception owes something to E. C. *Bentley's Philip Trent. In the first, *A Question of Proof* (1935), set in a preparatory school, the author draws on his experiences as a schoolmaster at Summer Fields School, Oxford, and Cheltenham Junior School. Among the best are *Thou Shell of Death* (1936; US title *Shell of Death*), *The Beast Must Die* (1938), *The Smiler with the Knife* (1938), *The Case of the Abominable Snowman* (1941; US title *The Corpse in the Snowman*), *Minute for Murder* (1947), *Head of a Traveller* (1949), *End of Chapter* (1957), and *The Worm of Death* (1961). As a translator he is noted for his versions of Virgil's *Georgics* (1940), *The Aeneid* (1952), and *The Eclogues* (1963) and for his highly acclaimed rendering of Valéry's *Le Cimetière Marin* (1946). *C. Day-Lewis: An English Literary Life* (1980) by his son Sean Day-Lewis reveals the uncertainties and complexities of attitude informing much of his writing.

Day of the Locust, see WEST, NATHANAEL.

Day of the Triffids, The, see WYNDHAM, JOHN.

DEANE, Seamus (1940–), Irish poet and cultural historian, born in Derry City, educated at Queen's University, Belfast, and at Cambridge University. In 1968 he began lecturing at University College, Dublin, where he became Professor of English and American Literature in 1980. His poetry, in which social and political themes combine tellingly with personal experience, is collected in *Gradual Wars* (1972), *Rumours* (1975), and *History Lessons* (1985); *Selected Poems* appeared in 1988. A founding member of the *Field Day Theatre Company, he edited the three-volume *Field Day Anthology of Irish Writing* (1991), the most comprehensive work of its kind to date. His principal scholarly works include *Celtic Revivals: Essays in Modern Irish Literature* (1985), *A Short History of Irish Literature, 1580–1980* (1986), and *The French Enlightenment and Revolution in England, 1789–1832* (1988).

Dean's December, The, see BELLOW, SAUL.

Death and the King's Horseman, see SOYINKA, WOLE.

Death Comes for the Archbishop, a novel by Willa *Cather, published in 1927. The novel is Cather's fictional tribute to the beauties and strengths of European Catholicism. (She never actually became a Catholic, as was popularly believed, but found in the Church an acceptable imaginative alternative to what she saw as the greedy, crass society of post-First World War America.) The novel takes two distinguished French servants of the Church, Bishop Jean Latour and his vicar Father Joseph Vaillant, who together carry out missionary work in New Mexico and organize the diocese there. Comrades in youth, they maintain their friendship throughout their life in America, complementing one another in their work and in their characters. Latour is intellectual, sensitive, and fundamentally solitary; Vaillant practical and warm-hearted. The novel ends with Latour's death, which takes place shortly after Vaillant's; his body lies in state in the cathedral at Santa Fe, his one great creation. The book reflects the author's feeling for New Mexico—cf. *The *Professor's House* (1925)—and the influence of certain painters, such as Puvis de Chavannes, on her style.

Death in the Family, A, a partially autobiographical novel by James *Agee, published in 1957. It tells the story of the shattering of a secure and happy family when the father is killed in a car crash. Agee's writings are marked by an exploration of his own past; this novel focuses on a young boy named Rufus, Agee's middle name. The book opens with 'Knoxville: Summer of 1915', a passage of descriptive prose by a mature man trying to reconstruct a child's perspective of a summer evening with his family. By juxtaposing passages in italics with ordinary print, the book details two times of the growth of Rufus, with the italicized sub-narrative weaving in and out of the main narrative providing a kind of psychological basis. The narrative then proceeds to Rufus's trip to a cinema with his father Jay, the stops they make on their way home at the bar and on a hillside, Rufus's confused understanding of the differences between his parents, and other thoughts. After hearing about his father's imminent death, Jay drives to his father's home and, upon returning, is killed in a car crash after driving recklessly along the mountain roads. The later part of the book is taken up with the preparations that Mary, Rufus's mother, makes for the funeral. The book was later dramatized under the title *All The Way Home* (1960; Pulitzer Prize) by Tad Mosel.

Death of a Hero, see ALDINGTON, RICHARD.

Death of a Naturalist, Seamus *Heaney's first collection of poems, published in 1966. The freshness and authenticity with which many of the poems made use of themes and imagery drawn from Heaney's rural upbringing were among the principal reasons for the book's enthusiastic critical reception. Poems like the title piece, 'The Barn', and 'Churning Day' display a Wordsworthian intensity of recollection in their sensuously detailed recreations of incidents in childhood. Elsewhere, the volume initiated Heaney's engagement with the larger communal past: the nineteenth-century Irish potato famine is harrowingly evoked in 'For the Commander of the "Eliza" ' and 'At a Potato Digging'; Ulster's troubled history is alluded to in 'Docker', a vignette of sectarian antagonism whose 'Oh yes, that kind of thing could start again' was to prove unhappily prophetic by the end of 1969. The volume also featured a distinctive group of love poems and firmly anticipated developments in Heaney's verse in 'Digging' and 'Personal Helicon'; the former establishes physical penetration of the earth as an extensible metaphor for poetry, heralding the imaginative excavations of myth and history in his treatments of the peat bogs (see NORTH); 'Personal Helicon' concludes the book by renouncing its preoccupation with childhood, the last lines indicating his subsequent concern with investigating personal identity in the statement 'I rhyme | To see myself, to set the darkness echoing'.

Death of a Salesman, a play by Arthur *Miller, published and performed in 1949. Described by Miller himself as 'Certain Private Conversations in Two Acts and a Requiem', it makes use of *Expressionist devices to present the life of Willy Loman and his relationship with his family up to the point at which he commits suicide. The action of the play proceeds both forwards and backwards and is remarkable both for its realistic portrayal of an American family and for its dramatic presentation of memory, fantasy, and trauma. It is also amongst the most powerful assaults on American materialism ever made and attacks the institutionalized expectations and behaviour patterns which sustain it: the cult of sport, the ambivalent relationship to honesty, the predatory attitude of men to women, and the corrosive consumerism of American society. Loman's enthusiastic acceptance of all this has tragic repercussions for his two sons, who stand very much at the centre of the drama. It is Biff, the sportsman turned kleptomaniac, who speaks the most appropriate epitaph for his father: 'He had the wrong dreams.' In the play, Miller counterpoints the materialistic fantasies of modern America with the pioneering ones of an older generation, to the detriment of the former.

Death of the Heart, The, a novel by E. *Bowen, published in 1938. Portia Quayne has had a vagrant, intimate childhood with her mother, who has died. The 16-year-old orphan has come to live with her half-brother Thomas and his cynical, egotistical, attractive wife Anna. Thomas's father made one late attempt to break free from the domineering Mrs Quayne (a powerful offstage figure) and fathered Portia, an intense, nervous, observant waif, whose arrival disrupts the exclusive, civilized life of Windsor Terrace. As her name suggests, she judges the Quaynes as much as they judge her, and the novel is in part a satire on the English middle classes of the 1930s, full of 'competitiveness and funk'. Portia falls naïvely, demandingly in love with Anna's unreliable protégé Eddie, comes to feel betrayed by him and the Quaynes, and runs away. Her drama (that of a heroine in a Gothic novel, but in a secular, sceptical setting) is overseen by two guardians, the sibylline housemaid, Matchett, and the loyal, shabby-genteel Major Brutt. It moves between the elegant Regency terrace and the robust vulgar seaside home of the Heccomb family, 'Waikiki'. As the disillusioned novelist St Quentin observes, the extreme demands of innocence will have to adapt to the compromised and treacherous grown-up world: 'We must live how we can.'

DE BERNIÈRES, Louis (1954–), British novelist, born in London, educated at the University of Manchester and the University of London. He taught in Columbia for two years and chose South America as the setting for some of his novels. The first of these, *The War of Don Emmanuel's Nether Parts* (1990), is set in an imaginary South American country run by gangsters and corrupt politicians and combines *magic realism with political satire. Also set in South America are *Señor Vivo and the Coca Lord* (1991), an indictment of the cocaine trade, and *The Troublesome Offspring of Cardinal Guzman* (1992), which deals with the persecution of certain members of a small town by a latter-day Inquisition. *Captain Corelli's Mandolin* (1994) focuses on the inhabitants of the Greek island of Cephalonia following the Italian invasion during the Second World War.

DE BOISSIÈRE, Ralph (Anthony Charles) (1907–), Australian novelist, born in Port of Spain, Trinidad, where he was educated at Queen's Royal College. In the 1920s de Boissière, who is of French Creole ancestry, was associated with a circle of politically radical young Trinidadian writers, such as Alfred H. *Mendes and C. L. R. *James, who contributed to the short-lived but highly influential monthly, *The *Beacon*. He emigrated to Australia in 1947, where he wrote all his novels, and became an Australian citizen in 1970. Among other jobs, he has worked as an auto assembler in Australia, and a bakery supplier in Trinidad. Drawing on his experience of life as a skilled worker, de Boissière's novels are panoramic epics on the struggles of unionized workers for a better life. The first two, *Crown Jewel* (1952) and *Rum and Coca Cola* (1956), investigate Trinidadian industrial relations during the turbulent 1930s and 1940s, a period punctuated by a series of bitter strikes and demonstrations, at first against the British and later against the Americans. Salman *Rushdie has said of *Crown Jewel* that 'the enormous appeal of this book lies not so much in its committed socialism as in its ability to integrate politics with the lives of its characters'. In *No Saddles for Kangaroos* (1964), de Boissière integrated Cold War politics and the Korean conflict with the private lives of Australian automobile workers in the early 1950s.

Decline and Fall, a novel by Evelyn *Waugh, published in 1928. Waugh's first novel, which was an immediate success, describes the misfortunes of Paul Pennyfeather, an innocent abroad in the decadent world of fashionable 1920s society. Sent down from Scone College, Oxford, after being wrongly accused of indecent behaviour, he is forced to give up his theological studies in order to become a schoolmaster (an episode which owes something to Waugh's own disastrous experiences as a preparatory school teacher) and arrives at Llanabba Castle, a minor public school. Here, his pupils include the son of Margot Beste-Chetwynde, a society beauty by whom Pennyfeather becomes infatuated, and who amuses herself by agreeing to marry him. On the eve of the wedding, however, Paul is arrested, though innocent, for having unknowingly become involved in Margot's activities in the white slave trade; he goes to prison, which he finds quite congenial, because 'anyone who has been to an English public school will always feel comparatively at home in prison'. His escape is eventually arranged by Margot, who has married Lord Metroland in the meantime. After faking his own death certificate, Paul returns under the same name but another identity—that of a 'distant cousin'—to Scone College, to resume his interrupted studies.

Deconstruction was not so much a movement as a practice of reading, a learned habit of scepticism. It was chiefly associated with the work of the French philosopher Jacques Derrida (notably *Writing and Difference*, 1967; *Of Grammatology*, 1967; *Margins*, 1972; *Dissemination*, 1972), which in turn was a critical revision of many of the propositions of *Structuralism. The architectural metaphors are not accidental. Structuralism sought to reveal the invisible articulation of literary and other buildings; Deconstruction questioned the building process. It was at first often spelled de-construction, which underlined the neologism (not demolition or destruction), and signalled its most active meaning: 'the unmaking of a construct' (Derrida). 'However negative it may sound,' Paul *de Man commented, 'deconstruction implies the possibility of rebuilding.' In theory Deconstruction might be applied to any kind of cultural object, but Derrida was most interested in the major movements of Western philosophy, which he saw as regularly blind to their own metaphors and strategies. They converted a need for origins, for example, into what they saw as the indispensable presence of those origins; they dreamed of immediacies of experience and meaning which no culture has ever known. Derrida sought to understand rather than simply to deny such needs and dreams, but thought it important to see how strongly and ubiquitously they are at work, even in unsuspected areas. Exported to America and elsewhere, Deconstruction became more literary, a matter of unravelling old conspiracies of agreed interpretation, an assault on supposed academic common sense. It came to seem unhistorical because it insisted on the textuality of all history; its defenders would say it was revising the idea of history rather than abandoning history itself. See also NEW CRITICISM.

DEEPING, (George) Warwick (1877–1950), English popular novelist, born in Southend, educated at Trinity College, Cambridge, where he read science and medicine. He achieved early success with popular historical romances such as *Uther and Igraine* (1903), *Bertrand of Brittany* (1908), and *The Red Saint* (1909). His most famous novel, and greatest critical success, was *Sorrell and Son* (1925), a tender account of the relationship between Captain Sorrell and his young son, Kit, whom he tries to protect from adversity. Deeping was often criticized for his sentimentality, but his novels (over seventy in all) remained popular and reflected Edwardian values. Later novels included *The Malice of Men* (1938), *The Dark House* (1941), and *Old Mischief* (1950).

DEIGHTON, Len (Leonard Cyril) (1929–), British thriller writer, called by Julian *Symons 'a kind of poet of the spy novel'; born in London, educated at the Royal College of Art. He served in the RAF and worked in a variety of professions before turning to authorship. His first book, *The Ipcress File* (1962), with its unnamed, working-class hero, elliptic narration, and emphasis on departmental rivalry in British intelligence, gave a new turn to the Cold War spy story. Seven more novels with the same hero followed—the best are perhaps *Horse Under Water* (1963), *Billion-Dollar Brain* (1966), *An Expensive Place to Die* (1967), and *Twinkle, Twinkle Little Spy* (1976; US title *Catch a Falling Spy*), but his later work, from *XPD* (1981) onwards, seems more conventional, possibly because his methods had now been imitated by others. Among his other thrillers is *SS-GB* (1978), which has *science fiction elements: the German invasion of 1941 has been successful, and Britain is an occupied country. Deighton has also written novels: *Bomber* (1970); short stories: *Declarations of War* (1971); historical studies of the Second World War: *Fighter: The True Story of the Battle of Britain* (1977), *Blitzkrieg: From the Rise of Hitler to the Fall of Dunkirk* (1979); and cookery books: *Où est le garlic?* (1965). Most recently he has returned to the subjects of espionage and departmental intrigue with a series of works about a British intelligence agent, Bernard Samson: *Spy Hook* (1988), *Spy Line* (1989), *Spy Sinker* (1990), *Faith* (1994), and *Hope* (1995).

Deirdre of the Sorrows, a play by J. M. *Synge; it was left unrevised at the dramatist's death and published posthumously, in 1910. The eponymous heroine, a foundling brought up to be his wife by Conchubor, High King of Ulster, rejects this unwanted marriage. Instead, she chooses Naisi for her husband, notwithstanding a prophecy that she will ruin him, and escapes with him and his brothers from Emain Macha to safety abroad in Alban. After seven years of intense happiness there, Conchubor sends an offer of peace and safe return home; and Deirdre accepts this, even though she does not trust it, because she is fearful of growing old, fearful that Naisi will tire of her, and fearful that their dream-like life will end. Back in Emain, the king does indeed renege on his promise. Naisi's brothers are attacked and, though Deirdre tries to stop him helping them, he goes out to his death. She then defies Conchubor, who still craves her, as 'an old man and a fool only', and stabs herself to death in what she, and Synge, suggest is the final triumph of love and beauty over reality.

DELAFIELD, E. M., pseudonym of Edmée Elizabeth Monica DASHWOOD (1890–1943), British novelist, born in Monmouthshire, the daughter of Count Henry de la Pasture and Mrs Henry de la Pasture, a popular novelist. She adopted the pseudonym 'E. M. Delafield', a loose translation of her French ancestral name, to avoid confusion between her own writing and her mother's. Her first novel, *Zella Sees Herself* (1917), was followed by over thirty others, including *The War Workers* (1918), *Humbug* (1922), *The Way Things Are* (1927), *What Is Love* (1928), *Woman Are Like That* (1929), *Thank Heaven Fasting* (1932), *Nothing Is Safe* (1937), and *Now No-one Will Know* (1941). She is best known for the series of novels, written in journal form, describing the day-to-day existence of a middle-class married woman living in a small country town during the 1930s and 1940s, beginning with *The Diary of a Provincial Lady* (1930) and including *The Provincial Lady Goes Further* (1932), *The Provincial Lady in America* (1934), and *The Provincial Lady in Wartime* (1940). Delafield's novels are characterized by an elegant and occasionally sardonic wit and by a refusal to sentimentalize the lives and conditions of her characters, most of them women whose circumstances, although relatively affluent, allow little room for intellectual or emotional development. Delafield also wrote three plays, *To See Ourselves* (1930), *The Glass Wall* (1933), and *The Mulberry Bush* (1935).

DE LA MARE, Walter (John) (1873–1956), British poet, born at Charlton in South East London, educated at St Paul's Cathedral Choir School; he subsequently worked as a clerk with the Anglo-American Oil Company in London. *Songs of Childhood*, his first volume of poetry, was published under the pseudonym 'Walter Ramal' in 1902. *Henry Brocken* (1904) was the first of his novels, its narrative of encounters with famous literary characters establishing the fantastic mode of much of his fiction. *Poems* (1906) consolidated his reputation and in 1908 he left his commercial employment to devote himself to writing. *The Listeners* (1912), his first widely successful volume, whose title-piece is perhaps his best-known poem, *Peacock Pie* (1913), *Motley* (1918), and *The Veil* (1921) are among the collections of verse that gained him a large popular readership. With Lascelles *Abercrombie and Wilfrid *Gibson he was a beneficiary of Rupert *Brooke's will, entitling him to considerable sums in royalties after 1915. Although his poetry has a certain narrowness of range in common with the work of many of the Georgian poets (see GEORGIAN POETRY) with whom he was associated, its compellingly imaginative character and flexible mastery of traditional forms won him the enduring respect of many discerning critics. Mortality and vague but incontrovertible apprehensions of the afterlife are central themes in many of his poems. The novels which gained him a high standing include the chilling parable of damnation in *The Return* (1910); and *Memoirs of a Midget* (1921), which recounts the frequently bizarre events in the life of its diminutive heroine, Miss M. *The Fleeting* (1933), in which the meditative and imaginative qualities of his verse are intensified, *Memory* (1938), and *The Burning Glass* (1945) are among his numerous further collections of poetry; the long discursive poems *The Traveller* (1946) and *Winged Chariot* (1951) form expositions of the philosophy of the interpenetration of the natural and the supernatural worlds that informs most of his work. *Collected Rhymes and Verses* (1944; reissued 1947, 1970, 1989) and *Collected Poems* (1942; reissued 1979) were compiled in accordance with de la Mare's division of his work into lighter and more serious modes; *Complete Poems* (1969) included a number of previously unpublished poems. *Collected Stories for Children* was published in 1947. His work as an anthologist is chiefly represented by *Come Hither* (1923), a collection for children which has remained popular, and *Behold This Dreamer* (1939), a compendious gathering of poetry and prose relating to sleep, dreams, and paranormal experience. In 1953 he was awarded the Order of Merit.

DELANEY, Shelagh (1939–), British dramatist, born in Salford; she left school at 16. Though she subsequently wrote *The Lion in Love* (1960) for the stage, and several screenplays, including *Dance with a Stranger* (1985), she is remembered primarily for her first play, *A Taste of Honey* (1958). This shows a working-class northern girl—pregnant by a black sailor, temporarily deserted by her nagging mother, and befriended by a homosexual art student—in the process of discovering her identity and accepting the impending birth of her baby. On its production in 1958, its unpretentious and often humorous realism was acclaimed as a vital contribution to the socially conscious or *'kitchen sink' school of playwriting then establishing itself in reaction to the drawing-room drama fashionable in the West End of London.

DELANY, Samuel R(ay) (1942–), American novelist and critic, born in New York City where he was educated at City College. His career began in the early 1960s with a number of *science fiction novels in which *space opera conventions were transformed by a baroque style. Most notable of these were *The Jewels of Aptor* (1962); the three novels assembled as *The Fall of the Towers* (1970); *Babel-17* (1966), whose linguistic speculations foreshadowed much of Delany's later criticism; and *The Einstein Intersection* (1967). From *Nova* (1968), one of his most sustained space operas, Delany's output became more ambitious. *Dhalgren* (1975), an experimental novel set in a ruined city, was followed by *Triton* (1976) and *Stars in My Pocket like Grains of Sand* (1984). His criticism, collected in *The Jewel-Hinged Jaw* (1977), *The American Shore* (1978), *Starboard Wine* (1984), and *The Straits of Messina* (1989), applies the methods of contemporary European theorists to the mapping of science fiction as a conceptually distinct genre.

DE LA ROCHE, Mazo (1885–1961), Canadian novelist, born in Newmarket, Ontario, brought up on a fruit and stock farm in Ontario, a background which was to appear in her fiction; she was educated at Toronto University and Toronto School of Art. Her novel *Jalna* (1927), the first novel in the 'Whiteoak Chronicles', distinguished her as the first Canadian to become an international bestseller. By 1949, it was estimated that 2,000,000 copies of her novels, translated into fifteen languages, had been sold. A subsequent twenty novels in the Whiteoak Chronicles narrated the deeds of the Whiteoak family, from the matriarch Ardeline to the handsome virile Renny.

DELDERFIELD, R(onald) F(rederick) (1912–72), English popular novelist and playwright, born in Greenwich, London. Many of his best-selling novels are family sagas with romantic overtones, often spanning the period between the First and Second World Wars and beyond. He often focused on middle-aged love between men and women, one of whom, at least, had already been married, or between a more experienced partner and a virtual novice. *God Is an Englishman* (1970) is perhaps his best novel, and its title was apparently not meant to be ironic. It chronicles the twists and turns of a marriage between an older man, Adam Swan, and his young, vulnerable wife, who strongly values her independence. Other novels include *Cheap Day Return* (1967; US title *Return Journey*, 1974), *The Green Gauntlet* (1968), and *Long Summer Days* (1974). His plays, which were more ephemeral than his novels, include *Peace Comes to Peckham* (1948), *The Old Lady of Cheadle* (1952), *The Mayerling Affair* (1958), and *Wild Mink* (1962). *Napoleon in Love* (1959), his best-known work of popular history, is one of several books he wrote about the French emperor. *For My Own Amusement* (1968) and *Overture for Beginners* (1970) are autobiographical works. See Sanford Sternlicht, *R. F. Delderfield* (1988).

DELILLO, Don (1936–), American novelist, born in New York, educated at Fordham University. Since he began publishing fiction in the early 1970s, he has established a reputation as a social satirist and critic of the 'American Dream', whose novels frequently incorporate disturbing and occasionally surreal metaphors of contemporary life. These include his first novel, *Americana* (1971), whose protagonist, David Bell, is a young and successful television executive who abandons his job and his New York life to make an experimental movie in a small Kansas town, becoming, in the process, increasingly divorced from reality; *End Zone* (1972), which constructs an elaborate parallel between the game of American football and nuclear warfare in order to investigate the underlying violence of American culture; *Ratner's Star* (1976); *Players* (1977); *The Names* (1982), which is set in Greece, the Middle East, and India and concerns a series of cult murders; and *White Noise* (1985), whose hero, a middle-class academic, becomes drawn into the violent sub-culture of the town in which he lives. *Libra* (1988) was an exploration of the Kennedy assassination which investigated the internal lives of the central figures in this crucial moment in recent history. In this, as in his other studies of the iconography of American life, historical fact is interwoven with fictional detail in a narrative whose chilling plausibility serves to reinforce its power. *Mao II* (1991) deals with the corrupting power of fame in its exploration of the life of a blocked writer, which, according to the author, was inspired by his reflections upon a photograph of the reclusive novelist J. D. *Salinger.

DE LISSER, Herbert George (1878–1944), Jamaican novelist and journalist, born in Falmouth, Jamaica. In 1904 he was appointed editor-in-chief of the *Daily Gleaner*, a position which gave him extensive knowledge of Jamaican society and an influential role in colonial politics. His allegiance was to a Fabian socialist, gradualist view of political development, similar to that of his lifelong friend, Sydney Oliver, one of the most liberal governors of Jamaica. His best-known novel, *Jane's Career* (1914), follows the fortunes of a country girl, and emphasizes her exploitation when she finds domestic work in urban Kingston, though she gradually learns how to climb up the social ladder. Most of de Lisser's other novels were initially published serially in *Planters' Punch*, edited by de Lisser, the unofficial mouthpiece of the Jamaica Imperial Association. Other novels of note include *Susan Proudleigh* (1915), and *Triumphant Squalitone* (1917), a political satire. Later novels tended to be either historical romances, such as *The White Witch of Rosehall* (1929), or satires of Jamaican society, like *Under the Sun* (1937).

DELL, Ethel M., see ROMANTIC FICTION.

DELL, Floyd (1887–1969), American novelist and radical journalist, born in Illinois. Dell established himself as a journalist in Chicago and became a leading light of the Chicago literary renaissance, where he furthered the careers of Sherwood *Anderson and Theodore *Dreiser. He moved to New York in 1914, and became involved with the bohemian radical intelligentsia of Greenwich Village. Here, he worked as a journalist and editor on *The *Masses* and *The Liberator* while also writing several one-act plays. He made his name with his first novel, *Moon-Calf* (1920), one of the first novels to explore the changing sexual and social mores of the disillusioned post-First World War American bohemian generation; he continued his portrait of the times in the sequel *The Briary-Bush* (1921). Further novels *Janet March* (1923), *Runaway* (1925), and *Love in Greenwich Village* (1926) continued to explore life amongst the unconventional in bohemian New York. During this time, he also wrote a study in child psychology, *Were You Ever a Child?* (1919); one of the earliest critical studies of the writings of Upton *Sinclair, *Upton Sinclair: A Study in Social Protest* (1927); the comic novel *An Unmarried Father* (1927); and a description of his views on sex in *Love in the Machine Age* (1930); he also edited an edition of Richard Burton's *Anatomy of Melancholy* in 1931 and wrote his autobiography *Homecoming* (1933), bringing him up to his thirty-fifth year, before moving to Washington, DC to work for the *Federal Writers' Project until his retirement in 1947.

DELORIA, Vine, Jr (1933–), Native American writer, born in South Dakota, educated at Iowa State University, the Lutheran School of Theology, and the University of Colorado. Deloria, a Sioux, is well known for his historical and ethnographical writings which present the Indian perspective upon modern history. His work gains great satirical power from the inversion of the official historical picture which Deloria uses with considerable wit. Deloria has been executive director of the National Congress of American Indians, Chair of the Institute for the Development of Indian Law, and professor of Native American studies and political science at the University of Arizona. Among his works are *Custer Died for Your Sins: An Indian Manifesto* (1969), a collection of essays which deals with, among other issues, Indian stereotypes and Indian humour, and *We Talk, You Listen: New Tribes, New Turf* (1970). Deloria has published a number of studies of Native American religions, most notably *God Is Red* (1973) and *The Metaphysics of Modern Existence* (1979), where he contrasts the Indian with the Judaeo-Christian worldview and argues that the new metaphysics can be modelled upon tribal cosmology. His works on the political and legal aspects of Indian–white relations include *Behind the Trail of Broken Treaties* (1974) and *American Indian Policy in the Twentieth Century* (1985). See also NATIVE AMERICAN LITERATURE.

DE MAN, Paul (1919–83), Belgian scholar and critic, born in Antwerp, educated at the University of Brussels and at Yale; he became Professor of Humanistic Studies at Johns Hopkins University and Professor of Humanities at Yale. His work on German, French, and English literature had a special emphasis on irony and rhetoric. He came to prominence with his book *Blindness and Insight* (1971), which offered English-speaking readers their first developed introduction to *Deconstruction and the work of Jacques Derrida; it argued that critical insights are characteristically accompanied by a matching blindness, and that all literary texts anticipate their own misreading. A literary text is one 'that implicitly or explicitly signifies its own rhetorical mode', and rhetoric is what makes interpretation indispensable and uncertain. Rhetoric is therefore language made visible, a revelation not only of strategy but of our deep entanglement in a medium we may think is at our service. De Man's later book, *Allegories of Reading* (1979), extended this idea through close commentary on works by Rousseau, Nietzsche, Rilke, and Proust; and de Man himself, in his later years, became America's chief apologist for Deconstruction, although fully aware of the ironies involved when a work of dismantling becomes a monument, when scepticism becomes a certainty. He was surprised by Deconstruction's academic success, and sought to correct the growing impression that the movement, or the practice, was unhistorical, or against history. De Man's posthumous *Resistance to Theory* (1986) sought to understand what had happened to literary study in the wake of modern critical and philosophical developments. He himself, or rather his memory, became the subject of a considerable controversy when it was discovered after his death that he had contributed many articles, some of them anti-Semitic, to a collaborationist journal in Belgium during the Second World War. Did this discovery discredit his later work, as his traditionalist opponents wished to think? Most readers thought not, but many deconstructive defences looked distinctly shaky.

DE MORGAN, William (Frend) (1839–1917), British writer and master potter, born in London, educated at University College, London, and the Royal Academy Schools. As a ceramicist, he came into close contact with William Morris (for whom he designed stained glass and decorative tiles) and other members of the Pre-Raphaelites. After illness and the failure of his firm de Morgan retired in 1905. In his late sixties he began producing expansive novels, the first and most successful being *Joseph Vance* (1906), a tragi-comic tale in autobiographical form told by a drunken builder whose Oxford-educated son becomes an inventor. He wrote eight more novels including *Alice-for-Short: A Dichronism* (1907), a ghost story, and *A Likely Story* (1911), a tale of magic; two posthumous novels, *The Old Madhouse* (1919) and *Old Man's Youth* (1921), were completed by his wife, Evelyn de Morgan, also an artist. The charm of his work lay in its originality and Dickensian style.

DENNIS, C. J. (Clarence Michael James) (1876–1936), Australian journalist, born in South Australia. He became editor of the Adelaide weekly *The Critic*, and eventually joined the Melbourne *Herald*. Having had little success with *Backblock Ballads and Other Verses* (1913), Dennis extracted four verse narratives from the collection and republished them as *Songs of a Sentimental Bloke* (1915), which achieved immediate popularity. *The Moods of Ginger Mick* (1916) recorded the antics of Bloke's friend during the war. This, with the earlier marching song 'The Australiaise' (1908), captured the prevailing mood of Australian nationalism. Both the Bloke and Ginger Mick were presented as caricatures of the irreverent, down to earth, good-humoured Australian. There is a shrewd sensitivity to human failings in Dennis's verse narratives which accounts for the folk stature they have acquired.

DENNIS, Nigel (Forbes) (1912–89), British novelist and dramatist, born in Bletchingley, Surrey, educated in Rhodesia, Austria, and Germany. He was an outstanding journalist and became co-editor of **Encounter*. Much of his first novel, *Boys and Girls Come out To Play* (1949), is set in America where he had worked as a journalist from 1931 to 1949. *Cards of Identity* (1955), which Dennis adapted for the stage in 1956, is widely regarded as his finest work; an extravagantly inventive satire on the shallowness of human identity in modern civilization, the novel culminates, in 'The Prince of Antioch', a sustained parody of Shakespeare. *A House in Order* (1960), set chiefly in a greenhouse from which the narrator observes a third world war, forms a tautly concentrated fable on the nature of human purpose. His other works as a dramatist include *The Making of Moo* (1957) and *August for the People* (1961). His love of the Mediterranean is expressed in *An Essay on Malta* (1972) and in *Exotics* (1970), a volume of poems set mainly in that region.

DESAI, Anita (1937–), Indian novelist and short-story writer, born in Mussoorie, educated in Delhi. Her novels of the 1960s signalled the emergence of a distinctive and original talent, but are now dismissed by the author as overwritten and melancholy. Her first work, *Cry, the Peacock* (1963), is compelling in its lyrical account of a frustrated young woman's madness and murder of her husband. Other novels, such as *Voices in the City* (1965) and the brief, pessimistic *Where Shall We Go This Summer?* (1975), explore the lives and sensibilities of the urban bourgeoisie from differing perspectives, usually those of young married women, while *Bye Bye Blackbird* (1969) is an attempt to cope with the realities of immigrants' lives in Britain. *Fire on the Mountain* (1977) brought Desai critical and popular acclaim; the novel reworks the tropes of innocence and experience in its depiction of the tense and ultimately violent relationship between an ageing Indian matron and her disturbed great-granddaughter. *Clear Light of Day* (1980) locates the experience of Partition and communal disharmony in the memories of an independent single woman attempting to come to terms with her life and relationships. The black comedy *In Custody* (1984) deftly intertwines linguistic and power politics, aesthetics, Hindu philosophy, and documentary realism in a tale of an idealistic Hindu teacher's obsession with the *œuvre* of a decadent but brilliant Muslim poet. *Barmgartner's Bombay* (1987) chronicles the life and murder of a Jewish refugee from Nazi Germany adrift in a changing India that simultaneously accepts and ignores him; contrasted with his are the experiences of an adventurous and exploitative German itinerant drug addict. In *Journey to Ithaca* (1995) Desai explores once again the encounter between East and West: a young European couple discover that an Indian saint and mystic was brought up in Egypt. Like Desai's other later novels, the book offers a subjective interpretation of much of this century's history. Other works include a novel for children, *Village by the Sea* (1982), and a collection of short stories, *Games at Twilight* (1978).

DESANI, G(ovindas) V(ishnoodas) (1909–), Indian novelist and dramatist, born in Nairobi, Kenya, educated privately; he came to England in 1926 and worked as a journalist. Throughout the Second World War he lectured on Indian Affairs for the Ministry of Information. From 1952 to the mid-1960s, he lived in monasteries in India and became a professor of Philosophy at the University of Texas, Austin, in 1968. Desani's most celebrated work is *All About H. Hatterr* (1951; revised 1970, 1972, 1986), originally published in 1948 under the title *All About Mr Hatterr, a Gesture*. Widely regarded as a comic masterpiece of the Absurd, the book recounts the fortunes of the worldly but philosophically disposed H. Hatterr with extraordinary stylistic and idiomatic mobility. The novel shares an underlying concern with illusion and reality displayed in Desani's *Hali* (1951), a poetic drama whose mystically exalted manner is in the traditions of classical Indian literature; it is collected with his shorter fictions in *Hali and Collected Stories* (1990). Desani became an American citizen in 1979.

DESHPANDE, Shashi (1938–), Indian novelist, born in Dharwar, North Karnataka, India, educated at Bangalore University. Both her first collection of short stories, *The Legacy* (1978), and her highly praised novel, *The Dark Holds no Terrors* (1980), signalled the arrival of an important new feminist voice in Indian fiction; through a network of familial relationships, and above all men and women, Deshpande explores contemporary India and illustrates the complex adjustments and social changes of the 1980s. Her honest treatment of sexuality, gender, and generational conflicts is evident in *Roots and Shadows* (1983); its intelligent, mature narrator, the journalist Indu, is a more independent, less tortured example of the modern urbanized Indian woman than some of Deshpande's other protagonists. In Deshpande's vision, liberation for the Indian woman is circumscribed by boundaries of class, social position, and marital status. Arguably her most accomplished novel, *That Long Silence* (1988) combines acerbic realism with subjective exploration, political awareness with Hindu philosophy. Deshpande has also written fiction for children, and two detective novels, *If I Die Today* (1982) and *Come Up and Be Dead* (1983).

Detective Fiction. Among the most enduring and widely read styles of popular writing in the twentieth century, the detective novel is a formulaic and conventionalized strand of crime fiction, emphasizing the 'puzzle' element. Within a restricted setting (often a country house or isolated rural community), a terrible crime is committed. There are several suspects, all variously plausible as the culprit. After a number of carefully stage-managed 'red herrings' and surprises, the mystery is eventually unravelled. The perpetrator is identified through a combination of deduction and intuition, in the person of the detective, who may be an amateur, and order is once again restored. The interest of such stories lies partly in the characterization and setting, partly in the reassuring sense that crime is soluble and manageable, but perhaps most importantly in the elaborate game of teasing and misleading the reader, who is encouraged to enter into a contest of wits with the detective, only to be thwarted by his or her superior ingenuity.

Precedents for the figure of the detective had been established in the nineteenth century, in Dickens's *Bleak House* (1852–3) and in Wilkie Collins's *The Moonstone* (1868), but the real progenitor of the detective story is commonly agreed to have been Edgar Allan Poe's 'Chevalier Dupin' stories ('The Murders in the Rue Morgue', 1841, and others). While *The Moonstone* has been claimed to be the first full-length detective novel in England, this title should in truth be given to A. C. *Doyle's *A Study in Scarlet* (1888). Drawing on Poe and Emile Gaboriau's *Monsieur Lecoq* (1869), Doyle created the brilliant but unstable Sherlock Holmes and his unimaginative but loyal assistant Dr Watson, constructing a paradigm for the genre much imitated by later writers. He also established the short story as the dominant form: in the hands of writers such as *Chesterton, *Freeman, and *Bramah, it maintained its ascendancy until E. C. *Bentley published *Trent's Last Case* (1913), which introduced in a full-length novel more characterization and the gentlemanly amateur detective with powers of ratiocination markedly inferior to those of Holmes and his successors, thus setting a pattern for the Golden Age of detective fiction in the 1920s and 1930s.

By the 1920s, rules of fair play between author and reader were formulated. In Monsignor Ronald Knox's 'Decalogue' (1928), the ten commandments for the detective writer, these conventions were listed and codified. Leading authors of the Golden Age were Agatha *Christie, whose Hercule Poirot, though obviously a metamorphosis of Holmes, also owes something to A. E. W. *Mason's Inspector Hanaud; *Rhode, H. C. *Bailey, *Berkeley, Michael Innes (pseudonym of J. I. M. *Stewart), Nicholas Blake (pseudonym of C. *Day Lewis); Dorothy *Sayers and Margery *Allingham, both of whom turned the gentlemanly detective into an aristocrat; Ngaio *Marsh, who made him a policeman as well; *Crofts, who kept closer to reality by creating the prototype of the solid police inspector who achieves results through attention to detail rather than deduction; and the Americans J. D. *Carr, S. S. *Van Dine, and Ellery *Queen, whose ever more ingenious and abstruse puzzles abandoned any pretence of characterization or realism.

Meanwhile in America the private eye novel, which differs from the classic detective story in that it is more violent, dynamic rather than static, and often does not follow the classic rule that the criminal must be introduced at the beginning of the story, had emerged in the 1920s and 1930s from the pulp magazine **Black Mask* (1920–36) and in the novels of Dashiell *Hammett, James M. *Cain, and Raymond *Chandler, who have been followed by a host of successors, most notably by R. *Macdonald. This *'Hard-boiled' fiction has been the dominant form in the USA since the 1930s, and after the Second World War began to establish itself in Britain, though attempts to transplant the genre generally failed. At the same time some British writers turned away from the snobbishness and nostalgia of the Golden Age and began writing increasingly realistic crime and spy novels which presented a less one-sided view of the conflict between justice and criminal and more interest in criminal psychology and social concerns. Writers who have remained more or less faithful to the classic detective novel, such as Edmund *Crispin, Michael Gilbert, Elizabeth Ferrars, H. *Keating, Ellis *Peters, and P. D. *James, have mostly abandoned the traditional amateur sleuth who is frequently replaced by a more plausibly drawn police officer, and exotic settings and realistic characterization have become more prevalent. In America, though Rex *Stout remained true to the Holmesian model, the scene has been dominated by the private eye novel, together with a variant on this type which might be called the tough police novel, exemplified by the work of authors such as Elmore *Leonard and Charles *Willeford. During the 1950s a new sub-genre, that of the 'police procedural', appeared in America under the influence of radio and television police series such as *Dragnet*. These novels portray a complete police unit investigating concurrently a series of separate crimes: chief exponents of the type are, in America, Ed *McBain, Hillary Waugh, and Elizabeth Linington; in Britain it has largely remained the preserve of television, though John *Creasey's J. J. Marric stories imitate the method. See Howard Haycraft, *Murder for Pleasure: The Life and Times of the Detective Story* (1942); Jacques Barzun and Wendell Hertig Taylor, *A Catalogue of Crime* (1971, revised 1989); Julian *Symons, *Bloody Murder: From the Detective Story to the Crime Novel, A History* (1972, revised 1985); Chris Steinbrunner and Otto Penzler, *Encyclopaedia of Mystery and Detection* (1976); John M. Reilly (ed.), *Twentieth Century Crime and Mystery Writers* (1980, 2nd edition 1985); and T. J. Binyon, *'Murder Will Out': The Detective in Fiction* (1989).

DEUTSCH, Babette (1895–1982), American poet, born in New York, where she was educated at Barnard College, after which she was secretary to the radical economist Thorstein *Veblen. From 1944 to 1971 she taught at Columbia University. *Banners* (1919), her first collection of verse, was followed by *Honey Out of the Rock* (1925), *Fire for the Night* (1930), and *Epistle to Prometheus* (1931), a long poem celebrating the Promethean spirit throughout human history. The emotional and intellectual energies which sustain her best work are held in balance by a discriminating free-verse technique and highly developed command of visual imagery. The social concerns in her verse are frequently allied to evocations of everyday life in New York. Later collections include *One Part Love* (1939), *Take Them Stranger* (1944), *Coming of Age* (1959), and *Collected Poems* (1969). Among Deutsch's novels are *A Brittle Heaven* (1926), a substantially autobiographical treatment of a woman who is a writer, wife, and mother; *In Such a Night* (1927), an experimental narrative about a woman giving birth at a dinner party; and *Mask of Silenus* (1933), based on the life of Socrates. Her critical writings on modern poetry include *Potable Gold* (1929) and *Poetry in Our Time* (1952). With her husband, Avraham Yarmolinsky, she translated much German and Russian verse, including works by Rilke, Pushkin, and Pasternak.

DEVANNY, Jean (1894–1962), New Zealand and Australian novelist, born Jane Crook in Ferntown, Nelson, the daughter of a miner; she left school at the age of 13. At 17 she married the militant miner and unionist Hal Devanny. Her first novel, *The Butcher's Shop* (1926), which dramatizes in romantic mode the argument for women's right to sexual autonomy, was banned in Australia and New Zealand for its sexual politics and its explicit descriptions of animal husbandry on a New Zealand farm. Devanny's subsequent fiction, with New Zealand settings, includes *Lenore Divine* (1926), *Old Savage and Other Stories* (1927), *Riven* (1929), and *Bushman Burke* (1930); after her move to Sydney in 1929 she produced several realist, Australian novels. Experience of the Depression in Australia stimulated Devanny's political activities and she became a member of the Australian Communist Party, although she often clashed with it on questions concerning women and cultural policy. Such themes are treated in her novels *Sugar Heaven* (1936) and *Cindie* (1949), which examined the plight of sugarcane workers in Queensland, and in her posthumously published autobiography *Point of Departure* (1986).

Devil's Disciple, The, the best-known of G. B. *Shaw's 'Three Plays for Puritans', first performed in Albany, New York in 1897 and published in 1901. It is set during the American War of Independence and primarily concerns Dick Dudgeon, regarded as demonic by his loveless mother and most of the other members of their conventional and pious New Hampshire community. When the British come to arrest the local minister, Anthony Anderson, Dick allows himself to be taken in his place. He is sentenced to be hanged by a military court—the proceedings watched over by the urbane General Burgoyne, who foresees the impending defeat of the British—and saved from the gallows only by the last-minute arrival of Anderson himself, now launched on a full-time career as an officer of the American militia. If the play were simply the melodrama it sometimes seems, there would doubtless be substance in the explanation of Dick's altruism offered by Anderson's wife Judith, that he has fallen in love with her. But that idea leaves him 'revolted'. He sacrificed himself because any other action would have affronted his sense of right and wrong: 'When it came to the point whether I would take my neck out of the noose and put another man's into it, I could not do it . . . I have been brought up standing by the law of my own nature; and I may not go against it.' The self-professed diabolist is thus one of Shaw's secular saints, a puritan in a profounder sense than the woebegone churchgoers of New England.

DE VRIES, Peter (1910–93), American novelist, born in Chicago, educated at Northwestern University. He was an editor of *Poetry* and in 1944 joined *The *New Yorker*. Connecticut and New York State form the background for many of the comic novels for which he became known, beginning with *But Who Wakes the Bugler?* (1940). The tales in *No, but I Saw the Movie* (1952) established him as a writer of verbal dexterity and exuberant imagination. His protagonists were God-fearing and vigorous but an underlying serious concern for religious and moral matters is evident in much of his work. Many of his novels evolved from stories previously published in *The New Yorker*. He parodied the style of writers such as *Faulkner, *Fitzgerald, and *Hemingway with great success in *The Tents of Wickedness* (1959). Other works include *Tunnel of Love* (1954), *Comfort Me with Apples* (1956), *The Mackerel Plaza* (1958), *Through the Fields of Clover* (1961), *Reuben, Reuben* (1964), *The Vale of Laughter* (1967), *The Prick of Noon* (1985), *Without a Stitch in Time* (1972; short stories), *Consenting Adults* (1980), and *Slouching towards Kalamazoo* (1983).

DEWEY, John (1859–1952), American philosopher and educationist, born in Burlington, Vermont, educated at the University of Vermont and Johns Hopkins University. After lecturing at the universities of Minnesota, Michigan, and Chicago, in 1905 he became a professor at Columbia University. The political and social stimuli to which he was exposed during his ten years in Chicago brought about the convergence of his socio-cultural and philosophical preoccupations. As Director of Chicago's School of Education he established the Laboratory School, in which he experimentally applied his principles of active and creative learning. Among his early works on education was *The Child and the Curriculum* (1902); the many publications which followed include *Moral Principles in Education* (1909), *Democracy and Education* (1916), and *Experience and Education* (1938). The extent of his influence on the theory and practice of education in America and beyond gives him pre-eminence among the educational reformers of the twentieth century. The emphasis on practicality in his educational writings reflects his philosophical pragmatism, which formed an extension of the work of William *James and was informed by his readings of Darwin. His doctrine of 'instrumentalism' viewed intellectual activity as a function of the instinct to adjust for survival in the human species. Among the expositions of his ideas which gained him a wide reputation as a philosopher were *Outlines of a Critical Theory of Ethics* (1891), *The Influence of Darwin on Philosophy* (1910), and *Reconstruction in Philosophy* (1920). *Experience and Nature* (1929) and *The Quest for Certainty* (1929) argued for a provisional and socially oriented conception of philosophy, challenging the traditional assumptions of academic philosophers concerning the abstract nature of knowledge. The concern with the spiritual dimensions of experience in his later work is most evident in *A Common Faith* (1934), in which he maintained a firm distinction between religious ideals and religious dogma. His many other publications include *Logic, the Theory of Enquiry* (1938), *Public Schools and Spiritual Values* (1944), and the collections of essays *Characters and Events* (1929) and *Problems of Men* (1946). George Dykhuizen's *The Life and Mind of John Dewey* appeared in 1973. See also BLACK MOUNTAIN WRITERS.

DHONDY, Farrukh (1944–), Indian playwright and novelist, born in Poona, India, educated at Pembroke College, Cambridge, and the University of Leicester. After working as a schoolteacher in London he was a freelance writer until 1985 when he became a commissioning editor for multicultural television programmes. His highly regarded works as a television dramatist include *No Problem*, which was written with Mustapha *Matura for broadcast in 1983, and *King of the Ghetto* (broadcast 1986). Among his other plays are *Mama Dragon* (produced 1980) and *Kipling Sahib* (produced 1982). His acclaimed first novel *Bombay Duck* (1990) forms a provocative treatment of conventional assumptions concerning black, white, and Asian cultural identities; its complex plot provides a context in which bizarre satirical elements can co-exist with a fundamental seriousness of purpose. Among his books for young people are *Come to Mecca* (1978) and *Black Swan* (1992). He is the editor of *Ranters, Ravers, and Rhymers* (1990), an eclectic anthology of verse by Caribbean, African, and Indian poets. Dhondy is also the author of *C. L. R. James* (1994), a biography.

Dial, The, a literary periodical founded in Chicago in 1880 by F. F. Browne. It was purchased by Scofield Thayer and J. S. Watson in 1919, following its move to New York in the previous year. Under Thayer's editorship it became the finest American magazine of literature and the arts of its day, publishing innovative work of the highest standard by leading American, British, and European writers. D. H. *Lawrence regularly contributed short stories, which were also supplied by Katherine *Mansfield, Sherwood *Anderson, and James *Stephens; among the notable poets whose work appeared were T. S. *Eliot, whose *The *Waste Land* had its first American publication in the journal, W. B. *Yeats, William Carlos *Williams, E. E. *Cummings, and Marianne *Moore, who became the editor in 1925. The *Dial* was of particular importance in fostering advances in criticism; essays and reviews by Kenneth *Burke, George *Saintsbury, Yvor *Winters, and other distinguished critics established new standards in textual analysis, anticipating the emergence of the *New Criticism. Notable European contributors included Thomas Mann, Maxim Gorky, Gerhardt Hauptmann, Anatole France, and Paul Valéry. Henry McBride was the principal art critic, and reproductions of work by leading European painters and sculptors were frequently featured. The *Dial* ceased publication in 1929, Marianne Moore later recording that a general falling off in enthusiasm had reduced the tasks of editorship to 'mere faithfulness to responsibility'.

DIBDIN, Michael (1947–), British novelist, born in Northern Ireland, educated at Sussex University and the University of Alberta, Canada. After completing his first novel, *The Last Sherlock Holmes Story* (1980), he spent four years teaching English at the University of Perugia; many of his novels have an Italian setting. *A Rich Full Death* (1986) was a murder story set in Florence, involving Robert and Elizabeth Barrett Browning and the poetry of Dante Alighieri. *Ratking* (1988), the first of his Aurelio Zen detective stories, won the Crime Writers Association Golden Dagger Award that year and was also set in Italy. It was followed by *The Tryst* (1989), *Vendetta* (1990), *Dirty Tricks* (1991), *Cabal* (1992), *The Dying of the Light* (1993), *Dead Lagoon* (1994), and *Dark Spectre* (1995).

DICK, Philip K(indred) (1928–82), American *science fiction novelist, born in Chicago, educated at the University of California. Of his more than thirty novels, the best-known include *Time out of Joint* (1959); *The Man in the High Castle* (1962), an alternative history; *The Three Stigmata of Palmer Eldritch* (1964), which depicts a society controlled by drug-induced fantasy and television; *Do Androids Dream of Electric Sheep?* (1968), later filmed as *Blade Runner*, set in a twenty-first century dominated by information technology; *Flow My Tears, The Policeman Said* (1976), which depicts a police state of the near future; and *A Scanner Darkly* (1977), a dystopian fantasy, set in California in the 1990s. These works express a blackly comic vision of late twentieth-century America, seen through the distorting glass of the future, depicting a technologically sophisticated, totalitarian society controlled by multinational corporations. Several early novels of a more conventional nature, written during the 1950s and published posthumously, express a similarly acerbic view of the modern world. They include *Puttering About in a Small World* (1985); *Humpty Dumpty in Oakland* (1986); *Mary and the Giant* (1987); and *The Broken Bubble* (1988).

DICKENS, Monica (1915–92), British novelist, born in London, educated at St Paul's Girls' School. During the 1930s she detached herself from her middle-class background and worked as a maid and a cook, an interlude providing the material for her first book, the lightly satirical autobiography *One Pair of Hands* (1939). Her earlier works include two further autobiographies, *One Pair of Feet* (1942), concerning her training as a nurse at the start of the Second World War, and *My Turn to Make the Tea* (1951), which draws on her experiences in journalism. Much of her fiction has a documentary aspect. *The Fancy* (1943) is directly informed by her wartime work in an aircraft factory, while *No More Meadows* (1953) and *Man Overboard* (1958) have a basis in her husband's career as an officer in the United States Navy. From the early 1960s onward, her novels assume a more serious sociological character. *The Heart of London* (1961) is a treatment of alcoholic destitution. She liaised closely with the NSPCC in researching child-abuse as the subject of *Kate and Emma* (1964). *The Listeners* (1970) reflects her work with the Samaritans, whose American branches she founded in 1974. Her numerous other novels include *Cobbler's Dream* (1963), *Enchantment* (1989), and *Scarred* (1991). *An Open Book* (1978) is a third volume of autobiography.

DICKEY, James (Lafayette) (1923–), American poet and novelist, born in Atlanta, Georgia, educated at Vanderbilt University. Having held posts at numerous American colleges and universities, he became Professor of English at the University of South Carolina in 1969. *Into the Stone* (1960) and *Helmets* (1964) are among his earlier collections of verse, which gained him wide notice as a powerfully direct poet of considerable conventional accomplishment. *Buckdancer's Choice* (1965) initiated the audacious formal experimentation which has remained a characteristic of his verse, much of which explores fundamental relations between man and his natural contexts. The value of the violent and bizarre aspects of his poetry has been the subject of critical controversy. His subsequent collections include *The Eye-Beaters, Blood, Victory, Madness, Buckhead and Mercy* (1970), *The Zodiac* (1976), *Puella* (1982), *The Eagle's Mile* (1990), in which a new purity of lyrical energy becomes evident; *The Early Motion* (1981), *The Central Motion* (1983), and *The Whole Motion* (1992) are collected editions. *Deliverance* (1970), the best-known of his novels, is the compelling story of four businessmen whose holiday journey to the wilds of Georgia develops into a struggle for survival. *Alnilam* (1987) describes a blind father's quest for knowledge of his son, whose death in a flying accident is linked with a secret society. *To the White Sea* (1993) concerns American airmen escaping through wartime Japan. Among Dickey's numerous other publications are the critical works *The Suspect in Poetry* (1964) and *Sorties* (1971), and the topographical writings of *The Starry Place between the Antlers* (1981) and *Wayfarer* (with photographs by W. A. Bake, 1988).

DICKINSON, Goldsworthy Lowes (1862–1932), British philosophical writer, born in London, educated at King's College, Cambridge, of which he was a fellow from 1887 onward. Among his early works is *The Greek View of Life* (1896), an introduction to classical Greek culture. There followed a series of ethical treatises using the form of the Socratic dialogues; these include *The Meaning of Good* (1901) and *Justice and Liberty* (1908). He was instrumental in formulating the League of Nations; the most notable of his several studies of the causes of the First World War is *The International Anarchy, 1904–1914* (1926). His numerous other publications include *After Two Thousand Years: A Dialogue between Plato and a Modern Young Man* (1930). Dennis Proctor edited *The Autobiography of G. Lowes Dickinson* (1973), written in 1927 but withheld from publication because of its disclosures concerning his homosexuality. E. M. *Forster's biography of Dickinson appeared in 1934.

DICKINSON, Patric Thomas (1914–94), British poet, born in Nasirabad, India, educated at St Catharine's College, Cambridge. After working as a schoolteacher he became a producer with the BBC and then a freelance writer and broadcaster. His first collection of poetry, *The Seven Days of Jericho*, appeared in 1948. Numerous succeeding volumes include *The Sailing Race* (1952), *The World I See* (1960), *A Wintering Tree* (1973), and *A Rift in Time* (1982). His poetry was characterized by its concise, conservatively innovative verse forms and by its unusual balance between a recurring note of tender intimacy and a sometimes sardonic, distancing wit. Although Dickinson's work frequently drew on classical sources, it remained firmly grounded in details of local and domestic experience. Notable among his translations are *The Complete Plays of Aristophanes* (2 volumes, 1971) and a version of *The Aeneid* (1961). He also worked extensively as a playwright for radio and stage; his published plays include *Theseus and the Minotaur* (1945) and *A Durable Fire* (1962). His autobiography entitled *The Good Minute* appeared in 1965.

DICKINSON, Peter (Malcolm de Brissac) (1927–), British writer, born in Zambia, educated at King's College, Cambridge. He is the author of a number of successful and original children's books, of which the best-known are perhaps the trilogy *The Weathermonger* (1968), *Heartsease* (1969), and *The Devil's Children* (1970). He has also written detective stories which are distinguished, above all, by a series of striking and memorable settings: the first, *Skin Deep* (1968; US title *The Glass-Sided Ant's Nest*), concerns the murder of the head of a New Guinea tribe installed in a Victorian house in London by a rich anthropologist. Equally unusual are *The Green Gene* (1973) and *The Poison Oracle* (1974), while *King and Joker* (1976) has as its characters an imaginary English royal family. His later novels, though often involving a crime, have moved away from the detective story genre (*The Last House Party*, 1982; *Skeleton-in-Waiting*, 1989).

DICKSON, Carter, see CARR, JOHN DICKSON.

DICKSON, Gordon R(upert) (1923–), American science fiction writer, born in Edmonton, Alberta, Canada, educated at the University of Minnesota. For many years he concentrated on *space opera tales but from the publication of *The Genetic General* (1960; enlarged as *Dorsai!*, 1976), the first of the Childe Cycle of novels, he embarked upon a more ambitious project. The theme of the Cycle, whose further volumes include *Necromancer* (1962), *The Final Encyclopedia* (1984), and *Other* (1994), is that the evolution of humanity is dependent on an upward physical and spiritual expansion to the stars towards a kind of Godhead. Novels written outside the series include *Time Storm* (1977), *The Far Call* (1978), *The Earth Lords* (1989) and, notably, *Wolf and Iron* (1990), an epic set in post-collapse America.

DIDION, Joan (1934–), American novelist and essayist, born in Sacramento, California, educated at the University of California at Berkeley. Didion was a features editor for *Vogue* magazine, a contributing editor for *The National Review*, and a columnist for the *Saturday Evening Post* before establishing herself as a freelance writer. Her novels include *Run River* (1963), *Play It as It Lays* (1970), *A Book of Common Prayer* (1977), and *Democracy* (1984), but she is better known for her journalism and her essays, notably the volumes *Slouching Towards Bethlehem* (1968) and *The White Album* (1979), which contain some of her most trenchant observations on contemporary America, particularly California in the 1960s and 1970s. Her other important works of non-fiction include *Salvador* (1983), based on her experiences in 1982 when she travelled through El Salvador, and *Miami* (1987). Later works include *Sentimental Journeys* (1993), a collection of essays, *After Henry* (1994), and *Joan Didion: Essays and Conversations* (1994). Her work in the essay form has been seen as an example of the *'new journalism' and compared with that of other 'journalists' such as Gay Talese and Tom *Wolfe, while her fiction has been described as *'post-modernist', though neither attribution does full justice to her literary talents. Mark Royden's *Joan Didion* (1989) is a useful introduction to her life and writings.

DIDSBURY, Peter (1946–), British poet, born in Fleetwood, Lancashire, educated at Balliol College, Oxford. Until 1981 he was a schoolteacher in Hull, since when he has been an archaeologist by profession. His poetry first attracted wide critical notice when it appeared in Douglas *Dunn's edition of *A Rumoured City: New Poets from Hull* (1982), which was published in the same year as his first collection, *The Butchers of Hull*. The imaginative and chronological juxtapositions in Didsbury's writing, coupled with shifts of discourse which have drawn comparisons with John *Ashbery, are among the qualities productive of appreciative but slightly bewildered critical responses typified by Ian Crichton Smith's reference to his 'extraordinarily bizarre, eloquent poems'. Personal experience is combined with literary and historical material in much of his best writing; the accessibility and intermittent humorousness of his poetry holds its complexity and seriousness, frequently of a theological order, in check. *The Classical Farm* (1987) and *That Old-Time Religion* (1994) extended the range and fluency of his work.

DILLARD, Annie (1945–), American writer, born in Pittsburgh, Pennsylvania, educated at Hollins College. Her first published work was a volume of poems, *Tickets for a Prayerwheel* (1974), but it was *Pilgrim at Tinker's Creek* (1974), her first work of prose—an extended meditation on nature—that established her reputation as a fine and original stylist, and gained her a Pulitzer Prize. Since then, Dillard has written a variety of prose works, including *Teaching a Stone to Talk* (1982), essays on nature and religion; *Living by Fiction* (1982), studies of such seminal writers as *Nabokov, Calvino, and Borges; an *An American Childhood* (1987), a partial autobiography, one of her most successful attempts to carve a new narrative form for herself which she has described as creative non-fiction. Her efforts to grapple with the meaning of creativity are detailed in the linked essays of *The Writing Life* (1989). Dillard turned to fiction with *The Living* (1992), a novel set in the late nineteenth century, about the experiences of frontier settlers in the American North West.

DINESEN, Isak, see BLIXEN, KAREN.

DI PRIMA, Diane (1934–), American novelist, playwright, and poet, born in New York City, educated at Swarthmore College, Pennsylvania. Di Prima's writings, particularly her verse, are frequently associated with both *Beat and confessional modes in modern American poetry and her poetic forms echo those of Beat contemporaries such as Allen *Ginsberg and Lawrence *Ferlinghetti. She was a contributing editor to *Kulchur* magazine in the early 1960s, a co-editor with LeRoi Jones (Amiri *Baraka) of the magazine *Floating Bear*, and from 1961 until 1965 was Director of the New York Poet's Theatre. Among her many volumes of verse are *This Kind of Bird Flies Backward* (1958), *Dinners and Nightmares* (1961), *Revolutionary Letters* (1969), *Selected Poems, 1956–1975* (1975), *Loba, Parts 1–8* (1978), *Pieces of a Song: Selected Poems* (1990), and *Seminary Poems* (1991). *Zip Code* (1993) is a volume of her collected plays, while *Memoirs of a Beatnik* (1969) is her most well-known novel. In a 1978 interview she spoke of the poet as 'the first person to begin the shaping and visioning of the new forms and the new consciousness when no one else has begun to sense it . . .' Di Prima has lived for many years in San Francisco and is one of the central figures in the city's vibrant poetic life. Her poem 'Brass Furnace Going Out', which describes her experience of undergoing an abortion, achieved some notoriety through its use by American anti-abortion groups, much to Di Prima's dismay.

Dirty Realist Fiction. A term used in Britain to describe the urbane minimalist fiction of a small group of American writers, notably Raymond *Carver, Richard *Ford, and Tobias *Wolff. Highly articulate and sophisticated in style, 'dirty realist' fiction eschewed slick metropolitanism in favour of the grimmer realities of small-town American life. It featured elliptical dialogue, seedy settings, with uncompromising descriptions of violence, sordid sex, and the dreary hopelessness of its downbeat characters. The expression became fashionable in Britain during the late 1980s following its inception in 1987 when Bill Buford, editor of *Granta, first used the term in an edition devoted to contemporary American fiction.

Disaffection, A, see KELMAN, JAMES.

DISCH, Thomas M. (1940–), American novelist, poet, and short-story writer, born in Des Moines, Iowa, educated at New York University. He has been a visiting lecturer at the universities of Minnesota, Michigan State, and Wesleyan. He is part of the 'New Wave' of writers which swept through *science fiction in the 1960s. *The Genocides* (1965) was quickly followed by *Mankind under the Leash* (1966), *102 H-Bombs* (1966), *Echo round His Bones* (1967), and *Black Alice* (1968). Disch made his reputation with his fourth novel, *Camp Concentration* (1968), which is, at one level, an allegory of the war in Vietnam. *Camp Concentration* imagines a world dominated by perpetual warfare between America and a host of Third World guerrillas. Its central character is Louis Sacchetti, an imprisoned poet and conscientious objector, who becomes the subject of a bizarre experiment to raise IQ, one of whose side-effects involves rapid physical deterioration. The book is a sustained meditation on the relationship between mortality and the Faustian will-to-power; alluding to Shakespeare, Rilke, *Joyce, and a host of other writers, its concerns are essentially metaphysical, though it never loses sight of the contemporary political situation. In similar fashion, *On Wings of Song* (1979) deals with the tension between Christian fundamentalism and artificially induced out-of-the-body experiences; its ending is a sombre and harrowing evocation of the gap between quotidian life and spiritual yearning. Disch concentrates not on heroes but on the forgotten victims of social control. *The Priest: A Gothic Romance* (1995), a long and sustained critique of the Catholic Church, continues the effort to expand his thematic range. Formally innovative and often densely written, his books challenge our preconceptions about the limitations of the science fiction genre.

Discourse is a word with three very different meanings in current critical and theoretical usage. First, it is a name for the flow of language, particularly dialogue and spoken language, in specific, practical situations. Discourse analysis attends to the structures and strategies by which we organize even our apparently unorganized verbal exchanges—interviews, for example, or gossip, or the succeeding speeches at a political rally. The second meaning of discourse arises chiefly from the work of the French theorist and intellectual historian Michel Foucault (1926–84), whose major works are *Madness and Civilization* (1961), *The Order of Things* (1966), *The Archaeology of Knowledge* (1969), *Discipline and Punish* (1975), and *The History of Sexuality* (1976, 1984). Foucault uses the term 'discourse' to indicate large-scale signifying practices, sometimes called discursive formations, that is, any historically identifiable pattern of verbal and non-verbal behaviour which transmits sets of propositions and implications. The discourse of medicine, for example, includes doctors' handwriting and nurses' uniforms, as well as the language of diagnosis and care. The discourse of the classroom includes the tone and manner of the teacher as well as what he or she says. Such discourses for Foucault are characteristically political: concerned with relations of power. Thus prison architecture and clinical definitions of madness are reflections of a culture's habits of social control, mirrors and instruments of its assumptions about normality and deviance. Finally, discourse is used to translate the Russian *sjuzet* (and the French *récit*), meaning the narrative arrangement of events in a story, as distinct from the events themselves prior to or outside the arrangement. (See PLOT.)

DISKI, Jenny (1947–), British novelist of Jewish descent, born in London. After being in institutional care when she was 14, she lived for four years with the novelist Doris *Lessing. In her early years she spent periods in psychiatric hospitals but subsequently trained as a teacher, and taught for five years before studying anthropology as a mature student. Her first novel, *Nothing Natural* (1986), a disturbing study of a sado-masochistic relationship, was followed by *Rainforest* (1987), in which a woman anthropologist journeys to the Malayan jungle in order to discover that civilization is only skin deep. The novel displayed her interest in the darker areas of the human psyche, which is also evident in her next novel, *Like Mother* (1989), a dialogue between a woman and her anencephalic baby. *Then Again* (1990) explores the Jewish past through the consciousness of Esther, an artist specializing in ceramics, and her disturbed teenage daughter. *Happily Ever After* (1991) concerns the love affair between Liam, a married, middle-aged alcoholic, and Daphne, an elderly woman who lives in the same building. As with all Diski's work, the novel explores the borderline between sanity and madness as well as the extremes of cruelty of which people are capable.

Dissociation of Sensibility, a term originated by T. S. *Eliot in his essay 'The Metaphysical Poets', which first appeared in 1921 as a review of H. J. C. *Grierson's edition of *Metaphysical Lyrics and Poems of the Seventeenth Century* (1921). Eliot's approval of the poetry of Donne and others, which was of considerable influence in establishing the high regard in which their work has since been held, emphasized their possession of 'a mechanism of sensibility which could devour any kind of experience'; the 'direct sensuous apprehension of thought' and the 're-creation of thought into feeling' characterizing the work of the Metaphysical Poets were lost in the course of the seventeenth century, when 'a dissociation of sensibility set in, from which we have never recovered'. As an example of the consequences, Eliot notes that 'Tennyson and Browning are poets, and they think; but they do not feel their thought as immediately as the odour of a rose'. The theory of dissociation of sensibility provoked much discussion and has been challenged as a misleadingly simple analysis of historical developments in English poetry; the phrase is, however, strongly indicative of the desire shared by Eliot, Ezra *Pound, and others to move beyond the debilitated conventions of the nineteenth century and establish a poetry capable of unifying a range of aesthetic, intellectual, and philosophical elements. Within the immediate context of the essay of 1921, Eliot's observations on the dissociation of sensibility and the limitations it imposes relate to his defence of a measure of obscurity in poetry: modern civilization's 'great variety and complexity . . . playing upon a refined sensibility, must produce various and complex results'; his own work of the period achieved such results in presenting unsettling and disjunctive emotional and mental states with the conviction of 'direct sensuous apprehension' he commended in the poets of the early seventeenth century.

DOBB, Maurice Herbert (1900–76), British economist and eminent Marxist scholar, educated at Pembroke College, Cambridge, and the London School of Economics, subsequently Fellow of Trinity College, Cambridge. Among his many books and articles, two stand out. The first is *Political Economy and Capitalism* (1937) which the obituary writer for the British Academy claimed marked 'the emergence of Marxist economics as a really serious economic discipline'. The second, *Studies in the Development of Capitalism* (1947), is an account of the transition from feudalism to capitalism in Western Europe. Dobb was a strong supporter of labour education, writing many pamphlets for the Workers' Education Association, and was active in British Communist Party circles between the wars. Towards the end of his life, he published a short and accessible book on the history of economic thought: *Theories of Value and Distribution since Adam Smith* (1973). In 1978 the *Cambridge Journal of Economics* published a memorial issue devoted to Dobb's life and work.

DOBSON, Rosemary (1920–), Australian poet, born in Sydney; she studied art at the University of Sydney. She spent some time in England and Europe where she became deeply interested in Greek antiquities and Italian paintings. Many of her poems first appeared in **Bulletin*, including the title poem of *The Ship of Ice* (1948) in which she reflects upon the timeless quality of art and its ability to capture moments suspended in time. These themes recur in much of her work, notably in 'Still Life', 'Young Girl in a Window', and in the title poem of *In a Convex Mirror* (1944). In *Child with a Cockatoo* (1955) and *Cock Crow* (1965) she introduces more personal themes. Her finely crafted poems display a cool lyricism and are frequently concerned with the processes and effects of art and the role of the artist. *Greek Coins* (1977) was inspired by the culture of ancient Greece, and *Over the Frontier* (1978) includes a series of poems celebrating the Greek traveller Pausanias. Her other collections include *Selected Poems* (1973; revised 1980), *The Three Fates* (1984), *Collected Poems* (1991), and *Untold Lives* (1992). She has also translated collections of Russian poetry, including *Seven Russian Poets* (1978; with David *Campbell), and has edited several anthologies including *Australian Voices* (1975) and *Sisters Poets* (1979).

DOCTOROW, E(dgar) L(awrence) (1931–), American novelist, born in New York, educated at Kenyon College and Columbia University. After working as a screenplay reader for Columbia Pictures, he wrote *Welcome to Hard Times* (1960; UK title *Bad Man From Bodie*, 1961) which examines the illusory foundations of the American myth of progress through the conventions of the Western. There followed the appearance of *Big as Life* (1966), a science fiction satire set in New York, and *The Book of Daniel* (1971), a fictional investigation of the impact of the Rosenberg trial on the children of the couple and employing that historical moment to study the traditions of the political left in America through the McCarthyite period to the 1960s. His major success came with *Ragtime* (1975), the story of Coalhouse Walker and his ever-escalating struggle against racism and injustice. Based on Kleist's Kolhaus legend, the novel examines the relationship of past and present by blending historical figures like Emma Goldman, Freud, Jung, and Ford, and fictional invention into a fast-moving and incisive narrative which moves to an explosive conclusion (see NEW JOURNALISM). He has continued to use this formula to considerable effect in later works, which include *Loon Lake* (1980), a novel about economic and political injustice in a searing portrait of the USA in the Depression, *World's Fair* (1985), *Billy Bathgate* (1988), and *The Waterworks* (1994). His other work includes the play *Drinks Before Dinner* (1979); the screenplay *Daniel* (1983); *Lives of the Poet, Six Stories and a Novella* (1984), which reflects upon the dual position of the writer as observer and participant in society; and *Poets and Presidents: Selected Essays 1977–1992* (1994).

Dodsworth, a novel by Sinclair *Lewis, published in 1929, dramatized by the author and Sidney Howard in 1934. A successful car manufacturer from the Midwestern city of Zenith, Samuel Dodsworth is unhappily married to Fran, a frivolous and pretentious snob. The pair visit Europe where Fran indulges in several flirtations, with an Englishman, Major Clyde Lockert, and in Paris with Arnold Israel. Fed up with this life of indulgence, Sam returns alone to America, but fearful of Fran's safety, rejoins her in Europe. Fran then falls in love with a German aristocrat, Kurt von Obersdorf. With an impending divorce, Sam wanders aimlessly in Europe and meets Edith Cortright, a mature

American widow who provides Sam with the companionship and intellectual stimulation he is seeking. Their marriage plans are interrupted when Fran's relationship is thwarted by Kurt's mother, and Sam is persuaded to return to America with his wife. However, recognizing that life with Fran will be intolerable, Sam notifies Edith that he will return to her on the next ship. The novel presents the familiar pattern of Lewis's fiction, wherein somebody glimpses a dream beyond the trivial actualities and stifling customs of daily life, and tries to make it real, with varying degrees of success.

DOERR, Harriet (1910–), American novelist, born in Pasadena, California. She resumed a discontinued education late in life, receiving a BA in history from Stanford University in 1977. Her first novel was the highly acclaimed and prize-winning *Stones for Ibarra* (1984); set in Mexico, which Doerr knows well, the novel tells the story of a couple's encounter with Latin American culture. The novel, which has been compared with the fiction of Marquez and K. A. *Porter, is actually composed of linked stories, several of which adopt Mexican perspectives. *Consider This, Señora* (1994) similarly treats expatriates in Mexico; delicately lyrical, the novel is, however, more sustained and compelling than Doerr's first, guaranteeing her a place in America's expatriate tradition.

DOMINIC, R. B., see LATHEN, EMMA.

DONLEAVY, J(ames) P(atrick) (1926–), Irish novelist and playwright, born in America. His literary reputation rests to a large extent on his first novel, *The Ginger Man* (1955), which was first published in Paris by the Olympia Press, well known as publishers of erotica. An expurgated version was published in New York in 1958 and a 'complete and unexpurgated' edition in 1965, also in New York. The novel describes the adventures of Sebastian Dangerfield, an American, ostensibly studying law at Trinity College, Dublin. He is, as the narrative makes clear, a lazy, lying, sponging philanderer, with a genius for getting himself out of impossibly difficult situations; his behaviour to everyone—wife, friend, mistresses, landlords, and shopkeepers—is outrageous, and he is particularly adept at exploiting women, financially and sexually. The action is seen from Dangerfield's point of view. Donleavy's prose has reminded some of *Joyce, especially in its loving evocation of Dublin and in its sexually frank language. Donleavy's first play, *Fairy Tales of New York*, opened in London in 1960. It consists of four loosely connected episodes in which a young man, Cornelius Christian, is involved in a bizarre situation, and may be considered an example of Theatre of the *Absurd. After beginning with such distinction, Donleavy's subsequent work has been perhaps less successful. The comic magic of *The Ginger Man* has proved unrepeatable. His other novels include *A Singular Man* (1961); *The Saddest Summer of Samuel S* (1966); *The Onion Eaters* (1971); *Shultz* (1980); *Leila* (1983); *Are You Listening, Rabbi Low?* (1987); and *That Darcy, That Dancer, That Gentleman* (1991). He has also published a collection of short stories, *Meet My Maker, the Mad Molecule* (1964). He has adapted a number of his novels, including *The Ginger Man*, for the stage. A love of Ireland is apparent in his work and in 1967 he became an Irish citizen. *The History of the Ginger Man* (1994) is chiefly a memoir of post-war Dublin, about the people and circumstances surrounding the making of the *Ginger Man*.

DOOLITTLE, Hilda (1886–1961), American poet (who wrote as 'H.D.'), the daughter of a professor of mathematics, born in Bethlehem, Pennsylvania, and educated at Bryn Mawr College. As a student she was closely associated with Marianne *Moore, W. C. *Williams, and Ezra *Pound, to whom she was briefly engaged and of whom she writes extensively in the autobiographical *End to Torment* (written in 1958, but not published until 1979). While holidaying in Europe in 1911 she met Pound in London, who styled her 'H.D.' when introducing her work to **Poetry*, Chicago, in 1912. She joined with Pound, *Flint, and *Aldington, whom she married in 1913 and separated from in 1919, to form the core of the *Imagist group. Her first collection of poems, *Sea Garden* (1916), is notable for the precision and clarity of its imagery, often derived from maritime settings, and for the slender, finely cadenced verse forms which remain characteristic of her poetry. *Hymen* (1921) and *Heliodora* (1924) followed, containing poems still identifiable as Imagist while initiating the engagement with classical mythology and the hieratic tone which are conspicuous features of her later work. Subsequent volumes include *Red Roses for Bronze* (1929) and *Helen in Egypt* (1961), the latter a lengthy and ambitious narrative also employing prose. *The Walls Do not Fall* (1944), *Tribute to the Angels* (1945), and *The Flowering of the Rod* (1946) were collected as *Trilogy* in 1973; this constitutes her most remarkable work, combining her experiences of wartime London and her intense imaginative involvement with ancient Egyptian and Judaeo-Christian myth and mysticism. An edition of her *Collected Poems* appeared in 1984. Among her novels are *Hedylus* (1928) and *Bid Me to Live* (1960), a *roman-à-clef* concerning her involvement with the *Bloomsbury circle during the years of the First World War; *Hermione* (1981) collects three stories on lesbian themes which she chose not to publish in her lifetime. Barbara Guest's *Herself Defined: The Poet H. D. and Her World* was published in 1984.

DORN, Ed(ward) (1929–), American poet, born in Villa Grove, Illinois, educated at the University of Illinois. Dorn's childhood in the Great Depression was marked by the transient migrant life of his impoverished mother and stepfather. He became disaffected from the orthodoxies of the state educational system, and went to *Black Mountain College, North Carolina, where he came under the influence of Charles *Olson, whose *A Bibliography on America for Ed Dorn* (1964) was written in response to Dorn's request for guidance in studying the American West. A wanderer by temperament, Dorn has taught at several universities in the USA and abroad. His first poems were published in the *Black Mountain Review*; his volumes of poems include *From Gloucester Out* (1964), *Geography* (1965, revised 1968), *The North Atlantic Turbine* (1967), *The Collected Poems 1956–1974* (1975; enlarged 1983), and *Abhorrences* (1990). He has published translations of Latin American poets, and Native American poets. His major prose works are *What I See in The Maximus Poems* (1960), a critical tribute to Charles Olson; *The Rites of Passage* (1965 and 1971; alternately issued as *By the Sound*), and *The Shoshoneans: The People of the Basin-Plateau* (1966). Dorn is a political poet, fiercely desiring the democracy that he finds lacking in the capitalist orthodoxy of American political and social institutions. He cherishes the Native Americans and their ancient culture, and mourns the loss of their ancestral lands. His *Gunslinger* (Parts 1 and 2, 1968–9; complete version, 1975) is an abrasive, witty grotesquery, mocking the myth of the West.

DORRIS, Michael A(nthony) (1945–), Native American novelist, critic, and anthropologist of the Modoc Tribe, born in Dayton, Washington, educated at Georgetown University and Yale; in 1983 he was appointed professor of Native American Studies at Dartmouth. In 1971 Dorris became the first unmarried man to adopt a child; the story of his son's life is juxtaposed with an account of the physical, mental, and social devastation caused by alcohol abuse in Native American communities in *The Broken Cord: A Family's Ongoing Struggle with Fetal Alcohol Syndrome* (1989). His first novel, *A Yellow Raft in Blue Water* (1987), deals with the lives of three generations of Native American women and explores the family tensions and social upheavals of the transition from reservation to urban living. Dorris has collaborated with his wife, Louise *Erdrich, and his first novel shares Erdrich's use of multiple narrators each of whom tells their story in their own idiomatic style. *The Crown of Columbus* (1991), the first novel to appear under both names, is a mystery thriller which follows the quest for Christopher Columbus's lost diary and his mythical crown. Among his other works are *Native Americans: 500 Years After* (1975), *A Guide to Research in Native American Studies* (1984), *Paper Trail: Essays* (1994), and the children's book *Morning Girl* (1992). See also NATIVE AMERICAN LITERATURE.

DOS PASSOS, John (Roderigo) (1896–1970), American novelist, poet, and playwright, born in Chicago, educated at Harvard. He contributed to various magazines whilst at Harvard, some of his college verse being published later in *Eight Harvard Poets* (1917). His father sought to prevent him from joining an American ambulance unit in 1916 by financing a year of architectural study in Spain, yet he enlisted in the famous Norton-Harjes ambulance unit and later served in Italy and France. These experiences became the basis of his first novel *One Man's Initiation – 1917* (1920; reissued as *First Encounter*, 1945). The war also provided the starting point for his second work, *Three Soldiers* (1921), which concerned the bureaucratic effects of warfare on the lives of three very different young men. After the war he became a freelance journalist, travelling extensively in Europe, the Near East, and Russia in the 1920s, as well as writing poetry (*A Pushcart at the Curb*, 1922) and critical essays on Spanish culture (*Rosinante to the Road Again*, 1922). He then produced *Streets of Night* (1923) and the novel that marked the beginning of the period of his major achievements, **Manhattan Transfer* (1925). During the next five years he became increasingly political, protesting at the Sacco and Vanzetti trial of 1927 in *Facing the Chair* (1927), and participating on the Dreiser committee which investigated the virtual state of civil war which surrounded the famous miners' strike in Harlan County, Tennessee, in 1931. He joined the executive board of the magazine the *New *Masses* in 1926, and was a writer for The New Playwrights' Theatre. He produced several plays, all demonstrating an acutely politicized consciousness, three of which were published as *Three Plays* (1934): *The Garbage Man* (1926), about a typical New York couple; *Airways Inc.* (1928), about corporate business and a building trades dispute; and *Fortune Heights* (1933), about the rise and fall of estate development. Further travel writings appeared, amongst them *Orient Express* (1927) and *In All Countries* (1934). Throughout his life he maintained a career as a novelist, playwright, and political reporter, though his major literary effort went into writing **U.S.A.* (1938), a trilogy which comprised *The 42nd Parallel* (1930), *1919* (1932), and *The Big Money* (1936). The trilogy *District of Columbia* (1952) is an examination of the political motivations of the New Deal and the Second World War, made up of *The Adventures of a Young Man* (1939), about Glenn Spotswood, a naïve communist who falls foul of the Party; *Number One* (1943), about Glenn's brother, Tyler; and *The Grand Design* (1949), about the boys' father. The first of these was the first real sign of a complete break with the left in the USA. There followed further fictional works, including *The Prospect Before Us* (1950); *Chosen Country* (1951); *Most Likely To Succeed* (1954), a satire on bohemians and socialists in the 1920s and 1930s; *The Great Days* (1958); and *Midcentury* (1961), a novel which takes the devices of *U.S.A.* and puts them to work in a defence of a battery of conservative values. As well as this considerable production of large novels, he also wrote reportage and critical essays about politics and culture, amongst which are *The Villages Are the Heart of Spain* (1937), *Journeys between Wars* (1938), *Tour of Duty* (1946), and *Brazil on the Move* (1963). However, the works for which he became most famous in the 1950s and 1960s were his historical studies relating to the problems of US democracy, including a series of biographies in *The Ground We Stand on* (1941) and *Prospects of a Golden Age* (1959), essays on early American leaders in *The Men Who Made the Nation* (1957), with other books including *Mr Wilson's War* (1963), and *The Shackles of Power* (1966) about the Jeffersonian era. In 1973, a volume of selections from his letters and diaries appeared under the title of *The Fourteenth Chronicle*.

DOUGHTY, Charles Montagu (1843–1926), British travel writer and poet, born in Suffolk; he studied geology at Caius College, Cambridge. In 1870 he began travelling in Europe, North Africa, and the Middle East; after a year in Damascus learning Arabic, he joined a pilgrimage to Mecca in 1876, undergoing much hardship before his journey concluded at Jedda in 1878. His experiences were recorded in *Travels in Arabia Deserta* (1888); apart from its topographical and anthropological interest, the work is remarkable for Doughty's cultivation of a richly poetic idiom based on the language of Chaucer and Spenser with additional elements derived from Arabic usage. D. H. *Lawrence, who wrote the introduction to the 1921 edition, and D. G. *Hogarth were among those on whom it made a deep impression. The book, in which Doughty terms himself a 'wandering anchorite in the fable of human life', anticipates the metaphysical preoccupations of his idiosyncratically ambitious poetry. *The Dawn in Britain* (six volumes, 1906–7), his best-known poem, forms a mythical allegory of national destiny. His verse also includes *Adam Cast Forth* (1908), a recasting of Biblical material, and *Mansoul* (1920), a mystical envisioning of man's quest to unite Heaven and Earth. Hogarth's biography of Doughty appeared in 1928.

DOUGLAS, Lord Alfred (Bruce) (1870–1945), British poet, born near Worcester, educated at Winchester and at Magdalen College, Oxford. In 1891 he was introduced to Oscar Wilde by Lionel Johnson. Douglas's father, the Marquis of Queensbury, disapproved of the relationship which developed and precipitated the sequence of events leading to Wilde's imprisonment in 1895. Douglas's translation from the original French of Wilde's *Salome* appeared with illustrations by Aubrey Beardsley in 1894. *Poems* (1896), his first collection of verse, was published in Paris. Subsequent volumes include *The City of the Soul* (1899), *In Excelsis* (1924), and *Sonnets and Lyrics* (1935). His work as a poet is highly conventional and often undistinguished. In addition to the lyrical and elegiac modes which predominate, he produced a substantial body of light verse. The sonnets he wrote in 1897 at his villa near Naples, where Wilde joined him following his release from prison, are his finest work. He edited the *Academy* from 1907 to 1910 and was jailed for a libel against W. S. *Churchill in 1923. His uncharitable view of Wilde in *Oscar Wilde and Myself* (1914) was largely retracted in *Oscar Wilde: A Summing Up* (1940). His self-revealing *Autobiography* appeared in 1929. *Bernard Shaw and Alfred Douglas: A Correspondence* (ed. Mary Hyde, 1982) covers the period 1931 to 1945. Biographies include *Lord Alfred Douglas* (1984) by H. Montgomery Hyde.

DOUGLAS, Ellen, pseudonym of Josephine HAXTON (1921–), American novelist, born in Mississippi, where she has spent most of her life. Her constant themes are the position of women and the relationship between black and white, using her considerable powers of observation of life in Mississippi to come to more universal conclusions. Her first novel, *A Family's Affairs* (1962), drawing on her own family, was followed by a volume of related novellas and stories, *Black Cloud, White Cloud* (1963). Subsequent books include *Apostles of Light* (1973) and *Where the Dreams Cross* (1986). *The Rock Cried Out* (1979) presents the South in the context of the Civil Rights period and relates it to the wider USA in the throes of the Vietnam War. *A Lifetime Burning* (1982) is a novel in the form of a journal, which shows the break-up of the narrator's marriage. The culmination of Douglas's honest and scrutinizing fiction must be *Can't Quit You, Baby* (1988), a novel about two women, one white, prosperous, protected (and also self-protecting), the other her black servant, a far more turbulent and emotionally honest person. Douglas has a deep interest in fairy-tale, and has also retold classic tales to illustrations by the visionary Mississippi artist Walter Anderson in *The Magic Carpet and Other Tales* (1987).

DOUGLAS, George, see BROWN, GEORGE DOUGLAS.

DOUGLAS, Keith (Castellain) (1920–44), British poet, born at Tunbridge Wells, Kent; he began writing poems at the age of ten. He was educated at Merton College, Oxford, where Edmund *Blunden was his tutor. From 1937 onwards his work appeared in a variety of periodicals, including Geoffrey Grigson's **New Verse*. He was posted to the Middle East in 1941 and became a tank commander in the North African Campaign, during which much of his finest poetry was written. He was killed soon after taking part in the D-Day landings in Normandy. *Alamein to Zem Zem*, his vividly documentary prose account of warfare in the desert, was published in 1946. The only volume of his poetry to appear in his lifetime was *Selected Poems* of 1943. His experiences of active service and wartime Cairo are presented through imagery of incisive clarity and a concentrated plainness of diction. The sometimes ruthlessly unsentimental quality of his work is intrinsic to the candour and detachment that are characteristics of his achievement. Although a *Collected Poems* was published in 1951, edited by G. S. *Fraser and J. Waller, interest in Douglas's poetry was comparatively slight until Ted *Hughes's selected edition of his work in 1964. Desmond Graham, whose biography *Keith Douglas: 1920–1944* appeared in 1973, produced a *Complete Poems* in 1979 and a miscellany of Douglas's prose in 1985. See also WAR POETRY.

DOUGLAS, (George) Norman (1868–1952), British travel writer and novelist, born at Thüringen in the Vorarlberg, Austria, a region he describes in the autobiographical *Together* (1923), educated at Uppingham School, which he found uncongenial, and Karlsruhe Gymnasium. Following a period in the British Foreign Service, from 1898 onward he lived chiefly in Capri and Florence. Between 1910 and 1916 he was in

London and spent three years as an associate editor of the *English Review*, becoming closely acquainted with D. H. *Lawrence—who based James Argyle in **Aaron's Rod* (1922) on Douglas—and with Joseph *Conrad and other notable writers of the day. *Siren Land* (1911), a vivid, erudite, and informative evocation of Capri and Sorrento, rapidly gained him a reputation that was enhanced by *Fountains in the Sand* (1912), on his experiences of Tunisia, and *Old Calabria* (1915), the account of Southern Italy that is sometimes regarded as his masterpiece. Prompted by Conrad, he wrote **South Wind* (1917), his first novel; the more formally structured narratives of *They Went* (1920) and *In the Beginning* (1927) lacked the attractive vitality of *South Wind* and by 1930 he had ceased writing fiction. His later works, which sustain the elegance, wit, and urbanity characteristic of his writing, include *Summer Islands* (1931), on Ischia and Ponza, and the autobiographies *Looking Back* (two volumes, 1933) and *Late Harvest* (1946). Among his numerous *jeux d'esprit* are *Some Limericks* (1928), originally published privately, and *Venus in the Kitchen* (1952), a selection of aphrodisiac recipes. Mark Holloway's *Douglas: A Biography* appeared in 1976.

DOVE, Rita (1952–), American poet, born in Akron, Ohio, educated at Miami University in Oxford, Ohio, the University of Tübingen in Germany, and the University of Iowa where she studied at the *Iowa Writers' Workshop. A professor of English at Arizona State University, Rita Dove won the Pulitzer Prize for Poetry in 1987 for her volume *Thomas and Beulah: Poems* (1986), an extended sequence of poems describing the lives of her grandparents. At 34 she was one of the youngest ever recipients of the prize and only the second African-American writer to win it. Her verse is characterized by both its lyric and narrative qualities, the latter being particularly evident in *Thomas and Beulah* which recounts the story of a black couple's life in the industrial Midwest in the first half of the twentieth century; the volume addresses one of Dove's persistent themes, that of displacement, or what Dove herself refers to as the sense of living in 'two different worlds, seeing things with double vision'. Her single most well-known poem, arguably, is 'Parsley' which is based on a massacre perpetrated by Rafael Trujillo in the Dominican Republic in 1957. Her other volumes of verse include *Ten Poems* (1977), *The Yellow House on the Corner* (1980), *Museum* (1983), *Grace Notes* (1991), and *Selected Poems* (1993). *Fifth Sunday: Stories* appeared in 1985 and was reprinted in 1990, while *Through the Ivory Gate* (1992) is a novel and *The Darker Face of the Earth* (1994) a play in verse. Rita Dove was named US poet laureate for the year 1993–4. Two valuable interviews with Dove in which she discusses her work are to be found in *Black American Literature Forum* (Fall 1986) and *Gargoyle* (1985).

Down and Out in Paris and London, an autobiographical work by George *Orwell, published in 1933. *Down and Out* was Orwell's first book, and its mixture of autobiographical insight, social criticism, and descriptive bravura make it an early index of the way his *œuvre* was to pull in a number of directions. The reflective asides on the social position of the Paris *plongeur* and of the British tramp are easily detached from a vigorous narrative of events, with occasional passages of dialogue that would not be out of place in a novel. At the centre of each of the two parts of the text is an appreciation of Orwell's companionship, first with Boris the Russian waiter, and then with Paddy the Irish tramp. In some ways the book is a study of the importance of friendship during Orwell's attempt to test his own endurance of harsh conditions. The characterization of Boris is particularly enthusiastic and Orwell's absorption in it is partly what turns the Parisian narrative into an account of an adventure rather than a pretext for social analysis. The London narrative has more campaigning purpose behind it and shows its author beginning to make inquiries about social structures and power relations in a manner that was to give his later projects their peculiar Orwellian stamp.

DOYLE, Sir Arthur Conan (1859–1930), British writer of *detective and historical fiction, of Irish descent, born in Edinburgh, educated at Stonyhurst and the University of Edinburgh, where he studied medicine. After a brief and unsatisfactory medical partnership with a friend in Plymouth—*The Stark–Munro Letters* (1895) gives a fictionalized account of the episode—he practised in Southsea from 1882 to 1890, and later served as an army physician during the Boer War, writing a history of the campaign (*The Great Boer War*, 1900) and an influential pamphlet 'The War in South Africa', which was much translated. He married Louise Hawkins (d. 1906) in 1885, and Jean Leckie, who survived him, in 1907. In the novel *A Study in Scarlet* (1888) he introduced the private detective Sherlock Holmes and his impercipient friend Dr Watson, the narrator in most of the stories, and with whom he resides at 221B Baker Street; the other Sherlock Holmes novels are *The Sign of Four* (1890), *The Hound of the Baskervilles* (1902), and *The Valley of Fear* (1914). Doyle's immense popularity, however, stemmed from the Sherlock Holmes short stories, published mainly in the *Strand Magazine*, where the first, 'A Scandal in Bohemia', appeared in 1891. Tiring of the character, he wrote of Holmes's death in 'The Final Problem' (1893), but vehement public protest forced a resurrection in 'The Empty House' (1903). The stories are collected in *The Adventures of Sherlock Holmes* (1892), *The Memoirs of Sherlock Holmes* (1894), *The Return of Sherlock Holmes* (1905), *His Last Bow: Some Reminiscences of Sherlock Holmes* (1917), and *The Case-Book of Sherlock Holmes* (1927). Undoubtedly the best-known and perhaps, too, the best of all fictional detectives, whose influence on later writers is demonstrated by such figures as *Freeman's Dr Thorndyke, or *Christie's Poirot, Holmes owes something to his predecessors, Poe's Dupin and Emile Gaboriau's Lecoq, while his deductive method is partly borrowed from Doyle's teacher at Edinburgh, Dr Joseph

Bell. There are over a hundred Sherlock Holmes films, the best-known being those of the 1940s with Basil Rathbone as the detective, a number of plays, two written by Doyle himself, and many radio and television adaptations. Doyle, however, set greater store by his historical fiction, which combines exciting adventure with carefully researched detail. The best works are *The White Company* (1891) and its successor, *Sir Nigel* (1906), set in the fourteenth century; *Rodney Stone* (1896), with a Regency prize-fighting background; and the light-hearted stories of a cavalry officer in Napoleon's army, *The Exploits of Brigadier Gerard* (1896). Also worthy of mention is *The Lost World* (1912), the first of a series of stories dominated by Professor Challenger. Doyle wrote many books on public themes, including a long history of the Flanders campaign in the First World War (6 volumes, 1916–19). His one-act play *Waterloo* provided Sir Henry Irving in 1894 with one of his most successful parts. In 1926 he published his *History of Spiritualism*, one of many books he wrote on the subject, in which he was greatly interested. His efforts to right miscarriages of justice resulted in the release of George Edalji in 1906 and of Oscar Slater in 1927, both wrongfully imprisoned. He published accounts of both cases. See lives by H. Pearson (1943), J. D. Carr (1949), and J. Symons (1979); and H. Keating, *Sherlock Holmes: The Man and His World* (1979).

DOYLE, Mike (1928–), poet, an Irishman born in Birmingham, and educated at Victoria University College, British Columbia, the University of New Zealand, and Auckland University; he served in the Royal Navy in 1945–54. For many years he was Associate Professor of English at the University of Victoria, British Columbia (and, prior to 1970, published under his original name, Charles Doyle). His first poetry collection, *A Splinter of Glass: Poems 1951–55* (1956), was published in New Zealand, where Doyle also worked with leading poets. He edited *Recent Poetry in New Zealand* (1965), which he intended as a 'work in progress' from younger writers rather than as an authoritative canon; to some extent the volume offered a deliberate alternative to the 1960 anthology by Allen *Curnow. Doyle's own approach to poetry is deceptively open, with his technical skills often concealed by an engagingly laconic familiarity and irreverence: 'A poet, if he can, should avoid too much literature. Like the verse of habit, it impedes observation.' *Stonedancer* (1976) is an impressive collection which also includes poems from previous volumes. Later works include *Steady Hand* (1982), *The Urge to Raise Hats* (1989), *Separate Fidelities* (1991), and *Intimate Absences: Selected Poems* (1993). He has also written studies of New Zealand poets R. A. K. *Mason (1970) and James K. *Baxter (1976), of William Carlos *Williams (1982), and a biography of Richard *Aldington (1989).

DOYLE, Roddy (1958–), Irish novelist and playwright, born in Dublin, educated at University College, Dublin. He became a teacher at Greendale Community School, Dublin, in 1980. Like his contemporary, Dermot *Bolger, Doyle is concerned with the people who live on the housing estates of north Dublin. However, his work differs from that of the more surreal Bolger in approaching its subject with a vibrant humour and gentleness which belie the 'honest language' and anarchic impulses of Doyle's highly memorable characters. His plays, such as *Brownbread* (1987) and *War* (1989), and his 'Barrytown' novels, *The Commitments* (1987) and *The Snapper* (1989) are, in essence, series of loud and fast conversations. His highly acclaimed novel *The Van* (1991), which continues the saga of the Rabbitt family begun in his first two novels, portrays the soccer madness which hit Dublin during Italia '90. All three novels were published as *The Barrytown Trilogy* in 1992. There are film versions of *The Commitments* (by Alan Parker) and *The Snapper* (directed by Stephen Frears). Doyle received the Booker Prize for *Paddy Clarke Ha Ha Ha* (1993); set in Dublin in 1968, the novel conveys the exuberance and bewilderment of its 10-year-old narrator and his estimation of his parents' floundering marriage. Doyle recreates the rhythm and langauge of childhood, together with the strange logic produced by a child's avid quest for information but partial understanding of the world. *The Woman Who Walked Into Doors* appeared in 1996.

DRABBLE, Margaret (1939–), British novelist, born in Sheffield, educated at The Mount School, York and Newnham College, Cambridge. She has lectured at home and abroad for the Arts Council and the British Council. Drabble's novels are traditional in form, displaying the author's allegiance to the *Realist tradition of George Eliot and Arnold *Bennett (of whom she published a biography in 1974), although latterly a note of ironic distance between the author and characters has become apparent. The early books, in which the protagonist is usually an educated and articulate young woman, often deal with the conflict between career and family life. These include *A Summer Birdcage* (1963), describing the sexual and intellectual rivalry between the protagonist, an Oxford graduate, and her elder sister; *The Garrick Year* (1965), which deals with the sexual intrigues of a group of actors in a small provincial town; *The Millstone* (1966), about the traumas undergone by a young academic who becomes pregnant after a casual sexual encounter; *Jerusalem the Golden* (1968), an early treatment of the North and South theme; and *The Waterfall* (1969), which describes the affair between a poet and her best friend's husband. Similar themes are explored in *The Needle's Eye* (1972), *The Realms of Gold* (1975), *The Ice Age* (1977), and *The Middle Ground* (1980). The later works are wider in scope, reflecting the writer's interest in the social upheavals of the post-war era. A trilogy (*The Radiant Way*, 1987; *A Natural Curiosity*, 1989; *The Gates of Ivory*, 1991) opens on New Year's Eve 1979 and follows its three main characters, Liz Headleand, Alix Bowen, and Esther Breuer, through the following ten years, touching on questions of social responsibility, the polarization of rich and poor, and the role of the educated middle class in contemporary Britain, as well as on universal themes such as the nature of genocide. Drabble's other works include a study of William Wordsworth (1966), *A Writer's Britain* (1979) and a biography of Angus *Wilson (1995). She also edited the fifth edition of *The Oxford Companion to English Literature* (1985). She married the actor Clive Swift in 1960. Her second husband is the biographer Michael *Holroyd. Her sister is the novelist A. S. *Byatt. Margaret Drabble was awarded the CBE in 1980.

Dream Songs, The, a body of 385 poems by John *Berryman, initially published as *77 Dream Songs* (1964) and *His Toy, His Dream, His Rest: 308 Dream Songs* (1968) and collected as *The Dream Songs* in 1969. Each poem consists of three six-line stanzas which make variable use of rhyme and employ a wide range of rhythmic effects. The sequence relies for its continuity on the presence of 'Henry', generally regarded as a quasi-autobiographical persona; pronominally referred to as 'I', 'you', or 'he', and frequently addressed by an anonymous interlocutor as 'Mr Bones', Henry provides *The Dream Songs* with their shifting centre, the basis for the poems' astonishingly fluid variations in tone and levels of discourse. Harshly demotic idioms are interchangeable, sometimes within the space of single poems, with baroquely erudite or urbanely conversational modes; the accumulating dramatic commentaries on himself and his times amount to Berryman's verbal mapping of the cultural, social, and existential contexts he inhabits. The tragic seriousness of which the work is capable is generally relieved by the play of his objectifying intelligence and remarkable wit, most pronounced in the blackly humorous 'Op. posth.' sections.

DREISER, Theodore (Herman Albert) (1871–1945), American novelist, born in Terre Haute, Indiana, into an impoverished Catholic family. Despite a largely negative and irregular pattern of formal education, he became a journalist for newspapers in St Louis, Chicago, Pittsburgh, and New York. He drew frequently on the social and economic vicissitudes of his own large family for the material of his early novels, and his powers of keen observation gave his fiction a vivid sense of accuracy and detail. Impressed by Herbert Spencer's writings on evolution, and inspired by the literary works of Balzac, Tolstoy, Zola, and *Hardy, his fiction arose from specific domestic situations in the context of precisely visualized social and economic circumstances. His first novel, **Sister Carrie* (1900), portrays the transformation of a poor working girl into a successful New York actress. Doubleday were reluctant to promote the novel because of the amoral behaviour of the heroine, and initially only 900 copies were sold. Public denunciations of the novel pushed Dreiser towards a breakdown, and he worked as an editor for magazines before completing his second novel **Jennie Gerhardt* (1991), which was given a similarly disapproving reception. Over the next fifteen years, however, he was to write the bulk of the work on which his considerable reputation rests. *The Financier* (1912) and *The Titan* (1914) were the first two volumes of a trilogy ultimately completed by the posthumous publication of *The Stoic* (1947). In these novels the unscrupulous tycoon Frank Cowperwood is subjected to a minute analysis deriving from Dreiser's fascination with extreme wealth and the vested interests which control it. *An *American Tragedy* (1925) shows the other pole within his work, namely his concern for the condition of the deprived. *The Genius* (1915) is the novel in which he works most closely with autobiographical material, and examines the problematic relationship between aesthetics and finance in modern society. The complex and sometimes contradictory philosophical thought in Dreiser's fiction has often been subsumed under the title of naturalism, but while he certainly believed in the power of society to shape individuals, he also believed in the capacities of individuals to shape the world in which they lived. The tension between abstract philosophizing and concrete, detailed description sometimes produces an ungainly prose style, as many critics have pointed out. Despite this, F. O. *Matthiessen's *Theodore Dreiser* (1951) makes a vigorous defence of his power as a writer, and Alfred *Kazin is also a strong advocate for his work. He also wrote many volumes of social criticism, including *Dreiser Looks at Russia* (1928) and *Tragic America* (1931); plays including *Plays of the Natural and the Supernatural* (1916) and the tragedy *The Hand of the Potter* (1918); poetry including *Moods, Cadenced and Declaimed* (1926); two volumes of memoirs, *A Book about Myself* (1922) and *Dawn: A History of Myself* (1931); volumes of essays, including *Hey Rub-a-Dub-Dub* (1920); and collections of short stories, including *A Gallery of Women* (1929). At the end of his life, the contradictions in Dreiser's thought were indicated by his joining of the Communist Party and the completion of his novel of religious faith lost and found, *The Bulwark* (published posthumously in 1946). A three-volume selection of *The Letters of Theodore Dreiser* was published in 1959.

DREWE, Robert (1943–), Australian writer, born in Melbourne. He travelled in China, India, the Philippines, the Pacific, and Japan as a journalist; he also worked as literary editor for the *Australian* and has written for the *Age* and the **Bulletin*. His first novel, *The Savage Crows* (1976), tells the story of Stephen, a young journalist researching into the life of the nineteenth-century Protector of Aborigines in Tasmania, George Augustus Robinson. Stephen's contemporary decline is alternated with passages from Robinson's diary: the novel's juxtaposing of its two different stories, told in two different styles, contrasts white disintegration with Aboriginal strength. In *A Cry in the Jungle Bar* (1979) Drewe explores Australian–Asian relations, placing an Australian water buffalo expert, a man of huge physique, in the middle of Asia, where he finds himself at a loss with the complexities of the culture and the politics. *The Bodysurfers* (1983) is a series of interlinked stories about three generations of one family. In these stories, which offer a kind of celebration of Australian hedonism, Drewe was one of the first to identify the dominant Australian cultural experience, which is drawn not from the bush, but from the beach. *Fortune* (1986), set partly in America, draws on the author's experience as a private eye in San Francisco and includes passages of journalistic 'faction'. A second collection of stories, *The Bay of Contented Men*, appeared in 1989. The novel *Our Sunshine* (1991) is a fictional portrait of Ned Kelly. Drewe is the editor of an anthology of stories, *The Picador Book of the Beach* (1994).

DRINKWATER, John (1882–1937), British poet and playwright, born in Leytonstone, Essex; he grew up in north Oxfordshire, whence the predominantly rural imagery of much of his poetry derives, and was educated at Oxford High School. He began writing poetry while working as a clerk in insurance offices in Nottingham and Birmingham, and became manager of the Birmingham Repertory Company upon its formation in 1913. He directed and acted in many productions and wrote a number of short verse-plays, among which are *Copethua* (1911) and *X = 0: A Night of the Trojan War* (1917), an allegorically effective statement against the Great War. His principal achievements as a playwright were his historical prose dramas: *Abraham Lincoln* (1918), *Oliver Cromwell* (1921), *Mary Stuart* (1922), and *Robert E. Lee* (1923). *Bird in the Hand* (1927) was a successful comedy in which Laurence Olivier and Peggy Ashcroft were given their first major roles. His *Collected Plays* appeared in two volumes in 1925. Drinkwater published over twenty books of poetry including *The Death of Leander and Other Poems* (1906), *Poems of Love and Earth* (1912), *Swords and Ploughshares* (1915), *From an Unknown Isle* (1924), and *Collected Poems* (3 volumes, 1923). His repute as a poet has declined with that of the *Georgian movement, whose mediocre rural sentimentalism is perhaps typified by much of his verse. Certain of his poems are, however, highly memorable, like 'Birthright' ('Lord Rameses of Egypt sighed | Because a summer evening passed . . .') and 'Moonlit Apples', and have secured him a place in the modern literary tradition. He wrote numerous critical biographies, including *William Morris* (1912), *The Pilgrim of Eternity: Byron* (1925), and *Pepys: His Life and Character* (1930); and two volumes of autobiography, *Inheritance* (1931) and *Discovery* (1932).

Drum, a South African magazine which began publication as *The African Drum* primarily for a white readership. Jim Bailey took over the journal in 1951. Under the editorship of Anthony *Sampson, and subsequently of Sylvester Stein (1956–7) and Tom Hopkinson (1958–61), *Drum* became almost legendary for its portrayal, addressed mainly to a black readership, of township life in and around Johannesburg, particularly Sophiatown. The journalists, much influenced by African-American writers like Langston *Hughes and Richard *Wright, were all black South Africans; Lewis *Nkosi, Es'kia *Mphahlele, and Bloke Modisane began their writing careers as journalists for *Drum*. The journal exposed injustices related to apartheid, and published fiction by Peter *Abrahams, Richard *Rive, and others. The magazine's photojournalism became world famous. Interviews with many of the contributors have been published in *A Good-looking Corpse* (1991) by Mike Nicol. Banned from 1965 to 1968, *Drum* never recovered its vigour, and was taken over by an Afrikaner publisher. See Anthony Sampson, *Drum: An African Adventure—and Afterwards* (1983).

DUBERMAN, Martin (1930–), American playwright and historian, born in New York City, educated at Yale. He began his career as an actor and playwright; many of his plays were Off-Broadway productions, such as *In White America* (1963). His other dramatic works include *Male Armor: Selected Plays 1968–1974* (1975), *Visions of Kerouac* (1977), and *Mother Earth: An Epic Play on the Life of Emma Goldman* (1991). Much of his early scholarly work, notably *Charles Francis Adams, 1807–1886* (1960) and *The Antislavery Vanguard: New Essays on the Abolitionists* (1965), reconsiders the history of the abolitionist movement in America. *Black Mountain: An Exploration in Community* (1972) is a seminal work on the development of postmodern American culture. More recently he has become known for his work in gay historiography. *About Time: Exploring the Gay Past* (1986) and *Hidden From History: Reclaiming the Gay and Lesbian Past* (1989; co-edited with Martha Vicinius and George Chauncey, Jr) are collections of documents presenting the history of homosexuals and homosexuality in America; *Cures: A Gay Man's Odyssey* (1991) and *Midlife Queer* (1996) are autobiographical works; and *Stonewall* (1993) is an oral history of the liberation movement. Duberman has taught at Princeton, Yale, and the City University of New York, among other universities, and became Executive Director for the Center for Lesbian and Gay Studies.

Dublin Magazine, The, a literary periodical begun in 1923 by James Starkey, who was known as editor and contributor under his pseudonym 'Seamus O'Sullivan'. It was conceived of as providing a point of cultural detachment from the upheavals which accompanied the emergence of the Irish Free State, and Starkey maintained his policy of political nonalignment throughout his thirty-five years as editor. The first issue of the magazine established its international tone: work by Gérard de Nerval and John *Masefield appeared alongside contributions from Irish authors, who included Padraic *Colum and James *Stephens; it continued to take an active interest in literature from various European countries, notably Italy and Portugal. In addition to its literary content, which took the form of poetry, fiction, critical articles, and the occasional publication of entire verse-dramas, the *Dublin Magazine* gave attention to developments in science and the graphic and plastic arts: Jack B. *Yeats and Augustus John were among the artists who supplied illustrations. The poets closely associated with the journal included Austin *Clarke, Patrick *Kavanagh, F. R. *Higgins, and Padraic *Fallon; verse by R. S. *Thomas and other Welsh poets was featured regularly during the 1940s. Arguably the best and certainly the longest-running Irish periodical of the twentieth century, the *Dublin Magazine* was discontinued after its editor's death in 1958.

Dubliners, a volume of fifteen short stories by James *Joyce. Begun in 1904, it was repeatedly rejected for publication, successively destroyed and then burnt by censorious printers, added to by its author, championed by George *Russell (AE), *Yeats, and *Pound, and finally published with reluctance by Grant Richards in 1914. Naturalistic in style and easily accessible by Joyce's standards, *Dubliners* represents his earliest efforts 'to betray the soul of that hemiplegia or paralysis which many consider a city'. After a century without its own parliament, Dublin had become a provincial backwater of the Union and the Empire, peopled by frustrated adolescents ('Araby'), jaded adults ('Clay'), and hack politicians ('Ivy Day in the Committee Room'). Written with a 'scrupulous meanness', these sparse, often beautiful, and occasionally humorous portraits of everyday life are connected by themes of entrapment, escape, and compromise, themes which culminate in the final story, 'The Dead', widely regarded as a masterpiece of its genre.

DU BOIS, W(illiam) E(dward) B(urghardt) (1868–1963), African-American historian, born in Great Barrington, Massachusetts, educated at Fisk University and Harvard. He began his academic career at Wilberforce University in 1894 and was subsequently a professor at Atlanta University. *The Suppression of the African Slave Trade* (1896), *Black Reconstruction* (1935), on the achievements of African-Americans in the aftermath of the Civil War, and *The World and Africa* (1947), an indictment of colonial exploitation, are among the most notable of his many works as a historian, which partake of the reforming zeal he applied to his endeavours as an activist against racial inequality. The essays of *The Souls of Black Folk* (1903) were enormously influential in stating the case for the extension of higher educational opportunities to blacks. A founder of the National Association for the Advancement of Colored People in 1909, he later disclaimed the organization as excessively conservative. From 1910 to 1936 he edited the magazine *The Crisis*, becoming a notable figure of the *Harlem Renaissance; from the 1930s onwards he adopted increasingly extreme positions. In 1960 he emigrated to Ghana, where he directed the planning of an *Encyclopaedia Africana*. His other works include the essays and reminiscences of *Darkwater* (1920) and the trilogy of novels collected as *The Black Flame* (1976), a dramatic treatment of conditions in the American South. *The Autobiography of W. E. B. Du Bois* appeared in 1968. The fullest of numerous biographical studies is *W. E. B. Du Bois: Radical Black Democrat* (1986) by Manning Marable.

Dub Poetry, a phrase coined by Black British poet Linton Kwesi *Johnson to denote poems written to be performed with musical accompaniment. Dub Poetry is invariably more readily available on records than in books, a situation which evolved through the collaboration between poets and West Indian, or Black British, disc jockeys. Populist in appeal, Dub Poetry is often political, and performed in Creole, or what Edward Kamau *Brathwaite has called Nation Language, in his important work *History of the Voice* (1984). Brathwaite argues that Nation Language stems from the oral tradition (chiefly African) and, when employed for poetry, displays musical rhythms, such as calypso and reggae, unlike the dominant iambic rhythms in much English poetry. Poems by dub poets such as Linton Kwesi Johnson and Benjamin *Zephaniah reflect, as James *Berry has observed, 'a collective psyche laden with anguish and rage'. Michael *Smith, a Jamaican Rastafarian, was the foremost dub poet in the West Indies, and the radicalism of his poetry, in both its 'subversive' political message and Nation Language style, was all too tragically confirmed, perhaps, when he was stoned to death during the Jamaican general election campaign of 1983. See also JAZZ POETRY.

DUCKWORTH, Marilyn (1935–), New Zealand novelist, sister of the poet Fleur *Adcock, born in Auckland, educated in England and Wellington, including part-time attendance at Wellington University. Her first novel, *A Gap in the Spectrum* (1959), a *science-fiction exploration of a woman's dependency, was published when she was 23 and established the fictional terrain of her early work: the constricting roles ascribed to women are seen to notable effect in *Over the Fence Is Out* (1969). Widowed once, and married four times, her career was punctuated by a long silence while she brought up her children. Her acclaimed novel *Disorderly Conduct* (1984), set during the 1981 Springbok tour protests, features a women with four children by three different fathers. Her other novels include *The Matchbox House* (1960), *A Barbarous Tongue* (1963), *Married Alive* (1985), *Rest for the Wicked* (1986), *Pulling Faces* (1987), *A Message from Harpo* (1989), and *Unlawful Entry* (1992). She has also published *Other Lovers' Children: Poems 1958–74* (1975) and *Explosions in the Sun* (1989), a volume of short stories. She was awarded the OBE in 1987.

DUDEK, Louis (1918–), Canadian poet, born in Montreal, Quebec, educated at McGill and Columbia Universities. In 1951 he began teaching at McGill University, where he became Professor of English in 1969. Throughout his career at McGill he initiated various publishing ventures, which include the McGill Poetry series (1956–66) and the Delta Canada Press (1967–). *East of the City* (1946) was his first collection of verse. The influence of Ezra *Pound and *Imagism becomes clear in *The Searching Image* (1952), which establishes exploratory free-verse forms and concentrated visual imagery as essential characteristics of his work. *Europe* (1954) was the first of his long sequences based on ideas of journeying, which also include *En Mexico* (1958) and *Atlantis* (1967); these ambitious poems form richly varied expositions of historical, cultural, and philosophical themes. His later collections include *Continuation 1* (1981) and *Zembla's Rocks* (1986); *Cross-Section* (1980) is a collected edition of his verse since 1940. Dudek's endeavours as a writer and publisher to establish an indigenous *modernist mode make him a figure of considerable importance in post-war Canadian literature. His critical writings include *The First Person in Literature* (1967) and *Technology and Culture* (1979). *DK—Some Letters of Ezra Pound* (1974) is an edition of the correspondence with Pound he began in the late 1940s.

DUFFY, Carol Ann (1955–), British poet, born in Glasgow; she grew up in Staffordshire, and studied philosophy at the University of Liverpool, a city reflected in a number of her poems. Two of her plays, *Take My Husband* and *Cavern of Dreams*, were produced at the Liverpool Playhouse in 1982 and 1984 respectively. She became poetry editor for *Ambit* magazine in 1983 and has worked as a writer-in-residence at various schools and colleges. *Standing Female Nude* (1985) was her first substantial collection of poetry. *Thrown Voices* followed in 1986, its title indicative of her ability in dramatic monologue forms; these are a principal feature of the collection *Selling Manhattan*, which won her considerable acclaim on its appearance in 1987, its numerous poems in the voices of dispossessed personae framing a penetrating critique of contemporary society. In both dramatic monologue modes and more directly personal idioms, Duffy's verse unites sensitive individuality of tone with starkly unsentimental objectivity. *The Other Country* (1990) and *Mean Time* (1993) display a broadening of technical and imaginative range; *Selected Poems* appeared in 1994.

DUFFY, Maureen (Patricia) (1933–), British novelist, poet, and playwright, born in Worthing, Sussex, educated at King's College, London. She worked as a schoolteacher and in adult education between 1951 and 1960, when she became a freelance writer. *That's How It Was* (1960), her substantially autobiographical first novel, was acclaimed for its portrayal of the relationship between an illegitimate child and her impoverished mother. Her reputation as an idiosyncratic prose stylist capable of bizarre amalgams of realism and fantasy is evident in the much-praised *Gor Saga* (1981), which is set in the future and deals with the consequences of an experiment in genetic engineering in which a scientist succeeds in producing a creature which is half-human, half-ape. Other novels include *The Microcosm* (1966) and *The Paradox Players* (1967), *I Want to Go to Moscow* (1973), *Housespy* (1978), *Londoners* (1983), and *Illuminations* (1991). A well-paced thriller, *Occam's Razor* (1993), the fourth of her novels to be set in London, was praised by Shena *Mackay, who confirmed Duffy as 'an imaginative poet of the city and someone who is committed to the cause of both human and animal rights'. Her poetry, written largely in carefully cadenced free verse with occasional ironic use of traditional rhyming forms, has in common with her prose its imaginative scope and disquieting emotional power; mythological, personal, and socio-political elements recur in her collections, among which are *Lyrics for the Dog Hour* (1968), *Evesong* (1975), *Memorials for the Quick and the Dead* (1979), and *Collected Poems, 1949–1984* (1985). A trilogy of plays, *Rites* (1969), *Solo* (1970), and *Old Tyme* (1970), is based on classical mythology; her dramatic works also include *A Nightingale in Bloomsbury* (1974), in which Virginia *Woolf considers her achievement prior to her suicide. Duffy's other publications include *The Erotic World Of Faery* (1972), a study of the supernatural in folklore and literature; *The Passionate Shepherdess* (1977), a biography of Aphra Behn, whose *Five Plays* (1990) she edited; *Men And Beasts: An Animal Rights Handbook* (1984); and a biography of *Henry Purcell* (1994) together with a play about the composer (1995). Duffy has played an active role in professional bodies such as the Writers' Guild of Great Britain and the British Copyright Council; she was one of the founder members, with Brigid *Brophy, Lettice *Cooper, and Francis *King, of the Writers' Action Group, vigorously campaigning for Public Lending Rights from 1972 to 1982; she chaired the Author's Lending and Copyright Society; and was appointed Vice-President of the European Writers' Congress.

DUGGAN, Alfred (Leo) (1903–64), British historical novelist, born in Buenos Aires, Argentina, educated at Balliol College, Oxford. Duggan wrote his first novel, *Knight With Armour* (1950), at the age of 47. Later, his keen interest in Crusader castles led him to write historical novels. Evelyn *Waugh praised his understanding of the Roman Empire and feudal Europe, and greatly admired his novel *Conscience of the King* (1951), which illuminates the role of Christianity in the early medieval world. Among his other novels are *The Lady for Ransom* (1953), about Roger the Norman and his exploits in the service of the Byzantine Empire; *Leopards and Lilies* (1954), which is entertaining in its depiction of chivalry; *The Cunning of the Dove* (1960), about Edward the Confessor's shrewd political manœuvres; *Family Favourites* (1961), which focuses on the notorious emperor Elagabalus; and *Count Bohemond* (1964), Duggan's last word on the First Crusade.

DUGGAN, Eileen (1900–72), New Zealand poet, born near Invercargill, educated at Victoria University College. Her verse collections, *Poems* (1924), *A Pioneer* (1929), *Poems* (1937), *New Zealand Poems* (1940), and *More Poems* (1951) show her talent for combining the demotic (and local detail) with the charm and regularity of rhymed verse form. Her themes are particularly of the privations and tragedies of ordinary lives. Duggan received a fellowship of the Royal Society of Literature in 1943 and her writing was published and widely read in the USA. In the 1950s, however, her reputation in New Zealand was somewhat eclipsed by the more modernist tendencies of the Caxton School and she was marginalized for what Allen *Curnow described as her 'Georgian decorum'. Duggan's work appears in most of the major anthologies.

DUGGAN, Maurice (1922–74), New Zealand short-story writer, born in Auckland, and educated at Auckland University. His first collection, *Immanuel's Land* (1956), contained work mostly written in Europe during 1949–53 and included the extended piece 'The Voyage'. *Summer in the Gravel Pit* (1965) contained the fine story 'Along the Rideout Road that Summer'. At his best Duggan showed mastery of a complex format of interrelated stories reflecting the fragility of human relationships, his focus usually being on finely sketched scenes of family life or memories of school-days and youth. He further extended his fictional range in *O'Leary's Orchard and Other Stories* (1970), three longer stories all reworked from earlier works published in **Landfall*. In 1966 Duggan described the challenge of writing as being the need to find a subject which was 'less a story than a prose celebration of a topography and a time that, in rediscovery and re-creation moved me strongly enough to force me away from what had become a habit of rhetoric'; he creates a flexible and sophisticated fictional form which conveys an unsettling vision of life at the same time as it precludes a straightforward narrative reading. C. K. *Stead edited his *Collected Stories* (1981), which included 'The Magsman Miscellany', and contributed a valuable Introduction.

DU MAURIER, Dame Daphne (Lady Browning) (1907–89), British novelist, born in London, educated in Paris, the granddaughter of George du Maurier, and daughter of Gerald du Maurier, the actor. Her first novel, *The Loving Spirit* (1931), began her successful career as a writer of popular novels and period romances. Many of them were set in Cornwall, including the best-selling *Jamaica Inn* (1936), a story of wreckers, and *Rebecca* (1938), her most popular novel. Other novels include *Frenchman's Creek* (1941), *Hungry Hill* (1943), *The King's General* (1946), and *My Cousin Rachel* (1951). She wrote several biographies including one of her father, *Gerald: A Portrait* (1934), as well as *The du Mauriers* (1937), *Mary Anne* (1954), *The Infernal World of Branwell Brontë* (1960), and *Golden Lads: A Study of Anthony Bacon, Francis and their Friends* (1975). Her writing often showed a strong sense of the macabre. Many of her novels were filmed, as were her two short stories, 'Don't Look Back' and 'The Birds'. See also ROMANTIC FICTION.

DUMMETT, Michael (Anthony Eardley) (1925–), British philosopher, born in London, educated at Winchester and at Christ Church, Oxford. In 1950 he was elected a fellow of All Souls College, Oxford, and was a senior research fellow from 1974 to 1979, when he was appointed Wykeham Professor of Logic at Oxford. He has also held numerous visiting posts in the USA and elsewhere. His early publications include *Frege and the Philosophy of Language* (1973), which established him as a leading interpreter of Frege's philosophy. Frege's methods form the basis for Dummett's analytical procedures in constructing a theory of linguistic meaning, which he believes must be a prerequisite for valid philosophical discourse. Among his further studies of Frege's work are *The Interpretation of Frege's Philosophy* (1981), *Frege: Philosophy of Mathematics* (1991), and the hitherto uncollected essays of *Frege and Other Philosophers* (1991). Dummett's writings on Frege are substantially vehicles for his own work in logic and the philosophy of mathematics, which has provoked controversy for its uncompromisingly technical character. He has stated that 'Philosophy must be either anecdotal or systematic; if one rejects the anecdotal as trivial, one will have to put up with the laboriousness of the systematic'. His other works include *Truth and Other Enigmas* (1978) and *The Logical Basis of Metaphysics* (1991); the historical treatise *The Game of Tarot* (1980) and the instructional *Twelve Tarot Games* (1980) regard the cards as exclusively recreational in function, dismissing the 'irrational' practices of occultists.

DUNBAR, Paul Laurence (1872–1906), African-American novelist, playwright, and poet, born in Dayton, Ohio, educated at Dayton High School. Dunbar was one of the most important black American writers of the late nineteenth and early twentieth centuries, in part because of his singular contributions to dialect verse. He began writing poetry whilst working as a lift operator in an office building in Dayton and his first volume of verse, *Oak and Ivy*, was privately published in 1893. His poetry came to the attention of William Dean *Howells whose defence of dialect poetry in his review of Dunbar's second volume, *Majors and Minors* (1895), transformed him from an obscure poet into a nationally known figure. Howells spoke of a 'direct and fresh authority' in the verse and it was this, coupled with Dunbar's ear for the rhythms and inflections of black speech, that gave the poetry such realism and sympathy. Among other volumes of verse published in his lifetime are *Lyrics of Lowly Life* (1896), *Lyrics of the Hearthside* (1899), *Poems of Cabin and Field* (1899), *Lyrics of Love and Laughter* (1903), *Li'l' Gal* (1904), *Lyrics of Sunshine and Shadow* (1905), and *Joggin' Erlong* (1906); the *Complete Poems* were published in 1913. Dunbar was prolific though less celebrated for his novels and plays; his play *Dream Lovers* (1898) was set to music by Samuel Coleridge Taylor. His novels include *The Uncalled* (1898) and *The Love of Landry* (1900), while *Folks from Dixie* (1898), *The Strength of Gideon and Other Stories* (1900), *In Old Plantation Days* (1903), and *The Heart of Happy Hollow* (1904) are collections of short stories. *The Dunbar Reader* (1975) was edited by Jay Martin and Gossie H. Hudson. Dunbar was an immensely successful reader of his own work in the USA, and he visited England in 1897. He served as an assistant in the Library of Congress between

1897 and 1898. See *A Singer in the Dawn: Reinterpretations of Dunbar* (1975), edited by Jay Martin.

DUNBAR-NELSON, Alice (1875–1935), African-American writer, born in New Orleans, educated at Straight University (now Dillard University). Dunbar-Nelson pursued many different careers in addition to her writing. She served as the secretary of the National Association of Colored Women; as an English teacher and the head of the English Department at Howard High School; she co-founded the Delaware Industrial School for Colored Girls; and was elected to membership of the Delaware Republican State Committee in 1920. Her first published work, *Violets and Other Tales* (1895), a volume of short stories and poetry, was followed by *The Goodness of St Rocque* (1898), a collection of stories. Dunbar-Nelson's early works, which often focused on Creole characters, evoked the language and settings of life in New Orleans. Some of her later stories, including 'The Stones of Village', explore darker, more troubling issues such as race relations and oppression. Much of Dunbar-Nelson's later work remained unpublished until the appearance of *The Works of Alice Dunbar-Nelson* (3 volumes, 1988; edited by Gloria T. Hull). Dunbar-Nelson was briefly married to Paul Lawrence *Dunbar.

DUNCAN, Robert (Edward) (1919–88), American poet, born in Oakland, California, educated at the University of California, Berkeley. As an editor of the *Experimental Review* in 1940 and 1941 he published work by Henry *Miller, Anaïs *Nin, Lawrence *Durrell, Kenneth *Patchen, and others. *Heavenly City, Earthly City* (1947), his first collection of verse, reflected his admiration for the work of George *Barker, whose mystical and rhetorical qualities are consonant with the tenor of much of Duncan's poetry. Contact with the poets associated with *Black Mountain College, where Duncan taught in 1956, led to the intensification of his interest in innovative forms that becomes apparent in *Caesar's Gate: Poems 1949–1955* (1956). Much of his later writing is remarkable for retaining a strong allegiance to European lyric and visionary traditions while adopting the *Projective Verse modes proposed by Charles *Olson, after whose death in 1970 Duncan became the leading practitioner of 'open field' composition. From the mid-1950s onward he was one of the principal figures in the *San Francisco Renaissance and was conspicuous among poets opposed to the Vietnam War during the 1960s (see VIETNAM WRITING); *Bending the Bow* (1968) contains 'Up Rising', one of the period's most notable poems of protest. The collection also begins the extended series of 'Passages', typographically dispersed poems offering highly flexible patterns of signification, which formed the main body of his subsequent work. Notable among his other volumes are *The Opening of the Field* (1960), *Roots and Branches* (1964), and the two volumes of *Ground Work* (1984, 1987). *Fictive Certainties* (1979) is a collection of essays having in common Duncan's idiosyncratically autobiographical approach to critical commentary.

DUNCAN, Ronald (1914–82), British poet and dramatist, born in Salisbury, Rhodesia, educated at Cambridge University. He gained wide recognition for the verse-drama *This Way to the Tomb* (1946), a 'masque and anti-masque' with music by Benjamin Britten, for whose opera *The Rape of Lucretia* (1946) he supplied a libretto; *Collected Plays* appeared in 1971. He was among the founders of the *English Stage Company in 1956. As a poet he displayed a high level of conventional accomplishment in modes ranging from humorous verse to philosophically ambitious meditations. Collections of his work include *The Mongrel* (1950) and *For the Fear* (1977); *Collected Poems* was published in 1981. He produced three volumes of provocative and entertaining autobiography, *All Men Are Islands* (1964), *How To Make Enemies* (1968), and *Obsessed* (1977).

DUNMORE, Helen (1952–), British poet and novelist, born in Beverley, Yorkshire, educated at York University. Her first volume of poems, *The Apple Fall* (1983), was praised for its rhythmical assurance which is a characteristic of her verse. *The Sea Skater* (1986) fuses personal and familial experience with more general socio-cultural themes, which are conveyed by precise and fluent successions of images. Further volumes include *The Raw Garden* (1988), *Short Days, Long Nights: New and Selected Poems* (1991), *Recovering a Body* (1994), and *Secrets* (1994). Dunmore also turned to writing fiction with *Zennor in Darkness* (1993), a novel in which the First World War is viewed through the eyes of two couples, one real (Frieda and D. H. *Lawrence), the other fictional. Her second novel, *Burning Bright* (1994), is an inventively constructed account of a young girl's gradual absorption into petty crime, and her relationship with her thuggish lover and the old lesbian neighbour who recounts her past in long monologues. *A Spell in Winter* (1995) is narrated in the first person by a girl drawn by loneliness into an incestuous love affair with her brother.

DUNN, Douglas (Eaglesham) (1942–), Scottish poet, born in Inchinnan, Renfrewshire, educated at the Scottish School of Librarianship in Glasgow and the University of Hull; he subsequently worked in the University's Brynmor Jones Library as an assistant librarian under Philip *Larkin, with whom he became well acquainted. He was a freelance writer from 1971 to 1991, when he was appointed to a professorship at the University of St Andrews. *Terry Street* (1969), his first collection of verse, contained acutely observed evocations of working-class life together with imaginative treatments of cultural and personal preoccupations which anticipated the thematic scope of *The Happier Life* (1972) and *Love or Nothing* (1974). The political concerns informing his earlier work become explicit in *Barbarians* (1979), which uses verse of great accomplishment to present parables of the deprivation inherent in the hierarchical structure of society. *St Kilda's Parliament* (1981) indicates a broadening of the imaginative compass of his writing in such pieces as the 'poem-films' 'Valerio' and 'La Route', and also contains notable examples of his highly developed abilities as a lyrical and discursive poet. He left Hull and returned to Scotland after the death in 1981 of his wife Lesley, whom he commemorates in *Elegies* (1985; Whitbread Book of the Year Award), which was acclaimed as the finest poetic embodiment of grief since Tennyson's *In Memoriam*. *Selected Poems: 1964–1983* appeared in 1986. *Northlight* (1988) combines an unusual range in treatments of local, political, historical, and aesthetic concerns with a striking degree of technical virtuosity. Further collections include *Dante's Drum-Kit* (1993). Among his other works are *Secret Villages* (1985) and *Boyfriends and Girlfriends* (1994), collections of short stories; and his verse translation of Racine's *Andromache* (1990). He has also edited numerous books, including *Two Decades of Irish Writing* (1975), *A Rumoured City: New Poets from Hull* (1982), and *The Faber Book of Twentieth-Century Scottish Poetry* (1992).

DUNN, Nell (Mary) (1936–), British novelist and dramatist, born in London, and educated at a convent school. Her collection of realistic interlinked short stories, *Up the Junction* (1963), and her novel, *Poor Cow* (1967), were considered sensational at the time. Both are about the constrained lives of independent-minded working-class women in London. The novel focuses on Joy, and her relationship with her husband, a professional thief, her lover (both of whom successively end up in prison), and her little son. Dunn co-authored the film version with director Ken Loach. Her other novels explore further aspects of women's lives, and include *The Incurable* (1971), *I Want* (1972; with Adrian *Henri), *Tear His Head off His Shoulders* (1974), and *The Only Child* (1978). Her play *Steaming* (1981), set in a council bath threatened with closure, also caused a sensation; the protagonists were all women, both working-class and middle-class, frequently (but quite naturally) in various states of undress. The play was acclaimed as an authentic slice of life, and an effective political protest. Another play, *The Little Heroine* (1988), portrays a heroin addict who successfully kicks the habit. *Grandmothers Talking to Nell Dunn* (1991) is a collection of interviews.

DUNNE, J(ohn) W(illiam) (1875–1949), British inventor and philosopher, educated privately; he served in the Anglo-Boer War (1899–1902). Dunne designed and built the first British military aeroplane (1906–7), but is best known for *An Experiment with Time* (1927), a book of scientific speculation. It challenged both Einstein on the nature of time, and Freud on the nature of dreams. Offering much practical advice about recording dreams, he considered them as precognitive clues to future events, and also as crucial in understanding time. His theory of 'serial time' was dramatized by one of his most enthusiastic supporters, J. B. *Priestley, in *Time and the Conways* (1937), and other plays. Dunne further elaborated his theories in *The Serial Universe* (1934), *The New Immortality* (1938), and *Nothing Dies* (1940). In *Man and Time* (1964), Priestley devoted an entire chapter to Dunne's controversial theories.

DUNNETT, Dorothy (1923–), Scottish portrait painter turned historical novelist, born in Dunfermline. With *Game of Kings* (1961) she began a series of six novels which, as the 'Lymond Chronicles', described the adventures of Francis Crawford, a sixteenth-century Scottish adventurer. This series gave her ample opportunity to display her gift for subtle narrative backed by meticulous research. *King Hereafter* (1982) was an ambitious attempt to identify the historical Macbeth. *Niccolo Rising* (1986) began another series, 'The House of Niccolo', set in the banking world of the fifteenth century and reaching from Bruges to Cyprus and Trebizond; it was followed by *The Spring of the Ram* (1987) and *Race of Scorpions* (1989). As Dorothy Halliday, she has written a series of contemporary comedy thrillers, featuring Johnson and his yacht, 'The Dolly', beginning with *Dolly and the Singing Bird* (1968).

DUNSANY, Lord (Edward John Moreton Drax Plunkett, 18th Baron) (1878–1957), Irish dramatist and short-story writer, of Anglo-Irish parentage, born in London, educated at Eton and Sandhurst. He was a friend of *Yeats, *Gogarty, and Lady *Gregory and others associated with the *Irish Revival. His first play, *The Glittering Gate* (performed 1909), was published in *Five Plays* (1914) together with other fantasies showing the influence of Maurice Maeterlinck; other plays appeared in *Plays of Gods and Men* (1917), *Plays of Near and Far* (1922), and *Seven Modern Comedies* (1928). His most successful play was *If* (1921), a dramatized Oriental tale. Many of his collections of mythological tales were illustrated with strange *fin de siècle* drawings by S. H. Sime, including *The Gods of Pegana* (1905), *Time and the Gods* (1906), and *Tales of Wonder* (1916). Set in a universe with its own mythology, these stories influenced popular American writers of fantasy such as H. P. *Lovecraft and F. *Leiber. His more realistic stories featuring Mr Jorkens and his remarkable adventures began with *The Travel Tales of Mr Joseph Jorkens* (1931) and continued in other volumes. He also wrote essays, verse, autobiographical works, and several novels including *The King of Elfland's Daughter* (1922), *The Blessing of Pan* (1927), and *The Last Revolution* (1951), a *science fiction work.

DURCAN, Paul (1944–), Irish poet, born in Dublin, educated at University College, Cork. His numerous collections of poetry have included *Teresa's Bar* (1976), *Jesus, Break His Fall* (1982), *Jumping the Train Tracks with Angela* (1983), *The Berlin Wall Café* (1985), *Going Home to Russia* (1987), *Jesus and Angela* (1988), and *Daddy, Daddy* (1990). The lavishly produced *In the Land of Punt* (1988) is a collaboration between Durcan and the noted Irish artist Gene Lambers. Durcan's poetry is highly idiosyncratic in its combination of 'an open Romanticism rare in contemporary poetry' (Edna Longley, introduction to *The Selected Paul Durcan*, 1982) with trenchantly satirical social commentaries, often employing bizarrely surreal narrative strategies. The accessibility and humour of his work, together with his striking vocal delivery, have made his readings widely popular. *Crazy About Women* (1991) and *Give Me Your Hand* (1994) are collections displaying Durcan's poetic responses to paintings in National Galleries of Ireland and Britain; new and selected poems appeared in *A Snail in My Prime* (1993).

DURRELL, Gerald (Malcolm) (1925–95), English writer and zoologist, born in Jamshedpur, India, the brother of Lawrence *Durrell. In 1928 his family returned to England, and from 1933 they lived mainly in Europe. Durrell's experiences on Corfu formed the basis for his comic autobiography, *My Family and Other Animals* (1956). His many zoological expeditions took him to the Cameroons, British Guiana, Sierra Leone, Paraguay, and Argentina, all of which he described in his numerous books. These include *The Drunken Forest* (1956), *The Overloaded Ark* (1957), *A Zoo in My Luggage* (1960), *Island Zoo* (1961), *Encounters with Animals* (1963), *Three Singles to Adventure* (1964), *Birds, Beasts and Relatives* (1969), *Catch Me A Colobus* (1972), *Beasts in the Belfry* (1973), and others. In 1959 he founded the Jersey Zoological Park, about which he wrote in *The Ark's Anniversary* (1990). In *The Aye-Aye and I* (1992) he recounted his experiences in Madagascar to save a rare mammal.

DURRELL, Lawrence (George) (1912–90), British novelist, poet, and travel writer, born in Julundur, India, educated at St Edmund's School. From 1934 onward he spent most of his life in Mediterranean locations, working as a journalist, for the British Foreign Service, and for the British Council between 1940 and 1957, when he achieved financial independence as a writer. His early novels, which include *Pied Piper of Lovers* (1935) and *Cefalû* (1947), attracted little attention; T. S. *Eliot thought highly of his experimental 'agon' *The Black Book* (Paris, 1938; London, 1973), which displays the influence of Durrell's close friend Henry *Miller: *The Durrell-Miller Letters 1935–1980*, edited by I. S. MacNiven, appeared in 1988. His international reputation was established with *Justine* (1957), the first part of *The Alexandria Quartet*, which was completed with *Balthazar* (1958), *Mountolive* (1958), and *Clea* (1960). The first three books of the work, which Durrell termed 'a four-dimensional dance, a relativity poem', reflect his interpretations of the theories of Einstein and Freud in using radically different narrative perspectives on a single set of events and personalities; *Clea* adopts a conventional chronological progression beyond the complex interactions of erotic, artistic, and political motifs in the earlier parts. Published in a single edition in 1962, *The Alexandria Quartet*, which has been both praised and condemned for the poetic opulence of its prose, anticipates the metaphysical critique of modern civilization central to its successors: *The Revolt of Aphrodite* (1974), consisting of *Tunc* (1968) and *Nunquam* (1970), concerns the resistance of individuals to the power of a multinational corporation; *Monsieur* (1974), *Livia* (1978), *Constance* (1982), *Sebastian* (1984), and *Quinx* (1985) are the five parts of *The Avignon Quintet*, a work whose extraordinarily mobile narrative extends from the suppression of the Knights Templars in the fourteenth century to the Nazi occupation of France. Durrell gained notice as a poet with *A Private Country* (1943). *The Tree of Idleness* (1955) and *The Ikons* (1966) are among his many subsequent collections; vivid and wittily imaginative treatments of people and places predominate in his poetry, which is fluently accomplished and has been preferred to his prose by numerous commentators. *Collected Poems 1931–1974* appeared in 1980. His travel books include *Prospero's Cell* (1945), on Corfu; *Reflections of a Marine Venus* (1953), dealing with Rhodes; *Bitter Lemons* (1957), a treatment of Cyprus during the conflicts of the 1950s; and *Caesar's Vast Ghost* (1990), a historically digressive work on Provence. A prolific and wide-ranging author, he also produced verse-dramas, literary criticism, and translations; *Antrobus Complete* (1985) collects the humorous stories he based on his experiences with the diplomatic corps.

Dutchman, a play by Amiri *Baraka (then known as LeRoi Jones), first performed in 1964 off-Broadway to immediate acclaim. Divided into two scenes, the play's setting is a New York subway carriage, 'In the flying underbelly of the city. Steaming hot, and summer on top, outside. Underground. The subway heaped in modern myth.' Clay, a respectable young black passenger, becomes a victim of a lynching. Lula, his white seductress, is a perverse allusion to Eve, as she gets on the train 'eating an apple, very daintily'. The action is based almost exclusively on the exchanges between these two, as Lula goads and baits Clay into his final outburst of anger in an affirmation of black history and culture, before the play moves towards its violent climax as Lula stabs him and dumps the body, aided by the carriage passengers. Resonating with a psychosexual tension behind the racial fear, the ideas, language, and actions examine interracial relationships in a drama which embraces fast-paced dialogue, vivid imagery, skilful dramatic timing, and a compelling interaction between its protagonists.

DUTTON, G(eoffrey) F(raser) (1924–), British poet, born on the Welsh borders, of Anglo-Scottish parentage. He has lived most of his life in Scotland and has published works on a variety of subjects, including enzymology and mountaineering. His first full-length collection, *Camp One* (1978), received a New Writing Award from the Scottish Arts Council. *Squaring the Waves* (1986), which attracted a wider critical response, was followed by *The Concrete Garden* (1991). The austere landscape around his home in a mountainous region of Perthshire and his active interest in the coastal and inland waters of Scotland are essential themes of his poetry. His style is extremely economical; a rigorous imagism is fashioned into slender, concentrated poems which often incorporate smooth mechanisms of rhyme and metre to highly unusual effect. He has also published a collection of short stories entitled *The Ridiculous Mountains* (1984).

DWORKIN, Andrea (1945–), American feminist writer, critical commentator, and political activist, born in Camden, New Jersey, educated at Bennington College. Active in women's campaigns throughout the USA, Dworkin has associated herself with the anti-pornography campaign. Her impassioned, and frequently controversial, writings attempt to lay bare the nature of patriarchal control; above all she sees such control expressed in acts of aggression against women. Her influential critical work *Pornography: Men Possessing Women* (1981) is a searing documentation of male violence against women, as is *Our Blood: Prophecies and Discourses on Sexual Politics* (1982). Dworkin has also written a fictional first-person account of a precarious female existence as a prostitute in New York's Lower East Side in her novel, *Ice and Fire* (1986), as well as a quasi-autobiographical novel about the female experience of rape, *Mercy* (1990). Equally controversial and even more polemical is *Intercourse* (1987). The control of women through domesticity and women's acceptance of male authority are discussed in *Right-Wing Women: The Politics of Domesticated Females* (1983). A decade of campaign speeches, interviews, and essays are collected in *Letters from a War Zone* (1988).

DYLAN, Bob (1941–), American songwriter and singer, born in Duluth, Minnesota, educated at the University of Minnesota. Originally named Robert Zimmerman, he became known as Bob Dylan in 1962. *The Freewheelin' Bob Dylan* (1963) and *The Times They Are A'Changin'* (1964) made him internationally famous as the leading 'protest singer' of the day. Much of his most impressive work was recorded on *Highway 61 Revisited* (1965) and *Blonde on Blonde* (1966), personal and socio-political themes combining in lyrics of considerable imaginative scope and incisiveness. Among his subsequent recordings are *Planet Waves* (1974), *Desire* (1975), *Street Legal* (1978), and *Saved* (1980), the last-named affirming the Christian beliefs he adopted in the late 1970s. Many of Dylan's songs exhibit great facility in rhyming and the ability to organize complex patterns of imagery into compelling lyrical structures. The poetic concentration of much of his writing has attracted the attention of several eminent literary critics, notably Christopher *Ricks. His disjunctively experimental novel *Tarantula* appeared in 1971; *Lyrics, 1962–1985* (1985) contains the words of his songs along with his drawings and other writings.

Dynasts, The, subtitled 'an epic-drama of the war with Napoleon, in three parts, nineteen acts and one hundred and thirty scenes': a verse-drama by Thomas *Hardy, published in three parts: 1904; 1906; and 1908. It is an extraordinary mixture of prose and poetry, epic and drama, incorporating narrative, theatrical, and even cinematic techniques. The first part of the work centres on the figure of Napoleon and concerns the events of the war with England, including the French invasion plans of 1805 and the battles of Ulm, Austerlitz, and Trafalgar. The second part describes the Prussian defeat at Jena; the meeting of Napoleon and Alexander at Tilsit; the battle of Wagram and the war in Spain; and Napoleon's divorce from Josephine, followed by his marriage to Marie Louise. Part III deals with the Russian campaign of 1812, the battle of Leipzig, Napoleon's abdication, and his eventual defeat at Waterloo. In each instance, the main historical events, narrated in a series of long and detailed scenes, are interspersed with short episodes describing the effect of each major political upheaval on the lives of ordinary people. In addition to this terrestrial commentary, a cast of supernatural beings—the Ancient Spirit of the Years, the Spirit of the Pities, the Spirits Sinister and Ironic, the Spirit of Rumour, and the Shade of the Earth—provide a Chorus on the affairs of the historical personages, amongst whom, apart from Napoleon himself, are included King George III, William Pitt, Charles James Fox, Horatio Nelson, and Thomas Masterman Hardy, Captain of the *Victory* and a distant relative of the author. Presiding over the entire drama is the Immanent Will, epitomizing the spirit of blind chance in human affairs, as it appears in many of Hardy's novels.

E

EAGLETON, Terry (1943–), British critic, born in Salford, educated at Trinity College, Cambridge; he became Warton Professor of English Literature at Oxford. A lively and committed literary reviewer, Eagleton's abiding interest, as a Marxist from a working-class Catholic background, has been in what he calls the politics of power, and more precisely, in the influence of buried or denied historical conditions on works of art and views of literature. In *Exiles and Emigrés* (1970) he makes connections between biographical facts and fictional themes in modern writing. Later work, like *Walter Benjamin* (1981) and *The Rape of Clarissa* (1982), elegantly combines Marxist thought with developing Continental literary theory and philosophy. Eagleton's best-known book, much read by students both tempted and baffled by the new terms of literary debate, is his witty and polemical *Literary Theory: An Introduction* (1983), a survey which is also a statement of theory's current account. Perhaps less widely read, but more substantial, is *The Ideology of the Aesthetic* (1990), a sustained pursuit of a sequence of ideas, from Kant to Adorno, to their various philosophical and literary lairs. A controversial figure, Eagleton has seen his role as that of challenging orthodoxies, including the orthodoxy of relativism, or of simple, unreflecting opposition to all versions of truth or order. Recent works include *Ideology: An Introduction* (1991), *Heathcliff and the Great Hunger* (1995), and the script for Derek Jarman's film *Wittgenstein* (1993). See also MARXIST LITERARY CRITICISM.

EARLE, Jean, the pseudonym of Doris BURGE (1909–), British poet, born in Bristol; she grew up in the Rhondda Valley of South Wales, which provides material for a number of her poems. Since 1937 she has lived in various parts of Wales. *A Trial of Strength* (1980), her first collection of poems, appeared when she was 71, following her resumption of writing many years after the publication of some of her stories and poems in various magazines. The volume suggests access to deep resources of memory and imagination in the disquietingly understated intensities of mood and deftly assured free-verse cadences of many poems. Her subsequent collections include *The Intent Look* (1984), *Visiting Light* (1987), and *Selected Poems* (1990). Much of her work explores the possibilities of affirmative significance in human and natural contexts she habitually views with sceptical intelligence. She has also written radio documentaries and worked as a literary journalist.

Earthly Powers, a novel by Anthony *Burgess, published in 1980. Narrated by Kenneth Toomey, an ageing homosexual and celebrated novelist, the story covers six decades and a vast geographical area. It is driven by a strong moral anger belied by the wit and humour of much of the book and the acknowledged decadence of its narrator. The first part portrays a society flawed and fallen, made evident in the developing tragedies of early twentieth-century Europe. The Catholic Church, though frequently invoked at points of suffering or squalor, is not presented as arbiter or remedy. Among the gallery of fictional and historical characters few are admired by Toomey, although his sister Hortense and his brother-in-law, the priest Carlo, become important. The first climax comes when the young Toomey meets Philip Shawcross, a doctor in a hospital in Malaya, and develops a strong, non-sexual love for him. Cursed by a Malay whose son dies at the hospital, Shawcross becomes dangerously ill. Carlo conducts an exorcism but the curse is lifted too late for Shawcross, who dies. Nevertheless, for the first time Toomey has acknowledged an intense non-sexual love, and for the first time—in the person of Carlo—human evil has been countered by religious certainties. This invasion of light into the darkness of the novel's world is one of its major structural pivots.

Carlo, ministering to his dying brother in Chicago, blesses a dying child, who recovers miraculously. Yet Burgess presents Carlo ambiguously: his rapid rise in the church is shown to be due to ambition, and Carlo appears to have little theological or pastoral insight. In strong contrast to Carlo is Godfrey Manning, leader of an extreme religious sect which he leads into an act of mass suicide/massacre. Toomey visits the sect in search of his niece who is a convert. The final ironic twist of the novel is that the child miraculously healed by Carlo in the Chicago hospital was none other than Godfrey Manning. Burgess refuses to portray good and evil in human beings as absolute. As Toomey ages in his own story and his sexual powers wane, evil is seen to be less what people *do* than what people *are*. By the inclusion of real events (the wartime broadcasts of P. G. *Wodehouse, the **Lady Chatterley* trial, etc.) and real people (Norman *Douglas, Rudyard *Kipling, etc.), the theological subtext is made contemporary and given currency.

EASTLAKE, William (1917–), American novelist, born in New York. He spent four years in the army, attended the Alliance Française in Paris, and later settled on a 300-acre cattle ranch in Cuba, New Mexico. There are three strands to his writing, the least important being his political work in *A Child's Garden of Verses for the Revolution* (1970) and *The Long Naked Descent into Boston* (1977). The second strand is his remarkable writing on the American West contained in *Go in Beauty* (1956), *The Bronc People* (1958), *Portrait of an Artist with Twenty-Six Horses* (1963), and *Dancers in the Scalp House* (1975). These books move from a concentration on the white experience of the West through to an accumulating sympathy for the plight of the Native American, registered most effectively in *Dancers*, whose linguistic experiments contort the American language in order to convey more accurately the scope and humanity of Indian thought. *Dancers* also presents with great anger and urgency an ecological viewpoint which Eastlake associates most closely with the patternings of Indian life. The third strand of his fiction deals with the reality of war; *Castle Keep* (1965) is a dense, formally innovative study of the Second World War, and *The Bamboo Bed* (1969) carries the same set of procedures into the war in Vietnam (see VIETNAM WRITING). His understandings of the power complex and his subtle investigations of memory help to turn these quasi-philosophical novels into important studies of the phenomenon of modern warfare.

EASTMAN, Charles (Alexander) (Ohiyesa) (1858–1939), Native American writer, born in Minnesota of mixed Sioux Indian and white parentage, educated at Dartmouth and Boston University Medical School. Eastman was one of the first Native American writers to achieve a mass popular audience through his magazine accounts of Indian life and customs, and volumes such as *Red Hunters and the Animal People* (1904) and *Old Indian Days* (1907). He has also inspired other Sioux to write, such as Luther *Standing Bear. *Wigwam Evenings* (1909; reissued as *Smoky Day's Wigwam Evenings*, 1910) was written in collaboration with his wife Elaine Goodale Eastman, herself a noted writer, whom he met and married when he was a government physician at Pine Ridge agency in South Dakota; there he witnessed the aftermath of the Wounded Knee Massacre. Eastman's influence has been felt most acutely through his autobiographical writing. *Indian Boyhood* (1902) describes his life to the age of 15 when he was sent to mission school. *From the Deep Woods to Civilization* (1916) describes his experience of white America, stresses the contribution of Indians to American society, and articulates a powerful criticism of the US government for its indifference towards the suffering of the Sioux people. In *The Soul of the Indian: An Interpretation* (1911), *Indian Child Life* (1913), *The Indian Today: The Past and Future of the American Indian* (1915), and *Indian Heroes and Great Chieftains* (1918), Eastman offers an appreciation of Indian culture. See also NATIVE AMERICAN LITERATURE.

EASTMAN, Max (Forrester) (1883–1969), American political writer and critic, born in Canandaigua, New York, educated at Williams College and Columbia University, where he taught philosophy between 1907 and 1911. In 1912 he became editor of the socialist periodical *The *Masses* and subsequently edited the pro-Soviet *Liberator*. His enthusiasm for the Soviet system was subdued by a visit to Russia during Stalin's ascendancy to power. *Since Lenin Died* (1925) was the first of a series of penetrating critiques of communism which also include *Marx and Lenin, the Science of Revolution* (1926) and *The End of Socialism in Russia* (1937). *The Enjoyment of Poetry* (1913), a valuable study of metaphor, is the best-known of his critical works; his antagonism to *Modernism becomes evident in *The Literary Mind* (1931), while *The Enjoyment of Laughter* (1936) opposes the claims of Freudian literary theory. *The Colours of Life* (1918) and succeeding volumes of his conventionally lyrical verse are collected in *Poems of Five Decades* (1954), which includes verse translations, chiefly from the Russian. From 1941 onward he travelled widely as a corresponding editor for *Reader's Digest*. *Heroes I Have Known* (1942) and *Great Companions* (1959) recount his associations with Mark Twain, Charlie Chaplin, John *Dewey, Ernest *Hemingway, and numerous others, including Lev Trotsky, whose *History of the Russian Revolution* (three volumes, 1932–3) he translated and of whom he produced a biography (1925). *Love and Revolution* (1965) is Eastman's autobiography.

East of Eden, see STEINBECK, JOHN.

EASTON ELLIS, Bret, see ELLIS, BRET EASTON.

EBERHART, Richard (1904–), American poet, born in Austin, Minnesota, educated at the universities of Minnesota, Dartmouth, Cambridge, and Harvard. Eberhart spent eight years as a school teacher in Southboro where one of his pupils was Robert *Lowell. At Cambridge in the late 1920s he became acquainted with the critical theories of William *Empson, and of I. A. *Richards who encouraged him as a poet. Eberhart's first book of poems, *A Bravery of Earth* (1930), was published in London. He has subsequently published nearly thirty volumes of poetry including *Selected Poems 1930–65* (1965; Pulitzer Prize), *Collected Poems 1930–76* (1976), and *The Long Reach: New and Uncollected Poems 1948–84* (1984). His *Collected Verse Plays* appeared in 1962. A traditionalist by conviction and a formalist in technique, Eberhart blends his traditional values with his visionary belief in the power of the imagination to inscribe the transcendental in the ordinary. Thus his deceptively simple poetry is impacted with a questioning complexity, and works through the juxtaposition of the commonplace and the allusive, effecting a union between reason and imagination.

Ebony Tower, see FOWLES, JOHN.

Echoing Grove, The, see LEHMANN, ROSAMOND.

EDEL, (Joseph) Leon (1907–), American biographer, born in Pittsburgh, Pennsylvania, educated at McGill University, Toronto, and the University of

Paris. During the 1930s he worked as a journalist and subsequently taught at New York University, where he became a professor in 1955. The five volumes of *Henry James* (1953–72), for which he received a Pulitzer Prize in 1963, established his eminence as a biographer. While avoiding the technical vocabulary of psychoanalysis, Edel's practice of biography makes extensive use of Freudian interpretative methods. His other works include *James Joyce: The Last Journey* (1947), *Bloomsbury: A House of Lions* (1979), *The Stuff of Sleep and Dreams* (1982), essays on literary psychology, and *Writing Lives* (1984), a discussion of biography, which he defends as 'a noble and adventurous art'. He is also noted for his editions of the writings of Henry *James, which include *The Complete Plays* (1949) and the four volumes of *Letters* (1974–84).

EDGAR, David (1948–), British playwright, born in Birmingham, the son of a television producer, educated at Manchester University. His first plays, mostly pieces of radical agitprop, were produced in Bradford while he was working there as a journalist; he continued in broadly the same vein until the mid-1970s, producing such work as the anti-Common Market *A Fart for Europe* (1972) and a Shakespearian parody about Richard Nixon, *Dick Deterred* (1974), usually for small socialist touring companies. But then came *Destiny* (1976), a study of racism and neo-fascism in modern Britain which, though clearly written from a left-wing stance, displayed an unexpected sensitivity, openness of mind, and interest in understanding his political enemies rather than straightforwardly condemning them. The same qualities have often marked his subsequent work, notably *The Jail Diary of Albie Sachs* (1978), about an imprisoned South African dissident; *Mary Barnes* (1978), a study of schizophrenia; *Maydays* (1983), a piece of epic sweep about the rise of the right wing in Britain; *Entertaining Strangers* (1985); *The Shape of the Table* (1990), a speculative picture of the mostly secret meetings and negotiations that brought about the radical changes in Eastern Europe in the late 1980s; and the ambitious *Pentecost* (1994), set in a Balkan country coming to terms with its new freedoms and, with its discovery of what may be a historically important fresco, raising questions about art and culture as well as nationalism, language, and the refugee problem. Edgar has also written for radio and television and made several adaptations for the stage, notably an eight-hour version of Dickens's *Nicholas Nickleby* which enjoyed great success when it was performed by the Royal Shakespeare Company in 1980.

EDGELL, Zee (1940–), Belizean novelist, born in Belize City, educated at Regent Street Polytechnic and the University of the West Indies. After working as a schoolteacher and newspaper editor, she became the Director of the Belizean administration's Department of Women's Affairs and has been an educational consultant since 1990. *Beka Lamb* (1982), her first novel and the first Belizean work of fiction to attract international notice, parallels the growth to maturity and independence of its female protagonist with the emergence and consolidation of Belize's sense of national identity. Like its predecessor, Edgell's second novel, *In Times Like These* (1991), conflates personal and national themes in its account of a well-educated Belizean woman's political involvements upon returning to her native country on the eve of Independence.

Edinburgh Review, The, a quarterly literary magazine begun in 1969 as the *New Edinburgh Review*, the title alluding to the *Edinburgh Review* (1802–1929), to which many of the major writers of the nineteenth and early twentieth centuries contributed. David Cubitt was the first editor of the *New Edinburgh Review*, which was published by students of Edinburgh University and contained poetry, short stories, and reviews of books and theatrical activities. By 1971 the journal had attracted work from numerous leading Scottish authors, including Hugh *MacDiarmid, George Mackay *Brown, and Norman *MacCaig. Under James Campbell's editorship from 1978 to 1982 the *Review* emerged as a literary periodical of repute, publishing work by a wide range of eminent writers who included Robert *Creeley, David *Daiches, Gavin *Ewart, Douglas *Dunn, William *Burroughs, and James *Baldwin. Allan *Massie, editor between 1982 and 1984, maintained the liveliness of tone and high standards Campbell had established, introducing James Naughtie as a political commentator and featuring stories by Muriel *Spark, William *Boyd, and Emma *Tennant. The present title was assumed in 1985. The magazine publishes prose fiction, poetry, reviews, and critical articles on literature, the graphic arts, and socio-cultural topics. Frank *Kuppner, James *Simmons, Tom *Leonard, Edwin *Morgan, and Alasdair *Gray are among the regular contributors.

EDMOND, Lauris (1924–), New Zealand poet, born in Hawkes Bay, educated there at Wellington Teachers' College and at Waikato University, Hamilton. Having married and produced five children Edmond was 51 when her first book appeared. Her collections include *In Middle Air* (1975), *The Pear Tree: Poems* (1977), *Wellington Letter* (1980), *Seven Poems* (1980), *Salt from the North* (1980), *Catching It* (1980), *Selected Poems* (1984), *Seasons and Creatures* (1986), and *Summer Near the Arctic Circle* (1988). A lyric poet with a bundle of obsessions that she has refined, developed, and duplicated in all her collections, her concerns are 'the interpenetrations of the domestic and the intellectual; observations of flora, fauna, families, lovers and loved ones; meditations on birth, love, separation, death ...' (Michele Leggott, in **Landfall*). One of New Zealand's most popular poets, Edmond is part of the literary scene in Wellington which includes Louis *Johnson and Vincent *O'Sullivan. She portrays herself as the poet and spokesperson of a generation of women effectively silenced by their responsibilities as wives and mothers; this is the tenor of her autobiographical works *Hot October: An Autobiographical Story* (1989) and *Bonfires in the Rain* (1991). A novel, *High Country Weather*, appeared in 1984.

EDMOND, Murray (1949–), New Zealand poet, playwright, and critic, born in Hamilton, educated at the University of Auckland. He has since worked in the theatre while continuing to write poetry. Edmond was published in **Landfall* while still at school, and in the early 1970s he was the editor of several issues of the 'messianic' and important though short-lived magazine *The Word is Freed*, which was very much the vehicle of a generation of young poets in the late 1960s which included Bill *Manhire and Ian *Wedde. Wedde describes Edmond's poems as 'rhapsodic and linguistically dense' and as having 'dramatic and narrative qualities which owe much to his life in theatre'. Edmond's interest in personal and domestic themes is related to wider intellectual concerns, such as the 'presence' of local histories, and indigenous and other literatures. Stylistically, Edmond shows an increasing commitment to innovation and experiment. Collections of poems include *Entering the Eye* (1973), *Patchwork* (1978), *End Wall* (1981), *Letters and Paragraphs* (1987), and *From the Word Go* (1992). *The Switch* (1994) is an experimental long poem in forty-nine parts on love and transience. He has also written short plays for children, a full-length musical *A New South Pacific*, and critical work on New Zealand drama and poetry; with Mary Paul he edited an anthology, *The New Poets: Initiatives in Recent New Zealand Poetry* (1987).

EDRIC, Robert, pseudonym of Gary Edric ARMITAGE (1956–), British novelist, born in Sheffield, educated at Hull University; he became a full-time writer in 1982. His novels *A Season of Peace* (1985) and *Across the Autumn Grass* (1986) were published under his original name. *Winter Garden* (1985), the first of his novels as Edric, won the James Tait Black Award, and displayed his masterful handling of the complex and sinisterly comic narratives often characteristic of his work. *In the Days of the American Museum* (1990) forms an extravagantly imaginative treatment of P. T. Barnum's celebrated exhibition of curiosities. *The Broken Lands* (1992) is a harrowingly bleak account of Sir John Franklin's search for the North West Passage. A small town in southern Germany in 1945 is the setting for the narrative of guilt and concealment in *Hallowed Ground* (1993). *The Earth Made Glass* (1994) deals compellingly with the arrival of an inquisitor in a remote village in seventeenth-century England. Edric's other novels include *A New Ice Age* (1986), *A Lunar Eclipse* (1989) and *Elysium* (1995).

Education of Henry Adams, The, an autobiography by Henry (Brooks) *Adams, privately printed in 1907 and posthumously published in 1918. Generally ranked as one of the most distinguished autobiographies, its subtitle, 'A Study of Twentieth-Century Multiplicity', describes Adams's purpose; he employs a series of selected moments from his life in order to illustrate his highly privileged existence and to set out his dynamic theories of history and philosophy. The book represents his long career as a failure, despite his successful achievements, because the USA was unable to equip him to meet the battles he had to face. His earlier work, **Mont-Saint-Michel and Chartres* (1904), studies Europe from the perspective of the thirteenth century, 'the point of history when man held the highest idea of himself as a unit in a unified universe' and thus contrasts with his description in *The Education* of the modern world as a 'multiverse'. This conception is best expressed in the chapter 'The Dynamo and the Virgin', in which he sees the mechanical dynamo, the symbol of electrical energy, as corresponding to the central symbol of the medieval world-view, the Virgin. Generated as it was by the World's Columbian Exposition of 1893 in Chicago, this idea also marked the geographical shift of ideas from the Eastern seaboard, which had been populated by generations of the Adams family, to the industrial heartlands of the Midwest. As such, it indicates the intellectual shift from the nineteenth century to a distinctively twentieth-century frame of thought.

EGAN, Desmond (1936–), Irish poet, born in Athlone, County West Meath, educated at University College, Dublin, afterwards becoming a teacher. In 1972 he founded the Goldsmith Press, which has since produced many editions, principally of poetry by Irish authors, including *Patrick Kavanagh: The Complete Poems* (edited by Peter Kavanagh, 1984). Egan's first collection of poetry, *Midland* (1973), was followed by subsequent volumes including *Song for My Father* (1989), *Seeing Double* (1991), and *In the Holocaust of Autumn* (1994); *Collected Poems* appeared in 1984, and *Selected Poems* in 1992, with an introduction by Hugh *Kenner. A keen interest in the possibilities of experimental poetic forms is evident throughout his work, which ranges thematically between outspokenly political poems and precisely observed lyrical verse. His other works include *The Death of Metaphor* (1989), a collection of his literary essays.

EGBUNA, Obi B(enue) (1938–), Nigerian novelist and short-story writer, educated at the University of Iowa and Howard University, Washington, DC. He lived in England from 1961 to 1973, where he became involved in the Black Power movement. Radical and impassioned, *Destroy This Temple: The Voice of Black Power in Britain* (1971) describes his spell on remand in Brixton Prison and the general political turmoil during this time. The problems he encountered when he returned to Nigeria are described in *The Diary of a Homeless Prodigal* (1978). His first novel, *Elina* (1978; first published as *Wind versus Polygamy*, 1964), caused great controversy in its sympathetic portrayal of a polygamous chief. Other novels include *The Minister's Daughter* (1975), which sets a young student against a corrupt government minister; and *The Madness of Didi* (1980) in which the eponymous former priest and college professor, a thinly disguised self-portrait, is a hero to the young, but due to his radical past faces suspicion when he returns to his native village. All Egbuna's novels display a sardonic sense of humour, as did his play *The Anthill* (1965). His collections of short stories include *Daughters of the Sun* (1970), *Emperor of the Sea* (1974), and *The Rape of Lysistrata and Black Candles for Christmas* (1980).

Egoist, The, a literary periodical strongly associated with the development of *Modernism in England from 1914 to 1919. Dora Marsden had formed the *Freewoman* in 1911, a magazine devoted to issues facing the 'new woman' and to philosophical discussion; in 1913 it became the *New Freewoman*, subtitled *An Individualist Review*, and attracted the attention of Ezra *Pound, who persuaded Marsden that innovative literary material should be included. The first issue under the title *The Egoist* appeared early in 1914; later that year Harriet Shaw Weaver succeeded Marsden as editor, the latter continuing to supply each issue with her singular philosophical essays. Richard *Aldington was assistant editor from 1914 to 1916, when his wife Hilda *Doolittle took over the position, which was occupied by T. S. *Eliot from 1917 to 1919. Pound ensured that *Imagism was strongly promoted in the magazine and contributed many critical articles cogently arguing in support of the writing he favoured; although he was responsible for the magazine's sometimes arrogant tone, he also arranged the publication of much of its best material: James Joyce's **Portrait of the Artist as a Young Man* was serialized in 1914 and 1915, and extracts from **Ulysses* were later published. Poetry from America was supplied by Marianne *Moore, W. C. *Williams, and others. Eliot's critical essays, which began appearing regularly in 1917, contained some of his most provocative and iconoclastic criticism; his 'Tradition and the Individual Talent' was featured in the last issue of *The Egoist*, which was discontinued as a result of increasing financial difficulties in 1919.

EKWENSI, Cyprian (Odiatu Duaka) (1921–), Nigerian novelist and short-story writer, born in Minna, Northern Nigeria, educated at the Universities of Ibadan and Ghana, and at the Chelsea School of Pharmacy, University of London. He has also been a lecturer and broadcaster, and has served with the Federal Ministry of Information, Lagos, and the Bureau of External Publicity in Biafra during the Nigerian Civil War. Ekwensi is generally recognized as an entertaining chronicler of the big city life in West Africa, and his novels are characterized by a vigorous, realistic style. His most famous novel, *Jagua Nana* (1961), follows the 'ageing African beauty' of the title, which refers both to Zola's original 'demimondaine' and the pidgin word for 'Jaguar' cars, in her quest for love and money in 'high life' Lagos. *People of the City* (1954), *Beautiful Feathers* (1963), and *Lokotown and Other Stories* (1966) are also all set in Lagos, and peopled with vivid characters in their hectic struggle to survive, or to shine. *Burning Grass* (1962), written as a children's story, deals with the Fulani cattlemen of Northern Nigeria, and is generally considered to be one of Ekwensi's most successful, though least characteristic, novels.

ELDERSHAW, M. Barnard, pseudonym of Marjorie BARNARD (1897–1987) and Flora ELDERSHAW (1897–1956), two Australian writers who worked in collaboration. Of their five novels the most successful was *A House Is Built* (1929), which traces the fortunes of a nineteenth-century Sydney family; the most ambitious was *Tomorrow and Tomorrow* (1947; unexpurgated version 1983), a satirical fantasy, set in Australia 400 years into the future. Other collaborations include *Phillip of Australia* (1938), *The Life and Times of Captain John Piper* (1939), and *My Australia* (1939), all historical works; *But Not for Love* (1989), a posthumous collection of short stories; and *Essays on Australian Fiction* (1938). Both women edited and published independent works. Eldershaw edited *The Peaceful Army* (1938), a collection of essays and poems by Australian women writers; Barnard published several more historical studies, critical essays for **Meanjin* and **Southerly*, a biography of Miles *Franklin, and *The Persimmon Tree* (1943), a collection of short stories.

Elder Statesman, The, a play by T. S. *Eliot.

ELIOT, T(homas) S(tearns) (1888–1965), American poet, critic, and dramatist, the son of a successful businessman of New England descent, born in St Louis, Missouri, where he attended the Smith Academy, contributing poems and stories to the school's magazine. In 1906 he entered Harvard, studying literature, history, and philosophy as an undergraduate and taking a master's degree in English Literature; among his teachers was Irving *Babbitt, whose repudiation of Romanticism and stress on the ethical functions of literature formed an abiding influence on Eliot's thought. In October 1910 he travelled to Europe, staying chiefly in Paris, where he attended lectures at the Sorbonne; 'Portrait of a Lady' and 'The Love Song of J. Alfred Prufrock' were completed before his return to Harvard to begin work on a Ph.D. in philosophy in the autumn of 1911. Having obtained a travelling fellowship, he went to England in 1914 to study at Merton College, Oxford. Conrad *Aiken, whom Eliot knew from Harvard, supplied him with an introduction to Ezra *Pound, who responded to his poetry by noting in a letter that 'he has actually . . . modernized himself *on his own*'; in the course of 1915 Pound introduced Eliot's poems to several magazines, notably **Poetry* and **Blast*, and included five in his *Catholic Anthology* of that year. Eliot had produced all the poems collected in **Prufrock and Other Observations* (1917), his first collection of verse, by the summer of 1915. His early work displayed striking originality and accomplishment, combining the suppleness of free verse with shrewd virtuosity in the use of rhythm and rhyme; imagery drawn from precise observation gained in poise and effectiveness from the detached irony of tone he had acquired at Harvard from his reading of Jules Laforgue (1860–87).

Marriage to Vivien Haigh-Wood in 1915, together with the stimulation and opportunities provided by his entry to the circle associated with the emergence of Anglo-American literary *Modernism, precluded his return to America to pursue the academic career he had formerly considered. His doctoral dissertation, published as *Knowledge and Experience in the Philosophy of F. H. Bradley* in 1964, was accepted by Harvard in 1916, but he did not complete the University's requirements for the degree. He worked as a schoolteacher, book reviewer, and tutor for the University of London Extension Board until he joined the Colonial and Foreign Department of Lloyd's Bank in 1917, when he also became assistant editor of the **Egoist*; the articles he produced for the magazine include numerous examples of his most vigorous and incisive criticism. By 1919 he was also reviewing regularly for the **Times Literary Supplement* and the **Athenaeum*; *The Sacred Wood* (1920) collected the best of his literary journalism from these years, including 'Tradition and the Individual Talent', in which he argued that 'the progress of an artist is . . . a continual extinction of personality', and 'Hamlet', in the course of which he coined the term *'objective correlative'. *Poems* (1919), published by the *Hogarth Press, demonstrated energetic technical and thematic advances; 'Whispers of Immortality' and 'Sweeney among the Nightingales' used rhymed quatrains of remarkable facility and concentration to achieve astringently witty presentations of their morbid social anatomies. *Ara Vos Prec* and the American edition of *Poems*, both of 1920, contained previously collected poems along with fresh material, notably 'Gerontion', a dramatically disquieting expression of his intensifying pessimism which displays the deepening historical and imaginative resonances commanded by his fluently allusive manner.

In 1921 both Eliot and his wife succumbed to nervous and emotional disorders; given three months' leave by his employers, he rested in Margate before going to Lausanne for treatment, on the recommendation of Lady Ottoline *Morrell. During this period he completed *The *Waste Land* (1922). The poem appeared in the first edition of the **Criterion*, of which Eliot remained editor, doing much to promote the acceptance of literary Modernism, until it ceased publication in 1939; the socio-cultural views in his editorials reflected the growing conservatism suggested by the assertion that he was 'classicist in literature, royalist in politics, and anglo-catholic in religion' in the preface to his essays in *For Lancelot Andrewes* (1928). He was received into the Church of England in 1927; in that year he also took British citizenship and composed *'Journey of the Magi', which established the importance of religious elements to most of his later work. *The Waste Land* having gained Eliot wide notice as a poet, his reputation was consolidated by *Poems 1909–1925* (1925); the only previously uncollected poem in the volume was 'The Hollow Men', the incantatory austerity of which anticipated the ritualistic qualities of much of his subsequent poetry. The book was the first of Eliot's to be issued by Faber and Gwyer (later *Faber and Faber), whose board of directors he joined in 1925; Pound, W. H. *Auden, Louis *MacNeice, Wallace *Stevens, Marianne *Moore, David *Jones, and Ted *Hughes are among the poets he secured for Faber's list. His work as a poet continued with *Ash Wednesday* (1930), a devotional meditation in six parts on self-denial and the possibility of redemption; it draws chiefly upon Dante and the Bible for its emblematic imagery, in which power and strangeness combine with great lucidity chiefly as a result of a new openness in the poem's language. The spirited children's verse of *Old Possum's Book of Practical Cats* (1939) forms a refreshing hiatus in the meditative seriousness of his later poetry, which culminates with **Four Quartets* (1943); with the exception of numerous minor poems, the sequence concluded his career as a poet.

The publications which gained him pre-eminence among the critics of his day include *The Use of Poetry and the Use of Criticism* (1933), *After Strange Gods* (1934), *Essays Ancient and Modern* (1936), *The Idea of a Christian Society* (1939), *Notes towards the Definition of Culture* (1948), and *On Poetry and Poets* (1957). His pervasive concern with the interdependence of literary tradition and modern cultural values decisively influenced the development of modern criticism through its appeal to F. R. *Leavis and his associates at **Scrutiny*; social and ethical issues assume growing importance in his critical writings in the course of the 1930s. In 1932 and 1933 Eliot lectured at various American universities. Upon his return to Britain he effected a separation from his wife, whose growing mental imbalance had reduced their marriage's hitherto meagre potential for success; Vivien was eventually committed to a psychiatric hospital, where she died in 1947. Eliot was married in 1957 to Valerie Fletcher, his secretary at Faber and Faber; their happiness is clear from the late poem 'A Dedication to my Wife'.

The uncompleted *Sweeney Agonistes* (1932), begun in 1923 and performed by the *Group Theatre in 1934, marked the beginning of his preoccupation with poetic drama; *The Rock* (1934), an ecclesiastical and historical pageant reflecting the social and political concerns of the early 1930s, was followed by **Murder in the Cathedral* in 1935. *The *Family Reunion* (1939) was the first of his attempts to align his underlying spiritual concerns with the conventions of the popular theatre; although the play was not a commercial success, he sustained the endeavour, in the belief that his art should serve a broad social purpose, with *The *Cocktail Party* (1950), *The Confidential Clerk* (1954), and *The Elder Statesman* (1959). Public enthusiasm for these plays was partly a result of Eliot's greatly increased prominence following the awards of the Nobel Prize and the Order of Merit in 1948. In his later years he enjoyed unrivalled celebrity and veneration as a literary and cultural figure; in terms of his combined importance to literature in English as a poet and critic, he remains the major figure of the twentieth century. His *Complete Poems and Plays* appeared in 1969 and *Selected Prose*, edited by Frank *Kermode, was published in 1975. The principal biographical studies are Peter *Ackroyd's *T. S. Eliot* (1984), and Lyndall Gordon's *Eliot's Early Years* (1977) and *Eliot's New Life* (1988); among the more interesting of many critical treatments are Hugh *Kenner's *The Invisible Poet* (1959), Bernard *Bergonzi's *T. S. Eliot* (1972), and Helen *Gardner's *The Composition of 'Four Quartets'* (1978). The first volume of Eliot's *Letters*, edited by his wife Valerie Eliot, was published in 1988.

ELKIN, Stanley (Lawrence) (1930–), American novelist and short-story writer, born in Brooklyn, New York City, educated at the University of Illinois. Elkin has been described as a 'major Jewish-American post-modernist' although his reputation has been somewhat eclipsed by other Jewish writers such as Saul *Bellow, Bernard *Malamud, and Philip *Roth. His first novel, *Boswell* (1964), revealed his striking talent for absurdist black humour and comic monologue, talents further developed in his first collection of short stories, *Criers and Kibitzers, Kibitzers and Criers* (1966), and in his second novel, *A Bad Man* (1967), where the humour is given a metaphysical edge in Elkin's meditations on the paradox of good and evil. *The Dick Gibson Show* (1971) received critical acclaim, while *Searches and Seizures* (1973; UK title *Eligible Men*, 1974) brought Elkin a wider audience through the cinematic adaptation of the first novella in the collection ('The Bailbondsman'), filmed as *Alex and the Gipsy*. Further novels include *The Franchiser* (1976), *George Mills* (1982), *The Magic Kingdom* (1984), *The Rabbi of Lud* (1987), and the *MacGuffin* (1991). *The Living End* (1979) contains three long stories, satirizing religion, and is notable for both its blasphemy and its vulgarity. Elkin took up an academic post in 1960 at Washington University in St Louis, becoming King Professor of Modern Letters in 1983, and has gained many academic awards.

ELLIOT, Alistair (1932–), British poet, born in Liverpool; he spent his childhood in the north of England and the USA, and was educated at Christ Church, Oxford. Among other posts, he has been a librarian in Britain, Europe, and the Middle East. The first of his principal collections of poetry, *Contentions* (1978), was followed by subsequent volumes including *Talking Back* (1982); *On the Appian Way* (1984), a long sequence recounting his journey on foot from Rome to Brindisi; *My Country* (1989), a collected edition; and *Turning the Stones* (1993). Elliot's poetry is characterized by its urbane informality of tone and its fluent use of rhymed traditional forms. His work draws equally on personal experience and on his considerable erudition, which is put to entertaining use in the numerous imaginative dialogues with historical figures in *Talking Back*. His numerous translations include a version of Heinrich Heine's *The Lazarus Poems* (1979) and Euripides' *Medea* (1993). Among the works he has edited is *Poems by James I and Others* (1970).

ELLIOTT, Janice (1931–95), British novelist, born in Derby, educated at St Anne's College, Oxford. She worked as a journalist in London until she became a freelance writer in 1962. She achieved wide recognition with her 'England Trilogy', *A State of Peace* (1971), *Private Life* (1972), and *Heaven on Earth* (1975), which depicts the social and cultural character of England in the years immediately following the Second World War with remarkable detail and authenticity. While a number of her books display a preoccupation with the psychological tensions beneath the rational surfaces of contemporary British middle-class life, her imaginative range was wide; esoteric political and mystical elements were ascendant in her later work, which includes *Dr Gruber's Daughter* (1986), in which Hitler lives out old age in an Oxford attic, and *The Sadness of the Witches* (1987), a bizarre fable set in Cornwall. *Summer People* (1980), *Secret Places* (1981), *Necessary Rites* (1990), *City of Gates* (1992), and *Figures in the Sand* (1994) are also among her twenty-two novels. She has also published *Noises from the Zoo* (1991), a collection of short stories, and five children's books.

ELLIS, Alice Thomas, pseudonym of Anna Margaret HAYCRAFT (1932–), British novelist, born in Liverpool, educated at Bangor Grammar School and Liverpool School of Art. The landscapes of North Wales, where she grew up, form the background to many of her short, poignant, and witty novels, the first of which was *The Sin Eater* (1977). Roman Catholicism, to which she is a convert, is an important influence on her vision, as is a strong sense of tragedy, which invariably leavens the fierce comedy that characterizes her fiction. Other novels include *The Birds of the Air* (1980), *The 27th Kingdom* (1982), *The Other Side of the Fire* (1983), and *Unexplained Laughter* (1985). Among her more celebrated works is the trilogy composed of *The Clothes in the Wardrobe* (1987), *The Skeleton in the Cupboard* (1988), and *The Fly in the Ointment* (1989); the latter, with its exotic and eccentric characters, including an anti-heroine who comes from Egypt, and its antics of infidelity and domestic betrayal, was filmed as *The Summerhouse* for television. *The Inn at the Edge of the World* (1990), with its island locale and allusions to Celtic myth, veers into the territory of fable. In *Pillars of Gold* (1992) Ellis explores, with customary wit, the urban anonymity and the unwholesomeness of life in the Britain of the 1990s. *The Evening of Adam* (1994) is a collection of short stories. Her 'Home Life' columns appear regularly in the *Spectator*.

ELLIS, Bret Easton (1964–), American novelist, born in Los Angeles, educated at Bennington College, Vermont. His first novel, *Less than Zero* (1985), was published while the author was still a student and portrayed disaffected 1980s' youth, preoccupied with drugs, casual sex, and money, against a background of affluent Los Angeles society. The book was subsequently made into a film. Similar themes recur in *Rules of Attraction* (1987), which deals with the psychological traumas of a group of middle-class students at a New England college. *American Psycho* (1991) caused widespread controversy for its portrayal of a middle-class Wall Street banker who is also a brutal killer; the novel was rejected by the author's American publisher for its excessive violence before being accepted by Picador. *The Informers* (1994), a collection of linked short stories, covered much the same territory. With

Jay *McInerney and Tama *Janowitz, Ellis has popularized a new style of American writing: laconic, cynical, and concerned with the decadent values of a materialistic generation.

ELLIS, (Henry) Havelock (1859–1939), British writer, born in Croydon, Surrey. His early travels to Australia were reflected in his novel *Kanga Creek* (1922). He later trained as a physician at St Thomas's Hospital, London. During this time he contributed to journals and edited the unexpurgated Mermaid Series of Elizabethan and Jacobean dramatists as well as the Contemporary Science Series. He was an energetic campaigner for a more liberal and open view of sex, and against censorship. A close friend of Olive *Schreiner, he was also associated with other progressive thinkers in the field of sexuality, including Edward *Carpenter, Arthur *Symons, the 'decadent' poet, and Margaret Sanger, the advocate of birth control. Among his many works on human sexual behaviour were *Sexual Inversion* (1897; with J. A. Symonds), which concerns homosexuality, and was to have formed part of *Studies in the Psychology of Sex* (1897–1928; 7 volumes), which was published in America, and until 1935, due to censorship, available in Britain only to members of the medical profession. The work was surreptitiously imported in large numbers, and gained Ellis many followers. Other works include *Affirmations* (1898, literary essays) and an autobiography, *My Life* (1939). A modern biography by P. Grosskurth appeared in 1980.

ELLIS, Steve (1952–), British poet and critic, born in York, educated at University College, London, gaining his Ph.D. in 1981 for a thesis which provided the basis for his first critical work, *Dante and English Poetry: Shelley to T. S. Eliot* (1983). In 1984 he took up an academic post at the University of Birmingham. His poetry, collected in *Home and Away* (1987) and *West Pathway* (1993), is notable for its lyrically incisive views of the unsettling implications of everyday events; long sociocultural perspectives are opened in the course of shrewd considerations of modestly anecdotal material. Samples of his work are included in the popular anthology *Poetry with an Edge* (1988, edited by Neil Astley). He completed a verse translation of Dante's *Hell* in 1991. *The English Eliot: Design, Language, and Landscape in Four Quartets* (1991) is a notable work of criticism.

ELLISON, Harlan (1934–), American short-story writer, born in Cleveland, Ohio, most of whose work is *science fiction or *fantasy. His short fiction has been published in many volumes including *Paingod* (1965), *I Have no Mouth and I Must Scream* (1967), *Over the Edge* (1970), *Deathbird Stories* (1975), *Shatterday* (1980), *The Essential Ellison* (1987), *Angry Candy* (1988), and *Mind Fields* (1994). The protagonists of his best stories find self-expression (often at fatal cost) in worlds more disturbing than most fantasy environments; for them the human and supernatural world becomes an arena in which survival of its punishing challenges is the only reward.

ELLISON, Ralph (Waldo) (1914–), African-American novelist and essayist, born in Oklahoma City, Oklahoma. He studied music at Tuskegee Institute, Alabama, and worked for some time as a jazz musician before going to New York City in the late 1930s to pursue a career in sculpture; there he met Richard *Wright, who encouraged him to write. In 1939 Ellison began to write in earnest with the New York *Federal Writers' Project, and in 1942 he edited *The Negro Quarterly*. After several early short stories like 'Slick Gonna Learn' and 'Mister Toussan', he published his novel **Invisible Man* (1952). Immediately fêted, Ellison soon became one of the most highly regarded black writers and was awarded several honorary degrees and guest professorships. He has lectured widely on black culture, folklore, and creative writing. His only other major publication is a volume of essays, *Shadow and Act* (1964), which range over literary issues, jazz and blues music, and African-American social and cultural conditions. Extracts from a projected second novel on religion and politics, appeared in several periodicals between 1960 and 1973, including the *American Review*, *Iowa Review*, and the *Quarterly Review of Literature*. In 1986, some of these writings appeared in *Going to the Territory*. See also ETHNICITY.

ELLMANN, Richard (David) (1918–87), American biographer and critic, born in Detroit, educated at Yale. In the course of a distinguished academic career he taught at Harvard and Northwestern University and was Goldsmith's Professor of English Literature at Oxford from 1970 to 1984. *Yeats: The Man and the Masks* (1948) established him as a critic of importance. His other works on W. B. *Yeats include *Eminent Domain* (1967), a study of the poet in relation to Oscar Wilde, James *Joyce, T. S. *Eliot, Ezra *Pound, and W. H. *Auden. He became widely known for *James Joyce* (1959, revised edition 1982), which is regarded by many as pre-eminent among modern literary biographies. The posthumous appearance of *Oscar Wilde* (1987) confirmed his reputation as a biographer. Among his other works are *Golden Codgers* (1973), biographical studies of leading exponents of literary *Modernism.

ELLROY, James (1948–),American crime novelist, born in Los Angeles. After serving in the US Army he drifted through a series of jobs, living for some time as a down-and-out before taking up writing. Perhaps the darkest of all *'hardboiled' writers, Ellroy's novels portray Los Angeles and its inhabitants since the 1940s. His vision of contemporary life, like that of James M. *Cain and Jim *Thompson, is one in which crime and madness are endemic, and in which sexual desire cannot be expressed satisfactorily. His early novels, *Blood on the Moon* (1984), *Because the Night* (1985), and *Suicide Hill* (1986), featured an ambivalent police detective, Lloyd Hopkins, whose investigations of homicides revealed monsters and psychopaths abounding. Ellroy's major work, a sequential history of Los Angeles articulated through a series of the most lurid crimes, begins with *The Black Dahlia* (1987) based on a famous murder case of 1947, and continues with *The Big Nowhere* (1988) about the McCarthyite 'Red scare' in Hollywood in the early 1950s, *L. A. Confidential* (1990) which deals with scandal in the movie industry and the sordid reality behind the 'dream factory', and *White Jazz* (1993). Ellroy embarked on a new series with *American Tabloid* (1995).

ELTON, G(eoffrey) R(udolph) (1921–94), British historian, born at Tübingen, Germany. After his family moved to Britain in the late 1930s he was educated at Rydal School, Colwyn Bay, and the University of London. Originally surnamed 'Ehrenberg', he adopted 'Elton' as his name in 1944 while serving with British military intelligence. From 1949 onward he taught at Cambridge University, where he became Regius Professor of Modern History in 1983. Among the works which established his reputation as a leading authority on the constitutional history of the English Reformation are *The Tudor Revolution in Government* (1953), *England under the Tudors* (1955), *Policy and Police* (1972), and *Reform and Reformation: England 1509–1558* (1977). His conservative and humanist philosophy as a historian is stated in the debate with R. W. Fogel in *Which Road to the Past?* (1983) and the lectures of *Return to Essentials* (1991). His other publications of note include *Reform and Renewal* (1973) and the collected essays of *Studies in Tudor and Stuart Politics and Government* (three volumes, 1974–82).

EMECHETA, (Florence Onye) Buchi (1944–), Nigerian-born British novelist, born in Lagos, educated at the University of London; she took up residence in Britain in 1962. Her first two novels, *In the Ditch* (1972) and *Second-Class Citizen* (1974), are semi-autobiographical. The first novel chronicles the struggles of Adah, Nigerian mother of five, to raise her children in poverty in North London, while working on a degree in Sociology, and separated from her husband. The second delves into Adah's childhood, her move to London, and her entrapment in a difficult marriage. These two novels established Emecheta's reputation as a feminist. An early version of *The Bride Price* (1976), a tragic love story set in the Igbo town of Ibuza in the early 1950s, was burned by Emecheta's husband. *The Slave Girl* (1977) and the ironically titled *The Joys of Motherhood* (1979), continue her scrutiny of traditional society and the difficulties that face women struggling to gain independence from male-dominated authority. Patriarchal values are seen at their worst in *Gwendolen* (1989), which examines the problems facing Caribbean immigrants in London and focuses on a sexually exploited Jamaican girl. Other novels include *Destination Biafra* (1981), a grim tale of civil war; *Double Yoke* (1982), about young Nigerians trapped between tradition and modernity; *The Rape of Shavi* (1983), a futuristic anti-colonial satire, and *Kehinde* (1994), a portrait of conflicting loyalties, in which a woman assesses the freedoms she will lose if she returns to Nigeria with her husband. *Head Above Waters* (1986) is an autobiography. Emecheta also writes children's books.

Eminent Victorians, see STRACHEY, LYTTON.

Emperor Jones, The, a play by Eugene *O'Neill, published in 1920. His first great success in the theatre, it is an experiment in theatrical expressionism, about the rise and fall of Brutus Jones, a former Pullman porter and escaped prisoner who flees to a West Indian island where he establishes himself as emperor. His regime is brutal, corrupt, and dictatorial, and he is warned by a white Cockney trader, Smithers, of impending revolt signalled by a drum beat which sounds throughout the play. Jones, who believes that he can be killed only by a silver bullet, is forced to take refuge in the forest where he is finally destroyed by his adversary Lem, whose troops shoot him with a silver bullet that Lem had especially made from melted down coins. One of the first American plays with a major role for a black actor, the initial success of *The Emperor Jones* had much to do with the performance of Charles Gilpin as Brutus, though O'Neill gave the part to the young Paul Robeson for the London production. Brutus Jones enacts a version of the black man's return to his native origins, but whose fatal display of the trappings of European militarism in a culture he no longer understands entails his fall from the heroic status he desires to that of a sacrificial victim to the local deities. O'Neill's play derives from an interest in African primitivism instigated by a book of photographs of African sculpture by Charles Sheeler.

Empire of the Sun, see BALLARD, J. G.

EMPSON, Sir William (1906–84), British poet and critic, born at Yokefleet Hall near Howden, Yorkshire, educated at Magadalene College, Cambridge, where he initially read mathematics and went on to study English. In lieu of essays, Empson was permitted by I. A. *Richards, his supervisor, to submit a dissertation which formed the core of **Seven Types of Ambiguity* (1930), the range and fluency of which established his reputation as a critic. A number of his best-known poems, including 'To an Old Lady', 'Arachne', and 'Legal Fiction', appeared in *Cambridge Poetry* of 1929. Between 1931 and 1934 he was Professor of English at Tokyo University; following a period of writing and study in London, in 1937 he took up a professorship at Peking National University, to which he returned after working in the BBC's monitoring department during the Second World War. From 1953 to 1971 he held the Chair of English at the University of Sheffield. Although he produced only two principal volumes of poetry, *Poems* (1935) and *The Gathering Storm* (1940), his acutely individual verse, which combines unsettling emotional power and great intellectual vitality, remains highly valued. His virtuosity in adapting traditional forms gave him particular command of the iambic pentameter as a uniquely flexible vehicle for the detached but quirkily insistent conversational tone he characteristically used. Despite the intimidating complexity of occasional poems like 'High Dive', in which mathematical, literary, and philosophical aspects of his intelligence are imaginatively conflated, his work invariably retains an identifiable centre of humane sensitivity. *Collected Poems* (revised edition, 1955) contains nothing later than 'Chinese Ballad' of 1952. The dry and ironically recondite manner of his verse is clearly echoed in some of the poetry of the *Movement, notably that of John *Wain, who remarked on Empson's 'passion, logic, and formal beauty'. Empson's career as a critic continued with *Some Versions of Pastoral* (1935); 'The Child as Swain', its concluding discussion of the extent to which Victorian anxieties inform Lewis Carroll's *Alice* books, memorably illustrates Empson's practice of relating literary works to their socio-cultural contexts. His minutely precise and revealing style of exegesis was influential in the emergence of the *New Criticism during the 1930s and 1940s; he argued against that school's exclusion of biographical factors in *Using Biography* (1984), a collection of essays. His other works include *The Structure of Complex Words* (1951), a wide-ranging exploration of levels of meanings, and *Milton's God* (1961), in which his antagonism to Christianity is most apparent. Empson's criticism constitutes a major contribution to modern literary discourse, its breadth of reference and analytical clarity attractively complemented by his stimulatingly speculative manner and talent for axiomatic succinctness. Among his numerous posthumously published collections of critical essays are *The Royal Beasts* (1986) and *Argufying* (1987), both edited by John Haffenden. *William Empson: The Man and His Work* (1974) is a collection of essays and memoirs edited by Roma Gill.

Encore, the most notable of the periodicals devoted to the theatre during the post-war decades. It was first published in 1954 by students of the Central College of Speech and Drama; Robert Pinker, Clive Goodwin, and Vanessa Redgrave were founding members of its editorial board. The magazine quickly attracted wide notice after it published Sean *O'Casey's controversial treatment of Beckett's **Waiting for Godot* and was acclaimed by Kenneth *Tynan in the *Observer*. In 1957 it became independent of the Central School under the management and patronage of Owen Hale. *Encore* energetically fostered the reputations of John *Osborne, Arnold *Wesker, Harold *Pinter, John *Arden, and other dramatists closely associated with the radical developments in British theatre during the late 1950s; in its commitment to the concept of socially concerned drama, it was equally vigorous in its denunciations of the commercial theatre of London's West End. First editions of numerous plays, including Pinter's *The *Birthday Party* (1958) and Anne *Jellicoe's *The Knack* (1962), were published by the magazine, which also ran a valuable series of interviews with many of the playwrights it supported. Charles Marowitz, Lindsay Anderson, Penelope *Gilliatt, and Tom Milne were among the principal contributors. *Encore* campaigned for the foundation of a National Theatre and was outspoken against the Lord Chamberlain's power of censorship. Having substantially succeeded in its objective of establishing a new British drama, the journal declined and was absorbed by *Plays and Players* in 1965.

Encounter, a magazine of political, cultural, and literary commentary begun in 1953 under the auspices of the Congress for Cultural Freedom (CCF), an organization opposed to communism, which intended *Encounter* as a forum for the expression of unified Anglo-American opinion. It was originally edited by Irving Kristol and Stephen *Spender, both of whom had renounced their former Marxism; Kristol was predominantly responsible for the magazine's concern with current affairs and politics while Spender determined its literary content. Albert Camus, Arthur *Koestler, Christopher *Isherwood, and C. P. *Snow, whose views on the *'Two Cultures' were expounded in the journal, were among the contributors of essays and articles during its earlier years; poets whose work was published included W. H. *Auden, Edith *Sitwell, Robert *Lowell, Ted *Hughes, and Christopher *Middleton. In 1958 Kristol was succeeded as co-editor by Melvin Lasky, who remained at *Encounter* until it ceased appearing in 1990 as a result of financial difficulties. Spender, who became American corresponding editor in 1966, resigned his post in 1967 after it was revealed that the magazine had received financial support from the CIA through channels supplied by the CCF. Frank *Kermode, Lasky's London co-editor, also resigned at this point. Subsequent co-editors included D. J. *Enright and Anthony *Thwaite. *Encounter* was noted for its authoritative discussions of all major international and domestic issues and for the high standard of critical and creative contributions from a wide range of leading writers from Britain, America, and Europe.

Endgame, a play by Samuel *Beckett, originally written in French and published and performed as *Fin de Partie* in 1957; it was translated into English by the author and published and performed under its present name in 1958. Its two main characters are the blind Hamm, who sits immobile in an armchair, and Clov, who may be his son and may simply be his servant. Its two subsidiary ones are Hamm's grotesque parents, Nagg and Nell, who live in dustbins and feed on dog biscuits. This hideous parody of a family, if family it is, appears to be on the point of disintegration and, in some cases, death. The tyrannical but impotent Hamm issues peremptory commands, demands, and threats, asking among other things for pain-killer, information about an apparently barren and desolate world outside, and 'my coffin'; he tells the story of how he rejected a man desperate for bread for his starving child ('use your head, can't you? You're on earth, there's no cure for that'); and finally he throws away his few props, including the whistle with which he has summoned Clov. Meanwhile, Clov resentfully plays the lackey, mourning his wasted life and confiding that he itches to kill a master whom, at the end, he seems about to desert. The play's meaning cannot be simply summed up; but it would seem that Hamm (perhaps the bloated, importunate body) and Clov (perhaps the tormented mind) are interdependent, and also that the first of them is painfully learning a necessary resignation. In one of his few comments on the play, Beckett said that Hamm is the 'king in a chess game lost from the start . . . Now at the end he makes a few senseless moves as only a bad player would. A good one would have given up long ago. He is trying to delay the inevitable end.' The setting, a bare room with two small, high windows shedding 'grey light', has been compared with the inside of a dying man's skull.

End of the Affair, The, a novel by Graham *Greene, published in 1951. Like much fiction concerned with wartime experience, it juxtaposes present loss and remembered fulfilment. These contrasts are sharpened by complexities of structure and point of view unusual in Greene's writing and owed, he suggests, to the influence of *The *Good Soldier* by Ford Madox Ford. Chapters in the first section enact the wish of the narrator—the novelist Maurice Bendrix—to 'turn back time': each opens with an account of his London life after the Second World War, then resumes memories of his affair with Sarah Miles which began before it and ended during a V-1 raid in 1944. A later section presents another version of the affair in Sarah's diaries, passed on to Bendrix by the private detective, Parkis, whom he hires to find the cause of her apparent desertion. They are a record of love and growing religious faith, in sharp contrast to Bendrix's hatred and envy, and reveal Sarah's promise to renounce their adulterous affair if God returns Bendrix to life after his apparent death in the raid. Later, after Sarah's own death and the miraculous events which seem to surround it, Bendrix tries to resist yet another version of events—the possibility that they were 'plotted' by a God whom he begins to see as a rival not only for Sarah's love, but in his craft as a novelist. This possibility adds to frequent self-reflexive discussion of his writing and the relation of fiction to reality. Despite revisions which emphasize mundane explanations for the apparent miracles, the novel has often been criticized as too influenced by Greene's Catholicism. In one way, its disparate narratives provide the fullest dramatization of his conflicting allegiances, around the time of the war, to the spiritual as well as the secular; to transcendence through religion as well as romance. Yet in another way, Sarah's religion functions simply as further confirmation of the problem Bendrix encounters in discovering her diaries—that 'no human being can really understand another'; that another individual is ultimately inaccessible, even when loved most intimately.

'End of the Tether, The', a story by Joseph *Conrad, serialized in *Blackwood's Magazine* (1902), and collected in *Youth, A Narrative; and Two Other Stories* (1902). Conrad's longest short story, it tells of the progressive deterioration of the character of Captain Whalley under the pressure of the financial needs of his beloved daughter and in the face of his oncoming blindness. The story emphasizes Whalley's heroic and honourable past, and it traces his moral corruption through a series of encounters: his lack of frankness with Captain Elliott; his fraudulent agreement with Massy; and his confession to Van Wyck. Through the temporal span of Captain Whalley's long career, the story reflects on the changes that have taken place in the Malay Archipelago, while the remorseless development of the narrative casts doubt upon Whalley's asserted 'boundless trust' in divine justice.

ENGEL, Marian (1933–85), Canadian novelist and short-story writer, born in Toronto; Engel spent her early years in Ontario and attended the Universities of McMaster, where she studied modern languages, and McGill, before winning a scholarship to study French literature in Aix-en-Provence. She subsequently worked in London and Cyprus, a period of her life which provided the inspiration for her novel *Monodromos* (1973; reissued as *One-Way Street*, 1974), a study of a divorced Canadian woman's attempt to find a new identity on a Greek island. Engel was a student of Hugh *MacLennan at McGill and her fiction has superficial affinities with the realist mode of MacLennan's writing, but in her best-known work, *Bear* (1976), she subverts the conventions of realism. The novel is centred on a woman's erotic relationship with a pet bear in the remote setting of the Lake Superior shoreline and suggests the liberating possibilities that both fantasy and the wilderness, usually presented as threatening in early Canadian writing, offer women. Engel also published *No Clouds of Glory* (1968), *The Honeymoon Festival* (1970), *Joanne* (1975), *The Glassy Sea* (1978), and two short story collections, *Inside the Easter Egg* (1975) and *The Tattooed Woman* (1985). She was the first Chairperson of the Writers' Union of Canada, which was founded in 1973.

English Patient, The, see ONDAATJE, MICHAEL.

English Review, The, a literary journal begun in 1908 by Ford Madox *Ford (then Hueffer) in association with various writers including Joseph *Conrad and H. G. *Wells. Increasingly dissatisfied with existing periodicals, Ford was motivated in founding the magazine when Thomas *Hardy's poem 'A Sunday Morning Tragedy' was rejected by other editors. The poem appeared in the first issue, along with work by Henry *James, Wells, Conrad, John *Galsworthy, and others. Under Ford's distinguished editorship, the *Review*'s contributors also included W. B. *Yeats, Violet *Hunt, Arnold *Bennett, and Hilaire *Belloc; among the emerging writers to whom he was hospitable were E. M. *Forster, Ezra *Pound, Wyndham *Lewis, D. H. *Lawrence, and F. S. *Flint. Ford's financial management of the magazine was not, however, satisfactory: his backer Arthur Marwood (a model for Christopher Tietjens in Ford's **Parade's End*) withdrew support and Sir Alfred Mond, a wealthy politician, acquired the *Review* as a platform for liberal reformist opinions; Austin Harrison was installed as editor in January 1910, maintaining literary standards with work from Aldous *Huxley, Herman Hesse, Katherine *Mansfield, Caradoc *Evans, and Bertrand *Russell. In 1923 Harrison was succeeded by Ernest Remnant, whose promotion of a conservative national ideal rendered the *Review* aridly political. Douglas Jerrold was editor from 1931 to 1935; with T. S. *Eliot among his reviewers, the magazine was noted for the quality of its commentaries on *Modernist writing. The *English Review* subsequently entered a period of decline and merged with the *National Review* in 1937.

English Stage Company, The, an organization established in 1955 at the Royal Court Theatre by George Devine (1910–66) and others. Its original aim was to encourage novelists and poets to write drama, and its first production was Angus *Wilson's *The Mulberry Bush*, but its primary purpose soon became the discovery of socially critical work by young, and usually left-wing, playwrights. Indeed, its presentation of John Osborne's **Look Back in Anger* in May 1956 is commonly regarded as the beginning of a British dramatic renaissance which the ESC continued to promote with productions of key work by *Wesker, *Arden, *Bond, *Jellicoe, *Hampton, *Hare, *Brenton, *Matura, *Churchill, and others. According to the then artistic director of the Royal Court, Max Stafford-Clark, the main function of the ESC in 1991 was still to present work 'urgently debating the nature of British society'.

ENRIGHT, D(ennis) J(oseph) (1920–), British poet, born in Leamington, Warwickshire, educated at Downing College, Cambridge. From 1947 onwards he taught at universities in Egypt, Japan, Germany, Thailand, Singapore, and Leeds. In 1971 he joined the publishers Chatto and Windus, becoming a director in 1974. His first collection, *The Laughing Hyena* (1953), was followed by a succession of volumes which include *Addictions* (1962), *The Terrible Shears* (1973), *Sad Ires* (1975), *Paradise Illustrated* (1978), *A Faust Book* (1979), *Collected Poems* (1981), *Selected Poems* (1990), *The Way of the Cat* (1992), and *Old Men and Comets* (1993); *Under the Circumstances* (1991) is a volume of 'poems and proses'. In *A Faust Book*, Enright exemplifies his characteristic ability to combine a theological seriousness with irreverent humour. His experiences of Egypt and the Far East provided material for many of his earlier poems, in which a sense of cultural detachment unites with an understated compassion in his quizzical and ironic reflections on human behaviour. Stylistically, Enright's poetry possesses an eloquent quality which is not diminished by an occasionally conversational tone. His prose autobiography, *Memoirs of a Mendicant Professor* (1969), is supplemented by *Instant Chronicles: A Life* (1985), a volume of autobiographical poetry of considerable candour and wit. Among his other prose works are *The World of Dew: Aspects of Living Japan* (1959), and the novels *Academic Year* (1955) and *Insufficient Poppy* (1960). As a critic and literary essayist Enright's publications include *The Alluring Problem: An Essay on Irony* (1986) and *Fields of Vision: Essays on Literature, Language, and Television* (1988). Among the works he has edited are *Poets of the Fifties* (1955), an early anthology of the *Movement; *The Oxford Book of Contemporary Verse: 1945–1980* (1980), in which he hoped 'to shake the notion that British poetry of the period has been discreditably or pitiably provincial or parochial'; and *The Oxford Book of the Supernatural* (1994). *Life by Other Means* (1990, edited by Jaqueline Simms) is a *festschrift* of essays marking Enright's seventieth birthday and the breadth of his contribution to literature.

Entertainer, The, a play by John *Osborne, first performed in 1957. It involves Archie Rice, a seedy music-hall comic who regards himself as 'dead behind the eyes . . . I don't feel a thing'. His plan to leave his long-suffering wife, Phoebe, for a much younger woman is aborted after her parents are informed of the affair by his father Billy, a comedian whom Osborne sees as representing the lost decencies of an older generation. Archie's son Mick, a soldier serving in Cyprus, is captured and killed by terrorists. This news brings Archie briefly back to emotional life, and he sings the same heartfelt blues he once heard an old black woman sing in a Canadian bar; but for most of the play he expresses a weary cynicism, whether with his family or when performing to audiences he thinks as dead as himself. His mock-patriotic songs, his advice to the audience not to clap too loud ('it's a very old building'), and a nude Britannia that materializes during his act, indicate that the decline of the music hall is to be identified with a national decline.

ERDRICH, Louise (1954–), American novelist and poet, born in Little Falls, Arizona, to a father of German origin and a Native American mother. She was educated at the Bureau of Indian Affairs boarding school, and later graduated from Dartmouth College. Erdrich's first and highly praised novel, *Love Medicine* (1984), was the richly poetic story of the interlinked destinies of two Chippewa families. Ranging from 1934 to 1984, it displayed Erdrich's formidable knowledge of Native American history and folklore, and was lauded as a new departure in contemporary American fiction, which was at the time marked by the minimalist trend. Her first collection of poems, *Jacklight*, also appeared in 1984. Erdrich's next novel, *The Beet Queen* (1986), covered the same period as its predecessor but was more an American rural novel in the grand tradition of *Faulkner, whose influence Erdrich acknowledges. It was enthusiastically received in Britain by such writers as John *Berger, Angela *Carter, and Marina *Warner, and Erdrich was widely held to be one of the most important American voices of the decade. *Tracks* (1988), the third volume of what loosely constitutes a tetralogy, presents an explicitly Native American vision of history. *The Crown of Columbus* (1991), co-authored by her husband, fellow Native American writer and frequent collaborator Michael *Dorris, employs the genre of the research novel and attempts to combine questions of significance to the history of the Americas and their native peoples in a robust adventure story. *The Bingo Palace* (1994) is the fourth in Erdrich's series of novels chronicling the lives and interlinked fortunes of several Native American and other families. It returns to the characters and situations of much of her previous work; its tone and technique are reminiscent of *Love Medicine* and *The Beet Queen*, though its range of voices and narrative span are considerably smaller. See also NATIVE AMERICAN LITERATURE and ETHNICITY.

Erewhon Revisited, Samuel *Butler's sequel to *Erewhon* (1872), published in 1901. The earlier work describes the experiences of its chief protagonist, whom *Erewhon Revisited* identifies as Thomas Higgs, in the remote land of Erewhon, the name being an anagram of 'nowhere'. The utopian society in which Higgs finds himself forms the basis for a succession of satires on the religious, social, and moral conventions of Victorian society. Higgs finally returns to England by balloon with his beloved Arowhena Nosnibor, the daughter of an Erewhonian merchant. *Erewhon Revisited* is narrated by John, the son of Higgs and Arowhena, from his father's records of a return to Erewhon after twenty years. Its central theme reflects Butler's scepticism in *The Fair Haven* (1873) about the miraculous content of Christianity: Higgs's ascent in the balloon has been mythologized into the official Erewhonian religion of 'Sunchildism', which is threatened with collapse when he reveals his identity during the opening of a new temple. He is arrested, but escapes back over the mountain range isolating Erewhon from the known world. The novel is less wide-ranging than *Erewhon*, partly as a result of its greater concern with consistency of characterization. Butler felt that difficulties over its publication arose from its potential offensiveness to the Church. George Bernard *Shaw introduced Butler to his publisher, who issued *Erewhon Revisited* to favourable reviews in October 1901.

ERICKSON, Steve (1950–), American novelist, born in Santa Monica, California, educated at the University of California at Los Angeles. Erickson wrote the 'Guerilla Pop' column for the *Los Angeles Reader* for three years, also writing for *Esquire* and *Rolling Stone*, and has worked as a freelance editor and writer in Europe and Los Angeles. His first novel, *Days between Stations* (1985), is a tale about Lauren and Michel's search for the latter's identity in a bleak futuristic setting, and establishes Erickson's shifting, surrealistic, near-cinematic style. A similar path, through a blend of science fiction, political fable, and fantastic love story is followed in his next novel *Rubicon Beach* (1986), in which the slippage of names and identities reinforces the dream-like narrative structure. *Tours of the Black Clock* (1989) combines past and future, history and fantasy in a narrative where Banning Jainlight becomes Adolf Hitler's pornographer. *Leap Year* (1989) is his account of the 1988 American presidential election and a parallel narrative about an eighteenth-century woman who chose to remain a slave to Thomas Jefferson in Paris in 1789. Among his recent novels is *Arc d'X* (1993). Erickson's work has received wide acclaim as examples of *post-modern fiction, especially from such peers as Thomas *Pynchon.

ERIKSON, Erik (Homburger) (1902–), American psychoanalytical author, born of Danish parents in Frankfurt, Germany. His eclectic education included a period as an art student in Munich, followed by study under Anna Freud at the Vienna Psychoanalytical Institute. In 1933 he emigrated to the USA, becoming a naturalized citizen in 1939. Despite his lack of formal qualifications he was welcomed at Harvard, where he conducted research and worked as an analyst at the university's Psychoanalytical Clinic. From 1939 to 1950 he taught at the University of California; he resigned in protest when required to swear an oath of loyalty to the USA as part of the attempted extirpation of communism in the immediate post-war period. He then spent ten years at the Austen Riggs Center in Massachusetts and became Professor of Human Development at Harvard in 1960. His works include *Observations on the Yurok: Childhood and World Image* (1943), which draws upon his perceptions of Native American culture; *Insight and Responsibility* (1964), a collection of essays; *Gandhi's Truth* (1969), a study of non-violent political action; and *Toys and Reasons* (1977), an investigation of the ritualization of experience. His biography *Young Man Luther* (1968) presents a sustained analysis of its subject's motivations and character in terms of critical events in his early life. Erikson, whose work is noted for its humane and imaginative character, claimed that he 'came to psychology from art'. Largely for his insistence on the significance of social determinants in the growth of the individual psyche, Erikson is regarded as one of the chief exponents of psychoanalytic theory since Freud. His use of the terms 'identity crisis' and 'life-cycle' in exploring his central concern with the developmental stages of the ego gave them centrality to the modern vocabulary of psychoanalysis.

Ern Malley Hoax, see ANGRY PENGUINS.

ERVINE, St John (Greer) (1883–1971), Northern Irish dramatist, born in Belfast of a long-established Ulster family. He made the province the setting of some of his earlier plays, among them *Mixed Marriage* (1911), about the love of an Orangeman for a Catholic girl, and *John Ferguson* (1915), about a fundamentalist Protestant farmer whose powerful faith is challenged by his daughter's seduction and the murder of the seducer by his son. Among Ervine's other works for the stage were *Jane Clegg* (1913), about a strong woman's marriage to a feckless philanderer; *The First Mrs Fraser* (1929), a drawing-room comedy which brought him his first substantial success in London's West End; and *Robert's Wife* (1937), about a woman doctor's battle to open a birth-control clinic. Ervine also practised as a drama critic in London and New

York and published several novels and biographies, including *Bernard Shaw: His Life, Work and Friends* (1956).

Essays in Criticism, a quarterly journal founded by F. W. *Bateson in 1951, which continues to be published from Keble College, Oxford. Early issues contained articles by numerous noted critics of varying persuasions, including W. H. *Auden, T. S. *Eliot, Kingsley *Amis, Raymond *Williams, Donald *Davie, John Middleton *Murry, Frank *Kermode, and Hugh *Kenner. In his 'The Function of Criticism' (1953) Bateson reasoned in favour of a critical approach that combined the explicatory precision of the *New Criticism with attention to socio-cultural context. The first of Bateson's 'Editorial Commentaries', which ran from 1953 to 1956, defended the journal against allegations that it lacked the binding purpose that had characterized **Scrutiny* in its earlier years; the limitations of F. R. *Leavis's critical practice were subsequently discussed by Fr Martin Jarrett-Kerr, prompting a reply from Leavis in 'The State of Criticism' in 1954. Robert *Graves, George *Steiner, Edwin *Morgan, William *Empson, C. S. *Lewis, and Geoffrey *Hill were among the contributors who sustained the journal's combination of work by established commentators and stimulating younger authors. From 1954 onward poetry was occasionally featured, work from members of the *Movement appearing repeatedly. In 1974, when Bateson retired to the position of advisory editor, joint editorship was undertaken by Stephen Wall and Christopher *Ricks.

ESSON, Louis (1879–1943), Australian playwright, born in Scotland and taken to Australia as a child. He worked as a journalist for the **Bulletin*, the *Socialist*, and other journals, and also published several volumes of verse, including *Bells and Bees* (1910) and *Red Gums* (1912). Following the performance of *The Woman Tamer* (perf. 1910; pub. 1976), a drama with a Melbourne setting, and the publication of two collections of plays, *Three Short Plays* (1911) and *The Time Is Not Yet Ripe* (1912), he went abroad for several years; on visiting the *Abbey Theatre in Dublin, he was encouraged by W. B. *Yeats to set up a national theatre in Australia. As a result of this encounter he established the short-lived but influential Pioneer Players in Melbourne in 1921. *Dead Timber and Other Plays* (1920) includes his one-act drama 'The Drovers', widely considered a classic of Australian bush literature; *The Southern Cross and Other Plays* (1946) is a collection of some of his better-known works.

Ethan Frome, an ironic novelette of repressed love in New England, by Edith *Wharton, published in 1911. The novel explores the rural decay of New England, and the way in which the poverty of the surroundings, the harsh climate, and the economic depression affect the lives of its inhabitants. The narrative is recounted by a young engineer, Ethan Frome, a sallow, embittered man, trapped by a strike in a small western Massachusetts town. He has remained with the family's failing farm to care for his father, then his mother, and finally his weak and dependent wife Zenobia (Zeenie). When her young cousin Mattie Silver arrives to stay, Ethan falls in love with her as she revives his life. Contemplating eloping with Mattie, he is prevented by his conscience. As Zeenie jealously orders Mattie out of the house, Ethan and Mattie confess their love for each other *en route* to the railway station, but recognize its hopelessness. However, after a careless accident with a snow sled, Mattie and Ethan are crippled and she returns with him to convalesce at the farm, where the three of them live out a strained and unpleasant existence.

Ethnicity. The word 'ethnic' has a long history. In the Bible it is used of the 'Gentiles', that is, all those who are not Israelites. Later, it is used to define all those nations who are not Christians or Jews, who are therefore categorized as 'heathens' or 'pagans'. In contemporary Western culture, the term is now used to describe a racial and cultural group, especially one that has migrated into a pre-existent other community, where the issue of integration between the two remains problematic. In this respect the old semantic association between 'ethnic' and 'heathen' or 'pagan' remains volatile, particularly where these terms are used as a vocabulary of discrimination from within the dominant community. Conversely, and especially in twentieth-century America, certain forms of ethnic expression celebrate the longevity of cultural roots in religions and myths held to be pre-Christian, as in the case of much contemporary Native American writing. The relationship between the ethnic and the dominant white Anglo-Saxon Protestant community in America is further complicated by the fact that the dominant community was itself originally an immigrant community; and the later history of European migration to America, of Dutch and German Protestants, Scottish Nonconformists, Irish and Italian Catholics, and East European Jews has made the ingredients of the dominant American culture of the twentieth century diverse and multi-faceted. None the less, from the perspective of other ethnic groups, the dominant white culture of America is seen as exclusionist, another form of the imposition of power over the ethnic citizenry. However, since the 1970s, there have been strenuous institutional efforts to erase the conflicts of otherness inherent in this situation, to enfold the plethora of ethnic experience within the consciousness of mainstream American cultural life. A good example of this is in the endeavour to place 'slave narratives', such as Frederick Douglass's *Narrative of the Life of Frederick Douglass* (1845, revised 1892), firmly within the canon of nineteenth-century American literature, to rescue them from the margin to which they have been consigned by a combination of political embarrassment and cultural indifference.

In contemporary America 'ethnic literature' commonly refers to the work produced by four large ethnic groups: African-Americans, Native Americans,

Latino-Americans, and Asian-Americans. African-American writing is by and about the community descended from the enslaved black peoples, now an extensive literature with a high cultural profile, particularly since the 1960s. If the history of African-Americans is first inscribed in slave narratives of the eighteenth and nineteenth centuries, and in abolitionist texts such as Harriet Beecher Stowe's *Uncle Tom's Cabin*, a remarkable manifestation of the vigour of African-American writing in the twentieth century came in the so-called *Harlem Renaissance of the 1920s, with the work of Countee *Cullen, Langston *Hughes, James Weldon *Johnson, Nella *Larsen, Claude *McKay, Jean *Toomer, and W. E. B. *Dubois. This first great wave of African-American writing was followed by important work in all the literary genres in the 1940s and 1950s; many are now rightly regarded not only as addressing that ethnic audience, but as major cultural documents for the whole American community; for example, Zora Neale Hurston's **Their Eyes Were Watching God* (1937), Ralph Ellison's **Invisible Man* (1952), and James Baldwin's **Go Tell It on the Mountain* (1953). More recently, the work of African-American writers such as Gayl *Jones, Toni *Morrison, Ishmael *Reed, and Alice *Walker, to name but a few, has achieved popular acclaim and recognition within the mainstream of contemporary American writing. African-American writing is now institutionalized as a subject for study in the universities, and there is a substantial community of scholars, both African-American and white, whose scholarly and critical commentaries on this ethnic writing are now published by the prestigious university presses.

This is also true for the other principal ethnic groups, even if their writing has a briefer historical reach than that of the African-Americans, and as yet a more regionalized presence as an institutionalized subject. The term 'Native American' displaces the white name 'Indians' for the indigenous peoples of North America (equal to the African-American displacement of the word 'negro'). Native American writing became increasingly prominent from the late 1960s, along with the challenge of this ethnic community to the legal and bureaucratic authority of the Bureau of Indian Affairs, and is evident in the Kiowan novelist N. Scott *Momaday's *House Made of Dawn* (1968), the Cheyenne Heyemeyohsts Storm's *Winter in the Blood* (1974), and the Laguna Leslie Marmon *Silko's *Ceremony* (1977), the novels of Louise *Erdrich, and the work of poets such as the Blackfoot James *Welch. Anthologies of these and other Native Americans, and scholarly and critical commentary on them, forms an increasingly substantial feature of the contemporary cultural scene in America, a situation also reflected in the new visibility of Latino-American and Asian-American writing. Werner Soller's *Beyond Ethnicity: Consent and Descent in American Culture* (1986) studies the whole corpus of issues raised by the concept of ethnicity, and the role of ethnic writing in the corporate culture of contemporary America. See also ASIAN-AMERICAN LITERATURE, LATINO/LATINA LITERATURE IN ENGLISH, and NATIVE AMERICAN LITERATURE.

Eustace and Hilda, a trilogy of novels by L. P. *Hartley, published in 1944, 1946, and 1947, and as a single volume in 1958. Hilda is the dominant older sister of Eustace: the trilogy describes their relationship throughout their lives. *The Shrimp and the Anemone* (1944) takes its title from the striking opening image, an episode in a characteristically observed childhood seaside holiday. Eustace is a gentle, reflective child with a disastrous willingness to submit to the extrovert and ardent Hilda and an overwhelming need to gain her love and approval. The novel shows the influence of Henry *James and also of Freudian psychology. The second novel, *The Sixth Heaven* (1946), opens with Eustace at Oxford, but neither financial independence nor the congenial atmosphere of Oxford can release him from Hilda's spell. Desperate to gain her approval, he encourages a love affair between her and his aristocratic friend Stavely, hoping that marriage will both fulfil Hilda and free himself. The final novel, *Eustace and Hilda* (1947), describes Stavely's betrayal of Hilda: having seduced her he abandons her. Eustace and Hilda are drawn even closer together by catastrophe. The obsessive, destructive nature of their relationship culminates in Eustace's death, seen as a sacrificial offering on his part, the only way in which Hilda can be released. The novel ends with a reference to the shrimp–anemone image. The trilogy, like the later *The *Go-Between*, is remarkable for its evocation of childhood, based on narrative and incident rather than nostalgia, and its exploration of the influence of childhood experience on adult personality. But it is the spiritual dimension of Eustace's sacrificial pursuit of his sister's fulfilment at the expense of his own—and the complexity of his dependence upon her—that gives the trilogy its place at the head of Hartley's fiction.

EVANS, (David) Caradoc (1878–1945), Welsh short-story writer and novelist, born in Llanfihangel-ar-Arth, Carmarthenshire, though associated with Rhydlewis, the Cardiganshire village where his mother worked a nine-acre smallholding. At 14 he became a draper's assistant. Following evening classes at the Workingmen's College, he began a career as a journalist which culminated in *T. P.'s Weekly*, which he and Con O'Leary co-edited, with Austin *Clarke as colleague. His stories in the **English Review*, collected in *My People* (1915), established him as a satirist of compelling originality. Fifteen pared-down stories exploded the myth of pastoral Wales, in a manner recalling fellow Celts, George Douglas *Brown and J. M. *Synge. In Wales his audacious treatment of local community influenced Dylan *Thomas and other writers, for whom *My People* became the founding text of modern *Anglo-Welsh literature. *Capel Sion* (1916) and *My Neighbours* (1920) continued the savage dissection. Controversy clung to Evans as theatre riots disrupted performances of his one play, *Taffy* (pub. 1924). His first novel, *Nothing to Pay* (1930), a Swiftian fable of money worship, charted the progress of its miserly anti-hero through the drapery underworld at the turn of the century. His later works include the novella *Morgan Bible* (1943), and the short story collections *Pilgrims in a Foreign Land* (1942) and *The Earth Gives All and Takes All* (1946). Reprints of *My People* (1987) and *Nothing to Pay* (1989) have been edited by John Harris, who has also compiled *Fury Never Leaves Us: A Miscellany of Caradoc Evans* (1985).

EVANS, Margiad, pseudonym of Peggy Eileen WHISTLER (1909–58), British novelist and poet, born in Uxbridge, London, to English parents of Welsh descent. Between 1920 and 1936 she lived at Bridstow, near Ross-on-Wye; following her marriage in 1940 she moved to Llangarron, near Ross, and later to Gloucestershire and Sussex. Her work is permeated with an awareness of her Welsh ancestry and a love of the Welsh Border country to which she felt she belonged. Her first novel, *Country Dance* (1932), was the story of a woman forced to choose between two lovers, one Welsh, the other English. Written in the form of a journal, it was followed by other idiosyncratic and poetic works, including *The Wooden Doctor* (1933), *Turf or Stone* (1934), and *Creed* (1936), each of which expresses, in one degree or another, the author's concern with human suffering and with man's relationship to God; each includes passages of lyrical and intense writing about love and sex as well as those depicting more violent passions. Her journals and essays were published in *Autobiography* (1943); short stories were collected in *The Old and the Young* (1948), and verse in *Poems from Obscurity* (1947) and *A Candle Ahead* (1956). In her second autobiographical work, *A Ray of Darkness* (1952), she wrote movingly and courageously about the onset of her epilepsy and her search for religious belief.

Everyman's Library, a series of 1,000 pocket-sized volumes established in 1906 by the publisher Joseph Malaby Dent, who envisaged it as 'the most complete library for the common man the world has ever seen'. Dent devised the project in consultation with the poet Ernest Rhys, who edited the series until his death in 1946. Fiction, poetry, drama, biography, philosophy, and history were among the thirteen original sections of the library, which was composed exclusively of reprints of masterpieces from the literatures of the world. Boswell's *Life of Johnson* was the first title to appear; other early volumes included works by Euripides, Plato, Francis Bacon, Coleridge, Jane Austen, and Tennyson. By 1939 more works by twentieth-century authors were included. In 1956 the fiftieth anniversary was marked by the publication of Aristotle's *Metaphysics* as the thousandth book in the series. Sales of the volumes making up the library since its inception were recorded as exceeding 60,000,000 in 1975. Everyman's Reference Library and Everyman's University Library were introduced in 1951 and 1971 respectively.

EWART, Gavin (Buchanan) (1916–95), British poet, born in London, educated at Christ's College, Cambridge. After active service in the Second World War, he worked in publishing and with the British Council before becoming an advertising copywriter in 1952. From the age of 17, when his poetry was first printed in Geoffrey Grigson's **New Verse*, he acquired a reputation for wit and accomplishment through such works as 'Phallus in Wonderland' and his skilful pastiches of *Auden, his principal influence, *Eliot, and *Pound. His first collection, *Poems and Songs*, appeared in 1939. The war disrupted his development as a poet, however, and he published no further volumes until *Londoners* of 1964. From then he produced many collections, which included *The Gavin Ewart Show* (1971), *No Fool like an Old Fool* (1976), *All My Little Ones* (1978), *The Ewart Quarto* (1984), and *Penultimate Poems* (1989). *The Collected Ewart: 1933–1980* (1980) was supplemented in 1991 by *Collected Poems: 1980–1990*. The intelligence and casually flamboyant virtuosity with which he framed his often humorous commentaries on human behaviour made his work invariably entertaining and interesting. The irreverent eroticism for which his poetry is noted resulted in W. H. Smith's banning of his *The Pleasures of the Flesh* (1966) from their shops. As an editor he produced numerous anthologies, including the *Penguin Book of Light Verse* (1980).

Executioner's Song, The, see MAILER, NORMAN.

Exiles (1918), a play by James *Joyce.

Expressionism, a tendency in the arts during the first three decades of the twentieth century, initially defined in relation to painting and subsequently applied to theatrical, literary, and cinematic works; the term denotes one of the many sub-divisions of *Modernism. Expressionism emerged as a coherent movement in the graphic arts in 1905, when the group named *Die Brücke* (literally 'the bridge') was formed in Dresden; Emil Nolde (1867–1956), Ernst Ludwig Kirchner (1880–1938), and Max Pechstein (1881–1955) were among its members, while precursors of the style included Vincent van Gogh (1853–90), Edvard Munch (1863–1944), and James Ensor (1860–1949). The evocation of traumatic and oneiric subjective conditions through disquieting heightenings and distortions of actuality in the works of these painters have their equivalents in Expressionist literature. As part of the widespread reaction against naturalism, such writing gave primacy to the projection of internal emotional and psychological states, often of aberrant intensity, resulting in the grotesque, disjunctive, and sometimes hysterical language and imagery typifying literary Expressionism. Essentially a European phenomenon, its most characteristic manifestations were theatrical; works by August Strindberg (1849–1912), Frank Wedekind (1864–1918), and Ernst Toller (1893–1939) disregarded the conventions of dramatic continuity, firmly influencing Bertolt Brecht's early plays and suggesting some of the techniques of his 'epic theatre'. Elmer *Rice's *The Adding Machine* (1923) was the first Expressionist dramatic work of significance in English. The plays of W. H. *Auden and Christopher *Isherwood, most notably *The Dog Beneath the Skin* (1935), absorbed much of the spirit of Expressionism through their adaptations of Brechtian practices. Other instances of the movement's impact on drama in English are found in the treatment of the First World War in Sean O'Casey's *The *Silver Tassie* (1929) and in Eugene O'Neill's *The *Emperor Jones* (1920). The works of Arthur *Miller and Tennessee *Williams retain elements of Expressionism. With reference to prose and poetry in English, the 'Circe' episode of James Joyce's **Ulysses* (1922) and passages in Wyndham *Lewis's novels employ the phantasmagoric and distorting effects associated with Expressionist literature; the poetries of Ezra *Pound and T. S. *Eliot occasionally suggest Expressionist qualities in exhibiting the deforming energies of emotional pressures, as, for example, in the more dissociative sections of *The *Waste Land*.

Eyeless in Gaza, a novel by A. *Huxley, published in 1936. Much criticized at the time for its pacifist ideology, it can now be read as an autobiographical, emotionally introspective work which marked Huxley's evolution from satirist to moralist. The carefully shuffled chronology of the novel is crucial in showing the development of Anthony Beavis, a detached observer of human behaviour insistent on his own freedom from commitment, to an awareness of his 'duties towards himself and others and the nature of things'. It opens on 30 August 1933, Beavis's forty-second birthday, then shifts back and forth between 1902 and 1935, covering the death of his mother and the suicide of his ascetic schoolfriend Brian Foxe; sexual affairs with Mary Amberley and subsequently her daughter Helen; the miraculous meeting with Dr Miller whilst in Mexico and consequent involvement in the peace movement. Miller, a vehicle for the ideas of Gerald Heard and F. M. Alexander, urges him to get beyond the ego and practise meditation, self-healing, and pacifism; such analytic musings are incorporated via Beavis's diary entries and reflect Huxley's almost contemporaneous adoption of the Reverend Dick Sheppard's Peace Pledge Union and the Alexander Technique of posture training. *Eyeless in Gaza*, which ends with a *stream-of-consciousness mystical perception of 'the unity of life', is indicative of the increasingly non-dramatic and prescriptive nature of Huxley's later works.

EZEKIEL, Nissim (1924–), Indian poet, born in Bombay to a Jewish family long resident in India, educated at the University of Bombay. He has held academic posts in Britain, Bombay, and America. Ezekiel's honest response to the challenge of expressing the cosmopolitan culture of which he is a product has made him the most respected of contemporary poets writing in English in India. He has an easy colloquial style, has experimented with Indian English, and varies his tone from a studied neutrality and ironic stance to themes that explore the mystical. Above all, Ezekiel is a poet of the city of Bombay, which is the landscape of all his work and a microcosm of contemporary urban experience. Among his volumes of poems are *The Unfinished Man* (1960), *The Exact Man* (1965), and *Hymns in Darkness* (1976). In *Latter Day Psalms* (1982), which also contains poems from earlier volumes, Ezekiel treats Old Testament psalms with irony, and explores his own Judaic background. His *Collected Poems, 1952–88* appeared in 1989. He has also published *Three Plays* (1969) and *Selected Prose* (1992). See Chetan Karnani, *Nissim Ezekiel: A Study* (1974).

F

Faber and Faber, a leading British publishing house of the twentieth century, especially notable for its contributions to the fields of poetry and drama. With Sir Maurice Gwyer (1878–1952), Sir Geoffrey Faber (1889–1961) founded Faber and Gwyer Ltd in 1925, the two having been in partnership since 1923 as directors of the Scientific Press Ltd. T. S. *Eliot was appointed to the board of directors in 1925, with the result that Faber and Gwyer took over publication of the **Criterion*; Eliot's acumen was indispensable in the building of the poetry list, which, in addition to his own collections, included much of the work central to the canon of twentieth-century verse: Ezra *Pound, W. H. *Auden, Louis *MacNeice, Stephen *Spender, Wallace *Stevens, Robert *Lowell, Philip *Larkin, Ted *Hughes, and Seamus *Heaney are among the many distinguished poets the company publishes. Following Gwyer's withdrawal in 1929, the name Faber and Faber was adopted; trade had been discouraging in the first four years, but steadily improved between 1930, when sixty titles were published, and 1940, when Faber and Faber issued 177 books. Dramatists whose work appears under the Faber imprint include Samuel *Beckett, Christopher *Hampton, N. F. *Simpson, Ann *Jellicoe, John *Osborne, and Tom *Stoppard. Latterly, the company has been increasingly noted for its contemporary fiction; it also publishes books on archaeology, art, history, literary criticism, music, travel, and a range of other subjects.

Faber Book of Modern Verse, The, an anthology of twentieth-century poetry, edited by Michael *Roberts, published in 1936. The only nineteenth-century poet included was Gerard Manley Hopkins; his influence following the first collection of his work in 1918 was integral to the book's attempt to define the modern movement in terms of technique and sensibility. Roberts's introduction argued that social and moral factors were significant in determining matters of form and content; he suggested that the alleged difficulty of much modern poetry resulted from its authenticity of relation between language, style, and experience in an age of rapid cultural change and religious uncertainty. Passages from Clough are cited as an English precedent for the ironically poised tone in the writings of Ezra *Pound, T. S. *Eliot, and others, and the value of a European literary perspective is emphasized. The introduction is a restrained polemic for what Roberts wished to establish as 'post-*Georgian' poetry; the phrase is used in his correspondence regarding the anthology with Eliot, who, favourably impressed with Roberts's editorship of *New Signatures* (1932) and *New Country* (1933), had commissioned him on behalf of Faber to undertake the project. W. H. *Auden, George *Barker, William *Empson, David *Gascoyne, and Dylan *Thomas were among the younger of the thirty-six contributors to the book, which also introduced the work of numerous American poets to a British readership. The anthology was directly instrumental in forming the tastes of succeeding generations of readers. Three revised editions containing additional material appeared under the editorships of Anne *Ridler (1951), Donald *Hall (1965), and Peter *Porter (1982), the last being intended as final.

Fabian Society, a group of socialist intellectuals dedicated to the principle of gradualist reform, which originated as a splinter group from Thomas Davidson's Fellowship of the New Life, a movement devoted to philosophical speculation. Its name was derived from the Roman general Quintus Fabius Maximus, whose delaying tactics in battle earned him the nickname 'Cunctator' or 'the Delayer'. In 1884 the Society was first addressed by G. B. *Shaw, whose *Manifesto* (1884) was characterized by his distinctive mixture of provocative statement and wit; other tracts arguing for reformist ideas, as opposed to the revolutionary methods advocated by Marxist and Anarchist groups of the period, were also published by Sidney *Webb and his wife, Beatrice, who joined the Fabians at Shaw's instigation in 1885. *Fabian Essays in Socialism* (1889), edited by Shaw, with designs by Walter Crane and May Morris, did much to popularize socialist ideas. Other early Fabians were Annie Besant, G. D. H. *Cole, E. Nesbit, Edward *Carpenter, Rupert *Brooke, Keir Hardie, Ramsay Macdonald, and Emmeline Pankhurst. Fabians have continued to attract distinguished members drawn from the socialist intelligentsia up to the present day, although its influence has declined with the rise of the Labour Party. Studies include: *The Story of Fabian Socialism* (1961), by Margaret Cole; *The First Fabians* (1977), by N. and J. Mackenzie. See also *Bernard Shaw*, vol. i (1988) by Michael *Holroyd.

Façade, see SITWELL, DAME EDITH.

Fahrenheit 451, see BRADBURY, RAY.

FAINLIGHT, Ruth (Esther) (1931–), American poet, born in New York; she attended schools in the USA and England, afterwards studying at Brighton and Birmingham Colleges of Art. *Cages* (1966), her first substantial collection of poetry, was followed by further volumes including *The Region's Violence* (1973), *Fifteen to Infinity* (1983), *Selected Poems* (1987), *The Knot* (1990), and *This Time of Year* (1993). Fainlight's essential qualities as a poet are indicated by her line 'fineness and toughness, my own special markings'; her work combines imagery of precision and delicacy with a resilient sensibility. Much of her poetry is concerned with the social and cultural constraints imposed on women. While her writing generally uses a contemporary realist mode, she has made recurrent use of mythology, most notably in *Sibyls and Others* (1980). Her translations include *Marine Rose* (1989), poems from the Portuguese of Sophia de Mello Breyner Andresen. Among her other publications are the volumes of short stories *Daylife and Nightlife* (1971) and *Dr Clock's Last Case* (1994). With her husband Alan *Sillitoe she wrote *All Citizens Are Soldiers* (1969), an adaptation of a play by Lope de Vega.

FAIR, A. A., see GARDNER, ERLE STANLEY.

FAIRBAIRNS, Zoe (1948–), British novelist, born in Tunbridge Wells, Kent, educated at St Andrews University, Scotland. Fairbairns read history at university, and a historian's sensibility may be detected in her preference for a large canvas which crosses time and place to intertwine the experiences of women from different generations and backgrounds. Fairbairns specializes in reworking popular genre from a feminist perspective. In her futuristic dystopia *Benefits* (1979), feminist revolution is suppressed by a government bent on returning women to their reproductive role. *Stand We at Last* (1983) adapts the family saga to encompass a century of women's struggles for emancipation. *Here Today* (1984) takes the crime thriller into the workaday world of the office 'temp'; *Closing* (1987) turns an ironic lens on the 'Superwomen' of blockbuster fiction; while *Daddy's Girls* (1991) examines three sisters' teenage years during three political periods. Her novels are notable for their capacity to make current feminist debates accessible to a wide audience. Her short stories have appeared in *Tales I Tell My Mother* (1978), by Fairbairns *et al.*, and *More Tales I Tell My Mother* (1987).

FAIRBURN, A(rthur) R(ex) D(ugard) (1904–57), New Zealand poet, born in Auckland and educated at the grammar school there, where he became friendly with R. A. K. *Mason. He travelled widely, doing various jobs, though his period in England from 1930 to 1932 was a disillusioning experience. Upon his return he was an editor, scriptwriter, and university lecturer, and was instrumental in awakening New Zealand sensibility and nationalism; though his status underwent critical reassessment in later years his achievement in this respect is unquestionable. *We New Zealanders* (1944) was a frank but committed portrait of his country ('This is my country, and I am very glad to belong to it—in spite of everything') while the two poetry collections *Strange Rendezvous* and *Three Poems*, both published in 1952, reflect Fairburn's ongoing engagement with issues of politics, humanism, and national identity; typical is the extensive verse satire 'Dominion', first published in 1938. Much important writing from the 1930s was not reprinted until the appearance of his *Collected Poems* (1966). There is a study, *Fairburn* (1984), by Denys Trussell, and his *Letters* (1984) were edited by Lauris *Edmond.

FAIRLIE, Gerard, see SAPPER.

FALKNER, John Meade (1858–1932), British novelist and topographical writer, born in Wiltshire, educated at Oxford University. He worked as a tutor to the children of Sir Alfred Noble, a partner in Armstrong's, the Newcastle armaments company. He was later Noble's secretary and was chairman of Armstrong's from 1915 to 1921. In 1925 he became Honorary Librarian at Durham Cathedral and Honorary Reader in Palaeography at the city's university. The first of his books to appear was *Handbook for Travellers in Oxfordshire* (1894); *Handbook for Berkshire* (1902) and *Bath in History and Social Tradition* (1918) are among his other topographical works, which draw directly on the antiquarian interests reflected in his fiction. *The Lost Stradivarius* (1896), a complex narrative of the supernatural, features detailed depictions of Oxford and Naples. *Moonfleet* (1898), which centres on smuggling along the Dorset coast, remains popular as an adventure story for younger readers. His most highly regarded novel is *The Nebuly Coat* (1903), an imaginatively disquieting account of an architect who is drawn into a murder investigation while conducting church restoration work. *Poems* (1930), the only collection of his verse, is memorable for its wistfully elegiac adaptations of ballad forms.

FALLON, Padraic (1905–74), Irish poet and playwright, born in Athenry, County Galway. He was a customs official, principally in Wexford, for forty years. Although his poems in anthologies and his writing for radio gained him a reputation as one of the most noteworthy Irish poets in the years following the death of W. B. *Yeats, no independent collection of his verse appeared until *Poems* (1974). His only other publication was a gathering of his short stories, *Lighting up Time* (1938). Fallon insisted that his numerous dramatic works, chiefly written for Irish radio, were integral to his achievement as a poet: they include *The Vision of MacConglinne*, *Steeple Jerkin*, and *The Hags of Clough*. His plays, which remain unpublished, were highly acclaimed and later productions were broadcast by the BBC and German and Dutch radio. The history, landscapes, and folklore of Galway inform much of his writing, which has the innate rhythmical and tonal musicality of poetry deriving something of its identity from Gaelic traditions. Although his writing frequently displays metaphysical concerns, it generally maintains a tone of conversational straightforwardness and grounds its imagery firmly in perceived actuality. *Collected Poems* (1990) is edited by

Brian Fallon, who also edited *Poems and Versions* (1983), which contains Fallon's verse translations of French poetry.

Family Reunion, The, a play by T. S. *Eliot, first performed in 1939, a modern variation on the Orestes story. Harry Lord Monchensey returns to his house, Wishwood, obsessed with the idea that he has killed the manic-depressive wife who was emotionally destroying him, and convinced that he is pursued by 'sleepless hunters that will not let me sleep'. In this loveless, ossified place, he eventually learns that it was his father, not he, who plotted to escape from an oppressive marriage through murder. He rejects the comfortable but stultifying roles offered him by his cold and powerful mother and the other members of his family, embraces the guilt he has inherited while renouncing the remorse he had felt, and leaves to become a missionary, encouraged by Furies he now realizes to be benign, not vindictive. Though the setting is the kind of upper-class drawing room all too familiar to London audiences of the first half of the twentieth century, the subject is a highly unusual one—spiritual self-discovery—and the form equally original. The dialogue consists almost entirely of poetry, itself notable for its bleak, chilly imagery; Harry's uncles and aunts are intermittently transformed into a chorus, commenting fearfully on the action in the Aeschylan mode; and the Furies themselves make a brief appearance. Though Eliot himself later wrote critically of these last two dramatic elements, and was never so adventurous in his subsequent drama, later performances of the play have shown that they may be readily accepted by a generation more accustomed to imaginative theatrical effects and incongruities of style.

Famished Road, The, see OKRI, BEN.

Fantasy. A term used to describe the vast range of non-realistic works frequently known as the 'literature of the Fantastic', a phrase which incorporates myths and legends, folklore and fairy tales, allegory, dream stories, *science fiction, utopias, and fantasy itself. Within this framework a fantasy can be described as an internally coherent story dealing with events and worlds which are impossible. This distinguishes fantasy from science fiction which deals with possible (though often improbable) events and worlds. It also distinguishes pure or full fantasy from most supernatural fiction (which includes ghost stories, occult romances, and tales of vampires and werewolves), because supernatural fiction also tends to claim that its subject-matter is occasioned by, or instructs, the real world.

At the heart of fantasy is the kind of story J. R. R. *Tolkien, its greatest exponent, called the fairy tale. By 'fairy' he did not mean small winged creatures, but 'Faerie' itself, the secondary world where marvels occur, a world impossible according to the rules of the real world, but internally coherent. Precursor versions of fully fledged secondary worlds can be found in the works of nineteenth-century writers such as George MacDonald and William Morris, and hints of Faerie illuminate many tales set mostly in the real world including much of the work of Lord *Dunsany. During the twentieth century, full secondary world fantasies have flourished. These include E. R. Eddison's Mercury, C. S. *Lewis's Narnia, and Tolkien's own Middle-Earth. Early American examples of full fantasies include Fritz *Leiber's Lankhmar, and Clark Ashton Smith's Zothique, while noteworthy recent examples have been created by Peter S. Beagle, Terry Brooks, John *Crowley, L. Sprague de Camp, Samuel R. *Delany, Robert Jordan, Ursula *Le Guin, Michael Swanwick, and Roger *Zelazny.

FANTE, John (Thomas) (1909–83), American novelist and short-story writer, born in Colorado; he attended a Jesuit boarding school, then Long Beach City College. His stories appeared in H. L. *Mencken's *American Mercury* and in popular magazines throughout the 1930s. *Wait Until Spring, Bandini* (1938) and *Ask the Dust* (1939) are picaresque novels featuring 'Arturo Bandini', an aspiring writer, the latter set amidst cheap hotels and racially mixed streets in Los Angeles. The stories in *Dago Red* (1940), rambunctious but with a streak of sentimentality prevalent in his work, offer boyhood angles on Catholicism, baseball, and Italian-American working-class family life. Employment as a Hollywood screenwriter, and diabetes, restricted Fante's output, though *Full of Life* (1952) was a commercial success. Rediscovery of his early fiction in the late 1970s, led by Charles *Bukowski, encouraged the now blind author to complete *The Brotherhood of the Grape* (1977), *Dreams of Bunker Hill* (1982), *The Road to Los Angeles* (1985), and a volume of letters to Mencken.

FANTHORPE, U(rsula) A(skham) (1929–), British poet, born in Lee Green, London, educated at St Anne's College, Oxford. In 1954 she entered schoolteaching, becoming Head of English at Cheltenham Ladies' College in 1962. She resigned in 1970 in order to further her writing, becoming, in her own words, 'a middle-aged drop-out'; she took temporary jobs and later worked as a clerk in a Bristol hospital. She held an Arts Council Writer's Fellowship between 1983 and 1985 and became Northern Arts Fellow at the Universities of Durham and Newcastle in 1987. Her first full collection, *Side Effects* (1978), rapidly gained her a considerable reputation for the assurance, originality, and wryly incisive intelligence her work consistently displays. Further volumes include *Standing To* (1982), *A Watching Brief* (1987), and *Neck-Verse* (1992). Fanthorpe's poems often form compellingly developed and sensitively observed treatments of everyday events and situations. Her work as a hospital clerk is the source of numerous poems in which an ironically poised objectivity and a deep compassion combine to great effect. She has also written a number of unusual and sometimes humorously engaging poems reflecting on religious subjects. *Selected Poems* appeared in 1986.

FARAH, Nuruddin (1945–), Somali novelist, born in Baidoa, in what was then Italian Somaliland, educated at Institution di Magistrale di Mogadishu, and the Universities of London and Essex. He has travelled widely and held academic posts in Europe, the USA, and Africa. His novels, written in English, have been described as political thrillers, but he uses the form to examine not only Somali society and politics, but also family relationships, and the complexities of life in zones of contention among the superpowers. He also analyses the dilemmas of women in traditional society, notably in his first novel, *From a Crooked Rib* (1970). In *A Naked Needle* (1976) a poor Somali teacher, 'proud and fanatical' in his simple views, undergoes traumatic disruption in his life when his former girlfriend proposes to return from England. *Sweet and Sour Milk* (1979), *Sardines* (1981), and *Close Sesame* (1983) form a trilogy entitled *Variations on the Theme of an African Dictatorship*, that of Siad Barre of the Somali Republic. *Maps* (1984) goes furthest in experimental narrative, but in the process loses none of Farah's political astringency. *Gifts* (1993) uses love-offerings as a metaphor to explore the psychology and culture of donations and gifts, and the obligations thus created.

Farewell to Arms, A, a novel by Ernest *Hemingway, published in 1929, dramatized in 1930. Set in Italy during the First World War, the novel is concerned with the developing relationship of an English woman and an American. Frederic Henry is wounded whilst serving as a volunteer in the Italian ambulance corps and falls in love with his nurse, Catherine Barkley. During his recovery and after an idyllic summer, she announces that she is pregnant. Refusing to marry him because she fears being sent home, they separate and he returns to the battlefield where he discovers his former comrades suffering from war-sickness. This is followed by a remarkable passage describing the retreat from Caporetto, at the end of which Henry deserts to rejoin Catherine in Stresa. Together they escape to Switzerland, where both she and their baby die during labour, leaving Henry to contemplate his loneliness.

FARMER, Beverley (1941–), Australian short-story writer and novelist, born in Melbourne, educated at the University of Melbourne. Following her marriage to a Greek she lived in Greece for several years before returning to Australia. Her first novel, *Alone* (1980), deals with the romantic, poeticized lesbian relationship of Shirley, a young woman afraid of heterosexual experience. It was followed by two volumes of short stories, *Milk* (1983) and *Hometime* (1985), most of which are about an outsider in the womb-like family nexus of a Greek village, and deal with the problems of being a woman in a patriarchal society and the tensions of a cross-cultural marriage. Her best stories are permeated with sensual impressions of life in a rural Greek community. *Place of Birth* (1990) contains a selection of stories from these volumes. *A Body of Water* (1990) was described by its publishers as a novel but is more like a diary, covering the period from February 1987 to February 1988 and incorporating passages of prose, poetry, criticism, and short fiction. The novel *The Seal Woman* (1992) is based on a Scandinavian legend of undying love; *The House in the Light* (1995) explores the emotional tempests unleashed by a woman's return to her husband's family in Greece.

FARMER, Philip José (1918–), American novelist of *science fiction and *fantasy, born in Terre Haute, Indiana, educated at Bradley University. His short-story collections such as *Strange Relations* (1960) and *The Alley God* (1960), and novels such as *Flesh* (1960) or *The Lovers* (1961), were considered daring for their metamorphosizing excursions into the physical nature of sexuality. His later work was more varied, moving from pastiches of J. Verne and K. *Vonnegut, to the sustained *Riverworld* series of adventures which take place on a long river where historic characters such as Mark Twain, Goering, and Jesus Christ mingle with others brought back to life; among these are *Riverworld* (1979) and *Gods of Riverworld* (1983).

FARNOL, Jeffrey (1878–1952), British novelist, born in Warwickshire. He went to the USA in 1902 where he wrote his first novel, *The Broad Highway* (1910), a picaresque adventure set in Georgian England. He returned to England where *The Amateur Gentleman* (1913), set in the Regency period, established his career as a best-selling author of more than forty titles, including *Beltane the Smith* (1913), *The Chronicles of the Imp* (1915), *Our Admirable Betty* (1918), *The Geste of Duke Jocelyn* (1920), *Black Bartelmy's Treasure* (1920), *The Quest of Youth* (1927), *Over the Hills* (1930), and *The Jade of Destiny* (1948). He had a great gift for story-telling, particularly in describing scenes of low life, but for modern tastes his women characters tend to be rather stereotyped figures of sweetness and virtue.

FARRELL, J(ames) G(ordon) (1935–79), Anglo-Irish novelist, born in Liverpool, educated at Rossall School and Brasenose College, Oxford. As well as travels to the USA, Europe, and the East, he spent several years teaching in France, the setting of his first novel, *A Man from Elsewhere* (1963). His next novel, *The Lung* (1965), centres on a victim of poliomyelitis, an illness which Farrell had contracted while at Oxford. *A Girl in the Head* (1967) is set in an English seaside resort. Farrell's reputation rests on his three major novels exploring Britain's imperial past, sometimes known as the 'Empire Trilogy'. The first of these, *Troubles* (1970), portrays the world of the ramshackle Anglo-Irish gentry in 1919 at the time of the Irish uprisings. In this, Farrell uses the crumbling Majestic Hotel as a symbol for the dying British Empire and a vanished way of life. *The Siege of Krishnapur* (1973; Booker Prize), a fable about the façade of British civilization, describes the siege of a British garrison holding a small town during the Indian Mutiny of 1857; the disintegration and the pompous absurdities of imperial protocol are described with characteristic wit and irony. *The Singapore Grip* (1978), set in 1942, depicts the collapse of the British Empire as a result of the Japanese invasion. As in all his novels, Farrell shows compassion to the wide range of characters caught up in the collapse, particularly those representing the dying order, doggedly maintaining due standards of decorum in situations of death and destruction, such as the chivalrous Major Brendan Archer who plays a major part in *Troubles*. Meticulously researched and skilfully narrated, Farrell's three major novels combine comedy with suspense, acute observation, and vivid characterization. Farrell was working on his posthumously published novel, *The Hill Station* (1981), at the time of his death in a drowning accident.

FARRELL, James T(homas) (1904–79), American author, born on the South Side of Chicago, where he lived until he was 27. He was educated at Chicago University, where he wrote the first parts of his famous *Studs Lonigan: A Trilogy* (1935): comprising *Young Lonigan* (1932), a *stream-of-consciousness narrative which records the youth as a baseball enthusiast and pupil at a Catholic school living in Chicago's seedy South Side; *The Young Manhood of Studs Lonigan* (1934), which follows the hero through his moral disintegration as the result of contact with the Chicago underworld; and *Judgement Day* (1935), which recounts his defeat and death. The chief influences on this work appear to be Proust, *Joyce, and *Dreiser, but it also shows interest in US social and economic inequalities. After moving to New York in 1931, Farrell remained constant to his theories of literary naturalism; these are discussed in his critical works *A Note on Literary Criticism* (1936), which defends his own brand of Marxism, *The League of Frightened Philistines* (1945), *Literature and Morality* (1947), and *Reflections At Fifty* (1954). This style is also evident in his later fictional five-volume series dealing with the life of Danny O'Neill, in *A World I Never Made* (1936), *No Star Is Lost* (1938), *Father and Son* (1940), *My Days of Anger* (1943), and *The Face of Time* (1953); and in a three-volume series, *Bernard Clare* (1946) and its sequels *The Road Between* (1949) and *Yet Other Waters* (1952), which deals with a gradually disillusioned New York writer and communist in the 1920s. Apart from these cycles, he wrote many other novels, including *Gas-House McGinty* (1933), *Tommy Gallagher's Crusade* (1939), *Ellen Rogers* (1941), *This Man and This Woman* (1951), and *What Time Collects* (1964), whilst *The Silence of History* (1963) began an uncompleted tetralogy featuring Eddie Ryan, a Chicago University student in 1926, who loses his faith in Catholicism. Farrell's novels often reflect the simple social and religious beliefs of hard-working Irish immigrants and how they are undermined in a later generation by the breakdown of the institutions designed to protect them, particularly the home and the Church. The books turn out as an angry but hopeless tirade against the material density and spiritual aridity of contemporary life. His volumes of short stories include *Calico Shoes* (1934), *Guillotine Party* (1935), *Can All This Grandeur Perish?* (1937), *$1,000 a Week* (1942), *To Whom It May Concern* (1944), *An American Dream Girl* (1950), *French Girls Are Vicious* (1956), and *Dangerous Women* (1957). His other writings include *My Baseball Diary* (1957), his perspective on the sport; a book about a visit to Israel, *It Has Come To Pass* (1958); and his *Collected Poems* (1965). See PROLETARIAN LITERATURE IN THE USA.

FARRELL, M. J., see KEANE, MOLLY.

FAST, Howard (1914–), American novelist, born in New York City; he spent two years at the National Academy of Design but, convinced that he would never be an artist, he embarked on a career as a writer. His first novel, *Two Valleys* (1933), established his forte for historical fiction used to promote radical, left-wing politics. *Two Valleys* is a tale of the American frontier during the Revolutionary War, a historical setting Fast revisited in *Conceived in Liberty: A Novel of Valley Forge* (1939), *The Unvanquished* (1942), *Citizen Tom Paine* (1943), and *The Proud and the Free* (1950). Like many American intellectuals of his generation Fast was a communist sympathizer during the 1930s, and joined the Party in 1943. His works were immensely popular in the Soviet Union (his novel *The Passion of Sacco and Vanzetti*, 1953, had an initial Soviet printing of 500,000 copies), but he resigned his membership of the Party in 1957, in part as a consequence of Premier Khrushchev's exposure of the barbarity of the Stalin years, and wrote a valuable account of his relationship to communism in *The Naked God: The Writer and the Communist Party* (1958); the story is enlarged in *Being Red: A Memoir* (1990). His other historical novels include *The Last Frontier* (1941), *Freedom Road* (1944), *The American* (1946), *Clarkton* (1947), and *Silas Timberman* (1954), all with American settings. *Spartacus* (1951), *Moses, Prince of Egypt* (1958), and *Agrippa's Daughter* (1964) were recreations of the ancient past, though some critics have argued that his attempts to find parallels between the distant past and the present are often anachronistic. Later novels include *The Outsider* (1984), *Immigrant's Daughter* (1985), *The Dinner Party* (1987), and *The Pledge* (1988). Fast also writes mystery fiction under the pseudonym E. V. Cunningham. See PROLETARIAN LITERATURE IN THE USA.

Father Brown stories, see CHESTERTON, G. K.

FAULKNER, William (1897–1962), American novelist, poet, and short-story writer, born in New Albany, Mississippi, educated at the University of Mississippi; he served with the Royal Air Force in Canada in 1918. Faulkner's great-grandfather, Colonel William Clark Falkner (Faulkner added the 'u' to his surname in 1924), commanded a Southern regiment during the American Civil War and wrote one of the most popular Southern novels of the nineteenth century, *The White Rose of Memphis* (1881), which went through thirty-six editions; his father owned a livery store and, in later years, became business manager of the state university of Mississippi. The family moved to Oxford, Mississippi in 1902; when Faulkner was five, and it was here that he was educated and spent most of his life. In 1918, after being rejected by the US military, he travelled to New York and, passing himself off as an Englishman, enrolled in the Royal Air Force and was sent to Canada for training; the First World War ended before Faulkner saw active service and he was discharged in December 1918, returned to Oxford, became a student at the University of Mississippi and, whilst there, published poems and drawings in the student newspaper, the *Mississippian*. Faulkner exerted considerable effort to get his poetry published in book form and, after two years of employment as the fourth class postmaster of the University of Mississippi and several publishers' rejections, he finally succeeded in placing a volume of verse, *The Marble Faun* (1924), with the Four Seas Company in Boston. By that time he had begun writing prose, and a meeting with Sherwood *Anderson, whose influence on young American writers was considerable, in New Orleans in November 1924 is thought by one biographer to be 'perhaps the single most important contact of his literary life' (Faulkner considered Anderson's 'I'm a Fool' second only, as a short story, to Conrad's **Heart of Darkness*). In January 1925 Faulkner began work on his first novel, *Soldier's Pay*, and in the summer of the same year he visited Europe, travelling through Italy, France, and, briefly, England before returning to Oxford at Christmas. With the publication of *Soldier's Pay* in 1926 Faulkner's career as a novelist and short-story writer had begun, and his brief and unsuccessful flirtation with verse, prompted in part by his reading of the French *symboliste* poets, was quickly forgotten.

Over the subsequent ten years Faulkner wrote a series of novels which have secured his critical reputation as the greatest American novelist of the twentieth century. The key works brought forward as evidence for this claim are *The *Sound and the Fury* (1929), **As I Lay Dying* (1930), **Sanctuary* (1931), **Light in August* (1932), and **Absalom, Absalom!* (1936), though there are many critics who would also admit later works such as *Go Down, Moses* (1942), *Requiem for a Nun* (1951), and the *Snopes Trilogy, *The Hamlet* (1940), *The Town* (1957), and *The Mansion* (1959), to the canon of his major achievements. In the 1930s, however, Faulkner did not enjoy great commercial success and in July 1933 he began working in Hollywood, a connection with the centre of the American film industry which was to continue, intermittently, until 1948; his most notable achievements are his screen adaptations of Ernest *Hemingway's *To Have and Have Not* and Raymond Chandler's *The *Big Sleep*, both for Howard Hawks. Faulkner was held in high esteem as a novelist in Europe, particularly in France where he was actively promoted by the novelist and philosopher Jean-Paul Sartre, but it was not until the publication in 1946 of *The Portable Faulkner*, edited by Malcolm *Cowley and containing an immensely influential introduction by Cowley, that his critical reputation in the USA began to grow. In recognition of his contribution to literature Faulkner was awarded the Nobel Prize for Literature in 1950. The last twelve years of his life were spent in the limelight that has sometimes attached to literary celebrity in the USA: he travelled on behalf of the State Department to Peru and Brazil in 1954 and to Japan, under the same auspices, in 1955; he was Writer-in-Residence at the University of Virginia and Charlottesville in 1957 and for part of each year from 1958 until his death in 1962. Faulkner was also the recipient of the French Legion of Honour, the O. Henry Award, the National Book Award, and the Pulitzer Prize.

As an imaginative artist Faulkner had an advantage enjoyed by few of his American contemporaries, that of having been born and raised in a complex society, the American South, at a critical period in its transition from a quasi-aristocratic agrarian community to a modern, industrial, and increasingly suburban society (see AGRARIANS). Those features of the 'Old South' which the modern South has slowly, and with varying degrees of success, sought to divest itself of—distinctions of class and race, a manorial social pattern, economic backwardness, one-party politics, a taste for the romantic and the sentimental coupled, contradictorily, with a predisposition to violence as a means of resolving disputes—were the features which provided such fertile soil for Faulkner's imagination. Like Thomas *Hardy, Faulkner began with a narrow corner of a previously uncharted world and peopled it with an immense gallery of characters, so much so that comparisons with the range of fictionally imagined lives in Balzac and Dickens seem entirely appropriate. His treatment of this world encompasses both the grandly tragic and the farcically comic (his prodigious gift for comedy is his most striking novelistic virtue). Much of the fiction of what might be called his 'middle years' is difficult and obscure, and his detractors have frequently criticized the exaggerated and inflated rhetoric of his prose in novels such as *The Sound and the Fury* and *Absalom, Absalom!*.

Faulkner's work has been the subject of more critical discussion than that of any other modern American writer, but many of the earlier studies remain the best introductions to his work, notably *William Faulkner: A Critical Study* (1952) by Irving *Howe, *William Faulkner: The Yoknapatawpha Country* (1963) by Cleanth *Brooks, and *The Achievement of William Faulkner* (1966) by Michael Millgate; Robert Penn *Warren's introduction to his edition of critical essays, *Faulkner: A Collection of Critical Essays* (1966), is one of the best short pieces. *Faulkner: A Biography* (2 volumes, 1974), by Joseph Blotner, is an immensely detailed account of the life, while *William Faulkner: American Writer* (1989), by Frederick R. Karl, is a biography containing much valuable critical commentary.

FAULKS, Sebastian (1953–), British novelist, born in Newbury, Berkshire, educated at Emmanuel College, Cambridge. He worked as a journalist for ten years, and in 1986 became Literary Editor of *The Independent*. His first novel, *A Trick of the Light* (1984), was followed by *The Girl at the Lion d'Or* (1989), a love story set in France during the 1930s, and *A Fool's Alphabet* (1992), in which the Anglo-Italian narrator explores significant moments in his life, chronicling them in the form of an alphabet. Faulks's lucid, understated style and his eye for the details of time and place are shown to advantage in his most ambitious novel, *Birdsong* (1994), about the First World War, which was widely acclaimed for its sensitive treatment of the central relationship between a young Englishman and a married Frenchwoman, and for its evocation of the horrors of trench warfare.

FAUSET, Jessie R(edmon) (1882–1961), African-American novelist, born in New Jersey, educated at Cornell University, the University of Pennsylvania, and the Sorbonne. She was a high-school teacher and, during 1912–26, an editor of *Du Bois's *The Crisis*, a periodical associated with the *Harlem Renaissance. As a novelist, she was primarily concerned with the African-American middle class, and its struggle for betterment and for a fair deal from American society. Her novels include *There Is Confusion* (1924), a romance in which an African-American woman (who wants to be a concert singer) helps her boyfriend in his struggle against racist obstacles to becoming a doctor; *Plum Bun* (1929), which contrasts the lives of two sisters, one living proudly in Harlem, the other unhappily 'passing for white' in Greenwich Village; *The Chinaberry Tree* (1931); and *Comedy: American Style* (1934). She was a pioneer in exposing the experience of African-American women, thereby anticipating such prominent later writers as Alice *Walker and Maya *Angelou.

Fear and Loathing in Las Vegas, see THOMPSON, HUNTER S.

FEARING, Kenneth (Flexner) (1902–61), American poet and novelist, born in Oak Park, Illinois, educated at the University of Wisconsin. The radical antagonism towards middle-class values expressed in *Angel Arms* (1929) and *Poems* (1935), his first two collections of verse, gained him eminence among the American socialist poets of the 1930s; his expansive free verse employs vigorously colloquial diction to frame its blackly humorous and sometimes surreally imaginative views of the desperation underlying normative urban existence. *Dead Reckoning* (1938) and *Afternoon of a Pawnbroker* (1943) sustain his tone of relentless disillusion and dissent with increasing deftness in the use of a range of topical idioms, among them the styles of police reports, newspapers, and the dialogue of popular films. His later verse in *Stranger at Coney Island* (1948) and *New and Selected Poems* (1956) exhibits a measure of lyrical detachment but remains fundamentally political in its themes. Fearing's bleak sociocultural vision informs the concern with hypocrisy and corruption central to his novels, the first of which, *Hospital* (1939), takes a highly sceptical view of medical ethics through its treatment of one hour in the life of a large hospital. *Dagger of the Mind* (1941) and *Clark Gifford's Body* (1942) are experimental murder mysteries, the latter's reworking of the story of John Brown forming an allegory of political revolution. *The Big Clock* (1946), his best-known novel, which hinges on a wealthy publisher's murder of his mistress, was adapted for the cinema in 1948 and has been frequently reprinted.

Fear of Flying, see JONG, ERICA.

Federal Theatre Project (1935–9). Founded by the Works Progress Administration (WPA), one of the most productive of Roosevelt's New Deal agencies, it was established to provide work for thousands of theatre workers made idle by the Depression. According to WPA director Harry Hopkins, its secondary aim was to provide 'free, adult, uncensored theatre', but censorship in the form of the House Un-American Activities Committee caused its early demise. The national director of the FTP was Hallie Flanagan, formerly director of the Vassar Experimental Theatre, and her book *Arena, the Story of the Federal Theatre* (1940) is a lively insider's account of its aims and accomplishments. A national organization of theatre groups which provided a wide variety of inexpensive and good theatre across the nation, its major impact was in New York City, where it drew huge audiences to its productions. FTP companies staged the classical and modern repertoire of plays, and encouraged new writing. Under its broad ethnic approach, black, Catholic, and Jewish projects flourished in New York, but its most successful and controversial achievement was in the *Living Theatre project, which derived from the models of revolutionary workers' theatre in Europe. Much of this work was politically radical, as in Arthur Arent's critique of housing provision *One Third of a Nation* (1938), Marc Blitzein's left-wing musical *The Cradle Will Rock* (1938), and Sinclair *Lewis and John Moffit's play about the risks of American fascism, *It Can't Happen Here* (1936). The extremism of these and other productions led powerful conservative forces to oppose it and Congress abolished the FTP in 1939.

Federal Writers' Project. A branch of President Franklin D. Roosevelt's Works Progress Administration (WPA), the Federal Writers' Project was established in 1935 to sponsor national projects for the relief of unemployed writers. The project employed some 4,500 to 5,000 people and produced a steady stream of books, pamphlets and 'issuances', including the series of guides to American cities and states (celebrated in John *Steinbeck's *Travels with Charley in Search of America*, 1962). The initiative was praised by W. H. *Auden who said that 'to consider in a time of general distress, starving artists as artists and not simply as paupers is unique to the Roosevelt administration'. It was the organized activities of the project that gave work to writers such as Nelson *Algren, Saul *Bellow, Richard *Wright, and others. The project was under the directorship of Henry G. Alsberg who received the active support of the President's wife, Eleanor Roosevelt, but it was not without its critics, some of whom saw it as a refuge for left-wing intellectuals and artists, or as an unnecessary public expenditure. Like many other New Deal projects the Federal Writers' Project did not survive the Second World War, and funding ceased in 1943. *The Dream and the Deal: The Federal Writers' Project, 1935–1943* (1972), by Jerry Mangione, is a history of the project.

FEDERMAN, Raymond (1928–), American novelist and critic, born in Paris, educated at Columbia University and the University of California at Los Angeles. Federman migrated to the USA in 1948 and took American citizenship in 1953. He is generally considered one of the central figures in the 'school' of *post-modernist, anti-realist fiction which began to dominate the American novel in the late 1960s and early 1970s, and his work is often discussed alongside that of contemporaries such as John *Barth, Robert *Coover, William *Gass, Thomas *Pynchon, and Ronald *Sukenick. In *Double or Nothing* (1971) the authorial role is distributed among a number of different voices, and *Take It or Leave It* (1976) makes much imaginative use of the typographical character of the printed page (notably in the novel's 'Pretext'); other novels include *The Voice in the Closet* (1979) and *To Whom It May Concern* (1990). *The Twofold Vibration* (1982), a work of political fiction, is generally considered his most innovative novel. His non-fiction prose is collected in *Surfiction: Fiction Now and Tomorrow* (1981) and *Critifiction: Postmodern Essays* (1993), while he has also written extensively on Samuel *Beckett, notably in *Journeys to Chaos: Samuel Beckett's Early Fiction* (1965) and *Samuel Beckett* (1976), and he has edited *Samuel Beckett: The Critical Heritage* (1979). He became a Professor of English at the State University of New York. See *The Novel as Performance: The Fiction of Ronald Sukenick and Raymond Federman* (1986) by Jerzy Kutnick.

FEINSTEIN, Elaine (1930–), British poet and novelist, born in Lancashire of Ukrainian Jewish descent, educated at Newnham College, Cambridge. After working as an editor and a university lecturer Feinstein made her reputation as a poet: her collections include *In a Green Eye* (1966), *The Magic Apple Tree* (1971), *The Celebrants and Other Poems* (1973), *The Feast of Euridice* (1980), and *City Music* (1990). Feinstein's early influences were Wallace *Stevens and William Carlos *Williams but her translations of Marina Tsvetayeva and other modern Russian poets became crucial in the development of her own lyrical and narrative voice; Feinstein's acclaimed biography of Tsvetayeva appeared in 1987. The themes of Feinstein's poetry—the individual's striving for identity, the conflicts between personal and public life—also recur in her novels. The first of these, *The Circle* (1970), is dominated by the consciousness of Lena, whose interior monologue explores the concept of freedom within the close interdependence of marriage. Exile and Jewish consciousness is central to *Children of the Ring* (1975) and the autobiographical *The Survivors* (1982). In *The Border* (1984), Feinstein examines the pressures in a marriage between a poet and a scientist; as Jews, they are in flight from the political oppressions of Austria in the 1930s. Feminism, always an important theme, is brought into sharp focus in *Mother's Girl* (1987). Lighter in style is *All You Need* (1989), a lively satire on Thatcher's London. *Loving Brecht* (1992) traces the fictitious history of one of Brecht's lovers. Other novels include *Dreamers* (1994), a love story, which portrays European Jewry in the mid-nineteenth century when enlightenment and industrial progress offered hope to the dispossessed, and *Lady Chatterley's Confession* (1995). A biography, *Lawrence's Women*, was published in 1993.

FELL, Alison (1944–), Scottish novelist and poet, born in Dumfries, Scotland; she trained as a sculptor in Edinburgh, and moved to London in 1970. Involved for several years with the women's movement, she was a member of the Spare Rib Collective. Her first published work was a novel for children, *The Grey Dancer* (1981). Her first adult novel, *Every Move You Make* (1984), was in the realist mode of confessional feminism. Her prize-winning collection of poems, *Kisses for Mayakovsky*, appeared in the same year. Fell's second novel, *The Bad Box* (1987), characteristically intertwines myth and realism; it deals with the coming-of-age sexual and creative fantasies of a Scottish teenager.

In the 1990s Fell emerged as one of the women, such as Michèle *Roberts and Marina *Warner, deliberately expanding the frontiers of the British novel. In *Mer de Glace* (1991) Fell is at her most compelling. Juxtaposing masculine and feminine perspectives, the novel explores an emotional triangle, in which the protagonists are an Irish writer, her American mountain-climbing lover, and the latter's wife. This complex, passionate account is framed in Alpine imagery and mythical allusions. *The Pillow Boy of the Lady Onogoro* (1994), though it presents Fell's familiar preoccupations with desire and dreams, is a stylistic departure: it is recounted in the manner of a medieval Japanese chronicle, and like the Arabian Nights tells many tales, delicate, cruel, and erotic, within the framework of its principal story. Here Fell indulges her gift for humour, pastiche, and fable, and lends her poet's skills to a celebration of Japanese (and Japanese-inspired) verse forms.

Female Eunoch, The, see GREER, GERMAINE.

Feminist Criticism. There were, of course, feminists and feminist criticism long before the terms were used with any frequency, but a convenient modern landmark is Virginia Woolf's *A *Room of One's Own* (1929), perhaps best read in conjunction with her less conciliatory **Three Guineas* (1938). Woolf addressed the question of women both as writers and as characters in works written by men, concluding that there was a huge discrepancy between the power of fictional or legendary women, like Cleopatra and Clytemnestra, and the powerlessness and virtual invisibility of most of their historical counterparts. Woolf thereby set the agenda for much feminist criticism to follow, whether by exploring and recovering the work of neglected women writers or by examining the (often wildly biased or deeply buried) assumptions behind the portrayal of women in literature. Kate *Millett's *Sexual Politics* (1971) took the second path with its acrid and funny exhibition of male mythologies in D. H. *Lawrence, Norman *Mailer and others, while Ellen *Moers's *Literary Women* (1976) and Elaine *Showalter's *A Literature of Their Own* (1977) revealed and pursued a female tradition of writing, along the lines of Woolf's suggestion that a woman writer can learn from her male predecessors, but cannot get *help* from them. Meanwhile Simone de Beauvoir, in her enormously influential *The Second Sex* (1949), had argued that the very idea of woman, as we experience it, is a male creation: an argument giving rise to the polemical claim of later feminists that language itself is masculine. Should women then seek to subvert this language or find a place within it; or should they (can they) form a language of their own? The idea of a specific *écriture féminine*, associated with the work of Hélène Cixous and Luce Irigaray, is still much debated: celebrated, questioned, parodied. Feminism has become a great force in the later twentieth century, but it is not a single movement: there are many feminisms. It has become customary, though, at least in the West, to think of two main strands of feminist criticism: the Anglo-American, which is practical and sceptical, inclined to view literary theory as a placebo, or institutional delaying tactic; and the French, strongly influenced by *Structuralism and psychoanalysis, inclined to believe that unless our theories are drastically revised, we can only shufffle the cards of the old order. There is little likelihood of an accommodation between the parties, but there are signs that younger feminists are able to take what they need from both sides. It is telling that the utopian project of deconstructing the very opposition between male and female, proposed in different ways by both Cixous and Julia Kristeva, should strongly resemble, at least in a certain reading, Woolf's argument for an ideal androgyny of the writing mind.

FENOLLOSA, Ernest (Francisco) (1853–1908), American orientalist and aesthetician, born in Salem, Massachusetts, educated at Harvard; in 1877 he began teaching at Tokyo University, where he developed a deep interest in Japanese painting. He was appointed Imperial Commissioner of Fine Arts by the Japanese administration in 1886. He subsequently lectured widely in the USA on art education and Japanese art. His numerous works include *Imagination in Art* (1894), a statement of his aesthetic philosophy, and *Epochs of Chinese and Japanese Art* (edited by M. Fenollosa, 1912). Ezra *Pound was given his papers in 1913, drawing upon them heavily for the translations of Chinese poetry in *Cathay* (1915) and in the writing of *'Noh' or Accomplishment: A Study of the Classical Stage of Japan* (1916). His versions of Noh dramas were used by Pound to prepare *Certain Noble Plays of Japan* (1916), which carries an introduction by W. B. *Yeats, himself much influenced by Fenollosa's work. In 1936 Pound edited Fenollosa's *The Chinese Written Character as a Medium for Poetry*, its theories of poetic imagery having informed the poetics of *The *Cantos* (1987). *Fenollosa: The Far East and American Culture* by L. W. Chisholm appeared in 1963.

FENTON, James (Martin) (1949–), British poet, born in Lincoln, educated at Magdalen College, Oxford. He worked at the **New Statesman* from 1971 to 1973, when began two years as a freelance correspondent in Indo-China; *All the Wrong Places* (1988) is a collection of his despatches from Cambodia during a time of great political and military turbulence. After a period as chief literary critic for *The Times* he returned to the Far East in 1986 as a correspondent for the *Independent.* As a poet, Fenton has gained a high reputation for the quality and range of his comparatively slender output; two pamphlets, *Our Western Furniture* (1968) and *Put Thou Thy Tears into My Bottle* (1969), were followed in 1972 by *Terminal Moraine*, a collection widely acclaimed for its originality of tone and conception. Several subsequent pamphlets include *A Vacant Possession* (1978), which contains numerous intensely atmospheric poems exemplifying his use of fictive modes. Among his other publications are *Dead Soldiers* (1981) and *A German Requiem* (1982), to which themes and narratives from his work as a foreign correspondent are central. *The Memory of War and Children in Exile: Poems 1968–1983* (1983) demonstrates the scope of his writing, which extends from the open compassion of the treatment of Cambodian refugees in 'Children in Exile' to the surreally disquieting humour of 'The Skip'. His talent for comic verse is displayed in *Partingtime Hall* (with John *Fuller, 1987), which is notable for its unusual blend of scurrility and erudition.

FERBER, Edna (1885–1968), American novelist, born in Kalamazoo, Michigan. She began her writing career as a cub reporter with a local paper but soon turned to fiction; her first novel, *Dawn O'Hara, the Girl Who Laughed*, was published in 1911. A prolific writer, she enjoyed popular success with such later novels as the family drama *So Big* (1924), set on a farm. The colourful *Showboat* (1926), with its tragic sub-plot of racism and miscegenation, has been filmed and continues to be revived on international musical stages, and is probably her main claim to lasting popularity. Often dismissed as sentimental and didactic—qualities that prevail in the works mentioned above—Ferber has nevertheless been praised for her socio-historical research and authentic portrayals of the American experience in romantic sagas such as *Cimarron* (1930) and *Saratoga Trunk* (1941). The immensely successful *Giant* (1952) is the epic story of a Texas family whose ranch serves as a metaphor for the oil-rich state; this, too, was successfully filmed, and probably influenced *popular culture in the shape of such long-running *soap operas as *Dallas*. Her last published work was an autobiography, *A Kind of Magic* (1963).

FERLINGHETTI, Lawrence (1920–), American poet, born in New York, educated at the University of North Carolina, Columbia University, and the Sorbonne. He was the fifth son of an Italian immigrant father and Portuguese mother; on his father's sudden death his mother went insane and was placed in an asylum. He was rescued from a New York orphanage by a relative, and taken to France for several years; after returning to America he was brought up by a family called Lawrence, from whom it appears he took his forename. A major figure in the *Beat movement, with Peter D. Maring he founded the City Lights bookstore in San Francisco in 1952, the first all-paperback bookstore in America, and began to publish City Lights Books and the Pocket Poets Series, and a mimeographed magazine called *Beatitude*, to denote the beatific dimensions of Beat poetry. He published the work of Allen *Ginsberg, Gregory *Corso, and other young poets, and through his public readings and publication of poems as broadsides did much to create a wider audience for poetry in the 1950s and 1960s. His own first book of poems was *Pictures from the Gone World* (1953), followed by *A Coney Island of the Mind* (1958), *Starting from San Francisco* (1961; revised 1967), *The Secret Meaning of Things* (1969), *Open Eye, Open Heart* (1973), *Landscapes of Living and Dying* (1979), and *Endless Life: The Selected Poems* (1981). His other works include a novel, *He-* (1960), translations, political satire, and experimental plays. Ferlinghetti composes in the open verse free forms characteristic of Beat poetry, and his subjects reflect his belief in states of ecstasy available through the spiritual teachings of Zen Buddhism, and the compulsions of love. An equally powerful strain in his work reflects his political disenchantment with American imperialism, and the squalor of its domestic politics. See also SAN FRANCISCO RENAISSANCE and UNDERGROUND POETRY.

FERMOR, Patrick (Michael) Leigh (1915–), born in London, educated at King's School, Canterbury. From 1935 to 1939 he travelled from Rotterdam to Istanbul; the first two books of a trilogy describing the journey, *A Time of Gifts* (1977) and *Between the Woods and the Water* (1985), form a richly evocative record of European social and cultural patterns destroyed by the Second World War. He received the OBE and DSO for his active service in Albania and Greece from 1939 to 1945; he spent two years in occupied Crete organizing guerrilla activities and led the party which captured General Kreipe, the island's German commander. Following a period as director of the British Institute in Athens, he became a freelance writer and translator. He rapidly achieved recognition as a travel writer through the idiosyncratic elegance and vividness of *The Traveller's Tree* (1950), an account of his experiences in the Caribbean, where his novel *The Violins of St Jacques* (1953) is set. His translations include *The Cretan Runner* (1955) by George Psychoundakis. *Mani* (1958), recording his travels in the Southern Peloponnese, and *Roumeli* (1966), which deals with Northern Greece, gained him eminence among the travel writers of his generation; the books display his characteristic ability to range fluently between a precisely erudite vocabulary and an energetically lyrical expression of his delight in what he encounters and perceives. Fermor's other works include *A Time To Keep Silence* (1953), his 'meditations on monastic life', and *Three Letters from the Andes* (1991), both of which originate in letters to his wife.

FIEDLER, Leslie A(aron) (1917–), American critic, born in Newark, New Jersey, educated at the universities of New York and Madison, Wisconsin. After war service he was, from 1947 to 1963, Professor of English at Montana State University and since then has taught at the University of New York, Buffalo. *An End to Innocence: Essays on Culture and Politics* (1955) showed Fiedler's polemical flair, and also included 'Come Back to the Raft Ag'in, Huck Honey' (*Partisan Review*, 1948) whose discussion of 'the erotic archetype' in Melville, Fenimore Cooper, and Twain anticipated his later approach. *Love and Death in the American Novel* (1960) was a critical landmark, owing as much to Freud as to D. H. *Lawrence in arguing the mythic and gothic status of classic American literature ('books which turn from society to nature or nightmare'). Fiedler's emphasis on the contexts of writing—and his energetic style, full of provocative generalizations—represented a turning away from the *New Criticism. After *Waiting for the End* (1964), the frontier mythology was examined in *The Return of the Vanishing American* (1968), ingeniously linking the legends of Pocahontas and 'Rip Van Winkle' to the New Westerns of *Barth, Thomas *Berger, and *Kesey. Fiedler's arrest on a marijuana charge in 1967 occasioned a partial autobiography, *Being Busted* (1970); he became a popular speaker often regarded, simplistically, as a spokesman for the counter-culture. The *Collected Essays* (2 volumes) appeared in 1971, *A Fiedler Reader* in 1977. Amongst the later works are *What Was Literature?* (1982) and *Fiedler on the Roof: Epistle to the Gentiles* (1991). His achievement has been to 'define the myths which give a special character to life and art in America'. Mark Royden Winchell's *Leslie A. Fiedler* was published in 1985.

Field Day Theatre Company, founded in Derry city by Brian *Friel and Stephen Rea in 1980. Since staging Friel's play **Translations* (1980), Field Day has reassessed the borders of its initial identity as a theatre company and has become a broader intellectual project seeking possible cultural and political solutions to the problems of Northern Ireland. With the addition of Seamus *Heaney, David Hammond, Tom *Paulin, and Seamus *Deane, the group inaugurated a series of pamphlets, including Heaney's *An Open Letter* (1983), Deane's *Civilians and Barbarians* (1983), and Terence Brown's *The Whole Protestant Community* (1985), which have sought to re-read Irish history in relation to the current crisis. Intellectuals at one or two removes from the immediate Irish scene, such as Fredric *Jameson, Terry *Eagleton, and Edward

*Said, have also contributed to this debate. More recently, *The Field Day Anthology of Irish Writing* (1991) has completed a long-term project intended to establish a distinct, heterogeneous, and alternative tradition to that of English Literature.

FIELDING, Gabriel, pseudonym of Alan BARNSLEY (1916–87), British novelist, born in Hexham, Northumbria, educated at Trinity College, Dublin; he practised as a doctor. A descendant of Henry Fielding, and a convert to Catholicism, much of Fielding's work is characterized by an intense feeling for a sinful man's desire for grace and for the battle between the flesh and the spirit. *Brotherly Love* (1954) introduces the Blaydons, a country clergyman's family; partly autobiographical, it centres on John, and his feelings for his elder brother, David, an Anglican priest who is also an incorrigible and destructive womanizer. The Blaydons reappear in other novels including *In the Time of Greenbloom* (1956) with its shocking story of the murder of John's young girlfriend. His most successful novel, *The Birthday King* (1962), set in Germany, reflected Fielding's study of the 'malignance of the Nordic mind' and depicted a riven family, much like the Krupps, who were servants of the Nazi state. Later works, such as *Gentlemen in Their Season* (1966), *New Queens for Old* (1972; novellas), *Pretty Doll-Houses* (1979), and *Women of Guinea Lane* (1986), were less successful.

FIERSTEIN, Harvey (1954–), American playwright, born in Brooklyn. He came to prominence with the 1981 Off-Broadway production of *Torch Song Trilogy* which won a Tony award for its 1982 Broadway production; the author starred in both the play and his screen adaptation of 1988. The trilogy consists of three previously produced one-act plays (*The International Stud*, 1978; *Fugue in a Nursery*, 1979; *Women and Children First!*, 1979) and depicts various aspects of gay life and culture. A prominent activist for both AIDS and gay rights, Fierstein also won the 1983 Tony award for his book of the musical version of *La Cage aux Folles* which, like Fierstein's other work for the stage and screen, explores the lives of the gay and lesbian community as a whole. *Safe Sex* was produced in New York in 1987. More recently, Fierstein has turned to acting, appearing in various guest roles on American TV, and in the Off-Broadway show *The Haunted Host* (1991). Among his works for television are *Tidy Endings* (1988) and *Cheers* (1992). His feature films include *Mrs Doubtfire* (1992), *White Lies* (1993), *The Harvest* (1992), and *Garbo Talks* (1984).

Fiesta, see SUN ALSO RISES, THE.

FIGES, Eva (1932–), British novelist and cultural critic, born in Berlin; her family moved to England in 1939. She was educated at Queen Mary College, University of London, and has worked as an editor for a number of publishers. Her novels focus on the subjective consciousness and show acute sensitivity to historical realities, and a debt to Kafka. In her rejection of external realism, Figes explains that 'The English social realist tradition cannot contain the realities of my lifetime, horrors which one might have called surreal if they had not actually happened.' The novels tend to be short, intensely poetic, and include *Equinox* (1966), her first novel; *Winter Journey* (1967); *Light* (1983), a portrait of a painter who searches for perfection in the midst of transience; *The Seven Ages* (1986), about women throughout history; *Ghosts* (1988), which treats time as a spectral phenomenon; *The Tree of Knowledge* (1990), a feminist version of the myth of Eden; *The Tenancy* (1993), a parable of urban disintegration set in a deteriorating house, where women struggle against various forms of intimidation; and *The Knot* (1996). As a feminist cultural critic, Figes's works include *Patriarchal Attitudes: Women in Society* (1970) and *Sex and Subterfuge: Women Novelists to 1850* (1982). She has edited *Women's Letters in Wartime: 1450–1945* (1993), a feminist anthology.

FIGUEROA, John (Joseph Maria) (1920–), Jamaican poet and educator, born in Kingston, and educated at St George's College, Kingston, Holy Cross College, Worcester, Massachusetts, and at London University. He has held academic posts in Britain, the Caribbean, and Nigeria. Religious imagery, occasional allusiveness, classical restraint, and a concern for the 'island folk' characterize much of his poetry, but it is also notable for its sensuousness and vivid painting of landscape. He often counterpoints Creole, Spanish, and Latin with English in poems asserting wide cultural dimensions. Spiritual introspection and sensitivity to the physical are inherent in his work, which has been published in *Blue Mountain Peak* (1943), *Love Leaps Here* (1962), and *Ignoring Hurts* (1976). *The Chase: A Collection of Poems 1941–1989* was published in 1992. He edited the pioneering anthology *Caribbean Voices* (1966; 1976).

FINDLATER, Mary (1865–1963) and Jane (1866–1946), Scottish novelists; they wrote separately, but their three novels written in collaboration (*Crossriggs*, 1908; *Penny Moneypenny*, 1911; and *Beneath the Visiting Moon*, 1923) exceeded their individual productions in both subtlety and intensity. Jane, whose much praised novel *The Green Graves of Balgowrie* (1896) has a ballad-like quality, endowed the books with their sense of the numinous and the tragic, while Mary provided the social analysis and comedy. *Crossriggs*, the study of interrelated lives in a village near Edinburgh, is distinguished by a wry humour, the constant play of poetry, and the presence of forces that overtake the individual, above all the sexual. This last is in evidence in *Penny Moneypenny*, the male protagonist of which is plainly based on Robert Louis Stevenson. Admired by Henry *James and Virginia *Woolf, among others, the Findlater sisters are now seldom read.

FINDLEY, Timothy (1930–), Canadian novelist, born in Toronto. He was an actor and a Hollywood dialogue writer before becoming a full-time author in the early 1960s. He has continued to write for the media, producing radio and television plays and documentaries, usually in collaboration with William Whitehead. Findley's fiction explores boundaries in 'the countries of our invention' between fiction, history, and truth. His first novel, *The Last of the Crazy People* (1967), is a study of a decadent southern Ontario family, seen through the eyes of an 11-year-old protagonist, who can only find love from a servant and his pet cats. *The Wars* (1977) and *Famous Last Words* (1981), the latter taking the form of the personal testament of Ezra *Pound's character Hugh Selwyn Mauberley, are powerful studies of the horrors of twentieth-century history, centred on the two World Wars. *Not Wanted on the Voyage* (1984) is a vividly inventive reworking of the story of the Great Flood. As Findley puts it, 'Everyone knows it wasn't like that' and ancient myth-making is replaced by contemporary fabulation. He has also published *The Butterfly Plague* (1969), *The Telling of Lies* (1986), and *Headhunter* (1994); a volume of short stories, *Dinner along the Amazon* (1984); a collection of autobiographical writings, *Inside Memory: Pages from a Writer's Workbook* (1990); a play, *Stillborn Lover* (1993); and *The Trials of Ezra Pound* (1995).

FINLAY, Ian Hamilton (1925–), Scottish poet, graphic artist, and sculptor; born in Nassau in the Bahamas, he grew up in Scotland. During the early 1950s he worked on farms in the Orkneys and began publishing short stories in the *Glasgow Herald*; *The Sea-Bed and Other Stories* (1958) contained work notable for its simplicity and symbolic power. *The Dancers Inherit the Party* (1960), a selection of his 'sophisticated folk poems', impressed critics through its formal economy and openness. In 1961 Finlay founded the Wild Hawthorn Press and produced *Glasgow Beasts, An a Burd*, a series of sometimes bizarre and amusing poems in Glasgow dialect. He has since published a great many books and pamphlets, among them *Stonechats* (1967), *Butterflies* (1973), *A Mast of Hankies* (1975), and *The Errata of Ovid* (1983). Jonathan *Raban noted his work's characteristic 'circumspect, private wit that resists condensation into fulsome generalizations'. In 1962 he developed an interest in *concrete poetry, of which he became a leading exponent. After settling at Stonypath in Dunsyre, Lanarkshire, in 1966, he commenced the landscaping of his celebrated 'garden temple', in which poems inscribed on slabs exist in aesthetic interaction with a range of other emblematic art objects, plants, and water. Finlay's productions, which have been widely exhibited, obviate the distinction between poems and graphic or sculptural art works. Both *A Wartime Garden* (1990; poems and graphics) and *The Garden, Little Sparta* (1992; prose and poetry) relate to his garden, which has become a *cause célèbre* through his legal disputes with the local council. *Ian Hamilton Finlay: A Visual Primer* (1985) by Yves Abrioux lavishly displays the extraordinary range and diversity of his work.

Finnegans Wake, an experimental prose work by James *Joyce, published in 1939. Written in a dense, richly textured, and allusive style, whose punning, fragmentary quality mirrors the free-associating nature of the dreaming mind, the book is perhaps the definitive and most extreme work of literary *Modernism. At once simple and complex, its narrative, which takes place in a single night but also incorporates the whole of human history, describes the relationships between Humphrey Chimpden Earwicker, an Everyman (H.C.E. translates as 'Here Comes Everybody') who is also Adam, his wife, Anna Livia Plurabelle, who is Eve and also the River Liffey, their daughter Iseult / Isobel, and their twin sons, Shem and Shaun, who are also Cain and Abel. Set in Dublin, the entire work is permeated with Irish legend and history, which is seen as an endless cycle of birth, dissolution, and renewal—a view Joyce derived, in part, from his reading of Vico's *Scienza Nuova* and which is implicit in the book's title, with its play on the dual meanings of the word 'wake'. The work is divided into four sections, corresponding, amongst other things, to the four seasons of the year and the Four Ages of Man, and offers a kind of guided tour around the 'museyroom' of the past, as well as a condensed history of language itself. It has given rise to a vast corpus of critical works and linguistic exegesis, focusing on every aspect of the work: from its use of children's nursery rhymes to its reworking of Homeric legend; from its exploration of the topography of Dublin—'Howth Castle and Environs'—to its exposition of the universal myth of fall and redemption. It is, in Joyce's succinct coinage, a 'funferal', offering, in the words of the Irish-American ballad from which it takes its title, 'lots of fun at Finnegan's wake'.

FIRBANK, (Arthur Annesley) Ronald (1886–1926), British novelist, born in London. His grandfather was a Durham miner who made his fortune as a railway contractor, his father a Unionist MP who was knighted on the accession of Edward VII. His childhood was spent in Chislehurst, a town whose connections with the exiled Empress Eugenie may have fed his enduring fascination with both royalty and Catholicism. His first book, containing the two tales 'Odette d'Antrevernes' and 'A Study in Temperament', was published in 1905. At Cambridge (1906–9) he took no degree but was received into the Catholic Church and pursued an interest in Oscar Wilde that is evident throughout his work. The war years, spent in isolation in Oxford, saw the publication of *Vainglory* (1915), *Inclinations* (1916), and *Caprice* (1917); *Valmouth* followed in 1919 and his play *The Princess Zoubaroff* in 1920 (first performed in 1951). Dandyish, frail, heavy-drinking, and intensely shy, he found it hard to readjust to society, and in 1919 for the sake of his health he resumed his pre-war nomadism in southern Europe, North Africa, and the Caribbean. After *Santal* (1921) came the three major novels of his maturity–like all his work, they are meditations on baffled aspiration and desire: *The Flower Beneath the Foot* (1923), set in an imaginary Vienna, combines an account of the youthful disappointments of a saint with a tart picture of English literary society in the run-up to a royal wedding; in *Prancing Nigger* (UK title *Sorrow in Sunlight*, 1924), set on a Caribbean island, Firbank's negroism finds its most concentrated expression in the sorry adventures of the Mouth family when, driven by Mrs Mouth's social ambitions, they move from the village to the city; in *Concerning the Eccentricities of Cardinal Pirelli* (1926), the moral and theological unorthodoxy of a great Spanish churchman leads to his exile and death. On his own death in Rome, Firbank left fragments of a novel, *The New Rythum* (1962), set in New York. From the early *The Artificial Princess* (posthumously published in 1934) on, his highly idiosyncratic work represents a radical and lonely experiment in form and technique: his books tend to an extreme brevity, his approach to plot is oblique and subversive, his construction seemingly fragmentary, though subject to a firm if baroque discipline. His manner is at once satirical and lyric, absurd and cryptically concentrated. It went largely unappreciated in his lifetime (he paid for the publication of all his books until *Prancing Nigger* made his name in the USA), but was to be a decisive influence on writers of the generation of Evelyn *Waugh, Anthony *Powell, and W. H. *Auden.

FIRST, Ruth (1925–82), South African journalist, political activist, and theorist, born in Johannesburg, educated at the University of Witwatersrand. She began her writing career as an investigative journalist exposing the grim working conditions of non-white and migrant labourers. She was killed by a letter bomb sent to the Centre for African Studies in Maputo, Mozambique, where she had been research director since 1978. Although she and her husband, Joe Slovo, a leading member of the Revolutionary Council of the African National Congress, were acquitted in the mass treason trials of 1956, during 1963 she was held in solitary confinement; this experience resulted in a classic work of political prison literature, *117 Days: An Account of Confinement and Interrogation under the South African Ninety-Day Detention Law* (1965). She later settled in London and was appointed Lecturer in Sociology at the University of Durham. *The Barrel of a Gun: Political Power in Africa and the Coup d'Etat* (1970), a work of acute political analysis, goes considerably beyond the narrow concerns of an academic specialist, and is one of the most revealing books about Africa in the twentieth century. With Ann Scott she wrote *Olive Schreiner* (1980), a biography. She is the mother of Gillian *Slovo.

First Men in the Moon, The, a novel by H. G. *Wells, published in 1901. In Wells's only interplanetary novel, two ill-assorted explorers, Mr Cavor and Mr Bedford—the pure scientist and the entrepreneur—travel to the moon in a sphere powered by the mysterious anti-gravity substance Cavorite. After experiencing weightlessness, the miraculous lunar sunrise, and the thinness of the moon's atmosphere, they are captured by the ant-like Selenites and taken below the surface. The moon, they discover, is hollowed out like a vast honeycomb. Bedford escapes and manages to return to earth, while his companion contrives to send back a series of radio messages describing the lunar civilization. *The First Men in the Moon* is a satiric comedy, much less apocalyptic in tone than Wells's earlier 'scientific romances', and showing his familiarity with the tradition of fantastic lunar voyages going back to Lucian. In its humour, idiosyncrasy, and apparent disregard of technological plausibility Wells's novel anticipates later British scientific fantasies, particularly C. S. *Lewis's *Out of the Silent Planet* (1938). However, his evocations of the lunar landscape and vegetation and of the sensations of space travel achieve a true sublimity. The final chapters containing Cavor's radio messages were not part of the author's original design. The Selenites' intricate and regimented society presided over by a vast disembodied brain, the Grand Lunar, is portrayed in terms of Swiftian satire, with the beleaguered and credulous Cavor taking the role of Gulliver. Nevertheless, the Grand Lunar's puzzlement on learning that the earth consists of warring nation-states without any co-ordinating world government echoes one of Wells's favourite themes.

First Statement, a Montreal magazine primarily devoted to poetry, founded in 1942 by John Sutherland in association with Robert Simpson, Keith MacLellan, and others. Sutherland is said to have been prompted to begin the journal in response to the rejection of his verse by **Preview*; a measure of sometimes antagonistic rivalry existed between the two in the earlier years of their comparatively short publishing histories. In 1945 the magazines merged to form *Northern Review*, which continued to appear until 1956, although it did not succeed in maintaining the energy and individuality of its predecessors. Whereas *Preview* favoured the examples of the leading British poets of the 1930s as models for advancing indigenous Canadian poetry, *First Statement*'s contributors were more characteristically influenced by the achievements of Ezra *Pound, William Carlos *Williams, and their followers. A. M. *Klein's work of the early 1940s is notable for satisfying the criteria of both magazines. Louis *Dudek, Irving *Layton, and Raymond *Souster were among the regular contributors of poetry, establishing it as the principal vehicle for the emergence of realist *Modernism in Canadian verse. After its fifth issue the magazine absorbed *The Western Free-Lance*, thereby significantly increasing its readership. Intended as a fortnightly, it was published irregularly in mimeographed form until Sutherland acquired a printing press in 1943; it subsequently increased in size to include regular book reviews and published short stories more frequently. First Statement Press continued after the journal merged with *Preview*, publishing numerous valuable editions of poetry, which include Souster's *When We Are Young* (1946) and Miriam *Waddington's *Green World* (1945).

FISH, Stanley (Eugene) (1938–), American critic, born in Providence, Rhode Island, educated at the University of Pennsylvania and at Yale. He subsequently held a succession of posts including Professor of English at the University of California and at Johns Hopkins University, Baltimore, and Arts and Sciences Distinguished Professor of English and Law at Duke University, Durham, North Carolina. *John Skelton's Poetry* (1965) was widely admired for its reading of Skelton's verse as a record of the poet's psychological and spiritual development. *Surprised by Sin: The Reader in 'Paradise Lost'* (1967) examined the centrality of individual responses in evaluating the poem; Fish's emphasis on the essentially subjective nature of literary interpretation was sustained in *Self-Consuming Artefacts: The Experience of Seventeenth Century Literature* (1972) and *The Living Temple: George Herbert and Catechizing* (1978). *Is There a Text in This Class: The Authority of Interpretive Communities* (1980) formed a wide-ranging critique of literary theory, which, Fish argued, offered an inflexible and reductive basis for critical discourse by discounting a reader's personal experience of a text; the book was equally provocative in challenging the traditional assumptions of liberal humanism, and gained Fish an international reputation. In *Doing What Comes Naturally: Change, Rhetoric and the Practice of Theory in Literary and Legal Studies* (1989) Fish's exposition centres on his belief that 'the troubles and benefits of interpretive theory . . . disappear in an enriched notion of practice'; the book's twenty-two essays are unified by the view that judgements in literature, law, philosophy, and psychoanalysis remain objectively valid while being necessarily subject to determination by their contexts. *There's No Such Thing as Free Speech: And It's a Good Thing Too* appeared in 1993; and *Professional Correctness: Literary Studies and Political Change* in 1995. See also READER-RESPONSE THEORY.

FISHER, Roy (1930–), British poet, born in Handsworth, Birmingham, educated at the University of Birmingham. He has held several teaching posts, including lecturer in American Studies at the University of Keele. The imaginative involvement with Birmingham in much of his writing pervades the impressionistic survey of *City* (1961), his first collection of poetry. Numerous subsequent volumes have included *The Memorial Fountain* (1967), *The Thing about Joe Sullivan* (1978), *Running Changes* (1983), *A Furnace* (1986), *Poems 1955–1987* (1988), and *Birmingham River* (1994). Each demonstrates Fisher's development of a highly individual modernist idiom: a commitment to the ethos of experimentation in modern American and European poetry is balanced by a fertile sensitivity to the moods and atmospheres of verse in the English tradition. The poetry which results is remarkable for combining intensely objective description with powerful indications of subjective emotion. A keen sense of the absurd is encountered in his occasional oblique satires. He is also noted for his prose poems, collections of which include *Metamorphoses* (1970) and *The Cut Pages* (1971). Anne Cluysenaar has remarked that 'Fisher inhabits a ground of perceptual precisions made taut by a heart-rending, though quiet, sense of inexplicable significance beyond'. He is increasingly recognized as one of the most valuably original British poets to emerge in the post-war era.

FITZGERALD, F(rancis) Scott (Key) (1896–1940), American novelist and short-story writer, born in St Paul, Minnesota. He entered Princeton University at the age of 17 where he took part in a variety of extra-curricular literary and dramatic activities and befriended campus intellectuals like Edmund *Wilson. He then joined the army and was posted to Montgomery, Alabama, where he fell in love with Zelda Sayre, a local belle, who refused to marry him when it transpired that he was unable to maintain her in her accustomed lifestyle. Fitzgerald went to New York City in 1919 determined to win her. Revising and completing a novel written at college, he published **This Side of Paradise* (1920) which was an immediate bestseller, and he became a celebrity overnight. A novel about college life, it was regarded as the voice of the younger generation and the jazz age, in a society increasingly preoccupied with the ideal of youth. A week later he married Zelda. However, their life together was difficult and they proved incapable of handling the pressures of living beyond their means. Living extravagantly at St Paul, Long Island, and New York, Fitzgerald published two collections of short stories, *Flappers and Philosophers* (1921) and *Tales of the Jazz Age* (1922), and a second novel, *The Beautiful and Damned* (1922), concerned with the extravagant and dissolute life led by a wealthy, aristocratic young artist and his wife. In 1924 the Fitzgeralds moved to Europe, and met such figures as *Hemingway, *Stein, and *Pound (see LOST GENERATION, THE). During this time he published his most acclaimed book, *The *Great Gatsby* (1925), and another book of short stories, *All the Sad Young Men* (1926). To support his failing standard of living he wrote hundreds of stories, many of them collected in *Taps at Reveille* (1935), *Afternoon of an Author* (1958), and *The Pat Hobby Stories* (1962). He became an alcoholic, while Zelda became mentally unstable until in 1930 she broke down, living most of the remainder of her life in mental institutions. In 1931 Fitzgerald returned permanently to the USA, living at first near Baltimore where Zelda was hospitalized. **Tender is the Night* (1934), like *The Great Gatsby*, investigates the illusions engendered by the 'American Dream', the materialist ethic, and the romantic alternatives. By 1937 Fitzgerald's alcoholism had worsened and he turned to Hollywood screenwriting, but his health was ruined and he died of a heart attack at the age of 44. His unfinished novel about a film mogul, *The *Last Tycoon* (1941), was posthumously published by Edmund Wilson, who also edited a miscellany of Fitzgerald's writings entitled *The Crack-Up* (1945). He also left behind a satirical play, *The Vegetable; Or, From President to Postman* (1923), and his *Letters* (1963).

FITZGERALD, Penelope (1916–), British novelist and biographer, born in Lincoln, educated at Somerville College, Oxford. Her father, Edward ('Evoe') Knox, edited *Punch* from 1932 to 1940; her uncles were Dillwyn Knox, the Greek scholar and cryptographer, and Wilfred and Ronald *Knox, the theologians. Fitzgerald worked at the BBC during the Second World War and began her writing career in her sixties. Her novels draw on her experiences of working as a journalist, in the Ministry of Food, in a Suffolk bookshop, at the Italia Conti Stage School, and at Westminster Tutors, and of living on a Thames barge. *The Golden Child* (1977) is an entertaining mystery story. *The Bookshop* (1978) is a wry, sad story of Florence Green's battle with a poltergeist, and with local enemies, when she opens the only bookshop in Hardborough, East Suffolk. *Offshore* (1979; Booker Prize) is a touching, funny account of the lives of the Chelsea houseboat people in the 1960s, especially the vulnerable Nenna James and her independent daughters Mattie and Tilda. *Human Voices* (1980) is a splendid comic satire on the BBC's baroque, high-minded wartime bureaucracy, centred engagingly on the new girl from Birmingham, Annie Asra, and her passion for the Recorded Programmes Director. *At Freddie's* (1982) is set in a 1960s London Stage School with a formidable proprietress. Two later novels move out from Fitzgerald's personal experience to 'a journey outside of myself': *Innocence* (1986) is set in a Florentine villa of the 1950s, whose family provides a vivid, tragi-comic version of post-war Italy; *The Beginning of Spring* (1988) is a poignant Anglo-Russian novel in which the sense of imminent momentous change presses in on the domestic concerns of its characters. Her next novel, *The Gate of Angels* (1990), was followed by *The Blue Flower* (1995) which deals with the idealized romantic relationship of the eighteenth-century German poet, Novalis, and his pubescent fiancée, Sophie. Fitzgerald has also written lives of *Edward Burne Jones* (1975), *The Knox Brothers* (1977), and of *Charlotte Mew and Her Friends* (1984). Fitzgerald writes short novels because she 'likes economy and compression'. Her style is subtle and subdued, and she writes about quiet characters, stoicism, failure, and misunderstandings. She is interested in peculiar, transitional communities, self-absorbed and on the point of vanishing, which she describes with great deftness, sympathy, and humour.

FITZGERALD, R(obert) D(avid) (1902–87), Australian poet, born in Sydney. A surveyor by profession, Fitzgerald was also involved in the production of the journal **Vision* in which his early work appeared. He won wide recognition with his second volume of poems, *To Meet the Sun* (1929), which contained 'The Greater Apollo' (published separately in 1927), a series of poems meditating upon the opposing themes of transience and reality. *Moonlight Acre* (1938) contained 'The Hidden Bole', an elegy on the ballet dancer Pavlova, and 'Essay on Memory' which was inspired by the theories of A. N. *Whitehead. *Heemskerck Shoals* (1949), a dramatic monologue by the seventeenth-century Dutch explorer Abel Tasman, and *Between Two Tides* (1952), a long narrative poem about a ship's boy from Tonga, exemplified the 'voyager poem' tradition of Australian literature. *This Night's Orbit* (1953) included 'The Face of the Waters', a meditation on the Creation, and 'The Wind at Your Door' which concerns the flogging of Irish convicts in 1804. Other collections include *Southmost Twelve* (1962), *Forty Years' Poems* (1965), *Product: Later Verses* (1977), and the prose writings in *Of Places and Poetry* (1976). Kenneth *Slessor regarded Fitzgerald's work as highly influential in the development of modern Australian literature but the philosophical complexity and occasional obscurity of much of his work has prevented Fitzgerald from becoming a popular poet.

FITZMAURICE, George (1878–1963), Irish playwright, born near Listowel, Co. Kerry; his father was a Church of Ireland clergyman and his mother a Catholic. He went to work for the Civil Service in Dublin in 1901, and lived in the city for most of his life, working at the Department of Agriculture. Though less renowned, Fitzmaurice ranks with *Synge and *O'Casey as one of the *Abbey Theatre's most important early dramatists. He began his writing career with peasant comedies. His first play, *The Country Dressmaker* (1907), was one of the Abbey Theatre's early successes, despite *Yeats's warning that it would bring more trouble than Synge's *The *Playboy of the Western World*. With his one-act plays *The Pie-Dish* (1908) and *The Magic Glasses* (1913), Fitzmaurice started to move away from realistic drama and into a realm of fantasy and experiment, a development which culminated in later works such as *The Dandy Dolls*, *The Enchanted Land*, and *The Ointment Blue*, which were published posthumously in *The Collected Plays of George Fitzmaurice* (1970). His strange and brilliant imagination is comparable with that of James *Stephens and Flann *O'Brien, but has been unfortunately neglected. Yeats, who never really approved of Fitzmaurice's work, seems to have made life difficult, rejecting several of his plays, including *The Moonlighters* (1970). After the Abbey's production of *Twixt the Giltinans and the Carmodys* (1923), Fitzmaurice, sensitive to criticism and more enamoured with fairyland, opted out of the theatrical scene and lived as a recluse. Since his death, the Abbey has recognized his significance and has staged several of his plays, some for the first time.

Fixer, The, a novel by Bernard *Malamud, published in 1967 and winner of the Pulitzer Prize. Malamud based his fiction on the arrest of Mendel Beiliss in 1911, on a charge of murdering a Russian boy. The novel is set in Tsarist Russia, and focuses on the life of a simple non-religious Jew, Yakov Bok, a handyman (or 'fixer'). He attempts to escape the *shtetl*, his Jewishness, and an unfaithful wife, and leaves for Kiev. There he rescues a man called Lebedev from a physical seizure and is rewarded with employment as an accountant at Lebedev's brickworks. Yakov is discovered living in a Christian area, and accused of the ritual murder of a Gentile child. He has been used as a scapegoat by officials in want of an excuse to start a pogrom. The book charts Yakov's changing emotions and perceptions, and the development of his Jewish and humanitarian consciousness that has resulted from his unjust arrest, prosecution, and torture in a Russian prison, and we are left with Yakov on his way to trial.

FLANAGAN, Mary (1943–), novelist and short-story writer, born in Rochester, New Hampshire, educated at Brandeis University. She moved to Britain in 1969, and the expatriate perspective she employs in some of her work has earned her the inevitable comparisons with Henry *James and *Wharton. Flanagan is, however, a resolutely contemporary writer, as her debut collection of stories, *Bad Girls* (1984), proved. She has been praised for her skill with the shorter form, in which she displays subtlety, irony, neat plotting, and stylistic economy. Her novels *Trust* (1987), a study of the relationships of two women and two men, and the modern *Bildungsroman Rose Reason* (1990) are, by contrast, large in scope and sprawling in structure, ranging over two continents and long timespans. With the whimsical, sometimes surrealistic short fictions collected in *The Blue Woman* (1994), Flanagan successfully returned to the form in which she made her name.

FLANNERY, Peter (1951–), British dramatist, born in Jarrow, educated at Manchester University. His first successful play, *Savage Amusement* (1978), involves the search for survival in the slums of a disintegrating Manchester at some unspecified date in the future, and his subsequent work has also been critically concerned with social and political subjects. This includes the epic *Our Friends in the North* (1982), about corruption in high places, and *Singer* (1989). The latter, generally regarded as Flannery's most impressive play, principally concerns a character, loosely based on the notorious Peter Rachman, who is incarcerated in Auschwitz, comes as a post-war refugee to Britain, and finds fortune and then disgrace as a slum landlord. But beyond this it is an ambitious attempt, written sometimes in realistic prose, sometimes in Shakespearian pastiche, to combine reflections on the Holocaust and the subject of revenge with satire both of the British upper class and of those who accumulated wealth and power under the Conservative government of Margaret Thatcher. Flannery has also written drama for television, including the series *Blind Justice*.

Flaubert's Parrot, a novel by Julian *Barnes, published in 1984. With its eclectic mixture of first-person narrative and scholarly digression (also used to effect in Barnes's later *The History of the World in 10½ Chapters*), the work displays the author's playfully postmodern approach to his subject, which in this instance is the life of Gustave Flaubert. Narrated by a retired doctor, Geoffrey Braithwaite, who is on holiday in France, the novel often reads like an eccentric lexicon of received ideas about Flaubert (an allusion, of course, to the absurd dictionary compiled by the eponymous characters in Flaubert's *Bouvard et Pécuchet*). Its chapters, which have titles such as 'The Train-Spotter's Guide to Flaubert' and 'The Flaubert Apocrypha', mingle extracts from Flaubert's journals and letters with speculation about the exact colour of Madame Bovary's eyes, the nature of Flaubert's relationship with his mistress Louise Colet, and the identity of the parrot in his short story *Un Coeur Simple*. Underlying this entertaining mixture of fact and fiction is a more sombre story: Braithwaite's wife, it transpires, has committed suicide, and one of the reasons for his pilgrimage to France is in order to unravel—and perhaps come to terms with—the reasons for this apparently irrational act.

FLECKER, (Herman) James Elroy (1884–1915), British poet, born in Lewisham, London, educated at Trinity College, Oxford, and at Caius College, Cambridge. Having written poetry since the age of 12, his style matured at Oxford, where he absorbed the influences of the aesthetic movement of the 1890s. *The Bridge of Fire* (1907) was his first collection of verse. In 1910 he entered the Consular Service and was vice-consul in Beirut from 1911 to 1913, when tuberculosis forced him to retire. He died two years later in a clinic at Davos, Switzerland. Among his other volumes of poetry are *The Last Generation* (1908), *Forty-Two Poems* (1912), and *The Golden Journey to Samarkand* (1913), which was widely acclaimed; the middle eastern exoticism of the enduringly popular title poem, given authenticity by his experiences of the region, appealed to the English taste established by Fitzgerald's *Rubaiyat of Omar Khayyam* (1859). While much of his work is characterized by a late romantic sensitivity to beauty and transience, a number of poems, notably 'Oxford Canal', are remarkable for the vividly documentary qualities of their imagery and diction. His verse was featured in the **Georgian Poetry* series. *Hassan* (1922), the best known of his plays, combines poetry, prose, dance, and spectacle and was staged with music by Delius in 1923. Among his other works is *The Grecians* (1910), a dialogue on education, and *The King of Alsander* (1914), an unusual and innovative novel. John Sherwood's biography of Flecker, *No Golden Journey*, appeared in 1973.

FLEMING, Ian (Lancaster) (1908–64), British thriller writer and journalist, educated at Eton and Sandhurst. He worked as a journalist, serving in Moscow, and during the Second World War worked for British Naval Intelligence. These experiences provided the background for his hugely successful series of James Bond novels, beginning with *Casino Royale* (1953) and including *Live and Let Die* (1954), *Diamonds Are Forever* (1956), and *On Her Majesty's Secret Service* (1963). Fleming's popularity was in part due to the wealth of detail in his novels, in accounts both of the world of espionage and also of exotic lifestyles, locations, and characters, all evoked with wit and expertise. The novels have a degree of self-mockery, which was carried much further in a series of James Bond films, such as *Dr No* (1962), *From Russia with Love* (1963), and *Goldfinger* (1964); owing very little to the novels on which they are based, they also omit the occasional philosophical passages that showed Bond to have had a fatalistic philosophy, a crude but dedicated sense of duty and patriotism, and a view of women and sex that is both exploitative and chauvinistic. Fleming wrote several other books, including *Chitty-Chitty-Bang-Bang* (1964), for children, which was also filmed. In his introduction to the anthology *The Seven Deadly Sins* (1962), Fleming revealed some of his personal philosophy. After his death others imitated the Bond style and formula, including Kingsley *Amis in *Colonel Sun* (1968).

FLEMING, (Robert) Peter (1907–71), British travel writer and military historian, born in London, the brother of Ian *Fleming, educated at Christ Church, Oxford. From 1931 onward he wrote for the **Spectator*; collections of his articles include *My Aunt's Rhinoceros* (1956) and *Goodbye to the Bombay Bowler* (1961). *Brazilian Adventure* (1933), his humorously understated account of an ill-managed expedition to find the lost explorer Colonel Fawcett, established his reputation as a travel writer. An assignment in China for *The Times* resulted in *One's Company* (1934), which contained a penetrating critique of communism. The best-selling *News from Tartary* (1936) is an urbane and self-deprecatingly witty record of his journey from Peking to Kashgar with the Swiss writer Ella Maillart; it exemplified the spirited amateurism which made Fleming an example to Eric *Newby and other succeeding travel writers. After wartime service in Norway, Greece, and India, Fleming turned to military history with *Invasion 1940* (1957), a study of Hitler's plans to conquer Britain; his subsequent works included *The Siege at Peking* (1959), on the Boxer Rebellion, and *The Fate of Admiral Kolchak* (1963), a study of incidents during the Russian Civil War. Duff Hart-Davis's biography of Fleming appeared in 1987.

FLETCHER, John Gould (1886–1950), American poet, born in Little Rock, Arkansas, educated at Harvard. In 1908 he moved to London and privately published five volumes of his poetry. Following the development of his firm friendship with Amy *Lowell, he emerged as a leading exponent of *Imagism. *Irradiations: Sand and Spray* (1915) and *Goblins and Pagodas* (1916) contained musically experimental verse rich in imagery of vivid precision. *Japanese Prints* (1918), which contained further examples of his Imagist verse, indicated his attraction towards Oriental painting and poetry. The increasingly philosophical concerns of his later work were accompanied by a gradual adoption of more traditional verse forms in a succession of volumes which include *Branches of Adam* (1926), *The Black Rock* (1928), *XXIV Elegies* (1935), and *Selected Poems* (1938; Pulitzer Prize). In 1933 he returned to Arkansas and became a dominant voice in the *Agrarian movement. The verse collected in *The Epic of Arkansas* (1936), *South Star* (1941), and *The Burning Mountain* (1946) indicates his imaginative commitment to the Agrarian vision of a self-sufficient regional culture. Among his prose works are *Paul Gauguin: His Life and Art* (1921); *The Two Frontiers* (1930), a comparison of Russian and American national ideals; and *Arkansas* (1947), a historical study. *Life Is My Song* (1937) is an autobiography.

FLINT, F(rank) S(tuart) (1885–1960), British poet, born in Islington, London; he left school at 13 and worked in various capacities before beginning his long and distinguished career in the Civil Service in 1904. By 1910, his intensive private study had gained him recognition as one of Britain's most highly informed authorities on modern French poetry. His first collection of poems, *In the Net of the Stars* (1909), consisted mainly of conventional love lyrics. His subsequent association with Ezra *Pound and T. E. *Hulme, together with his deepening knowledge of innovative French poetic techniques, radically affected his poetry's development; he became a leading spokesman for *Imagism and exemplified its methods in the concentration and clarity displayed by much of the work in *Cadences* (1915). *Otherworld*, his third and last collection, was published in 1920, its lengthy title poem responding to the desolation of the First World War in its meditations on more viable modes of existence. For some years after he ceased publishing poetry, Flint continued to contribute influential articles to the **Times Literary Supplement* and *The *Criterion*. He was also a prolific translator of prose works and poetry by French, German, and classical authors. With the exception of some short works arising from his activities as a civil servant, he ceased writing for publication entirely in the early 1930s.

FLYNN, Tony (1951–), British poet, born in Lancashire, educated at the Universities of Hull and Leicester, subsequently becoming a social worker in Walsall. His collections of poetry include *A Strange Routine* (1980) and *Body Politic* (1992); eighteen of his poems appeared in *A Rumoured City: New Poets from Hull* (1982, edited by Douglas *Dunn). Flynn's early work frequently employs minimalist strategies to produce poems of great concentration implying narratives derived from aspects of his working-class Catholic upbringing. The moral and emotional understatement in such writing is capable of moving effects. His later work exhibits an extended thematic range in its increased use of historical and European elements and its ready adoption of a variety of dramatic monologue modes.

Folding Star, The, see HOLLINGHURST, ALAN.

Fools of Fortune, a novel by William *Trevor, published in 1983. Divided into six sections of decreasing length, the novel is narrated alternately by William, a son of the Protestant Irish gentry, and by Marianne, his English cousin and lover. The third and sixth sections, told in the third person, focus on their daughter. The first section begins in 1918 with William relating the history of his family, the Quintons, who support Home Rule in spite of their Protestant heritage. Through the vicissitudes of local politics, William's father and two young sisters are murdered in an act of revenge, and his sensitive English mother succumbs to despair and alcoholism. The burden of tragedy, and the compulsion to avenge himself, form William's future. In the second section, Marianne tells the story of her adolescent love for William, which leads to pregnancy, separation from her family and roots, and the eventual recognition of the weight of retribution that lies at the core of her life, so closely intertwined through William with the destinies of the Quintons. Whereas in the first section Trevor uses William's voice to create a spare, evocative portrayal of the period described and its context, the second section, tinged with romantic lyricism, has the cadences and resonance of a traditional Celtic ballad. This skilled use of stylistic and narrative diversity is repeated in the third section in which the larger implications of the tragic past are revealed. The brutal reports of William's act of revenge, discovered by his daughter Imelda, who has never known her father, drive her to madness. This sacrifice to the past paves the way for the eventual reconciliation of William and Marianne, who are united in their old age. Their daughter, whose mental affliction is seen by the locals as a gift of healing, is the symbol both of their bond with the Ireland of their past, and their quiet integration into the Ireland of today.

FOOT, Michael (Mackintosh) (1913–), British politician, essayist, and biographer, born in Plymouth, educated at Wadham College, Oxford. He became editor of the *Evening Standard* before beginning his long and distinguished career as a Labour Member of Parliament in 1945. His historical and biographical studies include *The Pen and the Sword* (1957), on Jonathan Swift as a political pamphleteer; *Aneurin Bevan* (2 volumes, 1962, 1973); and *The Politics of Paradise* (1988), an investigation of Byron's libertarian philosophy. He is highly regarded for the unusual incisiveness and clarity of his essays, which are chiefly collected in *Debts of Honour* (1980), tributes to writers, politicians, and other figures who assisted or influenced him in various ways, and *Loyalists and Loners* (1986), biographical and critical appraisals of a wide range of statesmen, journalists, and literary figures. His biography of H. G. *Wells was published in 1995. *Michael Foot: A Portrait* by Simon Hoggart and David Leigh appeared in 1981. See also *Michael Foot* (1994) by Mervyn *Jones.

FORCHÉ, Carolyn (1950–), American poet, born in Detroit, educated at Michigan State and Bowling Green universities. *Gathering the Tribes* (1976), her first collection, was selected for the Yale Younger Poets series. *The Country Between Us* (1981) made a remarkable impact with its critique of regimes in Eastern Europe and El Salvador. The poems are frequently graphic in their details of imprisonment, torture, and mutilation: a sack full of human ears is spilled out onto a table ('The Colonel'); a boy-soldier peels the face from a corpse and hangs it from a tree ('Because One Is Always Forgotten'). A fine concluding poem, 'Ourselves or Nothing', characteristically balances political concerns with an undercurrent of sensuality. By Forché's own account, the free verse lyric-narratives of her earlier work have given way to a more discordant manner: 'broken, polyphonic, haunted'. This development is apparent in *The Angel of History* (1994), an intense meditation on the twentieth century's moral disasters, particularly the Holocaust and Hiroshima. Derek *Walcott has commended Forché for 'undertaking the responsibilities of conscience'. She has also edited an anthology by, for, and about the victims and survivors of political repression and violence, *Against Forgetting: Twentieth Century Poetry of Witness* (1993).

FORD, Ford Madox, formerly Ford Hermann HUEFFER (1873–1939), British novelist and editor, born in Surrey. The son of Dr Francis Hueffer, a music critic on *The Times*, and grandson of the Pre-Raphaelite painter Ford Madox Brown, Ford's earliest influences were the Pre-Raphaelite artists and writers of his parents' circle including Dante Gabriel Rossetti (about whom he wrote a study in 1902). Ford wrote of this period, '[I] came out of the hothouse atmosphere of Pre-Raphaelism where I was being trained for a genius' (in *Memories and Impressions*, 1911). His *The Pre-Raphaelite Brotherhood* (1907) offered further insights into the movement. *The Brown Owl* (1892), a collection of fairy tales, marked the beginning of a highly productive literary career. His influence on the development of modern literature is incalculable, both as an exponent of *Modernist techniques in his own writing, and as an editor whose generous encouragement of other writers and his eye for innovation helped to set the agenda for twentieth-century literature. Ford collaborated with *Conrad in three novels (*The Inheritors*, 1901; *Romance*, 1903; and *The Nature of a Crime*, 1924); during his association with Conrad, which began in 1898, Ford developed a fictional method and theory derived to an extent from Impressionism, but also linked to his reading of Flaubert and Maupassant. Ford published over thirty novels of great diversity, including historical romances, farces, comedies of manners, and studies of contemporary and political life. These include the *Fifth Queen Trilogy* (*The Fifth Queen*, 1906; *Privy Seal*, 1907; *The Fifth Queen Crowned*, 1908) about the rise and fall of Catherine Howard, the fifth wife of Henry VIII. He has also published volumes of verse, autobiographical works (including *Return to Yesterday*, 1931; and *It Was the Nightingale*, 1933), and many works of criticism (notably *The March of Literature*, 1938). As editor of *The *English Review* (1908–10) he was the first to publish D. H. *Lawrence and gave support to emergent *Vorticist writers such as *Pound and W. *Lewis. Ford's stormy marriage to Elsie Martindale, with whom he had eloped in 1894, resulted in a scandalous divorce after Ford became romantically involved with the novelist Violet *Hunt in 1908; unhappy marriages and adulterous liaisons were to feature in his major work, *The *Good Soldier* (1915), which is perhaps the most perfect expression of Ford's Impressionistic technique in his exploration of the 'dark forest' of the human heart. Ford's experience of active service in the First World War, during which he was wounded and sent home in 1917, provided the inspiration for his collection of poems of 1918 and his other major work, **Parade's End* (published separately as *Some Do Not*, 1924; *No More Parades*, 1925; *A Man Could Stand up*, 1926; and *The Last Post*, 1928), also known as the 'Tietjens Tetralogy' after its hero, Christopher Tietjens; Ford later wrote that his intention was to show the collapse of the social order in the aftermath of the cataclysm of the Great War. Having moved to Paris in 1922, Ford founded the **Transatlantic Review* in 1924, which published work by a wide variety of experimental and *Modernist writers (see LOST GENERATION, THE). His final years were spent in Europe and America where he influenced several younger writers, including Katherine Anne *Porter, William Carlos *Williams, and Eudora *Welty. See *Ford Madox Ford: A Dual Life* (1996) by Max Saunders.

FORD, Richard (1944–), American novelist and short-story writer, born in Jackson, Mississippi. Although Southern in origin he is more obviously associated with a group of writers emerging from the MidWest. His first novel, *A Piece of My Heart* (1976), concerns the quest of two men, one in search of a woman, the other trying to discover the truth about his own past. *The Sportswriter* (1986) is an evocative and moving study in the collapse and reconstruction of its central character. *Independence Day* (1995), its sequel, which finds the protagonist in his mid-forties, his so-called 'Existence Period', and now selling real estate, continues Ford's acute portrait of an ordinary man. His other work includes *Wildlife* (1990), set in Montana during the early 1960s, which deals with the underlying tensions of family life as perceived by 16-year-old Joe, whose parents are on the point of separating after his mother falls in love with another man; and stories, *Rock Springs* (1988). In Ford's work, dramatic and even violent incidents are conveyed with laconic understatement and a dryly ironic humour. This coolly detached style offsets the sordid or pathetic nature of the subjects described in a manner which recalls *Hemingway's short fiction. Ford has been associated with the '*dirty realist' group of writers of whom Raymond *Carver and Tobias *Wolff are the best-known exponents. Ford is the editor of *The Granta Book of the American Short Story* (1992).

Foregrounding is a term which was much used by the Russian Formalists (see FORMALISM), but also has a more general history. It refers to the emphasizing or making visible of particular features of a work, often its specifically literary or formal features. Rhyme foregrounds the possibilities of echoes in language, of clashes and consonances between sound and meaning; jokes foreground the role of play in interpretation; a plot full of coincidences reveals and foregrounds the controlling hand of the author. What is foregrounded—either by the writer or by the reader—is usually what was previously thought to be absent, or only a background element or a technical support system. A film, for example, might foreground the placing of the camera; a painting may foreground the painter's own presence in his or her work. We *see* the language and the labour, the medium, rather than simply use it or look through it.

FORESTER, C(ecil) S(cott) (Cecil Lewis Troughton SMITH) (1899–1966), British writer, born in Egypt; he studied medicine at Guy's Hospital, London. He is remembered as the creator of Horatio Hornblower, who appeared in *The Happy Return* (1937), the first of a long series of novels set in the Napoleonic Wars, outlining the career of an introspective naval officer, not always fortunate and seldom truly happy, who hates cruelty and loves the Navy, and who rises in rank to Admiral and eventually becomes Lord Hornblower. The Hornblower stories were collected in *The Hornblower Companion* (1964). Twenty other novels included *Brown on Resolution* (1929); *The Gun* (1933), set in the Peninsular War; *The African Queen* (1935); *The General* (1936); *The Captain from Connecticut* (1941); *The Ship* (1943), a story of the Second World War; and *The Sky and the Forest* (1948). Films were made of several of the Hornblower stories and of *The African Queen*, which became a classic film with Katherine Hepburn and Humphrey Bogart.

Formalism is a term generally applied to works of art or critical approaches which highlight formal properties—often, it is characteristically suggested, at the expense of the content of the object in question, so the term has acquired a faintly derogatory note. One solution to this problem has been to argue, as much modern criticism does, that form and content are inseparable, if not the same thing. This move seems to be an exaggerated and simplified version of the more subtle suggestion that form and content are intimately linked, that it is inadvisable to think for long about one without thinking of the other. Critics who cling to the idea of a thoroughly separable content are likely to see all such discussions as versions of the Trojan Horse, varieties of Formalism merely pretending to have an interest in subject matter. The Hungarian critic and philosopher Georg Lukács (1885–1971) suggested that while a little Formalism may lead us away from the content of a work, a more seriously pursued Formalism will bring us back; indeed he argued that form itself may be an aspect of content, that the narrative tactics of a novel, for example, are not merely a vehicle for meaning but are a part of the novel's meaning themselves. We read the form of the narration, whether it is first- or third-person, intimate or distanced, blinkered or omniscient, as a feature of what the narration says.

The most interesting critics and theorists who have been called Formalists—the Russian Formalists working in Moscow and St Petersburg/Leningrad both before and after the Revolution—provide strong support for this practice. They insist on language and form not to distract us from our daily reality but to return us to its particulars, to an awareness of all the details that have become blurred by our habits of perception. Victor Shklovsky (1893–), in a 1917 essay called 'Art as Technique', argued that it is the business of art to make objects unfamiliar, as if we were seeing them for the first time: 'art exists that one may recover the sensation of life'. By a curious paradox, an attention to what Shklovksy calls the 'artfulness' of the object allows us to see the object more rather than less clearly. Other Russian Formalists were Boris Eichenbaum, Boris Tomashevsky, and perhaps most notably Roman Jakobson (1896–1982). In a series of essays and lectures Jakobson developed a theory of the different functions of language, whereby a phrase may have referential, expressive, and poetic purposes, that is, it may refer to the world, express a speaker's feelings, or draw attention to language itself. The poetic function is a *foregrounding not of the message's meaning or mood but of the shape and nature of the message. All of these functions may be in play in the same utterance, although it is likely that one will be dominant at any given moment. The Russian Formalists were interested in what they called 'literariness', an earlier name for the poetic function, which they found in jokes and slogans as much as in high art. The literary/poetic occurs wherever there is visible linguistic play, an irony or pun or symmetry not *required* by the message. For this reason, as Jakobson insists in an influential paper called 'Linguistics and Poetics' (1958), critics of poetry must study more than poetry. And because poetry itself has other functions beside the poetic, they will need to look at mood and meaning in poetry too. Formalism is not, or does not need to be, an abstract or isolating practice. See also CHICAGO CRITICS.

FORNES, Maria Irene (1930–), American dramatist, born in Havana, Cuba, where she was educated in public schools; she went to the US in 1945 and became an American citizen in 1951. Initially trained as a painter, throughout the 1960s she served a long apprenticeship as a writer and director of Off-Off-Broadway theatre working in an experimental and anti-realist style, developing her distinctive voice within the Actors' Studio in the Judson Poets' Theatre. Her off-beat musical *Promenade* (1965) was a commercial success. *Fefu and Her Friends* (1977), widely regarded as her most important play, was performed by the New York Theatre Strategy, an association of women writers to which Fornes was central in the 1970s. Set in the 1930s, the play combines elements of conventional realism with highly innovative techniques to explore the interactive dynamics between eight women who meet in a New England country house to plan a fund-raising event to promote 'art as a tool for learning'. Her prolific subsequent work includes *Eyes on the Harem* (1979), *A Visit* (1981), *The Conduct of Life* (1985), *Lovers and Keepers* (1986), and *And What of the Night* (1989).

FORSTER, E(dward) M(organ) (1879–1970), British novelist, critic, and essayist. He was the only child of Edward Forster, an architect, who died nine months after the birth of his son, and Alice 'Lily' Whichelo. Forster's happiest childhood years were spent in Rooksnest, a house near Stevenage, where he was cared for by servants and a loving mother until they moved to Tonbridge in 1893, in order that Forster might attend Tonbridge School as a day boy. His education and post-University travels were financed by his great-aunt, Marianne Thornton, the other major influence on his childhood, who died in 1887, leaving £8,000 in trust for him. Marianne Thornton's father had been a member of the Clapham Sect, an organization whose philanthropic convictions formed part of Forster's liberal heritage. Forster hated Tonbridge School (which reappears as Sawston in his first two novels, and whose cultivation of the 'undeveloped heart' he later satirized in *Abinger Harvest*). At King's College, Cambridge, where he studied classics then history, he formed some of the friendships that were to sustain him personally and intellectually for most of his life. In 1901 he was elected to the *Apostles, an élite group of young men dedicated to the primacy of art, the intellect, and friendship. They included Bertrand *Russell, Lytton *Strachey, A. N. *Whitehead, Leonard *Woolf, and Desmond *MacCarthy, all of whom were influential in the *Bloomsbury Group, and Hugh Meredith, with whom Forster made his second great discovery: that of homosexual love (the first had been emancipation from the Christianity that had dominated his childhood).

On going down from Cambridge, Forster accompanied his mother on a year-long tour of Italy, taught briefly at the Working Men's College, Bloomsbury, then went on a tour of Greece, all of which provided him with material for his early novels, which satirize the pusillanimity of the English tourist abroad. His literary career began in 1903 with contributions to the *Independent Review*, launched by Cambridge friends including G. M. *Trevelyan, and in which his first short story, 'The Story of a Panic', was published in 1904. In 1905 he tutored the children of the Countess *von Arnim at Nassenheide before returning to England for the publication of his first novel, **Where Angels Fear To Tread*. In 1906 he and his mother established their home in Weybridge, where they spent the next twenty years. At this time he became tutor to Syed Ross Masood, a Muslim patriot with whom he developed an intense and passionate friendship. Forster's second novel, *The *Longest Journey* (1907), was followed by *A *Room with a View* (1908) and the novel that was to establish him as a leading literary figure, **Howards End* (1910). Deploying the strengths of realist forms, these novels examine the collision between philistine complacency and unguarded honesty and speak to the desire to 'only connect' rather than to live among fragments. The publication of a collection of short stories, *The Celestial Omnibus* (1911), brought this period of intense literary activity to a close. Forster was not to publish another book for more than ten years. The intervention of the First World War, two separate visits to India, and an influential meeting with Edward *Carpenter produced a troubled period in Forster's career as a novelist. In 1912 he went to India with R. C. Trevelyan, Goldsworthy Lowes *Dickinson, and G. H. Luce, but once there he travelled north to Aligarh, where Masood became his companion. During this journey he became friendly with the Maharajah of Dewas Senior and began his fictional critique of British colonial behaviour. This was unfinished on his return to England in 1913, when a visit to Edward Carpenter inspired him to write *Maurice*, his novel of homosexual love which, although circulated privately, was never published in his lifetime. In 1914, when war broke out, Forster spent some time as a fire-watcher and cataloguer in the National Gallery before removing himself from the mainstream of English culture by working for the International Red Cross in Alexandria. There he became close friends with the Greek homosexual poet Constantin Cavafy, whose work he introduced to the English-speaking world. Forster remained in Alexandria until 1919, when he returned to become literary editor of the left-wing paper the *Daily Herald*, and to contribute essays and reviews to various periodicals. In 1921 he returned to India as secretary and companion to the Maharajah of Dewas Senior. *Alexandria: A History and Guide* was published in 1922, although most of the stock was destroyed in a fire before circulation; the book was not republished (in revised form) until 1938.

In 1924 his last novel, *A *Passage to India*, was published and dedicated to Masood. 'What will he write next?' wrote Virginia *Woolf. That he published nothing more in novel form has been a persistent subject of enquiry. Of his friends who were also his literary contemporaries, Woolf thought he compromised himself as an artist: 'the poet is twitched away by the satirist; the comedian is tapped on the shoulder by the moralist.' D. H. *Lawrence, on the other hand, was teased by a sense of unrealized potential: 'There is so much more in him than ever comes out.' Katherine *Mansfield's verdict was less forgiving: '[he] never gets any further than warming the teapot.' Whether his reasons for abandoning the novel concerned form (realist or modernist: his main influences were Jane Austen, Samuel *Butler, and Marcel Proust) or sexuality (the difficulty in rendering the truths of the relationships most personally important to him in publishable fictional form), Forster thereafter turned to journalism and criticism. In 1927 the Clark Lectures, delivered at Cambridge, were published as *Aspects of the Novel*. In this highly equivocal commentary on realist techniques he issues the famous comment: 'Yes—oh dear, yes—the novel tells a story.' He outlines his description of 'flat' and 'round' characters, delineates features such as 'story' (dominated by the clock ticking in the background), 'plot' (in which the emphasis falls on causality rather than chronology), yet, on the other hand, identifies 'pattern' and 'rhythm', which draw attention to the underlying pulse of the novel rather than its narrative sequences. *The Eternal Moment*, a volume of short stories, was published in 1928, his biography of Goldsworthy Lowes Dickinson in 1934, and *Abinger Harvest*, a collection of essays, in 1936. Forster was offered an honorary Fellowship and a permanent home at King's in 1946, a year after his mother's death. In 1949 he worked with Eric Crozier on the libretto for Benjamin Britten's opera *Billy Budd*, and refused a knighthood. *Two Cheers for Democracy* ('there is no occasion to give three') was published in 1951 and *The Hill of Devi*, a portrait of India through letters and commentary, in 1953. His last book to be published in his lifetime was *Marianne Thornton* (1956), a biography of his great-aunt. Forster became a Companion of Honour in 1953; he received the Order of Merit in 1969. *Maurice* was finally published in 1971, a year after his death, and *The Life to Come*, a collection of short stories, also dealing with homosexuality, in 1972.

Forster has been championed as a kind of liberal saint. His treatment of East–West relationships helped to establish this, but it was confirmed by his activities for PEN, his firm stand against censorship, his campaign against the suppression of Radclyffe *Hall's *The Well of Loneliness* (1928), and his becoming the first president of the National Council for Civil Liberties in 1934. Late in his career, in 1960, he appeared as a defence witness in the trial against **Lady Chatterley's Lover*. Both F. R. *Leavis and Lionel *Trilling, although their terms are very different, admired him for his liberalism. Much of the earlier criticism of Forster is dominated by respect for his humanitarianism and his desire to transcend politics through love. Critics in the 1960s, such as Frank *Kermode, began to attend less to his humanism and more to the autonomy of his art, seeking out the formal unity in his texts, privileging their symbolism over their realism. The 1970s saw a new critical emphasis concerned more to unpick the apparent seamless unities, to *dis*connect. This was possibly informed by the appearance of P. N. Furbank's two-volume biography, *E. M. Forster: A Life* (1977–8), which openly explores his homosexuality. Later work has drawn considerably on the manuscripts held by the University of Texas and which arguably demonstrate the gaps and discontinuities that are part of the creative process. Later criticism has brought into play the perspectives of feminist and subaltern studies in an attempt to tease out the unacknowledged as well as the acknowledged sources of confusion in Forster's texts. Nicola Beauman's biography, *Morgan* (1993), draws on the textual work in the editions published by the Abinger Press, based on the Texas archive.

FORSTER, Margaret (1938–), British novelist and biographer, born in Carlisle, educated at Somerville College, Oxford. Ever since her early novels, *Dame's Delight* (1964), the story of a Northern scholarship girl's rebellion against male authority at Oxford, and *Georgy Girl* (1965), which examined seduction traps and sexual liberation, Forster has tended to use her own circumstances as a starting-point for her fiction, which explores local, domestic, and family conflicts, often using overlapping narratives and different points of view. Books such as *The Seduction of Mrs Pendlebury* (1974), which brings together the insecurities of the mother of a young child and the emotional isolation of an elderly widow in the neighbouring house, as well as *Mother Can You Hear Me?* (1979) and *Private Papers* (1986), both of which expose the hypocrisies which can be used to bolster family life, are characteristic of her work. Her examination of old age, *Have the Men Had Enough?* (1989), offers an unflinching account of how a family fails to cope with an 'elderly' woman, while a quest for custody raises further issues about the nature of the family in *The Battle for Christabel* (1991), and a violent assault provokes questions about the conflicting demands of mother-love in *Mother's Boys* (1994). Her interest in the domestic theatre and mother–daughter relationships lies behind *Significant Sisters: The Grass Roots of Active Feminism, 1839–1939* (1984), a collection of short biographies of eight feminist 'heroines'. It may also have started her interest in Elizabeth Barrett Browning, whose biography she wrote and whose poems she edited in 1988, and whose faithful but exploited maid Elizabeth Wilson is the subject of her novel *Lady's Maid* (1990). Her interest in nineteenth-century literature can be seen in her 'gothic' novel *The Bride of Lowther Fell* (1980) and also in her *tour de force* 'autobiography' of William Makepeace Thackeray (1978). She has also published an acclaimed biography, *Daphne du Maurier* (1993), which draws attention to du Maurier's bisexuality, and *Hidden Lives: A Memoir* (1995), a portrait of her own, her mother's, and her grandmother's past. Forster's feel for day-to-day existence and her perception for the way in which legend misrepresents reality informs all her writing.

Forsyte Saga, The, a sequence of novels by J. *Galsworthy, published in 1922. Previously published separately as three novels (*The Man of Property*) 1906; *In Chancery*, 1920; and *To Let*, 1921), and two interludes ('Indian Summer of a Forsyte', 1918, and *Awakening*, 1920), the sequence chronicles the social, financial, and emotional vicissitudes of the Forsyte family whose paterfamilias, Soames Forsyte, epitomizes both the shrewd entrepreneurial virtues and the sexual hypocrisies of late Victorian bourgeois society. *The Man of Property* opens as Soames, a prosperous solicitor, decides to marry the beautiful but impoverished Irene. As a wedding gift to his bride he commissions a young architect, Bosinney, to build a country house at Robin Hill: Irene, however, falls in love with Bosinney and the two begin an affair. Discovering that his wife feels only revulsion for him, Soames asserts his marital rights over his 'property' by raping her. She attempts to leave him but when Bosinney is killed in a street accident she is forced to return to Soames. *In Chancery* concerns the developing love between Irene and Soames's cousin, 'young Jolyon' (so named to distinguish him from his father, 'old Jolyon'), and Irene's decision to divorce Soames and marry Jolyon. Further complexities are introduced into the saga when Irene gives birth to a son, Jon, and Soames, who has married Annette Lamotte, becomes the father of a daughter, Fleur. In the final part of *To Let*, which is set in the 1920s, Fleur and Jon, both ignorant of their parents' unhappy histories, meet and fall in love. Before they marry, Jon learns of his mother's past from Jolyon and breaks off his engagement to Fleur. Bitterly hurt, she marries Michael Mont, a young aristocrat whom she does not love; Jon goes to America where, after Jolyon's death, Irene joins him. Soames meanwhile discovers that his wife, Annette, has been unfaithful and that Irene, the woman he still loves, is lost to him. In the novel's ironic closing episode he discovers that the house, Robin Hill, which has been the scene of so much unhappiness, is not 'to let'. *The Forsyte Saga* was adapted for television in 1967. A further Forsyte sequence was published as *A Modern Comedy* (1929).

FORSYTH, Frederick (1938–), British thriller writer, born in Ashford, Kent; he served in the RAF and worked as a journalist and BBC radio and television reporter. His first novel, *The Day of the Jackal* (1971), the account of an attempt to assassinate de Gaulle, was a runaway bestseller. It was innovatory in its use of detailed, factual accounts—closer to journalism than to fiction—of technical procedures and of illegal activity: for example, how to obtain a false British passport. Forsyth employed the same technique in subsequent, less successful novels (*The Odessa File*, 1972; *The Dogs of War*, 1974; *The Fourth Protocol*, 1984), and it has since been much imitated. His novel *The Fist of God* (1994) has the Gulf War as its subject. He has also written short stories and a novel, *The Shepherd* (1975). Most of his thrillers have been made into films.

Fortunes of Richard Mahony, The, a trilogy of novels by Henry Handel *Richardson, consisting of *Australia Felix* (1917), *The Way Home* (1925), and *Ultima Thule* (1929), published in one volume in 1930. Based largely on the life of the author's father, the work describes the central character's life from the early 1850s onwards. *Australia Felix* opens in 1852, and gives an account of the life of Richard Mahony, a 28-year-old immigrant of Irish extraction, formerly a medical student at Edinburgh University, who now runs a general store in Ballarat. It describes his marriage to Polly Turnham, and develops a panoramic picture of colonial Australian society, focusing on the reversals of fortune to which its members are subject, and ends with the departure of Mahony and his wife for England. *The Way Home* begins with the couple's arrival in England where Mahony establishes himself as a doctor, before becoming disillusioned with the restrictive social hierarchies of England. He returns to Australia, to find that his investments there have made him rich; after failing to settle into the wealthy society of Melbourne, he takes his family on a Grand Tour of Europe, only to learn that he has incurred financial ruin. *Ultima Thule* begins with Mahony's arrival back in Australia. After trying to establish a medical practice in Melbourne, he and family move to a small town in northern Victoria; but the practice fails, one of his daughters dies, and Mahony shows signs of mental instability. Eventually his wife leaves, taking the surviving children with her; Mahony follows her, but he deteriorates into madness and, after a period of incarceration in a mental asylum, dies.

Fortunes of War, see MANNING, OLIVIA.

For Whom the Bell Tolls, a novel by Ernest *Hemingway, published in 1940. A novel of the Spanish Civil War, in which an American volunteer in the Loyalist forces, Robert Jordan, has been sent into the mountains near Segovia to execute the bombing of a bridge. As he waits with a guerrilla band he encounters Maria, a victim of Fascist attack and rape, and they fall passionately in love. A sense of foreboding develops as the war moves closer and the political differences within the Loyalist camp are seen to be impeding the war effort. Ordered to retreat, Jordan nevertheless blows up the bridge but is wounded in the retreat. As he lies dying on a hillside he awaits the arrival of the Fascists, determined that he will shoot their leader. His final thoughts are: 'I have fought for what I believed in for a year now. If we win here we will win everywhere.' The book is remarkable for its scope and descriptive powers, and for Hemingway's attempt to reproduce the speech of the guerrillas. Its title derives from John Donne's sermon which contains the lines: 'No man is an Iland, intire of it selfe; every man is a peace of the Continent . . . And therefore never send to know for whom the bell tolls; It tolls for thee.'

FOSTER, David (1944–), Australian writer, born in Sydney, educated at the University of Sydney and the Australian National University. His work eschews realism for satirical allegory, parable, and comic pastiche and has attracted critical attention for its exuberant inventiveness. His first novel, *The Pure Land* (1974), centres on three generations of an Australian family beginning with Albert Manwaring, a photographer who leaves Australia for America in search of fulfilment; this is followed by the experiences of his daughter in England, and finally those of his grandson who returns to Australia. *Moonlite* (1981) is a political satire set partly in nineteenth-century Scotland and partly in the Australian colonies; *Plumbum* (1985) is a satire about 'The Last Great Heavy Metal Rock Band of the Western World'. *Dog Rock* (1985) is narrated by the postman of a country town and features a series of murders; the story continues in *The Pale Blue Crotchet Coathanger Cover* (1988). His other works include *The Adventures of Christian Rosy Cross* (1986), *Mates of Mars* (1991), and *A Slab of Fosters* (1994); *Testostero* (1987), a pastiche of Goldoni's *The Venetian Twins*; *Escape to Reality* (1977), short stories; *The Hitting Wall* (1989), two novellas; and *The Fleeing Atalanta* (1975), a collection of poems.

Four Quartets, the last of T. S. *Eliot's major poetic works, first published in its entirety in New York in 1943. Each of its four sections, which sustain a meditation on the temporal and eternal orders of reality, reflects one of the four seasons and draws concrete and associational imagery from the location whose name supplies its title: 'Burnt Norton' is a Cotswold house the poet initially visited in 1934; 'East Coker' is a Somerset village with which Eliot had ancestral connections; 'The Dry Salvages' is a rock formation off Cape Ann, Massachusetts, which served him as a marker when sailing as a boy; and 'Little Gidding' is the Huntingdonshire Manor where Nicholas Ferrar established his community in 1625. With the exception of 'Burnt Norton', which concluded Eliot's *Collected Poems, 1909–1935* (1936), the successive parts first appeared in the *New English Weekly* in 1940, 1941, and 1942 respectively. The poems' expression of the continuity of values amid the uncertainty of the Second World War gained them a wide readership and reinforced Eliot's reputation. The sequence originated in lines discarded from **Murder in the Cathedral* (1935), 'Time present and time past | Are both perhaps present in time future', which form the opening of 'Burnt Norton'; Eliot's theatrical work is also echoed in the restrained declamatory tone which gives the sequence the quality of a poised dramatic monologue enacting the shifting movement of thought. Each of the four parts has within it five divisions providing a structure for parallel developments from the opening statements of themes suggested by local context through to the hesitant resolutions of the conclusions; in the case of 'Little Gidding' the ending is more climactically affirmative, envisioning the moment out of time when 'the fire and the rose are one'. 'Little Gidding' is also notable for fusing evocations of wartime London with more purely imaginative elements, an achievement exemplified in its Dantean encounter with 'a familiar compound ghost' in deserted streets after an air-raid.

FOWLER, H(enry) W(atson) (1858–1933), English lexicographer and grammarian, born in Tonbridge, Kent, educated at Balliol College, Oxford. After retiring as a schoolmaster on an issue of principle, he wrote literary essays for periodicals, including those collected in *Popular Fallacies* (1904) and *Between Boy and Man* (1908). With his brother, Francis George Fowler (1870–1918), he wrote *The King's English* (1906), a popular work of grammar and lexicography, and compiled the *Concise Oxford Dictionary of Current English* (1911). The brothers joined the 'Sportsmen's battalion' in 1915, but Francis died of consumption before the war ended. Henry Fowler's best-known work, *Fowler's Dictionary of Modern English Usage* (1926), had been planned with his brother. The entries are short, occasionally idiosyncratic, essays illustrating the correct and incorrect usage of familiar words. He also compiled the *Pocket Oxford Dictionary of Current English* (1924). See Robert *Burchfield, *The Fowlers: Their Achievements in Lexicography and Grammar* (1979).

FOWLES, John (1926–), British novelist and essayist, born in Leighton-on-Sea, Essex, educated at New

College, Oxford. Fowles was a teacher in France and Greece (which resurface as landscapes in his fiction), there increasing his knowledge of classical and contemporary philosophies, and assimilating the French literary influences absorbed during his university years. His first novel, *The Collector* (1963), was a best-seller, and was made into a film by William Wyler two years later. His second published work, *The Aristos: A Self Portrait in Ideas* (1964), was an extended essay elucidating Fowles's evolving personal credo in the context of explorations of other philosophies, notably existentialism, which seems to have had some influence on him, as have the ideas of Jung. In spite of Fowles's avowed left-wing sympathies, the self-confessed élitism of his non-fictional debut has inspired some controversy, engaging as it does with the foundation of right-wing thought. Fowles continued his preoccupations in *The Magus* (1966; revised 1977), set on a vividly evoked Greek island. In an atmosphere of mystery, fantasy, and obsession, the novel concerns an Englishman, Nicholas Urfe, who obtains a teaching post on the island, and his involvement with an enigmatic Greek millionaire and his entourage; with its mythological dimension the novel suggests *magic realism, and in the agnostic fatalism of its ending point, Greek tragedy. Fowles's move to Lyme Regis in Dorset initiated the compelling sequence of images immortalized in his best-known work, *The *French Lieutenant's Woman*; the novel was filmed by Karel Reisz in 1981. His other works of fiction include *The Ebony Tower* (1974), a collection of short fiction, significant for its skilled craftsmanship; *Daniel Martin* (1977), a portrait of a modern man, with marked autobiographical overtones; *Mantissa* (1982), an erotic satire on Fowles's own previous imaginings of the artist and his anima / muse; and *A Maggot* (1985), an ambitious historical novel with a powerful element of fantasy. While not enjoying the success of *The French Lieutenant's Woman*, these novels nevertheless continue to be the focus of much literary debate. Fowles is also the author of such short works on natural history as *Islands* (1978) and *The Tree* (1980), and *A Short History of Lyme Regis* (1982).

Fox in the Attic, The, see HUGHES, RICHARD.

FRAME, Janet (1924–), New Zealand writer, born in Dunedin, educated at Otago University and Dunedin Teachers' Training College. Early stories were published in *The Lagoon* (1951, revised 1961). *Faces in the Water* (1961) drew creatively and with harrowing directness upon her many years of incarceration in institutions for the mentally ill. Frame left New Zealand in 1956, and lived for many years in England and the USA before returning to New Zealand. Her first novel, *Owls Do Cry* (1957), explored the borders of madness and 'reality' in a small-town New Zealand setting; *The Edge of the Alphabet* (1962) extended such concerns. Frame's writing has consistently pursued complex, indeed often by definition inexpressible, questions of human communication; later work includes *Intensive Care* (1970), *Daughter Buffalo* (1972), *Living in the Maniototo* (1979), and *You Are now Entering the Human Heart* (1983). Her three-volume autobiography, *To the Is-Land* (1983), *Angel at My Table* (1984), and *The Envoy from Mirror City* (1985), was widely acclaimed. In her largely New Zealand-set novel *The Carpathians* (1988), Frame again probes complex and profoundly disturbing issues of human identity, communication, and fulfilment in terms which also question the conventions and limits of the fictional form employed. Frame's poetry is collected in *The Pocket Mirror* (1967). Critical assessments are collected in Jeanne Delbaere's *Bird, Hawk and Bogie: Essays on Janet Frame* (1978), while two full-length studies of her work by Margaret Dalziel (1980) and Patrick Evans (1988) are complemented by a continuing international interest in her work, encouraged by the film *An Angel at My Table* (1990) which dramatizes her life.

FRAME, Ronald (1953–), Scottish novelist, short-story writer, and playwright, born in Glasgow, educated at Glasgow University and at Oxford. In his volumes of short stories Frame has displayed his gift for ironic counterpoint and the evocation of period. Among these are *Watching Mrs Gordon* (1985); *A Long Weekend with Marcel Proust* (1986), which contained short stories and a novella, 'Prelude and Fugue', about a young woman condemned to relive her experiences in the Blitz; and *A Woman of Judah* (1987), again containing short stories and a novella. His first novel, *Winter Journey* (1984), was followed by several others including *Sandmouth People* (1986), which dealt with one day in the life of a small seaside town during the 1950s, *Penelope's Hat* (1989), and *Bluette* (1990). His next novel, *Underwood and After* (1991), set in the 1950s, describes a young boy's infatuation with the sophisticated London 'set' presided over by the charming but sinister figure of Mr Chetwynd. Like several of his fictions, the novel focuses around a grand house (the eponymous 'Underwood'), whose symbolic meaning reflects the ambiguous nature of the society of which it is the centre. *The Sun on the Wall* (1994), a trio of novellas on related themes, contains similar ambiguities; its final story, also set in a large house in the Scottish Highlands, concerns the break-up of a family—undermined by its failure to confront the truth about the past.

FRANCIS, Dick (Richard Stanley) (1920–), British crime writer, born in Tenby, Pembrokeshire. He served in the RAF during the Second World War; from 1946 to 1957 he was a National Hunt jockey, becoming champion in 1953–4, and from 1957 to 1973 racing correspondent of the *Sunday Express*. His long series of novels, beginning with *Dead Cert* (1962), have enjoyed immense popularity and have been praised by, among others, Philip *Larkin. They are fast-moving thrillers, usually with a horse-racing background, though latterly the setting has become more varied. Among the best are *Flying Finish* (1966), *Enquiry* (1969), *Rat Race* (1970), *High Stakes* (1975), *In the Frame* (1976), and *The Danger* (1983). His autobiography, *Sport of Queens*, appeared in 1957 (revised editions 1968, 1974, 1982). He was awarded the OBE in 1984.

FRANK, Waldo (David) (1889–1967), American novelist, literary and social critic, born in Long Branch, New Jersey, educated at Yale University. A freelance writer for *The New York Times* and *Evening Post*, he was a co-founder and editor of *The *Seven Arts*, and also US correspondent for the *Nouvelle Revue Française*. Several early novels appeared, among them *The Unwelcome Man* (1917), *The Dark Mother* (1920), *Rahab* (1922), *City Block* (1922), *Holiday* (1923), and *Chalk Face* (1924), as well as a modernist play, *New Year's Eve* (1929). In addition, there were the critical essays and social studies in *Salvos* (1924), *Virgin Spain* (1926; revised 1942), and the travelogue *Dawn in Russia* (1932). He ranked as a literary radical and associated with Van Wyck *Brooks, H. L. *Mencken, and Lewis *Mumford. He was strongly influenced by Freud, and in the 1920s, along with other writers like Max *Eastman and John *Reed, was drawn to the dialectical materialism of Marx, which strongly moulded future works. During the 1930s, an editor of **New Republic* and *The *Masses*, and an active participant in the three Congresses of American Writers, Frank was at the centre of the debate over politics and culture. Novels such as *The Death and Birth of David Markand* (1934), *The Bridegroom Cometh* (1938), *Summer Never Ends* (1941), *Island in the Atlantic* (1946), and *The Invaders* (1948) addressed themselves directly to crucial social problems. All his fiction is characterized by an emotional style with a mixture of Marxism and a romantic conception of cosmic mysticism. Frank was well known for his work on Hispanic culture and contributed to inter-American understanding with such works as *Our America* (1919), *The Re-Discovery of America* (1928), *America Hispaña* (1931), *In the American Jungle* (1937), and *South American Journey* (1943). His other prose includes *Chart for Rough Water* (1940), *The Jew in Our Day* (1944), *Birth of a World* (1951), *Bridgehead* (1957), and *The Prophetic Island: A Portrait of Cuba* (1961). His *Memoirs* were published in 1973.

FRANKAU, Pamela (1908–67), British novelist, born in London. After refusing the offer of a place at Cambridge, she devoted herself to writing. Her first published novel, *The Marriage of Harlequin* (1927), appeared when she was 19 and was followed by over thirty others, including *She and I* (1930); *Tassell-Gentle* (1934), about a man losing his memory in an air crash; *The Devil We Know* (1939), which explores her feelings about her own Jewish ancestry in the character of Philip Meyer, an ambitious young screenwriter in the developing British film industry of the 1930s. This prolific period was interrupted by the war and by the death, in 1940, of her lover, Humbert Woolfe. *Shaken in the Wind* (1948) deals with her conversion to Catholicism. *The Willow Cabin* (1949), her most successful book, describes the relationship between Caroline Seward, a young actress, her lover, Michael Knowle, a man almost twice her age, and his wife, Mercedes, a Roman Catholic. The novel moves between London in the 1930s and during the Blitz to post-war America, incorporating the author's wartime experiences. Other novels include *The Winged Horse* (1953), a novel about a newspaper tycoon; *A Wreath for the Enemy* (1954), set in the South of France, which describes the relationship between the bohemian Wells family and the bourgeois Bradleys; and *The Bridge* (1957), which displays, in its treatment of the bisexuality of its central character, the author's uncompromising honesty. Her autobiography, *I Find Four People*, was published in 1935.

FRANKLIN, Miles (Stella Marie Sarah) (1879–1954), Australian novelist, born in New South Wales. Her early years were spent at Brindabella, her parents' remote farm in New South Wales, and later at Possum Gully which formed the background for her most famous work, *My Brilliant Career* (1901), a largely autobiographical novel about a young girl, Sybylla Melvyn, whose aspirations to become a writer are thwarted by the conventions and strictures of bush society. Franklin later moved to Sydney where she worked as a nurse and as a housemaid before becoming involved in a more literary milieu; she met Joseph *Furphy, Norman *Lindsay, and Henry *Lawson (who wrote the preface to *My Brilliant Career*) and became active in the Australian feminist movement. She then went to America and, after the outbreak of the First World War, to England, where she became involved in the war effort, returning to Australia in 1927. Other works include *All That Swagger* (1936), about an Australian pioneering clan based on her own family; *My Career Goes Bung* (1946), a sequel to her first novel, about her free-thinking life as a Sydney writer. She also published novels under the pseudonym 'Brent of Bin Bin' including *Up the Country* (1928), *Ten Creeks Run* (1930), *Back to Bool Bool* (1931), *Prelude to Waking* (1950), *Cockatoos* (1954), and *Gentlemen at Gyang Gyang* (1956), most of which project a romantic Australian nationalism and a celebration of pioneering life. She is as famous for her unconventional life and radical attitudes, held far in advance of her time, as she is for her fiction, despite attempts on the part of feminist critics to reassess her work.

Franny and Zooey, see SALINGER, J. D.

FRASER, Lady Antonia, née Pakenham (1932–), British biographer and historian, the daughter of Elizabeth *Longford and, since 1980, the wife of Harold *Pinter; she was born in London and educated at Lady Margaret Hall, Oxford. The diligent scholarship and imaginative sympathy with its subject of *Mary Queen of Scots* (1969) established her reputation as a biographer; among Fraser's subsequent biographical works are *Cromwell, Our Chief of Men* (1973), *King Charles II* (1979), and *The Six Wives of Henry VIII* (1992). *The Weaker Vessel* (1984) reviews the social and cultural positions of women in the seventeenth century, and *Boadicea's Chariot* (1988) is a historical survey of women who have exercised power. She has also written a series of detective novels featuring the elegant heroine 'Jemima Shore'; these include *Quiet as a Nun* (1977), *A Splash of Red* (1981), and *Political Death* (1994). The popular anthologies *Scottish Love Poems* (1975) and *Love Letters* (1977) were edited by Fraser.

FRASER, George MacDonald (1925–), British novelist, born in Carlisle, educated at Carlisle Grammar School and Glasgow Academy. He began working as a newspaper reporter in 1949 and was deputy editor of the *Glasgow Herald* from 1964 to 1969. *Flashman* (1969) was the first of a long succession of entertainingly eventful novels recounting the military career of the eponymous bully from *Tom Brown's Schooldays*; subsequent titles include *Flash for Freedom* (1971). *Flashman in the Great Game* (1975), *Flashman and the Mountain of Light* (1990), and *Flashman and the Angel of the Lord* (1994). Among his other works of fiction are the short-stories in *The General Danced at Dawn* (1970) and the novel *McAuslan in the Rough* (1974), both of which form spirited evocations of life in a highland regiment. Fraser's other publications include a history of the Anglo-Scottish Border Reivers entitled *The Steel Bonnets* (1971), and *Quartered Safe Out Here* (1992), a memoir of his experiences in Burma during the Second World War.

FRASER, G(eorge) S(utherland) (1915–80), Scottish poet and critic, born in Glasgow, educated at St Andrew's University. He was a journalist in Aberdeen until 1939, when he joined the Black Watch regiment; some of his most memorable poems are derived from his extended periods on active service in the Middle East. After working in various capacities, principally as a literary journalist, he became a lecturer at the University of Leicester. At the time of the appearance of his first collection of poems, *The Fatal Landscape* (1941), Fraser was numbered among the writers of the *New Apocalypse and wrote an introduction for *The White Horseman* (1941), the group's second anthology, edited by J. F. *Hendry and Henry *Treece. His early verse had, however, a degree of clarity and poise that distinguished it from the more turbulently expressive writing commonly associated with the movement. *Home Town Elegy* (1944) and *The Traveller Has Regrets* (1948) contained the war poetry upon which his reputation was principally established; the repeatedly anthologized 'Egypt' is a good example of the sceptically elegiac tone, precise imagery, and formal control characterizing the best of his work. Two further volumes, *Leaves without a Tree* (1956) and *Conditions* (1969), were followed by *Poems of G. S. Fraser*, a posthumous collected edition, in 1981. Fraser was widely respected as a critic for the judiciousness and generosity of his writings, which include *The Modern Writer and His World* (1953), *Vision and Rhetoric* (1960), and *Ezra Pound* (1961), which increased interest in that poet at a time when his achievement was somewhat neglected. Fraser's other works include the travel book *News from South America* (1949) and the autobiographical *A Stranger and Afraid*, written in 1949 but not published until 1983. Among his translations is Jean Mesnard's *Pascal: His Life and Works* (1952). With J. Waller, he edited *The Collected Poems of Keith Douglas* (1951).

FRAYN, Michael (1933–), British novelist and playwright; he was born, brought up, and educated in the South London suburbs, took a degree in moral philosophy at Emmanuel College, Cambridge, became proficient as a Russian speaker during his National Service, and became a journalist, writing humorous columns first for the *Manchester Guardian*, then for the *Observer*. His novels include *The Tin Man* (1965); *The Russian Interpreter* (1966); *Towards the Edge of the Morning* (1968), a comic picture of Fleet Street life and middle-class mores; *A Very Private Life* (1968), a wryly philosophical investigation of a utopia which promises total comfort and content; and *A Landing on the Sun* (1991), which concerns the mystery surrounding the death of a civil servant, Stephen Summerchild, rumoured to be working on a top-secret defence project for Harold Wilson's government in the early 1970s. He has also published a book of philosophic mini-essays and apophthegms, *Constructions* (1974). But it is for his plays that he has become best known. These include *Alphabetical Order* (1975), set in a newspaper library that becomes less chaotic and more orderly as the evening proceeds; *Donkeys' Years* (1976), about an unruly Cambridge college reunion; *Clouds* (1976), in which a group of journalists take a guided tour round modern Cuba, their relationship subtly shifting as they go; *Make and Break* (1980), set in and around a trade fair in Germany; *Noises Off* (1982), a highly successful farce showing disasters on-stage and off-stage during the provincial tour of a less successful farce; *Benefactors* (1984), about the embattled private and public life of a municipal architect; *Look Look* (1990), an attempt to explore the individual and collective psychology of members of a theatre audience; *Here* (1993), about a young couple's attempt to bring order both to their lives and to the tiny flat in which they live; and *Now You Know* (1995), the dramatic version of a novel of the same title published in 1994, which involves campaigners against government secrecy and investigates questions of openness and privacy on both public and private levels. Frayn's forte is comedy, sometimes high comedy, but comedy that always has serious and sometimes sombre resonances. His most characteristic theme is the difficulty of finding shape in or imposing order on a world that is complex, changeable, and often extremely disorderly. He has also made numerous translations and adaptations from the Russian, among them Tolstoy's *Fruits of Enlightenment*, Trifinov's comic picture of housing problems in Moscow, *Exchange*, and the plays of the dramatist he has admitted to regarding as his favourite, Chekhov.

FRAZER, Sir James George (1854–1941), British anthropologist, historian of religion, and classical scholar, born in Glasgow, where he obtained his MA at the University in 1874. In 1879 he became a fellow of Trinity College, where he remained in residence for most of his life. He was introduced to anthropology by his close friend Robertson Smith (1846–94), co-editor of the ninth edition of the *Encyclopaedia Britannica* (1875–89), for which Frazer wrote articles on 'Taboo' and 'Totemism' in 1885. Following the completion of *Totemism* (1887), his first independent publication of note, he began work on *The *Golden Bough* (1890–1915). His many other related works include *Totemism and Exogamy* (4 volumes, 1910), *The Belief in Immortality and the Worship of the Dead* (1913), *Folklore in the Old Testament* (1918), and *The Fear of the Dead in Primitive Religion* (3 volumes, 1933–6). Frazer proceeded very largely by collating materials from a wide range of secondary sources, his achievement consisting in the synthesis of his findings into impressively orchestrated wholes. His tactful but none the less persuasive demonstrations of the social and historical determination of all religious worship were widely influential in the growing secularization of culture from the 1890s onward. His highly regarded work as a classical scholar includes his editions, with translations and commentaries, of Pausanius's *Description of Greece* (6 volumes, 1898) and Ovid's *Fasti* (5 volumes, 1929). He also edited *The Letters of William Cowper* (1912), whom he admired above others as a poet. He was knighted in 1914. *J. G. Frazer: His Life and Work* by Robert Ackerman was published in 1987.

FREELING, Nicolas (1927–), British crime writer, born in London, educated at the University of Dublin. He worked as a cook in European hotels and restaurants from 1945 to 1960, and in 1962 published *Love in Amsterdam* (US title *Murder in Amsterdam*), the first of a series of crime novels—others include *The King of the Rainy Country* (1966) and *Strike Out where Not Applicable* (1967)—in which the detective is the Dutch policeman Van der Valk. Since Van der Valk's death in *A Long Silence* (1972; US title *Auprès de ma Blonde*) Freeling has moved the setting of his novels to provincial France, employing Henri Castang, also a policeman, as their hero (*Wolfnight*, 1982; *You Who Know*, 1994). Both characters obviously owe something in their conception to Georges Simenon's Maigret.

FREEMAN, Mary E(leanor) Wilkins (1852–1930), American writer, born in Randolph, Massachusetts. She is known primarily for her regional fiction set in her native Massachusetts and in Vermont where she lived. She wrote essays, plays, poetry, children's books, and novels, including *Pembroke* (1894) and *The Shoulders of Atlas* (1908), but she is best remembered for her short stories. Many of these appeared in magazines such as *Harper's Bazaar* and were first collected in *A Humble Romance and Other Stories* (1887). Her fiction characteristically concerns the lives of her contemporary New Englanders and evokes through careful description of scenery, dialect, and milieu a powerful sense of place and of regional character. Among the issues she explored are the pressure exerted upon the inherited social codes of small-town life by a changing urban world, the effect upon personal character of a decaying Puritan orthodoxy, the ambivalent position of unmarried women, and the potential power of the meek in society. In 1902 she married and moved to New Jersey; both the change of environment and life with an alcoholic husband affected the quality of her subsequent work. In 1926 she was awarded the William Dean Howells Gold Medal for Fiction, and in the same year became, with Edith *Wharton, the first woman honoured by the National Institute of Arts and Letters.

FREEMAN, R(ichard) Austin (1862–1943), British *detective story writer. The son of a Soho tailor, he studied medicine, entered the Colonial Service, and in 1887 was posted to the Gold Coast. Invalided home with blackwater fever in 1891, he turned to writing, producing *Travels and Life in Ashanti and Jaman* (1898), a classic in the travel genre. His first detective stories, *The Adventures of Romney Pringle*, written in conjunction with a friend, Dr J. J. Pitcairn, appeared under the pseudonym of Clifford Ashdown in 1902. These were followed by *The Red Thumb Mark* (1907), written under his own name, and in which his detective, Dr John Evelyn Thorndyke, first appears. Thorndyke, who is the central figure in twenty other novels—the last is *The Jacob Street Mystery* (1942)—and many short stories, probably commands more serious intellectual respect than any other fictional detective: his presence is imposing, his knowledge encyclopaedic, and his deductions have a logical rigour which is absent from those of his contemporary Sherlock Holmes. Freeman's first works passed unnoticed; he first made his name with the collection of short stories *The Singing Bone* (1912), in which he introduced the concept of the 'inverted tale', later much imitated. In the first half of these stories the reader is shown a crime being committed; in the second, how the detective arrives at its solution.

Free Verse, a poetic mode given wide currency from around 1910 onward by the emergence of *Imagism, whose practitioners sought, in F. S. *Flint's words, to 'compose in the sequence of the musical phrase, not in the sequence of a metronome'. The versions of the Psalms in the Authorized Version, Walt Whitman's incantationally flexible measures, and the *vers libre* of Jules Laforgue and others were among the precedents for the rejection of predetermined metres characterizing the advent of poetic *Modernism; in the attempt to make poetry more authentic in its relation to experience, the auditory rhetoric of strict forms was called into question along with the stock poetic diction and imagery of the nineteenth century. The achievement of T. S. *Eliot in the carefully modulated lines of 'The Love Song of J. Alfred *Prufrock' was among the finest early examples of the subtlety and effectiveness of free verse. While Robert *Frost stated that 'free verse is like playing tennis with the net down', Eliot insisted that the form did not involve an abandonment of discipline but rather increased the difficulty of satisfying the sensitive ear. Most verse describable as 'free' or 'cadenced' contains recurrent rhythmical effects which may be analysed in terms of traditional metrical feet and variations upon them. By 1936 Michael *Roberts noted in the introduction to *The *Faber Book of Modern Verse* that 'it is very hard to draw a sharp line . . . between "free" verse and *varied* regular verse', indicating the liberating effect of the development on poetic practice in general.

FRENCH, Marilyn (1929–), American novelist and literary critic, born in New York City, educated at Harvard. French established herself as a teacher and literary critic before embarking on a career as a novelist. Her *The Book as World: James Joyce's 'Ulysses'* (1976) is a study of *Joyce's great novel, while *Shakespeare's Division of Experience* (1984) explores what she sees as the division in Shakespeare's work between tragedy as the expression of the 'masculine principle' and comedy as the expression of the 'feminine principle'. However, it was her first novel, *The Women's Room* (1977), which brought her to the attention of a wider reading public and helped establish her as an important academic voice for the feminist movement. Her frequently trenchant essays on the place of women in society are collected in *Beyond Morals: Women, Men, and Morals* (1986) and *The War against Women* (1992). Her other novels include *The Bleeding Heart* (1980), *Her Mother's Daughter* (1987), and *Our Father* (1993).

French Lieutenant's Woman, The, a novel by John *Fowles, published in 1969. The narrative centres on a Victorian romance between Sarah Woodruff, a governess isolated by the local community for her reported former liaison with a French naval officer, and Charles Smithson, an aristocratic Victorian palaeontologist who is engaged to Ernestina Freeman, the daughter of a wealthy businessman. Sarah is dismissed from her post in Lyme Regis and moves to Exeter where the affair is eventually consummated. She becomes elusive; by the time Charles finds her, years later, she is a *New Woman and assistant to Dante Gabriel Rossetti. The novel, with its three alternative endings, heralded a new era of self-conscious writing in contemporary British fiction, hitherto held to be limited and parochial in scope. It is enriched by the formal innovations Fowles had borrowed, and reinvented, from the metafictional conventions of post-war European literature—the self-reflexive tones of the *nouveau roman* and its leading figure Robbe-Grillet—and the familiar outmoded traditions of Hardy and eighteenth-century English fiction. The lavish romanticism centred on the anima-like figure of Sarah, its misunderstood antiheroine, and her destructive passion for the conventional Charles, lend the novel lasting popular appeal, increased by Fowles's characteristic narrative energy and the period flavour captured in his skilful use of historical pastiche. Harold *Pinter wrote the screenplay for the 1981 film version by Karel Reisz.

Freudian Criticism, see PSYCHOANALITIC CRITICISM.

FRIEDMAN, Bruce Jay (1930–), American novelist and dramatist, born in the Bronx, New York City, educated at the University of Missouri. He served in the US Army, and then worked in publishing. Friedman is best known as a novelist and short-story writer, whose one successful play is the comedy *Scuba Duba*, produced at the New Theatre in New York in 1967. Like his novels, *Scuba Duba* is a witty comedy of the tensions of Jewish family life in which Harold Wonder's urbane world is shattered when his wife leaves him for a coloured lover. Friedman then brings in some of the statutory ingredients of this ethnic humour, with confrontations between the intellectual, liberal-minded Harold, his and her lover, his mother, and his psychiatrist. Friedman's novels include *Stern* (1962), *A Mother's Kisses* (1964), *The Dick* (1970), *About Harry Towns* (1974), *Tokyo Woes* (1985), and *The Current Climate* (1989). His short stories appear in volumes such as *Far from the City of Class* (1963), *Black Angels* (1966), and *Let's Hear It for a Beautiful Guy* (1984). His comic work of self-improvement, *The Lone Guy's Book of Life*, appeared in 1978.

FRIEDMAN, Milton (1912–), American economist, born in New York City, educated at Rutgers, and the universities of Columbia and Chicago, where he became Professor of Economics in 1946. Recipient of the Nobel Prize for Economics in 1977, he is the best-known advocate of the universal advantages of free-market capitalism and of monetarist economic policies, and is the foremost member of the so-called Chicago School of Economics. If the decline of Keynesian ideas (see KEYNES, JOHN MAYNARD) in economics circles (beginning in the mid-1970s) is to be traced to any one person, it would be to Friedman. It is through his more popular writings that Friedman reaches a more general audience. In *Essays in Positive Economics* (1953) Friedman launched a highly influential methodological programme designed to enlighten those who were otherwise being led to believe that unrealistic assumptions in economics diminished the usefulness of the science. He held instead that it was the predictive ability of theories that was really important. In *Capitalism and Freedom* (1962) democracy was identified with the workings of the free market. *Dollars and Deficits* (1968) sets out in intelligible and persuasive language some of his views on inflation, government deficit spending, and the balance of payments. *Free To Choose* (1980, with Rose Friedman), is a popular summing-up of his whole economic and political philosophy.

FRIEL, Brian (1929–), Northern Irish dramatist, born in Omagh, Co. Tyrone, educated in Derry and Belfast; he later became a teacher. His first substantial success was *Philadelphia, Here I Come* (1964), in which two actors embody the private and public frustrations of a young Irishman about to emigrate to America. This has been followed by many plays, some of them directly concerned with the agonies of Northern Ireland, such as the *Freedom of the City* (1974), about the shooting by British troops of the decidedly unheroic civil rights marchers who have inadvertently occupied Derry Town Hall, and *Volunteers* (1975), about political internees working on an archaeological dig;

but others are more indirectly and less obviously so. **Translations* (1980), widely regarded as his masterpiece, involves nineteenth-century linguistic imperialism, represented by a British army intent on replacing Gaelic place-names with English ones and goaded by the murder of a lovelorn young officer into retributory violence. Friel's more private plays include *The Loves of Cass McGuire* (1966) and *Lovers* (1968); *Faith Healer* (1976), four consecutive monologues describing the wanderings, apotheosis, and death of a modern medicine man clearly meant to represent the creative artist or writer; and *Aristocrats* (1979) and **Dancing at Lughnasa* (1990), two plays about family and social fragmentation, one occurring in the 1970s, and the other in the 1930s; *Wonderful Tennessee* (1993), about a group of dissatisfied Dubliners impotently trying to discover their pagan roots during an overnight trip out of town; and *Molly Sweeney* (1994), another series of monologues, this time involving a blind woman who feels more content in her darkness than in the sighted world to which she is briefly and disastrously returned. All four of these plays occur in or near Ballybeg, the exemplary Donegal village which Friel invented in the 1960s and where he continues to set much of his work. Overall, this is marked by a gentle scepticism about personal or political pretension, a wry, kindly humour, and a nostalgia for a world unscarred by the dislocation, loss, failure, and disillusion movingly shown in his plays. Friel has also made translations and adaptations, notably of Chekhov's *The Three Sisters* and Turgenev's *Fathers and Sons*. In 1980 he co-founded *Field Day, a touring theatre company centred on Derry.

FRIEL, George (1910–75), Scottish novelist, born and brought up in Glasgow, where he worked as a teacher. Of a poor background, Friel portrayed the lives of the underprivileged and uncharted, and his work is dense with the life of the poorer districts of Glasgow. He published *The Bank of Time* (1959), *The Boy Who Wanted Peace* (1964), *Grace and Miss Partridge* (1969), *Mr. Alfred MA* (1972), and *An Empty House* (1975). Of these, his reputation rests on *Mr. Alfred MA* whose central character is the unprepossessing schoolmaster, Mr Alfred, who is a failure. His ambitions of being a poet are wholly misplaced. He finds compensation in furtive association with tarts and in drinking, until he becomes obsessed by a girl pupil. The novel develops against an impressionistically rendered Glasgow, at a time of worsening poverty and the hideous escalation of gang life among the city youths. The novel enters the Scottish tradition of veiled use of the supernatural to resolve its complex themes: in his breakdown Mr Alfred encounters in an abandoned building the sinister Tod who, obviously, is one version of the Devil who has haunted Scottish fiction from James Hogg onwards.

From Here to Eternity, see JONES, JAMES.

FROST, Robert (Lee) (1874–1963), American poet, born in San Francisco; he grew up in Lawrence, Massachusetts, after the death of his father, a newspaper editor originally from New England, and was educated at Lawrence High school, where he was elected 'class poet' in his final year. He attended Dartmouth College in 1892 and, having worked as a cobbler, a farmer, and editor of a local newspaper, studied at Harvard from 1897 to 1899. Following the appearance of one of his poems in the *New York Independent* in 1894 he privately published *Twilight* (1894) and began to concern himself with making his reputation as a poet. Receiving no encouragement in America, he travelled to Britain in 1912 and became acquainted with a number of the poets associated with the *Georgian movement; he was closest to Edward *Thomas, encouraging him as a poet and later describing him as 'the only brother I ever had'. Two collections of his poetry, *A Boy's Will* (1913) and *North of Boston* (1914), which firmly determine the New England regionalism of his *œuvre*, appeared in England to favourable critical receptions; on his return to the USA in 1915 he was recognized as an established literary figure, a position he consolidated with the publication of *Mountain Interval* (1916). He took up residence on a farm in New Hampshire and between 1916 and 1950 recurrently held posts as a visiting professor of English and writer-in-residence at numerous American universities. His first three volumes contain a high proportion of his best-known work, including 'Mending Wall', 'Death of the Hired Man', 'Birches', and 'The Road Not Taken'; the conversational individuality of tone and diction in such poems remained his identifying characteristic. The tensions between the realism and directness of his verse and its loyalty to conventional forms make Frost's achievement one of unusually effective mediation between tradition and innovation. His many subsequent collections include *New Hampshire* (1923), in which political elements were added to his predominantly descriptive and contemplative idioms, *The Lone Striker* (1933), *Steeple Bush* (1947), *Aforesaid* (1954), and *In the Clearing* (1962). The *Complete Poems* was published in 1968. Frost enjoyed enormous popularity in America as a benevolent purveyor of versified common sense, rural lore, and evocations of natural order, impressions catered for by more anodyne poems like 'The Pasture'. Much of his work, however, reveals an imaginative attraction towards sinister depths of melancholy consistent with the fears of insanity and temptations to suicide apparent in his *Selected Letters* (1965, edited by Lawrance Thompson). Elsewhere, his sceptically fatalistic manner combines with a laconically unsentimental compassion to produce the many poems of which 'Out, Out —' is perhaps the typifying example. The verse-dramas *A Masque of Reason* (1942) and *A Masque of Mercy* (1951) are the principal manifestations of the theological and philosophical preoccupations evident in his work from the 1940s onward; he remained, however, capable of producing poems with the disturbing impact of 'The Draft Horse' to the end of his career. His standing in his later years is indicated by the fact that he won the Pulitzer

Prize three times, received more than forty honorary degrees, and served as President Kennedy's cultural emissary. Lawrance Thompson's biography of Frost appeared in three volumes in 1967, 1971, and 1977.

Frost in May, a novel by A. *White, published in 1933. It was described by Elizabeth *Bowen as not only a classic girls' school story, but a work of art: 'intense, troubling, semi-miraculous'. In 1908, nine-year-old Nanda Grey, the daughter of a convert, arrives at the Convent of the Five Wounds, where the creation of 'soldiers of Christ, accustomed to hardship and ridicule and ingratitude' is a governing principle. From descriptions of small but stringent religious demands on daily life through to passionate friendships nurtured by the very rules established to prevent them, the novel vividly creates this enclosed world. Though Nanda wholeheartedly accepts the Catholic Church, uncertainties surface: her First Communion lacks the spiritual climax she had anticipated; a retreat is hampered by the sense that some elements of religious life are a 'meaningless complication'. As a proof of faith, she begins a novel in which worldly behaviour will be exonerated by its characters' dramatic conversion in the final chapter. The unfinished manuscript is discovered and Nanda is despatched from the convent on her fourteenth birthday, without the opportunity to explain. Her father denounces her impurity; the Mother of Discipline affirms that by breaking her will, Nanda can be at one with God.

FRY, Christopher (Harris) (1907–), British poet and playwright, born in Bristol, the son of a Church of England lay preacher, educated at Bedford Modern School. He later adopted the name of his mother's Quaker family and served in a non-combatant unit in the Second World War. He was a schoolmaster, an actor, and a producer before writing a dramatic tale about St Cuthman, *The Boy with a Cart*, in 1938. Much of his subsequent work—for instance, his play about Moses, *The Firstborn* (1948), and the pacifist *A Sleep of Prisoners* (1951)—has an overt religious bent, aiming to evoke, in his words, 'a world which has deeps and shadows of mystery, in which God is anything but a sleeping partner'. All his plays reflect his belief that people have 'domesticated the enormous miracle' and failed to notice that reality is 'wildly, perilously, incomprehensibly fantastic'; these include *The *Lady's Not for Burning* (1949) and four 'seasonal' comedies: *A Phoenix Too Frequent* (1946), about the spring-like love that develops between a young widow and a despairing soldier; the autumnal *Venus Observed* (1950); the wintry *The Dark is Light Enough* (1954); and, belatedly representing summer, a play about renewal and reconciliation in post-war Siena, *A Yard of Sun* (1970). Throughout his career Fry has expressed his essential optimism in elaborately and sometimes playfully metaphoric verse and, with the more restrained T. S. *Eliot, was hailed as a leader of a renaissance of poetic drama: a claim and a trend that did not, however, survive the arrival of *'kitchen sink drama' in 1956. He has also written screenplays, notably for *Ben Hur*, and translated drama by Rostand, Anouilh, and Giradoux.

FRY, Roger (Eliot) (1866–1934), British art critic and painter, born in London, educated at King's College, Cambridge. Having read natural sciences Fry turned to painting and became interested in Renaissance art after visits to Italy. He was art critic of the *Athenaeum* in 1901, co-founded the *Burlington Magazine* in 1903, and was director of the Metropolitan Museum of Modern Art, New York, from 1905 to 1910. In 1910 he founded the Omega Workshops to produce well-designed and simple objects for daily use. His 1905 edition of Sir Joshua Reynolds's *Discourses* was highly acclaimed. On discovering Cézanne in 1906 his attention turned towards modern painting; in 1910 and 1912 he organized two celebrated exhibitions of Cézanne's work, together with that of Van Gogh, Gauguin, and other 'Post-Impressionists' (a term coined by Fry). His criticism, collected in *Vision and Design* (1920) and *Transformations* (1926), together with his monograph on *Cézanne* (1927), succeeded in stimulating immense enthusiasm for modern French painting. His *Last Lectures* appeared posthumously in 1939. An associate of the *Bloomsbury Group, Fry's biography was written by V. *Woolf (1940).

FRYE, (Herman) Northrop (1912–91), Canadian critic, born in Sherbrooke, Quebec, educated at Victoria College, University of Toronto; he studied theology at Emmanuel College, Canada, and literature at Merton College, Oxford. From 1940 Frye was a member of the faculty of the University of Toronto, becoming Chancellor of Victoria College in 1979. His early work on Blake (*Fearful Symmetry*, 1947) gained him instant notice, and his continuing work on Shakespeare (*A Natural Perspective*, 1965; *Fools of Time*, 1967) and on criticism and learning (*The Educated Imagination*, 1963; *The Stubborn Structure*, 1970; *The Critical Path*, 1971) has remained influential. Frye was above all interested in romance as a recurring structure of the imagination, a vision of probability in which magic, for example, becomes a metaphor for human generosity and capacity for renewal rather than a mere refusal of the real. Frye's major work is his ground-breaking *Anatomy of Criticism* (1957), which raised, with impeccable lucidity and much wit, indispensable questions about the teaching, evaluating, and classifying of literature. 'There is as yet,' Frye wrote in his 'polemical introduction', 'no way of distinguishing what is genuine criticism . . . from what belongs to the history of taste.' Frye urges us to understand literature as 'an order of words' rather than a pile of works, and to see criticism as a progressive, collaborative enterprise rather than simply 'leisure-class gossip'. *Anatomy of Criticism* contributes to this venture by its exposition of the problem, and through four long essays on different forms of criticism which Frye calls historical, ethical, archetypal, and rhetorical. Of these four forms, the archetypal attracted the most attention, with its concentration on underlying patterns in literature, and its anthropological background. There was a brief but widespread fashion for so-called myth criticism in the 1960s, when archetypes of all kinds, but particularly Christian ones, were found almost everywhere. Traces of this trend survive in talk of Christ-figures, and in the assumption that all apples in literature have something to do with the Garden of Eden.

FUGARD, Athol (Harold Lannigan) (1932–), South African playwright, born in Middleburg, Cape Province; he grew up in Port Elizabeth and was educated at Cape Town University. His father, of English descent, was a shopkeeper, and his mother an Afrikaner. Fugard became actively involved in theatre when he married Sheila Meiring, an actress and novelist, and both moved to Johannesburg, where his work as Clerk to the Native Commissioner's Court gave him first-hand experience of apartheid laws. His novel *Tsotsi* (1980), its title a name for township gangsters, grimly depicts the Sophiatown ghetto. His two naturalistic plays *No-Good Friday* (1958) and *Nongogo* (1959), published in *'Dimetos' and Two Early Plays* (1977), were also set in Sophiatown, a township which was later demolished, and its inhabitants expelled, under the Group Areas Act. *Three Port Elizabeth Plays* (1974) includes *The Blood Knot* (1961), about the difficulties faced by two coloured brothers; *Hello and Goodbye* (1965), which concerns a 'poor white' brother and sister; and *Boesman and Lena* (1968), about a frustrated married couple, whose relationship is strained by their struggle to survive as homeless coloured migrant workers, and the silent intrusion of a dying black. Much influenced by *Beckett and Camus, the 'Port Elizabeth' plays established Fugard as a dramatist of international stature. *Statements* (1974) includes the harrowing *Statements after an Arrest under the Immorality Act* (1974) and two plays written in collaboration with the actors John Kani and Winston Ntshona: **Sizwe Bansi Is Dead* (1972) and *The Island* (1973), a version of *Antigone* as presented by two political prisoners on the notorious Robben Island. *A Lesson from Aloes* (1980) turned to middle-class characters in a story about a liberal Afrikaner and his relationship with his wife and a coloured political activist. *'Master Harold' . . . and the Boys* (1982), based on Fugard's experiences as a teenager in Port Elizabeth, concerns a boy whose problematic relationship with his father leads him to ill-treat his two family servants. *The Road to Mecca* (1984), a powerful drama reminiscent of Ibsen in its exploration of the past of a woman artist and a Calvinist minister, is based on the tragic life of Afrikaner Helen Martins, a reclusive sculptor who lived in the arid Karroo region. In *My Children! My Africa!* (1989), portraying the dilemmas faced by a black schoolteacher, Fugard confronted the intransigence of politically militant Soweto schoolchildren. In *Playland* (1992), a black man and a white man have a revealing encounter in a travelling amusement park. *Valley Song* was performed in 1996. *Township Plays* (1993) collects several important plays including *The Coat* (1966). Fugard's film scripts include *The Guest: An Episode in the Life of Eugene Marais* (1977), *Marigolds in August* (1979), and the film version of *Boesman and Lena* (1972), with Fugard taking the part of Boesman. His private thoughts on the injustices of racialist politics, which his works vividly illuminate in public manner, are revealed in *Notebooks: 1960–1977* (1983), edited by Mary Benson. *Cousins: A Memoir* appeared in 1995. See Dennis Walder, *Athol Fugard* (1984).

Fugitive, The, see AGRARIANS, THE.

FULLER, Henry Blake (1857–1929), American novelist and playwright, born in Chicago, educated at Allison Classical Academy, Oconomowoc, Wisconsin. Fuller drew on his travels in Europe in 1879 and 1883 in his first book, *The Chevalier of Pensieri-Vani* (1890; revised 1892), a series of linked stories often with a Jamesian theme of the confrontation of American innocence and brashness with European sophistication, and pursued these interests in *The Chatelaine of La Trinité* (1892). In both works the analysis of American society, particularly the attack on its materialistic and industrial preoccupations, is a pervasive concern. These concerns were registered with intelligence and maturity in *The Cliff-Dwellers* (1893) and *With the Procession* (1895), both set in Chicago. Fuller turned to drama with 'O, That Way Madness Lies' (1895), a one-act fantasy, and published *The Puppet-Booth: Twelve Plays* (1896), influenced by the puppet theatre of Maurice Maeterlinck and the music of Richard Wagner. Subsequent novels include *The Last Refuge: A Sicilian Romance* (1900) and *Bertram Cope's Year* (1919). Despite his declared intention, in a letter to his friend Hamlin *Garland, to put up the 'shutters' on fiction, he wrote two more novels, *Gardens of This World* (1929) and *Not on the Screen* (1930). Although a relatively minor figure in American letters Fuller's place in the history of American literary realism is significant. See *Fuller of Chicago: The Ordeal of a Genteel Realist in Ungenteel America* (1974), by Bernard R. Bowron, Jr.

FULLER, John (Leopold) (1937–), British poet and novelist, born at Ashcroft in Kent, the son of Roy *Fuller, educated at New College, Oxford, where he won the Newdigate Prize for Poetry in 1960. In 1966 he became a fellow of Magdalen College, Oxford. His numerous volumes of poetry include *Fairground Music* (1961), *Cannibals and Missionaries* (1972), *Lies and Secrets* (1979), *Selected Poems: 1954–1982* (1985), *The Grey Among the Green* (1988), and *The Mechanical Body* (1991). Thematically and stylistically his work is wide-ranging, encompassing formally traditional lyric verse, wittily rhymed satires of contemporary social behaviour, and philosophically investigative poems in conversationally cadenced stanzas. The interaction of serious and comic elements in much of his writing is most evident in *The Illusionists* (1980). Fuller's practice frequently suggests a conception of poetry as a matter of ingenious verbal artificing, which, with the intelligence that permeates his work, identifies him as a disciple of *Auden. He has also produced several works of fiction, notably the novels *Flying to Nowhere* (1983) and *Look Twice* (1991); and short stories collected in *The Adventures of Speedfall* (1985) and *The Worm and the Star* (1993). In collaboration with James *Fenton, he wrote *Partingtime Hall* (1987), a collection of verse combining spirited scurrility and erudite allusiveness. Among Fuller's scholarly works are *A Reader's Guide to W. H. Auden* (1970) and his edition of John Gay's *Dramatic Works* (two volumes, 1983).

FULLER, Peter (1947–90), English art critic and broadcaster, born in Damascus, educated at Peterhouse, Cambridge. He was founder, editor, and publisher of the quarterly journal *Modern Painters*, which first appeared in 1988. Fuller particularly favoured the visionary British artists, such as Stanley Spencer and Cecil Collins. His art criticism at first showed the Marxist influence of his mentor, John *Berger, but he gradually came to argue for a spiritually transcendent art. His criticism appeared in a wide variety of publications and has been collected in *Art and Psychoanalysis* (1980) and *Aesthetics after Modernism* (1982). He also wrote about the American abstract artist *Robert Natikin* (1981). His last book, *Theoria: Art and Absence of Grace* (1988), focuses on John Ruskin's aesthetics, and its application to contemporary art.

FULLER, Roy (Broadbent) (1912–91), British poet, born at Failsworth in Lancashire, educated at Blackpool High School. An articled clerk from the age of 16, in 1934 he qualified as a solicitor, practising with a building society throughout his career. He was Oxford Professor of Poetry from 1968 to 1973. In the later 1930s he was a contributor to **New Verse*, producing poetry of social and political concern which indicated the influences of *Auden and *Spender. His early collections *The Middle of a War* (1942) and *A Lost Season* (1944) contain many poems memorable for their reflections of wartime atmospheres of loneliness, tedium, and fear. These volumes establish the contemplative detachment and urbanely ironic tone that predominate in much of Fuller's later writing. His numerous subsequent collections include *Brutus's Orchard* (1958), *Tiny Tears* (1973), and *Available for Dreams* (1989). *Collected Poems: 1936–1961* was published in 1962. Fuller's technical accomplishment is evident throughout his poetry, which makes fluent use of a wide range of traditional forms and innovative variations upon them. He also published a number of novels, among which are the imaginatively disquieting *Fantasy and Fugue* (1954) and *Image of a Society* (1956), which portrays personal interactions within a northern building society. Fuller's three volumes of memoirs, *Souvenirs* (1980), *Vamp Till Ready* (1982), and *Home and Dry* (1984) appeared under the title of *The Strange and the Good* in 1989. A further work of autobiography, *Spanner and Pen*, was published in 1991.

FURPHY, Joseph (1843–1912), Australian writer, born in Victoria, the son of Irish emigrants. He left school early to work on his father's farm and subsequently worked as a gold-digger, labourer, and teamster, before hardship forced him to work in his brother's foundry. A self-made but widely read individualist, Furphy possessed an idiosyncratic familiarity with the literary classics (including the Bible) which he used to great effect together with his wide experience of life on the land. *Such Is Life* (1903) was largely ignored on publication, but has since attained recognition for its innovative and sophisticated employment of shifting narrative and language techniques. It is also a rich and encompassing vision of Australian rural life, in all its mirth and hardship, though idiosyncratic in its focus and style. The work was originally published by the **Bulletin*, as were many of his earlier short stories (under the pseudonym 'Tom Collins'). Furphy produced two more books, *Rigby's Romance* (serialized 1905–6; published 1921; full version, 1946;) and *The Buln-Buln and the Brolga* (1948) from sections he had been asked to edit out from *Such Is Life*, but neither was published in his lifetime.

Futurism, a radically innovative movement in literature and the graphic arts begun in Italy by Filippo Tommaso Marinetti (1876–1944), whose *Futurist Manifesto* of 1909 called for the exalted participation of the arts in the dynamically mechanistic ethos of modernity. The *Manifesto of Futurist Painting* (1910) by Giacomo Balla, Gino Severini, and others emphasized flux and movement as essentials of representation. Marinetti's *Technical Manifesto of Literature* (1912) called for disruption of syntax and use of words for their sounds alone as methods of liberating language 'from the prison of the Latin sentence'. Russian Futurism was established in 1912 by Viktor Khlebnikov (1885–1922) and Vladimir Mayakovsky (1893–1930), whose manifesto entitled 'A Slap in the Face for Public Taste' rejected the validity of the nineteenth-century Russian literary tradition. Initially an active force in the cultural development of the revolution, the Russian Futurists were marginalized by official policy in the early 1920s. Futurism was a direct influence on *Dada and *Surrealism and the progenitor of numerous forms of poetic experimentation with sound and typography. Marinetti's controversial series of lectures in London in 1912 stimulated Wyndham *Lewis and Ezra *Pound to formulate *Vorticism; the first issue of **Blast* expressed their agreement with Futurism's basic aesthetics, but maintained that the movement was flawed in its fundamentally romantic attitude to mechanical dynamism.

G

GADDIS, William (1922–), American novelist, born in New York City, educated at Harvard. After a period of travel in Europe he published *The Recognitions* (1955), a complex, experimental, satirical novel whose settings range from nineteenth-century New England to Central America and contemporary New York, and whose central figure is the artist turned faker Wyatt Gwyon, who prostitutes his talent in the service of the demonic art dealer, Recktall Brown. In a book crowded with outlandish and sinister characters, incorporating a wide range of cultural and philosophical references, literary allusions, parodies of other works, and references to popular culture, Gaddis offers a bizarre and frequently disturbing portrait of contemporary society, in particular that of the shallow and self-seeking New York intelligentsia. It was highly acclaimed for its erudition and its originality. *JR* (1975) is an epistolary novel exploring the corruption and hypocrisy of the business world and centring on the ambitious young hero's quest for success. *Carpenter's Gothic* (1985) presents a bleak vision of America as a country in which the liberal decencies of the past have been eroded by reactionary fundamentalism and materialistic greed. Gaddis continues his assessment of contemporary society with *A Frolic of His Own* (1994), a satirical novel assessing the American legal system and the fashion for litigation.

GAINES, Ernest J(ames) (1933–), African-American novelist, born in Oscar, Louisiana, educated at San Francisco State College and Stanford University, California. Among other academic posts he was Professor of English at the University of Southwestern Louisiana, Lafayette. Gaines has been compared to William *Faulkner in his focus on one small area of the American South, describing the people of southern Louisiana including those of African descent, Cajuns of French descent, and mixed-race Creoles. In his most celebrated novel, *The Autobiography of Miss Jane Pittman* (1971), later made into a film, the recollections of a 110-year-old woman provide a highly personalized chronicle of the struggle for civil rights from the days of slavery to the emergence of Martin Luther King. *A Gathering of Old Men* (1983) is a study of lynch-mob psychology which focuses on the murder of a white farmer, and the manner in which eighteen elderly black men confound the racist authorities by each insisting on his own guilt; a film version directed by Volker Schlondorff appeared in 1987. Other novels include *Catherine Carmier* (1964), *Of Love and Dust* (1967), and *In My Father's House* (1978). *Bloodline* (1968) is a collection of short stories.

GAITSKILL, Mary (1954–), American writer, born in Lexington, Kentucky; she grew up near Detroit, and was educated at the University of Michigan. She had a troubled adolescence, absconding from home to live as a stripper in Manhattan at 16, and then led a rootless and insecure life sleeping rough. She established her reputation with *Bad Behaviour* (1988), a closely observed collection of short stories about the seedy side of New York City, and some of its marginalized inhabitants. Frequently dealing with the characters' desire for intimacy, the stories focus on drug abuse, self-abuse, and the link between romance and pornography in contemporary urban society. Following the huge success of the stories she published a novel, *Two Girls, Fat and Thin* (1991), an intense, compelling portrait of disturbance, seen through the relationship of a newspaper writer, Justine Shade, and her editor, Dorothy (both women were sexually abused as children) who are working on mysterious cult figure Anna Granite (based on Ayn *Rand).

GALBRAITH, J(ohn) K(enneth) (1908–), American *Keynesian economist, born in Ontario, Canada, educated at the universities of Toronto, California, and Cambridge. His distinguished career has ranged from academic posts (he was Professor of Economics at Harvard) to journalism (he edited *Fortune*), government service (he directed the Strategic Bombing Survey after the Second World War), and diplomat (he was United States Ambassador to India during the Kennedy administration). In his public interventions, he remains the foremost voice of a distinctive American brand of liberalism. In economics, his work is in the great tradition of American Institutionalism. Among the most widely read of his early publications are *The Great Crash* (1961), and his trilogy—*American Capitalism* (1952), *The Affluent Society* (1955), and *The New Industrial State* (1967)—in which disparities of power, wealth, and opportunity are eruditely exposed amongst other unpalatable realities of modern industrial society. Subsequent works include *Economics and the Public Purpose* (1973), *The Nature of Mass Poverty* (1979), *The Anatomy of Power* (1983), *The Culture of Contentment* (1992), and *A Journey through Economic Time* (1994). The lucidity with which he presents his subjects, combined with his wit, have contributed to his reputation as one of the most accessible and respected economists of the twentieth century; his television series of the mid-1970s, 'The Age of Uncertainty', brought him a wider audience and increased popularity.

GALE, Patrick (1962–), British novelist, born on the Isle of Wight, educated at Winchester and at New College, Oxford. His first novel, *The Aerodynamics of Pork* (1986), was followed by *Ease* (1986), and *Kansas in August* (1987), a romantic comedy involving a young gay man, his sister, and the lover they both share. Other novels include *Facing the Tank* (1988) and *Little Bits of Baby* (1989). In *The Cat's Sanctuary* (1990), Gale explores the antagonistic relationship between two sisters, one a successful writer, living with her female lover in a farmhouse in Cornwall, the other the widow of a diplomat killed by a terrorist bomb. More ambitious than his previous work, *The Facts of Life* (1995) is a three-generation saga focusing on the life of Edward Pepper, a Jewish composer exiled from Germany in his youth at the time of the Second World War. In this exuberant exploration of family ties and the nature of survival, Gale combines rich evocations of historical and contemporary situations with a precocious narrative fluency.

GALE, Zona (1874–1938), American novelist and short-story writer, born in Portage, Wisconsin, educated at the University of Wisconsin. Her imaginary hamlet in rural Wisconsin was the setting for a series of short stories, beginning with *Friendship Village* (1908), which dramatized the shifting patterns of small-town America as it faced the encroachments of modernity. Novels like *Birth* (1918) and *Miss Lulu Bett* (1920; Pulitzer Prize) exhibit a more critical perspective on American life. Her later fiction was more preoccupied with spiritualism and the occult. Gale also wrote plays, verse, and more volumes of stories, such as *Yellow Gentians and Blue* (1927) and *Bridal Pond* (1930). Her support for Senator Robert LaFollette's Progressive party in Wisconsin drew Gale to such reformist causes as women's rights, pacificism, and prohibition.

GALLANT, Mavis (1922–), Canadian writer, born in Montreal, brought up in Quebec, Ontario and the USA, before returning to Canada in 1941. She then worked with the National Film Board and became a feature writer with the *Montreal Standard*. During the 1950s she moved to Paris, but Canada frequently features in her writings. She has published several collections of stories, many of which first appeared in *The New Yorker* and *The New York Times Book Review*, including *The Other Paris* (1956), *My Heart Is Broken* (1964), and *From the Fifteenth District: A Novella and Eight Short Stories* (1979). *Home Truths* (1981) includes a perceptive and revealing introduction by Gallant herself, and has three sections, on Canada, on Canadians abroad, and the six stories featuring the young woman Linnet Muir in the Montreal of the 1930s and 1940s. Two novels, *Green Water, Green Sky* (1959) and *A Fairly Good Time* (1970), and the stories in *Overhead in a Balloon* (1985) and *In Transit* (1988) attest to Gallant's skill at evoking a special combination of location and memory with a poise born not from any dislocation from Canadian life and culture, but from dedication to her art. Her recent collections include *The Moslem Wife and Other Stories* (1993) and *Across the Bridge: Nine Short Stories* (1993). Gallant was made an Officer of the Order of Canada in 1981.

GALLOWAY, Janice (1956–), Scottish writer, born in Ayrshire, educated at Glasgow University; she has worked mainly as a teacher. Her first novel, *The Trick is to Keep Breathing* (1989), focuses on Joy Stone, a young drama teacher rendered almost insane by her lover's accidental death; written in a distinctive fragmentary style with an unusual use of typography, it powerfully evokes the suffering of a woman traumatized by grief. Galloway's talent for experimentation is further displayed in the short stories collected in *Blood* (1991), and in her novel *Foreign Parts* (1994), which follows Cassie and Rona, two Scottish welfare workers, through Northern France on a motoring holiday; interwoven with photographs of Cassie's past loves and extracts from travel guides, the novel is both a compassionate exploration of a friendship tested to its limits and a witty account of travelling abroad. The stories collected in *Where You Find It* (1996) are unsentimental examinations of the diversity of love.

GALSWORTHY, John (1867–1933), British novelist and playwright, born in Coombe, Surrey, the son of a wealthy solicitor; he studied jurisprudence at New College, Oxford. From 1890 to 1895, when he became a full-time writer, he practised as a barrister and travelled extensively; in the course of a voyage in 1892, he began a lasting friendship with Joseph *Conrad. His early works, all published under the pseudonym 'John Sinjohn', include the short stories of *From the Four Winds* (1897) and *Man of Devon* (1901) and the novels *Jocelyn* (1898) and *Villa Rubein* (1900); the last-named clearly displays the influence of Turgenev's humane realism, establishing the essential mode of Galsworthy's later work. Although respected in literary circles for his virtuosity in matters of form and style, he did not command a wider audience until 1906; in that year he published *The Man of Property*, the first of his novels to trace the fortunes of the Forsyte family, and enjoyed his first stage success with *The Silver Box*, which introduced the contrast between poor and privileged families as a recurrent feature of his dramatic writings. The astutely objective but penetrating projection of the values and manners of his own social class begun in *The Man of Property* was sustained with the continuing treatment of the Forsytes in *In Chancery* (1920) and *To Let* (1921); the books were collected with two additional lyrical 'interludes' as *The *Forsyte Saga* in 1922. A television serialization of the work made in 1967 was broadcast in over forty countries. *A Modern Comedy* (1929), consisting of *The White Monkey* (1924), *The Silver Spoon* (1926), and *Swan Song* (1928), registers the impact of the First World War on the society of the Forsytes in following a younger generation of the family to maturity. Other works centring on the lives and times of the Forsytes include *Soames and Flag* (1930), and the stories *On Forsyte Change* (1930). *Maid in Waiting* (1931), *Flowering Wilderness* (1932), and *Over the River* (1933), which present the history of the Charwells, rural cousins of the Forsytes, were collected as *End of the Chapter* (1934). Notable among Galsworthy's numerous other novels are *The Dark Flower* (1913), the most passionately lyrical expression of his erotic and romantic intuitions, and *Fraternity* (1909), to which the theme of the hypocrisy inherent in social conventions is central. The reservation of explicit moral judgement which characterized his novels is also a feature of his work for the stage, in which, however, his humanitarian concern with social justice is more conspicuously apparent. *Strife* (1909) dealt with the sufferings of workers and their families during a strike. Galsworthy's participation in campaigns for penal reform was reflected in **Justice* (1910), which was instrumental in swaying opinion against the widespread use of solitary confinement. *The Skin Game* (1920), exposing the aristocracy's jealous sensitivity to change, *Loyalties* (1922), attacking anti-Semitism, and *Escape* (1926), an experimentally episodic treatment of a prisoner's flight across Dartmoor, may also be mentioned out of the total of over thirty plays which gained him eminence among the dramatists of the day. In a career of prolific authorship, his other works include numerous volumes of essays, short stories, poetry, and some criticism, notably *Two Essays on Conrad* (1930). The Order of Merit was conferred on him in 1929, and he received the Nobel Prize for Literature in 1932. Although his novels have retained a substantial popular readership, adverse commentary by D. H. *Lawrence and Virginia *Woolf, who thought his work superficial, was a factor in the decline of his reputation among literary critics. His *Collected Works* appeared in twenty-six volumes between 1927 and 1934. Catherine Dupré's biography of Galsworthy was published in 1976.

GARDAM, Jane (Mary), née Pearson (1928–), British novelist, born in Coatham, Yorkshire, educated at Bedford College, London University. Her first published work, *A Few Fair Days* (1971), was a children's book based on her own childhood experiences on the north-east coast of England. She has written several other children's books; her novels *A Long Way from Verona* (1971), *The Summer After the Funeral* (1973), and *Bilgewater* (1977), all with teenage protagonists, are characterized by their combination of literary allusion and dramatic emotional scenes. Her adult novels, *God on the Rocks* (1978) and *Crusoe's Daughter* (1988), also depend on literary sources—Emily Brontë and Daniel Defoe—for their portrayal of the repressed romantic child at the mercy of her more worldly elders. This theme recurs in her short stories, *The Sidmouth Letters* (1980), *The Pangs of Love* (1983), and *Showing the Flag* (1989). The stories in *Going into a Dark House* (1994) are preoccupied with the familiar themes of death, the elderly, and ghosts through which Gardam observes commonplace suffering. Gardam uses her skills at economical scene-setting and local and period detail to dramatize contrasting milieux or class divisions. Recent novels include *The Queen of the Tambourine* (1991), an epistolary work transforming comedy into discomfort when a woman's obsessive concern for others heralds her undoing; and *Faith Fox* (1996).

GARDNER, Erle Stanley (1889–1970), American *detective story writer, born in Malden, Massachusetts, and after an adventurous youth admitted to the California Bar in 1911. From 1923 he combined law with writing, contributing hundreds of stories under many pseudonyms to pulp mystery and Western magazines. After the success of his first novel, *The Case of the Velvet Claws* (1933), which introduced his best-known detective, the Los Angeles lawyer Perry Mason, he devoted himself exclusively to writing, later settling on a ranch in Southern California, where he employed six full-time secretaries and produced over eighty Perry Mason stories, ending with *The Case of the Postponed Murder* (1977). Fast-moving, with crisp dialogue, and full of legal detail deployed with skill and ingenuity, these deservedly enjoyed immense popularity. His stories about a Californian district attorney, Doug Selby (*The D.A. Calls It Murder*, 1937) are less successful, but the twenty-nine novels about the private detective partners Donald Lam and Bertha Cool, originally published under the pseudonym of A. A. Fair (such as *The Bigger They Come*, published in Britain as *Lam to the Slaughter*, 1939) are fresh and amusing. In 1948 Gardner established the Court of Last Resort, a private organization which examined the cases of prisoners believed to have been unjustly convicted, and succeeded in obtaining a number of releases. Several films have been made of the Perry Mason stories, and a well-known television series in which he is portrayed by Raymond Burr.

GARDNER, Dame Helen (Louise) (1908–86), British scholar, critic, and editor, born in London, educated at St Hilda's College, Oxford, where she taught before becoming Oxford's Merton Professor of English Literature from 1966 until her retirement in 1975. Among her early works was *The Art of T. S. Eliot* (1949), a subject to which she returned in *T. S. Eliot and the English Poetic Tradition* (1965) and the highly regarded *The Composition of Four Quartets* (1978), the first such study to make use of the poet's working drafts. Her editions of Donne's *Divine Poems* (1952) and *Elegies, and Songs and Sonnets* (1965) superseded Sir Herbert *Grierson's editorial work on Donne's poetry and are unlikely to be surpassed for textual accuracy. Gardner's numerous other critical works include *Edwin Muir* (1961), *King Lear* (1967), and *Religion and Literature* (1971). *The Business of Criticism* (1959) and *In Defence of the Imagination* (1982) express her belief in maintaining the humanist traditions of criticism. She is most widely known as the editor of *The New Oxford Book of English Verse* (1972).

GARDNER, John (Champlin, Jr) (1933–82), American novelist, poet, short-story writer, editor, and critic, born in Batavia, New York, educated at De Pauw University, Washington University, and the University of Iowa. Gardner successfully combined the life of the teacher and scholar (particularly of medieval and classical literature) with those of novelist, editor, translator, and librettist. After finishing his doctorate at the University of Iowa (he submitted a novel, *The Old Men*, for his dissertation), Gardner took up his first teaching position at Oberlin College in Ohio in 1958 before moving to California State University at Chico where he taught from 1959 until 1962. His early writings are mainly editorial and critical: he co-edited *The Forms of Fiction* (1962), and his edition of *The Complete Works of the Gawain-Poet in a Modern English Version* (1965) was extremely well received. His first novel, *The Resurrection* (1966), was not successful, but his second, *The Wreckage of Agathon* (1970), which draws extensively on the literature of classical antiquity, brought him considerable critical attention. His most successful novel was *Grendel* (1971), in which Gardner reimagines the story of Beowulf from the point of view of the monster; the novel is simultaneously learned, comic, and, at times, deeply moving and offers powerful testimony to Gardner's critical view that literature should be 'wise, sane, and magical'. His later novels include *The Sunlight Dialogues* (1972), *Jason and Medea* (1973, a novel in verse), *Nickel Mountain* (1973), *October Light* (1976; National Book Critics Circle Award), *Freddy's Book* (1980), and *Mickelsson's Ghosts* (1982) thought by many critics to be his most demanding and ambitious novel. Gardner's fiction as a whole explores what he calls 'the nature and ramifications of man's two essential choices, affirmation and denial', and in an age when so much of the fiction of his contemporaries is characterized by submission to life's destructive forces his is notable for its affirmation of the transcendent power of art. His many other writings include one volume of poetry, *Poems* (1978); the critical studies *On Moral Fiction* (1978), which caused controversy for the charges of 'immorality' levelled at some of Gardner's contemporaries, and the posthumously published *The Art of Fiction: Notes on Craft for Young Writers* (1983), both valuable for their articulation of his theories of fiction; several volumes of writings for children, notably *A Child's Bestiary* (1977) and *The King of the Hummingbirds and Other Tales for Children* (1977); and three opera libretti, published as *Three Libretti* (1979). At the time of his death in a motorcycle accident Gardner was a Professor of English at the State University of New York at Binghamton. His fiction has received wide critical attention: among the better studies are David Cowart, *Arches and Light: The Fiction of John Gardner* (1983) and Dean McWilliams, *John Gardner* (1990).

GARFITT, Roger (1944–), British poet, born in Wiltshire, educated at Merton College, Oxford. He worked as a schoolteacher for several years before becoming a freelance writer. He was editor of **Poetry Review* from 1978 to 1981, and has contributed reviews and articles to most of Britain's leading literary magazines and journals. He has also been a presenter of BBC Radio 3's 'Poetry Now' series. He was married to the poet Frances *Horovitz until her death in 1983. In addition to his inclusion in numerous anthologies he has produced such collections as *Caught on Blue* (1970), *West of Elm* (1975), and *Given Ground* (1989). Many of his poems are notable for their precision and immediacy in presenting incidents and images from the natural world. His work is characterized by a scrupulous quality in its rhythms and diction. His later writing displays a deepening concern with socio-cultural themes, which are treated with the accuracy and integrity for which his earlier work was acclaimed.

GARIOCH, Robert (1909–81), Scottish poet, originally named Robert Garioch Sutherland; he was born in Edinburgh, where he was educated at the university. After a long career as a schoolteacher in England and the east of Scotland, in 1965 he returned to the University of Edinburgh as a lexicographer and transcriber in the School of Scottish Studies. Garioch's poetry is largely written in Scots, out of his stated intention of affirming the separate identity of the Scottish nation. *17 Poems for 6d. in Gaelic, Lowland Scots and English* (with Sorley *MacLean, 1940) was the first of numerous collections of his poetry, which include *Chuckies on a Cairn* (1949), a 'dramatic fantasy' entitled *The Masque of Edinburgh* (1954), *The Big Music* (1971), and *Doktor Faust in Rose Street* (1973). His considerable skills in versification combine with the high-spirited energies of his colloquial diction to remarkable effect in many of the comically satirical poems for which he is best known; recurrent targets were the municipal and cultural pretensions he identified in Edinburgh. He produced many translations into Scots from the works of Pindar, Belli, Apollinaire, and others. His four years as a prisoner of war in Italy and Germany are recorded in the prose memoir *Two Men and a Blanket* (1973). His *Complete Poetical Works*, edited by R. Fulton, was published in 1983.

GARLAND, (Hannibal) Hamlin (1860–1940), American novelist and short-story writer, born in West Salem, Wisconsin, educated at Cedar Valley Seminary, Osage, Iowa. Garland is an important figure in the history of American literary realism and one of the foremost exponents of 'local-colorism' or regionalism in American fiction at the turn of the century. In 1884 he moved to Boston where he began his literary and intellectual education, immersing himself in the poetry of Walt Whitman, the fiction of William Dean *Howells, the economics of Henry George, and the writings of evolutionary theorists such as Charles Darwin and Herbert Spencer. His first major publication, *Main-Travelled Roads: Six Mississippi Valley Stories* (1891), remains his most valuable contribution to American letters. The volume grew over subsequent editions; the final edition of 1922 (for which Garland wrote a preface) contains eleven stories which seek to challenge, and invert, the idyllic picture of life in the Midwest and the Great Plains that was inexorably becoming a powerful American myth. Four novels and a further collection of stories preceded *Crumbling Idols: Twelve Essays on Art* (1894) in which Garland sets out his theories of art and literature and describes his practice of 'veritism', a synthesis of the innovative ideas of literary impressionism, influenced by his reading of French critics, and the more established techniques of realism and naturalism. Garland attempted to sustain his theory in later works, notably *Rose of Dutcher's Coolly* (1895). The most important works of his later period are his four volumes of autobiography and family history; of these, *A Son of the Middle Border* (1917) and *A Daughter of the Middle Border* (1921) are an invaluable record of life on the frontier. His extensive literary friendships are recorded in *Roadside Meetings* (1930). See Joseph B. McCullough's *Hamlin Garland* (1978).

GARLICK, Raymond (1926–), British poet, born in London, educated at University College of North Wales. After working as a schoolteacher in Wales, he taught in the Netherlands from 1960 to 1967, when he became a senior lecturer at Trinity College, Carmarthen. In 1949 he founded the magazine *Dock Leaves*, later known as *The Anglo-Welsh Review*, which, until its disappearance in 1988, was one of the principal forums for *Anglo-Welsh poetry. His collections of poetry include *A Sense of Europe* (1968), *A Sense of Time* (1972), *Incense* (1976), *Collected Poems 1946–1986* (1987), and *Travel Notes* (1992). Much of his verse espouses pan-European republicanism, the moral and ideological context in which he locates his intense personal and cultural perceptions of Wales. His best work, much of it reflecting his experiences of France and the Netherlands, combines an energetic mobility of tone and rhythm with the emotional and intellectual force of his political convictions. The best-known of his critical works is *An Introduction to Anglo-Welsh Literature* (1970). With R. Mathias, he edited *Welsh Poetry: 1480–1990* (1993).

GARNER, Helen (1942–), Australian novelist and short-story writer, born in Victoria, educated at the University of Melbourne. Her dismissal from her teaching job in a Melbourne secondary school in 1972, for using explicit language when answering her pupils' questions about sex, became a *cause célèbre*. She later worked as a journalist, reviewer, and actress, and lived in Paris for a number of years. She achieved immediate success with her first novel, *Monkey Grip* (1977), which is set in Melbourne during the 1960s and focuses on the relationship between the narrator, Nora, and Javo, a heroin addict. The novel was later filmed. Her other works include two novellas, *Honour, and Other People's Children* (1980); a novel, *The Children's Bach* (1984), about the disintegration of a conventional, middle-class marriage; a collection of short stories, *Postcards from Surfers* (1985), widely acclaimed for its cool portrayal of diverse relationships; and *Cosmo Cosmolina* (1992), a novella and two linked stories, which make use of *magic realism.

GARNER, Hugh (1913–79), Canadian novelist and short-story writer, born in Batley, Yorkshire, and taken to Canada when he was six. Garner is regarded as one of the major exponents of realism in Canadian fiction. During the 1930s he travelled in the West, eking out a living from whatever temporary employment he could find, and fought for the Loyalists in the Spanish Civil War. His Second World War naval experiences provided the basis for his first novel, *Storm Below* (1949), which describes six days at sea in 1943. Garner's early life in Cabbagetown, a run-down inner city district of Toronto, underlay *Cabbagetown* (1950) which initially appeared in a heavily edited version; only when the full text was published in 1968 did it receive critical acclaim as one of Canada's finest social novels. It is written in the clear and direct prose style that characterizes all Garner's fiction and describes the hardship of Depression life in working-class Toronto and the lack of opportunity afforded to the district's youth. Garner's other novels include *The Silence on the Shore* (1962) and *The Intruders* (1975), which gives an account of the gentrification of Cabbagetown. His other works include volumes of short stories, three crime novels with Toronto settings (*The Yellow Sweater*, 1952; *Men and Women*, 1966; and *The Legs of the Lame*, 1967), and an autobiography, *One Damn Thing after Another* (1974). He is the subject of a critical biography by Paul Steuwe: *The Storms Below: The Life and Turbulent Times of Hugh Garner* (1988).

GARNETT, Constance (Clara) (1862–1946), British translator, born in Brighton, educated at Newnham College, Cambridge. A member of the *Fabian Society, she worked as librarian at the People's Palace in the East End of London. In 1889 she married Edward *Garnett, through whom she met Peter Kropotkin and other exiled Russian revolutionaries. From them she learned Russian in the months before the birth of her son, David *Garnett, in 1892. The following year she made her first journey to Russia, bearing money for the relief of famine in Nizhniy Novgorod and secret communications from her Russian friends in London; she met Tolstoy at Yasnaya Polyana. Upon returning to Britain, she began her monumental endeavour of translating some seventy volumes of Russian prose, including all the novels of Dostoevsky, Gogol, and Turgenev and most of the plays and stories of Chekhov. Her work did much to bring about the widespread influence of the Russian novel on English literature in the early decades of the twentieth century. Biographical material is contained in David Garnett's *The Golden Echo* (1953) and C. G. Heilbrun's *The Garnett Family* (1961).

GARNETT, David (1892–1981), British novelist and critic, born in Brighton, the son of E. and C. *Garnett, educated at the Royal College of Science. Prominent among the younger associates of the *Bloomsbury Group, he was involved in a famous *ménage à trois* with Duncan Grant and Vanessa Bell while working on the land as a conscientious objector during the First World War. He subsequently ran a bookshop in

Soho. His greatest success was his first novel, *Lady into Fox* (1922), a fantasy of metamorphosis in which a woman, transformed into a vixen, gradually becomes unmanageably wild. He continued his success with *A Man in the Zoo* (1924), in which a man unhappy in love successfully offers himself to a zoo as a human exhibit; *The Sailor's Return* (1925), in which a seaman attempts to live in a Dorset village with his black wife; *The Grasshoppers Come* (1931); and the biographical *Pocohontas: or the Nonpareil of Virginia* (1933). After many years he produced *Aspects of Love* (1955; later made into a musical by Andrew Lloyd Webber); the fantasies *Two by Two* (1963) and *The Master Cat* (1974); and the historical novel *The Sons of the Falcon* (1972). Garnett published three volumes of autobiography, *The Golden Echo* (1953), *The Flowers of the Forest* (1955), and *The Familiar Faces* (1962); he edited the letters of T. E. *Lawrence (1938), the novels of T. L. Peacock, and *Carrington: Letters and Extracts from her Diaries* (1979).

GARNETT, Edward (1868–1936), British writer, born in London, the son of Richard Garnett, husband of C. *Garnett, and father of D. *Garnett. For some time he was employed in the British Museum Reading Room. In the early 1900s he became known for his criticism, some of it being later collected as *Friday Nights* (1922), and plays, notably *The Breaking Point* (1907), banned by the Examiner of Plays; the play's publication, complete with an impassioned assault upon the Examiner and his principles, marked the start of the long campaign in England to abolish stage censorship. *Papa's War* (1919) was a collection of satirical fantasies. For many years he was a publisher's reader of great influence, doing much to advance the careers of J. *Conrad, D. H. *Lawrence, E. M. *Forster, and others.

GARRIGUE, Jean (1914–72), American poet, born in Evansville, Indiana, educated at the University of Chicago and the University of Iowa; she held a succession of posts as an instructor in English and poet-in-residence at numerous American colleges and universities, chiefly in the New York area. Her first collection of poetry, *The Ego and the Centaur* (1947), was acclaimed for the rich precision of diction and imagery which characterizes all her writing. A more confident lyricism emerged in the formally complex poems of *The Monument Rose* (1953). Her subsequent collections, *A Walk by Villa d'Este* (1959) and *Country Without Maps* (1964), drew on her extensive travels in Europe and Asia in poems remarkable for the brilliant acuteness of her descriptive talent. *New and Selected Poems* (1967) was followed by *Studies for an Actress* (1973), a collection of elegiac poignancy in which an element of radical political disaffection becomes evident. Her other publications include the novella *The Animal Hotel* (1966), *Essays and Prose Poems* (1970), and the short critical study *Marianne Moore* (1965). *Selected Poems* appeared in 1992.

GASCOYNE, David (Emery) (1916–), British poet, born in Harrow, Middlesex, educated at Salisbury Cathedral Choir School and Regent Street Polytechnic. His first collection of poetry, *Roman Balcony* (1932), appeared when he was 16. Advance royalties on his novel *Opening Day* (1933) enabled him to travel to Paris in 1933, where the work of the *surrealistes* made a profound impression upon him. His *A Short Survey of Surrealism* (1935), with his translations of Dali's *Conquest of the Irrational* (1935) and Breton's *What Is Surrealism?* (1936), established him as the leading British spokesman for the movement. His disjunctive and often unsettlingly sinister surrealist prose poems were collected in *Man's Life Is This Meat* (1936). His subsequent volume, *Poems 1937–1942* (1943), used richly musical adaptations of conventional verse forms to achieve its striking fusions of vividly observed imagery and visionary intuitions. The collection contains what is considered to be Gascoyne's finest work, much of it forming a powerfully imaginative response to the devastation of warfare. From 1947 until 1964 he lived mainly in France, a period during which his output as a poet underwent a drastic decline. His other works include *Night Thoughts* (1956), a 'radiophonic poem' commissioned by the BBC, and *The Sun at Midnight: Poems and Aphorisms* (1970). *Collected Poems*, with Gascoyne's autobiographical introduction, appeared in 1988. *Paris Journal 1937–1939* (1978) and *Journal 1936–1937* (1980), jointly published as *The Collected Journals* in 1990, form valuable accounts of his involvement in the political and artistic movements of the late 1930s. *Collected Verse Translations*, edited by R. Skelton and A. Clodd, appeared in 1970.

GASS, William H(oward) (1924–), American novelist, short-story writer, and literary critic, born in Fargo, North Dakota, educated at Kenyon College, Ohio Wesleyan University, and Cornell University. For three years he studied philosophy at Cornell where he attended seminars led by the philosopher Ludwig *Wittgenstein which he later referred to as 'the most important intellectual experience of my life'. In 1950 he took up a teaching post at the College of Wooster, Ohio, where he began writing short stories and his first novel, *Omensetter's Luck* (1966); when the novel was published Gass was fêted as one of the most gifted of the new generation of American writers. From Wooster he subsequently taught philosophy at Purdue University, Indiana. *In the Heart of the Heart of the Country* (1968; revised edition 1981) is a collection of five short fictional pieces which remains, arguably, Gass's most important work to date. In these stories Gass experiments with a variety of rhetorical styles, notably in the extravagant languages of their otherwise *naïf* narrators. *Fiction and the Figures of Life* (1970), a collection of Gass's critical and philosophical essays, contains his important meditation on the nature of fiction, 'The Concept of Character in Fiction'; included also are essays on Jorge Luis Borges, Gertrude *Stein, Robert *Coover, Vladimir *Nabokov, J. F. *Powers, and John *Updike. *Willie Masters' Lonesome Wife* (1971) is a work of 'mixed-media' fiction; *World Within the Word* (1978) and *Habi-*

tations of the Word: Essays (1985) are further volumes of essays. The essay *On Being Blue: A Philosophical Inquiry* (1976) show his great indebtedness to Gertrude Stein's theories of language. Though Gass has been resistant to the categorization of his writings as *'post-modernist' he is generally discussed in a context that includes other American post-modernist writers. *William Gass* (1990) by Watson L. Holloway is a critical study.

GATES, Henry Louis, Jr (1950–), African-American critic, born in Keyser in West Virginia, educated at Yale and at Cambridge University where his tutor was Wole *Soyinka. He became Professor of English at Duke University. Gates has contributed significantly to the increased accessibility of African-American writings, especially of the pre-twentieth-century period. In *Figures in Black: Words, Signs and the Racial Self* (1987), *Black Letters and the Enlightenment: On Race, Writing and Difference* (1986), and *The Signifying Monkey: Towards a Theory of Afro-American Literary Criticism* (1988), he explores the distinctive nature of black writing by looking to the linguistic and musical feature of black culture, especially the ritual function of language in black tradition. Gates's interest in literary theory seeks to evaluate the most appropriate theoretical approach to black writing. He explores literary expression in Africa and the Caribbean as well as America in the monographs *The History and Theory of Afro-American Literary Criticism, 1773–1881* (1978), *Black Literature and Literary Theory* (1984), *The Essential Soyinka* (1991), *Loose Canons: Notes on the Culture Wars* (1992), and *Colored People* (1993).

GÉBLER, Carlo (1954?–), Irish novelist, born in Dublin; he moved to London with his parents, the writers Ernest Gébler and Edna *O'Brien, at an early age. He graduated from the National Film School. His first novel, *The Eleventh Summer* (1985), like much of his work, is set in England and in Ireland; it evokes, in clear prose, the slowly changing countryside of Ireland through the childhood memories of Paul Weismann. His other novels include *August in July* (1986), *Work and Play* (1987), and *Life of a Drum* (1990). In *Malachy and His Family* (1991), he tells the story of a young boy who discovers his father's other family in America and a brother with the same name as himself. The novel is partly set in Ireland, as is a non-fictional volume about Enniskillen, *The Glass Curtain: Inside an Ulster Community* (1992). He is also the author of some children's fiction and a travelogue, *Driving through Cuba: An East–West Journey* (1988).

GEE, Maggie (Mary) (1948–), British novelist, born in Poole, Dorset, educated at Somerville College, Oxford. Her first novel, *Dying in Other Words* (1981), a blackly comic meditation on death focusing around a group of Oxford students, was followed by *The Burning Book* (1983), an apocalyptic vision of nuclear holocaust, which received widespread critical acclaim. In 1983 she was selected as one of the Book Marketing Council's Best Young British Novelists. *Light Years* (1985), which concerns a love affair between a rich London socialite and an impoverished writer, is given a certain resonance by its use of cosmic imagery, which links the lives of its protagonists to the movements of the planetary system. *Grace* (1988), a novel based on a real murder in Britain during the 1980s, of anti-nuclear campaigner Hilda Murrell, fuses political thriller, polemic, and lyrical description of childhood. The sombreness of this work was matched by *Where Are the Snows?* (1991), a love story which followed its two wilful and solipsistic protagonists, Alexandra and Christopher, across several continents and over several decades as they abandon the responsibilities of their life in London (including the care of Christopher's teenage children). Set against the background of ecological disaster and increasing international tension, the book offers a kind of parable about the selfishness of individual desires. *Lost Children* (1994) was a return to form with its account of the plight of homeless children in London, focused in its central drama about a mother in search of a lost daughter.

GEE, Maurice (1931–), New Zealand novelist, born in Whakatane in the North Island; educated at the University of Auckland. Gee's first story was published in *Landfall* in 1955; his first book, *The Big Season* (1962), showed his interest in New Zealand small town life which he later developed to great effect. His early fiction includes *A Special Flower* (1965), *My Father's Den* (1972), and *Games of Choice* (1976). In his trilogy, *Plumb* (1978), *Meg* (1981), and *Sole Survivor* (1983), a family study from three perspectives, Gee was able to explore in relentless and absorbing detail the complex interplay of history, politics, and religion in shaping the fortunes of one family's very different members; the final volume takes Gee's saga to the fifth generation. The trilogy remains a major addition to post-war New Zealand fiction; not least of its triumphs is its ability to accommodate sharply individual, if not eccentric, and more broadly international themes and issues. It was followed by the novel *Prowlers* (1987), a book of similar focus, while *Burning Boy* (1990) confirms Gee's craftsmanship and natural understatement. In *Going West* (1992) the narrator's unvarnished account of the life of his dead friend, a noted poet and ne'er-do-well, contrasts with the literary pieties of his biographer's version; the chilling *Crime Story* (1994) is set at the interface of politics, high finance, and the criminal underworld. Stories in *A Glorious Morning Comrade* (1974) were republished as *Collected Stories* (1986). David Hill's critical study *Introducing Maurice Gee* appeared in 1981.

GELBER, Jack (1932–), American dramatist, born in Chicago, educated at the University of Illinois. Gelber is chiefly famous for his play about drug addiction, *The Connection* (1959), produced by the *Living Theatre in 1959 when it ran for over 700 performances. His other plays are *The Apple* (1961), *Square in the Eye* (1965), *The Cuban Thing* (1968), *Sleep* (1972), *Barbary Shore* (adapted from Norman *Mailer's novel)

(1973), *Farmyard* (1975), *Rehearsal* (1976), and *Starters* (1980). Gelber is clearly influenced by Pirandello, Brecht, and Samuel *Beckett, most obviously in the way his plays experiment with the relationship between audience and performers within the context of the illusionist scenario of theatrical space. Thus in *The Connection*, the title refers not only to the user and pusher of the drug world, but also to the actors and audience in the theatre. The experimental, disruptive, sometimes baffling world of Gelber's plays makes no concession to the orthodoxies of the theatrical event, as in his use of Brechtian alienation techniques, and his persistent questioning of the distinction between fiction and reality.

GELLHORN, Martha (1908–), American novelist and journalist, born in St Louis, Missouri, educated at Bryn Mawr College, Philadelphia. Her career began as Paris correspondent for the **New Republic*. Her fiction, which is noted for its clarity and directness, is invariably informed by her experiences as a journalist and traveller. *The Trouble I've Seen* (1936), a set of four novellas, originated in her investigations of urban poverty during the American Depression. In 1937 she became a war correspondent with *Collier's* magazine and met Ernest *Hemingway (to whom she was married from 1940 to 1945) while covering the Spanish Civil War; the short stories in *The Heart of Another* (1941) portray American reporters in Spain. Her subsequent novels include *A Stricken Field* (1940), set in Prague on the eve of the Second World War; *His Own Man* (1961), on expatriate life in Paris; and *The Lowest Trees Have Tops* (1969), which is set in Mexico. Among her further collections of short stories are *The Honeyed Peace* (1954), *Two by Two* (1958), and *The Weather in Africa* (1978); *The Short Novels of Martha Gellhorn* appeared in 1991. Her journalism is collected in *The Face of War* (1959), reports from a succession of major conflicts in Europe and Asia, and *The View from the Ground* (1988), articles on a wide range of social and political topics. *Travels with Myself and Another* (1979) is an autobiography.

GEMS, Pam (1925–), British dramatist, born in Hampshire, educated at Manchester University. She was in her forties, and had worked as a gardener and a research assistant at the BBC, when she began to write plays. Her best work has involved the place of women in society—and especially that of the woman of passion and energy in a society hostile to those things—and combines feminist conviction with openness of mind and a sense of moral complexity. It includes *Dusa, Fish, Stas and Vi* (1976), a serious and sometimes moving comedy about disparate young women sharing a flât in London; *Queen Christina* (1977), about the great Swedish monarch; *Piaf* (1978), a tough, unsentimental portrait of the French singer; and a new version of *La Dame aux Camelias*, *Camille* (1984). The last three plays were first performed by the Royal Shakespeare Company, as was Gems's study of the French Revolution, *The Danton Affair* (1986). Other plays include *Aunt Mary* (1982); *Loving Women* (1984), about two young women's involvement with the same man; and *Deborah's Daughter* (1994), about the widow of an oil magnate who, with her daughter, gets caught up in a coup in an unnamed North African country. She has also written for television, and adapted Chekhov's *Uncle Vanya* (1979) and *The Cherry Orchard* (1982), Ibsen's *A Doll's House* (1980), and Lorca's *Yerma* (1993) for the stage.

Georgian Poetry: originally the title of a series of five poetry anthologies produced between 1912 and 1922, the term is more generally applied to predominantly rural and stylistically conventional verse of the kind the books tended to contain. The series was conceived by Edward *Marsh, who proposed to invigorate English poetry at a time when it remained dominated by late Victorian reputations; the title *Georgian Poetry* reflected the enthusiastic sense of a new era that accompanied the accession of George V in 1910. Rupert *Brooke, strongly favoured by Marsh and regarded as a leading Georgian, publicized the venture and Harold *Monro acted as publisher. In commercial terms the series was highly successful. The following were eminent among the total of thirty-six poets who contributed to the anthologies: Lascelles *Abercrombie, Gordon *Bottomley, W. H. *Davies, Walter *de la Mare, Wilfrid *Gibson, Ralph *Hodgson, James *Stephens, and Andrew *Young. While these and others produced work of note, the pedestrian rhythms, rural sentimentality, and imaginative banality of much of the verse has given 'Georgian' a distinct pejorative sense in the modern critical vocabulary. The blank verse dramas contributed by Abercrombie, Bottomley, and Gibson were among the most interesting material published in the series. Although the anthologies contained work by Edmund *Blunden, Robert *Graves, and Siegfried *Sassoon, the most talented of the younger Georgian poets, Marsh did not publish any of the more disturbing examples of their *war poetry; objections to the constraints imposed by his taste were voiced by Graves and Sassoon, the latter choosing not to be represented in the final volume of the series. D. H. *Lawrence was another contributor who disagreed with Marsh's fundamentally conservative views on questions of form and content. After Marsh discontinued the series in 1922, coincidentally but aptly the year in which *The *Waste Land* appeared, J. C. *Squire's *London Mercury* provided a platform for Georgian verse, and a target for its detractors, for whom it represented the antithesis to poetic *Modernism. F. Swinnerton's *The Georgian Literary Scene, 1910–1935* (1950) surveys the social and cultural contexts of Georgian poetry.

GERHARDIE (originally GAERHARDI), William (Alexander) (1895–1977), British novelist, born in St Petersburg. He served in the British embassy at Petrograd, and the British military mission in Siberia during the First World War, after which he was educated at Worcester College, Oxford. There he wrote *Anton Chehov* (*sic*) (1923), the first book on Chekhov to be written in English, and his first novel, *Futility: A Novel on Russian Themes* (1922), which enjoyed a considerable *succès d'estime*, winning the praises of H. G. *Wells and Edith *Wharton among others. The novel captured the mood of the 1920s and is remarkable for the informal, conversational manner with which great recent events—the Russian Revolution and its aftermath—are presented. Gerhardie led a very social life, with many love affairs, and enjoyed the friendship of Wells and *Beaverbrook. His second novel, *The Polyglots* (1925), concerns George Hamlet Alexander Diabologh, a young officer who, on a military mission in the Far East, encounters a highly eccentric Belgian family. The novel has a Chekhovian mingling of comedy and tragedy, of the inconsequential and the grave. *Pending Heaven* (1930) is the story of Paradise deferred for two literary friends who are also rivals in love. *Resurrection* (1934) derives from an actual experience of Gerhardie's when he felt his spirit rise from his body, and argues passionately for life after death. *Of Mortal Love* (1936) draws on Gerhardie's considerable amatory experience. His lively autobiography *Memoirs of a Polyglot* (1931) was followed by *The Romanovs* (1940), a historical biography of the Russian dynasty. For the rest of his life he lived increasingly as a recluse. Michael *Holroyd and Robert Skidelsky edited *God's Fifth Column* (1981), a biography. His name appeared as Gerhardie for the first time on the revised collected edition of his works, published in ten volumes in the early 1970s. There is a biography by Dido Davies (1990).

Getting of Wisdom, The, a novel by Henry Handel *Richardson, published in 1910. The novel is based on the author's experiences as a boarder at the Presbyterian Ladies College, in Melbourne, during 1883 to 1887. It consists in a series of ironically depicted scenes whereby Laura Rambotham, ostracized by her teachers and peers because of her name, unusual clothes, and forthright opinions, painfully acquires wisdom about herself and the world. Torn between a defiant individuality and the desire to gain approval, she learns that the 'unpardonable sin is to vary from the common mould'. Though personally immune to male appeal, she seeks to distinguish herself by inventing an intrigue with the local curate; new depths of rejection and misery result upon her exposure. A period of obsequiousness and caution is followed by a genuine friendship and acceptance into the school's prestigious literary society. Her final piece of wisdom comes when an appeal to God is apparently answered by an opportunity to cheat in her examinations; Laura takes the opportunity, subsequently resenting God as a double-dealing and pitiless being. Regarded as a classic portrait of the artist as an awkward adolescent, the novel was successfully produced as a film in 1977.

GHOSE, Zulfikar (1935–), Pakistani-American novelist and poet, born in Sialkot (now Pakistan); he lived in England from 1952 to 1969, and later became a professor at the University of Texas. He is the author of several volumes of poetry, including *The Loss of India* (1964), *The Violent West* (1972), and *A Memory of Asia* (1984); his *Selected Poems* were published in Pakistan in 1991. His first novel, *The Contradictions* (1966), was followed by *The Murder of Aziz Khan* (1969). Both works are set in the Indian subcontinent, but several others, including *The Beautiful Empire* (1975), *A Different World* (1978), *A New History of Torment* (1982), and *Figures of Enchantment* (1986) have a Latin American background; they have been described as 'picaresque prose epics of Brazilian history' and 'tales of the South American unknown'. In his novel *The Triple Mirror of the Self* (1992) Ghose juxtaposes his imaginative recreations of 'primitive' Latin America with pictures of recent Peruvian history and accounts of a boyhood in colonial India and a student's life in 1950s Britain. Whereas the segments that are set in the rainforest are mainly concerned with erotic fantasies, the Peruvian section is a convincing analysis of nationalism and expatriation. *The Triple Mirror* is a conflation of all Ghose's previous preoccupations and concerns, an exile's lyrical reclamation of lost sources, and a manifesto of the artist as dreamer and philosopher.

GHOSH, Amitav (1956–), Indian novelist, travel writer, and anthropologist, born in Calcutta, educated at Delhi University and at Oxford. His writings in all genres display his experiences of a variety of cultures. His first novel, *The Circle of Reason* (1986), was praised by some critics for its spontaneity and vitality, but others found it derivative of Rushdie's **Midnight's Children* and the school of *magic realism. His second, more original and accomplished novel, *The Shadow Lines* (1988), chronicles the intertwined destinies of an Indian and an English family over several decades and generations, and is particularly effective in its imagistic and documentary recreations of Ghosh's native Bengal. Though complex in structure and narrative technique, the novel indicates a return by younger Indian authors to a mode more sober than the flamboyant post-modernism of *Rushdie and his imitators. *In an Antique Land* (1992) conflates fictional techniques and historical research in an ambitious evocation of Egypt's richly eclectic past and its increasingly puritanical present. Ghosh's accounts of his travels have appeared in **Granta* magazine.

GIBBON, Lewis Grassic, pseudonym of James Leslie MITCHELL (1901–35), Scottish writer, born in Aberdeenshire; he grew up in Kincardineshire, the setting of his great trilogy, *A Scots Quair* (1932–4). He worked on the *Aberdeen Journal* and *Scottish Farmer* before joining the Royal Army Service Corps and the RAF, travelling extensively throughout Persia, India, and Egypt. His experiences enliven his early fiction, *Hanno* (1928), *Stained Radiance* (1930), and *The Calends of Cairo* (1931), and a further group of novels—*The Thirteenth Disciple* (1931), *Three Go Back* (1932), and *The Lost Trumpet* (1932)—express his interest in the then fashionable theory of Diffusionism. The three volumes of *A Scots Quair* (*Sunset Song*, 1932; *Cloud Howe*, 1933; and *Grey Granite*, 1934) comprise an epic account of the tensions and contradictions within Scottish history, seen through the life of a young woman, Chris Guthrie, voiced in a vigorously colloquial Scots. Chris's life takes her from country to town and city, and the narrative both intensifies a personal history and invests it with mythic resonance. The author's political sympathies are also prominent in *Spartacus* (1933). Gibbon was involved in various projects associated with Hugh *MacDiarmid, and he is a pivotal figure in the *Scottish Renaissance.

GIBBONS, Stella (Dorothea) (1902–89), British novelist and short-story writer, born in London, educated at University College, London. She worked for the *Evening Standard*, and as book reviewer for *The Lady*. The latter occupation presumably suggested the elements of literary parody that made her first novel, **Cold Comfort Farm* (1932), so successful. Its continuing popularity has obscured her other novels—she wrote over twenty, plus four collections of stories—though they tend to be sentimental comedies of manners involving a clash of social codes. In *Ticky* (1943), a dispute arises between the officers of a Victorian regiment and their hapless servants over possession of the Pleasure Grounds; as in *Cold Comfort Farm*, harmony is restored between the classes and celebrated by marriages. *Westwood* (1946) evokes wartime London, and *Here Be Dragons* (1956), life in Hampstead, both works in which a girl gains self-knowledge from contacts with another stratum of society. Gibbons, elected a Fellow of the Royal Society of Literature in 1950, retired from writing novels with *The Woods in Winter* (1970).

GIBSON, Graeme (1934–), Canadian novelist, born in London, Ontario, educated at the University of Edinburgh and the University of Western Ontario. He taught at Ryerson Polytechnic Institute, Toronto, from 1961 to 1968. Since 1973, he has lived with the novelist Margaret *Atwood. *Five Legs* (1969), his first novel, and its sequel *Communion* (1971), present an analysis of the cultural ills of modern Canada in their narratives of man's defective relations with nature and the worsening breakdown of social cohesion. Set in nineteenth-century Ontario, *Perpetual Motion* (1982) is widely regarded as his finest work; the chief protagonist's fanatical project of harnessing natural energies to run a perpetual motion machine allegorizes the modern world's obsessive exploitation of the environment. *Gentleman Death* (1995) is a more recent novel. Gibson's other works include the interviews collected in *Eleven Canadian Novelists* (1973).

GIBSON, Wilfrid (Wilson) (1878–1962), British poet, born at Hexham, Northumberland, the upland landscapes and communities of which strongly inform much of his writing. He became a social worker in the East End of London in 1912, when he met Edward *Marsh and Rupert *Brooke; he developed a close friendship with the latter, who bequeathed him a share in his posthumous royalties. With Lascelles *Abercrombie and John *Drinkwater, in 1912 he founded *New Numbers*, in which Brooke's celebrated *1914* sonnet sequence first appeared. His early collections included *Stonefolds* (1907), a series of short verse dialogues set in the Northumbrian fells, which also provide the setting for *Krindlesdyke* (1922), the most ambitious of his numerous verse-dramas. He established a firm reputation through his work's appearances in **Georgian Poetry*; his poetry is distinguished, however, from the sentimental pastoralism associated with the Georgians by the realism with which he presents the rigours of rural experience. *Battle* (1915) contains the majority of the poems relating to his period of active service on the Western Front, which remain his best-known work. The increasingly urban social consciousness that becomes evident in *Fires* (1912) is central to the long poems of *Livelihood* (1917), which base their narratives in documentary accounts of industrial conditions. *Collected Poems, 1905–1925* was published in 1926. His later collections, which continue to display his concern with the experiences of factory workers, include *Hazards* (1930), *The Alert* (1940), and *The Searchlights* (1943).

GIBSON, William (Ford) (1948–), American novelist and screenwriter, born in Conway, British Columbia, educated at the University of British Columbia. He became renowned as the main inventor of *Cyberpunk on the publication of his first novel, *Neuromancer* (1984), which is recognized as the seminal text of that movement. With this novel and its sequels *Count Zero* (1986) and *Mona Lisa Overdrive* (1988), Gibson has created a sense of the near future where Japanese corporations dominate a cybernetic universe in which its protagonists scramble for survival in an information network called 'cyberspace'. Clearly not himself computer literate, Gibson has succeeded in creating an environment existentially shaped by the information revolution. Beneath a polished exterior these works are highly romantic and show the influence of R. *Chandler's Philip Marlowe. *The Difference Engine* (1990), written with Bruce *Sterling, is an 'Alternate World' analysis of a nineteenth-century Britain transformed by the success of Charles Babbage's computer; *Virtual Light* (1993) is set in Near Future San Francisco. Gibson's short fiction has been collected in *Burning Chrome* (1986).

Gift, The, a novel by Vladimir *Nabokov, published in 1938. Generally considered the greatest of Nabokov's Russian works, *The Gift* was published as *Dar* in Paris (1937–8) under Nabokov's pseudonym of V. Sirin, though this edition lacked the fourth chapter which was not restored until the New York publication (again in Russian) in 1952; the English translation appeared in 1963. The novel explores one of Nabokov's great thematic preoccupations, the life of the *émigré* intellectual and writer (one that he himself lived), through the story of the poet and critic Fyodor Godunov-Cherdyntsev over three years of his life in Berlin in the 1920s. Each of the five long chapters enlarges the narrator's story while at the same time exploring what are, for Nabokov, important aspects of the Russian cultural and literary tradition. The second chapter is famous for its interweaving of details of the life of Fyodor's father with a biographical and critical account of the works of Alexander Pushkin. The fourth chapter, deleted from the first French edition, concerns the nineteenth-century social critic Nikolai Chernyshevsky and is reputed to have caused much offence to those Russian *émigré* writers and intellectuals who had read it.

GILBERT, Kevin (1933–), Australian part-Aboriginal writer, born in Condoblin, New South Wales. Orphaned at seven, and brought up in welfare homes and by relations, he worked as a labourer, and married early. Found guilty in 1956 of murdering his wife, Gilbert was sentenced to life imprisonment, and in this environment developed interests in both art and literature. On his parole in 1971, *The Cherry Pickers* (perf. 1971; pub. 1988), written in prison, was the first play by an Aboriginal writer to be performed in Australia. A book of verse, *End of Dreamtime* (1971), was heavily edited and changed without Gilbert's permission; an authorized version of his poems is *People ARE Legends* (1978), while *The Blackside* (1990) collects the best of Gilbert's past work, together with later verse to give a formidable impression of his talent, and a searing reflection on modern Australia. The experience of 'white' interference with Aboriginal texts was discussed by some of his subjects in the series of interviews, *Living Black: Blacks Talk to Kevin Gilbert* (1977) where the 'white' machinery of the tape recorder was suspect even in black hands. He has continued his work of promoting direct representation of Aboriginal literature in *Inside Black Australia: An Anthology of Aboriginal Poetry* (1988) and has written of the environmental and historical factors in contemporary Aboriginal culture in *Because a White Man'll Never Do It* (1994). He has also published books for children.

GILBERT, Martin (John) (1936–), British biographer and historian, born in London, educated at Magdalen College, Oxford. In 1962 he became a fellow of Merton College, Oxford. From 1968 to 1988 Gilbert was engaged in completing the biography of Sir Winston *Churchill, having formerly been research assistant to Randolph Churchill, the author of the first two volumes (1966, 1967); the subsequent six volumes appeared in 1971, 1975, 1976, 1983, 1986, and 1988. The work, which includes seven 'companion volumes' reprinting documents of historical importance, is regarded as the largest biography in the history of publishing; *In Search of Churchill* (1994) is an account of his experiences. Gilbert's numerous publications as a modern historian include *The European Powers, 1900–1945* (1965), *Exile and Return: The Emergence of Jewish Statehood* (1978), *The Holocaust* (1986), and *The First World War* (1993). *Shcharansky: Hero of Our Time* (1986) is among his other works as a biographer. *The Churchill War Papers* (vol. i) appeared in 1993.

GILCHRIST, Ellen (1935–), American short-story writer and novelist, born in Grace, Mississippi, educated at Millsaps College; she later worked in a variety of journalistic occupations. Though Gilchrist began her writing career as a poet, it was the publication of her first volume of stories, *In the Land of Dreamy Dreams* (1981), that placed her in the ranks of noted Southern women writers, inspired by Katherine Anne *Porter, Eudora *Welty, and Flannery *O'Connor, but more contemporary and less Gothic in tone. Her novel *The Annunciation* (1983) was followed by a second collection of short fiction, *Victory over Japan* (1984), which returned to the familiar Southern scenes of her first book; it was compared favourably with the work of Southern peers Anne *Tyler and Ellen *Douglas. Gilchrist excels in portrayals of Southern family life, through the perspectives of affluent middle-aged women, chronicling with zest and humour their affairs, preoccupations, and ambivalent relationships. Her third collection, *Drunk with Love* (1986), was praised for the limpid grace of its language, but her limitation of range and growing interest in 'New Age' terminology and thought, most particularly in the autobiographical *Falling Through Space: The Author's Journals* (1987) and the novel *The Anna Papers* (1988), the account of a cancer-ridden woman's celebratory suicide, has been less well received. *I Cannot Get You Close Enough* (1990) is a collection of linked novellas. Some of her best stories were collected in *The Blue Eyed Buddhist* in 1990.

Giles Goat-Boy; or, The Revised New Syllabus, a novel by John *Barth, published in 1966. *Giles Goat-Boy*, John Barth's fourth novel, depicts a world which has become a vast university divided into two 'campuses', East and West, each of which is controlled by huge, seemingly omnipotent computers. The novel is, in effect, an ambitious science-fictional spoof, and, despite its somewhat excessive length, is frequently immensely funny and merciless in its satire. The title refers to the novel's 'hero', Giles Goat-Boy, the world's first programmed man who, though the son of a computer, is reared by a herd of goats; the subtitle alludes to a kind of revised mythology, a new 'New Testament', which will replace the outmoded myths of the past. Giles Goat-Boy's adventures form the essentially picaresque framework which structures the novel.

GILL, (Arthur) Eric (Rowton) (1882–1940), British stone-carver, engraver, letter-cutter, and typographer, born in Brighton, educated at the Central School of Arts and Crafts, London. His home in Ditchling became the centre of a group of artists which included David *Jones. Having become a Roman Catholic in 1913, Gill carved the *Stations of the Cross* (1914–18) at Westminster Cathedral; this and *Prospero and Ariel* on Broadcasting House are among his most famous sculptures. Gill designed the printing types 'Perpetua' and 'Gill Sans-Serif' for the Monotype Corporation and typefaces for Robert Gibbings's Golden Cockerel Press, for which he also produced wood-carvings for many of its books including *The Four Gospels* (1941). In his books Gill frequently stressed the religious nature of artistic and physical beauty; they include *Christianity and Art* (1927), *Art-Nonsense and Other Essays* (1929), *The Necessity of Belief* (1936), and an *Autobiography* (1940). He also wrote a number of erotic works. A biography by Fiona MacCarthy of 1989 revealed some interesting and less pleasant aspects of his life including incestuous relationships with two sisters and two daughters.

GILLIATT, Penelope (1932–93), British novelist and short-story writer, born in London, educated at Queen's College. She worked at the Institute of Pacific Relations in New York before beginning her long career as a distinguished film critic with the *Observer* and the **New Yorker*; her criticism is collected in *Unholy Fools* (1971) and *Three Quarter Face* (1980). Her first novel, *One By One* (1965), gained wide notice for its wittily pessimistic evocation of a plague in modern London. The seriocomic element is common to all her fiction, as is her economy of style and acute social observation, notably of middle-class mores. *A State of Change* (1967), which concerns a Polish girl's displacement in London after the Second World War, was followed by *The Cutting Edge* (1978), a remarkable treatment of the emotional bond between two brothers in very different circumstances, *Mortal Matters* (1983), an ironic comparison of the values of succeeding generations, and *A Woman of Singular Occupation* (1988), a disquieting love-story set in Istanbul on the eve of the First World War. Her numerous collections of short stories include *What's It Like Out?* (1968), *Splendid Lives* (1977), *22 Stories* (1986), and *Lingo* (1990). Gilliatt also wrote several plays and the highly acclaimed screenplay for *Sunday Bloody Sunday* (1971). She was married to John *Osborne (1963–68).

GILMAN, Charlotte (Anna) Perkins (1860–1935), American novelist and social theorist, born in Hartford, Connecticut. After an insecure and unhappy childhood she studied art, and supported herself by teaching until her marriage to Charles Stetson in 1884. After recurrent periods of severe depression she left her husband, moved to California, and wrote 'The Yellow Wallpaper' (1892), a chilling fantasy of mental breakdown whose subtext is a powerful critique of women's enforced passivity under patriarchy. She became a dedicated champion of women's right to economic independence and 'world work'; several polemic studies, of which *Women and Economics* (1898) was the most famous, established her as a leading theorist of the early feminist movement. Happily married to her cousin George Gilman in 1900, she continued lecturing and writing on issues of gender and social organization, and popularized many of her ideas in fictional form: a stream of short stories and serialized novels, including *What Diantha Did* (1912) and *Benigna Machiavelli* (1914), appeared in her own monthly magazine *The Forerunner*. Though sometimes over-schematic, Gilman's fiction at its best, notably in the lively feminist utopia *Herland* (1915), conveys a challenging vision of alternative possibilities. Aged 75, she committed suicide rather than prolong a losing battle with cancer. See also UTOPIA AND ANTI-UTOPIA.

GILMORE, Dame Mary (1865–1962), Australian poet, born in New South Wales. After a childhood spent in the bush, she taught in mining towns and in Sydney, and became involved with contemporary radical movements. Her poetry first appeared in **Bulletin* from 1903 onwards, and in 1912 she published her first collection, *Marri'd and Other Verses*. This was followed by numerous others, including *The Passionate Heart* (1918), an indictment of war; *The Tilted Cart* (1925); *The Wild Swan* (1930); and *Under the Wilgas* (1932), in all of which she combined short, lyrical poems with polemical outbursts against injustice and inhumanity. *Battlefields* (1939) contains her most strongly radical verse. Her last volume, *Fourteen Men* (1954), published when she was almost 90, offers her calm reflections on death. She also published two volumes of reminiscences and anecdotes, *Old Days: Old Ways* (1934) and *More Recollections* (1935), both of which express her love of the Australian landscape and her concern for the Aboriginal people. She was created a Dame for her services to literature and society in 1936.

GILROY, Beryl (*c.*1925–), Guyanese novelist and autobiographical writer, born in Berbice, British Guiana (now Guyana). She moved to Britain in 1951, where she worked for the BBC Caribbean service. She later became a schoolteacher in London and a counselling psychologist. Her autobiographical book, *Black Teacher* (1976), hard-hitting, but often cheerful and humorous in tone, examines primary education and racial discrimination in Britain. Set in Guyana, her first novel, *Frangipani House* (1986), deals with 'Mama King', an elderly grandmother fighting to liberate herself from the eponymous 'home' for people like her, and also from her past. Compassionate, wry, and psychologically acute, yet fundamentally optimistic, the novel questions many current assumptions about old age. Her second novel, *Boy Sandwich* (1989), exposes how the elderly are treated in London. *Sunlight on Sweet Water* (1994) is a collection of short stories with an autobiographical undertone, set in British Guiana in the 1930s and 1940s. *Love in Bondage: Steadman and Joanna* (1991), a historical romance based on the journals of John Steadman, tells of the marriage of an eighteenth-century Dutch soldier to a slave-woman.

Ginger Man, The, see DONLEAVY, J. P.

GINSBERG, Allen (1926–), American poet, born in New Jersey, educated at Columbia University. After working in various capacities from 1948 to 1954, he settled in San Francisco where **Howl and Other Poems* was published in 1956, establishing him as the most widely noted participant in the *San Francisco Renaissance. The influence of William Carlos *Williams, whom he had known since the late 1930s, was apparent in a number of the collection's precisely observed and rhythmically flexible shorter lyrics. *Kaddish and Other Poems* (1961) confirmed his reputation as a poet of idiosyncratic accomplishment and direct emotional appeal. Taking its title from the Jewish form of prayer for the dead, the title poem mourns and celebrates Ginsberg's mother; the political perspective established by treatment of her socialist convictions provides the basis for the poem's continuation of his uncompromising critique of American society, which subsequently extended into his public role as a protester against the Vietnam War (see VIETNAM WRITING). During the later 1960s he was internationally pre-eminent among the proselytizers of 'flower power', a term of his coinage, and its associated cults of hallucinogenic drugs and Eastern mysticism. Among numerous subsequent collections are *Planet News* (1968), *The Fall of America* (1972), *Mind Breaths* (1978), *Plutonian Ode* (1981), *Collected Poems 1947–1980* (1985), *White Shroud* (1987), and *Cosmopolitan Greeting* (1994). Although Ginsberg occasionally uses rhymed forms, his most impressive work remains typified by rhythmically charged free verse, often conveying his visionary political philosophy or autobiographically discursive cultural commentary; in either mode he frequently demonstrates the disarming qualities, among them a highly developed sense of the absurd, which prompted Christopher *Ricks to classify him as 'a great comic poet'. His numerous other works include *The Yage Letters*, a correspondence with William *Burroughs (1963), and *Journals: Early Fifties–Early Sixties* (edited by Gordon Ball, 1977). *Allen Ginsberg* (1989) is a biography by Barry Miles. See also UNDERGROUND POETRY.

GIOVANNI, Nikki (Yolande Cornelia) (1943–), African-American poet, born in Knoxville, Tennessee, educated at Fisk University, Nashville, University of Pennsylvania School of Social Work, Philadelphia, and Columbia University, New York. She has held several academic appointments. Her poetry reflects the political turbulence, and African-American struggle for civil rights, of the late 1960s and early 1970s. Colloquial and expansive in style, the poems are notable for their revolutionary political rhetoric. *The Women and the Men* (1975) is generally considered to be her best volume. Other collections include *Black Judgement* (1968), *My House* (1972), and *Those Who Ride the Night Winds* (1983). Her other books include *Gemini: An Extended Autobiographical Statement on My First Twenty-Five Years of Being a Black Poet* (1971), *A Dialogue: James Baldwin and Nikki Giovanni* (1973), *A Poetic Equation: Conversations Between Nikki Giovanni and Margaret Walker* (1974), *Sacred Cows* (1988), a collection of essays, and *Racism 101* (1994), on African-American social conditions. *Grand Mothers* (1994) and *Knoxville, Tennessee* (1994) are poems for children. She is also a compelling performer of her own work, which is recorded in *Legacies* (1976) and *The Reason I Like Chocolate* (1976).

Giovanni's Room, a novel by James *Baldwin, published in 1956. The candour of Baldwin's treatment of homosexuality gave the novel something of a *succès de scandale*. Told in the first person by a young white American, it is a story of sexual evasion, infatuation, and betrayal. David, whose true inclinations are homosexual, arrives in Paris, where he encounters Giovanni, a young Italian waiter, with whom he falls in love. The feeling is reciprocated and David goes to live with Giovanni in a seedy little room which takes on the quality of a retreat for both the lovers. However, on holiday in Spain, David becomes involved with an American girl and, unable to stand the strain of being sexually unconventional, asks her to marry him, eschewing Giovanni and his milieu entirely. Giovanni, deeply hurt and now out of work, is forced to return to his former lover, a gross man who disgusts him and whom he eventually murders. When David learns of this terrible event, and that Giovanni is to die by the guillotine, he is shocked into some kind of emotional honesty. Despite its taut construction and vividly evoked background, the novel occasionally betrays its author's ambivalence towards his characters, and indeed his central theme, and is therefore, perhaps, not wholly successful; however, it deserves its reputation and its place in literary history for the sensitivity and tenderness with which homosexual love is rendered.

Girls of Slender Means, The, see SPARK, MURIEL.

GITTINGS, Robert (William Victor) (1911–92), British biographer and poet, born in Portsmouth, educated at Jesus College, Cambridge, where he was a supervisor in History from 1933 to 1940. He subsequently worked as a writer and producer with the BBC and became a freelance writer in 1963. His earlier collections of poetry include *Wentworth Place* (1952), the title sequence of which centres on incidents during the latter part of John Keats's life, and *Famous Meetings* (1953), which recreates encounters between historical personages; both make imaginative use of dramatic monologue forms. Among his further collections are *This Tower My Prison* (1961) and *American Journey* (1972), which contains 'In Memoriam of John Berryman', one of the finest tributes to that poet. A *Collected Poems* was produced in 1976. Although Gittings's poetry sustains a high level of technical competence and interest, his achievements as a biographer are more highly valued. *John Keats* (1968), *Young Thomas Hardy* (1975), and *The Older Hardy* (1979) have earned him wide recognition as one of the most eminent of modern literary biographers; *Claire Clairmont and the Shelleys* (1992) was written with his wife, Jo Manton. *The Makers of Violence* (1951) and *Out of This Wood* (1955) are amongst his plays.

GLASGOW, Ellen (1874–1945), American novelist, born in Richmond, Virginia, the first major novelist of the South. Her first novel, *The Descendant* (1897), was followed by *The Voice of the People* (1900), which began her long series of novels charting the social and political history of the South from the Antebellum through the Civil War to the ravages of the 'carpetbaggers' during the Reconstruction and the subsequent assimilation of the Southern states into the Union. Emulating Balzac, she divided her novels into different groups: 'Novels of the Commonwealth (dealing with the Virginian past)'; 'Novels of the Country'; and 'Novels of the City'. The earliest of these include *The Battleground* (1902), *The Deliverance* (1904), *The Wheel of Life* (1906), *The Ancient Law* (1908), *The Romance of a Plain Man* (1909), and *The Miller of Old Church* (1911). In *Virginia* (1913), a poignant study of a woman brought up to be nothing but a social ornament, and *Life and Gabriella* (1916), she focuses her powers of empathy and analysis on the condition of women. Three novels of political and social conflict followed: *The Builders* (1919), *Old Man in His Time* (1922), and **Barren Ground* (1925); and three penetrating satirical novels of manners: *The Romantic Comedians* (1926), *They Stooped to Folly* (1929), and *The *Sheltered Life* (1932). In *Vein of Iron* (1935), Glasgow returns to the theme of rural life, exploring the qualities of endurance necessary for survival in the harsh environment of which she writes. *In This Our Life* (1941; Pulitzer Prize) describes an aristocratic Virginian family fallen into decadence. Her posthumously published autobiography *The Woman Within* (1954) movingly describes her tormented emotional life and her aspirations for her fiction.

GLASPELL, Susan (1876–1948), American novelist and dramatist, born in Davenport, Iowa, educated at Drake University, Des Moines, Iowa. Glaspell wrote ten novels and many short stories but made her enduring reputation as a playwright. In 1913 she married George Cram Cook, writer, director, and moving spirit behind one of the most important theatre companies in modern American history, the Provincetown Players, who discovered Eugene *O'Neill. With Cook and O'Neill she wrote and acted for this company until Cook's death in 1924. Her best plays are *Trifles* (1920), *The Outside* (1920), *Inheritors* (1921), and *The Verge* (1924); her last play, *Alison's House* (1930), was a popular success. Of her novels, *Fidelity* (1915), *Brook Evans* (1928), *The Morning Is Near Us* (1939), and *Judd Rankin's Daughter* (1945) have survived best. Her autobiography *The Road to the Temple* appeared in 1927. As a dramatist her work is marked by a degree of formal experimentalism evident in the sparse settings and characterization of *The Outside*, and more obviously in her most extravagant work, *The Verge*. In this symbolist drama the heroine, Claire Archer (her name suggests both clarity and ambition), repudiates the roles of wife, mother, and finally, lover, in a desperate search for release into a new mode of being for which her amateur work as a scientific experimenter with hybrid plants acts as a metaphor. In her novels as in her plays, Glaspell's concern with the social role of women is repeatedly pictured through her representation of sexual deprivation and marital despair, often in a frontier landscape.

Glass Menagerie, The, a play by Tennessee *Williams, produced in 1944 and published in 1945. Partly expressionist in form, it is the play in which Williams came to terms with the emotional side of his own early life in St Louis, and in doing so, greatly extended the range of contemporary American theatre. Tom Wingfield, who stands for Williams himself and who also acts as narrator/chorus, lives with his mother, Amanda, and his crippled, withdrawn sister, Laura. Amanda, who has been deserted by her husband, dreams about her (largely fictitious) past as a Southern belle and projects her longing for fulfilment on to her children, demanding that Tom should get ahead in his job instead of brooding about becoming a writer, and that Laura should marry. She persuades Tom to bring home a friend, Jim O'Connor, in order to introduce him to Laura, and deludes herself into imagining a romantic connection between them. Jim wins Laura over by his warmth of manner and she, recognizing him as the boy she was attracted to in High School and incorporated into her innocent fantasies, shows him her collection of glass animals—the 'menagerie' of the title. Her favourite piece is a glass unicorn, and it is this which is damaged—its horn broken—when the two attempt to dance. Jim tells Laura that his private name for her during their schooldays was 'Blue Roses', after which he kisses her. However, the tenderness of the mood is broken when he reveals that he is already engaged to another girl. Amanda blames Tom for this disastrous outcome, and, furious at this injustice, he leaves home for good.

Glastonbury Romance, A, the most widely read of John Cowper *Powys's novels, first published in New York in 1932. Vividly pictorial and of a rich thematic and imaginative texture, the work runs to over 1,100 pages in standard editions. Some forty principal characters manifest the variousness of human life in its emotional, social, and, most importantly, spiritual aspects. As the book's central symbol, the Holy Grail denotes the essential substance of faith underlying all forms of religious belief. The narrative concerns events in Glastonbury following the founding by John Geard, a man with a 'superhuman mania for heightened life', of a spiritual cult fusing elements of paganism and Christianity. He is opposed by Philip Crow, whose pursuit of power is antithetical to all the Grail represents. The book ends with Crow's downfall and the death of Geard, who drowns in pursuit of higher levels of experience in the apocalyptic final chapter entitled 'The Flood'. *A Glastonbury Romance* is highly regarded for the powerful combination of drama and sensitivity characterizing its emotional and psychological realism. Its metaphysical content, centring on the need for a singleness of vision encompassing all physical and spiritual experience, tends to provoke the vague rhetoric of mystical assertion which has been a factor in the decline of Powys's reputation.

GLENDINNING, Victoria (1937–), British biographer and novelist, born in Sheffield, educated at Somerville College, Oxford, and the University of Southampton. She was a part-time schoolteacher from 1960 to 1969, when she became a psychiatric social worker; she was subsequently an editorial assistant at the **Times Literary Supplement* until 1978. *Eliza-*

beth Bowen: Portrait of a Writer (1977) argued persuasively for the importance of Bowen's contribution to modern fiction and established Glendinning's reputation as an authoritative and sensitive biographer. The book was the first of a series of treatments of literary women which continued with *Edith Sitwell: A Unicorn among Lions* (1981) and her acclaimed and popular work *Vita: The Life of Vita Sackville-West* (1983); Rebecca *West was deeply impressed by *Vita* and, shortly before her death, asked Glendinning to write her biography: *Rebecca West: A Life* appeared in 1987. *Anthony Trollope* (1992), her first extended study of a male author, was also published to wide acclaim. Her other works include *The Grown Ups* (1989), a humorous novel of sexual intrigue, and *Electricity* (1995), an account of a spirited young woman's adventures in the 1880s and the choices of her age: science versus religion, spiritualism or rationalism, gas or electricity. Glendinning married Terence de Vere *White in 1982.

GLOVER, Denis (1912–80), New Zealand poet, born in Dunedin, educated at Canterbury University College, where he later taught English. In 1936 he founded the Caxton Press, which was to have a distinguished role in New Zealand literature, especially poetry. Artistic respect for ordinary human endeavour informs Glover's work. He referred to his 'observational verse'; for one volume he described himself as 'enjoys talking, drinking and gesticulating. Dislikes writing and rhubarb.' In collections such as *The Wind and the Sand* (1945), *Sings Harry and Other Poems* (1951), and especially in the successful *Arawata Bill* (1952), Glover demonstrates his skill in the use of colloquial and ballad forms; the Arawata Bill persona (a lone gold prospector) proved an ideal device for the poet to reflect laconically upon ambiguous responses to New Zealand scenery and situations. *Hot Water Sailor* (1962) was an entertainingly informative autobiography. Selected poems were published as *Enter without Knocking* (1964; enlarged 1971), while *Diary to a Woman* (1971) comprised love poems. Later poems included *Dancing to My Tune* and *Wellington Harbour*, both published in 1974, *Come High Water* (1977), and *Selected Poems* (1981). There is a biographical and critical study, *Denis Glover* (1977), by John Thomson.

GLUCK, Louise (1943–), American poet, born in New York City, educated at Sarah Lawrence College and Columbia University. Like her contemporary Frank *Bidart, Louise Gluck is frequently described as a 'post-confessional' poet and in her early work the influence of Sylvia *Plath is strongly felt, notably in her first published volume, *Firstborn* (1969). Later volumes, among them *The House of Marshland* (1975) and *Descending Figures* (1983), reveal a sharpened, more intensified, if somewhat distanced, treatment of autobiographical experience. In *The Triumph of Achilles* (1985; National Book Critics Award), arguably her most distinguished collection, she writes with austere starkness about the death of her father, while *Ararat* (1990) shows a continuing preoccupation with the themes of family and family relationships; later volumes of verse include *The Wild Iris* (1992) and *The First Four Books of Poems* (1995). Her *Proofs and Theories: Essays on Poetry* (1992) draws together her critical writings on the art of poetry. Gluck taught at Goddard College in Vermont before taking up a teaching post at Warren Wilson College in North Carolina.

GLYN, Elinor (1864–1943), British novelist, born in Jersey; she was a prolific author of romantic and sensational books of which the first, *The Visits of Elizabeth* (1900), was a witty and sharply critical novel about the Edwardian upper classes. It was not until the publication of *Three Weeks* (1907) that she achieved notoriety through what was thought a shocking novel, describing the love affair of a Balkan queen who, desperate for an heir, takes as her lover a young English aristocrat; the novel shocked the Edwardians with its sensual imagery and its scenes on the famous tiger skin where the pair made love. In later life she lived in Hollywood and wrote screenplays. See also ROMANTIC FICTION.

Go-Between, The, a novel by L. P. *Hartley, published in 1953. Leo, now aged 60-plus, recalls the events of a childhood summer half a century earlier: invited to Brandham Hall in Norfolk, the country home of his schoolfriend Marcus Maudsley, he rapidly falls under the spell of Marcus's beautiful older sister Marian. He becomes the innocent courier of secret letters between Marian and local farmer Ted Burgess, only gradually realizing that he is the go-between in a clandestine love affair. Leo's developing respect for Marian's fiancé Lord Trimingham forces him to a moral crisis. He refuses to carry any more letters, but changes his mind when Marian accuses him of ingratitude. Later, on his thirteenth birthday, Marian's mother discovers Leo taking a letter. He refuses either to surrender it or to explain Marian's absence for the rest of the day, until Mrs Maudsley insists he accompany her on a search for her daughter: the conclusion of this is the discovery of Marian and Burgess making love in an outhouse. Later Ted Burgess commits suicide. The novel is a brilliant evocation of a social world and historical period. Richly complex, its theme is the individual's search for identity, and the relationship of childhood experience to adult problems. The narrative is framed by a prologue, in which the narrator confronts the challenge of the past's failed hopes and opportunities, and an epilogue in which he revisits Marian and agrees to go on one last errand—to her grandson, to give him his own version of the story—and thereby begins to resolve his personal emotional legacy of the past. Harold *Pinter wrote the screenplay for Joseph Losey's film of 1970.

GODBER, John (Harry) (1956–), British playwright, born in Upton, Yorkshire, educated at Bretton Hall College and the University of Leeds. After working as a schoolteacher, in 1984 he became artistic director of the Hull Truck Theatre Company, where he has directed the first productions of most of his plays. Predominantly in the mode of comic social commentary, Godber's plays often deal with events and activities within the common experience of the northern audiences that are his primary constituency. His remark that 'the dancer not the poet is the father of the theatre' reflects the emphasis on live performance that underlies his procedures as a writer-director who stimulates improvisation in bringing his works to production. *Up 'n' Under* (1984), *Bouncers* (1984), *Teechers* (1987), and *On the Piste* (1990) are among his best-known plays. He has also written extensively for several popular television shows and scripted the successful *The Ritz* (1987) series. His other plays include *Blood, Sweat, and Tears* (1986), *Happy Families* (1991), and *The Office Party* (1992).

GODDEN, (Margaret) Rumer (1907–), British novelist, born in Sussex; she spent her childhood in India and from the age of 12 was educated in various English schools. She returned to India to start a dancing school, married, and spent the war years alone in Kashmir with her small children. The predominant themes in her novels are the lives of foreigners in Eastern settings, the inner thoughts of children, and religious life. Her first novel, *Black Narcissus* (1939), focused on an Anglican Sisterhood in India, and was later filmed; a later work, *In This House of Brede* (1969), is set in an English Catholic nunnery written after she converted to Roman Catholicism. India formed the background of *The River* (1946), amongst others, and was filmed by Jean Renoir in 1950. Ballet featured in *A Candle for St Jude* (1948); her understanding of children was shown in *The Greengage Summer* (1958) and *The Battle of the Villa Florita* (1963), both filmed, and in her many books for children. In *A Fugue in Time* (1945) and *China Court* (1961) she skilfully draws in the past with the present. Among Godden's later fictions are the novels *Coromandel Sea Change* (1991), a fairy tale of romance and political connivery set in a lushly described, almost mythologized modern South India; and *Pippa Passes* (1994), the story of a young ballet dancer coming to terms with adulthood and her developing sexual desires. There are two volumes of autobiography, *A Time to Dance, No Time to Weep* (1987) and *A House with Four Rooms* (1989).

GODLEY, A(lfred) D(ennis) (1856–1925), British poet and classicist, born in Co. Leitrim, educated at Balliol College, Oxford; he became a fellow and tutor of Magdalen College. In 1910 he was appointed public orator of Oxford, an office he held until his death. His numerous volumes of translation include *The Histories of Tacitus* (1887, 1890) and *The Odes and Epodes of Horace* (1898). Among his other works are *Socrates and Athenian Society in His Day* (1896) and *Oxford in the Eighteenth Century* (1908). As a poet he is principally noted for his reflections in light verse on the life and institutions of Oxford University; in such examples as 'The Infant Scholar' and 'The Megalopsychiad' his great dexterity in versification combines to memorable effect with the engaging sense of the ridiculous that is frequently present in his humour. His five collections of poetry include *Verses to Order* (1892), *Lyra Frivola* (1899), and *The Casual Ward* (1912). In addition to his Oxford verses he wrote poetry out of his interests in mountaineering, archaeology, and Irish affairs, generally retaining his humorous emphasis. *Fifty Poems* (1927) is a selected edition prepared by C. L. Graves and C. R. L. Fletcher.

God that Failed, The: Six Studies in Communism, a book containing six autobiographical essays, edited and introduced by Richard Crossman, and published in 1950. The book, which grew out of a discussion between Crossman and Arthur *Koestler, made a great impact at the time and was considered one of the most effective intellectual weapons in the Western armoury of the Cold War. The six contributors were Koestler, Ignazio Silone, André Gide, Stephen *Spender, Richard *Wright, and Louis Fischer. Dr Enid Starkie, who suggested the title of the book, compiled and edited Gide's reminiscences from various sources, because he was too ill to provide an essay. All the contributors had been either communists or 'fellow-travellers' sympathetic to communism. Scrupulously honest about past motives, and from a disillusioned perspective, the essays all illuminate ideological commitment by intellectuals and artists in turbulent, crisis-ridden times when recollected in tranquillity. Crossman declared: 'We were not in the least interested in swelling the flood of anti-Communist propaganda or in providing an opportunity for personal apologetics.'

GOGARTY, Oliver (Joseph) St John (1878–1957), Irish poet and memoirist, born in Dublin, where he trained as a surgeon at Trinity College's medical school. In 1904 he and James *Joyce lived briefly in the Martello Tower at Sandymount that provides the setting for the start of **Ulysses*, in which Gogarty is cast as 'stately plump Buck Mulligan'. He was a senator of the Irish Free State for fourteen years and was well known in Irish public and literary life. His volumes of verse include *Hyperthuleana* (1916), *An Offering of Swans* (1923), and *Wild Apples* (1928). W. B. *Yeats thought highly of his poetry, featuring seventeen poems by Gogarty in his *Oxford Book of Modern Verse* (1936), a representation generally considered disproportionate to his importance as a poet. He possessed, however, a distinct lyrical talent and a sharply epigrammatic wit. *Collected Poems* appeared in 1951. The *Abbey Theatre produced several of his plays, among them *Blight* (1917) and *The Enchanted Trousers* (1919). In 1939 he moved to New York, occupying himself mainly with writing and lecturing. He is best known for the prose memoirs *As I Was Going Down Sackville Street* (1937) and *It Isn't this Time of Year at all* (1954); *Tumbling in the Hay* (1939) is a semi-autobiographical novel of considerable comic individuality. *Oliver St John Gogarty: Man of Many Talents* by J. B. Lyons was published in 1980.

Going After Cacciato, see O BRIEN, TIM.

GOLD, Herbert (1924–), American novelist, born in Cleveland, Ohio, educated at Columbia University and the Sorbonne. Gold's early novels, for example *Birth of a Hero* (1951) and *The Prospect before Us* (1954), are characteristic of much of the American realist writing of the 1950s, emphasizing the plight of the individual in a conformist society. His later novels, such as *The Optimist* (1959), are markedly less realist in their techniques and show a burgeoning preoccupation with parable and fable. *Salt* (1963) is a feverish portrait of the anonymity of New York City life executed through the points of view of the participants in a romantic triangle. *Fathers: A Novel in the Form of a Memoir* (1967) recounts Gold's family history over several generations and the process of 'Americanization' that the family underwent; *Family: A Novel in the Form of a Memoir* (1981) is a later reworking of the same technique, here again concerned with the history of a Jewish immigrant family. Other novels include *He/She* (1980), *True Love* (1982), and *Mister White Eyes* (1984). Gold is also an accomplished short-story writer and a witty, trenchant essayist; the early stories are collected in *Fifteen by Three* (1957) and *Love and Like* (1960), his essays in *The Age of Happy Problems* (1962) and *First Person Singular: Essays for the Sixties* (1963). His other works include *Fiction of the Fifties: A Decade of American Writing* (1959), *Stories of Modern America* (1961), *The Magic Will: Stories and Essays of a Decade* (1971), and an autobiography, *My Last Two Thousand Years* (1972).

GOLD, Michael, pseudonym of Itzok GRANICH (1893–1967), American novelist, playwright, and political journalist, born in New York City, educated at New York and Harvard Universities. Gold was one of the most important and influential members of the group of left-wing intellectuals associated with such publications as **Masses*, *The Liberator*, and the *New Masses* between 1916 and 1930. He was born to a poor immigrant Russian-Jewish family, brought up on New York's Lower East Side, and active in union politics from an early age. Subsequently, he became associated with the Provincetown Players, for whom he wrote three one-act plays and through whom he met Eugene *O'Neill. He co-founded the *New Masses* and was its editor from 1928 until 1947; through this journal Gold promoted a proletarian, neo-Stalinist view of the place of literature in society. He was actively involved in the leftward turn of the American intelligentsia in the early years of the New Deal. His first volume of stories was *The Damned Agitator and Other Stories* (1926); his best-known work of fiction was *Jews Without Money* (1930), a semi-autobiographical picture of New York ghetto life. Two of his plays, *Hoboken Blues* (1928) and *Fiesta* (1929), reflect his commitment in the possibilities of political drama, and his anthology *Proletarian Literature in the United States* (1935) is an important source-book for radical writing in the USA in the inter-war years (see PROLETARIAN LITERATURE IN THE USA). John Pyros's *Gold: Dean of American Proletarian Writers* (1979) is a useful study.

Golden Age; the term conventionally refers to the popular escapist crime fiction of the 1920s and 1930s, which avoided any attempt at social realism and offered in its place a highly stylized, closed setting mystery. Typically, a murder was solved by the intuitive and deductive skills of a personalized detective, entertaining the reader by a teasing display of false trails ('red herrings') before the revelatory final scene. The best examples of these 'clue-puzzle' stories came from Agatha *Christie and Dorothy L. *Sayers in the UK and S. S. *Van Dine in the USA. See also DETECTIVE FICTION.

Golden Bough, The, Sir James *Frazer's *magnum opus*, subtitled 'a study in magic and religion', first published in two volumes in 1890 and completed in twelve volumes which appeared between 1907 and 1915. A one-volume abridgement appeared in 1922, and a supplement, *Aftermath*, in 1936. *The Golden Bough* presents an enormously detailed anthropological thesis in accordance with Darwinian evolutionism: all religions, Frazer maintained, follow similar patterns of development, emerging from primitive magical belief towards increasingly comprehensive theological schemata, and having as their essential dynamic the biological imperative for survival; the advent of scientific wisdom in the West marks the final stage of this process of mental and institutional organization. The book develops out of Frazer's interest in the ancient priesthood of Nemi, the rule of which was that succeeding priests attained office by slaying their predecessors, having plucked 'the Golden Bough', to which the *Aeneid* alludes, before so doing. The work develops around two central questions: 'Why had the priest . . . to slay his predecessor? And why . . . had he to pluck the Golden Bough?' The first is answered in terms of ensuring the continuing vitality of the priesthood, the second by establishing that the Golden Bough, identified as mistletoe, magically embodied the priest's power. While the scientifically agnostic tones of Frazer's conclusion speak of 'the long tragedy of human folly and suffering which has unrolled itself before the readers of these volumes', his sensitivity towards his material is such that the work possesses considerable imaginative grandeur and dramatic power; 'at times he seems consumed with devout astonishment at his own subject-matter', remarks Robert Fraser, author of *The Making of The Golden Bough* (1990) and editor of the essays in *Sir James Frazer and the Literary Imagination* (1990). The latter examines the pervasive effect of Frazer's study on twentieth-century literature, to which it has contributed more meaningfully than to anthropology; T. S. *Eliot refers to it in the notes to *The *Waste Land* (1922) as 'a work . . . which has influenced our generation profoundly', indicating *The Golden Bough*'s significance for many writers, among whom are James *Joyce, W. B. *Yeats, John *Synge, Joseph *Conrad, D. H. *Lawrence, and Robert *Graves.

Golden Bowl, The, a novel by Henry *James, published in 1904. *The Golden Bowl* is the last of the three great final novels—the others are *The Wings of a Dove* (1902) and *The Ambassadors* (1903)—which many critics hold to be the pinnacle of his achievement in fiction. The plot, one of labyrinthine moral complexity, revolves, essentially, around Maggie Verver, the daughter of an American millionaire, who marries Prince Amerigo, an impoverished Italian aristocrat. One of Maggie's friends, another American, Charlotte Stant, with whom Amerigo has had an affair (they had not married because neither had enough cash), subsequently marries Maggie's father, Adam Verver (the chief motive being to free Maggie from any guilt that might attach to her having abandoned a father for a husband), but Charlotte continues her affair with Amerigo. The second half of the novel deals with Maggie's discovery of the liaison and her reactions to it, presented largely through the methods of 'interior narration' and point-of-view that characterize James's late works. The novel is, in part, a social comedy but its mood becomes increasingly dramatic as it progresses and many readers find its narrative strategies disconcertingly complex. James's 'Preface' to the first edition is an important account, both of its nature and of its composition. See Nicola Bradbury's *James: The Later Novels* (1979).

Golden Notebook, The, a novel by Doris *Lessing, published in 1962. Anna Wulf, a writer who has not published anything for some years, lives alone with her young daughter, surviving on the proceeds of her successful first novel, which she now condemns as a work of nostalgia. Five sections ironically entitled 'Free Women' present Anna and her close friend Molly in the third person, while the bulk of the book is taken from Anna's four notebooks, in which she writes about her self (as the younger woman in Africa, as the writer, the mother, the psychoanalyst's patient, the lover, the disenchanted communist) in various ways (memoir, political discussion, fiction, parody, daily record-keeping). She uses the notebooks to compartmentalize her experience, convinced for much of the book that it is impossible to write the whole truth and impossible to be whole. Finally, a period of breakdown, seen through the several mirrors of the notebooks and the 'Free Women' narrative, leads to a new creative purpose. In a new, golden notebook she writes the first sentence of her departing lover's novel, and he dictates the first sentence of hers, which is of course the first of this book. The conventional narrative ends as it began with Anna and Molly talking, amused and newly practical. Probably Lessing's best-known work, it is her most ambitious attempt to encompass the modern experience of fragmentation and impending destruction, and the three totems of communism, psychoanalysis, and feminism.

GOLDING, Sir William (Gerald) (1911–93), British novelist, born in Columb Minor, Cornwall, educated at Marlborough Grammar School and Brasenose College, Oxford. He worked as an actor and producer in small theatre companies before the Second World War when he joined the Royal Navy, becoming lieutenant in charge of a rocket ship; from 1945 to 1961 he was a schoolteacher. His early *Poems* were published in 1935. Golding won immediate critical acclaim with his first novel, **Lord of the Flies* (1954), a powerful narrative about a group of English schoolboys, stranded on an island after a plane crash, who resort to savagery. The harsh brutality of man is the underlying theme of this novel, a theme which he addresses in a diversity of historical contexts and settings in subsequent works. *The Inheritors* (1955) describes an episode when Neanderthal man is displaced by Cro-Magnon man and focuses on the doomed relationship of Lok and Fa; through his characters, who struggle to articulate their imaginative lives, Golding challenges the concept that 'new men' are intellectually and morally superior to those they supplanted. *Pincher Martin* (1956), which presents the last moments of a drowning man and his purgatorial reflections on his past life, demonstrates Golding's concern with fundamental moral contraries in man and his frequent use of the trick ending or dislocating shift of perspective. *Free Fall* (1959) investigates loss of innocence and the individual's moral destiny. The later *Darkness Visible* (1979) attempts to propose a solution to the moral darkness that most of his fiction discusses. Golding can be described as a profoundly religious novelist, although religion is not expressed in traditional Christian terms, even when describing clergymen as in *Rites of Passage* (1980). Much of his writing addresses the theological problem of Original Sin, yet few of his characters who witness evil are portrayed as really understanding it. *The Spire* (1964) concerns a dean who is gripped by an obsession that he has been chosen by God to build a huge spire on his cathedral; whether the dean is driven by human ambition or by a visionary desire to glorify God remains ambiguous. His next novel, *The Pyramid* (1967), was followed by *The Scorpion God* (1971), a collection of novellas set in antiquity, which includes the theme of ancient Egypt. **Rites of Passage* (1980; Booker Prize), with *Close Quarters* (1987) and *Fire Down Below* (1989), forms a trilogy entitled 'To the Ends of the Earth'; almost entirely set at sea, the trilogy chronicles a voyage from England to Australia during the nineteenth century. *The Paper Men* (1984) is an entertaining account of the pursuit of a famous English novelist by an industrious American academic researcher, which Golding has drawn from his own experiences as a literary celebrity. He has also published a play, *The Brass Butterfly* (1958), and two collections of essays, *The Hot Gates* (1965) and *A Moving Target* (1982). Later editions of *A Moving Target* include his speech on receiving the 1983 Nobel Prize for Literature. Golding was knighted in 1988.

GOLDMAN, Emma (1869–1940), American essayist, critic, and editor, born in Kovno, Lithuania, of Jewish parents, educated at the Realschule in Königsberg; she emigrated to the USA in 1885. She was 'radicalized' by the events surrounding the Haymarket Riot in Chicago in May 1886. Within a few years she had established herself as a leading advocate of anarchism in the USA, notably through her reading of Johann Most's anarchist newspaper *Die Freiheit*, with which she was later associated, and her familiarity with the writings of Bakunin and Kropotkin. She founded the anarchist monthly magazine *Mother Earth* in 1906 and became a well-known public speaker promoting such causes as anarchism, birth control, and feminism. Her *Anarchism and Other Essays* was published in 1910. During the First World War she was a prominent opponent of conscription and in June 1917 she was arrested and sentenced to two years in prison for conspiracy; *Mother Earth* was suppressed in the same year. In 1919 she was deported from the USA (her citizenship, obtained by marriage to Jacob Kershner in 1887, was rendered invalid by her divorce) and returned to Russia; here, her criticism of the centralization of the Soviet state took shape and gave issue to her important book, *My Disillusionment in Russia* (1922). She left Soviet Russia and lived for two years in England where she married James Colton, a Welsh miner. She subsequently took up residence in St Tropez in the south of France where she wrote her autobiography *Living My Life* (1931), and died. Her most important work of literary criticism is *The Social Significance of the Modern Drama* (1914). *Red Emma Speaks* (1972), edited by Alix Kates Shulman, is an anthology of her writings and speeches; Alice Wexler's *Emma Goldman: An Intimate Life* (1984) is a study of her anarchist years.

Gollancz (Victor Gollancz Ltd), the British publishing business founded in 1927 by Victor Gollancz (1893–1967) with the stated intention of steering between 'the Scylla of preciousness and dilettantism and the Charybdis of purely commercialised mass production'. The first list, announced in February 1928, was chiefly made up of histories, biographies, and fiction, with additional plays, volumes of poetry, and works on architecture; H. G. *Wells and Philip *Guedalla were the best-known of Gollancz's authors at the time. The company quickly established itself on a sound commercial footing, its editions becoming well known for their uniformly distinctive bright yellow dust-jackets. R. C. Sherriff's play **Journey's End* (1929) was the first of their conspicuously successful titles. Novelists published by Gollancz in its first ten years included Daphne *du Maurier, A. J. *Cronin, Michael Innes, Dorothy L. *Sayers, and George *Orwell. Throughout the early 1930s the firm was developing the specialization in socialist and pacifist books which resulted in the formation in 1936 of the *Left Book Club. From 1945 onward, a large proportion of Gollancz's books were by American authors, among them John *Updike, Vladimir *Nabokov, James *Agee, and John *Cheever. Since the early 1960s the company has been noted for its *science fiction publishing, authors having included J. G. *Ballard, Robert *Heinlein, Ursula *Le Guin, and Philip K. *Dick. Sheila Hodges's history of Gollancz, *The Story of a Publishing House, 1928–1978*, appeared in 1978.

GOMBRICH, Sir E(rnst) H(ans) (Josef) (1909–), British art historian, born in Vienna, where he obtained his Ph.D. in 1933. He emigrated to Britain in 1936, becoming a research assistant at the University of London's Warburg Institute; he remained at the Warburg Institute throughout his career, becoming its Director in 1959 and publishing a biography of its founder, Aby Warburg, in 1970. Gombrich's earliest major publication, *The Story of Art* (1950, 15th revised edition, 1989), which surveys the development of painting and sculpture from prehistory to the modernist era, is still widely regarded as the best introductory work available. His many more specialized studies include *Art and Illusion* (1960) and *The Sense of Order* (1979), which contain his influential writings on the psychology of pictorial representation and aesthetic values. Of central importance to Gombrich's *œuvre* is *Studies in the Art of the Renaissance*, which consists of *Norm and Form* (1966), *Symbolic Images* (1972), *The Heritage of Apelles* (1976), and *New Light on Old Masters* (1986). Among his other works are *Means and Ends* (1976), on the history of fresco painting, and *Oskar Kokoschska in His Time* (1986).

GOMES, Albert (1911–78), West Indian poet, editor, and politician, of Portuguese descent, born in Trinidad, educated at Granger Institute in Port of Spain. In 1930 he launched *The *Beacon*, an influential literary magazine, radical both politically and in its literary experimentation; his contributions of poems such as 'Reverie' and 'The Flesh' were among the freest from outmoded Victorian conventions still prevalent at the time. In 1942 he became President of the Federated Workers Trade Union, and later held various Cabinet posts in the Trinidad government. His autobiography, *Through a Maze of Colour* (1974), is an important document about literary and political activity, the two intimately related in the West Indies in the 1930s and 1940s. *Selected Speeches* (1944) foregrounds his anti-colonial political sentiments, which were of great consequence in his promotion of emancipated West Indian writing.

Gone with the Wind, see MITCHELL, MARGARET.

Goodbye to All That, Robert *Graves's autobiography of his early life, written at the age of 33 and published in 1929, the year of his departure for Majorca with Laura *Riding. Although the period covered extends beyond Graves's meeting with Riding, whose influence over him at the time of its composition was considerable, there is no reference to her in the text; Graves did not wish to include her in a work that was a conscious act of dissociation from his former life and its English social, cultural, and religious contexts. The book is principally noted for its vividly authentic treatments of trench warfare, which are presented with a bitter levelness of tone. The urgently laconic style throughout reflects the emotional compulsion under which Graves wrote. *Goodbye to All That* is classed with Sassoon's **Memoirs of an Infantry Officer* (1930) and *Blunden's *Undertones of War* (1928) as one of the three great memoirs of the First World War; by comparison with the air of casual immediacy Graves adopts, Sassoon's and Blunden's manners seem consciously literary. Graves's versions of many events were not accepted by Sassoon, who, having seen the book in a proof copy, drew up a list of over 200 inaccuracies and insisted on the deletion of passages referring to his mother. The first edition duly appeared with blank sections and sold exceptionally well. Numerous others were offended by the work, notably certain members of Graves's family, whom, it appears from *Robert Graves: The Years with Laura* (1990) by his son R. P. Graves, were treated unjustly and unreasonably.

Good-Bye, Mr Chips, see HILTON, JAMES.

Goodbye to Berlin, a collection of sketches and short stories by Christopher *Isherwood (1939). The work, taken as a whole, presents a unified picture of Berlin in the last years of Weimar. Isherwood, disguised in this book as Herr Issyvoo, lived in Berlin in 1929–33, supporting himself in the harsh economic climate by giving English lessons. The stories are technically brilliant but no less so in their insights into a society consciously disintegrating into dark chaos. 'Sally Bowles', the first novella, was published independently in 1937 and has remained perhaps the best-known story in the book, of a hopeless English *demi-mondaine* who comes to live with Herr Issyvoo's landlady (this inspired John Van Druten's play, *I Am a Camera*, 1951, and the immensely successful musical, *Cabaret*, 1968). Perhaps even more penetrating is the study of the Jewish family, 'The Landauers', magnates of a vast emporium. The pictures of Berliner working-class life are extremely lively and are all we have of Isherwood's once-intended vast novel about Germany, 'The Lost'. Nothing in the book has become more famous, as a declaration of authorial intent, than the words near the opening: 'I am a camera with its shutter open, quite passive, recording, not thinking. Recording the man shaving at the window opposite and the woman in the kimono washing her hair. Some day, all this will have to be developed, carefully printed, fixed.'

Good Companions, The, see PRIESTLEY, J. B.

GOODIS, David (1917–67), American crime novelist mainly associated with the *Hardboiled school of the 1940s, born in Philadelphia, educated at Indiana University, Bloomington, and Temple University, Philadelphia. Goodis benefited from the 1980s revival of interest in the darker styles of crime writing although his reputation in France has been consistently high. Like Jim *Thompson, Goodis presents a sombre and disillusioned portrait of the world, in which his solitary male protagonists search fruitlessly for meaning and significance in their lives. This mood is ironically and tersely expressed in his first novel, *Dark Passage* (1947); the brooding atmosphere of doubt and suspicion was memorably captured in the Delmer Davies film, starring Humphrey Bogart and Lauren Bacall. Throughout the 1950s his novels were consigned to the '*pulp' market. None the less, his work from this period is strikingly individual, with *The Burglar* (1953) and *The Moon in the Gutter* (1953) offering characteristic highly charged variants on the theme of nemesis. Goodis's gift for fast-paced narrative is best seen in *Down There* (1956), filmed by François Truffaut in 1962 as *Shoot the Piano Player*.

GOODISON, Lorna (1947–), Jamaican poet, born in Kingston, Jamaica, educated at the Jamaica School of Art and the Art Student League of New York. Her paintings have been widely exhibited and she is highly regarded as a book illustrator. She has worked as an art teacher and as a writer-in-residence at the University of the West Indies and at Radcliffe College, Massachusetts. Her principal collections of poetry are *Tamarind Season* (1980), *I Am Becoming My Mother* (1986), *Heartease* (1988), *To Us All Flowers Are Roses* (1990), and *Selected Poems* (1992). Many of her poems achieve powerfully imaginative effects through her use of domestic and natural imagery to evoke the interaction of psychological and material factors in women's experience of Caribbean history. Her work is notable for its accomplished fusions of elements of conventional versification with qualities integral to the oral traditions of Jamaica. Her other publications include *Baby Mother and the King of Swords* (1990), a collection of short stories forming compassionate explorations of the aspirations and fears of ordinary Jamaican individuals.

GOODMAN, (Henry) Nelson (1906–), American philosopher, born in Massachusetts, educated at Harvard. Among several academic posts he has held professorships in philosophy at Tufts College and at Brandeis University; in 1968 he was appointed Professor of Philosophy at Harvard. *The Structure of Appearance* (1951) gained him notice for its penetrating analysis of phenomenalistic systems of philosophy. His reputation increased with the appearance of *Fact, Fiction, and Forecast* (1954), in which he introduced the celebrated 'Goodman's paradox' as a linguistic mode for assessing the validity of philosophical inferences. His contributions to epistemology and the philosophies of science and language have in common his rigorous inductive methods, out of which he develops his valuable theory of projection for differentiating between confirmable and non-confirmable hypotheses; he is regarded as an uncompromising nominalist for his rejection of philosophical categories and his refusal to proceed on the basis of cases other than the particular and individual. Much of his later work has displayed a preoccupation with theories of representation, which he considers with regard to a wide range of instances, including painting, map-making, and musical scores. Among his other publications are *Languages of Art* (1968), *Ways of Worldmaking* (1978), and *Of Mind and Other Matters* (1984).

GOODMAN, Paul (1911–72), American novelist, playwright, poet, and social and educational commentator, born in New York City, educated at City College,

New York, and the University of Chicago. Although *Growing Up Absurd* (1960) brought Goodman a wide readership, his earliest writings, chiefly drama and verse, were published in the 1930s (the first volume of verse, *Ten Lyric Poems*, appeared in 1934) and he continued to publish poetry and plays throughout his long career as a scholar and a writer. His fiction dates from the 1940s and is notable for its articulation of the political radicalism that informs so much of his social and educational writings, particularly in *The Empire City* (1959) which is concerned with the life of New York City from about 1930 to 1950. His interest in the problems of the city, and urban life in general, is reflected in one of his major works of social philosophy, *Communitas: Means of Livelihood and Ways of Life* (1947; revised edition 1960), co-written with his brother Percival Goodman. This preoccupation with the terms and conditions of modern life is at the centre of *Growing Up Absurd*, where the study of youth and the associated problems of juvenile delinquency takes the form of a plea for a kind of intellectual and utopian anarchism which echoes Thoreau's belief that life is more ennobling and enriching when freed from the encroachments of the state; this work found its natural audience in the disaffected student radicals of the 1960s. Later important works of social thought include *Utopian Essays and Practical Proposals* (1962), *The Moral Ambiguity of America* (1966), and *New Reformation: Notes of a Neolithic Conservative* (1970). It is a testimony to the range and intellectual rigour of his thinking that his works in adjacent fields, such as *Gestalt Therapy* (1951) and *The Structure of Literature* (1954), are still read and admired. His verse has been collected in *Collected Poems* (1974), edited by Taylor Stoehr, and his short stories in four volumes of *Collected Stories* (1978–80), also edited by Taylor Stoehr. He taught at various colleges and universities, including the University of Chicago, Black Mountain College, Sarah Lawrence College, and the University of Wisconsin, and was film editor for *Partisan Review* and television critic for *New Republic*. See *Goodman* (1980), by Kingsley Widmer.

Good Soldier, The, a novel by Ford Madox *Ford, published in 1915, first serialized in **Blast* (1914) as *The Saddest Sotry*. The novel, in which the author perfected the allusive impressionistic style he had been moving towards in his earlier fiction, counterpoints themes of love and betrayal with masterly economy. Narrated in the first person by a wealthy expatriate American, John Dowell, it describes the relationships between Dowell, his wife Florence, and Edward and Leonora Ashburnham, an English couple whom they meet at a hotel in Nauheim in 1904. The ties which bind the foursome, ostensibly those of friendship and circumstance (both Florence and Edward suffer from heart trouble), gradually emerge as those of passion and intrigue. Edward and Florence become lovers and the latter is revealed as a liar, schemer, and blackmailer. In Nauheim, the spa which the foursome continue to visit, these events come to a head in 1913 with the arrival of Nancy Rufford, the Ashburnhams' young ward. Edward falls in love with Nancy and the distraught Florence kills herself. The Ashburnhams return to England with Nancy; Dowell, also in love with Nancy, returns to America to settle his affairs. Nancy is dispatched to her father in India and Edward, after receiving a heartless telegram from her, shoots himself in despair. The final scenes show Leonora remarried and Dowell acting as nurse to the now insane Nancy. Considered by Ford as his 'best book', the novel incorporates complex time shifts and subtle flashbacks and, in John Dowell, offers one of the best examples of the unreliable narrator in modern fiction.

GORDIMER, Nadine (1923–), South African novelist and short-story writer, born in Springs, Transvaal, educated at the University of Witwatersrand. Gordimer is known for her sensitivity to the repression of the black majority in South Africa. Her first novel, *The Lying Days* (1953), about a young woman growing up in a South African mining community, was followed by *A World of Strangers* (1958) and *Occasion for Loving* (1963), both portraying white protagonists open to relationships with blacks, but ostracized by their own people. Her distinctive realist style first emerged in *The Late Bourgeois World* (1966) with its depiction of a middle-class Johannesburg woman who looks back on past failures with her ex-husband, an ineffectual saboteur, and faces new challenges from a black friend involved in underground political struggle. *A Guest of Honour* (1971; James Tait Black Memorial Prize), set in an independent black African state, concerns a former English colonial official, who begins to question his most cherished liberal beliefs. *The Conservationist* (1974; joint winner of the Booker Prize) concerns the choices faced by a conscience-ridden South African industrialist. Gordimer's later novels reflect her perception of the narrowing of political options for the ruling white minority in South Africa. These include *Burger's Daughter* (1979), in which a young woman is haunted by the political legacy of her Afrikaner Marxist parents who died in prison; **July's People* (1981); and *A Sport of Nature* (1987), a picaresque novel about an independent young South African woman who travels throughout Africa and becomes involved in the process of liberation. *My Son's Story* (1990) deals with 'coloured', or mixed-race, protagonists; the central narrator attempts to come to terms with his father, who is forced to lead a life of clandestine deception due to his affair with a white mistress and his illegal political activities. As the son considers himself an aspiring writer, the novel comes closest to defining Gordimer's own complex role as a writer in South Africa on the eve of profound political and social change. *None to Accompany Me* (1994) is Gordimer's first novel after the free elections in South Africa; its chief protagonist is a woman lawyer whose personal life is politically impeccable but personally troubled. Some critics have judged it as irrelevant to the new South Africa. Gordimer's cool intellect is also evident in her many collections of short stories;

among the best are *The Soft Voice of the Serpent* (1953), *Friday's Footprint* (1960), *Selected Stories* (1975), *A Soldier's Embrace* (1980), and *Jump* (1991). She also wrote *The Black Interpreters* (1973), an introduction to various black South African writers, and *The Essential Gesture: Writing, Politics and Places* (1988), a collection of essays. She received the Nobel Prize for Literature in 1991. See Stephen Clingman, *The Novels of Nadine Gordimer: History from the Inside* (1986).

GORDON, Caroline (1895–1981), American novelist, short-story writer, and literary critic, born in Todd County, Kentucky, educated at Bethany College, West Virginia. She married the poet and critic Allen *Tate in 1924 and in 1928 went to Europe with Tate who was on a Guggenheim Fellowship; she herself was awarded a Guggenheim Fellowship in creative writing in 1929. In New York and in Paris she acted as Ford Madox *Ford's secretary and with his encouragement, and that of her husband, her writing career began in earnest. Her first novel, *Penhally* (1931), immediately established her as one of the foremost writers of what latterly has come to be called 'the Southern Renascence'. *Penhally* is a historical and dynastic novel following the declining fortunes of the Llewellyn family, the owners of the eponymous Kentucky estate. In 1934 her short story 'Old Red' won the O. Henry short story award, and her second novel *Aleck Maury, Sportsman*, was published. *None Shall Look Back* (1937) and *The Garden of Adonis* (1937) are novels about the Allard family, the first recording events during the American Civil War, the second bringing the family's history forward into the Depression years. *Green Centuries* (1941) concerns life on the Kentucky frontier during the American Revolution and is thought by many critics to be her finest. In 1947 Gordon converted to Catholicism and many of her later works arise from her growing preoccupation with religious and spiritual questions, notably *The Strange Children* (1951) and *The Malefactors* (1956). *The Collected Stories of Caroline Gordon* (1981) contains the best of her accomplished short stories. With Allen Tate she edited the widely used anthology *The House of Fiction: An Anthology of the Short Story* (1950; second edition, 1960) and her own theories of the art of fiction are eloquently expressed in *How To Read a Novel* (1957). Her familiarity with the writings of Ford Madox Ford resulted in *The Good Soldier: A Key to the Novels of Ford Madox Ford* (1963).

GORDON, Mary (Catherine) (1949–), American novelist, born in Long Island, of Jewish and Roman Catholic heritage, educated at Barnard College and Syracuse University. Gordon is often classified as a writer who conflates the concerns of feminism and Catholicism, but since her first novel, *Final Payments* (1978), which deals with a young woman's mourning for her father, she has proved to be a writer in the modern mainstream of American fiction, who combines domestic realism, satire, parody, and lyrical observation in her well-planned novels. *The Company of Women* (1981), a story set in a fashionable commune, shows the possible influence of Mary *McCarthy. Other novels of family life and social mores are *Men and Angels* (1985) and *The Other Side* (1989); short stories are collected in *Temporary Shelter* (1987). Among her finest works are the three novellas contained in *The Rest of Life* (1993), about women dealing with the vagaries of love; the title story examines the sensibility of an Italian migrant who spends 'the rest of life' dealing with the death of her lover, who committed suicide when he was 16 and she 15; in 'Immaculate Man' a social worker becomes the lover of a priest, which explores the conflict between flesh and church, a theme which continues in 'Living at Home', the story of an obsessive Italian reporter and his psychiatrist lover. *Good Boys and Dead Girls* (1991) is a collection of essays.

Gormenghast, see PEAKE, MERVYN.

GOSSE, Sir Edmund (William) (1849–1928), British critic, biographer, and essayist, born in London and privately educated. His childhood and difficult relations with his father, the eminent zoologist Philip Henry Gosse (1810–88), are recounted in his most highly regarded work, *Father and Son*, the autobiography which first appeared anonymously in 1907. Having become an assistant librarian in the British Museum in 1867, he developed a special interest in the literatures of the Scandinavian countries; his numerous publications in the field include *Studies in the Literature of Northern Europe* (1879). He did much to establish Ibsen's reputation in Britain, translating *Hedda Gabler* (1891) and *The Master Builder* (with William Archer, 1893); his biography of the playwright appeared in 1907. His works as a biographer also include *Thomas Gray* (1882), *The Life and Letters of John Donne* (two volumes, 1899), *Sir Thomas Browne* (1905), and *Algernon Charles Swinburne* (1917), the last-named having been his close friend. *Firdausi in Exile* (1885) is the most notable of his numerous collections of verse; *Collected Poems* appeared in 1911. Among his other works in a career of prolific authorship are the lectures of *From Shakespeare to Pope* (1885), which provoked John Churton Collins's attacks on his scholarship, and *Books on the Table* (1921), a collection of his literary journalism. Having emerged as a figure of considerable literary eminence in the course of the 1890s, in 1904 he became librarian to the House of Lords. Twelve volumes of his *Collected Essays* appeared in 1927. *Edmund Gosse: A Literary Landscape* (1984) is a biography by Ann *Thwaite.

Go Tell It on the Mountain, a novel by James *Baldwin, published in 1952. Baldwin was brought up by a stepfather who was a pastor and spent his formative years in an environment of Christian fanaticism. Baldwin draws heavily upon his own experiences which, along with its rapturous, lyrical prose heavily laden with biblical cadences, gives the book much of its authenticity and conviction. It tells the story of John Grimes, a Harlem boy, who at 14 is coerced by his father's religious zeal to embrace the Christianity his intimidating stepfather represents. Baldwin, who has written elsewhere of the roots of his own oppression within as well as outside the circle of the black family, here attempts to tap the sources of African-American religious practices by relating them to the collective racial tragedies from which they emerged. The novel has also been read as a symbolic portrayal of Baldwin's discovery of his own sexual preferences in which homoerotic desire is disguised as spiritual ecstasy.

GOUDGE, Elizabeth (1900–84), British novelist, born in Wells, Somerset; she studied art at Reading College. An only child, her father, Dr Henry Leighton Goudge, became Regius Professor of Divinity at Oxford; her mother was a descendant of a Guernsey Norman-French family. Goudge's first novel, *Island Magic* (1934), set in Guernsey, was followed by many others, including *A City of Bells* (1936), about an imaginary cathedral city based on Wells; and *Towers in the Mist* (1938), set in Elizabethan Oxford. Generally regarded as her best-known novels are *Green Dolphin Country* (1944), set in Guernsey and nineteenth-century New Zealand, a bestseller which was filmed in 1947; *Gentian Hill* (1949), a love story set in nineteenth-century Devon; and *The Child from the Sea* (1970), about Lucy Waters, the secret wife of Charles II. *The Bird in the Tree* (1940), *The Herb of Grace* (1948), and *The Heart of the Family* (1953), a trilogy of novels set in Devon, chronicles the lives of the Eliots of Dameroshay. Goudge's works are distinctive in style, incorporating lyrical descriptions of landscape with detailed historical background, and reflect her deep Christian beliefs. These qualities are also evident in her children's books. She has also published short stories, books on religious themes, and *The Joy of the Snow* (1974), an autobiography.

GOWERS, Sir Ernest (Arthur) (1880–1966), British civil servant and grammarian, born in London, educated at Clare College, Cambridge. In 1902 he entered the Civil Service, where he rose to become Chairman of the Board of Inland Revenue. *Plain Words: A Guide to the Use of English* (1948) was written at the suggestion of Sir Edward Bridges, the Head of the Civil Service, who admired the clarity of expression Gowers commanded. It was reprinted together with the subsequent *ABC of Plain Words* (1951) as *The Complete Plain Words* in 1954. The books remain invaluable for their emphasis on brevity and precision as cardinal virtues in the writing of factual matter in English. In 1965 Gowers produced a revised edition of H. W. *Fowler's *Modern English Usage*, applying his principles of clarification to some entries and adding articles on such topics as 'abstractitis', 'officialese', and 'sociologese'. His other publications include *A Life for a Life?* (1956), an influential work arising from his chairmanship of the Royal Commission on Capital Punishment, from which he emerged a convinced abolitionist.

GOYEN, William (1915–83), American novelist and short-story writer, born in Trinity, Texas, educated at Rice Institute. During the Second World War he served as an officer in the navy. Goyen's first novel, *The House of Breath* (1950), composed of the linked accounts of lives in a small town loosely connected by a first-person narrator, was distinguished by the voluptuous texture of its prose and its lush evocations of landscape. The elements of myth, fantasy, and lavish lyricism that characterize this novel are also evident in most of Goyen's short fiction, collected in *Ghost and Flesh* (1952), *Faces of Blood Kindred* (1960), *Collected Stories* (1975), and *Had I a Hundred Mouths* (1985), with a critical introduction by Joyce Carol *Oates, and in his novels *In a Farther Country* (1955), the picaresque tale of a Spanish-American woman's dream of a united Spain, and *Savata, My Fair Sister* (1963), in which the religious ardour of one sister is pitted against the vitality of another. The later novels were often dismissed as bizarre, plotless, and fantastic. The controversial *Come, the Restorer* (1974) conflates Christian symbolism with sexual imagery in a story of an entire town's projection of its quest for a saviour on the restorer of old photographs, Mr de Persia. A final novel, *Arcadio* (1983), the monologue of a hermaphrodite, raises contemporary issues of gender and sexuality in Goyen's customary frame of Latinized life in Texas and New Mexico.

GRACE, Patricia (1937–), New Zealand Maori writer, born in Wellington. Her collection of stories *Waiariki* (1975) was the first published by a Maori woman writer; later collections include *The Dream Sleepers* (1980), *Electric City and Other Stories* (1987), *Selected Stories* (1991), *The Sky People* (1994), whose stories are linked by the Maori myth of the title, and *Collected Stories* (1994). In addition to prize-winning children's books she has published the novels *Mutuwhenua/The Moon Sleeps* (1978), *Potiki* (1986), and *Cousins* (1992), which explore the special pressures to which contemporary Maori culture has to respond, especially in urban situations. The earlier novel reveals the conflicting attractions of home culture against the lure of the town through the relationship between Linda (who has dropped her Maori name) and Graeme. In *Potiki* similar tensions are sharpened through actual conflict between a Maori community and developers who employ every means (including violence) in an unsuccessful attempt to acquire ancestral land which they see simply as under-used real estate, while *Cousins* shows the resilience of three Maori women forced from the land into the city. Grace employs to great effect multiple perspectives on events, including untranslated passages in Maori, and her work furnishes a vivid and strongly Maori aspect on contemporary New Zealand culture.

GRAFTON, Sue (1940–), American crime writer, born in Louisville, Kentucky, educated at the University of Louisville; she is the daughter of C. W. Grafton, attorney and mystery writer. She published her first novel, *Keziah*, in 1967, the *Lolly Madonna War* (1969) was filmed in 1973, and from 1977 she wrote TV film scripts. By 1982, Grafton was a twice-divorced mother of three children who conceived *'A' Is for Alibi* (1982) in preference to murdering her ex-husband. She has now reached *'L' Is for Lawless* (1996) in her award-winning 'alphabet' series that has helped transform the predominantly male preserve of American crime writing. With Sara *Paretsky, Grafton has become one of the genre's most popular female writers. Her tightly paced mysteries are shaped by Kinsey Millhone, a feisty, self-sufficient private investigator who is appealingly candid, with a wry wit.

GRAHAM, Jorie (1951–), American poet, born in Italy, educated at the Sorbonne, New York University, and the University of Iowa. Graham's complex linguistic and cultural background (she was born of American parents, attended a French lycée in Rome, and is fluent in English, French, and Italian) provides much of the material for her intellectual, frequently erudite, verse. Graham's mother, the painter and sculptor Beverly Pepper, exposed her daughter at a young age to the cultural heritage of Italy, and many of Graham's poems, notably 'At Luca Signorelli's Resurrection of the Body' from her second volume of verse, *Erosion* (1983), reflect her preoccupations with the analogous expressive powers of poetic language and the visual arts. Graham herself speaks of the influence of the French *symbolistes*, particularly Baudelaire, Rimbaud, and Mallarmé, and of the American poet Elizabeth *Bishop, though her metrics recall those of William Carlos *Williams while her subject matter has much in common with that of Wallace *Stevens. Her other volumes of verse are *Hybrids of Plants and of Ghosts* (1980), *The End of Beauty* (1987), *Region of Unlikeness* (1991), and *Materialism: Poems* (1993); she has also published poetry in the **New Yorker* magazine. Graham undertook cinema studies at New York University (where she worked with the film director Martin Scorsese). Her teaching career has included posts at California State University, Columbia University, and Iowa University.

GRAHAM, W(illiam) S(ydney) (1918–86), British poet, born in Greenock, Renfrewshire, educated at Greenock High School. He subsequently studied at the Workers' Educational Association College, Newbattle Abbey, Edinburgh. After a period as a journeyman engineer he settled in Cornwall, often referring in his poetry to the topography around Zennor and his acquaintances in its community of artists. His early poetry, principally represented by *Cage without Grievance* (1942) and *2nd Poems* (1945), tended towards a cryptic compression indicative of Dylan *Thomas's influence. The work remained, however, perceptibly grounded in his experience of Clydeside's shipyards and countryside and possessed considerable verbal vitality. The assured individuality of tone and philosophical orientation characteristic of his later writing began to emerge in *The White Threshold* (1949). The long title-work of *The Nightfishing* (1955) forms the culmination of the use of maritime imagery in his verse, the literal and symbolic senses of the sea providing a focus for the poem's passionate fusion of elegy and contemplation. Although the book was favourably received, he published no further collections until *Malcolm Mooney's Land* in 1970, which was followed by *Implements in Their Places* (1977). *Collected Poems: 1942–1977* was published in 1979. Graham's later work shows a recurrent concern with the nature and functions of language and communication, such essentially abstract themes becoming entertainingly accessible through the incorporation of local elements and the subdued wit of his manner. A further edition entitled *Uncollected Poems* appeared in 1990.

GRAHAM, Winston (Mawdsley) (1910–), British novelist and writer of film scripts, born in Manchester; he left school at 16. He made his name as a writer of thrillers with subtle character observation and psychological undertones. *Marnie* (1961) was filmed by Alfred Hitchcock; films have also been made of *Take My Life* (1947), *Night without Stars* (1950), *Fortune Is a Woman* (1953), *The Sleeping Partner* (1956), and *The Walking Stick* (1967). He is best known for his historical novels set in eighteenth-century Cornwall and concerning the Poldark and Warleggan families, beginning with *Ross Poldark* (1945), and including *The Black Moon* (1973). There were two BBC television series during the 1970s based on the first seven books. He has also written non-fiction, including *The Spanish Armada* (1972) and *Poldark's Cornwall* (1983).

Grain of Wheat, A, a novel by *Ngugi, published in 1967. Set on the eve of Kenyan independence in 1963, the novel returns to the emergency period of the 1950s. The action centres on Mugo, a farmer; Mumbi and her carpenter husband Gikonyo; John Thompson, a British district officer; and Karanja, who once sympathized with the freedom movement. During preparations for Uhuru Day, it becomes clear how far people's lives and achievements have diverged from the ideals that inspired the dream of self-government. Karanja, as administrative chief of his area, becomes the servant of the British against his own people, rounding up Mau Mau suspects. Gikonyo, placed in a detention camp for his freedom-fighting activities, is unable to bear separation from his wife Mumbi; he forsakes his oath in order to return to her but, discovering that she has had a child by Karanja, he bitterly repudiates her love. Mugo, regarded as the leader of his village, is asked to deliver the main speech at the independence celebrations, in memory of his friend Kihika, a freedom fighter who was hanged by the colonial administrators. Mugo's refusal to make the speech is interpreted as an act of modesty but, on the contrary, he reveals himself as a traitor—the man who betrayed Kihika to his death. The major irony is that independence has left problems unsolved, and has in fact been achieved at the expense of all potential heroes.

Granta, originally *The Granta*, a periodical founded as the latest in a succession of Cambridge undergraduate journals by Murray Guthrie in 1889. Although the matter of whether or not women should be permitted to take degrees was earnestly debated in the 1890s, the magazine's tone was generally humorous and satirical; several writers associated with *The Granta*, notably A. A. *Milne, later contributed to *Punch*. After the First World War a more serious tone developed, and socio-cultural matters were treated with considerable gravity during the 1930s. In the 1950s and 1960s it concentrated on poetry, fiction, and literary criticism, publishing work by various distinguished students, including poems by Ted *Hughes and Sylvia *Plath. Having become moribund in the mid-1970s, it re-emerged as *Granta* in 1979 under Bill Buford's editorship to specialize in the publication of prose fiction and cultural commentary. In 1983 Granta Publications Limited entered into its continuing association with Penguin Books; work by eminent contributors including Martin *Amis, Ian *McEwan, James *Fenton, A. N. *Wilson, John *Berger, Salman *Rushdie, and Emma *Tennant combined with high production standards to make *Granta* the leading journal of its kind in Britain. Among the American authors whose work has been featured are John *Updike, Angela *Carter, George *Steiner, and John Herr. Since 1979 issues became devoted to particular themes or modes of writing; numbers 8 and 19, respectively subtitled '*Dirty Realism' and 'More Dirt', were principally devoted to recent American fiction.

GRANVILLE-BARKER, Harley (1877–1946), British playwright, scholar, and critic, born in London, the son of a property speculator; he rose to eminence in the Edwardian theatre. He created the character of Tanner in **Man and Superman*, played leading roles in other plays by *Shaw, and did much to prove the value of the repertory system during the period from 1905 to 1907, when he co-managed the Royal Court Theatre. In later years he turned to lecturing and writing, most importantly his *Prefaces to Shakespeare* (1927–47). On his death, Shaw described him as 'altogether the most distinguished and incomparably the most cultivated person whom circumstances had driven into the theatre at that time', meaning the first decade of the century, when all his major plays were written. These are *The Marrying of Ann Leete* (1901), about the daughter of an eighteenth-century politician who rejects a highly convenient aristocratic suitor for marriage to her father's gardener; *The Voysey Inheritance* (1905), in which a corrupt London solicitor dies, leaving his right-minded son to cope with the defalcations and debts he has inherited; *Waste* (1907), banned by the Lord Chamberlain for the candour with which it described the predicament of a leading politician whose mistress dies after an abortion; and *The Madras House* (1910), which uses the sale of a drapery store to air ideas about the place of women in Edwardian society. Granville-Barker's plays were criticized in their time for being too intellectual, subtle, and untheatrical. His later work, such as *The Secret Life* (1922) and *His Majesty* (1923), tends to substantiate that view. However, the four earlier plays have been successfully revived by the National Theatre and the Royal Shakespeare Company, winning general approval for the sweep and insight Granville-Barker brought to social and political themes seldom treated in the theatre of his day.

Grapes of Wrath, The, a novel by John *Steinbeck, published in 1939. Steinbeck's finest novel, *The Grapes of Wrath* is a fictional record of the migration of the 'Okies' (largely tenant farmers from Oklahoma and western Arkansas, though the term was used disparagingly of migrants from contiguous states such as Kansas, Missouri, and Texas) from the Southwestern states to California in the 1930s, a migration mainly brought on by the dust storms ('the dust bowl') of 1933 and 1935. Though the novel is almost Tolstoyan in scale—indeed, its use of intercalary, generalizing chapters is drawn from Tolstoy's *War and Peace*—it concentrates on the fortunes of the Joad family and through its protagonist, Tom Joad, it articulates a life-affirming 'mystical socialism' and speaks eloquently for the concerns of the deprived and the dispossessed. Peter Lisca's 1972 edition of the novel includes a number of critical documents which are indispensable to its study.

Graphic Novel is a term used to describe a long comic in book form containing a fictional or non-fictional narrative with a thematic unity. Since 1986 graphic novels have become increasingly popular. They are mainly about 50 pages in length, in full colour, and with card covers. Technically, for story-telling purposes, graphic novels depend on the characteristics of a traditional comic: they utilize a weave of text and image rather than a process of simply illustrating the text. However, the relationship of the graphic novel to the comic is that of the prose novel to the short story. Precedents can be traced to juvenile comics in the 1940s. Despite the fact that comics were stereotyped as a children's medium and were, therefore, produced in short and throwaway form, there were some extended narratives designed to be kept for longer. In Britain and America, the Classics Illustrated series, for example, which aimed to introduce classic works of literature to children in a palatable form, included several adaptations of more than 60 pages in length (including *A Tale of Two Cities*, 1942, and *Les Miserables*, 1943). Meanwhile, in Europe, longer comics with card covers had been produced from the late 1930s and were finding a mixed-age audience. The main continental hero was 'Tintin', an intrepid boy reporter, whose albums sold in their hundreds of thousands, and were first translated into English in 1958. But the roots of the graphic novel boom of the 1990s are in comics 'fandom', which developed in the 1970s and 1980s. This was, and remains, an organized network of fans and collectors of predominantly American comics, centring around 'fanzines' (a conflation meaning 'fan-magazines'), 'marts' (comic markets), and comics conventions. Out of this network emerged specialist shops, catering to collectors and selling solely comics. To service this market, publishers experimented with longer-lasting formats, including card covers. Moreover, because certain artists and writers were particularly popular, a system developed whereby lengthier collections of their work would be sold on the basis of their reputations. Thus, with some awareness of the large sale of album-comics currently being achieved in Europe, a culture based on comic albums and graphic novels began to develop.

Pioneering graphic novelists in this period included American Will Eisner, best known for his *A Contract With God* (1978), a series of semi-autobiographical vignettes about life in 1930s New York (the first book to be marketed as a 'graphic novel', thus establishing the term); Canadian Dave Sim, whose *Cerebus the Aardvark*, collected into albums from 1985, was both a parody of Conan the Barbarian and a complex satire; and British Bryan Talbot, whose *The Adventures of Luther Arkwright*, collected between 1982 and 1988, was a sophisticated science fiction odyssey. Although science fiction and fantasy were consistently the most popular themes, other subject matter was not uncommon.

In 1986–7, three outstanding titles were responsible for introducing the concept of the graphic novel to a much wider audience: *Maus* (1986), by Art Spiegelman, about the Nazi Holocaust, told in anthropomorphic terms—with Jews as mice, and Nazis as cats; *The Dark Knight Returns* (1986), by Frank Miller, a radical reworking of Batman mythology; and *Watchmen* (1987), by Alan Moore and Dave Gibbons, another adult revisionist superhero story. All three utilized the creative potential of the graphic novel to its optimum effect, and exhibited complex plotting and strong characterization. All had previously been serialized and became bestsellers in album form.

Mainstream book publishers soon began to publish graphic novels, particularly Penguin and Gollancz. Within a remarkably short time, they have become an established feature of the literary landscape, increasingly reviewed in the literary pages of the quality press, and even studied at some universities. Subject matter has expanded to include everything from Westerns (*Lieutenant Blueberry*, from 1989), horror (*Hellblazer*, from 1988), science fiction (*The Incal*, 1988), superheroes (*Marshal Law*, from 1988), autobiography (*The Playboy*, 1992), adaptations from classic literature (*Twelfth Night*, 1989), and political journalism (*Brought to Light*, 1989). In 1992 *Maus II*, Art Spiegelman's sequel to *Maus*, became the first graphic novel to be awarded a Pulitzer Prize for Literature. See *Adult Comics: An Introduction* (1993) by Roger Sabin. See also COMICS.

Grass is Singing, The, see LESSING, DORIS.

GRAU, Shirley Anne (1929–), American novelist, born in New Orleans, Louisiana, educated at Tulane University. Her first published work was a collection of stories, *The Black Prince* (1955); this, and the novels that followed—*The Hard Blue Sky* (1958) and *The House in Coliseum Street* (1961)—were well received by critics, who saw her as an exponent of the Southern school of writing. *Keepers of the House* (1964), a chronicle of three generations of the Howland family, was compared to the work of *Faulkner, and won the Pulitzer Prize. Other works include the novels *The Condor Passes* (1971) and *Evidence of Love* (1977), and two collections of stories, *The Wind Shifting West* (1973) and *Nine Women* (1985); in the latter, she extends her range to include, for example, the perspective of women of the new black middle class.

GRAVES, A(lfred) P(erceval) (1846–1931), Irish poet and editor, son of the Protestant Bishop of Limerick and the father of Robert *Graves; born in Dublin, where he was educated at Trinity College. Before taking his final examinations he left Dublin to become a clerk at the Home Office in London and in 1874 began his career with the Board of Education. In Dublin he had been encouraged as a poet by Sheridan Le Fanu, whose *Poems* he edited in 1896. *Songs of Killarney* (1872), his first collection of verse, set the consistently Irish tone of his work, the best-known being contained in *Irish Songs and Ballads* (1879) and *Father O'Flynn and Other Poems* (1889), the humorous title-piece of which was widely popular. *The Irish Poems of Alfred Perceval Graves* was published in two volumes with a preface by Douglas *Hyde in 1908. Graves was active in London's Irish Literary Society from its foundation in 1891, and was twice its president in later years. He produced numerous anthologies, including *Songs of Irish Wit and Humour* (1884) and *The Book of Irish Poetry* (1915). Welsh material was added to work of Irish provenance in later collections he edited, among them *A Celtic Psaltery* (1917). His autobiography *To Return to All That* (1930) appeared a year after the publication of Robert Graves's **Goodbye to All That* (1929).

GRAVES, Robert (van Ranke) (1895–1985), British poet, novelist, critic, and historian of mythology, born in Wimbledon, London, the son of A. P. *Graves, and educated at Charterhouse School. At the outbreak of the First World War he volunteered for active service and remained on the Western Front until invalided out in 1917. *Over the Brazier* (1916), *Goliath and David* (1916), and *Fairies and Fusiliers* (1917), his first three volumes of poetry, were published with the support of Edward *Marsh, in whose **Georgian Poetry* series his work repeatedly featured. He later suppressed most of the verse from these collections. The many war poems they contain appear in *Poems about War* (1988), edited by William Graves, his son; the volume is prefaced by Graves's essay 'Poetry of World War I', which is dismissive of 'war poetry' and accounts for his refusal to reprint a number of striking poems (see also WAR POETRY). His experiences of the conflict and the radical changes in his attitudes that it caused are described in his autobiography **Goodbye to All That* (1929). In 1918 he settled near Oxford, where he ran a grocery business with his first wife and studied at St John's College, gaining his B.Litt. in 1925 with the dissertation *Poetic Unreason and Other Studies*.

He became Professor of English at the University of Cairo in 1926; Laura *Riding, whom he had met the previous year, accompanied him and his wife to Egypt. *A Survey of Modernist Poetry* (1928), a critical collaboration with Riding, is regarded as a seminal work on poetic ambiguity. He separated from his wife in 1929 and went with Riding to Majorca, where they remained, running the Seizin Press, until 1936. Following their separation in 1939, for the rest of his life he lived chiefly in Majorca. Riding is widely credited with assisting Graves in the fuller realization of his talent.

The poetry he produced from the early 1930s onward, principally published in a number of collected editions, is characterized by the accomplishment and individuality of its fluently conversational use of traditional forms. His many love poems display the sceptical intelligence which makes his frequent treatments of metaphysical and supernatural subjects disquietingly credible. His verse frequently makes plain his dissent from social, political, and religious orthodoxies, and numerous poems, among them 'Ogres and Pygmies' and 'The Undead', form compelling and witty allegorical critiques of modern cultural conditions. *Collected Poems* (1986, edited by M. Seymour-Smith) is a recent edition. He was Professor of Poetry at Oxford between 1961 and 1966, publishing selections from his lectures in *Poetic Craft and Principle* (1967) and *The Crane Bag and Other Disputed Subjects* (1969). Having begun as a novelist with *My Head! My Head!* in 1925, Graves enjoyed continuing popularity after the publication of **I, Claudius* and *Claudius The God* in 1934. Among his numerous other novels are *The Story of Mary Powell, Wife to Mr Milton* (1943) and the widely read historical fictions *Sergeant Lamb of the Ninth* (1940) and *Proceed, Sergeant Lamb* (1941). His extensive writings on mythology and religion, which have in common a stimulatingly original approach to their materials, include *The Greek Myths* (1955) and *Mammon and the Black Goddess* (1965), the latter complementing *The *White Goddess* (1948).

Among his other works in some sixty years of prolific authorship were the biography *Lawrence and the Arabs* (1927) and many translations from various languages, including a controversial version of the *Rubaiyyat of Omar Khayyam* (1967). *The Assault Heroic* (1986) and *The Years with Laura* (1990) are the first two volumes of a biography by his son Richard Graves.

Gravity's Rainbow, a novel by Thomas *Pynchon, published in 1973. The novel is generally considered one of the most important works of post-war American fiction. Like Pynchon's other works its value as a work of art lies in its intellectual, linguistic, and philosophical complexity rather than its use of the conventional resources of realistic fiction. The principal metaphor is the German V-2 rocket, and its gravity-defined arc of aspiration and destruction. The novel is 'set' in London in the last days of the Second World War and its ostensible 'subject' is the German bombing of London by V-2 rockets, but it encompasses an immense intellectual landscape that incorporates much of twentieth-century scientific and technological history, its style ranging from philosophical discursiveness to linguistic and literary parody. As with Pynchon's other novels, *Gravity's Rainbow* is structured by assumptions about the ultimate impenetrability of what we take to be 'reality' and the conspiratorial nature of much social and scientific organization. Much has been made of Pynchon's use in the novel of cinematographic techniques but the novel is notable, chiefly, for its use of the full range of fictional devices; in this respect, it has been compared with both Melville's *Moby-Dick* and Joyce's **Finnegans Wake*.

GRAY, Alisdair (James) (1934–), Scottish novelist, short-story writer, and playwright, born in Glasgow, educated at Glasgow Art School. Prior to the publication of his 1981 novel **Lanark*, Gray lived mostly by teaching, painting, and writing and was best known for his lavish portraits and murals, and for more than a dozen television, radio, and stage plays. He has since become the outstanding figure in a Glasgow literary renaissance that also includes his friends James *Kelman, Liz *Lochhead, and Tom *Leonard. His second novel, *1982, Janine* (1984), is a *tour-de-force* combination of fantasy and political polemic taking place inside the head of 'Jock McLeish', an alcoholic security consultant holed up in a hotel bedroom; memories of school punishments and first love interchange with episodes of bondage, and diatribes on 'the matter of Scotland', the reverie frequently being interrupted by 'God' and other voices represented by graphic use of typeface. Gray's shorter fiction, often funny and fantastical, is gathered in *Unlikely Stories, Mostly* (1983)—including 'Five letters from an Eastern Empire', a masterly allegory set in Imperial China—*Lean Tales* (1985), and *Ten Tales Tall and True* (1993). A verse collection, *Old Negatives* (1989), and two novellas, *The Fall of Kelvin Walker* (1985) and *McGrotty and Ludmilla* (1990)—both previously plays—emerged out of a period in which he largely adapted already written material. This was also the case with his least well-received book, *Something Leather* (1990), whose pornographic passages attracted adverse reaction. *Poor Things* (1992) is another unlikely story, written in the form of Victorian memoirs 'edited' by Gray, concerning the surgeon 'Godwin Baxter' and his creation 'Bella'. In keeping with Gray's total authorship of his books, it has illustrations, a section of notes commenting on the text and its purported social history, exuberant pastiches, and even mock blurbs and reviews on the cover. A collection of informative essays on *The Arts of Alisdair Gray* was published in 1991.

GRAY, John (Henry) (1866–1934), British poet, born in Bethnal Green, London; he began publishing poems while working as a librarian at the Foreign Office. In 1890 he met Oscar Wilde, with whose support *Silverpoints*, his first collection of verse, appeared in 1893; the opulent exoticism of its imagery was complemented by a lavish binding designed by Charles Ricketts. The volume also contained translations of poems by French *Symboliste* poets and was hailed as epitomizing the aesthetic movement. The devotional sensibility occasionally discernible was channelled into *Spiritual Poems* of 1896, which signalled the end of his career as a decadent. He studied for the Roman Catholic priesthood and, following his ordination in 1901, devoted himself to his ministry in Edinburgh. His infrequent later publications as a poet include *The Long Road* (1926), which contained the allegorical 'The Flying Fish', his best-known poem. In 1931 he produced *Park: A Fantastic Story*, a futuristic novel envisioning a Catholic theocracy. *The Poems of John Gray*, edited by Ian Fletcher, was published in 1988. *In the Dorian Mode* (1983) is a biography by Brocard Sewell.

GRAY, Simon (1936–), British dramatist, born in Hampshire, educated at Dalhousie University, Halifax, Nova Scotia, and at Trinity College, Cambridge. He was for many years a lecturer in English at Queen Mary College, London. After achieving a modest success with *Wise Child* (1967), a dark comedy about a transvestite criminal on the run, he established himself with *Butley* (1971), about a witty, sadistic academic, and *Otherwise Engaged* (1974), about a publisher's attempts to escape the emotional demands and threats of those who insist on invading his privacy. Many of Gray's often sardonic but always humane comedies concern people of similar social background and calling: schoolmasters in *Spoiled* (1971; also a television play), *Dog Days* (1977), and *Quartermain's Terms* (1981); Cambridge graduates, former students and admirers of F. R. *Leavis, battling to keep a literary magazine afloat in *The Common Pursuit* (1984); publishers in *Melon* (1987) and *The Holy Terror* (1992), which are two alternative versions of the same tale of obsessive sexual jealousy; a literary agent and his novelist wife in *Hidden Laughter* (1990). *Molly* (1977), *The Rear Column* (1978), and *Cell Mates* (1995) are different in that they deal with, respectively, the Alma Rattenbury murder case, the events in the nineteenth-century Congo that gave rise to Conrad's **Heart of Darkness*, and the relationship of the spy George Blake with the petty criminal who organized his escape from prison, Sean Bourke; but they are similar in their concerns. At his best, Gray writes with wit, incisiveness, and an unsentimental sympathy about the darker, more secret aspects of human behaviour: sexual pain, compromise, betrayal, the sense of futility and failure, and the sheer struggle to survive the many personal and professional setbacks with which a difficult world presents people. He has also published four novels, written many plays for television, among them *Death of a Teddy Bear* (1967) and *An Unnatural Pursuit* (1985), and adapted Dostoevsky's *The Idiot* (1970) for the National Theatre.

GRAY, Stephen (Richard) (1941–), South African novelist, poet, and playwright, born in Cape Town, educated at the University of Cape Town, Queen's College, Cambridge, where he edited **Granta*, and Iowa State University. Before becoming a full-time writer in 1991, Gray was a professor of English at the Rand Afrikaans University, Johannesburg. His principal academic work is *South African Literature: an Introduction* (1979). Gray's poems display great versatility across a wide range of traditional and innovative forms. Collections of his verse, which is thematically dominated by his engagements with historical and socio-cultural aspects of South Africa, include *The Assassination of Shaka* (1974), *Hottentot Venus* (1979), *Apollo Café* (1989), *Season of Violence* (1992), and *Selected Poems, 1960–1992* (1994). *Local Colour* (1975), *Time of Our Darkness* (1987), *Born of Man* (1989), and *War Child* (1991) are among his numerous novels, which characteristically base their analyses of national identity in treatments of the everyday social realities of South Africa. *Schreiner: a One-Woman Play* (1983) is the most widely admired of his dramas. His works as an editor include *The Penguin Book of South African Stories* (1985). *Accident of Birth* (1993) is an autobiography.

Great Gatsby, The, a novel by F. Scott *Fitzgerald, published in 1925. *The Great Gatsby* is generally thought to be Fitzgerald's finest novel and one of the major achievements of twentieth-century American literature. The life of its eponymous hero, Jay Gatsby, is, in part, a merciless satire of the 'rags to riches' story, but Gatsby's accumulation of great wealth and a vast estate on Long Island is motivated not by greed but by the forlorn desire to reclaim a former lover, Daisy Fay, now married to Tom Buchanan, a wealthy Chicagoan also living on Long Island. It is through the novel's narrator, Nick Carraway, a cousin to Daisy, that Gatsby and Daisy are reunited, but the impossibility of their love is the novel's central thematic preoccupation. The novel is essentially tragic in mood and its climax is a series of scenes in which Myrtle Wilson, Tom's mistress, is accidentally killed when she is run down by Daisy who is driving Gatsby's car; Myrtle's husband, George, then kills Gatsby, mistakenly believing him to be the culprit, before taking his own life.

Nick Carraway, a 'middle-man' narrator, caught 'within and without, simultaneously enchanted and repelled by the inexhaustible variety of life', owes much to the influence of Joseph Conrad's Marlow of **Heart of Darkness* and **Chance*. Although the plot is not substantial, Fitzgerald's execution of it is a fine technical accomplishment. Above all, *The Great Gatsby* contains some of Fitzgerald's most beautiful and lyrical prose. See *Twentieth-Century Interpretations of 'The Great Gatsby': A Collection of Critical Essays* (1968), edited by Ernest Lockridge, and *The Achieving of 'The Great Gatsby': F. Scott Fitzgerald, 1920–1925* (1979), by Robert Emmet Long.

Great Hunger, The, a long poem by Patrick *Kavanagh, published in 1942. In fourteen parts, the poem is noted for its radical innovations in the treatment of rural material. The work exhibits great flexibility of style and form in sustaining its critique of the social and religious orthodoxy within which its chief protagonist, the peasant farmer Patrick Maguire, is confined. The intellectual, spiritual, imaginative, and sexual dimensions of his experience are charted with a harshly unsentimental but ultimately compassionate realism rooted in Kavanagh's personal knowledge of the circumstances of the small farmer. The poem modulates between lyrical, documentary, satirical, and dramatic idioms in achieving its concentrated presentation of Maguire's essentially static existence over several decades. Much of it implicitly repudiates the distortions of actuality perpetrated by the literature of the *Irish Revival; as Augustine Martin has written with reference to *The Great Hunger*, 'Kavanagh's most striking achievement in Irish poetry was to break the grip . . . of myth'. The poem's breach with the anodyne conventions of the modern pastoral drew it to the attention of the censor for its accounts of Maguire's sexual privations. In establishing a range of new registers for articulating the realities of rural life the work exemplified the potential of such subject matter for many succeeding Irish and British poets. It is widely regarded as one of the most successful long poems in English of the twentieth century.

GREEN, Henry, pseudonym of Henry Vincent YORKE (1905–73), British novelist, born in Tewkesbury, Gloucestershire, educated at Eton and at Magdalen College, Oxford. The third son of a wealthy family descended from the Earls of Hardwicke, he was brought up in a manor house in Gloucestershire, and sent to boarding school at the age of six. He joined the family business, H. Pontifex & Sons, Birmingham, beginning work in the stores, then on the shop-floor as a foundryman, and eventually becoming managing director. He married the Hon. Adelaide Biddulph in 1929. During the Second World War he served in the Auxiliary Fire Service. Green's nine novels and his 'interim autobiography', *Pack My Bag* (1940), are explorations of the English working and propertied classes across three decades. He began writing at school, and published his first novel, *Blindness* (1926), while still an undergraduate. He left Oxford without a degree, but in possession of a half blue for billiards. While serving his apprenticeship at his father's heavy engineering factory, he wrote to Neville Coghill, 'Some of the men are magnificent. The words they use even more so.' He drew on this experience for his second book, *Living* (1929), which Christopher *Isherwood described as 'the best proletarian novel ever written'. His close friend Evelyn *Waugh likened its style to 'those aluminium ribbons one stamps out in railway stations'. Green's novels of the war decade are his central achievement, a sequence of fiction which obliquely and movingly captures varied aspects of ordinary existence: *Party Going* (1939), a fable of social dislocation on the edge of war; *Caught* (1943), about fire-fighters preparing to cope with the approaching Blitz; *Loving* (1945), about the tensions above- and below-stairs in an Irish castle during wartime; and *Back* (1946), describing the traumatic return of prisoners-of-war to an England they do not recognize. *Concluding* (1948), set at the end of the millenium, is Green's vision of an over-administered future. His two final novels, *Nothing* (1950) and *Doting* (1952), depend increasingly on dialogue in the manner of Ivy *Compton-Burnett. *Surviving* (1992) collects his short stories, articles, and interviews. Like *Joyce, Green was dismissive of 'literary influences', only admitting, provocatively, to an admiration for Céline, and for the prose style of C. M. Doughty's *Arabia Deserta* (1888). His dialogue is careful of speech effects as inflected by class, and his descriptions are often lyrical and estranging. The reader has to take the measure of each character and situation, as if without any help from an author. Although he appeared to be uninterested in poetry, his statements about writing are those of a poet: 'Prose is not to be read aloud but to oneself at night, and it is not quick as poetry, but rather a gathering web of insinuations which go further than names however shared can ever go.' Many of his effects are sharply visual; a note to an exhibition of Matthew Smith's paintings, written in 1953, reveals the novelist's avidly graphic intelligence. Green's rewardingly strange prose ensured that sales of his novels were never very large, except for *Loving*, which briefly became a bestseller. But as the most genuinely innovative novelist of his generation he was read attentively by contemporaries such as Elizabeth *Bowen, W. H. *Auden, Angus *Wilson, Anthony *Powell, and John *Betjeman.

GREEN, Paul E(liot) (1894–1981), American dramatist, born in Lillington, North Carolina, educated at the University of North Carolina and Cornell University. He was a member of the Carolina Playmakers (which included Thomas *Wolfe), a writing and producing group founded at the University of North Carolina in 1918 by Frederick Koch. They had their own theatre, but also toured extensively through the Southern states, providing an influential model for the little theatre movement in regional and folk drama. Green's exploration of character through regional setting made a significant contribution to American drama, as in his first full-length play, *In Abraham's Bosom* (1926; Pulitzer Prize), influenced by Eugene O'Neill's **Emperor Jones*. His work is marked by a commitment to the underprivileged and dispossessed, both black and poor white, in a series of plays from the mid-1920s, culminating in his stage version of Richard Wright's novel **Native Son* (1941). His full-length plays include *Your Fiery Furnace* (1923), *The Field God* (1927), *Tread the Green Grass* (1929), *Roll, Sweet Chariot* (1934), and *The House of Connelly* (1931). He collaborated with Kurt Weill on a musical, *Johnny Johnson* (1937), and wrote a series of historical pageants which are performed annually at the venues for which they were written.

GREENE, (Henry) Graham (1904–91), English novelist, born in Berkhamsted, near London, educated at Berkhamsted School and Balliol College, Oxford. His father was the headmaster of Berkhamsted School; Greene has encouraged critics to see the divided loyalties which resulted as an origin of his fiction's distinctive antinomies and conflicting faiths—what he calls, quoting Robert Browning, its general concern with 'the dangerous edge of things | The honest thief, the tender murderer | The superstitious atheist'. Schooldays drove him close to breakdown and suicide—he was one of the first schoolboys in England to be psychoanalysed, in 1920—and Norman Sherry's *The Life of Graham Greene* (1989) has traced the cruelties of his fellow pupils as a source of the repeated interest of his fiction in fugitives, betrayal, secrecy, and lost innocence.

Oxford saw the publication of his only book of poems, *Babbling April* (1925), brief membership of the Communist Party, and a romance with Vivien Dayrell-Browning which required his conversion to Catholicism in 1926, before they married in 1927. Greene was by this time working as a sub-editor, first in Nottingham, later for *The Times*, an experience which may have encouraged the directness and economy which—along with brisk scenic construction perhaps learned from work as a film critic—marks much of his fiction. His first novel, however, *The Man Within* (1929), is a romantic period piece: like the two (later suppressed) which followed, *The Name of Action* (1930) and *Rumour at Nightfall* (1931), it bears traces of childhood admiration for authors such as Marjorie *Bowen, Rider *Haggard, John *Buchan, and a distant relation, Robert Louis Stevenson. *Stamboul Train* (1932) initiated his habitual setting in a contemporary world both highly realistic yet sufficiently idiosyncratic to have coined the critical description 'Greeneland'—a seedy domain of mean actions, disappointed hope, and the conviction that 'human nature is not black and white but black and grey'.

Greene cites personal financial anxiety as a factor encouraging realism at this time: it also disposed him to share the left-wing political perspective of the 1930s. This appears in the portrayal of the odious Swedish industrialist, Krogh, in *England Made Me* (1935); sympathy for Republican Spain in *The Confidential Agent* (1939); and questioning of the economic systems that create the depressed industrial landscapes of *It's a Battlefield* (1934) and *A Gun For Sale* (1936). Greene has suggested that he is a political writer rather than a Catholic one, though he has more often been critically assessed as the latter. Like that of his friend, Evelyn *Waugh, his Catholic faith was not apparent in his early writing: when it does appear, it is usually held in complex, often paradoxical tension with political or other secular values. These tensions began to figure centrally in **Brighton Rock* (1938), and continued through the other novels often held to be the core of Greene's achievement, *The *Power and the Glory* (1940), *The *Heart of the Matter* (1948)—drawing on wartime work for British Intelligence—and *The *End of the Affair* (1951).

With the exception of *A Burnt-Out Case* (1961), later fiction makes Catholicism a less central concern. Greene also renounced British settings until returning to Berkhamsted for the late spy story *The *Human Factor* (1978). Instead, in novels such as *The *Quiet American* (1955), **Our Man in Havana* (1958), *The Comedians* (1966), set in Papa Doc's Haiti, and *The Honorary Consul* (1973), a story of kidnapping in Argentina, Greene reflects the distant places and political conflicts he was drawn to in later years by his work as a journalist, or by friendships with world leaders such as Fidel Castro, Ho Chi Minh, Salvador Allende, and General Torrijos of Panama—or sometimes just by an urge to escape the boredom he claimed as a lifelong affliction. Though this later fiction typically uses 'the dangerous edge' of its setting to reflect and amplify stresses within its characters, central figues now often survive and even achieve a precarious enlightenment. From a tragic phase around the time of the Second World War, Greene's later writing sometimes moves towards romance and even comedy—darkly in *Doctor Fischer of Geneva* (1980) and his last published novel, *The Captain and the Enemy* (1988); more freely in *Monsignor Quixote* (1982) and *Travels with My Aunt* (1969).

Also including essays, literary criticism, plays, short stories, travel writing (*Journey Without Maps*, 1936; *The Lawless Roads*, 1939), autobiography (*A Sort of Life*, 1971; *Ways of Escape*, 1980), and screenplays (most notably *The *Third Man*, 1950), Greene's literary career spanned seven decades of the twentieth century and made him one of its most popular as well as critically admired authors. Though he described some of his earlier writing in the thriller genre as 'entertainment' to distinguish it from serious fiction, a particular achievement was his drawing together of the popular and the intellectual novel, reciprocally adding moral and psychological depth to the thriller, and, like his mentors Stevenson and Joseph *Conrad, elements of adventure to literary fiction. His appeal to a generally disillusioned age is also guaranteed by a continuing streak of romanticism which shows a credible if compromised heroism surviving in graceless, fallen worlds.

Green Hat, The, see ARLEN, MICHAEL.

Green Mansions, W. H. *Hudson's best-known work, first published in 1904. The novel takes its title from the words of its central protagonist, the political refugee Abel Guevez de Argensola, whose wanderings lead him to 'that wild forest, those green mansions where I . . . found so great a happiness'. Abel receives hospitality from an Indian tribe who live on the fringes of the tropical Venezuelan forest, but incurs disapproval by repeatedly visiting an area their superstitions forbid him to enter; there he is enchanted by 'a voice purified and brightened to something almost angelic', which belongs to Rima, a beautiful girl possessing magical affinities with the forest. An intense love develops between the two, but Rima is killed when she falls into a fire the Indians build around the base of a tall tree into which she has fled from them. Abel's grief and rage drive him to engineer the massacre of the tribe by their enemies;

bearing Rima's ashes, he returns to civilization stricken with guilt over his murderous actions. The book's success as an allegory of man's destructive violations of the beauty and sanctity of nature is largely a product of Hudson's vividly imaginative presentation of the forest; luxuriant imagery of dense vegetation in the constant play of light and shade forms a background to recurrent minutely observed descriptions of birds, snakes, and other creatures he had studied as a naturalist. Jacob Epstein's sculptural depiction of Rima is sited at the bird sanctuary in Hyde Park commemorating Hudson, which was opened in 1925.

Greenvoe, a novel by George Mackay *Brown, published in 1972. The island of Hellya and the village of Greenvoe which form the book's setting are imaginative adaptations of the Orkney landscapes and communities reflected throughout Brown's work. The main body of the novel presents a period of five days in the lives of the inhabitants of Greenvoe; the farming and fishing which form their principal occupations are evoked with detailed authenticity, as are the patterns of social interrelations on the island. From this episodic treatment a comprehensive portrait of a declining culture emerges and the presence of a stranger is explained in terms of his secret business on behalf of the government; the penultimate section of novel depicts the clearance and destruction of Greenvoe to make way for Black Star, a defence project which is eventually abandoned, leaving Hellya utterly desolate. In a brief concluding passage possible regeneration is symbolized when, ten years after the evacuation of the island, a band of villagers return and conduct a ceremony bringing 'light and blessing to the kingdom of winter'. The book forms an extended parable warning of the need to tend the inheritance from nature and history vital to the welfare of a society. Brown's stylistic register is wide, ranging from occasional passages in a richly poetic mode to the effective colloquial tone employed elsewhere. The account of the preparations for Black Star is written with a remarkable narrative economy that creates an emphatic impression of the swiftness of the catastrophe.

GREENWOOD, Walter (1903–74), British novelist and playwright, born in Salford, Lancashire. He left school at the age of 13 and, between long periods of unemployment, worked as an office boy, stable boy for a cotton millionaire, signwriter, chauffeur, warehouseman, and salesman. His early experiences of deprivation provided the background for his first and most famous novel, *Love on the Dole* (1933), which made a great impact at the time, and contributed significantly to the popular pressures which eventually led to the founding of the welfare state, through its descriptions of hardship brought about by the Depression, the humiliations imposed by the means test, and the desperation caused by mass unemployment. With Roland Gow, Greenwood adapted the novel into a successful play; it was also filmed in 1941. Greenwood also wrote the screenplay *No Limit* (1935) for the comedian George Formby, and wrote many other novels, including *His Worship the Mayor* (1934), which exposed corruption in local government. His plays include *My Son My Son* (1935), *The Cure for Love* (1951), and *Saturday Night at the Crown* (1953). *There Was a Time* (1967) is his autobiography. Randall Stevenson discusses Greenwood in *The British Novel Since the Thirties* (1986). Greenwood foreshadowed later Northern working-class novelists such as John *Braine and David *Storey.

GREER, Germaine (1939–), Australian feminist writer, born in Melbourne, educated at the universities of Melbourne, Sydney, and Cambridge. In 1964 she settled in Europe, spending much of her time in Britain and Italy. Among other academic posts she has been a lecturer at the University of Warwick and Director of the Tulsa Center for the Study of Women's Literature. She achieved worldwide fame with *The Female Eunuch* (1970) after its publication in the USA in 1971; the book questioned stereotypical depictions of, and assumptions about, women and achieved something of a cult status during the 1970s. *The Obstacle Race* (1979), *The Revolting Garden* (1979; under the pseudonym 'Rose Blight'), and *Sex and Destiny* (1984) extended her feminist concerns. Her other works include *The Mad Woman's Underclothes: Essays and Other Writings 1968–85* (1986), and *Daddy We Hardly Knew You* (1989), which explored her own family background. In *The Change: Women, Ageing and the Menopause* (1991) Greer argues passionately that the end of fertility can signal new freedoms for women. Greer studies the lives and work of poets including Sappho, Katherine Philips, and Aphra Behn in *Slip-Shod Sybils* (1995), arguing that because so few women wrote poetry in English before 1900, their work cannot be relied upon to be representative of women's sensibility and is often derivative and inauthentic. She has also edited *The Collected Works of Katherine Philips, The Matchless Orinda* (1993).

GREG, Sir W(alter) W(ilson) (1875–1959), British bibliographer, editor, and literary historian, born in Wimbledon, educated at Trinity College, Cambridge. In 1900 he completed his first work of bibliography, a finding list of plays written before 1643 and published before 1700. His unrivalled expertise in Elizabethan palaeography enabled him to produce his editions of Henslowe's *Diary* (1904) and *Papers* (1908). He also worked extensively with sixteenth- and seventeenth-century manuscripts as general editor for the Malone Society; *English Literary Autographs: 1550–1650* (1925–32), an edition of facsimiles and transcripts of documents, remains a primary tool for identifying the hands of various playwrights and scriveners. He is best known for *A Bibliography of the English Printed Drama to the Restoration* (four volumes, 1939–59), a work of great significance in the development of modern bibliographical studies. His numerous other publications include *The Editorial Problem in Shakespeare* (1942) and his widely admired dual-text edition of Marlowe's *'Doctor Faustus', 1604–1616* (1950).

GREGORY, Horace (Victor) (1898–1982), American poet and critic, born in Milwaukee, Wisconsin, educated at the University of Wisconsin at Madison. After graduation he moved to New York where he married the poet Marya *Zaturenska and published his first volume of poems, *Chelsea Rooming House* (1930); it was his evocation of the crowded slums of New York's lower west side that briefly associated him with Marxist and proletarian writers of the depression. His other volumes of verse include *No Retreat* (1933), *Chorus for Survival* (1935), *Poems, 1930–1940* (1941), *Selected Poems* (1951), *Medusa in Gramercy Park* (1961), *Collected Poems* (1964), and *Another Look* (1976). Like other modernist contemporaries, Gregory's verse frequently employs loose poetic structures and elliptical syntax, but his vision was more markedly social. From 1934 to 1960 he taught at Sarah Lawrence College (after retiring in 1961 he remained a Professor Emeritus until his death). Among his works as a distinguished translator from Latin are *The Poems of Catullus* (1931), Ovid's *The Metamorphoses* (1958), and *The Love Poems of Ovid* (1964). Notable among his works of literary and art criticism are *Pilgrim of the Apocalypse: A Critical Study of D. H. Lawrence* (1933) and *The World of James McNeill Whistler* (1959). He edited several anthologies, and with Marya Zaturenska published *A History of American Poetry, 1900–1940* (1946).

GREGORY, Lady (Isabella) Augusta (1852–1932), Irish playwright and folklorist, the youngest daughter of an Anglo-Irish landowner; she was born in Roxborough, Co. Galway. Following the death of her husband Sir W. H. Gregory in 1892, she took over the management of his estate at Coole Park, County Galway. A leading figure in the *Irish Revival, her close association from 1897 onward with W. B. *Yeats, who regularly stayed at Coole, resulted in the foundation of the *Abbey Theatre. Her account of the theatre's earlier history is contained in *Our Irish Theatre* (1913). Her skills in the written recreation of the dialects of western Ireland were used to assist Yeats in the writing of **Cathleen Ni Houlihan*, *The Pot of Broth*, performed in 1902, and other plays. She wrote some forty independent works as a playwright, including a series of dialect adaptations of Molière's work collected as *The Kiltartan Molière* (1910). The majority of her own works are one-act comedies, the best being contained in *Seven Short Plays* (1909); among her numerous further collections of plays are *New Comedies* (1913) and *Three Wonder Plays* (1922). Her other works include the translations from the Irish of *Gods and Fighting Men* (1904) and the compilations from Irish folklore published as *Poets and Dreamers* (1903), *A Book of Saints and Wonders* (1906), and *Visions and Beliefs in the West of Ireland* (1920). The many volumes of the Coole Edition of her works began appearing under the general editorship of Colin Smythe in 1970. Elizabeth Coxhead's *Lady Gregory: A Literary Portrait* appeared in 1961.

GRENFELL, Julian (Henry Francis) (1888–1915), British poet, the eldest son of Lord Desborough; he was educated at Balliol College, Oxford, after which he took a commission with the Royal Dragoons in 1910. A keen sportsman and much admired officer, he won the Distinguished Service Order for a courageous act of reconnaissance. He died of a head wound on 26 May 1915, the day upon which his poem 'Into Battle', sent to his mother the previous month, appeared in *The Times*; the *Morning Post* acclaimed it as 'the one incorruptible and incomparable poem which the war has yet given us' and Grenfell's name joined *Brooke's as a paragon of nobility and self-sacrifice. While 'Into Battle' has, like Brooke's work, been disparaged for its enthusiastic view of death in action, it is remarkable for the compelling accumulation of natural imagery through which it invokes the heroic spirit. Robert *Graves considered the poem an authentic expression of the 'overwhelming sense of natural beauty which a soldier is entitled to recognize as a premonition of death'. Grenfell's work was represented in T. Sturge Moore's edition of *Some Soldier Poets* (1919); no collection of his poetry has yet been published, although selections from it appear in *Julian Grenfell* (1976) by Nicholas Mosley.

GRENVILLE, Kate (1950–), Australian writer, born in Sydney, educated at Sydney University and the University of Colorado. She travelled in Europe and the USA for several years and has worked as a teacher, journalist, and film editor. Her first collection of stories, *Bearded Ladies* (1984), displayed her command of a variety of styles from black comedy to symbolism. *Lillian's Story* (1985) is a novel whose central character was based on a well-known Sydney street personality; the protagonist, oppressed by her father, takes refuge in food, only to court social and sexual ostracism, but she manages to survive despite her traumatic experiences. *Dreamhouse* (1986) is a psychosexual thriller set in Tuscany, describing a woman trapped in an unsatisfactory marriage and her eventual escape. The author's feminist convictions are also apparent in *Joan Makes History* (1988), which in comic mode argues that history has ignored women; the story of a modern Joan is linked to a series of other ordinary women, all named Joan, from earlier periods of history. *Writing Book* appeared in 1990. Her novel *Dark Places* (1994) is narrated by a misogynist who rapes the daughter who first appeared in *Lillian's Story*.

GREY, Zane, born Pearl Zane GREY (1872–1939), American novelist, born in Zanesville, Ohio, educated at the University of Pennsylvania. A youthful enthusiasm for dime novels and stories of his great-great-grandfather's heroic actions against the Indians gave rise to Grey's lasting conviction that literature and life were inextricably linked. He moved to New York ostensibly to practise dentistry, but in reality to get closer to the heart of publishing. In 1905 he married Lisa Elise Roth, who provided Grey with support as he strove to establish himself as a writer. *The Last of the Plainsmen* was published in 1908, but it was not until the publication of *Riders of the Purple Sage*

(1912) that he hit the bestseller lists. By pairing the civilizing heroine, Jane Withersteen, with Lassiter, the anarchic individualist, Grey ensured that the attraction they feel for each other is strong enough to indicate how each yearns for the other's strengths, thus initiating a dialogue of forces which is not resolved until the end of the book. This, combined with the book's narrative drive and intense, excitable language, indicates why *Riders* remains the most famous of all *Western novels. Grey wrote over sixty novels in all, but he never lost his love for the wilderness, returning frequently to the deserts which he felt constituted his real spiritual home.

GRIERSON, Sir Herbert (John Clifford) (1866–1960), British editor and critic, born in Quendale on the southern tip of Shetland, educated at King's College, the University of Aberdeen, and Christ Church, Oxford. In 1894 he became the first Professor of English Literature at Aberdeen and was subsequently Professor of Rhetoric and English Literature at the University of Edinburgh. Following his contribution of the chapter on John Donne to *The Cambridge History of English Literature* (edited by A. W. Ward and A. R. Waller, thirteen volumes, 1907–16), he produced his edition of *The Poems of John Donne* (two volumes, 1912). This work and his edition of *Metaphysical Lyrics and Poems of the Seventeenth Century* (1921), T. S. *Eliot's review of which gave rise to the celebrated phrase '*dissociation of sensibility', were strongly influential in the growth of critical interest in metaphysical poetry during the 1920s. His other publications include the critical study *Cross Currents in the Literature of the XVII Century* (1929) and the biography *Walter Scott, Bart.* (1938). He was knighted in 1936 for his services to literature.

GRIEVE, C. M., see MACDIARMID, HUGH.

GRIFFITHS, Trevor (1935–), British playwright, born in Manchester, the son of a labourer, educated at Manchester University. *Occupations* (1970), set during the 1920 Fiat strike in Turin, and focusing on arguments between a humane Gramsci and the ruthless Soviet apparatchik Kabak, was followed by two other plays written from a Marxist stance and asking how radical social change is best achieved: these were *The Party* (1973), in which a representative cross-section of leftists debate the student uprising in the Paris of 1968 while it unfolds on television, and **Comedians* (1975). Other works for the stage include *Sam, Sam* (1972), a semi-autobiographical piece about a young man who, for better or worse, remains trapped by his working-class roots while his brother makes an emotionally damaging journey into the middle class; *The Gulf Between Us* (1992), about English builders isolated in Iraq during the hostilities that followed the invasion of Kuwait; and *Thatcher's Children* (1993), which follows the lives of a group of friends from primary school in 1973 to the cruder, harder, more violent England we can expect to see in 1999. Griffiths has also adapted other people's work, freely transforming Chekhov's *Platonov* into the overtly socialist *Piano* (1990), and written plays for television, among them *Absolute Beginners* (1974), a drama about Lenin; *Through the Night* (1975), about a mastectomy patient in a notably impersonal hospital; and a series about a left-wing Labour politician, *Bill Brand* (1976).

GRIGSON, Geoffrey (Edward Harvey) (1905–85), British poet, critic, editor, and topographical writer, born at Pelynt, Cornwall, educated at St Edmund Hall, Oxford. He began his career as a journalist at the London office of the *Yorkshire Post* in 1927. In 1933 he founded **New Verse*, which provided the principal platform for his famously vehement style as a critic. During the war he worked at the BBC and subsequently became a freelance writer. His prolific output of literary journalism is represented by numerous collections of his critical writings which include *The Contrary View* (1974) and *Blessings, Kicks, and Curses* (1982). As an art critic, he was one of the first to recognize the achievements of Ben Nicholson and Henry Moore; *Samuel Palmer, the Visionary Years* (1947) prompted a revaluation of that artist's work. *The Englishman's Flora* (1955) and *The Shell Country Book* (1962) are among the best-known of his widely read works on the English countryside. His many collections of poetry include *Several Observations* (1939), *The Isles of Scilly* (1946), *A Skull in Salop* (1967), *Sad Grave of an Imperial Mongoose* (1973), and *Montaigne's Tower* (1984). Collected editions of his poems appeared in 1963 and 1982. The extent of Grigson's other activities have tended to obscure his stature as a poet. Much of his earlier verse, which displayed a laconically individual tone, was typical of the 1930s in its disquieted awareness of socio-cultural malaise. Throughout his career he avoided straightforwardly conventional forms, though his conversational manner frequently made rich use of subtle technical effects. His poems, which are invariably intelligent and fundamentally humane, range from lovingly particularized contemplations of the English countryside to scathingly funny satires of which 'White Tom's Position', on T. S. *Eliot, is the best known. His other notable publications include the autobiography *The Crest on the Silver* (1950) and *Recollections, Mainly of Writers and Artists* (1984).

GRISHAM, John (1955–), American novelist, born in Jonesboro, Arkansas, he studied law at Mississippi State University and the University of Mississippi and practised as a lawyer from 1981 to 1990. He also served in the Mississippi House of Representatives from 1984 to 1990. Grisham's fiction is informed by his knowledge of the American legal system. *A Time to Kill* (1989), his first novel, concerns the father of a rape victim who kills his daughter's attacker. *The Firm* (1991), which established him as a best-selling author, and its successors *The Pelican Brief* (1992) and *The Client* (1993), are treatments of individuals rendered vulnerable by their discoveries of corruption in legal and political circles. *The Chamber* (1994), which offers a deeply considered view of the death penalty, attracted more critical acclaim than its predecessors.

Sales of Grisham's books have reached levels at which his publishers style him 'the most popular author in the world'. *The Rainmaker* (1995) concerns a young lawyer who singlehandedly pursues an action against a major American insurance company.

GROSS, Philip (1952–), British poet, born in Cornwall, educated at the University of Sussex, subsequently training as a librarian. Gross's work first attracted wide notice when his poem 'The Ice Factory' won the Poetry Society's National Poetry Competition in 1982. His first collection, *Familiars* (1983), was followed by other volumes including *The Ice Factory* (1984), *Cat's Whisker* (1987), *The Son of the Duke of Nowhere* (1991), and *I.D.* (1994). Gross's poetry has an air of accessibility produced by its wealth of precise detail; the social and domestic incidents supporting many of his narratives provide events and images embodying the unsettling intuitions often developed in the course of his poems. His unobtrusive use of intricate schemes of rhyme and metre and a firm technical control is evident in all his writing. He collaborated with Sylvia *Kantaris to produce *The Air Mines of Mistila* (1988, illustrated by Kim Lewis), a poetic fantasy which may be read as a parable of Western civilization's destructive greed for valuable natural resources.

Group, The, a term denoting both a critical method forming a basis for the meetings of various writers, predominantly poets, and the name by which they came to be known as a loosely coherent movement. Philip *Hobsbaum initiated regular gatherings of poets in Cambridge in 1952 for discussions intended to bring F. R. *Leavis's principles of textual scrutiny to bear upon their work. In 1955 he convened a similar association of poets in London which became identified as the Group; Hobsbaum was its chairman until 1959, when he was succeeded by Edward *Lucie-Smith. Members, who joined at the chairman's invitation, submitted copies of their work for analysis and appraisal by their peers; disciplined experimentation, consciousness of poetry's social dimensions, directness of tone, and imaginative energy were among the qualities upon which a high value was placed, partly in reaction to what members perceived as the arid formalism of the *Movement. Notable among the writers concerned were Alan *Brownjohn, Martin *Bell, Peter *Porter, Peter *Redgrove, George *MacBeth, Fleur *Adcock, and B. S. *Johnson, whose wide range of styles and thematic preoccupations gave an eclectic character to *A Group Anthology* (1963), which Hobsbaum and Lucie-Smith edited. In 1965 the Group was more formally constituted as the Writer's Workshop, a development for which Martin Bell was significantly responsible, which met at the Poetry Society's premises in Earls Court. Hobsbaum introduced the Group's principles and practice to a series of meetings he held in Belfast during the early 1960s, which proved of great value to a number of the *Ulster poets. As the model for many subsequent forums for emerging writers and in terms of the achievement of some of its members, the Group occupies a position of considerable importance in post-war British poetry.

Group, The, see MCCARTHY, MARY.

Group Theatre (1931–41), American theatre company. Founded by Harold Clurman, Lee Strasberg, and Cheryl Crawford, and based in New York, it was an offshoot of the Theatre Guild, and planned as a permanent acting company committed to the highest ideals of professionalism in all aspects of theatre work. It encouraged new writers, and sought new plays which expressed some of the social and artistic ideals of its members. It took the Moscow Art Theatre as its model, and Lee Strasberg was particularly instrumental in introducing Konstantin Stanislavsky's theories of acting to the company, which he later expanded in the Actors' Studio where he taught the principles of 'Method' acting. Though the company failed to establish a permanent theatre, and was finally split apart by internal faction, it none the less had a powerful impact on the American theatre, and in its egalitarian organization, and its commitment to socialist politics, was a forerunner of the *Living Theatre and the *Open Theatre. The Group Theatre's most notable productions include Paul *Green's *The House of Connelly* (1931); John Howard Lawson's *Success Story* (1932); Sidney *Kingsley's *Man in White* (1933); three plays by Clifford *Odets, **Waiting for Lefty* (1935), *Awake and Sing!* (1935), and *Paradise Lost* (1935); and Paul Green and Kurt Weill's musical based on Erwin Piscator's *The Good Soldier Schweik*, under the title of *Johnny Johnson* (1937). It had an immense critical and popular success with Odets's *Golden Boy* (1937), and in its last three years produced new plays by Irwin *Shaw, *The Gentle People* (1938) and *Retreat to Pleasure* (1940–1), and William *Saroyan's *My Heart's in the Highlands* (1939). Harold Clurman's history of the Group Theatre, *The Fervent Years*, appeared in 1945.

Group Theatre, The, an experimental theatre company begun in 1932 by Rupert Doone to provide a focus for the activities of various actors, writers, and producers who were dissatisfied with the possibilities afforded by London's existing commercial facilities. The venture was also committed to working in broad alignment with the socialist doctrines pervasive in the arts during the 1930s. Doone, a ballet dancer and choreographer who had worked with Diaghilev and Cocteau in Paris, was assisted by the painter Robert Medley, the schoolfriend of W. H. *Auden's who had prompted him to become a poet in 1922, in organizing the basic membership. A commission to Auden eventually resulted in *The Dance of Death* (1933), which was given trial performances in 1934 and produced at the Westminster Theatre with T. S. *Eliot's *Sweeney Agonistes* in 1935. Eminent among the other poets involved were Stephen *Spender, whose *Trial of a Judge* (1938) the company produced, and Louis *MacNeice, who supplied his translation of *Agamemnon*

(1936) and *Out of the Picture* (1937). W. B. *Yeats and Eliot, who had written *The Rock* (1934) in association with members of the Group, led attempts to secure the Mercury Theatre, Notting Hill Gate, for performances after 1935; *The *Ascent of F6* (1936), one of the company's three plays by Auden and *Isherwood, was highly successful when staged there. The graphic artists associated with the theatre included Henry Moore and John Piper. Benjamin Britten composed incidental music for numerous productions. Having disbanded in 1939, the Group was revived from 1950 to 1954, their performances of Sartre's *The Flies* (1946) in 1951 being among the more memorable of later productions.

GROVE, Frederick Philip (1879–1948), Canadian novelist, born Felix Paul Greve in Radomno, Prussia (now Poland); he was brought up in Hamburg and subsequently attended university in Bonn and Munich. His picaresque early life involved associations with Stefan George and André Gide, a year in prison for fraudulently obtaining money from a friend, periods in Italy, Sicily, France, and Berlin, a host of translations, and the publication of a volume of poetry and a verse-drama. In 1909 he faked his death and fled to North America, where he invented a new identity for himself. Although he wrote an 'autobiography', *In Search of Myself* (1946), much of this work is fiction and it is hard to disentangle the facts of his 'real' life immediately after he settled in Canada. He probably worked as a farm labourer for a few years before later becoming a teacher in Manitoba. It was as Frederick Philip Grove, a writer of 'realistic' novels and a founding father of prairie fiction, that he became known. Perhaps his greatest fiction was himself. Grove's books include *Over Prairie Trails* (1922), a non-fiction account of travels in rural Manitoba, and the novels *Settlers of the Marsh* (1925), *Our Daily Bread* (1928), *Fruits of the Earth* (1933), and *The Master of the Mill* (1944). Despite his reputation as a realist, all his work contains passages in which romanticism intrudes.

GUARE, John (1938–), American playwright, born in Manhattan, educated at Georgetown University and at Yale. Much of Guare's work revolves around themes of family and success. His writing is recognized for its dark humour and his seemingly paradoxical romanticism. Among his best-known plays is *The House of Blue Leaves* (1971), the story of a would-be songwriter and his disastrous relationship with his family. *Landscape of the Body* (1978) relates events when Betty Yearn visits Greenwich Village to rescue her sister from life as a porn actress. In *Lydle Breeze* (1982) and *Gardenia* (1986), Guare uncharacteristically leaves the milieu of the present day for the post-American Civil War period. *Six Degrees of Separation* (1990; New York Drama Critics Award) is based on an incident in 1983 when a young con artist posed as Sidney Poitier and robbed various wealthy New Yorkers; Guare wrote the screenplay for the film of 1993. In addition to other screenplays such as *Taking off* (1971), in collaboration with Milos Forman and Jean-Claude Carrière, and *Atlantic City* (1981), Guare has also written musicals including *Two Gentlemen of Verona* (1971).

GUEDALLA, Philip (1889–1944), British historian and biographer, born in London, educated at Balliol College, Oxford. After he had repeatedly failed to become a Member of Parliament, *Supers and Supermen* (1920) established him as an author; its epigrammatically irreverent treatments of historical figures owed something to *Strachey's *Eminent Victorians* (1918). Similar in approach, *A Gallery* (1924) surveyed contemporary literary reputations. *The Second Empire* (1922), a study of France under Napoleon III, was his first historical work of note; engagingly biographical and impressively scholarly, it set the pattern for *Palmerston* (1926); *The Duke* (1931), a study of Wellington; and *The Queen and Mr Gladstone* (two volumes, 1933). His talent for vivid historical narrative was at its best in *The Hundred Years* (1936), which encompassed the century following Victoria's accession. His writings in support of the Allied cause during the Second World War include *Middle East 1940–1942: A Study in Air Power* (1944). Among Guedalla's other works are the accounts of his visits to North and South America respectively contained in *Conquistador* (1927) and *Argentine Tango* (1932).

Guerrillas, a novel by V. S. *Naipaul, published in 1976, based on a murder case involving Michael X which the author reported for the *Sunday Times Magazine* in May 1974 (his exploration of the true story is to be found in *The Return of Eva Perón and the Killings in Trinidad*, 1980). The novel is set in an unnamed recently independent Caribbean island that is being sustained by foreign interests, and the 'guerrillas' of the title are would-be revolutionary members of an agricultural commune led by the charismatic but dubious Jimmy Ahmed, whose racial and sexual ambiguities distort his political ideals. Another principal character is Peter Roche, an Englishman who acts as public relations officer for the local company that financially supports the commune in order to keep it under control. Roche's English girlfriend Jane accompanies him to the island, and her fascinated interaction with Ahmed builds towards a compelling picture of sexual and political violence and frustration in a disordered and despairing society. The Black Power revolution that Ahmed has been preparing for does not materialize, for when the opportunity comes no one rallies to his call. His grandiloquent fantasies culminate in his brutal sexual assault on Jane, after which he orders his homosexual partner to hack her to death. Roche finds himself in a position where he conspires to conceal her death (since she has managed to enter the country without a visa there is no official record of her presence there in the first place). Roche himself, as company scapegoat, must leave; and now that Ahmed's impotence is established, the government can dispense with him. There are no winners by the end of a novel that is a brilliant and brooding observation of psychological and political defeat.

GUNESEKERA, Romesh (1954–), Sri Lankan novelist and short-story writer, born in Sri Lanka; he lived in the Philippines and the USA before settling in England. Gunesekera's first collection of stories, *Monkfish Moon* (1992), was praised for its restrained, subtle prose. Set in Sri Lanka and in Britain, the stories explore, from a variety of perspectives, the violence, conflict, and strife prevalent in the author's native land, and the impact of ethnic and political mistrust on his characters' psyches. With his first novel, *Reef* (1994), Gunesekera established himself in the front rank of the singularly talented post-*Rushdie generation of expatriate South Asian writers (which includes the Indians Amitav *Ghosh, Sunetra *Gupta, and Amit *Chaudhuri, and the Pakistanis Aamer Hussein, Sara Suleri, and Nadeem Aslam). In *Reef*, which reads like a collection of stories linked by a single narrative perspective, Gunesekera employs the device of presenting complex political issues in a voice that grows from innocence to experience as the tale proceeds. Triton, a simple village boy, learns from his sympathetic master the ways of the world, witnesses the systematic dismemberment of his country, and finds himself and his destiny in exile in England. Though similar to his stories, the longer episodic form of *Reef* gives Gunesekera the opportunity to splice his account with metaphysical ruminations, and to display his gift for lyrical descriptions of landscape.

GUNN, Neil M(iller) (1891–1973), Scottish novelist and leading figure of the *Scottish Renaissance, born in Dalbeath, Caithness, the son of a fishing boat skipper and owner. All his work is set in the Scottish Highlands, particularly in Caithness and Sutherland. Gunn worked in the Customs and Excise from 1911 to 1937. His first stories and articles were published in 1923; the following year he met C. M. Grieve (Hugh *MacDiarmid) who influenced his work, although the two were later estranged. His first novel, *The Grey Coast* (1926), dealt with the fishing trade familiar from his childhood; it was followed by *Morning Tide* (1931), the story of a boy's growth from childhood to young manhood, set in the Highlands. *The Lost Glen* (1932) continued the exploration of Highland moors and the threat to them by 'foreign' usurpation of lands and rights; *Sun Circle* (1933) and *Butcher's Broom* (1934) were historical novels, the first an account of the Pictish communities, the second a recreation of the infamous Highland clearances. *Highland River* (1937), which follows its protagonist from boyhood to maturity, is informed by the numinous quality and by the sense of oneness with the natural world which is a feature of his work. *The Silver Darlings* (1941), *Young Art and Old Hector* (1942), *The Serpent* (1943), and *The Green Isle of the Great Deep* (1944) are works in which an anti-materialist philosophy and a sense of the mythic combine with an acute insight into the workings of a community. *The Drinking Well* (1947) is an ambitious work, incorporating a dialectic between urban and rural ways of life; it also shared an increasing didacticism with later novels such as *The Other Landscape* (1954). In his later years Gunn struggled with the complications of his own Nationalist position and moved eventually to an idiosyncratic Zen Buddhism. Other works include two collections of essays, *The Other Landscape* (1949) and the posthumous *Landscape and Light* (1987), edited by A. McCleery.

GUNN, Thom(son William) (1929–), Anglo-American poet, born in Gravesend, educated at Trinity College, Cambridge. From the mid-1950s he has lived chiefly in California, where he began lecturing at the University of California, Berkeley, in 1958. *Fighting Terms* (1954), his first substantial collection of verse, displayed the energetic engagement of experience that has remained a central characteristic of his verse throughout continuous stylistic developments; he has described his poetry as 'a debate between the passion for definition and the passion for flow'. The rational tone and accomplished use of conventional forms in his earlier work led to his association with the *Movement, in whose anthologies he was represented. *The Sense of Movement* (1957) emphasized his individuality in poetry unusual for the formal virtuosity of its treatments of themes derived from popular culture. With *My Sad Captains* (1961) his work became more conversationally flexible through the adoption of syllabic verse-lines, which are used alongside more traditional metres throughout *Touch* (1967) and *Moly* (1971). The latter indicates his participation in the Californian 'alternative culture' of the late 1960s and repeatedly invokes the effects of hallucinatory drugs. *Jack Straw's Castle* (1975) increased the exploratory freedom of his verse forms. The candour with which he had always used autobiographical material culminated in the open treatments of his homosexuality in *The Passages of Joy* (1982) and *The Man with Night Sweats* (1992), works of remarkable technical and thematic range. Among the numerous publications by *small presses which sustained his ethos of experimentation throughout the 1980s are *Undesirables* (1988) and *Death's Door* (1989). *Selected Poems: 1950–1975* appeared in 1979. *The Occasions of Poetry* (edited by Clive *Wilmer, 1982) is a collection of his critical and autobiographical essays; among his works as an editor are *Selected Poems of Fulke Greville* (1968).

GUPPY, Shusha (1939–), British memoirist and essayist of Persian origin, born and brought up in Tehran. She later studied Middle Eastern languages and philosophy at the Sorbonne, Paris, before moving to England where she established her career as a singer, songwriter, and recording artist, and as a critic, essayist, and travel writer. Her first book, *The Blindfold Horse* (1988), a memoir, tells the story of her scholarly Persian family against the deftly drawn backdrop of a dramatically changing mid-century Iran. Guppy's poetic, graceful writing style displays the influence of Karen *Blixen. Though her reminiscences adopt the mode of non-fiction, *The Blindfold Horse* has been compared with Isabel Allende's *House of Spirits* for its narrative energy and its evocation of a bygone age. *A Girl in Paris* (1991), its sequel, tells the story of

Guppy's years in France, her encounters with such figures as Prévert and Camus, and her discovery of herself as woman and artist. *Looking Back* (1993) consists of Guppy's dialogues with, and studies of, several eminent twentieth-century women of letters.

GUPTA, Sunetra (1965–), Indian novelist, born in Calcutta, educated at Princeton University and Imperial College, London. She was brought up mainly in Africa, and has spent much of her adult life in Britain. Her first novel, *Memories of Rain* (1992), tells the story of the Indian Moni's growing estrangement from her adulterous English husband and his native country. It was highly praised for its elaborate prose style, and she was compared to *Woolf and *Smart. Her fiction is dense with quotations from *Tagore, references to European literary giants, and allusion to Greek myth. *The Glassblower's Breath* (1993), her controversial second novel, takes more risks with the form; some critics took exception to its melodramatic character. Set in the span of a day, it follows the footsteps of a young Indian woman pursued by her several lovers; it shifts between past and present, memory, fantasy, and stream-of-consciousness, negotiating the disparate cultures, landscapes, and literary traditions of England, America, and India. In *Moonlight into Marzipan* (1995) Gupta intertwines the myth of Prometheus with a contemporary fable of scientific discovery. The novel, which is characteristically set in Britain and in India, shows a new and wide-ranging social awareness, and a considerable gift for mock-decadent satire.

GURNEY, Ivor (Bertie) (1890–1937), British poet and composer, born in Gloucester, educated at the Royal College of Music. He was on active service in Flanders from 1915 to 1918, when he was discharged after being wounded and gassed. He returned to the Royal College of Music in 1919. *Severn and Somme* (1917), his first collection of verse, was favourably reviewed; *War's Embers* (1919) was well received, though reservations were expressed over its colloquially direct diction. A third collection, provisionally entitled *Rewards of Wonder*, was rejected by his publisher in 1919. The more orthodox modes of the previous work, which often forms rich evocations of rural Gloucestershire, was superseded by new approaches suggested by his readings of Hopkins and Whitman. His increasingly idiosyncratic manner was manifest in juxtapositions of a passionate lyricism with strikingly factual documentation of conditions on the Western Front. During the period 1918 to 1922 his career in poetry and music progressed encouragingly: his poems appeared in influential journals and his first published compositions, *Five Elizabethan Songs* (1920), were highly acclaimed. *Ludlow and Teme* (1923) and *The Western Playland* (1926), his settings of verse by A. E. *Housman, and *Lights Out* (1925), his treatments of six poems by Edward *Thomas, were mainly written at this time. Following a deterioration of his mental health, which had been uncertain for some time, in 1922 he was committed to the City of London Mental Hospital in Dartford, where he remained until his death. He continued to compose music and poetry, though his output diminished after 1926. Five volumes of his songs were published between 1938 and 1980. *Collected Poems*, edited by P. J. *Kavanagh, appeared in 1982. *The Ordeal of Ivor Gurney*, a biography by Michael Hurd, appeared in 1978.

GUSTAFSON, Ralph (1909–), Canadian poet, born in the Eastern Townships of Quebec, educated at Bishop's University and Oxford University. He worked as a journalist in England, where his earliest verse was published in the 1930s, and subsequently in New York, during which time his early romanticism gave way to a verse more concerned with exploring social issues and the decline in moral values. After returning to Canada in 1960 he was a music critic for the Canadian Broadcasting Corporation and a professor of English at Bishop's University. Gustafson's interest in music informs his poetry of different periods. His later poetry employs a more *confessional tone and includes *Ixion's Wheel* (1969), *Fire on Stone* (1974), *Corners in the Glass* (1977), *Conflicts of Spring* (1981), and *The Moment Is All* (1983), a selection of his best work from 1944 to 1983. His numerous other volumes of verse include *The Golden Chalice* (1935), *Flight into Darkness* (1944), *Rivers among Rocks* (1960), and *Rocky Mountain Poems* (1960). Gustafson has also edited several anthologies of Canadian writing, including *Anthology of Canadian Poetry (English)* (1942) and *The Penguin Book of Canadian Verse* (1958; revised 1967). His short stories are collected in *The Brazen Tower* (1974) and *The Vivid Air* (1980).

GUY, Rosa (Cuthbert) (1925–), African-American novelist, born in Trinidad; she grew up in Harlem, New York. After working in a clothing factory, she attended New York University and began writing through her involvement with the American Negro Theatre; her play *Venetian Blind* was produced in 1954. She was one of the founders of the Harlem Writers' Guild in 1950. *Bird at My Window* (1966), her first novel, forms an uncompromising treatment of the despair engendered by conditions in the Harlem ghetto in the 1950s. Her most highly regarded work is *A Measure of Time* (1983), which registers social developments from the 1920s onward in its story of a black woman who leaves the oppression of Alabama to seek new opportunities in New York. Also well known as a writer for children, Guy edited *Children of Longing* (1970), a collection of revealing interviews with African-American children during the civil rights crises of the 1960s. *My Love, My Love: Or the Peasant Girl* (1985) is a retelling of Hans Christian Andersen's tale 'The Little Mermaid' newly set in the Caribbean.

H

HACKER, Marilyn (1942–), American poet, born in New York City, educated at Washington Square College of New York University and the Art Students League. In her first volume of poetry, *Presentation Piece* (1974; National Book Award, 1975), and in *Separations* (1976), Hacker begins to articulate her dissatisfaction with woman's traditional roles. *Taking Notice* (1980) and *Assumptions* (1985) contain reflections on the women in her life, including her mother, friends, and lovers. *Love, Death and the Changing of the Seasons* (1986), a poetic novel of a lesbian love affair, is an evocative and sensual work containing graphic sexual descriptions. In *Going Back to the River* (1990) the poet comes to terms with loss after the dissolution of a love affair as she writes of loves and life in Paris and New York. In *Winter Numbers* (1994) Hacker evokes memories linking the historical and personal disasters of her generation: the Holocaust, AIDS, and Hacker's own fight with breast cancer. *Selected Poems, 1965–1990* (1994), which contains work from five of her published books, reveals the many voices (lesbian, feminist, mother, Jew, intellectual) with which the poet speaks.

Hadrian the Seventh, a novel by Frederick *Rolfe, published in 1904. George Arthur Rose is, like Rolfe, a rejected candidate for the priesthood. The novel describes how he is called to be pope after a life of exemplary holiness and faithfulness to his vocation in obscurity and poverty. In a unique exercise in imaginative wish-fulfilment, Rolfe depicts Rose—now Pope Hadrian—embarking on a programme of papal reform: opening up centuries-old barriers between Church and world, renouncing any claim to temporal sovereignty, selling the Vatican treasures and giving the proceeds to the poor. He nevertheless denounces socialism and the doctrine of equality. The somewhat contrived ending of the book sees Hadrian assassinated by his enemies. The book is written in Rolfe's characteristic style, a mixture of rare exotic vocabulary and classically inspired coinings.

HAILEY, Arthur (1920–), British-Canadian novelist, born in Luton, Bedforshire, he left school at fourteen to work as a clerk and emigrated to Canada in 1947 after serving in the RAF throughout the Second World War. He worked in commercial capacities until 1956, when he became a full-time writer, initially of television plays. *Flight into Danger* (1956), his first novel, drew its factual authenticity from Hailey's experiences as a pilot. The detailed documentary character of his best-known works results from meticulous research into the social and professional spheres in which they are set. *Hotel* (1965) was followed by *Airport* (1968), which established him as a best-selling popular author. His subsequent books include *Wheels* (1971), a treatment of the automobile industry. *The Moneychangers* (1975), which deals with banking, *Strong Medicine* (1984), set in a major pharmaceuticals company, and *The Evening News* (1990), which concerns television journalism. Hailey's novels typically feature a proliferation of characters around whom a complex network of dramatic plots is woven. Among his other works are *The Final Diagnosis* (1959), *In High Places* (1962), and *Overload* (1979).

HALDANE, J(ohn) B(urdon) S(anderson) (1892–1964), British geneticist and writer, born in Oxford, educated at New College, Oxford; he was successively professor of genetics and of biometry at University College, London. His *The Causes of Evolution* (1932) was one of the most influential works on evolutionary theory of its day. During the 1930s he became a Communist and wrote brilliant articles for the Communist paper the *Daily Worker*, of which he was chairman of the editorial board (1940–9). The links between science and Marxism were persuasively explored in a series of lectures published as *The Marxist Philosophy and the Sciences* (1938). He resigned from the Communist Party *c.*1950 over Lysenko's theories and the course of Soviet genetics. Haldane was widely known as an imaginative popularizer of science, writing *Possible Worlds* (1927), which speculates on the future, and *Animal Biology* (1927; with Julian *Huxley); Aldous *Huxley drew on Haldane's theories in **Brave New World*. Haldane wrote a witty collection of children's stories, *My Friend Mr. Leakey* (1937), about a philanthropic magician, and his poem 'Cancer's a Funny Thing' is included in *Larkin's *Oxford Book of Twentieth Century Verse*. In 1957 he emigrated to India and was naturalized three years later. Haldane's sister was Naomi *Mitchison.

HALDEMAN, Joe (1943–), American science fiction writer, born in Oklahoma, educated at the University of Maryland. He received much acclaim for his first novel, *The Forever War* (1974), which transposes Vietnam into the mid-future and presents the world of war from the soldier's point of view. Other works on different themes have followed but the short stories collected in *Vietnam and Other Alien Worlds* (1993) return to the subject of his earlier work.

HALEY, Alex (Palmer) (1921–92), African-American writer, born in Ithaca, New York. After two years at college he served with the Coast Guard, and on retirement in 1959 became a freelance magazine writer and interviewer. He co-authored *The Autobiography of Malcolm X* (1965), based on intensive interviews with the famous Black Muslim leader. His lengthy foreword to the book is a shrewd and moving portrait of Malcolm X. His next book, *Roots* (1977; Pulitzer Prize), had a great international success, as did its popular television adaptation; it chronicles the lives of Kunta Kinte (one of Haley's ancestors who was brought to Virginia as a slave) and the six generations, both slaves and freed men, that followed. Haley sought and found his roots in The Gambia, West Africa, and his epic work is based on factual research. His novella *A Different Kind of Christmas* (1988) is a stirring story of the Underground Railway by which slaves were smuggled out to free territory in America.

HALL, Donald (Andrew, Jr) (1928–), American poet, essayist, and editor, born in New Haven, Connecticut, educated at Harvard University, Oxford University, where he won the Newdigate Prize for his poem 'Exiles', and Stanford University. He later became a professor at Michigan University. He has published poetry prolifically, from the more traditional metres, rhythms, and formalism of his early collections *To the Loud Wind, and Other Poems* (1955) and *Exiles and Marriages* (1955), to the freer forms of *The Dark Horses* (1958), poems about suburban life. There followed *A Roof of Tiger Lilies* (1964), the 'deep-image' inspired poems in *The Alligator Bride* (1969), *The Yellow Room* (1971), about a romance, and *A Blue Wing: Selected Poems, 1964–1965* (1975). These poems demonstrate a concise exactness in their style. He has stated that 'The listener doesn't have to understand this poem intellectually, but to enjoy it as a sensual object . . .' In addition to poetry, he has written an autobiography, *String too Short To Be Saved* (1961), plays, and essays on such topics as poetry, Henry Moore, Marianne *Moore, and how to write. He has also edited poetry anthologies, including the influential *The Faber Book of Modern Verse* (1965) and *Contemporary American Poetry* (1962; second edition 1972). He has acted as an editor on numerous journals and magazines, including the **Paris Review* (1953–62). More recent volumes of poetry are *Brief Lives* (1983), *The One Day: A Poem in Three Parts* (1988), and *Old and New Poems* (1990).

HALL, (Marguerite) Radclyffe (1880–1943), British novelist and poet, born in Bournemouth; she was privately educated and spent one year at King's College, London. She established herself as a minor poet of note with numerous collections of accomplished lyric verse, among which are *'Twixt Earth and Stars* (1906) and *Songs of Three Counties* (1913). Two of her early novels, *The Forge* (1924) and *A Saturday Life* (1925), are mild satires on married life. *Adam's Breed* (1926), her most widely acclaimed novel, has in common with much of her other work its thematic concern with the conflict between carnal love and an altruism rooted in her orthodox Christianity. She is best known for *The Well of Loneliness* (1928), which candidly reflects her homosexuality in its narrative of a lesbian novelist. Despite public statements of its merits from many eminent literary figures, it was banned after a prosecution for obscenity and was not republished until 1949; Vera Brittain's *Hall: A Case of Obscenity?* (1968) deals with the trial. Her other publications include *The Unit Lamp* (1924), centring on a daughter's subjection to her mother, and the stories of *Miss Ogilvy Finds Herself* (1934). *The Life and Death of Hall* (1961) is a biography by her partner Una Troubridge.

HALL, Rodney (1935–), Australian novelist and poet, born in England; he went to Australia after the Second World War and was educated at the University of Queensland. He was poetry editor of *The Australian* (1967–78), and has travelled widely in Europe, Asia, and the USA. His numerous volumes of poetry include *Penniless till Doomsday* (1962), *Forty Beads on a Hangman's Rope* (1963), *Eyewitness* (1967), *The Law of Karma* (1968), *Romulus and Remus* (1971), *A Soapbox Omnibus* (1973), *Black Bagatelles* (1978), and *The Most Beautiful World* (1981). His poetry, which is ironic, witty, and displays considerable technical virtuosity, is perhaps less well known than his fiction. Novels include *The Ship on the Coin* (1972), a satirical allegory attacking the apathy and cruelty of bourgeois society; *A Place among People* (1975); *Just Relations* (1982), set in a small Australian town with a gold-mining past, inhabited by a cast of ageing eccentrics; and *Kisses of the Enemy* (1987), a fable about the troubled relationship between Australia and the USA. Hall has been acclaimed for the scope and inventiveness of his 'Yandilli Trilogy' (published in one volume as *A Dream More Luminous Than Love*, 1994). The first volume, *Captivity Captive* (1988), about the solving of an 1888 murder, is based on an incident in Queensland; *The Second Bridegroom* (1991) deals with the early days of Australia's career as a penal colony; while *The Grisly Wife* (1993) is a gripping tale of cultism and murder.

HALL, Willis (1929–), British dramatist, born and educated in Leeds; he made his name with *The Long and the Short and the Tall* (1958), a realistic play about a group of soldiers in the Malayan jungle during the Second World War. That was followed by other works for the theatre, film, and television. Several of these have been written in collaboration with Keith *Waterhouse, among them the screenplays of *Whistle down the Wind* (1961) and *A Kind of Loving* (1961); stage and screen versions of Waterhouse's novel *Billy Liar* (1960), the story of a Yorkshire Walter Mitty unable to escape a dull family, job, and environment except through fantasy; *The Card* (1973), a musical version of Arnold *Bennett's novel of the same name; *Lost Empires* (1985; with Keith Waterhouse and music by Denis King), a play based on J. B. *Priestley's study of repertory theatres; and adaptations of plays by Eduardo de Filippo, *Saturday, Sunday, Monday* (1973) and *Filumena* (1977).

HALPER, Albert (1904–84), American novelist and short-story writer, born in Chicago. Halper was one of the proletarian realists and naturalists who emerged in the USA in the early 1930s. *Union Square* (1933) is a sociological cross-section of American society which shows some indebtedness to works such as John Dos Passos's **U.S.A.* Many of his works are autobiographical in nature, notably *On the Shore* (1934), *The Foundry* (1934), *Sons of the Fathers* (1940), and *The Golden Watch* (1953). *This is Chicago* (1952) is an anthology of Chicago stories, while *Atlantic Avenue* (1956) moves from Halper's usual Chicago setting to the violent world of the Brooklyn and New York waterfronts. As with many of his left-wing contemporaries Halper's writings found a large audience abroad, particularly in the Soviet Union, and were translated into a number of languages. See also PROLETARIAN LITERATURE IN THE USA.

HAMBURGER, Michael (Peter Leopold) (1924–), British poet and translator, born in Berlin of a Jewish family who emigrated to England in 1933; he was educated at Christ Church, Oxford. In addition to his work as a writer and translator he has held numerous visiting professorships in the USA. His verse translations of Hölderlin in *Poems* of 1943 brought the work of that poet to a wider English-speaking readership and established Hamburger as a translator of note. Among his many other translations are *Poems* (1966) by Hans Magnus Enzensberger, *Selected Poems* (1982) by Marin Sorescu, and *Poems of Paul Celan* (1988). His collections of poetry include *The Dual Site* (1958), *Travelling* (1969), *Real Estate* (1977), and *Roots in the Air* (1991); *Collected Poems* appeared in 1984. In the course of the 1960s the strict versification predominant in his earlier work gave way to the disciplined freedom of form in which most of his poetry is written. His underlying ethical and psychological concerns often relate to his complex sense of personal identity as a Jew of German birth and English upbringing. Among his critical works are the essays on German literature in *A Proliferation of Prophets* (1983) and *After the Second Flood* (1986).

HAMILTON, Hugo (1953–), Irish novelist, born in Dublin. His father was Irish and his mother German, and he worked as a journalist in Germany and Austria during the late 1970s before returning to Dublin. Hamilton is one of a growing number of contemporary Irish writers who are orientated towards more international themes and settings. Three of his short stories were included in Faber's *First Fictions* (1989). His first novel, *Surrogate City* (1990), set in Berlin before the fall of the Wall, was followed by *The Last Shot* (1991), whose action occurs towards the end of the Second World War in what was to become Czechoslovakia. *The Love Test* (1995) focuses on the marriage breakdown of an affluent young German couple after the re-unification of Germany, in which personal and political factors become inextricably interwoven in the husband's affair with a young East German woman who has been a victim of the security police.

HAMILTON, (Robert) Ian (1938–), British poet, critic, biographer, and editor, born in King's Lynn, Norfolk, educated at Keble College, Oxford. In 1962 he founded *The *Review*, one of the foremost periodicals of its day in the sphere of poetry and criticism. He became assistant editor of the **Times Literary Supplement* in 1965 and was poetry critic for *The Observer* from 1965 to 1970. In his editorial and critical capacities he exercised considerable influence over developments in British verse in the 1960s and 1970s. *A Poetry Chronicle* (1973) and *Walking Possession* (1994) are collections of essays and reviews. *The Visit* (1970), his first principal collection, appeared to widespread critical acclaim; the thirty short poems of this volume are characterized by their vivid economies of imagery and intense emotional candour, and were republished in *Fifty Poems* (1988) with twenty previously uncollected poems, which display an increased thematic range. As a biographer, he is highly regarded for his *Robert Lowell* (1982) and *In Search of J. D. Salinger* (1988). His other works include *Writers in Hollywood 1915–1951* (1990) and *Keepers of the Flame: Literary Estates and the Rise and Fall of Biography* (1992). He has also edited numerous works, including *Alun Lewis: Selected Poetry and Prose* (1966); *The Modern Poet* (1968), a collection of essays from *The Review*; *The Faber Book of Soccer* (1992); and *The Oxford Companion to Twentieth-Century Poetry in English* (1994).

HAMILTON, Patrick (Anthony Walter) (1904–62), English novelist and dramatist, born in Hassocks, Sussex, educated at Westminster School. He was described by *Priestley as 'above all the novelist of the *homeless*'; most of his novels focus on the seedier side of urban life and the dispossessed, and the shabby boarding-house setting of his novel *Craven House* (1926) was a characteristic background. A trilogy (*The Midnight Bell*, 1929; *The Siege of Pleasure*, 1932; and *The Plains of Cement*, 1934), later published as *Twenty Thousand Streets under the Sky* (1935), was set mainly in a pub, 'The Midnight Bell', near Euston station. *Impromptu in Moribundia* (1939), a fierce satire on British society, reveals Hamilton's Marxist sympathies. *Hangover Square* (1941), a psychological drama set in London in 1939, concerns the hopeless infatuation of an alcoholic for the beautiful but unfaithful actress whom he eventually murders. Hamilton's later novels, mainly thrillers, include *The Slaves of Solitude* (1947) and *The West Pier* (1951). Among his plays are the thrillers *Rope* (1929), which was made into a film directed by Alfred Hitchcock in 1938, and *Gas Light* (1938; US title *Angel Street*, 1939) which was filmed in 1944. A *Life* by Nigel Jones appeared in 1991.

HAMILTON-PATERSON, James (1941–), British novelist, born in Kent, educated at Exeter College, Oxford. He worked for several years as a teacher and journalist for the *New Statesman* and *The Sunday Times*. He received critical acclaim for *Gerontius* (1989; Whitbread Prize), a novel about the composer Edward Elgar. His subsequent novels include *The Bell Boy* (1990), set in south-east Asia, concerning the relationship between a middle-aged Englishwoman and a young Asian boy; *Seven-Tenths* (1992), about the Pacific Ocean; *Griefwork* (1993), set in an unnamed northern European city in the aftermath of the Second World War, and centring on the strange half-vegetable, half-human existence of Leon, the keeper of the Palm House in the city's botanical gardens; and *Ghosts of Manila* (1994), dealing with political corruption in the Philippines. Hamilton-Paterson is an elusive figure, who prefers to divide his time between the Far East and Italy; his novels are controlled and elegant exercises in style, structured around metaphorical conceits, which offer appealingly odd perspectives on the human condition.

HAMMETT, (Samuel) Dashiell (1894–1961), American crime writer, born in Maryland; he left school at 13, and from 1915 worked for Pinkerton's Detective Agency, first in Baltimore, then in San Francisco. He served in the US Army in the First World War, and again in the Second, when he was stationed in the Aleutian Islands. From 1923 he contributed short stories, originally under the name of Peter Collinson, to pulp magazines, especially **Black Mask*, where his first four novels were serialized. Later he worked in Hollywood as a screenwriter; there in 1930 he met the playwright Lillian *Hellman, his friend and companion until his death. After the 1930s he wrote little, devoting himself to political activities: as trustee of the Civil Rights Congress he spent five months in prison in 1951 for contempt of court, and two years later his Communist affiliations were investigated by the McCarthy sub-committee. The detective in most of his short stories and in the novels *Red Harvest* (1929), *The Dain Curse* (1929), and *$106,000 Blood Money* (1943; also published as *Blood Money* and as *The Big Knock-Over*) is the unnamed middle-aged, fat Continental Op, who works for an agency based on Pinkerton's. His best works are *The Maltese Falcon* (1930), filmed by John Huston in 1941 with Humphrey Bogart as the detective Sam Spade; *The Glass Key* (1931), probably his masterpiece, a story of political corruption in an American city; and *The Thin Man* (1934), a sparkling, semi-humorous crime novel, whose main characters, Nick and Nora Charles, were played by William Powell and Myrna Loy in a series of comedy thrillers of the 1930s and 1940s. Hammett writes in a bare, stripped-down style which in *The Glass Key* attains a complexity and subtlety that has led Julian *Symons to claim that it 'can stand comparison with any American novel of its decade'. *The Maltese Falcon* is one of the first, and best, of American private eye novels, rivalled only by *Chandler and Ross *Macdonald. There are biographies by Richard Layman (1981), William F. Nolan (1983), and Diane Johnson (1983). See P. Woolfe, *Beams Falling: The Art of Dashiell Hammett* (1980).

HAMMICK, Georgina (1939–), British short-story writer, born in Hampshire, educated in Kenya and England; she later attended the Academie Julian, Paris, and the Salisbury School of Art. Her first collection of stories, *People for Lunch* (1987), was acclaimed for its wit, irony, and compassion. The stories in *Spoilt* (1992), her second collection, return to the affectionately depicted parochial and suburban landscapes of the earlier work, and are characterized by Hammick's customary elegance of style; here, however, her skill with satirical dialogue and her narrative dexterity often conceal tragic depths, as in the superb 'The Dying Room'. Widely anthologized herself, Hammick has also edited an anthology, *The Virago Book of Love and Loss* (1992), which includes a number of influences and affinities—Elizabeth *Bowen, Sylvia Townsend *Warner, Elizabeth *Taylor, Alice *Munro.

HAMPSON, John, pseudonym of John SIMPSON (1901–55), British novelist, born in Birmingham into a theatrical family; he grew up in poverty and was educated at home. From 1914 to 1918 he worked as a billiard marker and a chef, amongst other jobs, and his knowledge of hotel life provided material for his fiction. His first novel, *Saturday Night at the Greyhound* (1931), set mainly in a Derbyshire pub, concerns the devotion of an introverted young man for his married sister. Other novels include *O Providence* (1932), about a large Midlands family, based on his own, and the relationship between an older and a younger boy; *Strip Jack Naked* (1934), which assembles its characters around the deathbed of a rich Birmingham widow; and *Care of the Grand* (1939). Hampson became one of the 'Birmingham Group' of novelists, which also included Walter *Brierley and Walter *Allen; most of his works provide insights into provincial life in the Midlands in a poetic, but realistic, manner. His last novel, *Bag of Stones* (1952), describing the murderous resentment of a mentally retarded boy towards his father, is based on Hampson's experience as tutor to a mentally handicapped boy. Hampson was a friend of E. M. *Forster, W. H. *Auden, Graham *Greene, and Louis *MacNeice.

HAMPTON, Christopher (James) (1946–), British dramatist, born in the Azores; he lived as a child in Aden and Egypt, was educated at Oxford University, and was still an undergraduate when his first play, *When Did You Last See My Mother?* (1964), was performed at the Royal Court Theatre in London. His subsequent work has included *Total Eclipse* (1968), about the relationship between Rimbaud and Verlaine; *The Philanthropist* (1970), about a well-meaning, self-doubting lecturer, temperamentally opposite to Molière's 'misanthrope', who vestigially inhabits a university itself detached from a Britain in which the Cabinet is slaughtered and writers are being picked off by terrorists; *Savages* (1973), about European atrocities against native Indian tribes and, more specifically, a British diplomat held hostage by South American revolutionaries; *Tales from Hollywood* (1982), about Brecht, Thomas and Heinrich Mann, and other European exiles in wartime California, most of them working for a philistine film industry; and *White Chameleon* (1991), a semi-autobiographical piece about an English boy who grows up in the troubled Egypt of the 1950s, and finds himself alienated from his compatriots when he is sent to school back home; and *Alice's Adventures Under Ground* (1994), a portrait of the troubled Charles Dodgson and the fantasy life he revealed under the guise of Lewis Carroll. Hampton's plays have been highly praised for their technical competence and for their warmth, gentle humour, and quiet, unpretentious humanity. He also wrote the book for Andrew Lloyd Webber's musical, *Sunset Boulevard* (1993), and has made many translations and adaptations, notably versions of Horvath's *Tales from the Vienna Woods* (1977), George Steiner's *The Portage to San Cristobal of A.H.* (1982), Laclos's *Les Liaisons Dangereuses* (1985), and several plays by Ibsen.

Handful of Dust, A, a novel by Evelyn *Waugh, published in 1934. The novel, whose title is from *Eliot's *The *Waste Land* and which is amongst Waugh's most savage portrayals of the idleness and decadence of the 'Bright Young Things', describes the deteriorating marriage of Lady Brenda Last, a beautiful but shallow young woman, and her husband Tony, who embodies the moral decency and respect for tradition the author clearly regarded as threatened by fashionable mores. Leaving Tony to pursue his duties as a local landowner, which includes the increasingly ruinous upkeep of Hetton Abbey, the Victorian Gothic mansion which is his chief preoccupation, Brenda begins an affair with a predatory younger man, John Beaver, who is attracted to her for her wealth and position. When her son, also called John, is killed in a hunting accident, Brenda at first imagines that it is her lover who is dead; her relief when it is revealed that this is not the case is one of the book's most chilling moments. The couple drift apart after the child's death and Brenda asks for a divorce in order to marry Beaver. Tony at first agrees to this, but when he realizes that the divorce settlement will mean selling his beloved Hetton he refuses to go through with it, and joins an expedition to the Amazon. Here he is saved from death and subsequently held captive by a madman, whom he is forced to entertain by reading aloud, each night, from the works of Dickens; after some time has elapsed, he is presumed dead and Brenda, abandoned by Beaver when it becomes clear that she will not inherit Tony's money, marries her former fiancé, Jock Grant-Menzies.

Handmaid's Tale, The, a novel by Margaret *Atwood, published in 1986. It is at once a feminist reworking of the traditional narrative mode of women's Gothic, and a cautionary tale in the manner of *Orwell, projecting its vision of a Christian fundamentalist dystopia on the America of the future. Offred, the narrator and heroine of the novel, is a woman whose ordinary life has been devastated by the radical overhaul of the political system. The present regime, relying on a reactionary reading of the Old Testament, has decreed that all women whose past morals fail to meet the standards required by the new fanaticism should become the concubines of leading officials with childless marriages. Atwood deftly interweaves images of woman-as-chattel (the concubines and surrogate mothers) and woman-as-collaborator (the powerful wives and teachers in charge of upholding prevalent patriarchal ideological institutions) in an ambitious philosophical meditation on the ruler and the ruled. Offred's narrative is interspersed with harrowing flashbacks of attempted escape and eventual capture, and images of incarceration and death by violence. Atwood succeeds in conveying a threatening premonition of a world at war with itself, destroyed by human—predominantly male—greed. This vision is all the more compelling for its reflection of contemporary political trends. The narrative nevertheless builds up to a conclusion that offers hope for the heroine and the future. See also UTOPIA AND ANTI-UTOPIA.

Hangover Square, see HAMILTON, PATRICK.

HANKIN, St John (1869–1909), British dramatist, born in Southampton, the son of a schoolmaster, educated at Oxford University. He became a journalist and dramatic critic with the aim eventually of writing for the stage, an ambition first fulfilled when his *The Two Mr Wetherbys* was performed in London in 1903. There followed *The Return of the Prodigal* (1905), *The Cassilis Engagement* (1907), and *The Last of the de Mullins* (1908), three plays highly critical of the upper classes and influenced by the earlier, more realistic work of *Shaw. By the time Hankin committed suicide in a fit of depression, he had established himself with *Granville-Barker and *Galsworthy as one of the more interesting of the Edwardian era's socially concerned dramatists.

HANLEY, James (1901–85), British novelist, short-story writer, and playwright, born in Dublin; he grew up in working-class Liverpool, which he vividly depicted in his most popular novel sequence, *The Furys* (1935). His formative years at sea in the merchant navy inspired his best work, bringing him early recognition for *Drift* (1930), *Hollow Sea* (1938), *The Ocean* (1942), and *Sailor's Song* (1944). His second book, *Boy* (1931), was successfully prosecuted in 1935 because of its frank account of a young sailor's sexual degradation; it remained out of print until 1990 when a new edition was published with an introduction by Anthony *Burgess. Praised by such diverse admirers as *Faulkner and E. M. *Forster, Hanley was very much a writer's writer and never achieved the recognition he deserved during his lifetime. Wartime London gave a powerful impetus to his imagination; the experimental *No Directions* (1943) is a complex portrait of an artist living through the Blitz, resolutely continuing to paint. *Levine* (1956), the story of a Polish sailor drawn towards murder, set in London in the 1940s, is perhaps his finest achievement. Hanley also wrote many plays for radio and television.

HANNAH, Barry (1942–), American novelist and short-story writer, born and brought up in Clinton,

Mississippi, educated at the University of Alabama. Hannah presents a world as dislocated and violent as William *Faulkner's, but without Faulkner's sustaining metaphysical beliefs. Lacking a sense of continuity, his characters live in an abrupt, staccato world over which they have little or no control. Hannah displays no reverence for the past, though his characters are often haunted by vivid fantasies of Civil War heroes whose exploits are completely at variance with their own horrified experiences of combat. *Airships* (1978), his most famous book, possesses a formidable range: alongside many grotesque vignettes of contemporary life, there are stories about the Civil War and about the future, all conveying the same blind atavistic impulses and desperate acts of honour which govern the behaviour of all his characters. This is the South as a kind of terminal fiction, doomed to repeat a series of disconnected routines entirely drained of meaning. Hannah's other books include *Geronimo Rex* (1972), *Nightwatchmen* (1973), *Ray* (1980), *Power and Light* (1983), *Hey Jack!* (1987), and *Never Die* (1991). He remains one of the most vibrant and compelling figures in contemporary fiction.

HANNAY, James Owen, see BIRMINGHAM, GEORGE A.

HANRAHAN, Barbara (1939–91), Australian writer and artist, born in Adelaide. She studied art in London and became an internationally known painter and print-maker. As a writer, she achieved recognition with her first book, *The Scent of Eucalyptus* (1973), an autobiographical work drawing on her memories of Adelaide from childhood to adolescence; it was followed by the sequel *Kewpie Doll* (1984). Her many novels include *Sea Green* (1974), *The Albatross Muff* (1977), *Where the Queens All Strayed* (1978), *The Peach Groves* (1979), *The Frangipani Gardens* (1980), *Dove* (1982), and *Annie Magdalene* (1986). Many of her novels, especially those dealing with different eras in the history of Adelaide, express her preoccupation with the contrast between prim respectability and sordid reality; she has described her native city as a 'terribly sinister place'. Among her later works are the novels *A Chelsea Girl* (1988), *Flawless Jade* (1989), *Good Night, Mr Moon* (1992), and *Michael and Me and the Sun* (1992), which is autobiographical. Her early short stories are collected in *Dream People* (1987); the stories in *Iris in Her Garden* (1992) also have an autobiographical basis.

HANSBERRY, Lorraine (1930–65), American playwright, born in Chicago, educated at the University of Wisconsin. She is best known for *A Raisin in the Sun* (1959), a play about an African-American family preparing to move from a Chicago ghetto to the suburbs. It focuses on the head of the family, Lena Younger, a widow determined to fulfil her dead husband's optimistic ambitions, which she shared, for the family against all the odds. It was made into a film in 1961, and a musical entitled *Raisin* in 1973. *The Sign in Sidney Brustein's Window* (1964) probes further into city life, with its large cast of Jewish-Americans, African-Americans, and others living in New York's Greenwich Village. *To Be Young, Gifted and Black* (1969) is a posthumous selection by her former husband, Robert Nemiroff, from her letters, diaries, and other unpublished material.

HANSEN, Joseph (1923–), American crime writer, born in Aberdeen, South Dakota, educated there and in Minneapolis. Like Barbara *Wilson, he belongs to that group of contemporary writers eager to exploit the form of the crime novel to investigate social issues, notably gender and sexuality. Southern California is the setting for these mysteries, and alongside Armistead *Maupin, Hansen is a witty chronicler of the fads and eccentricities of that life. His central figure is the private eye Dave Brandstetter, unapologetically homosexual, and from the first novel, *Fadeout* (1970) and onwards, the interaction between the investigator's private life and the mysteries he becomes embroiled in is compellingly handled; other novels in the Brandstetter series are *Death Claims* (1973) and *Early Graves* (1987). In narratives like *Gravedigger* (1982) and *Nightwork* (1984) his social commentary at times distracts from the momentum of the plot, but when engaged with the most challenging issues, he is a distinctive writer in the *Chandler tradition. Hansen also writes fiction outside the private eye genre, under his own name and as James Colton and Rose Brock.

HANSEN, Ron (1947–), American novelist and short-story writer, born in Omaha, Nebraska, educated at Creighton University, the University of Iowa, and Stanford University. Among other academic posts he was appointed Associate Professor at the University of California, Santa Cruz. Though he is not a prolific writer, Hansen's work depends upon a sustained immersion in the minute particularities of time and place; his books convey that history is not only strange but is also opaque, resistant to our attempts to understand it through generalization. *Desperadoes* (1979) enacts this theme by presenting the story of the Dalton gang as told in 1937 by Emmett Dalton who is both a real-estate broker and a scriptwriter for Western movies; his account is based on the immediacy of recollection and the distorting waves of his contemporary preoccupations. *The Assassination of Jesse James by the Coward Robert Ford* (1983) dispenses with the first-person voice and introduces the literally fantastic nature of the James family's life and belief structure; the book's rich and extravagant metaphors, which act to slow the pace, evoke a world coterminous with their life. His novel *Marietta in Ecstasy* (1991) deals with the enigmatic nature of spiritual revelation as experienced by a young postulant in 1906. *Nebraska* (1992) is his highly acclaimed collection of short stories.

HAN SUYIN (1917–), Chinese writer (naturalized British), born in Sinyang (Henan), China. Han has chronicled her experiences as a Eurasian in China, a medical practitioner in Asia, and a leading expert on contemporary Chinese politics, in a series of autobiographical works which conflate objective reportage and personal memoir. Her best-known works are probably *The Crippled Tree* (1965), *A Mortal Flower* (1967), and *Birdless Summer* (1968). In her novels, beginning with the popular classic *A Many-Splendoured Thing* (1952), Han has explored the space between documentary realism and subjective lyricism, articulating the concerns of a post-colonial Asian generation and depicting a cultural identity in a state of flux. Novels such as *And the Rain My Drink* (1956) and *The Four Faces* (1963), though firmly rooted in the political realities of their time, are highly imaginative experiments employing split perspectives, polyphonic narrative, word-games, and philosophical debates. The innovative *The Mountain Is Young* (1958) figures a woman in the act of writing her own sexuality; in its preoccupation with text and gender, it is a precursor of the feminist novels of the 1960s. Her collection of essays *Tigers and Butterflies* (1990) generated heated public debate for its reinterpretation of recent events in China.

Happy Days, a play by Samuel *Beckett, first performed in 1961; it involves Winnie, who spends the action with her shopping bag and parasol on a low mound in the hot and glaring sun, embedded in the first act up to her waist, and in the second to her neck. She is awoken by a piercing bell from off-stage, fiddles with a toothbrush, a handkerchief, her spectacles, and other domestic items, and even when she can no longer use her hands keeps up a brisk chatter, sometimes talking to herself, sometimes to her unresponsive husband, Willie, who has a 'tail', who 'crawls' and lives in a nearby 'hole', on 'straw'. Though she habitually affects a cheerful manner, and repeats the words 'great mercies, great mercies', her mood occasionally veers towards the angry, disgusted, or contemptuous: as well it might, given the wasted life and sorry marriage she inadvertently evokes. A revolver, which Winnie extracts from her bag and places 'conspicuously' beside her, indicates the only possibility of escape; and it may be towards this that Willie is reaching when, at the play's end, he appears in top hat and morning coat, only to slither to the bottom of the mound murmuring 'Win'. At this, Winnie herself declares 'oh this *is* a happy day' and launches smilingly into a song, 'it's true, it's true, you love me so'. The play would seem to be Beckett's sardonic but not unsympathetic comment on those who try to make the best of essentially frustrating lives.

HARBINSON, Robert, the pseudonym usually employed by Robert Harbinson BRYANS (1928–), Irish short-story writer and autobiographer, born in Belfast. He worked for a time on a dredger in Belfast Lough before deciding to become a medical missionary. He studied theology at the South Wales Bible College and subsequently taught in Canada and Venezuela. After giving up theology he took up diamond prospecting in Canada and South America. During the 1960s he wrote many travel books under his second pseudonym, Robin Bryans. Harbinson produced four volumes of autobiography, *No Surrender: An Ulster Childhood* (1960), *Song of Erne* (1960), *Up Spake the Cabin Boy* (1961), and *The Protégé* (1963), which recount his early life in working-class Belfast and portray Ulster as immutable and claustrophobic, permanently over-shadowed by the events of its distant past. Harbinson has also written two collections of short stories, *Tattoo Lily and Other Ulster Stories* (1961) and *The Far World and Other Stories* (1962), fictions based upon episodes from his life. In more recent years, he has worked as an opera librettist in London.

Hardboiled Fiction, a self-consciously tough and uncompromising school of crime writing originally associated with the American pulp magazine **Black Mask* (1920–36) and the novels of Dashiell *Hammett, James M. *Cain, and Raymond *Chandler. Unlike 'classic' British detective fiction, hardboiled writing avoids the reassuring pattern of puzzle and solution, and the cosy country house setting. In a vividly realized urban environment, it offers a dark view of crime as endemic rather than deviant, usually through the world-weary character of the narrator. At its most stylized, as described in Chandler's essay 'The Simple Art of Murder', the private eye narrator represents a slightly compromised standard of chivalry and heroism in a squalid and sordid universe. As well as developing a potent and influential style of delivery, the hardboiled novel, especially in the hands of Hammett, often became the vehicle of social criticism, offering a portrait of a world in which the forces of law and order were unreliable and often corrupt. Much of the energy of hardboiled fiction is expressed in the 'pulp' novels of Horace McCoy, Cornell *Woolrich, Charles *Willeford, and Jim *Thompson. Hardboiled fiction is also the basis of the genre of film known as *film noir*. More recently, hardboiled fiction has been appropriated in different ways by writers such as Elmore *Leonard and George V. *Higgins, and by such feminist writers as Barbara *Wilson and Sara *Paretsky as a way of reinvigorating the female presence in crime fiction. See DETECTIVE FICTION.

HARDWICK, Elizabeth (Bruce) (1916–), American novelist and critic, born in Lexington, Kentucky, educated at the University of Kentucky, Lexington, and at Columbia University. She contributed reviews and stories from the early 1940s onwards to **Partisan Review*, *Harpers*, and the **New Yorker*. Her first novel, *The Ghostly Lover* (1945), was followed by *The Simple Truth* (1955), concerning the murder trial of a college student. *Sleepless Nights* (1979) has a much less conventional narrative structure, a minor masterpiece of fictionalized autobiography whose narrator ('Elizabeth') moves in memory between Kentucky, New York, and Europe. Reflections range around time, death, disease, ageing, and 'the torment of personal relations'; characters encountered include Hardwick's one-time husband Robert *Lowell and Billie Holiday. She has commanded widespread respect as a critic over several decades, being a founder of the *New York Review of Books in February 1963, and influential in her appreciation of Mary *McCarthy and Susan *Sontag. Hardwick's stimulating essays are collected in *A View of My Own* (1962), dealing with literary and societal topics; *Seduction and Betrayal* (1974), which discusses women writers from the Brontës to Zelda Fitzgerald; and *Bartleby in Manhattan and Other Essays* (1983).

HARDY, Thomas (1840–1928), British novelist and poet, born at Higher Bockhampton, near Dorchester, Dorset, educated at the school in Dorchester run by the British and Foreign School Society. From 1856 to 1861 he was articled to a Dorchester ecclesiastical architect whose office was next door to the school run by William Barnes (1801–86), the Dorset dialect poet; with Barnes as his mentor, Hardy began writing verse at the age of 17. He worked for an architectural practice in London from 1862 to 1867, when he returned to his former position in Dorchester. Although he had formerly considered taking Holy Orders, at this time he became an agnostic. He completed *The Poor Man and the Lady*, his first novel, in 1868; the publishers Chapman and Hall showed interest, but their reader, George Meredith (1828–1909), advised against publication; the manuscript was eventually lost. *Desperate Remedies* (1871), his first novel to be published, was followed by *Under the Greenwood Tree* (1872) and *A Pair of Blue Eyes* (1873). *Far from the Madding Crowd* (1874), a work of great dramatic power and imaginative scope which deals with the destructive effects of sexual obsession, made clear his stature as a novelist. Its success enabled him to give up architecture for writing and to marry Emma Gifford, whom he had met on an architectural assignment at St Juliot, Cornwall, in 1874. Considerable strains eventually developed in the marriage; Emma's psychological instability, to which veiled allusions are thought to be made in the poem 'The Interloper', was among the causes. They took up residence in Max Gate, an imposing house near Dorchester built to Hardy's own design, in 1887. During its construction he worked on *The Mayor of Casterbridge* (1886), which marked an advance in his artistry in the authenticity of its social and economic dimensions and the deeply compelling characterization of its tragic hero Michael Henchard. The compassionate presentation of Tess as a victim of conventional Victorian morality in *Tess of the D'Urbervilles* (1891), often regarded as his finest novel, gave rise to the controversy with which the book was received; for some reviewers it established Hardy as the greatest novelist of the day, while others denigrated it as unhealthily pessimistic and immoral. Such hostility intensified with the publication of his uncompromising treatment of 'the modern vice of unrest' in *Jude the Obscure* (1895), in which the hero's unfulfilled desire for educational advancement is seen in the context of the decaying traditions of rural society. He later described the reception of *Jude the Obscure* as an 'experience completely curing me of further interest in novel-writing'; there are, however, grounds for concluding that he felt he had completed his work as a novelist and wished to devote himself to poetry, which he had continued to write throughout his career.

He defended the bleak vision of suffering and injustice in much of his writing with a line from the second poem of the 'In Tenebris' sequence, 'If way to the Better there be, it exacts a full look at the Worst', and based hope for gradual change on his belief in 'evolutionary meliorism'. Central to many of the novels, to the epic drama in verse and prose *The *Dynasts* (three volumes, 1904, 1906, 1908), and to much of his verse is the theme of man's subjection to the implacable and insentient 'Immanent Will that stirs and urges everything', as it is termed in the poem 'The Convergence of the Twain'. His first two collections of verse, *Wessex Poems* (1898) and *Poems of the Past and Present* (1902), contained a high proportion of early work, and each of his subsequent volumes included poems composed long before publication. After completion of *The Dynasts*, *Time's Laughingstocks* appeared in 1909.

In 1912 Emma died suddenly; Hardy revisited St Juliot and made a journey to her birthplace in Plymouth, brooding on their past in the landscapes of their courtship. 'Poems of 1912–13' resulted, the most concentratedly personal body of his poetry, which contains a number of his most memorable works, among them 'After a Journey', 'The Going', and 'The Voice'. In all, Hardy, for whom memory was an essential imaginative resource, produced over 100 poems concerning Emma and himself in the decades after her death. 'Poems of 1912–13' appeared in *Satires of Circumstance* in 1914, the year of Hardy's marriage to Florence Emily Dugdale, whose two-volume biography of Hardy (1928, 1930) was substantially of his own authorship. His subsequent collections were *Moments of Vision* (1917), *Late Lyrics and Earlier* (1922), and *Human Shows* (1925). *Winter Words* was published posthumously in 1928; *The Queen of Cornwall*, his only other verse-drama, appeared in 1923. *The Complete Poetical Works of Thomas Hardy* (three volumes, 1982, 1984, 1985) was edited by Samuel Hynes. The great individuality of his poetry is rooted in his native familiarity with the regional traditions of Dorset, which matured into a literary consciousness through his contact with William Barnes. Although Hardy did not continue to write dialect verse after his early experiments, the diction of his work remained fundamentally that of common spoken English. He thus anticipated *Modernism in breaking with the conventions of literary usage which increasingly constrained Victorian poetry. He was similarly independent in his attitudes to prosody, eschewing metres of mellifluous regularity in pursuit of his stated preference for 'poetic texture rather than poetic veneer'. His poetry's fidelity to ordinary patterns of speech is matched by the realism and accessibility with which he treats a remarkable range of subjects; he may be approached as a nature poet, a topographical poet (see TOPOGRAPHICAL POETRY), a poet of London, of rural custom, of love, and of grief. His achievement as a poet was not fully recognized until after his death.

Hardy may be said to occupy the unique position of being among the foremost novelists of the nineteenth century while occupying a position of the first importance as a poet of the twentieth century. In addition to his novels, poems, and dramas, he wrote many short stories which were collected in *Wessex Tales* (1888), *A Group of Noble Dames* (1891), *Life's Little Ironies* (1894), and *A Changed Man* (1913); although his short stories exhibit considerable stylistic and thematic variety, they have never been as highly regarded as his other works. He was awarded the Order of Merit in 1910.

Hardy devised the following classification for his novels and stories:

Novels of Character and Environment: *Under the Greenwood Tree*; *Far from the Madding Crowd*; *The Return of the Native* (1878); *The Mayor of Casterbridge*; *The Woodlanders* (1887); *Wessex Tales*; *Tess of the D'Urbervilles*; *Life's Little Ironies*; *Jude the Obscure*.

Romances and Fantasies: *A Pair of Blue Eyes*; *The Trumpet Major* (1880); *Two on a Tower* (1882); *A Group of Noble Dames*; *The Well-Beloved* (published serially 1892; revised edition 1897).

Novels of Ingenuity: *Desperate Remedies*; *The Hand of Ethelberta* (1876); *A Laodicean* (1881).

The Collected Letters of Thomas Hardy, edited by R. L. Purdy and M. Millgate, appeared in seven volumes between 1978 and 1988. Robert *Gittings's *Young Thomas Hardy* (1975) and *The Older Hardy* (1980) remain highly regarded among numerous biographical studies, including Millgate's *Thomas Hardy: A Biography* (1982) and Martin Seymour-Smith's *Hardy* (1994).

HARE, Cyril, pseudonym of Alfred Alexander Gordon CLARK (1900–58), British judge and *detective fiction writer, born in Mickleham, Surrey, educated at New College, Oxford; he was called to the Bar in 1924, where his practice was mainly in the criminal courts, joined the staff of the Director of Public Prosecutions in 1942, and in 1950 became a county court judge. A contributor to *Punch*, he wrote his first detective story, *Tenant for Death*, in 1937, and followed it with eight others and a number of short stories. His detectives, who usually appear together, are the policeman Inspector Mallett and the unsuccessful barrister Francis Petigrew. Well-written, civilized, and witty, Hare's books must be ranked high among classical detective stories. His masterpiece, and the author's favourite book, is *Tragedy at Law* (1942), one of the best of all detective stories with a legal background.

HARE, David (1947–), British playwright, born in Bexhill, Sussex, educated at Cambridge University. He began writing plays for Portable Theatre, a touring company he co-founded in 1968. His subsequent work has primarily concentrated on aspects of British politics and society since the Second World War, a period he regards as characterized by opportunism, avarice, corruption, and the betrayal of the hopes of those who defeated Hitler. Perhaps the most outstanding of these is *Plenty* (1978), about Susan Trahern who returns from working as a secret agent in occupied France believing in a glowing future; it presents a striking portrait of a woman destroyed by nostalgia, an uncompromising spirit, and other flaws and virtues. Other principal plays in this vein are *Knuckle* (1974), a parody of the Mickey Spillane thriller, with financiers and entrepreneurs as villains; *Teeth 'n' Smiles* (1975), about a rebellious rock singer and her disintegrating band at a Cambridge ball; *Map of the World* (1982), in which representatives of left and right come into conflict at an international conference; *The Secret Rapture* (1988), a more intimate piece, about an illustrator exploited by her associates, among them her Tory MP sister; *Racing Demon* (1990), a picture of a divided and confused Church of England; *Murmuring Judges* (1991), which looks at the workings of the law and order system in Britain, finding it anachronistic and inept where it is not actually corrupt; and *Absence of War* (1993), which involves the machinations within the Labour Party during a losing General Election campaign and contains a rich portrait of an Opposition leader in some respects indebted to the defeated Neil Kinnock. Under the title 'The Hare Trilogy', the last three of these plays have been presented in tandem by the National Theatre, the same theatre that presented the more intimate *Skylight* (1995), about a businessman's attempt to regenerate a love affair with a much younger schoolteacher. Hare has also written two plays in collaboration with Howard *Brenton: *Brassneck* (1973), about municipal corruption, and *Pravda* (1986), about the British press and the acquisition of newspapers by a right-wing entrepreneur. Like much of his and Brenton's solo work, these are stylistically innovative, combining epic sweep with cinematic jumps between often odd and unexpected locations. In addition to this, Hare has written some highly successful screenplays: on television, *Licking Hitler* (1978) and *Dreams of Leaving* (1980), the second of which he directed himself, as he did *Saigon: Year of the Cat* (1982), *Wetherby* (1985), and *Strapless* (1989) for the cinema.

HARE, R(ichard) M(ervyn) (1919–), British moral philosopher, born at Backwell near Bristol, educated at Balliol College, Oxford. He became an officer in the Royal Artillery in 1940 and was held prisoner-of-war by the Japanese from 1942 to 1945. In 1950 he began his academic career as a fellow and tutor of Balliol College; he was White's Professor of Moral Philosophy at Oxford between 1966 and 1983, when he was appointed Graduate Research Professor of Philosophy at the University of Florida. He is widely regarded as one of the most important British philosophers of the post-war decades. *The Language of Morals* (1952), *Freedom and Reason* (1963), and *Moral Thinking* (1981) contain the main expositions of his moral philosophy, which began as an extension of G. E. *Moore's critique of ethical naturalism and centres on the doctrine of 'universal prescriptivism'. Hare argues that moral evaluations are of an essentially imperative nature but are only valid as such if they are applicable in every case; he uses the expressions 'universalizability', and 'prescriptivity' to establish the basic conditions of moral judgement. Hare is a leading contemporary utilitarian in his belief that moral philosophy can be socially influential if it succeeds in its chief task of elucidating the meaning and implications of ethical terminologies. His deep concern with clarity of definition leads him to deprecate the citing of illustrative instances from literature in philosophical writing, a practice he views as tending towards obscurity. Among his other publications are *Essays on the Moral Concepts* (1971), *Applications of Moral Philosophy* (1972), *Essays in Ethical Theory* (1989), and *Essays on Political Morality* (1989).

HARIHARAN, Githa (1954–), Indian novelist, born in Coimbatore, educated at the Universities of Bombay and Fairfield, Connecticut. She came to writing after a career in editing, publishing, and reviewing. Her first novel, *The Thousand Faces of Night* (1992), won the Commonwealth Writers prize for the best first novel. Distinguished by its lyrical prose style, the novel charts the precarious course of three women's journeys through the routes of Indian social norms. *The Art of Dying* (1993), was described by *Coetzee as a collection of 'beautifully written stories about death and its place in life'. Hariharan changed direction in *The Ghosts of Vasu Master* (1994), an experimental work in which the story of a retired teacher's attempt to cure a strange child of his silence is used as a frame to tell inset stories which explore themes of teaching, healing, and the deceptive nature of reality.

HARJO, Joy (Foster) (1951–), Native American poet and script-writer of the Creek tribe, born in Oklahoma, educated at the University of New Mexico and the *Iowa Writers' Workshop. Harjo has been a consultant for Native American groups and a member of the Board of Directors of the National Association of Third World Writers, and has taught at the University of Arizona. Her interest in Native American women and their experience of change informs her poetry: *The Last Song* (1975), *What Moon Drive Me to This?* (1980), and *She Had Some Horses* (1983), which celebrates the survival of modern Indians but laments the difficulties and dangers of the urban Indian lifestyle. In *Mad Love and War* (1990) she moves away from the song structure to a freer prose form in which to explore racial injustice. Survival and regeneration are the twin concerns of Harjo's work. In 'Anchorage', dedicated to Audre *Lorde, she asks 'who would believe%thin; | %thin;the fantastic and terrible story of all our survival,%thin; | %thin;those who were never meant%thin; | %thin;to survive?' She has been involved with a number of films released by the Native American Broadcasting Consortium, most notably *The Origin of Apache Crown Dance* (1985), for which she wrote the script. See also NATIVE AMERICAN LITERATURE.

Harlem Renaissance, the term normally used to describe the upsurge of black American writing in the 1920s and 1930s. Though sometimes seen as a movement, it is better regarded as the more or less contemporary emergence of a number of writers who together make up the first modern generation of black American writers, a generation whose work, while often protesting about dispossession, poverty, and racial prejudice, is most significant for its articulation of a positive sense of black identity and its attempts to promote black consciousness. Harlem, viewed as a cultural matrix for blacks, provided a central focus for the activities of several of the writers who contributed to the Renaissance, or Awakening as it is sometimes also called, but others lived all or most of their lives elsewhere. Although there had been numerous earlier works that gave voice to the predicament of Americans of African descent, among them Frederick Douglass's *Narrative of the Life of Frederick Douglass* (1845), which is the best-known 'literary' example of the genre of slave narrative, Charles W. Chesnutt's *The Conjure Man* (1899), and James Weldon Johnson's *Autobiography of an Ex-Coloured Man* (1912), a work which is sometimes seen as a forerunner of the Awakening, the Renaissance is generally viewed as a major step forward. Figures instrumental in its formation included the sociologist W. E. B. *Du Bois, best known for his *The Souls of Black Folks* (1903), who rejected the integrationist approach of his famous contemporary Booker T. Washington, and the Jamaican-born Marcus Garvey, whose United Negro Improvement Association promoted an awareness of African origins and the possibility of an actual repatriation to Africa in Harlem in the 1920s. Other historical factors which contributed to the growth of a sense of distinctive racial identity and the emergence of an autonomous black literature in the 1920s included the racism from which many black Americans suffered when they served alongside their white compatriots in the First World War, the northward migration of blacks from the rural South, and the difficulties such newcomers experienced in adjusting to urban situations. The emergence of Du Bois's magazine *The Crisis* provided a forum in which black Americans could express their ideas without having to accommodate them to a white readership. When mainstream publishing outlets began to publish black writers shortly afterwards, a readership that was sympathetic to black causes was securely established. Jessie Redmon *Fauset, also an editor of *The Crisis*, Zora Neale *Hurston, and Dorothy *West were notable women figures of the Renaissance. The movement can be seen as having been ushered in by poems such as Claude *McKay's 'If We Must Die' (1919), Countee *Cullen's 'I Have a Rendezvous with Life', and Langston *Hughes's 'The Negro Speaks of Rivers' (both 1921). Among its most important works are McKay's *Harlem Shadows* (1922), *Banjo* (1929), and **Banana Bottom* (1933); Jean *Toomer's *Cane* (1923); Langston Hughes's *The Weary Blues* (1926) and *The Ways of White Folks* (1934); Countee Cullen's *Color*

(1925), *Copper Sun* (1927), and *The Black Christ* (1929); Rudolf Fisher's *The Conjure Man Dies* (1932); and Arna *Bontemps's *Black Thunder* (1935). Varied though these writings are, they illustrate the complexity and richness of black experience and in so doing demonstrate an emancipation from the cultural stereotyping from which blacks had continued to suffer in the Reconstruction period after the Civil War and subsequently. See also ETHNICITY.

Harlot's Ghost, see MAILER, NORMAN.

Harmonium, Wallace *Stevens's first collection of poetry, initially published in 1923; it contains seventy-four poems, including several lengthy sequences, written from approximately 1912 onward. A revised edition with fourteen further poems appeared in 1931. Its invigorating range extends from lengthy philosophical investigations like 'The Comedian as the Letter C' to the buoyant simplicity of 'Ploughing on Sunday' and numerous other poems related to the American folk tradition. Stevens's talent for presenting imagery of singular clarity, colour, and sharpness, an indication of his participation in *Imagism, is on display throughout the collection. Among its most vividly exotic poems are a number reflecting the landscapes and vegetation of Florida, which he recurrently visited. *Harmonium* is permeated by the preoccupation with the imagination as the only means of interpreting reality in a secular age that runs throughout Stevens's subsequent work (see THE MAN WITH THE BLUE GUITAR and NOTES TOWARD A SUPREME FICTION). 'The Emperor of Ice Cream', 'Sunday Morning', 'Thirteen Ways of Looking at a Blackbird', 'The Snow Man', 'Peter Quince at the Clavier', and 'Tea at the Palaz of Hoon' are among the well-known poems in the collection, which contains a remarkably high proportion of Stevens's most celebrated work.

HARPER, Michael S(teven) (1938–), African-American poet and critic, born in Brooklyn, educated at UCLA and the *Iowa Writers' Workshop at the University of Iowa. Among several important academic posts Harper was appointed Kapstein Professor at Brown University. His main interests are music, particularly jazz and blues, and history within both a national and a mythical framework; these themes he established in his first two volumes of poetry, *Dear John, Dear Coltrane* (1970) and *History Is Your Own Heartbeat* (1971). Other volumes include *Photographs: Negatives: History as Apple Tree* (1972), *Song: I Want a Witness* (1972), *Debridement* (1973), *Nightmare Begins Responsibility* (1974), *Images of Kin: New and Selected Poems* (1977), *Rhode Island: Eight Poems* (1981), and *Healing Song for the Inner Ear* (1985), and the recording *Hear Where Coltrane Is* (1971). The power of music to express the pain of racial history and to heal the psychological and spiritual wounds inflicted upon African-Americans provides Harper with a model for his art. His poetry seeks to witness and to remember the African-American experience in all its individual detail. Among the works he has edited are the anthology *Heartblow: Black Veils* (1975), *The Collected Poems of Sterling A. Brown* (1980), *Chant of Saints: A Gathering of Afro-American Literature, Art and Scholarship* (1979) with Robert Stepto, and *Every Eye Ain't Asleep: An Anthology of Poetry by Afro-Americans Since 1945* (1994) with Anthony Walton.

HARRIS, Frank (James Thomas) (1856–1931), British writer and critic, born in Galway. After early travels in America and Europe, he rose to fame as a dynamic editor of the *Evening News* (1882–6) and the *Fortnightly Review* (1886–94), but exerted most influence as editor of the *Saturday Review* (1894–8), publishing works by *Hardy, *Wells, *Beerbohm, and Arthur *Symons, with *Shaw as drama critic from 1895. As well as novels, volumes of short stories, and plays he wrote biographies of his friend Oscar Wilde (1916) and of Shaw (1931), completed by Shaw himself to benefit Harris's estate, and *The Man Shakespeare and His Tragic Life Story* (1909). Harris's reputation became tarnished by his continual assaults on Victorian values, and by his unashamed arrogance. Various rumours and his vainglorious and sexually explicit memoirs, *My Life and Loves* (four volumes, 1922–7) caused further scandal. There are biographies by Hugh Kingsmill (1932) and by Philippa Pullar (1975).

HARRIS, Macdonald, pseudonym of Donald W. HEINEY (1921–93), American writer and academic, born in California, educated at the University of Southern California; he taught for many years at the University of California, Irvine, and published literary criticism under his own name. After several early novels, such as *Private Demons* (1961), depicting modern American life, his range widened with *Bull Fire* (1973), a retelling of the story of the Minotaur and his birth in terms of psychosexual farce, with elements of *science fiction. *The Balloonists* (1976) described a late nineteenth-century balloon excursion to the North Pole; *Yukiko* (1977) recalls Japan in August 1945; *Pandora's Gallery* (1979) was set in the Venice of 1797 while *Herma* (1981) was set in the Belle Epoque; and *Screenplay* (1982) was a time-travel fantasy about Hollywood. His later works include *The Little People* (1986), a tale of American self-delusion in Europe; *Glowstone* (1988), a magic realist fable about Madame Curie; and *Hemingway's Suitcase* (1990), a clever reconstruction of the author's early years. Stories were collected in *The Cathay Stories and Other Fictions* (1988).

HARRIS, Wilson (Theodore) (1921–), Guyanese novelist, poet, and critic, born in New Amsterdam, educated at Queen's College, Georgetown, British Guiana. He was a land surveyor before leaving Guyana for England in 1959 to become a full-time writer. His exploration of the almost impenetrable forests, rivers, and vast savannahs of the Guyanese hinterland features prominently in many of his novels. Harris's novels are densely complex, alluding to diverse mythologies from different cultures, and eschew conventional narration in favour of shifting interwoven voices. His writing stems from a belief that in the West Indies the clash of widely different cultures has, at least potentially, made it possible for an almost universal consciousness to evolve. *The Guyana Quartet* (1985), made up of *Palace of the Peacock* (1960), his best-known novel, *The Far Journey of Oudin* (1961), *The Whole Armour* (1962), and *The Secret Ladder* (1963), a symbolic autobiographical work, together with *Heartland* (1964), chart Harris's first phase of novelistic exploration. His next four novels, also set in Guyana, explore the psyche and the workings of memory: *The Eye of the Scarecrow* (1965), *The Waiting Room* (1967), *Tumatumari* (1968), and *Ascent to Omai* (1970). Other novels in similar vein, but set in such diverse places as London, Edinburgh, and Mexico, include *Black Marsden* (1972), *Companions of the Day and Night* (1975), *Da Silva da Silva's Cultivated Wilderness* (1977), *Genesis of the Clowns* (1977), *The Tree of the Sun* (1978), and *The Angel at the Gate* (1982). *Carnival* (1985) is a Dantesque allegory, in which Heaven, Hell, and Purgatory are treated as states of mind about modern civilization. It is the first volume of 'The Carnival Trilogy'; the second is *The Infinite Rehearsal* (1987), based on Goethe's *Faust*. *The Four Banks of the River of Space* (1990) fragments the epic figure of Ulysses into several personalities who conduct self-analyses to redefine the nature and function of myth. *Resurrection at Sorrow Hill* (1993), a novel, recounts a river voyage into the depths of the rainforest. Harris's poems are collected in *Fetish* (1951) and *Eternity to Season* (1978). Critical writings include *Tradition, the Writer and Society* (1967), *Explorations* (1981), and *The Womb of Space* (1983). *The Radical Imagination* (1992) is a collection of essays. See Hena Maes-Jelinek, *Wilson Harris* (1982).

HARRISON, G(eorge) B(agshawe) (1894–91), British scholar and critic, born in Hove, Sussex, educated at Queens' College, Cambridge. In 1924 he began lecturing at King's College, University of London, subsequently holding professorships at Queen's University, Ontario, and the University of Michigan. Among his many works on Shakespeare and his period were *Shakespeare's Fellows* (1923), *Elizabethan Plays and Players* (1940), and *Shakespeare's Critics: From Jonson to Auden* (1964); *England in Shakespeare's Day* (1928) and *Shakespeare at Work* (1933) are highly regarded as introductions to the social and cultural contexts of Shakespeare's work. He also produced numerous editions of Elizabethan and Jacobean documents, notably Thomas Nashe's *Pierce Pennilesse, His Supplication to the Divell, 1592* (1924), *An Elizabethan Journal* (three volumes, 1928, 1931, 1933), *A Jacobean Journal* (two volumes, 1941, 1950), and *The Letters of Queen Elizabeth I* (1935). Harrison was general editor of the Penguin Shakespeare between 1937 and 1959. His other publications included *The Day before Yesterday* (1938), a journal for the year 1936; *Julius Caesar in Shakespeare, Shaw, and the Ancients* (1960); and *Profession of English* (1962), which reflects on the objectives and procedures of literary studies.

HARRISON, Jim (1937–), American novelist and poet, born in Grayling, Michigan, educated at Michigan State University. His early works are included in *Selected and New Poems, 1961–81* (1982), but it is as a novelist that he is best known. His first novel, *Wolf* (1971), was personal, angry, and confessional in tone. His second novel, *A Good Day to Die* (1973), more traditional in technique, has been called the first Vietnam novel. Other novels followed, including *Farmer* (1976), *Warlock* (1981), and *Sundog* (1985). But it is, perhaps, for his collections of novellas *Legends of the Fall* (1978) that he is most renowned: in these works, the rural setting he favours acquires a mythopoeic quality enhanced by the bleakness of his poetic prose. In *Dalva* (1989) he extends his range; speaking largely in the voice of a woman of Native American extraction, he vents his wrath at the treatment of Native Americans by the white race in his longest and most mellow work to date. In *The Woman Lit by Fireflies* (1991) he returns to the three-novella format. Though he has been cast as a Faulknerian regionalist, Harrison's allusive style and eclectic influences make him equally remote from the naturalistic tradition as from the 'dirty realism' or the fashionable post-modernist minimalism of his contemporaries. A further volume of verse, *The Theory and Practice of Rivers and New Poems*, appeared in 1989.

HARRISON, M(ichael) John (1945–), British novelist and writer of *science fiction. He came to notice through his science fiction stories in magazines; his first novel, *The Committed Men* (1971), displays the influence of J. G. *Ballard. His originality is increasingly evident in *The Pastel City* (1971), *A Storm of Wings* (1980), and *In Viriconium* (1982), a trilogy sustained by the imaginative adaptation of contemporary urban landscapes into the books' powerfully conceived setting, which also features in the stories of *Viriconium Nights* (1985). The compelling stories of *The Ice Monkey* (1984) are in predominantly naturalistic idioms. His widely acclaimed novel *Climbers* (1989) forms an intensely detailed evocation of the sub-culture of British rock-climbing. *The Course of the Heart* (1992), his subsequent novel, employs elements of the supernatural in its treatment of the longing for transcendence in a spiritually impoverished world. His other works include *The Centauri Device* (1974) and the stories of *The Machine in Shaft Ten* (1975).

HARRISON, Tony (1937–), British poet, translator, and dramatist, born in Leeds, educated at the University of Leeds, where he studied classics and did postgraduate work in linguistics. From 1962 to 1966 he taught at Ahmadu Bello University, Zaria, Nigeria, where he collaborated with James *Simmons on a version of Aristophanes' *Lysistrata* entitled *Aikin Mata* (1966), the first of his many adaptations of classical works. He subsequently lectured at Charles University in Prague and became an associate editor of **Stand* magazine in 1968. Among numerous visiting appointments he was resident dramatist at the National Theatre in 1977–8. His first substantial collection, *The Loiners* (1970), consistently displayed Harrison's virtuosity in adapting conventional forms to an energetically colloquial tone; treatments of his Leeds background and experiences of post-colonial Africa combined erotic candour, sardonic humour, and underlying political seriousness in a manner characteristic of much of his subsequent work. The distancing from his working-class origins brought about by education and the linguistic aspects of social conditioning receive concentrated attention in the Meredithian sonnets forming the title sequence of *The School of Eloquence* (1978); the work, whose main themes are central to Harrison's concerns as a poet, encompasses historical and socio-cultural material, autobiography, and movingly elegiac tributes to his parents and other relations. *Continuous* (1981) forms an extension of the sequence, to which additions are also made in the revised edition of his *Selected Poems* (1987). Harrison's other works as a poet include his versions of Palladus in *Poems* (1975); *A Kumquat for John Keats* (1981); *'*v.*' (1985), which provoked controversy when presented on television through its frequent use of language many considered obscene; *A Cold Coming* (1991), his poetic response to the Gulf War; *The Gaze of the Gorgon* (1992), poems reflecting modern European history; and *The Shadow of Hiroshima* (1995). As a writer for the theatre his works include an adaptation of Molière's *The Misanthrope* (1973); *Phaedra Britannica* (1975), a version of Racine's *Phedre*; his adaptation of *The Oresteia* (1981) of Aeschylus for the National Theatre; and *The Common Chorus: A Version of Aristophanes' Lysistrata* (1992). His verse-dramas achieve theatrical effectiveness through his liberating technical fluency across a wide range of idioms of speech and character; *Dramatic Verse, 1973–1985* appeared in 1985, and *The Trackers of Oxyrhyncus* was performed and published in 1990.

HARROD, Sir Roy Forbes (1900–78), British economist, born in London, educated at New College, Oxford. From 1923 until his retirement in 1967 he taught at Christ Church, Oxford. Harrod was one of a select group of younger economists from whom *Keynes solicited comments on his early drafts of the *General Theory* (1926), and was among those responsible for the propagation of Keynesianism in mainstream economic and political circles in the post-war world. His main contributions were to the theories of economic growth and imperfect competition. While most of these were published in academic journals, two books contain their results: *Towards a Dynamic Economics* (1948) and *Economic Essays* (1952). From the early 1950s Harrod turned more to practical policy matters. Here his books *Policy against Inflation* (1958), *Reforming the World's Money* (1965), and *Towards a New Economic Policy* (1967) stand out for their clarity and practical good sense. Harrod remained an advocate of Keynesianism to the end, despite that doctrine's fall from favour in the early 1970s. However, this adherence to Keynesianism did not lead him to a fixed commitment to any one political party—he advised Labour, stood for Parliament (unsuccessfully) as a Liberal in 1945, and later (with Churchill's help) sought (again unsuccessfully) nomination as a Conservative candidate. He is the author of *The Life of John Maynard Keynes* (1951), in which his unique and intimate knowledge of Keynes's economics, and of the man himself, combined to produce an intellectual biography of singular economic and literary quality.

HARROWER, Elizabeth (1928–), Australian novelist, born in Newcastle, New South Wales. She travelled in Europe and lived in London for several years. Her novels include *Down in the City* (1957), which traces the disillusionment of a middle-class woman married to a working-class businessman, who emerges as a racketeer and a bully; *The Long Prospect* (1958), which describes the adult world from the perspective of a child; and *The Catherine Wheel* (1960), set in London, which deals with the unsatisfactory relationship between a young Australian girl and her selfish and demanding lover. *The Watch Tower* (1966), perhaps her most ambitious novel, explores the tensions between three people: Felix Shaw, a cruel and tyrannical businessman, his wife, Laura, and her sister, Clare. As with all her fictions, it deals with the evil underlying apparent normality, and with the corrupting influence of power.

HARSENT, David (1942–), British poet, born in Devonshire. He worked as a bookseller and was a literary critic with the *Times Literary Supplement* and the *Spectator* before becoming editor-in-chief and director at André Deutsch in 1979. *A Violent Country* (1969), his first collection of poetry, established his reputation as a poet of unusual candour and emotional power. Its unflinchingly direct treatments of personal crisis were sustained in *After Dark* (1973). The exploratory use of poetic sequences in *Dreams of the Dead* (1977) culminated in *Mister Punch* (1984), the protagonist of the title providing a quasi-mythological vehicle for successive wittily disquieting treatments of a wide range of philosophical and religious themes. Subsequent volumes include *Selected Poems* (1989), *Storybook Hero* (1992), and *News from the Front* (1993). His rhythmical economy and the assured precision of his imagery allow poems of striking psychological intensity to remain 'focussed to a hard edge and convincingly lucid in their enigmatic contexts', as Craig *Raine wrote of *Dreams of the Dead*. Among Harsent's other works is the novel *From an Inland Sea* (1985).

HART, Moss (1904–61), American playwright and director, born in New York, where he was educated in public schools; he began his theatrical career working for the celebrated agent Augustus Pitou. With George S. *Kaufman he collaborated in *Once in a Lifetime* (1930), and many other successful theatrical comedies including *The Man Who Came to Dinner* (1939) which was also filmed. Hart collaborated with many of the major popular American composers of his day: with Irving Berlin (*Face the Music*, 1932; *As Thousands Cheer*, 1933); with Cole Porter (*Jubilee*, 1935);

with Richard Rodgers and Lorenz Hart (*I'd Rather Be Right*, 1937); with Ira Gershwin and Kurt Weill (*Lady in the Dark*, 1941). He also directed the Lerner and Loewe musicals *My Fair Lady* (1956) and *Camelot* (1960). His other works include the plays *Winged Victory* (1943) and *Light Up The Sky* (1947). Hart also served the interests of American theatre as president of the Dramatists' Guild (1947–55), and of the Authors' League (1955–61). *Act One* (1959) is his autobiography.

HARTLEY, L(eslie) P(oles) (1895–1972), British novelist, critic, and short-story writer, born at Whittlesey, Cambridgeshire, into a prosperous family and brought up at Fletton Towers, the family home near Peterborough; he was educated at Balliol College, Oxford. Throughout his literary career he was a fiction reviewer for the *Spectator*, the *Observer*, and many other journals. The first of his many volumes of short stories, a genre in which he excelled, was *Night Fears* (1924). Much of his adult life was spent in Venice, which formed the setting of his novella *Simonetta Perkins* (1925). His major work was his trilogy beginning with *The Shrimp and the Anemone* (1944), followed by *The Sixth Heaven* (1946) and **Eustace and Hilda* (1947), the latter providing the title for the trilogy as a whole. While the trilogy secured his reputation as a major novelist, his most critically successful work was *The *Go-Between* (1953). All four books share a magical evocation of childhood and of the recent past, and draw on the Norfolk landscape and comfortable circumstances of his own childhood; all are influenced by Freud's teachings on childhood character-formation. His other novels include *My Fellow Devils* (1951), set in the world of film; *A Perfect Woman* (1955); *The Hireling* (1957), which describes the sexually charged relationship between an aristocratic widow and her cynical driver; *Facial Justice* (1960), a science fiction fable of the future; *The Brickfield* (1964), and a sequel, *The Betrayal* (1966); *Poor Clare* (1968), which is set in Bloomsbury and in Italy; and *The Love Adept* (1969). In his later novels Hartley turned away from the evocative Edwardian backdrops of his major works, but his principal themes remained the same: the search for identity, the desire properly to confront the past, the influence of early life on the development of the adult character, and the mutually threatening class structures of British society and the dangerous allure of the inter-class sexual attraction. Over all is a deep concern for human and moral values. A volume of his critical essays, *The Novelist's Responsibility*, was published in 1968.

HARTMANN, Geoffrey (1929–), German-born scholar and critic, educated at Queens College, New York, Dijon University, France, and Yale. Hartmann is well known for his work on Romanticism (*The Unmediated Vision*, 1954; *Wordsworth's Poetry*, 1964); he was a close associate at Yale of Harold *Bloom and Paul *de Man. He shares Bloom's interest in problems of interpretation and immediacy, and was an important figure in the diffusion of *Deconstruction in America and elsewhere. He has controversially argued for criticism as a creative art, not a merely subservient mode of attention to literary work. More broadly he has urged the virtues of theory against the retrenchments of tradition and supposed common sense, bringing to the debate formidable learning and a strong philosophical interest. His *Criticism in the Wilderness* (1980) and *Saving the Text* (1981) explore what he calls (in the title of another book, 1975) the fate of reading, conceived as a difficult, dangerous art. *Minor Prophecies* (1991) recommends the refusal of apocalyptic imaginings and the acceptance of patient, continuing interpretation as faithful both to ancient traditions and to modern practices in scholarship and criticism. The volume also has a remarkable essay on Paul de Man and pays tribute to the old 'common language' of criticism, the idiom of Dr Johnson and the *Spectator*, while pointing out the always possible complacency in such a language, and the vast areas of literary inquiry it cannot, by its own definitions, begin to encompass. He edited *Holocaust Remembrance* (1994), recollections of the Holocaust.

HARTNETT, Michael (1941–), Irish poet, born in Newcastle West, Co. Limerick, educated at University College and Trinity College in Dublin. After living in London and Madrid, he returned to Limerick to teach at the National College of Physical Education. *Anatomy of a Cliché* (1968), his first collection of poetry, was followed by numerous volumes in both Irish and English. His works in Irish include *Adharca Broic* (1978) and *Do Nuala* (1984); *A Farewell to English* (1975), *Poems in English* (1977), *House of Moon* (1989), *The Killing of Dreams* (1992), and *Selected and New Poems* (1994) are his principal publications in English. *Cúlúide, The Retreat of Ida Cagney* (1975) and *A Necklace of Wrens* (1987) contain verse in both languages. His poetry reflects his deep involvement with Irish culture in its treatments of folklore, mythology, and the Catholic devotional sensibility. As a love poet he is capable of a lyrical intensity reminiscent of Lorca, whose *Romancero Gitano* he translated as *Gipsy Ballads* (1973). His acclaimed translation of the Gaelic poem *The Hag of Beare* appeared in 1969. A *Collected Poems* appeared in two volumes in 1985 and 1987.

HARWOOD, Gwen(doline Nessie) (1920–95), Australian poet, born in Brisbane. She studied music, which she later taught; her works include a number of librettos for contemporary Australian composers. Her first collection, *Poems* (1963), deals with themes of physical and emotional anguish, and includes the series of poems featuring 'Professor Eisenbart', an ageing nuclear physicist who is, to some extent, perhaps, an ironic projection of herself; it was followed by *Poems: Volume Two* (1968) which contains the satirical figure of 'Professor Krote', a frustrated, and alcoholic, musician. The collection expresses her preoccupation with the difficulties of personal fulfilment, with mortality, loss, and the demands of domesticity. Although her poems frequently reflect intensely personal and moving experiences, they are generally optimistic. Harwood has acknowledged

*Wittgenstein as an influence and has affirmed her belief in the 'power of poetry to infuse experience with value'. Other works include *Selected Poems* (1975; reissued as *Collected Poems*, 1992), *The Lion's Bride* (1981), and *Bone Scan* (1988). She has published work under a number of pseudonyms (including 'Walter Lehmann' and 'Francis Geyer') and has won numerous awards, including the Robert Frost Award (1977) and the Patrick White Award (1978). *Blessed City: The Letters of Gwen Harwood* (edited by Alison Hoddinot) appeared in 1990.

HARWOOD, Lee (Travers Rafe) (1939–), British poet, born in Leicester, educated at Queen Mary College, University of London. He has worked as a librarian, bookseller, and post office worker and has lectured periodically at New College, San Francisco, since 1985. *The White Room* (1968) was his first substantial collection of poetry. Subsequent volumes include *H.M.S. Little Fox* (1975), *All the Wrong Notes* (1981), *Monster Masks* (1985), *Rope Boy to the Rescue* (1988), *Crossing the Frozen River* (1988), and *In the Mists: Mountain Poems* (1993). The surrealist impenetrability evident in his earlier verse was superseded during the 1970s by a more fluently accessible manner. His sustained concern with recreating the immediacy of perception gives rise to the intense use of local imagery that characterizes much of his work; Brighton, Snowdonia, Italy, and New York are among the locations he has drawn on in poetry notable for the range and imaginative flexibility of its sense of place. He has also published several collections of short stories, which include *Dream Quilt* (1985).

HARWOOD, Ronald (1934–), South African playwright and novelist, born and educated in Cape Town; he trained for the stage at the Royal Academy of Dramatic Art, London. A prolific playwright, his first plays, *Country Matters* (1969, an adaptation of Evelyn *Waugh's *The Ordeal of Gilbert Pinfold* (1977)%thin;) and *A Family* (1978), were followed by his best-known play, *The Dresser* (1980), a picture of life behind the scenes with an actor based on Sir Donald Wolfit, with whom Harwood had worked in his youth. Among his later plays are *Tramway Road* (1984), set in the Cape Town of the 1950s, about an aspiring young actor whose hopes are shattered through his 'mixed-race' origins; *Interpreters* (1985), a romantic comedy with political overtones, about an English translator of Russian descent and a passionate Russian delegate; *Another Time* (1987), about a musician who grows up in South Africa and moves to London; *Poison Pen* (1994), involving the still-unexplained death of the critic Philip Heseltine, alias the composer Peter Warlock; and *Taking Sides* (1995), about the accusations of Nazism directed, in Harwood's view unjustly, at the conductor Wilhelm Furtwangler. At his best, as when he raises the relationship of art and politics in this last play, Harwood combines an interest in ideas with well-observed realism. Harwood has also written several novels, including *César and Augusta* (1978), about the French composer César Franck, and a biography of *Sir Donald Wolfit, CBE* (1971).

HASLUCK, Nicholas (1942–), Australian poet and novelist, born in Canberra, educated at the University of Western Australia. His first novel, *Quarantine* (1978), was followed by *The Blue Guitar* (1980), which deals with moral confusion in the world of commerce. *The Hand that Feeds You* (1982) is a political satire about a future corrupt republican Australia to which an innocent expatriate writer returns and gets elected to Parliament. *The Bellarmine Jug* (1984), perhaps his best novel, concerns the 1629 mutiny and massacre perpetrated in Australia by a party from a shipwrecked Dutch vessel. *Truant State* (1987) is set in Western Australia at the time of secession and involves the financial ruin of an English immigrant family. *The Country Without Music* (1990) is set in a group of islands, formerly a French penal settlement, and concerns the visit of a group of twentieth-century Australian businessmen, who plan to build a tourist centre there. *The Blosseville File* (1992) explores political corruption in a fictional ex-colony; *A Grain of Truth* (1994) is a crime story exposing influences on the law of political interests and the distortions of truth effected by skilful advocacy. Other works include *The Hat on the Letter O and Other Stories* (1978); *Anchor and Other Poems* (1976); *On the Edge* (1980; with William Grono); *Chinese Journey* (1985; with C. J. *Koch), a collection of prose writings; *Collage: Recollections of the Universe of Western Australia* (1987); and *Offcuts from a Legal Literary Life* (1993), autobiographical writings from his distinguished legal career.

HASS, Robert (1941–), American poet and editor, born in San Francisco, educated at St Mary's College, San Francisco and Stanford University. Hass is one of a group of younger American poets whose work came to critical attention in the early 1970s and who mark an important shift in poetic sensibility away from the *confessional and post-confessional lyric mode that dominated American poetry in the 1950s and 1960s, and from the intellectual nihilism of *Beat poetry. Hass's work owes much to the influence of Yvor *Winters, under whom he studied at Stanford: his early verse is intelligent, syntactically and grammatically uncluttered, but frequently elliptical and difficult. His feeling for the longer verse form, and a capacity to maintain it, is a characteristic of individual poems such as 'Maps' and 'Lament for the Poles of Buffalo', but he is equally at home in a more conventional lyric medium, as in 'Spring' or 'Child Naming Flowers'. Many of his poems make sympathetic use of Californian landscapes. He was a recipient of the Yale Younger Poets Award in 1972; his first volume of verse, *Field Guide* (1973), was followed by *Praise* (1978). *Twentieth Century Pleasures: Prose on Poetry* (1984) won the National Book Critics Circle Award. Later volumes include *Human Wishes* (1989) and *The Essential Haiku* (1994), the latter comprising 'versions', as he calls them, of Basho, Buson, and Issa. *Five American*

Poets (1979), edited by Michael Schmidt, contains a selection of his early verse.

HASSALL, Christopher (Vernon) (1912–63), British poet, librettist, and biographer, born in London, educated at Wadham College, Oxford; he subsequently became an actor. He produced highly accomplished lyrics for Ivor Novello's compositions, and gained financial success with their first musical, *Glamorous Night* (1939). His reputation as a poet increased with three sonnet sequences (*Crisis*, 1939; *S.O.S.—Ludlow*, 1940; and *The Slow Night*, 1949) drawing on his experiences of active service during the Second World War. The poems of *The Red Leaf* (1957) encompass a wide range of discursive and dramatically effective modes. The forty sonnets which form the title sequence of *Bell Harry* (1963) combine topographical and contemplative elements in an extended elegy on the death of his friend Frances *Cornford. As a librettist, he produced texts for William Walton's *Troilus and Cressida* (1954) and Prokofiev's *The Fiery Angel* (1965). Among his verse-dramas are *Christ's Comet* (1937) and *The Player King* (1953). Hassall's works as a biographer include *Edward Marsh* (1959); he had been encouraged by *Marsh early in his career as a poet. His other biographies include *Rupert Brooke* (1964).

HASTINGS, Michael (Gerald) (1938–), British playwright and novelist, born in Lambeth, London, and brought up in Brixton; he was educated at Alleyn's School. He subsequently trained as an actor and writer at the Royal Court Theatre in London where many of his plays were produced. His interest in the dramatic presentation of biography is best displayed in *Tom and Viv* (1984), a haunting study of T. S. *Eliot's marriage to his first wife, Vivienne Haigh-Wood. *Three Plays* (1980) contains: *Gloo Joo* (1978), an acerbic comedy of Caribbean manners; *For the West (Uganda)* (1977), about Ugandan dictator Idi Amin; and *Full Frontal* (1979), a monologue by a West Indian. His other plays include *Lee Harvey Oswald* (1966), published in *Three Political Plays* (1990); and *Carnival War/Midnite at the Starlite* (1981), which contains a powerful examination of the annual Notting Hill Carnival, in London, and a sardonic account of competitive ballroom dancing. *The Emperor* (1987) was an adaptation by Hastings and Jonathan Miller of Ryszard Kapuscinski's book about the fall of Haile Selassie, Emperor of Ethiopia. *Unfinished Business* (1994) depicts support for Hitler among the British upper classes. Hastings has also written several novels, and biographies of Rupert *Brooke (1967) and Sir Richard Burton (1978).

HAU'OFA, Epeli (1939–), Papua New Guinean novelist and short-story writer, born in Salamo, Papua New Guinea, educated at the University of New South Wales, McGill University, Montreal, and the Australian National University, Canberra. Following a succession of university appointments and a period as the deputy private secretary to the King of Tonga, he became Professor of Sociology at the University of the South Pacific, Fiji, in 1983. The twelve robustly humorous stories in *Tales of the Tikongs* (1983) are set on the imaginary island of Tiko; the social and cultural chaos produced by the collision of Western values and the island's indigenous traditions mirrors the absurdities wrought by accelerated change in the South Pacific. His novel *Kisses in the Nederends* (1987), a picaresque narrative of the protagonist's search for relief from his perianal afflictions, similarly reflects the difficulties inflicted on the Pacific states by colonialism and its legacy of continuing exploitation. Hau'ofa's works as a sociologist and anthropologist include *Our Crowded Islands* (1977) and *Mekeo: Inequality and Ambivalence in a Village Society* (1981).

HAWKES, Jacquetta (1910–96), English archaeologist and novelist, born in Cambridge, educated at Newnham College, Cambridge. She worked for UNESCO during 1943–8 and 1964–79. She was particularly well known for her popular books on archaeological topics. Notable among these is *A Land* (1951, with colour plates by Henry Moore), which she described as 'the story of the creation of what is at present Britain'; other works in this vein include *Archaeology of Jersey* (1939), *Early Britain* (1945), *Guide to the Prehistoric Monuments of England and Wales* (1951), *Man on Earth* (1954), *The Dawn of the Gods* (1968), *The First Great Civilizations* (1973), and *The Shell Guide to British Archaeology* (1986). She was married to Christopher Hawkes with whom she wrote *Prehistoric Britain* (1952), and to J. B. *Priestley with whom she collaborated in the play *Dragon's Mouth* (1952). Her other works include *Symbols and Speculations* (1948; poems), *Fables* (1953; stories), *King of the Two Lands* (1966; novel), *A Quest of Love* (1980), a semi-autobiographical novel, and *Mortimer Wheeler* (1982), a biography.

HAWKES, John (Clendennin Burne, Jr) (1925–), American novelist, born in Connecticut, educated at Harvard; he spent his formative years in Alaska. His experience as an ambulance driver in Italy and Germany during the Second World War was to mark his early fiction, including the novel *The Cannibal* (1949), which was viewed by many critics as an allegory of German fascism. Hawkes is often compared to the masters of avant-garde and post-modernist fictional technique, and his lavish prose style, imagistic virtuosity, and skilled use of the first-person narrative voice echo *Nabokov and Djuna *Barnes. Hawkes's novels include *The Beetle Leg* (1951), set in the American West; *The Lime Twig* (1961), a parody of the detective novel, marked by Hawkes's characteristic emphasis on violent and occasionally misogynistic sexuality; *The Blood Oranges* (1971), which reworks Ford's *The *Good Soldier*; *Death, Sleep and the Traveler* (1974), a drama of sexual exchange and infidelity; and *Travesty* (1976), the monologue of an ageing writer driving the lover of his wife to death and himself to suicide. In later work Hawkes has experimented with female voices and semi-pornographic themes. The highly praised *Virginie: Her Two Lives* (1982), rich with allusions to the writings of de Sade, is narrated by a girl of 11, living parallel lives in two centuries, the eighteenth and the twentieth. *Adventures in the Alaskan Skin Trade* (1985) uses autobiographical material, though the narrator, Sunny, is a woman. Rich with detailed descriptions of Alaska, the novel is Hawkes's most uncharacteristic work, and has been seen by some critics as his mandatory attempt to write the 'Great American Novel'. Other works include the novels *Second Skin* (1964), *The Passion Artist* (1979), and *Whistlejacket* (1988). Hawkes's early short fiction, located in an Italy set between fact and fantasy, was collected in *Lunar Landscapes: Stories and Short Novels '49–'63* (1969). Hawkes is much admired by academics for his experimentalism and unashamed literariness.

Hawksmoor, a novel by Peter *Ackroyd, published in 1985. The double narrative of this combination of suspense, horror, and social history unfolds in the early eighteenth century and in the present day. The chapters set in the skilfully evoked London of the past are narrated by an architect named Nicholas Dyer, whose mastery of his craft is accompanied by a fervent belief in the esoteric and the supernatural. His plan to build seven churches in the City of London is underwritten by arcane symbolism and the ritual murder of vagabonds, children, and, eventually, his adversaries. In the chapters set in the present, a similar series of ritualistic murders of children and tramps, on the sites of the churches built by Dyer, links the alternating narratives. The murders are brought to the attention of Nicholas Hawksmoor, a senior detective in the CID. This surly, reclusive man eventually traces a pattern connecting the murders to the past and to Nicholas Dyer; the scepticism of his colleagues parallels the dismissal of Dyer's esoteric speculations by his peers and fellow architects, including Sir Christopher Wren. Hawksmoor is taken off the unsolved case, just as Dyer, in the past, was superseded by his contemporaries. Hawksmoor's unsuccessful attempts to unravel the mystery of the ritual murders, with their strong implication of the unseen and supernatural, eventually lead him to a state of hallucinatory obsession and despair. His name refers to the real architect responsible for six of the churches in the novel, and upon whose career Dyer's is partly based.

HAYDEN, Robert (1913–80), African-American poet, born in Detroit, educated at Wayne State University and the University of Michigan; he taught English at Fisk University before returning to the University of Michigan in 1968. In 1976 Hayden became the first African-American to be appointed Consultant in Poetry to the Library of Congress. He worked as a researcher for the *Federal Writers Project of the Works Progress Administration (1936–8) and the facts of African-American history with which he dealt formed the substance of much of his later poetry. Prominent historical black figures like Harriet Tubman, Frederick Douglass, and Nat Turner combine with more recent figures like Malcolm X, Paul Robeson, and Bessie Smith and with personal recollections. 'Elegies for Paradise Valley' is a sequence of poems that recreate the Detroit neighbourhood in which Hayden grew up. The historical imagination is central to Hayden's work, especially in poems like 'Middle Passage', a collage which dramatizes through multiple voices a range of accounts of slavery focusing upon the conditions aboard the slave ship *The Armistad* and the slave-led rebellion that symbolizes the conflict between oppression and the indomitable desire for freedom. Hayden deliberately wrote of themes other than racial conflict and African-American history and culture: he adhered closely to the belief that poetry should speak universally and that the representation of a particular political moment should be such that it carries universal relevance. His collections include *Heart-Shape in the Dust* (1940), *Figures of Time: Poems* (1955), *A Ballad of Remembrance* (1962), *Selected Poems* (1966), *Words in the Mourning Time* (1970), *Angle of Ascent: New and Selected Poems* (1975), *American Journal* (1978), *Collected Prose* (1984), and *Collected Poems* (1985).

Hay Fever, a comedy by Noël *Coward, performed in 1925. The main characters are Judith and David Bliss, respectively an actor and a writer, and their adult children, Simon and Sorel. Unknown to the others, each has asked a guest to the house for the weekend, but each proceeds to pay attention to someone other than the person he or she has invited. So unnerved are the visitors by the family's ceaseless histrionics that, the morning after a lively evening, they creep away unnoticed. The play is slight, but elegantly plotted and full of humorous characterization. The National Theatre's revival in 1964, with Edith Evans and Maggie Smith in leading roles, did much to re-establish Coward's reputation, which had been adversely affected by the arrival of the socially aware drama associated with **Look Back in Anger*.

HAZZARD, Shirley (1931–), Australian writer, born and educated in Sydney. Since leaving Australia at the age of 16 she has travelled to Hong Kong, New Zealand, Europe, and America. She married Francis Steegmuller, became an American citizen, and divides her time between the USA and Italy. In 1976 she wrote an influential account of Australia for the **New Yorker*, for which she had also written short stories, later collected in *Cliffs of Fall and Other Stories* (1963). Having worked with the United Nations (1952–62) she became a vocal opponent of that institution, about which she wrote in *Defeat of an Ideal: A Study of the Self-Destruction of the United Nations* (1973) and *Countenance the Truth: The United Nations and the Waldheim Case* (1990), and in *People In Glass Houses* (1967), a sharply satirical novel, analysing life within the UN walls. *The Evening of the Holiday* (1966), set in Florence, is about the love of a young Anglo-Italian woman for an older Italian architect. *The Bay of Noon* (1970) is narrated by a woman who fled to Naples to escape a triangular relationship, only there to be drawn into a similar situation. Her highly acclaimed *The Transit of Venus* (1980) is a romantic novel concerning a young Australian woman who travels to England with her sister, her entanglement with a feckless Englishman, and her rescue from despair by a middle-aged American. Hazzard's writings are mostly a sensitive exploration of the infinite aspirations, manifestations, and memories of human love. A finely wrought simplicity of style and structure lends her work unusual powers of evocation and analysis.

H.D., see DOOLITTLE, HILDA.

HEAD, Bessie (1937–86), South African novelist, born in Pietermaritzburg, and educated at a mission school. She worked as a teacher, and as a journalist for **Drum* magazine in South Africa, before she moved to Botswana due to political pressures associated with the trial of a friend. The pain of exile and alienation permeates her first three novels, all set in Botswana. They are also infused with the tensions between rural and urban values, and those caused by racism, traditionalism, male chauvinism, and tribal particularism. In *When the Clouds Gather* (1969) a black South African nationalist and an English agricultural expert encounter opposition from a local chief who is suspicious of the modern methods. *Maru* (1971) focuses on the new teacher, Margaret Cadmore, who is taken for a 'Coloured' by villagers, and treated respectfully until she reveals herself to be a member of a despised tribe. *A Question of Power* (1973) extends these themes and reaches for new values, opposed to both traditional and dominant modern ones. *Serowe: Village of the Rain Wind* (1981) and *A Bewitched Crossroad* (1984) explore the past, depicting aspects of Botswana history culled from the oral tradition. Her collection of stories *The Collector of Treasures* (1977) contains tales of village life, very much in the spirit of oral storytelling and didactic parable.

HEALY, Dermot (1947–), Irish novelist and writer of short stories, born in Co. Westmeath. He has worked as a labourer, insurance underwriter, actor, director, and editor of *The Drumlin*, a magazine of literature and local history based in Co. Cavan. Much of Healy's work has concerned the divided communities of Ireland's border counties, a setting which offers metaphors with which to cross the divide between past and present. His short story collection *Banished Misfortune* (1982), and his novels *Fighting with Shadows; or Sciamachy* (1984) and *The Goats' Song* (1990), incorporate diverse styles of expression while producing an ironic effect of realism.

HEANEY, Seamus (Justin) (1939–), Irish poet and critic, born in Castledawson, Co. Derry, educated at Queen's University, Belfast, where he began lecturing in 1966. During the early 1960s he was part of the Belfast writers' group run by Philip *Hobsbaum and was closely associated with the emergence of *Ulster poetry. He moved to Glanmore in County Wicklow in 1972 to devote himself to writing. Following a succession of visiting appointments at American universities, he became Boylston Professor of Rhetoric and Oratory at Harvard in 1986 and was elected Oxford Professor of Poetry in 1989. His first two collections of verse, **Death of a Naturalist* (1966) and *Door into the Dark* (1969), reflect his agricultural background with an immediacy and authenticity for which the poetry of Patrick *Kavanagh supplied a rural Irish precedent. Throughout his career he has continued to make remarkably full and varied use of themes and images drawn from his native locality. Ireland's troubled history and Heaney's uneasy identity as an Irish Catholic writer with firm allegiances to the English literary tradition assume increasing significance in his earlier volumes. The outbreak of sectarian violence in Ulster in 1969 was registered deeply in *Wintering Out* (1972). The collection initiated the imaginative engagement with the landscape of the peat bogs as a means of comprehending contemporary events which is sustained and intensified in **North* (1975). His sense of personal implication in Ulster's upheaval was explored at this time through the recollections of childhood in the prose poems of *Stations* (1975). A more private and lyrically meditative manner is resumed in *Field Work* (1979); the volume contains several memorable elegies for victims of sectarian killings, anticipating some of the Dantean dialogues with the dead in the title sequence of *Station Island* (1984). The collection contains a wide range of material amounting to a thorough survey of all his principal concerns; the twelve poems of 'Station Island' involve him in an ordeal of confronting his origins and obligations, repeatedly through dramatically imagined encounters with the dead, who include the ghosts of Kavanagh and James *Joyce. The book concludes with a new assertion of artistic freedom which is maintained in the liberating imaginative scope and heightened technical virtuosity of *The Haw Lantern* (1987) and *Seeing Things* (1991). His *New Selected Poems, 1966–1987* appeared in 1990. Other works by Heaney include *Sweeney Astray* (1983), a version of the medieval Irish *Buile Suibhne*, of which a revised illustrated version appeared as *Sweeney's Flight* (1993). He has also gained a high reputation as a critic, showing a wide knowledge of European and American, as well as English and Irish, poetries in the collected essays of *Preoccupations* (1980) and *The Government of the Tongue* (1988). Heaney won the Nobel Prize for Literature in 1995.

HEARNE, John (1926–95), Jamaican novelist, born in Montreal, Canada, but brought up in Jamaica; educated at Jamaica College and the University of Edinburgh. He has been a teacher and journalist, and a researcher working for Prime Minister Michael Manley of Jamaica. Conservative in outlook, his novels are notable for their depiction of the Jamaican professional classes, and antagonisms based on racial and class difference. His first novel, *Voices Under the Window* (1955), is narrated entirely in flashback, and focuses on a young lawyer at the point of death reflecting on his ultimately lethal involvement in Jamaican politics and his racial origins. *Stranger at the*

Gate (1956), *The Faces of Love* (1957), *The Autumn Equinox* (1959), and *The Land of the Living* (1961), set in an imaginary exotic 'Cayuna', concentrate on the personal dilemmas of romantic love and middle-class alienation, though underlying political factors persist. More symbolic and allegorical, *The Sure Salvation* (1981), set in a slave ship, is marked by pessimism about both politics and personal relationships.

Heartbreak House, a play by G. B. *Shaw, published in 1919 and performed in 1920, though it was probably written in 1916–17, largely in response to the Great War, an event addressed in an unwontedly sombre preface. The plot to this 'fantasia in the Russian manner on English themes' is given a semblance of unity through the character Ellie Dunn, daughter of the idealistic Mazzini Dunn. She is invited to the household of the aged Captain Shotover by his younger daughter, Hesione Hushabye, a woman of bohemian inclination, said to have been partly modelled on Virginia *Woolf. There, Ellie admits to being in love with Marcus Darnley, who turns out to be Hesione's husband Hector in one of his many romantic guises. Disillusioned and hardened, Ellie announces her intention of marrying Boss Mangan, a rich and influential financier. Later, she rejects the prospect of wealth and proclaims herself spiritually wed to Shotover, in what appears to be a union of vitality and wisdom. With Hesione's sister Ariadne Utterwood, the conventional wife of a colonial bureaucrat, and her brother-in-law, the feeble Randall, all these characters have contributions to make to what becomes a dramatized debate about an England Shaw regarded as hopelessly divided between the representatives of 'Heartbreak House' (meaning the cultured but self-absorbed and politically irresponsible) and those of what his preface calls 'Horseback Hall' (meaning Ariadne and the other aggressive philistines). Shotover, a self-mocking portrait of Shaw himself, delivers the key warning about the future of the ship of state: 'The captain is in his bunk, drinking bottled ditchwater; and the crew is gambling in the forecastle. She will strike and sink and split. Do you think the laws of God will be suspended in favour of England because you were born in it?' In an ambiguous ending, a bomber kills the capitalist Mangan and leaves Hesione, Hector, and Ellie radiant at the prospect of a second air-raid, even though it may destroy them.

Heart is a Lonely Hunter, The, see MCCULLERS, CARSON.

Heart of Darkness, a novel by Joseph *Conrad, published in 1902 together with 'Youth' and 'The End of the Tether' (serialized in *Blackwood's Magazine*, 1899). The framing narrative is set on board the *Nellie*, on the lower reaches of the Thames, where Charlie Marlow is relating an episode from his earlier life to professional companions, a Director of Companies, an Accountant, a Lawyer, and the anonymous narrator who opens and concludes the narrative. Marlow recalls his experience captaining a tin-pot steamboat up an unnamed central African river in search and rescue of Mr Kurtz, a renowned ivory collector employed by the Belgian company for which Marlow is temporarily working. Marlow's journey down the African coast to the Company's Outer Station headquarters and trek inland to the Central Station to take charge of his boat has already exposed him to the brutal realities of colonial military and economic exploitation. Marlow becomes increasingly disillusioned by his complicity with the 'pilgrims of progress' who represent European civilization, while his simultaneous fascination with and dread of the 'monstrous and unearthy, inscrutable' jungle and its native inhabitants grow as he struggles upriver towards Kurtz. Kurtz himself has achieved almost god-like authority over the native tribesmen, who seek to fight off the approaching steamboat. The row of severed heads on stakes surrounding Kurtz's encampment intimate something of the 'unspeakable rites' which Kurtz has embraced with Nietzschean audacity. Back in Europe, Marlow's final lie to Kurtz's Intended—that on his deathbed Kurtz uttered her name and not his appalling ambiguous cry, 'The horror! The horror!'—consolidates one of Conrad's major thematic preoccupations: that consciousness of deeper truths is painful and that 'the surface truths' of things ('luckily! luckily!') hides their reality. Much of Conrad's powerful insight was gained on his own trip up the Congo river some ten years earlier (cf. *Congo Diary*) and through his friendship with R. B. *Cunninghame Graham. A vast body of critical commentary has mined the dense richness and consciously paradoxical quality of this seminal modernist work, with its modern version of a Dantean journey into the Inferno, its Faustian figure of Kurtz provoking ambivalently fascinated horror, and Marlow's characteristically modernist self-conscious story-telling. Remarkably varied analyses exploit mythical, Freudian, formalist-narratological, feminist, deconstructionist, and Marxist approaches; insights generated by notions of the cultural/racial Other (cf. Chinua *Achebe and Edward *Said) have provided eloquent critiques. The influence of *Heart of Darkness* can be traced in writers as diverse as T. S. *Eliot, André Gide, H. G. *Wells, Achebe, William *Golding, Graham *Greene, V. S. *Naipaul, and George *Steiner, while Francis Coppola's film *Apocalypse Now* taps some of its rich imaginative possibilities by transposing it to the Vietnam War.

Heart of the Matter, The, a novel by Graham *Greene, published in 1948, set in West Africa, where Greene worked for British Intelligence during the Second World War. Greene's title echoes Joseph Conrad's **Heart of Darkness*, though his novel shows Africa not as a dark continent so much as one suffused with the greyness he sees as universally part of human nature. Its stale, sticky background of vultures, rats, and cockroaches reflects and extends loneliness and despair in a snobbish, bickering society of colonial administrators. Only the assistant police commissioner, 'Scobie the just', tries to live by black-and-white moral principles. He is destroyed by the attempt, driven to suicide by compromised religious beliefs and his 'terrible sense of responsibility'—for his lover Helen Rolt, a young widow from a torpedoed ship; and for his wife Louise, whose unhappiness drives him to borrow from the corrupt Syrian trader Yusef, who blackmails him. *The Heart of the Matter* is part of a phase of strong Catholic interest in Greene's writing, and there has been much debate about whether Scobie's mortal sins truly exclude him from God's mercy. Greene has disclaimed interest in the issue: like most of his fiction, the novel is concerned less with orthodox doctrines and ideals than with their tension with ordinary nature under the pressures of modern history. This is emphasized by a scene in which Scobie finds that the only reading material available to entertain another young victim of the torpedoing is the outdated, idealistic missionary tract *A Bishop among the Bantus*. He transforms it into a racy tale of betrayal and detection in which the secret agent A. Bishop pursues bloodthirsty 'Bantu' pirates. The episode is paradigmatic of Greene's fiction: like Scobie, he challenges and reshapes conventional concepts of virtue and heroism, also showing in this novel the pride—even foolishness—as well as courage of trying to adhere to them at all in an uncertain, unfaithful age.

Heat and Dust, a novel by Ruth Prawer *Jhabvala, published in 1975, and winner of the Booker Prize. It tells the interlocked stories of two Englishwomen, divided by time and era, but related by family ties and by their experience of India. An unnamed narrator—whose diary part of the novel purports to be —travels to India in search of the elusive Olivia, her grandfather's first wife (whose life is revealed in fragments and flashbacks to 1923); captivated by the vitality concealed within the post-colonial decay of India, she, like Olivia before her, decides to remain there. Olivia, however, as the wife of a colonial officer, had known a more exotic and opulent India; she was seduced by an Indian prince whose mistress she then became, causing a scandal in the bigoted Anglo-Indian society of the time. The narrator, however, in an age when history has overtaken the Raj and the imperial past is regarded as something of an irrelevance, becomes pregnant by the petty clerk in whose house she boards and is left to deal with her life as best she can on her own resources. Jhabvala deftly contrasts the imperial with the colonial, the East with the West; the similarity that recurs across gaps of time and culture is, however, in the harsh treatment of women, whether by exclusion and ostracism, marginalization, or mere indifference. As in much of her fiction, Jhabvala indicates an implicit parallel between cultural diversity and gender difference. *Heat and Dust* was successfully filmed by the Merchant-Ivory-Jhabvala team in 1983.

HEATH, Roy (1926–), Guyanese novelist, born in British Guiana where he attended Central High School, and worked as a civil servant, before emigrating to England in 1950. Although he was called to the English Bar in 1964 Heath never practised law, but worked as a schoolteacher in London. His first novel, *A Man Came Home* (1974), is concerned with the day-to-day activities of the urban, middle-class Guyanese who form the subject of most of Heath's fiction. In such novels as *The Murderer* (1978) and the Armstrong trilogy (*From the Heat of the Day*, 1979; *One Generation*, 1981; and *Genetha*, 1981) Heath explores the psychological, financial, and sexual implications of life in a Guyanese landscape where the extended family structure, unaffected social relations, explicit speech and gestures, and frank reliance on the supernatural lend an air of complete authenticity to his writing. In *The Shadow Bride* (1988) Heath focuses on the Indian community in Guyana. His work is marked by comprehensive social observation, penetrating psychological analysis, and vigorous, picaresque action. *Shadows Round the Moon* (1990) is a volume of autobiography.

HEATH-STUBBS, John (Francis Alexander) (1918–), British poet, born in London, educated at Worcester College for the Blind and at Queen's College, Oxford, where he formed a close friendship with Sidney *Keyes. He has held a succession of visiting posts at universities in Britain and overseas. *Wounded Thammuz* (1942), his first collection of verse, was followed by numerous volumes, which include *The Charity of the Stars* (1949), *The Watchman's Flute* (1978), *Collected Poems 1943–1987* (1988), *The Game of Love and Death* (1990), and *Selected Poems* (1990). Much of his work is characterized by a wry individuality of tone and skilful manipulation of rhythmical effects. 'Send for Lord Timothy', a purposefully ludicrous satire of the cult of nostalgia in the English detective novel, is one of the best-known examples of the marked comic strain in his work. Many of his poems arise from his preoccupation with mythological and historical subject matter, of which *Artorius* (1972), a treatment in twelve parts of Arthurian legend, is the most sustained manifestation. Of his translations, *Poems from Giacomo Leopardi* (1946) is particularly highly valued. Among his other publications are the plays collected in *Helen in Egypt* (1958); the monograph *Charles Williams* (1955); *The Darkling Plain* (1950), his charting of the 'later fortunes of romanticism', and a prose autobiography, *Hindsights* (1993).

HEAT MOON, William Least (1939–), American author, born in Kansas City, Missouri, educated at the University of Missouri. Originally named William Trogdon, he adopted his Native American name, which translates as 'Least Heat Moon'. He taught in Columbia, Missouri, from 1965 to 1978, when, reacting against the uniform materialism of modern American life, he embarked on a three-month journey around the USA in a van; the widely popular *Blue Highways: A Journey into America* (1982) forms an abundantly detailed record of the landscapes and societies he passed through. In 1991 Heat Moon published *PrairyErth*, his attempt to construct a 'deep map' of

Chase County, Kansas, through the collation of an extraordinary range of information on the human and natural characters of the area.

Heat of the Day, The, a novel by E. *Bowen, set in wartime London between 1942 and 1944, published in 1949. Stella Rodney, an attractive widow in her forties, is having a passionate wartime affair with Robert Kelway, who works at the War Office. Stella is approached by the sinister Harrison, a secret agent of sorts, who has come into his own in this 'crooks' war'. He tells her that Robert is a spy, selling secrets to the enemy, and that if Stella will allow Harrison into her life, he will leave Robert 'on the loose'. Stella gradually discovers that this is the truth about Robert; he explains his treachery by a loathing of English democracy derived from a stifling mother-dominated childhood (his gloomy suburban home, Holme Dene, is the scene of grotesque comedy) and from his experience at Dunkirk ('army of freedom queuing up to be taken off by pleasure boats'). Stella refuses his arguments, and Robert is killed escaping pursuit. Two minor characters, Louie Lewis, an 'ordinary' soldier's wife living in London with her friend Connie, and Stella's son Roderick, who has inherited an Anglo-Irish house, Mount Morris, contrast with Robert's disaffection. The plot is implausible, but Stella's predicament is painfully vivid, Harrison is impressive, and the novel's atmosphere is a remarkable achievement, the best evocation of the unreality and excitement of London in the Blitz.

Heaven's My Destination, see WILDER, THORNTON.

HECHT, Anthony (Evan) (1923–), American poet, born in New York, educated at Bard College and Columbia University. Having held a succession of posts at various American universities, including Kenyon College, where he worked with John Crowe *Ransom, he became Professor of Poetry and Rhetoric at Rochester University in 1967. His early collections of poetry, which display his considerable accomplishment in traditional verse forms, include *A Summoning of Stones* (1954), *The Seven Deadly Sins* (1958), and *A Bestiary* (1962). The ornate intricacy of many of the poems in these books was superseded by the plainer and more immediate manner characteristic of much of the best work in *The Hard Hours* (1967; Pulitzer Prize), *Millions of Strange Shadows* (1977), and *The Venetian Vespers* (1979). The poems these volumes contain range from precisely observed anecdotal treatments to the philosophically encompassing title sequence of *Venetian Vespers*, which forms the culmination of the historical, cultural, and metaphysical preoccupations of his preceding work. Hecht published no further collections of poetry until *The Transparent Man* (1990), in which the long poem 'See Naples and Die' is a self-revealing companion piece to the stoically pessimistic vision of 'Venetian Vespers'. *Collected Earlier Poems* also appeared in 1990. His literary criticism is principally represented by the essays collected in *Obbligati* (1986), and *The Hidden Law: The Poetry of W. H. Auden* (1993). Among his numerous works as a translator are his version of Voltaire's *Poem upon the Lisbon Disaster* (1977) and the translations of poems by Joseph *Brodsky in *The Venetian Vespers*. See also CONFESSIONAL POETRY.

HECHT, Ben (1894–1964), American novelist and dramatist, born in New York and brought up in Wisconsin. Hecht eventually settled into a bohemian orthodoxy in the literary world of Chicago after the First World War where he edited the *Chicago Literary Times* (1923–4), a *little magazine that espoused a *fin de siècle* aestheticism in a spirit of modernist iconoclasm. He wrote numerous plays of which the best known are two gritty comedies written in collaboration with Charles *MacArthur, *The Front Page* (1928) and *Twentieth Century* (1932), which was adapted for cinema by Howard Hawks in 1934. *The Front Page* deals with Chicago newsmen and the duplicitous manœuvres of an editor who will go to any lengths to prevent a young reporter, who has just scooped a story, escaping to marriage and New York. Set in the newsroom of the paper, *The Front Page* is the precursor of contemporary newspaper television serials, and has been made into a film several times: by Lewis Milestone in 1931, by Howard Hawks under the title *His Girl Friday* in 1940, and by Billy Wilder in 1974. Hecht's autobiography *A Child of the Century* appeared in 1954.

HEINLEIN, Robert A(nson) (1907–88), American writer, born in Missouri, educated at the University of Missouri and at Annapolis. After naval service was brought to an end by illness, he began writing *science fiction; within a few years of publishing his first story in 1939 he became widely known, and for fifty years his work dominated American science fiction. His many novels and stories generally featured a series of 'Competent Men'; argumentative, tough, numerate, and bright, they explored and exploited the solar system, against the constraints of timid bureaucrats. The future history Heinlein created in the 1940s for these heroes are collected in *The Past through Tomorrow* (1967) which provided a model for this imaginative domestication of the future. His *Stranger in a Strange Land* (1961) was the first science fiction novel to become a bestseller. It has been suggested that the series of children's novels culminating in *Starship Troopers* (1959) represented Heinlein at his best, but his adult novels, such as *Double Star* (1956), *The Door into Summer* (1957), and *The Moon is a Harsh Mistress* (1966), are similarly accomplished. Among the many critical studies on the author is H. B. Franklin's (1982).

HEJINIAN, Lyn (1941–), American poet, born in San Francisco. She taught herself letterpress printing and edited the Tuumba series of chapbooks in which many of the *Language poets appeared. Since then she has been an editor of *Poetics Journal* with Barrett *Watten. She is best known for her longer book-length works, *Writing Is an Aid to Memory* (1978), *My Life* (1980/1987), *Oxota: A Short Russian Novel* (1991), and *The Cell* (1992). Like Ron *Silliman and Barrett Watten she works with generative frameworks (each section of the second edition of *My Life* has forty-nine sentences and the same number of sections, her age at the time of writing) and favours structures built from complete but varyingly disjunctive sentences: 'one must be careful not to read any sequence of sentences as a series of substitutes or cancellations.' *The Cell* is a self-exploratory phenomenology of consciousness that avoids confessionalism. *My Life* combines rigorous introspective attention to memory with a steady observation of a woman's experience of everyday life.

HELLER, Joseph (1923–), American novelist, born in Brooklyn, educated at New York, Columbia, and Oxford Universities. Heller published short stories, becoming a full-time writer in 1961 after having worked for *Time* and *Look* magazines. His experiences in the US Army Air Force during the Second World War led to his first novel and major success with **Catch-22* (1961), which depicted the absurdity and chaos of warfare through a group of memorable characters, with a plot based on the military bureaucratic mind. The book's immense success during the years of the Vietnam War led to its title becoming a common phrase in modern usage to express an impossibly frustrating position. His next fiction was *Something Happened* (1974), which investigates the alienation suffered by a commercial functionary, Robert Slocum, by surrounding the central and eponymous event with a mass of detail to describe the tedium of his life as he becomes a victim of his own psychological paralysis. With *Good as Gold* (1979), Heller made an effective return to satire with this cruelly humorous portrait of Washington political life, with the focus on the Jewish professor Bruce Gold, who 'sells out' to material, sexual, and literary opportunism. Other works include *God Knows* (1984), about the Biblical hero David, albeit from the alternative confessional perspective of David the cocky Jewish child and one-time crony of God; *No Laughing Matter* (1986), with Speed Vogel, a narrative about suffering and recovering from an illness; and *Picture This* (1988), a novel that looks at the differing frames of reference of Renaissance Holland and Ancient Greece, as it examines Rembrandt's picture 'Aristotle Contemplating the Bust of Homer'. With the elaborately structured *Closing Time* (1994), Heller returns to the cast of *Catch-22* who are now fighting the battle against old age. In addition, he has written several screenplays, among them *Sex and the Single Girl* (1964), *Casino Royale* (1967), and *Dirty Dingus Magee* (1970).

HELLMAN, Lillian (1905?–84), American playwright and memoirist, born in New Orleans, Louisiana, educated at the Universities of New York and Columbia. Her first play, *The Children's House* (1934), written under the tutelage of her companion Dashiell *Hammett, was the sensitive account of two teachers accused by a malicious student of concealing a lesbian relationship; the play had allusions to the misuse of power which acquired new resonances during the period of McCarthy's anti-communist witchhunts. Hellman's next play, *Days To Come* (1936), a drama of unionism, was followed by her highly successful *The Little Foxes* (1939), which established her as one of the leading playwrights of her generation. The central theme of the play—the rise to power of the *petit bourgeois* class, the rapacity of the newly rich—is subordinated to its melodramatic blend of blackmail, sibling rivalry, sexual manipulation, and murder, and to the powerful character of its evil protagonist, Regina Hubbard. Hellman was said to have drawn largely on memories of her mother's Southern family, which increased the appeal of the play; she returned to the Hubbard family in *Another Part of the Forest* (1946), which has been compared to the minor works of Shakespeare, and its emphasis on violence seen as an attempt to foreground the powerful themes of good and evil that continued to preoccupy her. During the Second World War her plays *Watch on the Rhine* (1941) and *The Searching Wind* (1944) were both highly topical, dealing with the fascist menace, and Hellman's reputation was assured for posterity. Later plays, *The Autumn Garden* (1951) and *Toys in the Attic* (1960), pay more attention to plot, technique, and psychology than to melodrama, and in this phase she has been compared to Chekhov. The settings of these plays were contemporary and drew again in part on Hellman's family. Hellman's reminiscences, *An Unfinished Woman: A Memoir* (1969) and *Pentimento: A Book of Portraits* (1973), earned the highest praise for their accounts of an unexpectedly heroic life. A third volume, *Scoundrel Time* (1976), raised a storm of controversy; Hellman's testimonial of her difficult position during the McCarthy trials was held to be inaccurate by such contemporaries as Mary *McCarthy and Diana Trilling. Her last book, *Maybe: A Story* (1980), published as fiction, attempts to illustrate her technique of interweaving fiction and documented fact, memory, and imagination, and of turning life into text as she had done in the memoirs and the plays.

Héloïse and Abélard, see MOORE, GEORGE.

HELPRIN, Mark (1947–), American novelist, born in Ossining, New York, educated at Harvard and at Oxford University; he was raised beside the Hudson River and grew up in the British West Indies. His experiences serving in the British Merchant Navy and in the Israeli Air Force find resonance in much of his fiction. Helprin has published work in the **New Yorker* and the *Atlantic Monthly*. In his epochal *A Soldier of the Great War* (1991), the savagery of war is projected and interpreted prismatically through a range of characters who are affected by its physical and psychic tolls. In both his novels and his stories, Helprin confronts morally complex issues, of love, war, and death, with lyricism, charm, and fierce acuity. His other works of fiction include *A Dove of the East and Other Stories* (1975) and *Ellis Island and Other Stories* (1981); and the novels *The Life and Adventures of Marshall Pearl, a Foundling* (1977), *Winter's Tale* (1983), *Swan Lake* (1989), and *A Memoir from the Antproff Case* (1995).

HELWIG, David (1938–), Canadian writer, born in Toronto, educated at the Universities of Toronto and Liverpool. Helwig first attracted attention as a poet whose work moved between domestic themes and a concern with violent, anti-social behaviour. His long poem *Atlantic Crossings* (1974) offers an individual perspective on Canadian history through an examination of four archetypal journeys to the Americas. *A Book of the Hours* (1979) is centred on the figure of the scholar Thomas Bullfinch. His many other volumes of verse include *The Sign of the Gunman* (1969), *The Best Name of Silence* (1972), and *The Hundred Old Names* (1988). Helwig's best-known fictional work is a tetralogy of novels set in Kingston: *The Glass Knight* (1976), *Jennifer* (1979), *It Is Always Summer* (1982), and *A Sound of Laughter* (1983). These deal with the complexities of supposedly ordinary lives and, like his later novel *The Only Son* (1984), are notable for their perceptive rendition of gender relations. His other fiction includes *The Streets of Summer* (1969), *The Day before Tomorrow* (1971), *The King's Evil* (1981), *The Bishop* (1986), *A Postcard from Rome* (1988), *Old Wars* (1989), a spy story, and *Of Desire* (1990). Helwig has worked as literary manager of Canadian Broadcasting Corporation television and has written several radio plays, including *You Can't Hear What I'm Saying* (1978), *Moving In* (1980), and *Everybody Has Something To Hide* (1983).

HEMINGWAY, Ernest (Miller) (1899–1961), American novelist and short-story writer, born in Oak Park, Illinois. Whilst refusing to become a doctor like his father, Hemingway nevertheless took to his father's love of outdoor pursuits. After an education in various public schools, he began work as a reporter on the Kansas City *Star*, where he received a valuable vocational training. He volunteered as an ambulance driver in the First World War, seeing action in Italy before being wounded in 1918 on the Austro-Italian front. After a brief return home, he became the Toronto *Star*'s foreign correspondent in Paris. Here he moved with a large number of other expatriate writers and artists, including Gertrude *Stein, F. Scott *Fitzgerald, Ford Madox *Ford, and Ezra *Pound (see LOST GENERATION, THE). With their encouragement, he published *Three Stories and Ten Poems* (1923) in Paris; and then his first collection of stories in New York, *In Our Time* (1925), which attracted critical acclaim for the objective, understated style which was to become so famous. Returning to New York, with the help of Sherwood *Anderson he published a little-known satirical work, *The Torrents of Spring* (1926). From Gertrude Stein he also acquired the epigraph for his first novel, *The *Sun Also Rises* (1926; UK title, *Fiesta*, 1927) which narrates the journey of a group of aimless Paris-based American expatriates to Pamplona for the bullfights. The 'lost generation' of the epigraph are conjured up in almost biographical detail in this work, which balances preoccupations of sexuality and power with the developing sparse and yet resonant use of language which was to characterize the subsequent works. He returned to war in his second novel, *A *Farewell to Arms* (1929); Hemingway's commitment to his craft is indicated by the number of versions which exist of the closing paragraphs of this work as he strove for a precision in language. For the next fifteen years this technique steadily tightened, as displayed in short story collections *Men Without Women* (1927) and *Winner Take Nothing* (1933), an account of big-game hunting in *Green Hills of Africa* (1935), and the novel *To Have and Have Not* (1937), set in and near Key West during the Depression era. Throughout his life, Hemingway energetically pursued personal adventure and enjoyment; his increasing interest in bullfighting resulted in *Death in the Afternoon* (1932), where the fight is perceived more as a tragic ritual than a sport. Hemingway raised money for the Spanish Loyalists against Franco's uprising and wrote a play, *The Fifth Column* (1935), set in besieged Madrid; this was later published in *The Fifth Column and the First Forty-Nine Stories* (1938), which included the famous short stories 'The Short Happy Life of Francis Macomber' and 'The Snows of Kilimanjaro'. His largest novel, **For Whom the Bell Tolls* (1940), was also based on an incident during the Spanish Civil War and is clearly sympathetic to the Loyalist cause. After being actively involved with counter-espionage exploits during the Second World War, his next novel, *Across the River and Into the Trees* (1950), about an army officer who dies whilst in Venice, was a disappointment. He restored his reputation with *The *Old Man and the Sea* (1952; Pulitzer Prize), and won the Nobel Prize in 1954. The last years of his life produced no new major work and the inexorable deterioration of his physical and mental health ended when he took his own life. Since his death several posthumous works have been published, including *A Moveable Feast* (1964), an often scurrilous collection of anecdotes about his apprentice years in Paris; the novels *Islands in the Stream* (1970), three related stories of his memories of life in the Caribbean and Cuba, and *The Garden of Eden* (1987); and another bullfighting work, *The Dangerous Summer* (1985). In addition he produced a considerable quantity of journalism and poetry, the latter posthumously edited as *Eighty-Eight Poems* (1979). An authoritative biography entitled *Ernest Hemingway: A Life Story*, by Carlos Baker, was published in 1969.

Hemlock and After, see WILSON, SIR ANGUS.

HENDERSON, Hamish (1919–), Scottish poet, born in Blairgowrie, Perthshire, educated at Downing College, Cambridge. After serving in North Africa in the Second World War, he became a lecturer at the University of Edinburgh in 1951. *Elegies for the Dead in Cyrenaica* (1948), his best-known work, is recognized as one of the major poetic testimonies to emerge from the Second World War; its eleven sections constitute a sustained meditation on the war's moral ambivalence and the distortions of human values that make such conflicts possible. All aspects of Henderson's experiences as a soldier, from the raging height of battle to the minutiae of commonplace tedium, are presented in verse forms indebted to the modernist examples of T. S. *Eliot and Hugh *MacDiarmid. Henderson is also highly regarded as a folklorist and songwriter; some of his songs may be found in his edition of *Ballads of World War II Collected by Seumas Mor Maceanruig* (1947). His *Collected Essays* appeared in 1990. See also WAR POETRY.

Henderson the Rain King, a novel by Saul *Bellow, published in 1959. The novel opens with Eugene Henderson, a New England millionaire playboy in a state of torment despite his prosperous background, explaining the abandonment of his fortune due to his embroilment in social, domestic, and personal problems. The novel depicts a desperate hero in a world where the dissolution of the family and other economic factors have enforced an increased isolation of the individual in an overwhelmed existence, but which causes agony and comedy simultaneously. Henderson journeys to Africa on an impulse, yearning for some new forms of satisfaction, and drifts off the beaten track. With Romilayu his guide, he causes a disastrous mishap in trying to help an African village cleanse its water supply, leaving in disgrace. He reaches another village where he befriends the local chief Dahfu, and is declared Sungo the official rainmaker after 'causing' a deluge by moving the goddess of the clouds. Henderson becomes involved in the tribal rites of the chief's succession, becoming the chief after Dahfu's death. Fearing for their safety, Henderson and Romilayu escape from the village, and Henderson returns home having successfully brought new horizons to his life.

HENDRIKS, A(rthur) L(emière) (1922–), Jamaican poet, born in Kingston, Jamaica, educated at Jamaica College and Ottershaw College, Surrey. After working as General Manager of the Jamaica Broadcasting Company he became a television director in London. He became a freelance writer in 1971. His early collections of verse, which include *On This Mountain* (1965) and *These Green Islands* (1971), made use of rigorously economical forms to frame their imaginative commentaries on a wide range of personal and social concerns. The long title sequence of *The Islanders* (1983), a vivid evocation of the human and natural aspects of the Caribbean, marked the emergence of more musically flexible modes of verse. His principal subsequent collections are *The Naked Ghost* (1984) and *To Speak Simply* (1988), a selected edition of his poetry containing much previously uncollected material. Much of his best work from the early 1980s onward achieves striking dramatic effectiveness through his accomplished use of Jamaican patois. Among his other publications is the historical survey *Great Families of Jamaica* (1984).

HENDRY, J(ames) F(indlay) (1912–86), British poet, born in Glasgow, educated at the Universities of Paris and Glasgow. After military service from 1939 to 1946, he worked as a translator and became Professor of Modern Languages at Laurentian University, Ontario, in 1965. He edited *The *New Apocalypse* (1939), an anthology of poetry, stories, and criticism announcing the identically named literary movement, which was sustained by two further anthologies, *The White Horseman* (1941) and *The Crown and the Sickle* (1944), jointly edited by Hendry and Henry *Treece. *The Bombed Happiness* (1942) was his first collection of verse, which contained numerous powerfully imaginative treatments of warfare. A further volume, *The Orchestral Mountain* (1943), was followed by a long hiatus in his career as a publishing poet, which resumed with *Marimarusa* (1978) and *A World Alien* (1980). These displayed his interest in the more purely musical aspects of poetic technique. His other works include the novel *Fernie Brae* (1949), which is explicitly modelled on Joyce's **Portrait of the Artist as a Young Man*, a biography of Rilke entitled *The Sacred Threshold* (1983), and his edition of *The Penguin Book of Scottish Short Stories* (1970).

HENLEY, Beth (1952–), American dramatist, born in Mississippi, educated at Southern Methodist University and the University of Illinois. Henley achieved instant success with her first full-length play, *Crimes of the Heart* (1978; Pulitzer Prize), which was first performed by the Actors' Theatre of Louisville, Kentucky; a tale of three distressed sisters in a Mississippi family down on its luck, the play is clearly influenced by Chekhov though the oral tradition of Southern story-telling is equally resonant. Her other plays include *The Miss Firecracker Contest* (1981), *The Wake of Jamey Foster* (1982), *The Lucky Spot* (1986), *The Debutante Ball* (1987), *Abundance* (1989), and *Control Freaks* (1992). She wrote the book for a 1940s musical, *Parade* (1975), and the screenplay for Bruce Beresford's 1986 film version of *Crimes of the Heart* starring Diane Keaton, Jessica Lange, and Sissy Spacek. At her best, Henley manages an adroit fusion of comedy and pathos in her depiction of characters caught irresolutely in a world apparently determined to blight their lives.

HENRI, Adrian (Maurice) (1932–), British poet and painter, born in Birkenhead. He settled in Liverpool in 1957 where he, Roger *McGough, and Brian *Patten became prominent as The *Liverpool Poets in the 1960s and 1970s. His poetry was influenced at various times by popular and rock music (from 1967 to 1970 he was the leader of the poetry/rock group 'The Liverpool Scene'), American beat culture and jazz, and absurdist and other art and literature movements: in the 1960s he did much to familiarize British audiences with the works of French eccentric Alfred Jarry. His poetry is eclectic in style, influenced by the 'cut-ups' of William *Burroughs, but consistently returns to sequences of fragmentary observations often provocatively juxtaposed. The joys and tribulations of love are a recurring theme, but expressed more in the imagery of pop music than in either the lyricism of Patten or the irony of McGough. The *Mersey Sound* anthology (1967) established him as a poet. By 1983, and the sequel *New Volume*, McGough and Patten had left Liverpool. Henri's output since the 1960s is prolific. It includes fiction (*I Want*, with Nell *Dunn, 1972); verse and prose for children (*Eric the Punk Cat*, 1987; *Rhinestone Rhino*, 1989); *Box and Other Poems* (1990) for teenagers; and several plays for stage and television including *The Wakefield Mysteries* (1988). Henri's published work can be *confessional and personal in tone, as in the collection *Autobiography* (1971) and the elegiac *Wish You Were Here* (1990). *Collected Poems* appeared in 1986, and *Not Fading Away: Poems 1989–1994* in 1994.

HENRY, O., pseudonym of William Sidney PORTER (1862–1910), American short-story writer, born in Greensboro, North Carolina. Following his mother's death in his early childhood, he was brought up by his grandmother and aunt, before going to Texas at the age of 19. After a series of jobs, he began a newspaper called *The Rolling Stone* in 1894, which embraced political satire, ethnic humour, and parody of small-town life. The paper collapsed after a year and he was tried for embezzlement; after having skipped jail and gone into exile in Honduras, he returned and was sentenced for five years in 1897. Whilst in Ohio Penitentiary, he began writing stories under a variety of pen-names before he settled on O. Henry. After prison he moved to New York City, where his stories appeared in various well-known magazines. In 1904 he published his first book of stories about Honduras, entitled *Cabbages and Kings*; this was followed by stories about New York, *The Four Million* (1906). With his reputation now established, there followed a stream of collections: *Heart of the West* (1907); *The Gentle Grafter* (1908); *The Voice of the City* (1908); *Options* (1909); *Roads of Destiny* (1909); *Strictly Business* (1910); *Whirligig* (1910); *Sixes and Sevens* (1911); *Stones* (1912); *Waifs and Strays* (1917); *O. Henryana* (1920). Despite his contrived endings, sentimentality, and repetition, his famous stories such as 'The Furnished Room', 'Mammon and the Archer', and 'The Gift of the Magi' demonstrate a keen eye for detail, and a sympathy for the underdog. Various other posthumous publications appeared including *Postscripts* (1923), *O. Henry Encore: Stories and Illustrations* (1939), *The Complete Works of O. Henry* (1953), and the *Collected Stories of O. Henry* (1979). His name has been appropriated for the American annual short story prize.

HERBERT, A(lan) P(atrick) (1890–1971), British writer, born in Surrey, educated at New College, Oxford. Herbert drew on his First World War experiences in *The Secret Battle* (1919), and satirized the legal system in *Misleading Cases in the Common Law* (1929), a collection of mock law reports. An urbane writer, a leading contributor to *Punch*, he also campaigned for several causes; one of these was reform of divorce law which resulted in a novel, *Holy Deadlock* (1934), and the Matrimonial Causes Bill, which became law in 1938. *Independent Member* (1950) reflects his experience as an Independent Member of Parliament for Oxford (1935–50). An affection for rivers and boats is evident in his libretto for *Riverside Nights* (1926) and in his best-known novel, *The Water Gypsies* (1930). Other works include *A Book of Ballads; Being the Collected Light Verse of APH* (1931; revised edition 1949) and *APH: My Life and Times* (1970), his memoirs. He was knighted in 1945.

HERBERT, Frank (Patrick) (1920–86), American *science fiction writer, born and educated in the Pacific Northwest. From the publication of *Dune* (1965; later filmed), public perception of his career was dominated by this vast novel and its sequels, *Dune Messiah* (1969), *Children of Dune* (1976), *God-Emperor of Dune* (1981), *Heretics of Dune* (1984), and *Chapter House Dune* (1985). Over the course of the sequence, the desert planet Dune with its stern society becomes a venue for complex speculations about ecology, kingship, biology, godhood, and the nature of human societies. Some of his later work, such as *Hellstrom's Hive* (1973) and *The White Plague* (1982), expansively expressed biological and ecological concerns. Throughout his career Herbert succeeded in combining modern intellectual disciplines with the fertile plot-patterns of science fiction. See also SPACE OPERA.

HERBERT, James (1943–), British writer of horror fiction, born in London, educated at Hornsey College of Art. He worked in advertising from 1963 to 1977, when he became a full-time writer. *The Rats* (1974), his highly successful first novel, is a dystopian fantasy rooted in his childhood familiarity with parts of London devastated by wartime bombings. The city also provides the background for *The Fog* (1975), *The Dark* (1980), and *Domain* (1984). Herbert's appeal as the best-selling contemporary British horror writer draws on his ability to base the grotesquely imaginative elements of his work in narratives reflecting aspects of common experience. Much of his writing features specifically English settings and idioms; *James Herbert's Dark Places* (1993) records the locations and legends informing his work. His other novels include *Fluke* (1977), *The Jonah* (1981), *The Magic Cottage* (1986), *Portent* (1992), and *The Ghosts of Sleath* (1994).

HERBERT, Xavier (1901–84), Australian novelist, born in Port Hedland, Western Australia. After working in a pharmacy and studying medicine in Melbourne he led a varied existence in Australia, the Pacific, and Britain. His novel *Capricornia* (1938) was a vivid portrait of the Northern Territory; completed in 1932, it was an indictment of white Australians' abuse of land and of the Aboriginal peoples from the 1880s to the 1930s, detailing in particular the difficulties experienced by half-castes. *Seven Emus* (1958), with its eccentric experiment in punctuation, explored similar themes. These Herbert expanded in the monumental *Poor Fellow My Country* (1975) with its epic treatment of the period 1936 to the late 1970s. Outstanding in both its scope and its passion, the book won considerable praise and brought Herbert national recognition. Herbert's writing early engaged issues now increasingly seen as central to contemporary Australian culture and identity, and his recognized mastery (despite spectacular lapses) of narrative and setting have assured him a place in the history of Australian writing. His other work includes *Soldiers' Women* (1960), about wartime Sydney; *Larger than Life* (1963), collected stories; and *Disturbing Element* (1963), an impressive autobiographical account to the year 1925. Herbert's short stories from 1925 to 1934 were edited by Russell McDougall in *South of Capricornia* (1991).

HERBST, Josephine (Frey) (1897–1969), American novelist, born in Sioux City, Iowa, educated at the University of California at Berkeley. Herbst worked in New York as an editorial reader for the influential literary magazines *Smart Set* and *The *American Mercury*, and lived for three years in Europe. In 1925 she married the left-wing writer John Herrmann (they were divorced in 1940) and in the early years of the Depression she became an increasingly visible figure on the American literary left. Her first two published novels, *Nothing is Sacred* (1928) and *Money for Love* (1929), were influenced by her years of European expatriation. Her best-known work, the trilogy comprising *Pity Is Not Enough* (1933), *The Executioner Waits* (1934), and *Rope of Gold* (1939), traces the story of the Trexler family through eight decades of American history, beginning in 1868 and ending with the sit-down strikes of 1937. Much of the trilogy is concerned with the growth of union organizations and the emerging class antagonisms of the Depression years. Herbst was also a notable journalist: she was a special correspondent for the *New York Post* in Germany in 1935, went to Cuba in the same year, and covered the Spanish Civil War in 1937. Her other novels of note are *Satan's Sergeants* (1941) and *Somewhere the Tempest Fell* (1947); her non-fiction writings include *The Unknown Americas* (1939), a socio-economic study of Latin America, and *New Green World* (1954), a biography of the naturalist John Bartram. Elinor Langer's *Josephine Herbst: The Story She Could Never Tell* (1985) is an invaluable biography. See also PROLETARIAN LITERATURE IN THE USA.

HERGESHEIMER, Joseph (1880–1954), American novelist, born in Philadelphia, educated at the Pennsylvania Academy of Fine Arts in Philadelphia. He studied art in Italy before writing his first novel, *The Lay Anthony* (1914), and between 1915 and 1938 he was a regular contributor to *The Saturday Evening Post*. His early novels were historical romances, often with an exotic setting as, for example, in *Java Head* (1919), but later works explore the manners and milieu of America in the 1920s in a way that bears comparison with the novels of F. Scott *Fitzgerald. *Linda Condon* (1919) and *Cytherea* (1922), the latter probably his best-known novel, survey the post-war world with a combination of ironic detachment and an extravagant, almost luxuriant, style. Alfred *Kazin labelled Hergesheimer an 'exquisite', while Clifton Fadiman spoke of him as 'the Sargent of the modern American novel', thus capturing perfectly the attention to detail and colour in his prose. He was elected to the American Academy in 1921 but by the early 1930s was something of a figure of fun for an increasingly earnest, left-wing intelligentsia. He wrote two volumes of autobiography, notably *The Presbyterian Child* (1923), several works of non-fiction, and a screenplay, *Flower of Night* (1925). An interesting study is *Hergesheimer* (1921) by James Branch *Cabell.

Hermeneutics is the study of the art of interpretation, evolved as a separate object of interest through German theology and philosophy towards the end of the nineteenth century. The leading figure in this movement was Wilhelm Dilthey (1833–1911); distinguished later theorists are Paul Ricoeur and Hans Georg Gadamer, and Frank *Kermode makes a subtle contribution to the debate in *The Genesis of Secrecy* (1979). Interpretation has many meanings and occasions, but it also has recurring features which can be described and explored; it seeks to adjust texts to the needs of their readers, to build bridges, for example, between the communities of the Gospels and later communities wishing to lead their lives in accordance with Gospel precepts. Hermeneutics characteristically addresses questions about where interpretation starts, what assumptions it makes, and which assumptions are indispensable. More recently, through the work of Roland Barthes and others—in *S/Z* (1970) Barthes identifies a 'hermeneutic code' in narrative, a strand which involves the ravelling and unravelling of an enigma—'hermeneutic' has come to designate the practice of deriving meaning from a text, as distinct from, say, studying its origins or its rhetoric. See also SEMIOTICS.

HERR, Michael, see VIETNAM WRITING.

HERRICK, Robert (Welch) (1868–1938), American novelist and educator, born in Cambridge, Massachusetts, educated at Harvard. Among several academic posts he was Professor of English at the University of Chicago from 1905 to 1923. He published his first book, *Literary Love Letters and Other Stories*, in 1897, but it was his third work, *The Gospel of Freedom* (1898), which revealed Herrick's strengths as a progressive critic of commercial and materialistic society, notably of Chicago, and which established his intellectual kinship with other social realists such as Theodore *Dreiser and Frank *Norris. In *The Web of Life* (1900) the protagonist, a doctor, is tempted by the financial advantages offered to him as a society physician, but rejects them and refuses the hand of a capitalist's daughter until she renounces her inheritance. *The Memoirs of an American Citizen* (1905) follows the career of a Chicago meat-packer who rises to a position of great financial and political power. Of his later novels, *Together* (1908), *One Woman's Life* (1913), and *The End of Desire* (1932) are of interest for their treatment of modern marriage, sexual liberation, and feminism. His 1914 essay 'The Background of the American Novel' is an important document in the history of American literary realism. Blake Nevius's *Robert Herrick: The Development of a Novelist* (1962) is a critical study.

HERSEY, John (Richard) (1914–), American writer, born in China, educated at Yale. He rose to fame through his Second World War reportage, most notably with *Hiroshima* (1946), an intense humanitarian analysis of the dropping of the first nuclear bomb; its initial publication occupied a whole issue of *The *New Yorker*. Novels such as *A Bell for Adano* (1944; Pulitzer Prize) and *The Wall* (1950) are near-apocalyptic visions of the world during the 1940s. Some of his later work is *science fiction; *The Child Buyer* (1960) is a dystopian satire on government and commerce, while *White Lotus* (1965), set in an alternative reality, posits a world dominated by China. Both books show a disappointed response to modern America.

Herzog, a novel by Saul *Bellow, published in 1964. Moses Elkanah Herzog, a frustrated moderately successful university lecturer on the brink of divorce from Madeleine, his attractive yet destructive second wife, reaches a point of near insanity and neurosis. In an effort to explore his failure to be happy, he bombards his friends, his family, even famous people dead and alive like Napoleon, the American President, and Spinoza (with whom Herzog closely identifies), with a stream of letters on current public issues. Feeling that he is trapped as a 'prisoner of perception, a compulsory witness', he negotiates with a changing self-image which centres particularly on his Jewish heritage. Having been totally assimilated into Western Christian culture, the disintegration of his life causes Herzog to reconsider his present existence in relation to his past tradition. Labouring under the illusion that Madeleine and her lover are mistreating his daughter, Herzog rushes to Chicago determined to murder his ex-wife. Frustrated in his plans, he returns to New England and lapses into a pervading and satisfactory quietness based on silence towards the issues of the day, the novel closing with the words, 'At this time he had no messages for anyone. Nothing. Not a single word.'

HEWETT, Dorothy (1923–), Australian playwright and poet, born and brought up on an isolated farm in Western Australia, educated at the University of Western Australia. Her experience working in factories in Sydney provided material for her only novel *Bobbin Up* (1959). She had published some early poems in **Meanjin* and subsequently produced several collections including *Windmill Country* (1968), *Rapunzel in Suburbia* (1975), *Greenhouse* (1979), *Journeys* (1982), and *Alice in Wormland* (1987). Frequently *confessional and romantic in tone, she also makes use of humour and a variety of verse forms to create poems which directly engage with themes of ideology, sexuality, ageing, and personal experience. Her first play, *This Old Man Comes Rolling Home* (perf. 1967; pub. 1976), is about working-class life in a poor suburb of Sydney. Other plays include *The Chapel Perilous* (perf. 1971; pub. 1972), *Bon-Bons and Roses for Dolly* (perf. 1972; pub. 1976), *The Golden Oldies* (1976), *The Tatty Hollow Story* (perf. 1974; pub. 1976), *The Man from Mukinupin* (1979), *The Fields of Heaven* (1983), and *Golden Valley* (1985). *Wild Card: An Autobiography 1923–1958* (1990) displays much of the vigour of her drama and verse.

HEWITT, John (Harold) (1907–87), Northern Irish poet, born in Belfast, where he was educated at Queen's University. In 1930 he began working in Belfast Museum and Art Gallery and was for many years Art Director of the Herbert Art Gallery and Museum, Coventry. *Conacre* (1941) and *No Rebel Word* (1948) established the rationally discursive manner of his best-known verse, which makes accomplished use of rhymed traditional forms. His numerous further collections include *Collected Poems* (1966), *Out of My Time* (1974), *The Rain Dance* (1978), and a volume of autobiographical verse entitled *Kites in Spring* (1980). His poetry, in which Seamus *Heaney discerned an 'Augustan poise married to an inward elegiac note', recurrently displays his concern with the historical and cultural identity of Northern Ireland's Protestant communities. Among his prose writings, selections from which make up *Ancestral Voices* (edited by Tom Clyde, 1987), are numerous essays advancing regionalism as a viable solution to the divisions within Ulster. Hewitt's work provided an important precedent for the emergence of *Ulster poetry in the 1960s. *The Collected Poems of John Hewitt* (1991) were edited by Frank *Ormsby.

HEWLETT, Maurice (Henry) (1861–1923), English novelist, poet, and essayist, born in Kent. He was called to the Bar but never practised, and during 1897–1900 he was Keeper of Land Revenue Records. Instant success came with his first novel, *The Forest Lovers* (1898), a historical romance set in medieval England. He wrote numerous other historical novels and romances including *Richard Yea-and-Nay* (1900), about Richard the Lionheart; *The Queen's Quair* (1904), about Mary, Queen of Scots; *Gudrid the Fair* (1918), about the Viking discovery of North America; and *Mainwaring* (1921). His comic novels about modern life in which a wandering scholar, John Maxwell Senhouse, features prominently include *Halfway House* (1908), *Open Country* (1909), and *Rest Harrow* (1910). Hewlett is now particularly remembered for *The Song of the Plow* (1910), a long narrative poem about the plight of the agricultural labourer from the Norman Conquest onwards. Hugh *Walpole observed that 'it was as a poet that he made in his last years his passionate declarations of belief in the English peasantry as the only hope for England'. *Wiltshire Essays* (1921), *Extempore Essays* (1922), and the posthumous *Last Essays* (1924) display his often leisurely style to advantage. *The Letters of Maurice Hewlett* (1926) were edited by Laurence *Binyon.

HEYER, Georgette (1902–74), British writer of historical novels and detective stories, born in London. A best-selling author for more than fifty years, she was an expert on the Regency period, owning a reference library of more than 1,000 books on all aspects of its history. The most popular of her Regency romances include *Devil's Cub* (1934), *Regency Buck* (1935), *Faro's*

Daughter (1941), *Venetia* (1958), and *Lady of Quality* (1972), which were written with considerable charm and humour. Interspersed were historical novels of other periods, such as *The Conqueror* (1925), *Simon the Coldheart* (1925), and *Royal Escape* (1938). Her fifty-seventh novel, *My Lord John* (1975) about John, Duke of Bedford, brother to Henry V, was unfinished and unrevised at her death. See *Daphne du Maurier* (1993) by Margaret *Forster. See also ROMANTIC FICTION.

HEYWARD, DuBose (1885–1940), American novelist, dramatist, and poet, born in Charleston, South Carolina. He was an insurance salesman before his great success with *Porgy* (1925); its fatalistic story of a beggar driven to murder is set among a community of African-Americans in a ghetto area of Charleston immortalized as Catfish Row. In 1927 Heyward and his wife, Dorothy, collaborated on a popular dramatic version which won the Pulitzer Prize, and was published in 1928; *Porgy and Bess* (1935), the famous musical version of the novel, was composed by George Gershwin. *Mamba's Daughters* (1929) deals with an African-American family, its members struggling for economic betterment over three generations; a dramatized version, again in collaboration with his wife, was produced in 1939. Other novels include *Peter Ashley* (1932), a Civil War saga; and *Star Spangled Virgin* (1939), set in the Virgin Islands and notable for its scepticism about New Deal attempts to better the lot of African-Americans. His poems, steeped in Southern folklore, and exploring similar terrain to the novels, have been collected in *Carolina Chansons* (1922), *Skylines and Horizons* (1924), and *Jasbo Brown* (1931). See Frank Durham, *Heyward, the Man who Wrote Porgy* (1965).

HIBBERD, Jack (1940–), Australian playwright and novelist, born in Victoria, educated at the University of Melbourne. He became a leading figure in the alternative theatre of the 1960s, writing and directing plays for the Australian Performing Group at La Mama. The new 'rough-theatre' made energetic use of vernacular idiom, social satire, audience participation, and declining censorship; his introduction to *Three Popular Plays* (1976) describes his approach to popular drama. Early plays, such as *White with Wire Wheels* (perf. 1967; pub. 1970), employ an abrasive direct style, frequently exploring the nature of cultural stereotypes, particularly those associated with the Australian male. *Dimboola* (perf. 1969; pub. 1974) satirizes the behaviour of Australians at a wedding. *A Stretch of the Imagination* (perf. 1971; pub. 1973) is about an old man facing death with irascible humour and courage. *The Overcoat* (1977) is an adaptation of Gogol's story of the same name. Other plays include *The Les Darcy Show* (perf. 1977), *A Toast to Melba* (perf. 1975), *Mothballs* (1980), *Breakfast at the Windsor* (1981), *Glycerine Tears* (1982), and *Squibs* (1984). His first novel, *Memoirs of an Old Bastard* (1989), is a picaresque Rabelaisian tale in which an eccentric millionaire travels to Melbourne in search of his lost daughter; *The Life of Riley* (1991) has a similarly picaresque, comic structure. *Perdita* (1992), the companion volume to his first novel, traces an abandoned girl's quest for her lost father.

HICHENS, Robert (Smythe) (1864–1950), British novelist, short-story writer, and music critic, born in Kent, educated at the Royal College of Music, London. He is best remembered for *The Green Carnation* (1894), a sub-Wildean novel of fashionable London society, and for the best-selling *Garden of Allah* (1904), a romance of the desert, set in North Africa and combining sex and religion in equal measure. It was followed by *Call of the Blood* (1906), a story of contemporary Edwardian life, set in Sicily and North Africa, and by another novel displaying a fascination with Arab life and with the mystery and romance of the desert, *Bella Donna* (1909), whose wicked heroine comes to a bad end in Egypt.

HICKS, Sir John (Richard) (1904–89), British economist, born in Warwick, educated at Balliol College, Oxford. He became Professor of Economics and a Fellow of All Souls, received the Nobel Prize for Economics (1972), and was knighted in 1964. *Value and Capital* (1939), his greatest theoretical work, presented the first sophisticated approach to the integration of micro-economics and macro-economics—though not fully taken up by the economics profession until after the war, its arguments now underpin much of modern macro-economic thinking. Hicks was also the inventor of the so-called IS-LM interpretation of the ideas of *Keynes; its simple diagrammatic apparatus has since been adopted as the standard textbook presentation of Keynesian economics. *A Theory of Economic History* (1969) is probably his most accessible work; in it, the development of markets, their increasing sophistication and pervasiveness, is taken to be effectively synonymous with progress and improvement. He published an essay diagnosing what he called *The Crisis in Keynesian Economics* (1974); and a short book on economic methodology under the title *Causality in Economics* (1979).

HIGGINS, Aidan (1927–), Irish novelist and short-story writer, born in Celbridge, Co. Kildare, educated at Clongowes Wood College. After various jobs, he toured Europe and then Southern Africa with a puppet theatre company. He has lived in Spain, Germany, England, and, more recently, Ireland. Higgins belongs to that significant minority of Irish writers, such as *Joyce and *Beckett, who have been prepared to experiment. His first collection of short stories, *Felo de Se* (1961; revised and retitled, *Asylum and Other Stories*, 1978), attempts to avoid the provincial realism of Sean *O'Faolain and Frank *O'Connor by moving in setting from Ireland to Europe and developing a more continental complexity. This contradiction between the insular and the worldly is central to much of Higgins's work and most evident in his first novel, *Langrishe, Go Down* (1966); an avant-garde exercise in nostalgia, the novel experiments with the 'Big House' of Anglo-Irish fiction while being reluctant to undermine its prevalence. His next novel, *Balcony of Europe* (1972), is a long, solipsistic first-person narrative which begins and ends in Ireland but is mainly set in Andalusia and focuses on an adulterous affair between Dan Ruttle, an Irish artist, and Charlotte Bayless, an American Jewess; in this experimental work Higgins uses quotations from *Yeats, Joycean symbolism, and a narrative technique of repetition and grammatical manipulation, reminiscent of Beckett. In *Scenes from a Receding Past* (1977), Dan Ruttle and characters from his earlier fiction reappear. Higgins combines a modern artistry with a talent for the more traditional techniques of character and recollection in *Bornholm Night-Ferry* (1983). By contrast, *Lions of Grünewald* (1993) is a picaresque novel about an Irish professor's lavishly funded sabbatical in Berlin in the late 1980s prior to the reunification of Germany. Higgins's other works include *Helsingør Station and Other Departures* (1989), a volume of short stories; *Ronda Gorge and Other Precipices* (1989), a travel work; and *Donkey's Years: Memoirs of a Life as a Story Told* (1995), an autobiographical work.

HIGGINS, Brian (1930–65), British poet, born in Batley, Yorkshire, educated at the University of Hull. During the 1950s and early 1960s he travelled extensively in Europe and worked in various capacities, including as an aero-elastician, railway clerk, and schoolteacher. Prior to his unexpected death in 1965, he was increasingly productive as a freelance literary journalist. His first collection of poetry, *The Only Need* (1960), was followed by two further volumes, *Notes while Travelling* (1964) and *The Northern Fiddler* (1966). Higgins's work characteristically displays a depth of innate technical ability which enabled him to combine fluent use of rhyme and metre with great colloquial vigour. While his weaker writing might be described as 'the higher doggerel', the majority of his poems are distinguished by anarchic imaginative energies and a penetratingly lucid intelligence. Thematically, his work drew repeatedly on his personal experiences, which he adapted to a range of treatments, including ironic social commentaries and idiosyncratic metaphysical or lyric modes. Though largely neglected latterly, his poems were widely admired and featured in numerous influential anthologies, including *The Faber Book of Twentieth Century Verse* (edited by David Wright and John *Heath-Stubbs, 1965).

HIGGINS, F(rederick) R(obert) (1896–1941), Irish poet, born at Foxford, County Mayo, he became a clerk for a builders' merchant at the age of 14 and was subsequently active as an official in the emergent Irish trades union movement. The fervent interest in the Irish folk tradition that runs throughout his work is evident in his early collection *Island Blood* (1925), though the conventional lyricism of the poems lacks the more imaginative qualities apparent in *The Dark Breed* (1927); with its emphatic sense of the relation between the localities of the far west of Ireland and the essentials of national identity, this volume secured Higgins's reputation among the generation succeeding the writers of the *Irish Revival. *Arable Holdings* (1933) displayed an accomplished use of the assonantal traditions of Gaelic poetry as Higgins's preoccupation with the purely musical aspects of his writing increased. In 1935 he met *Yeats, who sought his assistance in editing material for the Cuala Press, appointed him a director of the *Abbey Theatre, and generally extended the approval that made Higgins his chief protégé in Ireland during the two years between Yeats's death and his own. In *The Gap of Brightness* (1941), his last and most widely acclaimed collection, Higgins's style is at its most refined.

HIGGINS, George V(incent) (1939–), American lawyer and crime writer, born in Brocton, Massachusetts, educated at Stanford University and Boston Law School. A former newspaper reporter and Boston district attorney, Higgins has used his knowledge of criminal life, law, and local politics to good effect in a series of critically acclaimed and successful novels set in and around Boston whose characters, for the most part, come from the Boston Irish. The first of these, *The Friends of Eddie Coyle* (1972), is wholly original: the narration is carried forward almost completely through conversation and monologue, rich in colloquial and criminal expressions, and which imitate, almost exaggeratedly, the repetitions and hesitations of everyday speech. Higgins continued in the same vein with *The Digger's Game* (1973), *Coogan's Trade* (1974), and *The Judgement of Deke Hunter* (1976). In *A Year or So with Edgar* (1979), *Kennedy for the Defense* (1980), *A Choice of Enemies* (1984), and *Penance for Jerry Kennedy* (1985), Higgins explored individual lives in the police, the press, the law, and the judiciary. He returned to low-life in *Impostors* (1986), *Outlaws* (1987), and *Wonderful Years, Wonderful Years* (1988), where a whole complex of issues surrounding personal and political integrity are uncovered with precision and scepticism. More recently, with works such as *Trust* (1989), which explores the multiple mendacities and deceptions of an ex-jailbird turned used car salesman, Higgins appears to have moved away from the crime novel to depict a section of contemporary American life frequently seen in the novels of *dirty realist writers such as Richard *Ford or Raymond *Carver.

HIGHSMITH, (Mary) Patricia, née Plangman (1921–95), American writer of mixed German and English-Scots parentage, born in Fort Worth, Texas, educated at Barnard College, New York. Her first crime novel, *Strangers on a Train* (1950; filmed by Alfred Hitchcock, 1951) was an immediate success, and was followed by a number of novels and short stories which are hard to categorize, but which usually involve crime; often based on a sensational idea, they are subtle psychological studies of weak characters attracted by violence, or of couples linked together by the idea of crime. Her heroes are often criminals, whom she sees as free individuals, able to escape the constraints of society: 'Criminals are dramatically interesting, because for a time at least they are active, free in spirit, and they do not knuckle down to anyone', she wrote. Her best-known character of this type, portrayed with a distinctive black humour, is the seemingly charming but completely amoral young American Tom Ripley, like the author, resident in France, who appeared first in *The Talented Mr Ripley* (1955; filmed by René Clement as *Plein Soleil* with Alain Delon, 1959; UK titles *Purple Noon* and *Lust for Evil*) and later in *Ripley Under Ground* (1970), *Ripley's Game* (1974), and *The Boy who Followed Ripley* (1980). Among her other works, not all of which are crime novels, are *The Blunderer* (1954; also published in the USA as *Lament for a Lover*), *Deep Water* (1957), *The Two Faces of January* (1964), *The Glass Cell* (1964), *The Story-Teller* (1965; UK title *A Suspension of Mercy*), *The Tremor of Forgery* (1969), *Edith's Diary* (1977), and *People Who Knock on the Door* (1983). Her last novel, *Small g: A Summer Idyll* (1995), is, as the title suggests, optimistic in mood and very unlike her previous work. Collections of short stories include *The Snail Watcher and Other Stories* (1970; UK title *Eleven*), *Slowly, Slowly in the Wind* (1979), and *The Black House* (1981). Critically more esteemed in France and in Britain than in America, she was called by Julian *Symons 'the most important crime writer at present in practice'.

High Wind in Jamaica, A, see HUGHES, RICHARD.

HIJUELOS, Oscar (1951–), American writer, born in New York City, the son of Cuban immigrant parents, educated at the City College of the City University of New York. He worked for several years in the advertising industry before turning to writing. In a remarkably short time, Hijuelos established an important critical reputation; some reviewers have compared him to Gabriel Garcia Marquez in his stylistic use of *magic realism as a way to merge history, myth, and the fantastic. His lyrical writings explore the immigrant experience, Cuban displacement, and the Latin American community. Hijuelos's highly acclaimed *The Mambo Kings Play Songs of Love* (1989) won a Pulitzer Prize and was made into a successful film. His other novels include *Our House in the Last World* (1983), *The Fourteen Sisters of Emilio Monez O'Brien* (1993) and *Mr Ives' Christmas* (1995). See LATINO / LATINA LITERATURE IN ENGLISH.

HILL, (John Edward) Christopher (1912–), British historian, born in York, educated at Balliol College, Oxford; he became a fellow of the college in 1938 and its Master in 1965. *Puritanism and Revolution* (1958), *Intellectual Origins of the English Revolution* (1965), and *The World Turned Upside Down* (1972) are among the publications which established his reputation as the leading historian of the Civil War period. Hill's socialist convictions inform his writings, which encompass a broad spectrum of human experience through comprehensive attention to the political, economic, and religious dimensions of the era. Literary sources are widely used in his work; *Milton and the English Revolution* (1977) examines the poet's responses to the failure of the Commonwealth, while the writings of Marvell and others are surveyed in *The Experience of Defeat* (1984). His numerous other books include *Antichrist in Seventeenth Century England* (1971), *A Nation of Change and Novelty* (1990), the three volumes of his *Collected Essays* (1985–6), and *The English Bible and the Seventeenth-Century Revolution* (1993).

HILL, Errol (1921–), Trinidadian playwright, poet, actor, and theatre director, born in Trinidad, educated at the Royal Academy of Dramatic Art, London, and at the Yale School of Drama. His first version of his best-known play, *Man Better Man*, in vernacular prose, was first performed in Jamaica in 1957. The second version, written in calypso-inspired verse and music, was first performed in 1960. The play celebrates the legendary 'stickfighters' who fought fierce duels at carnival time, the rules of engagement for this sport, known as 'calinda', being as elaborate as those of medieval jousting. It was published in *Plays for Today* (1985), with a play by Derek *Walcott and another by Dennis *Scott. He has also edited the two volumes of critical essays entitled *The Theatre of Black Americans* (1980), an important source book of scholarship on African-American drama. His short plays, mainly comedies, include *The Ping-Pong*, *Wey-Wey*, *Square Peg*, *Dilemma*, and *Oily Portraits*, all published in 1966, and *Dance Bongo* (1972). Other books include *The Trinidad Carnival: Mandate for a National Theatre* (1972), and *Shakespeare in Sable: A History of Black American Actors* (1984).

HILL, Geoffrey (1932–), British poet, born in Bromsgrove, Worcestershire, educated at Keble College, Oxford. He taught at the University of Leeds from 1954 to 1980, when he became a university lecturer in English at Cambridge. *For the Unfallen* (1959), his first substantial collection of verse, displayed his virtuosity in the use of traditional forms. His preoccupations with religious and historical themes are expressed in verse of resonant grandeur in the 'Funeral Music' sequence in *King Log* (1968). The collection's concern with disjunctions between power and morality remains central to the prose poems of *Mercian Hymns* (1971); the volume's treatment of the life and times of King Offa is wittily enlivened by anachronistic intrusions of modernity into ancient Mercia. *Tenebrae* (1979) contains his most unequivocally religious writing in the disquietingly intense sonnets of the 'Lachrimae' sequence. The thirteen sonnets of 'An Apology for the Revival of Christian Architecture in England' are equally impressive for the lucidity and their complex discourse on history. *The Mystery of the Charity of Charles Péguy* (1983), Hill's meditation on the French author, reflects aspects of his own philosophy. His *Collected Poems* appeared in 1985 and 1994. His essays were collected in *The Lords of Limit* (1984); *The Enemy's Country* (1991) is a critical work on language and its contexts.

HILL, Reginald (1936–), British crime writer, born in Durham, educated at St Catherine's College, Oxford. His crime stories fall into two groups: the first, beginning with *A Clubbable Woman* (1970), are police novels, set against a well described Yorkshire background, in which the detectives are the ill-matched pair Superintendent Dalziel and Sergeant (later Inspector) Pascoe; the second, of which perhaps the best is *The Spy's Wife* (1980), are not connected with one another, and though crime stories, do not necessarily contain an element of detection. Hill has also written a series of thrillers under the pseudonym Patrick Ruell, and, in his early career, science fiction and comic historical novels.

HILL, Selima (1945–), British poet, born in London, educated at New Hall, Cambridge University. She was assistant manager of a London bookshop until 1985, when she became a freelance writer and teacher of writing in schools. *Saying Hello at the Station* (1984), her first collection of poems, gained wide notice for its unusually striking imagery and individual directness of tone. It was followed by *My Darling Camel* (1988), a collection rich in exotic elements derived from sources which include Eskimo culture and ancient Egyptian mythology. The imaginative and emotional intensity characterizing much of her work is most fully apparent in *The Accumulation of Small Acts of Kindness* (1989), a long sequence reflecting the experience of a young girl undergoing a period of acute psychological disturbance. The three parts of the poem make highly inventive use of altering poetic forms to reflect the fragmentation of the consciousness evoked. Subsequent collections include *A Little Book of Meat* (1993) and *Trembling Hearts in the Bodies of Dogs: New and Selected Poems* (1994).

HILL, Susan (1942–), British novelist, short-story writer, and playwright, born in Scarborough, educated at King's College, University of London. A regular reviewer and broadcaster, her reputation as a writer was established with a series of novels displaying a powerful and versatile imagination and a gift for exploring the bonds people form between themselves, particularly within families. *Gentlemen and Ladies* (1968) is one of the more humorous of these, in which middle-aged Hubert manages to free himself and his mother from their long dependence on one another. In *A Change for the Better* (1969), the newly widowed Flora Carpenter also attempts to attain independence, by contrast with the much younger Deirdre Fount, who feels stifled by her relationship with her late mother. *I'm the King of the Castle* (1970; Somerset Maugham Prize, 1971) is a novel told from a child's point of view about the difficult, and finally fatal, relationship of two young boys whose lives coincide when the father of one, a widower, employs as his housekeeper the widowed mother of the other. Written from a male point of view, *Strange Meeting* (1972) vividly recreates the atmosphere of the trenches during the First World War in a story focusing on the love between a young subaltern and a second lieutenant. *The Bird of Night* (1973) also depicts a friendship between men, which is marred by madness. *In the Springtime of the Year* (1974) deals with the nature of loss and grief, themes echoed in Hill's frighteningly effective ghost story, *The Woman in Black* (1983), later adapted for stage and television. After an eight-year pause appeared *Air and Angels* (1991), which tells the story of an eminent middle-aged cleric's obsessive love for the enigmatic and much younger Kitty. Lyrical and complex in pattern, the novel is set in both India and England. *The Mist in the Mirror* (1992) is another ghost story. *Mrs de Winter* (1993) is Hill's much-publicized sequel to *Du Maurier's *Rebecca*, recounting in the first person the experiences and travails of the earlier work's timid narrator. The short stories collected in *The Albatross* (1971), *The Custodian* (1972), and *A Bit of Singing and Dancing* (1973) reflect many of Hill's preoccupations in haunting miniature. Hill's non-fiction works include *The Magic Apple Tree: A Country Year* (1983) and *Family* (1989), both autobiographical, as well as collected essays and two illustrated books. She has also written plays for radio and television and has published several books for children.

HILLERMAN, Tony (1925–), American crime novelist, born in Sacred Heart, Oklahoma, educated among Pottawatomie and Seminole Indians and at Oklahoma State University. After distinguished war service with the US Army, he became a journalist and later taught journalism at the University of New Mexico. The main purpose of Hillerman's tales of mystery and suspense is to engage readers with the religions, cultures, and values of Navajo and Pueblo Indians. At the heart of each novel lies a conflict between the circumspect and oblique customs of Indian life and the harsh demands of modern existence. Since 1970, Hillerman has produced a series of deftly written police procedural novels set in the Navajo reservations in Arizona, featuring two members of the Navajo Tribal police. Lieutenant Joe Leaphorn stands between his original culture and its more 'sophisticated' rival, while Sergeant Jim Chee makes greater efforts to reintegrate himself into the more traditional Navajo way of life. He constantly returns to Indian beliefs and fears, with witchcraft dominating *The Blessing Way* (1970) and *Skinwalkers* (1988). The sense of loss and oppression is dramatized in *A Thief of Time* (1988) through the exploitation of Indian artefacts, and in *Talking God* (1990) Navajo life is seen as an increasingly sterile museum piece. In *Dance Hall of the Dead* (1973) and *The Ghostway* (1985) Indian dances and ceremonies are elaborately described and integrated within the plot. *Sacred Clowns* (1994) is a recent Leaphorn novel.

HILLYER, Robert (Silliman) (1895–1961), American poet, born in East Orange, New Jersey, educated at Harvard, where he taught from 1919 until his retirement as a professor in 1945. *Sonnets and Other Lyrics* (1917) and *The Five Books of Youth* (1920), his first two collections of verse, demonstrated the fluent accomplishment in traditional forms which characterizes his poetry. Arthur *Machen's introduction to *The Halt in the Garden* (1925) emphasized the neoplatonism central to Hillyer's aesthetic and philosophical preoccupation with beauty and transience. His numerous subsequent collections include *In Time of Mistrust* (1939), *The Death of Captain Nemo* (1949), a lengthy narrative poem, and *The Relic* (1957); *Collected Verse* (1933; Pulitzer Prize) was superseded by *Collected Poems* (1961). Hillyer's richly lyrical rural imagery and nostalgic sensibility give his verse affinities with typifying examples of *Georgian poetry. Among his other works are the novel *My Heart for Hostage* (1942), a semi-autobiographical evocation of Paris after the First World War, and the critical studies *First Principles of Verse* (1938) and *In Pursuit of Poetry* (1960).

HILTON, James (1900–54), British novelist, born at Leigh, Lancashire; he grew up in Walthamstow, London, and was educated at Christ's College, Cambridge, where he produced his first novel, *Catherine Herself* (1920). During the 1920s he worked as a journalist in London and Dublin, writing eleven further novels, among them *Storm Passage* (1922) and *The Dawn of Reckoning* (1925), before *Lost Horizon* made him famous in 1933; this utopian romance of an earthly paradise in the Himalayas gave the term 'Shangri-La' to the language. Commissioned to write a story for the *British Weekly*, he quickly completed the work published independently as *Good-Bye, Mr Chips* (1934), a disarmingly sentimental account of the life and death of a schoolmaster, which was informed by Hilton's impressions of his father's career in teaching. In 1935 he was invited to Hollywood to participate in the filming of these enormously successful books and remained there for the rest of his life writing for the film industry; he received an Academy Award in 1942 for his work on the film *Mrs Miniver*. A number of his subsequent novels were adapted for the cinema; these include the story of an amnesiac officer returned from the First World War in *Random Harvest* (1941) and the narrative of a small Lancashire community in *So Well Remembered* (1947), which were released as films in 1942 and 1947 respectively. Other later works include *Nothing So Strange* (1948) and *Time and Time Again* (1953).

HIMES, Chester (1909–84), African-American crime writer, born in Jefferson City, Missouri, educated at Ohio State University. Convicted of armed robbery in 1926, he served seven years in Ohio State Penitentiary. In 1953 he moved to Europe and, on the suggestion of a French publisher, wrote a detective story set in Harlem. *La Reine des pommes* (1958; published in the USA as *For Love of Imabelle*, 1959; also as *A Rage in Harlem*) won the Grand Prix Policier in that year, and was followed by nine more 'Harlem domestic detective stories', as Himes termed them. All but one appeared originally in French, and all except two have as heroes the two black police detectives Coffin Ed Johnson and Gravedigger Jones. Written with great verve and panache, they are both exceedingly violent and exhilaratingly comic, full of grotesque characters and surreal incidents. As the series progresses, the novels, and the detectives themselves, become ever more bitter and cynical about the future of black urban life in America; in the last novel—which Himes did not write—the detectives were to have been killed trying to prevent a black revolution. Himes also wrote novels, including *If He Hollers Let Him Go* (1945), and two volumes of autobiography: *The Quality of Hurt* (1972) and *My Life of Absurdity* (1976).

HINDE, Thomas (1926–), pseudonym of Sir Thomas Willes CHITTY, British novelist, born in Felixstowe, Suffolk, educated at University College, Oxford. After working as a civil servant and subsequently as an executive of the Shell Company, he became a full-time author in 1960. His numerous novels include *Mr Nicholas* (1952), *A Place Like Home* (1962), *Ninety Double Martinis* (1963), *Generally a Virgin* (1972), and *Daymare* (1980). His fiction is noted for the originality and inventiveness of the social realist modes through which it addresses a range of urgently contemporary themes. Among his other publications are *Stately Gardens of Britain* (1983), the biography *Capability Brown* (1986), and *Tales from the Pumproom* (1988), a history of Bath. *Sir Henry and Sons* (1980) is autobiographical.

Hindle Wakes, see HOUGHTON, STANLEY.

HINES, (Melvin) Barry (1939–), British novelist, born in Hyland Common, near Barnsley, the son of a miner, educated at Ecclesfield Grammar School. He played football for Barnsley, while working variously as an apprentice mining surveyor, a labourer, and a blacksmith's assistant, then attended Loughborough College of Education. Hines emerged as a writer in the wake of northern working-class novelists like *Sillitoe and *Braine, and his realism and political concerns are those of the '*angry young men'. His first novel, *The Blinder* (1966), considers professional football as a means of escape from working-class life. *A Kestrel for a Knave* (1968), better known as *Kes*, the title under which it was filmed and reprinted in 1974, is set in a working-class environment in the West Riding of Yorkshire, and shows a deprived young boy, Billy Casper, lavishing care on a hawk; Billy's life is developed in a series of flashbacks in which he comes constantly into conflict with authority but, in his struggle to remain himself, there is a dignity and a fragile optimism. *The Gamekeeper* (1975) follows the daily round of a gamekeeper, George Purse, on a ducal estate in the north of England; despite his escape from the degrading industrial world, Purse cannot escape from the web of social hierarchy and has, in his heartless pursuit of poachers and collusion with the Duke, turned against his own class. *The Price of Coal* (1979) is a satirical account of a Royal Visit to a colliery. Hines continues his themes of traditional working-class communities in the north of England coming to terms with change in *Looks and Smiles* (1981), which centres on the problems of three young people faced with poverty during the Thatcher years; *Unfinished Business* (1983); and *The Head of It* (1994).

HINOJOSA (-SMITH), Rolando (1929–), Chicano short-story writer, novelist, and poet, born in

Mercedes, Texas, educated at the University of Texas, Highlands University, and the University of Illinois, Urbana. A master of humour, irony, and subtlety, Hinojosa weaves the tales of his characters with the history of his fictional Rio Grande Valley town, Klail City. The first of the Klail City death trip series, *Estampas del valle y otras obras* (1973), is composed of *estampas*/sketches and focuses on the shared traditions, language, and history of the Chicano community. The second novel in the series, *Klail City y sus alredores* (1976), introduced new characters to the cultural geography of Klail City, which by now was being compared to William *Faulkner's fictional Yoknapatawpha County. Further novels in the series include *The Useless Servants* (1993), which uses Hinojosa's collage technique to depict Chicano life and the way it copes with the separate Anglo world. His first collection of poems, *Korean Love Songs from Klail City Death Trip* (1980), was based on earlier experiences while serving in Korea. Hinojosa continues to focus on the urban experience and socio-economic condition of Chicanos with *Mi Querido Rafa* (1981), *Rites and Witnesses* (1982), *Partners in Crime: A Rafe Buenrostro Mystery* (1985), *Claros Varones de Belken* (1986), and *Becky and Her Friends* (1988). Hinojosa was appointed Professor of English at the University of Texas, Austin. See LATINO/LATINA LITERATURE IN ENGLISH.

HIPPOLYTE, Kendel (1952–), Caribbean poet and dramatist, born in Castries, St Lucia, educated at the University of the West Indies; he teaches at St Mary's College, St Lucia, where he is closely involved as a playwright and director with the Lighthouse Theatre Company. Much of his drama is experimental and improvisational. *Drum-maker*, his best-known work for the stage, was published in Keith Noel's edition of *Caribbean Plays for Playing* (1981). The play's uncompromising use of idiomatic Caribbean language and its concern with the political context of indigenous Caribbean culture are equally characteristic of his poetry. Collections of his verse, which rejects the formal traditions of European lyric poetry in favour of the freer models provided by American *modernism, include *Island in the Sun, Side Two . . .* (1980), *Bearings* (1986), and *The Labyrinth* (1991). Hippolyte is the editor of the anthologies *Confluence: Nine Saint Lucian Poets* (1988) and *So Much Poetry in We People* (1990).

HIRSCH, Edward (1950–), American poet, born in Chicago, educated at Grinnell College and the University of Pennsylvania. He taught at Wayne State University from 1979 to 1982, when he became an associate professor at the University of Houston, then Professor of English there in 1988. *For the Sleepwalkers* (1981), his first collection of poetry, received considerable acclaim for the combination of emotional power and formal accomplishment which have remained characteristic of his verse. The collection's compassionate focus on aspects of human suffering in urban situations is sustained in *Wild Gratitude* (1986) and *The Night Parade* (1989); the latter volume makes use of more flexible verse forms for its narrative treatments of Hirsch's personal and familial background in its retrospective evocations of Chicago. *Earthly Measures* (1994) displays an elegiac concern with the moral and spiritual impoverishment of contemporary society's materialistic and secular culture.

HIRSCHMAN, Albert Otto (1915–), American economist, born in Berlin, educated at the Sorbonne, the London School of Economics, and the University of Trieste. An active anti-fascist in the 1930s, he fled Nazi-occupied France for the USA in 1941, subsequently holding academic posts at Yale, Columbia, Harvard, and Princeton. In *The Strategy of Economic Development* (1958) Hirschman first displayed that independent turn of mind which became the hallmark of his approach to economics; in discussing underdevelopment, he rejected both the solution of leaving the problem entirely to the market and also that of entrusting it to extensive state co-ordination and control of economic activity. In *Exit, Voice and Loyalty* (1970) the subject was individuals' responses to 'disorder' in their social lives. Starting from the simple observation that free people could either leave ('exit') or complain ('voice') in such situations, he indicated how certain conditions of the economic and political world acted either to constrain or foster these possibilities (which he thought of as basic rights). In *The Passions and the Interests* (1977) he turned to the history of social thought to see what he might learn about civilization and its discontents from previous arguments for and against 'capitalism'. In later years Hirschman has been preoccupied with exposing the pretensions of economists who think their science gives unambiguous answers to the questions it asks (*Rival View of Market Society and Other Essays*, 1986).

Historical Novel, a novel set in a specific historical period, in which some attempt at accurately describing the customs of the period has been made. Sir Walter Scott is generally recognized as the father of the modern historical novel; novels such as *Rob Roy* (1817), *Ivanhoe* (1819), *Kenilworth* (1821), *Redgauntlet* (1824) and others were widely admired and imitated by writers such as Thackeray, Dickens, George Eliot, and *Hardy, for their imaginative portrayal of actual events, using both fictional and historical characters in narratives of great power and excitement. In the 1920s and afterwards the historical romance, as exemplified by the novels of *Orczy, *Weyman, *Farnol, and *Heyer, achieved widespread popularity for their extravagant plots, dashing and colourful characters, and love of romantic incident. Other writers in this tradition included *Forester, whose Hornblower novels established a fashion for romances about warfare and male camaraderie. In the 1950s Mary *Renault set a new standard of historical accuracy with her novels of Ancient Greece and Rome, which have been widely influential. The novels of J. *Tey, R. Sutcliffe, H. *Treece, and others belong to this category of historical fiction, which is scholarly in tone and realistic, rather than romantic in style. In more recent times the appeal of the form as a mode for serious fiction has declined, but several attempts to revive it have been made by writers such as R. *Macaulay, William *Golding, Rose *Tremain, and Timothy *Mo. Its greatest following is now in the popular market.

History Man, The, see BRADBURY, MALCOLM.

History of Mr Polly, The, a novel by H. G. *Wells, published in 1910. The story of a small shopkeeper who rebels against his station in life, *The History of Mr Polly* is a unique mixture of social realism, romance, and vivacious and exuberant comedy. Alfred Polly is the archetypal Wellsian 'little man', an oppressed, frustrated, and highly imaginative individual who can find no outlet for his dreams and desires until he sets fire to his shop, fails to execute a carefully planned suicide attempt, and disappears to take up the life of a tramp. 'If the world does not please you, *you can change it*' is Wells's optimistic message. The experiences of lower-middle-class life that drive Polly to spiritual imprisonment and despair, and his adventures on the road once he has obtained his release, are portrayed with a combination of scathing social insight and Dickensian jauntiness. Polly's gift of romanticizing the drabbest and most mundane circumstances is displayed through his habit of creative malapropism and linguistic deformation, a technique in which Wells sometimes seems to anticipate *Joyce. Formally, however, this is one of the most traditional of Wells's novels, reflecting his impatience with the self-conscious craft of his more modernist contemporaries and his affection for the narrative freedoms of the eighteenth century. The book begins with Polly's chronic indigestion, with the rumblings in his stomach being viewed as a form of industrial unrest or internal civil war; leaving political symbolism behind, it ends with the hero's digestion restored after his victory in a mock-epic battle for the Potwell Inn, a homely, rural English version of the earthly paradise.

History of the World in 10½ Chapters, A, see BARNES, JULIAN.

Hitch-Hiker's Guide to the Galaxy, The, see ADAMS, DOUGLAS.

HOAGLAND, Edward (1932–), American writer, born in New York, educated at Harvard University. He has taught at several universities including Iowa and California, Davis. His first novel, *Cat Man* (1956), about life in the circus, was followed by others, often focusing on the struggles faced by society's outcasts. Characters whose occupations require physical strength recur in his fiction, including *The Circle Home* (1960), which concerns the world of boxing and a prize-fighter's failure to become a champion or to make a success of his marriage. *Seven Rivers West* (1986) is set in Canada during the late nineteenth century when white settlers were building the railroad in hitherto Indian territory; interwoven with descriptions of the feelings of the indigenous people and the struggles faced by the settlers are vivid evocations of the wild landscapes of the Canadian west. Hoagland is also a leading essay writer, his subjects ranging from city and country life to the natural world and ecology; his collections include *The Courage of Turtles* (1971), *Heart's Desire: The Best of Edward Hoagland* (1990), and *Balancing Acts: Essays* (1992). His travel books include the highly acclaimed *African Calliope: A Journey to the Sudan* (1979). Hoagland's compelling observations on life and his powerful narrative voice have won much critical praise.

HOAR, Stuart (1957–), New Zealand playwright, born in New Plymouth, Taranaki, educated largely in Auckland. His dramatic influences are Brecht and British dramatists such as Howard *Barker, Howard *Brenton, and Caryl *Churchill. His first full-length stage play, *Squatter* (1988), startled audiences and readers with its determinedly non-naturalistic exposition of a crucial moment in New Zealand history, the Liberal era of the 1890s when the Squattocracy that had commandeered enormous land holdings in Canterbury was dismantled by government reforms. *Exile* (1990) satirically represents the formative figures of New Zealand literature as an endlessly self-editorializing group of literati. Hoar has also written for radio, television, and film.

HOBAN, Russell (Conwell) (1925–), American novelist and children's writer, born in Pennsylvania; he settled in London in 1969. Trained as an illustrator, he worked in television and advertising before becoming a full-time writer of great originality. His first novel for adults, *The Lion of Boaz-Jachin and Jachin-Boaz* (1973), introduces the themes and symbols common to all his fiction, yet every one of his novels is unique in subject and approach. Jachin-Boaz and Boaz-Jachin are a father and son who rediscover one another with the aid of a comically incongruous mythic beast. *Kleinzeit* (1974), self-mockingly surreal, concerns an advertising copywriter sent to hospital with a slipped hypoteneuse and other mathematical complications; what really ails him (and all his companions in Ward A4) is the urge to write. *Turtle Diary* (1975) is, by contrast, a conventional novel with an eccentric plot about two sea turtles rescued from London Zoo. His fourth novel required a yet more radical shift. Set 2,000 years after a nuclear holocaust in what remains of Kent, *Riddley Walker* (1980) is narrated in truncated and wholly reinvented English by the young riddler, or priest-figure, of a primitive people puzzling over the relics of our civilization. *Riddley Walker* is so far the ultimate expression of Hoban's fascination with word-play and with language as both a limiting and a liberating factor in human thought. In *Pilgermann* (1983), which draws on the history of the Crusades for a story of Jews, Muslims, and Christians, he explores the human craving for pattern and religion. All these preoccupations are evident in his novel *The Medusa Frequency* (1987), the story of a writer searching for inspiration and plagued by visions of Orpheus, Eurydice, and the Medusa. Hoban has become a prolific writer of children's fiction. *The Moment Under the*

Moment (1992) is a collection of stories, essays, and a libretto. *Fremden* (1996) is a *space opera.

HOBSBAUM, Philip (Dennis) (1932–), British poet and critic, born in London, educated at Downing College, Cambridge, where he studied under F. R. *Leavis, and Sheffield University, where William *Empson supervised his Ph.D. In 1962 he began his academic career at Queen's University, Belfast; in 1985 he commenced a professorship at Glasgow University. He was the founder of the *Group in 1955 and, with Edward *Lucie-Smith, edited *A Group Anthology* (1963). He convened a further writing group in Belfast during the 1960s, which stimulated the emergence of *Ulster poetry; Seamus *Heaney has recorded his gratitude for the 'energy, generosity, belief in the community' with which Hobsbaum encouraged him and others. His collections of poetry include *The Place's Fault* (1964), *In Retreat* (1966), *Coming out Fighting* (1969), and *Women and Animals* (1972). His work is notable for its accomplishment in combining traditional patterns of rhyme and metre with witty and conversationally candid accounts of personal experience. He also produced a number of verse satires of academic life, some of which display a Lawrentian invective against the repression of creative spontaneity he identifies in higher education. His works of criticism include the provocative *Tradition and Experiment in English Poetry* (1979) and *A Reader's Guide to Robert Lowell* (1988).

HOBSBAWM, Eric (John Ernest) (1917–), British historian, born in Alexandria, Egypt, educated at Cambridge University. Throughout his academic career he has taught at London University, where he became Professor of Economic and Social History in 1970. *Primitive Rebels* (1959), *Labouring Men* (1964), and *Industry and Empire* (1968) were among the publications that gained him recognition as a leading historian of the working classes. His subsequent works as a meticulous historian of British and European economic and social history include the trilogy *The Age of Revolution, 1789–1848* (1962), *The Age of Capital, 1848–1875* (1975), *The Age of Empire, 1875–1914* (1987), and *Echoes of the Marseillaise* (1990), which examines how interpretations of the French Revolution have progressed over 200 years; *The Age of Extremes* (1994) is a work on twentieth-century history. While his writing consistently displays a socialist orientation, his willingness to challenge the traditional assumptions of the Left is clear from *Politics for a Rational Left* (1989), a collection of provocative essays on British society during the 1980s. His other works include *The Jazz Scene* (1959), published under the pseudonym 'Francis Newton'. *Culture, Ideology and Politics* (1983) is a *festschrift* for Hobsbawm edited by Raphael Smith and Gareth Stedman Jones.

Hobson's Choice, a comedy by Harold *Brighouse, performed in 1916. The best-known product of the so-called 'Manchester School' of realistic drama, this principally involves Henry Horatio Hobson, owner of a Salford shoe shop but a drinker and a drone, dependent on his three daughters for the running of his business. Maggie, the ablest and least sentimental of the three, decides to marry her father's bootmaker, Willie Mossop, and set up in business with him. Through talent and hard work, this enterprise thrives while Hobson's shop declines; and by the end Mossop and Maggie have taken benign control both of Hobson and of his business. Maggie also takes advantage of a drunken mishap involving her father to ensure that he gives her sisters permission to marry, and handsome dowries as well. Thanks mainly to Brighouse's lively characterization of the blustering, self-pitying Hobson, a role that has attracted actors of the calibre of Charles Laughton and Michael Redgrave, the play has been regularly revived throughout the twentieth century.

HODGE, Jane Aiken (1917–), British writer, born in Massachusetts, one of the daughters of Conrad *Aiken (her sister is the writer Joan *Aiken). She has written more than twenty historical novels, set mainly in the late eighteenth or early nineteenth century. Her novels often have unusual backgrounds: the American War of 1812 in *Here Comes a Candle* (1961); the Greek War of Independence, in which Byron died, in *Greek Wedding* (1970); and Georgia after the Napoleonic Wars in *Savannah Purchase* (1971). *Shadow of a Lady* (1974) touches on the life of Emma Hamilton, and *Polonaise* (1981) is set in Poland during Napoleon's occupation. She has also written two biographies, *The Double Life of Jane Austen* (1972) and *The Private World of Georgette Heyer* (1984).

HODGE, Merle (1944–), Caribbean novelist, born in Trinidad, educated at the University of London. She travelled widely in Europe before becoming a lecturer in French at the University of the West Indies in Jamaica. Her novel *Crick Crack Monkey* (1970) is set in rural Trinidad, and traces the growth of the narrator, Tee, through childhood to maturity. Close family relationships within a stable rural community exist uneasily beside a middle-class world in which feudalistic values of race, colour, and class provoke unsettling but familiar Caribbean preoccupations with issues of personal identity and cultural nationality. These preoccupations are blended with warmth and humour that suggest a vision of tempered compassion. Hodge worked for the ill-fated Bishop regime in Grenada, but returned to Trinidad after it was overthrown. *Crick Crack Monkey* remains a novel of vibrant social manners and gratifying optimism despite its lack of recognition outside the Caribbean.

HODGINS, Jack (1938–), Canadian novelist and short-story writer, born on Vancouver Island, educated at the University of British Columbia. Hodgin's fiction shows the influence of Latin American *magic realism, but expresses a strong sense of regional cultural identity. Like much contemporary Canadian fiction, his novel *The Invention of the World* (1977) dramatizes a quest for origins; employing a broad range of narrative modes, it examines the Irish roots of a Vancouver Island community, showing how its mythic inheritance has been based on the ambivalent legacy of a founder figure who has 'swindled' his people with promises of a New World Eden. However, as in his short stories, collected in *Spit Delaney's Island* (1976) and *The Barclay Family Theatre* (1981), any superficial pessimism is mitigated by a resilient vision of human potential. Other novels include *The Resurrection of Joseph Bourne* (1980), which explores a folk community's capacity for fabulation; *The Honorary Patron* (1987), in which a Vancouver Island art historian returns home from Switzerland, after an absence of forty years, as patron of an arts festival; and *Innocent Cities* (1990), in which an English widow visits her sister's family in Australia. Other work includes *Over Forty in Broken Hill: Unusual Encounters Outback and Beyond* (1992), travel writing and anecdotes of the Australian Outback, and *A Passion for Narrative* (1994), a discussion of fiction techniques.

HODGSON, Ralph (Edwin) (1871–1962), British poet, born in Darlington, County Durham. His life is not well documented due to the reclusiveness of his later years; he is known to have worked as a scene-painter in New York and as an illustrator in London prior to the appearance of *The Last Blackbird* (1907), his first collection of verse. Under the imprint of 'The Sign of the Flying Fame' he became a publisher in 1913, producing editions noted for their typographical individuality. He was acquainted with numerous leading literary figures of the period and contributed to the **Georgian Poetry* series. *Poems* (1917) gained him a firm reputation for his ability to combine precise natural description with a visionary element reminiscent of Blake in its luminous simplicity. He became friendly with T. S. *Eliot, who addressed the fourth of his 'Five Finger Exercises' (1933) to him. In 1924 he began lecturing at Sendai University in Japan and settled on a farm near Minerva, Ohio, in 1938. No further substantial collection of his verse appeared until *The Skylark and Other Poems* (1958), which contained 'To Deck a Woman', the most powerful of his numerous statements against man's savage exploitation of animals. *Collected Poems* was published in 1961.

HODGSON, William Hope (1877–1918), British writer, born in Essex. His experience serving at sea during 1891–9 provided the material and imagery for most of his books, including the two novels *The Boats of the 'Glen Carrig'* (1907) and *The Ghost Pirates* (1909) and most of the stories collected in *Men of the Deep Waters* (1914) and *The Luck of the Strong* (1916). He is remembered for his two major supernatural novels: *The House on the Borderland* (1908), which conflates traditional horror story material with an apocalyptic vision of the future; and *The Night Land* (1912), a futuristic fantasy set in a dying Earth whose only human inhabitants huddle together in great steel 'redoubts', and who encounter fantastic creatures as they await humanity's demise. Hodgson served throughout the First World War and died at Ypres.

HOFF, Harry Summerfield, see COOPER, WILLIAM.

HOFMANN, Michael (1957–), poet, born in Freiburg, Germany, the son of Gert Hofmann, a distinguished German novelist; he grew up in England and was educated at Magdalene College, Cambridge, the University of Regensburg, and Trinity College, Cambridge. Since 1983 he has been a freelance writer, and taught creative writing at the University of Florida in 1990. *Nights in the Iron Hotel* (1983), his first collection of poetry, gained him notice for its tone of detached disenchantment and the restrained inventiveness of his forms and imagery. *Acrimony* (1986), *K. S. in Lakeland: New and Selected Poems* (1990), and *Corona, Corona* (1993) are among his subsequent collections. His understated elegance and studied flatness of manner are particularly appropriate to the treatments of disjunctive relationships in various poems. Numerous poems in *Acrimony* deal with his complex attitudes towards his father in a sometimes movingly direct manner. His other works include an adaptation of Brecht's *The Good Person of Sichuan* (1989), and translations of Kurt Tucholsky's *Castle Gripsholm* (1985) and Joseph Roth's *The Legend of the Holy Drinker* (1989).

HOGAN, Desmond (1950–), Irish writer, born in Co. Galway, educated at University College, Dublin. His first novel, *The Ikon Maker* (1976), was set in a remote part of Galway and depicted the obsessional relationship between a mother and son. *The Leaves on Grey* (1980) was a lyrical account of three friends growing up in 1950s' Dublin. This was followed by *A Curious Street* (1984), in which a young man remembers his father, who has died by his own hand; and *A New Shirt* (1986), in which the protagonist leaves his native Ireland for America and is overcome with longing for his homeland. In his poetically charged novel *A Farewell to Prague* (1995), Hogan uses montage, memory, and vignettes in a journey across the cities of Eastern Europe that also refers back to Ireland. Two collections of short stories, *The Mourning Thief* (1987) and *Lebanon Lodge* (1988), deal with similar themes of exile and loss, incorporating elements of Irish history and contemporary detail in a richly textured prose. *The Edge of the City: A Scrapbook, 1976–1991* (1993) is a collection of travel writings.

HOGARTH, David George (1862–1927), British archaeologist and writer on the Middle East, born at Barton-on-Humber, educated at Winchester and at Magdalen College, Oxford. His early work in Asia Minor, Cyprus, Egypt, and elsewhere is described in the autobiographical *Accidents of an Antiquary's Life* (1910). The richly evocative descriptions of *A Wandering Scholar in the Levant* (1897) gained him the reputation as a travel writer which he maintained with *The Nearer East* (1902), *The Penetration of Arabia* (1904), *Ionia and the East* (1909), and other works. Following a period as director of the British School of Archaeology in Athens, in 1900 he returned to Oxford, where he was Keeper of the Ashmolean Museum from 1908 till his death; his acquisitions for the museum reflected his interest in the Hittite civilization, on which he produced numerous books including *Hittite Seals* (1920) and *Kings of the Hittites* (1926). In 1915 he was sent on government service to Cairo, where he assumed great influence in the determination of British policy as director of the Arab Bureau; he recruited T. E. *Lawrence, whom he had known and influenced at Oxford, into the Arabian Campaign. Among his other works are *Excavations at Ephesus: The Archaic Artemisia* (1908), *The Ancient East* (1914), and *The Life of Charles M. Doughty* (1928).

Hogarth Press, The, a publishing house begun in 1917 by Leonard and Virginia *Woolf with a hand-press at Hogarth House, their Richmond residence. An edition of 150 copies of their jointly written *Two Stories* (1917) was encouragingly received and in 1918 a list of subscribers was established. The success of Katherine *Mansfield's *Prelude* (1918) led to the adoption of commercial printing methods. T. S. *Eliot's *Poems* and Virginia Woolf's *Kew Gardens* followed in 1919. The subscription system having been replaced by arrangements with booksellers in 1923, the Woolfs and the press moved to Tavistock Square, London, in 1924. They became the publishers of Freud's works in English and subsequently published much important European writing in translation. Robert *Graves, C. *Day Lewis, Christopher *Isherwood, E. M. *Forster, J. M. *Keynes, Harold Laski, and H. G. *Wells were among the authors who gave the press its reputation for publishing books of the highest intellectual and literary value. John *Lehmann was part-owner from 1938 to 1946, when the press, having published 527 titles since its inception, was incorporated into Chatto and Windus. J. Howard Woolmer's *A Checklist of the Hogarth Press* appeared in 1986.

HOGGART, Richard (1918–), British scholar and critic, brought up in Leeds, educated at Leeds University. Among many important posts, he was Professor of English at Birmingham from 1962, deputy Director-General at UNESCO (1970–5), and warden of Goldsmiths' College, London (1976–84). His most influential work, *The Uses of Literacy* (1957), about his childhood and his experience of working-class culture between the wars, did much to widen interest in the study of literature, education, communications, and *popular culture. His autobiographical volumes include *A Local Habitation* (1988), *A Sort of Clowning* (1990), and *An Imagined Life* (1992). Other works on social questions and on literature include *Auden* (1951), *Higher Education: Demand and Response* (1969), *Only Connect* (1972; Reith Lectures), and *English Cultural Studies* (1987). His topographical work *Townscape with Figures: Farnham, Portrait of an English Town* appeared in 1994.

HOLBROOK, David (Kenneth) (1923–), British poet, critic, and novelist, born in Norwich, educated at Downing College, Cambridge, where he was appointed Director of English Studies in 1981. His collections of poetry include *Imaginings* (1961), *Against the Cruel Frost* (1963), *Object Relations* (1967), *Chance of a Lifetime* (1978), and *Selected Poems 1961–1978* (1980). He has stated that in his poetry and prose fiction he is 'trying to find what meaning there might be in normal, everyday existence'. Many of his poems combine emotional candour and lyrical tenderness in their treatments of domestic incidents which form the basis for wider philosophical speculation. His novels include *A Play of Passion* (1978), *Flesh Wounds* (1987), *A Little Athens* (1990), *Jennifer* (1991), and *Even if They Fall* (1994). *Dylan Thomas: The Code of Night* (1972) and *Sylvia Plath: Poetry and Existence* (1976) reflect his urgent concern to identify viable cultural values. His opposition to what he has termed the 'new Barbarism' of contemporary society is clear in such books as *Sex and Dehumanization* (1972) and *Education, Nihilism, and Survival* (1977). Amongst recent critical works are *The Skeleton in the Wardrobe* (1990), an exploration of the fantasy world of C. S. *Lewis; *Where D. H. Lawrence was Wrong about Women* (1991); *Edith Wharton and the Unsatisfactory Man* (1991); *Charles Dickens and the Image of Woman* (1993); and *Creativity and Pop Culture* (1994).

HOLDEN, Molly (1927–81), British poet, born in Peckham, London; she grew up in Surrey and Wiltshire, and was educated at King's College, London. Having had poems published in leading periodicals as a student, she resumed writing during the early 1960s when she became increasingly disabled with multiple sclerosis. The privately published *A Hill Like a Horse* (1963) was her first collection of verse. Her reputation was established with *To Make Me Grieve* (1968). Two more volumes of her poetry were published, *Air and Chill Earth* (1971) and *The Country Over* (1975), before her illness prevented her from writing. The considerable personal candour of much of her finest verse is balanced by the rigorously objective treatments of natural phenomena; she attributed the penetrating clarity of such imagery to the opportunities for concentrated observation produced by her confinement to a wheelchair. Her accomplished style is typically based on conversational adaptations of conventional forms. She also wrote novels for children. A *Selected Poems*, with the addition of previously uncollected material, was published in 1987.

HOLDEN, Ursula (1921–), British novelist, born in Dorset; she has lived in Egypt, Dublin, and London. She published her first novel, *Endless Race* (1975), when she was 54. Her austere, almost staccato style and fast-moving narrative contrasts with the dreamy fairy-tale quality of many of her books. The unease and the black humour which she cultivates comes partly from this contrast and also from the sudden unveiling of the brutal realities behind family relationships and divisions in social class. In *Eric's Choice* (1984) the marriage between a middle-class schoolmaster and his spoiled working-class student proves disastrous because neither of them can tolerate any reality other than the one into which they have been born. Her trilogy of novels, *Tin Toys* (1986), *Unicorn Sisters* (1988), and *A Bubble Garden* (1989), about three sisters abandoned by their glamorous mother to a succession of nannies and relatives and a run-down boarding school, juxtaposes extremes of innocence and sexual knowingness. A more recent novel is *Help Me Please* (1991).

HOLLAND, Cecelia (Anastasia) (1943–), American novelist, born in Nevada, educated at Pennsylvania State University. Most of her novels are based on historical subjects including her first, *The Firedrake* (1966), which explores past history from the fall of Rome onwards. *The Death of Attila* (1973) and *The Belt of Gold* (1984) encompass the Dark Ages; *Until the Sun Falls* (1969) is set in Mongol Asia; *The Earl* (1971) and several companion volumes deal with medieval Europe; and *Home Ground* (1981) is set in the contemporary world, as is *Pacific Street* (1992). Even her first science fiction tale, *Floating Worlds* (1976), unfolds an environment which seems to reflect some actual domain.

HOLLANDER, John (1929–), American poet and critic, born in New York City, educated at Columbia University and Indiana University. Allen *Ginsberg was a fellow student and friend at Columbia, though their poetry is entirely antithetical. Hollander has taught at Harvard, Connecticut College, Hunter College, and at Yale. His first book, *A Crackling of Thorns* (1958), had an Introduction by W. H. *Auden, who praised the 'literariness' of Hollander's work. Later books include *Movie-Going and Other Poems* (1962), *Visions from the Ramble* (1965), *Jiggery-Pokery: A Compendium of Double Dactyls* (1967; with Anthony *Hecht and others), *Philomel* (1968), *Types of Shape* (1969), *The Night Mirror* (1971), *Tales Told of the Fathers* (1975), *Reflections on Espionage* (1976), *Spectral Emanations: New and Selected Poems* (1978), *Blue Wine and Other Poems* (1979), and *Powers of Thirteen* (1984). His literary criticism in *The Untuning of the Sky: Ideas of Music in English Poetry 1500–1700* (1961) and *Vision and Resonance: Two Senses of Poetic Form* (1975) underscores his own commitment to a poetry based on formal verse. Hollander's own work has always sought the refuge of form, a quality of self-restraint unlike the open forms frequently found in twentieth-century American poetry.

HOLLERAN, Andrew (1948–), American novelist, educated at Harvard and at the University of Iowa. Little is known of his life or his real name, although Holleran has intimated that the white, affluent milieu of his novels reflects his own life. His first novel, *Dancer from the Dance* (1978), was a major breakthrough in mainstream gay fiction. Narrated by the campy Sutherland, it describes the rise and fall of Malone, a young gay man old before his time, prodded into the frantic underground of parties, drugs, and promiscuity in Manhattan and on Fire Island. *Nights on Aruba* (1983) chronicles the life of Paul from his birth in Aruba through middle age; written as extended flashback triggered by an impending visit to parents in Florida, he negotiates between his overtly homosexual New York life and the straight mask worn for his family. While neither novel explicitly touches on the impact of AIDS, they are permeated with a sense of metaphorical doom which lies at the core of gay existence. The essays in *Ground Zero* (1989) do reflect Holleran's responses to the disease and to the deaths of those around him. Holleran was a member of the 'Violet Quill', an important collective of gay male writers, including Felice Picano, Edmund *White, and Robert Ferro, whose correspondence with Holleran can be found in *The Violet Quill Reader* (1994).

HOLLINGHURST, Alan (1954–), British novelist, born in Stroud, educated at Magdalen College, Oxford. He has taught at the universities of Oxford and London, and has worked on the staff of the *Times Literary Supplement*. His first published work was a collection of poems, *Confidential Chats with Boys* (1982). Hollinghurst's highly praised and controversial novels are, on one level, depictions of gay life in contemporary Europe, replete with graphic descriptions of casual sexual transactions; on another level, they grapple with the nature of sexual desire and artistic creation, and the complex relationship between the two. In *The Swimming Pool Library* (1988), which is set in a vividly evoked underground London of bars, pools, and discotheques, the handsome young narrator is a modern *flâneur* who finds, amidst his relentless cruising, the time to befriend a harried aristocrat who represents an older generation of more diffident and yet more daring homosexuals. The novel's casual juxtaposition of formal, allusive prose with its transgressive subject matter did much to rescue gay fiction from generic ghettos. *The Folding Star* (1994), ambitious in its range and autumnal in tone, is set in the gay milieu of a Belgian city; here, a somewhat less attractive narrator pursues a similar search for love—the object of his desire is a 17-year-old boy. In this novel, described as a triptych, Hollinghurst explores the fine line between lust and love, returns to his narrator's past to examine the sense of loss that haunts him, and introduces the parallel theme of a Belgian symbolist painter's infatuation with an actress. An element of mystery prevails during the proceedings. While the influence of *Firbank is evident in Hollinghurst's first novel, his second ironically evokes Mann.

HOLMAN, Robert (1952–), British dramatist, born in Guisborough, Cleveland, the son of a farmer, educated at the local grammar school. His most successful plays are marked by a strong sense of atmosphere, usually that of his native north Yorkshire, and the understated style in which he evokes ordinary people and their relationships. Among these are *Mud* (1974) and *German Skerries* (1977), set on a cliff overlooking the North Sea and involving the birdwatchers who gather there; *Rooting* (1979), set on a pig farm and touching on the subject of rural depopulation; *The Estuary* (1980), about a father and son's fishing expedition and, by extension, their family's troubles; and the more ambitious *Other Worlds* (1983), about the impact on a farming and fishing community of the threat of Napoleonic invasion. Since then his plays, though still quiet and unpretentious in tone, have grown in political and social resonance. They include *Examples Are Today* (1984), a look at the pre-Second World War period through the experience of men who went to fight in the Spanish Civil War; *The Overgrown Path* (1985), set on the Greek island of Tinos and mainly involving the expatriate professor who helped develop the H-bomb; the trilogy *Making Noise Quietly* (1986), several of whose characters have been touched by war and violence; and *Across Oka* (1989), about the edgy relationship of an English and a Russian boy entrusted with taking the fertilized egg of the near-extinct Siberian crane to its natural habitat. He has also written for television, notably *Chance of a Lifetime* and *This Is History, Gran*.

HOLME, Constance (1881–1955), English regional novelist, born in Milnthorpe, Westmorland, where most of her fiction is set. Her most famous novel, *The Lonely Plough* (1914), was described by her as 'the story of a landed estate, and of a big flood on a northern marsh bringing out the loyalty of the north-country character, not only to the living but to the dead'. Feudal relationships between landlord, agent, and tenant are also portrayed in her first novel, *Crump Folk Going Home* (1913), and in *The Old Road from Spain* (1916) in which the landscape, social life, and rural traditions of the region are vividly evoked. Many novels, such as *Beautiful End* (1918), *The Splendid Fairing* (1919), and *The Things which Belong* (1925), focus on the daily lives of working people of the area. Other novels include *He-Who-Came* (1930), and *The Trumpet in the Dust* (1921), the title of which was taken from a poem by Rabindranath *Tagore, with whom Holme felt some kinship.

HOLMES, John Clellon (1926–88), American novelist and journalist, born in Holyoke, Massachusetts, educated at Columbia University and the New School for Social Research. He was credited by some authorities with coining the phrase 'the *Beat Generation'. He contributed articles to such magazines as *Harper's*, **Partisan Review*, **Poetry*, and the *New York Times Magazine*, and later held posts at various American universities. Although his initial publications after university were poetry, his only collection was the later *The Bowling Green* (1977), and he rapidly turned to fiction. *Go* (1952; UK title *The Beat Boys*, 1959), about the intellectual drifters in the New York City of the Beat Generation, and *The Horn* (1958), about the declining days of a black saxophonist, are very much novels of the 'Beat' movement, soaked in jazz and the atmosphere of the 1950s. Later works, such as *Get Home Free* (1964), are less confident in their evocation of the period. Whilst he never achieved the status of *Ginsberg or *Kerouac, the essays collected in *Nothing More To Declare* (1967), regarded as a succinct and accurate representation of the Beat movement, and his memoir *Visitor: Jack Kerouac in Old Saybrook* (1980), are useful resources for the study of one of the important strands of post-war American literature.

HOLMES, Richard (1945–), British biographer, born in London, educated at Churchill College, Cambridge. *Shelley: The Pursuit* (1974) was written in the course of travels in England, Wales, Switzerland, France, and Italy, which he undertook to reconstruct Shelley's journeyings from 1811 onward. *Coleridge* (1982), a valuable critical introduction, was succeeded by *Coleridge: Early Visions* (1989), the first volume of an ambitious biography providing a comprehensive treatment of Coleridge's psychology and personal relationships. *Footsteps: Adventures of a Romantic Biographer* (1985) was Holmes's imaginative autobiographical account of the itineraries of his researches between 1964 and 1976; the book also conveys its author's interest in Gérard de Nerval, about whom he wrote a radio play entitled 'Inside the Tower', which was broadcast in 1977. His other works include *My Fantoms* (1976), his translations of stories by Théophile Gautier; an edition of *A Short Residence in Sweden* (1987) by Mary Wollstonecraft and William Godwin; and *Dr Johnson and Mr Savage* (1993), a biographical study.

HOLROYD, Michael (de Courcy Fraser) (1935–), British biographer, born in London; he was educated, as he states in *Who's Who*, at Eton and Maidenhead Public Library. In the latter he discovered the works of Hugh Kingsmill, the subject of his first biography (1964) and of his edition of *The Best of Hugh Kingsmill* (1971). *The Unknown Years* (1967) and *The Years of Achievement* (1968), his two-volume biography of Lytton *Strachey, won considerable acclaim for its remarkable attention to detail and was instrumental in reviving interest in the *Bloomsbury Group; a revised edition, *Lytton Strachey: The New Biography* appeared in 1994. *The Years of Innocence* (1974) and *The Years of Experience* (1975) are his two-volume biography of the painter Augustus John. *The Search for Love* (1988), *The Pursuit of Power* (1989), *The Lure of Fantasy* (1991), *The Last Laugh* (1992), and *The Shaw Companion* (1992; including a list of source references), his work on George Bernard *Shaw, confirmed his reputation as a major biographer. His other publications include the novel *A Dog's Life* (1969) and *Unreceived Opinions* (1973), a collection of essays; he has also written scripts for radio and television. In 1982 he married the novelist Margaret *Drabble.

HOLTBY, Winifred (1898–1935), British novelist and journalist, born in Yorkshire. Her studies at Somerville College, Oxford, were interrupted by the First World War, during which she served with the WAAC in France. At Oxford, her lifelong friendship with Vera *Brittain began. Between the wars, Holtby became an influential journalist in London, writing for the *Manchester Guardian*, the *Yorkshire Post*, the *Daily Herald*, and *Time and Tide*. Feminism and pacifism were amongst the issues she covered. She also produced poetry, short stories, and a study of *Virginia*

Woolf (1932). It is as a novelist that she is best remembered. The first of six novels, *Anderby Wold* (1924), explores the clash between traditional values and social change, and prefigures her final work. *The Crowded Street* (1925) was one of her most successful books; with its heroine's search for independence counterpointed by a portrait of middle-class Edwardian society and the First World War that devastated it, the novel echoes Brittain's *Testament of Youth*. In style, Holtby followed the nineteenth-century realist school, focusing on domestic and social issues; the exception was *Mandoa! Mandoa!* (1933), a satire on Western industrialized society. Set in an imaginary African state, it enabled Holtby to pursue her concern for racial justice. The posthumously published *South Riding* (1936; James Tait Black Memorial Prize) was Holtby's finest work. A chronicle both of a Yorkshire community and of an idealistic young headmistress within it, it was described by Brittain as a 'testament of its author's undaunted philosophy'.

Homage to Catalonia, a mixture of personal memoir and political analysis of the Spanish Civil War, by George *Orwell, published in 1938. *Homage to Catalonia* includes some of Orwell's most moving and finely judged writing. It is restlessly balanced between an enduring commitment to the ideals of socialism and a growing dismay at the inefficiencies and factionalism of the Republican campaign against Franco. The book opens memorably with a vivid account of the squalor, confusion, and high hopes of revolutionary Barcelona in December 1936, and proceeds to an unflinching portrayal of conditions on the Aragon front during the ensuing winter and spring. Orwell reveals a completely unforced enthusiasm for the social equality that existed briefly in the city and more lingeringly among the left-wing militias: 'I had dropped more or less by chance into the only community of any size in Western Europe where political consciousness and disbelief in capitalism were more normal than their opposites.' At the same time, his impatience with the lack of weapons and training and the talent for incompetence he encountered among Republicans modulated into a form of despair on his return to Barcelona after a nearly fatal throat wound ended his active service career. The final episode in the book deals with the savage infighting among socialist and anarchist organizations and the subsequent outlawing of the Trotskyist party to whom Orwell was affiliated. The shock of the experience threw him into a passionate commitment to the good faith of individuals caught up in the partisan conflict, as well as a growing awareness of the corruptibility of all revolutionary movements.

HOME, William Douglas (1912–92), British dramatist, born in Edinburgh, son of the 13th Earl of Home, educated at New College, Oxford, and the Royal Academy of Dramatic Art. After working as an actor, and serving as a captain in the Royal Armoured Corps, he came to public notice in 1947 with *Now Barabbas*, set in a prison as a murderer waits to be executed. His subsequent work has included drawing-room comedies, notably *The Chiltern Hundreds* (1947), in which an earl's socialist son is beaten in an election by his father's butler; *The Reluctant Debutante* (1955), about the pressures of the London 'season'; and *The Secretary Bird* (1968); and 'straight' plays, including *The Thistle and the Rose* (1949), about the events preceding Flodden; *The Queen's Highland Servant* (1967), about Queen Victoria's relationship with John Brown; and *The Dame of Sark* (1974), about the German occupation of the smallest of the Channel Islands. Critically, Home became a prime victim of the reaction against 'mandarin' boulevard drama, but he continued to write prolifically, achieving modest public success with *Lloyd George Knew My Father* (1972), a serious comedy about a deadening marriage, and *The Kingfisher* (1977), about an old man's attempt to marry the woman who rejected him fifty years before. He published one autobiography, *Half Term Report*, in 1954 and another, *Mr Home Pronounced Hume*, in 1979.

Homecoming, The, a play by H. *Pinter, performed and published in 1965. One of its author's darkest dramas, the play involves the homecoming of Teddy, an academic living in America, with his English wife Ruth, once a photographic model, born in the same north London area where his family still lives. Their welcome is far from conventional. Teddy's widowed father, Max, is alternately insulting, bullying, and ingratiating, and his brothers, Joey and Lenny, make sexual advances to Ruth, who calmly accepts them. By the end of the play, Teddy departs for America and for his young children, leaving Ruth ostensibly the creature of father and brothers who have decided to make her a prostitute, but actually their surrogate mother, in full command of the household. As often in Pinter, seemingly banal or irrelevant speeches and exchanges carry great emotional weight, helping to explain behaviour that at first seems motiveless. The result is a picture, probably Pinter's most shocking, of family politics at their most intricate, disturbing, and overwhelming.

Honest Ulsterman, The, a quarterly journal of poetry and criticism begun in 1968 by James *Simmons, who promoted an ideal of cultural and personal individuality in his editorials. In its early years the magazine was an invaluably non-sectarian platform for the growing reputation of *Ulster poetry. Derek *Mahon, Seamus *Heaney, Michael *Longley, Ciaran *Carson, Tony *Harrison, and Iain Crichton *Smith have been among the regular contributors. Frank *Ormsby maintained the magazine's eclectically authoritative ethos as editor from 1969 to 1989, when he was succeeded by his assistant Robert Johnstone. A 'Business Section' under the authorship of 'Jude the Obscure' has appeared in each issue since 1970, often providing the vehicle for penetrating critical articles on a wide range of writers and literary topics. The *Honest Ulsterman* has produced pamphlets by numerous contributing poets, which include titles by Tom *Paulin, Peter *Porter, Paul *Muldoon, Gavin *Ewart, and Carol *Rumens.

HOOD, Hugh (1928–), Canadian novelist and short-story writer, born to English and French-Canadian parents in Toronto, educated at the University of Toronto. He became a professor of English in Connecticut and Montreal. His Catholicism informs his fiction, which habitually investigates issues of conscience and moral dualities. He first achieved recognition for a volume of Montreal sketches, *Around the Mountain* (1967). Subsequent short-story volumes include *The Fruit Man, the Meat Man and the Manager* (1971), *Dark Glasses* (1976), *None Genuine without This Signature* (1980), *August Nights* (1985), *A Short Walk in the Rain* (1989), *The Isolation Booth* (1991), and *You'll Catch Your Death* (1992). Hood's novels include *White Figure, White Ground* (1964); *The Camera Always Lies* (1967), set in the film world; *A Game of Touch* (1970); and *You Can't Get There from Here* (1972), a satirical novel set in a fictional African country whose two peoples evoke the cultural divisions between anglophone and francophone Canadians. His most ambitious work is his 'New Age' cycle, a projected series of twelve novels, which began with *The Swing in the Garden* (1975). By focusing on a particular protagonist and family, it aims to provide a viewpoint on moral and social issues from the 1880s to the year 2000, and continued with *A New Athens* (1977), *Reservoir Ravine* (1979), *Black and White Keys* (1982), *The Scenic Art* (1984), *The Motor Boys in Ottawa* (1986), *Tony's Book* (1988), and *Property and Value* (1990). He has also published a collection of literary and cultural essays, *Unsupported Assertions* (1991).

HOOKER, (Peter) Jeremy (1941–), British poet and critic, born in Warsash, Hampshire, educated at the University of Southampton. The prevailing concern in Hooker's verse with the interactions of man, place, and history was established in *The Elements* (1972) and *Soliloquies of a Chalk Giant* (1974), his first two collections of verse. *Solent Shore* (1978) explored the personal, familial, and communal significances of his native Hampshire landscape. In *Englishman's Road* (1980) his absorption in the implications of Welsh culture became apparent. *Master of the Leaping Figures* (1987) reflects the historical, religious, and mythical dimensions of his experience of Winchester, where he had taught. The fluid free verse Hooker generally employs is highly appropriate to the extended sequences which predominate in his work. *A View from the Source: Selected Poems* appeared in 1982. His critical works include *John Cowper Powys* (1973) and *John Cowper Powys and David Jones: A Comparative Study* (1979); the essays of *Poetry of Place* (1982) and *The Presence of the Past* (1987) are thematically centred on the treatments of local elements and ideas of nationality in the work of a range of British and American poets.

HOPE, A(lec) D(erwent) (1907–), Australian poet and critic, born in New South Wales, educated at Sydney and Oxford Universities. Indefatigable defender and articulator of the central role of poetry in life, Hope has also directed his erudite wit at individuals, institutions, and values which, he believed, threatened such vital elements. Hope's writing was first collected in *The Wandering Islands* (1955), by which time he already had a reputation as a poet. Subsequent verse includes *Collected Poems: 1930–1965* (1966), *Collected Poems: 1930–1970* (1972), *Antechinus: Poems 1975–1980* (1981), *The Tragical History of Dr Faustus* (1982), and *The Age of Reason* (1985). *The Drifting Continent, and Other Poems* (1979) included several comic bush ballads. His works of literary criticism include *The Cave and the Spring* (1965), *Native Companions* (1974), which gathered articles over forty years, and *The New Cratylus* (1979). As a poet and critic Hope's position has always been enigmatic: learned and traditional in his references, techniques, and symbolism, he has also demonstrated an iconoclastic relish in social and moral matters. Much of his energy in all his writings has been devoted to reinvigorating Australian life through imaginative access to the enduring and life-enhancing patterns of myth and symbolism as well as the literature and forms of the past.

HOPE, Christopher (1941–), South African novelist and poet, born in Johannesburg, educated at the universities of Witwatersrand and Natal; he moved to London in 1976. Hope's first novel, *A Separate Development* (1981), which was banned in South Africa, fiercely ridiculed apartheid and satirized fears of miscegenation. It is narrated by the adolescent Harry Moto who, due to a sexual misdemeanour, is forced to disguise himself as a black person. *Kruger's Alp* (1984; Whitbread Prize) is an allegorical novel which targets the legacy of Paul Kruger, leader of the Afrikaners during the Anglo-Boer War (1899–1902). *The Hottentot Room* (1986), about political exiles in London, comically scrutinizes fashionable assumptions about race and power politics. His novella *Black Swan* (1987) is a bleak, hard-hitting parable which portrays a black township boy called 'Lucky' who becomes obsessed with classical ballet. *My Chocolate Redeemer* (1989), set in France, is narrated by Bella, an intellectually precocious nymphet. Much comic irony and satirical scorn are generated by her relationships with an exiled African dictator, and her atheistic uncle, who dabbles in racialist politics. *The Love Songs of Nathan J. Swirsky* (1993) is a comic novel set in South Africa. In *Serenity House* (1992) Hope moves the scene to London, to recount the blackly satirical mystery of the identity of Max Montfalcon, a denizen of an old people's home who may or may not be an erstwhile Nazi exterminator. *Darkest England* (1996), a Swiftean satire on England, follows David Mungo Booi from Africa to contemporary Britain. Hope's other works include the poems in *Cape Drives* (1974), *In the Country of the Black Pig* (1981), and *Englishmen* (1985); *Private Parts and Other Tales* (1981); *White Boy Running* (1988), a memoir; and *Moscow! Moscow!* (1990), a travel book about Gorbachev's Russia.

HOPKINS, John (Richard) (1931–), British dramatist, born in London, educated at Cambridge University. He first came to notice for his work for television, which included no fewer than fifty-three scripts for the police series *Z Cars* between 1962 and 1965, several 'one-off' plays, and the critically admired tetralogy *Talking to a Stranger* (1966), which looked at the events of one painful and finally disastrous day from the stance of each member of a family of four. He has continued to write for the medium, scripting an adaptation of John *le Carré's *Smiley's People* in 1982; but is also the author of plays for the stage, notably *This Story of Yours* (1968), about an emotionally troubled policeman who, disgusted yet fascinated by the horrors of his profession, beats to death a child rapist; *Find Your Way Home* (1970), an early example of the 'coming out of the closet play', in which a married man acknowledges his homosexuality and 'finds his way home' to what promises to be a long-term relationship with a younger man; *Economic Necessity* (1973), in which a man gives up a job he thinks pointless, only to discover, when his wife takes a lover and his family rejects him, that he was more financially than emotionally important to his nearest and dearest; and *Next of Kin* (1974), which presents three generations of a suburban family, all of them actuated by avarice and other vices. As this suggests, Hopkins's work has been marked by a sweeping and sometimes brutally intense scepticism about human relationships.

HOPKINS, Pauline (1859–1930), African-American novelist, short-story writer, and journalist, born in Portland, Maine, educated at the prestigious Girls' High School in Boston. In 1900 Hopkins co-founded the first US black press literary magazine, *Colored American Magazine*, which serialized three of her novels (*Hagar's Daughter: A Story of Southern Caste Prejudice*; *Winona: A Tale of Negro Life in the South and Southwest*; and *Of One Blood: Or, the Hidden Self*); her stories and articles also appeared in *Colored American Magazine* and in *Voice of the Negro*. Her first novel, *Contending Forces: A Romance Illustrative of Negro Life North and South* (1900), which chronicles the enslaved lives of several generations of an African-American family, links antebellum violence against slaves to post-Reconstruction practices of lynching, rape, and segregation. The Schomburg Library's 1988 republication of the novel and *The Magazine Novels of Pauline Hopkins* has ignited an often contradictory US critical response to Hopkins's work: some argue that Hopkins's impassioned fictional preoccupation with racial justice none the less betrays strongly assimilationist or élitist impulses, while recent historicist criticism details a more theoretically complex engagement between Hopkins's texts and both contemporaneous literary conventions and such pop-culture discourses as Jamesian psychology.

HOPLEY, George, see WOOLRICH, CORNELL.

Horizon, a literary periodical founded by Cyril *Connolly in association with Stephen *Spender, who was assistant editor, and Peter Watson, who acted as art editor. Connolly intended it for readers formerly served by the **Criterion*, the **London Mercury*, and **New Verse*, all of which had ceased publication in 1939. In the first issue of January 1940 he stated that 'Our standards are aesthetic and our politics are in abeyance'; the magazine's opposition to Nazism was, however, invariably clear. The authors who gained *Horizon* its high reputation included Graham *Greene, Sean *O'Faolain, Evelyn *Waugh, Henry *Miller, W. H. *Auden, Louis *MacNeice, Dylan *Thomas, Patrick *Kavanagh, and Alun *Lewis. Work by numerous distinguished American and European writers was also regularly featured. In commercial terms the magazine was moderately successful, though its sales never exceeded 10,000 copies. In 1950 the final issue's editorial voiced Connolly's sense of cultural beleaguerment in his remark that 'it is closing time in the gardens of the West'.

HORNUNG E(rnest) W(illiam) (1866–1921), British novelist, born in Middlesborough. He is chiefly remembered as the creator of Raffles, the gentleman burglar. Educated at Uppingham, Hornung spent two years of his youth in Australia. His first novel, *A Bride from the Bush* (1890), was followed by *Raffles* (1899), his greatest success, in which the eponymous hero carries out a series of daring jewel robberies, admiringly described by his former school fellow, 'Bunny'. It was followed by *Stingaree, a Thief in the Night* (1905), an attempt to recreate a Raffles character in an Australian setting, and by a sequel to the earlier bestseller, *Mr Justice Raffles* (1909). His other novels include *Notes of a Camp Follower* (1919). See 'Raffles and Miss Blandish' by G. *Orwell.

HOROVITZ, Frances (1938–83), British poet, born in London, educated at the University of Bristol and the Royal Academy of Dramatic Art. In 1964 she married Michael *Horovitz. She became a noted reader of poetry on radio and worked widely as a teacher of creative writing. *Poems* (1967) and *The High Tower* (1970), pamphlet editions of her verse, were followed in 1980 by *Water Over Stone*, a substantial collection drawing much of its imagery from the remote part of the Cotswold Hills where she lived from 1971. *Snow Light, Water Light* (1983) reflects the topography and history of the Irthing Valley in Northumbria, where she went in 1980 to work on *Wall* (1981), a collaborative treatment of Hadrian's Wall by a group of writers and graphic artists. Anne *Stevenson's remark on Horovitz's 'effortless synthesis of self and nature' indicates the imaginative fusions of mood and closely observed particulars of landscape which characterize her best work. The rhythms and diction of her verse frequently produce effects of great delicacy. *Collected Poems* (1985) was edited by Roger *Garfitt, whom she married shortly before her death from cancer.

HOROVITZ, Michael (1935–), British poet, born in Frankfurt, Germany; he grew up in London, and was educated at Brasenose College, Oxford. In 1959 he founded **New Departures*. His desire to reinstate poetry as a popular art form gave rise to Live New

Departures, a touring company combining poetry with musical and theatrical activities. His early publications include *Declaration* (1963), *Nude Lines for Barking* (1965), and *High Notes from when I Was Rolling in Moss* (1966). His stated desire to unite 'pre-Renaissance inspirations with contemporary fact' is demonstrated in his work's fusions of a celebratory lyricism with socio-political critiques. During the 1960s he was central to the emergence of *underground poetry and edited the popular and controversial anthology *Children of Albion: Poetry of the 'Underground' in Britain* (1969). His most highly regarded works are *The Wolverhampton Wanderer* (1971) and *Midsummer Morning Jog* (1985, with illustrations by Peter Blake); the discursive style of these long poems modulates energetically between wide-ranging contemplation and incisively polemical elements. His most substantial collections include *Growing Up: Selected Poems and Pictures 1951–1979* (1979) and *Wordsounds and Sightlines: New and Selected Poems* (1994). Among his other works are his experimental combinations of textual and graphic elements in *Bop Paintings, Collages, Drawings & Picture-Poems* (1989) and a further anthology entitled *Grandchildren of Albion* (1992), which contains a wide range of verse by younger British poets.

Horse's Mouth, The, see CARY, JOYCE.

HOSAIN, Attia (1913–), Indian writer, born in Lucknow, India, educated at La Martinière School and Isabella Thoburn College, Lucknow. Along with her liberal English education, she absorbed the courtly values and traditions of her aristocratic Muslim family, and studied Persian and Arabic as well as her native Urdu. Hosain moved to Britain in 1947, and worked for many years for the BBC. She has had considerable influence on Indo-Anglian fiction, and her work is admired for its lyrical prose and its carefully delineated social, historical, and political perspectives. The stories collected in *Phoenix Fled* (1953) focus mainly on the dispossessed, the underclass, and the peasantry; her imagistic prose evokes the cadences of her native Urdu, and a strong current of anti-colonial nationalism links her work to that of her progressive contemporaries in indigenous languages. Her novel *Sunlight on a Broken Column* (1961) articulates the personal dilemmas of a woman, a daughter of the ruling classes, caught between the demands of tradition and change; the background of events leading to the independence of India and the creation of Pakistan add depth to the novel.

HOSPITAL, Janette Turner (1942–), Australian novelist and short-story writer, born in Melbourne, educated at the University of Queensland. She has travelled widely in America, Europe, and India; since 1971 she has lived mainly in Canada. Among other occupations she has worked as a librarian at Harvard, and as a lecturer in universities in Canada, America, and Australia. Her first novel, *The Ivory Swing* (1982), is a personal and psychological drama involving a young Canadian woman who finds herself in India accompanying her academic husband on sabbatical. *The Tiger in the Tiger Pit* (1984) concerns an elderly couple reaching their golden wedding, and focuses on the wife's attempts to draw together the disparate threads of her ever-increasing family. *Borderline* (1985) skilfully exploits conflicting levels of narration and plot, in reconstructing an international story of differing flights and concealments; Hospital deploys the interrelating tensions of alternative truths to construct a work which traces the borderlines between both political and existential worlds through blending the conventions of thriller and psychological drama. *Charades* (1988) is the story of an Australian girl, Charade Ryan, travelling the world in search of her lost father; the novel moves between Boston, Toronto, Melbourne, and Queensland, and shifts backwards and forwards in time (from Cook to Quantum Physics). *The Lost Magician* (1992) continues in the tradition of its predecessors: similarly dense, lyrical, and multi-layered, it investigates, through the intertwined destinies of its protagonists—a Chinese photographer, a self-destructive prostitute, and the idealistic son of a rich judge among others— political corruption in high places and the seething lowlife of contemporary Australia. The stories in *Dislocations* (1986), set in Queensland, America, and India, all explore disruption of ordinary life, or separation from a known environment. The stories in *Isobars* (1990), set in different places and times, are linked by isobars of the imagination.

Hostage, The, a play by Brendan *Behan.

Hotel du Lac, see BROOKNER, ANITA.

HOUGHTON, Stanley (1881–1913), British playwright, born in Cheshire, educated at Manchester Grammar School. He went into his father's cotton business, hoping eventually to become a professional writer. Though he wrote a classic short play in *The Dear Departed* (1908), and though there is dramatic merit in the longer *The Younger Generation* (1909) and *The Perfect Cure* (1911), he did not achieve his ambition until the year before he died of meningitis. *Hindle Wakes*, which came with great success to London in 1912, remains one of the most striking achievements of the so-called 'Manchester School' of playwrights associated with that city's Gaiety Theatre. It is a lively comedy on Houghton's favourite theme, the right to personal freedom of the young, here represented by the weaver who appals the older generation by choosing independence rather than marriage to the mill owner's son who has made her pregnant. Houghton is clearly attacking 'double standards' of morality and showing the little town of Hindle, in the words of the ambiguous title, 'waking' to the twentieth century; he achieves this through humorous observation of character and of Lancashire.

House for Mr Biswas, A, a novel by V. S. *Naipaul, published in 1961. Set against the backdrop of multiethnic Trinidad, it tells, in mock-epic mode, the story of the struggles of Mohun Biswas, a journalist of

Indian origin, from his birth to his death (from a heart attack). The character of Biswas affords Naipaul an opportunity to portray the conflicts between resilience and hope on the one hand, and disappointments, dread, and defeats on the other; the former ultimately triumph, if only in a moral sense. The house of the title comes to symbolize the freedoms that Biswas, besieged by adversity in his personal and his professional life, longs for: from the problems of love (and the lack of it), identity, class, and social prestige. The tale is recounted with ease and humour, allowing Naipaul to create a representative gallery of cleverly drawn types (including the Tulsis, Biswas's rapacious in-laws) that present a panoramic view of Caribbean attitudes. Naipaul's whimsical treatment of his theme betrays the influence of *Narayan.

HOUSEHOLD, Geoffrey (Edward West) (1900–88), British writer, born in Bristol, educated at Clifton College and at Magdalen College, Oxford. He achieved recognition as a writer of adventure stories with *Rogue Male* (1939), which establishes the characteristic Household protagonist (a solitary, self-reliant English gentleman) and sets him against an unnamed but recognizably Nazi European dictator and his regime. The pursuit continues in its sequel *Rogue Justice* (1982). These and other works such as *Watcher in the Shadows* (1960) and *Dance of Dwarfs* (1968) are similar in tradition to the work of J. *Buchan. *The Third Hour* (1937) was a utopian discourse set in South America. Several late novels, including *The Sending* (1980), *Summon the Bright Water* (1981), and *Arrows of Desire* (1985), attempted fantasy themes with some success.

House of Mirth, The, a novel by Edith *Wharton, published in 1905, a social satire depicting manners in New York society. Lily Bart, despite her beauty and high social connections, remains unmarried at 29. Among her suitors are the rich financier Simon Rosedale, and Lawrence Selden, a lawyer, who is her real love but is without the means to support her. She unwittingly falls into the power of Gus Trenor in a gambling game, who advances her money to cover her debts. He seeks repayment by demanding physical attention, but Lily escapes and promises to repay the money. Later, her reputation in fashionable society is ruined through being framed as George Dorset's mistress by his wife, who is seeking to cover her own love affair. As Lily goes down in the world, so Simon Rosedale rises to the top, winning social acceptance by a shrewd manipulation of his increasing wealth. Lily becomes a milliner, and after a final declaration of her love to Selden, she returns to her boarding-room and commits suicide. Upon Selden's arrival to request her hand in marriage, he discovers that Lily has put aside her aunt's entire bequest to pay her debt to Trenor. Lily is thus destroyed by the very society whose decorative but inhumane specifications her upbringing had designed her precisely to meet.

House with the Green Shutters, The, see BROWN, GEORGE DOUGLAS.

HOUSMAN, A(lfred) E(dward) (1859–1936), British poet, born near Bromsgrove, Worcestershire, educated at St John's College, Oxford, where, for reasons which remain unclear, he failed his final examinations. During the ten years of his subsequent employment in the Patents Office in London he published papers on Propertius, Juvenal, Ovid, and other classical authors, establishing the reputation that gained him the Chair of Greek and Latin at University College, London, in 1892. He became Kennedy Professor of Latin at Trinity College, Cambridge, in 1911. The most substantial of his works of textual scholarship was his edition of Manilius, which appeared in five volumes between 1903 and 1930. Housman appears to have intensified his very private practice of poetry after the departure of his intimate friend Moses Jackson for India in 1887. *A *Shropshire Lad*, published at his own expense in 1896, gradually drew wide critical acclaim. Successive commercial editions were printed and by 1912 Housman was widely known. The *Georgian Poets venerated him as the progenitor of their predominantly rural mode. In 1922 he published *Last Poems*, a series of forty-one verses sustaining his pessimistic lyricism. *Praefanda* (1931), his miscellany of obscene passages from Latin sources with an ironically erudite introduction, was published in Germany. Apart from his more orthodox writings on classical authors, he published only one other work in his lifetime, the text of his Cambridge lecture *The Name and Nature of Poetry* (1933), which declared poetry to be 'physical rather than intellectual' in origin. The posthumous *More Poems* (1936) was supplemented by eighteen further poems in *A. E. H.* (1937) by his brother Laurence *Housman. Christopher *Ricks's edition of Housman's *Collected Poems and Selected Prose* was published in 1988. *A. E. Housman: The Scholar Poet* (1979) is a biographical study by R. P. Graves.

HOUSMAN, Laurence (1865–1959), British writer, born near Bromsgrove, Worcestershire, the brother of A. E. *Housman; he studied painting in London and became a highly regarded illustrator. His first successful publication was *An Englishwoman's Love Letters* (1900), an ingenious parody of romantic fiction. *Trimblerigg: A Book of Revelation* (1924), a comically effective political satire directed against Lloyd George, and *The Duke of Flamborough* (1924) are the best-known of his novels. The protagonists of his plays, collections of which include *The Little Plays of St Francis* (1922) and *Victoria Regina* (1934), were recurrently based on biblical personages and English royalty, with the result that his work repeatedly incurred the Lord Chamberlain's ban. Among his earlier collections of poetry are *Green Arras* (1896) and *Spikenard* (1898); a *Collected Poems* was published in 1937. As a poet, he tended towards conventional sentimentality, though he was capable of memorably epigrammatic effects. A prolific author, his other works include fairy tales with his own illustrations, art criticism, and treatises on prison reform and the emancipation of women. *A. E. H.*

(1937) contained his memoir of A. E. Housman, together with eighteen previously uncollected poems and a selection of letters. *The Unexpected Years* (1937) is an autobiography. *Laurence Housman*, an illustrated critical biography by Rodney Engen, was published in 1973.

HOUSTON, Douglas (Norman) (1947–), British poet, born in Cardiff, educated at the University of Hull. Sixteen of Houston's poems appeared with work by other *Hull poets in Douglas *Dunn's anthology *A Rumoured City* (1982). Peter *Porter described him as 'an *Auden-like artificer of great accomplishment'. *With the Offal Eaters* (1986) and *The Hunter in the Snow* (1994) are among his collections of poems. Houston's poetry is frequently characterized by the tensions established between succinctly defined social settings and the radically fictional nature of the situations and personae which emerge. Such strategies involve a range of effects extending from the grotesquely humorous to the sombrely elegiac. His work is featured in *Poetry with an Edge* (1988, edited by Neil Astley) and in Meic Stephen's edition of *The Bright Field* (1991), a selection of notable work produced since 1965 by *Anglo-Welsh authors.

HOUSTON, Libby (1941–), British poet, born in North London, educated at Lady Margaret Hall, Oxford. During the 1960s she became a popular performer of her work. *A Stained Glass Raree Show* (1967), her first collection of poetry, was followed by *Plain Clothes* (1971), *At the Mercy* (1981), and *Necessity* (1988). Many of her poems succeed in combining an intention to entertain with an understated moral or philosophical seriousness. The title poem of her widely acclaimed collection, *At the Mercy*, formed an extended meditation on the death in 1974 of her first husband, the artist Mal Dean. While she is frequently concerned with aspects of fable and legend, anecdotal treatments drawn from everyday experience are equally characteristic of her work. *All Change* (1993) is a substantial collection containing mainly children's verse. Since the early 1970s, she has contributed poetry programmes to BBC broadcasts for schools.

HOVE, Chenjerai (1956–), Zimbabwean poet and novelist, born near Zvishavane in central Zimbabwe, educated at the University of Zimbabwe. He was Chairman of the Zimbabwe Writers' Union. In the late 1970s, he taught at rural schools and witnessed horrific aspects of the war of liberation, an experience registered in the anger and compassion pervading *Up in Arms* (1982), his first collection of poetry. In *Red Hills of Home* (1985), he extends the range of his verse to include celebratory and critical responses to conditions among the rural population in the immediate aftermath of Independence. The war of liberation is also central to *Bones* (1988), Hove's highly regarded first novel; its poetically experimental narrative evokes unrest in pre- and post-Independence Zimbabwe through acutely psychological characterization. A subsequent novel, *Shadows* (1991), also adopts an imaginatively internalized approach to the struggles of ordinary Zimbabweans in both urban and rural settings. Hove's other works include the stories of *Shebeen Tales: Messages from Harare* (1995). He has also published a body of fiction in the Shona language.

HOWARD, Elizabeth Jane (1923–), British novelist, born in London; she originally trained as an actress, but left the repertory circuit to work as a model, secretary, book reviewer, editor, and finally a full-time writer. Her first novel, *The Beautiful Visit* (1950), introduces one of Howard's central themes: an intelligent woman's search for the security denied her in a painfully inadequate childhood. *The Long View* (1956) is a well-crafted novel which begins with the break-up of a marriage in 1950, then dissects the 25-year relationship backwards through time. In subsequent novels (*The Sea Change*, 1959; *After Julius*, 1965; *Something in Disguise*, 1969; *Odd Girl Out*, 1972; *Getting It Right*, 1982) she has expanded her range to include less genteel characters and more complex, sometimes quietly comical, situations. *The Light Years* (1990), *Marking Time* (1991), *Confusion* (1993) and *Casting Off* (1995) form 'The Cazalet Chronicle', about a large English family from 1937 onwards. She has also written several screenplays, television and radio plays, and a collection of short stories (*Mr Wrong*, 1975), and has compiled *Green Shades: An Anthology of Plants, Gardens and Gardeners* (1991). With Fay Maschler, she has written *Cooking for Occasions* (1994, previously entitled *Howard and Maschler on Food*, 1987). She was formerly married to Kingsley *Amis.

HOWARD, Richard (1929–), American poet and translator, born in Cleveland, Ohio, educated at Columbia University and the Sorbonne. After working as a lexicographer, he became a freelance translator and critic in 1958; in 1988 he became Rhodes Professor of Comparative Literature at the University of Cincinnati. *Quantities* (1962) and *Damages* (1967), his first two collections of poetry, displayed his characteristic virtuosity in finely regulated discursive forms. *Untitled Subjects* (1969; Pulitzer Prize) established the dramatic monologue as the dominant mode of his verse; poems in the voices of writers and artists, among them Goethe, Browning, Wilde, Ibsen, *Auden, and Rodin, form the most consistently impressive work in *Findings* (1971), *Two-Part Inventions* (1974), and *Fellow Feelings* (1976). His later collections, in which an increasingly rich imaginative dimension is evident, include *Misgivings* (1979), *Lining Up* (1984), *No Traveller* (1989), and *Like Most Revelations* (1994). Howard's poems are frequently written in strict syllabic forms of great precision and elegance. He is the translator of over 150 works of literature, chiefly from the French, and is credited with introducing much modern French fiction to an American readership. His other publications include *Alone With America: Essays on the Art of Poetry in the United States Since 1950* (1969).

Howards End, a novel by E. M. *Forster, published in

1910. It is an ambitious, multi-layered novel, which indicates its message through its epigraph, 'only connect': class conflicts can be sublimated in personal relationships. Forster's goal is to examine the 'State of the Nation' of England; this he does on a variety of levels. On the social level, the relationships of the urban intellectual Schlegel sisters with the affluent Wilcox family and the lower-class, downwardly mobile Basts represent the shifting values of the time. Through the symbolic device of the house of the title—based on Forster's early home, Rooksnest—the author explores the decay of moral and spiritual values, and the hope of future regeneration. Margaret Schlegel, who does not know that the house has been bequeathed to her, marries the widower of Mrs Wilcox, her friend and its erstwhile owner, and ultimately comes to possess Howards End as an indirect result of the murder of Bast, her sister Helen's lover; thus, Helen and Bast's illegitimate child symbolizes the reconciliation of antagonistic classes. Bast's wife, a former prostitute, reveals the worthy Wilcox as a fornicator, allowing Forster to criticize, albeit obliquely, the rising business classes. Margaret's early compassion for Bast turns to dismay when, immersed in her dreams of newly acquired privilege, she sees her stubbornly idealistic sister too closely involved with his fortunes; it is only his tragic, accidental death and Helen's unwitting complicity in it that reveals to her the extent of her own participation in the Basts' downfall. Deftly concealing its didactic and moralizing purposes in intricate narrative and metaphoric structure, *Howards End* works well both as romance and as realist drama; this was skilfully conveyed in the screen adaptation (1993) by *Jhabvala.

HOWATCH, Susan (1940–), British novelist, born in Surrey; she studied law but turned to writing, achieving success with her first novel, *Penmarric* (1971), a family saga set in Cornwall, which utilizes the 'double' technique she has used elsewhere, particularly in her historical fiction, relocating the story of Henry II to a different time and place. *Cashelmara* (1974), similarly, incorporates two different historical periods; *The Sins of the Fathers* (1980) tells the story of Julia, daughter of the Emperor Augustus, but sets it in the contemporary world. *Glittering Images* (1987) was the first in a series of novels devoted to the influence of individual talents and powerful personalities on the Church of England, using the same double technique. The novel, which was loosely based on the life of Bishop Herbert Hensley Henson, was followed by several others, including *Glamorous Powers* (1988), which refers to the writings of Dean Inge; *Ultimate Prizes* (1989), based on Charles Raven's religious thought; and *Scandalous Risks* (1990), which deals with the repercussions in the Church of Dr John Robinson's book, *Honest to God. Mystical Paths* (1992) and *Absolute Truths* (1994) complete the series. She has also conceived, selected, and introduced *The Library of Anglican Spirituality* (1994), eight reissues of classic theological texts.

HOWE, Irving (1920–93), American historian and literary critic, born in New York City, educated at the City College of New York. Howe enjoyed a distinguished career as a critic, historian, and anthologist as well as being one of the leading intellectual figures on the American left for much of the latter half of the twentieth century (he was for many years co-editor of the socialist quarterly *Dissent*). His first book was a work of American labour history, *The UAW and Walter Reuther* (1949), co-authored with B. J. Widick, but his second, *Sherwood Anderson: A Critical Biography* (1951), marked the beginning of a developing interest in modern American literature. His *William Faulkner: A Critical Study* (1952) remains one of the best studies of *Faulkner's fiction. In a literary climate dominated by the *New Criticism and its attempts to eschew what were considered 'extraneous' factors in the creation of a work of art, Howe's criticism was notable for its insistence, quasi-Marxist in character, on the historicity of literary texts and his synthesis of criticism and history. His particular preoccupation with the place of politics in literature led to his important work of literary criticism, *Politics and the Novel* (1957), notable for its treatment of the works of a number of nineteenth-century realists. Other notable works of literary criticism include *Thomas Hardy* (1967), *Decline of the New* (1971), *Celebrations and Attacks: Thirty Years of Literary and Cultural Commentary* (1979), and *The American Newness: Culture and Thought in the Age of Emerson* (1986). Among his other political writings are *Steady Work: Essays in the Politics of Democratic Radicalism, 1953–1966* (1966), *Trotsky* (1978), and *Socialism and America* (1985). Howe's interest in the history of Jewish migration to the USA led to *World of Our Fathers: The Journey of the East European Jews to America and the Life They Found and Made* (1976) for which he received the National Book Award for History. *Selected Writings, 1950–1990* (1990) is an introduction to the range of his work while *A Margin of Hope* (1982) is a volume of autobiography. Howe taught at several American universities, including Brandeis and Stanford, and was a Professor of English at Hunter College in New York City (1963–86).

HOWE, Susan (1937–), American poet, born in Ireland, raised in Cambridge, Massachusetts; she became a visual artist in New York in the 1960s, working increasingly with texts, until a decision in the early 1970s to concentrate on poetry culminating in her first volume, *Hinge Picture* (1974). Since then she has emerged as one of the most original and widely praised of the *Language Poets, although her work significantly diverges from Language Poetry because of its attention to a thematics of American history, puritanism, myth and legend, and its clear roots in three precursors, Emily Dickinson, H.D. (Hilda *Doolittle), and Charles *Olson. She has written a book on Emily Dickinson, *My Emily Dickinson* (1985), and essays 'unsettling the wilderness in American literary history' collected in *The Birth Mark* (1993). Her poetry is a true *hermeneutics of early America, interweaving preoccupations with language, myth, and history in an understated style which frequently uses noun phrases lacking the assertiveness of propositional statements. It is an intent poetry of immense learning, which can shade off into *concrete poetry or into expository prose. Her avowed wish to 'tenderly lift from the dark side of history, voices that are anonymous, slighted—inarticulate' points to a strong feminist theme throughout her work. 'A poet is a foreigner in her own language', she writes. Books include *A Secret History of the Dividing Line* (1978); two collections of earlier work, *Singularities* (1990) and *The Europe of Trusts* (1990); and *The Non-Conformist's Memorial* (1993).

HOWE, Tina (1937–), American playwright, born in New York, educated at Sarah Lawrence College, Columbia University, and the University of Chicago. Her early one-act plays, *The Nest* (1969) and *In Birth and After Birth* (1973), were followed by *Museum* (1976), in which several characters wander round a museum discussing the exhibits and the role of women in the arts, a theme also explored in *The Art of Dining* (1979), which concerns the struggles of a young couple to operate a restaurant in New Jersey. *Painting Churches* (1983) is a largely autobiographical work about a female painter's relationship with her ageing parents. *Coastal Disturbances* (1986) is a comedy about relationships that occur on a private beach in Massachusetts' North Shore in late August; another comedy, *Approaching Zanzibar* (1989), centres on the Blossom family and their journey across the USA. Other plays include *Appearances* (1982) and *Swimming* (1993). Published collections of her plays include *Three Plays by Tina Howe* (1984) and *Approaching Zanzibar: Four Plays by Tina Howe* (1989).

HOWELLS, William D(ean) (1837–1920), American novelist, critic, essayist, and editor, born in Martin's Ferry, Ohio. He came to have a profound impact upon the growing, serious middle-class American readership of the late nineteenth and early twentieth centuries. By 1860 Howells had published two books, a poem entitled 'Poems of Two Friends' (1860) with J. J. Piatt, and was contributing to the *Atlantic Monthly*. He worked for the *Ohio State Journal* at Columbus (1857–61), and met such writers as Lowell, Emerson, and Hawthorne. After writing a successful campaign biography of Lincoln, he was rewarded with the American consulship in Venice; in Italy, he wrote a variety of travel sketches, and later published *Modern Italian Poets* (1887). Returning to New York in 1865 he worked for *The Nation*, and by 1871 he had become editor of the *Atlantic Monthly* where he become an influential writer promoting the cause of realism in American fiction. The first of his thirty-five novels, *Their Wedding Journey* (1872), is a travel narrative loosely based on his own travels in 1870 from Boston to Canada. Thereafter, he wrote prolifically, publishing *A Chance Acquaintance* (1873), a further travel narrative which introduced Kitty Ellison, a figure similar to Henry *James's Daisy Miller. There followed *A Foregone Conclusion* (1875), *The Lady of the Aroostock* (1879), and *The Undiscovered Country* (1880), all uncomplicated narratives which eschewed the more action-packed plots of some of his contemporaries. His most acclaimed fiction appeared in the 1880s and early 1890s, and includes *A Modern Instance* (1882), which examined the social and psychological disintegration in post-Civil War America; a study of women and social values in Boston in *A Woman's Reason* (1883); and his best-known novel, *The Rise of Silas Lapham* (1885), which focuses on the *nouveau riche* Silas Lapham, and the comedy of manners involved in the awkward relationships with the aristocratic Bostonian family, the Coreys. After *Indian Summer* (1886), a comedy of manners, his increasing awareness of ugly social forces and economic anomalies began to permeate his fiction, in the 'economic' novels about class differences: *Annie Kilburn* (1888), *A Hazard of New Fortunes* (1890), and *The World of Chance* (1893). Other novels of this period include *Minister's Charge* (1887) and *April Hopes* (1888), as well as the utopian romance *A Traveller From Altruria* (1894), with its sequel *Through the Eye of the Needle* (1907). For part of this time he contributed critical essays to *Harper's* 'Editor's Study', which continued his championing of Critical Realism, some of which are collected in *Criticism and Fiction* (1891), and produced his penetrating essay 'Novel-Writing and Novel-Reading' (1891), *My Literary Passions* (1895), and *Literature and Life* (1902). He also wrote shorter novels which explored individual consciousness: *The Shadow of a Dream* (1890), and *An Imperative Duty* (1892), a study of miscegenation. Later novels include *The Landlord at Lion's Head* (1897), *The Son of Royal Langbrith* (1904), *Editha* (1905), *The Leatherwood God* (1916), *Years of My Youth* (1916), and the posthumously published *The Vacation of the Kelwyns* (1920). He was elected President of the American Academy of Arts and Letters in 1910. In 1960 his correspondence with Mark Twain was published; in 1974, a first volume of a projected five volumes of his letters was published. His thirty-six plays appeared in the *Complete Plays* (1960) and his *Complete Poetry* appeared in 1974.

How Green Was My Valley, see LLEWELYN, RICHARD.

Howl, a long poem by Allen *Ginsberg, forming the title work of *Howl and Other Poems* (1956), his first collection of verse, for which William Carlos *Williams supplied an enthusiastic foreword. The poem is chiefly written in long free-verse lines whose duration is intended to correspond to the individual breaths of the reader. The compellingly incantational effects produced suggest similarities with the work of Whitman and the lyrical parataxis of the Old Testament. *Howl* is unified thematically by the apocalyptic vision of America's materialist post-war society as the devouring Moloch against which the poem is raised in outraged protest and attempted exorcism. The inviolability of extremes of individual experience, mystical, sexual, psychotic, and drug-induced, is affirmed against the repression, persecution, and mechanistic consciousness imputed to the culture of Moloch. The concluding 'Footnote to Howl' is an extravagantly exalted invocation of the cosmic forces of holiness and benevolence. Widespread publicity accompanied the unsuccessful prosecution of Ginsberg's publisher, Lawrence *Ferlinghetti, for the poem's alleged obscenity. *Howl* was rapidly accorded the status of the manifesto of the *Beat Generation and remains the most compelling single work to emerge from the *San Francisco Renaissance.

How Late It Was, How Late, see KELMAN, JAMES.

HOYLE, Sir Fred (1915–), British writer and astronomer, born in Bingley, Yorkshire, educated at Emmanuel College, Cambridge. His *science fiction works, written with the authority his scientific eminence justifies, have consistently misled readers into the assumption that it was scientifically based; however, novels such as *The Black Cloud* (1957), *Ossian's Ride* (1959), and *October the First is Too Late* (1966) were in fact speculative romances dealing with subjects like time travel. The novels written in collaboration with his son, Geoffrey Hoyle, were fast-paced excursions into metaphysical and political wish-fulfilment; *Fifth Planet* (1963), *Seven Steps to the Sun* (1970), and *The Inferno* (1973) are among the most intriguing (and eccentric) demonstrations available of the scientific mind at loose in the world.

HUDSON, W(illiam) H(enry) (1841–1922), British naturalist and novelist, born of American parents at Quilmes, near Buenos Aires, Argentina; he spent much of his boyhood working on his father's farm, where he developed his abiding interest in ornithology. Left unfit for farming by a serious illness, he began writing and moved to London in 1874. *The Purple Land that England Lost* (two volumes, 1885), a collection of exotic stories with South American settings, was followed by *The Crystal Age* (1887), a novel envisioning an era of harmony attained through mankind's transcendence of sexuality. *Argentine Ornithology* (1888) was the first of his authoritative works of natural history, which also include *The Naturalist in La Plata* (1892), *Birds in London* (1898), and *Nature in Downland* (1900). In 1901 he met Edward *Garnett, who greatly admired the stories of *El Ombu* (1902) and encouraged him to complete **Green Mansions* (1904); its widespread success gained him the financial security required for the travels throughout the south of England which resulted in a succession of works, including *Afoot in England* (1909) and *A Shepherd's Life* (1910), an elegiac reconstruction of the traditional order in South Wiltshire. Among his later publications are *Far Away and Long Ago* (1918), his highly regarded autobiography of his early years, and *The Birds of La Plata* (1920). The precise descriptive powers with which he communicated his intense love for nature gained him great critical and popular acclaim. A twenty-four volume edition of his *Works* was produced in 1922–3. *W. H. Hudson: A Biography* by Ruth Tomalin appeared in 1982.

HUEFFER, Ford Hermann, see FORD, FORD MADOX.

HUGHES, David (John) (1930–), English novelist, born in Alton, Hampshire, educated at Christ Church, Oxford, where he edited *Isis*. Hughes served in the Royal Air Force (1949–50), worked as an editor in London, wrote film scripts in Sweden (his first wife was the Swedish actress Mai Zetterling), and lived in France for several years. He has also been a film critic and a regular reviewer of fiction. In his own fiction war and its effects on individuals is a dominant theme. An ingenious story-teller adept at creating memorable characters, Hughes has written several novels of deceptive power including *Memories of Dying* (1976) and *The Imperial German Dinner Service* (1983). His most significant book is *The Pork Butcher* (1984), the affecting story of a man from Thomas Mann's Lübeck, dying from cancer and plagued with guilt of his wartime past. Suffused with irony, it is a remarkable study of individual and international hopelessness. *But for Bunter* (1985) continues the theme. The semi-autobiographical novel, *The Little Book* (1996), is a compelling book of revelations heightened by elements of the surreal.

HUGHES, Glyn (1935–), British poet and novelist, born in Middlewich, Cheshire, educated at the Regional College of Art, Manchester. He worked as an art teacher from 1956 to 1973, when he became a full-time writer. His principal collections of verse are *Neighbours* (1970), *Rest the Poor Struggler* (1972), *Alibis and Convictions* (1978), and *Best of Neighbours: New and Selected Poems* (1979). His poetry, like much of his fiction, is characterized by the depth of its imaginative involvement with social, historical, and topographical aspects of the Pennine regions of Yorkshire and Lancashire. *Where I Used To Play on the Green* (1982), his first novel, is based on the life of William Grimshaw, the eighteenth-century Yorkshire Methodist; *Mary Hepton's Heaven* (produced in 1984) is his adaptation of the book for the stage. His subsequent novels include *The Hawthorn Goddess* (1984) and *The Rape of the Rose* (1987), treatments of the social upheaval wrought by the Industrial Revolution, and *Roth* (1992), the main protagonist of which is an emotionally disturbed painter. Among his other works is *Millstone Grit* (1975), a guide to the Pennines.

HUGHES, (James Mercer) Langston (1902–67), African-American writer, born in Joplin, Missouri, educated at Columbia and Lincoln Universities. Hughes was an important figure in the *Harlem Renaissance, who sought to capture the dominant oral and improvisatory traditions of black culture in written form. In the 1920s he drifted around Europe and North America with a variety of jobs; he wrote and published poetry continuously, including eleven poems in an anthology entitled *The *New Negro* (1925). Some of his early poetry was published in *Crisis* and *Opportunity*, two leading black journals of the 1920s. After being noticed by some culturally sympathetic white benefactors, his first collection, *The Weary Blues*

(1926), was published, which characteristically employed jazz rhythms to investigate black experience. Other volumes of poetry followed, including *Fine Clothes to the Jew* (1927), *Dear Lovely Death* (1931), *The Negro Mother* (1931), *The Dream Keeper and Other Poems* (1932), and *Scottsboro Limited: Four Poems and a Play in Verse* (1932). A novel, *Not Without Laughter* (1930), consolidated his reputation, and he was soon known as the 'Negro Poet Laureate'. During and after the activist 1930s, Hughes's writing took on a political militancy. He worked as a journalist and produced newspaper sketches of the popular black hero Jesse B. Semple, later collected in *Simple Speaks His Mind* (1950) and *Simple Stakes a Claim* (1957). He founded black theatres in Harlem, Los Angeles, and Chicago and published collections of black writing, including *The Poetry of the Negro* (1949) and *The Book of Negro Folklore* (1958). He wrote autobiographies, screenplays, and plays like *Mulatto* (1936) and *Black Nativity* (1961); and continued to write poetry, with the volumes *A New Song* (1938), *Shakespeare in Harlem* (1942), *Fields of Wonder* (1947), and *One Way Ticket* (1949), including such famous anthems of the civil rights movement as 'I, Too, Sing America' and 'Freedom Train'. He is probably best known for his collection of short stories entitled *The Ways of White Folks* (1933), in which he investigates black/white relations with an acute eye for detail. *The Big Sea* (1940) and *I Wonder as I Wander* (1956) are two volumes of autobiography. His later poetry appeared in *Montage of a Dream Deferred* (1951), *Ask Your Mama* (1961), *The Panther and the Lash: Poems of Our Times* (1967), and an edition entitled *Good Morning Revolution: Uncollected Social Protest Writings by Langston Hughes* (1973). His other prose includes some short stories about Negro urban experiences and problems in *Laughing to Keep from Crying* (1952) and *Fight for Freedom* (1962), about the National Association for the Advancement of Colored People. A collection of some of his letters appeared in *Arna Bontemps–Langston Hughes. Letters 1925–1967* (1980), edited by C. H. Nichols. See also ETHNICITY.

HUGHES, Richard (Arthur Warren) (1900–76), British novelist, playwright, and poet, of Welsh descent, born in Weybridge, Surrey, educated at Oriel College, Oxford. Living mainly in Wales from 1923, he was Vice-President of the Welsh National Theatre (1924–36). As an undergraduate he produced a volume of poems, *Gipsy Night* (1922), and his first play, *The Sisters' Tragedy* (1922), which anticipates later work in its theme of the destruction of the innocent and the violence inherent in nature. Other plays include *The Man Born To Be Hanged* (1923) and *A Comedy of Good and Evil* (1924), and the first-ever commissioned radio play, *Danger* (1924), about three people trapped in a coal mine by a roof-fall. In his first novel, *A High Wind in Jamaica* (1929; US title *The Innocent Voyage*), a family of children in the earlier nineteenth century leave their Jamaican home for Britain, to be captured by pirates. The children respond only arbitrarily to events; Hughes thus turns notions of innocence on their head, the charming girl, Emily, being capable of a terrible murder. *In Hazard* (1938) is the story of a tramp steamer in a freak hurricane which pits its assorted characters against brute Nature. *The Fox in the Attic* (1961), the first volume of what was to be called 'The Human Predicament', was received with enormous critical acclaim. Opening in rural Wales, shortly after the end of the Great War, the novel shows us Augustine, the innocent young hero shocked out of his squirearchic and deliberately reclusive life by the inexplicable death of a very young child, and deciding to visit relations in Germany. The fictional characters mingle with real ones, most ambitiously of all Hitler, in whose abortive Munich *putsch* the novel culminates. The second volume, *The Wooden Shepherdess* (1973), contains a real *tour de force* in its account of the murder of Röhm, the 'Night of the Long Knives', and a vivid and poetic presentation of Prohibition America.

HUGHES, Robert (1938–), Australian art critic and writer, born in Sydney, educated at Sydney School of Architecture. He published *The Art of Australia* (1966) and *Heaven and Hell in Western Art* (1969), and in 1970 became art critic for *Time* magazine. *The Shock of the New: Art and the Century of Change* (1980) was based on a successful BBC television series. *The Fatal Shore* (1988) was a vivid, at times rather over-written, but hugely successful reassessment of Australia's brutal convict past. Published to coincide with Bicentennial year, it continued Hughes's longstanding interest in the relationship between society and sensibility and provoked informed reviews and debate on what was once a much-suppressed aspect of Australia's (and Britain's) history. The idea for it grew from Hughes's realization that 'like nearly all other Australians' he 'knew little about the convict past' of his own country. Not until the publication in 1962 of the first volume of *A History of Australia* by Manning Clark did Hughes recall gaining any glimpse of the darker side of history; his own book is important for its popular and evocative presentation of the central facts. Other critical work includes *Frank Auerbach* (1990), *Nothing if Not Critical* (1990), and *Barcelona* (1992), a historical and cultural portrait, emphasizing the city as the chief seat of Spanish art nouveau, and coinciding with the Olympic Games in that city. Hughes provoked much debate and a strong critical response with *The Culture of Complaint: The Fraying of America* (1993), three long essays on contemporary American culture which he perceives as dominated by politically correct notions of art and literature as therapeutically functional.

HUGHES, Ted (Edward James) (1930–), British poet, born in Mytholmroyd in West Yorkshire, an area drawn upon in much of his poetry; he was educated at Pembroke College, Cambridge. In 1956 he married Sylvia *Plath, with whom he spent two years in the USA. He returned to Britain in 1959 and eventually settled in Devon, where he has latterly divided his time between writing and farming. The hyperbolic vigour and innate accomplishment evident in *The*

Hawk in the Rain (1957), his first collection of verse, rapidly established him as one of the most interesting younger poets of the late 1950s; its treatments of animal subjects were particularly striking, vividly affirming the natural forces of vitality with which modern civilization has diminished contact. The book was seen by numerous critics as embodying an alternative to what they perceived as the arid intellectualism of the *Movement; Charles *Tomlinson remarked that 'Hughes has . . . a sense of nature, a sense of that other England which the London-bound writer has forgotten about'. His second volume, **Lupercal* (1960), displayed increased technical control and imaginative power. The insistence on the inseparability of beauty and brutality in the collection challenged pastoral idealizations of nature and anticipated the more extreme vision of **Wodwo* (1967). The apocalyptic metaphysics adumbrated in that collection link it with the parables of survival and destruction in **Crow* (1970), which forms the summation of the violence apparent in much of Hughes's preceding writing. A more socially realistic milieu forms the setting for the long prose poem *Gaudete* (1977); its bizarre narrative centres on events in a rural parish where supernatural agents bring about a revival of ancient fertility rites. *Remains of Elmet* (1979, with F. Godwin) contributes to the tradition of *topographical poetry in its comprehensive poetic and photographic evocation of the human and natural characters of his native region of the Pennines; the perceptions of decay, transience, and stoical endurance in his previous poetry of the area strongly inform the collection. Local elements are also central to the long title sequence of *Moortown* (1979; revised edition 1989), which draws with great immediacy on his experiences as a farmer. *Wolfwatching* (1989) retrieves the imaginative energies and thematic range of earlier volumes, extending the overall scope of his work through the emotional directness and clear social orientation of several notable poems. Other collections by Hughes include *Season Songs* (1976), *The River* (1983, with P. Keen), and *Rain-Charm for the Duchy* (1992). *New Selected Poems: 1957–1994* appeared in 1995. Hughes's critical prose and essays have been collected in several volumes, including *Shakespeare and the Goddess of Complete Being* (1992), *A Dancer to God: Tribute to T. S. Eliot* (1992), and *Winter Pollen: Occasional Prose* (1994; ed. William *Scammell). He has also written many books of verse and prose for children and juveniles and worked prolifically as a dramatist; among his plays are a version of Seneca's *Oedipus* (1968) and *Orghast* (1971). He was appointed Poet Laureate in 1984.

HUGO, Richard (Franklin) (1923–82), American poet, born in an impoverished district of Seattle; he saw wartime service in the US Air Force then studied at the University of Washington with Theodore *Roethke, an important early influence. After working for the Boeing Company, Hugo became director of the Writing Program at the University of Montana from 1964 until his death. Very much a regionalist, whether writing of his native Pacific north-west or his adopted Montana, he nevertheless employed a fictive rather than a literal approach. *A Run of Jacks* (1961) and *The Death of the Kapowsin Tavern* (1965) have a hard, somewhat isolated masculine stance counterpointed by a rich imagery of natural beauty, as in his much-admired poem 'Duwamish', about a boy wandering beside a trout stream. Roethke's legacy is also evident in the formal qualities of sound and rhythm which greatly enhance the slow interior drama of Hugo's best work. This is exemplified by 'Degrees of Gray in Philipsburg', from *The Lady in Kicking Horse Reservoir* (1973), also typical in its viewing of a small, dismal town as a wider symbol of personal and psychological tension. The poems in *31 Letters and 13 Dreams* (1977), written in the aftermath of Hugo's need to seek treatment for alcoholism, address friends such as Denise *Levertov and James *Wright from specific towns, on a journey in search of self-reconciliation. His final poems are in *Making Certain It Goes On: The Collected Poems of Richard Hugo* (1984). A work of autobiography, *The Real West Marginal Way*, also appeared posthumously in 1986. The best criticism of Hugo's achievement is *We Are Called Human* (1982) by Michael S. Allen.

HULL, Maud, see ROMANTIC FICTION.

Hull Poets: a group of poets active in that city between 1975 and 1981; their work was collected in Douglas *Dunn's edition of *A Rumoured City* (1982), for which Philip *Larkin wrote a foreword. Dunn was closely involved in the emergence of much of their writing. Of the poets featured in *A Rumoured City*, Tony *Flynn and Peter *Didsbury had published substantial collections shortly before the anthology's appearance; Sean *O'Brien, Douglas *Houston, Frank Redpath, and T. F. Griffin subsequently produced volumes to favourable critical receptions, and work by Ian Gregson, Margot K. Juby, Tony Petch, and Genny Rahtz has been widely published in periodicals. Other poets closely associated with the above include George Kendrick, whose *Bicycle Tyre in a Tall Tree* (1974) won high acclaim, and Julian Smith, whose *Sampler* appeared in 1992. No clear similarities of manner are identifiable in the work of the Hull Poets, though their best work is noted for its imagination and technical accomplishment in both traditional and innovative verse forms. The eclectic periodical *Bête Noire*, edited by John Osborne, has sustained a high level of poetic activity in the city through the successful series of poetry readings which commenced in 1985.

HULME, Keri (1947–), New Zealand writer of Maori, Scots, and English ancestry, born in Christchurch, educated at Canterbury University. Among other employment she has worked in the postal service and as a director for New Zealand television. *Silences Between: Moeraki Conversations* (1982) was a collection of poetry and prose. Hulme achieved international fame with *The Bone People* (1983; Booker Prize), a dazzlingly powerful modern fable of epic scope and passionate commitment. As Hulme herself is well aware, the book in many respects defies categorization in its exploitation of techniques and expectations drawn as much from the thriller as from a wide range of consciously national and mythic writing. Violent, amusing, and fiercely independent in many ways, the book has aroused much healthy debate about its author's status as a Maori writer and about the range of personal, national, and mythopoeic claims it stakes. She has since become recognized as an important new voice in New Zealand literature. *The Windeater/TeKaihau*, a collection of prose and poetry, and *Lost Possessions* both appeared in 1985. A further collection of poetry, *Strands*, was published in 1992. She has also published *Homeplaces* (1989), essays on New Zealand's South Island, with photographs by Robin Morrison.

HULME, T(homas) E(rnest) (1883–1917), British philosopher and aesthetician, born at Endon, Staffordshire, educated at St John's College, Cambridge, from which he was sent down in 1904. He subsequently studied privately in London and Belgium. In 1909 he convened meetings of a group of poets which included Ezra *Pound and F. S. *Flint. Hulme's rejection of Romanticism and his emphasis on clarity and precision in poetic imagery provided the theoretical basis for *Imagism. His 'Complete Poetical Works' of five poems, intended to illustrate his innovative conceptions, were published in the **New Age* in 1912. His translation of *Introduction to Metaphysics* by Henri Bergson, who was a major influence on his thought, appeared in 1913. After joining the army in 1914, his 'war notes' were published in the *New Age*, expressing his opposition to pacifism and its philosophical implications. He was killed near Nieuport in 1917. The stress on discipline and austerity and the subscription to the idea of Original Sin which characterize Hulme's combination of *Modernism and conservatism were widely influential; in 1924 T. S. *Eliot, whose intellectual and ethical position came to resemble Hulme's closely, described him in a **Criterion* editorial as 'classical, reactionary and revolutionary . . . the antipodes of the eccentric, tolerant and democratic mind of the end of the century'. Herbert *Read edited two volumes of Hulme's works, *Speculations* (1924) and *Notes on Language and Style* (1929); *Further Speculations*, edited by S. Hynes, was published in 1955. Biographical and critical studies include Michael *Roberts's *T. E. Hulme* (1938) and Alun R. Jones's *The Life and Opinions of T. E. Hulme* (1960).

Human Factor, The, a novel by Graham *Greene, published in 1978. A return late in Greene's career to the genre of spy fiction, *The Human Factor* partly resembles **Our Man in Havana* (1958). 'We have our own country', remarks Maurice Castle's black South African wife, Sarah: as in the earlier novel, Secret Service chiefs appear cynical, absurd Machiavels, and it is love and loyalty to individuals, rather than states or systems, which is most valued. *The Human Factor* differs, however, in ending bleakly, with Castle isolated from Sarah at the end of a broken telephone line, in a glacial Moscow to which he defects after—as readers very gradually discover throughout—years of passing secrets to the Russians in recompense for Communist assistance in rescuing Sarah from the South African secret police.

Greene talks of attempting in this novel a spy story free of conventional violence and glamour, and extensive detail of ordinary life in drab, contemporary Britain helps establish MI6 almost as an ordinary job for a Berkhamsted commuter. Like Castle himself, *The Human Factor* is not 'James Bond minded'; its complex plot, plausible characters, and interest in the intricate power balances of the Cold War place it closer to the work of Greene's admirer John *le Carré than to Ian *Fleming. While making the spy genre naturalistic, Greene also makes of the 'traitor', Castle, an entirely natural, engaging figure. Greene was a friend of Kim Philby, one of his chiefs during his own Secret Service work: sometimes referred to as 'The Third Man' when he defected to Moscow in 1963, Philby quoted Greene's *The Confidential Agent* (1939) in defence of his actions. Greene denies Philby's relevance to *The Human Factor*, but records abandoning the novel (begun in the 1960s) until his defection was partly forgotten, and critics continue to assume a connection. Biographical or not, its well-tried themes of loyalty, betrayal, and individual responsibility within a heartless history make it among the best of Greene's late novels.

Humboldt's Gift, a novel by Saul *Bellow, published in 1975, winner of the Pulitzer Prize. Set in the affluent suburbs of Chicago where even the wives of mafiosi are taking Ph.D.s, the book places two generations of writers at its centre. One is represented by the anguished modernist, Von Humboldt Fleischer, an intellectually omnivorous poet who dies in poverty. The other is exemplified by his disciple Charlie Citrine, a famous dramatist who succeeds in becoming wealthy in the Chicago of the materialist 1970s. The novel is related from Citrine's perspective, reminiscing about his friendship with Von Humboldt. However, Citrine refuses to succumb to the chaos of the materialist world and its emptiness of morality, by adopting a gnosticism in late life. Citrine clings to his memories of Von Humboldt as a means of fending off the harassment and demands of a variety of people, moving inward to protect himself from the threats of physical violence, and the pressures of materialism and mere physicality. Endeavouring to fuse a transcendental philosophy with modern commercial America, the novel was a mixed success, while the combination of the fantastic and the realistic produced a varied response from contemporary reviewers.

HUMPHREY, William (1924–), American novelist, born in Clarksville, Texas. Humphrey's first work of fiction, *The Last Husband and Other Stories*, was published in 1953; his novel *Home from the Hill* (1958) was a best seller and was made into a film. His fiction is very much associated with his native Texas; both *Home from the Hill* and his later novel, *The Ordways* (1965), are preoccupied with Texan history and culture. *The Collected Stories of William Humphrey* (1976) brings together the best of his short fiction; other novels of note include *A Time and a Place* (1968) and *Proud Flesh* (1973).

HUMPHREYS, Emyr (1919–), Welsh novelist, poet, and critic, born in Prestatyn, the son of a Flintshire schoolmaster, educated at the University of Aberystwyth. In 1939 he signed on as a conscientious objector to work on farms in Pembrokeshire and North Wales. Later he worked as a teacher, drama producer, and lecturer. His first novel, *The Little Kingdom* (1946), established the grave, inquiring, yet often lyrical tone of later work. Pre-eminent among his earlier novels is *A Toy Epic* (1958), which interweaves the first-person stories of the lives of three Welsh boys (a vicar's son, a farmer's son, and an urban working-class boy) up to the threshold of manhood, all forming a paradigm of Welsh life. The novel is indebted to Virginia Woolf's *The *Waves*. Other novels of note are *A Man's Estate* (1955), *Outside the House of Baal* (1965), and *Jones* (1984). At his best Humphreys has great poetic insight into the puritan and into the ordinary but serious mind. *The Taliesin Tradition* (1983) is a study of the Welsh character over the centuries. *Salt of the Earth* (1985) opens a sequence of novels about Welsh social and political life from the 1920s onwards.

HUNT, (Isobel) Violet (1866–1942), English novelist and biographer, born in Durham. The daughter of the minor painter William Albert Hunt, she studied art, and grew up among the Pre-Raphaelites of the 'Rossetti circle'. A renowned society hostess, who encouraged D. H. *Lawrence among others, and a friend of H. G. *Wells and Henry *James, she wrote much literary journalism and later campaigned actively for women's suffrage. Her close friendship with Ford Madox *Ford is recorded in her autobiography, *The Flurried Years* (1926; US title *I Have This To Say*). She was probably the model for Florence in Ford's *The *Good Soldier* (1915), and the two collaborated on *Zeppelin Nights* (1915), a book of historical sketches. She is best known for *The Wife of Rossetti* (1932), a biography of the tragic Elizabeth Siddal, based on her own memories. Her many novels include *The Maiden's Progress* (1894), *Sooner or Later* (1904), based on one of her love affairs, *The White Rose of Weary Leaf* (1908), and *The Tiger Skin* (1924). She also wrote the macabre *Tales of the Uneasy* (1911).

HUNTER, Evan, see MCBAIN, ED.

HURSTON, Zora Neale (1901–60), American novelist and folklorist, born in the all-black township of Eatonville, Florida, which was to provide a basis for episodes in her best-known work, **Their Eyes Were Watching God* (1937). Hurston left home in her teens and worked as a maid and wardrobe girl for a touring Gilbert and Sullivan troupe before becoming a part-time student at Howard University. During her twenties she published several short stories and essays, gaining the attention of leading figures of the *Harlem Renaissance. Along with a number of these black writers, including Langston *Hughes, she was instrumental in the founding of the short-lived literary magazine *Fire!*, which took the view that black writing should not be exclusively preoccupied with confronting the problem of racial oppression. In the late 1920s and 1930s she became involved in anthropological field work on the living conditions of black Americans and in 1935 published *Mules and Men*, an anthropological study of black American folklore. This was followed by a similar study of Caribbean folklore, *Tell My Horse* (1938). It is, however, as a writer of fiction that Hurston is best known, and her finest novel, *Their Eyes Were Watching God*, a work which has grown in reputation since her death, is an important contribution to writing that asserts the independent selfhood of black women. Hurston also published *Jonah's Gourd Vine* (1934, her first novel); *Moses, Man of the Mountain* (1939), a novel which is as much concerned with the importance of Moses in black mythologies as in the Old Testament; *Seraph on the Suwanee* (1948), a novel about white characters; and *Dust Tracks on a Road* (1942), an 'autobiography', whose factual accuracy has been called into question. During her later years illness affected her ability to support herself and she died in comparative poverty. See also ETHNICITY.

HUTCHINSON, (William Patrick Henry) Pearse (1927–), Irish poet, born in Glasgow of Irish parents; he grew up in Dublin, where he was educated at University College. In 1951 he became a translator with the International Labour Organization, and was a drama critic for Irish radio and television from 1957 to 1968. His first collection of poetry, *Tongue Without Hands* (1963), was followed by a volume of poems in Irish entitled *Faoistin Bhacach* (1969; lit. 'imperfect confession'). There followed *Expansions* (1969), *Watching the Morning Grow* (1973), *The Frost Is All Over* (1975), *Climbing the Light* (1985), and *The Soul that Kissed the Body* (1990), a selection of his verse in Irish accompanied by his own translations. Hutchinson's early poetry was predominantly written in strict forms and was notable for its vivid reflections on his Irish background and his experiences of Spain, where he lived in the 1950s. Social preoccupations are treated in his later work, in which more relaxed and expressive verse forms are developed. His sustained critique of modern Ireland is most intense in the satires of *Climbing the Light*. Among his other works are the translations of Galaico-Portuguese love poetry in *Friend Songs* (1970).

HUTCHINSON, R(ay) C(oryton) (1907–75), English novelist, born in London, educated at Oriel College, Oxford. A fastidious craftsman, he wrote seventeen novels in all, but is best known for *Testament* (1938), his epic work about the Russian Revolution. Though conservative in outlook, his imaginative sympathy brought home to many readers the great significance, particularly their spiritual implications, of revolutionary changes in the Soviet Union. Early novels include *The Unforgotten Prisoner* (1933), set in Weimar Germany; *Shining Scabbard* (1936); *The Fire and the Wood* (1940), which focuses on Dr Josef Zepichmann, a young idealist straight from medical school facing persecution from the Nazis; and *Elephant & Castle* (1949). Later novels include *The Stepmother* (1955); *A Child Possessed* (1964), which deals sympathetically with a mentally defective child; and *Rising* (1976), his last novel, which is set in a Latin American country and, like *Testament*, deals with revolutionary politics from a conservative viewpoint.

HUXLEY, Aldous (Leonard) (1894–1963), English novelist, essayist, and short-story writer, born in Godalming, Surrey, into a family distinguished by scientific and literary attainments; Matthew Arnold was a great-uncle, T. H. Huxley his grandfather, the novelist Mrs Humphry Ward an aunt, and the biologist Julian *Huxley his brother. He was educated at Eton and at Balliol College, Oxford, where, in spite of severely restricted vision, he took a First in English in 1916 and published a volume of poems, *The Burning Wheel*. He began contributing reviews and articles to *The Athenaeum*, edited by John Middleton *Murry, later writing on diverse subjects for *Vanity Fair* and other magazines. Huxley's stories in *Limbo* (1920) and *Mortal Coils* (1922) were well received, but he came to prominence as a satirical novelist to whom the epithets 'witty' and 'cynical' were invariably applied. Between 1921 and 1939 he wrote the novels on which his literary reputation mainly rests, analysing the ideas, mores, and personalities of the age with iconoclastic virtuosity. **Crome Yellow* (1921) is a Peacockian 'discussion novel' informed by Huxley's acquaintance with Lady Ottoline *Morrell's set at Garsington; **Antic Hay* (1923) shocked and delighted its audience with a debunking tone, fashionable despair, and open treatment of infidelity, drugs, jazz, and drunkenness amongst London's artistic bohemia; *Those Barren Leaves* (1925) is another Country House satire, but located in Italy. Huxley subsequently found his ideal form in the discussion-novel-of-ideas, especially in **Point Counter Point* (1928), a kaleidoscopic novel orchestrating multiple viewpoints. **Eyeless in Gaza* (1936) signalled a conversion to more spiritual interests. Between these large, ambitious books was a most influential work, **Brave New World* (1932), which combined scientific prophecy with a parable about a future World State (see UTOPIA AND ANTI-UTOPIA). Huxley's pacifism led him to join the Peace Pledge Union in the mid-1930s, and he addressed the causes of war in essays collected in *Ends and Means* (1937). He left Europe in 1937 for a lecture tour of the USA with his friend Gerald Heard and remained in Southern California from then on, meeting *Isherwood and becoming fascinated by Eastern religious mysticism. His first novel set in America, however, *After Many a Summer Dies the Swan* (1939), characteristically depicts the oddities of people he encountered, a Hearst-like millionaire ('Joe Stoyte') and Heard as the mystic 'Propter'. Huxley wrote screenplays for Hollywood, including *Jane Eyre* and *Pride and Prejudice*, and continued to operate in a variety of genres. Although increasingly his best work tended to be non-fiction, his concern above all was the communication of ideas. He discussed modern technology in *Science, Liberty and Peace* (1946), the aftermath of nuclear war in the novel *Ape and Essence* (1948), and studied supposed diabolic possession and the priest Urban Grandier in *The Devils of Loudun* (1952). Huxley experimented with hallucinogenic drugs, including mescalin and LSD, and elaborated on their aesthetic and moral implications, their potential for access to visionary experiences, in *The Doors of Perception* (1954) and *Heaven and Hell* (1956). His Californian home burnt down in 1961, but Huxley rescued the manuscript of *Island* (1962), a final attempt to frame utopian themes within a novelistic format. The most common critique of Huxley has been a charge of artistic and emotional inadequacy, that he fell away from his early incisive mode of satire towards a more nebulous later one of mysticism. Frequently labelled a 'novelist of ideas' or a representative of the 1920s, Huxley's literary standing declined during the 1950s, with his style tending towards prolixity, his encyclopaedic approaches inviting parody. But Isaiah *Berlin called him 'one of the major intellectual emancipators' of his generation, and the books produced up to 1939 assure Huxley of a place amongst the major English social satirists.

HUXLEY, Elspeth (Josceline) (1907–), British writer, born in London, brought up mainly in Kenya; her studies at the universities of Reading and Cornell were recorded in *Love among the Daughters* (1968). She has served on the Empire Marketing Board and the BBC Advisory Council and travelled widely in Africa and America with her husband, Gervas Huxley (a cousin of Aldous *Huxley). Among her many books on African history, politics, and agriculture are *White Man's Country: Lord Delamere and the Making of Kenya* (1935), *African Dilemmas* (1948), *Livingstone and His African Journeys* (1974), *Out in the Midday Sun: My Kenya* (1985), and *The Nine Faces of Kenya* (1990). Perhaps her greatest achievements are *The Flame Trees of Thika* (1959) and *The Mottled Lizard* (1962; US title *On the Edge of the Rift: Memories of Kenya*), which vividly describe the life of her family and fellow British settlers in Africa. Her novels include *The Walled City* (1948) and *A Thing to Love* (1954), both reflecting cultural and political tensions among native and European communities in Africa; and several entertaining detective novels, mainly with African settings, such as *Murder at Government House* (1937), *Murder on Safari* (1938), *Death of an Aryan* (1939; reprinted as *The African Poison Murders*, 1986), and *The Merry Hippo* (1963; US title *The Incident at the Merry Hippo*).

HUXLEY, Sir Julian (Sorrell) (1887–1975), British biologist and writer, brother of Aldous *Huxley, born in

London, educated at Eton and at Balliol College, Oxford. Of his many public appointments he was professor of zoology at King's College, London (1925–7), secretary of the Zoological Society (1935–42), and Director-General of UNESCO (1946–8). With his rare gift for communicating the findings of science to the layreader without compromising scientific exactitude he became widely known through his broadcasts and for several books that have lasted despite subsequent scientific advance. These include *Essays of a Biologist* (1923), *Animal Biology* (1927; with J. B. S. *Haldane), *The Science of Life* (1929; with G. P. and H. G. *Wells), *Soviet Genetics and World Science* (1949), and *Evolution in Action* (1953). *Bird-Watching and Bird Behaviour* (1930) and *The Captive Shrew and Other Poems of a Biologist* (1932), amongst other works, reveal his fascination for the natural world.

HWANG, David Henry (1957–), American playwright and screenwriter, born in Los Angeles, educated at Stanford University. His first play, *F.O.B* (1979), which won an Obie Award for the best Off-Broadway play of 1980–1, was followed by *The Dance and The Railroad* (1980), concerning a strike by Chinese railroad labourers in 1867, and *Family Devotions* (1981), which satirizes dogmatic religious faith in its portrayal of a wealthy, fundamentalist Chinese-American family in conflict with their newly arrived Chinese relatives. *Sound and Beauty* (1983), a double bill, marked a departure from Hwang's Chinese-American themes: the first part, *The Sound of a Voice*, was set in seventeenth-century Japan; the second, *The House of Sleeping Beauties*, placed Nobel Prize-winner Yasunari Kawabata in the setting of his own novella and was published together with Hwang's first three plays in *Broken Promises: Four Plays* (1983). *Rich Relations* and *As The Crow Flies* were produced in 1986. His play *M. Butterfly* won the 1988 Tony Award for the best Broadway play and was later filmed; loosely based on a real event, the play focuses on the revelation that a French diplomat had had a twenty-year relationship with a woman who was not only a spy for the Chinese government but a man. Hwang collaborated with composer Phillip Glass in *1000 Airplanes on the Roof* (1988) and wrote the libretto for Glass's opera *The Voyage* (1992). His most recent work has included several screenplays and the plays *Bondage* (1992) and *Face Value* (1993). See also ASIAN-AMERICAN LITERATURE.

HYDE, Douglas (1860–1949), authority on Gaelic and leader of the *Irish Revival, born near Castlerea, Co. Roscommon, where he learned Gaelic as a youth; he was educated at Trinity College, Dublin. His early publications include the Gaelic miscellany *Leabhar Sgeulaigheachta* (lit. 'the book of story-telling') (1889) and *Beside the Fire* (1890), his translations of traditional stories. He was the principal founder in 1893 of the Gaelic League, of which he remained president until 1915. *Love Songs of Connacht* (1893), which contained verse translations of Gaelic poems alongside the original texts, was widely influential, offering many writers imaginative access to Irish poetic idioms. In *The Story of Early Gaelic Literature* (1895) and *A Literary History of Ireland* (1899) he established the historical authenticity of Irish literary culture. In 1909 he became the first professor of Modern Irish at the National University. The best-known of his numerous plays in Gaelic, which were translated into English by Lady *Gregory, is *Casadh an tSugain* ('The Twisting of the Rope') (1901). Several of his works were staged at the *Abbey Theatre, of which he was vice-president. In 1938 he was elected the first president of the Republic of Ireland.

HYDE, Robin, pseudonym of Iris Guiver WILKINSON (1906–39), New Zealand novelist and poet, born in Cape Town, South Africa, shortly before her parents settled in Wellington, New Zealand, where she was educated at Wellington Girls' College. Her novels *Passport to Hell* (1936) and *Nor the Years Condemn* (1938) are sharp historical portraits of New Zealand life in the early twentieth century, and *Check to Your King* (1936) is a remarkable recreation of the life and times of Charles de Thierry, 'Sovereign Chief of New Zealand'. She regarded *Wednesday's Children* (1937) as her first 'straight' novel. It was *The Godwits Fly* (1938), a complex and moving study of colonial sensibility through the fortunes of a settler family not unlike her own, which was to be her finest work, and the novel is now recognized as an important treatment of this enduring New Zealand theme. Her journey through China during the Sino/Japanese War and *en route* to England, in 1938, produced the fine book *Dragon Rampant* in 1939, the year she took her own life. *Houses by the Sea and the Later Poems* (1952) was a posthumous verse collection, also reprinting the best of her early verse from *Persephone in Winter* (1937). *Selected Poems* and the autobiographical fragment *A Home in This World* were both published in 1984.

I

I, Claudius, a novel by Robert *Graves, published in 1934. The book charts the unlikely fortunes of Claudius, who succeeds in surviving the reigns of Tiberius and Caligula before reluctantly becoming emperor in its closing stages. The narrative purports to be the emperor's lost autobiography, and is continued in *Claudius the God*, which appeared in the same year. Graves read very widely in preparation for the book's composition, conceiving of it as a reconstruction of Rome in the first century AD and intending as great a degree of authenticity as possible: Tacitus, Suetonius, Seneca, and Josephus are among the authors to whom he referred for details relating to Roman customs, politics, law, trade, and military affairs. The result is notable for its unrelenting portrayal of vice, corruption, and horror at various levels in Roman society; Claudius's tone as narrator resembles the cool and laconic manner Graves developed in **Goodbye to All That*. Although he and Laura *Riding tended to dismiss the work as a pot-boiler, it is remarkably well crafted and maximizes the effect of its strong plot and richness of historical detail; it was awarded the Hawthornden Prize and the James Tait Black Memorial Prize in 1935 and hailed as a masterpiece. Constantly in print since 1934, *I, Claudius* enjoyed a period of enormous popularity when it was adapted for television in 1976. Randall *Jarrell called it 'a good book singular enough to be immortal'.

Iceman Cometh, The, a play by Eugene *O'Neill, produced in 1946. The play marked O'Neill's return to the theatre after a twelve-year absence, and though widely heralded as a masterpiece, many critics felt it to be too long. A brilliant revival in 1956 did much to establish its reputation as one of O'Neill's greatest plays. In a seedy tavern run by the ironically named Harry Hope, a group of down-and-outs nurse their illusions with alcohol, bound together by the camaraderie of collective failure and hopeless pipe-dreams of the future. They are joined by a familiar companion, Theodore Hickman, an outwardly successful hardware salesman, commonly known as Hickey. Hickey's customary joke used to secure his drinking with the others is that his wife is with the iceman, but on this occasion he has come to threaten their composure with the news that he has given up drink. With a new-found peace of mind, Hickey discards his former illusions and advises the others to follow his example. As the play unfolds, Hickey reveals that he has murdered his wife Evelyn, out of hatred and marital despair, and that the 'iceman' is Death. When the police come for Hickey his companions fall on the idea that he is insane, and bolstered by this latest illusion, return to their customary world of alcohol and pipe-dreams. The immediate source of this starkly realistic drama was O'Neill's short story of 1917, 'Tomorrow', though it also draws on his knowledge of European theatre, of Gorky, Ibsen, and Strindberg.

IHIMAERA, Witi (Tame) (1944–), New Zealand Maori novelist and short-story writer, born at Gisborne, educated at Auckland University, and at Victoria University, Wellington. Ihimaera worked for many years for the Ministry of External Affairs and has held posts in many countries. His story collection *Pounamu, Pounamu* (1972) was the first collection of stories by a Maori writer to be published, and has proved popular in furnishing an image of Maori culture and identity. *Tangi* (1973), the first novel by a Maori writer, and *Whanau* (1974) continue his exploration of his people's rural culture; *Whanau* was also the basis for his 1984 opera *Waituhi—The Life of the Village*. With *The New Net Goes Fishing* (1977) Ihimaera began a new trilogy treating Maoris in an urban setting. He edited, with D. S. Long, *Into the World of Light: An Anthology of Maori Writing* (1982). Later fiction includes *The Matriarch* (1986), *The Whale Rider* (1987), *Dear Miss Mansfield: A Tribute to Katherine Mansfield* (1989, short stories), and *Bulibashi: King of the Gypsies* (1994). *Introducing Witi Ihimaera* (1984), by Richard Corballis and Simon Garrett, provides a valuable perspective of his work. He is also editor of *Te Ao Marama* (from 1992), a series of anthologies of contemporary Maori writing.

IKE, (Vincent) Chukwuemeka (1931–), Nigerian novelist, born in Eastern Nigeria, educated at Government College, Ibadan, and Stanford University, California. He has produced the authoritative *University Development in Africa: The Nigerian Experience* (1976), and has held several important administrative academic posts in Nigeria. Most of his novels are satirical and deftly comic exposés of university life in West Africa, and could be described as African versions of the *campus novel. Ike's novels of university life, which have wide social significance and display a radically populist stance, include *Toads for Supper* (1965), about a philandering undergraduate; *The Naked Gods* (1970), which focuses on academic intrigues among British and American expatriates; and *The Chicken Chasers* (1980). Other novels include *The Potter's Wheel*

(1976), about a boy's spartan regime in a Nigerian school; *Expo 77* (1980), a detective story which investigates examination leaks; and *Sunset at Dawn* (1976), which explodes myths about the Nigerian Civil War (1967–70) in its sympathetic portrayal of Dr Kanu, a Biafran official, and Fatima, his northern Nigerian wife.

I Know Why the Caged Bird Sings, the first volume of a multi-volume autobiography by Maya *Angelou, published in 1970. The book broke ground for African-American women writers in terms of critical acclaim and large sales. It is a powerful and often painful evocation of Angelou's childhood in the 1930s and 1940s, mostly in the black community of the US Deep South. As the book opens, the author—then Marguerite Johnson, lonely, shy, self-conscious—and her older brother Bailey, aged three and four respectively, offspring of a failed marriage, travel from California with a note entrusting them to the care of their grandmother in Stamps, Arkansas. They little understand adult codes or the harsh realities of segregated society, and the world to which they become used is disrupted four years later when they are reunited with their mother in St Louis. There begins a sequence of events central to the author's journey towards adolescence: the eight-year-old Marguerite is raped by her mother's lover Mr Freeman, but at a subsequent trial the confused child denies it. When Freeman is later found murdered, Maya is so traumatized by the belief that she is to blame for lying that she becomes a voluntary mute, and is banished back to Stamps, where after five years Mrs Flowers, 'the aristocrat of Black Stamps', helps release her from silence by encouraging her love of reading. In 1941, the children join their mother and her new husband in San Francisco, where Maya learns the ghetto ethic of survival and begins to take power over her own destiny. An exploration of her sexuality leaves her pregnant at 16, but the birth of her son brings an ability to assume control of her own life and creativity, free at last from a caged existence.

ILES, Francis, see BERKELEY, ANTHONY.

Illywhacker, see CAREY, PETER.

Imagism, the first of numerous concerted movements associated with Anglo-American poetic *Modernism. T. E. *Hulme was influential in the emergence of Imagism's aesthetic and technical characters, which were summed up in the tripartite declaration of aims formulated by Ezra *Pound and F. S. *Flint and published in **Poetry* (Chicago) in 1913: '1) Direct treatment of the "thing", whether subjective or objective; 2) To use absolutely no word that does not contribute to the presentation; 3) As regarding rhythm: to compose in the sequence of the musical phrase, not in the sequence of a metronome.' Pound coined the term in his preface to 'The Complete Poetical Works of T. E. Hulme', which appeared as an appendix to his *Ripostes* in 1912: 'As for the future', he wrote, '*Les Imagistes* . . . have that in their keeping.' In its clarity, concentrated precision, and disciplined formal freedom, the best work of the Imagists was highly successful as an antidote to the debilitated poetic conventions of the nineteenth century and to the subjective excesses of the Symboliste poets. *Des Imagistes* (1914), edited by Pound, was the movement's first anthology, containing work by himself and ten other poets, among whom were Hilda *Doolittle, Flint, Richard *Aldington, Amy *Lowell, W. C. *Williams, F. M. *Ford, and James *Joyce. Pound wrote of the image as an 'intellectual and emotional complex in an instant of time', conceiving of Imagism as a bodying forth of subjective states in externally apprehended particulars; these ideas are illustrated by his 'In a Station of the Metro', a well-known example of the mode's characteristic brevity and incisiveness, which reads in its entirety as follows: 'The apparition of these faces in the crowd; | Petals on a wet, black bough.' Doolittle's early poetry is frequently regarded as the *locus classicus* of Imagism for its crystalline descriptive concision in which imaginative and emotional energies are actively inherent. Three further anthologies all entitled *Some Imagists* were published in 1915, 1916, and 1917, under the editorship of Amy Lowell, who became the principal promoter of the movement and created growing interest in it in America. For Pound and others, however, Lowell brought about the degeneration of Imagism to 'Amy-gism'. The essential flowering was over by 1916, the year in which Doolittle's *Sea Garden* and Pound's *Lustra* appeared, which, with Flint's *Cadences* (1915), contain the best examples of Imagist poetry. In its emphasis on the primacy of the poetic image and its dedication to purging poetry of imprecise diction, metrical predictability, and tendencies to vague abstraction, Imagism's influence over poetry in English in the twentieth century has been pervasive and enduring. *Imagist Poetry* (1972), edited by Peter Jones, contains extracts from the movement's theoretical statements and prefaces as well as selections from the work in their *anthologies.

Inadmissible Evidence, a play by John *Osborne, performed in 1964, published in 1965. The central character, Bill Maitland, is a London solicitor suffering a middle-age crisis that threatens to become a mental, emotional, and spiritual breakdown. The play begins with his nightmare, in which he is in court accused of having published an obscenity, namely his life, and continues with confrontations, in the flesh and on the telephone, with his clerks, his mistress, his daughter, his wife, and others. He ends rejected by almost everybody, including himself, awaiting a visit from the Law Society, which is investigating his dubious professional ethics. Though Maitland was originally seen by critics largely as an ageing version of Jimmy Porter in **Look Back in Anger*, and the play as a critique of Britain in the 1960s, subsequent revival has tended to suggest that its principal merit is Osborne's rich characterization of a protagonist variously actuated by anger, self-pity, self-hatred, and the need for love.

In Cold Blood, see CAPOTE, TRUMAN.

Index on Censorship, a monthly journal established in 1972 by Writers and Scholars International, a group dedicated to recording and analysing the extent and effects of state censorship throughout the world; Stephen *Spender and the Soviet dissident Pavel Litvinov were directly instrumental in the formation of the organization in 1971. Having begun under Michael Scammell's editorship as *Index*, in 1975 it became known by its present title. South Africa, Central and Eastern Europe, South America, and China have supplied many of the detailed case histories of censorship which form an essential feature of the magazine. It also publishes examples of prose fiction, drama, poetry, and documentary writing by authors whose work has been suppressed in their own countries. Václav Havel, Alexander Solzhenitsyn, Andrei Voznesensky, and Wole *Soyinka have been among the contributors with direct experience of censorship. Other leading authors who have supplied essays and articles are Arthur *Miller, George Seferis, Adewale *Maja-Pearce, Nadine *Gordimer, Samuel *Beckett, and Noam *Chomsky. The subjects of the interviews which occasionally appear have included Graham *Greene, Salman *Rushdie, and Joseph *Brodsky.

INGE, William (Motter) (1913–73), American dramatist, born in Independence, Kansas, educated at the University of Kansas and the George Peabody College for Teachers. Inge worked as a general arts critic for the St Louis *Star-Times* when he met Tennessee *Williams, with whose encouragement he wrote his first play, *Farther off from Heaven* (1947). His second play, *Come Back, Little Sheba* (1950), was a popular success on Broadway; equally successful were *Picnic* (1953; Pulitzer Prize), *Bus Stop* (1955), and *The Dark at the Top of the Stairs* (1957). He won an Oscar for the screenplay of his film *Splendour in the Grass* (1961). His subject was the sexual repression of small-town Midwesterners; but his failure to move away from this dominant concern led to his decreasing popularity from the 1960s onwards and, convinced he had lost his gift, Inge committed suicide at the age of 60. Several of his plays were successfully adapted for the screen: *Come Back, Little Sheba* (1953) starred Shirley Booth and Burt Lancaster, *Picnic* (1956) starred William Holden, Rosalind Russell, Kim Novak, and Susan Strasberg, and *Bus Stop* (1956) provided Marilyn Monroe with one of her most celebrated roles.

Inheritors, The, see GOLDING, WILLIAM.

Inklings, The, see CARPENTER, HUMPHREY.

INNES, Michael, see STEWART, J. I. M.

Inspector Calls, An, a play by J. B. *Priestley, first performed in Moscow in 1945. Although the play is set in 1912, it clearly reflects the anti-establishment views of an author committed to the election of a socialist party. A man claiming to be a local policeman, Inspector Goole, arrives at the house of Arthur Birling, wealthy Conservative industrialist and ex-Lord Mayor of Brumley, who has been playing the host at a private dinner to celebrate the engagement of his daughter, Sheila. Goole announces that he has come to investigate the suicide of an impoverished, pregnant young woman, Eva Smith, and proceeds to demonstrate that those present are responsible for it. The chain begins with Birling, who sacked her for helping to organize a strike for higher wages; continues with Sheila, who successfully demanded her dismissal after unfairly losing her temper with the girl, then an assistant in a department store; passes through Sheila's fiancé, Gerald Croft, who made her his mistress; and ends with Birling's son Eric and wife Sybil, who respectively made her pregnant and persuaded a charity committee to refuse her help as 'undeserving'. Having shamed the younger characters, and left Birling terrified of a scandal that will deprive him of his promised knighthood, Goole exits remarking that if people will not learn that they are responsible for each other they will be 'taught it in fire and blood and anguish'. It is then discovered that there is no Inspector Goole and no dead girl in the local hospital, revelations whose irrelevance to the moral issues raised only Sheila and Eric seem to see; but the rejoicing is interrupted by a phone call from the police station, revealing that a girl has just committed suicide and an inspector is on his way to the Birlings. On that somewhat cryptic note the play ends, its attack on the smug, spoiled, and myopically selfish complete. *An Inspector Calls* is a cautionary thriller, written in a conventional naturalistic style, but a highly praised 'expressionistic' revival at the National Theatre in 1992 gave it more scope and weight, leaving one critic acclaiming it as 'an eloquent attack on the sins of the century'.

Insular Possession, An, see MO, TIMOTHY.

Interzone, a *science fiction magazine founded in 1982 by a collective board of eight editors who, after the demise of **New Worlds* (which last appeared regularly in the mid-1970s), felt that there was need for a genre magazine in Britain. *Interzone* began first as a quarterly then appeared every two months; in 1990 it became a monthly. The magazine published works of well-known British science fiction writers as well as newer writers of the genre.

Invisible Man, a novel by Ralph *Ellison, published in 1952. The novel charts the 'progress' of its narrator, a young Southern black, from his early days in a black college (modelled on Ellison's own college, Tuskegee Institute in Alabama; the portrait in the novel of President Bledsoe, the college president, is loosely based on Tuskegee's founder, Booker T. *Washington), through his travels north to New York City where he is appropriated by the Brotherhood (resembling the American Communist Party of the 1930s) who seek to make him a mouthpiece for the party line, his experiences with Ras the Exhorter, a black separatist who vows to kill the narrator for betraying his race (Ras is loosely drawn from the nationalist leader Marcus Garvey) and with Rinehart, a 'spiritual technologist', and on to his final political disillusionment and his retreat into a world of symbolic invisibility. The structure, both of narrative and of philosophical ideas, is taken, in part, from Dostoevsky's *Notes from Underground* (though the influence of post-war existentialist thinking is also significant). Despite the reverence, even awe, in which Ellison's novel has been held it created considerable controversy, and a younger generation of African-American writers has been critical of its surrealist narrative methods and its refusal to espouse any political ideology. *Invisible Man* won the National Book Award in 1953. See *Twentieth Century Interpretations of 'Invisible Man'* (1970), edited by John M. Reilly, and Ellison's *Shadow and Act* (1964).

Iowa Writers' Workshop, the first (its origins go back as far as 1922) and most prominent of the large number of American university graduate programmes in creative writing, in Iowa City. These degrees, especially the Masters programmes, have had an enormous, yet hard to define, influence on contemporary American writing, especially poetry and fiction.

According to one estimate more than a quarter of the best-known writers in America have studied at Iowa at some point in their career. These former students include Flannery *O'Connor, Raymond *Carver, Jayne Anne *Phillips, John *Gardner, James *Tate, Robert *Bly, Donald *Justice, W. D. *Snodgrass, William *Stafford, Mark *Strand, W. D. Kinsella, Sandra *Cisneros, and T. Coraghessan *Boyle. Teachers have included Paul Engle, Frank *Conroy, Norman *Mailer, John *Irving, Philip *Roth, Robert *Stone, William *Kennedy, and Grace *Paley.

As this list might suggest, there is no Iowa School or movement, although the workshop is associated, rightly or wrongly, with the first-person lyric narrating an event. Fiction produced by workshop graduates might be categorized as an almost documentary realism narrated in a highly transparent style that eschews any foregrounding of language or narrative convention. Critics like Robert Peters (*Hunting the Snark*, 1989) claim that the preferred poetic style has tended to be bland, semi-autobiographical, cute pastoral ('poets seem to boast perpetually of farm origins'). Yet the allegation of uniformity is misleading, since writers now associated with radical schools of poetry and fiction have also attended Iowa.

Iowa Writers' Workshop is recognized as the most salient location of the appropriation of literary apprenticeship by the educational establishments. The distinctive feature of programmes like Iowa is that they focus almost exclusively on the act of composition (hence the term 'workshop'). For further discussion see Andrew Levy, *The Culture and Commerce of the American Short Story* (1993) and Stephen Wilbers, *The Iowa Writers' Workshop* (1980).

IRELAND, David (1927–), Australian novelist, born in Sydney. After a wide range of employment and experiences, he became a full-time writer in 1973. His informing concern with humankind's aspirations and self-deceptions warrants comparison with Peter *Carey. A working method of scenes/passages written on filing cards enables Ireland to 'shuffle' his novel in construction to achieve the careful disconnectedness central to his purpose. In *The Unknown Industrial Prisoner* (1971), Ireland drew upon his own experience of work in an oil refinery to construct from this intricate, and apparently self-referential, world a powerful image for human fallibility, both collective and individual. An existential concern with the outcast is reflected in the part-Aboriginal family of *Burn* (1974), and with the escapist yet regenerative male community of the public bar in *The Glass Canoe* (1976). In contrast, *A Woman of the Future* (1979) employed surreal devices of allegory in exploring potentially ideal or disastrous options for a future Australia, while *City of Women* (1981), set in Sydney, explored the spiritual aspirations of the lesbian central character. In common with Patrick *White, Ireland uses everyday images and occupations to express questions which explore the very essence of that materialistic fulfilment which Australia is often taken to exemplify. The two novels *Archimedes and the Seagle* (1984) and *Bloodfather* (1987) maintained Ireland's reputation for challenging conventions. A critical study by Helen Daniel, *Double Agent*, was published in 1982.

IRISH, William, see WOOLRICH, CORNELL.

Irish Revival, The, a major movement of cultural nationalism in Ireland which began in the 1880s and retained much of its energy until the late 1920s. Standish O'Grady (1846–1928) is regarded as its principal progenitor, his two-volume *History of Ireland* (1878, 1880) having made much of Ireland's ancient mythical and legendary material widely available. Other precursors of the Revival include the poets of the Young Ireland movement of the 1840s, whose popular anthology *The Spirit of the Nation* (1843) contained sentimentally patriotic verse; Samuel Ferguson (1810–86), William Allingham (1824–89), and Thomas Moore (1779–1852) had also produced poetry of an emphatically Irish character. John O'Leary (1830–1907), a former Fenian activist, became the mentor of W. B. *Yeats and others whose verse was collected in *Poems and Ballads of Young Ireland* (1888), the publication of which inaugurated the Irish Revival. Yeats's *The Wanderings of Oisin* (1889) and Douglas *Hyde's translations of traditional stories in *Beside the Fire* (1890) contributed to the movement's emergence. The fall of Parnell in 1891 left Ireland politically directionless, with the result that nationalist commitment was diverted into cultural channels. In 1892 Yeats was pre-eminent in the formation of the Irish Literary Society in London and the National Literary Society in Dublin; these bodies provided a focus for the activities of Yeats, Hyde, George 'AE' *Russell, Lady Augusta *Gregory, Katharine *Tynan, and others, whose writings reflected their common belief that authentically Irish qualities remained present in the indigenous rural communities. Hyde founded the Gaelic League in 1893, which widely promoted the

Irish language and other cultural pursuits. By the late 1890s the Irish Revival had a broad popular base in the many societies and clubs to which it had given rise. A further significant development was the establishment of the Irish Literary Theatre in 1899, which became the Irish National Theatre Society in 1903 and was known as the *Abbey Theatre Company from 1904 onwards; works by Yeats, John *Synge, Sean *O'Casey, G. B. *Shaw, and Padraic *Colum made drama the predominant form of Irish Revival literature from 1900 onwards, while George *Moore's *The Untilled Field* (1899) initiated the growth of its prose fiction. The nationalist consciousness generated by the movement culminated in the political events by which Ireland secured independence in 1921. During the later 1920s writers began to react against the Revival's conventions of Irishness, which nevertheless provided a starting point for the works of numerous notable authors, among them Flann *O'Brien, Austin *Clarke, Patrick *Kavanagh, and Frank *O'Connor. Critical surveys of the Irish Revival include R. Fallis's *The Irish Renaissance* (1977) and W. I. Thompson's *The Imagination of an Insurrection* (1967).

Iron Heel, The, a novel by Jack *London, published in 1907. A bleak pessimism pervades this dystopic narrative, rejected even by contemporary socialists because of its horrific representation of the future. It is written in the form of a diary kept by the wife of a proletarian leader, Ernest Everhard, annotated as a manuscript discovered several centuries later. Part love story, part social satire, the novel begins with set-piece debates at bourgeois dinner-tables, as Everhard argues the socialist position with various representatives of capitalist power. The novel proceeds to describe the rise of organized labour and the collapse of capitalism, the advent of a tyrannical oligarchy which seeks to protect its material interests, and a brutal civil war waged over three centuries of dictatorial government. It portrays the ruthless dehumanization and enslavement of the working class, inhabitants of labour ghettoes and utterly degraded as the abject waste of a society. Although the novel received poor reviews when published, with the emergence of the Fascist and Communist dictatorships, critics reconstrued it as a proleptic vision of the political machinations of oligarchic powers. See also UTOPIA AND ANTI-UTOPIA.

IRVING, John (1942–), American novelist, born in Exeter, New Hampshire, educated at the universities of Pittsburgh, Vienna, New Hampshire, and Iowa. Irving's first novel, *Setting Free the Bears* (1969), was followed by *The Water-Method Man* (1972) and *The 158-Pound Marriage* (1974), but it was his fourth novel, *The World According to Garp* (1978), which established both his considerable critical reputation and his commercial success. The novel, with its oblique self-referentiality and intellectual subversiveness, was quickly appropriated for the world of fictional post-modernism, and later novels such as *Hotel New Hampshire* (1981) and *The Cider House Rules* (1985) serve to confirm Irving's place alongside other American 'post-modernists' such as John *Barth, Donald *Barthelme, William H. *Gass, and Thomas *Pynchon. Irving has a prodigious gift for inventive, comic narrative but his novel *A Prayer for Owen Meany* (1989), which many critics consider his best, with its serio-comic tale of the consequences of an accident at a 'Little League' baseball game, is evidence of a more profound register in his fiction. Later works include *Trying to Save Piggy Sneed* (1993; stories and essays), *A Son of the Circus* (1994; a novel), and *The Imaginary Girlfriend* (1996; a memoir).

ISHERWOOD, Christopher (William Bradshaw) (1904–87), British novelist, born in Cheshire, educated at Corpus Christi College, Cambridge. Isherwood knew W. H. *Auden at his preparatory school, and Edward *Upward (Allen Chalmers) at Repton and Cambridge; later he enjoyed a close friendship with Auden's Oxford friend, Stephen *Spender, and played a strong creative part in the development of their poetry. His first novels, *All the Conspirators* (1928) and *The Memorial* (1932), are works revealing the moral bankruptcy of the English upper-middle class and its tendency to retreat into sickness and daydream. **Mr Norris Changes Trains* (1935), a short novel, and **Goodbye to Berlin* (1939), a sequence of short stories, reflect his years in Berlin during 1929–33 and are excerpts from a long novel of interconnected Berlin lives, 'The Lost', which was never completed; the novels are incomparable renderings of a society at the point of disintegration. *Goodbye to Berlin* contains the memorable 'Sally Bowles' (published separately, 1937) which was adapted for the stage by John Van Druten as *I Am a Camera* (1951) and as a musical (*Cabaret*, 1968). The memoir *Lions and Shadows* (1938) anatomizes his own and his friends' imaginations as they attempt to live with the demands of the larger world and to overcome the tensions imposed on their psyches by upper-class England. During the 1930s Isherwood collaborated with Auden on three plays, *The Dog Beneath the Skin* (1935), *The *Ascent of F6* (1936), and *On the Frontier* (1938); *expressionist presentations of Freudian and Marxist ideas; and *Journey to a War* (1939), the fruits of their journey to China together. In 1939 Auden and Isherwood left for America; Isherwood received American citizenship in 1946. As a leading anti-Fascist writer, his departure from England was often seen as a defection. Isherwood settled near Hollywood, where he worked on film scripts, and associated with Aldous *Huxley and Gerald Heard, whose pacifism he had come to share. His study of Hindu wisdom resulted in a translation, with Swami Prabhavananda, of the *Bhagavad-Gita* (1944) and *Vedanta for the Western World* (1945). *The World in the Evening* (1954), which contains a memorable account of a homosexual relationship, provides the first literary discussion of the term 'camp'. The stories in *Down There on a Visit* (1962) carry frankness about homosexuality further still. This was followed by *A Single Man* (1964), *A Meeting by the River* (1967),

Kathleen and Frank (1972), and the memoir *Christopher and His Kind* (1977). *My Guru and His Disciple* (1980) is a persuasive presentation of his religious re-education.

ISHIGURO, Kazuo (1954–), British novelist, born in Nagasaki, Japan, of 'middle-class samurai parents'; he moved with his family to England at the age of six where he was educated at the universities of Kent and East Anglia. Ishiguro has written short stories and television plays but it was his first three dazzling short novels that brought him recognition. Though he did not return to Japan until a brief visit in 1989, these novels have a Japanese setting or atmosphere. In *A Pale View of Hills* (1982) Etsuko, a Japanese widow, living alone in an English village, being visited by the Westernized daughter of her second, English marriage, is haunted by the suicide of her older daughter Keiko. *An Artist of the Floating World* (1986; Whitbread Prize) is also a retrospective novel, this time set entirely in post-war Japan. Masuji Ono, a once-distinguished painter, who is trying to get his younger daughter married, and is being visited by his older daughter and her little boy, looks back on a career which now seems to him discredited. His move from the 'floating world' of traditionally sensual Japanese art to imperialist propaganda is tainted, retrospectively, by his country's shame and defeat. The comedy of the family relationships is held in balance with Ono's self-deception and despair. *The Remains of the Day* (1989; Booker Prize) is set in England at the time of Suez, 1956, but keeps the Japanese theme of the loyal servant. Stevens, butler at Darlington Hall, sacrificed his emotional life for the sake of 'greatness' in his profession. But the later Lord Darlington is a disgraced figure who was a dupe of the Nazis, and Stevens's life of service is revealed as a catastrophic self-betrayal. In all three books, the self-deceptions and evasions of the central figure are presented through a cryptic, formal narrative which seems to pick its way through landscapes of lost opportunities and stifled emotions. *The Unconsoled* (1995), his most experimental work, is set in an unnamed Eastern European city, where the central character, a pianist named Mr Ryder, arrives in order to perform at some unspecified cultural event. He is then involved in a series of no less vague and frustrating encounters—a reception in his honour at which he is obliged to appear in his dressing-gown; a photo-call for which he is equally unprepared—in the course of which he meets people from his past, including his wife and stepson, his parents, and various old school friends, all of whom relate their stories. The enigmatic mood of the novel, with its conscious echoes of *Joyce, Kafka, Borges, Calvino, and other practitioners of the all-encompassing fable, is sustained to the end.

IYAYI, Festus (1947–), African novelist, born in Nigeria, educated there and at the University of Bradford. His parents were farmers, who experienced considerable deprivation. A master of hard-hitting social realism, his first novel, *Violence* (1979), is a stark indictment of the Nigerian social system, and its misuse of oil wealth. Its story of a day-labourer, Idemudia, and his wife, Adisa, who struggle desperately to survive in harsh contrast to their employers, Olufun and Queen, prosperous hotel proprietors, highlights the exploitation of the former by the latter. It was followed by *The Contract* (1982). Iyayi gained particular prominence with *Heroes* (1986; Commonwealth Writers Prize) which focuses, through the eyes of a journalist, Osime, on the brutalities and corrupting influence of the Nigerian Civil War (1967–70).

J

JACKSON, Shirley (1919–65), American writer, born in San Francisco, educated at the University of Rochester. An acclaimed practitioner of the neo-gothic mode, she is best remembered for the title story of the collection *The Lottery* (1948), which introduces an element of horror into seemingly calm parochial surroundings—the title refers to the selection of a victim for a ritual sacrifice. In novels such as *The Haunting of Hill House* (1959; successfully filmed in 1963) and *We Have always Lived in the Castle* (1963), Jackson uses settings to create a sense of pervasive chill; the horror largely exists in the tormented minds of her protagonists. Traditional in her technique and manner of expression, Jackson, though long superceded by practitioners of more radical genres of horror, continues to be respected as a skilled exponent of the well-made tale of unease. Representative samples of her work can be found in *The Magic of Shirley Jackson* (1966).

JACOB, Naomi (1884–1964), British novelist and biographer, born in Yorkshire. She had a long association with the stage, making her first appearance as an actress in 1920. Her first novel, *Jacob Ussher* (1926), was followed by several others before the very successful *Four Generations* (1934), a story of a wealthy family of English Jews. Of her many other novels the most notable are *The Lenient God* (1937), *This Porcelain Clay* (1939), and *They Left the Land* (1940), a study of three Yorkshire generations. She also wrote a series of autobiographies, the last of which, *Me—and the Stage* (1964), was published a month before she died, and a biography of Marie Lloyd, *Our Marie* (1936).

JACOBS, W(illiam) W(ymark) (1863–1943), British writer, born in the docklands of Wapping in East London, the son of a wharf manager. While still employed in the Civil Service, his work appeared in Jerome K. *Jerome's *The Idler*; in 1895 he joined *Strand Magazine* where he began producing the comic tales of sailors, bargees, dockers, and other shore-workers, for which he became renowned. *Many Cargoes* (1896), his first collection of stories, was followed by many others including the 'Claybury' stories featuring the bucolic ne'er-do-wells of village life inspired by East Anglia. He also wrote tales of the macabre and the supernatural, notably 'The Monkey's Paw', which appeared in *The Lady of the Barge* (1902) and was dramatized. Other collections include *Sea Urchins* (1898), *Light Freights* (1901), and *Sea Whispers* (1926), in which maritime themes develop a deeper nostalgia. His novels include *A Master of Craft* (1900), *At Sunwich Port* (1902), *Dialstone Lane* (1904), and *Salthaven* (1908).

JACOBSON, Dan (1929–), South African novelist and short-story writer, born in Johannesburg. In 1980 he became Reader in English at University College, London. Jacobson's naturalistic earlier novels, *The Trap* (1955), *A Dance in the Sun* (1956), *The Price of Diamonds* (1958), *The Evidence of Love* (1960), and *The Beginners* (1966), illuminate different aspects of the human condition in South Africa. *The Wonder-Worker* (1973) and *The Confessions of Joseph Baisz* (1977) focus on lonely, alienated figures, and examine unstable states of mind. The first is set in contemporary London, but the second creates an imaginary Kafkaesque country bearing some resemblance to South Africa, in which 'Joseph Baisz' is fated to love only those he has first betrayed. *The Rape of Tamar* (1970) is a modern retelling of the power struggle between King David and his sons. *Her Story* (1987), the most subtle and enigmatic of Jacobson's fictional works, is an elaborate, extended parable, which examines the story of the Virgin Mary, but in the context of a world plagued by guerrilla war, intense suffering, and ironic futurology. In *Hidden in the Heart* (1991), a young white South African in England is emotionally exploited by his older English lover; *The God-Fearer* (1992) is set in a fictionalized medieval central Europe in which Judaism is the dominant religion and the Christian minority persecuted by a demagogue. His other works include the short stories in *A Long Way from London* (1958), *Through the Wilderness* (1968), and *Inklings* (1973); *Time and Time Again: Autobiographies* (1985); *Adult Pleasures* (1988), essays on literature; and *The Electronic Elephant* (1994), about a journey through post-apartheid South Africa.

JACOBSON, Howard (1942–), British novelist, born in Manchester, educated at Cambridge University; he has taught English at Selwyn College, Cambridge, Sydney University, and Wolverhampton Polytechnic. His first novel, *Coming from Behind* (1983), was set at the fictional West Midlands institution of Wrottesley Polytechnic and concerned the exploits of Sefton Goldberg, a young Jewish academic obsessed with the notion that he is a failure; written in a dryly comic style, the novel pays ironic homage to the *campus novels of M. *Bradbury and D. *Lodge and is also reminiscent, in its use of farce and slapstick, of the novels of T. *Sharpe. *Peeping Tom* (1984) was equally satirical in its portrayal of the morbid fixations of its protagonist, Barney Fugelman, whose West Country idyll is disturbed by his fantasies about Thomas *Hardy and his conviction that his wife is betraying him. *Redback* (1987) was set in Australia (the title refers to a venomous Australian spider). He has also published a travel book, also about Australia, *In the Land of Oz* (1987). A more recent novel, *The Very Model of a Man* (1992), considered the Jewish experience in the light of the story of its most famous family—Adam and Eve and their sons, Cain and Abel.

Jacob's Room, an early novel by V. *Woolf, published in 1922, and written as an elegy for her brother Thoby, who died young in 1906. The novel tries to extend the fluid narrative method of her early short stories, using interconnected images (butterflies, a sheep's skull) carefully patterned. It is strongly influenced by her reading of Greek literature. The factual 'biography' of Jacob moves from his childhood on holiday in Cornwall with his widowed mother Betty Flanders and his two younger brothers. Jacob grows up in Scarborough, learns Latin from Mr Floyd (who also proposes to his mother), collects butterflies, and goes to Cambridge in October 1906, aged 19, where he meets Richard Bonamy and Tim Durrant, whose sister Clara he is attracted to. After Cambridge he lives in elegant eighteenth-century rooms in London, has affairs, goes to parties and operas, writes essays, visits Europe, and is killed in the war—which proves to be the novel's hidden subject—at the age of 26. But these facts are presented indirectly through impressions and conversations. Jacob is an elusive, absent shadow or ghost. Conventional biographical techniques cannot 'catch' him. His own youthful, Wordsworthian resistance to the hard realities of modern life resemble Woolf's own attempt to change the conventions of fiction.

JAMES, Clive (Vivian Leopold) (1939–), Australian writer and broadcaster, born in Kogarah, New South Wales, Australia, educated at Sydney University and Pembroke College, Cambridge. Collections of his early work as a literary journalist with the *Times Literary Supplement* and other leading periodicals include *The Metropolitan Critic* (1974). *Visions Before Midnight* (1977) collects samples of his work as television critic for the *Observer* from 1972 to 1982. During the 1980s he emerged as a well-known television personality and cultural commentator. *Other Passports: Poems 1958–1985* (1986) displays his accomplishment in traditional verse forms and contains numerous memorable parodies. His other works include the mock-heroic poem *Charles Charming's Challenges on the Pathway to the Throne* (1981) and the novels *Brilliant Creatures* (1983), *The Remake* (1987), and *Brrm Brrm!* (1991). His three volumes of autobiography, *Unreliable Memoirs* (1980), *Falling towards England* (1985), and *May Week Was in June* (1990), have enjoyed considerable success. *Fame in the Twentieth Century* (1993) is a tie-in for a TV series.

JAMES, C(yril) L(ionel) R(obert) (1901–89), Trinidadian historian, political theorist, and novelist, born in Tunapuna, near Port of Spain, Trinidad, educated at Queen's Royal College. In the early 1930s he was involved in the publication of two influential literary and political magazines, **Trinidad* and **The Beacon*. In 1932 he moved to Britain where he became cricket correspondent for the *Manchester Guardian*, and later the *Glasgow Herald*. In this period he published his only novel, **Minty Alley* (1936), which had a great influence on modern Caribbean fiction, and *The Black Jacobins: Toussaint L'Overture and the San Domingo Revolt* (1938). A prolific writer, and a political activist and publicist, James was much involved in the struggles for independence in the West Indies, and in Africa, initially from a Trotskyist, but later from an independent, and always anti-Stalinist perspective: he translated Boris Souvarine's critical biography of *Stalin* (1939). He stayed in the USA after a lecture tour in 1938, but was interned in Ellis Island in 1952, and expelled in 1953 for his Marxist political activities. His other major works included a study of Herman Melville, *Mariners, Renegades and Castaways* (1953); *Notes on Dialectics* (1980); *Nkrumah and the Ghana Revolution* (1977); and his delightfully autobiographical book on cricket, *Beyond a Boundary* (1963). Most of his essays have been collected in *The Future in the Present* (1971), *Spheres of Existence* (1980), and *At the Rendezvous of Victory* (1984). See Paul Buhle, *C. L. R. James: The Artist as Revolutionary* (1988).

JAMES, Henry (1843–1916), American novelist and author of short stories, critical essays, and plays, born in New York, son of the Swedenborgian philosopher Henry James, Sr, brother of William *James. He spent many of his formative years in Europe, residing in Geneva, London, Paris, and Boulogne in 1855–8 and 1859–60, until returning to live in Newport, Rhode Island in 1860. He entered Harvard Law School in 1862. With encouragement from William Dean *Howells, with whom he developed a lifelong friendship, he devoted himself to writing. He contributed short stories and book reviews to the *Nation* and *Galaxy* in 1865, his first short story appearing in the *Atlantic Monthly* in 1868. In 1869 James returned to Europe and spent some time travelling in England, France, and Italy; this provided him with his observations of Americans adrift in Europe and the 'international' theme of the collision and collusion between Europe (especially Britain) and the USA that was to preoccupy his fiction in future years. Back in Cambridge, Massachusetts, his first novel *Watch and Ward* was serialized in the *Atlantic Monthly* in 1871, and appeared in book form in 1878. His first significant short story, 'The Passionate Pilgrim', also appeared in 1871, later published in *A Passionate Pilgrim and Other Tales* (1875). These early tales reflect the influence of the realism of Dickens, Balzac, Hawthorne, and George Eliot. After living in Boston writing reviews, short stories, and art criticism, he returned to Europe in 1872 and spent the next two years in Italy working on his first long work, *Roderick Hudson* (1875), a novel whose description of the disintegration of the life of a young American sculptor in Rome, hopelessly in love with an Italian girl, appears to suggest that love and passion are detrimental to the aesthetic vocation. After returning to America in 1874, he spent a year in Paris during 1875–6, where his friendship with Ivan Turgenev introduced him to a literary circle which included Gustave Flaubert, Guy de Maupassant, Emile Zola, Alphonse Daudet, and de Goncourt; he settled in London in 1876, where he lived for twenty years. He completed *The American* (1877), *The Europeans* (1878), *Daisy Miller* (1879), a short story about an American girl's experiences of the inflexibility of European social politeness and behaviour, and the two novelettes *An International Episode* (1879) and *Confidence* (1880), all of which continued his investigation of the cultural, social, and historical relationships between Europe and the USA. A collection of short stories also appeared at this time, *The Madonna of the Future and Other Tales* (1879). This period also brought James's first major works of criticism, *French Poets and Novelists* (1878) and *Hawthorne* (1879); these were followed in 1888 by *Partial Portraits* which included the classic essay 'The Art of Fiction', which laid down many of the aesthetic precepts for much of his work.

The 1880s saw several important achievements: *Washington Square* (1881), a novel about the isolated and hemmed-in social and cultural aspirations of the young American woman Catherine Sloper; *The Bostonians* (1886), which deals with the emerging feminist movement and different social and gender reactions to its demands; and *The Princess Casamassima* (1886), a tale about London revolutionaries, which brings back the Italian girl from *Roderick Hudson*. His abiding theme of analysing the American character with a group of Europeans occurred again in the book acknowledged as his first masterpiece, *The Portrait of a Lady* (1881). Its detailed and extended analysis of the characters involved in the story makes the book a triumph of understated psychological realism. During this period there were also several attempts at playwriting, with a dramatization of *Daisy Miller* (1883), but his later unsuccessful *Guy Domville* (1895) was booed off the stage. Several novelettes were also written, including *The Reverberator* (1888) and *The Aspern Papers* (1888), the latter about a critic's attempt to acquire a famous poet's correspondence. There followed *The Tragic Muse* (1890), which was set in London and focused on the lives of an artistic circle; *What Maisie Knew* (1897), describing the break-up of a marriage through the eyes of a young girl; an unsuccessful melodrama, *The Other House* (1896); and *The Spoils of Poynton* (1897), dramatizing the mean-mindedness of the occupants of a magnificent house, and a complex set of relationships based on acquisitiveness and a chain of personal pressures.

As well as writing these successful full-length novels, throughout his career James also produced a steady stream of outstanding short stories and novellas, including the collections *A London Life* (1889), *The Lesson of the Master* (1892), *The Private Life* (1893), *The Wheel of Time* (1893), *Terminations* (1895), *Embarrassments* (1896) which contains the tale 'The Figure in the Carpet', *In The Cage* (1898), *The Two Magics* (1898) which contains 'The Turn of the Screw', a ghost story of subtle horror, *The Altar of the Dead* (1909), and *The Finer Grain* (1910). In 1897 he purchased Lamb House in Rye, where he lived for the remainder of his life. The novel *The Awkward Age* appeared in 1899, about Nanda Brookhouse and her adolescent experiences in the materialistic and cut-throat New York salon society; and *The *Sacred Fount* in 1901, a novelette which satirizes the 'detached observer' of James's novels, and ranges over the distinction between masks and 'reality', the ageing process, the invulnerability of art, the 'madness of art' which insists on seeing more than the immediate 'real', and the vulnerability of love.

Although the majority of James's fiction was written in the nineteenth century, he reached the peak of his career in the early 1900s with three massive novels: *The *Wings of the Dove* (1902), a masterpiece of ironic character portrayal; *The *Ambassadors* (1903); and *The *Golden Bowl* (1904). In 1904 he returned to the USA, where he stayed with Henry *Adams, and his generally dyspeptic and pessimistic analysis of the country and culture was expressed in *The American Scene* (1907). For the two years after the publication of this volume, he worked on the enormous New York Edition of his works, which eventually appeared complete with the new prefaces on the art of fiction. Although criticized by some for the labyrinthine complexity of his style, James's prose is usually regarded as second to none for subtlety of phrase and perception, with a reputation for sophistication, and his attention to textual detail and nuance is clearly evident in the revisions occasioned by this publishing enterprise. Between 1910 and 1914 he completed two volumes of a projected five-volume autobiography: *A Small Boy* (1913) and *Notes of a Son and Brother* (1914). He also began two novels, *The Sense of the Past* and *The Ivory Tower* (both published in 1917), and a volume of autobiography, *The Middle Years* (1917), all of which remained incomplete. His final years were scarred by his brother William's and sister Alice's deaths, and the outbreak of the First World War, which he described as 'the plunge of civilization into the abyss of blood and darkness'. In 1915 he acquired British citizenship and was awarded the Order of Merit. James also published several travel books, principally *Transatlantic Sketches* (1875), *Portraits of Places* (1883), *A Little Tour in France* (1900), and *Italian Hours* (1909). Other works of criticism were *Picture and Text* (1893), *Notes on Novelists* (1914), and *Within the Rim and Other Essays* (1918). F. O. *Matthiessen edited James's *Notebooks* (1947), and four volumes of his *Letters* (1974–84) were edited by Leon *Edel. Edel has also written an authoritative five-volume biography, *The Life of Henry James* (1953–72), all of which confirm James's place as one of the most self-reflective artists to have ever lived.

JAMES, M(ontague) R(hodes) (1862–1936), British writer and scholar, born at Goodnestone, Kent, educated at King's College, Cambridge. In the course of a long academic career, he was Vice-Chancellor of Cambridge (1913–15) and Provost of Eton College (1918–36). He possessed an unrivalled knowledge of mediaeval illuminated manuscripts and was a leading authority on Biblical *Apocrypha*. He is best remembered for *Ghost Stories of an Antiquary* (1904), *More Ghost Stories of an Antiquary* (1911), *A Thin Ghost* (1919), and *A Warning to the Curious* (1926), four volumes of supernatural fiction which established him as a leading exponent of the ghost story. From an early age he had been much influenced by the surreal ghost stories of Sheridan Le Fanu, whose works he edited. Unlike almost all earlier supernatural fiction, which depended upon exotic backgrounds and gothic language, James's tales of revenge and dislocation were set in a calm and everyday world. Only slowly, as in his greatest story, 'Oh, Whistle, and I'll Come to You, My Lad', would a horror emerge to colour the scene and the reader's consciousness. The theme which eventually manifests itself is the intrusion into the conscious mind of that which it has repressed, and it is this which continues to be of central importance in the contemporary ghost story. His *Collected Ghost Stories* appeared in 1931. In addition to his many works as a scholar, editor, and translator, he published the autobiographical *Eton and Kings: Recollections, Mostly Trivial 1875–1925* (1926).

JAMES, Lady P(hyllis) D(orothy) (1920–), British crime writer, born in Oxford, educated at Cambridge High School. Before turning to authorship, James held various appointments in hospital administration and was later a senior civil servant in the police and criminal policy departments of the Home Office, and a Justice of the Peace. She has used her experience to good effect in a series of detective novels beginning with *Cover Her Face* (1962), which introduced the Scotland Yard policeman and poet Adam Dalgliesh, who appears in most of her books. She has also written of a female private detective, Cordelia Gray (*An Unsuitable Job for a Woman*, 1972). She has been seen as the successor of Dorothy L. *Sayers, but her approach is more harsh and realistic and is perhaps seen at its best in *Death of an Expert Witness* (1977). In her later novels (*The Skull Beneath the Skin*, 1982; *A Taste for Death*, 1986; *Devices and Desires*, 1989; *Original Sin*, 1994) she has attempted to write on a much larger scale than that of the conventional detective story, and the detection element has receded into the background in favour of description and delineation of character. Her best-known novel, *Innocent Blood* (1980), is not a detective story, but the account of an adopted girl's search for her real parents. Amongst other public appointments, she has been Chairman of the Society of Authors, a governor of the BBC, and Chairman of the Arts Council Literature Advisory Panel. She was awarded a life peerage in 1991.

JAMES, William (1842–1910), American psychologist and philosopher, the brother of Henry *James the novelist, born in New York. He gained his MD in 1870 at Harvard University, where he taught from 1872 to 1907 and established a laboratory of psychology in 1876, carrying out the extensive programme of research that resulted in *The Principles of Psychology* (2 volumes, 1890); its opening statement that 'Psychology is the Science of Mental Life, both of its phenomena and their conditions' asserts his intention of transforming psychology from a part-time activity of philosophers into an autonomous empirical science. He was among the first to recognize the import of Sigmund Freud's theories of the unconscious. *The Will to Believe* (1897), his first major contribution to philosophy, defined his position as 'radical empiricist'; in its correlation between the truth of a belief and its results in terms of experience, the essay initiated the development of his influential philosophical pragmatism, which derived from the work of Charles *Peirce. Among his other publications as a philosopher are *Pragmatism* (1907); *The Meaning of Truth* (1909), a response to criticisms of his pragmatist doctrine; *A Pluralistic Universe* (1909), which contained the principal exposition of his metaphysics; and *Essays in Radical Empiricism* (1912). The last-named advanced the hypothesis of 'neutral monism', according to which mental and physical experience constituted distinct aspects of a single universal substance, a theory extended by Bertrand *Russell in his *Analysis of Mind* (1921). James's work as Gifford Lecturer in Natural Religion at Edinburgh in 1901 and 1902 resulted in *Varieties of Religious Experience* (1902), his enduringly important account of the psychological character of subjective religious states. F. H. Burkhardt was general editor of *The Works of William James* (7 volumes, 1975–9). R. B. Perry's *The Thought and Character of William James* appeared in two volumes in 1935.

JAMESON, Fredric (1934–), American scholar and critic, born in Cleveland, Ohio, educated at Haverford College and Yale. Perhaps the most distinguished English-language Marxist literary theorist of the post-Second World War period, Jameson has taught at Yale, the University of California, and Duke University. His initial engagement was with Sartre and with French philosophy and literature, but he also confronted the work of Georg Lukács and the Russian Formalists (see FORMALISM). His early books, *Marxism and Form* (1971) and *The Prison-House of Language: A Critical Account of Structuralism and Russian Formalism* (1972), chart with great intelligence and rigour the political and literary implications of *Structuralism and its forebears and descendants. Jameson has also written interestingly on Wyndham *Lewis (in *Fables of Aggression*, 1979), and on film (*Signatures of the Visible*, 1990; *The Geopolitical Aesthetic: Cinema and Space in the World System*, 1992) and other contemporary modes of cultural production. *The Political Unconscious* (1981) remains faithful to Marxism while incorporating a number of other strands of modern European thought (see MARXIST LITERARY CRITICISM). Jameson's later work includes several volumes of theoretical essays, and *Postmodernism: The Cultural Logic *of Late Capitalism* (1991) where an intricate and ambiguous cultural climate is explored through a persistent belief in the continuing flexibility and force of materialist accounts of the world. See also CULTURAL MATERIALISM and POST-MODERNISM.

JAMESON, (Margaret) Storm (1891–1986), British writer, born in Whitby, Yorkshire, the daughter of a sea captain, educated at Leeds University. Yorkshire forms the background of much of her work including her two trilogies, 'The Triumph of Time' (*The Lovely Ship*, 1927; *The Voyage Home*, 1930; *A Richer Dust*, 1931) and 'Mirror of Darkness' (*Company Parade*, 1934; *Love in Winter*, 1935; *None Turn Back*, 1936), which chronicle the fortunes of a Yorkshire shipbuilding family from the middle of the nineteenth century to the 1920s. In these and in her other works such as *Women against Men* (1933, stories) and *The Early Life of Stephen Hind* (1966) there is a slight dourness which underlies much of her work. She also published poems, biographies, and several volumes of literary criticism including *Modern Drama in Europe* (1920) and *The Georgian Novel and Mr Robinson* (1929). Her autobiographical works include *Journey from the North* (1969) which describes, amongst other events, her years as president of PEN during the Second World War.

JANOWITZ, Tama (1957–), American writer, born in San Francisco, educated at Columbia University. Her first novel, *American Dad* (1981), an ironic *Bildungsroman*, was followed by the bestselling *Slaves of New York* (1986), a collection of short stories which chronicle the efforts of a number of failed artists, writers, and film-makers in New York's Lower East Side to find fame, fortune, and happiness. *A Cannibal in Manhattan* (1987), a black comedy about a cannibal chief's visit to the wilder shores of America, was an ambitious portrayal of the absurdities of metropolitan life. *The Male Cross-Dresser Support Group* (1992), like her other work, is set in New York, and offers a familiar mix of farcical incident, wry observation, and lurid description of low-life scenes, culminating in a car chase across America in which the heroine is accompanied by a small boy dressed as a girl, and a severed head.

JARRELL, Randall (1914–65), American poet and critic, born in Nashville, Tennessee, educated at Vanderbilt University. He also wrote essays, a novel, children's stories, and translated Chekhov, Goethe, and Rilke. His academic career began in 1937 at Kenyon College, where he was a close friend of Robert *Lowell and became influenced by J. C. *Ransom and the *New Criticism; from 1947 until his death in a road accident, he taught at the Women's College at the University of North Carolina. Jarrell was one of the last Americans for whom literature, as distinct from some particular branch of literature, was a passion and a vocation. His prose is witty, shrewd, unassuming, serious, perhaps at its best in his book *Poetry and the Age* (1953); other notable prose collections are *A Sad Heart at the Supermarket* (1962) and *The Third Book of Criticism* (1969). He was a gifted and agile reviewer, able to turn apparently casual remarks into major insights. 'He has taken all culture for his province,' Jarrell said of Ezra *Pound, 'and is naturally a little provincial about it.' Jarrell felt he lived in a time of criticism rather than creation, but was energetic rather than despairing about this plight. Critics, he argued, are 'the bane of our age' not because they are not useful or (sometimes) talented but 'because our age so fantastically over-estimates their importance and so willingly forsakes the works they are writing about for them'. Readers, he added, 'real readers are almost as wild a species as writers . . .' Jarrell's poetry is fluent, idiomatic, experimental, and wide-ranging, much of it regularly anthologized. He wrote about childhood, war, illness, animals, books, time, loneliness, and above all loss: lost children, lost love, lost lives, a lost world. There are echoes of Frost and *Auden in his writing, but a certain mixture of jauntiness and pathos is all his own. He liked to experiment with verse forms, but was always faithful to a certain traditional lilt and music. Among his collections are *Blood for a Stranger* (1942), *Little Friend, Little Friend* (1945), *The Seven-League Crutches* (1951), *The Woman at the Washington Zoo* (1960), perhaps his best-known volume, and *Complete Poems* (1969). His comic novel *Pictures from an Institution* (1954) is a glancing satirical portrait of American academic life which caused reviewers to think not only of Oscar Wilde but also of the Marx Brothers.

Jazz, see MORRISON, TONI.

Jazz Poetry, a form established in the 1950s in the USA involving the reading of poetry to jazz accompaniments. Kenneth *Rexroth, Lawrence *Ferlinghetti, Jack *Kerouac, and Kenneth *Patchen were among the leading exponents of the idiom, which was established in San Francisco in 1957. The *Black Mountain poets' emphasis on the importance of the vocal aspects of poetry and the increased interest in readings fostered by the *Beat poets created the context in which jazz poetry emerged. In 1958 Christopher *Logue and others adopted the mode in Britain; Logue regarded it as a possible means of reinvigorating poetry at a time when it was perceived by many to have lost any breadth of appeal to a popular audience. In 1959 he collaborated with the jazz musicians Tony Kinsey and Bill Le Sage to broadcast *Red Bird Dancing on Ivory* on BBC radio and to present *Jazzetry* at the Royal Court Theatre. The success of these ventures led to considerable interest in jazz poetry; Michael *Horovitz, Bob *Cobbing, Pete Brown (1940–), and Roy *Fisher were among those who performed their work widely with musical ensembles throughout the 1960s. Proponents of the genre viewed it as a revival of the traditional association of poetry and music. Notable among twentieth-century precedents for jazz poetry are Edith *Sitwell's *Façade*, performed with William Walton's pastiches of popular dance music in 1923, and Langston *Hughes's experimental readings of his verse, which had affinities with blues lyrics, to musical accompaniments in the late 1930s. Jazz poetry was influential in the development of further fusions of music and verse, including the frequent performances by the *Liverpool poets with the guitarist Andy Roberts and the readings to rock or reggae accompaniments by numerous subsequent poets. See also DUB POETRY.

JEFFERS, (John) Robinson (1887–1962), American poet, born in Pittsburgh, Pennsylvania, educated at Occidental College in California. In 1913 he settled at Carmel, California, its mountainous coastal landscape becoming the principal source of imagery for his verse. Central to much of his work is the philosophy he termed 'Inhumanism', the belief in the superiority of nature to man; 'I'd sooner . . . kill a man than a hawk' in 'Hurt Hawks' is the best-known statement of his dismissive and often contemptuous attitude to humanity. *Tamar and Other Poems* (1924) established him as a poet of importance, its powerfully direct and carefully cadenced free verse, often in lines of unusual length, emerging as the characteristic form of his best work. The title poem's treatment of the theme of incest uses a modern Californian setting for its adaptation of elements from the biblical story of Tamar. The collection also contains the first of his many versions of classical narratives in 'The Tower beyond Tragedy', based on the *Oresteia* of Aeschylus. His *Medea* (1946), a version of the work by Euripides, was successfully produced on Broadway in 1947. The poems of *Tamar* were reprinted in *Roan Stallion, Tamar, and Other Poems* (1925), the new title piece drawing on the Californian folk tradition for its incipiently mythological celebration of feral energy. Numerous subsequent collections, typically dominated by lengthy narrative title poems, include *The Women at Point Sur* (1927), *Cawdor and Other Poems* (1928), and *Thurso's Landing* (1932). *Selected Poems* appeared in 1938. Following the death of his wife in 1950 he became reclusive and published no further collections after *Hungerfield and Other Poems* (1954). The first two volumes of a projected four-volume edition of his *Collected Poetry* appeared in 1988 and 1989. *The Stone Mason of Tor House* (1966) is M. B. Bennett's biography of Jeffers.

JELLICOE, (Patricia) Ann (1927–), British playwright, born in Middlesborough; she trained as an actress at the Central School of Speech and Drama, and worked as a theatre director before turning to writing. She made her name with *The Sport of My Mad Mother* (1958), a fantasy about teenage violence, and *The Knack* (1962), a whimsical comedy about sexual prowess, male rivalries, and the limitations of a young English Casanova eventually bettered by his awkward, unconfident flatmate. *Shelley: Or the Idealist*, a documentary drama which takes a somewhat sceptical view of the poet and his circle, followed in 1966. Since the West End failure of *The Giveaway* (1969), a comedy about the emotional tribulations of a family which has won a decade's supply of breakfast cereal, she has written plays for children, translated work by Ibsen and Chekhov, and become active as a director, producer, and general creative force in community theatre in the West Country, presenting (among other plays) the world première of David *Edgar's *Entertaining Strangers* in Dorchester.

JENKINS, Alan (1955–), British poet, born in London, educated at the University of Sussex. In 1980 he began working on the *Times Literary Supplement*, of which he subsequently became deputy editor. He received an Eric Gregory Award for his poetry in 1981 and a selection of his work appeared in *New Chatto Poets* in 1986. *In The Hothouse* (1988), his first collection of verse, gained him wide notice as a strikingly individual and deftly accomplished poet. *Greenheart* (1990) and *Harm* (1994) are his principal subsequent publications. Jenkins is a poet of considerable imaginative scope, most evident in the unsettlingly inventive narrative of the title poem of *Greenheart*, and urgently contemporary concerns, notably in the acerbic reflections of metropolitan life in *Harm*. Powerfully candid treatments of personal relationships, often with a strong erotic component, are a recurrent feature of his poetry. He is the editor of *Essential Reading* (1986), a selection from Peter *Reading's poetry.

JENKINS, (John) Robin (1912–), Scottish novelist, born in the village of Flemington in Lanarkshire, educated at Hamilton Academy and Glasgow University. After working as a schoolteacher in Scotland, he taught from 1957 to 1968 in Afghanistan, Spain, and the East Indies, which respectively provide the settings for his novels *Dust on the Paw* (1961), *The Sardana Dances* (1964), and *The Holy Tree* (1969). *So Gaily Sings the Lark* (1951) was the first of many novels, the majority of which are characterized by the authenticity and detail of their reflections of his Scottish background: others include the quasi-autobiographical *Happy for the Child* (1953); *The *Cone-Gatherers* (1955); *The Changeling* (1958), a compassionately ironic treatment of class distinctions; *A Very Scotch Affair* (1968); *A Toast to the Lord* (1972), which draws upon issues raised by the US submarine base at Holy Loch; and *Fergus Lamont* (1973), the most successfully comic of his works. Among his later novels are *The Awakening of George Darroch* (1985), a historical work which centres on the schism in the Church of Scotland in 1843, and *Poverty Castle* (1991). The underlying moral purpose informing all Jenkins's writing is evident in the consistency with which he engages the themes of loss of innocence and the interaction of creative and destructive impulses in human relations at personal and social levels. The conditioning of Scottish culture by a repressive Calvinist ethos, class prejudice, and the spiritual poverty engendered by material privation are also recurrent concerns in his work.

Jennie Gerhardt, a novel by Theodore *Dreiser, published in 1911. Jennie's poor immigrant family is characterized by her father's Lutheranism and her mother's brave attempts to sustain the home. Whilst working in a hotel in Columbus, Ohio, Jennie meets

Senator George Brander, who becomes infatuated with her. He helps her family and declares his wish to marry her; Jennie, grateful for his benevolence, agrees to sleep with him, but ill fortune intercedes and the Senator dies, leaving her pregnant. She gives birth to a daughter, Vesta, and moves to Cleveland where she finds work as a lady's maid to a prominent family. Consequently, she meets Lester Kane, a prosperous manufacturer's son. Jennie falls in love with him, impressed by his strong will and generosity: she leaves her daughter behind and they visit New York together. Kane, unaware that Jennie has a child, wishes to marry her, but, anticipating his family's disapproval, decides instead that she shall become his mistress. They live together successfully in Chicago, even through Jennie's revelation after three years that Vesta is her daughter. Kane does not yield to his family's pressure to leave Jennie, but after his father's death discovers that he will not inherit a substantial part of the family business unless he discards her. They visit Europe together, where Kane's attention shifts from Jennie to a woman of his own class, Letty Gerald. On hearing the will's terms, it is Jennie who demands that they separate: Kane, after providing for her, marries Letty and resumes his former social status. Jennie loses her daughter to typhoid and adopts two orphans, but through it all, continues to love him. Kane becomes ill, tells Jennie he still loves her, and she tends him until his death, mourning secretly at his funeral.

JENNINGS, Elizabeth (1926–), British poet, born in Boston, Lincolnshire, educated at St Anne's College, Oxford. Before becoming a freelance writer in 1961, she worked as an assistant at the Oxford City Library and as a publisher's reader. Her first substantial collection of poetry, *A Way of Looking* (1956), was followed by numerous subsequent volumes including *The Mind Has Mountains* (1966), *Moments of Grace* (1979), *Extending the Territory* (1985), *Collected Poems 1953–1985* (1986), *Tributes* (1989), *Times and Seasons* (1992), and *Familiar Spirits* (1994). Jennings's technical accomplishment, together with the restrained urbanity and intelligence characteristic of her work, gained her inclusion in Robert Conquest's **New Lines* anthology of 1956; she thus became associated with the *Movement, although the metaphysical preoccupations evident in her poetry were not among that group's distinguishing traits. Much of her writing combines visionary intensity and meditative poise in its concern with the religious dimensions of her experience. She has produced a number of memorable poems drawing on the lives of Christian mystics, which include treatments of St John of the Cross and St Teresa of Avila. Among her prose works are *Every Changing Shape* (1961) and *Christianity and Poetry* (1965), which consider relations between mysticism, religion, and poetry. In 1961 her translations of *The Sonnets of Michelangelo* were published. She has also edited numerous anthologies, including *The Batsford Book of Religious Verse* (1981), and published books of poetry for children.

JEROME, Jerome K(lapka) (1859–1927), British writer, born in Walsall, educated at Marylebone Grammar School, leaving at 14 to become a railway clerk. Later he worked as a schoolmaster, actor, and journalist. *On Stage and Off* (1884) and *The Idle Thoughts of an Idle Fellow* (1886) were both collections of humorous essays. *Three Men in a Boat* (1889), about a trio of young men and their dog on a boating holiday on the Thames, was immediately successful; *Three Men on the Bummel* (1900) recounted a tour of Germany with the same characters. *Paul Klever* (1902) was an autobiographical novel. *My Life and Times* was published in 1926. Of his many plays his best-known is *The Passing of the Third Floor Back* (1907). He co-founded the humorous magazine *The Idler* in 1892, which published the work of several leading comic writers. Jerome's work is predominantly comic, in the tradition of 'the English clerk at play', but there is a sombre side that surfaces frequently, even in his funniest books: of the many reflective passages in *Three Men in a Boat*, some are genuinely tragic in feeling (e.g. the woman suicide), and in *Three Men on the Bummel* Jerome's judgements on the German character have an ironic thrust seen against nineteenth- and twentieth-century history. In this respect he resembles the later Mark Twain, though his view of human nature is more optimistic.

Jewel in the Crown, The, see RAJ QUARTET, THE.

JHABVALA, Ruth Prawer (1927–), British novelist, born in Cologne of Polish parents. She emigrated to England as a refugee in 1939, and was educated at Queen Mary College, London. Between 1951 and 1975 she lived in India and has since lived in New York. Her first two novels, *To Whom She Will* (1955) and *The Nature of Passion* (1956), express the author's fascination with the country of her adoption, exploring Western traditions and conflicts within the framework of domestic comedy. In *Esmond in India* (1958) she introduced the theme with which she was to be identified, the encounter between East and West. *The Householder* (1960), on the other hand, is an entirely Indian novel in subject matter and treatment; this portrait of a marriage was made into a successful film by Merchant Ivory Productions with whom Jhabvala has since frequently worked, writing innovative original screenplays such as *Shakespeare Wallah* (1973), *The Guru* (1968), and *Hullaballoo over Georgie and Bonnie's Pictures* (1978). She has also adapted several contemporary classics for the same company, notably *Rhys's *Quartet* (1981), *James's *The Bostonians* (1984), and Forster's *A *Room With a View* (1986). Jhabvala's novels of the 1970s signalled a deeper, richer phase of her writing. *A New Dominion* (1972) examines the mystic Hindu cults that began to proliferate in the 1960s, and their systematic and unscrupulous exploitation of Western *naïveté*. **Heat and Dust* (1975; Booker Prize) is perhaps her finest novel. In the novels published since her departure from India, such as *In Search of Love and Beauty* (1983), *Three Continents* (1987), *Poet and Dancer* (1993), and *Shades of Memory* (1995),

Jhabvala has attempted to reconcile her ambivalent fascination with Indian themes and her experience of contemporary America, linking her subjects with a distinctive expatriate sensibility. Jhabvala is also the author of several volumes of short stories including *Out of India* (1987).

John Bull's Other Island, a play by G. B. *Shaw, first performed in 1904, mainly set in its author's native Ireland. Larry Doyle, an Irish civil engineer settled in London, returns to his own island with his business partner, a sentimental, self-satisfied, but practical Englishman named Thomas Broadbent. Doyle, who regards Ireland as a land of frustrated dreamers and futile cynics, is at first seen by the priest and other community leaders as a possible parliamentary candidate; but his views are too unorthodox, and perhaps too Shavian, for them. Broadbent, who thinks that 'Home Rule will work wonders under English guidance', manages to express his complacent Liberal Party beliefs in an acceptable way; and ends up winning the local heiress, somehow turning a comical car trip with a pig to his political advantage, and preparing to bring hotels and golf links to the undeveloped countryside. The play, though full of humorous observation and entertaining argument, shows Shaw's feelings of alienation when he reflected on Ireland. Aspects of the dramatist are to be found both in the bitter Doyle, who is clearly more comfortable in England, and in the ex-priest Peter Keegan, who speaks with sombre power about his 'ignorant and oppressed land' and with ringing pessimism of his conviction that the world itself is 'hell'.

JOHNSON, Amryl (*c.*1948–), British poet, born in Tunapuna, Trinidad; she has lived in Britain since the age of 11. She was educated at the University of Kent, became a teacher of arts education at the University of Warwick, and is a popular performance poet. Many of the poems in *Long Road to Nowhere* (1985) make extensive use of imagery inspired by the Trinidad Carnival. Whether politically charged, or more personal, her poems are invariably distinctive in the expression of thought and feeling. The encounter described in 'Black Coral' is very much about the 'urgency of longing', yet it also displays a strong sense of individual, and politically defined, identity. 'The New Cargo Ship' powerfully and ironically merges collective memories of past slavery with present-day emigration. Some of her poems also make skilled use of Creole dialect, such as the humorous 'Peanut Vendor'. An earlier collection also entitled *Long Road to Nowhere* (1982) contains only one poem reprinted in the later work. *Tread Carefully in Paradise* (1991) collects poems from the two earlier works. *Gorgons* (1992) consists of poems that use the myth of the Gorgon as a unifying motif. *Sequins for a Ragged Hem* (1988), a prose work, describes her return to Trinidad for a visit in 1983, which she found to be a 'haunting' experience.

JOHNSON, B(ryan) S(tanley William) (1933–73), British writer and film-maker, born in London, educated at King's College, London. His first novel, *Travelling People* (1963), was an experimental work employing a diversity of styles; the influences of J. *Joyce, S. *Beckett, F. *O'Brien, and L. Sterne can be discerned in the deliberate fragmentation of the narrative and in the use of typographical devices to suggest breaks in continuity. This playful experimentation continued in the novels *Albert Angelo* (1964) and *Trawl* (1966; Somerset Maugham Award, 1967), the latter of which was described by the author as 'all interior monologue, a representation of the inside of my mind but at one remove', but reached its most extreme form in his celebrated 'novel in a box', *The Unfortunates* (1969), in which the twenty-seven loose-leaf sections could be arranged in any order. In this work, which dealt with the narrator's feelings on the death of a close friend from cancer, the author's intention was to 'create an alternative to the enforced consecutiveness of the conventional novel' and to offer the reader a metaphor for the randomness of experience. *House Mother Normal: A Geriatric Comedy* (1971) displayed the vein of black comedy running throughout Johnson's work. *Consequences: A Novel* (1972) was followed by *Christie Malry's Own Double-Entry* (1973); in this novel the author himself intrudes into the narrative in order to converse with the character. *See the Old Lady Decently*, the first part of the projected but never completed 'Matrix' trilogy on the theme of motherhood (other sections were to have been entitled *Buried Although* and *Amongst Those Left Are You*), was published posthumously in 1975. Other publications include a collection of short stories, *Statement against Corpses* (1964), published with Zulfikar *Ghose; *Street Children* (1964), illustrated with photographs by Julia Trevelyan Oman; two volumes of poems published in 1963 and 1972; and *The Evacuees* (1968), a collection of personal narratives, which he made into a film of the same name for the BBC. *The Unfortunates* was also filmed for television. Other cinematic works include *You're Human Like the Rest of Them*, produced for the British Film Institute in 1967, and *Up Yours Too, Guillaume Apollinaire!* (BFI, 1968). Several of Johnson's plays were performed, including *Whose Dog Are You?* (1971), *One Sodding Thing after Another* (1967), and *Entry*, produced in 1965 for BBC radio. Consistently experimental in all his chosen media, Johnson attempted to deconstruct conventional narrative forms, to reflect what he saw as the multi-levelled nature of human experience.

JOHNSON, Charles R(ichard) (1948–), African-American novelist, essayist, short-story writer, and screenwriter, born in Evanston, Illinois, educated at Southern Illinois University and the State University of New York. He began his artistic career as a cartoonist, and published two collections of comic art: *Black Humor* (1970) and *Half-Past Nation Time* (1972). His writings, both fiction and non-fiction, reflect his assiduous study of world philosophies. Johnson's first published novel, *Faith and the Good Thing* (1974), explores Faith's search for the meaning of life, the 'good thing'. *Oxherding Tale* (1982), set in the nineteenth century, also concentrates on the search for enlightenment and liberation; *Middle Passage* (1990; National Book Award), a fictionalized slave narrative also set in the nineteenth century, is a metaphysical journey leading the protagonist, Rutherford Calhoun, on a quest for knowledge and self-revelation of which Johnson wrote the screen adaptation. *The Sorcerer's Apprentice* (1986) is a volume of short stories. His collection of essays *Being and Race: Black Writing Since 1970* (1988) asserts the importance of diverse philosophical fiction in contemporary African-American literature. He became Professor of English at the University of Washington.

JOHNSON, Colin, see MUDROOROO.

JOHNSON, Denis (1949–), American writer, born in Munich, Germany, educated at the University of Iowa. His work combines harsh realism with allusions to myth and Christian symbolism, in an American tradition that includes Jim *Harrison, Louise *Erdrich, and Jayne Ann *Phillips. His first novel was *Angels* (1984), in which a pair of outcasts, a sailor and a convict, engage in bank robbery and murder. This was followed by the futuristic *Fiskadoro* (1985), a surreal evocation of forgotten wars and global crises; *The Stars at Noon* (1989); and *Resuscitation of a Hanged Man* (1991), in which the protagonist falls in love with a lesbian. *Jesus' Son* (1992) is a collection of linked stories narrated by a heroin addict. Johnson's poetry is collected in *New and Collected Poems* (1995).

JOHNSON, Georgia Douglas (Camp) (1886–1966), African-American poet, born in Atlanta, Georgia, where she was educated at the University. After teaching in Alabama, she moved to Washington, DC in 1909 and subsequently served with numerous government agencies. The passionate lyricism of *The Heart of a Woman* (1918), her first collection of verse, established her as one of the first black woman poets to achieve recognition in the USA. Her concern with racial issues was clearly stated in *Bronze* (1922), which displayed her accomplishment in making inventive use of traditional verse forms. *An Autumn Love Cycle* (1928), in which she began using free verse extensively, marked a return to the more private concerns of her earlier work. A final collection entitled *Share My World* appeared in 1962. During the 1920s a number of her plays were produced, most notably *Blue Blood* (1927), which controversially dealt with the rape of a black woman by white men.

JOHNSON, James Weldon (1871–1938), American poet, songwriter, and critic, born in Jacksonville, Florida, educated at Jacksonville and Columbia Universities. In 1901 he and his brother, John Rosamond, moved to New York, where they collaborated on successful musical comedies. He was General Secretary of the National Association for the Advancement of Colored People from 1920 to 1930, and served as a US diplomat in Venezuela and Nicaragua (1906–13). He also held many academic posts. His poetry draws heavily on the African-American folk and religious traditions. Very biblical in style, his best-known collection, *God's Trombones* (1927), consists of seven sermons by an old-time black preacher; his other collections include *Fifty Years and Other Poems* (1917) and *St. Peter Relates an Incident of the Resurrection Day* (1930). His only novel, *The Autobiography of an Ex-Colored Man* (1912), was a landmark in African-American fiction. *Along This Way* (1933), his autobiography, has become a classic. *The Book of American Negro Poetry* (1922, revised edition 1931), which he edited, was the first anthology of its kind, and was prefaced by 'An Essay on the Negro's Creative Genius'. Together with his brother, he also edited *The Book of American Negro Spirituals* (2 volumes, 1940). See also ETHNICITY and HARLEM RENAISSANCE.

JOHNSON, Linton Kwesi (1952–), British poet, born in Chapeltown, Jamaica; he moved to London in 1963, and was educated at Goldsmiths' College, University of London. Among other posts, he has worked as an Education Officer. Together with Benjamin *Zephaniah and John *Agard, he is one of the foremost *dub poets, all of whom write poetry primarily for performance. Political and social protest, with accompanying demotic rhetoric and articulate anger, are strong elements in Johnson's poems. Even in cold print, their powerful, mesmerizing rhythms demand attention. He is also successful in adapting English rhyme to West Indian speech patterns, as in this stanza from 'Reggae fi Dada': 'o di grass | turn brown | soh many trees | cut doun | an di lan is ovahgrown'. His collections include *Voices of the Living and the Dead* (1974), *Dread Beat an' Blood* (1975, recorded 1978), and *Inglan Is a Bitch* (1980). His recorded works included *Forces of Victory* (1979), *Bass Culture* (1980), and *Making History* (1984). *Tings and Times: Selected Poems* (1991) was released as both a book and a recording.

JOHNSON, Louis (1924–88), New Zealand poet, born in Wellington; he grew up in the rural areas of the North Island, and was educated at the Teachers' Training College in Wellington. Johnson spent some time in America during the 1970s, and in Melbourne, as a freelance writer, before returning to New Zealand in the 1980s. In the 1950s his poetry was important for its affirmation of the value and validity of ordinary suburban life in a period when this representative New Zealand experience was often ignored, if not derided. Like James K. *Baxter and Mike *Doyle, with both of whom he edited the magazine *Numbers* (1954–60), Johnson did not espouse the nationalistic reading of New Zealand imaginative history promulgated by Allen *Curnow. His acknowledged influences were *Pound and *Auden. Johnson's first collection, *Stanza and Scene* (1945), struck a representative prophetic tone, which *The Sun among the Ruins: Myths of the Living and the Dead* (1951) continued. Later collections include *The Dark Glass* (1955); *Bread and a Pension* (1964), a collection which included an experimental section; *Fires and Patters* (1976), which won the first New Zealand Poetry Book of the Year Award;

Coming and Going (1982); *Winter Apples* (1984); and *Confessions of the Last Cannibal* (1986). Johnson's *Last Poems* appeared posthumously in 1990.

JOHNSON, Pamela Hansford (1912–81), English novelist, critic, and playwright, born in London, educated at Clapham School and the Société Européenne de Culture. She subsequently taught at various universities, including Yale. London is the background for several of her works, including her first novel, *This Bed Thy Centre* (1935), which was published when she was 22 and was followed by more than twenty others, including *Blessed Above Women* (1936), *Girdle of Venus* (1939), *Too Dear for My Possessing* (1940), *The Trojan Brothers* (1944), *An Impossible Marriage* (1954), and *An Error of Judgement* (1962). Most of her novels have love as a central theme, although she also focused on the relationship between her characters and contemporary society. In her fiction and critical writing she was renowned for her delicately malicious wit. Her best-known work is perhaps the 'Dorothy Merlin' trilogy, a satire on the literary world, consisting of *The Unspeakable Skipton* (1959), *Night and Silence, Who Is Here* (1962), and *Cork Street, Next to the Hatter's* (1965). Later works include *The Good Listener* (1975) and *The Bonfire* (1981). She also published collections of poetry, including *Symphony for Full Orchestra* (1934), and plays, such as *Spare the Rod* (1951), as well as critical studies of I. *Compton-Burnett (1951) and C. P. *Snow (1983), whom she married in 1950. In 1975 she received the CBE. There is a biography by I. Quigley (1968).

JOHNSON, Terry (1955–), British playwright, born in Hillingdon, Middlesex, educated at Birmingham University; he was brought up in Watford, near London, where his father was a builder. His first successful play, later made into a film, was *Insignificance* (1982), a satiric fantasy which brings Einstein, Marilyn Monroe, the baseball player Joe DiMaggio, and the politician Joseph McCarthy into the same New York hotel room. Subsequent pieces have included *Unsuitable for Adults* (1984), about alternative comedians and other cabaret performers combatively at work and play in a London pub; *Cries from the Mammal House* (1984), which involves a group of mutually estranged people trying to save a zoo from collapse, among them a conservationist who goes to Mauritius and returns with a live dodo; *Tuesday's Child* (1986; with Kate Lock), about the appearance of what seems to be a pregnant virgin in an Irish village; *Hysteria* (1993), in which Freud, spending his old age in Hampstead, is visited by phantasms, notably the painter Salvador Dali, and accusing memories of former clinical cases; and the highly successful *Dead Funny* (1994), which involves both troubled marriages and the obsessive people who belong to groups dedicated to the appreciation of Benny Hill and other comedians. Johnson's work, usually comic but sometimes sombre in tone, is marked by a Stoppardian delight in ideas and unexpected imaginative connections.

JOHNSTON, Sir Charles (Hepburn) (1912–86), British poet, born in London, educated at Balliol College, Oxford. In 1936 he began his career in the British Diplomatic Service. After a succession of postings in various capitals, including Tokyo, Cairo, Madrid, and Bonn, he became High Commissioner in Australia in 1965. Much of his poetry draws richly on the landscapes of his diplomatic experiences. During the war he was interned by the Japanese, which gave rise to some of his most memorable and complex poetry in the Spenserian stanzas of *Towards Mozambique* (1947). It was published under the pseudonym 'Charles Hepburn', which he also used for *For Leagros and Other Poems* (1940), his first collection of verse. A poet of polished accomplishment in traditional modes, he first gained wide notice with his translation of Pushkin's *Eugene Onegin* (1977). Among his subsequent collections are *Rivers and Fireworks* (1980) and *Talk about the Last Poet* (1981), which typically consist of further translations, principally of Pushkin and Lermontov, interspersed with original work. He also wrote a number of books on the countries to which he was posted, including *The Brink of Jordan* (1972) and *The View from Steamer Point* (1964), an account of his time in Aden. As a writer of fiction, he produced *Mo and Other Originals* (1971). His *Selected Poems*, with an introduction by Roy *Fuller, appeared in 1985.

JOHNSTON, (William) Denis (1901–84), Irish dramatist, born in Dublin, educated at Christ's College, Cambridge, and the Harvard Law School. He was a member of the Board of the Dublin Gate Theatre (1931–6). His experiences as war correspondent for the BBC in the Middle East and Europe (1942–5) are chronicled in *Nine Rivers from Jordan* (1953). His most celebrated play, *The Moon in the Yellow River* (1932), produced at the *Abbey Theatre in 1931, confronts extreme republicanism in a post-Civil War Ireland. His other plays, which Johnston characterized as 'in various ways historical', include *The Old Lady Says 'No'!* (1929), *A Bride for the Unicorn* (1933), *The Dreaming Dust* (1940), and *The Scythe and the Sunset* (1958), which is a riposte to *O'Casey's *The Plough and the Stars* (1926). His *Collected Plays* (2 volumes, 1960) contain informative prefatory remarks. His other books include the highly controversial *In Search of Swift* (1959); *John Millington Synge* (1965); and *The Brazen Horn* (1968; revised edition 1976), a meditative autobiography. He was the father of Jennifer *Johnston.

JOHNSTON, Dorothy (1948–), Australian novelist, born in Geelong, Victoria, educated at the University of Melbourne. She was a founding member of the Seven Writers group, which jointly wrote *Canberra Tales* (1988). Her works include *Tunnel Vision* (1984), a short novel set in a massage parlour; and *Ruth* (1986), a story of a middle-aged woman who leaves her husband and lives with her children at a women's refuge. *Maralinga, My Love* (1988) examines the British atomic tests in South Australia and their devastating effects; the novel also explores the neo-colonial relationship between Britain and Australia during that period, figured in terms of oedipal relationships between the male characters.

JOHNSTON, George Benson (1913–), Canadian poet, born in Hamilton, Ontario, educated at the University of Toronto. Johnston is a comparative rarity among Canadian poets as a writer of comic verse. His apparently simple metres and traditional subjects often conceal layers of technical complexity and irony that are not always obvious on a first reading. His interest in middle-class suburban Canadian life has placed him outside the mainstream of contemporary Canadian poetry, but he has explored his chosen poetic terrain with considerable skill and perspicacity, frequently blending compassion with a sharp, satirical eye. His volumes of verse include *The Cruising Auk* (1959), *Home Free* (1966), *Happy Enough: Poems 1935–72* (1972), *Taking a Grip: Poems 1972–78* (1979), and *Auk Redivivus* (1981). A scholar of Old Norse, Johnston has also produced important translations of sagas and *Rocky Shores* (1981), a verse translation of work by modern Faroese poets.

JOHNSTON, George Henry (1912–70), Australian novelist, born in Melbourne. A journalist, reporting from several battle zones, he wrote five books about different aspects of the Second World War. He was appointed European editor for the Sydney *Sun* in 1950, and from 1954 he spent ten years in Greece. The trilogy of novels published at the end of his career constitute his best work; largely autobiographical, they also show an important shift in Australian consciousness. *My Brother Jack* (1964) summarizes, in Jack, the epitome of the Australian male in the nationalist and post-Anzac period; it is the intellectual, David, second-rate by that standard, who succeeds, lionized for his war journalism. *Clean Straw For Nothing* (1969) records disillusioning, expatriate, middle years. The unfinished *A Cartload of Clay* (1971) reconciles the returned expatriate to the limitations of his land. Johnston wrote thrillers as 'Shane Martin', and also two travel books and three novels with his wife, the journalist Charmian Clift. Johnston and Clift's stories were collected in *Strong Man from Pireaus* (1984).

JOHNSTON, Jennifer (1930–), Irish novelist, born in Dublin into a theatrical family (her father was Denis *Johnston), educated at Trinity College, Dublin. Her first novel, *The Captains and the Kings* (1972), established Johnston as one of the foremost chroniclers of the Northern Irish experience. Issues of class and religion, the decaying fortunes of the Anglo-Irish gentry, and the conflicting loyalties of successive Irish generations are Johnston's major fictional preoccupations. Her fictions fall into three overlapping categories: *The Gates* (1973), *The Old Jest* (1980), and *Fool's Sanctuary* (1987) feature female protagonists, usually adolescents, embodying the divided loyalties of class and nation that link them to the male protagonists of *The Captains and the Kings* and of *How Many Miles to Babylon?* (1974), novels which depict relationships between members of the Anglo-Irish gentry and the Catholic underclass. The third category, represented by *Shadows on Our Skin* (1978), concentrates exclusively on the urban working class. *The Railway Station Man* (1985) reiterates all Johnston's fictional concerns with her combination of compassion and objectivity, incorporating a philosophical meditation on the relationship between art and mourning. An unusual departure is *The Christmas Tree* (1982), the story of a dying woman's love for a survivor of the Holocaust. In her novel *The Invisible Worm* (1991), Johnston reworks her theme—the Big House in Ireland—to include more overtly sexual imagery; the heroine is sexually and emotionally abused by her politician father. The *Illusionist* (1995) is a love story set partly in London.

JOLLEY, Elizabeth (1923–), Australian short-story writer and novelist, born in Birmingham; she went to Western Australia in 1959. After early success as a radio dramatist she published two volumes of short stories later collected in *Stories* (1984). In *Woman in a Lampshade* (1983) the stories reveal Jolley's growing interest in odd characters and disconcerting situations. Her first novel, *Palomino* (1980), was followed by two novels about eccentric old people: *The Newspaper of Claremont Street* (1981), concerning a cleaning woman known as 'Newspaper' for her command of gossip; and *Mr Scobie's Riddle* (1983), about a squalid old people's home from which Mr Scobie bravely and madly attempts to escape. *Miss Peabody's Inheritance* (1983) is a novel about a woman who works in an office and cares for her sick mother; her life is enhanced by letters from an Australian novelist, concerning 'work in progress', in whose imaginary world Miss Peabody lives. *Sugar Mother* (1988) is a black comedy about the Virgin birth in a modern setting. Jolley's distinctive talent is for a world of outwardly reassuring normality in which disturbingly powerful conflicts of morality and social relations surface to challenge the comfortable complacencies of both the individual and the community. Other novels include *Milk and Honey* (1984), *Foxybaby* (1985), *The Well* (1986), *My Father's Moon* (1989), and *Cabin Fever* (1990).

JONES, (Walter) David (Michael) (1895–1974), British poet and graphic artist, born in Brockley, Kent, educated at Camberwell School of Art and Westminster School of Art. He enlisted for military service in 1915 and was wounded in 1916 at Mametz Wood, the setting for the conclusion of *In Parenthesis* (1937), his first publication of note, which was acclaimed by T. S. *Eliot as 'a work of genius'. Parts of the book, which develops chronologically around the experience of Jones's persona 'Private John Ball', resemble a straightforward memoir of the war; much of it, however, modulates between idiosyncratically mannered free verse and richly lyrical prose. The documentary content fuses with Jones's historical, mythical, and metaphysical concerns as the work moves towards its concluding vision of redemptive transcendence. Throughout the 1920s Jones worked with Eric *Gill in Sussex and Wales. His conversion to

Catholicism in 1921 was of essential importance to both his graphic art and his writing, which are deeply imbued with his devotional sensibility. Examples of his work as a graphic artist are on permanent exhibition in the Tate Gallery, the Victoria and Albert Museum, and other leading galleries. *The Anathemata* (1952), which W. H. *Auden referred to as 'probably the finest long poem written in English this century', again moves freely between poetry and prose; its eight parts centre on Jones's concern to relieve the spiritual and cultural impoverishment of the modern era by re-establishing contact with Christian and pre-Christian systems of meaning and symbol. The work, which carries a remarkably extensive apparatus of notes, is densely inlaid with linguistic and archaeological references to Welsh, classical, biblical, and ancient British sources. His opposition to centralized control in modern cultures is stated in *The Sleeping Lord and Other Fragments* (1974), the title piece of which forms a compelling accumulation of topographical and mythical imagery identifying indigenously sacramental values as sources of possible regeneration. *Epoch and Artist* (1959) and *The Dying Gaul* (1974) are collections of his essays and other prose writings. *Dai Greatcoat* (1980, edited by R. Hague) is subtitled 'a self-portrait of David Jones in his letters'; *David Jones: Artist and Writer*, a biography by D. Blamires, appeared in 1971.

JONES, Gayl (Amanda) (1949–), African-American novelist and poet, born in Lexington, Kentucky, educated at Connecticut College and Brown University; she later taught at the University of Michigan. Her disturbing first novel, *Corregidora* (1975), like her subsequent fictions *Eva's Man* (1976) and the short-story collection *White Rat* (1977), explores the psychology and sexual identity of her characters, often women doubly oppressed by racism and sexism, who are caught up in emotionally violent relationships. The language used is at times correspondingly raw and is rooted in the traditions of black speech and music patterns. Her writing also has a ritualistic and historical aspect that reflects her study of the African presence in Brazil and Mexico in past centuries, which is particularly evident in her poetry such as *Song for Anninho* (1981), an extended ballad about an eighteenth-century slave revolt in Brazil, and *Xarque and Other Poems* (1985). She is the author of the critical work *Liberating Voices: Oral Tradition in African American Literature* (1991). See also ETHNICITY.

JONES, Henry Arthur (1851–1929), British dramatist, born in Grandborough, Buckinghamshire, the son of a farmer; he left school early to become a draper's assistant and a commercial traveller. In 1878 he gave up regular employment to try his luck as a writer, had *A Clerical Error* performed in London the following year, and scored a huge success with the melodrama *The Silver King* in 1882. Gradually, he established himself as a major figure in the late nineteenth-century theatre, second only to *Pinero as an exponent of the well-made play. He wrote several lively comedies: among them, *The Case of Rebellious Susan* (1894); a satiric attack on provincial puritanism, *The Triumph of the Philistines* (1895); and the witty, cynical *The Liars* (1897). However, his reputation in his own era depended primarily on 'problem plays' which, like those of Pinero, and from a stance fundamentally as conventional, treated such subjects as the woman with a dubious past and double standards of sexual behaviour. *Mrs Dane's Defence* (1900) remains the most effective of these, but the same theme intrudes in *Saints and Sinners* (1884) and *Michael and His Lost Angel* (1895), two plays in which the protagonist is a clergyman afflicted by scandal. The latter was praised by *Shaw, as much an admirer of Jones as he was hostile to Pinero, as 'genuinely sincere and moving'; but posterity has judged the playwright's serious work more harshly.

JONES, James (1921–77), American novelist, born in Robinson, Illinois. Jones served in the US Army in the Pacific during 1939–44, an experience which informs his most famous novel, *From Here to Eternity* (1951), and two later novels, *The Pistol* (1958) and *The Thin Red Line* (1962). From 1958 to 1974 he lived in Paris, and wrote a novel about the May 1968 riots, *The Merry Month of May* (1971). Jones was never to match the authoritative intimacy and scope of his portrait of army life in *From Here to Eternity*, which has been compared with Norman Mailer's *The *Naked and the Dead* (1948), and was made into a popular film, directed by Fred Zinneman, starring Burt Lancaster, Deborah Kerr, Montgomery Clift, and Frank Sinatra. The novel is set in an army barracks on the eve of the Japanese attack on Pearl Harbor, but is not strictly a war novel. It uses the impending arena of battle as the setting for the conflict of individualism between its central characters, Private Robert E. Lee Prewitt (named after the Confederate general) and Sergeant Milton Warden, whose job it is to enforce the military orthodoxies of absolute loyalty and service to the system. It is a novel of brutal events, of moral and sexual betrayal, ending in suicide and murder. Jones's other works are the novels *Some Came Running* (1958), *Go to the Widow-Maker* (1967), *A Touch of Danger* (1973), and *Whistle* (1974–8); *The Ice-Cream Headache and Other Stories* (1968); and his diary of a visit to Vietnam in 1973, *Viet Journal* (1974).

JONES, Leroi, see BARAKA, AMIRI.

JONES, Madison (Percy, Jr) (1925–), American novelist, born in Nashville, Tennessee, educated at Vanderbilt University and the University of Florida. Jones was influenced by the ideology of regionalism of the *Agrarians, especially Donald *Davidson and Andrew *Lytle. In the 1940s he was a farmer and a horse-trainer, and in 1956 became a teacher at Auburn University, Alabama. The regionalism is most evident in his first novel, *The Innocent* (1957), which deals with the life and experiences of Duncan Welsh, whilst *Forest of the Night* (1960) continued the interest in American innocence by placing it within the context of the wilderness of frontier life in the 1800s. *A Buried Land* (1963) described the flood damage and destruction of farms and communities by the Tennessee Valley Authority in the 1930s. After *An Exile* (1967; filmed as *I Walk the Line*, 1970), came his most widely received book, *A Cry of Absence* (1971), about the shock waves caused in a Southern community by the brutal murder of a black man. *Passage through Gehenna* (1978) was about fundamentalist religion, while *Season of the Strangler* (1982) drew together twelve stories through the central symbolic figure of a local strangler, and is a series of portraits of people who strangle their own lives. *Last Things* (1989) explores the corrupt life of a Southern village, as the aspiring young writer Wendell Corbin sinks into a life of drug-running and racketeering. Jones's fiction focuses on traditional themes, such as Southern small-town values, fundamentalism, moonshine, racial tension, loyalty to the Confederacy, and the ramifications of historical change for small, insular societies.

JONES, Mervyn (1922–), British novelist, short-story writer, and journalist, son of Ernest Jones, the biographer of Freud; he is a former assistant editor of *Tribune* (1955–60) and of the *New Statesman* (1966–8). The background of his fiction reflects twentieth-century social and political issues, which are examined from a left-wing perspective, whilst the stories themselves focus on human relationships. A prolific writer, his work has an underlying commitment to the struggle of the working class. It includes *No Time To Be Young* (1952), *The Last Barricade* (1953), *John and Mary* (1966), and, notably, *Holding On* (1973, adapted for television), which portrays the heroic struggles of a family in the East End of London and the breakdown of their culture as they endure the major economic and social changes of the century. Later novels include *Today The Struggle* (1978), *Coming Home* (1986), and *That Year in Paris* (1988). He has also written the biographies *A Radical Life: The Biography of Megan Lloyd George, 1902–1966* (1991) and *Michael Foot* (1994).

JONG, Erica (1942–), American novelist and poet, born in New York City, and educated at Barnard College (New York), Columbia University, and Columbia School of Fine Arts. She has since held a number of academic posts. *Fear of Flying* (1973), her first, and most famous, novel, focuses on the sexual fantasies of the heroine, Isadora Wing, writer and New Yorker. Her frustrated, but adventurous, open-ended, and sexually experimental quest for self-knowledge struck a chord with many readers and critics. She appeared to herald a new kind of liberated, literary heroine. Its sequels are *How To Save Your Own Life* (1977), *Parachutes and Kisses* (1984), and *Any Woman's Blues* (1990). In a sense, Jong has revived the genre of picaresque fiction (long a male preserve) and given it a feminist edge. Her talent for literary and historical pastiche, successfully transformed into her own fictive vision, is reflected in *Fanny, Being the Adventures of Fanny Hackabout Jones* (1980) and *Serenissima: A Novel of Venice* (1987), perhaps her best novel. Her collections of verse, mainly *confessional, include *The Poetry of Erica Jong* (1976), *At the Edge of the Body* (1979), *Ordinary Miracles* (1983), and *Becoming Light: Poems New and Selected* (1991). *Fear of Fifty: A Mid-Life Memoir* (1994) is an autobiographical account. She is also the author of *The Devil at Large: Erica Jong on Henry Miller* (1993), a biographical and critical reassessment of *Miller and his works, relying on the author's acquaintance with her subject.

JORDAN, June (1936–), American poet and essayist, born in New York City, where she was educated at Barnard College. Since the 1960s, when she was active in the civil rights movement, she has taught at various colleges throughout the USA and became Professor and Afro-American Studies and Women's Studies at the University of California, Berkeley, in 1989. Jordan's work testifies to her belief in the inseparability of personal and political realities through its characteristic grounding of her statements against racism and sexism in her own emotional and social experiences. Her poetry, noted for the lyrical energy of its free verse forms, has appeared in numerous collections which include *Some Changes* (1971), *Things That I Do in the Dark* (1977), and *Living Room* (1985); *Naming Our Destiny: New and Selected Poems* was published in 1989. *Civil Wars* (1981), *Moving towards Home* (1989), and *Technical Difficulties: African-American Notes on the State of the Union* (1992) are among the collections of her essays, which often combine vivid reportage with the powerful expression of her political creed.

JORDAN, Neil (1951–), Irish short-story writer, novelist, and film director, born in Sligo, educated at University College, Dublin. He worked as a labourer and a teacher until he founded the Irish Writers' Co-operative in Dublin in 1974. Although more widely known for his films, Jordan has made significant contributions to contemporary Irish writing. His first collection of short stories, *Night in Tunisia and Other Stories* (1976), plays with literary genre and history in a way which is characteristic of *post-modern fiction. His novels include *The Past* (1980), *The Dream of a Beast* (1983), and, most notably, *Sunrise with Sea Monster* (1995), an exuberant narrative set in Ireland in the 1930s, and Spain, where the chief protagonist is a prisoner in the Spanish Civil War. Jordan has written and directed several feature films, including *Angel* (1982), *A Company of Wolves* (1984), adapted from the story by Angela *Carter, *Mona Lisa* (1986), *High Spirits* (1990), and *The Crying Game* (1992), most of which have been critically acclaimed.

JOSEPH, Jenny (Jenefer Ruth) (1932–), British poet, born in Birmingham, educated at St Hilda's College, Oxford. She has worked as a journalist and as a lecturer in adult education. *The Unlooked-For Season*, her first collection of verse, appeared in 1960. She produced no further volumes until *Rose in the Afternoon* (1974), which was followed by *The Thinking Heart* (1978), *Beyond Descartes* (1983), *Beached Boats* (1991), *Selected Poems* (1992), and *Ghosts and Other Company*

(1995). Much of her poetry strikes an unusually effective balance between its qualities of statement and its carefully observed imagery. Her work is also notable for its witty and energetic sense of philosophical enquiry into everyday events. *Persephone* (1986), her experimental fiction in prose and poetry, won the James Tait Black Memorial Prize; the Greek myth provides a basis for a complex treatment of self-discovery and the relations between mother and daughter. She has also written numerous books for children.

JOSEPH, M(ichael) K(ennedy) (1914–81), New Zealand poet and novelist, born in London, educated at University College, Auckland, and at Oxford University. After serving in the Second World War, he returned to New Zealand to teach at the University of Auckland where he later became Professor of English. His first novel, *I'll Soldier No More* (1958), an impressive exploration of service life as well as a statement of his Christian values, established his reputation. Later novels were challenging in their choice of contemporary subject matter: *A Pound of Saffron* (1962) focuses on a Machiavellian academic while *The Hole in the Zero* (1967) is set in the future. Joseph continued to be fascinated by his war experience, and his last novel, *A Soldier's Tale* (1976; also filmed), returned to this setting in a romance in Second World War France. A selection of Joseph's poems, collected in *Inscriptions on a Paper Dart* (1974), show his wide range of verse form, styles, and voices, and reveal particularly his talent for pastiche and parody.

Joseph Vance, see DE MORGAN, WILLIAM.

JOSIPOVICI, Gabriel (David) (1940–), British writer, born in France; he grew up in Egypt and moved to England in 1956. He became a lecturer in literature at Sussex University in 1963, and a part-time professor in 1984. In both his novels and his plays he is concerned with identity, memory, and the nature of perception. Often abandoning the traditional fictional structures, his work reconstructs the world rather than imitating it. His novels include *The Inventory* (1968), *Words* (1971), and *The Present* (1975). His concern with the difficulties of individual communication has led some critics to regard the characters in his novels as descendants of the isolated beings of Samuel *Beckett. *Contre-Jour* (1986) is a study of the relationship between a painter (based on Pierre Bonnard), his estranged wife, and their imaginary daughter. *The Big Glass* (1991), whose title is an allusion to Marcel Duchamp's celebrated work, is a fictionalized account of the artist's life. Later novels include *In a Hotel Garden* (1993) and *Moo Pak* (1994). His plays include *Mobius and the Stripper* (1974) and *Vergil Dying* (1977). Amongst his works of literary criticism are *The Lessons of Modernism* (1977), *The Book of God: A Response to the Bible* (1988), his edition of *The Modern English Novel: The Reader, the Writer and the Book* (1975), and *Text and Voice* (1992).

'Journey of the Magi, The', a poem by T. S. *Eliot, published in 1927 as the eighth of the Ariel poems, a series of illustrated pamphlets issued by Faber and Gwyer (later *Faber and Faber). The poem's directness of statement and religious content became central characteristics of his later work. It forms a monologue spoken by one of the Magi, who describes the rigours of the journey to the infant Christ and concludes by reflecting disquietedly on the passing of 'the old dispensation'. Appearing shortly after Eliot's reception into the Anglican Communion, the poem serves to allegorize an entry into faith that has involved an arduous transition from spiritual death to birth. The inverted commas enclosing the first five lines indicate their direct derivation from a sermon by Lancelot Andrewes (1555–1626), to whom Eliot dedicated the collection of essays he published in 1928.

Journey's End, a play by R. C. *Sherriff, first performed in 1928. It is set in the trenches late in the First World War, in which the author himself served as a subaltern. Captain Stanhope returns from leave, to find to his dismay that a new lieutenant, Raleigh, who hero-worshipped him at school, has inveigled his way into his company. But it is soon apparent to the boy, as to everybody else, that the heavy drinking of which Stanhope is ashamed has not compromised his competence as an officer. For instance, he deals highly effectively with a frightened lieutenant, Hibbert, who tries to report sick. Raleigh successfully captures a prisoner in a raid on the German lines, but Osborne, Stanhope's second-in-command, is killed. Raleigh, too, dies of wounds, this time in the big enemy offensive that continues as the play ends. Sherriff makes no direct condemnation of the war; but his unpretentiously authentic observation of ordinary and mostly unprotesting men helplessly trapped in an intolerable predicament carries its own message.

JOYCE, James (Augustine Aloysius) (1882–1941), Irish novelist, short-story writer, and poet, born in Dublin, educated, despite his father's declining fortunes, at Jesuit schools: Clongowes Wood College, Co. Kildare, and Belvedere College, Dublin where he, in turn, considered the priesthood and rejected the Roman Catholic faith. Attending University College, Dublin, to read modern languages, he wandered from the curriculum, developed an aesthetic based upon his interpretation of Aquinas, and chose to have no part with either Irish nationalism or the *Irish Literary Revival (though he later welcomed assistance from *Russell ('AE'), *Yeats, and Lady *Gregory). Instead, he looked to the writers of continental Europe for his influences; his first published work, 'Ibsen's New Drama', precocious and outspoken, attracted a warm response from the Norwegian playwright. Upon graduating in 1902, Joyce left for Paris where he lived in poverty, ostensibly studying medicine, actually reading his way through the literature section of the Bibliothèque Nationale. In April 1903, news of his mother's imminent death recalled him to Dublin. Supporting himself by teaching, he remained there for eighteen restless months and began to write short stories and an autobiographical novel, *Stephen Hero*

(1944). He lived briefly with Oliver St John *Gogarty in the Martello Tower at Sandycove, contemplated his failure as an artist, and then met Nora Barnacle, the woman with whom he would share the rest of his life. Within months of their first walk together on 16 June 1904, they left Ireland for Europe from where they would seldom and, eventually, never, return. While they led an almost nomadic existence pursuing teaching positions in Zurich, Trieste, Pola, and Rome, their two children were born: Georgio in Trieste in 1905 and then Lucia in 1907, again in Trieste. The family managed to stay there until 1915, when the First World War forced them to move to Zurich.

Between 1904 and 1906 Joyce composed the majority of the love poems collected in *Chamber Music* (1907), his first published book; due to his loss of enthusiasm for the work, the final arrangement of the thirty-six poems was made by his brother Stanislaus. Dowland and Jonson are recalled by the exquisite lyrical refinement of the collection, the title of which reflects the proliferation of images relating to music; 'I hear an army charging upon the land . . .', the last of the sequence, was included in *Des Imagistes* (1914; see IMAGISM). A later volume, *Pomes Penyeach* (1927), contained thirteen strikingly concentrated poems mostly composed in Trieste and Zurich between 1912 and 1918; predominantly in rhymed forms of great originality and flexibility, many of the poems form powerfully imaginative records of significant moments of autobiographical experience. *Poems And Shorter Writings* (edited by Richard *Ellmann and others, 1991) contains the well-known 'Ecce Puer' and seventy-two 'Occasional Poems', many remarkable for their wittily brilliant informality; the volume also collects the 'Epiphanies', fragments of dialogue and description written from 1901 onwards.

In **Dubliners*, a collection of fifteen short stories, Joyce displayed the blend of lyricism and realism that was to remain characteristic of his work, even at its most experimental. The stories, which he began writing in Dublin in 1904, were completed with the final story, 'The Dead', in 1907, and published, after numerous rejections and difficulties, in 1914. By this time Joyce's work had attracted the attentions of *Pound and Harriet Shaw Weaver, editor of *The *Egoist*, who took up the cause of the exiled Irish writer and exerted a deciding influence in his favour.

The serialization of his first novel, *A *Portrait of the Artist as a Young Man*, a more complex and ironic version of the previously abandoned *Stephen Hero*, in *The Egoist* (1914–15) led to its publication in New York in 1916. A play, *Exiles* (1918), was produced unsuccessfully in Munich in 1919 and did not reach a London stage until 1926. The effects of such disappointments, Joyce's financial insolvency, and his rapidly deteriorating eyesight were alleviated by the level-headed support of his brother, Stanislaus, and the generosity of friends. Through the efforts of Yeats and *Pound to ensure recognition of his work, Joyce obtained a grant from the Royal Literary Fund in 1915 and from the Civil List soon afterwards. After the war, Joyce and his family left Zurich and returned to Trieste from where they moved to Paris in 1920. In Paris, Joyce became the centre of the expatriate literary community (see LOST GENERATION), which included G. *Stein, *Hemingway, R. *McAlmon, and Pound, through whom he met T. S. *Eliot and W. *Lewis, an encounter amusingly described in Lewis's memoirs, *Blasting and Bombardiering* (1937).

Relatively free to work, Joyce came near to finishing the novel that would make his name. **Ulysses* was serialized in *The Egoist* in 1919 and continued in *The *Little Review* in 1920 until it was prosecuted by a US court for obscenity. The scandal meant that no publisher in the English-speaking world would touch the complete book. In the end, *Ulysses* was published in 1922 by Sylvia Beach under the imprint of her Paris bookshop, Shakespeare and Co., but the first UK edition did not appear until 1936. It was Joyce's honest depiction of sexuality and some of the more mundane of human functions that upset the sensibility of the day. He had developed the *'stream of consciousness' technique to such a degree that no detail was spared, no thought omitted from the minds of his characters. The reaction from other writers was mixed: Eliot, for example, welcomed the use of *The Odyssey* to draw meaning from modern life and acknowledged its influence on *The *Waste Land* (1922); *Woolf was less impressed, believing *Ulysses* to be 'the book of a self-taught working man'; Stein felt her own position as arch-experimentalist challenged by Joyce's success. Samuel *Beckett, with whom Joyce had become friendly during this period, undertook the French translation of part of the novel.

During the seventeen years he spent on his next novel, Joyce released fragments of what he called 'Work in Progress' to a small, expectant, and frequently puzzled audience, which included *Ford, W. C. *Williams, and Beckett. **Finnegans Wake*, as the work was eventually titled, moved from the waking consciousness of *Ulysses* to a world of dream and nightmare. Though again set in Dublin, the streets evoked so particularly in previous works were now unrecognizable. Completed in 1932 but not published in its final form until 1939, *Finnegans Wake* remains one of the greatest and most uncompromising works of the *Modernist period. With *The Waste Land* and Pound's **Cantos*, the book epitomizes what M. *Bradbury has described as 'an émigré art of linguistic pluralism', reflecting the fragmentation and discontinuity of the post-war era. 'I have put the language to sleep', Joyce wrote of *Finnegans Wake* in a letter to Harriet Weaver; as he explained to Max *Eastman, 'In writing of the night, I really could not . . . use words in their ordinary connections . . . When morning comes of course everything will be clear again . . . I'll give them back their English language. I'm not destroying it for good.'

The influence of Joyce's work on his contemporaries, such as Woolf and Beckett, and on subsequent literature (in the work of writers as diverse as

S. *Bellow, J. *Updike, T. *Pynchon, J. *Barth, and A. *Burgess) has been enormous. His books have given rise to a vast body of critical commentary and disputes over authorial intention. One example was the controversy surrounding the 'Corrected Text' of *Ulysses*, edited by Hans Walter Gabler, Professor of English at Munich University, which was published in 1986 as a 'new copyright' version. This supposedly corrected many of the mistakes and corruptions of the earlier (1961) edition, but in 1988 an American academic, John Kidd, of the University of Virginia, claimed in an article in the *New York Review of Books* that the revised version was inaccurate and introduced errors not present in the 1961 edition.

Joyce and Nora Barnacle were married during a visit to London in 1931. Their lives, however, continued to be troubled. Joyce suffered from iritis and glaucoma; and their daughter, Lucia, who had been mentally unstable since her teens, was diagnosed as schizophrenic in 1932. In 1939 the family was once more compelled to move away from war. They returned to Zurich where Joyce failed to recover from an operation on a duodenal ulcer. He is buried in Fluntern Cemetery. There is a biography by R. Ellmann (1959; 2nd edition 1982). Also of interest are *The Letters of James Joyce*, published in three volumes: vol. i, edited by S. Gilbert (1957), vols. ii and iii, edited by R. Ellmann (1966); and *Selected Letters*, edited by R. Ellmann (1975).

Joy Luck Club, The, see TAN, AMY.

July's People, a novel by Nadine *Gordimer, published in 1981. To escape from a situation of siege, a white South African couple, Bam and Maureen Smales, leave their urban home with their children to seek refuge with their erstwhile servant, July, in his remote village. Their encounter with the realities of black South African life transforms entirely their hitherto limited perspective, forcing them to examine their relationship to privilege, to the comforts of 'civilized' life, and above all to July. The bond of servant and master is reversed as the Smaleses become entirely dependent upon July. Balanced subtly between critical realism and tensely constructed futuristic allegory, *July's People*, with its immediate predecessor, *Burger's Daughter*, marks a radical turning point in Gordimer's career. Liberalism, once central in her fictional discourse, has reached its limits and failed as a solution for racial equality and harmony; individual compassion is inadequate, and a total reconstruction of society is required. The fragmentation of Maureen's family serves as a metaphor for the dismantling of antiquated Eurocentric structures. Whereas the protagonists of other fictions by Gordimer choose revolutionary political activism as their only escape from the ossified situation they encounter, Maureen, at the chilling climax of the novel, is seen escaping from the harsh reality of village life to an uncertain future symbolized by the appearance of a helicopter in the distance.

Jumpers, a play by Tom *Stoppard, performed and published in 1972. Perhaps Stoppard's most original attempt to reconcile intellectual ideas with what he has called 'the theatre of audacity', this play begins with a song, some striptease by a girl on a chandelier, and dogged acrobatics by yellow-suited university dons, one of whom is shot dead as he piles into a human pyramid. What follows, though packed with diverting jokes and parody, mainly involves the forlorn attempts of George, a Professor of Moral Philosophy, to compose a paper defending his belief in God and to maintain a relationship with his wife Dottie, a *chanteuse* disoriented by the moral implications of men landing on the Moon. Eccentric invention proliferates as the play continues, but is somehow subordinated to a serious overriding purpose, which is to attack modern materialist philosophy, primarily represented here by the unnamed university's opportunist vice-chancellor, Sir Archie Jumpers. Stoppard himself has described the result as 'a theist play written to combat the arrogant view that anyone who believes in God is some kind of cripple'.

Jungle, The, a novel by Upton *Sinclair, published in 1906. *The Jungle* is Sinclair's best-known novel and one of the most tractarian works of fiction in American literature. It tells the story of Jurgis Rudkus, a Lithuanian immigrant, and of his family and their life in Chicago, particularly the 'Packingtown' district of the city which borders Chicago's infamous stockyards. The great power of the novel lies in its evocation of the progressive degradation of Jurgis and his family, brought on by their experience of urban America: he loses his job as a meat packer; his child, little Antanas, is drowned in the thick mud that surrounds their wooden-frame house; and Jurgis becomes a tramp. This narrative of events, in effect, occupies the first half of the novel; the second half is largely tendentious and polemical as Sinclair uses Jurgis's experiences to provide a justification for socialist agitation and social and industrial reform. The novel had enormous political impact: President Theodore Roosevelt read *The Jungle* and immediately ordered an investigation of the Chicago slaughterhouses; in June 1906 the Pure Food and Drug Act became law, soon after Doubleday had published Sinclair's novel. Some historians have gone so far as to suggest that *The Jungle* was the cause of a relative decline in meat consumption in the USA for about two decades.

Juno and the Paycock, a play by Sean *O'Casey, performed in 1924, published with *The *Shadow of a Gunman* in *Two Plays* (1925). The plot, set in a Dublin tenement during the civil war of 1922, involves the disintegration of the Boyle family. Jack Boyle, the 'paycock', is the wastrel father told he has inherited £2,000. The family gets heavily into debt, only to discover that a fault in the will's wording means it will receive nothing. The new furniture is repossessed. Bentham, the clerk responsible for the bad will, abandons Boyle's daughter, Mary, whom he has made pregnant. Boyle's son Johnny, an IRA quartermaster who has betrayed the commandant of his battalion, is shot. Mary and her mother, Juno, then leave Jack, who ends the play obliviously drunk with his crony, Joxer Daly. At root, this is a painful tale of destruction inflicted from outside and inside, by political nemesis, sexual exploitation, and paternal fecklessness. It also contains a memorable portrait of the self-sacrificial matriarch in Juno Boyle. Yet, as often with O'Casey, an unsentimental humour is everywhere, and notably in the depiction of the ingratiating Joxer and the shiftless, self-important Jack Boyle, at once a callous, greedy liar, a flamboyant dreamer, and the victim of a poverty-stricken environment.

Jurgen: A Comedy of Justice, a novel by James Branch *Cabell, published in 1919. *Jurgen* is the best-known novel from the ambitious, 18-volume 'Biography of the Life of Manuel', also known as the 'Poictesme cycle', that occupied Cabell from 1905 until 1929. The novel tells the story of Jurgen, a poetical pawnbroker, whose marriage to Dame Lisa is a distinctly soulless affair. Dame Lisa is spirited away to a cave by the Devil; Jurgen, somewhat reluctantly, follows her into the cave where he has many adventures, some of them romantic. The adventures are used by Cabell to dramatize a host of mythical creatures and stories (at one point Jurgen marries a vampire), and, in part, a good deal of the interest of the novel is anthropological and historical. *Jurgen* was something of a *cause célèbre*, for on publication it was suppressed for two years by the Comstock Society on grounds of obscenity and indecency; however, the suppression, of course, did much to promote interest in the novel, and the critic H. L. *Mencken remarked that 'every flapper in the land has read *Jurgen* behind the door; two-thirds of the grandmothers east of the Mississippi have tried to borrow it from me'.

Justice, a play by John *Galsworthy, first performed in 1910. It involves a weak young lawyer's clerk, William Falder, who steals money from his employers in order to run off with a married woman, and is apprehended, convicted, and sent to prison for three years. On his release he finds it impossible to obtain work, commits a new crime by forging a reference, and, on being traced by the police, defenestrates himself. Galsworthy uses this unglamorous and unsensational story as a case study through which to explore everyday 'justice', showing the workings of the courts and the prison system in what was described at the time as a 'cinematographic' style, one which eschewed special pleading or easy sympathies and antipathies. The counsel for the prosecution and the judge do no more or less than their duty, and the prison governor is a notably humane man. As Max *Beerbohm argued at the time in the *Saturday Review*, such fairness and impartiality give extra force to the implied argument: which is that, notwithstanding the good intentions of individuals, justice is, in Galsworthy's words, 'a blind goddess . . . quite unable to fit punishment to crime—a disproportionate creature blundering along in obedience to the herd instinct to stamp out . . . the weak and diseased'. *Justice* is one of the few plays which have influenced public policy: the scene in which Falder is shown pacing his cell and dementedly beating on its door may be credited with ending the practice of putting felons into solitary confinement at the start of their sentences; and the last act helped bring about reforms in the ticket-of-leave system.

JUSTICE, Donald (Rodney) (1925–), American poet, born in Miami, Florida, educated at the University of Miami, the University of North Carolina, Stanford University, California, and the University of Iowa. From 1955 onward he held a succession of senior posts at various American universities and became Professor of English at the University of Florida, Gainsville, in 1982. *The Summer Anniversaries* (1960), his first collection of verse, established him as a poet of unostentatious virtuosity. *Night Light* (1967) and *Departures* (1973) displayed an increasing technical flexibility, which extended in the latter volume to experimentation with random methods of composition. *Selected Poems* (1979; Pulitzer Prize) confirmed his stature. *The Sunset Maker* (1987) contains a memoir of childhood and two short stories in addition to a substantial body of previously uncollected poems; the wryly elegiac confrontation with personal and cultural desolation which pervades much of his work is especially effective in the poems concerning a fictive protagonist named 'Tremayne'. In its detached habituation to a nearly tolerable despair, his poetry sometimes recalls that of Weldon *Kees, whose *Collected Poems* (1960, revised edition 1975) Justice edited. *A Donald Justice Reader* (1991) is a selection of poetry and prose.

K

KABBANI, Rana (1958–), Syrian cultural historian, born in Damascus, educated at the American University of Beirut and Jesus College, Cambridge. After working as an art critic in Paris and as a publisher's editor in London, she became a full-time writer in 1986. *Europe's Myths of the Orient: Devise and Rule* (1986) evaluated Western perceptions of Islamic culture with particular reference to the formulation of erotic stereotypes in literature and painting; the book was later republished as *Imperial Fictions: Europe's Myths of the Orient* (1994). The increase in hostility towards Islam produced by events following the publication of Salman Rushdie's *The *Satanic Verses* prompted Kabbani to clarify the religious and cultural character of the Muslim world in *A Letter to Christendom* (1989). Her other works include her translations from the Arabic of Mahmoud Darweesh's *Sand and Other Poems* (1986) and her editorship of *The Passionate Nomad: Diaries of Isabelle Eberhardt* (1987).

Kailyard School, The, originally referring to the work of a number of Scottish novelists, notably J. M. *Barrie, Ian Maclaren (pseudonym of John Watson, 1850–1907), and S. R. Crockett (1859–1914), the term 'Kailyard' has latterly been descriptive of the tendency to sentimentally hackneyed Scottishness in books, newspapers, and other media. The expression, which means 'cabbage-patch' in the Scots vernacular, was first used to denote critical disparagement by J. H. Millar (1864–1929) in attacking the sentimentality, moral platitudinousness, and banal characterization of these authors' presentations of Scottish village life. Typifying examples of the genre are Maclaren's stories in *Beside the Bonnie Briar Bush* (1894) and Crockett's *The Stickit Minister* (1893). Such fiction was highly popular during much of the 1890s; its deficiencies prompted a reaction initiated by George Douglas *Brown, whose *The House with the Green Shutters* (1901) repudiates the endemic cosiness of the Kailyard idiom through its harshly realistic treatment of the village of Barbie. While the mode remains current in certain forms of popular fiction, it has been regarded as the epitome of all that serious Scottish literature in the twentieth century has sought to avoid. See also SCOTTISH RENAISSANCE.

KALDOR, Nicholas (1908–86), Hungarian-born economist; he became Baron Kaldor of Newnham in 1974. Kaldor taught at the London School of Economics and at Cambridge University, where he became a Fellow of King's College and Professor of Economics. In addition to his major theoretical contributions—principally to the theory of economic growth and to monetary and fiscal policy—Kaldor was an active and influential economic adviser to home and foreign governments. Although beginning his career at the London School of Economics, Kaldor soon fell under the spell of *Keynes's economics, and established connections with a group of younger Keynesians at Cambridge, including Joan *Robinson. He was an early advocate of the taxation of expenditure rather than income (*An Expenditure Tax*, 1955) and in his Inaugural Lecture at Cambridge, *Causes of the Slow Rate of Economic Growth of the United Kingdom* (1966), he developed the influential idea of 'cumulative causation': namely, that the structure of manufacturing industry was such that failure (or success) tends to be self-perpetuating. In the 1970s Kaldor became a formidable defender of Keynesian ideas in the decade which saw them coming under increasing attack from monetarist economists like Milton *Friedman. *The Scourge of Monetarism* (1982) reveals Kaldor the polemicist at his most pure and devastating.

Kangaroo, a novel by D. H. *Lawrence, published in 1923. *Kangaroo* was written at great speed during Lawrence's three-month stay in Australia in 1922. The book is set in and around Sydney but its central characters, Richard Somers, a writer, and his wife Harriet, are English. Indeed, the main issues in the book are transposed versions of European concerns, and in 'The Nightmare', one of the most powerfully written chapters, Richard Somers is given Lawrence's own haunting wartime experiences. The plot concerns Somers's involvement with 'Kangaroo', the *nom-de-guerre* of the charismatic leader of The Diggers, a fascist political group. Somers is drawn by Kangaroo's personal magnetism but, never fully committed and half-attracted, half-repelled by the violence which surrounds him, breaks free into the prickly individualism which was Lawrence's general political stance. None the less, *Kangaroo* is, with **Aaron's Rod* and *The *Plumed Serpent*, one of three uncomfortable books by Lawrence which deal directly with themes of male bonding and political authoritarianism. One of the striking things about *Kangaroo* is the clarity of Lawrence's understanding of the social origins of fascism which he had experienced in the early 1920s in Italy. Lawrence was a gifted travel writer, and *Kangaroo* contains fine descriptions of a frighteningly unsolacing natural world. The novel as a whole is pervaded by a feeling of rootlessness as Somers searches for a commitment which will make sense of a drifting life. Another of the novel's themes—marriage—is subjected to similar scrutiny as the Somerses' relationship becomes strained. All these ideas reflect Lawrence's own circumstances, and Somers is another of his ironic self-portraits. An interesting feature of the book is the way Harriet's point of view is emphasized to undercut the male bonding. This device, begun in *The *Rainbow*, also appears in **Lady Chatterley's Lover*.

KANTARIS, Sylvia (1936–), British poet, born in Grindleford, Derbyshire, educated at Bristol University and the University of Queensland. Her collections of poetry include *Time and Motion* (1975), *The Tenth Muse* (1983), *The Sea at the Door* (1985), *Dirty Washing: New and Selected Poems* (1989), and *Lad's Love* (1993). She has also produced two books in collaboration with other poets: *News from the Front* (1983), written with D. M. *Thomas, deals candidly with failures of communication in an erotic relationship; *The Air Mines of Mistila* (1988), her work with Philip *Gross, is a highly imaginative parable of man's greed for natural resources, set in a fictitious South American territory. Much of Kantaris's writing has a refreshing vitality and directness; seriousness of purpose and a ready wit frequently co-exist in the treatments of personal relations, natural phenomena, and social contingencies that form the basis of many of her poems.

KAUFMAN, George S(imon) (1889–1961), American playwright and director, born in Pittsburgh, Pennsylvania, educated at the Pennsylvania Law School. Kaufman gave the Broadway musical an air of sophistication and urbanity. He was also an important figure in a distinctively Jewish-American tradition of comic writing. His collaborations include *Merton of the Movies* (1922) and *Beggar on Horseback* (1924), with Marc *Connelly; *June Moon* (1929), with Ring *Lardner; *The Royal Family* (1927), *Dinner at Eight* (1932) and *Stage Door* (1936), with Edna *Ferber; *The Cocoanuts* (1925), with Irving Berlin; *Business is Business* (1925), with Dorothy *Parker; *Strike Up the Band* (1932) and *Of Thee I Sing* (1931, Pulitzer Prize), with Morrie Ryskind and George and Ira Gershwin; *You Can't Take it With You* (1936, Pulitzer Prize), *The Man Who Came to Dinner* (1939) and *George Washington Slept Here* (1940), with Moss *Hart; and *Park Avenue* (1946; lyrics by Ira Gershwin) and *Silk Stockings* (1955; music by Cole Porter), with Nunnally Johnson. In addition to screenplays for the Marx Brothers' *Night at the Opera* (1935) and *Star Spangled Rhythm* (1942), he was the director of the films *The Senator Was Indiscreet* (1947) and *Guys and Dolls* (1950).

KAVAN, Anna, pseudonym of Helen WOOD (1901–68), British novelist, born in Cannes, France, of English parentage. She spent her childhood in Europe, California, and England, and began writing novels under her married name, Helen Ferguson, while living with her first husband in Burma. These novels, later dismissed as merely competent examples of the predominant 'home counties' feminine novel, contain some sensitively reworked autobiographical material and, in *Let Me Alone* (1930) and *A Stranger Still* (1935), present an authorial alter ego, Anna Kavan, the name the author would use for her best works. These traditional early novels focus on lonely women in search of love and creativity and resemble the works of Jean *Rhys and Kay *Boyle; a notable example is the transitional *Change the Name* (1941). Kavan's new persona entailed a radical change of style, and her consequent discovery of Kafka revolutionized her vision. *Asylum Piece* (1940) contains hallucinatory, apocalyptic short fictions based on her own experiences of madness and lifelong drug addiction. Her short stories are collected in *I Am Lazarus* (1945), haunted by the psychological impact of the war, *A Bright Green Field* (1958), *Julia and the Bazooka* (1970), and *My Soul in China* (1975), the title novella of which resembles the novel *Sleep Has His House* (1947), in which fragments of the narrator's life are spliced cinematically with detailed re-enactments of disturbing dreams. *Who Are You* (1963) is an obvious precursor of **Wide Sargasso Sea* and is reminiscent, in tone and structure, of Robbe-Grillet and the *Nouveau Romanciers*; here the customary vulnerable, victimized Kavan woman fights the terrors of a strange land, Burma, and her sexually violent and sadistic husband. *Ice* (1967), Kavan's most famous novel, was designated by Brian *Aldiss as science fiction because of its landscape, in which nuclear testing has brought about the freezing of the world, a setting which serves to heighten the sense of Kavan's female protagonist as she escapes, from country to country, the attentions of her two sadistic lovers. Novels recently discovered for publication include *Mercury* (1995) and *The Parson* (1995); there is a biography, *The Case of Anna Kavan* (1992), by David Callard.

KAVANAGH, Patrick (1905–67), Irish poet, born near Iniskeen, County Monaghan; he left school at 14 and worked on farms in his native locality. In 1929 his poetry attracted the attention of George 'AE' *Russell and began appearing in *The Irish Statesman*, which Russell edited. *Ploughman and Other Poems* (1936), Kavanagh's first collection of verse, drew in some measure on the idealized rural idioms of the *Irish Revival, but frequently displayed a refreshing individuality of tone and a keen sense of realism in its imagery. *The Green Fool*, a memorably lyrical prose autobiography, was published in 1938, but was withdrawn after a libel action arising from unintentionally offensive references to Oliver St John *Gogarty. It has similarities with *Tarry Flynn* (1948), a novel derived from Kavanagh's experiences as a young man of his native community. In 1939 he moved to Dublin, working as a journalist and film critic, and published *The *Great Hunger*, generally regarded as his most important work, in 1942. *Lough Derg* of 1942, published in 1978 with a foreword by Paul *Durcan, is an ambitious but unfinished long poem, as is 'Why Sorrow?', also composed in 1942; both contain incisive critiques of institutionalized religion. Among his other publications are the volumes of poetry *A Soul for Sale* (1947) and *Come Dance with Kitty Stobling* (1960). The latter contained some of his finest lyrics, chosen from 'The Canal Bank Poems', an exuberantly affirmative body of work produced during his convalescence from cancer in the mid-1950s. A *Collected Poems* was produced in 1964, followed by *Collected Pruse* (*sic*) of 1967, which included selections from *Kavanagh's Weekly*, a periodical produced in collaboration with his brother, Peter Kavanagh, in 1952. Much of Kavanagh's later poetry is written with a headlong conversational spontaneity which lapses at times into doggerel, a recurrent tendency in the satires arising from his frequently antagonistic relations with many other Irish writers. With Flann *O'Brien and Brendan *Behan, he was a dominant literary presence in Dublin throughout the 1950s. In forging new possibilities for a realist poetry of Irish rural experience Kavanagh gave confidence to many younger writers, amongst whom Seamus *Heaney is pre-eminent. *Complete Poems* was published in 1984, edited by Peter Kavanagh, whose *Sacred Keeper* (1986) is a biography.

KAVANAGH, P. J. (Patrick Joseph Gregory) (1931–), British poet and novelist, born in Worthing, educated at Merton College, Oxford. He lectured in Barcelona and Jakarta in the 1950s; from 1959 to 1970 he worked as an actor. *One and One*, his first collection of poems, appeared in 1960. *The Perfect Stranger* (1966), his prize-winning autobiography, is an account of his life until 1958, when his first wife Sally, the daughter of Rosamond *Lehmann, died unexpectedly of poliomyelitis in Java; it was widely acclaimed for its remarkable fusion of humour and moving forthrightness. Numerous further collections of Kavanagh's poetry include *Edward Thomas in Heaven* (1974), *Life before Death* (1979), *Presence* (1987), and *An Enchantment* (1991). His verse displays an overall development from the more descriptive and discursive modes of earlier work towards the humanity and imaginative breadth which increasingly characterized his work from the mid-1970s. *Collected Poems* was published in 1992. Kavanagh's novels, *A Song and Dance* (1968), *A Happy Man* (1972), *People and Weather* (1979), and *Only by Mistake* (1986), have enjoyed popular and critical success. Among his other prose works are *Finding Connections* (1990), an account of his travels in Australia and New Zealand in the course of investigating his family's past, into which much personal retrospection is woven. *People and Places* (1978) is a wide-ranging collection of essays. His works as editor include *Collected Poems of Ivor Gurney* (1982), *The Bodley Head G. K. Chesterton* (1985), and *A Book of Consolations* (1992). He has also worked as a broadcaster and written documentary dramas for television, including 'William Cowper Lived Here' (1971). *Voices in Ireland: A Traveller's Literary Companion* appeared in 1994.

KAY, Jackie (1961–), British poet, born in Edinburgh; she grew up in Glasgow and was educated at Stirling University. In addition to her activities as a writer and performer of her poetry, she has worked in publishing, child-care, and arts administration. Her work first came to notice in *A Dangerous Knowing: Four Black Women Poets* (1984), edited by Prathiba Parma. *The Adoption Papers* (1991), her acclaimed first collection of poems, is strongly informed by her background as a black child adopted by white parents. A second collection, *Other Lovers* (1993), appeared in 1993. Kay's compassion and humour temper the strong political and feminist engagement in her work, which frequently deals with race and sexuality. She has also written two plays, *Chiaroscuro* (1986) and *Twice Over* (1988). Her other works include the children's poetry in *Two's Company* (1992) and the television 'poetry documentary' *Twice Through the Heart* (1991), a highly original treatment of a murder case.

KAYE-SMITH, Sheila (1887–1956), British novelist, born at St Leonard's-on-Sea, Sussex. Following the publication of her first novel, *The Tramping Methodist* (1908), she left Sussex to live for a time in London where she was to meet Alice *Meynell, D. H. *Lawrence, Dorothy *Richardson, Thomas *Hardy, and Mary *Webb. *Sussex Gorse* (1916) attracted considerable notice, and following the war three further books confirmed her reputation as a Sussex novelist, in particular *Joanna Godden* (1921). Her popularity as a regional novelist during the 1920s has not endured and, like Mary *Webb, she was among the writers satirized by Stella Gibbons in **Cold Comfort Farm*. Religion was also a central theme in her work; following her conversion to Roman Catholicism in 1929 she wrote a study of four Roman Catholic heroines, *Quartet in Heaven* (1953). Among her other works are *Talking of Jane Austen* (1943) and *More Talk about Jane Austen* (1950), both written in collaboration with Gladys Bertha Stern; and three volumes of autobiography (*Three Ways Home*, 1937; *Kitchen-Fugue*, 1945; *All the Books of My Life*, 1956).

KAZANTZIS, Judith (1940–), British poet, born in Oxford, educated at Somerville College, Oxford. She worked as a home tutor with the Inner London Education Authority and was poetry reviewer with *Spare Rib* magazine for six years during the 1970s. *Minefield* (1977) was her first collection of poetry; her principal subsequent collections are *The Wicked Queen* (1980), *Let's Pretend* (1984), *Flame Tree* (1988), and *The Rabbit Magician Plate* (1992). Her earlier work recurrently dealt with injustices inherent in the contemporary situation of women through adaptations of materials from mythology, folklore, and history. Since the mid-1980s the political scope of her verse has expanded to address economic oppression in the Third World, particularly in the countries of Central America, which she has repeatedly visited. Her poetry is notable for combining passionate conviction with exuberant wit and flamboyantly imaginative use of closely observed local detail. The freshness and vitality of her language is equally apparent in poems drawing directly on her personal experience. She edited *Women in Revolt: The Fight for Emancipation: A Collection of Contemporary Documents* (1968).

KAZIN, Alfred (1915–), American critic, born in Brooklyn of Russian immigrant parentage, educated at City College, New York, and Columbia University. During a wide-ranging academic career he taught at *Black Mountain, Harvard, and Amherst, at Cambridge as Fulbright lecturer in 1951, becoming Professor of English at Stony Brook, and latterly Stanford. Kazin began as a freelance teacher, convinced socialist, and student of *Modernism. Working in public libraries on the 'dark seedtime' of modern American writing, he produced a magisterial survey of the period 1890 to 1940, published as *On Native Grounds* (1942). His interpretation stressed the evolution from W. D. *Howells and *Dreiser through to *Hemingway, *Faulkner, and the socially conscious novelists of the 1930s, and encompassed figures such as Van Wyck *Brooks, Thorstein *Veblen, and H. L. *Mencken, arguing their 'absorption in every last detail of their American world together with a deep and subtle alienation from it'. The book established Kazin's critical reputation and he became a Contributing Editor of *The New Republic* and *Fortune* in the mid-1940s; but he also wrote for numerous other magazines, the essays collected in *The Inmost Leaf* (1955) and *Contemporaries* (1962), the latter volume including his astute critique of JFK, 'The President and Other Intellectuals'. The autobiographical trilogy, *A Walker in the City* (1951), *Starting Out in the Thirties* (1965), and *New York Jew* (1978) includes sketches of the cultural luminaries he encountered. Kazin's other major study of prose fiction is *Bright Book of Life: American Novelists and Storytellers from Hemingway to Mailer* (1974), an integrated account of writers prominent since the war, concluding with a chapter on *Nabokov. With Lionel *Trilling, Irving *Howe, and Leslie *Fiedler, he joined the vital mid-century move of Jewish-American literary intellectuals into the mainstream. He championed the Liberal Imagination alongside Trilling, and his friend Edmund *Wilson.

KEANE, John B(rendan) (1928–), Irish playwright, born in Listowel, Co. Kerry, educated at St Michael's College, Listowel. He owns a successful public house in the town and has become the most vociferous supporter of the Listowel Writers' Week. Keane's first play, *Sive* (1959), began his career as a dramatist much admired by the Irish public; with its theme of arranged marriage, Keane manages momentarily to revive the peasant drama of the early *Abbey Theatre. *Many Young Men of Twenty* (1961) saw the beginning of his attempts to address modern Ireland and the demise of its rural communities. Although it is a musical, its serious main theme is emigration caused by permanent economic recession. Keane's best-known play, *The Field* (1965), presents a man, 'The Bull' McCabe, on the edge of destitution, resorting to savagery and murder in order to survive; the play also provides a fascinating portrayal of the local people, their distrust of authority, in the guise of police and priests, and their instinct to protect their own. *The Field* was produced as a successful feature film in 1991. Keane's plays have become central to the repertoire at the Abbey Theatre. His other plays include *The Year of the Hiker* (1963), *Big Maggie* (1969), *Moll* (1971), *The Buds of Ballybunion* (1978), and *Chastitude* (1980). More recently Keane has concentrated more on fiction with the novels *Durango* (1992) and *The Contractors* (1993), and the collection of stories *Death Be Not Proud* (1994). He has also published collections of essays, and a series of letters (*Letters to an Irish Priest*, 1970; and *Letters of a Matchmaker*, 1975).

KEANE, Molly (1904–96), Irish novelist, born in Co. Kildare into 'a rather serious Hunting and Fishing and Church-going family' who were not assiduous about seeing that she was properly educated. She chose her pseudonym, 'M. J. Farrell', to hide her literary side from her sporting friends. Following her first novel, *The Knight of the Cheerful Countenance* (1921), written for Mills & Boon when she was 17, she wrote ten novels under her pseudonym, including *Taking Chances* (1929), *Mad Puppetstown* (1931), *Conversation Piece* (1932), *Devoted Ladies* (1934), *The Rising Tide* (1937), *Two Days in Aragon* (1941), and *Loving Without Tears* (1951). She was also a successful playwright whose drawing-room comedies, in the opinion of James *Agate, were comparable to those of Noël *Coward; her plays with John Perry, invariably directed by John Gielgud, include *Spring Meeting* (1938), *Ducks and Drakes* (1941), *Treasure Hunt* (1949), and *Dazzling Prospect* (1961). Keane stopped writing for more than twenty years until 1981, when she re-emerged, under her own name, with *Good Behaviour*. This precipitated the reprinting of many of her earlier novels and was followed by *Time after Time* (1983) and *Loving and Giving* (1988). The world of which Keane writes has now vanished—a society where servants were faceless, while dogs were 'little people'; where a good day's hunting earned a girl the ultimate accolade: 'That girl Rowley's a proper bit of stuff. In fact I think she's a real live human being.' Though part of such a social environment, Molly Keane was also something of a subversive. She wrote about not just the beauty of the sheltered world of big houses and field sports, but also the riveting selfishness of people whose prolonged loyalty was the exclusive preserve of their unpleasant pet dogs. The story is incidental in her novels, the characters are all-important, and the sense of location and dislocation is endemic throughout her fiction. The humour is mordant, her observation of manners and sexual shenanigans acute, and the aftertaste, bitter-sweet.

KEATES, Jonathan (1946–), British novelist, travel writer, and biographer, born in Paris, educated at Magdalen College, Oxford. His early works as a topographical writer include *The Companion Guide to the Shakespeare Country* (1979) and *Historic London* (with

Angelo Hornak, 1979). He received the James Tait Black Memorial Prize and the Hawthornden Prize for *Allegro Postillions* (1983), a collection of four stories set in nineteenth-century Italy, which also provides the background for his novel *The Strangers' Gallery* (1987); his fiction is highly regarded for its stylistic elegance, psychological authenticity, and rich historical allusiveness. *Handel: The Man and His Music* (1985) ranks among the finest biographies of the composer. His other works include *Tuscany* (with Charlie Waite, 1988), *Italian Journeys* (1991), *Stendhal* (1994), *Venice* (1994), and *Purcell* (1995). Keates also writes regularly on music, art, and literature for the *Observer*, the *Independent*, and the *Times Literary Supplement*.

KEATING, H(enry) R(aymond) F(itzwalter) (1926–), British crime writer, born in St Leonards, educated at Trinity College, Dublin. He worked as a journalist and during 1967–83 reviewed crime novels for *The Times*. His first four books are original, occasionally almost surrealist, detective stories (for example, *Zen There Was Murder*, 1960; *A Rush on the Ultimate*, 1961), but in 1964 he published *The Perfect Murder*, the first of a long and successful series of semi-humorous novels, set mainly in India, in which the detective is Inspector Ganesh Ghote of the Bombay CID. Other titles include *Inspector Ghote's Good Crusade* (1966), *Filmi, Filmi, Inspector Ghote* (1976), *Inspector Ghote Draws a Line* (1979), *Dead on Time* (1988), and *The Iciest Sin* (1990). His best novel, however, is probably *The Murder of the Maharajah* (1980), set in the India of the 1930s and in which Ghote does not appear. Keating is also the author of many short stories, and has written widely on *detective fiction (*Murder Must Appetize*, 1975; *Sherlock Holmes: The Man and His World*, 1979).

KEEFFE, Barrie (1945–), British playwright, born in the East End of London, educated at East Ham Grammar School. He was an actor with the National Youth Theatre, and worked as a journalist while he was establishing himself as a dramatist. After *Only a Game* (1973), about a waning soccer star, he wrote *A Sight of Glory* (1975), about boxers in the East End, and *Scribes* (1976), about newspaper workers during a strike. His first substantial success, however, was *Gimme Shelter* (1975–7), a dramatic trilogy about deprived, frustrated, and alienated working-class youth. His other work, equally critical of British society, especially in its dealings with young people, has varied from the realistic *Abide with Me* (1976), *Killing Time* (1977), *Sus* (1982), *Wild Justice* (1990), and *Not Fade Away* (1990) to the musical play *Bastard Angel* (1980) and *Chorus Girls* (1981), in which the Prince of Wales is captured by a troupe of vaudeville performers and converted into a spokesman for the unemployed. In the same vein of scurrilously exuberant satire is his updated version of Middleton's *A Mad World, My Masters* (1977), in which East End criminals seek to compromise the sexually indiscreet industrialist whose conquests, in the revision Keeffe made in 1984, include the then Prime Minister. He has also written drama for television, notably the play *Gotcha* and the series *No Excuses*, as well as the screenplay of the film *The Long Good Friday* (1981).

Keep the Aspidistra Flying, a novel by George *Orwell, published in 1936. The only one of Orwell's novels about a writer, *Keep the Aspidistra Flying* is most autobiographical in its admission of the fear driving its protagonist, Gordon Comstock, to abandon his poetic vocation for the sake of financial security. Its epigraph is an adaptation of I Corinthians xiii: 'And now abideth faith, hope, money, these three; but the greatest of these is money'. Lack of money vitiates all of Gordon's most important relationships, with his mother, his sister, and especially with his fiancée, Rosemary, whom he is unable to marry, or even make love to, owing to his poverty: 'It is not easy to make love in a cold climate when you have no money.' Although Orwell's text contains a vehement rejection of the cash nexus, it also betrays a horror of insolvency that associates the life of the poor with regression to a primeval state: 'to sink down, down into the ultimate mud.' Throughout the novel, the image of the aspidistra occurs to symbolize the resilience of the British desire for respectability. Although Gordon makes repeated attempts to kill the aspidistras he encounters, the indestructibility of these plants found everywhere represents the overwhelming nature of the forces pitted against him. As with his counterpart Winston Smith in **Nineteen Eighty-Four*, the resistance of this nonconformist individual is slowly but surely whittled away. But whereas the later novel ends on a tragic note, the narrator of *Keep the Aspidistra Flying* assesses Gordon's final capitulation with a sour contempt. The novel is in many ways Orwell's most embittered work.

KEES, Weldon (1914–55), American poet, born in Beatrice, Nebraska, educated at the University of Nebraska. After a period as a research librarian in Denver, he moved to New York in 1943, the year in which *The Last Man*, his first collection of poetry, appeared, and worked as a journalist and scriptwriter. During the 1940s he also achieved recognition as an abstract expressionist painter. Following his move to San Francisco in 1951 he was variously active as a critic, film-maker, composer, and jazz pianist. He collaborated with Jurgen Ruesch in the writing of the psychological study *Non-Verbal Communication* (1956), for which Kees also supplied photographs. He disappeared while beset by personal difficulties in 1955 and is assumed to have committed suicide by drowning. He published two further volumes of verse, *The Fall of the Magicians* (1947) and *Poems, 1947–1954* (1954). His most characteristic achievements are fraught with the tension between his pervasive and often harrowingly elegiac pessimism and a tone of equably understated directness. 'Aspects of Robinson' and 'Robinson at Home', two of his best-known poems, exemplify his use of sharply realized urban detail to create contexts for imaginative treatments of ethical and existential futility. His work attracted new interest in the 1980s following the appearance of a revised edition of his *Collected Poems*, edited by Donald *Justice, in 1975. Kees's letters were published in 1986 under the title *Weldon Kees and the Midcentury Generation*, edited by R. E. Knoll.

KEILLOR, Garrison (Edward) (1942–), American novelist and short-story writer, born in Anoka, Minnesota, educated at the University of Minnesota. He worked for radio stations in Minneapolis, becoming host and principal writer for a famous weekly programme 'A Prairie Home Companion', a throwback to the Golden Age of Radio. It incorporated a variety of country and blues music, and Keillor's stories about the inhabitants of his fictional town, Lake Wobegon, Minnesota, 'the little town that time forgot and the decades cannot improve'. He contributed stories for the *New Yorker*, the *Atlantic Monthly*, and other magazines, which were collected in *Happy to Be Here* (1981, revised 1983). Keillor's major fictional success came with *Lake Wobegon Days* (1985), a series of narratives centred on a number of second-generation Scandinavian immigrant families and characters living in Lake Wobegon. Usually beginning each story with 'It has been a quiet week in Lake Wobegon', they combine pathos and comedy with his characteristic down-to-earth style and ironic wit. Subsequent stories, in *Leaving Home* (1987) and *We Are Still Married* (1989), return to many of the Lake Wobegon characters and act as vehicles for comments on contemporary American society and culture. His first novel, *Radio Romance* (1991), describes the rise and fall of a radio station in Minneapolis. Later works include stories collected in *The Book of Guys* (1993), the theme of which is American manhood, depicted here as gentle and neglected, and *Cat, You Better Come Home* (1995).

KELLY, George (Edward) (1890–1974), American dramatist, born in Philadelphia; Kelly was the uncle of the actress Grace Kelly, later Princess Grace of Monaco. He began as an actor playing juvenile roles, and performed his own sketches in vaudeville. His first success was with *The Torch-Bearers* (1922), a satire on the little theatre movement. His fourth play, *Craig's Wife* (1925; Pulitzer Prize), was a social melodrama in which a wife's obsessive propriety spoils her marriage and isolates her and her husband, a theme played with variations in his next successful play, *Behold the Bridegroom* (1927), about the self-destructiveness of a wealthy, self-indulgent woman. His later plays are *Maggie the Magnificent* (1929), *Philip Goes Forth* (1931), *Reflected Glory* (1936), *The Deep Mrs Sykes* (1945), and *The Fatal Weakness* (1946). Kelly's insistent probing at human vanity and weakness proved less and less congenial to audiences, and he was never to repeat the success of *Craig's Wife* and *Behold the Bridegroom*.

KELLY, Robert (1935–), American poet, born in Brooklyn, educated at Columbia University. Kelly is a prolific poet who has published over forty books. Ezra *Pound, William Carlos *Williams, and the *Black Mountain poets are central influences on his work; these, together with his work on medieval and German language and literature, have helped him to create a processive, visionary poetry of great formal variety. Together with Jerome *Rothenberg, he coined the term 'deep image' in order to convey the sense of a mystical presence underpinning each section of his work, a presence which cannot be directly visualized but which may be intuited in the twists and turns of his syntax. His long poems include *The Loom* (1975) and *The Common Shore* (1969), the latter taking America as the principal feature of his concerns. *Red Actions* (1995), selected poems, offers a useful introduction to Kelly's work. Collections of shorter material include *Lunes* (1965), *Songs I–XXX* (1968), *Kali Yuga* (1970), *Kill the Messenger Who Brings Bad News* (1979), and *Spiritual Exercises* (1981). *The Scorpions* (1969) is a novel, and *In Time* (1971) is a collection of essays.

KELMAN, James (1946–), Scottish novelist, born in Govan, Glasgow, one of five sons of a frame-maker and picture restorer. He left school at 15 to serve an apprenticeship as a compositor, but abandoned it two years later when his family emigrated to America. He soon returned to Scotland and subsequently worked in Glasgow, Manchester, and London in a variety of manual jobs, interspersed with periods of unemployment. At 28, he studied English and Philosophy at Strathclyde University, but left during the third year. Kelman began writing seriously in his early twenties, but had no success with British publishers. His first book, *An Old Pub Near the Angel and Other Stories*, was published by a small American press in 1970, and *Not Not While the Giro* (1983), a collection of stories, was brought out by Polygon, Edinburgh University's student-run publishing company. Recognition of his uncanny ability to translate the workings of the mind and the spoken language of Glasgow people on to the page was gradual. His first published novel, *The Busconductor Hines* (1984), is a compassionate, but challenging, narrative, tracing the daily grind of a young man working on the Glasgow buses. It was ridiculed by some sections of the English literary establishment, and *A Chancer* (1985) fared little better, but Kelman nevertheless acquired a cult following. The reception was warmer for the volume of scurrilously funny short stories, *Greyhound for Breakfast* (1987), and *A Disaffection* (1989), a beautifully sustained evocation of the life of disenchanted schoolteacher, was widely acknowledged as a work of linguistic virtuosity. *The Burn* (1991) collects stories of Scottish life in Kelman's inimitable style; *Some Recent Attacks* (1993) contains essays and journalistic pieces that range from aspects of the *Rushdie affair to the abuse of workers' rights in insanitary factories. *How Late It Was, How Late* (1994; Booker Prize), his most acclaimed novel, follows an ex-convict on his blundering—literally, as he suffers from a loss of sight after a drinking bout—path down Glasgow's meanest streets. Customary echoes of *Beckett and Kafka are leavened by Kelman's own brand of dour Glasgow humour and his distinctive use of argot and dialect.

KEMELMAN, Harry (1908–), American crime writer, born in Boston, educated at Boston University and Harvard. He is the author of a number of detective stories set in a small town in Massachusetts. The first, *Friday the Rabbi Slept Late* (1964), was followed by *Saturday the Rabbi Went Hungry* (1966), *Sunday the Rabbi Stayed Home* (1969), and others with similar titles. In all the hero is the local rabbi, David Small, who solves mysteries by the application of *pilpul*, or Talmudic logic. Kemelman has written that his purpose is 'to explain—via a fictional setting—the Jewish religion'.

KENEALLY, Thomas (Michael) (1935–), Australian novelist of Irish Catholic extraction, born in New South Wales. He trained for the Catholic priesthood but was never ordained; a fascination with spiritual and moral failure may owe something to this early training. His first novel, *The Place at Whitton* (1964), a murder mystery set in a seminary during a retreat, was followed by many others including *The Fear* (1965), *Bring Larks and Heroes* (1967), *Three Cheers for the Paraclete* (1968), *The Survivor* (1969), and *A Dutiful Daughter* (1971). *The Chant of Jimmie Blacksmith* (1972) is an examination of the relationship between European and Aboriginal in which the eponymous hero first attempts to become assimilated into white society and is later driven to murder. Keneally's most characteristic subject is that of the individual in a hostile environment, frequently finding himself (or herself) in opposition to religious, political, or social systems. *Blood Red, Sister Rose* (1974), a novel about Joan of Arc (a figure who recurs in several of his books), was followed by *Gossip from the Forest* (1975), *A Season in Purgatory* (1976), *A Victim of the Aurora* (1977), *The Confederates* (1979), *Passenger* (1979), and *Cut-Rate Kingdom* (1980). His best-known work, **Schindler's Ark* (1982), caused controversy because it was originally commissioned as a work of non-fiction, but was later reclassified as a novel by its editors and subsequently won the Booker Prize; the film version, *Schindler's List*, appeared in 1994. Later novels include *A Family Madness* (1985), which inserts flashbacks of a Belorussian family's wartime experience into an account of their lives in post-war Australia; *The Playmaker* (1987), about a performance of Farquhar's *The Recruiting Officer* by a group of convicts in Sydney Cove; *Towards Asmara* (1989), about Eritrean resistance to the Ethiopian government; *Flying Hero Class* (1991), about the hijacking of an American aircraft whose passengers include an Aboriginal dance troupe; *Woman of the Inner Sea* (1992), an allegory of the impoverishment of contemporary values versus the simple life of an earlier era; *Jacko the Great Intruder* (1994), which explores the dominance of television-oriented culture via a New York chat show host; and *A River Town* (1995), about a quest for justice for the remains of an unknown dead woman in a small Australian town, circa 1900. His playscripts include *Halloran's Little Boat* (1966; an adaptation of *Bring Larks and Heroes*) and a dramatization of *Gossip from the Forest* (1983), as well as several plays: *Childermas* (1968), *An Awful Rose* (1972), and *The Bullie's House* (1980). He has also published two travel books: *Now and in Time to Be: Ireland and the Irish* (1991) and *The Place Where Souls are Born* (1992), which traces the southwestern desert regions of America and their inhabitants. His autobiographical works include *Memoirs from a Young Republic* (1993), which expresses a Republican polemical view of twentieth-century Australia, and *Homebush Boy: A Memoir* (1995). Keneally was elected Fellow of the Royal Society of Literature in 1972.

KENNEDY, Adrienne (1931–), African-American dramatist, born in Cleveland, Ohio, educated at Ohio State University. She began working as a playwright during a visit to West Africa during 1960–1, which gave her a sense of connection with African culture and introduced her to the work of Chinua *Achebe and Wole *Soyinka. In *Funnyhouse of a Negro* (1962), her first play, Kennedy uses a scenic idiom in which the dream-scape of hallucination and nightmare voices is developed through the impersonation of several historic personalities, Queen Victoria, the Duchess of Hapsburg, Jesus Christ, and Patrice Lumumba. The play's rejection of conventional realism and its challengingly imaginative treatment of black American issues are characteristic of her work of the 1960s, which also includes *The Owl Answers* (1963), *A Rat's Mass* (1966), *A Lesson in a Dead Language* (1968), and *Boats* (1969). Among the most notable of her many subsequent plays are *Evening with Dead Essex* (1973), *A Movie Star Has to Star in Black and White* (1976), *She Talks to Beethoven* (1988), and *The Deadly Triplets* (1990). Her other works include *The Lennon Play: In His Own Write* (1967), a dramatic adaptation of John Lennon's writings, and *Sun: A Poem for Malcolm X Inspired By his Murder* (1968). An autobiography, *People Who Led to My Plays* (1987), maintains the surreal quality which underlies much of her work.

KENNEDY, A(lison) L(ouise) (1965–), Scottish novelist and short-story writer, born in Dundee, educated at Warwick University. Her highly acclaimed first collection of stories, *Night Geometry and the Garscadden Trains* (1990; John Llewelyn Prize), concerns the 'small lives' of the 'silent majority'. *Now That You're Back* (1994) contains the caustic story 'Mouseboks Family Dictionary' in which a writer describes her craft as 'Warming my hands and telling lies'. Kennedy's first novel, *Looking for the Possible Dance* (1993; Somerset Maugham Award), concerns a young woman, her father, and her lover, the victim of an appalling act of brutality in the novel's climax. Kennedy was selected as one of the twenty Best of Young British Novelists in 1993. In *So I Am Glad* (1995), which combines Swiftian satire, allegory, and love story, Cyrano de Bergerac steps into the life of a professional enunciator who has retreated from urban disaffection and memories of abuse into emotional dislocation and sadism. Guilt, loss, and violence inform Kennedy's much acclaimed work. Her intensely focused prose, shaped by austerity and economy, balances tenderness with despair.

KENNEDY, Margaret Moore (1896–1967), British novelist, born in London, educated at Cheltenham Ladies' College and Somerville College, Oxford. Her first novel, *The Ladies of Lyndon* (1923), was followed by a popular success, *The Constant Nymph* (1924), about a gifted musician and the fate of his talented, unruly children; it was adapted for the theatre, and followed by a sequel, *The Fool of the Family* (1930). Other novels include *The Midas Touch* (1938); *The Feast* (1950), a modern version of the Seven Deadly Sins; *Lucy Carmichael* (1951), set in a provincial university; and *Troy Chimneys* (1953), set in Regency England, which won the James Tait Black Memorial Prize. She wrote five plays, including *Escape Me Never* (1934). Her biography of Jane Austen appeared in 1950.

KENNEDY, William Joseph (1928–), American novelist, short-story writer, journalist, and film critic, born in Albany, New York State. Kennedy's first novel, *The Ink Truck* (1969), a study of resistance, features a columnist named Bailey, and deals with a prolonged newspaper strike. His next two novels established a reputation for a grittily realist fiction which investigated the lives of those who have lost in some degree in the race to pursue the 'American Dream'. *Legs* (1975) portrayed the life of the noted gangster Jack 'Legs' Diamond. *Billy Phelan's Greatest Game* (1978), narrated by reporter Martin Daugherty, focuses on the seedy and doomed characters in the isolated dives of Albany's Broadway. Francis Phelan, Billy's father, is the central figure in *Ironweed* (1983, Pulitzer Prize), a harrowing story of the Depression years, which intertwines his past with the present relationship with his Vassar-educated hobo girlfriend, and the results of being brought face-to-face with his old house, wife, and children. It was subsequently filmed in 1987, starring Jack Nicholson and Meryl Streep. Much of Kennedy's writing is centred on the seedy side of New York state's capital city, Albany; he has also written a series of essays and articles on Albany, most notably *O Albany! An Urban Tapestry* (1983). *Quinn's Book* (1988) focuses on the residents of pre-Civil War Albany, notably Daniel Quinn and his experiences with 'Maud the Wondrous'. In 1984 Kennedy co-authored the screenplay of *The Cotton Club* with Francis Ford Coppola, which deals with the gangsters of the 1930s and the stars of the Harlem night-club scene.

KENNELLY, (Timothy) Brendan (1936–), Irish poet, born in Ballylongford, County Kerry, educated at Trinity College, Dublin, and the University of Leeds. He became Professor of Modern Literature at Trinity College in 1973. His numerous collections of poetry include *My Dark Fathers* (1964), *A Drinking Cup: Poems from the Irish* (1970), *Salvation, the Stranger* (1972), *The Islandman* (1977), *The Boats Are Home* (1980), and *Breathing Spaces* (1992), a collection of early poems. Much of this work draws on Kennelly's rural background for its harshly objective lyricism. The range of his poetry is extended by the use of dramatic monologues, a technique culminating in *Cromwell* (1983). This remarkable sequence of over 250 poems takes place in the uneasy consciousness of a modern Irishman named M. P. G. M. Buffun; his 'various forms of dream and nightmare, including the nightmare of Irish history' are dominated by Cromwell, who phlegmatically conflates history and the present in his recollections of atrocities. *The Book of Judas* (1991) contains a further extended sequence demonstrating Kennelly's ability to encompass imaginatively a formidable range of cultural and historical materials. *Time for Voices: Selected Poems 1960–1990* appeared in 1990. *Journey Into Joy* (1994) contains selected prose. His novels include *The Crooked Cross* (1963) and *The Florentines* (1967). Among numerous works he has edited is *The Penguin Book of Irish Verse* (1970, revised and enlarged 1972, 1981).

KENNER, (William) Hugh (1923–), Canadian critic, born in Peterborough, Ontario, educated at the University of Toronto and at Yale. After holding a succession of academic posts he became Franklin Professor and Callaway Professor at the University of Georgia. *Paradox in Chesterton* (1947), his first critical study, was followed by *The Poetry of Ezra Pound* (1951), which affirmed that poet's importance when his reputation was at its nadir; *Wyndham Lewis* (1954); and *The Invisible Poet* (1959), an interpretation of T. S. *Eliot's work. Kenner is widely considered the pre-eminent critical commentator on literary *Modernism, particularly since *The Pound Era* (1971); its comprehensive treatment of *Pound and his circle was described by Guy *Davenport as amounting to 'a new kind of book in which biography, history, and the analysis of literature are . . . harmoniously integrated'. Notable among his many other works are *The Stoic Comedians* (1962), a study of the fictions of Flaubert, *Joyce, and *Beckett; *A Homemade World* (1975), on twentieth-century American modernist writers; and *A Colder Eye: The Modern Irish Writers* (1983). In *A Sinking Island* (1988), a provocative analysis of British literature from 1895 to the 1980s, Kenner argues that the vitality of the modernist tradition has been supplanted by a resumption of bourgeois literary mediocrity. *Mazes* (1989) and *Historical Fictions* (1991) are collections of his essays. His works as an editor include *The Translations of Ezra Pound* (1970). *Chuck Jones: A Flurry of Drawings* (1994) is a biography of the celebrated cartoonist.

Kenyon Review, The, a quarterly journal founded at Kenyon College, Gambier, Ohio, in 1939 by John Crow *Ransom, who edited it until 1959. His advisory editors were R. P. *Blackmur, Allen *Tate, Mark Van Doren, and Robert Penn *Warren. Among the contributors of critical articles during the 1940s and 1950s, when the review was the pre-eminent organ of the *New Criticism, were Cleanth Brooks, John Peale *Bishop, William *Empson, Harry Levin, and Yvor *Winters. In addition to its primary concern with the textual analysis of poetry, it published essays on music, aesthetics, and the graphic and plastic arts in general. Following the closure of the *Southern Review* in 1942, Ransom arranged for its subscription list to be taken over by his magazine. The *Kenyon Review* was subsequently enlarged to accommodate samples of contemporary prose fiction and featured work by a number of the *Southern Review*'s former writers. Its interest in poetry was, however, always more pronounced and work from Louis *MacNeice, Marianne *Moore, Delmore *Schwartz, John *Berryman, and other leading poets appeared regularly during its earlier years. The editorship was taken over in 1959 by Robie Macauley, who introduced a new emphasis on broader cultural commentary and increased the standard of prose fiction with work from contributors who included John *Barth, Thomas *Pynchon, and Flannery *O'Connor. In 1970 the review was suspended, but resumed publication in 1979. Anthologies of material from the *Kenyon Review* appeared in 1951 and 1966.

KER, W(illiam) P(aton) (1855–1923), British scholar, born in Glasgow, educated at Glasgow University and Balliol College, Oxford. In 1879 he was elected a fellow of All Souls College. Among other academic posts Ker was Chair of English at the newly formed University College of Wales in Cardiff, and Quain Professor of English Language and Literature at University College, London (UCL); between 1920 and 1922 he was Oxford Professor of Poetry, publishing his lectures as *The Art of Poetry* (1923). His early publications include his edition of *Froissart's Chronicles* (6 volumes, 1901–3; translated by Lord G. H. Berners); *The Dark Ages* (1904), his first work of historical criticism; *Essays on Mediaeval Literature* (1905); *English Literature: Mediaeval* (1912); and his best-known work, *Epic and Romance* (1897). From 1917 onward he was active in establishing the Department of Scandinavian Studies at UCL. He was the leading authority of his day on the history and development of poetic forms, a specialization he applied across a remarkable range of English, Scottish, and Scandinavian literatures; the posthumous *Form and Style in Poetry* (1928) was edited by R. W. *Chambers, who succeeded Ker to the Quain Chair. His work was of seminal importance in the formation of English studies as a university discipline. Ker's *Collected Essays*, edited by C. Whibley, were published in 1925.

KERMODE, (John) Frank (1919–), British scholar and critic, born in Douglas, Isle of Man, educated at the University of Liverpool. Among other academic posts, he was appointed King Edward VII Professor of English at Cambridge in 1974. His principal academic field is the English Renaissance, but he is widely known as a reviewer of great range. His *Romantic Image* (1957) was an influential rethinking of the aesthetic theory and practice of the French Symbolists and the Anglo-American Modernists. His later work, like *The Classic* (1975) and *The Genesis of Secrecy* (1979) (see HERMENEUTICS), often started out as lecture series, and retained the fluent, speculative, open style of the mode of discussion. *The Sense of an Ending* (1967), a brilliant exploration of fictions of finality, anticipated much *reader-response theory and *narratology by reintroducing the notions of time and narrative into a criticism which had for some two decades privileged spatial metaphors. (See also APOCALYPTIC LITERATURE). Kermode was influential in furthering the consideration of *Structuralism in the English-speaking world, and in making connections between the arts of theological and literary interpretation. His agile intelligence and his thoughtful curiosity, combined with his resistance to dogmas of all kinds, made him an unusual figure in contemporary literature, at least until the arrival of the *New Historicism. Since its inception in 1979 he has been a member of the advisory board of the **London Review of Books*. He has edited the *Selected Prose of T. S. Eliot* (1975) and, with Robert Alter, *The Literary Guide to the Bible* (1988), and in 1990 published *The Uses of Error*.

KEROUAC, Jack (1922–69), American novelist, born Jean Louis Lebrid de Kerouac of French-Canadian parents in Lowell, Massachusetts, educated at Columbia University and the New York School for Social Research. Following service in the US Merchant Marine, he worked in various capacities in New York while writing his first novel, *The Town and the City* (1950). The book's elaborate adaptation of his personal experience and familial history drew comparisons with the fiction of Thomas *Wolfe; the ending, in which the principal protagonist leaves the city in his quest for more authentic values, links the work with his famous novel of restless journeying, **On the Road* (1957). The conventionally disciplined manner of *The Town and the City* was henceforth superseded by what Kerouac termed 'spontaneous prose', the urgently paced and fluently discursive idiom of his best-known work. His principal novels form quasi-autobiographical narratives of his highly mobile experiences from around 1949 onward; titles include *The Dharma Bums* (1958), an account of striving for purity of being through Zen Buddhism, in which Gary *Snyder is portrayed as 'Japhy Ryder'; *The Subterraneans* (1958), evoking the San Francisco literary milieu of the early 1950s; *Doctor Sax* (1959), concerning the adolescence of his persona 'Jack Duluoz'; and *Visions of Gerard* (1963), an elegiac treatment of the death of a spiritually gifted child in which Kerouac's Roman Catholic sensibility is most clearly apparent. After the remarkable success of *On the Road* he was exposed to intense publicity, emerging in the public consciousness as the leader of the *Beat Generation; *Big Sur* (1962) announced his increasing withdrawal from the identity his writing had conferred on him. *Desolation Angels* (1965), his last major work, forms a wistfully retrospective account of the earlier years of the Beat movement. Among his numerous other publications are *Visions of Cody* (1970), the most freely improvisatory demonstration of 'spontaneous prose'; *Maggie Cassidy* (1959) and *Tristessa* (1960), both centring on love affairs; the travel sketches of *Lonesome Traveller* (1960); and the lyrical and experimental poetry of *Mexico City Blues* and *Scattered Poems* (1971). The fullest of several biographies of Kerouac is Gerald Nicosia's *Memory Babe* (1983). See also BLACK MOUNTAIN WRITERS and SAN FRANCISCO RENAISSANCE.

KERR, Philip (1956–), British novelist, born in Edinburgh, educated at the University of Birmingham, where he studied Law. His first novel, *March Violets* (1989), set in Germany during the 1930s, features the detective Bernie Gunther; two further novels in this sequence are *The Pale Criminal* (1990) and *A German Requiem* (1991). In *A Philosophical Investigation* (1992), set in a future dystopia, Kerr used the detective genre to explore ideas about the nature of reality, making ingenious use of references to the writings of *Wittgenstein and T. S. *Eliot. His next novel, *Dead Meat* (1993), a detective story set in post-Communist St Petersburg, was dramatized for television as *Grushko*. *The Gridiron* (1995), set in Los Angeles, is a chilling thriller about a new hi-tech building totally controlled by computers designed by the architechnologist protagonist, Ray Richardson; the novel explores the grim potential of new technology. Kerr has also edited *The Penguin Book of Lies* (1990) and *The Penguin Book of Fights, Feuds and Heartfelt Hatreds* (1992).

KERSH, Gerald (1911–68), British writer, born in Middlesex; he lived in the USA and became an American citizen in 1959. Much of his work was set in the East End of London, including *Night and the City* (1938), which evocatively reflects this background during the pre-war period, and *Fowler's End* (1957), a later and more humorous account. He served in the Second World War, and in *They Die with Their Boots Clean* (1941) and several other works he vividly engaged with the horrors of war. Other works include *The Weak and the Strong* (1945), a thriller; *Prelude to a Certain Midnight* (1947), a detective novel; *The Great Wash* (1953), science fiction; and stories collected in *The Horrible Dummy* (1944), *The Brighton Monster* (1953), and *Men without Bones* (1955).

KESEY, Ken (1935–), American novelist, born in La Junta, Colorado, educated at the University of Oregon and Stanford University, where one of his teachers was Malcolm *Cowley. In the late 1950s he was introduced to the drug LSD through acting as a paid volunteer for government drug experiments in a California hospital, where he later worked as a ward attendant. These experiences provided the background for his first published novel **One Flew over the Cuckoo's Nest* (1962), an instant critical and popular success, which became one of the cult books of the 1960s; the film version of 1975 starring Jack Nicholson won five Academy Awards. Another novel, *Sometimes a Great Notion* (1964), is the story of feuding brothers in an Oregon lumber town. *Kesey's Garage Sale* (1973), with an introduction by Arthur *Miller, is a collection of essays, drawings, letters, interviews, and prose fiction by and about Kesey. His celebrated lifestyle as the West Coast trend-setter for drug-induced radical experience, a pursuit of the numinous through the senses, is recorded in Tom *Wolfe's *The Electric Kool-Aid Acid Test* (1968). Sections of Kesey's projected novel provisionally entitled *Seven Prayers by Grandma Whittier* appeared in his book *Kesey* of 1977. In his personal lifestyle, and in his most successful novel, Kesey embodies the social rebel, a role honoured in American national mythology.

KESSON, Jessie (1915–94), Scottish novelist and playwright, born in Inverness. She never knew her father, and her mother was disowned by her respectable farming family, so that her early upbringing in Elgin was plagued by poverty. At eight years old Kesson was taken away to an orphanage in Skene, Aberdeenshire, and received a good education. At 16 she was sent into service. She married in 1934, living initially in a tent, and then settling on a farm with her husband. Kesson, who had written since childhood, met the Scottish novelist Nan Shepherd on a train and was encouraged by her to enter a short story competition. She won first prize. Her first published story was in *The People's Friend* in the 1930s. She moved to London in 1949 and, while working in a variety of other jobs, began writing radio plays for the BBC. Much of her work has been autobiographical, capturing the speech and landscape of the north-east of Scotland, and evoking the inter-war years. Her novels include *The White Bird Passes* (1958), which tells of her destitute early years; *Glitter of Mica* (1963), set in the farming communities of Aberdeenshire; and *Another Time, Another Place* (1983), describing the effect on those communities of the arrival of Italian prisoners of war in the 1940s. A collection of short stories, *Where the Apple Ripens*, was published in 1985, and her work has been adapted for television and the cinema.

***Kestrel for a Knave, A* or *Kes*,** see HINES, BARRY.

KEYES, Sidney (Arthur Kilworth) (1922–43), British poet, born in Dartford, educated at Queen's College, Oxford. As a student he edited the *Cherwell* and, with Michael *Meyer, *Eight Oxford Poets* (1941), to which Keith *Douglas, John *Heath-Stubbs, and Keyes himself were the most notable contributors. *The Iron Laurel*, his first collection of verse, appeared in 1942, the year in which he enlisted in the army. He was killed after being captured while on patrol in Tunisia. He was posthumously awarded the Hawthornden Prize for a further collection entitled *The Cruel Solstice* (1943). His absorbing interest in myth and legend is reflected in much of his writing. *Yeats was eminent among his declared influences, who also included Wordsworth, Rilke, and Jung. In the lengthy sequences 'The Foreign Gate' and 'The Wilderness' he aspired to a poetry that would embody a comprehensive metaphysical philosophy. His best work is, however, less consciously ambitious, holding his mystical intuitions in balance with sharply observed imagery drawn from English landscapes. Keyes's *Col-*

lected Poems (1945) is prefaced with a memoir by Michael Meyer, who also edited *Minos of Crete: Plays and Stories* (1948), a gathering of Keyes's early work. *Sidney Keyes: A Biographical Enquiry* by John Guenther appeared in 1967. See also WAR POETRY.

KEYNES, John Maynard, first baron Keynes of Tilton (1883–1946), British economist, the single most important and influential economist of the twentieth century: born in Cambridge, son of economist John Neville Keynes, educated at Eton and King's College, Cambridge, of which he became a Fellow. He married Russian dancer Lydia Lopokova (1925) who had come to London with Diaghilev's company. In 1942 he became Baron Keynes of Tilton. In 1919 Keynes resigned from the Treasury over his differences with the official British line at Versailles. His masterful polemic, *The Economic Consequences of the Peace* (1919), propelled him to international notoriety. At Cambridge, especially in the 1920s and 1930s. Keynes's influence on economists was all-pervasive; it was felt by Sir Dennis Robertson, Piero *Sraffa, Richard Kahn, Joan *Robinson, Sir Austin Robinson, James Meade (subsequently Nobel Laureate in 1977), Sir Richard Stone (Nobel Laureate, 1984), and many foreign graduate students. Keynes was also a legendary Bursar of King's College from 1924; it is said that he claimed that his investment activities had made for the College three fortunes, and lost two. Keynes was a member of the Royal Commission on Indian Finance and Currency (1913–14), and gave evidence before the Committee on Currency and Foreign Exchanges (known as the Cunliffe Committee, 1918); he was a key member of the Committee on Finance and Industry (known as the Macmillan Committee, 1931), the Economic Advisory Council (1930–9), and the British Delegation to Bretton Woods (1944).

Keynes's contribution to economic analysis proper was enormous. His first book, *Indian Currency and Finance* (1913), reflected his involvement in the administration of that country. He was dominant in the debates over the Versailles Treaty and reparations, Britain's return to the gold standard in 1925, policies to promote full employment in the 1920s and 1930s, wartime finance, and the establishment of the IMF and World Bank. A selection of these can be found in his *Essays in Persuasion* (1931). His two books on monetary theory, *A Tract on Monetary Reform* (1923) and *A Treatise on Money* (1930, 2 volumes), carried the orthodox quantity theory of money to its limits (a theory he later repudiated). He wrote exemplary biographical accounts of the life and works of economists: some of these are collected in his *Essays in Biography* (1933). But Keynes's crucial work is *General Theory of Employment, Interest and Money* (1936), a book that changed the way we look at the economic world. Keynes was also closely connected with literature and the arts. He was a prominent member of the *Bloomsbury Group. In 1917 he raised £20,000 from the Chancellor of the Exchequer for the National Gallery (of which, in 1941, he became a Trustee) for the purchase of items from Degas' private collection, which have become the backbone of the Gallery's collection of modern French painting. Keynes was chiefly responsible for setting up the London Artists' Association; he became Treasurer of the financially troubled Comargo Ballet Company (1931) and handed it over to the Vic-Wells Ballet four years later, financially solvent; he conceived, founded (1936), and managed the Arts Theatre in Cambridge; he was a Chairman of the Committee for the Encouragement of Music and the Arts (1942) and later of its successor, the Arts Council (1945). The Royal Economic Society has published thirty volumes of his collected writings. There are biographies by Sir Roy *Harrod (1951) and Robert Skidelsky (2 volumes: 1983, 1992).

KEYNES, Sir Geoffrey Langdon (1887–1982), British surgeon, bibliographer, and editor, born in Cambridge, the brother of J. M. *Keynes, whose *Essays in Biography* (1951) he edited; he was educated at Pembroke College, Cambridge. He qualified as an MD in 1918 after serving with the Royal Army Medical Corps throughout the First World War; his *Blood Transfusion* (1922), the first British textbook on the subject, resulted from the pioneering work he carried out during the conflict. He was a surgeon at St Bartholomew's until his retirement in 1952. *A Bibliography of the Works of Dr John Donne* (1914) was the first of the many bibliographies he compiled; others include those of the works of Sir Thomas Browne (1924), Jane Austen (1929), William Hazlitt (1931), and Siegfried *Sassoon (1962). His best-known work as an editor is *Complete Writings of William Blake* (1966). His critical essays on the poet and his circle were collected as *Blake Studies* (1949). Among his other works as an editor are John Evelyn's *Memoirs for My Grandson* (1926), and the *Poetical Works* (1946) and *Letters* (1968) of Rupert *Brooke. His *Life of William Harvey* (1966) won a James Tait Black Award. *The Gates of Memory* (1981) is Keynes's autobiography.

KHALVATI, Mimi (1944–), British poet of Iranian origin, born in Tehran; she moved to Europe at an early age and was educated on the Isle of Wight, at the University of Neuchâtel, Switzerland, and the Drama Centre in London. Khalvati worked in the theatre in Iran before the revolution. The poems in her first collection, *In White Ink* (1991), are distinguished by their technical sophistication and subtle but vivid imagery; prevalent motifs are exile and expatriation, childhood and family, and passionate tributes to her native culture and its poets. The collection is dominated by the magnificent long poem 'Plant Care', which combines a feminist sensibility with a tragic universal symbolism which is at once secular and syncretic. Khalvati's second collection, *Mirrorwork* (1993), is dominated by three long poems; their sustained perspective and narrative persona is that of a woman, alone in London, battling with memories of a past elsewhere. Contemplative and restrained, the poems proffer a new politics of peace in coming to terms with oneself and with the world. The shorter poems with which these are interspersed are often allusive and playful.

KHAN, Ismith (1925–), Trinidadian novelist of Pathan ancestry, born in Port of Spain, educated at Queen's Royal College, Trinidad, Michigan State University, the New School for Social Research in New York City, and Johns Hopkins University. His novella *The Crucifixion* (1988) originated as a thesis submission of Johns Hopkins. Khan's high reputation as a writer rests chiefly on his two novels, *The Jumbie Bird* (1961) and *The Obeah Man* (1964). Both are set in colonial Trinidad, and focus on the experience of East Indians, most of whom first came to the island as indentured labourers. In *The Jumbie Bird* three successive generations of East Indians come to terms with the harshness of life in a colonial environment. Its keynote is expressed by the main character, Rahim; of the second generation, and born in Trinidad, he nevertheless cries out in anguish: 'We ain't belong to Hindustan, we ain't belong to England, we ain't belong to Trinidad.' *The Obeah Man* focuses on Zampi, a diviner, spiritual guide, and herbal physician through whom are embodied the human possibilities denied to most of the other characters. This story of blighted lives is enriched by the novelist's unerring ear for street language. *A Day in the Country* (1994) is a collection of short stories.

KIELY, Benedict (1919–), Irish short-story writer, novelist, and critic, born in Dromore, Co. Tyrone. He began studying to be a Jesuit priest but, after a serious illness, he decided to leave the Society. He completed his education at University College, Dublin. Between 1945 and 1964 he worked as a journalist in Dublin, and then taught creative writing at universities in the USA until returning to Ireland in 1968. As a literary editor he was responsible for *The Penguin Book of Irish Short Stories* (1981) and *The Small Oxford Book of Dublin* (1983). Kiely's first published work was *Counties of Contention* (1945) in which he criticizes the creation of Northern Ireland. His other works of non-fiction include *Poor Scholar* (1947), a study of William Carleton, and *Modern Irish Fiction: A Critique* (1950). Kiely's fiction, particularly his short stories, belongs to the tradition of Frank *O'Connor and Sean *O'Faolain in the way it experiments with form and insists upon autobiographical content. His novels include *Land without Stars* (1946), *Honey Seems Bitter* (1952), *Dogs Enjoy the Morning* (1955), *Nothing Happens in Carmincross* (1985), and *Proxopera* (1977) which, like Val *Mulkerns's *Antiquities* (1978), attacks the brutality of contemporary republicanism. Among his short-story collections are *A Journey to the Seven Streams* (1963), *A Ball of Malt and Madame Butterfly* (1973), *The State of Ireland* (1980), and *A Letter to Peachtree* (1987).

KILROY, Thomas (1934–), Irish playwright and novelist, born in Callan, Co. Kilkenny, educated at University College, Dublin. From 1962 to 1965 Kilroy taught at various American universities, then returned to Ireland and lectured in English at University College, Dublin. In 1977 he was appointed play editor of the *Abbey Theatre, and from 1979 to 1989 he was Professor of English at University College, Galway. He is a fellow of the Royal Society for Literature and a member of the Irish Academy of Letters. Kilroy's first play, *The Door*, was broadcast by the BBC in 1967. His first important work, *The Death and Resurrection of Mr. Roche* (1968), presents the economic, cultural, and spiritual failure of Irish society in the late 1960s through the tale of a group of drunken bachelors who apparently murder the enigmatic 'Mr. Roche'. After the production of *The O'Neill* (1969), Kilroy turned successfully to fiction with *The Big Chapel* (1971), a novel which recreates anti-clerical riots that occurred in Kilkenny in the nineteenth century. Kilroy returned to drama with *Tea and Sex and Shakespeare* (1976), followed by *Talbot's Box* (1977). His radio play *That Man, Bracken*, broadcast by the BBC in 1986, led to the stage play *Double Cross* (1986), which compares the lives of two Irishmen, Brendan Bracken and William Joyce, and examines the relationship between the act of treason and the idea of personal identity. *The Madame McAdam Travelling Show* was produced in 1991, and *Gold in the Streets* in 1993.

Kim, a novel by Rudyard *Kipling, published in 1901. The story of an Irish orphan's adolescence in late nineteenth-century India, *Kim* is a rich blend of *Bildungsroman*, spy fiction, and boy's adventure story which is now recognized as one of the most important fictions dealing with imperialism. Initially brought up in the bazaar by a native foster-mother, Kim takes up with a Lama searching for enlightenment. Early in their journey Kim establishes contact with his father's former regiment and is taken on as a trainee in counter-intelligence. From then on Kim combines his role as apprentice spy with aiding the Lama. During their journey to the Himalayas, Kim foils an attempt by foreign spies to foment discontent with British rule. Kim's travels, and his relationship with the Lama, allow Kipling to celebrate India's spirituality, diversity, and vitality in a picaresque and strongly pictorial mode.

Critics of *Kim* generally divide into two camps, according to how they interpret the ending of the novel. One group argues that Kim will take his place as a full-time member of the secret service, policing opposition to British rule. This implies that Kim betrays the Lama and that Kipling's apparently non-judgemental 'anthropological vision' of Indian culture is a façade behind which he reaffirms Britain's fitness to rule the sub-continent. The second group, by contrast, argues that Kipling leaves the novel unresolved (certainly it does not end in the manner one might expect of the stereotypical imperial adventure story). From this perspective, Kim is deemed to be unable to resolve his conflict of loyalties between India and Britain, or to attain the secure sense of cultural identity that would enable him to act effectively as a model member of the imperial class. In these readings, the Lama's mystical and compassionate vision remains an authoritative counter-weight to official imperial ideology. Such critics suggest that the ideological ambivalence of *Kim* is reinforced by both the unstable positioning of the narrative voice and Kipling's extensive borrowings from Indian vernacular narrative; these produce a text which is radically hybrid, both formally and thematically.

KINCAID, Jamaica (1949–), Antiguan novelist and short-story writer, originally named Elaine Potter Richardson, born in St John's, Antigua, and educated at Antigua Girls' School. In 1966 she emigrated to New York and joined the staff of the **New Yorker* in 1976. *At the Bottom of the River* (1983), her first collection of stories, was acclaimed for the lyrical originality of its treatments of everyday events in a Caribbean setting. More factual in manner, her novel *Annie John* (1985) dealt with the tensions between a mother and daughter as the latter moves away from the traditional Antiguan culture in pursuit of professional opportunity. *Lucy* (1990) displays her increasing deftness of characterization and narrative in its account of a young Antiguan woman coming to New York as an *au pair*. Kincaid's other works include *A Small Place* (1988), which investigates the social and economic results of Antigua's emergence from its colonial past, and *Autobiography of My Mother* (1994).

Kind of Loving, A, a novel by Stan *Barstow, published in 1960. Vic Brown, the narrator-protagonist of Barstow's first novel, is the son of a solidly respectable mining family enjoying the post-war years of prosperity and full employment. Set in Cressley, a fictitious industrial town in the West Riding of Yorkshire, the novel creates a convincing picture of a society adapting its strictly moral and hierarchical past to a more liberal future, and absorbing the manifestations of a burgeoning popular culture. Caught up in the middle ground between the old and the new, the naïve and self-absorbed Vic drifts into a purely physical relationship and ends up in a loveless marriage to a girl he has made pregnant. Despite the barely restrained savagery and anguish of its later episodes, the novel ends positively with Vic finally accepting responsibility for his own actions and determined to make something of his unpromising future.

KING, Francis (Henry) (1923–), British novelist, short-story writer, and critic, born in Switzerland, educated at Shrewsbury School and Balliol College, Oxford. His early years were spent in Switzerland and India and in 1949, after the publication of *To the Dark Tower* (1946) and *An Air that Kills* (1948), he began working abroad for the British Council. Subsequent novels include *The Dividing Stream* (1951), a study of English, Americans, and Italians in post-war Florence; *The Dark Glasses* (1954) and *Man on the Rock* (1957), both of which offer insights into the Greek character; *The Widow* (1957); and a novel with a Japanese background, *The Custom House* (1961). After his return to Britain in 1963, King's fiction became more intense in its imaginative and psychological investigation of human behaviour. Thus the central character of *The Needle* (1977) is a compulsive paedophile, and *Act of Darkness* (1983) deals with the murder of a small boy. King has always sought to explore the homosexual predicament: *A Domestic Animal* (1970) is a moving scrutiny of the obsessive feelings a handsome young Italian philosopher arouses in a rather repressed English writer. King's interest in the psychology of older women finds fictional expression in *Voices in an Empty Room* (1984) and *The Woman Who Was God* (1988). *Punishments* (1989) tells of a young English medical student in the bombed Germany of 1948 and his sexual involvement with Jurgen, a young German whose object is to make him suffer for what the British did to his country. *Visiting Cards* (1990) draws on his experience of British Council activities. Again, set in Florence immediately after the Second World War and based on King's own experiences, *The Ant Colony* (1991) concerns an innocent young Englishman who is exposed to an intense spectrum of new sexual and cultural experiences. In *The One and Only* (1994) a respectable middle-class man finds evidence of a very doubtful act in his past when reading a friend's autobiography; the novel is a haunting examination of the dark forces beneath English respectability and the vulnerability of identity. King's volumes of short stories include *The Brighton Belle and Other Stories* (1968), *Hard Feelings and Other Stories* (1976), and *One Is a Wanderer* (1985). In his social comedy, his use of other cultures as points of reference in the dissection of his own, and in his recognition of homosexuality as an incontestable force, King stands very much in the tradition of E. M. *Forster, though he is in fact a far more conservative writer, both formally and in his values. His other works include *Florence: A Literary Companion* (1991) and *Yesterday Came Suddenly* (1993), an autobiography.

KING, Stephen (1948–), American writer of horror stories, born in Portland, Maine, which formed the setting of most of his best stories, and educated at the University of Maine. He published short fiction in the 1960s, and became a best-selling author with his first novel, *Carrie* (1974), which, like many of his books, was filmed. King has perhaps absorbed in his fiction some of the excesses of the horror movies of the time. With increasing sophistication and growing complexity he has integrated this material into a vision of modern rural and small town America in works such as *Salem's Lot* (1975), *The Shining* (1977, filmed by Stanley Kubrick), *Firestarter* (1980), *Cujo* (1981), *Christine* (1983), *Pet Sematary* (1983), and *It* (1986). *The Stand* (1978) moves to an apocalyptic future, and *The Dead Zone* (1979) endows its psychic protagonist with a genuine pathos. *Misery* (1987) and *The Dark Half* (1989) inwardly depict their writer protagonists whose personalities mask a deadness of the heart. With later novels such as *Needful Things* (1991) and *Insomnia* (1994), King's use of the supernatural has decreased. See also BESTSELLERS.

KINGSLEY, Sidney (1906–), American dramatist, born in Philadelphia, educated at Cornell University. Kingsley had a brief career as an actor before concentrating on writing, directing, and producing plays. His first success was *Men in White* (1933; Pulitzer Prize), produced at the Group Theatre, which dramatized the conflict faced by a young hospital doctor forced to choose between marriage to a wealthy woman and his medical vocation. Kingsley twice won the New York Drama Critics Circle Award, first for *The Patriots* (1943), a historical chronicle about the political conflict between Thomas Jefferson's democratic idealism and Alexander Hamilton's federalism, and later for his adaptation of Arthur Koestler's novel **Darkness at Noon* (1951). His other plays include *Dead End* (1935), about New York street gangs; *Ten Million Ghosts* (1936), an anti-war propaganda play; *The World We Make* (1939); *Detective Story* (1949); *Lunatics and Lovers* (1954); and *Night Life* (1962). With the exception of the light-hearted *Lunatics and Lovers*, Kingsley's plays are intense dramas of moral and social engagement.

KINGSTON, Maxine Hong (1940–), Chinese-American writer, born in Stockton, California, to first-generation immigrant parents from Southern China, educated at the University of California, Berkeley. Her experiences of growing up bilingual and bicultural in a Californian Chinatown are reflected in *The Woman Warrior, Memoirs of a Childhood among Ghosts* (1976), and its sequel, *China Men* (1980). Both works are characterized by structural fragmentation, poetic diction, and lavish use of Chinese folklore, often transplanted to American settings. In Britain, Kingston was praised by such eminent voices as Salman *Rushdie and Marina *Warner for her innovative formal experiments and her charting of new thematic territory; while in North America, she has been acclaimed as the leading figure of a new wave of writing by immigrants, particularly Asian-Americans, including Amy *Tan and Bharati *Mukherjee, exploring roots and chronicling family histories. *Tripmaster Monkey: His Fake Book* (1989), about the would-be poet and visionary Whitman Ah Sing, is a biting satire on Chinese-American male attitudes, and is remarkable for its sustained linguistic dexterity and its imaginative transformation of Chinese myth to American metaphor. The works of Kingston are featured in Amy Ling's *Between Worlds: Women Writers of Chinese Ancestry* (1990). See also ASIAN-AMERICAN LITERATURE.

KINNELL, Galway (1927–), American poet, born in Providence, Rhode Island, educated at Princeton University and the University of Rochester. Since the early 1950s he has held a succession of visiting posts at universities in Europe, the Middle East, and America; he became director of the Squaw Valley Community of Writers in 1979. His earlier verse, represented by *What a Kingdom It Was* (1960) and the belatedly published *First Poems 1946–1954* (1970), combined a straightforwardly reflective tone with fluent use of complex traditional forms. The vivid and imaginative presentation of natural imagery in these volumes remains an essential feature of his later work, collections of which include *Flower Herding on Mount Monadnock* (1964), *Body Rags* (1969), *The Book of Nightmares* (1971), *Mortal Acts, Mortal Words* (1980), *Selected Poems* (1982), *The Past* (1985), and *When One Has Lived a Long Time Alone* (1990). Throughout the 1970s his verse became increasingly experimental in conveying his encompassing vision of the fundamental unity of the human and natural world. The most notable of his many poems addressing social and historical injustice is the long title work of *The Avenue Bearing the Initial of Christ into the New World*, a collected edition of his verse published in 1974. Among his other works is the novel *Black Light* (1966) and numerous translations, which include *The Poems of François Villon* (1965) and *The Lackawanna Elegy* (1970) by Yvan Goll.

KINSELLA, Thomas (1928–), Irish poet, born in Dublin, where he was educated at University College. After a successful career in the Irish Civil Service, he began teaching at American universities in 1965 and became Professor of English at Temple University, Philadelphia, in 1970. *The Starlit Eye* (1952) was his first collection of verse. His reputation was established by the highly accomplished work in *Poems* (1956). The experimental character of his later poetry emerged in the sombrely lyrical *Another September* (1958). *Nightwalker* (1967), the long poem widely regarded as an important advance in Irish *Modernism, conducts its penetrating analysis of Ireland's socio-cultural situation through a psychologically revealing treatment of Kinsella's responses to his country's past and present. His later collections include *Notes from the Land of the Dead* (1972), *Songs of the Night and Other Poems* (1978), *Collected Poems: 1956–1973* (1980), *One Fond Embrace* (1981), *Blood and Family* (1988), which contains work previously issued by Peppercanister, the publishing house he founded in Dublin in 1972, and *From Centre City* (1994). Kinsella is also noted for his translation of the Irish epic poem *The Tain* (1968). His works as an editor include *The New Oxford Book of Irish Verse* (1986). His prose work *Dual Tradition* (1995) focuses on poetry and politics in Ireland.

KIPLING, Rudyard (1865–1936), English novelist, poet, and short-story writer, born in Bombay, India, the son of John Lockwood Kipling, art teacher and illustrator, and Alice, sister-in-law of Sir Edward Burne-Jones, the Pre-Raphaelite painter. As a young child, Kipling was left in England with foster-parents for several years, a traumatic experience of abandonment which was reworked notably in his important short story 'Baa Baa, Black Sheep'. His secondary education was at the United Services College—an experience which forms the basis for *Stalky and Co* (1899). Returning to India at the age of 16, Kipling worked (1882–9) as a journalist on two leading Indian newspapers, and began to publish short fictions as a means of leavening their staple fare of official reports and home news. These were subsequently collected in a series of volumes for a local readership before being discovered by London publishers. *Plain Tales from the Hills*

(1888), *Soldiers Three* (1889), and *Life's Handicap* (1891) are the most notable collections of Indian tales.

Kipling returned to London in 1889 to find himself a celebrity, though he soon experienced a severe mental breakdown—a central theme in his first published novel, *The Light that Failed* (1890). While in London, Kipling struck up a friendship with a young American, Wolcott Balestier, with whom he collaborated on another unremarkable novel, *The Naulakha* (1892). On Wolcott's sudden death, Kipling married his sister Carrie, with whom he had three children. The eldest daughter, Josephine, died in 1899 and Kipling's son John was killed in action in 1915. To these events are often attributed the growing melancholy of Kipling's writing after 1900, an almost pathological desire for privacy—his autobiography *Something of Myself* (1937) must be one of the most unrevealing specimens of the genre—and an increasing interest in the supernatural. For several years the Kiplings were unsettled, moving between Vermont, the west of England, and South Africa. This wandering lifestyle did not inhibit Kipling's creativity; in this period he produced novels such as *Captains Courageous* (1897) and **Kim* (1901), collections of short stories, including *Many Inventions* (1893) and *The Day's Work* (1898), and a considerable body of verse. In 1902 the Kiplings settled in Sussex, where Kipling enjoyed productive friendships with a number of neighbouring writers such as *Conrad and Rider Haggard.

Because of the Indian short stories and *Kim*, generally considered to be his only successful novel, Kipling is generally identified as 'the laureate of empire', to use *Orwell's phrase. However, there is an enormous range of subject matter, genre, styles, and tones in Kipling's prose work, including fables, science fiction, war stories, ghost stories, and a range of material written for children, such as *The Jungle Books* (1894–5), *Just So Stories* (1902), *Puck of Pook's Hill* (1906), and *Rewards and Fairies* (1910). Kipling is also an underrated travel writer, with *From Sea to Sea* (1899) his most notable work in this mode. Three major volumes of short stories appeared in the twentieth century, but these are considered less even in quality than earlier collections. Kipling was also a prolific writer of poetry throughout his career; this ranges from light-hearted early satires like *Departmental Ditties* (1886) to gravely prophetic, moralizing explorations of national and international problems, such as 'Recessional' and the notorious 'White Man's Burden'. Stylistically, Kipling's verse is most notable for its experiments in popular forms and dramatic voice, particularly *Barrack-Room Ballads* (1892).

Kipling's reputation has fluctuated wildly. Early in his career, he was hailed as the greatest new talent since Dickens, and Henry *James saw in him the potential to become 'an English Balzac'. His reputation abroad was such that in 1907 he became the first English recipient of the Nobel Prize for literature. However, his vigorous support for the British effort in the Great War, an increasing public distaste for empire, together with the advent of the experimental writing associated with *Modernism, led to a rapid eclipse of his reputation by the time of his death. While Kipling began to receive sympathetic critical attention again after the publication of Charles Carrington's biography (1955), his reputation remains mixed. Many critics continue to upbraid Kipling for his allegedly supremacist views on race and empire. Others, however, suggest that attention to the complex forms of Kipling's narrative prove that his ideological positions are much more ambivalent than is often recognized. Kipling is undoubtedly one of the great short-story writers in English and the subtlety of his early narrative technique has led some to claim him as a proto-Modernist. Latterly Kipling's work has been republished in major new critical editions, and there has been a serious engagement with the enormous body of his poetry for the first time since T. S. *Eliot's efforts in the 1940s—notably by Ann Parry, Peter Keating, and Andrew Rutherford. Biographies by Angus Wilson (1977) and Martin Seymour-Smith (1990) attest to the undiminished interest in Kipling's enigmatic and elusive personality and private life.

Kipps, a novel by H. G. *Wells, published in 1905. This romantic comedy, drawing on Wells's early experiences as a draper's assistant, established its author as one of the leading Edwardian novelists. Today it survives principally as a period piece. The opening chapters, in which the young, illegitimate Artie Kipps enters Shalford's emporium in Folkestone, contain Wells's fullest and bitterest description of the apprentice's life. The drapery trade is represented as a lifelong dead end, but Kipps escapes miraculously when it turns out that he is heir to a fortune. He then embarks on a comic journey through the English class system, living the life of a gentleman as prescribed by a contemporary etiquette book, *Manners and Rules of Good Society*. He tries to amend his uncouth behaviour and accent, and becomes engaged to the genteel Helen Walshingham, unwisely entrusting his investments to her crooked brother. Just as snobbery and social pretension seem to have ensnared him as effectively as the drapery had done, he rebels and returns to his childhood sweetheart, Ann Pornick. He ends up comfortably as a small bookseller. The most memorable of a large cast of minor characters is the bohemian Chitterlow, who becomes a successful playwright. *Kipps*, a deliberate melodrama, was itself adapted for the stage in 1912, and filmed in 1922 and 1941. A later musical version, *Half a Sixpence*, appeared on both stage and screen. Wells described the novel as a fragment of a much larger design, part of which survives in draft form; this was published posthumously as *The Wealth of Mr Waddy* (1969).

KIRKUP, James (1923–), British poet, playwright, and travel writer, born in South Shields, County Durham, educated at Durham University. He has held posts at universities in Britain, Europe, America, and Japan. He has also worked extensively as a translator. Among his earlier collections of poetry is *A Correct Compassion* (1952), the title poem of which is perhaps his finest single work, developing its rhymed narrative of cardiovascular surgery with a remarkable combination of documentary objectivity and understated dramatic tension. His many subsequent publications as a poet include *Descent into the Cave* (1957), *The Bewick Bestiary* (1971), *Scenes from Sesshu* (1978), *The Guitar Player of Zuiganji* (1985), and *Throwback: Poems Towards an Autobiography* (1992). In 1977 Kirkup's poem 'The Love that Dares To Speak Its Name', which presents Christ as the object of homosexual love, resulted in a successful prosecution for blasphemous libel. Among his numerous plays are *An Actor's Revenge* (1979) and *The Damask Drum* (1984). He has produced several volumes of autobiography, including *The *Only Child* (1957), *Sorrows, Passions, and Alarms* (1959), *I, of All People* (1988), *A Poet Could Not But Be Gay* (1991), and *Me All Over: Memoirs of a Misfit* (1993). His many travel books include *These Horned Islands* (1962), on his early experiences of Japan, *Filipinescas* (1968), and *Hong Kong and Macao* (1970).

Kitchen Sink Drama, a term applied in the later 1950s to the often abrasive realistic plays, with working-class or lower-middle-class settings, that were then challenging the drawing-room dramas of *Coward and *Rattigan for critical approval—and finding it, notably in the reviews of Kenneth *Tynan. Examples of the genre would include Osborne's **Look Back in Anger*, set in a cluttered bed-sitter; *Delaney's *A Taste of Honey*, set in a 'comfortless flat' in Salford; and *Wesker's *The Kitchen*, which actually occurs in the chaotic kitchen of a busy restaurant.

KITCHIN, Clifford (Henry Benn) (1895–1967), British novelist, born in Harrogate, educated at Exeter College, Oxford; he became a barrister and a stockbroker. His two first novels, *Streamers Waving* (1925) and *Mr Balcony* (1927), have the wit, fantasy, and mannered artifice associated with *Firbank. The first presents a useless-seeming spinster, with an eccentrically developed inner life, the second a man who decides to deprive himself of his normality by having himself castrated on a visit to Africa. Subsequent novels include *The Birthday Party* (1938), *The Secret River* (1956), and *The Auction Sale* (1949), generally agreed to be his masterpiece with its awareness of the significance of possessions and its quiet sense of ecstasy. Kitchin also wrote four detective stories, the first, *Death of My Aunt* (1929), soon achieving classic status. Their sleuth, Malcolm Warren, is a stockbroker, and the novels manage to be comedies of manners as well as whodunnits.

KIZER, Carolyn (1925–), American poet, born in Spokane, Washington, educated at Sarah Lawrence College, Columbia University, and the University of Washington. In 1959 she founded the magazine *Poetry Northwest*, which she edited until 1965. Her verse is personal, reflecting love, loss, family life, and the courage of women. Among her earlier volumes are *The Ungrateful Garden* (1961), *Knock upon Silence* (1965), and *Midnight Was My Cry: New and Selected Poems* (1971). Although much of her work is woman-centred, it is almost entirely free of didacticism or stridency. Her awareness of the inherent tensions between male and female is voiced in the complementary volumes *Mermaids in the Basement: Poems for Women* (1984) and *The Nearness of You: Poems for Men* (1986). Another volume, *Yin* (1984), contains autobiographical material. Kizer has lived in Pakistan, and her interest in the verse forms of the Urdu language is reflected both in her translations and in her own writings. Japanese and Chinese influences are also discernible in her work. Her best translations from these languages and others have appeared in *Carrying Over* (1988), which includes translations from the work of the popular woman poet of Mainland China, Shu Ting. Her interest in interrelationships between male and female, and between conflicting cultures, is balanced in characteristic Taoist fashion.

KLEIN, A(braham) M(oses) (1909–74), Canadian poet, born in the Ukraine and taken to Montreal in 1910, educated at McGill University and the Université de Montreal. Klein practised at the Bar from 1933 until 1954. His writings explore Jewish culture from a rich Canadian perspective with both learning and wit. *Hath Not a Jew . . .* (1940) explored issues relating to Palestine and to religious uncertainty, and was followed by *Poems* and *The Hitleriad*, both published in 1944. The latter was a highly satirical mock-epic, through which Klein intended to highlight the horror of Hitler's rise. *The Rocking Chair* (1948) drew on the French-Canadian background of Montreal and reflects his own sharp sense of a Canadian identity. *The Second Scroll* (1951) was inspired by a visit to Israel, and in 'poetic novel' form reflects both a literal and a spiritual odyssey in modern times. His short fiction was collected in *Short Stories* (1983). Always politically attuned, Klein's work encompasses a vision of Canada's relationship to a wider world.

KNIGHT, G(eorge) (Richard) Wilson (1897–1985), British critic, born in Sutton, Surrey, educated at St Edmund Hall, Oxford. He became Professor of English at the University of Leeds in 1956. *The Wheel of Fire* (1930) immediately gained him an international reputation. His concern with the underlying metaphorical structures of Shakespeare's plays transcended the constraints of more conventional approaches of the sort typically associated with A. C. *Bradley, which tended to concentrate on linear developments of character and plot. His numerous other Shakespearian studies include *The Imperial Theme* (1931), which deals with the Roman plays; *The Shakespearian Tempest* (1932); *The Crown of Life* (1947), on the late plays; and *The Mutual Flame* (1955), a treatment of the poems. He also produced and acted in a number of Shakespeare's plays and presented a one-man show entitled 'Shakespeare's Dramatic Challenge'. *Principles of Shakespearian Production* (1936) was among his influential books on the staging of the plays. Among his other works are *The Starlit Dome* (1941), a study of the Romantic poets; *Lord Byron:*

Christian Virtues (1952); and *Laureate of Peace* (1954), his highly regarded book on Pope. *Atlantic Crossing* (1936) is autobiographical.

KNIGHTS, L(ionel) C(harles) (1906–), British critic, born in Grantham, Lincolnshire, educated at Selwyn College and Christ's College, Cambridge. A founder of **Scrutiny* in 1932, he was its most eminent contributor in the field of Shakespearian studies. He held successive professorships at Sheffield, Bristol, and Cambridge Universities. His essay 'How Many Children Had Lady Macbeth?' (1933), collected in *Explorations* (1946), opened with a provocative review of the state of Shakespearian criticism, very much at the expense of the orthodoxy represented by A. C. *Bradley; the second part conducted a detailed thematic interpretation in the manner demonstrated by G. Wilson *Knight. His further works on Shakespeare's plays include *Some Shakespearean Themes* (1959) and *An Approach to Hamlet* (1960). He also produced numerous works considering literature from a sociological perspective, among them *Drama and Society in the Age of Jonson* (1933) and *Public Voices* (1971), a study of literature and politics with particular reference to the seventeenth century. Additional collections of his essays include *Further Explorations* (1965), *Explorations 3* (1976), and *Hamlet and Other Shakespeare Essays* (1981).

KNOX, Monsignor Ronald (Arbuthnott) (1888–1957), British writer, born at Kibworth, Leicestershire, educated at Balliol College, Oxford. At the age of 18 he enjoyed considerable success with *Signa Severa* (1906), a collection of epigrammatic light verses in English, Latin, and Greek. He entered the ministry in 1911 and became Chaplain of Trinity College, Oxford, in 1912. *Absolute and Abitofhell* (1913) is the most notable of his versified attacks on latitudinarianism. In 1917 he became a Roman Catholic, accounting for his conversion in the autobiographical *A Spiritual Aeneid* (1918). He was chaplain to the Roman Catholic undergraduates at Oxford from 1926 to 1939, when he resigned in order to concentrate on his translation of the Bible, which appeared in a single edition in 1955; *The Trials of a Translator* (1949) describes his preparations for this task. His other translations include the *Autobiography* of St Thérèse of Lisieux (1958). His other works include *Enthusiasm* (1950), a study of religious vagaries, and *Let Dons Delight* (1939), which traces the disintegration of a common culture through a sequence of imaginary conversations between Oxford dons from the sixteenth century onward. *The Three Taps* (1927) and *Double Cross Purposes* (1937) are among his numerous detective stories. His close friend Evelyn *Waugh published *The Life of the Right Reverend Ronald Knox* in 1959.

KOCH, C(hristopher) J(ohn) (1932–), Australian novelist, born in Hobart, educated at the University of Tasmania. His work, which draws on his experiences in Europe, America, and Asia, reflects a preoccupation with the political and cultural relationships between Australia and the Far East. His first novel, *The Boys in the Island* (1958; revised 1974) was acclaimed for its sensitive account of growing up in Tasmania and Melbourne. *Across the Sea Wall* (1965; revised 1982) was set in India and Australia and centres on the relationship between an Australian man and a Latvian girl. Its visionary quality and its themes of disillusionment and the corruption of idealism characterize subsequent works. *The Year of Living Dangerously* (1978) was widely admired for its complex and dramatic evocation of Jakarta in 1965 on the eve of Sukarno's fall; a film based on the novel appeared in 1982. *The Doubleman* (1985) vividly evokes the spirit and landscapes of Tasmania. *Crossing the Gap: A Novelist's Essays* (1987) showed him to be a perceptive social and political observer and offers an illuminating account of his Tasmanian background.

KOCH, Kenneth (1925–), American poet, born in Cincinnati, Ohio, educated at Harvard and Columbia Universities. Koch served for three years in the US Army as a rifleman in the Pacific theatre of war. He has taught at several colleges and became resident poet at Columbia. Koch is a founding member of the '*New York School of Poets', with John *Ashbery and Frank *O'Hara. His books include *Poems* (1953), *Ko, or a Season on Earth* (1959), *Permanently* (1961), *Thank You and Other Poems* (1962), *When the Sun Tries to Go On* (1969), *Sleeping with Women* (1969), *The Pleasures of Peace and Other Poems* (1969), *The Duplications* (1977), *Sleeping on the Wing* (1982), *Selected Poems* (1985), *On the Edge* (1986), and *On the Great Atlantic Railway* (1994). Like the other New York poets, Koch has also written for the experimental theatre; his dramatic work is collected in *A Change of Hearts: Plays, Films and Other Dramatic Works, 1951–1971* (1973). More recently he has published *One Thousand Avant-Garde Plays* (1988). As a young man, Koch lived for a time in France and Italy, and in Paris became enthralled with the surrealist poetry of Jacques Prévert; much of his own work seeks to capture what he calls the 'incomprehensible excitement' he found in French poetry. A surreal ironist and parodist, guided by the pleasure principle rather than the admonitory compulsions of the satirist, Koch is an accomplished craftsman who disdains what he calls the postures of high seriousness. He has also published a collection of essays and short stories, *Hotel Lamboga* (1993).

KOESTLER, Arthur (1905–83), Anglo-Hungarian novelist and journalist, born in Budapest, educated at the University of Vienna. Koestler served in the Spanish Civil War as war correspondent for the *News Chronicle*, was arrested by Franco's Nationalists in 1937, and finally freed by the intervention of the British government. The experience resulted in *Spanish Testament* (1937) which, like all his books before 1941, was written in German. *Scum of the Earth* (1941), his first major work in English, records his imprisonment in a French concentration camp in 1940, from which he escaped to England. He became a naturalized British subject in 1948. His other autobiographical works include *Arrow in the Blue* (1952) and *The Invisible Writing* (1954). **Darkness at Noon* (1940), his masterpiece, made an enormous impact in its exposure of the sham, brutality, and sheer horror behind Stalin's show trials. *Arrival and Departure* (1943) examines neurosis as the possible root of revolutionary politics. His other novels include *Thieves in the Night* (1946), about the Zionists in Palestine; *The Age of Longing* (1951), a parable about a nuclear-threatened future; and *The Call-Girls* (1972), a satire about high-powered, mainly male, intellectuals. *Twilight Bar: An Escapade in Four Acts* (1945), his only play, was produced in Paris and Baltimore in 1946. His wide-ranging collections of essays include *The Yogi and the Commissar* (1945), *The Trail of the Dinosaurs* (1955), and *Drinkers of Infinity* (1958). He also wrote many speculative books on scientific topics, including *The Ghost in the Machine* (1967) and *The Roots of Coincidence* (1972). Koestler suffered from terminal illness and with his devoted third wife, Cynthia Jefferies, died in a suicide pact. Their last days are movingly recorded in the jointly written *Stranger on the Square* (1984).

KOGAWA, Joy (1935–), third-generation Japanese-Canadian writer, born in Vancouver. She was interned with her family during the Second World War and transported to the ghost town of Slocan in the Rockies of British Columbia, and then to Alberta. Her writings provide an invaluably complex vision of the 'Canadian' experience from her own unique perspective, at the same time writing into the nation's imaginative history aspects of its politics it might well prefer to forget. *The Splintered Moon* (1967), her first poetry collection, was followed by *A Choice of Dreams* (1974), *Jericho Road* (1977), and *Woman in the Woods* (1985). Her novel *Obasan* (1981, adapted for children as *Naomi's Road*, 1986), which disturbingly compounds fiction and documentary in defining truth, traces the fate of a third-generation Canadian family of Japanese origin in the face of Canadian Government internment policies during the Second World War. The novel is a moving exploration of the complexities of cultural diversity in a largely immigrant culture such as Canada's. Its sequel *Itsuka* (1992) follows the family's campaign to obtain redress from the Canadian authorities for their suffering.

KOPIT, Arthur (1937–), American dramatist, born in New York, educated at Harvard. He won his reputation with a student play, *Oh Dad, Poor Dad, Mamma's Hung You in the Closet, and I'm Feelin' So Sad* (1961). Written in the idiom of European theatre of the *Absurd, *Oh Dad* is at once imitative and parodic of fashionable avant-garde theatre of the 1960s, and features a woman who keeps her husband's corpse in a wardrobe and dominates her son. Of Kopit's many other plays, the most highly regarded are *Indians* (1968), concerning white American imperialism, which fuses the narratives of the erasure of the North American Indian tribes from their ancestral homelands with America's involvement in Vietnam (see VIETNAM WRITING), and *Wings* (1978), a poetic drama about a woman recovering from a stroke, whose fractured world is revealed through her interior monologue. A writer of considerable versatility in a variety of theatrical idioms, Kopit's work shows many European influences, especially those of Brecht and Pirandello. In 1982 he wrote the book for a musical, *Nine*, based on Federico Fellini's film *8½*, and adapted from the Italian by Mario Fratti, and in 1984 wrote a new translation of Ibsen's *Ghosts*. Several of his plays have been made into films, most notably *Oh Dad* (1967) with Rosalind Russell and Jonathan Winters, and *Buffalo Bill and the Indians, or Sitting Bull's History Lesson* (1976), based on *Indians*, and made by Robert Altman.

KOPS, Bernard (1926–), British dramatist, born in Stepney, London, educated at Stepney Jewish School. He worked as a docker, chef, salesman, waiter, and barrow-boy before writing his first play, *The Hamlet of Stepney Green* (1959), about a young dreamer who, having sworn to take revenge on behalf of a father 'poisoned' by an unfulfilling world, instead falls in love with the local Ophelia. Subsequent stage work, much of it notable for its exuberance of observation, hostility to convention, and delight in freedom and eccentricity, has included *The Dream of Peter Mann* (1960), a loose reworking of Ibsen's *Peer Gynt*; *Enter Solly Gold* (1962), about a conman who, disguised as a rabbi, brings happiness to a bored, materialistic household; and *The Lemmings* (1963), which ends with a zombiesque British nation, including the only couple who still have a little spirit, walking into the sea. Kops, who has also published novels and poetry, as well as an autobiography, *The World Is a Wedding* (1964), wrote little for the theatre between the mid-1960s and 1981, when *Ezra*, his study of Ezra *Pound, was performed. Subsequent plays have included *Simon at Midnight* (1985); *Sophie* (1990); *Playing Sinatra* (1991), about a man who lives in childlike isolation with his more restless sister; *Who Shall I Be Tomorrow?* (1992), another study of recluses, this time a suicidal actress and her homosexual neighbour; and an adaptation of *The Diary of Anne Frank* (1992).

KOSINSKI, Jerzy (Nikodem) (1933–91), Polish-born American novelist, born in Lodz, Poland, educated at the University of Lodz, (Polish) State Academy of Sciences, and Columbia University. Separated from his parents at the age of six, Kosinski spent the years of the Second World War wandering through Russia and Poland, living on his wits in alien communities before being reunited with his parents in 1945. This extraordinary experience caused Kosinski to lose the power of speech for some years, which he recovered through a skiing accident in 1947. Radically at odds with the totalitarian society of post-war Poland, he managed to get himself 'invited' to study in the USA by a complete hoax. He became a graduate student at Columbia University in 1958, and at the New School for Social Research in 1962. His first two books were sociological studies of the fate of the individual in totalitarian societies, *The Future Is Ours, Comrade*

(1960), and *No Third Path* (1962), published under the name Joseph Novak. His first novel was *The Painted Bird* (1965), a fictionalized account of his boyhood experiences during the German occupation of Poland and Russia; this and his next four novels, *Steps* (1968), *Being There* (1971), *The Devil Tree* (1973), and *Cockpit* (1975), form a five-novel cycle, whose common theme is that of an individual completely isolated in his social world, alienated from his own past and the contemporary culture he inhabits. Of his later novels, *Blind Date* (1977) and *Passion Play* (1979) employ the picaresque form as the one most appropriate to Kosinski's conversion to the philosophy of chance, in which the development of an individual's life as the expression of a consistent personality is abandoned in favour of the variousness of contingent experiences, each of which allows a different sense of self to develop. This preoccupation with the unreliability of a socially conceived and imposed identity also informs his novel *Pinball* (1982).

KOTZWINKLE, William (1939–), American novelist and short-story writer, born in Scranton, Pennsylvania, educated at Penn State University. Kotzwinkle is a prolific writer, dividing his attention equally between books for adults and for children. His transparent style and his stress on the primacy of illusion derive from his Buddhist conception of the universe, which also gives his novels their curious combination of playfulness and seriousness. *Fata Morgana* (1977), *Herr Nightingale and the Satin Woman* (1978), and *The Hot Jazz Trio* (1989) are all fantasy novels, underpinned by close attention to archetypal configurations. *Jack in the Box* (1980) and *Queen of Swords* (1984) satirize the clash between libido and social convention. *E.T. the Extra-Terrestrial* (1982), *Superman III* (1983), and *E.T.: The Book of the Green Planet* (1985) stem from his affiliation to the world of film, whose dislocation from reality he chillingly presents in *The Exile* (1987). The contrast between his most sombre book, *Swimmer in the Secret Sea* (1975), and the slapstick comedy of *The Fan Man* (1974) and *The Midnight Examiner* (1989), vividly illustrates the spread of his abilities. Though he has a reputation of being a cult novelist, he is too detached to cater to the interests of a specific minority. In terms of tone and vision, the best of his work stands comparison with that of Kurt *Vonnegut and Richard *Brautigan.

KRAMER, Larry (1935–), American playwright and novelist, born in Bridgeport, Connecticut, educated at Yale University. He worked as an executive in the film industry, first in London and later in New York. In 1970 he wrote and produced the screenplay for Ken Russell's acclaimed adaptation of D. H. Lawrence's **Women in Love*. His controversial novel *Faggots* (1978) was praised by some for its forthright account of the New York–Fire Island gay circuit in the free-wheeling 1970s, but others criticized the novel for its seemingly moralistic tone towards the gay sub-culture in which Kramer had himself participated. With the advent of AIDS, Kramer's confrontations against the political and medical establishment won the approval of many in the gay world. In 1981 he founded the Gay Men's Health Crisis in New York, and in 1988 he helped to form ACT-UP (the AIDS Coalition to Unleash Power). Kramer later broke with both organizations and himself contracted AIDS. *The Normal Heart* (1985) is the first drama to deal directly with the AIDS crisis, which is also the subject of essays in *Reports from the Holocaust: The Making of an AIDS Activist* (1989). *The Destiny of Me* (1991) is an autobiographical play dealing with Kramer's family and coming out.

KRANTZ, Judith, see ROMANTIC FICTION.

Krapp's Last Tape, a play by Samuel *Beckett, written in 1957 for the actor Patrick Magee. It shows a 69-year-old man listening to a tape-recording he made thirty years before. In this, he is variously heard talking of his beliefs and spiritual health, complaining of his evidently chronic constipation, remembering a vaguely sexual encounter while his mother lay dying, and mocking the worthy 'aspirations' and 'resolutions' that he has found recorded on a still earlier tape, one he made when he was a 'young whelp' in his twenties. Cynicism had evidently begun to set in then, and is infinitely more marked now. The reaction of the aged Krapp, who shuffles about eating bananas and drinking wine, is mostly one of impatience and boredom with what, in the new tape he begins to record, he dismisses as the pointless ramblings of a 'stupid bastard'—'hard to believe I was ever as bad as that'. But one part of the old tape fascinates him, and he replays it obsessively. It describes being in a boat on a lake with a woman: 'We lay there without moving. But under us all moved, and moved us, gently, up and down, and from side to side.' Eventually he throws away his new tape, listens again to his memory of the incident, and then to his 39-year-old self's closing words: 'Perhaps my best years are gone. When there was a chance of happiness. But I wouldn't want them back. Not with the fire in me now. No, I wouldn't want them back.' The 69-year-old Krapp is left 'motionless staring before him', a visible example of the vanity of human wishes.

KREISEL, Henry (1922–), Canadian novelist, born in Vienna, where he spent his first sixteen years, before fleeing to England to escape the Nazi occupation. Interned as an 'enemy alien' at the beginning of the Second World War, he was sent to Canada in 1940 and remained interned there for a further eighteen months. He subsequently studied at the Universities of Toronto and London and became a Professor of English at the University of Alberta in Edmonton. His fiction is less concerned with the predicament of New World immigrants than with alienation more generally. *The Rich Man* (1948) tells the story of a Jewish-Canadian immigrant who returns to his native Austria in the 1930s, pretending to be rich, but forced to acknowledge his dissimulation when his family is struck by tragedy and he is unable to assist them. *The Betrayal* (1964) is a moral fable centred on an encounter in Edmonton between a young Jew who has narrowly escaped Nazi persecution and his former betrayer. It contrasts the New World innocence of Western Canadian life with the horrific recent history of middle Europe and poses complex ethical questions about responsibility, conscience, and revenge. Kreisel has also published a collection of short stories, *The Almost Meeting* (1981).

KRIPKE, Saul A(aron) (1940–), American logician and philosopher, born in Bayshore, New York State, educated at Harvard, where he was subsequently an associate professor. In 1972 he became Professor of Logic and Philosophy at Rockefeller University, New York, and in 1977 he was appointed McCosh Professor of Philosophy at Princeton University. His numerous visiting posts include his appointment as Locke Lecturer at Cambridge in 1973. Kripke's early work established him as a valued contributor to developments in mathematical logic; 'Semantic Considerations on Modal Logic' (1963) suggested possibilities for mediating between different interpretations of necessity. In *Naming and Necessity* (1973) his thinking on modal logic extended to a critique of existing theories of reference. He introduced the term 'rigid designation' in arguing for the integrity of relationship between proper names and the entities to which they refer; the proposition's implications for concepts of identity were linked to his work on linguistic philosophy in 'Outline of a Theory of Truth' (1975). Kripke's most valued publication is *Wittgenstein on Rules and Private Languages* (1982), in which the paradoxes proposed by scepticism in considering meaning are resolved by a persuasive appeal to the nature of language as phenomenon verified by practice within a linguistic community; the book contains a 'Postscript' examining thought on the sceptical problem of meaning from the eighteenth century onward.

KROETSCH, Robert (1927–), Canadian novelist, poet, and critic, born in Heisler, Alberta, educated at the Universities of Alberta, McGill, and Iowa. His work as a critic is informed by a strong interest in American *post-modernism and an attempt to relate this to the Western Canadian environment. His novels are particularly concerned with gender issues and the cultural identity of Prairie communities; they habitually employ quest patterns. In *The Studhorse Man* (1969) a Swiftian narrator, who writes naked in a bathtub, provides an ambivalent elegy for Western manhood. In *Gone Indian* (1973) an American graduate student deserts academic life by following in the steps of 'Grey Owl', the Englishman-turned-Canadian Indian Archie Belaney. *Badlands* (1975) combines a fictional account of a 1916 archaeological expedition with a contemporary feminist quest narrative, in which the daughter of the expedition's leader liberates herself from her father's stultifying psychological influence. Kroetsch's other novels include *The Words of My Roaring* (1966), the magical realist *What the Crow Said* (1978), and *Alibi* (1983). His volumes of verse include *The Stone Hammer Poems* (1975), *The Ledger* (1975), *Seed Catalogue* (1977), and *The Sad Phoenician* (1979), and have been collected together to form a gradually accumulating poetic autobiography, *Field Notes* (vol. i, 1981; vol. ii, 1985). *Completed Field Notes* (1989) concludes the project and includes *Advice to My Friends* (1985), *Excerpts from the Real World: A Prose Poem in Ten Parts* (1986), and later writings. He has also published a collection of essays and literary criticism, *The Lovely Treachery of Words* (1989). *Labyrinths of Voice* (1982), a book-length interview with Kroetsch, provides the best introduction to his literary theories.

KUMIN, Maxine (Winokur) (1925–), American novelist, poet, and short-story writer, born in Philadelphia, educated at Radcliffe College. Kumin is well known as a writer of children's literature. She is also a gifted, if underestimated, poet whose verse is frequently *confessional, like much post-war American poetry. She won the Pulitzer Prize for Poetry in 1973 for her volume *Up Country: Poems of New England* (1972), though the best introduction to her poetry is *New and Selected Poems* (1982); *Looking for Luck: Poems* appeared in 1992. *Why Can't We Live Together Like Civilized Human Beings* (1982) is an impressive collection of short stories, while *The Passions of Uxport* (1968) is among her best-known novels. She was a close friend of the American poet Anne *Sexton, with whom she wrote two books for children; 'How It Was', her preface to *The Collected Poems of Anne Sexton* (1981), is one of the most sensitive essays on the poet and her work. The essay by Elaine *Showalter and Carol Smith, 'A Nurturing Relationship: A Conversation with Anne Sexton and Maxine Kumin', in *Women's Studies* (April 1976), offers many insights into both writers. *Women, Animals and Vegetables: Essays and Stories* was published in 1994.

KUNENE, Mazisi (Raymond) (1930–), South African poet, born in Durban, educated at Natal University and at London University's School of Oriental and African Studies. After a period as Director of Education for the South African United Front, he was the chief representative of the African National Congress in Europe and the USA and subsequently became Professor of African Literature and Language at the University of California, Los Angeles. Kunene composes his poetry in Zulu and makes his own translations into English. The resonantly imaginative treatments of the interactions of man and nature in *Zulu Poems* (1970), his first collection of verse, were strongly informed by Zulu oral traditions. *Emperor Shaka the Great* (1979), a verse narrative based on nineteenth-century history, and *Anthem of the Decades* (1981), an adaptation of tribal myths concerning the coming of death to mankind, are works of epic dimensions. His political concerns are most apparent in *The Ancestors of the Sacred Mountain* (1982), which contains reflections on conditions in South Africa in addition to lyrical and meditative poetry rooted in his Zulu cultural inheritance.

KUNITZ, Stanley (1905–), American poet, born in Worcester, Massachusetts, educated at Harvard.

Kunitz worked in New York editing the *Wilson Library Bulletin*, and, with Howard Haycraft, four biographical dictionaries of major English and American authors. He taught at various American colleges and in 1969 became editor of the Yale Series of Younger Poets. His first book of poems, *Intellectual Things* (1930), was followed by *Passport to the War* (1944). He achieved prominence with his *Selected Poems, 1928–1958* (1958; Pulitzer Prize). His later work includes *The Testing Tree* (1971), *The Poems of Stanley Kunitz, 1928–1978* (1979), *The Wellfleet Whale & Companion Poems* (1983), and *Next to Last Things* (1985). He has also translated Andrei Voznesensky's *Antiworlds* (1967, with others) and Anna Akhmatova's *Poems* (1970). Kunitz is a formalist whose early poetry, chiefly inspired by the seventeenth-century English Metaphysical poems, is both cerebral and passionate, densely patterned, and full of intellectual conceits. His later poetry is more relaxed in manner, where his self-reflective voice ponders on his own isolation as a symptom of a widely experienced condition. Among his prose works is *A Kind of Order, A Kind of Folly: Essays and Conversations* (1975).

KUPPNER, Frank (1951–), Scottish poet, born in Glasgow, where he read English and German at the University, and later qualified as an electronics engineer. His principal collections of poetry are *A Bad Day for the Sung Dynasty* (1984) and *The Intelligent Observation of Naked Women* (1987). Much of his attractively unorthodox verse takes the form of long and highly discursive sequences whose fluent free-verse lines are strictly arranged into four-line stanzas. The range of the exploratory and sometimes enigmatically disjunctive meditations which result is very wide. The recurrence of domestic, erotic, historical, and astronomical themes, together with the occasional introduction of narrative elements, are among the methods by which continuity is sustained. Vividly particular imagery and a keen sense of humour are also characteristic of his writing. His other works include *Ridiculous! Absurd! Disgusting!* (1989), which contains both poetry and prose, and *A Very Quiet Street* (1989), an imaginative investigation of a Glasgow murder trial of 1908.

KUREISHI, Hanif (1954–), British novelist and screenwriter, born in London, educated at King's College, London. In 1981 he received the George Devine award for his play *Outskirts* (pub. 1983), and he was writer-in-residence at the Royal Court Theatre in 1982. Other published plays include *Borderline* (1981) and *Birds of Passage* (1983). He achieved fame as author of the screenplay of *My Beautiful Laundrette* (pub. 1986), which focused on the enterprising immigrant community from Pakistan; it caused great critical controversy, though the film was an international popular success. It was evident that Kureishi's satirical targets went far beyond citizens of Pakistani descent in Britain. Even more controversial was his screenplay for *Sammy and Rosie Get Laid* (pub. 1988), which depicts contemporary London riven with street violence, dereliction, and casual racism. Both films were highly critical, sexually explicit, and satirical about life in Britain under the Thatcher government in the 1980s. He also wrote the screenplay of *London Kills Me* (1991), in which two young people who wish to escape their lives of petty drug-dealing are prevented by the poverty-trap from finding work. He directed the film himself. *The Buddha of Suburbia* (1990), Kureishi's first novel, satirizes English suburban life in the 1970s, and draws upon his upbringing in Bromley, Kent. In *The Black Album* (1995), his second, Kureishi explores the dilemma of a young Asian student torn between sensual gratification and the call of Islamic fundamentalism. The former triumphs, at the fag-end of the 'glorious' 1980s. He also edited, with Jon Savage, *The Faber Book of Pop* (1995).

KUSHNER, Tony (1956–), American playwright, born in New York, educated at Columbia and New York University. His first play, *A Bright Room Called Day* (1984), concerns the dissolution of a small circle of friends under pressures created by the Nazis' rise in Germany during the last months of the Weimar Republic. He came to prominence with his seven-hour, two-part epic, *Angels in America*: Part I, *Millenium Approaches* (1991) won him a Tony Award and a Pulitzer Prize in 1993; Part II, *Perestroika* (1992), won him a Tony Award in 1994. In his alumni magazine *Columbia* (Sp. 93) Kushner is quoted as saying that *Angels* 'is nothing less than a fierce call for gay America to seize the strings of power in the war for tolerance and against AIDS'. His adaptations include *A Dybbuk* (1994), by Corneille, and *The Good Person of Szetchuan* (1994), a version of Brecht's *The Good Woman of Szetchuan*. He also wrote a dance theatre piece, *La Fin de la Baleine: An Opera for the Apocalypse* (1982). His work *Slavs! Thinking About The Longstanding Problems of Virtue and Happiness* (1994) contains much material left out of *Angels*.

L

Lady Chatterley's Lover, a novel by D. H. *Lawrence, first published in 1928. The novel is inseparable from its notoriety. The plot centres on the unhappy marriage of Sir Clifford Chatterley and his wife Constance, and her affair with the gamekeeper Oliver Mellors in the years after the First World War. Sir Clifford's wartime wounds have left him paralysed, and his physical and psychological injuries symbolize for Lawrence the debilitated state of post-war Britain. Sir Clifford, who is both a writer and an industrialist, owns the mines whose environmental damage contrasts with the sexual regeneration of Connie and Mellors. The novel contrasts the slowly flourishing affair between Connie and her lover, in the pastoral woodlands around Sir Clifford's estate, with the sexual and cultural hollowness represented by the country house. Written in the wake of the General Strike of 1926, which Lawrence witnessed, the book is an argument about both political debility and sexual renewal, and ends on a note of uneasy, but forward-looking poise as, socially ostracized and expecting a child, Connie and Mellors are temporarily separated. The novel is fiercely iconoclastic, with fulsome sexual descriptions and a free use of four-letter words through which Lawrence tried to rescue a non-prurient language for sexuality. None the less, the novel was calculated to offend the sexual, social, and literary decorums of the day, and it is unlikely that Lawrence seriously expected it to be published in Britain in a period of intense Home Office scrutiny of 'immoral' publications during which his poems and paintings were seized by the police in London. So the novel was privately published in Italy in 1928 and an expurgated version appeared in Britain in 1932, after his death. However, the first British edition of the full text was not published until 1960 when Penguin Books, with the support of many leading writers of the day (including E. M. *Forster, Richard *Hoggart, and Helen *Gardner), won a celebrated trial, one of whose long-lasting consequences was the popular reputation Lawrence acquired as a merely erotic writer. Lawrence, in fact, took great literary pains with *Lady Chatterley's Lover*. The novel exists in three distinct versions, and the first two are published as *The First Lady Chatterley* and *John Thomas and Lady Jane*. However, his original title, 'Tenderness', gives a good sense of the positive effect he looked for despite the novel's deliberate political and erotic challenge which he defended in 1930 in one of his best essays, *À Propos of Lady Chatterley's Lover*.

Lady's Not for Burning, The, a play by Christopher *Fry, first performed in 1948. Set in a small English town in 1400 'either more or less or exactly', this involves Thomas Mendip, a profoundly disillusioned soldier who unsettles the local authorities by demanding to be hanged, and Jennet Jourdemayne, a scientifically minded young woman sentenced to die as a witch. Thanks to the feelings of love she excites in him, her growing awareness of the complexity and mystery of God's world, and the reappearance of the rag-and-bone merchant he claims to have murdered and she is accused of bewitching, both end up saved: he from despair, she from both the pyre and her exorbitant rationalism. The principal conflicts are between death or the death-wish and the life-force, and between the emotionally exceptional and the dull and mundane, represented by a bureaucratic mayor, his domestically minded sister, and her son, a town councillor 'respectable on the surface and lustful below'; and both are resolved positively, in verse whose metaphoric verve itself reflects the play's optimistic tenor.

LA GUMA, Alex (1925–85), South African novelist, born in Cape Town. He was arrested in the Treason Trial of 1956–61, partly as a consequence of his activities with the Communist Party and the Coloured People's Congress, and from 1962 to 1965 he was under continual house arrest, having previously been on the staff of *New Age*, a progressive newspaper. *A Walk in the Night* (1962) is a grimly realistic, and intensely psychological, short novel. It evokes one desperate and fear-ridden night in the life of Michael Adonis, a recently dismissed young factory worker, as he angrily prowls the streets of District Six—a multiracial ghetto—in Cape Town. Other novels include *And a Threefold Cord* (1964), also set in District Six; *The Stone Country* (1967), a stark depiction of conflicts among political, and other, prisoners and their warders; *In the Fog of the Season's End* (1972), and *Time of the Butcherbird* (1979), both of which deal with overt political resistance to apartheid, and its tragic consequences.

LAING, B(ernard) Kojo (1946–), West African novelist and poet, born in Kumasi, Ghana, educated in Ghanaian and Scottish schools and at the University of Glasgow. He has worked in Ghanaian central and local government and since 1985 has helped to manage a private school established by his mother. His first two novels have drawn much praise for their linguistic ebullience; both contain glossaries which include Ghanaian words and 'author's neologisms'. Laing's flamboyant style and more positive approach to African modernity contrast sharply with the grimy realism and bitter pessimism of his fellow Ghanaian novelist, Ayi Kwei *Armah. Epic in sweep, his first novel, *Search Sweet Country* (1986), explores city life in Accra, in the process defining a modern African identity. Employing elements of *magic realism, and firmly rooted in Asante folklore, *Woman of the Aeroplanes* (1988) pits two communities, one Ghanaian and the other Scottish, but both 'immortal', in a trading contest. It reads like a parable of economic relations between Africa and the West. With the publication of *Major Gentl and the Achimota Wars* (1992), a futuristic novel set in AD 2020 which deals with the battle for the control of a city between a compassionate leader and a ruthless militarist, Laing was credited with being the exemplary African modernist novelist. *Godhorse* (1989) is a collection of poems.

LAING, R(onald) D(avid) (1927–89), British psychiatrist and author, born in Glasgow, where he obtained his M.D. in 1951 and worked as an instructor in psychological medicine at the University. He moved to London in 1956 to practise psychiatry. In 1964 he founded the Philadelphia Association to experiment with more humane treatments of mental illness. *In The Divided Self* (1960) and *The Self and Others* (1961; revised, 1969), Laing advanced his controversial views concerning the social and familial aetiology of schizophrenia, which he argued was a mode of adaptation to extreme circumstances rather than a meaninglessly aberrant condition. The political and cultural implications of his theories were expanded upon in *The Politics of Experience* (1967), re-issued with *The Bird of Paradise* in 1967, which saw his emergence as leading figure in the radical movements of the 1960s. Among his subsequent writings, which include poetry and transcripts of recorded conversations, are *The Politics of the Family* (1971), *Do You Love Me?* (1976), *Conversations with Children* (1978), and *Sonnets* (1980). The autobiographical *Wisdom, Madness, and Folly: the Making of a Psychiatrist* appeared in 1985.

Lake Wobegon Days, see KEILLOR, GARRISON.

LAMBERT, (Leonard) Constant (1905–51), British composer and writer on music, born in London, educated at Christ's Hospital and the Royal College of Music. A close associate of the Sitwells, he shared the speaking parts with Edith *Sitwell in the first production of her *Façade* in 1922. *The Rio Grande* (1929), his extravagant setting for Sacheverell *Sitwell's poem of that title, reflects his keen interest in jazz and Latin American idioms. His compositions for ballet include *Romeo and Juliet* (1926), which was commissioned by Diaghilev, *Horoscope* (1938), and *Tiresias* (1951), both for the Sadler's Wells company, of which he became musical director in 1930. Among his other well-known works are the choral masque *Summer's Last Will and Testament* (1936) and *Aubade Heroique* (1942). His principal work as a writer is *Music Ho!: A Study of Music in Decline* (1934), a wittily tendentious and critically penetrating survey of contemporary developments in music. Richard Shead's biography of Lambert appeared in 1973.

LAMMING, George (1927–), Barbadian novelist, poet, lecturer, and trade union activist, born in Barbados. Apart from writing, he has produced programmes for the BBC and travelled and lectured widely. Lamming's first novel, *In the Castle of My Skin* (1953), explores quintessential Caribbean themes of cultural displacement and fragmentation, and the relationship between nationality and colonial or political subjection. It is a multi-layered novel which, at its most obvious level, depicts what the author calls 'the sprawling dereliction' of a boy's growth and development into adolescence in colonial Barbados during the 1930s and 1940s. At a more symbolic level, through its intensively lyrical language and poetic evocation of West Indian history, the novel provides a rich and deep meditation on the African origin of West Indians, the damage of slavery, and the prospect for spiritual and political regeneration. When it first appeared, the novel provided the most complete account of West Indian experience that then existed in fiction. Issues of West Indian history, culture, and politics are further considered in *The Emigrants* (1954), *Of Age and Innocence* (1958), and *Season of Adventure* (1960). Lamming's non-fiction work, *The Pleasures of Exile* (1960), was regarded as an authoritative and far-reaching study of West Indian colonialism. Two more novels appeared in 1972, *Natives of My Person* and *Water with Berries*. In later years, Lamming devoted his energies entirely to lectures and essays, and is regarded as one of the most perceptive commentators on the West Indies.

Lanark: A Life in Four Books, a novel by Alisdair *Gray, published in 1981. After belated publication, sections being written between 1952 and 1976, the book's magisterial qualities established Gray as both a leading *post-modernist and exemplary Scottish artist. Two narratives are interwoven over 560 pages. Books I and II recount the fraught early life of 'Duncan Thaw', an art student growing up in post-war Scotland, while Books III and IV recount his after-life as 'Lanark', who becomes an ambassador travelling from The Institute (a research centre and seat of political power) through the Inter-calendrical Zone to the threatened city of Unthank, phantasmagoric twin of Glasgow. The structure is ordered so that Thaw's *Bildungsroman* is contained within Lanark's epic fantasy; the novel signalled Gray's characteristic mix of social history, polemic, fantasy, and pastiche with other devices highlighting his authorship—illustrations, facetious notes, and typographical extravagances. In a comical epilogue, 'Lanark' confronts his creator, alongside an 'index of diffuse and imbedded Plagiarisms' semi-seriously pointing out the book's wealth of references to international literature. The serious subtext of *Lanark* is an elaborate allegory of political power and its human consequences, but what remains most striking is the density of inventiveness and visual imagination derived from Gray's complementary career as a painter.

LANCASTER, Sir Osbert (1908–86), British cartoonist and writer on travel and architecture, born in London, educated at Lincoln College, Oxford, and trained in stage design at the Slade School of Art; he was a noted designer of sets for opera and ballet. He became well known for his cartoons in the *Daily Express* from 1939 to 1981, which voiced his idiosyncratically satirical views on social and political events through the upper-middle class Maudie Littlehampton and her circle; *The Life and Times of Maudie Littlehampton* (1984) is the fullest of the many collections which appeared. Among his humorously informative commentaries on architecture are *Homes, Sweet Homes* (1940) and *Here of All Places* (1959). *Classical Landscape with Figures* (1947) and *Sailing to Byzantium* (1969) are based on his travels in Greece and the Eastern Mediterranean. His other books include the autobiographies *All Done from Memory* (1953) and *With an Eye to the Future* (1967).

Landfall, New Zealand's most notable and longest established literary journal, founded in 1947 by the poet Charles *Brasch, who remained its editor until 1966. The magazine was of central importance in fostering an independent literary culture in New Zealand during the 1950s and 1960s; in addition to the publication of work by established New Zealand writers like Brasch, Frank *Sargeson, and Allen *Curnow, it actively encouraged the emergence of younger poets and authors of prose fiction, among whom were C. K. *Stead, James K. *Baxter, and Maurice *Duggan. Its literary articles and reviews made it the country's principal forum for critical writing and space was regularly devoted to coverage of the arts in general and current affairs. Lauris *Edmond, Fleur *Adcock, Robin Healey, Elizabeth Hill, and Albert *Wendt have been among later contributors; since the mid-1980s *Landfall* has published an increasing amount of work by British authors, including Craig *Raine and David *Lodge. From the outset, the magazine has been noted for its colourful covers, which have frequently displayed reproductions of paintings by many of New Zealand's best artists.

LANGLEY, Lee (1940?–), British novelist of Scottish descent, born in Calcutta. She spent her childhood travelling widely in India, an experience that shapes some of her best fiction, such as the autobiographical *Changes of Address* (1987), which analyses the relationship of a daughter with her volatile, alcoholic mother. Langley began her career as a novelist in 1973 with the publication of *The Only Girl* and later published *From the Broken Tree* (1979) and *The Dying Art* (1983). She made her mark as a novelist with the Indian trilogy initiated by *Changes of Address*. The second volume, *Persistent Rumours* (1992), is set, both in the past and in the present day, in the Andaman Islands, an old British penal colony; it comments on British colonialism and middle-class values. *A House in Pondicherry* (1995), which completes the trilogy, is narrated mostly from the perspective of Oriane, who combines French origins with a (suppressed) Indian heritage, and explores several generations and historical aspects of life in French India. Taken together, the novels provide a valuable account, with telling psychological insights, of the clash and the blend of European and Indian world-views and sensibilities.

Language Poetry, a literary movement which emerged in the USA in the early 1970s. It began in a series of small magazines and poetry presses outside the mainstream which was then dominated by the first-person autobiographical poem. It was probably more of a reaction to the waning power of the existential dramas of *projective verse, *Beat poetry, and the *New York School, than a direct hit at what had become the default style for academic and popular verse. Charles *Olson died in 1970, Robert *Duncan stopped publishing poetry, Robert *Creeley published little for several years, and some of the most influential poets of the avant-garde, notably Frank *O'Hara and Jack *Spicer, had died several years earlier. This vacuum was matched by another significant social change, the end of the Vietnam War and the consequent loss of direction for the political culture of opposition it had engendered. Women's Liberation and Black Power movements then became the most active forms of alternative political organization, developing a strong cultural practice, including poetry, for constituencies that largely excluded white male writers. Such libertarian activism appeared to require the immediacy of expression provided by linguistically recognizable, and therefore already known, modes of poetry, which in practice were similar to those of the mainstream. Radical formal and linguistic experiment was sidelined. A few poets with a radical political agenda became convinced that language itself was a political and ethical arena, and began experimenting with forms of writing which might also be political actions in themselves. They drew on diverse precedents, including *Dada and *Surrealism, Russian Zaum poetry, Constructivism, Gertrude *Stein, Samuel *Beckett, Louis *Zukofsky, and John *Ashbery's book *The Tennis Court Oath*, and produced writing which, like abstract painting, made its own processes its subject, keeping 'the reader's attention at or very close to the level of language, that is, most often at the sentence level, or below' (Ron *Silliman). The aim was to avoid external validation either by an authentic authorial voice as in so much poetry of the time, or by an objective reality to which the poem pointed. These poets also took for granted the abandonment of metrical forms by their immediate free verse precursors. The result was an explosion of innovative writing whose structures ranged from patterns of complete sentences to sequences of broken syllables, experimenting with epigrammatic phrases, evocative and unfinished lines, startlingly conjoined words, staccato implosive phrases, and vocabularies hitherto unknown in poetry. Much of the poetry therefore read as if it were non-communicative and non-referential, its words arranged in abstract patterns for their own sake. Some Language Poets subsequently justified this abstraction of the communicative utility of language as a direct political challenge to a society in which the productive processes of language had become reified into falsely objective realities of hierarchy, inequality, and exploitation. By halting the reader's rush into meaning the text could help a rebirth of the reader's anaesthetized capacity for taking responsibility for cultural meaning.

Language Poetry has been largely an urban phenomenon, closely tied to about six major cities, especially San Francisco and New York, amongst poets who had few academic affiliations until the late 1980s, but did have a fascination with the various linguistic turns in recent philosophy, literary theory, and the social sciences, especially *post-structuralism. However, it would be a mistake to read Language Poetry as an application of post-structuralist ideas rather than a contribution to the wider debate of which French semiotic philosophy was part. Nor did Language Poetry ever operate in the fashion of André Breton's surrealist movement. There was no formula for Language Poetry, no one defining politics or aesthetics of the heterogeneous groups of poets included in the anthologies or magazines. The name, which many of the poets find discomfiting, was thrown at them by critics who read the key magazine *L-A-N-G-U-A-G-E*, edited by Bruce *Andrews and Charles *Bernstein, as if it were a manifesto instead of a discussion forum for poets. Nevertheless Language Poetry has definitely had a collective character, so that even a brief history needs to list a substantial number of writers: Charles Bernstein, Bruce Andrews, James Sherry, P. Inman, Peter Seaton, Ray Di Palma, and Ted Greenwald in New York; Robert Grenier, Barrett *Watten, Lyn *Hejinian, Bob *Perelman, David Melnick, Alan Davies, Leslie Scalapino, Kit Robinson, Ron Silliman, Rae Armantrout, Carla Harryman, Steve Benson, Michael Davidson, Tom Mandel, David Bromige, and Stephen Rodefer in California; and a few others such as Steve McCaffery and Diane Ward, based elsewhere. Alongside these poets a few others who were already working in this mode, or whose work, although appearing alongside the Language Poets, is quite distinct, must also be mentioned: Clark *Coolidge, Jackson Maclow, Susan *Howe, Fanny Howe, Michael Palmer, Marjorie Welish, and Keith and Rosemarie Waldrop.

Critical reception has been at least as volatile as that which greeted earlier avant-garde movements. The poetry has been dismissed as 'word salad', 'too easy to write', randomly and therefore meaninglessly polysemic, or as an unresisting mirror of the fragmented space-time of *post-modernism. Defenders argue that the poetry is rarely, if ever, non-referential, that it demonstrates many traditional virtues in new ways, and represents a complex, insightful engagement with the media age. Language Poetry has certainly intensified attention to many traditional dimensions of poetry, especially sound, structure, and lexis, and made visible the assumptions behind the dominant poetic paradigm's validating trinity of voice, narrative, and realist diegesis.

The most representative anthology of Language Poetry, *In the American Tree* (1986), edited by Ron Silliman, gives a good picture of its radical experimentation. The most comprehensive is the excellent *From the Other Side of the Century* (1994), edited by Douglas Messerli, which places the poetry in a wider historical context showing affinities with earlier generations of post-war poets. *Postmodern American Poetry* (1994), edited by Paul Hoover, contains useful brief biographical and critical comment, as well as some poets' essays. Writing on poetics by the poets can be found in *Code of Signals* (1983), edited by Michael Palmer; *The L-A-N-G-U-A-G-E Book* (1984), edited by Bruce Andrews and Charles Bernstein; *Writing/Talks* (1985), edited by Bob Perelman; *The Politics of Poetic Form* (1990), edited by Charles Bernstein; and in journals such as *Poetics Journal* (1982–), edited by Barrett Watten and Lyn Hejinian, *Jimmy and Lucy's House of K* (1984–9), edited by Andrew Schelling and Benjamin Friedlander, as well as *L-A-N-G-U-A-G-E*. Like most poetry, it is dependent on magazines for its circulation, and it is in the magazines that its energies can be best understood. Of those not already mentioned, *This* (1972–82), *Temblor* (1985–9), and *o blek* (1987–) provide a good sense of the range of activity.

LARDNER, Ring(old Wilmer) (1885–1933), American journalist and short-story writer, born in Niles, Michigan, educated at Armour Institute of Technology, Chicago. He first established himself as a sportswriter and journalist for various newspapers, notably the *Chicago Tribune* for which he wrote the column 'In the Wake of the News'. In 1919 he moved to Long Island, taking up a syndicated column for the Bell Syndicate. Lardner devoted much of his short literary life to the perfection of the short story, particularly the short story in vernacular mode. The earliest of these, which appeared in *Redbook* and *The Saturday Evening Post*, included a sequence of six stories of an apprentice baseball player recounting his experiences of big league baseball in letters to his home-town friend, Al, subsequently collected as *You Know Me, Al: A Busher's Letters* (1916). Edmund *Wilson said of Lardner that he had 'an unexcelled, a perhaps unrivalled, mastery' of the American language, and his friend F. Scott *Fitzgerald wrote of 'some of the most uproarious and inspired nonsense since Lewis Carroll'. (See Fitzgerald's essay 'Ring' in *The Crack-Up*.) Other successful collections include *The Real Dope* (1919) and *How to Write Short Stories (with Samples)* (1924); *The Big Town* (1921) is a sequence of five stories which mercilessly dissect American society in the post-war years of boom and prosperity. In 1926, Lardner was diagnosed as having tuberculosis and he became pessimistic and world-weary. *The Best of Ring Lardner* (1984) was edited by David *Lodge, with a stimulating introduction. See also *Ring Lardner: A Biography* (1956) by Donald Elder.

LARKIN, Philip (Arthur) (1922–85), British poet and novelist, born in Coventry, educated at St John's College, Oxford. In 1943 he began his career in librarianship at Wellington in Shropshire; after working at University College, Leicester, and Queen's University, Belfast, he became Librarian of the Brynmor Jones Library at the University of Hull in 1955, a post he held until his death. *The North Ship* (1945), his first collection of poetry, was republished in 1966 with an introduction in which Larkin spoke of 'the predominance of *Yeats' among the influences governing his early verse; he concluded by noting the emergence of his great admiration for Thomas *Hardy's poetry, a development which led towards the controlled conversational manner of his mature work. *Jill* (1946), the first of his two novels, is partially autobiographical in its account of the experiences of a young man on a scholarship at Oxford in wartime. *A Girl in Winter* followed in 1947, anticipating a recurrent motif in his poetry in its narrative of a solitary figure stoically confronting existence in an English provincial town. In 1955 his reputation as a poet was firmly established with the appearance of *The *Less Deceived*. Robert *Lowell remarked of the collection that 'No post-war poetry has so caught the moment', indicating the widespread regard in which Larkin came to be held as the most distinguished and representative poet of his day. His contribution to **New Lines* in 1956 brought him added notice as a leading member of the *Movement, whose shrewdly colloquial tones and understated technical virtuosity are epitomized in his verse. *The *Whitsun Weddings* (1964), his most highly valued collection, characteristically combined a pessimistically sceptical outlook, often tempered by a dry wit, with deeply apprehended affirmations of shared human values. His last collection of verse, *High Windows* (1974), employed a tone of great directness to heighten the emphasis on mortality underlying much of his previous work. Anthony *Thwaite edited Larkin's *Collected Poems* (1988), which contains much previously unpublished material, and *Selected Letters: 1940–1985* (1992). *Required Writing* (1983) is a collection of his essays and reviews, revealing his distaste for *Modernism, which he saw as excluding the general reader. His reviews of jazz records, written for the *Daily Telegraph* during the 1960s, are contained in *All What Jazz* (1970). His chief work of editorship is *The Oxford Book of Twentieth Century English Verse* (1973). *Philip Larkin: A Writer's Life* (1993) is a biography by Andrew *Motion.

Lark Rise to Candleford, see THOMPSON, FLORA.

LARSEN, Nella (Imes) (1893–1964), African-American novelist, born in Chicago to a Danish mother and a black father from the Virgin Islands. She was educated at Fisk University and at university in Copenhagen, and returned to the USA where she trained as a nurse. Her two published novels deal with identity and marginality and are pioneering works in raising issues of black female sexuality. *Quicksand* (1928), described by W. E. B. *Du Bois as 'the best piece of fiction that Negro America has produced since the heyday of Chesnutt', tells of the search for self of Helga Crane, a mixed-race woman trapped between middle-class respectability and sexual fulfilment. *Passing* (1929) is ostensibly about black people who 'pass' for white, but also about the desire of one woman for another. In the wake of a controversy about her 1930 story 'Sanctuary' resembling another writer's, she left the literary scene and died in near obscurity. See also ETHNICITY.

LASKI, Marghanita (1915–88), British novelist and critic, born in London, educated at Somerville College, Oxford. A journalist, broadcaster, and contributor to the *Oxford English Dictionary*, she became Vice-Chairman of the Arts Council of Great Britain in 1982 and was Chairman of its Literature Panel from 1980 to 1984. Her novels *Love on the Supertax* (1944), *To Bed With Grand Music* (under the pseudonym 'Sarah Russell', 1946), *Tory Heaven* (1948), and *The Village* (1952) offer critical analyses of class issues with particular reference to the situations of their women protagonists; *Little Boy Lost* (1949) centres on a father's search for his son in France after the Second World War. Her best-known work of fiction is *The Victorian Chaise-Longue* (1953), a sombre horror story about a woman trapped in the body of a dying Victorian. *Mrs Ewing, Mrs Molesworth, and Mrs Hodgson Burnett* (1950), and *Victorian Tales for Girls* (1947), a study of idealizing tendencies in Victorian literature, are among Laski's critical works. Her other publications include the play *The Offshore Island* (1959), a polemic for nuclear disarmament, and *Ecstasy: a Study of Religious and Secular Experience* (1961).

Last Exit to Brooklyn, see SELBY, HUBERT JR.

Last Poems and Plays, the last major collection of *Yeats's poetry, which appeared posthumously in January 1940. The volume, which amalgamated the contents of the Dublin editions of *New Poems* (1938) and *Last Poems and Two Plays* (1939), formed a substantial gathering of work produced between 1936 and 1939; 'The Black Tower' and 'Cuchulain Comforted' were written in the last two weeks of his life, the latter forming what Seamus *Heaney has called 'a strange ritual of surrender, a rite of passage from life into death'. Other poems, notably 'Beautiful Lofty Things', 'The Municipal Gallery Revisited', and 'The Man and the Echo', intimate an awareness of death's approach in their qualities of retrospective summation, while 'Under Ben Bulben' offers the text of his epitaph: '*Cast a cold eye | On life, on death. | Horseman, pass by.*' Among the other well-known poems in the volume are 'Lapis Lazuli', 'Long-Legged Fly', 'News for the Delphic Oracle', and 'The Circus Animals' Desertion'. The magnificent complexity and concentration of which 'The Statues' is perhaps the best example is complemented by numerous memorably straightforward works in ballad forms, among them 'Come Gather Round Me Parnellites', 'Roger Casement', and 'The O'Rahilly'; these and other poems constitute Yeats's most unequivocal affirmation of the heroic dimensions of modern Irish political history. The plays in the volume were 'Purgatory' and 'The Death of Cuchulain', both of which sustain the development of Yeats's dramatic verse in the new freedom and flexibility they exhibit.

Last Puritan, The, a novel by George *Santayana, published in 1935. Santayana's only novel, *The Last Puritan* is a study of the conflict between puritanism and hedonism intended as a fictional epitaph for New England puritanism which both attracted and repelled Santayana, and whose historical roots and culture he had philosophically analysed. Partly autobiographical, it tells the story of Oliver Alden, the heir of a wealthy New England family, whose father, Peter, substituted ceaseless travel for the life of genuine human engagement. Peter marries Harriet because she represents a comfortable solution to a social problem rather than because he loves her; their child Oliver is nurtured without deep love, and fussed over by his effusive German governess, Irma Schlote, whose romantic idealism has no place in the late Calvinist atmosphere of the Aldens' family home. Oliver, a withdrawn and dutiful child, is introduced to the pleasures and dangers of emotional sympathy by Jim Darnley, the captain of his father's ocean-going yacht. Familiarly known as 'Lord Jim' for his murky past in the British Navy, Darnley is a study in self-serving hedonism, whose moral laxity further serves to attenuate Oliver's emotional life, though Oliver manages to persuade himself that he is in love with Jim's sister, Rose. As Jim fades from the centre of the novel, he is replaced by the real oppositional force to Oliver's rectitude in the person of his cousin Mario Van de Weyer, born and bred in Europe, educated at Eton, and representative of an unrepentant hedonism, which seeks to give pleasure rather than to receive. Recklessly un-selfregarding, Mario is a social gadfly at Harvard, where he and Oliver are fellow students, and elsewhere in the conventional life of the American ruling classes. The novel ends with Oliver and Mario serving in the First World War; the dilettante Mario flourishes heroically in service, whereas Oliver, born and bred to duty and self-sacrifice, is a sad failure as an officer. He is killed not in combat but in a motor accident, a day after the Armistice is declared. In a final irony, Rose Darnley, the girl he intended to marry, has always loved Mario, whose warmth of spirit had captured her love years before. *The Last Puritan* is very much a philosopher's novel, where the principle of 'either/or' allows very little shading of its dominant colours of elective sympathy.

Last Tycoon, The, a novel by F. Scott *Fitzgerald, published in 1941. The novel, which Fitzgerald began writing in 1939, was left unfinished on his death in December 1940 and it was the critic Edmund *Wilson who assembled the text (including an extensive apparatus of notes) for publication. The novel draws on Fitzgerald's familiarity with Hollywood and concerns Monroe Stahr (a character loosely based on the MGM producer Irving Thalberg), an autocratic and influential film producer. Much of the novel is narrated from the point of view of Cecilia Brady, the daughter of one of Stahr's partners, and hopelessly in love with Stahr, but Fitzgerald's handling of her is not particularly accomplished and there are unsatisfactory shifts from first to third person in the text which, no doubt, Fitzgerald would have sought to revise had the novel been completed. *The Love of The Last Tycoon* (1994), edited by Matthew J. Bruccoli, offers an authoritative, scholarly edition of Fitzgerald's text.

Late Call, see WILSON, SIR ANGUS.

LATHEN, Emma, pseudonym of Mary J. LATSIS (*c.*1917–) and Martha Henissart (*c.*1929–), the American authors of a series of detective stories, beginning with *Banking on Death* (1961), in which the central figure is John Putnam Thatcher, senior vice-president of the Sloan Guaranty Trust in New York. The plots, which usually turn on some point of financial fraud or chicanery, obviously owe much to the authors' experiences: Latsis has been an economist, working for the United Nations Food and Agricultural Organisation in Rome, and Henissart was employed in corporate banking and finance. The best of their many novels are perhaps *Accounting for Murder* (1964), *Death Shall Overcome* (1966), *Murder Makes the Wheels Go Round* (1966), *Come to Dust* (1968), and *Ashes to Ashes* (1971). Under the name of R. B. Dominic they have also written a less successful series with a political background (*Murder Sunny Side Up*, 1968; *The Attending Physician*, 1980).

Latino/Latina Literature in English. Traditional views of American literary history have often emphasized the westward expansion of the United States and have tended to overlook the Spanish settlement of the American southwest. Since a number of American Latino communities were established over three hundred years ago, well before the advent of the United States, it is difficult to place their literature within the dominant perspective of American literary history. Substantial sections of US Latinos/as cannot be considered immigrants to the United States in the traditional sense and their cultural history is therefore set apart from other ethnic groups. The earliest examples of US Latino/a literature might include such examples as Alvar Nunez Cabeza de Vaca's *La Relacion* (1542), a story of exploration and survival in Florida, or *La Historia de la Nueva Mexico* (1610), an epic poem of New Mexico by Gaspar Perez de Villagra.

As a result of the cultural *mestizaje* between indigenous and Spanish peoples, US Latino/a literature is often the product of a cultural hybridity that is derivative of European, American, and Afro-Caribbean cultures. If there is a cultural thread linking these hybridizations, it is the prevalence of spoken and written Spanish in US Latino communities, whether identified as Mexican, Mexican-American, Chicano, *Puertorriquenos*, Nuyorican, or *Cubanos*. However, the impact of cultural hybridity on the production of their literature has been quite different, and the particularities of their experiences are often overlooked in an attempt to homogenize these literatures. The Puerto Ricans' story of assimilation is different from that of the Mexican-Americans: Puerto Ricans, along with Cuban-Americans, have come to the mainland and are considered immigrants, while Mexican-Americans argue that the US 'came to them'.

When the 'melting-pot' theory of assimilation was still in vogue, the desire to diminish cultural differences was more prevalent; influenced by this sensibility US Latino/a writers attempted to articulate the process of assimilation. Works like *The Memoirs of Bernardo Vega* (1984; edited by A. Iglesias, translated by J. Flores), Pedro Juan Labarthe's *The Son of Two Nations* (1931), and Jesus Colon's *A Puerto Rican in New York and Other Sketches* (1961) spoke to the Puerto Rican/Nuyorican split experience, while Celedonio Gonzalez's *Los Primos* (1971) chronicled the Cuban diaspora and the post-Fidel Castro Cuban society.

Current US Latino/a writing focuses on the renewed importance of Latino culture and history. For many US Latinos/as, the rejection of the old world is not as easy as it might have been for European immigrants. Mexican-Americans in California often visit Mexico during the weekend and Puerto Ricans can easily take a flight home. Only the Cuban-Americans have had strong political obstacles barring their return home, which strongly inform such works as Cristina Garcia's *Dreaming in Cuban* (1992), Roberto Fernandez's *Raining Backwards* (1988) , and Gustavo Perez-Firmat's *Next Year in Cuba* (1995).

Spanish is often the language of choice for US Latino/a writers, even for those who read and write in English. As a result, there is a considerable element of linguistic diversity in the literature. Rolando *Hinojosa's 'Klail City Death Trip' series (1972–82) about Chicanos in Texas was originally written chiefly in Spanish, with sections that later appeared in English, while the magnificent *bildungsromans* by Nicholasa Mohr (*Nilda*, 1986) and Judith Ortiz-Cofer (*Line of the Sun*, 1989), portray the Nuyorican experience in English. Although many Latino/a writers lost their fluency in Spanish and recognized that their sensibility was affected by assimilation, the widely-felt importance of preserving and celebrating the sounds of the Spanish language is exemplified by Josephina Niggli's *Mexican Village* (1945). Opposition to the retention of cultural memory, as the work of Richard Rodriguez shows (*Hunger of Memory*, 1981; *Days of Obligation*, 1992), often invokes the 'melting-pot' era to reinforce arguments for the rapid assimilation of immigrants. While Rodriguez argues that he is first an American, and only secondly a Mexican-American, the Mexican-American cultural memory clearly dominates his autobiographical narratives. Yet Rodriguez's writing style is affected by his intercultural understanding of US history as much as Sandra *Cisneros's writing (*House on Mango Street*, 1984, and *Woman Hollering Creek*, 1991) reflects her learning at the *Iowa Writers' Workshop. Likewise, Judith Ortiz-Cofer's *Terms of Survival* (1987) reflects her professorship at the University of Georgia, and the poet Martin Espada's *Trumpets from the Islands of their Eviction* (1988) and *City of Coughing and Dead Radiators* (1993). evinces his legal training as an attorney. Similarly, in works like Gary *Soto's novel *Jesse* (1994) and Lorna Dee Cervantes's poetry collections (*Emplumada*, 1984, and *From the Cables of Genocide*, 1992), Chicanos/as celebrate their ethnic differences while affirming their American identities. In this sense, their work resembles that of the Puerto Rican American poets Tato Laviera (*La Carreta Made a U-Turn*, 1984) and Victor Hernandez-Cruz (*Red Beans*, 1991), whose work also exhibits a desire to preserve cultural history.

Although many Latino/a writers share the concern expressed by Roberto Fernandez that the market for their work is small, and limited to the Latino community, mainstream publishers have begun to publish works such as Ana Castillo's *So Far From God* (1992), Rudolfo *Anaya's *Zia Summer* (1995), Julia *Alvarez's *In the Time of the Butterflies* (1994), Sandra Cisneros's *Woman Hollering Creek* (1991), and Oscar *Hijuelos's *The Mambo Kings Play Songs of Love* (1989; Pulitzer Prize). One of the obstacles to be overcome in gaining a wider readership for US Latino/a literature in English is the misperception that it is mostly autobiographical. While the autobiographical form initially dominated nearly all emergent ethnic literatures in America, Latino/a writers outgrew this genre-specific model some time ago. Oscar Zeta *Acosta's *Autobiography of a Brown Buffalo* (1972) imaginatively parodies autobiography, while Gloria *Anzaldúa's *Borderlands* (1987) and Terri de la Pena's *Margins* (1991) are the observations of skilled Chicana writers on Chicana lesbian culture and identity. In its increasing variety of forms, the canon of US Latino/a writing in English continues to grow each year, valuably augmenting the power and vitality of American literary culture.

LAURENCE, Margaret (1926–87), Canadian novelist of Scots ancestry, best known for her 'Manawaka' novels, a sequence set in a fictional version of Neepawa, the small Manitoba town where she was born and grew up. Mainly written in England, where Laurence lived between 1962 and 1972, the Manawaka novels are about the problems encountered by women in provincial Canada. They began with *The Stone Angel* (1964), a classic study of old age in which a 90-year-old Scots Presbyterian woman attempts to come to terms with both her past and her present. *A Jest of God* (1966) deals with the conflicts experienced by a 34-year-old spinster schoolteacher; *The Fire-*

Dwellers (1969) is centred on this heroine's married sister. The final novel of the sequence, *The Diviners* (1974), is a longer and technically more complex work that departs from the social realism of Laurence's earlier work. It is both an investigation of aspects of Western Canadian history, which dramatizes the neglect of Scots and Métis culture, and an account of the writer-protagonist's quest for identity, as she journeys from Manawaka to Winnipeg, Toronto, Vancouver, London, and Scotland, before finally settling in Ontario, where Laurence spent the latter part of her life living in another small town, Lakewood. The novel is also notable for its complex interweaving of past and present and its rendition of the problem of writing about the past, whether personal or public. Laurence also published a volume of short stories about Manawaka, *A Bird in the House* (1970), and both fiction and non-fiction about Africa, where she lived, in Somalia and Nigeria, between 1950 and 1957.

LAVIN, Mary (1912–96), Irish short-story writer and novelist, born in East Walpole, Massachusetts, and moved to Ireland at the age of ten; she was educated at University College, Dublin, and at the National University of Ireland. Lavin's talents for characterization, dialogue, and succinct description are best displayed in her short stories, of which she published more than a dozen collections since *Tales from Bective Bridge* (1942), and which earned her comparisons with Chekhov. Set against the backdrop of a changing Ireland, these stories employ a range of narrative perspectives, often those of children. The collections *The Shrine* (1977) and *A Family Likeness* (1985) reveal a wider range wherein family memoirs present a microcosmic view of several Irish and immigrant generations, and the Protestant–Catholic divide is examined through the contrasting viewpoints of adolescents. In her two novels, *The House in Clewe Street* (1945) and *Mary O'Grady* (1950), Lavin explored in some depth the themes of her shorter fiction. Her stories have been collected in three volumes (1964–85).

LAWLER, Ray(mond Evenor) (1921–), Australian playwright, born in Melbourne; he left school at the age of 13, and later began working as an actor with the National Theatre Company of Melbourne. He received widespread fame with his play *The Summer of the Seventeenth Doll* (1955), a tragi-comic drama about two sugar-cane cutters, Barney and Roo, and their Melbourne girlfriends whom they visit annually, during the summer 'lay-off' period, bringing with them their traditional gift of a kewpie doll; on the seventeenth summer the men are faced with the reality that their women no longer find the arrangement acceptable. The play was regarded as a milestone in Australian drama for its examination of cultural and sexual stereotypes and its reassessment of the myth of the bush; it was made into a film in 1960 and was later complemented by two related plays, *Kid Stakes* (1975) and *Other Times* (1976). Other plays on similar themes include *The Piccadilly Bushman* (1959) and *The Unshaven Cheek* (1963). A later play, *Godsend* (1982), has a religious theme and is set in England.

LAWLESS, Emily (1845–1913), Anglo-Irish novelist, poet, and biographer, daughter of the 3rd Baron Cloncurry, born in Co. Kildare and educated privately. While her success as a writer brought her public prominence and close connections with the British government, her personal life was one of suffering. The suicides of her father and her two sisters, coupled with her intense disillusionment with the development of a strong Home Rule movement in Ireland, drove her to England, where she lived in seclusion until her death. Lawless's most renowned novel, *Grania* (1892), uses the Aran Islands as a romantic setting while portraying political conflict during the Land War of the late nineteenth century. Although a loyalist, Lawless consistently expressed her belief in the need for land reform in Ireland and her work was recognized by Gladstone as essential to his own understanding of the 'Irish Question'. Her fictional portrayals of local conditions, particularly in her novel *Hurrish* (1886), and her consciousness of a distant and uninitiated audience, connect her to the Anglo-Irish literary tradition of William Carleton and Maria Edgeworth. Indeed, her biography of Edgeworth, published in 1904, is symptomatic of the fact that she was only ever at ease with Ireland's past and found its desire to reject a colonial identity extremely discomforting. Lawless's finest work concerns the past, such as her novel *Maelcho* (1894), and *With the Wild Geese* (1902), a collection of verse whose form and content derive from an imagined history of Ireland. Thus, her significance for twentieth-century literature is assured by her influence upon the preoccupations of the Irish literary renaissance (see IRISH REVIVAL).

LAWRENCE, D(avid) H(erbert) (Richards) (1885–1930), British novelist, short-story writer, poet, playwright, critic, and essayist, born in Eastwood, Nottinghamshire. Lawrence had one of the most extraordinary yet representative twentieth-century literary careers in its fierce alienation from mainstream British culture. He was the fourth son of a coal-miner and a mother who had trained as a schoolteacher and whose family had wider cultural and social aspirations. Despite their early attraction, Lawrence's parents were not well matched, and his mother encouraged the early evidence of his gifts as a way of fulfilling her own frustrated ambitions. Lawrence was educated locally and, on a scholarship, at Nottingham High School, before working for a brief period as a clerk in a surgical appliance factory. He then became a pupil-teacher and, in 1906, entered University College, Nottingham to train as a teacher. During this youthful period he had a close relationship with Jessie Chambers, a farmer's daughter, to whom he became engaged and whom he controversially portrayed as Miriam in **Sons and Lovers*. (They separated in 1910.) Jessie Chambers and other local friends encouraged his literary aspirations, and she sent some of his poems to Ford Madox Hueffer (*Ford), which were published in the **English Review* in 1909. Lawrence was thus introduced to the metropolitan literary world. He began work as a schoolteacher in Croydon in 1908, but his teaching career was cut short by illness—he had suffered from bouts of pneumonia since childhood—and he resigned in 1912. Meanwhile his first novel, *The White Peacock*, was published in early 1911, though too late to be seen by his mother who had died two months earlier. His second novel, *The Trespasser*, was published in 1912, but he had long been at work on an autobiographical novel eventually published as *Sons and Lovers* (1913). This established his name and remains his early masterpiece. Throughout his career, Lawrence used the details of his own life and those of his friends for his fiction, and *Sons and Lovers* tells a skewed version of his family history (he came to regret the portrait of his father in particular) and early sexual experience. The final version of the novel was written to some extent under the influence of his German wife-to-be, Frieda Weekley (née von Richthofen), the wife of his former tutor at Nottingham, Ernest Weekley, with whom she had three children. Lawrence and Frieda eloped in 1912 and married after her divorce in 1914. She introduced Lawrence to a range of continental thought, including Freud's psychoanalysis. He later rejected Freud's ideas fiercely, but the theory of the 'Oedipus Complex' provides, in part, the narrative shape for *Sons and Lovers*. Its publication closed the first stage of Lawrence's career.

*The *Rainbow* (1915) opened the next. By now Lawrence was moving in avant-garde circles which included Bertrand *Russell, Lady Ottoline *Morrell, E. M. *Forster, Katherine *Mansfield, and John Middleton *Murry. *The Rainbow* established him as both talented and controversial. Published during the war, the book was immediately banned and the next few years were some of the worst of his life. Rejected from the army on health grounds, unable to publish, with a German wife and a suspect reputation, Lawrence lived a marginalized, poverty-stricken life. They settled in Cornwall for a time but were mistrusted by the locals and subject to police and military surveillance. Eventually, they were ordered to leave under suspicion of being German agents. Thereafter, for the duration of the war, they lived in some hardship, often dependent on the charity of patrons and family. Lawrence opposed the war totally, and for the first time began to formulate his life-long hostility to industrial culture. For him, the war was butchery on an industrial scale and symptomatic of a general cultural disease. None the less, he fell out with Russell and other anti-war dissidents and began to stake out a lonely and not altogether coherent critique of all forms of modern collective life. From this point his vision is predominantly individualistic. His best-known novel of this period is **Women in Love* (1920 USA; 1921 UK), an embittered and in many ways pessimistic indictment of the culture of the war years which grew directly from *The Rainbow*. After the war the Lawrences left Britain and thereafter, except for three brief visits to Europe in the mid-1920s, lived a globe-trotting life. They went first to Italy where Lawrence spent three creative and productive years from 1919, travelling widely and living for an extended period at Taormina, Sicily. Work produced in this period includes *The Lost Girl* (1920), *The Sea and Sardinia* (1921), **Aaron's Rod* (1922), many of the stories in *England, My England* (1922), and the novellas *The Ladybird, The Fox and The Captain's Doll* (published together in 1923). In 1922 the Lawrences went to Ceylon (now Sri Lanka), then Australia (where he began **Kangaroo*), and then to the USA, settling in Taos, New Mexico for a brief period. Trips to Mexico in 1923 and 1924 inspired *The *Plumed Serpent*, and Lawrence, preoccupied by themes of violent conversion away from Western lifestyles, also wrote the long stories *St Mawr* (1925) and *The Woman Who Rode Away* (1928). After returning to Europe following a temporary estrangement from Frieda, he settled with her at the Kiowa Ranch outside Taos (given in return for the *Sons and Lovers* manuscript) where he cherished hopes, entertained since the war, of founding a visionary community he called 'Rananim'. However, after several serious illnesses, diagnosed as tuberculosis, Lawrence returned to Europe in late 1925, visiting England twice (on one occasion witnessing the General Strike of 1926) and Germany, but settling in Italy for his final years, first at Sportono and then at the Villa Mirenda outside Florence. He died, of tuberculosis, in a sanatorium in Vence, France in March 1930.

Lawrence's fiction in his last period falls into two overlapping groups, and he continued to write poems and shorter pieces, plays, travel books, and other non-fictional work in great quantities, in addition to taking up painting seriously for the first time since his youth. Novels such as *The Lost Girl* (1920), the newly recovered *Mr Noon* (written 1920–1), and *Aaron's Rod* (1922), as well as novellas such as *The Fox* (1922) and *The Virgin and the Gypsy* (1926) are preoccupied with themes of renewal and the need to break from inhibiting cultural and social environments. As in much of his work, this search is conducted through complex, ambiguous portraits of sexual relationships. Other works, like *Kangaroo* (1923) and *The Plumed Serpent* (1926), however, deal with more explicit political issues related to the rise of fascism, and, despite his explicit loathing of Mussolini, Lawrence has been accused of leaning towards the irrationalist Right and the cult of male violence in this period. However, his final work, **Lady Chatterley's Lover* (originally entitled 'Tenderness'), reverses this trend sharply.

The variety of Lawrence's work has often not been fully acknowledged and there is now substantial critical interest in his stories and poems where he is recognized as a major figure. The stories, which often do not have the doctrinal attack which became a feature of his longer work, include the collections *The Prussian Officer* (1914), *England, My England* (1922), and the posthumous *Love Among the Haystacks and Other Pieces*

(1933). The range of Lawrence's poetry is also considerable, from satirical squibs and polemical pieces to his best work which displays a mastery of tone, free-verse rhythm, and an under-appreciated complexity of emotion and argument. Like many of his generation, Lawrence was influenced by the American poet Walt Whitman whose rangy, personal verse liberated Lawrence from the conventional poetic structures with which he began. These freer forms suited his insouciant outlook and modes of composition. Often, in his best poems about the natural world, Lawrence combines an observational detail with the ability to develop associations of meaning which give a mythological grandeur and depth to the exploration of often startlingly mundane experiences. As with many of the leading *modernist writers of his generation, the reworking of classical and Christian myths to speak to contemporary concerns was a matter of major interest. Some of his finest poetry is to be found in the volume of wartime verse, *Look! We Have Come Through!* (1917), and in *New Poems* (1920), *Birds, Beasts and Flowers* (1923), and *Pansies* (1929), while the substantial *Complete Poems* were published in 1964.

Lawrence is also an underestimated playwright; his range includes naturalistic pieces about the lives of miners, such as *The Daughter-in-Law* and *The Widowing of Mrs Holroyd* (both 1913), and later work with mythological themes like *David* (1925). Many of these are still performed. Lawrence's speculative non-fiction and criticism is also a key part of his *œuvre*, particularly that written after the war when he turned to non-fiction as publishers closed the door on his novels. Often this work shows the influence of the nonconformist sermon tradition, and, in essays like 'The Whistling of Birds' (1919), he displays his talent for turning stylistic and formal convention inside out. This venture in the Edwardian nature essay becomes a rhapsodic meditation on death to provide an extraordinary commentary on the aftermath of the war. He was later to bring the same gifts to some splendid travel writing, including three books about Italy, *Twilight in Italy* (1916), *The Sea and Sardinia* (1921), and *Etruscan Places* (1927), and *Mornings in Mexico* (1927). Particularly in the later works, this writing mixes rapt meditation and a vividly observant, often comic, eye for detail with engaged political concerns. Lawrence's longer non-fictional prose can appear disordered and hectoring by comparison with his shorter pieces. But his two dissertations on psychoanalysis, *Psychoanalysis and the Unconscious* (1921) and *Fantasia of the Unconscious* (1923), are interesting rejections of Freud and reformulations of some key psychoanalytic positions. Essentially, though, Lawrence was not a measured writer in this vein and his discursive books are sometimes only loosely tied to their subject, though in fact this is the source of their interest now. They offer free-wheeling, assertive, characteristically Lawrentian meditations on a variety of topics including the influential *Studies in Classic American Literature* (1923), *Movements in European History* (1924), and *Apocalypse* (1931), a loosely conceived exercise in biblical criticism.

Frequently Lawrence's best work, in all genres, moves effortlessly and disconcertingly from the banal to the metaphysical. It is a risky way of writing and can court disaster, but it is also the source of some of his best and most knowingly ironic effects. In developing this style Lawrence was trying to find a language for experiences the prevailing literary language could not accommodate, in particular that of sex, but more generally a sense of the unconscious depths of personality and behaviour and their intersection with cultural and social norms. As a result he ran into persistent difficulties with the authorities who sought to ban not just *The Rainbow* and *Lady Chatterley's Lover*, but also his poems and paintings. Since his death, Lawrence has remained a controversial figure, as the famous trial over the eventual publication of *Lady Chatterley's Lover* as late as 1960 amply demonstrates, but his reputation has swung sharply. Censored and vilified by the establishment in his own time, he was later valued as a moralist and spokesman for stifled instinct by a range of major critics and writers after the Second World War when his work became for many a cornerstone of the twentieth-century canon. Subsequently, however, he has been revalued by feminists troubled by what is seen as his male-centredness.

John Worthen's *D. H. Lawrence: The Early Years 1885–1912* (1991) is the first volume of a definitive biography, and the scholarly Cambridge Edition of the collected works and letters is well on the way to completion. All but the last volume of letters have been published. Full scholarly editions of the novels, with the exception of *Lady Chatterley's Lover*, are available, although a number of these have been controversial in seeking to restore unmolested what the editors have taken to be Lawrence's intended text. In the case of *Sons and Lovers*, for example, this has added a substantial amount of material to the novel which Lawrence himself, admittedly under pressure, participated in deleting. Whatever the merits of these changes, all the Cambridge editions give superb notes and textual apparatus. There are stimulating general critical books on Lawrence by Frank Kermode, *Lawrence* (1973), Keith Sagar, *D. H. Lawrence: Life into Art* (1985), and Tony Pinkney, *D. H. Lawrence* (1990), while Keith Brown (ed.), *Rethinking Lawrence* (1990) and Peter Widdowson (ed.), *D. H. Lawrence: A Critical Reader* (1992) are useful collections of essays. An illuminating, more specialized work is Paul Delany's *D. H. Lawrence's Nightmare: The Writer and His Circle in the Years of the Great War* (1979).

LAWRENCE, T(homas) E(dward) ('Lawrence of Arabia') (1888–1935), British soldier and writer, born at Tremadoc, Caernarvonshire, the illegitimate son of an Anglo-Irish baronet and a governess, educated at Oxford High School and Jesus College, Oxford; his undergraduate dissertation on the military architecture of the Middle East was published with a collection of his letters as *Crusader Castles* (two volumes, 1936). In 1910 he was sent to assist with the excavations at Carchemish, on the banks of the Euphrates, by D. G. *Hogarth, from whom he had acquired his interest in Middle Eastern archaeology as a student. He worked at the Carchemish site until 1914, achieving some conversational fluency in Arabic, acquiring a taste for the food and clothing of the Arabs, and becoming active on behalf of British military intelligence. The report of his survey of the Negev region in 1914 was published as *The Wilderness of Zin* (with C. L. Woolley, 1915). Following the formation in 1915 of Hogarth's Arab Bureau in Cairo, Lawrence liaised between the British and the Arabs, organizing a highly effective campaign of guerrilla warfare against the Turkish army in Syria which culminated in his forces' entry into Damascus in 1918. *The *Seven Pillars of Wisdom: A Triumph*, his celebrated autobiographical account of the conflict, was privately printed in 1926 and posthumously published in a commercial edition in 1935; an abridgement appeared in 1927 under the title *Revolt in the Desert*. Despite its sometimes cumbrously ornate style, the work remains a compelling and self-revealing testimony to Lawrence's deep admiration and affection for the Arabs and their culture. He attended the Versailles Peace Conference on behalf of the Arab States and in 1921–2 served under W. S. Churchill as an adviser to the Middle Eastern Department of the Colonial Office, resigning out of his disillusionment with Britain's policy in the Middle East, which he saw as manipulating Arab interests. From 1922 onward he sought anonymity, repudiating the fame generated by his heroic reputation as 'Lawrence of Arabia' and serving as an enlisted man in the RAF and the tank corps under the successive pseudonyms 'J. H. Ross' and 'T. E. Shaw'; he legally adopted the latter in 1927. His documentary record of conditions in the ranks appeared as *The Mint* in 1936. Lawrence died of injuries following a crash on his motorcycle shortly after he left the RAF. Notable among his other writings are a prose translation of *The Odyssey* (1932), which Maurice *Bowra admired, and the *Letters* (edited by D. Garnett, 1938); his correspondents included Thomas *Hardy, John *Buchan, E. M. *Forster, Siegfried *Sassoon, and George Bernard *Shaw, the last-named's wife Charlotte becoming Lawrence's confidante; *Oriental Assembly* (edited by A. W. Lawrence, 1939) is a miscellany of previously uncollected pieces. The powerful appeal of his profoundly ambivalent and intriguingly complex personality has made Lawrence the subject of many biographical treatments, among which B. H. Liddell Hart's *T. E. Lawrence in Arabia and After* (1934), John Mack's *A Prince of Our Disorder* (1976), and J. M. Wilson's voluminous *T. E. Lawrence* (1989) may be mentioned. The numerous imaginative works which are strongly informed by their authors' conceptions of Lawrence include Shaw's *Too True To Be Good* (1932), W. H. Auden's *The *Ascent of F6* (1936), and Terence Rattigan's *Ross* (1960).

LAWSON, Henry (1867–1922), Australian short-story writer and poet, born in the goldfields of New South Wales. Lawson published his first poems in journals such as the *Republican* and **Bulletin*. In 1892–3 he spent eighteen months in Bourke in New South Wales; this harsh experience of bush life was the source of much of his prose and verse. His first collection of verse, *In the Days When the World was Wide* (1896), contained some of his best bush ballads, such as 'The Roaring Days', and protest poems, including 'Faces in the Street'. His use of dynamic rhythms and colloquial speech generated a wide readership and critical acclaim. Other collections of poems include *Popular Verses* (1900), *Humorous Verses* (1900), *When I Was King* (1905), *The Skyline Riders* (1910), *For Australia and Other Poems* (1913), *My Army, O, My Army* (1915), and *Song of the Dardanelles* (1916). Lawson is now remembered for his short stories, which appeared in many collections. His work was amongst the first to formulate the character of Australian experience in the late nineteenth century, in stories such as 'The Drover's Wife', 'The Bush Undertaker', and 'The Union Buries Its Dead'. Lawson was the first Australian writer to be accorded a state funeral. His unfinished autobiography, written in 1903 and edited by Colin Roderick in 1972, contains some of his best and most immediate writing.

LAWSON, John Howard (1894–1977), American dramatist, born in New York, educated at Williams College. A committed socialist writer, Lawson's theatrical work spanned the years from 1923 to 1937; thereafter, he abandoned the theatre for Hollywood and an important screenwriting career until he was blacklisted in the McCarthy era. *Roger Bloomer* (1923) and *Processional* (1925) are notable examples of *expressionism, the first about a young rebel's rejection of bourgeois society, the second about a miners' strike in the West Virginia coalfields. *Loud Speaker* (1927) is a political farce; *The International* (1928) projects a world-wide workers' revolution; *Success Story* (1932) is about a man who loses his soul for material power; and *Marching Song* (1937) returns to the theme of strikers and strikebreakers. In 1936 he published his *Theory and Technique of Playwriting*.

LAYTON, Irving (1912–), Canadian poet, born in Neamtz, Romania, and taken to Montreal at the age of one; originally named Lazarovitch, he has used the name Layton since 1937. After war service he studied economics at McGill University, Montreal; he was Professor of English at York University, Toronto, from 1969 to 1978. Layton has published many volumes of verse in addition to critical, political, and general writings. Always deliberately outspoken on politics, sex, and other issues such as Canadian anti-American cultural tendencies, Layton is as revered by some as he is disliked by others. *Collected Poems* (1971) contained 385 titles exploring a broad range of themes; *Selected Poems* appeared in 1974. *Engagements: The Prose of Irving Layton* (1972) brought together his views on life and love, while *Uncollected Poems, 1936–1959* (1976) further demonstrated his tireless energy in grappling with issues both personal and international. A similarly wide-ranging selection of worldly comment was gathered in *Taking Sides: The Collected Social and Political Writings* (1977), while *Waiting for the Messiah* (1985) told his life up to 1946. *A Wild Peculiar Joy: Selected Poems 1945–82* appeared in 1982, and *Final Reckoning: Poems 1982–1986* in 1987. Layton was made a Companion of the Order of Canada in 1976. *Irving Layton: A Portrait* by Elspeth Cameron appeared in 1985.

LEACOCK, Stephen (1869–1944), Canadian humorist, born at Swanmore in Hampshire; he was taken to Canada when he was six. He grew up in Ontario and was educated at the universities of Toronto and Chicago; he lectured in political economics at McGill University from 1903 to 1936. His first book was *Elements of Political Science* (1906), but it was *Literary Lapses* (1910) that launched him on the career as a humorist that made him a household name. Often viewed as Canada's Mark Twain, Leacock's comic range is considerable, varying from the inspired nonsense of a piece like 'Guido the Gimlet of Ghent: A Romance of Chivalry', in which, like Twain, he makes fun of romance conventions, to more serious satires such as 'My Financial Career'. Most of his books are collections of sketches, but some of the finest of them have more overall unity, such as *Sunshine Sketches of a Little Town* (1912), which offers a part-sentimental, part-satirical account of life in the small Canadian town of 'Mariposa' (based on Orillia, Ontario, where Leacock had a summer home). *Arcadian Adventures with the Idle Rich* (1914) is a more trenchant satire attacking North American capitalism. *My Discovery of England* (1922), which grew out of a lecture tour that Leacock made to England in 1921, impishly reverses the method of many European travel writers by judging the metropolis according to provincial standards. His other books include *Nonsense Novels* (1911), *Moonbeams from the Larger Lunacy* (1915), *Frenzied Fiction* (1918), *Winnowed Wisdom* (1926), *My Unremarkable Uncle* (1942), *Last Leaves* (1945), and *The Boy I Left Behind Me*, an uncompleted autobiography. He also published works such as *Humor: Its Theory and Technique* (1935) and *Humor and Humanity* (1937), which argue for the place of humour in a humanitarian society.

LEAVIS, F(rank) R(aymond) (1895–1978), British literary critic, born in Cambridge, where he was educated at Emmanuel College, gaining his doctorate in 1924 for work on the relationship between literature and journalism. As a probationary lecturer at Cambridge from 1927 to 1931 he was censured for introducing students to James Joyce's **Ulysses*, which was banned at the time. From 1932 onward he was occupied in establishing **Scrutiny* in collaboration with his wife Q. D. Leavis (1906–81), author of *Fiction and the Reading Public* (1932), an analysis of cultural tendencies since the seventeenth century; she remained centrally involved with *Scrutiny* and is credited with making significant contributions to some of her husband's best-known works. His critical methods derived from the work of I. A. *Richards, whose influence he absorbed as a postgraduate. He combined Richards's techniques of detailed textual analysis with an emphasis on the socio-cultural context and ethical responsibilities of literature. His sense of cultural crisis following upon the 'technologico-positivist or Benthamite enlightment' is the principal theme of *Mass Civilization and Minority Culture* (1930), *For Continuity* (1933), and *Education and the University* (1943). *New Bearings in English Poetry* (1932), his first major publication, dismissed the legacy of Victorian verse and argued forcefully for the recognition of Ezra *Pound, T. S. *Eliot, and Gerard Manley Hopkins as exemplary modern poets. In *Revaluation* (1936) he prescribed a radical and iconoclastic reordering of the canon of English poetry in favour of 'the line of wit' stemming from Donne and against what he considered the mechanically rhetorical tradition of Milton. His preoccupation with the novel from the mid-1940s onward arose from his view that 'in the nineteenth century and later the poetic and creative strength of the English language goes into prose fiction'; *The Great Tradition* (1948) concentrated on the works of Jane Austen, George Eliot, Henry *James, and Joseph *Conrad, which he saw as exemplifying the morally educative qualities of literature. His early *D. H. Lawrence* (1930), whom he also numbered as a vessel of 'the great tradition' for the deeply affirmative spirit of his work, was superseded by *D. H. Lawrence: Novelist* (1955), which did much to advance Lawrence's reputation. *Dickens the Novelist* (1970, with Q. D. Leavis) revised his views on that author, whose achievement Leavis had formerly tended to belittle. The essays collected in *The Common Pursuit* (1952) indicate the scope of his criticism in their commentaries on a diverse range of writers which includes Bunyan, Shakespeare, Swift, Wyndham *Lewis, and E. M. *Forster.

LEAVITT, David (1961–), American writer, born in Pittsburgh, Pennsylvania; he grew up in California, and was educated at Yale. His two collections of stories, *Family Dancing* (1984), which has been praised for its evocative studies of modern American family life, and *A Place I've Never Been Before* (1990), earned him a reputation as a fashionable minimalist. His first novel, *The Lost Language of Cranes* (1986), is expansive in structure and style, and deals with the complex, often tormented relationship of a father and son, both homosexual. (Gay life in the post-AIDS world also surfaces as a theme or sub-plot in Leavitt's short fiction.) Though the portrayal of the son fits fairly easily into the conventions of gay fiction of the 1980s, it is in his depiction of the father, a middle-aged married man uneasily coming to terms with his sexual nature and forced to seek advice from his son, that Leavitt displays uncommon perception and breaks new ground. *Equal Affections* (1989) returns to the theme of homosexuality and the family: here one of the leading female protagonists is gay.

LE CARRÉ, John, pseudonym of David John Moore CORNWELL (1931–), British writer of spy fiction, born in Poole, Dorset, educated at Sherborne School, Berne University, and Lincoln College, Oxford; he taught briefly at Eton before joining the Foreign Office in 1959. His first novel, *Call for the Dead* (1961; filmed by Sidney Lumet as *The Deadly Affair*, 1967; republished with this title), introduced the British intelligence agent George Smiley, who also features in *A Murder of Quality* (1962), a more traditional detective story. *The Spy Who Came in from the Cold* (1963; filmed by Martin Ritt, 1965), a harsh, bleak Cold War novel of loyalty and betrayal, written as a reaction to the then fashionable James Bond spy novels of I. *Fleming (which le Carré has stigmatized as 'candyfloss'), was an immense success, enabling the author to leave the Foreign Office and devote himself to writing. It was followed by *The Looking-Glass War* (1965), *A Small Town in Germany* (1968), and an unsuccessful novel, *The Naive and Sentimental Lover* (1971). *Tinker, Tailor, Soldier, Spy* (1974), his best work, reintroduced the figure of Smiley; his duel with the Russian spymaster Karla, which ends with Smiley's victory, is the subject of this novel and its two successors, *The Honourable Schoolboy* (1977) and *Smiley's People* (1980). In these novels he constructs a new vocabulary to describe the technical details of intelligence operations: many of its terms have since passed into the jargon of real life intelligence agencies. Later works are *The Little Drummer Girl* (1983), in which he turns from the Cold War to Palestinian terrorism; *The Perfect Spy* (1986); *The Russia House* (1989), set in post-glasnost Russia; and *The Secret Pilgrim* (1991), in which Smiley returns once more. Together with *Deighton, le Carré has revolutionized the spy story; both devote much attention to departmental intrigues within the intelligence service, but le Carré, whose work has been much imitated, combines grim and realistic detail with Byzantine elaboration of plot. His novels deal with conflicts of loyalty, between that owed to the individual and that owed to the country, and the divergent claims of morality and duty. The collapse of the Soviet Union seemed to deprive him of his main subject, and later novels—*The Night Manager* (1993), *Our Game* (1995)—though bestsellers, were critically less well received. See D. Monaghan, *The Novels of John le Carré: The Art of Survival* (1985), and A. Bold, *The Quest for le Carré* (1988).

LEDWIDGE, Francis (1891–1917), Irish poet, born in Slane, Co. Meath; he received elementary education and worked as a copper miner and an overseer of roadworks for the local council. Despite his strong nationalist sympathies, he joined the Royal Inniskilling Fusiliers soon after the outbreak of the First World War, partly out of disappointment in love, and was killed on the Western Front. A number of his poems express regret that he was unable to participate in the Easter Rising of 1916. In 1912 he sent some of his verses to Lord *Dunsany, whose patronage secured the publication of *Songs of the Fields* (1915) and *Songs of the Peace* (1917); Dunsany also produced the posthumous *Last Songs* (1918) and *Complete Poems* (1919). Many of Ledwidge's poems form contemplative and precisely observed treatments of the landscapes around Slane, which also serve as the setting for his distinguished love poems. His work was featured in **Georgian Poetry: 1913–1915* (1915). Themes from Irish legend and motifs from classical mythology entered his verse after his introduction to Dublin's literary milieu. His later work exhibits a deepening preoccupation with religious experience. *Complete Poems* (1974) was edited by Alice Curtayne, whose biography of Ledwidge appeared in 1972.

LEE, (Nelle) Harper (1926–), American author, born in Monroeville, Alabama, educated at the University of Alabama. She worked for the reservations department of an international airline before she began writing, but has since become somewhat reclusive. Her reputation rests upon the unanimous acclaim accorded to her novel *To Kill a Mockingbird* (1960; Pulitzer Prize), which presents the sensational trial of Tom Robinson, a black man accused of raping a white woman, through the eyes of the daughter of the white defence lawyer, Atticus Finch. We are presented with a series of the experiences and obsessions of his son and daughter, Scout and Jem Finch, through which they lose their innocence, as the novel traces the reactions of the inhabitants of Maycomb, a small Southern town, who become engrossed and scandalized by the entire case. A screenplay by Horton Foote was filmed in 1962.

LEE, Laurie (1912–), British writer and poet, born and educated in Gloucestershire. *The Sun My Monument* (1944), Lee's first collection of verse, contained numerous responses to the Spanish Civil War; these form some of his best work as a poet in their imaginative sensings of tensions between the lyrical vitality of nature, a dominant theme in all his verse, and man's fatally destructive proclivities. Subsequent volumes of poetry, including *My Many-Coated Man* (1957) and *Selected Poems* (1983), present evocations of the natural world drawn from a wide range of English, European, and Asian settings. His prose work *A Rose for Winter* (1955) describes his travels in Franco's post-war Spain. The publication of *Cider with Rosie* (1959), an account of his boyhood in a Cotswold village, brought him world-wide popular and critical acclaim; the work remains one of the outstanding evocations of childhood in English, conveying its experiences with memorable freshness and clarity. The childhood so convincingly recreated ends with the narrator's first taste of cider and the kisses of Rosie, a village girl. A sequel, *As I Walked Out One Midsummer Morning* (1969), follows the narrator on foot from Gloucestershire to London, and in Spain where he remains, supporting himself by playing his fiddle, until the outbreak of the Civil War. His other works include *The Firstborn* (1964), an essay on the birth of his daughter; *I Can't Stay Long* (1975), a collection of short pieces; *Two Women* (1983), a photographic essay on his wife and daughter, and *A Moment of War: A Memoir of the Spanish Civil War* (1991).

LEE, Vernon, pseudonym of Violet PAGET (1856–1935), British writer, born in France to English

Parents. She lived mainly in Italy, whose history and culture were the subject of most of her works. *Studies of the Eighteenth Century in Italy* (1880) and its numerous sequels were praised for their scholarship. A prolific and versatile writer, her other works include *Genius Loci* (1899) and *The Tower of Mirrors* (1914), both travel works; *The Handling of Words* (1923); and *Music and Its Lovers* (1932). She is best remembered for her fiction, which includes the novel *Miss Brown* (1884), satirizing London literary and artistic circles. Her supernatural stories published in her three main collections, *Hauntings* (1890), *Pope Jacynth* (1904), and *For Maurice* (1927), are elegiac tales mainly rooted in Italy, where the past exercises a haunting dominance over the drab and shallow present, and a sense of loss resounds throughout. A biography by P. Gunn was published in 1964.

Left Book Club, The, a scheme for the dissemination of politically educative literature begun in 1936 by the publisher Victor Gollancz in collaboration with Harold Laski and John Strachey. Members received books and the journal *Left Book Club News* on a monthly basis. While the doctrinaire character of the majority of the publications was apparent, all shades of opinion on the political left were represented and the intellectual standard was often high. Titles included *Days of Contempt* (1936) by André Malraux, Stephen *Spender's *Forward from Liberalism* (1937), J. B. S. *Haldane's *A. R. P.* (1938), Leonard *Woolf's *Barbarians at the Gate* (1939), and Arthur *Koestler's *Scum of the Earth* (1941); George Orwell's *The *Road to Wigan Pier* (1937) was criticized by Gollancz in his foreword for its ambivalent attitude to the working classes and was reissued in an abridged form. By 1939 the Club had over 56,000 subscribers and some 1,500 affiliated 'left discussion groups' throughout Britain; several major rallies were held at the Albert Hall. The Nazi–Soviet Pact and the outbreak of war in 1939 initiated a rapid decline in membership; G. D. H. *Cole's *The Meaning of Marxism* (1948) was the last of its publications.

Left Review, a monthly journal of politics and literature founded in 1934 as the platform of the British section of the pro-Soviet Writers' International. Until December 1935 it was edited by a group in which Montague Slater's was the dominant voice. Early issues were preoccupied with defining the functions of writers as instruments of revolutionary socialism. Although much of the content of *Left Review* justifies Bernard *Bergonzi's remark on its 'simplistic sentimental Russophilia', contributions from W. H. *Auden, Edward *Upward, Stephen *Spender, C. *Day Lewis, and Christopher *Caudwell give it some centrality to literary developments of the period. From January 1935 to June 1937 Edgell *Rickword was principal editor. A series of critically astute articles by Rex *Warner, C. Day Lewis, and Rickword himself applied socialist literary theory to the works of Dickens, Swift, Spenser, Hopkins, Shakespeare, and Blake. Rickword regularly published work by European contributors and made the magazine the principal forum for British writers in support of the Republican forces in the Spanish Civil War. During Randall Swingler's editorship, which continued until the magazine closed in May 1938, the Communist Party exerted increasingly rigid control, to the marked diminishment of *Left Review*'s literary quality.

LE GALLIENNE, Richard (1866–1947), British poet and memoirist, born in West Derby, near Liverpool, educated at Liverpool College. Encouraged as a poet by Oliver Wendell Holmes, he published *My Ladies' Sonnets* in 1887. In 1888 he moved to London and became a publisher's reader. *Volumes in Folio* (1889) established his reputation as a poet, its refined sensuality manifesting the influence of Oscar Wilde, with whom he was acquainted. A frequent contributor to *The Yellow Book*, he enjoyed considerable success throughout the 1890s; his recollections of the period were published as *The Romantic Nineties* (1926). His other prose works include the mildly scandalous novel *The Golden Girl* (1896) and the topographical reflections of *Travels in England* (1900). He moved to New York in 1901, where he worked as a journalist. Among his later volumes of poetry are *The Lonely Dancer* (1913) and *The Silk-Hat Soldier* (1915), an ill-judged assortment of responses to the First World War. From 1927 onward he lived in France. *From a Paris Garret* (1936) records his contact with *Joyce, *Pound, *Hemingway, and others. *The Quest of the Golden Boy* (1960) is a biography by R. W. Egan and G. Smerdon.

LE GUIN, Ursula K(roeber) (1929–), American *science fiction writer, born in Berkeley, California, educated at Radcliffe College and Columbia University. *Rocannon's World* (1966) and *City of Illusions* (1967) demonstrated her literary talents which she firmly established with *The Left Hand of Darkness* (1969), a serene narrative in which a human ethnologist visits a new planet whose humanoid trans-sexual inhabitants challenge his innately gender-bound view of reality. *The Lathe of Heaven* (1971) presented metaphysical questions about the nature of reality. The highly acclaimed *The Earthsea Trilogy*, written for children (*The Wizard of Earthsea*, 1968; *The Tombs of Atuan*, 1971; and *The Farthest Shore*, 1972) envisages an oceanic world dominated by magic; it was followed by a sequel, *Tehanu* (1990). Her most characteristic and best-known work is *The Dispossessed: An Ambiguous Utopia* (1974), in which two contrasting worlds reveal a yin-and-yang principle to which Le Guin has been much attracted. Subsequent works include *Orsinian Tales* (1976) and *Malafrena* (1979), both set in an almost contemporary Europe; *The Beginning Place* (1980), concerning adolescent rites of passage; and *Always Coming Home* (1985), which combines feminist goals with Native American values. Among her collections of short stories are *Buffalo Gals, and Other Animal Presences* (1987) and *A Fisherman of the Inland Sea* (1994). Her critical works include *The Language of the Night* (1979) and *Dancing at the Edge of the World* (1989). See also UTOPIA AND ANTI-UTOPIA.

LEHMANN, (Rudolph) John (Frederick) (1907–87), British poet and editor, born at Bourne End in Buckinghamshire, the brother of Rosamond *Lehmann, educated at Trinity College, Cambridge. He joined the *Hogarth Press as an assistant in 1931 and became a partner in the venture in 1938. *Thrown to the Woolfs* (1978) contains his reminiscences of Leonard and Virginia *Woolf. In 1936 he established **New Writing*, which was succeeded by *The Penguin New Writing* (1940–50). He was founding editor of **London Magazine* from 1954 to 1961. In these periodicals he published work by almost every poet of note over a period of twenty-five years. His own publications as a poet include *A Garden Revisited* (1931) and *The Sphere of Glass* (1944), which collect the work that gained him a high reputation in the 1930s; *Collected Poems* (1963) was followed by *New and Selected Poems* (1985). His three volumes of autobiography, *The Whispering Gallery* (1951), *I Am My Brother* (1960), and *The Ample Proposition* (1966), form a valuable account of literary life during the years of his greatest activity. His other works include *A Nest of Tigers* (1968), his study of the *Sitwells, and two novels, *Evil Was Abroad* (1938) and *In the Purely Pagan Sense* (1976).

LEHMANN, Rosamond (Nina) (1901–90), British novelist, born in Buckinghamshire, educated at Girton College, Cambridge; she married her first husband, Leslie Runcimann, in 1924. Her first novel, *Dusty Answer* (1927), a frank account of a young woman's first emotional involvement, brought her instant success, tinged with scandal; *A Note in Music* (1930) was less enthusiastically received. *Invitation to a Waltz* (1932) and its sequel *The Weather in the Streets* (1936) centre on the figure of Olivia—with whom Lehmann, in later life, explicitly identified herself. An ingenuous adolescent in the first book, in the second she painfully acquires maturity after an adulterous love affair, the collapse of her marriage, and a traumatic backstreet abortion. The novel was far ahead of its time in its honest, unsentimental treatment of the truths of women's lives. Lehmann continued to explore feminine experience in her only collection of short fiction *The Gipsy's Baby* (1946), and the novel *The Ballad and the Source* (1944), which introduces the enigmatic and compelling figure of Mrs Jardine. An innovative reworking of the myth of Demeter and Persephone forms the structural core of the novel: Lehmann herself ascribed her use of myth to the writer's connection to the collective unconscious and its symbols as theorized by Jung, in whose works she later developed an interest. Lehmann's second marriage to the Communist peer Wogan Phillips had dissolved in 1940, and she had started a long, happy relationship with Cecil *Day Lewis; her own favourite work, *The Echoing Grove* (1953), was written in the aftermath of the end of this relationship. The novel concerns the love of two sisters for the same man, to whom one of them is married, and brilliantly displays Lehmann's imaginative transformation of personal pain. The death of her daughter Sally in 1958 led to a long silence broken by the publication of *The Swan in the Evening* (1967), fragments of autobiography which revealed her growing preoccupation with spiritualism and psychic phenomena. *A Sea-Grape Tree* (1967), which reintroduces the figure of Mrs Jardine, is also permeated with insights into the occult. Neither of these works were received with the enthusiasm of her earlier novels which had long been out of print, as the fashion for social realism, political comment, or avant-garde experimentalism had placed her incandescent explorations of sensibility at the margins. The republication of her major works by Virago Press once again brought her renown. A new generation of critics and readers finally recognized Lehmann's contribution to literature and hailed her as one of the century's foremost English novelists. In her long life she received many honours: she was a Vice-President of International PEN, a Fellow of the Royal Society of Literature, and in 1982 was made a Commander of the British Empire.

LEIBER, Fritz (Reuter, Jr) (1910–92), American short-story writer and novelist, born in Chicago, educated at the University of Chicago. Most of his work has been fantasy, though he is highly regarded for his occasional science fiction novels. He is perhaps best known for his 'Sword and Sorcery' tales (a term which he coined) involving two characters, Fafhrd (a self-portrait) and Gray Mouser (based on a long-time friend), but his other works, distinguished by humanitarianism, sexual daring, and frequent formal experiments, are highly regarded within the field. *The Wanderer* (1964) concerns a planetary disaster, while *Our Lady of Darkness* (1977) is a ghost story set in the richly observed heart of San Francisco where Leiber lived for many years. Other novels include *Gather, Darkness!* (1950), *Conjure Wife* (1953), *The Green Millennium* (1953), and *A Spectre is Haunting Texas* (1969). Some of the best of his earlier short stories were collected in *Ship of Shadows* (1979) but among his best achievements are the autobiographical fantasies gathered in *The Ghost Light* (1984).

LEIGH, Mike (1943–), British dramatist, born and educated in Salford, where his father was a doctor, and trained as an actor and a designer in London. He has become known as a pioneer of 'improvised' drama: that is, of work that emerges in rehearsal with actors and is then scripted under his or her name by the director. In the theatre, the most successful have been somewhat pessimistic comedies about lonely people. They include *Bleak Moments* (1970), centring on the empty life of a young woman who lives with her sister, who has Down's syndrome; *Babies Grow Old* (1974), which among other things shows the despair of a doctor who feels he is 'prolonging suffering in order to make money for the drug companies'; *Abigail's Party* (1977), about the loveless pleasures of *nouveau-riche* people on a London housing estate; the ironically titled *Ecstasy* (1979), about the woes of bedsit existence; *Goose-Pimples* (1981), centring on a Saudi Arabian who mistakes a London flat, peopled by xenophobic opportunists, for a brothel; and *Greek Tragedy* (1990), about expatriate Greeks in Australia. *It's a Great Big Shame* (1993) was more obviously ambitious, consisting as it did of two parts, one set in nineteenth-century London and involving an unhappy marriage and its violent consequences, the other their equally troubling contemporary counterparts. Leigh's many improvised plays for television include a version of *Bleak Moments*, *Nuts in May* (1976), and *Home Sweet Home* (1982). Notwithstanding the creative participation of many different actors, his work has been marked by a distinctively wry and mordant humour and a sharp eye for telling social detail, as well as sympathy for the mainly frustrated inhabitants of the urban wilderness.

LEITCH, Maurice (1933–), Northern Irish novelist, born in Muckamore, Co. Antrim, educated at Stran Mills Training College, Belfast. He taught in secondary schools for several years before joining BBC Northern Ireland in 1960 as a producer. In 1970 he moved to London where he was head of BBC radio's drama feature department until 1989. Leitch's first novel, *The Liberty Lad* (1965), is characteristic of his continuing portrayal of life in Ulster as dark, stagnant, and isolated. In *Poor Lazarus* (1969) Leitch explores the sectarianism which permeates Northern Irish society through the short-lived and uneasy relationship between an Ulster Protestant and a Catholic Irish-Canadian. This was followed by *Stamping Ground* (1975), *Silver's City* (1981), *Chinese Whispers* (1987), *Burning Bridges* (1989), and *Gilchrist* (1994), a psychologically compelling narrative in which an evangelist who absconds to Spain, in response to a sexual entanglement, confronts his past through a meeting with a sinister *doppelgänger*. Leitch has also written several plays for television, including the acclaimed *Rifleman* (1980), and a collection of short stories, *The Hands of Cheryl Boyd* (1987).

LEITHAUSER, Brad (1953–), American poet, born in Detroit, Michigan, educated at Harvard, obtaining a doctorate in jurisprudence in 1980. From 1980 to 1983 he was a research fellow at Kyoto Comparative Law Centre, Japan. *Hundreds of Fireflies* (1982) and *The Cats of the Temple* (1986), the latter strongly informed by his impressions of Japan, gained him wide notice for their fusions of great descriptive precision with personal and contemplative elements. His first two books were reprinted as *Between Leaps: Poems, 1972–1985* (1987), the first British edition of his work. A further collection entitled *The Mail from Anywhere* (1990) draws on his experiences of Britain and Iceland. Leithauser's poetry is refreshing for its meticulous but supple sense of form and the skill with which his rich elaborations of imagery are sustained. His works of fiction include *The Line of Ladies* (1975; short stories) and novels, including *Equal Distance* (1985) and *Hence* (1989), richly particularized adaptations of autobiographical material which constitute statements on the attitudes of his generation. *Penchants and Places* (1995) includes essays and criticism.

LEONARD, Elmore (1925–), American crime novelist, born in New Orleans, educated at the University of Detroit. After writing Westerns and screenplays, Leonard emerged as a foremost practitioner of the modern crime novel (see DETECTIVE FICTION). In a range of astringent novels about urban life he has used crime to present a distinctive and sophisticated vision of the world. His principal settings are Miami and Detroit (although *Pronto*, 1994, is set in Italy), and his terse, laconic prose style encompasses the entire social range from ghetto to penthouse to condominium. His early crime novels, *Fifty-Two Pickup* (1974), *Unknown Man No. 89* (1977), and *The Switch* (1978), are enlivened by crisp dialogue. In subsequent novels like *Gold Coast* (1980), *Split Images* (1982), and *Cat Chaser* (1982) the plot becomes less important than the creation of compelling minor characters in vividly realized contexts. Leonard's plots are not mysteries in the conventional sense, but confrontations between flawed male protagonists and more vital agents of cynicism and violence. This conflict of good and evil is vividly presented in *City Primeval* (1980) and in the unrepresentative *Touch* (1987) where the religious background is expressed. Leonard's reputation rests with *La Brava* (1983), *Glitz* (1985), *Bandits* (1987), and *Freaky Deaky* (1988); in a variety of settings these narratives juxtapose the world of business and that of crime. *Killshot* (1989), *Get Shorty* (1990), and *Maximum Bob* (1991) continued this diversity.

LEONARD, Hugh, pseudonym of John Keyes BYRNE (1926–), Irish playwright, born in Dublin, educated at Presentation College, Dun Laoghaire. He worked as a civil servant before becoming a prolific dramatist and, in later years, programme director for the Dublin Theatre Festival. Among the work that followed his first play, *The Big Birthday* (1956), was *The Poker Session* (1964), *The Au Pair Man* (1968), *The Patrick Pearse Motel* (1971), and *Da* (1973), a striking exploration of a young man's ambiguous feelings for his dead father. Leonard has also written a great deal of original drama, and adapted several novels, for television, and produced two volumes of autobiography, *Home before Night* (1979) and *Out after Dark* (1988).

LEONARD, Tom (1944–), Scottish poet, born in Glasgow, where he was educated at the University. In addition to his activities as a writer, he has worked in a variety of clerical capacities. *Poems* (1973) confirmed his reputation as a poet of stylistic versatility and seriocomic power. While much of Leonard's poetry is written in Glasgow dialect, the highly inventive and politically outspoken character of his work is equally apparent in his use of standard English. His other collections of poems include *Bunnit·Husslin* (1975), *Ghostie Men* (1980), *Situations Theoretical and Contemporary* (1986), *Intimate Voices* (1984; collected verse from 1965 to 1983), and *Sane Words Rhyme* (1994). *Satires and Profanities* (1984), *Two Member's Monologues* (1989), and *On the Mass Bombing of Kuwait, Commonly Known as the 'Gulf War'* (1992) are among Leonard's satirical and polemical prose writings, which share his poetry's passionate concern with political ethics and social justice; *Reports from the Present: Selected Work 1982–94* (1995) contains poetry, prose, and performance pieces. *Places of the Mind* (1993) is a critical biography of James Thomson.

LEPAN, Douglas (1914–), Canadian writer, born in Toronto, educated at Toronto and Oxford Universities. LePan has moved between careers as a diplomat and politician, as an academic in London and Washington, and as a professor of English at Queen's University and the University of Toronto. His published writing includes the poetry collections *The Wounded Prince* (1948), *The Net and the Sword* (1953), and *Something Still to Find* (1982); and *The Deserter* (1964), a novel centred on the figure of a hunted man and a quest for faith. The poetry is characterized by its use of sharply realized sensual impressions and a concern with Canadian identity at home and abroad. Like his novel, it inveighs against the destruction of war. *Bright Glass of Memory* (1979) engages with the problematics of writing autobiography.

LERNER, Laurence (David) (1925–), British poet, critic, and novelist, born in Cape Town, South Africa, educated at the University of Cape Town and at Pembroke College, Cambridge. After holding a succession of academic posts in Africa and Britain, he became a professor at Vanderbilt University, Nashville, USA, in 1985. His collections of poetry include *Domestic Interior* (1959), *Selves* (1969), *The Man I Killed* (1980), and *Rembrandt's Mirror* (1987). *Selected Poems* appeared in 1984. The restrained rationalism and formal accomplishment of his earlier work conformed to the conventions established by the *Movement. Successive volumes retained his characteristic qualities of intelligence and directness while revealing adventurously imaginative developments. The element of wit in his work is most evident in *A.R.T.H.U.R.: The Life and Opinions of a Digital Computer* (1974) and *A.R.T.H.U.R. and M.A.R.T.H.A.: Or, the Loves of the Computers* (1980), his verse dialogues for computers. His novels include *A Free Man* (1968) and *My Grandfather's Grandfather* (1985). Among his numerous works of criticism are *The Uses of Nostalgia* (1972), *Essays on Literature and Society* (1982), and *The Frontiers of Literature* (1988).

Less Deceived, The, the second of Philip *Larkin's principal collections of verse, published in 1955. The book's title, taken from the poem 'Deceptions', suggests its recurrent critique of what 'Next Please' terms the 'bad habits of expectancy' fostered by romantic ideals of fulfilment or escape; conventional notions of emotionally significant attachment of particular persons or places are repudiated in several poems, notably 'Places, Loved Ones' and 'I Remember, I Remember'; the defunctness of organized religion as a counter to the increasingly secular and materialist cultural order evinced in numerous poems is a principal theme in 'Church Going', the collection's longest and best-known poem. 'If, My Darling' extends Larkin's assessment of the diminished quality of life to his own imaginative experience; in defining the tension between 'meaning and meaning's rebuttal' in a consciousness for which 'the past is past and the future neuter' the poem indicates the book's pervasive distrust of received ideas, complacencies of memory, and illusory expectations. The bleak tenor of much of *The Less Deceived* is offset by the unsentimentally affirmative lyricism informing numerous poems, particularly 'Wedding Wind', 'Coming', and 'At Grass'; Larkin's scepticism is also frequently qualified by his wryly ironic wit and the subversive effects of occasional humorous colloquialisms. Virtuosity in the highly individual use of rhyme, metre, and stanzaic structure and resonantly effective use of imagery drawn from precise observation are apparent throughout the collection, which established Larkin's reputation among the foremost poets of the 1950s.

LESSING, Doris (May), née Tayler (1919–), British novelist and short-story writer, born in Persia of British parents who moved when she was five to a farm in Southern Rhodesia. She left school at 15 and worked as a nursemaid, then as a shorthand typist and telephone operator in Salisbury. After the break-up of her first marriage she became involved in radical politics. She remarried in 1945, but in 1949 left for England with her youngest child; soon afterwards she was declared a Prohibited Immigrant, and barred from Rhodesia until the advent of black majority rule in 1980. Her first published novel, *The Grass is Singing* (1950), is the story of a white farmer's wife and her black servant, and the violent conclusion of their relationship; the novel presages Lessing's continuing fascination with misfits and madness and shows the psychological insight of her later work. Her quintet 'Children of Violence' (*Martha Quest*, 1952; *A Proper Marriage*, 1954; *A Ripple in the Storm*, 1958; *Landlocked*, 1965; and *The Four-Gated City*, 1969), traces the history of Martha Quest from her childhood in Rhodesia, through post-war Britain, to an apocalyptic ending in AD 2000. *The *Golden Notebook* (1962), a lengthy and ambitious novel, was hailed as a landmark by the Women's Movement. In the 1970s Lessing experimented with science or 'space fiction', intrigued by the possibilities that genre affords for 'seeing ourselves as others see us'. *Briefing for a Descent into Hell* (1971) features a classics professor confined to a psychiatric hospital, embarked on a visionary voyage to planet Earth. *The Memoirs of a Survivor* (1975) explores the breakdown of society after 'it', an unmentionable, catastrophic war. With the five volumes of *Canopus in Argos: Archives* (*Re: Colonised Planet 5, Shikasta*, 1979; *The Marriages Between Zones Three, Four and Five*, 1980; *The Sirian Experiments*, 1981; *The Making of a Representative for Planet 8*, 1982; *Documents Relating to the Sentimental Agents in the Volyen Empire*, 1983), Lessing invents a whole universe. She returned to traditional realism with *The Diary of a Good Neighbour* (1983), which was submitted to her usual British publishers under the pseudonym Jane Somers, and rejected. When the novel was reissued with its sequel, *If the Old*

Could (1984), in one volume bearing Lessing's own name (*The Diaries of Jane Somers*, 1984), both books were praised for their unflinching description of how it is to be old in contemporary Britain. *The Summer Before the Dark* (1973) deals with some of the same themes. Later novels include *The Good Terrorist* (1985), a disturbing portrayal of a young woman mothering a houseful of squatters and progressing from radical politics to terrorism; *The Fifth Child* (1988) about a couple who stake their happiness on breeding children only to lose all because Harriet refuses to reject her monstrous fifth child; and *Love, Again* (1996) about a woman who falls in love at the age of sixty-five. Lessing's many other works of fiction, non-fiction, and drama display her interest in politics, Sufism, and the changing destiny of women. Her range and versatility is demonstrated in her many other publications which include *Collected Stories* (2 volumes, 1978), *Particularly Cats, and More Cats* (1989; with paintings by Anne Robinson), *London Observed: Stories and Sketches* (1992), *African Laughter: Four Visits to Zimbabwe* (1992), and most notably *Under My Skin: Volume One of My Autobiography, to 1949* (1994) which was considered by Hilary *Mantel, to be 'her greatest work of art'.

LE SUEUR, Meridel (1900–), American poet, novelist, and journalist, born in Murray, Iowa; she dropped out of high school, then lived in New York where she studied at the American Academy of Dramatic Art. Known for her political radicalism, she contributed to *The New Masses* and *The Daily Worker*. The stories and reportage collected in her early works, *Salute to Spring* (1940) and the novel *The Girl* (written in 1939 and published in 1978), reflect a concern for the outcasts, predominantly women, among whom Le Sueur lived for a time on the fringes of society. *Annunciation* (1935), written in the form of a journal, records Le Sueur's response to the execution of the anarchists Sacco and Vanzetti. *North Star Country* (1945) and *Crusaders* (1955) are accounts of Le Sueur's own family history and that of her native Midwest. Her later poetry, *Rites of Ancient Ripening* (1975), seeks to enact feminist principles by developing a vocabulary with which to describe landscape while resisting the male attitude of dominance. In place of masculine possessiveness, Le Sueur uses Native American motifs as representative of communal feminine experience. Le Sueur continually encountered difficulty in publishing her work. Her stories are collected in *Harvest and Song for My Time* (1977); *Ripening* (1982; edited by Elaine Hedges) is a selection from all her work.

Levant Trilogy, The, a trilogy of novels by Olivia *Manning consisting of *The Danger Tree* (1977), *The Battle Lost and Won* (1978), and *The Sum of Things* (1980). It is the second trilogy of a six-volume sequence entitled 'The Fortunes of War', the first being *The *Balkan Trilogy*.

The Danger Tree opens with the arrival in Cairo in 1942 of Simon Boulderstone, a young lieutenant in the British Army. After reporting for duty, he fulfils a commission from his brother, Hugo, to visit the latter's girlfriend, Edwina Little, an attractive young English woman of somewhat dubious reputation, at her house in Garden City, in the suburbs of Cairo. There, amongst a group of Edwina's friends and admirers, he encounters Harriet Pringle who is waiting to hear news of her husband, Guy, still in Alexandria. After a visit to the pyramids, the group go to the house of Desmond Hooper, a British Embassy official. Whilst they are there, his wife returns from a painting expedition with the body of the couple's young son, who has been killed by a grenade. Shaken by the scene, Simon and Harriet fall into conversation and Harriet recalls her last meeting with Hugo Boulderstone, whom she is convinced has been killed, although she says nothing to Simon of this. Harriet eventually persuades Guy to join her only to find that he has little time to spare from his teaching duties and complicated social life to care for his ailing and unhappy wife. The scenes describing the Pringles' difficult marriage alternate with those detailing the desert campaign and the Battle of El Alamein.

The Battle Lost and Won opens with Simon on leave in Cairo following the news of his brother's death in battle; calling to see Edwina, he meets Harriet again and is comforted by her. As in the earlier novel, scenes describing the desert war (in particular, a powerfully imagined night attack) alternate with those focusing on the Pringles' unhappy marriage and on the hedonistic and decadent social life of Cairo. Harriet falls ill, but after agreeing under pressure from Guy to return to England, she suddenly changes her mind and decides to accept a lift to Damascus.

The Sum of Things opens as Simon, seriously wounded in an explosion which killed his driver, is recovering in hospital. Guy Pringle has learned that the ship on which Harriet sailed for England has been torpedoed and that she is not amongst the survivors; Harriet, meanwhile, arrives in Damascus and attempts unsuccessfully to find a job, convinced that her marriage is over. After learning that Guy believes her dead, she decides to return to Cairo to confront him with the truth and to salvage her relationship with him. The couple are reunited at Edwina's wedding, where Simon, now recovered from his wounds, celebrates Harriet's return from the dead and his own release from his unhappy love for Edwina.

As with *The Balkan Trilogy*, the work mingles elements of contemporary history (including a detailed knowledge of the practices of modern warfare), colourful descriptions of exotic locations, satirical vignettes of life amongst the multinational expatriate community, and a—somewhat unconventional—love story.

LEVERSON, Ada (née Beddington) (1862–1933), British novelist, born in London. Through her contributions to *Punch* and other periodicals, she came to the notice of Oscar Wilde, who named her 'Sphinx' and declared her the wittiest woman in the world.

Aubrey Beardsley, Walter Sickert, John Singer Sargent, Mrs Patrick Campbell, and Max *Beerbohm were all *habitués* of her salon. In the 1890s she published two stories in *The Yellow Book*. At the time of Wilde's trial in 1895, the Leversons distinguished themselves by sheltering him in their son's nursery. She published six elegant comedies of 1890s' society including *Love's Shadow* (1908), *Tenterhooks* (1912), and *Love at Second Sight* (1916). They were published in one volume in 1962 as *The Little Ottleys* with a foreword by Colin *MacInnes. Her later years were spent in the company of Harold *Acton, William Walton, and the *Sitwells. She wrote a memoir of Wilde, *The Last First Night in the Criterion* (1926); her daughter, Violet Wyndham, in turn wrote a memoir of her, *The Sphinx and Her Circle* (1963).

LEVERTOV, Denise (1923–), American poet, born in Ilford, Essex, and privately educated. Her experiences as a nurse during the Second World War inform her first collection of verse, *The Double Image* (1946), which showed affinities with the poetry of the *New Apocalypse. After moving to New York, she took American citizenship in 1955. During the 1950s she was associated with the *Black Mountain poets. She began teaching at American universities in 1965 and became Professor of English at Stanford University in 1981. Her reputation was established by *Here and Now* (1957) and *Overland to the Islands* (1958), which displayed her originality of tone in free verse of great suppleness. The lyrical concern with essentially spiritual values in *With Eyes at the Back of Our Heads* (1959) and *The Jacob's Ladder* (1961) combined with energetic opposition to the Vietnam War in *The Sorrow Dance* (1967), *To Stay Alive* (1971), and *Footprints* (1972). Her political convictions and feminist beliefs remain characteristic of subsequent work. Her numerous later collections include *The Freeing of the Dust* (1975), *Candles in Babylon* (1982), *Breathing the Water* (1987), and *A Door in the Hive* (1989). *Collected Earlier Poems, 1940–1960* appeared in 1979. Her critical writings are collected in *The Poet in the World* (1973) and *Light up the Cave* (1981), which also contains autobiographical material.

LEVI, Peter (Chad Tigar) (1931–), British poet, born in Ruislip, London, educated at Campion Hall, Oxford. He was ordained as a Roman Catholic priest in 1964 and lectured at Campion Hall from 1965 to 1977 when he resigned from the priesthood and became a fellow of St Catherine's College, Oxford. His collections of poetry include *The Gravel Ponds* (1960), *Death Is a Pulpit* (1971), *Collected Poems 1955–1975* (1976), *Private Ground* (1981), *The Echoing Green* (1983), *Shadow and Bone* (1989), and *The Rags of Time* (1994). Much of Levi's poetry is characterized by his highly developed descriptive powers which provide a firm basis in vivid imagery, often drawn from landscape and natural phenomena, for his wide-ranging meditations on religious, philosophical, and social themes. His other publications include the autobiographical *The Flutes of Autumn* (1983) and the travel writings of *The Light Garden of the Angel King* (1972), recording his experiences of Afghanistan, and *The Hill of Kronos* (1981), an account of Greece. As a biographer his works include the highly regarded *Boris Pasternak* (1990), as well as *Tennyson* (1993) and *Edward Lear* (1995). He was Oxford Professor of Poetry from 1984 to 1989, and his lectures appeared in *The Art of Poetry* (1991).

LEVINE, Norman (1923–), Canadian short-story writer and novelist, born to Polish-Jewish parents in Ottawa, educated at Cambridge and McGill Universities. Levine settled in England, where he lived mainly in the artistic community of St Ives, Cornwall, from 1949 to 1980, when he returned to Canada. The experience of his early years is examined in *Canada Made Me* (1958), a work which documents his ambiguous feelings as a Canadian expatriate writer. Levine's spare, understated prose style is seen at its best in his short stories. Predominantly first-person narratives, they exhibit a keen eye for external details, but their prime concern is with the subjective experience of the outsider. His collections include *One Way Ticket* (1961), *I Don't Want to Know Anyone Too Well* (1971), *Thin Ice* (1979), *Champagne Barn* (1984), *Why Do You Live So Far Away?* (1984), and *Something Happened Here* (1991). He has also published two novels, *The Angled Road* (1952) and *From a Seaside Town* (1970; reissued in 1975 as *She'll Only Drag You Down*, and two volumes of verse, *The Tightrope Walker* (1950) and *I Walk by the Harbour* (1976), which largely deals with St Ives.

LEVINE, Philip (1928–), American poet, born in Detroit, educated at Wayne State University and at the *Iowa Writers' Workshop at the University of Iowa. Levine was awarded a Fellowship in Poetry at Stanford University in 1958. His books include *On the Edge* (1961), *Silent in America: Vivas for Those Who Failed* (1965), *Not This Pig* (1968), *Red Dust* (1971), *Pili's Wall* (1971), *They Feed They Lion* (1972), *1933* (1974), *The Names of the Lost* (1976), *Ashes: Poems Old & New* (1979), *7 Years from Somewhere* (1979), *One for the Rose* (1981), *Selected Poems* (1983), *Sweet Will* (1985), *A Walk with Tom Jefferson* (1988), *New Selected Poems* (1991), and *What Work Is* (1992). In 1985 he published *Off the Map: Selected Poems by Gloria Fuertes*, which he edited and translated with Ada Long. A child of the Depression years who grew up with the social deprivation of the cities and townships of the MidWest, Levine's poetry speaks for and about the marginalized and dispossessed, and those who stand defiantly beyond the social spectrum. In narrating these lives Levine uses the idioms of common speech, catching the verbal and experiential poverty of his subjects in a vocabulary of vigorous simplicity; but he also possesses an inventive power, especially evident in the incantatory rhythms of his most celebrated collection, *They Feed They Lion*.

LEWIS, Alun (1915–44), Welsh poet, born in Cwmaman, Glamorgan, educated at the Universities of Aberystwyth and Manchester. After prolonged indecision due to his pacifist views, he joined the army in 1940 and served as an officer in India and Burma. He died at Arakan after the discharge of his own revolver in circumstances which remain unclear. The elegiac lyricism and descriptive acuteness of *Raiders' Dawn* (1942), his first collection of poems, gained him a reputation which was consolidated by *The Last Inspection* (1943), a volume of ironically factual and carefully structured short stories. Many of the poems and stories convey the tedium and isolation of life in army training camps in England. *Ha! Ha! Among the Trumpets* (1945), a posthumous collection of poetry with an introduction by Robert *Graves, was followed by the selections from his correspondence in *Letters from India* (1946) and a further volume of stories entitled *In the Green Tree* (1948). The inhospitable landscapes of India and Burma and the fatalistic philosophies of their inhabitants strongly inform his later verse, in which love and death are prevailing themes. Ian *Hamilton's edition of his *Selected Poetry and Prose* appeared in 1966. A biography by John Pikoulis was published in 1984. See also WAR POETRY.

LEWIS, C(live) S(taples) (1898–1963), British literary scholar, critic, Christian apologist, and novelist, born in Belfast, educated at University College, Oxford. Among several academic posts he was Fellow of Magdalen College, Oxford and Professor of Medieval and Renaissance English at Cambridge. His literary reputation was established in the 1930s, after his conversion to Christianity, partly reflected in *The Pilgrim's Regress* (1933). *The Allegory of Love* (1936) was the first of several significant critical works, which include *A Preface to Paradise Lost* (1942), *English Literature in the Sixteenth Century* (vol. 3 in the *Oxford History of English Literature*, 1954), and *The Discarded Image* (1964). Lewis, though a theological layman, became widely known as a Christian writer; books such as *The Problem of Pain* (1940), *Miracles* (1947), and *The Four Loves* (1960) were highly influential, as were his general and apologetic writings such as *The Screwtape Letters* (1940)—letters from a senior to a junior devil—and *Letters to Malcolm: Chiefly on Prayer* (1964). Lewis's extensive reputation was largely due to his popular radio talks on religious themes, collected in *Mere Christianity* (1952). *Out of the Silent Planet* (1938) was the first volume of an uneven *science fiction trilogy, followed by *Perelandra* (1943; retitled *Voyage to Venus*, 1953) and *That Hideous Strength* (1945). Much more consistent are the seven children's novels about the imaginary world of Narnia, beginning with *The Lion, The Witch, and the Wardrobe* (1950) in which the lion Aslan, a representation of God, is introduced. Both series are broadly allegorical and owe much to Lewis's friendship with J. R. R. *Tolkien and Charles *Williams. All three were members of the Inklings, a circle meeting in Oxford (1939–62) for the purpose of mutual literary criticism and conversation. In 1956 Lewis married Joy Davidman, an American author on Christian subjects, to guarantee her residency rights in Britain. This marriage of convenience deepened into a real love affair and a second, Christian wedding took place in 1957 when Joy was in hospital suffering from cancer; she died in 1960. *Shadowlands*, a play by William Nicholson, tells the story of their relationship, and Lewis—writing as 'N. W. Clerk'—published *A Grief Observed* (1961), describing his own pilgrimage of grief after bereavement. Among several critical assessments and biographical works is A. N. *Wilson's *C. S. Lewis: A Biography* (1990).

LEWIS, Janet (1899–), American writer, born in Chicago, educated at Lewis Institute and the University of Chicago. Her early travels in Europe, particularly France, had a considerable influence on her writings. Her first novel, *The Invasion* (1932), is an imaginative creation of Native American life (Lewis herself is of part-Indian origin). Lewis is best known for her three historical novels based on Phillips's *Famous Cases of Circumstantial Evidence* (1873). *The Wife of Martin Guerre* (1941), set in sixteenth-century France, recounts the story of the return of a vanished young husband; *The Trial of Sören Qvist* (1947), set in seventeenth-century Denmark, deals with the repercussions of the return of an assumed murder victim and the execution of the wrongly accused pastor Qvist; *The Ghost of Monsieur Scarron* (1956), set in France, concerns an honest publisher wrongly accused of producing scurrilous pamphlets about Louis XIV and his present mistress. *Against A Darkening Sky* (1943) was an experiment in contemporary realism and social comment, and chronicles the fortunes of one rural family in California during the Depression. All her novels are characterized by her economical, elegant and evocative prose style. Her other works include *Goodbye Son* (1946; stories); volumes of verse, including *Poems Old and New 1918–1978* (1981) and *Last Offerings* (1988); and librettos for *The Wife of Martin Guerre* (1956; music by William Bergsma), and Alva Henderson's opera of James Fenimore Cooper's *The Last of the Mohicans* (1976). Lewis was married to Yvor *Winters.

LEWIS, Norman (1918–), British travel writer and novelist, born in London, educated at Enfield Grammar School. His experiences of active service in Italy during the Second World War were drawn upon in *Naples '44* (1978), a documentary treatment of the city in wartime, and the novel *Within the Labyrinth* (1950). Lewis's reputation as a travel writer was established with *A Dragon Apparent* (1951) and *Golden Earth* (1952), which deal respectively with Indo-China and Burma. *Voices of the Old Sea* (1984), a lyrically retrospective account of the Mediterranean coast of Spain in the late 1940s, *A Goddess in the Stones* (1991), a vivid record of his journeys in India, and *An Empire of the East* (1993), recounting his travels in Indonesia, are among the most widely acclaimed of his works. His novels, which include *A Single Pilgrim* (1953), *A Small War Made to Order* (1966), and *Cuban Passage* (1982), are generally informed by the political and social characters of countries in which he has travelled. *The Sicilian Specialist* (1974) is a fictionalized treatment of the Mafia's involvement in the assassination of President Kennedy. Lewis's autobiography entitled *Jackdaw Cake* appeared in 1985.

LEWIS, (Harry) Sinclair (1885–1951), American novelist, born in Sauk Center, Minnesota, educated at Yale University; he was the son of a country doctor of Welsh descent whose life provided details for some of his later fiction. Lewis held a variety of jobs, mostly connected with publishing; for a short time, he worked as the janitor of Upton *Sinclair's socialist colony, Helicon Hall, in New Jersey. In 1916, after publishing the two novels *Our Mr. Wrenn* (1914) and *The Trail of the Hawk* (1915), and several short stories in periodicals, he became a freelance writer. He produced several further novels including *The Job* (1917), *The Innocents* (1917), and *Free Air* (1919). He achieved an international reputation with **Main Street* (1920), a satiric caricature detailing the drabness, conformity, and materialism of small town middle America. The ensuing decade saw the emergence of his best fiction. **Babbitt* (1922) portrayed a *petit-bourgeois* businessman in a middle-sized Midwestern city, who vainly attempts to break out of a stifling conformity to achieve his own freedom. Next came *Arrowsmith* (1925), a study of the medical profession which is contrasted with an idealized view of scientific research; *Mantrap* (1926); *Elmer Gantry* (1927), an extravagantly comic satirical attack on the Protestant ministry; *The Man Who Knew Coolidge* (1928); and **Dodsworth* (1929), a satirical perspective of the American businessman abroad. He continued his prolific writing during the 1930s with a scrutiny of the career woman in *Ann Vickers* (1933); a look at the hotel industry in *Work of Art* (1934); and *It Can't Happen Here* (1935), a study of fascism. These works lacked the satiric power and intensity of his earlier works as Lewis became increasingly conservative. His later novels include *Prodigal Parents* (1938), about radical and irresponsible children; *Bethel Merriday* (1940), about the education of a young actress; an attack on organized philanthropy in *Gideon Planish* (1943); *Cass Timberlane* (1945), an account of an American marriage; an unconvincing parable about racial issues in *Kingsblood Royal* (1947); *The God-Seeker* (1949), about the early settlement days in Minnesota; and *World So Wide* (1951). He wrote two plays entitled *Hobohemia* (1919) and *Jayhawker* (1934), and his letters were edited by Harrison Smith in *From Main Street to Stockholm* (1952). He refused the Pulitzer Prize for *Arrowsmith* in 1926, but he was the first American to be awarded the Nobel Prize for Literature in 1930.

LEWIS, (Percy) Wyndham (1882–1957), British artist, novelist, and critic, the son of an American father and an English mother; he was born on his father's yacht off the coast of Nova Scotia and spent his early childhood in New England. In 1888 his parents, who separated when he was 11, moved to England. Lewis was educated at a succession of schools, and later studied at the Slade School of Art. Between 1902 and 1908 he travelled extensively in Spain, Germany, and France, where he established himself as a painter. His early short stories were published in *The *English Review*. In 1914, after a celebrated falling-out with Marinetti, the leader of the *Futurists, Lewis edited **Blast: The Review of the Great English Vortex*, a satirical analysis of the state of contemporary art and letters, which was the manifesto for his *Vorticist movement. A second, 'War Number', was published shortly before Lewis's departure for the Western Front. His first novel, **Tarr* (1918), was admired by *Pound who described it as 'the most vigorous and volcanic English novel of our time'. *The Wild Body* (1927; short stories) was followed by *The *Childermass* (1928), the first volume of a proposed tetralogy entitled *The Human Age*, which was set in the Afterlife and included a sustained parody of *Joyce's *work in progress* (later published as **Finnegans Wake*). Lewis first met Joyce in 1920 (the occasion is described in his memoir, *Blasting and Bombardiering*, 1937) and was also associated, through Pound, with T. S. *Eliot. Both Joyce and Eliot are amongst the figures satirized in Lewis's notorious *roman-à-clef*, *The *Apes of God* (1930). *Bloomsbury never forgave him for his satirical portrayal of its foibles, and during the 1930s and afterwards he was increasingly ostracized by the literary establishment; his isolation was compounded when, in 1931, he published a book expressing his admiration for Hitler. *Auden described him as 'that lonely old volcano of the Right', but in spite of his damaged reputation Lewis produced some of his best work during the late 1930s and early 1940s. *The *Revenge for Love* (1937), an intricately plotted thriller set at the time of the Spanish Civil War, and *The Vulgar Streak* (1941), set in Italy on the eve of the Munich crisis, show Lewis's incisive style at its best. Lewis spent the war years in self-imposed exile in Canada, a period chronicled in his novel *Self Condemned* (1954), which describes the gradual alienation from society of Dr Rene Harding, a historian whose brand of anti-democratic élitism parallels Lewis's own. *The Human Age*, his projected four-part reworking of *The Divine Comedy*, remained unfinished, although the surreal narrative begun in *The Childermass* was developed in *Monstre Gai* (1955), which follows its protagonists Pullman and Sattersthwaite to Purgatory and, in *Malign Fiesta* (1955), to Hell. Critical and polemical works include *The Art of Being Ruled* (1926); *Time and Western Man* (1927), which contains his celebrated attack on Joyce's **Ulysses*; *The Lion and the Fox: The Role of the Hero in the Plays of Shakespeare* (1927); *Men Without Art* (1934); and *The Writer and the Absolute* (1952). In *Rude Assignment* (1950) he attempted to set the record straight concerning some of the exigencies of his career. His extreme and aggressively proclaimed views, together with his own propensity for the role of the 'Enemy' (the title of one of the *little magazines he started in the late 1920s), contributed towards his isolation at the end of his life. *'The Enemy'* is also the title of a biography of Lewis, by Jeffrey Meyers (1980).

Life and Letters, a literary periodical initially edited by Desmond *MacCarthy, who began it in 1928. During its early years it frequently included work by MacCarthy's associates in the *Bloomsbury Group;

Virginia *Woolf, Lytton *Strachey, J. M. *Keynes, Clive *Bell, and E. M. *Forster were among the contributors. Writing by D. H. *Lawrence, Cyril *Connolly, and Evelyn *Waugh was also featured. Following the end of MacCarthy's editorship in 1934, the new authors whose work appeared included W. H. *Auden, Louis *MacNeice, Stephen *Spender, Frank *O'Connor, and Graham *Greene. In 1935 it became known as *Life and Letters Today* under the co-editorship of Petrie Townshend and Robert Herring. It absorbed the **London Mercury* and *Bookman* in 1939 and reverted to the title *Life and Letters* in 1945. During the Second World War the magazine gave extended attention to the social implications of the conflict and favoured the *New Apocalypse. From 1945 onward it was noted for its attention to European writing. It closed unexpectedly in 1950.

Light in August, a novel by William *Faulkner, published in 1932. The central character, Joe Christmas, is the son of Milly Hines and a circus man. Milly's father, Eupheus Hines, murders Milly's lover, believing him to be partly negro, and she dies in childbirth. On Christmas (the origin of Joe's surname) night Hines leaves his hated baby grandson on the steps of an orphanage for white children. At the age of five, Joe is forced to leave the home after witnessing two staff members making love. He then goes to the household of an obsessedly puritanical farmer, McEachern, who beats him. When he is 18, Joe quarrels with McEachern, perhaps killing him. After fifteen years of wandering, he arrives in Jefferson and becomes the lover of a reclusive white woman, Joanna Burden. He also becomes involved with a fellow vagrant, Joe Brown (also called Lucas Burch). Joanna's attempts to convert Joe to religion so enrage him that he cuts her throat and sets fire to her house. Lena Grove arrives in Jefferson in search of Burch by whom she has become pregnant ('Light in August' is a country expression for pregnancy.) She is led to Byron Bunch (due to his name's similarity to Burch) who befriends her. Meanwhile both Burch and Joe Christmas are wanted by the police after the murder of Joanna Burden. Confronted with Lena and the child, Burch flees, while Joe Christmas is caught, and his old grandfather, steadfast in his hatred of him, stirs up a mob to lynch him. Joe Christmas takes refuge in the house of Hightower, the clergyman, but is shot and castrated by Percy Grimm, a crazed racist. Byron Bunch and Lena stay together and journey on through the Southern countryside.

LIM, Shirley Geok-lin (1944–), Malaysian poet, born and raised in Malacca, Malaya, educated at the University of Malaya, and Brandeis University in the USA. She has continued to live in America, with frequent sojourns in Asia, but her work in all genres reflects her fascination with her heritage as a Chinese woman in Malaysia and a permanent foreigner in the country of her adoption. The choice of English as her language of expression, fraught with political ambiguities, is also a crucial issue in her writings. She is the author of several collections of poems, the first and best known of which is *Crossing the Peninsula* (1980). Her subsequent volumes include *No Man's Grove* (1985) and *Modern Secrets: New and Selected Poems* (1989); *Monsoon History* (1994) is a retrospective selection of her work. A well-known critic and scholar of Asian literature in English, Lim produced the pioneering anthology of women's writing *The Forbidden Stitch* (1990). Her most representative work is *Writing South East/Asia in English: Against the Grain* (1994), which contains autobiographical essays, critiques of writings by Asians such as *Das and *Mo, and theoretical reflections on being a literary migrant. See also ASIAN-AMERICAN WRITING.

LINDSAY, David (1876–1945), British writer, born in Blackheath, south-east London, educated in Scotland. He is remembered for his first novel, *A Voyage to Arcturus* (1920), ostensibly a tale of interplanetary romance, but in fact a highly disciplined philosophical foray into an imagined wonderland, where the protagonist undergoes a transformative rite of passage. The influence of Lindsay's Calvinist upbringing and his study of German philosophy evident in this work distinguishes it from other *science fiction works. Notable among his other novels is *The Haunted Woman* (1922), a supernatural work posing moral questions of good and evil.

LINDSAY, Jack (1900–90), Australian writer, born in Melbourne, educated at Brisbane University. His early work includes a volume of poetry, *Fauns and Ladies* (1923), with illustrations by his father, Norman *Lindsay. His energy was the driving force behind the creation of the periodical **Vision* (1923–4). He left for London in 1926 where he edited several journals, including *The London Aphrodite*, and had considerable success as founder of the Fanfrolico Press, an experience later described in his autobiographical work *Fanfrolico and After* (1962). In addition to distinguished political works from a Marxist position, he wrote a wide-ranging series of classical, historical, and art studies, acclaimed biographies of artists, and literary studies of *William Blake* (1927 and 1978), *Mulk Raj Anand* (1948), *Dickens* (1950), and *Meredith* (1956). He published 169 books including thirty-eight novels and twenty-five volumes of translations (from Latin, Greek, Polish, and Russian). *Betrayed Spring* (1953), *A Local Habitation* (1957), and *All the Never-Never* (1961) were novels focusing on the British. *Decay and Renewal* (1976) gathered critical writings on Australian and other literatures; *Life Rarely Tells* (1958; reprinted 1982) and *The Roaring Twenties* (1960) were absorbing and revealing autobiographies.

LINDSAY, Norman (1879–1969), Australian artist and writer, born in Victoria. He left home at the age of 16, and subsequently led a bohemian life in Melbourne where he established his reputation as an artist and illustrator. This period is reflected in his first novel, *A Curate in Bohemia* (1913). In 1901 he began his long association with the Sydney-based **Bulletin* as artist, reviewer, and contributor of essays and fiction. His paintings and drawings, often condemned by the establishment as immoral, aroused much controversy for their overt sexuality. He was the main driving force behind *Vision*, a magazine edited by his son Jack *Lindsay and Kenneth *Slessor. *Creative Effort* (1920) and *Madam Life's Lovers* (1929) express his aesthetic credo. Deeply influenced by Rabelais and Nietzsche, his novels also aroused protest for his revolutionary ideas and their sexual explicitness. *Redheap* (1930; US title *Every Mother's Son*), banned in Australia until 1958, was the first part of his trilogy which also included *Saturdee* (1933) and *Halfway to Anywhere* (1947); these novels, with their sexually vigorous young protagonists, comically depict small town life. Novels in similar vein include *The Cautious Amorist* (1932), also banned, and *The Age of Consent* (1938). Other works include *The Magic Pudding* (1918), a classic children's book; *Norman Lindsay's Book, No. I* (1912) and *Norman Lindsay's Book, No. II* (1915), sketches and stories; and *My Mask* (1970), an autobiography.

LINDSAY, (Nicholas) Vachel (1879–1931), American poet, born in Springfield, Illinois. After studying art in New York he began the years of vagrancy described in the prose of *Adventures while Preaching the Gospel of Beauty* (1914) and *A Handy Guide for Beggars* (1916); *The Tree of Laughing Bells* (1905) and *Rhymes To Be Traded for Bread* (1912) were among the pamphlets of verse he bartered for food and shelter. His characteristic combination of religious fervour and political liberalism became apparent in the verse of *General William Booth Enters into Heaven* (1913); the title piece typifies the heavily syncopated rhythms of much of his work. *The Congo* (1914) gained him wide notice as a radically innovative poet. He was actively involved in the resurgence of American literary culture associated with the **Seven Arts*. Subsequent collections of his poetry, which exhibit a gradual decline in his formerly intense imaginative energies, include *The Chinese Nightingale* (1917), *The Golden Whales of California* (1920), and *Going-to-the-Sun* (1923), which contained many of his unusual line drawings. His increasing eccentricity led him to retreat to Springfield in the late 1920s, where he took his life by drinking poison in the house in which he had been born. His other publications include *The Art of the Motion Picture* (1915), one of the earliest studies of the cinema, and *The Golden Book of Springfield* (1920), which envisions a utopia of social and aesthetic harmony. Dennis Camp edited *The Poetry of Vachel Lindsay* (two volumes, 1984). Biographical material includes *Vachel Lindsay: A Poet in America* (1935) by his friend Edgar Lee *Masters.

Lines Review, a literary magazine begun as an eight-page poetry broadsheet entitled *Lines* in 1952. Norman *MacCaig, Sydney Goodsir *Smith, and Hamish *Henderson were among the poets represented. Alan Riddell was its editor until 1954, when the name *Lines Review* was adopted; he resumed the editorship in 1962. Primarily a magazine of poetry and criticism, *Lines Review* was almost exclusively concerned with Scottish verse up to 1967; under Robin Fulton's editorship from 1967 to 1977 it began devoting attention to European literature, and occasionally published prose fiction. In addition to the publication of original work and translations in English, it has frequently featured poetry in Scots by Smith, *MacDiarmid, and others, and Gaelic writing by contributors who have included Iain Crichton *Smith and Sorley *MacLean. Among the other distinguished authors whose work has appeared in *Lines Review* are Douglas *Dunn, George Mackay *Brown, Naomi *Mitchison, Edwin *Morgan, and Burns *Singer.

LINKLATER, Eric (Robert Russell) (1899–1974), Scottish writer, born in Wales and brought up in the Orkney Islands, educated at Aberdeen University. Many of his novels were set in Scotland, including *White Maa's Saga* (1929), *Poet's Pub* (1929), *The Men of Ness* (1932), *Magnus Merriman* (1934), *Laxdale Hall* (1951), and *The Dark of Summer* (1956). *Juan in America* (1930) and *Juan in China* (1937) are picaresque novels recounting the adventures of an English Don Juan. *Private Angelo* (1946) humorously describes its protagonist's attempts to escape from his military commitments during the campaign in Italy. A versatile writer, noted for the elegance of his prose, Linklater's works reflect his interest in Scottish history, Norse saga, and the British army. He has also published dramatic works, poetry, essays, children's stories, and official histories. *The Man on My Back* (1941) and *A Year of Space* (1953) were autobiographies.

LIPPMANN, Walter (1889–1974), American essayist, journalist, and social commentator, born in New York City, educated at Harvard. Lippmann's career as an analyst and critic of American social and political affairs began at the end of the First World War and ended with the traumas of the Vietnam War and Watergate. In 1913 he joined the **New Republic* at the invitation of Herbert Croly. His first book, *A Preface to Politics* (1913), was strongly influenced by Croly's espousal of big government and strong leadership as ways of combating the powers of big business and special interest groups. In 1918 Lippmann was commissioned as a captain in US military intelligence and was delegated to provide the official commentary on Woodrow Wilson's 'Fourteen Points' speech. He joined *Vanity Fair* in 1920, the New York *World* in 1922, and the New York *Herald Tribune* in 1931. During the USA's increasing involvement in Vietnam Lippmann was attached to the *Washington Post* syndicate and, as a columnist, to *Newsweek*. During this period he had risen to become the most respected liberal columnist in the USA, but despite his liberal proclivities, Lippmann was an excoriating critic of the New Deal, dismissing Franklin D. Roosevelt as an 'amiable boy scout' and supporting Wendell Willkie's candidacy for the Republican nomination for the Presidency. He supported the broad objectives of US foreign policy during the Cold War period, but was frequently a trenchant critic of those who administered the policy.

His other major works are *Drift and Mastery* (1914), *The Good Society* (1937), and *Essays in the Public Philosophy* (1955). See also *Walter Lippmann and the American Century* (1980), by Ronald Steel.

Listener, The, a weekly journal begun by the BBC in 1929 to publish broadcast talks and to promote its work in adult education. Richard Lambert was its first editor. In its early years the texts of broadcasts included work by Desmond *MacCarthy, Herbert *Read, and Julian *Huxley; Vita *Sackville-West and Edwin *Muir were the principal book reviewers. Under J. R. *Ackerley's literary editorship from 1935 to 1959 the *Listener* became an important forum for new poetry, publishing verse by W. H. *Auden, Dylan *Thomas, Louis *MacNeice, Stephen *Spender, and other notable poets of the period. Throughout the Second World War, when the publication of *Churchill's speeches attracted a wide readership, circulation rose steadily to a peak of 150,000 in 1949. In the 1960s and 1970s the *Listener* maintained its literary and intellectual standards while keeping abreast of an increasingly eclectic cultural environment. Following a marked decline in circulation from 1980 onward, it was discontinued in December 1990.

Literary Review, The, a periodical founded in Edinburgh in 1979 by Anne Smith, who remained editor until 1981, when she sold it to the publisher Naim Attallah. Under Smith's editorship the magazine published reviews, articles, short stories, poetry, and interviews; Anthony *Burgess, Doris *Lessing, Angus *Wilson, William *Trevor, Geoffrey *Grigson, and David *Lodge were among the contributors. In 1982 it absorbed **Quarto* and was henceforth published from London. Its reviewers included Derek *Mahon, Michael *Hofmann, P. J. *Kavanagh, and Germaine *Greer; poetry was contributed by Andrew *Motion, David *Harsent, Peter *Reading, Edwin *Morgan, and others. In 1986 the editorship passed to Auberon *Waugh, whose wittily sceptical 'From the Pulpit' column introduces each issue. Under his direction the journal has been increasingly devoted to reviewing with the aim of being intelligently informative to the general reader and free of any political bias. Jeremy *Reed, Colin *Wilson, Paul *Theroux, Tom *Sharpe, Peter *Levi, and Victoria *Glendinning have been among the more recent contributors of reviews.

Little Foxes, The, see HELLMAN, LILLIAN.

Little Magazines, a term denoting periodicals whose specialized concern with aspects of literature or art generally places them beyond the ambit of commercial publishing. Numerous examples existed in the nineteenth century or earlier, notably *The Germ*, the organ of the Pre-Raphaelite Brotherhood founded in 1850, *The Savoy*, and *The Dome*, both associated with the coteries of the 1890s; principally because of their major contribution to the dynamics of *Modernism, however, little magazines are considered an essentially twentieth-century phenomenon: Malcolm *Bradbury has written that 'the "little magazine" . . . has been a central and primary feature of the modern movement in literature', noting that between 1912 and 1947 some 600 appeared in England and America, of which approximately 100 may be considered of importance. These include **Blast*, *The *Dial*, *The *Egoist*, **Horizon*, *The *Little Review*, **New Verse*, **Poetry London*, *Rhythm*, and **Transatlantic Review*. Instances of the little magazines' value to modern literature include the initial appearance of Joyce's **Portrait of the Artist as a Young Man* and substantial extracts from **Ulysses* in *The Egoist* and *The Little Review* respectively, the early promotion of *Imagism in **Poetry* (Chicago), and the centrality of *New Verse* to the poetry of the 1930s. The work of the above publications was often characterized by an energetic sense of radical cultural revaluation that is largely absent from the little magazines of the present day. They remain, however, very numerous, as Peter Finch's *Small Presses and Little Magazines of the U.K. and Ireland* (1988, sixth revised edition) indicates in listing over 300; among the more notable and long-established are **Agenda*, **Ambit*, **Honest Ulsterman*, **London Magazine*, **New Departures*, **Poetry Review*, **Poetry Wales*, and **PN Review*. Ian *Hamilton's study *The Little Magazines* appeared in 1976.

Little Review, The, a periodical founded by Margaret Anderson (1893–1973) in Chicago in 1914 and based in New York from 1917 to 1922. The magazine quickly achieved notoriety for promoting Nietzschean philosophy and anarchist political opinions. By 1916, when Jane Heap joined Anderson as assistant editor, the *Little Review* had begun supporting *Imagism; Ezra *Pound, European editor from 1917 to 1919, exercised a large measure of control and supplied work by W. B. *Yeats, T. S. *Eliot, F. M. *Ford, and Wyndham *Lewis. In 1918 the serialization of extracts from James Joyce's **Ulysses* began and continued until a prosecution for obscenity in 1920. Ernest *Hemingway, W. C. *Williams, Wallace *Stevens, Hart *Crane, and E. E. *Cummings were also among its contributors. In 1922 Anderson and Heap moved to Paris, where the *Little Review* was henceforth published irregularly. Heap assumed increasing editorial responsibility, favouring the more esoteric forms of European *Modernism. After 1927 it was effectively defunct until the final issue of 1929, which carried statements by both editors expressive of deep disillusionment.

LIVELY, Adam (1961–), British novelist, born in Swansea, educated at Cambridge University. His works display a preoccupation with history and philosophy as well as music, politics, and the genesis of creativity. His first brief novel, *Blue* (1988), is the story of an eighteenth-century musician and scientist who is projected into the New Orleans of the future, where he discovers the rhythms of black music. *The Burnt House* (1989) focuses on a well-known American TV personality who seeks redress from his painful memories in the anonymity of British life. The novella *The Snail* (1991), set in 1940, tells of the quest of Morgan, an English journalist, for two Czech Jewish refugees, the

16-year-old Antonin and his uncle, whom he has helped to escape from their war-torn country. *I Sing The Body Electric* (1993) is set in the future in an unnamed European land, in which, through the perspective of the celebrated composer Paul Clearwater, he explores the nature of artistic creativity and its relationship to life and experience. In 1993, Lively was amongst those chosen as the best of Britain's young writers. He is the son of Penelope *Lively.

LIVELY, Penelope (1933–), British novelist and children's writer, born in Cairo, educated at St Anne's College, Oxford. Her childhood in Egypt is vividly evoked in *Oleander, Jacaranda* (1994), an autobiography of her early years. Beginning with *Astercote* (1970), Lively has written over twenty well-received books for children. Her first novel for adults, *The Road to Lichfield* (1977), and her subsequent novels are rewarding for their sensitivity to character, their intelligent humour, their admission of tragedy, and their historical insights. *Treasures of Time* (1979) explores the painfully conflicting memories uncovered by a television documentary about a dead archaeologist who had had an adulterous affair with his wife's sister. In *Judgement Day* (1980) Lively comes closest to a statement of faith, not in any established religion, but in love that is very much human and in the power of words. *According to Mark* (1984) presents a biographer learning as much about himself as about the blustering and deceptive great man who is his subject. In *Moon Tiger* (1987; Booker Prize) an uncompromising old lady relives her past; different voices reveal the complexities and chronic misunderstandings of their relationships, including those of her long-buried wartime lover, who speaks through his diary, and their daughter who has always irritated her mother, partly because she is the child of the wrong man. What passes between mothers and children is central to her work, which shows how easily, through neglect of language as of feeling, those relationships can falter. *Passing On* (1989) considers the lifelong effects of such distortion, as a woman in her fifties struggles to free herself after the death of her inescapable mother. *City of the Mind* (1991) interweaves vignettes from London's past and present with a narrative about an architect's marriage breakdown and his hopes for a new future. Historical and contemporary concerns are again featured in *Cleopatra's Sister* (1993), recounting a romance between a female journalist and a palaeontologist who are drawn together in the fictional North African state of Callimbia during a time of political crisis. Lively has also written plays, screenplays, and several volumes of stories, including *Pack of Cards: Stories 1978–86* (1986). Her non-fiction works include a work on landscape history, *The Present and the Past* (1976).

Liverpool Poets, the name given to a group of three poets, Adrian *Henri, Roger *McGough, and Brian *Patten, who came together in the early 1960s in the euphoria generated in part by the success of the *Beatles. *The Liverpool Scene* (1967) gave the term currency; achieving unusually high sales for a poetry anthology, it was eclipsed by the astonishing success of the 1967 Penguin anthology *The Mersey Sound* and of collections by, in particular, Patten. But the major impact was in performance. All three were involved in performance poetry in 1961, and later in 'happenings' (about 1963), performances with musicians, poetry recordings (e.g. *The Incredible New Liverpool Scene*, Henri/McGough, 1967), theatre, and broadcasting. Their work was public and accessible, a statement against academic and 'establishment' poetry, subversive, and often surreal. It drew its imagery from the urban landscape, usually precisely located in Liverpool. The three styles were distinct: Patten was one of the outstanding lyric poets of the 1960s; McGough's often-imitated punning word-play used domestic urban images; Henri's impressionist poetry bizarrely juxtaposed contemporary images, making frequent use of techniques such as William *Burroughs's 'cut-ups'. Different styles reflected sharply differing literary backgrounds. Patten's sensuous musical lyricism stands in a clearly recognizable tradition, McGough's pungency and wit likewise in the line of English comic verse; Henri, by contrast, intercut the Liverpool landscape with that of the European avant-garde, American *Beat culture, rock music, and political anarchy.

By 1970 Patten had left Liverpool and the group's identity changed, though it remained influential for the rest of the decade. A final anthology, *New Volume* (1983), covered the period since the publication of *The Mersey Sound. The Liverpool Scene* generated a poetry climate in which several other poets became well known, including Matt *Simpson, Henry Graham (co-editor of **Ambit*), and Willy *Russell (later a successful playwright).

LIVESAY, Dorothy (1909–), Canadian poet, born in Winnipeg, educated at the University of Toronto and at the Sorbonne, Paris. She subsequently worked in France, the USA, and Zambia, before holding various posts at Canadian universities from 1966. From early and predominantly lyrical collections such as *Green Pitcher* (1928) and *Signpost* (1932) her work increasingly reflects social and political issues. *Selected Poems* (1956) confirmed her abiding concern with capturing the interplay of idealism and passion. *The Colour of God's Face* (1965) contained poems shaped by her experience in Africa. *Collected Poems: The Two Seasons* (1972), which demonstrated the range and consistency of her work, explored tensions between individual aspirations and the pressures and demands of communal life. Her autobiographical volume of short stories, *A Winnipeg Childhood* (1973), contained work from 1953 onwards; *Right Hand Left Hand* (1977), which was 'A True Life of the Thirties', was subtitled 'Paris, Toronto, Montreal, The West and Vancouver. Love, politics, the depression and feminism', and covered the period 1928–39. Always politically highly aware, Livesay worked for the Communist Party during the 1930s and was a feminist in her broad commitments long before the feminist revival of the 1960s. Her later poetry includes *The Phases of Love* (1983) and *Selected Poems: The Self-Completing Tree* (1986).

Living Theatre, American theatre company. Founded in New York City in 1947 by Judith Malina and her husband Julian Beck, it was originally committed to poetic drama and *modernist plays that had little chance of commercial success, such as Gertrude *Stein's *Doctor Faustus Lights the Lights*, T. S. *Eliot's *Sweeney Agonistes*, Alfred Jarry's *Ubu the King*, Paul *Goodman's *Faustina*, Jean Cocteau's *Orpheus*, and William Carlos *Williams's *Many Loves*. The most pioneering company of avant-garde theatres, and the one that survived longest, it elected the most extreme forms of experimentalism in its productions, was structured as an egalitarian organization, and was proto-anarchist in its political colouring. From its earliest makeshift locations, it was eventually established at a former department store on Sixth Avenue and Fourteenth Street in New York, and its theatre named as The Fourteenth Street theatre, also called the Living Theatre Playhouse. The 1959 production of Jack *Gelber's *The Connection*, and the 1963 production of Kenneth Brown's *The Brig*, brought it widespread critical acclaim and financial success. The Fourteenth Street theatre was eventually closed in 1963 by the Inland Revenue Service because of back taxes owed by the Becks. In 1964 the company moved to Europe and, with brief return visits to the USA, went into exile in Europe and Latin America for the next twenty years. Throughout this time it was increasingly committed to subversive social politics, matching its unorthodox productions, which included at one time a willingness only to give street performances, so as to dissociate itself from the inherent cultural elitism of the conventional theatre. In Europe its success was based on a sequence of other brilliant productions, such as *Mysteries* (1964), *Frankenstein* (1965), *Antigone* (1967), and, above all, *Paradise Now* (1968). Since the early 1970s the political extremism of the company has been modified by its interest in theatre–audience relations, and the consequent ideal of a communal challenge to the imperialist politics of the American mainstream. In the mid-1980s Julian Beck left the company to work in motion pictures, television, and off-off-Broadway theatre, and Judith Malina composed a video documentary on the Living Theatre, *Signals Through the Flames*.

LIVINGS, Henry (1929–), British dramatist, born in Prestwich, Lancashire, educated at Liverpool University. He worked in the theatre as an actor before writing several comedies whose anti-heroic heroes are usually the resilient, if slightly gormless, members of an oppressed Northern working class. These plays are often, though not invariably, written in a quirky, somewhat surreal style that itself reflects their author's anti-authoritarian instincts and love of eccentricity. They include *Stop It Whoever You Are* (1961), *Big Soft Nellie* (1961), *Nil Carborundum* (1962), and *Eh?* (1964), whose protagonist is the quintessential Livings character Valentine Brose, a boiler-man who pays less attention to the exotic machinery it is his task to tend than to the narcotic mushrooms he is growing in its vicinity. Other work has included the powerful *Kelly's Eye* (1964), about the brutality and violence of the 1930s as exemplified not just by a society soon to go to war, but by the protagonist, himself destroyed after murdering his best friend; *The Ffinest Ffamily in the Land* (1970), a comedy about the sexual adventures of the cartoon Lancastrians who inhabit some high-rise flats; a version of Kleist's *The Shattered Jug* called *Jug* (1975); and the sombre *Stop the Children's Laughter* (1990), based on a true case of child murder in Victorian Lancashire.

LIYONG, Taban Lo (1939–), East African essayist, poet, and short-story writer, born in Northern Uganda, educated at the National Teachers' College, Kampala, and in the USA at Howard University, Knoxville College, and the University of Iowa. His great interest and research studies in oral literature have resulted in *Eating Chiefs: Lwo Culture from Lolwe to Malkal* (1960) and, as editor, *Popular Culture of East Africa* (1972). His satires, parables, and moral tales in *Fixions and other Stories* (1969), and his poetry, are very much inspired by the oral tradition, but also by Nietzsche and modernist poets such as *Eliot and *Pound, while the more overtly modernistic stories in *The Unfinished Man* (1971) reflect the breakdown of that tradition in 'fragmented images'. Liyong's poems defy stylistic convention, and reinforce his roles as both social critic and literary experimenter. Poetry collections include *Frantz Fanon's Uneven Ribs* (1971), *Another Nigger Dead* (1972), and *Ballads of Underdevelopment* (1976). Essay collections include *The Last Word* (1969) and *Thirteen Offensives Against Our Enemies* (1973), which also contains poems. *Meditations in Limbo* (1970) and *Meditations of Taban Lo Liyong* (1978) are autobiographical works in similar essayistic vein.

Liza of Lambeth, see MAUGHAM, W. SOMERSET.

LLEWELLYN, Richard (1907–83), Welsh novelist and dramatist, born in St David's, educated in Cardiff and London. During the 1930s he worked in the film industry, but a slump forced him to turn to drama, resulting in the popular psychological thriller *Poison Pen* (1937). After war service he lived abroad, mainly in North America and Argentina. His first novel, *How Green Was My Valley* (1939), was a bestseller which charted the rise of the ambitious Huw Morgan in a Welsh mining community and is renowned for its lyrical evocation of family life in the Welsh valleys. It was made into a Hollywood film. Its sequels are *Up, Into the Singing Mountain* (1960), *Down Where the Moon is Small* (1966), and *Green, Green My Valley Now* (1975). His novels about Cockney low life in the London slums, *None But the Lonely Heart* (1943) and *A Few Flowers for Shiner* (1950), were less successful. Among other works he wrote spy novels, and *A Night of Bright Stars* (1979), a novel set in *fin de siècle* Paris.

LOCHHEAD, Liz (1947–), Scottish poet and dramatist, born in Motherwell, Lanarkshire, educated at

Glasgow School of Art. Her first two collections of verse, *Memo for Spring* (1972) and *The Grimm Sisters* (1981), established her as a poet whose refreshing humour and directness were combined with a shrewdly understated technical accomplishment. Her subsequent volumes, in which an increasingly feminist perspective is evident, are *Dreaming Frankenstein, and Collected Poems* (1984), *True Confessions and New Clichés* (1985), and *Bagpipe Muzak* (1991). Much of her poetry, of which she is a noted performer, makes especially vigorous use of the speech idioms of the Glasgow area. The recurrence of dramatic modes in her verse links it with her work as a playwright, which began with her treatment of Mary Shelley in *Blood and Ice* (1982). Her numerous other plays include *Silver Service* (1984) and *Mary Queen of Scots Got Her Head Chopped Off*, an exuberant and provocative exploration of history and the female psyche, which was published with her version of *Dracula* in 1989; her translation into Scots of Molière's *Tartuffe* (1985) was widely acclaimed.

LOCKE, Alain (LeRoy) (1886–1954), American philosopher and cultural critic, born in Philadelphia, educated at the Philadelphia School of Pedagogy, Oxford University, the University of Berlin, and Harvard. Among other academic appointments, he was Professor of Philosophy at Howard University. Throughout his teaching and writing career he promoted African-American culture and the arts, most notably as editor of an anthology of writing by Langston *Hughes and other contributors associated with the *Harlem Renaissance, *The *New Negro: An Interpretation* (1925). His many other books include *A Decade of Negro Self-Expression* (1928), *The Negro in America* (1953), and *The Negro in Art* (1940).

LOCKLIN, Gerald (Ivan) (1941–), American poet, short-story and novella writer, born in Rochester, New York, educated at the University of Arizona. In 1965 he took up an academic post at California State University, Long Beach, where he became a Professor of English. Among the best-known of his early works are *The Toad Poems* (1970), *Poop and Other Poems* (1972), and *The Criminal Mentality* (1976); with a characteristic anecdotal ease and playfulness, facetious literary and filmic references are blended into an unpretentious language. A substantial collection, *The Firebird Poems*, was published in 1992. Like his friend and mentor Charles *Bukowski, Locklin offers candid reports on relations between the sexes, usually (though not always) deflating chauvinism by self-deprecating humour. He adopts a casual, discursive manner in ranging over West Coast mores and urban perils; sex, fatherhood, and domestic skirmishes; teaching, drinking, and the pursuit of all the essential human appetites. Notable among other works are *The Case of the Missing Blue Volkswagen* (1984), a spoof detective genre novella, and *The Gold Rush* (1989), a substantial collection of stories. The prolificness of his verse and prose, frequent live readings, and above all his encouragement of younger talents, have made him a central figure in the vitality of Los Angeles writing through the 1980s.

LODGE, David (1935–), British novelist and critic, born in London, educated at University College, London, and the University of Birmingham where, from 1976 to 1987, he was Professor of Modern English Literature. He is best known for his alert and funny *campus novels, *Changing Places* (1975), *Small World* (1984), and *Nice Work* (1989), in which English and American academics encounter the well-observed follies of each other's professional and cultural climates. Lodge's other novels include *The Picturegoers* (1960), *Ginger, You're Barmy* (1962), *The British Museum Is Falling Down* (1965), *Out of the Shelter* (1970), *How Far Can You Go?* (1980), and *Paradise News* (1991); their themes, as Lodge says, include 'lower middle-class life in the inner suburbs of South East London; a wartime childhood and a post-war "austerity" adolescence; Catholicism; education and the social and physical mobility it brings; military service, marriage, travel etc.' *Therapy* (1995), whose hero, Tubby Passmore, is a successful writer of television 'sit-coms' suffering from a mid-life crisis, recapitulates many of the author's prevailing concerns with Catholicism, with sexual guilt, with academic jargon, and (increasingly) with the horrors of middle age. Tubby's quest for a solution to the 'angst' with which he finds himself afflicted leads, unsurprisingly, to an encounter with the works of Søren Kierkegaard—a comic juxtapositioning of incongruities which is typical of Lodge's witty and irreverent fiction. Lodge is also a critic interested in contemporary theoretical developments; in *The Language of Fiction* (1966) and *The Modes of Modern Writing* (1977), for example, he incorporates his readings of stylistics and linguistics into a determinedly pragmatic literary approach. *Working with Structuralism* (1981) and *After Bakhtin* (1990) are informed and open-ended responses to bodies of thought and practice many Anglo-American critics have found intractable, and Lodge's two influential anthologies, *Twentieth Century Literary Criticism* (1972) and *Modern Criticism and Theory* (1988), are lucid and well-balanced guides to difficult and often mystified territories.

LOGUE, Christopher (1926–), British poet and playwright, born in Portsmouth, educated at Portsmouth Grammar School. His early collections of poetry include *Wand and Quartet* (1953), which indicates the accomplishment in traditional lyric forms underlying less orthodox subsequent work. During the later 1950s, he was among the leading performers of poetry to jazz accompaniments (see JAZZ POETRY) and was closely involved with the *English Stage Company. His dramatic works include the Brechtian musical *The Lily White Boys* (1960, with H. Cookson) and the plays collected in *Trials by Logue* in 1960. *Songs* (1959) was highly regarded and established the emphatically socio-political and satirical character of his verse; later volumes include *New Numbers* (1969), *Abecedary* (1977), and *Ode to the Dodo: Poems from 1953–1978* (1981).

Logue's most concentrated achievement is generally considered to be *War Music* (1981), his versions of Books XVI to XIX of the *Iliad*, in which historical and modern conflicts are conflated to project an imaginative condemnation of warfare; he continued the project with *Kings* (1990), his adaptations of Books I and II, and *The Husbands: An Account of Books III and IV of Homer's Iliad* (1994). See also UNDERGROUND POETRY.

Lolita, a novel by Vladimir *Nabokov, published in 1955. Fear of the possibility of prosecution for obscenity made both American and British publishers unwilling to accept the novel and it was first published in Paris by the Olympia Press; American publication followed in 1958 and British in 1959. The subject of the novel is the passion of the narrator, Humbert Humbert, for a 12-year-old girl, Lolita, the daughter of his second wife, Charlotte, a widow. She, fortuitously, is killed in a road accident after only a few weeks of marriage to Humbert (he had intended to kill her himself) and the now orphaned Lolita falls into his care. The sexual adventures of Humbert and Lolita are presented in minute detail but the novel is never obscene or pornographic, in large part because much of the eroticism is comic, but also because Nabokov's preoccupation with the transforming power of art and the expressive properties of language enable him to invest the nympholepsy which is at the centre of the novel with a rapturousness that is rare in modern fiction. *Lolita* has been much discussed and is seen, variously, as Nabokov's supreme realization of American suburban life, his most eloquent rejection of the limitations of social realism, and the most verbally playful of his 'American' novels. Its virtues, however, are considerably easier to enumerate: *Lolita* tells a fascinating story, is beautifully written, and offers much penetrating psychological characterization. Alfred Appel's *The Annotated Lolita* (1971) attempts to explicate many of the 'problems' of the text.

Lolly Willows, see WARNER, SYLVIA TOWNSEND.

LOMAS, Herbert (1924–), British poet, born in Todmorden, West Yorkshire, educated at Liverpool University. He has held lectureships at the Universities of Helsinki and London. His collections of poetry include *Chimpanzees Are Blameless Creatures* (1969), *Public Footpath* (1981), which attracted wide notice, *Fire in the Garden* (1984), and *Letters in the Dark* (1986). His disciplined free verse often generates unusual rhythms in its shifts between hesitancy and fluency, an effect consistent with the understated but insistent tone of much of his poetry. He is also accomplished in the use of traditional verse forms, which form the basis of *Letters in the Dark*, an ambitious and often challenging religious meditation whose fifty-two poems range between acutely personal commentary and philosophical speculation. Among his other publications is a work on social and economic factors entitled *Who Needs Money?* (1972). His highly regarded works as a translator include the anthology *Contemporary Finnish Poetry* (1992).

LONDON, Jack (John Griffith) (1876–1916), American novelist, essayist, and social activist; he was born in San Francisco and led an irregular childhood living on the waterfront. After leaving school at 14, he continued this way of life and eventually sailed for Japan and the Arctic aboard a sealer, before returning to America where he also travelled extensively. In 1894 he joined Kelly's Industrial Army, which was to join forces with Coxey's Army, to form a massive crusade across America against unemployment and poverty before arriving in Washington DC; this event drew together his developing interests in both writing and socialism. He studied briefly in Oakland High School and for a semester in the University of California before heading for the Klondike in March 1897. He failed as a prospector and became ill, but wrote of his experiences for periodicals and in *The Son of the Wolf* (1900), a collection of stories. He used similar material for his famous dog stories, *The *Call of the Wild* (1903), in which a dog escapes civilization to lead a wolf pack, and its counterpart, *White Fang* (1906), in which a wild dog is domesticated, and for his celebrated short story 'To Build a Fire', published in the volume *Lost Face* (1910), where a man endures the seeming cruelties of the natural environment. He was influenced by his reading of Darwin and Marx, and became a committed socialist, writing *People of the Abyss* (1903), based on his first-hand experience of British slum-dwellers 'dying miserably at the bottom of the social pit called London', and *The *Iron Heel* (1908), a futuristic work predicting a fascist dictatorship which would later give way to a socialist paradise. However, London also applied the writings of Herbert Spencer and Frederick Nietzsche to his faith in the primordial power of individualism, and much of his writing tends towards fantasies of a superman or woman especially fitted to survive and adapt. This tension between collectivism and Social Darwinism is reflected in novels like *The *Sea-Wolf* (1904), about a ruthless captain of a sealing ship; *The Game* (1905), the tale of a boxer; *Before Adam* (1906), the story of a primordial human society; and **Martin Eden* (1909), an autobiographical novel about the development of a writer. Later works include *The Valley of the Moon* (1912), expressing outright admiration for the Aryan race; *Smoke Bellew* (1912), stories about a journalist in the Yukon; and *John Barleycorn* (1913), which was subtitled 'Alcoholic Memoirs', and drew largely on London's own drink problem which began when he was 15. The contradictory influences of Marx and Nietzsche are well illustrated in two posthumously published works: *The Human Drift* (1917), a socialist treatise, and *Jerry of the Islands* (1917), a fantasy of an Irish setter pup in the South Sea Islands.

London Fields, see AMIS, MARTIN.

London Magazine, The, a periodical founded in 1954 by John *Lehmann as a monthly journal of poetry, prose fiction, and criticism. During its early years contributors included Graham *Greene, V. S. *Pritchett, Edwin *Muir, Robert *Graves, William *Plomer, and Louis *MacNeice. Lehmann also regularly published work by European writers. From the mid-1950s onward poets associated with the *Movement were much in evidence. In 1961 the editorship passed to Alan *Ross, under whom the *London Magazine* has been noted for the breadth of its coverage of the arts in general. London Magazine Editions was established as the magazine's book imprint in 1965. Ross's catholic editorial policy has resulted in the appearance of writing by young or comparatively unknown authors alongside work from well-known contributors. Douglas *Dunn, Jonathan *Raban, Hugo *Williams, who was for a time Ross's assistant editor, Peter *Redgrove, and Selima *Hill are among those whose work has been featured from the earliest stages of their careers.

London Mercury, The, a monthly publication begun in 1919 by J. C. *Squire, whose policy of presenting accessible *belles-lettres* in an attractively produced magazine made it remarkably popular throughout much of the 1920s. Poetry, essays, and fiction were supplied Robert *Frost, Thomas *Hardy, W. B. *Yeats, Edmund *Gosse, G. K. *Chesterton, Virginia *Woolf, and Katherine *Mansfield. Squire's editorial stance was characterized by his disparagement of *Modernism, which he regarded as an 'orgy of undirected abnormality'; his conservative preferences made the magazine a forum for those associated with **Georgian Poetry*. Following a period of decline, the editorship passed to R. A. Scott-James in 1934; an immediate shift leftwards in the *Mercury*'s political position was accompanied by the publication of more progressive writing by authors who included W. H. *Auden, C. *Day Lewis, Mervyn *Peake, Christopher *Fry, and Frank *O'Connor. After absorbing the *Bookman* in 1935, the *Mercury* was incorporated into **Life and Letters* in 1939.

London Review of Books, The, a fortnightly literary periodical which began appearing as part of the **New York Review of Books* in October 1979, when the **Times Literary Supplement* had temporarily ceased publication. In May 1980 it became an independent publication. Karl *Miller was founding editor and continued to edit the journal until 1992. The editorial advisory board includes Ian *Hamilton, Frank *Kermode, and V. S. *Pritchett, each of whom has been a frequent contributor. The high standards of its reviews have firmly established it among the principal literary and intellectual journals of its time. Karl Miller described the *LRB*, as it is generally known, as 'not the sort of literary journal which prefers to be silent about public matters', seeing it as a 'paper of the democratic Left'. George *Steiner, Christopher *Ricks, Angela *Carter, and A. J. P. *Taylor have been among the most eminent of its regular contributors. Notable poets whose work has been featured include Craig *Raine, Ted *Hughes, Seamus *Heaney, Tony *Harrison, and Derek *Walcott.

Loneliness of the Long Distance Runner, The, a collection of thematically linked stories by Alan *Sillitoe, published in 1959. The highly praised title story tells of a boy in Borstal who, when chosen to run a race, uses it to subvert the control of the authorities whose power he resents. Told in the first person in the authentic vernacular voice of a working-class youth, the story sets the pace for the rest of the collection, which is a realistic record of the minds and lives of the English working class, and pays tribute to the restless, rebellious, and resilient spirits it occasionally produces.

Lonely Passion of Judith Hearne, The, see MOORE, BRIAN.

Long Day's Journey into Night, a play by Eugene *O'Neill, produced and published posthumously in 1956, but written in 1940–1. The play takes place in the New England household of a retired actor, James Tyrone. His attractive wife, Mary, has recently been released from a home to cure her drug addiction. The day seems to begin cheerfully enough, with Tyrone and Mary teasing one another and their sons Jamie, aged 35, and Edmund, aged 25, laughing over the table, but in fact it is apparent at the outset that the banter masks deep tensions, which gradually emerge as the day progresses. Tyrone, a rich man who possibly could have been a great actor, is the victim of his own close-fistedness, attributable to a hard childhood in Ireland. He has made others suffer for it, though he is, in many respects, a wastrel, while Edmund has ruined his health in nervous dissipation, partly to emulate his loved older brother, partly to overcome the difficulties of home. Edmund learns that he has tuberculosis, and this releases pent-up feelings and sadness. Mary becomes nostalgic about past dreams of success but it also becomes apparent that her addiction began when a quack doctor, chosen by her mean husband, treated her with morphine following the birth of Edmund. Jamie drunkenly reveals his love for Edmund, and hate for his being responsible for their mother's drug addiction; Mary appears lost to the world dragging her wedding gown and dreaming of a brighter past. The play is the most autobiographical of O'Neill's works, drawing directly from his own family life as a young man and described by him as a 'play of old sorrow, written in tears and blood'.

Longest Journey, The, a novel by E. M. *Forster, published in 1907. Its central character, Rickie Elliot, is a young man handicapped in his dealings with others as much by his sensitivity and intelligence as by the fact that he is lame; he is first seen at Cambridge, where his circle of friends include the philosopher, Ansell. He is befriended by Herbert and Agnes Pembroke, a brother and sister: Herbert runs a school; Agnes is engaged to Gerald Dawes, whom Rickie recognizes as the bully who had terrorized him during their school days. When Gerald is killed during a football match, Rickie comforts Agnes; he falls in love with her and proposes marriage, despite Ansell's attempts to discourage him. He takes Agnes to visit his aunt, Emily Failing, at Cadover, her Wiltshire estate, where he encounters Stephen Wonham, her somewhat uncouth but good-natured protégé. There, Rickie learns that Stephen is in fact his half-brother—a circumstance which has been kept from Stephen himself. The scene shifts to Sawston School, where Rickie, having relinquished his earlier hopes of becoming a writer, works as a schoolmaster. He is bitterly unhappy in his new life and his marriage has proved a disappointment: Agnes is revealed as shallow and commonplace, and their child is born with a club foot and later dies. Stephen Wonham arrives at Sawston, intending to confront him with the knowledge that he and Rickie are brothers. Agnes, supposing that he intends to blackmail her husband, offers him money to leave Rickie in peace; horrified at this suggestion, Stephen disappears. It emerges that he has fallen out of favour with his aunt, partly as a result of Agnes's spiteful interference, and that he is the son not of Rickie's hated father, but of his adored mother. Attempting to bring about a reconciliation, Rickie eventually finds his brother in Wiltshire; when he tries to save Stephen, who has fallen asleep in a drunken stupor on the railway line, Rickie is injured and dies a few days later. A postscript to the story informs the reader that Rickie's stories have now found a publisher, and that he has achieved, posthumously, the success which evaded him during his lifetime. The novel, whose title is an allusion to Shelley's *Epipsychidion*, was Forster's own favourite amongst his works and contains, particularly in its portrayal of its central character and in its affectionate depiction of Cambridge life, an autobiographical element found to the same degree only in some of his short fiction and in his novel **Maurice* (1971).

LONGFORD, Elizabeth (Pakenham, Countess of Longford) (1906–), British historian and biographer, born in London, educated at Lady Margaret Hall, Oxford. During the 1930s she worked as a tutor with the Workers' Educational Association and served on the Paddington and St Pancras Rent Tribunal from 1947 to 1954. As a journalist she produced material for the *Daily Express* and *The Sunday Times* between 1953 and 1962. She emerged as a respected historian with her controversial study *Jameson's Raid* (1960) and, having gained access to the Royal Archives at Windsor, published the compendious *Victoria R.I.* in 1964. Her numerous subsequent works include *Years of the Sword* (1969) and *Pillar of State* (1972), the two parts of her life of Wellington; *The Life of Byron* (1976); *A Pilgrimage of Passion* (1979), her biography of Wilfred Scawen *Blunt; and *Elizabeth R.* (1983). She is the editor of *The Oxford Book of Royal Anecdotes* (1989). *The Pebbled Shore*, her autobiography, appeared in 1986.

LONGLEY, Michael (1939–), Northern Irish poet, born in Belfast, educated at Trinity College, Dublin. He became Director for Literature and the Traditional Arts with the Arts Council of Northern Ireland in 1970. His first publication of note was *Ten Poems* (1965), which appeared during the Belfast Festival of 1965 with pamphlets by Seamus *Heaney and Derek *Mahon, marking the emergence of *Ulster poetry. His collections of verse include *No Continuing City* (1969), *An Exploded View* (1973), *Man Lying on a Wall* (1976), *The Echo Gate* (1979), *Poems 1963–1983* (1985), *Gorse Fires* (1991), and *Ghost Orchid* (1995). Longley's work displays a high degree of technical assurance in a wide variety of forms. His thematic range extends from harrowingly direct responses to sectarian strife in Northern Ireland to richly detailed treatments of remote natural environments, often in the far west of Ireland. His many poems on birds and animals achieve an emblematic power through their poise and clarity of description. A phantasmagorically imaginative quality is apparent in a number of his most memorable poems, which include the serenely disquieting view beyond death of 'Obsequies'. Among the books Longley has edited are Louis *MacNeice's *Selected Poems* (1988).

LONSDALE, Frederick (1881–1954), British dramatist, born Lionel Frederick Leonard in Jersey. The son of a seaman, he was himself a page-boy on a transatlantic liner and a sailor before enlisting in the army for five years. He became the leading exponent of drawing-room comedy in the 1920s, known for his urbanity and sophisticated cynicism, his nonchalant dialogue, and his neatly constructed plots. Among his successes were *Aren't We All?* (1923), in which a young wife waxes indignant about her husband's *amour*, only to be deflated by the revelation that she has flirted with the same temptation; *The Last of Mrs Cheyney* (1925), about a jewel thief masquerading as a society lady; the witty picture of trial marriage, *On Approval* (1927); and *Canaries Sometimes Sing* (1929), about two ill-suited couples who unsuccessfully swap partners. Before turning to the legitimate theatre, he wrote the librettos for several musical plays, among them *The Balkan Princess* (1910) and *The Maid of the Mountains* (1917).

Look, Stranger!, a collection of verse by W. H. *Auden, published in 1936. It contains a number of his best-known poems, including those later given the titles 'On This Island', 'Our Hunting Fathers', and 'A Bride in the 30's'. His social and political preoccupations of the earlier 1930s remain apparent, most obviously in 'Brothers, who when the sirens roar . . .'; the references to communism which were contained in earlier versions of that poem were, however, deleted for its appearance in *Look, Stranger!* Such textual changes, and the non-inclusion of other explicitly political material that was available to him, indicate the withdrawal from a doctrinaire ideological position that is a characteristic of Auden's development at the time. The concern with spiritual values that dominates his thinking from 1938 onwards becomes discernible in the collection, particularly in 'A Summer Night' and 'Paysage Moralisé'. The volume is also memorable for the imaginative panoramas of landscape and history which open up in the contemplative poems 'Prologue' ('O Love, the interest itself in thoughtless Heaven . . .') and 'Here on the cropped grass of the narrow ridge I stand . . .'; these pieces typify the rather self-consciously vatic manner exhibited in parts of *Look, Stranger!* Auden was unhappy with the book's title, chosen by his publisher while he was in Iceland, and remarked that it sounded 'like the work of a vegetarian lady novelist'; the American edition of 1937 was entitled *On This Island*.

Look Back in Anger, a play by John *Osborne, produced in 1956, published in 1957. The plot concerns Jimmy and Alison Porter, he of working-class origins, she from an upper-middle-class background, who share a room as uncomfortable as their marriage is turbulent. The arrival of Alison's old friend Helena enrages Jimmy and, after he has left to attend the deathbed of the mother of one of his own friends, she allows her father, a retired colonel, to take her back to the parental home. There she loses the child she was expecting, while Jimmy launches into an unexpected affair with Helena. This ends with Alison's return and a tentative resumption of the marriage. The play has a plot in many respects conventional, but it was nevertheless felt to mark a significant break with the drama fashionable in the 1950s. That was partly because of its drably realistic setting but mainly because of the forceful impression made by Jimmy, an anti-hero from an unprivileged background given to blistering denunciations of the social status quo. He became known as the archetypal '*Angry Young Man' and the play itself an important contribution to *kitchen sink drama.

Look Homeward, Angel, a novel by Thomas *Wolfe, published in 1929. Subtitled 'A Story of the Buried Life', it is the first of a series of novels about the Gant family. In this youthful semi-autobiographical work Wolfe appears as Eugene Gant, an artist growing up in Altamont, a small Southern town in the state of Old Catawba. He is caught in the cross-currents of his parents' stormy relationship, between his mother's practicality and his father's romantic passion. The novel charts his education from school, where he is persecuted for being a loner, to university where, after an awkward start, he develops into a major figure on the campus. It tells of his encounters with a prostitute, events on the campus, an unhappy love affair, concluding with the death of his brother as he decides to leave the town behind. The novel deals with the revolt of the individual from the constrictions of the provincial American small town South, in the same vein as novels by Sherwood *Anderson and Sinclair *Lewis. In a style marked by topographical detail and imagery, this romantic and often satiric portrait reveals Wolfe's stylistic debts to the modernist influences of *Joyce, *Dreiser, and other contemporaries.

Loot, a play by Joe *Orton, first performed in 1965. It takes what its author called 'a farcical view of things normally treated as tragic', prime among them death and bereavement. Mrs McLeavy's coffin is used by her son Hal and his lover Dennis to hide the money they have stolen from the local bank. The body itself is planted upside down in a cupboard, then taken out, stripped, and disguised as a sewing dummy, in an effort to outwit the detective on the case, Truscott. A traffic accident on the way to the funeral brings the loot back to the house, where it is transferred to the casket that held Mrs McLeavy's viscera, which have exploded. Truscott discovers it there, only to agree to divide it with Hal, Dennis, and Fay, the mass-murdering nurse whose latest victim turns out to have been Mrs McLeavy. The only conventional character in the piece, the widower McLeavy, is dispatched to jail, where he too will be quietly killed. The play is notable for its witty and often scurrilous exposure of the greed and callousness that Orton thought was concealed by moral and religious pretension.

LORDE, Audre (1934–92), African-American feminist poet and essayist, born in Harlem of West Indian parentage, educated at Hunter College, Columbia University School of Library Science, and the University of Mexico. *The First Cities* (1968) was her first volume of poetry; other volumes include *Cables to Rage* (1970), *From a Land where Other People Live* (1973), *New York Head Shop and Museum* (1975), *Between Ourselves* (1976), *Coal* (1976), *The Black Unicorn* (1978), *Chosen Poems—Old and New* (1982), and *Our Dead Behind Us* (1987). She was outspoken on matters personal and political—racism, sexism, and sexual identity—in her works of non-fiction, autobiography, and what she called 'biomythography' (fiction combining elements of biography and history of myth), which include *Uses of the Erotic: The Erotic as Power* (1978), *The Cancer Journals* (1980), a powerful pamphlet based on a diary kept during her battle with breast cancer, and *Zami: A New Spelling of My Name* (1982). Her essays are collected in *Sister Outsider* (1984) and *A Burst of Light* (1988).

Lord Jim, a novel by Joseph *Conrad, published in 1900, serialized in *Blackwood's Edinburgh Magazine* (1898–1900). Probably Conrad's most popular and accessible work, the novel concerns a young Englishman who decides on a career at sea 'after a course of light holiday literature'. However, the sea does not live up to his romantic expectations. The crisis comes when the *Patna*, with its 800 passengers, collides at sea, while Jim, the chief mate and officer on watch, had been day-dreaming about heroic adventures. Not only does Jim fail to live up to his own romantic self-image, he fails in his duty as an officer. In the second half of the novel he is given another chance and, in the romantic world of Patusan, he is allowed to realize his romantic expectations until the arrival of the piratical Gentleman Brown confronts him with a second crisis. Apart from its engagement with Conradian concerns of isolation, identity, betrayal, solidarity, and moral tests, the novel also marked a development in Conrad's narrative method both in its handling of narration and in its use of time-shift. After four chapters recounted by an omniscient narrator, the English sea-captain Marlow takes over the narration. Introduced at the 'official inquiry' into the incident in Bombay, Marlow then conducts his own investigations. He interrogates a succession of witnesses who act as moral touchstones and interpreters of Jim: the impeccable Captain Brierly; the honourable French lieutenant; the disreputable Chester; and finally the romantic Stein, who suggests sending Jim to Patusan. Before Marlow is introduced, however, Conrad effects one of his most significant time-shifts, when he jumps a month from the moment of collision to the time of the Inquiry (and thus conceals from the reader the events that followed immediately after the collision).

Lord of the Files, a novel by W. *Golding, published in 1954. A party of schoolboys are the only survivors of an aeroplane crash during a nuclear war. Stranded on a desert island, they attempt to recreate the structures of democracy from which they came, but by the end of the book have descended to savagery. By the time Golding introduces his *deus ex machina*, two of the boys have been killed. Golding makes the island story a parable of events in the larger world, and places it in a religious perspective: Ralph and Simon both demonstrate Christ-like attributes, and the social catastrophe is explicitly blamed upon mankind's incapacity to control its own human nature. The moral argument of the book, however, is more complex than merely a discourse on Original Sin, and many questions—such as whether the 'civilized' world to which the boys will return is morally any better than the island society of the boys—are deliberately left unresolved. On several levels, *Lord of the Flies* rejects the optimism of R. M. Ballantyne's *The Coral Island* (1858), from which Golding borrows several names and themes.

Lord of the Rings, The, see TOLKIEN, J. R. R.

Lost Father, The, see WARNER, MARINA.

Lost Generation, The, the term for the American and British writers who chose to live in Europe, chiefly in Paris, during the 1920s. The designation was supplied by Gertrude *Stein; her remark that 'You are all a lost generation' was used by Ernest *Hemingway, a leading member of the group, to preface *The *Sun also Rises* (1926), which forms a vivid fictionalized account of the milieu and attitudes of the literary expatriates thus described. Hemingway's *A Moveable Feast* (1964) consists of a series of factual reminiscences of his associates in Paris, among them F. Scott *Fitzgerald, Ezra *Pound, Ford Madox *Ford, and James *Joyce; other notable members of the Lost Generation include Malcolm *Cowley, Robert *McAlmon, Archibald *MacLeish, John Dos *Passos, E. E. *Cummings, and Hart *Crane. *Being Geniuses Together* (1938) contains McAlmon's impressions of the period. Cowley's *Exile's Return* (1934, revised edition 1951) examines the psychology of the young American authors who migrated to Europe from 1920 onward; their dissent, he concludes, was personal and aesthetic rather than political in motivation, but was none the less indicative of a thoroughgoing dissatisfaction with the socio-economic and cultural climate of the USA after the First World War. The deep disillusionment with which Pound left Britain in 1920 is expressed in *Hugh Selwyn Mauberley* (1920). *Broom* (1921–4), *Secession* (1922–4), **transition*, the **Transatlantic Review*, and, in its later years, the **Little Review* are the principal magazines associated with the writers of the Lost Generation, most of whom had returned to their countries of origin or gone elsewhere by 1930.

Lost Lady, A, a novel by Willa *Cather, published in 1923. The first of her highly wrought symbolic novels, which are nevertheless rooted in closely observed life, it tells the story of beautiful Marion Forrester from the point of view of the gentle Niel Herbert, whose adoration of her makes it hard for him to accept the truth, which is that she leads a double life. This refined beauty, who illuminates the house of her husband, the Captain, and entertains his fellow members of the Nebraska Railroad aristocracy, is also promiscuous, with a taste for alcohol and a compulsive attraction towards low company. After the Captain's death she takes up with Ivy Peters, a coarse-grained braggart who, as is made apparent early in the book, is capable of wanton cruelty. Marion Forrester's eventual destiny is, however, more mysterious than this scenario suggests: it is implied that she comes to know a modest salvation. Her decline and fall symbolizes both the fate of the West, which has been opened up and exploited, and the way of life which characterized its communities, at once attractive and doomed, self-confident and weak.

LOVECRAFT, H(oward) P(hillips) (1890–1937), American writer of horror stories, born in Providence, Rhode Island. The best of his stories promulgated a malign universe with its roots aeons deep in the Chaos prefiguring human occupancy of the planet; these stories of the Chthulhu Mythos, the best of which were collected in *The Outsider and Others* (1939), articulated his psychic distress in unforgettable terms. Lovecraft's was the distress of the fragile schizoid personality for whom the world externally threatens engulfment. The powerful effect of his work, despite its stylistic limitations, has influenced many subsequent authors who have written stories within the Chthulhu precepts. His complete short stories can be found in *The Dunwich Horror* (1963), *At the Mountains of Madness* (1964), and *Dagon and Other Macabre Tales* (1965). His one novel, *The Lurker at the Threshold* (1945), was less impressive.

Love in a Cold Climate, see MITFORD, NANCY.

LOVELACE, Earl (1935–), West Indian novelist and playwright, born in Trinidad, where he studied agriculture. His first novel, *While Gods Are Falling* (1965), shows acute awareness of the economic deprivation and cultural fragmentation caused by colonialism in Trinidad. *The Schoolmaster* (1968), set in a remote Trinidadian village, considers the same subject through a story of suspense, violation, disintegration, and reintegration. His third novel, *The Dragon Can't Dance* (1979), is again concerned with colonial damage and efforts at rehabilitation; it was adapted as a play by the author and performed in London in 1990. *The Wine of Astonishment* (1982) confirmed Lovelace's skill for creating plots with vigorous action, much suspense, and a rather melodramatic denouement. Altogether Lovelace's fiction is notable for its persistent commentary on the poverty, disorganization, and inertia caused by colonialism. All four novels also demonstrate the need for stable communities, and focus on psychological rehabilitation or the quest for selfhood, asserting values that have been discredited by colonial history. *Jestina's Calypso and Other Plays* (1984) collects Lovelace's work for the theatre. He is also the author of *A Brief Conversation and Other Stories* (1988). Apart from brief travels in the USA and England, Lovelace has always lived in Trinidad.

Love on the Dole, see GREENWOOD, WALTER.

'Love Song of J. Alfred Prufrock, The', see PRUFROCK AND OTHER OBSERVATIONS.

LOWELL, Amy (Lawrence) (1874–1925), American poet and critic, born in Brookline, Massachusetts, of the influential New England family to which Robert *Lowell also belonged; she was educated at private schools in Boston. She engaged in travel and voluntary work from the age of 16 until 1902, when she acquired the intense interest in poetry which thereafter dominated her life. Following the appearance of her first collection of conventionally accomplished lyric verses, *A Dome of Many-Coloured Glass* (1912), she met Ezra *Pound during a visit to England and became actively associated with the development of *Imagism. Her poetry rapidly took on the movement's identifying attributes of free-verse forms and visually precise imagery and was represented in Pound's edition of *Des Imagistes* (1914), the anthology that brought the school to public attention. Lowell edited three subsequent volumes entitled *Some Imagist Poets* (1915, 1916, 1917), emerging as the doyenne of what Pound termed 'Amy-gism', an enervated version, he claimed, of the mode he had formerly championed. The Imagist tendency having been firmly established in her collection *Sword Blades and Poppy Seed* (1914), the experimental impulse was sustained in *Men, Women, and Ghosts* (1916), in which she first used 'polyphonic prose', a rhythmically and musically enriched prose style she claimed to have learned from the French poet Paul Fort. *Can Grande's Castle* (1918) consisted of four narratives written entirely in polyphonic prose, which lent itself well to Lowell's opulently exotic descriptive manner. The refined and delicate imagery of *Pictures of the Floating World* (1919), which resulted in part from her attention to Chinese and Japanese poetry, constitutes her finest lyrical work; *Fir-Flower Tablets* of 1921 contained her translations of Chinese verse. Several posthumous collections included *What O'Clock* (1925; Pulitzer Prize). The *Complete Poetical Works* (1955) was edited by Louis Untermeyer. Lowell also published a valuable body of critical works, among which are *Six French Poets: Studies in Contemporary Literature* (1915) and *Tendencies in Modern American Poetry* (1917); her *A Critical Fable* (1922), which appeared anonymously, is a verse satire on the American literati of the day modelled on *A Fable for Critics* (1848) by James Russell Lowell, her distinguished forebear. Notable among her other works is the compendious biographical study *John Keats* (1925), in which she made use of materials hitherto neglected by commentators on Keats's life and works. Of numerous biographies of Lowell, S. Foster Damon's *Amy Lowell: A Chronicle* (1935) remains the most highly regarded.

LOWELL, Robert (Traill Spence) (1917–77), American poet, born in Boston of the distinguished New England family whose earlier generations include James Russell Lowell (1819–91) and Amy *Lowell. He entered Harvard University in 1935 but left during his second year, and spent several months near Nashville with Alan *Tate, whose stylistic example determined the strict formalism of Lowell's earlier verse. In 1938 he enrolled at Kenyon College, Gambier, Ohio, where he absorbed the influence of John Crowe *Ransom and the *New Criticism and became a Roman Catholic; these developments are reflected in the complex textures and religious preoccupations of *Land of Unlikeness* (1944) and *Lord Weary's Castle* (1946), his first two volumes of poetry. After further study at Louisiana State University, Lowell joined a publishing company in New York and was imprisoned in 1943 as a conscientious objector to military service. His subsequent career was dominated by his activities as a poet, in addition to which he intermittently taught at various American and British universities. *Poems, 1938–1949* (1950) demonstrated the accomplishment and passionate sincerity of his verse throughout the 1940s. *The Mills of the Kavanaughs* (1951) was less well received; its historical dramatic monologues lacked the urgency of the dialogue between faith and doubt through which Lowell had previously voiced his generation's sense of post-war disillusionment. From the mid-1950s onward he sought greater directness, modifying some of his poems to increase their accessibility, and achieving the more conversationally flexible idiom of *Life Studies* (1959). The book contained numerous candid treatments of Lowell's departure from Catholicism, marital problems, and mental instability, establishing the mode subsequently identified as *confessional poetry. *For the Union Dead* (1964) and *Near the Ocean* (1967) confirmed his stature through the authority and imagination with which many poems conflate his personal, historical, and socio-political concerns. During the late 1960s, when Lowell publicly opposed the Vietnam war (see VIETNAM WRITING), he produced the many metrically free fourteen-line poems published in *Notebook 1967–1968* (1968) and *History* (1973). His last two volumes, *The Dolphin* (1973), which made controversial use of letters relating to his disordered marriage, and *Day by Day* (1977), characterized by deeply elegiac retrospection, tended to amalgamate the various stylistic approaches he had evolved since the early 1950s. His habits of continually revising and reprinting poems from volume to volume have to date precluded the production of a collected edition of his poetry. *Collected Prose* (1987, edited by Robert Giroux) includes fragments of an unfinished autobiography in addition to a wide range of critical writings. Among Lowell's other works are *Imitations* (1961), his admired verse translations of classical and European poetry. Ian *Hamilton's biography of Lowell appeared in 1982.

LOWES, John Livingston (1867–1945), American scholar and critic, born in Decatur, Indiana, educated at the universities of Leipzig and Berlin, and at Harvard, where he was Professor of English from 1918 to 1930. Greatly admired as a teacher, Lowes lectured throughout the USA and was the first holder of the Eastman Visiting Professorship at Balliol College, Oxford, in 1930–1. Among his earlier works are editions of Shakespeare's *All's Well that Ends Well* (1912) and *Hamlet* (1914). *Convention and Revolt in Poetry* (1919), an authoritative survey of tensions between tradition and innovation in the development of English verse, extended his reputation, which was greatly enhanced by *The Road to Xanadu* (1927); this 'study in the ways of the imagination', widely regarded as one of the highest critical achievements of the twentieth century, establishes an enormous frame of reference in its charting of Coleridge's creative processes in the writing of 'Kubla Khan' and 'The Rime of the Ancient Mariner'. Lowes was also respected as a commentator on the poetry of Chaucer, his principal publications in this field being *The Art of Geoffrey Chaucer* (1931) and *Geoffrey Chaucer and the Development of His Genius* (1934). His collections of essays include *Of Reading Books* (1930) and *Essays in Appreciation* (1936). Among the other books Lowes edited is Amy *Lowell's *Selected Poems* (1928).

LOWRY, (Clarence) Malcolm (1909–57), English novelist, born in New Brighton, Cheshire, the son of a Liverpool cotton broker. After working as a deckhand on a tramp steamer he continued his education at St Catharine's College, Cambridge. These early experiences at sea led to his first novel, *Ultramarine* (1933); highly experimental in technique, with Conrad *Aiken and *Joyce as two of several models, this autobiographical work concerns a boy attempting to prove himself in the rough world of a freighter. Subsequently, Lowry led a nomadic life in Spain, Paris, New York, and Hollywood, until settling with his second wife, and later his literary executor, Margerie Bonner, among a community of squatters on Dollarton Beach, Vancouver, in 1940. His second novel, **Under the Volcano* (1947), which took many years to write and underwent many revisions, is a classic of twentieth-century fiction. Set in Mexico, during the 'day of the dead', the novel focuses on Geoffrey Firmin, an alcoholic former British consul who resembles Lowry himself. Lowry never completed his other major works, which were published posthumously. Also set in Mexico, **Dark as the Grave wherein My Friend Is Laid* (1968), edited by Douglas Day and Margerie Lowry, is a thinly fictionalized account of Lowry's struggles in writing and publishing *Under the Volcano*. *Lunar Caustic* (1968), edited by Earle *Birney and Margerie Lowry, was based on the collapse of Lowry's first marriage, and consequent detention as an alcoholic patient. Margerie also edited *October Ferry to Gabriola* (1970), another unfinished novel. His collection of stories, *Hear Us, O Lord, from Heaven Thy Dwelling Place* (1961), contains 'The Forest Path to the Spring', set in British Columbia, which was intended as a sketch of the Paradiso to the Purgatorio of *Under the Volcano*. His attachment to British Columbia made many regard him as an honorary Canadian novelist; indeed, he was the posthumous recipient of the Governor-General's Award, Canada, in 1962. Sadly, he and his wife had left Canada in 1954 when they were evicted to make way for a public park. Other posthumous publications include *Selected Poems* (1962; edited by Earle Birney and Margerie Lowry) and *Selected Letters* (1965; edited by Harvey Breit and Margerie Lowry). Lowry died 'of misadventure' near Lewes in East Sussex. See Douglas Day, *Lowry: A Biography* (1973).

LOY, Mina (1882–1966), British/American poet, artist, and polemicist, born Mina Gertrude Lowy in London. She was an artist before she began to write and changed her surname to Loy in 1903. Loy published her first piece of *modernist writing, 'Aphorisms on *Futurism', in *Camera Work* journal (1914). Her plays and manifestos (including her important 'Feminist Manifesto') are significant for their formal experimentation and their dialogue with Futurism, a movement rarely associated with women. These, and her avant-garde poetry and drawings, were published in the experimental *little magazines. Her poetry was highly regarded by, among others, William Carlos *Williams and Loy's close friends Djuna *Barnes and Gertrude *Stein. The only collections of poetry to appear in her lifetime were *Lunar Baedeker* (1923) and *Lunar Baedeker and Time-Tables* (1958). Of particular interest are her 'Love Songs'; her satires, which were greatly admired by Yvor *Winters; and her longest poem, the difficult 'Anglo-Mongrels and the Rose'. Her collected works appeared as *Last Lunar Baedeker*, edited by Roger L. Conover, in 1982.

LUBBOCK, Percy (1879–1965), British editor, biographer, and critic, born in London, educated at King's College, Cambridge. In 1906 he became librarian of the Pepys Library at Magadalene College, Cambridge, which supplied the materials for his biography of Samuel Pepys (1909). His editions of the *The Middle Years*, *The Sense of the Past*, and *The Ivory Tower*, the unfinished novels of his friend Henry *James, appeared in 1917. He also edited *The Letters of Henry James* (two volumes, 1920) and the thirty-five volumes of James's *Novels and Stories* (1921–3). James's precepts concerning the structural principles of the novel are central to Lubbock's *The Craft of Fiction* (1920), his most influential critical work. *Roman Pictures* (1923), a humorously fictionalized account of an Englishman's visit to Rome, is more successful than his only novel, *The Region Cloud* (1925), a diffuse treatment of the artistic sensibility. *Earlham* (1922) and *Shades of Eton* (1929) are autobiographies of his early life. His other works include *Elizabeth Barrett Browning in Her Letters* (1906), an edition of the *Diary* of A. C. Benson (1926), and *Portrait of Edith Wharton* (1947), the most notable of his biographies.

LUCAS, E(dward) V(errall) (1868–1938), British journalist, essayist, travel writer, and novelist, born in Eltham, Kent; he received an irregular education before starting work at a bookshop in Brighton where he began to read widely. After working as a journalist in Sussex and London, he joined the staff of *Punch*, of which he became assistant editor. *The Open Road* (1899) was followed by well over a hundred titles. His travel writings are principally represented by his *A Wanderer In* . . . series, which covered London (1904), Holland (1905), Paris (1909), Florence (1912), and other towns and countries in Britain and Europe. His light and urbanely fluent style, which he claimed to have developed by translating Maupassant, was adequate to essays on a remarkable range of subjects; collections of such pieces include *Listener's Lure* (1905), *Old Lamps for New* (1911), and *A Rover I Would Be* (1928). He also published introductory studies of painters, among which are *Vermeer of Delft* (1922) and *John Constable the Painter* (1924). *Over Bemerton's* (1908), the most notable of his numerous novels, draws on his experience of the book trade. He produced the standard edition of *The Works of Charles Lamb and Mary Lamb* (7 volumes, 1903–5) and wrote the authoritative *Life of Charles Lamb* (2 volumes, 1905). *Reading, Writing, and Remembering* (1932) is an autobiography.

LUCAS, F(rank) L(aurence) (1894–1967), British critic, novelist, and poet, born at Hipperholme in Yorkshire, educated at Trinity College, Cambridge. He was elected in 1920 to a fellowship at King's College, Cambridge, where he lectured until 1962. His early publications include *Seneca and Elizabethan Tragedy* (1922), *Euripides and His Influence* (1924), and his edition of *The Complete Works of John Webster* (4 volumes, 1927). From the mid-1920s onward he wrote prolifically across the wide range of his literary interests. Among his more notable works are *Authors Dead and Living* (1926), *Eight Victorian Poets* (1930), and *The Decline and Fall of the Romantic Ideal* (1936), which vividly reflects the intellectual history of the 1930s. As a critic he was hostile towards the new modes of criticism associated with **Scrutiny* and defended traditional notions of sound judgement in *The Search for Good Sense* (1955) and *The Art of Living* (1959). *Delights of Dictatorship* (1938) and *Journal under the Terror, 1938* (1938) are political commentaries written in response to the worsening international situation on the eve of the Second World War. Following the favourable reception of his semi-autobiographical novel *The River Flows* (1926), he produced a succession of historical fictions, which include *Cecile* (1930) and *Dr Dido* (1938). *Time and Memory* (1929), *Marionettes* (1930), and *Poems 1935* (1935) are his principal collections of verse; his poetry, which uses conventional forms, frequently displays a romantic extravagance of imagery and is sometimes sharply epigrammatic. Among his other works are a study of Ibsen and Strindberg (1962) and numerous translations from the Greek, which include a version of the *Iliad* (1950) and the anthology *Greek Poetry for Everyman* (1951).

LUCIE, Doug (1953–), British dramatist, born in Chessington, educated at Worcester College, Oxford. His first play, *John Clare's Mad Nuncle* (1975), was followed by subsequent works which have been widely admired for their sardonic portrayal of Britain in the 1980s, a place and period he sees as corrupt, acquisitive, and callous. Key plays include *Hard Feelings* (1982), about bright young Londoners not above harassing the Jewish lodger of the flat they share; *Progress* (1984), which primarily concerns the pretension of modern liberals, among them a consciousness-raising group of 'non-sexist' men; and *Fashion* (1987), about the world of advertising and, specifically, the cynical tycoon who hopes to remodel the image of the Conservative Party at the next election. With *Grace* (1993), however, the satiric attack switched to born-again religion as represented by an American 'televangelist' whose attempt to set up his European headquarters in an English mansion was, surprisingly for Lucie, seen as menacing a Britain which, though morally damaged by the 'Thatcher years', still embodied some traditional decencies. His more familiar cynicism reasserted itself in the melodramatic *Gaucho* (1994), about a decent man alienated enough by a malign British establishment to become a drugs smuggler, arms dealer, and international villain.

LUCIE-SMITH, (John) Edward (Mackenzie) (1933–), British poet and art historian, born in Kingston, Jamaica, educated at Merton College, Oxford. He was an advertising copywriter from 1956 to 1966, when he became a freelance writer. He was a prominent member of the *Group and, with Philip *Hobsbaum, co-edited *A Group Anthology* (1963). His principal collections of poetry are *A Tropical Childhood* (1961), *Confessions and Histories* (1964), *Towards Silence* (1968), and *The Well-Wisher* (1974). The conventional accomplishment of his earlier work was superseded by the growing imaginative range apparent in his use of dramatic monologue modes. His later work displays a leisured intensity appropriate to the meditatively erotic content of many poems. He is a prolific author of authoritative works on art history, among which are *Eroticism in Western Art* (1972), *Art Deco Painting* (1990), *Art and Civilization* (1992), *British Art Now* (1993), and *Elisabeth Frink* (1994). His numerous translations include highly regarded versions of Paul

Claudel's *Five Great Odes* (1967). Among his other works are *The Dark Pageant* (1977), a novel based on the life of Gilles de Rais, and an autobiography entitled *The Burnt Child* (1975). The many works he has edited include the popular *The Liverpool Scene* (1967) (see LIVERPOOL POETS), and *The Faber Book of Art Anecdotes* (1992).

Lucky Jim, a novel by Kingsley *Amis, published in 1954. Amis's first novel established him as one of the most anarchic and irreverent comic writers of his generation; like *Osborne's Jimmy Porter, his protagonist, Jim Dixon, epitomized the iconoclasm of the '*Angry Young Men'. The novel opens as Dixon, a young lecturer in medieval history much given to pulling faces and to practical jokes, is attempting to ingratiate himself with Professor Welch, the Head of the History Department at the provincial university where they both work, in order to improve his chances of gaining security of tenure. With this aim in mind, he accepts an invitation to one of Welch's cultural weekends, which proves to be a disaster. Dixon manages to offend just about everyone he meets, including Welch's obnoxious artist son, Bertrand, and his girlfriend, Christine Callaghan. Dixon is attracted to Christine, who appears to reciprocate his interest, but is prevented from establishing the relationship on a more intimate footing by his sense of obligation towards Margaret Peel, a fellow lecturer, whose previous involvement with a man ended in her attempted suicide. A closer understanding between Dixon and the attractive Christine is precipitated, however, by a series of comic events, culminating in the end-of-term lecture he gives to the assembled university whilst under the influence of a considerable amount of alcohol. He finds himself out of a job, but Fate—in the person of Christine's wealthy art historian uncle, Julius Gore-Urquhart—intervenes, and Dixon's problems with Margaret are resolved in time for a reconciliation with Christine, in the closing pages of the book.

Lupercal, a collection of poetry by Ted *Hughes, published in 1960. The volume maintained the confidence and energy which had distinguished his first book, *The Hawk in the Rain* (1957), but displayed greater stylistic control and fluency across an increased thematic range; Al *Alvarez's statement that 'Hughes has found his own voice . . . and has emerged as a poet of the first importance' is indicative of the highly favourable critical response to *Lupercal*, which established Hughes as the most noteworthy of the younger poets of the day. Conventional modes of rhyme and metre, which Hughes later tended to eschew, are adapted with great accomplishment in numerous poems, most notably in the 'Lupercalia' sequence with which the collection concludes; Hughes's imaginative concern with the sustaining power of the vital principle is expressed with concentration and eloquence in the poem's narrative of ancient Roman fertility rites. Elsewhere, the volume is rich in his more characteristic imagery of wild natural surroundings: 'November', 'Crow Hill', and 'Mayday on Holderness' are among the poems in which precise local detail takes on considerable emotional and metaphorical force. *Lupercal* also contained a number of memorable poems celebrating the instinct for survival embodied in certain creatures, 'the bullet and automatic | purpose' central to much of Hughes's writing; these include 'Pike', 'Thrushes', 'Hawk Roosting', 'Esther's Tomcat', 'The Bull Moses', and 'An Otter', each of which is among Hughes's best-known works.

LURIE, Alison (1926–), American writer, born in Chicago, educated at Radcliffe College. Lurie has chronicled contemporary North American life in her elegantly composed and witty novels. Like Malcolm *Bradbury and David *Lodge, Lurie shows great skill in relating the idiosyncrasies of university life and charting intellectual fashions. *Love and Friendship* (1962) concerns the rivalries within a small New England campus community; *Imaginary Friends* (1967) features the attempts of two sociologists to penetrate a religious cult in upstate New York; and *The War between the Tates* (1974) describes marital strife alongside student unrest. The world of writers and artists is examined in novels such as *Real People* (1969), set in an artistic community, and *The Truth about Lorin Jones* (1988), which casts an ironic eye over the New York art establishment and feminist movement, as an art historian finds her identity entwined with that of her research subject. Although most of Lurie's novels are concerned with the East Coast, *The Nowhere City* (1965) depicts the initial estrangement from, and gradual assimilation into, California life of a far from West Coast couple, and *Foreign Affairs* (1984) is set in London where several Americans find themselves tested by their stay in England; they include a professor interested in children's folk-rhymes and a waste disposal engineer in search of his ancestors. In *Only Children* (1979) Lurie wryly observes the behaviour of several adults, mainly through their children's eyes, on a rural holiday during the Depression. Other works include *The Language of Clothes* (1981), and *Not in Front of the Grown-Ups* (1990), a study of children's literature and children's books. She has also edited *Clever Gretchen and Other Forgotten Folktales* (1991) and *The Oxford Book of Modern Fairy Tales* (1993).

Luther, a play by John *Osborne, first performed in 1961, tracing the religious reformer's life from 1506, when he is received into the Augustinian order, to 1530, when he is living with his wife, a former nun, and their young son. Between these years, he is seen castigating the practice of selling indulgences, nailing his theses to the church door in Wittenberg, rejecting the authority of the Pope for that of scripture, being excommunicated by Leo X (whom he describes, in characteristically scatological style, as 'an over-indulged jakes' attendant to Satan himself, a glittering worm in excrement'), and refusing to give his support to the peasant uprising he has indirectly inspired. A picture emerges of a rebel in conflict with his father, God, his own anguished mind and intransigent body, a venal Church, and the corruption, smugness, and superficiality of a world Osborne seemed to wish his audiences to identify with their own.

LYTLE, Andrew (Nelson) (1902–), American novelist and critic, born in Tennessee, educated at Vanderbilt University where he was associated with the Fugitive group, in particular Allen *Tate (see AGRARIANS). He shared their vision of the need for the South to assert its cultural and spiritual independence and refuse collusion with the materialistic industrial world. He contributed to the magazine *The Fugitive* and to the movement's anthology, *I'll Take My Stand* (1936). Lytle farmed for a time in northern Alabama. Later he taught at the University of the South at Sewanee and edited *The *Sewanee Review*. His first book was a study of the controversial Civil War general, Bedford Forrest (1931); *The Long Night* (1936) was the first of his novels dealing with the Southern past. Of these the most successful is *The Velvet Horn* (1956), set in rural Tennessee in the mid-nineteenth century; it is partly an account of a boy's initiation into manhood, and partly a study of an incestuous relationship. It reflects Lytle's Jungian knowledge of myth and his (Episcopalian) Christianity. His essays are collected in *The Hero with the Private Parts* (1966). *A Wake for the Living* (1975) is a family memoir.

M

McALMON, Robert (1896–1956), American author and publisher, born in Clifton, Kansas; he attended the University of Southern California and subsequently lived in New York. With William Carlos *Williams, he founded *Contact* (1920–3), a *little magazine which contributed valuably to the development of American literary *Modernism. In 1921 he married Winifred Bryher, who later became Hilda *Doolittle's companion. They settled in Paris where, with William Bird, he established Contact Editions and the Three Mountains Press, which published works by a number of distinguished members of the '*Lost Generation'. His own publications include *Village* (1924), an impressionistic evocation of youth in a typical Midwestern American community, and the poetry of *The Portrait of a Generation* (1926); it contains the ambitious long poem 'The Revolving Mirror', which includes a revealing portrait of James *Joyce, with whom he was closely acquainted. He returned to America in 1929. *Being Geniuses Together* (1938) is an account of Paris in the 1920s, written with Kay *Boyle. *McAlmon and the Lost Generation* (1962) consists of autobiographical fragments prepared by Robert E. Knoll, whose *Robert McAlmon: Expatriate Writer and Publisher* appeared in 1959.

MacARTHUR, Charles (1895–1956), American dramatist, born in Scranton, Pennsylvania. MacArthur worked for the Hearst newspapers as a journalist in Chicago in the 1920s. He made his name in the theatre with a play about a black prostitute, *Lulu Belle* (1926), written in collaboration with his uncle, the playwright Edward Sheldon. MacArthur is best known for his association with Ben *Hecht with whom he collaborated on *The Front Page* (1928), an acerbic comedy about the world of newsmen, and *Twentieth Century* (1932), in which the machinations of a failing Hollywood producer are laid bare. His other collaborations with Hecht were for the musical *Jumbo* (1935), the play *Ladies and Gentlemen* (1939), written as a vehicle for MacArthur's wife, the actress Helen Hayes, and *Swan Song* (1946). His solo play *Johnny on a Spot* (1942) was an unsuccessful political satire. Like Hecht, he was also a successful screenwriter.

McAUGHTRY, Sam (1921–), Northern Irish short-story writer, born in Belfast. He left school at the age of 14, joined the Royal Air Force in 1940 and eventually became a flying officer. Immediately after the war he worked as a builder in London; he returned to Belfast in 1947 and joined the Ministry of Agriculture. McAughtry came to the attention of the Irish public with his first book *The Sinking of the Kenbane Head* (1976), an autobiographical novel which he has described as his 'memorial to a loved brother and my tribute to a cruelly exploited generation of Irish mothers. It is also a researched account of a famous sea battle, and an acknowledgement of the bravery of merchant seamen in wartime.' He followed this with three collections of short stories, *Play It Again Sam* (1978), *Blind Spot and Other Stories* (1979), and *Belfast No. 1* (1981). McAughtry has also worked as a journalist for *The Irish Times* and has become a well-known broadcaster on both radio and television in Ireland.

MACAULAY, Dame (Emelie) Rose (1881–1958), British novelist, essayist, and travel writer, a cousin of the historian Lord Macaulay, born in Rugby, educated at Somerville College, Oxford; her early life was spent in Italy, Aberystwyth, and Cambridge. Her novels began with *Abbots Verney* (1906), a *Bildungsroman* set in Rome, 'Verney' being the first of numerous androgynously named central characters in her fiction. During the First World War she worked briefly as a nurse; effects of shell-shock are depicted in *Non-Combatants and Others* (1916), in which 'Alix' comes to appreciate her forceful mother's pacifist campaigning and contemplates a religious faith. Macaulay gained a wide readership in the 1920s for her topical novels with a liberal social ethos, characterized by an ironic, sometimes flippant, tone. *Potterism* (1920) was a bestseller, and dealt with the excesses of popular journalism; *Dangerous Ages* (1921) studied the problems of four generations of women within a family; and *Crewe Train* (1926) satirized London literati and society life. A busy woman of letters, Macaulay was often in contact with the likes of E. M. *Forster and Virginia *Woolf, and produced accomplished works within a number of genres. Her fascination for the seventeenth century resulted in an important historical novel of the Civil War period, *They Were Defeated* (1932), as well as a biography of Milton in 1934. *They Went to Portugal* (1946) and *Fabled Shore* (1949) are delightfully quirky travel books, and her scholarly interest in archaeology informs *Pleasure of Ruins* (1953). Macaulay's last novel is perhaps the best known: *The Towers of Trebizond* (1956), the story of a fruitless missionary jaunt around Turkey aboard an erratic camel; its narration contains many entertaining digressions on religion (particularly Anglicanism), culture differences, and the eccentricities of human behaviour. A more serious sub-plot concerns a long-standing adulterous relationship, conflicts of desires that keep 'Laurie' ultimately outside the 'magical and mystical' Byzantine city of Trebizond, which comes to symbolize Christianity for her. Macaulay's fictions mostly explore women's social roles and some are now period pieces, but her civilized wit and oblique feminist perspectives remain of contemporary interest. Jane Emery's *Rose Macaulay: A Writer's Life* (1991) is a sympathetic account, while *Eros and Androgyny* (1988) by Jeanette N. Passty offers a detailed critique of sexual identity within her works.

McAULEY, James (Phillip) (1917–76), Australian poet and critic, born in Lakemba, New South Wales, educated at the University of Sydney. Wartime experience in New Guinea led to a series of distinguished articles in the 1940s and 1950s on that country's life and culture. His first verse collection, *Under Aldebaran* (1946), was followed by *A Vision of Ceremony* (1956), *Selected Poems* (1963), *Collected Poems 1963–1970* (1971), *Music Late at Night: Poems 1970–1973* (1976), and *Time Given: Poems 1970–1974* (1976). An unswerving classicist in his poetic practice, McAuley's disdain of certain modernist practices led to his perpetration, with fellow writer Harold Stewart, of the now-legendary 'Ern Malley Hoax'; their jointly concocted 'poem' was duly published by the radical and modernist journal **Angry Penguins*. The event did little to advance the cause of modernism in Australia, while some of 'Ern Malley's' lines have lived to haunt Australian culture. McAuley's most evocative work is *Captain Quiros* (1964), which recreates the search of the Portuguese explorer Pedro Fernandez de Quiros for the Great South Land. The poem fitted with other explorer-centred writings of the period. As an editor and critic, his chief volumes are *The End of Modernity* (1959), *The Personal Element in Australian Poetry* (1970), and *The Grammar of the Real* (1975).

McBAIN, Ed, pseudonym of Evan HUNTER (1926–), American writer, born Salvatore A. Lombino in New York, educated at Hunter College; he served in the US Navy in the Second World War and worked briefly as a teacher. Under his own name Hunter has written a large amount of popular fiction, plays, and screenplays, including the celebrated novel *The Blackboard Jungle* (1954), which depicts the violence and racial tension in the New York school system. He is perhaps best known, however, for the long and successful series of detective stories, beginning with *Cop Hater* (1956), which describe the work of the policemen of the 87th precinct in a fictional city, recognizable as New York. These were among the first, and are still among the best, of what have been called police procedural novels. The numerous titles include *Lady Killer* (1958), *Killer's Wedge* (1959), *Give the Boys a Great Big Hand* (1960), *Hail, Hail the Gang's All Here!* (1971), *Poison* (1987), and *Romance* (1995). McBain has also written a series of crime novels about a Florida attorney, Matthew Hope (*Goldilocks*, 1978; *Cinderella*, 1986; *There Was a Little Girl*, 1994), and other fiction under the pseudonyms Curt Cannon, Hunt Collins, Ezra Hannon, and Richard Marsten.

MacBETH, George (Mann) (1932–92), British poet and novelist, born in Shotts, Lanarkshire and brought up in Yorkshire, educated at New College, Oxford. He was a producer of features on poetry and the arts for BBC radio, a teacher, and broadcaster. A member of the *Group in the late 1950s, MacBeth's early work, most substantially represented in *The Broken Places* (1963), showed great accomplishment in the adaptation of conventional techniques. In subsequent collections, including *The Night of Stones* (1969), *The Burning Cone* (1970), and *The Orlando Poems* (1971), he experimented widely with innovative forms and procedures, and was associated in the later 1960s with the growth of interest in 'performance poetry'. Reflecting on MacBeth's stature as a seminal experimenter, Peter *Porter referred to him as 'the most inventive poet of his generation in Britain'. Among his later collections, which display a gradual return to traditional modes, are *Poems of Love and Death* (1980), *The Cleaver Gardens* (1986), *Anatomy of a Divorce* (1988), *Collected Poems 1958–1982* (1989), and *Trespassing* (1991). Although MacBeth has ranged widely through the possibilities of poetic practice, his work's engagement with primal areas of experience, notably death, sex, power, and vulnerability, has remained constant throughout his career; his poetry's capacity to disturb is more than matched by its honesty and individuality of tone. His numerous novels, which have thematic similarities with his verse, include *The Samurai* (1976), *The Seven Witches* (1978), and *Anna's Book* (1983). MacBeth has also produced a volume of autobiography entitled *A Child of the War* (1987) and edited numerous works including *The Penguin Book of Victorian Verse* (1969). See also UNDERGROUND POETRY.

McCABE, Eugene (1930–), Irish playwright and fiction writer, born in Glasgow, educated at University College, Cork. He ran his family's dairy farm in Co. Monaghan for ten years and has subsequently become one of Ireland's most talented, but least prolific, playwrights. *King of the Castle* (1964), his powerfully realistic play about the corrupting effects of wealth in rural Ireland, won the first Irish Life Drama Award. This was followed by the unremarkable *Breakdown* (1966) and *Swift* (1969); it was not until *Cancer* in 1976, a trilogy of plays for television, that McCabe regained both critical and popular attention. He published the 'Victims' section of this trilogy as a novel in 1977; 'Cancer' and 'Heritage' appeared as short stories in *Heritage* (1977). McCabe's novel *Death and Nightingales* (1992), set in rural Ireland in 1883, with Parnell in the ascendancy, offers a disquieting evocation of the violence of rural existence and a sense of foreboding about Ireland's future. *Christ in the Fields* (1993), a trilogy of novellas, explores the impasse between Protestant and Catholic cultures and identities.

MacCAIG, Norman (Alexander) (1910–96), Scottish poet, born in Edinburgh, where he was educated at the Royal High School and the University. He was a schoolteacher and latterly a headmaster from 1937 to 1970, when he became a reader at the University of Stirling. During the 1940s MacCaig was associated with the *New Apocalypse and his early work, collected in *Far Cry* (1943) and *The Inward Eye* (1946), partook of the movement's wildly energetic romanticism. A new fluency and discipline emerge as stylistic characteristics in *Riding Lights* (1955), in which his enduring concern with interpreting the nature of perception is established. Subsequent collections include *The Sinai Sort* (1957) and *A Common Grace* (1960). The poised conversational manner developed in his work of the 1950s and its thematic preoccupation with the north-western highlands of Scotland are sustained in later writing. Many poems isolate fundamental human values in their views of the lives of crofters. His imaginative sensitivity to the landscapes of lochs and mountains produces much striking visual imagery. From the mid-1960s onward he began to dispense with the strict forms he had formerly used; freer verse of great buoyancy, informality of tone, and musical effectiveness is increasingly evident in his numerous later collections, among which are *Rings on a Tree* (1968), *Tree of Strings* (1977), *The Equal Skies* (1980), *A World of Difference* (1983), and *Voice-Over* (1988). The marked individuality of his poetry results in part from the unusually gentle ironic tone he frequently adopts. His *Collected Poems* of 1985 appeared in a revised and enlarged edition in 1990, containing many poems hitherto unpublished. After the death of *MacDiarmid in 1978, MacCaig was widely regarded as Scotland's most eminent poet. See also TOPOGRAPHICAL POETRY.

McCARTHY, Cormac (1933–), American novelist, born in Rhode Island but brought up in Knoxville, Tennessee, educated at the University of Tennessee. McCarthy is a reclusive writer who presents a dark vision of America. His prose style is an extraordinary hybrid which intermingles *Faulkner and Melville, *Joyce and Stephen Crane. Resonant and imagistic, it focuses upon an almost exclusively masculine universe, marked by the curse of violence and satanic dissent. There is nothing pleasant about his collection of outcasts and degenerates; Lester Ballard, the central figure in *Child of God* (1973), is an utterly estranged necrophiliac, his perversion representing the only form of contact left to him by a society which has taken his land and abrogated his most basic human rights. *Suttree* (1979) focuses on the squalor and violence surrounding a pack of outcasts living by the Tennessee River; its hero nevertheless reserves a dignity based on his refusal to acquiesce to the compromises of mainstream society. McCarthy's masterpiece, *Blood Meridian, or the Evening Redness in the West* (1985), presents a vision of the American West as a kind of Hell, ruled by an insane appetite for destruction and presided over by the Ahab-like Judge, nihilist philosopher of this Dantesque Inferno. *Blood Meridian* is essentially a non-realistic novel; even the detailed landscape is perceived as an active participant in the drive towards apocalypse. Its central figure is an etiolated Ishmael, an orphan cast adrift in a cruel world; though he finally tries to extricate himself from his immersion in evil, its influence is too pervasive and he is eventually destroyed. McCarthy confirms the landscape of the Mexican/US border as his own in *All the Pretty Horses* (1992), the first novel in his highly regarded 'Border Trilogy' and his first work to attain popular success. A horseback journey of exploration and discovery for two boys, as well as a love story, it captures the romanticism and menace of wilderness culture. *The Crossing* (1994), a bleaker novel, recounts the quests of its young protagonist who ventures into the same elemental terrain, initially with a wolf he plans to return to her native hills. Each novel conveys the sense of man alone.

MacCARTHY, Sir (Charles Otto) Desmond (1878–1952), English critic and journalist, born in Plymouth, educated at Trinity College, Cambridge, where he was closely associated with the *Bloomsbury Group, though not of its inner circle. He served with the Red Cross during the First World War, and was knighted in 1951. Throughout his journalistic career he edited a number of periodicals, including the *New Statesman*, for which he also wrote articles under the pseudonym 'Affable Hawk'; he was also a principal book reviewer for the London *Sunday Times*. An early book, *The Court Theatre 1904–1907: A Commentary and a Criticism* (1907), provides a valuable record of the famous Harley *Granville-Barker seasons, which also included première productions of Bernard *Shaw's plays. MacCarthy also wrote portraits of Shaw, Henry *James, *Conrad, and Leslie Stephen (father of V. *Woolf), among others. Undoubtedly one of the most entertaining and perceptive of critics, his collections of essays, reviews, and reminiscences include *Portraits* (1931), *Criticism* (1932), *Experience* (1935), *Drama* (1940), *Shaw's Plays in Review* (1951), *Memories* (1953), *Humanities* (1954), and *Theatre* (1955).

McCARTHY, Mary (Therese) (1912–89), American novelist, essayist, and teacher, born in Seattle, Washington. Her parents died when she was six, and she was brought up by relatives, in Minneapolis, Seattle, and Tacoma. McCarthy's early life is recorded in *Memoirs of a Catholic Girlhood* (1957). She attended Vassar College, where she knew Muriel *Rukeyser and Elizabeth *Bishop. She taught literature at Sarah Lawrence and Bard Colleges and became theatre critic for **Partisan Review*. Among other journals she wrote reviews for *The *New Republic* and *The *Nation*, which were collected in *Sights and Spectacles* (1956). Through her involvement with the non-Stalinist left, she married (and later divorced) Edmund *Wilson. Her short stories of this period are collected in *Cast a Cold Eye* (1950). She achieved early success with her first book, *The Company She Keeps* (1942), a novel which experiments with narrative perspective and concerns young New Yorkers in the political and social milieu of Greenwich Village. This was followed by *The Oasis* (1949; UK title, *Source of Embarrassment*, 1950), a satire about the failure of liberalism; *The Groves of Academe* (1952), a cutting depiction of a college president struggling with the politics of his English department; and *A Charmed Life* (1955), about retirement from the world into a life of aestheticism. After producing two art histories, *Venice Observed* (1956) and *The Stones of Florence* (1959), she published her most famous work, *The Group* (1963), a fictionalized account of a group of friends who met at Vassar, whose diverse histories are unified by the story of Kay Strong, and marked by McCarthy's characteristic acidic satire and sharp observation. Her strong political views are recorded in essays collected in *On the Contrary* (1961), and in a trilogy about the US involvement in Vietnam (see VIETNAM WRITING): *Vietnam* (1967), *Hanoi* (1968), and *Medina* (1972). Her final novels, *Birds of America* (1971) and *Cannibals and Missionaries* (1979), deal with the crisis of liberal and humanitarian values in the face of violent activists and terrorism. A further volume of critical essays about the state of the USA during these years appeared under the title *The Writing on the Wall* (1970), while other aspects of the modern political world, particularly Watergate, figure in *The Mask of State* (1974) and *The Seventh Degree* (1974). In her later years, she was involved in a bitter controversy with Lillian *Hellman. Her later works which demonstrated her balanced commitment to fiction and critical prose, include *The Hounds of Summer and Other Stories* (1981), *Occasional Prose: Essays* (1985), and the autobiographical works, *How I Grew* (1987) and *Intellectual Memoirs* (1992).

McCLURE, James (Howe) (1939–), British crime writer, born in Johannesburg; he worked on newspapers in South Africa and, after 1965, in Edinburgh and in Oxford. His novels, often broadly comic, are for the most part set in the South African town of Trekkersburg—which can be identified with Pietermaritzburg, in Natal—and have as detectives the Afrikaner Lieutenant Tromp Kramer and the Zulu Sergeant Zondi. The depiction of South African society in *The Steam Pig* (1971) and others has been compared to that of Alan *Paton and Nadine *Gordimer, but the approach seems closer to that of Tom *Sharpe's early works. McClure has also written non-fictional studies of police work in Liverpool (*Spike Island*, 1980) and San Diego (*Copworld*, 1984).

McCLURE, Michael (Thomas) (1932–), American poet, born in Marysville, Kansas, educated at the University of Wichita and San Francisco State University. In 1962 he commenced teaching at the California College of Arts and Crafts, Oakland. His reputation as a poet was established during the *San Francisco Renaissance; collections of his earlier verse, which repeatedly displays violently passionate imagery and language, include *Passage* (1956), *Hymns to St Geryon* (1959), and *The New Book: A Book of Torture* (1961). His beliefs concerning the physical origins of poetry directly inform the experimentation with oral modes in *Ghost Tantras* (1964). Among his later collections, in which a more meditative tone and a sustained ecological concern become apparent, are *Star* (1971), *Jaguar Skies* (1975), *Antechamber* (1978), and *Fragments of Perseus* (1983); *Selected Poems* appeared in 1986. The best-known of McClure's dramatic works, which frequently centre on bizarrely imaginative conceptions, is *The Beard* (1965), an erotic dialogue between Jean Harlow and Billy the Kid; his other plays include *Gargoyle Cartoon* (1971), *Gorf* (1976), and *Josephine the Mouse Singer* (1980). Among his other publications are the novels *The Mad Cub* (1970) and *The Adept* (1971) and the collections of essays *Meat Science Essays* (1963), *Scratching the Beat Surface* (1982), and *Specks* (1985). See also UNDERGROUND POETRY.

McCRAE, Hugh (1876–1958), Australian poet, born in Melbourne, where he was articled to an architect. He then became a freeland writer and moved to Sydney in 1904. *Satyrs and Sunlight* (1909) was described by Kenneth *Slessor as the beginning of modern Australian poetry. Creating a mythical landscape of satyrs, centaurs, and unicorns, he departed from the nationalist-realist school of the 1890s. The titles of subsequent collections, *Colombine* (1921), *Idyllia* (1922), *The Mimshi Maiden* (1938), *The Forests of Pan* (1944), and *Voice of the Forest* (1945), are indicative of their pastoral and mythological content. Contemporaries, from Mary *Gilmore to Judith *Wright, delighted in his vision and technique but subsequent criticism has deplored its excesses and logical weaknesses. Nevertheless, his poetry is not pure pastoral: the tension between the decorative surface and the sexual impact of his descriptions is its distinctive strength. His importance in Australian literature is that in 1909 he anticipated, perhaps influenced, the development of the Vision school and later contributed to their magazine **Vision*. Other works include *My Father and His Friends* (1935), a biography of George Gordon McCrae, containing memories of Marcus Clarke, Henry Kendall, and Adam Lindsay Gordon.

McCRUM, Robert (1953–), British novelist and editor, born in Cambridge, educated at Cambridge University. His novels, several of which have political themes, include *In the Secret State* (1980); *A Loss of Heart* (1982); *The Fabulous Englishman* (1984), set in Czechoslovakia during the Prague Spring of 1968 and concerning the affair between a young Englishman and his Czech lover; and *Mainland* (1991), a political thriller exploring the nature of betrayal, in which the protagonist, engaged on a politically sensitive mission in an occupied territory, encounters a beautiful journalist and is drawn into a nightmarish world of violence and corruption. Political corruption also surfaces in *The Psychological Moment* (1993), set in Cape Cod. McCrum is also the author of several books for children and of the award-winning BBC series, *The Story of English* (1985). As Editor in Chief of Faber & Faber, he has been instrumental in publishing, amongst others, the work of the Czechoslovakian novelist, Milan Kundera.

McCULLERS, Carson (Smith) (1917–67), American novelist, short-story writer, and playwright, born in Columbus, Georgia, educated at Columbia and New York Universities and the Juilliard School of Music. She suffered a series of crippling strokes in her twenties which left her partially paralysed and confined to a wheelchair towards the end of her life. Her reputation was established with *The Heart Is a Lonely Hunter* (1940), immediately acclaimed for its moving portrait of a deaf-mute, Mr Singer, who listens to the stories and confessions of his neighbours, and who is deprived of his closest friend, an obese, half-witted mute, and forced to reconstruct his life as best he can by seeking help from those around him. Described by McCullers as an 'ironic parable of fascism', the book establishes the principal preoccupations of her fiction: the lonely individual's search for love and acceptance, and the focus on people who are psychologically or physically abnormal. Her next novel, *Reflections in a Golden Eye* (1941), set in a peacetime army post in Georgia, dissects the relationships of a repressed homosexual captain and his nymphomaniac wife, and a strange man who likes riding horses naked. *The Member of the Wedding* (1946) continued with Southern settings, a description of the lonely teenager Frankie Addams's emotions on the occasion of the marriage of her older brother, and was subsequently dramatized by McCullers in 1950 and made into a movie in 1952. After the plays *The Twisted Trinity* (1946) and *The Square Root of Wonderful* (1958) she returned to the novel with *Clock Without Hands* (1961), which recounts the final days of a pharmacist dying of leukaemia, and looks at racial problems in the South. She also published two collections of short stories, *The Ballad of the Sad Café* (1951), which tells of a complicated series of love relationships between odd characters, and which was dramatized by Edward *Albee in 1963, and the posthumous *The Mortgaged Heart* (1971). Her novels are a macabre and sombre exploration of love, frustration, and isolation, which often verge on the comic, even when the material turns to tragedy.

MacDIARMID, Hugh, pseudonym of Christopher Murray GRIEVE (1892–1978), Scottish poet, critic, and Scottish nationalist, born at Langholm, Dumfriesshire, educated at Broughton Student Centre and the University of Edinburgh. In 1912 he began his career as a journalist in Scotland and South Wales. He became involved in 1920 in the movement to revive indigenous Scottish culture and edited three editions of *Northern Numbers* (1920, 1921, 1922), an anthology of Scottish poetry (see SCOTTISH RENAISSANCE). His first collection of verse, *Annals of the Five Senses*, appeared in 1923. Intent on evolving a form of written Scots adequate to the concerns of the twentieth century, he reinforced the dialect of his native region with vocabulary and usages from literary and etymological sources. Conscious of the degenerative influence of sub-Burnsian sentimentality, he promoted Dunbar as exemplifying a vigorous poetry in Scots. *Sangschaw* (1925) and *Penny Wheep* (1926) contain many poems demonstrating the appropriateness of MacDiarmid's linguistic idiom to his energetic and imaginative abilities as a poet; the thematic range of the collections extends from erotic lyricism to theological speculation. *A Drunk Man Looks at the Thistle* (1926), a work of epic dimensions and great stylistic scope, fuses his vision of Scottish nationhood with his broader philosophical and cultural preoccupations. In 1928 he was among the founders of the National Party of Scotland, which he was asked to leave in 1933. He subsequently joined the Communist Party, from which he was expelled in 1938 for 'national deviation'. His persistently controversial political attitudes involved him in numerous unsuccessful parliamentary candidatures. Ideological concerns became dominant in his poetry with *To Circumjack Cencrastus* (1930) and the emphatically polemical *First Hymn to Lenin* (1931). English emerged as the principal language of his later work in *Stony Limits* (1934), which contained 'On a Raised Beach', the fullest exposition of his metaphysical beliefs. His later collections include *In Memoriam James Joyce* (1954) and *The Kind of Poetry I Want* (1961), which indicate his increasing intellectual and technical eclecticism. By the 1950s he was internationally recognized as a major poet and made visits to Russia and China. *Collected Poems* appeared in two volumes in 1978, with a revised edition in 1982. Among his numerous prose works are the essays of *At the Sign of the Thistle* (1934) and *The Uncanny Scot* (1968) and the autobiography *Lucky Poet* (1943). *MacDiarmid: The Terrible Crystal* (1983) is a biography by Alan *Bold, who also edited *The Letters of Hugh MacDiarmid* (1984).

MacDONAGH, Donagh (1912–68), Irish poet and playwright, born in Dublin, the son of Thomas *MacDonagh, educated at University College, Dublin. He was a barrister from 1935 to 1941, when he became a District Justice in Wexford and Dublin. As a student he published *Twenty Poems* (with Niall Sheridan, 1934) and mounted the first Irish production of T. S. Eliot's **Murder in the Cathedral*. His own plays are either verse-dramas or ballad-operas, for which he provided new lyrics to traditional tunes. His greatest success was *Happy as Larry* (1946), which was produced in London and New York. Among his other plays, most of which remain unpublished, are the comedy *Step-in-the-Hollow*, *God's Gentry*, the best of his ballad-operas, and numerous works for radio. His accomplishment as a versifier is evident in *Veterans and Other Poems* (1941), *The Hungry Grass* (1947), and *A Warning to Conquerors* (1968), his principal collections of poetry, which reflect his deep interest in Gaelic culture in their many translations of early Irish lyrics. With Lennox *Robinson, MacDonagh edited *The Oxford Book of Irish Verse*, published in 1958.

MacDONAGH, Thomas (1878–1916), Irish poet and playwright, born in Cloughjordan, County Tipperary, educated at University College, Dublin. In 1908 he became a teacher at Patrick Pearse's St Enda's School. His first play, *When the Dawn Is Come*, was produced by the *Abbey Theatre in 1908, after revisions suggested by *Yeats and *Synge had made its nationalist content more explicit. Yeats was later satirized in another of MacDonagh's plays, *Metempsychosis*, produced in 1912. In 1913, by which time he was a lecturer in English at University College, Dublin, he joined the Irish Volunteers, devoting himself wholeheartedly to the movement; he was executed in May 1916 as one of the leaders of the Easter Rising. His collections of poetry include *Through the Ivory Gate* (1902), *Songs of Myself* (1910), and *Lyrical Poems* (1913). His later verse displays a confident directness of tone and imagery of accomplished clarity. Numerous translations of Gaelic poems and works by Catullus were included in *The Poetical Works of Thomas MacDonagh* (1916). Among his other writings is *Literature in Ireland* (1916), a work important for its identification of Anglo-Irish literature as a distinct cultural category.

McDONALD, Ian (1933–), Trinidadian poet, novelist, and editor, born in Trinidad to a colonial family, educated at Queens Royal College and Cambridge University. He is best known for his novel *The Hummingbird Tree* (1969), which powerfully evokes childhood scenes and gives rare insight into the attitudes and reactions of both white and Indian Trinidadians. When he later moved to Guyana, McDonald produced *Mercy Ward* (1988), a collection of poems that reflects the mixed quality of Guyanese life. These poems reveal acute powers of observation, wide sympathies, and great technical skill. Other collections of poems include *Essequibo* (1992), which explores aspects of Guyanese culture and landscape, and *Jaffo the Calypsonian* (1994). He is the editor, with Stuart Brown, of *The Heinemann Book of Caribbean Poetry* (1992).

MacDONALD, John D(ann) (1916–86), American crime writer, born in Pennsylvania; he studied at the Harvard Business School and served (1940–6) with the OSS in the US Army in the Far East, rising to the rank of lieutenant-colonel. After contributing many short stories in a variety of genres to *pulp magazines under his own name and a number of pseudonyms, he published his first novel, *The Brass Cupcake*, in 1950. It was followed by many others, often dealing with corporate swindles and involving greed and violence; titles include *Dead Low Tide* (1953), *Murder in the Wind* (1956; UK title *Hurricane*), *The Only Girl in the Game* (1960), *A Key to the Suite* (1962), and *Condominium* (1977). He is best known, however, for the immensely popular long series of novels featuring Travis McGee, a Florida 'salvage consultant', an original reworking of Raymond *Chandler's knightly hero. The best of the series, all of which have a colour adjective in the title, are *The Deep Blue Good-by* (1964), *A Deadly Shade of Gold* (1965), *Bright Orange for the Shroud* (1965), *Darker than Amber* (1966), *One Fearful Yellow Eye* (1966), *Pale Gray for Guilt* (1968), *Cinnamon Skin* (1982), and *The Lonely Silver Rain* (1985).

MacDONALD, Philip (1899–1981), British crime writer, grandson of George MacDonald, born in London; he served in Mesopotamia in a cavalry regiment in the First World War, and in 1931 moved to Hollywood where he worked as a scriptwriter—working on, among many other films, Alfred Hitchcock's version of Daphne *du Maurier's *Rebecca*—and bred Great Danes. One of the many detective story writers who appeared in the 1920s, he brought out his first novel, *The Rasp*, in 1924; its hero, who was to appear in most of his books, is Colonel Anthony Gethryn. Others are *The White Crow* (1929), *The Link* (1930), and *The Nursemaid Who Disappeared* (1938; US title *Warrant for X*). Of his other crime stories the best are *Rynox* (1930; also entitled *The Rynox Mystery*; US title *The Rynox Murder Mystery*) and *X v Rex* (1933, originally published under the pseudonym of Martin Porlock; also entitled *The Mystery of Mr X*; US title *Mystery of the Dead Police*). His last Gethryn novel, *The List of Adrian Messenger* (1959), was made into a film by John Huston.

MacDONALD, Ross (Kenneth Millar) (1915–83), American crime writer, born in Los Gatos, California, raised in Canada, educated at the University of Western Ontario; he has held posts at the universities of Toronto and Michigan. Within a mainly California setting, MacDonald's series of mystery novels featuring private eye Lew Archer successfully reproduce the style of Raymond *Chandler and the political sensibility of Dashiell *Hammett. In a fluent style, MacDonald uses Archer to investigate crimes which the official agencies of law and order prefer to overlook. In the earliest of this sequence, *The Moving Target* (1949), Archer demonstrates that the lines between good and evil are not clearly drawn, and that almost everyone has darkness within—an explicit statement of the central principle of *'hardboiled' fiction. Behind the protective coating of irony, Archer remains a heroic figure, like Chandler's Philip Marlowe, engaged in a personal crusade against social evil. In the best of these novels, *The Drowning Pool* (1950), *The Zebra-Striped Hearse* (1962), and *The Goodbye Look* (1969), the evils uncovered are seen as social and psychological. In *Find a Victim* (1954) the recurrent theme of police corruption is raised, a topic which recurs in many of MacDonald's novels.

MACDONELL, A(rchibald) G(ordon) (1895–1941), British novelist, born in India, educated at Winchester. Following two years of active service in Flanders, he was invalided out of the army in 1918 and rapidly established himself as a freelance journalist, becoming drama critic for the **London Mercury* in 1919. From 1922 to 1927 he was a member of staff with the League of Nations; he subsequently produced a succession of thrillers using the pseudonyms 'Neil Gordon' and 'John Cameron'. *England, Their England*, the first of his books to appear under his own name, was published in 1933; the work's good-humoured but incisive satire of a wide range of English institutions appealed to the prevailing disillusionment of the time and earned Macdonell considerable renown. Class pretensions and political insincerity were among the chief targets of the elegantly written and memorably comic novel *Autobiography of a Cad* (1938). His numerous other works include the historical study *Napoleon and His Marshalls* (1934), the short stories of *The Spanish Pistol* (1939), and the novels *How Like an Angel* (1934), *What Next Baby?* (1939), and *The Crew of the Anaconda* (1940). Macdonell also contributed regularly to the *Observer* and made a highly valued series of broadcasts for the BBC's Empire Service in 1940, applying his keenly satirical sense of the absurd to undermining the claims of Nazi propaganda.

McELROY, Joseph (Prince) (1930–), American novelist, born in Brooklyn, New York, educated at Williams College and Columbia University. McElroy is one of several highly regarded contemporary American novelists such as William *Gaddis, William *Gass, Thomas *Pynchon, and Don *DeLillo, who make few concessions to the ordinary reader. His first novel, *A Smuggler's Bible* (1966), was followed by *Hind's Kidnap* (1969), *Ancient History* (1971), *Lookout Cartridge* (1974), *Plus* (1977), *Ship Rock* (1980), *Women and Men* (1987), and *The Letter Left to Me* (1988). These novels illustrate McElroy's explorations into fictional form, where character, plot, setting, atmosphere, language, and narrative devices are used with a high degree of self-conscious artifice, to reflect the post-modernist fascination with information theory, with technology, and all the contemporary analogues for human memory, speech, and gesture. In *A Smuggler's Bible*, the title refers to a hollowed-out bible used by an American writer, David Brooke, to conceal his autobiographical manuscripts which he carries on a trans-Atlantic voyage with his English wife. The use of a smuggler's bible as a metaphor is characteristic of McElroy's preoccupations with the ambivalent relationship between narrator, story, and reader, and our compulsion for coherence in a world where incoherence and dysfunction are proposed as common conditions of experience.

McEWAN, Ian (Russell) (1948–), British novelist and short-story writer, born in Aldershot, Hampshire educated at the Universities of Sussex and East Anglia. He created something of a stir with his first book, *First Love, Last Rites* (1975, Somerset Maugham Award), a collection of stories startling in their cool portrayal of ordinary people caught up in ordinary nightmares; masturbation, incest, castration, and the bewildering potency of adolescent sexual urges are the themes of this collection and his next, *In Between the Sheets* (1978). His first novel, *The Cement Garden* (1978), describes a family of four children who bury their mother in concrete rather than admit her (natural) death to the authorities. *The Comfort of Strangers* (1981) shuts four adults in an ultimately violent nightmare of their own. McEwan's three children were born in the interval between this and his third novel, *The Child in Time* (1987), which is warmer, broader, and considerably more committed than his previous fiction, dealing as it does with politics and parenthood, loss and desire. *The Innocent* (1990) uses a historical espionage venture, the CIA/MI6 tunnel dug in 1955–6 to tap the telephone lines of East Berlin, as the basis for an exquisitely crafted story of misplaced machismo and farcical deceit. *Black Dogs* (1992) is a fable about the nature of evil, whose central event—an encounter between a young woman on holiday with her husband in post-war France and the black dogs referred to in the title—has a clear political symbolism. The novel, which moves between this event and a contemporary setting, deals with changes in political allegiances in the aftermath of the Cold War, and asks some pertinent questions about the possible resurgence of Fascism in such a climate. In this, as in other more recent works, McEwan has moved from the purely psychological focus of his early stories towards a broader concern with social and political issues, and the ways in which these impinge on individual lives. McEwan's political instincts and distrust of patriarchal values are equally evident in his libretto for Michael Berkeley's oratorio, *Or Shall We Die?* (1983), as well as in his television plays and his screenplay for *The Ploughman's Lunch* (produced 1983, published 1985).

MacEWEN, Gwendolyn (1941–87), Canadian poet, novelist, and short-story writer, born in Toronto; her poetry first appeared in **Canadian Forum* several years before she left school at the age of eighteen to devote herself to writing. *The Rising Fire* (1963), her first substantial collection of verse, was followed by eight further volumes, which include *A Breakfast for Barbarians* (1966), *The Armies of the Moon* (1972), *The T. E. Lawrence Poems* (1982), *Earthlight: Selected Poems* (1982) and *Afterworlds* (1987); MacEwen's poetry combines great rhythmical and tonal vitality with imagery that is at once vividly particular and resonantly imaginative. Much of her work seems to create a mythology of transcendent order out of the experiences and language of the everyday. Her novels *Julian the Magician* (1963), a treatment of hermeticism in the early Renaissance, and *King of Egypt, King of Dreams* (1971), based on the life of the pharaoh Akhenaton, are similarly concerned with transcending limited conceptions of reality. Her collections of short-stories *Noman* (1972) and *Noman's Land* (1985) place their magician protagonist in a contemporary Canadian setting. In addition to her work for children and the travel book *Mermaids and Ikons: A Greek Summer* (1978), MacEwen wrote verse-dramas, the best-known being *Terror and Erebus* (contained in *Afterworlds*), a treatment of Franklin's attempt to find the Northwest Passage, and a radical adaptation of Euripides' *The Trojan Women* (performed 1978, published 1979).

McGAHERN, John (1934–), Irish novelist and short-story writer, born in Dublin, educated at St Patrick's Training College, Dublin. He achieved immediate fame with his first book, *The Barracks* (1963), for its depiction of Irish rural life, its attention to detail, and its elegant prose, but *The Dark* (1965), with its uncompromising attitude to sex and its scabrous language, fell foul of the puritanical 1929 Censorship of

Publications Act, and was banned in Ireland. The author was subsequently dismissed from his teaching post by the Archbishop of Dublin and went to Spain where for several years he lost his urge to write. In 1970 appeared a collection of stories, *Nightlines*, many of which were previously published in the **New Yorker*. His next novel, *The Leavetaking* (1974), was followed by *The Pornographer* (1979), in which a writer of pornographic fiction creates an ideal world of sex in his imagination while he mismanages his own entanglement with an older woman who has the misfortune to fall in love with him. Though located in the late twentieth century it is a timeless and strikingly unsentimental work. His novel *Amongst Women* (1990) is a poignant story of a moribund old man living with his second wife and three daughters in the Irish countryside and remembering his days of glory as a Republican fighter in the War of Independence. McGahern's sensitivity to the lives of ordinary people is evident throughout his harsh yet poetic *Collected Stories* (1992) in which everyday incidents both reveal and conceal emotion. A play, *The Power of Darkness*, was published in 1991.

McGEE, Greg (1950–), New Zealand playwright, born in Oamaru in the South Island, educated at the University of Otago, Dunedin. Both McGee's experience as a law student and his time as a Junior All Black (rugby player) contributed to the creation of his successful first play *Foreskin's Lament* (1979/81). Its first half is set in the changing shed on practice night; the action is about young Foreskin's unsuccessful attempt to introduce some altruism into a brutal team strategy. The play was welcomed as a questioning of the values of the wider society. McGee's other stage plays continue strategic attacks on contemporary values; both *Tooth and Claw* (1984) and *Out in the Cold* (1984) deal with issues of sexism and racism. *Whitemen* (1986) was less successful. McGee has also produced original screenplays, and adaptations, for television. These include *Free Enterprise* (1982); the series *Mortimer's Patch* (1984) and *Roche* (1985); and a dramatization of the controversial inquiry into the aircrash on Mt Erebus in Antarctica.

McGILL, Patrick (1891–1963), Irish poet and novelist, born in Glenties, Co. Donegal; he left school at the age of 12 to work locally as a farm labourer, and emigrated to Scotland when he was 14, where he worked as a potato picker and a navvy. Writing from his own experience, McGill became the voice of the Irish immigrant worker. His early collections of poetry, *Songs of a Navvy* (1911) and *Songs of the Dead End* (1912), are reflections on the hard life that the Irish in Scotland were forced to live. The First World War served to deepen his sense of outrage and strengthened his resolve to speak out for those who had been wasted for the sake of a society from which they had been excluded. During the war, McGill served with the London Irish Rifles and recounted his experiences in *The Amateur Army* (1915). His most memorable works are five novels, *Children of the Dead End* (1914), *The Rat Pit* (1915), *Glenmornan* (1919), *The Glen of Carra* (1934), and *Helen Spenser* (1937), in which he employed his experiences of Donegal and Scotland to write angry and uncompromising narratives of social protest.

McGINLEY, Patrick (1937–), Irish novelist, born in Donegal; he was educated at Galway University and spent several years teaching in Ireland before moving to London where he took up a career as a publisher. His first novel, *Bogmail* (1978), centred on the hard-drinking philosophers of his home country and was much admired for its earthiness and exuberant language. Its successor, *Goosefoot* (1982), marked an ambitious development, being the story of a young girl's life told from her point of view. Notable among later works are *Foggage* (1984) and *The Bed Men* (1987), in which eccentric, weird, and sometimes violent events, usually located in rural Ireland, are related with rapacious audacity and the blackest of humour. *The Devil's Diary* (1988) is a novel set in contemporary rural Ireland and centres on the conflict between a priest and a property developer whose plans threaten the local culture and landscape. *The Lost Soldier's Song* (1994), whose innocent protagonist joins the IRA during the Irish War of Independence and emerges with his ideals shattered, presents a bleak vision of brutality and inhumanity on both sides of the conflict.

McGOUGH, Roger (1937–), British poet, born in Liverpool, educated at the University of Hull. He was a teacher in Liverpool from 1960 to 1964. With work by Adrian *Henri and Brian *Patten, McGough's poetry was first published in *The Mersey Sound* (1967), which introduced the work of the three, collectively the *Liverpool Poets, to a remarkably wide readership. He subsequently became a member of the recording group 'The Scaffold', for which he wrote lyrics. Collections of his verse include *Watchwords* (1969), *Holiday on Death Row* (1979), *Waving at Trains* (1982), *Defying Gravity* (1992), and *Lucky* (1993). The majority of his poems contain humorous elements, which range from the ingeniously surreal to the blatantly burlesque. His comic abilities are also employed for occasional poems of satirical social commentary and to establish an ironic detachment from the underlying seriousness of elegiac treatments of transience and human frailty. *Selected Poems 1967–1987* (1989) was supplemented in 1991 by *You at the Back*, a further selected edition. He has also written numerous plays, which include *Zones* (1971) and *Lifeswappers* (1980), and several volumes of children's verse.

McGRATH, John (1935–), British dramatist, born in Birkenhead, educated at Oxford University. His early plays, notably *Events while Guarding the Bofors Gun* (1966) and *Bakke's Night of Fame* (1968), about a murderer on the eve of his execution, brought an element of complexity to social subjects. His work has become simpler and more didactic, though always also robust and humorous, since 1971, the year he founded the 7:84 Theatre Company. This derived its name from a statistic which claimed that 7 per cent of the British population owned 84 per cent of the national wealth, and has remained dedicated to bringing radical ideas directly to the working class. Among the McGrath plays that have been presented by either the English or the Scottish sections of this troupe are *Fish in the Sea* (1972), about the occupation of a factory being 'rationalized' by a multinational corporation; *The Cheviot, the Stag and the Black, Black Oil* (1973), about the exploitation of the Scottish Highlands by the rich and ruthless; *Little Red Hen* (1975), in which a fiercely socialist Scotswoman gives her granddaughter a lesson in politics by way of weaning her from her attachment to Scottish nationalism; *Blood Red Roses* (1980), another exemplary tale about an attempt to resist international capitalism on the shop floor; and *The Garden of England* (1984), about the coalminers' strike of 1984. McGrath is also the co-author, with Richard Norton Taylor, of *Half the Picture* (1994), a dramatic digest of the evidence given to Sir Richard Scott's official inquiry into the question of whether and why British arms were sold to Iraq in the period before the Gulf War.

McGRATH, Thomas (Matthew) (1916–90), American poet, born near Sheldon, North Dakota, educated at the University of North Dakota, Louisiana State University, and New College, Oxford. After working as a writer of scripts for documentary films he became Associate Professor of English at Moorhead State College, Minnesota, in 1969. Much of his verse is informed by a political radicalism originating in his early involvement with militant socialist movements in the 1930s. He first achieved recognition as a poet with *Longshot O'Leary's Garland of Practical Poesie* (1949), which reflects his engagement in trade union activities on the New York waterfront. *Witness to the Times* (1954) and *Figures from a Double World* (1955) established the fusion of angry dissent, wit, and thematically encompassing lyricism that distinguishes his major work, *Letter to an Imaginary Friend*, parts of which appeared successively in 1962, 1970, and 1985. The poem's comprehensive survey of America since the 1920s is authenticated by its sustained autobiographical orientation; the landscapes and townships of North Dakota supply a wealth of vivid imagery emblematic of social and cultural conditions throughout the USA. Other collections of verse by McGrath include the sixty short poems of *Open Songs* (1977); *Echoes inside the Labyrinth* (1983); and the posthumously published *Death Song* (1991), which complements outspoken political testimony with transcendent lyrics of natural phenomena. *Selected Poems 1938–1988* appeared in 1988. Among his other works is the novel *This Coffin Has no Handles* (1984), which is based on the New York longshoremen's strike of 1945.

McGUANE, Thomas (1941–), American novelist, short-story writer, and essayist, born in Michigan, educated at Michigan State University, the Yale School of Drama, and Stanford. None of his first three novels is set exclusively in the West, though they all borrow ingredients from its traditional Western, most notably in their portrayal of lonely, disaffected individuals who court violence and who deliberately flout convention. *The Sporting Club* (1969), *The Bushwhacked Piano* (1971), and *Ninety-Two in the Shade* (1973) feature paired characters who are mirror images of each other's strengths and weaknesses. They are locked into a cycle of misunderstandings whose consequences are disastrous, yet their rebellion is based on an often incisive view of the society through which they move. *Panama* (1978), which marks a turning point in his fiction, repeats the scenario of his early novels, but dispenses with paired characters in favour of a more naked concentration on the relationship between father and son, which arguably underlies the kind of psychological malaise found in his previous three books. His next three novels, *Nobody's Angel* (1981), *Something To Be Desired* (1984), and *Keep the Change* (1989), all concern the attempt to return home, an attempt which always ends in failure, though this time his characters gather an increasing store of wisdom. *Nothing But Blue Skies* (1993) is an exuberantly comic novel, despite its concentration on mania and loss. *To Skin a Cat* (1986) is a collection of stories, and *An Outside Chance* (1980) is a notable collection of essays on sport. He has written the film scripts for *The Missouri Breaks*, *Rancho DeLuxe*, and *Ninety-Two in the Shade*, which he also directed.

McGUCKIAN, Medbh (1950–), Irish poet, born in Belfast, where she was educated at Queen's University. In 1974 she began teaching at St Patrick's College, Knock, Belfast, and in 1986 became the first woman to be appointed writer-in-residence at Queen's University. Her principal collections of verse, *The Flower Master* (1982), *Venus and the Rain* (1984), and *On Ballycastle Beach* (1988) have established her as a writer of note. Her technical accomplishment and vividly precise imagery contribute to the finely textured surfaces of poetry which is equally characterized by the presence of less accessible underlying significances. In response to allegations of obscurity, she wrote of allowing 'the intensity of images to shadow-paint the inner life of the soul', stating of her work that 'its territory is the feminine subconscious'. Later collections include *Marconi's Cottage* (1991) and *Captain Lavender* (1994). Twenty-three of her poems are included in Paul *Muldoon's edition of *The Faber Book of Contemporary Irish Poetry* (1986). She is the editor of *The Big Striped Golfing Umbrella* (1985), a compilation of poems by young people from Northern Ireland.

McGUINNESS, Frank (1956–), Irish playwright, born in Buncrana, Co. Donegal, educated at University College, Dublin. Since the *Abbey's production of his play *The Factory Girls* (1982), McGuinness has been of crucial importance to contemporary Irish drama. His reputation was confirmed with *Observe the Sons of Ulster Marching toward the Somme* (1985), a play which follows the thoughts and friendships shared between eight Ulster soldiers as they await the Battle of the

Somme. McGuinness confronts their individual bravery and collective loyalty with the futility of their probable deaths. Furthermore, by recalling that 1 July 1916 was the anniversary of the Battle of the Boyne in 1690, the play questions the link between their story and the history of the Ulster Protestant victory with which they identify and are determined to emulate. McGuinness is eclectic in his interests and this is reflected in the variety of his work. His other dramatic works include *Innocence* (1986), about the life of Caravaggio; *Carthaginians* (1988); *Mary and Lizzie* (1989), which explores the lives of two sisters and their relationship with Friedrich Engels; and *Someone Who'll Watch Over Me* (1992), a hostage drama set in Beirut. *Booterstown* (1994), McGuinness's first collection of poems, was praised for its lyricism and candid tone. McGuinness has produced a translation of Lorca's *Yerma* (1987) and versions of Ibsen's *Rosmersholm* (1987) and *Peer Gynt* (1988), and Chekhov's *Three Sisters* (1990).

MACHEN, Arthur (originally Arthur Llewellyn JONES) (1863–1947), British short-story writer, born in Caerleon, Monmouthshire, educated at Hereford Cathedral School. He was the only son of a Welsh Anglican clergyman. His early immersion in Welsh myth and legend disposed him toward the esoteric; following his move to London in 1880 he worked as a cataloguer of arcane and cabbalistic literature and joined the Order of the Golden Dawn, of which W. B. *Yeats was the best-known member. The stories of *The Chronicle of Clemendy* (1888) marked the start of his career as a prolific author of grotesquely imaginative supernatural and mystical fiction. The better known of his subsequent works include *The Great God Pan* (1894), *The Three Impostors* (1895; stories), *The House of Souls* (1906; stories), and *The Hill of Dreams* (1907). A later tale, *The Angel of Mons* (1915), created an apocryphal legend of the First World War. Other works include translations of *The Heptameron* (1886) and *The Memoirs of Casanova* (1893); *Hieroglyphics* (1902, criticism); and two volumes of autobiography, *Far Off Things* (1922) and *Near and Far* (1923).

McILVANNEY, William (Angus) (1936–), Scottish novelist and poet, born in Kilmarnock, the son of a miner; he attended Glasgow University and became an English teacher before taking up creative writing fellowships in Scotland and overseas. McIlvanney's novels often feature 'hard men' who have to reckon with the tensions of their working-class inheritance, as well as their own violence, in order to define a sense of integrity. Such themes, suggested in *Remedy is None* (1966) and *A Gift from Nessus* (1968), received authoritative development in *Docherty* (1975), focusing on a miner's courage and endurance during the Depression years, as seen by his son. His best-known book is *The Big Man* (1985; later made into a film), in which Dan Scoular, an unemployed family man living in a decaying pit community, is offered the challenge of making money in bare-knuckle fights. McIlvanney has also produced several volumes of poetry, movingly elegizing the victims of famine and the Depression in *The Longships in Harbour* (1970), plus the award-winning crime thrillers *Laidlaw* (1977) and *The Papers of Tony Veitch* (1983). In its incisive portrayal of Scottish working-class masculinity, his work has some affinities with that of James *Kelman. McIlvanney's other publications include a book of short stories, *Walking Wounded* (1989); a collection of journalism, *Surviving the Shipwreck* (1991); and a novel, *Strange Loyalties* (1991).

McINERNEY, Jay (1955–), American writer, born in Hartford, Connecticut, educated at Williams College and Syracuse University. His first novel, *Bright Light, Big City* (1983), dealing with the decadent habits of a group of middle-class New Yorkers, initiated a trend in American fiction of the early 1980s, which was characterized by a certain metropolitan brittleness, sexual cynicism, and a concern with the conspicuous consumerism of the Reagan years; McInerney also wrote the screenplay for the film adaptation. *Ransom* (1985) is about an American expatriate in Japan, and *Story of My Life* (1988) returns to a New York setting and a cast of somewhat jaded Bright Young Things. The more ambitious in scope *Brightness Falls* (1992), set in New York in the 1980s, concerns a group of ambitious young professionals including Russell Calloway, a publisher who becomes embroiled in financial difficulties; his wife, Corinne, a high-flying businesswoman torn between the demands of her career and her longing to have a child; and Jeff Pierce, a successful writer who seems intent on destroying himself with drugs. The novel offers a jaundiced view of contemporary American society, which emerges as morally bankrupt and obsessed with material gain. McInerney edited *Cowboys, Indians and Commuters* (1994), a collection of short stories on modern American life by various writers.

MacINNES, Colin (1914–73), British novelist and essayist, born in London, brought up in Australia; he was the son of popular novelist Angela *Thirkell. His first novel, *To the Victor the Spoils* (1950), which chronicled a Field Security unit in occupied Europe, was followed by *June in Her Spring* (1952), an adolescent love story set in the Australian outback. His best-known work, an informal trilogy about bohemian London, consists of *City of Spades* (1957), a satirical view of the black immigrant community; *Absolute Beginners* (1959), about troubled teenagers; and *Mr. Love and Justice* (1960), an allegorical tale in which a young, over-zealous policeman confronts a sailor turned pimp. Other novels include *Westward to Laughter* (1969), *Three Years to Play* (1970), and *Loving Them Both* (1973). Praised for their gritty realism in his own time, his novels now seem mannered, even romantic. Other works include *England, Half English* (1961), a collection of essays; and *Sweet Saturday Night* (1967), a history of the British music hall.

MACINTOSH, Elizabeth, see TEY, JOSEPHINE.

McKAY, Claude (1890–1948), Jamaican/American novelist and poet, born in the Clarendon region of Jamaica. McKay was influenced by the English folklorist Walter Jekyll, who introduced him to poetry and encouraged him in the writing of local 'dialect' verse. His collections *Songs of Jamaica* (1911) and *Constab Ballads* (1912) mark an important step forward in anglophone Caribbean verse, being the first volumes of West Indian verse to employ a Creole voice as the main register. However, in the year of their publication, McKay left Jamaica for the USA, where he spent most of the remainder of his life. After attending the Tuskegee Institute and Kansas State University, he migrated north to New York, where he became an important figure in the *Harlem Renaissance. During the 1920s McKay became a communist and travelled to the USSR where he met Lenin and Trotsky and addressed the Third Internationale as a representative of the American Workers' Party. Back in America he turned to prose fiction, publishing *Home to Harlem* (1928); *Banjo* (1929); *Gingertown* (1931), a volume of short stories set in Jamaica; and **Banana Bottom* (1933), acknowledged as his finest novel. McKay also published *Spring in New Hampshire and Other Poems* (1920); *A Long Way from Home* (1937), an autobiography that provides personal testimony of American racial prejudice; and the non-fiction *Harlem: Negro Metropolis* (1940). In his later years he was converted to Catholicism. He occupies an important place in the African-American literary canon, but his contribution has a particularly Caribbean quality to it. See also ETHNICITY.

MACKAY, Shena (1944–), Scottish writer, born in Edinburgh, educated at Tonbridge Girls' Grammar School and Kidbrooke Comprehensive School. She left school at 16, and at 17 wrote her first short novel, *Dust Falls on Eugene Shlumberger*, which, along with *Toddler on the Run*, was published in 1964. *Music Upstairs* (1965) is an evocative account of life in the Earl's Court Road in the early 1960s. The novels *Old Crow* (1967) and *An Advent Calendar* (1971) established her reputation as a witty and innovative writer with a particular gift for simile and telling metaphor. *Babies in Rhinestones* (1983), a collection of stories, broke a long and significant silence, demonstrating Mackay's mastery of the short form. Other volumes of stories (*Dreams of Women's Handbags*, 1987, and *The Laughing Academy*, 1993) display the flamboyant imagery and surreal humour that characterize her best work; her *Collected Stories* were published in 1994. Mackay's novels of the 1980s, *A Bowl of Cherries* (1984) and *Redhill Roccoco* (1987), are set in the suburban background she has made her own; they deal, like many of her stories, with jealousy and morbid obsession. The theme of women fighting their way out of poverty and bad marriages to bond with each other is significant. Mackay's reputation reached its peak with the massive and ambitious *Dunedin* (1992), which follows the fortunes of the Mackenzie family in its progress from Scotland at the turn of the century to the urban hell of contemporary London. Bizarre comedy combines with lavish lyricism, political parable, and myth; the notion of redemption in love counterpoints what is essentially a bleak, tragic, and cautionary vision of *fin-de-siècle* London. Contemporaries drew parallels with *Firbank's decadent symbolism and Dickens's carnivalesque canvasses; but the overall uniqueness of Mackay's narrative technique has placed her among Britain's finest contemporary writers of fiction.

MacKAYE, Percy (Wallace) (1875–1956), American playwright, born in New York, educated at Harvard; he was the son of Steele MacKaye, an important figure in the modernization of nineteenth-century American theatre. Percy MacKaye wrote many plays in a variety of modes including the tetralogy *The Mystery of Hamlet, King of Denmark; or, What We Will* (1949), imagining events which preceded Shakespeare's play. His single success, *The Scarecrow* (1911), based on Nathaniel Hawthorne's tale 'Feathertop', is a dark fantasy of amatory vengefulness, in which a New England scarecrow is brought to life by the Devil and a seventeenth-century witch, Goody Rickby, to be the agent of revenge against the man who had been Goody's lover. MacKaye is highly regarded by theatre historians, even though attempts to stage his historical dramas and political satires have never proved successful. He anticipates the convictions of later twentieth-century American playwrights such as Arthur *Miller and Edward *Albee in his belief in the ideal of a subsidized non-commercial theatre, and wrote about these issues in *The Playhouse and the Play* (1909), *The Civic Theatre* (1912), and *Community Drama* (1917).

MACKENZIE, Sir (Edward Montague) Compton (1883–1972), British novelist, born in West Hartlepool, County Durham, educated at Magdalen College, Oxford. Following successes with the novels *The Passionate Elopement* (1911) and *Carnival* (1912), he was acclaimed as a major novelist for *Sinister Street* (two volumes, 1913, 1914), a psychologically penetrating narrative of a young man's passage through Oxford towards moral dissolution in the East End of London. After wartime service in the Dardanelles, Mackenzie lived in Capri for much of the 1920s, associating with D. H. *Lawrence and Norman *Douglas; 'Sirene', a fictionalized version of the island, forms the setting for *Vestal Fire* (1927) and *Extraordinary Women* (1928), which were considered scandalous for their erotic content. *Greek Memories* (1932), the last of the series of memoirs of his wartime experiences, resulted in a prosecution for disclosing classified information, to which he reacted with *Water on the Brain* (1933), a farcical satire on the intelligence services. Thereafter, he produced a succession of comic novels which include *The Red Tapeworm* (1941), the highly successful *Whisky Galore* (1947), *Rockets Galore* (1957), and *The Lunatic Republic* (1959). The most notable of his other novels is *The Four Winds of Love* (six volumes, 1937–45), an encompassing panorama of cultural and political developments throughout the earlier decades of the twentieth century. His many other publications include *Reaped and Bound* (1933), a collection of essays; *All over the Place* (1948), on his travels; and *Wind of Freedom* (1943), an account of the invasion of Greece in 1940. *My Life and Times*, his entertaining autobiography, appeared in ten volumes from 1963 to 1971.

MacLAVERTY, Bernard (1942–), Northern Irish novelist and short-story writer, born in Belfast. From 1960 to 1970 he worked as a laboratory technician before taking an English degree at Queen's University, Belfast. Upon graduating he moved to Scotland and taught there until 1981, when he became a full-time writer. MacLaverty's fiction has tended to concern themes of victimization, loneliness, and the destruction of desire by glacial social forces: as in *Secrets* (1977), his first collection of short stories. *Lamb* (1980), his first novel, portrays the efforts of a disillusioned Christian Brother to rescue both himself and a young boy from the brutal indifference of a remote institution. MacLaverty's second novel, *Cal* (1983), which has been produced successfully as a film, deals with the consequences of political violence and guilt upon the individual and succeeds in representing an intensely human aspect of the contemporary crisis in Ulster. MacLaverty's further volumes of short stories include *A Time to Dance and Other Stories* (1982), *The Great Profundo and Other Stories* (1987), and *Walking the Dog and Other Stories* (1994).

McLAVERTY, Michael (1907–), Irish novelist and short-story writer, born in Carrickmacross, Co. Monaghan, educated at Queen's University, Belfast. McLaverty taught mathematics in Belfast, becoming headmaster of St Thomas's School on the Falls Road. He has published several novels and collections of short stories. In his first novel, *Call My Brother Back* (1939), he explores the attitudes of Ulster people towards the land against the background of the sectarian violence which accompanied the creation of Northern Ireland. Subsequent novels include *Lost Fields* (1941) and *In This Thy Day* (1945), both of which portray the conflicts and loyalties of marginalized rural families. His first collection of short stories, *The Game Cock and Other Stories* (1947), illustrates McLaverty's belief in a simple and unpretentious prose style which develops from the nature of its subject matter. He rarely engages large political or social issues directly. His *Collected Short Stories* were published in 1978. McLaverty has been noted for the encouragement he gave to several 'younger' Ulster writers, such as Seamus *Heaney and John *McGahern.

MacLEAN, Alistair (Stuart) (1922–88), British popular novelist, born in Glasgow, educated at the University of Glasgow. His first novel, *H.M.S. Ulysses* (1955), was a bestseller; briskly narrated, it celebrates the endurance of the men who risked their lives on the hazardous 'Murmansk run', during the Second World War, to supply Soviet Russia. Most of his many books are witty adventure thrillers, many of which have been made into blockbuster Hollywood films. His best-known works include *The Guns of Navarone* (1957), *South by Java Head* (1958), *Fear is the Key* (1961), *Ice Station Zebra* (1963), and *Where Eagles Dare* (1967). Commando operations feature prominently in many of the novels, most notably in *Force 10 from Navarone* (1968) and *Partisans* (1982), both of which ingeniously exploit the complex allegiances of Yugoslav guerrilla factions during the Second World War.

MacLEAN, Sorley (Somhairle MacGill-Eain) (1911–), Gaelic poet, born in Osgaig on the island of Raasay, educated at the University of Edinburgh. He was a schoolteacher, and latterly a headmaster, subsequently becoming writer-in-residence at the University of Edinburgh and at the Gaelic College in Skye. In 1940 he was conscripted into the army and fought at the Battle of El Alamein where he was severely wounded. His experiences in wartime inform numerous poems, notably the compassionate study of a dead German soldier in 'Glac a' Bhàis'. MacLean wrote poetry in English until the early 1930s, having been stimulated by exposure to the work of *Eliot and *Pound; he decided, however, to write primarily in Gaelic, his first language and the tongue in which the rich cultural traditions of his family were rooted. His first publication was *Seventeen Poems for Sixpence* (1942), a collaboration with Robert *Garioch to which MacLean contributed eight Gaelic poems; a substantial collection entitled *Dàin do Eimhir* appeared in 1943, a work of the greatest significance in terms of its revitalization of literature in Gaelic. The title sequence of forty-eight elegiac love poems, translated as *Poems to Eimhir* (1971) by Iain Crichton *Smith, is accompanied by thirty-one other pieces on a wide range of themes and subjects comprehending responses to literature and music as well as autobiographical and political elements. MacLean characterized his language as possessing 'a sensuousness chiefly of the ear' in a letter to Hugh *MacDiarmid, whose close friend he remained after their first meeting in 1934. The elegiac realism of his use of landscape, the luminous precision of much of his imagery, and what Seamus *Heaney has described as his 'naturally genealogical imagination' are most memorably evident in 'Hallaig'; this long poem on the Highland clearances is included in *Reothairt is Contraigh/Spring Tide and Neap Tide* (1977), a collected edition with his own translations. *O Choille gu Bearradh/Collected Poems* (1989) displays the scope, political incisiveness, emotional sensitivity, and intellectual rigorousness of his work. His other books include *Ris a' Bhruthaich* (1985), a collection of critical essays centring on considerations of the Gaelic songs of the sixteenth and seventeenth centuries. See also SCOTTISH RENAISSANCE.

MacLEISH, Archibald (1892–1982), American poet and dramatist, born in Glencoe, Illinois, educated at Harvard; he practised as a lawyer until 1923, when he moved to Paris. He remained there for five years, associating with members of the *'Lost Generation' of American expatriate authors and developing innovative verse techniques under the influence of T. S. *Eliot and Ezra *Pound. *The Pot of Earth* (1925), *Streets in the Moon* (1926), and *The Hamlet of A. MacLeish* (1928), his principal collections of the period, form extended philosophical investigations of psychological and cultural themes. *Nobodaddy* (1926), the first of his verse-dramas, is an idiosyncratic treatment of fundamental metaphysical questions. Following his return to the USA, the concern with American nationhood in *New Found Land* (1930) set the pattern for much of his subsequent verse, which often emphasizes the disparity between America's democratic ideals and social actualities. The violent contrasts of European and Aztec orders in the long narrative poem *Conquistador* (1932) are emblematic of the cultural divisions accentuated by the Depression. The verse-dramas *Panic* (1935), *The Fall of the City* (1937), and *Air Raid* (1938) are imaginatively urgent responses to contemporary events in America and Europe. From 1939 to 1949, when he became Boylston Professor at Harvard, MacLeish held numerous important administrative posts, notably as Librarian of Congress and Assistant Secretary of State. Notable among his later collections of poetry are *Actfive* (1948), which evokes his sense of the challenge of the post-war years, and *Songs for Eve* (1954), in which a more personal and wide-ranging lyricism is evident. *New and Collected Poems, 1917–1982* appeared in 1985. His reaction to the anti-communist hysteria of the early 1950s took the form of the radio broadcast in 1952 of *The Trojan Horse*, a verse-drama collected with his earlier works in the genre in *Six Plays* (1980). His renewed interest in dramatic forms also resulted in *J. B.* (1958), a modernized version of the Book of Job which was produced on Broadway. The best known of his critical works is *Poetry and Experience* (1960), which centres on his conceptions of the social functions of poetry. The essays and memoirs of *A Continuing Journey* (1968) and *Riders on the Earth* (1978) incorporate much autobiographical material.

MacLENNAN, (John) Hugh (1907–90), Canadian novelist, born in Glace Bay, Cape Breton Island, educated at Dalhousie University (Halifax), Oxford University, and Princeton. One of Canada's best-known novelists, MacLennan was primarily a writer of allegorical fiction with a humanist message and a strong commitment to exploring the changing nature of Canadian identity. He took a complex view of his country, seeing Canada as occupying a middle ground between Old World classical humanist values and New World materialism. His first novel, *Barometer Rising* (1941), was set in Halifax in the First World War and centred on a devastating explosion in the city's harbour, which he views in the novel as signalling the end of the colonial era in Canada. *Two Solitudes* (1945) is set in Quebec and explores the social, cultural, and linguistic separateness of francophone and anglophone Canada. *The Watch that Ends the Night* (1959) contrasts the intersecting careers of two representative Canadian figures, the morally serious stay-at-home narrator and an adventurous and flamboyant internationalist. *Voices in Time* (1980), a science fiction novel set in a post-nuclear holocaust Montreal, reviews twentieth-century Western history and may be read as MacLennan's ultimate statement on the decline of Western civilization. Other works include *The Precipice* (1948), *Each Man's Son* (1951), *Return of the Sphinx* (1967), and three volumes of highly regarded essays.

McLUHAN, Marshall (1911–80), Canadian critic and theorist of popular culture and media, born in Edmonton, Alberta, educated at the universities of Manitoba and Cambridge. In the 1960s, when he was director of the University of Toronto's Center for Culture and Technology, his teasing publications on the history and contemporary cultural significance of technological developments in communications achieved controversial status internationally. *McLuhan Hot and Cool* (1967), with essays by Susan *Sontag, Tom *Wolfe, George *Steiner, and others, and responses by McLuhan, was described by *Harper's* as 'a philosophical discotheque'. His most important works are *The Mechanical Bride: Folklore of Industrial Man* (1951), *The Gutenberg Galaxy: The Making of Typographical Man* (1962), *Understanding Media* (1964), and *War and Peace in the Global Village* (1968). The central perception of McLuhan's world-view was that 'any technology gradually creates a totally new human environment'. McLuhan's most important contribution to the continuing debate was his emphasis upon how the controlling power of global media may have rendered outmoded our very sense of identity, with profound moral and psychological consequences for society. He foresaw how the media explosion of the 1970s and 1980s would challenge traditional social and academic divisions, and in *The Medium Is the Message* (1967) he stressed the impossibility of unmediated access to 'reality'. Later works include *Culture Is Our Business* (1970), *The Interior Landscape: The Literary Criticism of Marshall McLuhan, 1943–62* (1969; edited by Eugene McNamara), and *Letters of Marshall McLuhan* (1987; edited by Matie Molinaro and Corinne McLuhan, his widow, and annotated by William Toye).

MacMAHON, Bryan (1909–), Irish short-story writer, novelist, and playwright, born in the literary town of Listowel, Co. Kerry, which was also the birthplace of George *Fitzmaurice, John B. *Keane, and Maurice Walsh. He was educated at St Patrick's Teacher Training College, Dublin. During the Second World War he worked in factories in England, an experience he used to write about in his 'Plain People of England' column for *The *Bell* magazine. McMahon has turned his hand to poetry, fiction, balladeering, translation, scripts for radio and television, and books for children. His first collection of short stories, *The Lion-Tamer* (1948), predicted his ascendancy as one of the few masters of the Irish short story to emerge in the wake of Frank *O'Connor and Sean

*O'Faolain. Other collections include *The Red Petticoat* (1955). *The Honey Spike* (1967), generally regarded as his most accomplished novel, was adapted for the stage and performed at the *Abbey Theatre.

MacMANUS, Francis (1909–65), Irish novelist, born in Kilkenny, educated at University College, Dublin. He joined Radio Eireann as general features editor in 1948, in which capacity he introduced the Thomas Davis lectures series. His first novel, *Stand and Give Challenge* (1934), is the first volume of a trilogy about life in eighteenth-century Ireland; *Candle for the Proud* (1936) and *Men Withering* (1939) completed the trilogy, which is unified by the central figure of the poet Donnacha Ruadh MacConmara. His second trilogy, based on the fictional rural town of Drombridge, is set in the Kilkenny of his experience; *This House Was Mine* (1937), *Flow On, Lovely River* (1941), and *Watergate* (1942) deal with the established themes of Irish rural life: obsessions with land, sexual frustration, and the trials of emigration and return. He wrote three other novels in the early 1940s: *The Wild Garden* (1940), a study in the emotions of childhood; *The Greatest of These* (1943), concerning religious conflict in nineteenth-century Kilkenny, a theme similar to that of *The Big Chapel* (1972) by Thomas *Kilroy; and *Statue for a Square* (1945), his one (unsuccessful) attempt at being humorous. In his last two novels, MacManus descended into the depths of theological debate; *The Fire in the Dust* (1950) was followed by *American Son* (1959), a remarkable dialogue between conflicting modes of belief which, none the less, reveals the strong influence of Roman Catholicism on its author.

McMURTRY, Larry (1936–), American novelist, born in Wichita Falls, Texas, educated at North Texas State in Denton and at Rice University in Houston. McMurtry's father and grandfather were both cattlemen; his books reveal a nostalgia for the values of the Old West, though he is shrewdly aware that its reputation has been inflated by myth, a process he has attempted to reverse in books like *Anything for Billy* (1988), which presents Billy the Kid as an inept gunman living in a world of senseless violence. On the other hand, he has little time for the modern age, most memorably represented in the figure of Hud in *Horseman, Pass By* (1961); Hud is a self-centred, amoral man with no respect for anything but commercial profit. Although *Lonesome Dove* (1985; Pulitzer Prize) and its sequel, *Streets of Laredo* (1993), concentrate on the mixed glories of the Texas past, books like *Moving On* (1970) and *The Desert Rose* (1983) deal with the bittersweet realities of the modern-day survivor. *The Late Child* (1995) and *Dead Man's Walk* (1995) are recent novels. His books belong to the mainstream aesthetic of the realist novel; although he is not a literary innovator, he has shown a curiosity about other kinds of aesthetic, as seen in his portrayal of a writer in *All My Friends Are Going To Be Strangers* (1972). Many of his books have been filmed, including *Hud* (1961) and *The Last Picture Show* (1966).

McNAMARA, Brinsley, pseudonym of John WELDON (1890–1963), Irish novelist, short-story writer, and playwright, born in Delvin, Co. Westmeath. In 1910, while studying in Dublin for a career with the Customs and Excise, he joined the Abbey Players and accompanied them on their first tour of the USA. His first, and most notorious, novel, *The Valley of the Squinting Windows* (1918), is a vituperative study of the narrow-mindedness and religious orthodoxy of a rural community; it was burned in Delvin and vilified from pulpits throughout Ireland. In 1924 he became registrar of the National Gallery of Ireland, succeeding James *Stephens. He was also a founding member of the Irish Academy of Letters and, for a brief period in 1935, a director of the *Abbey Theatre; ironically, he resigned in protest over the production of *O'Casey's *The Silver Tassie* (1935). The reaction to his first novel did not deter McNamara's satiric impulse, and in *The Clanking of Chains* (1919) and *The Irishman* (1920) he undermined the Irish pastoral which had been made fashionable by Lady *Gregory. He began writing fiction and his novels became increasingly self-reflective until he wrote his experimental masterpiece, *The Various Lives of Marcus Igoe* (1929). McNamara's other works include the novels *Return to Ebontheever* (1930) and *Michael Caravan* (1946); a novella, *The Story of XYZ* (1951); and two collections of short stories, *The Smiling Faces* (1929) and *Some Curious People* (1946). As a playwright, his connections with the Abbey saw the production of nine of his plays between 1919 and 1945, including *The Glorious Uncertainty* (1923), *Look at the Heffernans* (1926), and *Margaret Gillan* (1933).

MacNAMARA, Gerald, the pseudonym of Harry C. MORROW (1866–1938), Northern Irish playwright and actor, born in Belfast, where he ran a decorating business in addition to his theatrical activities, which remained on an amateur basis throughout his career. MacNamara was a leading writer and actor with the *Ulster Literary Theatre, which produced twelve of his plays, chiefly comedies making incisive commentaries on the Northern Irish situation. Among the more notable are *Suzanne and the Sovereigns* (performed 1907), a satire on sectarian rivalries; *The Mist that Does Be On the Bog* (performed 1909), a parody of the *Abbey Theatre's 'peasant play' genre; and *No Surrender* (performed 1924), which satirizes aspects of Ulster society. *Thompson in Tir-na-nOg* (1918), his only published work, presents the transportation of a dull-witted Ulsterman to the Gaelic Land of Youth.

MacNEICE, (Frederick) Louis (1907–63), British poet, born in Belfast, educated at Merton College, Oxford, where he began friendships with W. H. *Auden and Stephen *Spender. After lecturing at the University of Birmingham and London University from 1930 to 1940, he was a writer and producer with the BBC from 1941 until his death. Among the many plays for radio he produced were a number of his own works, of which *Christopher Columbus* (1944) and *The Dark Tower* (1947) are considered classics of the genre. *Blind Fire-*

works (1929), his first volume of poetry, appeared in his final year at Oxford. Although the social concern in his verse of the 1930s is apparent, it lacks the doctrinaire political tone occasionally encountered in the work of Auden, Spender, and C. *Day Lewis, with whom he was closely associated. His collections of the period include *Poems* (1935), *The Earth Compels* (1938), containing some of his most memorable love poems, and *Autumn Journal* (1938), a topical meditation on events leading up to the Munich crisis. His numerous later collections of verse include *Springboard* (1944), *Holes in the Sky* (1948), *Visitations* (1957), and *The Burning Perch* (1963). *Collected Poems*, edited by E. R. Dodds, appeared in 1966. Both his lyric poetry and his more discursive verse are characterized by what Geoffrey *Grigson termed the 'certainty and peculiarity and delicacy of his rhythms'. His work often has an idiosyncratic lightness of touch allowing imagery of unusual vividness to border on fantasy without diminishing an underlying seriousness. His Belfast origins and the presence in his work of Irish themes and tones have latterly identified him as a precursor of the Ulster poets (see ULSTER POETRY) who emerged in the mid-1960s. Among his many other publications are *Letters from Iceland* (1937), his entertaining collaboration with Auden; the autobiographical *The Strings Are False* (1965); and *The Poetry of W. B. Yeats* (1941), the best-known of his critical works. There is a definitive biography, *Louis MacNeice* (1995) by Jon *Stallworthy.

McNEILL, Anthony (1941–), Jamaican poet, born in St Andrew, near Kingston, Jamaica, educated at Nassau Community College, Johns Hopkins University, and the University of Massachusetts. He has worked as a journalist and a university teacher and was Assistant Director of Publications for the Institute of Jamaica from 1976 to 1981. His principal collections of poetry are *Hello Ungod* (1971), *Reel from 'The Life-Movie'* (1975), and *Credences at the Altar of Cloud* (1979). Much of his work makes highly imaginative use of vivid natural imagery in the creation of disquieting treatments of socially and psychologically alienated states. His disciplined free verse combines rhythmical suggestions of Jamaica's oral traditions with the Standard English in which his work is chiefly written. With Neville Dawes, he edited *The Caribbean Poem* (1976), an anthology of verse by fifty West Indian poets.

McNICKLE, D'Arcy (1904–77), Native American writer of mixed Cree/Salish and white descent, born in St Agnatius, Montana, educated intermittently at universities in Montana, Oxford, and Grenoble. Active in Indian affairs throughout his life, McNickle worked for the Bureau of Indian Affairs (1936–52) and was chair of the Division of Social Sciences of the University of Saskatchewan, Regina (1965–71); he co-founded the National Congress of American Indians, and was the first director of the Center for the History of the American Indian at the Newberry Library. The experience of federal government Indian policy informs his three novels, and each deals with the conflict between white and tribal cultures from different perspectives. *Surrounded* (1936) describes the impact of the loss of tribal lands upon the values and communal identity of the tribe. In this work, and in *Runner in the Sun* (1954), his second novel, McNickle uses a lone figure who finds himself an embodiment of his tribal heritage. *Wind from an Enemy Sky* (1978) contrasts traditionalist and assimilationist world-views, expressing McNickle's pessimistic view of intercultural relations. He published a number of Native American histories, including *They Came Here First* (1949), *The Tribes of the United States* (1962), and *Native American Tribalism* (1973). *Indian Man* (1971) is a biography of Oliver La Farge. See NATIVE AMERICAN LITERATURE.

McPHERSON, James A(lan) (1943–), African-American story-writer, born in Savannah, Georgia, educated at Morris Brown College (Atlanta), Morgan State College (Baltimore), Harvard, and *Iowa Writers' Workshop. His considerable reputation rests upon two highly accomplished volumes of short stories, *Hue and Cry* (1969; Pulitzer Prize) and *Elbow Room* (1977), which received unstinting praise from Ralph *Ellison. McPherson's strengths lie in his angle on quotidian black life, city or country, past or present. In *Hue and Cry* stories like 'On Trains' and 'A Solo Song: For Doc' assume the voice of legendary black Pullman porters and waiters, historic elders from a classic American railway era; 'Cabbages and Kings' calls up the era of Civil Rights in terms of a remembered love gone awry across racial divides. In *Elbow Room* a story like 'Why I Like Country Music' has a black New Yorker harking back to his Southern boyhood in the image of a girl he once partnered at a country dance; 'The Story of A Dead Man' recreates a feisty, black, mythic figure out of black folklore; and 'I Am An American' tells of a young American black couple making their 'innocents abroad' entrance into the white metropolitan world of London. McPherson's distinctiveness lies in his command of an irony full of nuance yet never intrusive.

MACPHERSON, Jay (Jean) (1931–), Canadian poet, born in London; from 1940 onward she grew up in Canada, principally in Ottawa. She was educated at McGill University and at the University of Toronto, where she became Professor of English at Victoria College in 1974. The contents of *Nineteen Poems* (1952), published by Robert *Graves's Seizin Press, and *O Earth Return* (1954), issued by Emblem Books, Macpherson's own small press (see SMALL PRESSES), were incorporated into *The Boatman* (1957; expanded 1968) which gained her a considerable reputation. Dedicated to Northrop *Frye and his wife, the collection reflects Frye's emphasis on the mythic and archetypal properties of poetry. Macpherson's other major collection, *Welcoming Disaster* (1974), employs more complex forms to pursue its quest for meaning; the poems frequently succeed in maintaining imaginative contact with social reality while extending Macpherson's essential concern with psychological and metaphysical conditions. *The Boatman* and *Welcoming Disaster* were reissued together as *Poems Twice Told* (1981). Her other works include *Four Ages of Man* (1962), adaptations of classical myths for younger readers; and *The Spirit of Solitude* (1982), a highly regarded study of the elegiac and pastoral traditions from the seventeenth century onward.

McTAGGART, John (McTaggart Ellis) (1866–1925), British philosopher, born in London, educated at Trinity College, Cambridge. An idealist philosopher concerned with developing Hegelian notions of metaphysics, religion, and personal identity, McTaggart spent his academic life in Cambridge. Eager to reinforce 'a conviction of harmony between ourselves and the universe at large', yet critical of conventional, institutionalized religion and of Christianity, McTaggart's main text is the dense and paradoxical *The Nature of Existence* (2 volumes, 1921, 1927). Like fellow idealist F. H. *Bradley, who strongly influenced T. S. *Eliot, McTaggart was much concerned with the philosophy of time and matter, both concepts being seen by him as illusions, or systematic misperceptions of reality. By destabilizing the notion of time, McTaggart arrived at a version of immortality, whereby individuals existed timelessly, however much their appearances changed. In the end, McTaggart employed rational processes of deduction to reach towards a mystical vision of universal love. His main arguments are extraordinarily intricate and taxing. Like other British idealist writers (T. H. Green, B. Bosanquet, and Bradley), McTaggart's influence sharply waned after the emergence of logical positivism and its vehement distrust of metaphysics. His main works include *Studies in the Hegelian Dialectic* (1896), *Studies in Hegelian Cosmology* (1901), and *Some Dogmas of Religion* (1906).

McTeague, see NORRIS, FRANK.

McWILLIAM, Candia (1955–), Scottish novelist, born in Edinburgh, educated at Girton College, Cambridge. Her first novel, *A Case of Knives* (1988), a deftly plotted account of a triangular love affair involving an eminent heart surgeon, his male protégé, and the girl he selects as his beloved's future wife, was acclaimed for its sinister wit and stylistic inventiveness. *A Little Stranger* (1989), a black comedy about the uneasy relationship between an upper-middle-class woman and her child's nanny, also displays the writer's gift for sardonic observation. *Debatable Land* (1994) is set on board a yacht sailing from Papeete to Moorea, Tonga, and thence to New Zealand, and examines with characteristic subtlety the relationship between a group of characters of Scottish extraction, all of whom are haunted by aspects of the past. These include Logan Urquhart, a wealthy Glaswegian American who owns the boat, his second wife, Elspeth, who comes from the 'Debatable Land' of the Scottish borders immortalized by Stevenson; Alec, an Edinburgh artist; and Gabriel, a young girl who is taken on as a cook. McWilliam's distinctive style, which combines an almost pedantic precision with sharp observation of detail, gives her writing an intensely poetic quality.

MADDEN, Deirdre (1960–), Irish novelist, born in Co. Antrim, educated at Trinity College, Dublin and the University of East Anglia. Her novella *Hidden Symptoms* (1988) was published in Faber's *First Fictions* anthology. She won critical acclaim and the Somerset Maugham Prize for *Birds of the Innocent Wood* (1988), set in Ireland during the 1970s. *Remembering Light and Stone* (1992), which moves between Ireland and Italy, concerns its narrator's attempts to resolve her feelings of estrangement from her native country and to find some kind of reconciliation with her own past. *Nothing is Black* (1994), set in County Donegal, is about the relationship between three women—a painter, Claire, her cousin Nuala, who is prone to kleptomania, and Anna, a Dutch woman consumed by her thwarted desire for motherhood. In this, as in her earlier novels, Madden depicts the lives of her characters by focusing on the apparently inconsequential: details of their possessions, the meals they eat, and the daily tasks they perform are described with loving attentiveness, building up a complex and believable psychological portrait.

MADGE, Charles (Henry) (1912–96), British poet and sociologist, born in Johannesburg, South Africa, educated at Magdalen College, Oxford. Kathleen *Raine was his first wife. After working as a journalist, in 1937 he joined T. Harrisson and H. Jennings in founding *Mass-Observation, an organization for the collation of sociological data supplied by widespread observers. With Harrisson, he edited four compilations of reports, which include *Britain By Mass Observation* (1938). In 1950 he became Professor of Sociology at the University of Birmingham. Among his works as a sociologist are *War-Time Pattern of Saving and Spending* (1943) and *Society in the Mind* (1964). Having gained wide notice for his contributions to leading periodicals, he published *The Disappearing Castle*, his first collection of verse, in 1937. *The Father Found* (1941) was his last volume of poetry until *Of Love, Time, and Places* (1994), a selected edition containing numerous uncollected poems. His poetry characteristically combines considerable intellectual energy with a fluent and accessible style. Elsewhere a witty surrealism enlivens his socio-political concerns. His poem 'Letter to the Intelligentsia', which states 'there waited for me in the summer morning | Auden . . .', is frequently cited as evidence of W. H. *Auden's impact on his generation.

Magic Realism, a term coined in 1928 by the art critic Franz Roh to describe a school of German painting, has been most frequently used in the discussion of modern Latin American fiction. Writers who have been gathered under the label include the Guatemalan Miguel Angel Asturias (1899–1974), the Cuban Alejo Carpentier (1904–80), the Colombian Gabriel García Márquez (1928–), and the Chileans José Donoso (1924–) and Isabel Allende (1942–).

The term itself seems to signal confused, if not contradictory, attributes. On the one hand it indicates a form of writing which seeks to catch the extraordinary, magical-seeming properties of reality itself—of a (particularly South American) world which looks fantastic but isn't. This is what Carpentier meant by his phrase 'the marvellous real', *lo real maravilloso*. The realism mirrors reality, the idea of magic is a metaphor for the writer's delighted surprise. On the other hand, much of this fiction deals with events which are magical by any standards, even in South America—levitation, clairvoyance, sundry miracles, imaginary diseases, deaths without cause or reason, ghosts, lives of Biblical longevity—and the realism concerns the tone in which these events are reported. The narrative treats them as quite ordinary, not to be distinguished from the most mundane occurrences. Magic is written as if it were real, as if the fantastic had simply vanished from the world. It is the second mode which seems dominant, although the British practitioners of magic realism—notably Angela *Carter and Salman *Rushdie—manage to put both modes together with some success. For them reality, even domestic reality and especially political reality, is fantastic; but their narrative voices, although less studiously neutral than that of García Márquez, for example, remain ironic rather than agitated, expressive of hilarity and dismay but not astonishment. Carter's chief works in this vein are *The Infernal Desire Machines of Doctor Hoffman* (1972), *The Passion of New Eve* (1977), and *Nights at the Circus* (1984); Rushdie's are **Midnight's Children* (1981), *Shame* (1983), and *The *Satanic Verses* (1988).

Magus, The, see FOWLES, JOHN.

MAHAPATRA, Jayanta (1928–), Indian poet, born in Cuttack, Orissa, educated at Ravenshaw College, Cuttack, and Patna University. He has worked as a lecturer in physics at a succession of colleges, chiefly in the Orissa region. *Close the Sky, Ten by Ten* (1971), his first significant publication as a poet, was followed by numerous collections which include *A Rain of Rites* (1976), *Life Signs* (1983), *Burden of Waves and Fruit* (1988), and *Temple* (1989); *Selected Poems* appeared in 1987. His work is notable for the poise with which disquieted alienation and deep attachment are held in tension in his perceptions of the traditional patterns of Indian life. The intense privacy which gives rise to haunting effects of mood in much of his verse is complemented by vivid use of closely observed imagery drawn from his urban and natural surroundings. Among his other publications is the topographical prose work *Orissa* (1987).

MAHON, Derek (1941–), Northern Irish poet, born in Belfast; he grew up in Glengormley, Co. Antrim, and was educated at Belfast Institute and Trinity College, Dublin. After teaching in Belfast and Dublin, he became the **Listener*'s drama critic in 1971 and subsequently held editorial positions with *Vogue* and the **New Statesman*. He has also worked as a writer-in-residence in Britain and America and as a television scriptwriter. His first significant publication as a poet was *Twelve Poems*, produced along with pamphlets of work by Seamus *Heaney and Michael *Longley for the Belfast Festival in 1965 (see ULSTER POETRY). *Night Crossing* (1968) was followed by numerous collections which include *Lives* (1972), *The Snow Party* (1975), *Poems 1962–1978* (1979), *The Hunt by Night* (1982), *Antarctica* (1985), *Selected Poems* (1991), and *The Yaddo Letter* (1992). Much of Mahon's poetry draws its economically precise imagery from various Irish localities. Considerable power and originality are evident in his imaginative confrontations with social and cultural conditions in Northern Ireland; 'Rage for Order' and 'Last of the Fire Kings' address the extreme predicament of the poet in Ulster in energetic and disciplined free verse. His later work is more contemplative in tone and is distinguished by the subtlety and accomplishment of its verse forms. *High Time* (1984) and *The School for Wives* (1986) are his adaptations of plays by Molière; *The Bacchae* is adapted from the play by Euripides. His works as a translator include Nerval's *The Chimeras* (1982) and *Selected Poems* (1988) of Jaccottet.

MAILER, Norman (1923–), American novelist, essayist, and journalist, born in Long Branch, New Jersey, he grew up in Brooklyn and was educated at Harvard. Mailer served with the armed forces in the Pacific during the Second World War, which provided the background for his highly successful first novel, *The *Naked and the Dead* (1948). His following novels, *Barbary Shore* (1951) and *The Deer Park* (1955), were poorly received. At this time, Mailer was moving philosophically towards a particularly personal version of existentialism, which received expression in numerous of the essays and short stories collected in *Advertisements for Myself* (1959), the most notable of which were 'The White Negro', 'The Time of Her Time', and 'The Man Who Studied Yoga'. This collection describes his turbulent career in the decade after the war: marriage and divorces; disillusionment with left-wing politics; experiments with drugs and with new fictional styles. During the 1960s he produced mainly journalism and essays, and he was one of the driving forces behind what became '*New Journalism' with its blurring of the boundaries between fiction and fact. The work of this period includes *The Presidential Papers* (1963), a varied selection of past writings; *Cannibals and Christians* (1966); *Why Are We in Vietnam?* (1967); and *The *Armies of the Night: History as a Novel, the Novel as History* (1968), his report of the huge 1967 anti-Vietnam War march on the Pentagon (see VIETNAM WRITING). His most notorious work is *An American Dream* (1965). Stephen Rojack, the hero-as-hipster, murders his wife and sexually abuses her maid, in a book which is often gruesome in its depiction of violence and which has been regarded as autobiographical fantasizing. It marked the beginning of a series of collisions between Mailer and the leading members of the Women's Liberation Movement, which he did nothing to ameliorate by writing *The Prisoner of Sex* (1971), a polemical attack on Kate *Millett and an account of his belief that the Women's Liberation Movement was intellectually feeble. During this time, Mailer ran unsuccessfully for mayor of New York in 1969, and acted in a number of films, including *Maidstone* (1968). Other books include *A Fire on the Moon* (1970), on NASA's first lunar spaceflight; a biography of Marilyn Monroe, *Marilyn* (1973); *The Fight* (1975), an account of the Foreman–Ali heavyweight fight in Zaire; and *Genius and Lust: A Journey Through the Major Writings of Henry Miller* (1976). In addition, other collections of essays and miscellaneous material on culture, politics, sport, sex, rocketry, speeches, lectures, and manifestos are to be found in *Miami and the Siege of Chicago* (1968), *St. George and the Godfather* (1972), *Existential Errands* (1972), *Some Honorable Men* (1975), and *Pieces and Pontifications* (1982). His work and life continued to provoke controversies, often caused by the aggressive and idiosyncratic critical positions he has adopted. His later works include *The Executioner's Song* (1979), a lengthy study of Gary Gilmore's criminal life; *Ancient Evenings* (1983), a vast 'historical' novel set in Egypt; *Tough Guys Don't Dance* (1984); *Harlot's Ghost* (1991), a huge novel about the CIA, and the intricate network of deceptions, double-crossings, and espionage of secret agents, in the world of intelligence and counter-intelligence; *Oswald's Tale: An American Mystery* (1995); and *Pablo and Fernande: Portrait of Picasso as a Young Man: An Interpretative Biography* (1995).

Main Street, a novel by Sinclair *Lewis, published in 1920, dramatized in 1921. Carol Milford, an unremarkable though quick-witted girl, upon graduation from college marries Will Kennicott, a kindly and hardworking doctor from Gopher Prairie, Minnesota. Carol yearns for a free and gracious life, but when she attempts to put her vague aspirations into action by improving village life, finds herself thwarted by the intolerant, smug, and complacent attitudes of the villagers. The novel dramatizes a clash between Carol's naïve idealism and the reality of habitual and standardized dullness. Certain characters like the repressed yet energetic schoolteacher Vida Sherwin, the local lawyer Guy Pollock, and the Swedish vagabond Miles Bjornstam, appear to escape the trammels of this stultifying existence, although they are equally inadequate rebels. Carol becomes attracted to Erik Valborg and moves to Washington to forge her own life. However, when Kennicott comes for her two years later, she returns with him to Gopher Prairie. In the end, Kennicott's middle-class values of steady complacency triumph, as does the Middle West and the middle brow. The impulse to escape class conventions, to flee the humdrum, turns into a partial success and then compromise with convention.

MAIS, Roger (1905–55), Jamaican novelist, poet, painter, and playwright, born in Kingston, Jamaica. Although he belonged to the well-to-do middle class, Mais had a lively social conscience that inspired lifelong interest in the poorer classes of his black countrymen. Sharp social criticism in an article he wrote for the People's National Party newspaper *Public Opinion* in 1944 earned him a six-month jail sentence, where he experienced the appalling conditions in Jamaican prisons during British colonial rule. These conditions are vividly portrayed in his first novel, *The Hills Were Joyful Together* (1953), which consists of loosely assembled episodes giving a stark portrait of denizens of a slum in Kingston, Jamaica; but this bleakness is relieved by ribald humour and self-mockery. Similar themes are treated in **Brother Man* (1954), his best-known work. *Black Lightning* (1955) explores the spiritual failure of a blacksmith carving a lifesize statue of Samson; like Samson, he is destroyed by pride. The strong biblical language and references in Mais's writing suggest that he was as much concerned with spiritual regeneration as with political ideology and patriotism. He also published two collections of stories and completed two unpublished novels. In 1978 he was posthumously awarded the Order of Jamaica.

MAITLAND, Sara (1950–), British novelist and short-story writer, born in London, educated at Oxford University, where she became interested in reconciling feminist principles with Christianity. Her first novel, *Daughter of Jerusalem* (1978; Somerset Maugham Prize, 1979), was a feminist reworking of Old and New Testament stories and concerned women and fertility. Feminist themes were similarly explored in her novel *Virgin Territory* (1984) and in a collection of essays, *A Map of the New Country* (1983), examining the role of women in the Christian Church. *Three Times Table* (1990) is set in a London house during a single night, in which three women of different generations reflect upon the choices they have made and the significant options open to them. *Home Truths* (1993), which probes the dynamics of a large family and unravels self-deceipt, was followed by *Hagiographies* (1996). Maitland has also published several volumes of short stories, including *Telling Tales* (1983), which includes a feminist version of the Creation myth and an account of the life of a female Pope, *A Book of Spells* (1987), and *Women Fly when Men Aren't Watching* (1993). She has also published a book of Greek myths, *Pandora's Box* (1995).

MAJA-PEARCE, Adewale (1953–), British-Nigerian writer, born in London of British and Yoruba parents; he grew up in Lagos and was educated at the University College of Wales, Swansea, and London University's School of Oriental and African Studies. He became a researcher for **Index on Censorship*. *Loyalties and Other Stories* (1986) are short stories drawing on his experiences of Nigeria. He has subsequently made the documentary essay his principal medium, in the belief that it is most suited to his investigations of the British and Nigerian cultures he has inherited. His most highly regarded works are *In My Father's Country*

(1987), an account of his travels in Nigeria, and *How Many Miles to Babylon?* (1990), on racial consciousness in contemporary Britain. His other publications include *Who's Afraid of Wole Soyinka?: Essays on Censorship* (1991), an examination of censorship in Africa, and *A Mask Dancing: Nigerian Novelists of the Eighties* (1992). He edited *Christopher Okigbo: Collected Poems* (1986) and *The Heinemann Book of African Poetry in English* (1990).

MAJOR, Clarence (1936–), American novelist and poet, educated at the Art Institute of Chicago, the New School for Social Research, the State University of New York, and the Union for Experimental Colleges and Universities; amongst other teaching posts he became Professor at the University of California at Davis. Widely recognized to be at the experimental forefront of African-American poetry and fiction, he has made a special forte of using popular culture in his work—African-American and American-at-large. Although he began as a poet, he won his early reputation with a novel, *All-Night Visitors* (1969), an urbane, and at times strikingly erotic, inter-racial story. Verse, fiction, essays, short stories, and anthologies have followed in profusion. His other works of fiction include the novels *NO* (1973), a kind of literary detective story; *Reflex and Bone Structure* (1975), a model of reflexivity; *Emergency Exit* (1979), again an experiment in voice and design; *Such Was The Season* (1987), an intimate, more conventional, story-memoir of black middle-class life in Atlanta; and a short-story collection, *Fun and Games* (1990). Among his volumes of poetry are *Swallow The Lake* (1970), *Symptoms and Madness* (1971), *Private Line* (1971), *The Cotton Club* (1972), *Inside Diameter: The France Poems* (1985), and *Surfaces and Masks* (1988). He has also written a *Dictionary of Afro-American Slang* (1970).

Major Barbara, a play by Bernard *Shaw, performed in 1905, published in 1907. This portrays a wager and a moral conflict between Barbara, a major in the Salvation Army, and her father Andrew Undershaft, a wealthy and powerful manufacturer of armaments. Each undertakes to give up his or her calling if the other's work proves sufficiently impressive. On a visit to the East End shelter where she works, he undermines her belief in the Army by exposing the extent to which it is dependent on the economic system which creates the poverty it helps to relieve. Barbara then visits her father's arms factory with her conventional mother and brother, Lady Britomart and Stephen Britomart, and her fiancé, a Professor of Greek named Adolphus Cusins. All are impressed by the model community Undershaft has created, and Cusins agrees to enter (and eventually inherit) his business after allowing himself to be convinced that arms, war, and violence have the power to change the social system the Salvation Army is perpetuating. Barbara consents to become part of this arrangement, in what Shaw suggests is a synthesis of the spiritual and the practical, religion and the promise of political change. Undershaft, at first a Mephistophelean tempter and capitalist villain, has by now been transformed into an exemplary embodiment of the evolutionary appetite and the 'life force'. Shaw subtitled the play 'a discussion in three acts' in wry acknowledgement of the increasingly common accusation that he was more interested in debating ideas than in dramatizing action; but frequent revivals attest to its humour, tension, and other theatrical strengths.

MALAMUD, Bernard (1914–86), American novelist, born in Brooklyn to first-generation Russian immigrant parents, educated at Columbia University. The recipient of many writing awards and honours, as a popular Jewish-American writer he has contributed influentially to the ethnic consciousness of American literature. His first novel, *The Natural* (1952), adapted as a film in 1984, parodies both the pretensions of those who see baseball as a metaphor for heroism and the idea of the existence of the 'great American novel'. His second, *The *Assistant* (1957), a more serious work, explores the collision between emotional bonds and cultural barriers in its depiction of the tensions and connections between the Jewish and Italian communities in New York. Thereafter, Malamud's work vacillates between these two poles of satire and serious moral commentary. His next novel, *A New Life* (1961), charts the life of Sam Levin from loser to father, a development of the responsibility of the individual but also of disillusionment. Malamud's best-known novel, *The *Fixer* (1967, Pulitzer Prize), was followed by *Pictures of Fidelman: An Exhibition* (1969), a picaresque novel which examines the innocent American abroad as Fidelman travels through Italy, and *The Tenants* (1971), an experimental novel which looks at the complex relationships between blacks and Jews in mid-twentieth-century America. His final novels were *Dubin's Lives* (1979), about a middle-aged biographer torn between passion and honesty, and *God's Grace* (1982), about a sole survivor of a nuclear holocaust. Many of the themes of satire, seriousness, and examination of the qualities and trials of being Jewish in the USA are concentrated into his collections of short stories which include *The Magic Barrel* (1958), *Idiots First* (1963), and *Rembrandt's Hat* (1973). Here, as in the rest of his work, the continuing concern with the strains between cultural and ethnic specificity, and with the conception of the USA as a 'melting pot', is interrogated at length.

Malgudi Days, see NARAYAN, R. K.

MALOUF, David (1934–), Australian poet and fiction writer, born in Brisbane. Malouf first established his reputation with *Bicycle and Other Poems* (1970), while *Neighbours in a Thicket* (1974) revealed an early interest in European history. The poems in *First Things Last* (1980) explored the contours of landscapes of the mind; *Selected Poems* appeared in 1980 and *New and Collected Poems* in 1991. The shift from the apparently autobiographical *Johnno* (1975) to *An Imaginary Life* (1978), which with extraordinary power recreated the inner and outer worlds of the poet Ovid in exile on the Black Sea, revealed Malouf as a talented fiction writer. *Child's Play* (1982; published with *Fly Away Peter*, 1982) drew on Malouf's perceptions of contemporary Italy in its exploration of the links a terrorist perceives between himself and the writer who is his intended victim. *Fly Away Peter* was set in Queensland before the First World War, juxtaposing its peaceful lush landscape with the destructive horrors of the European trenches. *Harland's Half Acre* (1984), an acclaimed family saga set in rural Australia, presented the central character, painter Frank Harland, as a visionary exile. *Antipodes* (1985) was a collection of short stories, while *12 Edmonstone Street* (1985) discerningly explored four different, but complementary, pasts, from childhood Brisbane to Tuscany where Malouf lived from 1977. His first play, *Blood Relations* (1988), is about a Christmas gathering and the tensions it releases. Returning to fiction in *The Great World* (1990) Malouf used differing reactions to war to evoke a wide-ranging picture of Australian life. He was highly acclaimed for his detailed evocation of a past age in *Remembering Babylon* (1993), a novel charting a young boy's struggle to accept the white culture he is restored to after spending sixteen years with Aborigines. He has also written *Baa Baa Black Sheep: A Jungle Tale* (1993), a libretto for an opera by Michael Berkeley, based on work by Rudyard Kipling. Malouf has demonstrated an impressive range of voices and interests, and in international review articles has shown himself to be an important cultural critic.

MALTZ, Albert (1908–85), American dramatist and novelist, born in Brooklyn, New York, educated at Columbia University and Yale Drama School. At Yale Maltz attended George Pierce *Baker's influential drama workshop where he befriended George Sklar; the friendship resulted in Sklar's collaboration with the writing of Maltz's influential early plays, *Merry-Go-Round* (1932) and *Peace on Earth* (1933). Maltz was quickly adopted by the American literary left which had come to prominence in the Depression years. The first play under his sole authorship, *Black Pit* (1935), with its tale of a coal miners' strike, is openly propagandistic and tendentious, as is *Private Hicks* (1936), with its fictionalized treatment of the breaking of a strike at the Electric Auto-Lite Company in Toledo, Ohio, in 1934. Maltz then turned to fiction with *The Way Things Are* (1938), a collection of short stories, and novels such as *The Underground Stream* (1940) and *The Cross and the Arrow* (1944). He achieved notoriety with his infamous article in the *New Masses* in 1946, 'What Shall We Ask of Writers?', a rejection of most contemporary American left-wing writing and of the 'art as weapon' theory that sustained it. His prominence on the left brought him further trouble when he was numbered among the 'Hollywood Ten' by the House Committee on Un-American Activities, cited for contempt, and subsequently blacklisted. His work for the cinema includes *This Gun for Hire* (1942), *Destination Tokyo* (1944), and *Pride of the Marines* (1945). See also PROLETARIAN LITERATURE IN THE USA.

MAMET, David (1947–), American dramatist, born in Flossmore, Illinois, educated at Goddard College, Vermont. Mamet moved to Chicago and helped found the St Nicholas Theatre Company which subsequently staged the first productions of many of his early plays including *Duck Variations* (1972), *The Poet and the Rent* (1974), *Squirrels* (1974), and *Reunion* (1976). From the mid-1970s Mamet developed a close relationship with the Goodman Theater in Chicago, where *American Buffalo* was first produced in 1975, followed by *A Life in the Theater* (1977), *The Woods* (1977), and *Lone Canoe, or The Explorer* (1979). Mamet's involvement with the Chicago theatres has meant that his work is often premièred in that city before opening in New York. He is a tirelessly productive writer who has written a great many full-length plays and short plays, several screenplays and adaptations, and a collection of essays entitled *Writing in Restaurants* (1986). His best-known plays are *Sexual Perversity in Chicago* (1974), *American Buffalo*, *Glengarry Glen Ross* (1983; Pulitzer Prize), which was made into a film, and *Speed the Plow* (1988). Mamet has also written the screenplays for Bob Rafelson's remake of *The Postman Always Rings Twice*, Sidney Lumet's *The Verdict*, and Brian De Palma's *The Untouchables*. More recently, in *House of Games* (1987), *Things Change* (1987), and *Homicide* (1990), Mamet has become director of his own screenplays, and has quickly developed a reputation as a talented film-maker. Mamet uses speech as a means to anatomize the discontents of the American psyche, especially in relation to the conflicts of desire between men and women, and the unrealizeable dreams of success which animate Americans in their workaday world. His characters are endowed with a vituperative rhetoric which is not unlike John *Osborne's theatrical idiom. Mamet, who has also been compared with Harold *Pinter, acknowledges a deep respect for Chekhov, not only in the way in which the Russian master uses language as a mode of revelation to and through his characters, but also in his consummate stagecraft. And like Chekhov and Pinter, Mamet is very much a man of the theatre and with Arthur *Miller, Edward *Albee, and Sam *Shepard, is one of the luminaries of the contemporary American theatre. A more recent play, *Oleana* (1992), is a controversial drama where issues of gender politics and linguistic hierarchy are crystallized in the charged tutorial encounter between a male professor and one of his female students. Though seen by many as a topical and misogynist diatribe against the agenda of contemporary feminism, the play's wider concern with the use and abuse of power gives it an interest beyond the anxieties of present-day sexual politics. *The Cryptogram* (1994), by contrast, is a short, intense family drama of betrayal and duplicity featuring an abandoned wife and young son; the play has invoked comparisons with Pinter in Mamet's investigation of the uses we make of language to deceive others and ourselves, especially within the bedrock of family life. *David Mamet* (1985) by C. W. E. Bigsby is a critical study.

Man and Superman, a play by Bernard *Shaw, first published in 1903, first performed (without Act 3) in 1905; Act 3, *Don Juan in Hell*, was first presented, as a one-act play, in 1907. This is a witty variation on the Don Juan story, in which the brilliant John Tanner, a progressive thinker with distinct similarities to Shaw himself, is relentlessly if slyly pursued by a woman determined to make him her husband, Ann Whitefield. When Tanner is made aware of her intentions by his chauffeur Straker (an example of H. G. *Wells's 'new man') he flees by motor-car to Spain, where he is captured by brigands and discovered by Ann, who has followed him. The play ends with her announcing their engagement and his surrendering to a fate he realizes is inevitable. There is also a sub-plot, involving Ann's tough-minded friend Violet and her secret marriage to the son of an American millionaire, Hector Malone. The story is full of coincidences and melodramatic happenings, but there is invariably something ironic or paradoxical about them. The brigands, for instance, are political thinkers. The heroine, not the hero, takes all the romantic initiatives. Tanner's emotional defeat by Ann is also the victory of one 'life-force' over another, of the female need to perpetuate the species over the male desire for intellectual accomplishment. Still more incongruously, Act 3 is a dream-debate, 'Don Juan in Hell', in which Tanner, or Juan, puts the case for the aspiring intellect and the Devil for conventional happiness. The play as a whole is heavily imbued with Shavian metaphysics, and this particular sequence was described by its author as 'a new book of Genesis for the Bible of the Evolutionists'.

MANDEL, Eli(as Wolf) (1922–), Canadian poet and critic, born in Esteven, Saskatchewan, educated at the Universities of Saskatchewan and Toronto. Mandel began publishing verse in small magazines in the early 1950s; his first notable collection, 'Minotaur Poems', appeared along with poems by Phyllis Webb and Gael Turnbull in *Trio* (1954). His first individual volume was *Fuseli Poems* (1960), where the title pays homage to the eighteenth-century Swiss-English poet, whose tragic subjects and Gothic landscapes provided an inspiration for Mandel's own reflections on human suffering and the harshness of the natural world. It was followed by *An Idiot Joy* (1967) and *Stony Plain* (1973), in which his Jewish background and the horrors of twentieth-century Jewish history first become overt subjects. Later work has included *Out of Place* (1977), which deals with his Jewish Saskatchewan origins in a mode which questions the referential quality of language, and *Life Sentence* (1981), a collection inspired by his travels in Latin America and India, which interrogates the autobiographical form. Mandel has moved from a dense and opaque allusiveness to a more colloquial and accessible style, with recent work adopting more experimental modes. Other volumes of poetry include *Black and Secret Man* (1964), *Crusoe: Poems Selected and New* (1973), and *Dreaming Backwards: Selected Poems* (1981). Mandel has also edited several important anthologies of Canadian poetry, including *Poets of Contemporary Canada: 1960–1970* (1972). His critical writing, which is informed by the same questioning approach to language as his poetry, includes *Irving Layton* (1969), *Another Time* (1977), and *The Family Romance* (1986).

Mandelbaum Gate, The, a novel by M. *Spark, published in 1965. Set in Jerusalem in the early 1960s, the novel opens with the reflections of a middle-aged British expatriate, Freddie Hamilton, a bachelor and amateur poet, concerning the arrival of a British schoolmistress, Barbara Vaughan, who has enlisted his help in order to visit certain religious sites on the Jordanian side of the Mandelbaum Gate, which marks the division between the Arab and Jewish quarters of the city. The situation is complicated by the fact that Miss Vaughan, a Catholic convert, is half Jewish; and the political tension between the Arab and Israeli states makes her intended pilgrimage seem fraught with danger. To add to the complexity, Barbara Vaughan is waiting to hear from her fiancé, Harry Clegg, an archaeologist working on the Dead Sea Scrolls excavation, as to whether he has succeeded in having his marriage annulled. In a scene of great suspense, Barbara visits Jordan disguised as an Arab serving-woman; while she is there she contracts scarlet fever and then disappears. Freddie Hamilton, meanwhile, who has engineered this escapade, finds himself back in the Jewish part of the city, with no memory of events leading up to her disappearance and fearing that his headstrong countrywoman is in mortal danger. The novel deals compellingly with issues of religious and political identity, and makes the story of its protagonist's quest for the reconciliation of the two cultural and religious traditions to which she belongs as exciting as any thriller.

MANDER, Jane (1877–1949), New Zealand novelist, born near Auckland. A family timber-milling background is reflected in her powerful and sensitive depiction of the wild North Island landscape as spiritually as well as physically challenging, as in *The Story of a New Zealand River* (1920). Both *The Passionate Puritan* (1922) and *The Strange Attraction* (1922) evoked sexual as well as colonial tensions; in this respect Mander was ahead of her time, and endured much hostile criticism of her writing. Her best novel, *Allen Adair* (1925), charted terrain that later New Zealand writers were to see as central issues of personal and national identity but was largely ignored in New Zealand on publication: regrettably, as Mander's work represents an important women's perspective on a culture whose myths have too often been defined in male terms. *The Besieging City: A Novel of New York* was published in 1926. She lived in London from 1923 and returned to Auckland in 1932 intending to write of that country she had once described as being 'in my bones', but she died without realizing her ambition. *Jane Mander* (1972) by Dorothea Turner is a critical study.

Man for All Seasons, A, see BOLT, ROBERT.

Manhattan Transfer, a novel by John *Dos Passos, published in 1925. *Manhattan Transfer* was the most experimental of Dos Passos's early novels and in it he employed narrative techniques which he was to develop in the subsequent novels that make up the **U.S.A.* (1938) trilogy. As its title—a reference to the 'transfer' stations on the New York subway system—indicates, the novel is concerned with life in New York City in the years around the First World War and uses a series of characters through whom the urban experience is reflected. The novel dispenses with plot and narrative as traditionally understood and uses the resources of impressionism, newsreel, popular song, and journalistic reportage to mimetically recreate a 'montage' of New York life. In its technical features it is one of the most innovative American novels of the 1920s and was admired by many of Dos Passos's contemporaries, in both the USA and Europe. Like many of his early works, *Manhattan Transfer* is also important as a document of his political radicalism. See also PROLETARIAN LITERATURE IN THE USA.

MANHIRE, Bill (1946–), New Zealand poet and short-story writer, born in Invercargill, educated at the University of Otago and at University College, London. His early work appeared in the seminal magazine *Freed*, along with that of Ian *Wedde and Murray *Edmond. As Reader in the Department of English at Victoria University, Wellington, Manhire inaugurated a creative writing course which has had a strong influence on the work of younger poets and novelists. His collections *The Elaboration* (1972), *How To Take Off Your Clothes At a Picnic* (1977), *Good Looks* (1982), *Zoetropes: Poems 1979–82* (1984), and *Milky Way Bar* (1991) are characterized by restraint in language and a minimalist but playful surface. He includes unusual and complex extremes in his poems. Uncertainty and humour are also characteristic of Manhire's tone, along with a bemused use of cliché and a sense that language will always fall short of what the poet is attempting to convey. Manhire has also produced the short stories *The New Land: A Picture Book* (1990) and *South Pacific* (1994). *The Brain of Katherine Mansfield* (1989) is a quirky collection of prose pieces.

MANNING, Olivia (1908–80), British novelist, born in Portsmouth. She spent much of her youth in Ireland, where her first novel, *The Wind Changes* (1937), is set; the book explores the relationships between a young woman, her Irish Republican lover, and the middle-aged English writer who fascinates them both, and displays the interest in political themes she was later to develop in her most famous work. She studied art in Portsmouth and moved to London in her early twenties, where she was employed for a time as a furniture painter—a period described in her autobiographical novel *The Doves of Venus* (1955), which also contains a portrait of her friend Stevie *Smith. She married R. D. Smith, a British Council lecturer, on the eve of the Second World War, and accompanied him to Bucharest and later to Greece, Egypt, and Jerusalem, experiences which were to form the basis of *The *Balkan Trilogy* (*The Great Fortune*, 1960; *The Spoilt City*, 1962; *Friends and Heroes*, 1965) and *The *Levant Trilogy* (*The Danger Tree*, 1977; *The Battle Lost and Won*, 1978; and *The Sum of Things*, 1980). The novels powerfully evoke the vicissitudes of life in wartime and give a vivid sense of place and period. Manning wrote several other novels, including *Artist Amongst the Missing* (1949), set in Cairo; *School for Love* (1951), set in a Jerusalem boarding house; *A Different Face* (1953), about a schoolmaster in Portsmouth; *The Play Room* (1969), also set in Portsmouth; and *The Rain Forest* (1974), set on an imaginary North African island. She also published two volumes of short stories, *Growing Up* (1948) and *A Romantic Hero* (1966); a travel book about Ireland, *The Dreaming Shore* (1950); and a biographical study of Stanley in Africa, *The Remarkable Expedition* (1947). *The Balkan Trilogy* and *The Levant Trilogy* were televised in 1987 under the overall title of *Fortunes of War*.

Man of the People, A, a novel by Chinua *Achebe, published in 1966. This satire deals with corruption and the cult of personality in a newly independent African state. The two main protagonists are government minister Chief Nanga, 'the most approachable politician in the country', and his idealistic former pupil Odili, who narrates the story in a style characteristic of the author, effectively blending African proverbs and pidgin English with evidence of the encroachment of Western mores. Invited to stay with Chief Nanga, Odili finds himself in an unfamiliar but seductive social world, where Nanga enjoys an opulent *arriviste* lifestyle while at the same time subscribing to traditional customs, including polygamy. Things take a turn for the worse for Odili when his sometime girlfriend succumbs to Nanga's charms, leaving Odili smarting with resentment and hatching plans for revenge. He sets out to influence Nanga's intended second wife, Edna, away from Nanga though in the process he begins to value her qualities. At the same time Odili, on behalf of a dissident political party, decides to contest Chief Nanga's seat at the coming election, and the repercussions have adverse effects not only for Odili's friends and family but for his whole village. The two rivals clash publicly and physically at Nanga's inaugural campaign meeting, as a result of which Odili is hospitalized and briefly arrested on a trumped-up charge. Although Odili's political ambitions come to an abrupt end, and Nanga is re-elected, by the end of the book the corrupt government—'a regime which inspired the common saying that a man could only be sure of what he had put away safely in his gut'—has fallen, and Odili has won Edna.

MANSFIELD, Katherine, pseudonym of Kathleen Mansfield BEAUCHAMP (1888–1923), British short-story writer, born in Wellington, New Zealand, educated at Queen's College, London between 1903 and 1906. Returning to New Zealand in 1906 she rapidly tired of staid colonial society and returned to London. She became involved in a series of unsatisfactory affairs and a short-lived marriage in 1909 to George Bowden. The despondency caused by a pregnancy by another man, which had resulted in a miscarriage in Bavaria, was reflected in many of her early stories, first published in A. R. Orage's **New Age*, and later collected as *In a German Pension* (1911). In 1911 she met John Middleton *Murry, but could not marry him until 1918, and began contributing stories to *Rhythm* of which Murry was editor. Through Murry, and as a result of her growing literary reputation, she became associated with the *Bloomsbury Group, although she was never entirely accepted by the circle; Virginia *Woolf, in particular, betrayed an envious dislike of Mansfield in her journals. Mansfield and Murry developed a friendship with D. H. *Lawrence and his wife Frieda, but a period spent in neighbouring cottages in Cornwall in 1915 ended in the near-rupture of the relationship. In 1915, Mansfield's younger brother Leslie arrived from New Zealand but soon after enlisting was killed on the Western Front. Devastated by her brother's death, Mansfield was determined to recreate, through her fiction, the experiences of their shared childhood. Her fine story 'The Aloe', later revised and published by the *Hogarth Press as *Prelude* (1918), was one result and displays the sharp observation of character and impressionistic detail of her mature fiction. The story was later published in the collection *Bliss* (1920) which includes some of her best work, including the title story first published in 1918 in *The *English Review*, in which a young married woman exults in a moment of perfect happiness, only to feel it shattered by the realization that her husband has been betraying her. Mansfield's own sense of the fragility of contentment had been sharpened, in 1918, by the diagnosis of the pulmonary tuberculosis which was eventually to kill her. Despite her failing health, she published a third collection of stories, *The Garden Party*, in 1922. Many of the stories written during this period reflect an awareness of mortality and the ephemeral nature of human relationships. After Mansfield's death at the Gurdjieff Institute at Fontainebleau, where she had gone in search of remission from her illness, Murry collected work from her last months, some of which remained unfinished. Two posthumous collections, *The Dove's Nest* (1923) and *Something Childish* (1924), confirmed her reputation as a distinctive and innovative writer, and showed her allegiance to Chekhov. Murry also published her *Journal* (1927; revised 1954) and the two-volume *Letters* (1928). *The Scrapbook of Katherine Mansfield* appeared in 1939, and *Letters to John Middleton Murry* in 1951, but Murry's selective rearrangement of material only became apparent after his death in 1957. A fuller collection, *The Letters and Journals of Katherine Mansfield* (edited by C. K. *Stead, 1976), gives a more accurate picture of her turbulent emotional life, her ambiguous attitude towards her native country, and her difficult and often strained relationship with Murry. A biography by A. Alpers appeared in 1953 (revised 1980); Alpers also edited *The Stories of Katherine Mansfield* (1984). Her *Collected Letters* (1983– ; edited by V. O'Sullivan and M. Scott) corrected earlier omissions and alterations. Claire Tomalin's biography, *Katherine Mansfield: A Secret Life*, and her edition of *The Critical Writings of Katherine Mansfield* both appeared in 1987.

MANTEL, Hilary (1952–), British novelist, born in Derbyshire, educated at the London School of Economics and Sheffield University. She worked in Africa and the Middle East for eight years, and in 1987 became film critic for *The Spectator*. Her novels are noted for their acerbic wit, their exposure of hypocrisy, and their fascination with the grotesque and with madness and obsession. *Every Day Is Mother's Day* (1985), a blackly comic tale about a disturbed woman and her mentally handicapped daughter, was followed by *Vacant Possession* (1986) and *Eight Months on Ghazzah Street* (1988). A mill town in the north of England during the 1950s is the setting for *Fludd* (1989), a kind of contemporary fairy tale in which an alchemist posing as a curate transforms the desolate lives of a nun and a priest and brings a spiritual and sensual awakening to the village. More panoramic in scope, *A Place of Greater Safety* (1992) is set during the French Revolution and concerns the rise and fall of three committed revolutionaries, Camille Desmoulins, Danton, and Robespierre. The novel was widely admired for the vividness with which it dramatized historical events, and for its convincing portrayal of character. *A Change of Climate* (1994), set in the early 1980s, concerns a missionary and his wife, who have returned after many years in Africa to the north of England. *An Experiment in Love* (1995) is a psychological drama depicting the rivalry between two poor but respectable Catholic girls who compete, as schoolgirls and later as students at London University in the 1960s, for moral and academic superiority.

Man Who Was Thursday, The, see CHESTERTON, G. K.

Man with the Blue Guitar, The, a collection of poetry by Wallace *Stevens, first published in 1937. The title sequence of thirty-three short poems in couplets is among the best-known of his works. The book also contained two shorter pieces, the satirical 'A Thought Revolved' and the elegiac 'The Men that Are Falling', and an abridged version of 'Owl's Clover', which had originally appeared in 1936; this lengthy sequence, widely regarded as the least successful of Stevens's poems, formed a rhetorically complex attempt to define the poet's place in the bleak social context of the 1930s. By comparison, 'The Man with the Blue Guitar' employs language of marked, though sometimes enigmatic, lucidity and exactness in conducting its extended meditation on relations between imagination and actuality. 'The man bent over his guitar' of the first poem invokes the painting 'The Old Guitarist' by Picasso, who is specifically referred to in poem XV.

As Stevens's symbol of the poetic imagination, the blue guitar must give forth an art that simultaneously transmutes and remains faithful to reality; the philosophical and aesthetic issues thus raised are identified and evaluated in the course of the poem, which moves towards a tentative reconciliation of the apparently conflicting demands of life and art as it concludes.

MAPANJE, Jack (1945?–), dissident Malawian poet, born of Yao and Nyanja parents in Kadango village in the south of the country. He received his university education in Malawi and in London, and went on to become the best-known of the disproportionate number of outstanding poets to have been produced by this small landlocked African country. Mapanje's first collection of poems, *Of Chameleons and Gods* (1981), shows his keen sense of observation and distinctive allusive handling of imagery. In his brief introduction to the volume he states: 'The verse in this volume spans some ten turbulent years in which I have been attempting to find a voice (or voices) as a way of hanging on to some sanity. Obviously where voices are too easily muffled, this is a difficult task to set oneself. This explains why the product of these energies sometimes seems to be too cryptic to be decoded.' However, the Malawian government banned the book and arrested the author, who was at the time Head of the Department of Language and Literature at the University of Malawi. He was imprisoned without charge or trial—the implication being that he was accused of 'teaching subversion in the classroom'—from September 1987. His release in May 1991 came after a vigorous international campaign by many prominent individuals and human rights organizations. In 1988 he won the Poetry International Award. His second collection of poems is *The Chattering of Wagtails in Mikuyu Prison* (1993).

Mapp and Lucia, see BENSON, E. F.

MARCUS, Frank (1928–), British dramatist and critic, born in Breslau, Germany, educated at Bunce Court School, Kent, and St Martin's School of Art; he was an actor, director, and antiques dealer before becoming a professional writer. His most successful play remains *The Killing of Sister George* (1965), a warm and humorous study of a lesbian love affair between a young woman and the fading star of a radio *soap opera. His other original work for the stage includes *The Formation Dancers* (1964), a witty comedy about adultery and pretended adultery; *Mrs Mouse, Are You Within?* (1968), a more darkly humorous play at whose centre is an emotionally exploited and embattled woman pregnant by a Black Power militant; and *Notes on a Love Affair* (1972), about a blocked writer who organizes an affair between her former lover and a dentist's assistant in order to observe their reactions. Marcus has also adapted Molnár, Hauptmann, and Schnitzler for the theatre, and was the drama critic of the *Sunday Telegraph* from 1968 to 1978.

MARECHERA, Dambudzo (1955–87), African novelist and short-story writer, born in Rhodesia (now Zimbabwe), educated in a mission boarding school, and at Oxford University. Subsequently, he lived on the edge of insolvency in London, Cardiff, and Oxford, before returning to a newly independent Zimbabwe. *The House of Hunger* (1979), a collection of short stories, portrays the brutalities of life in a pre-independence Zimbabwean township. The stories unforgettably reveal how frustration results in futile, self-inflicted violence among the oppressed. His novel *Black Sunlight* (1980) focuses on a photographer caught between recording violence, and being involved in it; he can escape neither the fortunes of an urban guerrilla group, nor a society in the process of disintegration, and Marechera's experimental style highlights the nightmarish options. *Mind Blast* (1984) is a collection of short fiction, drama, poems, and essays. Posthumous publications include *The Black Insider* (1990), a novella, three stories, and two poems; and *Cemetery of Mind: Collected Poems of Dambudzo Marechera* (1992). The latter is edited by Flora Veit-Wild, who has also compiled biographical and critical material, with selections of his writings, in the companion volume, *Dambudzo Marechera: A Source Book on His Life and Works* (1992).

MARKANDAYA, Kamala (1923–), British novelist, born and educated in India. Her first novel, *Nectar in a Sieve* (1954), was variously described as a rural tragedy, a portrait of the clash between tradition and change in modern India, and a convincing depiction of a deprived woman's life. As both anglophone and expatriate, Markandaya was criticized for her bourgeois rendition of a peasant woman's sensibility and her inaccurate representation of rural traditions and mores. In novels such as *Some Inner Fury* (1955) and *Possession* (1963), she explored the relationship between the colonized Indians and their British masters using sexual encounters as a metaphor for cross-cultural interaction. In other novels, such as *The Coffer Dams* (1969) and *Pleasure City* (1982), she presents a comprehensive picture of Western technologists attempting to modernize India, usually in the service of their own selfish ends. The 1970s saw Markandaya at the height of her imaginative powers. *The Nowhere Man* (1972) is the account of an elderly Indian immigrant's savage annihilation. *Two Sisters* (1973) examines sexuality in an updated feminist idiom in rural South India. *The Golden Honeycomb* (1977) is arguably her most ambitious work: turning to the historical past, she circumvented the now mandatory criticism of her detached and distanced expatriate perspective. Ironically, Markandaya is best known in her native India as an expatriate novelist, and in her adopted Britain as an Indian writer and a pioneer of Indian women's writing.

MARKHAM, E(dward) A(rchibald) (1939–), British poet, born in Monserrat, West Indies; he emigrated to Britain in 1956 and was educated at Kilburn Polytechnic, London, and Saint David's University College, Lampeter. Since 1968 he has held numerous positions as a lecturer, writer-in-residence, and arts administrator in Britain, the West Indies, and Papua New Guinea. In 1980 he became assistant editor of **Ambit* and edited *Artrage* magazine from 1985 to 1991. Among the numerous early collections of his work to appear from British small presses are *Cross-Fire* (1972), *Master Class* (1977), and *Family Matters* (1984). *Human Rites: Selected Poems 1970–1982* (1984) gained him wider notice for the originality of tone and wry humour with which his verse covers a wide range of personal and socio-political themes; the diffidently detached personae of 'Lamchops' and 'Philpot' are vehicles for many of the most effective poems. Subsequent collections include *Living in Disguise* (1986), *Towards the End of the Century* (1989), *Letter from Ulster and the Hugo Poems* (1993) which confirm Gavin *Ewart's statement that Markham is 'a writer of great intelligence and vitality'. He has also written several plays, and published collections of short stories including *Something Unusual* (1986) and *Ten Stories* (1994).

MARKHAM, Edwin (Charles Edward Anson) (1852–1940), American poet, born in Oregon City; he grew up in Southern California, and was largely self-educated before his enrolment at the Christian College in Santa Rosa. He became Principal of the Tompkins Observatory School in Oakland in 1890. The socialist character of his early verse, which appeared in William Morris's *Commonweal* and other journals from around 1886 onward, culminated in 'The Man with the Hoe', a response to Millet's painting of the same title; the poem, whose blank verse powerfully envisioned the rise of the working classes, appeared in the *San Francisco Examiner* in 1899 and was widely reprinted throughout the USA. *The Man with the Hoe and Other Poems* (1899) was followed by *Lincoln and Other Poems* (1901), which emphasized the American democratic idealism inherent in his views of social progress. Subsequent collections include *The Shoes of Happiness* (1915), *The Gates of Paradise* (1920), and *New Poems: Eighty Poems at Eighty* (1932); *Collected Poems* appeared in 1940. His reputation as a poet of social concern provided the basis for his career as a lecturer, essayist, and participant in programmes of reform. With B. B. Lindsay and G. Creel, he produced *Children in Bondage* (1914), a sociological study which advanced the campaign against child labour. Among his works as an editor was his voluminous and eclectic *The Book of Poetry* (ten volumes, 1926). He is believed to have supplied the model for Presley, the sincere but politically ineffectual poet, in Frank Norris's *The *Octopus* (1901).

MARLATT, Daphne (1942–), Canadian poet, born in Melbourne, Australia; she moved with her family to Vancouver in 1951, later attending the Universities of British Columbia and Indiana. Marlatt's poetry is influenced by French feminist linguistic theory and the work of some of her Quebec women contemporaries; her concern with showing how personality and gender identity are constructed by language is particularly evident in *Touch to My Tongue* (1984). *Steveston* (1974) is a discontinuous long poem that, in part, offers a social history of a small Japanese fishing town in British Columbia, but at the same time questions the very mode of documentary that it employs by constantly emphasizing the writer's involvement in creating the world of the poem. Much of Marlatt's work, including her Mexican 'novel' *Zocalo* (1977) and *How Hug a Stone* (1983), an account of a journey to England with her son to rediscover the maternal side of her family, mixes travel-journal and autobiography with literary forms traditionally more associated with creativity to suggest the factitious nature of all writing and constructs of the self. Marlatt's other works include *Frames* (1968), *Leaf/leafs* (1969), *Rings* (1971), *Vancouver Poems* (1972), *Our Lives* (1975), and *Here and There* (1981).

MARRIC, J. J., see CREASEY, JOHN.

MARSH, Sir Edward (Howard) (1872–1953), British editor, patron of the arts, and translator, born in London, educated at Trinity College, Cambridge. Having entered the Civil Service in 1896, he became private secretary to Winston S. *Churchill in 1905. In association with his close friend Rupert *Brooke, he launched the **Georgian Poetry* series in 1912; Marsh edited each of the five volumes, though to most of their large readership he was known only as 'E.M.', the initials appended to his prefaces. He prepared the posthumous editions of Brooke's *Letters from America* (1916) and *Collected Poems* (1918); the introduction to the latter was separately published in 1918 as *Rupert Brooke: A Memoir*. Marsh shared his considerable royalties from the *Georgian Poetry* anthologies with his contributors and was noted for his generosity to many artists and writers, including James *Joyce, for whom he secured a Civil List pension at Ezra *Pound's suggestion. As a translator, he produced versions of *The Fables of Jean De La Fontaine* (two volumes, 1931), the *Odes of Horace* (1941), and *The Sphinx of Bagatelle* (1951) by Princess Marthe Bibescu. *Minima* (1947) contains examples of his own poetry. *A Number of People* (1939) is a volume of his reminiscences. He was knighted in 1937. Christopher *Hassall's *Edward Marsh* appeared in 1959.

MARSH, Dame (Edith) Ngaio (pron. Ny-o) (1899–1982), New Zealand detective novelist, born in Christchurch, New Zealand, where she studied art and worked in the theatre as an actress and producer. In the 1940s she produced many plays at Canterbury University in Christchurch, was made an honorary lecturer in drama, and published two books on the subject: *A Play Toward* (1946) and *Play Production* (1948). In 1962 a new theatre at the university was given her name and in 1966 she was awarded the DBE for her work. Her interest in the theatre is reflected in her detective novels, many of which have a stage background; a number are set in New Zealand. The first, *A Man Lay Dead* (1934), was written during her first visit to England, when she worked as an interior decorator in London. It introduced her detective, Roderick Alleyn of Scotland Yard, who features in all her thirty-two novels. The charge of snobbishness has been brought against her work, which has possibly worn less well than that of her contemporaries, *Christie, *Allingham, and *Sayers. The earlier books are to be preferred, and include *Enter a Murderer* (1935), *The Nursing-Home Murder* (1935; in collaboration with Henry Jellett), *Death in Ecstasy* (1936), *Artists in Crime* (1938), *Death in a White Tie* (1938), *Overture to Death* (1939), *Surfeit of Lampreys* (1941; published in the USA as *Death of a Peer*, 1940), and *Opening Night* (1951; US title *Night at the Vulcan*). An autobiography, *Black Beech and Honeydew*, appeared in 1965 (revised 1981), and a life by Margaret Lewis in 1991.

MARSHALL, Paule (1929–), American writer, born in New York to Barbadian immigrant parents, educated at Brooklyn College. Her first novel, **Brown Girl, Brownstones* (1959), was followed by *South Clap Hands and Sing* (1961), a collection of novellas. These early works display the commitment and maturity that characterize all her writings, as she examines from various perspectives the central issues of race, class, and gender. Her books, underwritten by her conviction that women embody the power principle as easily as men, are the forerunners of a movement of black and feminist writing that gained prominence a decade later. *The Chosen Place, the Timeless People* (1969) examines in depth her major philosophical and political preoccupations: colonialism and neocolonialism, the crippling effects of economic imperialism, and the black experience of deracination. Her third novel, *Praisesong for the Widow* (1983), concerns the perspective of one woman, Avatara Johnson, a member of the new black bourgeoisie; it presents through her eyes the roots and branches of the black experience in Africa and the New World, and stresses the reclamation of a heritage alive in oral lore and memory. Her collection *Merle and Other Novellas* (1983) includes a series of semi-fictional texts that reveal the course of her development, the depth of her perception, and the considerable though underrated impact of her ideas on her younger contemporaries. *Daughter* (1991), Marshall's long-awaited novel, tells the story of a young woman who attempts to come to terms with her American present, her father's Caribbean heritage, and her African-American mother's notions of justice and redemption. The novel spans several decades and is set both in the USA and in an imaginary but recognizable Caribbean island. Marshall returns to the ambitious sweep of her early works, combining political analysis of the post-colonial world with her interest in characterization and feminist issues.

MARS-JONES, Adam (1954–), British writer and critic, born in London, educated at Westminster and Trinity Hall, Cambridge. He became film critic and reviewer for *The Independent*. His first collection of short stories, *Lantern Lecture* (1981; Somerset Maugham Award, 1982), was widely praised for its stylistic elegance and surreal wit. *A Darker Proof* (1986; with Edmund *White) is a collection of stories dealing with the AIDS crisis; while describing with unflinching honesty the experience of living with death, the stories are enlivened by touches of satirical humour. A novel, *The Waters of Thirst* (1993), also concerns themes of illness and mortality, but makes only oblique reference to the AIDS crisis. The central character, a gay actor specializing in television voice-overs, is suffering from kidney disease and is obliged to undergo renal dialysis; his observations on his experience are related with the dry humour for which the author is renowned. Whatever his ostensible subject, Mars-Jones is pre-eminently a stylist, with an acute sensitivity for nuances of behaviour and expression which transforms even his most sombre material.

MARSON, Una (Maud) (1905–65), Jamaican poet, playwright, and broadcaster, born in Jamaica, and educated there and at Hampton School, Malvern. She went to England in 1932, where she became secretary to the League of Coloured Peoples, and private secretary to Haile Selassie, the exiled Ethiopian Emperor. During her second period in England (1938–47) she was a broadcaster with the BBC. As an author, she is best known for her poetry, which was published in *Tropic Reveries* (1930), *Heights and Depths* (1931), and *The Moth and the Star* (1937). Her collection *Towards the Stars* (1945) includes many of the poems of earlier collections. She experimented to great effect in vernacular and 'blues' poems, but was equally fluent in more formal style, such as the tersely epigrammatic 'Politeness'.

Martian Poetry, James *Fenton's term for a mode of composition characterized by the use of startlingly unusual metaphors and similes produced by imaginative transpositions of visual data. The heyday of Martian poetry began in 1979, when Craig *Raine's *A Martian Sends a Postcard Home* appeared, the title poem of which is the *locus classicus* of the idiom; its opening lines provide an example of the procedures by which everyday objects, in this instance books, are metaphorically estranged: 'Caxtons are mechanical birds with many wings | and some are treasured for their markings'. Occasionally, familiarity is so thoroughly displaced by Martian strategies that the reader must endeavour to establish correspondences between images presented and the actualities from which they derive; success affords a satisfaction akin to that experienced upon solving crossword puzzles. Eminent among the other poets of the school are Christopher *Reid, whose *Arcadia* (1979) and *Pea Soup* (1982) exhibit great dexterity in the manipulation of detail, and David Sweetman, whose *Looking into the Deep End* (1981) was noted for the acuity and strangeness of its imagery. *The Penguin Book of Contemporary British Poetry* (1982, edited by A. *Motion and Blake *Morrison) accorded significance to the Martians, whose characteristic tone of detachment is indicated in the Introduction's view of them as 'not inhabitants of their own lives so much as intrigued observers'. The movement, although little heard of after about

1985, was of value in stimulating new interest in the imaginative aspects of poetry and had a subtle but pervasive influence on the techniques of image formation in the work of numerous poets.

Martin Eden, a novel by Jack *London, published in 1909. The narrative begins with Martin Eden, an uncouth sailor and labourer, entering the luxurious house of a cultured friend. Although uneasy in the cultivated company, he craves knowledge and life, and the narrative describes the quest upon which Eden's intellectual curiosity leads him. At the house he falls in love with Ruth Morse, an educated society woman who represents the values to which he aspires and who finds Eden both attractive and repellent. Eden becomes an unsuccessful writer, only finding understanding from his friend Russ Brissenden, a socialist poet, who gradually educates Eden in politics. After Eden is falsely reported as a socialist in the newspapers, his fiancée Ruth and her family desert him. Yet when one of his books belatedly makes him wealthy and famous, Ruth seeks to resume their previous engagement. Eden sees through her hypocrisy, and with Brissenden's suicide and his own increasing social isolation, he leaves home to travel in the South Seas. Having lost all self-respect and any will to live, he jumps from the ship and drowns. Eden's journey of self-education through the apparently high-thinking life of the bourgeoisie has distinct biographical parallels with London's own endeavours.

MARTYN, Edward (1859–1924), Irish playwright, born in Co. Galway, educated in Dublin and at Christ Church College, Oxford. His family were wealthy Catholics who had gained exemption from the Penal Laws in 1709. After his return to Ireland, he took an active interest in music and in the revival of the Irish language. He founded the Palestrina Choir in Dublin's Pro-Cathedral, and helped to establish the Feis Cheoil, an annual festival of traditional Irish music. In 1898, with W. B. *Yeats, George *Moore, and Lady *Gregory, Martyn founded the Irish Literary Theatre which was to become the *Abbey Theatre. His own peasant dramas, including *The Heather Field* (1898) and *Maeve* (1899), were among the first plays to be produced by the new theatre company. *The Dream Physician* (1914) is Martyn's attempt at revenge upon his 'friend' George Moore who had mocked him as 'dead Edward' in *Hail and Farewell* (1911–14). In 1914 Martyn withdrew from the Abbey and set up the short-lived Irish Theatre with Joseph Plunkett and Thomas *MacDonagh.

Marxist Literary Criticism begins with Marx, who was interested in the way the contradictions of capitalism are revealed in a writer like Balzac, of prodigious gifts and rightist sympathies. With the success of the Russian Revolution, and above all with the ascent to power of Joseph Stalin, a regimented and highly prescriptive Marxist literary criticism developed, devoted to so-called Socialist Realism; but there were always other currents, notably represented by Georg Lukács, whose *Theory of the Novel* (1971) predates his conversion to communism but nevertheless anticipates his later work (*The Historical Novel*, 1962; *Studies in European Realism*, 1950), where formal and moral questions are intricately related, and where realism is celebrated as a fidelity to underlying historical and economic truths rather than a mere reflection of surfaces. The Frankfurt School, led by T. W. Adorno and Max Horkheimer, elaborated a powerful, non-Stalinist mode of cultural criticism on the basis of Marx's insights into the relation of language and ideology to the material bases of production. Closely associated with this school, although not always an assiduous pupil, was Walter Benjamin, perhaps the most brilliant of all Marxist critics. In a series of essays written in the 1920s and 1930s, Benjamin explored the work of Proust, Kafka, and the Surrealists, and the potentially drastic aesthetic implications of the inventions of photography and the cinema. Shortly before he died, in 1940, Benjamin wrote a remarkable brief study in the philosophy of history, proposing a history that would remember the vanquished as well as, or more than, the victors; unless we can learn to do this, he memorably said, not even the dead will be safe. It is a perspective which looks towards the 'archaeology' of Michel Foucault, the study of unspoken or suppressed communities, and also towards the *New Historicism, with its attention to neglected detail. Meanwhile in Britain Christopher *Caudwell, in *Illusion and Reality* (1937), sought to domesticate and rethink Marxist assumptions about the social bases of art; and much criticism in the 1930s, whether openly Marxist or not, accepted the materialist presuppositions of Marx's agenda. Later critics like Fredric *Jameson and Terry *Eagleton have complicated but not abandoned these Marxist premisses, and the debt to Marxism of critics as different as Lionel *Trilling and Raymond *Williams is perfectly clear. Marxism remains, for literary and social criticism, an optic rather than a doctrine, a way of connecting, beyond all narrow determinisms, the aesthetic and the political; and is present, at least in vestige, in all the many current criticisms of ideology, whatever their particular impulse or angle. It is very much alive in *Cultural Materialism, a British movement in criticism associated with the work of Jonathan Dollimore, Alan Sinfield, and Peter Stallybrass, and which takes the material context of culture as both unavoidable and often thoroughly disguised by an idealizing conservative consensus.

MASEFIELD, John (Edward) (1878–1967), British poet, born in Ledbury, Herefordshire; from the age of 13 he trained for a career in the merchant navy. After a crossing to New York in 1895, he deserted ship and remained in America for two years, where he began writing poetry. Shortly after returning to Britain in 1897 he formed a friendship with W. B. *Yeats, to whom he paid tribute in *Some Memories of W. B. Yeats* (1940). His reputation as a poet was established with the appearance of *Salt-Water Ballads* (1902); the collection's maritime lyricism was sustained in *Ballads and Poems* (1910), which demonstrated his growing virtuosity and imaginative reach. The first of his long narrative poems was *The Everlasting Mercy* (1911), which was controversial for the dramatic use of profanely colloquial language in its account of the spiritual regeneration of the labourer Saul Kane. The realism of setting and characterization he aspired to are further developed in numerous subsequent verse narratives, which include *The Widow in the Bye Street* (1912) and *Dauber* (1913), a psychologically compelling treatment of a sailor with artistic instincts. *Collected Poems* of 1923 sold over 200,000 copies. In 1930 he succeeded Robert *Bridges as Poet Laureate and received the Order of Merit in 1935. He was also highly regarded as a playwright and published *Prose Plays* and *Verse Plays* in 1925. Shorter narratives of country life and lyrical evocations of the natural world predominate in his later collections of poetry, which include *The Country Scene in Poems* (1937), *On the Hill* (1949), and *The Bluebells* (1961). His many other publications include *The Midnight Folk* (1927), his celebrated story for children, and the popular adventure novels *Sard Harker* (1924) and *Live and Kicking Ned* (1939). *So Long To Learn* (1952) and *Grace before Ploughing* (1966) are autobiographical.

MASON, A(lfred) E(dward) W(oodley) (1865–1948), British novelist, born in Dulwich, educated at Oxford University. After failing as an actor he became a successful novelist; he was also a Member of Parliament (1906–10). He is best remembered as the author of *The Four Feathers* (1902; filmed 1939) in which the protagonist, Harry Feversham, redeems himself as a hero against accusations of cowardice by his fellow officers. He also wrote historical novels, including *Fire over England* (1936), filmed with Laurence Olivier, Vivien Leigh, and Flora Robson in 1937; *Konigsmarck* (1938), the story of the Swedish lover of Sophie Dorothea, wife of King George I (also filmed); and *Musk and Amber* (1942), a tale of the world of the castrato singer in the late eighteenth century. His many other popular works include the series of novels featuring Inspector Hanaud, a French detective, which began with *At the Villa Rose* (1910).

MASON, Anita (1942–), British novelist, born in Bristol, educated at Oxford University. Her first novel, *Bethany* (1981), was followed by *The Illusionist* (1983), perhaps her best-known work; through the enigmatic figure of Simon of Samaria, known as the Magus and the 'Angel of Satan', and said to have inspired the legend of Faust, the novel explores the growth of Christian doctrine, the conflicts that arose within it, and the gnostic cults assimilated or rejected by it. Her style is lucid and the structure of her novels is conventional but her themes are consistently adventurous. *The War against Chaos* (1988) is a dystopia set in an unnamed city in an unspecified future, seen through the eyes of the dispossessed John Hare; *The Racket* (1990) employs a Brazilian background and characters.

MASON, Bobbie Ann (1940–), American novelist, short-story writer, and critic, born in Mayfield, Kentucky, educated at the University of Kentucky, the State University of New York at Binghamton, and the University of Connecticut. Mason describes her work as 'Southern Gothic going to the supermarket', a phrase by which she captures both her indebtedness to great Southern writers of the first half of the century, notably William *Faulkner, and her considerable distance from them. She published two critical books, *Nabokov's Garden: A Nature Guide to 'Ada'* (1974), a study of Vladimir *Nabokov's long novel, and *The Girl Sleuth: A Feminist Guide to the Bobbsey Twins, Nancy Drew, and Their Sisters* (1975), a title characteristic of her intellectual playfulness, but latterly her interests have turned towards creative writing. After several unsuccessful attempts at getting published she finally succeeded in placing her first story, 'Offerings', in the *New Yorker* in 1980. Her first volume of stories, *Shiloh and Other Stories* (1982; Ernest Hemingway Award), depicts life in rural Kentucky. Her first novel, *In Country* (1985), concerning a young woman whose father was killed in Vietnam, received considerable critical praise, as did *Spence & Lila* (1988), which focuses on an elderly woman facing treatment for cancer. Both novels explore family relationships, articulating the feelings of ordinary Kentucky people at times of crisis. Her third novel, *Feather Crowns*, appeared in 1993.

MASON, Bruce (1921–82), New Zealand playwright, born in Wellington, educated at Victoria University College, Wellington. Of Mason's early plays, *The End of the Golden Weather* (1962), and his 'Maori plays', particularly *The Pohutukawa Tree* (1960) and *Awatea* (1969), were of most interest. *The End of the Golden Weather* became synonymous with the New Zealand intellectual culture of the 1960s, as Mason toured the country presenting the multiple faces of his childhood in a *tour de force* of solo performance. The play presents a nostalgic view of an eccentric and often intolerant small community. It was later revamped (1989/90) as a production for many players. The so-called 'Maori plays' collected together under the title *The Healing Arch* (1987) now appear to represent a rather ethnocentric use of Maori society, ritual, and customs; the most successful of them, *The Pohutukawa Tree*, continued to be popular and much produced. *Blood of the Lamb* (1981), about a lesbian couple who raise a child, also received much attention. Critical writings and reviews were collected together under the title *Every Kind of Weather* in 1986.

MASON, R(onald) A(llison) K(ells) (1905–71), New Zealand poet, born near Auckland, educated at the University of Auckland. His early interest in Latin writers became a lasting influence on his own work. Mason lived most of his life in Auckland. A committed Marxist, and politically active during the Depression of the 1930s, he was an important influence on other writers, though he wrote but little himself; Charles *Brasch, A. R. D. *Fairburn, and Allen *Curnow were among those who knew him well, and in 1964 he introduced the first volume by the Maori poet Hone *Tuwhare. Early volumes *The Beggar* (1924) and *No New Thing* (1934) were not a success and later books fared little better. Among several plays are *Squire Speaks* (1938), a satire for radio, and *To Save Democracy* (1938), an essay-like drama which explored the treatment of New Zealand's conscientious objectors during the First World War. *This Dark Will Lighten: Selected Poems, 1923–41* (1941) appeared when much of Mason's energy was devoted to trade union activities, but exemplified his effective blend of harshly understated realism and lyric grace. Mason's *Collected Poems* (1962) includes a valuable introduction by Curnow.

Masses, The, a monthly magazine founded in 1911 by Piet Vlag in New York as a platform for socialist views; Thomas Seltzer was the first editor. Following a financial crisis, Vlag resigned his interest early in 1912 and Max *Eastman assumed the editorship. The political content, consistently of a socialist and pacifist character, was supplied by Eastman, John *Reed, Floyd *Dell, James Oppenheim, and others; birth control, racial equality, and feminism were among the issues discussed. Eastman's hospitality to work from a range of younger writers gives the *Masses* considerable importance among the journals of the day: Carl *Sandburg, Sherwood *Anderson, Amy *Lowell, Vachel *Lindsay, William Carlos *Williams, and Bertolt Brecht were among the contributors of poetry and fiction. Outspoken opposition to America's entry into the First World War led to the trial of Eastman and his editorial associates for conspiracy; the jury disagreed and a re-trial was ordered, with the same inconclusive result. The magazine was resumed in 1918 as the *Liberator*; an increasingly doctrinaire socialist stance became apparent and in 1924 it merged with *Labour Herald* and *Soviet Russia Pictorial* to form *Worker's Monthly*. In 1926 the *New Masses* was founded in an attempt to revive the lively eclecticism of the original magazine. Michael *Gold was sole editor from 1928 until it was re-formed as a weekly journal in 1934; its literary content subsequently diminished as a result of its intensifying ideological preoccupations. Joseph North was chief editor between 1938 and the magazine's closure in 1949 as a result of difficulties imposed by the Cold War. Robinson *Jeffers, Theodore *Dreiser, Carl *Rakosi, Kenneth *Fearing, Lola *Ridge, and Van Wyck *Brooks were among the contributors of poetry, fiction, and criticism in its earlier years; documentary reportage by Dorothy *Parker, Erskine *Caldwell, and Ernest *Hemingway appeared. *New Masses: An Anthology of the Rebel Thirties* (1969) was edited by North. See also PROLETARIAN LITERATURE IN THE USA.

MASSIE, Allan (1938–), Scottish novelist, biographer, and historian, born in Singapore, educated at Trinity College, Cambridge. His first novel, *Change and Decay in All Around I See* (1978), was an absurdist pastiche in which the well-educated Atwater, determined to fulfil no one's expectations, drifts through London from pub to betting-shop. *The Last Peacock* (1980) tells the story of Belinda, another drifter, who returns to Scotland after a bad marriage to witness her grandmother's death. *The Death of Men* (1981) owes much to Massie's personal experience of Italy and to newspaper reports of Aldo Moro's kidnapping, but it is an original and finely crafted political novel about terrorism. *One Night in Winter* (1984) returns to the theme of the deracinated Scot, in this case the self-muzzled antiques dealer Dallas, reliving at last his youthful encounter with a wild Scottish Nationalist. *Augustus* (1986) is entirely different: the mock memoirs of the Roman emperor, a frequently ironic, but vivid, fiction clearly inspired by Massie's historical work on *The Caesars* (1983). His novel *A Question of Loyalties* (1989) was followed by *The Sins of the Fathers* (1991) which describes the relationship between Franz Kestner, a young man of German extraction, and Becky Szinner, who is half English, half German Jewish; the couple meet in Argentina during the 1960s and fall in love, only to discover the terrible truth about their respective pasts. For Franz's father is a former Nazi, guilty of appalling crimes against humanity, and Becky's father, a survivor of the Holocaust, is the man who eventually denounces him. Returning to the Roman world, *Tiberius* (1991) presents a fictional autobiography of the Emperor in a psychologically revealing portrait of tyranny, while *Caesar* (1993) is a retelling of Caesar's story from the crossing of the Rubicon to the Ides of March by Decimus Junius Brutus, and a wry treatment of political intrigues. In *These Enchanted Woods* (1993) the narrative focuses on a millionaire returning to Perthshire after 20 years to reclaim the woman he loved. *The Ragged Lion* (1994) is a fictional version of the life of Sir Walter Scott. Massie has also written biographies of *Muriel Spark* (1979), *Colette* (1986), and *101 Great Scots* (1987); a study of five Victorian murders in Edinburgh, *Ill Met By Gaslight* (1980); a *Portrait of Scottish Rugby* (1984); a book on *Byron's Travels* (1988); and a historical work on *Edinburgh* (1994).

Mass-Observation originated in 1937 as a social survey group under the leadership of Tom Harrisson (an anthropologist), Charles *Madge (leftist poet/journalist), and Humphrey Jennings (documentary film-maker), with the project of producing 'the anthropology of ourselves'. As such it pre-empted in its interests (if not methodology) some of the concerns now studied as *popular culture. It was characteristic of a growing commitment among politically and socially aware 1930s writers and intellectuals to 'experience' and document how 'ordinary people' lived, worked, and thought and, as such, bears comparison with George *Orwell (**Down and Out in Paris and London*, 1933, and *The *Road to Wigan Pier*, 1937), *Auden and *MacNeice (*Letters from Iceland*, 1937, and the former's collaboration with the documentary film-maker John Grierson), and *Isherwood (*Goodbye to Berlin*, 1939). Using a team of 'fly-on-the-wall' investigators (students, artists and writers, photographers and unemployed workers) and recruiting volunteer (self-)'observers' from all over Britain and many walks of life to keep regular diaries and respond to questionnaires on specific topics, Mass-Observation applied documentary reportage techniques to pioneer a study of British 'everyday life' from 1937 until well after the Second World War. A mass of ephemera—press cuttings, leaflets, posters, sketches, and photographs—was also collected to supplement 'observations' on such subjects as Air Raids, Anti-Semitism, Capital Punishment, Children's Games and Toys, Commodities, Dreams, Drink, Graffiti, Propaganda, Pub Life, Sexual Behaviour, War Grumbles, and Women in War-Time. Among its more noted contributors/observers are to be counted William *Empson (who investigated sweet-shop windows), J. B. S. *Haldane, Naomi *Mitchison, and Kathleen *Raine. The photographic documentation of Bolton and Blackpool by Humphrey Spender (*Worktown*, 1937/8) is seminal and also signals the paradoxical roots of the project in British Surrealism. But despite leftist-surrealist origins, M-O was essentially positivist and reformist, not radical, in tendency, as its wartime Government work reporting on civilian morale and its name suggest. Since 1970 the M-O archives have been housed at the University of Sussex, which in 1981 revived earlier projects to document the daily lives of observers through the 1980s, including responses to Royal Weddings, the Falklands Crisis, and unemployment. See *Speak for Yourself: A M-O Anthology, 1937–49*, edited by A. Calder and D. Sheridan (1984), and Humphrey Spender's photographs of *Worktown* (Bolton) (1977).

MASTERMAN, C(harles) F(rederick) G(urney) (1874–1927), British writer on social conditions, born in Wimbledon, educated at Christ's College, Cambridge. The zealous social concern produced by his Christian idealism and liberal political principles led him to take up residence in one of the poorest parts of south-east London in 1900, where he planned *The Heart of Empire* (1901); subtitled 'Discussions of modern city life in England', the book contained contributions from a number of his associates, including G. M. *Trevelyan, in addition to his own survey of urban deprivation. *From the Abyss* (1902) contrasted the extremes of poverty and affluence which co-existed in London. *The Condition of England* (1909), his best-known work, addressed the absence of effective social reform with persuasive conviction. He was elected to Parliament in 1906 and held various positions in Liberal Governments until 1915, when he lost his seat in the House of Commons. He supplied the model for the politician Waterhouse in *Parade's End* (1924–8) by his friend Ford Madox *Ford (then Hueffer). His other works include *In Peril of Change* (1905) and *England after War* (1922). There is a biography by his wife Lucy Masterman (1939).

MASTERS, Brian (1939–), British writer, born in London, the son of Cockney parents, educated at University College Cardiff and the University of Montpelier in France. Having written several studies on French authors, Masters became interested in the aristocracy through his friendship with the Marquess of Londonderry and went on to write *The Dukes* (1975), a history of the origin and ennoblement of all the dukedoms. Several biographies followed, including *Now Barabbas was a Rotter* (1978), a life of Marie Corelli, and a highly acclaimed life of E. F. *Benson (1991). *The Passion of John Aspinall* (1988), about the gambler and zoo-keeper, involved the author in many hours of research in a cage of gorillas. Masters attracted wide attention with *Killing for Company* (1985; Gold Dagger Award for non-fiction), an objective and humane account of the mass-murderer Dennis Neilsen which Beryl *Bainbridge described as 'a bloody masterpiece'. Murder was also the subject of *The Shrine of Jeffrey Dahmer* (1993), about the US serial-killer and cannibal convicted in 1991, while *On Murder* (1994) considers the phenomenon chiefly with regard to the psychology of motivation and predisposition; *The Evil that Men Do* appeared in 1996. Masters has been praised for his elegant prose, his meticulous research, and the compassion with which he treats his subjects.

MASTERS, Edgar Lee (?1868–1950), American poet, novelist, and biographer, born in Garnett, Kansas; he grew up in a remote part of Illinois, conceiving the dislike for rural American culture which informs much of his poetry. From 1891 to 1920 he was a partner in a successful Chicago legal practice, after which he devoted himself to writing. He published eleven books, which include *A Book of Verse* (1898) and the blank-verse drama *Maximilian* (1902), before the appearance of his most celebrated work, *Spoon River Anthology*, in 1915. The collection consists of 214 short dramatic poems in free verse spoken by deceased inhabitants of Spoon River, an imaginary small town in Illinois. The malevolence, greed, and violence revealed in the poems stood in direct contrast to the conventions of piety dominating early twentieth-century literature of rural America. An underlying moral seriousness and compassion for victims of misfortune lent conviction to the poetry's indictments of pettiness and corruption. The less successful *The New Spoon River* (1924) transferred his critique of American society to the degeneration of urban values. Among his many subsequent volumes of poetry are *The Fate of the Jury* (1929), *The New World* (1936), and *Poems of the People* (1937). He produced several novels based on memories of his youth, which include *Mitch Miller* (1920) and *Skeeters Kirby* (1923). His iconoclastic *Lincoln, the Man* (1930) was followed by biographies of Vachel *Lindsay (1935), Walt Whitman (1937), and Mark Twain (1938). *Across Spoon River* (1936) is his autobiography.

MASTERS, John (1914–83), British novelist, born in India, educated in England. After attending Sandhurst Military Academy he joined the Indian Army in 1934, retiring in 1948 having served in Burma and the Middle East during the Second World War. He began a series of novels with *Nightrunners of Bengal* (1951), about the Indian Mutiny, describing the history of the Savage family, which was based on his own. This was followed by *The Deceivers* (1952), also with an Indian theme; *The Lotus and the Wind* (1953); and *Bhowani Junction* (1954), which was perhaps his best-known novel, set at the time of Indian Independence. *Coromandel* (1955) and *Far, Far the Mountain Peak* (1967) completed the Savage family saga. There were many other novels, some set in the USA, where he lived from 1949, as well as two volumes of autobiography, *Bugles and A Tiger* (1956) and *The Road Past Mandalay* (1961).

MASTERS, Olga (1919–86), Australian writer, born in New South Wales. At the age of 15 she worked on a local newspaper and later edited the *Manly Daily*. Her journalism has been collected in *Olga Masters: Reporting Home* (1991). In her late fifties she began writing fiction. *The Home Girls* (1982), a collection of short stories set in small towns during the Depression, examined the cruelty and loneliness of the domestic environment; *Loving Daughters* (1984), set in the same period, explored the repressed sexual feelings of two sisters who fall in love with the same young clergyman; *A Long Time Dying* (1985) is a collection of linked stories about the inhabitants of a small community during the 1930s. Hypocrisy, petty malice, and silent pain are sharply registered in her fiction. *Amy's Children* (1987) is a novel about an abandoned woman who leaves her three children in order to start a new life. *The Rose Fancier* (1988) was the collection of stories on which she was working at the time of her death.

MATHERS, Peter (1931–), Australian novelist, born in Fulham, London; he moved to Australia in infancy. He studied at Sydney Technical College and held various jobs until 1964, when he left Australia to live in Britain and the United States, returning in 1968. *Trap* (1966), his first novel, established him as an important voice in Australian fiction. Its part-Aborigine protagonist Jack Trap embodies an iconoclastic ambivalence to both the white and indigenous cultures of Australia and provides the focus for a narrative expansion that encompasses two centuries of its violent colonial history. *The Work Papers* (1972) combines an intricate network of individual destinies and versions of modern Australian identity in its treatments of a father and son whose exploratory journeys chart the state of the continent from the 1930s onward. Both novels are seriocomic *tours de force*, employing an extraordinary range of stylistic and narrative modes. The experimental tendency in Mathers's writing is at its most pronounced in the pervasive word-play and cryptic compression of the short stories in *A Change for the Better* (1984). A number of his plays, including *Mountain King* (1985) and *Grigori Two* (1987) have been produced by Melbourne theatre companies.

MATHEWS, Aidan (Carl) (1956–), Irish poet, playwright, and novelist, born in Dublin, educated at University College, Dublin and Trinity College, Dublin. He gained the Teaching Fellowship of Creative Literature at Stanford University, California, between 1981 and 1983, then returned to Ireland, and became a producer for Radio Telefis Eireann. His plays include a version of *Antigone* (1984), *The Diamond Body* (1985), and *Exit/Entrance* (1988). His other works include two significant collections of poetry, *Windfalls* (1977) and *Minding Ruth* (1983); collections of short stories, *Adventures in a Bathyscope* (1988) and *Lipstick on the Host* (1992); and the novel *Muesli at Midnight* (1990). Mathews is of a generation of Irish writers more likely to identify with the international traveller rather than the emigrant or exile.

MATHEWS, Harry (1930–), American novelist, born in New York; he studied music at Harvard, then at the Ecole Normale de Musique in Paris, and has lived mainly in France since 1952. A friend of John *Ashbery, Mathews edited *Locus Solus*, the magazine of the New York school of poets, from 1960 to 1962. He was the only American member of OULIPO, or Workshop of Potential Literature, an experimental group including Queneau, Perec, and Calvino. Out of these mainly Francophile interests, extending back to Apollinaire, Roussel, and *Dada, came his dandified early works with their witty blend of intellectual fantasy and flamboyant games-playing. From Raymond Roussel in particular he drew absurd logic, a highly artificial manner, and texts-within-texts, incorporating maps, musical scores, indices, footnotes, and word games. Each of his first three novels involves complicated quests. The narrator of *The Conversions* (1962) has to solve three strange riddles in order to inherit a fortune; *Tlooth* (1966) is a travelogue-adventure imbued with eccentric erudition. Mathews's preoccupation is with the nature of the fictive, working in reflections on language, imagination, and reality. In *The Sinking of the Odradek Stadium* (1975) he manipulates the conventions of the epistolary novel; a series of letters concerning a search for treasure also becomes a rewrite of Poe's story *The Gold Bug*. Mathews continued his experimentation in *Cigarettes* (1987) with its interlocking narratives about well-to-do American characters. *A Mid-Season Sky: Poems 1954–1991* (1992) is characteristically fuelled by humour, experiment, and linguistic virtuosity.

MATHEWS, John Joseph (*c.*1894–1979), Native American writer, born in Pawhuska, Oklahoma, educated at the University of Oklahoma. He is known for his literary autobiography, *Talking to the Moon* (1945), written in the tradition of Thoreau's *Walden*. After a life of international study and travel which began in France with the Signal Corps during the First World War and took him to Oxford University, the School of International Relations in Geneva, and to North Africa, Mathews returned in 1929 to Pawhuska where he built a cabin and lived for the next decade, recording his personal development as he rediscovered his tribal identity. The narrative develops a pattern of contrast and comparison between the Osage people and white Americans, the natural environment and

Native American culture, the continuance of tribal values and the disruptive violence represented by the Second World War. Mathews's novels concern the impact of assimilationist policies on the lives of individuals and the effects of reservations on traditional Indian culture; these themes are explored in *Wah'Kon-Tah* (1932) and *Sundown* (1934). Mathews also published a biography, *Life and Death of an Oilman: The Career of E. W. Marland* (1951), and a personal history of his tribe, *The Osages: Children of the Middle Waters* (1961). See also NATIVE AMERICAN LITERATURE.

MATTHIESSEN, F(rancis) O(tto) (1902–50), American critic, born in Pasadena, California, educated at Yale and at Harvard, where he became Professor of English in 1942. His initial specialization in Elizabethan literature, represented by *Translation: An Elizabethan Art* (1931), was supplanted by the interest in American writing stimulated by his reading of Van Wyck *Brooks's works in the late 1920s. *Sarah Orne Jewett* (1929), his first treatment of an American author, was followed by *The Achievement of T. S. Eliot* (1935), the earliest study of *Eliot's work to appear in the USA. *American Renaissance* (1941), Matthiessen's most influential publication, establishes a comprehensive perspective on the historical and intellectual backgrounds to the writings of Emerson, Whitman, Melville, Thoreau, and Hawthorn. *Henry James: The Major Phase* (1944) was the first work to make use of material from James's notebooks, the first edition of which Matthiessen produced with Kenneth B. Murdock in 1947. *The James Family* (1947) considered creative interactions between Henry *James, William *James, and their father, the philosopher Henry James, Sr. After teaching in Prague, he published *From the Heart of Europe* (1948), which posited a radical vision of Europe as a united social democracy. His edition of *The Oxford Book of American Verse* appeared in 1950, the year in which his suicide was precipitated by his growing despair at cultural conditions. Matthiessen's last years form the basis of May *Sarton's novel *Faithful Are the Wounds* (1955). *F. O. Matthiessen: The Critical Achievement* by Giles Gunn was published in 1975.

MATTHIESSEN, Peter (1927–), American novelist and travel writer, born in New York City, educated at Yale University. In 1953 he was co-founder of the **Paris Review*. His early novels *Race Rock* (1954), *Partisans* (1955), and *Raditzer* (1961) have in common the theme of the disjunctions between thought and action. *Wildlife in America* (1959) initiated his career as a writer on natural history and travel. His many expeditions to remote areas of the world are described in a succession of books which include *The Cloud Forest* (1961), on the South American wilderness and its inhabitants; *The Snow Leopard* (1978), an account of an arduous trek in the Himalayas; and *Baikal, Sacred Sea of Siberia* (1992). The concern evident in such work over technology's threats to the natural order informs his later fiction. *At Play in the Fields of the Lord* (1965), his most highly regarded novel, deals with the effects on an Amazonian tribe of a group of American missionaries. *Far Tortuga* (1975), an experimental montage of dialogue, description, and folk-tales, depicts the lives of Caribbean fishermen. *Killing Mr Watson* (1990) is a partly fictional account of the killer of Belle Starr, the outlaw. Matthiessen's other works include *In the Spirit of Crazy Horse* (1983), which investigates an incident of armed conflict between Native Americans and the FBI in 1975.

MATURA, Mustapha (1939–), Trinidadian dramatist, born in Port of Spain, Trinidad, where he was educated at Belmont Boys Roman Catholic Intermediate School. After working in various capacities, he emigrated to Britain in 1961 and became a full-time writer in 1968. He co-founded the Black Theatre Co-operative with Charles Hanson in 1978. Internationally regarded as pre-eminent among contemporary West Indian dramatists, his principal published plays are *As Time Goes By* (1972), *Play Mas* (1974), *Nice Rum and Cola and Welcome Home Jacko* (1980), and *Independence and Meetings* (1982), which were collected as *Six Plays* in 1992. His work displays a fundamental concern with the psychological and political effects on the individual produced by the decay of the indigenous cultures of the Caribbean. The satirical tenor of much of his writing gains impact from the wry humour and quirky individuality which are recurrent features of his characterizations. Among his other plays are *The Playboy of the West Indies* (1984), *Trinidad Sisters* (1988), and *The Coup* (1991).

MAUGHAM, W(illiam) Somerset (1874–1965), English novelist, short-story writer, and playwright, born in Paris, the sixth and youngest son of the solicitor to the British Embassy. His adored mother died of TB when he was eight years old, and the trauma of the event apparently stayed with him until his own death at the age of 91. Following the death of his father two years later, Maugham was sent to live in Whitstable, Kent with a middle-aged childless uncle and aunt. The sudden uprooting and change of language and lifestyle left the young Maugham lost and miserable, a state which worsened when he was sent to King's School, Canterbury, where his stammer caused him much pain and embarrassment. In 1891 Maugham spent nine months in Heidelberg, attending lectures at the University and enjoying his first taste of freedom and intellectual excitement. In 1892 he enrolled as a medical student at St Thomas's Hospital, London, and although he concentrated on private reading and writing, he succeeded in qualifying. He never practised as a doctor, but his experiences delivering babies in the slums of Lambeth were put to use his first novel, *Liza of Lambeth* (1897), the story of a Cockney factory girl whose romantic ambitions lead her to a hopeless relationship with an older married man. The grim realism of his portraits of slum life showed the influence of Zola. Relying on an income of £150, left to him by his father, Maugham then travelled to Seville, returning after nine months with a travel book and the first sketch of what would become *Of Human Bondage (1915). For the next five years Maugham lived in London and wrote without any great success. He published several novels, including *The Hero* (1901), *Mrs Craddock* (1902), and *The Merry-Go-Round* (1904). He also continued to write plays and *A Man of Honour* was produced in 1903 by the Stage Society. Maugham moved to Paris and lived a bohemian life in the company of painters and writers, a period of his life he was to recall in *The Moon and Sixpence* (1919).

In 1907 Maugham's fortune turned when his play *Lady Frederick*, put on as a last-minute stop-gap at the Royal Court, turned out to be a huge success. Within a year, Maugham had four plays running simultaneously in the West End—*Lady Frederick*, *Jack Straw*, *Mrs Dot*, and *The Explorer*. For the next thirty years, Maugham produced fashionable comedies of manners, and well-made plays with a gentle irony. The best of these are *The Circle* (1921) and *The Breadwinner* (1930).

In 1911 Maugham left the theatre temporarily to write *Of Human Bondage*, correcting the proofs while serving as an ambulance driver in France during the Great War. In 1915 he was recruited into Military Intelligence, and sent to Geneva; when his tour of duty ended, he travelled to the USA and then to Tahiti in the company of Gerald Haxton, his long-term companion and secretary. On his return, despite the blossoming of his relationship with Haxton, he married his mistress, Syrie Wellcome. Recruited once more into the Secret Service, Maugham travelled to Russia. After the war, Maugham continued to travel and write. *The Moon and Sixpence* (1919), an exploration of the creative genius, based on the life of Paul Gauguin, confirmed his reputation as a novelist, and headed the long list of works inspired by the author's travels in the South Seas. *The Trembling of a Leaf* (1921) was his first, highly popular collection of stories of the Far East, and *The Painted Veil* (1925), a story of adultery and redemption, was set in Hong Kong. In 1927 Maugham and his wife were divorced and he went to live in the Villa Mauresque on Cap Ferrat, the narrow peninsula between Nice and Monte Carlo. This beautiful and luxurious villa, filled with works of art, was to become one of the Riviera's great pilgrimage points, where social and literary celebrities were entertained in Maugham's exacting style. On the gatepost was inscribed a Moorish device against the evil eye which his father had brought back from abroad, and which appears on the covers of the uniform edition of his works.

In 1928 *Ashenden*, the cycle of stories based on his war experiences, was published. The urbane narrator, Willie Ashenden, became a kind of alter ego for Maugham and reappears in other writings, including *Cakes and Ale* (1930). This witty and moving novel was followed by a stream of successful but less exceptional publications which, like so much of his work, pleased the public but not the critics. Despite his unrivalled position as the most popular and financially successful writer of his time, Maugham never enjoyed critical acclaim. His middle-brow label adhered, due in part to a verbal predictability and shallowness of characterization, but also perhaps to his unrivalled readability.

With the outbreak of the Second World War, Maugham left France and stayed in the USA. During this time *The *Razor's Edge* (1944) was published, and filmed in the following year. In 1946 he returned to the Villa Mauresque. Gerald Haxton had died in 1944, and his place was taken by Alan Searle who would stay with Maugham until his death. The author's later life was enlivened by the making of film versions of some of his excellent short stories, *Quartet* (1948), *Trio* (1950), and *Encore* (1951), introduced by the author in person. He was made a Companion of Honour in 1954, and in 1962 he published *Looking Back*, a volume of memoirs which contained a vindictive and pointless attack on his deceased ex-wife, and which lost him many friends.

MAUPIN, Armistead (1944–), American journalist and novelist, born in Washington DC, educated at the University of North Carolina. From the mid-1970s Maupin has published short, witty accounts of the hedonistic lifestyles of some of San Francisco's citizens in the *San Francisco Examiner*. These pieces, with engaging recurrent characters, form a continuous chronicle that has been published in the form of successive novels. *Tales of the City* (1978) and *More Tales of the City* (1980) describe a world of joyful and frequent sexual encounters, against a background of California bath-houses, holidays in Mexico, and desert whorehouses. Although full of comic incident, the novels *Further Tales of the City* (1982) and *Babycakes* (1986) feature a less carefree attitude in Maupin's creations as he describes the careerism of the Reagan years, and shows how AIDS is beginning to take its tragic toll on the gay community. *Significant Others* (1988) revels in a modern-day war between the sexes, as a separatist Women's camp finds itself pitched beside a weekend retreat for wealthy Californian men. *Sure of You* (1990) is less anarchic and, in elegiac and compassionate mood, contrasts the brave new world of the late 1980s with the more pleasurable times of the decade before. *Maybe the Moon* (1993) focuses on Cadence ('Cady') Roth, a midget actress who starred as an elf, totally covered in rubber, in a successful film. The book evinces Maupin's anger at prejudices and stereotyping and was praised for its stylish wit and fluent plotting; it is dedicated to the late Tamara de Treaux, the diminutive actress who was inside the E.T. suit in Spielberg's film *E.T.*

Maurice, a novel by E. M. *Forster, published in 1971. Written in 1914, the novel remained unpublished for over fifty years, on account of its subject: the homosexual relationship between two young men, one of whom eventually conforms to social convention by marrying, the other of whom remains unmarried and unrepentant about his sexual inclinations. The novel opens with the latter, Maurice Hall, on the point of leaving his preparatory school to go to public school:

its opening chapter includes the very funny account of the rather rudimentary sex education the boy receives from a well-meaning but misguided master, which results in his subsequent abhorrence of sexual relations with women. The next few chapters follow Maurice's career at school and at Cambridge University, where he first encounters the young man with whom he is to fall so disastrously in love, Clive Durham. Despite the fact that it is Clive who first confesses his love for Maurice, it soon becomes apparent that it is the latter who feels more strongly about the relationship, even risking being sent down because of it. The love affair—by now rather one-sided—continues for a few years after the two young men leave Cambridge, although it becomes clear that there is no longer any sexual dimension to the relationship. Then, in an outburst of candour, Clive tells Maurice of his intention to marry. Maurice, devastated by his friend's betrayal, at first attempts to 'cure' himself of his own homosexual feelings by undertaking a course of psychotherapy, which proves unsuccessful. Just as he is contemplating suicide or flight to the Continent, he meets Alec Scudder, one of the gamekeepers on Clive's estate, with whom he is at last able to reach some kind of emotional and sexual equilibrium.

MAURICE, Furnley, pseudonym of Frank WILMOT (1881–1942), Australian poet, born in Melbourne. He was on the advisory board of the Commonwealth Literary Fund, and in 1922 he assisted in the foundation of the influential Pioneer Players. Following an anonymous collection, *Unconditioned Songs* (1913), he produced two collections, *To God: From the Warring Nations* (1917) and *Eyes of Vigilance* (1920), in which he decried both war and Australia's alignment with Europe's activities. His poems are exuberant and he engages with colloquial speech patterns to pleasing effect. Further collections include *Ways and Means* (1920), *The Gully and Other Verses* (1929), and *Odes for a Curse-Speaking Choir!* (1933). *Romance* (1922) presented an early account of an Australian poet's response to new movements in poetry in Europe and America, and in *Melbourne Odes* (1934) the influence of *Modernism became apparent; in the preface Maurice expressed the need for new developments in Australian poetry.

MAVOR, Osborne Henry, see BRIDIE, JAMES.

Maximus Poems, The, an epic poem by Charles *Olson. Conceived of in 1945, but not started until 1950, *The Maximus Poems* occupied the last twenty years of Olson's life. Ezra Pound's *The *Cantos* and William Carlos Williams's **Paterson* were the most insistent contemporary influences, though Olson, in *Mayan Letters* (1954), objected to Pound's egotism and Williams's historical naïvety. He also felt that Pound had not gone back far enough in human history, stopping within a Western framework that essentially inhibited what Olson took to be the necessary growth of a modern epic. Olson's debt to Melville, to Sufism, to Alfred North *Whitehead, and to Carl Jung also helped to distinguish his achievement from that of his forebears. Each of the first two volumes of Maximus consists of three books, some of which were published separately, such as *Maximus 1/10* (1953) and *Maximus 11/12* (1956). *The Maximus Poems* (1960) is the volume most explicitly concerned with the local history and politics of Olson's adopted city of Gloucester, Massachusetts (the focus also of T. S. Eliot's 'Dry Salvages' of the **Four Quartets*, though Olson characteristically railed against Eliot's use of symbolism which for him obliterated the actualities of the place). *Maximus Poems IV, V, VI* (1968) widens the scope of his epic: its saturation in myth and world history complements and extends the materials of the first volume. It constitutes the major rite of passage in the poem, a submersion into the problematics of self and world which has much in common with Melville's *Moby-Dick*. Ending with an allusion to Ishmael's fate in Melville's novel, the volume paves the way for the posthumously published *The Maximus Poems: Volume Three* (1975). This last volume, though tinged by sadness, has an air of spiritual acceptance and rootedness, parallel with Walt Whitman's later writings. Extensively edited and revised by George F. Butterick, the poem was published as a whole in 1983; Butterick's *A Guide to the Maximus Poems of Charles Olson* remains an expert and invaluable guide to this great twentieth-century epic poem.

MAXWELL, Gavin (1914–1969), British writer on travel and natural history, born at Elrig, Wigtown; his aristocratic family background is described in the autobiographical *The House of Elrig* (1965). He was educated at Hertford College, Oxford. *Harpoon at a Venture* (1952), his first book, describes the commercially unsuccessful shark fishery he opened in 1944 on the Hebridean island of Soay. During the 1950s he travelled widely, recording his experiences of Sicily in *God Protect Me from My Friends* (1956) and *The Ten Pains of Death* (1959). A journey to Iraq with Wilfred *Thesiger in 1956 produced *A Reed Shaken by the Wind* (1957), his acclaimed treatment of the country's Marsh Arabs. The otter he brought back from Iraq and another he subsequently acquired provided material for his best-known work, *Ring of Bright Water* (1960), an absorbing and lyrically detailed account of the creatures and the interactions of their lives with his. *The Otter's Tale* (1962) and *The Rocks Remain* (1963) continue his narrative of the otters. His other publications include *Lords of the Atlas* (1966), a study of the violent rise to power of the Glaoua dynasty in Morocco.

MAXWELL, Glyn (Meurig) (1962–), British poet, born in Welwyn Garden City, educated at Worcester College, Oxford, and the University of Boston, where he studied Creative Writing under Derek *Walcott and George Starbuck. In 1988 he commenced work as a freelance publishing editor and literary journalist. *Tale of the Mayor's Son* (1990), his first collection of verse, gained him wide notice for its idiosyncratically effective handling of narrative and lyric modes. A further volume entitled *Out of the Rain* appeared in 1992; its title sequence offers the most impressive example of his consistently successful use of longer forms. Much of Maxwell's poetry offers richly particularized but imaginatively detached commentaries on the moral and cultural complexion of contemporary society. His writing frequently combines a fluently conversational tone with unusual patterns of syntax. Among his other publications is *Gnyss the Magnificent* (1993), which contains three of the verse-plays he has staged at his home in Welwyn Garden City.

MAYNE, Rutherford, pseudonym of Samuel WADDELL (1878–1967), Northern Irish playwright and actor, born in Japan, brother of Helen *Waddell. Mayne became as important to the *Ulster Literary Theatre, which he joined in 1904, as Lennox *Robinson was to the *Abbey. His first play, *The Turn of the Road* (1906), is a serious satire whose target is the Protestant fanaticism which Mayne found so distasteful. This was followed by his best-known play, *The Drone* (1907), a comedy which attacks the puritanical beliefs of Protestants in rural County Down. Having written nine plays for the Ulster Literary Theatre, Mayne turned his attentions to the Abbey in Dublin, where *Peter* (1930) and *Bridgehead* (1934) were produced. More adventurous than his earlier work, these plays show signs of the influence of Lennox Robinson.

MAYOR, F(lora) M(acdonald) (1872–1932), British novelist and short-story writer, born in Kingston-upon-Thames, educated at Newnham College, Cambridge. Her collection of stories *Mrs Hammond's Children* (1901) attracted little attention but *The Third Miss Symons* (1913), introduced by John *Masefield, was highly praised; it is the story of a single woman circumscribed by late Victorian society, and could be described as a classic 'spinster novel'. It was followed by *Miss Browne's Friend—A Story of Two Women*, serialized in the *Free Church Suffrage Times* (1914–15). Her finest work was *The Rector's Daughter* (1924), in which simplicity of structure belies a rigorous exploration of social and emotional truths. A mature expansion of her earlier theme, it was duly acclaimed: Rebecca *West pronounced Mayor's immense superiority to *Galsworthy; E. M. *Forster and Virginia *Woolf wrote admiringly to her. Other publications include the novel *The Squire's Daughter* (1924) and a posthumous collection of stories, *The Room Opposite* (1935).

Meanjin, an Australian cultural journal with a special interest in new poetry and prose and literary criticism. 'Meanjin' is the Aboriginal word for Brisbane; its first editor, Clem Christesen, poet and journalist, founded the magazine there under the title *Meanjin Papers* in 1940. It subsequently adopted the titles of *Meanjin* (1947–60), *Meanjin Quarterly* (1960–76), and *Meanjin* again from 1977. With Christesen the journal moved to the University of Melbourne in 1945. The journal expanded to include the visual arts and writing from other countries, comparative commentary and, later, Australian multicultural writing. The distinctive school of Australian criticism which it developed saw literature as part of a larger social and cultural context. Christesen edited *Meanjin* until 1974, and succeeding editors have maintained its traditions. *On Native Grounds* (1967) was a selection from the journal's first twenty-five years. *The Temperament of Generations* (1990) is a selection from fifty years of publication.

MEHTA, Ved (Parkash) (1934–), Indian journalist and autobiographical writer, born in Lahore, educated at Balliol College, Oxford and at Harvard. For many years he wrote for the *New Yorker* and in 1975 he became an American citizen. *Walking the Indian Streets* (1960; revised edition 1971) describes his return to India, together with his compatriot Dom *Moraes. Mehta is best known for his autobiographical memoirs which include *Face to Face* (1957), *Daddyji* (1972), *Mamaji* (1979), *Vedi* (1982), and *The Ledge Between the Streams* (1984); as well as combining acute descriptions of everyday life in India, and shrewd analysis of Indian society, the memoirs also reveal with great pathos and humour the courageous confrontations with life of one who has been blind from childhood. *Fly and the Fly-Bottle* (1963) was based on articles in the *New Yorker* about his meetings with various British intellectuals, including I. *Berlin, A. J. *Ayer, and A. J. P. *Taylor. His novel *Delinquent Chacha* (1967) is a satirical comedy set in London and Oxford. *Up at Oxford* (1993) is a memoir of his student days in the late 1950s. Other works include *Portrait of India* (1970), *Mahatma Gandhi and his Apostles* (1977), *The New India* (1978), *Sound-Shadows of the New World* (1986), *Three Stories of the Raj* (1986), *The Stolen Light* (1989), and *Rajiv Gandhi and Rama's Kingdom* (1994).

Member of the Wedding, The, see MCCULLERS, CARSON.

Memoirs of a Fox-Hunting Man, the first part, published in 1928, of Siegfried *Sassoon's 'Sherston Trilogy', the others being **Memoirs of an Infantry Officer* (1930) and *Sherston's Progress* (1936). The three books were published as *The Complete Memoirs of George Sherston* in 1937, describing Sherston's life from infancy to the years immediately after the First World War. Although the trilogy is closely based on Sassoon's personal history, the use of the 'Sherston' persona permits minor alterations and major omissions; there is, for example, little reference to his schooling, his time at Cambridge, and his literary ambitions in *Memoirs of a Fox-Hunting Man*, which deals with the period between childhood and Sherston's early experiences at the Western Front. Sassoon later stated that 'Sherston was a simplified version of my "outdoor self". He was denied the complex advantage of being a soldier poet.' The ten parts of *Memoirs of a Fox-Hunting Man* portray Sherston's preoccupation with the 'tremendous trivialities' of life; his is a world of great affluence in which a shy boy grows into a young man devoted to riding, fox-hunting, cricket, and golf. The book is rich in evocations of the Kent landscapes of his upbringing; as an elegy for the innocence and ease of the Edwardian era any tendency to sentimentality is balanced by the ironic tinge with which the retrospective narrative regards Sherston and his social milieu. The work is primarily successful in terms of its enormously attractive style; Sassoon writes with great clarity and simplicity, and frequently employs a dry humour, in following his main concern with the quality of youthful experience and its gradual transition into emerging maturity.

Memoirs of A Midget, see DE LA MARE, WALTER.

Memoirs of an Infantry Officer, the second part of Siegfried *Sassoon's quasi-autobiographical 'Sherston Trilogy'; published in 1930, it followed **Memoirs of a Fox-Hunting Man* (1928) and preceded *Sherston's Progress* (1936). The books offer a selective and lightly fictionalized version of the period between Sassoon's infancy and the years immediately after the First World War; other aspects of his earlier life are dealt with in the straightforwardly autobiographical *The Old Century and Seven More Years* (1938), *The Weald of Youth* (1942), and *Siegfried's Journey* (1945). *Memoirs of an Infantry Officer* begins on the Western Front in 1916, the point at which *Memoirs of a Fox-Hunting Man* ends. Sherston's progress towards moral responsibility, fuller social awareness, and personal maturity continues towards 'Independent Action', the title of the last of the ten parts; an account is given of Sassoon's actions and their consequences when he issued 'A Soldier's Declaration' in 1917 to protest against the prolongation of the war. Although Sherston's attitudes to the war change radically in the course of *Memoirs of an Infantry Officer*, the development from uneasy idealism to angry disillusionment is gradual and not emphasized for dramatic effect; Sherston's feelings are thoroughly integrated into the highly detailed view of the life of a young subaltern, presented in the companionable tone generated by Sassoon's fluently modulated prose. The book is regarded as Sassoon's greatest success and forms, in George Fraser's words, 'the classic personal account of the First World War in English'.

MENCKEN, H(enry) L(ouis) (1880–1956), American journalist, editor, and critic, born in Baltimore; he began his career in journalism in 1899 as a reporter for the *Baltimore Herald* group, becoming a full editor by 1906. *George Bernard Shaw: His Plays* (1905) and *The Philosophy of Friedrich Nietzsche* (1908), the first American studies of their subjects, gained Mencken the notice that led to his appointment as literary editor of *The Smart Set*, the self-styled 'magazine of cleverness', in 1908. From 1914 to 1923 he co-edited the journal with George Jean *Nathan, raising it to importance among the literary forums of the day; D. H. *Lawrence, James *Joyce, Ezra *Pound, Amy *Lowell, Sherwood *Anderson, and Theodore *Dreiser were among the contributing writers. *A Book of Prefaces* (1917) collects the literary criticism he was producing at the time. Mencken's association with the Baltimore *Sunpapers* resulted in wide circulation for 'The Free Lance', the column which established his reputation as an iconoclastic commentator on current affairs; as a foreign correspondent during the First World War, from 1916, his support for Germany aroused fierce controversy. With Nathan, he founded the **American Mercury* in 1924, of which he became sole editor in 1925; among the authors he published were F. Scott *Fitzgerald, Sinclair *Lewis, Willa *Cather, and Ben *Hecht, whom he regarded as exponents of an authentic modern American literature. His other publishing ventures included *The *Black Mask*, a magazine of *detective fiction begun with Nathan in 1920. The 1920s were the zenith of Mencken's fame; his devastatingly cynical and wittily opinionated articles in the *American Mercury* and elsewhere, collected in six volumes of *Prejudices* (1919–27), appealed to the widespread scepticism of the post-war era through their attacks on the pretensions he saw as intrinsic to almost every social and cultural institution. *The American Language* (1919, revised editions 1921, 1923, 1936; supplements 1945, 1948), was an impressive work of popular scholarship distinguishing between British and American English and defending the rich variety of the latter. The *New York Times*'s description of him as 'the most powerful private citizen in the United States' was, however, no longer apt by the early 1930s, when socio-economic factors determined a graver cultural atmosphere than that in which Mencken had thrived. *A Treatise on the Gods* (1930) and *A Treatise on Right and Wrong* (1934), his respective treatments of religion and ethics, were unsuccessful and, after the demise of the *American Mercury* in 1933, he was principally occupied as a political journalist for the remainder of the decade. He regained a measure of his former celebrity with *Happy Days* (1940), *Newspaper Days* (1941), and *Heathen Days* (1942), three volumes of humorously unreliable autobiography which appeared together as *The Days of H. L. Mencken* in 1947. Illness prevented him from writing from 1950 onward. Among his many other works are *A Book of Burlesques* (1916), *In Defense of Women* (1918), and *A Dictionary of Quotations on Historical Principles* (1942). Selections of his shorter writings include *A Mencken Crestomathy* (1949), his own compilation, and *The Gist of Mencken* (edited by M. DuBasky, 1990). Carl Bode's *Mencken* (1969) is the best of several biographies. Other biographical sources include *Letters of H. L. Mencken* (edited by G. J. Forgue, 1961) and *The Diary of H. L. Mencken* (edited by C. Fecher, 1989).

MENDELSON, Edward (1946–), American scholar and editor; born in New York, educated at the University of Rochester and at Johns Hopkins University. He began his academic career at Yale in 1969 and became Professor of English at Columbia University in 1983. In the course of his doctoral research he had numerous meetings with W. H. *Auden, who chose him to be his literary executor. His edition of Auden's *Collected Poems* appeared in 1976. He subsequently published *The English Auden* (1977), which contains poetry, essays, and dramatic writings from the years 1927 to 1939; the poems appear without any of Auden's later alterations and are supplemented by a valuable appendix presenting many uncollected texts. *Early Auden* (1981) is a critical companion to *The English Auden*, providing a lucid exposition of the ideas and influences characterizing the initial stages of Auden's career. *W. H. Auden and Christopher Isherwood: Plays* (1989) and *Libretti and Other Dramatic Writings by W. H. Auden, 1939–1973* (1993) are two volumes of his projected complete edition of Auden's works. Other publications he has edited include *Thomas Pynchon: A Collection of Critical Essays* (1978).

MENDES, Alfred H(ubert) (1897–), Trinidadian novelist and short-story writer, born in Trinidad, educated at Hitchin Grammar School in England. During the 1920s and 1930s he published short stories and essays, in **Trinidad* and *The *Beacon* amongst other journals. In the 1930s he spent some time in America, where work on the *Federal Writers' Project brought him into contact with black American writers such as Langston *Hughes and Countee *Cullen. His first novel, *Pitch Lake* (1934), was published with an introduction by Aldous *Huxley; the novel focuses on Joe da Costa, of Portuguese descent, who is torn between the sterility of middle-class life and a woman belonging to the 'barrack-yard' or poorer section of Trinidadian society. His other novel, *Black Fauns* (1935), is set entirely in the 'barrack-yard' milieu and has been praised for its focus on strong women characters.

MERCER, David (1928–80), British dramatist, born in Wakefield, the son of an engine driver. After leaving school at 14 he worked as a laboratory technician, then went to King's College, Newcastle, first to study chemistry, then to take a degree in fine arts. After some years spent teaching he became a full-time writer, achieving recognition with a series of television plays, including *Where the Difference Begins* (1961), *A Climate of Fear* (1962), and *A Suitable Case for Treatment* (1962), which was later filmed as *Morgan* (1965). Subsequently he produced many works for TV, helping to establish that medium as an important forum for serious drama, and several for the stage, including *Ride a Cock Horse* (1965), *Flint* (1970), *After Haggerty* (1970), and *Cousin Vladimir* (1978), about a Soviet dissident's appalled reaction to a morally derelict Britain. Mercer's work, though written from a Marxist stance, tended to concentrate on individuals desperately trying to discover themselves and achieve wholeness in a world he found bewildering, oppressive, and painful on both personal and public levels.

MEREDITH, William (Morris, Jr) (1919–), American poet, born in New York, educated at Princeton University, where he was three times Resident Fellow in Creative Writing between 1947 and 1966. From 1955 to 1983 he taught at Connecticut College, New London, becoming Professor of English in 1965. The most impressive work in *Love Letter from an Impossible Land* (1944), his first collection of poetry, and *Ships and Other Figures* (1948) displayed technical accomplishment and emotional understatement in verse reflecting his wartime experiences as a naval airman. His naval background remains an important imaginative resource in *The Open Sea* (1958) and *The Wreck of the Thresher* (1964); the title poem of the latter volume is an elegiac meditation of remarkable scope prompted by the loss of an American submarine. Meredith's work has been compared to Robert *Frost's for its unostentatious formal strength and poised conversational tone. His later collections, in which his verse forms display increasing flexibility, include *Earth Walk: New and Selected Poems* (1970), *Hazard the Painter* (1975), and *Partial Accounts: New and Selected Poems* (1987; Pulitzer Prize, 1988). Among his other publications is *Poems Are Hard to Read* (1991), an entertainingly varied collection of memoirs and essays.

MERRILL, James (Ingram) (1926–95), American poet, born in New York, educated at Amherst College, Massachusetts. *First Poems* (1951) attracted favourable notice for its concentration and technical accomplishment. Successive volumes, among them *The Country of a Thousand Years of Peace* (1959), *Water Street* (1962), *Nights and Days* (1966), and *The Fire Screen* (1969), displayed his increasing ability to combine personal experience, vivid local description, and imaginative elements in verse of remarkable sonority and refinement. A selected edition entitled *From The First Nine: Poems, 1947–1976* appeared in 1982. *The Divine Comedies* (1976) contained 'The Book of Ephraim', the first part of a trilogy completed by *Mirabell: Books of Number* (1978) and *Scripts for the Pageant* (1980), which was published in its entirety of over 500 pages as *The Changing Light at Sandover* (1982). The three books, which range widely through history, science, cosmology, and metaphysics, purport to owe their composition to Merrill's experiments with a ouija board; much of the material is presented as a symposium consisting of transcriptions of communications from supernatural agents. The work constitutes a remarkable achievement in terms of its intellectual audacity, overall organization, and encompassing thematic scope. Merrill's novels, *The Seraglio* (1957) and *The (Diblos) Notebook* (1965), draw on his experiences as a traveller and reflect the affluent family background to which much of his poetry also alludes. He has also written plays, which include *The Immortal Husband* (1956) and *The Bait* (1960). *Late Settings* (1985) and *The Inner Room* (1988) marked the return of his poetry to more conventional lyric modes, though numerous poems make imaginatively effective use of the interpenetration of myth and subjective experience.

MERWIN, W(illiam) S(tanley) (1927–), American poet, born in New York City, educated at Princeton University where he established an enduring friendship with Galway *Kinnell. His books of poems include *A Mask for Janus* (1952), *The Dancing Bears* (1954), *Green with Beasts* (1956), *The Drunk in the Furnace* (1960), *The Moving Target* (1963), *The Lice* (1967), *The*

Carrier of Ladders (1970; Pulitzer Prize), *Writings to an Unfinished Accompaniment* (1973), *The Compass Flower* (1977), *Finding the Islands* (1982), *Opening the Hand* (1983), and *The Rain in the Trees* (1988). Like his earliest mentor Ezra *Pound, Merwin is a student of Romance languages, and has become one of the most accomplished translators of poetry in the second half of the twentieth century with versions of *The Poem of the Cid* (1959), *The Satires of Perseus* (1961), *The Song of Roland* (1963), *Transparence of the World: Poems of Jean Follain* (1969), *Voices: Selected Writings of Antonia Porchia* (1969), *Pablo Neruda, Twenty Love Poems and a Song of Despair* (1969), and *Selected Poems of Osip Mandelstam* (with Clarence Brown, 1974). Merwin's prose works include *Regions of Memory, Uncollected Prose, 1949–1982* (1987), edited by Ed Folsom and Cary Nelson. Merwin's central subject is language itself, both in terms of the necessary precision required to write at all, and the difficulties of naming the parts of the world without making that process an act of appropriation. A major poet of great technical virtuosity, his vision of the human condition is not reassuring, though his search for the means to relate our experiential world to that of nature, myth, and primary creation is bleakly impressive.

Metafiction is a term which became current in the 1960s and fashionable in the 1970s and 1980s. It refers to writing which reflects on its own fictional status, fiction about fiction. Such work is not necessarily concerned with fiction as opposed to reality, or its own techniques as opposed to the world beyond the book; it does necessarily acknowledge the presence in the text of a fiction-making mind. John *Barth's *Lost in the Funhouse* (1969) is an oft-cited example, and Barth in turn was much influenced by Jorge Luis Borges's *Ficciones* (1944). The writing of Samuel *Beckett can be thought of as metafictional throughout, and more recently the term has been taken up in film studies, to describe the work of, among others, David Lynch and Woody Allen. Early instances of metafiction would be Sterne's *Tristram Shandy* (1760–7) and Diderot's *Jacques le fataliste* (written 1773–5, published 1796), and there is much metafictional comment in Fielding's *Tom Jones* (1749). The most brilliant recent example of the mode is probably Italo Calvino's *If On a Winter's Night a Traveller*... (1979).

Metalanguage. *Meta* is a Greek term which in English suggests, apparently on the basis of a misunderstanding of the etymology of the word 'metaphysics', going beyond or above a particular domain—see METAFICTION for a similar use of the prefix. Metalanguage accordingly is a language which discusses language. A dictionary, for example, is almost all metalanguage in relation to the words it defines; descriptive grammar is another metalanguage. More generally, criticism is often taken to be a metalanguage with respect to the texts it addresses, and it is of course possible for literary works to contain their own metalanguage, to look at themselves as if in a mirror. This occurs in *Hamlet*, for instance, when the prince compares his situation to that of the actors, thereby reminding an audience that they are watching (at least) two plays: one representing a fictional life in Elsinore, one taking place now, wherever the work is staged. Hamlet's speech to the players is both language (within the play) and metalanguage (about the play). Roman Jakobson (see FORMALISM) reminds us that ordinary speech is full of metalanguage in the form of hints and explanations: 'Do you understand what I am saying?'; 'What I really meant was . . .'; '*Jerk* is a slang expression for . . .'. These phrases point indirectly to the meaning of a conversation and directly to its articulation; they clarify the way the language works.

METCALF, John (1938–), Canadian novelist and short-story writer, born in Carlisle, England, educated at the University of Bristol; he emigrated to Canada in 1962. After teaching in Loyola College in Montreal he became a full-time writer in 1971. His abiding reputation as one of the finest prose stylists in contemporary Canada was established with the vividly observed and imaginatively disquieting stories collected in *The Lady Who Sold the Furniture* (1970). His first novel, *Going Down Slow* (1972), centres on the personal and professional conflicts surrounding a school teacher whose artistic and political idealism sets him at odds with a prevailingly materialistic cultural order. A similar disaffection characterizes *General Ludd* (1980), Metcalf's second novel, which satirizes the pretensions pervading contemporary higher education. *The Teeth of my Father* (1975), *Girl in Gingham* (1978), and *Adult Entertainment* (1986) are further collections of the short-stories and novellas which are often regarded as his best work; *Selected Stories* appeared in 1982. Metcalf's critical writings, which include *Kicking Against the Pricks* (1982) and *Freedom from Culture* (1987), frequently castigate Canadian literature for what he considers its provincial orientation. *Writers in Aspic* (1988) and *The New Story Writers* (1992) are among the numerous anthologies of fiction he has edited.

METCALF, Paul (1917–), American prose writer, born in Cambridge, Massachusetts, educated at Harvard; he is the great-grandson of Herman Melville. Since his mother was Melville's literary executor, Metcalf's home was constantly visited by scholars, one of whom was Charles *Olson, who later had a profound influence on the development of Metcalf's writing. Metcalf has led an independent existence, refusing to be tied to any particular institution; while living in North Carolina, he visited *Black Mountain College but made no attempt to affiliate himself to it. His books offer beautifully composed alternative histories of America, written from the native American viewpoint of writers like William Carlos *Williams and composers like Charles Ives. Metcalf employs montage to great effect, weaving together both fictional and non-fictional material, the latter drawn from a wide range of sources, including history, biology, mythology, and geography. While

Genoa (1965) concentrates primarily on Melville, it also includes Christopher Columbus, the war in the Pacific, and a pair of fictionalized brothers; *Patagonia* (1971) places Henry Ford alongside Peruvian Indians; *Both* (1982) pairs Edgar A. Poe with John Wilkes Booth. These strange and unusual combinations yield surprisingly central understandings; Metcalf's achievement in *Genoa* rivals Olson's in *Call Me Ishmael*. Particularly from *Apalache* (1976) onwards, his books are composed in a symphonic manner, a process which culminates in *Waters of Potomac* (1982), a long and moving account of America's tragic descent into waste, divisiveness, and pollution. *Enter Isabel: The Herman Melville Correspondence of Clare Spark and Paul Metcalf* (1991) testifies to Metcalf's lifelong meditation on his great grandfather's influence and centrality.

MEW, Charlotte (Mary) (1869–1928), British poet and short-story writer, born in Bloomsbury; she attended lectures at University College, London. Following the appearance in 1894 of her story 'Passed' in *The Yellow Book*, she contributed poems and stories to numerous periodicals. *The Farmer's Bride* (1915), her first collection of poetry, displayed the austerely lyrical tone and preoccupation with torment and grief that characterize much of her verse. Her recurrent treatments of mental imbalance, of which 'On the Asylum Road' is a memorable example, have a disquieting intensity related to the fact that she had a brother and a sister who were confined in private asylums. She killed herself in a London nursing home, fearing that the breakdown she had undergone following the deaths of her mother and one of her sisters marked the advent of insanity. A second volume of poetry, *The Rambling Sailor*, appeared in 1929, the title poem typifying the curious and imaginative effects she achieved through her idiosyncratic adaptations of traditional forms. Hilda *Doolittle and Virginia *Woolf were among her admirers; *Hardy believed her to be unquestionably the best woman poet of her day and, with the support of *De La Mare and *Masefield, obtained a Civil List pension for her in 1923. Her skilfully structured short stories are notable for their sustained concern with women's attitudes and experiences. V. Warner's edition of *Collected Poems and Prose* appeared in 1981; *Charlotte Mew and Her Friends*, by Penelope *Fitzgerald, was published in 1984.

MEYER, Michael (1921–), British biographer and translator, born in London, educated at Oxford University. From 1947 to 1950 he was a visiting lecturer in English at the University of Uppsala, where he learned the Scandinavian languages. He has written two major biographies, of Ibsen (2 volumes, 1967, 1971) and of Strindberg (1985), and has also translated many of their works for the stage. His memoirs, *Not Prince Hamlet* (1989), record his long and lively involvement with British theatre and his own 'love affair with Sweden'.

MEYNELL, Alice (née Thompson) (1847–1922), British poet and essayist, born in Barnes, London. She became a Roman Catholic in 1868, which determined the devotional character of much of her poetry. *Preludes* (1875), her first collection of verse, was much admired by the author and editor Wilfrid Meynell (1852–1948), whom she married in 1877. In 1891 they rescued Francis Thompson from destitution and secured him literary recognition. Her subsequent volumes include *Poems* (1893), *A Father of Women* (1917), and *Last Poems* (1923). Frederick Page edited the complete edition of her verse (1940). By 1900 she enjoyed widespread critical and popular esteem, largely founded on the impression of lyrical piety generated by her work. Her later verse is more rigorous in tone and sometimes makes use of precisely observed detail. Certain of her poems, notably 'Christ in the Universe', display impressive imaginative power. Her essays, originally published in a range of influential periodicals, were collected in numerous volumes, among which are *The Rhythm of Life* (1893) and *The Spirit of Place* (1899); *The Wares of Autolycus* (edited by P. M. Fraser, 1965) is a selection of her essays. A biography by J. Badeni appeared in 1981.

Michael Robartes and the Dancer, see YEATS, W. B.

MICHENER, James A(lbert) (1907–), American novelist, born in New York City, educated at the University of Northern Colorado, and the University of St Andrews, Scotland. His *Tales of the South Pacific* (1947; Pulitzer Prize, 1948) was later made into the Rodgers and Hammerstein musical, *South Pacific*. His many bestselling novels include *Sayonara* (1954), later made into a film with Marlon Brando; *The Bridge at Andau* (1957); *Hawaii* (1959); and *Chesapeake* (1978). His most accomplished novel is generally considered to be *Centennial* (1974), a grand epic of the opening up, or 'taming', of the American West. Other novels, reflecting Michener's ongoing concern and engagement with politics and world affairs, include *The Covenant* (1980), an epic treatment of South African history; *Legacy* (1987), a fictional look at the Iran / Contra affair; and *The Novel* (1991), set in the publishing world. *The World Is My Home* (1992) is an autobiography, and *Literary Reflections* (1993) is a collection of essays.

MICHIE, James (1927–), British poet and translator, born in Weybridge, Surrey, educated at Trinity College, Oxford. He began his successful career in publishing in 1951. He is well known for the elegant accomplishment and accuracy of his verse translations, which include *The Odes of Horace* (1964), *The Poems of Catullus: A Bilingual Edition* (1969), and *The Epigrams of Martial* (1973). *Possible Laughter* (1959) and *New and Selected Poems* (1983), his collections of original verse, display a singularity of tone integral to their relaxed formality of technique. His poetry, which invariably succeeds in combining entertainment and underlying seriousness, is often characterized by the complex inventiveness of its metaphors. The wit permeating much of his work can be disquietingly macabre. *Collected Poems* appeared in 1994. He has also edited numerous works, which include *The Bodley Head Book of Longer Short Stories* (1975) and, with P. J. *Kavanagh, *The Oxford Book of Short Poems* (1985).

Middle Age of Mrs Eliot, The, see WILSON, SIR ANGUS.

MIDDLETON, (John) Christopher (1926–), British poet, born in Truro, Cornwall, educated at Merton College, Oxford. After lecturing at Zurich University and King's College, University of London, in 1966 he became Professor of Germanic Languages and Literature at the University of Texas. *Torse 3: Poems 1949–1961* (1962), his first major collection of poetry, was followed by numerous succeeding volumes including *Our Flowers and Nice Bones* (1969), *The Lonely Suppers of W. V. Balloon* (1975), *111 Poems* (1983), *Two Horse Wagon Going By* (1986), and *The Balcony Tree* (1992). Middleton, whose work is firmly aligned with the traditions of European *Modernism, is regarded by many as the best of the English poets of the present day dedicated to working in experimental modes; George *Steiner noted his 'characteristic tautness, sinewy elegance, and reach of invocation'. Much of his verse displays the remarkable flexibility and power of his historical imagination, which ranges freely between the Roman era and the twentieth century. *Selected Writings* (1989), which contains poems, short fiction, and essays, is a representative collection of his work. His other publications include the collections of essays *Bolshevism in Art and Other Expository Writings* (1978) and *The Pursuit of the Kingfisher* (1983). Among his many works as a translator are *Selected Letters* (1969) of Nietzsche; *The Spectacle at the Tower* (1985), a novel by Gert Hofmann; and *Andalusian Poems* (1993).

MIDDLETON, Stanley (1919–), British novelist, born in Bulwell, Nottingham, educated at University College of Nottingham. For many years he worked as a teacher, becoming Head of the English Department at High Pavement College, Nottingham. Teachers are among the characters who inhabit his acutely observed novels about provincial life in the Midlands. His novels focus on the emotional dilemmas that beset articulate, middle-class people, and the reverberations these have on the lives of those around them. Middleton's style is quiet, precise, and, for all its fidelity to ordinary life, not without a kind of poetry, which transfigures the mundane world of the often determinedly conventional people of his fictions. His ability to let complex characters unfold is evident in *The Daysman* (1984), where the protagonist is a headmaster addicted to altruistic-seeming interference in the affairs of others and incapable of appreciating the moral narcissism of which he is guilty. Middleton's method serves him well in the portrayal of marital difficulties and in describing the relations between men and women generally; *Holiday* (1974; Booker Prize) offers a good example of this. His agnostic humanism is apparent in his treatment of loneliness, old age, and death. Among his many other novels are *Two Brothers* (1978), *An After-Dinner's Sleep* (1986), *After a Fashion* (1987), *Recovery* (1988), *Vacant Places* (1989), *Changes and Chances* (1990), *Beginning to End* (1991), and *Married Past Redemption* (1993).

Midnight's Children, a novel by Salman *Rushdie, published in 1981 and winner of the Booker Prize. This highly innovative novel was the forerunner of a new genre of writing from India, other Asian countries, and Africa, combining the *magic realism of Latin American novels with political comment, satire, and dissertations on contemporary history in the context of decolonization. It is narrated entirely in the voice of Saleem Sinai, one of the 1,001 gifted children born at midnight, 15 August 1947, the moment of India's formal declaration of its independence from Britain. Saleem's life reflects the vagaries and changes of the Indian political situation, and is intertwined with the fates of midnight's other children. Saleem, himself the changeling child of an Englishman and a street-singer, reflects the confused pluralism of contemporary South Asian society. As Rushdie himself had done, Saleem grows up in a Kashmiri Muslim family; born and brought up in Bombay, he moves to Karachi in the late 1950s. Both Bombay and Karachi are portrayed as microcosmic representations of post-colonial India and Pakistan—the latter, like Saleem, the changeling child of England and India—and allow Rushdie to satirize the political, social, and sexual scandals of the time. The latter part of the novel deals with the tumultuous events of the 1971 war and the creation of Bangladesh, and the controversial period of Mrs Gandhi's rule. Rushdie virtually erases the thin line between documentary realism, journalistic analysis, and fable. Elements of Hindu myth and Islamic legend are evident in the naming of the novel's characters. Padma, Saleem's semi-literate lover, is a personification of the Indian popular spirit and imagination. Saleem, himself the artist of compromise, deceit, and subterfuge, mirrors the failed hopes, ideals, and aspirations of a new generation expected to accelerate the radical process of decolonization.

Midwich Cuckoos, The, see WYNDHAM, JOHN.

MILLAR, Margaret (1915–), American writer, born in Canada, educated at the University of Toronto. She was married to Kenneth Millar (Ross *Macdonald). During the 1940s she worked as a screenwriter and wrote a number of unmemorable novels and detective stories in some of which, including *The Invisible Worm* (1941), the detective is Dr Paul Prye, a whimsical psychiatrist. *Beast in View* (1955), however, was the first of five brilliant and unusual mystery novels, of which the last, *How Like an Angel* (1962), in which an ex-policeman becomes involved with the True Believers, a strange Californian religious cult, is the best. The others are *An Air That Kills* (1957; UK title *The Soft Talkers*), *The Listening Walls* (1959), and *A Stranger in My Grave* (1960). Her later books are less successful. An autobiography, *The Birds and the Beasts Were There*, appeared in 1968.

MILLAY, Edna St Vincent (1892–1950), American poet and writer, born in Rockland, Maine, educated at Barnard and Vassar Colleges. Millay gained her reputation by voicing the spirit of rebelliousness and liberalism in the 1920s. She worked as an actress, becoming associated with the Provincetown Playhouse and the Theatre Guild, and writing several satirical verse-plays, *The Princess Marries the Page* (1918, published 1932), *Aria da Capo* (1920), *The Lamp and the Bell* (1921), and *Two Slatterns and a King* (1921). Her first book of poetry, *Renascence and Other Poems* (1917), demonstrated technical mastery and verve. This was followed by two volumes which vacillated between the lightly cynical and the morbidly tragic, *A Few Figs from Thistles* (1920) and *Second April* (1921), both of which displayed a highly personal lyricism and a conscious use of archaism. After a period in Europe, she settled on a farm in upstate New York and published many more volumes of poetry, including *The Harp Weaver and Other Poems* (1923, Pulitzer Prize), which is notable for a deeper disillusionment than her earlier work; and several volumes which demonstrated an acclaimed sonnet technique and a lyric directness, *The Buck in the Snow* (1928), *Fatal Interview* (1931), and *Wine from These Grapes* (1934). She took part in public affairs, being arrested and jailed in Boston for her support for Sacco and Vanzetti in 1927. During the 1930s she wrote anti-totalitarian verse, radio plays, and speeches. Her increased social consciousness is evident in the dramatic narrative *Conversation at Midnight* (1937), and several other volumes: *Huntsman, What Quarry?* (1939), *Make Bright the Arrows* (1940), and *Murder of Lidice* (1942), a radio poem. She wrote the libretto for *The King's Henchmen* (1927), an opera by Deems Taylor. Her *Collected Sonnets* appeared in 1941, her *Collected Poems* in 1956, and her *Letters* in 1952.

MILLER, Arthur (1915–), American dramatist, born in New York, educated at the University of Michigan. Miller is widely regarded as one of America's foremost playwrights, whose accomplishment bears comparison with Eugene *O'Neill and Tennessee *Williams. After the success of his earliest work, there followed a ten-year period of apprentice work with eight plays which were not commercially successful, but laid the foundations of Miller's increasing mastery of his art, culminating in two decades of work which earned him widespread critical and popular acclaim, beginning with **All My Sons* (1947), **Death of a Salesman* (1949; Pulitzer Prize), *The *Crucible* (1953), *A *View from the Bridge* (1955), and *After the Fall* (1964). In 1959 the American National Arts and Letters Institute awarded Miller the Gold Medal for Drama. Though he has maintained a high level of productivity from the mid-1960s onwards with another dozen plays, his greatest successes in this time have been in revivals of *Death of a Salesman*, *After the Fall*, and *All My Sons* which, along with *The Crucible*, have long been established as modern classics of the American theatre. In 1984 Miller wrote an account of a memorable production of *Death of a Salesman* in Beijing (formerly Peking), called *'Salesman' in Beijing*.

Miller's other plays include *The Great Disobedience* (1938), *The Golden Years* (1939–40), *The Man Who Had All the Luck* (1944), *That They May Win* (1945), *A Memory of Two Mondays* (1955), *Incident at Vichy* (1961), *The Price* (1968), *Fame* (1970), *The Reason Why* (1970), *The Creation of the World and Other Business* (1972), *Up From Paradise* (1974), *The Archbishop's Ceiling* (1977), *The American Clock* (1980), *Two-Way Mirror* (1984), *I Can't Remember Anything* (1987), and *Clara* (1987). In 1950 he wrote an adaptation of Ibsen's *An Enemy of the People*; he also wrote the screenplays for Kingsley-International's film *The Witches of Salem* (1958), and for John Huston's film *The Misfits* (1961), starring Clark Gable and Marilyn Monroe. Among his non-dramatic writings are the novel, *Focus* (1949), many short stories, and several critical essays about the theatre and its uses, later collected in an edition by Robert A. Martin, *The Theatre Essays of Arthur Miller* (1978). Miller has been extensively interviewed by journalists and academics, and thirty-seven of the most significant of these interviews are gathered in Matthew Roudane's collection, *Conversations with Arthur Miller* (1988).

Miller has always been a writer of high seriousness, a moralist whose adversarial view of American society has earned him much respect. His achievement in *Death of a Salesman* reflects his capacity to dramatize the failure of the American dream through a narrative of ordinary people, where the temptations of the dream of material success are most persistently realized. The relationship between the private and public arenas of the moral life forms the basis of *All My Sons* and *The Crucible*, in the first where a war veteran son discovers his father's dishonesty in selling defective aeroplane parts to the Government, and the latter based loosely on the seventeenth-century witchcraft trials in Salem. *A View from the Bridge* is about the consequences of sexual jealousy in the family of a New York longshoreman, whilst *After the Fall* is a semi-autobiographical play about Miller's marriage to Marilyn Monroe.

Miller's contribution to American theatre may be measured not only in his work as a playwright, but also in his tireless quest for a theatre which addresses the social issues of the day in a medium and in venues accessible to the ordinary public. These preoccupations are voiced in such essays as 'Art and Commitment' (1960), 'Broadway, from O'Neill to Now' (1969), 'When Life Had at Least a Form' (1972), 'Politics as Theatre' (1972), and 'Every Play Has a Purpose' (1979). His antagonism to the brash commercial values of Broadway forced his abandonment of Broadway from the 1960s, since when his plays have been produced at the Lincoln Center in New York, the Kennedy Center in Washington DC, and off-Broadway. His despair of the conditions of production, for actors, audiences, and writers in the American theatrical scene compelled him to bring *The Ride Down Mount Morgan* (1990), a play about marital infidelity and bigamy, to London for its première, where his work has always been well received and produced. Other more recent plays include *The Last Yankee* (1991), about personal relationships focused on two men who meet in a mental hospital where their wives are inpatients, and *Broken Glass* (1994). Miller's autobiography *Timebends* was published in 1987.

MILLER, Henry (Valentine) (1891–1980), American author, essayist, and painter, born in New York. At the age of 33 he went to Paris and began chronicling his own seedy life there while working as an editor for various periodicals. For their treatment of intense personal experiences and sexual relations, as a teenager in Brooklyn and as an expatriate in France, *Tropic of Cancer* (1934; USA 1961), *Black Spring* (1936; USA 1963), and *Tropic of Capricorn* (1939; USA 1962) were charged with being pornographic and were held up by the US censors upon their publication in Paris. Miller's basic notion that the sexual drive in man is a form of necessary self-expression has caused much debate; one of his most vehement critics is Kate *Millett in *Sexual Politics* (1970). Other writings of this time were *Aller Retour New York* (1935), *Max and the White Phagocytes* (1938), essays and short stories in *The Cosmological Eye* (1939), and *The Wisdom of the Heart* (1941). In 1939, Miller's travels to Greece issued forth *The Colossus of Maroussi* (1941). With the beginning of the Second World War he returned to the USA and produced two other autobiographical works, *The Air-Conditioned Nightmare* (1945) and its sequel *Remember to Remember* (1947). Before the war ended he settled in Big Sur, California, which he later described in *Big Sur and the Oranges of Hieronymous Bosch* (1957). At this point he began expanding *Tropic of Capricorn*, which resulted in a trilogy entitled *The Rosy Crucifixion*, comprising *Sexus* (1949), *Plexus* (1953), and *Nexus* (1960). During the 1950s he largely turned away from the *risqué* style towards an increasingly straightforward non-fiction, of which *The Time of the Assassins* (1956), a lengthy essay on Rimbaud, is a notable example. Other publications of this time include *The Angel Is My Watermark!* (1944), *Obscenity and the Law of Reflection* (1945), *Patchen: Man of Anger and Light* (1946), and the short stories and narratives in *Nights of Love and Laughter* (1955) and *Quiet Days in Clichy* (1956). Miller began to concentrate on his watercolour painting, and published a variety of works on painting and a collection of his own watercolours in *The Paintings of Henry Miller* (1982). Other essays and narratives have appeared in *Stand Still Like the Hummingbird* (1962), whilst there have also been two volumes of *Selected Prose* (1965); an autobiography, *My Life and Times* (1971); and *Sextet* (1977), a collection of previous miscellaneous writings. Large collections of his correspondence with Lawrence *Durrell, Anaïs *Nin, and Michael Fraenkel have been published; later publications include *Letters to Emil* (1991), and the posthumous publications of a novel entitled *Crazy Cock* (1991), another autobiography *Nothing but the Marvellous* (1990), and a study of the socially marginalized in *On the Fringe: The Dispossessed in America* (1991).

MILLER, Karl (Fergus Connor) (1931–), British critic and editor, born in Edinburgh, educated at Downing College, Cambridge. He became literary editor of the **New Statesman* in 1961 and edited the **Listener* from 1967 to 1973. In 1979 he founded the **London Review of Books*, which he edited until 1992. From 1974 to 1992 he was Lord Northcliffe Professor of Modern English Literature at University College, London. He won a James Tait Black Award for *Cockburn's Millenium* (1975), the first major study of the Scottish judge and memoirist Lord Henry Cockburn (1779–1854), whose vividly informative *Memorials of His Time* (1974) Miller edited. His principal publications as a critic are *Doubles* (1985), an investigation of the literary theme of the *Doppelgänger*, and a wide-ranging collection of essays entitled *Authors* (1989). The various books he has edited include *Memoirs of a Modern Scotland* (1970), a collection of essays, and two anthologies of writing from the *Listener* (1970 and 1973). *Rebecca's Vest* (1993) is an autobiography.

MILLER, Walter M(ichael), Jr (1922–), American *science fiction writer, born in New Smyrna Beach, Florida, educated at the University of Texas. He is best known for *A Canticle for Liebowitz* (1960); this novel was constructed according to a typical science-fiction practice from magazine stories published earlier. It focuses on the Abbey of Liebowitz somewhere in the deserts of a post-disaster America. Over a Dark Age of 1,200 years the monks preserve something of human culture, until a new barbarism leads to another nuclear war. It was Miller's only novel, and was influential within the genre of science fiction. His short stories written in the 1950s have been collected in *Conditionally Human* (1962) and *The View from the Stars* (1965).

MILLETT, Kate (Katherine Murray) (1934–), American feminist cultural analyist and novelist, born in St Paul, Minnesota, educated at the University of Minnesota and St Hilda's College, Oxford. She has lectured in literature and philosophy, is an accomplished sculptor and now divides her time between New York and her Poughkeepsie farm in upper New York State. *Sexual Politics* (1970), her rigorous literary and cultural study of patriarchial bias, became an immediate best-seller and is one of the most important and pioneering books about the relationship between the sexes. Closely examining the work of Jean Genet, D. H. *Lawrence, Norman *Mailer, and Henry *Miller, together with history, sexual theory, and psychoanalysis—Freud and beyond—it is a feminist classic. Millett's concern with the political importance of autobiography is reflected in her documentary film *Three Women* (1970) and in *The Prostitution Papers* (1978), which give voice to her subjects' own words; in her candid autobiographical novels, *Flying* (1974) and *Sita* (1977); and in *The Loony Bin Trip* (1991). The latter is a courageous account of her struggle with the stigma of mental illness which followed her international success in the 1970s also analyses the criminalization of psychosis, arguing against the definition and institutionalization of madness. Millett has also published *The Basement: Meditations on a Human Sacrifice* (1979), *Elegy for Sita* (1979), *Going to Iran* (1982), and *The Politics of Cruelty: An Essay on the Literature of Imprisonment* (1994). See also FEMINIST CRITICISM.

MILLHAUSER, Steven (1943–), American novelist, born in New York City, educated at Brown University, Providence, Rhode Island. Millhauser worked as a copywriter in New York before attending Brown University where he studied Medieval and Renaissance Literature. He came to critical attention in 1972 with the publication of his first novel, *Edwin Mullhouse: The Life and Death of an American Writer, 1943–1954, by Jeffrey Cartwright* which, like much contemporary American post-modernist fiction, wilfully breaks down the traditional distinctions between fiction and non-fiction, biography, and autobiography. Millhauser's writings have been compared with those of *Nabokov and a Nabokovian playfulness and invention is to be found in later writings such as *Portrait of a Romantic* (1977), the novella *In the Penny Arcade* (1985), *From the Realm of Morpheus* (1986), *The Barnum Museum* (1990), a volume of stories, and *Little Kingdoms: Three Novellas* (1993).

MILLIN, Sarah Gertrude (1889–1968), South African novelist, born in Lithuania, educated in Kimberley. Her obsession as a novelist was with the supposed dire consequences of miscegenation. As J. M. *Coetzee has shown in *White Writing* (1988), though she was Jewish her assumptions about race were derived from Victorian anthropologists and Social Darwinists like Herbert Spencer. Yet this discredited outlook, so widespread at the time, did not prevent her from writing some good novels with genuine tragic pathos, such as *God's Stepchildren* (1924), with its haunted, 'mixed-blood' protagonist, Barry. Despite her racialism Millin was vehemently anti-Nazi and attacked Nazi ideology in *The Herr Witchdoctor* (1941). As well as many novels, including *Adam's Rest* (1922), *The Sons of Mrs. Aab* (1931), and *King of the Bastards* (1950), she wrote autobiographical memoirs, war diaries, short stories, and two distinguished biographies, *Rhodes* (1933) and *General Smuts* (1936). In such non-fiction as *The South Africans* (1926, revised edition 1934), she addressed the potential for racial conflict.

Mills and Boon, a publishing company founded in 1909 by Gerald Mills and Charles Boon, both of whom had previously worked for Methuen. They quickly established themselves on a successful basis, with Hugh *Walpole, P. G. *Wodehouse, and Jack *London among the authors on their early lists. During the 1920s their sales declined, with the result that the company began to concentrate on supplying the commercial circulating libraries with light romances, a strategy which determined their emergence as Britain's chief purveyors of such fiction. Mills and Boon also published educational and technical books from 1961 to 1980, when they sold their non-fiction list and concentrated exclusively on romances. In association with Harlequin Enterprises, Toronto, they issue some 500 new titles each year with sales reaching hundreds of thousands of copies annually. Their stories tend to be closely aligned with prevailing contemporary assumptions concerning gender relations and desirable modes of social and material gratification; they have therefore come to constitute a useful index to socio-cultural developments since the 1920s. See also ROMANTIC FICTION.

MILNE, A(lan) A(lexander) (1882–1956), British playwright, novelist, essayist, and writer of short stories and poems, born in St John's Wood, London, educated at Trinity College, Cambridge. Though known today primarily for his children's books, Milne acquired several large and distinct audiences in his lifetime. His weekly contributions to *Punch* (as 'A.A.M.') in 1908–18 were collected into several popular volumes including *The Day's Play* (1910), *Once a Week* (1914), and *The Sunny Side* (1921): selections from these appeared as *Those Were the Days* (1929) and *The Pocket A.A.M.* (1941). *If I May* (1920) was a selection of non-*Punch* journalism; *The Red House Mystery* (1922) was a detective novel. After the early plays *Worzel-Flummery* (1917) and *Belinda* (1918), *Mr. Pym Passes By* (1920) launched Milne into a successful theatrical career; other plays include *The Dover Road* (1922), *To Have the Honour* (1924), and a pantomime-fantasy, *Make-Believe* (1918). In 1924, *When We Were Very Young* appeared to instant success. This collection of poems for children, based on his son, Christopher Robin, captures the joyful innocence of childhood while retaining its vulnerability and the sometimes frightening largeness of the adult world—elements present also in the outstandingly popular *Winnie-the-Pooh* (1926) and *The House at Pooh Corner* (1928), and a second collection of poems, *Now We Are Six* (1927). Milne claimed that the popularity of his children's books eclipsed his other writings, which included novels and essays for adults. His most successful play was *Toad of Toad Hall* (1929), a faithful adaptation of Kenneth Grahame's *The Wind in the Willows* (1908). Of many dramatic presentations of the children's novels, Alan *Bennett's sympathetic readings for the BBC in the early 1980s are especially notable. An autobiography, *It's Too Late Now*, appeared in 1939.

MINHINNICK, Robert (1952–), Welsh poet, born in Neath, Glamorgan, educated at University College, Cardiff. He worked as a postman, a clerk, a schoolteacher, and in other capacities before becoming involved in environmental education in 1984. He is also active as a writer-in-residence for schools and residential courses. His collections of poetry include *A Thread in the Maze* (1978), *Native Ground* (1979), *Life Sentences* (1983), *The Dinosaur Park* (1985), *The Looters* (1989), and *Hey Fatman* (1994). Minhinnick's poems display his strong concern with poetic craft; the sometimes constraining pentameters which tended to dominate his earlier work have been superseded by a more personally cadenced prosody. Much of his work is in a compassionately social-realist mode, which is most provoking and effective when combined with imaginative elements. The increasingly ambitious and flexible character of his poetry is evident in *The Looters*, which contains two substantial and challenging sequences, 'The Hot House' and 'Fairground Music'. *Watching the Fire Eater* (1992) is a collection of essays.

Minty Alley, C. L. R. *James's only novel, written before he left Trinidad in the mid-1930s, published in London in 1936. Set in a 'barrack-yard' in a poor part of Port of Spain, it is the story of Haynes, a young black man from a lower middle-class background, who on his mother's death has to find cheaper lodgings. He takes a room at No. 2, Minty Alley, a community of working-class people dominated by women: the landlady Mrs Rouse; her spirited niece Maisie; the Nurse, who is having a clandestine affair with Mrs Rouse's lover of eighteen years, Benoit; Miss Atwell, another lodger; and the trusted East Indian maid Philomen. Minty Alley's day-to-day dramas are seen from the perspective of Haynes, who has little previous experience of 'real life'. Initially a voyeuristic outsider, but increasingly a participant in events, he becomes a confidant and authority figure for the other inhabitants, who defer to his superior education and seek his guidance and judgement. By the time the Minty Alley group breaks up and Haynes moves on, he has undergone a change, and acquired a new maturity. In his treatment of the estrangement of the West Indian intellectual from the common people, James reflects a unique identification with the vitality of those at the bottom of society, and his pioneering concern for class, colour, and race relations in the Caribbean was to become central to the works of writers who were to follow.

Miss Lonelyhearts, a story by Nathanael *West, published in 1933, described as a 'modernized, faithless Pilgrim's Progress'. The nameless protagonist, a middle-aged son of a Baptist minister, is a reporter who writes an agony column for a New York newspaper under the name 'Miss Lonelyhearts'. Disillusioned, anxiety-ridden, and alienated in a world of irrational violence and capitalist indifference, and suffering from what he calls his 'Christ complex', he variously turns to sexual love, other human relationships, and popular culture. As these all gradually appear to be arid, empty, and unsatisfactory, Miss Lonelyhearts heads for a spiritual crisis. Negotiating the cynicism of his bullying editor Shrike, the lack of understanding by his unsympathetic girlfriend Betty, and his desperate lust for the deprived Mrs Fay Doyle, coupled with his sympathy for Fay's crippled husband, Peter, he becomes suicidal. Peter, feeling ambivalent towards Miss Lonelyhearts, plans to shoot him with a gun concealed in a package. In an ending of black comedy and irony, Miss Lonelyhearts is shot accidentally. In a blend of allegory, pastiche, stereotype, and a surrealist juxtaposition of striking imagery, West offers a stark critique of modern existence.

Mister Johnson, see CARY, JOYCE.

MISTRY, Rohinton (1952–), Indian novelist and short-story writer, born in Bombay; he was educated at the University of Bombay and, following his emigration to Canada in 1975, at the University of Toronto. Mistry's reputation was established with the interlinked short-stories of *Tales from Firozsha Baag* (1987), which deal with the Parsi inhabitants of a Bombay block of flats. The stories' thematic concern with personal and communal identity is extended in the treatment of the Parsi community in his prize-winning novel *Such a Long Journey* (1991); the novel sets up a compelling interaction between the fortunes of its hapless chief protagonist and the workings of history, as events draw him into political and financial intrigues surrounding the creation of Bangladesh. Similar themes are explored in his second novel, *A Fine Balance* (1996).

MITCHELL, Adrian (1932–), British poet and playwright, born in London, educated at Christ Church, Oxford. After graduating, he worked as a journalist until 1959, when he became a freelance author. *Poems* (1964), Mitchell's first substantial collection, gained him recognition as a persuasively original writer on social and political themes. Subsequent volumes include *Out Loud* (1969), *Ride the Nightmare* (1971), *The Apeman Cometh* (1975), and *On the Beach at Cambridge* (1984). *For Beauty Douglas: Collected Poems 1953–1979* appeared in 1982; a selection from his work was published under the title *Adrian Mitchell's Greatest Hits* in 1991. A forceful and idiosyncratic use of rhyme and rhythm characterizes his most memorable poems, in which the earnestness of political and ethical elements often co-exists with considerable humorous and imaginative energy. Among his numerous dramatic works are *U.S.* (1966), centring on American military activity in Vietnam; *Tyger* (1971), a celebration of the life and works of William Blake; and *Man Friday* (1973), his adaptation of the story of Robinson Crusoe. Mitchell has also published several novels, including *If You See Me Comin'* (1962) and *Wartime* (1973). See also UNDERGROUND POETRY.

MITCHELL, Gladys (Maude Winifred) (1901–83), British crime writer and schoolteacher, born in Cowley, Oxfordshire. She published some seventy detective stories, beginning with *Speedy Death* (1929), in all of which the central figure is the psychiatrist Mrs Beatrice Lestrange Bradley. Though her work has its partisans, others find that the frequent intrusion of the occult—in the shape of witchcraft, the supernatural, or folk superstitions—detracts from its merit as detective fiction. Her best books are perhaps *Laurels Are Poison* (1942), *Tom Brown's Body* (1949), *Watson's Choice* (1955), and *Spotted Hemlock* (1958). She also wrote several novels as Stephen Hockaby and other crime fiction as Malcolm Torrie.

MITCHELL, Julian (1935–), British novelist and playwright, born in Epping, Essex, educated at Wadham College, Oxford. His novels include *Imagi-*

nary Toys (1961), *The White Father* (1964), and the more experimental *The Undiscovered Country* (1968), in which a narrator, 'Julian Mitchell', in an apparently straight autobiographical mode, tells the story of his school and university days, describing his relationship with a boyhood friend who, on his suicide, leaves him the manuscript of a novel he then proceeds to transcribe. Subsequently, Mitchell has turned his hand to television and stage drama, adapting the novels of Ivy *Compton-Burnett for the theatre and producing original plays in *Half-Life* (1977), *The Enemy Within* (1980), and *After Aida* (1986), as well as the highly successful *Another Country* (1981), about the alienating effects of public school life on two intellectually gifted boys in the 1930s, and the transformation of one into a Marxist radical and of the other into a potential spy, akin to the late Guy Burgess.

MITCHELL, Margaret (1900–49), American novelist, born in Atlanta, educated at Smith College; she is the author of America's most celebrated bestseller, *Gone With the Wind* (1936). The daughter of an attorney who was president of the Atlanta Historical Society, she grew up with stories of the Civil War. These, combined with her grandmother's reminiscences of the South and her own early disastrous marriage to a bootlegger, 'Red' Upshaw, were later to provide the background to the novel, which took her ten years to write. *Gone with the Wind* is set in Georgia at the time of the American Civil War. Its heroine, Scarlett O'Hara, is determined to keep her beloved family home at Tara, despite war, poverty, and frustrated passions. Scarlett, who loves the unattainable, is the epitome of the headstrong heroine who ruins her life, eventually driving the hero, Rhett Butler, to the immortal rejection—'My dear, I don't give a damn'. The clamour of publicity after the novel's publication locked the author in the legend she had created and for years afterwards, until her death in a road accident at the age of 49, her life was taken up with lengthy correspondence with the book's admirers. See also ROMANTIC FICTION.

MITCHELL, W(illiam) O(rmond) (1914–), Canadian novelist, born in Saskatchewan, educated at the Universities of Manitoba and Alberta. His best book, *Who Has Seen the Wind* (1947), a novel about a Prairie boyhood, captures vividly 'moments when an enquiring heart seeks finality, and the chain of darkness is broken'. Margaret *Laurence has said of his 'Jake and the Kid' stories published in *Maclean's* in the 1940s (and later translated to radio and film): 'these stories were among the first that many of us who lived on the prairies had ever read concerning our own people, our own place and our own time.' Thirteen of the stories were published in *Jake and the Kid* (1961). Their oral flavour helped to bring a new dimension into Canadian literature. Later works include *The Kite* (1962), *The Vanishing Point* (1973), and *How I Spent My Summer Holidays* (1981). The successful 1967 musical *Wild Rose* (with Norris Surdin) marked a new departure, while the play *Back to Beulah* (1973) reflected his sure perception of small town life; *Dramatic W. O. Mitchell* (1982) collected five plays, including *The Devil's Instrument* from 1949. The novel *Since Daisy Creek* was published in 1984, and *Ladybug, Ladybug...* in 1988.

MITCHISON, Naomi (Mary Margaret) (1897–), British novelist, born in Edinburgh, educated at St Anne's College, Oxford. Her brother was J. B. S. *Haldane. She married G. R. Mitchison, barrister and later Labour MP and a life peer, and became active in many progressive causes. Mitchison is best known for her early historical novels, including *The Conquered* (1923), *Cloud Cuckoo Land* (1925), *The Corn King and the Spring Queen* (1931), *The Blood of the Martyrs* (1939) and *To the Chapel Perilous* (1955). Her historical novels are notable for bold use of modern language and their considerable psychological insights. *Memoirs of a Spacewoman* (1962) is one of her best science fiction novels. She has also published biographies; short story collections; memoirs such as *Small Talk: Memories of an Edwardian Childhood* (1973), *You May Well Ask: A Memoir 1920–1940* (1979), and *Mucking Around: Five Continents Over Fifty Years* (1981); and *The Wartime Diaries of Naomi Mitchison 1933–45* (1985), which was originally written for *Mass-Observation.

MITFORD, Jessica (Lucy) (1917–), Anglo-American memoirist, social critic, and journalist, born in Gloucester, the daughter of Lord and Lady Redesdale. Her sisters were Nancy *Mitford, Unity, well-known as a Nazi sympathizer, and Diana, who married Sir Oswald Mosley, leader of the British Union of Fascists. Jessica was always closer to the left of the political spectrum. Her first husband, Esmond Romilly, was killed during the Battle of Britain in 1941. She became an American citizen in 1944, and settled in California with her second husband and family in 1947. Her successful first book, *Hons and Rebels* (1960; US title *Daughters and Rebels*), is a lively chronicle of her early years at the secluded family estate of Swinbrook, and her first marriage; 'Hons' refers to the 'Society of Hons', a fantasy world invented by the Mitford sisters. Her other books include *The American Way of Death* (1963), a devastating attack on the funeral business in the USA; *The Trial of Dr. Spock* (1969), about the conspiracy charges against the famous child psychologist, and other anti-Vietnam War activists; *Kind and Usual Punishment: The American Prison Business* (1973); *The Making of a Muckraker* (1979; US title *Poison Penmanship: The Gentle Art of Muckraking*), a collection of journalistic articles which includes her interview in prison with George Jackson, an African-American political activist killed shortly afterwards by the prison authorities; and *The American Way of Birth* (1992).

MITFORD, Nancy (1904–73), British novelist and biographer, the eldest of the seven children (six daughters and a son) of the second Lord Redesdale. In *The Pursuit of Love* (1945), the novel which made her name, she gives an almost detached view of her extraordinary family with her father appearing as 'Uncle Matthew'. Of her sisters, Jessica *Mitford became a communist, Diana married the British fascist Oswald Mosley, and Unity became an admirer of Hitler. English aristocratic family circles, their eccentricities and amatory escapades, are at the centre of her next novel, *Love in a Cold Climate* (1949). After the war she settled in France, about which she wrote in *Don't Tell Alfred* (1960), a *roman-à-clef* about the British Embassy in Paris. Her biographies include *Madame de Pompadour* (1954; revised edition, 1968), *Voltaire in Love* (1957), and *Frederick the Great* (1970). She edited the comically snobbish *Noblesse Oblige: An Enquiry into the Identifiable Characteristics of the English Aristocracy* (1956) in which she gives currency to the expressions 'U' (upper-class) and 'non-U' to describe traits in speech and comportment of the upper classes and their counterparts. Her amusing light satires, with their acute observations of social nuances and caricatures of bohemian aristocrats, were highly popular in their day but in later years became dated.

MITTELHOLZER, Edgar (1909–65), Guyanese novelist, born in British Guiana (now Guyana) from where he moved to Trinidad before emigrating to England in 1948. His first novel, *Corentyne Thunder* (1941), describes the impoverished and degraded living conditions of Indian peasants in British Guiana during the 1930s. The Kaywana trilogy, which consists of *The Children of Kaywana* (1952), *The Harrowing of Hubertus* (1954; republished as *Hubertus*, 1955, and again as *Kaywana Stock*, 1968), and *Kaywana Blood* (1958; republished as *The Old Blood*, 1958), deals with the continuous history of Guyana from its settlement by Europeans in the seventeenth century to 1953, when the colony had its first elections under universal adult suffrage. These three novels reveal formidable powers of invention, historical reconstruction, and psychological insight. His novels are characterized by much physical violence, eroticism, and sensational action; many of them, for example *Shadows Move Among Them* (1951), also deal with abnormal psychology, sexual deviation, the supernatural, and the occult. Other novels reveal a similar iconoclasm aimed at the restrictive conventions and inhibitions of bourgeois society. Mittelholzer also produced *With a Carib Eye* (1958), a travel book; and *A Swarthy Boy* (1963), an autobiography. He pioneered the treatment of political, psychological, and philosophical themes in West Indian literature which suffered a tragic loss when he took his own life.

MLA. The MLA (Modern Language Association) is the main professional organization of teachers of modern languages and their literatures (predominantly English) in America. As Article II of its constitution states: 'The object of the association shall be to promote study, criticism, and research in the more and less commonly taught modern languages and their literatures and to further the common interests of teachers of the subject.' These common interests do not imply conditions of work or salary, which is generally left to the AAUT (the American Association of University Teachers).

The MLA was founded in 1883, and held its first meeting on 27 and 28 December, at Columbia University, New York. (The annual convention has, ever since, been held in the interval between Christmas and New Year, since the 1940s in large, metropolitan hotels.) The impulse behind the formation of the association was the desire of professors 'in different institutions in the Eastern state' to meet with colleagues and discuss matters 'pertaining to Modern Language study'. Forty members (out of a membership of 126) attended the first convention. There were four plenary meetings on pedagogic and curricular topics. At this first meeting, there was 'animated discussion' on 'methods', with sharp disagreement between modernists and traditionalists—a split that would enliven meetings of the association over the next hundred years, reaching explosive dimensions in the 1960s. The first president was Franklin Carter, followed, in 1887, by the better-known James Russell Lowell of Harvard. Initially, presidents held office for a number of years; nowadays, they are elected by the membership (in keenly contested elections) for one year only. In the first decade, membership of the association reached some 3,000–4,000, and attendance at the conventions was about half that. The character of the association was male, WASP, and Ivy League. Meetings were at colleges up and down the Eastern seaboard. Attendance at the annual conventions gradually increased, breaking the 1,000 mark in 1930 and the 5,000 mark in 1959. Then, with the post-war expansion of higher education, it leapt to 12,300 in 1966 with an all-time high of 14,000 attendees at the epochal New York convention of 1968 (this represented half the 28,000 registered members—in more recent decades, average attendance has varied between a sixth and a third, depending on the attractiveness, and the remoteness, of the host city to the convention).

The late 1960s were the era of anti-war demonstration, campus protest, and riotous political assemblies. At the 1968 MLA there was chaos, with the arrest of three demonstrating participants, and the threatened arrest of scores of others. As a result, the next year's venue was switched from Chicago (tainted by Mayor Daley's 'police riot' against demonstrators at the Republican Convention) to Denver. 1968 also saw a qualitative change in the MLA programme. A decision was taken to go for growth: 'Faced with its constant expansion in size and activity', the ruling committee reported, 'the MLA cannot realistically escape its responsibilities by a nostalgic quest for the serene and intellectually exclusive meetings of the distant past.' As a result, sessions (four at the first meetings in 1883) hovered between the 700 and 800 mark in the 1990s. One of the most effective committees of the MLA, that on the status of women in the profession, was set up in 1970. The late 1960s and early 1970s witnessed the clearest split between old and young in the MLA (fanned by 'theory' which had taken root in a seminal conference at Johns Hopkins, in 1967). Maynard Mack's presidential address in 1970 was elegiac: 'What is very clear in December 1970', he declared, 'is that we who teach the oncoming generation have arrived at some kind of watershed beyond which the familiar landscapes look different, or even begin to fade away.'

From its inception, the association published its proceedings, and its members' scholarly articles, in a learned journal, *Publications of the Modern Language Association* (*PMLA*). Only members might publish in the journal, and members received quarterly copies free, as part of their subscription. Early contributions to the journal concentrated on philology, grammar, and curriculum issues. Over the years *PLMA* has evolved into the best-selling literary journal in the English-speaking world, with a circulation of between 30,000 and 40,000. Since the 1980s submission has been 'blind' (i.e. papers are read by assessors with all evidence of authorship suppressed). The MLA also issues a 'style sheet', which instructs members on how to prepare and present scholarly work. One of the earliest practical initiatives of the MLA was to create a list of member institutions and personnel. This provided an arena in which continentally separated colleagues might meet, debate, and, not infrequently, dispute among themselves. Over the decades, the MLA has been the glue that holds together teachers and scholars of English and Modern Languages at the tertiary level. It has also been the platform on which the profession's conflicted views on political 'relevance', affirmative action, 'cultural studies', ethnic studies, and 'theory' have been debated. The MLA awards prestigious prizes to academic publications (notably the William Riley Parker prize, for the outstanding article of the year in *PMLA*, and the James Russell Lowell prize, for the best academic book of the year). The convention has increasingly become the site where 'faculty exchange' (i.e. hiring) takes place.

MO, Timothy (1950–), Anglo-Chinese novelist, born in Hong Kong, educated at Oxford. His fiction is traditionalist in form, reflecting a wide range of interests and extensive travels in the Far East and in America. Dickensian characterization and fine comic writing distinguishes his first novel, *The Monkey King* (1978), a study of a domestic tyrant, the wealthy Hong Kong merchant Mr Poon. *Sour Sweet* (1982) explores Chinese society in Britain during the 1960s, through the fortunes of Chen, an ambitious young restaurant owner, whose attempts to establish his own business involve him in the dubious affairs of one of the powerful Triad societies; Ian *McEwan wrote the screenplay for the 1987 film version of the novel. The author's vivid realization of historical events is displayed in *An Insular Possession* (1986), set in 1833 in Canton, Portuguese Macao, and Hong Kong, drawing on contemporary newspaper accounts, letters, and diaries in its account of the Opium Wars. With a cast of memorable characters, the central story concerns two young Americans, Walter Eastman and Gideon Chase, who establish a weekly newspaper as an outlet for their campaigning journalism. *The Redundancy of Courage* (1991), narrated by the effete American-educated Chinese hotel owner Adolph Ng, describes the invasion of an island—clearly inspired by East Timor—in the Indonesian archipelago by a brutal military regime based on Suharto's, and the heroic resistance of the freedom fighters with whom Adolph takes refuge. Mo published *Brownout on Breadfruit Boulevard* (1995) himself, as a protest against the editorial and financial policies of the publishing establishment. After the epic scale of his most recent works, *Brownout* is a smaller, sharper performance; it is, however, equally distant from the domestic comedy of his early novels. Set in the Philippines, it adopts the perspectives of Asians and Westerners to analyse the vicissitudes of international politics and cultural clashes. Dominating the fictional proceedings is a conference in which a right-wing German academic 'speaks his mind' about race, religion, and culture: some races, including the Filipinos, are simply backward and inferior. Thus, Mo's novel has been read by some critics as a fine example of right-wing satire. But, in spite of its caricatures of white liberals and Third World intellectuals, its controversial portrayal of the German professor as a coprophiliac (faecal matter is a persistent metaphor throughout) who sexually exploits Asian prostitutes, invites a more complex reading of cultural and imperial domination.

Modernism, a term encompassing numerous movements characterizing international developments in literature, music, and the graphic and plastic arts from the late nineteenth century onward. Most commentators consider literary Modernism's typifying manifestations in English to have appeared between 1890 and 1930. Among the authors most frequently cited are Joseph *Conrad, T. S. *Eliot, William *Faulkner, Ford Madox *Ford, James *Joyce, D. H. *Lawrence, Ezra *Pound, William Carlos *Williams, Virginia *Woolf, and W. B. *Yeats; European writers associated with Modernism include Bertolt Brecht, André Gide, Franz Kafka, Thomas Mann, Vladimir Mayakovsky, Marcel Proust, and Rainer Maria Rilke, while Charles Baudelaire, Gustav Flaubert, and Arthur Rimbaud are regarded as three of its principal progenitors. The experimental qualities thought of as essentially Modernist are found in the writings of many of the above; others are more traditional in their stylistic and narrative practices. All, however, respond acutely to the radical shifts in the structures of thought and belief that were brought about in the fields of religion, philosophy, and psychology by the works of Sir James *Frazer, Charles Darwin, Friedrich Nietzsche, Sigmund Freud, and others. The moral cataclysm of the First World War accentuated the senses of general cultural catastrophe and individual spiritual crisis apparent in the writings of novelists and poets already sensitive to such disruptions in the humanist tradition. Pound's *Hugh Selwyn Mauberley* (1920), Eliot's *The *Waste Land* (1922), Woolf's **Jacob's Room* (1922), and Joyce's **Ulysses* (1922) are among the works which indicate the breach with the conventions of rational exposition and stylistic decorum in the immediate post-war period.

Experimental techniques become a distinguishing trait of Modernist texts between approximately 1912 and 1930, the period of what is sometimes referred to as 'High Modernism'. Among the strategies used to reinterpret experience in the novel were the '*stream of consciousness' mode, narrative discontinuities, shifting authorial perspectives, and effects of montage and collage comparable to innovations in the cinema and painting. Similar procedures were introduced into poetry through the extended poetic engagements with personal experience, history, and contemporary conditions in *The Waste Land* and Pound's early drafts of *The *Cantos* (1917–33). These works demonstrated the possibilities for poetry's freedom from the constraints of orthodox thematic development, metrical determination, and the distinctions between lyrical and expository idioms. *Imagism's emphasis on clarity, concentration, and the essential functions of the image revised poetic theory and practice in Britain and America from around 1912 onward. The use of myth as a structural device is common to numerous definitive texts, most notably *Ulysses*, *The Waste Land*, and *The Cantos*; the energetic stylistic mobility evident in each of these exemplifies the high degree of aesthetic self-consciousness of literary Modernism. Edith *Sitwell, Pound, and Wyndham *Lewis were among the Modernist writers noted for polemical hostility towards conservative authors, a quality often evident in the *little magazines with which they were associated; the vigour with which they rejected conventional literature arose from the urgency of the need they felt to sever connections with a culture the war had proved a failure. The Modernists' disregard of the expectations of a common readership resulted in allegations of obscurity and élitism which remain central to critical debate. Modernism has been, and remains, widely pervasive in its influence; it has engendered a multiplicity of approaches to matters of literary form and content that have affected writing in English, whether obviously or subtly, on almost every level.

A Survey of Modernist Poetry (1927) by Robert *Graves and Laura *Riding, which established a firm distinction between 'modern' and 'modernist', is one of the earliest extended studies of literary modernism. *The Modern Tradition: Backgrounds of Modern Literature* (1965, edited by R. *Ellmann and C. Feidelson) remains valuable as an anthology of Modernist documents. *Modernism* (1976, edited by M. *Bradbury and J. McFarlane) offers a comprehensive critical survey. Among the many studies available are H. Kenner's *The Pound Era* (1971), S. Schwartz's *The Matrix of Modernism* (1985), A. Gelpi's *A Coherent Splendor: The American Poetic Renaissance, 1910–1950* (1988), and B. Bergonzi's *The Myth of Modernism and Twentieth Century Literature* (1986). See also SURREALISM.

Modern Utopia, A, see UTOPIA AND ANTI-UTOPIA.

MOERS, Ellen (1928–79), American literary critic, born in New York, educated at Columbia University, Radcliffe, and Vassar. She taught at the University of Connecticut and the CUNY Graduate School. Like Elaine *Showalter, Moers was important in founding Anglo-American feminist critical practice (see FEMINIST CRITICISM). *Literary Women* (1976) provides an illuminating literary history of women's writing; in this expansive and highly individual work Moers speculates upon common concerns, literary influences, and female expectations of American and European women writers. She was also author of the critical works *The Dandy: Brummel to Beerbohm* (1960) and *Two Dreisers* (1969), as well as a contributor to numerous journals and magazines, including *The New York Review of Books* and *Harper's*.

MOGGACH, Deborah (1948–), British novelist, born in London, educated at the University of Bristol. She lived in Pakistan for two years, where she worked as a journalist, an experience reflected in *The Hot Water Man* (1982), which is set in Karachi. Its central character, Christine Manley, torn between her feminist convictions and her desire to have a child, and increasingly attracted by a culture she does not understand, is a typical Moggach heroine: self-doubting, well-intentioned, but occasionally misguided in her actions. Her other fiction, which frequently engages with issues affecting women's lives, includes *Porky* (1983), a study of an incestuous relationship; *Driving in the Dark* (1989); *Stolen* (1990), which was adapted for television, and concerns a woman's struggle to regain her children after they have been abducted by her ex-husband; *The Stand-In* (1991); *The Ex-Wives* (1993); and *Seesaw* (1996). Her collections of short stories include *Smile* (1988) and *Changing Babies* (1995).

MOLE, John (1941–), British poet, born in Taunton, Somerset, educated at Magdalene College, Cambridge. Since 1964 he has worked as a schoolteacher and is well-known as a presenter of poetry broadcasts for BBC radio. With Peter *Scupham, he is co-editor of the Mandeville Press, which has produced numerous limited editions of his verse. His collections of poetry include *The Love Horse* (1974), *From the House Opposite* (1979), *Feeding the Lake* (1981), *Homing* (1987), and *Depending on the Light* (1993). The fluent accessibility and energetic wit of much of Mole's verse, which recurrently deals with the theme of childhood, make it unusual in its appeal to both adult readers and a younger audience; D. W. Hartnett remarked that 'In his best work poet and child participate in a dance of disquieting complicity.' *Once There Were Dragons* (1979) and *Boo to a Goose* (1987) are among his collections of verse for children. His later work shows increasing scope in its confrontations with problematic aspects of human behaviour and its imaginative engagement with social and political concerns.

MOLLOY, M(ichael) J(oseph) (1917–), Irish playwright, born in Co. Galway; he trained for the priesthood until illness forced him to end his studies. Molloy's plays concern the decay of the West of Ireland caused by emigration and economic deprivation. In dealing with the violent consequences of this destitution, he anticipates the finest work of Tom *Murphy and John B. *Keane. Molloy also recalls *Synge in the way he dramatizes individual suffering while avoiding the temptation of questioning its historical and political causes. His tone, reflected in the characters he creates, tends to be mournful and fatalistic. His first play, *The Old Road* (1943), staged at the *Abbey Theatre, reveals the beginnings of his continuing preoccupation with emigration, as well as his characteristic use of local dialect and eccentricity. After *The Visiting House* (1946), Molloy wrote his best-known and most powerful play, *The King of Friday's Men* (1948). This was followed by *The Wood of the Whispering* (1953), *The Will and the Way* (1955), and *Daughter from Over the Water* (1962).

MOMADAY, N(avarre) Scott (1934–), Native American writer, born in Lawton, Oklahoma, of Kiowa Indian ancestry, educated at the University of New Mexico and at Stanford University, where he was taught by Yvor *Winters. He has taught at several American universities. He won a Pulitzer Prize for his first published novel, *House Made of Dawn* (1969), about a young Native American unable to feel acceptance either in the white American world, or in that of his ancestral community; his second novel, *The Ancient Child* (1989), focuses on a Kiowa artist in San Francisco who was raised as an Anglo and, like the first novel, deals with questions of identity. His much admired retelling of Kiowan legends, *The Way to Rainy Mountain* (1969), explored, in relation to Momaday's own youth, his sense of their significance as part of the central American heritage. His other works include two books of poems, *Angle of Geese* (1973) and *The Gourd Dancer* (1976); a biographical memoir, *The Names* (1976); and *In the Presence of the Sun: Stories and Poems, 1961–1991* (1992). Momaday has played a major part in bringing the work of contemporary Native American writers to the notice of a wider public. His achievement is to have placed the Native American experience within the main frame of the contemporary American novel, especially in the context of narratives whose organizing principle is the search for social identity where ancestral ethnic values conflict with those of conventional society. See also ETHNICITY and NATIVE AMERICAN LITERATURE.

MONETTE, Paul (1945–95), American novelist, born in Lawrence, Massachusetts, educated at Yale. Monette's early novels, such as *Taking Care of Mrs. Carroll* (1978) and *The Gold Diggers* (1979), were mostly traditional romances in which gay characters replaced straight characters. He is best known for *Becoming A Man: Half A Life Story* (1992; National Book Award), an autobiography covering childhood to graduation, and *Borrowed Time: An AIDS Memoir* (1988), describing the excruciating physical decline and subsequent death of his first lover, Roger Horwitz, and one of the first books to document the devastating psychological and social impact of AIDS. *Afterlife* (1990) and *Halfway Home* (1991) both present gay protagonists dying of AIDS. Another important contribution to AIDS literature is *Love Alone: 18 Elegies for Rog* (1988) in which Monette experiments with various forms to express his grief and fury. Many of the essays in *Last Watch of the Night* (1993) were written while Monette was seriously ill with AIDS, and represent his own slow shift towards death. His last work, *West of Yesterday, East of Summer* (1994), is a collection of new and selected poetry.

Money, see AMIS, MARTIN.

MONRO, Harold (Edward) (1879–1932), British poet and publisher, born in Brussels; he moved to Somerset in 1886, and was educated at Caius College, Cambridge. After a period of poultry farming in Ireland, he established the Samurai Press in Haslemere, Surrey; its publications include his prose treatise *Proposals for a Voluntary Nobility* (1907) and verse by John *Drinkwater and Wilfrid *Gibson. His subsequent travels in Europe resulted in *The Chronicle of a Pilgrimage* (1909), an account of a journey from Paris to Milan on foot. In 1911 he settled in London and founded **Poetry Review* in 1912. He opened The Poetry Bookshop in Bloomsbury in 1913 to serve as a publishing house, a retail outlet, and a venue for readings; the best-known of its many publications is the **Georgian Poetry* series. Monro came to be regarded as a spokesman for poetry and was much in demand as a public speaker. Much of his poetry is classifiable as Georgian in its descriptive celebrations of the countryside as a liberating antidote to the dispiriting effects of London. Numerous poems are, however, based on unsentimental social observations of the city. His collections include *Poems* (1906), *Before Dawn* (1911), *The Earth for Sale* (1928), and *Elm Angel* (1930). *Collected Poems* (1933) carried an introduction by T. S. *Eliot, who wrote of Monro's 'sincere and tormented introspection', a quality most apparent in the harrowingly phantasmagoric late poem 'Bitter Sanctuary'. Joy Grant's *Harold Monro and the Poetry Bookshop* (1967) is a biographical and critical study.

MONROE, Harriet (1860–1936), American poet and editor, born in Chicago, where she spent most of her life. Monroe came to public notice with *Columbian Ode* (1892), a poem in celebration of the World's Columbian Exposition in Chicago; her *Valerie and Other Poems* (1892) was followed by a book of five verse-plays, *The Passing Show* (1903). Monroe's main claim to fame is through her editorship of **Poetry: A Magazine of Verse*, devoted exclusively to poetry, which she founded in 1912. The most influential *little magazine in modern American literary history, *Poetry* provided a venue for the emergent modernist poetry of Ezra *Pound, Wallace *Stevens, Hart *Crane, T. S. *Eliot, Robert *Frost, and many others, and created an audience responsive to this new work. Monroe was equally content to publish more conventional poets, especially her Chicagoan peers such as Carl *Sandburg, Vachel *Lindsay, and Edgar Lee *Masters, thus exhibiting an openness of editorial policy which ultimately led Pound to resign his role as 'foreign' editor of *Poetry*. With Alice Corbin Henderson, her valuable deputy on *Poetry*, Monroe published *The New Poetry* (1932), an anthology of twentieth-century verse; her autobiography *A Poet's Life* appeared in 1937.

MONSARRAT, Nicholas (John Turney) (1910–79), English novelist, born in Liverpool, educated at Winchester and at Trinity College, Cambridge. His early childhood was spent on Merseyside, but it was at the family country home in Anglesey that he developed his love of the sea and sailing which he was subsequently to employ to such fruitful effect in his fiction. His novels of the 1930s include *This is the Schoolroom* (1938). During the Second World War, he responded to an advertisement for 'gentlemen with yachting experience' to join the Royal Naval Volunteer Force, and within weeks was on a corvette in the Atlantic. This experience formed the background to his best-seller *The Cruel Sea* (1951), a vivid account of mid-ocean life during war-time. Though he held various public offices after the war, he could now afford to devote himself to writing. A stream of books appeared, the most memorable of which are *The Kapillan of Malta* (1973) and *The Master Mariner* (two volumes, 1978 and 1980, unfinished). Monsarrat also published two volumes of autobiography (1966, 1970).

MONTAGUE, C(harles) E(dward) (1867–1928), Anglo-Irish novelist, essayist, and journalist, born in London, educated at Balliol College, Oxford. He was journalist for the *Manchester Guardian* from 1890 to 1925. His first novel, *A Hind Let Loose* (1910), a satire on various aspects of journalism in the Edwardian period, was followed by *Dramatic Values* (1911), a collection of drama reviews, and *The Morning's War* (1913), a celebration of mountaineering. Montague's experience of service during the First World War provided material for his most memorable writing: *Disenchantment* (1922), a collection of combative essays; and *Rough Justice* (1926), his best-known novel, and a powerful indictment of the war. He also produced *The Right Place* (1924), essays on lighter subjects; *Fiery Particles* (1923) and *Action* (1928), collections of short stories; and *A Writer's Notes on His Trade* (1930). Oliver Elton's *C. E. Montague, A Memoir* (1929) contains extracts from his war diaries.

MONTAGUE, John (Patrick) (1929–), Irish poet, born in Brooklyn, New York; he returned as a child to his family's farm at Garvaghey, Co. Tyrone. He was educated at University College, Dublin, and at the Universities of Yale and Iowa, USA. After working as a journalist in Dublin and Paris, he became Lecturer in Poetry at the University of Cork in 1972. His collections of poetry include *Forms of Exile* (1958), *Poisoned Lands* (1961), *The Rough Field* (1972), *The Great Cloak* (1978), *Selected Poems* (1982), *Mount Eagle* (1988), *New Selected Poems* (1990), and *Time in Armagh* (1993). Investigation of the connections between individual identity and Irish culture and history is a central concern in his writing. Much of his poetry takes the form of extended sequences in which his richly particularized vision of Ireland's heritage combines imaginatively with treatments of his personal and political preoccupations. Montague was responsible for introducing innovative procedures into Irish poetry during the 1960s, when he and Thomas *Kinsella emerged as the principal successors to Austin *Clarke and Patrick *Kavanagh. His prose works include the short stories of *Death of a Chieftain* (1964) and the novella *The Lost Notebook* (1987). He edited *The Faber Book of Irish Verse* (1974).

MONTGOMERY, L(ucy) M(aud) (1874–1942), Canadian novelist, born on Prince Edward Island, educated at Dalhousie University, Halifax. She was brought up by her maternal grandparents after her mother died when she was only two; these early experiences provided the basis for most of her fiction. Her first novel, *Anne of Green Gables* (1908), which brought her international fame, deals with the growing pains of its heroine, the spirited and impressionable Anne Shirley, Montgomery's most enduring creation; among numerous sequels are *Anne of Avonlea* (1909), *Anne of the Island* (1915), *Anne's House of Dreams* (1917), *Rainbow Valley* (1919), and *Anne of Windy Poplars* (1936), which follow the heroine into adulthood and life as a teacher, wife, and mother. In the short stories of *The Story Girl* (1911), *Chronicles of Avonlea* (1912), and *Further Chronicles of Avonlea* (1920), the main focus shifts from Anne to a range of local characters. In the 1920s Montgomery wrote a trilogy of novels about another young female protagonist, Emily, which are generally considered more autobiographical than the 'Anne' books. A brief incursion into adult fiction in the novels *The Blue Castle* (1926) and *A Tangled Web* (1931) was followed by a return to adolescent subjects in the novels *Pat of Silver Bush* (1933) and *Jane of Lantern Hill* (1937).

Month in the Country, A, see CARR, J. L.

Mont-Saint-Michel and Chartres, a historical study by Henry (Brooks) *Adams, privately printed in 1904 and published in 1913. Conceived of as the companion volume to *The *Education of Henry Adams*, Adams saw the book as being the start of a larger study of the role of historical forces and motions. By focusing on the period 1150 to 1250, he chose 'the point of history when man held the highest idea of himself as a unit in a unified universe' and thus provided a point of contrast with his own times. Through a detailed description of the powerful and magnificent architecture of Mont-Saint-Michel, he presents the dominant intellectual and theological attitude of the period as being committed to a unified reaction to the universe. This is best expressed by his understanding of the Virgin as a symbol of unity. This unity is then related to other works of the time: the soaring Gothic cathedrals, especially that of Chartres, and their stained glass windows; the metaphysics of Thomas Aquinas; the *Chanson de Roland*; the tradition of courtly love; and the work of prominent figures of the time, among them Eleanor of Aquitaine, Peter Abelard, and St Francis of Assisi. This effort to synthesize different manifestations of the same phenomenon is not only remarkable in itself, but also symptomatic of one of the larger American intellectual ambitions of the twentieth century.

MOODY, Anne (1940–), American author, born in Centreville, Mississippi, educated at Tougaloo College. Moody worked for the Congress of Racial Equality in Washington DC from 1961 to 1964, when she became a civil rights project co-ordinator at Cornell University. *Coming of Age in Mississippi* (1968) forms a richly detailed autobiographical account of her impoverished childhood in racially segregated Mississippi and her subsequent involvement in the emergent civil rights movement from the late 1950s onward. It is regarded as one of the most valuable testimonies to the condition of African-American women in the two decades after the Second World War. Moody concludes the book by indicating her disaffection with the civil rights movement, which she began to view as too narrow in its aims to benefit oppressed minorities at a global level. *Mr Death*, a collection of her short stories, appeared in 1975.

MOODY, William Vaughan (1869–1910), American dramatist, born in Spencer, Indiana, educated at Harvard. Moody later taught English at Harvard and then at the University of Chicago. He was both poet and playwright, and his earliest plays were blank-verse dramas, *The Masque of Judgment* (1900) and *The Fire Bringer* (1904), neither produced in his lifetime. The first debates man's rightful exercise of free will which leads him to rebel against God's authority; the latter deals with rebellion through the narrative of Prometheus. A third such play, *The Death of Eve*, remained incomplete at Moody's death: it was to deal with the reconciliation of God and man through the creation of woman. *The Great Divide* (1906), originally produced under the title *A Sabine Woman*, was an important realization of a crucial issue in American culture, the conflict between puritanical repression and the liberated individualism of the frontier West. *The Faith Healer* (1909) deals with a man who seeks to recover the healing powers he lost when he gained the earthly love of a woman. Moody has long been regarded as the precursor of Eugene *O'Neill in the depth of his understanding of the interior landscape of the American psyche.

Moon and Sixpence, The, see MAUGHAM, W. SOMERSET.

MOORCOCK, Michael (1939–), British writer and editor, born in Mitcham, Surrey. Having published several 'sword-and-sorcery' tales he first came to notice as one of the most prominent of the 'New Wave' *science fiction writers when he was editor of *New Worlds* from 1964 to 1971; others, including B. *Aldiss, J. G. *Ballard, M. John *Harrison, Thomas M. *Disch, Keith *Roberts, and John *Sladek, published their experimental work in the magazine. He firmly established himself with *Behold the Man* (1969) and with four linked novels, *The Final Programme* (1968), *A Cure for Cancer* (1971), *The English Assassin* (1972), and *The Condition of Muzak* (1977), which described the adventures of Jerry Cornelius, the ravaged 1960s hero and Moorcock's most famous character; the series was described by Aldiss as a meeting point of 'the worlds of Ronald Firbank and Ian Fleming'. Other novels include *An Alien Heat* (1972), the first volume of a fantasy trilogy entitled 'The Dancers at the End of Time', the other volumes of which are *The Hollow Lands* (1974) and *The End of All Songs* (1976); *Breakfast in the Ruins* (1972); and *The Entropy Tango* (1981). A graver note could be heard in novels such as *Gloriana: Or, The Unfulfill'd Queen* (1979), an intricate alternate-world vision of the first Queen Elizabeth. *The Brothel in Rosenstrasse* (1982) was a lament on the perils of romantic obsession. In the 1980s, having written more than sixty genre books, Moorcock increasingly turned to ambitious novels which rarely contained elements of fantasy. *Byzantium Endures* (1981) and *The Laughter of Carthage* (1984) shared in Colonel Pyat a protagonist whose reminiscences of life in Russia, Europe, and America were a litany of the twentieth century's self-inflicted ills. *Mother London* (1988) was both a paean to the vanishing metropolis and an imaginative reconstruction of the ideal City.

MOORE, Brian (1921–), Irish novelist, born in Belfast, educated there at St Malachy's College. Moore emigrated to Canada in 1948, taking Canadian citizenship; he later moved to New York and thence to California, where he settled and worked on film scripts. The uprooted individual is a recurring theme in his fiction, and the confusion of values consequent on expatriation has elicited some of his most powerful and original writing. *Judith Hearne* (1955; US title *The Lonely Passion of Judith Hearne*, 1956), set in Belfast during the early 1940s, deals with a despairing Belfast spinster who becomes an alcoholic. Also set in Belfast during the early 1940s are *Feast of Lupercal* (1958; republished as *A Moment of Love*, 1965), about a repressed Catholic schoolmaster's infatuation with a sexually experienced Protestant girl, and *The Emperor of Ice-Cream* (1965), which centres on the 17-year-old Gavin, one of Moore's most sympathetic, and autobiographical, heroes. The first of his North American novels, *The Luck of Ginger Coffey* (1960), describes the struggles of an Irish immigrant in Montreal and his dreams of wealth and social success; *An Answer from Limbo* (1962) is set in New York and concerns an egoistic hack-writer and his old mother whom he brings to America. *I Am Mary Dunne* (1968), a first-person narration, shows Moore's sympathy with the female psyche and with the split personality, interests further developed in *Fergus* (1970) and *The Doctor's Wife* (1976). From the 1970s onwards came a change of direction from the larger-scale novel of social conflict of his earlier work to novels which could be loosely described as *genre* fiction. This development has not been accompanied by a diminution of the literary artistry or the intellectual range of his work. *Catholics* (1972), *The Great Victorian Collection* (1975), and *Cold Heaven* (1983) partake of fantasy. *The Mangan Inheritance* (1979) owes something to the Gothic mode and is in part based on the tragic life of the nineteenth-century Irish poet J. C. Mangan. *The Temptation of Eileen Hughes* (1981) returned to a concentration on the interaction of complex yet culturally conditioned people that was so notable in Moore's early work. *Black Robe* (1985) is a historical novel, set in what is now French Canada in the seventeenth century, and contrasts the French with their narrow proselytizing faith with the Algonquin Indians whose religion embraces communion with the dead. *The Colour of Blood* (1987), an account of a brave yet compromising cardinal in a communist state, has overtones of the thriller, as does *Lies of Silence* (1991) which returns to Belfast and concerns a hotel manager whose involvement with IRA terrorists wreaks havoc on his life. *No Other Life* (1993), a disturbing adventure story concerning a coup on a fictionalized Haiti, drew comparisons with Graham *Greene. His recent novel, *The Statement* (1995), is a tale of public and private morality, and crimes against humanity in post-war France.

MOORE, George (Augustus) (1852–1933), Irish novelist, born in Ballyglass, Co. Mayo, the eldest son of a landowner and racehorse breeder. After his father's death in 1870, he inherited the family estate with which he subsidized seven years in Paris, studying art and literature. Due to his absence and the effects of the Land War in Ireland, he suffered a financial crisis in 1880 and had to leave Paris. He became a professional writer of fiction, intent on introducing the ideas of Zola, Balzac, and Flaubert to the English novel. His first published work, *A Modern Lover* (1883), which concerns the relationship between artistic compromise and sexual prostitution, was critically condemned as immoral and banned by the powerful circulating libraries. In reaction, Moore began a prolonged attack on the handful of critics and businessmen who controlled the reading habits of late Victorian England. The novels which followed refused to pander to prudery or the contemporary distrust of French narrative technique. In *A Mummer's Wife* (1884), which influenced Arnold *Bennett, and *A Drama in Muslin* (1886), a novel about the landed gentry in Ireland, Moore experimented with Zola's theory of authorial detachment. His autobiographical portrayal of Parisian artists, *Confessions of a Young Man* (1888), recounts his conversion to naturalism: 'The idea of a new art based upon science, . . . an art that should explain all things and embrace modern life in its entirety . . . filled me with wonder.' Moore's financial problems were solved by the success of his most renowned novel, *Esther Waters* (1894), which tells the story of a servant girl's misfortunes and her struggle to protect her child. Esther is illiterate and her condition restricts her ability to reflect upon her suffering. In choosing to narrate the novel through a figure of low social rank, Moore exceeded the efforts of Thomas *Hardy in *Tess of the d'Urbervilles* (1891) to represent a mind of limited understanding.

In his later novels, Moore continued to run counter to contemporary tastes; *The Brook Kerith* (1916) and *Héloïse and Abélard* (1921), an imaginative reconstruction of life in the Middle Ages, experiment successfully with historical epic, while *Celibate Lives* (1927) pays homage to the aesthetics of Flaubert. In 1901 Moore moved to Dublin and, with W. B. *Yeats, Lady *Gregory, and Edward *Martyn, helped to establish the Irish National Theatre, later the *Abbey Theatre. His contribution to Anglo-Irish literature continued with a collection of short stories, *The Untilled Field* (1903), with which, Frank *O'Connor has argued, 'the Irish short story became a fact'. *Vale* (1914), the third and final volume of his autobiography, *Hail and Farewell* (1911–14), brilliantly satirizes the excesses of the *Irish Literary Revival, though Moore never relinquished his belief in the renewal of Irish culture and identity. See *The Life of Moore* (1936), by J. M. Hone; *George Moore: A Reconsideration* (1955), by Malcolm Brown; and *George Moore in Perspective* (1983), by Janet Dunleavy. A new edition of the letters of George Moore, 1900–1933, *George Moore on Parnassus* (1988), was edited by Helmut E. Gerber.

MOORE, G(eorge) E(dward) (1873–1958), British moral philosopher and epistemologist, born in London to a Quaker family, educated at Dulwich College and Trinity College, Cambridge. He lectured at Cambridge where he became professor of philosophy and logic (1925–39). From 1921 to 1947 he was editor of the academic journal *Mind*. Moore's *Principia Ethica* (1903), alongside his associate Bertrand *Russell's *Principia Mathematica* (1903), established a style and set an agenda for British analytic philosophy which remained intact for nearly seventy years. Although now unfashionable, Moore exerted great contemporary influence on the *Bloomsbury Group, particularly on Clive *Bell, Lytton *Strachey, and Virginia *Woolf. In direct reaction to the prevailing current of utilitarianism, and the emergent beliefs of Marxism, he argued that 'good' could not be broken down into another meaning (such as 'pleasurable' or 'beneficial'). Like J. L. *Austin and Gilbert *Ryle, he sought to lodge his conclusions in the linguistic usage of upper middle-class speakers of standard English, and to legitimize a certain perception of the world. Although Moore's influence can still be found in the writings of Iris *Murdoch he is perhaps now best known as the vehicle for a number of mistaken-identity jokes in Tom Stoppard's play **Jumpers* (1972). His other important works are *Ethics* (1912), *Philosophical Studies* (1922), and the posthumous collection *Philosophical Papers* (1959).

MOORE, Lorrie (1957–), American novelist, born in Glen Falls, New York, educated at St Lawrence College and Cornell University; she then taught English at the University of Wisconsin in Madison.

Her first book, *Self-Help* (1985), was a collection of stories characterized by their wit, polish, and experimental zeal; Moore employs the title's reference to pop psychology as a metaphor and thematic link between her stories. Her first novel, *Anagrams* (1987), looked at one woman's life from a variety of perspectives and parallel narrative strategies. Her second collection of stories, *Like Life* (1992), which focuses on the difficulties of male–female relationships, is distinguished by its unusual themes, settings, and imagery (which verges on the surreal). Her second novel, *Who Will Run the Frog Hospital?* (1995), is the story of a woman's adolescence, marriage, and relationships with other women, told mostly in flashback. Simple but subtle in execution, it displays, in its brief span, the skill and maturity of her best stories.

MOORE, Marianne (Craig) (1887–1972), American poet, born in St Louis, Missouri, educated at Bryn Mawr College; she grew up in Carlisle, Pennsylvania. Her specialization in biology informs the many poems based on her observations of animals, which occasionally employ items of scientific vocabulary. In 1916 she became acquainted with W. C. *Williams and the group of poets associated with the New York magazine *Others*; in 1918 she moved to New York where she lived for the rest of her life. She worked as a teacher, a secretary, and a librarian from 1911 to 1925, when she became editor of *The *Dial*, in which her poetry had been published regularly. From 1915 onward her verse appeared frequently in *The *Egoist*; her contributions to the magazine were assembled into a first collection without her knowledge by Winifred Ellerman and Hilda *Doolittle, who had been her classmate at Bryn Mawr, and published in London as *Poems* by the Egoist Press in 1921. *Observations* followed in 1924, after which no further volume appeared until her *Selected Poems* of 1936, which, with its introduction by T. S. *Eliot, initiated a wider recognition of her idiosyncratic achievements. Her numerous subsequent collections included *The Pangolin* (1936), *Nevertheless* (1944), *O To Be a Dragon* (1959), and *The Arctic Ox* (1964); a revised edition of her *Complete Poems* (1959) was produced in 1981. The intricate syllabic forms and deftly unobtrusive uses of rhyme she developed early in her career are essential to the poised combination of control and spontaneity with which her poems conduct their urbanely informal discourses. The philosophical optimism of much of her writing is enacted in the exuberance and precision of her descriptive imagery. Among her other works are her verse translations of *The Fables of La Fontaine* (1954). Her critical writings, which include the essays on her favourite writers in *Predilections* (1955), are collected in *Complete Prose* (1986).

MOORE, Merrill (1903–57), American poet, born in Columbia, Tennessee; he studied medicine at Vanderbilt University, Nashville, Tennessee. Whilst a student, Moore submitted some of his poems to the magazine *The Fugitive*, and his poetic career was soon associated with the *Agrarians who published the journal. A massively prolific writer of sonnets, he reinvented and adapted that form for the American idiom. He then became a practising psychiatrist in Boston, but continued to publish poetry using the sonnet form with great fluency and flexibility. His collections include *The Noise that Time Makes* (1929), *It Is a Good Deal Later than You Think* (1934), *Six Sides to a Man* (1935), *M: One Thousand Autobiographical Sonnets* (1938), *Some Poems for New Zealand* (1945), *Clinical Sonnets* (1949), *Illegitimate Sonnets* (1950), and *More Clinical Sonnets* (1953).

MOORE, Nicholas (1918–1986), British poet, born in Cambridge, the son of the philosopher G. E. *Moore; he was educated at Trinity College, Cambridge. As a leading contributor to the anthologies of the *New Apocalypse, his reputation was considerable during the 1940s. *A Wish in Season* (1941), his first book of poetry, was followed by seven further early collections, the contents of which are represented by *The Glass Tower: Poems, 1936–1943* (1944) and *Recollections of the Gala: Selected Poems, 1943–1948* (1950). Moore published no further collections until *Identity* (1969), after which he produced several further volumes, including *Spleen* (1973), which contained thirty-one ingeniously different versions of Baudelaire's 'Je suis comme le roi d'un pays pluvieux'. *Longings of the Acrobats* (edited by Peter Riley, 1988) is a selection from his work. His earlier poetry often suggests the examples of W. H. *Auden's lighter verse and more sinister lyrics. American experimental poetry became a prevalent influence in his later verse, which has been admired by a younger generation of British poets seeking alternatives to the central English traditions.

MOORE, T(homas) Sturge (1870–1944), British poet and illustrator, born in Hastings, Sussex, the brother of the philosopher G. E. *Moore; he was privately educated. His collections of verse include *The Vinedresser and Other Poems* (1899), *The Little School: A Posy of Rhymes* (1905), *The Sea Is Kind* (1914), and *The Unknown Land and a Dozen Odd Poems* (1939). Among his highly regarded verse-dramas are *Aphrodite against Artemis* (1901), *Marianne* (1911), and *Tragic Mothers: Medea, Niobe, Tyrfing* (1920). He was also noted for his long narrative poems based on material from classical and Judaeo-Christian scriptural sources. *The Poems of T. Sturge Moore: A Collected Edition* appeared in four volumes between 1931 and 1934. Ezra *Pound and W. B. *Yeats admired the musical refinement and lyrical fluidity of his poetry. His 'In Time of War' is among the finest traditionally elegiac responses to the Great War. One of the leading illustrators of his day, he produced cover illustrations for Yeats's *The *Tower* (1928) and *The Winding Stair* (1933); *W. B. Yeats and T. Sturge Moore: Their Correspondence 1901–1937*, edited by Ursula Bridge, appeared in 1953. Among his numerous other publications is *Armour for Aphrodite* (1929), a treatise on aesthetics.

MOOREHEAD, Alan (McCrae) (1919–83), Australian journalist and historian, born in Melbourne, where he was educated at the University and spent six years with the Melbourne *Herald*. He arrived in Britain in 1936 and joined the *Daily Express*. The courage and distinction with which he worked as a war correspondent from 1939 to 1945 gained him an international reputation. His accounts of the North African campaigns were collected as *African Trilogy* (1944); *Eclipse* (1945) deals with the war in Europe. After a period in Florence, during which he produced the novel *The Rage of the Vulture* (1948), he established himself as a modern historian with *Gallipoli* (1956). *The Russian Revolution* (1958) and *No Room in the Ark* (1959), reflecting on post-war developments in Africa, followed before the appearance in 1960 of his most widely acclaimed work, *The White Nile*, on the nineteenth-century expeditions to find the source of the Nile. Notable among his numerous other publications are *Cooper's Creek* (1963), dealing with the first crossing of the Australian continent, and *The Fatal Impact* (1966), a treatment of the cultural and ecological effects of the arrival of Europeans in the South Pacific. The autobiography *A Late Education* (1970) was the only work he published after suffering a stroke in 1966. *Alan Moorehead* (1990) is a biography by T. Pocock.

MOORHOUSE, Frank (1938–), Australian fiction writer, born in Nowra on the southern coast of New South Wales. He initially worked as a journalist (and in 1972 was one of a Sydney group which founded the alternative magazine *Tabloid Story*). His first story was published in *Southerly* in 1957. Moorhouse's fascination with the subcultures and sexual prowlings of urban society made publication difficult, but *The Americans, Baby* (1972) won acclaim. In subsequent collections Moorhouse refined his preferred technique of 'discontinuous narrative' in which characters and incidents recur in an apparently unstructured, but actually carefully planned, manner to allow the reader cumulative understanding. *Days of Wine and Rage* (1980), a series of 1970s writings edited by Moorhouse, provides a valuable glimpse of his Sydney cultural and intellectual context at that time, and complements both *Futility and Other Animals* (1969) and *The Americans, Baby*. The progressive Americanization of Australia, a phenomenon explored differently by Peter *Carey, features also in *The Electrical Experience* (1974) and in *Conference-ville* (1976), a caustically hilarious account of the academic circuit. In *Tales of Mystery and Romance* (1977) the traditional structure and status of the family furnishes the source of ironic humour; the collection *Room Service* was published in 1985, and *Forty-Seventeen*—another 'discontinuous narrative'—in 1988. The latter text subtly interweaves previous and new material to construct a wide-ranging work of great pathos and hilarity. In *Lateshows* (1990) two of the three sequences are clearly autobiographical while the third parodies literary, cultural, and political behaviour. His novel *Grand Days* (1993) portrays a young officer of the League of Nations and her sexual and political awakening in Geneva and Paris of the 1920s and 1930s.

MOORHOUSE, Geoffrey (1931–), British travel writer and historian, born in Bolton, Lancashire, educated at Bury Grammar School. From 1952 to 1970, when he became a freelance author, he was a journalist, travelling widely from 1963 onward as chief features writer with the *Guardian*. His earlier works include the sociological *Britain in the Sixties: The Other England* (1964) and *Against all Reason* (1970), his widely acclaimed investigation of monastic life. *Calcutta* (1971), a richly textured evocation of the city, was the first of his publications as a travel writer. Subsequent books include *The Fearful Void* (1974), his psychologically revealing account of a journey across the Sahara by camel; *To the Frontier* (1984), which records his experiences of north-western Pakistan; and *Apples in the Snow* (1990), on travels in Central Asia. As a historian, Moorhouse is admired for *India Britannica* (1983), his accessible and concentrated account of British India. In *Hell's Foundations* (1992) he examines the part played by soldiers from Bury in the Dardanelles Campaign in 1915 and assesses its social and cultural effects on the town. His highly regarded books on sport include *The Best-Loved Game* (1979), a celebration of cricket, and *At The George* (1989), a collection of essays on Rugby League.

MORAES, Dom(inic) (1938–), Indian poet and writer, born in Bombay, educated at Jesus College, Oxford; he is the son of the writer Frank Moraes. Moraes has held a variety of editorial and journalist posts. His reputation as a leading Indo-Anglian poet rests largely on the enthusiastic reception of his first collection, *Beginnings* (1957). His work reflects Western influences and mentors in its idiom, sensibility, and subject matter. Later collections include *John Nobody* (1965) and *Bedlam Etc.* (1966), which explore universal classical and philosophical themes, usually within the context of European literature, and *Absences* (1983). Moraes has been criticized for not encompassing the realities of his Indian surroundings in his poems but as a prolific writer of miscellaneous prose he has attempted to examine various aspects of contemporary Indian life. His prose writings include *Gone Away* (1960), a personal travel journal; *Mrs Gandhi* (1980), a portrait of the controversial leader in which Moraes reports on his own difficult encounters with his subject; *My Son's Father* (1969), an autobiography; *From East to West* (1971), a collection of essays; and several volumes of travel writing and journalism.

MORAGA, Cherrie (1952–), Chicana writer, born in Whittier, California, educated at San Francisco State University. Moraga was one of the first writers to explore Chicana lesbianism. She co-edited *This Bridge Called My Back: Radical Writings by Women of Color* (1981) with Gloria *Anzaldúa and began establishing her own voice as a literary critic, particularly in her examination of the key differences between white feminism and the feminism practised by women of colour. As a lesbian who is half Chicana and half Anglo, is her first individual work, *Loving in the War Years* (1983), Moraga articulated her complex bicultural relationship to Anglo and Chicano culture. In her play *Giving Up the Ghost* (1986), the Chicana heroine embraces the potential of her lesbianism, rather than rejecting it. *The Last Generation* (1993) is a compelling collection of prose and poetry that displays her continuing commitment to the advancement of the Chicano people; like her other works, the book is highly politicized and moves across literary genres in a bilingual method of expression that reconsiders ideas surrounding gender, sexuality, and ethnic identity.

MORGAN, Charles (Langbridge) (1894–1958), British novelist and drama critic of *The Times* (1926–39), educated at Osborne and Dartmouth naval colleges and at Brasenose College, Oxford. He won critical acclaim with *Portrait in a Mirror* (1929), his third novel, and maintained his reputation with such novels as *The Fountain* (1932), which described his war experiences in Holland; *Sparkenbroke* (1936); *The Voyage* (1940; James Tait Black Memorial Prize); and *The Judge's Story* (1947). The concept of honour and the need to defend principles are a central theme in many of Morgan's books. His non-fiction works include an *Ode to France* (1942; verse); *Reflections in a Mirror* (1947) and *Liberties of the Mind* (1951), collections of essays; plays, such as *The Flashing Stream* (1938); and a stage version of his novel *The River Line* (1949; dramatized 1952), about the French resistance. Regarded as a master of prose in his own day, his reputation declined in later years.

MORGAN, Edwin (George) (1920–), Scottish poet and translator, born in Glasgow; he was educated at the University of Glasgow, where he taught from 1947 until his retirement as Professor of English in 1980. The interplay between actuality and imagination that is a consistent feature of his writing was already apparent in *The Vision of Cathkin Braes* (1952), his first collection of poetry. Among his many subsequent volumes are *The Second Life* (1968), *From Glasgow to Saturn* (1973), *Themes on a Variation* (1988), and *Hold Hands among the Atoms* (1991). A *Collected Poems* appeared in 1990. Ian *Hamilton has remarked that Morgan 'is unconfinable to any single mode': accomplished in the use of traditional forms, he has also experimented widely with *concrete and sound poetries. Much of his work is pervaded by a disquietingly surreal comic sense and he is one of the few poets to have made significant use of the imaginative idioms of *science fiction; the compassionate social realism he frequently employs is well represented by the 'Glasgow Sonnets', a densely detailed evocation of harsh conditions in the city that forms the background to much of his writing. A fundamentally optimistic humanism underlies the eclecticism of his achievement. *Rites of Passage* (1975) is a collection of his translations, which include versions of poetry by Montale and Neruda. A wide range of material is collected in *Nothing not Giving Messages* (1990) to form a 'critical autobiography' reflecting on his life and work.

MORGAN, Kenneth O(wen) (1934–), British historian, born in London; he was educated at Oriel College, Oxford, and lectured at University College, Swansea from 1958 to 1966, when he became a fellow of Queen's College, Oxford. In 1989 he became Principal of University College, Aberystwyth. *Keir Hardie* (1967) and *Consensus and Disunity* (1979), a study of the coalition government from 1918 to 1922, were among the works which gained him eminence as a historian of British politics in the twentieth century. He has latterly concentrated on the decades following the Second World War, most notably in *Labour in Power, 1945–1951* (1984) and *The People's Peace* (1990), which traces the social, political, and cultural history of Britain from 1945 to 1990. His other publications include *Labour People* (1987), a collection of brief biographies of figures in the history of the Labour Party, and *Rebirth of a Nation: Wales, 1880–1980* (1981), one of a number of works on which his reputation as a leading historian of modern Wales is based.

MORRELL, Lady Ottoline (Violet Anne) (1873–1938), British literary hostess and memoirist, born in London; she studied briefly at Somerville College, Oxford. In 1902 she married Philip Morrell, who became Liberal Member of Parliament in 1906. Her activities as a hostess and patron of the arts began in 1908 at her home in Bedford Square, London. Her hospitality entered its most celebrated phase after her move to Garsington Manor, Oxfordshire, in 1915. Among her visitors there were Bertrand *Russell, Augustus John, with both of whom she had affairs, W. B. *Yeats, Virginia *Woolf, Lytton *Strachey, Siegfried *Sassoon, John Maynard *Keynes, and T. S. *Eliot, with whom she sustained a long friendship. D. H. *Lawrence used her as the model for the repellent 'Hermione Roddice' in *Women in Love* (1921). She is also recognizable in the figure of 'Priscilla Wimbush' in Aldous *Huxley's *Crome Yellow* (1921). Robert Gathorne-Hardy edited two volumes of her memoirs (1963, 1974). *Ottoline* (1976) is a biography by S. J. Darroch.

MORRIESON, James Ronald Hugh (1922–72), New Zealand novelist and short-story writer, born and lived all his life in the small North Island town of Hawera where he was a music teacher. His first novel, *The Scarecrow* (1963), a blackly comic thriller heavily influenced by cinema, and *Came a Hot Friday* (1964) were the only novels to appear in his lifetime; two others, *Predicament* (1974) and *Pallet on the Floor* (1976), were published posthumously. The vulgarity of Morrieson's work, which initially alienated New Zealand critics and audiences, was reassessed in Peter Simpson's monograph on Morrieson (1982) which explains the crudely drawn 'black' characters in, for instance, *The Scarecrow* as a manifestation of the young narrator's fears about sexuality and 'adult life'. Other critics have characterized Morrieson's work as delightfully voyeuristic and perverse.

MORRIS, Jan (formerly James Morris) (1926–), British travel writer, born at Clevedon, Somerset, educated at Christchurch, Oxford. Morris became a journalist in 1947 after a period of military service. He held successive posts as a foreign correspondent with *The Times* and the *Guardian* from 1951 to 1962. He travelled with the 1953 Everest expedition, becoming widely known for his reports of the ascent; *Coronation Everest* (1958) forms an account of his experiences. Among the works which established Morris's reputation as a culturally and historically authoritative travel writer are *Coast to Coast* (1956), drawing on visits to the USA, *Venice* (1960, revised edition 1983), and *The Presence of Spain* (1964, revised edition 1988). His comprehensive and accessible trilogy on the British Empire in the nineteenth century consists of *Pax Britannica* (1968), *Heaven's Command* (1973), and *Farewell the Trumpets* (1978). In 1972 the sex change for which Morris had been preparing since 1964 was completed and from 1973 onward her books were published under her present name; the autobiographical *Conundrum* (1974) is widely regarded as the best account of transsexuality available. Among Morris's later publications are *Hong Kong* (1988) and *Sydney* (1992); the experimental *Letters from Hav* (1985) describes an imaginary city. Morris has also written extensively on Wales, where she chiefly resides, in *The Matter of Wales* (1984) and *A Machynlleth Triad* (1993).

MORRIS, Mervyn (1937–), Jamaican poet, born in Kingston, Jamaica, educated at the University of the West Indies and St Edmund Hall, Oxford. In 1970 he began lecturing at the University of the West Indies, where he was subsequently appointed a Reader in West Indian Literature. The principal collections of his verse are *The Pond* (1973), *On Holy Week* (1976), *Shadowboxing* (1979), and *Examination Centre* (1992). His earlier verse, which made idiosyncratic use of conventional verse forms, commented wryly on a wide range of social issues raised by his personal experiences. The most notable development in his work has been towards the concentration and flexibility evident in *Shadowboxing*, in which poems of marked brevity are capable of a disturbing power of imaginative implication. His work as an editor includes *Seven Jamaican Poets* (1971) and *The Faber Book of Contemporary Caribbean Short Stories* (1990).

MORRIS, Wright (1910–), American novelist, born in Central City, Nebraska, educated at Crane College, Chicago, and Pomona College, Claremont, California. Despite considerable praise from many influential critics and writers, Morris remains one of the most neglected of major American writers. He travelled extensively in Europe before returning to the USA in 1934 to begin his literary career; he also established a complementary career as a photographer. Morris's first published novel was *My Uncle Dudley* (1942), a charming, largely autobiographical work, showing stylistic affinities with *Hemingway and peopled with characters reminiscent of those in *Steinbeck's fiction; his second novel was *The Man Who Was There* (1946). A 15,000-mile tour of the USA in 1940–1 provided him with photographic material for *The Inhabitants* (1946), an earlier version of which was published by James Laughlin in *New Directions in Prose and Poetry* (1940); *The Inhabitants* was the first of a projected series of five volumes of 'photo-text' (complementary fiction and photography), published by Charles Scribner's Sons in New York, of which the only other volume to be published was *The Home Place* (1948) (*The World in the Attic*, intended for the series, was published in 1949 without photographs). Both texts bespeak Morris's imaginative preoccupation with the landscape, both natural and man-made, of the American West and, in particular, of his home state of Nebraska. *Man and Boy* (1951) marked a slight shift of direction, the novel having Eastern settings in suburban Philadelphia and the Brooklyn Navy Yard, and later novels, notably *Love among the Cannibals* (1957) and *What a Way To Go* (1962), reveal a talent for irony and social satire absent from the earlier writings. *Ceremony in Lone Tree* (1960), however, with its Nebraskan setting, is more characteristic of Morris's style and vision, and it remains, arguably, his most impressive work of fiction. Other works include the novels *Fire Sermon* (1971) and *A Life* (1973); *Collected Stories, 1948–1986* appeared in 1986. *The Territory Ahead* (1958) is a collection of essays on American literature; *Structure and Artifacts: Photographs 1933–1954* and *Morris* (1981) are representative photographic portfolios, while *God's Country and My People* (1968) is an autobiographical essay with photographs. *Wright Morris* (1964) by David Madden and *The Novels of Morris: A Critical Interpretation* (1978) by G. B. Crump are critical studies.

MORRISON, Bill (1940–), Northern Irish playwright, born in Ballymoney, Co. Antrim, educated at Queen's University, Belfast. He has worked as an actor, BBC radio drama producer, and theatre director. As an Ulster playwright, Morrison is by no means unique in feeling that his work must respond to the recent troubles in Northern Ireland. His own response has involved comedy and farce arising from the belief that apparent chaos may represent the complexities of Northern Ireland. At first, Morrison's experimentations with dramatic form in plays such as *The Love of Lady Margaret* (1972) and *Ellen Cassidy* (1974) were produced only on radio. Eventually, he found access to the stage with *Flying Bird* (1977) and *Scrap* (1982), works in which he continued to approach tragedy through farce. His other plays include *Maguire* (1979), *Shergar* (1986: for TV), *Be Bop a Lula* (1988), and *Force of Duty* (1992).

MORRISON, (Philip) Blake (1950–), British poet and critic, born in Burnley, Lancashire, educated at the University of Nottingham and University College, London. He was poetry and fiction editor with the *Times Literary Supplement* from 1978 to 1981, when he joined the staff of the *Observer*. In 1990 he became literary editor of the *Independent on Sunday*. *Dark Glasses* (1984), his first collection of verse, contained work of impressive range, including numerous inventive treatments of domestic and personal material. *The Ballad of the Yorkshire Ripper* appeared in 1987;

its title poem, which incorporates elements of Yorkshire dialect, forms a remarkable critique of the misogyny implicit in traditional male attitudes and assumptions. Other poems in the book demonstrated his increasing skill in the use of startlingly original imagery of the type associated with *Martian poetry. Among his critical writings are *The Movement: English Poetry and Fiction of the 1950s* (1980), the most definitive consideration of its subject available, and the monograph *Seamus Heaney* (1982). With Andrew *Motion, he edited *The Penguin Book of Contemporary British Poetry* (1982). A memoir, *And When Did You Last See Your Father?*, appeared in 1994.

MORRISON, John (Gordon) (1904–), Australian writer, born in Sunderland, England; he settled in Australia in 1923. He has been a jackeroo, swagman, dock worker, and gardener. He published stories in **Meanjin* and **Overland*, about fellow workers, union activities, the people he met on the tram to work, and social conditions. Morrison published two novels, *The Creeping City* (1947) and *Port of Call* (1949), and several collections of stories, including *Sailors Belong Ships* (1947), *Black Cargo* (1955), *Twenty-Three* (1962), *North Wind* (1982), *Stories of the Waterfront* (1984), and *This Freedom* (1985). His style and technique can be described as Australian social realism with polished devices derived from European realist story writers. Stories such as 'The Incense Burner', in which a sick sailor, unable to work his passage home, burns gum leaves in his lonely room, reflect Australian nostalgia. Others, including 'North Wind', a description of fighting a bush fire, display a narrative power which have contributed to his reputation as a master of his craft. He has also published a collection of essays, *The Happy Warrior* (1990).

MORRISON, Toni (Chloe Anthony Wofford) (1931–), American novelist, born in Lorain, Ohio, educated at Howard and Cornell Universities. Since graduation, she has worked as a teacher at various American universities, and as a senior editor at Random House Press, editing the work of several of her contemporaries. Her own fiction, using a blend of realism, history, myth, folktale, and poetic fantasy, attempts to describe the different political realities of black America and the influence of sexual divisions within black experiences. Her first novel, *The *Bluest Eye* (1970), presents a bleak world through the perspective of two adolescent girls in which the social unhappiness of the black population is conditioned by white ideology. *Sula* (1974) shatters black female stereotypes in its powerful exploration of the friendship between Sula and Nel and the demise of the community they inhabit. Then came **Song of Solomon* (1977), a haunting study of racism and its effects on several generations of a family. The exploration of the relationship between blacks and whites is the central focus of *Tar Baby* (1981), which traces a sophisticated black model's educational experience at the Sorbonne, supported by white benefactors. Morrison's acclaimed novel **Beloved* (1987) is a dense and complex investigation of family commitments and ties set in the years immediately before and after Reconstruction; its blend of realistic description of sexuality and violence, and its fantastic evocation of the influence of the past, make it one of the finest novels of its period. *Jazz* (1992) is set in Harlem, in 'the City', in spring 1926, and presents the story of Joe and Violet Trace, a middle-aged married couple. Joe's murder of his young lover Dorcas initiates an eruption of memories through which the narrator 'traces' the movement of blacks from the poor rural South to the dangerously hypnotic North, showing an intolerable crisis in individual lives. In an avowedly political fiction, Morrison's novels continue to be concerned with the retrieval and archaeology of black experience and history, particularly that of black women. She was awarded the Nobel Prize in 1993, the first African-American writer to be so honoured; her *Nobel Prize Speech* was published in 1994. Recent critical work includes *Race-ing Justice, Engendering Power* (1993) and *Playing in the Dark* (1993). See also ETHNICITY.

MORROW, John (1930–), Northern Irish novelist and short-story writer, born in Belfast. Having left school at the age of 14, he followed various occupations. He began to write short stories in the 1960s, contributing some of his early work to *The *Honest Ulsterman* and *The Irish Press*. His novels include *The Confessions of Prionias O'Toole* (1977) and *The Essex Factor* (1982). Among his short-story collections are *Northern Myths* (1979) and *Sects and Other Stories* (1987). Morrow prefers a realistic and witty, if facetious, undermining of political rhetoric and 'idealism' to the more conventional attempts at serious artistic analysis. His anecdotal, comic style exaggerates petty ambitions and libidinous habits as the common denominators between the conflicting sides in Northern Ireland. His main characters tend to be simple, self-serving humans who remain blissfully unaware of the layers of historical irony with which Morrow surrounds them.

MORTIMER, John (Clifford) (1923–), British novelist, short-story writer, and playwright, born in Hampstead, London, educated at Harrow and Brasenose College, Oxford. He was a practising barrister for many years, and became a Queen's Counsel in 1966. He had published several novels before turning to the theatre, where he achieved popular recognition with plays such as *The Dock Brief* (1957), about the relationship between an inept lawyer and the client he is defending; *The Judge* (1967), about the private uncertainties of a professional dispenser of justice; *A Voyage Round My Father* (1970), a portrait of a blind barrister, based on his own father; and *Heaven and Hell* (1976), two short theological comedies. He has written film scripts, radio and television plays, including a six-part life of Shakespeare, and adaptations of his own Rumpole stories, about an eccentric barrister; he also wrote the screenplay for the adaptation of Waugh's **Brideshead Revisited*. His later, and more successful, novels include *Paradise Postponed* (1985), which charts the rise of Leslie Titmuss, an aspiring politician, from his deprived childhood to his eventual triumph as Conservative Member of Parliament; the novel was adapted for television. *Summer's Lease* (1988), a murder mystery set in the Chianti area of Tuscany (or 'Chiantishire', as it is nicknamed to reflect the minority population of British expatriates who have settled there), was also televised. *Titmuss Regained* (1990), a sequel to *Paradise Postponed*, in which the eponymous hero falls in love with the widow of a socialist Oxford don, was published with its companion volume as *The Rapstone Chronicles* (1991). His novel, *Dunster* (1992), centres on a libel action arising from allegations of war crimes. Apart from his novels, Mortimer has published numerous collections of short stories concerning the lovably irascible Horace Rumpole; these include *Rumpole of the Bailey* (1978), *The Trials of Rumpole* (1979), *Rumpole for the Defence* (1981), *Rumpole and the Age of Miracles* (1985), *Rumpole and the Angel of Death* (1995), and a collection of stories, *The Best of Rumpole* (1993). An autobiography, *Clinging to the Wreckage* (1982), was widely acclaimed for its honesty and its dry wit. *Murderers and Other Friends* (1994) is a memoir of Mortimer's legal career. He is the editor of *The Oxford Book of Villains* (1992). Mortimer was formerly married to Penelope *Mortimer.

MORTIMER, Penelope (1918–), British novelist, born in Wales, the daughter of a clergyman, and educated at University College, London. Her novels tend to focus on destructive relationships between men and women, notably *The Pumpkin Eater* (1962), the story of a woman harried by the breakdown of her marriage, who obsessively uses motherhood to define her identity; it was made into a film with the screenplay written by Harold *Pinter in 1964. *Daddy's Gone a'Hunting* (1958; published in the USA as *Cave of Ice*, 1959) tells of a mother and her daughter combining surreptitiously against the brutish 'head' of the family. In *My Friend Says It's Bullet-Proof* (1967) the protagonist, a woman, adjusts to life after a breast-cancer operation through a liaison with a man. Later novels are *The Home* (1971), *The Handyman* (1973), and *Long Distance* (1974). Her other books include *Saturday Lunch with the Brownings* (1960), a collection of short stories; *Queen Elizabeth: A Life of the Queen Mother* (1986); and her volumes of autobiography, *About Time: An Aspect of Autobiography* (1979) and *About Time Too: 1940–1978* (1993). She was formerly married to John *Mortimer.

MORTON, H(enry Canova) V(ollam) (1892–1979), British travel writer, born in Ashton-under-Lyme; he grew up in Birmingham, where he began reporting for local newspapers before becoming a sub-editor on the *Daily Mail*. After active service in the First World War, he resumed his journalistic career in 1919 and produced his first book, *The Heart of London*, in 1925; by the end of 1926, he had published four further books about London. An *In Search of*... series followed, the first, *In Search of England*, appearing in 1927; its successors dealt with Scotland (1929), Ireland (1930), and Wales (1932). Morton's buoyant and richly descriptive manner made him one of the most respected popular authors of his day. In 1942 he accompanied *Churchill to the Atlantic Charter negotiations with President Roosevelt, giving his account of events in *Atlantic Meeting* (1943). Among his many other travel books are *Through Lands of the Bible* (1938), one of a number with a devotional orientation, *In Search of South Africa* (1948), *A Stranger in Spain* (1954), and *A Traveller in Rome* (1957). *I, James Blunt* (1942) is Morton's fictionalized autobiography.

MORTON, J(ohn) (Cameron Andrieu) B(ingham) (Michael) ('Beachcomber') (1893–1979), British humorist, born in London; he went from Harrow to Worcester College, Oxford, but left after his first year due to family difficulties. Following service on the Western Front and in intelligence during the First World War, he joined the staff of the *Sunday Express*. In 1924 he took over as 'Beachcomber' on the *Daily Express* from D. B. Wyndham Lewis; he continued to write the column daily until the early 1970s, peopling it with such bizarrely humorous creations as 'Mr Justice Cocklecarrot' and 'Dr Strabismus (Whom God Preserve) of Utrecht', who respectively provided vehicles for his satires on the British legal system and modern science. Some twenty 'Beachcomber' selections were published, among them *A Diet of Thistles* (1938) and *The Tibetan Venus* (1951); Michael *Frayn edited *The Best of Beachcomber* (1963, revised 1991). Morton produced a wide range of other writing: his novels include *The Barber of Putney* (1919), drawn from his experiences on the Western Front, and *Maladetta* (1932); several early essays were collected as *Vagabond* (1934); *Sobieski: King of Poland* (1932) and *Marshall Ney* (1958) are among the numerous histories and biographies he regarded as his most valuable work. He was a close friend of Hilaire *Belloc, of whom he produced a memoir in 1955; as a member of J. C. *Squire's literary circle, he is portrayed as 'Mr Huggins' in A. G. *Macdonnell's *England, Their England* (1933).

MOSLEY, Nicholas, 3rd Baron Ravensdale (1923–), British novelist and biographer, born in London, educated at Eton and at Balliol College, Oxford. Since the publication of his first novel, *Spaces of the Dark* (1951), Mosley's fiction has responded to, and experimented with, ideas. He is an uncompromising writer who has sought narrative forms which reflect intellectual debate rather than succumbing to the rewards of a recognizable style. His early novels, including *The Rainbearers* (1955) and *Corruption* (1958), are realistic works. Subsequent novels became more self-reflective, preoccupied with the divorce between fiction and reality. *Accident* (1965), which was filmed by Joseph Losey with a screenplay by Harold *Pinter, is set in Oxford and concerns academic play with marriage and adultery. *Impossible Object* (1969) is a series of eight stories connected by the changing viewpoints of different narrators. Eight years after *Natalie, Natalia* (1971) Mosley produced his experimental *Catastrophe Prac-*

tice: Plays Not for Acting, and Cypher: A Novel (1979). Intended to be the first volume of a sequence of seven novels, it is written in the form of three plays and a novella and appropriates Catastrophe Theory as a science which yields metaphors for the construction of meaning out of chaos. *Imago Bird* (1980), *Serpent* (1981), and *Judith* (1986) followed as the next novels in the sequence of seven. Then came *Hopeful Monsters* (1990), a novel of ideas comparable to certain works by Aldous *Huxley and Doris *Lessing, which traces the interconnecting lives of an English physicist and a German radical as they move through the political, philosophical, and scientific development of the twentieth century. *Children of Darkness and Light* (1996) focuses on a group of children in Cumbria. *Rules of the Game* (1982) and *Beyond the Pale* (1983) are biographical works about this father, Sir Oswald Mosley; *Efforts at Truth* (1994) is an autobiography.

MOSLEY, Walter (1952–), African-American novelist, born in Los Angeles, where most of his works are set, educated at Johnson State College and City College of the City University of New York. His first novel, featuring the black detective Ezekiel 'Easy' Rawlins and his sidekick Mouse, was *Devil in a Blue Dress* (1990) in which the protagonist searches for a missing woman in post-1948 Los Angeles and becomes involved in an organized crime ring. Others in the series include *A Red Death* (1991), *White Butterfly* (1992), and *Black Betty* (1994), all of which are set in the 1950s and deal, in varying degrees, with the position of black people in post-war American society. Mosley has been compared to R. *Chandler, and there are obvious similarities, both in the choice of setting and in the laconic and witty style employed by both writers to which Mosley adds the rhythms and imagery of African-American speech. In *RL's Dream* (1995), Mosley moves away from crime in a novel which focuses on an elderly blues guitarist.

MOTION, Andrew (1952–), British poet, biographer, and critic, born in London, educated at University College, Oxford, where he won the Newdigate Prize for Poetry in 1975. After lecturing at the University of Hull, he edited *Poetry Review* until 1983, when he entered publishing, becoming an editor with *Faber and Faber in 1989. In 1995 he succeeded Malcolm *Bradbury as Chair of Creative Writing at the University of East Anglia. *The Pleasure Steamers*, his first substantial collection of poetry, appeared in 1978. Subsequent volumes include *Secret Narratives* (1983), *Natural Causes* (1987), *Love in a Life* (1991), and *The Price of Everything* (1994); a collected edition of his verse entitled *Dangerous Play* was produced in 1984. His characteristic technique of suggesting narrative coherence through imaginative correspondences of imagery and atmosphere was established early in his work. The suppleness and economy of his style is highly appropriate to the detached elegiac tenor of much of his verse. *Natural Causes* contains 'This Is Your Subject Speaking', a finely judged elegy for Philip *Larkin, whom Motion knew at Hull; *Philip Larkin: A Writer's Life*, his highly regarded biography of Larkin, appeared in 1993. His works as a critic include *The Poetry of Edward Thomas* (1980) and *Philip Larkin* (1982). His novels *The Pale Companion* (1989) and *Famous for the Creatures* (1991) successively chart the growth to early adulthood of a main protagonist named Francis Mayne. Among his other publications is the biographical study *The Lamberts: George, Constant, and Kit* (1986). With Blake *Morrison, he edited *The Penguin Book of Contemporary British Poetry* (1982).

MOTLEY, Willard (Francis) (1912–65), African-American novelist, born and raised in Chicago; he spent several nomadic years during the Depression as a migrant labourer and freelance journalist. His first and most successful work was *Knock on Any Door* (1947), a grim narrative of urban poverty, vice, and violence in the naturalistic tradition of *Dreiser, J. T. *Farrell, and Richard *Wright. Like Wright in **Native Son*, Motley saw crime as environmentally determined, and drew on sociological research and actual criminal trials for his portrait of a slum youth's inexorable progress towards the electric chair. *We Fished All Night* (1951) and *Let No Man Write My Epitaph* (1958) continue to explore the social pathology of inner-city Chicago. It is significant that none of the novels depicts a black protagonist: focusing on Italian, Polish, and Hispanic Americans, Motley is one of the few black writers whose protest against social injustice is not concerned with the specific determinants of colour and race prejudice. While some critics applauded this as a step in the direction of 'universality', others saw it as a regrettable betrayal of the distinctive concerns of black America. His last novel, *Let Noon Be Fair* (1966), is set in Mexico, where he lived as an expatriate for the last twelve years of his life.

MOTTRAM, R(alph) H(ale) (1883–1971), British novelist, born in Norwich. For some years he worked as a bank clerk but with encouragement from John *Galsworthy, who was to be the subject of the later work *For Some We Loved* (1956), he turned to writing. His first novel, *The Spanish Farm* (1924), with a preface by Galsworthy, reflected his experiences in France and Flanders during the First World War; it was followed by *Sixty-four, Ninety-four* (1925) and *The Crime at Vanderlyden's* (1926) which together formed 'The Spanish Farm Trilogy'. The trilogy gives a vivid account of military life, both from the view of the British servicemen and from that of the peasants who lived near the battle front. His autobiographical account of the war period appeared as *Three Personal Records of the War* (1929). As well as many novels, including *To Hell with Crabb Robinson* (1962), he also wrote collections of short stories, such as *The Headless Hound* (1931); autobiographical essays contained in *The Window Seat* (1954) and *Another Window Seat* (1957); as well as *A History of Financial Speculation* (1929) and *A History of the East India Company* (1940).

Mourning Becomes Electra, a dramatic trilogy by Eugene *O'Neill, produced and published in 1931, comprising *Homecoming*, *The Hunted*, and *The Haunted*. Reflecting O'Neill's absorption in Greek tragedy and Freud, the work transposes the situations and events of the *Oresteia* of Aeschylus to America at the close of the Civil War, with Brigadier Ezra Mannon as O'Neill's Agamemnon, his wife Christine as Clytemnestra, and his son and daughter, Orin and Lavinia, as Orestes and Electra. Lavinia, whose obsessional state of mind reflects important aspects of the American psyche, is at the centre. Ezra Mannon returns from the war to his New England home, in which Christine has been unfaithful to him with a sea-captain, Adam Brant, who is Mannon's socially outcast nephew intent on family revenge. Lavinia, who hates her mother, discovers the affair. Christine, who adores her son, Orin, vows never to submit to her husband's advances again. Pretending to succumb, she enters the bedroom where she poisons Ezra with supposed medicine supplied by Brant. On Orin's return from the war Lavinia, aware of her mother's act and Brant's complicity, drives her brother to avenge his father's death. Orin, reluctant at first, overhears Christine and Brant conspiring on Brant's moored ship; he kills Brant, whereupon Christine commits suicide. Lavinia and Orin leave for the South Seas. There Lavinia comes to accept that she has inherited her mother's fierce sensuality, while Orin becomes the victim of guilt and sorrow, of the puritan conscience, like his father. Back in America, neither brother nor sister can find satisfaction; Orin commits suicide after a temptation to incestuous relations with Lavinia who proceeds to immure herself in the Mannon family mansion. O'Neill combines the exploration of basic human drives with the tyranny of the family. Largely due to his secure placing of the characters in the tormented post-bellum years, they speak and act with the dignity of a historical predicament upon them, in the manner of Aeschylus, thus transcending their often sordid and compulsive speeches and acts.

MOURNING DOVE, see NATIVE AMERICAN LITERATURE.

Movement, The, a group of young poets of the 1950s 'announced', as Ian *Hamilton writes in his essay 'The Making of the Movement', 'to be in concerted reaction against the tangled and pretentious neo-romanticism' of the *New Apocalypse and their immediate successors. The name was coined in an unsigned leading article in the *Spectator* in October 1954 which stressed the sceptically intelligent, accessible, and robustly commonsensical attitudes of the poets; two of them, Kingsley *Amis and John *Wain, were already enjoying considerable success with their first novels. D. J. *Enright and Robert *Conquest, themselves numbered among the Movement poets, respectively edited the group's principal anthologies, *Poets of the 1950s* (1955) and **New Lines* (1956); the other poets represented were Donald *Davie, Thom *Gunn, John Holloway, Elizabeth *Jennings, and Philip *Larkin. Conquest's introduction claimed their poetry was characterized by 'rational structure and comprehensible language' and 'negative determination to avoid bad principles'. The poets were designated 'the New Augustans' in recognition of the accomplishment with which they used traditional verse forms and the logically discursive development typifying many of their poems. Their detractors found their work intellectually arid and elitist in its habits of erudite allusion, factors associated with the preponderance of university lecturers among the Movement poets. Blake *Morrison's study *The Movement* (1980) identified F. R. *Leavis, George *Orwell, and William *Empson as precursors of various aspects of the poets' theory and practice. Davie's *Purity of Diction in English Verse* (1952) stated the critical assumptions underlying much of the group's poetry. Briefly alluding to the Movement in the introduction to his *Oxford Book of Contemporary Verse* (1980), which contains work by six of the group, Enright later noted 'the nonchalance with which, after a brief period of cohesiveness, its members went their separate ways'; the Movement had, however, a decisive influence on poetry in English for many years.

MPHAHLELE, Es'kia, formerly known as Ezekiel Mphahlele (1919–), South African novelist, essayist, and short-story writer, born in Pretoria, educated at the University of South Africa and the University of Denver. In *Down Second Avenue* (1959) Mphahlele gives an impassioned account of his impoverished childhood in Pretoria. He left South Africa for Nigeria in 1957. Together with Wole *Soyinka and Ulli Beier he edited the literary journal *Black Orpheus* (1960–4). After a period as Professor of English Literature at the University of Pennsylvania, he returned to South Africa in 1977 and became Senior Research Fellow at the African Studies Institute of the University of Witwatersrand. Some of his best fiction, brusque in style and angry in tone, is in his short stories about life in the South African ghettoes, collected in *Man Must Live* (1947), *The Living and the Dead* (1961), and *In Corner B* (1967). His novels, which frequently deal with themes of exile, dispossession, and corruption in African politics, include *The Wanderers* (1971), *Chirundu* (1979), and *Father Come Home* (1984). Other works include *The Unbroken Song* (1981), short stories; *Afrika My Music: An Autobiography 1957–83* (1984); and *The African Image* (1962) and *Voices in the Whirlwind* (1973), two influential volumes of literary and social criticism.

Mr Biswas, see HOUSE FOR MR BISWAS, A.

Mr Britling Sees It Through, a novel by H. G. *Wells, published in 1916. Set on the eve of the First World War, the novel concerns Hugh Britling, a well-known author resembling Wells himself, who presides over a pleasant and well-run household in the Essex village of Matching's Easy. Here he is visited by an American friend, Mr Direck, to whom he confides his view that war is by no means inevitable, as long as the spirit of rationality prevails, and that, as a civilized country, Germany can have no real intention of severing its connections with the rest of the civilized world. The pamphlet he writes, expressing this entirely logical but misguided point of view, is entitled *And Now War Ends*—an allusion to Wells's own work, *The War That Will End War* (1914). Britling's optimism proves ill-founded and he becomes increasingly disillusioned. His son enlists and is later killed in action, his death further undermining Britling's idealistic belief in the coming of a new world order. The novel ends with Britling's painful attempts to resurrect his optimism about the future by writing another pamphlet, *The Better Government of the World*, about post-war reconstruction. In the context of the novel, this is seen as a brave, but perhaps futile, exercise.

Mr Fortune's Maggot, see WARNER, SYLVIA TOWNSEND.

Mr Norris Changes Trains, a novel by Christopher *Isherwood, published by the *Hogarth Press in 1935, which firmly established his reputation as a novelist of importance. Set in Berlin, it is strongly informed by Isherwood's experiences of living in the city from 1929 to 1933, Hitler's ascendancy becoming increasingly apparent in the latter stages of the narrative. The book draws its episodic structure from the encounters of William Bradshaw, Isherwood's semi-autobiographical narrator, with Arthur Norris, a ruthlessly unprincipled but eccentrically charming con-man who introduces Bradshaw to Berlin's criminal and political underworld; the dissolute homosexual journalist Gerald Hamilton, whom Isherwood met in Berlin in 1931, was the model for the figure of Norris. Bradshaw's moral sensibility develops in the course of the narrative towards the realization that private and public morality are not readily separable, an awareness that frees him from his admiration for Norris. Stylistically, the work marks a considerable advance on Isherwood's earlier novels, initiating the fluently straightforward and objectively economical manner that is sustained in its sequel *Goodbye to Berlin* (1939).

Mr Polly, see HISTORY OF MR POLLY, THE.

Mrs Dalloway, a novel by V. *Woolf, published in 1925. A day in the life of a middle-aged upper-class London woman planning her party is Woolf's first completely successful *modernist novel, and one of her finest books. She arrived at it through experimenting with new forms of narrative in her earlier novels and through what she called her 'tunnelling process' (*Diary*, 15 Oct. 1923), digging out 'beautiful caves' (*Diary*, 30 Aug. 1923) behind her characters. The fluid narrative moves between different minds and memories and times, using a rhythmical, patterned prose, structured by connecting images and repeated strikings of 'the hours' (the book's working title). The technique owes something to J. Joyce's **Ulysses*. Clarissa Dalloway, wife of the MP Richard Dalloway (they appeared in *The Voyage Out*) walks up Bond Street on a post-war June morning ('What a lark! What a plunge!'), buys her flowers, goes home, is jealous that Richard has been invited out to lunch, sews her dress, is visited unexpectedly by her old lover Peter Walsh, back from India and about to be married, remembers their painful courtship at her family home, Bourton, and her passionate friendship with Sally Seton, and is jealous of her daughter Elizabeth's friendship with the religious, oppressive Miss Kilman. Richard lunches with Lady Bruton and takes Clarissa some flowers. Peter, much moved by seeing Clarissa, walks through London, follows a beautiful girl, and sleeps in the park. Elizabeth sheds Doris Kilman and takes a pioneering omnibus ride up Fleet Street. This narrative is adjacent to the agonizing story of Septimus Warren Smith and his Italian wife Lucrezia. He is 'insane', a shell-shock victim, hallucinating the return of his dead friend Evans. The couple are observed by Peter Walsh. Rezia takes Septimus to see the hateful Harley Street doctor Sir William Bradshaw. In the late afternoon, after a moment's tranquillity together, they are visited by the bullying Dr Holmes, and Septimus jumps out of the window. Peter Walsh sees the ambulance. The two stories join at the party, when Clarissa's social ambitions (the Prime Minister is a guest) and her past (Sally Seton arrives, disappointingly changed) seem insignificant beside the news of the young man who has killed himself. Woolf was anxious that Clarissa might seem too 'stiff, too glittering and tinselly' and that the novel would seem 'disjointed because of the mad scenes not connecting with the Dalloway scenes'. This difficult structural problem is resolved through the politics of the novel, in that Clarissa and Septimus both want to resist 'coercion', and both are, differently, outsiders in society.

Mrs Warren's Profession, a 'play unpleasant' by G. B. *Shaw, completed in 1893, published in 1898, but refused a licence by the Lord Chamberlain. Though it was privately performed by the Stage Society in 1902, it was not seen on the public stage in London until 1926. The main reason for the ban was that the play presents a brothel madame, Kitty Warren, with understanding and a degree of sympathy. As Mrs Warren explains to her daughter Vivie, a well-educated and capable *'new woman', she saw her half-sister die of industrial lead poisoning and felt justified in escaping the poverty of her environment by entering the only trade that offered a chance of prosperity: prostitution. Vivie is impressed, but soon afterwards discovers from the amorous Sir George Crofts, her mother's business partner, not only that the young man who wishes to marry her may be her half-brother but that Mrs Warren still runs a chain of 'houses' on the Continent. At the end Vivie, now working as an accountant, rejects Mrs Warren on the grounds that she hypocritically behaves as a respectable person and conventional mother while continuing to exploit needy women. The play is simultaneously a defence of that much-anathematized Victorian character, the 'Woman with a Past', and an attack on a society that mistreats the poor and 'fallen' while tolerating those who profit from their misery, such as Crofts and the now-wealthy Mrs Warren.

Mr Weston's Good Wine, see POWYS, T.F.

MTSHALI, (Mbuyiseni) Oswald (1940–), South African poet, born in Vryheid, Natal, where he attended Inkamana High School. After working in various capacities, he became a columnist with the *Rand Daily Mail* and entered Columbia University, New York, in 1974. On his return to South Africa in 1980 he was appointed Deputy Headmaster of the Pace Commercial College, Jabulani, Soweto. *Sounds of a Cowhide Drum* (1971), his first collection of verse, was highly acclaimed for the understated force of its commentaries on conditions among the black communities. His best work combines documentary qualities with an innate lyricism conveyed by the sensitivity and precision of its imagery. A further collection entitled *Fireflames* (1980), which was banned in South Africa, contained more explicitly political material and poems drawing on his experiences of America. He is the editor of *Give Us a Break* (1988), a compilation of extracts from the diaries of Soweto schoolchildren.

MUDROOROO (formerly known as Colin Johnson, he has also adopted the names Mudrooroo Narogin and later the name Mudrooroo Nyoongah) (1938–), part-Aboriginal Australian novelist, born in Beverley, Western Australia, and brought up in an orphanage. He spent several years from 1965 in India, part of the time as a Buddhist monk. *Wild Cat Falling* (1965), the first published novel by an Aboriginal writer, presented a stark portrait of the problems for Aboriginal people in modern Australian society. The novel *Long Live Sandawara* (1979) followed the failed attempts of a part-Aboriginal youth to organize Aboriginal resistance in Perth. *Doctor Wooreddy's Prescription for Enduring the Ending of the World* (1983) explores the tragic history of race relations in Tasmania. *Doin' Wildcat: A Novel Koori Script* (1988) employed skilful interweaving of original text, film adaptation, and authorial commentary. *Master of the Ghost Dreaming* (1991) concerns two Cockney missionaries and their relationship with an Aborigine who is trying to recreate the spirit of his tribe. *The Kwinkan* (1993) reveals the cancer of political corruption and suspicion in white society via a paranoiac white narrator who believes an Aboriginal conspiracy has sabotaged his career. Johnson's verse collections include *The Song Circle of Jacky and Selected Poems* (1986), *Dulwurra: The Black Bittern. A Poem Cycle* (1988), and *The Garden of Gethsemane* (1991); the sequence showed the effectiveness of traditional concepts and forms in embracing a search for spirit and heritage that is international in scope. A critical work, *Writing from the Fringe: A Study of Modern Aboriginal Literature,* was published in 1990. *Aboriginal Mythology* (1994) is a cultural history.

MUGO, Micere (Githae) (1942–), Kenyan poet, critic, and playwright, born in Baricho in the Kiriyaga District of Kenya; she was educated at Makerere University, Uganda, and at the Canadian universities of New Brunswick and Toronto. Her Ph.D. thesis formed the basis of *Visions of Africa* (1978), her best-known critical work, which considers treatments of Africa in the writings of several women novelists. Having been Dean of the Faculty of Arts at the University of Nairobi, she was exiled for political reasons and became Professor of Literature at the University of Zimbabwe in 1982. Her plays include *The Long Illness of Ex-Chief Kit*, a treatment of political and cultural disunity among the Kenyan people, and *Disillusioned*, dealing with racist hypocrisy in religion, which were published together in 1976. *Daughter of My People, Sing* (1976), the principal collection of her verse, is strongly informed by her Marxist and feminist views in its imaginative articulation of her passionate concern with the future of post-colonial Africa.

MUIR, Edwin (1887–1959), Scottish poet, critic, and translator, born at Deerness in Orkney, educated at Kirkwall Grammar School. In 1901 the family moved to Glasgow, where Muir lost both his parents and two of his brothers in five years and himself experienced physical and mental ill-health. This period of privation informed his work as an imaginative antithesis to the vision of purity of being he strove to manifest in his verse. In 1919 he married Willa Anderson and moved to London to join the staff of the **New Age*; the socialist verse-polemics and Nietzschean aphorisms he had contributed to the periodical since 1913 were published under the pseudonym 'Edward Moore' as *We Moderns: Enigmas and Guesses* (1918). Muir began producing the poetry for which he is remembered between 1921 and 1924, when he and his wife travelled in Europe following his submission to psychoanalysis; their collaboration as translators, which resulted in their well-known versions of many of Kafka's works, also began at this time. *First Poems* (1925) contained numerous pieces reflecting his experiences of Germany, Austria, and Czechoslovakia. His subsequent collections of verse include *Chorus of the Newly Dead* (1926), *Journeys and Places* (1937), *The Labyrinth* (1949), and *One Foot in Eden* (1956); by the mid-1930s he was recognized as a poet whose essentially traditional manner did not compromise the radical originality of his mythopoeic imagination. The increasingly visionary character of his later verse is exemplified by the evocation of spiritual and material renewal in 'The Transfiguration'. After teaching for the British Council in the 1940s, he was warden of the college at Newbattle Abbey near Edinburgh, where he encouraged George Mackay *Brown, and held a visiting professorship at Harvard in 1955–6. His critical works include *The Structure of the Novel* (1928) and *Scott and Scotland* (1936), which estranged him from Hugh *MacDiarmid for its views on the unviability of Scots as a literary language. Among the collections of his essays are *Latitudes* (1924), *Transition* (1926), and *Essays on Literature and Society* (1949). His novels, *The Marionette* (1927), *The Three Brothers* (1931), and *Poor Tom* (1932), are not as highly regarded as the lyrically autobiographical prose of *Scottish Journey* (1935) and *The*

Story and the Fable (1940), the latter revised as *An Autobiography* in 1950. *Collected Poems* (1960) is edited by Willa Muir and J. C. Hall. P. H. Butter's *Edwin Muir: Man and Poet* appeared in 1966.

MUKHERJEE, Bharati (1940–), American novelist and short-story writer, born in Calcutta, educated at the universities of Calcutta, Baroda, and Iowa, where she obtained her doctorate in 1969. She has held many academic appointments including a professorship at the University of California at Berkeley. Of Bengali background herself, Mukherjee's stories and novels, which often employ shock tactics, focus on the experience of immigrants from the Indian sub-continent in America, emphasizing the fractured, disorientated, and insecure nature of their lives. Her third novel, *Jasmine* (1989), chronicles the odyssey of Jasmine Vijh; widowed at 17, she flees her constricted Indian village to emigrate to America, where she eventually marries a middle-aged banker in Iowa, and adopts a Vietnamese refugee, her name metamorphosed into Jane Ripplemeyer. Other novels include *The Tiger's Daughter* (1972) and *Wife* (1975). Together with her husband, Canadian writer Clark Blaise, she also wrote *Days and Nights in Calcutta* (1977), which records their stay there for over a year. *The Middleman and Other Stories* (1988) won the National Book Critics Circle Award. A recent novel, *The Holder of the World* (1993), attempts a feminist reworking of romantic historical formulae, intertwining the stories of two American women: one reaches a position of power in Mogul India; the other, married to an Indian, researches her life several centuries later. See also ASIAN-AMERICAN LITERATURE.

MULDOON, Paul (1951–), Northern Irish poet, born in Co. Armagh, educated at Queen's University, Belfast, where Seamus *Heaney was among his lecturers. He worked as a radio producer with the BBC in Northern Ireland until 1986. After holding a succession of posts as writer-in-residence in Britain and America, he became a lecturer at Princeton University in 1990. His considerable reputation was established by the freshness and stylistic individuality evident in *New Weather* (1973), his first substantial collection of poetry; subsequent volumes include *Mules* (1977), *Why Brownlee Left* (1980), *Quoof* (1983), *Meeting the British* (1987), *Madoc* (1990), *The Annals of Chile* (1994), and *The Prince of Quotidian* (1994). The long title poem of *Madoc*, which conflates real and imagined histories of North America, forms the culmination of his interest in the possibilities of narrative experimentation. An uneasy sense of the tensions between his inherited Irishness and his immediate Ulster background informs much of Muldoon's earlier work. The imaginative deftness and buoyant openness of tone with which he handled such material gained his verse recognition as an innovative extension of *Ulster poetry. *Selected Poems: 1968–1983* appeared in 1986. Muldoon is the editor of *The Faber Book of Contemporary Irish Poetry* (1986). *Shining Brow* (1993) is an opera libretto about Frank Lloyd Wright.

MULGAN, John (1911–45), New Zealand writer, born in Christchurch, educated at Auckland and Oxford universities. Experience of the 1932 Auckland unemployment riots awakened him to a political commitment reflected in his journalism from England during 1936. In 1938 Mulgan edited an anthology, *Poems of Freedom*, to which E. M. *Forster contributed an appreciative preface. His sole work of fiction, *Man Alone* (1939), an outstanding portrait of New Zealand life between the wars traced through the life of an immigrant, reflects Mulgan's experience of European political events during this crucial period. Mulgan took his own life in 1945. The posthumous *Report on Experience* (1947) drew profoundly upon his wartime experiences in Egypt and Greece in commenting on New Zealand and English society and politics during the 1930s, and on Mulgan's shifting responses to his own country.

MULKERNS, Val (1925–), Irish novelist and short-story writer, born in Dublin, educated at the Dominican College, Dublin. She was an associate editor of *The *Bell* from 1952 to 1954, and has worked as a journalist, reviewer, and lecturer. Her first novel, *A Time Outworn* (1952), a simple well-observed story of young love, was followed by *Peacock Cry* (1954), but it was not until the late 1970s that Mulkerns wrote with confidence and distinction. Her collection of connected short stories, *Antiquities* (1978), finally established her reputation as a significant Irish writer; the stories concern the history of a single family through which Mulkerns traces the decay of republicanism into a form of apolitical brutality. Mulkerns's other books include *An Idle Woman* (1980), *The Summerhouse* (1984), *Very Like a Whale* (1986), and *A Friend of Don Juan* (1988).

MUMFORD, Lewis (1895–1990), American cultural critic, born in Flushing, Long Island, New York, educated at Columbia and New York universities. He taught at several colleges and universities. His first work, *The Story of Utopias* (1922), was followed by *Sticks and Stones* (1924), which considered American life through its architecture. His many books have challenged modern life from a perspective deeply rooted in a respect for the individual. Among the subjects of his scathing critiques are the organization of city life and the design of basic implements of living. Such themes are developed in the group of related volumes which extends from *Technics and Civilisation* (1934), through *The Culture of Cities* (1938) and *The City in History* (1961), to the two-volume *The Myth of the Machine* (1967, 1970). Other notable works are *The Condition of Man* (1944), *The Conduct of Life* (1951), and a study of Thomas Jefferson's contribution to American architecture in *The South in Architecture* (1941). Several earlier works were devoted to a study of literature, in which he made a significant contribution to the critical analysis of the role of puritanism in American culture and the establishment of the canon of nineteenth-century literature as we now understand it. These include *The Golden Day* (1926), a book on

New England themes; *Herman Melville* (1929), a psycho-critical biography; and *The Brown Decades* (1931), a study of artistic development from the Civil War until 1895. Other works are *Faith for Living* (1940), *In the Name of Sanity* (1954), and *Transformations of Man* (1956). Mumford's greatest achievement is a study of civilization and world history through the perspective of the development of cities in *The City in History* (1961) and *The Highway and the City* (1963). Later works include *The Urban Prospect* (1968), *Interpretations and Forecasts* (1973), and a series of autobiographical and personal memoirs in *Findings and Keepings—Analects for an Autobiography* (1975), *My Works and Days* (1979), and *Sketches from Life: The Autobiography of Lewis Mumford* (1982).

MUNGOSHI, Charles (Muzava) (1947–), Zimbabwean novelist and short-story writer, born near Enkeldoorn in the Manyene Tribal Trust Land, educated at St Augustine's Secondary School. After working with the Rhodesian Forestry Commission and as a clerk in a book-distribution company, he entered publishing in 1975 and became Literary Director of the Zimbabwe Publishing House in 1981. Mungoshi is the most eminent Zimbabwean author writing in both English and Shona. *Waiting for the Rain* (1975), his only novel in English to date, is widely regarded as the masterpiece of fiction by a Zimbabwean writer; its portrayal of an educated son's alienation from his family powerfully evokes unrest and malaise in the decade before Zimbabwean Independence in 1980. His short stories, which combine a strong element of political protest with their vividly imaginative use of landscape, are collected in *Coming of the Dry Season* (1972), which was banned before Independence, and *Some Kinds of Wounds* (1980); a selection from these books is contained in *The Setting Sun and the Rolling World* (1980). His three novels in the Shona tongue (1970, 1975, 1983), like much of his writing in English, are concerned with the tensions accompanying cultural change.

MUNRO, Alice (1931–), Canadian short-story writer and novelist, born in Wingham in southwestern Ontario, educated at the University of Western Ontario; she subsequently lived in British Columbia before returning to Ontario. Munro has been described as one of the finest living short-story writers and is acclaimed for her ability to dissect the contradictory passions of relationships. Her fictional territory is mainly provincial Ontario, a locale as extensive as *Faulkner's Yoknapatawpha County or *Joyce's Dublin, and the emotional lives of its women, whose expectations and disappointments she unravels in supple prose. Her style appears to be naturalistic, but draws connections between 'ordinary' and 'bizarre' events, suggesting that the everyday and the extraordinary are frequently no more than different aspects of the same phenomenon. Her fiction is also notable for its dramatization of a range of other themes including the ways in which identity is shaped by popular culture, and the importance of fiction-making in day-to-day perceptions and activities. Her works include *Lives of Girls and Women* (1971), a novel; *Who Do You Think You Are?* (1978; UK title *The Beggar Maid*), a collection of linked short stories set in British Columbia which centres on the same protagonist and comes close to being a novel; and *Open Secrets* (1994), stories of which two are set outside Canada (one in Albania and the other in Australia). Further volumes of stories include *Dance of the Happy Shades* (1968), *Something I've Been Meaning to Tell You* (1974), *The Moons of Jupiter* (1982), *The Progress of Love* (1987), and *Friend of My Youth* (1990).

Murder in the Cathedral, the first of T. S. *Eliot's major verse-dramas, published in 1935; it deals with the martyrdom of Thomas Becket and was first performed in 1935 in the Chapter House of Canterbury Cathedral, close to the site of Becket's death, after which it ran successfully in London and on tour. The work resulted from a suggestion by the Bishop of Chichester, who had been favourably impressed by Eliot's ecclesiastical pageant *The Rock* (1934), that he should write a play for the Canterbury Festival. Its first part establishes the conflicts between Church and State which determine Becket's martyrdom; by overcoming the Four Tempters, who respectively offer pleasure, political power, treason, and spiritual pride, he accepts that his death will accord purely with God's purposes. In the second part, Becket is murdered by the Four Knights, whose subsequent prose speeches argue for 'a just subordination of the pretensions of the Church to the welfare of the State' and conclude that Becket, 'a monster of egotism', effectively engineered his own death. The play ends with a prayer of praise and supplication by the Chorus of Women of Canterbury, whose commentaries throughout are the medium for Eliot's richest poetic effects. It is arguably his most theatrically effective play, Becket's murder providing a central action which his later dramas lack. E. Martin Browne, who collaborated on the play's production and later wrote *The Making of T. S. Eliot's Plays* (1966), recommended the excision of certain passages, one of which beginning 'Time present and time past . . .' opens 'Burnt Norton', the first of the **Four Quartets*.

MURDOCH, Dame Iris (Jean) (1919–), British novelist and philosopher, born in Dublin of Anglo-Irish parents, educated at Badminton School, at Somerville College, Oxford and later at Newnham College, Cambridge. She became a Fellow of St Anne's College, Oxford, and a lecturer in philosophy. From her first novel, *Under the Net* (1954), Murdoch has followed a highly productive career as a novelist. Although filled with incident and vivid detail, her novels often seem like dramatized philosophical debates on the nature of good and evil, on the conflict between rationality and sexuality, and on free will and determinism. Many of her books have a dream-like quality, heightened by her frequently elaborate use of symbolism. Their settings are usually contemporary, although the prevailing impression is one of timelessness. Her characters, almost always drawn from the intelligentsia or from literary, artistic, and theatrical circles, are often memorably eccentric. Perhaps because of their combination of narrative exuberance and philosophical seriousness, her novels have resisted categorization. *The Sandcastle* (1957) involves a relationship between a schoolmaster and a young artist; *The Bell* (1958) concerns the extraordinary events in a lay community surrounding the consecration of a new bell; *A Severed Head* (1961; dramatized in 1963 by J. B. *Priestley) is a blackly comic farce about infidelity; *The Black Prince* (1973; dramatized by the author) focuses on a middle-aged writer suffering from a 'block'; *The Sea, The Sea* (1978; Booker Prize) describes the obsessional love of the narrator for his childhood sweetheart; *The Good Apprentice* (1985) has a fairytale quality and deals with the themes of disintegration and reconciliation; *The Book and the Brotherhood* (1987) concerns the moral and ideological dilemmas confronting a group of Oxford intellectuals; and *The Message to the Planet* (1989), her twenty-fifth novel, focuses on a magus-like figure, as do many of her works, and displays the author's fascination with the inhuman power of the exceptional individual, whose effect on the lives of others is seldom benign and frequently catastrophic. In *The Green Knight* (1993), a fictionalized philosophical dialogue, a man who has accidentally been killed 'returns', demanding restitution and retribution of his assailant in an echo of the medieval tale. Despite their preoccupation with the macabre and with extremes of human behaviour—suicide, incest, jealousy, and attempted murder all feature in her books—their overall mood is comic, rather than tragic, displaying an amused tolerance towards the absurdities of sexual relationships as well as a profound humanism. Her many other novels include *The Flight from the Enchanter* (1955), *An Unofficial Rose* (1962), *The Unicorn* (1963), *The Italian Girl* (1964), *The Red and the Green* (1965), *The Time of Angels* (1966), *The Nice and the Good* (1968), *Bruno's Dream* (1969), *A Fairly Honourable Defeat* (1970), *An Accidental Man* (1971), *The Sacred and Profane Love Machine* (1974), *A Word Child* (1975), *Henry and Cato* (1976), *Nuns and Soldiers* (1980), *The Philosopher's Pupil* (1983), and *Jackson's Dilemma* (1995). Amongst her philosophical works are *Sartre: Romantic Rationalist* (1953), *The Sovereignty of Good* (1970), *The Fire and the Sun: Why Plato Banned the Artists* (1977), *Acastos: Two Platonic Dialogues* (1986), and *Metaphysics as a Guide to Morals* (1992). She has also written several plays and published a volume of poetry, *A Year of the Birds* (1978). In 1956 she married the literary critic John Bayley, and became a DBE in 1987.

MURNANE, Gerald (1939–), Australian writer, born in Melbourne. The rural landscape of Victoria is evoked in several of his novels. *Tamarisk Row* (1974) concerns a father who attempts to win a fortune with his racehorse while his son retreats into a world of fantasy; in subsequent novels escapism becomes a compulsive search for inner fulfilment. A strong sense of landscape pervades Murnane's work, notably in *A Lifetime on Clouds* (1976) where a youth travels the landscapes of America but dreams of a past Australia. *The Plains* (1982), narrated by a film-maker, concerns the inner worlds of the nameless inhabitants of a fertile area of central Australia. *Inland* (1988) continues the use of imaginary worlds. *Landscape with Landscape* (1985) is a series of six stories, and *Velvet Waters* (1990) is a collection of short stories offering an oblique commentary on Australia's cultural past and present. His most recent fiction includes *Emerald Blue* (1995).

MURPHY, Dervla (Dervilla Maria) (1931–), Irish travel writer, born at Cappoquin, Co. Waterford, Ireland; she was educated at the Ursuline Convent, Waterford, until the age of 14, when she began nursing her invalid mother. Following her mother's death, she cycled to India, where she worked with Tibetan refugees; her experiences are recorded in *Full Tilt: Ireland to India by Bicycle* (1965) and *Tibetan Foothold* (1966), which established her reputation as an energetically original travel writer. Her subsequent works, the majority of which describe journeys to remote regions made with her daughter, who was five years old when she became Murphy's fellow traveller, include *Where the Indus Is Young* (1977), *Eight Feet in the Andes* (1983), *Muddling Through in Madagascar* (1985), and *Cameroon with Egbert* (1989). The humane concern with conditions of existence among the peoples she encounters informs her accounts of deprived areas of Birmingham and Bradford in *Tales from Two Cities* (1987). Among her other works are *Race to the Finish* (1981), a survey of issues relating to nuclear weapons, and the autobiography *Wheels Within Wheels* (1979). Recent travel works include *Transylvania and Beyond* (1992) and *The Ukimwi Road: From Kenya to Zimbabwe* (1993).

MURPHY, Richard (1927–), Irish poet, born in Co. Galway; he spent much of his childhood in Sri Lanka, where his father was the last British mayor of Colombo. He was educated at Magdalen College, Oxford, and the Sorbonne. He was skipper of the fishing boat described in his poem 'The Last Galway Hooker' from 1960 to 1967, after which he held a succession of visiting posts at American universities. His collections of poetry include *Sailing to an Island* (1963), *The Battle of Aughrim* (1968), *High Island* (1974), *The Price of Stone* (1985), and *New Selected Poems* (1989). Much of his best poetry is in the form of extended sequences through which he pursues his concern with personal and cultural identity. A productive tension exists in his work between his sense of his Protestant Ascendancy background and a broader Irish cultural heritage. The persistence of history in the landscapes of his verse is richly suggested by his keenly observed imagery of artefacts and natural features. Murphy's accomplishment in traditional forms is suited to his urbane levelness of tone. Freer verse is used in *The Mirror Wall* (1989), which contains his versions of ancient Sri Lankan poems. He edited *The Mayo Anthology* (1990), stories and poems about County Mayo.

MURPHY, Tom (1935–), Irish playwright, born in Tuam, Co. Galway, educated at the Vocational Teachers' Training College, Dublin. He taught at a local vocational school from 1957 until 1962, when he moved to London and became a full-time writer. His first play, *A Whistle in the Dark,* having been rejected by the *Abbey in 1960, was produced at the Theatre Royal in 1961. Kenneth *Tynan described it as 'the most uninhibited display of brutality that the London theatre has ever witnessed'. The play portrays the destruction of an Irishman living in Coventry during the 1950s, dramatizing the conflict between his bitter sense of displacement and his father's romantic illusions of identity and 'home'. *Famine* (1968) concerns a community facing its own decimation and the real, historical destruction of its identity. *A Crucial Week in the Life of a Grocer's Assistant* (1969) goes to the heart of Murphy's experience of stagnant rural existence. The experimental and disturbing *The Morning after Optimism* (1971) is a fantasy which presents an ageing whore and her pimp who meet their idealized alter egos in a magical forest, and murder them. Murphy was a director on the board of the Abbey from 1973 until 1983. *The Sanctuary Lamp* (1975) concerns three fighting down-and-out circus performers who spend the night in a church recounting their personal histories; *The Blue Macushla* (1980) is an unsuccessful attempt at tackling an overtly political theme. *The Gigli Concert* (1983) is a demanding play which portrays the breakdown of a millionaire builder, who has fulfilled his dreams of success but finds he cannot go on: not only has God deserted him, he has deserted himself. He pursues the healing order of music, developing a mad desire to sing like Gigli. *Conversations from a Homecoming* and *Bailegangaire* (Town-without-Laughter), produced in 1985, continue Murphy's concern with contemporary Ireland's loss of identity. His plays have been published individually and in collections, such as *After Tragedy: Three Irish Plays* (1988), *A Whistle in the Dark and Other Plays* (1989), *Plays: One* (1992), *Plays: Two* (1993), and *Plays: Three* (1994). His first novel, *The Seduction of Morality* (1994), is rich in digressions of rural story-telling tradition, and highly comic in its portrayal of female rivalries and family conflict over an inheritance.

MURRAY, Sir James A(ugustus) H(enry) (1837–1915), British lexicographer and philologist, born at Denholm, Roxburghshire, and educated in local schools. After a period as a schoolmaster, he moved to London in 1864. He worked for the Chartered Bank of India until 1870, when he took a teaching post at Mill Hill School. Having joined the London Philological Society, he became a respected associate of those involved in compiling the Society's *New English Dictionary*, out of which developed *The Oxford English Dictionary*. His earlier publications as a philologist include *The Dialect of the Southern Counties of Scotland* (1873). In 1879 the Clarendon Press at Oxford contracted to publish the *New English Dictionary* and appointed Murray as editor. He moved to Oxford in 1885. Although he estimated in 1884, when 'A–Ant' was published as the first part, that it might be completed by 1896, it was not until 1928 that C. T. *Onions and William *Craigie finally finished the main text. In terms of the methodology he developed, *The Oxford English Dictionary* is largely Murray's creation; as the 'Historical Introduction' to the *OED* states, 'to Murray belongs the credit for giving it, at the outset, a form which proved to be adequate to the end'. *Caught in the Web of Words* (1977) is a biography by his granddaughter, K. M. E. Murray. He was knighted in 1908.

MURRAY, Les (1938–), Australian poet, born at Nabiac, New South Wales, educated at Sydney University. Murray worked as a translator before becoming an influential critic, reviewer, and poet. His challenging view on the importance of the land in the mythology of Australians, both indigenous and settler, is expressed in the essay 'The Human Hair Thread' (first published 1977) in his critical collection *Persistence in Folly* (1984). Murray's first collection, *The Ilex Tree* (1965, with Geoffrey Lehmann), established his distinctive concerns: the shaping rituals of the everyday, and a powerful and almost instinctive empathy for the quiddities of rural life and labour. His belief in the necessity, and possibility, of 'cultural convergence' between settler Australian and Aboriginal values posits themes of great import for contemporary Australian society, themes extended with impressive poetic versatility in subsequent collections: *The Weatherboard Cathedral* (1969), *Poems against Economics* (1972), and *Ethnic Radio* (1977). Murray's stature and versatility is demonstrated in *The Vernacular Republic: Poems 1961–1981* (1982; revised and enlarged 1988) and *Selected Poems* (1987). *The Peasant Mandarin* (1978) and *Blocks and Tackles: Articles and Essays 1982–1990* (1990) collected stimulating prose writings; *The Paperbark Tree: Selected Prose* appeared in 1993. *The Boys Who Stole the Funeral: A Novel Sequence* (1980) unusually employed a sequence of 140 sonnets to narrative effect. Other works include *The Daylight Moon* (1988), *The Dog Fox Field* (1990), and *Translations from the Natural World* (1992). His *Collected Poems* were published in 1991. Murray has also edited the *New Oxford Book of Australian Verse* (1986) and an *Anthology of Religious Poetry* (1987).

MURRAY, (Anna) Pauli(ne) (1910–85), African-American author and lawyer, born in Baltimore; she worked as a schoolteacher before studying law at Howard University and the University of California, Berkeley. Active in the causes of racial equality and women's rights, in 1946 she became the first black woman to hold the office of Deputy Attorney of California and was admitted to the bar of the Supreme Court of the United States in 1966. She was also the first black American woman to be ordained as an Episcopalian priest. As a writer she is best known for her autobiographies *Proud Shoes* (1956; revised edition 1978) and *Song in a Weary Throat* (1987), which form a moving and spirited record of social and cultural developments among America's black population in the twentieth century. *Dark Testament* (1970) is a collection of poems reflecting on her personal and professional experiences. Murray also published numerous works of jurisprudence, which include *Human Rights U.S.A., 1948–1966* (1967), and, with Leslie Rubin, drafted *The Constitution and Government of Ghana* (1961).

MURRAY, T(homas) C(ornelius) (1873–1959), Irish playwright, born in Co. Cork, educated at St Patrick's Teacher Training College, Dublin, where he also taught. Murray became a leading writer with the *Abbey Theatre Company. His first play, *Wheel of Fortune* (1909), a comedy, was produced at the Cork Little Theatre which Murray had founded with Con O'Leary, Terence MacSwiney, and Daniel *Corkery. His plays *Birthright* (1910), *Maurice Harte* (1912), and *Spring* (1918) reflect rural Ireland's fear of disinheritance, poverty, and social disgrace. Murray's work, set in rural Cork, is realistic and concentrates upon the frustration caused by social and religious pressures. For the characters in plays such as *Aftermath* (1922), *Autumn Fire* (1924), and *Michaelmas Eve* (1932) there appears to be no choice but to conform to these pressures, a potent symbol of which are incompatible but 'necessary' marriages between young women and older men with money. Murray's intense religiosity is reflected in the dark and fatalistic tone of his plays.

MURRY, John Middleton (1889–1957), British critic and editor, born at Peckham in London, educated at Brasenose College, Oxford, where he founded the magazine *Rhythm*; his insistence as editor on the direct relationship between art and society established the central emphasis of his career. Through the magazine he met Katherine *Mansfield, whom he married in 1918, and D. H. *Lawrence, with whom he sustained a troubled but intense friendship; *Son of Woman* (1931) is his tribute to Lawrence. *Fyodor Dostoevsky* (1917) was the first of his many critical studies. He edited the **Athenaeum* from 1919 to 1921. *The Problem of Style* (1922) established him as a critic of note. He remained dedicated to Mansfield's memory after her death in 1923 and edited a succession of her works. From 1923 to 1930 he was editor of the **Adelphi*. *Keats and Shakespeare* (1925) confirmed him as an astute and provocative critic, while *To the Unknown God* (1924) and *The Life of Jesus* (1925) indicated the increasingly religious tenor of his thought. His Marxist tendencies throughout the 1930s are clear from *The Fallacy of Economics* (1932) and *The Necessity of Communism* (1932). *The Pledge for Peace* (1938) followed his conversion to pacifism in 1936; during the Second World War he lived in a pacifist agrarian commune and edited *Peace News*. His later works include *Jonathan Swift* (1954) and *Love, Freedom, and Society* (1957), a comparative study of Lawrence and Albert Schweitzer. *Between Two Worlds* (1935) is an autobiography of his earlier life. F. A. Lea's *Life of John Middleton Murry* (1959) and *Beloved Quixote* (1986) by his daughter Katherine Middleton Murry are the principal biographical studies.

MWANGI, (David) Meja (1948–), Kenyan novelist, born in Nanyuki, Kenya, educated at Kenyatta College. His novels, which focus on Kenyan social problems, are brisk, sometimes humorous, and written in a meticulously realist style. *Carcase for Hounds* (1974) and *Taste of Death* (1975) deal with the anti-colonial Mau Mau insurgency of the 1950s; they are distinguished by emphasis on the 'impersonal mechanism', as he put it, of guerrilla warfare. *Carcase for Hounds* formed the basis of a film, *Cry Freedom* (1981). Urban squalor is explored in *Kill Me Quick* (1973), which charts the descent into petty thievery of two desperate young men; *Going Down River Road* (1976) exposes low-life in Nairobi. *The Cockroach Dance* (1979), set in an opulent housing estate, highlights an impoverished meter reader's slow-burning, but inexorable, fuse of rebellion. A thriller, *The Bushtrackers* (1979), examines such evils as big-game poaching, gun-running, and protection rackets. Other novels include *Bread of Sorrow* (1987), another socially concerned thriller; *Weapon of Hunger* (1989); *The Return of Shaka* (1989), set in the USA; and *Striving for the Wind* (1990), which treats the despair of small farmers in contemporary rural Kenya.

My Antonia, a novel by Willa *Cather, published in 1918. It is the author's most popular novel, which has been studied by generations of young Americans for its lyrical appreciation of pioneer life. The novel is related by Jim Burden, who looks back on his early years in Nebraska, seeing Antonia Shimerda as a symbol of them and what was significant about them. Antonia's father was tricked into buying poor land which, dreamy and devoted to music as he is, he cannot work. Despite the help he receives from Jim's family he gives in to despair, eventually committing suicide. Antonia, herself only an adolescent, finds work as a domestic help, yet retains her dignity in the face of this and other assaults on her pride. Jim, who ends up going to college and later to Harvard, hears of her subsequent elopement with a man who deserts her and their child and of her eventual return, in disgrace, to work on her brother's farm. But, in spite of these setbacks, it is a fulfilled married woman he meets twenty years on, who embodies the strongest and most life-enhancing virtues of her 'race'. The novel is in the pastoral mode of **O, Pioneers* (1913) but its art is more refined; indeed, despite the robustness of its characters and the life they lead, the book is characterized by a singular delicacy.

My Beautiful Laundrette, see KUREISHI, HANIF.

My Brilliant Career, see FRANKLIN, MILES.

MYERS, L(eo) H(amilton) (1881–1944), British novelist, son of the poet and psychical researcher F. W. H. Myers (1843–1901), born in Cambridge, educated at Eton and at Trinity College, Cambridge. A private income enabled him to occupy himself solely with writing, with the exception of a period during the First World War when he worked as a clerk in the Board of Trade. *Arvat* (1908), a verse-drama, was his first publication. *The Orissers* (1922), his first novel, establishes the conflict between spiritually affirmative and trivially materialistic attitudes to life as the sustaining theme of his subsequent work. The tetralogy forming his major achievement, *The Near and the Far* (1929), *Prince Jali* (1931), *The Root and the Flower* (1935), and *The Pool of Vishnu* (1940), is set in sixteenth-century India at the court of the Mogul emperor Akbar. Published in one volume as *The Near and the Far* in 1943, the books use their exotically idealized setting to project a profoundly imaginative treatment of modern spiritual impoverishment. The work contains Myers's satire on the *Bloomsbury Group in its portrayal of the self-important aesthetes who congregate in 'The Pleasance of the Arts'. His other novels are *The Clio* (1925), in which the aristocratic protagonists are estranged from their complacency on an Amazonian yachting adventure, and *Strange Glory* (1936), which sets its analysis of social and cultural values in the Louisiana swamps. Myers's espousal of communism as a possible route to the spiritually integrated society he sought to define is clearest in *The Pool of Vishnu* and *Strange Glory*. After suffering intermittently from severe depression, he committed suicide in 1944.

MYLES NA GOPALEEN, see O BRIEN, FLANN.

Myra Breckenridge, see VIDAL, GORE.

MYRDAL, Gunnar (1898–1987), Swedish economist, born in Gustafs, Sweden, recipient of the Nobel Prize for Economics (1974), and Swedish parliamentarian. As a young economist, Myrdal was a leading member of the so-called Stockholm School of Economics (which included Erik Lindahl and Dag Hammarskjöld, later Secretary-General of the United Nations), and which is sometimes seen as having anticipated certain of *Keynes's ideas. His theoretical book, *Monetary Equilibrium* (1939, originally published in Swedish in 1931), is one of the classics produced by that group. Turning his attention to broader social analysis, Myrdal published *An American Dilemma* (1944, 2 volumes), an insightful but controversial indictment of race relations in the USA (the outcome of a four-year project undertaken in that country). After serving on the United Nations Economic Commission for Europe, in 1958 he embarked upon a decade of study of the problem of underdevelopment and poverty in the Third World. This led to the publication of *Asian Drama* (1968, 3 volumes), which remains the most systematic study of the tensions between the Western ideals of modernization and those of indigenous culture and society. He also published *The Political Element in the Development of Economic Thought* (1953, originally published in German in 1932).

My Son's Story, see GORDIMER, NADINE.

N

NABOKOV, Vladimir (1899–1977), American novelist, born in St Petersburg, educated at Trinity College, Cambridge. Nabokov enjoyed a privileged childhood, interrupted by the Russian Revolution when his father, who had been a leading member of the Russian Constituent Assembly, evacuated the family south to Yalta to avoid the Red Army. In 1919 Nabokov left Russia, never to return. In 1922 he rejoined his family in Berlin for a short-lived reunion; later in that year his father was assassinated by a Russian monarchist gunman. Nabokov's earliest writings predate the revolution: *Stikhi* (*Poems*) was privately published in 1916, but his more mature writings are a product of his Berlin years: his early plays such as *Smert* (*Death*) and *Polyus* appeared in *Rul* (*The Rudder*) magazine in 1923 and 1924, and his first novel, *Mashenka*, was published in Berlin in 1926 (translated by the author and Michael Glenny as *Mary* in 1970). Despite his sojourn in Germany, Nabokov continued to write in Russian, using the pseudonym V. Sirin for novels including *Korol, Dama, Valet* (*King, Queen, Knave*, 1928), *Zashchita Luzhina* (*The Defense*, 1930), *Kamera Obskura* (*Camera Obscura*, also known as *Laughter in the Dark*, 1932), and *Otchayanie* (*Despair*, 1936). In 1937 Nabokov moved his family to Paris where *Dar* (translated as *The *Gift*, 1963) appeared in an incomplete version in 1936 and *Priglashenie na Kazn* (translated by the author and Dimitri Nabokov as *Invitation to a Beheading*) in 1938. In Paris Nabokov wrote his first novel in English, *The Real Life of Sebastian Knight* (1941). In 1940 he moved to the USA where he held academic posts at Stanford University, and later at Wellesley College in Massachusetts; throughout this period he was also a part-time research fellow at the Museum of Comparative Zoology at Harvard where he pursued his passion for lepidoptery. Having taken US citizenship in 1945 Nabokov was now, in effect, an American writer and *Bend Sinister* (1947), despite its European setting, was, like the subsequent major fiction, written in English. In 1948 Nabokov took up a position in Comparative Literature at Cornell University in Ithaca, New York, and rose to become a professor. At Cornell he wrote **Lolita* (1955), his best-known novel. Much criticism of Nabokov has sought to understand the significance of his early Russian writings in relation to the later works, particularly with regard to the themes and devices they share. Both *Pnin* (1957) and **Pale Fire* (1962) seek to assimilate Russian experience to that of the USA. The American writings, in particular, have been appropriated by the critics of *post-modernism and Nabokov is now commonly discussed alongside other American 'anti-realists' such as Robert *Coover, John *Hawkes, and Thomas *Pynchon (whom he taught at Cornell) who make much use of the techniques of fractured chronology, collage effects, unreliable narrators, and varieties of sexual degradation. But Nabokov was also influenced by European modernism and writers such as Franz Kafka and Thomas Mann, and by the nineteenth-century 'romantic realists', in particular Nikolai Gogol, of whom he wrote a valuable critical study, *Nikolai Gogol* (1944). Nabokov's last three novels were **Ada or Ardor: A Family Chronicle* (1969), *Transparent Things* (1972), and *Look at the Harlequins!* (1974); at his death, however, he left an incomplete manuscript for *Original of Laura*, which his only son, Dimitri, claims would have been his most brilliant novel. In addition he wrote one of the great volumes of twentieth-century autobiography, *Speak, Memory* (1966), parts of which had earlier appeared as *Conclusive Evidence* (1951), and several works of translation and criticism, the most important of which are his translations of *The Song of Igor's Campaign* (1960) and Pushkin's *Eugene Onegin* (1964). Julian Moynahan's *Vladimir Nabokov* (1971) and Tony Sharpe's *Vladimir Nabokov* (1991) are short introductions to his work; *Vladimir Nabokov: The Russian Years* (1990), and *Vladimir Nabokov: The American Years* (1991) is a two-volume biography by Brian Boyd.

NAGEL, Thomas (1937–), American philosopher, born in Belgrade, Yugoslavia; from 1939 onward he lived in the USA, of which he became a naturalized citizen in 1944. After studying at Cornell and Oxford, he obtained his Ph.D. at Harvard in 1963, when he became an assistant professor at the University of California, Berkeley. He subsequently held a succession of posts at Princeton University before becoming Professor of Philosophy at New York University in 1980. *Mortal Questions* (1979) gained wide notice for its examination of a number of the central themes of human existence, including death, sexuality, and socio-political issues. Nagel's quest for 'a philosophical method that aims at personal as well as theoretical understanding' was fulfilled by the book's success in combining analytical rigour with a breadth of appeal to common experience. The humane orientation of his work was sustained in *The View from Nowhere* (1986), a compellingly lucid analysis of the tensions between the subjective and objective aspects of intellection and identity; the quasi-instinctual desire to achieve objectivity is seen as fundamental to the central preoccupations of philosophy in the course of the wide-ranging development towards a concluding treatment of major ethical problems. Nagel's engagement of experientially urgent matters which have been obscured in the highly technical writings of many philosophers prompted Charles Taylor to recommend the book to 'all . . . who are bored with or in despair about philosophy'. Other works by Nagel include *What Does It All Mean* (1987), a stimulating survey of nine essential topics for beginners in philosophy, and *Equality and Partiality* (1991), in which he discusses questions of justice.

NAHAL, Chaman (1927–), Indian novelist, born in Sialkot, formerly in India and now in Pakistan, educated at the University of Delhi and the University of Nottingham. Since 1949 he has taught in a succession of universities in India; he became Professor of English at the University of Delhi in 1980. *My True Faces* (1973), his first novel, was followed in 1975 by *Azadi*, a compelling narrative of the divisive effects of Partition in 1947, which is widely regarded as his finest work. A trilogy, *The Crown and the Loincloth* (1981), *The Salt of Life* (1990), and *The Triumph of the Tricolour* (1993), sustains his engagement with the modern history of India through their psychologically penetrating treatments of Gandhi and his career. His other novels, which are noted for the realism with which they present the Indian middle classes, include *Into Another Dawn* (1977), a love story largely set in America, and *The English Queens* (1979), a highly imaginative satire of India's English-speaking élite. Among his numerous critical studies is *D. H. Lawrence: An Eastern View* (1971).

NAIPAUL, Shiva(dhar) (Srinivasa) (1945–85), Trinidadian novelist, born in Port of Spain, educated at Queen's Royal College, Trinidad, and at University College, Oxford. His first two novels, *Fireflies* (1970) and *The Chip-Chip Gathers* (1973), focus on wealthy Indian families, particularly the women, and the inexorable disintegration of their Hindu culture in modern Trinidad. In his autobiographical essay 'Beyond the Dragon's Mouth', Naipaul describes this process at work in his own family: 'The clannish, hierarchical Hindu past known to the older members of my family (a gap of nearly twenty-five years separates my eldest and youngest sisters) had all but dissolved by my day, been split up into its various, often warring, fragments, each of which rigorously pursued its own interests.' While these early novels balance comedy and elegiac feeling, *A Hot Country* (1983) is much bleaker in its despairing vision of post-colonial politics, as suggested by its US title, *Death in a Hot Country* (1984). His other books include: *North of South* (1978), an acerbic travelogue about Africa; *Black and White* (1980), reportage on the mass suicides of religious fanatics in Jonestown, Guyana; and *Beyond the Dragon's Mouth* (1984), which contains short stories and autobiographical pieces. He was the younger brother of V. S. *Naipaul, and his last book, *An Unfinished Journey* (1986), which contains more autobiography and reportage, includes 'My Brother and I', as well as one of his most devastating diatribes, 'The Illusion of the Third World'.

NAIPAUL, V(idiadhar) S(urajprasad) (1932–), Trinidadian novelist and travel writer, born in Trinidad, educated at Queen's Royal College, Trinidad, and at University College, Oxford. After graduation, Naipaul remained in England where he became known as a witty and satirical novelist through such works as *The Mystic Masseur* (1957), a story of religious and political charlatanism: *The Suffrage of Elvira* (1958), an account of electioneering trickery and fraudulence; and *Miguel Street* (1959), fictional sketches that expose absurdities of life in colonial Trinidad. A longer novel, *A *House for Mr Biswas* (1961), won Naipaul acclaim both for its study of colonial displacement and disorder, and for its insight into twentieth-century alienation. Other works, such as *The Mimic Men* (1967) and *In a Free State* (1971; Booker Prize), confirmed Naipaul's reputation as a major novelist. But while his reputation rose in Europe and the USA, Naipaul became increasingly vilified in the Caribbean and Third World countries for his unflattering portraits of colonial disorder and despair, both in his fiction as well as in such non-fictional works as *The Middle Passage* (1962), in which the assertion that 'nothing was ever created in the West Indies' achieved wide notoriety. *An Area of Darkness* (1964) and *India: A Wounded Civilisation* (1977) are travel books considered hostile to India, but in his third book on the country, *India: A Million Mutinies Now* (1990), his tone is more mellow, allowing Indians wide scope to speak for themselves. Some of his other notable works include *Guerillas* (1975), a bleak novel which culminates in a squalid 'revolutionary' murder; *A *Bend in the River* (1979), where he echoes *Conrad with regard to modern Africa: and *Enigma of Arrival* (1987), set in the English countryside, obliquely autobiographical, and his most introspective novel. *A Way in the World* (1994) is a novel composed of nine interlinked sections which draw together, in many voices, narratives of personal experience, aspects of history, and socio-political factors. It combines Naipaul's imaginary and documentary approaches, unified by the theme of Trinidad and its place in the Caribbean. *The Overcrowded Barracoon* (1972) and *The Return of Eva Peron* (1980) are collections of essays and articles. He has received numerous awards, including the Trinity Cross, Trinidad's highest award, and a knighthood in Britain. Even those who do not admire the views and attitudes in Naipaul's writing admire its technical distinction, lucid analysis, and freedom from cant and hypocrisy. It is the unsparing honesty of his writing that is regarded as harshness and hostility in some quarters. Yet Naipaul's study of Caribbean homelessness and insecurity is consistent and authentic, and is increasingly accepted as a perceptive examination of the central preoccupations of our time.

Naked and the Dead, The, a novel by Norman *Mailer, published in 1948. It is a realistic and naturalistic pseudo-historical narrative about the lives of some soldiers who survive the battle for the Japanese-held island, Anopopei, in the Pacific during the Second World War. General Cummings leads the invasion to attack the garrison of General Tayaku, a battle which takes on symbolic significance in the eyes of the American soldiers. However, through the series of portraits, it becomes evident that the battles with most at stake are principally those within the self: in the locking of wills between Red Vaslen and Sergeant Croft; in Goldstein's defence of his Jewish integrity against the rest of the platoon's anti-semitism; in the psychic struggle of mind and personality between the proto-fascist General Cummings and his liberal Lieutenant Hearn; between Hearn and Croft for the effective leadership of the platoon while climbing Mount Anaka, the geographical and symbolic centre of Anopopei. The soldiers are represented as deprived and twisted by the disintegrative and totalitarian forces and counterforces of the world, the forces which caused the war they are fighting. Whilst it is a war novel, Mailer has described it as expressive of 'death and man's creative urge—all kinds of things you never dream of separating and stating so baldly'.

Naked Lunch, The, a novel by William *Burroughs, published in 1959; subsequently republished in 1962 as *Naked Lunch*. Burroughs explained in an interview that much of his novel, in form both hallucinatory and disorganized, was written under the influence of specific drugs, particularly cannabis. The novel has no plot and makes few concessions to social or psychological realism, though many of its evocations of a world dominated by drugs, perverted forms of sexuality, and death are powerfully realized and deeply disturbing. 'The Sickness' to which Burroughs refers in his introduction is, locally, that of drug addiction, but, as critics have suggested, this sickness is also one of the soul and of society in general, so much so that Burroughs's response to what we might call the 'real world' is frequently apocalyptic and atavistic. *Naked Lunch* is a major text of the '*Beat Movement' and is often discussed in the context of other 'Beat' writings, notably those of Allen *Ginsberg and Jack *Kerouac. See *Contemporary Literary Censorship: The Case History of Burroughs' 'Naked Lunch'* (1981), by Michael B. Goodman.

NAMIER, Sir Lewis (Bernstein) (1888–1960), British historian, born near Warsaw, educated at the London School of Economics and Balliol College, Oxford. He became a British subject in 1913 and was variously engaged in business activities, historical research, and work on behalf of the Zionist movement before his appointment as Professor of Modern History at Manchester University in 1931. His reputation as a political historian of originality and distinction was established by *The Structure of British Politics at the Accession of George III* (1929) and *England in the Age of the American Revolution* (1930), which displayed his characteristic attention to minute detail. Having undergone psychoanalysis in Vienna in the early 1920s, he applied Freudian principles to his work, seeking to disclose the motives underlying the rational appearances of policies and decisions. Collections of his articles and reviews include *Personalities and Powers* (1955) and *Vanished Supremacies* (1958). Among his other works are *Diplomatic Prelude* (1948), on the background to the Second World War, and the three volumes of *The History of Parliament: The House of Commons, 1745–1790* (with John Brooke, 1964). Linda Colley's *Namier* appeared in 1989.

Napoleon of Notting Hill, The, see CHESTERTON, G. K.

NARAYAN, R(asipuram) K(rishnaswami) (1906–), Indian novelist and short-story writer, born in Madras, educated mostly in Mysore. He worked as a teacher and as a journalist before the publication of his first novel, *Swami and Friends* (1935). This evocation of a South Indian middle-class childhood attracted the attention of Graham *Greene, who recommended it for publication in Britain. A number of novels followed, all set in the imaginary town of Malgudi, a microcosmic representation of India. Some of his early novels, including *The Bachelor of Arts* (1937), *The English Teacher* (1945), *Mr Sampat* (1949), and *The Financial Expert* (1952), draw heavily on his own life's experiences, including the tragic early death of his wife, on the struggle for independence with its Gandhian ideology and inspiration, and on Mysore where Narayan has lived most of his life. These works signal the evolution of his distinctive vision, with its blend of comedy and tragedy, conservatism and irony, mythical analogies and social satire. Central to this vision is the unending struggle between the creative, self-willed, and iconoclastic Narayan heroine (or anti-heroine) and the forces of society, embodied in the phlegmatic or feckless males she encounters, and the patriarchs, who represent order, conservative tradition, and the unchanging values of a once-stable hierarchical India. In *The Guide* (1958), the passionate encounter of the eponymous narrator with the talented tormented dancer Rosie leads to prison, despair, and loss of love and roots. In *The Vendor of Sweets* (1967) and *The Painter of Signs* (1976) social changes are figured as encounters between men devoid of the certainties of tradition, and women committed to the destruction of ancient, repressive mores. These women, with their outlandish names, are all outsiders: family-planning experts, professionals who refuse to submit to socially determined roles and expectations, or simply foreigners who, while struggling to assimilate the rules of their husbands' milieu, similarly import new ways antithetical to the pious sensibilities of the preceding generation. Narayan is possibly the Indian novelist best known and loved abroad, though in his native country his influence has been largely disclaimed by his younger contemporaries, who accuse him of tailoring his fictions to suit the West's increasing appetite for exotic colours and quaintness. Critics in the West, while noting an attenuation of creative energy in his later fiction, *Talkative Man* (1985) and *The World of Nagaraj* (1990), continue to compare his work to that of Chekhov and Katherine *Mansfield, and to praise his elevation of the local and particular to the universal in his portrayal of Malgudi and its archetypal inhabitants. His collection of short stories, *Malgudi Days* (1982), is set against the backdrop of a semi-imaginary city in South India and portrays characters from every walk of urban Indian life, usually in the throes of some crisis that will transform their destinies or lead to a moment of enhanced perception. This, and short stories, collected in volumes such as *An Astrologer's Day and Other Stories* (1947), *Lawley Road* (1956), and *A Horse and Two Goats* (1970), together with the novellas in *The Grandmother's Tale* (1993), display similarities of theme and characterization with his novels. *My Days* (1975) is an autobiography.

NAROGIN MUDROOROO, see MUDROOROO.

Narratology is the study of narrative methods and strategies. It assumes that story-telling is a fundamental human activity which can be explored in different cultures and different modes which will reveal common, or at least comparable, features and habits. Narratologists examine fairy tales, myths, detective stories, classic novels, films, epic poems, gossip, jokes, advertising, comic strips—it is the management of the story that interests them, rather than the genre or the status of the text. Their characteristic questions concern time and structure, point of view, recurring themes. Are there flashbacks in a narrative, for example? Does it look forward to its own conclusion? Are characters arranged in pairs, do certain events mirror each other? An early influential work in this field is V. Propp's *Morphology of the Folk Tale* (1928); a major study is Roland Barthes's *S/Z* (1970), and Gérard Genette's *Narrative Discourse* (1972), although largely dedicated to the work of Marcel Proust, is lucid and helpful about more general technical matters.

NASH, Ogden (1902–71), American poet, born in Rye, New York; he attended Harvard University in 1921 and 1922. He established himself as a successful writer of light verse in the early 1930s, when he was a member of the editorial staff of the **New Yorker*. *Free Wheeling* and *Hard Lines* of 1931 were followed at regular intervals by many further collections, which include *I'm a Stranger Here Myself* (1938), *The Face Is Familiar* (1940), *You Can't Get There from Here* (1957), and *There's Always Another Windmill* (1968). *I Wouldn't Have Missed It* (1975) is the fullest of the various collected editions of his work. His highly idiosyncratic verse, much of which formed a sophisticated extension of the gauche idioms of naïve American poets in the folk tradition, enjoyed enormous popularity. Although he produced many polished epigrams, his most characteristic effects were achieved through the use of unusually long lines concluding with audaciously ingenious rhymes. His humour was often turned to incisive purpose in verse exposing aspects of social injustice or the underlying complacencies of American culture. He also wrote prolifically for children and completed *The Scroobius Pip* (1968), which Edward Lear left unfinished at his death. Among his other works was the collaboration with S. J. *Perelman and Kurt Weill on the musical comedy *One Touch of Venus*, which was successfully produced on Broadway in 1943.

NATHAN, George Jean (1882–1958), American drama critic and essayist, born in Fort Wayne, Indiana, educated at Cornell University. After working as a journalist and drama critic, in 1908 he joined the staff of the *Smart Set*, which he co-edited with H. L. *Mencken from 1914 to 1923. Collections of Nathan's essays and reviews from this period include *Mr George Jean Nathan Presents* (1917), *The Popular Theatre* (1918), and *Materia Critica* (1924). In collaboration with Mencken he wrote the plays *The Artist* (1912) and *Heliogabalus* (1920); his principal dramatic works of sole authorship are *The Eternal Mystery* (1913) and *The Avon Flows* (1937). In 1924 he founded the **American Mercury* with Mencken; disagreements led to his resignation as editor in 1925, although he continued to supply reviews. In association with Theodore *Dreiser and others, he began the *Spectator* in 1932. Throughout the 1920s and 1930s Nathan was the most influential commentator on contemporary American drama, attracting hostility from controlling interests in the commercial theatre for his authoritatively iconoclastic denigrations of many productions. Among the playwrights whose reputations he fostered were Eugene *O'Neill, William *Saroyan, Arthur *Miller, and Sean *O'Casey. Numerous further books of his criticism include *Art of the Night* (1928), *Passing Judgements* (1934), *The Entertainment of a Nation* (1942), and *The Theatre in the Fifties* (1953). *The Autobiography of an Attitude* (1925) and *The Intimate Notebooks of George Jean Nathan* (1932) are witty collections of reminiscences.

NATHAN, Robert (Gruntal) (1894–1985), American novelist and screenwriter, born in New York. Most of his books were satirical fantasies, including his most famous, *Portrait of Jennie* (1940), which was based on the time theories of J. W. *Dunne. Few of his many works are novels of action, and Nathan was never a popular creator of commercial fantasies. Writing in delicate prose, Nathan tended to fabricate worlds which were resonant with loss, such as in *The Puppet Master* (1923). Other works include *The Road of Ages* (1935), which prophetically describes a new Jewish diaspora; and *The Weans* (1960), which takes the form of an archaeological report written in the distant future, and gently satirizes contemporary America.

Nation, an independent journal published fortnightly in Australia from 1958 to 1972. It was founded and funded by T. M. Fitzgerald, Financial Editor of the *Sydney Morning Herald*. His contributors were 'free to say anything they wished' as long as they substantiated it by fact or argument. *Nation* was liberal but essentially middle-class, commenting freely on all aspects of culture as well as domestic and international politics and business matters. The journal began to lose ground at the beginning of the 1970s. Its importance was in providing the main independent comment on politics, economics, and culture in Australia throughout the 1960s.

Native American Literature. While Native American literature in English does not significantly predate the early nineteenth century, it is intimately linked to the rich oral traditions of the tribes whose ancestors migrated to the continent over 28,000 years before. The oral cultures of the Native Americans remain vigorously current in their principal forms of song, a category encompassing many forms of poetry, ritual drama, and story-telling. Although highly diversified in terms of language, religious beliefs, and sociocultural patterns, the oral art forms tend to have in common an emphasis on physical and spiritual harmony between humanity and the natural environment and the maintenance of a viable sense of community within the structures of the tribe. As the dominant oral genre for entertainment and exposition, story-telling has had the greatest influence over twentieth-century Native American writing in English, in which the narrative modes of the novel and autobiography are prevalent.

Autobiographical writings are of central importance to the establishment from the mid-nineteenth century onward of Native American literature in English. The blending of personal life history and ethnography found in the writings of William Apes (Pequot, 1798–?), George Copway (Ojibwa, 1818–*c.*1863), and other nineteenth-century writers is sustained in the works of Charles *Eastman (Sioux), whose autobiographies *Indian Boyhood* (1902) and *From the Deep Woods to Civilization* (1916) display the persistence and vitality of the oral traditions. *Mourning Dove: A Salishan Autobiography*, the personal testimony of Mourning Dove (1888–1936), one of the earliest Native American women novelists, appeared in 1990 under Jay Miller's editorship. The best-known of the many life histories recorded from oral accounts is *Black Elk Speaks* (1932), narrated by *Black Elk, a Sioux medicine man, to the author John G. *Neihardt. In the autobiography *Talking to the Moon* (1945) by John Joseph *Mathews (Osage), elements of the oral tradition combine with conventional literary accomplishment in anticipation of the work of N. Scott *Momaday (Kiowa). Momaday's *The Names* (1976) is a straightforwardly autobiographical account of his ancestry and early life. His innovative and influential *The Way to Rainy Mountain* (1969) imaginatively frames the emergence of a personal quest for tribal origins within a broad exploration of Kiowa culture in its contemporary context. Notable among later autobiographies are *Interior Landscapes* (1990) by the versatile and prolific novelist and poet Gerald *Vizenor and *Lakota Woman* (1990) by Crow Dog (Lakota; also known as Mary Brave Bird), a first-person account of the American Indian movement from the 1960s onward.

The earlier development of the Native American novel in the twentieth century is marked by recurrent treatments of mixed-blood protagonists seeking to secure their individual and communal identities through discussions between tribal traditions and American modernity. Mourning Dove (Okanogan-Colville) wrote *Co-ge-we-a, the Halfblood* (1927), a novel based on Okanogan oral stories, which was among the first works to address sociocultural displacement in the post-reservation era; she also published *Coyote Stories* (1933). In John Joseph Mathews's *Wah'Kon-Tah* (1932) and *Sundown* (1934), and *Surrounded* (1936) by D'Arcy *McNickle (Cree-Salish), the breakdowns in traditional social structures are dramatically realized in patterns of crisis in individual lives. Other Native American novelists of the 1930s are John Oskison (Cherokee), whose *Brothers Three* (1935) contributes to American regionalism in narrating the attempts of a Cherokee family to re-establish themselves in their Oklahoma homeland, and Todd Downing (Choctaw), the author of ten mystery novels which include *Murder on Tour* (1933) and *Night Over Mexico* (1937).

The emergence of a highly productive new generation of Native American writers was inaugurated with the publication of N. Scott Momaday's *The House Made of Dawn* (1968), an affirmative treatment of the quest to renew contact with tribal values which is also central to his *The Ancient Child* (1989). The ultimately optimistic emphasis on the vitality and diversity of Native American culture in *Ceremony* (1977) by Leslie *Silko (Laguna) is shared by *Between Two Rivers* (1987) and *Humors and/or Not So Humorous* (1988), the best-known works of Maurice Kenny (Mohawk). Other novels which suggest the viability of the ritual quest for Native American identity include *A Good Journey* (1977) by Simon *Ortiz (Acoma) and *Medicine River* (1990) by Thomas King (Cherokee). Further treatments of the recuperation of tribal culture are offered by Duane Niatum (Klallum) in *Digging Out the Roots* (1977) and *Songs for the Harvester of Dreams* (1981), and Jim Barnes (Choctaw) in *The American Book of the Dead* (1982).

A harsher realism engaging alienation and displacement as fundamental to Native American experience is encountered in *The Death of Jim Loney* (1979) by Jim *Welch (Blackfeet-Gros Ventre), *What Moon Drove Me to This* (1979) by Joy *Harjo (Creek), and *Fire Water World* (1988) by Adrian Louis (Paiute), a devastating treatment of alcoholism and substance abuse in the reservations; Barney Bush (Shawnee) uses mordantly ironic humour to deal with the disintegration of Native American culture in *My Horse and a Jukebox* (1979) and *Inherit the Blood* (1985). Other novels notable for their contemporary realism include *Winter of the Salamander* (1980) by Ray A. Youngbear (Mesquakie) and *The Light on the Tent Wall* (1990) by Mary Tallmountain (Athabascan). Personal alienation and cultural dispossession are salient themes in *Mean Spirit* (1990) by Linda Hogan (Choctaw) and *Dawnland* (1993) by Joseph Bruchac (Abenaki), two of the principal historical novels written by Native Americans. *The Lone Ranger and Tonto Fist Fight* (1993), by Sherman Alexie (Spokane) contains linked stories reflecting the complex density of life in the Spokane Indian Reservation. The importance of women and the family in Native American life is central to many works by contemporary authors, most notably those of Louise *Erdrich (Chippewa), who has dealt with complex familial relationships in *Love Medicine* (1984), *Beet Queen* (1986), and *Tracks* (1988), and Paula Gunn *Allen (Laguna), author of *The Woman Who Owned the Shadows* (1983) and *The Sacred Hoop* (1986). *A Yellow Raft on Blue Water* (1987) by Michael *Dorris (Modoc) deals with tensions of belonging and division among three generations of Native American women, while Janet Campbell Hale (Coeur d'Alene) forcefully presents an alcoholic female protagonist in *The Jailing of Cecilia Capture* (1985). Other novels with a feminist perspective include *One More Shipwreck* (1981) by Luci Tapahonso (Navajo) and *White Corn Sister* (1977) by Peter Blue Cloud (Mohawk); while *The Grass Dancer* (1994) by Susan Power (Sioux/Dakota) contains linked stories covering several generations of Native American women.

In the late 1960s, many Native American writers began producing poetry in English enriched by the traditions of the oral culture and vitalized by a keen sense of experimental possibilities. Among the authors referred to above who have produced poetry covering a wide range of themes and forms are Paula Gunn Allen, Jim Barnes, Louise Erdrich, Joy Harjo, Linda Hogan, Duane Niatum, Leslie Silko, and Gerald Vizenor. Other genres not widely adopted by twentieth-century Native American writers in English include satire, in which the 'Fux Fixico Letters' (1901) of Alexander Posey (Creek) and *Rogers-isms; The Cowboy Philosopher at the Peace Conference* (1919) by Will *Rogers (Cherokee) anticipate the detached satirical stance in much of Gerald Vizenor's work. With regard to drama by Native American authors, Lynn Riggs (Cherokee) was probably the best-known playwright prior to the 1960s; his celebrated folk-drama *Green Grow the Lilacs* (1931) provided the basis for the musical *Oklahoma!* (1954). During the 1970s Hanay Geiogamah (Kiowa/Delaware) emerged as the most notable Native American playwright, chiefly through the success of his best-known work, *Body Indian* of 1972; he founded the American Indian Theatre Ensemble (now the Native American Theatre Ensemble) in 1972. Gerald Vizenor, Tom King, and Linda Hogan have also written drama and screenplays.

In the field of non-fiction Vine *Deloria, Jr (Sioux) has emerged as the most prolific and respected author since the appearance of his controversial interpretation of historical transitions in *Custer Died for Your Sins* (1969). Other writers who have challenged settled views of Native American history include Robert Conley (Cherokee) in *Mountain Windsong* (1992), Clifford Trafzer (Wyandot) in *The Kit Carson Campaign* (1981), and Pueblo tribal historian Joe Sando (Jemez) in *Nee Hemish* (1982). Studies of issues relating to environmental and sociocultural resources form a substantial contribution to contemporary Native American writing, notable examples being the treatment of repatriation in *Ghost Singer* (1988) by Anna Walters (Otoe/Pawnee), *Termination and Relocation* (1985) by Donald Fixico (Creek), and *American Indian Societies* by Duane Champagne (Chippewa). Major critical studies by Native Americans include *Other Destinies* (1992), a remarkable interpretation of the modern Native American novel by Louis Owens (Choctaw/Cherokee), and *Gerald Vizenor: Writing in the Oral Tradition* (1996) by Kimberley Blaeser (Chippewa).

Native Son, a novel by Richard *Wright, published in 1940. Bigger Thomas, a black youth from the rat-infested squalor of Chicago's South Side ghetto, is hired as chauffeur by the wealthy white Dalton family. Late the first night, having been coerced into socializing with his employers' daughter Mary and her communist boyfriend, he has to help the intoxicated girl to her bedroom; when blind Mrs Dalton appears, Bigger, terrified of being discovered, accidentally smothers Mary while trying to keep her quiet. In a series of desperate stratagems, he stuffs her body into the basement furnace, fakes a misleading kidnap note, hides out briefly, and brutally murders his own girlfriend Bessie before he is hunted down. At the trial, his communist attorney blames society, arguing that the crimes were an inevitable outcome of racial and economic oppression. The prosecution's inflammatory case, however, secures a conviction, and Bigger is sentenced to death. A landmark of black American fiction, the novel has been variously regarded as social protest in the deterministic mode of Dreiser's *An *American Tragedy*, as a blistering manifesto of race hostility, as communist propaganda, and as an existential drama of self-realization. While the use of contemporary court records and newspaper reports, the tense foreshadowing of inexorable destiny, and the grimly realized urban landscape reflect Wright's literary naturalism, it was his Marxist ideology which shaped an understanding of Bigger's behaviour as both typical and predictable, given the material and psychic stresses of a dehumanizing environment. Since this analysis underpins the argument of Bigger's defence counsel, it is often assumed that the trial scene is a vehicle for Wright's own communist conclusions. But the novel's central perspective is Bigger's, and ultimately it is *his* reality, rather than his lawyer's interpretations, which Wright endorses. Refusing all socio-political excuses and explanations, Bigger embraces his monstrous violence as the affirmation of a long-suppressed identity: 'What I killed for, I *am*.' If this anticipates the existential themes of Wright's later work, it also embodies, as his preface warns, a more immediate social truth: 'the moral horror of Negro life in the United States'.

NAUGHTON, Bill (1910–92), British playwright, born in Co. Mayo, raised in Lancashire. After leaving school he was variously employed as a lorry driver, weaver, and coal-bagger before turning seriously to drama. His first plays were for the radio, but two of them, *My Flesh, My Blood* (1957) and *Alfie Elkins and His Little Life* (1962), were subsequently adapted by him for the stage, and respectively became the highly successful *Spring and Port Wine* (1964), about family stresses in a patriarchal northern household, and *Alfie* (1963), about the sexual adventures of a spry yet clearly somewhat inadequate Don Juan. Like *All in Good Time* (1963), about the difficulties a young couple have in consummating their marriage, these are both comedies, in the tradition of such other Lancashire playwrights as Harold *Brighouse and Stanley *Houghton; and they are notable for their good-humoured yet unsentimental observation of working-class life. Naughton has also published several novels, including a version of *Alfie* in 1966, some short stories, and two volumes of autobiography, *A Roof over Your Head* (1945) and *Pony Boy* (1966).

NAYLOR, Gloria (1952–), African-American novelist, born in New York City, educated at Brooklyn College and Yale. Her novels focus imaginatively on aspects of the black experience within the wider American context. Her reputation was firmly established with the appearance of her first work of fiction, *The *Women of Brewster Place*. As one of the emergent generation of black American writers, her work displays the liberating influence of such seminal figures as Toni *Morrison; she is able to depict such phenomena as the rise of the black middle class in a manner that permits a combination of fantasy and folklore with stringent, if controlled, social comment. *Linden Hills* (1985) employs a *magic realism mode influenced by Morrison's **Song of Solomon*, recovering, through the experiences of two black youths, the representative histories of systematic abuse concealed within a seemingly affluent black household. *Mama Day* (1988) alternates male and female narrative voices to contrast reason with faith, rationality with superstition, and heedless social conformism with the recognition of the past's undeniable heritage. It is also a moving and tragic love story, notable for its sensitive understanding of the construction of black male identity, though black women are represented as the repositories of culture and tradition. *Bailey's Café* (1992) employs Naylor's familiar device of unity of location; the surrealistic café of the title is the meeting-place for a variety of eccentric characters who exchange their stories, moving back and forth in time and—as always in Naylor's work—unveiling hidden black histories.

NAZARETH, Peter (1940–), Ugandan novelist, critic, and dramatist, born in Kampala, educated at Uganda's Makerere University College and the University of Leeds. Following a period in public service in Uganda, the success of *In a Brown Mantle* (1972), his first novel, gained him a Seymour Lustman Fellowship at Yale University. In 1973 he began teaching at the University of Iowa, where he became Associate Professor of English in 1980. Nazareth first achieved notice as a dramatist, his play *Brave New Cosmos*, contained in *Origin East Africa* (edited by David Cook, 1965), being the first work by a Ugandan dramatist to be broadcast by the BBC's African service. His other plays, which have been chiefly performed on radio, include *The Hospital* (1976) and *X* (1976). A second novel, *The General is Up*, appeared in 1984. Nazareth's creative and critical works have in common their urgent concern with the vulnerability and cultural and economic potential of Africa and the Third World during the immediate post-colonial era. His critical writings, which include *Literature and Society in Modern Africa* (1972), *An African View of Literature* (1974), *The Footnote Man* (1980), and *Literature of the African People* (1984), confront the ethical assumptions of much contemporary African writing.

NDEBELE, Njabulo (1948–), South African writer and president of the Congress of South African Writers (COSAW); born in Johannesburg, he grew up there and in Charleston Location, Nigel. He earned a reputation as an outstanding poet in the late 1960s, being widely published in South African journals such as **Staffrider*, *Contrast*, *Classic*, and *Izwi*. As editor of the student literary journal *Expression* he emerged as a leading literary theoretician of the Black Consciousness Movement, and he has subsequently played a crucial role in directing and shaping critical discourse around South African literature. He received wide acclaim for his first book *Fools and Other Stories* (1985). Lyrical and vibrant in their telling, the five short stories in this collection deal with childhood and the experience of growing up in the black urban locations in which Ndebele was himself raised. Their thrust stems from his belief that too much of the imaginative lives of Africans has been given away to the oppressor and his deeds. The author explained in an interview that 'the book was an attempt on my part to focus attention on the quality of life in its creative aspects in the townships'. His *South African Literature and Culture: Rediscovery of the Ordinary* was published in 1994.

NEIHARDT, John G(eisenau) (1881–1973), American poet, born near Sharpsburg, Illinois, brought up in Wayne, Nebraska and educated at Nebraska Normal College. He finished his first book, *The Divine Enchantment* (1900), when he was only 16 and started his major work, the five-part *A Cycle of the West* (1949), in 1912, after having spent the years from 1901 to 1907 collecting stories on the Omaha Indian Reservation. In 1921 he was declared Poet Laureate of Nebraska and in 1923 he became Professor of Poetry at the University of Nebraska. From 1926 to 1938 he was literary editor of the St Louis *Post-Dispatch*, during which time he recorded a series of conversations with *Black Elk which were eventually published as *Black Elk Speaks* (1932). In 1936 the National Poetry Center awarded him its gold medal of honour, signifying that he was the foremost poet of the nation. From 1949 to 1965 he was poet in residence and lecturer in English at the University of Missouri. Neihardt's poetry is relatively conventional in form, but its content reveals a profoundly mystical sense of the world which has much in common with Native American thought and religious observance; though his mysticism predated his contact with them, Native Americans provided him with concrete, living examples of mysticism in action, as well as a tragic history of neglect and abuse.

NEILSON, John Shaw (1872–1942), Australian poet, born at Penola, South Australia, the son of the poet John Neilson (1842–1922); he received an elementary education in Minimay, Victoria, and spent most of his adult life as an itinerant labourer. Having achieved recognition as a poet, he was awarded a pension from the Commonwealth Literary Fund in 1922 and held a sinecure with the Melbourne County Roads Board from 1928 onward. In 1896 his verse began appearing in periodicals and his first volume of poetry, *Old Granny Sullivan*, was published in 1916. His subsequent collections include *Heart of Spring* (1919), *Ballads and Lyrical Poems* (1923), and *Beauty Imposes* (1938). *Witnesses of Spring* (edited by J. Wright and others, 1970) and *Green Days and Cherries* (edited by M. Anderson and L. J. Blake, 1981) were assembled posthumously; *The Poems* (1965) is a collected edition produced by A. R. Chisholm. The refined musicality of Neilson's verse and its austere lyrical clarity have established him as one of the most noteworthy of Australia's poets of the early twentieth century. The best of his poetry displays a visionary depth of response in its elegiac and celebratory treatments of the natural world. *The Folly of Spring* (1990) is a study of Neilson by Cliff Hanna.

NEMEROV, Howard (Stanley) (1920–), American poet, novelist, and critic, born in New York City, educated at Harvard; he subsequently served as a pilot in the Second World War, an experience informing many of his poems. After holding a succession of posts at American colleges and universities, he became Distinguished University Professor at Washington University, Missouri, in 1976. From 1988 to 1990 he was Poet Laureate of The United States. *The Image and the Law* (1947), *Guide to the Ruins* (1950), and *The Salt Garden* (1955), his first three collections of verse, established his reputation as a poet capable of combining accomplishment in the use of conventional forms with an urgency of address to a wide range of personal, social, and cultural themes. His numerous subsequent volumes include *The Next Room of the Dream* (1962), *The Blue Swallows* (1967), *Sentences* (1980), and *War Stories* (1987). *Collected Poems* appeared in 1977. The urbanely ironic and sometimes scathingly satirical wit that is frequently encountered in his poetry is a dominant characteristic of his novels, which form modern comedies of manners emphasizing the moral ambiguities and social pressures of middle-class American life; *The Melodramatists* (1949) centres on the dissatisfactions of a Boston family, *Federigo, or the Power of Love* (1954) is a complex farce of adultery, and *The Homecoming Game* (1957) concerns a university professor whose values collide with the workings of the educational system. He also published two collections of short stories, *A Commodity of Dreams* (1959) and *Stories, Fables and Other Diversions* (1971). Nemerov's other works include *Journal of the Fictive Life* (1965), an autobiographical examination of the psychology of writing; *Poetry and Fiction* (1963), *Reflexions on Poetry and Poetics* (1972), and *Figures of Thought* (1978) are collections of his literary essays.

NEVILLE, Jill (1933–), Australian-born novelist, playwright, and poet who has spent most of her life in London. Her novels include *Fall Girl* (1966), a picaresque novel about an Australian adrift in London; *The Girl Who Played Gooseberry* (1968), the study of a philanderer, a leap in literary style and range; *The Love Germ* (1970), which captures the euphoria of Paris in 1968; *The Living Daylights* (1974), shimmering fragments of interlocking lives; *Last Ferry to Manly* (1984), a much-praised novel on the classic Australian theme: the return of the *émigré*; and *Swimming the Channel* (1993), a story of passionate love and betrayal in London and Paris. In *The Day We Cut the Lavender* (1995), another novel about the return of the long-absent wanderer, the protagonist, Norah, flies back to Sydney to raise money for her addict daughter now drying out in a London clinic; as she visits her old lover, and enters the family web, she is haunted by an earlier Antipodean escapee, Katherine *Mansfield. As in all her novels, Neville's style is spare, enlivened by a wiry wit and often startling imagery.

New Age, The, journal originally founded as a liberal weekly in 1894; it was not a success until it was acquired by A. R. *Orage in association with G. B. *Shaw and Holbrook Jackson in 1907. Subsequently announcing itself as 'an independent socialist review of politics, literature, and art', it became one of the leading periodicals of its day. Although firmly aligned with the *Fabian Society, the *New Age* avoided a narrowly political emphasis through Orage's determination as editor to give it broad cultural scope and authority; in addition to literary contributions from H. G. *Wells, J. C. *Squire, Arnold *Bennett, W. B. *Yeats, Katherine *Mansfield, and other writers of note, essays on drama, the graphic arts, aesthetics, and philosophy were regularly featured. F. S. *Flint, who supplied numerous articles on poetry, attracted T. E. *Hulme to the magazine in 1909 as a writer on philosophical topics; Hulme in turn introduced work by Ezra *Pound, who published poetry and literary criticism in the *New Age* and contributed reviews of art and music under the pseudonyms 'B. H. Dias' and 'William Atheling'. The First World War weakened Orage's motivating belief in the socially transformative power of cultural and socio-political discourse; from 1918 onward the magazine was increasingly dominated by his interests in economic theory and more mystical meliorative doctrines, leaving the *New Statesman* as the principal organ of Fabian Socialism. The editorship passed to Arthur Moore in 1922 when Orage departed for the Gurdjieff Institute in Paris. Although valuable work from Edwin *Muir, Oliver St John *Gogarty, and Herbert *Read appeared during the 1920s, the *New Age* entered a slow decline and was discontinued in 1938.

New Apocalypse, The, a group of writers, predominantly poets, who cohered closely as a movement from the appearance in 1939 of *The New Apocalypse: An Anthology of Criticism, Poems and Stories*, edited by J. F. *Hendry, until the later 1940s. With Henry *Treece, Hendry edited two further anthologies, *The White Horseman* (1941) and *The Crown and the Sickle* (1944); the former is prefaced with a passage from *Apocalypse* (1931), D. H. *Lawrence's radical critique of cultural and religious orthodoxy, with which the movement made its alignment apparent in its choice of name. G. S. *Fraser's introduction to *The White Horseman* declares the group's 'ruthless scepticism about political thought' and defends the intense imaginative subjectivity characteristic of much of its writing; Fraser rejected the rationally discursive 'classicism' felt to be typified by the poetry of *Auden and his associates, describing the New Apocalypse as a 'dialectical development of Surrealism' in its reliance on the deep creative resources of the individual psyche. While their poetry was sometimes capable of registering the moral turmoil of wartime, its violent excesses of imagery and tendency to formal indiscipline prompted the anti-romantic reaction typified by the *Movement in the post-war years. Freudian and Marxist thought strongly informed the group's philosophy, and Dylan *Thomas was their principal exemplar in poetry. The first two anthologies featured work by Hendry, Treece, Fraser, Nicholas *Moore, Norman *MacCaig, Vernon *Watkins, and others; *The Crown and the Sickle* indicated the start of the movement's decline, being largely made up of writing by less distinguished contributors.

NEWBOLT, Sir Henry (John) (1862–1938), British poet, born in Bilston, Staffordshire, educated at Corpus Christi, Oxford; he became a barrister in 1887. The enormous success of *Admirals All and Other Verses* (1897), his forthrightly patriotic first collection of verse, prompted him to retire from the bar and devote himself to literature. His numerous popular collections of poetry include *The Island Race* (1898), *The Sailing of the Long-Ships* (1902), and *Songs of Memory and Hope* (1909). His considerable public standing was increased by *The Year of Trafalgar* (1905), a history written for the battle's centenary. He also wrote historical novels, notably *The New June* (1909). As a critic, he lent support to the **Georgian Poetry* series in *A New Study of English Poetry* (1917). Famous for viewing the British military spirit in terms of 'Play up! play up! and play the game' ('Vitai Lampada'), his verse was inadequate to the mood of the First World War, and he produced little poetry after 1918; *Poems: New and Old* (1912, enlarged 1919), is the principal collection of his verse. He remained prominent as a public figure until his death. *My World as in My Time* (1932) is a volume of his memoirs.

NEWBY, (George) Eric (1919–), British travel writer, born in London, educated at St Paul's School. After two years with an advertising agency he became an apprentice seaman on a Finnish sailing-vessel in 1938; his experiences at this time form the basis of *The Last Grain Race* (1956). In 1939 he began a period of active service in the Second World War; from 1942 to 1945 he was a prisoner of war in Italy, an interlude reflected in *Love and War in the Appenines* (1971). He subsequently worked in the fashion industry, an occupation described in *Something Wholesale* (1962), and as a publicist with a London publisher before becoming travel editor with the *Observer* in 1964. The casual elegance and ironic wit integral to Newby's style do not diminish the lyrical profundity of his descriptions or his capacity for evoking the emotional and philosophical dimensions of his travels. *A Short Walk in the Hindu Kush* (1958), his most celebrated, and perhaps his most insistently humorous, work, recounts an adventurous and inadequately equipped journey to Nuristan. *Slowly down the Ganges* (1966), describing an expedition on which he was accompanied by his wife Wanda, and *The Big Red Train Ride* (1978), his account of the Trans-Siberian railway, are among his other notable books. His publications also include *Great Ascents* (1977), a history of mountaineering informed by his own enthusiasm for the activity; *On the Shores of the Mediterranean* (1984); and *What the Traveller Saw* (1989), a collection of photographs taken on his travels. *A Traveller's Life*, Newby's vividly anecdotal autobiography, appeared in 1982.

NEWBY, P(ercy) H(oward) (1918–), British novelist, born in Crowborough, Sussex, educated at Hanley Castle Grammar School, Worcester, and St Paul's College, Cheltenham. His experiences as a lecturer in English at Fouad I University in Cairo (1942–6) strongly inform his fiction, in which Egyptian and Mediterranean settings recur. In 1949 he joined the BBC as a producer in the Talks Department, rising to become Managing Director of Radio before his retirement in 1978. The themes of the struggle for self-knowledge and the clash of mutually incomprehensible cultures in *A Journey to the Interior* (1946), his first novel, remain central to much of his subsequent work. *Agents and Witnesses* (1947), *The Picnic at Sakkara* (1955), *A Guest and His Going* (1959), and *Something to Answer For* (1968), for which he received the first Booker Prizer in 1969, reflect the turbulent post-war politics of Egypt and the Arab world in narratives successfully combining farce and underlying seriousness. More subdued forms of humour interact with analysis of middle-class attitudes in his novels with British settings, which include *The Snow Pasture* (1949), *A Season in England* (1951), *The Barbary Night* (1964), and *One of the Founders* (1965). His numerous other novels include *Revolution and Roses* (1957), *Kith* (1977), *Leaning in the Wind* (1986), and *Coming in With the Tide* (1990). Notable among Newby's other publications are the historical works *The Warrior Pharaohs* (1980) and *Saladin in His Times* (1980). The autobiographical *Feelings Have Changed* (1981) is an account of his experiences at the BBC.

New Criticism, a movement in American literary criticism associated with a group of poets and critics who were strongly influenced by the ideas and practice of I. A. *Richards and William *Empson. It received its name from the book of that title published by John Crowe *Ransom in 1941; the group also included Allen *Tate, Robert Penn *Warren, and Cleanth *Brooks (see AGRARIANS). The New Criticism was not a tightly knit school or programme, and was considerably less consistent than its opponents have often imagined. It was chiefly a response to the new poetry of the first part of the century, the work of *Eliot, *Pound, *Yeats. It was interested in irony and ambiguity, hostile to sentimentality and paraphrasable statement. It was devoted to the principle of close reading, to a sense of 'the words on the page', and this was often taken to imply an indifference or resistance to history, to everything in literature that seems to take place around rather than in a text. In fact none of the New Critics was as anti-historical as this—indeed, since they were mostly Southerners, and largely conservative, it may be that they were not so much resisting history as refusing the progressive liberal consensus American history seemed to have become by the 1940s. New Criticism, or at least its practice of close reading, was eminently teachable and had far-reaching effects in schools and universities in Britain and especially America. It was firmly opposed to what it regarded as an unquestioned tradition of old-fashioned 'literary history' and it has been seen as preparing the ground for *Deconstruction. A notable reaction to its supposed indifference to context and history is the *New Historicism. See also PRACTICAL CRITICISM.

New Departures, a magazine founded by Michael *Horovitz in 1959, since when issues have appeared at irregular intervals. At its best, *New Departures* has fulfilled its editor's original intention of making it a forum for all the arts: poetry by leading authors from various parts of the world has been accompanied by graphic and photographic work of high quality, and musical scores by eminent experimental composers have also been published; W. H. *Auden, Samuel *Beckett, Charles *Olson, Jack *Kerouac, Ezra *Pound, John *Berryman, Yevgeny Yevtushenko, Seamus *Heaney, and Ted *Hughes have been among its contributors, who have otherwise tended to be drawn from the '*underground poetry' movement. David Hockney is notable among the artists who have supplied illustrations; composers whose work has been featured include John Cage and Cornelius Cardew. The energies of Horovitz and his associates were diversified in the magazine's early stages into the 'Live New Departures Roadshows', the principal platform for the performance of poetry in combination with music (see JAZZ POETRY) and drama throughout the 1960s and 1970s. Many poems from the magazine's earlier issues were included in Horovitz's edition of *Children of Albion: Poetry of the 'Underground' in Britain* (1969).

New Edinburgh Review, see EDINBURGH REVIEW.

New Historicism. The term was coined by Stephen Greenblatt to describe a development in American literary scholarship and criticism which sought to combine the acquisitions of contemporary theory with a return to a historical perspective felt to have been too long and too carelessly abandoned by the *New Criticism and its descendants. Walter Benjamin is a (remote) predecessor, and Michel Foucault is a powerful influence. The most distinguished early work in New Historicism, characteristically mingling close reading with an attention to historical details often neglected by historians, was done in Renaissance studies, notably in Greenblatt's own *Renaissance Self-Fashioning* (1980) and *Shakespearean Negotiations* (1988), but there have also been impressive and well-grounded arguments by Marjorie Levin, Jerome McGann, and others, inviting major revisions of Romanticism. New Historicism shares much terrain with its British cousin *Cultural Materialism but remains rather more aloof politically, less dedicated to particular programmes of social or cultural change. See also MARXIST LITERARY CRITICISM and WILLIAMS, RAYMOND.

New Humanism, The, a movement promoted by numerous eminent American scholars and critics from the early 1920s onward to counter what they saw as the threatened dissolution of ethical and artistic standards. Irving *Babbitt's works, attacking the fallacies of Romanticism and appealing to Hellenistic values, were central to the New Humanism; its leaders also included Paul Elmer More (1864–1937), whose *Shelburne Essays* (eleven volumes; 1904–21) often concurred with Babbitt's views, Norman Foerster (1887–1972), whose *Toward Standards* (1930) is one of the movement's notable documents, and Stuart Sherman (1881–1926), who argued for stable criteria of literary judgement in *Matthew Arnold: How To Know Him* (1917) and *On Contemporary Literature* (1917). Babbitt's 'inner principle of restraint' was an essential tenet in the New Humanism's call for curbs upon the moral and cultural laxity he and his associates saw as the legacy of Romanticism. Their philosophical and theological emphasis was on man's unique and ethically autonomous position between God and nature, in accordance with which they commended reason, discipline, and general cultivation of the higher faculties and gave primacy to the ethical functions of literature. They were antagonistic to scientific materialism and strongly disapproved of many aspects of literary *Modernism. Norman Foerster edited *Humanism and America: Essays on the Outlook of*

Modern Civilization (1930), a symposium to which T. S. *Eliot contributed; Eliot had, however, already expressed doubts concerning the claims of the New Humanism in an article of 1927, and eventually rejected it as an inadequate surrogate for religion. The opponents of the movement, who included Edmund *Wilson, Malcolm *Cowley, Kenneth *Burke, Lewis *Mumford, and Allen *Tate, quickly responded to *Humanism and America* with *The Critique of Humanism* (1930); H. L. *Mencken made the New Humanists a frequent target for his satire throughout the 1920s. During the 1930s interest in the New Humanism declined as political solutions for America's ills assumed priority.

New Journalism, The, is generally considered to have begun in the 1960s with the debate generated by the publication of Truman *Capote's *In Cold Blood* (1965) and Tom *Wolfe's *Kandy Kolored Tangerine-Flake Streamline Baby* (1965). This debate focused on the new blending of literary technique with journalistic fact. Also referred to as the 'nonfiction novelists', these writers combined the 'objective credibility' of journalism with the subjective self-reflection of fiction, exploring meanings beyond the media-constructed 'reality'. As Tom Wolfe described in his 'manifesto' *The New Journalism* (1973), exponents reacting against the assumed 'objective' perspective of orthodox journalism and its reliance on official, often hidden, sources, asserted that they needed to go beyond the constraints of conventional journalism in order to represent contemporary events. These writers were also partly reacting to the shocking events of the 1960s—political assassination, the Vietnam War, the moon-walk—as much as to the new media. Such works as Norman Mailer's **Armies of the Night* (1968), *Of a Fire on the Moon* (1970), and *Executioner's Song* (1979), Hunter S. *Thompson's *Hell's Angels: A Strange and Terrible Saga* (1967), Tom Wolfe's *Electric Kool-Aid Acid Test* (1968), an account of the rise of the drug culture in California in the 1960s, and *The Right Stuff* (1979), and Michael Herr's *Dispatches* (1974) (see VIETNAM WRITING), exemplify the self-reflective movement from innocence to experience. These writers often ally themselves with the fictional work of writers like Thomas *Pynchon, Kurt *Vonnegut, Donald *Barthelme, and others whose writing experiments suggest that modern 'reality' is so extraordinary and absurd that the methods of conventional realistic narration are no longer adequate. Other writers like Joan *Didion, Mary *McCarthy and her works on the Vietnam War, George Plimpton, Seymour Krim, and Gay Talese, also react against the pre-packaged, formulaic, and anonymously constructed journalistic methods. Other examples of 'new journalism' might include Robert *Coover's *The Public Burning* (1977), and E. L. *Doctorow's novels *Welcome to Hard Times* (1960), *The Book of Daniel* (1971), and *Ragtime* (1975).

New Lines, an anthology of verse by the poets central to the *Movement, published in 1956 under the editorship of Robert *Conquest, who supplied eight poems. The other contributors were Kingsley *Amis, Donald *Davie, D. J. *Enright, Thom *Gunn, John Holloway (1920–), Elizabeth *Jennings, Philip *Larkin, and John *Wain. With clear reference to the poets of the *New Apocalypse, Conquest's introduction dismissed much of the poetry of the 1940s as 'diffuse and sentimental verbiage or hollow technical pirouettes'; claims that his contributors' work displayed a 'certain unity of approach' in its formal regularity and straightforwardness were borne out by the pervasive technical accomplishment and characteristic tone of sceptically intelligent informality. While *New Lines* found favour with the majority of the critics, Charles *Tomlinson reviewed it in terms of its 'suburban mental ratio' and 'lack of real poetic talent and ambition'. Al *Alvarez echoed these remarks by stating that 'gentility . . . reigns supreme' in the verse of the Movement in his introduction to *The New Poetry* (1963), which espoused more vigorous modes. *New Lines* rapidly established its contributors as representatives of an enduringly dominant tendency and provoked an early reaction in the form of *Mavericks* (1957), an anthology edited by Dannie *Abse and Howard Sergeant, whose introduction enumerated the Movement's limitations. Although Conquest subsequently produced *New Lines 2* (1963), the original group of poets took no pains to sustain a corporate identity. (See also ANTHOLOGIES).

New Machiavelli, The, a novel by H. G. *Wells, published in 1911. Wells's first-person narrator, Richard Remington, resembles the author of *The Prince* in being a politician in exile, his career in ruins, dreaming of a strengthened and more perfect state. The narrative traces his intellectual and emotional formation and his adventures among the Edwardian political intelligentsia. Graham Wallas, Sidney and Beatrice *Webb, and Arthur Balfour are among those who appear under thin disguises. Remington marries the politically ambitious Margaret, becomes a Liberal Member of Parliament, and founds a political weekly. As a member of a cross-party dining club, the Pentagram Circle (modelled on the Coefficients Club to which Wells had belonged), he comes under the influence of the Tory imperialists and changes sides at the time of the 1909 Budget. His platform of feminism, universal education, and a 'trained aristocracy' has some populist appeal, but neither his wife nor his new allies are very convinced by it. Finally, he abruptly abandons politics and leaves England with his new lover, Isabel Rivers. The novel offers vivid commentary on the London political scene, and portrays with considerable insight the mixture of power-lust, sexual indulgence, and public censoriousness which has led to the downfall of prominent British politicians both before and after Wells's time. It is one of the very few twentieth-century novels of high politics to transcend the limitations of the 'political thriller'. Unfortunately, *The New Machiavelli*'s weakest point, in an avowed 'discussion novel', is the woolly, sentimental sloganizing of what are offered as Remington's ideas.

New Masses, see MASSES, THE.

New Men, The, a novel by C. P. *Snow, published in 1954. Like other novels in the series *Strangers and Brothers* this book is narrated by Lewis Eliot, the Cambridge tutor who moved from Cambridge to work for the British government. The central character of the novel is Lewis's brother Martin who is involved in the manufacture of the atomic bomb. The narrative starts before the outbreak of the Second World War, and ends after its conclusion when Martin returns to Cambridge to do pure research, having refused the opportunity to remain in charge of government research into the bomb. Martin's wife Irene is unfaithful to him, and this private conflict mirrors the various difficulties characters in this novel have about loyalty. Many of the scientists, including Martin and Walter Luke, an important character in *The Masters*, have doubts about the morality of exploding the bomb. Luke's assistant Sawbridge betrays the atomic secrets to the Russians, and with Martin's assistance the government forces him to confess. Snow records the mixture of motives which drive his characters into certain positions, although he is perhaps better at investigating self-interest and love of power than at exploring genuine moral concern.

New Negro: An Interpretation, the title of an anthology of African-American writing and art edited by Alain *Locke, published in 1925. It was Paul U. Kelly, the editor of *The Survey*, a journal devoted to social problems, who initially made the book-length anthology possible as a special 'Harlem Number' with Locke as guest editor. Most of the contributors were writers associated with the *Harlem Renaissance. Locke's foreword speaks of 'a fresh spiritual and cultural focusing'. Among poets, Langston *Hughes, Jean *Toomer, Countee *Cullen, James Weldon *Johnson, and Claude *McKay all contributed important work. Jessie *Fauset contributed a dramatic vignette, 'The Gift of Laughter'. Essays which illuminate the state of African-American arts, culture, and society at the time include 'The New Negro' by Alain Locke, 'The Negro in American Literature' by W. S. *Braithwaite, 'Harlem: The Cultural Capital' by James Weldon Johnson, and 'The Negro Mind Reaches Out' by W. E. B. *Du Bois.

New Poetry, The, an anthology of verse edited by Al *Alvarez, first published by Penguin Books in 1962. Alvarez's controversial introduction argued that since the decline of *Modernism 'the machinery of modern English poetry seems to have been controlled by a series of negative feed-backs'; the latest of these, the reaction against the excesses of Dylan *Thomas and his followers, had established traditionalism and gentility as dominant characteristics of post-war poetry. To this extent, the anthology proposed itself as a corrective to the *Movement's 'academic-administrative verse, polite, knowledgeable, efficient, polished' that had been promoted by *New Lines* in 1956. *The New Poetry* espoused a more urgent and vigorous poetic engagement with a broader spectrum of experience. Six of the *New Lines* poets nevertheless featured in Alvarez's selection, along with fourteen further British poets, including R. S. *Thomas, Norman *MacCaig, Christopher *Middleton, Ted *Hughes, and David *Holbrook, and two Americans, John *Berryman and Robert *Lowell. Sylvia *Plath, Peter *Porter, and Ian *Hamilton were among the eight poets added to the revised edition in 1965. Although the introduction's claims were at odds with the sober tone of much of the verse, the anthology marked an important development in introducing the work of numerous significantly innovative poets to a wide public.

New Republic, The, a weekly magazine devoted to domestic and international current affairs, reviews of the arts, and commentary on a wide range of social and cultural topics. It was founded in New York in 1914 by Willard D. Straight, with Herbert D. Croly as editor. Croly was succeeded in 1930 by Bruce Bliven. The magazine subsequently came under the control of an editorial board. Malcolm *Cowley, Robert *Pinsky, and Edmund *Wilson have been among its literary editors. Although the prevailing political orientation of the *New Republic* has always been perceptibly, and sometimes radically, liberal, it is remained hospitable to a wide spectrum of views. It assumed authority and influence early in its career; its failure to censure the Bolsheviks after the Russian Revolution generated controversy and it was instrumental in swaying opinion towards the Senate's repudiation of President Wilson's signature to the Treaty of Versailles. In the course of the 1920s it became one of the most highly regarded of the more widely circulated periodicals of quality in America and Britain, featuring work from distinguished writers on both sides of the Atlantic: Walter *Lippmann, Thomas *Wolfe, George *Santayana, John Maynard *Keynes, George Bernard *Shaw, and Virginia *Woolf were among the contributors of articles; reviewers included Llewellyn *Powys, Sean *O'Faolain, Lewis *Mumford, Robert Penn *Warren, and Louise *Bogan, who also supplied poems, as did Edith *Sitwell, Edna St Vincent *Millay, and Elinor *Wylie. From 1930 onward the increasing urgency of the journal's political concerns resulted in some diminishment of its literary content. In the post-war decades it regained its reputation for the excellence of its book reviews, and is also noted for its coverage of the cinema and theatre.

New Review, see REVIEW, THE.

News from Tartary, see FLEMING, PETER.

New Statesman, The, a weekly magazine founded in 1913 to 'deal with all current political, social, religious, and intellectual questions'. Originally associated with the *Fabian Society, it has remained a vehicle for views from the political left, while retaining its independence of restrictively doctrinaire affiliations. Early issues featured a serialization of 'What Is Socialism?' by Beatrice and Sidney *Webb. G. B. *Shaw, Leonard and Virginia *Woolf, T. S. *Eliot, Arnold *Bennett, and Bertrand *Russell were among the notable contributors under Clifford Sharp's editorship from 1913 to 1930. In 1931 the *New Statesman* absorbed the *Nation* and was edited by Kingsley Martin until 1963; subsequent editors have included Paul Johnson (1965–70), Richard Crossman (1970–2), and Hugh Stephenson (1982–6). Since 1988, when it merged with *New Society*, it has appeared under the title *New Statesman and Society*. It is noted for the consistently high standards of its coverage of current affairs and political issues. Although the space devoted to poetry and other forms of creative writing has diminished since the early 1980s, the *New Statesman* formerly published verse by many leading poets, including W. B. *Yeats, Edward *Thomas, Robert *Graves, Stephen *Spender, D. J. *Enright, and Donald *Davie.

New Verse, a periodical described by Ian *Hamilton as 'the toughest and most entertaining of all the *little magazines'; it was founded in 1933 by Geoffrey *Grigson, who remained editor until 1939. Grigson's enthusiasm for the work of W. H. *Auden and his fellow poets of the early 1930s, to whom Michael *Roberts's *New Signatures* anthology of 1932 had given a corporate identity, motivated him to establish *New Verse*; from 1933 to 1937 it was the only periodical devoted exclusively to the interests of poetry. Wyndham Lewis's **Blast* was greatly admired by Grigson, who strove to emulate its uncompromising tone in his editorial denunciations of 'Pure Poetry-ism'; the political and academic positions exemplified respectively by Roberts and F. R. *Leavis were both repudiated by Grigson, who fiercely maintained his belief in the assessment of poetry in terms of its relation to objective reality. By 1934 *New Verse* had gained a reputation for vitriolic criticism (mostly composed by Grigson). Edith *Sitwell, dubbed 'the old Jane', Laura *Riding, and Robert *Graves were among the writers upon whom memorable attacks were launched; poets closely associated with the magazine were not spared its intelligent ridicule when their work failed to meet Grigson's exacting standards. Between 1934 and 1936 *New Verse* was actively interested in surrealism, featuring poetry by David *Gascoyne, Philip O'Connor, Paul Eluard, and Hans Arp; it had rejected the movement by 1937, when the poetic implications of *Mass Observation became its specialization. Auden was the poet most frequently published in *New Verse*, a double issue in 1937 being devoted to celebrating his thirtieth birthday; Dylan *Thomas, Gavin *Ewart, Norman *Cameron, and Charles *Madge also contributed repeatedly. The magazine's energies began to diminish in 1938 and it was discontinued in 1939.

New Woman, a term used to describe a new generation of active women, who believed in women's suffrage, equal educational opportunities for women, sexual independence, and what they called rational dress. New Women figure in Virginia Woolf's **Night and Day* and in the works of *Schreiner, *Shaw, *Wells, Rebecca *West, and others. Sarah Grand is said to have coined the phrase in the *North Atlantic Review* in 1894.

New Worlds, a *science fiction magazine founded in 1946. For many years, under the editorship of Ted Carnell, it was the only influential British journal in its field. After 1964, when M. *Moorcock became editor, *New Worlds* was slowly transformed into one of the most challenging fiction magazines of the 1960s. It became controversial through its promoting of 'New Wave' or experimental fiction. J. G. *Ballard, B. W. *Aldiss, T. M. *Disch, and J. T. *Sladek were among those whose most vigorous and searching work appeared in the magazine. In about 1970, after the W. H. Smith bookselling chain refused to stock the journal, and after Moorcock resigned to concentrate on his own work, the magazine ceased to command a large audience. In the early 1970s some further issues appeared in quarterly format, but publication was intermittent and the last numbers appeared in 1979. In 1991, with Moorcock's co-operation, *New Worlds* once again appeared, this time as a serial anthology.

New Writing, a periodical founded in 1936 by John *Lehmann. Although Lehmann stated in the first issue that *New Writing* 'is first and foremost interested in literature and is independent of any political party', its opposition to fascism made it hospitable to writers well known for their socialist convictions; poetry by Stephen *Spender, C. Day *Lewis, and W. H. *Auden appeared and early issues included prose by Edward *Upward and Rex *Warner. Regarding **New Verse* as the primary forum for poetry, Lehmann was predominantly concerned with publishing fiction and documentary articles in *New Writing*; George *Orwell, V. S. *Pritchett, Christopher *Isherwood, Virginia *Woolf, and E. M. *Forster were notable contributors, who also included numerous foreign authors: work by Jean Paul Sartre and Federico Garcia Lorca appeared, and Mulk Raj *Anand was among the writers from various parts of the Commonwealth who were featured. In 1940 the title was changed to *Folios of New Writing*, announced as 'a laboratory where the writers of the future may experiment'; a decline in the level of interest became apparent until 1942, when the moribund *Daylight* was incorporated to form *New Writing and Daylight*, which continued until 1946. In addition to new fiction, the regular 'reports from the front' restored the journal's documentary aspect; articles by Raymond *Williams, Philip *Toynbee, and Arthur *Koestler contributed to the articulate commitment to humanist values maintained throughout the war. From 1940 to 1950 Lehmann also edited *Penguin New Writing*, which appeared as a quarterly paperback; editions of up to 100,000 copies were sold within weeks of publication. *Penguin New Writing* originally consisted chiefly of material from *New Writing*, but increasingly published new work by British, European, American, and Commonwealth authors.

New Yorker, The, a weekly magazine established in 1925 by Harold Ross, who remained its editor until his death in 1951, and the publisher Raoul Fleischman; James *Thurber was managing editor in the publication's early years and contributed material throughout his career. The combination of scrupulously accurate reportage, urbanely humorous and satirical articles, lively reviewing, short stories, and poetry established by Ross and his colleagues ensured the magazine's success after an initial period of uncertainty; its influence over American journalism and humorous writing was considerable during its first twenty-five years. Edmund *Wilson, John *O'Hara, Truman *Capote, John *Updike, John *Cheever, J. D. *Salinger, S. J. *Perelman, and Dorothy *Parker are among the writers whose work has been regularly featured; the wide range of American and British poets who have contributed includes Ogden *Nash, Robert *Frost, John *Ashbery, Ted *Hughes, Douglas *Dunn, and Seamus *Heaney. Among the artists who have supplied the distinctive cartoons which are indispensable to the *New Yorker* have been Charles Addams, Gluyas Willimas, Willima Steig, and Mary Petty. William Shawn, the editor since 1952, was controversially replaced by Robert Gottlieb in 1985 when the periodical was acquired by S. I. Newhouse, owner of the Condé Naste and Random House publishing groups. *Here at The New Yorker* (1975, revised edition 1990) is Brendan Gill's detailed memoir of his long association with the magazine.

New York Review of Books, The, a fortnightly literary periodical founded on a provisional basis in 1963, when a printers' strike resulted in the suspension of New York's principal book-reviewing pages through the temporary closure of the *New York Times* and the *Herald Tribune*. It was favourably received and began regular publication under the continuing joint editorship of Robert B. Silvers, formerly a member of the editorial board of the **Paris Review*, and Barbara Epstein. Among the reviewers have been D. J. *Enright, James *Baldwin, Gore *Vidal, Frank *Kermode, V. S. *Pritchett, and contributors of articles have included W. H. *Auden, Noam *Chomsky, Richard *Ellmann, Andrei Sakharov, Claude Lévi-Strauss, and Mary *McCarthy. Like its British descendant, the **London Review of Books*, the journal is noted for the high standards of its extended review essays and is a leading literary and intellectual organ of the democratic Left. During the Vietnam War and the Watergate affair it was in the vanguard of articulate protest against the American administration. The celebrated caricatures of literary and political figures by the artist David Levine are a perennial feature of its pages. Most issues devote space to poetry; among the notable British and American poets whose work has been represented are Robert *Lowell, John *Berryman, Ted *Hughes, John *Ashbery, and Richard *Wilbur.

New York School of Poets, a name loosely applied to a number of poets working in New York between about 1950 and 1975. Two American cities have given their names to groups of poets, San Francisco and New York, and both in a somewhat ironic style. The poets of the *San Francisco Renaissance mockingly adopted the name of one of their main sources of intellectual inspiration, although their activities hardly constituted a renaissance in the ordinary sense of the term, and the New York School was a name invented by a gallery director who published a series of poets from 1952 onward. The school had its origins in a friendship between Frank *O'Hara, John *Ashbery, James *Schuyler, and Kenneth *Koch that began in the early 1950s, based on a common interest in painting, urban life, and recent European poetry. Emerging at the same time that New York became a centre for the artistic avant-garde in the 1950s, the name stuck although the poets themselves never tried to create a school in the usual sense of the term. Unlike other groups of poets such as the *Black Mountain poets or the *Language poets, they have produced little in the way of writing about their poetics. The best-known essay to emerge from the group, 'Personism: A Manifesto' by Frank O'Hara, is a parody of the genre.

Their poetic style is urbane, witty, discursive, surreal, and above all fascinated with surfaces of all kinds. References to popular culture, especially the cinema, abound, as well as an acute awareness of the aesthetics of their painter contemporaries. Their poems offer wonderfully inventive displays of metaphor, image, quick changes of tone and theme, and often seem devoted to a conscious celebration of the artificial inventions of the imagination. They developed a cosmopolitan voice in their poetry which concealed its artfulness so well that it became the most imitated feature of their work. A second generation soon emerged, so that *An Anthology of New York Poets* (ed. Ron Padgett and David Shapiro, 1970) included twenty-three poets, and even then made some omissions. Notable second-generation poets would include Anne *Waldman, Ted Berrigan, Alice Notley, and Bernadette Mayer. The New York School has arguably produced a third generation in the Language Writers who originated in New York.

What has most changed the status of the New York School since the 1960s has been John Ashbery's extraordinary success as a poet since **Self-Portrait in a Convex Mirror* (1975), a success which has taken him away culturally and stylistically from any grouping. For many poets his early book *The Tennis Court Oath* (1962) was the most characteristic of the school. Its poems seem to press against the limits of what is possible in poetry, notably 'Europe' which is a series of 111 short sections in which fragments of popular fiction, stray images, gnomic remarks, grids, and disjunctive phrases, seem to be united only by occasional explicit references to European culture. Frank O'Hara's early death in 1966 has also affected subsequent perception of the style of these poets, creating an aura around some of his poems, especially those that recreate walks in downtown Manhattan, that has been hard to see beyond. In some ways it is actually the least well-known of the originating poets, James Schuyler, whose brilliant poetry deserves to be much better known, and most conforms to the idea of a New York school. His awareness of New York as a city of census-takers, 'unpedimented lions', fire escapes, 'capless tubes of unguents', whose inhabitants look at nature and ask 'is this lichen, this stuff here? | And these leaves, are they oak leaves?' (*Freely Espousing*, 1969), permeates his surprisingly meditative poems.

Many of the poets were homosexual, and Geoffrey Ward argues that although homosexuality is rarely the explicit theme of their work, they employ a repertoire of poetic attitudes and devices which result from 'seeing from the edge of things where the excluded go'. Ward's book *Statutes of Liberty* (1993) is the one major critical study of the school, although there are numerous books on Ashbery, and a smaller number on O'Hara.

New York Trilogy, The, see AUSTER, PAUL.

NGCOBO, Lauretta (1931–), South African novelist, born in Ixopo, Natal, educated at Fort Hare University. Forced into exile as a member of the banned Pan-African Congress, she arrived in Britain in 1970 and began working as a teacher in London. *Cross of Gold* (1981), her first novel, drew on her memories of the violent turbulence in South Africa from the 1950s onward; her difficulties in writing about the political experience of black South African women led her to feature a male activist as the book's central protagonist. *And They Didn't Die* (1990) succeeds in giving centrality to female characters, dramatically evoking the efforts of Jezile, a black domestic maid, to free herself from both white racism and the constraints of her people's traditional culture. Ngcobo is the editor of *Let It Be Told* (1987), a collection of essays by black women writers living in Britain, and the children's book *Fiki Learns to Like Other People* (1993).

NGUGI wa THIONG'O, formerly known as James T. NGUGI (1938–), Kenyan novelist, dramatist, and essayist, born in Limuru, Kenya, educated at Makerere University College and at the University of Leeds. Ngugi's experiences as a Kikuyu adolescent during Kenya's struggle for independence from white colonial domination inform his first two novels. *Weep Not, Child* (1964), set mainly during the Mau Mau Rebellion of the 1950s, was the first novel in English by an East African writer. *The River Between* (1965), his second novel, but the first to be written, deals with religious divisions in two rural communities. In both novels, social injustice, dispossession, economic and cultural disintegration, are perceived through youthful and messianic protagonists. *A *Grain of Wheat* (1967) and **Petals of Blood* (1977) are Ngugi's most critically acclaimed novels in English. *Secret Lives* (1975) is a collection of stories. His plays include *The Black Hermit*, written for Uganda's Independence celebrations in 1962; *The Trial of Dedan Kimathi* (1976; with Micere *Mugo): and *This Time Tomorrow* (1970) which includes 'The Rebels', and 'The Wound in the Heart'. His first work in the Gikuyu language, the play *Ngaahica Ndeenda* (1977; translated as *I Will Marry When I Want*, 1982), co-authored by Ngugi wa Mirii, is a community drama addressed to peasants and workers. It was banned by the authorities as subversive and Ngugi was arrested, and spent a year in prison, an experience vividly recorded in *Detained: A Writer's Prison Diary* (1981). While in prison he wrote his first novel in Gikuyu, which was published in 1980, and translated as *Devil on the Cross* (1982). He has argued ever since that the duty of African writers is to write primarily in local languages as an urgent political, social, and cultural necessity. His second novel in Gikuyu, *Matigari* (1989; translated by Wangui wa Goro), focuses on a former Mau Mau fighter, the novel's eponymous protagonist, and his eventual realization that a new liberation struggle has to be initiated. It was immediately banned in Kenya. Books of essays, invariably combative, include *Homecoming* (1972), *Writers in Politics* (1981), *Barrel of a Pen* (1983), and *Decolonizing the Mind* (1986). *Moving the Centre: The Struggle for Cultural Freedoms* (1993) studies twentieth-century African literature and posits the need to find African modes independent of European ones. See David Cook and Michael Okenimkpe, *Ngugi wa Thiong'o: An Exploration of His Writings* (1983).

NICHOL, b p (Barrie Phillip) (1944–), Canadian writer, born in Vancouver, educated at the University of British Columbia. Nichol first achieved recognition for 'concrete' poems which express their thought through physical shape. All his work explores the way in which language operates to construct meaning, and his poetry frequently questions the premises on which verse has traditionally been based by breaking down barriers between the literary and the oral and between art and popular culture. His best-known work, the multi-volume poem *The Martyrology* (books 1–8, 1972–90), which has been described as the longest of contemporary Canada's many long poems, is a present-tense autobiography which attempts to document in language how mental and physical processes work. Nichol has also written a considerable body of sound poetry and *stream-of-consciousness prose. His other works include *Dada Lama* (1968), *Two Novels* (1969), *The Cosmic Chef* (1970), *Still Water* (1970), *The True Eventual Story of Billy the Kid* (1970), *Craft Dinner* (1978), and *Journal* (1978). Nichol's *Selected Writings* were published in 1994; he is also a noted author of books and television scripts for children. *Sons of Captain Poetry* (1970) is a film about his early sound poetry, made by Michael *Ondaatje.

NICHOLS, Grace (1950–), Guyanese poet, born in Georgetown, where she was educated at the University of Guyana. After working as a schoolteacher and journalist, she emigrated to Britain in 1977. *I Is a Long-Memoried Woman* (1983), her first collection of poetry, for which she received the Commonwealth Poetry Prize, formed a cycle of poems surveying the oppressed history of Caribbean women and celebrating their capacity for survival. The purposeful humour which emerges as a characteristic of her work in *The Fat Black Woman's Poems* (1984) is integral to the wide-ranging poetic commentaries on the contemporary culture of the Caribbean in *Lazy Thoughts of a Lazy Woman* (1989). Her verse, which uses both Jamaican patois and Standard English, is rich in subtly musical qualities of rhythm and rhyme. Among her other works is the novel *Whole of a Morning Sky* (1989), which draws on her childhood memories of growing political turmoil in Guyana from the late 1950s onwards. She has also published numerous stories for children, including *Give Yourself a Hug* (1994), and edited several anthologies of verse.

NICHOLS, Peter (Richard) (1927–), British playwright, born and educated in Bristol; he worked as an actor and a teacher before achieving success with his first stage play, *A Day in the Death of Joe Egg* (1967), a dark comedy about the pains and pressures of bringing up a severely disabled child. His subsequent work includes *The National Health* (1969), *The Freeway* (1974), and *Born in the Gardens* (1979), which respectively use a hospital ward, a traffic jam on a motorway, and a Bristol household to make general comments on what their author sees as the decline of England; three pieces with autobiographical aspects, *Forget-Me-Not-Lane* (1971), a nostalgic picture of a West Country childhood notable for its wry portrayal of an eccentric father, *Privates on Parade* (1977), about an ENSA troupe in Malaya, and *A Piece of My Mind* (1988), about a somewhat embittered playwright unsuccessfully trying to write an autobiographical novel; *Chez Nous* (1974) and *Passion Play* (1981), plays about the strains of marriage, the latter using four performers to embody the different aspects of a fastidious yet sensual husband and a seemingly calm but distraught wife; and a musical about the opium trade and British imperialism, *Poppy* (1982). Nichols's œuvre, which at its best is marked by stylistic daring, a sense of social responsibility, and a sardonic yet compassionate humour, also includes television plays, notably *The Gorge* (1968), and the autobiography *Feeling You're Behind* (1984).

NICHOLS, Robert (Malise Bowyer) (1893–1944), British poet, born at Manningtree, Essex, educated at Trinity College, Oxford. He was on active service on the Western Front from 1914 until he was invalided out after the Battle of the Somme in 1916. His responses to the war are contained in *Invocation* (1915) and *Ardours and Endurances* (1917), which established him as one of the most highly acclaimed younger poets of the day. 'The Assault', his best-known poem of the conflict, evokes the destructive havoc and emotional turbulence of an attack in verse of unusual freedom and energy. Much of his poetry combines documentary elements with a vestigially romantic attitude. From 1921 to 1924 he preceded Edmund *Blunden as Professor of English at Imperial University, Tokyo. He published two further volumes of poetry, *Aurelia* (1920), in which rural lyricism predominates, and *Fisbo, or the Looking Glass Loaned* (1934), a satirical fantasy. His other publications include the novel *Under the Yew* (1927) and the play *Guilty Souls* (1922). Fragments of his ambitious unfinished works 'Don Juan Tenorio the Great' and 'The Solitudes of the Sun' appear in *Such Was My Singing* (1942), a selected edition of his verse.

NICHOLSON, Norman (Cornthwaite) (1914–87), British poet, born in Millom, Cumberland, where he was educated at local schools and remained all his life. He was a schoolteacher for many years before becoming a full-time writer. Nicholson first attracted notice as a poet when his work appeared alongside poetry by J. C. Hall and Keith *Douglas in *Selected Poems* (1943). *Five Rivers* (1944), his first independent collection, was followed by numerous further volumes which include *Rock Face* (1948), *The Pot Geranium* (1954), *A Local Habitation* (1972), in which freer verse-forms emerge in his work, and *Sea to the West* (1981). Nicholson's engagement with his native locality is pervasive; the topography, geology, and urban and industrial aspects of his surroundings provide themes and imagery for poems combining descriptive and contemplative elements in a fine balance. 'The Pot Geranium', one of his best-known poems, states the belief in the interpenetration of the near-at-hand and the cosmically inclusive that informs his best work. *Selected Poems: 1940–1982* was published in 1982. The Christian metaphysics discernible in many poems are also integral to his verse-dramas, notably *The Old Man of the Mountains* (1946), and his critical writings, among which are *Man and Literature* (1943) and *William Cowper* (1951). His other works include a biography of H. G. *Wells (1950), numerous books on the Lake District, and the novels *The Fire of the Lord* (1944) and *The Green Shore* (1947). An autobiography entitled *Wednesday Early Closing* appeared in 1975. See also TOPOGRAPHICAL POETRY.

NI CHUILLEANAIN, Eilean (1942–), Irish poet, born in Cork, educated at University College, Cork, and at Lady Margaret Hall, Oxford. In 1966 she became a lecturer at Trinity College, Dublin, and was a founding editor of *Cyphers*, one of the city's leading literary periodicals. *Acts and Monuments* (1972), her first collection of poetry, was followed by subsequent volumes including *Site of Ambush* (1975), *The Rose-Geranium* (1981), *The Second Voyage* (1986), *The Magdalene Sermon* (1989), and *The Brazen Serpent* (1994). Her remark that 'The problem of addressing the special (Irish) audience in a special (female) voice remains unsolved and many of my poems are attempts to solve it' indicates the deep concern with identity which underruns much of her work. Gaelic and classical material is fused with intensely personal imaginative responses in a number of her poems. The characteristic clarity of her imagery, often conveying mysteriously evocative qualities, is sensitively used in portraying disregarded aspects of her native city in *Cork* (1977), her collaboration with the artist Brian Lalor.

NICOLSON, Sir Harold (George) (1886–1968), British author, diplomat, and politician, born in Tehran where his father was serving with the British Legation, educated at Balliol College, Oxford. He held diplomatic postings in Europe and the Middle East from 1909 to 1929, drawing on his experiences of the diplomatic service in the satirical novel *Public Faces* (1932). During this period he produced *Some People* (1927), nine humorously fictionalized portraits of 'real people in imaginary situations', and several critical biographies, which include *Paul Verlaine* (1921) and *Byron, the Last Journey* (1924). He was Member of Parliament for West Leicester from 1935 to 1945. Among his later works are the biographies *Curzon, the Last Phase* (1934) and *King George V: His Life and Reign* (1952), and the urbanely witty essays of *The English Sense of Humour* (1947). Nicolson's *Diaries and Letters* (three volumes, 1966–8) were edited by his son Nigel *Nicolson, author of *Portrait of a Marriage* (1973), an account of his father's unorthodox but ultimately well-founded relationship with Vita *Sackville-West. There is a biography of Nicolson by James Lees-Milne (two volumes, 1980, 1981).

NICOLSON, Nigel (1917–), British biographer and editor, the son of Harold *Nicolson and Vita *Sackville-West, born in London, educated at Balliol College, Oxford. His first publication was *The Grenadier Guards, 1939–1945* (1949), an official history of the regiment with which he served throughout the Second World War. In 1948 he became a director of a publishing house, and was MP for Bournemouth and East Christchurch from 1952 to 1959. His most widely acclaimed works are *Alex* (1973), the biography of Field Marshall Earl Alexander of Tunis, and *Portrait of a Marriage* (1973), a sensitive and revealing account of his parents' unusual but fundamentally stable relationship. Among his other publications are the biographical studies *Mary Curzon* (1977) and *Napoleon, 1812* (1985), and the topographical books *The Himalayas* (1975) and *Kent* (1988). He is the editor of his father's *Diaries and Letters* (three volumes, 1966–8) and, with Joanne Trautmann, *The Letters of Virginia Woolf* (six volumes, 1975–80).

NIEDECKER, Lorine (1903–70), American poet, born at Fort Atkinson, near Madison, Wisconsin, the region in which she spent most of her life; educated at Beloit College. She worked for Madison University's WHA radio station and as a librarian until deteriorating eyesight led her to seek other employment, chiefly as a domestic assistant in a Madison hospital. She dated her development as a poet from the beginning of her contact with her 'friend and mentor' Louis *Zukofsky, with whom she initiated a long correspondence after reading the 'Objectivists' (see OBJECTIVISM) issue of **Poetry* which he edited in 1931. *New Goose* (1946), her first collection of verse, was followed by *My Friend Tree* (1962), *North Central* (1968), and *Tenderness and Gristle* (1970), a collected edition. Much of her flexibly structured poetry combines remarkable concentration and fluency; successions of short poems rich in assonance, alliteration, and unobtrusive rhyme form an affirmative and precisely detailed evocation of her remote natural surroundings. 'Lake Superior' and 'Wintergreen Ridge' are longer sequences drawing on the botanical and geological elements of her landscapes for imagery typifying the 'undistractable clarity' Ed *Dorn identified in her work. Cid *Corman edited *Blue Chicory* (1976) and *The Granite Pail* (1985); *'Between You and Me'* (edited by L. P. Faranda, 1986) collects letters she exchanged with Corman. Her other collections of verse include *Harpsichord & Saltfish* (edited by J. Penberthy, 1991). Peter Dent's edition of *The Full Note* (1983) contains poems and letters by Niedecker and a range of tributes from her associates and admirers. *From This Condensery* (edited by R. Bertholf, 1985) is a full edition of her work.

Nigger of the Narcissus, see CONRAD, JOSEPH.

Night and Day, V. *Woolf's second novel and her most conventional in form (criticized by K. *Mansfield for being 'a lie in the soul'), published in 1919. It is a four-sided love story which is at once comical, melancholy, and awkwardly formal. The tone is Jane Austen-like satire, with a Mozartian, operatic structure of quest and resolution, and a strong ingredient of Shakespearean comedy. There are four main, young characters from different backgrounds. Katharine Hilbery is the granddaughter of a famous nineteenth-century poet and belongs to an intellectual aristocracy; her mother, the fey, stage-managing Mrs Hilbery, makes her guard the poet's shrine, but Katharine would rather escape into the abstractions of mathematics. She is engaged to the prissy, conventional William Rodney, but falls in love, in a tentative, almost asexual way, with a solicitor's clerk, Ralph Denham, who is loved by Katharine's suffragist friend, Mary Datchet. These four allow for a consideration of the social and sexual choices for women. A desire is felt for an alternative, utopian world where incoherent fragments might be unified; but the narrative has difficulty in expressing these concepts.

'Nightfall', see ASIMOV, ISAAC.

Nightwood, see BARNES, DJUNA.

NIN, Anaïs (1903–77), American diarist, literary critic, and novelist, born near Paris, of a Spanish-Cuban father and a Danish-French mother. At the age of 11 she moved with her mother to New York. She trained as a psychoanalyst under Otto Rank, and practised briefly. The publication in Paris of her first book, *D. H. Lawrence: An Unprofessional Study* (1932), brought her into contact with Parisian artistic circles and *émigrés* such as Lawrence *Durrell, Henry *Miller, and William Carlos *Williams, and with *la groupe surrealiste*. In her later years she lived mainly in the USA where she became renowned as a speaker on women's creativity and art for the US women's movement. Her ever-changing life is meticulously documented in her *Early Diaries* (2 volumes, 1978, 1982) and *Journals* (7 volumes, 1966–80), collected by Gunther Stuhlmann, which provide a fascinating first-hand description of American and French literary circles. Nin's interest in dreams, unconscious desires, and her overriding concern with female identities are interwoven in her works, including her prose poem *House of Incest* (1936) and her novel *A Spy in the House of Love* (1954). Other novels include *Children of the Albatross* (1947), *Solar Basque* (1958), and *Seduction of the Minotaur* (1961). Her short stories, collected in *Under a Glass Bell* (1948) and other volumes, demonstrate her gift as a story-teller, a talent that is sometimes overwhelmed by the opacity of her poetic imaginings and private mythologies in her more extended novels. Her critical works include *The Novel of the Future* (1968). Nin also produced several volumes of erotic fiction such as the stories published as *Delta of Venus* (1969). Letters between Nin and Henry Miller from 1932 to 1953 have been collected as *A Literate Passion* (1987).

Nineteen Eighty-Four, a novel by George *Orwell, published in 1949. *The Last Man in Europe* was the working title of Orwell's most celebrated novel, which projects a totalitarian future from the austerities of the early Cold War. Orwell worked on the manuscript during a protracted stay on the remote Scottish island of Jura; he had none of the usual distractions of his editing, reviewing, and broadcasting routine and, as a result, the narrative has a much clearer sense of direction than his other fiction. The hero, Winston Smith, lives in a box-like flat in London, the 'Airstrip One' of the new super-power, Oceania. The texture of his daily life, with its bad food, chronic shortages, faulty goods, ambient propaganda, and inescapable surveillance is composed of selective features of life in post-war Europe but it has also become the model for many subsequent fictions, literary and cinematic, which pit the individual against the system, the advocate of free speech against the operatives of the secret society. Winston is employed in the misnamed Ministry of Truth, where he is forced to rewrite history in accordance with the official line of Ingsoc, or English Socialism: the Party. His inevitable act of rebellion is focused on a forbidden love affair with Julia, another Party member. Together, they attempt to get in touch with the Brotherhood, a quasi-Trotskyist underground movement, but choose the wrong channel in O'Brien, a high-ranking Party official who successfully uses torture to make them betray each other. The book is most famous for its creation of Big Brother, the Thought Police, and its image of a hopeless future: 'If you want a picture of the future, imagine a boot stamping on a human face—for ever'. But perhaps its most disturbing prediction concerns the less sensational but more profoundly undermining corruption of language by Newspeak, a deliberately impoverished version of English which by systematically removing, rather than adding, items of vocabulary and forms of speech, drastically reduces the scope of thought and feeling of its speakers. See also UTOPIA AND ANTI-UTOPIA.

NIVEN, Larry (Lawrence Van Cott Niven) (1938–), American *science fiction writer, born and educated in California. He combined an erudite style with a sound scientific basis in a series of novels and stories about Known Space beginning with *World of Ptavvs* (1966). Perhaps the best-known of these are *Ringworld* (1970), which argued the efficacy of constructing an artificial world in the shape of a sun-encircling ring, and *Protector* (1973); other volumes in the sequence were *Neutron Star* (1968) and *The Shape of Space* (1969), which espoused the romantic aspects of technological extrapolation. He collaborated with J. Pournelle in a series of novels including *The Mote in God's Eye* (1974), *Lucifer's Hammer* (1977), *Oath of Fealty* (1981), and *Football* (1985). His best short fiction is published in *N-Space* (1990) and *Playgrounds of the Mind* (1992).

NKOSI, Lewis (1936–), South African essayist and novelist, born in Natal. After writing for *Drum* magazine and other publications, in 1960–1 he studied journalism at Harvard, but was prevented by the South African authorities from returning to his own country. Living in exile he has held various academic posts, and in London he was literary editor of *New African*. One of the foremost African literary and cultural critics, Nkosi is best known for his magisterial essays, which vigorously demonstrate the relevance and importance of African literature in the modern world; these are collected in *Home and Exile* (1965) and *The Transplanted Heart* (1975). In *Tasks and Masks: Themes and Styles of African Literature* (1981) African culture and society, resistance to remnants of colonialism, and the development of modern African literature are all examined with vitality and impartial urgency. Nkosi's novel *Mating Birds* (1986), a spare, laconically eloquent first-person account by a young South African Zulu on death row for allegedly raping a white woman, explores the psychological dimensions of apartheid. His play *The Rhythm of Violence* (1965), set in Johannesburg in the early 1960s, deals with a group of young African, English, and Afrikaner students who become tragically involved in violent resistance against the apartheid regime.

NOLAN, Christopher (1965–), Irish writer, born in Mullingar, Co. Westmeath, educated at Trinity College, Dublin. He suffered severe brain damage at birth, which left him paralysed and unable to communicate clearly; at the age of 11 he began typing by movements of his head transmitted through a 'unicorn stick' after treatment with a new drug had increased his muscular control. The title of *Dam-Burst of Dreams* (1981), a collection of the poetic, dramatic, and prose pieces he had produced by the age of 14, indicates the sense of accumulated energies evident in much of the writing. His poetry, which often combines social, religious, and personal elements, is characterized by flamboyantly idiosyncratic constructions that recall the styles of Hopkins and *Joyce. His compelling autobiography, *Under the Eye of the Clock* (1987; Whitbread Prize, 1987), displays his rich use of language, ranging stylistically between a ribald realism and passages of impressionistic prose.

No Laughing Matter, see WILSON, SIR ANGUS.

No Man's Land, a play by Harold *Pinter, first performed in 1975. The play mainly involves the relationship between the rich and reclusive alcoholic Hirst and the shabby *soi-disant* poet, Spooner, roles respectively played by Sir Ralph Richardson and Sir John Gielgud in the original production at the National Theatre, in London. Hirst brings Spooner home, having apparently met him on Hampstead Heath. He plies him with whisky and, himself more and more affected by drink, proceeds to identify and almost certainly misidentify him as 'Charles', a friend from a past clearly more alive for him than the present. There follows a bizarre conversation about their sexual adventures, in which Spooner accuses Hirst of having seduced his wife. This appears to be part of the former's attempt to inveigle his way into the latter's memories, hence into his life, hence into a position of security and power in his household. This becomes overt when Spooner suddenly asks Hirst to 'let me live with you and be your secretary': a request never answered, but not at all to the liking of Hirst's tough-talking servants, Foster and Briggs, who have reacted to Spooner's intrusion by harassing him both physically and verbally. Whatever the eventual outcome, Hirst himself will clearly remain locked in a past that is real, imaginary, or both: 'no man's land, which never moves, which never changes, which never grows older, but which remains forever, icy and silent'.

NOONUCCAL, Oodgeroo, traditional name-form adopted by Kath WALKER (1920–93), part-Aboriginal poet and writer, of the Noonuccal tribe of Stradbroke Island, near Brisbane. Formally educated only to primary level, she worked as a domestic servant from the age of 13, racist regulations barring her from the nursing profession. Her first volume of verse, *We Are Going* (1964), established both her talent and her committed stance and was followed by *The Dawn Is at Hand* (1966); these works were collected in *My People: A Kath Walker Collection* (1970) together with new poems and prose. *Kath Walker in China* (1988), a further collection of verse, affirmed her belief in the power of people to effect positive change. *Stradbroke Dreamtime* (1972) explored traditional stories from Aboriginal folklore. *Legends and Landscapes* (1990) was also a collection of Aboriginal stories, each located in its area of origin by maps and photographs, and organized by tribal groups. Writing was always part of Walker's long and distinguished campaign for Aboriginal rights. Overall her work, and life, was a passionate and articulate expression of wrongs inflicted upon Australian Aboriginal people and of the Aboriginal's indomitable will not only to survive but to flourish.

NORMAN, Marsha (1947–), American dramatist, born in Louisville, Kentucky, educated at the University of Louisville. Her first play, *Getting Out* (1977), was produced by the Actors' Theatre of Louisville where she became a playwright in residence. *Third and Oak* (two one-act plays) was produced there in 1978, as was *Circus Valentine* and a workshop production of *Holdup*, which had its full première in San Francisco in 1983. Norman's most celebrated play, *'night, Mother* (1981; Pulitzer Prize) is an extended dialogue between a widowed mother and her divorced daughter who announces her intention to commit suicide; she also wrote the 1986 screenplay for the film version directed by Tom Moore. The play was followed by *Traveler in the Dark* (1984) and *Sarah and Abraham* (1988). Her first novel, *The Fortune Teller*, appeared in 1987. Norman's plays focus on women and issues of female identity, as in the mother–daughter relationship, sisterhood, and women's autonomy. However, she has been attacked by feminists for her conservatism and apparent indifference to feminist ideology, especially in her refusal to propose social prescriptions which may help to improve conditions for women. More recently she has written an adaptation of Frances Hodgson Burnett's *The Secret Garden* (1991) with music by Lucy Simon.

NORRIS, (Benjamin) Frank(lin) (1870–1902), American novelist, born in Chicago, educated at the University of California at Berkeley, and at Harvard. He is among the important exponents of American literary naturalism at the end of the nineteenth century, whose number also included Stephen *Crane and Theodore *Dreiser. After a grand tour of Europe in 1887, Norris remained in Paris to study painting at Atelier Julien. His first book, written while at Berkeley, *Yvernelle: A Legend of Feudal France* (1892), is a narrative verse romance, showing the influence of Sir Walter Scott and the *Chronicles* of Jean Froissart. At Harvard he came under the influence of Lewis E. Gates, an English teacher to whom he was to dedicate his best-known novel, *McTeague* (1899); this work concerns an unqualified San Francisco dentist who marries one of his patients, Trina Sieppe, and charts their decline with a remorseless intensity that owes much to Zola and the author's familiarity with Social Darwinism. In 1895 he joined the staff of the San Francisco *Chronicle* and then travelled to South Africa to cover the Uitlander insurrection. His next novel, *Moran of the Lady Letty: A Story of Adventure off the California Coast* (1898), was followed by *Blix* (1899) and *A Man's Woman* (1900). By late 1899 Norris was planning a more ambitious fictional project. Drawing on the models of Balzac's *Comédie Humaine* and Zola's Rougon-Macquart series, he conceived a cyclical work of three novels, 'The Epic of the Wheat', which, in his own words, 'will in no way be connected with each other save only in their relation to (1) the production, (2) the distribution, (3) the consumption of American wheat'. Only the first two volumes, *The *Octopus* (1901) and *The *Pit* (1903), were published; the projected final volume, *The Wolf*, was never begun. *The Pit* was for a long time his most successful work and saw both stage and screen adaptation, but *The Octopus*, with its range and skilful fusion of the seemingly contradictory aspects of Norris's art—his enthusiasm for both the romantic and the naturalistic—is regarded by many critics as one of the most remarkable American novels of the early twentieth century. Posthumous publications include *The Responsibilities of the Novelist and Other Literary Essays* (1903) and *Vandover and the Brute* (1914), a novel probably begun while Norris was at Harvard. *Frank Norris: A Biography* (1932, 1963) is a biography by Franklin Walker. *The Novels of Frank Norris* (1966) by Donald Pizer is a critical study.

NORRIS, Leslie (1921–), Welsh poet and short-story writer, born in Merthyr Tydfil, educated at the City of Coventry College and the University of Southampton. After lecturing at Bognor Regis College of Education, in 1973 he began teaching at American universities and became a professor at Brigham Young University, Provo, Utah, in 1985. His collections of poetry include *Tongue of Beauty* (1941), *Finding Gold* (1967), *Islands off Maine* (1977), and *A Sea in the Desert* (1989). *Walking the White Fields* (1980) is a collected edition of his verse. His volumes of short stories include *Sliding* (1978) and *The Girl from Cardigan* (1988). Both his poetry and his prose display remarkably rich powers of description. An elegiac intensity of concern with memories of his boyhood in Wales characterized much of his earlier writing. His imaginative response to a wide variety of landscapes and weathers forms a valuable contribution to the modern traditions of rural poetry. Among his other works is his edition of *The Mabinogion* (1980).

North, Seamus *Heaney's fourth collection of poems, published in 1975. The book consists of two parts, the second of which addresses aspects of the Troubles in Northern Ireland in verse of conversational directness; 'Whatever You Say Say Nothing' forms an urgently topical expression of anger and frustration, while the 'Singing School' sequence deals with the sectarian conditioning of Heaney's upbringing and confronts the difficulties of artistic detachment. The importance of *North* is generally considered in terms of its longer first part. Its eighteen loosely sequential poems, mostly in stanzas of lapidary concentration, have at their centre a group pursuing the implications of 'The Tollund Man' in *Wintering Out* (1972), his preceding collection; that poem establishes imaginative parallels between deaths in the course of Ireland's struggle for nationhood and the body of an Iron Age victim sacrificed to the earth goddess, then preserved in a Danish peat-bog. Like 'The Tollund Man', 'Bog Queen', 'The Grauballe Man', 'Strange Fruit', 'Punishment', and other poems draw on P. V. Glob's *The Bog People* (1969) to present what Heaney designates, in a phrase from *Yeats's 'Meditations in Time of Civil War', 'befitting emblems of adversity'. 'The goddess' of *North*, who 'swallows our love and terror', is broadly equivalent to Yeats's *Cathleen Ni Houlihan and other feminine personifications of Ireland. The poems constitute a compassionate but sometimes shockingly clear-sighted acknowledgement of the force of territorial and cultural imperatives in human affairs, locating the Troubles within a historical and mythological frame of reference.

North American Review, The, one of the most eminent of the American periodicals of the nineteenth and early twentieth centuries. It was edited from its inception in 1815 by William Tudor; his numerous successors included James Russell Lowell, Charles Eliot Norton, and Henry *Adams. Ralph Waldo Emerson, Walt Whitman, Henry Wadsworth Longfellow, and Anthony Trollope were among the authors whose work was published. Originally a journal of the literary and intellectual circles of Boston and Harvard, in 1878 it moved to New York and became actively, and sometimes controversially, involved in socio-political debate. The early years of the twentieth century were a distinguished period in the *Review*'s history, when its contributors included Mark Twain, H. G. *Wells, Alan *Seeger, Maeterlinck, D'Annunzio, and Tolstoy; fiction by Henry *James and Joseph *Conrad appeared when serialized novels became a regular feature. From 1918 onward the publication began to decline and, despite attempts to revitalize it, it expired in 1939. The title was revived in 1963 by Cornell College, Iowa, later the University of Northern Iowa, where it continues to be published as a quarterly.

Nostromo, a novel by Joseph *Conrad, published in 1904 (serialized in *T. P.'s Weekly*, 1904) shortly after the secession of Panama from Colombia. Regarded by many critics as Conrad's masterpiece, the novel is set in the fictional South American republic of Costaguana. It traces the history of the town and province of Sulaco from the time of Spanish rule under the Conquistadores to the period of its secession from Costaguana with the encouragement of European and American capital. The central characters are 'Nostromo', an Italian sailor who has come ashore and become the Capataz de Cargadores (the leader of the port's dockers), and Charles Gould, the owner of a silver mine, which becomes the dominant economic and political force in the province. Reference to Gould's grandfather, uncle, and father outline the relations between the mine and successive Costaguanan governments. Together these create the personal and political context that determines Gould's decision to make a success of the mine. In contrast to Gould, 'the Idealist-creator of Material Interests', 'Nostromo', to begin with, is interested only in his reputation. Gradually, it becomes clear that he aspires to the status of folk hero, but the action upon which he pins this hope, the transporting of a boat-load of silver, ends with his questioning the ideal. Conrad asserted that 'Nostromo' was not intended as the hero of the novel; silver was 'the pivot of the moral and material events, affecting the lives of everybody in the tale'. The narrative is constructed through constant shifts in time, place, and point of view to produce a complex patterning of echoes and anticipations, affinities and contrasts. This technical virtuosity is necessitated by the nature of his thematic concerns: the innumerable intersecting forces that create the historical event, that are involved in the processes of historical and social change.

Notes Toward A Supreme Fiction, a long poem by Wallace *Stevens, first published in an edition of forty-six pages in 1942. Its three parts, 'It Must Be Abstract', 'It Must Change', and 'It Must Give Pleasure', contain some of his richest and most lyrically fluid poetry. Like much of Stevens's most impressive earlier work, the poem meditates on the creative imagination's interpretations of reality in an era faced with the obsolescence of traditional religious belief; poetry must conceive of and realize a 'supreme fiction', a focus for human aspirations and understanding equivalent to that formerly offered by religion. The first part reviews the fundamentals of man's imaginative capacities and considers images of the human condition; the second part celebrates change, variousness, and renewal through unions of opposites as essentials of the human and natural orders; the final section emphasizes inclusiveness and balance as attributes of the 'supreme fiction' before concluding with praise of the world's lovely ordinariness. A coda beginning 'Soldier, there is a war . . .' intensifies the poem's underlying moral urgency by relating it to its contemporary background of warfare. Mindful of the work's tentative and fragmentary character as 'notes', Stevens stated that 'in projecting a supreme fiction, I cannot imagine anything more fatal than to state it definitely and incautiously'.

Notes Towards the Definition of Culture (1948), T. S. *Eliot's best-known work of social criticism, which began with a series of articles entitled 'Notes Toward a Definition of Culture' in the *New English Weekly* in 1943; these were revised as 'Cultural Forces in the Human Order', his essay in *Prospect for Christendom* (edited by M. B. Reckitt, 1945), and, with further revisions, formed 'The Three Senses of Culture', the first chapter of *Notes Towards the Definition of Culture*. The 'three senses' relate to individuals, social groups, and whole societies, though their interdependence is such that cultural health requires 'an overlapping and sharing of interests, by participation and mutual appreciation'. Eliot considers decline in religious belief, which he identifies as the ultimate embodiment of a civilization's values, as the chief cause of cultural decay. The family is viewed as the 'primary channel of transmission of culture' within a coherent society, which will also be characterized by a stable class structure, sound systems of government and education, and some aspects of regionalism. An appendix, 'The Unity of European Culture', locates his arguments in an international context. The 'definition of culture' remains rather imprecise; at one point he states that it 'may even be described simply as that which makes life worth living'. George *Orwell's remark that the book's emphasis on 'class privilege . . . conflicts with certain moral assumptions Mr Eliot appears to share' indicates an element of contradiction between its evidently hierarchical view of culture and its democratic concern for the common good. (See POPULAR CULTURE.)

Not I, a play by Samuel *Beckett, first performed in 1973, a 20-minute monologue, highly unorthodox in form and character. All the audience sees are spotlit lips, whose owner is identified only as Mouth. She delivers what at first seems to be a wild, incoherent babble, but on closer inspection turns out to be a muddled account, told throughout in the third person, of a long, sad, and lonely life, surely her own. She was born in a 'godforsaken hole', left with a strong sense of sin and guilt by the religious who ran the orphanage where she was raised, and seems to have done little as an adult but tramp the countryside, occasionally visit shops and, on one occasion, be taken to court for an unspecified offence. Mostly she is silent, but once or twice a year gets an urge to 'tell': which presumably explains the 'steady stream' of 'mad stuff' that now culminates in her confused memories of a quasi-mystical experience she had in a field, involving a moving ray of moon-like light. Five times she interrupts the verbal flow with a cry of 'what? who? no! she!' The significance of this is uncertain, but may be that, though pushed into a new articulacy by the ray, she still thinks of herself as an object and cannot acknowledge that it is she, not someone else, who has lived this empty, loveless life. Equally debatable is the purpose of an 'Auditor', a cowled figure who listens silently, his arms rising and falling in 'a gesture of helpless compassion' in reaction to what Beckett's stage directions call Mouth's 'vehement refusal to relinquish third person'.

Now and Then, a periodical begun as a house magazine by the publishers Jonathan Cape in 1921, the year in which the company was formed. It contained reviews, articles on authorship and various aspects of the literary life, poetry, and occasional short stories, and was frequently illustrated with photographs and wood-cuts. Among the contributors to earlier issues were Hugh *Walpole, H. G. *Wells, George Bernard *Shaw, G. K. *Chesterton, Virginia *Woolf, and H. E. *Bates; poems by W. H. *Davies were regularly featured and verse by Amy *Lowell also appeared. During the 1930s, the period in which *Now and Then* achieved its greatest distinction, contributors included W. H. *Auden, Graham *Greene, E. M. *Forster, Anthony *Powell, V. S. *Pritchett, and Michael *Roberts. Although Cape's own authors were invariably in the majority as contributors and the subjects of reviews, the journal tended to subordinate its promotional interests to its functions as a periodical of high literary standing. Despite various changes in design the magazine assumed a mediocre character in the 1950s and, after diminishing to little more than a pamphlet, ceased publication in 1961. *Then and Now* (1935) is a selection of work from its first fifty issues.

NOWLAN, Alden (1933–83), Canadian poet, born in Windsor, Nova Scotia. One of Maritime Canada's most important poets, Nowlan found the distinctive voice of his early work in *The Rose and the Puritan* (1958), a collection of short, formally traditional lyrics, mainly focusing on an episode in the life of a New Brunswick small-town resident and culminating in some kind of 'moral' revelation. Much of this early poetry is concerned with family relationships and the deleterious effects of puritanism. It is influenced by Edwin Arlington *Robinson, Edgar Lee *Masters, Charles *Olson, and William Carlos *Williams. Identity as well as formal structure is seen as less stable in the later Nowlan, and in the prose memoir *Various Persons Named Kevin O'Brien* (1973), a fictionalized account of his own life, people, places, and past memories are all seen to exist in a state of flux. His volumes of poetry include *The Things Which Are* (1962), *Bread, Wine and Salt* (1967), *The Mysterious Naked Man* (1969), *Playing the Jesus Game* (1970), *Between Tears and Laughter* (1971), *I'm A Stranger Here Myself* (1974), and *Smoked Glass* (1977). Nowlan's plays, written in collaboration with Walter Learning, include *Frankenstein* (1976) and a Sherlock Holmes story, *The Incredible Murder of Cardinal Tosca* (1978).

NOWRA, Louis (1950–), Australian playwright, born in Melbourne, educated at La Trobe University. An anti-naturalistic writer, he has attracted considerable attention for his structural skill, his emblematic effects, and his exploration of isolated individuals. *Albert Names Edward* (1976) deals with the manipulation of an amnesiac; *Inner Voices* (1977) concerns Ivan, heir to the Russian throne who has been kept prisoner since infancy by his mother Catherine II; *Visions* (perf. 1978; pub. 1979) centres on a nineteenth-century Paraguayan dictator. All these plays concern powerful figures who control language and information to further their ambitions. Later plays have dealt with the relationship between European and Aboriginal culture; these include *Sunrise* (1983), and *The Golden Age* (1985) which concerns the discovery and subsequent destruction of a lost tribe of white Europeans in Tasmania. More recent plays include *Summer of the Aliens* (1992, for radio), about a boy growing up in working-class Melbourne; *Cosi* (1992), concerning an attempt to perform *Cosi Fan Tutte* in a psychiatric hospital; *The Temple* (1993), which satirizes 1980s Australian consumer excess; *Radiance* (1993), about three Aboriginal sisters who reunite to bury their mother; and *Crow* (1994). *The Cheated* (1979) is a collection of newspaper reports of catastrophes. A novel, *The Misery of Beauty* (1976), is narrated by a grotesque character called Frogman and describes his relationship with his master, a magician named Earl.

NOYES, Alfred (1880–1958), British poet, novelist, and critic, born in Wolverhampton, educated at Exeter College, Oxford, where he was much influenced by Ernest de *Selincourt. *The Loom of Years* (1902), his first collection of poems, established the reputation he consolidated with a succession of volumes, among them *The Flower of Japan* (1903) and *Drake: An English Epic* (two volumes, 1906, 1908). The last-named secured him a popular readership whose tastes had been formed by the heartily patriotic verse of Sir Henry *Newbolt and others. Other examples of his historical narrative verse include *Forty Singing Seamen* (1907) and *The Golden Hynde* (1908). He held a professorship in English at Princeton University until 1923. The increasing preoccupation with religion which led to his conversion to Roman Catholicism in 1925 is reflected in *The Watchers of the Sky* (1922), *The Book of Earth* (1925), and *The Last Voyage* (1930); these works, published together as *The Torch-Bearers* in 1937, form a poetic trilogy attempting to reconcile the claims of science and religious belief. *Collected Poems* was published in 1950. 'The Highwayman', which remains a standard piece for children, is the most enduring of his poems. *The Unknown God*, his widely read work of Christian apologetics, appeared in 1934. His biography *Voltaire* (1936) was received with hostility by certain Catholic churchmen for its sympathetic treatment of its subject's theism. Noyes was an outspoken opponent of *Modernism, having a particular detestation of Joyce's **Ulysses* (1922); his poetic practice and his critical writings, which include *Some Aspects of Modern Poetry* (1924), indicate his firm commitment to Victorian literary conventions. Among his novels, most of which he described as fantasies, are *Walking Shadows* (1918) and *The Last Man* (1940). *Two Worlds for Memory* (1953) is autobiographical.

NOZICK, Robert (1938–), American philosopher, born in Brooklyn, New York, educated at Columbia University and at Princeton, where he was an assistant professor until 1965. Before being appointed to a professorship at Harvard in 1969, he held several posts, including an associate professorship at Rockefeller University; in 1985 he became Harvard's Arthur Kingsley Porter Professor of Philosophy. Nozick's reputation was established with *Anarchy, State, and Utopia* (1974); this constituted the most persuasive critique of John *Rawls's highly influential *A Theory of Justice* (1971), which Nozick opposed for its collective view of social organization. It remains his most noted contribution to political philosophy for its formulation of the 'entitlement theory' of social justice and its strong arguments for the ethical necessity of defending libertarian ideals. In *Philosophical Explanations* (1981) he develops his celebrated conditional theory of knowledge, which unifies *a priori* and *a posteriori* conditions of knowing, in the course of refuting the sceptical philosophical position; the book also demonstrates his work's breadth of reference in its expansive discussions of central questions relating to free will, ethics, and personal identity. Nozick's other works include *The Normative Theory of Individual Choice* (1990) and *The Examined Life* (1989), in which he locates sexual relations and other fundamental areas of personal experience within a comprehensive system of existential values.

NUTTALL, A(nthony) D(avid) (1937–), British philosophically minded critic and professor at

Oxford; he was born in Hereford, and educated at Merton College, Oxford. His *A Common Sky* (1974) explored the curious consequences, in philosophy and literature, of the restriction of what we think of as secure knowledge to what the senses tell us; above all the resulting isolation of the hesitant and suspicious consciousness. Writers from Sterne to *Eliot were seen as grappling with, refuting, acting out, and succumbing to this problem in different ways. *Two Concepts of Allegory* (1967) offers illuminating readings of romance and allegory in Shakespeare, and *A New Mimesis* (1983) seeks to establish the continuing claims of realism against a whole host of continental (and other) modes of scepticism. Much of Nuttall's later work, always lively and inquisitive, has been engaged with what he sees as the extravagances of theory. His project is the defence of the given world not against reasonable doubt but against fashionable confusion, and against what he sees as the frivolity of much would-be sophistication. His other works include *Pope's Essay on Man* (1984), a critical commentary; *The Stoic in Love: Selected Essays on Literature and Ideas* (1989); *Openings: Narrative Beginnings from Epic to the Novel* (1992); and an edition of William Shakespeare's *Timon of Athens* (1989).

NUTTALL, Jeff (1933–), British poet and novelist, born in Clitheroe, Lancashire, educated at Hereford School of Art and Bath Academy of Art. He became Head of Fine Art at Liverpool Polytechnic in 1981. Nuttall was eminently involved with the *underground poetry movement in Britain in the 1960s and 1970s and became its principal apologist with *Bomb Culture* (1968). His first substantial collection of poems, *Poems I Want To Forget* (1965), was followed by many others including *Journals* (1968) and *Sun Barbs* (1976). His *Selected Poems* and *Poems 1962–69* were both published in 1970. The anarchically experimental ethos of Nuttall's poetry is indicated by his remark that 'I am hardly at all concerned with direct verbal/syntactical "meaning".' Among his numerous novels are *Oscar Christ and the Immaculate Conception* (1968) and *The Gold Hole* (1978). *Performance Art: Memoirs and Scripts* (two volumes, 1979) collects his writings for the theatre. *The Bald Soprano* (1989) is an impressionistic portrait of the musician Lol Coxhill.

NWAPA, Flora (Nwanzuruaha) (1931–), Nigerian novelist and short-story writer, born in Oguta, educated at University College, Ibadan, and the University of Edinburgh. She has held several administrative posts in Nigerian educational institutions, and cabinet posts in her home state, including the Ministry of Health and Social Welfare. She was the first Nigerian woman novelist to be published, and is best known for her novels *Efuru* (1966) and *Idu* (1970). Both deal with village life, and focus on eponymous heroines, *Efuru* having a strong element of parable about the pivotal role of women in society, and *Idu* celebrating conjugal love. In *Never Again* (1976) the woman narrator, Kate, supports the Biafran side during the Nigerian Civil War (1967–70), but with awareness of the shortcomings in her own people. Collections of short stories include *This Is Lagos* (1971) and *Wives at War* (1980).

NYE, Robert (1939–), British novelist and poet, born in London, educated in Surrey and Essex; he left school at 16. He began to publish his poems as early as 1961. *A Collection of Poems 1955–1989* appeared in 1989, and *Collected Poems* in 1995. Nye was poetry editor of the *Scotsman* from 1967 and of *The Times* from 1971. His first novel, *Doubtfire* (1967), was followed by *Tales I Told My Mother* (1969), a collection of stories inspired by the actual lives of literary figures; the device of reworking extant stories, historical or legendary, has been adopted by Nye in subsequent novels. These include *Falstaff* (1976), *Merlin* (1979), and *Faust* (1980), which focus on these quasi-mythical figures; *The Voyage of Destiny* (1982), *The Memoirs of Lord Byron* (1989), *The Life and Death of My Lord Gilles de Rais* (1990), and *Mrs Shakespeare* (1992), all of which are historical. Nye explores the iconic power of these figures in the popular cultural imagination, often from the perspective of peripheral figures. His novels combine a historian's researched erudition with a raconteur's earthy humour and a fantasist's ability to evoke the ineffable.

OAKLEY, Barry (1931–), Australian novelist and playwright, born in Melbourne, educated at the University of Melbourne. His three picaresque novels are *A Wild Ass of a Man* (1967), a satirical comedy about a luckless young man named Muldoon; *A Salute to the Great McCarthy* (1970), about a star football player, which was later filmed; and *Let's Hear It for Prendergast* (1970), an iconoclastic satire about a Melbourne poet. A more recent novel, *The Craziplane* (1989), is similarly picaresque and tells of a young novelist who goes to Sydney to write the biography of the (fictional) greatest living Australian playwright and becomes comically entangled in his life. *Walking through Tigerland* (1977) is a collection of short stories. His numerous plays include *From the Desk of Eugene Flockhart* (1966), a comedy set in a Canberra public services office; *Witzenhausen Where Are You?* (1967), about a mystic messenger in a large car company, who causes disruption by locking himself in the lavatory, passing subversive messages written on pieces of toilet paper under the door; *A Lesson in English* (1968); *It's a Chocolate World* (1968); *The Feet of Daniel Mannix* (1971); *Beware of Imitations* (1972, published 1987); and *Scanlan* (1978). Later works include *Buck Privates* (1980), *The Hollow Tombola* (1980), a satire of Patrick *White's *The Solid Mandala* (1966), *Politics: A Farce* (1980), *The Great God Mogadon and Other Plays* (1980), and *Marsupials* (1981). A collection of essays, *Scribbling in the Dark*, appeared in 1985.

OATES, Joyce Carol (1938–), American novelist, playwright, short-story writer, and essayist, born in Lockport, New York, educated at Syracuse and Wisconsin Universities. Oates began her prolific literary career with *By the North Gate* (1963), a collection of short stories. Her first novel, *With Shuddering Fall* (1964), ushers in many of the concerns of her subsequent novels. Set, as is much of her work, in the fictional 'Eden County' which is largely modelled on her birthplace, the book explores an obedience and love which might transcend good and evil. Though mainly concerned with the redemptive power of love, madness, violence, and lust also figure in bizarre forms in her fiction. Experimenting with a variety of points of view and styles—realism, gothic horror, metafiction, and parodies of forms—her work frequently explores the corruption beneath the surface of normality, which is both socially and individually generated. Her further novels include *A Garden of Earthly Delights* (1967); *Expensive People* (1968); *Them* (1969); *Wonderland* (1971), a surrealistic narrative in the manner of Lewis Carroll's *Alice's Adventures in Wonderland*; *Do with Me what You Will* (1973); *The Assassins* (1975); *The Childwold* (1976); *Son of the Morning* (1978); *Unholy Loves* (1979); *Cybele* (1979); *Bellefleur* (1980); and *A Bloodsmoor Romance* (1982), *Mysteries of Winterthurn* (1984), and *Solstice* (1985). *Marya: A Life* (1986) and the monumental *You Must Remember This* (1987), both set in upstate New York, are more openly autobiographical. As well as the later novels *American Appetites* (1989), *Because It Is Bitter, and Because It Is My Heart* (1991), *The Rise of Life on Earth* (1991), and *I Lock My Door upon Myself* (1991), she has written many collections of short stories including *The Wheel of Love* (1970), *Marriages and Infidelities* (1972), *Crossing the Border* (1976), *Heat: And Other Stories* (1991), *Haunted: Tales of the Grotesque* (1994), and *Will You Always Love Me? and Other Stories* (1995). Among her plays are *Sunday Dinner* (1970), *Miracle Play* (1974), *Presque Isle* (1984), and *Twelve Plays* (1991). She has written much non-fiction and criticism, including *The Hostile Sun: The Poetry of D. H. Lawrence* (1973); produced such essay collections as *Contraries* (1981), *The Profane Art* (1983), *On Boxing* (1987), and *(Woman) Writer: Occasions and Opportunities* (1988); and edited *The Best American Essays Nineteen Ninety-One* (1991). She has also published many collections of poetry.

Objective Correlative, a term introduced in the essay 'Hamlet' by T. S. *Eliot, which appeared in the **Athenaeum* in 1919 and was subsequently collected in *The Sacred Wood* (1920). Eliot maintained that *Hamlet* is 'an artistic failure' because it is 'full of some stuff that the writer could not drag to light, contemplate, or manipulate into art'; the play is 'dominated by an emotion which is inexpressible, because it is in *excess* of the facts as they appear'. These deficiencies are explained as the result of Shakespeare's inability to find 'an "objective correlative" . . . a set of objects, a situation, a chain of events which shall be the formula for that *particular* emotion'. In defining the need for internal states to be manifest in external equivalents, the expression achieved axiomatic status in the criticism of poetry; as a critical generalization, it encompasses both Stéphane Mallarmé's description of Symbolisme as the art of 'evoking an object so as to reveal a mood' and Ezra *Pound's account of the image as 'an intellectual and emotional complex' in the poetics of *Imagism. The term may be considered a product of Eliot's creative preoccupations in the period immediately after the First World War, which centred on the need to achieve imaginative integration in poetry which dealt with problematic intensities of emotion; to this extent, the objective correlative is related to his concept of '*dissociation of sensibility'. Both expressions are suggested by Eliot's reference to 'a few notorious phrases which have had a truly embarrassing success in the world' in the lecture 'The Frontiers of Criticism', given to an audience of 14,000 at the University of Minnesota in 1956.

Objectivist Poetry: an influential movement in American verse of the early 1930s which stressed the importance of concrete detail and the spatial integrity of the poem; its practitioners avoided metaphorical devices as tending to diffuseness. Louis *Zukofsky was the principal spokesman for the group, of which George *Oppen, Charles *Reznikoff, and Carl *Rakosi were other leading members, and produced **Poetry*'s 'Objectivists' special issue in 1931; Ezra *Pound was instrumental in the editorial arrangements, and Basil *Bunting and Kenneth *Rexroth were also among the contributors. William Carlos *Williams's theories concerning the poem's status as an autonomous entity resulting from the relationship between the perceiving consciousness and objective reality were of great significance in the formulation of the Objectivists' tenets; Zukofsky wished to regard the poem as an 'object in process', its images indissociable from a formal entirety that would not merely record events but constitute a primary phenomenon of itself; he was insistent that the term 'Objectivism' should not be applied to his poetic theories in order to avoid confusion with the philosophical meanings of the word. Objectivist verse was in part an attempt to purge *Imagism of affectations it was felt to have developed since its beginnings. *An 'Objectivists' Anthology* (1932) was published under Zukofsky's editorship by the press Oppen had established at Le Beausset in France; the two then formed the Objectivist Press which produced numerous valuable editions, including Williams's *Collected Poems, 1921–1931* in 1934. The theories of the Objectivists and their use of innovative typographical procedures anticipated important features of later American poetry, notably the *Projective verse of Charles *Olson and his followers.

O'BRIAN, Patrick (1914–), British historical novelist and biographer, born in Ireland; he is best known for his series of novels set during the Napoleonic wars, which chronicle the exploits of Captain 'Lucky' Jack Aubrey, a courageous and brilliant naval officer, and his friend and colleague, Stephen Maturin. The first of these books, *Master and Commander* (1970), describes the initial meeting between the two characters in Minorca in 1800; it was followed by *Post Captain* (1972), *H M Surprise* (1973), *The Mauritius Command* (1977), *Desolation Island* (1978), *The Fortune of War* (1979), *The Surgeon's Mate* (1980), *The Ionian Mission* (1981), *Treason's Harbour* (1982), *The Far Side of the World* (1984), *The Reverse of the Medal* (1986), *The Letter of Marque* (1988), *The Thirteen Gun Salute* (1989), *The Nutmeg of Consolation* (1991), *Clarissa Oakes* (1992), *The Wine-Dark Sea* (1993), and *The Commodore* (1994). These novels display a profound knowledge of naval history and of the natural world as well as a certain psychological depth in their portrayal of the central characters. Each novel deals with a different aspect of the naval campaign. Their settings range from the Baltic to the Mediterranean and from Nova Scotia to the penal colonies of Australia. O'Brian's non-fiction includes biographies of Picasso (1976) and of the eighteenth-century naturalist, Sir Joseph Banks (1987).

O'BRIEN, Conor Cruise (1917–), Irish literary critic and political commentator, born in Dublin, where he was educated at Trinity College. After joining the Irish Civil Service in 1942, he held numerous senior posts and became a special representative of the United Nations in 1961. From 1969 to 1977 he was a member of the Dail Eirann, becoming Minister for Posts in 1973, and was subsequently a member of the Senate. He has also held various university appointments and was Editor-in-Chief of the *Observer* from 1979 to 1981. Having achieved notice as a critic for his work with *The *Bell*, his first collection of essays, *Maria Cross: Imaginative Patterns in a Group of Modern Catholic Writers*, appeared under the pseudonym 'Donat O'Donnell' in 1952. Later studies include *Writers and Politics* (1965), *Camus* (1970), and *Edmund Burke* (1981). The analysis of sectarianism and nationalism in *States of Ireland* (1972) initiated the fusion of political, historical, and cultural perspectives that is sustained in *Herod: Reflections on Political Violence* (1978), *Religion and Politics* (1984), *Passion and Cunning* (1988), *God Land: Reflections on Religion and Nationalism* (1988), and *Ancestral Voices* (1994). *To Katanga and Back* (1962), *The United Nations: Sacred Drama* (1968), and *The Siege: the Saga of Israel and Zionism* (1986) are among his writings on international politics. O'Brien's many other publications include *The Great Melody* (1993), his acclaimed biography of Burke.

O'BRIEN, Edna (1932–), Irish novelist and short-story writer, born and brought up in the village of Tuamgraney, Co. Clare, the daughter of a farmer, educated at the Convent of Mercy in Loughrea, Co. Galway. At 16 she worked in a chemist's shop in Dublin and attended evening classes at the Pharmaceutical College. In 1959 she moved to London where she wrote her first novel. *The Country Girls* (1960) begins the bitter-sweet story of Caithleen and Baba, two girls brought up in the close-knit, cruel world of a small Irish village. Narrated by the soft and sympathetic Caithleen, and confessional in tone, the novel traces her development from a naïve schoolgirl—afraid of her drunken father and used by the confident, malicious Baba—into a no less naïve young woman, flirting with disaster in the alien environment of Dublin. In *The Lonely Girl* (1962; reprinted as *Girl with Green Eyes*, 1964), and *Girls in Their Married Bliss* (1964), set in Dublin, the narration switches from the gentle Caithleen to the bold Baba; these three novels appeared together in *The Country Girls Trilogy* *and Epilogue* (1986). The ego/alter ego relationship is a recurring theme in O'Brien's work, and in *August Is a Wicked Month* (1965) she internalizes the conflict in the character of Ellen whose responsible side is left behind when she goes on a hedonistic trip to the Riviera; the death of her son while on holiday with her estranged husband leaves Ellen unable to reconcile the two sides of her personality. The realistic evocation of Ireland and the Irish has been one of the great strengths of O'Brien's fiction. Her other novels include *Casualties of Peace* (1966), *Night* (1972), *Johnny I Hardly Knew You* (1977), and *The High Road* (1988). In the 1990s O'Brien enjoyed increasing success. In *Time and Tide* (1992), Nell, the protagonist of earlier novels, is seen as the mother of adult sons, coping with despair and bereavement. Even more accomplished and critically acclaimed was the controversial *The House of Splendid Isolation* (1994), the tragic tale of a lonely widow's encounter with an IRA terrorist on the run. Arguably O'Brien's most ambitious novel, it is also the most overtly politically engaged of her works. O'Brien has published several collections of short stories including *The Love Object* (1968), *A Scandalous Woman and Other Stories* (1974), *Mrs Reinhardt and Other Stories* (1978), *Returning* (1982), and *Lantern Slides* (1989); these, like her novels, contain gentle, yet painful considerations of love, guilt, and loss. She has written several plays, including *Virginia* (1981), a study of Virginia *Woolf, and writes for film and television.

O'BRIEN, Flann, the principal pseudonym of Brian O'NOLAN, otherwise O'Nuallain (1911–66), Irish novelist and humorist, born at Strabane in Co. Tyrone; from the age of 13 he grew up in Dublin, where he was educated at Blackrock College and University College. In 1935 he entered the Department of Local Government in Dublin, where he remained until his retirement through ill-health in 1953. **At Swim-Two-Birds* (1939), his highly unusual first novel, was favourably received. He was deeply discouraged by his publishers' rejection of *The *Third Policeman* (1967), the posthumously published novel which is widely regarded as his masterpiece. In consequence, he resorted to journalism as a channel; under the pseudonym 'Myles na Gopaleen', his 'Cruiskeen Lawn' column appeared in the *Irish Times* from 1940 until the year of his death. The articles, initially in Gaelic and subsequently in English, became celebrated for their wittily acerbic commentaries on Irish affairs in general and the cultural life of Dublin in particular; na Gopaleen's columns are collected as *The Best of Myles* (1968), *Further Cuttings from Cruiskeen Lawn* (1976), and *The Hair of the Dogma* (1977). He also wrote for a number of other Irish newspapers under a range of pseudonyms including 'George Knowall' and 'Lir O'Connor'. In 1943 three of O'Brien's plays were produced in Dublin, two of which, *Thirst* and *Faustus Kelly*, are included in *Stories and Plays* (1973). *An Beal Bocht* (1941), a novel in Gaelic issued under the na Gopaleen pseudonym and translated by P. C. Power as *The Poor Mouth* (1974), is among the finest of his works; its assault on the Free State's institutionalized versions of Gaelic culture takes the form of a hyperbolically unrelenting portrayal of life in the far west of Ireland as a rain-sodden ordeal of privation. The acclaim which greeted *At Swim-Two-Birds* upon its reissue in 1960 had a stimulating effect on O'Brien, who had long felt disregarded as a novelist. *The Hard Life* (1961) conducts its 'exegesis of squalor' with characteristically mordant humour and bizarre narrative developments; although considered the weakest of his books, *The Dalkey Archive* (1964), in which James *Joyce is found to be alive and working as a barman, is rich in fantastic strategies. His reputation as one of the most important Irish writers of fiction to succeed Joyce now seems assured. Of a number of books published on O'Brien the fullest and most authoritative is the biography *No Laughing Matter* (1989) by Anthony *Cronin.

O'BRIEN, Kate (1897–1974), Irish novelist, born in Limerick, educated at University College, Dublin. Originally known as a playwright, with *Distinguished Villa* (1926) and *The Bridge* (1927), she found huge popularity with her first and in many respects weakest novel, *Without My Cloak* (1931). When depicting the conflict between religion (Catholicism) and the sensibility of the artist, her work is at its best. *The Land of Spices* (1942) is among the best novels of convent life ever written in English and was deemed immoral by the Irish Censorship Board. Like many Irish girls, she spent time in Spain as a governess, an experience which formed the basis of her novel *Mary Lavelle* (1936). But her interest in Spain and its history is most memorably employed in *That Lady* (1946), her fictional portrayal of the Castilian princess Ana de Mendoza. *Music and Splendour* (1958) is of interest for its depiction of love between women. She also wrote travel books, including *Farewell Spain* (1937), and a monograph on *Teresa of Avila* (1951). Other notable novels include *The Ante Room* (1934) and *The Last of Summer* (1943). Despite early success, she died in poverty, and never received her just due as one of Ireland's finest novelists.

O'BRIEN, Sean (1952–), British poet, born in London, educated at Cambridge, Birmingham, and Hull Universities. In 1989 he became Fellow of Creative Writing at the University of Dundee. Following the enthusiastic reception of his work when it appeared in Douglas *Dunn's edition of *A Rumoured City: New Poets from Hull* (1982), he has produced several collections including *The Indoor Park* (1983: Somerset Maugham Award), *The Frighteners* (1987), *Boundary Beach* (1989), *H.M.S. Glasshouse* (1991), and *Ghost Train* (1995), which have sustained his reputation as an astute stylist of considerable technical virtuosity. The imaginative compass of O'Brien's poetry is expansive, with social, historical, personal, and elegiac elements often coalescing into unsettling fictions whose settings range from the squalidly urban to the exotically remote. In the best of his work, intricate rhythmical textures become inseparable from compelling continuities of imagery. *The Deregulated Muse* (1995) are critical essays on contemporary poetry. With Simon *Armitage and Tony *Harrison, he edited *Penguin Modern Poets: 5* (1995).

O'BRIEN, (William) Tim(othy) (1946–), American novelist and journalist, born in Austin, Minnesota, educated at Malacaster College, Minnesota, and Harvard. O'Brien served with the US Army in Vietnam. Wounded and discharged in 1970, he subsequently became a reporter on the *Washington Post*; many of his journalistic pieces were collected in *If I Die in a Combat Zone, Box Me Up and Ship Me Home* (1973; revised 1979). Written from the perspective of an ordinary foot-sol‹ er, these articles and his fictional works boldly confront the truth about Vietnam and vividly portray some of its worst aspects. *Going After Cacciato* (1978; National Book Award) is among the most outstanding fictional narratives of the Vietnam War. Narrated by a foot-soldier, Paul Berlin, the novel interweaves his horrific memories over the preceding five months with the imaginary adventures of a group of soldiers in pursuit of the deserter Cacciato in an epic journey across Asia and Europe to the Paris Peace Talks. This fusion of reality and fantasy is again used to great effect in *The Things They Carried* (1990). Other works of fiction include *Northern Lights* (1975), which explores the relationship of two brothers, one a veteran of Vietnam, who find themselves in the hostile environment of Arrowhead country in Minnesota; *The Nuclear Age* (1981), concerning a middle-aged man's paranoia about nuclear war; and *In the Lake of the Woods* (1994). See also VIETNAM WRITING.

O'CASEY, Sean (John Casey) (1880–1964), Irish playwright, born in Dublin, the son of Protestant parents; he was brought up in circumstances of great poverty, with eight of his twelve siblings failing to survive infancy. From the age of 14 he took a variety of menial jobs, ranging from caretaking to hod-carrying. He became politically active, joining the Gaelic League and the clandestine Irish Republican Brotherhood, then involving himself in the trade union movement, and eventually committing himself to the Socialist Party of Ireland. He also developed an interest in the arts, especially the drama and Shakespeare, though not until 1923 did his own creative writing receive recognition. In that year, *The *Shadow of a Gunman* was performed at the *Abbey Theatre, followed by **Juno and the Paycock* (1924) and *The *Plough and the Stars* (1926) which, like *The *Playboy of the Western World* (1907), provoked nationalist riots in the theatre. The theme of these plays, generally regarded as his masterpieces, is akin to that which preoccupied *Synge, the contrast of romance and reality. All three look at major events in recent Irish history from the view of the residents of slum tenements, a stance which subverts high-flown sentiment and demythologizes patriotic rhetoric.

In 1926 O'Casey left Ireland and took up permanent residence in England, a move often used to explain the general decline of his work. Though he continued to draw most of his subject matter from his native country, his alienation from it became complete when the Abbey rejected *The *Silver Tassie* (1928) which combined his customary naturalism with a new *Expressionism in order to expose the immediate terrors of, and the suffering left by, the First World War. Later work worthy of note includes *Within the Gates* (1933), a morality play in which various religious and intellectual interests battle for the soul of a prostitute; *Purple Dust* (1930), a satiric piece involving pompous Englishmen in Ireland; *The Star Turns Red* (1940), a didactic play in which O'Casey seeks to reconcile a somewhat unorthodox communism with a somewhat unorthodox Christianity; *Red Roses For Me* (1942), in which he treats political unrest in Dublin, but without the scepticism about heroes and heroics that marked his first plays; and *Cock-a-Doodle Dandy* (1949) and *The Bishop's Bonfire* (1955), two sprightly attacks on parochialism, philistinism, and religiosity in Ireland. It has been well said that, just as a reader or spectator is giving up O'Casey as sententious, laboured, and dull, he will introduce a line, a note, or a sentiment that brings his work freshly to life. Nothing matches the observation of slum life that marks his 'Abbey' plays; but he never lost his wry eye for human absurdity, his quirky humour, or his gift for sparkling, imaginative dialogue. Biographies include *Sean O'Casey: The Man and His Work* (1960) by David Krause, and *Sean* (1971) by Eileen O'Casey. See also *Letters* (4 volumes; 1975–92), edited by David Krause.

O'CONNOR, Flannery (1925–64), American novelist and short-story writer, born in Georgia, educated at the University of Iowa. Though she is now viewed as belonging firmly to the Southern tradition of American literature, O'Connor was a Roman Catholic, and the paradox of being a Catholic writer in one of the most fanatically Protestant societies in the world was tackled directly by her in letters and essays, including 'The Catholic Novelist in the Protestant South' (collected in *Mystery and Manners*, 1969). It is in this area of Southern life that O'Connor finds the characters and situations of her novels and stories. **Wise Blood* (1952) concerns a young man who tries to establish a Church Without Christ in his Southern town; ironically he repeats the terrible martyrdom of the early Christians. *The Violent Bear It Away* (1960) centres round the struggle between the boy Tarwater, brought up by his crazed grandfather to think of himself as a prophet, and his liberal uncle over the baptism of the latter's idiot son; the novel abounds in the macabre and the darkly, crazily ecstatic. These qualities are to be found too in O'Connor's short stories, in which her best work appears. There are two collections, *A Good Man Is Hard to Find* (1955) and the posthumously published *Everything that Rises Must Converge* (1965). O'Connor has been accorded cult status, particularly in her native South; other critics, while admiring the intensity of vision and literary judgement of her work, find her obsession with cruelty, pain, and punishment revelatory of a certain unacknowledged imaginative sadism. Her essays were edited by her friends Robert and Sally Fitzgerald as *Mystery and Manners* (1969), and her letters as *The Habit of Being* (1979), by Sally Fitzgerald.

O'CONNOR, Frank, pseudonym of Michael Francis O'DONOVAN (1903–66), Irish short-story writer, critic, and novelist, born in Cork into a poor family. He left school at 12 and was largely self-educated, making good use of a spell of imprisonment in 1923 after he had taken the Republican side in the civil war. The Irish language was of early and lasting importance to him, and on his release he became a teacher of Irish. Subsequently he started a theatre group in Cork, then began to write, working as a librarian to support himself. His first volume of stories, *Guests of the Nation* (1931), was fired with Republican romanticism and the thrill of idealistic combat, although by this time O'Connor was disillusioned with de Valera's leadership of the nationalists. In the early 1930s he began to contribute to the *Irish Statesman* and, along with Sean *O'Faolain and Liam *O'Flaherty, rapidly became a prominent figure in the literary world of Dublin. Over the following decade O'Connor produced another collection of stories; two novels; *The Big Fellow* (1937), a biography of Michael Collins; a volume of poetry; several plays; and three volumes of verse translated from Irish Gaelic. At the same time he was contributing articles and stories to newspapers, and was on the Board of Directors of the *Abbey Theatre. In 1939 he resigned from the Abbey after a feud over censorship, married a young Welsh actress, and moved to Wicklow. His most interesting work from this time appeared in *Crab Apple Jelly* (1944), an appropriate title for a diverse collection of bittersweet stories; in *Irish Miles* (1947), a lively record of cycling trips across the country in search of historical sites; and in *The *Bell*, the important literary magazine published by O'Faolain, of which O'Connor became poetry editor, and to which he contributed stories, letters, articles, and poems. In 1951 O'Connor left Ireland to teach in America. Having gained a reputation for unpatriotic and iconoclastic writing, he had suffered the pressures of the censor and subsequent financial difficulties. In the USA he published some of his most charming stories, based on his childhood, and produced his two fine volumes of literary criticism, *The Mirror in the Roadway* (1956) and *The Lonely Voice* (1963). In 1967 he published *The Backward Look*, a history of Irish literature, and a personal appraisal of his native culture. O'Connor returned to Ireland in 1961, and despite suffering a stroke he continued to write. *A Set of Variations* (1969) was published posthumously and in its simplicity and intensity recalled his finest short stories. Like all his work, they are deeply rooted in the Irish landscape and character.

O'CONNOR, Joseph (1963–), Irish novelist, born in Dublin, the older brother of the Irish rock star Sinead O'Connor; he was educated at University College, Dublin, and worked for the British Nicaraguan Solidarity Campaign before becoming a full-time writer in 1988. *Cowboys and Indians* (1991), his first novel, is a vivid and anarchically humorous treatment of a young Irishman who goes to London to pursue a career in rock music. The short stories of *True Believers* (1991) comment with imaginative acuteness on social and cultural conditions in Britain and Ireland. *Desperadoes* (1994), a novel of considerable scope and seriocomic power, draws on his experiences of Nicaragua in its narrative of the disappearance of an Irish musician in Central America. O'Connor's fiction is marked by stylistic economy and directness in combination with deft handling of narrative complexities and vigorously demotic dialogue. His other works include *The Secret World of the Irish Male* (1994), a collection of iconoclastic essays on contemporary Ireland, and *Even the Olives Are Bleeding* (1992), a biography of the Irish poet Charles Donnelly.

Octopus, The, a novel by Frank *Norris, published in 1901, the first volume of a projected trilogy, 'The Epic of the Wheat', of which the only other volume is *The *Pit* (1903). Generally considered his greatest novel, it dramatizes the struggle between California wheat ranchers and the railroad, the 'octopus' of the title, which transports the wheat. Norris drew directly on the events of the Mussel Slough 'massacre' of May 1880 when tensions between the agents of the Southern Pacific Railroad and the wheat farmers of Tulare County in the San Joaquin Valley erupted in open battle. In the novel the railroad is all-powerful and all-encompassing: it raises transport rates without explanation, cuts wages despite its healthy profit margins, controls the local newspapers, and, to all intents and purposes, controls the courts and state government. The major character is Presley, an outsider who has come to California in the hope of writing a great poetic epic of America's Indian and Spanish past. Presley is a friend of many of the younger wheat ranchers, notably Harran Derrick and Annixter, and is inevitably drawn into the conflict between the farmers and the railroad; he puts aside his epic project and for much of the novel acts as the main commentator on the events of the story. Presley's role in the novel is balanced against that of Vanamee, a romanticized 'shepherd prophet' who provides a kind of Whitmanian overview of the action and whose interpretation of what he has seen, particularly in his final conversation with Presley, is echoed by Norris at the end of the novel. *The Octopus* has a number of subplots but at its centre is the confrontation between farmer and railroad which Norris imagistically renders as a battle between the wheat, 'a mighty world force', and the railroad, 'a vast power, huge, terrible . . .'. Among the novel's many impressive set scenes is the brilliantly realized pitched battle at the end and the death of S. Behrman, the railroad agent, in a hold of wheat.

ODETS, Clifford (1906–63), American playwright, born in Philadelphia, but brought up in New York City. He left school early to become an actor, initially in radio and later with the Theatre Guild. At 25, he was a founder member of the *Group Theatre, together with Harold Clurman, Lee Strasberg, and Cheryl Crawford: for the Group he later wrote his first major work, **Waiting for Lefty* (1935), which deals with a taxi drivers' strike and the desperation of the strikers' lives. *Awake and Sing!*, *Till the Day I Die*, and *Paradise Lost* were also produced in the same year. *Till the Day I Die*, written to be performed on Broadway with *Waiting for Lefty* and sharing with it the characteristics of agit-prop theatre, celebrates communist resistance to the German Nazi Party. *Awake and Sing!* is a Depression play centred on the Bergers, a poor Jewish family in the Bronx. Jacob Berger commits suicide so that his grandson Ralph may receive the insurance money; Ralph, however, gives the money to his family and dedicates himself to radical campaigning. Subsequently, Odets developed a more realistic style in the successful *Golden Boy* (1937) and *Rocket to the Moon* (1938); the former presents the life and death of Joe Bonaparte, who renounces violin-playing for wealth as a boxer, and who dies in a car crash, having lost his talent, his lover, and his integrity. Odets was briefly a Communist Party member, but in the post-war period took a 'co-operative' stance in his testimony to the House Un-American Activities Committee, and wrote drama rather less concerned with overtly political themes. These included *The Big Knife* (1949), *The Country Girl* (1950)—a commercial success—and *The Flowering Peach* (1954), a retelling of Noah's story.

O'DONNELL, Peadar (1893–1986), Irish novelist, editor, and political activist, born in Meenmore, Co. Donegal, educated at St Patrick's Teacher Training College, Dublin. After working for the Irish Transport and General Workers' Union in 1918, he joined the IRA in 1919 and fought in the War of Independence. Opposing the Treaty of 1921, he took the side of the republicans in the Civil War, was captured in 1922, and imprisoned for two years. Throughout his life, O'Donnell remained true to his republican and socialist beliefs, the determined practice of which are recorded in the three volumes of his autobiography, *The Gates Flew Open* (1932), *Salud! An Irishman in Spain* (1937), and *There Will Be Another Day* (1963). O'Donnell's career as a novelist began with *Storm* (1925), *Islanders* (1927), and *Adrigoole* (1929), works whose portrayal of the deprived and decimated communities of the west of Ireland cry out for the advent of social justice. His other novels include *The Knife* (1930), which concerns the poverty caused by the seasonal and necessary migration of Irish workers to Scotland. O'Donnell edited *The *Bell* from 1946 until its demise in 1954.

O'DONOVAN, Gerald, pseudonym of Jeremiah O'DONOVAN (1871–1942), Irish novelist, born in Co. Down. He entered the seminary at Maynooth and was ordained a Catholic priest in 1895. Posted to a parish in Loughrea, Co. Galway, he became active in the Gaelic League and the Irish Agricultural Organisation Society. Through his connections with key figures in the Irish cultural revival, such as Edward *Martyn, O'Donovan enlisted the support of Jack B. *Yeats in the building of a new cathedral. His prominence and popularity made him a strong candidate for the bishopric of Tuam but, disillusioned by the Church's reluctance to modernize, he left the priesthood in 1904, moving to Dublin and then to London, signifying a desire to break with the past by calling himself Gerald O'Donovan. His first and most renowned novel, *Father Ralph* (1913), is a largely autobiographical work about a young priest's inability to accept the papal encyclical against reform. His other novels include *Waiting* (1914), *How They Did It* (1920), and *The Holy Tree* (1922) which portrays a character based upon his close friend, Rose *Macauley. O'Donovan's novels have been recognized for their unique representation of a pre-Independence Ireland.

O'DONOVAN, Michael Francis, see O'CONNOR, FRANK.

O'DOWD, Bernard (1866–1953), Australian poet, born in Beaufort, Victoria, educated at the University of Melbourne. He was Assistant Librarian at the Supreme Court in Melbourne from 1887 to 1913 and became State Parliamentary Draughtsman in 1931. Much influenced by Walt Whitman, with whom he corresponded, in his visionary concern for the development of his country, O'Dowd's hopes and anxieties for Australia were central to *Dawnward?* (1903), his first collection of verse. *The Bush* (1912), generally considered his finest achievement as a poet, foresaw the future of Australia in terms of its equivalence to Greece and Rome in the classical era. Among his other collections of poetry are the mystically speculative *The Silent Land* (1906), *Dominions of the Boundary* (1907), and the sexually candid *Alma Venus!* (1921). *Collected Poems* appeared in 1944. His other publications include *Poetry Militant: an Australian Plea for the Poetry of Purpose* (1909), an exposition of his socialist conceptions of the functions of verse.

O'DUFFY, Eimar (Ultan) (1893–1935), Irish novelist, born in Dublin, educated at University College, Dublin, where he qualified as a dentist. He became involved in the Irish cultural and nationalist movement, contributing a few unsuccessful plays to Edward *Martyn's Irish Theatre, while joining the Irish Republican Brotherhood and becoming a captain in the Irish Volunteers prior to the 1916 Rising. O'Duffy's first novel, *The Wasted Island* (1919), is deeply critical of the ideologies and protagonists behind the 1916 Rising, and guaranteed that he would share in the 'damnation' reserved for writers such as James *Joyce and Brinsley *McNamara who had dared express their disillusionment with Ireland. In *Printer's Errors* (1922) and *Miss Rudd and Some Lovers* (1923), O'Duffy managed to be more light-hearted while maintaining his impulse to satirize Irish society before and during the Easter Rising and the War of Independence. He worked as a teacher and then at the

Department of External Affairs in Dublin until his outspoken views led to the loss of his job and his move to England in 1925. His Cuandine trilogy (*King Goshawk and the Birds*, 1926; *The Spacious Adventures of the Man in the Street*, 1928; and *Asses in Clover*, 1933) is an inventive and highly ironic portrayal of modern Ireland which reveal O'Duffy's belief that capitalism negates the vitality of a developing nation. Late in his short life, illness and financial difficulties forced him to try writing detective stories, a venture which failed miserably.

O'FAOLAIN, Julia (1932–), Irish novelist and short-story writer, born in London, the daughter of Sean *O'Faolain, educated at University College, Dublin, with further study at the University of Rome and the Sorbonne in Paris. *We Might See Sights! and Other Stories* (1968) is a multifarious collection set in Ireland and Italy, and varying in tone from the tender and gently humorous to the acid and gruesome. Her first novel, *Godded and Codded* (1970), is the comic tale of an innocent Irish girl at large in Paris. The stories collected in *Man in the Cellar* (1974) displayed her characteristic ironic black humour. *Women in the Wall* (1975), which marked a new departure, is set in and around a convent in sixth-century Gaul, and revolves around a group of characters, some historical, some invented, who struggle against the social mores and mysticism of the time. *No Country for Young Men* (1980) is set in present-day Ireland, but recalling the Troubles of the 1920s. *The Obedient Wife* (1982) concerns a conventional young Italian wife who becomes involved with a Catholic priest. *The Irish Signorina* (1984) is the story of an Irish girl who goes to stay with the Italian Marchesa for whom her mother worked many years before. *Not in God's Image* (1973) is a documentary history of women in the West written by O'Faolain and her husband, the American historian Lauro Martines. *The Judas Cloth* (1992) chronicles the transformation of Pius IX from the progressive 'Angel Pope' to the loathed reactionary; rich in period detail, the novel recreates the intrigue and factionalism of post-revolutionary papal Rome.

O'FAOLAIN, Sean (John Francis WHELAN) (1900–91), Irish writer, born in Cork, the son of a policeman, educated at the National University of Ireland; after a period with the Irish Republican Army during the Troubles, he went to Harvard for three years (1926–9). He lectured at St Mary's College, Strawberry Hill, until his return to Dublin in 1933. His first published collection of short stories, *Midsummer Night Madness and Other Stories* (1932), is marked by a romantic lyricism, and reflects his experience as a revolutionary. His three early novels, *A Nest of Simple Folk* (1933), *Bird Alone* (1936), and *Come Back to Erin* (1940), figure youthful, idealistic protagonists, in search of freedom and fulfilment, who eventually rebel against the strictures of the lower middle class, to which they belong. As in his stories, O'Faolain here intertwined individual choice and destiny with an exploration of the collective malaise of a stunted post-revolutionary society. Further collections of stories (*A Purse of Coppers*, 1937; and *Teresa*, 1947) display a growing pessimism, as O'Faolain mercilessly examined Irish eccentricities and religious foibles. In his later work, this pessimism was replaced by humour and tolerance; the protagonists were often average and apolitical. Collections such as *The Talking Trees* (1971), *Foreign Affairs and Other Stories* (1976), and the novel *And Again?* (1979), subordinate specific social or moral issues to the philosophical issues of age and time, permanence and change. O'Faolain was regarded as Ireland's leading short-story writer. His fictional *œuvre* represents the painstaking craftsmanship and disciplined writing of an Irish school to which a younger generation of writers such as William *Trevor and Mary *Lavin also belong. Like Lavin, O'Faolain was often compared with Chekhov in the early years; later critics found comparisons with *Nabokov more apt. His collected stories were published in three volumes between 1980 and 1983. O'Faolain's involvement with the world of letters extended beyond the boundaries of his distinguished career as a writer of fiction. As editor of *The *Bell* (1940–6) he was in a position to encourage new Irish writing, develop existing talents, and expound his own liberal views. Between the 1930s and the 1960s O'Faolain also published several notable works of non-fiction in various genres: literary criticism, travelogues, social histories, cultural commentary, and perhaps most importantly, historical biographies of leading Irish figures such as Daniel O'Connell (1938), De Valera (1939), and Hugh O'Neill (1942). The range of his written work reflected his concern and engagement with all aspects of Irish life, and his vast knowledge of the structures of the society that formed him as a writer and thinker.

OFEIMUN, Odia (1950–), Nigerian poet, born in Pruekpon in the Bendel State of Western Nigeria, educated at the University of Ibadan, where he began contributing verse to the magazine *Opon Ifa*. He was personal assistant to the Nigerian politican Chief Obafemi Awolo before joining the editorial board of the Lagos *Guardian* and subsequently became general secretary of the Association of Nigerian Authors. In 1989 he left Nigeria to work with Adzido, the leading African dance company in Britain. Following the appearance of his work in *Poems of Black Africa* (1975), edited by Wole *Soyinka, Ofeimun generated considerable controversy with his first collection of verse, *The Poet Lied* (1981; revised and enlarged, 1989), which condemned the platitudinous attitudes of established Nigerian writers. His poetry is characterized by a fusion of emotional commitment and political intensity. Its rhetorical and imaginative force are often accompanied by an underlying good humour. *A Handle for the Flutist*, his second collection, appeared in 1986.

Of Human Bondage, a novel by W. Somerset *Maugham, published in 1915. Inspired by Goethe and Samuel *Butler, Maugham's lengthy *Bildungsroman* was written in an attempt to free himself from the worries and obsessions which he carried into adulthood from his difficult early years. He described it as an autobiographical novel, and his protagonist, Philip Carey, suffers the same childhood misfortunes as Maugham himself: the loss of his mother, the break-up of his family home, and his emotionally straitened upbringing by elderly relatives. In addition, Carey has a club foot, a handicap which commentators equate with either Maugham's stammer or his homosexuality. The novel traces Carey's miserable schooldays, his happy escape to the University of Heidelberg, and his decision to become a painter in Paris. Failing to achieve artistic success, he returns to London to study medicine. His progress is a continual struggle against the sense of alienation engendered by his physical disability and against the women who entrap him, particularly Mildred Rogers, a shallow, dishonest girl who attracts Carey by her very indifference to him. Carey's eventual escape from Mildred and decision to marry the wholesome Sally Anthelny signifies his release from a sado-masochistic view of love, and a new enthusiasm for life.

O'FLAHERTY, Liam (1897–1984), Irish novelist and short-story writer, born on Inishmore, the largest of the Aran Islands where his father farmed a few, bare acres. He was educated at the Dublin diocesan seminary, but decided not to take Holy Orders. He spent one year at University College, Dublin, before enlisting in the Irish Guards in 1915. He fought in France and was invalided out in 1917; during a year's convalescence from shell-shock, he began writing stories. For the next three years he travelled widely, working as a stoker, deckhand, beachcomber, and lumberjack, on three continents. He returned to Dublin as a communist in 1921, joined the Republican side in the civil war, and in 1923 he fled to London. His first novel, *Thy Neighbour's Wife* (1923), is a detailed description of life on the land on Aran. It attracted the attention of Edward *Garnett, the critic and editor of D. H. *Lawrence, who helped O'Flaherty with his subsequent novel, *The Black Soul* (1924), which was also set on Aran. He married at this time, and travelled between Ireland, France, and England. *The Informer* (1925) made a great impact with its lurid portrayal of Republican terrorism, and has lasting interest as a study of rebellion. It was successfully filmed in 1935. *Mr Gilhooley* (1926), *The Assassin* (1928), and *The Puritan* (1931) all centred around men alienated by their urban environments. *The Return of the Brute* (1929), based on his army experiences, *The Martyr* (1933), which satirizes civil war, and *Insurrection* (1950), dealing with the Irish struggle, all relate to specific historic events but have a timeless concern with human dilemmas and reactions. Among his finest novels are *Skerrett* (1932), the sorry tale of a courageous Aran schoolmaster, and *Famine* (1937), which follows the Kilmartin family through the famine of the 1840s. He wrote over 150 short stories, the best of which concentrate on the characters and natural life of Aran. He wrote two volumes of autobiography, *Two Years* (1930), about his youthful travels, and *Shame the Devil* (1934). Throughout his life, O'Flaherty continued to travel, dividing his later years between America and Ireland; his most recent stories were written in the early 1960s.

Of Mice and Men, a short novel by John *Steinbeck, published in 1937 and dramatized in 1937 by the author. The principal figure, George Milton, is a resourceful and independent itinerant labourer, with a dream of finding some future security on a farm of his own. He is limited by having assumed the guardianship of Lennie Small, a drastically incapable person, with the mind of a retarded child in a physically powerful man's body. Lennie's tragedy lies in his mental inability to control his physical behaviour, as he kills soft things which he loves to fondle. While they are working on a ranch in Salinas Valley, California, the provocative attentions of the ranch boss's wife attract Lennie's interest, but he accidentally kills her when she resists his caresses. Compelled to run away, he is hunted by a mob led by Curley, the enraged ranch boss, whilst George hurries to find Lennie first before the posse reaches him, to shoot him in an act of kindness, thereby shattering their idyllic dream.

OGOT, Grace (Emily Akinyi) (1930–), Kenyan novelist and short-story writer, born in Butere in the Luo-speaking Central Nyanza district of Kenya; she studied midwifery at St Thomas's Hospital in London. She was Principal of the Women's Training Centre at Kismu, Kenya, before becoming a delegate to the General Assembly of the United Nations in 1975. Following her election to the Kenyan Parliament in 1985 she was appointed Assistant Minister for Culture and Social Services. Her work as a novelist is pervaded by her perceptions of tensions between indigenous tradition and scientific modernity in contemporary Kenyan life. Her first novel, *The Promised Land* (1966), a treatment of the persistence of tribal enmities, was the first work of imaginative literature to be published in English by a Luo. The best-known of her other novels is *The Graduate* (1980), which deals with the depletion of Kenya's intellectual and creative resources through the attractions of emigration. The principal collections of her short stories, which are noted for the poetic intensity of their language, are *Land Without Thunder* (1968), *The Other Woman* (1976), and *The Island of Tears* (1980). Among her other works is *The Strange Bride* (1989), her translation of her Luo novel *Miaha* (1985).

O'HANLON, Redmond (Douglas) (1947–), British travel writer, born in Dorset, educated at Marlborough and at Merton College, Oxford. *Joseph Conrad and Charles Darwin: The Influence of Scientific Thought on Conrad's Fiction* (1984) was his first major work. In 1981 he became an assistant editor with the **Times Literary Supplement*. *Into the Heart of Borneo* (1984) recounts a journey with the poet James *Fenton through tropical forests in search of a rare breed of rhinoceros. An unusual combination of humorous detachment and high-spirited fortitude is apparent in O'Hanlon's attitude to the hazards encountered; Eric *Newby called it 'the funniest travel book I have ever read'. Similar in tone, *In Trouble Again* (1988) describes an expedition across the Amazon basin; a strong sense of fellowship develops between O'Hanlon and the tribespeople he encounters, admitting him to a range of extraordinary experiences. His often irreverent manner is complemented by his lyrically eloquent responses to the threatened cultures and natural environments he visits.

O'HARA, Frank (1926–66), American poet, born in Baltimore, educated at the New England Conservatory of Music, Harvard, and the University of Michigan. He lived mostly in New York City, and was one of the leading figures of the *New York School of Poets, which included John *Ashbery, Barbara Guest, Kenneth *Koch, Ted Berrigan, and James *Schuyler. An art critic and professional curator, O'Hara worked for the Museum of Modern Art in New York and was responsible for major exhibitions of the Abstract Expressionist painters, especially Robert Motherwell and Jackson Pollock. He wrote plays for the avant-garde theatre, and worked as playwright in residence at the Poet's Theatre, Cambridge, Massachusetts, which he had helped to found whilst at Harvard. His books of poems are *A City Winter and Other Poems* (1952), *Second Avenue* (1960), *Odes* (1960), *Lunch Poems* (1964), *Love Poems: Tentative Title* (1965), *In Memory of My Feelings* (1967), *The Collected Poems of Frank O'Hara* (1971), and *Poems Retrieved* (1977). His *Art-Chronicles 1954–66* appeared in 1974, and *Selected Plays* in 1978. O'Hara was an accomplished commentator on the New York art scene when he was killed in a bizarre accident at the age of 40, run over by a beach taxi. As a poet he repudiated the aesthetic conventions of late romanticism, high modernism, and the competing contemporary schools of confessionalism and Charles *Olson's projectivism. His manifesto 'Personism ' argues his belief in poetry as a spontaneous product, responsive to change, alert to the electrical magnetism of New York city life, nourished by the surface experience of objects and events. O'Hara celebrated the accidental, the contingent, and the ordinary, and often took simple social occasions as the instigation of his poems, as *Lunch Poems* suggests. At his best he catches the sense of being at the lived moment with real power, in celebration and in lament, as in his famous elegy for Billie Holiday, 'The Day Lady Died'.

O'HARA, John (Henry) (1905–70), American novelist, playwright, and screenwriter, born in Pottsville, Pennsylvania. One of the most prolific of twentieth-century American writers, O'Hara never attended college or university, but his literary apprenticeship on small-town newspapers provided him with a rich repository of anecdote and incident upon which he drew over his literary career; a fine eye for detail and an understanding of how detail can be made fictionally significant are gifts that give his major novels their precise realism and their value as social documents. He began writing stories for the *New Yorker* in 1928 but his first novel, *Appointment in Samarra* (1934), established him as a novelist of considerable potential; it remains one of the most distinguished American novels of the inter-war years. The historian Allan Nevins said of his subsequent novel, *Butterfield 8* (1935), that no one could hope to understand the world of 1930s America without reading it. Both novels draw on O'Hara's familiarity with Pennsylvania and New York; his third novel, *Hope of Heaven* (1938), moves to Hollywood (O'Hara was a scriptwriter for Paramount, and other studios, from 1934). His third collection of short stories, *Pal Joey* (1940), was adapted for the musical theatre by Richard Rodgers and Lorenz Hart and filmed in 1958. During the Second World War, O'Hara was a war correspondent; he returned to the novel with *A Rage to Live* (1949), set in the Harrisburg area of Pennsylvania during the first two decades of the twentieth century, and over the next twenty-one years he added another twelve novels and several collections of short stories to his *oeuvre*. The most important of his later works are *From the Terrace* (1958), *Ourselves to Know* (1960), *Elizabeth Appleton* (1963), *The Lockwood Concern* (1965), and the two posthumously published works, *The Ewings* (1972) and *The Second Ewings* (1977). He was frequently criticized for the superficial realism of his fiction and the sometimes disproportionate attention he gives to minor detail, but he had admirers in contemporaries such as F. Scott *Fitzgerald and John *Steinbeck, who considered him the most underrated writer in the USA. See *The O'Hara Concern: A Biography* (1975) by Matthew J. Bruccoli; *O'Hara* (1983) by Robert Emmet Long is a critical study.

OKADA, John, see ASIAN-AMERICAN LITERATURE.

OKAI, (John) Atukwei (1941–), African poet, born in Accra, Ghana, educated there and at the Gorki Institute in Moscow, and the University of London where he studied Russian literature. He is very much a performance poet, and his poems are rooted in the oral tradition, virtually inseparable from traditional African music and dance. The poems are also politically radical and socially conscious, one of his great concerns being Pan-Africanism. Among his collections of verse are *Flowerfall* (1969), *Oath of the Fontonfrom and Other Poems* (1971), and *Logorligi Logarithms* (1974). The last title juxtaposes the Ga and English words for the same mathematical concept, thus indicating Okai's parallel traditional and modern consciousness as a poet.

OKARA, Gabriel (Inomotimi Gbaingbain) (1921–), Nigerian poet and novelist, born in Bumoundi in the Niger delta, educated at Government College, Umuahia, Yaba Higher College, and Northwestern University, USA. He became a book-binder, and wrote plays and features for broadcasting. Later, he was employed as Information Officer for the Eastern Nigerian Government Service. Together with Chinua *Achebe, and at the time of the Nigerian Civil War, he was roving ambassador for Biafra's cause during part of 1969. His poetry appeared in *Black Orpheus* and major anthologies for many years, before the publication of his first collection, *Fisherman's Invocation* (1978; Commonwealth Poetry Prize, 1979), which is partly based on the Ijaw oral tradition. *The Voice* (1964), a short novel which experiments with rendering Ijaw speech patterns into English, made a great impact in its depiction of the doomed 'hero' Okolo, a charismatic and prophetic figure, undergoing Kafkaesque trials in his quest for truth and integrity (*it*) in the modern world.

OKIGBO, Christopher (1932–67), Nigerian poet, born in Ojoto in Eastern Nigeria, educated at the University of Ibadan, where he read Classics. He was killed in action on the Nsukka battlefront during the Nigerian Civil War, in which he fought as a major in the Biafran army. Among other posts he was Private Secretary to Nigeria's Federal Minister of Research and Information, and librarian at the University of Nsukka. His densely allusive poetry, which bridges African and European culture, is characterized by striking symbolism, liturgical ritual, sheer musicality, and often anguished tone. The posthumous collection *Labyrinths* (1971) also includes all the poems in *Heavensgate* (1962) and *Limits* (1964). 'Path of Thunder' in the same collection is a direct, prophetic sequence in which allusiveness gives way to the rhetoric of approaching war.

OKPEWHO, Isidore (1941–), Nigerian novelist and critic, born in Abraka in midwestern Nigeria, educated at the University of Ibadan and the University of Denver, Colorado. In 1992 he was appointed Professor of Afro-American and African Studies at Binghampton University, New York. His critical works include *The Epic in Africa: Towards a Poetic of the Oral Performance* (1979), *Myth in Africa: A Study of its Aesthetic and Cultural Relevance* (1983), and *African Oral Literature: Backgrounds, Character and Continuity* (1992). *The Victims* (1970), Okpewho's first novel, deals with the constraining effects of traditional superstitions on Africa's emergence into economic and cultural modernity. A subsequent novel, *The Last Duty* (1976), draws on the Nigerian Civil War for its bleak treatment of a woman's struggle to survive in a territory rendered hostile by the conflict. *Tides* (1993) centres on the Nigerian government's complicity with international oil interests in the despoliation of the natural environment and the dispossession of indigenous peoples from their homelands.

OKRI, Ben(jamin) (1959–), Nigerian novelist, poet, and short-story writer, born in Lagos, educated at Urhobo College, Warri, and at the University of Essex. His first novel, *Flowers and Shadows* (1980), focuses on an adolescent boy living a cocooned existence until he discovers his father's ruthless business dealings; the consequences become explosive for the entire family. *The Landscapes Within* (1981) deals with an artist whose protests in his paintings against squalor and inhumanity rebound disastrously on him. The narrator of his novel *The Famished Road* (1991; Booker Prize) is a 'spirit-child', determined to stay on earth 'to make his mother smile', rather than die early and return to the spirit world. As a result, Okri achieves a haunting parable of social and economic conditions in Africa, and illuminates its complex, often brutal realities. *Songs of Enchantment* (1993), a briefer work, is its sequel, continuing the narrative of the spirit-child Azaro; *Astonishing the Gods* (1995) is a parable-like novel in which a traveller, finding himself on an island with invisible inhabitants, learns to question distinctions between mental and physical experience; *Dangerous Love* (1996) sets a love story into a realistic portrayal of Lagos during the early 1970s. His short stories, collected in *Incidents at the Shrine* (1986) and *Stars of the New Curfew* (1988), are also underpinned by a corrosive disillusionment on the part of key protagonists, together with strong social comment, but stylistically they go further, often generating a phantasmagoric realism. Okri's poems are collected in *An African Elegy* (1992).

Old Man and the Sea, The, a short novel by Ernest *Hemingway, published in 1952. This simple yet powerful tale of the endurance of a Cuban fisherman, Santiago, is also a parable of man's engagement with the natural world. Once accompanied by a young assistant with whom he discussed better days and baseball, Santiago is now aged and alone. After searching the Gulf Stream for marlin for 84 unsuccessful days, he finally hooks a giant marlin, with which he wrestles for two days and a night. Having at last secured the fish to his boat, he is robbed of his prize by marauding sharks which consume the marlin and reduce it to a skeleton as Santiago sails for home. Defeated but not humbled, he is found asleep in his hut, dreaming of the past, by the other fisherman who marvel at his catch.

OLDS, Sharon (1942–), American poet, born in San Francisco, educated at Stanford and Columbia; she has lectured at several colleges, and taught creative writing at New York University. By her own commentary, Olds 'began by working in close forms, then more and more wanted a line-break and poem-shape which felt more alive to me'. What distinguishes her verse, however, is not formal qualities but the humanity and vigour with which she writes. Her debut, *Satan Says* (1980), made an immediate impact with its candid views of motherhood, mother–daughter relations, sexuality, and adolescence. Hers are strong, writing-the-body poems, triumphantly so in perhaps her most admired poem 'The Language of the Brag'. *The Dead and the Living* (1984) and *The Gold Cell* (1987) continued to view human dramas with compassion. 'The Girl' concerns the rape and murder of a teenager, 'What If God' maternal incest, and 'Summer Solstice, New York City' depicts a potential suicide being enveloped by the roof-top efforts to save him. Winner of the National Book Critics Circle Award, Olds has earned a reputation as one of the vital talents in contemporary American poetry. A selected poems, *The Sign of Saturn*, appeared in 1991 followed by *The Father* (1992).

Old Times, a play by Harold *Pinter, performed and published in 1971. This characteristically enigmatic play involves a reunion between Kate, now married to Deeley and living quietly in the country, and Anna, an old friend who knew her well when they were young women in London but has not seen her for some years. Gradually, it becomes apparent that, under the polite conversation, Deeley and Anna harbour hostile and jealous feelings towards each other. The conflict is seldom open and never acknowledged, but it becomes an increasingly ugly and passionate battle for the mastery of the abstracted, inscrutable Kate, in which memories, or purported memories, are used as weapons. In a somewhat surreal ending, Kate appears to reject both combatants and assert her independence. The play is full of charged silences, unpretentiously pregnant lines, and a feeling that these hidden and unassertive characters are fighting for their emotional survival. In its combination of strong feeling, understatement, and mystery, it is a good example of Pinter's ability to show molehills and suggest mountains.

Old Wives' Tale, The, a novel by Arnold *Bennett, published in 1908. Generally considered Bennett's masterpiece, this is the epic story of two sisters, Sophia and Constance Baines, daughters of a draper of Bursley (Burslem, one of the Five Towns). It charts their progress from their girlhood over the shop to old age, contrasting the dull, patient, stay-at-home Constance, who marries the shop's assistant Samuel Povey, with the spirited and rebellious Sophia, who elopes to Paris with the dashing but feckless commercial traveller, Gerald Scales, whom she has to bully into marriage. Constance lives for her husband, and, after his death (hastened by family scandal), for her son Cyril; the dramas and passions of small town provincial life are drawn with feeling and accuracy. Sophia, deserted by Gerald, survives in Paris as the ruthless and efficient mistress of a highly respectable boarding-house; there is a lively description drawn from newspaper and eyewitness accounts of Paris during the siege of 1870–1. (Sophia's French admirer Chirac departs by balloon and is never seen again.) At length the two long-estranged sisters are reconciled and Sophia returns as an old woman to her childhood home in Bursley. One of the finest passages in the book describes Sophia's emotions as, summoned too late to his deathbed, she sees the aged corpse of Gerald Scales, who has died poverty-stricken and alone in lodgings: she reflects on the impenetrable riddle of Time, in terms that reflect Bennett's own agnostic and stoic wonder at the mystery of life.

'OLIVIA' (Dorothy STRACHEY) (1866–1960), British novelist and translator. Sister of Lytton *Strachey, friend and translator of André Gide, Strachey would merit no more than a footnote in literary history were it not for a single, pseudonymous work. *Olivia* (1949) is set in a French girls' boarding school, where the eponymous English heroine falls in love with her schoolteacher. The novel hints at Mlle Julie's lesbianism, but Olivia's passion for her is both wildly erotic and 'innocent'. *Olivia* draws on the author's memories of the Strachey household and of her own teacher, the charismatic Marie Souvestre. It is a highly charged, compressed, and beautifully controlled study of the psychological turmoil of first love. *Olivia* was filmed in 1950, directed by Jacqueline Audry.

OLIVIER, Edith (1872–1948), British novelist of Huguenot descent, born in Wilton, Wiltshire, one of the ten children of the autocratic and conservative Rector (later Canon) of Wilton, educated at St Hugh's College, Oxford. At the age of 55 she produced her first novel, *The Love-Child* (1927), a vivid, strange, absorbing story of the neurotic, possessive spinster Agatha, haunted by an imaginary child, the bold, alluring Clarissa, who gradually becomes visible to others and whose loss Agatha terribly fears. The novel is a minor classic, strongly influenced by Jane Austen and Nathaniel Hawthorne, and is one of a genre of fantasy novels popular at the time. From 1924, Olivier's life was changed by a deep friendship with Rex Whistler, then a 19-year-old art student. She became a well-loved confidante and hostess in the aesthetic, upper-class homosexual circles centred on country life in Wiltshire, which included Siegfried *Sassoon, Osbert *Sitwell, and Cecil Beaton. Olivier's four other novels drew on her family background for their emotions and their atmosphere, and showed a curious interest in split personalities: *As Far As Jane's Grandmother's* (1928), *The Triumphant Footman* (1930), *Dwarf's Blood* (1930), and *The Seraphim Room* (1932). Olivier also wrote a biographical work, some local studies of places and people, and an autobiography, *Without Knowing Mr. Walkley* (1938). See Penelope Middleboe, *Edith Olivier* (1989), and *The Love-Child* (Virago, 1981), with an introduction by H. Lee.

OLSEN, Tillie (1913–), American poet, novelist, short-story writer, critic, and activist, born in Omaha, Nebraska, she grew up in a poor household. She left school early, and as a teenager wrote various sketches and musical dramas for the Young People's Socialist League; in 1932 she was imprisoned for her leafleting activities. Her early work, much of which described her life as an industrial worker in her home state of Nebraska, was published in **Partisan Review*, including versions of the opening chapters of *Yonnondio: From the Thirties* (1974); the title is from the American Indian word for 'lament for the lost', and the novel displays a powerful awareness of the ruling social forces and a sensitivity to individual aspirations. With the pressures of family and domestic life, she ceased writing until the early 1960s. A collection of essays and extracts entitled *Silences* (1965) is an impassioned blend of personal memories and socio-historical observations, focusing on the stultification of individual expression owing to the restrictions imposed by class, race, or gender. A few stories, including 'Requa I' (1970), were collected as *Tell Me a Riddle* (1961), and her 1972 essay 'One out of Twelve: Women Who Are Writers in Our Century' was incorporated in the 1978 edition of *Silences*. Her other works include a collection of women's writings entitled *Mother to Daughter, Daughter to Mother* (1984). Her sensitivity to the politics of class and gender has inspired such women writers as Margaret *Atwood, Adrienne *Rich, Maxine Hong *Kingston, and Ellen *Moers.

OLSON, Charles (1910–70), American poet, born in Worcester, Massachusetts, educated at Wesleyan University and Harvard. Olson obtained an MA in 1933 with a thesis on Herman Melville: his investigation of Melville's library was later acknowledged by F. O. *Matthiessen in *American Renaissance*. His exploration of Melville's annotations of Shakespeare was of particular importance; entering Harvard in 1939 as a graduate student and teaching assistant, he published 'Lear and Moby-Dick' and finished a first draft of a book on Melville, a book whose prose was initially influenced by Edward *Dahlberg. His first poems were written in 1940, but he spent most of the Second World War working first for the American Civil Liberties Union and then the Foreign Language Information Service, from which he resigned in protest in 1944. *Call Me Ishmael* (1947) was written in 1945, a classic study of American culture which rivals D. H. *Lawrence's *Studies in Classic American Literature* in importance. From 1946 to 1948 he visited Ezra *Pound in St Elizabeth's, finally breaking off contact when Pound's fascism grew too abhorrent. In 1948 he wrote *Stocking Cap* (1966) and *The Fiery Hunt* (1978) and also gave his first lectures at *Black Mountain College; he returned to Black Mountain in 1949 and 1951, first as a faculty member, then rector, eventually closing the college in 1956. *Y and X* was published in 1949, initiating an intense period of productivity; the first **Maximus* poem, his long correspondence with Robert *Creeley, and the publication of '*Projective Verse' all occurred in 1950. In 1951 he spent six months in Lerma, Campeche and helped to put together the first edition of Cid *Corman's magazine *Origin*. *In Cold Hell, In Thicket*, and *Maximus 1/10* (see MAXIMUS POEMS, THE) were published in 1953, followed by *Mayan Letters* (1954) and *Maximus 11/22* (1956). His lecture series, *A Special View of History*, was delivered in 1957. 1960 saw the publication of Donald Allen's *The New American Poetry* and of the first major book of the *Maximus* poems: Olson's revolution in poetry was clearly beginning to consolidate itself, a process which continued with the Vancouver Poetry Conference of 1963 and the Berkeley Poetry Conference of 1965, during which time Olson was a visiting Professor of English at the State University of New York at Buffalo. Olson's last years were a mixture of extreme isolation and frenzied activity; his second wife was killed in an automobile accident in 1964 and Olson, lacking to some extent the collective focus of Black Mountain, led a somewhat dispersed life, despite commanding the respect and attention of a large number of students. Nevertheless, *Human Universe* was published in 1965, *Selected Writings* in 1967, *Maximus IV, V, VI* in 1968, and *Letters for Origin* in 1969, the year in which he was Visiting Professor at the University of Connecticut. He died in New York in 1970, declaring that he had finished the *Maximus* poems of which *The Maximus Poems: Volume Three* was published in 1975, then revised for a complete edition in 1983. The volume is his life's greatest achievement, extending as it does the tradition of the long American poem initiated by Whitman, Williams, and Ezra Pound.

Omeros, a poem in seven books by Derek *Walcott, published in 1990 in an edition of 325 pages. 'Omeros' is the Greek for Homer, whose *Iliad* is echoed in the names of the poem's chief protagonists, the St Lucian fishermen Achille and Hector; their rivalry for the love of Helen, the beautiful servant girl emblematically identified with the island, is central to the poem's development. Odysseus has a counterpart in the poem's narrator, whose wanderings through America and Europe in Books IV and V before returning to his birthplace in St Lucia are in close alignment with Walcott's autobiographical experience. Among the poem's most imaginatively intense sections are the visionary survey of the island upon which Omeros conducts the narrator in the final book and the spiritual return of Achille to the Africa of his ancestors in Book III. Predominantly written in intermittently rhymed tercets, the poetry consistently displays Walcott's gift for rhythmical effects of great suppleness and strength. The sea is both a principal source of the poem's wealth of natural imagery and a unifying principle in the exposition of its vast historical and geographical scope.

OMOTOSO, Kole (1943–), Nigerian novelist, dramatist, and critic, born in Akure, educated at the Universities of Ibadan and Edinburgh. His early novels are characterized by a cool, unsentimental lucidity of style which belies the remorseless approach of tragedy: *The Edifice* (1971) concerns the slow disintegration of the marriage between Dele, a Nigerian overseas student, and Daisy, an English girl, when he takes her to Nigeria; *The Combat* (1972) is a parable of the Nigerian Civil War, focusing on two brothers engaged in futile conflict. Omotoso has described his *Fella's Choice* (1974) as the first Nigerian detective novel. *Just Before Dawn* (1988), a Nigerian tragedy, has been described as his finest novel and compared, in its 'historical' sweep', to **Midnight's Children*. *Miracles and Other Stories* (1973) contains grim, realistic tales about children. His plays, *The Curse* (1976) and *The Scales* (1976), are satirical and focus on the inequalities in Nigerian society; his most powerful drama is the four-act *Shadows on the Horizon* (1977), subtitled 'a play about the combustibility of private property'. Critical works include *The Form of* *the African Novel* (1979) and *The Theatrical into Theatre: A Study of Drama and Theatre in the English-Speaking Caribbean* (1982), and *Achebe or Soyinka? A Reinterpretation and a Study in Contrasts* (1995).

ONDAATJE, Michael (1943–), Canadian poet and fiction-writer, born in Colombo, Ceylon (now Sri Lanka) of Dutch ancestry, educated at Dulwich College, from 1954. He moved to Canada in 1962 and attended the University of Toronto and Queen's University, Kingston, Ontario, before subsequently teaching at the University of Western Ontario and Glendon College in Toronto. His work is difficult to categorize since it frequently confounds conventional generic distinctions, but it none the less occupies an important place in recent Canadian post-modernist writing. Although his subject matter is mainly non-Canadian it is centrally concerned with the making of cultural mythologies and the problems inherent in writing about both personal and public pasts, issues which figure prominently in the work of many of his Canadian contemporaries, such as Robert *Kroetsch, Margaret *Laurence, and Rudy *Wiebe. *The Collected Works of Billy the Kid* (1970) is a discontinuous narrative, written in both verse and prose and with photographs interspersed, about the life of the legendary Western outlaw. Like much of Ondaatje's work, it questions notions of normality, at times suggesting that the psychotic Billy is no more crazed than his adversary, the 'sane' sheriff Pat Garrett. American mythologies are also central in *Coming Through Slaughter* (1979), a treatment of the pioneer New Orleans Jazz musician, Buddy Bolden. In *Running in the Family* (1982), another discontinuous narrative, which contains elements of both the travel journal and the family memoir, Ondaatje returns to his native Sri Lanka and, again mixing prose, verse, and photographs, offers a meditation on the subject of 'historical relations', both those of his own privileged and highly eccentric family and those of the country more generally. Less dependent on historical fact is *In the Skin of a Lion* (1987), which focuses on the lives of marginalized immigrant communities in Toronto and Southwestern Ontario from 1900 to 1940 through the perspective of its protagonist. *The English Patient* (1992; joint winner of the Booker Prize) is his most ambitious work. Returning to some of the characters of *In the Skin of a Lion*, the novel is set as the Second World War ends. Through the intertwined lives of four characters including a badly burned Englishman and a young idealistic Indian soldier, the novel examines the morality of war and politics, and the role of colonial subjects in the Allied victory. Ondaatje's other works include the poetry collections *The Dainty Monsters* (1967), *The Man with Seven Toes* (1969), *Rat Jelly* (1973), *There's a Trick with a Knife I'm Learning to Do* (1979), and *The Cinnamon Peeler* (1989).

One Flew Over the Cuckoo's Nest, a novel by Ken *Kesey, published in 1962. The narrative is told by Chief Bromden, so named for his Native American descent, an inmate in a psychopathic ward of an Oregon mental hospital, where he has chosen the guise of a mute to defend his alienation from a society he cannot tolerate. Bromden tells of the eruption into the ward of Randle Patrick McMurphy, an ebullient convict serving time for rape, who has stage-managed his release from prison by pretending insanity. McMurphy's exuberant vitality challenges the ruthless efficiency of the Head Nurse, Miss Ratched, known as Big Nurse, whose mechanistic control of her patients has terrorized them into a state of lifeless docility. McMurphy, who uses laughter and irreverence as instruments of defiance, encourages his fellow patients to recover their selfhood and rebel against Big Nurse's sadistic authority. His success in this leads to his own sacrifice, culminating in repeated electric shock therapy and a lobotomy that reduces him to a vegetable state. The novel ends as Chief Bromden smothers McMurphy as an act of mercy, and then escapes, redeemed by what he has done, into the outer world. The novel struck a chord with the radically motivated young people of the 1960s who found McMurphy's anarchic vitality an inspiring resource to set against the orthodoxies of a suffocating materialism in domestic policy, and the rampant imperialism of American foreign policy.

O'NEILL, Eugene (Gladstone) (1888–1953), American dramatist, born in New York, the son of James O'Neill, a well-known romantic actor. After a fragmented education, including a Catholic boarding-school and a year at Princeton, O'Neill led an adventurous life as a gold prospector, beachcomber, seaman, and actor. In 1912 he suffered a physical breakdown and the enforced rest turned him to drama. His earliest work was written in association with George Pierce *Baker's '47 Workshop', and after 1916 with the Provincetown Players. Many of his early one-act plays reflect his experiences on ships and among outcasts, and his growing vision of life which entails a deep rejection of conventionally organized society. Success came with **Beyond the Horizon* (1920), a play about two brothers, which displays the sombreness of mind that was to distinguish O'Neill's best work. From this point onwards he was preoccupied with writing plays embodying man's deep reflections on religion. Among his most significant works of this period are *Chris Christopherson* (1920), rewritten as *Anna Christie* (1921), a naturalistic drama of a prostitute and her redemption; the symbolic expressionist plays *The *Emperor Jones* (1920) and *The Hairy Ape* (1922), whose brutal protagonist, Yank, is shown, in a society incorrigibly wedded to machines, with no real kin other than an ape; the more naturalistic *All God's Chillun Got Wings* (1924), a tragedy of a black man's marriage to an arrogant white woman; and *Desire Under the Elms* (1924), a study of puritanism and thwarted sexuality set in New England in 1850. With *The Great God Brown* (1926), O'Neill's interest in the multiple personality is first given major expression. *Lazarus Laughed* (pub. 1927; perf. 1928) uses masked choruses to affirm life in this presentation of the story of Lazarus who, resurrected from the dead, brings news of all-important love and the 'laughter of God'. *Marco Millions* (pub. 1927; perf. 1928) attacks American materialism in its reworking of the story of Marco Polo. **Strange Interlude* (1928; Pulitzer Prize), one of the dramatic masterpieces of O'Neill's career, demonstrates his absorption in both Freud and the Greek drama, as does his great trilogy, **Mourning Becomes Electra* (1931), in which Aeschylus's *Oresteia* is transposed to New England at the close of the Civil War as O'Neill explores the tormented relations of the Mannon family. The work can be compared with the great plays of Ibsen and Strindberg, both of whom O'Neill admired. After *Days Without End* (1934), with its theme of the search for faith, O'Neill was silent for some years. In 1936 he was awarded the Nobel Prize for Literature. *The *Iceman Cometh* (1946) is a long naturalistic tragedy set in a Bowery bar. **Long Day's Journey into Night* (written 1940; pub. and perf. 1956), perhaps his greatest work, was published posthumously, as were *A Moon for the Misbegotten* (1953) and two in a projected eleven-play cycle, 'A Tale of Possessors Self-Dispossessed', *A Touch of the Poet* (1957) and *More Stately Mansions* (1964). See also EXPRESSIONISM.

ONIONS, C(harles) T(albut) (1873–1965), British lexicographer and grammarian, born in Edgbaston, Warwickshire, educated at Mason College, Birmingham. In 1895 he met James A. H. *Murray, who invited him to join the staff of the *New English Dictionary* (later the *Oxford English Dictionary*) at Oxford, where Onions remained for the rest of his life. In 1914 he became a co-editor of the Dictionary and was independently responsible for the entries 'Su–Sz', 'Wh–Worling', 'X', 'Y', and 'Z'. *A Shakespeare Glossary* (1911) formed a by-product of his lexicography and drew extensively on his native knowledge of Warwickshire dialect. He was a reader in English philology at Oxford from 1927 to 1949. In 1922 he became editor of *The Shorter Oxford English Dictionary* (1932) and subsequently worked with William *Craigie as co-editor on the *Supplement* (1933) to *OED*. *The Oxford Dictionary of English Etymology* (1966) was his major independent work. His other publications include the frequently reprinted *An Advanced English Syntax* (1904).

ONIONS, Oliver (1873–1961), British writer, born in Bradford. Having studied art in London, he turned to fiction with the publication of *The Compleat Bachelor* (1900). This was followed by many other novels including two historical novels, *The Story of Ragged Robin* (1945) and *Poor Man's Tapestry* (1946), and *A Shilling to Spend* (1965). He is now remembered principally for the eloquent ghost stories contained in *Widdershins* (1911), *Ghosts in Daylight* (1924), and *The Painted Face* (1929). The subtle interplay of manifestation and psychosis in his most famous single story, 'The Beckoning Fair One' (in *Widdershins*), is couched in an elegant prose which characterizes much of his work. He was married to the romantic novelist Berta Ruck (1878–1978).

Only Child, The, James *Kirkup's 'autobiography of infancy', published in 1957. The book was highly acclaimed for its remarkably effective recreations of the atmospheres and particulars of Kirkup's life up to the age of six, when his family left the two-room flat in South Shields, County Durham, which forms the principal setting. The authenticity with which the consciousness of a child is conveyed is partly the result of restricting the autobiography's compass to the flat and the street immediately outside it; only towards the end does the local frame of reference expand, when the child becomes aware of a local park and then of the River Tyne as features of a world beyond the end of the street. Kirkup's methods permit occasional touches of sentimentality to offset the neutral objectivity of much of the writing; the strategy is valuable in characterizing a child who might otherwise seem over-serious in his precocious sensitivities, which confer a sense of separateness from the everyday concerns of others. The book has a documentary value in its detailing of the life of a working-class family in the 1920s; periods of hardship are common as a consequence of the occasional unemployment of Kirkup's father, whose work as a joiner at the shipyards fluctuates.

O'NOLAN, Brian, see O'BRIEN, FLANN.

On The Black Hill, see CHATWIN, BRUCE.

On the Road, Jack Kerouac's best-known novel, published in 1957. The original draft was written with great rapidity in 1951, following the development of the improvisatory style Kerouac described as 'spontaneous prose'; accordingly, it was typed onto a continuous roll of paper to avoid the interruptions necessary for the changing of separate sheets. The often headlong narrative, which is structured around the successive journeys made by 'Sal Paradise', Kerouac's autobiographical persona, enacts the novel's existential creed of the pursuit of fulfilment through indiscriminate immersion in experience; this affirmative and quasi-religious philosophy is most fully realized in the person of 'Dean Moriarty', the pseudonym for Kerouac's friend Neal Cassady, with whom he underwent the events informing the book. An ungovernable appetite for physical and mental stimulation drives Moriarty to the transcendent extreme of 'BEAT—the root, the soul of beatific'; this usage and the values and attitudes thus comprehended resulted in the adoption of the term '*Beat Generation' to describe Kerouac and, *inter alia*, Allen *Ginsberg and William *Burroughs, both of whom appear in the work under the respective names 'Carlo Marx' and 'Bull Lee'. The radically anti-authoritarian tone and enthusiastic accounts of cannabis smoking and other modes of intoxication were among the reasons for the rejection of *On the Road* by the publishers of Kerouac's comparatively conventional first novel, *The Town and the City* (1950); during the years that elapsed before its publication the original text was abridged and emended, a process in which Malcolm *Cowley was instrumental in his capacity as a reader for the Viking Press, who issued the book in 1957. In the previous year the controversy surrounding the appearance of Ginsberg's *Howl (1956) had prepared the way for *On the Road*, which gained a wide popular readership among those disaffected with the socio-cultural climate of post-war conformity.

OODGEROO, see NOONUCCAL, OODGEROO.

Open Field Composition, see PROJECTIVE VERSE.

Open Theatre, New York City, an American theatre company; with *Living Theatre, one of the two most respected avant-garde theatre companies in recent American history. From its inception in February 1963, the Open Theatre was committed to experimentation in non-naturalistic modes of theatre. Although a non-hierarchical organization, the Open Theatre is inextricably linked with the name of Joseph Chaikin, a Living Theatre actor, who became its leader and sole director in 1973, the year it closed. Its members regarded the Open Theatre as both a production company and an experimental laboratory, and held its workshop innovations to be as important as its public productions. It staged one-act and full-length plays by members of the company and others, but its most memorable work was in five full-length collaborative plays, *Viet Rock*, principally written by Megan *Terry, *The Serpent* by Jean-Claude van Itallie, *Terminal*, *Mutation Show*, and *Nightwalk*, co-authored by Megan Terry, Sam *Shepard, and Jean-Claude van Itallie. The Open Theatre was conceived as a non-commercial agency, a vital experiment in communal theatre which did not pay its members, nor charge its audience for its workshop performances. The commercial success of the above five productions finally led Chaikin to propose its demise, and its final performance was of *Nightwalk* at the University of California, Santa Barbara, on 1 December 1973.

O Pioneers!, a novel by Willa *Cather, published in 1913. The novel, with a title taken from Walt Whitman, celebrates the courage and transfiguring stoicism of immigrants in Nebraska, where Cather grew up. After the death of her father, Alexandra Bergson assumes responsibility for the family farm since her mother lacks the ability to do so and her brother, Emil, is too young. Alexandra finds in herself the qualities to build up the farm, qualities which the author sees as contributing significantly to the civilization the early settlers created for themselves out on the prairie. Not entirely satisfied by work alone, and deploring the descent into materialistic meanness of some members of her community, much of Alexandra's emotional attention is given to the sensitive and intelligent Emil, until he and the young married woman with whom he is having an affair are killed by her jealous husband. As a result of this terrible tragedy, Alexandra decides to marry her old friend, Carl Lindstrum. The novel is distinguished by beautiful incidental descriptions evoking life in the Nebraskan prairie, and is the earliest example of the American pastoral which Cather sought and practised in her work.

OPPEN, George (1908–84), American poet, born in New Rochelle, New York, he grew up in California. From 1930 to 1933 he lived at Le Beausset in France, where he and his wife founded To Publishers, producing editions by various poets associated with Objectivism, including Louis *Zukofsky's *An 'Objectivists' Anthology* in 1932 (see OBJECTIVIST POETRY). His first collection of poetry, *Discrete Series* (1934), for which Ezra *Pound supplied a preface, conveyed responses to his urban surroundings in austere verse characterized by a stark clarity of imagery and a mutedly emphatic tone. In 1935 he joined the Communist Party, after which his work as a poet was for many years subordinated to his political activities. He was wounded on active service during the Second World War and subsequently established himself as a cabinet-maker in Los Angeles, moving his business to Mexico in 1950 due to anti-communist agitation. From 1958 onward he lived in San Francisco, publishing his second volume, *The Materials*, in 1962; his remarkable ability to suggest passionate moral and emotional conviction through images of great concrete particularity is clearest in the poems drawing on his trade as a skilled woodworker. His further collections include *This in Which* (1965), *Seascape* (1973), and *Primitive* (1978), after which he contracted Alzheimer's disease and effectively ceased writing. *Of Being Numerous* (1968; Pulitzer Prize), widely considered his finest achievement, is permeated by his stoically affirmative belief in 'survival's | Thin, thin radiance'; each of the forty sections of the title sequence functions both as an autonomous poetic unit and as a development of the whole, which amounts to a vividly realized confrontation with the significances of urban existence. A *Collected Poems* appeared in 1975. *Meaning a Life: An Autobiography* (1978) is by the poet's wife Mary Oppen.

ORAGE, A(lfred) R(ichard) (1875–1934), British editor and critic, born at Dacre in Yorkshire; he taught in Leeds after training at a college in Culham, Oxfordshire. His interest in the cultural implications of socialism led him to found the Leeds Arts Club with Holbrook Jackson. His early publications include the monograph *Friedrich Nietzsche* (1905). In 1906 he became a journalist in London and took over the **New Age* in association with Jackson in 1907. His critical writings for the periodical emphasize the ethical and social functions of literature and contain close textual readings which anticipate the development of analytical criticism in the 1920s. The *New Age* remained a central forum for literary discourse until around 1920, when Orage became immersed in the teachings of Gurdjieff, whose *Meetings with Remarkable Men* (1963) he translated. Between 1922 and 1930 he was active as a fund-raiser for the Gurdjieff Institute in Fontainebleau. In 1931 he founded the *New English Weekly*, the chief organ of the Social Credit movement. His *Political and Economic Writings* (1935) were edited by Montgomery Butchart. *'The New Age' under Orage* (1967) is by Wallace Martin, who edited *Orage as Critic* (1974), a selection of his critical work.

Orators, The, the second of W. H. *Auden's books, published in 1932, with revised editions in 1934 and 1966. Sub-titled 'An English Study', the work is in three parts, 'The Initiates', 'The Journal of Airman', and 'Six Odes', the first two of which are predominantly written in prose. Its disjunctive development, experimental formal strategies, and pervasive sense of combined personal and cultural crises identify it as Auden's most typically Modernist (see MODERNISM) work. The 'radical uncertainty of tone' which Edward *Mendelson notes partially accounts for Auden's later view of the work as 'a fair notion fatally injured'; this characteristic is, however, a function of the multiplicity of personae and contexts employed, as well as being intrinsic to the sustained thematic concern with uncertainties of identity and intention. The ascendancy of European fascism strongly informs the political urgency embodied in the doomed figure of the Airman; other important elements in the complex conceptual fabric of the work are provided by Auden's reading in psychology and anthropology. The book's stylistic mobility is remarkable: aridly dialectical passages modulate into blackly humorous burlesque, parodies of platitudinous rhetoric fade into stretches of gnomic pronouncement, and lyrically descriptive elements are juxtaposed with the Airman's telegraphese; as Mendelson has stated, *The Orators* 'has a pungency and extravagance that he never equalled'. Soon after its initial publication Auden began expressing his severe misgivings about the work; six of its poems survive in *Collected Poems* (1976), while the entire 1934 edition is to be found in *The English Auden* (1977).

ORCZY, Baroness (Mrs Montague Barstow) (1865–1947), Hungarian-born novelist, educated in Brussels, Paris, and London, where she studied art. She became immediately famous with her romantic novel *The Scarlet Pimpernel* (1905), which followed a dramatic version written with her husband Montague Barstow, performed in Nottingham in 1903 and with great success in London in 1905. The romance follows the adventures of the fearless Sir Percy Blakeney, leader of the League of the Scarlet Pimpernel, a band of Englishmen committed to rescuing the endangered victims of the Reign of Terror in Paris. He valiantly outwits his opponents with ingenious disguises and conceals his identity from his friends in England. Several sequels followed, such as *The Elusive Pimpernel* (1908) and *The Way of the Scarlet Pimpernel* (1932). She also wrote several other historical romances and volumes of detective stories, but they did not match the success of her major work.

Orlando: A Biography, a work by V. *Woolf, published in 1928, dedicated to her friend Vita *Sackville-West, as a witty love offering. Fantastical, comical, light and whimsical, it also makes a serious inquiry into the status and treatment of women in English history and the possibility of an 'androgynous' personality which could be 'a mixture of man and woman, one being uppermost and then the other'. It is also a skilful pastiche of conventional biography, showing 'what a phantasmagoria the mind is and meeting-place of dissemblables', and how resistant to the dull plod of chronology. Orlando begins the book as a seductive 16-year-old Elizabethan boy, trying to write poetry, inheritor of a great country house (based on the Sackville house, Knole), and madly in love with a Russian princess. His picaresque journeys take him through a sex change, a romantically adventurous relationship with 'Marmaduke Bonthrop Shelmerdine', and three vividly caricatured centuries till s/he reaches the 'present day'.

ORMOND, John (1923–90), Welsh poet, born at Dunvant, near Swansea, educated at University College, Swansea. After working as a journalist, he began a career with the BBC in 1955, becoming a distinguished director and producer of documentary films. Following the appearance of his verse in *Indications* (with James *Kirkup and John Bayliss, 1942), he was advised by Vernon *Watkins to publish no more poetry before he was 30; he consequently developed prohibitively exacting standards of self-criticism, with the result that his first independent collection, *Requiem and Celebration*, did not appear until 1969. His other principal publications are *Definition of a Waterfall* (1973) and *Selected Poems* (1987), which contained much previously uncollected material. Ormond's formidable technical abilities are frequently used to provide lucid structures for his exploratory treatments of problematic personal and social concerns. The dramatically effective visual qualities of many of his poems suggest an imaginative continuity between his writing and his work as a film-maker. His films include *A Bronze Mask* (1968), on Dylan *Thomas, and *The Fragile Universe* (1969), on Alun *Lewis.

ORMSBY, Frank (1947–), Northern Irish poet, born in Eniskillen, Northern Ireland, educated at Queen's University, Belfast. He edited **Honest Ulsterman* from 1969 to 1989. *A Store of Candles* (1977), his first substantial collection of verse, was widely acclaimed for its unobtrusive technical accomplishment and the candour with which he dealt with domestic and local material. *A Northern Spring* (1986) showed him to have built ambitiously on his previous achievements. The long title sequence of thirty-six poems forms a richly imaginative treatment of the Second World War presented through a wide range of voices and incidents; the Ulster settings common in his earlier writing are used as points of departure for work which develops its themes in a wide European context. He has edited numerous books, including *Northern Windows* (1987), a collection of excerpts from the autobiographies of Ulster-born writers, and *A Rage for Order* (1992), an anthology of poetry relating to the conflict in Northern Ireland.

O'ROURKE, P(atrick) J(ake) (1947–), American humorist, born in Toledo, Ohio, educated at Miami University and Johns Hopkins University. Working at first for underground newspapers in the 1960s, including *Baltimore Harry* (1968–71), he soon moved towards the mainstream, first with the *New York Herald* (1971–3), then as editor with *The National Lampoon* (1973–81), and head of the international affairs desk of *Rolling Stone* in 1981. O'Rourke is essentially a hedonist of the 1980s, fiercely opposed to the liberal agenda and proud of his affiliation to republican causes. Although he claims to share concerns with a wider, more conventional audience, his stance is restricted and his humour often dependent on a highly selective presentation of detail: for instance, the essay in which he attempts to convince his audience that the massacre at Mutlaa Ridge was really an apocalypse of consumer durables. His books include *Republican Party Reptile* (1987), *Parliament of Whores* (1991), *Give War a Chance* (1992), and *All the Trouble in the World: The Light Side of Famine, Pestilence, Destruction and Death* (1994).

ORTIZ, Simon J. (1941–), Native American poet and short-story writer, born in Albuquerque, New Mexico; he was brought up within the Acoma Pueblo community and was educated at the universities of New Mexico and Iowa. Ortiz has taught at various educational institutions and edited the Navajo publication *Rough Rock News*. His collections of verse include *Naked in the Wind* (1970), *Going for the Rain* (1976), and *A Good Journey* (1977); two further volumes, *A Poem is a Journey* and *From Sand Creek: Rising in This Heat which Is Our America*, appeared in 1981. Ortiz aligns his work with the oral traditions of Native American storytelling; fundamental to his purposes is a celebration of mankind's relationship with Nature and the continuity of the earth. The speaker of 'My Father's Song' recalls planting corn, and the passing of knowledge between generations. His poems often movingly juxtapose white manifestations—missionaries, IBM cards, motels, Western philosophies—with the native ideal of rootedness in crafts, ritual, and a sense of place. Ortiz's collections of stories include *Howbah Indians* (1978) and *Fightin': New and Collected Stories* (1983). He has also written *Fightback: For the Sake of the People, for the Sake of the Land* (1980), reflecting a strong advocacy of Native American culture and civil rights. See NATIVE AMERICAN LITERATURE.

ORTON, Joe (1933–67), British playwright, born in Leicester, the son of a municipal gardener; he left school to train as an actor. He wrote several lively short comedies for both the stage and television, including *The Erpingham Camp* (1967), a variation on Euripides' *The Bacchae* in which rioting holidaymakers punish the arrogant owner of a seaside camp. His only full-length plays, however, were *Entertaining Mr Sloane* (1964), about a genteel brother and sister who bribe and blackmail their psychopathic lodger into becoming their sexual slave; **Loot* (1965); and the posthumously performed *What the Butler Saw* (1969), about a series of farcical misunderstandings, confusions, disguises, and subterfuges in a private asylum run by an amorous psychiatrist. Although the first of these pieces is more realistic than the other two, all are black, witty, and marked by a contempt for conventional institutions and values, especially sexual values, and by an anarchic glee in their subversion of exposure as fraudulent. Orton was battered to death by his long-time companion, Kenneth Halliwell: the tragic climax of a life well described by John Lahr in the biography *Prick Up Your Ears* (1978).

ORWELL, George, pseudonym of Eric Arthur BLAIR (1903–50), British novelist and social critic, born in Bengal, educated at Eton; he was the son of Richard Blair, an opium agent in the Indian Civil Service, and his much younger wife Ida. Relations between father and son were virtually non-existent for the first eight years of Orwell's life, as he and his mother and older sister Marjorie moved to England in 1904, leaving Richard on his own in India until his retirement in 1911. Orwell was educated at St Cyprian's Preparatory School under the regime of a Mr and Mrs Wilkes, whom he later portrayed as brutally unjust in 'Such, Such Were the Joys'. Here he befriended Cyril *Connolly, with whom he was also subsequently at Eton. He had no university education, but spent his early adulthood in Burma as an officer of the Imperial Office. It was this experience that led to the texts 'Shooting an Elephant', 'A Hanging', and *Burmese Days* (1934).

In 1927, after an attack of dengue fever, he returned to Europe and a succession of poorly paid jobs in Paris and London. He began the experiment of living for short periods among the homeless and deprived while trying to establish himself as a professional writer. For his first major publication, **Down and Out in Paris and London* (1933), which reflected this period of impoverishment, he adopted the pen-name of George Orwell. After a spell as a teacher, and during his employment with a London bookseller in 1935, he met Eileen O'Shaughnessy, who was to be his first wife. By this time he had completed two novels, *Burmese Days* and *A Clergyman's Daughter* (1935). His publisher for these was Victor Gollancz who had a phobia about libel and asked for numerous changes, but he also commissioned *The *Road to Wigan Pier* (1937), the book in which Orwell found his authentic voice and the kind of politically aware approach that has been associated with him ever since. At the time of its publication Orwell was already in Spain, fighting for the Republicans as a member of the P.O.U.M. militia. His account of the Spanish Civil War, in which he was wounded in the throat, focused on his experiences in Barcelona and at the Aragon front, but when the book was first offered for publication, the two chapters dealing with the political infighting on the Republican side were antagonistic to the orthodox Left in Britain, and Gollancz declined to publish Orwell's version of events. It was left to Fredric Warburg, of the then 'midget' publishing firm of Secker and Warburg, to bring out **Homage to Catalonia* (1937).

After returning from Spain, and until the London blitz of 1940, Orwell and Eileen spent most of their time in a cottage in Wallington, Hertfordshire, where they kept animals, planted a vegetable garden and opened a village shop. Soon after the outbreak of war they moved to London where Orwell began reviewing films and drama, contributing regularly to Cyril Connolly's **Horizon* and to the American **Partisan Review*, and composing some of his finest political journalism, including 'Inside the Whale', 'My Country, Right or Left', and 'The Lion and the Unicorn'. Despite the ambitious scope of his fiction in **Keep the Aspidistra Flying* (1936) and **Coming Up for Air* (1939), his reputation as a novelist was only securely established with **Animal Farm* (1945), which enjoyed worldwide success. The financial rewards came too late for Orwell to share with Eileen, who died of a heart attack after reacting adversely to anaesthetic during an operation. Orwell was left to bring up their newly adopted son Richard with the help primarily of his younger sister Avril. He spent the best part of his remaining years on the remote farm in Jura where he completed his most formidable work of fiction, **Nineteen Eighty-Four* (1949). Even before he finished the typescript of this he became gravely ill, and after being diagnosed as tubercular, was more or less hospitalized for the last year of his life. His wedding to Sonia Brownell took place at his bedside in University College Hospital. By the time of his death, he had been judged a major author by critics on both sides of the Atlantic, and his value as a cultural critic has been increasingly widely recognized. His warnings against ideological manipulations of language, as in 'Politics and the English Language' (1946), have become increasingly pertinent. The collection of journalistic pieces *The Lion and the Unicorn: Socialism and the English Genius* (1941), elucidating his own non-conformist brand of patriotism, received high critical acclaim for its clarity and colloquial style. His essays were collected in *Inside the Whale and Other Essays* (1940), *The Lion and the Unicorn: Critical Essays* (1946), *Shooting an Elephant and Other Essays* (1950), and *Such, Such Were the Joys* (1953). The four volumes of Orwell's *Collected Essays, Journalism and Letters* (1968) were edited by Sonia Orwell and Ian Angus. See *Orwell* (1971) by Raymond *Williams, *George Orwell* (1980; revised edition, 1981) by Bernard *Crick, and *George Orwell: The Authorised Biography* (1991) by Michael Shelden. See also UTOPIA AND ANTI-UTOPIA.

OSBORNE, John (James) (1929–94), British playwright, born in London, the son of a commercial artist; he was educated at Belmont School, Devon. The first volume of his autobiography, *A Better Class of Person* (1981), describes his unhappy childhood and his years as an actor in provincial repertory, during which he wrote *Epitaph for George Dillon* in collaboration with Anthony Creighton. This study of alienation and ennui was not, however, performed until 1958, by which time its author's name had been made by a vastly more eloquent and influential play, **Look Back in Anger* (1956). The late 1950s and early 1960s proved to be Osborne's most fruitful period, producing as they did *The *Entertainer* (1957), which brought Laurence Olivier from the classical to the contemporary stage as Archie Rice, a shoddy survivor of the great days of music hall; **Luther* (1961), based on the life of (as Osborne saw him) a troubled yet inspiriting rebel in conflict with his father, his God, his own inadequacies, and a decadent Church and world; **Inadmissible Evidence* (1964); and *A Patriot for Me* (1965), about the rise and fall of an officer with the misfortune to be both bourgeois and homosexual in the Austro-Hungarian military élite. All Osborne's work was highly critical of those aspects of contemporary society he thought damaging to the emotionally alive individual. Often, he selected a single character to give what he called 'lessons in feeling' in opposition to or in conflict with apathy, triviality, stupidity, cupidity, or other manifestations of an uncaring world. Osborne's later work, starting with *Time Present* (1968) and *The Hotel in Amsterdam* (1968), was, however, more sweeping in its vituperation and perhaps less discriminating in its choice of targets. In *West of Suez* (1971), *A Sense of Detachment* (1972), and *Watch It Come Down* (1976), it also became increasingly nostalgic for civilized decencies he believed had been lost in 'the whole, hideous, headlong rush into the 20th century'. Though the divide between the two was never as absolute as it might at first seem, the archetypal *Angry Young Man became a somewhat more conservative older one: a change explicit in Osborne's *Deja Vu* (1992), which showed Jimmy Porter, the protagonist of *Look Back in Anger*, in rancorous late middle age, denouncing contemporary liberalism as forthrightly as he had earlier attacked the old-fashioned, reactionary, and out-of-date.

Oscar and Lucinda, see CAREY, PETER.

OSOFISAN, (Baba) Femi (Adeyemi) (1946–), Nigerian dramatist and novelist, born in Ijebu Ode, Western Nigeria, educated at the universities of Ibadan, Dakar, and Paris. Inspired to some extent by Wole *Soyinka, and respecting his achievement, Osofisan nevertheless departs from the older dramatist in providing more emphatic social and political commitment in his own plays, and greater scepticism about the liberating effects of myth and ritual. His plays are usually premièred at the University of Ibadan, where he became a lecturer, and staged by Osofisan's own theatre group. Published plays include *A Restless Run of Locusts* (1975), about political violence; *The Chattering and the Song* (1977), dedicated to Wole Soyinka and Christopher *Okigbo, which deals with the role of artists and intellectuals in bringing about political change; and *Who's Afraid of Solarin?* (1978), a satirical work adapted from Gogol's Russian political farce, *The Government Inspector; Morountodun and Other Plays* (1982); *Birthdays are Not For Dying and Other Plays* (1988); and *Yungba Yungba and the Dance Contest* (1995). His novel *Kolera Kolej* (1975) satirizes post-independence politics in Africa.

O'SULLIVAN, Vincent (Gerard) (1937–), New Zealand poet, fiction writer, playwright, and editor, born in Auckland, educated at the Universities of Auckland and Oxford. The earliest of his poetry collections, *Our Burning Time* (1965) and *Revenants* (1969), rework classical themes to explore relationships and states of mind, while his 'Butcher' sequences (*Butcher and Co*, 1977, and *The Butcher Paper*, 1982) in their often macabre portraits of 'the ordinary man' demonstrate O'Sullivan's dramatic and satiric talents. Later collections include *From the Indian Funeral* (1976), *Brother Jonathan, Brother Kafka* (1980), and *The Pilate Tapes* (1986). *Miracle, A Romance* (1976) is a satire on rugby and the sexual mores of a provincial culture. The latter is a favourite theme of this firmly realist writer who frequently uses his work to comment on New Zealand as a territory of division and conformity. His *Selected Poems* appeared in 1992. Collections of short stories include *The Boy, The Bridge and the River* (1978), *Dandy Edison for Lunch and Other Stories* (1981), *Survivals and Other Stories* (1985), *The Snow in Spain* (1990), and *Palms and Minarets: Selected Short Stories* (1993). Among his plays are *Shuriken* (1985), *Jones and Jones* (1989), and *Billy* (1989). O'Sullivan edited *The Oxford Anthology of New Zealand Poetry* (1970), *The Oxford Book of New Zealand Writing Since 1945* (1983; with MacDonald P. Jackson), *The Collected Letters of Katherine Mansfield* (1984; with Margaret Scott), an edition of Katherine Mansfield's poems, and *The Oxford Book of New Zealand Short Stories* (1993).

OSUNDARE, Niyi (1947–), Nigerian poet, born in Ikere-Ekiti, educated at the University of Ibadan, the University of Leeds, and York University, Toronto. He returned to Nigeria to work as a university lecturer and journalist. Since 1985 he has taken poetry to a wide audience through his regular column in the *Tribune* newspaper. One of the most prolific and highly regarded of Nigeria's contemporary poets, Osundare's work uses a wide range of vernacular and literary idioms to frame its lyrical and satirical concern with social justice. His principal collections of verse include *Songs of the Marketplace* (1984), *Waiting Laughters* (1990), *Songs of the Season* (1990), *Selected Poems* (1992), and *Midlife* (1993). *The Eye of the Earth* (1986) won both the Association of Nigerian Authors' Poetry Prize and the Commonwealth Poetry Prize. He is a celebrated performer of his poetry, which has affinities with Nigeria's oral traditions.

Our Man in Havana, a novel by Graham *Greene, published in 1958, described by its author as 'a Secret Service comedy' and drawing on his experience of intelligence work in Sierra Leone and London during and after the Second World War. Tracing 'the absurdities of the Cold War' through louche, decadent Havana, shortly before Fidel Castro's revolution ended Batista's rule, the novel shows a British agent, Hawthorne, recruiting a local vacuum-cleaner salesman, Wormold. His pious but profligate daughter, general shortage of money, and extravagance of imagination drive Wormold to create a complex world of plots and sub-agents to satisfy his London paymasters, Hawthorne proving too embarrassed to suggest to them that drawings of supposed installations in the Cuban hills actually represent much-enlarged vacuum-cleaner parts. Though Wormold's scheme is inevitably discovered in the end, he is allowed to escape—despite the attention of the sinister local police chief, Captain Segura, and his murder of a rival agent—into a romantic second marriage with his new secretary, who shares his beliefs that 'kingdoms, republics, powers' matter less than individual loyalties.

Greene later regretted minimizing the terrors of Batista's Cuba to gain lightness of effect, though *Our Man in Havana* also has a serious side. Greene uses Wormold's fabrication of plots and agents—and the way they alarmingly seem to come alive—to resume some of the questions about the relation of fiction and reality which he first raised seriously in *The *End of the Affair* (1951). Such questions were strangely extended in another way by the Cuban Missile Crisis of 1962, initiated by the discovery of installations not unlike those Wormold invents. Even with experience of the Secret Service, Greene could scarcely have guessed how prescient—as well as summary—of the deepening anxieties of the Cold War and the Atomic Age this comedy about fiction, espionage, and the absurdities of world politics would prove.

Our Town, a play by Thornton *Wilder, produced and published in 1938 when it won the Pulitzer Prize. It portrays the everyday lives of the Gibbs and Webb families in Grover's Corners, New Hampshire, a typical American small town, during 1901–13. Act One, 'Daily Life', presents the activities of an ordinary day: milk delivery, cooking, gossip, school and family problems. The second act, 'Love and Marriage', charts the courtship between George Gibbs and Emily Webb. In the final act, 'Death', Emily dies in childbirth. The central character of the play is the stage manager, who in a manner reminiscent of Brecht's dramatic techniques, speaks to the audience, introduces characters, comments upon the action, and plays various minor roles. The absence of scenery seeks to suggest that human experience is eternal and universal, transcending time and place. It was produced as a film in 1940.

Outsider, The, the title of novels by Colin *Wilson and Richard *Wright.

Overland, an Australian journal, the motto of which is 'Temper democratic, bias Australian' (Joseph *Furphy). After the failure of *The Realist Writer* in 1954, Stephen Murray-Smith, its editor, immediately reconstituted it under the title *Overland*. In 1956 many Australian communists were disillusioned by Russia's handling of the uprising in Hungary, among them Murray-Smith, who subsequently left the Party in 1958. By 1962, *Overland* seemed to have moved almost completely away from the early commitment to nationalism and social realism, seeing new directions for Australian arts in the work of Patrick *White and Randolph *Stow, and Albert Tucker and Sydney Nolan. As well as stories, poems, graphics, and book reviews, there are features on literary figures of Europe, America, South America, and other countries, together with regular articles surveying current trends in poetry and prose.

OWEN, Wilfred (Edward Salter) (1893–1918), British poet, born at Plas Wilmot, Oswestry, Shropshire, the son of a railway official; he was educated at Shrewsbury Technical School. Having failed to win a scholarship to London University, in 1911 he became a lay assistant to the vicar of Dunsden, near Reading, and subsequently taught English in Bordeaux. He volunteered for active service in 1915 and was eventually commissioned into the Manchester Regiment. After sustaining shell-shock in the Battle of the Somme, he was sent to Craiglockhart Hospital near Edinburgh in 1917, where he edited *The Hydra*, the hospital's magazine, and became friendly with Siegfried *Sassoon, who later introduced him to Robert *Graves. In August 1918 he returned to France and was awarded the Military Cross in the following month for gallantry under fire; he was killed one week before the Armistice in November 1918. Although Owen saw only four of his poems in print, in *The Hydra*, *The Bookman*, and *The Nation*, he had written much accomplished poetry, frequently reflecting his devoted admiration for Keats, before he joined the army. He worked intensely on his poetry of the war at Craiglockhart Hospital, where Sassoon assisted him in developing his harrowing realism. Certain poems, among them 'Inspection' and 'The Chances', adopt the dramatically straightforward manner Sassoon devised to shock the complacent into awareness of conditions in the trenches. The emotional and imaginative range of his finest work is, however, much greater than Sassoon's. 'Dulce et Decorum Est', 'Futility', 'Anthem for Doomed Youth', and 'Strange Meeting' are among the best-known of his richly elegiac evocations of the horror, futility, and pity of the war, their understated moral outrage inseparable from a compassionate depth of appeal to the humane instincts of the reader. His poetry is also remarkable for the power of its imagery and the great virtuosity of its metrical and musical effects. The editions of his poems prepared by Sassoon in 1920 and *Blunden in 1931 established him as a major poet. *The Complete Poems and Fragments* (two volumes, 1983) was edited by Jon *Stallworthy, whose biography of Owen appeared in 1974; the *Collected Letters* (1967) was edited by John Bell and Harold Owen, the poet's brother, whose *Journey from Obscurity* (1963–5) is a three-volume memoir of his family. See also WAR POETRY.

OZICK, Cynthia (1928–), American novelist and short-story writer, born in New York City, educated at New York and Ohio State Universities. In her essay 'Towards a New Yiddish: Note' in *Art and Ardor: Essays by Cynthia Ozick* (1983), Ozick describes herself as 'a third-generation American Jew . . . perfectly at home and yet perfectly insecure, perfectly acculturated and yet perfectly marginal'. Her imaginative expression of the sense of the ambiguous status of the Jew in America has made Ozick one of the most provocative of contemporary Jewish American writers. Her first work of fiction was a novel, *Trust* (1966), but it was her stories, particularly 'The Pagan Rabbi', 'Bloodshed', and 'Usurpation', which brought her to the attention of the reading public. She has more recently been preoccupied with the problems of Jewish aestheticism, and has expressed in her non-fiction prose the conviction that, for the Jew, art is an idolatrous activity. Despite this, she continues to write fiction of a consistently high standard of intelligent, creative expression. Her early stories are collected in *The Pagan Rabbi and Other Stories* (1971); other important works of fiction include *Bloodshed and Three Novellas* (1976), *Levitations: Five Fictions* (1982), *The Cannibal Galaxy* (1983), *The Messiah of Stockholm* (1987), and *The Shawl* (1989). Among her non-fiction works are *Metaphor and Memory* (1988), *What Henry James Knew and Other Essays on Writers* (1993), and *Portrait of the Artist as a Bad Character and Other Essays on Writing* (1994). Sanford Pinsker's *The Uncompromising Fiction of Cynthia Ozick* (1987) is a study of her fiction which emphasizes her interests in mysticism and spiritualism.

P

Paddy Clarke Ha Ha Ha, see DOYLE, RODDY.

PAGE, P(atricia) K(athleen) (1916–), Canadian poet, born in Swanage, Dorset; she grew up in Canada from 1919 onward and was educated at St Hilda's School for Girls in Calgary, Alberta. She was among the founders of **Preview* magazine in 1942. From 1953 to 1964 she lived in Australia, Brazil, and Mexico, where her husband was successively Canadian Ambassador. *As Ten as Twenty* (1946), her first collection of verse, displayed the political concern shared by many of the poets associated with *Preview*; more personal and compassionate treatments of social themes were presented in *The Metal and the Flower* (1954), which contained vivid treatments of spiritual and material impoverishment in urban settings. She published no further collections until *Cry Ararat!* (1967); the subdued pessimism of earlier work is supplanted by an affirmative heightening of her visual responses in poems inspired by her experiences of Brazil and Mexico. These qualities develop into the visionary clarity apparent in *Evening Dance of the Grey Flies* (1981). *The Glass Air* (1985) is a selected edition which includes previously uncollected material. Among her other works are the autobiographical *Brazilian Journal* (1987) and the highly imaginative short stories of *The Sun and the Moon, and Other Fictions* (1973).

PAINTER, George D(uncan) (1914–), British biographer, born in Birmingham, educated at Trinity College, Cambridge. From 1938 to 1974 he worked in the Department of Printed Books at the British Museum, where he became an assistant keeper in charge of fifteenth-century material in 1954. *Studies in Fifteenth Century-Printing* (1984) collects his internationally respected writings as a bibliographer and incunabulist. *André Gide* (1951) was the first of his biographies; Gide's *The Chelsea Way* (1967), a parody of Proust, is among the numerous works he has translated. His reputation as one of the foremost biographers of the twentieth century was established with *Marcel Proust* (2 volumes, 1959, 1965); the product of eighteen years' writing and research, it combines scholarship of immense meticulousness with a lucidly developed narrative. Painter's other biographies include *William Caxton* (1976), which draws on his specialized knowledge of fifteenth-century printing, and *Chateaubriand* (1977), the first part of a projected three-volume study.

Pale Fire, a novel by Vladimir *Nabokov, published in 1962. *Pale Fire* is Nabokov's fictional *tour de force*, a 'novel' comprising the foreword to a 999-line poem, 'Pale Fire' by John Shade, the text of the poem itself, a commentary on the poem by Charles Kinbote, Shade's editor, and an index. The commentary forms by far the longest part of the novel and it is here that Kinbote, who had befriended Shade, his neighbour, over the past few months of Shade's life, purporting to offer a disinterested exegesis and interpretation of the poem provides, instead, a veiled, self-serving autobiography and a biographical allegory about the exiled King of Zembla ('a distant northern land' which one takes to be Nabokov's Russia). In part the novel is a sustained parody of academic scholarship, but it is also one of Nabokov's most philosophical and metaphysical works and one in which his meditations on the fictional universe and its ambiguous relationship to 'reality' find their most penetrating and imaginative expression. The novel is considered one of the most important and formative works of American *post-modernism, notably for its use of a wholly unreliable narrator, and has been the subject of extensive commentary.

PALEY, Grace (Goodside) (1922–), American short-story writer and poet, born of Russian-Jewish immigrant parents in the Bronx, New York City, educated at Hunter College and New York University. She has taught at Sarah Lawrence College and Columbia University. She is widely regarded as a quintessentially New York writer, the city's environment and its rich variety of spoken idioms being integral to her work. Her stories began to appear in *Esquire, Atlantic,* and the *New American Review* in the mid-1950s. *The Little Disturbances of Man* (1959), her first collection, established her typifying mode in its moving reflections of lives of paradigmatic ordinariness. Much of her writing displays remarkable concentration, some of her stories being equivalent to prose poems in their brevity and imaginative impact. Stylistic developments towards more impressionistic narrative structures were evident in her second book, *Enormous Changes at the Last Minute* (1974); a prominent pacifist since the time of the Vietnam War, her dissenting politics were discernible in the feminist and pacifist perspectives in some of the stories. A further collection, *Later the Same Day* (1985), contains some of the finest examples of her characteristic fusions of comic and elegiac tones. Although she had published little poetry for many years, *New and Collected Poems* (1992) presents work she had accumulated since the early

1950s, which has thematic similarities with her fiction.

PALMER, Nettie (1885–1964), Australian literary journalist, born in Victoria, educated at the University of Melbourne. After travels in Europe she and her husband Vance *Palmer devoted themselves to nurturing Australian literature. Her works include *The South Winds* (1914) and *Shadowy Paths* (1915), poetry collections; *Modern Australian Literature* (1924), a survey of Australian literature between 1900 and 1923; the essays in *Talking It Over* (1932); and her studies of *Henry Handel Richardson* (1950) and *Bernard O'Dowd* (1954; with Victor Kennedy). As well as the above, she was the first to promote Miles *Franklin, Katharine *Prichard, M. Barnard *Eldershaw, and Barbara *Baynton. Her journal, *Fourteen Years* (1948), reveals Palmer as an influential figure at the centre of an expanding literary network. Her criticism was collected in *Nettie Palmer: Fourteen Years: Extracts from a Private Journal, 1925–39; including Poems, Reviews and Literary Essays* (1988) by Vivian Smith.

PALMER, Vance (Edward Vivian) (1885–1959), Australian writer and critic, born in Queensland. He travelled widely and for some years he lived in London, where he came under the influence of A. R. *Orage and married Nettie *Palmer in 1914; he finally settled in Melbourne. As well as collections of verse and several plays he wrote fifteen novels, including the trilogy *Golconda* (1948), *Seedtime* (1957), and *The Big Fellow* (1959), set in Queensland, and several volumes of short stories, notably *Let Birds Fly* (1955) and *The Rainbow Bird* (1957). With his wife he believed in the 'spirit' of Australia and its realization in literature, and devoted his critical powers to its promotion. Among his works are *National Portraits* (1940), studies on individual writers including the playwright Louis *Esson (1948), and *The Legend of the Nineties* (1954), a seminal text on Australian national realism. He pioneered the rediscovery of Joseph *Furphy's *Such Is Life* (1903) and compiled *Old Australian Bush Ballads* (1951).

Parade's End, a tetralogy of novels by Ford Madox *Ford, also known as the *Tietjens Tetralogy* after its central character, and originally published as *Some Do Not . . .* (1924), *No More Parades* (1925), *A Man Could Stand Up* (1926), and *Last Post* (1928). The work is set at the time of the Great War and attempts to show the interaction between public and private events, so that Ford's hero, Christopher Tietjens, a Yorkshire landowner with an unhappy past, 'must go through the public affairs of distracted Europe with that private cannonball all the time dragging at his ankle'. Tietjen's 'private cannonball' is his disastrous marriage to his beautiful but unstable wife Sylvia, whose vindictiveness towards him increases the more honorably and unselfishly he treats her. In the first volume, he takes her back after she has been unfaithful to him; he himself, although he is in love with another woman, does not betray her. Shortly after the outbreak of war he enlists, although his wife's campaign to discredit him in the eyes of his commanding officers pursues him to France; later, suffering from shell-shock, he returns to England. Tietjens's wartime experiences up to Armistice Day are described in the middle two volumes of the tetralogy, in which he also resolves, after suffering repeated injustices at his wife's hands, to leave her and establish a life with the woman he loves, Valentine Wannop (a scenario perhaps based on Ford's own unhappy marriage and his relationship with Violet *Hunt). In the final novel, Tietjens and Valentine are living together; Valentine is pregnant and Sylvia, after a final attempt to ruin her husband's happiness, agrees to relinquish her claims over him. Despite the ambitious scope of the work and its many characters, which include portraits of luminaries from the artistic, political, and intellectual circles in which Ford moved, he compared it with his finest work *The *Good Soldier*, declaring 'I think the Tietjens books will probably "date" a good deal, where the other may—indeed need—not.'

PARETSKY, Sarah (1947–), American crime novelist, born in Ames, Iowa, educated at the universities of Kansas and Chicago. Paretsky's private eye novels, featuring the plausible character of V. I. Warshawski, represent the impact of feminist thinking on a traditionally male form. With Barbara *Wilson, Amanda *Cross, and others, Paretsky uses the crime novel to investigate the role of women in American society and to uncover its widespread injustices. Following Ross *MacDonald, she emphasizes the investigative and revelatory side of private eye writing, and her novels offer a powerful critique of the politics and civic practices of her setting, Chicago. Her first novel, *Indemnity Only* (1982), offered an analysis of corruption in the labour unions. *Deadlock* (1984) showed the squalid practices of corporate business structures. Novels such as *Killing Orders* (1985), *Bitter Medicine* (1987), *Blood Shot* (also known as *Toxic Shock*) (1988), *Burn Marks* (1990), *Guardian Angel* (1992), and *Tunnel Vision* (1994) construct a detailed human context for the analysis of issues through the dilemmas and struggles of the fallible central figures.

PARGETER, Edith, see PETERS, ELLIS.

PARINI, Jay (Lee) (1948–), American poet, novelist, and biographer, born in Pittston, Pennsylvania, educated at Lafayette College and the University of St Andrews. After teaching at Dartmouth College, New Hampshire, he became Professor of English at Middlebury College, Vermont, in 1982. *Singing in Time* (1972), *Anthracite Country* (1982), and *Town Life* (1988) are collections of his poetry, which is highly regarded for its classical poise and emotional directness. His verse draws recurrently on the Pennsylvania mining country where he grew up; his novel *The Patch Boys* (1988) is set in the area in the 1920s. *The Last Station* (1990), his widely acclaimed novel, portrays Tolstoy during the last year of his life. The first of his works as a literary biographer is *Theodore Roethke: An American Romantic* (1979), which was followed by *John Steinbeck*

(1994), the fullest account of its subject available. His other publications include *The Love Run* (1980), his first novel, and the textbook *An Invitation to Poetry* (1987).

Paris Review, The, an international literary periodical begun in Paris in 1953 by Peter *Matthiessen and Harold Humes and latterly published in Paris and New York. Matthiessen remains prominent among the unusually numerous editorial personnel, as do George Plimpton and Donald *Hall, who joined him on the second issue in 1953. *The Paris Review* was founded to pursue a policy of filling its pages with all forms of creative writing and graphics, deliberately eschewing what its editors viewed as the constraining *gravitas* of critical and socio-political material. Its emphasis has always been on publishing the best contemporary writing available while encouraging authors in the early stages of their careers; its contributors have included Jack *Kerouac, Samuel *Beckett, Philip *Larkin, Robert *Creeley, Jorge Luis Borges, Simone Weil, V. S. *Naipaul, Terry Southern, Wole *Soyinka, Edna *O'Brien, and William *Burroughs, a list indicative of its vigorously eclectic tendency. The magazine is particularly noted for its regular interviews with leading authors: E. M. *Forster, Robert *Frost, T. S. *Eliot, Ezra *Pound, Boris Pasternak, Robert *Lowell, and Marianne *Moore were among the subjects in its earlier years; more recently, interviews with Doris *Lessing, William *Trevor, Maya *Angelou, and Tom *Stoppard have appeared. Graphic artists whose work has been published include Marc Chagall, Pablo Picasso, Willem de Kooning, and Raoul Duffy.

PARKER, Dorothy (1893–1967), American writer, born in West End, New Jersey and raised in New York City. After an education in convents and exclusive girls' schools, she worked for a procession of the most famous magazines, publishing poems in *Vogue* in 1916, and becoming the drama critic for *Vanity Fair* in 1917. She married Edwin Parker, whose surname she kept after their divorce. She achieved fame among New York society circles for her sharp observation and wit; her first book, a collection of poems entitled *Enough Rope* (1926), was a bestseller. This was later reissued with *Sunset Gun* (1928) and *Death and Taxes* (1931), as *Not so Deep as a Well* (1936), which enhanced her reputation through a display of self-mockery, humour, and acerbic wit. Her later work as a literary and dramatic critic for the **New Yorker* gave her a near-legendary status. Her short stories and sketches were collected in *Laments for the Living* (1930), *After Such Pleasures* (1933), and *Here Lies* (1939). An active anti-fascist before the Second World War, she also worked as a newspaper correspondent during the Spanish Civil War and was a leading member of the Anti-Nazi League. In 1933 she went to Hollywood, and in 1941 wrote the screenplay for Lillian *Hellman's *The Little Foxes*. After the war, she worked as a screenwriter and collaborated on a number of plays, among them *Ladies of the Corridor* (1953). A selection of her writing, *The Portable Dorothy Parker* (1944), was reissued in an expanded version edited by her close friend Lillian Hellman in 1977.

PARKER, Robert B(rown) (1932–), American crime novelist, born in Springfield, Massachusetts, educated at Boston University; he has taught in various American colleges. Working firmly within the tradition of Raymond *Chandler, Parker's first novel, *The Godwulf Manuscript* (1974), introduces the central character of Spenser, almost a caricature of the traditional private eye—an efficient boxer, a crack shot, a man of letters, and a lover of women. Parker combines tough and sensitive characterization with a gift for narrative momentum. Spenser's cases often involve uncovering a conspiracy—*The Judas Goat* (1978), *Looking for Rachel Wallace* (1980), and *A Catskill Eagle* (1985) all take this form, and in *Valediction* (1984) he is up against a sinister religious cult. In most of the later novels, Spenser is aided by a ruthless black assistant, Hawk, and his life is complicated by his relationship with his lover, the impossibly perfect Susan Silverman. Among Parker's best books are *God Save the Child* (1974), *Mortal Stakes* (1975), and *Promised Land* (1976). He has published the completion of Chandler's fragment *Poodle Springs* (1989), and a sequel to *The *Big Sleep* entitled *Perchance to Dream* (1991).

PARKER, (James) Stewart (1941–88), Northern Irish playwright, born in Belfast, educated at Queen's University, Belfast. Between 1965 and 1969 he lectured in the USA. Following the publication of two collections of poetry, *The Casualty's Meditation* (1966) and *Maw* (1968), Parker began writing plays for radio and television. His first play for the theatre, *Spokesong* (1975), concerns the efforts of a young man to save his family's bicycle shop from the ageless sectarian violence and twentieth-century urban progress of Belfast. This play, like his 'Caribbean-Irish Musical Comedy', *Kingdom Come* (1978), is typical of his enigmatic and optimistic approach to the 'Troubles' in Northern Ireland. Though influenced by Sam *Thompson, Parker's work differs from the 'Thompson School' of Ulster drama in opening up both the history and the present problems of Northern Ireland to an eccentric range of dramatic ideas. In the 1980s Parker developed the dramatic and intellectual possibilities of an individual voice speaking from Ireland's political and literary past. *Nightshade* (1980) was followed by *Northern Star* (1984), a play about Henry Joy McCracken, the Protestant hero of the abortive United Irishmen rebellion in 1798, relaying his thoughts through a series of parodies of Irish dramatists such as Wilde, *Shaw, and Boucicault; *Heavenly Bodies* (1986), whose main character is Boucicault; and *Pentecost* (1987), which was first produced by the *Field Day Theatre Company in Derry.

PARKS, Tim (1954–), British novelist, born in Manchester, educated at Cambridge and Harvard Universities. He received instant critical acclaim with his first two novels, *Tongues of Flame* (1985; Somerset

Maugham Award), a powerful study of a family torn apart by the confusions of religious and sexual hysteria; and *Loving Roger* (1986), which deals with an obsessional love affair that ends in death. The author's ambivalent attitude to the origins of evil, his compassion and precision, give his created world an awful credibility. *Home Thoughts* (1989) is set in Italy; *Family Planning* (1990), gives an account of the madness which overtakes Raymond Baldwin, an eldest son, and examines the influence of family life on mental breakdown. As in all his work, moral responsibilities are brought under the author's scrutiny and the result is a disturbing analysis of an appalling dilemma. In *Cara Massimina* (1990, originally published as *John MacDowell*), set in Italy, a kidnap is the prelude to several murders; these continue in *Mimi's Ghost* (1995) which shares a protagonist now confirmed as a serial killer in an attempt to cover the tracks of his first crime. *Goodness* (1991), an exploration of euthanasia, centres on a self-obsessed careerist faced with the birth of a severely disabled daughter. *Shear* (1993) offers a vivid psychological study of personal disintegration through the portrait of a man engulfed in an unmanageable emotional and sexual life. Parks has lived in Italy since the early 1980s where he has translated works by Italian writers, including Alberto Moravia's *Erotic Tales* (1983), and Italo Calvino's *The Road to San Giovanni* (1993) and *Numbers in the Dark* (1995). His *Italian Neighbours: An Englishman in Verona* appeared in 1992.

PARSONS, Clere (Trevor James Herbert) (1908–31), British poet, born in India, educated at Christ Church, Oxford, where he was a contemporary of W. H. *Auden, and was recognized as one of the most promising young poets of his day. He edited the annual *Oxford Poetry* anthology for 1928; this was prefaced with his 'Plea For Better Criticism', which rejected *Georgian poetry as 'the swan-song of Victorian poetry' and argued in favour of verse capable of confronting urban modernity with intellectual integrity. The four poems Parsons contributed to this volume are distinctly experimental. Following his early death his sole volume, *Poems*, appeared in 1932. The eighteen works making up the collection display considerable accomplishment in his skilful adaptations of conventional forms. His detached urgency of tone occasionally recalls the manner of Auden's early verse.

Partisan Review, The, a periodical founded in New York in 1934 and run by an editorial board whose members included Philip *Rahv and Dwight MacDonald. The magazine originally had strong affiliations with the Communist Party and espoused the cause of *proletarian literature; literary standards were often subordinated to ideological evaluations of the poetry, prose, and criticism featured. Following its reconstitution in 1937, it declared independence of the Communist Party and became committed to publishing work of quality. Delmore *Schwartz (who joined the editorial board in 1943), Wallace *Stevens, Edmund *Wilson, James T. *Farrell, and James *Agee were among its new contributors. In 1940 MacDonald left after a bitter disagreement with Rahv over the magazine's publication of T. S. *Eliot's 'East Coker'. The *Review* subsequently aligned itself with the national consensus in support of America's war effort from 1941 onward. Its political concerns were gradually displaced by its growing reputation for the quality of its criticism of literature and art. In the course of its continuing career, its many distinguished contributors have included W. H. *Auden, Theodore *Roethke, Randall *Jarrell, George *Orwell, Robert *Lowell, Norman *Mailer, Saul *Bellow, and Philip *Roth.

PARTRIDGE, Eric (Honeywood) (1894–1979), Australian lexicographer and etymologist, born in Waimata Valley, New Zealand, educated at the Universities of Queensland and Oxford. He founded the Scholartis Press; its failure led him to specialize in books about slang and bawdy. He is best known for *A Dictionary of Slang and Unconventional English* (1937) and *Shakespeare's Bawdy* (1947). While serving with the propaganda department of the Royal Air Force (1942–5) he wrote *Usage and Abusage* (1942) and *A Dictionary of RAF Slang* (1945). His apparently haphazard methods of compiling his dictionaries have aroused some criticism, but one of his most stringent critics, Robert *Burchfield, has singled out *Origins: A Short Etymological Dictionary of Modern English* (1958) and *A Dictionary of Catch Phrases: British and American from the Sixteenth Century to the Present Day* (1977) as works of lasting value. See David Crystal (ed.), *Eric Partridge in His Own Words* (1980).

PARTRIDGE, Frances (Catherine) (1900–), British diarist and translator, born in Bloomsbury, London, educated at Bedales School and Newnham College, Cambridge, after which she worked in a bookshop from 1921 to 1928. Having become well acquainted with Lytton *Strachey and other members of the *Bloomsbury Group, in 1933 she married Ralph Partridge, whose *ménage à trois* with Strachey and Dora Carrington had ended with the deaths of both in the preceding year. With her husband, she assisted in the completion of Strachey's unfinished work, *The Greville Memoirs* (edited by L. Strachey and R. Fulford, 8 volumes, 1938), and subsequently began her career as a translator of French and Spanish literature. Her autobiographical account of the 1920s and 1930s in *Love in Bloomsbury: Memories* (1981) is supplemented by her photographic memoir in *A Bloomsbury Album* (1987). She began publishing her diaries in 1978 with *A Pacifist's War* (1978), continuing to cover the years 1945 to 1970 with *Everything to Lose* (1987), *Hanging On* (1990), *Other People* (1993), and *Good Company* (1994). Apart from their acknowledged value as contributions to social and cultural history, the works form a vivid testimony to the author's buoyancy of spirit and her faith in the sustaining ethos of friendship. Her other publications include *A Portrait of Julia Strachey* (with Julia Strachey, 1983).

Passage to India, A, a novel by E. M. *Forster, published in 1924. The novel, which drew on the author's experiences in India in 1912 and 1921–2, when he was personal secretary to the Maharajah of Dewas, describes the class-ridden and fundamentally unstable society which existed under the British Raj, foreshadowing the eventual decline of British imperialism and the rise of Indian nationalism with extraordinary prescience; consequently the book was widely criticized in Anglo-Indian circles for what was regarded as its anti-British bias. The plot deals with a scandal involving a young Indian doctor, Aziz (a sympathetic portrait of great subtlety), and Adela Quested, a plain, spinsterish Englishwoman who has come out to India in order to marry and finds herself overwhelmed, in more than one sense, by the experience. The novel opens with a description of the city of Chandrapore, where much of the action takes place, and moves to a meeting between Aziz and Mrs Moore, the elderly Englishwoman whose son, Ronnie, the City Magistrate, is engaged to marry Miss Quested, and who has accompanied her future daughter-in-law to India. After an initial wariness on Aziz's part, a friendship develops, as a result of which he invites the two ladies to tea and subsequently offers to show them the celebrated Marabar Caves. He goes to great lengths to plan this expedition and himself acts as guide, although Mrs Moore feels unwell at the last moment and does not accompany Aziz and Adela into the Caves; she is therefore unable to provide crucial evidence in support of Aziz, whom she stubbornly believes to be innocent, after he is accused by Miss Quested of indecent assault. Aziz is arrested and put on trial; assumed guilty by most of the British contingent, he is defended by Mrs Moore (who is despatched home by her son and dies on the way) and by Fielding, the Principal of the Government College, who befriends him. Feelings run high on both sides, and an anti-British riot seems almost inevitable when, in a scene of intense excitement, Adela Quested withdraws her accusation and Aziz is released. Humiliated and exhausted by her courtroom ordeal, her engagement broken off, she returns to England. Fielding follows her, some time later, and the two become friends; he later marries Mrs Moore's daughter, Stella. A final reconciliation takes place between Fielding and Aziz years later, on the former's return to India, where the young doctor, now working in another part of the country, encounters his former friend and learns something which helps to mitigate the bitterness he has felt against the British as a result of the 'Marabar Case'. The novel ends with his realization that he and Fielding can only truly be friends once India is free: 'India shall be a nation! No foreigners of any sort! Hindu and Moslem and Sikh and all shall be one! Hurrah! Hurrah for India!'

PATCHEN, Kenneth (1911–72), American poet, born in Niles, Ohio, briefly attended the University of Wisconsin and the Commonwealth College, Arkansas, but did not complete his studies. Patchen was an abstract expressionist painter as well as a poet. His first book of poems was *Before the Brave* (1936), followed by *The Teeth of the Lion* (1942), *Pictures of Life and Death* (1946), *Because It Is* (1960), *Collected Poems* (1968), and *There's Love All Day: Poems* (1970). His prose poems were collected as *Panels for the Walls of Heaven* (1947) and *The Famous Boating Party* (1954). His prose work includes *The Journal of Albion Moonlight* (1941), and two novels, the satirical *Memoirs of a Shy Pornographer* (1945) and *See You in the Morning* (1948). Reflecting his membership of that disaffected anti-establishment culture that came to maturity in the post-Depression years, there are two dominant strains in Patchen's work. The first is that of the social polemicist raging against the brash materialism of American common culture and the way it condemns its citizens to a life of social and imaginative impoverishment. In this mode, Patchen's tone is deliberately strident, attacking the enemy in its own vulgar tongue. His other mode shows a greater continuity between his poetry and his painting, where his free verse forms seem to seek the consolations of some other, almost transcendental or symbolist reality, to set against the impoverishments of the personal life and social world.

Paterson, William Carlos *Williams's compendious poem in five books presenting the social, topographical, cultural, and historical characters of a typical American industrial community; the work takes its title and local and historical particulars from Paterson, New Jersey, a large town not far from Williams's home in Rutherford. Books I to III appeared in 1949, Book IV in 1951, and Book V in 1958; a single edition of all five books was published in 1963. Williams's insistence on the poem's immediate relation to the flux and continuity of life came to preclude any intention of ending it; a sixth book was in progress at the time of his death in 1963. The overarching sense of the interpenetration of the locality and its human constituents is embodied in the quasi-mythological figure of 'Dr Paterson', who simultaneously represents the town as a physical entity and the consciousness that perceives it. After the opening's geographical and social survey of the area, the poem enters upon a sustained recognition of the abuses of power and consequent suffering, prior to the celebration of vitality and the vision of potential regeneration in Book V. In comprehending the multifariousness of his subject Williams employs techniques of literary collage by incorporating documents relating to various aspects of the locality; unabridged letters from Ezra *Pound and others are also among the materials used. The scope of the poem is enormous, extending to discussions of, for example, African-American patois, economic theory, medieval tapestries, and the customs of tribal societies. *Paterson* marked the fullest realization of Williams's belief in the inexhaustible resources of local experience as the truest basis for poetry. The poem exerted a prevailing influence on the works of many of his successors, most notably Charles *Olson, whose methods form an extension of those originated in *Paterson*.

PATERSON, A(ndrew) B(arton), commonly known as 'Banjo' (1864–1941), Australian writer, born on a bush station in New South Wales; he trained as a solicitor. The author of 'Waltzing Matilda', he grew up in the bush and had first-hand acquaintance with drovers, teamsters, shearers, horsemen, and other outback figures which he vividly portrayed in his ballads and stories. The publication of *The Man from Snowy River* (1895) brought him instant fame with its dynamic rhythms and its celebration of such legendary characters as 'Clancy of the Overflow' and 'Saltbush Bill'. His collection of *Old Bush Songs* (1905) is a seminal book in Australian balladry. He also wrote *An Outback Marriage* (1906) and *The Shearer's Colt* (1936), both novels; *Three Elephant Power* (1917), short stories; and *Happy Dispatches* (1934), autobiographical reminiscences. His *Collected Verse* appeared in 1923, and his *Complete Works* in 1983. *A Vision Splendid* (1990) presents all the verse of 'Australia's national poet' in one volume.

PATON, Alan (Stewart) (1903–88), South African novelist, educator, and biographer, born in Pietermaritzburg, educated at Natal University College, where he studied mathematics and physics. Though he was National President of the South African Liberal Party until it was declared illegal in 1968, Paton's profound knowledge of South African society and the apartheid system stems not only from his political activities, but also from his experience as a teacher and Principal of Diepkloof Reformatory in the Transvaal for thirteen years. Some of the short stories in *Debbie Go Home* (1961) are directly based on this experience. His first novel, **Cry, the Beloved Country* (1948), was an international bestseller; it was later filmed by Alexander Korda, and made into an opera by Maxwell Anderson and Kurt Weill entitled *Lost in the Stars* (1950). Equally powerful, but formally more accomplished, is *Too Late the Phalarope* (1953). Paton's biographies of personal friends who were publicly involved in the tragedies of South African politics are generally considered to be scrupulously objective, and include *Hofmeyr* (1964) and *Apartheid and the Archbishop: The Life and Times of Geoffrey Clayton, Archbishop of Cape Town* (1973). His third novel, *Ah, but Your Land Is Beautiful* (1981) is less emotionally intense than his earlier fiction, but its unflinching chronicle of the struggle against apartheid in the 1950s employs a vigorous semi-documentary style of writing to most compelling effect. See Edward Callan, *Alan Paton* (1982).

Patriot's Progress, A, see WILLIAMSON, HENRY.

PATTEN, Brian (1946–), British poet, born in Liverpool, where he was educated at Sefton Park Secondary School and worked as a reporter on the *Bootle Times*. Prior to the enormous success of *The Mersey Sound* (1967), as a result of which Patten, *McGough, and *Henri became collectively well known as the *Liverpool Poets, he had published *Portraits* (1962) and *Maud* (1965). His numerous subsequent volumes include *Little Johnny's Confession* (1967), *Notes to the Hurrying Man* (1969), *Vanishing Trick* (1976), *Love Poems* (1981), *Storm Damage* (1986) and *The Magic Bicycle* (1993); a selected edition of his work entitled *Grinning Jack* appeared in 1990. Much of Patten's work has an entertaining directness appropriate to his popularity as a performer of his poetry. He is widely regarded as the most interesting of the Liverpool Poets for the tonal range of his work, which extends from the sceptical tenderness of his love poetry to the sometimes scathingly ironic manner of his satirical and socially critical writing. *Gargling with Jelly* (1985) and *Thawing Frozen Frogs* (1990) are among the collections which have gained him a high reputation as a writer of poetry for children. His works for the theatre include *The Sly Cormorant*, produced in 1977.

PATTERSON, Orlando (1940–), Jamaican novelist, born in Jamaica, educated at Kingston University and the London School of Economics; he subsequently taught at Harvard University. In his first novel, *The Children of Sisyphus* (1964), Patterson, like Roger *Mais, exposes the squalor, violence, and dehumanization of Jamaican slum dwellers, but he also suggests Sisyphus-like defiance and resilience especially through the story of Dinah, a prostitute who attempts to escape from her degrading circumstances. In the process, he paints a sympathetic portrait of the Rastafarians, millenarian cultists who regarded the former Ethiopian emperor Haile Selassie as divine. *An Absence of Ruins* (1967) turns from social documentation to the psychological analysis of alienation in an educated, black Jamaican. *Die the Long Day* (1972) puts the author's researches to good effect by portraying a slave plantation in eighteenth-century Jamaica. Patterson's reputation as a novelist rests largely on his first novel, while his fame as a scholar grew with such books as *The Sociology of Slavery* (1967) and *Slavery and Social Death* (1982). *Freedom in the Making of Western Culture* (vol I, 1991) is the first of a two-volume analysis of concepts of freedom from sixth-century Greece onwards. In 1971 Patterson was awarded an honorary degree from Harvard University.

PAULIN, Tom (Thomas Neilson) (1949–), Northern Irish poet and critic, born in Leeds; he grew up in Belfast and was educated at the University of Hull and Lincoln College, Oxford. In 1972 he became a lecturer at the University of Nottingham. *A State of Justice* (1977), his first collection of poetry, was followed by *The Strange Museum* (1980), *The Book of Juniper* (1981), *Liberty Tree* (1983), *Fivemiletown* (1987), *Selected Poems, 1972–1990* (1993), and *Walking in Line* (1994). Stylistically, Paulin's poetry has developed from the disciplined brevity of his earlier work towards the more conversationally idiosyncratic manner that emerged in *The Liberty Tree*. There is a distinct continuity in his concern to comprehend and define socio-political conditioning and the possibilities of independence. The analytical dimensions of his writing take on emotional urgency from his sense of personal implication in the fraught culture of Northern Ireland. *Fivemiletown* is remarkable for the interplay of a sombrely sceptical realism and a lucidly playful candour. His critical works include *Thomas Hardy: The Poetry of Perception* (1975) and *Minotaur: Poetry and the Nation State* (1992). Among his dramatic works are *The Riot Act* (1985), an adaptation of the *Antigone* of Sophocles, which was staged by the *Field Day Theatre Company in Londonderry, of which he is a director. He is the editor of *The Faber Book of Political Verse* (1986) and *The Faber Book of Vernacular Poetry* (1990).

Pawnbroker, the, see WALLANT, EDWARD LEWIS.

p'BITEK, Okot (1931–82), Ugandan poet, born in Gulu, educated at King's College, Budo, Bristol University, and the University College of Wales, Aberystwyth. The subject of his thesis at the Institute of Social Anthropology in Oxford was Acoli and Longo traditional songs. Among other posts he was Director of Uganda's National Theatre, and a Lecturer in Literature at Nairobi University. His most famous work, *Song of Lawino* (1966), was written originally in Luo, and later rendered into English. It is a dramatic monologue in which a wife laments, and sarcastically describes her Westernized husband's cultural and personal inadequacies. *Song of Ocol* (1970), the husband's reply, reveals him to be just as predictably inadequate as his wife had declared. In *Two Songs* (1971) p'Bitek made further use of dramatic monologue and Acoli story-telling techniques to denounce, sombrely through a political prisoner ('Song of Prisoner'), and humorously through a prostitute ('Song of Malaya'), post-independence injustices. *Horn of My Love* (1974) contains traditional Acoli poetry in his own translations. Preoccupations of traditional culture and modernity were elucidated in *African Religions in Western Scholarship* (1971) and *Africa's Cultural Revolution* (1973). See G. A. Heron, *The Poetry of Okot p'Bitek* (1976).

PEAKE, Mervyn (Laurence) (1911–68), British novelist, poet, and artist, born in China, the son of a medical missionary, educated at the Royal Academy Schools in London. Originally an illustrator, art teacher, and writer of verse and stories for children, Peake became a war artist in the Second World War; his experiences of the horrors of war and a visit to Belsen in 1945 deeply affected him. His best-known work is his Gormenghast trilogy (*Titus Groan*, 1946; *Gormenghast*, 1950; and *Titus Alone*, 1959), a Gothic fantasy which chronicles the life of Titus, 77th Earl of Groan, within the vast castle of Gormenghast. Reflecting the traditional landscape of the Gothic romance and peopled by a gallery of grotesques and eccentrics, Gormenghast is a closed world bound by ritual and threatened by a destructive evil. There are also implications of anti-clericalism and a dualistic view of good and evil, which are more clearly evident in *Mr Pye* (1953) and in the sinister novella *Boy in Darkness* (1956). Peake's verse includes *The Glassblowers* (1952), *The Rhyme of the Flying Bomb* (1962), and the posthumously published *A Book of Nonsense* (1972). His illustrations for his own books, and those for Coleridge's *The Rime of the Ancient Mariner* (1943) and Stevenson's *Treasure Island* (1949), and his various exhibitions established his reputation as an artist. The memoir by Peake's widow Maeve Gilmour, *A World Away* (1970), describes their life together and the struggle in his later years against Parkinson's disease.

PEARSON, (Edward) Hesketh (Gibbon) (1887–1964), British biographer, born at Hawford, Worcestershire, educated at Bedford Grammar School; he worked in a shipping office and spent two years in America before beginning his career as an actor in 1911. He continued to work successfully in the theatre until 1931, when he became a full-time writer. Pearson's early works include *Modern Men and Mummers* (1921), sketches of well-known figures in the theatre, and the short stories of *Iron Rations* (1928). *Doctor Darwin* (1930), a biography of Erasmus Darwin, was the first of the many works which made him the leading popular biographer of his day. Among his subsequent publications are *Smith of the Smiths* (1934), a treatment of Sydney Smith, *Conan Doyle* (1943), *Dickens* (1949), and *Henry of Navarre* (1963). He collaborated on several books with Hugh Kingsmill; *Skye High* (1937) recorded their expedition along the route taken by Boswell and Johnson in the latter's *A Journey to the Western Isles of Scotland* (1775). The autobiographical *Hesketh Pearson, by Himself* appeared in 1965.

PEIRCE, Charles Sanders (1839–1914), American philosopher, born in Cambridge, Massachusetts, educated at Harvard; he was a lecturer at Johns Hopkins University between 1879 and 1884. Peirce is considered to be the founder of pragmatism, in which he took truth to be the sum total of the conceivable effects of a particular object, as he states in his well-known axiom: 'Consider what effects, that might conceivably have practical bearings, we conceive the object of our conception to have. Then, our conception of those effects is the whole of our conception of the object.' Peirce's essays on logic, epistemology, and metaphysics were published posthumously in the eight-volume *Collected Papers* (1931–1958) and in *Letters to Lady Welby* (1953). With the developments in *structuralism by such theorists as Roman Jakobson and Umberto Eco, Peirce has recaptured philosophical interest owing to his pioneering work on signs and *semiotics. Few writers have dedicated such effort to the definition of 'the meaning of meaning' than Peirce, who believed that he was dealing with the foundations of logic, since he perceived logic to be the science of the basic laws of signs. The motivation behind his semiotic analyses was the attempt to provide better grounds for belief and disbelief, and to teach us how to clarify our ideas sufficiently to verify their truthfulness. His framework for the existence of knowledge derives from the triad of signs: *icon*, *index*, and *symbol*. Since all signs include some aspects of the signifying functions of this triad, Peirce developed a complex system of the classification of signs upon this basis. Since a sign can function in one or more modes of signification, the ultimate nature of a sign's dominant mode will finally depend on its *context*. Peirce's semiotic theories are increasingly being used as a means to investigate and to explicate the mutations in language and culture, clarifying both the sense of grammar and the sense of change.

Penguin Books, a paperback publishing venture, whose intention was to make good reading available cheaply, begun by Allen Lane (1902–70) in 1935, when its first ten titles appeared; priced at sixpence each, they included *A Farewell to Arms* by Ernest *Hemingway, *The Unpleasantness at the Bellona Club* by Dorothy L. *Sayers, *Ariel* by André Maurois, and *Poet's Pub* by Eric *Linklater. By the end of 1936, the year in which Penguin Books was formed as an independent company, one million books had been sold. Having begun trading from a disused church crypt in Euston Road, London, in 1937 the company moved into specially built premises in Harmondsworth. The literary quality of Penguins, together with their high standards of book production and typography, established paperback publishing as a central aspect of the British book trade. The non-fiction Pelican series launched in 1937 was the first of numerous subsidiary initiatives, which also include the Penguin Shakespeare (1937–), Puffin Books (1941–), the imprint for children's literature, and the Penguin Classics (1946–), which has published over 750 major works from the literatures of the world. The publication of D. H. Lawrence's **Lady Chatterley's Lover* in 1960 gave rise to the twentieth century's most celebrated trial for alleged obscenity. By the 1980s international sales of Penguin titles were in the region of 50 million copies annually. *Fifty Penguin Years* (1985) is a copiously illustrated history of the company.

Penguin New Writing, see NEW WRITING.

PERCY, Walker (1916–90), American novelist, born in Birmingham, Alabama, educated at the University of North Carolina. Percy studied medicine at Columbia University and while working in New York's Bellevue Hospital contracted tuberculosis; during his long stay in a sanatorium, he decided to be a writer and moved towards an existential Catholicism, joining the Catholic Church in 1946. His first novel, *The Moviegoer* (1961), set in New Orleans, established him as one of the leading writers from the American South. Its central figure and narrator, Binx Bolling, is the first of Percy's alienated heroes: an outsider, who finds himself unable to participate in the aspirations and activities of those around him. *The Last Gentleman* (1966) concerns Will Barrett, who suffers from curious amnesiac attacks or 'fugues' in which he is unable to identify people or places. *Love in the Ruins* (1971), a work of fantasy, was followed by the very successful *Lancelot* (1977), the confession of an inmate of a mental hospital. *The Second Coming* (1980) is again about Will Barrett, now middle-aged; a quasi-apocalyptic work, set in North Carolina, it describes the protagonist's gradual realization of the hollowness of his comfortable, affluent existence and his involvement with a girl afflicted with aphasia. *The Thanatos Syndrome* (1987) is a more extrovert novel, about the dangers of libertarianism. Percy also wrote several works of philosophical and theological speculation, including *The Message in the Bottle* (1975) and *Lost in the Cosmos* (1981), which reflect his immersion in *Phenomenology.

PERELMAN, Bob (1947–), American poet, born in Youngstown, Ohio, educated at the University of Michigan and the Ohio Writers' Workshop; after various jobs he took a Ph.D. and became a Professor of English at the University of Pennsylvania. He was editor of *Hills* magazine and the centrally important series of Talks at the Langton Street Gallery, some of which are collected in *Hills* (1981) and *Writing/Talks* (1985). He writes poetry with an acute sense of poetic traditions both modern and classical, and some of the most amusing satires on contemporary ideologies of wealth, innovation, and power. Echoing Alexander Pope, he begins 'The Family of Man' saying: 'Hey I know one: The proper study of mankind is what? | Why is there money, Daddy? And why is there daddy, Money?' (*Face Value*, 1988). These concerns are also evident in his major study of the cult of genius in modernist poetry, *The Trouble with Genius* (1994), where he argues for a *rapprochement* between the writing and critical reading of poetry. See also LANGUAGE POETRY.

PERELMAN, S(idney) J(oseph) (1904–79), American humorist, playwright, screenwriter, and cartoonist, born in Brooklyn, educated at Brown University. He established himself as a writer and cartoonist with *Judge*, a New York magazine of humour and satire. His humour is characterized by his ear for puns and the absurd meanings generated by words used in false contexts, a gift that he exploited to startling effect in his screenplays for the Marx Brothers, particularly *Monkey Business* (1931) and *Horse Feathers* (1932). Perelman described himself as a *feuilletoniste* and from 1934 was a regular contributor to the **New Yorker*. In an interview for the *New York Times Magazine* (26 January 1969) he said of humour that 'its chief merit is the use of the unexpected, the glancing allusion, the deflation of pomposity, and the constant repetition of one's helplessness in a majority of situations'. Throughout a long career Perelman produced a series of consistently inventive essays and sketches in twenty-five volumes of prose. *The Best of Perelman* (1947) and *The Most of Perelman* (1958) are selections of his writings. In 1929 he married Laura West, the sister of Nathanael *West.

Periodicals: the proliferation of literary magazines and reviews from the mid-nineteenth century onward had important consequences for twentieth-century literature. The popularity of serialized fiction in many periodicals fostered the emergence of the novel as the pre-eminent modern literary form. Critical methods were advanced through the abundant production of essays and reviewing to a high general standard. During the 1890s the primacy accorded to aesthetic values in *The Yellow Book* (1894–7) and *The Savoy* (1896) anticipated the advent of the '*little magazines', which were central to the development of literary *Modernism in the early decades of the century; the most frequently cited examples include the **Little Review*, **Poetry* (Chicago), the **Egoist*, and **Blast*. Their ethos of experimentalism was transmitted to a succession of later American periodicals among which are *Contact* (1920–32), edited by William Carlos *Williams and Robert *McAlmon, Ezra *Pound's *Exile* (1927–8), Robert *Bly's *The Fifties* (1958–), and Robert *Creeley's *Black Mountain Review* (1954–7).

Of the smaller British magazines begun before the First World War, *Rhythm* (1911–13), the *Blue Review* (1913), both edited by John Middleton *Murry, and the **English Review* were also hospitable to innovative writing. *New Numbers* (1914) and **Poetry Review* were the main periodicals of the time to publish work by the Georgian poets (see GEORGIAN POETRY), whose verse later appeared regularly in the **London Mercury*. *The *Dial* and T. S. Eliot's **Criterion* in the 1920s were strongly instrumental in the legitimation of Modernism, while the **Adelphi* and **Life and Letters* also maintained an active interest in progressive writing. Critical writing of a high standard characterized the **Times Literary Supplement* from its formation in 1902. Between 1925 and 1927 *The *Calendar of Modern Letters* set new standards in textual exegesis, providing an example followed by **Scrutiny*, the most celebrated of the century's critical periodicals. In America, criticism of similar quality appeared in John Crowe Ransom's **Kenyon Review* (1939–) and in the **Sewanee Review* (1892–) after Allen *Tate became editor in 1944.

The combining of attention to politics and literature in the **New Statesman* and the **New Age* became an essential feature of numerous well-known periodicals of the 1930s; **New Verse* and **New Writing* were discernibly opposed to fascism and favoured writing exhibiting social concern, while the **Left Review* and **Partisan Review* were frequently preoccupied with Marxist evaluations of literature. The growing sense of internationalism in the 1920s is reflected in the establishment in Paris of the **Transatlantic Review* and **transition*; later magazines of a markedly international character include the multilingual **Botteghe Oscure* and the eclectic **Paris Review* and **Antaeus*.

The closure of numerous important publications in the late 1930s supports the widely held view that by 1940 the heyday of the literary periodical was over. Despite the rationing of paper and the dispersal of contributors caused by the Second World War, **Horizon* and **Poetry London* continued to publish new writing throughout the conflict. The 1950s and 1960s saw the formation of **London Magazine*, *The *Review*, **Stand*, **Agenda*, and **Ambit*; these sustain the tradition of the little magazines in publishing what their editors consider to be the best work available by new and established authors while surviving with comparatively low circulations. The numerous regional magazines of distinction which appeared during the 1960s include the **Honest Ulsterman*, **Lines Review*, the *New *Edinburgh Review*, and **Poetry Wales*. Temporary closure of the *Times Literary Supplement* in 1978–9 engendered a crop of new periodicals, of which the **London Review of Books* and the **Literary Review* have proved the most enduring.

In terms of their value to notable authors in the early stages of their careers and their continual critical assessment of literary developments, periodicals have been, and remain, of enormous importance to twentieth-century literature. *The British Literary Magazines* (four volumes, 1982–6), edited by Alvin Sullivan, and *The Little Magazine* (1946, reprinted 1967), edited by F. J. Hoffmann, C. Allen, and C. Ulrich, are indispensable guides to their subjects. (See also the ATHENAEUM, BANANAS, the BELL, the CONTEMPORARY REVIEW, the CORNHILL MAGAZINE, the CRITICAL QUARTERLY, the DUBLIN MAGAZINE, ENCORE, ENCOUNTER, GRANTA, LANDFALL, the LISTENER, NEW DEPARTURES, the NEW YORKER, the NEW YORK REVIEW OF BOOKS, NOW AND THEN, PLANET, PN REVIEW, QUARTO, the SPECTATOR, TIME AND TIDE.)

Petals of Blood, a novel by *Ngugi, published in 1977. A disturbing, passionately political book that also works as a thriller, the story begins after a fire in a brothel has killed three prominent, corrupt African directors of the foreign-owned brewery in Ilmorog, a traditional village now transformed into a sprawling modern industrial town. Held for questioning are the novel's four important characters—Munira, Karega, Abdulla, and Wanja—who have all striven in vain to reach accommodation with the New Kenya, where unbridled capitalism has altered the balance of social forces. Their interlocking backgrounds, hidden lives and loves, come to light in a series of flashbacks. Munira went to Ilmorog to be headmaster of the school but, twelve years later, worldly contradictions have driven him to religious fanaticism. Abdulla, disillusioned shopkeeper and barman, was once a guerrilla fighter in the freedom struggle. The attractive and resourceful Wanja was employed as his barmaid, but latterly has turned to prostitution. Karega was an untrained teacher until Munira's jealousy of his relationship with Wanja led to his dismissal; returning to Ilmorog as a militant trade unionist, he has tried to organize the exploited brewery workers. The profound changes wrought in the fabric and character of Ilmorog are related to the arrival of the Trans-Africa Highway; and the factory brewing of Theng'eta, a potent native drink, epitomizes the uncompromising new spirit of enterprise. The three dead men belong to a latter-day élite of businessmen and politicians who reap the profits; and though it transpires that the four murder suspects each had motive enough to have sought revenge, it is Munira who reveals himself as the arsonist. Characteristically, Ngugi goes for an ending that allows hope for the dispossessed.

PETERS, Ellis, pseudonym of Edith (Mary) PARGETER (1913–95), British crime writer and historical novelist, born in Shropshire, served in the WRNS during the Second World War, under her own name the author of a number of historical novels (*Hortensius, Friend of Nero*, 1937) and a prolific translator from Czech. Her first detective story, *Fallen into the Pit* (1951), featured the policeman George Felse and his family, who appear in most of her novels up to *Rainbow's End* (1979). With *A Morbid Taste for Bones: A Medieval Whodunnit* (1977), she began a series of detective novels set in and around the Benedictine abbey at Shrewsbury in the twelfth century, which have enjoyed great popularity. Typically they combine a detailed portrayal of medieval life with the investigation of a crime and a romantic sub-plot: in later novels this last element has tended to gain in importance. The central figure and detective in all is the monk Cadfael, a former crusader, who tends the abbey's herb garden. Among the titles are: *One Corpse Too Many* (1979), *Saint Peter's Fair* (1981), *The Virgin in the Ice* (1982), *The Devil's Novice* (1984), *The Raven in the Foregate* (1987), *The Confession of Brother Haluin* (1988), and *The Heretic's Apprentice* (1989).

PETERS, Lenrie (Wilfred Leopold) (1932–), Gambian poet, born in Bathurst, Gambia; he studied medicine at Trinity College, Cambridge, and worked as a surgeon at Northampton General Hospital before returning to Gambia in 1969 to practise at Banjul. *Poems* (1964), his first collection of verse, was followed by *Satellites* (1967) and *Katchikali* (1971); *Selected Poems* appeared in 1981. Much of his verse is notable for the urbane detachment with which it conducts its incisive meditations on a wide range of social and cultural themes, often with reference to contemporary conditions in Africa. Many of his metaphors and images are drawn from his experiences as a surgeon, which are also the basis for numerous moving poems about mortality. His novel *The Second Round* (1965) deals with the return of a doctor from Europe to his native Sierra Leone, where he is confronted by the unreality of his sense of belonging.

PETRY, Ann (Lane) (1908–), African-American novelist, short-story writer, journalist, and children's author, born in Old Saybrook, Connecticut. She studied pharmacy at the state university and worked in her parents' drugstore until marriage took her to Harlem in 1938. As a roving reporter for two Harlem newspapers, she was confronted by the endemic deprivation and despair of the black ghetto, and her response to what Sterling *Brown called 'the tribulations of the slum-shocked' informs the bleak social vista of *The Street* (1946) and the novella *In Darkness and Confusion* (1947). Although Petry's stress on the determining pressures of race and poverty has much in common with the naturalism of Richard *Wright, *The Street* makes a distinctive contribution to black protest fiction in the 1940s by focusing on the experience of a female protagonist. In *The Country Place* (1947), *The Narrows* (1953), and *Miss Muriel and Other Stories* (1971), Petry turns from urban nightmare to the more humdrum frustrations of small-town New England life. She has also written books for children including *Harriet Tubman* (1955) and *Tituba of Salem Village* (1964).

PEVSNER, Sir Nikolaus (Bernhard Leon) (1902–83), British historian of art and architecture, born in Leipzig, educated at the universities of Leipzig, Berlin, Frankfurt, and Munich. His first book, *Leipziger Barock* (1928), dealt with the baroque houses of his native city. Of Jewish descent, he was forced by Nazi regulations to resign his lectureship at the University of Göttingen in 1933, the year he moved to Britain. The reputation he gained with *Pioneers of the Modern Movement* (1936), on the origins of modern architecture, and *Academies of Art* (1940), one of the earliest social histories of art, was internationally confirmed by *An Outline of European Architecture* (1942), which proved widely influential for its innovative philosophical approach to architectural form. From 1942 to 1969 Pevsner taught at Birkbeck College, London, becoming Professor of the History of Art in 1959; he also held professorships at Oxford and Cambridge and was knighted in 1969. In 1941 he began a long association with *Penguin Books; he edited the King Penguin series and the *Pelican History of Art* and produced *The Buildings of England* (46 volumes, 1951–74), the exhaustive architectural survey which is his greatest achievement. Other important works in his remarkably prolific career include *The Englishness of English Art* (1956) and *A History of Building Types* (1976).

Phenomenology is a philosophical movement most frequently associated with the work of Edmund Husserl (1859–1938) and Maurice Merleau-Ponty (1900–61). It seeks to ground human understanding in perception rather than abstraction, and devotes particular attention to the workings of consciousness. Its chief literary application has been through the so-called Geneva School, led by Georges Poulet, whose followers have included, in France, Jean-Pierre Richard, and in America, J. Hillis Miller (1928–). The phenomenological approach to literature seeks to understand an author from the inside, not as a collection of biographical incidents but as a mind making sense of itself and the world around it. It characteristically reads the works, letters, jottings of an author as a single, seamless text, a lifelong writing project rather than a series of individual books or communications. Poulet's *Studies in Human Time* (1949) brilliantly reconstructs what we may call the mentalities of major writers from Montaigne to Proust; Richard takes us into the universes of Mallarmé, Baudelaire, and others; Hillis Miller offers new orderings of the worlds of Dickens, and of modern English and American poets.

PHILLIPS, Caryl (1958–), West Indian playwright and novelist, born in St Kitts, West Indies, brought up in Leeds, educated at Queen's College, Oxford. His plays, including *Strange Fruit* (1981) and *Where There Is Darkness* (1982), are tense, naturalistic dramas dealing with Caribbean families who have settled in Britain. His novels *The Final Passage* (1985) and *A State of Independence* (1986) are more expansive and coolly detached than the plays, focusing on other aspects of the Afro-Caribbean experience both in Britain and in the West Indies. More experimental in style, *Higher Ground* (1989) explores three different periods of history in the collective experience of Africans, and descendants of Africans. The film script of *Playing Away* (1987) sets a Brixton cricket team against a Home Counties team, thereby satirizing certain aspects of race relations in Britain. In *Cambridge* (1991) Phillips evokes a nineteenth-century slave plantation through a travel diary written by a young Englishwoman, and also a contrasting account by the ironically named slave, Cambridge. *Crossing the River* (1993) sustains Phillips's literary mission to explore and make sense of the African diaspora, showing the legacy of broken heritages resulting from the slave trade. Composed of four sections across a broad historical and geographical framework, the novel is reminiscent in structure of *Higher Ground*, though even more complex. His other works include *The Wasted Years* (1985), a radio play, and *The European Tribe* (1987), a travel book.

PHILLIPS, Jayne Anne (1952–), American novelist and short-story writer, born in West Virginia, educated at the University of Iowa. Her first collection of stories, *Black Tickets* (1979), consists largely of monologues, experiments in voice and narrative, and innovative prose pieces; it was praised by Margaret *Atwood and Ian *McEwan. Her evocation of the mores of small-town America and the vagrant lifestyle of its young has earned her a reputation as one of the *Dirty Realists. Her first novel, *Machine Dreams* (1984), is the story of the Hampson family; in the foreground is the daughter Danner's journey to adulthood during the troubled years of the Vietnam War, to which she loses her beloved brother Billy. Her second collection of stories, *Fast Lanes* (1987), returns to the wanderers, vagrants, and grim landscapes of her earlier works. Phillips has spoken of her admiration for Eudora *Welty, and the story 'Bess', set largely in the past, fits into a timeless tradition of rural fictions by American women writers such as Welty, Katherine Anne *Porter, and Flannery *O'Connor. In *Shelter* (1995) two young girls encounter evil and despair; dense and multi-layered, it confirms Phillips's reputation as one of the most unusual and gifted American writers of her generation.

PHILLIPS, Stephen (1864–1915), British poet and verse-dramatist, born at Somerton, near Oxford, educated at Peterborough Grammar School. He became an actor with a Shakespearian company run by his cousin Frank R. Benson and played leading roles in numerous tragedies. His earlier collections of poetry include *Eremus* (1894) and *Christ in Hades* (1896); *Poems* (1898) gained him a considerable reputation and was reprinted fourteen times by 1904. Phillips's shorter poems tend towards the morbidly sensual lyricism of the Decadents. His longer narrative works frequently display the melodramatic fatalism typified by his 'The Woman with the Dead Soul'. Among his later collections were *The New Inferno* (1911) and *Panama* (1915). *Paolo and Francesca* (1898) was the first of his numerous verse-dramas; its considerable success led to increasingly spectacular and highly successful productions of his subsequent plays, which include *Herod* (1901), *Ulysses* (1902), and *Nero* (1906). His adaptation of Goethe's *Faust* (1908, with J. C. Carr) was, however, considered excessively extravagant in production and his fortunes entered a decline. He resumed his activities as a poet and took over the editorship of *Poetry Review* from Harold *Monro in 1913, dying in greatly reduced circumstances in 1915.

PHILLPOTTS, Eden (1862–1960), British writer, born in India, educated in Plymouth, Devon. He abandoned a stage career and worked for ten years in an insurance office before embarking on a reclusive career as a writer. He wrote 250 books, many of them set in Devon, including the novels *Children of the Mist* (1898) and *Widecombe Fair* (1913), both set in Dartmoor. His novel *The Farmer's Wife* (1917) in a dramatized version written in collaboration with his daughter, Adelaide Phillpotts, met with great success on the London stage in 1924, as did *Yellow Sands* (1926) by the same authors. He wrote several other plays (some in collaboration with Arnold *Bennett and J. K. *Jerome), volumes of verse, essays, several detective novels, including *A Voice from the Dark* (1925), and science fiction, such as *The Apes* (1929), *Saurus* (1938), and *Address Unknown* (1949).

PICKARD, Tom (1946–), British poet, born in Gateshead, Newcastle upon Tyne; he attended local schools until the age of 16. In 1963 he founded the Morden Tower Book Room, where many notable poetry readings were held. He was directly instrumental in ending the obscurity that surrounded Basil *Bunting, whom he sought out for advice when he began writing poetry. *High on the Walls* (1967) was his first collection of poems; among his succeeding volumes are *The Order of Chance* (1971), *Dancing under Fire* (1973), and *Custom and Exile* (1985), which contains 'Spring Tide', his fine elegy for Bunting. *Hero Dust* (1979) is a selected edition containing much previously uncollected work, including poems from *The Jarrow March*, his radio documentary broadcast in 1976. His early work was widely admired for its precise imagery, its sensitive musicality, and its remarkable fusions of political and personal concerns. The mythic dimensions of *Dancing under Fire* demonstrated an increase in imaginative range. His later verse displays a widening cultural frame of reference. *Tiepin Eros: New and Selected Poems* appeared in 1994. His other works include *Guttersnipe* (1972), a collection of largely autobiographical prose pieces.

PIERCY, Marge (1936–), American novelist, poet, and political activist; born in Detroit, she received a Jewish upbringing. She was educated at the University of Michigan and Northwestern University, and her political engagement formed in the context of student unrest during the 1960s. Piercy suffered physical abuse from the authorities during political demonstrations in New York City; such an attack is described in *Vida* (1980), a novel which documents the fate of student activists in the increasingly conservative America of the 1970s. In this work and in novels such as *Going Down Fast* (1969) and *Dance the Eagle Asleep* (1971), Piercy explores the relationships between sexual liberation and political radicalism through characters who seek to reform American society. *Woman on the Edge of Time* (1976) presents a Utopian vision of a society untouched by sexism or racism (see UTOPIA AND ANTI-UTOPIA). Other novels include the autobiographical *Braided Lives* (1982), *Fly Away Home* (1984), and *Gone to Soldiers* (1987) which chronicles the pervasive effects of the Second World War. Her poems, characterized by the voice of a radical socialist feminist, have been collected in *Hard Loving* (1969), *The Moon is Always Female* (1980), *My Mother's Body* (1985), and *Available Light* (1988). Her essays have appeared in *The Grand Coolie Dam* (1970) and *Parti-Colored Blocks for a Quilt* (1982).

Pilgrimage, see RICHARDSON, DOROTHY M.

Pincher Martin, see GOLDING, WILLIAM.

PINCKNEY, Darryl (1953–), African-American writer, educated at Columbia University. Like the unnamed hero of *High Cotton* (1992), the novel which established his reputation, Pinckney grew up the son of a monied African-American family. 'High Cotton' refers to cotton easy to pick—the implication being that the black bourgeoisie, the 'Also Chosen', has been able to sidestep much of America's racial dispensations. To an extent, Pinckney's unnamed hero bears this out; he has means, a good education, time to loaf, an initial readiness to assimilate. But he also has old-time Southern kin, notably his preacher grandfather Eustace who, though he graduated from Harvard and Brown, helps him see the fuller context of his blackness. He finds himself forced to rethink black Dixie, the black legacy of the 1960s, and above all, himself as modern African-American. The novel reads as much as a meditation as a fictional autobiography. Although Pinckney continues to write for journals like *The *New York Review of Books* and **Granta*, it is *High Cotton* which has marked him out as a radically gifted stylist.

PINERO, Sir Arthur Wing (1855–1934), British dramatist, born in Islington, London; he received a scanty and spasmodic education, acquiring a knowledge of law in the office of his father, a London solicitor, and of elocution at the Birkbeck Institute. After an unsuccessful period as an actor—a Birmingham critic described his King in *Hamlet* as 'the worst Claudius the city has ever seen'—he turned to writing at the instigation of Sir Henry Irving and gradually established himself as the period's most accomplished exponent of well-made drama. His first play, *£200 a Year* (1877), was followed by a series of highly successful farces, notably *The Magistrate* (1885), *Dandy Dick* (1887), and *The Schoolmistress* (1887). His reputation as a major dramatist, however, derived from the serious plays he wrote in the 1890s and 1900s, many of them about the sufferings inflicted by society on women who commit sexual indiscretions. These included not only *The Second Mrs Tanqueray* (1893), the best-known of the genre, but *The Notorious Mrs Ebbsmith* (1895), *Iris* (1901), *Letty* (1903), and *Mid-Channel* (1909). Such pieces, criticized by *Shaw in their time as 'conventional' and even 'pornographic' reworkings of Ibsen's drama of ideas, have inevitably dated. Pinero's farces are, however, still remembered and sometimes revived, as is his affectionate picture of a dramatist based on T. W. Robertson, *Trelawney of the 'Wells'* (1898), and three comedies of a more robust nature: *The Gay Lord Quex* (1899), *His House in Order* (1906), and *The Thunderbolt* (1908).

PINSKY, Robert (1940–), American poet, born in New Jersey, educated at Rutgers and Stanford Universities, where he studied with Yvor *Winters. Pinsky taught at Wellesley College, and later became Professor of English at the University of California, Berkeley. His books of poems include *Sadness and Happiness* (1975), *An Explanation of America* (1979), and *History of My Heart* (1984). His critical writing includes a study of the British poet Walter Savage Landor, *Landor's Poetry* (1968), and a polemical study *The Situation of Poetry* (1977). He became poetry editor of the **New Republic*. Pinsky is a celebrant of the ordinary and the commonplace, whose deceptively simple poems acknowledge our desires for larger meanings beyond the insistent visibility of the ordinary world of daily reality.

PINTER, Harold (1930–), British playwright, born in East London, the son of a tailor, educated at Hackney Downs Grammar School; he became a professional actor, performing in provincial repertory under the name David Baron. His first work, *The Room*, a one-act play, staged in Bristol in 1957, was followed by *The Dumb Waiter* (1958) and the London production of his first full-length work, *The *Birthday Party*. This puzzling, somewhat Kafkaesque piece, though now regarded as a minor classic, found little favour with critics or the public; and Pinter suppressed *The Hothouse*, a stylistically similar satire on bureaucratic callousness and incompetence he wrote at roughly the same time, not permitting it to be performed until 1980. Instead, he moved his writing in a more realistic direction, achieving major successes with *The *Caretaker* (1960) and *The *Homecoming* (1965). The short plays *The Collection* (1960), *The Lover* (1963), and *Tea Party* (1965), all written for television but subsequently staged, also belong to this phase. At the end of the decade came another shift of style with the appearance of the ruminative *Landscape* (1968) and *Silence* (1969), in which characters relive their key memories, mostly in fragmented monologues. These were followed by **Old Times* (1971) and **No Man's Land* (1975), full-length works in which Pinter succeeded in reconciling aspects of his earlier and his later creative self. Neither play was fully realistic, and both largely consisted of characters' memories; but, since the accuracy of those memories was a matter of dispute, the dramatic conflict that had marked Pinter's more conventional work made a reappearance. In *Old Times*, in particular, the past became a battleground and memories weapons in attempts to seize control of the present.

Since *Betrayal* (1978), a triangle-drama told backwards, so that the play ends with the genesis of the love affair shown in collapse at the beginning, Pinter has written more sparingly for the stage, and, with the possible exception of the 80-minute *Moonlight* (1993), never at what's conventionally considered full length. *A Kind of Alaska*, inspired by *Awakenings*, Dr Oliver Sacks's case-studies of people afflicted by the epidemic of encephalitis lethargica that struck the world between 1916 and 1926, was performed in 1982 in conjunction with two still shorter plays, *Family Voices* and *Victoria Station*, under the overall title of *Other Places*. Since then, Pinter has written screenplays, directed his own and other people's work on the stage, and has become publicly identified with many radical and libertarian causes. For some ten years his only original plays were *One for the Road* (1983), the 17-minute *Mountain Language* (1988), and *Party Time* (1992): all three about political oppression and the violent abuse of human rights, all reflecting his involvement with Amnesty International and, with the exception of parts of *Party Time*, all somewhat less subtle than his previous work. However, *Moonlight* did seem to represent a return to what many commentators would regard as his best, most distinctive manner, concerning as it did family fragmentation (specifically, a dying man's conflicts with his wife and alienation from their grown-up sons) and written as it was in dialogue that mixed the colloquial with the poetic and the exact with the enigmatic.

Pinter's most original work combines powerful conflict with a sense of mystery. His characters are commonly battling for territory, power, sex, security, or survival itself, but rarely do so openly or directly. The key transactions occur either beneath the simple, colloquial, and, as it sometimes seems, barely relevant dialogue or during the silences for which Pinter has become famous. The result is a drama full of menace and danger, the more unsettling for their lack of specificity.

PIRSIG, Robert M(aynard) (1928–), American writer, born in Minneapolis, educated at the University of Minnesota. Pirsig became a technical writer for various firms, and a member of the board of directors of the Minnesota Zen Meditation Center in 1973. His enormously influential *Zen and the Art of Motorcycle Maintenance* (1974), a journey of self-discovery permeated by philosophical discussion, and startlingly original and disturbing imagery, was based on an autobiographical account of a journey across the USA on a motorbike undertaken with his son in 1968; the shifts between narrative, analogy, and philosophical meditation have prompted several critics to see this work as a latter-day *Moby-Dick*. Since then, he has been engaged in 'anthropological research, intended to relate the metaphysics of quality, as defined in the first book, to cultural problems today'. He became more peripatetic in later years, and a recent edition of *Zen and the Art of Motorcycle Maintenance* contains a postscript written in Sweden, in which he attempts to come to terms with the murder of Chris, the son with whom he made the journey. His next novel, *Lila: An Inquiry into Morals* (1991), is another journey of philosophical exploration, in which Phaedrus, the protagonist of his earlier novel, travels down the Hudson River on a sailboat as winter closes in. He picks up Lila as a travelling companion in a riverside bar, but her desperate sexuality, madness, and hostility begin to threaten his life, and their relationship forces him to rethink the entire philosophical basis of his existence.

Pit, The, a novel by Frank *Norris, published in 1903, the second volume in Norris's projected trilogy, 'The Epic of the Wheat', the first volume of which is *The *Octopus* (1901). Norris drew on historical fact for his story: the attempt in 1897 of Joseph Leiter to corner the Chicago wheat market. In the novel Leiter becomes Curtis Jadwin, a tycoon with a farm background who has made a fortune in real estate and now wants to dominate the Chicago wheat market of the city's Stock Exchange, 'the pit' of the title. In Jadwin, Norris's intention seems to have been to offer a study of the financier along the lines of William Dean *Howells's *The Rise of Silas Lapham* (1885) or Theodore *Dreiser's later novel *The Titan* (1914), but most critics find that the novel comes alive most in the treatment of Jadwin's wife, Laura, as Norris follows her from Massachusetts to Chicago, marriage to Jadwin, and the inevitable decline of their relationship as Jadwin ignores her to indulge his growing passion for speculation in wheat futures. Laura is Norris's finest female creation, and the consequence of this is that *The Pit* becomes more a domestic tragedy than a coherent part of the planned trilogy. The wheat, the great life force which Norris intended as the central theme of his trilogy, plays a somewhat subordinate role in the novel. *The Pit* was adapted for both stage and screen. The planned third volume of the trilogy, *The Wolf*, was never written.

PITTER, Ruth (1897–92), English poet, born in Ilford, Essex. Among other occupations, she painted giftware and furniture for a London business in which she was a partner, and worked as a broadcaster and popular journalist. In 1955 she became the first woman to receive the Queen's Gold Medal for Poetry. Pitter's early poems were published in the *New Age* in 1911. *First Poems* (1920) appeared with a preface by Hilaire *Belloc; her numerous succeeding volumes include *Persephone in Hades* (1931), *A Mad Lady's Garland* (1934), *The Spirit Watches* (1939), *The Ermine: Poems 1942–1952* (1953), *End of Drought* (1975), and *Collected Poems* (1990) with an introduction by E. *Jennings. Much of her verse displays her great accomplishment in complex traditional forms, while elsewhere she writes in more conversationally cadenced modes. While her poetry sometimes exhibits a strong element of social critique, it consistently reveals a celebratory and essentially religious attitude towards experience; her affirmations range from the pure visionary qualities represented by 'Sudden Heaven' to the coarser delight memorably expressed in 'The Rude Potato'.

PITT-KETHLEY, Fiona (1954–), British poet, born in Edgware; she studied at Chelsea College of Art and subsequently worked as a film extra, theatre usherette, and bric-à-brac dealer. Her earlier publications as a poet include *London* (1984), *Rome* (1985), and *The Tower of Glass* (1985); their historical orientation differs considerably from the emphatically modern idioms of her better-known work. *Sky Ray Lolly* (1986) brought her wide notice, with its uncompromisingly sexual content that remains a clear characteristic of her verse in *Private Parts* (1987) and *The Perfect Man* (1989). Many of her poems present acerbically humorous anecdotes illustrative of sexual attitudes and social behaviour she sees as typifying contemporary hypocrisies. A robust blank verse is her most frequently used form. Later collections of poems include *Dogs* (1993) and *A School for Life* (1993). Her other publications include *Journeys to the Underworld* (1988), an account of her travels in Italy while investigating the myths of the sibyls; *The Pan Principle* (1994), exploring Greece and its mythology; and *The Misfortunes of Nigel* (1991), a novel satirizing the London literary scene. She is the editor of *The Literary Companion to Sex* (1992) and *The Literary Companion to Low Life* (1995).

PLAATJE, Sol(omon) T(shekiso) (1878–1932), South African novelist, linguist, journalist, and statesman, born near Boshof, Orange Free State. He served as an interpreter with the British Army during the Anglo-Boer War (1899–1902). *The Boer War Diary of Sol T. Plaatje* (1973), written during the siege of Mafeking, is an important document about the experience of black Africans in that conflict. From 1901 to 1908 Plaatje lived in Mafeking and edited a Setswana weekly journal whose title translates as *The Tswana Gazette*. During the First World War he led an unsuccessful delegation in London to protest against the Natives' Land Act, forerunner of later apartheid legislation. In the same period he wrote a pamphlet, *The Mote and the Beam* (1920), which exposed racism in South Africa, and a historical novel, *Mhudi* (1930). It was the first novel in English published by a black African and deals with violent conflict between the Barolong and the Matebele tribes, and the encroachment of the Boers. Tim Couzens in his introduction to the 1975 reprint draws attention to Plaatje's use of proverb and fable in his fiction, a practice which was to be followed by many later African novelists writing in European languages, notably *Achebe. Plaatje produced a scholarly work, *Native Life in South Africa* (1916), a compilation of *Sechuana Proverbs* (1916), and translations of Shakespeare into Tswana.

PLAIDY, Jean, pseudonym of Eleanor HIBBERT (*c.*1910–93), British historical novelist, whose other pseudonyms included Eleanor Burford, Ellalice Tate, Elbur Ford, Victoria Holt, and Philippa Carr. Her first novel (as Eleanor Burford), *Daughter of Anna* (1941), was followed by many others. As Victoria Holt, her later works include *The Silk Vendetta* (1987), *The India Fan* (1988), and *The Captive* (1990). As Philippa Carr her novels include *The Pool at St Branock* (1987), *The Changeling* (1989), and *The Black Swan* (1990). As Jean Plaidy, her first published work was *Together They Ride* (1945). Thereafter she produced numerous books, including *Passage to Pontefract* (1981), *The Sun in Splendour* (1982), *Myself My Enemy* (1983), *Queen of the Realm* (1984), *Victoria Victorious* (1985), *The Lady in the Tower* (1986), *The Courts of Love* (1987), *In the Shadow of the Crown* (1988), *The Queen's Secret* (1989), and *The Reluctant Queen* (1990). These are mostly popular and well-researched works of historical fiction, although as Victoria Holt she also wrote Gothic romance. See also ROMANTIC FICTION.

Planet, a literary and political periodical begun in 1970 by Ned Thomas, who remained its editor until 1990. During the 1970s its cultural perspective was determined by its prevailing concern with Welsh nationalism, which extended to an active interest in the affairs of other European linguistic minorities. The magazine's campaigns, which repeatedly made it the subject of controversy, included support for broadcasting in Welsh and the formation of separate legislatures for Wales and Scotland. Among the contributors of articles were Dannie *Abse, John *Wain, Anthony *Cronin, Iain Crichtor *Smith, and Edwin *Morgan, who was the principal Scottish correspondent. Work by R. S. *Thomas, Leslie *Norris, John *Tripp, John *Ormond, and other Anglo-Welsh (see ANGLO-WELSH POETRY) poets and short-story writers was regularly featured. In 1979 *Planet* closed after its fiftieth issue; publication was resumed in 1985, since when it has appeared every two months. While its interest in various aspects of the Welsh national identity remains pronounced, it has emerged as a forum of wide-ranging commentary on literary, socio-cultural, and ecological matters. Robert *Minhinnick, Jan *Morris, Sheenagh *Pugh, and Les *Murray are among the writers who have contributed articles and essays, while the poets featured have included Gillian *Clarke, Lauris *Edmond, George Mackay *Brown, and Pablo Neruda.

PLANTE, David (1940–), American novelist, born in Providence, Rhode Island. He attended the University of Louvain in Belgium. His first novel, *The Ghost of Henry James* (1970), was followed by *Slides* in 1971; both paid tribute to the great masters of American literature such as *James and Hawthorne. Much of his fiction, such as the autobiographical series of novels *The Francoeur Family*, including *The Family* (1978), *The Woods* (1981), and *The Country* (1987), reflects his background (he is of French colonial and Blackfoot Indian descent) as well as his Roman Catholic upbringing.

His novels range from the experimental mode of early works such as *The Darkness of the Body* (1974) and *Figures in Bright Air* (1976) to the more direct confessional tone of *The Foreigner* (1984) and *The Catholic* (1986). These later works add to themes of religion and the family that of desire and complex emotional/sexual relationships; the connecting factor is often guilt. The discovery of homosexual desire is a recurrent theme. He is also the author of *Difficult Women* (1983), a memoir of his friendship with three illustrious women including Jean *Rhys. He has contributed short fiction to anthologies such as *God* (1992).

PLATER, Alan (Frederick) (1935–), British playwright, born in Jarrow-on-Tyne, he was educated at King's College, Newcastle-on-Tyne. His early work for television includes the plays *The Referees* (1961) and *See the Pretty Lights* (1963) and the scripting of eighteen episodes of the popular *Z Cars* series between 1963 and 1965. *Charlie Came to Our Town* (1966) was the first of the works for the stage he wrote with the composer Alex Glasgow; his other collaborations with Glasgow include *Close the Coalhouse Door* (1968), their celebrated 'musical documentary' about the mining communities in the north-east of England, and *Simon Says* (1970), a satire on the British class system. Among his many other works for television are *The Crystal Spirit: Orwell on Jura* (1983), *Edward Lear: On the Edge of the Sand* (1985), and *Misterioso* (1987). Plater has also written screenplays, notably for D. H. *Lawrence's *The Virgin and the Gipsy* (1970), and numerous popular novels which include *The Beiderbecke Affair* (1985) and *Oliver's Travels* (1994).

PLATH, Sylvia (1932–63), American poet and novelist, born in Boston, Massachusetts, educated at Wellesley High School and Smith College. She was appointed a student guest-editor for *Mademoiselle* magazine in 1953, an interlude which strongly informs her novel *The *Bell Jar* (1963). In 1955 she took up a Fulbright Scholarship to Newnham College, Cambridge, where she met Ted *Hughes. They were married in 1956 and went to America in the following year. Plath taught for a time at Smith College and subsequently attended a writers' group in Boston supervised by Robert *Lowell, to whose influence the emergence of confessional (see CONFESSIONAL POETRY) elements in her verse has been attributed. In 1959 she and her husband returned to England, settling in Devon prior to their separation in 1962. Her first collection of poetry, *The Colossus* (1960), displayed her accomplishment in the use of conventional forms, while 'Suicide off Egg Rock' prefigured the disquieting intensities of her later writing. In 1963 she killed herself in London after a remarkably prolific period of composition, the results of which Philip *Larkin described as 'a prolonged high-pitched ecstasy like nothing else in literature'. **Ariel*, her best-known collection, appeared to enormous critical acclaim in 1965. Great originality and skill are evident in the forms and rhythms of the poetry, which also displays an incisive directness of tone, dramatic power, and imagery of startling clarity and precision. The fascination with mortality and extreme states of mind increasingly evident in her work after 1960 is emphatic in a number of the collection's best-known poems, among them 'Lady Lazarus', and 'Daddy'. Two further volumes, *Crossing the Water* and *Winter Trees*, were published in 1971 and a *Collected Poems* edited by Hughes appeared in 1981. Hughes also edited *Johnny Panic and the Bible of Dreams* (1977), a selection of diary excerpts and prose-pieces. Her mother, A. S. Plath, produced an edition of her correspondence entitled *Letters Home* (1975), and F. McCullough edited *The Journals* (1982). *Sylvia Plath* (1987) by Linda Wagner-Martin and *Bitter Fame* (1989) by Anne *Stevenson are biographical studies.

PLATT, Charles (1945–), British *science fiction writer, born in Hertfordshire. His best novels, *Garbage World* (1967), *The City Dwellers* (1971; much revised in 1977 as *Twilight of the City*), and *Silicon Man* (1991), are sharp, anti-heroic, and satirical, qualities which have also characterized his polemical essays on science fiction. The interviews assembled in *Dream Makers* (1980) and *Dream Makers II* (1983) are perhaps the best ever conducted of a group of science fiction writers. Platt was involved with **New Worlds* magazine, and edited or co-edited its various incarnations from 1970 to 1974.

Playboy of the Western World, The, a play by J. M. *Synge, first performed and published in 1907. This involves the impact on a drab, remote Irish village of Christy Mahon, a frightened young man on the run after giving his father what he believes to have been a death-blow with a hoe, and the impact on him of the village's admiration of this supposedly heroic act. Pegeen Mike, daughter of the local publican and fiancée of the cowardly Shawn Keogh, persuades her father to hire him as potboy and proceeds to fall in love with him. The Widow Quin also fêtes him, as do the village girls; and a newly confident Christy triumphs in the local sports. Then Old Mahon, bandaged but not dead, comes in pursuit of his son, who tries a second time to kill him, only to find that the villagers react with disgust to violence they could mythologize in abstract: 'there's a great difference between a gallous story and a dirty deed'. Pegeen Mike rejects Christy, but he finds he has at last established mastery over his domineering father, who has once again survived the attack; and he leaves the village a changed man, 'a likely gaffer in the end of all'. Showing as it does Christian savages romanticizing not just murder, but the sin of patricide, the play's first production roused nationalist feelings and provoked serious riots at Dublin's *Abbey Theatre.

PLOMER, William (Charles Franklyn) (1903–73), South African poet and novelist, born in Northern Transvaal, educated at Rugby School. After returning to South Africa, he founded the magazine *Voorslag* ('Whiplash') with Roy *Campbell in 1926. He eventually settled in England and became the principal reader for the publishers Jonathan Cape in 1937. *Turbott Wolfe* (1926), his first novel, was remarkable for its angry denunciations of racism. His other novels, which have been compared to the works of *Joyce and *Forster for their fluent lucidity of style, include *The Case Is Altered* (1932), *The Invaders* (1934), and *Museum Pieces* (1952). Among his collections of poetry are *The Family Tree* (1929), *The Dorking Thigh and Other Satires* (1945), *Taste and Remember* (1966), *Celebrations* (1972), and *Collected Poems* (1960, revised 1973). Although Plomer was a lyrical and meditative poet of distinction, he is best known for the incisive wit and technical virtuosity of his satirical verse. Among his other works are a number of librettos for compositions by Benjamin Britten, notably *Gloriana* (1953) and *The Prodigal Son* (1968), and his *Autobiography* (1975). The many publications he edited include *Kilvert's Diary* (3 volumes, 1938–40) and *A Message in Code: The Diary of Richard Rumbold, 1932–1960* (1964). Peter F. Alexander's *William Plomer: A Biography* appeared in 1989.

Plot and Story need to be thought of together, since even in conflicting current uses the words continue to function as a pair. Sometimes they are used interchangeably, as simple synonyms: 'retelling the story' would be exactly the same as a 'plot summary'. At other times they are clearly distinguished. E. M. *Forster, in *Aspects of the Novel* (1927), thought a plot was 'an organism of a higher type' than a story. A story was a mere sequence of events, but a plot 'demands intelligence and memory', it is a structure of events, the 'logical intellectual aspect' of a narrative, 'the emphasis falling on causality'. Aristotle said the plot was the soul of the story, and Coleridge particularly admired the plots of *Oedipus Rex*, *The Alchemist*, and *Tom Jones* ('the most perfect plots ever planned'). Complicated plots were much in favour in the nineteenth century and perhaps mirrored a world felt to be full of complex and multiple interrelations. Plot was scorned by early modern writers, but has made a comeback in later fiction, notably that which leans towards *magic realism. Translators and followers of the Russian Formalists (see FORMALISM) use 'story' and 'plot' to represent *fabula* and *sjuzet*, literally fable and subject. This usage is not the same as Forster's, but it is not incompatible with it; indeed, there is a certain overlap. The story/*fabula* in a narrative is the events as they would have occurred or did occur in time, the linear progression of one thing after another. The plot/*sjuzet* is the arrangement of events in the story as we read or hear it. Since even the simplest stories are arranged to some degree, and apparently simple stories often turn out to have very complicated narrative organizations, the story in effect is always reconstructed, while the plot is what we actually perceive but often forget. 'I saw her when she was on her way to the bank' and 'She was on her way to the bank when I saw her' are sentences with the same story but (slightly) different plots. *Sjuzet* has sometimes been translated as *discourse in order to separate its meaning from older and looser uses of the word 'plot'.

Plough and the Stars, The, a play by Sean *O'Casey, performed and published in 1926. Set in a Dublin tenement during the nationalist uprising of Easter 1916, this tragi-comedy centrally involves Nora Clitheroe, a young wife who loses both her baby and her mind when her husband, Jack, is killed in the fighting. However, the play's tone and meaning are largely determined by such characters as Fluther Good, Ginnie Gogan, Peter Flynn, and Bessie Burgess: braggarts, drunks, and wastrels who share the building, are constantly engaged in arguments and quarrels, and, many of them, use the conflict as an opportunity to loot the local shops. Characteristically, O'Casey contrasts patriotic pretension with the reality of life in the slums. In the second act, set in a pub, a voice akin to that of Padraig Pearse is heard hailing bloodshed as a 'cleansing and sanctifying thing' while a prostitute touts for custom. The anti-heroic thrust is obvious, and led to serious disturbances at the *Abbey Theatre, where the play was first staged; but O'Casey is also at pains to show, not without irony, the unpretentious heroism of some of his low-life scavengers. Prime among these is Bessie Burgess, a quarrelsome, violent Protestant and loyalist who spends much of the play bawling promises of grisly retribution at her Catholic neighbours, yet puts herself into serious danger and eventually loses her life in her efforts to protect Nora.

Plumed Serpent, The, a novel by D. H. *Lawrence, published in 1926. Lawrence's Mexican novel was begun in spring 1923 and finished in February 1925. Lawrence wrote it whilst travelling through Mexico and the USA. Today it is perhaps his most controversial work and certainly his most openly ideological. After its publication there is evidence that he regretted many of the opinions in it, and his next and last book, **Lady Chatterley's Lover*, reverses many of its ideas. The novel concerns Kate Leslie, an Irishwoman mourning the death of her republican husband. Like many of Lawrence's characters in this period she is emotionally and socially adrift and travels to Mexico in a footloose but directionless searching. There she meets Ramón Carrasco and Cipriano Viedma who are attempting to revive the religious cults of the ancient Aztecs. Attracted by Cipriano, a native Indian, Kate is gradually drawn into Ramón's effort to revitalize Mexican culture against the influence of American modernization. She joins the group, which begins to catch the imagination of the nation. At the close Kate and Cipriano are married with full ritual and she accepts, a little restively, the passive role which 'The Men of Quetzalcoatl' believe proper to women. The political context of the novel is the turbulent series of violent revolutions and *coups d'état* in Mexico around the turn of the century; in it Lawrence makes clear his hostility to both socialism and American capitalism. The cult of Quetzalcoatl is an attempt to found a ritualistic politics based on ideals of mass communion with ancient wisdom. But the disturbing violence and irrationalism of some of the ceremonials, the book's emphasis on race, and its heavily authoritarian message about sexual relations, trouble some readers. There are powerful moments, such as the opening scene at a bullfight in Mexico City, and the descriptions of the environment are, as ever in Lawrence, extraordinarily graphic. But the attempt to fabricate a ritualized, incantatory language is stylistically more awkward.

PN Review, a British-based periodical dedicated to the publication and criticism of poetry, begun by C. B. Cox and Michael *Schmidt in 1973 in twice-yearly hardback form as *Poetry Nation*; the first issue stated the editors' intention of providing 'a magazine that expresses and explores the growing consensus among poets' in favour of 'clearly formal writing, a common bridling at vacuous public and private rhetoric'. In 1977 the present title was assumed and large-format paperback presentation adopted; under Schmidt's general editorship, *PN Review* now appears on a bimonthly basis. Eminent among the critics associated with the magazine was Donald *Davie; one of its most frequent contributors from the outset, he led a debate on the nature and value of *post-modernism which ensued in its pages. Poetry and criticism by C. H. *Sisson, Charles *Tomlinson, Michael *Hamburger, Clive *Wilmer, and Jeremy *Hooker have also been featured repeatedly. *PN Review* has succeeded in maintaining what the first issue described as its 'responsibilities to a vital linguistic and formal heritage' while remaining keenly interested in more experimental approaches to poetry. During the 1970s and 1980s the magazine printed work by almost every contemporary poet of note; Christopher *Middleton, John *Heath-Stubbs, Thom *Gunn, F. T. *Prince, and Les *Murray have been among its contributors.

Poetry, 'a magazine of verse', as its subtitle states, founded in Chicago in 1912 by Harriet *Monroe, the author of several collections of verse, who had organized a highly efficient programme of funding in 1911. Her advance publicity for the venture drew it to the attention of Ezra *Pound in time for him to be listed as the magazine's foreign correspondent in its first issue. By 1913 Pound had established *Poetry* as the principal platform for *Imagism, introducing work by Hilda *Doolittle, Richard *Aldington, Amy *Lowell, and others; the sixth issue featured F. S. *Flint's statement of Imagist poetics and Pound's 'A Few Don'ts By An Imagist'. He also supplied poems by W. B. *Yeats, Robert *Frost, and F. M. *Ford. Pound's international and experimental emphases were at odds with Monroe's more conservative sense of the magazine's essentially American identity; he had to exert considerable pressure in persuading her to print T. S. *Eliot's 'The Love Song of J. Alfred *Prufrock' in 1915. Although Pound remained associated with *Poetry* until 1919, his involvement diminished as his interest in the **Little Review* increased. In 1919 Monroe affirmed her patriotic intentions of dedicating the magazine to 'the imaginative life of the nation'. Until the end of her editorship in 1935 *Poetry* was primarily concerned with the work of American poets; Wallace *Stevens, Marianne *Moore, and W. C. *Williams were among those who dispelled the mediocrity which occasionally prevailed. Monroe's successors include Karl *Shapiro, who edited *Poetry* from 1950 to 1955. It continues to appear, its contributors having included almost every American poet of note and many European, Israeli, and dissident Russian poets.

Poetry London, a magazine founded in 1939 by *Tambimuttu in collaboration with Anthony Dickens, Keidrych Rhys, and Dylan *Thomas, and generally regarded as the most important forum for new poetry of the 1940s. Tambimuttu edited the first fifteen editions. His eclectic editorial policy, which Geoffrey *Grigson viewed as an enthusiastic lack of discrimination, made *Poetry London* hospitable to work by a remarkable range of poets, many central to the literary history of the period; the tendency to favour poetry by writers associated with the *New Apocalypse was balanced by the generous representation of material by poets having no links with the movement. Graphics by Henry Moore, Graham Sutherland, and others added to the periodical's distinction. Editions Poetry London, formed in 1943, published some seventy books and pamphlets, including works by Keith *Douglas, G. S. *Fraser, Henry *Miller, Vladimir *Nabokov, and Kathleen *Raine, before it was discontinued in 1951. After Tambimuttu's departure for New York in 1947, the magazine was edited by Nicholas *Moore and Richard March; it was felt, however, to lack its former vitality and ceased appearing in 1949. A five-volume reprint of the series was produced in 1971. Tambimuttu continued to use the name in his subsequent publishing ventures, which included *Poetry London—New York* (1953) and *Poetry London/Apple Magazine* (1979).

Poetry Nation, see PN REVIEW.

Poetry Review, the magazine of the Poetry Society, founded by W. G. Kyle in 1909, when the *Poetical Gazette* was introduced to disseminate information about readings and other events. In 1911 Harold *Monro was approached by the Society, who wished him to edit the *Gazette*; Monro was out of sympathy with the marked conservatism of the senior members, who included Sir Henry *Newbolt and Herbert *Trench, and proposed forming *Poetry Review* as an independent journal incorporating the *Gazette*. The first issue appeared in January 1912. Due to disharmony between himself and the Society, Monro's editorship lasted only a year; he gave the magazine a refreshingly eclectic character, favouring verse by the leading *Georgian poets but admitting work by more innovative writers at the suggestion of F. S. *Flint and Ezra *Pound, who supported the venture. Stephen *Phillips was the editor from 1913 to 1915; his preferences for verse-dramas and late Victorian poetry determined *Poetry Review*'s reactionary tone. Between 1916 and 1947 W. G. Kyle assumed editorship, appointing Alice Hunt Bartlett as American associate editor in 1923; poems and articles by American writers were regularly featured throughout the 1920s and 1930s and sales increased through Kyle's skill in attracting a popular readership. The quality of the work published tended, however, to be unexceptional. Muriel *Spark's editorship from 1947 to 1949 enlivened the magazine. Since then it has developed into an essential forum for contemporary poetry in Britain, featuring verse and criticism by the leading writers of successive decades while remaining hospitable to work by newer writers.

Poetry Wales, a magazine of poetry and criticism founded in 1965 by Meic Stephens, who wished to strengthen the cultural identity of the English-speaking Welsh and to provide a forum for the publication and critical evaluation of *Anglo-Welsh poetry; the *Anglo-Welsh Review* was already in existence, but was felt by Stephens and others of nationalist sympathies to be insufficiently Welsh in character. Stephens was editor from 1965 to 1967 and from 1969 to 1973. Raymond *Garlick, Vernon *Watkins, John *Tripp, Leslie *Norris, John *Ormond, and Anthony *Conran were among the poets whose work recurrently appeared in early issues. Under J. P. Ward's editorship between 1975 and 1980 *Poetry Wales* began publishing contributions from poets working outside Wales, who included C. H. *Sisson, Roy *Fisher, and Seamus *Heaney. More recently, the magazine has displayed an active interest in writing from Eastern Europe, the Caribbean, and Sweden, in addition to the regular inclusion of poems from other parts of Britain. Among the authors to whom special issues have been devoted are David *Jones, R. S. *Thomas, Henry Vaughan, and Alun *Lewis. Mike Jenkins became editor in 1986, since when *Poetry Wales* has appeared in a larger format and remained hospitable to a wide range of contributors. Poetry Wales Press, latterly Seren Books, was established in 1980; the many poets whose collections it has published include Tony *Curtis, Jean *Earle, Robert *Minhinnick, and Sheenagh *Pugh.

POHL, Frederik (1919–), American *science fiction writer, born in New York, educated at schools in the Brooklyn area. After working as a publisher's editor and literary agent, he became a freelance writer in 1953. Pohl's earliest novels, *The Space Merchants* (1953), *Search the Sky* (1954), and *Gladiator-at-Law* (1955), all written with C. M. Kornbluth, are entertaining futuristic satires on American society. Among his other works of the 1950s are the novel *Slave Ship* (1957) and the short stories of *Alternating Currents* (1954) and *The Man Who Ate the World* (1960). Space exploration motivated by greed is a recurrent theme in his later novels, notable examples being *The Gold at the Starbow's End* (1972), *Gateway* (1977), and *JEM* (1979); among *Gateway*'s numerous sequels are *The Annals of Heechee* (1988) and *The Gateway Trip* (1990). Pohl's other publications include *Turn Left at Thursday* (1961), *Syzygy* (1981), *Years of the City* (1984), and *The Voices of Heaven* (1994). *The Way the Future Was* (1978) is an autobiography.

Point Counter Point, a novel by A. *Huxley, published in 1928. Generally viewed as Huxley's fictional masterpiece, for its masterly interplay of discussions about the *Zeitgeist* and a sophisticated structural technique, it became a contemporary bestseller and remains the best example of the discussion-novel-of-ideas which he appropriated as an ideal satiric vehicle. Like **Antic Hay*, though on a larger scale, the book is filled with artists, scientists, socialites, politicos, and literati, who represent and argue through problems and philosophies of the time. Continuing Huxley's penchant for writing *à clef*, the disputatious 'Mark Rampion' has many of the traits of D. H. *Lawrence, and 'Lucy Tantamount' ('Living modernly's living quickly') of Nancy Cunard; John Middleton *Murry appears unsympathetically as the magazine editor 'Burlap'. 'Everard Webley', leader of the fascistic British Freemen, who pursues 'Elinor Quarles' and is eventually murdered, is clearly modelled on Oswald Mosley. The novel proceeds by what the writer 'Philip Quarles' (a stand-in for Huxley himself) calls a 'musicalisation of fiction': theme, variation, and counterpoint in which contrasting or complementary characters, singly or in combinations, dramatize a multiplicity of perspectives. This contrapuntal form operates by short scenes and often abrupt transitions between sets of characters, and incorporates extracts from Philip Quarles's Notebook which meditate upon fiction, biology, and motivations of personalities encountered.

POLIAKOFF, Stephen (1952–), British dramatist, born in London, educated at Cambridge University. After achieving a modest success with *Clever Soldiers* (1974), about public schoolboys and Oxford undergraduates in somewhat confused conflict with a society that eventually leads them to the killing fields of the Great War, he produced a series of highly distinctive plays, wryly melancholy in tone. Typically, they involve contemporary urban culture in its concrete-and-plastic aspects and those making (usually vain) attempts to defy its encroachment. The more notable of these are *Hitting Town* (1975), *City Sugar* (1975), *Shout Across the River* (1978), *American Days* (1979), *The Summer Party* (1979), *Favourite Nights* (1981), and *Siena Red* (1992), pieces whose settings respectively include an underground car park, a local radio station, a recording studio, a five-storey pub-palace with a disco club in the basement, a pop concert, a particularly soulless London casino, and a large do-it-yourself store. Among his other works are *Strawberry Fields* (1977), about two young fascists on a terrorist mission in a characteristically charmless Britain; *Breaking the Silence* (1985), about an inventor escaping from the Bolsheviks after the revolution, and based on the experiences of Poliakoff's Russian-Jewish grandfather; *Coming in To Land* (1987), about a Polish woman's attempts to settle in Britain and, by inference, about the relationship of East and West;

and *Playing with Trains* (1989), also about an inventor, but this time concentrating on his unsettled relationship with his British family. Poliakoff's television plays include *Bloody Kids* and *Caught on a Train*.

POLLOCK, Sharon (1936–), Canadian dramatist, born in Fredericton, educated at the University of New Brunswick. Pollock is generally regarded as a prairie dramatist. Her plays employ the documentary mode as a means of exploring social issues and forcing a reassessment of them. She first achieved recognition for *Walsh* (1973), which, like much of her later work, is about the mistreatment of minorities; it deals with the Canadian attempt to force the Sioux, who came north after the Battle of Little Big Horn, back into the USA. *The Komagata Maru Incident* (1976) addresses another historical instance of supposed Canadian racism, when a group of Sikh immigrants were prevented from landing in Vancouver in 1914. *Blood Relations* (1979) shows a shift to a concern with the negative stereotyping of unconventional women in its sympathetic representation of the folk figure Lizzie Borden, acquitted of the axe murder of her father and stepmother in New England in 1892, but subsequently condemned in the popular imagination. Other plays include *A Compulsory Option* (1971), *Generations* (1979), *One Tiger to a Hill* (1980), *Whiskey Six* (1983), *Doc* (1984), and *Saucy Jack* (1994).

Polyglots, The, see GERHARDIE, WILLIAM.

Polyphonic Prose, see LOWELL, AMY.

Poor White, a novel by Sherwood *Anderson, published in 1920. In the introduction to the novel, Anderson wrote that the actual 'hero' of the book was a small Ohio town, Bidwell, and that the people of the town, even the central character, Hugh McVey, the 'poor white' inventor, were additional. Hugh McVey, the shy telegraph operator, invents several mechanical items which are exploited by Steve Hunter who makes millions and establishes Bidwell as a booming industrial town. Despite his new-found wealth, McVey still finds it difficult to communicate with people, but eventually marries Clara Butterworth after she recognizes his worthiness. As prosperity reaches Bidwell, so it is followed by industrial struggles between bosses and labourers, and finally, McVey recognizes the corrupting effect that he has had upon the town and its inhabitants. The narrative is principally concerned with the devastating effects of the modernization of a rural Midwestern town, and the disappearance of a pioneer democracy as it is swamped by class values based on material wealth.

POPE-HENNESSY, (Richard) James (Arthur) (1916–74), British biographer and writer on travel and history, born in London, the younger brother of Sir John *Pope-Hennessy, educated at Balliol College, Oxford. He was secretary to the Governor of Trinidad and Tobago in 1939 and served in the Intelligence Corps throughout the Second World War. After two years as literary editor of the **Spectator*, he became a full-time writer in 1949. *West Indian Summer* (1943) and *The Baths of Absalom* (1954) draw on his experiences of the West Indies. His other works as a travel writer include *London Fabric* (1939), a characteristically eloquent account of little-known areas of the city; *Aspects of Provence* (1952); and *Half-Crown Colony* (1969), a historical and topographical treatment of Hong Kong. *The Years of Promise* (1949) and *The Flight of Youth* (1951), the volumes of his life of Richard Monckton Milnes (1809–85), established his reputation as a biographer; among his numerous further works are *Lord Crewe, the Likeness of a Liberal* (1955), *Anthony Trollope* (1971), and *Robert Louis Stevenson* (1974). *Verandah* (1964), a study in colonial history which traces the career of his ancestor Sir John Pope Hennessy (1834–91), and *Sins of the Fathers* (1967), a harrowing history of the Atlantic slave trade from 1441 to 1807, are often regarded as his best works. His homosexuality gave rise to the circumstances in which he was murdered in his London flat. *A Lonely Business* (edited by Peter *Quennell, 1974) is a collection of autobiographical fragments.

POPE-HENNESSY, Sir John (Wyndham) (1913–94), British art historian, born in London, the older brother of James *Pope-Hennessy, educated at Balliol College, Oxford. In 1938 he joined the staff of the Victoria and Albert Museum, becoming Keeper of the Department of Architecture and Sculpture in 1954 and Director and Secretary in 1967. After two years as Director of the British Museum, he was appointed Professor of Fine Art at New York University in 1977. Largely self-taught in art history, he was generally regarded as a foremost authority on Italian painting and sculpture. His earlier works include *Giovanni di Paolo* (1937), *Sassetta* (1939), and *Sienese Quattrocento Painting* (1947). *Italian Gothic Sculpture* (1955), *Italian Renaissance Sculpture* (1958), and *Italian High Renaissance and Baroque Sculpture* (1963) are the three volumes of *An Introduction to Italian Sculpture*, upon which his wider reputation was established. *Cellini* (1985), one of the most highly acclaimed of his publications, takes its underlying structure from the artist's *Autobiography*, of which Pope-Hennessy produced an edition in 1949. Among his other works are *Luca Del Robbia* (1980), *Donatello: Sculpture* (1993), and *Paradiso: The Illuminations to Dante's Divine Comedy by Giovanni di Paolo* (1993). His autobiography, *Learning to Look*, appeared in 1991.

POPPER, Sir Karl R(aimund) (1902–94), British philosopher of science and political philosopher, born in Vienna, educated at the University of Vienna. He was acquainted with Rudolf *Carnap and other members of the Vienna Circle of logical positivists, with whom he disagreed over the status of inductive reasoning. He left Vienna as the ascendancy of Nazism intensified and lectured at Canterbury University College, Christchurch, New Zealand. In 1945 he became a reader at the London School of Economics, where he was Professor of Logic and Scientific Method from 1949 to 1969. Widely regarded as the twentieth century's most eminent philosopher of science, he was knighted in 1964. His first major work, *Logik der Forschung* (1935), translated as *The Logic of Scientific Discovery* (1959), was centrally concerned with the task of distinguishing science from the pseudo-sciences. Popper rejected induction as the identifying characteristic of science, arguing that scientists did not proceed on the basis of pure observation but were actively creative in bringing anticipatory hypotheses to their work. He proposed the principle of falsifiability as a fundamental criterion of authentic science; the theorist's concern, he maintained, should be with the establishment of instances which negate a statement rather than with attempts at confirmation. The pseudo-sciences, among which he numbered Marxism and psychoanalysis, were by comparison beyond the scope of logical falsification. He criticized rational empiricism for its fallacious desire to substitute an infallible theoretical system for the former absolutes of theology. His critiques of social and historical determinisms in *The Open Society and Its Enemies* (1945) and *The Poverty of Historicism* (1957) are similarly based on his refusal to endorse the quest for certainty. Popper's other works include *Objective Knowledge* (1972), *A World of Propensities* (1990), and the autobiography *Unended Quest* (1976, revised edition 1986).

Popular Culture often overlaps, and/or is confused with, 'folk culture', 'working-class culture', 'mass culture', 'consumer culture', and 'sub-culture'. The history of changing and contested semantics of the term 'popular culture' tracks not only the complex social and historical developments from so-called 'traditional' communities ('pre-industrial', 'oral') through the industrial revolution to late capitalism. Its usage also registers the more or less conscious ways in which the links between culture and society in their broadest senses have been defined and analysed, largely within the framework offered by Marxist theories of ideology and 'cultural production' (Walter Benjamin, Gramsci, and Raymond *Williams).

To trace the changes which the word 'popular' has undergone from its original (Latin) legalistic and political sense of 'belonging to the people', to modern senses of 'well-liked by many people', and the more derogatory sense of 'seeking favour with the people', is to map very complex ground. Conjoined with 'culture', the term has come to adopt roughly three differing meanings. First, it refers to a body of 'texts' and genres from a wide range of media (folk-songs, chapbooks, detective fiction, the Romance novel, Hollywood movies, TV soap operas, etc.) produced either '*for* the people', or (and this crucial difference colours much dissenting debate) '*by* the people', which stands in contradistinction to the canon of established classic 'great works' representing a 'High Culture' of a ruling élite. Secondly, it refers more broadly to a whole way of life, set of beliefs and values, codes of social behaviour, that 'the common people' share. This sense finds its origins in ethnography and sociology and is close in its range of reference to the (ethnically or historically confined) traditional 'folk-culture'. Thirdly, 'popular culture' has been recognized as a field of study within the academy: with the rise in interdisciplinary theoretical interests which bring together methodologies and disciplines embracing cultural and social history, literary textual criticism, semiotics, and (particularly French) psychoanalytical studies of the construction of the subject, a very fertile field of enquiry concerning everyday life, both past and present, is being explored. Theoretical articulations about the nature of ideological formations and cultural production and consumption (particularly the relation of 'dominant' to 'subordinate' cultures within societies) have been greatly enriched by the Marxist thinking of Benjamin, Gramsci, Althusser, and Williams. Simultaneously, from a critical perspective which tends to identify contemporary 'popular culture' with a capitalist (manipulative and debased) 'mass culture', the Frankfurt School (Adorno and Horkheimer), among others, has sought to identify a reactionary (if populist) aspect of the terrain. Cultural historians, some of the French 'Annales' School, have greatly enlarged the historical range of the subject into the medieval and early modern 'Everyday'; while the work of Barthes on *Mythologies* (1957) and Bakhtin (*Rabelais and His World*, 1965) on carnival have proven seminal in offering an account of the complex relations of cultural hegemony, accommodation, and resistance existing between social groups and classes.

In Britain, those involved in *Mass-Observation in the 1930s and writers as different as George *Orwell (with essays on seaside postcards and boys' comics) and T. S. Eliot (**Notes Towards the Definition of Culture*, 1948) had come to recognize the regional and class diversity inherent in the idea of a national culture, which the study of popular culture has elaborated. More recently, E. P. *Thompson's work on plebeian and working-class cultures (*The Making of the English Working Class*, 1963), along with Richard Hoggart's ground-breaking *The Uses of Literacy* (1957) (a 'left-Leavisite' intervention) and Raymond Williams's works, have been crucial in establishing popular culture as a discipline within the academy. Dissatisfaction, though, with the gender-blindness inherent in much of the theory and procedures of these positions has led to an uneasy but productive dialogue with feminist historians and theorists (e.g. Coward, *Female Desires*, 1984).

Porcupine, The, see BARNES, JULIAN.

PORTER, Hal (1911–84), Australian writer, born in Melbourne. A stylish detachment characterizes his short stories, the first volume of which was published in 1942. Of six collections, *A Bachelor's Children* (1962), *Mr Butterfry, and Other Tales of Japan* (1970), and *Fredo Fuss Love Life* (1974) received most critical attention. Sharp, extravagant of detail, the stories are realistic depictions of everyday life. Porter's first novel, *A Handful of Pennies* (1958; revised 1980), is about

Australians with the occupation forces in Japan, the children of whom Porter had taught in 1949–50. *The Tilted Cross* (1961), set in colonial Hobart, gives a fictional account, through the artist Vaneleigh, of the story of Thomas Wainewright, a historical convict. *The Right Thing* (1971) is set in a coastal town in Victoria of the 1960s. His autobiography *The Watcher on the Cast Iron Balcony* (1963), which recorded his childhood, is recognized as his major work and was continued in two sequels: *The Paper Chase* (1966), which conveys the subsequent period of recognition of the conditions of his vocation; and *The Extra* (1974), in which the author appears as observer of the world and includes some memoirs of fellow writers. His non-fictional works include *The Actors* (1968), a study of modern Japan; *Bairnsdale: Portrait of an Australian Country Town* (1977), a history of his own town; three books of verse, and several plays.

PORTER, Katherine Anne (1890–1980), American fiction writer, born in Indian Creek, Texas. Though her output was slim, Porter is widely acclaimed as one of the finest American prose stylists of her generation. Porter lived a richly picaresque life that has become the stuff of legend, even though she herself took the view that writers' biographies are of little importance. She supported herself as an entertainer in Texas, worked as a bit-part film actress in Chicago, and studied art in Mexico. She eloped from school at the age of 16 and was divorced at 19; had a tragic love affair, which provided a background for her story 'Pale Horse, Pale Rider', in her twenties; and in later life was twice more married. Until the publication of her novel *Ship of Fools* (1962), which she spent twenty years writing, she was best known as the author of the short-story volumes *Flowering Judas* (1930), *The Leaning Tower* (1944), and *The Old Order: Stories of the South* (1944), and the three novellas of *Pale Horse, Pale Rider* (1939). Influenced by the James *Joyce of *Dubliners* and the stories of Katherine *Mansfield, Porter achieved a subtlety and suggestiveness rarely equalled in short fiction. As with *Faulkner, the 'Old South' and its replacement by new social forces provided the subject matter for much of her finest work. Moral concerns are always to the fore in her fiction, particularly the conflicts between commitment and detachment, and nature and civilization. Her masterpiece *Ship of Fools* is a moral allegory, in which the passengers of a ship, journeying from Mexico to Germany in the early 1930s, provide a microcosm of the many types that make up the human race. Porter's other works include *Hacienda: A Story of Mexico* (1934), and an account of the notorious Sacco–Vanzetti case entitled *The Never-Ending Wrong* (1977). Her *Collected Stories* (1965) added some new pieces to her previously published work; a volume of *Collected Essays* appeared in 1970.

PORTER, Peter (Neville Frederick) (1929–), Australian poet, born in Brisbane, where he became a reporter with the *Courier-Mail* in 1947. In 1951 he emigrated to Britain and worked in various capacities until 1968, when he became a freelance writer and broadcaster. The disciplined experimentation and social orientation of his early work reflected his association with the *Group. *Once Bitten, Twice Bitten* (1961) and *Poems Ancient & Modern* (1964) contained numerous poems that gained him notice as an incisive satirist; more typical of subsequent developments is the recurrent sense of an imaginative tension between a debased contemporary culture and the traditions of European art, to which he alludes throughout his collections. *A Porter Folio* (1969), *The Last of England* (1970), and *Preaching to the Converted* (1972) display an increase in stylistic and thematic confidence; elliptical narratives, dramatic monologues, and outrageously humorous registrations of the absurd are among the modes employed. The considerable reputation he had gained by the early 1970s was consolidated by *Living in a Calm Country* (1975) and *The Cost of Seriousness* (1978), in which increased use of local elements and an intensified elegiac sense are encountered; the latter collection contains his most acutely personal poetry, written in response to the death of his wife in 1974. The greater directness of manner that emerges in the volume is accompanied by a new urgency in his differentiations between art and life. The Australian critic Jeff Doyle has noted that 'discrimination of all gradations of meaning becomes a moral pursuit' in Porter's work. The remark is appropriate to the ethical preoccupations of *English Subtitles* (1981), *Fast Forward* (1984), and *The Automatic Oracle* (1987), which often feature poetry of considerable complexity; the baroque richness of such writing and the constant play of wit annul objections to obscurity, while many poems form candidly straightforward addresses to intellectual and emotional concerns. *Possible Worlds* (1990), *The Chair of Babel* (1992), and *Millenial Fables* (1994) demonstrate his imaginative range in the creation of elaborate fictions as vehicles for sweeping socio-cultural critiques. Among his other works are four collaborations with the Australian graphic artist Arthur Boyd; the latest, *Mars* (1988), forms a powerful denunciation of war. His satirical abilities and humorous command of contemporary idioms are memorably deployed in the versions from the Latin of *After Martial* (1972). *Collected Poems* was published in 1983.

Portnoy's Complaint, a novel by Philip *Roth, published in 1969. An immediate bestseller, this novel scandalized moralists with its focus on a protagonist who displays an insatiable desire for sexual adventure and erotic novelty. It further caused anger among Jewish circles with its unflattering contemporary clichés about Jews. The novel charts Alexander Portnoy's attempt to break the Oedipal bond with his mother, Sophie, and her overbearing, claustrophobic Jewish domestic ethos. Endeavouring to fight what his upbringing has taught him is irreconcilable, 'to be bad—and to enjoy it', Alexander concludes that masturbation is his sole release and this leads him to the kinkiest of schemes, albeit constantly torn by his conscience. The entire novel takes place as the rambling confessions of Alex on the psychoanalyst's couch, and this highlights the novel's concerns with psychological and sexual conflict and repression. As a satire on Jewish-American life, this Freudian tale of arrested development is bizarrely comic, yet also frustrated and angry.

'Portrait of a Lady', see PRUFROCK AND OTHER OBSERVATIONS.

Portrait of the Artist as a Young Dog, a collection of ten stories by Dylan *Thomas, published in 1940. Predominantly in an idiom of straightforward comic realism, much of the material derives from Thomas's autobiographical experience; 'The Peaches', among the funniest and most moving of the stories, evokes a visit in childhood to the farm in Carmarthenshire which Thomas later made the setting for the poem 'Fern Hill'. 'The Fight', 'Where the Tawe Flows', 'Old Garbo', and 'One Warm Saturday' are explicitly set in Swansea, his home town: their swift economy of imaginatively heightened description most clearly demonstrates the technique of 'illuminated reporting' he claimed was the method of the stories in a letter to Vernon *Watkins; it is in these pieces that the 'young dog' is most directly portrayed during his schooldays and brief career as a journalist. The conception of centring the book on Swansea was partly a response to *Joyce's example in **Dubliners*; Thomas's title, with its obvious Joycean allusion, was suggested to him by his friend Richard *Hughes. The remark by Constantine Fitzgibbon, Thomas's biographer, that '*Portrait of the Artist as a Young Dog* . . . is surely his happiest and most successful prose work' represents the general consensus of opinion on this enduringly popular collection.

Portrait of the Artist as a Young Man, A, a novel in five chapters by James *Joyce. The novel began its life in 1904 as *Stephen Hero*, which Joyce abandoned and partly destroyed in 1907 and subsequently rewrote in full by 1914. With the help of *Yeats, *Pound, and Harriet Shaw Weaver, it was serialized in *The *Egoist* and, after difficulties similar to those experienced with **Dubliners*, published in the USA in 1916. Apparently autobiographical, it narrates significant episodes from the childhood, adolescence, and early adulthood of Stephen Dedalus, which is also the name of one of the main characters in **Ulysses*. Born in Ireland towards the end of the nineteenth century, Dedalus inherits the weight of its codes and traditions, service to family, Roman Catholic dogma, Irish history, and nationalist politics. It is in Stephen's negotiation of the conflict between these nets of received wisdom and the open skies of creative freedom that Joyce portrays the development of his artist. Detached and compassionate, the author employs the details of his own life with the irony of hindsight and charts the ways in which an aspiring writer can be both duped and inspired by words. Dedalus's confusion in the midst of opposing interests, countered by his few moments of clarity, serve Joyce as an explanation for his own lifelong exile from a city and a country which he never left alone.

Possession, see BYATT, A. S.

Post-modernism is a term that was used by the American critic R. P. *Blackmur and others as early as the 1950s, but became fashionable, indeed ubiquitous, in the late 1980s. It was employed to describe not only architecture, literature, and music but haircuts, habits, jokes, states of mind. Its general connotations are irony, self-mockery, allusiveness, parody, immersion in *popular culture, refusal to believe in or even worry about grand ideas or gestures, amused acceptance of everything that caused anguish to the Modernists. It is not entirely clear that anyone or any thing actually *is* Post-modernist—perhaps the paintings and films of Andy Warhol are. The condition seems to be a generalized projection of what are felt as scattered but unmistakable tendencies in the West since 1945. There are two quite different ways of thinking about the condition, one broader and more historical than the other. In the first, Post-modernism is the name of what comes after *Modernism in the arts, whatever follows Modernism's exhaustion. This might in some areas be *post-structuralism, or certain aspects of it, a development of the questioning, disintegrational possibilities of Modernism; or it might be a reaction against Modernism, a return to older values. In the broader sense Post-modernism is the name of the overall cultural climate of late capitalism, the way we think, feel, write, build, play, sing, act in the multinational, high-technology, consumer-directed economic order of the second half of the twentieth century. We are Post-modern whether we know it or not; our art and culture are our reflection, displayed in entertaining but revelatory mirrors. Both usages assume what future historians may doubt: that Modernism is over, that a new mode or period has arrived. Yet another way of thinking of Post-modernism, therefore, is to see it as a particular variety of Modernism rather than its successor: late Modernism rather than beyond Modernism. Interesting discussions of the whole question can be found in J.-F. Lyotard's *The Postmodern Condition* (1984), D. Harvey's *The Condition of Postmodernity* (1990), and F. *Jameson's *Postmodernism* (1991). See also ADAPTATION.

Post-structuralism is often taken to be synonymous with *Deconstruction, and it is true that Deconstruction has seemed to be the main form that Post-structuralism has taken. Without *Structuralism, Deconstruction would not have been possible; and it does offer both a continuation and a reversal of Structuralism's assumptions and practices, seeking gaps, lapses, and inconsistencies where Structuralism sought rules and patterns of coherence. Post-structuralism more broadly is any practice or way of looking which does the same: it might go 'beyond structure' without being interested in dismantling the structure. As Jonathan Culler suggests in his *Barthes*

(1983), we should not exaggerate or make too tidy the differences between Structuralism and its successor. Structuralism posited a general science of signs and conventions, but often focused on exceptional cases; Post-structuralism puts everything into question, but needs the concept of the general rule in order for the questioning to become visible. Roland Barthes's *S/Z* (1970), often taken as a key work of Post-structuralism, can be seen to look both ways: towards the rules of narrative and social signification and away from them. Other writers and thinkers who were Structuralists before they came to be regarded as Post-structuralists are Jacques Lacan, Michel Foucault, and Julia Kristeva. More avidly Post-structuralist are Gilles Deleuze and Félix Guattari, notably in their *Anti-Oedipus* (1972), which seeks to reclaim schizophrenia as a political arm against totalizing systems.

POTTER, Dennis (1933–95), British dramatist, born in the Forest of Dean, the son of a miner, educated at Oxford University; he subsequently worked as a journalist and critic. Starting in 1965, when his semi-autobiographical plays *Vote, Vote, Vote for Nigel Barton* and *Stand Up, Nigel Barton* were transmitted, he established himself as an original, inventive, and prolific television dramatist. His work for the medium includes an evocation of childhood, *Blue Remembered Hills* (1979), and the serials *Pennies from Heaven* (1978), *The Singing Detective* (1986), *Christabel* (1988), and *Blackeyes* (1989). He also adapted some of his television plays for the stage, among them a portrait of Christ, *Son of Man* (1969), and *Brimstone and Treacle* (1977), which was banned by the BBC because of a scene in which a mentally damaged young woman is raped by a satanic visitor.

POTTER, Stephen (Meredith) (1900–69), English humorist and radio producer, born at Clapham in South London, educated at Merton College, Oxford. His early works include *D. H. Lawrence: A First Study* (1930), *Coleridge and S. T. C.* (1935), and *The Muse in Chains* (1937), an irreverent attack on the teaching of English literature in universities. In 1938 he became writer and producer in the Features Department of the BBC; among other programmes, he is remembered for the 'How' series of wryly amusing commentaries on everyday matters written in collaboration with Joyce Grenfell. *The Theory and Practice of Gamesmanship; Or the Art of Winning Games without Actually Cheating* (1947) was the first of the urbanely humorous treatises on the strategies of success that made him well known in Britain and America; subtly satirical in its revelation of social pretensions, the book set the pattern for *Some Notes on Lifesmanship* (1950), *One-Upmanship* (1952), and *Supermanship* (1958), which jointly donated the '—manship' suffix to the language and were collected along with the original *Gamesmanship* in *The Complete Upmanship* (1970). Other works in a similar vein include *Christmas-ship; Or the Art of Giving and Receiving* (1956). *Steps to Immaturity* (1959) is Potter's highly regarded autobiography of boyhood and youth. Alan Jenkins's *Stephen Potter* appeared in 1980.

POUND, Ezra (Weston Loomis) (1885–1972), American poet, born in Hailey, Idaho; he grew up in Philadelphia where his father worked as an assayer with the US mint. His study of Romance Languages at the University of Pennsylvania had an important bearing on the development of his poetry, which was initially influenced by the works of Swinburne and Rosetti. As a student he began his long friendship with William Carlos *Williams and was briefly engaged to Hilda *Doolittle. In 1906 he lectured at Wabash College, Indiana, and subsequently travelled in Spain, France, and Italy. In 1908, the year in which *A Lume Spento*, his first collection of verse, was published in Venice, he came to London to renew his acquaintance with W. B. *Yeats, whom he had met in the USA in 1903. His debt to Yeats, who employed him as his secretary in 1913 and 1914, is indicated in *Personae* (1909), a work which shows the influence of the dramatic monologues of Browning. Yeats also benefited from their working relationship, the new directness of voice in **Responsibilities* (1914) resulting in part from revisions suggested by Pound. In 1908 he taught at the Regent Street Polytechnic, adapting his lectures to form *The Spirit of Romance* (1910). His later critical writings include *A B C of Reading* (1934) and *Guide to Kulchur* (1938).

Ripostes (1912), in which his well-known translation of 'The Seafarer' appeared, established him as the spokesman of the *Imagists, whose anthology *Des Imagistes* he edited in 1914. The free-verse forms introduced in *Ripostes* become dominant in *Lustra* (1916) which contains his most characteristically Imagist poems, the two lines of 'In a Station of the Metro' having been frequently cited as epitomizing the mode. In 1913 he came into possession of the papers of Ernest *Fenollosa, which provided the basis for the majority of the translations from the Chinese in *Cathay* (1915). His growing interest in Chinese culture expanded his work's cultural frame of reference, which had already encompassed French, Italian, English, and Classical antecedents, and led him towards the 'Ideogrammatic Method' of *The *Cantos*, published in numerous sections from 1925. He subsequently produced many versions from the Chinese and other languages, selections of which appeared as *The Translations of Ezra Pound* (1970). *Cathay* made him 'the inventor of Chinese poetry for our time', as *Eliot stated in his introduction to Pound's *Selected Poems* (1928). The two had met in 1914, by which time Pound was an established figure in the literary life of London; he was also influential in the USA as European editor of **Poetry*, Chicago, through which he promoted the poetry of Robert *Frost and others. Eliot respected him greatly, particularly for his remarkable sensitivity to the musical and rhythmical aspects of verse; having increased Eliot's confidence as a poet through his advice and encouragement, Pound secured publication of **Prufrock and Other Observations* with the Egoist

Press in 1917. Among the other writers whom he assisted was James *Joyce, whose *Portrait of the Artist as a Young Man* was serialized in *The *Egoist* magazine in 1914 and 1915. In 1922 Eliot sought his assistance in finalizing his draft of *The *Waste Land*; Pound's extensive excisions and alterations determined the form in which the work was published.

He moved to Paris in 1920; *Hugh Selwyn Mauberley* (1920) testifies to his disillusionment with the 'botched civilization' of Georgian England, which he saw as ridden with false values and shadowed by the massive futility of the First World War. The book, thought by many to be his finest, frames its acerbically elegiac synopsis of English cultural history from the mid-nineteenth century onwards in verse of great deftness and originality. In 1924 he settled at Rapollo in Italy, devoting himself henceforth to *The Cantos*. His conception of the work as a unifying structure for the diversity of his preoccupations was informed by the *Vorticist aesthetics of Wyndham *Lewis and Henri Gaudier-Brzeska, with whom he had collaborated to produce **Blast* in 1914; his *Gaudier-Brzeska: A Memoir* (1916) describes how his sense of poetic form developed in response to the sculptor's use of contrasting masses and interrelated planes, which find their equivalents in the thematic juxtapositions and correspondences of *The Cantos*.

During the 1930s his obsession with economic theories led him to express distinctly anti-Semitic views in criticizing usury as the basis of international capitalism. Feeling his ideas were in broad conformity with the fascism of Mussolini, whom he had met and been impressed by in 1933, in 1941 he began broadcasting material hostile to the USA's wartime interests on Rome Radio. He was arrested in 1945 and, after some months in abject conditions of captivity near Pisa, was taken to Washington to stand trial for treason. Considered unfit to plead, he was committed to a New York psychiatric hospital until 1958. He then returned to Italy, where he remained, continuing *The Cantos*, until his death.

While Pound's stature is clouded by the intimidating complexity and ideological implications of *The Cantos*, his earlier work is recognized as an achievement of great distinction. Eliot, who was directly instrumental in securing his release from confinement in 1958, indicated Pound's centrality to modern literature in stating that he was 'more responsible for the XXth Century revolution in poetry than any other individual'. *The Letters of Ezra Pound, 1907–1941*, edited by D. D. Paige, were published in 1950; biographical studies include N. Stock's *The Life of Ezra Pound* (1970) and H. Carpenter's *A Serious Character* (1988). See also BLACK MOUNTAIN WRITERS, OBJECTIVIST POETRY, and PROJECTIVE VERSE.

POWELL, Anthony (Dymoke) (1905–), English novelist, born in London, educated at Balliol College, Oxford. At his prep school in Kent he met Henry Yorke (later the novelist, Henry *Green) and both subsequently attended Eton and Oxford. Their chance meeting, Powell acknowledged, foreshadowed a constant theme in his fiction, the part that coincidence and chance play in life. At Eton his contemporaries included George *Orwell, Harold *Acton, Robert *Byron, and Cyril *Connolly; at Oxford, Maurice *Bowra and Evelyn *Waugh. He started work for Duckworth's, the publishers, in 1926, a period evoked in *What's Become of Waring* (1939), which amusingly explores the belief that 'Authorship is only impressive to those in the book business'. In 1934 he married the authoress Lady Violet Pakenham. His first novel, *Afternoon Men* (1931), with its background of supper dances and country houses, nightclubs, pubs, and London office life, was followed by *Venusberg* (1932), set in a mythic Baltic capital; *From a View to a Death* (1933), about village society; and *Agents and Patients* (1936), a farcical work about a diffident young man of means who emerges, after experiences with a film man and a psychiatrist, as master of his fate. These works, with their distinctive black humour and laconic delivery, distinguished Powell as one of the most promising novelists of his generation. During the Second World War he served in the Welch Regiment and the Intelligence Corps while working on his biography of John Aubrey (1948). Powell's 12-volume opus, *A *Dance to the Music of Time* (1951–75), is recognized as one of the great fiction achievements of the twentieth century. Its title is drawn from Poussin's painting of the same name and echoes Proust's *A la recherche du temps perdus*. Both *roman-à-clef* and *Bildungsroman*, the sequence is narrated by the elusive Nicholas Jenkins, whose story begins in *A Question of Upbringing* (1951) and ends in *Hearing Secret Harmonies* (1975). At the core of a cast of hundreds, drawn in the main from the upper echelons of society, is Kenneth Widmerpool, son of a liquid manure manufacturer. All the characters are carefully choreographed dancers moving 'slowly, methodically, sometimes a trifle awkwardly, in evolutions that take recognizable shape: or (break) into seemingly meaningless gyrations, while partners disappear only to reappear again, once more giving to the pattern'. Powell has subsequently concentrated on his four-volume autobiography, *To Keep the Ball Rolling* (1976–82), a testimony to his obsession with genealogy, and which gives considerable insights into the creation of his masterpiece. His later fiction includes *O, How the Wheel Becomes It!* (1983) and *The Fisher King* (1986). *Miscellaneous Verdicts: Writings on Writers, 1946–1989* (1990) and *Under Review: Further Writings on Writers, 1946–1989* (1991) are collections of essays; Powell's *Journals, 1982–1986* were published in 1995.

Power and the Glory, The, a novel by Graham *Greene, published in 1940, a time when conflicts between religious and secular or political imperatives frequently shape his writing. In this novel, these are played out between individual characters, named only as the Priest and the Lieutenant—Greene later used similar tactics, though much more lightly, in

Monsignor Quixote (1982). As in the later novel, he tries to ensure that his protagonists are of equal appeal. The Lieutenant is a 'figure of hate'—engaged in the kind of persecution of the clergy Greene witnessed on his visit to Mexico and describes in *The Lawless Roads* (1938)—but there is also a 'secret of love' in his political idealism and care for children and the poor. Though the Priest has an illegitimate child and also regularly gives way to the temptations of alcohol, he has the courage, or pride, to continue as the last servant of an outlawed religion in his province. His capture by the Lieutenant's forces and later death, arranged by a kind of Judas figure, have strong overtones of Calvary. Greene admitted the novel was 'written to a thesis', and it has been criticized for allegorical qualities which can seem facile and schematic. The whisky priest, however, is of interest less as an allegoric figure than as a very ordinary one who, nevertheless, achieves an exalted status. As in several of Greene's novels, interest of this kind is emphasized by references to an analogous but more conventionally heroic story. The Priest is first contrasted but eventually amalgamated in a child's imagination with a more obviously heroic martyr described in a piece of Catholic propaganda. In this and other ways, *The Power and the Glory* suggests a kind of sanctity still accessible to fallible mortals; a heroism still achievable in a mundane world whose difficulties are much emphasized in this case by the novel's fetid, chaotic Mexican background.

POWERS, James Farl (1917–), American novelist and short-story writer, born in Jacksonville, Illinois, educated at Northwestern University, Evanston, Illinois. Powers's writings are notable for their preoccupation with Catholicism, a theme that emerged in his first collection of short stories *The Prince of Darkness and Other Stories* (1947) and subsequently in a second collection, *The Presence of Grace* (1956). *Morte D'Urban* (1962), a novel, follows the fortunes of a Chicago priest, Father Urban, who tries to improve the financial position of his order, the Clementines, through a series of comically realized business contacts. *Wheat That Springeth Green* (1988) continues the exploration of the ambiguous relationship between faith and modernity. Powers has been much esteemed in Britain, particularly by Evelyn *Waugh and John *Wain who have written admiringly of his wit and mordancy.

POWYS, John Cooper (1872–1963), British novelist, poet, and polemicist, born in Derbyshire, educated at Corpus Christi College, Cambridge. The son of a clergyman and brother of Llewelyn and Theodore *Powys, he spent his boyhood in the West Country, which was later to feature in many of his novels. Between 1904 and 1934, he lived in the USA before settling in North Wales. He published *Odes* (1896) and *Poems* (1899), but only with his first novel *Wood and Stone* (1915) did he discover an appropriate form in which to express his idiosyncratic vision. Focusing on the relationships between the members of a small, rural community, the work contains many of the preoccupations—the conflict between pagan and Christian elements, and sex and sensuality—developed in his later work. *Rodmoor* (1916), set in a small town, deals with the complex relationships between pairs of lovers, and is written in a highly charged, symbolic language which mirrors the disintegration into madness of the novel's main protagonist, Adrian Sorio. *Ducdame* (1925) counterpoints the stories of the protagonists, mirroring the struggle between death wish and life force, a theme to which Powys's fiction frequently returns. *Wolf Solent* (1929) follows its eponymous hero from London to Dorset, where he takes up a post as secretary to the eccentric Squire Urquhart, falls in love with the innocent Christie Malakite, but ends up marrying the sensual but faithless Gerda Torp. *A *Glastonbury Romance* (1932), his best-known novel, was followed by *Weymouth Sands* (1934, NY; published in Britain as *Jobber Skald*, 1935, for libel reasons but later republished under its original title), which deals with the violent attraction of Jobber Skald for Perdita Wane and his equally violent hatred for Dogberry Cattistock. The novel displays characteristics associated with Powys's mature work, including subjects such as vivisection, mental illness, and sexual energy. *Maiden Castle* (1936), set in Wessex, concerns the 'death quest' of its protagonist, Dud No-Man, in order to 'solve the meaning of death itself'. *Morwyn* (1937), in the form of a letter from the narrator to his son, describes a descent into Hell, where Torquemada, Socrates, and Rabelais are amongst those encountered. *Owen Glendower* (1940), set in fifteenth-century Wales, concerning the Welsh uprising against the English, was followed by *Porius* (1951), which incorporates the author's reworking of Welsh mythology, Arthurian romance, and Blakean symbolism. Other later works include *The Inmates* (1952); *Atlantis* (1954); *The Brazen Head* (1956); and *All or Nothing* (1960). Visionary, strange, and idiosyncratic, Powys's novels question orthodoxies of all kinds, offering, in place of the life-denying limitations of modern, technological society, a celebration of individual potential and cosmic wholeness. As an essayist and polemicist, he is best remembered for *In Defence of Sensuality* (1930) and *A Philosophy of Solitude* (1934). His critical works include *The Enjoyment of Literature* (1938), and he also published a revealing *Autobiography* (1934). See *The Demon Within* (1973) by John Brebner and *The Brothers Powys* (1983) by R. P. Graves.

POWYS, Llewelyn (1884–1939), British essayist, born in Dorchester, the brother of J. C. *Powys and T. F. *Powys, educated at Corpus Christi College, Cambridge. In 1909 he learned he was suffering from tuberculosis and entered a sanitorium in Davos-Platz, Switzerland; his illness is memorably dealt with in *Skin for Skin* (1925). He subsequently travelled in Europe and began a period as a farmer in Kenya in 1914. From 1920 to 1928 he lived mainly in New York and California; his essays on African subjects for the *New York Evening Post*, together with earlier work, provided material for *Ebony and Ivory* (1923) and *Black Laughter* (1924). Much of his later writing reflected his extensive travelling in Europe, Palestine, and the West Indies. His further collections of essays include *Earth Memories* (1930), *A Pagan's Pilgrimage* (1931), *Dorset Essays* (1935), and *Swiss Essays* (1947), which contain much highly evocative topographical writing. He also wrote numerous books presenting his unorthodox religious and philosophical views: *The Pathetic Fallacy* (1930) accuses the Church of distorting Christ's teachings, while *Impassioned Clay* (1931) and *Damnable Opinions* (1935) express his idealistically materialist belief that the purpose of life lies in the attainment of happiness. He returned to the sanitorium in Davos-Platz for the last three years of his life, anticipating his death in the lyrical 'imaginary autobiography' *Love and Death* (1939). His other works include the novel *Apples Be Ripe* (1930) and *The Cradle of God* (1929), an idiosyncratic interpretation of the Old Testament. His *Letters* (1943) are edited by Louis Wilkinson; there is a biography by Malcolm Elwin (1946).

POWYS, T(heodore) F(rancis) (1875–1953), British novelist, born at Shirley in Derbyshire, the brother of John Cowper and Llewelyn *Powys, educated at Sherborne School. Much of his fiction draws on the social and natural characters of his surroundings at East Chaldon, Dorset, where he lived from 1904 to 1940. A deeply religious sensibility pervades his writing; his idiosyncratic metaphysical views are outlined in *An Interpretation of Genesis* (1907) and *Soliloquies of a Hermit* (1917). *The Left Leg*, his first collection of stories, appeared in 1923. The rich simplicity of his style, which suggests the influence of Bunyan, is highly appropriate to the function of many of his narratives as parables of the human capacities for good and evil. *Mr Weston's Good Wine* (1927), widely regarded as his finest achievement, forms an allegorical meditation on the nature and purposes of God, manifest as the travelling wine-salesman named in the title. Its fundamentally affirmative vision has its counterpart in the disquieting bleakness of *Unclay* (1931), the most notable of his other novels. During his lifetime he published eight collections of stories and eight novels, which also include *Mr Tasker's Gods* (1925), *Kindness in a Corner* (1930), perhaps his most purely comic work, and the late short stories of *God's Eyes a-Twinkle* (1947). Among his posthumously published works are *The Strong Wooer* (1970) and *Father Adam* (1990). H. Coombes's critical and biographical study *T. F. Powys* appeared in 1960.

Practical Criticism, a term used by I. A. *Richards at Cambridge University to illustrate his experiment in criticism, described in his Introduction to *Practical Criticism: A Study in Literary Judgement* (1929) as 'a piece of fieldwork in comparative ideology'; it revealed, by asking a group of readers to respond to unidentified texts, how much they assumed about authors and reputations, and how little they were accustomed to attend to the words on the page. It was effectively a call for a new schooling of reading, and it lay at the heart of the *New Criticism. 'The lesson of all criticism', Richards wrote, 'is that we have nothing to rely upon in making choices but ourselves. The lesson of good poetry seems to be that, when we have understood it, in the degree in which we can order ourselves, we need nothing more.' 'Practical' for Richards was not opposed to 'theoretical', but was meant to carry a strong sense of hard scientific work, an aura of the laboratory. See also SCRUTINY.

Prancing Nigger, see FIRBANK, RONALD.

PRATCHETT, Terry (1948–), British fantasy novelist whose career began with science fiction parodies of L. *Niven and other writers of modern American 'hard sf', but who has become known for a series of comic fantasies set on a Discworld supported by four elephants riding through space on a giant tortoise. Pratchett's verbal facility, the balance of his plots, and his humour distinguish these novels in a genre not famous for comedy. The series includes *The Colour of Magic* (1983), *The Light Fantastic* (1986), *Equal Rites* (1987), *Mort* (1987), *Sourcery* (1988), *Wyrd Sisters* (1988), *Pyramids* (1989), *Guards! Guards!* (1989), *Eric* (1990), *Moving Pictures* (1990), *Reaper Man* (1991), *Witches Abroad* (1991), *Small Gods* (1992), *Lords and Ladies* (1992), *Men at Arms* (1993), *Soul Music* (1994), *Interesting Times* (1994), and *Masakerade* (1995).

PRATT, E(dwin) J(ohn) (1882–1964), Canadian poet, born in Newfoundland, educated at the University of Toronto. The son of a Methodist minister, Pratt was also ordained himself, but subsequently pursued an academic career. Although often considered Canada's finest writer of narrative verse of the twentieth century, much of his work is concerned with Victorian conflicts, such as the collapse of faith and humanity's relationship with nature more generally; thus the collision between the ship and the iceberg in *The Titanic* (1935) exemplifies the limitations of technological 'progress'. His best-known works, *Brébeuf and his Brethren* (1940) and *Towards the Last Spike* (1952), are poems of epic scope with subjects drawn from Canadian history: the former treats the massacre of a group of early French missionaries by the Iroquois and, more generally, the problem of establishing a European culture in Canada; the latter takes the building of the transcontinental railroad, a metaphoric as well as a physical expression of national unity, as its subject. Pratt's poetry employs a wide range of metrical forms, demonstrating considerable technical assurance in all of them. His other works include *Newfoundland Verse* (1923), *The Witches' Brew* (1925), *The Iron Door* (1927), *Verses of the Sea* (1930), *The Fable of the Goats* (1937), and *Still Life* (1943). His *Collected Poems* appeared in 1958.

Precious Bane, see WEBB, MARY.

Preview, a Canadian journal largely devoted to poetry and short stories, founded in Montreal in 1942 by an editorial group which included Patrick

Anderson, F. R. *Scott, P. K. *Page, and Bruce Ruddick. It was intended as a platform for innovative and socially concerned literature and stood in opposition to the more traditional and conservative modes which *Canadian Poetry Magazine* was felt to espouse. The critical and ideological essays featured in *Preview* testified to the essentially socialist persuasions of its editors, who had declared themselves in the first issue's editorial in the following terms: 'all anti-fascists, we feel that the existence of a war between democratic culture and the paralysing forces of dictatorship only intensifies the writer's obligation.' Although intended as a monthly, the magazine was published irregularly, twenty-three issues appearing in all. It was, however, strongly instrumental in affecting the course of Canadian literature through its refusal to comply with any narrowly nationalistic conceptions of indigenous poetry. The character of the work it favoured tended to reflect the examples of W. H. *Auden, Dylan *Thomas, and other leading British poets of the 1930s. Its role in the fostering of new modes in Canadian verse was complementary to that of **First Statement*, which favoured the models provided by American *Modernism; in 1945 the two magazines merged to form *Northern Review*, which continued to appear until 1956.

PRICE, Reynolds (1922–), American author, born in North Carolina, educated at Duke University. His first novel, *A Long and Happy Life* (1962), set like almost all his fiction in his native state, centres on a young girl of small-farming background who discovers she is pregnant by her errant boyfriend. The girl's family reappears in the long story 'A Chain of Love' in *The Names and Faces of Heroes* (1963) and in *A Generous Man* (1973), a ritualistically constructed novel about young Milo Mustian's loss of virginity. *The Surface of Earth* (1975) is a novel of enormous scope and emotional depth centring on Rob Mayfield, son of a brief, doomed union, and his quests for his parents, for himself, and for spiritual rest. A *Palpable God* (1978) contains an essay on, and translations of portions of, the Bible, including St Mark's Gospel, with reflections on the art of narrative. *The Source of Light* (1981) continues the story of Hutch Mayfield, Rob's son, taking him to Oxford and Europe. *Kate Vaiden* (1986) is a moving account of both the destructive and restorative powers of love in a woman conditioned by the tragedy of her parents' love. *Good Hearts* (1988) returns to the Mustian family, now in middle age. Later novels include *The Tongues of Angels* (1990) and *Blue Calhoun* (1992). Other works include *Things Themselves* (1972), a collection of essays; *Clear Pictures: First Loves, First Guides* (1989), an autobiographical memoir; *The Use of Fire* (1990), a collection of poems; *New Music* (1990); a trilogy of plays, *Full Moon and Other Plays* (1993), and *The Collected Stories of Reynolds Price* (1993).

PRICHARD, Katherine Susannah (1883–1969), Australian writer, born in Fiji. Prichard was a founder member of the Communist Party of Australia; her writing dealt with social injustice and frequently included idealized portraits of working people. *The Pioneers* (1915), a bush romance, was followed by numerous other novels including *Windlestraws* (1916), a melodramatic romance about the theatre, set in London; *The Black Opal* (1921), a study of a mining community oppressed by capitalist entrepreneurs; *Working Bullocks* (1926), which concerns the exploitation of teamsters in Western Australia; *Conardoo* (1929), an informative account of cattle station workers; and *Haxby's Circus* (1930), about an acrobat deformed in an accident. A trilogy (*The Roaring Nineties*, 1946; *The Winged Seeds*, 1948; and *Golden Miles*, 1950) presents a history of a gold-mining community from the 1890s to the 1940s through the life of its heroine, Sally Gough. Prichard also published two volumes of poetry, an autobiography, and a book on Russia.

PRIEST, Christopher (McKenzie) (1943–), British novelist, born in Manchester; he left school at 16 and became an accountant. He began as a writer of *science fiction with speculative novels such as *Indoctrinaire* (1970), *Fugue for a Darkening Island* (1972), *Inverted World* (1974), and *A Dream of Wessex* (1977). In his later work futuristic projections gave way to settings more or less contemporary and familiar, but distorted by the psychological confusions and manipulations of the characters. *The Glamour* (1984) describes a number of invisible people who may or may not be delusions. *The Quiet Woman* (1990) uses plausible elements—the murder of an elderly CND campaigner, a nuclear accident that has polluted southwest Britain, the violent fantasies of a schizophrenic and unreliable narrator—to build a disturbingly open-ended story of deceit and individual helplessness. He has also written short stories, film scripts, and a book for children about film-making.

PRIESTLEY, J(ohn) B(oynton) (1894–1984), British novelist, playwright, critic, and essayist, born in Bradford, educated at Trinity Hall, Cambridge, after serving throughout the First World War. The short essays of *Brief Diversions* (1922) impressed J. C. *Squire, who assisted Priestley to establish himself as a journalist in London. Among his other early publications are the critical study *Figures in Modern Literature* (1924) and the essays of *Apes and Angels* (1928). He became well known with the novel *The Good Companions* (1929), a picaresque narrative of a travelling theatre troupe, which was enormously popular in Britain and America. Among the more notable of his more than thirty novels are *Angel Pavement* (1930), a treatment of London on the eve of the Depression; *Daylight on Saturday* (1943), set in a wartime aircraft factory; and *Bright Day* (1946), a Jungian allegory of the quest for psychic integration. *Out of Town* (1968) and *London End* (1968), the two parts of *The Image Men*, present his good-humouredly pessimistic view of modern mass communications. Following the stage adaptation of *The Good Companions* in 1930, Priestley began his career as one of the most highly regarded playwrights of his day; among the best-known of his many plays are the comedies *Laburnum Grove* (1934) and *When We Are Married* (1938), and the morality parables of *Johnson over Jordan* (1939) and *An *Inspector Calls* (1947); *Dangerous Corner* (1932), *Time and the Conways* (1937), and *I Have Been here before* (1937), which he discusses in *Three Plays about Time* (1947), reflect his preoccupation with the theories of J. W. *Dunne. During the Second World War Priestley made distinguished contributions to national morale through his broadcasts, collections of which include *Britain Speaks* (1940) and *All England Listened* (1968). His many other publications include the travel books *English Journey* (1934) and *Russian Journey* (1946); the ambitiously synoptic critical work *Literature and Western Man* (1960); and the trilogy of historical studies *The Prince of Pleasure and His Regency* (1969), *Victoria's Heyday* (1972), and *The Edwardians* (1970). *Thoughts in the Wilderness* (1957) and *Outcries and Asides* (1974) are among the collections of his post-war journalism, much of which is strongly informed by his socialist convictions. *Midnight on the Desert* (1937), *Rain upon Godshill* (1939), *Margin Released* (1962), and *Instead of Trees* (1977) are autobiographical. He was awarded the Order of Merit in 1977. A biography by Vincent Brome appeared in 1988.

Prime of Miss Jean Brodie, The, a novel by Muriel *Spark, published in 1961. The rise of fascism in Europe during the 1930s is one of the book's underlying themes, although its ostensible subject, the relationship between an eccentric and highly strung Edinburgh schoolmistress, Jean Brodie, and her acolytes, a group of adolescent schoolgirls, seems at first sight far removed from such a theme. As the novel progresses the parallels become more apparent: Miss Brodie, it emerges, is something of a dictator, employing her considerable charm and intelligence to fascinate her susceptible charges. One of them is so inspired by her teacher's admiration for Franco that she runs away to join the Civil Guard in the Spanish Civil War, and is killed in the attempt. Miss Brodie's malign influence extends to other areas of her pupils' experience: she tries to promote an affair between Rose Stanley, the prettiest member of the Brodie 'set', and Teddy Lloyd, the married art master, with whom she herself has had an affair; the plan goes wrong and Sandy Stewart, the intellectual of the group, becomes his mistress. Sandy, from whose point of view the action is seen, is a classic Spark protagonist—torn between her love for Miss Brodie and her equally strong desire for revenge against her. It is Sandy who eventually denounces her teacher to the authorities, for her alleged sympathies with Hitler; the novel is in fact an extended flashback in which Sandy, now Sister Helena of the Transfiguration, recalls these traumatic events and the loss of innocence that accompanied them.

PRINCE, F(rank) T(empleton) (1912–), British poet and scholar, born in Kimberley, South Africa, educated at Balliol College, Oxford, and at Princeton. He began his academic career in 1946 at the University of Southampton, where he was Professor of English from 1957 to 1974. *Poems* (1938), his first collection of verse, was followed by *Soldiers Bathing* (1954), the title piece of which is one of the most widely anthologized poems of the Second World War; its emotional candour and fluent interweaving of contemplative and observational elements are representative of Prince's manner in much of his work. His subsequent volumes include *The Doors of Stone: Poems 1938–1962* (1963), *Drypoints of the Hasidim* (1975), and *Later On* (1983). In addition to many fine shorter poems, his achievements include several dramatic monologues which sustain an eloquence appropriate to the grandeur of their imagined speakers; among them are 'Michelangelo in Old Age', 'Words from Edmund Burke', and 'An Epistle to a Patron', the last in the voice of Leonardo da Vinci. Prince excluded many poems he considered inadequate in quality from his *Collected Poems* (1979). *Walks in Rome* (1987) exemplifies the urbanely lyrical mode of his later work in its extended meditation on his ambiguous attitude to religious faith. Among his critical writings are *The Italian Element in Milton's Verse* (1954) and *William Shakespeare: The Poems* (1963). His numerous works as an editor include texts of Milton's *Samson Agonistes* (1957) and the New Arden edition of Shakespeare's poems (1960).

PRITCHETT, Sir V(ictor) S(awdon) (1900–), British novelist, critic, and short-story writer. Born in Ipswich, son of a travelling salesman with religious ambitions, Pritchett was educated at Alleyn's School, Dulwich, which he left at 15 to work in the leather trade. His early immersion in the heterogeneous life of the city has proved perhaps his greatest asset as a writer, his powers of observation being greatly developed also by persistent travel in early manhood. At 21 he went to Paris, then embarked on his long career as a journalist. He wrote for the *Christian Science Monitor* in Ireland and in Spain, and this paper published his first extended pieces, the essay sequence 'The Appalachian Mountains', based on his walks in America. Pritchett's first full-length book was another travelogue, *Marching Spain* (1928); it has had several distinguished successors, including *The Spanish Temper* (1954). *Clare Drummer* (1929) was the first of several novels whose number includes *Dead Man Leading* (1949), centring on an explorer with obvious affinities to T. E. *Lawrence, and *Mr Beluncle* (1959) which, in its portrait of a restless, overweening father with a mania for embracing religious sects, drew on personal memories. Pritchett's greatest achievement lies in the short story, to which form he has made one of the most considerable contributions of the twentieth century. Stories range from portraits of (often quirky) individuals such as 'The Saint' to poetic renderings of epiphanic episodes (e.g. the famous 'Many Are Disappointed'), from the humorously anecdotal such as 'Sense of Humour' to complex presentations of inter-relationships within a group, of which 'When My Girl Comes Home', one of his greatest productions, can stand as example. Collections include *The Spanish Virgin and Other Stories* (1930), *You Make Your Own Life* (1938), *When My Girl Comes Home* (1961), and *The Camberwell Beauty* (1974). Two volumes of *Collected Stories* appeared in 1982 and 1983, and an even larger edition to commemorate his ninetieth birthday in September 1990. He has also written two books of autobiography, *The Cab at the Door* (1968), dominated by its portrait of his parents, and *Midnight Oil* (1971). In his later years Pritchett has continued to refine his art. His collection *A Careless Widow* (1989) contains the story 'Cocky Olly' (the title is the name of a children's game), a remarkable portrait of two children in post-Second World War Britain and their confused understanding of the adult society around them. *At Home and Abroad* (1990) is a collection of travel pieces. Pritchett's reputation as a critic rests chiefly on the exemplary clarity and precision of his literary essays, which are collected in *The Myth Makers* (1979), *The Tale Bearers* (1980), and *Man of Letters* (1986); *The Complete Essays* appeared in 1991. His highly regarded critical and biographical monographs include *Balzac* (1974), *The Gentle Barbarian: the Life and Work of Turgenev* (1977), and *Chekhov: A Spirit Set Free* (1988).

Private Lives, a comedy by Noël *Coward, performed and published in 1930. Probably its author's best-known play, it primarily involves Amanda and Elyot, whose turbulent marriage ended in divorce and who have just married steadier, more conventional people, Victor and Sibyl. When they discover that their honeymoons are coincidentally occurring in the same Riviera hotel, they first quarrel with their new spouses, then leave together for Paris. There, a violent row coincides with the arrival of the indignant Victor and Sibyl, who themselves eventually launch into a quarrel of their own, which this time coincides with Amanda and Elyot's *rapprochement* and surreptitious departure. The play has been admired for the deft parallelism of its plotting, as well as for its sophisticated humour and amusing portraiture of people who find it difficult to live either with or without each other.

Professor's House, The, a novel by Willa *Cather, published in 1925. The novel is intricately constructed and symbolic at many different levels. Its central figure, Professor St Peter, is a man in late middle age, who is about to leave the house where he has lived all his married life and where he has done his finest work (he is an authority on the Spanish in America). As the novel opens, he is very aware that he has arrived at a new and bleak stage of his life, when he must perhaps learn to live without joy. Both his daughters are married, one to a rather sycophantic worldling, the other to a hopeless and embittered journalist. Both couples are preoccupied with materialistic concerns—another reason for the Professor's increasing feeling of isolation. This is exacerbated by the memory of one of his students, the brilliant Tom Outland, who was killed in the Great War. Ironically, it is he who has enabled the family to live as well as they do, since the money from his patented discovery has been bequeathed to St Peter's daughter, Rosalind. Outland's story, describing his discovery, as a boy, of a mesa village in the New Mexico desert, and his subsequent attempts to defend it against exploitation, is inset into the novel. It is perhaps his memories of Outland which eventually help the Professor to come to terms with life, although not before he has attempted suicide by allowing himself to fall asleep in a room full of gas. But as the novel ends, it is apparent that this self-destructiveness will not be permitted to recur, and that the protagonist has gained a new spiritual strength from his reflections. Both the Professor's predicament and Tom Outland's story reflect the changes—the capitulation to materialism and the loss of the pioneer spirit—which Cather felt were overcoming America itself.

Projective Verse, the theory and practice of poetry described in Charles *Olson's essay 'Projective Verse', which appeared in *Poetry New York* in 1950; it was collected in Olson's *Selected Writings* (edited by Robert *Creeley, 1966). Olson's conceptions, which extended the developments chiefly associated with the work of Ezra *Pound and William Carlos *Williams (see also IMAGISM, OBJECTIVIST POETRY, and FREE VERSE), centred on his belief that the dynamics of a poem in its making should be the prime determinant of its form; he defined poetic structure in terms of 'kinetics', the qualities of the poem as 'a high-energy construct and . . . an energy discharge', 'principle', summarized in the statement that 'form is never more than an extension of content', and 'process', the generative continuity by which one perception leads directly to another. No rigid presuppositions concerning technique or subject would be imposed on the poem; composition would constitute an 'open field', capable of admitting elements apprehended during the act of writing, which would, in Creeley's words, thus 'move in the field of its recognitions' and become an 'intensely specific revelation of one's own content'. Olson divided the governing properties of verse into syllable and line, indicating their essentiality in the words 'the HEAD, by way of the EAR, to the SYLLABLE | the HEART, by way of the BREATH, to the LINE'. His views and the practical demonstrations offered in his writing were felt by many to be of enormous benefit in liberating American poetry from the constraining conservatism of the immediate post-war era; Williams, who quoted extensively from 'Projective Verse' in his *Autobiography* (1950), called the essay 'an advance of inestimable proportions'. Projective verse, or 'open field composition', became the characteristic mode of the poets associated with *Black Mountain College in the early 1950s and had seminal influence in increasing the flexibility of form and thematic inclusiveness of poetry in English in succeeding decades.

Proletarian Literature in the USA. The beginnings of the proletarian 'tradition', sometimes termed 'movement', in twentieth-century American letters can be dated to the first appearance of *The *Masses* magazine in 1911. Founded by Piet Vlag but most influential from 1913 onwards under the editorships of Max *Eastman and Floyd *Dell, *The Masses* espoused an exhilarating mixture of avant-gardism, anarchism, and radical socialism. By 1918 the increasingly left-wing affiliation of the weekly magazine and its open support of the Russian revolution (Eastman had published Lenin's 'Letter to American Workingmen' and had defended Bolshevism against the attacks of Walter *Lippmann in the **New Republic*) brought it under the scrutiny of the US government and it was suppressed in December 1918. In just six years, however, *The Masses* had established an intellectual and political climate on which a later generation of writers, notably those of the Depression years, could build. *The Masses* was succeeded by *The Liberator* (1918–1924), and when the latter folded the openly Marxist *The New Masses* came in to fill the space left by its demise. Through the boom years of the 1920s *The New Masses* offered a sustained critique of American capitalism but did so in a climate that was more literary than political.

The leftwards shift in American culture in the late 1920s and 1930s is more a mark of the affiliations of the literary intelligentsia than of American society in general. Influenced, particularly, by Lenin's remarks on the place of literature in society and the emphasis on the closer identification of the creative writer with the worker's cause, many American writers sought to create imaginative works which were simultaneously a criticism of the worst excesses of advanced capitalist society and, to varying degrees, a call to arms. Novels, therefore, such as John Dos Passos's **Manhattan Transfer* (1925) and Theodore Dreiser's *An *American Tragedy* (1925), though not tendentious in the Leninist sense, have distinct affinities with later, more overtly political, proletarian writings.

By 1935, with the USA deep in recession, *The New Masses* published a call for an American Writers' Congress, and Waldo *Frank's address to the first congress in May 1935 spoke of the inevitability of communism and the plight of the American writer under a capitalist system. Other significant papers read at the congress included those of Malcolm *Cowley and Joseph Freeman; Cowley, in particular, in his paper 'What the Revolutionary Movement Can Do for a Writer', sought to give the term 'proletarian novel' a specific American character and definition. Writers whose works are closely associated with the proletarian literature of the Depression years include Robert *Cantwell, Michael *Gold, James T. *Farrell, Howard *Fast, Albert *Halper, Josephine *Herbst, Albert *Maltz, Upton *Sinclair, and John *Steinbeck, while among critics V. F. Calverton, Granville Hicks, and Edwin Seaver, as well as Cowley and Gold, acted as important proselytizers.

By 1940 the movement was, to all intents and purposes, dead, the victim of internal contradiction and disagreement, and of external events such as the Hitler–Stalin pact and evidence of purges within the Soviet Union which had, collectively, eroded the movements' intellectual and political credibility; many of the writings of those associated with American proletarianism, however, continue to have value whilst others have little more than historical interest. Daniel Aaron's *Writers on the Left* (1961) remains the best general study of the left-wing proclivities in American writing in the inter-war years, whilst Walter B. Rideout's *The Radical Novel in the United States, 1900–1954* (1956) is more narrowly concerned with proletarian fiction. Joseph Freeman's edition of *Proletarian Literature in the United States* (1935) is the most valuable contemporary anthology of the literature.

PROULX, E(dna) Annie (1935–), American novelist, born in Connecticut, educated at the University of Vermont. She has worked as a journalist, travelled to the Far East, lived in New York City, and has spent most of her life in Vermont. Her collection of stories *Heartsongs and Other Stories* (1988) and her novels *Postcards* (1991) and *The Shipping News* (1993; Pulitzer Prize, 1994) have received high acclaim. Set in an almost mythical Newfoundland, *The Shipping News* tells the story of Quoyle, a frustrated journalist who moves there from New York with an aunt and two eccentric daughters when an accident kills his wife. Proulx's witty, sharp, and evocative prose style, her sense of North American history and landscape, and her resolutely unspectacular post-modern stance appeal to critics and general readers alike; she is a comic writer in a growing feminine tradition which includes such figures as Anne *Tyler.

Prufrock and Other Observations, T. S. *Eliot's first collection of poems, published in 1917 under the imprint of the **Egoist* magazine. Ezra *Pound undertook arrangements for publication and assisted with the costs of printing. Its forty pages contained work Eliot had produced between 1911 and 1915 while variously resident in Paris, Boston, and Oxford. The following poems appeared in the order given: 'The Love Song of J. Alfred Prufrock', 'Portrait of a Lady', 'Preludes', 'Rhapsody on a Windy Night', 'Morning at the Window', 'The Boston Evening Transcript', 'Aunt Helen', 'Cousin Nancy', 'Mr Appolinax', 'Hysteria', 'Conversation galante', and 'La Figlia che Piange'. 'The Love Song of J. Alfred Prufrock' offers the fullest demonstration of the radical newness of style and technique Eliot had achieved: like most of the poems, it combines the flexibility of *free verse with a highly disciplined irregularity in the use of rhyme; it constitutes an encompassing projection of a sensibility defined through interactions of mood, perceptions, preoccupations, and other cognitive events. Although classifiable as a dramatic monologue, it breaks with the conventions of the mode by dispensing with orthodox narrative or thematic continuity, enacting Prufrock's incapacitating self-consciousness and intellectual doubt in the modulations of its mannered and artfully digressive development. 'Portrait of a Lady' proceeds similarly, transposing Prufrock's social anxieties into a darker study of disjunctions and superficialities in human relationships; both poems ironically subvert the traditions of lyric verse, a characteristic of the volume most evident in the treatments of romantic love in the humorously evasive 'Conversation galante' and the estrangingly detached 'La Figlia che Piange'. Vividly economical imagery pervades the collection and is used to particular effect in the evocative urban realism of 'Preludes'. The mildly satirical concern with order and morality in 'Aunt Helen' and 'The Boston Evening Transcript' anticipates the moral revulsion which culminates in *The *Waste Land*.

PRYNNE, J(eremy) H(alward) (1936–), British poet, born in Kent, educated at Jesus College, Cambridge. In 1962 he became a fellow of Gonville and Caius College, Cambridge, where he also became a lecturer and College Librarian. Prynne's numerous collections of poetry include *Kitchen Poems* (1968), *The White Stones* (1969), *Brass* (1971), *High Pink on Chrome* (1975), *The Oval Window* (1983), and *Word Order* (1989); *Poems* (1982) presents work from twelve preceding books with the addition of previously uncollected material. His elegantly cadenced poetry creates an appearance of urbane discourse, but consistently challenges his readers' assumptions concerning meaning through a range of strategies that make much of his work resistant to paraphrase. A vibrant precision of imagery and strong suggestions of mood and atmosphere are among the qualities by which his verse commands interest. Frequent use of terminologies from science and economics gives Prynne's idiosyncratic writing an impressionistic breadth of reference to social and cultural concerns. The relationship between money and personal identity is imaginatively analysed in two of his more accessible poems, 'Die a Millionaire' and 'A Sketch for a Financial Theory of the Self'. He is regarded as a leading exponent of poetic *postmodernism.

Psychoanalytic Criticism. Psychoanalysis is both a theory of the mind and a practice of interpretation. Its early applications to literature, by Freud himself and by disciples like Marie Bonaparte and Ernest Jones, concentrated on the presumed psychology of the writer, on the repressed or displaced psychic material uncovered by textual analysis and recombination. This work was often reductive, too eager to crack the case, and none too faithful to psychoanalysis' own best clinical practice, which insists on the patient's collaboration, and the fullest, most carefully constructed context for each individual instance, seen as quite different from all others. Far more influential in the long run was Freud's sense of large forces other than conscious ones at work in literature, and elsewhere. Criticism learned to listen for the half-said and the unsaid, and works like William *Empson's *Seven Types of Ambiguity* and *Some Versions of Pastoral*, although not obviously psychoanalytic in tendency, are very much indebted to Freud. To make the story of *Alice in Wonderland* sound Freudian, Empson said, one has only to tell it. Psychoanalysis, as deployed in Freud's *Interpretation of Dreams* (1900) and elsewhere, was also a method of *reading*, and much contemporary literary criticism is psychoanalytic in the sense of being influenced by this method: seeking not the unconscious of a writer or of a character but something like the unconscious of the text, whatever is revealed in those places where the text misspeaks or contradicts itself, or appears to get agitated without cause. Psychoanalysis in this form, through the writing of Jacques Derrida, has made common ground with *Deconstruction. In his clinical and theoretical work, Jacques Lacan gave psychoanalysis a French face and manners and home, and an alliance with *Structuralism was forged. 'The unconscious is structured like a language', Lacan memorably (and cryptically) said, meaning among other things that the concept of structure may take us further, and dominate us more imperiously, than we are inclined to think. In Britain the work of Juliet Mitchell and Jacqueline Rose has been of great importance in exploring and furthering these insights, particularly in relation to the politics of feminism. Julia Kristeva's *Black Sun* (1987) considers poetry and novels and paintings, and constitutes a brilliant revision of Freud's great themes of melancholy and mourning.

PUDNEY, John (Sleigh) (1909–77), British poet, born in Langley, Buckinghamshire, educated at Gresham's School, Holt, Norfolk. After working as a producer with the BBC, he began a career in publishing in 1950. *Spring Encounter*, his first collection of poems, appeared in 1933. During the Second World War he gained a wide readership with a succession of volumes reflecting his experiences of active service with the RAF. The six collections he published between 1939 and 1945 include *Dispersal Point* (1942), *Beyond This Disregard* (1943), and *Almanack of Hope* (1944). He produced many poems which were felt to speak for the majority of those serving in the armed forces; 'For Johnny' exemplifies the profound elegiac simplicity of his best work. Pudney was a prolific author, publishing works on aviation and historical subjects, in addition to numerous novels, biographies, and collections of short stories. Among the volumes that sustained his reputation as a poet were *Low Life* (1947), *The Trampoline* (1959), and *Selected Poems: 1967–1973* (1973), which contained more flexibly innovative work. *Collected Poems* appeared in 1957. *Thank Goodness for Cake* (1978) is his autobiography. See also WAR POETRY.

PUGH, Sheenagh (1950–), British poet, born in Birmingham, educated at the University of Bristol. *Crowded by Shadows* (1977), her first collection of poems, established the sceptical levelness of tone and wryly understated wit which characterize much of her work. Her subsequent volumes, in which an increasingly flexible technique is evident, are *What a Place to Grow Flowers* (1980), *Earth Studies and Other Voyages* (1983), *Beware Falling Tortoises* (1980), and *Sing* *for the Taxman* (1993); much previously uncollected material appears in her *Selected Poems* (1990). Her work is notable for its unusual range, which extends from erudite use of historical materials to urgently topical treatments of social and political themes. *Prisoners of Transience* (1985) are translations of several little-known seventeenth-century German poets.

PULLINGER, Kate (1961–), Canadian writer, born in Cranbrook in the Rocky Mountains; she briefly attended McGill University before moving to England in 1982. Her first published book, *Tiny Lies* (1988), was an acclaimed collection of stories which blended comedy and satire with insight into the lives and dreams of single young women. Her first novel, *When The Monster Dies* (1989), was set in a rundown, contemporary South London milieu; its protagonists, migrants from Britain's former colonies, are examples of the empire striking back in eccentric and subversive ways. Her second novel, *Where Does Kissing End?* (1992), explores unspoken sexual needs, desires, and fantasies by reworking vampire legends in a postmodern vein. Pullinger collaborated in the novelization of Jane Campion's celebrated film *The Piano* (1994). Resolutely international in her perspective, and fascinated with travel, escape, and dislocation, she has edited *Border Lines* (1993), an anthology of original stories by writers such as Janette Turner *Hospital, Romesh *Gunesekera, Audrey *Thomas, and Aamer Hussein. A recent novel, possibly her most complex and ambitious, is *The Last Time I Saw Jane* (1996).

Pulp Magazines. These popular American magazines, most evident in the later 1920s and the 1930s, dealt with sensationalist crime writing, often of a highly charged erotic nature, and helped evolve the laconic 'tough guy' style of writing. The most influential was **Black Mask*, but other lasting titles include *Popular Detective* and *Dime Detective Magazine*.

Pumpkin Eater, The, see MORTIMER, PENELOPE.

PURDY, Al(fred) (1918–), Canadian poet, born in Wooler in rural Ontario. He led a nomadic early life, working at a variety of jobs and travelling extensively, but though the eclecticism of his poetry reflects the diversity of his experience of life, its central locus is 'the country north of Belleville', Ontario, which provided a title for one of his best-known poems. The main preoccupation of his work is the effect that the Canadian landscape has had on the formation of the country's psychic identity. While his first collection of verse appeared in 1944, Purdy did not discover his distinctive poetic voice until the 1960s, though there are hints of it in *The Crafte So Longe To Lerne* (1959), where the title alludes to his sense of having taken a long time to reach maturity as a poet. Then, in volumes like *Poems for All the Annettes* (1962) and *The Cariboo Horses* (1965), he began to write in the idiomatic vein that established his reputation as one of the finest Canadian poets of his generation. His other volumes of verse include *North of Summer* (1968), *In Search of Owen Roblin* (1974), and *The Stone Bird* (1981). Most of his best work is collected in *Being Alive: Poems 1958–78* (1978). He has also written radio and television plays.

PURDY, James (1923–), American novelist and short-story writer, born in Ohio, educated at the University of Ohio and the University of Puebla, Mexico. His work is often set in West Virginia or in New York where he has spent most of his life. Purdy established his dominant theme of a lost boy, casually encountered by the narrator in his first extended fiction, *63 Dream Palace* (1956). *Malcolm* (1959, dramatized 1965 by Edward *Albee) concerns another lost boy, searching for his father in a corrupt adult world; in *The Nephew* (1960), a spinster decides to write a commemorative booklet about her loved nephew presumed dead in Korea, and in the process discovers his hatred for society and his homosexuality. *Cabot Wright Begins* (1964) is a satirical novel about a rapist himself inveigled into becoming a victim by publishers who want to turn his deeds into money. *Eustace Chisholm and the Works* (1967), set in Depression Chicago, is far more explicit about homosexual relations than previous work and also presents more markedly the prelapsarian–postlapsarian antithesis stemming from a heterodox Christianity so central to subsequent work. *I am Elijah Thrush* (1972) and *In a Shallow Grave* (1975) are poetic extravaganzas. The trilogy *Sleepers in Moon-Crowned Valleys* (*Jeremy's Version*, 1970; *The House of the Solitary Maggot*, 1974; *Mourners Below*, 1981) offers Purdy's profoundest insights into the dreams and urges of people placed in a convention-bound milieu. *Narrow Rooms* (1978), his most audacious work, presents tragic homosexual relationships between four young men in a remote West Virginia community and culminates in acts of appalling violence which stand as re-enactments of religious myth. Subsequent works include the novels *On Glory's Course* (1983), *In the Hollow of His Hand* (1987), *Garments the Living Wear* (1989), and *Out With the Stars* (1992); *Children Is All* (1962), stories and two plays; *The Candles of Your Eyes* (1988), stories; and *Collected Poems* (1990).

Pursuit of Love, The, see MITFORD, NANCY.

Pygmalion, a play by Bernard *Shaw, performed in 1913 in Vienna, published and performed in London in 1916. This amusing piece, which was eventually to achieve popular renown as the musical *My Fair Lady* (1957), describes the reconstruction of the Cockney flower-girl Eliza Doolittle by the arrogant phonetician Henry Higgins. Her education falls into three stages. At first she says the wrong things in the right accent, bewildering the respectable. Then she learns how to be a plausible 'lady', triumphing at a fashionable ball. Finally, she realizes that being a lady without an income leaves her with little option but to find a husband to support her: 'I sold flowers, I didn't sell myself, but now you've made a lady of me I'm not fit to sell anything else.' For Higgins, this insight at last changes her from a 'millstone' to a 'woman', meaning a self-sufficient individual. Though Shaw wrote a postscript suggesting that Eliza married the devoted but dim Freddy Eynsford-Hill, and set up a flower shop with him, the play itself does not resolve the questions it raises. It remains Shaw's critique of the obstacles to self-discovery and self-realization caused by class.

Pylon School, a term loosely applied to numerous poets of the 1930s whose work contained imagery reflecting the impact of industry and technology upon Britain's landscape and culture. It was used from about 1935 onward, often disparagingly; Julian *Symons, for example, expressed relief in the first issue of *Twentieth Century Verse* (1937) that Dylan *Thomas was not 'a Pylon-Pitworks-Pansy poet'. Pylons feature in several well-known poems written early in the decade: W. H. *Auden refers to them in 'Get there if you can and see the land you once were proud to own . . .' and 'The chimneys are smoking, the crocus is out on the border . . .', as do Cecil *Day Lewis in 'Look west, Wystan, lone flyers' of *The Magnetic Mountain* (1933) and Charles *Madge in 'Instructions'; Stephen *Spender's 'The Pylons' is the definitive specimen, and, arguably, the most vulnerable to ridicule for its 'Pylons, those pillars | Bare like nude, giant girls that have no secret'. Other poets classifiable as members of the Pylon School are Louis *MacNeice, A. S. J. *Tessimond, John *Lehmann, and Michael *Roberts, all of whom make significant use of industrial modernity as a source of imagery in some of their work of the period. Wilfrid *Gibson's poetry from *Livelihood* (1917) onwards prefigures such writing in its social concern and its frequent allusions to mechanical processes. Roberts's *New Country* anthology of 1933 was rich in references to machinery, factories, and modes of power and transport; among such features, the pylon was emphatically up-to-date, the completion of Britain's National Grid having been achieved in 1933. In *British Writers of the Thirties* (1989) Valentine Cunningham discusses the pylon's function as a symbol of technological progress and considers the influence of *Futurism and related Modernist (see MODERNISM) modes on the use of such imagery by British poets of the 1930s.

PYM, Barbara (Mary Crampton) (1913–80), British novelist, educated at St Hilda's College, Oxford. Pym's first published novel was *Some Tame Gazelle* (1950), followed by *Excellent Women* (1952); *Jane Prudence* (1953); *Less Than Angels* (1955); *A Glass of Blessings* (1958); and *No Fond Return of Love* (1961). These are wry comedies of middle-class life, often with tragic undertones, extraordinarily observant and with a breadth of emotional and psychological content that the classical and ironic style of presentation would not, at a casual reading, seem to suggest. Her father was a Shropshire solicitor and Pym's world is that of members of the professions, drawing also on her experience of anthropological circles, and centring to a considerable degree around the Anglican Church. Her protagonists are often single women of a certain age, frequently suffering the pangs of unrequited love. The appearance in a Pym novel of characters from a previous one heightens the effect of a real, mapped society. In 1963 her publisher rejected *An Unsuitable Attachment*—the beginning of a long period of neglect. Then in 1977 the *Times Literary Supplement* invited contributors to name the most undervalued writers of the century; when Lord David *Cecil and Philip *Larkin nominated Barbara Pym, that led to a reversal of fortune. The novels which appeared after that renascence are more sombre in tone. *Quartet in Autumn* (1977), a poignant and melancholy study of ageing and death, was followed by *The Sweet Dove Died* (1978), a study in selfishness and self-deception, and *A Few Green Leaves* (published posthumously, 1980). *An Unsuitable Attachment* was eventually published in 1982. Since then, Pym's friend, Hazel Holt, has edited her journals and letters, published as *A Very Private Eye* (1984). Admirers compare Pym with Jane Austen; detractors see her growing posthumous reputation as an index of British contempt for the experimental and intellectual in fiction.

PYNCHON, Thomas (1937–), American novelist and short-story writer, born on Long Island, New York, educated at Cornell University. Pynchon is regarded by many as the archetypal post-modern novelist, whose work has been the expression of an America suspended between chaos and systematic paranoia. Since he has been one of the most determinedly private of writers, biographical information rests on rumours and apocrypha. He spent some time in Greenwich Village, New York, writing short stories and working on a first novel. His earliest stories, written between 1958 and 1964, are collected in *Slow Learner* (1984), which are early explorations of ideas that later became crucial to his subsequent novels. In 1960 he was hired as a technical writer for Boeing Aircraft Corporation in Seattle, but left two years later. **V* (1963) is a novel about a quest by a large and varied band of characters for the elusive, supernatural adventuress known only as 'V', who appears in various guises at critical moments in European history. This was followed by the more compact *The *Crying of Lot 49* (1966), another quest narrative. Pynchon's construction of a situation where the act of reading parallels the protagonists' acts of deciphering an encoded world emerges with most sophistication in **Gravity's Rainbow* (1973), a *tour de force* of twentieth-century writing, which employs a variety of narrative modes to investigate an extraordinary range of phenomena, exploring the dilemmas of humanity in modern industrial capitalism. Pynchon's novels are complex and erudite, often in the form of anti-detective stories, where mystery rather than solution is highlighted. One is led through an interface between the different discourses of science, politics, popular culture, technology, metaphysics, religion, and epistemology, as well as the labyrinth of the individual psyches of his characters. After a long silence which bred much speculation about his whereabouts,

Pynchon published *Vineland* (1990). The quest in this novel is for Frenesi Gates, the estranged wife of Zoyd Wheeler. Having rejected her counter-cultural background, she has the love of Brock Vond, a Justice Department official. Set in the Nixon–Reagan era, the hidden antagonist in the narrative is Reagan himself, and the book shows all Pynchon's qualities of complex plotting and his allusive knowledge of his surroundings. He has also written an essay entitled 'Journey into the Mind of Watts' on Los Angeles (1966) and an article 'Is It O.K. To Be a Luddite?' (1984). *Deadly Sins* appeared in 1993.

Q

Quadrant, a journal of the Australian Association for Cultural Freedom (part of the International Congress for Cultural Freedom, an anti-communist organ of the 1950s). It was established in 1956 under the editorship of James *McAuley, who saw it as a vehicle for his essentially European and traditionalist vision. Modelled on Britain's **Encounter*, it was intended as a political, social, and literary magazine to rival the left-wing Australian journal **Overland*, and the nationalist bias of **Meanjin*. By the 1960s *Quadrant* had become a forum for conservative but liberal discourse, drawn from participants at home and abroad. McAuley was sole editor until 1964 when he was joined by Donald Horne. Under their editorship, together with Vivian Smith as literary editor, *Quadrant* became a major literary journal and has maintained its standing. It has a preference for high quality poetry of fairly traditional form, and for mainly autobiographical prose. *Quadrant: Twenty Five Years* (1982) is a celebratory anthology.

Quare Fellow, The, a play by Brendan *Behan, first performed in 1956. It is set in an Irish prison on the night before, and morning of, the hanging of a murderer. Though the atmosphere is carefully and often humorously evoked, the conversation of the characters never wanders far from an execution. Even the 'quare fellow's' last trip from the condemned cell to the gallows comes in the form of a parody horse race, with a prisoner providing a breezy commentary from a window. The characters include the alcoholic old lags, Dunlavin and Neighbour; the hangman, a convivial publican brought over from England; the governor, who is anxious the condemned man should get a good last breakfast; and Regan, a warder notorious among his harder colleagues for his dislike of 'neck breaking and throttling' and for his habit of asking murderers to pray for him. The impression finally given is of a macabre ritual somehow made worse by everybody's determination to carry it out with humane efficiency.

Quarto, a monthly journal edited by Richard Boston and John Ryle which appeared between 1979, when it was formed during the temporary closure of the **Times Literary Supplement*, and 1982, when it was absorbed by the **Literary Review*. During its comparatively brief career *Quarto* attracted contributions from many of the leading literary and intellectual figures of the period, its scope extending to coverage of music, psychoanalysis, socio-political tendencies, and the theatre. Michael Tippett, Craig *Raine, Tom *Paulin, James *Fenton, George *Steiner, and Seamus *Heaney were among the authors of articles and reviews; poems by numerous emerging writers who later established substantial reputations appeared under Peter *Porter's poetry editorship, as did verse from leading poets who included Ted *Hughes, John *Updike, Douglas *Dunn, and John *Betjeman. Among the subjects of the interviews which were regularly featured were Michael *Frayn, Geoffrey *Hill, John *Ashbery, William *Golding, and Thom *Gunn.

QUEEN, Ellery, pseudonym of Frederic DANNAY (1905–82) and Manfred Bennington LEE (1905–71), American writers of *detective fiction featuring the author/detective Ellery Queen. The earliest stories followed the mannered 'Golden Age' style of S. S. *Van Dine, and showed the erudite amateur sleuth using intuition and intelligence to outwit the plodding forces of law and order. In the best of these, *The Roman Hat Mystery* (1929), *The Greek Coffin Mystery* (1932), *The Egyptian Cross Mystery* (1932), and *The Spanish Cape Mystery* (1935), a successful formula was evolved with all the ingredients of a puzzle laid before the reader. The stories were adapted for numerous films and a long-running radio series (1939–48). By this time the authors had turned to the short story. *Ellery Queen's Mystery Magazine* (1941–82) became an outlet for Dannay and Lee and for a host of other crime writers. Among notable later Queen novels are *Calamity Town* (1942) and the final *A Fine and Private Place* (1971).

Queer Theory, see SEDGWICK, EVE KOSOFSKY.

QUENNELL, Peter (Courtney) (1905–93), British biographer, critic, and essayist, born at Bickley, Kent, educated at Balliol College, Oxford. From 1925 to 1930 he wrote for the **Criterion* and other leading periodicals. After holding a professorship in Tokyo, which gave rise to *A Superficial Journey through Tokyo and Peking* (1932), he returned to literary journalism. He edited the **Cornhill Magazine* between 1944 and 1951, when he began *History Today*, which he co-edited until 1979. The narrative fluency and stylistic accomplishment of *Byron: The Years of Fame* (1935), *Byron in Italy* (1941), and *Caroline of England* (1939) established his reputation as a biographer. *Four Portraits* (1945), his highly regarded treatment of Sterne, Boswell, Wilkes, and Gibbon, and *Alexander Pope: The Education of Genius* (1968) are among his other biographical studies. His critical works include *Baudelaire and the Symbolists* (1929) and *The Profane Virtues* (1945), an assessment of eighteenth-century literature. Among his numerous collections of essays are *The Singular Preference* (1952) and *Casanova in London* (1971). *The Marble Foot* (1976) and *The Wanton Chase* (1980) are autobiographical.

Quiet American, The, a novel by Graham *Greene, published in 1955 and set during France's military struggle to retain Vietnam, which Greene witnessed during trips to the country as a journalist in the early 1950s. His nearly lifelong antipathy to the USA and readier sympathy for communist regimes figure in the novel's prescient warning about early American infiltration of Vietnam. This focuses on Alden Pyle, a young diplomat naïvely convinced of the validity of American foreign policy, free to draw on extensive military resources, and eventually unrepentantly responsible for horrifying civilian casualties in Saigon. Readers know from the novel's first pages that Pyle himself has been killed, but it is only gradually, in his account of earlier events, that the narrator, Thomas Fowler, reveals his complicity in this murder—a teasing unravelling which adds conviction to Greene's view that *The Quiet American* is more successful technically than *The *End of the Affair* (1951). The use of Fowler—like Greene, a seasoned foreign correspondent—also helps explain the novel's extensive reportage: its detail and restrained clarity communicate military violence with some of the hard immediacy of Ernest *Hemingway. The detachment of the reporter, however, eventually gives way, through Fowler's contact with Pyle, to a conviction that 'one must take sides'—a position complicated by Pyle's appropriation of Fowler's Annamite mistress Phuong. Although Catholicism has faded as an interest since *The End of the Affair*, apart from occasional echoes in Pyle's debates with Fowler, the ambivalence of the latter's narrative ensures that the novel remains highly complex morally. Its issues of political engagement and responsibility share repeated concerns of 1950s writing: later generations of critics interested in post-colonial literature may concentrate on Greene's vivid depiction of late colonial conflict and his use of this political struggle as a context for the examination of individuals' moral concerns.

QUILLER-COUCH, Sir Arthur (Thomas) (1863–1944), British novelist, critic, and editor, born in Bodmin, Cornwall, educated at Trinity College, Oxford, where he adopted the pseudonym 'Q' under which much of his later writing appeared. *Dead Man's Rock* (1887) was the first of his many adventure novels; others include *The Ship of Stars* (1899) and *Poison Island* (1907). His fiction was collected in the thirty volumes of *Tales and Romances* (1928–9). He became King Edward VII Professor of English Literature at Cambridge in 1912; *On the Art of Writing* (1916) and *On the Art of Reading* (1920) collect his lectures, which tend to promote his beliefs in the uncomplicated enjoyment of literature. He was chiefly responsible for the establishment in 1917 of Cambridge's honours school of English. Among his other works of criticism are the three volumes of *Studies in Literature* (1918–29). In 1921 publication of his *New Cambridge Shakespeare* began, which was eventually completed under John Dover *Wilson's editorship. His many other works of editorship include *The Oxford Book of English Verse* (1900). From the 1890s onward his home was at Fowey in Cornwall, of which he became Mayor in 1937. He was knighted in 1910, substantially as a result of his journalistic services to the Liberal Party. *Memories and Opinions* (1944) is his unfinished autobiography. See also F. Brittain's *Arthur Quiller-Couch: A Biographical Study of Q* (1947), and *Quiller-Couch, a Portrait of Q* (1988), by A. L. *Rowse.

QUIN, Ann (Marie) (1936–73), British novelist, born in Brighton. She won acclaim with her first novel, *Berg* (1964), a psychological drama set in an out-of-season seaside town where a man plots the murder of his father. *Three* (1966) is an exploration of a triangular relationship between a married couple, Ruth and Leonard, and 'S', a young girl whose death by drowning prefigures the author's own. *Passages* (1969), as experimental in tone as the earlier works, deals with the nature of identity and the relationship between reality and fantasy in its account of a woman's search for her lost brother. *Tripticks* (1972) follows its narrator/hero across America, in pursuit of his ex-wife. The work is a collage of styles and perspectives, incorporating cinematic techniques (Quin acknowledged the influence of the 'nouvelle vague' cinema on her writing) and images reminiscent of Pop Art.

QUINE, W(illard) V(an) O(rman) (1908–), American philosopher, born in Akron, Ohio, educated at Harvard, where he held a succession of appointments throughout his academic career. His doctoral studies were supervised by A. N. *Whitehead. In 1932 he visited Vienna, Warsaw, and Prague, where he began a lasting association with Rudolf *Carnap; their letters are collected in *Dear Carnap, Dear Van* (edited by R. Creath, 1990). His early publications, which established him as one of the first American exponents of logical positivism, include *A System of Logistic* (1934) and *Mathematical Logic* (1940). His eventual doubts concerning logical positivism's conceptions of meaning led to the critique formulated in 'Two Dogmas of Empiricism', an essay reprinted in *From a Logical Point of View* (1953); acknowledging a debt to Pierre Duhem (1861–1916), he rejected the grounding of logical analysis in singular terms, affirming that 'our statements about the world face the tribunal of experience not individually but as a corporate body'. His challenge to the traditional assumptions of philosophy continued in *Word and Object* (1960), which contained the theory of the 'indeterminacy of radical translation'; his view that singular concepts have no real power of signification was extended to cast doubt on the convertibility of meaning between languages. His other publications include *Ontological Relativity* (1969), *The Roots of Reference* (1974), and *The Pursuit of Truth* (1989), which sustain his lively and provocative contributions to symbolic logic and the philosophy of language. His informal autobiography *The Time of My Life* appeared in 1985.

R

RABAN, Jonathan (1942–), British travel writer, born at Fakenham in Norfolk, educated at Hull University. He lectured at University College, Aberystwyth, and the University of East Anglia from 1965 to 1969, when he became a full-time writer. His early publications include the critical essays of *The Technique of Modern Fiction* (1968) and *The Society of the Poem* (1971), his stimulating study of post-war poetry. *Soft City* (1974), an entertaining socio-cultural investigation of living in London, was followed by *Arabia through the Looking Glass* (1979), which established his reputation as an incisively original travel writer. *Old Glory: An American Voyage* (1981) is an often mordantly humorous treatment of a journey by boat down the Mississippi. Autobiographical retrospection combines with keenly observed social commentary in the account of a voyage around Britain in *Coasting* (1986). *Hunting Mister Heartbreak* (1990) describes his improvisatory itinerary through the USA in an attempt to recreate the experience of early emigrants. His other works include the novel *Foreign Land* (1985), in which an expatriate returns to England to encounter alienating change, and *For Love and Money* (1987), a record of his life as a writer which is interspersed with selections from his articles and essays. He is the editor of *The Oxford Book of the Sea* (1992).

Rabbit Tetralogy, The, a sequence of novels by John *Updike, comprising *Rabbit Run* (1960), *Rabbit Redux* (1971), *Rabbit Is Rich* (1981; Pulitzer Prize), and *Rabbit at Rest* (1990; Pulitzer Prize), which chronicles the life of Harry 'Rabbit' Angstrom from his adolescence to middle age. In *Rabbit Run*, Harry rebels against the constraints of his society and impulsively flees from his domestic responsibilities (from his wife Janice and son Nelson) to indulge his sexual feelings for the one-time prostitute Ruth Leonard. Harry rejects his dreary job, selling the MagiPeel peeler, for the countryside and a new job as a gardener. Yet he is called back to Janice when she is in labour. A calamity occurs when Janice, while drunk, accidentally drowns their daughter Rebecca while Harry is away with another woman. After much anguish about who is guilty for Rebecca's death, a new predicament emerges when Harry discovers that Ruth is pregnant. Unable to face his obligations, 'Rabbit' is on the run again: 'he runs. Ah: runs. Runs.'

Rabbit Redux is more overtly political. Set between July and October 1969, it refers to the Apollo moon shot, civil rights protests, the rise of 'alternative' culture, and Chappaquiddick, amongst other events. Now involved in the media as a linotyper, Harry lives his life by outdated rules and attempts to evade the news of Janice's adultery with the Greek salesman Stavros, but ultimately accepts their relationship. Harry meets the rich hippy Jill, who reshapes his sensual life, before she takes in a young Vietnam veteran, the black activist and fugitive Skeeter, whom Harry shelters. While this new relationship politicizes Harry's life, the neighbours become increasingly intolerant with the *ménage à trois*, and the house is burned down with Jill inside. In the fourth section, Rabbit's sister Mim arrives and organizes his reconciliation with Janice.

Rabbit Is Rich is about the 1970s, the American Dream of the 1950s and 1960s having now gone sour. At 46, Rabbit is a Toyota dealer, and happily married with Janice. A father–son tension develops with his son Nelson, now 22 and a college drop-out, who marries a secretary whom he has made pregnant, then abandons. Rabbit gradually realizes that he cannot escape to a transcendence, what he called 'it', recognizing that he is trapped in time and space. In *Rabbit at Rest*, Nelson returns to his wife and runs the car business, while Harry and Janice live in Florida. But with Nelson getting into trouble over drugs, Harry returns to rescue the car business, and in so doing revisits his old flames. Living the good life in the Reagan years, he is now suffering from heart attacks, and he eventually dies as he leaps to pitch a basketball.

RABE, David (1940–), American dramatist, born in Dubuque, Iowa, educated at Villanova University, Pennsylvania. Rabe served in Vietnam in 1965–7, an experience which informs much of his early drama. A controversial trilogy of plays about Vietnam established his reputation—*The Basic Training of Pavlo Hummel* (1971), *Sticks and Bones* (1971), and *Streamers* (1976). His other plays include *The Chameleon* (1959), *The Orphan* (1973), *Boom Boom Room* (1973), *Goose and Tomtom* (1982), and *Hurlyburly* (1984). Like Sam *Shepard and David *Mamet, Rabe is equally drawn to screenwriting, and wrote the screenplay for Robert Altman's 1983 film version of *Streamers*. His career in the 1970s forms part of the history of the New York Shakespeare Festival/Public Theatre, founded by Joseph Papp in 1954, who staged five of Rabe's plays, and did much to enhance Rabe's reception in a series of brilliant productions. Rabe's native pessimism was deepened by his Vietnam experiences which he turned to rich account in his use of the military scenario as expressive of the nihilism at the heart of most human endeavour. His more recent works include the screenplay *Casualties of War* (1989), about Vietnam; and the plays *Those the River Keeps* (1991) and *Crossing Guard* (1995). See also VIETNAM WRITING.

Ragged Trousered Philanthropists, The, a novel by Robert *Tressell, published in 1914. 'I have invented nothing. There are no scenes or incidents in the story that I have not witnessed either myself or had conclusive evidence of', said Tressell of his pioneering novel, and the great strength of the work is its authentic portrayal of Edwardian society and its insights into the misery and extortion which formed the backbone of this great British age. The novel concerns the working lives of a group of painters and decorators, and their gradual realization that it is not so much their employers and social betters who cause their poverty and poor working conditions, but the system itself. The guiding metaphor of the novel is the decoration of Mayor Sweater's house, for which paint is watered, work skimped, and wages cut, to allow for the owner's profits. Only the Moorish Room is properly prepared and painted by Frank Owen, a signwriter and socialist, whose painstaking work suggests the pleasure to be gained from labour well done and properly rewarded. Despite its didactic tone, the novel is genuinely funny and deeply moving. The book became a popular success after the First World War, and has been frequently dramatized.

Ragtime, see DOCTOROW, E. L.

RAHV, Philip (1908–73), American literary critic and editor, born in Kupin, Ukraine, educated at Brown University. He migrated to the USA in 1922 and within little more than a decade had made an important contribution to American culture: his founding, with William Phillips, in 1934 of the **Partisan Review*, the most distinguished journal of radical thought in contemporary American letters. When he resigned from the journal in 1969 a chapter in the history of the American left effectively came to an end. Rahv was strongly influenced by many of the key figures of European *modernism, notably T. S. *Eliot, James *Joyce, Franz Kafka, and D. H. *Lawrence, and his literary criticism reflects his heterogeneous intellectual alliance of the Old World with the New, particularly in his edition *Discovery of Europe: The Story of American Experience in the Old World* (1947), and in *The Myth of the Powerhouse* (1965), a collection of essays on European and American writers. His collection of essays *Image and Idea* (1949) includes 'Paleface and Redskin', an influential article in which he argues that American literature is characterized by a competition between Western 'redskin' writers—for example, Mark Twain—and Eastern 'palefaces', amongst whom he would number Henry *James, whose American critical reputation he had helped establish with his edition of *The Great Short Novels of Henry James* (1944). His other important works include *Literature in America* (1957) and *Literature and the Sixth Sense* (1969), a volume of collected essays. Rahv was for much of his adult life a Professor of English at Brandeis University. His formative role in the development of the intellectual left in the USA is assessed in James B. Gilbert, *Writers and Partisans: A History of Literary Radicalism in America* (1968).

Rainbow, The, a novel by D. H. *Lawrence, published in 1915. Begun in early 1913, *The Rainbow* had a tormented compositional and publishing history and was suppressed by Court Order on grounds of obscenity. It is now regarded, with **Sons and Lovers* and **Women in Love*, as amongst his best work. The novel is written to a classic generic pattern—the three-generation family saga—and there is evidence that Lawrence initially thought of it as a pot-boiler. It is, by his standards, complexly plotted and tells the overlapping stories of the Brangwen family beginning on the Nottinghamshire family farm. The first part deals with Tom Brangwen's marriage to Lydia Lensky, a Polish exile. The second recounts the relationship of Will Brangwen, Tom's nephew and a craftsman carpenter, with Anna, Lydia's daughter by her first marriage. The final and longest part concerns Will and Anna's daughter Ursula and takes her from girlhood through the beginnings of a vividly described career in teaching and her early relationships, including a lesbian affair. The novel ends with Ursula looking positively to the future after a miscarriage and the break up of her engagement to Anton Skrebensky, an upright army officer. Originally the novel was to have taken the story further but Lawrence split the material in 1915 and Ursula's story is continued in *Women in Love*. *The Rainbow* deals with the arrival of the modern world. It starts on the land in the late nineteenth century and moves, through the experiences of an artisan craftsman, to the situation of a modern woman working in an urban school. Throughout Lawrence is interested in the tension between the traditional and the new. But the novel is also notable for its controversial descriptions of sexuality and individual scenes of extraordinary power which are typical of Lawrence's best work. The novel is stylistically highly original with a resonant, symbolic style which would reflect Lawrence's developing concern with unconscious physical and psychological forces.

RAINE, Craig (Anthony) (1944–), British poet, born in Bishop Auckland, County Durham, educated at Exeter College, Oxford. After lecturing at various Oxford colleges from 1971 to 1979, he held a succession of editorial posts in London before returning to Oxford as a fellow of New College in 1991. *The Onion Memory* (1978), his first collection of poems, rapidly established his reputation as an imaginatively inventive stylist. His characteristic device of basing images and metaphors on improbable but surprisingly accurate correspondences culminated in the bravura performance of the title poem of his second volume, *A Martian Sends a Postcard Home* (1979), which earned him recognition as progenitor of the *Martian school of poetry. *Rich* (1984), while continuing to display a rewarding fascination with the possibilities of imagery, suggests a growing assurance in the handling of emotional experience. His idiosyncratic sense of humour is also encountered more frequently. The collection contains 'A Silver Plate', a prose memoir of childhood, which is in part a mutedly affectionate portrayal of his father. *The Electrification of the Soviet Union* (1986), a poetic drama commissioned by Glyndebourne as a libretto for music by Nigel Osborne, is an adaptation of Pasternak's novella *The Last Summer*; the work is the fullest demonstration of Raine's accomplishment in the use of conventional verse forms. His other works include *1953* (1990), a version of Racine's *Andromache*; and *Haydn and the Valve Trumpet* (1990), a substantial collection of his critical writings. *History: The Home Movie* (1994) is a novel-sized poem of twentieth-century history (the histories of his and his wife's families, the Raines and the Pasternaks).

RAINE, Kathleen (Jessie) (1908–), British poet and critic, born in London; much of her childhood was spent in Northumberland. She was educated at Girton College, Cambridge, where she became a research fellow in 1955. She was the first wife of the poet and sociologist Charles *Madge. Her poems were featured in **Poetry London*, which published her first collection entitled *Stone and Flower*, illustrated by Barbara Hepworth, in 1943. Numerous later volumes of her verse have included *The Pythoness* (1949), *The Year One* (1952), *The Hollow Hill* (1965), and *The Oracle in the Heart* (1980). *Collected Poems* (1981) was followed by a new selected edition in 1988. Raine's early poetry was marked by the lyrical effectiveness and precision of its botanical and geological imagery. A neoplatonic mysticism pervades much of her work and provides a basis for her outspoken denunciations of modern *cultural materialism. In many poems, notably those concerned with her sense of exile from her Northumbrian landscapes of childhood, visionary elements are held in balance with attractively particularized local observation. Among her extensive critical writings, which exhibit a sustained concern with her quasi-religious view of poetry, are *Blake and Tradition* (1969, 2 volumes), an exhaustive analysis of Blake's symbolism, and the collections of essays *Defending Ancient Springs* (1967) and *The Inner Journey of the Poet* (1976). *Farewell Happy Fields* (1973), *The Land Unknown* (1975), and *The Lion's Mouth* (1977) are autobiographical.

Raj Quartet, The, four novels by Paul *Scott, published between 1966 and 1974. Set between 1939 and 1947, these inter-connected novels gradually bring to light the corruption and bigotry within the Anglo-Indian community, and trace the roots of the violence following on the British departure and the Partition of India. The books share a complex narrative structure which incorporates letters, conversations, reports, and memories, presenting the same events from different, and conflicting, viewpoints. The first two novels—*The Jewel in the Crown* (1966) and *The Day of the Scorpion* (1968)—centre on two main events: the attack on Miss Crane, an elderly school supervisor, and, in the Bibighar Gardens at Mayapore, the multiple rape by Indians of an English girl, Daphne Manners. Characters and scenes from the first novel are seen in a harsher, less edifying light in the second, particularly the imprisonment of the English-educated Hari Kumar by the sadistic police superintendent, Ronald Merrick. *The Towers of Silence* (1972), set in the hill station of Pankot, covers a similar period, but introduces new characters, notably Barbara Batchelor, a retired missionary teacher, who suffers the insults and snobbery of the class-conscious British wives. The lengthy final novel, *A Division of the Spoils* (1974), concentrates on the two years leading up to Partition. Through several interwoven stories, and the fresh eyes of Guy Peron, it views both the tragic and comic elements of Britain's ignominious retreat and the ensuing explosion of violence between Muslim and Hindu.

RAKOSI, Carl (1903–), American poet, born in Berlin; in 1910 he emigrated to the USA, where he was educated at the Universities of Wisconsin, Chicago, and Texas. In 1932 he began a career in social work and was Director of the Jewish Family and Children's Service in Minneapolis from 1945 to 1968. He has held numerous posts as a writer-in-residence. Rakosi was eminent among the *Objectivist poets and was represented in the 'Objectivists' special issue of *Poetry* (1931) and *An 'Objectivists' Anthology* (1932), both edited by Louis *Zukofsky. His early verse made highly selective and economical use of concrete detail to imply his underlying social concerns, in which he was immersed to an extent that curtailed his activities as a poet between 1941, when his *Selected Poems* appeared, and 1965. He has subsequently produced numerous collections, including *Amulet* (1967), *Ex Cranium, Night* (1975), *History* (1981), *Meditation* (1985), and *Collected Poems* (1986). Rakosi's later verse is noted for the mobility with which it covers a remarkable range of intellectual and perceptual registers; an equivalent flexibility of tone characteristically succeeds in uniting an essential seriousness with his idiosyncratic wit. Among his other works is the *Collected Prose* of 1984.

RAMANUJAN, A(ttinat) K(rishnaswami) (1929–93), Indian poet, born in Mysore, educated there and at Indiana University. Long resident in the USA, he was appointed Professor of Linguistics and of South East Asian Languages and Civilization at the University of Chicago. More austere in style than fellow 'Indo-Anglian' poets like Dom *Moraes and Nissim *Ezekiel, his poems are particularly notable for applying Indian sensibilities to American culture. 'Death and the Good Citizen', a powerful and uncompromising poem, for instance, starkly contrasts Indian and American attitudes to death. He has written of his cultural background: 'English and my disciplines give me my "outer" forms—linguistic, metrical, logical and other such ways of shaping experience; and my first thirty years in India, Tamil, and the classics and folklore give me my substance, my "inner" forms, images and symbols.' He has also translated much from Kannada, including devotional lyrics rendered as *Speaking of Siva* (1972), and from Tamil and Malayalam. His poetry collections in English include *The Striders* (1966), *Relations* (1971), *Selected Poems* (1976), and *Second Sight* (1986).

RAND, Ayn (1905–82), American novelist, essayist, and pamphleteer, born in St Petersburg, Russia, educated at the University of Petrograd; she emigrated to America shortly afterwards. Her first novel, *We the Living* (1936), was the melodramatic account of a woman's emotional involvement with two men, one communist, one not; it was largely dismissed by the critics, as was *Anthem* (1938), a futuristic fantasy. A self-styled philosopher who attempted, through her fiction, to theorize her belief in the supremacy of rationalism, individualism, and entrepreneurial capitalism, Rand built her reputation on the enormous popular success of her novels *The Fountainhead* (1943) and *Atlas Shrugged* (1957). Her works appealed to the imagination not only of a mass readership but of a group of intellectuals who detected in her narratives the seeds of a right-wing ideology of monetarism and hegemony. After 1957 she abandoned fiction in pursuit of a quasi-academic career. As well as publishing books such as *For the New Intellectual* (1961), which collects some of her essays, *The Virtue of Selfishness* (1965), and *The Romantic Manifesto* (1969), she promoted her theories, now labelled Objectivism, in a series of tracts, pamphlets, articles, and journals. There is a biography, *The Passion of Ayn Rand* (1986), by Barbara Branden; a novel by Mary *Gaitskill, *Two Girls, Fat and Thin* (1991), skilfully satirizes her theories and considerable influence.

RANSOM, John Crowe (1888–1974), American poet and critic, born in Pulaski, Tennessee, educated at Vanderbilt University, Nashville, and at Christ Church, Oxford. He taught at Vanderbilt from 1914 to 1937, when he was appointed Carnegie Professor of Poetry at Kenyon College and began the **Kenyon Review*. *Poems about God* (1919), his first collection of verse, has much in common with the distinctively ironic manner of his subsequent poetry, which Randall *Jarrell described as 'detached, mock-pedantic, wittily complicated'. He did not include any poems from the volume in the selected editions of his work, regarding *Chills and Fever* (1924) and *Two Gentlemen in Bonds* (1927) as his principal collections. His poetry is remarkable for its almost unremitting concern with man's divided nature; tensions between the intellectual and instinctual faculties, the 'two gentleman' in the title of his 1927 volume, and the paradoxical inseparability of life and death are recurrent themes. *Selected Poems* of 1945 was revised in 1963 and 1969. He was a founding editor of the *Fugitive* (1922–5), a Nashville journal notable for the standards of its poetry and criticism. Its contributors included Allen *Tate, Robert Penn *Warren, and Laura *Riding. The concern with the literary identity of the Southern states shared by the *Fugitive* group culminated in the emergence of the *Agrarian movement; Ransom contributed the 'Statement of Principles' to *I'll Take My Stand* (1930), the Agrarian manifesto, which declared their commitment to a unified regional culture. His ideas are expanded in the defences of art, myth, and ritual against the ascendancy of scientific technology, which he dismissed as a mode of interpreting human experience, in *God without Thunder* (1930) and *The World's Body* (1938). As a critic he exercised wide influence with *The *New Criticism* (1941), in which he argued for methods of literary analysis adequate to the imaginative, philosophical, and emotional complexes embodied in poetry. Among his other critical works are *Poetics* (1942) and the essays of *Beating the Bushes* (1972). T. D. Young's *Gentleman in a Dustcoat* (1976) is a biography of Ransom.

RANSOME, Arthur (Michell) (1884–1967), British writer, journalist, and illustrator, born in Leeds, educated at Rugby. He rose from office boy for the publisher Grant Richards to reporter for the *Daily News* and the *Manchester Guardian*. In 1913 he visited Russia and later returned to report the Revolution for the *Daily News*. His interest in Russia resulted in *Old Peter's Russian Tales* (1916), a collection of legends and fairy tales, and *Racundra's First Cruise* (1923), which describes his exploration of the Baltic by boat. *Missie Lee* (1941) draws on Ransome's knowledge of China gained during extensive travel in the 1920s. *Swallows and Amazons* (1930) was the first of his twelve children's stories which recount the adventures of the Walker family (the Swallows) and the Blackett family (the Amazons) and their friends. Set mainly in the Lake District and Norfolk, and vividly evoking Ransome's love of country pastimes and sailing, the novels include *Pigeon Pie* (1936), *We Didn't Mean To Go to Sea* (1938), *The Big Six* (1940), and *Great Northern?* (1947). His other books include *Mainly about Fishing* (1959) and *The Autobiography of Arthur Ransome* (edited by R. Hart-Davis, 1976).

RAO, Raja (1909–), Indian novelist, born in Hassan, Karnataka, educated in Hyderabad and Aligarh, before attending the universities of Montpellier and the Sorbonne in France. In 1965 he became a Professor of Philosophy at the University of Austin, Texas. Rao's first novel, *Kanthapura* (1938), foregrounded the Gandhian struggle for national independence, but is remarkable for its narrative voice—a village grandmother—and its reworking of the English idiom in a lyrical Indian mode. In its interweaving of myth and legend with politicized realism, the novel foreshadows the *magical realist trend evident in the work of later Indian novelists. Rao's best-known novel, *The Serpent and the Rope* (1960), an account of the disintegration of a marriage, allows its narrator, an intellectual Brahmin whose wife is French, to reflect not only on the polarities between Hindu and Western attitudes but on philosophy, religion, history, and literature. Later novels include *The Cat and Shakespeare* (1965), a metaphysical treatise lightly disguised as fiction, and *Comrade Kirilov* (1976), which parodies the Marxist pretensions of a Westernized advocate of Indian national independence; both novels are characterized by their brevity and satirical tone. The range of his fictional concerns is also effectively displayed in his short stories collected in *The Cow of the Barricades* (1947), *The Policeman and the Rose* (1978), and *On the Ganga Ghat* (1989).

RAPHAEL, Frederic (Michael) (1931–), American novelist, born in Chicago, educated St John's College, Cambridge; he has lived chiefly in England as a full-time writer. His early novels include *The Limits of Love* (1960) and *A Wild Surmise* (1961), which display the moral and psychological concern with relations between the individual and a larger community that pervades his writing. *The Trouble with England* (1962) and *The Graduate Wife* (1962) are understated satires ironically invoking British middle-class values. *Lindmann* (1963) won widespread acclaim for its narrative of a British civil servant seeking to atone for his treatment of Jewish refugees during the Second World War. Individuals constrained by moral dilemmas inherent in their social and cultural circumstances feature prominently in his work of the 1970s, which includes *Like Men Betrayed* (1970) and *California Time* (1975), the latter reflecting his familiarity with the motion picture industry; his screenplays include *Darling* (1965) and *Far from the Madding Crowd* (1967). Among his subsequent novels are *Richard's Things* (1973), an elegiac study of transience and loss; *The Glittering Prizes* (1976), tracing the fortunes of a group of Cambridge graduates, which was successfully serialized for television; and *A Double Life* (1993), a psychologically acute account of a retired French diplomat taking stock of his life. Other novels by Raphael include *The Earlsdon Way* (1958), *Orchestra and Beginners* (1967), *Heaven and Earth* (1985) and *Old Scores* (1995). *Sleeps Six* (1979) and *The Latin Lover* (1994) are collections of short stories. Notable among his numerous works as a translator is *Aeschylus* (1991), the two-volume edition of the plays he produced with Kenneth McLeish.

Rates of Exchange, see BRADBURY, MALCOLM.

RATTIGAN, Sir Terence (1911–77), British dramatist, born in London, the son of a diplomat, educated at Trinity College, Oxford. From the age of 25 he was one of England's commercially most successful playwrights. *French without Tears* (1936), a comedy set in a language school, was followed by plays both serious and humorous: among them, *Flare Path* (1942), a tribute to the RAF at war; *The *Winslow Boy* (1946), about a father's battle to clear his naval-cadet son of allegations of theft; *The *Browning Version* (1948), a sympathetic study of an unpopular schoolmaster; dramatic biographies of (respectively) Alexander the Great, T. E. *Lawrence, and Lady Hamilton, *Adventure Story* (1949), *Ross* (1960), and *A Bequest to the Nation* (1970); *The Deep Blue Sea* (1952), whose protagonist is a judge's wife unhappily in love with a pilot; the Ruritanian frolic *A Sleeping Prince* (1953); *Separate Tables* (1954), two short plays set in a hotel, the better of which involves a phoney 'major' accused of indecency in a cinema; *In Praise of Love* (1973), in which a writer keeps from his wife the news that she is dying, by maintaining a pose of ill humour; and *Cause Célèbre* (1977), about Alma Rattenbury, who scandalized the nation when her youthful lover murdered her elderly husband. Rattigan said he aimed his work at an archetypal middle-brow theatregoer he called Aunt Edna, a claim that helped to damage his reputation in the 1950s and 1960s, the period of the *Angry Young Men and the *Kitchen Sink Drama. However, in later years it became increasingly recognized that, despite his traditionalism of form and accessibility of content, he had a distinctive and original voice, characterized by a sympathy for the victims both of their own overpowering feelings and of the disapproval of conventional society.

RAVEN, Simon (Arthur Noel) (1927–), British novelist, born in London, educated at Charterhouse and at King's College, Cambridge. After a career as an officer in the British Army, Raven began his successful literary career with *The Feathers of Death* (1959), a novel about homosexuality in the army. A sequence of ten linked novels, 'Alms for Oblivion' (1964–75), which includes *Friends in Low Places* (1965), *The Judas Boy* (1968), and *Sound the Retreat* (1971), humorously portray the outrageous behaviour of upper-class British society and also reveal an underlying concern with the decline of British power and influence. A second sequence of novels, 'The First Born of Egypt', including *Morning Star* (1984), *The Face of the Waters* (1985), *Before the Cock Crows* (1986), and *The Troubadour* (1992), confirmed his reputation as a writer of sardonic comedy. Embellished with exotic setting, scandal, and sex, Raven's novels also deal with traditional subjects like cricket and public schools. His adaptations for television include novels by Aldous *Huxley, Iris *Murdoch, Nancy *Mitford and, notably, Trollope whose *Palliser* novels he dramatized in 1974. Among his non-fiction works are *The English Gentleman* (1961; US title *The Decline of the Gentleman*, 1962), *Shadows on the Grass* (1982), and the memoirs *The Old School* (1986) and *Bird of Ill-Omen* (1989).

RAWLS, John (Bordley) (1921–), American philosopher and political theorist, born in Baltimore, educated at Princeton and Cornell Universities. Following military service during the Second World War, he began his academic career; in 1960 he became a professor at Harvard, where he was made James Bryant Conant University Professor in 1979. 'Justice as Fairness' (1958) and 'Legal Obligation and the Duty of Fair Play' (1964) were among the articles preceding the publication of his *A Theory of Justice* (1971), which gained him pre-eminence among political philosophers of the day. Rawls bases his concepts of political values on individual rights, stating that members of a society should enjoy 'the most extensive basic liberty compatible with a similar liberty for others'; his 'difference principle' requires that economic inequalities should be arranged in a manner permitting the greatest possible benefits to accrue to the least advantaged. His argument for the rational necessity of social equality entails a persuasive critique of utilitarian views of justice. *A Theory of Justice* provoked a general reassessment of political philosophy; Rawls's most notable opponent is Robert *Nozick, whose *Anarchy, State and Utopia* (1974) framed a 'radical libertarian' argument defending the individual's rights of acquisition.

RAWORTH, Tom (Thomas Moore) (1938–), British poet, born in Bexleyheath, Kent, educated at the University of Essex, and the University of Granada, Spain. Since 1969 he has worked as a writer-in-residence at numerous universities in the UK and the USA. He founded the Matrix and Goliard Presses in 1959 and 1965 respectively (see SMALL PRESSES). From the outset, his poetry displayed a striking independence of both conventional verse forms and existing experimental techniques. His early volumes, which include *Weapon Man* (1965) and *The Relation Ship* (1966), contained numerous disquieting and occasionally quasi-surreal studies of disregarded aspects of domestic routine; subsequent collections include *Ace* (1974), *Sky Tails* (1978), *Tottering State* (1983; revised 1987), *Lazy Left Hand* (1986), and *Catacoustics* (1991). Much of Raworth's best-known poetry achieves a cinematic quality through rapid accumulations of imagery recreating shifts of mood and perception. His other works include *A Serial Biography* (1969), which arose from his extensive correspondence with Ed *Dorn.

RAYMOND, Ernest (1888–1974), British novelist, essayist, and biographer, born in France, educated at Chichester Theological College; he was ordained into the Anglican Church in 1914 and resigned in 1923. His first and most popular novel, *Tell England* (1922), was based upon his experiences in the First World War, when he served as a clergyman. His long series of novels, entitled *A London Gallery*, dealt frequently with a search for personal faith. This topic perhaps drew him to the Brontës, Keats, and Shelley, writers on whom he wrote popular biographies. His own autobiographical volumes, *The Story of My Days* (1968), *Please You, Draw Near* (1969), and *Good Morning, Good People* (1970), are a useful insight into the values of mid-twentieth-century England and explain why Raymond's novels, which were once so fashionable, are now so dated.

Razor's Edge, The, a novel by W. Somerset *Maugham, published in 1944. This was the first work in which the narrative voice is identified as Maugham's by name. Written after much painstaking research into Eastern philosophy and mysticism, *The Razor's Edge* is Maugham's twentieth-century manifesto for human fulfilment. In it he mercilessly satirizes American and European materialism, and holds up the figure of the spiritual seeker as a model for those searching for meaning in existence. Maugham's serious observations on the nature of being are complemented with a brilliantly realized portrait of Paris in the 1920s, and a gallery of closely observed characters who in their various ways point up the vacuity of the social values of the time. The finest of these are Elliot Templeton, an American *arriviste* who devotes himself to social niceties with religious fervour, and his niece Isabel Maturin, whose desire for material wealth blinds her to the possibilities of a different and deeper kind of happiness. These are affectionate portrayals, and Maugham's narrative voice is at its most warmly urbane as it wanders through the drawing-rooms and bohemian cafés of Paris. The character of Larry Darrell is less convincing, but the skilful unfolding of his mysterious quest makes his spiritual journey compelling, if not inspirational.

READ, Sir Herbert (Edward) (1893–1968), British poet and critic, born in Kirbymoorside, Yorkshire, educated at the University of Leeds. His experiences on active service during the First World War are reflected in the prose works *In Retreat* (1925) and *Ambush* (1930) and in the verse collected in *Songs of Chaos* (1915) and *Naked Warriors* (1919). He became an Assistant Keeper at the Victoria and Albert Museum in 1922. His subsequent works as a poet include *The End of a War* (1933) and *Moon's Farm* (1955). The influences of T. E. *Hulme, whose essays Read edited in *Speculations* (1924), and of *Imagism are apparent in the economically precise imagery of his verse. *Collected Poems* appeared in 1966. A close associate of T. S. *Eliot's, Read's work for the **Criterion* established him as a critic of note; his advocacy of *Modernism in literature and art stressed the need for effective mediation between tradition and innovation. Among his principal works of literary criticism are *Reason and Romanticism* (1926) and *The Literature of Sincerity* (1968). He was best known for his many influential works of socially oriented art criticism, which include *Art and Industry* (1934) and *Education through Art* (1947). With Roland Penrose, he founded the Institute of Contemporary Arts in 1947. His novel *The Green Child* (1935) allegorizes his aesthetic philosophy. *The Innocent Eye* (1933) and *The Contrary Experience* (1963) are autobiographical.

READ, Piers Paul (1941–), British novelist, born in Beaconsfield, Buckinghamshire, educated at St John's College, Cambridge; the son of Sir Herbert *Read. His first novel, *A Game in Heaven with Tussey Marx* (1966), was followed by *The Junkers* (1969), a study of Nazism and the Holocaust. Political and moral preoccupations predominate in Read's novels, notable among which are *The Professor's Daughter* (1971), *The Upstart* (1973), *The Villa Golitsyn* (1982), and *A Patriot in Berlin* (1995). The influence of Graham *Greene is discernible, as demonstrated in *Monk Dawson* (1970), in which the eponymous protagonist turns his back on a hostile, decadent, and materialistic society to seek refuge in ascetism. His settings are wide in range: *The Free Frenchman* (1986) employs the backdrop of the Second World War; in *A Season in the West* (1989), Western capitalistic decadence is contrasted with the Eastern European communist ethos through the eyes of a dissident Czechoslovakian intellectual; *On the Third Day* (1991) conflates politics, Christian historical speculations, and the Arab–Israeli conflict. Read's non-fiction reflects the concerns of his novels; *Alive! The Story of the Andes Survivors* (1974) chronicles the now legendary case of survivors of a plane crash who were forced to resort to cannibalism when stranded in the wilderness.

Reader-Response Theory. This approach to criticism derives from *Hermeneutics, a discipline which places at its centre the practice of interpretation rather than particular results. In such a perspective, the reader of a literary text, so long ignored or taken for granted, makes a dramatic reappearance as the focus of meaning, the site of the construction of significance, if not always the actual constructor. Hans Robert Jauss developed what he called an 'aesthetics of reception', and Wolfgang Iser, in a book entitled *Der Implizite Leser* (1972), explored the concept of the implied or implicit reader, that is, the reader called for by a specific text, a reader we may recognize without wishing, or being able, to identify entirely as ourselves. For Stanley *Fish, in *The Self-Consuming Artifact* (1972) and *Is There a Text in this Class?* (1980), the very mistakes we make as readers are an integral part of the reading process, and indeed the notion of a 'mistake' is problematic for him. Fish's answer to the apparent suggestion of anarchy in his approach is the concept of the 'interpretive community': we agree (or we can discuss) an interpretation, or different ages and cultures have agreed or discussed interpretations, not because we have settled on a permanent truth of the text but because we speak the same language, because we are able to make our interpretations intelligible to those who share our idiom. Literary history therefore is the story not of progress and correction but of changing communities and sets of assumptions. For Roland Barthes, the death of the Author (the title of a well-known essay of 1968) was to be the price of the birth of the reader; but it is important to note that his Author is capitalized, a tyrannical old literary deity to be dethroned, not a mere writer, and that the reader has a small r and is (implicitly) plural, a liberated but not irresponsible collaborator with the text's proposals.

READING, Peter (1946–), British poet, born in Liverpool, educated at the Liverpool College of Art, where he lectured from 1968 to 1970. He then moved to Shropshire and worked as a weighbridge operator at an agricultural feed mill before becoming a freelance writer. His first substantial collection of poetry was *For the Municipality's Elderly* (1974), which established his enduring concern with lives overlooked by the social consensus. His subsequent collections, which include *Tom O' Bedlam's Beauties* (1981), *Ukelele Music* (1985), *Stet* (1986), and *Final Demands* (1988), gained him wide notice as a highly individual poet whose work makes use of innovative and sometimes startlingly arbitrary forms. *Essential Reading* (1986) is a selected edition compiled by Alan *Jenkins, who characterizes the poetry as 'mordant and elegiac, hilarious and heartbreaking'. The humour in his work frequently results from his use of found materials suggesting the inherently absurd aspects of modern society. His reporting of overheard conversations rich in malapropisms and highly eccentric attitudes also achieves remarkable effects. *Perduta Gente* (1989) is a harrowingly factual account of London's terminally dispossessed tramps and dossers. His verse has engendered controversy over the value of its unrelenting disgust at the violence, vacuous materialism, political dishonesty, and ignorance he perceives in contemporary life. In response to critics who find his poetry repellent, he has denounced what he sees as a poetic orthodoxy of soporific aestheticism and is noted for the sometimes scathing rigour of his work as a critic. His recent collections include *Evagatory* (1992), *Last Poems* (1994), and *Collected Poems 1: 1970–1984* (1995).

Realism is a word with many meanings and uses, in philosophy, history of art, literary criticism, and ordinary language. In literature it is most often used to describe the great achievements of the European novel in the nineteenth century: the work of, for instance, Balzac, Tolstoy, and George Eliot. This writing characteristically depicts a large and complex social world from the point of view of a shared sanity. Author, reader, and characters inhabit the same implied universe, what Raymond *Williams calls a knowable community. The heroes and heroines of realist novels are often idealists rather than realists themselves, but they are disappointed in their hopes, if not actually destroyed, and learn to come to terms with the limits of historical possibility. Realism in fiction is thus related to the ambition of nineteenth-century (and other) historians to describe things 'as they really are'—a laudable but problematic programme—and to the philosophical concept of the way things 'usually' look, on an ordinary day to ordinary eyes in ordinary lighting. When the notion of the ordinary becomes questionable, when the world we live in no longer seems knowable, or discussable in terms that can count on being understood, realism in this sense is usually abandoned for another mode. Grandly proclaiming that Dostoevsky was not a novelist, the critic Georg Lukács meant, among other things, that Dostoevsky had begun to leave the shared world of realism behind. In nineteenth-century painting realism refers to the work of Courbet and others, and reflects a new interest in ordinary life and in working people, a reaction against the grandiose historical subjects which had dominated earlier art. Inherent in all forms of realism is the idea of a corrected view or assumption, a response to an exaggerated romanticism, idealism, or sentimentalization.

Realism, even in vague and everyday uses, is always an argument, suggesting that some form of unreality is in the ascendancy and needs combatting. Whenever we hear it we need to ask, as the philosopher J. L. *Austin suggests, which particular lack of reality is being attacked or remedied.

REANEY, James (Crerar) (1926–), Canadian poet and playwright, born in Ontario, educated at the University of Toronto. He worked under Northrop *Frye for his doctorate, and shares his interest in the mythic dimension of poetry. From 1960 to 1971 he edited the magazine *Alphabet*, dedicated to the 'iconography of the imagination', and has retained a commitment to experimentation. His early poetry demonstrated a formidable range of both subject matter and technique, from dark satire to contemporary pastoral. *The Red Heart* (1949) was his highly acclaimed first volume of poetry; *A Suit of Nettles* (1959) employed a Spenserian mode, while *Twelve Letters to a Small Town* (1962) struck a tranquil note. *Collected Poems* appeared in 1973, and *Selected Longer Poems* in 1976. His best-known early play is *The Killdeer*, performed in 1960 (published in *The Killdeer and Other Plays*, 1962). Drama became Reaney's chief interest, and he achieved acclaim with his trilogy *The Donnellys* (produced 1973–5), published individually as *Sticks and Stones* (1975), *The St Nicholas Hotel* (1976), and *Handcuffs* (1977), and as a trilogy in 1988. These plays recreate the events of an 1880s murder in Ontario, and its repercussions over a 36-year period. *Wacousta!* (1979) and *The Canadian Brothers* (1984) were both melodramas based on early nineteenth-century works by Major John Richardson. A libretto for a murder mystery opera, *Crazy to Kill*, was published in 1989.

RECHY, John (Francisco) (1934–), American novelist, born in El Paso, Texas, educated at Texas Western College and the New School for Social Research, New York. His first novel, *City of Night* (1963), was a celebrated exploration of a homosexual underworld and the rootlessness of big city life. Its narrator moves from El Paso to Chicago, New York, and Los Angeles, encountering gay prostitution and drug-taking in bars and cheap hotels, describing hustlers, drag queens, and the police in a tone between sympathy and detachment. The book's subject matter attracted controversy, and praise, at a time of legal action surrounding William Burroughs's *The *Naked Lunch* and the first US publication of works by Jean Genet and Henry *Miller; it was followed by a sequel, *Numbers* (1967). Rechy's creation of an alternative gay world in opposition to the representatives of 'straight' society and moral order recalls Genet, especially the fascination with ambiguities of eros, criminality, and violence. His subsequent novels include *This Day's Death* (1970), *The Fourth Angel* (1973), *Rushes* (1979), *Bodies and Souls* (1983), and *Marilyn's Daughter* (1988). He is the author of two plays based on his novels, and *The Sexual Outlaw* (1977), a documentary account of urban homosexual lifestyles. His tenth book, *The Miraculous Day of Amalia Gomez*, appeared in 1991.

Rector's Daughter, The, see MAYOR, F. M.

REDGROVE, Peter (William) (1932–), British poet and novelist, born in Kingston, Surrey; he read Natural Sciences at Queens' College, Cambridge and subsequently worked as a scientific journalist. He was a founding member of the *Group in 1956. After holding visiting posts at the University of New York and the University of Leeds from 1961 to 1965, he became poet-in-residence at Falmouth School of Art. He married Penelope *Shuttle in 1980; among the works they have written in collaboration are *The Wise Wound* (1978), a study of the psychology of menstruation; *Alchemy for Women* (1995); and *The Terrors of Dr Treviles* (1974), a novel whose elements of fantasy and occultism are equally characteristic of Redgrove's prose fictions, which include *In the Country of the Skin* (1973) and *The Beekeepers* (1980). His first collection of poetry, *The Collector* (1960), was followed by numerous volumes, notably *The Force* (1966), *Dr Faust's Sea-Spiral Spirit* (1972), *The Weddings at Nether Powers* (1979), and *Dressed as for a Tarot Pack* (1990). *The Moon Disposes: Poems 1954–1987* appeared in 1987. His earlier work contained numerous treatments of domestic themes which identified tensions between the rational surfaces of events and latent senses of fear and wonderment. Disquieting dramatic monologues achieved prominence in *The Force*, anticipating his subsequent preoccupation with mystical and magical themes. His poetry is notable for its imaginatively flamboyant imagery and disciplined technical originality. Recent collections of poems include *Under the Reservoir* (1992) and *My Father's Trapdoors* (1994). Selected short stories appeared in *The Cyclopean Mistress* (1993).

Redundancy of Courage, The, see MO, TIMOTHY.

REED, Henry (1914–86), British poet and radio dramatist, born in Birmingham, educated at Birmingham University. After periods as a teacher and a journalist, he worked in the Foreign Office and Naval Intelligence during the Second World War and began his prolific career as a writer for radio in 1945. Five of his many verse-dramas are collected in *The Streets of Pompeii and Other Plays* (1971); selections from his humorous prose writings for radio are contained in *Hilda Tablet and Other Plays* (1971). His reputation as poet is based on *A Map of Verona* (1946), the only substantial collection published in his lifetime, which consistently displays his exceptional originality and accomplishment. He is best known for the remarkable sequence consisting of 'Naming of Parts', 'Judging Distances', and 'Unarmed Combat'; among the most frequently anthologized poems of the Second World War, they exemplify Reed's keenly developed and purposeful sense of the absurd. *A Map of Verona* also features 'Chard Whitlow', his celebrated parody of T. S. Eliot's manner in **Four Quartets*. *Collected Poems* (1991), edited by Jon *Stallworthy, contains much previously unpublished work. Other works by Reed include the critical study *The Novel since 1939* (1948).

REED, Ishmael (Scott) (1938–), American novelist and poet, born in Chattanooga, Tennessee, educated at the University of Buffalo. Highly innovative and experimental, Reed's novels weave American myths and legends into a playful pattern of parody which satirizes many aspects of contemporary America, and radically re-evaluates its past. His first novel, *The Free-Lance Pallbearers* (1967), parodies early African-American autobiographical narratives in order to set up a confrontation between its folk hero, HARRY SAM, and the repressive authority of the American state, personified by a dragon. Other novels include *Yellow Back Radio Broke-Down* (1969), about a black cowboy; *Mumbo-Jumbo* (1972), set in 1920s New Orleans and Harlem, with a multiple and mythic text, which includes drawings, photographs, and collages; *The Last Days of Louisiana Red* (1974), his idiosyncratic vision of student political activism at Berkeley in the 1960s; *Flight to Canada* (1976), an attack on the slavery and Civil War periods of American history; and *The Terrible Twos* (1982). Other novels satirizing aspects of American life—feminist extremism, Reaganist eccentricity, the politics of the campus—are *Reckless Eyeballing* (1986), *The Terrible Threes* (1989), and *Japanese by Spring* (1993). Often typographically playful, his books of poetry include *Catechism of D Neoamerican HooDoo Church* (1970), *Conjure: Selected Poems 1963–1970* (1972), and *New and Collected Poems* (1988). His essays are collected in *Shrovetide in Old New Orleans* (1978), *God Made Alaska for the Indians* (1982), and *Airing Dirty Linen* (1993). See also ETHNICITY.

REED, Jeremy (1951–), British poet, born in Jersey, educated at Essex University. *Bleecker Street* (1980), his first substantial collection, established acute observation, imaginative range, and literary allusion as essential characteristics of his poetry. *By the Fisheries* (1984) and *Nero* (1985) brought him prominence among younger British poets, initiating controversy over the merits of his verse; Kathleen *Raine declared him to be 'the most imaginatively gifted poet since Dylan *Thomas', while others saw his work as technically glib and repetitive in its dramatizations of his sensitivities. Further volumes of his poetry include *Selected Poems* (1987), *Nineties* (1990), *Red-Haired Android* (1992), and *Black Sugar: Trisexual Poems* (1992), with drawings by Jean Cocteau. Reed's eclecticism is such that rock music and eighteenth-century poetry are equally available to him as material for poems. Among his other writings are the novels *Blue Rock* (1987), *Red Eclipse* (1989), and *When the Whip Comes Down* (1992), a novel about de Sade. *Madness: The Price of Poetry* (1989) is a study of mental imbalance in the lives and works of various poets. *Lipstick, Sex, and Poetry* (1991) is an autobiography. Remarkably prolific, his publications in 1994 included two novels (*Chasing Black Rainbows* and *Diamond Nebula*), two collections of poems (*Pop Stars* and *Kicks*), and a biography of the rock star Lou Reed (*Waiting for the Man*).

REED, John (1887–1920), American journalist, born in Portland, Oregon, educated at Harvard. Rejecting his wealthy background, he became one of the USA's most famous radical journalists and the only American to be buried in the Kremlin Wall. With the aid of Lincoln Steffens, the famous radical journalist, he began his career with *The American Magazine*, but finding it politically restrictive he began to write for other journals, including *The *Masses*. He achieved national recognition with his hard-hitting coverage of the Paterson mill strike, and of the Mexican Revolution, *Insurgent Mexico* (1914), which condemned America's interference in Mexican domestic affairs. As part of the radical literary bohemia, he wrote articles, small vignettes of New York life, and some modernist poetry for *The *Seven Arts* and other *little magazines, meeting such leading figures as Floyd *Dell and Eugene *O'Neill. He covered the war in Europe, and his eye-witness account of the events of the October Revolution, *Ten Days that Shook the World* (1919), is among the finest reportage of the century; it combines a sense of the historical importance of the events with an anecdotal quality which uses small incidents to illustrate the extent of the changes taking place. Praised by Lenin, the book won him international renown. He participated in the founding of the Communist Labour Party of America in 1919, then returned to Russia where he became a member of the Executive Committee of the Communist International, dying prematurely of typhus. The John Reed Clubs were established in 1929 to encourage proletarian writing and to encourage an awareness of the political nature of all culture.

REEMAN, Douglas (1924–), British writer and former naval officer, born in Thames Ditton, Surrey. His first book, *A Prayer for the Ship* (1972), was set in the navy during the Second World War. As Alexander Kent he writes historical novels, set at the time of the Napoleonic wars, about the life and career of a young naval officer, Richard Bolitho, following his rise from Midshipman to Admiral. The first of these many novels was *To Glory We Steer* (1974); more recently he has published *Beyond the Reef* (1992) and *The Darkening Sea* (1993). In each of his books he displays his understanding of the realities of life in the eighteenth-century navy and his ability to convey an exciting and absorbing story. His other novels, many with a Second World War setting, include *The Torpedo Run* (1981), *Badge of Glory* (1982), *The Iron Pirate* (1986), *In Danger's Hour* (1988), *The White Guns* (1989), and *Killing Ground* (1991).

REEVES, James (1909–78), British poet, born in London, educated at Jesus College, Oxford. From 1932 to 1952 he taught English in a number of schools and teachers' training colleges, subsequently becoming a freelance author and editor. His first collection of poems, *The Natural Need*, was published in 1936 by the Seizin Press, run by Robert *Graves and Laura *Riding, whose work Reeves's early poetry sometimes resembles. Numerous further volumes include *The Imprisoned Sea* (1949), *The Talking Skull* (1958), and *Poems and Paraphrases* (1972); *Collected Poems* of 1974 is the fullest edition of his verse. His best work characteristically combines intensity of mood with an understated manner to distinctive and sometimes haunting lyrical effect. The rural descriptiveness of his less distinguished poetry is elsewhere the vehicle for an ironic pastoralism voicing his disaffection with urban modernity. His popular books of poetry for children were collected as *The Wandering Moon and Other Poems* (1973). As an editor, Reeves was prolific, producing many anthologies of prose and poetry, as well as selections from the work of Donne, Hopkins, Clare, and others.

Regional Poetry, verse reflecting certain essential aspects of specific geographical areas, generally approximating in size and distinctness of cultural identity to counties. Although there are numerous earlier examples of poets firmly associated with particular districts or landscapes, John Clare and Thomas *Hardy among them, the term is primarily applicable to work produced from the late 1950s onward; at this time regional loyalties were emerging as a force in Britain's internal political and administrative affairs in reaction to increasing economic and cultural centralization in the post-war era. Social, linguistic, topographical, historical, and mythical characteristics of various areas are among the factors informing work by a number of distinguished poets with pervasive regional qualities: Basil *Bunting and Tom *Pickard are associated with Northumberland, Tony *Connor, Tony *Harrison, Glyn *Hughes, and Cliff *Ashby with Yorkshire, Norman *Nicholson with Cumberland, and Jack *Clemo and A. L. *Rowse with Cornwall; although John *Hewitt wrote from the standpoint of an Ulster regionalist, other *Ulster poets are not readily thus designated. Similarly, some poets have been referred to as 'regional' who are more properly regarded as Welsh, Scottish, or Irish, respective examples being R. S. *Thomas, Norman *MacCaig, and John *Montague. The last-named published the poem 'Regionalism' in 1960, displaying a wittily ironic consciousness of the implications of the term; these include the substitution of 'regional' for 'provincial' in the Arnoldian sense of remoteness from a 'centre of ... correct judgement, correct taste'. While a self-congratulatory attitude to its own local indigenousness is evident in some verse, regional writing forms an important dimension of poetry in English in recent decades. In his essay 'Englands of the Mind' (1980), Seamus *Heaney extends the term's validity in noting of Geoffrey *Hill, Ted *Hughes, and Philip *Larkin that 'all three treat England as a region—or rather treat their region as England'.

REID, Alastair (1926–), British poet and translator, born in Whithorn, Scotland, educated at the University of St Andrews. He has held numerous visiting posts at universities in the USA and elsewhere. He became a staff writer and correspondent with *The *New Yorker* in 1959. His collections of poems include *To Lighten My House* (1953), *Oddments Inklings Omens Moments* (1961), and *Weathering* (1978), which carried a preface suggesting he had ceased writing verse. His poetry has an attractive lightness of touch that enables him to deal accessibly with paradoxically complex aspects of human experience. He has written numerous memorable poems of Scottish and American landscapes. He has translated the poetries of Pablo Neruda and Jorge Luis Borges, including Neruda's *Isla Negra* (1982) and Borges's *The Gold of the Tigers* (1979). His other publications include the travel writings of *Passwords* (1963) and *Whereabouts* (1987). *An Alastair Reid Reader* (1994) contains selected poetry and prose.

REID, Christopher (1949–), British poet, born in Hong Kong, educated at Exeter College, Oxford, where Craig *Raine was his tutor. In 1991 he was appointed to an editorial position with *Faber and Faber. *Arcadia* (1979) and *Pea Soup* (1982), his first two collections of poetry, gained him a reputation as one of the leading exponents of the *Martian manner. The intense clarity and spatial economies apparent in the best of the poems suggest an almost transcendent quality. 'Charnel' and 'Magnum Opus' make explicit an elegiac sense of the absence of the numinous in modern secular culture. *Katerina Brac* (1985) deceptively purports to contain translations from the verse of a little-known Eastern European poet. As dramatic monologues the poems display very little of the Martian imagery common in Reid's earlier poetry. *In the Echoey Tunnel* (1991) and *Universes* (1994) renew the elegantly idiosyncratic wit characteristic of his verse and indicate a broadening scope.

REID, Forrest (1875–1947), Ulster novelist, born in Belfast where he spent most of his life, educated at Cambridge University. His work combines a sense of the numinous with an appreciation of the mundane, particularly as evidenced in bourgeois provincial Ulster life. His first book, *The Kingdom of Twilight* (1904), was followed by *Garden God: A Tale of Two Boys* (1905), dedicated to his admired Henry *James who would not acknowledge it, presumably because of its homoeroticism. Subsequent novels include *Following Darkness* (1912), a rich account of a sensuous and appreciative boy growing up in Ulster and experiencing intimations of the life of the spirit (this was later reworked into *Peter Waring*, 1937); *Demophon* (1927), which recreates a Greek mythic world; and *Brian Westby* (1934), a study of an estranged father and son in an Ulster seaside resort implicitly representing a Socratic ideal. His trilogy *Uncle Stephen* (1931), *The Retreat* (1936), and *Young Tom* (1944) moves backwards in time so that the final volume portrays the central figure, Tom Barber, as a boy enjoying an intense rapport with Nature. Reid was also the author of an autobiography, *Apostate* (1926), and its sequel, *Private Road* (1940), which describes the genesis of his novels, with critical studies of W. B. *Yeats and Walter *de la Mare.

REID, Graham (1945–), Northern Irish playwright, born in Belfast, of a Protestant working-class family, educated at Queen's University, Belfast. His first two plays, *The Death of Humpty-Dumpty*, produced at the *Abbey Theatre in 1979, and *The Closed Door* (1980), deal with the effects of the violence in Belfast upon innocent bystanders and examine how these victims are forced to realize their own involvement. *The Hidden Curriculum* (1982) and *Remembrance* (1984) have been successfully performed. Reid is best known for *Billy* (1982), a trilogy of plays for television concerning personal difficulties occurring within the context of civil disorder. *Ties of Blood*, first broadcast in 1985, explores the implications of the British Army's presence in Northern Ireland for marital and familial relationships.

REID, John MacNair (1895–1954), Scottish poet and novelist, born in Glasgow, where he later worked as a journalist. In 1936 his wife accepted a medical post in the Highlands, and Reid spent virtually the rest of his life there. Though he published two books of poems, and though two novels were issued posthumously, his reputation rests on his remarkable novel *Homeward Journey* (1934). This is a study of the relationship between two young people, David, the diffident, determinedly virtuous son of a minister, and Jessie, the first girl he has really known, encountered on his one night out on the town with an office mate. Jessie is anxious to get away from her poor and unsatisfactory family situation, a bedridden mother, a hopeless and at times truculent father. To effect her escape she is capable of telling and acting lies, and manipulating her power of sexual attraction. However, Reid eschews conventional moralism; his penetration into the secret hopes and desires of his protagonists, who are also defined by their social contexts, owes something perhaps to the Russian and French novelists he so admired.

REID, Victor (1911–87), Jamaican novelist, journalist, and editor, born in Jamaica, educated at Kingston Technical High School. His first novel, *New Day* (1949), reconstructs the history of Jamaica, as narrated by 87-year-old John Campbell, from his childhood days to 1944, when Jamaica gained internal self-government from Britain. The novel is written entirely in a version of Jamaican English, and interweaves episodes from Jamaican history with incidents involving individuals in Campbell's family. Reid's stated aim is to 'transfer to paper some of the beauty, kindliness and humour of my people'. This is also the aim in later works of fictionalized history written mainly for younger readers, for example *Sixty-Five* (1960), which deals with the Morant Bay uprising of 1865, and *The Young Warriors* (1967), which is concerned with the maroons, African slaves who escaped from their Spanish rulers during the Spanish period of Jamaica's history. Reid's second novel, *The Leopard* (1958), is a poetic evocation of the Mau Mau war for independence in Kenya, and was written before the author even visited Africa. In spite of this imaginative feat, Reid's lifelong preoccupation was with Jamaican history and culture, and the destiny of the Jamaican people, about which he wrote in several other books including a biography of the Jamaican politician Norman Manley. Reid was awarded the Order of Jamaica in 1980.

Remains of the Day, The, see ISHIGURO, KAZUO.

RENAULT, Mary, pseudonym of Mary CHALLANS (1905–83), British novelist, born in London, educated at St Hugh's College, Oxford. She settled in South Africa after the Second World War. Her first five books were romantic novels. Travels in Greece led her to the work for which she is best known: eight carefully researched historical novels set in ancient Greece and Asia Minor. Her usual method—familiar, but in her case vividly effective—was to invent a fictional first-person narrator close to the great men of his age. *The King Must Die* (1958) and *The Bull from the Sea* (1962) retell the legend of Theseus. *The Last of the Wine* (1956), *The Mask of Apollo* (1966), and *The Praise Singer* (1979) conjure up the politicians, philosophers, dramatists, and poets of ancient Athens. *Fire from Heaven* (1970), *The Persian Boy* (1972), and *Funeral Games* (1981) together make up her most cohesive work, recreating the life and death of Alexander the Great, who was also the subject of her biography, *The Nature of Alexander* (1975).

RENDELL, Ruth (1930–), British crime writer, born in London; she worked briefly for an Essex newspaper. With *From Doom with Death* (1964) she began a long series of police novels set in the mid-Sussex town of Kingsmarkham, with Detective Chief Inspector Wexford as their central character. Though these have similarities in method with the classical pre-war detective story, they differ from it in their subjects, which include, for example, transvestism and sexual obsession and frustration. Among the best are *Some Die and Some Lie* (1973), *Shake Hands for Ever* (1975), *A Sleeping Life* (1978), and *The Speaker of Mandarin* (1983). More interesting and more unusual are her other novels, which have led critics to compare her work with that of Patricia *Highsmith. These are usually studies of abnormal psychology—often sexual perversion—leading to violence and crime, such as *A Demon in My View* (1976), *A Judgement in Stone* (1977), *The Killing Doll* (1984), *The Tree of Hands* (1984), and *Crocodile Bird* (1993). Under the name of Barbara Vine she has also written a number of novels in which the interest is again psychological, although crime is usually less in evidence (*A Dark-Adapted Eye*, 1986; *A Fatal Inversion*, 1987; *The House of Stairs*, 1988; *Gallowglass*, 1990). Rendell edited *The Reason Why: An Anthology of the Murderous Mind* (1995).

RENEE, pen-name of Renee TAYLOR (1929–), New Zealand playwright, born in Napier, educated at Massey University and at the University of Auckland. Her first full-length play, *Setting the Table* (1984), was followed by *Wednesday to Come* (1985), the first play of a trilogy, which established Renee's reputation. The play draws on both feminist and working-class perspectives in a family drama which takes place in a house situated on the path of a national unemployment march, where four generations of women battle with the repercussions of a husband's suicide brought about as the consequence of the Depression of the 1930s. The story of this family of strong women enduring and triumphing over the bleakest circumstances continues in *Pass It On* (1986), set during the 1951 watersiders' confrontation with the government, and in *Jeanie Once* (1990), which is set in Dunedin in the 1890s. Renee's published plays are naturalistic dramas but some of her most successful productions, for example *Born To Clean* (1987), have minimal scripts and rely on the skills of women actors and singers in ensemble production. Her fiction includes *Willy Nilly* (1990) and *Daisy and Lily* (1993).

Responsibilities, a collection of poems by W. B. *Yeats, published in 1914, which completes the gradual development away from the melancholy romanticism of the *Celtic Twilight in his early work. The most striking advances are achieved in a group of poems placed near the opening of the book which include 'To a Wealthy Man . . .', 'September 1913', and 'To a Shade'; these and others are remarkable for the combative directness of tone with which they denounce what Yeats perceived as the debased attitudes prevailing among his contemporaries in Dublin. The emergence of a clear public voice anticipates much of his best work of the next decade, while 'The Magi' and 'The Dolls' are forerunners of his later philosophical poetry. Although Yeats's interest in Irish legend survives in pieces like 'The Grey Rock' and 'The Two Kings', his treatments of such material are stripped of the decorative and mysterious qualities that characterized much of his former work. With reference to 'A Coat', the volume's penultimate poem which rejects 'embroideries | Out of old mythologies', Louis *MacNeice remarked that in *Responsibilities* Yeats 'abdicates the throne of the twilight'. Among the factors leading to the changes of attitude and manner evident in the book was the disillusionment with the idea of a worthwhile national culture which resulted in part from his involvements with the *Abbey Theatre. The stylistic chastening in *Responsibilities* is to some extent attributable to the influence of Ezra *Pound; as Yeats's secretary in 1913, Pound argued for the concentration essential to his conceptions of *Imagism and was instrumental in effecting revisions to certain poems.

Restoration, see TREMAIN, ROSE.

Return of the Soldier, The, see WEST, DAME REBECCA.

Revenge for Love, The, a novel by Wyndham *Lewis, published in 1937. Set at the time of the Spanish Civil War, the novel opens in the Spanish gaol where its central character, Percy Hardcaster, an English revolutionary fighting for the Communists, is incarcerated following his capture by the Civil Guard. He attempts to escape, but is shot and repatriated, after losing a leg—a war wound which gives him great cachet amongst the fashionably left-wing intelligentsia by whom he is taken up on his return to London. These include Tristram and Gillian Phipps, an upper-middle-class couple who run a kind of salon for impoverished artists and aspiring revolutionaries, and Victor Stamp, a mediocre painter, who forges Old Masters for a living. Percy is at first fêted as a hero of the proletariat by the Phippses and their hangers-on; later, when he reveals his political pragmatism to Gillian, during an amorous encounter, she is incensed, and encourages another of her admirers, Jack Cruze, to beat him up. Recovering from the beating, Percy decides to involve himself once more in politics, and to this end inveigles Victor Stamp and his common-law wife, Margot, into a dubious scheme running guns over the border to the Communist rebels in Spain. Victor and Margot are killed in the attempt, and Percy, once more in prison, is left with the realization that his political ideals have achieved nothing, except the deaths of two innocent people. The novel—whose original title, *False Bottoms*, was rejected by the publishers as too salacious—contains some of Lewis's most spare and powerful writing.

Review, The, a magazine of poetry and criticism founded by Ian *Hamilton in 1962. As editor, Hamilton sought to establish 'a new lyricism, direct, personal, concentrated'; the sometimes acerbic tone of its reviewing recalled that of Geoffrey *Grigson's **New Verse*, which like *The Review* was the leading poetry periodical of its decade. Contributors of criticism included Clive *James, Peter *Porter, and Alan *Brownjohn. From the fifth issue onward Hamilton wrote a concluding article under the pseudonym 'Edward Pygge', humorously disparaging verse which failed to win his approval. David *Harsent, John *Fuller, Hugo *Williams, and Douglas *Dunn were among the poets regularly featured, their work tending to exemplify the scrupulous modes *The Review* favoured. Several leading American poets, notably John *Berryman and Robert *Lowell, had their reputations in Britain consolidated by the magazine's support for their verse; it also published much work by European poets. *The Review* having closed in 1972, Hamilton began *The New Review* as a monthly publication in 1974; although many of the poets and critics associated with the earlier journal continued to write for *The New Review*, its frame of reference broadened considerably with the regular inclusion of fiction, profiles of leading authors, reports from foreign correspondents, and attention to a range of socio-cultural topics. Martin *Amis, David *Lodge, Malcolm *Bradbury, Saul *Bellow, Jean *Rhys, and Nadine *Gordimer were among the contributors of fiction and essays; emerging poets whose work appeared included Craig *Raine, Peter *Reading, and Andrew *Motion. From 1976 onward the magazine encountered financial difficulties and ceased appearing in 1978.

REXROTH, Kenneth (1905–82), American poet and essayist, born at South Bend, Indiana; he grew up mainly in Chicago, where he studied at the Art

Institute. *An Autobiographical Novel* (1966) recounts his precocious involvement in a range of *Modernist movements in literature and the graphic arts. From 1927 he lived principally in San Francisco, working as a journalist and latterly as a visiting lecturer at various universities. His early verse was eventually collected in *The Art of Worldly Wisdom* (1949) and *A Homestead Called Damascus* (1963). His involvement in the emergence of *Objectivist poetry in 1931 is most clearly reflected in the verse of *The Phoenix and the Tortoise* (1944). His socialist activities in the 1930s are indicated by the political tenor of *In What Hour* (1940), his first published collection. Subsequent collections, in which his work is broadly divided into polemical and lyrical verse, include *The Dragon and the Unicorn* (1952), a verse-journal of travel in post-war Europe, *In Defense of the Earth* (1956), *The Heart's Garden, The Garden's Heart* (1967), and *The Morning Star* (1979). Rexroth's later work is informed by his familiarity with Oriental poetry and has its thematic centre in his desire to reconcile Christianity and Taoism. In the 1950s he was popularly termed 'Godfather of the *Beats' and is portrayed in Jack *Kerouac's *The Dharma Bums* (1958) as 'Rheinhold Cacoethes'. Collected editions of his shorter (1967) and longer (1968) poems have been produced. Among his collections of literary essays and cultural speculations are *Bird in the Bush* (1959), *With Eye and Ear* (1970), and *The Elastic Retort* (1973). His extensive *œuvre* also encompasses numerous verse-dramas and translations of Chinese, Japanese, French, and classical Greek poetry. The remarkable scope of his interests is well represented by the selections in *The Rexroth Reader* (edited by Eric Mottram, 1972). See also BLACK MOUNTAIN WRITERS and SAN FRANCISCO RENAISSANCE.

REYNOLDS, Oliver (1957–), Anglo-Welsh poet, born in Cardiff, educated at the University of Hull. In his first collection of poetry, *Skevington's Daughter* (1985), the cultural concerns of his native South Wales were clearly apparent in the final section; the book's verbal ingenuity and visually codified imagery identified it, however, as *Martian poetry rather than *Anglo-Welsh literature. *The Player Queen's Wife* (1987) extended the emotional and imaginative range of his elegantly accessible though often complex style. The highly economical narrative developments characteristic of much of Reynolds's writing are exemplified by the treatment of events and atmospheres in a psychiatric hospital in 'Rorschach Writing'. A later collection is *The Oslo Tram* (1991).

REZNIKOFF, Charles (1894–1976), American poet, born in Brooklyn, New York, educated at the School of Journalism of the University of Missouri and at New York University, where he gained his LL.B. in 1915. His early publications as a poet include *Rhythms* (1918), *Uriel Acosta* (1921), and the verse-dramas of *Chatterton, The Black Death, and Meriwether Lewis* (1922). The terse compression of his mature style emerged in *Five Groups of Verse* (1927). In 1932 his poetry was featured in Louis *Zukofsky's *An 'Objectivists' Anthology*; the concrete precision of his imagery and his emphatic exclusion of metaphorical and rhetorical effects exemplify the tenets of *Objectivist poetry. Among his other collections are *In Memoriam* (1934), *Separate Way* (1936), and *Inscriptions* (1959), in which an increasing concern with Jewish culture is evident. *Testimony: The United States (1885–1915)* (3 volumes, 1965, 1968, 1979) forms a social history compiled entirely from law reports. Materials from the Nuremberg trials form the basis of *Holocaust* (1975), in which his habitually factual tone is harrowingly effective in presenting documentary details of genocide. Seamus Cooney's complete edition of Reznikoff's poems appeared in two volumes in 1978. *By the Waters of Manhattan* (1930), the first of Reznikoff's novels, fuses his love for New York with his elegiac sense of exile from the central traditions of Judaism. In the historical novel *The Lionhearted* (1944) he recreates the experience of the Jewish communities in medieval England. *The Manner Music* (1977) is a fictionalized account of his efforts to continue writing in the midst of discouragement in the 1930s, the period covered in the composite biography of members of his family in *Family Chronicle* (1963).

RHODE, John, pseudonym of Major Cecil John Charles STREET, MC, OBE (1884–1965), British crime writer, commissioned in the Royal Artillery in 1903; under this name and that of Miles Burton he wrote over 140 detective stories between 1924 and 1961. The central figure of the Rhode stories is the polymathic scientist Dr Priestley (*The Paddington Mystery*, 1925), and of those written as Burton the amateur detective Desmond Merrion (*The Secret of High Eldersham*, 1930; US title *The Mystery of High Eldersham*). As Rhode he also wrote on true crime (*The Case of Constance Kent*, 1928) and under his own name on European history and politics (*Hungary and Democracy*, 1923; *President Masaryk*, 1930) and translated Halevy's *Vauban, Builder of Fortresses* (1924).

RHONE, Trevor (1940–), Jamaican playwright, born in Kingston, Jamaica; he studied drama at the Rose Bruford College in Kent. In 1965 he founded 'Theatre 77', which performed at the Barn Theatre in Kingston, for which Rhone wrote *The Gadget* (1969). His published plays include *Old Story Time and Other Plays* (1981), which also contains *Smile Orange* and *School's Out*, and *Two Can Play and School's Out* (1986). Set in a 'third-rate' beach hotel, *Smile Orange* (1971, filmed and directed by Rhone in 1974) is a deceptively gentle satire on the insidious corruptions of the tourist industry, while *School's Out* (1975) draws on Rhone's experiences as a schoolmaster, and questions many current assumptions about education. Rhone's most popular play, *Old Story Time* (1979), in which 'Pa Ben', the old story-teller, recounts forty years of Jamaican life, reveals the playwright's comic vision at its most luminous. Rhone's realistic comedies about Jamaican life all combine serious social criticism with buoyant humour, and are acutely sensitive to a wide variety of dialects and modes of speech. *If: A Tragedy of* *the Ruled* (1983) and *Hopes of the Living Dead* (1988) are both historical allegories set in turn-of-the-century Nigeria. He also co-authored and produced the internationally successful film *The Harder They Come* (1972).

RHYS, Jean (Ella Gwendolyn Rees Williams) (1890–1979), British novelist, born in Roseau, Dominica, of Welsh descent; she moved to Britain in 1907. Her shifting life as a chorus girl, her years in Paris, her difficult first marriage, and her encounter with Ford Madox *Ford gave her ample material for her early fiction. Her first two novels, *Postures* (1928, reprinted as *Quartet* in 1969) and *After Leaving Mr Mackenzie* (1930), present the story of the recognizable Rhys heroine, a lost woman struggling to survive in a hostile masculine world. With *Voyage in the Dark* (1934) Rhys found her distinctive voice: her assumption of the first person, her foray into painful reminiscences of her Caribbean childhood, her growing disregard for conventions of plot and characterization, and the soaring, controlled beauty of her prose, render the novel one of the finest of its time. Rhys had intuitively adopted the procedures of *modernist writing; her next novel, *Good Morning Midnight* (1938), was far ahead of its time, a precursor of women's novels of the 1960s in its account of its middle-aged protagonist's struggle with her life, her sexuality, and her pessimism. Rhys's masterpiece, **Wide Sargasso Sea* (1966), signalled a new understanding of her fiction. Here, she struggles with the canons of English literature to claim the figure of Bertha Mason (renamed Antoinette in this novel), placed by Charlotte Brontë at the villainous periphery of *Jane Eyre*, as the subjective centre of a distinctively Caribbean work. Rhys counterpoints the voices of Bertha and Rochester to present two contrasting world-views—male and female, imperial and colonial, Northern and Southern. This double process of decolonization and recolonization places Rhys's mature work at the centre of post-colonial 'English' literary politics. Two collections of short stories, *Tigers are Better Looking* (1968, including stories from her first collection, *The Left Bank*, 1927) and *Sleep It off, Lady* (1976), display a potential widening of range; some stories, notably 'Let Them Call It Jazz', with its black narrator, can be included among Rhys's finest work and display her knowledge of Caribbean culture along with her ambiguous sensitivity to matters of race and colour. However, years of poverty, neglect, and silence had exhausted her, and she died in 1979, leaving her autobiography, *Smile Please*, published in the year of her death, incomplete. Her *Letters 1931–66*, edited by F. Wyndham and D. Melly, appeared in 1984.

RICE, Elmer (1892–1967), American playwright, novelist, and producer, born Elmer Reizenstein in New York, educated at the New York Law School. His first successful play, *On Trial* (1914), a courtroom melodrama and murder mystery, employed the 'flashback' technique and a revolving stage. His later plays are also characteristically experimental in form and subversive in content, notably *The Adding Machine* (1923), an expressionistic play satirically illustrating the dehumanizing effects of mechanization. This was followed by *Wake Up, Jonathan* (1928; written with Hatcher Hughes), *Close Harmony* (1924; written with Dorothy *Parker), and the mystery *Cock Robin* (1928; written with Philip *Barry). *The Subway* (1929) was followed by *Street Scene* (1929, Pulitzer Prize), a vivid drama of life outside a New York tenement house, subsequently adapted as a musical by Kurt Weill and Langston *Hughes in 1947. The focus on social injustice and the plight of the oppressed continued in *We, the People* (1933), about unemployment and racism; *Judgement Day* (1934), concerning the burning of the Reichstag building; *Between Two Worlds* (1935); *American Landscape* (1938); *Two on an Island* (1940); *Flight to the West* (1941); and *A New Life* (1943). Mainly farces and melodramas, his other plays include *See Naples and Die* (1929), *The Left Bank* (1931), *Counsellor-at-Law* (1931), *Black Sheep* (1932), *Not For Children* (1936), *Dream Girl* (1945), *The Grand Tour* (1951), and *Love among the Ruins* (1963). His few novels include *A Voyage to Purilia* (1930), a satire about the film industry, and one about New York entitled *Imperial City* (1937). A collection of his essays and writings on the theatre appeared as *The Living Theatre* (1959). His autobiography, *Minority Report* (1963), detailed his work as a lawyer through to his involvement in the theatre, which included the directorship of the New York *Federal Theatre Project and helping to establish the Playwright's Producing Company. See also EXPRESSIONISM.

Riceyman Steps, generally considered the best of the late novels of Arnold *Bennett, published in 1923. It is the tale of a miserly second-hand London bookseller, Earlforward, who marries a neighbouring shopkeeper in Clerkenwell, the trim and efficient Mrs Arb. She becomes more and more shocked by his pathological meanness (he even tries to sell the dust from his vacuum cleaner) and eventually both fall ill and die, nursed with devotion by Earlforward's loyal charwoman Elsie. It is a grim and convincing psychological study, and a vivid and sympathetic portrait of one of London's poorest quarters. Elsie proved such a success with the novel's readers that Bennett reintroduced her in a less authentic but interesting long short story, 'Elsie and the Child' (1924), in which Elsie tries to better herself and become a proper maidservant.

RICH, Adrienne (Cecile) (1931–), American poet, born in Baltimore, educated at Radcliffe College. She has held posts at numerous American universities and became Professor of English and Feminist Studies at Stanford University in 1986. *A Change of World* (1951), her first collection of verse, was notable for the restraint with which her accomplished versification conveyed an underlying sense of vulnerability and impermanence. Strongly implied concern with the cultural distortions of women's experience in *The Diamond Cutters* (1955) anticipated the emergence of her characteristically feminist idiom in *Snapshots of a Daughter-in-Law* (1963). The collection also initiated the use of richly musical free verse as the essential form of her poetry. The candour with which the title sequence used autobiographical elements led various critics to classify her as a *Confessional poet. *Necessities* (1966), *Diving into the Wreck* (1972), *The Dream of a Common Language* (1978), *Your Native Land, Your Life* (1986), and *Atlas of the Difficult World* (1991) are among the numerous subsequent collections throughout which she has sustained a tone of uncompromising directness in poetry reflecting her radical feminism and urgent dissatisfaction with America's political status quo. *The Fact of a Doorframe: Poems Selected and New 1950–1984* appeared in 1984. *Of Woman Born* (1976), an examination of the natural and social significances of motherhood, established Rich as an influential theorist of feminism; selections from her essays are contained in *On Lies, Secrets, and Silence* (1979) and *Blood, Bread, and Poetry* (1986).

RICHARDS, I(vor) A(rmstrong) (1893–1979), English critic, born in Cheshire, educated at Magdalene College, Cambridge. He was a teacher of enormous importance for the development of modern methods of reading and thinking about literature. *Principles of Literary Criticism* (1925) was acclaimed by T. S. *Eliot not only for changing the course of criticism but for altering the meaning of the term, and there were many who thought Richards had reinvented the very notion of reading. With Richards, Allen *Tate said, it became a matter of reading poetry 'with all the brains one had and with one's arms and legs, as well as what may be inside the rib cage'. In **Practical Criticism* (1929) Richards effectively engendered the *New Criticism through his alarming (and alarmed) discovery that much of what we call reading is merely an agglomeration of prejudice and blindness. Richards had asked his students and others to comment on poems not identified by date or author, and had received some very strange judgements and preferences in response. He concluded that we needed to *learn* to read literature—closely, as if for the first time. 'The lesson of all criticism', he said, 'is that we have nothing to rely upon in making choices but ourselves. The lesson of good poetry seems to be that, when we have understood it, in the degree in which we can order ourselves, we need nothing more.' Richards found models for the ordering of the self in Coleridge (*Coleridge on the Imagination*, 1935) and in the Chinese philosopher Mencius (*Mencius on the Mind*, 1932). His early work with C. K. Ogden in semantics (*The Meaning of Meaning*, 1923) remains influential, and Richards's writing and example were important for William *Empson, who was Richards's pupil at Cambridge. Richards's attacks on vagueness and sentimentality found an echo in F. R. *Leavis. Richards later moved from England to a distinguished career at Harvard. He wrote verse, and continued to reflect tirelessly on questions of language and thought. His career remains the model of what rationality may hope to do in a complex and largely unreasonable age.

RICHARDSON, Dorothy M(iller) (1873–1957), British novelist, born in Abingdon, Oxfordshire. An important and long-neglected British *modernist, Richardson is best known for her influential and original work *Pilgrimage*, which was published in parts, as eleven separate novels, between 1915 and 1935, then reissued as a single novel, in four volumes, comprising twelve 'chapter novels' (Richardson's own term) in 1938. A thirteenth novel, probably unfinished, was added to the posthumous edition in 1967. Closely based on Richardson's own life, *Pilgrimage* is the story of Miriam Henderson from the early 1890s, when she is 17, until 1915, when she is about 40 and just beginning her career as a writer. Miriam has grown up in a wealthy family in which her father has sold the inherited family business to live as a 'gentleman'. When the novel begins the family is nearly bankrupt, and Miriam is leaving to begin a life of supporting herself in poorly paid 'women's work'—as a teacher, governess, and dental secretary. She is also involved in various political groups, attending lectures, reading widely, and exploring her perceptions of the physical and social world around her. Later, she lives in a Quaker community and becomes interested in notions of communication through silence (Richardson published two studies of Quaker ideas in 1914). Several of the male characters want to marry her, but Miriam remains single. Her most intense emotional relationship is with another woman. *Pilgrimage* is also a novel about the act of writing. The first literary work to be described as using '*stream of consciousness' techniques (a term which Richardson herself rejected), it employs complex narrative strategies which change considerably over its 2,000 pages. Richardson also wrote for various journals, such as *Life and Letters*, and film journals such as *Close Up*. Her stories and autobiographical sketches were collected and republished under the title *Journey to Paradise* (1989). Described as 'a writer's writer', Richardson was at the forefront of modernist innovation in narrative. *Pointed Roofs*, the first book of *Pilgrimage*, was written in 1912–13 and is almost contemporaneous with key works of *Joyce and Proust, with which Richardson's writing is often compared. Her friends included H. G. *Wells (who is portrayed as Hypo Wilson in *Pilgrimage*), *Bryher, Hilda *Doolittle, and John Cowper *Powys. Contemporary feminist critics find her work particularly interesting for its exploration of gender, subjectivity, and narrative.

RICHARDSON, Henry Handel (born Ethel Florence Lindesay RICHARDSON) (1870–1946), Australian novelist, born in Melbourne. In 1888, accompanied by her mother and sister, she travelled to Europe and studied music at the Leipzig Conservatorium. In Germany she read widely in European literature and also met her future husband, J. G. Robertson, who later became Professor of German Literature at the University of London. She settled in London in 1903. Her first novel, *Maurice Guest* (1908), concerning a young musician studying in Leipzig who is finally destroyed by his obsessive love for a selfish woman, was favourably received by the critics and by Somerset *Maugham; it was made into a film, *Rhapsody* (1954), starring Elizabeth Taylor. *The *Getting of Wisdom* (1910) is based on Richardson's own experiences as a pupil at a Melbourne boarding school. For the next twenty years she devoted herself to writing the trilogy *The *Fortunes of Richard Mahony* (1930) which consists of *Australia Felix* (1917), *The Way Home* (1925), and *Ultima Thule* (1929); the trilogy chronicles the rise to prosperity and subsequent ruination and disgrace of its central character, who is modelled on Richardson's father. It is widely regarded as one of the major works of Australian literature, exploring themes of personal and cultural alienation and offering a complex and detailed picture of late nineteenth-century colonial life. Her other works include *Young Cosima* (1939), a novel about Cosima von Bulow and Richard Wagner; and *Two Studies* (1931) and *The End of Childhood* (1934), both collections of short stories. *Myself when Young* (1948), an unfinished autobiography, and *The Adventures of Cuffy Mahony* (1979), a collection of previously unpublished short fiction, appeared posthumously. *Ulysses Bound* (1973), by Dorothy Green, is a study of her life and work.

RICHLER, Mordecai (1931–), Canadian novelist and short-story writer, born in Montreal, educated at Sir George Williams University. From 1951 to 1972 he was in Britain—'I wasn't going somewhere as much as getting to hell out of Montreal'; an uneasy, though productive, coming to terms with memories of the now-vanished Montreal Jewish ghetto of his childhood colours much of his best writing, notably *Son of a Smaller Hero* (1955) and *The Apprenticeship of Duddy Dravitz* (1959), the tragi-comic story of a young would-be entrepreneur, who betrays all who are close to him. Other novels include *The Incomparable Atuk* (1963), *Cocksure* (1968), *St Urbain's Horseman* (1971), *Joshua Then and Now* (1980), in which Richler again explored the Montreal St Urbain street world, and *Solomon Gursky Was Here* (1989), epic in scope, which demonstrates the distinctive quality of his writing and is regarded by many as his finest novel. Journalistic work was collected in *Hunting Tigers under Glass* (1968), *Notes on an Endangered Species* (1974), and *Home Sweet Home: My Canadian Album* (1984), a bitter-sweet collection of essays originally published in such journals as **Encounter*, *The *New York Review of Books*, and *Maclean's*. In the opening essay, typically entitled 'Home Is where You Hang Yourself', Richler comments of his motives for returning to Canada: 'too many other expatriate Commonwealth writers, writers I respected, had been driven in exile to foreign fictions set in the distant past, the usually dreaded future, or, indeed, nowhere.' In the essay 'My Father's Life' he concludes movingly that with his father's death he is left with 'unresolved mysteries. A sense of regret. Anecdotes for burnishing.' More recently he has published *Broadsides: Reviews and Opinions* (1990), *Oh Canada! Oh Quebec!: Requiem for a Divided Country* (1992), and *This Year in Jerusalem* (1994), an autobiographical account of his journey to Israel to clarify his origins and discern the meaning of being a Canadian Jew.

RICKS, Christopher (1933–), British critic, born in London, educated at Balliol College, Oxford. After teaching at the universities of Oxford, Bristol, and Cambridge, in 1986 he became Professor of English at Boston University. His edition of the poems of Tennyson which appeared in 1969 is the fullest available text of that poet's work; his *Tennyson's Methods of Composition* (1966) and *Tennyson: A Biographical and Critical Study* (1972) are also highly regarded. Notable among his many other publications are *Milton's Grand Style* (1963), *Keats and Embarrassment* (1974), *The Force of Poetry* (1984), and *T. S. Eliot and Prejudice* (1988). He is noted for the penetrating and revealing analyses of poetry achieved by his remarkably close attention to the textual fabric of works under consideration; the results are invariably stimulating and sometimes provocatively tendentious. The scope of his interests is unusually wide, extending from John Gower to Bob *Dylan. His other works as an editor include *The Brownings: Letters and Poetry* (1970), *The New Oxford Book of Victorian Verse* (1987), *A. E. Housman: Collected Poems and Selected Prose* (1988), and *The Faber Book of America* (1992; with William M. Vance). The texts of his Clarendon lectures of 1990 were published as *Beckett's Dying Words* (1993).

RICKWORD, (John) Edgell (1898–1982), British poet and critic, born in Colchester, Essex, educated at Pembroke College, Oxford. His experience of active service on the Western Front from 1916 to 1918 is reflected in numerous poems in *Behind the Eyes* (1921), his first volume of verse. During the early 1920s he established his reputation as a critic through his contributions to leading literary periodicals. His *Rimbaud: The Boy and the Poet* (1924) was the first authoritative treatment of that author to be published in Britain. From 1925 to 1927 he co-edited, with Douglas Garman, *The *Calendar of Modern Letters*. He compiled two volumes of *Scrutinies* (1928, 1931), a series of essays from the journal which preceded F. R. *Leavis's **Scrutiny* and influenced the latter in the development of his critical practices. Increasingly political in his cultural attitudes, Rickword was subsequently editor of *The *Left Review* from 1934 to 1938 and of *Our Time* between 1944 and 1947. He published two further collections of verse, *Invocation to Angels* (1928), which contains his finest work, and the predominantly satirical *Twittingpan and Some Others* (1931). The technical refinement and concentrated fusions of thought and feeling in his best verse recall the work of Donne and Marvell while remaining distinctly individual in tone. *Behind the Eyes: Collected Poems and Translations* appeared in 1976. Two volumes of his *Essays and Opinions* (1974, 1978) were edited by A. Young. There is a biography by Charles Hobday entitled *Edgell Rickword: A Poet at War* (1989). His *Collected Poems* (1991) were edited by Charles Hobday.

Riddle of the Sands, The, see CHILDERS, ERSKINE.

Riddley Walker, see HOBAN, RUSSELL.

Riders to the Sea, a play by J. M. *Synge, first performed in 1904. It remains one of the few one-act pieces to be widely regarded as a tragedy. Set on an island off the west coast of Ireland, it tells with grim simplicity of the bereavement of Maurya, who has already lost a husband and four sons to the sea. The bundle of clothes brought in by the priest, taken from a drowned man in Donegal, turns out to belong to one of her two surviving sons, Michael; and the other, Bartley, who insists over her protests on going to a fair, is thrown by his pony to his death in the surf. As the body of the latter is brought in, and her daughters and the other village women keen over it, she expresses her resignation: 'They're all gone now, and there isn't anything more the sea can do to me . . . No man at all can be living for ever, and we must be satisfied.'

RIDGE, Lola (Rose Emily) (1871–1941), American poet, born in Dublin. At the age of 16 she accompanied her mother to New Zealand; they eventually settled in Sydney, Australia, where she attended Trinity College and studied art at the Academie Julienne. Following her mother's death, in 1907 she travelled to the USA and settled in New York, working as an artist's model and an advertising copywriter. She became identified as a poet of political dissent through the publication of her verse in Emma *Goldman's *Mother Earth*, America's leading anarchist journal in the years before the First World War. The title sequence of *The Ghetto* (1918), her first collection of poems, employed a social realist mode to celebrate the lives and occupations of typifying examples of New York's working classes. Her disciplined free-verse forms and emphatic use of concrete detail, which showed her affinities with *Imagism, were sustained in *Sun-Up* (1920) and *Red Flag* (1927), both of which reflected her socialist views. With Edna St Vincent *Millay and others, Ridge devoted much energy to the unsuccessful campaign to prevent the executions of Sacco and Vanzetti, whose deaths are symbolically central to the impassioned lyricism of her version of the Crucifixion in *Firehead* (1929). The religious and mythical aspect of her work intensified in *Dance of Fire* (1935), in which she displays impressive skill in the use of traditional verse forms; although intended as the first part of an epic celebration of human development, no further sections were published.

RIDING, Laura (1901–91), American poet, born in New York, educated at Cornell University. She first attracted notice as a poet through her association with J. C. *Ransom and other contributors to the *Fugitive* (1922–5; see AGRARIANS, THE), in which her verse repeatedly appeared. From 1925 to 1939 she lived with Robert *Graves, with whom she produced the seminal critical work *A Survey of Modern Poetry* (1927). *Contemporaries and Snobs* (1928) and *Anarchism Is not Enough* (1928) are the best-known of her other critical works. The *Hogarth Press published *The Close Chaplet* (1926), her first collection of verse; subsequent volumes include *Love as Love, Death as Death* (1928), *Poet: A Lying Word* (1933), and *The Second Leaf* (1935). Her poetry is remarkable for the suppleness of its verse forms and its tendency to combine lyrical simplicity with intellectually complex meditations. *Collected Poems* (1938) effectively marked the end of her career as a poet. The reasons for her renunciation of poetry, which centre on her belief in its inadequacy as a medium for truth, are discussed in prefaces to *Selected Poems* (1973) and *The Poems of Laura Riding* (1980). Among her other publications are *Lives of Wives* (1939), a collection of biographical fictions, and *The Telling* (1973), an exposition of her philosophy. Posthumous publications of her works include *First Awakenings: The Early Poems of Laura Riding* (1992) and *A Selection of the Poems of Laura Riding* (1994). A biography, *In Extremis: The Life of Laura Riding*, by Deborah Baker, appeared in 1993.

RIDLER, Anne (1912–), British poet, born in Rugby, Warwickshire, educated at King's College, the University of London. She worked in the editorial department of *Faber and Faber from 1935 to 1940, after which she was fully occupied with motherhood and writing. Her first collection of verse was *Poems* (1939); subsequent volumes include *The Nine Bright Shiners* (1943), *A Matter of Life and Death* (1959), *Some Time After* (1972), *New and Selected Poems* (1988), and *Collected Poems* (1994). Much of her finest poetry projects the insights of a visionary religious sensibility into treatments of familial and domestic experience. Ridler has also written a number of plays, notably the verse-drama *The Trial of Thomas Cranmer* (1956), and *The Jesse Tree* (1972), a masque in verse with music by Elizabeth Maconchy. Among her other works are the biography *Olive Willis and Downe House* (1967) and English libretti for operas by Monteverdi, Cavalli, Cesti, Handel, and Mozart. She has edited numerous books, including a collection of Charles *Williams's essays entitled *The Image of the City* (1958), and *Poems and Letters of James Thomson* (1963).

RILEY, Joan (1958–), Jamaican novelist, born in St Mary, Jamaica, educated there and at the universities of Sussex and London. Her novels, dealing primarily with the experiences of women who have moved from the West Indies to Britain, are notable for their scrupulous realism and sensitive characterization. Her first, *The Unbelonging* (1985), is about an 11-year-old girl, Hyacinth, who finds herself abruptly cut off from her exuberant life in the back streets of Kingston when her father summons her to Britain. The novel chronicles her struggle to adjust to 'the gloom of inner-city life'. *Waiting in the Twilight* (1987) focuses on another immigrant, Adela, formerly a talented seamstress but latterly a grandmother crippled by a stroke, who looks back and assesses her hard life. *Romance* (1988), set in Croydon, is about two sisters, one romantically escapist, and the other realistically down-to-earth, and tellingly contrasts the imagined world of a '*Mills and Boon' romance with a real romance. In *A Kindness to the Children* (1992), Riley's most accomplished and complex novel, three women—a second-generation British Caribbean, a first-generation migrant, and a local Jamaican housewife—represent different facets of Caribbean reality. The tragic end of one of the characters is contrasted with the others' relative success to offer a kaleidoscopic view of post-colonial politics.

RILEY, John (1937–78), British poet, born in Leeds, educated at Pembroke College, Cambridge. In 1966, he founded the Grosseteste Press with Tim Longville, a leading British *small press noted for its editions of poetry. Riley's first collection of verse, *Ancient and Modern* (1967), showed originality and accomplishment in the use of closely regulated forms. His other publications include *What the Reason Was* (1970), *Ways of Approaching* (1973), and *That is Today* (1978), which display an increasing concern with religious intuitions. While his mature poetry suggests modern American influences in the openness of its forms, the elegant cadencing and lyrical restraint of his best work seem firmly in the English tradition. Riley was killed by muggers in Leeds in 1978. His *Collected Works*, edited by Tim Longville, and a *Selected Poems*, edited by Michael Grant, appeared in 1980 and 1995 respectively.

Rites of Passage, a novel by W. *Golding, published in 1980 and awarded the 1980 Booker Prize. Edmund Talbot, an immature dandy, is travelling by ship to Australia to take up a prestigious post; his journal of the voyage forms the text of the novel. The community of passengers and crew includes Zenobia, who seduces him, and Prettiman, the free-thinker, but the main storyline concerns the clergyman Colley, ridiculed and abused by all from the Captain downwards. The book's climax describes the sexual humiliation of Colley when drunk, and his death from shame. The ship is portrayed by Golding as the world in small, with Captain Anderson presiding like a god—a metaphor that is often underlined. The miniature society is maintained on board more successfully than in **Lord of the Flies*, but the same darkness threatens it. The title therefore has a double thrust: Talbot has matured by the end of the novel, but more literally, Colley's downfall is precipitated by the approaching ceremony of Crossing the Line, the 'rites of passage', when the anti-religious fury of most of the characters comes to the surface. The novel ends with the ship still at sea. Golding's two sequels, *Close Quarters* (1987) and *Fire Down Below* (1989), complete the story of the voyage.

RIVE, Richard (1931–89), South African novelist and short-story writer, born in District Six, Cape Town, educated at the University of Cape Town, Columbia University (New York), and Magdalen College, Oxford. Rive lived mainly in South Africa, and held various teaching and academic appointments. Like his compatriot Alex *La Guma, he chronicled the squalor and tension of township life arising directly from apartheid legislation in South Africa. He was particularly concerned with District Six, which was demolished by government fiat, and its mainly mixed-race population driven out. His short stories are collected in *African Songs* (1963) and *Advance Retreat: Selected Short Stories* (1983). Other stories, as well as plays and essays, are included in *Selected Writings* (1976). His first novel, *Emergency* (1964), told in flashback, traces the events which led to the Sharpeville massacre, and their effect on a young schoolteacher. Its sequel, *Emergency Continued* (1991), was published posthumously. Another novel, *Buckingham Palace: District Six* (1986), richly distils the author's vision of life, as experienced by the marginalized and dispossessed. *Writing Black* (1981) is an autobiographical memoir. Rive also edited *Modern African Prose* (1964), and *The Letters of Olive Schreiner*, vol. 1, *1871–1899* (1988).

RIVERA, Tomás (1935–84), Chicano novelist and poet, born in Crystal City, Texas, educated at the University of Oklahoma. He is best known for the novel *. . . y no se lo trago la tierra / And the Earth Did Not Part* (1971), a story-cycle recounted as the dying words of a Chicano elder who recalls through the persona of an unnamed child the racial conflicts that have shaped the identity of his ethnic community. The novel is characterized by a fragmented style which shifts from realism to dream sequences to portray the life of an anonymous migrant farmworker from the protagonist's highly subjective point of view. The relationship between the solitary life of the individual and a growing collective sense of solidarity among dispossessed workers is powerfully dramatized. The novel represents a successful literary response to the Chicano civil rights movement of the late 1960s. It was reconstructed with added material, according to Rivera's original intention, by Rolando *Hinojosa-Smith and published as *This Migrant Earth* (1985). Other works include *Always and Other Poems* (1973) and *The Harvest Stories* (1989), a posthumous volume of short fiction.

Road, The, a play by Wole *Soyinka.

Road to Wigan Pier, The, a polemical work by George *Orwell, published in 1937. This powerful indictment of grim living conditions in the mining communities of the north of England established Orwell's credentials as a left-wing commentator but also aroused suspicion and hostility in the communist press. The reception of his text did much to confirm an inclination towards political independence that had grown so strong by 1946 that even a reporter in *Vogue* could acknowledge it: 'Orwell is a defender of freedom, even though most of the time he violently disagrees with the people beside whom he is fighting.' The complaints made in the *Daily Worker* were directed at Orwell's middle-class sensibility. Despite the fact that his detractors wilfully distorted what he had actually said, there is something in this. A fastidious recoil from the physical realities of working-class culture can be found throughout his *œuvre* and suggests that one explanation for his insistent need to go on tramping expeditions was a recurrent attempt to overcome his distaste. But the book also draws on feelings of sincere indignation over the dilapidation and overcrowding of the slums, the meagre diet, the injustice of the means test, the devastating effect of unemployment, and the appalling rate of deaths and disabilities among miners. Parts of the book are delivered in the neutral tones appropriate to the documentation of representative cases, and there are disquisitions on class consciousness and on the relationship between socialism and mechanization that are presented as dispassionate inquiries; but, as always with Orwell, the most telling moments have a sharply personal flavour.

Road to Xanadu, The, see LOWES, JOHN LIVINGSTON.

ROBBINS, Harold, see BESTSELLERS.

ROBBINS, Lionel Charles (1898–1984), British economist, who became Baron Robbins of Clare Market in 1961, born in Middlesex, educated at the London School of Economics where he later became Professor of Economics. Between the wars he was an active anti-Keynesian (something he later declared to have been 'the greatest mistake of my professional career' in his *Autobiography of an Economist*, 1971). He chaired a committee on higher education (known as the Robbins Committee) which is credited with setting in motion the great expansion of the British system of higher education which took place in the 1960s and 1970s. In his classic *Essay on the Nature and Significance of Economic Science* (1932), Robbins proposed a definition of the subject matter of economics: the economic problem, and therefore the proper subject of the discipline, is the allocation of scarce resources among competing ends. Just how far his position on government intervention had altered since the war is evident in his *Theory of Economic Policy in English Classical Political Economy* (1952), which argued that even famous 'free-marketeers' like Adam Smith and Jeremy Bentham were in fact *not* dogmatic proponents of *laissez-faire*.

ROBBINS, Tom (Thomas Eugene) (1936–), American novelist, born in Blowing Rock, North Carolina, educated at Lee University and the University of Washington. He first published the biography *Guy Anderson* (1965), and remained relatively unknown until his two novels *Another Roadside Attraction* (1971) and *Even Cowgirls Get the Blues* (1976) were republished in paperback. His hugely popular novels embrace the counter-cultural attitudes of personal freedom, transcendence through Eastern mysticism, and escape from the urban to the pastoral Pacific Northwest common to the 'West Coast' school of writing and authors like Ken *Kesey and Richard *Brautigan. *Another Roadside Attraction* is about some eccentrics who get involved with the mummified body of Christ which appears at the Captain Kendrick Memorial Hot Dog Wildlife Reserve; whilst *Even Cowgirls Get the Blues* narrates the adventures of Sissy Hankshaw, an extraordinary hitchhiker endowed with oversize thumbs. Less well received was *Still Life with Woodpecker* (1980), but success returned with *Jitterbug Perfume* (1984), about a waitress called Priscilla who devotes her life to inventing the ultimate perfume. Robbins has maintained his reputation for anarchical attitudes to traditional narrative forms, and his love of word-play, puns, and black humour, in *Skinny Legs and All* (1990). His novel *Half Asleep in Frog Pajamas* appeared in 1994.

ROBERTS, Sir Charles G(eorge) D(ouglas) (1860–1943), Canadian poet and writer, born in Douglas, New Brunswick, educated at the University of New Brunswick. Roberts is sometimes regarded as the father of Canadian poetry, chiefly because the favourable reception of his early and best work, which blends late Romantic poetic modes with an attempt to encompass Canadian themes, proved an inspiration to other poets of his generation. He is generally classified as one of the 'Confederation Poets', the group of turn-of-the-century Canadian writers who did much to establish a local tradition in poetry. His landscape verse ultimately turns away from the English models in which it finds its origins by legitimizing Canadian wilderness settings as proper subjects for poetry. His later work is influenced by *Modernism and the changing social and ideological climate of the inter-war years. Roberts published 21 volumes of poetry, of which *Orion* (1880), *In Divers Tones* (1886), *Songs of the Common Day* (1893), and *The Iceberg* (1934) are among the best-known. Along with Ernest Thompson *Seton, he helped to establish the animal story as a highly popular Canadian form. His work in this genre reflects his belief that humanity should live closer to nature, and includes *Earth's Enigmas* (1896), *The Kindred of the Wild* (1902), *The Watchers of the Trails* (1904), and *The Feet of the Furtive* (1912).

ROBERTS, Keith (John Kingston) (1935–), British writer of *science fiction and fantasy, born in Kettering, Northamptonshire, educated at Leicester College of Art. Most of his work is set in southern England; *Pavane* (1968), his first success, presented an alternate history of England in which the Spanish Armada won, and an intriguingly different culture ensued; a bleaker alternate history governed the England of *Kiteworld* (1985). Many of his novels are linked stories, as in *The Chalk Giants* (1974) in which an apocalyptic abyssal future is inhabited by strange characters. Roberts seems most concerned with the mysteriousness of men and women deeply rooted in self and landscape; the short stories of *Machines and Men* (1973), *The Grain Kings* (1976), *Ladies from Hell* (1979), *The Lordly Ones* (1986), and *Winterwood* (1989) are a series of character portraits of the unknowable; even the voluble protagonist of *Kaeti & Company* (1986) remains an enigma. A powerful ambivalence about relations between the sexes affects the dystopian *Molly Zero* (1980), and is best articulated in *Grainne* (1987).

ROBERTS, Michael (William Edward) (1902–48), British poet, critic, and editor, born in Bournemouth, educated at King's College, London, and Trinity College, Cambridge. After working as a schoolteacher, he joined the BBC's European Service during the Second World War, and became Principal of the College of St Mark and St John in Chelsea in 1945. As the editor of *New Signatures* (1932) and *New Country* (1933) he gave a corporate identity to the group of poets whose leading members were W. H. *Auden, Stephen *Spender, and C. *Day Lewis. In 1936 he edited *The *Faber Book of Modern Verse*. His own poetry, initially tending towards the restrained accomplishment of *These Our Matins* (1930), his first collection, grew more individual in tone and technically freer with *Poems* (1936) and *Orion Marches* (1939). An ability to combine intellectually contemplative and observational elements characterizes the best of his verse. His experiences as a climber provided imagery for many of his poems, including the memorable 'La Meije 1937' and 'The Secret Springs'. *Collected Poems* was published in 1958. He also produced several wide-ranging and challenging books on cultural concerns, notably *The Recovery of the West* (1941), an analysis of the inadequacy of prevailing social attitudes, and *The Estate of Man* (1951, edited by J. B. A. Smith), which anticipates the urgent ecological concerns of later generations. Among his other works are the critical studies *Critique of Poetry* (1934) and *T. E. Hulme* (1938).

ROBERTS, Michèle (1949–), British novelist, born in Bushey, Hertfordshire, educated at convent school and at Somerville College, Oxford. Her mother was a French Catholic and her father an English Protestant. Roberts's early novels, *A Piece of the Night* (1978) and *The Visitation* (1983), earned her a reputation as a leading feminist novelist. In *The Wild Girl* (1984) she turned to myth and archetype, a lasting preoccupation, to tell the story of Mary Magdalene. The novel, with its perspective reminiscent of the Gnostic Gospels, earned its author some censure from orthodox religious groups. In *The Book of Mrs Noah* (1987) Roberts combines her fascination with myth, both biblical and Greek, with a post-modernist zest of metatextual commentaries on the related arts of story-telling and textuality, feminizing these issues in a manner that parallels the literary/linguistic explorations of gender practised by her French contemporaries, Hélène Cixous, Luce Irigaray, and Julia Kristeva. Her interest in contemporary literary theory and her exuberant inventiveness are again evident in *In the Red Kitchen* (1990), an entertaining juxtaposition of Egyptian legend and Victorian charlatanism. *Daughters of the House* (1992), a critical and commercial success, revealed a new and simpler facet of Roberts's talent: based, in part, on a true incident, the novel relocates a reported sighting of the Virgin to the setting of the Second World War, and tells, in straightforward narrative, of the impact of these happenings on the lives and future fantasies of two young girls. *During Mother's Absence* (1993) collects stories which reveal her joy in richly textured depictions of sensuous pleasures. In *Flesh and Blood* (1994), a novel composed of cruel tales set in various centuries, she returns to the style and concerns of earlier fictions. Roberts's poems, which appeared in *Touch Papers* (1982; with Judith *Kazantzis and Micheline Wandour), *The Mirror of the Mother* (1986), and *Psyche and the Hurricane* (1990), are included in *All the Selves I Was: New and Selected Poems* (1994).

ROBERTSON, E. Arnot (Eileen Arbuthnot) (1903–61), British novelist, broadcaster, lecturer, and film critic, born in Surrey. A popular novelist of the 1920s and 1930s, her first novel, *Callum* (1928), was a study of obsessive love. Her concern for the effects of 'civilization' on the free spirit of childhood is expressed in her second novel, *Three Came Unarmed* (1929). Her finest and most enduring work is *Ordinary Families* (1933), a classic portrayal of British family life, sibling rivalry, and the complexities and betrayals that lie below the surface of a healthy boating family. She published nine novels in all, including *Four Frightened People* (1931), in which one woman and two men are stranded together in the Malayan jungle, and *Devices and Desires* (1954), in which she drew upon her experiences of Greece during the Greek Civil War. She was married to H. E. Turner, general secretary of the Empire and Commonwealth Press Unions, whose death in a boating accident in 1960 precipitated her suicide the following year.

ROBINSON, Edwin Arlington (1869–1935), American poet, born in Maine, educated at Harvard. During his early life Robinson struggled to attain recognition as a poet, finally achieving it with *The Man against the Sky* (1916), which began his most prolific and successful period. During the years that followed he produced numerous volumes of verse including *Merlin* (1917), *Lancelot* (1920), *The Three Taverns* (1920), *The Man who Died Twice* (1924), *Dionysus in Doubt* (1925), and *Tristram* (1927). This period saw a development in his work from short dramatic and reflective poems to longer narrative works written in blank verse and demonstrating a greater psychological complexity. Robinson's early verse is characterized by a quasi-Wordsworthian attempt to write poetry about everyday subjects in ordinary language and usually attempting to tell the story of humdrum existences. This and an alleged reputation for pessimism denied him the recognition he deserved until a change in the social and cultural climate after the First World War and a movement towards greater sophistication in his verse found him a more appreciative audience. Though difficult, his poetry of this period is devoid of hermetic *Modernist symbolism. Robinson's later years saw a decline in both the quality of his work and in his reputation. His other volumes of verse include *The Children of the Night* (1897), *Captain Craig* (1902), *The Town Down the River* (1910), *The Glory of the Nightingales* (1930), and *Collected Poems* (1937). He also published the prose plays *Van Zorn* (1914) and *The Porcupine* (1915).

ROBINSON, Joan Violet (1903–83), British economist, born in Camberley, Surrey, educated at Girton College, Cambridge. She was one of the group of younger economists at Cambridge which was instrumental in staging the so-called Keynesian Revolution. Her first book, *The Economics of Imperfect Competition* (1933), launched an entire revolution of its own in thinking about the theory of the firm—but she later disowned it (as a wrong turning). She was successively a Fellow of Girton and of Newnham College, Cambridge, subsequently becoming Professor of Economics (1965). Never shy of controversy, Robinson took on cherished economic dogmas with a near-crusading zeal, and to devastating effect; among her many targets were the textbooks of orthodox economics, certain converts to 'Keynesianism' in the post-war years she dubbed 'bastard Keynesians', aspects of Marxian economics, the marginal productivity theory of distribution, and the doctrine of *laissez-faire*. Among her massive published output are *An Essay on Marxian Economics* (1942), *Economic Philosophy* (1962), *Freedom and Necessity* (1970), and *Aspects of Development and Underdevelopment* (1979). Both when she was right and when she was wrong, Robinson's style often infuriated her adversaries.

ROBINSON, Kim Stanley (1962–), American *science fiction writer, born in Waukegan, Illinois, educated at the Universities of California, San Diego, and Boston. He has been praised for a thematic trilogy of novels set in three different versions of Orange County, California: *The Wild Shore* (1984), set after a nuclear holocaust, subjects the pastoral utopias typical of science fiction to ironic scrutiny; *The Gold Coast* (1988) sees America becoming further entangled in the consequences of the military-industrial complex; and *Pacific Edge* (1990) guardedly envisions some small-scale utopian solutions. *Icehenge* (1984) is a metaphysical *space opera; *Escape from Kathmandu* (1989) comically depicts American climbers in Nepal. The widely praised *Red Mars* (1992) explores in cogently realistic terms the possibilities of human survival within this solar system. *Green Mars* (1993) continues the sequence. *Remaking History* (1994) is a selection of Robinson's short stories.

ROBINSON, Lennox (1886–1958), Irish playwright and theatre director, born in Douglas, Co. Cork, the son of a Church of Ireland clergyman, and educated at Bandon Grammer School. After the popular success of his first play, *The Clancy Name* (1908), he was invited by W. B. *Yeats to manage the *Abbey Theatre, a position he held from 1910 to 1914 and then from 1919 to 1923, subsequently serving as an influential member of the theatre's board of directors until 1956. His popular comedies *The Whiteheaded Boy* (1916) and *Crabbed Youth and Age* (1922) helped the Abbey during an extended period of financial difficulty. In *The Lost Leader* (1918) and *The Big House* (1926) he showed that he was also capable of tackling more serious themes arising from Irish political life. Following *The Far-Off Hills* (1928), Robinson returned to lighthearted comedy with *Drama at Inish* (1933; retitled *Is Life Worth Living?*), a play which is a pragmatic portrayal of middle-class rural life appealing to the insularity of Ireland in the 1930s and 1940s. Perhaps Robinson's greatest contribution was as a director and theatrical mentor. Having founded the Dublin Drama League in 1919, he helped bring the experimentations of *Realism and *Expressionism to the Irish stage; he has also been accredited with discovering Sean *O'Casey.

ROBINSON, Peter (1953–), British poet, born in Salford, educated at the Universities of York and Cambridge; he taught at the University College of Wales, Aberystwyth, and at Cambridge before becoming a lecturer at Tohoku University, Japan, in 1989. Robinson's poetry was first collected in the *small press editions *The Benefit Forms* (1978), *Overdrawn Account* (1980), and *Anaglypta* (1985). His principal collections include *This Other Life* (1988), *More About the Weather* (1989), and *Entertaining Fates* (1992). Many of his poems explore aspects of everyday experience and personal relationships with a restrained lyrical intensity that owes much to the skill with which he inlays rhyme unobtrusively into the patterns of ordinary speech. *Leaf-Viewing* (1992) consists exclusively of poems reflecting his first two years in Japan. Robinson's other publications include the critical essays of *In the Circumstances* (1992). He is the editor of *The Collected Poems of Adrian Stokes* (1981).

ROCHE, Billy (1949–), Irish dramatist, born in Wexford, Ireland, the son of a publican, educated in the same town. He worked in a car-seat factory, then went to England in an unsuccessful attempt to make his living as a folk-singer, but achieved some success when he returned to Ireland and formed his own touring rock band. A novel, *Tumbling Down* (1986), was followed by three plays which, like the novel, take place in his native Wexford. They are *A Handful of Stars* (1988), set in a pool hall and involving a young drifter slipping into crime; *Poor Beast in the Rain* (1989), set in a betting shop owned by a man whose wife has run off with a local 'wild man', Danger Doyle, to what has turned out to be a sad, lonely life in London; and *Belfry* (1991), set in a church and involving a sacristan who launches into a love affair with a married woman. After these plays, performed with great success in London in 1992 as the 'Wexford trilogy', came *Amphibians* (1992), about the decline of the same town's fishing industry and its traditions, and *The Cavalcaders* (1993), another elegiac comedy, this time involving a group of cobblers who have formed themselves into a barber-shop quartet during their spare hours. Roche's work is notable for its sympathetic, humorous, yet critical portrayal of a community that is both nourishing and stultifying and of the individuals whose lives are both positively and negatively shaped by those profoundly ambivalent roots.

RODGERS, W(illiam) R(obert) (1909–69), Northern Irish poet, born in Belfast, where he was educated at Queen's University. In 1935 he was ordained as a Presbyterian minister. He resigned from the ministry in 1946, after an opportunity with the BBC in London arose through his association with Louis *MacNeice, whom he commemorated in the fine elegy 'A Last Word'. Transcripts of his broadcasts on eminent Irish writers were published as *Irish Literary Portraits* (1972). From 1966 until his death in Los Angeles he taught at various Californian colleges. His first volume of poetry, *Awake! and Other Poems* (1941) was followed by *Europa and the Bull* (1952). Their contents, together with previously uncollected work, made up his *Collected Poems* (edited by Dan Davin, 1971). Rodgers's earlier work is remarkable for the extravagant musical energies it generates in imitation of the vitality of natural phenomena. His poetry was also unusual in its day for its imaginative evocations of the sinister tensions he perceived in Northern Irish society. Vivid recreations of biblical incidents are a recurrent feature of his later work. Darcy O'Brien's *W. R. Rodgers* (1972) is a critical and biographical study.

ROETHKE, Theodore (Huebner) (1908–63), American poet, born in Saginaw, Michigan, where his father, a wholesale florist, owned the greenhouses which became a major source of imagery in Roethke's poetry. Educated at the University of Michigan, he began his academic career in 1931 at Lafayette College in Pennsylvania and was Professor of English at the University of Washington from 1948 until his sudden death in 1963. His first collection, *Open House* (1941), displayed a lyrical concentration that anticipated the psychological intensity of later work. Radical stylistic advances in *The Lost Son* (1948) established disciplined free verse as the characteristic form of his verse. The volume included the first of his poems to use memories of the fecundity and decay in the greenhouses of his childhood as a medium for exploring the underlying structures of consciousness. *Praise to the End!* (1951) displayed the increasingly visionary aspect of his concern with the nature of individual identity. *The Waking* (1953; Pulitzer Prize) and *Words for the Wind* (1958) contain verse from preceding volumes with hitherto uncollected material. The last collection to be published in his lifetime, *I Am! Says the Lamb* (1961), featured poetry of childlike simplicity charged with symbolic and mystical implication. *The Far Field* (1964), arguably his most impressive collection, maintained a poised balance between elegy and celebration in its imaginatively expansive responses to the natural world. *Collected Poems* (1966) shows the range of Roethke's *œuvre*, in which many ebulliently humorous poems complement the gravity of much of his best-known writing. *On the Poet and His Craft* (1965), a selection of his criticism, and *Selected Letters of Theodore Roethke* (1968) are edited by Ralph J. Mills Jr; *Straw for the Fire* (edited by D. Waggoner, 1972) is a collection of extracts from his voluminous notebooks. The fullest of several biographies of Roethke is *The Glass House* (1968) by Alan Seager.

ROGERS, Jane (1952–), British novelist, born in London, educated at Cambridge University. Her first novel, *Separate Tracks* (1983), traces with imaginative boldness the lives of Emma, an undergraduate of enlightened middle-class parents, and Orph, a working-class youth brought up in care. *Her Living Image* (1984) deals with a split personality, Carolyn Tanner, who is both conventional wife and mother and, as Caro, a radical feminist with like-minded friends. *The Ice Is Singing* (1987) is an account of a woman running away from her husband and writing stories to fend off self-confrontation. *Mr Wroe's Virgins* (1991) recreates the world of John Wroe, a Bradford religious fanatic who, in the 1820s, founded a Christian Israelite Church in Ashton-under-Lyme, near Manchester, and who in 1830 asked for, and was given, seven virgins to live in this household. The novel is told by four of the virgins, and explores their contrasting relationships with Wroe, and the tensions between the spiritual, sexual, and societal lives within the artificial circumstances of an extreme Puritan community. *Promised Lands* (1995) interweaves the story of William Dawes, naval officer and astronomer and part of the 1788 British expeditionary force that founded Sydney, with the contemporary first-person narratives of a teacher and his wife, to create a novel exploring exile, colonialism, creativity, and motherhood.

ROGERS, Will(iam Penn Adair) (1879–1935), American humorist, born in Oologah, Oklahoma. In the 1920s and early 1930s Rogers was one of America's most popular humorists. He was already acquiring an international reputation when he joined Ziegfeld's Follies in 1915. He made his first motion picture in 1918 (*Laughing Bill Hyde*) and in 1919 published the first two collections of his jokes, *Rogersisms: The Cowboy Philosopher on the Peace Conference* and *Rogersisms: The Cowboy Philosopher on Prohibition*, following which his reputation as a humorous commentator on American political affairs grew rapidly. Between 1925 and 1928 he travelled widely in the USA on lecture tours; he reported on the Democratic Convention of 1928 for the *New York Times*, at the same time offering himself as the candidate for the 'Anti-Bunk' party. He made a series of popular films in the late 1920s and early 1930s, including *A Connecticut Yankee*, *Young as You Feel*, and *State Fair*.

ROHMER, Sax, pseudonym of Arthur Henry SARSFIELD (Ward) (1883–1959), British popular writer and author of songs and comedy sketches for the music hall, born in Birmingham. His experiences as a crime reporter in London's Limehouse district provided the material for his best-known work, the long series of stories in which the villain is the sinister Chinaman Dr Fu-Manchu, whose diabolical schemes are constantly thwarted by the noted Orientalist Sir Denis Nayland Smith: *The Mystery of Dr Fu-Manchu* (1913; US title *The Insidious Dr Fu-Manchu*) was followed by *The Devil Doctor* (1916; US title *The Return of Dr Fu-Manchu*) and others; the later are less successful. Rohmer's *The*

Romance of Sorcery (1914) is a standard reference work on the occult.

ROLFE, Frederick William (1860–1913), British novelist, essayist, painter, and calligrapher, self-styled variously as Baron Corvo and 'Fr Rolfe', born in London. Rolfe's desire to enter the Roman Catholic priesthood was never fulfilled; he converted to Roman Catholicism from a dissenting background and trained for Holy Orders, but his vocation was rejected. Six retellings of folk legends of the Catholic saints, *Stories Toto Told Me* (1898), were first published in *The Yellow Book*, and a collection of twenty-six were published as *In His Own Image* (1901). Rolfe's obsession with Renaissance Italy and the Borgias is displayed in his *Chronicles of the House of Borgia* (1901), the idealized self-portrait **Hadrian the Seventh* (1904), *Don Tarquinio* (1905), and *Don Renato* (1909). Rolfe, perpetually dogged by poverty, was supported by friends in Italy who were appalled to see their generosity repaid by scathing pen-portraits in *The Desire and Pursuit of the Whole* (published posthumously in 1934) and *Nicholas Crabbe* (1958). His prima-donna attitude to publishers and patrons, his obscure subject matter, and his falling foul of libel and homosexuality laws all ensured that he died in poverty. *The Quest for Corvo* (1934), A. J. A. *Symons's 'experiment in biography', found him the audience that had eluded him in life; symposia such as *New Quests for Corvo* (1961; edited by Cecil Woolf and Brocard Sewell) were published for what had become a Corvo cult.

Roman Spring of Mrs Stone, The, a novel by Tennessee *Williams.

Romantic Fiction. The antecedents of popular Romantic Fiction can be found in the Gothic romances of Sir Walter Scott, with their powerfully drawn heroes and villains and their complex and sympathetically drawn heroines, and in the eighteenth-century novels of manners, such as Samuel Richardson's *Clarissa* (1748), which focused on a contest of wills between its eponymous heroine and her sexually attractive but ruthless seducer. The novels of Jane Austen, particularly *Pride and Prejudice* (1813), anatomized similar conflicts between men and women which ended, however, not with the heroine's death but with her marriage. By the mid-nineteenth century, novels such as Charlotte Brontë's *Jane Eyre* (1847) and Emily Brontë's *Wuthering Heights* (1847) explored the complexities of sexual attraction and—in the characters of their respective heroes, Mr Rochester and Heathcliffe—provided archetypes for much that was to follow.

The early part of the twentieth century saw a burgeoning of popular romantic fiction. It was never explicitly sexual, although the novels of Ethel M. Dell (1881–1939) and Elinor *Glyn offered a frisson of eroticism. In Glyn's best-known novel, *Three Weeks* (1907), for example, a naïve young Englishman learns about sexual pleasure from a mysterious woman who seduces him on a tiger skin in Venice. Dell's *The Way of an Eagle* (1912) was similarly exotic. Set on the North-West Frontier of India, it concerns the romance between a brigadier's daughter and a masterful but cold-blooded hero. The sado-masochistic element implicit in these novels is even stronger in Edith Maud Hull's *The Sheik* (1919), which became an international bestseller after it was filmed with Rudolf Valentino in the title role. The story concerns an English girl who is kidnapped and seduced by an Arab sheik, with whom she eventually falls in love and marries, after discovering that he is, in fact, a member of the British aristocracy. From the 1920s onward, romantic novels began to use more realistic settings (although exotic backgrounds remained popular), in which the heroine—frequently an impoverished, though well-bred, young woman—attained social advancement with love. Romances with a historical setting, such as the Regency novels of Georgette *Heyer, also achieved a wide following. Bestsellers of the period include Margaret *Mitchell's *Gone with the Wind* (1936) and Daphne *du Maurier's *Rebecca* (1938), both of which were made into popular films. In more recent times, Dame Barbara Cartland (1901–) has enjoyed great popular success with her romantic fiction, much of it also with a historical setting, and has written over 500 books.

Contemporary romantic fiction can be divided into several categories. These include the short, formulaic novels published by *Mills and Boon and Robert Hale; their authors often write three or four books a year under different names and are unknown outside their own readership. Higher up the scale are the genre novels, published by mainstream publishers. These books have, on the whole, more original settings, as well as better characterization and plot development than the average Mills and Boon romance. Catherine *Cookson, for example, has written many novels incorporating romantic plots into the realistic settings of her native North-East of England. Jean *Plaidy (who also wrote as Philippa Carr and Victoria Holt) displayed an extensive knowledge of different historical periods in her books. In her 'Wideacre' books, Philippa Gregory writes for a younger readership who prefer a more sexually explicit narrative. A recent phenomenon in genre fiction is the 'sex and shopping' saga, of which the leading exponents are the writers Jackie Collins, Judith Krantz, Shirley Conran (1932–), and Sally Beauman (1940–).

ROMER, Stephen (1957–), British poet, born in Bishop's Stortford, educated at Trinity Hall, Cambridge. *Idols* (1986), his first full collection of poetry, attracted wide critical notice. Derek *Mahon's commendation of Romer's 'emotional candour and intellectual clarity' summarizes the essential qualities of his work. *Plato's Ladder* (1992) further demonstrates his ability to express intimate and intense personal experience while retaining the impress of a complex and erudite sensibility. He has also produced translations, including *The Growing Dark* (1981), his versions of poems by Jacques Dupin.

Room at the Top, a novel by John *Braine, published in 1957. Hardened by war service and the loss of his parents, Joe Lampton arrives in the Yorkshire town of Warley convinced of the supremacy of materialistic values, and intent on making his way into the upper echelons of bourgeois society. Braine's self-assured, iconoclastic hero serves as a sardonic observer of the personalities and politics of a provincial town as he makes his way in this world, aided by his respectable, middle-class landlady, his prowess in amateur dramatics, and his professional pursuit of Susan Brown, daughter of the richest man in Warley. Braine's rather schematic plot, which sets Lampton's social success against his genuine love affair with a married woman named Alice Aisgill, and demands that he choose between the two, is saved by the knowing humour of his style and occasional passages of genuine power, particularly the scene of hopeless low life in the working-class quarter of Warley where Joe seeks woeful comfort after his rejection of Alice and her subsequent suicide. Achieving his goal of marriage to Susan Brown and acceptance by the plutocrats of Warley, Lampton finally realizes the emptiness of his achievement and the terrible sacrifice of his integrity.

Room of One's Own, A, a feminist essay about women's education, exclusion, and writing, by V. *Woolf, published in 1929 and based on two lectures on 'Women and Fiction' given in October 1928 to Newnham and Girton Colleges, Cambridge. Woolf describes the educational, social, and financial disadvantages and prejudices against which women have struggled throughout history. The history of women's writing is a slowly accumulating inheritance emerging from poverty, discouragement, and exclusion. But, once 'a room of one's own and £500 a year' (a shorthand for education, independence, a career, and an income) have been acquired, women should not discard the obscure history of their literary 'mothers'. Their 'alien and critical stance' should be preserved. What civilization needs is the writing of 'outsiders', which can be indifferent to sexual grievance, free from personal bias, and interested instead in the relation of individual to 'the world of reality'. She pays tribute to women writers of the past (including Aphra Behn, Jane Austen, and the Brontës). She projects a future in which increasing equality would enable women to write about friendships with each other and to be poets as well as novelists. In the last chapter she discusses the concept of 'androgyny'. This famous utopian ideal, borrowed from Coleridge, does not apply to a mind which has discarded its femaleness or dissolved it into a kind of sexual melting-pot, but a mind which retains its difference while discarding anger or egotism. The tone of the essay is diplomatically urbane and witty, with its own anger concealed under amusing anecdotes. The argument of a society of 'outsiders' was resumed more aggressively in **Three Guineas* (1938). See also FEMINIST CRITICISM.

Room with a View, A, a novel by E. M. *Forster, published in 1908. The opening scene takes place in the Pensione Bertolini, in Florence, where Lucy Honeychurch, a charmingly naïve young Englishwoman, her chaperone, Miss Bartlett, and an assortment of other English visitors are staying. Amongst these are the unconventional Mr Emerson and his son George, who, learning that the room which Lucy and her companion are sharing has no view of the city, offer to exchange rooms—a gesture which, in Miss Bartlett's opinion, is somewhat indelicate. Lucy, however, persuades her to accept, and a relationship develops between the two young people, which culminates in the moment when, on an excursion to Fiesole, George kisses Lucy. Other guests at the pensione include the lady novelist Miss Lavish and the clergyman Mr Beebe, whom the ladies encounter on their return to Lucy's parents' home in the Surrey village of Summer Street, where he is the local vicar. Here, Lucy becomes engaged to Cecil Vyse, a cultivated, but essentially effete, dilettante. When the Emersons appear in the village, having taken a house there for a few months, Lucy gradually comes to realize that it is not Cecil she loves, but George. Constrained both by her innocence in affairs of the heart and by a feeling of obligation towards Cecil, she is prevented from telling George of her feelings until it is almost too late; only a timely intervention by Miss Bartlett brings matters to a satisfactory conclusion. The novel ends, with fitting symmetry, in the Pensione Bertolini, where George and Lucy are staying on their honeymoon.

Roots, see HALEY, ALEX.

ROSENBERG, Isaac (1890–1918), British poet and painter, the son of a Russian-Jewish *émigré*, born in Bristol; from the age of seven he grew up in Stepney, London. He worked as an apprentice engraver before becoming a student at the Slade School of Art, and began his career as an artist in 1913. Examples of his work are on permanent exhibition in the Tate Gallery and the National Portrait Gallery in London. His early poetry is collected in *Night and Day* (1912) and *Youth* (1915), which display considerable accomplishment in the use of traditional forms and marked originality in the compression and imaginative force of much of the verse. Edward *Marsh was impressed by his work and encouraged him to attempt verse-drama. Of the several plays and fragments he produced, *Moses* (1916), an ambitious adaptation of biblical material, is the best-known; an excerpt formed his sole contribution to the **Georgian Poetry* series. In 1916 he volunteered for active service. The poetry he wrote as a private on the Western Front prior to his death in action near Arras is characterized by the concrete particularity of its imagery, its angrily unsentimental tone, and its freedom from the constraints of traditional versification; 'Break of Day in the Trenches', 'Dead Man's Dump', 'Louse Hunting', and others are among the finest and most realistic of the poems of the First World War. His achievement was not widely appreciated until the publication of the *Collected Works* of 1937, edited by Gordon *Bottomley and

D. W. Harding. Ian Parsons's comprehensive edition of the poems, plays, essays, and letters, which contains plates of fifty of Rosenberg's paintings and drawings, was published in 1979. Biographical studies include Jean Liddiard's *The Half Used Life* (1975) and Joseph Cohen's *Journey to the Trenches* (1975). See also WAR POETRY.

Rosencrantz and Guildenstern Are Dead, a play by Tom *Stoppard, performed and published in 1966. This, the play that first established its author as a significant voice, brings to the centre of the stage the two 'attendant lords' from *Hamlet*. Beginning with a scene in which they encounter the players on their way to Elsinore, they play word-games, exchange banter and ideas, and from time to time move into the action of Shakespeare's play itself. Indeed, they come to believe themselves trapped by its—to them—inscrutable plot; and though they read the death warrant Hamlet has substituted for the one given them by Claudius, they go consciously to a fate they now feel has been pre-ordained by some hostile power beyond their understanding or control. With its emphasis on ontological bewilderment and helplessness, the play has marked similarities to Beckett's **Waiting for Godot*, but is written with a deft wit particular to Stoppard himself.

ROSS, Alan (1922–), British poet and editor, born in Calcutta, educated at St John's College, Oxford. His wartime experiences on the Murmansk convoys are memorably dealt with in the verse of *Something of the Sea* (1954). In 1945 and 1947 he was in Germany with the Naval Staff; *The Derelict Day: Poems in Germany* (1947) reflects the atmospheres of defeat and bewilderment he encountered. In 1961 he became editor of *The *London Magazine* and founded London Magazine Editions in 1965. His numerous later collections of poetry include *To Whom It May Concern* (1958), *African Negatives* (1962), *Poems 1942–1967* (1967), *The Taj Express* (1973), and *Death Valley* (1980). Much of his verse, in which rigorously objective description combines to incisive effect with a mood of disenchanted detachment, draws on his extensive travels in Europe, Africa, America, and elsewhere. He has also written travel books, among them *Time Was Away: A Notebook in Corsica* (1948) and *The Bandit at the Billiard Table* (1954), an account of Sardinia. His numerous works on sport include *The West Indies at Lords* (1963) and, as editor, *The Cricketer's Companion* (1960) and *The Turf* (1982). *Blindfold Games* (1986) and *Coastwise Lights* (1988) are autobiographical.

ROSS, (James) Sinclair (1908–), Canadian novelist and short-story writer, born near Prince Albert, Saskatchewan. He was a bank employee throughout his working life. After retirement he travelled to Europe, where he lived in Athens, Barcelona, and Malaga, before returning to Canada and settling in Vancouver in 1980. Ross is often regarded as a one-book novelist. His masterpiece, *As for Me and My House* (1941), is a classic study of the constraints of small town prairie life during the Depression years, as experienced by a minister who is an artist *manqué* and his equally thwarted wife, whose diary is the narrative medium of the tale and who is one of Western Canadian fiction's most complex and ambiguous characters. Two of his other novels, *The Well* (1958) and *Whir of Gold* (1970), juxtapose Montreal and Saskatchewan values by relocating a character from one of these environments in the other. His fourth novel, *Sawbones Memorial* (1974), is centred on a retirement party for a Saskatchewan doctor with the action confined to a single evening, and again focusing on the hypocrisies of small town prairie life. *The Lamp at Noon* (1968) and *The Race and Other Stories* (1982) are collections of short stories.

ROSSNER, Judith (1939–), American novelist, born in New York, educated at City College, New York. Her first novel, *To the Precipice* (1966), is the story of a Jewish woman's marriage to a gentile, and her slow progress towards maturity. Her first major success was *Looking for Mr Goodbar* (1975), the harrowing account of a Catholic woman's relentless search for pleasure and release in random sexual encounters, a journey which ultimately results in her death. *Attachments* (1975) deals with two women married to Siamese twins. Rossner handles similarly sensational material with restraint, clarity, and candour, in much of her work. *Emmeline* (1980) retells a true story from the nineteenth century; here the eponymous heroine inadvertently marries her son. *August* (1983) tells of the relationship between an analyst and her patient; *His Little Women* (1990), with its allusion to the innocent Alcott children's classic, is a family psychodrama set in the rapacious world of Hollywood.

ROTH, Henry (1906–95), American author, born in Tysmenica, Austria-Hungary, educated at the City College, New York. His reputation rests on one book, *Call It Sleep* (1934), which was little known until the 1960s, when it was chosen as the 'most neglected book' of twentieth-century American literature by Alfred *Kazin and Leslie *Fiedler. The target of several vigorous attacks and defences from both right and left, it concentrates on Jewish immigrant life in Brooklyn and the Lower East Side of New York told from a child's perspective. Influenced by James *Joyce, its *stream of consciousness combines Jewish myth and urban reality, and as part of its realist strategy, the language of the novel is a fascinating blend of English narrative, Yiddish speech, and street idioms. After the Second World War, he became a water-fowl farmer and later a teacher in New England. He published no more works until *Shifting Landscapes* (1987), a collection of miscellaneous writings. A multi-volume series of autobiographical novels entitled *Mercy of a Rude Stream* began to appear in 1994.

ROTH, Philip (1933–), American novelist, born in Newark, New Jersey, educated at Bucknell and

Chicago Universities. He taught creative writing at Iowa and Princeton Universities before becoming a full-time writer. His collection of an eponymous novella and five short stories, *Goodbye Colombus* (1959), won him immediate success for its sensitive portrayal of the problems facing young Jewish-Americans. Many novels followed, including *Letting Go* (1962) and *When She Was Good* (1967). **Portnoy's Complaint* (1969) brought him notoriety with its focus on masturbation and its generally acerbic view of the levels of alienation faced by the occupants of Jewish-American society. *Our Gang* (1971) was a vicious satire of Richard Nixon's presidency, whilst *The Breast* (1972) was a Freudian allegory about a professor of comparative literature who turns into a massive female breast. *The Great American Novel* (1973), a long spoof of all things American, parodied the general political climate through the allegory of the decline and fall of a baseball team. In *My Life as a Man* (1974) the devastations of a failed marriage become the focus. *The Professor of Desire* (1977) is another novel about a search for the solutions to a failed world in sexual adventure. There followed his semi-autobiographical Nathan Zuckerman sequence, in which a Jewish-American writer comes to terms with personal failure and the wider implications of being Jewish in a post-Holocaust world. The sequence comprises *The Ghost Writer* (1979), *Zuckerman Bound* (1981), and *The Anatomy Lesson* (1983), which, together with *The Prague Orgy* (1985), were republished as *Zuckerman Bound: A Trilogy and Epilogue* (1985). After *The Counter-Life* (1986), a novel which presents a vertiginous display of 'post-modern' games with signification, appeared *The Facts: A Novelist's Autobiography* (1989), an autobiography. *Deception* (1990) focuses on the adultery of an illicit love affair between Philip and his mistress that takes place in a bare room. He has also written two plays, *Heard Melodies Are Sweet* (1958) and *The President Addresses the Nation* (1973). In addition to promoting the work of many Eastern European writers through his efforts as an editor, he has ventured into writing critical essays in *Reading Myself and Others* (1975), which produced many useful insights into his creative life. His latest works include *Operation Shylock: A Confession* (1993) and *Sabbath's Theater* (1995).

ROTHENBERG, Jerome (Dennis) (1931–), American poet, born in New York City, educated at the City College of New York and at the University of Michigan. He held various visiting academic posts throughout the USA before becoming a professor at the University of California, San Diego, in 1988. *White Sun, Black Sun* (1960), his first publication as a poet, displayed an allegiance to *Imagism in the concentrated forms of its meditative lyrics. The compass of his work has subsequently expanded to reflect his interests in Japanese literature, North American Indian culture, *Dada, and his familial connections with the Jewish communities of Eastern Europe. His many collections of verse, which display his commitment to continuous experimentation, include *The Seven Hells of the Jigoku Zoshi* (1962), *A Seneca Journal* (1978), *Vienna Blood* (1980), *That Dada Strain* (1983), *Poland/1931* (1974), *New Selected Poems, 1970–1985* (1986), and *Gematria* (1993); *Khurbn* (1989) constitutes his fullest confrontation with the tragic modern history of the Jewish people. He is the editor of the anthologies *Technicians of the Sacred* (1985) and *Shaking the Pumpkin* (1986), which contain a range of ethnic poetries from Africa, America, Asia, and Oceania.

ROTIMI, Ola (1938–), Nigerian dramatist, born in eastern Nigeria, educated at the Methodist Boys' High School in Lagos, Boston University, and at Yale, where his first play, *Our Husband Has Gone Mad Again*, won the Yale Major Play of the Year award in 1966. In *The Gods Are Not To Blame* (1968), first performed during the Nigerian Civil War, Yoruba King Odewale, an African Oedipus, is tragically defeated, not so much by the gods as by tribal conflicts which he cannot resolve; his failure of leadership, rather than inexorable fate, is a modern version of the Oedipus myth for an African audience, and exhorts Africans not to blame the 'gods' (i.e. the superpowers) for their own political shortcomings. Rotimi's historical tragedies, *Kurunmi* (1969) and *Ovonramwen Nogbaisi* (1971), focus on the personal and political dilemmas of traditional chiefs in the nineteenth century: one headed the Yoruba empire of Oyo, and the other that of Benin. His experimental play *Holding Talks* (1979), eschews both tragedy and history.

ROWBOTHAM, Sheila (1943–), British feminist historian, born in Leeds, educated at St Hilda's College, Oxford. During the 1960s and 1970s she taught with the Workers' Educational Association. In 1968 she joined the editorial staff of the radical socialist journal *Black Dwarf*. She has also held several academic posts. Her endeavour to establish the historical provenance of the women's movement of the 1970s began with *Women, Resistance and Revolution* (1972) and continued in a succession of works which includes *Hidden from History: 300 Years of Women's Oppression and the Fight against It* (1973), the biographical study *A New World for Women: Stella Browne, Socialist Feminist* (1977), *Dreams and Dilemmas: Collected Writings* (1983), *Women in Movement: Feminism and Social Action* (1992), and *Homeworkers Worldwide* (1993). Rowbotham's work is notable for the close interaction of her socialist views and her deep imaginative commitment to the implications of feminism. *The Past Is Before Us* (1989), her survey of the development of feminism in recent decades, gains authority from her personal experience as an activist for political and social change. Her other publications include *Socialism and the New Life* (with Jeffrey Weeks, 1977), a study of Havelock *Ellis and Edward *Carpenter.

ROWSE, A(lfred) L(eslie) (1903–), British poet and historian, born at St Austell, Cornwall, educated at Christ Church, Oxford. From 1925 to 1974 he was a fellow of All Souls College, Oxford. Rowse's remark that 'Places speak to me rather than people and are apt to mean more to me' indicates the emphatically local quality of much of his poetry, which draws widely on the landscapes of Cornwall and Oxford (see TOPOGRAPHICAL POETRY). His numerous collections of verse include *Poems of a Decade: 1931–1941* (1941), *Poems of Deliverance* (1946), *Poems of Cornwall and America* (1967), and *The Road to Oxford* (1978); *A Life: Collected Poems* appeared in 1981, followed by the *Selected Poems* of 1990. The tension between faith and doubt in much of his verse and his accomplished use of traditional forms give his work affinities with that of Sir John *Betjeman, whom he admires. His range extends from ballads of disarming simplicity to poetry of challenging intellectual rigour. Rowse has written prolifically on the history and literature of the sixteenth and seventeenth centuries; his works, which have frequently provoked controversy, include *The England of Elizabeth* (1950), *William Shakespeare: A Biography* (1963), *Milton the Puritan* (1977), and *Four Caroline Portraits* (1993). *The Annotated Shakespeare* (3 volumes, 1978) and *The Sayings of Shakespeare* (1993) are among his works as an editor. Among his other publications are the autobiographical works *A Cornish Childhood* (1942), *All Souls in My Time* (1993), and *Histories I Have Known* (1995). His critical biographies include *The Poet Auden* (1987) and *Quiller-Couch, a Portrait of 'Q'* (1988).

ROY, Namba (1910–61), Jamaican novelist, born in Kingston, Jamaica; he spent much of his childhood among the Maroons, the descendants of escaped African slaves, in the mountainous northern area of the island known as 'the Cockpit Country'. The region's cultural traditions strongly inform *Black Albino* (1961), his first novel, which is based on an episode of violent disunity among the Maroons during the eighteenth century. Following his discharge from the Merchant Navy in 1944 he lived in London, working in various capacities and producing his highly regarded paintings and sculptures. A further novel entitled *No Black Sparrows* appeared posthumously in 1989; its narrative of abandoned children who live as pedlars on the streets of Kingston compellingly evokes the society of colonial Jamaica in the 1930s.

RUBENS, Bernice (Ruth) (1928–), British novelist, born in Cardiff, educated at University College, Cardiff. She taught English at a boy's grammar school in Birmingham, and has since worked as a documentary film writer and director for the United Nations and other organizations. Her first novel, *Set on Edge* (1960), displayed the elements of outrageous comedy and keen observation of the family unit which emerge in different combinations in much of her subsequent work; like *Madame Sousatzka* (1962) and *Mate in Three* (1965), it is an explicitly Jewish novel, exploring the particular idiosyncrasies of the Jewish character and family and their potentially tragic repercussions. Her fourth novel, *The Elected Member* (1969; Booker Prize), inspired by the work of R. D. *Laing, is a searingly honest examination of the emotional damage caused by a Jewish matriarch's exaggerated expectations of her family, and showed that Rubens is as much at home in the psyche as the sitting room. Rubens stepped outside the claustrophobic Jewish household in her next novel, *Sunday Best* (1971), a suspense story whose central character is a transvestite, yet she continues to focus on airless settings which allow examination of intense relationships: the expatriate community of *The Ponsonby Post* (1977), and the passengers on a cruise in *Birds of Passage* (1981). She took a much broader canvas in *The Brothers* (1983), tracing six generations of a Jewish family and their survival through hundreds of years of antagonism and racial hatred. Rubens's narratives are written in a precise, straightforward style which accommodates her extremes of imagination and quirky humour. Her books are not descriptive of appearances, and the colour of surfaces is replaced in her fiction by brilliant flights of fancy which can invent a fiddle-playing foetus in *Spring Sonata* (1979) and a Deity who leaves messages on an answering machine in *Our Father* (1987). Other works include *A Solitary Grief* (1991); *Mother Russia* (1992), a historical saga; and *Autobiopsy* (1993). In *Yesterday in the Back Lane* (1995), an elderly woman reflects on her past and the murder she committed at the age of seventeen when threatened with rape. Rubens also writes for the stage and television, and two of her novels have been filmed.

RUDD, Steele (1868–1935), Australian short-story writer and novelist, born Arthur Hoey Davis in Drayton, Queensland; he received a rudimentary education and worked as a shearer before taking clerical employment in Brisbane in 1885. He took the name Steele Rudd for the spuriously autobiographical stories about the typically Australian Rudd family which he began contributing to the Sydney **Bulletin* in 1895. Following the success of *On Our Selection* (1899), his first collection of sympathetically humorous stories about the Rudds and their smallholding, he produced some fifteen books about the Rudds, which include *Dad in Politics* (1908), *Grandpa's Selection* (1916), *The Old Homestead* (1917), and *Me and th' Son* (1924). Subsequent adaptations of *On Our Selection* for the stage (1912) and cinema (1932) were also highly successful. Among Rudd's novels, which are generally considered inferior to his shorter works, are *The Romance of Runnibede* (1927) and *The Green Homestead* (1934). His other collections of sketches and stories include *On Emu Creek* (1923) and the substantially autobiographical *The Miserable Clerk* (1926).

RUDKIN, (James) David (1936–), British playwright, born in London, educated at St Catherine's College, Oxford; he worked for a time as a schoolteacher. He came to prominence with *Afore Night Come* (1962), a powerful drama in which a scapegoat, an inoffensive Irish tramp, is ritually murdered by his fellow fruit-pickers in an orchard in the contemporary Midlands. His later work includes *Cries from Casement as His Bones Are Brought to Dublin* (1973), an attempt to find parallels between modern Irish history and that of the period when the main character was hanged as a traitor; *Ashes* (1974), about a couple's increasingly desperate attempts to overcome their childlessness and, less directly, about what Rudkin sees as the sterile agonies of Ulster; *Sons of Light* (1977), about an attempt to bring enlightenment to an island variously inhabited by dour Christian stoics, helot zombies, and vicious scientists; and *The Saxon Shore* (1986), set near Hadrian's Wall at the time of the collapse of the Roman empire and involving settlers transformed by night from good Christians into werewolves. Rudkin's plays show an interest, unusual for a contemporary dramatist, in myth, legend, and the unconscious, especially in its darker, more primitive aspects. He has also written drama for television, adapted other writers' work, notably Euripides's *Hippolytus* (1979) and Ibsen's *Peer Gynt* (1983), translated Schoenberg's opera *Moses and Aaron*, and written a version of *Hansel and Gretel* (1981) for the Royal Shakespeare Company.

RUELL, Patrick, see HILL, REGINALD.

RUKEYSER, Muriel (1913–80), American poet and biographer, born in New York, educated at Vassar College, where she founded the *Student Review* with Elizabeth *Bishop and Mary *McCarthy, and at Columbia University. She subsequently undertook research at the Roosevelt Aviation School, which provided material central to *Theory of Flight* (1935), her first collection of poetry. From the outset Rukeyser's verse is marked by the political concern which made her active in a succession of causes; she was jailed for her part in protests against the Vietnam War, to which her lyrically elegiac 'Delta Poems' form a response. Her numerous collections of verse include *U. S. 1* (1938), *Beast in View* (1944), *Body of Waking* (1958), *The Speed of Darkness* (1968), *The Gates* (1976), and *Collected Poems* (1978). The polemical qualities of her earlier work were gradually superseded by the more flexibly individual tone around which she developed the free-verse forms of her best-known poems. Her impassioned idealism is conveyed by vividly precise imagery, frequently drawn from her perceptions of natural phenomena. Her biographical works include *Willard Gibbs: American Genius* (1942), a study of the noted nineteenth-century scientist; *One Life* (1957), which combines verse, prose, and documentary material for its account of the American business magnate Wendell Willkie; and *The Traces of Thomas Hariot* (1971), on the life of the Elizabethan mathematician. Among Rukeyser's other works are *The Orgy* (1965), a novel centring on events at the annual Puck Fair in Kerry, and *The Life of Poetry* (1949), a collection of her essays on socio-cultural and literary themes which includes autobiographical material.

RULE, Jane (1931–), Canadian novelist, born in Plainfield, New Jersey, educated at Mills College (California), University College (London), and Stanford University. Her first and best-known novel, *Desert of the Heart* (1964), tells, in alternating narrative voices, the story of two women who break away from heterosexual constraints to find fulfilment in a lesbian relationship. *This Is not for You* (1970) is limited to a single perspective and treats its lesbian theme with less optimism. Other novels—which include *Against the Season* (1972), *The Young in One Another's Arms* (1977), *Contract with the World* (1980), *Memory Board* (1987), and *After the Fire* (1989)—adopt multiple points of view to examine various social and psychological issues and aspects of North American life. Short stories are collected in *Theme for Diverse Instruments* (1975) and *Inland Passages* (1985). Rule's fiction consistently explores the subjectivities of a wide range of women and men, both hetero- and homosexual, with compassion and insight. Her reflections on lesbian themes in fiction are collected in her popular and accessible critical work, *Lesbian Images* (1975).

RUMENS, Carol (1944–), British poet, born in Lewisham, London, educated at Bedford College, University of London. She became poetry editor of the **Literary Review* in 1982; she is also active as a teacher of creative writing. *A Strange Girl in Bright Colours* (1973) was her first collection of poetry; subsequent volumes include *A Necklace of Mirrors* (1978), *Unplayed Music* (1981), *Star Whisper* (1983), *Direct Dialling* (1985), *Selected Poems* (1987), *From Berlin to Heaven* (1989), and *Thinking of Skins: New and Selected Poems* (1993). Many of her earlier poems combined precisely observed imagery, sardonic humour, and remarkable candour in their treatments of domestic and suburban experience. From *Star Whisper* onward her work displays an intensifying imaginative involvement with modern European history; numerous memorable poems of suffering and persecution include the tragically elegiac treatments of the Nazi Holocaust in 'Outside Osweicim' and 'A New Song'. *Plato Park* (1987), her first novel, is largely set in Moscow. Among her other publications is *Jean Rhys: A Critical Study* (1985). She edited *Making for the Open: The Chatto Book of Post-Feminist Poetry* (1987), and *New Women Poets* (1990).

RUNCIMAN, Sir (James Cochran) Steven(son) (1903–), British historian, born in Northumberland, educated at Eton and at Trinity College, Cambridge, of which he was a fellow between 1927 and 1938. He subsequently held a succession of senior academic posts in Europe and America and was President of the British Institute of Archaeology in Ankara from 1960 to 1975. His earlier publications include *The Emperor Romanus Lecapenus* (1929) and *The First Bulgarian Empire* (1930). *The Eastern Schism* (1955), *The Fall of Constantinople* (1965), *The Last Byzantine Renaissance* (1970), and *Mistra: Byzantine Capital of the Peloponnese* (1980) are among the works which established his reputation as a foremost authority on Byzantine civilization. *A Traveller's Alphabet* (1991) contains Runciman's informative and entertaining autobiographical recollections of the wide range of countries and cultures he has experienced. His other works include the highly regarded *A History of the Crusades* (3 volumes, 1951–4). He was knighted in 1958.

RUNYON, (Alfred) Damon (1884–1946), American writer, born in Manhattan, Kansas. Runyon won fame for his stories of Broadway life, turning the gamblers, gangsters, and high-rollers of the 1920s and 1930s into exotic characters, whose inventive slang vocabulary captured the imagination of his audience. Many of these stories were later gathered in collections such as *Guys and Dolls* (1932) and *Take It Easy* (1938). A theatrical farce called *A Slight Case of Murder* (1935) was co-authored with Howard Lindsay. One of the stories from *Guys and Dolls*, 'The Idyll of Miss Sarah Brown', formed the basis for Frank Loesser's famous musical version of *Guys and Dolls* of 1950 and was later made into a movie starring Jean Simmons, Frank Sinatra, and Marlon Brando. Runyon belongs to a long tradition of American writers of comedy whose work occasionally transcends the limitations of the comic mode to accomplish a work of durable pleasure and fascination. John Mosedale's *The Men Who Invented Broadway: Damon Runyon, Walter Winchell and Their World* (1981) is the standard biography.

RUSHDIE, (Ahmed) Salman (1947–), Anglo-Indian novelist, born in Bombay, educated at Rugby School, and King's College, Cambridge. He worked as an actor and as an advertising copywriter before taking up writing full-time after the great success of his second novel, **Midnight's Children* (1981; Booker Prize, and the James Tait Black Memorial Prize). His first published novel, *Grimus* (1975), a fantasy inspired by a twelfth-century Sufi narrative poem, *The Conference of the Birds* (the 'birds' of the traditional fable transformed into a group of science fiction 'illuminati' conspiring to live forever), experiments in exuberant manner with the *magic realism so prominent in his subsequent novels. *Midnight's Children* exploits complex narrative techniques of allegory, fable, fantasy, and textual self-consciousness, coupled with detailed realism in the depiction of personal relationships and certain key historical events, to illuminate what, in Rushdie's view, has gone wrong in India since Independence, particularly attacking the Nehru–Gandhi dynasty. **Shame* (1983) ruthlessly probes the state of Pakistan and the political manipulation of fundamentalist Islam by a military despot modelled on General Zia, who ruled at the time. Rushdie himself said about *Shame* in an interview that 'in Pakistan the numbers of people who settle the fate of the nation are very small, so that it is a kind of domestic story about kitchen tyranny'. Both novels generated much controversy, and banning-orders, but it was *The *Satanic Verses* (1988) which made the author an international *cause célèbre*. Following demonstrations in Britain against the book for alleged blasphemy, particularly by Islamic fundamentalists, Rushdie found himself the recipient of a death sentence pronounced by the late Ayatollah Khomeini, then ruler of Iran, and was forced into hiding under police protection. Yet, ironically, the novel, as Malcolm *Bradbury has pointed out, 'is surely less about Islam than about a time of racial despair and psychic conflict in a multi-ethnic age'. It is also about existential transformation, and perpetual change, with contemporary Britain as its focus, its model in this respect being Ovid's *Metamorphoses*. Rushdie's next novel, *The Moor's Last Sigh* (1995), tells, in the voice of a narrator of Christian and Jewish origin, the story of two centuries of a family's history, moving from India to Spain, and analysing in Rushdie's customary dense, rich, and erudite style, the problems of sectarian warfare that eternally recur in the pages of history, whether Eastern or Western. Other works by Rushdie include *The Jaguar Smile: A Nicaraguan Journey* (1987) and *Is Nothing Sacred?* (1990), the text of his Herbert Read Memorial Lecture, which was delivered by Harold *Pinter. Rushdie's first children's book, *Haroun and the Sea of Stories* (1990), is like an extended parable about the dangers and responsibilities of story-telling. *Imaginary Homelands* (1991) is a collection of Rushdie's essays, which also records his developing attitude towards Islam. See Lisa Appignanesi and Sara *Maitland (eds), *The Rushdie File* (1989).

RUSS, Joanna (1937–), American *science fiction writer and critic, born in New York City, educated at Cornell University and Yale University School of Drama. Her first novel, *Picnic on Paradise* (1968), reverses the sexual stereotyping endemic to much popular science fiction, and *The Female Man* (1975) constructs a series of alternate visions of female potential. Similar feminist issues are explored in *We Who Are About To . . .* (1977) and *The Two of Them* (1978). *How To Suppress Women's Writing* (1983) savagely cross-examines the American literary and publishing establishment for bias against women writers. Her short fiction, which varies from conventional science fiction to daunting experimental meditations, includes *The Zanzibar Cat* (1983) and *The Hidden Side of the Moon* (1987).

RUSSELL, Bertrand (Arthur William) (1872–1970), 3rd Earl Russell, British philosopher, born in Trellech, Gwent, educated at Trinity College, Cambridge. He published prolifically on a wide range of social, philosophical, and cultural issues and was instrumental in leading modern British philosophy in an anti-Idealist direction. This trend is evident in *The Analysis of Matter* (1921) and *The Analysis of Mind* (1927), where the principal thesis is that mind and matter are differing constructions of the same 'neutral' material. In *The Principles of Mathematics* (1903), and the three-volume *Principia Mathematica* (1910–13; with A. N. *Whitehead), Russell outlined his idea that the language of logic provides the building blocks for any theorems produced in pure mathematics. This assertion might be perceived as part of Russell's larger philosophical quest to pare human knowledge down to its barest and simplest forms of expression, and is explored in *An Inquiry into Meaning and Truth* (1940) and *Human Knowledge, Its Scope and Limits* (1948). This thrust is similarly evident in his development of Logical Atomism, a theory which proposes that the world consists of atomic facts and that these can be successfully represented by basic propositions. The value of Logical Atomism appears to lie less in its individual success than in prompting fresh philosophical and poetic attempts to construct a language consonant with the world, such as, for instance, the writings of Ezra *Pound and Ludwig *Wittgenstein's *Tractatus Logico-Philosophicus* (1922). Russell was an active radical in politics and published several pamphlets on pacifism and anti-nuclear statements during and after the two world wars, establishing the Campaign for Nuclear Disarmament in 1958. He published *A History of Western Philosophy* (1945) and in 1950 he was awarded the Nobel Prize for Literature. His final years were marked by broadcasts on BBC radio and the publication of his scandalous *Autobiography* (1967–9). *The Life of Bertrand Russell* (1975), by R. W. Clark, describes his relationships with such figures as Ottoline *Morrell, Wittgenstein, D. H. *Lawrence, and G. E. *Moore. See also A. J. *Ayer's *Russell* (1972), and Nicholas Griffin's edition of *The Selected Letters of Bertrand Russell* (1992).

RUSSELL, George William ('AE') (1867–1935), Irish poet, editor, and agronomist, born in Lurgan, Co. Armagh, of an Irish Protestant family, educated at Dublin's Metropolitan School of Art, where he began a lasting friendship with his fellow student W. B. *Yeats. 'AE', as he was generally known, was an abbreviated form of 'Aeon', a pseudonym he had once used. Yeats was influenced by Russell's wide knowledge of esoteric philosophies and Irish mythology; *The Candle of Vision* (1918) is the fullest exposition of his mystical beliefs. His first collection of verse, *Homeward: Songs by the Way* (1894), contained numerous fusions of Theosophy and Irish mythology. His subsequent collections include *The Earth Breath* (1897), *The Divine Vision* (1904), *Voices of the Stones* (1925), and *Midsummer Eve* (1928). *Collected Poems* appeared in 1913. While much of his verse is of a rather nebulously visionary character, occasional pieces form attractively simple adaptations of folk themes; elsewhere, touches of wry humour and idiosyncratically precise diction produce memorable effects. A leader of the *Irish Revival, Russell was involved in the establishment of the *Abbey Theatre, which produced his play *Deirdre* in 1902. Between 1905 and 1923 he was editor of *The Irish Homestead*; he wrote prolifically on cultural and agricultural topics, outlining his ideas on rural economy in *Co-operation and Nationality* (1912). From 1923 to 1930 he edited *The Irish Statesman*, a literary and political journal which encouraged numerous distinguished authors. Although a proponent of Irish independence since his youth, and latterly an eminent public figure, he declined the invitation to become a senator of the Irish Free State. His later publications include *The Avatars* (1933), a prose fantasy based on his mystical conceptions of evolution, which forms his most compellingly imaginative work. H. Summerfield's biography *That Myriad-Minded Man* appeared in 1975.

RUSSELL, Willy (1947–), British dramatist, born in Whiston near Liverpool, the son of a factory worker; he left school at 15 and became a hairdresser. Later, however, he went to St Katharine's College of Education and gained the qualifications to launch on a brief career as a teacher. His first success was a musical play about the *Beatles, *John Paul George Ringo . . . and Bert* (1974). That was followed by other plays wryly and observantly celebrating the energy and resilience of the often oppressed inhabitants of his native city: *Breezeblock Park* (1975), about family life on a housing estate; *Stags and Hens* (1978), set in the ladies' and gentlemen's lavatories of a Liverpool club and involving a couple holding separate parties on the eve of their wedding; *Educating Rita* (1980), about the relationship between a university teacher and a ladies' hairdresser in search of a degree; another musical play, *Blood Brothers* (1983), about the inadvertent reunion, the friendship, and the fate of twins separated at birth and brought up in very different social circumstances; and *Shirley Valentine* (1988), about a Liverpool housewife who escapes her humdrum life and unfulfilling marriage to find liberation in Greece.

RYGA, George (1932–87), Canadian dramatist, born in Alberta. He grew up on a homestead farm and received only an elementary schooling. Youthful communism gave way to a more loosely held socialist belief after 1956, when his disillusionment over the Hungarian uprising caused him to leave the party. Ryga's drama deals with social outsiders and is written in a vein of protest. His early plays, *Indian* (1964) and his best-known work *The Ecstasy of Rita Joe* (1967), focus on the isolation of Indians in white society. Other works include *Grass and Wild Strawberries* (1969); *Captives of the Faceless Drummer* (1971); *Sunrise on Sarah* (1973); *Paracelsus* (1974); *Ploughman of the Glacier* (1976); *Seven Hours to Sundown* (1977); and *A Letter to My Son* (1982), in which Ryga went back to his Ukrainian roots for a study of the older generation's isolation. Ryga's theatre employs a wide variety of dramatic modes, ranging from realism to the use of expressionist dream sequences. He also published the novels *Hungry Hills* (1963), *Ballad of a Stonepicker* (1966), and *Night Desk* (1976).

RYLE, Gilbert (1900–76), British analytic philosopher, born in Brighton, educated at Queen's College, Oxford. He was Wayneflete Professor of Metaphysical Philosophy (1945–68) at Oxford, and succeeded G. E. *Moore as editor of *Mind* (1947–71). Like J. L. *Austin and Ludwig *Wittgenstein, Ryle was interested in scrutinizing the workings of language, and in demonstrating how everyday linguistic idioms could create inappropriate beliefs and theories. His first major book, *The Concept of Mind* (1949), was an influential and elegant attack on Cartesian dualism, the notion that every human being has both a body and a mind. The mind, according to Ryle, is not to be defined as a series of inner events or as consciousness, to which each individual has privileged access, but rather as a disposition or liability to behave in certain ways. Ryle's desire to demystify human action makes him the philosophical counterpart of behavioural psychologists like J. B. Watson and B. F. Skinner, and an inheritor of the sceptical tradition in British philosophy. Although Ryle's arguments have always been contested, his sophisticated manner of presentation set the terms of reference for academic philosophy in most British universities throughout the 1950s and 1960s. His most notable works include *Locke on the Human Understanding* (1933), *Dilemmas* (1954), *Collected Papers* (1971), and *On Thinking* (1979).

S

SĂ, ZITKALA-, see ZITKALA-SĂ.

SABATINI, Rafael (1855–1924), British novelist, born in Jesi, Italy, educated in Switzerland and Portugal. An enthusiastic popular historian and biographer of Cesare Borgia, Sabatini is best remembered for his swashbuckling historical romances and stories of piracy. His most enduring novels combine an imaginative reconstruction of actual historical events with adventure and fantasy. Perhaps the best examples of his technique are the Captain Blood novels: *Captain Blood, His Odyssey* (1922), *The Chronicles of Captain Blood* (1931), and *The Fortunes of Captain Blood* (1936). His romance of the French Revolution, *Scaramouche* (1921), gave another enduring fictional character to the worlds of popular literature and cinema. Other successful works include *The Sea-Hawk* (1915), *The Black Swan* (1915), and *Mistress Wilding* (1924), all tales of piracy; *The Banner of the Bull* (1915), a fictionalized account of life under the Borgias; and the ambitious two-volume *Historical Nights' Entertainments* (1919–37).

SACKVILLE-WEST, Hon. Victoria ('Vita') Mary (1892–1962), British poet and novelist, born at Knole, in Kent, which provided the setting and inspiration for much of her writing, including *The Edwardians* (1930) and *The Heir* (1922). Her parents were first cousins; her father became the 3rd Baron Sackville and her mother was the illegitimate daughter of Lionel Sackville-West and the Spanish Flamenco dancer, Pepita de Oliva, about whom she wrote a book published in 1937. In 1913 she married Harold *Nicolson, with whom she travelled extensively during his diplomatic career. In 1918 she began a passionate affair with her schoolfriend Violet Keppel (later Trefusis), daughter of Alice Keppel: their three-year liaison is fancifully portrayed in her novel *Challenge* (1923). Her subsequent friendship with Virginia *Woolf, whom she met in 1922, was to be the inspiration of Woolf's novel **Orlando* (1928); *The Letters of Vita Sackville-West to Virginia Woolf* appeared in 1984 (edited by L. DeSalvo and M. Leaska). In 1930 the Nicolsons moved to Sissinghurst Castle in Kent, where they created their famous garden. She wrote books on travel, biography, history, and on literary and gardening topics. Her poetry includes the pastoral poem *The Land* (1926, Hawthornden Prize), *Collected Poems* (1923), and *The Garden* (1946). Her novels are uneven, but include some fine work, in particular *All Passion Spent* (1931), the story of a woman finding freedom from the constraints of society and marriage in old age; *Seducers in Ecuador* (1942), in which the influence of Virginia Woolf can be detected; and *No Signposts in the Sea* (1961). Her unusual marriage was described by her son Nigel *Nicolson in *Portrait of a Marriage* (1973).

Sacred Fount, The, a novelette by Henry *James, published in 1901. This is the last of a series of tales of curiosity and wonder, in which James explores the extent to which humans live by their own fabricated 'realities' of the mind. During a houseparty at Newmarch, an English country house, the narrator reports his observations and theories to the reader. Moving among the guests, he is struck by the fact that Grace Brissenden who had married Guy, a man much younger than herself, has grown remarkably young. Later he notices that Guy has grown appreciably older. Out of this observation, the narrator evolves his hypothesis: that people are capable of draining each other, in a vampire-like manner. This theory gains further credence when he meets another guest, Gilbert Long, previously of a dull and banal disposition, now alert, witty, and intelligent. The narrator's weekend becomes a quest for the 'sacred fount' which has ministered to Long. Whilst judging the others as suspects in a detective story, he picks out one May Server, a once beautiful and intelligent woman, now apparently drained of life and hiding an emotionally broken and unhappy existence. However, his whole hypothesis is thrown into turmoil when Mrs Brissenden accuses the narrator of being 'crazy', as she rebuffs his veiled notions. The novel remains unclear as to whether his repudiation is due to her lies or his fanciful imagination. The novel examines the distinction between masks and reality, but it also deals with the ageing process, the invulnerability of art, and the vulnerability of love.

SADLEIR, Michael (formerly Sadler) (1888–1957), British bibliographer and novelist, born in Oxford, educated at Balliol College, Oxford. A keen interest in the Victorian era and nineteenth-century books resulted in two important bibliographies, *Excursions in Victorian Bibliography* (1922) and *Nineteenth Century Fiction* (2 volumes, 1951). This interest is evident in his best-known novel, *Fanny by Gaslight* (1940), which was also filmed; set in the 1870s, it tells the story of young Fanny Hooper's experience in London, with strong emphasis on authentic descriptions of parts of the city, and period styles of narrative. As well as novels, essays, and other prose works, he also wrote *Trollope: A Commentary* (1927), *Trollope: A Bibliography* (1927), and a memoir (1949) of his father, the educationalist Michael Sadler. Sadleir became a director of the publishing house Constable and Co. in 1920.

SAHGAL, Nayantara (1927–), Indian memoirist, novelist, and political analyst, born in Allahabad, India, educated there and at Wellesley College, Massachusetts. The fascinating events that formed her intellect are chronicled in two autobiographical works, *Prison and Chocolate Cake* (1954) and *From Fear Set Free* (1963). Sahgal grew up in the heart of India's struggle for independence; her mother was Vijayalaxmi Pandit and her uncle the renowned Jawaharlal Nehru, and her childhood experiences were of political struggle, ideological debate, and even imprisonment. Her first novel, *A Time To Be Happy* (1958), attempts to deal with the concerns and sensibilities of an emergent post-colonial generation uneasily enthusiastic about the future and unable to dispense with the burden of the past. Many of her novels, including *This Time of Morning* (1966), *Storm in Chandigarh* (1969), and *The Day in Shadow* (1971), reflect Sahgal's intimate knowledge of the complex machinations of Indian politics and her abiding concern with the status of women in contemporary India. *A Situation in New Delhi* (1977) fictionalizes the aftermath of the death of Nehru. *Rich Like Us* (1985) intertwines the first-person narrative of an independent, strong-willed, and motivated woman with the story of a family's systematic eradication of the opponent—an ageing Englishwoman—in their midst; *Plans For Departure* (1986) imaginatively recreates the world of the Raj; and *Mistaken Identity* (1988) gives a richly entertaining account of an aristocratic family's struggle for independence.

SAID, Edward (1935–), Palestinian critic, born in Jerusalem, educated at Princeton and Harvard. In 1970 he became Professor of Comparative Literature at Columbia University, New York. Said has written widely and forcefully on literature, politics, and music. His first book was on Joseph *Conrad and he continues to work on the major Anglo-British *Modernists, but much of his reputation rests on his engagement with European philosophy and theory—on his revision of the work of Jacques Derrida (1930–) and Michel Foucault (1926–84), for example, in the direction of a resistance to European cultural domination. *Beginnings* (1975) asks a series of difficult questions about origins and lineages, exploring the relevance of Freud, Marx, and Nietzsche to contemporary critical and theoretical questions. *Orientalism* (1978), Said's major work, examines in detail the discourse the West has constructed about and around the East, the role of this discourse in Western political and literary culture, and its implications for the hidden or ignored inhabitants of this mythified domain. The work is both historical—an account of how the East has in fact been seen by travellers and others, from Dante to the State Department—and polemical, charging contemporary politicians and scholars with using the myth of the East to blind themselves to much they would rather not know. *Orientalism* has had a great influence on cultural studies, where the East itself may not be in question but the difficulties and dangers of constructing 'otherness' are. Said has also written passionately about the current fortunes of his native land in *The Question of Palestine* (1979) and *The Politics of Dispossession* (1994), and a moving personal memoir, with photographs by Jean Mohr, entitled *After the Last Sky* (1986). Later critical works include *The World, the Text, and the Critic* (1983) and *Culture and Imperialism* (1993). *Musical Elaborations* (1992) studies classical music, particularly opera and the piano repertoire, in the cultural and political context of its performance and dissemination. *Representations of the Intellectual* (1994) represents the texts of his Reith Lectures of 1993.

SAIL, Lawrence (Richard) (1942–), British poet, born in London, educated at St John's College, Oxford. His collections of poetry include *Opposite Views* (1974), *The Kingdom of Atlas* (1980), and *Devotions* (1987); *Out of Land* (1992) is a selected edition which includes previously uncollected work. His combination of a relaxed urbanity with strictly regulated verse structures is sometimes reminiscent of W. H. *Auden's manner. Much of his poetry succeeds in maintaining a fundamentally affirmative tone while conducting unflinching explorations of suffering and grief in social and personal contexts. His imaginative visual responses to landscapes and paintings are apparent in numerous memorable poems. He edited *First and Always: Poems for the Great Ormond Street Children's Hospital* (1988), which contained work by a wide range of eminent poets.

ST AUBIN DE TERÁN, Lisa (1953–), British novelist, the daughter of an English mother and Guyanese father, born and brought up in London. She settled for seven years in the Venezuelan Andes where she managed her husband's sugar plantation and avocado farm, the subject of her first acclaimed novel, *The Keepers of the House* (1982). In *The Slow Train to Milan* (1983) she draws on her travels through Italy with a group of Venezuelan exiles. Her lush, highly wrought prose is infused with a South American imagination. Her ability to employ *magic realism convincingly is notable in *The Tiger* (1984). Her other novels include *The Bay of Silence* (1986), *Black Idol* (1987), *Joanna* (1990), and *Nocturne* (1992), part odyssey, part obsessive love story, set in Italy. Her short stories in *The Marble Mountain* (1988) reveal the versatility and range of this writer in pieces that range from high gothic to an understated humour. Her other works include *The High Place* (1985; poems), *Off the Rails: Memoirs of a Train Addict* (1988), *Venice: The Four Seasons* (1992), with photographs by Mick Lindberg, and *A Valley in Italy: Confessions of a House Addict* (1994).

St Joan, a play by G. B. *Shaw, first performed in 1923 and published in 1924. Written in an idiomatic and at times light-hearted style, with the characters saying (in Shaw's words) 'the things they actually would have said if they had known what they were really doing', this traces Joan of Arc's story from Vaucouleurs to Rouen. She charms and chivvies the local squire, Baudricourt, into sending her to Chinon, where she cannily picks the Dauphin out from his courtiers and persuades him to give her the power that results in the storming of Orleans. The Earl of Warwick plots with the Bishop of Beauvais, Cauchon, to capture and try her as a heretic; she is rejected by the Dauphin, whom she has just crowned, and warned by her other 'friends' that she cannot rely on them. Then comes her capture, a trial that Shaw is at pains to suggest was scrupulously fair, and her burning; this is followed by an epilogue, a dream sequence in which Joan's posthumous admirers, including a modern Vatican bureaucrat, 'spring to their feet in consternation' at her suggestion that she might return from the dead. As Shaw sees her, she represents a vitalist rebellion against every aspect of the status quo, military, political, social, sexual, ecclesiastic, and spiritual; but she is also a vividly realized individual, gauche and jaunty at first, arrogant later, but always single-minded in her pursuit of what she regards as God's will and plain common sense.

ST OMER, Garth (1931–), West Indian novelist, born in St Lucia, where his major works are implicitly set; he was educated at the University of the West Indies at Mona, Jamaica, and at Princeton. His reputation as a writer rests chiefly on a small number of novellas. A masterly practitioner of the form, St Omer employs a method of narrative in which intense introspection and striking imagery predominate over conventional story-telling. His first novella, *Syrop* (published in Faber's *Introduction Two: Stories by New Writers*, 1964), is a dramatic depiction of an adolescent boy's short journey to manhood and death. Other novellas, all displaying a harsh and bleakly fatalistic vision of life, include *A Room on the Hill* (1968), *Shades of Grey* (1968), which contains 'Light on the Hill' and 'Another Place, Another Time', *Nor Any Country* (1969), and *J-, Black Bam and the Masqueraders* (1972).

SAINTSBURY, George (Edward Bateman) (1845–1933), British critic, born in Southampton, educated at Merton College, Oxford. The second volume of his *Scrap-Book* (3 volumes, 1922–4) contains his recollections of Oxford. After working as a schoolteacher in Guernsey, he settled in London in 1876 and began his prolific career as a journalist and author. His first book, *A Primer of French Literature* (1880), established the historically descriptive mode of much of his writing. His further studies of French literature include *A Short History of French Literature* (1882) and *The History of the French Novel* (1917–19). During the 1880s he wrote numerous books on English literature, among them *Dryden* (1881) and *A History of Elizabethan Literature* (1887). He also produced biographies, notably *Marlborough* (1885), and a new edition of Sir Walter Scott's *Works of Dryden* (18 volumes, 1882–93). Appointed in 1895 to the Regius Professorship of English at Edinburgh, he concentrated upon his literary histories, among which are *A Short History of English Literature* (1898), *History of Criticism* (1900–4), and *A History of English Prosody* (1906–10). He exercised a wide influence in the emergence of English studies as an academic discipline. He supplied twenty-one chapters for *The Cambridge History of English Literature* (edited by A. W. Ward and A. R. Waller, 13 volumes, 1907–16). The best-known of his many other works is *Notes on a Cellarbook* (1920), an attractively whimsical record of his pleasures as a connoisseur of wines. A biography by A. Blyth Webster was published in 1977.

SAKI, pseudonym of Hector Hugh MUNRO (1870–1916), British writer, born in Burma, educated in England; after his mother's death when he was an infant he was brought up in North Devon by two aunts. He served in the Burmese military police, and from 1900 wrote political satire for the *Westminster Gazette*. During 1902–8 he was correspondent for the *Morning Post* in Poland, Russia, and Paris. He is best remembered for the mercilessly alienated stories published in *Reginald* (1904), *Reginald in Russia* (1910), *The Chronicles of Clovis* (1911), *Beasts and Super-Beasts* (1914), *The Toys of Peace* (1919), and *The Square Egg* (1924). Satirical and occasionally macabre, his tales frequently used wolves, tigers, cats, and bulls to enact revenge on mankind; his works influenced writers as diverse as R. *Firbank, N. *Coward, and J. *Collier. *The Unbearable Bassington* (1912) displays the author's characteristic irony. *When William Came: A Story of London under the Hohenzollerns* (1913) is one of his finest admonitory novels on political themes published during the troubled decades before the Great War; it presents the moral conundrums attendant upon England's imagined defeat, and stands as his most sustained analysis of a dying world. In 1914 he enlisted as a trooper and was killed in France while resting in a shallow crater.

SALINGER, J(erome) D(avid) (1919–), American novelist and short-story writer, born in New York, educated at Valley Forge Military Academy, New York University, and Columbia University. *The *Catcher in the Rye* (1951), his first published book, had enormous success, particularly with the young who were able to identify with the young hero/narrator, Holden Caulfield. Owing something to Mark Twain's *Huckleberry Finn*, Holden relates his adventure in a racy vernacular (which was to affect the idiom of generations of readers). *Nine Stories* (1953, UK title *For Esme with Love and Squalor and Other Stories*) collects earlier stories from 1948 onwards; its first, 'A Perfect Day for Banana Fish', and others, introduce the Glass family, by whom Salinger was to become increasingly obsessed. The Glass family, resident in New York, but of Irish and Jewish descent (Salinger's own position), are headed by Bessie and Les, distinguished vaudeville artists. *Franny and Zooey* (1961) presents the youngest two members of the family at crisis moments of their early lives. Franny, a college senior, goes up to Boston to visit her boyfriend for a football weekend, but suffers a nervous attack through her realization of the hollowness of ordinary life when contrasted with the religious and inner life. Zooey, her handsome young actor brother, attempts to give her spiritual ease. Both stories are related by Salinger's self-confessed alter ego, Buddy Glass, and have a marvellously acute ear for the inconsequential logic of ordinary conversation. *Raise High the Roof Beams, Carpenters* and *Seymour: An Introduction* (1963) is a single volume made up of two Glass family stories originally printed in *The New Yorker* (1955, 1959). In the first, Buddy Glass tells of his return to New York during the War to attend his brother Seymour's wedding, and goes on to describe Seymour's jilting of his bride and later elopement with her. The second story is Buddy's anguished brooding on his loved and admired brother's suicide. Salinger began to lead an increasingly isolated country life in New Hampshire, and blocked any attempt to draw him out of it, including a book to which he originally appeared to give some kind of consent (*In Search of J. D. Salinger* by Ian *Hamilton, 1988).

SALKEY, (Felix) Andrew (Alexander) (1928–95), Jamaican novelist and poet, born in Colon, Panama, educated at St George's College in Jamaica, and the University of London. His first novel, *A Quality of Violence* (1959), set in rural Jamaica during the drought of 1900, focuses on the desperately violent rituals of the Pocomania cult. Subsequent novels featured alienated middle-class protagonists who asserted themselves through violent personal confrontations, predatory sexuality, and destructive manœuvres for power, which exposed the social and racial tensions in Jamaica: they include *Escape to an Autumn Pavement* (1960), *The Late Emancipation of Jerry Stover* (1968), *The Adventures of Catullus Kelly* (1969), and *Come Home, Malcolm Heartland* (1976). *Anancy's Score* (1973) is a collection of short stories featuring a modern, urban version of the folkloric spider-trickster; Anancy reappears in *One* (1985), a political fable satirizing Guyanese politics; in *Anancy Traveller* (1992), more short stories; and in *Brother Anancy* (1993), stories for children. *Jamaica* (1973), a long impassioned narrative poem, argues in favour of revolutionary change. As well as volumes of verse, including *In the Hills where Her Dreams Live* (1979) and *Away* (1980), Salkey has written stimulating and controversial travel books such as *Havana Journal* (1971) and *Georgetown Journal: A Caribbean Writer's Journey from London via Port of Spain to Georgetown, Guyana, 1970* (1972), and children's books.

SALTER, James (1923–), American novelist, born in New York City, educated at Georgetown University and West Point Military Academy; he then served in the United States Air Force for twelve years. He lived briefly in France and numbers modern French writers such as André Gide and Jean Genet among those who have influenced his own writing. Salter's fiction arises very much out of his own experiences; his first two novels, *The Hunters* (1956) and *The Arm of Flesh* (1961), reflect his Air Force years while both *A Sport and a Pastime* (1967) and *Solo Faces* (1979) draw upon his familiarity with France. *Light Years* (1975) contains some of his most effective impressionistic prose. Salter has enjoyed neither commercial nor academic success but his writings have been highly praised by contemporary novelists such as Saul *Bellow, Graham *Greene, John *Irving, and Irwin *Shaw.

SAMUELSON, Paul Anthony (1915–), American economist, born in Gary, Indiana, educated at Chicago and Harvard Universities, recipient of the Nobel Prize for Economics (1970). Samuelson is known to generations of students as the author of a best-selling introductory textbook, *Economics* (1st edition 1948). He spent his academic career as Professor of Economics at the Massachusetts Institute of Technology. As a student in the 1930s, *Keynes's *General Theory* came to him as a breath of fresh air. With the possible exception of Alvin Hansen (one of his teachers), Samuelson was chiefly responsible for introducing generations of economists in the USA to their own brand of Keynesianism—he called it the 'neo-classical synthesis' (namely, a means of combining Keynesian arguments with older, more orthodox ones, in a manner which made both more acceptable). Samuelson was also a great proponent of the use of mathematical methods in economics, exemplified in his *Foundations of Economic Analysis* (1947). He contributed a regular three-weekly column for *Newsweek* between 1966 and 1981, selections from which were collected in *Economics from the Heart* (1983). His scientific papers are collected in five volumes; there is an assessment of his life and work in *The New Palgrave* (1987).

SANCHEZ, Sonia (1934–), American poet, born in Birmingham, Alabama, educated at Hunter College, New York. From 1967 onwards she held posts at numerous colleges and universities and became Professor of English at Temple University, Philadelphia, in 1979. *Homecoming* (1969), *WE a BaddDDD People* (1970), and *Liberation Poem* (1970), her early collections of verse, established Sanchez as an outspoken and verbally inventive poet of African-American experience. Her work is noted for its uncompromising use of the speech forms of urban black communities, which extends across a wide stylistic and thematic range. Her membership of the Nation of Islam in the early 1970s is reflected in *A Blues Book for Blue Black Magical Women* (1974), which indicates her dissatisfaction with Islamic attitudes to women. *I've Been a Woman: New and Selected Poems* (1978), *Under a Soprano Sky* (1987), and *Wounded in the House of a Friend* (1995) are among her later collections of poetry. Her plays include *Uh, Uh: But Do It Free Us?*, produced in 1975, which deals with misogyny within black culture. *A Sound Investment* (1979) contains her short stories.

Sanctuary, a novel by William *Faulkner, first published in 1931, and, in what has become known as 'the original text', in 1981. *Sanctuary*, Faulkner's sixth novel in order of publication, though written before **As I Lay Dying* (1930), the fifth to appear, exists in two quite distinct versions. The novel, said by the author to be 'the most horrific tale I could imagine' and 'deliberately conceived to make money', was written in the early summer of 1929 and initially rejected by his publishers, Cape and Smith; some eighteen months later he thought it a 'terrible' novel, and, before the New York publication in 1931, undertook extensive revisions to the manuscript. *Sanctuary: The Original Text* (1981), edited by Noel Polk, restores the unrevised text of the novel.

Sanctuary is numbered among Faulkner's most violent novels and it contains many scenes of great dramatic and symbolic power as well as instances of his prodigious gift for comedy. It concerns a group of social misfits, chief among whom are Temple Drake, the daughter of a judge, and Popeye, a Memphis hoodlum, and the drama is played out against the background of the degenerating society of Frenchman's Bend in Faulkner's fictional Yoknapatawpha County, Mississippi. The impotent Popeye's rape of Temple with a corncob, which he uses as his instrument of sexual conquest, is one of the most disturbing images in Faulkner's fiction. Moral authority is embodied in the character of the lawyer, Horace Benbow, who finds his idealism and his belief in human reason defeated by what one critic calls 'the horrifying power of evil' which the novel depicts. Critical opinion of *Sanctuary* remains deeply divided, some critics seeing it as little more than a commercially motivated exercise in *grand guignol*, others as a tragedy of almost classical proportions. Both *William Faulkner: The Yoknapatawpha Country* (1963), by Cleanth *Brooks, and *The Achievement of William Faulkner* (1966), by Michael Millgate, contain intelligent assessments of the novel.

SANDBURG, Carl (August) (1878–1967), American poet, born in Galesburg, Illinois; he left school at 13 and spent several years travelling before serving in the Spanish-American War. After study at Lombard College, Galesburg, in 1902 he became a reporter and was on the staff of the *Chicago Daily News* from 1917 to 1930. *In Reckless Ecstasy* (1904) and *The Plaint of a Rose* (1905) contained lyrically sentimental poems he discounted in preparing future collections of his work. He was politically active while living in Milwaukee, where he was secretary to the first socialist mayor from 1910 to 1912. The political sympathies informing his poetry are apparent in the vigorously democratic affirmation of 'Chicago', which appeared in the March issue of **Poetry* in 1914. With the publication of *Chicago Poems* (1916) and *Cornhuskers* (1918), he gained wide notice as a radically new voice in American poetry, extending the achievement of Whitman, whose sweeping verse forms his own resembled, to emphatically contemporary treatments of urban subjects. *Smoke and Steel* (1920), an incantational celebration of industrial endeavour, was followed by his optimistic envisionings of America's enormous human and natural resources in *Slabs of the Sunburnt West* (1922) and *Good Morning, America* (1928); the latter's expansive panorama of American life set the pattern for his ambitious populist epic entitled *The People, Yes* (1936), which declared his belief in the ultimate indomitability of America's common humanity. In 1919 Sandburg began working on his biography of Abraham Lincoln, whom he regarded as a heroic embodiment of the American ideal: *The Prairie Years* (2 volumes, 1926) was followed by *The War Years* (4 volumes, 1939), which received the Pulitzer Prize for History. His later collections of poetry include *The Sandburg Range* (1957) and *Honey and Salt* (1963); *Complete Poems* appeared in 1970. Among his other publications are the highly regarded body of children's stories in his *Rootabaga* volumes (1922, 1923), the novel *Remembrance Rock* (1948), which chronicles three centuries of American history, and *Always the Young Stranger* (1952), his autobiography of his earlier years. North Callahan's *Carl Sandburg: His Life and Works* (1987) is the most detailed of several biographies.

SANDOZ, Mari (1896–1966), American historian, biographer, and novelist, born to Swiss immigrant homesteaders on the northwestern Nebraska frontier. Her childhood memories, her Native American neighbours, and the region of the western Plains inspired her work. From her earliest success, *Old Jules* (1935), a biography of her father doubly marked by the brutality of his character and the rawness of the Nebraska frontier, Sandoz had difficulties convincing Eastern readers that her presentation of the West was accurate. *Slogum House* (1937) and *Capital City* (1939) are allegorical novels, responding to the threat of fascism developing in Europe. *Crazy Horse: The Strange Man of the Oglalas* (1942) is her Indian-narrated biography of the regional struggles between the native people and the US government, culminating in the murder of the revered Sioux hero. Following her anti-war novel *The Tom Walker* (1947), Sandoz returned to Native American themes with *Cheyenne Autumn* (1953), a biography of chiefs Little Wolf and Dull Knife. *The Buffalo Hunters: The Story of the Hide Men* (1954), *The Cattlemen: From the Rio Grande Across the Far Marias* (1958), and *The Beaver Men: Spearheads of Empire* (1964), all focus on plains animals while her novels, *Miss Morissa: Doctor of the Gold Trail* (1955) and *Son of the Gamblin' Man: The Youth of an Artist* (1960), feature fictionalized figures from the West, including in the latter work the painter Robert Henri.

San Francisco Renaissance, an interlude of heightened literary activity based in San Francisco which is generally considered to have begun with a poetry reading in October 1955 at which Kenneth *Rexroth introduced Allen *Ginsberg, Michael *McClure, Gary *Snyder, Philip *Whalen, and Philip Lamantia; Jack *Kerouac recorded his impressions of the reading in *The Dharma Bums* (1958). Although frequently associated with the activity of the *Beat Generation, it cannot be considered synonymous with that movement, as certain notable participants, including Robert *Duncan and Jack *Spicer, did not identify with the Beats. Other participating poets include Gregory *Corso and Lawrence *Ferlinghetti, whose City Lights Bookshop and activities as the publisher of City Lights Books were intrinsic to the cohesion of interests the Renaissance represented. Much of the writing produced shared an anarchic and pacifist ideology as a basis for rejecting the increasingly uniform collective experience of post-war American society; Zen Buddhism and neo-romantic conceptions of the purity of nature are also essential to its philosophical character. The dissenting energies of the San Francisco Renaissance were of importance in the emergence of the protest movement against the Vietnam War and the general cultural liberalism of the later 1960s. Michael Davidson's *The San Francisco Renaissance* appeared in 1989. See also NEW YORK SCHOOL OF POETS and BLACK MOUNTAIN WRITERS.

SANSOM, William (Norman Trevor) (1912–76), British short-story writer and novelist, born in Camberwell, London, educated at Uppingham School. He joined the National Fire Service at the outbreak of war and witnessed the bombing raids on London. At the time, he contributed short stories to **New Writing* and **Horizon*. Many of the stories in his first collection, *Fireman Flower* (1944), display documentary realism, while others are in the surreal vein of Kafka. The stories tend to evoke a drab, seedy post-war London, and often reproduce the distortion of perception suffered by those under severe stress. Among other collections of stories are *South* (1948), *The Passionate North* (1950), and *The Stories of William Sansom* (1963), with an introduction by Elizabeth *Bowen. His novels include *The Body* (1949), *a tour de force* which plunges the reader into the deranged mind of a married middle-aged barber consumed with obsessive jealousy; *A Bed of Roses* (1954); *The Loving Eye* (1956); *The Cautious Heart* (1958); and *The Last Hours of Sandra Lee* (1961). He also wrote *Westminster in War* (1947), and the travel books *Away to It All* (1964) and *Grand Tour Today* (1968).

SANTAYANA, George (1863–1952), Spanish-American philosopher, born in Madrid, educated at Harvard. Christened Jorge Ruiz de Santayana y Borrais, he used the English form of his name after he was taken to the USA in 1872. Santayana is now best remembered for his cultural analyses of the American character. He formulated a materialist philosophy in his major early work, *The Life of Reason* (5 volumes, 1905–6), in which he argued that matter was the only reality. *Scepticism and Animal Faith* (1923), the prolegomena to a new theory of philosophy, was intended to modify and supplement his materialist ideas, which appeared under the collective title of *The Realms of Being* (1927–40). In these books, Santayana investigated what he called the realms of essence, matter, truth, and spirit, and argued that knowledge consists of faith in the unknowable, which is symbolically manifest to us through essences. His first publications were literary and aesthetic, beginning with *Sonnets and Other Verses* (1894); a treatise on aesthetics, *The Sense of Beauty* (1896); a verse play, *Lucifer: A Theological Tragedy* (1899); *Interpretations of Poetry and Religion* (1900); the poems *A Hermit of Carmel* (1901), and the collected *Poems* (1923). His other publications include *Three Philosophical Poets* (1910), studies of Lucretius, Dante, and Goethe; *Philosophical Opinion in America* (1918); *Character and Opinion in the United States* (1920), which addresses the conflict of materialism and idealism in American life; and *The Genteel Tradition at Bay* (1931), an analysis of Calvinism and Transcendentalism. His only novel, *The *Last Puritan*, appeared in 1935. His lectures, essays, and reviews were collected in *Obiter Scripta* (1936), and his collected *Works* appeared in fourteen volumes (1936–7). Santayana made a major contribution to American intellectual life throughout the first half of the twentieth century. He was also the subject of a tribute from Wallace *Stevens, whose poem 'To an Old Philosopher in Rome' is one of the few poems Stevens openly addressed to an identifiable figure.

SAPPER, pseudonym of Herman Cyril MCNEILE (1888–1937), British popular writer, a regular army officer who served in the Royal Engineers and retired as a lieutenant-colonel in 1919; he is best known for his stories about Captain Hugh Drummond, in most of which the villains are Carl Peterson and his daughter Irma. *Bull-Dog Drummond: The Adventures of a Demobilized Officer Who Found Peace Dull* (1920) was followed by *The Black Gang* (1922), *The Third Round* (1924; US title *Bulldog Drummond's Third Round*), and others; after McNeile's death the series was continued by Gerard Fairlie (1899–1983), the original model for the character.

SARGESON, Frank (1903–82), New Zealand short-story writer and novelist, born in Hamilton, educated at the University of New Zealand, Auckland. Experience of the 1930s Depression shaped his early work which displayed a mastery of a highly individual monologue style, and an accurate rendering of laconic New Zealand expression in the face of adversity. These early stories were collected in *Conversations with My Uncle and Other Sketches* (1936) and *A Man and His Wife* (1940). The novel *I for One* (1952) marked a new departure in format and range while the picaresque *Memoirs of a Peon* (1965) allowed even greater freedom of treatment in its combination of satire and social comment. *Joy of the Worm* (1969) and *Man of England Now* (1972, three novellas) explored in Sargeson's adroit tragi-comic manner the increasingly complex and contradictory world of twentieth-century England/New Zealand relations. A rich introduction to Sargeson's concerns and character is provided by the autobiographical trilogy *Once Is Enough* (1972), *More than Enough* (1975), and *Never Enough* (1978), published in one volume as *Sargeson* in 1981; with their irreverent vitality the novels testify to Sargeson's insatiable fascination with the intricacies of human relationships in New Zealand provincial life. Other novels include *Sunset Village* (1976) and *En Route* (1979). *The Collected Stories of Frank Sargeson* (1964) was expanded and republished as *The Stories of Frank Sargeson* (1973) and reissued in 1982 with an additional story. Sargeson's essays *Conversations in a Train and other Critical Writing*, edited by Kevin Cunningham, were collected in 1983. His varied and sustained output has established Sargeson as an influential figure in post-war New Zealand fiction. Critical essays appeared in *The Puritan and the Waif* (1954; edited by Helen Shaw). A critical study by H. Winston Rhodes was published in 1969; more recent studies include R. A. Copland's *Frank Sargeson* (1976) and *Frank Sargeson in His Time* (1976) by D. McEldowney.

SARO-WIWA, Ken (1941–95), Nigerian novelist, dramatist, and political writer, born in Bori, Nigeria, educated at the University of Ibadan. He lectured at the University of Lagos and held government office before founding Saros International Publishers in 1973. In 1994 he was arrested for his leading role in the violent campaign against the dispossession of the Ogoni people by the development of Nigeria's oil resources. The following year he was sentenced to death and executed with eight other activists amid protests from governments throughout the world. Saro-Wiwa's early works include the radio plays *The Transistor Radio* (1972) and *Bride by Return* (1973). His best-known dramatic writings are contained in *Four Farcical Plays* (1989). These exuberantly humorous satires on the unscrupulous materialism pervading modern Nigerian culture are derived from the 'Basi and Company' television series he scripted from 1985 to 1990. The Basi series also gave rise to numerous children's books and the novel *Basi and Company: A Modern African Folktale* (1987). His first novel, *Sozaboy: a Novel in Rotten English* (1985), deals with the Nigerian Civil War and forms a passionate denunciation of the cultural myths sustaining militarism. The novels, *Prisoners of Jebs* (1988) and *Pita Dumbrok's Prison* (1991), are outspoken satires on the corruption and ineffectuality of African politics. The short-stories in *Forest of Flowers* (1987) and *Adaku* (1989) deal with the everyday life of Nigerian people. His political writings, which sustain an uncompromising critique of post-Civil War Nigeria, include *On a Darkling Plain: an Account of the Nigerian Civil War* (1989), *Nigeria: the Brink of Disaster* (1991), and *Genocide in Nigeria: the Ogoni Tragedy* (1992). Among Saro-Wiwa's other works are the poems of *Songs in a Time of War* (1985), *Similia: Essays on Anomic Nigeria* (1991), and *The Singing Anthill: Ogoni Folk Tales* (1991).

SAROYAN, William (1908–81), American short-story writer and dramatist, born in Fresno, California, to Armenian-American parents. Saroyan won early fame with his short stories. His play *My Heart's in the Highlands* (1939), a paean to the simple life, was followed by *The Time of Your Life* (1939), which deals with a group of down-and-outs at a seedy San Francisco waterfront bar, whose essential goodness the play reveals: it won a Pulitzer Prize, which Saroyan quixotically refused. His other plays include *Love's Old Sweet Song* (1940); *The Beautiful People* (1941); a double bill, *Across the Board on Tomorrow Morning* and *Talking to You* (1942); *Hello, Out There* (1942); *Get Away Old Man* (1943); and *The Cave Dwellers* (1957). Saroyan produced and directed many of his own plays off Broadway; his rhapsodic impressionistic writing is at its best in the evocation of mood and the creation of character.

SARTON, (Eleanor) May (1912–95), American poet and novelist, born at Wondelgem in Belgium; from 1916 onward she grew up in Cambridge, Massachusetts, where she was educated at the Latin School. From 1937 she taught creative writing at American colleges and universities. *Encounter in April* (1937), her first collection of verse, established the meditative and descriptive concerns central to much of her poetry; in both free verse and strict traditional forms, her work explores relations between art and nature, its often impassioned lyricism subdued by her restrained directness of tone. Subsequent collections include *The Lion and the Rose* (1948), *Land of Silence* (1953), *A Private Mythology* (1966), *Letters from Maine* (1984), and *The Silence Now* (1988); *Collected Poems 1930–1973* appeared in 1974. Tensions between individual values and the demands of political necessity form a recurrent theme in her numerous novels, which include *The Bridge of Years* (1946), depicting the impact of the First World War on a Belgian family; *Faithful Are the Wounds* (1955), which culminates in the suicide of an eminent professor placed under intolerable pressures during the McCarthy investigations; and *Mrs Stevens Hears the Mermaids Singing* (1965), a parable of the situation of the female artist. Among Sarton's autobiographical publications are *I Knew a Phoenix* (1959), *Plant Dreaming Deep* (1968), and *At Seventy: A Journal* (1984).

SASSOON, Siegfried (Louvain) (1886–1967), British poet, born in Brenchley, Kent, educated at Clare College, Cambridge. He was on active service in Flanders throughout much of the First World War and is generally recognized as the first poet to record the horrors and privations of life in the trenches. *The Old Huntsman*, the first volume of his war poetry, appeared in 1917, the year in which he threw away his Military Cross and published his open letter 'A Soldier's Declaration' denouncing the administration of the war. Robert *Graves deflected a possible court martial and Sassoon was sent to Craiglockhart Hospital in Edinburgh to be treated for shell-shock. There he met Wilfred *Owen, whom he greatly influenced; their friendship forms the subject of S. MacDonald's *Not about Heroes* (1983). He returned to active service in Flanders, publishing *Counter-Attack* (1918), in which the element of anti-war polemic becomes emphatic. *Picture Show* (1919) was the last of his volumes predominantly concerned with the war. After a period as literary editor of the *Daily Herald* he gradually resumed his pre-war life as a country gentleman. His quasi-autobiographical prose trilogy **Memoirs of a Fox-Hunting Man* (1928), **Memoirs of an Infantry Officer*

(1930), and *Sherston's Progress* (1936), published as *The Complete Memoirs of George Sherston* in 1937, follows Sherston's fortunes through an undemanding adolescence to a shocking precipitation into maturity on the Western Front. He subsequently wrote three parallel volumes of autobiography, *The Old Century and Seven More Years* (1938), *The Weald of Youth* (1942), and *Siegfried's Journey* (1945), which describe his life up to 1920. His verse sustained its tone of strenuous dissent well into the 1930s: his socialist opinions are clear in *Satirical Poems* (1926) while *The Road to Ruin* (1933) warns against failure to learn from the First World War in its envisioning of a more terribly destructive conflict. His austerely contemplative later collections include *Vigils* (1935) and *Sequences* (1956). R. Hart-Davis edited two volumes of his *Diaries* (1981, 1983). *Collected Poems, 1908–1956* was published in 1961. See also WAR POETRY.

Satanic Verses, The, a novel by Salman *Rushdie, published in 1988. This complex, polyphonic novel is an ambitious attempt to conflate the harsh realities of migrants' lives in Britain's inner cities with the cultural fantasies that inhabit them and constitute another, phantasmagoric dimension of reality. These conflicting levels of consciousness are embodied in the antithetical characters of Saladin Chamcha, an Anglicized Indian and minor actor, and Gibreel Farishta, Bombay's leading cinematic icon and superhero. The two men's lives connect when they survive the bombing of a plane over the English Channel. Though their journeys separate them, their destinies will intertwine, illustrating different aspects of the immigrant experience, at a political and an allegorical level. Saladin, whose life has hitherto been lived in the precarious cocoon of painfully achieved assimilation, is transformed into a monster, the author's metaphor for the plight of the dispossessed and their objectification by the Other's gaze. Gibreel, on the other hand, becomes angel-like and prone to visions and revelations. The dream-like state in which he faces an alien world is the source of the novel's most controversial sections, in which the histories and traditions of Islam, notably the life of Muhammad, are rewritten from the perspective of a schizophrenic's distorted imagination. In other visions, Gibreel—whose roles in these hallucinations is that of his namesake, the angel Gabriel—leads a charismatic young woman in rural India to guide her gullible followers to a projected pilgrimage that will end in their self-annihilation by drowning. Khomeini, too, makes an appearance in yet another dream. If these sections articulate Rushdie's critique of faith's easy transformation into manipulation, hegemony, and superstition, the parallel account of Saladin's decline and fall into the world of inner-city immigrant lives allows Rushdie to comment on the state of Britain today. These sections stress the celebratory aspects of hybridization, multiple identities, and cultural collisions. A novel that concerns itself above all with the nature of change—in spite of its implicitly avowed trajectory, the examination of the nature and relativity of good and evil—*The Satanic Verses*, in its concluding sections, reflects its own project by changing into a Shakespearian melodrama of suspected adultery, pathological jealousy, and murder. A paradoxically affirmative ending sees Saladin reconciled with the memory of his father, with his own heritage, and, it is implied, with the actuality of his double existence as Indian and expatriate.

SATCHELL, William (1860–1942), New Zealand novelist, born in England, educated partly in Germany. He emigrated to New Zealand in 1883 and worked at various occupations, from storekeeper to stockbroker, and published, among other novels and journalistic works, *The Land of the Lost* (1902) and *The Greenstone Door* (1914). Both were pioneering examples of the imaginative exploration of New Zealand landscape and history in fictional terms. The mythic resonance that Satchell attained in *The Land of the Lost* was to inspire later New Zealand writers; republished in 1971 with a perceptive Introduction by Kendric *Smithyman, the book predates the writings of Jane *Mander in its use of bleak North Island landscapes as a testing ground for spiritual as well as physical endurance. *The Greenstone Door* explored aspects of New Zealand history in the second half of the nineteenth century through the childhood recollections of a hero who is cared for by a Maori chief after his father is killed. The critical study *William Satchell* by Phillip Wilson appeared in 1968.

Saturday Night and Sunday Morning, a novel by Alan *Sillitoe, published in 1958. Arthur Seaton, the bullish young hero of Sillitoe's first novel, is a worker in a Nottingham bicycle factory, whose week is spent in grinding repetition at the lathe, and who erupts into hedonistic action in his evenings and weekends. Rebelling against the hypocritical conventions and morality of society, he lives according to his own rules and values. The novel follows in his confident footsteps through the pubs and night-time streets of Nottingham, showing the sordid realities of his frantic drinking sessions and affairs with married women. Through matter-of-fact description and realistic dialogue, Sillitoe creates a sense of the narrow, retributive world of the Nottingham working class, within which Arthur's relish for explosions of violence and excesses of drunken, garish entertainment is both understandable and attractive. Sillitoe imparts a strong sense of the hero's unspent energies and his fear of entrapment. The book ends with Arthur on the verge of marriage, preparing for the Sunday morning of reckoning which must follow the Saturday night of his riotous youth

SAUNDERS, James (1925–), British dramatist, born in Islington, educated at Southampton University; he worked as a chemistry teacher before writing *Next Time I'll Sing to You* (1962), an attempt to uncover the motives of a modern hermit. His subsequent work, often notable for its sympathy for those who find it difficult to fit in with a society intolerant of oddity or strong emotion, includes *A Scent of Flowers* (1964), a dramatic post-mortem on a girl who has been driven to suicide by her family's lack of understanding and compassion; *The Borage Pigeon Affair* (1969), a satire on small town hypocrisy and squalor; *Bodies* (1977), on one level a tale about the infidelities of two couples, on another an attempt to put the case for the turbulent and neurotic over the rational, placid, and contented; *Fall* (1984), about the reunion of three sisters respectively seeking fulfilment in Zen Buddhism, left-wing politics, and the hippie life; *Making It Better* (1992), about a BBC producer who, breaking with her homosexual husband, launches into affairs with two Czechoslovakians, one a down-at-heel *émigré*, the other a young, ruthless representative of the newly liberated Eastern Europe; and *Retreat* (1995), a psychological thriller involving a confrontation between a reclusive journalist who has killed his wife and maimed his daughter in a car crash, and the daughter of two of his old friends, themselves recently killed in a plane accident. Saunders has also written drama for television and radio and adapted Vaclav Havel's *Redevelopment* for the stage in 1991.

Savacou, a Caribbean literary journal in the tradition of **Bim*. It was first published in 1970 (between then and 1989 eleven issues were produced), taking its name from the bird-god in Carib mythology with control over thunder and strong winds. Announced as the Journal of the Caribbean Artists' Movement, which had been started in London a few years earlier, it was edited initially by Edward *Brathwaite in Jamaica, academic and critic Kenneth Ramchand in Trinidad, and Jamaican writer Andrew *Salkey in London, bringing together the work of creative writers, academics, and theoretical thinkers and providing a forum for artistic expression and thought in the Caribbean. Its advisory committee included Lloyd King, Gordon Rohlehr, Orlando *Patterson, Sylvia *Wynter, John La Rose, Paule *Marshall, and Wilfred Cartey, and among early contributors were C. L. R. *James, Michael *Anthony, Louis James, Derek *Walcott, George *Lamming, Martin *Carter, and John *Figueroa. It was the first Caribbean publication to devote a special issue (in 1977) to writing by women, including work by Merle *Hodge, Lorna *Goodison, Jean Goulbourne, Marjorie Thorpe, Opal Palmer, and Christine Craig. The Savacou name also appears as a publishing imprint.

SAYER, Paul (*c.*1956–), British novelist, born in South Milford, near Leeds. He was working as a staff nurse in a psychiatric hospital when his first novel, *The Comforts of Madness* (1988; Whitbread Prize), was published. It is the moving first-person account of a speechless, catatonic patient in a hospital therapy unit, and displays its author's intimate knowledge of hospital life, the world of the mentally ill, and the workings of the disturbed mind. His second novel, *Howling at the Moon* (1990), is another exploration of obsessive states, delusions, and the effects of childhood deprivation and traumas on the adult psyche; Sayer's spare, unemotional style and his portrait of a modern marriage destroyed by paranoid jealousy are compelling. In *The Absolution Game* (1992), the story of a social worker's personal dilemmas, and *The Storm-Bringer* (1994), the account of the tragic secrets that lie behind a marriage's apparently calm surface, Sayer continues his quiet investigation of contemporary norms and mores.

SAYERS, Dorothy L(eigh) (1893–1957), British detective novelist, born in Oxford, the daughter of the headmaster of Christ Church Cathedral choir school, educated at Somerville College, Oxford. She published two volumes of verse while teaching modern languages at a girls' school in Hull; in 1921 she moved to London and worked as a copy-writer for Benson's advertising agency (where she considerably influenced the style of contemporary advertising), marrying a journalist, O. A. Fleming (1881–1950), in 1926. Her first detective story, *Whose Body?* (1923), introduced her detective, Lord Peter Wimsey, who appears in all her novels with the exception of *The Documents in the Case* (1930; in collaboration with Robert Eustace). Of the ten other Wimsey novels the best are perhaps *Unnatural Death* (1927; US title *The Dawson Pedigree*), *Strong Poison* (1930), *The Five Red Herrings* (1931; US title *Suspicious Characters*), and *Have His Carcase* (1932), though all exhibit ingenious plotting and well-researched backgrounds and have, too, an intellectual weight which is rare in the genre. In later works—*Gaudy Night* (1935) and *Busman's Honeymoon* (1937)—she tried, in her words, to make the detective story 'more a novel of manners than a crossword puzzle', but critics have found these long-winded and snobbish. She also wrote a number of detective short stories (*Lord Peter Views the Body*, 1928; *Hangman's Holiday*, 1933; *In the Teeth of the Evidence*, 1939), and edited several collections of crime stories (*Great Short Stories of Detection, Mystery and Horror*, 3 volumes, 1928–34; US title *The Omnibus of Crime: Tales of Detection*, 1936): the introductions are excellent short discussions of the genre. She also wrote religious plays, mainly for broadcasting, and her learning, wit, and pugnacious personality made her a formidable theological polemicist. Her last years were devoted to a translation of Dante's *Divina Commedia* (3 volumes, 1949–62). See J. Hitchman, *Such a Strange Lady: An Introduction to Dorothy L. Sayers* (1975) and J. Brabazon, *Dorothy L. Sayers: the Life of a Courageous Woman* (1981).

SCAMMELL, William (1939–), British poet, born in Hythe, Hampshire; he left school at the age of 15 and worked in various capacities, including as a journalist and as a photographer aboard the *Queen Mary*, before entering the University of Bristol. In 1975 he became a lecturer at the University of Newcastle. His collections of verse include *Yes and No* (1979), which established his reputation as a poet of considerable technical accomplishment, *Jouissance* (1985), *The Game: Tennis Poems* (1992), *Bleeding Heart Yard* (1992), and *Five Easy Pieces* (1993). The range of his work is impressive, extending as it does from translations of the Latin poetry of Ronsard and Milton featured in *A Second Life* (1982) to the imaginatively expansive accounts of his experiences of America in *Eldorado* (1987). Whether in conversationally cadenced free verse or in elaborately traditional forms, his verse invariably displays an attractive vitality and accessibility. Among the works published under his editorship is *Between Comets* (1984), a distinguished collection of poems and essays to commemorate Norman *Nicholson's seventieth birthday. Scammell's other books include the critical and biographical study *Keith Douglas* (1988).

SCANNELL, Vernon (1922–), British poet and novelist, born in Spilsby, Lincolnshire, educated at the University of Leeds after active service in the Second World War and a period as a professional boxer. He was a schoolteacher from 1955 to 1962, when he became a freelance writer. His numerous collections of poetry include *Graves and Resurrections* (1948), *The Masks of Love* (1960), *The Winter Man* (1973), *Funeral Games* (1987), *Soldiering On* (1989), and *A Time for Fires* (1991). *New and Collected Poems 1950–1980* was published in 1980, and *Collected Poems, 1950–1993* in 1993. Scannell's poetry, which generally combines an informality of tone with accomplished use of traditional forms, recurrently draws on his background as a boxer, soldier, teacher, and parent. Mortality is a frequent theme, which he treats with a characteristic combination of pessimism, wit, and compassion. Among his novels are *The Big Chance* (1960), *Ring of Truth* (1983), acclaimed for the authenticity of its treatment of boxing, and *Argument of Kings* (1987), which is closely based on his wartime experiences. *The Tiger and the Rose* (1971), *A Proper Gentleman* (1977), and *Drums of Morning: Growing Up in the Thirties* (1992) are autobiographies. His critical works include *Not without Glory* (1976), a study of British and American poetry of the Second World War. He has edited several anthologies of poetry and prose, notably the popular *Sporting Literature* of 1987.

Scarlet Pimpernel, The, see ORCZY, BARONESS.

Scenes from Provincial Life, see COOPER, WILLIAM.

SCHAEFFER, Susan Fromberg (1941–), American novelist, born in Brooklyn, New York, educated at the University of Chicago. Influenced by both her literary studies (her Ph.D. dissertation was on the novels of *Nabokov) and her familial experience of the Jewish Holocaust experience, Schaeffer is most frequently classified as a Jewish-American writer. She has enriched the genre of the family saga by adding a growing awareness of feminist issues, a critical consciousness, and interest in linguistic play to her writing. She writes sweeping historical novels and shorter novels of domestic and psychological realism with equal ease, such as *Mainland* (1985), in which a married woman writer recovering from an eye operation discovers, in her relationship with a Chinese immigrant, new depths of sensitivity and compassion; and *The Injured Party* (1986), about the dilemma of a woman faced with her lost and dying lover. *Buffalo Afternoon* (1989), a long novel set during and after the Vietnam War, adopts a male perspective. Her other works include the novels *Falling* (1973), *Anya* (1975), *The Madness of a Seduced Woman* (1983), and *First Nights* (1993); collections of poetry, *The Witch and the Weather Report* (1972), *Alphabet for the Lost Years* (1976), and *The Bible of the Beasts of the Little Field* (1980); and the short stories in *The Queen of Egypt* (1980).

SCHAMA, Simon (Michael) (1945–), British historian, born in London, educated at Christ's College, Cambridge, where he was a fellow and Director of Studies in History from 1966 to 1976. He became Professor of History at Harvard University in 1980. His early works include *Patriots and Liberators* (1977), a study of Dutch political radicalism in the Napoleonic era, and *The Two Rothschilds and the Land of Israel* (1979). He is best known for *The Embarrassment of Riches* (1987), his analysis of the cultural, economic, and social character of the Netherlands in the seventeenth century, and *Citizens* (1989), a reinterpretation of the French Revolution as the result of the *ancien régime*'s loss of control of the progressive ethos it had fostered. Among his other works is the experimental *Dead Certainties (Unwarranted Speculations)* (1991), a pair of 'historical novellas' investigating the disparity between events and their subsequent narration. *Landscape and Memory* (1995) ties in with a TV series.

Schindler's Ark, a novel by Thomas *Keneally, published in 1982 (Booker Prize). An epic account of the Second World War, the novel, based on extensive research and interviews with survivors of concentration camps, questions the boundaries between the genres of historical documentation and imaginative fiction. Set in Nazi Germany, and based on a real person, it tells the story of Oskar Schindler, an amoral and profligate though ambitious German entrepreneur who moves to Cracow to profit from the collapse of Jewish-run businesses as anti-Semitic fervour accelerates. The seemingly unscrupulous profiteer becomes an unlikely protector of Polish Jews, to be revered as a hero by Israel and by Jews all over the world. As the narrative progresses, Schindler demonstrates his wit and courage, using his factory and connections to save the beleaguered and the threatened from extermination by their Nazi oppressors. He eventually succeeds in his mission of rescuing a band of women and children prisoners from Auschwitz-Birkenau. Keneally painstakingly reconstructs historical fact to present a convincing portrait of a variety of individuals—particularly women—and their great resilience when faced with the fear of imminent destruction. Underlying the account is his fascination with the central figure's psychology, and with the circumstances of destiny which lead similar individuals to do good or evil, to preserve or destroy. Due to its historical dimension the book was a contentious winner of the Booker Prize for fiction. The novel was published in the USA as *Schindler's List* which was the title of the film version by Steven Spielberg of 1994.

SCHLESINGER, Arthur (Meier) Jr (1917–), American historian, born in Columbus, Ohio, educated at Harvard, where he began his academic career; in 1966 he became Albert Schweitzer Professor in Humanities at the City University of New York. He was special assistant to Presidents Kennedy and Johnson from 1961 to 1964. *The Age of Jackson* (1945) won a Pulitzer Prize; its rejection of widely held assumptions on the early nineteenth-century development of the USA established his reputation as an admired and provocative historian. *The Age of Roosevelt*, generally regarded as the most authoritative history of the USA from 1930 to 1945, comprises *The Crisis of the Old Order* (1957), *The Coming of the New Deal* (1959), and *The Politics of Upheaval* (1960). He received a second Pulitzer Prize for *A Thousand Days* (1965), a study of the Kennedy administration; his disillusionment with the course of American politics under Johnson is clear from the critique of American involvement in Vietnam in *The Bitter Heritage* (1967) and the essays collected as *The Crisis of Confidence* (1969). Notable among his many other works are *Robert F. Kennedy and His Times* (1978), and *The Cycles of American History* (1986), essays on the fluctuations of American liberalism.

SCHMIDT, Michael (Norton) (1947–), poet, born in Mexico City, educated at Harvard and at Wadham College, Oxford. In 1969 he became managing director of the Carcanet Press. He was Gulbenkian Fellow in Poetry at the University of Manchester from 1972 to 1975 and became editor of the literary periodical *Poetry Nation* in 1984. His first full collection was *Bedlam and Oakwood* (1970). Subsequent volumes have included *My Brother Gloucester* (1976), *A Change of Affairs* (1978), and *Choosing a Guest: New and Selected Poems* (1983). His earlier poetry, in which meditative and lyrical elements predominate, is characterized by its disciplined avoidance of technical or rhetorical ostentation. *The Love of Strangers* (1989), a sequence of twenty extended verse-memoirs, is strongly autobiographical in its accounts of meetings with individuals who influenced his intellectual and artistic growth. Schmidt has edited numerous anthologies of poems, most notably *Some Contemporary Poets of Britain and Ireland* (1983), and several collections of essays, including *British Poetry since 1960* (1972). Among his other writings are two novels, *The Colonist* (1980) and *The Dresden Gate* (1986).

SCHREINER, Olive (Emilie Albertina) (1855–1920), South African writer, born in Cape Colony, the daughter of a German missionary and an English mother. Her first published novel, *The Story of an African Farm* (1883), is a classic of modern South African literature. In its intense and poetic evocation of mood and landscape the novel shows the influences of *Hardy and of Emily Brontë's *Wuthering Heights*. Set in the Bible-belt veld in the 1860s, on a lonely ostrich farm, the novel follows the lives of a group of white characters, notably Tant' Sannie, a widowed Boer woman, Lyndall and Em, two orphaned cousins who grow up under her guardianship, Waldo, the idealistic son of the farm's devout German overseer, and the roguish smooth-talking conman Bonaparte Blenkins. The very different outlooks of the two young women provide the novel's main interest: Lyndall, brilliant, beautiful, and rebellious, is a doomed and unforgettable heroine, who rejects marriage, gives birth to an illegitimate child, and subsequently dies; Em is a more typical example of traditional womanhood, who eventually runs the farm with her husband Gregory. Schreiner's treatment of women, particularly Lyndall with her passionately held unconventional views, a pioneer *New Woman, established her as an important early writer for feminists. Published under the pseudonym 'Ralph Iron' the novel received instant acclaim. When the author's female identity was revealed, Schreiner was courted by literary and progressive London where she had gone in 1881, returning to South Africa in 1889, and she formed lasting friendships with Havelock *Ellis and E. *Carpenter. Her other novels are the shorter, allegorical *Trooper Peter Halket of Mashonaland* (1897), which denounced the expansionist designs of Cecil Rhodes; *Man to Man* (1926), described by the author as 'the story of a woman, a simple childlike woman, that goes down, down'; and *Undine* (1929), written when she was 18, the first novel she wrote. As a pioneer feminist, and an early critic of incipient apartheid and of British colonialism, she wrote *An English South African's View of the Situation* (1898), which attacked British anti-Boer policies; *A Letter on the South African Union and the Principles of Government* (1909), an indictment of policies towards the black majority; *Woman and Labour* (1911), regarded by early British feminists as the 'Bible of the Women's Movement'; and *Thoughts on South Africa* (1923). Schreiner's health declined rapidly in her final years, and she died alone in a Cape Town boarding house. The definitive edition of the *Olive Schreiner Letters* (vol. 1, 1988) was edited by Richard *Rive. Biographies include *The Life of Olive Schreiner* (1924), by her husband Samuel Cron Cronwright, a South African politician, and *Olive Schreiner* (1980), by Ruth *First and Ann Scott.

SCHULBERG, Budd (Wilson) (1914–), American novelist and screenwriter, born in New York City, educated at Dartmouth College. The son of a Hollywood screenwriter and producer, Schulberg has always been intimately associated with the film industry, largely through the commercial success of his first novel, *What Makes Sammy Run* (1941), a frenzied account of how its hero, Sammy Glick, rises from an inauspicious beginning on New York's Lower East Side to a position of power and influence in Hollywood. During his years as a screenwriter in Hollywood between 1936 and 1939, he met F. Scott *Fitzgerald, about whom he was to write an important biographical essay, 'Old Scott: The Myth, the Masque, the Man', first published in *Esquire* in 1961 and reprinted in *The Four Seasons of Success* (1972). Fitzgerald's last years inspired Schulberg's portrait of the suffering writer in his third novel, *The Disenchanted* (1950). He achieved recognition from the world of film for his screenplay for Elia Kazan's *On the Waterfront* (1954); a novel, *The Waterfront*, followed in 1955. *The Harder They Fall* (1947), his second novel, is set in the world of boxing and presents an analysis of criminal entrepreneurship. Schulberg has been active in the promotion of creative writing programmes, notably in his founding of the Douglass House Watts Writers' Workshop in Los Angeles shortly after the 1965 Watts riots, and in his involvement with the New England Theatre Conference and the Frederick Douglass Creative Arts Center in New York City. His more recent works include *Love, Action, Laughter and Other Sad Tales* (1990) and *Sparring with Hemingway* (1995).

SCHUMACHER, E(rnst) F(riedrich) (1911–77), German economist, journalist, and economic adviser, born in Bonn, educated at Oxford University. Schumacher became a guru of the so-called 'New Age' movement late in his life thanks largely to the impact of his best-selling *Small Is Beautiful* (1973). He worked and studied in Britain and the USA during much of the 1930s, and eventually returned to research at Oxford after being released from internment in Britain as an 'enemy alien' during the Second World War. After a visit to Burma in 1955 he developed a deep interest in the process of economic development in the Third World. In this field his emphasis on the importance of 'intermediate technology' has been influential in moving official thinking towards the contemplation of rather more 'appropriate' development strategies. In Burma he also came under the sway of Buddhism, to which he actually converted. This conversion provides a key to understanding his growing scepticism as to the utility of familiar Western capitalist values (such as acquisitiveness and consumerism) as a means to human happiness and fulfilment. From there it was but a short step to the idea that 'intermediate technology' might be the solution not only to the problems of the Third World, but also to those of all the world. *A Guide for the Perplexed* (1977) is a further collection of essays.

SCHUMPETER, Joseph Alois (1883–1950), Austrian-born economist, born in Triesch, Moravia, Austria-Hungary, educated at the University of Vienna. His *The Theory of Economic Development* (1934), although written first in German (1912), was influential when it appeared in English for introducing into the discussion of the dynamics of the economic process the centrality of innovation and investment undertaken by 'heroic entrepreneurs'. In probably his best-known book outside economics circles, *Capitalism, Socialism and Democracy* (1942), Schumpeter translated what had been principally a theoretical economic argument into a full-blown account of the history of Western civilization and of its future prospects. Its basic argument was that capitalist society was inexorably tending towards a socialist future, in which democratic participation would amount to no more than periodically choosing between specialist managers from the same élite class: a future upon which Schumpeter looked out with regret and dismay. Schumpeter was the author of numerous essays, articles, biographical sketches, and reviews, some of which are collected in his *Ten Great Economists* (1951) and *Essays* (1969). The monumental (and unfinished) *History of Economic Analysis* (1954) was published posthumously, and quickly became a standard reference.

SCHUYLER, James (1923–91), American poet and novelist, born in Chicago, educated at Bethany College, West Virginia. Schuyler lived in Italy for some years, but spent much of his life in New York working for the Museum of Modern Art and, like other members of the *New York School such as John *Ashbery and Frank *O'Hara, wrote for *Art News* and other art journals. His books of poems include *Salute* (1960), *May 24th or So* (1966), *Freely Espousing* (1969), *The Crystal Lithium* (1972), *Hymn to Life: Poems* (1974), *The Morning of the Poet* (1980; Pulitzer Prize), and *Selected Poems* (1988). His novels include *Alfred and Guinevere* (1958), *Nest of Ninnies* (1969), written with John Ashbery, and *What's for Dinner* (1979). Schuyler's poetry is resonant with a lifetime spent working with and writing about pictures, and it is a pictorialist's eye which he turned on the world. His poems are filled with the apparently casual iconography thrown up by urban and pastoral scenes though these visual signs of the outer world were usually accommodated to some reflective purpose, arrived at in a mood of quiet acceptance.

SCHWARTZ, Delmore (1913–66), American poet, born in Brooklyn, New York, educated at Harvard and at New York University. Schwartz published his first book of poems, *In Dreams Begin Responsibilities*, in 1938. He was poetry editor for the **Partisan Review* and the **New Republic* and taught writing at numerous colleges. A man of wide-ranging intellect, a brilliant teacher and conversationalist, he partook of a life of bohemian excess in Greenwich Village. His collections *Genesis I* (1943) and *Vaudeville for a Princess* (1950) were followed by *Selected Poems: Summer Knowledge* (1959). A victim of mental ill-health, he published little poetry after the success of *Selected Poems*, and died in isolation in a Times Square hotel. His *Selected Essays* appeared in 1970, followed by *Last and Lost Poems* (1979), and a selected edition of his *Letters* in 1984. His translations of Rimbaud's *A Season in Hell* appeared in 1939. Schwartz once wrote that the subject of poetry 'is experience not truth', yet his own early work is animated by an oppositional dialectic familiar to the philosophic mind, where the binaries of mind and body, appearance and reality, flesh and spirit, Heaven and Hell become the focus of his quest to relate his sense of the individual 'I' to all that lies beyond it. The power of his early poems had much to do with his use of traditional forms. In later years, his use of the newly fashionable long lines of open form was ultimately fatal to his reputation.

Science Fiction is a term used in two broadly conflicting senses, and no single definition, for this reason, has ever satisfied any student of the form. The first is ostensibly descriptive and refers to a body of literature defined as science fiction by those Americans who invented the term in the 1920s, and who published what they called scientifiction or science fiction in *pulp magazines dedicated to the form. Within a few years of the creation of the term a cohesive sub-culture had evolved, composed of writers, editors, reviewers, and fans; stories and novels written within this sub-culture shared certain intrinsic assumptions as well as distinctive linguistic and thematic codes. This complex of ideas, and not just the fictional texts which initially gave rise to it, came to be called science fiction. The second of the two senses is prescriptive, and is restricted to texts. There can be no doubt that it is the first of these two senses which continues to dominate most writers of the form and the markets to which they must sell their works. However, American science fiction in 1930, as written by authors like E. E. *Smith, M. Leinster, E. Hamilton, J. *Williamson, J. W. Campbell Jr and others, was principally a body of tales set in the future: this was the great innovation of the form.

Throughout the nineteenth century, hundreds of texts were published which later prescriptive definitions of the form have plausibly designated as science fiction, because in one way or another their settings or scientific assumptions were *displaced* from the normal world. But almost invariably these displacements were horizontal, through space rather than time; and if a story were set at some future date, that future world was usually seen either as substantially identical with the present, or as a mirror in which the present could be regarded in utopian or dystopian form. Even the futures promulgated in H. G. Wells's *The Time Machine* (1895) or *When the Sleeper Wakes* (1899) can be seen, in this sense, as reflective (see UTOPIA AND ANTI-UTOPIA). This was all changed with the American pulp writers two decades later. With a fine disregard of didacticism, writers such as Smith, in his *Lensman* sequence, created future environments for tales of adventure and exploration. The effect of this liberation of futuristic fictions from the constraints of allegory was, in literary terms, explosive. From it derives the kinetic vivacity of early American science fiction, the love of new inventions for their own sake, the readiness to believe in superheroes, and the leap into space itself. From this freeing of the future derives the characteristic flavour of American science fiction: its ease with scale, technology, and gear; its richness of narrative device; and its secret impatience with reason. For writers like R. A. *Heinlein, I. *Asimov, A. E. *Van Vogt, and T. *Sturgeon, who came to maturity in the 1930s and 1940s, the naïve tradition into which they had been born seemed both all-encompassing and natural; and for many readers, the work of this generation of writers remains the only genuine science fiction. So compelling a myth of origin, shaped as it was by writers still alive, called for definition. In 1952, for instance, Asimov suggested that science fiction was 'That branch of literature which is concerned with the impact of scientific advance upon human beings'. K. *Amis wrote of the genre in 1960 as 'That class of prose narrative treating of a situation that could not arise in the world we know, but which is hypothesized on the basis of some innovation in science or technology, or pseudo-science or pseudo-technology, whether human or extraterrestrial in origin.' H. *Ellison in 1971 defined it as 'Anything that deals in even the smallest extrapolative manner with the future of man and his societies.'

In 1973, in *Billion Year Spree*, Brian *Aldiss broke new ground by arguing that science fiction began neither with American pulp magazines nor with H. G. Wells, but with M. Shelley's *Frankenstein* (1818); Aldiss defined the form as a child begotten upon Gothic romance by the industrial and scientific revolution of the early nineteenth century. Whether or not this argument was entirely plausible, it was undeniably influential in its undercutting of earlier claims that science fiction derived from an early twentieth-century American blend of populist rhetoric and positivism. More abstract was Darko Suvin's definition from 1979: science fiction was 'A literary genre whose necessary and sufficient conditions are the presence and interaction of estrangement and cognition, and whose main formal device is an imaginative framework (or 'Novum') alternative to the author's empirical environment.' However, Suvin's definition significantly failed to encompass American science fiction, in which the framework is almost always alternative to our world, but in which estrangement tends significantly to be absent. In 1987, K. S. *Robinson described science fiction as 'an historical literature. . . . In every sf narrative, there is an explicit or implicit fictional history that connects the period depicted to our present moment, or to some moment of our past.' See also APOCALYPTIC LITERATURE.

Scoop, a novel by E. *Waugh, published in 1938. Mistaken identity is the central plot device in the novel, which satirizes the cynical opportunism of Fleet Street journalists in search of a story as well as Waugh's more familiar target of contemporary morality. William Boot is a naïve young man who lives with his parents and a large extended family of grandparents and elderly retainers on the decaying estate of Boot Magna. When, mistaken for the fashionable novelist John Boot, he is sent by the editor of the *Daily Beast* (a newspaper owned by the powerful magnate Lord Copper) to cover the civil war in the imaginary African republic of Ishmaelia, he is horrified at the thought of relinquishing his rural idyll (his only journalistic experience is as the *Beast*'s nature columnist) and spends the rest of the novel trying to get himself recalled by the newspaper. He is hindered in this endeavour by a beautiful German girl, Katchen, whom he meets at the Pension where he is staying. Prevented by his involvement with Katchen from following the other special correspondents on a wild goose chase into the desert, William encounters the mysterious 'Mr Baldwin', to whom he had previously offered some assistance, who reciprocates by providing him with his 'scoop', a sensational account of a Russian plot to overthrow the Ishmaelian government. As a result of this, William becomes the hero of the hour and it is with the greatest difficulty that he manages to avoid attending the banquet given in his honour, at which his uncle Theodore, in a final case of mistaken identity, takes his place. Waugh drew on his own experiences as a war correspondent in Abyssinia during the 1930s for the book, one of the few of his novels to have a (relatively) happy ending.

Scots Quair, A, see GIBBON, LEWIS GRASSIC.

SCOTT, David (1947–), British poet, born in Cambridge; he studied theology at the University of Durham and at Cuddleston College, near Oxford, before entering the Anglican Ministry. In 1980 he became vicar of Torpenhow and Allhallows, near Wigton, Cumbria. His poetry attracted notice when his 'Kirkwall Auction Mart' won the *Sunday Times*/BBC poetry competition in 1978. *A Quiet Gathering* (1984), his first collection of verse, was followed by *Playing for England* in 1989; both books are illustrated with drawings by Graham Arnold, a member of the Brotherhood of Ruralists. Much of Scott's poetry employs an engagingly subdued tone for its treatments of his clerical duties and events in the lives of his parishioners. He has also produced numerous impressively concise poems on literary and ecclesiastical figures; these include 'A Walk with St Teresa of Avila', notable for the interplay of a witty spiritual surrealism with his characteristically precise use of local detail. His other works include *How Does It Feel?* (1989), a collection of poems for children, and a number of plays for the National Youth Music Theatre, including *Bendigo Boswell*, which was televised in 1983.

SCOTT, Dennis (1939–91), Jamaican poet and playwright, born in Kingston, educated at the University of the West Indies at Mona and the University of Newcastle-upon-Tyne. He was Director of the Jamaica School of Drama, and was Visiting Associate Professor of Playwriting at the Yale School of Drama. His play *An Echo in the Bone* (1974) was published, together with a play by Derek *Walcott and another by Errol *Hill, in *Plays for Today* (1985), edited by Errol Hill. The phrase 'echo in the bone' refers to racial memories of oppression, and the play, structured ritualistically around the 'nine-night' ceremony preparing the dead for burial, powerfully condenses a particular phase of Jamaican history. The 'dead man' in the play is a living fugitive peasant on the run from killing a white estate owner. Scott's poetry tends to be complex and dense with shifting voices, often focusing on the self, and its continual search for emotional and political stability. He was awarded the Commonwealth Poetry Prize for *Uncle Time* (1973). Among other publications are *Dreadwalk: Poems 1970–78* (1982), an edition of *Sir Gawain and the Green Knight* (1978), and a short play, *Terminus* (1966).

SCOTT, Duncan Campbell (1862–1947), Canadian poet, born in Ottawa. With Charles G. D. *Roberts, Archibald Lampman, and Bliss Carman, he is usually grouped as one of the 'Confederation Poets'. He collaborated with Lampman on 'At the Mermaid Inn', a column published in the *Toronto Globe* in 1892 and 1893. His occupation as a civil servant in the Department of Indian Affairs led to his travelling in remote parts of Canada, which gave him contact with Native peoples and provided the impetus for his particular brand of reflective topographical poetry, which responded directly to local nature. Though fascinated by the wilderness, Scott remained a Victorian in his desire to bring civilization to 'primitive' Canada. His life-long interest in music can be seen in the lyric sensibility that informs his poetry and in its stress on the aural. After retiring in 1932 he travelled to Europe, where he found new subjects for his verse. Among his volumes of poetry are *The Magic House* (1893), *Labor and the Angel* (1898), *New World Lyrics and Ballads* (1905), *Lundy's Lane* (1916), *The Green Cloister* (1935), and *The Circle of Affection* (1947). He also published the short-story collections *In the Village of Viger* (1896) and *The Witching of Elspie* (1923).

SCOTT, F(rancis) R(eginald) (1899–1985), Canadian poet, born in Quebec, educated at Bishop's College, Lennoxville, Quebec, and at Magdalen College, Oxford. Scott followed a distinguished dual career as practising lawyer and as cosmopolitan and satiric poet; from the 1920s his energies were often devoted to promoting the cause of modern poetry and to satirizing what he saw as the tedious solemnity of much Canadian poetry of the period. Scott's experience of the Depression years in the 1930s changed his priorities, and his legal skills were increasingly devoted to fighting for an amelioration of the human condition; he co-edited *Social Planning for Canada* in 1935, and was National President of the League for Social Reconstruction for two years. In 1936 he edited with A. J. M. *Smith the influential poetry anthology *New Provinces*, and they were later to co-operate again on the satirical anthology *The Blasted Pine* (1957). Scott's own poetry collections include *Overture* (1945), *Selected Poems* (1966), and *Collected Poems* (1980). *Essays on the Constitution* (1977) brought together essays and papers written between 1928 and 1971, and the *Collected Stories of F. R. Scott* appeared in 1981. Scott developed a keen interest in French Canadian writing; his highly acclaimed translation of *Poems of French Canada* appeared in 1977. *A New Endeavour: Selected Political Essays, Letters and Addresses* (1986) was edited by M. Horn.

SCOTT, Geoffrey (1883–1929), British architectural historian and poet, educated at New College, Oxford, where he won the Newdigate Prize for his poem 'The Death of Shelley' and the Chancellor's Prize for his essay 'The National Character of English Architecture'. During a tour of Italy with John Maynard *Keynes in 1906 he met Bernard *Berenson, who subsequently employed him as a secretary and librarian. Berenson's theories of art informed Scott's *The Architecture of Humanism* (1914, revised 1924), which is regarded as a seminal work for its extension of the critical vocabulary and its advocacy of the baroque. He returned to England in 1925 following the collapse of his marriage after an affair with Vita *Sackville-West, one of several celebrated liaisons which fostered his reputation for remarkable charm and exceptional good looks. The formal elegance and opulent imagery of *A Box of Paints* (1923), his first collection of poems, combines with a rigorous contemplative element in the posthumous *Poems* (1931), from which W. B. *Yeats made selections for his *Oxford Book of Modern Verse* (1936). In 1925 he published *The Portrait of Zelide*, his witty biography of Madame de Charrière; among her suitors had been James Boswell, whose papers Scott began editing in 1927. His 18-volume edition of *The Private Papers of James Boswell from Malahide Castle* (1928–34, vols vii–xviii with Frederick Pottle) was in an advanced state of preparation at the time of his death.

SCOTT, Paul (Mark), (1920–78), British novelist, born in north London, educated at Winchmore Hill Collegiate School, the second son of a family of freelance commercial artists. Despite early ambitions as a poet he began training in accountancy (passing exams with ease thanks to his photographic memory). In 1940 he was called up to work in the British Intelligence Department in London, and in 1943 he was transferred to the Indian Army, arriving just after the critical 'Quit India' resolution of 1942. The three years he spent as an Officer Cadet in India, Burma, and Malaya fuelled his writing for the following two decades. On his return to London he was employed in publishing and subsequently as a literary agent while also working on his own writing. He published a volume of his poetry in 1941, wrote several radio plays, was a regular reviewer for *Country Life*, and contributed articles to *The Times*. His first published novel, *Johnnie Sahib* (1952), is a war story concerning the tensions within a small group of men, the personnel of an air supply unit of the kind in which Scott himself served. Seven novels rapidly followed, four of them with Indian settings. The exceptions are *A Male Child* (1956), an account of a man's quest for a purpose in life after he is invalided out of the war in the East and rejected by his wife; *The Bender* (1963), a picaresque comedy about a drifter with money troubles; and *The Corrida at San Feliu* (1964), an intricate book, set in Spain and exploring the novelistic process of making fiction from reality. The latter novel introduced the fragmentary narrative which Scott would subsequently employ in *The *Raj Quartet*.

The novels set in India show a gradual broadening of Scott's canvas from wartime India to the entire history of the Anglo-Indian relationship. *The Alien Sky* (1953), *The Mark of the Warrior* (1958), and *The Chinese Love Pavilion* (1960) were followed by *The Birds of Paradise* (1962), which explores the mercurial nature of the past and suggests the genesis of Scott's later interest in multiple perspectives. In 1964 Scott returned to India, at the expense of Heinemann, his publishers, living with an Indian family and researching Anglo-Indian history. This visit bore copious fruit in the creation of *The Raj Quartet*, the complex and exhaustive fictional survey of India under British rule until Partition in 1947, of which the individual novels are *The Jewel in the Crown* (1966), *The Day of the Scorpion* (1968), *The Towers of Silence* (1971), and *A Division of the Spoils* (1975). Scott's final work was *Staying On* (1977; Booker Prize), a poignant coda to *The Raj Quartet* concerning an English couple, Colonel 'Tusker' Smalley and his wife Lucy, who live out their isolated retirement in India after Independence; their existence in the crumbling annexe of Smith's Hotel is a sad final comment on the long relationship between Britain and India. Scott returned again to India in 1972 on a British Council lecture tour. In 1976 and 1977 he was Visiting Lecturer at Tulsa University, Oklahoma. He was a retiring man who never sought publicity, and despite a warm reception for *The Jewel in the Crown*, Scott barely figured on the literary scene until *Staying On* won the Booker Prize in 1977. He was too ill to receive the prize in person, and died from cancer less than six months later. In 1981 *Staying On* was adapted for television, and in 1984 *The Raj Quartet* was successfully televised as *The Jewel in the Crown*.

SCOTT, Robert Falcon (1868–1912), British explorer, born in Devonport; he became a naval cadet in 1880 and received his first command as leader of the Antarctic expedition which left Britain in 1900. *The Voyage of the 'Discovery'* (1905) contains his account of the expedition. In 1910 he set sail for the Antarctic again in the *Terra Nova*, reaching the South Pole in January 1912 to find the Norwegian expedition led by Roald Amundsen had been the first to reach it less than a month before. Scott and his four companions all perished in extremely severe weather on the return journey. Stephen Gwynn's *Captain Scott* (1930) and Reginald Pound's *Scott of the Antarctic* (1977) are among the many biographies. His journals of 1910–12 were published under the title *Scott's Last Expedition* (edited by L. Huxley, 1913).

Scottish Renaissance, a term coined by the French critic Denis Saurat in 1924 to describe the contemporary revival in consciousness and culture in Scotland, between the World Wars, which is now more loosely associated with the writing of Hugh *MacDiarmid, Lewis Grassic *Gibbon, Edwin *Muir, and Neil M. *Gunn. This creative resurgence was prompted partly by the growth of national consciousness and political turbulence in Scotland after the First World War, and partly by a self-conscious literary reaction against the prevailing sentimental '*Kailyard' trend in late nineteenth-century Scottish writing. Exploiting the arguments about the distinct nature of Scottish sensibility found in Professor Gregory Smith's *Scottish Literature:*

Character and Influence (1919), and recognizing the success of the recent *Irish Literary Revival, MacDiarmid's periodical *The Scottish Chapbook* (1922) first took on the role of promoting a separate Scottish literature which would return to the irreverent spirit of Robert Burns and William Dunbar. Although the tireless MacDiarmid kept reiterating the slogan 'Not Traditions—Precedents!', the literature of the Renaissance is less concerned with *Modernist experimentation than with capturing the combination of the spectral and the practical thought to individuate the Scots psyche—'the Caledonian anti-syzygy'. MacDiarmid's early collections of lyric poetry *Sangshaw* (1925) and *Penny Wheep* (1926) drew on vernacular traditions expressed in 'synthetic Scots', a stylized and elaborated version of Scots dialect. The purpose of writing in Scots (sometimes called 'Lallans') was at once democratic (to revive and dignify the language of the home and the hearth) and European (to create an authentic indigenous, non-English literature). The first major work of this movement was MacDiarmid's long poem *A Drunk Man Looks at the Thistle* (1926), a *stream-of-consciousness monologue in Scots combining the influences of Burns, Whitman, and the Russian philosopher Shestov, to produce an invigorating combination of mundanity and sublimity. MacDiarmid's poetry of the 1930s also conveys his willingness to experiment, as does Lewis Grassic Gibbon's vigorous prose trilogy *A Scots Quair* (1932–4), conducted in Scots, which presents an anatomy of Scottish experience during the first three decades of the century through the life of its heroine. With the completion of the trilogy the Scottish Renaissance reached its peak, but by the middle 1930s the sense of communal purpose had dispersed, and although the most interesting work of Neil Gunn and the Gaelic poet Sorley *MacLean was still to come, the first wave of the resurgence was over. MacDiarmid continued to produce copious verse, less frequently in Scots, and some critics identify a second wave of creativity in the 1940s, and yet a third in the 1970s. Roderick Watson's *The Literature of Scotland* (1984) offers a useful survey of developments, and Christopher Harvie's *No Gods and Precious Few Heroes: Scotland 1914–1980* (1981) provides a clear account of the social context.

SCOTT-MONCRIEFF, C(harles) K(enneth) (1889–1930), Scottish translator, born in Stirlingshire, educated at the University of Edinburgh. Best known for his inspired translations from the French, beginning with *The Song of Roland* (1919, *Chanson de Roland*), his letters, collected in *C. K. Scott-Moncrieff: Memories and Letters* (1931, edited by J. M. Scott-Moncrieff and L. W. Lunn), reveal his own accomplishment as a writer. After working as a private secretary to Lord Northcliffe, and writing for *The Times*, he began his famous translations of Proust's *Remembrance of Things Past* (*A la recherche du temps perdu*): *Swann's Way* (1922), *Within a Budding Grove* (1924), *The Guermantes Way* (1925), *Cities of the Plain* (1927), *The Captive* (1929), and *The Sweet Cheat Gone* (1930). He died before completing the work (later revised by Terence Kilmartin), but Scott-Moncrieff's great translation is generally recognized as itself a masterpiece of the art, some reviewers declaring it even superior to the original. He also translated Stendhal, including *The Red and the Black* (*Le rouge et le noir*, 1926), Pirandello, and *Beowulf*, and edited *Marcel Proust: An English Tribute* (1923).

SCOVELL, E(dith) J(oy) (1907–), British poet, born in Sheffield, educated at Somerville College, Oxford. She was a secretary and journalist before her marriage in 1937 to the biologist Charles Elton, whom she accompanied as field assistant on expeditions in South America. Her first collection of poems, *Shadows of Chrysanthemums* (1944), was followed by *The Midsummer Meadow* (1946) and *The River Steamer* (1956). Subsequent volumes include *The Space Between* (1982), *Listening to Collared Doves* (1986), *Collected Poems* (1988), and *Selected Poems* (1991). Her poetry's gently idiosyncratic rhythms and factually meditative tenor are among its most attractive qualities. The fusion of precisely observed natural imagery with a readily accessible visionary element in much of her best writing is exemplified by the pellucidly mysterious quality of 'The River Steamer'.

Screenwriting. In its early days, true to the etymology of the word 'photography', the cinema was described as a form of 'writing with light'. Much later, the French director and critic Alexandre Astruc coined the concept of the *caméra-stylo*, the camera as a pen. But the relations between writers and film have characteristically been bumpier than these images suggest, and Hollywood mythology is in large part constituted by writers like Nathanael *West and F. Scott *Fitzgerald who converted their frustration with the industry into full-scale metaphors for a failing America. Other distinguished writers, like William *Faulkner, took Hollywood more lightly and were, on the whole, associated with better films and directors. The professional screenwriter, in any case, was a very different figure, fast-thinking, hard-working, and a person who had learned his or her trade in the cinema rather than outside: Ben *Hecht and Leigh Brackett are good examples. But 'writing with light' fully comes into its own, perhaps, only in the work of the writer-director, the figure who holds (or at least directs) the camera *and* the pen. Erich von Stroheim and Chaplin were powerful early instances, and most of the directors of the French New Wave—Truffaut, Godard, Chabrol—wrote their own films. Orson Welles also wrote his scripts, although there is continuing discussion about how much of *Citizen Kane* (1941) is his and how much belongs to Hermann Mankiewicz. Beyond this, of course, lies the whole vexed question of who the 'author' of any film is. Playwrights like Tom *Stoppard and David *Hare have become successful directors, but perhaps the best example of the writer as master of quite different media is Harold *Pinter, whose screenplays, chiefly for Joseph Losey (*The Servant*, *Accident*, *The Go-*

Between, and others), are models of the craft and quite unlike any of Pinter's work for the theatre.

Scrutiny, a critical periodical produced at Cambridge University from 1932 to 1953 which, in the words of its chief editor F. R. *Leavis, accomplished 'a comprehensive revaluation of English literature' through its rigorously maintained standards of textual analysis and evaluation. Leavis and his wife Q. D. Leavis were the principal contributors and dominant in the editorial group; their collaborators included D. W. Harding, Denys Thompson, and L. C. *Knights. Leavis and his associates had admired the **Calendar of Modern Letters*, its 'Scrutinies' section, noted for its high level of critical discourse, suggesting their choice of title. Q. D. Leavis's *Fiction and the Reading Public* (1932) defined a crisis in the quality of literacy which motivated *Scrutiny* in its task of upholding critical values relevant to the cultural health of the era. Concern with the social implications of literary criticism was apparent in the attention given to educational matters; it was opposed to the neutrality of linguistic and historically annalistic approaches to literature and decried what it viewed as the indulgent aestheticism of the *Bloomsbury Group. *Scrutiny*'s textual methods derived from those developed by I. A. *Richards, J. C. *Ransom, and other exponents of the *New Criticism; while their work outlined the procedures of *Practical Criticism, *Scrutiny* was the first journal to apply such methods consistently to a broad historical range of poetry, drama, and prose fiction. Eminent contributors included D. A. Traversi who, with L. C. Knights, effected a major revision of Shakespeare studies, John Speirs, Edgell *Rickword, William *Empson, and D. J. *Enright, whose work on German authors was important in sustaining the attention to European literature in later issues. *Scrutiny*'s weakness lay in its failure to achieve balanced evaluations of contemporary writing; Graham *Greene, Virginia *Woolf, W. H. *Auden, and Dylan *Thomas were among the authors somewhat peremptorily dismissed and Leavis found the later poetry of W. B. *Yeats disappointing. After the dispersal of its central contributors during the Second World War, Leavis was unable to muster stable support for *Scrutiny*, which was discontinued in 1953. The achievement of the journal itself and the many valuable books based on material it had published had very considerable influence on the methods and content of literary studies throughout the post-war period. A complete set of the nineteen volumes of *Scrutiny* was issued by Cambridge University Press in 1963.

SCUPHAM, (John) Peter (1933–), British poet, born in Liverpool, educated at Emmanuel College, Cambridge. He began his career as a schoolteacher in 1957. Since 1974 he has owned the Mandeville Press, specializing in limited editions of new poetry. His first full collection, *The Snowing Globe* (1972), was followed by numerous volumes of poetry, including *The Hinterland* (1977), *The Air Show* (1988), *Selected Poems* (1990), *Watching the Perseids* (1990), and *The Ark* (1994). The reputation he established with his earlier work gained him inclusion in *The Penguin Book of Contemporary Verse* (1982, edited by Andrew *Motion and Blake *Morrison) and *Some Contemporary Poets of Britain and Ireland* (1983, edited by Michael *Schmidt). Scupham's writing invariably displays a high degree of technical polish. His tendency to formal complexity combined with refractions of personal experience has produced work of an enigmatic quality. Domestic and local detail frequently provide the contexts for the emotional and intellectual elements in his poetry.

SEABROOK, Jeremy (1939–), British writer and journalist, born in Northampton, educated at Northampton Grammar School and Cambridge University. He has worked as a teacher and a social worker, written a play (*Life Price*, 1969, with Michael O'Neill), and contributed frequently to *New Society*, the *Guardian*, and other periodicals, on social, political, and ecological issues. His books include *The Unprivileged* (1967), a sympathetic account of working-class culture, and *What Went Wrong: Working People and the Ideals of the Labour Movement* (1978). His autobiographical *Mother and Son* (1979) is a vivid evocation of his own childhood as a twin in a single-parent family and a classic description of the social problems and intellectual successes of a post-war generation of state-educated children. His work combines a concern with the nature and causes of poverty and unusual delicacy of observation.

SEARLE, John (1932–), American linguistic philosopher, born in Denver, Colorado; he became Professor of Philosophy at the University of California, Berkeley, in 1959. Searle's influence first became apparent in his 1959 study of the philosophical problems arising from the use of proper names, a highly specialized topic which had implications for wider issues. In his most important work, *Speech Acts* (1969), he developed J. L. *Austin's notion of the 'performative utterance'. For Searle these 'illocutionary' acts can form the basis for a theory of meaning and communication, in opposition to the prevailing ideas of Frege. Searle substantiates his claim by distinguishing five different types of speech act: the representative, the directive, the commissive, the expressive, and the declaration. By trying to break down Austin's distinction between the performative and the constative Searle is moving from the problematic referential notion of truth. Searle's influence lies in narrowing the gap between philosophy and linguistics, and his arguments have permeated the school of literary criticism called 'affective stylistics', associated with Stanley *Fish. One of the few Anglo-American philosophers to have any point of contact with Continental developments, Searle has been extensively discussed by French linguistic philosophers, notably Michel Foucault and Jacques Derrida. His other works include *Expression and Meaning* (1979), *Intentionality* (1983), and *The Foundations of Illocutionary Logic* (1985).

Sea-Wolf, The, a novel by Jack *London, published in 1904. The delicate aesthete Humphrey Van Weyden, who has led a sheltered existence, is cast adrift from a ferryboat in San Francisco Bay after a collision with a steamer. He is picked up by Wolf Larsen, captain of the *Ghost*, a sealing schooner. Larsen is a man of immense strength, amoral, and contemptuous of society's morality of servitude. Although something of an intellectual, he is also described as 'a primitive man'. Van Weyden works on the ship until the *Ghost* picks up survivors from a sea-wreck off Japan, amongst whom is a poetess, Maud Brewster. A struggle over her ensues between Van Weyden and Larsen. Van Weyden and Brewster escape and are marooned on a desert island, on which the wreck of the *Ghost* is later washed up. Larsen, abandoned by his crew, is on board, but goes blind owing to mental illness and is doomed to die of paralysis. Brewster and Van Weyden escape from the island back to civilization, but the unsubdued Larsen dies. A novel about a callous 'superman', it delineates a somewhat archetypal struggle between civilized morality and a ruthless, amoral primitivism.

Secret Agent, The, a novel by Joseph *Conrad, published in 1907. The misleading subtitle—'A Simple Tale'—signals the profoundly ironic tone with which Conrad treats the familial relations of Verloc, the secret agent who runs a seedy Soho shop as cover for his political activities, and his wife Winnie, who wilfully blinds herself to Verloc's shady dealings in a marriage she suffers for the sake of her simpleton younger brother Stevie. 'Things', she feels, 'do not stand much looking into', and the motifs of willed false perceptions, self-interested deception, and hollow rhetoric pervade the duplicitous atmosphere of the novel. As anarchist agitator but also paid informer to the Russian First Secretary Vladimir at the London embassy of an autocratic Central European state, Verloc is pressured by the latter into perpetrating an 'anarchist outrage' at Greenwich with the aim of provoking a reactive clamp-down on *émigré* anarchist revolutionaries by the all-too-tolerant British Government. As accomplice Verloc recruits Stevie, whose barely articulate sense of social injustice—'Bad world for poor people'—has been excited by overhearing the fiery talk of Verloc's sham revolutionary friends Michaelis, Ossipon, and Yundt. When Winnie discovers from Chief Inspector Heat of Scotland Yard (another beneficiary of Verloc's confidences) that Stevie has been blown to pieces, tripping while carrying the bomb, she wreaks a furiously cool vengeance on the porcine Verloc, murdering him with a carving knife. Her attempted escape by Channel ferry is both encouraged then betrayed by Ossipon, who nevertheless accepts her misplaced affection and all her bank balance. Her suicide by drowning relieves her of the dread of the gallows. The novel is based on an actual (failed) anarchist attack on the Greenwich Observatory in 1894. The melodramatic plot is brilliantly rendered and rescued through Conrad's scorching black-humorous exploration of the cynical and self-interested parts that almost all his protagonists play. His ironic tone, along with the fractured chronological structure of the novel, forces the reader constantly to reassess the stability of judgements made and knowledge held. From the eloquent and ineffectual anarchists and their upper-class patrons, to the illustrious members of the British Establishment protected by Heat and his Whitehall superiors, to the agents of foreign governments—all, Conrad sceptically suggests, are in the same game of duplicity and self-duplicity. With the moral innocence of Stevie obliterated, only the Professor, the bomb-carrying nihilist, the seeker after the literal and metaphorical 'perfect detonator' which will ignite the world, chillingly walks out of the novel unscathed.

Secret Destinations, a book of poetry by Charles *Causley, published in 1984. The short stanzaic units, traditional, rhythms, and subtly mannered tones prevalent in his earlier work were displaced in *Secret Destinations* by more capacious forms whose longer verse-lines were suited to a mode more suggestive of the cadences of speech. The quasi-mythological colouring which his treatments of the past had tended to take on through his use of ballad forms was annulled by the detailed realism in his poems of local and familial history. A widening of his poetry's cultural and geographic compass was effected by the emergence of a European frame of reference and the inclusion of material produced by his experiences of Australia and Canada. The collection was acclaimed for its breadth of subject matter, technical originality, and the poise of its sombrely retrospective poems, in which Peter *Porter found 'powerful images of disquiet'.

'Secret Sharer, The', a story by Joseph *Conrad, published in *Harper's Magazine* (Aug.–Sept. 1910), then in *'Twixt Land and Sea* (1912). This enigmatic tale, with haunting *Doppelgänger* motif, is set in the Malay Archipelago, where Conrad's own maritime experiences provided crucial source material. The story is told in the first person by a youthful, apparently law-abiding, sea captain on his first command. His routine is shattered by Leggatt, a fugitive who emerges from the water and confesses to the captain that he has murdered a mutinous fellow sailor. In thoroughly uncanny ways the young captain's mirror-image, Leggatt's appearance challenges the captain's sense of professional and moral duty as he secretly protects Leggatt and engineers his dramatic escape at almost fatal risk to his own ship and crew. Though courting disaster, the captain paradoxically achieves his moral and professional coming of age through this clandestine test of will, solidarity, self-knowledge, and sheer nerve.

SEDGWICK, Eve Kosofsky (1950–), American theoretician, born in Dayton, educated at Yale. She became a professor of English at Duke University and a key figure in the emergence of 'queer theory' as an academic discipline. Her two most influential texts, *Between Men: English Literature and Male Homosocial Desire* (1985) and *Epistemology of the Closet* (1990), argue that the homosexual–heterosexual binary develops as an instrument to support heterosexuality and male dominance. *Between Men* traces the changes in the imagining of male–male relations with respect to a third term, woman, in standard 'canonized' English writers, for example Shakespeare, George Eliot, Thackeray, and Dickens. She describes a 'homosocial triangle' in which two men vie for a woman as a way to repress their desire for each other. In *Epistemology of the Closet*, she describes how the 'closet' supports heterosexual dominance by imagining a homosexual secret that is lurking in all male relationships. Looking at texts by Henry *James, Proust, Melville, and Wilde, she suggests that homosexuality is not a minor aspect of culture, but rather central to Western constructions of gender and sexuality. Her work has had profound effect on numerous critical and theoretical writers interested in sexuality and gender by opening up areas of inquiry, most notably the study of male homosexuality in Western culture. Her other works include *Tendencies* (1993), a collection of critical essays; *Fat Art, Thin Art* (1994), a collection of poems; and *The Coherence of Gothic Conventions* (1980), an early study.

SEEGER, Alan (1888–1916), American poet, born in New York City, educated at Harvard, where he contributed poems to the *Harvard Monthly*, which he edited in his final year. He went to Paris in 1912 to pursue a bohemian existence and was among forty Americans who joined the French Foreign Legion at the outbreak of the First World War. He gained wide notice in America following the publication of 'Ode in Memory of the American Volunteers Fallen for France' in the **North American Review*. In 1916 he was killed in the Battle of the Somme and was posthumously awarded the Croix de Guerre and the Medaille Militaire. *Poems of Alan Seeger* (1916), his only collection of verse, included examples of his early poetry in addition to the body of work drawing on his experiences of the conflict; contrasting images of natural beauty and the ravaged landscapes of Flanders are used to memorable effect in 'I Have a Rendezvous with Death', his best-known poem, which expresses the lyric fatalism recurrent in his work. *The Letters and Diary of Alan Seeger* was published in 1917. For some time after his death his reputation was equivalent to that of Rupert *Brooke in England.

SELBY, Hubert Jr (1928–), American novelist and short-story writer, born in Brooklyn, New York. Selby left school to join the Merchant Marines in the Second World War but he contracted TB and was hospitalized for three years, during which time he developed a dependency on morphine which was to teach him much about the horrors of addiction. His work began to appear in the 1950s in magazines like *Black Mountain Review* and *Kulchur* but it was not until the publication of *Last Exit to Brooklyn* in 1964 that he achieved wider recognition. Prosecuted for obscenity in Britain, Selby's novel is in fact a profoundly moral book, exploring the broken lives of the urban poor with a taut Christian compassion. This unwavering but anguished moral base runs through all his writings, complementing and widening the accuracy with which he observes the lives of his subjects. His books are meticulously constructed, following with geometrical precision the inevitable descent of his characters into the nightmare underworld of the American dream. *The Room* (1971) revolves around the fantasies of a prisoner who dreams of exacting retribution for his mistreatment at the hands of the system; *The Demon* (1976) concentrates on a sexual malaise which drives its subject inexorably into the hell of demonic possession; *Requiem for a Dream* (1978) traces the lives of two drug addicts and their pitiful collapse into a world of extreme degradation. His short stories are collected in *Song of the Silent Snow* (1986). Selby settled in Los Angeles, where he helped to supervise a film version of *Last Exit to Brooklyn*.

SELF, Will (1961–), British novelist, born in London, educated at Oxford University. The blackly comic stories collected in *The Quantity Theory of Insanity* (1991) offered a bizarre vision of contemporary life. *Cock & Bull* (1992) consisted of two linked novellas, both dealing with sexual transformation and the concomitant blurring of identity. In his novel *My Idea of Fun* (1993) the narrator, Ian Wharton, aided by his eidetic memory and apparently at the instigation of his unscrupulous alter ego, 'The Fat Controller', is able to visualize himself engaged in various violent and immoral acts. *Grey Area* (1994) is another collection of short stories. Perhaps inevitably, Self's writing has been compared to that of M. *Amis—who admires Self's work—both in its concerns, which are frequently grotesque, and in the comic surrealism of its style. *Junk Mail* (1995) is a collection of journalism.

Self-Portrait in a Convex Mirror, a collection of poems by John *Ashbery, published in 1975, which achieved the unprecedented distinction of winning all three of America's principal book awards, the Pulitzer Prize, the National Book Award, and the National Book Critics' Circle Award. It consists of thirty-four shorter poems, 'Grand Galop', 'Hop O'My Thumb', and 'The One Thing That Can Save America' being among the best-known, and the lengthy title work, which was largely responsible for the acclaim the volume generated. As an extended meditation on a self-portrait by the Renaissance painter Parmigianino, the poem exemplifies the scope and imaginative power of the visual aesthetic which informs much of Ashbery's writing. Ranging between scholarly detachment and passionate conviction in its subtle tonal modulations, its chief concerns are the relations between art and actuality and the interactions of personal and public experience in 'a society specifically | Organized as a demonstration of itself'. The sense of social engagement apparent in the title poem and a number of the shorter pieces was welcomed as an indication of Ashbery's emergence from the often opaquely private idioms of his earlier verse.

SELINCOURT, Ernest de (1870–1943), British scholar and literary critic, born in Streatham, London, educated at University College, Oxford. He became Professor of English Language and Literature at Birmingham University in 1908 and was Oxford Professor of Poetry from 1928 to 1933. At both universities he made an essential contribution to the emergence of English studies as an independent academic discipline. His first notable works of scholarship, *The Poems of John Keats* and *Hyperion: A Facsimile of Keats's Autograph Manuscript*, were published in 1905. He is best known for his editorial work on the writings of William and Dorothy Wordsworth, which includes editions of *The Prelude* (1926), *The Letters of William and Dorothy Wordsworth* (4 volumes, 1935–9), *The Poetical Works of William Wordsworth* (2 volumes, 1940–4), and Dorothy Wordsworth's *Journals* (2 volumes, 1941). His biography of Dorothy Wordsworth appeared in 1933. Among his other publications are the collected essays of *Wordsworthian and Other Studies* (1947), and *English Poets and the National Ideal*, a series of lectures published in 1915.

SELVON, Samuel (Dixon) (1923–94), Trinidadian novelist, short-story writer, poet, and playwright, born in Trinidad, educated at Naparima College in southern Trinidad. He worked briefly as a journalist on the *Trinidad Guardian* before emigrating in 1950 to England; in 1975 he left for Canada and later became a Canadian citizen. His first novel, *A *Brighter Sun* (1952), paints a loving portrait of Indian peasants engulfed by squalor and deprivation in southern Trinidad during the period of the Second World War. This novel and others by such writers as Edgar *Mittelholzer and George *Lamming arrived in a blaze of literary productivity that, by the end of the 1950s, brought West Indian writing into international focus. Selvon's second novel, *An Island Is a World* (1955), considered themes of cultural mixing, nationality, and exile which recur in more than a dozen works of fiction that were to follow. These themes are evident in his third novel, *The Lonely Londoners* (1956), which brilliantly evokes the bitter-sweet experiences of West Indian immigrants living in London in the early 1950s: their cultural rootlessness, economic deprivation, and outgoing manners produce exactly the right combination for Selvon's comic art. His fiction combines humorous handling of West Indian language, speech, and idioms with affectionate insight into West Indian character and cultural forms. His use of one narrator in three novels, *The Lonely Londoners*, *Moses Ascending* (1975), and *Moses Migrating* (1983), confirms Selvon's undiminished skill in the sustained ironic treatment not only of West Indian immigrants, but of black power advocates, institutions of white power, and the fickleness of human nature in general. His poems and plays are less well known compared with his fictional output, which made Selvon one of the most popular and enduring of West Indian writers. Other works are *Foreday Morning* (1989), a collection of short stories and essays; *Highway in the Sun and Other Plays* (1988) and *Eldorado West One* (1989), a further collection of plays. A critical study, *Critical Perspectives on Sam Selvon* (1989), was edited by Susheila Nasta.

Semiotics is the study of signs and of systems of signs. It has a dual origin in the work of the American philosopher C. S. *Peirce and the Swiss linguist F. de Saussure (1857–1913: see also STRUCTURALISM). The word is used more or less interchangeably with semiology, although we can, if we are anxious to make a distinction, see semiotics, following Peirce, as something pragmatic, the study of signs at work, and semiology, following Saussure, as the general science of signs. Language is the chief sign-system of most cultures, but other signs are all around us, from traffic lights to body language, from high fashion to football crowd behaviour. The impulse of semiotics is to see the human being as above all a signifying creature, one that makes meanings, and has a need to find meanings everywhere. In this sense it is related to *Hermeneutics, although semiotics tends to be interested in the structure and performance of signs rather than the process of their interpretation. For the semiotician the sign is purely conventional (Saussure used the word 'arbitrary', which is misleading in English, since it suggests that a sign can mean anything we like), taking its sense from its place in a pattern, not from a natural link to its referent. Hence what is studied is always a signifying system: a cluster of sentences, for example, rather than individual words; the flow of traffic rather than the routes of separate cars.

SENIOR, Olive (1943–), Jamaican writer, born in the rural Trelawney district of Jamaica, educated at Montego Bay High School and at Carleton University, Ottawa. After working as a publications officer at the University of the West Indies, she became the managing director of the Institute of Jamaica Publications and editor of the *Jamaica Journal*. Her early works include *The Message Is Change* (1972), a survey of the 1972 Jamaican General Election. *Summer Lightning* (1986) and *The Arrival of the Snake Woman* (1989), her collections of short stories, draw on the oral traditions of her rural background for their moving and sometimes disarmingly humorous evocations of conditions among the working-class inhabitants of Jamaica. Her poetry, collected in *Talking of Trees* (1985), conveys her imaginative sense of the interactions of the past and present in the island's communities. Among her other publications is *Working Miracles* (1991), a sociological survey of women in the Caribbean.

SEPAMLA, Sipho (Sidney) (1932–), South African poet and novelist, born in Krugersdorp. He trained as a teacher, has been highly active in promoting writing and the arts in the South African townships, and has edited two journals, one of which covered black theatre. His own writing focuses on fear, tension, and political resistance in township life. Books of poetry include *Hurry up to It!* (1975), *The Blues Is You in Me* (1976), described by David *Wright as 'spare, ironic, pungent and deadpan', and *The Soweto I Love* (1977), which voices the anger and frustration of black South Africans after the Soweto disturbances of 1976. His novel *The Root Is One* (1979) chronicles the ruthless politics behind the forcible removal of residents from one township (near Johannesburg) to another. His second novel, *A Ride in the Whirlwind* (1981), about Soweto, was banned in South Africa. Other novels exploring aspects of public and private life in South Africa are *Third Generation* (1986) and *Scattered Survival* (1989). *From Gore to Soweto* (1988) collects poems with the experience of townships as their central theme.

Serjeant Musgrave's Dance, a play by John *Arden, first performed in 1959 and published in 1960. The title character, once 'the hardest sergeant of the line', is now a deserter from the Victorian army, impelled by the atrocities he has witnessed in the colonies to take exemplary reprisals in Britain. To this end he comes, with three fellow observers, to a colliery town during a lock-out, planning to use a fake recruiting meeting to shoot those he believes ultimately responsible for the 'corruption', specifically the local mayor, constable, and parson. The resistance of a pacifist comrade and the arrival of dragoons are among the reasons Musgrave fails in his endeavour; but Arden's more fundamental suggestion, in a play notable for its moral intricacy, is that the sergeant is trying to impose his own over-simple logic on a situation whose complexities and contradictions he has not understood.

SEROTE, Mongane Wally (1944–), South African poet, born in Sophiatown, educated in Soweto and later at Columbia University. Together with Oswald *Mtshali and Sipho *Sepamla, he is among the most prominent South African township poets. Serote's poems contain a strong element of political protest; he was tested to the limits of endurance in 1969 when he spent nine months in solitary confinement, though in the end was released without being charged. His books of poetry include *Yakhal'inkomo* (1972), the title of which refers to the 'cry of cattle at the slaughterhouse'; *Tsetlo* (1974), which was banned by the South African authorities; *No Baby Must Weep* (1975), dramatically framed as a long monologue to a silent mother; and *Behold Mama, Flowers* (1978) and *The Night Keeps Winking* (1981), both of which experiment with jazz-like rhythms. *A Tough Tale* (1987) and *Third World Express* (1992) are long poems, the former documenting the sufferings of black South Africans and envisioning apocalyptic change; the latter a more affirmative extension of earlier sociocultural preoccupations. *Come and Hope With Me* (1994) is a collection of poems. His novel *To Every Birth Its Blood* (1981), set in the Alexandra Township, articulates the militant aspirations of young blacks in South Africa. *On the Horizon* (1990) is a collection of essays on literature, culture, and politics.

SERVICE, Robert William (1874–1958), Canadian poet, born in Preston and raised in Glasgow; he emigrated to Canada in 1895. His collection *Songs of a Sourdough* (1907) included the ballads 'The Shooting of Dan McGrew' and 'The Cremation of Sam McGee', both of which drew upon his personal experience of the Yukon gold rushes and which became popular classics. A sequel volume was *The Spell of the Yukon* (1907). His *Collected Verse* was first published in 1930 and has been reprinted innumerable times. Later volumes were *More Collected Verse* (1955) and *Later Collected Verse* (1960). Service himself was somewhat embarrassed by the extraordinary success of his ballads, and in the autobiographical volumes *Ploughman of the Moon* (1945) and *Harper of Heaven* (1948), as well as in the earlier *Why Not Grow Young? Or, Living for Longevity* (1928), sought to secure his privacy by providing an edited version of his life. Having served as a reporter in the Canadian Army during the First World War he then lived in the South of France. *The Poisoned Paradise* (1922) describes the Monte Carlo of the time; it was filmed in Hollywood and was a great critical and financial success.

SETH, Vikram (1952–), Indian poet and novelist, born in Calcutta, educated in India and at the universities of Oxford and Stanford. His experiences as a student and traveller in China, where he researched economic demography, are chronicled in *From Heaven Lake* (1983). His first collection of poems, *The Humble Administrator's Garden* (1985), earned him a reputation as a skilled and witty poet. His reputation was greatly enhanced by the publication of his novel-in-verse, *The Golden Gate* (1986), a deft combination of metre and narrative in the manner of Pushkin. Set entirely in California, this multi-voiced satirical 'novel' wittily characterizes middle-class Californian social and sexual mores and anxieties. His second volume of poetry, *All You Who Sleep Tonight* (1990), was acclaimed for its bristling wit and technical virtuosity. Seth has also produced translations of classical Chinese love lyrics. Entirely different in tone and technique is Seth's second work of prose fiction, *A Suitable Boy* (1993), the popular success of which exceeded the considerable critical acclaim it gathered. Set in the years immediately following Partition, the novel follows the linked destinies of several families, both Hindu and Muslim, commenting through their viewpoints on the confluence of public and private histories. While the names of Tolstoy and Trollope have been invoked in Seth's praise, the novel is very much a literary artifact of the late twentieth century: careful to avoid omniscient commentary, self-consciously unselfconscious in its appropriation of uncomplicated narrative means to achieve its ends. At its best, it also works well as a compendium of a vital and turbulent historical and cultural moment.

SETON, Ernest Thompson (1860–1946), Canadian naturalist and writer, born in England at South Shields and taken to Canada in 1866. He studied art in Canada, London, and Paris and educated himself as a naturalist, subsequently combining his two interests as a writer and illustrator of books about birds and animals. Throughout his life he published serious naturalist studies, but he is best known for his animal stories, the first collection of which was the immensely popular *Wild Animals I Have Known* (1898). *Lives of the Hunted* (1901) and *Animal Heroes* (1905) are among the best of his subsequent collections. He was known in his own day as the founder, along with Sir Charles G. D. *Roberts, of the realistic animal story, and was post-Darwinian in his stress on affinities between animals and humans. In *Survival* (1972) Margaret *Atwood sees Seton's animal stories as typifying the victim consciousness which she argues is central to Canadian literature. Seton spent the last sixteen years of his life in Santa Fe and became an American citizen in 1931.

Seven Arts, The, a magazine founded in November 1916 by James Oppenheim, with Waldo *Frank and Van Wyck *Brooks as associate editors; their enthusiastic commitment to the idea of an American cultural renaissance was shared by Robert *Frost, Louis Untermeyer, Robert Edmond Jones, and others who lent their support to the venture from the outset. Oppenheim's first editorial made clear his sense of national purpose and announced that '*The Seven Arts* is not a magazine for artists, but an expression of artists for the community'. As the chosen title suggests, music and the graphic and plastic arts, as well as dance and architecture, were all within the journal's compass, although its central concern was with literary criticism, prose fiction, and poetry. Frank, Oppenheim, and Brooks were the most regular contributors of criticism, whose number also included H. L. *Mencken and Willard Huntington Wright. Sherwood *Anderson, John Dos *Passos, S. N. *Behrman, and Eugene *O'Neill were among the comparatively unknown writers whose short stories were featured, and Frost, Amy *Lowell, Carl *Sandburg, and Stephen Vincent *Benét supplied poetry. With a circulation in the region of 5,000, the magazine was the foremost journal of its kind until its opposition to America's involvement in the First World War led to the withdrawal of financial support by its sponsors. Although it ran for only a year, *The Seven Arts* proved a powerful stimulant to American culture and established the standards subsequently maintained by the **Dial*, to which a number of its leading contributors transferred their loyalties.

Seven Pillars of Wisdom, The, T. E. *Lawrence's largely autobiographical account of the Arab Revolt against the Turks during the First World War, upon which his reputation as a writer chiefly rests. A lavishly produced limited edition of the book appeared at Lawrence's expense in 1926, leaving him with substantial debts. He rapidly completed a severe abridgement, excising much moral speculation and troubled examination of his motives, with the result that *Revolt in the Desert* achieved commercial success in the following year. A trade edition of the complete text was published in 1935. The book describes events between Lawrence's arrival in Jidda in October 1916 and the establishment of an Arab government in Damascus two years later. Episodic, vividly descriptive, accounts of the actions of the highly mobile campaign and the desert landscapes in which it took place form the essential substance of the work. Much controversy has surrounded the matter of Lawrence's accuracy as a military historian, which is considered to have been diminished by his desire to convey a heroic impression of the Arab people and himself. Lawrence was assisted by G. B. *Shaw and E. M. *Forster in the composition of the book, which he began in 1919. The title *The Seven Pillars of Wisdom*, which has no clear relation to the content, was originally that of a work he had formerly projected on the seven principal cities of the Middle East.

Seven Types of Ambiguity, the book which established William *Empson's reputation upon its appearance in 1930. It formed the first major product of the mode of close textual analysis initiated in the mid-1920s at Cambridge University by I. A. *Richards, under whose supervision Empson originally drafted the work as a student. At the time, the Cambridge journal *Experiment* promoted a scientifically rational view of literature in the spirit of *Wittgenstein's critique of the metaphysical dimensions of language in the *Tractatus* (1922); Empson partook strongly of such attitudes in *Seven Types of Ambiguity*, dissociating himself as a critic from any responsibility to produce moral or aesthetic judgements with regard to the value of literature. His purpose in the book was rather to demonstrate the workings of the 'machinery for analysis' in order for readers to have available an objective method of validating their own responses to texts. This was achieved by pursuing the implications of language in a wide range of poetry with great sensitivity of response to verbal nuance and occasional displays of brilliant ingenuity in establishing more remote extensions of meaning. In the preface to the second edition (1947) Empson admitted to having shown a tendency to 'trail my coat' and altered some of the more provocative passages. The term 'ambiguity' was central to his methodology, which admitted any linguistic event 'which gives room for alternative reactions to the same piece of writing'. Metaphor, paronomasia, and Freudian indications of mental division were among his varieties of ambiguity, which he qualified with the statement that 'sometimes... the word may be stretched absurdly far'. The scope of the poetry considered is very wide, comprehending verse by most of the major poets from Chaucer to T. S. *Eliot.

Sewanee Review, The, a quarterly journal of literature and criticism founded in 1892 at the University of the South, Sewanee, Tennessee, with Telfair Hodgson as editor. In its earlier years it was largely devoted to descriptive criticism and essays on history and biography. George Herbert Clarke, the editor from 1920 to 1925, introduced the publication of poetry, for which the magazine subsequently became an important forum, printing verse by John Crowe *Ransom, Laura *Riding, Theodore *Roethke, and Wallace *Stevens. Under William S. Knickerbocker's editorship from 1926 to 1942 it emerged as one of America's foremost academic periodicals. Allen *Tate was editor from 1944 to 1946 and a frequent contributor. Under his direction the journal joined the **Kenyon Review* as a leading organ of the *New Criticism; among the critics whose work was featured were Ransom and R. P. *Blackmur. *The Sewanee Review* continues to appear regularly and is decades ahead of its nearest rival as the longest established journal of its kind in the USA. More recently its editors have included Andrew *Lytle and George Core.

SEXTON, Anne (1928–74), American poet, born in Newton, Massachusetts. She worked as a fashion model in the 1950s and, after establishing herself as a poet, held various visiting appointments at American universities. She was encouraged to write poetry by the psychoanalyst who treated her for depressive illness. She also acknowledged W. D. *Snodgrass's *Heart's Needle* (1959), widely regarded as one of the first works of '*confessional poetry', as an enabling example for the unsettlingly candid treatments of her difficulties in *To Bedlam and Part of the Way Back* (1961) and *All My Pretty Ones* (1962), her first two collections. *Live or Die* (1966), which won a Pulitzer Prize, contains her best-known work, exemplifying her technical originality and imaginative energy in its evocations of sinister dimensions of the psyche. *Love Poems* (1969) was followed by *Transformations* (1971), her adaptations of stories by the Grimms. Her characteristic autobiographical directness and ironic neutrality of tone were resumed in *The Death Notebooks* of 1974, the year of her suicide. The metaphysical orientation which emerges in her later work is most explicit in the guardedly affirmative vision of *The Awful Rowing towards God* (1975). Her description of herself as 'an imagist who deals with reality and its hard facts' is appropriate to the clarity and force of much of her writing. *Complete Poems* was published in 1981. *A Self-Portrait in Letters* (1977) was edited by L. G. Sexton, her daughter, and Lois Ames. Diane W. Middlebrook's biography of Sexton appeared in 1991.

SEYMOUR, Alan (1927–), Australian playwright and film and theatre critic, born in Perth. Seymour achieved recognition with his surreal play *Swamp Creatures* (1957), which is set in a Gothic mansion and concerns two sisters, one of whom experiments in the creation of monster insects. More naturalistic, and less characteristic, is his best-known play, *The One Day of the Year* (1960), which takes place on Anzac Day and explores themes of national identity and social change through the conflicting views of different generations of an Australian family; it was adapted as a novel in 1967. *The Gaiety of Nations* (1965), about the Vietnam War, was followed by other plays including *A Break in the Music* (1966), *The Pope and the Pill* (1968), *The Shattering* (1973), and *The Float* (1980). His novel *The Coming Self-Destruction of the United States* (1969) concerns racial questions in America. In Britain he received acclaim for his television adaptations of L. P. Hartley's **Eustace and Hilda*, Antonia White's **Frost in May*, and John *Masefield's *The Box of Delights*.

SEYMOUR, A(rthur) J(ames) (1914–90), Guyanese poet and civil servant, born in British Guiana (now Guyana), educated at Queen's College. He was deputy chairman of the Department of Culture, editor of the influential literary journal *Kyk-over-al* from 1945 to 1961, among other posts, and launched the pamphlet series of 'Miniature Poets' (1951–3), two of whose prominent authors were Wilson *Harris and Martin *Carter. Seymour was a prolific poet, but only with his seventh collection, *The Guiana Book* (1948), did he begin to have a distinctive voice of his own. His later poetry meditates on the blood-drenched history of the Caribbean and the crucible of forces, particularly the effects of the slave trade, which have moulded the present Guyanese identity. *Water and Blood* (1952), *Monologue* (1968), *Patterns* (1970), *Italic* (1974), *Mirror* (1975), *Images of Majority* (1978), and *Selected Poems* (1983) are only a few of his many other subsequent collections. Autobiographical volumes include *Growing Up in Guyana* (1976), *Pilgrim Memories* (1978), and *Thirty Years a Civil Servant* (1982). See Ian McDonald (ed.), *AJS at 70* (1984).

SHADBOLT, Maurice (1932–), New Zealand novelist and short-story writer, born in Auckland, educated at the University of Auckland. The sequence of stories in *The New Zealanders* (1959) reflected his closeness to New Zealand society; a further collection, *Summer Fires and Winter Country* (1963), traced mostly the response of urban dwellers to the imaginative pull of the country, and to tensions rooted in their own pasts. *The Presence of Music* (1967; three novellas) was followed by the novels *This Summer's Dolphin* (1969); *An Ear of the Dragon* (1971), which charted New Zealand life from the perspective of an immigrant writer; *Strangers and Journeys* (1972), which chronicled society of two generations; and *Danger Zone* (1975). Here Shadbolt drew upon his own experience of helping to sail a yacht into the French atomic test zone off Mururoa atoll to produce a work of direct relevance to the modern Pacific. By contrast *Figures in Light: Selected Stories* (1979) was seen by some as rather outmoded in its focus largely on rural settings. Later fiction includes *The Lovelock Version* (1980) and *Among the Cinders* (1984). *Season of the Jew* (1987), one of New Zealand's finest historical novels, *Monday's Warriors* (1990), and *The House of Strife* (1993), each examine the New Zealand Wars of 1845–72, against Maori uprisings, and blend fiction with historical fact. The play *Once on Chunuk Bair* (1982) used the experiences of one day in the trenches to explore the significance in New Zealand's national memory of the terrible losses at Gallipoli during the First World War campaign in the Dardanelles. *One of Ben's: A New Zealand Medley* (1993) is an autobiography and family memoir.

Shadow-Line, The, a novel by Joseph *Conrad, published in 1917 (serialized in *English Review*, and *Metropolitan Magazine* 1916–17). Commonly regarded as the masterpiece of his final years, the novel draws, like **Lord Jim* and 'The *Secret Sharer', on Conrad's maritime experiences in the Far East in the late 1880s. It treats of the themes of isolation and community, of youthfulness and maturity gained through the testing extremes of experience; and it does so through a predominantly sombre tone and vision which endorses a morality of unsung heroism and dogged endurance in the face of the absolute indifference of the natural elements. The first-person narrator takes unexpected charge of his first maritime command, and is forced to cope with a becalmed sailing-ship, manned by a crew bedevilled by sickness, whose former captain, in his death-throes, has betrayed and tricked them, with near-fatal consequences. Echoes of *Hamlet* and 'The Rime of the Ancient Mariner' suggest the struggles of self-doubt, evil, and responsibility. The realities and metaphors of disease, stasis, and guilt prevail. But through this rite of passage is won self-knowledge and ultimate confirmation of human dignity and solidarity.

Shadow of a Gunman, The, a play by Sean *O'Casey, first performed in 1923. It is set in a Dublin slum three years earlier, at a time when conflict between the Irish Republican Army and the British 'Black and Tans' was tearing apart the populace. The self-professed poet Donal Davoren, harassed by his landlord for his rent, allows himself to be mistaken for an IRA gunman on the run both by a pretty young neighbour, Minnie Powell, and by other tenement-dwellers, some of whom seek his help in pursuing their petty grievances. 'What danger can there be in being a shadow of a gunman?', he asks himself at the end of Act One, after kissing Minnie; he receives his answer in Act Two. A bag left in his room by a friend of his pious fellow-lodger, Seumas Shields, turns out to be full of bombs; Minnie takes it out to conceal it from the Black and Tans, who are raiding the tenement; she is arrested, and shot while trying to escape. Donal ends self-indulgently lamenting his guilt: 'Oh Davoren, Donal Davoren, poet and poltroon, poltroon and poet!' *The Shadow of a Gunman* was the first of O'Casey's plays to be staged; and like those that followed it, **Juno and the Paycock* and *The *Plough and the Stars*, deromanticizes twentieth-century Irish history by looking at major events in wry, tragi-comic style, from the stance of the city poor.

SHAFFER, Peter (Levin) (1926–), British playwright, born in Liverpool, educated at Cambridge University. He made his name with *Five Finger Exercise* (1958), a drama about growing up in oppressive family circumstances. His other plays include *The Royal Hunt of the Sun* (1964), an epic drama about the conquest of Peru and, more specifically, the curious meeting of minds between the rough yet inquisitive Pizarro and the Inca god-king Atahuallpa; the brilliant farce *Black Comedy* (1965); and *The Battle of Shrivings* (1970), a metaphysical debate between a rationalist philosopher and a poet who takes a more sceptical view of man's nature. *Equus* (1970), a drama clearly indebted to the theories of R. D. *Laing, concerns a psychiatrist's relationship with a boy who has blinded the six horses he loved and identified with an all-powerful, all-watchful God; it would seem that the boy knew a kind of ecstasy with the horses and that they are frightening symbols of the repressed energies of a young man. *Amadeus* (1979), another psychological study, concerns the slow and sly destruction of Mozart by his envious fellow composer Salieri. Shaffer's later plays include the biblical epic *Yonadab* (1985), in which the title character, part-idealist and part-voyeur, encourages Amnon to rape his half-sister, Tamar; *Lettice and Lovage* (1987), a nostalgic comedy about two women with a shared hatred of the banality of contemporary urban life, especially its architecture; and *The Gift of the Gorgon* (1992), about a wild Russian-Welsh dramatist and his disastrous marriage. It has been said that Shaffer writes philosophical, humanist plays for middle-brow audiences, concentrating particularly on the significance of art, the nature of creativity, the importance of the imagination, and man's yearning, often self-destructive, for ecstasy and rapture.

His twin brother, Anthony Shaffer, is also a playwright, best known for a bravura thriller, *Sleuth* (1970), but also the author of *Murderer* (1975).

SHAH, Idries (Sayed) (1924–), Afghani Oriental scholar and novelist, born in India. In 1966 Shah became Director of Studies at the Institute for Cultural Research, London. An authority on Sufi thought, his works have helped introduce Islamic philosophy to the West, and had an influence on the speculative fictions of Doris *Lessing. They include *Oriental Magic* (1956), *Destination Mecca* (1957), *The Way of the Sufi* (1968), *The Sufis* (1969), and *Neglected Aspects of Sufi Study* (1977). Like many of his works, *A Perfumed Scorpion* (1978) contains a mixture of humour, aphorisms, and verse inspired by Sufi philosophy. He also compiled and translated *The Exploits of the Incomparable Mulla Nasrudin* (1966), *Tales of the Dervishes* (1967), and *The Subtleties of the Inimitable Mulla Nasrudin* (1973). *Kara Kush* (1986), an epic novel about popular resistance to the Soviet invasion of Afghanistan, was a bestseller. *Darkest England* (1987) and *The Natives Are Restless* (1988) look at Britain; *The Commanding Self* (1993) is a work on Sufi wisdom in Shah's familiar vein.

Shame, a novel by Salman *Rushdie, published in 1983. Like its precursor, **Midnight's Children*, it deals with contemporary realities in the turbulent subcontinent but is even more directly linked to documentary realism since the events it chronicles—the imprisonment and hanging of Pakistan's prime minister, Zulfiqar Ali Bhutto (caricatured here as Iskandar Harappa), and the takeover of power by the military—had occurred some four years before its appearance; Zia-ul-Haq (represented as Raza Hyder) was still in power, radically altering Pakistani society, and Benazir Bhutto (who appears as the Virgin Ironpants) was developing her political persona. The major figure, Omar Khayyam, is the son of three mothers, an allusion to Rushdie's three countries, India, Pakistan, and Britain; the daughter of Raza Hyder, the general who deposes Harappa, symbolizes the country's collective dementia. There are significant differences in narrative method; Rushdie here employs a shifting perspective, introducing a voice that is a metafictional echo of his own to comment on the philosophical sub-texts of the novel, a device that adds a gravity in direct contrast to the satirical levity of the novel.

SHANGE, Ntozake (1948–), African-American experimental dramatist and poet, born in Trenton, New Jersey, educated at the University of Southern California, Los Angeles. In 1983 she became Associate Professor of Drama at the University of Houston. She achieved wide recognition for her innovative fusion of poetry, theatre, and dance when *For Colored Girls Who Have Considered Suicide/When the Rainbow Is Enuf* (1976) was produced on Broadway in 1975. The work consists of verse monologues spoken by seven women and shares its celebratory emphasis on the qualities of black womanhood with her other plays, among them *A Photograph: Lovers-In-Motion*, *Boogie Woogie Landscapes*, and *Spell #7*, which were collected as *Three Pieces* in 1981. Her collections of poetry, which employ energetically rhythmical free verse, include *Nappy Edges* (1978), *From Okra to Greens* (1984), *A Daughter's Geography* (1985), *The Love Space Demands* (1991), and *I Live in Music* (1994). Other works include the novels *Sassafrass, Cypress and Indigo* (1982), a lyrical account of the lives of three women; *Betsey Brown* (1985), a semi-autobiographical treatment of the late 1950s and the beginnings of civil rights campaigning; and *Liliane: Resurrection of the Daughter* (1995); *See No Evil: Prefaces, Essays and Accounts 1976–83* (1984); and *Ridin' the Moon in Texas: Word Paintings* (1987).

SHAPCOTT, Thomas (1935–), Australian poet and writer, born near Brisbane, educated at the University of Queensland. From 1983 to 1990 he was Director of the Literature Board of the Australia Council, of which he wrote a history in 1988. Early poetry collections such as *Time on Fire* (1961), *A Taste of Salt Water* (1967), and *Inwards Towards the Sun* (1969) established Shapcott's poetic gift for blending traditional forms and themes with a willingness to experiment. He confirmed this position in his editions of *New Impulses in Australian Poetry* (1968; with Rodney Hall), *Australian Poetry Now* (1970), and *Contemporary American and Australian Poetry* (1976), all influential collections in confirming possible new directions for Australian poets. In 1981 he edited *Consolidation: The Second Paperback Poets Anthology*. Shapcott's lasting fascination with his childhood background found expression in *Shabbytown Calendar* (1975). Later collections of verse include *Turning Full Circle* (1979), *Welcome!* (1983), *Travel Dice* (1987), *Selected Poems 1956–1988* (1989), *In the Beginning* (1990), and *City of Home* (1995). His writing ranges from children's fiction, through experimental 'prose inventions', to his best-known novel, *The White Stage of Exile* (1984), a closely researched study of the exile of an art collector after the failure of his museum in Budapest; another novel, *The Search for Galina* (1989), concerns the narrator's search for a Russian poet. *Mona's Gift* (1993) is a love story set in war time Sydney, told via letters and diaries. *What You Own* (1991) is a collection of short stories. *Biting the Bullet: A Literary Memoir* (1990) includes essays, speeches, and reviews. He has also written a monograph (1967) and a biography (1990) of the painter Charles Blackman.

SHAPIRO, Karl (Jay) (1913–), American poet, born in Baltimore, educated at the University of Virginia, Johns Hopkins University, and the Pratt Library School, Baltimore. He held a succession of appointments at American universities until his retirement as Professor of English at the University of California, Davis, in 1984. From 1950 to 1956 he was the editor of **Poetry*. His early publications as a poet include *Person, Place and Thing* (1942) and *V-Letter* (1944), which received a Pulitzer Prize; the latter volume was strongly informed by his experiences as a soldier during the Second World War, which were occasionally subject to ironic qualification by Shapiro's ambivalent sense of his Jewishness. His numerous subsequent collections, which sustain an unsettlingly witty critique of the cultural pretensions of post-war America in verse of supple virtuosity, include *Trial of a Poet* (1947), *Poems of a Jew* (1958), *White-Haired Lover* (1968), *Adult Bookstore* (1976), *Collected Poems* (1978), *Love and War, Art and God* (1984), *New and Selected Poems, 1940–1986* (1987), and *The Old Horsefly* (1992). The prose poems of *The Bourgeois Poet* (1964), which explore the human capacity for embodying absurd contradictions, form the culmination of the experimental tendencies in his verse of the 1950s. Among his other works is the novel *Edsel* (1971), a satire of American academic life. His highly regarded collections of essays include *Beyond Criticism* (1953), *To Abolish Children* (1968), and *The Poetry Wreck* (1975). *The Younger Son: Poet* (1988) and *Reports of My Death* (1990), which are written entirely in the third person, are the first two parts of a projected autobiographical trilogy.

SHARPE, Tom (1928–), British novelist, born in London, educated at Pembroke College, Cambridge. He was a lecturer in Cambridge and a photographer in South Africa prior to becoming a novelist. Sharpe's savage farces often feature grotesque characters and incidents, and deal with a wide range of political and cultural assumptions. *Riotous Assembly* (1971) and *Indecent Exposure* (1973), his first two novels, had South African settings and dealt with aspects of the country's political regime. *Porterhouse Blue* (1974) was set in an imaginary Cambridge college and focused on the progressive zeal of the new dispensation of academics; it was televised and later followed by a sequel, *Grantchester Grind* (1995). *Blott on the Landscape* (1975) satirized the notion of progress for its own sake in its explorations of the building a new motorway and was also filmed for television. *Wilt* (1976) concerned the nightmarish experiences of Henry Wilt, a college lecturer suspected of murder, whose story continued in *The Wilt Alternative* (1979). Other novels include *The Great Pursuit* (1977), *The Throwback* (1978), *Ancestral Vices* (1980), *Vintage Stuff* (1982), and *Wilt on High* (1984).

SHAW, (George) Bernard (1856–1950), Irish dramatist, born in Dublin, the youngest child of an alcoholic corn merchant; he did poorly at school. The best account of his parents' troubled marriage and his own unhappy upbringing and self-education, as of his later life, is to be found in Michael *Holroyd's massive biography (*Bernard Shaw*, 4 volumes, 1988–92). In 1876 he followed his mother to London, where he struggled to make a living. He wrote five unsuccessful novels and a great deal of music, book, and art criticism. He was also a proselytizer for socialism, composing tracts and delivering lectures on that and other political, social, and ethical subjects and, in 1884, becoming a co-founder and highly influential member of the *Fabian Society. But it was not until 1892 that his first play, *Widowers' Houses*, was produced, and then for only two performances to 'advanced' audiences. This was written under the influence of Ibsen, whom Shaw had already made the subject of a book, *The Quintessence of Ibsenism* (1891), and was enthusiastically to promote when he served as the *Saturday Review*'s drama critic from 1895 to 1898 (eventually publishing his reviews under the title *Our Theatres in the Nineties*, 3 volumes, 1932). *Widowers' Houses* transforms a conventional love story into an attack on slum landlordism and, like much of his earlier drama, may be said to have given the well-made play a socialist twist. It was eventually published as one of his 'Plays Unpleasant', along with *The Philanderer* (written 1893, prod. 1905) and **Mrs Warren's Profession* (written 1893, prod. 1902), which fell foul of the dramatic censor because of its suggestion that prostitution was the inevitable result of social injustice. During the 1890s he also wrote the three 'Plays Pleasant', so called because they were comedies and concentrated on the 'follies' rather than the 'vices' of society. These were *Arms and the Man* (1894), Shaw's attack on the romantic pretensions of love and war; *Candida* (1895), in which a 'muscular' yet inwardly weak Christian minister and an effete-seeming but actually strong poet compete for the emotional allegiance of the title character; and *You Never Can Tell* (1898). The 'Three Plays for Puritans'—*The *Devil's Disciple* (1897), *Captain Brassbound's Conversion* (1900), *Caesar and Cleopatra* (1901)—also belong to a phase of Shaw's career when he was using traditional styles of drama to reclaim values from what he regarded as the moral stupidities of society and its institutions. In its published form, each set of plays came complete with prefaces exploring the ideas he had dramatized. Throughout his long career, he continued to use this device to clarify and broaden his didacticism.

Increasingly, however, the plays themselves became more intellectually explicit. Extreme examples would include *Getting Married* (1908), *Misalliance* (1910), and **Heartbreak House* (1920); but his portrait of Ireland, **John Bull's Other Island* (1904), and **Man and Superman* (1905) and **Major Barbara* (1905), though all relatively generous with lively character and event, also helped win Shaw the reputation of writing dialogues or debates rather than drama. This trend was by no means straightforward. *Androcles and the Lion* (1913), **Pygmalion* (1913), and **St Joan* (1923) have proved lastingly popular with audiences at least as much because of the pull of their stories as because of their larger implications. *John Bull's Other Island* was amusing enough to give Shaw his first substantial success in the London theatre. But it has been well argued, most cogently by the critic Eric Bentley, that the mature Shaw invented a new kind of drama, not merely one in which the importance of a character was the ideas he represented, but one which substituted conflict of ideas for conflict of character and other traditional sources of tension.

Shaw's wit, humour, and ability to create entertaining characters, often verging on Dickensian caricature, remained undiminished throughout his career. He was often accused of frivolity and emotional superficiality; but his own view was that, by provoking laughter, he could ensure his audience's attention while demolishing their moral and social preconceptions. His views did, however, change with time and with his own growing conviction that radical social change was unlikely to occur through the reform of existing institutions. Hence his promotion of what he called 'creative evolution', a philosophy most clearly dramatized in the 'metabiological pentateuch' **Back to Methuselah* (1922), which emphasized man's ability himself to will his destiny and his progress towards 'omnipotence and omniscience'. Hence, too, the impatience with parliamentary democracy and the fascination with 'supermen' which link *Caesar and Cleopatra* and *Major Barbara* with such late work as *The *Apple Cart* (1929), *On the Rocks* (1933), and *Geneva* (1938). Shaw had no sympathy with Hitler or Nazism, but his regard for Mussolini and, in particular, Stalin is well attested.

Other works worth discovering include *The Perfect Wagnerite* (1898), *Common Sense About the War* (1914), *The Intelligent Woman's Guide to Socialism and Capitalism* (1928), as well as the plays *The Doctor's Dilemma* (1906), a serio-comic attack on the medical profession; *Fanny's First Play* (1911), which gently mocks theatre critics; and *Too True to Be Good* (1932), which debates sex, the generation gap, the death of traditional values, and other topics. As this suggests, Shaw expressed strong views about many matters from experiments on animals, vaccination, and meat diets (which he deplored) to euthanasia and the extermination of the morally or mentally 'unfit' (which he favoured). Though he had numerous love affairs as a young man, the marriage he made in 1898 to Charlotte Payne-Townshend seems to have been platonic.

Certainly, his work shows increasing contempt for the 'greasy commonplaces of flesh and blood', meaning all supposedly over-close relationships, and a growing belief that 'the intellect is a passion as much as sex, with less intensity but lifelong permanency'. Some have been tempted to see in his traumatic childhood an explanation for his Manichaeism, as for the imperviousness to human suffering and lack of a 'sense of horror' that has troubled his critics; but the intellectual coherence of his ideas cannot be doubted. It was in recognition of a size of achievement unmatched in contemporary drama that he won the Nobel Prize in 1925. His music criticism has been collected in *Shaw's Music* (3 volumes, 1981, ed. Dan H. Laurence).

SHAW, Bob (1931–), British *science fiction writer, born in Ulster. From his first novel, *Night Walk* (1967), he became renowned for the dexterity of his action-filled *space opera tales; his early works, such as *The Palace of Eternity* (1969), featured protagonists of human warmth and complexity. Novels like *Other Days, Other Eyes* (1972) and *Orbitsville* (1975), which featured highly inventive scientific extrapolations, also demonstrated a growing humaneness. Later novels included *Vertigo* (1978), *Fire Pattern* (1984), and the three tales *The Ragged Astronauts* (1986), *The Wooden Spaceships* (1988), and *The Fugitive Worlds* (1989), set in an alternative universe whose physics permit an hour-glass-like air bridge between twin planets.

SHAW, Irwin (1914–), American novelist, playwright, and short-story writer, born in Brooklyn, New York, educated at Brooklyn College. Shaw enjoyed his greatest commercial success with *The Young Lions* (1948), a long and ambitious novel (subsequently filmed) about the Second World War which seeks to dramatize the military and moral experience of both American and German combatants. From the mid-1930s Shaw began to establish himself as a screenwriter in Hollywood. His early plays, notably *Bury the Dead* (1936) and *The Gentle People: A Brooklyn Fable* (1939), are characteristic of much of the left-wing writing of the period in their emphases on the dangers of fascism and their appeal for pacifism. His early volumes of short stories reveal a talent for social realism. His second novel, *The Troubled Air* (1951), explores the dilemma of the liberal mind in its treatment of a radio show producer who is asked to fire several members of his cast in view of their alleged communist sympathies. Significant later novels include *Lucy Crown* (1956), *Two Weeks in Another Town* (1960), *Voices of a Summer Day* (1965), and *Acceptable Losses* (1982). His short stories are collected in *Stories of Five Decades* (1982).

Sheik, The, see ROMANTIC FICTION.

Sheltered Life, The, a novel by Ellen *Glasgow, published in 1932. Set in Queensborough (a fictional version of Glasgow's native Richmond, Virginia), this novel represents its author's profoundest speculations on the interrelationship of sexuality and society. Its all-pervasive central figure is a former Southern beauty, Eva Birdsong, married to the weak, amoral George, of whose relationships with others she is obsessively jealous. We see Eva through the eyes of her neighbour, a young girl, Jenny Blair Archibald, and her grandfather, a distinguished Southern (Confederate) General, David Archibald. Jenny's great devotion to Eva does not prevent her falling in love with George who, for his part, responds to her, albeit a little reluctantly. At the climax of the novel Eva finds George and Jenny in each other's arms; Jenny flees into the garden and George kills both his wife and himself. The novel shows, with irony and with a genuine sense of the tragic, how Southern society has become over-inward in its life; emotions turn on themselves and prove destructive.

SHEPARD, Lucius (1950–), American novelist, short-story writer, and rock musician, born in Virginia. His *science fiction works engage powerfully with contemporary concerns. His first novel, *Green Eyes* (1984), raises ethical questions about medical research in Southern Gothic mode. *Life During Wartime* (1987) grotesquely illuminates American wars from Vietnam to Panama. The stories collected in *The Jaguar Hunter* (1987) and *The Ends of the Earth* (1991) are a promising display of his virtuoso ability.

SHEPARD, Sam, born Samuel Shepard ROGERS, Jr (1943–), American dramatist, born in Illinois. Shepard is a prolific and hugely successful playwright as well as film actor, screenwriter, and film director. His first play, *Cowboys* (1964), was followed by a stream of plays most of which were produced in New York in off-Broadway theatres. Widely regarded as the leading American avant-garde playwright of the late twentieth century, Shepard's work has inspired some antagonism from critics who do not share his preoccupation with popular culture, and from feminist critics who regard his treatment of women in his plays as characteristic of the worse excesses of male authority and power. Shepard's work falls into two phases. Until the mid-1970s his work was experimental in form, explorations in the possibility of non-naturalistic theatre, influenced by the work of Joseph Chaikin in the *Open Theatre; he has also acknowledged the influence of Samuel *Beckett and Peter Handke. His early plays are highly charged with imagistic vocabulary derived from rock music, Hollywood, particularly the Western movie, television, the drug scene, and the politics of revolt. Among these are *Chicago* (1965), *Icarus's Mother* (1965), *Red Cross* (1966), *La Turista* (1967), *Forensic and the Navigators* (1967), *Operation Sidewinder* (1970), *The Tooth of the Crime* (1972), and *Action* (1974). From *The Curse of the Starving Class* (1977) Shepard's plays have a more conventional shape, reflecting his desire for a sparer theatrical idiom closer to *O'Neill's realism. Their major focus is that of family relations, even though these remain essentially conflictual and destructive. The language of these plays, if frequently abrasive in the idiomatic use of obscenity, is equally poetic in the power to evoke the gravity of human despair and isolation. Among the later plays are *Buried Child* (1978; Pulitzer Prize), *True West* (1980), *Fool for Love* (1983), *Lie of the Mind* (1985), *States of Shock* (1991), and *Simpatico* (1994). In addition, he wrote the screenplay for Michelangelo Antonioni's *Zabriskie Point* (1972), the film about Bob Dylan, *Renaldo and Clara* (1978), Wim Wender's *Paris, Texas* (1984), and his own *Fool for Love* (1985).

SHERRIFF, R(obert) C(edric) (1896–1975), British playwright, born in Kingston-on-Thames. He followed his father into a local insurance office, and wrote what became his best-known play, **Journey's End* (1928), to raise money for his rowing club. Though he subsequently wrote eight others, ranging from the rustic comedy *Badger's Green* (1930) to the moral ghost story *The White Carnation* (1953), none matched the success he achieved with this sensitive, unsentimental portrait of unheroic heroism as he himself had experienced it as a captain in the trenches of the First World War.

SHERWOOD, Robert E(mmet) (1896–1955), American dramatist, born in New Rochelle, New York State, educated at Harvard, where he followed George Pierce *Baker's course in the history of the theatre. His successful first play, *The Road to Rome* (1927), shows Hannibal turning away from his march on Rome, an anti-war gesture designed to express Sherwood's disillusion with the international politics which had led to the First World War. Sherwood's most successful period as a playwright was in the 1930s, with *Reunion in Vienna* (1931), *The Petrified Forest* (1935), *Idiot's Delight* (1936, for which he won the first of his four Pulitzer Prizes), *Abe Lincoln in Illinois* (1938), and *There Shall Be No Night* (1940). With S. N. *Behrman and others, Sherwood was a founder member of the Playwrights' Company (1938), designed to set high standards of writing and production in the contemporary theatre. His play *Waterloo Bridge* (1930), about an English prostitute who preserves the ideals of an American soldier by refusing to give herself to him, was well received in London, and a cleaned-up version—in which the prostitute becomes a ballerina—was made into a film by Mervyn Leroy in 1940, starring Robert Taylor and Vivien Leigh (with screenplay by Behrman), and later remade as *Gaby* (1956), directed by Curtis Bernhardt with Leslie Caron as the female lead. Sherwood's pacifism, founded on his First World War disillusionment, informed much of his writing.

SHIEL, M(atthew) P(hipps) (1865–1947), British novelist, son of an Irish Methodist minister, born in Montserrat in the West Indies; on his fifteenth birthday he was crowned by his father as king of Redonda, a small neighbouring island. He was educated at Harrison College, Barbados, and King's College, London; he studied medicine at St Bartholomew's Hospital, London, but then turned to literature, publishing novels and short stories in a variety of genres, predominantly mystery, crime, and *science fiction. His style, which has been compared to that of George Meredith, aimed at 'an elaborate simplicity that can be called biblical': it is extravagant, archaic, complex, and ornate. His best works are *Prince Zaleski* (1895), a collection of detective stories which show the influence of Edgar Allan Poe; the crime novels *How the Old Woman Got Home* (1927), *Dr Krasinki's Secret* (1929), and *The Black Box* (1930); and the science fiction fantasy *The Purple Cloud* (1901; revised 1929), one of the best of the 'last man' novels. The books written in collaboration with Louis Tracy, published under the pseudonym Gordon Holmes, are considerably weaker. He spent his last years writing a biography of Christ, which remained unfinished.

Shield of Achilles, The, a collection of poetry by W. H. *Auden, published in 1955. The title poem is among his finest, its bitterly elegiac view of the modern human condition tempered by its depth of imaginative compassion and the resonant accomplishment of its form. The volume also includes two of Auden's major poetic sequences, 'Bucolics' and 'Horae Canonicae'. The former consists of seven vividly illustrated and technically inventive meditations on various landscapes and natural phenomena. In a tone combining philosophical seriousness and witty informality, the poems consider the ethical implications of man's interactions with nature. The sections of 'Horae Canonicae' follow the order of the Church's seven traditional hours of prayer to present an encompassing statement of the individual's complicity in the acts of his civilization, the 'lying self-made city' to which he belongs. The poems acknowledge human fallibility and guilt as the fundamental basis of true community as an ordinary day is shown to contain a judicially ordered death emblematically equivalent to the Crucifixion. The sequence is the most powerful of Auden's poems that draw directly on his radical Protestant theology. 'Ode to Gaea' and 'The Truest Poetry Is the Most Feigning' are among the other notable poems in *The Shield of Achilles*, which is widely regarded as the most valuable of Auden's later collections.

SHIELDS, Carol (1935–   ), Canadian-based novelist, born in Oak Park, Illinois, educated at Hanover College and the University of Ottawa. She settled in Canada in 1957. Though none of her novels had previously appeared in Britain, the publication of *Mary Swann* in 1990 gained her a reputation as one of the decade's significant novelists. With its intricate exploration of a poet's life, her death at her husband's hand, her subsequent reputation and posthumous mythologization, the book has been compared with A. S. *Byatt's *Possession* published in the same year. Frequently compared to *Munro and *Atwood, Shields displays a characteristic gift of combining commonplace domestic themes with post-modernist techniques of considerable sophistication. *The Republic of Love* (1992) recounts the love affair of Fay Macleod, a folklorist, with the radio personality Tom Avery; an elaborate symbolic structure adds lustre to what is essentially the material of Hollywood romance. In *The Stone Diaries* (1993), Shields returns to the complexity of *Mary Swann* with the story of Daisy Goodwill, from her birth in 1905 to her death eight decades later, recounted in a variety of voices. The one pinnacle in Daisy's life is her short residency as a local paper's gardening correspondent and only as she ages are the traces of her natural intellect revealed to her intimates. Reissues of Shields's previous neglected works include *Happenstance: The Husband's Story* (1980) and *Happenstance: The Wife's Story* (1982). A collection of stories, *Various Miracles*, appeared in 1994.

SHIELS, George (1886–1949), Northern Irish playwright, born in Ballymoney, Co. Antrim. After being educated locally, he emigrated to Canada where he was permanently crippled in a railway accident. He returned to Ireland and began to write, initially using George Morshiel as a pseudonym. His first plays, *Bedmates* and *Insurance Money*, were produced at the *Abbey Theatre in 1921, but it was with *Paul Twyning* in 1922 that Shiels had his first real success. Subsequently, the Abbey staged one of his plays annually until 1948. His instinct appears to have been for popular and entertaining plays, typical examples of which are *Paul Twyning* and *Professor Tim* (1925), in which roaming, picaresque characters manage to evade problems through their wit and guile. His comedies are deceptively relativistic. As *Yeats remarked of *Cartney and Kervney* (1927), Shiels's plays present immoral actions while suspending any trace of moral comment. In *The Passing Day* (1936) the entire cast quarrels over the contents of a will, cynically appealing to every ideal of behaviour, while Shiels remains sublimely indifferent. His more serious plays, *The Rugged Path* (1940) and *The Summit* (1941), reflect upon the conflict between the deep-rooted suspicions of Irish rural communities and the 'progressive' values of the modern world.

SHINEBOURNE, Jan(ice) (1947–), Guyanese novelist, born in British Guiana (now Guyana) and educated there; she later became resident in London. Her first novel, *Timepiece* (1986), focuses on Sandra Yansen, a young woman who leaves her village to work as a reporter in Georgetown. Her experiences reflect the position of women and racial conflict in Guyanese society. *The Last English Plantation* (1988) charts similar territory, but also explores political turbulence in British Guiana in the 1950s. Wilson *Harris commended the work for psychologically exploring 'the *inner* landscape of a colonial age'.

SHINER, Lewis (1950–), American writer, born in Oregon; he grew up in Arizona, New Mexico, Georgia, and the Sudan. He has written a variety of short stories, and a first novel entitled *Frontera* (1985). He has travelled widely throughout the USA and Mexico, and worked at a host of different jobs, ranging from rock musician to house decorator, clerk, and construction worker. He received much praise for his novel *Deserted Cities of the Mind* (1988), which recounts various factual events—the Mexico City earthquake, the border riots of 1986—within a narrative of surreal events and actions taking place in a fictitious Central American setting. In a plot with an apocalyptic tone and perspective, the novel details US government corruption in backing a guerrilla army with Iran-Contragate funds, and the wranglings of the drug culture. He has since published several further novels: *The Edges of Things* (1991), *Slam* (1991), *When The Music's Over* (1991), and *Glimpses* (1993).

Ship of Fools, see PORTER, KATHERINE ANNE.

SHIPTON, Eric (Earle) (1907–77), British writer on mountaineering, born in Ceylon; he received an irregular education in the course of a highly mobile childhood. Having made the first ascent of Kamet, at that time the highest mountain ever climbed, in 1931, his four attempts on Mount Everest (1933, 1935, 1936, 1938) established him as the foremost Himalayan climber of the day. His distaste for large expeditions is said to have cost him the leadership of the successful 1953 Everest expedition, for which he surveyed the route, publishing *The Mount Everest Reconnaissance Expedition* in 1952. *Nanda Devi* (1936), an account of the exploration of the approaches to Nanda Devi, is among the most highly regarded mountaineering books of the century. His works, characteristically unassuming and witty in style, include *Blank upon the Map* (1938), on his 1937 Shaksgam expedition; *Upon That Mountain* (1943), an autobiography; *Mountains of Tartary* (1951), a record of climbs in Central Asia; and *Land of Tempest* (1963), on exploration and climbing in Tierra del Fuego; all the above titles were collected as *The Six Mountain Books* in 1985. Among Shipton's other publications is the autobiographical *That Untravelled World* (1973).

SHOWALTER, Elaine (1941–), American cultural and feminist critic, born in Cambridge, Massachusetts, educated at Bryn Mawr College and the University of California. She became Professor of English at Princeton University. Showalter is best known for *A Literature of Their Own* (1977; revised edition 1982), an examination of women novelists from Charlotte Brontë to Doris *Lessing in which many critically neglected writers of the period are recovered. Showalter's other major critical works, *The Female Malady: Women, Madness and English Culture, 1830–1980* (1987) and *Sexual Anarchy* (1990), continue her interdisciplinary investigations of female experience in the modern period. In both these books, she extends her concerns beyond women writers and looks at the contradictions and tensions that shape women's social, psychological, and sexual development. Showalter's area of scrutiny in *Sister's Choice* (1991) is the cultural specificity of American women's writings and crafts. She has also edited several valuable collections of essays, including *The New Feminist Criticism* (1985) and *Speaking of Gender* (1989), as well as offering a re-reading of Louisa M. Alcott in *Alternative Alcott* (1985). In 1993 she published *Daughters of Decadence: Women*

Writers of the Fin de Siède, a collection of stories from the period. See also FEMINIST CRITICISM.

Shropshire Lad, A, A. E. *Housman's first collection of verse, published in 1896, consisting of sixty-three poems united by their profound lyrical melancholy and the Shropshire setting suggested by the recurrence of various place-names. The poems also have in common their consummate fluency of versification in traditional forms; Housman's virtuosity as a metricist produces results of remarkable elegance within the narrow confines of the ballad stanzas which predominate. He referred to Shakespeare's songs, the Scottish border ballads, and the poetry of Heinrich Heine as precedents for the fusion of simplicity and sophistication the poems characteristically exhibit. Although the volume was first published at his own expense, by 1900 it enjoyed considerable commercial success. Imaginative retrospection on the 'blue remembered hills' to the west in Housman's Worcestershire childhood creates an arcadia blighted by the romantic unhappiness and repeatedly fatal misfortunes of the youthful protagonists; love and war are leitmotifs in many poems, which share their stark philosophical pessimism with much of Thomas *Hardy's writing. The epigrammatic economy and stoical austerity of the work are indications of Housman's classical orientation; George *Orwell remarked on the 'bitter, defiant paganism' that gave the book a marked appeal to his generation in its adolescence. The archetypally English 'land of lost content' of the poems, inhabited by 'lads that will die in their glory and never be old', appealed profoundly to the public's temperament during the First World War; *A Shropshire Lad* became ineradicably impressed upon the national consciousness and has since been constantly in print. Several of the poems have also, to Housman's dislike, been set to music by many composers including Ralph Vaughan Williams, George Butterworth, and Ivor *Gurney.

SHUTE, Nevil, pseudonym of Nevil Shute NORWAY (1899–1960), British writer, born in Middlesex, educated at Balliol College, Oxford. Shute worked as an engineer in an airship factory, and in 1931 founded an aircraft manufacturing firm of which he became a director in 1938. By this time he had established himself as a writer of traditional tales of romance and adventure with such novels as *Marazan* (1926), *So Disdained* (1928), *Lonely Road* (1932), and *Ruined City* (1938). *The Pied Piper* (1942) concerns the rescue of a group of children from the Nazis. His interest in aeronautics is reflected in many of his novels, such as *No Highway* (1948). He later emigrated to Australia, where much of his later fiction was set, including his best-known novel, *A Town like Alice* (1949), a romance set in Alice Springs in the barren centre of Australia. His other works include *The Far Country* (1952), *On the Beach* (1957, later filmed), and *The Trustee from the Toolroom* (1960).

SHUTTLE, Penelope (Diane) (1947–), British poet and novelist, born in Staines, Middlesex, where she was educated at Matthew Arnold County Secondary School. She is the wife of Peter *Redgrove, with whom she has collaborated on several works, among them the novel *The Terrors of Dr Treviles* (1974); a study of the cultural significances of menstruation entitled *The Wise Wound* (1978); and *Alchemy for Women* (1995). Her collections include *The Orchard Upstairs* (1980), *The Child-Stealer* (1983), *The Lion from Rio* (1986), *Adventures with My Horse* (1988), and *Taxing the Rain* (1992). Her statement that 'I am writing to repair the degradation of women's experience' indicates the feminist orientation of much of her work, which explores the erotic, maternal, social, and spiritual aspects of womanhood. The disciplined energies of her free verse cover a range of styles from the extravagantly lyrical to the domestically factual. Her novels include the widely acclaimed *Wailing Monkey Embracing a Tree* (1973) and *The Mirror of the Giant* (1980), which have in common with her verse their highly imaginative vividness of imagery.

SIDHWA, Bapsi (1938–), Pakistani novelist, born in Karachi, a member of the tiny Parsi (Zoroastrian) community; Sidhwa grew up in Lahore, where she was educated. Her first published novel, *The Crow Eaters* (1978), is the carnivalesque chronicle of three generations of a Parsi family, an ambitious blend of satire, farce, social history, and *magic realism. A far more sober tale, *The Bride* (1983) is a reworking of an earlier, unpublished novel, telling of the tragic marriage of a working-class Lahore woman to a youth from the underdeveloped regions of the North-West Frontier. Like all Sidhwa's work, the novel contains a rich undercurrent of legend and folklore. *Ice-Candy-Man* (1988) combines Sidhwa's affectionate admiration for her own community with a compassion for the dispossessed. Her own childhood memories of the tragedies of the Partition of India—a preoccupation which underwrites much of her work—give the novel further depth and resonance.

Siege of Krishnapur, The, see FARRELL, J. G.

SILKIN, Jon (1930–), British poet, editor, and critic, born in London, educated at Dulwich College. In 1952 he founded **Stand*, the literary magazine he has continued to edit with his wife Lorna Tracy. He has held a succession of posts as a writer-in-residence at universities in Britain, Israel, and the USA. His numerous collections of poetry include *The Peaceable Kingdom* (1954), *The Re-Ordering of the Stones* (1961), *Nature with Man* (1965), *The Principle of Water* (1974), *The Psalms with Their Spoils* (1980), *The Ship's Pasture* (1986), *Selected Poems* (1988; revised 1993), and *The Lens-Breakers* (1992). Stylistically, his verse ranges from an unambiguous directness of statement to cryptically compressed experimental forms. His concerns are primarily ethical and humanitarian. Many of his finest poems form dramatic monologues spoken by victims of historical events; 'The People', a long blank-verse sequence, is notable for the detached compassion and imaginative sensitivity of its detailed account of the

Nazi concentration camps. Among his critical writings is *Out of Battle: Poetry of the Great War* (1972). He has edited numerous anthologies, including *Poetry of the Committed Individual* (1973) and *The Penguin Book of First World War Poetry* (1979).

SILKO, Leslie Marmon (1948–), American novelist, short-story writer, and screenwriter, born in Albuquerque, New Mexico, educated at the University of New Mexico. Silko's writing is rooted in her complex heritage, part Mexican, part Pueblo Indian, part white; she has said of her work that 'at the core of my writing is the attempt to identify what it is to be a half-breed or mixed blooded person; what it is to grow up neither white nor fully traditional Indian'. Her first published story, 'The Man to Send Rain Clouds' (1969), published in the *New Mexico Quarterly*, arose from a college writing assignment. A selection of her poems was published as *Laguna Women* (1974), Laguna being the name of the pueblo on which Silko was raised. She won high critical acclaim for *Ceremony* (1977), a novel about a Second World War veteran which immediately established her as one of the foremost writers in contemporary Native American literature. A later novel, *Almanac of the Dead* (1991), was praised for its historical and moral insights of the Americas told from a Native American perspective. *Storyteller* (1981) is an assembly of poems, legends, stories, and photographs; *The Delicacy and Strength of Lace* (1985), edited by Anne Wright, is a collection of letters between Silko and the poet James Wright. *Black Elks* is a screenplay written for Marlon Brando. *Leslie Marmon Silko* (1980) by Per Seyersted is a critical introduction to her work. See also ETHNICITY and NATIVE AMERICAN LITERATURE.

SILLIMAN, Ron (1946–), American poet, born in Pasco, Washington. Residing in the San Francisco area, he has worked as a political organizer, an editor of *Socialist Review*, a teacher and college administrator, and in the computer industry. His influential essays (collected in *The New Sentence*, 1987) on the economic and political conditions of poetry argue that language has been commodified in the West. Referentiality helps maintain existing power relations by making them seem real and natural: 'My intention is to incite a riot in the "prison house of language".' He coined the phrase 'the new sentence' in an essay which describes his own and others' practice as the use of sentences and syntax in such a way that they obstruct a reader's easy assimilation into larger structures, and therefore focus attention at the level of the sentence. His long works *Ketjak* (1978), *Tjanting* (1981), *What* (1989), and *The Alphabet Book* (only parts, notably *From Demo to Ink*, 1992, have yet been published), are based on large-scale generative structures (*Tjanting* uses the Fibonacci series), and consist of autobiographical sentences in a disjunct structure, depicting the Bay Area, politics, everyday life, and the act of writing in an elegant, often epigrammatic manner. (See LANGUAGE POETRY.)

SILLITOE, Alan (1928–), British novelist and poet, born in Nottingham, the son of a labourer in a cycle factory. He left school at 14 to become a factory worker and then an air-control assistant. He was a wireless operator with the RAF in Malaya (1946–9), and began to write during an eighteen-month convalescence from TB. He lived in France and Spain during the 1950s, and has continued to travel widely, although his work tends to be set in and around Nottingham. His first novel, **Saturday Night and Sunday Morning* (1958), remains his best-known. Its unsentimental portrait of working-class life in Nottingham and the rebelliousness of the young factory worker, Arthur Seaton, caught the mood of the time, and it was successfully filmed. The title story of *The Loneliness of the Long Distance Runner* (1959) is a finely crafted realization of Sillitoe's social philosophy. Following the thought processes of a Borstal boy as he runs a long-distance race against a local public school, it traces the evolution of the boy's own set of values which persuade him to lose the race deliberately in the face of the governor's flawed notions of rehabilitation into a competitive society. *The General* (1960) is a political fable in which a general captures an entire orchestra and allows them to play one final concert. The music destroys the soldier in him, however, and he begins to lose his war. Sillitoe's third novel, *Key to the Door* (1961), focuses on Arthur Seaton's elder brother Brian, whose rebellion is a quieter, more intellectual affair. Tracing the family history through the Depression of the 1930s, it is a powerful and moving account of working-class life. Frank Dawley, the protagonist of *The Death of William Posters* (1965), *A Tree on Fire* (1968), and *The Flame of Life* (1974), is a Nottingham factory worker who abandons his wife and children and ends up running guns in Algeria. His commitment to communism is used in the novel to explore the notion of working-class revolution. The roles are reversed in *Her Victory* (1982), a soul-searching novel in which a woman abandons her boorish husband after twenty years of marriage, and escapes to London and more meaningful relationships. His more recent novels include *The Open Door* (1989), whose hero is Brian the brother of Arthur Seaton, who overcomes TB in order to realize his ambition as a writer; *Last Loves* (1990), about two veteran army comrades who revisit the scene of conflict in Malaya forty years later; *Leonard's War: A Love Story* (1991), a tale of sexual obsession set in Nottingham during the Second World War; and *Snowstops* (1993), about twelve people thrown together in a remote hotel in the Pennine Peak District. Sillitoe has published several volumes of short stories, including *The Ragman's Daughter* (1963), *Guzman Go Home* (1968), *The Far Side of the Street* (1988), and *Collected Stories* (1995), which reveal his ability to reproduce the texture of restricted lives in a compassionate, uncondescending way. He has also published seven collections of poetry, and an autobiography, *Life Without Armour* (1995).

SILVERBERG, Robert (1935–), American writer, born in New York, educated at Columbia University. Silverberg is best known for his science fiction. His early work includes *Revolt on Alpha C* (1955), his first novel, and *The 13th Immortal* (1957), the first of a long series of *space operas. During much of the 1960s he concentrated mainly on non-fiction but with *Thorns* (1967), *Hawksbill Station* (1968), *The Masks of Time* (1968), and *Nightwings* (1969) he received acclaim, and consolidated his reputation with such novels as *Downward to the Earth* (1970), *Tower of Glass* (1970), *The World Inside* (1971), *A Time of Changes* (1971), *Son of Man* (1971), *The Book of Skulls* (1971), and *Dying Inside* (1972). Both *The Stochastic Man* (1975) and *Shadrach in the Furnace* (1976) anatomized science fiction and rewrote its themes with ferocious intensity. Among several collections of stories are *Moonferns and Starsongs* (1971) and *Capricorn Games* (1976). After a long break Silverberg published a collection of stories, *The Conglomeroid Cocktail Party* (1984), and several novels of interest including *Tom O'Bedlam* (1985), which reflects his abiding interest in religious transcendence and the charisma of charlatanism, and *Hot Sky at Midnight* (1994), which analyses the near future in apocalyptic terms.

Silver Tassie, The, a play by Sean *O'Casey, published in 1920 and performed in 1929. This principally involves Harry Heagan, a Dublin footballer whose skill wins his club the 'silver tassie', or cup, three years running. But he is seriously wounded in the Great War, losing both the use of the lower half of his body and his fiancée, Jessie. He ends up in a wheelchair at the football club dance. At first, he bitterly confronts Jessie and her new lover, Barney, who earned the VC rescuing him under fire; but then he discovers resignation and a deeper heroism—'what's in front we'll face like men'. Though most of the play is naturalistically written, and some of it marked by O'Casey's characteristically humorous observation of Irish eccentricity and fecklessness, the second act attempts to evoke the war's horror and suffering in a heightened, liturgical style. It was mainly because of this that *The Silver Tassie* was rejected for performance by Dublin's *Abbey Theatre, thus accelerating O'Casey's alienation from his native country. It was, however, much admired by G. B. *Shaw, who described it as 'a new drama rising from unplumbed depths to sweep the nice little bourgeois efforts of myself and my contemporaries into the dustbin'.

SIMAK, Clifford D(onald) (1904–88), American *science fiction writer and journalist, born in Millville, Wisconsin, where he set many of his stories. Simak created what might be described as a pastoral form of science fiction espousing a resilient humanism that eschewed sentimentality, as presented in novels such as *City* (1952), which is not about a city, *Way Station* (1963), *All Flesh Is Grass* (1965), and *A Choice of Gods* (1972). Later works included the fantasies *The Fellowship of the Talisman* (1978) and *Where the Evil Dwells* (1982).

SIMIC, Charles (1938–), American poet, born in Yugoslavia; he went to the USA in 1949, and was educated at the University of Chicago and New York University. Simic became professor of English and director of the creative writing programme at the University of New Hampshire. His first book of poems was *What the Grass Says* (1967); his other books include *White* (1970), *Dismantling the Silence* (1971), *Return to a Place Lit by a Glass of Milk* (1974), *Charon's Cosmology* (1977), *Classic Ballroom Dances* (1980), *Austerities* (1982), *Weather Forecast for Utopia & Vicinity* (1983), and *Unending Blues* (1986). His translation of I. Lalic's poems (with C. W. Truesdale) as *Fire Garden* appeared in 1970, followed by translations of Vasko Popa's *The Little Box* (1970), *Four Modern Yugoslav Poets* (1970), Vasko Popa's *Homage to the Lame Wolf* (1979, 1987), and I. Lalic's *Rollcall of Mirrors: Selected Poems* (1988). *The Uncertain Certainty: Interviews, Essays, and Notes on Poetry* appeared in 1985. Simic's memory of his wartime European childhood of devastated cities and landscapes gives a dimension of the surreal to his work, which he blends with the tradition of American gothic, so that his poems are often haunted by a stark humour. Simic uses figures and locations from ancient myth and rituals, biblical, pagan, and legendary, as a way of placing our present preoccupations in a wider frame of historical and social reference.

SIMMONS, Dan (1948–), American *science fiction and fantasy writer, formerly a teacher of gifted children; he became a full-time writer in 1989, following the success of *The Song of Kali* (1985), a horror novel centring on an Indian cult. *Hyperion* (1989) and its sequel *The Fall of Hyperion* (1990), which sustain an apocalyptic narrative of a doomed civilization, gained him a firm reputation as a science fiction author. *Carrion Comfort* (1990), set in contemporary America, and *Children of the Night* (1992), which takes place in Romania after the fall of Ceausescu, both employ imaginative variants on the theme of vampirism. Simmons's other novels include *Phases of Gravity* (1989), *The Hollow Man* (1992), *Summer of Night* (1991), and *Fires of Eden* (1994). *Prayers for Broken Stones* (1990) and *Lovedeath* (1993) are collections of his short stories.

SIMMONS, James (Stewart Alexander) (1933–), Northern Irish poet, born in Londonderry, educated at the University of Leeds. After teaching at Ahmadu Bello University in Nigeria, in 1968 he became a lecturer at the New University of Ulster, Coleraine. In 1968 he founded the poetry magazine *The *Honest Ulsterman*. Simmons's *Ballad of a Marriage* was published along with pamphlets by Seamus *Heaney and others to mark the Belfast Festival of 1965, initiating the emergence of *Ulster poetry. His collections include *Late but in Earnest* (1967), *The Long Summer Still To Come* (1973), *Judy Garland and the Cold War* (1976), *From the Irish* (1985), *Poems 1956–1986* (1986), *Sex, Rectitude and Loneliness* (1993), and *Mainstream* (1994). His poetry is noted for its humour, candour, and fluently accessible use of traditional forms. The 'generous democracy of response' Edna Longley noted in Simmons's work forms a basis for the forceful rejection of cultural élitism in his 'No Land Is Waste, Dr Eliot'. His treatments of sectarian violence in Northern Ireland include 'Lament for a Dead Policeman', which exposes the complexity of social, credal, and familial loyalties in the region's troubled culture. Among his other publications is the critical work *Sean O' Casey* (1983).

SIMON, Neil (Marvin) (1927–), American dramatist, born in the Bronx, New York, of Jewish parentage, educated at New York University. Simon began his career as a radio and television script writer and it is often held that the mark of writing for these media persists in his plays where his use of the one-line joke is a frequent device. His first play, *Come Blow Your Horn* (1961), was the first of a long line of major popular successes, and he has since proved to be the most commercially successful playwright of his time. Amongst his plays are *Barefoot in the Park* (1963), *The Odd Couple* (1965), *The Star-Spangled Girl* (1966), *Plaza Suite* (1968), *Last of the Red-Hot Lovers* (1969), *The Gingerbread Lady* (1970), *The Prisoner of Second Avenue* (1971), *The Sunshine Boys* (1972), *The Good Doctor* (1973), *God's Favourite* (1974), *California Suite* (1976), *Chapter Two* (1977), *I Ought To Be in Pictures* (1980), *Fools* (1982), *Actors and Actresses* (1983), *Brighton Beach Memoirs* (1983), *Biloxi Blues* (1985), and *Broadway Bound* (1986). In addition, Simon has collaborated on six musicals of which the most famous are probably *Heidi* (1959), *Sweet Charity* (1966), and *They're Playing Our Song* (1978). He has also written the screenplays for many of his plays as well as original screenplays. He is a writer of popular comedies, rooted in such themes as marriage, sexual awakening, infidelity, and divorce, alert to the comic potential of how the young learn to make their way in the world.

SIMPSON, Helen (1958?–), British writer, born in Bristol, educated at Oxford University; she grew up in London and worked for several years as a journalist. Her first collection of stories, *Four Bare Legs in a Bed* (1990), was acclaimed for the unsparing humour with which she dissected the lives of women, their domestic turmoils, and the realities and fantasies of their sexual relationships. The same year saw the publication of a novella, *Flesh and Grass*, a suspenseful comedy with a vegetarian heroine; this appeared with Ruth *Rendell's *The Strawberry Tree* under the general title *Unguarded Hours*. Simpson was listed as one of Granta's Best of Young British Novelists before she actually produced a novel. Her second book, *Dear George and Other Stories* (1995), explores, with comedy and verbal flair, issues similar to her earlier collection, with increasing confidence and a subtler, more restrained technique.

SIMPSON, Louis (Aston Marantz) (1923–), American poet, born in Kingston, Jamaica; from 1940 onward he lived in the USA where he was educated at Columbia University. He taught at the University of California, Berkeley, from 1959 to 1967, when he became Professor of English at the State University of New York. His early collections of verse, which include *The Arrivistes* (1949) and *A Dream of Governors* (1959), made accomplished use of conventional verse forms to frame their incisive meditations on a wide range of social and cultural themes. He has been widely recognized as a poet of importance since *At the End of the Open Road* (1963; Pulitzer Prize); its disquietingly bleak survey of American values made highly imaginative use of imagery drawn from close observation and displayed marked individuality of tone through a disciplined freedom of technique. His numerous subsequent volumes include *Adventures of the Letter I* (1971), *Caviare at the Funeral* (1981), *Collected Poems* (1988), and *In the Room We Share* (1990). His best work is characterized by the impressive plainness of manner with which its profound lyrical and elegiac effects are achieved. Among his critical works are *Three on a Tower* (1975), studies of T. S. *Eliot, Ezra *Pound, and William Carlos *Williams, and the collected essays of *A Company of Poets* (1981). His other publications include the novel *Riverside Drive* (1962), which reflects his early experiences of New York, and the autobiographical works *Air with Armed Men* (1972) and *The King My Father's Wreck* (1994).

SIMPSON, Matt (1936–), British poet, born in Bootle, Lancashire, where he grew up amid the maritime traditions informing much of his poetry; he was educated at Cambridge University. He has taught at various schools and colleges and in 1966 became a lecturer in English at the Liverpool Institute of Higher Education. Simpson's poetry appeared in four pamphlet editions before the publication of his first full collection, *Making Arrangements* (1982). The volume was widely praised for its individuality and its authentic evocations of the social, local, and historical perspectives of Merseyside. Among his stylistic qualities is his ability to synchronize a firm rhythmical pulse with a dramatically effective conversational tone. His further collections include *An Elegy for the Galosherman: New and Selected Poems* (1990), which contained 'Collecting Beetles', Simpson's laconically humorous account of the experiences of a Liverpudlian in Cambridge during the 1950s, and *Catching Up With History* (1995).

SIMPSON, Mona (Elizabeth) (1957–), American writer, born in Green Bay, Wisconsin, educated at Berkeley and Columbia Universities. She has published stories in *Harper's*, the **Paris Review*, and literary journals like the *Iowa Review* and *Ploughshares*; one story, 'Approximations', was included in the anthology *Twenty under Thirty* (1985). She received wide acclaim for her first novel, *Anywhere but Here* (1986), which concerned an eccentric mother–daughter relationship. Adele August and her daughter Ann travel from the Midwest to Beverly Hills so that Ann can become a child star. Once in Beverly Hills, life pales and illusions set in as the dream sours, and the novel charts the way the relationship grows apart as Ann desires more independence from her mother. Simpson's second novel, *The Lost Father* (1991), describes Ann's adult life. Now known as Mayan Stevenson, she is finally on her own, leading a normal life and attending medical school. However, her life-long obsession with the father she never knew grows, and the novel follows her literal and metaphorical search for him.

SIMPSON, N(orman) F(rederick) (1919–), British dramatist, born in London, educated at London University; he became a schoolmaster. He became fashionable in the late 1950s for plays that were widely regarded as distinctively English contributions to a Continental European movement, the Theatre of the *Absurd. The most notable of these were *A Resounding Tinkle* (1957), about a suburban couple called the Paradocks whose day brings the delivery of an elephant and a request to form a government, and *One-Way Pendulum* (1959), in which a young man teaches speak-your-weight machines to sing the Hallelujah Chorus while his father is put on trial in the replica Old Bailey he has built in his living room. Though the surreal inventiveness of these plays, as well as that of *The Hole* (1958), *The Cresta Run* (1965), and *Was He Anyone?* (1972), earned him comparison with the work of Eugene Ionesco, they now seem lighter and less purposeful, more akin to the quirky exuberance of the comedian Spike Milligan and the radio programme *The Goon Show*.

SINCLAIR, Andrew (Annadale) (1935–), British novelist, biographer, and cultural historian, born in Oxford, educated at Eton, at Harvard, and at Cambridge, where he became a don. His first novel, *The Breaking of Bumbo* (1959), based on his experiences in the army, was made into a film. *My Friend Judas* (1959), a comic novel set in Cambridge, describes the anarchic activities of its hero, Ben Birt; *The Hallelujah Bum* (1963; US title *The Paradise Bum*) is a sequel. Other fiction includes *The Project* (1960), a futuristic fantasy about nuclear weapons; *The Raker* (1964), a historical novel; *A Patriot for Hire* (1978), a political satire set in Britain in the near future; and *The Facts in the Case of E. A. Poe* (1979), a mixture of fiction and biographical fact. Perhaps his best-known work is his 'The Albion Triptych': *Gog* (1967), a panoramic account of English history from the building of Stonehenge to the Second World War, incorporating elements of Druidic myth, Arthurian legend, and surreal fantasy; *Magog* (1972), a satire about political corruption; and *King Ludd* (1988), which moves from Cambridge in the 1930s to London in the late 1980s. The protagonists are George Griffin ('Gog'), a Cambridge undergraduate, and his corrupt and self-seeking half-brother Magnus Ponsonby ('Magog'), whose nicknames recall the giants of Ancient British legend. *The Far Corners of the Earth* (1991) is the first novel in his 'Empire Quartet', a fictionalized account of the history of the Sinclairs from the Highland Clearances onwards; *The Strength of the Hills* (1992) follows his ancestors' lives in India and Canada prior to the First World War. Sinclair's numerous works of biography include volumes on Dylan *Thomas (1975), Jack *London (1977), and Francis Bacon (1993). Other works include *War Like a Wasp: The Lost Decade of the Forties* (1989), a study of Fitzrovia during the period; *The Need to Give* (1990), an account of arts patronage through the ages; *The Naked Savage* (1991), a portrait of the savage as myth and reality in history; *The Sword and the Grail* (1993), about the Knights Templars' role in the discovery of America; and a memoir of the 1960s, *In Love and Anger* (1994).

SINCLAIR, Clive (1948–), British writer, born in London, educated at the Universities of East Anglia and California. The stories collected in *Hearts of Gold* (1979) and *Bedbugs* (1982), like much of his subsequent fiction, are characterized by an acerbic humour and a fascination with the nature of Jewish identity. *For Good and Evil* (1991) is a selection of stories from his previous volumes. His novel *Blood Libels* (1985) focuses on Jake Silkstone, a Jewish writer who becomes unwittingly involved in the activities of an anti-Semitic sect, 'The Children of Albion', and whose attempts to atone for his error implicate him in the political complexities of the state of Israel. Similar themes are explored in the blackly comic *Cosmetic Effects* (1989). With *Augustus Rex* (1992) Sinclair meshed history and fairy tale with imaginative skill; Strindberg, who had formerly made a pact with Beelzebub, the narrator of the novel, is resurrected in 1960s Sweden and, as Augustus Rex, rescues the nation through his alchemical abilities. *Diaspora Blues* (1987) is a travel book.

SINCLAIR, Iain (1943–), British poet and novelist, born in Cardiff, educated at the London School of Film Technique and at Trinity College, Dublin. From the late 1960s onward he lived in London, the topography, history, and legends of which inform much of his writing. Since 1970 his work has been published chiefly by various British *small presses; collections include *Back Garden Poems* (1970), *The Penances* (1977), *Fluxions* (1980), and *Significant Wreckage* (1988). *Lud Heat* (1975) gained him considerable notice for its powerful interaction of factual and imaginative elements; the lengthy prose section entitled 'Nicholas Hawksmoor, His Churches' has been acknowledged by Peter *Ackroyd as a significant influence in the conception of **Hawksmoor* (1985). *Flesh Eggs and Scalp Metal* (1989) is a selected edition of Sinclair's poetry from 1970 to 1987, much of which is concerned with his intuitions of sinister and corrupt forces active beneath the surfaces of modern culture. *White Chappell: Scarlet Tracings* (1987) won him acclaim as a novelist for its compellingly phantasmagoric narrative. The panoramically episodic structure of *Downriver; Or, The Vessels of Wrath* (1991) sustains his disquieting vision of London's docklands. The complex, intricate *Radon Daughters* (1994) also makes use of a shadowy East End. A comic epic of mysticism and degeneracy, the novel concerns an attempt to retrieve a lost sequel to William Hope *Hodgson's *The House on the Border-*

land, and features characters from *Downriver*. Sinclair's description of his texts as 'baroque realism' suits his inventive manipulation of language and form. His other works include *The Kodak Mantra Diaries* (1971), an account of Allen *Ginsberg's visit to Britain in 1967, and *Lights Out for the Territory* (1995), a celebration of London.

SINCLAIR, May (Mary Amelia St Clair) (1863–1946), British novelist, born in Cheshire, and educated mainly at home. She was the youngest child and only daughter of a shipping magnate whose business went bankrupt and who became an alcoholic. Sinclair lived with her mother after her parents separated and looked after her brothers while pursuing a formidable private course of study. After the publication of her first novel, *Audrey Craven* (1897), she moved to London. From 1908 she worked actively for Women's Suffrage and mixed with many of the leading writers of the day. The influence of Freud and Jung was evident in *The Divine Fire* (1904), about a Cockney poet and his relationship with a refined intellectual woman. Among her finest novels, which again manifest the author's interest in psychology, are *The Three Sisters* (1914), deriving from the lives of the Brontë sisters, *Mary Olivier: A Life* (1919), and *Life and Death of Harriett Frean* (1922). In *Harriett Frean*, the author makes use of a '*stream-of-consciousness' technique; the central character is mentally and spiritually trapped by the role society accords her, and not only accepts but almost rejoices in this restriction of emotional possibilities. *Mary Olivier*, which has many features in common with the author's life, depicts its heroine's longing for knowledge, her Platonist sense of the richness of life from which she has been excluded because of her sex. During the last fifteen years of her life May Sinclair suffered from Parkinson's disease.

SINCLAIR, Upton (Beall) (1878–1968), American novelist, born in Baltimore; he paid his way through the City College of New York by writing novels, an activity which also financed his graduate work at Columbia. His first major work was *The *Jungle* (1906) in which he exposed the appalling conditions prevalent in the meat-packing industry and which resulted in legislation for reform. The novel also marked his first open and avowed commitment to the cause of socialism, closing as it does with a sequence celebrating the presidential campaign of Eugene V. Debs. The proceeds from the novel were used to found Helicon Hall, a utopian community for socialist living and education. His continuing commitment to socialist ideas shaped his writing and political activity for the next thirty years, producing a stream of novels and pamphlets which exposed the iniquities of American society. Of the non-fiction, perhaps *The Profits of Religion* (1918), *The Brass Check* (1919), *Mammonart* (1925), and *Money Writes!* (1927) were the most successful, whilst from the novels *The Metropolis* (1908), *King Coal* (1917), *Oil!* (1927), *Boston* (1928), and *The Flivver King* (1937) are the major achievements. *King Coal* is partly based on sworn testimony drawn from the Colorado coal strike enquiry of 1914–15, and tells of a college boy's experience of mining work and his subsequent agitation for improved working conditions and union representation. *Oil!* reveals the corruption within the oil industry, politics, and public life, and ends with the hero 'Bunny' Ross's realization that only socialism can cure society's ills. Sinclair moved to California in 1915, and later, in 1934, he campaigned for the governorship of the state, and was a leading figure in the EPIC (End Poverty in California) Coalition in the Depression years. *World's End* (1940) was to be the first of a series of ten novels recounting in international terms the state of politics from 1913 up to and including the 1940s. The protagonist Lanny Budd, after whom the sequence is sometimes named, is also the hero of the sequel, *The Return of Lanny Budd* (1953). Sinclair produced well over 100 books which sold in millions world-wide, and in his eighties published a selection of his correspondence, *My Lifetime in Letters* (1960), and an *Autobiography* (1962), which, despite the relative lack of acclaim in America, demonstrated the extraordinary range of his contacts. See also PROLETARIAN WRITING IN THE USA.

Singapore Grip, The, see FARRELL, J. G.

SINGER, Burns (James Hyman) (1928–64), Scottish poet, born in New York of Scottish parents; he grew up in Glasgow, where he attended the University. He travelled widely in the late 1940s and sought out W. S. *Graham in Cornwall for guidance in the development of his writing. After working as a research assistant in a marine laboratory, he became a highly regarded literary journalist and broadcaster in London. He resumed his work in marine biology shortly before his death. His substantial collection entitled *Still and All* (1957) included his earlier publications *The Gentle Engineer* (1952) and *Sonnets for a Dying Man* (1957). *Collected Poems*, edited by W. A. S. Keir, and *Selected Poems*, edited by Anne Cluysenaar, were published in 1970 and 1977 respectively. Singer's scientific training and his studies of philosophy and linguistics influenced the character of much of his poetry. At its best, his work achieves a highly original synthesis of intellectual speculation, imaginative elements, and precise observation. He also wrote *Living Silver* (1957), a documentary fiction based on his experiences of the fishing industry, which inform numerous poems, and was editor and translator, with Jerzy Peterkiewicz, of *Five Centuries of Polish Poetry* (1960).

SINGER, Isaac Bashevis (1904–91), American novelist, short-story writer, and playwright, born in Leoncin, Poland, educated at Tachkemoni Rabbinical Seminary, Warsaw. Singer (the surname is anglicized from Zynger and the middle name is a pseudonym taken from his mother's name, Bathsheba) emigrated to the USA in 1935 and took American citizenship in 1943; apart from some early works written and published whilst he was studying in Warsaw almost all his major fiction was written in Yiddish and published in the

USA, and it was the subsequent translation of his Yiddish writings into English that secured him the reputation of being the most widely read of Yiddish writers—indeed, one of the most popular of post-war American authors. In Warsaw Singer was an associate editor for *Globus*; when he moved to New York he quickly became associated with *Vorwarts*, the *Jewish Daily Forward*, writing for it under both his own name and the assumed names of Varshavsky and Segal. In 1950, however, with the publication of *The Family Moskat*, Singer in effect began his career as an 'English' writer, the novel appearing simultaneously in both Yiddish and English. In *The Family Moskat* Singer writes within a largely realistic tradition, the novel depicting that point in contemporary Jewish history when the settled traditions of a confined *shtetl* life were under threat, from both Nazi tyranny and the pace of social and economic change; other works of a similarly sociological kind include *The Manor* (1967) and *The Estate* (1969). It was his short stories, though, that did most to establish his popularity, notably the collections *Gimpel the Fool and Other Stories* (1957), some of which were translated by Saul *Bellow, *The Spinoza of Market Street and Other Stories* (1961), *Selected Short Stories* (1964, edited by Irving *Howe), *The Seance and Other Stories* (1968), and *A Friend of Kafka and Other Stories* (1970). Novels such as *Satan in Goray* (1935; translated in 1955) and *The Magician of Lublin* (1960) embody that blend of the realistic and the mysterious which gives such symbolic depth to much of his major fiction. Other volumes of stories include *Short Friday and Other Stories* (1964), *A Crown of Feathers and Other Stories* (1973), *Old Love* (1979), and *The Collected Stories* (1982); among his other novels are *The Slave* (1962), *Enemies: A Love Story* (1972), and *The Penitent* (1983). His autobiographical works, particularly *In My Father's Court* (1966), *A Day of Pleasure: Stories of a Boy Growing Up in Warsaw* (1969), and *A Little Boy in Search of God: Mysticism in a Personal Light* (1976), combine a lyrical evocation of a Hasidic childhood in Eastern Europe with accounts of Singer's intellectual and spiritual 'awakenings'. Singer also wrote several plays, numerous volumes of stories for children, and was an assiduous translator of distinguished foreign fiction into Yiddish, notably works by Gabriele D'Annunzio, Knut Hamsun, Thomas Mann, and Erich Maria Remarque. He was honoured by many American colleges and universities and received many awards for his fiction, amongst them the Nobel Prize for Literature in 1978 (his *Nobel Lecture* was published in 1979). *A Singer Reader* (1971) is a useful introduction to his writings, and *Conversations with Singer* (1985) is valuable for its anecdotes and its insights into his art. *Critical Views of Singer* (1969), edited by Irving Malin, draws together some intelligent critical essays whilst David N. Miller's *Fear of Fiction: Narrative Strategies in the Works of Singer* (1985) subjects his fiction to post-modernist analyses; further critical commentary can be found in *The Achievement of Singer* (1969), edited by Marcia Allentuck, and *Singer and His Art* (1970) by Askel Schiotz.

SINGH, Khushwant (1915–), Indian writer, critic, journalist, and translator, born in Hadali in the Punjab (now in Pakistan), educated in Delhi and Lahore, before attending King's College, University of London. Called to the Bar in 1938, Singh practised at the Lahore High Court in the 1940s. After a career in public service, including a period with the Ministry of External Affairs, he became a journalist and editor, establishing a reputation as one of India's leading cultural commentators. His vast erudition and understanding of India's history, political systems, and literary heritage is reflected in his prose works which included a history of his own community, the Sikhs, published in 1963. His novels, which are deeply rooted in the recent history and political situation of contemporary India, include *Train to Pakistan* (1954), one of the most compelling (quasi-documentary) accounts of the Partition of India in 1947; *I Shall Not Hear the Nightingale* (1961); and *Delhi* (1989), a picaresque history of India's capital narrated by a eunuch. Singh has translated into English the works of Iqbal (1981), and the celebrated Urdu novel *Umrao Jan Ada* (as *The Courtesan of Lucknow*, 1961); he has also introduced the works of the Sikh poetess Amrita Pritam to an English-speaking audience.

Sinister Street, see MACKENZIE, SIR COMPTON.

SISSON, C(harles) H(ubert) (1914–), British poet and translator, born in Bristol, where he read Philosophy and English at the University. He began his career in the Civil Service in 1936 and retired as Assistant Under-Secretary of State in 1973. He co-edited **PN Review* from 1976 to 1983. He first gained wide notice with *The Spirit of British Administration* (1959), a study of administrative and constitutional issues. The title poem of *The London Zoo* (1961), his first substantial collection of poetry, forms an acerbic satire on the habits and attitudes of middle-class commuters. Among his subsequent volumes are *Numbers* (1965), *In the Trojan Ditch: Collected Poems and Selected Translations* (1974), *Exactions* (1980), *God Bless Karl Marx!* (1987), and *Antidotes* (1991); *Collected Poems 1943–1983* was published in 1984. Much of his earlier poetry exhibited a bleak philosophical outlook, giving rise to many laconically epigrammatic pieces and longer poems of a sombrely lyrical tone. From the mid-1970s onward his verse displays an increasing preoccupation with religious and contemplative themes, which are dealt with in a style of trenchant plainness. Notable among his translations are versions of Dante's *Divine Comedy* (1980) and Virgil's *Aeneid* (1986). He has also produced two novels, *An Asiatic Romance* (1953) and the highly acclaimed *Christopher Homm* (1965). His several collections of essays, noted for their outspokenness against poetic practices he opposes, include *The Avoidance of Literature* (1978) and *In Two Minds* (1990). A 'partial autobiography' entitled *On the Look Out* appeared in 1989.

Sister Carrie, a novel by Theodore *Dreiser. It was first published in 1900 but not promoted by Doubleday, on the grounds of its alleged immorality. It was reissued in 1912, the year after the publication of *Jennie Gerhardt*, although the unexpurgated edition of the novel did not appear until 1981. Caroline Meeber, the eponymous heroine, is a naïve girl from a country town who arrives in Chicago to stay with her sister and brother-in-law and look for employment. Only casual and low-paid factory work is available, and after an illness she suffers unemployment and depression. In this condition, she permits Charles Drouet, a travelling salesman, to make her his mistress but as her circumstances improve, so her regard for Drouet diminishes, and in his absence she becomes drawn to his friend George Hurstwood, an unhappily married manager of a popular restaurant. Hurstwood embezzles $10,000 from the company safe and tricks Carrie into eloping, first to Montreal and then to New York, where they run a saloon and live together for three years. He loses the saloon and, driven to desperate measures, becomes a strike-breaker attacked by striking trolley-workers. Meanwhile Carrie finds employment as a chorus-girl and attempts to support Hurstwood. She becomes increasingly successful as his condition deteriorates, and finally she leaves him. As her theatrical renown grows, so he falls victim to complete destitution and ultimately kills himself. However, Carrie's remarkable rise to fame and her material success do not prevent her from feeling the pain of isolation.

SITWELL, Dame Edith (Louisa) (1887–1964), British poet, born in Scarborough, the sister of Osbert and Sacheverell *Sitwell; she grew up at Renishaw Hall in Derbyshire, the seat of her aristocratic family. Her early collections of poetry include *The Mother and Other Poems* (1915), notable for its unusually violent title piece; *Twentieth Century Harlequinade* (1916), one of several collaborations with Osbert; and *Clowns' Houses* (1918), which established rhythmically extravagant experimentation as a characteristic of her verse. She edited **Wheels* from 1916 to 1921. *Façade*, a radically innovative suite of predominantly unparaphrasable poems, provoked controversy when it was performed with music by William Walton in 1923. The attention she and her brothers attracted throughout the 1920s caused F. R. *Leavis to remark that the Sitwells 'belong to the history of publicity rather than that of poetry'. Her poetry grew more ethically purposeful with *Gold Coast Customs* (1929), which denounced the habits of affluent society through the creation of parallels with the rites of African tribes. *Street Songs* (1942), *Green Song* (1944), and *The Song of The Cold* (1945), won her wide respect for their stoically transcendent treatments of the suffering and destruction wrought by the Second World War. The resonantly rhetorical title poem of *The Shadow of Cain* (1947), a response to the atomic bombing of Hiroshima, indicates her affinities with Dylan *Thomas, whom she was among the first to acclaim. She was made a Dame Grand Cross of the Order of the British Empire in 1954. *Collected Poems* was produced in 1957. Her numerous prose works include the critical study *Aspects of Modern Poetry* (1934) and the popular biography *Victoria of England* (1936); *Taken Care of* (1965) is autobiographical. John *Lehmann's *A Nest of Tigers* (1968) is a study of the three Sitwells; Victoria *Glendinning's biography *Edith Sitwell* appeared in 1981.

SITWELL, Sir (Francis) Osbert (Sacheverell) (1892–1969), British poet, novelist, and autobiographer, born in London, the brother of Edith and Sacheverell *Sitwell; he grew up at Renishaw Hall, his family's seat in Derbyshire. He was educated at Eton, which he described in the novel *The Man Who Lost Himself* (1923) as 'that wasteful, antiquated, rather beautiful machine'. His early collections of poetry, which include *The Winstonburg Line* (1919) and *Argonaut and Juggernaut* (1919), contain some incisive satires of official attitudes to the First World War, during which he served with the Grenadier Guards. From 1919 onward he devoted himself to authorship. The best-known of his numerous novels is *Before the Bombardment* (1926), a fictionalized treatment of the artillery attack on Scarborough in 1914. During the 1920s he joined with Edith and Sacheverell in zealously promoting *Modernism and disparaging the *Georgian literary establishment. His later poetry was noted for its elegant wit, which frequently gave offence. *Collected Satires and Poems* appeared in 1931; *England Reclaimed* (1927), *Wrack at Tidesend* (1952), and *On the Continent* (1958) were collected as *Poems about People* in 1965. His travel writings include *Winters of Content* (1932), an account of Italy, and *The Four Continents* (1954). His most highly regarded work remains his five-volume autobiography—*Left Hand! Right Hand!* (1945), *The Scarlet Tree* (1946), *Great Morning!* (1948), *Laughter in the Next Room* (1949), and *Noble Essences* (1950)—from which his father, the eccentric Sir George, emerges as a comic figure of Shandean proportions.

SITWELL, Sir Sacheverell (1897–1988), British poet and art historian, born in Scarborough, the brother of Edith and Osbert *Sitwell; he grew up at Renishaw Hall in Derbyshire and was educated at Balliol College, Oxford. His collections of poetry, notable for their delicate musicality and precise yet often mysterious imagery, include *The People's Palace* (1918), *Exalt the Eglantine* (1926), *Dr Donne and Gargantua* (1930), and *An Indian Summer* (1982); *Collected Poems* appeared in 1936. His principal work of fiction is *Far from My Home* (1931), a collection of 'long and short stories'. Less of a public figure than Edith and Osbert, he proved a more prolific author than either, producing a long succession of books in which his interests in travel and art were combined; among the most valuable of these are *Southern Baroque Art* (1924), *German Baroque Art* (1927), and *Spanish Baroque Art* (1931), which did much to generate interest in the baroque period. His most notable single work as an art historian is the comprehensive *British Architects and Craftsmen* (1945). *The Dance of the Quick and the Dead* (1936) and *Journey to the*

Ends of Time (1959) are erudite and imaginatively disquieting meditations on art, literature, and mortality; together with the opulently textured 'autobiographical fantasy' *All Summer Long* (1926), they form what is arguably his finest achievement. Biographies of each of the Sitwells are contained in *Facades* (1978) by John Pearson.

Sizwe Bansi Is Dead, a play by Athol *Fugard, performed in 1972, published in *Statements: 3 Plays* (1974). Styles, a photographer in the South African town of New Brighton, Port Elizabeth, sees the studio of which he is the proprietor as a 'strong room of dreamers', and his vocation as the immortalization of the simple people who are never mentioned in the history books and who 'never get statues erected to them'. One such simple dreamer, who identifies himself as a Xhosa named Robert Zwelinzima (the surname means 'suffering land'), wanders into his studio; persuaded by Styles to commission more than the one photograph he originally required, he dictates a letter to the wife he has left behind, in which the secret of his identity is revealed. Sizwe Bansi, as he was originally called, came to the town in search of work but, because he did not have the necessary papers, was ordered to leave. During a night of drunken revelling with a friend, he came across the corpse of the man whose identity he has now assumed. Through the night-long crisis of consciousness he has undergone, Bansi—or Zwelinzima—becomes aware of the plight of the urban worker and the internal migrant in a South Africa oppressed by the laws of apartheid. Names are interchangeable, jobs almost impossible to find, and life cheap. Bansi's loss of name and identity serves as a metaphor for the slow erosion of a way of life, and the story of his success is a story of compromise, pain, and loss of self; the only path available to the oppressed and deprived is that of subterfuge and trickery.

Sjuzet, see PLOT.

Skin of Our Teeth, The, see WILDER, THORNTON.

SLADEK, John T(homas) (1937–), American novelist and short-story writer, born in Waverley, Iowa, educated at the University of Minnesota. Most of his work can be described as *science fiction. After *The Muller-Fokker Effect* (1970), which features the deconstruction of a human personality into separate computer tapes, his science fiction novels *Roderick* (1980) and its continuation *Roderick at Random* (1983), *Tik-Tok* (1983), and *Bugs* (1989) all dealt with the conundrums and abysses of artificial intelligence often personified by robots. His short fiction, which is among the funniest ever written in the genre, was collected in *The Steam-Driven Boy* (1973), *Keep the Giraffe Burning* (1977), *Alien Accounts* (1982), and *The Lunatics of Terra* (1984). Other works include the detective novels *Black Aura* (1974) and *Invisible Green* (1977); *The New Apocrypha* (1973), which has been highly esteemed for its analysis of beliefs such as Scientology; and *Arachne Rising* (1977), a book-length spoof of astrology, which creates a thirteenth sign of the zodiac.

SLAUGHTER, Carolyn (1946–), British novelist, born in India, educated in South Africa and in England; she worked as a copywriter in London until 1976. Her first novel, *The Story of the Weasel* (1976), was praised for its sensitive treatment of fraternal incest in Victorian England and for its subtle poetic prose. *Columba* (1977) again displayed a preoccupation with pathological mental states, impossible love, and loneliness, with compassion and lyricism. *Magdalene* (1978) explores the myths of early Christianity from an entirely subjective perspective in impassioned tones and poetic prose reminiscent of Elizabeth *Smart. With *Dreams of the Kalahari* (1981) Slaughter turned to South Africa for inspiration, combining the personal with the political in a series of more accessible novels. In *The Banquet* (1983) Slaughter returns to a controversial theme, but the novel's extended metaphor of cannibalistic desire verges on the lurid and sensationalistic. Slaughter became a resident of America. Other novels include *A Perfect Woman* (1984) and *The Widow* (1989).

Slaughterhouse-Five; or, The Children's Crusade, a novel by Kurt *Vonnegut, Jr, published in 1969. *Slaughterhouse-Five* is perhaps the most successful of Vonnegut's novels. Its hero, Billy Pilgrim, a chaplain's assistant in the American army during the Second World War, is captured and imprisoned in Dresden (in the 'slaughterhouse-five' of the title) where he witnesses the infamous Allied fire-bombing of the German city. After the war he becomes a successful optometrist and on the evening of his daughter's wedding is hijacked by a flying saucer and taken to the planet Tralfamodore where he is mated in a public zoo with the actress Montana Wildhack. The plot of Vonnegut's novel, his characteristic mixture of the realistic and the science-fictional, largely functions as a framework for a series of mordant and satirical comments on human nature, and, more particularly, on war and life in the USA. The novel is markedly autobiographical—Vonnegut was a prisoner-of-war and saw at first hand the Dresden air-raid—and, in part, is concerned with the difficulty he had trying to erase his experience of Dresden from his memory and the process by which he came to fictional terms with it. *Slaughterhouse-Five* established Vonnegut as one of the most important of post-war American novelists. *City of Words* (1971) by Tony *Tanner contains a valuable essay on Vonnegut which includes extended consideration of the novel.

SLESSOR, Kenneth (1901–71), Australian poet, born in New South Wales. He was a journalist and became joint editor with Norman *Lindsay of **Vision*, in which his earliest poems appeared. His experience as official war correspondent in 1940–4 resulted in 'Beach Burial', one of his finest war poems. Early poems, such as those contained in *The Thief of the Moon* (1924) and *Earth Visitors* (1926), made effective use of imagery and were often romantic in tone. He began to experiment with form in *Cuckooz Contrey* (1932) which contained 'Captain Dobbin', celebrating an eccentric seaman. His 'Five Visions of Captain Cook' (in *Trio*, 1931) was one of the finest and earliest of the 'voyager' poems in Australian literature. In the title poem of *Five Bells* (1939) Slessor weaves into a complex structure personal responses to a drowned friend with haunting images of Sydney harbour. His collection *One Hundred Poems 1919–1939* (1944) was reissued as *Poems* (1957) with two additional poems. Although he wrote no new poetry after 1944, Slessor remained active in literary life, editing the journal **Southerly* from 1956 to 1961, as well as several anthologies, including *Australian Poetry* (1945) and *The Penguin Book of Australian Verse* (1958). Posthumous publications include *War Diaries* (1985, edited by Clement Semmler), *War Despatches of Kenneth Slessor* (1988), and *Sea Poems of Kenneth Slessor* (1991).

SLOCUM, Joshua (1844–?1909), American travel writer, born in Wilmot Township, Nova Scotia; he received an irregular education before going to sea as a cook at the age of 12. A naturalized American citizen, from 1869 onward he was captain of a succession of vessels sailing out of San Francisco. *The Voyage of the Liberdade* (1890), his first book, describes a shipwreck and the voyage to safety in a boat constructed from salvage. *The Voyage of the Destroyer* (1894) is an account of his unhappy command of a warship being delivered to Brazil. In 1898 he became the first man to achieve a single-handed circumnavigation of the globe; the enormously successful *Sailing Alone around the World* (1900), his laconically engaging record of the three years and 46,000 miles the journey covered, was for decades a set text in many British schools. Slocum was never seen again after setting sail for South America in 1909. His life and work were assessed in the 1950s by Walter Teller, who wrote a biographical account, *The Search for Captain Slocum* (1959), and edited *The Voyages of Captain Slocum* (1958), which collects Slocum's three books along with various literary fragments.

SLOVO, Gillian (1952–), South African novelist, born in Johannesburg, the daughter of the ANC leaders Joe Slovo and Ruth *First; she grew up in Britain from 1964, following her parents' departure from South Africa as political fugitives. She has worked as a journalist and film producer. Her detective novel *Morbid Symptoms* (1984) introduced Kate Baeier, virtuoso saxophonist and private investigator, whose adventures continue in *Death by Analysis* (1986), *Death Comes Staccato* (1990), *Catnap* (1994), and *Close Call* (1995). *Ties of Blood* (1989) traced South African history from 1900 to the 1980s through its expansive narrative of familial loyalties and antagonisms. Suspicions of treachery within the ANC generate the atmospheres of tension and violence in her psychologically penetrating political thriller *The Betrayal* (1991); *Façade* (1993) is a family drama, with the London stage and the world of International Aid as a backdrop. Among her other works is her contribution to *Subverting Apartheid* (with J. Corrigall and E. Unterhalter, 1990), which considers alternative strategies for education, information, and culture during emergency rule in South Africa.

Small Presses fulfil an astonishing variety of functions, some of them marginal, others as crucial as Sylvia Beach's publication of James Joyce's **Ulysses*, the Gaberbocchus Press's editions of Alfred Jarry's work, or the Marvell Press's publication of Philip Larkin's **The Less Deceived*. The present significance of small presses as outlets for work of value neglected by established publishing houses began as a phenomenon of the 1960s; numerous small presses emerged at this time with a specific agenda, fostered in part by a strong reaction against certain insular and regressive tendencies imputed to the pervasive influence of the *Movement poets of the 1950s. Some notable British and American Modernist (see MODERNISM) poets remained unpublished, a situation which Stuart Montgomery's Fulcrum Press remedied by issuing work by David *Jones, Basil *Bunting, Lorine *Niedecker, George *Oppen, Ed *Dorn, Robert *Duncan, and others. Asa Benveniste founded Trigram Press and produced an edition of Louis *Zukofsky's *A-22/23*. Tom *Raworth, Barry Hall, and Nathaniel Tarn, editors of Goliard Press (later Cape Goliard), published the work of Charles *Olson, John *Wieners, Robert *Kelly, and Allen *Ginsberg. Equally important was the publishing of British extensions and revisions of this already varied modern American tradition: as well as issuing the work of Robert *Creeley, Gael Turnbull's Migrant Press produced books by Ian Hamilton *Finlay and Roy *Fisher, while Goliard and Trigram published Raworth and Fulcrum published Lee *Harwood, Tom *Pickard, and Spike Hawkins.

The death of Charles Olson in 1970 seems a symbolic end to this initial period of energetic activity by the small presses; while American concerns like Black Sparrow and New Directions continue to publish many of the poets named above, more experimental American work has latterly received diminished attention in Britain from both established publishing houses and small presses. Two recent anthologies offer a comprehensive summary of what has been taking place in British small press publishing since the early 1970s. *The New British Poetry* (1988), edited by Gillian Allnutt, Fred *D'Aguiar, Ken Edwards, and Eric Mottram, has a wide range, including both feminist and black British poetries, together with a catholic selection of work from younger writers. A narrower view is offered by *A Various Art* (1987); edited by Andrew Crozier and Tim Longville, the anthology stems in the main from their publishing activities with the Ferry and Grosseteste Presses, which issued work by Peter Riley, John Riley, Douglas Oliver, Anthony Barnett, and J. H. *Prynne. Crozier, Fisher, Peter Riley, John James, Iain *Sinclair, and Ralph Hawkins are represented in both these anthologies. The contributors to *A Various Art* insist on opacity in poetry because they are intent on examining the opacity of language itself. In this, their work has similarities to the *Language Poetry now well established in America and shares with that movement an acknowledgement of the inevitably political nature of most forms of communication. *The New British Poetry* reminds us of possibilities which remain marginalized, for example Bob *Cobbing's and Bill Griffiths's energetic experimentation in sound-poetry and other modes. If anything unites these two anthologies, it is the sense of disaffiliation from any orthodox definition of literary culture which is central to the motivations of the small presses. Both collections constitute interesting responses to a fundamental difficulty facing contemporary poetry: in the 1960s there was a perceptible continuity of effort which was sharpened and enriched by the tension between 'mainstream' and 'alternative' work; Thom *Gunn's respect for William Carlos *Williams and Robert *Duncan or Donald *Davie's keen interest in *Pound and the *Black Mountain poets bear witness to the productive element in the midst of disagreement.

No such productive dialogue existed in the 1980s, while poets continued to feel the need to broaden their horizons still further. More generally, as boundaries of gender and race begin to erode, the range of competing voices has begun to extend beyond hope of confinement, a situation for which the small presses are uniquely well suited; desk-top publishing of the 1990s stands ready to take over the role of the mimeograph machines of the 1960s, its rapid and inexpensive dissemination of material providing the small presses with a technology adequate to the challenges of our rapidly evolving times.

SMART, Elizabeth (1913–86), Canadian novelist and poet, born in Ottawa, Ontario, educated at private schools in Canada and at King's College, University of London. During the 1930s she wrote for the *Ottawa Journal*. Most of her later life was spent in Britain. She worked as a journalist for *Vogue* and *Queen* and as an advertising copywriter. She is best known for the novel **By Grand Central Station I Sat Down and Wept* (1945), a celebration of the beginning of her long relationship with the poet George *Barker, by whom she bore four children. Smart published no further books until *A Bonus* of 1977, her first collection of poetry, which contains free verse of great conversational directness; her clarity and descriptive vitality as a poet are most evident in the *Imagist precision of the 'Nature Notes' sequence. Her other works include *Eleven Poems* (1982), *In the Mean Time* (1984), which contains poems and short prose pieces, and the short autobiographical novel *The Assumption of the Rogues and Rascals* (1978), a concentrated account of her life from the 1950s onward. *Necessary Secrets* (1986), a collection of her journals, and *Early Writings* (1987) were both edited by Ann Van Wart. *By Heart*, Rosemary Sullivan's biography of Smart, appeared in 1991.

SMEDLEY, Agnes (1892–1950), American writer and reporter, born in North-West Mississippi; she grew up in circumstances of rural poverty. Her autobiographical novel *Daughter of Earth* (1929)—recognized as a feminist-proletarian classic—recounts, with power and depth, her struggle to liberate herself from the confines of her background, her self-education, her escape to Europe, and her encounter with the politics of Indian nationalism in the person of her lover, the revolutionary 'Anand' (a portrait of the Indian nationalist Virendranath Chattopadhyaya.) Here Smedley adopts a fictional persona, Marie Rogers, and the events of her life are altered and telescoped to accommodate the demands of fiction. However, in her subsequent major autobiographical work, *Battle Hymn of China* (1943), she abandons narrative masks and fictive strategies. Summarizing the facts behind the novel's fictions in ten pages, she links it to her 'real' life, and proceeds to document her discovery of, and her commitment to, the Chinese Revolution-in-process, and her friendships with several of its seminal political and literary figures, including Mao himself. Smedley's exemplary non-doctrinaire political commitment also illuminates her various works on China such as *Chinese Destinies* (1933), *China Fights Back* (1934), the posthumous *The Great Road* (a biography of Chu Teh, 1956); and *Portraits of Chinese Women in Revolution* (1976), edited and introduced by her biographers, Jan and Steve Mackinnon.

SMILEY, Jane (1951?–), American novelist, born in Los Angeles, educated at Vassar and the University of Iowa. Her fiction is notable for the range of its techniques and subject matter. Her first novel, *Barn Blind* (1980), is set in Iowa, where she became resident; it is the tragic story of a woman's obsessive love of horses. A collection of quietly controlled stories, *The Age of Grief* (1987), was followed by the epic *The Greenlanders* (1988), a long saga set in the fourteenth century which is also the story of one family, the Gunnarsons. It was *A Thousand Acres* (1992), an inventive contemporary recasting of *King Lear* in her favoured setting of rural Iowa, that raised her to the front ranks of American writers, earning her, among other prizes, the Pulitzer. The novel presents its tragic theme with an array of domestic detail in the prevalent American feminine tradition; the modern Lear is an incestuous hog farmer. Smiley followed this great success with a move to light comedy in the academic satire *Moo* (1995).

SMITH, A(rthur) J(ames) M(arshall) (1902–80), Canadian editor, critic, and poet, born in Montreal, educated at McGill and Edinburgh Universities. He played an important role in what became known as 'the Montreal Group', the most significant avant-garde Canadian literary movement of its day. In association with F. R. *Scott, A. M. *Klein, and E. J. *Pratt he produced *New Provinces: Poems of Several Authors* (1936) and went on to become extremely influential as an editor. His anthologies include *The Book of Canadian Poetry: A Critical and Historical Anthology* (1943), *The Oxford Book of Canadian Verse in English and French* (1960), *Modern Canadian Verse* (1967), and two collections of criticism, *Masks of Fiction* (1961) and *Masks of Poetry* (1962). Smith also produced a significant body of criticism, collected in *Towards a View of Canadian Letters* (1973) and *On Poetry and Poets* (1977), and poetry, written in a range of styles—lyrical, satirical, metaphysical, and parodic. His verse seldom deserts the controlled, urbane tone which is its dominant voice. It has been published in *News of the Phoenix* (1943), *A Sort of Ecstasy* (1954), *Collected Poems* (1962), *Poems New and Collected* (1967), and *The Classic Shade* (1978), with each new volume subsuming and polishing poems from earlier collections.

SMITH, Bernard (1916–), Australian art historian and cultural critic, born in Sydney where for many years he was Power Professor of Fine Art at Sydney University. He retired to Melbourne in 1977. Best known for his complementary pioneering studies *European Vision and the South Pacific: A Study in the History of Art and Ideas* (1960) and *Australian Painting 1788–1960* (1962), he has also completed outstanding editorial work relating to the voyages of Captain Cook, and the artists who sailed with him. Throughout a long and distinguished career he committed himself to many challenging causes, including urban conservation and Aboriginal Land Rights. The prize-winning first volume of his autobiography, *The Boy Adeodatus: The Portrait of a Lucky Young Bastard* (1984), charts his hard early life and education in Sydney in rewarding detail. *The Death of the Artist as Hero: Essays in History and Culture* and *The Critic as Advocate: Selected Essays 1941–1988* (both 1988) well represent his scholarly and forthright contributions on a wide range of important issues.

SMITH, Dave (Jeddie) (1942–), American poet, born in Portsmouth, Virginia, educated at the University of Virginia, Southern Illinois, and Ohio University. Among several distinguished academic and editorial posts, Smith has served as literary editor of the *Rocky Mountain Review*, editor of *Southern Review*, and in 1982 became Professor of English at Virginia Commonwealth University. His work is characterized by his Virginian identity, together with an ability to contemplate the history, locality, and experience of the South. Influenced formally by the verse narratives of Robert Penn *Warren, Smith began by writing about Poquoson, a fishing village bordering the Chesapeake Bay, in *Bull Island* (1970). In *The Fisherman's Whore* (1974) and *Cumberland Station* (1976) he continues to view the area's ruination, poverty, and pollution with a bitter compassion. Helen Vendler has praised Smith's 'passionately Southern descriptiveness', qualities especially evident in the powerful sequence *Gray Soldiers* (1983); 'On a Field Trip at Fredericksburg', which memorializes the Civil War dead in contemporary terms, and 'Night Fishing for Blues' are among his most admired poems. His collections include *In the House of the Judge* (1983) and *Cuba Night* (1990). *Night Pleasures: New and Selected Poems* appeared in 1992.

SMITH, Dodie (1896–1990), British dramatist and novelist, born in Whitefield, Lancashire, educated at St Paul's School and the Royal Academy of Dramatic Art. Until 1935 she wrote under the name C. L. Anthony. Her first play, *Autumn Crocus* (1931), was followed by several others, including *Service* (1932), *Touch Wood* (1933), *Call It a Day* (1935), *Bonnet over the Windmill* (1937), *Lovers and Friends* (1942), *Letter from Paris* (1952), and *These People, Those Books* (1957). The best-known of her plays is *Dear Octopus* (1938), a loving dissection of a family, which was successfully revived in 1967. Six novels followed, including the delightfully romantic *I Capture the Castle* (1949), which she later dramatized, *The New Moon with the Old* (1963), *The Town in Bloom* (1965), *A Tale of Two Families* (1970), and *The Girl from the Candle-lit Bath* (1978), as well as numerous books for children, of which *One Hundred and One Dalmations* (1956) is the most famous and has become a classic. The book was later made into a Disney cartoon film. Four volumes of autobiography comprise *Look Back With Love* (1974), *Look Back with Mixed Feelings* (1978), *Look Back with Astonishment* (1979), and *Look Back with Gratitude* (1985).

SMITH, E(dward) E(lmer) (1890–1965), American *science fiction writer and chemist, born in Sheboygan, Wisconsin, educated at George Washington University. He is known as Doc Smith, a central figure in the creation of modern American *space opera. As created by Smith (with E. Hamilton), space operas are morally simplified dramas of conflict (usually military) with dynamic plots which take place in vast galaxy-spanning venues. In Smith's first series, the *Skylark* books which began to appear in magazines from 1928 and were published (in volume form) from 1946 to 1966, the increases in scale were simply linear, and his hero an implausible tinkerer; in his second, the *Lensman* series, published in magazines from 1934 and in volume form as *Triplanetary* (1948), *First Lensman* (1950), *Galactic Patrol* (1950), *Gray Lensman* (1951), *Second Stage Lensman* (1953), and *Children of the Lens* (1954), he created one of the most successful of space opera stories. The action of each novel, though independent in itself, turns out only to be a local action in the greater war engaged upon in its successor; the final war, between two ancient species, takes billions of years to reach a climax.

SMITH, Iain Crichton (1928–), Scottish poet and novelist, born in Glasgow, educated at the University of Aberdeen. He was a schoolteacher in Glasgow and Oban from 1952 to 1977. A prolific author in both English and Gaelic, *The Long River* (1955) was his first collection of verse; among his subsequent volumes in English are *The Law and the Grace* (1965), *From Bourgeois Land* (1969), *Love Poems and Elegies* (1972), *The Exiles* (1984), *Selected Poems* (1985), *The Village* (1989), and *Ends and Beginnings* (1994). *A Life* (1986) is a long autobiographical poem. *Collected Poems* was published in 1992. Smith's belief in 'a poetry of fighting tensions and not in a poetry of statement' is consistent with his rejection of dogmatic ethical, religious, and social codes in numerous memorable poems, among them 'Lenin' and 'The Law and the Grace'. The landscapes and communities of the Scottish highlands provide much of his imagery and subject matter. His novels, notable for their shrewdness of characterization and vigorous dialogue, include *Consider the Lilies* (1968), *Goodbye, Mr Dixon* (1974), *The Tenement* (1985), *The Dream* (1990), and *An Honourable Death* (1992). His works in Gaelic, published under the name Iain Mac A' Ghobainn, include the poems of *Biobuill Is Sanasan Reice* (1965, lit. 'bibles and advertisements'), the play *An Coileach* (lit. 'the cockerel'), which was produced in 1966, and several books of short stories, among them *An t-Adhar Amaireaganach* (1973, lit. 'the American sky'); it is as a short-story writer that he is considered to have made his most valuable contribution to Gaelic culture. Among his volumes of short stories in English are *Selected Stories* (1990) and *Listening to the Voice* (1993). Among his other works is *Towards the Human* (1986), a collection of critical essays, and his translation of Sorley *MacLean's *Poems to Eimhir* (1971).

SMITH, Ken(neth John) (1938–), British poet, born in Rudston, Yorkshire, educated at the University of Leeds. In 1963 he became a co-editor of **Stand* magazine. He has worked widely as a teacher of creative writing in Britain and the USA; his experiences as writer-in-residence at Wormwood Scrubs prison from 1985 to 1987 resulted in the prose account of prison life in *Inside Time* (1989). *The Pity* (1967), his first collection of poetry, was well received, the assured cadences of its bleak lyricism indicating the individuality of tone that characterizes his work. Subsequent collections include *The Poet Reclining: Selected Poems 1962–1980* (1982), *Terra* (1986), *Wormwood* (1987), *The Heart, the Border* (1990), and *Tender to the Queen of Spades* (1993). Smith's writing sustains its concern with human behaviour and the interactions of the individual and society through a wide range of emotional and imaginative registers. His publications also include *Berlin: Coming in from the Cold* (1990), a documentary study of the aftermath of the opening of the Berlin Wall.

SMITH, (Lloyd) Logan Pearsall (1865–1946), American essayist, born in Millville, New Jersey, educated at Harvard and at Balliol College, Oxford, where he set the stories in his first book, *Youth of Parnassus* (1895). With his sister Mary and Bernard *Berenson, whom she later married, he produced a periodical entitled *The Golden Urn* in 1897–8, contributing short prose sketches of a wittily aphoristic character. These formed the beginnings of his *Trivia* (1902, revised edition 1918) which was collected with *More Trivia* (1922), *Afterthoughts* (1931), and *Last Words* (1933) as *All Trivia* in 1933. *The English Language* (1912), a treatise on usage displaying his elegantly mannered style, was among the works that drew him into association with Robert *Bridges for the formation of the Society for Pure English in 1913. His numerous critical works include *The Prospects of Literature* (1927) and *Milton and His Modern Critics* (1940), in which he was hostile to T. S. *Eliot and Ezra *Pound for their denigration of Milton. *The Life and Letters of Sir Henry Wotton* (1907) remains a standard work on that author. *Unforgotten Years* (1938) is autobiographical. Robert Gathorne-Hardy's *Recollections of Pearsall Smith* appeared in 1949.

SMITH, Michael (1954–83), Jamaican poet, born in Kingston; his father was a mason and his mother a factory worker. By the time he graduated from the Jamaica School of Drama in 1980 he was one of the most popular *Dub performance poets in Jamaica. Smith's poetry is so uncompromisingly demotic and instinctively dramatic that, had he lived, he would have been the natural successor to Louise *Bennett. Proverbs, biblical cadences and allusions, Rastafarian spirituality, and, above all, complete identification with ordinary people are characteristic of the poems, making him one of the best and closest to the oral tradition of the 'Dub' poets. 'Me Cyaan Believe It', which is also the title of his LP record, is his most famous poem. It is a devastating and relentlessly sardonic indictment of how ends never meet for the poor. *It a Come* (1986) is his only book of poetry. Smith was stoned to death by four hired thugs during the Jamaican general election campaign of 1983.

SMITH, Pauline (Janet) (1882–1959), South African novelist and short-story writer, born in Oudtshoorn, Cape Province, educated in Britain from the age of 13. She wrote only one novel, *The Beadle* (1926), and a collection of short stories, *The Little Karoo* (1925; expanded edition 1930). Her work is generally acknowledged to be a sensitive and accurate depiction of the harsh, acquisitive, and oppressively patriarchal life of Calvinistic Afrikaner farmers in the desolate Little Karoo region, where she grew up, and where her English father was a physician. *The Beadle* treats of a love affair between a self-sacrificing Afrikaner woman and an amiable, hedonistic Englishman. Like the stories, the novel achieves a poignant balance between nostalgia for a vanished way of life and realism about its difficulties, even cruelties. Her most prominent literary mentors in England were the critic John Middleton *Murry, who first published her stories in *The Adelphi*, and Arnold *Bennett, who greatly encouraged her. Her generous tribute to the novelist, *A.B.* (1933), appeared two years after his death. See Geoffrey Haresnape, *Pauline Smith* (1969).

SMITH, Stevie (Florence Margaret) (1902–71), British poet and novelist, born in Hull, the daughter of a shipping agent. From the age of three she grew up with her mother and her aunt in Palmers Green, London, where she remained for most of her life. After attending the North London Collegiate School for Girls, she worked as a secretary for the magazine publishers Newnes-Pearson until 1953, when she became a freelance writer and broadcaster. Her first book was *Novel on Yellow Paper* (1936); she published two further prose fictions, *Over the Frontier* (1938) and *The Holiday* (1949). All her novels are substantially autobiographical;

their discursive narratives are rich in the wittily heightened sense of the absurd which is strongly present in her verse. *A Good Time Was Had by All* (1938) introduced her as a poet and she gradually established a considerable reputation with her seven succeeding volumes, which include *Harold's Leap* (1950), *Not Waving but Drowning* (1957), and *Scorpion and Other Poems* (1972). She also gained an enthusiastic following as a reader of her work. A *Collected Poems* appeared in 1975. Her poetry ranges freely through a gamut of modes from the charmingly whimsical to the theologically serious; it frequently displays her sometimes deeply ironic sense of humour and is highly idiosyncratic in tone. Her technical procedures are similarly unusual; while most of her work rhymes, in a wide variety of forms often suggesting an element of improvisation, it is equally effective in the free verse she occasionally employed. *Some Are more Human than Others* (1958) contains a selection of the sketches, reminiscent of James *Thurber's drawings, with which she illustrated her collections. Among the numerous works she edited are *T. S. Eliot: A Symposium on His Seventieth Birthday* (1958). *Me Again* (1981, edited by J. Barbera and W. McBrien) contains selections from her uncollected prose writings. Several biographical works on Smith include *Ivy and Stevie* (1971) by Kay Dick and Frances Spalding's *Stevie Smith* (1988).

SMITH, Sydney Goodsir (1915–75), Scottish poet, born in Wellington, New Zealand, the son of an emigrant Scottish academic, educated at the University of Edinburgh, after which he pursued a career as a journalist, broadcaster, and teacher. Smith and Robert *Garioch are generally considered *MacDiarmid's most distinguished successors as modern poets writing in Scots. His reputation as a poet was established with *Skail Wind* (1941), which displayed his fluency and accomplishment in a range of lyrical modes; subsequent collections, in which his political concern with Scottish national identity become apparent, include *The Deevil's Waltz* (1946), *Cokkils* (1953), and *Girl with a Violin* (1968); *Collected Poems, 1941–1975* appeared in 1975. He used the rhythms and vocabulary of spoken Scots throughout a wide range of poetic modes, frequently to witty or ironic effect. *Under the Eildon Tree* (1954) is generally regarded as his finest achievement. Its twenty-four elegies combine vigorously colloquial diction and complex verse forms in sustaining their treatment of unhappiness in love. Thomas the Rhymer, Cuchulain, and Orpheus are among the personae introduced in the course of the poem's widely allusive development. Among Smith's other works is the novel of fantasy entitled *Carotid Cornucopius* (1947), an often outrageous *jeu d'esprit*, and *The Wallace* (1960), a five-act play of a patriotic character. He also edited numerous volumes, including *Gavin Douglas: A Selection from His Poetry* (1959) and *A Choice of Burns's Poems and Songs* (1966).

SMITHYMAN, (William) Kendrick (1922–), New Zealand poet, born in Northland, educated at Auckland University and Teacher's College. He was a primary school teacher before becoming a tutor at Auckland University. Described as a poet craftsman and, in *Auden's phrase, as a 'contriver of verbal contraptions', Smithyman's volumes of poetry include *Seven Sonnets* (1946), *Inheritance* (1962), *Flying to Palmerston North* (1968), *Dwarf with a Billiard Cue* (1978), *Are You Going to the Pictures?* (1987), *Selected Poems* (1989), and *Auto/Biographies* (1992). His poems explore themes of history and geography, obsessively embracing the detail of local events and the ironies of their juxtaposition; their form is characterized by complex syntax, a love of curious vocabulary, and elaboration. A compassionate tone and wry humour accompany what some critics have seen as excesses of detail. *A Way of Saying* (1965) is a collection of essays focusing on New Zealand poetry.

SNODGRASS, W(illiam) D(e Witt) (1926–), American poet, born in Wilkinsburg, Pennsylvania, educated at the University of Iowa, where he studied with Robert *Lowell in the *Iowa Writers' Workshop. Snodgrass achieved immense success with his first book of poems, *Heart's Needle* (1959; Pulitzer Prize), which established his reputation as a leading *Confessional poet. The poems in the sequence entitled 'Heart's Needle' were addressed to and are about his daughter Cynthia, the child he lost with the collapse of his first marriage. The controlled lyric gravity of these poems reflects the intensity of his loss, while America's engagement in the Korean War provides a broader metaphorical frame and a focus on contemporary political events; the 'cold war' of the military campaign is seen as a public echo of the desolation of his private landscape, pictured through the frozen wastes of his marriage. His other collections include *After Experience: Poems and Translations* (1968), *The Fuhrer Bunker: A Cycle of Poems in Progress* (1977), *Six Minnesinger Songs* (1983), and *Selected Poems 1957–1987* (1987). *In Radical Pursuit* (1975) is a collection of his essays on poetry.

Snopes Trilogy, The, a trilogy of novels by William *Faulkner, comprising *The Hamlet* (1940), *The Town* (1957), and *The Mansion* (1959), and dominated by the family which lends its name to the title. In his prefatory note to *The Mansion* Faulkner speaks of a 'work conceived and begun in 1925'; among the earliest manifestations of the trilogy are the short stories 'The Hound' (the Ernest Cotton of the story becomes Mink Snopes in the trilogy) from 1930 and 'Spotted Horses' (generally thought one of Faulkner's greatest comic achievements) from 1931, which was subsequently incorporated into *The Hamlet*. The trilogy is set in and around Frenchman's Bend and Jefferson (both in the fictitious Yoknapatawpha County in Mississippi) and follows the progress of the Snopes family who represent a new kind of South in which greed, profit, and a bogus respectability have replaced the older, more agrarian order.

SNOW, C(harles) P(ercy), Baron Snow of Leicester (1905–80), British novelist and essayist, born in

Leicester, educated at University College, Leicester, and Christ's College, Cambridge. In the early stages of his career he was committed to science. He held many important public and academic posts, and was created Baron in 1964. Most of Snow's novels form part of an eleven-volume sequence entitled *Strangers and Brothers*, narrated by Lewis Eliot, a character whose career follows fairly closely to that of the author, who rose from an obscure background. Power and the abuse of power, possessive love, and the bureaucracy of organized groups are central themes in much of his work. The first volume of the sequence, originally *Strangers and Brothers* (1940) and retitled *George Passant* (1973), is set mainly during Eliot's youth, and introduces the eccentric utopian character of the title. Others include *Time of Hope* (1949), describing Eliot's childhood and early life as a lawyer and his marriage to Sheila Knight; *The Masters* (1951), perhaps Snow's best-known novel, concerning a Cambridge college involved in a dispute over the election of a new Master; *The New Men* (1954), in which Eliot's brother, Martin, examines a group of scientists developing the atomic bomb; *Homecomings* (1956); *The Affair* (1960); *Corridors of Power* (1964), set in Parliament and which introduced the catchphrase for the workings of civil servants and parliamentarians; and *The Sleep of Reason* (1968), centring on the trial of the Moors murderers. Novels outside the sequence include *New Lives for Old* (1934) and *The Malcontents* (1972). The most notable, and controversial, of his non-fiction works is his 1959 Rede Lecture, *The *Two Cultures and the Scientific Revolution* (1959). He has written many other works including plays, often in collaboration with his wife Pamela Hansford *Johnson, and a life of Trollope (1975). His essays on the need for education in science were influential for a time.

SNYDER, Gary (Sherman) (1930–), American poet, born in San Francisco, educated at Reed College, Portland, and the University of California, Berkeley, from 1953 to 1956, the period of his association with various writers of the *Beat Generation; Jack *Kerouac's portrayal of him as 'Japhy Ryder' in *The Dharma Bums* (1958) makes clear the central importance of Zen Buddhism to Snyder, who spent eight years in Japan as a student of Zen between 1956 and 1968. In 1985 he became Professor of English at the University of California, Davis. The remarkable immediacy, clarity, and economy with which Snyder's poetry evokes landscapes and natural phenomena was fully apparent in his first major collection, *Riprap, and Cold Mountain Poems* (1965). While Snyder's disciplined free verse and acute use of detail relate to the modern tradition of *Imagism, his Buddhist belief in the sacredness of physical actuality forms an aesthetic principle underlying the precision of his work's perceptual notations. His subsequent collections include *Six Sections from Mountains and Rivers without End* (1965, enlarged edition 1970), offering extracts from a major sequence upon which he continues to work, *The Back Country* (1967), *Regarding Wave* (1970), and *Manzanita* (1972). The urgency of his concern for the natural environment and his fears for a human culture that 'alienates itself from the very ground of its own being' are forcefully conveyed in the verse and prose of *Turtle Island* (1974), which received a Pulitzer Prize. *Axe Handles* (1983) is rich in the celebratory treatments of work, family life, and other aspects of everyday experience which recur in his writing. *Left out in the Rain* (1986) contains over 200 hitherto uncollected poems written from 1947 onward. *No Nature: New and Selected Poems* appeared in 1993. Among Snyder's prose works, which sustain the ecological and spiritual themes of his verse, are *Earth House Hold* (1969), *The Old Ways* (1977), and *The Practice of the Wild* (1990); Scott McLean edited *The Real Work* (1980), a collection of Snyder's interviews and talks. See also SAN FRANCISCO RENAISSANCE.

Soap Opera, a form of popular television entertainment that has its origins in the 1930s' serialized radio dramas. It was initially aimed at women audiences who were targeted as potential buyers of the advertised products. Some scholars can see predecessors of the soap opera in eighteenth-century sentimental novels like *Pamela* (1740) by Samuel Richardson, which were also aimed at female audiences and employed similar narrative techniques. The soap opera came to fruition with the rise of post-war consumerism and developed, in terms of both content and form, into a distinct mode of popular entertainment. It was mainly concerned with 'women's themes' and always upheld traditional and conservative values. Formally, it relied on old and well-tested narrative devices like the never-ending story, slow pace, and constant repetition. As in the oral tradition of story-telling, most of the story-line progressed through narration rather than action. Its mode of production differed from that of other television programmes as well; usually filmed on a daily basis and transmitted almost immediately, speed, cost efficiency, and its potential to shape viewers' consuming habits were seen as its main guidelines. As a consequence, it lacked artistic merit and attracted very little serious criticism.

The situation has changed since the late 1970s. With the rise of cultural studies and feminism, the study of soap operas as a form of mass communication becomes more prevalent. The soap operas themselves seem to have given rise to many and varied forms of television entertainment programmes. Traditionally, soaps were broadcast during the day and aimed at women's audiences; during the 1970s and particularly the 1980s, new forms of soaps appeared which were no longer aimed solely at women. Instead of daytime, they made up what came to be called prime-time viewing (early evening). Soap operas like *Dynasty* or *Dallas* were concerned with power and money, but still remained within the traditional context of the family saga. At the same time, daytime soaps continued to flourish. Soap operas like *The*

Guiding Light (USA) have managed to survive three generations of the genre; originally broadcast on radio in 1937, it was the only serialized radio drama to transfer successfully to television (in 1952). The various off-shoots of the soap opera all partake in the deep-bred traditionalism and conservatism that is characteristic of the genre. However, this, too, has been contested lately. Programmes like the BBC's *East Enders* seem to share qualities of both television drama and soap opera: while applying some of the narrative devices of the soap opera, it lacks its conservative and consolidating content. Indeed, programmes like *East Enders* or the Australian *A Country Practice* have come to be known as quality soaps. More recently, there have been attempts to upgrade soap operas artistically; David Lynch's *Twin Peaks* (1990) was a post-modern reworking of the 1950s and 1960s style soaps (particularly *Peyton Place*, 1964–9, USA), in a style that consciously celebrates the soap opera as an artistic mode in its own right.

Socialist Realism, a term used to describe the official artistic doctrine adopted at the Congress of Soviet Writers in 1934, and approved by Stalin, Gorky, Bukharin, and Zhdanov. It required that the creative artist should serve the Revolution by presenting positive images of socialist possibility; it denigrated the bourgeois artist and all forms of experimentalism and formalism as degenerate, subjective, and pessimistic. (The works of *Joyce were singled out for particular condemnation.) The doctrine presented problems for philosophical Marxist critics like Lukács, who opted for the study of nineteenth-century realism and kept silent about most of his contemporaries. After the hard Stalinist period the use of the term was modified to cover the works of such artistic innovators as Brecht and Mayakovsky; but it is still seen in the Western world as a denial of creativity and freedom of expression, above the freedom to represent darkness or despair. 'Social realism' is a distinct term, used loosely to describe a purportedly objective, yet socially aware and detailed representation of reality.

SOFOLA, 'Zulu (Nwazulu) (1938–), Nigerian dramatist, born in Issele-Uke, Nigeria, educated at Virginia Union University and the Catholic University of America, Washington DC, where she gained her MA with a thesis on Igbo ritual. She returned to Nigeria in 1966 and taught at the University of Ibadan before becoming Head of the Department of Theatre Arts at the University of Ilorin. She has also worked as a producer of plays for stage and television. Among the works which established her reputation as Nigeria's most notable woman playwright are *Wedlock of the Gods* (1970), *King Emene* (1974), *The Sweet Trap* (1977), *Old Wines Are Tasty* (1981), and *Song of a Maiden* (1991). Her plays range from farce to high tragedy and combine elements of traditional African ritual with devices from the Western dramatic tradition. Local dialects and standardized English co-exist to ironic effect in her satirically incisive social comedies.

SOMERVILLE and ROSS, joint pseudonym of Anglo-Irish novelists Edith Oenone SOMERVILLE (1858–1949), born in Corfu and brought up at Castletownshend, Co. Cork, and Violet Florence MARTIN (1862–1915), born at Ross House, Co. Galway. They collaborated on around thirty books, most of which were set in Ireland; which of them held the pen was 'wholly fortuitious', Edith later wrote. Their first novel, *An Irish Cousin* (1889), was followed by many others, including *Naboth's Vineyard* (1891) and *The Real Charlotte* (1894), about the rivalry between Francie Fitzpatrick, a beautiful Dublin girl, and the malevolent Charlotte Mullen, set against a background of Ireland's Great Houses. *Some Experiences of an Irish RM* (1899), a collection of stories in which the Anglo-Irish 'resident magistrate', Major Yeates, confronts the eccentricities of rural Irish life and indulges his passion for hunting, achieved widespread popularity. It was followed by a sequel, *Further Experiences of an Irish RM* (1908) and by a third volume of stories, *In Mr Knox's Country* (1915). Other collections of stories and occasional pieces include *All on the Irish Shore* (1903) and *Some Irish Yesterdays* (1906). After Violet's death, Edith commemorated their friendship in *Irish Memories* (1917) and continued to publish novels under their joint name, including *Mount Music* (1919), *An Enthusiast* (1921), and *The Big House at Inver* (1925).

SONE, Monica, see ASIAN-AMERICAN LITERATURE.

SONG, Cathy (1955–), Hawaiian poet, born in Honolulu, Hawaii; she grew up in the small sugar town of Wahaiwa, and was educated at the University of Hawaii, Wellesley College, and Boston University. She has taught creative writing in many institutions. Her first book, *Picture Bride* (1983), was chosen for the Yale Younger Poets Prize by the poet Richard *Hugo. Two later collections, *Frameless Windows, Squares of Light* (1988) and *School Figures* (1994), extend the range of her finely observed compositions which aspire to the condition of the visual aesthetics of the painters she celebrates, the Japanese printmaker Kitagawa Utamaro and the American painter Georgia O'Keeffe. She has also co-edited a collection of fiction and poetry by women from Hawaii, *Sister Stew* (1991). Widely anthologized, her poems draw upon Korean and Japanese Hawaiian cultural sources and address multicultural, familial, and highly personal themes. At their best they are sensuously drawn, marked by a respect for tradition and unforced imagery. See ASIAN-AMERICAN LITERATURE.

Songlines, see CHATWIN, BRUCE.

Song of Solomon, a novel by Toni *Morrison, published in 1977. One of the author's most impressive novels, *Song of Solomon* explores Milkman Dead's return to both his American and African roots in a journey from his Northern middle-class city home to the Southern rural community where his family began. In its account of Milkman Dead's fantastic genealogy the novel contains elements of *magic realism and shows the influence of contemporary

South and Central American authors such as Isabel Allende, Alejo Carpentier, and Carlos Fuentes. Through Morrison's use of African-American folk-tales depicting escaping slaves, she weaves a parable of transcendence through self-discovery.

Sons and Lovers, a novel by D. H. *Lawrence, published in 1913. Freely based upon events in his own life, Lawrence's third novel *Sons and Lovers* was his first clear success. It adapts the popular nineteenth-century form of the *Bildungsroman* to recount the early life of Paul Morel. The novel is set in a small Nottinghamshire mining community where Paul's mother's social and cultural aspirations separate her from her hard-drinking husband. The rift within the family, the tragic death of the eldest son William, and Paul's growing alienation from his father and community occupy the first part of the book. The second part is largely concerned with Paul's early work experiences in a Nottingham factory, and the legacy of his unusually close relations with his mother as seen in two doomed love affairs: the first with a girl of his own age, Miriam Leivers, and the second with an older, married feminist, Clara Dawes. The novel ends with the death of Paul's mother and the collapse of his relationship with Clara, who returns to her estranged husband. Paul's own situation at the close is left carefully uncertain. Although the novel is in part autobiographical, it is also very much a work of its period and is often compared to Joyce's *A *Portrait of the Artist as a Young Man* published only a year later. Both novels use the budding artist's experience (Paul is a talented painter) as a way of exploring the strains and limits of provincial communities and, as in many works of the period, the dynamics of the family are a particular object for scrutiny. Lawrence himself was keen that the novel be understood in general terms. He changed its original title—'Paul Morel'—to the more wide-ranging *Sons and Lovers*, and, as has often been noted, Paul's relations with his mother correspond closely to those described by Freud in his exactly contemporary work on the 'Oedipus Complex'. Lawrence knew something of Freud's work through his German wife, Frieda. In literary terms, *Sons and Lovers* is in many respects stylistically innovatory. It emphasizes moments of sharp personal conflict and intense psychological process which is conveyed in the charged, symbolic prose characteristic of Lawrence's best work.

SONTAG, Susan (1933–), American novelist, critic, and film-maker, born in New York City, educated at the Universities of California, Chicago, and Harvard. She grew up in Tucson, Arizona, and Los Angeles, California. Though Sontag is best known for her prolific and influential cultural criticism, she sees herself primarily as a writer of fiction. Her first novel, *The Benefactor* (1963), is an ambitious work in which a male, European narrator, Hippolyte, examines, in elegantly austere prose, his experiences and sensibilities, and often outrageous dreams. The novel's disquisitions on absurdity and aesthetics caused critics to discern the influence of Kafka, *Beckett, Sartre, and Camus, but Sontag has recast her European borrowings in a distinctive, contemporary American mould; this is evident in her next novel, *Death Kit* (1967), which again focuses on a male figure, the American Diddy, and in its bold and occasionally violent style bears a comparable relationship to the *nouveau roman*. Style was of primary importance to Sontag in the first decades of her fame; her essays on literature, cinema, photography, and other art forms are collected in several volumes, including *Against Interpretation* (1966), *Styles of Radical Will* (1969), and *Under the Sign of Saturn* (1980). But, since the mid-1970s, her writings indicate a slight shift in position; she has stated that she now realizes the importance of a historical perspective. Her moral preoccupations are evident in her book-length essays: 'On Photography' (1977), 'Illness as Metaphor' (1978), inspired by her own encounter with cancer, and 'Aids as Metaphor' (1989). Sontag's reputation as a writer of fiction was built largely on her innovative, quirky stories, collected in *I, etcetera* (1977). However, her later novel *The Volcano Lover* (1992) signalled a new phase in her career. Ostensibly a historical romance inspired by the lives of William (the volcano lover of the title) and Emma Hamilton, this ambitious polyphonic work—told in first-, second-, and third-person voices by a variety of narrators both central and peripheral—conflates Sontag's thoughts on aesthetics and history, revolution and feminism, destiny and passion with intelligence, wit, and, above all, style.

Sophie's Choice, see STYRON, WILLIAM.

SORLEY, Charles Hamilton (1895–1915), Scottish poet, born in Aberdeen, where his father was Professor of Moral Philosophy, educated at Marlborough College. He was noted for the confidence and critical maturity of his addresses to the college's literary society; its magazine, the *Malburian*, published twelve of his poems in 1913. His experiences of the Wiltshire Downs, where he was fond of running, inform much of his work, most notably the celebrated 'Song of the Ungirt Runners'. In 1914 he went to Germany and spent a term at the University of Jena. Briefly held under arrest as a spy after the outbreak of the war, upon returning to England he applied for a commission. The poetry he wrote during training anticipates active service with a fatalistic pantheism that is clearest in the unsettlingly spirited 'All the hills and vales along', with its refrain of 'So be merry, so be dead'. He was killed at the Battle of Loos in October 1915. His brief exposure to the realities of the Western Front gave rise to a number of poems, including 'When you see millions of the mouthless dead' and 'Such, such is Death: no triumph: no defeat', which form emphatically bitter repudiations of *Brooke's *1914* sequence. Sorley's *Marlborough and Other Poems* appeared in 1916. Despite the book's success and the claims made for his work by *Graves, *Bridges, and *Blunden, Sorley received little attention for several decades; T. B. Swann's biography *The Ungirt Runner* was published in 1965, since when there have been several editions of his writings, principally *Collected Poems* (1985) and *Collected Letters* (1989), both edited by Jean Moorcroft Wilson.

SORRENTINO, Gilbert (1929–), American novelist and poet, born in Brooklyn, educated at Brooklyn College. Sorrentino has lived in New York City all his life and his prose and poetry are saturated with the idioms and rhythms of urban life. His first volume of poetry, *The Darkness Surrounds Us* (1960), which shows the influence of *Black Mountain poets, was followed by a second volume, *Black and White* (1964). Sorrentino's first novel, *The Sky Changes* (1966), largely autobiographical in nature, marks the beginning of his increasing preoccupation with prose fiction. *Steelwork* (1970), a series of 'snapshots' of Brooklyn life between 1935 and 1951, reveals subtle shifts in theme and mood. *Imaginative Qualities of Actual Things* (1971) explores the literary and artistic world of New York in the late 1930s and 1940s, orchestrated through the voices of eight characters. *Splendide-Hotel* (1973) follows the essentially episodic structure of his earlier fiction in employing twenty-six sections (titled with the letters of the alphabet) which, collectively, form a kind of homage to the French poet Rimbaud but seen through the language and idiom of William Carlos *Williams. *White Sail* (1977) marks a return to a more lyrical poetic voice. His novel *Mulligan Stew* (1979), with its philosophical play on the ontology both of art and of characters (some of whom are 'borrowed' from other authors), is regarded as one of the most important works of American fictional *post-modernism. *Selected Poems, 1958–1980* appeared in 1981, and *Something Said: Essays* in 1984. Later works include *Under the Shadow* (1991), *Aberration of Starlight* (1993), and *Red the Fiend* (1995).

SOTO, Gary (1952–), Chicano poet and prose writer, born in Fresno, California, educated at California State University, Fresno, and the University of California, Irvine. During his childhood he worked as a migrant farm labourer. Soto's social concerns and poetic style have led to comparisons with Philip *Levine, his former teacher at Fresno, who also deals with the plight of the American worker. Others have noted that Soto's writing transcends social commentary and represents a shift within Chicano literature towards a more personal and less political agenda. Soto has insisted that although he addresses Mexican themes in his earlier poetry and in the collection of prose memoirs *Living up the Street: Narrative Recollections* (1985), his writing also focuses on the suffering that poverty engenders. Many of his poems, such as those in his second volume of poems, *The Tale of Sunlight* (1978), celebrate a childlike and consolatory imagination. Soto's later work expands to include issues of friendship, love, and parenthood. In the 1990s he produced several short works of fiction centring on youthful protagonists confronting typical adolescent dilemmas. *New and Selected Poems* appeared in 1995. He became a professor of Chicano studies and English at the University of California, Berkeley. See LATINO / LATINA LITERATURE IN ENGLISH.

Sot-Weed Factor, The, a novel by John *Barth, published in 1960. The novel, in excess of 800 pages, tells the story of Ebenezer Cooke, a poet, who is made poet laureate of Maryland in the New World and who is commissioned to write a commemorative epic poem for the state, *The Marylandiad*. His journey to the New World and his adventures there, often political and sexual, provide the loose, picaresque framework on which the novel is constructed. The novel is particularly memorable for its style, a richly inventive and exuberant pastiche of late seventeenth-century English prose, and like many of Barth's novels it has been appropriated for the critical language of fictional *post-modernism for its use of fabulation and its interrogation of the very nature of fictional representation. See *Barth* (1970) by Gerhard Joseph.

Sound and the Fury, The, a novel by William *Faulkner, published in 1929. Many critics consider it Faulkner's finest novel and it is generally thought to be among the greatest works of twentieth-century American literature. The story of the decaying Compson family in the early years of the twentieth century is told in the interior monologues of three Compson brothers, Benjy, Quentin, and Jason; only the fourth section of the novel adopts an authorial point of view, though even here much of what is reported is seen through the black servant, Dilsey, who, in effect, represents compassion, order, and moral integrity. The decline of the Compsons is the decline of a once great Mississippi plantation family, and while Faulkner's delineation of the social background is not detailed the novel is regarded as one of his most profound commentaries on the conflict between traditional values and a modern society. The structure of recollected memories, particularly those of Benjy, the idiot son, and Quentin, who commits suicide while at Harvard University, a structure which makes up the body of the novel, is deliberately fragmented and achronological, a consequence of the combined influences of Joseph *Conrad and James *Joyce, and the placing of 'present' events around the Easter weekend of 1928 has tempted some critics to see Faulkner's novel as an elaborate Christian allegory. Much of the drama concerns the character of the brothers' sister Caddy, a 'fallen' woman, though it is one of the striking aspects of the novel that she is presented only through the observations and recollections of her immediate family. *The Sound and the Fury* is also seen as Faulkner's testimony to the transforming and ennobling power of art and its concluding images, at once naturalistic and aesthetic, offer some respite from the degeneration and disorder the novel so powerfully enacts. The title is taken from Macbeth's famous soliloquy ('She should have died hereafter') in Act 5 of Shakespeare's play. The novel has been the subject of a great deal of critical discussion; *The Most Splendid Failure: Faulkner's 'The Sound and the Fury'* (1976), by André Bleikasten, is an invaluable full-length study. See also STREAM OF CONSCIOUSNESS.

Sour Sweet, see MO, TIMOTHY.

SOUSTER, (Holmes) Raymond (1921–), Canadian poet, born in Toronto, where he was educated at the Humberside Collegiate Institute; he worked in a Toronto bank from 1939 until his retirement in 1984. While serving in Nova Scotia with the Royal Canadian Air Force during the Second World War, he began the magazine *Direction* (1943–6), which was succeeded by *Contact* (1952–4) and *Combustion* (1957–60). *Shake Hands with the Hangman: Poems 1940–1952* (1953) indicates his early tendency towards the lyrical and thematic conventions of Romanticism. His subsequent writing reflects his admiration for the work of William Carlos *Williams in its conversational free-verse forms and rich use of concrete imagery drawn from his urban surroundings in Toronto. Although many of his poems are of substantial length and thematic range, he is best known for the many witty and compassionate shorter works which cumulatively form a densely textured treatment of the city's social character. His numerous collections include *Crepe-Hanger's Carnival* (1958), *Ten Elephants on Yonge Street* (1965), *Change-Up* (1974), *Jubilee of Death: The Raid on Dieppe* (1984), *Asking for More* (1988), and *Running Out the Clock* (1991). *Collected Poems 1940–1989* appeared in six volumes between 1980 and 1989. *The Winter of the Time* (as 'Raymond Holmes', 1949) and *On Target* (as 'John Holmes', 1973) are novels drawing on his wartime experiences.

SOUTAR, William (1898–1943), Scottish poet, born in Perth, educated at Perth Academy and the University of Edinburgh. The spinal disease he contracted on naval service during the First World War left him bedridden from 1930 onwards. Although he had published a collection of verse entitled *Gleanings of an Undergraduate* (1923) in his final year at University, it was not until his illness disabled him that he began his sustained work as a poet in English and Scots. *Conflict* (1931), *The Solitary Way* (1934), and the posthumous *The Expectant Silence* (1944) are among his collections of poetry in English, which is characterized by its concentrated fusions of descriptive precision, contemplative intelligence, and understated wit. An associate of *MacDiarmid's, whom he affectionately satirized in 'The Thistle Looks at a Drunk Man', he was a partisan of the revival of poetry in Scots, producing rhythmically compelling verse notable for its imaginative range. *Seeds in the Wind* (1933) contains many of his 'bairnrhymes', Scots children's poems of great simplicity and vigour. His other volumes include *Poems in Scots* (1935) and *Riddles in Scots* (1937). *Collected Poems* with an introduction by MacDiarmid was published in 1948. His extensive prose journals are represented by *Diaries of a Dying Man* (1954), edited by A. Scott, whose *Still Life* (1958) is a biography of Soutar.

Southerly, the journal of the Sydney affiliation of the English Association, first published in 1939, edited by R. G. Howarth. For the first five years the journal covered English and American literature. Australian publishers Angus and Robertson, who became involved in 1944, and its second editor, Kenneth *Slessor, turned *Southerly* into 'A Review of Australian Literature'. Distinguishing itself from what was seen as the 'sociological' or 'semi-literary' commentary of **Meanjin*, the journal required of its contributors impartial criticism of work perceived as standing in its own right, similar to the *New Criticism in the USA. *Southerly* has excluded reviews of other arts and European literature; its commitment to Australian literature remains complete.

SOUTHERN, R(ichard) W(illiam) (1912–), British medieval historian, born in Newcastle-upon-Tyne, educated at Balliol College, Oxford, where he became a fellow and tutor in 1937. He was Chichele Professor at All Souls College from 1961 to 1969, when he was elected President of St John's College. *The Making of the Middle Ages* (1953), his first major work, has been widely translated and remains an essential text on the period. Southern's subsequent publications, noted for their fluently accessible mastery of complex bodies of knowledge, include *Western Views of Islam in the Middle Ages* (1962), *Western Society and the Church in the Middle Ages* (1970), and *Robert Grosseteste* (1986), a study of its subject's enormous contributions to science and philosophy in the thirteenth century. *St Anselm: A Portrait in a Landscape* (1990) supersedes *St Anselm and His Biographer* (1963), Southern's previous work on the saint and his follower Eadmer, author of *Vita Anselmi*.

South Riding, see HOLTBY, WINIFRED.

South Wind, Norman *Douglas's most widely read work and sole success as a novelist, published in 1917. Nepenthe, the island setting, is a fictional equivalent to Capri, though, in accordance with Douglas's remark that 'I have taken what liberties I pleased with the place', much natural detail is taken from other Mediterranean locations he knew well. The narrative concerns twelve days spent on the island by Thomas Heard, a bishop returning to England from his diocese in Africa. During this time his moral rigour yields to various influences, chiefly the mysterious action of the *sirocco*, the south wind of the title, and his talks with the local residents; the amoral Mr Keith is the principal channel for the exposition of the philosophical hedonism which pervades much of Douglas's writing. Essentially a novel of conversation, its characters' wittily eloquent digressions provide vehicles for Douglas's opinions on a remarkable variety of topics. The candour with which sex is discussed made the book seem scandalous to many at the time of publication. It was staged in London in 1923 in an adaptation by Isabel C. Tippett.

SOYINKA, (Olu) Wole (Akinwale) (1934–), Nigerian dramatist, poet, and novelist, born in Abeokuta, educated at the universities of Ibadan and Leeds. His first play, *The Swamp-Dwellers* (1958), was followed by the most successful of his early plays, *The Lion and*

Jewel (1959), a sardonic comedy dramatizing the clash between Lakunle, a young, priggish schoolteacher of Westernized disposition, and Baroka, an ageing but physically agile and politically wily traditional chief, in their courtship of Sidi, the belle of the village. Mime and dance, inspired by traditional Yoruba theatre, pervade the play in performance. *A Dance of the Forests* (1960), produced in Lagos as part of the Nigerian independence celebrations, is an extravaganza of folk myth and African history. *The Trials of Brother Jero* (1960) introduced the conman Jero, one of Soyinka's finest comic creations; in *Jero's Metamorphosis* (1974) he becomes more sinister than comic, in line with the dramatist's bleak view of Nigerian society under military rule. Plays targeted against African dictators include *Kongi's Harvest* (1965) and *A Play of Giants* (1984). Chicanery, corruption, and deception at various levels of society were satirized in *Opera Wonyosi* (1977), adapted from Brecht's *The Three-Penny Opera* (1928). Most of his dramatic works are published in *Collected Plays* (2 volumes, 1973, 1974) and *Six Plays* (1984). In *The Man Died: Prison Notes* (1972) Soyinka gives an impassioned account of his period in solitary detention for allegedly pro-Biafran activities during the Nigerian Civil War (1967–70). His bitterly anti-war satire *Madmen and Specialists* (1970), the poems in *A Shuttle in the Crypt* (1971), and his second novel, *Season of Anomy* (1973), are all informed by Soyinka's reaction to the conflict. Yoruba mythology and religious ritual are powerful undercurrents of poetic symbolism in his drama, particularly in *The Road* (1965) and *Death and the King's Horseman* (1975), a tragedy which focuses on Elesin, the 'king's horseman': shortly after the death of his master, the King of Oye, he is prevented from committing ritual suicide by the colonial District Officer, a disastrous humiliation for both himself and his society. The situation is ultimately redeemed by the courageous self-sacrifice of his son. The play fuses both ancient Greek and Yoruba concepts of tragedy, which Soyinka discussed in *Myth, Literature and the African World* (1976), the fullest statement of his aesthetics. More recent plays include *From Zia With Love; and A Scourge of Hyacinths* (1992) and *The Beatification of Area Boy* (1995). Critical comments are collected in *Art, Dialogue and Outrage: Essays on Literature and Culture* (1988). His use of traditional symbols, transformed by a modernist sensibility, is particularly evident in his two novels, *The Interpreters* (1965) and *Season of Anomy* (1973), his densely allusive poetry, and his adaptation of *The Bacchae of Euripides* (1973). His books of poetry include *Idanre and Other Poems* (1967), *Ogun Abibiman* (1976), and *Mandela's Earth* (1989). *Ake* (1981) is about his childhood, and *Isara: A Voyage Around Essay* (1989) an affectionate portrait of his father. An autobiographical work is *Ibadan: The Penkelemes Years: A Memoir, 1946–1965* (1994). Soyinka was awarded the Nobel Prize for Literature in 1986.

Space Opera, a *science fiction term applied to novels and tales usually set in interstellar space. The classic space opera has its roots in the nineteenth-century dime novel and in other popular forms of romance which emphasized extravagant action, an imperial condescension to 'lesser' races, and the eventual triumph of good over evil. Although space operas were written in Europe at the turn of the century, from 1925 the genre was developed by American science fiction writers into a dominant form of popular literature. Authors like Edgar Rice *Burroughs, Ray Cummings, Edmond Hamilton, Murray Leinster, and, notably, E. E. *Smith wrote innumerable tales set in the future and in armed spaceships; beyond the frontiers of human space lay the unknown, populated by aliens for whom surrender was the only choice. As science fiction matured, with Olaf *Stapledon's metaphysical space operas, the form began to reflect a more complex vision of the universe. The galactic empires of Isaac *Asimov, from the 1940s, helped rationalize the form; and later writers, like James *Blish, Frank *Herbert, and Gene *Wolfe, augmented it with complex ironies. Outside the genre, the term 'space opera' is often used pejoratively to designate science fiction as a whole.

'Spanish Farm Trilogy', see MOTTRAM, R. H.

SPARK, Muriel (1918–), British author, born in Edinburgh; her father was Jewish and born in Scotland, her mother was English and Anglican. Spark was educated at James Gillespie's School for Girls in Edinburgh, on which her novel *The *Prime of Miss Jean Brodie* was based, and which she claimed was 'more progressive than I realised' (*Scotland on Sunday*, 16 Sept. 1990). In 1937 she married Oswald Spark and they moved to Africa where their son, Robin, was born. The marriage soon failed but Spark did not return to Britain until 1944 when she began working for the Foreign Office. In 1947 she became secretary of the Poetry Society and edited its **Poetry Review*, but two years later she was sacked. At this time she saw herself as a poet, and published her first collection, *The Fanfarlo and Other Verse*, in 1952. Meanwhile, in 1951, she won the *Observer* short story competition and was asked to write a novel. She was reluctant at first, finding the novel a lesser art. In 1954 she became a Roman Catholic which, she claimed, enabled her to speak with her own voice, and many of her works deal, obliquely or directly, with metaphysical and moral questions. In her first novel, *The Comforters* (1957), her protagonist, Caroline Rose, a Catholic convert, reflects on the 'exorbitant' and 'outrageous' demands Christianity makes on its adherents. Other early novels, such as the blackly comic *Memento Mori* (1959) and the bizarre morality tale *The Ballad of Peckham Rye* (1960), reflect on the nature of death and the existence of evil with characteristic sang-froid. *The Prime of Miss Jean Brodie* (1961) reflects on the corrosive power of guilt, told from the point of view of a nun looking back on her childhood involvement with the woman whose influence has shaped her life. In 1962 Spark became what she describes as 'an international exile'; she first moved to New York, and in 1966 she settled in Italy where several of her novels have been set. Her other novels include *The Girls of Slender Means* (1963), a tragi-comedy set in a Kensington hostel in 1945, which deals with themes of good and evil later to recur in a novel with a similar setting, *A Far Cry from Kensington* (1988); *The *Mandelbaum Gate* (1965), set in Jerusalem; *The Public Image* (1968), about a beautiful but shallow actress living in Rome; *The Driver's Seat* (1970), in which a woman travels to Naples to keep an appointment with death; *The Abbess of Crewe* (1974), a satirical fantasy about the political machinations of a power-mad ecclesiastic, written in the aftermath of the Watergate affair; *The Take-Over* (1976), also set in Italy; *Loitering with Intent* (1981), narrated by a young writer whose involvement with an 'Autobiographical Association' provides material for her first novel; *Symposium* (1990) deals with the complex psychological and sexual relationships of a group of wealthy socialites, first encountered at an Islington dinner party. Apart from *The Mandelbaum Gate* her novels are short, and despite the seriousness of many of their themes they are witty, satirical, eccentric, and often macabre. Spark's fascination with the demonic and with the perverse aspects of human behaviour manifests itself in many of her books. Her distinctive elegant style, her use of the device of narrative omniscience, and the element of fable or parable often introduced into her fictions has influenced a whole generation of post-war writers. As well as novels, several of which have been dramatized and filmed, and poems (*Collected Poems 1*, 1967), she has also published short stories (*Collected Stories 1*, 1967 and 1994), plays for the radio, juvenilia, and critical works, including *Child of Light: A Reassessment of Mary Shelley* (1951), *Emily Brontë: Her Life and Work* (1953, with Derek Stanford), and *John Masefield* (1953, revised 1992). She has edited *A Tribute to Wordsworth* (1950, with Derek Stanford), *A Selection of Poems* (1952) by Emily Brontë, *My Best Mary: The Letters of Mary Shelley* (1953, with Derek Stanford), *The Brontë Letters* (1954), and *Letters of John Henry Newman* (1957); *The Essence of the Brontës: A Compilation with Essays* (1993) brings together Spark's earlier work on the Brontës. In 1992 she published *Curriculum Vitae—Autobiography*. Among several critical studies are those by Alan Bold (1986) and Norman Page (1990). See also Ruth Whittaker's *The Faith and Fictions of Muriel Spark* (1982).

Spectator, The, a weekly review of politics, current affairs, and the arts begun in 1828 by Robert Stephen Rintoul, whose choice of title invoked the illustrious example of the early eighteenth-century periodical. Following Rintoul's retirement in 1858, a succession of editors maintained the moderate radicalism of the journal, regarded by William Gladstone as 'one of the few papers which are written in the fear and love of God'. Although current affairs were its principal concern in the early 1900s, much space was devoted to book reviews and Katharine *Tynan, Henry *Newbolt, Siegfried *Sassoon, and Ivor *Gurney were among the authors of the poems featured every week. From 1922 to 1938 a literary supplement was produced; its reviewers included Richard *Aldington, V. S. *Pritchett, Stephen *Spender, and *Michael Roberts. Edith *Sitwell, Patrick *Kavanagh, William *Plomer, Edwin *Muir, and Edmund *Blunden were among the poets whose work appeared in its pages in the 1920s and 1930s. Louis *MacNeice and Graham *Greene respectively wrote regular reviews of the theatre and cinema in the earlier years of J. Wilson Harris's editorship from 1932 to 1954, when Sir Ian Gilmour became owner and editor. Since then the *Spectator* has been among the liveliest journals of political commentary, Bernard Levin and Auberon *Waugh having contributed much to its incisive and sometimes irreverent tone.

SPENCER, Elizabeth (1921–), American short-story writer and novelist, born in Carrollton, Mississippi, educated at Vanderbilt University. Her early novels, *Fire in the Morning* (1948) and *This Crooked Way* (1952), explored Southern themes from perspectives ignored by her contemporaries; *The Voice at the Back Door* (1956), detailing an unscrupulous lawyer's conflict with a rough but highly principled athlete, was an honest examination of the racial question. Spencer's move to Italy introduced a new landscape to her fiction. The highly successful novella *The Light in the Piazza* (1960) was the first of her fictions to explore the sensibilities of expatriates, usually women, in search of themselves in a Europe always fascinating but often indifferent to them, and elicited comparisons with the work of Henry *James. *Knights and Dragons* (1965), the interior monologue of a divorcee, juxtaposes images of Rome with lyrical meditations on the nature of love and loss. Her other novels include *The Snare* (1972), set in New Orleans, and the unusually compelling *The Salt Line* (1984), which returns to the Mississippi locations of her early fictions. Spencer's short stories also display her fascination with place, ranging from the American South and Europe to Canada; collections include *The Stories of Elizabeth Spencer* (1981) and *Jack of Diamonds* (1988).

SPENDER, Dale (1943–), Australian feminist critic and literary theorist, born in Newcastle, New South Wales, educated at the universities of Sydney, New England, and London. Spender's importance was established with *Man Made Language* (1980), in which she argued that male cultural dominance extended to a patriarchal bias inherent in spoken and written communication. Among her subsequent works are *Invisible Women: The Schooling Scandal* (1982), a study of the limitations in women's educational opportunities; *There's Always Been a Women's Movement This Century* (1983), a social and historical survey based on interviews with leading feminists; *Mothers of the Novel* (1986), a critical and biographical view of 100 women authors preceding Jane Austen; and *Writing a New World* (1988), on Australian women writers since the eighteenth century. *The Diary of Elizabeth Pepys* (1991), of which Spender is ostensibly the editor, entertainingly extends her concern with the centrality of women to social and literary history into the realm of fiction. The numerous publications she has edited include *Men's Studies Modified* (1981) and *An Anthology of British Women Writers* (with Janet Todd, 1989).

SPENDER, Sir Stephen (Harold) (1909–95), British poet and critic, born in London, educated at University College, Oxford. As a student he began his lasting friendship with W. H. *Auden, whose poems were first collected in an edition of thirty copies hand-printed by Spender in 1928. While at Oxford he also produced a pamphlet of his own poems entitled *Nine Experiments* (1928), which was followed in 1930 by *Twenty Poems*. After graduating in 1929, he travelled in Germany with Christopher *Isherwood and drafted his novel *The Temple*; originally rejected by his publisher as pornographic, the book did not appear until 1988, having been reworked to form a substantially autobiographical evocation of the Weimar Republic at the time of Hitler's ascendancy. The inclusion of his poetry in Michael Roberts's *New Signatures* (1932) and *New Country* (1933) gained him notice as a member of the group of politically conscious poets which also included Auden, Louis *MacNeice, and C. *Day Lewis; Spender's poem 'The Pylons', typifying the group's tendency to employ emphatically contemporary imagery, suggested the term '*Pylon Poets'. With Auden, Isherwood, and MacNeice, he was associated with the *Group Theatre, which produced his play *Trial of a Judge* (1938). *Poems* (1933) contains much of his best-known verse, which frequently displays his ability to fuse documentary realism with a resonantly idealistic tone of lyrical exaltation. His political preoccupations are apparent in the critical study *The Destructive Element* (1935), which acclaims the writings of Auden and Edward *Upward for their respective exemplification of the socio-political mode in poetry and prose fiction. He was a propagandist for the Republicans during the Spanish Civil War, an interlude which resulted in numerous memorable poems collected in *The Still Centre* (1939). A member of the Communist Party in 1936 and 1937, he argued that communism was an authentic extension of the liberal tradition in *Forward from Liberalism* (1937), one of the *Left Book Club's most noteworthy publications. From 1939 to 1941 he assisted Cyril Connolly in the editorship of **Horizon*. He was a member of the National Fire Service in London between 1941 and 1944; his experiences of the bombings inform poems in *Ruins and Visions* (1942), in which the increasingly meditative and personal nature of his verse becomes apparent. His disengagement from doctrinaire socialism is already discernible in *Life and the Poet*, a critical work of 1942, and is clearly recorded in the autobiographical *World within World* (1951), a central document in the intellectual history of the 1930s. The critical study *The Creative Element* (1953) establishes the position of philosophically affirmative humanism which forms the basis of all his later work. He was co-editor of **Encounter* from 1953 to 1966 and a founder of **Index on Censorship* in 1972. In 1970 he became Professor of English at University College, London. His post-war collections of poetry include *Poems of Dedication* (1947), *The Edge of Being* (1949), and *Sirmione Peninsula* (1954). His subsequent output as a poet is largely represented by additions to successive collected editions of his work, among them *Collected Poems 1928–1985* (1985). The volume contains much new verse marked by a refreshing directness of tone and shrewdly understated accomplishment. A subsequent volume of poems, *Dolphins*, appeared in 1994. Among Spender's other publications, which include books on art, travel, short stories, and numerous translations, chiefly of German works, are *Love–Hate Relations: A Study of Anglo-American Sensibilities* (1974) and the personal and cultural recollections of *The Thirties and After* (1978); his *Journals, 1939–1983* appeared in 1985. He was knighted in 1983.

SPICER, Jack (1925–65), American poet, born in Los Angeles, educated at the University of California, Berkeley. Spicer lived most of his life in California, combining poetry with the professional study of linguistics. Spicer and Robert *Duncan were equally energetic in their responses to the writings of others; despite their shared interest in the occult, however, there were many differences between them, particularly regarding Spicer's increasingly Manichaean view of the world. The completion of *After Lorca* in 1957 was the major turning point in his development as a poet, serving as it did to commit Spicer entirely to the composition of serial poems, a decision honoured by Robin Blaser in his posthumous edition of *The Collected Books of Jack Spicer* (1975), a volume which also included such notable work as *Billy the Kid* (1959), *The Heads of the Town up to the Aether* (1962), *The Holy Grail* (1964), *Language* (1965), and *Book of Magazine Verse* (1966). As the Vancouver lectures in 1961 demonstrate, *After Lorca* also persuaded Spicer that the true poem had utterly mysterious origins, which he sometimes likened to messages from outer space, inevitably scrambled by the imperfections implicit in the language we use to translate them. The more esoteric resonances of this belief were offset by Spicer's use of American vernacular language. Spicer's witty, tough-minded, and surreal poetry frequently rewrites mythology in the light of his own conception of the doom of homosexual love, an approach which gives particular poignancy to his version of *Billy the Kid*. Spicer's alcoholism ensured an early death, but his work continues to exert a central influence on the development of American poetry. See also SAN FRANCISCO RENAISSANCE.

SPINRAD, Norman (Richard) (1940–), American *science fiction writer, born in New York City, educated at City University, New York. He is best known for two novels both of which proved controversial within the genre for their sexual outspokenness and sharp satirical view of contemporary events, not usually characteristic in the field of science fiction. The first novel, *Bug Jack Barron* (1969), presciently argued that media heroes were well-placed to become President; the second, *The Iron Dream* (1972), is an alternative history in which Adolf Hitler becomes a popular writer of pulp science fiction. Other works include *The Last Hurrah of the Golden Horde* (1970, short stories), *The Void Captain's Tale* (1983), and *Deus X* (1993), which confronts traditional religion with the metaphysical implications of cyberspace.

Spire, The, see GOLDING, SIR WILLIAM.

SPIVAK, Gayatri Chakravorty (1942–), Indian writer, critic, literary theorist, and academic, born in Calcutta, where she was educated. She later studied in America, where she has held several important academic posts. In 1976 she translated Derrida's *Of Grammatology*, which was instrumental in disseminating the theories of *deconstruction in America and in Britain. In her own critical practice, Spivak expands the methodology of deconstruction to introduce Marxist and feminist perspectives. Her influential work of cultural theory, *In Other Worlds* (1987), is a collection of essays which analyse contemporary ideas and ideologies from psychoanalysis and social theory to subaltern history and Eurocentric feminism. Though Spivak's rhetorical style is often abstruse and recondite, her original contribution to contemporary critical theory lies not only in her radical examination of the relationship between language, women, and culture, but also in her introduction of a pro-Third World perspective with an emphasis on the marginalized subject of cultural discourse. The essays in *Inside in the Teaching Machine* (1993) continue her deconstructive trajectory and display her deepening involvement with Third World affairs and their literary manifestations. *Imaginary Maps* (1995) contains her translations of three stories by the radical Bengali woman writer Mahasweta Devi, accompanied by critical essays on the work and a long interview with the author by Spivak.

SPRING, (Robert) Howard (1889–1965), British novelist, born in Cardiff; he left school at the age of 12 and became a message-boy with the *South Wales Daily News*. He subsequently worked as a journalist in Bradford, Manchester, and London. *Shabby Tiger* (1934) was his first novel. *O Absalom!* (1938), published in the USA and later in Britain as *My Son, My Son!*, gained him a wide readership. *Fame is the Spur* (1940), which narrates the rise to power of a Labour politician, increased his reputation. He retired to Cornwall in 1939, which supplies the settings for a number of his later novels, including *Hard Facts* (1944), *The Houses in between* (1951), and *I Met a Lady* (1961). His work is noted for its straightforwardly compelling narratives and humane characterizations. *Heaven Lies about Us* (1939), *In the Meantime* (1942), and *And Another Thing . . .* (1946) were collected as *The Autobiography of Howard Spring* (1972).

SPURLING, (Susan) Hilary (1940–), British biographer, the wife of playwright John *Spurling, born in Stockport, educated at Somerville College, Oxford. She was theatre critic with the *Spectator* from 1964 to 1970, when she became a freelance writer. *Ivy when Young* (1974) and *Secrets of a Woman's Heart* (1984) are the two parts of her biography of Ivy *Compton-Burnett, which gained her a high reputation among contemporary biographers for its imaginatively intense treatment of an externally uneventful life. *Ivy: The Life of Ivy Compton Burnett* appeared in 1995. *Paul Scott* (1990) is also highly regarded for its revealing analytical study of Scott's complex personality and its detailed depiction of his social milieu. Spurling's other works include *Elinor Fettiplace's Receipt Book* (1986), a practical guide to Elizabethan cookery, and her 'handbook' to Anthony Powell's *A *Dance to the Music of Time*, which was originally published in 1977 and reissued in 1992 as *An Invitation to the Dance*.

SPURLING, John (1936–), British dramatist, born in Kisumu, Kenya, educated at Oxford University, after which he worked as a plebiscite officer in the Cameroons, a BBC radio announcer, and a freelance radio and book critic. The National Theatre's production of his *MacRune's Guevara* (1969), which sceptically examines disparate attitudes to the guerrilla and folk hero, was followed by other plays notable for their intellectual curiosity, their diversity of cultural and political interests, and their feeling for contradiction and complexity, prime among them *In the Heart of the British Museum* (1971), *Shades of Heathcliff* (1971), *On a Clear Day You Can See Marlowe* (1974), *Antigone through the Looking Glass* (1979), *The British Empire Part One* (1980), and *Coming Ashore in Guadeloupe* (1982). Spurling, who was the *New Statesman*'s art critic from 1976 to 1988, has also written radio and television plays and a novel, *The Ragged End* (1989).

SQUIRE, Sir J(ohn) C(ollings) (1884–1958), British poet and editor, born in Plymouth, educated at St John's College, Cambridge. He began his career as a literary journalist with the **New Age*, being, like its editor A. R. *Orage, a convinced *Fabian socialist. In 1917 he became editor of the **New Statesman* and founded the **London Mercury* in 1919. In the course of the 1920s he emerged as a man of considerable literary influence. He was unofficial leader of a group of poets and critics sharing an antipathy to *Modernism, whom their detractors, notably the *Sitwells, referred to as 'the Squirearchy'. Among his collections of poetry are *The Three Hills* (1913), *American Poems* (1923), and *A Face in the Candlelight* (1932). *Collected Poems* (1959) carried an introduction by John *Betjeman, whose work Squire had been among the first to publish. While much of his verse is indifferently conventional, he produced numerous memorable poems, including the well-known 'Winter Nightfall', which typifies the disquiet frequently present in his finest work, and 'The Stockyard', a harrowing account in free verse of a visit to a Chicago abattoir. His many other publications include the short stories of *The Grub Street Nights' Entertainment* (1924) and two volumes of memoirs, *The Honeysuckle and the Bee* (1937) and *Water-Music* (1939). *Squire: Most Generous of Men* (1963) is a biography by P. Howarth.

SRAFFA, Piero (1898–1983), Italian economist, born in Turin, educated at the University of Turin. Sraffa fled the persecution of Mussolini's Italy to come to Britain (with the help of*Keynes) in the late 1920s. He became a Fellow of Trinity College, Cambridge. Sraffa's decisive influence on *Wittgenstein's later philosophical investigations is legendary; he also became a close friend of Antonio Gramsci (a friendship that sustained Gramsci during his political imprisonment). He wrote a dissertation on post-war monetary reconstruction in Italy which anticipated many of the arguments that Keynes was to propound a little later in the *Manchester Guardian* 'Reconstruction Supplements' (1922). Apart from a few brief notes and comments in professional journals, after coming to Cambridge Sraffa published just three more works, each of which has become a modern classic: an essay on the theory of the firm (*Economic Journal*, 1926); the definitive edition of the works of David Ricardo (1951–73); and an austere 100-page book on pure economics, *Production of Commodities by Means of Commodities* (1960). In *The New Palgrave* (1987), Paul *Samuelson doubted whether any scholar had had so great an impact on economic science as Sraffa did, in so few writings. In 1988 the *Cambridge Journal of Economics* published a memorial issue devoted to his life and work. Sraffa was also the greatest economics book collector of the century; his library was bequeathed to Trinity College.

STABLEFORD, Brian M(ichael) (1948–), British *science fiction writer and sociologist, born in Shipley, Yorkshire, educated at the University of York. His first novel, *Cradle of the Sun* (1969), was followed by many others which develop a not entirely unmerited reputation for misanthropic levity. Some novels of the 1970s, such as *Man in a Cage* (1975), *The Realms of Tartarus* (1977), and *The Walking Shadow* (1979), are more contemplative in tone. *The Empire of Fear* (1988) is an alternative history of a Europe dominated by benign vampires. A later trilogy comprising *The Werewolves of London* (1990), *The Angel of Pain* (1991), and *The Carnival of Destruction* (1994) is a philosophical examination of the nature of reality. His critical works in science fiction have been acute, and *Scientific Romance in Britain* (1985) offers a deceptively quiet, revisionist analysis of the true nature of the genre.

STACPOOLE, H(enry) de Vere (1863–1931), novelist of Irish descent, born in Kingstown, Co. Dublin; he studied medicine at St George's and St Mary's Hospitals, London. He travelled as a ship's doctor on several voyages to distant places and many of his fifty novels had a romantic island setting. His early novels showed the influence of the *fin de siècle* writers surrounding *The Yellow Book* with whom he associated. They include *The Crimson Azalea* (1907), set in Japan, and his best-known novel, *The Blue Lagoon* (1908), which tells a story of innocence mixed with sex, involving two cousins marooned on a tropical island at the age of eight, who grow up, fall in love, produce a baby, and die a romantic death. Tropical backgrounds also featured in *The Ship of Coral* (1911), *The Pearl Fishers* (1915), and *The Reef of Stars* (1916). In 1942 his autobiography, *Men and Mice*, was published.

STACTON, David (Derek) (1923–68), American novelist, born in San Francisco, educated at the University of California. Stacton spent much of his writing career abroad. His early novels, of which the most significant are *Dolores* (1954), *A Ride on a Tiger* (1954), and *The Self-Enchanted* (1956), were first published in Britain and only latterly in the USA. Many of his better-known writings are historical novels, notably *Remember Me* (1957), a novel about King Ludwig II of Bavaria; *A Dancer in Darkness* (1960), about the Duchess of Malfi; and *Sir William* (1963), which fictionally reimagines the famous affair between Lord Nelson and Lady Hamilton. Despite his proclivity for the historical, Stacton's style gravitates towards the gothic and melodramatic, though his characterizations are often powerfully psychological.

STAFFORD, Jean (1915–79), American novelist and short-story writer, born in Covina, California, but grew up in Colorado; she was educated at the University of Colorado and the University of Heidelberg. In 1940 she married the poet Robert *Lowell, the first of her three husbands; their marriage and divorce are the source of some of her most incisive short fiction. Her first novel, *Boston Adventure* (1944), is a long, confessional account of a young woman's search for love among the privileged classes. Her second novel, *The Mountain Lion* (1947), entirely different in tone and texture, with its rural Colorado setting, colloquial narrative voice, and subtle intertwining of myth and symbolism with realism, received much praise as did her third novel, *The Catherine Wheel* (1952). Stafford is best remembered as a highly skilled writer of short fiction; her collection *Children Are Bored on Sunday* (1954) brought her renewed acclaim, and her *Collected Short Stories* (1969) won the Pulitzer Prize. She produced only one further full-length prose work, *A Mother in History* (1966), a controversial portrait of Lee Harvey Oswald's mother, which confirmed her reputation as a leading stylist. A biography by David Roberts was published in 1989.

STAFFORD, William (1914–), American poet, born in Hutchinson, Kansas, educated at the universities of Kansas and Iowa. Stafford has been one of the most prolific of twentieth-century American poets, though much of his work has appeared in *little magazines or been published by *small presses, and he has not enjoyed the fame of some of his contemporaries. He is frequently associated with the American tradition of transcendentalism exemplified by the writings of Emerson and Thoreau, but there is also in his work the kind of sturdiness and linguistic clarity which entered American poetry through the influence of Robert *Frost. He is, to some extent, a regional poet exploiting the landscapes of the Midwest and far West, though he is able to invest what is familiar to him with a sense of universal significance. Among his many volumes of verse are *West of Your City* (1960), *Travelling Through the Dark* (1962; National Book Award, 1963), *The Rescued Year* (1966), *Temporary Facts* (1970), *Going Places* (1974), *Stories That Could Be True: New and Collected Poems* (1977), *The Quiet of the Land* (1979), *Things That Happen When There Aren't Any People* (1980), *A Glass Face in the Rain: New Poems* (1982), *Smoke's Way: Poems from Limited Editions* (1983), *Listening Deep* (1984), *Annie-over: Poems* (1988), *Passwords* (1991), *The Darkness Around Us Is Deep: Selected Poems* (1993), and *Learning to Live in the World: Earth Poems* (1994). As a consequence of his religious beliefs Stafford was a conscientious objector during the Second World War and his experiences of his work in a labour camp are recorded in a prose memoir, *Down in My Heart* (1947). His poetry criticism includes *Friends to This Ground: A Statement for Readers, Teachers, and Writers of Literature* (1967). See *Understanding William Stafford* (1989) by Judith Kitchen.

Staffrider, a South African cultural magazine (taking its name from the young men who ride 'staff' on the crowded commuter trains from Johannesburg's black townships, by climbing on the carriage roofs or standing on the steps), which first appeared in March 1978, produced by the radical book publishing house Ravan Press. The magazine's first editorial stated its aim as being 'not to impose "standards" but to provide a regular meeting place for the new writers and their readers, a forum which will help to shape the future of our literature'; its policy was 'to encourage and give strength to a new literature based on communities, and to establish important lines of communication between these writers, their communities, and the general public'. Controlled by an informal editorial collective, and drawing on a wide range of contributions—poetry, fiction, drama, interviews, reviews, photography, and graphic art—it went on to become one of the most successful literary journals in South Africa and has played a crucial role in the spread of a democratic culture, interacting with all the significant political and historical developments over the years since its inception. Its non-élitist orientation has meant that it has been an outlet for young and often inexperienced writers, as well as for well-known names such as Njabulo *Ndebele, Nadine *Gordimer, Es'kia *Mphahlele, Miriam *Tlali, Mongane Wally *Serote, Lionel Abrahams, Mothobi Mutloatse, and Mtutuzeli Matshopa.

STALLWORTHY, Jon (Howie) (1935–), British poet, biographer, editor, and critic, born in London, educated at Magdalen College, Oxford, where he won the Newdigate Prize in 1958. He was John Wendell Anderson Professor of English at Cornell University, New York, until 1977, when he became a fellow of Wolfson College, Oxford. *The Astronomy of Love* (1961), his first collection of poetry, displays the highly developed technical accomplishment that is a constant feature of his work. Subsequent volumes include *Out of Bounds* (1963), *Root and Branch* (1969), *Hand in Hand* (1974), and *A Familiar Tree* (1978); a selected edition containing many previously uncollected poems was published as *The Anzac Sonata* in 1986. Much of his verse displays the vividness of his historical imagination, which issues in a finely detailed account of his family's history from the mid-eighteenth century in the sequence entitled 'The Marquesas'. The balanced fusion of description and contemplation characterizing many poems is exemplified by 'Toulouse Lautrec at the Moulin Rouge'. Stallworthy is widely known for his work on Wilfred *Owen, whose biography he published to considerable acclaim in 1974. He is the editor of the definitive edition of Owen's poetry, *The Complete Poems and Fragments* of 1983; the elegiac 'Goodbye Wilfred Owen' is one of the finest of his short poems. He has since published the much praised biography of *Louis MacNeice* (1995). Among his other works are the critical studies *Vision and Revision in Yeats's 'Last Poems'* (1969) and *Poets of the First World War* (1974).

Stand, a magazine of poetry, criticism, and prose fiction begun in mimeographed form by Jon *Silkin in 1952. Silkin's early editorials established *Stand*'s abiding concern with the social functions of literature, a topic which has been vigorously discussed within its pages by contributors with differing views; in 1979 the magazine entered into a debate with **PN Review* over the political implications of various modes of poetry. Raymond *Williams and E. P. *Thompson are among the notable authors who have supplied articles of socio-cultural commentary; in 1967 Terry *Eagleton became the principal reviewer of new poetry. Silkin, who continues to edit *Stand*, has published verse by many poets in the early stages of their careers as well as featuring poems from established authors, including Michael *Hamburger, Douglas *Dunn, Geoffrey *Hill, Jeffrey *Wainwright, Tony *Harrison, and George *MacBeth. B. S. *Johnson, Tom *Pickard, and Angela *Carter are among the authors whose prose has been featured. The magazine is valued for its international perspective, which has resulted in special attention to writing from Eastern Europe, Peru, Turkey, Holland, and elsewhere. Based in Newcastle-upon-Tyne since 1965, *Stand* is published quarterly. Silkin edited an anthology of poems from the magazine's first twenty years entitled *Poetry of the Committed Individual*, which appeared in 1973.

STANDING BEAR, Luther (Ota K'te) (*c*.1868–1939), Native American writer, born in South Dakota; he was among the first students of Carlisle Indian School, established in 1879. Later he joined Buffalo Bill's Wild West Show, touring the USA and England in 1902. After settling in California, he became a movie actor and developed an active role in Indian causes. Standing Bear is best known for his autobiographical works, *My People, the Sioux* (1928), and *Land of the Spotted Eagle* (1933), which describe Indian life from the point of view of one who witnessed the historical transition from a traditional tribal lifestyle to reservation life; both works were written with E. A. Brininstool. The latter work gives detailed descriptions of Sioux culture and is particularly critical of white America and its attitude towards Indians. *Stories of the Sioux* (1934) is a collection and recreation of traditional Sioux narratives, and *My Indian Boyhood, by Chief Luther Standing Bear, Who Was the Boy Ota K'te (Plenty Kill)* (1931) is for children.

STAPLEDON, (William) Olaf (1886–1950), British *science fiction writer and philosopher, born in Cheshire, educated at Oxford and at Liverpool University, where he taught after the First World War. He was the most formidable figure in the field of British science fiction after H. G. *Wells; though his audience was not wide, the extraordinary conceptual sweep of his fictional discourses upon future history had a powerful impact upon other writers. His five major books, *Last and First Men* (1930), *Last Men in London* (1931), *Odd John* (1935), *Star Maker* (1937), and *Sirius* (1944), provide blueprints for the rigorous shaping in fictional form of speculative thought about evolution, man's ethical place in the universe, cosmogony, and the nature of God. Writers as dissimilar as B. W. *Aldiss, G. *Bear, A. C. *Clarke, and Stanislaw Lem were influenced by his work. The eighteen evolutionary stages of humanity encompassed in *Last and First Men* provide an unrivalled conspectus of the futures that can be conceived for this species; *Odd John* relentlessly examines the concept of the Superman; and *Star Maker* ascends from the first book to a stringent, evolutionary vision of a God. At the same time, in all his fiction, and in straightforward speculative texts like *Waking World* (1934), an abiding frustration at the strictures of mortal man suffuses his most enthralling vistas with melancholy. See also UTOPIA AND ANTI-UTOPIA.

STARK, Dame Freya (Madeline) (1893–1993), British travel writer, born in Paris; she was domiciled for most of her life in Italy. After attending the School of Oriental and African Studies, London, she went to Baghdad in 1930, publishing *Baghdad Sketches*, her first book, in 1933. She subsequently travelled widely in the Middle East, describing her hazardous expeditions to remote areas in *The Valley of the Assassins* (1934) and *The Southern Gates of Arabia* (1936). During the Second World War she served in diplomatic capacities in various countries, a period described in the autobiographical *Dust in the Lion's Paw* (1961); her accounts of her earlier life are contained in *Traveller's Prelude* (1950), *Beyond the Euphrates* (1951), and *The Court of Incense* (1953). From the late 1940s onward her interest in the eastern extensions of ancient Greek civilization resulted in a succession of books which include *Iona: A Quest* (1954), *Alexander's Path* (1958), and *Riding to the Tigris* (1959). *Rome on the Euphrates* (1966) deals with the Asian frontiers of the Roman Empire. Eight volumes of her letters appeared between 1974 and 1982; *Over the Rim of the World* (1988), a selection of her correspondence, was edited by Caroline Moorehead, author of the biography *Freya Stark* (1985).

State of the Language, The, an encyclopaedic work made up of contributions by well-known writers and academics, on various aspects of the English language and its current usage. First published in 1980 and edited by Christopher *Ricks and Leonard Michaels, the book was sponsored by the English-Speaking Union (San Francisco Branch). The second edition, published in 1990, opens with a combative essay by David *Dabydeen, 'On Not Being Milton: Nigger Talk in England today'. J. Enoch Powell's contribution, entitled 'Further Thoughts: Grammar and Syntax', bemoans 'the loss of Latin as an obligatory element in school education'. 'Further Thoughts: They Can't even Say It properly now', by Kingsley *Amis, attacks 'fashionable malapropisms'. Other notable contributions include Marina *Warner on 'Fighting Talk', Michael Rogers on 'Computers and Language: An Optimistic View', and Walter J. Ong on 'Subway Graffiti and the Design of the Self'.

STEAD, C(hristian) K(arlston) (1932–), New Zealand critic, editor, poet, and novelist, born in Auckland, educated at Auckland University College and Bristol University. He first made an impact with *The New Poetic: Yeats to Eliot* (1964), a text on modernist poetics which has been widely used in British and American universities. He has also produced volumes of verse including *Queseda* (1978), *Walking Westwards* (1978), *Geographies* (1982), *Between* (1988), and *Voices* (1990), as well as short stories, *Five for the Symbol* (1981). In his novels Stead has drawn on exaggerated conflicts within New Zealand society in order to create a dramatic story-line. They include *Smith's Dream* (1971), which depicts a possible rural guerrilla movement tearing the country apart; *All Visitors Ashore* (1984), an evocation of the literary scene of the 1950s (including a portrait of Janet *Frame); *The Death of the Body* (1986), which dramatizes the culture of the university; *Sister Hollywood* (1989); and *End of the World at the End of the Century* (1992), praised for its portrait of a middle-aged woman's psyche. Stead was a Professor of English at the University of Auckland for twenty years before retiring in 1986. A writer who enjoys controversy, in his later years Stead became a polemicist of what might be called 'the cultural right', standing up to perceived orthodoxies of bi-culturalism and feminism which he saw as threatening to swamp the New Zealand literary scene. Other works include *In the Glass Case* (1981) and *Answering to the Language* (1989), both collections of essays; and *Pound, Yeats, Eliot, and the Modern Movement* (1985). He is the editor of *The Faber Book of Contemporary South Pacific Stories* (1994).

STEAD, Christina (Ellen) (1902–83), Australian novelist and short-story writer, born in Rockdale, New South Wales, educated at Sydney Teachers' College. In 1928 she left Australia. She and William J. Blake, the American writer and Marxist economist, whom she later married, travelled a great deal, living in the USA, Britain, and Europe. Her first publication, *The Salzburg Tales* (1934), written while working in a Paris bank, and structured like the *Decameron*, were tales supposedly told by a group of international visitors to a music festival. Her first novel was *Seven Poor Men of Sydney* (1934), an evocation of her home environment and the social and political climate of that time. *The Beauties and the Furies* (1936) returned to Paris, as did *The House of All Nations* (1938). *The Man Who Loved Children* (1940), though set in America, is largely an account of the circumstances of Stead's childhood and her teenage struggle against a patriarchal parent. *For Love Alone* (1944) gives a closely autobiographical version of her determination to leave Australia, her arrival in England, her disappointment with the young man she had followed, and her subsequent meeting of her future husband. This was followed by *Letty Fox: Her Luck* (1946), *A Little Tea, a Little Chat* (1948), and *The People with the Dogs* (1952). After a period of silence, Stead published *Cotter's England* (1967; US title, *The Dark Places of the Heart*, 1966), set in England during the Cold War, which is a study of Nellie Cotter, a left-wing journalist, and the extent of her self-deception. *I'm Dying Laughing* (1986) was written largely in the 1940s and concerns McCarthyite Hollywood in the 1930s. Her other works include *The Little Hotel* (1973) and *Miss Herbert* (1976), both novels; *The Puzzleheaded Girl* (1967), a collection of four novellas; and the posthumous *Ocean of Story* (1985), short stories. The 1965 reprint of *The Man Who Loved Children* brought her belated recognition in Australia as the country's greatest female novelist.

STEGNER, Wallace (Earle) (1909–), American novelist, historian, and biographer, born in Lake Mills, Iowa, educated at the University of Utah and the State University of Iowa. After teaching at Harvard, he held a professorship at Stanford University, California, from 1945 to 1976. His early novels, which establish the concern with identity, individuality, and community that runs throughout his work, include *Remembering Laughter* (1937) and *Fire and Ice* (1941). *The Big Rock Candy Mountain* (1943), an expansive treatment of a family's wanderings through the Midwest and Canada, brought him wide notice as a novelist. Notable among his numerous subsequent novels are *The Preacher and the Slave* (1950), based on the life of the radical Joe Hill, *A Shooting Star* (1961), in which powerful female protagonists predominate, and *Angle of Respose* (1971), which won a Pulitzer Prize for its rendering of the life of the writer Mary Hallock Foote (1847–1938). *The Spectator Bird* (1976) and *Recapitulation* (1979) conduct retrospective evaluations of change in the twentieth century through their chief protagonists' recreations of their pasts. His works as a historian include *Mormon Country* (1941), *The Gathering of Zion* (1964), an account of the Mormon migration of 1846–7, and *Wolf Willow* (1962), which combines an autobiographical view of the Saskatchewan town where he grew up with a conventional history of the community. The most highly regarded of his works of non-fiction is *Beyond the Hundreth Meridian* (1954), his biography of the explorer and naturalist John Wesley Powell (1834–1902), whose writings Stegner has edited. His other publications include the essays collected in *One Way to Spell Man* (1982) and *Where the Bluebird Sings* (1992), a study of living and writing in the American West.

STEIN, Gertrude (1874–1946), American novelist, poet, playwright, and critic, born in Allegheny, Pennsylvania, educated at Radcliffe College and Johns Hopkins Medical School, Baltimore. As a child, Stein lived in Vienna, Paris, and Oakland in California before taking an undergraduate degree in philosophy at Harvard where she studied under William *James, who was later to remark that she was among the brightest students he had ever taught. Her interests were in experimental psychology, and she enrolled in a course in pre-medicine at Johns Hopkins University as a prelude to what she hoped would be a career in psychology. In 1902 she travelled with her brother Leo first to London and then, in 1903, to Paris where her subsequent fame as an American expatriate, patroness of the arts, and arbiter of taste was established (see LOST GENERATION). With Leo she began to collect modern paintings, notably those of Braque, Cézanne, Matisse, and Picasso (who painted a well-known portrait of her in 1906), and she actively encouraged the careers of other artists. Her own writings were a linguistic response to the 'discoveries' of Cubism, and her first published work, the stories in **Three Lives* (1909), experimented with various narrative perspectives. When she parted from her brother in 1912—by which time she was living with her lifelong companion, Alice B. Toklas—she quickly became an established figure of literary and artistic life in Paris. She was visited by Roger *Fry, Clive *Bell, and Wyndham *Lewis, and later by American writers, notably Ezra *Pound, who took an instant dislike to her, Sherwood *Anderson, who spoke frequently of her influence on his work, Ernest *Hemingway, and F. Scott *Fitzgerald. The publication of *Tender Buttons* (1914), a volume of prose poems, marks the beginning of her systematic investigation of the elements of language, particularly its grammatical, syntactical, and semantic properties. While her own creative writings are frequently difficult to read, it is her interest in the formal roots of language which she was to bequeath to her American protégés. William Carlos *Williams wrote that she tackled 'the fracture of stupidities bound in thoughtless phrases, in our calcified grammatical constructions, and in the subtle brainlessness of our meter and favourite prose rhythms—which compel words to follow certain others without precision of thought'. Her linguistic experimentation is best seen in one of her most important works, *The Making of Americans, Being a History of a Family's Progress*, published in 1925 though written between 1906 and 1908. Her autobiography, *The *Autobiography of Alice B. Toklas* (1933), written as if it were the autobiography of her close friend, became one of her most successful and popular works. A lecture tour to the USA followed in 1934, and the transcripts of *Lectures in America* were published in 1935.

She wrote prolifically through the 1930s, particularly plays and opera libretti (often for music by Virgil Thomson), and a number of non-fictional prose works, notably *Narration: Four Lectures* (1935), *The Geographical History of America* (1936), a further volume of autobiography, *Everybody's Autobiography* (1937), and her portrait of *Picasso* (1938). During the Second World War her care of American servicemen brought her further public distinction. She continued to write over the last few years of her life and *Wars I Have Seen* (1944) is among the more readable of her late narratives; other important works were published after her death. There are two valuable anthologies of her writings, *Selected Writings of Gertrude Stein* (1946), edited by Carl *Van Vechten, and *Look at Me Now and Here I Am: Writings and Lectures, 1911–1945* (1967), edited by Patricia Meyerowitz. See *Gertrude Stein: Her Life and Her Work* (1957) by Elizabeth Sprigge and *Gertrude Stein* (1961) by Frederick J. Hoffman.

STEINBECK, John (Ernst) (1902–68), American novelist, born in Salinas, California, educated at Stanford University. He held various odd jobs before publishing his first work, *A Cup of Gold* (1929), a pirate romance about the buccaneer Henry Morgan. *Tortilla Flat* (1935), an affectionate portrait of the Mexican-American 'paisanos', set in Monterey, established him as a master of the realistic novel of contemporary life. In similar vein was *In Dubious Battle* (1936), focusing on the fraudulent and brutal practices of the Californian land monopolists, and **Of Mice and Men* (1937; dramatized, 1938), a narrative about two itinerant workers in California. The short stories in *The Red Pony* (1937) and *The Long Valley* (1938) also featured Southern Californian workers. The concern for the victims of the Depression expressed in these works came to fruition in his masterpiece, *The *Grapes of Wrath* (1939; Pulitzer Prize). During the Second World War Steinbeck worked as a journalist and writer for the Office of War Information, a period which produced the anti-fascist short novel and play *The Moon Is Down* (1942), and *Bombs Away* (1942), the story of a bomber team. There followed *Cannery Row* (1945), also set in Monterey, which traces the lives of characters such as Doc the marine biologist, Mack and the Boys, the girls from the Bear Flag whorehouse, and Lee Chong the grocer. Among other works he wrote *The Wayward Bus* (1947), a satire on the modern businessman; *The Pearl* (1947), a parable; *Burning Bright* (1950); *East of Eden* (1952), the history of one family from the Civil War to the First World War; *Sweet Thursday* (1954), in which the characters in *Cannery Row* reappear; *The Short Reign of Pippin IV* (1957), a satirical novel of French politics; and *The Winter of Our Discontent* (1961), about a man struggling against the pressures of the modern world. He also wrote several books of travel and commentary such as *The Log from the Sea of Cortez* (1950), on a biological expedition; *Once There Was a War* (1958); *Travels with Charley in Search of America* (1962), a narrative about a trip made with his dog; and several film scripts including *The Forgotten Village* (1941). A notable statement of his socio-philosophical beliefs is contained in *The Sea of Cortez* (1941), written with his friend and mentor Ed Ricketts. Steinbeck was awarded the Nobel Prize in 1962. *Steinbeck: A Life in Letters* (1975) is a comprehensive selection of his correspondence. See also PROLETARIAN LITERATURE IN THE USA.

STEINEM, Gloria (1934–), American activist, journalist, and lecturer, born in Toledo, Ohio, educated at Smith College. She became known as a journalist, first as an editor and political columnist with *New York* magazine, and as co-founder and editor of *Ms* magazine, which has played a powerful role in bringing feminist issues to a wide audience. A powerful and stirring public lecturer, Steinem's influence was manifest in the formation of consciousness-raising groups across the USA during the early 1970s. Among her works are the prize-winning essay 'After Black Power, Women's Liberation' (1969); *Marilyn* (1986), a biographical study dealing with the personal and public implications of media manipulation; *Outrageous Acts and Everyday Rebellions* (1983), a collection of Steinem's writings; *Revolution From Within: A Book of Self Esteem* (1992); and *Moving Beyond Words* (1994), a volume of essays that includes a reassessment of Freud.

STEINER, (Francis) George (1929–), American critic, born in Paris of Austrian-Jewish parents; from 1940, when his family fled France, he grew up in America. He was educated at the University of Chicago, Harvard, and Balliol College, Oxford. In 1961 he became a fellow of Churchill College, Cambridge, and was appointed Professor of English and Comparative Literature at the University of Geneva in 1974. Much of Steiner's writing is deeply informed by loss of faith in the civilizing power of liberal humanism as a result of modern history's barbaric record of major wars, ruthless totalitarianism, and, most notably, the Nazis' treatment of the Jewish people. His view of literature as inseparable from its broader cultural contexts was clear from *Tolstoy or Dostoevsky* (1959), his first major publication, which challenged the claims of the *New Criticism that social and historical factors are not relevant to literary analysis. *Language and Silence* (1967) examined the effects of science and mass communications on language and literature, concluding that silence may be the only supportable option for a writer confronted with the twentieth century's moral abnegation. *After Babel: Aspects of Language and Translation* (1975), widely regarded as his most important work, surveys a remarkable range of literary and linguistic theory in proposing that the intrinsic differences between languages and cultures are of greater significance than their apparent similarities. His other works include *Real Presences* (1989), in which he argues that meaning in literature and the other arts is ultimately of a moral and metaphysical nature. His best-known work of fiction is *The Portage to San Cristobal of A. H.* (1979), in which Adolf Hitler, an aged fugitive in South

America, speaks in defence of his actions; it was adapted for the stage by Christopher *Hampton in 1982.

STEPHENS, James (1882–1950), Irish poet and story-writer, born in Dublin. He came from a poor family and began writing while working as a clerk in a solicitor's office. The poems and articles he contributed in *Sinn Fein* brought him to the notice of George *Russell ('AE') with whose encouragement Stephens published *Insurrections* (1909), one of several volumes of poems culminating in *Collected Poems* (1926; revised 1954). His first novel, *The Charwoman's Daughter* (1912), was a portrait in miniature of Dublin seen through the day-dreams of Mary Makebelieve, which reflected the poverty that Stephens had experienced in his formative years. Much of his less whimsical works have been overshadowed by his major novel, *The Crock of Gold* (1912), a fantasy combining Irish legend and folklore with parable and parody; it centres on two philosophers, their wives and two children, who live in a pine wood and encounter leprechauns, the god Pan, policemen, and others, in their search for happiness. Other novels include *The Demi-Gods* (1914) and *Deirdre* (1923). *The Insurrection in Dublin* (1916) manifests his fervent support for Irish independence. With his mastery of Irish literature and mythology Stephens did much to encourage a revival of interest in the Gaelic language; his many volumes of short stories include *Irish Fairy Tales* (1920; illustrated by Arthur Rackham). In later years, Stephens became a widely known broadcaster. A biography by A. Martin appeared in 1977.

STERLING, Bruce (1954–), American science fiction writer, born in Brownsville, Texas, educated at the University of Texas. He is one of the better-known advocates of *Cyberpunk (see GIBSON, WILLIAM) which he sees as the only form of science fiction capable of confronting the near future; he edited *Mirrorshades: The Cyberpunk Anthology* (1986). Some of his later works, such as *Schismatrix* (1985), *Islands in the Net* (1988), and the stories collected in *Crystal Express* (1989), demonstrate his sense that the future will comprise an ineradicable complexity of networks from computer webs to shared identities. *Heavy Weather* (1994) deals with environmental catastrophes in the next century.

STERN, G(ladys) B(ertha) (1890–1973), British novelist, born in London, educated at schools in London, Germany, and Switzerland. Her first novel, *Pantomime* (1914), was followed by over forty others. The best-known of these are the series based on her own family, of which the first three volumes were published as *The Rakonitz Chronicles*. These include *Tents of Israel* (1924; later published as *The Matriarch*), *A Deputy Was King* (1926), *Mosaic* (1930), *Shining and Free* (1935), and *The Young Matriarch* (1942). They chronicle the fortunes of a wealthy, cosmopolitan Jewish family and are set against the background of fashionable 1930s' London. Her literary circle during this period included Noël *Coward, Rebecca *West, and Somerset *Maugham. She also wrote short stories, plays, and biographies of Jane Austen and Robert Louis Stevenson, as well as an autobiography, *All in Good Time* (1954), which describes her conversion to Catholicism.

STERN, James (Andrew) (1904–93), Irish writer, born in Co. Meath, educated at Eton. His career began as a journalist on the **London Mercury* and he also travelled widely. His first volume of short stories, *The Heartless Land* (1932), established him as a distinctive voice and was followed by several other collections, including *Something Wrong* (1938) and *The Man Who Was Loved* (1952). His work was praised by contemporaries such as M. *Lowry, W. H. *Auden, and C. *Isherwood, who, writing in 1952, described Stern as 'the most unjustly neglected writer of short stories today'. His stories were later collected as *The Stories of James Stern* (1968) and display his lucid style and ear for dialogue in their treatment of themes connected with childhood, loss of innocence, and the dispossessed. He was also a distinguished translator of German and Eastern European writers such as Mann, Kafka, Brecht, and Broch. *The Hidden Damage* (1947; reprinted 1990) is a study of life in Germany during the summer of 1945.

STEVENS, Wallace (1879–1955), American poet, born in Reading, Pennsylvania, educated at Harvard and at New York University Law School. After working as a lawyer in New York, in 1916 he joined the Hartford Accident and Indemnity Company, of which he was Vice-President from 1934 until his death. **Harmonium* (1923), his remarkably assured first collection of poetry, drew little acclaim from the critics of the day; Stevens retained a special regard for the book, which is rich in what he termed 'the essential gaudiness of poetry', a phrase suggesting the colourful imagery, wit, and flamboyance of gesture displayed by much of his writing. With the exception of an expanded edition of *Harmonium* produced in 1931, he published no further collections until *Ideas of Order* in 1935. A more purposeful tone emerged in this volume, which formalized his enduring preoccupation with relations between the creative imagination and objective reality, a theme achieving memorable expression in 'The Idea of Order at Key West'. Several further collections included *The *Man with the Blue Guitar* (1937), **Notes toward a Supreme Fiction* (1942), *Auroras of Autumn* (1950), and *Collected Poems* (1954). *Opus Posthumous* (1957, revised and enlarged 1990) contains three plays in addition to numerous essays and many previously unpublished poems. Stevens's work successfully combines aspects of Romanticism, notably his identification of the imagination as the supreme human faculty, with an exploratory attitude to aesthetics and philosophy characteristic of *Modernism. Marianne *Moore's remark on his 'infallible mastery of pause and tone' indicates the deftness and poise evident throughout his poetry, which is equally accomplished in conventional metres and highly disciplined free verse. His principal prose work is *The Necessary Angel: Essays on Reality and Imagination* (1960). Holly Stevens, his daughter, edited *Selected Letters* (1966). The two volumes of Joan Richardson's biography of Stevens were published in the USA in 1986 and 1988. See also SYMBOLISM.

STEVENSON, Anne (Katherine) (1933–), American poet, born in Cambridge, England, of American parents; she grew up in the USA and was educated at the University of Michigan. After working as a schoolteacher in England and the USA, she settled in Britain in the early 1960s. She has held posts as writer-in-residence at various colleges and universities throughout Britain. *Living in America* (1965) and *Reversals* (1969), her first two collections of verse, established her as a poet of candour and intelligence capable of combining sharp observation and imaginative energy in her subtle critiques of American culture and society. *Correspondences* (1974) forms a sustained investigation of the American past through the medium of a fictitious sequence of letters. The landscapes of the north-east coast of Scotland provide settings for the stoical lyricism of *Enough of Green* (1977), which contains some of the most notable examples of her characteristic ability to fuse perceptual and contemplative qualities. Local observation, chiefly of the Welsh border country, forms the basis for much of *Minute by Glass Minute* (1982), in which her philosophical questionings centre on the individual's search for clarity of vision in the midst of the distractions presented by the past and the present. Subsequent collections, including *The Fiction-Makers* (1985), *The Other House* (1990), and *Four and a Half Dancing Men* (1992), extend her concern with the interactions of the imagination and objective reality. She has also published a succession of pamphlets which include *Turkish Rondo* (1982) and *Black Grate Poems* (1984). *Selected Poems: 1956–1986* appeared in 1987. Among her other works are the critical monograph *Elizabeth Bishop* (1966) and *Bitter Fame* (1989), a biography of Sylvia *Plath.

STEWART, Douglas (1913–85), New Zealand poet, born in Taranaki Province, New Zealand; he settled in Australia in 1938. As the influential editor of the Red Page of the **Bulletin* and a publisher's editor he did much to encourage younger poets. His early volumes of verse, *Green Lions* (1936) and *The White Cry* (1939), were lyrics celebrating the beauty of New Zealand landscapes. *Elegy for an Airman* (1940) and *Sonnets to the Unknown Soldier* (1941) were volumes of war poems. *The Dosser in Springtime* (1946) displayed his effective use of the ballad form, for which he became renowned. The collections *Glencoe* (1947) and *Sun Orchids* (1952) were followed by *The Birdsville Track* (1955), a sequence of poems evoking the landscapes, birds, and animals of Australia's outback, which also formed the commentary for the documentary film *Back of Beyond*. His *Collected Poems 1936–1967* appeared in 1967. His verse-dramas include *Ned Kelly* (1940), about the famous bushranger, and *The Fire on the Snow* (1941), about Captain Scott's expedition to the South Pole. His stories, many about the New Zealand of his youth, are collected in *A Girl with Red Hair* (1944). *Springtime in Taranaki* (1983) was an autobiography. *The Flesh and the Spirit* (1948) and *The Broad Stream* (1975) are critical works.

STEWART, J(ohn) I(nnes) M(ackintosh) (1906–94), British academic, critic, and novelist, born in Edinburgh, educated at Edinburgh Academy and Oriel College, Oxford. Among several academic posts, he was Tutor and Reader in English Literature at Oxford during 1949–73. He has written a critical biography of *Hardy (1971), and studies of Shakespeare (1949), *Joyce (1957), Peacock (1963), *Kipling (1966), and *Conrad (1968), while his *Eight Modern Writers* (1963) is the final volume of the *Oxford History of English Literature*. He is also the author of some twenty novels—*Mark Lambert's Supper* (1954) is the first—five of which (*The Gaudy*, 1974; *Young Pattullo*, 1975; *A Memorial Service*, 1976; *The Madonna of the Astrolabe*, 1977; and *Full Term*, 1978), entitled collectively *A Staircase in Surrey*, depict with some comedy the way of life in an Oxford college. He is best known, however, for the many successful detective stories and thrillers written under the pseudonym of Michael Innes. The first, *Death at the President's Lodging* (1936; US title *Seven Suspects*), introduced his detective, John Appleby of Scotland Yard. Other titles include *Hamlet, Revenge!* (1937), *Stop Press* (1939; US title *The Spider Strikes*), *Appleby on Ararat* (1941), *A Private View* (1952; in USA also as *One-Man Show* and *Murder is an Art*), and *Appleby at Allington* (1968). These are full of high spirits, though the conversation, stuffed with recondite literary allusions and quotations, often seems to take precedence over the detection. Among his thrillers, which show the influence of Stevenson and *Buchan, are *The Journeying Boy* (1949; US title *The Case of the Journeying Boy*), *Operation Pax* (1951; US title *The Paper Thunderbolt*), and *The Man from the Sea* (1955; also in USA as *Death by Moonlight*). The autobiographical *Myself and Michael Innes: A Memoir* appeared in 1987.

STEWART, (Lady) Mary (Florence Elinor) (1916–), British novelist, born in Sunderland, educated at Durham University where she subsequently lectured in English, before becoming a full-time writer. Many of her novels are romantic adventures in contemporary settings, including her first novel, *Madam Will You Talk?* (1955), *Touch Not the Cat* (1976), and *Thornyhold* (1988). *The Crystal Cave* (1970) was the first of several books retelling the legends of Arthur and Merlin on a plausible human scale; *The Hollow Hills* (1973), *The Last Enchantment* (1979), *The Wicked Day* (1983) and *The Prince and the Pilgrim* (1995) continue the epic. Her books for children include *Ludo and the Star Horse* (1974), winner of the Scottish Arts Council Award.

STOKER, Bram (Abraham) (1847–1912), Anglo-Irish novelist and short-story writer, born in Clontarf, near Dublin, educated at Trinity College, Dublin. His experiences as a civil servant in Dublin resulted in *The*

Duties of the Clerks of Petty Sessions in Ireland (1879). He was also drama critic for the *Dublin Mail*, and contributed to other Irish newspapers. In 1878 he left for England, where he became manager of Henry Irving's Royal Lyceum Theatre in London. *A Glimpse of America* (1886) records a tour with Irving and his company, and he also wrote the two-volume *Personal Reminiscences of Henry Irving* (1906). Stoker is best known for his gothic horror novel *Dracula* (1897), the most famous of all tales of vampirism; Dracula, with his 'mocking smile', his long white blood-sucking teeth, and his eerie castle in Transylvania, has inspired numerous film and stage versions of the novel, including those by Bela Lugosi, Christopher Lee, and Klaus Kinsky; the most memorable and haunting was F. W. Murnau's *Nosferatu* (1922) starring the cadaverous Max Schreck. Stoker's many other horror novels and collections of short stories include *The Lair of the White Worm* (1911), a gruesome tale of the eponymous monster from ancient Mercia emerging from a bottomless well, and *The Water's Mou'* (1895), inspired by his visits to Cruden's Bay in Scotland. *Dracula's Guest and Other Weird Stories* (1914), with a preface by his widow, Florence, was published posthumously, and contains his finest short fiction, including 'The Squaw' and 'The Judge's House'. See Christopher Frayling and Daniel Farson, *The Man Who Wrote Dracula* (1975).

STOKES, Adrian (Durham) (1902–72), British art critic and poet, born in London, educated at Rugby and Magdalen College, Oxford. During the 1920s he visited Rapallo in Italy, where he came to know Ezra *Pound, who was instrumental in shaping his thought and who introduced his work to the **Criterion*. From his studies of fifteenth-century Italian sculpture and architecture in *The Quattro Cento* (1932) and *Stones of Rimini* (1934), Stokes developed his fundamental distinction between carving as the releasing of form innate in the medium and modelling as the imposing of form onto the medium. *Colour and Form* (1937), *Art and Science* (1949), *Smooth and Rough* (1951), *Painting and the Inner World* (1963), and *Reflections on the Nude* (1963) are among the subsequent studies in which his ideas take on a broader cultural relevance. His poetry, which displayed a remarkable vividness of imagery and considerable strengths of rhythm and form, was included in *Penguin Modern Poets: 23* (with Edwin *Muir and Geoffrey *Grigson, 1973) and *Collected Poems*, edited by Peter *Robinson, appeared in 1981. Three volumes of *The Critical Writings of Adrian Stokes*, edited by Lawrence Gowing, appeared in 1978.

STONE, Lawrence (1919–), British historian, born in Epsom, Surrey, educated at the Sorbonne and at Christ Church, Oxford. From 1963 to 1990 he was Dodge Professor of History at Princeton University. *An Elizabethan: Sir Horatio Palavicino* (1956), a study of its subject's career in commerce and espionage, displayed the meticulous scholarship and attention to the domestic and personal dimensions of history for which Stone became widely noted. A succession of subsequent works on the altering structures of social organization in the sixteenth and seventeenth centuries included *The Crisis of the Aristocracy, 1558–1641* (1965) and *The Causes of the English Revolution, 1529–1642* (1972). Among Stone's later works, which have shown an intensified concern to define social values with reference to individual cases, are *The Family: Sex and Marriage in England, 1500–1800* (1977), *An Open Elite? England, 1530–1880* (1984), and *Road to Divorce: England, 1530–1987* (1990).

STONE, Louis (1871–1935), Australian writer, born in England; he left for Australia in 1884. He attended Sydney University and subsequently worked as a primary school teacher in the remote areas of New South Wales and in Sydney. Stone is remembered for his naturalistic novel *Jonah* (1911), about Sydney urban life; in the character of Jonah he popularized the Australian 'larrikin' (a street urchin) who struggles to survive in the city slums. A new edition of the novel, published in 1988, stimulated a revival of interest in Stone's work. Another novel, *Betty Wayside* (1915), was followed by the plays *The Lap of the Gods* (1923) and *The Watch That Wouldn't Go* (1926), both of which displayed his gift for vivid characterization. A progressive nervous illness brought a premature end to his literary career.

STONE, Robert (Anthony) (1937–), American novelist, born in Brooklyn; he worked for the *New York Daily News* while attending New York University. At Stanford he met Ken *Kesey, becoming an associate of his during the mid-1960s. Drugs and alcohol are prominent in Stone's novels, sometimes represented by hallucinatory passages, as in *A Hall of Mirrors* (1967) in which three drifters come to New Orleans and are involved in violence following a right-wing rally. In 1971 Stone went to Vietnam as a journalist; American moral and military defeat forms the backdrop to his most celebrated work, *Dog Soldiers* (1974, National Book Award), in which an ex-marine returning from Vietnam agrees to smuggle heroin, and is pursued to a shoot-out on the Mexican/Californian border by dubious narcotics agents. Fine detailing of the drug culture gives conviction to Stone's metaphors of individual and state corruption. *A Flag for Sunrise* (1981) also attracted much praise, the diverse motivations and connected fates of three Americans in 'Tecan' reflecting upon the USA's ambiguous involvement in Central America. A novel satirizing Hollywood, *Children of Light* (1986), was less successful. *Outerbridge Reach* (1992) was controversial for the use of material concerning the real-life disappearance of the lone yachtsman Donald Crowhurst during a round-the-world race. None the less, Stone's position as a leading novelist has been well earned for the skill with which he imbues the novel of action with moral and political dimensions. See also VIETNAM WRITING.

STOPPARD, Tom (1937–), British dramatist, born in Czechoslovakia, the son of a company doctor who was killed when the Japanese invaded Singapore; he came to England after the war, and took his British stepfather's name. Stoppard left school at 17 to become a journalist, seeing his first play, *A Walk on the Water* (later, the stage play *Enter a Free Man*), televised in 1963, and a novel, *Lord Malquist and Mr Moon*, published in 1965. In 1967 **Rosencrantz and Guildenstern Are Dead* moved to the National Theatre from the Edinburgh Festival's Fringe, establishing him as a dramatist of rare wit and intellectual curiosity. His major stage plays since have included **Jumpers* (1972); **Travesties* (1974); *Every Good Boy Deserves Favour* (1977), set in a Soviet mental hospital and simultaneously involving an authentic lunatic and a dissident pronounced mad by the authorities; *Night and Day* (1978), about the threat to freedom of restrictive practices in journalism; *The Real Thing* (1982), a comedy about love and adultery; *Hapgood* (1988), which brings together quantum physicists and secret agents for an elaborate dramatic exploration of the nature of reality; **Arcadia* (1993); and *Indian Ink* (1994; an expanded stage version of the earlier radio play *In the Native State*), which moves between 1930 and 1985, following the fortunes of a young poetess on a visit to India and showing her trip's long-term results, in the process raising questions about colonialism, culture, language, and nationality. Stoppard has written other pieces for radio and television, notably *Professional Foul* (televised in 1977), about the predicament of dissidents in his native Czechoslovakia. He has also adapted the work of European playwrights, notably Nestroy's *Einen Jux will er sich machen* into *On the Razzle* (1981), and Molnár's *The Play at the Castle* into *Rough Crossing* (1984). Some of Stoppard's more recent work has concerned the abuse of human rights, especially in Eastern Europe, but his most admired plays involve large and less specific matters, up to and including the moral nature of the universe and the significance of life itself. He has said that his aim is 'to achieve the perfect marriage between ideas and farce or high comedy', and his plays characteristically use parody, puns, conceits, visual jokes, and the bravura yoking together of apparently heterogeneous material in a fundamentally serious quest for truths which are felt always to be elusive. Stoppard has also said that he writes plays 'because dialogue is the most respectable way of contradicting myself', and that 'the dislocation of an audience's assumptions' is a major part of his purpose. What matters is intricately to pose, not definitively to answer, questions of cultural, ethical, and philosophic import. His work has sometimes been accused of being excessively cerebral, a slur that does, however, overlook his continuing and compassionate concern with human vulnerability. The complaint has become even harder to sustain since *Arcadia* and *Indian Ink*, both of which involve able, attractive, and highly sympathetic young women who die before being able wholly to fulfil their considerable talents.

STOREY, David (1933–), English novelist and dramatist, born in Wakefield, the son of a miner, educated at the Slade School of Fine Art, London. His early novels reflect the working-class background of his Yorkshire upbringing, and his displacement to the intellectual milieu of the South. His experience as a professional rugby player for Leeds formed the background to his first novel, *This Sporting Life* (1960), in which the protagonist struggles against the confining effects of his working-class roots; in *Flight into Camden* (1960) a miner's daughter, involved with a married man, is torn between the values inherited from her parents and her uneasily assimilated urban attitudes. *Radcliffe* (1963) examines class conflicts in a dramatic and partly allegorical portrayal of an obsessive homosexual relationship between an aristocrat and a working-class protagonist which ends in murder; it was followed by the play *The Restoration of Arnold Middleton* (1966), about the mental collapse of a schoolmaster. Storey's subsequent work for the stage has been stylistically unpredictable, varying from the Ibsenesque realism of *In Celebration* (1969), about an uneasy family reunion, and the Chekhovian *The Contractor* (1970) in which a tent is raised and lowered by a gang of social misfits, to the grotesque farce of *Mother's Day* (1976); but it has been thematically more consistent, concentrating on the loss of roots, emotional mutilation, disintegration, and the elusiveness of human wholeness. Other plays include *Home* (1970), about two old men in an asylum; *The Changing Room* (1972), a behind-the-scenes picture of the players during a rugby match; *Life Class* (1974), set in an art school; *Sisters* (1978); *Early Days* (1980), about a famous politician in his unruly old age; *The March on Russia* (1989); and *Stages* (1992), about a writer looking unhappily back on the many confusions and contradictions of his life. Storey's novels of the 1970s and 1980s include *Pasmore* (1972), about a lecturer's desertion of his wife and children, and his psychic disintegration; *A Temporary Life* (1973), narrated by a painter and teacher of art; *Saville* (1976; Booker Prize), an epic of Yorkshire miners' lives; *A Prodigal Child* (1982); and *Present Times* (1984), which chronicles the life of a rugby professional.

Story, see PLOT.

Story of an African Farm, The, see SCHREINER, OLIVE.

STOUT, Rex (Todhunter) (1886–1975), American crime writer, born in Noblesville, Indiana, educated at the University of Kansas. After working as a bookkeeper and hotel manager, Stout became a full-time writer in 1927. He produced several orthodox novels before turning to detective fiction and publishing *Fer-de-Lance* (1934), the first of a long series of novels and short stories in the majority of which the central figure is the private detective Nero Wolfe, Montenegrin by birth, a gourmet who weighs a seventh of a ton, and rarely leaves his house on West 35th Street in New York. The stories are narrated by Wolfe's assistant, Archie Goodwin. The best of the novels is possibly *Some Buried Caesar* (1938; alternative US title *The Red Bull*), but *Too Many Cooks* (1938), *The Silent Speaker*

(1946), *And Be a Villain* (1948; UK title *More Deaths than One*), *The Second Confession* (1949), and *Gambit* (1962) are also excellent.

STOW, Randolph (1935–), Australian poet and novelist, born in Geraldton, Western Australia, educated at the University of Western Australia. In 1966 he settled in England. Stow's early poetry, *Act One* (1957), *Outrider: Poems 1956–1962* (1962), illustrated by Sydney Nolan, and *A Counterfeit Silence* (1969), mainly private letters, received wide acclaim as did his spiritually challenging and strongly atmospheric novels *A Haunted Land* (1956), *The Bystander* (1957), and *To The Islands* (1958, revised with an important Preface in 1982). His writing, both prose and poetry, demonstrates formidable technical virtuosity combined with great diversity of influence and reference, such as *Tourmaline* (1963), which draws on Chinese Taoism. The autobiographical novel *The Merry-Go-Round by the Sea* (1965) is a sensitive exploration of the development of a young boy from childhood in Western Australia to adolescence. In his best-selling book for children, *Midnite* (1967), Stow combines adventure and scholarship with literary satire and infectious good humour. *Visitants* (1979), set in Papua New Guinea, spanned anthropology, science fiction, and the thriller in drawing on Stow's own time in the Trobriand Islands. *The Girl Green as Elderflower* (1980) fused his sure knowledge of Suffolk with medieval myth, while *The Suburbs of Hell* (1984) recreated the atmosphere of John Webster in contemporary Old Harwich, where Stow lived, to produce a taut and disturbing book. Stow's is a distinguished and individual voice, his concerns the unchanging ones of life (and death) through different ages and cultures, but the forms and conventions are assuredly his own. *Strange Country: A Study of Randolph Stow* (1986) is by Anthony J. Hassal.

STRACHEY, (Giles) Lytton (1880–1932), British biographer, essayist, and critic, born in London, educated at Leamington College, Liverpool University, and Trinity College, Cambridge, where he was elected to the *Apostles and established lasting friendships with J. M. *Keynes, E. M. *Forster, and others with whom he was later identified as a member of the *Bloomsbury Group. His first publications were the volumes of poetry *Prolusiones Academicae* (1902) and *Euphrosyne* (1905). His early work as a literary journalist for the **Spectator* and other periodicals is represented by *Spectatorial Essays* (1964). In *Landmarks in French Literature* (1912) he drew the attention of a wider British readership to the writings of Racine. The wittily iconoclastic portraits of Dr Thomas Arnold, Florence Nightingale, General Gordon, and Cardinal Manning in *Eminent Victorians* (1918) made him well known and had a marked influence on the subsequent course of *biography. His other principal works as a biographer are *Queen Victoria* (1921), which displays an ironically poised sympathy for its subject, and *Elizabeth and Essex* (1928), a vivid and melodramatic treatment in which a Freudian analytical tendency is clearly discernible. Strachey also wrote many biographical essays which are collected in *Portraits in Miniature* (1931) and *Characters and Commentaries* (1933). The vitality and precision of his style and his ability to deal with ethical and psychological complexities while maintaining a brisk narrative pace have gained his work lasting recognition. Michael *Holroyd, author of *Lytton Strachey* (2 volumes, 1967, 1968) and *Lytton Strachey: The New Biography* (1994), edited *Lytton Strachey by Himself* (1971), a collection of autobiographical fragments.

STRAND, Mark (1934–), American poet, born on Prince Edward Island, Canada, educated at Antioch College, Ohio, and Yale Art School. He has taught at Iowa, Yale, Brandeis, and Columbia Universities and became a writer-in-residence at the University of Utah in Salt Lake City. His poetry collections include *Sleeping with One Eye Open* (1964), *Reasons for Moving* (1968), *Darker* (1970), *The Story of Our Lives* (1973), *The Late Hour* (1978), *Selected Poems* (1980), *Rembrandt Takes a Walk* (1987), and *Dark Habor: A Poem* (1993); *Mr and Mrs Baby* (1985) is a collection of short stories and *The Monument* (1978) a collection of assorted prose pieces. Strand is an active advocate of the work of other poets and has edited *The Contemporary American Poets: American Poetry Since 1940* (1969), *New Poetry of Mexico* (1970), and, with Charles *Simic, *Another Republic: 17 European and South American Writers* (1976), as well as translating the work of his contemporaries, notably in *The Owl's Insomnia: Selected Poems of Rafel Alberti* (1973) and *Souvenir of the Ancient World: Carlos Drummond de Andrade* (1976). Strand's verse is characterized by its deceptive simplicity, its cultivated anti-romanticism and its affinities with American abstract painting, and he shares with many of his contemporaries an interest in magic, his verse sometimes slipping effortlessly from the real to the surreal and spiritual (a characteristic which suggests the influence of Latin American writers). One of his finest works is the frequently anthologized 'Elegy for My Father', a poem which employs chanted litanies in its re-engagement with, and recreation of, childhood experience. He is a regular contributor of poetry to the *New Yorker* and during 1990–1 was the US Poet Laureate.

Strange Interlude, a play by Eugene *O'Neill, produced in 1928. A highly successful play which earned O'Neill a sizeable fortune and a Pulitzer Prize, it was immediately popular for its frank airing of sexual issues presented through a Freudian investigation of its characters' psychology. It tells the story of Nina Leeds and the men in her life, including her possessive father who persuaded her fiancé, Gordon Shaw, not to marry her before he went to France in the Great War, where he was killed. Nina laments not having given herself to Gordon, and disowns her father for his interference. She becomes a nurse in a military hospital where three men fall for her: Charles Marsden, a novelist devoted to his mother, Dr Edmund Darrell, who represses his love for her, preferring the safety of his scientific career, and Sam Evans, the weakest of the three, whom she is persuaded to marry. Once pregnant by Sam, she is told by his mother that there is a history of insanity in the family, and she has an abortion which she conceals from Sam. She then has a son by Edmund Darrell, whom Sam believes to be his, and, inspired by his apparent fatherhood, he becomes a confident and successful businessman. Nina refuses Darrell's plea that she divorce Sam and marry him, and they part. When they meet again eleven years later, their son, Gordon, named after her dead fiancé, has grown up preferring Sam to his real father, and is increasingly alienated from his possessive mother. Nina now realizes that she has lost both Gordon and Darrell, and Sam dies before she can tell him the truth about Gordon. She is left with the logical Charles Marsden, whom she then marries. The concluding lines of the play, when Nina says 'our lives are merely strange dark interludes in the electrical display of God the Father', may be interpreted as an expression of bitter irony or of patient acceptance. The action of *Strange Interlude* takes place over twenty-five years, but the sense of narrative continuity is deliberately fractured by O'Neill's concentration on the significant interludes in the lives of these characters.

Strange Meeting, see HILL, SUSAN.

Strangers and Brothers, see SNOW, C. P.

STRAUB, Peter (1943–), American novelist, born in Milwaukee, educated at the University of Wisconsin, Columbia University, and University College, Dublin. His first books were acute psychological studies, but he is best known for his horror novels such as *If You Could See Me Now* (1977), and *Ghost Story* (1979), which has been filmed. In these books, he manipulated the horror genre's crude obsession with the past into a subtle series of confrontations of guilt-ridden protagonists with their own ancient fears. *Shadow Land* (1980) and *Floating Dragon* (1983) were fantasies, as was *The Talisman* (1984), written with S. *King. *Koko* (1988), *Mystery* (1989), and *The Throat* (1993) were complex thrillers in which the supernatural rhetoric of his earlier work is less marked.

STRAWSON, Sir P(eter) F(rederick) (1919–), British philosopher, born in London, the son of a schoolmaster, educated at St John's College, Oxford. After military service between 1940 and 1946, he began teaching philosophy at University College of North Wales, Bangor; from 1947 onward he lectured at Oxford, becoming Wayneflete Professor of Metaphysical Philosophy in 1968. He was knighted in 1977 for his contributions to philosophy, which have been chiefly concerned with theories of language and metaphysics. *Introduction to Logical Theory* (1952) gained wide notice for its extension of what is termed 'ordinary language philosophy' to an exacting consideration of its implications for formal logic. Strawson maintained that the techniques of logical analysis were not equipped to deal with the complexity and range of normal usages; his attention to the nature of linguistic functions in relation to truth led to an insistence on the distinction between the active and descriptive capacities of language. During the mid-1950s he developed his ideas on 'descriptive metaphysics', a designation he introduced to differentiate his work from speculative metaphysics, which he viewed as preoccupied with establishing conceptual systems. *Individuals, an Essay in Descriptive Metaphysics* appeared in 1959, comprehensively examining the structures of thought by means of which we apprehend reality and identifying particular material objects as the basis for theories of knowledge; the book is regarded as having re-established metaphysics as a branch of philosophical discourse. Among Strawson's other works are *The Bounds of Sense* (1966), his provocative commentary on Kant's *Critique of Pure Reason* (1781); *Freedom and Resentment* (1974), a study of moral and relational attitudes; and *Skepticism and Naturalism, Some Varieties* (1985), four lectures out of which a flexible mode of naturalism emerges in the course of a concentrated review of his work to date.

Stream of Consciousness, the literary technique whereby an author attempts to render the internal verbal, imaginative, and perceptual activities of a character. William *James coined the term in *Principles of Psychology* (1890) to designate the continual succession of cognitive events that take place in the mind. Increasing use of lengthy passages of introspection in the novels of Henry *James, Fyodor Dostoevsky, and others preceded the emergence of the stream of consciousness method. Early examples of the mode, which is also referred to as 'interior monologue', are found in *Les Lauriers sont coupés* (1888) by Edouard Dujardin (1861–1949); this novel is believed to have suggested possibilities to James Joyce, whose **Ulysses* (1922) remains the most memorable demonstration of stream of consciousness writing. The book's narrative is developed primarily through the depictions of the internal workings of the minds of its three main characters; Molly Bloom's forty-page monologue forming the conclusion bears only one punctuation mark, indicating the distortions of conventional syntax and usage which are frequently a feature of the technique. Dorothy *Richardson's monumental *Pilgrimage* (1915–67) contains striking early uses of stream of consciousness procedures, which are also central to Virginia Woolf's *The *Waves* (1931) and William Faulkner's *The *Sound and the Fury* (1931). The technique has latterly become a comparatively commonplace device in prose fiction and has its equivalents in poetry, notable examples being found in W. H. Auden's *The *Age of Anxiety* (1948) and the title poem of Ted Hughes's **Wodwo* (1967).

Streetcar Named Desire, A, a play by Tennessee *Williams, produced and published in 1948. Blanche DuBois, her life in ruins and her family home, *Belle Reve*, compulsorily sold and the proceeds frittered away, arrives in the Elysian Fields district of New Orleans, a virtual slum, to stay with her sister Stella and brother-in-law Stanley Kowalski. Blanche finds the coarseness of Stanley and his pals, most of them 'Polacks' (of Polish origin), hard to take. An understanding begins between her and a friend of Stanley's, the more sensitive Mitch. Blanche is hardly justified in her contempt for Stanley for she has left behind in Mississippi a promiscuous past. Stanley finds out about this and disabuses Mitch of the illusions he has built up around her. He then forces himself upon Blanche physically with the words: 'We've had this date with each other from the beginning', finally arranging for her commitment to a lunatic asylum. Stella, though distressed at her sister's plight, finds consolation in her husband's renewed physical attentions. Blanche represents the South in the twentieth century, backward-looking, at once degenerate and over-refined, proud, and whorish.

STRONG, L(eonard) A(lfred) G(eorge) (1896–1958), Anglo-Irish novelist and poet, born in Plymouth, educated at Wadham College, Oxford. He was a school master in Oxford where he befriended the young C. *Day Lewis. Strong worked as an editor in publishing houses and was a director of Methuen (1938–58). He received critical acclaim with his first novel, *Dewer Rides* (1929), set in Dartmoor. This was followed by many others, displaying the writer's predilection for the macabre and violent. Of these, several have an Irish background, including *Sea Wall* (1933). *Travellers* (1945; James Tait Black Memorial Prize, 1946) was amongst his many volumes of short stories. His critical works include *The Sacred River: An Approach to James Joyce* (1949) and *Personal Remarks* (1953; essays) containing studies on *Synge and *Yeats. Strong also wrote dramatic works, biographies, poems, including the collection *The Body's Imperfections* (1957), and an autobiography, *Green Memory* (1961).

Structuralism, a movement of thought which developed from the linguistic theory of Ferdinand de Saussure (1857–1913) and the practice of the Russian Formalists (see FORMALISM). It was chiefly a French phenomenon, although it had far-reaching effects elsewhere, and rose to international prominence with the anthropological work of Claude Lévi-Strauss (1908–): *Structural Anthropology* (1958), *The Savage Mind* (1962), and *Totemism* (1965). The brilliant literary and cultural criticism of Roland Barthes (1915–1980), notably *Writing Degree Zero* (1953), *Mythologies* (1957), and *On Racine* (1963), was also immensely influential. Saussure argued that the linguistic sign is purely conventional, functioning only as part of the system to which it is assigned; the Formalists sought to direct attention to the *foregrounding of artistic means. Together, these two suggestions invited a new emphasis on structures rather than textures, on codes and systems rather than contents and meanings. In a famous example of Saussure's, what identifies a train is the journey it makes and its place in a time-table, not the engine and the rolling-stock. In marriage exchanges even people become a form of currency. Structuralism proposed that much human activity, even seemingly improvised activity, is in fact a game or a ritual, and that all games and rituals have rules which can be uncovered and described. One effect of this proposition for literature was a rediscovery of rhetoric as a mode of analysis, and the work of Tzvetan Todorov (1940–) and Gérard Genette (1930–) in particular offers excellent examples of what highly formalized close investigation of a text can yield. Structuralism gave way to *post-structuralism when writers and scholars began to feel that the rule-bound world of their enquiries was not so much too abstract as too intelligible, too perfect in its inevitable coherence.

STUART, Francis (1902–), Irish novelist, born in Queensland, Australia, brought up in Ireland, and educated in England. He married Iseult Gonne (Maud Gonne's daughter) in 1920, and his early poetry, which appeared in *We Have Kept the Faith* (1923), was praised by W. B. *Yeats. Stuart was a man of action, keen on sports, and his early novels *The Coloured Dome* (1932), *Pigeon Irish* (1932), and *Try the Sky* (1933) reflect an interest in flying. During the Second World War he was in Germany, at first as a lecturer at the University of Berlin, but he became better known for his weekly broadcasts supporting Irish neutrality. *Black List, Section H* (1971), perhaps his best-known novel, deals intensively with this period; similar themes are explored in *The Pillar of Cloud* (1948) and *Redemption* (1949) which, with *The Flowering Cross* (1950), formed a trilogy. *Memorial* (1973), *A Hole in the Head* (1977), and *The High Consistory* (1981) deal with Irish political themes. An impassioned plea for the artist's independence of spirit is apparent in much of his work. *A Festschrift for Francis Stuart on his 70th Birthday* (1972), edited by W. J. McCormack, attests to the growth of his reputation in the years since the war.

STURGEON, Theodore (Hamilton) (1918–85), American short-story writer and novelist of fantasy and *science fiction, born Edward Hamilton Waldo, in Staten Island, New York; his name was changed to Sturgeon when he was adopted in 1929. His most famous work, *More Than Human* (1953), is a collection of three closely linked novellas presenting a transpersonal *Gestalt*. His first novel, *The Dreaming Jewels* (1950), expressed with equal power the adolescent dream of secret omniscience. *Venus Plus X* (1960) integrated a utopian discourse within a pulp narrative. Sturgeon's best stories, which are highly charged, ingenious, and romantic, appeared in *Without Sorcery* (1948), *E Pluribus Unicorn* (1953), *Caviar* (1955), *A Way Home* (1955), *A Touch of Strange* (1958), and *Beyond* (1960). He influenced writers such as S. R. *Delany and R. *Zelazny.

STYRON, William (1925–), American novelist, born in Newport News, Virginia, educated at Duke University. He has served in the US Marine Corps. His first novel, *Lie Down in Darkness* (1951), the story of a young Southern woman's madness and eventual suicide, is indebted to *Faulkner. The relatively brief

The Long March (1956), set against the backdrop of the Korean War in which he served, is considered by some critics to be his finest work of fiction. In *Set This House on Fire* (1960) Styron inhabits the consciousness of another Southerner, an expatriate artist who wanders around France and Italy in search of the creativity that, because of his heavy drinking and the lack of real love in his life, continues to elude him. He is also the author of *The *Confessions of Nat Turner* (1967) and the famous *Sophie's Choice* (1979), which examines, through the eyes of a newcomer to New York (a convincing autobiographical portrayal), the lives of the fascinating and enigmatic Polish refugee Sophie and her Jewish lover who is seemingly brilliant but actually quite insane. Set in part in the Nazi concentration camps in which Sophie claims to have suffered, the novel is a searching account of strategies of survival and ensuing guilt, and raised some controversy for its provocative handling of tangled moral issues.

SUI SIN FAR, see ASIAN-AMERICAN LITERATURE.

Suitable Boy, A, see SETH, VIKRAM.

SUKENICK, Ronald (1932–), American novelist and critic, born in Brooklyn, New York City, educated at Brandeis University. Ever since his involvement with the Fiction Collective, which he helped to establish in 1970, Sukenick has come to be regarded as one of the central figures in contemporary American *postmodernist fiction. Like Raymond *Federman, Sukenick is as much interested in the iconic or visual character of fiction as he is in the worlds it dramatizes and his writing makes extensive use of variable typographical faces. His novels include *Up* (1968), *Out* (1973), *98.6* (1975), *Long Talking Bad Conditions Blues* (1979), *Blown Away* (1986), and *Down and In: Life in the Underground* (1988). *The Death of the Novel and Other Stories* (1969) draws together his early short stories while *In Form: Digressions on the Art of Fiction* (1985) is a collection of critical writings. He has also written on the American poet Wallace *Stevens, notably in *Wallace Stevens: Musing the Obscure* (1967). Sukenick became Director of Creative Writing at the University of Colorado at Boulder. See *The Novel as Performance: The Fiction of Ronald Sukenick and Raymond Federman* (1986), by Jerzy Kutnick.

Sula, see MORRISON, TONI.

SUMMERSON, Sir John (Newenham) (1904–92), British architectural historian, born in Darlington, educated at University College, London. From 1934 to 1941 he edited *The Architect and Building News* and subsequently held lectureships at various colleges in Britain and America. He was Slade Professor of Fine Art at Oxford (1958–9) and Cambridge (1966–7) and was curator of the Sir John Soane Museum from 1945 to 1984; *Sir John Soane* (1952) is his appreciation of the architect and his work. The essays of *Heavenly Mansions* (1949) were among the early works that brought Summerson to notice as a writer on architecture. His major studies include *Architecture in Britain, 1530–1830* (1953), *The Classical Language of Architecture* (1964, revised edition 1980), *Inigo Jones* (1966), and *The Life and Work of John Nash, Architect* (1981). His later essays were collected in *The Unromantic Castle* (1990). He was knighted in 1958.

Summoned by Bells, an autobiographical poem in blank verse by John *Betjeman, first published in 1960; *The Illustrated Summoned by Bells*, with paintings and drawings by the author's friend Sir Hugh Casson, appeared in 1990. The text is in nine parts occupying more than 100 pages, and its sales exceed those of any poem of comparable length in the twentieth century. Betjeman used blank verse for the work, his most extended piece of autobiographical writing, as a compromise between prose and poetry; the style he adopts is deliberately more prosaic than that of other poems he wrote in blank verse and proves highly appropriate to the rapid development of the narrative. A variety of rhymed verse forms are used at certain points throughout the poem for occasional effects of lyrical emphasis. In addition to the wealth of information imparted about Betjeman himself and his family, *Summoned by Bells* contains many passages of architectural interest, the subject emerging as a leitmotif after his interest in it is seen to intensify at Marlborough College. The topographical predilections evident elsewhere in his poetry are also apparent in the numerous treatments of places and landscapes, most notably north London, Cornwall, Wiltshire, and Oxford. The poem covers the period between infancy and the commencement of Betjeman's brief spell in the teaching profession following his ignominious departure from Oxford after failing in Divinity; it forms a valuable contribution to the social and cultural histories of the late Edwardian and Georgian eras, and alludes to numerous well-known figures with whom Betjeman had contact.

Sun Also Rises, The, a novel by Ernest *Hemingway, published in 1926; published in Britain as *Fiesta* in 1927. The original title derives from a passage in Ecclesiastes, which concludes that 'the earth abideth forever'. Its epigraph, 'you are all a lost generation' (see LOST GENERATION), comes from a story told to the author by Gertrude *Stein, but was later described by Hemingway as laughable after a disagreement with Stein. The novel opens with Jake Barnes, the emasculated narrator, in Paris. Among the cast of characters assembled in the city is Lady Brett Ashley, a sexually ambiguous Englishwoman who is awaiting a divorce in order to marry Michael Campbell. After a fishing trip with his friend Bill Gorton, the description of which is an early indication of Hemingway's completely mature style, Barnes arrives in Pamplona in time for the fiesta. The others follow, and the central section of the novel is devoted to detailed accounts of their fascination with the mysterious ritual of the bullfight. Brett shuns the attentions of Robert Cohn, a Jewish novelist, falls in love with Romero, a toreador, and then abandons him in order to return to

Campbell because he is one of her kind. This motley crew disbands acrimoniously and despairingly, and at the end Brett and Jake are alone in a taxi to act out an epitome of the empty relationships which have dominated the book throughout.

Surfacing, a novel by Margaret *Atwood, published in 1973. A young Canadian divorcee travels with three friends—one of them her lover—to her childhood home, in search of clues to the disappearance of her father from a remote island in a large lake in Northern Quebec. This outward search takes her back to her childhood and her past, inducing her to face the unresolved questions of her life as a woman. Motherhood, sexuality, and identity are dissolved in a crucible of mysticism verging on madness, as she plunges into visions of the supernatural and the mythological, described in spare, poetic language that evokes the wonder and the horror of the Canadian wilderness. Natural imagery is employed by Atwood as a metaphor for inner states in this novel of quest, which, while reflecting contemporary works by Doris *Lessing and some of the theories of R. D. *Laing, is nevertheless innovative and unique in its fusion of language and vision and its depiction of psychological states. The triumphant conclusion, in which the narrator emerges in full possession of her powers as a woman, is a masterpiece of feminist epiphany, and the novel sets forth several of the themes of Atwood's later poetry and of her prose, both fictional and critical.

Surrealism was a European movement in the arts, centred on the proclamations and activities of André Breton (1896–1966) in Paris. It included work in film, painting, and literature, although it was opposed to the very notion of art as irredeemably bourgeois. The Surrealists sought immediate, uncensored contact with the unconscious and the unintelligible, and the principle of automatic writing was at the heart of their enterprise. They were interested in dreams, Freud, political revolution, whatever seemed to them to deny or overturn conventional rationality. 'The marvellous is always beautiful', Breton said in the first *Surrealist Manifesto* (1924); 'anything marvellous is beautiful; indeed, only the marvellous is beautiful.' In spite of the anarchy of their ambitions, the Surrealists produced some notable art in several areas: what remains is not the gesture of rebellion but an eerie sense of the revelation of repressed or neglected material, the continuing threat which apparent nonsense poses to apparent order. In painting René Magritte produced haunting work, and there are still surprises in the over-produced dreamscapes of Dali. Buñuel and Dali's films *Un Chien andalou* (1929) and *L'Age d'or* (1930) remain powerful and disturbing. In prose, Breton's *Nadja* (1928) and Aragon's *Le Paysan de Paris* (1926) eloquently evoke the mood of the movement; its most gifted and memorable poets were Paul Éluard and Robert Desnos. Surrealism was very much an expression of the period between the wars, a French cousin of Anglo-American *Modernism, although its politics were very different. It was a response to the sense of betrayal widely felt in Europe after the First World War, and it faded as the approach of the Second World War brought to the fore a new order of anxieties and needs.

SUTHERLAND, Efua (Theodora Morgue) (1924–), Ghanaian playwright, born in Cape Coast, Ghana; she trained as a teacher at Homerton College, Cambridge, and subsequently entered London University's School of Oriental and African Studies. In 1951 she returned to Ghana to teach. She founded the Ghana Drama Studio in Accra in 1957, a seminal resource which was superseded by the National Theatre in 1990; she also established the School of Performing Arts at the University of Ghana in 1964. Her plays include *Foriwa* (1962), a plea for the acceptance of social change; *Edufa* (1967), a dramatization of tensions between inherited belief and modernity; and *The Marriage of Anansewa* (1975), which presents a comic fable of cultural manipulation. Much of her writing attempts to fuse traditional Ghanaian dramatic conventions and urgently contemporary themes. Her other works include the documentary essays of *The Roadmakers* (1961) and *The Original Bob* (1970), a biography of the celebrated Ghanaian comedian Bob Johnson.

SWEENEY, Matthew (1952–), Irish poet, born in Donegal, educated at University College, Dublin, the Polytechnic of North London, and Freiburg University. He was Fellow in Creative Writing at the University of East Anglia in 1986. He has also worked as an organizer of events and publicity officer for the Poetry Society. His collections of poetry include *A Dream of Maps* (1981), *A Round House* (1983), *The Lame Waltzer* (1985), *Blue Shoes* (1989), and *Cacti* (1992). A laconic but confiding tone permeates much of his writing, which is remarkable for the idiosyncratic wit and economy of its narrative and anecdotal treatments. Many of his poems form imaginatively disquieting fables of the precariousness of existence. A high degree of technical accomplishment underlies the effects of rhyme and rhythm which unobtrusively enrich the textures of his verse. He is also noted for his books of poetry for children, which include *The Chinese Dressing Gown* (1987).

SWENSON, May (1919–), American poet, born in Logan, Utah, educated at Utah State University. Swenson's first volume of poetry, *Another Animal*, was published in 1954 but it was several decades later that she secured her standing as one of the most significant of post-war American women poets. Despite the semantic simplicity of her verse her poems are often abstruse and elliptical. Like many of her contemporaries she sees poetry as a kind of magic and she frequently draws on mythological and necromantic imagery to suggest the intractable mysteries of being. The verse frequently suggests equations between natural landscapes and the human body, notably in 'Sketch for a Landscape'. Her second volume, *A Cage* *of Spines* (1958), was followed by *To Mix with Time: New and Selected Poems* (1963), which combines earlier poems with new poems resulting from her travels through France, Italy, and Spain in 1960 and 1961. Other volumes include *Half Sun Half Sleep* (1967), *Iconographs: Poems* (1970), *The Guess and Spell Coloring Book* (1976), *New and Selected Things Taking Place* (1978), *In Other Words: New Poems* (1987), *The Love Poems of May Swenson* (1991), and *Nature: Poems Old and New* (1994); she has also written several volumes for younger readers, particularly *Poems to Solve* (1966), *More Poems to Solve* (1971), and *The Complete Poems to Solve* (1993). In addition she has translated *Windows and Stones* (1972) from the Swedish of Thomas Transtromer. See *Alone With America: Essays on the Art of Poetry in the United States Since 1950* (1971), by Richard Howard.

SWIFT, Graham (1949–), British novelist, born in London, educated at the University of East Anglia. His first novel, *The Sweetshop Owner* (1980), was followed by the psychological thriller *Shuttlecock* (1981; Geoffrey Faber Memorial Prize, 1983), which traces the narrator's gradual discovery of the truth about his father's wartime past; and by a collection of short stories, many of them with a London setting, *Learning to Swim* (1982). In 1983, Swift was one of those chosen as the Best Young British Novelists by the Book Marketing Council. His novel *Waterland* (1983), a study of an obsessional relationship, set in the East Anglian Fenlands, was widely acclaimed for its detailed recreation of the Norfolk landscape and for its skill at conveying disturbed states of mind. Narrated by a middle-aged history teacher, Tom Crick, it describes the traumatic events which took place many years before in his boyhood home, and incorporates reflections on a wide variety of subjects, including the French Revolution, the history of the East Anglian drainage system, the life-cycle of the eel, and the development of brewing techniques. *Out of This World* (1988) consists of three linked narratives: that of Harry Beech, a war photographer, his daughter Sophie, and his war-hero father, murdered by terrorists in front of his son and granddaughter. *Ever After* (1992) is narrated in the first person by a middle-aged academic, Bill Unwin, whose account of his own life, ranging from post-war Greece to 1950s Soho, is interspersed with details of the life of his Victorian ancestor, Matthew Pearce, pieced together from notebooks. In *Last Orders* (1996) the friends of Jack Dobbs, a Bermondsey butcher, honour his last request by scattering his ashes on the sea at Margate. During their car journey through Rochester, Chatham and Canterbury, the characters (a second-hand-car dealer, an insurance clerk, a fruit and vegetable trader) tell their very different stories. The novel demonstrates great technical skill in its use of alternate narrators and confirms Swift's reputation as a consistently accomplished writer, most at ease when he is exploring the intricacies of psychological motivation, but also displaying an acute sensitivity towards details of place and atmosphere. Apart from his fiction, Swift has also co-edited (with David Profumo) *The Magic Wheel: An Anthology of Fishing in Literature* (1985).

Swimming Pool Library, The, see HOLLINGHURST, ALAN.

SWINNERTON, Frank (1884–1982), British novelist and critic, born in London. After leaving school at the age of 14 he worked as an office boy, and eventually became an editor at Chatto and Windus. Early novels, such as *The Merry Heart* (1909) or *The Happy Family* (1912), emulated the Edwardian world of A. *Bennett, whom he admired, but with *Nocturne* (1917) he achieved critical acclaim. A prolific writer, his subsequent novels included *Young Felix* (1923), *Harvest Comedy* (1937), and *Death of a Highbrow* (1961). Among his non-fiction works were biographies of *George Gissing* (1912), *R. L. Stevenson* (1914), and *Arnold Bennett: A Last Word* (1978). As literary critic of *Truth and Nation*, the *Evening News*, and the *Observer* he was a central figure in London literary circles; *The Georgian Literary Scene* (1934) provided an interesting account of the period, as did his autobiographies, *Swinnerton: An Autobiography* (1937) and *Reflections from a Village* (1969).

Sword of Honour, a trilogy of novels by Evelyn *Waugh, published in 1965; originally published as *Men at Arms* (1952), *Officers and Gentlemen* (1955), and *Unconditional Surrender* (1961). *Men at Arms* concerns the attempts of its hero, Guy Crouchback, to get a commission at the outbreak of the Second World War, partly to distract himself from the memory of his ex-wife, Virginia Troy, whom he still loves. He enlists in the Royal Corps of Halberdiers and is sent to West Africa, where his comrades-in-arms include the eccentric Apthorpe. When Apthorpe is taken ill with a tropical fever, Guy gives in to his urgent request for a bottle of whisky—only to find that his gift has fatal consequences. Disgraced, Guy returns to England. *Officers and Gentlemen* finds Guy on a remote Hebridean island, training with a commando unit. Action in Alexandria is followed by a disastrous and humiliating campaign in Crete, from which the troops are withdrawn after suffering heavy losses. Other characters include the social-climbing Captain 'Trimmer' McTavish, formerly a hairdresser, who has an affair with Virginia. *Unconditional Surrender* finds Guy, disgusted by the futility of the war, confined to a desk job at HOO HQ (Hazardous Offensive Operations Headquarters); attempting to relieve this bureaucratic tedium, he learns to parachute, injuring himself in the process. Virginia visits Guy in hospital and later tells him that she is pregnant by Trimmer, whom she now loathes. Guy offers to marry her in order to give a father to her child. He does so, shortly before being sent to Yugoslavia where he learns that Virginia has been killed in an air-raid. Her child survives and Guy remarries after the war.

Symbolism is present wherever an object or gesture stands for or suggests something beyond itself, and in this sense is littered about ordinary life, something we engage in all the time. In literature it refers to the technique of relying heavily on master images, as in the drama of Ibsen or Maeterlinck, and more importantly, to a movement in poetry and aesthetics in France at the end of the nineteenth century. The leading Symbolist poet was Stéphane Mallarmé (1842–1898), whose poems and theories had a very strong influence on certain developments in English and American literature, notably the work of W. B. *Yeats and Wallace *Stevens. For Mallarmé it was the business of the poet to 'paint not the thing but the effect it produces', a form of Impressionism. What words evoked was not what they named but what they could not name, the implied, always absent perfection being supplied by the mind of the reader. Mallarmé also believed that the poet should disappear from his verse as a person, 'yielding the initiative to the words'. His own work was delicate, difficult, and highly formal, although it included experiments with typography and in prose. His precursor was Charles Baudelaire (1821–1867); he shared a number of poetic preoccupations with Arthur Rimbaud (1854–1891) and Paul Verlaine (1844–1896); Edgar Allan Poe, whom he translated, was also important to him. His chief successor was Paul Valéry (1871–1945), who saw poetry as a form of dance of the intelligence. Symbolism was introduced into Britain by Arthur Symons's *The Symbolist Movement in Literature* (1899), widely read by poets and critics; a good early account of Symbolism as a European movement, more or less identical with what was later to be called *Modernism, is *Axel's Castle* (1931), by Edmund *Wilson. A. G. Lehmann's *The Symbolist Aesthetic in France* (1950) is an excellent analysis of the intricacies of Symbolist thought.

SYMONS, A(lphonse) J(ames) A(lbert) (1900–41), British biographer and bibliophile, born in London; he left school at the age of 14. His involvements in book-dealing led him to establish the First Editions Club in 1922, which he ran until his death. An authority on the literature and bibliography of the 1890s, he produced his widely read *Anthology of 'Nineties' Verse* in 1928. Through his bibliographical activities he developed a compelling interest in F. W. *Rolfe ('Baron Corvo'); *The Quest for Corvo: An Experiment in Biography* (1934), his best-known work, advanced *biography through its strategy of making the author a principal protagonist in an investigative narrative. He failed to complete his ambitious biography of Oscar Wilde, parts of which appear in *Essays and Biographies* (1969), edited by his brother Julian *Symons. He also wrote short biographies of H. M. Stanley (1928) and Emin Pasha (1933) and produced numerous penetrating essays on other figures whose idiosyncratic characters appealed to him. He was a founding member of the Sette of Odde Volumes Dining Club, to which he addressed a number of his essays. Julian Symons's *A. J. A. Symons: His Life and Speculations* was published in 1950.

SYMONS, Julian (Gustave) (1912–94), British poet, biographer, social historian, crime novelist, and critic, born in London, the brother of A. J. A. *Symons; he worked as an advertising copywriter before the Second World War, but in 1945 became a freelance writer and critic. He founded and edited *Twentieth Century Verse* (1937–9), an important magazine which published most of the young poets outside the immediate *Auden circle. He published several collections of verse (*Confessions about X*, 1939; *The Second Man*, 1943; *The Object of an Affair*, 1974), and wrote much on poetry of the 1930s. The subjects of his biographies include his brother (1950), Dickens (1951), Carlyle (1952), Horatio Bottomley (1955), Poe (1978), and *Doyle (1979), while among his works on British social history in the 1920s and 1930s are *The General Strike: A Historical Portrait* (1957) and *The Thirties: A Dream Revolved* (1960; revised 1975), together with many articles. He wrote on true crime (*A Reasonable Doubt: Some Criminal Cases Re-examined*, 1960; *Crime and Detection: An Illustrated History from 1840*, 1966, US title *A Pictorial History of Crime*), and prolifically on crime fiction, which he reviewed for the *Sunday Times* for a number of years: *Bloody Murder* (1972, revised 1985; US title *Mortal Consequences*) is an authoritative history of the genre. His first work of crime fiction, *The Immaterial Murder Case* (1945), an accomplished parody of the detective genre, was followed by many novels and short stories. *The Man Who Killed Himself* (1967) and *The Plot against Roger Rider* (1973) are highly ingenious detective stories, but his best novels are perhaps those which combine crime with a critical view of contemporary society (*The Colour of Murder*, 1957; *The End of Solomon Grundy*, 1964; *The Players and the Game*, 1972; and *Playing Happy Families*, 1994), or of late Victorian hypocrisy (*The Blackheath Poisonings*, 1978; *Sweet Adelaide*, 1980; and *The Detling Murders*, 1982, US title *The Detling Secret*). The autobiographical *Notes from Another Country* (1972) deals with his early life.

SYNGE, John Millington (1871–1909), Irish playwright, born in a Dublin suburb, the son of a barrister. After graduating in languages, including Celtic, from Trinity College, Dublin, he travelled in Europe and settled for some years in Paris. There, W. B. *Yeats advised the aspiring writer to go to the Aran Islands, off the west coast of Ireland, in search of 'a life that has never found expression'. Accordingly, he stayed there annually from 1898 to 1902, describing the peasant world he discovered in the non-fiction *The Aran Islands* (1907) and finding in it both language and inspiration for the plays he proceeded to write. The first, *The Shadow of the Glen* (1903), is a sombre one-act comedy in which an elderly husband feigns death, then leaps from his winding sheet and banishes the neglected young wife who has started discussing marriage with a local farmer. The equally short **Riders to the Sea* (1904), one of the few modern plays which can claim to be called a tragedy, involves the death of the sixth son of an old woman who has already lost all his brothers and her own husband to the sea. *The Well of the Saints* (1905) is a sardonic comedy about a beggar and his wife who, given their sight by a holy man, elect to resume their former blindness rather than cease pretending that they are both of exceptional physical beauty. *The *Playboy of the Western World* (1907), which caused serious rioting at Dublin's *Abbey Theatre on its first performance, was the last play Synge himself saw on the stage. He died of cancer at only 37, leaving unperformed the short *Tinker's Wedding* (1908) and the longer **Deirdre of the Sorrows* (1910), in which the title character, having eloped with the beautiful Naisi, is lured home and destroyed by the lustful King Conchubor.

Synge's is a slim *œuvre*, but a distinctive and distinguished one, partly because of the lyricism and simple power of his language, but mainly because of the grim yet ecstatic view of life his plays convey. Their overriding theme, and usually the source of dramatic tension, is the contrast between illusion, dream, fantasy—an Irish imagination he found 'fiery, magnificent and tender'—and the more numbing aspects of an often sordid Irish reality.

SZIRTES, George (1948–), British poet, born in Budapest, Hungary; his family came to London after the uprising of 1956. He studied fine art at Leeds College of Art, where Martin *Bell encouraged him in his early work as a poet. After working as an art teacher in various schools and colleges, he became a freelance writer in 1987. In addition to his considerable reputation as a poet, he is highly regarded as a graphic artist and has exhibited his work widely. With his wife Clarissa Upchurch, he runs the Starwheel Press, which specializes in finely illustrated limited editions of verse. His first full collection of poetry, *The Slant Door* (1979), was followed by subsequent publications including *November and May* (1981), *Short Wave* (1983), *The Photographer in Winter* (1986), *Metro* (1988), *Bridge Passages* (1991), and *Blind Field* (1994). His verse is characterized by the striking precision and clarity of its imagery and the originality and assurance of his use of rhyme and metre. His later collections reveal his intense imaginative concern with modern European history and its effects on his immediate family. His many translations of Hungarian poetry include Imre Madách's *The Tragedy of Man* (1988), and poems by Zsuzsa Rakovsky in *New Life* (1994).

T

TAGORE, Rabindranath (1861–1941), Bengali poet, novelist, and playwright, born in Calcutta, educated privately and at University College, London, from 1878 to 1880. In India, Tagore is highly regarded as one of the great figures of modern literature for his innovations in poetry, prose fiction, and drama in his own language, Bengali. The current reassessment of his work depends entirely on recent translations of his work and the republishing of translations of the ingeniously constructed novel *The Home and the World* (tr. 1919), upon which Satyajit Ray based a successful film. However, he first achieved international renown as a sort of mystic and sage, praised by literary dignitaries like *Yeats and *Pound, when he produced his own English renditions—now considered woefully inferior to the Bengali originals—of such works as *Geetanjali* (1912), presented as a series of prose poems, which earned him the Nobel Prize in 1913, *The Gardener* (1913), and *Lover's Gift, and Crossing* (1918). However, his English works are out of print and he is best appreciated in translation. A notable novel is *Gora* (tr. 1924). *Rabindranath Tagore, Poet and Dramatist* (1926) is a critical biography by Edward *Thompson who translated his works. See also *Alien Homage: Edward Thompson and Rabindranath Tagore* (1993) by E. P. *Thompson.

Tamarack Review, a quarterly journal of poetry, prose fiction, essays, and criticism established in 1956 in Toronto by Robert Weaver in association with Kildare Dobbs, Anne *Wilkinson, William Toye, and others. Weaver and Toye remained as editors of the magazine throughout its career. The discontinuation of *Northern Review* (see FIRST STATEMENT and PREVIEW) in 1956 was a motivating factor in the founding of *Tamarack Review*, which declared its commitment to literary merit as the sole criterion for publication of work by new and established writers; the maintenance of such standards resulted in adverse criticism of the magazine's apparent neglect of writing favoured by more emphatically nationalist literary factions. Its concern with aesthetic quality was also evident in its consistently attractive design and production and it rapidly achieved an international reputation as the finest Canadian literary periodical of its day. F. R. *Scott, A. J. M. *Smith, and Irving *Layton were among the recognized writers whose verse was recurrently featured; it helped to foster the careers of Jay *Macpherson, Leonard *Cohen, and other notable Canadian poets of the 1960s, while Mordecai *Richler and Alice *Munro were among the emerging writers who contributed prose fiction. In 1982 it ceased publication. Robert Weaver edited *The First Five Years* (1963), an anthology of work which demonstrated the healthily eclectic character of the magazine.

TAMBIMUTTU, (Meary James Thurairajah) (1915–83), Ceylonese editor and poet, generally known by his surname alone, born of an aristocratic English-speaking family in Ceylon (now Sri Lanka). He left Ceylon for Britain in 1937. Once in London, he rapidly established himself as a significant member of the literary and artistic circles of Soho and Fitzrovia, and was among the founders of **Poetry London* in 1939. He edited the magazine until his departure for the USA in 1947, where he began the short-lived *Poetry London–New York* in 1956. His versions of traditional Indian erotic lyrics were published with a series of prints by John Piper in an opulently produced limited edition entitled *India Love Poems* (1977). His numerous other works as an editor include a Festschrift for the sixtieth birthday of T. S. *Eliot, who approved of his endeavours in the 1940s and commissioned him to edit *Poetry in Wartime* (1942); *Natarajah* (1949), also in celebration of Eliot's birthday, and *Out of this War* (1941) are his principal publications as a poet. *Tambimuttu: Bridge between Two Worlds* (1989) is a collection of memoirs edited by Jane Williams.

TAN, Amy (1952–), Chinese-American novelist, born in Oakland, California, educated in California and Switzerland, and at the San José State University. Tan's parents were immigrants from mainland China and her fictions are inspired, in part, by the history of her own family. In her first novel, *The Joy Luck Club* (1989), her mother's experiences of semi-feudal China, of the Civil War, and of the advent of the Communist Revolution are refracted through the perspectives of the first-generation immigrant mothers of resolutely, if ambivalently, American daughters. *The Kitchen God's Wife* (1991), concentrating on the relationship between a mother and daughter, explores the position of women in pre-revolutionary China; it was followed by *The Hundred Secret Senses* (1996). Tan's recurring theme—the contrast between the Chinese past and the American present—and the exotic imagery she employs in her prose place her within a tradition of Asian-American writing closely identified with Maxine Hong *Kingston. Her novels, which bridge the gap between the literary and the popular, have also been compared to the novels of Louise *Erdrich, Bharati *Mukherjee, and Isabel Allende.

TANNER, Tony (1935–), British critic, born at Richmond in Surrey, educated at Jesus College, Cambridge. In 1964 he became Director of English Studies at King's College, Cambridge, and was appointed Professor of English and American Literature at Cambridge in 1989. *The Reign of Wonder: Naivety and Piety in American Literature* (1965), his first major critical work, investigates the quality of wonderment as an essential characteristic of American literature from the era of the Trancendentalists to the *Modernism of Ernest *Hemingway, Gertrude *Stein, and others. *City of Words: American Fiction, 1950–1970* (1970), which established his reputation in the vanguard of contemporary criticism, examines the ethical and aesthetic dilemmas of various post-war American authors and considers the development of 'style as a defensive strategy'. His other publications include *Adultery in the Novel* (1979), *Henry James* (1985), *Jane Austen* (1986), and the wide-ranging collection of essays entitled *Scenes of Nature, Signs of Men* (1987). Among the numerous texts Tanner has edited are Henry James's *Hawthorne* (1968) and Hermann Melville's *Moby-Dick* (1988).

Tarka the Otter, see WILLIAMSON, HENRY.

TARKINGTON, (Newton) Booth (1869–1946), American novelist, born in Indianapolis, Indiana, educated at Purdue and Princeton Universities. He was a popular and prolific author, writing over forty novels, over thirty plays and screenplays, and several collections of short stories in a career that began with his first novel, *The Gentleman from Indiana* (1899). Popular success was secured with his second novel, *Monsieur Beaucaire* (1900), an eighteenth-century romance. He twice won the Pulitzer Prize, for *The Magnificent Ambersons* (1918) and *Alice Adams* (1921). The former, the second part of his trilogy *Growth* (1927), remains his best-known novel, mainly due to the brilliant film adaptation by Orson Welles in 1942. A regional realist, Tarkington celebrates the simple democratic values of the rural Midwest, particularly those of Indiana, a state which he briefly served politically in the Indiana House of Representatives between 1902 and 1903. His writings, however, are perceptively alert to the effects of the rapid industrialization of the Midwest and to the increasing heterogeneity of American life in the early years of the twentieth century. In an age which looked for greater sophistication and experimentation in fiction he was viewed rather disdainfully; Vernon Louis Parrington in *The Beginnings of Critical Realism in America, 1860–1920* (1930) called him 'the dean of American middle-class letters . . . a purveyor of comfortable literature to middle-class America'. A standard study is *Booth Tarkington: Gentleman from Indiana* (1955) by James Woodress.

Tarr, a novel by Wyndham *Lewis, published in 1918, revised in 1928. Set in Paris in the early 1900s, the novel describes the relationships within a group of 'bourgeois-bohemians' in the café society of Montmartre. The opening conversation between Frederick Tarr, a talented young English painter, and Alan Hobson (a satirical portrait of Roger Fry), about Tarr's intentions towards his fiancée Bertha Lunken, a German art student, results in Tarr's decision to break off his engagement. Finding himself unable to carry out his resolution, and in order to cure himself of his sentimental attachment to Bertha, he resolves to practise a Nietzschean code of 'indifference', but his cynical resolution is shaken when he encounters the beautiful Anastasya Vasek whose sexual and intellectual appetites match his own. Anastasya already has an admirer, Otto Kreisler, a failed painter and fervent believer in the Nietzschean concept of the *'Übermensch'*, who represents the nihilistic centre of the book. Through a series of bizarre accidents, Kreisler becomes involved in a duel over Anastasya with another of her admirers, Louis Soltyk, whom he kills; he rapes Bertha, who becomes pregnant, and finally hangs himself. Tarr, who no longer loves Bertha, agrees to marry her, but true to his contempt for the bourgeois institution of marriage, continues his affair with Anastasya and with other women. The novel in its original form was intended as an expression of Lewis's 'Vorticist' principles of art; in its revised form, the hard-edged *Modernism of its style was somewhat modified, although the main elements of the story remained the same. See also VORTICISM.

Taste of Honey, A, see DELANEY, SHELAGH.

TATE, (John Orley) Allen (1899–1979), American poet, novelist, and critic, born in Kentucky, educated at Vanderbilt University in Nashville, Tennessee, where he associated with the *Agrarians. With John Crowe *Ransom, Robert Penn *Warren, and Andrew *Lytle, he believed that the South should reject the materialistic, industrially based modern world and turn to its own roots; Tate edited the magazine *The Fugitive* (1922–5), contributed to the Fugitive/Agrarian symposium *I'll Take My Stand* (1930), and wrote interpretative biographies of Stonewall Jackson (1938) and Jefferson Davis (1929). His intellectual, neo-metaphysical poetry was collected in *Mr Pope and Other Poems* (1928), *Poems 1928–1931* (1932), and *The Mediterranean and Other Poems* (1936). The poem sequence 'Season of the Soul' (1944), while not rising to the heights of 'Ode to the Confederate Dead', contains beautiful meditations on time and contemporary history. *The Swimmers and Other Poems* (1971) contained more personal poems; *Collected Poems* appeared in 1977. His only full-length novel, *The Fathers* (1938, revised edition 1977) is narrated by an old man, Lacy Buchan, recalling the terrible events of his youth at the onset of the Civil War; the novel shows how the divisions between Unionist and Confederates within the same family reflect divisions of a cultural and psychic nature in any human society. Two remarkable short stories are 'The Immortal Woman' (1933), relating to *The Fathers*, and 'The Migration' (1934), an account of pioneers crossing the Blue Ridge Mountains. As a critic Tate subscribed to many of the tenets of the *New Criticism as seen in *Essays of Four Decades* (1969) and *Memoirs and Opinions* (1975).

TATE, James (1943–), American poet, born in Kansas City, Kansas, educated at the University of Iowa. Tate won the Yale Younger Poets competition whilst still a student at the *Iowa Writers' Workshop and he was quickly recognized as one of the most inventive, and prolific, of that younger generation of American poets born towards the end of the Second World War. His early volumes of verse, *The Lost Pilot* (1967) and *The Oblivion Ha-Ha* (1970), reveal an essentially comic and frequently sardonic voice within structures that are loosely surrealistic, but later poems seem tempered by a more mature, contemplative intelligence. His other volumes include *Hints to Pilgrims* (1971), *Absences* (1972), *Hottentot Ossuary* (1974), *Viper Jazz* (1976), *Riven Doggeries* (1979), *Constant Defender* (1983), *Reckoner* (1986), and *Distance From Loved Ones* (1990). In 1970 he took up a teaching post at the University of Massachusetts at Amherst.

TAWNEY, R(ichard) H(enry) (1880–1962), British economic historian and political philosopher, born in Calcutta, educated at Balliol College, Oxford; he became Professor of Economic History at the London School of Economics (1931). He was also a long-time supporter of the Workers' Educational Association in Lancashire and North Staffordshire, and was for sixteen years President of the Association. His best-known book, *Religion and the Rise of Capitalism* (1926), is an analysis of the impact of economic expansion on the development of religious thought in England in the sixteenth and seventeenth centuries. In contrast to Max Weber's *The Protestant Ethic and the Spirit of Capitalism*, from which it is often wrongly said to have been derivative, Tawney was concerned to chart how religious opinion on economic and social questions was materially adjusted to suit new social realities. It was in *The Agrarian Problem in the Sixteenth Century* (1912), his first book, that Tawney first displayed his mastery of the historical method that he was to deploy in *Religion and the Rise of Capitalism*. Although deeply influenced by Marx, it was not Marxist in any orthodox sense; the great divide between the economic 'base' and the political and religious 'superstructure', which had become the cornerstone of orthodox Marxist historiography, was dismantled by Tawney in the course of his analysis. In two other books, *The Acquisitive Society* (1921) and *Equality* (1931), Tawney set out his own opinion of capitalism, which he found anathema. He was fond of quoting *Keynes to the effect that modern capitalism was 'absolutely irreligious, without internal union, without much public spirit, often, though not always, a mere congeries of possessors and pursuers'.

TAYLOR, A(lan) J(ohn) P(ercivale) (1906–90), British historian, born in Birkdale, Lancashire, educated at Oriel College, Oxford. From 1928 to 1930 he worked with the Austrian historian A. F. Pibram in Vienna, gathering material for his book *The Italian Problem in European Diplomacy 1847–1849* (1934). After lecturing at Manchester University for eight years, he became a fellow of Magdalen College, Oxford, in 1938, where he taught till 1963. His preoccupation with German nationalism as a force in modern history gave rise to a succession of books which include *Germany's First Bid for Colonies* (1938), *The Habsburg Monarchy* (1941, revised edition 1948), one of his most highly regarded works, and *The Course of German History* (1945), which was explicitly condemnatory in tone. During the 1950s and 1960s he became known to a wide public through his journalism and celebrated television lectures, which were collected in 1980 as *Revolutions and Revolutionaries*. *The Origins of the Second World War* (1961) provoked a heated controversy through its reinterpretation of the extent to which Hitler was individually responsible for the conflict. Taylor's other works in a career of prolific authorship include *The Struggle for Mastery in Europe* (1954), *English History 1914–1945* (1965), his last major publication, and the biographies *Bismarck* (1955) and *Beaverbrook* (1972); his socialist convictions inform the sympathetic treatment of nineteenth-century radicals in *The Trouble Makers* (1957). *Personal History* (1983) is his wittily iconoclastic autobiography.

TAYLOR, C(ecil) P(hilip) (1927–82), British dramatist, born in Glasgow of Russian-Jewish immigrant parents, educated in the same city. He worked as an electrician, a television engineer, and a salesman before writing a series of plays which, though written from a broadly socialist stance, were notable for their gentle mockery of moral and political attitudinizing, as well as their warmth of characterization. Among them were *Allergy* (1966), *Bread and Butter* (1966), and *The Black and White Minstrels* (1972). His later work included *And a Nightingale Sang* (1979), a nostalgic comedy set in wartime Newcastle-upon-Tyne. *Good* (1981), probably his finest work, concerns Halder, a German writer and academic of the 1930s; maddened by his senile mother, he publishes a novel sympathetic to euthanasia, whereupon he finds himself courted by Nazis in search of intellectual respectability. He is persuaded to exercise his 'humane' scruples first in a subnormality hospital, then in a concentration camp, and ends up a functionary at Auschwitz, having successfully convinced himself that the Jews have brought their sufferings on themselves. Throughout his abbreviated career Taylor was unusually prolific, and wrote many television plays, as well as an adaptation of Sternheim's *Schippel* (1974).

TAYLOR, Elizabeth (1912–75), British novelist and short-story writer, born and educated in Reading, Berkshire, where she worked as a governess and librarian. In 1936 she married John Kendall Taylor, with whom she spent the rest of her life, mostly in the Buckinghamshire village of Penn, the kind of prosperous rural setting which was to provide the background for many of her novels. Her first novel, *At Mrs Lippincote's* (1945), described the effects of war on the lives of a group of middle-class English people. *Palladian* (1946) and *A View of the Harbour* (1947) were followed by *A Wreath of Roses* (1949), about the liaison between a young schoolteacher and the handsome but unreliable man who ensnares her. It was the first of an unbroken series of perceptive, poetic, and witty novels, including *A Game of Hide and Seek* (1951); *The Sleeping Beauty* (1953); *Angel* (1957), about a popular romantic novelist; *In a Summer Season* (1961), about a woman married to a man ten years her junior, whose encounter with a friend from her past prefaces dramas that reveal loving to be tragic as well as tender; and *The Soul of Kindness* (1964), a portrait of a self-deluding do-gooder. Her novels are constructed as a series of vignettes, showing the tensions and hidden dramas of the superficially comfortable and respectable world she depicts. Many of her books deal with the collapse of order (often symbolized by the breakdown of marital or sexual relationships) which is perceived as essentially fragile; the restraint with which her characters convey their feelings heightens, rather than diminishes, the emotional intensity. Later novels include *The Wedding Group* (1968), about a bohemian artistic community perhaps based on that of Eric *Gill; *Mrs Palfrey at the Claremont* (1971); and the posthumously published *Blaming* (1976). She published four acclaimed collections of short stories: *Hester Lilly* (1954), *The Blush* (1958), *A Dedicated Man* (1965), and *The Devastating Boys* (1972). *Dangerous Calm*, a selection of her stories, including hitherto unpublished and uncollected work, edited by Lynn Knight, appeared in 1995. She also published a children's story, *Mossy Trotter* (1967).

TAYLOR, Peter (1917–), American short-story writer and novelist, born in Trenton, Tennessee, educated at Vanderbilt University, Nashville, Southwestern College, Memphis, and Kenyon College, Ohio. Taylor has explored the tensions and nuances of Tennessee life, particularly in its upper and middle classes. He had published several volumes of short stories prior to *Collected Stories* (1969). The title stories of *In the Miro District and Other Stories* (1977) and *The Old Forest and Other Stories* (1985) are explorations of changing sexual mores in the traditionalist South. Other collections include *For Good or Evil* (1991), praised for its outrageous black humour, and *The Oracle at Stoneleigh Court* (1993), the title story of which concerns the irreversible effects on young lives of tarot card predictions and spiritualism. Taylor's art as a short-story writer relates, on his own admission, to a gossip's; anecdotal and attentive to the rhythms of ordinary, educated speech, the tales convey by inference the inner assumptions and confusions of a particular world. *A Summons to Memphis* (1986; Pulitzer Prize) and his subsequent novels exhibit the same qualities of restraint and subtlety that distinguish the stories. *In the Tennessee Country* (1994), set in the fading world of US southern aristocracy in the early twentieth century, is narrated by an art historian who is obsessed by his grandfather's illegitimate son.

TEMPLETON, Edith (1916–), British novelist, born in Prague, educated at the French Lycée and Prague Medical University; she settled eventually in England and married a doctor, later moving with her husband to India, where he was appointed physician to the King of Nepal. Her first story was published at the age of ten; her first novel, *Summer in the Country* (1950), is set in her native Bohemia, where an impoverished minor noble family quarrels amongst itself and ignores a murder. Further novels include *Living on Yesterday* (1951), *The Island of Desire* (1952), set in Prague and Paris, and *This Cheering Pastime* (1955), set mainly in Sicily. Her sophisticated novels often concern ignorant, wilful, and passionate young women, who are the victims of demanding and impossible men. She has also written many short stories and articles for *Vogue*, *Harper's*, and the **New Yorker*, as well as a fascinating book of memoirs and travels, *The Surprise of Cremona* (1954).

Ten Days that Shook the World, see REED, JOHN.

Tender Is the Night, a novel by F. Scott *Fitzgerald, published in 1934 and, in a revised version by Malcolm *Cowley, in 1948. Set, predominantly, on the French Riviera during the 1920s, the novel is both a social history of American expatriate life in France after the First World War and a study of the decline of an individual, Dick Diver, a gifted psychiatrist, whose marriage to the wealthy Nicole Warren (who is brought to him for treatment after an incestuous relationship with her father) precipitates his degeneration. Fitzgerald said of the novel that he wanted to 'show a man who is a natural idealist . . . giving in for various causes to the ideas of the *haute bourgeoisie*, and in his rise to the top of the social world losing his idealism, his talent, and turning to drink and dissipation', though some critics have argued that Diver's 'fall' is insufficiently motivated and explained.

The novel took some eight years to write, but Fitzgerald seems to have been dissatisfied with it. His notebooks indicate revisions to the text, primarily structural, that he might have effected and it was in the light of Fitzgerald's suggestions that the critic Malcolm *Cowley edited the revised edition of 1948. Where Fitzgerald's original text utilized a fragmented, achronological construction (for example, in the beginning, the life of the Divers on the Riviera is seen through the eyes of Rosemary Hoyt, a young actress with whom Dick has an affair), the revised edition assembles the story in a chronological sequence of events; critical opinion tends to favour the original edition. See *The Composition of 'Tender Is the Night'* (1963) by Matthew J. Bruccoli, and *'Tender Is the Night': A Critical Guide* (1986) by Kathleen Parkinson.

TENNANT, Emma (1937–), British novelist, born in London, educated at St Paul's Girls' School. In 1975 she founded and edited the experimental literary magazine **Bananas*. Her novels include *The Time of the Crack* (1973; republished as *The Crack*, 1978), an apocalyptic fantasy; *The Last of the Country House Murders* (1974), a surreal detective story; *Hotel de Dream* (1976), in which the waking lives of the lodgers at a seedy boarding-house are increasingly taken over by their dreams; *The Bad Sister* (1978), in which a young woman surrenders her identity to her murderous alter ego; and *Two Women of London: The Strange Case of Ms Jekyll and Mrs Hyde* (1989), a surreal murder story involving changes of identity. Tennant's work is blackly comic in mood, favouring bizarre events and extremes of human behaviour, and is generally described as *magic realist. *The House of Hospitalities* (1987) and *A Wedding of Cousins* (1988) are the first two volumes of a projected sequence entitled 'The Cycle of the Sun' following the fortunes of Jenny Carter, an impoverished upper-middle-class protagonist with a penchant for bohemian aristocrats. Among her other novels are *Wild Nights* (1979), *Alice Fell* (1980), *Queen of Stones* (1982), *Woman Beware Woman* (1983), *Black Marina* (1985), *The Adventures of Robina by Herself* (1986), and *Sisters and Strangers* (1990). Tennant's later work has focused on the rewriting and reworking of classical texts—fables, legends, and novels—from a feminist perspective. Her strategies range from pastiche of canonical women writers such as Jane Austen in *Pemberly—A Sequel to Pride and Prejudice* (1993) and *An Unequal Marriage—Pride and Prejudice Continued* (1994), to the feminization of myth in *Faustine* (1991). *Tess* (1993) locates, around the figure of Hardy's heroine, a series of other characters of the author's period, historical and semi-fictional, to provide a feminist interpretation of the story.

TENNANT, Kylie (1912–88), Australian novelist and historian, born in New South Wales, educated at Sydney University. Her experiences as a journalist, reviewer, lecturer, and bee-keeper, among other jobs, provided material for her novels. Her books frequently concern dispossessed sections of society and offer lively evocations of working lives. *Tiburon* (1935) was a novel about poverty during the Depression years, as was *The Battlers* (1941), which focused on agricultural day-workers at that time. A vigorous humanitarianism is demonstrated in many of her works including *Foveaux* (1939), about slum dwellers, and *Ride on Stranger* (1943). As well as novels, such as *Time Enough Later* (1943), *Lost Haven* (1946), *The Joyful Condemned* (1953; retitled *Tell Morning This*, 1967), *The Honey Flow* (1956), and *Tantavallon* (1983), she also published *Australia: Her Story* (1953); *Speak You so Gently* (1959), a study of Aboriginal collectives; and children's books. Her autobiography, *The Missing Heir*, appeared in 1986.

TERKEL, Studs (Louis) (1912–), American social historian, interviewer, critic, and radio and television broadcaster, born in New York, educated at the University of Chicago and Chicago Law School. In what remains his best known work, *Division Street America* (1966), Terkel says that 'I was out to swallow the world' . . . 'The world was my city', and in over sixty interviews with residents of Chicago he sought to represent the frequently inarticulate trials and vexations of those whom he saw as representative spokesmen and spokeswomen of urban America. The result was a literary species he called 'guerilla journalism' and *Division Street America* became an American bestseller. He deployed the same techniques of oral history, and with similar success, in *Hard Times: An Oral History of the Great Depression* (1970), *Working* (1974), *American Dreams: Lost and Found* (1980), *The Good War: An Oral History of World War II* (1985; Pulitzer Prize), and *The Great Divide: Second Thoughts on the American Dream* (1988). His other works include *Giants of Jazz* (1956), a volume of jazz criticism; *Amazing Grace* (1959), a play; *Talking to Myself: A Memoir of My Life and Times* (1977); *Chicago* (1986); and *Race: How Blacks and Whites Think and Feel About the American Obsession* (1992).

TERRAINE, John (Alfred) (1921–), British historian, born in London, educated at Keble College, Oxford. In 1944 he began working at the BBC, becoming associate producer and chief scriptwriter for the television series *The Great War* in 1963. In 1964 he became a freelance author. His reputation as a historian of the First World War was established with *Mons: The Retreat to Victory* (1960), the first of numerous studies of the conflict; subsequent works include *Douglas Haig: The Educated Soldier* (1963), *Impacts of War, 1914 and 1918* (1970), *The Road to Passchendaele* (1977), *To Win a War: 1918, the Year of Victory* (1978), and *White Heat: The New Warfare, 1914–1918* (1982). By his sometimes controversial but scrupulous interpretations of previously neglected sources, Terraine tends to qualify the general view of the First World War as an agonizingly extended exercise in deadlock and futility. Among his other publications are *The Mighty Continent* (1975), a survey of Europe in the twentieth century, and *Business in Great Waters* (1989), an account of submarine warfare from 1916 to 1945.

TERRY, Megan (1932–), American dramatist, born in Seattle, educated at the University of Washington. She is a central figure in contemporary American alternative theatre, and has been hailed as the mother of American feminist drama. She was a founding member of the *Open Theatre with Joseph Chaikin, the New York Theatre Strategy, and the Women's Theatre Council, and in 1974 was made playwright-in-residence of the Omaha Magic Theatre. In each of these contexts, she has freely engaged in formal experimentalism and the politicization of the theatrical event, especially in relation to women in society and in the theatre. Eight of her plays were produced by the Open Theatre including *Eat at Joe's* (1963), *Keep Tightly Closed in a Cool Dry Place* (1965), *Calm Down Mother* (1965), and most notably *Viet Rock* (1966), subtitled a 'Folk War Movie', which gave full expression to the transformational idiom of the Open Theatre's work, in which they sought a theatre of 'ritual, myth, illusion, and mystery' as opposed to the theatre of behavioural or psychological realism. In her work with the Omaha Magic Theatre, Terry has explored a version of 'community theatre' in which plays are created in response to the social and domestic problems of the small townships of the central Midwest plains, such as *100,001 Horror Stories of the Plains* (1976),

Goona Goona (1979), about spouse and child abuse, and *Kegger* (1982), about alcohol abuse amongst the young. Her other plays include *The Gloaming, Oh My Darling* (1965), *Approaching Simone* (1970, a version of the life of French philosopher Simone Weil), *Hothouse* (1974), *Do You See What I'm Saying* (1990), *Body Leaks* (1990), *Breakfast Serial* (1991), and *Sound Fields: Are We Hear* (1992).

TERSON, Peter, pseudonym of Peter PATTERSON (1932–), British dramatist, born in Newcastle-upon-Tyne; he started writing plays while working as a games and physical education teacher in the West Midlands, and took his pseudonym when he was resident dramatist at the pioneering theatre-in-the-round at Stoke-on-Trent in the 1960s. There, he composed several works notable for their lively observation of rural people, notably *A Night to Make the Angels Weep* (1964) and *The Mighty Reservoy* (1964), about the relationship between the hard-drinking custodian of a reservoir and a frustrated young teacher. Later, he became associated with the National Youth Theatre, writing *Zigger Zagger* (1967), an attempt to understand the so-called 'football hooligan'; *The Apprentices* (1968), set in a factory yard; *Fuzz* (1969), about a variety of dissident students, from anarchists to anti-Vietnam activists; and *Good Lads at Heart* (1971), about Borstal boys. In general, Terson's work has been marked by its humorous observation of and unsentimental sympathy for people, often young people, whose ebullient energy he contrasts with the attitudes and behaviour more conventionally found in a lacklustre society. In later years his output diminished, though he achieved some success with *Strippers* (1984), about women pluckily earning a difficult living in a dreary Northern club.

TESSIMOND, A(rthur) S(eymour) J(ohn) (1902–62), British poet, born in Birkenhead, Cheshire, educated at Charterhouse, to which he refused to return at the age of 16. After a period in London, he entered the University of Liverpool. By the age of 25 he had begun to distinguish himself as a poet; *The Walls of Glass*, his first collection of verse, appeared in 1934. *Voices in a Giant City* (1947) contained much of his finest work. The sombrely ironic lyricism with which the shabbier aspects of London are depicted makes incisive use of his sharply economical descriptive abilities. Tessimond's manner ranges between occasional poems of baldly outspoken statement and more characteristic subtleties of mood sometimes giving rise to attractively mysterious qualities. *Selection* (1958) contained material from his earlier volumes along with previously uncollected verse. A posthumous collection entitled *Not Love Perhaps . . .* appeared in 1978. *Collected Poems* (1985), edited and introduced by Hubert Nicholson, includes translations from the French poetry of Jacques Prévert.

Testament, see HUTCHINSON, R. C.

Testament of Youth, see BRITTAIN, VERA.

TEY, Josephine, pseudonym of Elizabeth MACKINTOSH (1897–1952), British crime writer and dramatist, born in Inverness. During the 1920s she worked as a school physical education teacher. She wrote eight excellent detective stories most of which feature Inspector Alan Grant, on whom Ngaio *Marsh's Roderick Alleyn appears to be modelled. The first, originally published under the pseudonym Gordon Daviot, is *The Man in the Queue* (1929; alternative US title *Killer in the Crowd*), which was followed by, among others, *A Shilling for Candles: The Story of a Crime* (1936), *Miss Pym Disposes* (1946), *To Love and Be Wise* (1950), *The Singing Sands* (1952), and *The Daughter of Time* (1952), in which Grant re-examines the supposed murder by Richard III of his two nephews in the Tower of London. *The Franchise Affair* (1948) is a fictional adaptation of the famous eighteenth-century Elizabeth Canning case. As Gordon Daviot she wrote novels (*Kif: An Unvarnished History*, 1929); a biography, *Claverhouse* (1937); a fictionalized life of the buccaneer Henry Morgan (*The Privateer*, 1952); and a number of plays for the stage and for radio, of which the best-known is *Richard of Bordeaux*, first produced in London in 1932 with John Gielgud in the title role. See S. Roy, *Josephine Tey* (1980).

Their Eyes Were Watching God, a novel by Zora Neale *Hurston, published in 1937; it tells the story of an independently minded black woman. As a girl the heroine Janie Crawford is taught by her grandmother to seek more than the life of drudgery that is the usual fate of women in her society. As an adult Janie leaves a loveless marriage to a husband who owns land and joins up with Joe Starks, a confident smooth-talking man who takes her to an all-black Florida town, where he hopes to find an environment where he can achieve independence. Though Joe achieves the kind of self-esteem he desires through becoming the mayor of the town, their marriage proves unfulfilling for Janie. Joe expects her to be subordinate to him and she rebels against this. When he dies she finds greater fulfilment in a third marriage to a younger man, Tea Cake, with whom she falls deeply in love. Her happiness is, however, short-lived. The couple enjoy a brief idyll working in the Florida Everglades, but, fleeing from a hurricane, Tea Cake is bitten by a rabid dog. Driven mad by his illness, he attempts to shoot Janie, who kills him in self-defence; she is tried for murder but acquitted by an all-white jury. Though sometimes melodramatic, *Their Eyes Were Watching God* has considerable emotional power and is notable for its sensual and organic imagery. Ahead of its time in its uncompromising representation of racial and gender oppression, the novel has gradually acquired an impressive reputation and today it is seen as a forerunner of the work of contemporary African-American women writers like Alice *Walker and Toni *Morrison.

THEROUX, Paul (Edward) (1941–), American novelist and travel writer, born in Medford, Massachusetts, educated at the University of Massachusetts. He lectured in English in Malawi, Uganda, and Singapore. Africa provides the background for three of his early novels, *Fong and the Indians* (1968), *Girls at Play* (1969), and *Jungle Lovers* (1971), which display a common concern with the morally deforming tensions between Western and African cultures. *Saint Jack* (1973), centring on prostitution in Singapore, was his first major success as a novelist; subsequent novels include *The Family Arsenal* (1976), a story of terrorism in London; *The Mosquito Coast* (1981; stage production by David Glass, 1995), on an American family's attempt to inhabit a South American jungle; *Chicago Loop* (1990), a violent anatomy of social disorder and sexual obsession; and *Millroy the Magician* (1993), about a children's entertainer turned TV evangelist preaching healthy eating as the route to salvation. As a travel writer specializing in extended rail journeys, Theroux has published *The Great Railway Bazaar* (1975), on his crossings of Europe and Asia; *The Old Patagonian Express* (1979), an account of North and South America; *The Imperial Way* (1985), on a journey from Pakistan to Bangladesh; and *Riding the Iron Rooster* (1988), which describes his experiences of China. Among his other travel books are *The Kingdom by the Sea* (1983), a record of his itinerary around the British coast, *The Happy Isles of Oceana* (1992) on travels in the Pacific, and *The Pillars of Hercules* (1995) about a Mediterranean tour. *Sunrise with Seamonsters* (1985) is a collection of essays on his travels from 1964 to 1984.

THESIGER, Wilfred (Patrick) (1910–), British travel writer, born in Addis Ababa, Ethiopia, where his father was British Minister, educated at Magdalen College, Oxford. In 1933 he travelled to the interior of the Danakil Desert in Ethiopia, becoming the first European to gain the confidence of the region's inhabitants. He was attached to the Sudan Political Service till 1940, when he began his distinguished military career, winning the DSO for his part in the Desert Campaigns. After the war he travelled with the Bedouin in remote parts of Southern Arabia for five years, a period recounted in his first book, *Arabian Sands* (1959). *The Marsh Arabs* (1964) describes the eight years he spent from 1950 onward living in Southern Iraq. He subsequently continued to travel widely and settled for some years with the Samburu in Kenya. In addition to their sensitive evocations of the human and natural characters of the places experienced, the books are informed by the critique of modernity which emerges from Thesiger's dismissal of contemporary society's mechanistic conceptions of progress. The vigour and forthrightness of his prose reflects similar qualities in the works of *Kipling, *Buchan, and *Churchill, whom he has identified as stylistic models. His photographic records of his journeys are contained in *Desert, Marsh and Mountain* (1979) and *Visions of a Nomad* (1987). *A Life of My Choice* (1987) and *My Kenya Days* (1994) are autobiographical works. See *Thesiger: A Biography* (1994) by Michael Asher.

Things Fall Apart, see ACHEBE, CHINUA.

Third Man, The, a novel by Graham *Greene, published in 1950. Much of Greene's fiction has been filmed, but none so successfully as *The Third Man*, directed in 1949 by Carol Reed, with haunting zither music by Anton Karas, and Orson Welles as the cynical racketeer Harry Lime. The film is able to exploit more fully than Greene's text the darkly atmospheric background of the city of Vienna, ruined by the Second World War and divided between Russian and Western control. Reed uses this context particularly powerfully to communicate Rollo Martins's disillusion with Lime, a friend and boyhood hero. Martins fully realizes the truth about Lime's blackmarketeering and faked death when he appears accidentally illumined in a street doorway. He plunges in pursuit into the subterranean, rushing world of the Vienna sewers—a movement emblematic of his sudden immersion into a universe darker and more complex than any anticipated by someone who had 'never really grown up'.

Greene considered the film 'the finished state of the story', and his text no more than 'raw material'. Nevertheless, it marks a stage in his development as a novelist—his earliest sustained use of first-person narrative, later developed more successfully in *The *End of the Affair* (1951) and *The *Quiet American* (1955). The narrator, Major Calloway, the policeman pursuing Lime, sometimes enters implausibly far into other characters' private thoughts and feelings, but his initially limited understanding makes him a good vehicle for a story of unfolding discovery. Like Martins, though less naïvely, he underestimates the depths of Lime's malign ingenuity: their discovery of truths even darker than they had supposed makes *The Third Man* a kind of paradigm for the feelings of an age whose faiths and sanctities had so recently been ruined by the Second World War and the opening hostilities of the Cold War which followed. It is also typical of repeated movements in Greene's fiction towards underworlds of disillusion and destroyed innocence.

Third Policeman, The, a novel by Flann *O'Brien, first published posthumously in 1967. The work, a disquieting and richly comic imaginative and stylistic *tour de force*, is recounted by an anonymous narrator, who describes events leading up to and following his killing of an elderly farmer. His self-possession is gradually eroded by the intensely strange phenomena he witnesses after entering the world of police sergeants MacCruiskeen and Pluck, quasi-mythological figures obsessed with bicycles and atomic physics. The narrator is immersed to a similar extent in the work of the metaphysician de Selby, whose extremely eccentric writings on the illusory nature of reality are dwelt on at length in the text and its footnotes. Having escaped and encountered the elusive third policeman, Sergeant Fox, who bears a disturbing similarity to the man he has killed, the narrator momentarily realizes he is dead; in a state of deep bewilderment, he returns to the point at which his experiences with the policemen recommence. O'Brien described the novel as 'happening in a sort of hell . . . where none of the rules and laws (not even the law of gravity) holds good'.

THIRKELL, Angela (Margaret) (1890–1961), English novelist, born in London, educated at St Paul's Girls' School. The mother of Colin *McInnes, she was related to Edward Burne-Jones, Rudyard *Kipling, and Stanley Baldwin. Her first book, *Three Houses* (1931), an entertaining memoir of her Edwardian childhood, was followed by over thirty novels about life among the country gentry, which were very popular in the 1930s and 1940s. These include *Wild Strawberries* (1934), *Pomfret Towers* (1938), *The Brandons* (1939), and *Cheerfulness Breaks In* (1940), which focused on the fortunes (both fateful and financial) of families in Barsetshire, the fictional county borrowed in tribute to Trollope. After the Second World War, Thirkell faithfully recorded the rancour of the upper-middle classes against austerity measures, egalitarian attitudes, and the Labour Government in novels such as *Peace Breaks Out* (1946), *Private Enterprise* (1947), *Love Among the Ruins* (1948), and *Coronation Summer* (1953).

This Side of Paradise, a novel by F. Scott *Fitzgerald, published in 1920. Initially called *The Romantic Egoist*, it appeared at the outset of the 'roaring Twenties' and immediately became a bestseller and a cult work for the younger generation of the jazz age, in a society increasingly attracted to the ideal of youth. The young protagonist, Amory Blaine, exemplifying the post-war dandy, makes his life the egotistical pursuit of sexual adventure and social ambition. After a sheltered and spoilt childhood, he goes to Princeton where he throws himself into literary pursuits, writing for the university journal, joining the Triangle Club, and championing the English poets of decadence. Amory gets involved with Princeton's social set and the beautiful and wealthy, and is narcissistically intrigued with his own emotional states. Following a series of abortive love affairs, he goes to France as an officer; upon his return he finds his mother dead and his financial circumstances straitened. He becomes an advertising writer, has a few more unsatisfactory affairs, and gradually grows poor and unemployed. At the end of the novel Amory is left contemplating the limited summation of his experiences at the age of 24.

This Sporting Life, see STOREY, DAVID.

THOMAS, Audrey (1935–), Canadian-based novelist and short-story writer, born in Binghamton, New York, educated at Smith College and the University of British Columbia. From 1964 to 1966 she lived in Ghana, a source for some of her subsequent fiction, before settling in British Columbia. Her first collection of short stories was *Ten Green Bottles* (1967); others include *Ladies and Escorts* (1977), *Real Mothers* (1981), and *Goodbye, Harold, Good Luck* (1986). Her novels are essentially feminist in outlook, exploring the changing nature of male–female relationships in the contemporary world in post-modernist modes. In *Mrs Blood* (1970) the protagonist is the distraught victim of a miscarriage in Ghana. *Songs My Mother Taught Me* (1973) is about a girl's growing up in New York State. *Blown Figures* (1974) employs a collage technique to express the schizophrenia from which its heroine is suffering. Thomas's other novels include *Latakia* (1979), set in Greece and the Middle East, and *Intertidal Life* (1984), set on Galiano Island, the British Columbian Gulf island where Thomas herself had settled many years earlier. *The Wild Blue Yonder* (1990) is a further collection of short stories.

THOMAS, Augustus (1857–1934), American dramatist, born in St Louis, Missouri. Thomas worked for some time as a journalist before turning to the theatre. One of the most prolific American dramatists, he wrote more than sixty plays, beginning with *Editha's Burglar*, originally a one-acter but turned into a full-length play for its Broadway production in 1889. His most important work is in a series of plays designed to depict various aspects of the American character in a regional setting, such as *Alabama* (1891), about an unrepentant Confederate father and his more nationalistic son, *In Mizzoura* (1893), *The Capitol* (1895), *Arizona* (1900), and *The Copperhead* (1918), about a Northerner with Southern sympathies. His many other plays deal with the conflict between the demands of individual liberty and the constraints of social or ideological conditioning.

THOMAS, Bertram (Sidney) (1892–1950), British Arabist and travel writer, born in Easton-in-Gordano, Somerset; he left school at the age of 16 to work for the Post Office. Following military service in Mesopotamia during the First World War he entered Trinity College, Cambridge, and subsequently returned to the Middle East on administrative work. He was responsible for the mapping of formerly uncharted regions of Southern Arabia and was the first European to cross the Rub Al Khali Desert; an account of the expedition is given in *Arabia Felix* (1932), his best-known work, for which T. E. *Lawrence supplied a foreword. *Alarms and Excursions in Arabia* (1931) also records his travels, while *The Arabs* (1937) is a history of the Arab peoples. Thomas's other publications include his linguistic studies, among which are *Four Strange Tongues from Southern Arabia—The Hadara Group* (1938).

THOMAS, D(onald) M(ichael) (1935–), British poet, novelist, and translator, born in Redruth, Cornwall; he spent much of his childhood in Australia. He was educated at New College, Oxford. His collections of poetry include *Symphony in Moscow* (1974), *Love and Other Deaths* (1975), *The Honeymoon Voyage* (1978), *Dreaming in Bronze* (1981), and *Selected Poems* (1983). Much of his earlier verse combined elements of science fiction and eroticism in an entertaining manner. From the mid-1970s onward he concentrated increasingly on psychologically penetrating examinations of emotional states and personal relationships. *News from the Front* (1983), a collaboration with Sylvia

*Kantaris, examines tensions in a sexual liaison with remarkable candour. Latterly, he has considered himself 'a poet who *mainly* writes novels'. His first, *The Flute-Player* (1979), forms a tribute to the spirit of Russian artists oppressed by totalitarian policies. The bizarre narrative of *Birthstone* (1980) combines humour, elements of the occult, and erotic fantasy in a Cornish setting. *The *White Hotel* (1981) is his most celebrated work. *Ararat* (1983) is the first part of his *Russian Nights* sequence, an impressionistically encompassing survey of political and cultural conditions in post-war Eastern Europe, which continues with *Swallow* (1984), *Sphinx* (1986), *Summit* (1987), and *Lying Together* (1990). Among his numerous translations are versions of Alexander Pushkin's *The Bronze Horseman* (1982) and *Boris Godunov* (1985). His other works include the novel *Pictures at an Exhibition* (1993) and an experimental autobiography entitled *Memories and Hallucinations* (1988).

THOMAS, Dylan (Marlais) (1914–53), Welsh poet, born in Swansea, Glamorgan, educated at Swansea Grammar School. Much of his verse originates in a series of notebooks dating from his schooldays, which have been published as *Poet in the Making: The Notebooks of Dylan Thomas* (edited by Ralph Maud, 1968; revised 1989). In 1931 he became a reporter with the *South Wales Daily Post*. *18 Poems* (1934) was published in the year of his move to London. *Twenty-Five Poems* (1936) established his reputation as a poet of importance, partly as a result of Edith *Sitwell's favourable review in the *Sunday Times*. Thomas's rhythmically compelling early verse explores the themes of birth, sex, and death through imagery he described as 'derived . . . from the cosmic significance of the human body'. His influence was considerable during the later 1930s, most notably upon the poets of the *New Apocalypse. *The Map of Love* (1939), a collection of poems and lyrical prose pieces, was followed by the humorously realistic short stories of **Portrait of the Artist as a Young Dog* (1940). A further collection of stories, *Adventures in the Skin Trade* (1955), has as its title piece Thomas's unfinished picaresque novel. *Collected Stories* was published in 1984. From 1934 to 1940 he worked intermittently as a literary journalist and acquired his enduring reputation for extravagant behaviour. Following his marriage to Caitlin MacNamara, in 1938 he began living in Laugharne, Carmarthenshire, which became his permanent home in 1949. The locality is reflected vividly in the coastal imagery of much of his later poetry. In 1940 he started working as a writer and reader for the BBC in London, where his friends Louis *MacNeice and Roy *Campbell were producers; selections from his work for radio, which prompted him to write his 'play for voices' **Under Milk Wood* (1954), were published under the title *Quite Early One Morning* (1954). *Deaths and Entrances* (1946), in which his poetry displays a more fluently lyrical manner, gained him exceptional acclaim. Between 1950 and 1953 he made four reading-tours of the USA, where he was enthusiastically received, particularly after the enormous success of his *Collected Poems* (1952). The period is documented in J. M. Brinnin's *Dylan Thomas in America* (1955). His death in New York was precipitated by a combination of alcohol and drugs administered for exhaustion. While opinion concerning the value of his work is divided, he remains one of the most widely read poets of the twentieth century. His *Collected Letters*, edited by Paul Ferris, was published in 1985; Walford Davies and Ralph Maud produced a new edition of *Collected Poems* in 1988. Constantine Fitzgibbon's *The Life of Dylan Thomas* (1965) is regarded as the standard biography.

THOMAS, (Philip) Edward (1878–1917), British poet, critic, and topographical writer, born in Lambeth, London, educated at Lincoln College, Oxford. His earliest publication of note was *The Woodland Life* (1897), a peripatetic account of rural locations in the manner of Borrow and Jefferies; his enthusiasm for these writers is clear in the biographical studies *George Borrow: The Man and His Books* (1912) and *Richard Jefferies: His Life and Work* (1909). *Beautiful Wales* (1905), *The Heart of England* (1906), and *The Ickneild Way* (1913) are among his numerous subsequent topographical works, which combine contemplative elements with a closely observed sensitivity to natural phenomena. Although Thomas was self-effacing about his prolific work as a literary journalist, he was consistent in supporting *Yeats, *de la Mare, and *Masefield when their reputations were uncertain and was among the first to acclaim the poetry of Ezra *Pound. His critical works include *Walter Pater* (1913), which reveals his distaste for the artificiality of late Victorian writing. The fluent plainness of his own prose anticipates the conversational idiom he later developed as a poet. While recovering from a breakdown in 1911, he planned to extend the creative range of his writing. After long discussions with Robert *Frost, with whom he began a close friendship in 1913, he began producing poetry in 1914. In 1915 he enlisted in the army and continued to produce verse until his death at Arras, at which time a collection was being prepared under the pseudonym 'Edward Eastaway', the name used for the publication of *Six Poems* in 1916. Of the numerous editions of his work that have succeeded *Poems* of 1917, the most definitive is *Collected Poems* (1978), edited by R. George Thomas. The 'fidelity to the postures which the voice assumes in the most expressive intimate speech' which Thomas discerned in Frost's poetry is equally characteristic of his own work's rhythmical restraint and avoidance of poetic rhetoric. His imaginative handling of natural imagery provides vividly realized contexts for his poetry's subtly disquieting evocations of psychological states. The fusion of muted lyricism and elegiac detachment in much of his verse produces a tone of great individuality and poise. F. R. *Leavis was one of the first to accord Thomas's work a high critical evaluation in *New Bearings in English Poetry* (1932). Biographical material includes *As It Was* (1926) and *World* *without End* (1931) by his widow Helen Thomas, and R. George Thomas's *Edward Thomas* (1985).

THOMAS, Elean (1947–), Jamaican writer, born in St Catherine, Jamaica, educated at the University of the West Indies and Goldsmiths' College, London. Active for many years in the women's struggles in the Caribbean, she participated in the movement for national independence and was a founder and International Secretary of the Workers Party of Jamaica. She has made her reputation primarily as a poet, although she says: 'I call my pieces Word-Rhythms. I honestly believe it is pretentious to call them poems. They are merely word-sketches, word-photographs, word-drawings, word-paintings, word-beats.' Her works include two collections of poetry with some prose stories, *Word Rhythms from the Life of a Woman* (1986) and *Before They Can Speak of Flowers: Word Rhythms* (1988) with a foreword by *Ngugi and an introduction by Benjamin *Zephaniah, and a novel, *The Last Room* (1991).

THOMAS, Sir Keith (Vivian) (1933–), British historian, born in Wick, Glamorgan, educated at Balliol College, Oxford. Throughout his career he has taught at Oxford, where he became President of Corpus Christi in 1986 and Pro-Vice-Chancellor of the University in 1988. Thomas is eminent among contemporary authorities on the social and intellectual history of England between the sixteenth and eighteenth centuries. In discerning developments from the superstitious culture of the Tudor period towards the era of scientific rationalism he draws on materials from a remarkable range of sources. His major works are *Religion and the Decline of Magic* (1971) and *Man and the Natural World* (1983), his widely read study of changing perceptions of nature between 1500 and 1800. Among his other publications is *History and Literature* (1988), in which he addresses the debate over the value of literary texts as resources for the historian. He was knighted in 1988.

THOMAS, R(onald) S(tuart) (1913–), Welsh poet, born in Cardiff; he read Classics at the University College of North Wales, Bangor, and received his theological training at St Michael's College, Llandaff. He ministered in a succession of Welsh parishes from 1937 until his retirement in 1978. His first three volumes of poetry, *The Stones of the Field* (1946), *An Acre of Land* (1952), and *The Minister* (1953), a verse-drama for radio, established the harshly unsentimental concern with remote rural landscapes and their inhabitants that is dominant in his writing until the early 1960s. *Song at the Year's Turning* (1955), a substantial collection of his work, gained him a considerable reputation as a poet of uncompromisingly original vision. Among his numerous subsequent volumes are *Pieta* (1966), *Frequencies* (1978), *Experimenting with an Amen* (1986), *Counterpoint* (1990), and *Mass for Hard Times* (1992), throughout which the theological element discernible in many earlier poems gradually assumes primacy. The intellectual rigour and passionate restraint of Thomas's broodings on the Incarnation, the problems of pain and suffering, and other major religious themes produce verse of great fluency and sureness of tone. Eminent among the proponents of Welsh cultural and linguistic nationalism, his writings in Welsh, which he uses only for prose, include *Neb*, literally 'no one', his autobiography of 1976. *Selected Poems 1946–1968* (1973), *Later Poems: A Selection* (1983), and *Collected Poems, 1945–1990* (1993) are his major collections.

THOMAS, Ross (Elmore) (1926–), American novelist, born in Oklahoma City, educated at the University of Oklahoma. He worked as a journalist, public relations director, and consultant to the US government until 1966, when he became a full-time writer. Much of his writing is informed by his professional experience of managing political campaigns. His suspense novels dealing with political corruption include *Cast a Yellow Shadow* (1967), *The Seersucker Whipsaw* (1967), *The Fools in Town Are on Our Side* (1970), *If You Can't Be Good* (1973), and *Briarpatch* (1984). *The Porkchoppers* (1972) and *Yellow-Dog Contract* (1976) centre on sinister aspects of American labour organizations. He is highly regarded for his considerable stylistic range and fluent handling of complex plots. Other works by Thomas include *The Cold War Swap* (1966), *The Backup Men* (1971), *Twilight at Mac's Place* (1990),and *Ah, Treachery* (1994). *The Brass Go-Between* (1969) and *The Procane Chronicle* (1972) are among the thrillers he has published under the pseudonym Oliver Bleeck.

THOMPSON, Edward (John) (1886–1946), British poet, translator, historian, and novelist, born in Bath, educated at Oxford University and the University of London. *The Knight Mystic* (1907) was his first collection of verse. In 1909 he became a Methodist minister and worked as an educational missionary in Bengal. His experiences as an army chaplain from 1916 to 1918 are reflected in the vivid and moving poems of the Palestinian and Mesopotamian Campaigns in *Mesopotamian Verses* (1919), which established his reputation as a poet. Stylistically, his verse remained firmly traditional throughout his career. *John in Prison* (1912) is the most impressive of his repeated treatments of devotional subjects. After the appearance of *Collected Poems* (1930), he concentrated principally on cultural and historical works about India, among which are *Ethical Ideals in India Today* (1942) and *The Making of the Indian Princes* (1943). He also published a number of novels, which include *Introducing the Arnisons* (1935) and *John Arnison* (1939). The most successful of his numerous plays was *Elizabeth and Essex* (1943). He was a translator of the writings of Rabindranath *Tagore and published the critical biography *Rabindranath Tagore, Poet and Dramatist* in 1926.

THOMPSON, E(dward) P(almer) (1924–93), British historian, born in Oxford, educated at Corpus Christi College, Cambridge. After a period at Leeds and Warwick Universities he became Professor of the Institute for Advanced Research in the Humanities at

Birmingham University. *William Morris: Romantic to Revolutionary* (1955), his first major publication, considered the interactions between its subject's artistic and political careers. His most enduringly influential book is *The Making of the English Working Class* (1963) (see POPULAR CULTURE), a study of political, religious, and cultural manifestations of the working class's growing cohesion between 1780 and 1832; the remarkable range and diligence of its attention to formerly neglected sources was widely emulated by succeeding historians. His other notable works include *Whigs and Hunters* (1975), on political ferment in the eighteenth century; *Family and Inheritance: Rural Society in Western Europe, 1200–1800* (1976); and *Customs in Common* (1991; social history, 1688–1901). The socialist commitment which informs his historical writings is central to his essays and polemical articles, many of which relate to his activities as a founder member of the Campaign for Nuclear Disarmament; collections include *Zero Option* (1982) and *The Heavy Dancers* (1985). His other works include a novel, *The Skyaos Papers* (1988), a dystopian fantasy; *Alien Homage: Edward Thompson and Rabindranath Tagore* (1993); and *Witness against the Beast: William Blake and the Moral Law* (1993).

THOMPSON, Flora (1876–1947), British autobiographical novelist, born in Juniper Hill, Oxfordshire, faithfully described in her major novels as 'Lark Rise'. The eldest of ten children of a stonemason and a former housemaid, she left school at the age of 12 to become a clerk at the post office in the village of Fringford, then at Greyshott in Surrey. In 1900 she married John Thompson, also a post office clerk, and moved first to Bournemouth, then to Liphook in Hampshire, and eventually to Dartmouth. Her early stories and articles appeared in various periodicals including the *Daily News*, and in 1920 she contributed a series of monthly nature notes for the *Catholic Fireside* (later known as *The Peverel Papers*). Her first publication was a collection of poems, *Bog-Myrtle and Peat* (1921). In 1937 she began a sequence of sketches about her childhood in the *Lady* and *The Fortnightly Review* which were to form part of her autobiographical trilogy: *Lark Rise* (1939), *Over to Candleford* (1941), and *Candleford Green* (1943), published together as *Lark Rise to Candleford* (1945). Narrated by Laura, her memories of childhood and youth are interwoven with acutely observed, unsentimental evocations of pre-industrial rural England with its slowly vanishing crafts and traditions. Together, the novels form a history of the social, economic, and cultural change that took place at the end of the nineteenth century. In her posthumously published *Still Glides the Stream* (1948) Thompson returns to Juniper Hill, described this time as 'Restharrow', and seen through the eyes of the elderly Charity Finch. *A Country Calendar and Other Essays* (1979) is a collection which includes the autobiographical novel *Heatherley*, written in the mid-1940s. This novel's description of the early struggles of a female intellectual of humble origins, in an age when such disqualifications were almost crippling, is evidence of Thompson's importance as a social historian.

THOMPSON, Hunter S(tockton) (1939–), American journalist, writer, and novelist, exponent of the *New Journalism, born in Louisville, Kentucky. Thompson began as a sportswriter and freelance reporter with *The Reporter* and *The National Observer*. He made his mark in the mid-1960s with an assignment for *The Nation*, covering a Hell's Angel motorcycle group, later published as *Hell's Angels: A Strange and Terrible Saga* (1967), in which he developed what he calls 'gonzo journalism'. Thompson's journalistic works are closely linked to the *post-modern experiments in fiction of such writers as Kurt *Vonnegut, Thomas *Pynchon, Robert *Coover, and Donald *Barthelme. In *Fear and Loathing in Las Vegas: A Savage Journey to the Heart of the American Dream* (1971), Thompson creates disorientating effects when fact becomes indistinguishable from fantasy. The persona Raoul Duke relates his failure to cover two events in Las Vegas, the Fourth Annual 'Mint 400' motorcycle desert race and the National Conference of District Attorneys Seminar on Narcotics and Dangerous Drugs. The novel is a narrative of his hallucinations and fantastic adventures, and the exploration of his chaotic mind becomes a metaphor for the state of the American nation. *Fear and Loathing: On the Campaign Trail '72* (1973) appeared while he was working for the magazine *Rolling Stone*; it is a loosely episodic account of the presidential campaign and the attempt to remove Nixon from the White House in 1972. Other works are the retrospective collection of articles *The Great Shark Hunt: Strange Tales from a Strange Time* (1979); *The Curse of Lono* (1983), which recounts his antics during a visit to Hawaii with his longtime illustrator Ralph Steadman; *Generation of Swine: Tales of Shame and Degradation in the Eighties, Gonzo Papers Vol. II* (1988); *Songs of the Doomed: More Notes on the Death of the American Dream, Gonzo Papers, Vol. III* (1990); and *Better Than Sex: Confessions of a Political Junkie* (1994). Hunter's self-parody has itself been famously parodied by Garry Trudeau as the figure of 'Uncle Duke' in the 'Doonesbury' cartoon.

THOMPSON, Jim (1906–77), American crime novelist, born in Oklahoma, educated at the University of Nebraska. Little-known in his lifetime, in later years Thompson was reassessed as a classic 'pulp' writer, a genre now being revived. Like Charles *Willeford or John D. *MacDonald, Thompson wrote a great many crime stories which are now seen as collector's items in the '*hardboiled' school. His most characteristic style is first-person narrative, in which an abnormal or psychopathic character laconically relates a bizarre career. Thompson's mixture of melodrama, irony, and black humour is used with tremendous skill in *The Killer Inside Me* (1952), *Savage Night* (1953), *The Nothing Man* (1954), *A Hell of a Woman* (1954), *After Dark, My Sweet* (1955), and *Pop. 1280* (1964). Frequent film versions of his novels, including Sam Peckinpah's

The Getaway (1972) and Stephen Frear's version of *The Grifters* (1990), have gained him prominence.

THOMPSON, Sam (1916–65), Irish playwright, born in Belfast; he was a tradesman and trade unionist who turned to writing during the 1950s. His first plays were written for radio and originate in his concern for the poverty and violence of the society to which he belonged. Thompson's significance is assured by his play *Over the Bridge* (1960), portraying sectarian prejudice in Belfast and the inevitability of its violent consequences. Considered controversial, the play was withdrawn by the Ulster Group Theatre before production; Thompson had to form his own theatre company and wait three years before it was performed at the Empire Theatre in Belfast. In the fifty years that had elapsed since St John *Ervine's *Mixed Marriage* (1911) had touched upon the nerve of factional hatred, Thompson was the only playwright who had dared to present Ulster's sectarian problems on stage. Set in the Belfast shipyards, and against a background of an IRA bombing, it concerns the victimization of a Catholic worker and the efforts of his union representative, who is a Protestant, to protect him. As well as being historically significant, *Over the Bridge* also provided a dramatic precedent for playwrights such as John *Boyd and Graham *Reid, who were to portray the same problems. Thompson's only other full-length plays to be produced were *The Evangelist* (1961) and *Cemented with Love* (1964).

Three Guineas, V. *Woolf's second feminist essay, published in 1938 (cf. *A *Room of One's Own*); it grew from a lecture, 'Professions for Women' (1931), and from the early version of *The *Years*. Writing a response to three requests for a guinea—one for preserving peace, one for helping women's education, and one for enhancing their professional opportunities—she evolves a startling comparison between Victorian patriarchy and fascism. Women, she says (or more narrowly, 'the daughters of educated men'), are as alien to the propagandist, war-making, male-dominated modern world as they were oppressed in the Victorian home. They should form an 'anonymous and secret Society of Outsiders' which would challenge tyranny through ridicule and scepticism and a refusal to 'join'. This utopian argument involves a wide-ranging attack on the cultural and educational establishment, the media, the Church, psychiatry, and science. Woolf's friends and critics alike took fright at the essay's radical stance and it was dismissed or neglected for many years before becoming an important influence on feminist thinking. See FEMINIST CRITICISM.

Three Lives, a book of three stories by Gertrude *Stein, published in 1909. *Three Lives: Stories of the Good Anna, Melanctha, and the Gentle Lena*, the full title, was Stein's first published work and one of her most successful. The stories are character studies of three women: Anna, a German servant, Melanctha, an uneducated black girl, and Lena, a German maid, written in response to the differing influences of Gustave Flaubert and Paul Cézanne (her initial title was 'Three Histories', an echo of Flaubert's *Trois Contes*). 'Melanctha', in particular, is notable for its use of a variety of narrative perspectives and is evidence of Stein's interest in trying to bring the techniques of Cubist painting to fictional narrative. See *The Making of a Modernist: Stein from 'Three Lives' to 'Tender Buttons'* (1984), by Jayne L. Walker.

Three Soldiers, see DOS PASSOS, JOHN.

THUBRON, Colin (Gerald Dryden) (1939–), British travel writer and novelist, born in London, a descendant of John Dryden (1631–1700), educated at Eton College. He worked in publishing and travelled widely as a film-maker for the BBC from 1959 to 1965, when he became a freelance author. *A Mirror to Damascus* (1967), his first work as a travel writer, was followed by *The Hills of Adonis* (1968), an account of Lebanon, *Jerusalem* (1969), and *Journey into Cyprus* (1975). In addition to the lyrical eloquence of their descriptions, the books displayed his capacity for historically resonant evocations of the places visited. The perceptive humanity and depth of response to social and cultural conditions in *Among Russians* (1983), the result of a 10,000-mile journey by road through the USSR; *Behind the Wall* (1987), a record of his experiences in China; and *The Lost Heart of Asia* (1994), on Central Asia, have established him among the foremost travel writers of the post-war era. *Emperor* (1978), the first of Thubron's novels to be widely acclaimed, forms an imaginative reconstruction of events leading up to Constantine's triumphant entry into Rome in AD 312; other novels include *A Cruel Madness* (1984), a skilful treatment of insanity and delusion set in a psychiatric hospital, and *Turning Back the Sun* (1991), in which the chief protagonist is a European doctor enduring the tensions between duty, love, and the sense of exile in a town on the edge of an African wilderness.

THURBER, James (Grover) (1894–1961), American humorist, born in Columbus, Ohio, educated at Ohio State University. Thurber initially became well known through the pages of the **New Yorker*. The combination of mordant prose with understated illustration was the dominant feature of his work. His first publication, *Is Sex Necessary?* (1929), in collaboration with E. B. *White, was a satirical attack on the 1920s vogue for sex manuals. After the work of the 1930s, which included *The Owl in the Attic and Other Perplexities* (1931), *The Seal in the Bedroom and Other Predicaments* (1932), amusing reminiscences in *My Life and Hard Times* (1933), *The Middle-Aged Man on the Flying Trapeze* (1935), *Let Your Mind Alone!* (1937), a parable of war in *The Last Flower* (1939), and *Fables for Our Time* (1940), his writing took on a somewhat quieter tone. This is best seen in the essays, sketches, and stories in *My World—and Welcome to It* (1942), which contained 'The Secret Life of Walter Mitty', in which a thoroughly ordinary character escapes from his mundane life by the use of a constant stream of fantasies. Beneath the humorous surface there was always a sense of a perception under siege by irrationality and falsity. Other works include *Men, Women and Dogs* (1943), *The Thurber Carnival* (1945), *Thurber Country* (1953), *Further Fables for Our Time* (1956), *Alarms and Diversions* (1957), and the essays in *Lanterns and Lances* (1961). He also wrote children's books. *The Years with Ross* (1958) was a personal reminiscence of his life with the *New Yorker* and its editor, Harold Ross. A selection of his letters was published in 1981.

THWAITE, Ann (1932–), British writer, born in Hampstead, London, educated at St Hilda's College, Oxford. Her experiences of Tokyo, where she travelled with her husband Anthony *Thwaite in 1956, gave rise to her first book, *The Young Traveller in Japan* (1958). Her early works for younger readers include *The House in Turner Square* (1960) and *Toby Stays with Jane* (1962), the first of a series of successful 'Toby and Jane' stories. *Waiting for the Party* (1974), her biography of Frances Hodgson Burnett, was followed by the highly acclaimed *Edmund Gosse: A Literary Landscape* (1984), which placed her in the first rank of contemporary biographers, and *A. A. Milne: His Life* (1990). Thwaite has also edited various books, which include *My Oxford* (1977) and *Portraits from Life* (1991) by Edmund *Gosse.

THWAITE, Anthony (Simon) (1930–), British poet, born in Chester, educated at Christ Church, Oxford. After lecturing in Tokyo for two years, he became a producer for BBC radio in 1957, working under Louis *MacNeice, a period alluded to in his poem 'For Louis MacNeice'. He subsequently held a succession of editorial positions with *The *Listener*, **New Statesman*, and **Encounter* and became editorial director with André Deutsch publishers in 1986. Collections of his poetry include *Home Truths* (1957), *The Owl in the Tree* (1963), *Inscriptions* (1973), *Victorian Voices* (1980), *Letter from Tokyo* (1987), *Poems, 1953–1988* (1989), and *The Dust of the World* (1994). The restraint and accomplishment of his early work indicate his association with the *Movement; the detached disenchantment in poems reflecting ordinary urban experience suggests particular affinities with the poetry of Philip *Larkin, whose *Collected Poems* (1988) and *The Selected Letters of Philip Larkin* (1992) Thwaite edited. In *The Stones of Emptiness* (1967), which reflects his experiences of living in Libya, the imaginative use of historical materials emerges as a characteristic of his verse; 'The Letters of Synesius', a sequence largely in the phlegmatic voice of a fourteenth-century bishop, anticipates his growing use of the dramatic monologue. *Victorian Voices* forms a detailed recreation of nineteenth-century social and cultural conditions in the monologues of a series of fictitious and historical Victorian figures. Among his travel books are a work on Libya entitled *The Deserts of Hesperides* (1969) and *Odyssey: Mirror of the Mediterranean* (1981). His critical writings include *Poetry Today 1960–1973* (1973) and *Twentieth-Century English Poetry* (1978).

'Tietjens Tetralogy', see PARADE'S END.

TILLER, Terence (Roger) (1916–87), British poet, born at Truro in Cornwall, educated at Jesus College, Cambridge. After lecturing at Cambridge he held an appointment at Fuad University in Cairo from 1939 to 1946. He subsequently became a highly regarded and prolific writer and producer for BBC radio; his more notable achievements included an adaptation of *The Vision of Piers Ploughman* (broadcast 1980; published 1981). *Poems* (1941), his first collection of poetry, was followed by *The Inward Animal* (1943) and *Unarm, Eros* (1947), which are generally thought to contain his best work; his experiences of Egypt during the war gave rise to lyrics of great formal accomplishment and sensuously precise imagery which drew upon the tensions latent in his ambivalent sense of himself as a non-combatant expatriate. *Reading a Medal* (1957), *Notes for a Myth* (1968), and *That Singing Mesh* (1979), which carried a preface announcing his intention to cease writing poetry, sustained his reputation for highly wrought verse of elegant complexity. Among his other works is *Confessio Amantis (The Lover's Shrift)* (1963) by John Gower, which he translated and edited.

TILLYARD, E(ustace) M(andeville) W(etenhall) (1889–1962), British scholar and critic, born at Cambridge, where he was educated at Jesus College and lived throughout his life. He worked as an archaeologist in Athens before returning to Cambridge to lecture. His involvement in the emergence of the Cambridge School of English during the 1920s is recalled in his late work *The Muses Unchained* (1958). The works of Milton and Shakespeare were his chief interests: *Milton* (1930), which established his reputation as a scholar, was followed by *The Miltonic Setting* (1938); his trilogy *Shakespeare's Last Plays* (1938), *Shakespeare's History Plays* (1944), and *Shakespeare's Problem Plays* (1950) was highly regarded. He is best known for *The Elizabethan World-Picture* (1943), which widely influenced literary studies through its emphasis on the centrality of 'the chain of being' to Elizabethan thought. His other works include *The English Epic and Its Tradition* (1954) and *The Personal Heresy* (1939), a collaboration with C. S. *Lewis.

TILMAN, H(arold) W(illiam) (1898–?1977), British writer on mountaineering and sailing, born in Wallasey, Cheshire; he attended the Royal Military Academy, after which he was on active service in Flanders from 1916 to 1918. Following a period as a coffee-planter in Kenya, where he began his celebrated climbing partnership with Eric *Shipton, he devoted himself chiefly to mountaineering, becoming one of the leading climbers of his day. His absorbing accounts of expeditions in Africa, the Himalayas, the Karakoram, and the Chinese Pamirs are collected in *The Seven Mountain-Travel Books* (1983). From the early 1950s until his disappearance after sailing out of Rio in 1977, Tilman voyaged in a succession of small boats, most notably his cutter *Mischief*, to remote mountainous areas in the Arctic and Antarctic. The books which resulted are collected as *The Eight Sailing/Mountain-Exploration Books* (1987). *High Mountains and Cold Seas* (1980) is J. R. L. Anderson's biography of Tilman.

TILSLEY, Frank (1904–57), British novelist, born in Lancashire; he grew up in Manchester, where he was educated at Chapel Street Council School, Levenshulme. After working in various capacities, including as an accountant's clerk and a schoolteacher, he became a full-time author following the success of his first novel, *Plebeian's Progress* (1933). The work was highly valued for the authenticity of its critical depiction of working-class conditions in a period of economic depression. He published some twenty subsequent novels, which based their robustly straightforward narratives on detailed reportage of contemporary social conditions. Titles include *She Was There Too* (1938), *Pleasure Beach* (1944), *Champion Road* (1948), *Heaven and Herbert Common* (1953), and *Brother Nap* (1954). Tilsley was also a frequent radio broadcaster and from 1950 onward won considerable acclaim as a television dramatist.

Time and Tide, a weekly magazine of literature and current affairs begun in 1920 by Margaret Haig Thomas (1883–1958), Viscountess Rhondda, who appointed Helen Archdale as editor. Well received from the outset for its witty and politically independent tone, in its earlier years the magazine published prose fiction by Virginia *Woolf, Sylvia Townsend *Warner, and Katherine *Mansfield, poems by D. H. *Lawrence, W. H. *Davies, and Vita *Sackville-West, and essays by G. B. *Shaw, Bertrand *Russell, Aldous *Huxley, and G. K. *Chesterton. In 1926 Thomas assumed the editorship, thereafter remaining in personal control of *Time and Tide*. The 1930s saw the peak of the journal's success. Having absorbed *Foreign Affairs* in 1931, its coverage of international events became increasingly authoritative. Work by leading American and European writers was regularly featured. After Thomas's death in 1958 the magazine gradually declined and, having become *Time and Tide and Business World* in 1966, ceased publication in 1979.

Time's Arrow, see AMIS, MARTIN.

Times Literary Supplement, The, the most notable of the British literary journals of the twentieth century. It originated in the introduction of additional book-reviewing to *The Times* in 1902 as a means of filling space created by the absence of parliamentary reports during the summer recess. The literary supplement thus created was distributed as part of the newspaper until 1914, when the *Times Literary Supplement* became an independent weekly publication. Sir Bruce Richmond, the editor from 1902 until 1937, consolidated its standing as a journal of quality and authority, recruiting the best literary journalists and scholars available; the scope of its reviews and articles quickly extended to include history, archaeology, philosophy, politics, and the arts in general. T. S. *Eliot, Virginia *Woolf, Edgell *Rickword, F. S. *Flint, John Middleton *Murry, Lewis *Namier, Sir James *Frazer, and G. M. *Trevelyan were among the authors whose work appeared under Richmond's editorship. The *TLS*, as it came to be known, was the last major periodical to preserve the anonymity of its contributors, a procedure which was not dispensed with until John Gross assumed the editorship in 1974. Industrial action by journalists resulted in the closure of the *TLS* for fifty-one weeks in 1978 and 1979, a period in which several new literary periodicals were launched to cater for its readership. In addition to reviewing between thirty and sixty books each week, the journal publishes essays and poems by leading authors.

TINDALL, Gillian (1938–), British novelist and freelance writer, born in London, educated at Oxford University. Tindall's wide-ranging output has included journalism, translation, history, literary criticism, and biography. Her first novel, *No Name in the Street*, appeared in 1959. *The Youngest* (1967), *Someone Else* (1969), and *Fly Away Home* (1971) deal with the educated woman's journey towards self-knowledge. Violent, sudden, or anticipated death provides the point of departure in her fiction, initiating a probing reassessment of the apparently familiar. In 1964 Tindall translated René Masson's *Number One*, a fictionalized study of the mass murderer Henri Landru, and her novels return continually to the thin line between the 'normal' and the 'criminal'. In *The Youngest*, a mother kills her malformed child; in *The Traveller and His Child* (1975), a divorced father abducts a substitute son. The theme finds its most concentrated exploration in *Give Them All My Love* (1989), the confessional narrative of a middle-aged man in prison for murder. *Spirit Weddings* (1992), set in a fictional Far Eastern country which has experienced a variety of cultural and political regimes, enquires whether character is predetermined or shaped by events. In *Celestine: Voices from a French Village* (1995) she uses a cache of letters she found, dating from the 1800s, to piece together a woman's life and construct the social history of a village. She has also published *Journey of a Lifetime and Other Stories* (1990) and *Countries of the Mind: The Meaning of Place to Writers* (1991).

TIPTREE, James, pseudonym of Alice Bradley SHELDON (1915–87), American *science fiction author, born in Chicago, educated at the University of California and George Washington University. After working in photo-intelligence for the CIA, from 1955 to 1968 she taught experimental psychology in Washington DC at the American University and George Washington University. She killed herself after shooting her husband, who was suffering from Alzheimer's Disease. Her reputation as a powerfully imaginative and emotionally disquieting science fiction author rests chiefly upon the short stories collected in *Ten Thousand Light Years from Home* (1973), *Warm Worlds and Otherwise* (1975), *Star Songs of an Old Primate* (1978), and *Out of Everywhere* (1981). Her academic training in psychology and anthropology informs her stories' concern with death, sex, and other fundamentals of human experience. Her other publications include the novels *Up the Walls of the World* (1978) and *Brightness Falls from the Air* (1985). *Her Smoke Rose Up Forever* (1990) is a collected edition of her stories.

Titus Groan, see PEAKE, MERVYN.

TLALI, Miriam (1933–), South African novelist, born in Doornfontein, Transvaal. She spent two years at Witwatersrand University; when it was closed to black students, she completed her studies at the National University of Roma, Lesotho. Her experiences as a clerk in a hire-purchase business formed the basis for her first novel, *Muriel at Metropolitan* (1976), which is regarded as the first treatment in English of the cultural and political conditions afflicting black women. *Amandla* (1981) dealt with the schoolchildren's rebellion in Soweto in 1976; both novels were banned in South Africa until the lifting of apartheid. She was among the founders of **Staffrider*, South Africa's leading forum for black writers, for which she wrote the 'Soweto Speaks' column, and has been a noted contributor to the *Rand Daily Mail*; some of her journalism is collected in *Mihloti* (1984), which also contains interviews and samples of her travel writing. *Footprints in the Quag* (1989), published in Britain as *Soweto Stories* (1989), is a collection of stories and dialogues which reflect her increasing interest in the resources of an oral culture.

TODD, Ruthven (1914–78), British writer, born in Edinburgh, educated at Edinburgh College of Art. He is best remembered for his two allegorical and surreal quest novels, *Over the Mountain* (1939) and *The Lost Traveller* (1943), in which a strayed wanderer is sentenced by the minions of a faceless state to an impossible task, and is ultimately sacrificed. Both were indebted to books such as Wyndham *Lewis's *Childermass* (1928) and Rex *Warner's *The Wild Goose Chase* (1937), but introduced a monitory political note reflecting a period of uncertainty. The essays collected in *Tracks in the Snow* (1946) offered some interesting analysis of the allegorical writings of William Blake and Henry Fuseli. He has also written a series of science fiction novels for children including *Space Cat* (1952), and several detective novels under the name R. T. Campbell, such as *Take Thee a Sharp Knife* (1946).

TÓIBÍN, Colm (1955–), Irish novelist, born in Wexford, educated at University College, Dublin. He has worked as a journalist and columnist for *The Dublin Sunday Independent*, *Esquire*, and the *London Review of Books*. His first novel, *The South* (1990), deals with the encounter of Katherine Proctor, an Irish Protestant, with the Spanish Civil War activist Miguel in the aftermath of the events of 1939. Praised for its restraint and its subtlety of style, the novel foregrounds Tóibín's twin historical preoccupations with twentieth-century Spain and his native Ireland. *The Blazing Heather* (1992), Tóibín's second novel, was even more enthusiastically received; it tells, with compassion, intensity, and characteristic compression, of the relationship of a judge with his wife following his retirement. Though Tóibín displays evident similarities with his Irish contemporaries and predecessors, his nevertheless remains a fresh and original voice: less melodramatic than N. *Jordan's, less mandarin than *Banville's, and more attuned to the present than *Trevor's. Tóibín was awarded the E. M. Forster Prize from the American Academy of Arts and Letters in 1995. An eloquent essayist and writer of travelogues, he is also the author of the nonfiction works *Walking Along the Border* (1987), *Homage to Barcelona* (1990), and *The Sign of the Cross* (1995), his observations on Catholic Europe.

To Kill a Mockingbird, see LEE, HARPER.

TOLKIEN, J(ohn) R(onald) R(euel) (1892–1973), British writer and academic, born in South Africa; he came to England at the age of three and was educated at Exeter College, Oxford. From 1945 he was Merton Professor of English Language and Literature at Oxford. Among his early works are *A Middle-English Vocabulary* (1922), an edition of *Sir Gawain and the Green Knight* (1925; with E. V. Gordon), and *Beowulf: The Monsters and the Critics* (1936). While serving in the trenches in the First World War, he began, for consolation and pleasure, to create tales set in a 'Secondary World'. The theoretical foundations for this 'subcreation' were presented in 'On Fairy-Stories', the definitive form of which appeared in *Essays Presented to Charles Williams* (1947); with Tolkien and C. S. *Lewis, who edited the volume, Charles *Williams was a leading member of the Inklings, at whose meetings in the 1930s Tolkien began to read the draft excerpts from the Secondary World tales which later became *The Lord of the Rings* (3 volumes, 1954–5). This World was partially glimpsed in *The Hobbit* (1937), a children's novel and the first published tale of Middle-earth; even the enormous (but meticulously constructed over a 40-year period) epic narrative contained in *The Lord of the Rings* only hinted (in long appendices) at the extraordinary substrata of created mythology surrounding Frodo the Hobbit's long soul-searching quest to return the Ring of Power to its immemorial source. The events in this novel were rooted in an extended history of Middle-earth, of which some details appeared in *The Silmarillion* (1977), *Unfinished Tales of Numenor and Middle-Earth* (1980), and *The Book of Lost Tales* (2 volumes, 1983–5); the languages of human and elf and Orc quoted in the text were samples of tongues Tolkien had created. After several years of moderate sales, Tolkien's works became vastly popular and influential. Among the many studies are Humphrey Carpenter's biography *J. R. R. Tolkien* (1977) and T. A. Shippey's *The Road to Middle-earth* (1982).

TOMALIN, Claire (1933–), British biographer, born in London, educated at Newnham College, Cambridge. After working as a publisher's editor, in 1968 she joined the staff of the *New Statesman*, becoming literary editor in 1974, and was subsequently literary editor of the *Sunday Times* until 1986. Her reputation as a distinguished biographer was established with *The Life and Death of Mary Wollstonecraft* (1974; Whitbread Prize). Her extensive research for *Katherine Mansfield: A Secret Life* (1987) disclosed much that had been overlooked by previous biographies. Her play *The Winter Wife* (1991) deals with Mansfield's relationship with her intimate friend Ida Baker. *The Invisible Woman* (1990; James Tait Black Memorial Prize, and Hawthornden Prize), is a remarkable investigative study of the actress Nelly Ternan and her clandestine liaison with Charles Dickens; the work, which contributes valuably to the social history of the Victorian era, has been acclaimed as a masterpiece of feminist biography. Tomalin also received high praise for *Mrs Jordan's Profession* (1994) a biography of the actress Dorothy Jordan, the mistress of William IV. She is married to Michael *Frayn.

TOMLINSON, (Alfred) Charles (1927–), British poet and graphic artist, born in Stoke-on-Trent, educated at Queens' College, Cambridge, and the University of London. In 1957 he became a lecturer at the University of Bristol, where he was appointed Professor of English in 1982. *The Necklace* (1955), his first substantial collection of verse, was more favourably received in the USA than in Britain. His numerous subsequent volumes include *A Peopled Landscape* (1963), *The Way of a World* (1969), *The Shaft* (1974), *Notes from New York* (1984), *Collected Poems* (1985), *The Door in the Wall* (1992), and *Jubilation* (1995). Tomlinson has stated that he aspires to 'a phenomenological poetry' giving 'objects their own existences', indicating the affinities with *Objectivist Poetry to which his prose work *Some Americans: A Personal Record* (1981) attests. The primacy of visual responses in his verse results in patterns of imagery that combine striking clarity with scrupulous complexity of structure. Some of his later work makes explicit the metaphysical and celebratory impulses underlying his conceptions of poetry. The visual refinement of his writing accords with his work as a graphic artist, which is published in *In Black and White* (1975). His other publications include *Translations* (1983), containing his versions of the poetry of Octavio Paz and Antonio Machado, and *Poetry and Metamorphosis* (1983), a collection of his lectures.

TOMLINSON, H(enry) M(ajor) (1873–1958), British travel writer and novelist, born in East London; he left school at the age of 12 and worked as a shipping clerk till 1904, when he began his career as a journalist. His assignments included a series of voyages to remote locations; the journey up the Amazon he made in 1909 was recorded in his first and most celebrated book, *The Sea and the Jungle* (1912). After three years as a war correspondent in France he became literary editor of the *Nation* in 1917. His travel writings also include *South to Cadiz* (1934) and the essays on the Dutch East Indies in *Tidemarks* (1924) and *Malay Waters* (1950). *Gallions Reach* (1927), the first of his novels to gain wide notice, draws heavily on his experiences of the seas and jungles of South-East Asia. The most highly regarded of his many works of fiction is *All Our Yesterdays* (1930), a compelling narrative of the First World War which echoes his explicit polemic against warfare in *Mars His Idiot* (1935); *The Trumpet Shall Sound* (1957), his last novel, was acclaimed for its portrayal of a London family during the air-raids of the Second World War. Among the numerous collections of Tomlinson's essays, in which his stylistic accomplishment is most readily evident, are *London River* (1921), *Gifts of Fortune* (1926), and the autobiographical pieces of *A Mingled Yarn* (1953).

Tono-Bungay, a novel by H. G. *Wells, published in 1909. Described by its author as a Balzacian 'social panorama', this is Wells's most ambitious and sweeping indictment of Edwardian England. Its form is that of a *Bildungsroman* narrated by George Ponderevo, the son of the housekeeper at Bladesover House in Kent. George studies science in London, but his prospects are transformed when he joins his uncle Edward in exploiting the latter's invention of a patent medicine, Tono-Bungay, which takes both men to fame and fortune. Edward's swaggering career as a manufacturer, tycoon, swindler, and eventual bankrupt parallels his more puritanical nephew's growing experience of social and moral disillusionment. The tale of the Ponderevo's rise and fall is accompanied by George's astringent sociological commentary, exposing both the corruption of the old 'organic' English class system by the new forces of corporate wealth and greed, and the confusion and unhappiness of individuals caught up in a degenerate society. But if the England of *Tono-Bungay* appears ripe for revolution, the novel is far from offering any blueprint for an alternative social organization. George's detailed confession of his moral compromises and sexual entanglements shows his inability to detach himself from the life he rejects. Leaving his uncle's business in disgust, he turns to aeronautical engineering, designing and building the airship which enables his uncle to escape from his creditors. As a last irony, this novel with its vivid representation of social history concludes with a symbolic vision of the passing of traditional England, as seen from the bridge of a naval destroyer.

TOOLE, John Kennedy (1937–69), American novelist, born in New Orleans, educated at Columbia University, New York City. His reputation rests almost entirely on one novel, the posthumously published *A Confederacy of Dunces* (1980) which won the Pulitzer Prize for fiction in 1981. The novel was written in the early 1960s and Toole's failure to place it with a publisher is generally thought to be one of the reasons behind his suicide. In 1976, Toole's mother contacted Walker *Percy who acted as Toole's agent; excerpts from the novel appeared in the *New Orleans Review* in 1979 prior to its publication by Louisiana State University Press. The novel's protagonist, Ignatius J. Reilly of New Orleans, is an intellectual *picaro*, with similarities to Saul *Bellow's Herzog, who conducts a one-man assault on the excesses of modernity; his Big

Chief tablets (like Herzog's letters) are the occasions for his synoptic philosophizing and provide a kind of internal monologue which operates in counterpoint to the richly inventive comic action of the novel. The title rephrases part of a sentence by Jonathan Swift: 'When a true genius appears in the world, you may know him by this sign, that the dunces are all in confederacy against him.' The novel was both a commercial and a critical success and many critics hold that, had Toole lived, he would be numbered among the most important writers of post-war Southern literature.

TOOMER, Jean (1894–1967), American novelist, born in Washington, DC to parents of Louisiana Creole stock, educated at the University of Wisconsin and at City College, New York. Toomer began publishing poems and sketches in 1918 and in 1922 went to Georgia, where he worked in schools, an experience which provided material for the first part of *Cane* (1923), the book on which his reputation rests. Around 1923 his interest in mysticism brought him under the influence of the Russian Gurdjieff and he spent part of the summer of 1926 at his Institute in Fontainebleau, France; in 1931, in his quest for an alternative lifestyle, he organized an experiment in communal living with eight friends in Portage, Wisconsin. *Cane* is a modernist text that defies easy categorization. Though it has been called a 'novel', it is a miscellany that brings together short stories, poetry, and dramatic scenes and blends realistic detail with a lyrical narrative mode. The first part is set in Georgia, the second in Washington and Chicago; it concludes with a longer story, 'Kabnis', which employs a primarily dramatic mode to explore the educated northern African-American's quest for self. Many of the stories in *Cane* deal, in restrained and compassionate style, with protagonists who are the victims of their mixed racial identity. Toomer also published *Essentials* (1931), which expounds his philosophy of human possibility, and a number of plays. A fair-skinned man whose 'coloured' maternal grandfather Pickney Bentor Stewart Pinchbeck was acting governor of Louisiana during the Reconstruction era, Toomer's exact racial identity remains unclear. He himself consistently argued that his humanity transcended his origins—'I am of no particular race. I am of the human race'—but today he is generally regarded as a seminal figure in the African-American literary renaissance of the 1920s, albeit for his artistic innovation rather than any propagandist message. See ETHNICITY and HARLEM RENAISSANCE.

Topographical Poetry, a mode of verse which in its essential form is an eighteenth-century phenomenon, typified by works like John Dyer's *Grongar Hill* (1726) and James Thomson's *The Seasons* (1726–30); much of its character survives, however, in the prevalence of local description and landscape imagery in a substantial body of twentieth-century poetry. Dr Johnson defined topographical poetry as 'a species of composition . . . of which the fundamental subject is some particular landscape', adding that 'embellishments may be supplied by historical retrospection, or incidental meditation'. Its emphatically visual and descriptive nature was much modified by Wordsworth, who made landscape the medium for his moral, imaginative, and spiritual intuitions; approaches to topographical poetry in the twentieth century generally follow his example in avoiding the constraints of being exclusively concerned with locality *per se*. Many of Thomas *Hardy's poems are sufficiently rich in details drawn from his Wessex surroundings to function on one level as topographical poetry. In the work of various *Georgian poets, notably Andrew *Young, local description predominates. The ascendancy of *Imagism from around 1910 onward tended to promote the visual dimension intrinsic to topographical writing. Numerous poems by authors strongly associated with *Modernism have distinct topographical aspects: Basil Bunting's **Briggflatts* (1966), the **Four Quartets* (1935–42) of T. S. Eliot (who also produced a series entitled 'Landscapes'), and William Carlos Williams's **Paterson* (1946–58) are sustained to a large extent by local elements. Sir John *Betjeman's work is perhaps closest to topographical poetry in its strict sense, displaying a high incidence of poems remarkable for their detailed fidelity to specified English locations. Others notable for poetry making extensive use of landscape include Charles *Causley, Ted *Hughes, Norman *MacCaig, Norman *Nicholson, and A. L. *Rowse, some of whom are also describable as *regional poets.

To the Lighthouse, a novel by V. *Woolf, published in 1927, frequently judged to be her best work, and one of the finest achievements of English *Modernism. Family comedy, elegy, symbolic prose poem, and meditation on the artist's responsibility all in one, it was planned (in 1925) 'to have father's character complete in it; & mother's; & St Ives; & childhood', and was felt by her sister Vanessa Bell to have 'given a portrait of mother which is more like her to me than anything I could ever have conceived of as possible'. The Stephen family in their holiday home in Cornwall is transformed into the Ramsay family at 'Finlay', on the Isle of Skye in the Hebrides. Mr Ramsay, a philosopher whose best work is done and who fears he will never 'reach R' in the alphabet of the mind's journey, is passionate-tempered, rationalist, comically tyrannical, eccentric, and demanding of admiration and female sympathy. Mrs Ramsay holds the family together, loves children, believes in marriage, comforts the dying, is short-sighted, queenly, beautiful, and manipulative, and in her private self profoundly melancholy. The relationship is examined through a narrative which moves between their thought processes and those of the onlookers at the house. These are the painter Lily Briscoe, in love with Mrs Ramsay and the whole family, but determinedly independent; the fastidious objective bachelor William Bankes, a scientist, with mixed feelings about family life; Charles Tansley, a working-class self-made scholar, awkward and aggressive; Augustus Carmichael, a sleepy, opium-taking, inscrutable poet; and the stupid, attractive young couple Paul and Minta. Of the eight Ramsay children, Cam, wild and intractable, and the youngest, James, hating his father, are the most prominent. In the first section, 'The Window', Mr Ramsay tells James he won't be able to go to the lighthouse the next day, Mrs Ramsay reads him the story of 'The Fisherman and his Wife', while Lily tries to paint them, observed by Mr Bankes; Paul and Minta get engaged on the beach, Mrs Ramsay gives dinner ('bœuf en daube') for fourteen people and feels she has created something momentarily 'immune from change', and the Ramsays are seen alone together. In the middle section, 'Time Passes', a 'solitary sleeper' contemplates the advent of war, the house is deserted, the deaths of Mrs Ramsay and of her two oldest children, Prue and Andrew, take place shockingly in parentheses, and after ten years two charladies, Mrs McNab and Mrs Bast, resuscitate the house. The last section, 'The Lighthouse', is divided between Lily's strenuous attempt to start her painting again as a way of remembering Mrs Ramsay and of balancing the opposing forces of the Ramsays, and the journey to the lighthouse, in which Cam and James move from resentment of their father's tyranny to admiration of his heroism. Lily's vision ends (and is analogous with) the novel.

Tower, The, a collection of verse by W. B. *Yeats, published in 1928, which contains a number of his best-known poems and marks the beginning of the final and most masterly phase of his work. The volume also exemplifies the fineness of production characteristic of many of his books; the green cover, designed by T. Sturge *Moore, is inlaid with a stylized illustration in gold of Thoor Ballylee, the tower near Coole Park which Yeats lived in after his marriage in 1917. The tower and its surroundings are repeatedly alluded to, notably in the title poem and 'Meditations in Time of Civil War', a sequence conflating Yeats's direct observations of the conflict in Ireland in 1922 and 1923 with the pessimistic historical prognosis he set out in *A *Vision* (1925). The twenty-one poems also include 'Among School Children', 'Leda and the Swan', 'Nineteen Hundred and Nineteen', 'All Souls' Night', and 'Sailing to Byzantium'. Rhymed forms are adjusted with great virtuosity to the rhetorically heightened conversational idiom of the collection to establish the prevailing manner of his later work. The poetry also gains depth and range from the constant interplay between personal experience and larger philosophical or public themes. As A. Norman Jeffares remarked in *W. B. Yeats: Man and Poet* (1949), 'The poetry of *The Tower* period is rich because of the fullness of Yeats's life, because his style was reaching maturity at the same time as his life.'

Towers of Trebizond, The, see MACAULAY, DAME ROSE.

TOWNSEND, Sue (1946–), British novelist and playwright, born in Leicester. She is the author of *Three Plays* (1984), consisting of *Bazaar and Rummage*, *Gasping for Words*, and *Womberang*. She achieved her greatest success with *The Secret Diary of Adrian Mole Aged 13¾* (1982), which examines British society in the 1980s through the eyes of its precocious teenaged narrator, whose voice Townsend captures with authenticity and humour. *The Growing Pains of Adrian Mole* followed in 1984. Adrian Mole has appeared as the hero of a stage play and a successful television serial, both scripted by the author. She has since written, in similarly satirical vein, the novels *Rebuilding Coventry* (1988), which tells the story of a woman who escapes from a small town to London's 'cardboard city' of the homeless after murdering a man, and *The Queen and I* (1992). She is also the author of the non-fiction work *Mr Bevan's Dream: Why Britain Needs Its Welfare State* (1989).

TOYNBEE, Arnold (Joseph) (1889–1975), British historian, born in London, educated at Balliol College, Oxford, where he was a tutor until 1915. He became a professor at London University in 1919 and was Director of the Royal Institute of International Affairs from 1925 until he retired in 1955. *A Study of History* (10 volumes, 1934 and 1954) took some twenty major civilizations as examples upon which Toynbee based his argument that a cycle of emergence, development, and ultimate dissolution was inevitable in societies and cultures; the onset of the final phase had, he maintained, begun in the modern world. Prolonged controversy arose with regard to the value of his conclusions and the generalizing energies of his methods. The abridgement by D. C. Somervell, published in two parts in 1946 and 1960, commanded a wide popular readership. In its call for a universal spiritual code as the channel for possible cultural regeneration, *A Study of History* displays the religious sensibility also evident in Toynbee's *An Historian's Approach to Religion* (1956) and *Mankind, Whence and Whither?* (1966). Among his works in his original field as a classical historian, which remain highly regarded, are *Greek Historical Thought* (1950) and *Hannibal's Legacy* (1965). His prolific career as an author also gave rise to numerous accounts of his travels, the best-known of which is *Between Oxus and Jamna* (1961). *Acquaintances* (1967) and *Experiences* (1969) are volumes of his memoirs. He was the father of Philip *Toynbee, with whom he wrote *Comparing Notes: A Dialogue across a Generation* (1963).

TOYNBEE, (Theodore) Philip (1916–81), British novelist, poet, critic, and diarist, born in Oxford, educated at Christ Church College, Oxford. His early novels reflected his leftist political sympathies, but with *Tea with Mrs Goodman* (1947; US title *Prothalamium*) and *The Garden to the Sea* (1953) his novels became both experimental and psychologically subtle, the latter exploring the collapse of a marriage partly due to the strains of war. *Friends Apart: A Memoir of Esmond Romilly and Jasper Ridley in the Thirties* (1954) concerns friends who died in the war. *Comparing Notes: A Dialogue across a Generation* (1963) was written with his father, Arnold *Toynbee. Latterly he produced a series of verse novels (in seven parts), entitled 'Pantaloon', which includes *Pantaloon or the Valediction* (1961), *Two Brothers* (1964), *A Learned City* (1966), and *Views from a Lake* (1968); primarily comic in vision, the sequence explores the 1914–46 period through the shifting memories and perspectives of its old hero, Dick Abberville. Toynbee's journals, *Part of a Journey* (1981) and *End of a Journey* (1988), chronicle his return to the Christian faith, and his final meditations on art and life. From 1950 he was a highly influential reviewer for the *Observer*. See Jessica *Mitford, *Faces of Philip: A Memoir of Philip Toynbee* (1984).

Transatlantic Review, The: (1) a literary journal begun in Paris in 1923 by Ford Madox *Ford. James *Joyce, Ezra *Pound, and Ernest *Hemingway were closely associated with the magazine and supported it as both contributors and editorial advisers. Basil *Bunting was Ford's assistant editor. Hilda *Doolittle, E. E. *Cummings, F. S. *Flint, Gertrude *Stein, William Carlos *Williams, and Djuna *Barnes were among the noted *Modernist authors whose writing was featured. The inclusion of graphic work by Georges Braque and Man Ray and the publication of surrealist poems by Tristan Tzara and others emphasized the cosmopolitan tone Ford cultivated in the magazine. The fourth issue contained Joyce's 'Work in Progress', which constituted the first appearance in print of material relating to **Finnegans Wake* (1939). Disagreements between Ford and Hemingway over the *Review*'s literary aesthetics were among the reasons for its closure in January 1925.

(2) J. McCrindle began another periodical under the title *Transatlantic Review* in 1959, which was noted for the quality of its prose fiction; its contributors included William *Trevor, Edna *O'Brien, Samuel *Beckett, John *Updike, William *Burroughs, and Ian *McEwan. It also published interviews with Joe *Orton, Tom *Stoppard, Edward *Bond, and other leading dramatists. B. S. *Johnson was its poetry editor from 1965 until his death in 1973; notable among the poets whose work appeared were W. H. *Auden and Ted *Hughes. McCrindle's *Transatlantic Review* ran for sixty issues before its closure in 1977.

transition, an international literary journal begun in Paris in 1927 by Eugene Jolas as a 'laboratory of the word'. Assisted by his wife Maria, who translated contributions, Jolas remained editor until the last issue in 1938. Manifestos affirming 'The Revolution of the Word' and the advent of 'Vertigralism', Jolas's quasi-mystical aesthetic of 'primitive grammar', were characteristic of *transition*'s radical tone. James *Joyce's 'Work in Progress', which culminated in **Finnegans Wake* (1939), exemplified Jolas's ideas of linguistic innovation; extracts were regularly published in the magazine from its inception onward. Predominantly in English, the magazine also published writing in French and German and contained work by many eminent contributors. The first translations of stories by Franz Kafka appeared in its pages in 1927, and 'Metamorphosis' was serialized in 1936. Dylan *Thomas, Gertrude *Stein, Anaïs *Nin, W. C. *Williams, and Samuel *Beckett also supplied stories, which Jolas termed 'paramyths'. Contributors of essays included S. M. Eisenstein, Herbert *Read, and C. G. Jung, whose theories of the collective unconscious were of great interest to *transition*. Hart *Crane, Laura *Riding, Paul Éluard, Randall *Jarrell, and Yvor *Winters were among the poets whose work was featured. *transition* was also noted for its coverage of the graphic and plastic arts and was produced with covers designed by Picasso, Miro, and other artists of distinction.

Translations, a play by Brian *Friel, performed in 1980, and published in 1981. This is set in 1833 in a Donegal 'hedge school', a place where Latin, Greek, myth, and history are taught to the Irish-speaking peasantry. But it is also a time when British sappers are passing through the region, translating the ancient place-names into English. There is inevitable conflict between the old and the new, a poor but imaginative populace and the forces of a sort of cultural imperialism, Irish 'backwardness' and English confidence. The play ends with the promise of reprisals as a result of the disappearance and probable death of an officer, Lieutenant Yolland, who has attempted to cross the barriers of nationality and fallen in love with a local girl, Maire. Though some critics have expressed doubt about the plausibility of this romance, there has been general admiration for the vitality and complexity with which Friel handles his theme, the nature and importance of language.

TRANTER, John (1943–), Australian poet, born in New South Wales, educated at the University of Sydney. He has worked as a publisher's editor and a producer for the Australian Broadcasting Commission. He was one of a generation of poets, during the late 1960s, whose aims were to introduce *Modernism into Australian poetics; according to one critic, Tranter is 'contemptuous of gum-tree-laden poetry, poetry of assertion and poetry that is not essentially about language itself'. *Parallax* (1970) frequently deals with distorted perception and is perhaps more traditional than his subsequent works, which are progressively experimental; these include *Red Movie* (1972), *Crying in Early Infancy* (1977), *Dazed in the Ladies Lounge* (1979), *Under Berlin: New Poems* (1988), and *Days in the Capital* (1992). In some of his works, such as *The Alphabet Murders* (1976), Tranter examines the poetic process itself. *The Floor of Heaven* (1992) consists of four narrative poems in which four characters, interlinked between poems, reveal the core of their lives. He was the editor of *Poetry Australia's Preface to the 70s* (1970) and *The New Australian Poetry* (1979).

TRANTER, Nigel (1909–), Scottish writer of historical novels, born in Glasgow. Tranter writes mainly on Scottish themes; his books are rich in character and action. His trilogies include 'The Master of Gray' (*The Master of Gray*, 1961; *The Courtesan*, 1963; *Past Master*,

1965), 'The Bruce Trilogy' on Robert the Bruce, 'The Stewart Trilogy', and 'The MacGregor Trilogy'. Other works include two novels on Montrose (*The Young Montrose*, 1972; *Montrose, the Captain General*, 1973) and many others on aspects of sixteenth- and seventeenth-century Scotland, such as *Warden of the Queen's March* (1989) about Mary, Queen of Scots, and *Children of the Mist* (1992) concerning the conflicts between the Campbells and the MacGregors. *Druid Sacrifice* (1993) focuses on Thanea, niece of King Arthur and mother of St Mungo, and the clash between pagan traditions and early Christianity. He has also written children's books and non-fiction works on Scottish history. *Footbridge to Enchantment* (1992) contains his articles, observations, and anecdotes about his home ground near Aberlady in East Lothian.

TRAPIDO, Barbara (1941–), British novelist, born in Cape Town, South Africa, educated at the University of Natal and the University of London. After working as a schoolteacher in London, she published *Brother of the More Famous Jack* (1982), her first novel, a highly polished satirical romance whose complex plot ranges over fifteen years in the life of a well-educated but naïve young woman. Strongly informed by Trapido's South African background, *Noah's Ark* (1984) follows the social and emotional chaos surrounding its heroine's attempts to deal with her past. *Temples of Delight* (1990) was praised for the Dickensian vigour of characterization in its treatment of social and cultural mobility from a restricted *nouveau riche* milieu to international bohemian circles. Its sequel, *Juggling* (1992), adapts the structure of Shakespearean comedy to frame its elaborate and sometimes sexually disquieting narrative of two sets of twins growing up in New York. Trapido's novels are noted for their opulently sensual descriptions and their success in sustaining an aspect of psychological and emotional seriousness amid their predominant comedy.

TRAVERS, Ben (1886–1980), British playwright, born in Hendon, London, educated at Charterhouse School. He joined the family sugar business and worked for a time in Malaya, then turned to publishing, and began to write novels. One of these he adapted into *A Cuckoo in the Nest* (1925), the first of a long series of 'Aldwych farces', so-called after the London theatre in which they were staged. Others included *Rookery Nook* (1926), in which a pretty girl is given sanctuary from her Prussian stepfather by a newly married man and his cousin; *Thark* (1927); *Plunder* (1928); and *Turkey Time* (1931). *Banana Ridge* (1938), probably the best of Travers's later farces, is set in Malaya and involves a group of men presented with a boy who may be the son of one of them, and who proves irresistible to their wives. The laughter in these plays invariably derives from deceit, misunderstanding, and embarrassment, and usually occurs when strong and anarchic sexual impulses, somewhat camouflaged for the benefit of the censor, come into conflict with a morally inflexible society, often represented by an aggressive, puritanical woman. This tension was more open in *The Bed before Yesterday*, a comedy successfully produced in 1975, Travers's ninetieth year.

Travesties, a play by Tom *Stoppard, performed in 1974, published in 1975. Though there are occasional jumps to a later period, the play occurs mainly in Zurich during the First World War, at a time when Lenin, *Joyce, and the Dadaist Tristan Tzara were living in the city. They all appear, as does a British consular official named Henry Carr, who sued Joyce for the cost of a pair of trousers in a production of *The Importance of Being Earnest* in 1917. Out of this historical curiosity, Stoppard builds a wild extravaganza which includes Wildean pastiche, limericks, striptease, and a lecture in Marxist theory, while simultaneously discussing a subject on which all his main characters have strong opinions, the place of the artist in society.

TREECE, Henry (1911–66), British poet and novelist, born in Wednesbury, Staffordshire, educated at the University of Birmingham. He was a schoolteacher until 1959, when he became a full-time writer. In 1938 he met J. F. *Hendry, with whom he became co-founder of the *New Apocalypse and co-editor of two of its anthologies, *The White Horseman* (1941) and *The Crown and the Sickle* (1943). Treece's *How I See Apocalypse* (1946) formed the principal critical apologia for the movement. *38 Poems* (1940) was his first independent collection; numerous volumes followed, including *The Black Seasons* (1945) and *The Exiles* (1952), his last book of poetry. *Collected Poems* was published in 1946. While some of his poems are identifiably of the New Apocalypse in their unrestrained use of grotesque imagery, his rhythmical control and regularity of structure give his work a durably traditional character. His religious poems exhibit the historical tendencies of his imagination which are most apparent in his fiction. His numerous historical novels, which include *The Dark Island* (1952), *Electra* (1963), and *The Queen's Brooch* (1966), are vividly imagined and compellingly developed. Treece also produced much historical fiction for juveniles and a number of mystery stories with contemporary settings. His critical works include *Dylan Thomas: 'Dog among the Fairies'* (1949), the first substantial study of the poet's work.

Tree of Man, The, a novel by Patrick *White, published in 1956. Beginning in the 1880s and ending in the 1930s, this is the epic story of a New South Wales farmer, Stan Parker, and his wife, Amy. Their lives and destinies are shaped by their hazardous relationship with the land and the forces and disasters of nature. Their neighbours, too, influence the course of their eventual emotional separation. Amy finds solace in rearing her late-born children, in fantasizing about the lives of her glamorous neighbours, and eventually, to Stan's despair, in a casual affair with a passing stranger. Stan, now a veteran of the First World War, retreats into his own poetic fantasies, which draw him still further away from his wife. Their son, Ray, a delinquent, is shot in a fight, leaving behind him his wife, Elsie, and a son. Amy finds an emotional outlet in her relationships with Elsie and the child: her daughter, Thelma, has chosen an arid urban life. In his old age Stan sees his farm engulfed by ugly suburban developments, and dies disillusioned and unfulfilled, after a negative epiphanic experience. But the novel ends with the indication that his yearning for poetic expression will be fulfilled by his grandson, who dreams of writing a masterpiece.

TREMAIN, Rose (1943–), British novelist and playwright, born in London, educated at the Sorbonne, and the University of East Anglia where she became a lecturer in creative writing. Her first novel, *Sadler's Birthday* (1977), looks back on the life of an ageing butler and dealt with themes of old age and death to which the writer was to return. *Letter to Sister Benedicta* (1979), in which a middle-aged woman writes a letter to the nun who brought her up at a convent in India, and *The Cupboard* (1982), which reflects on an ageing writer's past, both offered variations on this theme. *The Swimming Pool Season* (1985), which depicts the relationships between a number of expatriates in a remote village in the South of France, displayed her gift for ironic observation, also seen to advantage in her two collections of short stories, *The Colonel's Daughter* (1983) and *The Garden of the Villa Mollini* (1987). The novel *Restoration* (1989) marked a new departure in her fiction. Set at the time of Charles II's restoration to the throne, the novel is an ambitious work, exploring themes of exile and restoration on a number of different levels. The story is narrated by the hero, Robert Merivel, a fat, hedonistic student of anatomy and court favourite, now disgraced, whose attempt to regain royal favour and to find happiness are chronicled with a certain bawdy humour tinged with melancholy. *Sacred Country* (1992; James Tait Black Memorial Prize) was set in Norfolk during the 1950s and dealt with themes of sexual identity through the medium of its transsexual narrator. *Evangelista's Fan* (1994) was a collection of short stories with various settings, ranging from medieval France to contemporary America. The title story, about an eighteenth-century clockmaker who falls in love with an unknown woman and then convinces himself that his beloved (whose face he has only glimpsed) must be terribly disfigured, is characteristic of the collection, which displays the versatility of Tremain's writing and the diversity of her concerns.

TRENCH, (Frederic) Herbert (1865–1923), British poet and dramatist, born at Avoncore, Co. Cork, educated at Keble College, Oxford. He entered the Civil Service in 1891. His early publications as a poet, which include *Deirdre Wed* (1900) and *New Poems* (1907), gained him a considerable reputation. He was director of the Haymarket Theatre from 1911 to 1913. He subsequently lived mainly at Settignano, near Florence, which is vividly evoked in much of his later verse. His ambitions as a dramatist were most substantially realized in *Napoleon* (1919); during the play's successful production Trench sustained injuries from which he never fully recovered. *Talleyrand* was to have been his *magnum opus* for the theatre, but remained unfinished at his death. Among his later publications are *Ode from Italy in Time of War* (1915) and *Poems, with Fables in Prose* (1918); a three-volume *Collected Works* was produced in 1924. Although the title poem of *Deirdre Wed* is markedly Irish in character, his verse is typically written in a rhetorically grandiose late Victorian style. His most interesting work is the long poem 'Apollo and the Seaman', which achieves an unusual combination of spirited ballad form and philosophically speculative content.

Trent's Last Case, see BENTLEY, E. C.

TRESSELL, Robert, pseudonym of Robert NOONAN (1870–1911), Irish novelist, born in Dublin into a middle-class family. He emigrated to South Africa in the early 1890s, where he married and had a daughter. After the death of his wife, he sailed to England and settled in Hastings. He had been politically active in Africa, and once in Britain he joined the Social Democratic Foundation, a Marxist forerunner of the Independent Labour Party. In 1904, while working long hours as a housepainter and signwriter, he found time to start his novel *The *Ragged Trousered Philanthropists*, basing it closely on the working conditions and attitudes he encountered at first hand. The completed work was turned down by all the publishers to whom it was sent. The despairing Tressell consigned the manuscript to the fire, from which it was rescued by his daughter, Kathleen. By 1910 worsening health had persuaded Tressell to emigrate to Canada, and he travelled to Liverpool in an attempt to find work to pay his passage. He became ill, died in a workhouse of bronchial pneumonia, and was buried in a pauper's grave. *The Ragged Trousered Philanthropists* was published in an abridged version in 1914; the full-length version was not published until 1955.

TREVELYAN, G(eorge) M(acaulay) (1876–1962), British historian, born in Stratford-on-Avon, the son of Sir George Otto Trevelyan (1838–1928), educated at Trinity College, Cambridge; he was appointed Regius Professor of Modern History at Cambridge in 1927 and was Master of Trinity College from 1940 to 1951, when he became Chancellor of Durham University. Following the appearance of numerous studies, notably *England under the Stuarts* (1904), he came to general notice with the trilogy on the *Risorgimento* which comprised *Garibaldi's Defence of the Roman Republic* (1907), *Garibaldi and the Thousand* (1909), and *Garibaldi and the Making of Italy* (1911). The work, which is pervaded by the liberalism informing much of his writing, exemplifies the dramatic and descriptive qualities intrinsic to his belief that 'The art of history remains always the art of narrative'. The most widely read historian of his day, his most popular books were *A History of England* (1926) and *English Social History* (1944), both of which offer authoritatively encompassing surveys. *Blenheim* (1930), *Ramillies and the Union with Scotland* (1932), and *The Peace and the Protestant Succession* (1934), the three volumes of *England under Queen Anne*, are often regarded as his essential contribution to historical scholarship. Among his many other works in a career of prolific authorship are the biographies *A Life of John Bright* (1913) and *Grey of Falloden* (1937) and *An Autobiography and Other Essays* (1949). *G. M. Trevelyan* (1980) is a biographical memoir by his daughter Mary Moorman.

TREVELYAN, Raleigh (1923–), British author, born in Port Blair in the Andaman Islands; he spent his early years in India and Kashmir and was educated at Winchester College. From 1942 to 1946 he was on active service and drew on his experiences of combat in Italy for *The Fortress: Anzio and After* (1956) and *Rome '44: The Battle for the Eternal City* (1981); both were widely acclaimed for combining authoritative military history with vivid and emotionally compelling personal recollection. In 1948 he took up the first of his many senior positions in publishing. His extensive familiarity with Italy is reflected in *Princes under the Volcano* (1972), an account of Sicily, and the treatment of the destruction of Pompeii in *The Shadow of Vesuvius* (1976). The informatively accessible study of the artistic movement in *A Pre-Raphaelite Circle* (1978) draws on records of his family, as does *The Golden Oriole* (1987), a wide-ranging treatment of the British in India based on five journeys to places he knew in childhood. His other publications include *A Hermit Disclosed* (1960), a sympathetic portrait of an Essex recluse, and *Grand Dukes and Diamonds* (1991), about the mining magnate Sir Julius Wernher and his descendants.

TREVOR, William, born William Trevor COX (1928–), Anglo-Irish novelist and short-story writer, born in Mitchelstown, Co. Cork, educated at Trinity College, Dublin. His early novels were a combination of allegory, farce, and acute social observation, and displayed a singular sensitivity to the plight of the old, the lonely, and the ill-adjusted, particularly women. In novels such as *The Old Boys* (1964), *The Boarding House* (1965), *The Love Department* (1966), and *The Children of Dynmouth* (1976), institutions such as beach resorts, boarding schools, and hostels serve as miniature representations of the larger world. A wide range of characters, usually drawn from the English middle and lower middle classes, are portrayed in these and novels such as *Mrs Eckdorf at O'Neill's Hotel* (1969), *Miss Gomez and the Brethren* (1971), *Elizabeth Alone* (1973), and *Other People's Worlds* (1980). With **Fools of Fortune* (1983), *The Silence in the Garden* (1988), the short-story collection *The News from Ireland* (1986), and the novella *Nights at the Alexandra* (1987), Trevor reclaims the grand tradition of the Anglo-Irish novel. He shares with Elizabeth *Bowen an insider's knowledge of the great mansions and the fading traditions of the Irish gentry, but reverses nostalgia and romanticism to reveal a world in the terminal stages of decline. His protagonists are burdened with the weight of their own historical guilt, and determined to make reparation by finding their appropriate place in Ireland's changing social structure. Trevor's stories often have the impact of short novels; his later collections employ a variety of European settings, particularly Italy. The development of narrative technique demonstrated in his novels is matched by an increasing mastery of style; though his fiction retains a strong link with traditional forms, its exquisitely worked, subtly experimental surfaces employ the collagist, fragmented modes of *Modernism to great effect. *Two Lives* (1992) consists of two novels, *Reading Turgenev* and *My House in Umbria*, telling of the importance of fiction in the solitary imagination of lonely women; this, and the prize-winning *Felicia's Journey* (1994), in which a simple Irish woman migrates to England, considerably enhanced Trevor's popular reputation as a man of letters. *The Collected Stories* (1992) bear witness to his consistent proficiency in the short form.

TREVOR-ROPER, Hugh (Redwald) (1914–), British historian, born in Glanton, Northumberland, educated at Christ Church, Oxford, where he was a research fellow before becoming Regius Professor of Modern History in 1957. His earlier publications include *Archbishop Laud* (1940), which established him as a leading historian of the seventeenth century, *The Last Days of Hitler* (1947), and *The Gentry, 1540–1640* (1953). *The Rise of Christian Europe* (1965), encompassing developments from the Roman era to the Middle Ages, *Princes and Artists* (1976), on the Habsburgs' exercise of patronage between 1517 and 1633, and *A Hidden Life* (1976), a study of the reclusive Sir Edmund Backhouse (1873–1944), are among the works which demonstrate the unusual scope of his scholarship. His highly regarded collections of historical essays include *Religion, the Reformation, and Social Change* (1967), *Renaissance Essays* (1985), and *From Counter-Revolution to Glorious Revolution* (1992). He was created Baron Dacre of Glanton in 1979.

TRILLING, Lionel (1905–75), American critic, born in New York, educated at Columbia University. Among other academic posts, he taught at the University of Wisconsin and Hunter College, and rose to Professor of English at Columbia. One of the most subtle and reflective of American critics, his continuing concern was the fate of culture in troubled times, and the possibilities of contestation and rejuvenation represented by distinguished literary work. His touchstones were Jane Austen, Wordsworth, Arnold, and Tolstoy, and his critical project was an extension of the great themes of the liberal Enlightenment, to be found in an early, optimistic form in Diderot, and played out in a tragic mode in Freud as Trilling read him. Trilling's first books concerned the humanism of Arnold and *Forster; his late work *Sincerity and Authenticity* (1972) explored and separated two terms often taken to be synonymous. Trilling was closely associated with the best of the American literary journals, like *The *Partisan Review*, and most of his books were made up of essays and prefaces written for discrete occasions. *The Opposing Self* (1955) and *Beyond Culture* (1965) are substantial works of this kind, but Trilling's most enduring work is perhaps *The Liberal Imagination* (1950), which contains essays on Wordsworth, Freud, American literature, American literary history, and some profound reflections on the European novel. Shadows too are part of reality, Trilling said, and the recognition of sadness was an important part of his optimism—hence the attraction of Freud as the great modern poet of the cost as well as the triumph of culture. We shall all do better, meet with kindlier judgements, Trilling said, if Tolstoy rather than Dostoevsky is right about the world. It is characteristic of Trilling's tact that he should think this was a reason for wanting to prefer Tolstoy, not a proof that others should. See also MARXIST LITERARY CRITICISM.

Trinidad, a literary magazine edited by Alfred H. *Mendes and C. L. R. *James. Its only appearances, in Christmas 1929 and Easter 1930, did much to stimulate new styles of West Indian writing, most notably the 'barrack-yard' stories written by the editors. Stories such as James's 'Triumph' and Mendes's 'Her Chinaman's Way' caused a great furore at the time because of their supposedly sordid portrayal of life in the barrack-yards. *Trinidad* set the example for Albert *Gomes to found *The *Beacon*, a more broadly based literary periodical. The short stories in *Trinidad* are preserved in *From Trinidad: An Anthology of Early West Indian Writing* (1978), edited by Reinhard W. Sander and Peter K. Ayers.

TRIPP, John (1927–86), Welsh poet, born in Bargoed, Glamorgan; he spent most of his childhood in Cardiff. He worked for the BBC from 1943 to 1957 and was subsequently a press assistant at the Indonesian Embassy. In 1969 he returned to Cardiff to become a full-time writer. His first collection, *Diesel to Yesterday*, appeared in 1966, followed by *The Loss of Ancestry* (1969) and *The Province of Belief* (1971). These volumes were conspicuously concerned with the aspirations of Welsh nationalism and contained numerous striking dramatic monologues recreating events in Welsh history. More personal and lyrical subject matter became dominant in his work with *Bute Park* (1971), after which he produced several further volumes, including *The Inheritance File* (1973), *For King and Country* (1980), and *Passing Through* (1984). *Collected Poems 1958–1978* appeared in 1978. The social-realist idiom characteristic of much of his verse is frequently enhanced by richly elegiac effects. His angry indignation at economic and environmental decay in South Wales is recurrently tinged with mordant comedy through his use of ironic understatement. He also produced numerous memorable treatments of artists and writers. *John Tripp: Selected Poems*, edited by John Ormond, was published in 1989. His other works include a collection of short stories entitled *Last Day in England* (1979). Nigel Jenkins's *John Tripp* (1989) is a critical and biographical study.

TROLLOPE, Joanna (1943–), British novelist, born in Gloucestershire, educated at St Hugh's College, Oxford, a descendant of the Trollope family. Trollope worked in the Foreign Office and then taught English. Her first historical novel, *Eliza Stanhope* (1978), covered the Regency period. Several others have followed, with a variety of settings; eighteenth-century India for *Parson Harding's Daughter* (1979), the Crimean War for *Leaves from the Valley* (1980), Burma in the 1880s for *The City of Gems* (1981), and the Boer War for *The Steps of the Sun* (1983). All are carefully researched, well-written novels of people troubled by the times in which they live. In *The Choir* (1988) she used a contemporary setting, following it with *A Village Affair* (1989), a closely observed, witty account of English country life. *The Best of Friends* (1995) deals with adulterous betrayal and marital breakdown in a small country town and focuses on the relationships between two couples, exploring the ways in which longstanding friendships are tested by the strains of romantic involvement. Darker in mood than her earlier work, the novel offers the same mix of socially accurate observation and wry humour which have made her books so widely popular.

Tropic of Cancer and ***Tropic of Capricorn,*** see MILLER, HENRY.

Troubles, see FARRELL, J. G.

TUCHMAN, Barbara (1912–89), American historian, born in New York, educated at Radcliffe College, Harvard. Before 1962 she published under her maiden name of Barbara Wertheim. Her earlier works include *The Lost British Policy* (1938), on relations between Britain and Spain since 1700, and *The Bible and the Sword* (1956), a study of British involvement in the formation of the state of Israel. She attracted a wide readership with the compelling narrative style and diligent research of *The Zimmermann Telegram* (1958), an account of communications between Germany and Mexico which were instrumental in bringing the USA into the First World War. *The Guns of August* (1962; Pulitzer Prize) deals with the opening weeks of the First World War, while *The Proud Tower* (1965) surveys the decades preceding the conflict. Parallels between the remote past and recent history are drawn in *A Distant Mirror* (1978), a study of the upheavals of fourteenth-century Europe, and *The March of Folly* (1984), an investigation of political error from the siege of Troy to the Vietnam War. Tuchman's other works include *Stilwell and the American Experience in China* (1971), an account of an American military officer's activities in China from 1911 to 1945, for which she received a further Pulitzer Prize; *The First Salute* (1989), on the American War of Independence; and the essays of *Practicing History* (1981).

TUOHY, (John) Frank (1925–), British novelist and short-story writer, born in Uckfield, Sussex, educated at King's College, Cambridge. He has lectured in Finland, Sweden, Brazil, Poland, and Japan and his work is distinguished by his depth of knowledge of different societies. Set in Brazil, his first novel, *The Animal Game* (1957), gives a harrowing description of pigs imprisoned in a truck during a bitter railway strike and turning to cannibalism with vultures waiting overhead. *The Warm Nights of January* (1960) presents people of different nationalities united by their foreignness and focuses on the emotional life of a bohemian French *émigrée*, Bella Magnard, and her relationship with her Brazilian lover, Hadriano. In *The Ice Saints* (1964), Rose, a young snobbish Englishwoman, visits her sister and brother-in-law, an ambitious but undistinguished Polish academic in Biala Gora, and brings news of an inheritance to their son; the despair and corruption that follows offers a paradigm of Polish life under Gomulka. Among Tuohy's volumes of stories are *The Admiral and the Nuns* (1962), *Fingers in the Door* (1970), *Live Bait* (1978), and *The Collected Stories* (1984).

TURNER, W(alter) J(ames) (Redfern) (1889–1946), British poet, born in Melbourne, Australia, where he was educated at Scotch College before emigrating to London in 1907. His subsequent travels in Europe and South Africa inform much of his poetry. *The Hunter* (1916) and *The Dark Fire* (1918) reflect his experiences on the Western Front. In 1918 he joined the staff of the **Spectator* and became its literary editor in 1942. He enjoyed a brief success as a playwright with *The Man Who Ate the Popomack* (1922). *The Seven Days of the Sun* (1925), an experimental series of free-verse meditations, demonstrates his work's affinities with poetic *Modernism. More conventional verse is contained in *In Time Like Glass* (1921), *Landscape of Cytherea* (1923), *Songs and Incantations* (1936), and *Fossils of a Future Time* (1946). His best work is marked by the luminous brilliance of imagery characteristic of his evocations of exotic landscapes. Several of his poems indicate his friendship with W. B. *Yeats, with whom he shared a strong poetic interest in metaphysical speculation; Yeats represented him generously in his *Oxford Book of Modern Verse* (1936). His other works include the critical biographies *Beethoven: The Search for Reality* (1927) and *Berlioz: The Man and His Work* (1934), and the quasi-autobiographical novels *Blow for Balloons* (1935) and *Henry Airbubble* (1936).

TUROW, Scott (1949–), American novelist, born in Chicago, educated at Amherst College, Stanford University, and Harvard University. His first book, *One L.: An Inside Account of Life in the First Year at Harvard Law School* (1977), remains widely read by students. He was an assistant United States attorney in Chicago from 1978 to 1986, when he joined a Chicago legal practice; he divides his time between writing and legal work. *Presumed Innocent* (1987) established him as a best-selling author. Its narrative of municipal corruption and lack of judicial integrity derives authenticity from Turow's knowledge of the American legal system, as do *The Burden of Proof* (1990), in which a defence lawyer finds himself enmeshed in intrigues and duplicity after his wife's murder, and *Pleading Guilty* (1993), which centres on the disappearance of a large sum of money from the accounts of a legal practice.

TUTUOLA, Amos (1920–), Nigerian novelist, born in Abeokuta, educated at the Anglican Central School in that town; he was a founder member of the Mbari Club, a group of influential writers and publishers including Wole *Soyinka in their membership. Tutuola's novels are written in highly idiosyncratic English which initially caused much controversy, particularly on the first publication of *The Palm-Wine Drinkard* (1952); this was translated into many languages, and was followed by another visionary novel with symbolic and allegorical overtones, *My Life in the Bush of Ghosts* (1954). Highly individual in style, these novels owe something to the Yoruba oral tradition, and the Yoruba writings of D. O. Fagunwa. Other novels include *Simbi and the Satyr of the Dark Jungle* (1955), *The Brave White Huntress* (1958), *Ajaiyi and His Inherited Poverty* (1967), and *Pauper, Brawler, and Slanderer* (1987). In most of these a hero with supernatural powers or support goes forth on a quest and triumphs over suffering. *Yoruba Folktales* (1986) and *The Village Witch Doctor and Other Stories* (1990) are volumes of short fiction.

TUWHARE, Hone (1922–), New Zealand Maori poet, born in Kaikohe, educated at technical colleges in Otahuhu, near Wellington. After army service he was a boilermaker and was active in union affairs and in politics. The title poem of his successful initial collection, *No Ordinary Sun* (1964), referred to atomic testing in the Pacific. Later collections include *Sap-Wood and Milk* (1972, illustrated by the Maori artist Ralph Hotere); *Something Nothing* (1974), which included an outstanding poem inspired by the death of 'Hemi', fellow poet James K. *Baxter; and *Making a Fist of It* (1978; poems and short stories). Tuwhare published his *Selected Poems* in 1980 and *Year of the Dog—Poems New and Selected* in 1982. The volume *Mihi: Collected Poems* (1987, again illustrated by Ralph Hotere) allowed Tuwhare's poetic achievement to be properly assessed for the first time and demonstrated his great ability to evoke and question both traditional and contemporary Maori life through a sure sense of the speaking voice. Tuwhare's poetry included from the start a severe and accurate, if often wry, rendering of the contemporary industrial and labour life he knew at first hand. *Short Back and Sideways* (1992) is a later collection; *Deep River Talk: Collected Poems* appeared in 1994.

Two Cultures, The, a phrase supplied by the title of C. P. *Snow's *The Two Cultures and the Scientific Revolution* (1959) which became widely current in describing the separation of science and literature. The essay, originally Snow's Rede Lecture at Cambridge in 1959, lamented the 'gulf of mutual incomprehension' between scientists and writers, contrasting the formers' sometimes arrogant self-confidence with the diffidence displayed by literary intellectuals; Rutherford and *Eliot served as his respective cases in point. Snow attributed the isolation of science and literature from one another to the specialization characteristic of the British educational system, which he compared unfavourably with those of the USA and USSR. A heated controversy ensued, as a result of which Snow published *The Two Cultures and a Second Look* in 1964, defending his views and enlarging on his belief in the need to make science more widely accessible through changes in educational practice. Among Snow's leading antagonists was F. R. *Leavis, whose *Two Cultures? The Significance of C. P. Snow* (1962) and '"Literarism" versus "Scientism"' (*Times Literary Supplement*, 4 April 1970) accused Snow of abusing the concept of culture and of grossly undervaluing the importance of literature as the chief channel for the transmission of traditional values.

TYLER, Anne (1941–), American novelist, born in Minneapolis, Minnesota, but grew up in Raleigh, North Carolina; she graduated from Duke University and undertook post-graduate research in Russian studies at the University of North Carolina. Tyler rejected her early novels, *If Morning Ever Comes* (1964) and *The Tin Can Tree* (1965), written in her early twenties, but with *A Slipping-Down Life* (1970) and *The Clock Winder* (1972) she earned a reputation as a skilful novelist working in the Southern mode perfected by Carson *McCullers. Tyler disclaims any Southern influences except that of Eudora *Welty, who taught her to recognize the importance of the seemingly mundane in fiction. In further novels, she continued to paint domestic interiors and portray family life, though on a wider canvas and with more intensity. *Celestial Navigations* (1974) tells the story of an artist through the varied perspectives of the women in his life; *Searching for Caleb* (1976) chronicles four generations of the eccentric Peck family; *Earthly Possessions* (1977), one of Tyler's most unusual novels, is the first-person account of the journey of a woman held hostage by a bank robber on the run; *Morgan's Passing* (1980) tells the story of the adventures of a likeable misfit. With *Dinner at the Homesick Restaurant* (1982) she established herself as the leading literary voice of the urban South. One of her most compelling works, the novel is the story of the two sons and one daughter of an abandoned mother, employing the viewpoint of all its characters. *The Accidental Tourist* (1985) repeated the formula perfected in early novels, focusing on the figure of a male misfit and his loves; it was extremely successful, and was made into a film. *Breathing Lessons* (1989; Pulitzer Prize) recounts a day in the life of a woman whose wish to transform the lives of family and friends entangles her in lies, deceit, and petty disasters. *Saint Maybe* (1991) tells the story of yet another misfit whose guilty involvement in the undoing of his family leads him to charismatic Christianity and doomed attempts at expiation. *Ladder of Years* (1995), described by Joyce Carol *Oates as Tyler's most conventional novel so far, is the story of a married woman who leaves her life of boredom to find herself unequipped for an autonomous existence; she returns to her discarded past.

TYNAN, Katharine (1861–1931), Irish poet and novelist, born in Clondalkin, Co. Dublin, educated at the convent school of St Catherine of Drogheda. She gained a reputation as a poet with her first volume, *Louise de la Vallière and Other Poems* (1885). Like *Yeats, who was her close friend for many years, she was a disciple of John O'Leary's in matters of literary nationalism, and was represented in *Poems and Ballads of Young Ireland* (1888); the anthology initiated the *Irish Revival, of which she was the leading female exponent. Her numerous subsequent collections include *Ballads and Lyrics* (1890), *Cuckoo Songs* (1894), and *A Lover's Breast Knot* (1896). Folktales, some making use of dialect speech, and lyrical celebrations of the natural world predominate in her poetry. An element of Catholic piety distinguishes her verse from the more characteristically pagan tone of Irish Revival writing, and *The Flowers of Peace* (1914) consists entirely of devotional verse. Yeats selected the contents of her *Twenty One Poems* (1907); a *Collected Poems* was published in 1930. Following her marriage in 1893 she moved to London where she wrote over 100 works of romantic fiction, the majority resulting from her need to generate an income after her husband's death in 1919. Among her earlier novels are *The Sweet Enemy* (1901) and *The Adventures of Alicia* (1906), which share the concern with women's rights and the consciousness of social injustice evident in her extensive journalism. She also produced four volumes of autobiography, *Twenty-Five Years* (1913), *The Middle Years* (1916), *The Years of Shadow* (1916), and *The Wandering Years* (1922). R. McHugh's edition of Yeats's *Letters to Katharine Tynan* appeared in 1953.

TYNAN, Kenneth (Peacock) (1927–80), English drama critic and theatre producer, born in Birmingham, educated at Magdalen College, Oxford. As one of the most influential drama critics of his time, his reviews for the *Observer* were notable for their wit and stylistic brilliance. He promoted the early plays of John *Osborne, Arnold *Wesker, and, most notably, Tom *Stoppard. In 1963 Sir Laurence Olivier appointed Tynan literary manager of the newly founded National Theatre. Tynan's production of *Oh! Calcutta!* (1969), with sketches on erotic themes by himself and various established writers and celebrities of the time, caused a sensation in London and New York for decisively breaking the barriers against nudity on stage. His reviews are collected in *Curtains* (1961), *Tynan Right and Left* (1967), *A View of the English Stage* (1975), and *The Sound of Two Hands Clapping* (1975). *Show People* (1980) contains his finest essays, particularly the profiles of leading actors. He also wrote a book about *Alec Guinness* (1953). His second wife, Kathleen Tynan, wrote *The Life of Kenneth Tynan* (1987).

'Typhoon', a story by Joseph *Conrad, first published in *Pall Mall Magazine* (1902) and collected in *Typhoon and Other Stories* (1903). The story of a steamship, the *Nan-Shan*, carrying 200 Chinese coolies from Fu-chau to their homes in Fo-kien, 'Typhoon' focuses on the two tests with which the captain is confronted during the voyage: the typhoon itself and the problem of apportioning the coolies' money and possessions, which have become confused during the typhoon. Conrad tells part of 'Typhoon' through letters from the three main characters: Captain MacWhirr; Mr Jukes, the first mate; and Mr Solomon Rout, the chief engineer. At the centre of the story is the contrast between the unimaginative Captain MacWhirr and his imaginative first mate, and the story both invites an evaluation of Captain MacWhirr's performance and explores the advantages and disadvantages of imagination.

U

Ulster Literary Theatre, The, was founded by Bulmer Hobson and David Parkhill in Belfast in 1902. Although Hobson and Parkhill had been strongly influenced by the Irish Literary Theatre, later the *Abbey Theatre, which had been founded by *Yeats, *Moore, *Martyn, and Lady *Gregory, Yeats gave little support to its Ulster equivalent. In reaction, Hobson is said to have exclaimed: 'Damn Yeats, we'll write our own plays!', which they did, developing an Ulster variant of the Abbey's style of peasant drama. Hobson and, in particular, Parkhill (who used the pseudonym Lewis Purcell) wrote several of the theatre's early plays. Their beginnings, however, were not as pioneering as they had hoped, with the productions of Yeats's **Cathleen Ni Houlihan* in 1902 and, after a long period of silence, *Deirdre* by George *Russell ('AE') in 1904. The company still called itself the Ulster Branch of the Irish Literary Theatre but, eventually, the original group in Dublin took exception to this and demanded that they changed their name. They became the Ulster Literary Theatre and quickly began to develop a distinctive character, in both the performance and the writing of plays. Hobson's *Brian of Banba* and Purcell's *The Reformers* were produced towards the end of 1904. Purcell wrote two amusing parodies of the Abbey's style which attracted the interest and talents of Gerald *McNamara, who added *The Mist that Does Be on the Bog* in 1909, a hilarious send-up of the peasant plays so popular in Dublin at that time. Rutherford *Mayne became the company's most successful playwright; his comedy *The Drone* (1908) was a huge success with Northern audiences and became central to the company's repertoire. The Ulster Theatre, as it had become in 1915, provided first production opportunities to playwrights such as George *Shiels and St John *Ervine. The Ulster Theatre had to disband in 1934 due to financial difficulties and the strains of its nomadic existence, but its important contribution to Irish drama remains significant.

Ulster Poetry, the corporate designation for the work of a number of distinguished poets of Northern Irish birth who came to prominence from the mid-1960s onward. Seamus *Heaney, Michael *Longley, Derek *Mahon, Paul *Muldoon, Frank *Ormsby, Tom *Paulin, and James *Simmons are the principal writers classifiable as Ulster poets. The oldest among them, James Simmons, was born in 1933 and the youngest, Paul Muldoon, in 1951; all produced their first substantial collections of poetry after 1966, when the appearance of Seamus Heaney's **Death of a Naturalist* began to generate interest in the new poetic talents of the Province. Simmons's *Late but in Earnest* (1967), Mahon's *Night Crossing* (1968), and Longley's *No Continuing City* (1969) followed, impressing critics through their accomplishment and originality of tone. Over the next ten years a succession of volumes from these poets contained much of the finest poetry written in English during the 1970s. Seamus Heaney's essay 'Belfast' in *Preoccupations* (1980) describes the stimulating effect on young writers in the city of the writing group begun by Philip *Hobsbaum in the early 1960s; Heaney and his fellow poets had begun to attract attention by the time of the Belfast Festival in 1965, in which their work was featured. The onset of the Troubles in Northern Ireland in 1969 added urgency to the poetry being produced there; although the Ulster poets rejected the expectations of certain commentators concerning the directness with which they should confront the strife, military and sectarian violence became a clear theme in much of their writing. The examples of the *Movement and the *Group informed the earlier work of the Ulster poets, all of whom had a keen awareness of post-war developments in English poetry. Patrick *Kavanagh's precedents in the treatment of Irish rural material were important in the emergence of Heaney's poetry, and Louis *MacNeice's poems on Northern Irish themes indicated possibilities for Mahon and Longley.

Ulysses, a novel by James *Joyce, one of the most notorious, celebrated, and influential works of the twentieth century. Early chapters appeared in *The *Egoist* in 1919 and then, in 1920, in *The *Little Review* which was prosecuted by a New York court for publishing obscene matter. It was eventually published in full by Shakespeare and Co., a Paris bookshop, on 2 February 1922. After a long and now legendary saga involving confiscations by British Customs, a burning by the US postal authorities, and the clandestine efforts of Joyce and friends to publish and distribute his masterpiece, the first British edition finally appeared in 1936. Originally an idea for a short story to be included in **Dubliners*, *Ulysses* became a massive and complex gesture to encompass the concerns of mankind within a single book, a small city, and a single day. Taking its name from the Roman translation of 'Odysseus', it transposes the Homeric myth to the events which unfold during eighteen hours in Dublin on 16 June 1904 (a date dubbed 'Bloomsday' by Joyceans). Parallels with Homer focus upon themes such as fatherhood and betrayal, which are universal to both past and present; they also poke an ironic stick at the disparity between the ancient heroic and the modern mundane. The novel's three central characters, Stephen Dedalus, a struggling writer reincarnate from *A *Portrait of the Artist as a Young Man*, Leopold Bloom, a Dublin Jew, cuckold and seller of advertising, and Molly Bloom, wife, adulterer, and part-time *chanteuse*, hardly resemble Telemachus, Odysseus, and Penelope. And yet modern life requires its own form of heroism: the heroic effort of the mind to distract itself while it endeavours to reconcile its conflicts. It is in the forms of such distraction that the body of the novel takes place: from Dedalus's philosophical ruminations on Dollymount Strand and Bloom's voyeuristic walk before breakfast, to the chaos of both their subconscious minds in a Dublin brothel and Molly's final 'soliloquy' which alone can keep all things together in one, unpunctuated breath. The action of *Ulysses* occurs internally, through a '*stream of consciousness'; externally, nothing extraordinary happens. Dedalus and Bloom wander through their day unconnected, their paths occasionally crossing, until they meet without consequence. From a realistic beginning, Joyce gradually reveals a labyrinth of allusion, erudition, parody, and linguistic experiment until what was apparently insignificant becomes unfamiliar and difficult to understand. In places, the reader might benefit from an awareness of *The Odyssey*, *Hamlet*, Irish history, the history of English literature, medical science, or the topography of Dublin. But these are only a few of the ways through a richly rewarding, hilarious, and moving novel about being human.

Underground Poetry, the term for the work of poets identified with the radical cultural attitudes of the 1960s. The American *Beat poets were the immediate predecessors of underground poetry in the USA and Britain, which was characterized by rejection of conventional forms in favour of conversational and rhetorical modes immediately accessible in performance. William Blake was frequently invoked as the visionary progenitor of the spirit of romantic rebellion espoused by many poets in the movement. The poetry was generally ideological in tone, its strong element of protest and repudiation of political orthodoxy arising from reaction to the Vietnam War; the opposition to nuclear weapons mobilized by the Campaign for Nuclear Disarmament in the late 1950s was also an important element in the work of many writers of the time. Underground poetry in Britain became established as a recognized genre with the reading by Allen *Ginsberg, Lawrence *Ferlinghetti, Michael *Horovitz, George *MacBeth, Christopher *Logue, Alexander Trocchi, and numerous others in the Royal Albert Hall in 1965. Ed Sanders, Tuli Kupferberg, Bob *Cobbing, Adrian *Mitchell, Michael *McLure, Jeff *Nuttall, and Pete Brown are also among the poets associated with 'the underground'. The peak of the cultural activity of which underground poetry was a part was in 1968, when student riots occurred in Paris and elsewhere and the 'Dialectics of Liberation' congress was held over two weeks in London. The lyrics of many of the popular music groups of the period, notably some of the work of the *Beatles and the Rolling Stones, gave wide currency to the dissenting idealism typifying underground poetry. Michael Horovitz's edition of *Children of Albion: Poetry of the 'Underground' in Britain* (1969), and *Bomb Culture* (1968), a study of cultural tendencies by Jeff Nuttall, are two of the principal texts of the movement.

Under Milk Wood, Dylan *Thomas's 'play for voices', evoking the passage of a single spring day in the village of Llareggub through the accounts given by some sixty characters of their daily activities, dreams, memories, and relationships. Thomas's involvement with radio and film from 1940 onwards led him to begin the work in 1945, when he wrote 'Quite Early One Morning', which anticipates *Under Milk Wood* in the use of imagined voices independent of its principal speaker. Although a version of the play was published in **Botteghe Oscure* under the title *Llareggub: A Piece for Radio perhaps* in 1952, Thomas continued to work on it until just before its three performances in the USA in 1953, the first of which was a solo reading at Harvard, followed by two productions with a cast of actors in New York. Its dramatic structure is unconventional in taking its central dynamic from the rapid interaction of the lyrically humorous dialogue between the many voices, conspicuous among which are those of Captain Cat, the Reverend Eli Jenkins, and Polly Garter. 'Llareggub' (which may be read backwards) and its inhabitants constitute a caricature of the community in Laugharne, Carmarthenshire, where Thomas lived from 1949. *Under Milk Wood* was first broadcast by the BBC in 1954, since when it has been performed many times and remains a popular work.

Under the Volcano, a novel by Malcolm *Lowry, published in 1947. The opening sequence takes place on the Day of the Dead in November 1939, in the Mexican city of Quauhnahuac. Jacques Laruelle, a French expatriate film-maker, reflects on the tragic events which occurred exactly a year before, in the same place, in which the main protagonists were Geoffrey Firmin, former British Consul in Quauhnahuac, his estranged wife, Yvonne, and Firmin's half-brother, Hugh. The narrative involves numerous flashbacks and shifts of viewpoint. Yvonne, who has been away for a year, following the breakdown of her marriage to the Consul, returns with the intention of giving her husband another chance. She finds him recovering from the previous night's alcoholic excesses. The couple establish an uneasy rapport, and it becomes apparent that they still love one another, but this is upset with the arrival of Hugh. Firmin starts drinking heavily and the situation deteriorates further when Firmin, Yvonne, and Hugh are invited for drinks at Laruelle's house, and the Consul is confronted with the unpleasant recollection of Yvonne and Laruelle's brief affair, also a factor in their estrangement. An excursion is proposed to a nearby village, where a carnival is in progress. The Consul becomes separated from Hugh and Yvonne; he finds solace in a drinking binge, which takes him from one sordid cantina to the next in a downward spiral that ends only when he is shot as a spy by a member of the local secret police. Meanwhile Yvonne and Hugh have become lost in the nearby forest; during a thunderstorm, Yvonne is accidentally killed by a riderless horse, terrified by the lightning. The novel is permeated with symbolism, and with allusions to Greek drama, Jacobean tragedy, and the poetry of Baudelaire and Swinburne, as well as to jazz and the cinema. The atmosphere of brooding menace is intensified by powerfully evocative descriptions of the Mexican landscape, of which the most distinctive features are the volcanoes Popocatepetl and Ixtaccihuatl, which give the novel its name.

Under Western Eyes, a novel by Joseph *Conrad, published in 1911 (serialized in the **English Review* and the **North American Review*, 1910–11). The novel is narrated by an unnamed English Teacher of Languages living in Geneva, who is privy to the private diaries of Razumov, a student of philosophy in St Petersburg. Haldin, a revolutionary fellow-student and self-confessed political assassin, seeks help from Razumov. Questions of loyalty to the Czarist Russian state and the mixed motives of self-interest vie with Razumov's conscience. His betrayal of Haldin to the authorities and his subsequent interrogation with the head of counter-espionage, the cynical Councillor Mikulin, result in Razumov's despatch as state informant to Geneva, where he is welcomed as Haldin's brave collaborator by a group of Russian revolutionaries-in-exile. Razumov's involvement with the deception of this group, his growing sense of cynicism and non-identity, his developing affection for Haldin's innocently idealistic sister, Natalia, and his conversations with co-revolutionary Sophia Antonovna force upon him a despairing guilt and self-recognition, and he confesses his complicity. Torture and brutal deafening conclude Razumov's story but paradoxically his self-exposure signals a spiritual self-redemption. Complexities of narrative form—radical chronological disruptions, ironic juxtapositions of scene between Russia and Geneva, unsignalled shifting sources of narrative focus and information (letters, diaries, conversations heard and imagined)—contribute to the reader's sense of the unreliable interpretability of the world. 'Truth-telling', 'trust', 'vision', 'loyalty': all fall subject to a testing Conradian sceptical irony. This irony also embraces the often naïvely pompous Western European liberal democratic Teacher of Languages whose function as imaginative composer and interpellator helps highlight the self-reflective modernist concern for the nature of language: 'Words are the great foes of reality'. Conrad's equivocal attitude to revolutionary alternatives to the evil Russian autocracy is reflected in the range of motives, self-deceptions, and moral qualities enjoyed by the revolutionary exiles. Their leader, Peter Ivanovitch, has mystic 'feminist' revolutionary ideas, but these sit ill with his exploitation of his idealistic secretary and serving-woman Tekla, and of his financial patron and bourgeois salon-revolutionary Madame de S—. His radical henchman, Nikita, Razumov's torturer, turns out to be another Czarist secret agent. But Natalia's burning revolutionary utopianism and her compassion for Razumov, and Sophia Antonovna's undiminished resilience, escape Conrad's pessimistic scorn. Stylistic innovation matches the intricacies of political and psychological theme to produce a work frequently compared (indeed indebted) to Dostoevsky's *Crime and Punishment* for its profound treatment of identity, betrayal, social morality, and self-confession.

Union Street, see BARKER, PAT.

UNSWORTH, Barry (1930–), British novelist, born in Durham, educated at Manchester University. Since the early 1960s he has lived in Greece, Turkey, Finland, and Italy, dividing his time between university lecturing and writing. His first novel, *The Partnership* (1966), deals with the pretensions of an artists' colony in Cornwall; subsequent earlier works include *The Greeks Have a Word For It* (1967), which reflects his experiences in Athens, *The Hide* (1970), a treatment of betrayal anticipating the moral dynamics of his later work, and *Mooncranker's Gift* (1973), in which a historical dimension becomes integral to his fiction. *Pascali's Island* (1980) and *The Rage of the Vulture* (1982), which centre on the collapse of the Ottoman Sultanate, establish Unsworth's abiding concern with the theme of empire. Ethical expediency and economic power in the Venetian Republic are dealt with in *Stone Virgin* (1985), while the history of slavery underlies the treatment of depressed contemporary Liverpool in *Sugar and Rum* (1990). *Sacred Hunger* (1992), joint winner of the Booker Prize, brought the great imaginative scope and moral authority of Unsworth's historical fiction to wider notice through its harrowing narrative of the eighteenth-century British slave trade. Set in fourteenth-century England, *Morality Play* (1995) uses the re-enactment of a murder by a group of players to present a fable of art's relations with truth.

UPDIKE, John (Hoyer) (1932–), American novelist, born in Shillington, Pennsylvania, educated at Harvard. Updike worked for the **New Yorker*, where many of his short stories appeared before their collection and publication in such volumes as *The Same Door* (1959), *Pigeon Feathers* (1962), *Too Far To Go* (1979), *The Beloved* (1982), *Trust Me* (1987), and, more recently, *The Afterlife and Other Stories* (1994). His first novel, *Poorhouse Fair* (1959), develops around a single day upon which the inmates of a county poorhouse are allowed to host a fair for local citizens, and focuses on the tension between a patient and an administrator. After *The Magic Flute* (1962) came *The Centaur* (1963), which presents the dual narratives of the realistic memories of Peter Caldwell's student days, and an adaptation of the Greek tale of Chiron the centaur. The companion volume, *On the Farm* (1965), focuses on a middle-aged son's attempts to come to terms with a difficult parent. *Couples* (1968) is a scrutiny of marriage which focuses on the religious crisis and womanizing of Piet Hanema; in an analysis of affluent American suburbia, the novel considers whether the physical and sexual can replace the strength lost by a decline in faith. *Marry Me: A Romance* (1970) provides a similar scrutiny by focusing on the life of Jerry Conant. It is, however, with two sequences that Updike's major work has been achieved: *The *Rabbit Tetralogy*, comprising *Rabbit Run* (1960), *Rabbit Redux* (1971), *Rabbit Is Rich* (1981; Pulitzer Prize), and *Rabbit at Rest* (1990; Pulitzer Prize), and the Bech sequence, *Bech: A Book* (1970) and *Bech Is Back* (1982), which provides a comic portrait of an American writer caught between desiring recognition and wanting to be left alone. Among his other novels are *Bottom's Dream* (1969), *The Coup* (1978), the trilogy *Month of Sundays* (1975), *Roger's Version* (1986), and *S* (1988), a contemporary treatment of Nathaniel Hawthorne's *The Scarlet Letter*, *Brother Grasshopper* (1990), and *Brazil* (1994). His best-known work is probably *The Witches of Eastwick* (1984), a profoundly satirical novel in which the inhabitants of a small New England town receive a visitation from a character who may well be the devil incarnate. Among his collections of verse are *The Carpentered Hen and Other Tame Creatures* (1958), *Seventy Poems* (1963), *Telephone Poles and Other Poems* (1963), *The Angels* (1968), *Tossing and Turning* (1977), *Spring Trio* (1982), *Jester's Dragon* (1984), and *Taming Nature* (1985), poems which frequently celebrate language in comic verse. His essays have made a further analysis of American marriage and of domestic and family life, among other subjects, and have appeared in *On Meeting Authors* (1968), *Picked up Pieces* (1975), *Hugging the Shore* (1983), *Emersonianism* (1984), and *Just Looking: Essays on Art* (1989).

UPFIELD, Arthur W(illiam) (1888–1964), Australian crime writer, born in Gosport; he emigrated to Australia in 1911, where he was a cook, boundary rider, itinerant worker, and miner, before publishing *The Barakee Mystery* (1929; US title *The Lure of the Bush*), the first of twenty-nine novels in which the detective is Inspector Napoleon Bonaparte, a part-Aboriginal Australian. Though the writing is stiff, the setting of the novels (the Australian outback) is impressive: among the best are *The Bone Is Pointed* (1938), *The New Shoe* (1951), *Death of a Lake* (1954), *Sinister Stones* (1954; UK title *The Cake in the Hatbox*), and *The Will of the Tribe* (1962).

UPWARD, Edward (Falaise) (1903–), English novelist and short-story writer, born in Romford, educated at Corpus Christi College, Cambridge. A schoolmaster in London from 1928 to 1962, during the 1930s he was a member of the Communist Party and closely associated with Christopher *Isherwood, Stephen *Spender, and W. H. *Auden. His novel *Journey to the Border* (1938) examines Marxism through the interior monologues of a middle-class young man employed as a tutor in the house of a rich man. Both this novel and the title story of *The Railway Accident and Other Stories* (1969) were inspired by an imaginary world, the village 'Mortmere' created by Upward and his friend Isherwood when they were undergraduates at Cambridge. Upward left the Communist Party in 1948 due to ideological disagreements. The conflict between political commitment and artistic fulfilment is examined in his semi-autobiographical trilogy *The Spiral Ascent* (1977), made up of *In the Thirties* (1962), *The Rotten Elements* (1969), and *No Home but the Struggle* (1977), which portray several decades in the life of a middle-class poet and schoolteacher, Alan Sebrill. Later volumes of stories are *The Night Walk and Other Stories* (1987) and *An Unmentionable Man* (1994). *The Mortmere Stories* (1994) collects stories written with Christopher Isherwood in the 1920s.

U.S.A., a trilogy of novels by John *Dos Passos, first published in a single volume in 1938. *U.S.A.* comprises three novels that were separately published: *The 42nd Parallel* (1930); *Nineteen Nineteen* (1932); and *The Big Money* (1936). Dos Passos had as his objective a panoramic depiction of American life in the first thirty years of the twentieth century and the scale of his endeavour forced him to refine and enlarge the narrative techniques he had employed in earlier novels, such as **Manhattan Transfer* (1925), where he had successfully mixed fiction with documentary fact. In *U.S.A.* three fictional devices are used: the narrative elements, which are fifty-two in number and concentrate on the lives of twelve major characters (many of whom appear in more than one novel), are 'punctuated' by 'Newsreel' and 'Camera Eye' sections, the former montages of newspaper headlines, advertisements in shops or on billboards, and popular songs, the latter largely made up of autobiographical reminiscence or authorial commentary on public events. The three novels, in part, record the shifting moods of Dos Passos's political leanings: the first two volumes evince his commitment to a socialist understanding of American society and the concomitant attractions of Marxism while the third volume shows the influence of the American sociologist Thorstein *Veblen and his theories of 'conspicuous consumption' and the creation of a 'leisure class'. *U.S.A.* presents certain preliminary difficulties for the uninitiated reader of Dos Passos, but it remains one of the most remarkable technical achievements in modern American literature. *Dos Passos' Path to 'U.S.A': A Political Biography, 1912–1936* (1972), by Melvin Landsberg, is valuable for its reading of the novel in the light of the evolution of Dos Passos's politics.

Uses of Literacy, The, see HOGGART, RICHARD.

Utopia and Anti-Utopia. Modern literary utopianism emerges out of the divided heritage of the nineteenth-century socialist utopia, with its antithetical images of the future represented, in the English-speaking world, by Edward Bellamy and William Morris. Bellamy's *Looking Backward* (1888) portrays a scientific-industrial state of the collectivist or 'totalitarian' type that would be satirized in the two most influential twentieth-century anti-utopias, Aldous Huxley's **Brave New World* and George Orwell's **Nineteen Eighty-Four*. The pastoral communism of Morris's *News from Nowhere* (1890) anticipates aspects of the ecological and feminist utopianism of the late twentieth century. Both the collectivist and the ecological utopia share a futurological orientation inherited from the tradition of scientific socialism.

Although he was the author of several utopian future-history novels, H. G. *Wells's major formal utopia, *A Modern Utopia* (1905), is set on a parallel world in the present day. Wells's version of the scientific-industrial state includes universal welfare benefits, a centralized bureaucracy, and a meritocratic hierarchy reflecting the fascination with élites that recurs throughout utopian thought. The Wellsian utopia was parodied in E. M. *Forster's 'The Machine Stops' (1909), and in *Brave New World* where eugenics and behaviour control are used to perpetuate social stratification. *A Modern Utopia* remains influential for two main reasons. As a deliberate summing-up and synthesis of the earlier tradition—a work of 'utopography' as well as a utopia—it reflects the interdisciplinarity of utopian thought, and anticipates the more recent emergence of utopian studies as an intellectual field. Wells's acknowledgement of the difficulty (and yet the necessity) of combining didactic exposition with imaginative narrative exemplifies the formal problem of utopian fiction, a much-maligned genre. Also influential is his championship of the dynamic as against the static utopia. Each 'hopeful stage' of society is provisional rather than definitive, and at the heart of his Utopia Wells places a scientific élite, the Samurai—the modern descendants of Plato's Guardians—part of whose function is to destabilize Utopia and promote further progress.

The possibility of endless progress held out by modern scientific cosmology found its most far-reaching embodiment in Olaf *Stapledon's *Last and First Men* (1930), a narrative of the next two billion years. Here the subject is not the perfect society but the successive evolutionary transformations of the human stock. Stapledon's successors are to be found in the future-history cycles of science-fiction authors such as Isaac *Asimov and Arthur C. *Clarke, with their diffused utopianism, rather than in the utopian genre more narrowly conceived (see SCIENCE FICTION). The near-future utopia, by contrast, typically shows the quality of life improved by measures of rational planning, political reorganization, or behaviour control, sometimes confined to a small community as in B. F. Skinner's *Walden Two* (1948). In Aldous Huxley's *Island* (1962), the people of Pala practise Buddhism and enjoy the fruits of intermediate technology until invaded by a rapacious neighbour backed by the multinational oil companies. Ursula K. *LeGuin's Anarres in *The Dispossessed* (1974) and Ernest Callenbach's breakaway North American republic in *Ecotopia* (1975) provide further examples of the strictly regulated, bounded utopia. The feminist utopia, from Charlotte Perkins *Gilman's *Herland* (1915) to Marge *Piercy's *Woman on the Edge of Time* (1976) and Octavia *Butler's *Xenogenesis* trilogy (1987–9), relies either on sexual segregation or on control of reproductive methods. Of all these societies it may be asked whether the intellectual daring that went into setting them up can continue to flourish within them. By contrast, the value of mental and emotional freedom remains paramount in the fictional anti-utopia, a genre whose warnings about the threats posed by scientific and industrial progress are heard throughout the century, from Jack London's *The *Iron Heel* (1907) to Margaret Atwood's *The *Handmaid's Tale* (1985). See *Utopia and Anti-Utopia in Modern Times* (1987), by Krishan Kumar, and *Utopian and Science Fiction by Women: Worlds of Difference* (1995), edited by Jane L. Donawerth and Carol A. Kolmerten.

UYS, Pieter-Dirk (1945–), South African playwright and satirist, born in Cape Town, educated at the University of Cape Town and the London Film School. He has written, directed, and acted in many plays, mainly for the Space Theatre (Cape Town) and the touring Syrkel Theatre Company, and is also well known as a satirical impersonator of South African politicians. His plays are darkly satirical comedies about how apartheid corrupts the self-regarding white middle classes. What he has said about one of his plays, *God's Forgotten* (1975), can be applied to most of them: 'It is a black comedy or a white tragedy—depending on whose side you're on.' Two other plays, *Paradise Is Closing Down* (1977; rewritten in 1987) and *Panorama* (1987), have been collected in *Paradise Is Closing Down and Other Plays* (1989). Other plays include *Scorched Earth* (1989) and *Just Like Home* (1989); *No-one's Died Laughing* (1986) is an autobiographical look at how he developed his political satire.

V

v., a long poem by Tony *Harrison, first published in 1985. The title is the abbreviation for 'versus', indicating the work's thematic concern with 'all the versuses of life', the political, cultural, and personal conflicts characterizing the society of the mid-1980s on which the urgently topical work reflects. Its opening describes Harrison's visit to his parents' grave in a Leeds cemetery where many of the monuments have been desecrated by graffiti. His anger at the semi-literate perpetrators is tempered in the course of surveying the social conditions which make such acts understandable responses to the boredom and frustration of unemployment. A heated debate between the poet and an imagined youth representing the graffitists forms the centre of the work, which subsequently moves towards its conclusion with a meditation on change and the centrality of love to any viable scheme of human values. Drawing dramatic power from its strong charge of personal emotion and encompassing a wide range of acute socio-cultural commentary, *v.* ranks with the most important longer poems of the post-war era. Its 112 rhymed quatrains consistently display Harrison's technical virtuosity. The frequent use of obscene language which is essential to the work's documentary aspect caused widespread protest when it was presented on television.

V, a novel by Thomas *Pynchon, published in 1963. Like many of his other works of fiction, *V* is structured by a search (or quest), here for the mysterious being 'V' which, while having some of the attributes of a woman, also has metal dentures and detachable feet. The novel has a wide historical range, encompassing events from late nineteenth-century and contemporary America, largely through two characters, Stencil and Benny Profane, who occupy, in effect, different historical times though they are brought together and travel to Malta at the time of the Suez crisis. The plotting is complex and defies brief summary, but the novel reveals many of Pynchon's characteristic qualities, notably his fictional inventiveness and his immense resources of satire and parody.

VANCE, Jack (John Holbrook VANCE) (1916–), American writer of *science fiction and fantasy, born in San Francisco, educated at the University of California; he has also written some *detective fiction under other names. Some of his best work is contained in the linked stories published as *The Dying Earth* (1950), in which he transposed the interplanetary romance of E. R. *Burroughs to the distant future. 'Dying Earth' novels have since become numerous, but even the most sophisticated are directly indebted to Vance. Vance went on to create a large number of planetary landscapes filled with sentient beings, some of them human, in novels such as *Big Planet* (1957), *The Dragon Masters* (1963), *The Blue World* (1966), *Trullion: Alastor 2262* (1973), and *Maske: Thaery* (1976) which variously promulgate a universe teeming with difference. In *Lyonesse* (1983) and its sequels his landscape moves to Earth's own past.

VAN DER POST, Sir Laurens (Jan) (1906–), South African writer, born in Philippolis, South Africa, educated at Grey College, Bloemfontein. Together with Roy *Campbell and William *Plomer, he founded in 1926 the short-lived anti-racialist magazine *Voorslag*. He served in the British Army with distinction during and after the Second World War. Van der Post is best known for his vivid accounts of expeditions into remote parts of Africa in travel books such as *Venture to the Interior* (1952), *The Lost World of the Kalahari* (1958), and *The Heart of the Hunter* (1961). These works, which share with his novels much visionary speculation about the nature of man, were derived from the theories of C. G. Jung about whom he wrote in *Jung and the Story of Our Time: A Personal Experience* (1975). His first novel, *In a Province* (1934), dealt with racial antagonism and the dehumanizing effects of Marxism in South Africa; other works of fiction include *The Face Beside the Fire* (1953), *Flamingo Feather* (1955), *The Hunter and the Whale* (1967), and *A Mantis Carol* (1975). The three linked stories in *The Seed and the Sower* (1963) concern the experiences of two characters in a Japanese prisoner-of-war camp. Among other works are *The Dark Eye in Africa* (1955); the travel books *Journey into Russia* (1964), *A Portrait of all the Russias* (1967), and *A Portrait of Japan* (1968); *The Night of the New Moon* (1970); the semi-autobiographical *Yet Being Someone Other* (1982); and *A Walk with a White Bushman* (1986), which contains wide-ranging conversations with broadcaster Jean-Marc Pottiez. *About Blady: A Pattern Out of Time* (1991) blends fact and fiction and is substantially autobiographical; *The Voice of the Thunder* (1993) is a collection of essays; *Feather Fall: An Anthology* (1994) is a selection of other writings.

VAN DINE, S. S., pseudonym of Willard Huntington WRIGHT (1888–1939), American art critic and detective novelist, born in Virginia, educated at Harvard. He was editor of the magazines *Smart Set* and *The International Studio*, published works on modern art and on Nietzsche, and became known for a savage attack on the *Encyclopaedia Britannica* (*Misinforming a Nation*, 1917) before forming—during a two-year convalescence after a breakdown—a theory of *detective fiction which he put into practice in twelve novels written between 1926 and 1939 and which enjoyed immense success. In all of them the detective is Philo Vance, a rich young man-about-town and polymathic aesthete, of whom Ogden *Nash wrote 'Philo Vance | Needs a kick in the pance'. His first two books, *The Benson Murder Case* (1926) and *The Canary Murder Case* (1927), both based on actual crimes, are perhaps his best, but the most characteristic is *The Bishop Murder Case* (1929), which contains a series of murders based on nursery rhymes.

VAN DUYN, Mona (1921–), American poet, born in Waterloo, Iowa, educated at the University of Iowa. She has been characterized as both a Midwesterner and 'a poet of the suburbs'. From her initial collections onwards, *Valentines to the Wide World* (1959) and *A Time of Bees* (1964), her work has been popular and widely published. To influential admirers such as Richard *Howard and the critic Robert von Hallberg, her 'simple, human subjects' and skill within traditional forms (often quatrains or rhymed/offrhymed couplets) are what constitutes her appeal. In 1971 she won the National Book Award for *To See, To Take*, having received the Bollingen prize the previous year; decisions loudly deprecated at the time by Allen *Ginsberg. But, as von Hallberg pointed out in *American Poetry and Culture 1945–1980* (1985), Van Duyn's inclination 'is always to resist the visionary, even at the cost of being known as a . . . complacent representative of "domestic mediocrity"'. *Letters From a Father, and Other Poems* (1982), written in memory of her aged parents, contains one of her best-known poems, 'The Stream'. She has continued to produce well-received if somewhat conservative volumes, including *Near Changes* (1990).

VAN HERK, Aritha (1954–), Canadian novelist, born in Wetaskiwin, Alberta, educated at the University of Alberta; she teaches at the University of Calgary. The geography and landscapes of northern and western Canada form the background of her uncompromisingly feminist narratives of women's quests for autonomous identities. In her first novel *Judith* (1978), the protagonist leaves her urban background to re-define herself on a remote farm in Alberta. The heroine of *The Tent Peg* (1981) is the only woman on a mining expedition to the Yukon, whose inhospitable terrain becomes a proving ground for her values. *No Fixed Address* (1986) recounts the extensive journeying of a travelling saleswoman whose sense of personal integrity is inseparable from her actively independent sexuality. Van Herk's more recent work in *Places Far From Ellesmere* (1990), *A Frozen Tongue* (1991), and *In Visible Ink* (1991) are remarkable *post-modernist fusions of literary criticism, topographical writing, and imaginative and autobiographical material.

VANSITTART, Peter (1920–), British novelist, born in Bedford, educated at Worcester College, Oxford. He worked as a schoolteacher for twenty-five years before becoming a full-time writer. His first work, *I Am the World* (1942), is a metaphysical fiction on utopian themes in the manner of R. *Warner. Several of his novels, such as *The Friends of God* (1963), *The Lost Lands* (1964), *Pastimes of a Red Summer* (1969), and *The Wall* (1990), are erudite historical studies; others, like *A Verdict of Treason* (1952), *Orders of Chivalry* (1958), *Landlord* (1970), *Quintet* (1976), and *Aspects of Feeling* (1986), are anatomies of contemporary English life. Among his most striking works are a series of novels, including *The Story Teller* (1968), *Lancelot* (1978), *The Death of Robin Hood* (1981), and *Parsifal* (1988), in which fantasy fruitfully engages with historical detail. A more recent novel, *A Safe Conduct* (1995), depicts fifteenth-century Germany. His non-fiction includes *Green Knights, Black Angels: The Mosaic of History* (1969); *Worlds and Underworlds: Anglo-European History Through the Centuries* (1974); a memoir, *Paths from a White Horse* (1985); and *In the Fifties* (1995), a portrait of the decade.

VAN VECHTEN, Carl (1880–1964), American novelist, music critic, and reviewer, born in Cedar Rapids, Iowa, educated at the University of Chicago. Van Vechten was one of the most influential and visible literary figures of the 1910s and 1920s. He began his career in journalism as a reporter, then in 1906 joined *The New York Times* as assistant music critic and later worked as its Paris correspondent. His early reviews are collected in *Interpreters and Interpretations* (1917 and 1920) and *Excavations: A Book of Advocacies* (1926). His first novel, *Peter Whiffle: His Life and Works* (1922), a first-person account of the salon and bohemian culture of New York and Paris and clearly drawn from Van Vechten's own experiences, was immensely popular. *The Blind Bow-Boy* (1923) is a satirical novel after the manner of Max *Beerbohm and Anatole France, whose works were widely admired in the USA in the years around the First World War. Van Vechten's most important work of fiction is *Nigger Heaven* (1926), notable for its depiction of black life in Harlem in the 1920s and its sympathetic treatment of the newly emerging black culture. Two further novels followed, *Spider Boy: A Scenario for a Moving Picture* (1928) and *Parties: Scenes from Contemporary New York Life* (1930), the latter containing a rather ill-disguised portrait of Zelda and F. Scott *Fitzgerald, before Van Vechten turned away from fiction and towards photography. His photographs are the basis of many important documentary collections at the Museum of Modern Art in New York and elsewhere. An important literary patron, he established the James Weldon Johnson Memorial Collection of Negro Arts and Letters at Yale University. His friendships with Mabel Dodge Luhan and Gertrude *Stein, among others, are recorded in *Sacred and Profane Memories* (1932), a series of autobiographical essays. He was elected to the American Academy in 1961. See *Carl Van Vechten* (1965) by Edward Lueders.

VAN VOGT, A(lfred) E(lton) (1912–), Canadian-born *science fiction writer, born in Winnipeg, Manitoba, resident in the USA from 1944. Together with I. *Asimov and R. A. *Heinlein, he dominated American science fiction for a decade from 1939. His first novel, *Slan* (1940, in *Astounding Science Fiction*; final revised edition 1951), adopted for young magazine readers the idea of the solitary superman. More ambitious were two sets of linked novels, *The Weapon Shops of Isher* (1951) and *The Weapon Makers* (final form 1952), a *space opera in which the solar system is created as an afterthought, and *The World of A* (1948) and *The Pawns of Null-A* (1956), which attempted to relate the principles of Count Alfred Korzybski's General Semantics to the politics and intellectual processes of an immortal superman. Some of his best stories, many of them featuring savage but engrossing aliens, were collected in *The Voyage of the Space Beagle* (1950), *Away and Beyond* (1952), and *Destination: Universe* (1952). For a period Van Vogt's energies were diverted by R. Hubbard's Dianetics (later Scientology), but in the 1970s he was again producing prolifically, though novels such as *The Battle of Forever* (1971) lacked the haunting momentum of his earlier work.

VASSANJI, Moyez G(ulamhussein) (1950–), Kenyan novelist, born in Nairobi, a member of Kenya's long-established Indian community; he emigrated to the USA in 1970, where he was educated at the Massachusetts Institute of Technology and the University of Pennsylvania. In 1978 he began working as a nuclear physicist with Atomic Energy of Canada, then taught at the University of Toronto until 1989. *The Gunny Sack* (1989), his highly acclaimed first novel, uses a richly textured episodic form to recount the movements of four generations of his family following their migration from India to East Africa in the mid-nineteenth century. Its successor, *No New Land* (1991), forms a powerful treatment of exile and dispossession in the lives of an immigrant community in Toronto following their flight from political upheaval in Africa. *The Book of Secrets* (1994) encompasses the historical, political, and cultural history of East Africa from the First World War to the late 1980s through the interweaving of its many narrative elements. His other works include the short stories of *Uhuru Street* (1991). Vassanji is the editor of the *Toronto South Asian Review*, which he founded in 1982.

VEBLEN, Thorstein (Bunde) (1857–1929), American economist and social commentator, born in Cato, Wisconsin, educated at Johns Hopkins University and Yale. From 1891 onward, he held posts at the University of Chicago, Stanford University, the University of Missouri, and the New School for Social Research, New York. *The Theory of the Leisure Class* (1899), his first and best-known work, offered a critical analysis of affluence as a major determinant of social values. The treatment of the price system in *The Theory of Business Enterprise* (1904) established the distinction between production and control of production that is central to *The Instinct of Workmanship* (1914), *The Vested Interests and the State of the Industrial Arts* (1919), and *Absentee Ownership and Business Enterprise* (1923). In *The Place of Science in Modern Civilization* (1919) and *The Engineers and the Price System* (1921) he denounced capitalism as parasitic upon labour and scientific development, and envisioned a technocratic future in which politicians and financiers would cease to exercise control. Much of Veblen's thought, expressed in an accessible and ironically persuasive style, has become integral to modern sociological analysis. David Riesman's *Thorstein Veblen* appeared in 1953.

Vers libre, see FREE VERSE.

Victim, The, a novel by Saul *Bellow, published in 1947. Asa Leventhal is left alone by his wife, who has gone south to her mother's, to fend for himself in the sweltering New York summer. He is assailed by an acquaintance, Allbee, who accuses him of having brought about the loss of his job, this crime being linked, with increasing vehemence, to Leventhal's Jewishness. Leventhal is bemused, angry, upset, yet Allbee awakens certain buried emotions in him, above all a guilt in his relationship to all the hopeless in society (Allbee is a drinker). The story of Leventhal's relationship with Allbee, a shifting and at times desperate affair, is counterpointed with that of his relationship with his brother's family, and with his mortally ill son, Mickey. *The Victim* displays Bellow's gift for compassionate dissection of situation and its effect on character, and his humanist belief in some deep common factor linking disparate individuals at a psychic level. It is a work of great power and literary authority, a study of anti-Semitism and of a Jew's response to it that both illuminates and transcends its particular subject.

Victory, a novel by Joseph *Conrad, published in 1915, serialized in *Munsey's Magazine* (1915). Its central character, Axel Heyst, a Swedish aristocrat, lives on an island in the Malay Archipelago. Influenced by the sceptical philosophy of his father, and trying to avoid forming any attachments, his way of life is challenged when he rescues Lena, who has been touring the islands as part of a Ladies' Orchestra, from the sexual harassment of the hotelkeeper, Schomberg. The novel explores their relationship and the difficulties precipitated by the arrival of the devilish 'Mr Jones' and his two companions. The novel is divided into four parts. In Part I, Heyst and his flight from Sourabaya with Lena is presented by an unnamed narrator who has no privileged access to Heyst's inner thoughts and feelings. In Part II, Heyst's flight is presented first from his own point of view and then from Schomberg's. Part III is similarly split between a first half devoted to Heyst's developing relationship with Lena and a second half that sets up Heyst's confrontation with Jones. In the final part, these various relations interact to produce a violent and tragic conclusion. The novel explores such typical Conradian concerns as isolation, identity, and the relations between fathers and sons, but it also displays Conrad's interests, in his late novels, in relations between men and women, in concepts of masculinity, and in the construction of female identity. Apart from the repeated shifts in narrative perspective, the novel is also of interest for the way in which it superimposes various mythic and literary patterns: for example, the characters and events on the island are clearly variations and adaptations of characters and events in Shakespeare's *The Tempest*.

VIDAL, Gore (1925–), American writer, born in West Point, New York, educated in New Mexico and at the University of New Hampshire; he served in the US army from 1943 to 1946. His first novel, *Williwaw* (1946), a Second World War story, was derivative of *Hemingway; however, Vidal employed this influence to good effect in *The City and the Pillar* (1948). Telling the story of a homosexual's obsession with his childhood companion, the novel is distinguished by its honesty and lack of self-pity; the central figure is unexceptional in every respect but his sexual choices. Vidal published his sixth novel, the original and entertaining *A Search for the King* (1950), when he was 25; set in the time of Richard Cœur de Lion, it displayed the imaginative interest in the reconstruction of history that characterizes so much of his mature work. One of his most successful forays into the historical is *Julian* (1964); in the manner of Yourcenar's *Memoirs of Hadrian*, by which it is possibly influenced, this novel is presented as the autobiography of a renowned emperor of Rome. Vidal's fascination with the ancient world is exuberantly displayed in *Creation* (1981), which examines, through the encounters of its central figure, the Persian Cyrus Spitama, with their originators, the growth of such eastern creeds as Zoroastrianism, Buddhism, and Confucianism, and their formative impact on culture and history. Always a versatile and bold novelist, and almost impossible to categorize successfully, Vidal does, however, produce fictions that can be loosely defined in two genres: the bizarre and satirical—such as the cult favourite *Myra Breckenridge* (1968), a farce involving transsexuality, male rape, and Vidal's favoured setting, Hollywood; its sequel, *Myron* (1975); and *Duluth* (1983); and the epic, including *Creation*; *1876* (1976); and *Lincoln* (1984), a portrait of the American president, considered by many to be his masterpiece. In later works such as *Hollywood* (1990) and *Golgotha* (1992) the modes occasionally combine, though the documentary element, rich with Vidal's impressive understanding of the vagaries of American (and world) politics, is usually privileged. The scale and ambition of Vidal's writings occasionally obscure the fact that he is a lucid and elegant stylist, a fact that is amply proved by the occasional prose essays and reviews, which display his erudition as a cultural commentator, collected in such volumes as *Pink Triangle and Yellow Star and Other Essays 1976–1982* (1982) and *Armageddon and Other Essays 1983–1987* (1987). *Palimpsest: A Memoir* appeared in 1995.

Vietnam Writing. The Vietnam War spawned a great range of cultural, poetic, and literary representations, as people sought to articulate the experiences of the conflict. The works frequently make new projections of mythic consciousness as attempts to extend the collective memory into new contexts of perception about the war. Among the dramatic works several plays have emerged by David *Rabe, amongst them *The Basic Training of Pavlo Hummel* (1973), *Sticks and Bones* (1973), and *Streamers* (1977), all of which seek to explore the effects of the Vietnam War on American life. Arthur *Kopit's *Indians* (1969) was a symbolic exploration of the war's relationship to a larger body of collective mythic assumptions, set as it is in Buffalo Bill's America with the killing and hunting down of American Indians. Various books of poems have been published, including two anthologies of poems by veterans, *Demilitarized Zones: Veterans after Vietnam* (1976) and *Winning Hearts and Minds* (1972), together with Michael Casey's *Obscenities* (1972), D. C. Berry's *Saigon Cemetery* (1972), John Balaban's *After Our War* (1974), and Bruce Weigl's *A Romance* (1979) among the more prominent works. In addition, there are the protest poems of the anti-war demonstrators like Robert *Bly, Allen *Ginsberg, Denise *Levertov, Robert *Duncan, Robert *Lowell, and Walter Lowenfels. Among the many documentaries and analyses of the war is Michael Herr's *Dispatches* (1977), an account of the war which is represented as a venture into a strange midworld suspended somewhere between 'reality' and 'art'; *Dispatches* has become one of the most influential literary texts of the war and an important example of the *New Journalism and of post-modernism. Other works in this area are C. D. B. Bryan's *Friendly Fire* (1976), which depicts the anguish of an Iowa family over the loss of a son killed by his own artillery; Gloria Emerson's *Winners and Losers* (1976), which goes directly to the experiential heart of the war in an angry polemical work; Norman *Mailer's *Why Are We In Vietnam?* (1967); and Mary *McCarthy's trilogy of books dealing with Vietnam. The fiction has been prolific, notable examples of which are Tim *O'Brien's *If I Die in a Combat Zone* (1973), an account of a young infantryman's passage through a year at war rendered as an odyssey through cultural myths; Robert *Stone's *Dog Soldiers* (1974), which demonstrates how the war anger spread into the American landscape with returning soldiers; the soldier memoirs of Ron Kovic's *Born on the Fourth of July* (1976) and Philip Caputo's *A Rumour of War* (1977); and the oral histories in Mark Baker's *Nam* (1981) and Al Santoli's *Everything We Had* (1981). Other more traditional combat novels include David Halberstam's *One Very Hot Day* (1967); Josiah Bunting's *The Lionheads* (1972); Ronald Glasser's short narratives in *365 Days* (1971); Robert Roth's *Sand in the Wind* (1973); Charles Durden's *No Bugles, No Drums* (1976); William Pelfrey's *The Big V* (1972), a story about three college boys' attitudes and initiation into war; Larry Heinemann's *Close Quarters* (1977); Gustav Hasford's *The Short-Timers* (1979), about the experiences of members of an infantry platoon; Stephen Wright's *Meditations in Green* (1983); and James Webb's *Fields of Fire* (1978). In William *Eastlake's *The Bamboo Bed* (1969) and Tim O'Brien's *Going after Cacciato* (1978), the war is represented as a surreal fantasy and nightmare.

View from the Bridge, A, a play by Arthur *Miller, published in 1955, revised in 1956. Reminiscent of a Greek tragedy, it is set amongst the longshoremen of New York, and deals with episodes in the life of a single family, which are described by the lawyer Alfieri, taking the role of 'chorus'. Eddie and his wife give hospitality to two illegal Italian immigrants, Marco and Rodolpho, who are brothers of very different temperaments. Eddie takes to Marco but is suspicious of Rodolpho, whom he suspects of homosexual inclinations. His contempt turns to active hatred as Rodolpho makes advances to Catherine, Eddie's beloved niece, with a view to marriage. He convinces himself that Rodolpho is only interested in marrying her as a means of getting an American passport, and informs on the Italians. When the immigration authorities arrive to arrest the brothers, Marco springs to the attack and stabs Eddie to death. Much of the play's power derives from the extent to which the audience is left in doubt as to the true nature of events: we never know, for example, how far Eddie's suspicions about Rodolpho are correct and whether he himself has felt some attraction towards the other man. Miller's use of stagecraft is also singularly inventive and disciplined.

Vile Bodies, a novel by Evelyn *Waugh, published in 1930. Following the success of **Decline and Fall*, his chronicle of the empty hedonism of the 'roaring Twenties', Waugh introduced many of the same themes and characters, including the brittle, amoral Margot Metroland, into his second novel. The book opens with an account of a Channel crossing undertaken by a group of 'Bright Young Things' including the hero, Adam Fenwick-Symes, together with other social luminaries such as the American evangelist Mrs Melrose Ape, the disgraced former Prime Minister Walter Outrage, the sinister Jesuit priest Father Rothschild, and the society beauty Agatha Runcible. All these characters reappear at the various social gatherings which punctuate the narrative, where other characters, including Lady Metroland, Miles Malpractice, and Nina Blount, Adam's fiancée, are introduced. One of the book's running jokes is the alternate breaking-off and reinstatement of Adam's engagement to Nina, as his finances dwindle or increase. Eventually, Nina marries Ginger Littlejohn, her childhood sweetheart, but continues her illicit liaison with Adam. The surreal tone of the work is epitomized in its closing scenes, in which war is declared and Adam, now a war hero, reads his last letter from Nina on the field of battle—a prescient image of the impending cataclysm.

VINE, Barbara, see RENDELL, RUTH.

Virginian, The: A Horseman of the Plains, a classic *Western novel by Owen *Wister, published in 1902. An important influence on later Westerns, *The Virginian* established a formula that was to become popular for the whole genre through its depiction of a laconic stranger who rides into a community and helps maintain law and order by taking on and defeating the forces of evil. It anticipates such later novels as Jack Schaeffer's *Shane* and numerous Hollywood Western films. The novel is set in the wide open spaces of Wyoming and, in its concern with the ethics of frontier society, proposes the transplantation of 'civilized' values into the wild, 'natural' environment of the West: far from being a rough Westerner himself, its hero is from the cultured East. While generally regarded as a pioneer Western novel, *The Virginian* has obvious antecedents in the fiction of James Fenimore Cooper, which is equally concerned with the role of chivalric values in the world of the frontier. Central episodes include the protagonist's early quarrel with the villain Trampas, when the latter accuses him of cheating in a poker game, and the duel, said to be the first use of this motif in a Western novel, in which he eventually kills Trampas. *The Virginian* is narrated by a tenderfoot figure who gradually matures during its course, as does the Virginian himself. Ultimately it is an elegy for a way of life that is seen as having recently vanished and belongs, with such works as Cooper's Leatherstocking Series and Twain's writing about life on the Mississippi in the ante-bellum South, to a genre of writing that is both concerned with mythologizing the freedom offered by the frontier and at the same time lamenting its loss.

Vision, a short-lived Australian journal (1923–4), but of major importance in Australian letters. It was a challenge to **Bulletin*, which had dominated the Australian literary scene in its promotion of the nationalist strain of Australian writing. It was not the 'Vision' school's intention, however, to create an outpost in Australia for European modernism. Printing mainly the work of such poets as Kenneth *Slessor, Jack *Lindsay, R. D. *Fitzgerald, and Hugh McRae, with illustrations by Norman *Lindsay, their intention was to create a renaissance in Australia by returning to the influences of classical and Romantic literature. *Vision* subscribed to a Coleridgean theory of the imagination and was also inspired by Nietzschean ideas.

Vision, A, a prose work by W. B. *Yeats, originally published privately in 1925 and made generally available in considerably revised form in 1937. In *A Packet for Ezra Pound* (1929), which was included in the 1937 edition as an introduction, Yeats described how the book's system of twenty-eight historical and cultural phases was communicated to him by spirits through his wife's automatic writing. The phases, which together form a recurrent cosmic cycle, ordain the content of history, the nature of religious and ideological belief, and the dispositions of individuals. Yeats's favourable interest in Irish fascism in the early 1930s may be regarded as a product of the rigidly determinist philosophy of history in the original text. Refinements in the second edition admitted the possibility of circumventing historical determinism. For many, *A Vision* must be, in Louis *MacNeice's words, 'the most ingenious, the most elaborate, and the most arid of his writings'. Its centrality to Yeats's later verse is, however, undeniable. Transcripts of the automatic writings and other original materials relating to the work are contained in *Yeats's 'Vision' Papers* (3 volumes, 1992), edited by George Mills Harper, author of *The Making of Yeats's 'A Vision'* (2 volumes, 1987).

Vivisector, The, see WHITE, PATRICK.

VIZENOR, Gerald (1934–), American writer of mixed French and Chippewa descent, born in Minneapolis, educated at the University of Minnesota; he became Professor of Literature and American Studies at the University of California at Santa Cruz. Vizenor's work is concerned with the social, psychological, and spiritual difficulties experienced by Americans of mixed blood. Among his volumes of poetry are *Raising the Moon Vines: Original Haiku in English* (1964), *Seventeen Chirps: Haiku in English* (1964), and *Matsushima: Pine Islands* (1984). He achieved critical acclaim with his second novel, *Griever: An American Monkey King in China* (1987), in which the trickster figure of tribal stories, who appears throughout Vizenor's writing, is presented in Chinese guise as the Monkey King. The trickster god provides the model for liberation for the hero, a mixed-blood Indian teaching in China, who finally triumphs over Chinese bureaucracy. The quest for ritual knowledge also provides a structuring principle in *Darkness in Saint Louis Bearheart* (1978; retitled *Bearheart: The Heirship Chronicles*, 1990) and *Trickster of Liberty: Tribal Heirs to a Wild Baronage* (1988). A later novel is *Heirs of Columbus* (1991). The interweaving of white and tribal motifs, which characterizes Vizenor's fiction, is matched by the mixing of fictional with historical elements in volumes such as *Earthdivers: Tribal Narratives on Mixed Descent* (1981) and *Tribal Scenes and Ceremonies* (1976, expanded 1990). Other non-fiction works include *The Everlasting Sky: New Voices from the People Named the Chippewa* (1972) and *Interior Landscapes: Autobiographical Myths and Metaphors* (1990). See also NATIVE AMERICAN LITERATURE.

VOLLMANN, William T(anner) (1959–), American novelist and short-story writer, born in Los Angeles, educated at Cornell University. His researches have taken him to many parts of the world, frequently to places engaged in political turmoil: he covered the war in Afghanistan and was wounded in Sarajevo. His first novel, *You Bright and Risen Angels* (1987), used the picaresque form, robust humour, and fascination with power found in Thomas *Pynchon, although there were already signs here of an individual vision, particularly in his treatment of sexuality. Subsequent volumes deepen and extend the historical research, journalism, experiential testing, and fascination with mythology that can be found in the first novel. *The Rainbow Stories* (1989) and *Thirteen Stories and Thirteen Epitaphs* (1991) are volumes of interconnected short stories; *Butterfly Stories* (1993) is a novel which focuses on both AIDS and Cambodia. His most ambitious work to date, 'Seven Dreams', is a projected sequence forming a 'symbolic history' of North America; the Norse discovery is dealt with in the *Ice-Shirt* (1990), the Jesuits in *Fathers and Crows* (1992), and Franklin's attempt to find the north-west passage in *The Rifles* (1994). The latter volume, being written out of sequence, is the sixth dream and, like the others, holds a prodigious array of materials within the gaze of a disabused yet passionate individual.

VON ARNIM, Elizabeth (1866–1941), British novelist who wrote under the pseudonym 'Elizabeth', born Mary Annette BEAUCHAMP in Sydney, Australia, but brought up in England. In 1890 she married Count Henning August von Arnim-Schlagenthin, who appears as 'The Man of Wrath' in her best-known work, *Elizabeth and Her German Garden* (1898); it is a witty, slightly eccentric portrayal of her family life and the garden she created at Nassenheide in Pomerania, where E. M. *Forster and Hugh *Walpole numbered amongst her children's tutors. Debt forced the von Arnims to England in 1908, where the count died two years later. Fleeing a cheerless Britain, she built a chateau in Switzerland; at the outbreak of the First World War she returned to England, where she was briefly married to Earl Russell, brother of Bertrand *Russell. Two of her finest and most complex novels came from intensely painful liaisons: *Vera* (1921) is a harrowing but brilliant portrayal of her marriage to Earl Russell, and *Love* (1925) poignantly and humorously describes a middle-aged woman's relations with a man decades her junior. *The Pastor's Wife* (1914) and *Father* (1931) are other psychologically complex novels.

VONNEGUT, Kurt Jr (1922–), American novelist, born in Indianapolis; he studied biochemistry at Cornell University, and after serving in the Second World War studied anthropology at the University of Chicago. His first novel, *Player Piano* (1952), attacks the post-war conformity and standardization he had witnessed while working for a giant corporation. His two dystopic works, *The Sirens of Titan* (1959), a novel which envisages the entire history of the human race as an alien accident, and *Cat's Cradle* (1963), in which a complex narrative of human selfishness causes the end of the world, helped to establish *science fiction as a genre in which serious social problems might be addressed. *Mother Night* (1962, reissued 1967), explored the questions of war-crime guilt and anti-Semitism in a narrative about espionage in the Second World War, whilst *God Bless You, Mr Rosewater* (1965) depicted an alcoholic millionaire's realization that the only practical utopia lies in aiding and understanding the world's wretched, lonely, and ignorant. There followed his most celebrated work, **Slaughterhouse-Five* (1969), a post-modern anti-war novel. Subsequent works include *Happy Birthday, Wanda Jane* (1971) and *Between Time and Timbuktu, or Prometheus Five: A Space Fantasy* (1972), two plays, both of which have fast and funny dialogue; *Breakfast of Champions, or Goodbye Blue Monday* (1973), which touched on various subjects including ecology, racism, and politics; *Slapstick* (1978); *Jailbird* (1979); and *Deadeye Dick* (1982), a series of horrific episodes interspersed with recipes by the eponymous protagonist. Vonnegut's progressively pessimistic tone, barely alleviated by black comedy, is exemplified in *Galapagos* (1985), which narrates an inversion of evolution as the only means to peace, as a group of humans stranded on the Galapagos Islands turn into turtles. Then came *Bluebeard* (1987), which uses the myth of Bluebeard in Rabo Karabekian's autobiography about life amongst the Abstract Expressionists. *Hocus Pocus* (1990), a work set in the near future, treats of Armageddon with Vonnegut's usual black comic outlook. He has produced a wide variety of other writings including collections of short stories in *Canary in a Cat House* (1961) and *Welcome to the Monkey House* (1968); and the essays in *Wampeters, Foma, and Granfalloons: Opinions* (1974), *Palm Sunday: An Autobiographical Collage* (1981), and *Fates Worse than Death* (1991). In charting the struggle of the individual against a hostile universe, Vonnegut's fiction frequently travesties 'high culture' in a satiric and wryly humorous voice, and he shares with such writers as John *Barth, Donald *Barthelme, William *Burroughs, and Joseph *Heller a perspective of the modern world as an absurd, fantastic, apocalyptic farce. His latest works include *Timequake* (1994) and *Three Complete Novels* (1995).

Vortex, The, a play by Noël *Coward, performed in 1924. It tells of Florence Lancaster, a fading beauty who cannot accept the march of time, and her drug addict son, Nicky. She mixes with mostly idle, futile people, and neglects her husband, David, for younger and more glamorous admirers, the latest of whom is Tom Veryan. Nicky returns from Paris having just become engaged, but his fiancée, Bunty, rejects him for the less neurotic Tom; and Florence goes into a tantrum when she discovers her lover's disloyalty. The climactic scene comes in Florence's bedroom, with Nicky accusing her of ruining his father's life with her yearning for flattery, of neglecting him, and causing them both to 'swirl in a vortex of beastliness'. The play ends with her promising to change and the two of them in each other's arms. Its relative candour won Coward great notoriety in its day; but critics now tend to dismiss it as a period melodrama.

Vorticism, a *Modernist movement in British art and literature, linked to *Imagism and *Futurism, as promulgated by the Italian impresario Marinetti. Its leading figure was the writer and painter Wyndham *Lewis; the term 'vortex' was first coined by Ezra *Pound, in an essay on the sculptor Henri Gaudier-Brzeska, and was adopted by Lewis to describe the concentrated energy of the new movement. In October 1913, after a quarrel with Roger *Fry, Lewis broke away from the *Bloomsbury-dominated Omega Workshops to set up the Rebel Art Centre, where he was joined by a number of artists, including Frederick Etchells, Edward Wadsworth, C. R. W. Nevinson, Jacob Epstein, and Gaudier-Brzeska, as well as Pound, Richard *Aldington, and others. In June 1914 **Blast: The Review of the Great English Vortex* appeared, edited, illustrated, and largely written by Lewis, although with significant contributions from Pound; its most distinctive feature was the 'Manifesto of the Great London Vortex' with its catalogue of 'Blasts' and 'Blesses'. Its aim was to promote hard-edged abstraction in the visual arts and a corresponding anti-Romantic emphasis in literature, of which the best examples can be found in Lewis's own productions, such as his 1912 *Timon of Athens* series, his *Composition* (1913), and *Workshop* (1915); his *Expressionist play *Enemy of the Stars*, which appeared in *Blast II* (1915), and the first version of his novel **Tarr* (1918) are also Vorticist in style. Jacob Epstein's *Rock Drill* (1913), David Bomberg's *In the Hold* (1913–14), and Gaudier-Brzeska's *Hieratic Head of Ezra Pound* (1913) are other examples. A Vorticist Exhibition was held at the Doré Gallery in 1915; but the First World War effectively brought the movement to an end.

Voss, a novel by Patrick *White, published in 1957. Inspired by the true story of Ludwig Leichardt, *Voss* is the epic account of the German explorer Johann Voss, a visionary who planned to cross the Australian continent in 1845, in a Nietzschean attempt to transform himself into a superman. His encounter with the emancipated Laura Trevelyan before his departure develops into a mystical, telepathic bond strengthened by his absence. Voss's attempt to conquer the desert is doomed from the outset; he experiences hunger, robbery, desertion by companions, and sickness on his quest. His sufferings are eventually and brutally curtailed by one of his travelling companions, the aboriginal Jackie, who decapitates him. Laura, in Sydney, is ravaged by fever, in a psychic reflection of Voss's experiences. Voss lives on in collective memory, variously iconized as a martyr, revered as a hero, or reviled as a madman. Only Laura perceives the truth of Voss's existence; like all mortals, Voss was the meeting-place of good and evil.

Voyage Out, The, see WOOLF, VIRGINIA.

WADDELL, Helen (Jane) (1889–1965), British medievalist, born in Tokyo, where her father was a missionary; from the age of 10 onward she grew up in County Down, Ulster, and was educated at Queen's University, Belfast. Having studied under George *Saintsbury, with whom she remained friendly, she produced *Lyrics from the Chinese* (1913), the first of her numerous works of translation; her play *The Spoiled Buddha* (1919) was produced in Belfast in 1915. Following a period of study at Somerville College, Oxford, she secured a travelling scholarship with Saintsbury's assistance and was in Paris from 1923 to 1925, pursuing her consuming interest in medieval culture at the Bibliothèque Nationale. Her researches resulted in *The Wandering Scholars* (1927), which remains of value as an introduction to medieval Latin literature. *Medieval Latin Lyrics* (1929) contains her creative but sometimes erratic translations. The two publications gained her a wide reputation for accessible and imaginatively stimulating scholarship which she consolidated with the novel *Peter Abelard*, her best-known work, in 1933. From 1945 her health began to deteriorate; *Poetry in the Dark Ages* (1948), the texts of her W. P. *Ker lectures at Glasgow, was her last publication of any note. Her other works include a translation of *Manon Lescaut* (1931) by Antoine-François Prévost. There is a biography (1986) by F. Corrigan, who edited Waddell's *More Latin Lyrics from Virgil to Milton* (1976).

WADDINGTON, Miriam (1917–), Canadian poet, the daughter of Russian-Jewish immigrants, born in Winnipeg, educated at the University of Toronto. After many years as a social worker in Montreal, in 1964 she began lecturing at York University, Toronto, where she became Professor of English in 1973. During the early 1940s she was closely associated with the magazines *First Statement* and *Preview*. The lyrical reflections on personal experience in *Green World* (1945), her first collection of verse, and its successor *The Second Silence* (1955) made precise and energetic use of natural imagery. Social concerns emerge as a dominant aspect of her verse in *The Season's Lovers* (1958). Her subsequent collections include *The Glass Trumpet* (1966), in which greater economies of form become apparent, *Say Yes* (1969), *The Price of Gold* (1976), and *The Visitants* (1982); her *Collected Poems* appeared in 1986. Her wide experience in social work underlies the compassion and anger with which she presents her often harrowingly realistic views of the casualties of urban modernity. A taut and persuasive directness of tone and vividly particular imagery are characteristic of much of her verse. Among her other publications are the short stories of *Summer at Lonely Beach* (1982), which extend her concern with lives on the margins of society, and the critical essays collected in *Apartment 7* (1989).

WADE, Henry, pseudonym of Sir Henry Lancelot Aubrey FLETCHER, 6th baronet, DSO, Croix de Guerre (1887–1969), British writer, born in Leigh, Surrey, educated at Eton and New College, Oxford. He served with the Grenadier Guards in the First and Second World Wars, was High Sheriff and Lord Lieutenant of Buckinghamshire, and wrote, under his mother's maiden name, some twenty classic detective novels and a number of short stories. Among the best are *Mist on the Saltings* (1933), *Constable, Guard Thyself!* (1934), *Heir Presumptive* (1935), *Bury Him Darkly* (1936), and *Lonely Magdalen* (1940). Under his own name he published *A History of the Foot Guards to 1856* (1927).

WAIN, John (Barrington) (1925–94), British poet, novelist, and critic, born in Stoke-on-Trent, educated at St John's College, Oxford. His first substantial publication was the novel *Hurry on Down* (1953), which charts the fortunes of its disaffected hero through a range of occupations, legitimate and illicit. Among his subsequent novels are *Strike the Father Dead* (1962), a further treatment of youthful rebellion, and *A Winter in the Hills* (1970), in which his comic spirit is most evident. *Where the Rivers Meet* (1988), *Comedies* (1990), and *Hungry Generations* (1994) form a trilogy set in Oxford between the wars. In 1956 his poetry appeared in Robert Conquest's **New Lines* anthology; *A Word Carved on a Sill* (1956) was his first independent collection. The understated intensities, technical accomplishment, and ironic rationality of his verse exemplified the attributes of the *Movement. His subsequent collections, which display an increasing inventiveness of form and manner, include *Weep before God* (1961), *Wildtrack* (1965), *Feng* (1975), and *Open Country* (1987). *Poems, 1949–1979* was published in 1981. The most highly regarded of his numerous scholarly works is the biography *Samuel Johnson* (1974; James Tait Black Memorial prize); his intense affinity with Johnson resulted in a play, *Johnson Is Leaving* (1994), written for one voice, about the last years of Johnson's life. From 1973 to 1978 he was Oxford Professor of Poetry, publishing his lectures under the title *Professing Poetry* (1978).

WAINWRIGHT, Jeffrey (1944–), British poet, born in Stoke-on-Trent, educated at the University of Leeds. After teaching at University College, Aberystwyth, and Long Island University, New York, he became a lecturer at Manchester Polytechnic in 1973. *The Important Man* (1970) was his first independent publication as a poet. His work attracted critical acclaim when it appeared in Jon *Silkin's edition of *Poetry of the Committed Individual* (1973) and Faber's *Poetry Introduction: 3* (1975). *Heart's Desire* (1978), *Selected Poems* (1985), and *The Red-Headed Pupil and Other Poems* (1994) are among his principal collections of verse. Wainwright's poetry invariably displays a compelling stylistic economy which gives his brief lyric treatments of personal experience an unsettling intensity. His imaginatively concentrated presentations of historical subject matter are among his finest work; 'Thomas Muntzer', a sequence of dramatic monologues in the voice of the sixteenth-century German revolutionary, is deeply informed by Wainwright's own political and spiritual beliefs. His other works include an adaptation of Charles Péguy's *The Mystery of the Charity of Joan of Arc* (1986), which was produced by the Royal Shakespeare Company in 1984.

Waiting for Godot, the first play by Samuel *Beckett; it was published in French as *En Attendant Godot* in 1952, staged in French in Paris in 1953, and performed in Beckett's own English translation in 1955. One of the key works of the twentieth century, it is set on and around a country road and involves two days in the life of Estragon and Vladimir, both tramps and both awaiting the arrival of the mysterious title character. He never appears, notwithstanding the promises of a small boy who enters at the end of each act, claiming to be his emissary. Meanwhile, Vladimir (the more optimistic and energetic) and Estragon (the more pessimistic and self-pitying) pass the time by playing verbal games, reminiscing, bickering, philosophizing inconsequentially, speculating about the future, and reacting to two other characters: the arrogant Pozzo and his slave, Lucky. Each act ends with the same exchange: 'well, shall we go?'; 'yes, let's go', followed by the stage direction, 'they do not move'. Beckett's aim is evidently to represent in symbolic terms the inscrutability of the universe, the uncertainties of human existence, and the vanity of human effort, which explains why the play is regarded as a seminal contribution to The Theatre of the *Absurd. Though humour is often present, it is of a kind that shows the folly as much as the resilience of human beings. Again, though Beckett himself said that the play is 'striving all the time to avoid definition', the thrust seems well summed up by Pozzo, who has been inexplicably struck blind between his two appearances: 'One day we were born, one day we shall die, the same day, the same second . . . they give birth astride of a grave, the light glimmers an instant, and then it's night once more.'

Waiting for Lefty, by Clifford *Odets, his most famous short play, first produced by the *Group Theatre on 6 January 1935 at a benefit for striking cab drivers. Framed by an introduction and conclusion are six memory scenes (later five), which, on a darkened stage, reveal the injustices of working people's lives. At a strike meeting, taxi drivers await their leader, Lefty Costello, while a corrupt union boss, Harry Fatt, supported by an armed thug, advises against industrial action. He permits the six committeemen to address the workers, and their personal circumstances are dramatized in the following scenes. First, Edna persuades Joe to strike for their children's sake, then, in 'The Lab Assistant', Miller refuses to make poison gas for the government; in 'The Young Hack and His Girl', Sid and Florrie realize that they cannot marry without a living wage, while in 'Labor Spy Episode', Fatt introduces a cab driver who is then exposed as a company stooge. 'The Young Actor' includes a reference to *The Communist Manifesto*, and was later dropped from the play. 'Interne Episode' attacks anti-Semitism, and shows how medicine is sacrificed to capitalist interests. Finally, Agate Keller urges collective action, and on hearing that Lefty has been murdered, the meeting, including the actors in the audience, cries out 'STRIKE, STRIKE, STRIKE!!!'

WAKEFIELD, Tom (1935–96), British novelist and short-story writer, born into a mining family in Staffordshire, educated at the University of London. *Forties Child* (1980) is a poignant recreation of his early years. Wakefield was the author of a number of novels which celebrate the sensitive person trapped by the conventions that society demands. The stubborn strength in a homosexual attachment is the subject of *Mates* (1983) where the ironical ending casts a transfiguring light on the relationship at the centre of the book. *The Discus Throwers* (1985) is a moving blend of the comic-grotesque and the near-tragic, and confers nobility on its characters through its ending. The central character of *The Variety Artistes* (1987) is an elderly widow, Lydia Poulton, who is determined to enjoy her old age, despite attempts on the part of her family to make her conform to conventional ideas of widowhood. *Lot's Wife* (1989) deals with similar themes and displays Wakefield's characteristic humour. *War Paint* (1993) is a portrait of a Midland's mining community during the Second World War. *Drifters* (1984) is a collection of short stories, and 'The Other Way' a touching novella concerning a lonely Englishwoman holidaying in North Africa (published in the triptych *Secret Lives*, 1991, together with novellas by Wakefield's friends Patrick *Gale and Francis *King). He edited an anthology of stories, *The Ten Commandments* (1992), to which he also contributed.

WAKOSKI, Diane (1937–), American poet, born in Whittier, California, educated at the University of California at Berkeley. Wakoski has taught at several universities. A prolific poet, her first publication was *Coins and Coffins* (1962). She established her reputation with *Discrepancies and Apparitions* (1966); later notable collections include *The George Washington Poems*

(1967), *Inside the Blood Factory* (1968), *The Motorcycle Betrayal Poems* (1971), *Virtuoso Literature for Two and Four Hands* (1976), *Waiting for the King of Spain* (1977), and *Cap of Darkness* (1980). She continues to develop her long poem 'Greed', the first two parts of which appeared in 1968, and which has been published as *The Collected Greed, Parts 1–13* (1984). Wakoski has written of herself as a didactic poet, whose subject is that unique body of knowledge—herself. She dissociates herself from the *Confessional poets such as Sylvia *Plath and Anne *Sexton, and allies herself with the tradition of William Carlos *Williams and Allen *Ginsberg, which, for all Williams's interest in modern aesthetics, has its origins in Whitman's poetry as 'psalms of self'. Her poems are self-expressive rhapsodies, in celebration and in vehement repudiation of all that has sought to damage that unique self.

WALCOTT, Derek (Alton) (1930–), West Indian poet and playwright, born in Castries, St Lucia, educated at the University College of the West Indies; he worked as schoolteacher before pursuing a career in journalism from 1956 onward. In 1959 he founded the Trinidad Theatre Workshop, where a number of his plays were first performed. From 1981 he has held a succession of visiting professorships at American universities. *In a Green Night* (1962), the first widely distributed collection of his poetry, was acclaimed for the fluency with which he applied traditional verse forms to richly perceptive treatments of Caribbean experience. His numerous subsequent volumes, in which an increasing flexibility is evident in his virtuosity as a versifier, include *The Castaway* (1965), *The Star-Apple Kingdom* (1979), *The Fortunate Traveller* (1981), *The Arkansas Testament* (1987), and **Omeros* (1990). Much of his writing coheres around his concern to define his identity as a product of both the indigenous traditions of the West Indies and the European culture by which he is equally sustained. His verse is characterized by the lucid particularity of its imagery and the great variety and power of its rhythmical effects. *Collected Poems 1948–1984* appeared in 1986. The integrity and range of his engagement with moral and spiritual themes of universal significance have gained him an international reputation as one of the finest poets of his generation. His work as a dramatist began with numerous treatments of Caribbean history, of which *Henri Christophe* (1950) is the best-known. Drawing deeply on West Indian folklore, his plays combine verse and prose and make extensive use of Creole vocabulary. *The Dream on Monkey Mountain and Other Plays* (1970) was his first major publication as a playwright, the title work forming a mythical exposition of the relevance of the past to the present. Among his other plays are *The Last Carnival*, dealing with effects of political radicalism on a French-Creole family; *A Branch of the Blue Nile*, which centres on conflicts within a small drama company; and *Beef, no Chicken*, a treatment of municipal corruption; these were collected as *Three Plays* in 1986. His stage version of *The Odyssey* was published in 1993. Walcott received the Nobel Prize for Literature in 1992; his Nobel Lecture was published as *The Antilles: Fragments of Epic Memory* (1993).

WALDMAN, Anne (Lesley) (1945–), American poet, born in Millville, New Jersey; she attended Bennington and from 1968 onwards was the director of a community arts project at St Mark's Church-in-the-Bowery. Organizing readings and workshops, co-editing *Angel Hair* magazine and books, being involved with John Giorno's experimental sound recordings, her activities there were integral to the younger generation of the *New York School of Poets. Reflecting this, the poems in *Giant Night* (1968), *Baby Breakdown* (1970), and *No Hassles* (1972) are exuberant and playful; full of references to friends, drugs, travel, parodies ('13 Tanka in Praise of Smoking Dope'), games with poetic forms ('How the Sestina (Yawn) Works'), and collaborations with the likes of Ted *Berrigan, Ron Padgett, Joe Brainard, Lewis Warsh, and visual artists Larry Fagin and George Schneeman. In 1974 Waldman joined Allen *Ginsberg in founding the Jack Kerouac School of Disembodied Poetics at the Buddhist Naropa Institute in Boulder, Colorado. The title poem of *Fast Speaking Woman and Other Chants* (1975), her best-known volume, is a *tour de force*, read with driving impetus by Waldman in public and on recordings, reiterating a woman's acts of self-definition and self-liberation. Among her subsequent collections are *Journals and Dreams* (1976), *Make-Up on Empty Space* (1984), and *Helping the Dreamer: Selected Poems* (1989). She has also edited, with Marilyn Webb, *Talking Poetics from Naropa Institute* (2 volumes, 1978–9), lectures and interviews by visiting writers, many of them associated with the *Beats or the New York School. See also LANGUAGE POETRY.

WALEY, Arthur (David) (1889–1966), British poet and translator, born in Tunbridge Wells, educated at King's College, Cambridge. In 1913 he became *Binyon's assistant in the Sub-Department of Oriental Prints and Drawings at the British Museum. In the course of his work he learned Chinese and Japanese and developed a strong interest in the poems incorporated into paintings he dealt with. In 1917 a large number of his verse translations appeared in the *Bulletin* of the newly formed School Of Oriental Studies, where he later lectured. At this time he was closely acquainted with T. S. *Eliot and Ezra *Pound; the latter's translations from the Chinese had appeared in *Cathay* of 1915, which, according to W. B. *Yeats, 'created the manner followed with more learning but less subtlety of rhythm by Arthur Waley'. *One Hundred and Seventy Chinese Poems* (1918) proved popular with a wide readership. He developed a verse-line in which stresses were matched to the occurrence of the Chinese monosyllables in his originals. The concrete precision of his imagery produces results which resemble the best poetry of *Imagism. His many other translations include *The Tale of the*

Genji (6 volumes, 1925–33), his version of *Genji Monogatari*, the eleventh-century Japanese novel by Murasaki Shikibu. Among his numerous historical and biographical studies are *The Opium War through Chinese Eyes* (1958) and *The Poetry and Career of Li Po* (1951). His wife Alison Waley published a memoir entitled *A Half of Two Lives* in 1982.

WALKER, Alice (Malsenior) (1944–), American novelist, poet, and short-story writer, born in Eatonton, Georgia, educated at Spelman College and Sarah Lawrence College. After graduating from Sarah Lawrence College, where she wrote her first novel (*The Third Life of Grange Copeland*, 1970), Walker taught writing and African-American literature at Jackson State College and Tougaloo College in Mississippi. She has also taught at Wellesley College, the University of Massachusetts, and Yale University, as well as serving as an editor on *Ms.* magazine and *Freedomways*. During the summer of 1966 she was a volunteer on voter registration drives in Mississippi and she has made much of the interplay between her political, cultural, educational, and maternal experiences in her writings. One of the earliest short stories, 'To Hell With Dying', was published in the influential edition by Langston *Hughes of African-American short stories, *The Best Short Stories by Negro Writers* (1967). Walker's first collection of short stories, *In Love and Trouble* (1973), helped establish her very considerable reputation in African-American literature; further collections include *You Can't Keep a Good Woman Down* (1981) and *The Complete Stories* (1994). Her second novel, *Meridian* (1976), draws on her experience of the Civil Rights movement in the 1960s. She is best known for *The Color Purple* (1982), for which she was the first African-American woman to receive a Pulitzer Prize. An epistolary novel set in the segregated South between the wars, it offers a haunting portrait of abuse and oppression. The novel became a bestseller and was filmed by Steven Spielberg in 1985. *The Temple of My Familiar* (1989), which contains some of her most impressive prose, traces a history of the dispossessed in epic form and is underpinned by her awareness of African-American spirituality. More recently she has published *Possessing the Secret of Joy* (1992), which examines the subject of female circumcision and is linked, through its characters, with *The Color Purple*. She has published several volumes of poetry, including *Once: Poems* (1968), *Revolutionary Petunias and Other Poems* (1973), *Good Night, Willie Lee, I'll See You in the Morning* (1979), *Horses Make a Landscape Look More Beautiful* (1984), and *Her Blue Body Everything We Know: Earthling Poems 1965–1990* (1991). She defines her prose as 'womanist', stating, 'Womanist is to feminist as purple is to lavender'. Her essays have been collected in *In Search of Our Mothers' Gardens: Womanist Prose* (1983) and *Living by the Word: Selected Writings 1973–1987* (1988). *I Love Myself When I Am Laughing*... (1979) is her anthology of the writings of Zora Neale *Hurston whom she cites as an influence on her work. See also ETHNICITY.

WALKER, Kath, see NOONUCCAL, OODGEROO.

WALKER, Margaret (Abigail) (1915–), African-American poet and novelist, born in Birmingham, Alabama, educated at Northwestern University and the University of Iowa. She began her academic career at Livingstone College, North Carolina, in 1941 and was Professor of English at Jackson State College, Mississippi, from 1949 to 1979. *For My People* (1942), her first collection of verse, was widely acclaimed; in addition to its powerful free-verse affirmations of the indomitable dignity of black Americans, it contained ballads drawing on the black folk tradition and sonnets displaying a high degree of conventional accomplishment. Her subsequent collections include *Prophets for a New Day* (1970), a celebration of the spiritual energies of the Civil Rights movement, and *This Is My Century: New and Collected Poems* (1989). Her well-known novel *Jubilee* (1966) describes the effects of the Civil War on a family in slavery; the book drew on her great-grandmother's memories of the period for its remarkable wealth of detail, as Walker records in *How I Wrote Jubilee* (1972). Among her other works are the biography *The Daemonic Genius of Richard Wright* (1982) and *Black Women and the Liberation Movements* (1981).

WALKER, Ted (Edward Joseph) (1934–), British poet, born in Lancing, Sussex, educated at St John's College, Cambridge. In 1962, with John *Cotton, he founded the magazine *Priapus*. His first full collection, *Fox on a Barn Door* (1965), rapidly established him as a formidable talent extending the tradition of English nature poetry. The essential landscapes of his work, the Sussex coastline and remote inland locations, were defined in this volume and have sustained much of his subsequent writing. Several further collections have included *The Solitaries* (1967), *Gloves to the Hangman* (1973), and *Burning the Ivy* (1978). Walker's poetry is capable of an economy and impact of imagery that make his treatments of the brutality he apprehends in nature disturbing and memorable. His earlier poetry was often tautly musical in its habitual use of strict forms, though sometimes an element of constraint ensued. After *The Night Bathers* (1970), his third collection, a more colloquial and discursive tone emerged in his writing. *Hands at a Live Fire: Selected Poems* appeared in 1987. *The High Path* (1982) is a prose work combining autobiography and Walker's impressions of his native West Sussex. He has also published a collection of short stories entitled *You've never Heard Me Sing* (1983), and written plays for television and radio. *The Last of England* (1992) is an autobiography.

WALLACE, (Richard Horatio) Edgar (1875–1932), British novelist, short-story writer, poet, and journalist, probably the most popular mystery and crime writer of all time. Born in Greenwich, the illegitimate son of an actor and actress, he was adopted by a fish porter, joined the army, and served in South Africa during the Boer War, writing war poetry and acting as a correspondent for Reuters and London newspapers. His first mystery and best-known work, *The Four Just Men* (1905), was promoted by a vast advertising campaign, and was followed by a stream of novels (173 in all), short stories, and plays; these earned him a fortune, yet he left vast debts when he died in Hollywood while working on the screenplay of *King Kong*. Much of his work is worthless: from it, however, can be singled out the novels *The Man Who Bought London* (1915), *The Tomb of Ts'in* (1916), *The Crimson Circle* (1922), and the short stories which feature J. G. Reeder, an original detective (*The Mind of Mr J. G. Reeder*, 1925; US title *The Murder Book of Mr J. G. Reeder*, and others), together with those set in West Africa (*Sanders of the River*, 1911, and others). See M. Lane, *Edgar Wallace: The Biography of a Phenomenon* (1938, revised 1964).

WALLACE-CRABBE, Chris(topher) (1934–), Australian poet, born in Richmond, Victoria, educated at the University of Melbourne. From 1965 to 1967 he was Fellow in Creative Writing at Yale University and subsequently taught at the University of Melbourne, where he became Professor of English in 1988. *The Music of Division* (1959), *In Light and Darkness* (1964), and *The Rebel General* (1967) established his reputation as one of the most valuable Australian poets of his generation, his accomplishment in conventional forms providing the basis for work of compassionate socio-political awareness and philosophical rigour. Further collections include *Selected Poems 1955–1972* (1973), *The Foundations of Joy* (1976), *The Amorous Cannibal* (1985), *For Crying out Loud* (1990), *Rungs of Time* (1993), and *Selected Poems, 1956–1994* (1995). The energetically experimental qualities in much of his later writing result from his stated interest in discovering 'how far lyrical, Dionysian impulses can be released without loss of intelligence'. Although his concerns are frequently abstract, his work remains rich in objective detail, much of it drawn from his natural surroundings in Australia. Among his works as a critic are the collections of essays *Melbourne or the Bush* (1973), *Toil and Spin* (1979), and *Falling into Language* (1990). His novel *Splinters* (1981) is set in Melbourne during the late 1960s and reflects the sense of cultural change prevalent at that time. As an editor his works include *The Golden Apples of the Sun: Twentieth Century Australian Poetry* (1980).

WALLANT, Edward Lewis (1926–62), American novelist, born in New Haven, Connecticut, educated at the University of Connecticut, at the Pratt Institute, and the New School for Social Research, New York. His first novel was *The Human Season* (1960), followed by *The Pawnbroker* (1961). His other two novels, *The Tenants of Moonbloom* (1963) and *The Children at the Gate* (1964), were published posthumously, following his early death from a coma brought on by a tumour. The keynote of Wallant's writing is his preoccupation with the ordinary characters who inhabit his fictional world, and whose native dignity survives their material impoverishment. Wallant's deep faith in the power of human bonding to overcome the tribulations of personal suffering is perhaps best reflected in *The Pawnbroker*, which was made into a highly successful film by Sidney Lumet in 1965. The eponymous pawnbroker is Solomon Nazerman, an emotionally anaesthetized survivor of the Nazi concentration camps. Against his desire for isolation from the mess of humanity, epitomized for him in the concentration camps, is his young assistant, Jesus Ortiz, whose 'volatile innocence' has a strange power to break through Sol's self-protective indifference to his customers. In a dramatic but unsentimental conclusion, in which Ortiz dies in the act of saving Sol's life, Sol is restored to a knowledge of human affections. The sombre mood of this novel is enlivened by the gaiety of a panoply of minor characters whose buoyant individualism attests to the power of human survival in a hostile world. *The Tenants of Moonbloom* reiterates these preoccupations in a more overtly comic vein.

WALMSLEY, Leo (Lionel) (1892–1966), British regional novelist, born in Shipley, West Yorkshire. His semi-autobiographical novels *Foreigners* (1935) and *The Sound of the Sea* (1959) are set in a fictional 'Bramblewick' which closely resembles Robin Hood's Bay in North Yorkshire where Walmsley spent much of his childhood. His service in East Africa during the First World War resulted in his war memoir, *Flying and Sport in East Africa* (1920). He is best known for his realistic novels about Yorkshire fishermen and their families, including *Phantom Lobster* (1933), *Sally Lunn* (1937, adapted for the stage by Walmsley in 1944), and, notably, *Three Fevers* (1932), which was filmed as *Turn of the Tide* (1936), the first picture made by J. Arthur Rank. His later novels, largely autobiographical, and deeply sensitive to landscape and seascape, include *Love in the Sun* (1939), *The Happy Ending* (1957), *Paradise Creek* (1963), and *Angler's Moon* (1965). *So Many Loves* (1944) is his autobiography. See Peter J. Woods, *The Honey-Gatherers: Leo Walmsley and the Autobiographical Novel* (1991).

WALPOLE, Sir Hugh (Seymour) (1884–1941), British novelist, born in New Zealand, educated at Emmanuel College, Cambridge, the son of a canon who became bishop of Edinburgh in 1910. Like E. M. *Forster he was a tutor to the children of Elizabeth *von Arnim; he also taught at a preparatory school for a short time, which provided the background for his novel *Mr. Perrin and Mr. Traill* (1911). His First World War experiences, serving with the Red Cross and with a British propaganda unit in Russia, were reflected in *The Dark Forest* (1916) and *The Secret City* (1919). A sequence of three stories about a young boy, beginning with *Jeremy* (1919), introduced the cathedral city of Polchester which provided the setting for *The Cathedral* (1922); it also showed the influence of Trollope about whom he wrote in *Anthony Trollope* (1928). A darker current emerged in his two fantastic horror thrillers, *The Old Ladies* (1924) and *Portrait of a Man with Red Hair: A Romantic Macabre* (1925). From 1924 Walpole lived in Cumberland, the setting of his

'Herries Chronicle' (*Rogue Herries*, 1930; *Judith Paris*, 1931; *The Fortress*, 1932; and *Vanessa*, 1933). As well as numerous novels he wrote critical works, plays and screenplays, and *Joseph Conrad* (1916, revised 1924). Walpole was a popular figure in literary circles of his time and a friend of Henry *James, but he was concerned that his work lacked the innovation of contemporary modernist writers such as his friend, V. *Woolf. There is a life by R. Hart-Davis (1952).

WALWICZ, Ania (1951–), Australian poet and playwright, born in Swidnica, Poland, she emigrated to Australia in 1963 and was educated at Melbourne's Victorian College of Arts and the University. She has been a writer-in-residence at Australian universities and is well-known for performances of her work. She is widely admired for her highly experimental poetry, which rejects the conventional structures of free-verse in favour of the prose-poem form, but creates energetic rhythms through patterns of grammatical and tonal recurrence. Walwicz's principal collections include *Writing* (1982), re-issued as *Travel/Writing* in 1989, *Boat* (1989), and *Red Roses* (1992). Her theatrical pieces include *Girlboytalk* (1986), *Dissecting Mice* (1989), and *Elegant* (1990).

WARNER, Marina (1946–), British cultural historian, novelist, and critic, born in London to an English father and an Italian mother, educated at Lady Margaret Hall, Oxford. Her first published work, *The Dragon Empress* (1972), a biography of Tzu Hsi of China, was praised for its lavishly detailed recreation of a significant period of Chinese history. With *Alone of All Her Sex: The Myth and Cult of the Virgin Mary* (1976), Warner initiated a feminist project of studying the mythology, symbolism, allegories, and icons surrounding the feminine in history; this innovative work combined analyses of religion and history with art and literary criticism. Two further studies of male mythologization of the feminine were *Joan of Arc: The Image of Female Heroism* (1981) and *Monuments and Maidens: The Allegory of the Female Form* (1985). Her work has been praised for its erudition and its adventurous reinterpretation of female symbolism. Her novels *In a Dark Wood* (1977) and *The Skating Party* (1983) reflect the concern with legend and folklore displayed in her works of non-fiction. Her most successful novel, *The Lost Father* (1988), set in Southern Italy in the opening decades of the century, was inspired by Warner's own Italian heritage. The central figure, Anna, is an archivist collecting material on her enigmatic grandfather, whose slow decline, caused by a bullet lodged in his skull in the aftermath of an atavistic duel, can be read as a metaphor for the corruption of Italian politics during the Fascist regime. References to opera, legend, and history permeate this opulent work which has been compared to the Italian masterpiece *The Leopard*, by Lampedusa, for its conflation of history and political analysis with adventurous romance. Shakespeare is the inspiration for the dense and highly ambitious *Indigo* (1992); this rewrites the characters and archetypes of *The Tempest* in order to explore the terrain of Caribbean history and the guilt-laden legacy of empire from a perspective of post-colonial theoretical insight. The short fictions of *The Mermaid in the Basement* (1993) look at the feminine through figures from myths both popular and classical, and particularly from the Old Testament, in the light of deconstructivist critical theory. Warner's preoccupations with the power of myth, fable, and fairytale, and the complicity of women in their creation, are again evident in *Wonder Tales* (1994), a collection of French *contes* introduced and edited by Warner, and in the multi-faceted essay *From the Beast to the Blonde* (1994).

WARNER, Rex (1905–86), British poet, novelist, and translator, born in Gloucestershire, educated at Wadham College, Oxford. Much of Warner's *Poems* of 1937 was in recognizable alignment with the more declamatory writing of W. H. *Auden and C. *Day Lewis, whom he met at Oxford; in 'Light and Air' his political beliefs were inextricably linked to his vision of the benign energies of nature. Other poems related to his experiences of Egypt or formed celebratory studies of ornithic subjects. In the revised edition entitled *Poems and Contradictions* (1945), the 'Contradictions' sonnet sequence constitutes an intricate exposition of the elemental power of love. Warner's best-known novels show the influence of Kafka, particularly in their use of parable and symbolic action. *The Wild Goose Chase* (1937) contains an allegorical presentation of fascism in the form of a rugger match of which the outcome has already been decided; *The Professor* (1938), set in Central Europe, concerns a liberal humanist professor unable to challenge fascist forces, and resembles Stephen *Spender's verse play *Trial of a Judge* (1938); and *The Aerodrome: A Love Story* (1941) is an allegory of fascism set in an English village. Warner also translated Aeschylus, Euripides, Plutarch, and George Seferis, among others.

WARNER, Sylvia Townsend (1893–1978), British novelist and poet, born in Harrow where her father was a schoolmaster at Harrow School. Her first published work was a volume of poems, *The Espalier* (1925), and she continued to write verse throughout her life; *Collected Poems* appeared in 1982. She is best known as a writer of prose fiction. Her first novel, *Lolly Willows* (1926), the story of a witch who makes an uneasy pact with the devil, achieved great success for its whimsical mood, eliciting comparisons with the fictions of David *Garnett and T. F. *Powys. Warner's next two novels were *Mr Fortune's Maggot* (1927), a fable of the encounter of Christianity with paganism in the South Seas, with marked homoerotic undertones; and *The True Heart* (1929), a reworking of the myth of Cupid and Psyche in a Victorian setting. The underlying seriousness of her vision was scarcely perceived until the publication of *Summer Will Show* (1936), set in 1848 against the backdrop of the two revolutions in Paris. The story of the relationship of two women, an aristocratic Englishwoman and her husband's Jewish mistress, the novel reaches its climax in the conversion of the former to communism and reflects Warner's own growing belief in Marxist theory and ideology. Her political commitment also inspired *After the Death of Don Juan* (1938), which the author intended as an allegory of the rise of fascism in Franco's Spain. Appropriating the Molière play and the Mozart opera for its own ends, the novel is a celebration of the tragic beauty of Spain and a testament to the eternal struggle of the peasantry against exploitation by ruthless landlords. Less explicitly motivated by politics, but equally concerned with history, were *The Corner that Held Them* (1948), set entirely in a fourteenth-century Benedictine convent, and *The Flint Anchor* (1954), the story of a merchant and his family in nineteenth-century Yorkshire, inspired in part by Warner's family history. Warner was also a highly skilled and acclaimed writer of short stories, most of which appeared in *The *New Yorker*. In her last years she wrote a short series of narratives about elves, collected in the volume *Kingdoms of Elfin* (1977). A representative selection of her short fiction appeared as *Selected Stories* in 1988. Sylvia Townsend Warner's *Letters* (1982) are a testament to both her talent and her gift for friendship, which illuminates her work. She is the subject of a biography by Claire Harman (1989), who also edited her diaries (1994).

War Poetry; although poetic treatments of armed conflict have been written at almost every stage in the history of English literature, the term is taken to denote work produced in response to the First and Second World Wars. Furthermore, 'war poetry' most typically arises from active experience of battle and other aspects of military life, and does not, therefore, include a poem like *Binyon's 'For the Fallen', despite its firmness of relation to warfare. The most distinguished poetry of the First World War, written by Wilfred *Owen, Siegfried *Sassoon, Robert *Graves, Isaac *Rosenberg, and Edmund *Blunden, is also noted for its emphatic realism; this characteristic, most obvious in the gruesome physical details of slaughter in, for example, Owen's 'Dulce Et Decorum Est', constituted a conscious repudiation of the idealistic poetry of the war exemplified by the verse of Rupert *Brooke, which had been feverishly acclaimed in 1915. Charles Hamilton *Sorley was among the first to react in opposition to Brooke's famous sonnets. After the futile carnage on the Somme in 1916 Sassoon produced many poems whose documentary qualities were intended to disabuse the public of the attitudes he believed were prolonging the war; although the work was not enthusiastically received in Britain, it had widespread influence on his fellow poets. These developments forced a breach with the sedate conventions of *Georgian poetry, the prevailing poetic mode of the time, with which many of the war poets had been associated. The investment of emotion and imagination in celebrations of the English countryside in the work of the Georgians was continuous with the patriotic sentiment of the poetry written in the early years of the war; the aggressive realism and hostility towards the institutions of nationalism in the wartime and post-war writings of Sassoon, Graves, and others contributed significantly to the major changes in the literary climate between 1910 and 1930.

Brian Gardner's *Up the Line to Death* (1964), featuring work by seventy-two poets, is the best of numerous anthologies of the poetry of the First World War; *The Terrible Rain* (1966), in which 119 poets of the Second World War are represented, is also edited by Gardner, who states in his introduction: 'The First War produced the greater poetry: but there is a great deal more good poetry of the Second War.' No radical changes of poetic orientation were precipitated by the conflict of 1939–45; the fact that the poets brought few patriotic illusions to their experiences as soldiers was part of their inheritance from their predecessors in the Great War. Rather than having to evolve new idioms to replace a stock of defunct conventions, they had a range of possibilities at their disposal as a result of the impact of *Modernism and the ethos of experimentation that had permeated the 1930s. Keith *Douglas wrote a number of the most striking poems of active service, the extreme lucidity and concentration of his style constituting an idiosyncratic technical advance. The reputations of Alun *Lewis, Hamish *Henderson, John *Pudney, and Sidney *Keyes are also largely based upon the poetry they produced during the war. Certain works by Dylan *Thomas, Edith *Sitwell, Louis *MacNeice, and others are immediately classifiable as war poems for the force with which they register the atmospheres and emotions of the air-raids. Many of the finest poets of both world wars died on active service, often, as was the case with Owen, Rosenberg, Douglas, and Lewis, shortly after their talents had begun to mature; what they might have gone on to achieve remains the saddest imponderable in English literature. See also *The Oxford Book of War Poetry* (1984), edited by Jon *Stallworthy.

WARREN, Robert Penn (1905–89), American poet and novelist, born in Guthrie, Kentucky, educated at Vanderbilt University, where he was a student of John Crowe *Ransom's, the University of California, and Oxford University. After holding a succession of posts at American universities, he became Professor of English at Yale in 1962. His metaphorically elaborate early verse in *Thirty Six Poems* (1936) and *Eleven Poems on the Same Theme* (1942) displays considerable formal accomplishment. He published little further poetry until *Promises* (1957; Pulitzer Prize). The book initiated the use of the free forms and conversational idioms characterizing his numerous later collections, which include *You, Emperors, and Others* (1960), *Incarnations* (1968), *Now and Then* (1978; Pulitzer Prize), *Chief Joseph of the Nez Perce* (1983), and *New and Selected Poems* (1985). He described his methods as 'moralized anecdote', revealing his deeply ambivalent regard for the American South through the ironic narratives on which many poems are based. Powerful effects are achieved through his imaginative uses of natural imagery to suggest primal qualities in the human psyche. His career as a novelist began with *Night Rider* (1939), based on the 'tobacco war' in Kentucky in the 1900s; the treatment of financial power and ethical negligence in *At Heaven's Gate* (1943) anticipated the study of political corruption in the highly successful *All the King's Men* (1946), which received a Pulitzer Prize, making Warren the only author to have earned the award for both poetry and fiction. His other novels include *Band of Angels* (1955), in which the theme of miscegenation extends into a searching examination of personal and racial identity, and *A Place to Come* (1977), which voices his elegiac sense of irreversible change in his native region through the retrospection of an ageing scholar. With Cleanth *Brooks, he was co-author of several critical studies, notably *Understanding Poetry* (1938) and *Understanding Fiction* (1943), which promulgated the *New Criticism. His many other works include *The Legacy of the Civil War* (1961), an assessment of the enduring sociocultural effects of the conflict. In 1986 he became the first Poet Laureate of the United States.

WASHINGTON, Booker T(aliaferro) (1856–1915), African-American leader and writer, born in Hale's Ford, Franklin County, Virginia, educated at Hampton Institute, Virginia, and Wayland Seminary, Washington, DC. Washington was born on a Virginia plantation, the son of a slave woman and an unidentified white slave-owner; in his autobiography, *Up from Slavery* (1901), he recalls in the first chapter the years of his childhood and, in particular, the occasion in 1865 when, at the end of the Civil War, the Emancipation Proclamation was read to the assembled family of slaves and slave-owners. At the end of the Civil War he moved with his mother and stepfather to Malden, West Virginia, where he attended elementary school and was employed as a domestic servant. It was with his 500-mile journey to Hampton Institute in Virginia, a school expressly established for the education of Southern black children, that Washington began his remarkable rise to prominence in American political life. In 1881 he moved to Tuskegee Normal School in Alabama and by 1893 had become principal of the school, now renamed as the Tuskegee Institute. In 1895 he came to national attention when he addressed the Atlanta Exposition; his speech, which later became known as 'The Atlanta Compromise', spoke a nineteenth-century gospel of thrift, industry, and self-help, but it is the conciliatory approach to black–white relations with its implicit acceptance of the doctrine of segregation and the social inferiority of the black American that attracted much attention, and later black leaders and intellectuals were openly critical of Washington's position. However, the position advocated had just the effect on the white audience that he had intended. He was later a guest at a dinner given by President Theodore Roosevelt, received honorary degrees from Dartmouth College and Harvard University for his services to black America, and by the time of his death was known as the 'Moses of his race'. In 1900 Washington recounted his life story for *Outlook* magazine, and the serialization became the basis for his most famous work, *Up from Slavery*. In addition he wrote a biography of Frederick Douglass, *Frederick Douglass* (1907), *The Story of the Negro* (1909), and many other works. The definitive biography is that of Louis R. Harlan in two volumes, *Booker T. Washington: The Making of a Black Leader, 1856–1901* (1972) and *Booker T. Washington: The Wizard of Tuskegee, 1901–1915* (1983).

WASSERSTEIN, Wendy (1950–), American playwright, born and raised in New York City, educated at the City College of New York, and Yale School of Drama. During the late 1970s and 1980s Wasserstein produced her plays in off- and off-off-Broadway venues. Her early work, in which she experimented with chronology, language, and form, showed her at her most innovative. *Uncommon Women and Others* (1975) is a compelling work about a reunion of five college friends; the scene moves between 1978, the year they meet, and the year they graduate, shifting through various conversations as they attempt to reconcile their present with their past. She came to prominence with *The Heidi Chronicles* (1989; Pulitzer Prize) which centres on an art historian and her imaginary visits to the many people who have influenced her life; the play examines Heidi's disenchantment with the progressive women's movement, charting its history through the 1970s and early 1980s. Her other works include *When Dinah Shore Ruled the Earth* (1975; with Christopher Durang), *Isn't It Romantic* (1981), *Tender Offer* (1983), and *The Sisters Rosenweig* (1993), which is reminiscent of Chekhov's *The Three Sisters*. *Bachelor Girls* (1990) is a collection of essays.

Waste Land, The, T. S. *Eliot's most celebrated work, first published in the **Criterion* in 1922; later that year an edition was produced in New York, to which notes were added to clarify allusions to or quotations from the works of some thirty-five authors, among them Ovid, Dante, Shakespeare, Marvell, and Baudelaire. The notes indicate the importance to Eliot's conception of J. L. Weston's *From Ritual to Romance* (1920). In discussing the Grail legend, Weston refers to the realm of the Fisher King as the 'Waste Land', arid and sterile as a result of the sexual wound he has sustained; the Fisher King is identifiable at several points in the poem, which projects a vision of a moribund culture whose pathology is primarily sexual in its causes and symptoms. 'The Fire Sermon', the third section, presents a series of corrupt or futile sexual relationships observed by the hermaphroditic figure of Tiresias, to whom the notes accord central significance; his incomplete masculinity gives him some equivalence to the Fisher King. The view that the work has its roots in Eliot's gravely unsatisfactory relations with his first wife is supported by his statement in the first volume of his *Letters* (edited by V. Eliot, 1988) that 'To her the marriage brought no happiness . . . to me, it brought the state of mind out of which came *The Waste Land*'. The poem's five parts, 'The Burial of the Dead', 'A Game of Chess', 'The Fire

Sermon', 'Death by Water', and 'What the Thunder Said', combine impressionistic juxtaposition, precisely evocative imagery, and powerful effects of language to present a succession of episodes suggestive of cultural collapse and spiritual sterility. The first and final sections enclose the whole within their vividly symbolic renderings of 'the dead land'; the apocalyptic conclusion suggests possibilities of divinely ordained regeneration and looks forward to the religious tenor of Eliot's later verse in its adaptations of events from the Gospels. *The Waste Land*'s continuities of mood, imagery, and poetic texture give it a cohesion independent of narrative or thematic progression; F. R. *Leavis noted that 'The unity the poem aims at is that of an inclusive consciousness: the organization it achieves . . . may, by analogy, be called musical'. For many, *The Waste Land* forms the definitive expression of the bitter disillusionment and widespread sense of cultural failure that followed the First World War; Eliot, however, preferred to regard it as 'the relief of a personal and wholly insignificant grouse against life . . . just a piece of rhythmical grumbling'; the statement is taken from *The Waste Land: A Facsimile and Transcript* (edited by V. Eliot, 1971), which presents the original text of the poem along with the many suggestions for changes and excisions made by Ezra *Pound, whose advice Eliot followed in drastically abridging the work for publication. Pound's remark that it was 'About enough . . . to make the rest of us shut up shop' anticipated the enormous impact of *The Waste Land* as the exemplary work of poetic *Modernism and the most enduringly compelling poem of the twentieth century for succeeding generations of critics and general readers.

WATERHOUSE, Keith (Spencer) (1929–), British novelist, playwright, and journalist, born in Leeds, educated at Osmondthorpe Council School. During the Second World War he served in the Royal Air Force. A prolific and seemingly effortless craftsman, mordant farce is his *métier*. His first novel, *There Is a Happy Land* (1957), typifies his irreverent response to life; a boy plays at being blind, drunk, or maimed, mimics all elders, and delights in impudence or in embarrassing adults. He is best known for *Billy Liar* (1959), which he successfully adapted for the stage and the cinema; typically anarchic and fantastical, it is simultaneously a paean to and an attack on parochial England. It was followed by a sequel, *Billy Liar on the Moon* (1975). In subsequent novels, *The Bucket Shop* (1968), *Office Life* (1978), and *Maggie Muggins* (1981), London is the dominant milieu, a world of anonymity where people are drifters, and where redundancy and alcoholism are tests of survival. More recently he has published *Unsweet Charity* (1992). Recognized as an authority on correct usage, he was a member of the Kingman Committee on the Teaching of the English Language, and is the author of influential books on newspaper style, including *Waterhouse on Newspaper Style* (1989), and *English Our English* (1991), a lively book on correct usage. *Sharon and Tracy and the Rest* (1992) is a collection of his columns for the *Daily Mail*. *City Lights: A Street Life* (1994) and *Streets Ahead* (1995) are autobiographies.

Waterland, see SWIFT, GRAHAM.

WATERMAN, Andrew (1940–), British poet, born in London, educated at Leicester and Oxford Universities. His collections of poems include *The Living Room* (1974), *From the Other Country* (1977), *Over the Wall* (1980), *Out for the Elements* (1981), *Selected Poems* (1986), and *In the Planetarium* (1990). The long title poem of *Out for the Elements* has been regarded as his finest single work; Waterman succeeds in making this imaginative itinerary through England and Ireland the vehicle for a rich fusion of personal reflections on the cultural condition of contemporary Britain. His writing frequently sustains a vigorous spoken idiom within precisely crafted arrangements of rhyme and metre. His residence in Northern Ireland, as lecturer at the New University of Ulster, Coleraine, has given rise to some penetrating commentaries on sectarian and political aspects of the Province. A keen chess player, he edited the anthology *The Poetry of Chess* (1982).

WATKINS, Vernon (Phillips) (1906–67), Welsh poet, born in Maesteg, Glamorgan, educated at Repton School. He left Cambridge after one year at Magdalene College and worked at a bank in Cardiff until he underwent a severe breakdown. He described this interlude as a 'revolution of sensibility' and determined to devote himself as a poet to 'the conquest of time'. From this intention stems the cohesiveness of his *œuvre* as a sustained celebration of the imperishable essences of experience. Two years later he resumed his duties as a bank clerk in Swansea, where he remained, refusing promotion, until his retirement in 1965. He subsequently travelled widely as a lecturer and died while playing tennis in Seattle. His numerous collections of verse include *The Ballad of the Mari Lwyd* (1941), *The Lady with the Unicorn* (1948), *The Death Bell* (1954), *Cyprus and Acacia* (1959), and *Affinities* (1963). The visionary emphasis in his poetry led to his association with the writers of the *New Apocalypse in the 1940s; his lucid neo-Platonism and fluent accomplishment in traditional forms was distinct, however, from the undisciplined tendencies of that movement, as Philip *Larkin noted in his contribution to *Vernon Watkins, 1906–1967* (edited by Leslie *Norris, 1970). While many of his poems are rooted in immediate perceptual experience, his work frequently invokes Welsh history and mythology, most notably in his recurrent adoptions of the persona of Taliesin, who provides a mouthpiece for his metaphysical view of poetry in 'Taliesin and the Spring of Vision'. His *Collected Poems*, edited by Ruth Pryor, appeared in 1986. Among the translations he produced is *The North Sea* (1955), his version of two sequences by Heine. His long friendship with Dylan *Thomas, whom he commemorated in the elegy 'A True Picture Restored', is recorded in *Dylan Thomas: Letters to Vernon Watkins* (1957).

WATMOUGH, David (1926–), Canadian novelist, born in London, educated at King's College, University of London. He grew up on a farm in Cornwall, leaving Britain in the late 1940s for Paris, New York, San Francisco, and finally Vancouver. He writes that his 'persistent literary impulse probably derives from a Cornish / Celtic youthful pre-occupation with familial unity, plus the further impetus coming from a sexually marginalized man who still thinks "family"'. All his fiction, from the early collections *Love and the Waiting Game* (1975) and *From a Cornish Landscape* (1975) onwards, is concerned with the pressures exerted by conflicting relationships between individuals. His work has been described by critics as conforming with a wider trend in Canadian writing towards domestic social realism. *The Time of the Kingfishers* (1994), which is set against Vancouver's changing social and cultural landscape, concentrates on the lives of three markedly different couples, all approaching middle age, as they discuss their lives together. His autobiographical work *Thy Mother's Glass* (1992) traces forty years in the life of Davey Bryant, and slowly unveils Davey's gay identity while navigating the fraught love that exists between a mother and a son who don't understand each other. From childhood in Cornwall, and travels through Europe, the Middle East, and South Africa, he finally ends up in San Francisco on the eve of Stonewall, the riot that sparked the Gay Liberation movement.

WATSON, Colin (1920–82), British crime writer and journalist, born in Croydon; he wrote a number of richly comic satires of contemporary English life in the form of detective stories set in the imaginary East Anglian town of Flaxborough, beginning with *Coffin, Scarcely Used* (1958). The best is possibly *The Flaxborough Crab* (1969; US title *Just What the Doctor Ordered*), but *Bump in the Night* (1960), *Lonelyheart 4122* (1967), and *Broomsticks over Flaxborough* (1972; US title *Kissing Covens*) are also excellent. Watson is also the author of *Snobbery with Violence* (1971; revised 1979), a study of twentieth-century crime fiction.

WATSON, Ian (1943–), British *science fiction writer, born in North Shields, Northumberland, educated at Balliol College, Oxford. Among the most intellectually adventurous practitioners of the genre, Watson's work has been compared to that of O. *Stapledon and A. C. *Clarke. In his first and best-known novel, *The Embedding* (1973), an analysis of the meaning of language unites three separate plots into one complex argument. *The Jonah Kit* (1975) uses the transcendent suicide of the planet's whales as its climax. His other works include *The Martian Inca* (1977), *Deathhunter* (1981), *The Book of the River* (1984), *Whores of Babylon* (1988), *The Fire Worm* (1988), *Lucky's Harvest* (1993), and *The Fallen Moon* (1994). Of his several story collections, the most engaging and memorable are perhaps *The Very Slow Time Machine* (1979), *Salvage Rites* (1989), and *The Coming of Vertumnus* (1994).

WATSON, Sheila (1909–), Canadian novelist, born in New Westminster near Vancouver, educated at the Universities of British Columbia and Toronto. Her doctorate, on Wyndham *Lewis, was supervised by Marshall *McLuhan. Watson's experience teaching in the Cariboo region of the British Columbia interior provided the basis for her highly acclaimed novel *The Double Hook* (1959), sometimes described as the first modern Canadian novel; it is a complex archetypal work, which intersperses Biblical echoes with Western Canadian Indian mythology, particularly in the use of the trickster figure of Coyote, and blends the conventions of folk tale and modernist fiction. Notable for its fragmentary, elliptical narrative method and absence of authorial moral commentary, the novel nevertheless works as a quasi-religious allegory about the redemptive power of community and communion. Watson's only other work is a volume of *Four Stories* (1979) and an individually published story, 'And the Four Animals' (1980), a remarkably wide-ranging but concise fable about the genesis of faith and cultural transformation. Her influence has been acknowledged by several later Canadian writers, including Robert *Kroetsch and Rudy *Wiebe.

WATSON, Sir (John) William (1858–1935), British poet, born at Burley-in-Wharfedale, Yorkshire; he grew up near Liverpool. Two volumes of verse, *Prince's Quest* (1880) and *Epigrams of Art, Life, and Nature* (1884), preceded his move to London, where he established himself as a literary journalist. *Wordsworth's Grave* (1891), the title piece of which is arguably his best poem, gained him wide notice, and *Lachrymae Musarum* (1892), his elegies on the death of Tennyson, made him the favourite of the literary establishment of the day. The moral rectitude of his verse gained him acclaim as a champion of the traditional poetic virtues threatened by the decadent poets of the 1890s, towards whom he was publicly hostile. He was firmly proposed for the laureateship, but became ineligible as a result of untoward behaviour during a severe breakdown in 1892. He regained his standing in 1894 with *Odes and Other Poems*, which included the accomplished 'Vita Nuova', expressing gratitude for his recovery. *The Year of Shame* (1896), a versified critique of British foreign policy, and *For England* (1903), for which he was accused of voicing 'Pro-Boer' sentiments, made him a figure of controversy. He was knighted in 1917, allegedly as a result of good personal relations with Lloyd George. His espousal of Irish independence in *Ireland Unfreed* (1919) sustained his reputation for contention. A collected edition of his verse appeared in 1936. Jean Moorcroft Wilson's critical biography *I Was an English Poet* was published in 1982.

WATTEN, Barrett (1948–), American poet, born in Berkeley, educated at M.I.T., *Iowa Writers' Workshop, and at Berkeley. He became editor of *This* press, which produced a magazine and books that helped shape the development of *Language Poetry in the

1970s and early 1980s, and of *Poetics Journal* with Lyn *Hejinian, a key opportunity for theoretical and critical writing on the aesthetics and politics of the new poetry. His collection of essays *Total Syntax* (1985) helped trace the sources of Language Poetry in earlier avant-gardes, including Surrealism, Russian formalism, and the artists of the 1960s, particularly Robert Smithson and the Art-Language group. This book and his other essays and interviews present some of the most original thinking about self-expression, form, and the relations between public and private spheres in contemporary poetics. Like other West Coast Language Poets his poetic texts employ disjunct sentences and clauses as units whose complex relations form the structure of the work. A philosophical and political meditation on language emerges in witty epigrams, images, and structures in such books as *1–10* (1980), *Progress* (1985), *Conduit* (1988), and *Under Erasure* (1991). After working as a managing editor for *Representations* for some years he then became a professor of English at Wayne State University, Detroit.

WAUGH, Alec (Alexander Raban) (1898–1981), English novelist, born in London, educated at Sherborne School, Dorset, which provided the background for his first novel, *The Loom of Youth* (1917), which caused a scandal for its allusions to homosexuality in a public school. This novel and *Three Score and Ten* (1929), also about schoolboys, later provoked Wyndham *Lewis's attack on Waugh and others in *The Doom of Youth* (1932), which had to be withdrawn due to libel threats. Alec Waugh was considerably more liberal-minded than his elder brother, Evelyn *Waugh. His greatest critical and commercial success, *Island in the Sun* (1956), set in the West Indies, was made into a film starring Harry Belafonte. Later works include *A Spy in the Family* (1970), 'an erotic comedy', and *The Fatal Gift* (1973). Waugh's many autobiographical works include *Myself when Young* (1923), *The Early Years of Alec Waugh* (1962), and *The Best Wine Last* (1978).

WAUGH, Auberon (Alexander) (1939–), British journalist, critic, and novelist, born in Somerset, the eldest son of Evelyn *Waugh, educated at Downside School and Oxford University. His lasting antagonism towards the British public school system is expressed in his amusing first novel, *The Foxglove Saga* (1960). He wrote three further satirical novels, *Path of Dalliance* (1963), about Oxford in the 1950s; *Who Are the Violets Now?* (1965), about Fleet Street; and *Consider the Lilies* (1968), his best and funniest novel, about an agnostic rural clergyman with a difficult wife. His career as a journalist began in 1960 with the *Daily Telegraph*, after which he joined the Mirror Group as a 'special writer'. In 1967 he became political correspondent of the **Spectator*; he was dismissed from this post in 1970 by the editor, Nigel Lawson, and won an action for wrongful dismissal. Since then he has worked variously as columnist, reviewer, and polemicist on several journals and newspapers including *The Times*, *Private Eye*, the *New Statesman*, the *Evening Standard*, and the *Independent*. In 1986 he became editor of the **Literary Review*.

WAUGH, Evelyn (Arthur St John) (1903–66), English novelist, born in Hampstead, London, the second son of the publisher and literary critic Arthur Waugh, and brother of Alec *Waugh. He was educated at Lancing and at Hertford College, Oxford, where he read Modern History and cultivated an outrageous persona; through his friendship with H. *Acton, he was drawn into a literary and artistic circle which included C. *Connolly, A. *Powell, H. Yorke (Henry *Green), and the celebrated aesthete B. Howard (later portrayed as Ambrose Silk in *Put Out More Flags* and as Anthony Blanche in **Brideshead Revisited*). He left Oxford with a third-class degree and worked as a schoolmaster for a time, which he loathed. His first published work, a life of Dante Gabriel Rossetti (1927), was followed by his highly successful first novel, **Decline and Fall* (1928), which portrayed, in the character of Paul Pennyfeather, an innocent caught up in the decadent games of fashionable London society. In 1928 he married Evelyn Gardner but the couple were divorced in 1930, the year in which Waugh was received into the Catholic Church. **Vile Bodies* (1930) pursued his fascination with the hedonism and amorality of the 'Bright Young Things'. The novels of this period are Waugh's *Comedie Humaine*, capturing the brittle cynicism of the post-war generation and containing some memorably flamboyant characters. They include *Black Mischief* (1932), written after a trip to Africa (about which Waugh also published a travel book, *Remote People*, in 1931), which introduced the unscrupulous figure of Basil Seal, a dilettante and adventurer, who becomes embroiled in the politics of an imaginary African country; *A *Handful of Dust* (1934), perhaps his darkest work; and **Scoop* (1938), his comic account of Fleet Street corruption, based on Waugh's experiences as a war correspondent during the Italian invasion of Abyssinia in the 1930s, about which he also wrote in his collection of essays *Waugh in Abyssinia* (1936). Other travel writings include his account of a trip to the Mediterranean, *Labels* (1930), and his description of a journey through South America, *Ninety-Two Days* (1934). In 1937 he married Laura Herbert, a cousin of his first wife, and established himself as a man of property at Piers Court in Gloucestershire and later at Combe Florey in Somerset. In 1938 the first of his six children was born. With the outbreak of war in 1939 Waugh was commissioned as an officer in the Royal Marines, later transferring to the Royal Horse Guards, in which he served in the Middle East and Yugoslavia. *Put Out More Flags* (1942), which is set in London in the early months of the war, offers a valediction to the glamorous, if shallow, world depicted in the early novels. Perhaps his most famous evocation of the *fin de siècle* mood of the period appears in *Brideshead Revisited* (1945). His later novels also include *The Loved One* (1948), a macabre comedy about Californian funeral practices, and *The Ordeal of Gilbert Pinfold* (1957), about the terrifying paranoid delusions suffered by a middle-aged Catholic novelist on a Pacific cruise. The latter novel is Waugh's most self-revealing work of fiction, although a more complete picture of the man emerges from his *Diaries* (1976; edited by M. Davie) and his *Letters* (1980; edited by M. Amory). His wartime experiences were chronicled in the **Sword of Honour* trilogy, which appeared in 1965 and was originally published as *Men at Arms* (1952), *Officers and Gentlemen* (1955), and *Unconditional Surrender* (1961). Waugh's character, in his later years, was increasingly that of the irascible reactionary, renowned as much for the crusty anti-egalitarianism of his views as for his fiction. His novels offer a more subtle range of ideas; whilst they are, on one level, an excoriation of the follies of literary London between the wars, they are also a celebration of it. His other works include a collection of short stories, *Work Suspended* (1943), and the autobiographical sketch *A Little Learning* (1964), which deals with his childhood and youth at Oxford.

WAUGH, Harriet (1944–), British novelist, born in Somerset, the daughter of Evelyn *Waugh. She has worked as a publisher's reader and written several distinctive and original blackly comic novels of domestic intrigue among affluent middle-class families. Her first, *Mirror, Mirror* (1973), described by Timothy *Mo as 'a very fine piece of black fantasy', was followed by others including *Mother's Footsteps* (1978), which portrays, with ironic twists of plot, a feckless mother-in-law who is detested by both her daughter (herself constantly on the edge of a nervous breakdown) and her highly conventional, but devious, son-in-law. *Kate's House* (1983) is a *tour de force* in its portrayal of a peculiarly malevolent 4-year-old, who succeeds in manipulating, in fantastic manner, all the characters in the novel.

Waves, The, a novel by V. *Woolf, published in 1931. It takes as far as possible her method of expressing character and states of mind through a poetic language of recurrent images and rhythmical repetitions. It traces the lives of a group of friends (Bernard, Susan, Rhoda, Neville, Jinny, and Louis) from childhood to late middle age. Each character speaks his or her thoughts in a formalized direct speech, stylistically undifferentiated but each consisting of recognizable patterns of images, preoccupations, and turns of phrase. Bernard is the writer, Susan is rural and maternal, Jinny is sensual, Rhoda is lonely and unstable, Louis is a solitary businessman, Neville is a homosexual. 'Factual' information (Susan marries a farmer, Louis and Rhoda are lovers for a time) is given less prominence than their states of mind. The 'speech' of the characters is intercut with italicized sections of lyrical prose describing the rising and sinking of a near-allegorical sun (which keeps pace with their lives) over a seascape of waves and shore. The long last section is spoken by Bernard to an imaginary listener, the reader. There is one additional character, Percival, who does not 'speak'. He is the focus for all the characters' desires and ambitions, and, because of his early death in India, for their fears and defiance of death and mortality.

Way of All Flesh, The, Samuel *Butler's semi-autobiographical novel, published posthumously in 1903. Butler began the work in 1873 and had completed his last revisions by 1884. He chose to leave it unpublished during his lifetime, chiefly because it displays what Robert *Bridges termed 'his bitter onesided almost venomous regard for his own family'; in doing so, it functions on a more general level as a revelation of the subtly sadistic hypocrisy and stifling conventionality of middle-class Victorian family life. The early chapters deal with the family background and childhood of the chief protagonist, Ernest Pontifex, whose unhappiness under his parents' regime of punitive harshness and repressive religious zeal closely resembled Butler's own. In accordance with his father's wishes, Ernest is ordained as an Anglican minister; socially and sexually naïve, he makes a disastrous pass at a respectable woman during a pastoral visit, as a result of which he is imprisoned for indecent assault. A violent breach with his social and familial conditioning thus effected, he makes a bad marriage and runs a second-hand clothes shop in London. He is released from his circumstances when his alcoholic wife's bigamy is disclosed and his Aunt Alethea, the only member of his family of whom he was fond, leaves him £70,000. Ernest retires to a cynically atheistic bachelorhood and occupies himself with writing. George Bernard *Shaw, E. M. *Forster, Leonard *Woolf, John *Galsworthy, H. G. *Wells, and Lytton *Strachey were among those who led the gradual recognition of *The Way of All Flesh* as a novel of the first importance.

Weather in the Streets, The, see LEHMANN, ROSAMOND.

WEBB, Beatrice (Martha) (1858–1943) and Sidney (James) (1859–1947), British writers on sociology and political reform. Beatrice, née Potter, born in Standish, Gloucester, was encouraged in her intellectual development by Herbert Spencer (1820–1903), a friend of her wealthy family. She witnessed conditions among the poor while collecting rents on family properties in London and assisted Charles Booth (1840–1916) with research for *Life and Labour of the People of London* (17 volumes, 1891–1902). The son of a shopkeeper, Sidney was born in London and educated at the City of London College; he was a civil servant from 1878 to 1892, the year in which he married Beatrice and became a member of London County Council. Both were energetic members of the *Fabian Society. *The History of Trade Unionism* (1894) initiated their prolific collaboration as writers, which, with their political activities, was a major factor in the development of the Labour Party and the formulation of its policies. Among their many publications are *Industrial Democracy* (2 volumes, 1897), *The State and the Doctor* (1910), *The Decay of Capitalist Civilization* (1923), and *English Local Government* (9 volumes, 1906–29). They were closely involved in the founding of the London School of Economics in 1895 and of the *New Statesman in 1913. H. G. *Wells, with whom they had a long association, unflatteringly based the self-regarding Baileys of *The *New Machiavelli* (1911) on the Webbs. Sidney became Lord Passfield in 1929 after some years as a Member of Parliament. Beatrice produced two volumes of autobiography entitled *My Apprenticeship* (1926) and *Our Partnership* (1948); N. and J. Mackenzie edited her *Diary* (4 volumes, 1982–6). *Beatrice and Sidney Webb, Fabian Socialists* by Lisanne Radice appeared in 1984.

WEBB, Francis (1925–73), Australian poet, born in Adelaide, educated at Sydney University. Webb later moved to Canada, then to England where he suffered his first mental breakdown. His subsequent attempts to overcome schizophrenia and to resolve questions of identity are reflected in many of his poems in which, with his combination of surrealist imagery and religious intensity, he created powerful lyrical effects. *A Drum for Ben Boyd* (1948) is a sequence of linked poems in which a merchant adventurer is celebrated; *Leichardt in Theatre* (1948) focused on an eccentric explorer and his spiritual search. The title poem in *Birthday* (1953) is a verse-drama about the final days of Adolf Hitler in the Berlin bunker; another poem deals with Francis of Assisi. In his later poetry, Webb explores the role of the artist and considers his own experiences as a psychiatric patient. *Socrates and Other Poems* (1961) and *The Ghost of Cock Walk* (1964) contain some of his most innovative and eloquent work. His *Collected Poems* (1969) assured his reputation. Webb considerably influenced the development of Australian poetry during the 1960s and 1970s.

WEBB, Mary, née Meredith (1881–1927), British novelist and poet, born in Shropshire, where she spent most of her life and which she celebrated in her novels; she was educated mainly at home. Her novels include *The Golden Arrow* (1916), *Gone to Earth* (1917), *The House in Dormer Forest* (1920), *Seven for a Secret* (1922), and *Amour wherein He Trusted* (1929). Her most famous novel, *Precious Bane* (1924), set in North Shropshire after the Napoleonic Wars, tells the story of Prue Sarn, a sensitive and gentle young woman stigmatized as a witch in her local community, because she has been born with a hare-lip. The novel epitomizes the qualities for which Webb's writing became renowned during her short life: its fervent, pantheistic celebration of nature, its somewhat fatalistic sympathy for the innocent and the dispossessed, and its exploration of the nature of female consciousness and sexuality. Her work has been compared with that of Thomas *Hardy and with the rustic novels of Sheila *Kaye-Smith. Both Webb and Kaye-Smith were amongst the writers satirized in Stella *Gibbons's comic work, *Cold Comfort Farm*. A collection of nature poems and essays, *The Spring of Joy* (1928), appeared posthumously.

WEDDE, Ian (1946–), New Zealand poet, novelist, critic, and editor, born in Blenheim, New Zealand, educated mainly in England and at the University of Auckland. Wedde's evocative clarity of image and lyricism were already evident in his early poem sequence *Homage to Matisse* (1971), published while he was briefly resident in London. *Made Over* (1974) showed the influence of William Carlos *Williams's poetics. Wedde's publications tend to be 'stations' of his life; *Earthly: Sonnets for Carlos* (1975) was written after the birth of his first son, while the long poem *Pathway to the Sea* (1975) is a local protest against the ecological destruction of an untouched beachline by an aluminium smelter. More sinister visions and extended form characterize the later collections *Castaly* (1980) and *Tales of Gotham City* (1984), written in the 1970s when Wedde was also creating theatre scripts and co-editing a tabloid, *Spleen*. Other collections of poems are *Georgicon* (1984), *Tendering* (1989), *Driving into the Storm* (1987; selected poems), and *The Drummer* (1993). Wedde's experimental novel *Dick Seddon's Great Dive* (1976) was followed by the comic *Survival Arts* (1981) and the much acclaimed *Symmes Hole* (1986). His editions (co-edited) of *The Penguin Book of New Zealand Verse* (1985) and of *The Penguin Book of Contemporary New Zealand Poetry* (1989) seek to make a genuine intervention in New Zealand culture, particularly in their inclusion of poems in Maori and in their reassessment of some previously undervalued women poets. A collection of writings, *How to Be Nowhere: Essays and Texts, 1968–1993* was published in 1995.

WEDGWOOD, Dame C(icely) V(eronica) (1910–), British historian, born in Northumberland, educated at Lady Margaret Hall, Oxford. A specialist of the seventeenth century, her books include *Strafford* (1935), *William the Silent* (1944; James Tait Black Memorial Prize), her highly acclaimed volumes on the Civil War (*The King's Peace*, 1955; *The King's War*, 1958; *The Trial of King Charles*, 1964), a book of essays (*Velvet Studies*, 1946), and the lives of Oliver Cromwell (1939), Montrose (1952), and Milton (1969). To her scholarship and mastery of the period is added an ability to bring the characters she writes about vividly to life. She was created a Dame in 1968.

WEISS, Theodore (Russell) (1916–), American poet, born in Reading, Pennsylvania, educated at Muhlenberg College, Allentown, Pennsylvania, and Columbia University, New York. He began his academic career in 1941 at the University of Maryland. After holding a succession of posts at American universities, he was a Professor of English at Princeton from 1967 to 1987. *The Catch* (1951), his first collection of poetry, was followed by *Outlanders* (1960), *Gunsight* (1962), and *The Medium* (1965); *The World Before Us: Poems 1950–1970* appeared in 1970. Weiss's early work, in which a formal debt to W. C. *Williams is evident, is dominated by his interest in the longer poem as a vehicle for exploring his motivating psychological and cultural preoccupations. His later collections, which display an increasingly fluid lyricism, include *Fireweeds* (1976), *Recoveries* (1982), *A Slow Fuse* (1984), *A*

Sum of Destructions (1994), and *From Princeton One Autumn Afternoon: Collected Poems* (1987). Weiss is also highly regarded for his critical writings, among which are *The Breath of Clowns and Kings: A Study of Shakespeare* (1971) and *The Man from Porlock* (1982), a collection of his essays.

WELCH, (Maurice) Denton (1915–48), British novelist and essayist, born in Shanghai, educated at Repton School and Goldsmith's School of Art, London. As a consequence of a serious bicycle accident in 1935 he became a partial invalid. All Welch's books, some of them illustrated by himself, are strongly autobiographical. *Maiden Voyage* (1943) recaptures with sensory richness his running away from school and going to China to join his father. *In Youth Is Pleasure* (1944) conveys the physical confusions of pubescence. Posthumously published were *Brave and Cruel, and Other Stories* (1949), mostly narrated in the first person, reflecting different experiences of the author's short life; *A Voice through a Cloud* (1950), a powerful recollection of his accident and the indignity he suffered as an invalid; and *The Last Sheaf* (1951; edited by Eric Oliver), a collection of stories, pictures, and poems. In his *Journals* (1952; unexpurgated version 1984, edited by Michael De-la-Noy) he lays bare with brave honesty his own neurotic and difficult personality as well as conveying, again with sensory detail, the texture of life in the English countryside, particularly during the Second World War.

WELCH, James (1940–), Native American writer of mixed Blackfoot and Gros Ventre descent, born in Montana, educated at the University of Montana; he has taught Native American literature at the University of Washington and Cornell University. Welch describes himself less as a traditional story-teller and more as a novelist within the Western, European-American tradition, dealing with characters in a situation of psychological crisis. *Winter in the Blood* (1974) and *The Death of Jim Loney* (1979) both focus on characters who seek release from alcoholism and alienation through the recovery of a tribal consciousness; in the latter work, Jim Loney, unable to control his life, finally takes control of the manner of his death. *Fools Crow* (1986) is a historical novel set in the 1860s, describing the various responses of avoidance and resistance of members of a Blackfoot band experiencing the impact of white settlement. Welch's poetry is collected in *Riding the Earthboy 40* (1971). See ETHNICITY and NATIVE AMERICAN LITERATURE.

WELDON, Fay (1933–), British novelist, dramatist, and television screenwriter, born in Alvechurch, Worcestershire, educated at the University of St Andrews. She began her career as a copywriter in an advertising agency and wrote several plays for radio and television. Her novels, which frequently deal with aspects of women's experience, including the demands made upon them by marriage and motherhood and the unreasonable expectations of men, established her as a spokeswoman for the emerging feminist movement. Her first novel, *The Fat Woman's Joke* (1967), originally written for television, displays a sardonic wit which characterizes her work. *Down among the Women* (1971), which casts a satirical eye on a group of women friends, their marriages, and love affairs, was followed by a number of others with a similar theme, including *Female Friends* (1975) and *Remember Me* (1976). *Praxis* (1978) was a more sombre work, following the career of its central character from her childhood through to her final apotheosis as a feminist heroine. *Puffball* (1980) dealt with themes of witchcraft and the supernatural touched on elsewhere in the author's work, as well as the often devastating effects of pregnancy and child-rearing on women's lives. *The Lives and Loves of a She-Devil* (1983) is a fable about female power and powerlessness, telling the story of Ruth, an ugly woman married to a philandering man, who transforms herself by sheer strength of will into the image of her hated rival; this and *The Heart of the Country* (1987), about the horrors of a loveless marriage, were made into films for television. Other novels include *The Hearts and Lives of Men* (1987), *Leader of the Band* (1988), *Darcy's Utopia* (1990), *Growing Rich* (1992), *Life Force* (1992), *Affliction* (1993), and *Splitting* (1995), a triumphant comedy in which a divorced wife with several personalities enables Weldon to explore the many roles women play. She has published two collections of short stories: *Moon over Minneapolis* (1991) and *Wicked Women* (1995). *Angel, All Innocence* (1995) is a selection of her shorter fiction, compiled by Giles Gordon.

WELLER, Archie (1957–), Australian part-Aboriginal writer, born in Subiaco, Western Australia; he grew up in bush country just south of Perth. As a teenager he lived in East Perth, a poor area of 'bikies, methos, migrants and Aboriginal families'. He went through secondary education, and studied for a year at the Western Australian Institute of Technology (now Curtin University of Technology), Perth, but left to write *The Day of the Dog* (1981). A biting account of contemporary urban poverty and violence, it also captures the desperate humour that is the last resort of those whom society ignores. *Going Home* (1986), a collection of short stories, captures the life and language of its characters with force and confidence. Weller has also written commissioned poems, plays, and film scripts, including the screenplay *First Citizen* (1988) about the famous Aboriginal artist Albert Namatjira. He is the editor, with Coleen Francis-Glass, of *Us Fellas: An Anthology of Aboriginal Writing* (1987).

WELLESLEY, Dorothy (Violet) (1889–1956), British poet, born at Heywood Lodge, White Waltham, Berkshire; she was privately educated. Her numerous collections of verse include *Early Poems* (1913), *Lost Lane* (1925), *Matrix* (1928), *Lost Planet* (1942), and *Desert Wells* (1946). From 1934 onwards she was W. B. *Yeats's close friend; some of his letters to her were published as *Letters on Poetry* in 1940. He valued her work highly for the 'passionate precision' with which it displayed her intuitive understanding of the mystical philosophy he had laboured to expound. She was generously represented in his *Oxford Book of Modern Verse* (1936). Fusions of observational and imaginative elements give much of her verse its compelling vividness. Her weaker work tends towards historical and mythological portentousness. A collected edition entitled *Early Light* was produced in 1955. She was the wife of Lord Gerald Wellesley, who became the Seventh Duke of Wellington in 1943. Her other publications include the biography *Sir George Goldie: Founder of Nigeria* (1934) and *Far Have I Travelled* (1952), a volume of autobiography.

Well of Loneliness, The, see HALL, RADCLYFFE.

WELLS, H(erbert) G(eorge) (1866–1946), English novelist, social critic, and educator, born in Bromley, Kent, the third son of Joseph Wells, an unsuccessful small shopkeeper, and his wife Sarah, a former lady's maid. In 1880 Wells's mother left home to become resident housekeeper at Uppark, a large country house in Sussex, while her son began a series of apprenticeships, including two years at a drapery emporium. He had to work a thirteen-hour day, and slept in a dormitory above the shop. At 16 he managed to escape from the drapery trade and became a student assistant at Midhurst Grammar School, and a year later he won a government scholarship to the Normal School of Science, South Kensington, where he studied biology under T. H. Huxley. He spent three years as a science student, failing his final examinations, though he eventually took his BSc in 1890. From 1887 he worked as a science teacher and correspondence tutor, until chronic ill-health forced him to give up teaching for a precarious life as a literary journalist. His first marriage, to his cousin Isabel, broke down in 1893; two years later he married his former student Amy Catherine Robbins. In 1895 he burst on the literary scene with *The Time Machine* and with the first of several volumes of short stories. There followed in quick succession *The Island of Doctor Moreau* (1896), *The Invisible Man* (1897), *The War of the Worlds* (1898), and *The *First Men in the Moon* (1901). These 'scientific romances', arguably his finest works, have had an incalculable influence on modern literature and popular culture; their cosmic sweep and haunting pessimism have influenced most subsequent *science fiction. By the turn of the century Wells had produced his first semi-autobiographical novel, *Love and Mr Lewisham* (1900), while his reputation as a social and political prophet was nurtured by *Anticipations* (1901), *The Discovery of the Future* (1902), and *A Modern Utopia* (1905; see UTOPIA AND ANTI-UTOPIA). His growing international fame and his friendships and correspondence with Arnold *Bennett, Joseph *Conrad, George Gissing, Henry *James, and Bernard *Shaw made him a central figure in Edwardian literature. His membership of, and spectacular quarrel with, the *Fabian Society influenced the development of modern socialism. He drew on his experiences as a draper in his comic novels **Kipps* (1905) and *The *History of Mr Polly* (1910). In 1909 he published **Tono-Bungay*, a panoramic critique of Edwardian plutocracy, and his controversial 'suffrage novel' **Ann Veronica*. *The *New Machiavelli* (1911), set in the world of high politics, reflects the atmosphere of scandal surrounding his numerous extra-marital liaisons (including his long relationship with Rebecca *West, with whom he had a son, Anthony West). In later life his main fictional vehicle was the 'discussion novel' or novel of ideas, a form most successfully deployed in his best-selling war novel **Mr Britling Sees It Through* (1916). Wells had anticipated the First World War in futuristic romances such as *The War in the Air* (1908). In 1914 he published *The World Set Free* with its prophecy of the atomic bomb; Winston S. *Churchill, remembering Wells's story 'The Land Ironclads' (1903), also credited him with the invention of the tank. He lived to regret the slogan he coined in August 1914—'The War that Will End War'—and became increasingly concerned with peace-making and propaganda for world government. *The Outline of History* (1920) gives his view of universal history, ending characteristically with a plea for world peace. Here Wells summed up the human outlook as a 'race between education and catastrophe'. During the next two decades he pursued global political influence through his meetings with Lenin, Roosevelt, and Stalin. He reacted sharply against the rise of fascism, and was the leading spirit behind the Sankey Declaration of the Rights of Man. Artistically, however, he was widely regarded as a spent force; his later novels were ridiculed by younger rivals such as D. H. *Lawrence and Virginia *Woolf. In some respects the heir of the great Victorian cultural prophets, Wells's writing, like Thomas Carlyle's, became prolix, repetitive, and, at times, Cassandra-like. (His *Experiment in Autobiography*, 1934, and his short fable *The Croquet Player*, 1936, are exceptions to this.) He collaborated with Alexander Korda to produce the epic future-war movie *Things to Come* (1936). He stayed in London throughout the Second World War, and died there shortly after the founding of the United Nations and the onset of the nuclear age at Hiroshima—two events which sum up Wells's hopes and fears for humanity. See *H. G. Wells: Desperately Mortal* (1986), by David C. Smith, *H. G. Wells* (1987), by Michael Draper, *The History of Mr. Wells* (1995), by Michael *Foot, and *H. G. Wells: The Critical Heritage* (1972), edited by Patrick Parrinder.

WELLS, Robert (1947–), British poet and translator, born in Oxford, educated at King's College, Cambridge. Wells has worked as a forester on Exmoor, and much of his best writing is characterized by its depth and immediacy of response to the natural world. With work by Dick *Davis and Clive *Wilmer, his poetry was featured in *Shade Mariners* (1970), which demonstrated the survival of traditional verse forms. His collections of poems include *The Winter's Task* (1977) and *Selected Poems* (1986), which incorporated new work and extracts from his highly regarded translations of Virgil's *Georgics* (1982) and Theocritus's *Idylls* (1988). The sensory vividness with which he writes of landscapes and other natural phenomena in conventional forms gives his poetry a rare freshness and originality. He has written numerous lyrics of considerable poise and clarity in freer styles of verse.

WELSH, Irvine (1958–), Scottish novelist, born in Edinburgh where he was brought up on a housing estate in Muirhead. He left school at sixteen, lived in London in the 1980s, then became a training officer in Edinburgh Council's housing department, gaining an MBA at Heriot Watt University. His first novel, *Trainspotting* (1993; filmed with screenplay by John Hodge, 1996), swiftly became a cult for its uncompromising portrayal of Edinburgh's underclass. Written in the vernacular of Scotland's East Coast, Welsh's raw depiction of the wrecked lives of a group of young drug addicts is relieved by humour and ironic insights into the drug-user's self-obsessed world. The stories of *The Acid House* (1994) deal with violence, sexual perversion, and drug addiction, themes which also feature in the novel *Marabou Stork Nightmares* (1995), narrated by a semi-conscious football casual, Roy Strang, whose hallucinations shift between bitter reality, rave culture, and ornithological adventure in Africa. In *Ecstasy* (1996; three novellas), grotesque events are described in characteristic laconic vein.

WELTY, Eudora (1909–), American short-story writer and novelist, born in Jackson, Mississippi, educated at the University of Wisconsin. She worked with the Works Progress Administration, travelling throughout Mississippi and taking photographs later collected in *One Time, One Place* (1971) and *Photographs by Eudora Welty* (1989). Her first short stories, championed by Katherine Anne *Porter, appeared in *A Curtain of Green* (1941) and *The Wide Net* (1943) and mostly derive from her experience and observations during this period; the latter includes 'First Love' and 'A Still Moment', which imaginatively recreate the past and show her heightened poetic apprehension of place. Keenly interested in the past of the American South, she set her first novel, *The Robber Bridegroom* (1942), in the Natchez Trace country during the last years of Spanish rule, capturing through the medium of a reworked folktale the sense of doubleness she felt peculiarly as a feature of pioneering culture. *Delta Wedding* (1946), a more orthodox novel, assembles diverse but related characters in a Plantation house in the Mississippi Delta country on the occasion of a wedding. *The Golden Apples* (1949) is a sequence of linked short stories; it not only portrays a country community (Morgana, Mississippi) from the beginning to the middle of the twentieth century but makes a lyrical assault on time itself, as it translates and consumes a group of interconnected people. *The Ponder Heart* (1954) carries on Welty's tradition of letting people reveal themselves as they relate events of which they have only partial knowledge and understanding; the novel also shows the author's humour and her affection for the eccentric or displaced person. *Losing Battles* (1970) covers three generations of a family who gather together one Sunday in the early 1930s, to celebrate the grandmother's ninetieth birthday. *The Optimist's Daughter* (1972) is a short novel which, in the antagonism between a judge's daughter and her younger stepmother, explores new emotional territory—that of hatred. Her collection of essays, *The Eye of the Story* (1978), contains reflections on the art of the short story, and the seminal essay 'Place in Fiction'. *One Writer's Beginnings* (1984) is an autobiography. Though admired by many different writers and critics, Welty did not achieve wide recognition until the publication of her *Collected Stories* (1980). See Louise Westling's *Eudora Welty* (1989), *The Still Moment: Eudora Welty, Portrait of a Writer* (1994) by Paul Binding, and *A Writer's Eye: Collected Book Reviews* (1994), edited by Pearly A. McHatlaney.

WENDT, Albert (1939–), Western Samoan writer, born in Western Samoa, educated at Victoria University, Auckland. He returned to Auckland in 1987 as the first Professor of New Zealand Literature at Auckland University. His novel *Sons for the Return Home* (1973) was the first by a Western Samoan and, like all his work, explores the complexities of Pacific culture in the present day. *Flying Fox in a Freedom Tree* (1974) consisted of 'modern fables' set in Samoa. In the title poem of *Inside Us the Dead: Poems 1961–1974* (1976) Wendt charted with a moving blend of wit and honesty his own mixed European/Pacific ancestry and heritage. *Leaves of the Banyan Tree* (1978) was a major novel of epic scope, and an important imaginative document in the accommodation of traditional and 'Western' influences, both religious and secular, in the Pacific. In *Ola* (1991) his heroine journeys with her father to the Holy Land where she attempts to come to terms with her situation as a partially dispossessed contemporary Samoan woman. The fast-paced *Black Rainbow* (1992) offers an *Orwellian vision of New Zealand in the near future. The poetry collection *Shaman of Visions* appeared in 1984, and *The Birth and Death of the Miracle Man and Other Stories* in 1986; Wendt edited and introduced *Lali* (1980), an anthology of Pacific writing, and *Nuana—Pacific Writings in English Since 1980* (1995). Always an articulate and passionate critic of those who subject the complex and diverse populations of the Pacific to the demeaning and constricting stereotypes of 'South Pacific' life, Wendt is sharply aware of the political, religious, and cultural inheritance he has gained through living, as he once put it, 'in a stone castle in the South Seas'.

WERTENBAKER, Timberlake, British dramatist born of Anglo-American parents; she was educated in France and America. Her first significant play was *New Anatomies* (1981), about the life of the nineteenth-century explorer Isabelle Eberhardt, who managed to travel in Islamic countries by adopting male Arab dress. Her subsequent work has been variously marked by a concern for women in a male-dominated society, a belief in the power of the creative imagination, and an interest in Greek myth. It includes *The Grace of Mary Traverse* (1985), about an inquisitive young woman who leaves her father's house to discover the perils and pains of eighteenth-century

London; *Our Country's Good* (1988), adapted from Thomas *Keneally's novel *The Playmaker*, which involves convicts in a brutal Australian settlement who put on a production of Farquhar's *The Recruiting Officer*; *The Love of the Nightingale* (1989), about the rape of Philomele by Tereus and the vengeance taken by his wife Procne; and *Three Birds Alighting on a Field* (1991), whose characters (including one identified with Philoctetes) variously display a financial, a socially snobbish, and an authentic interest in painting, thus raising questions about the value of art itself. *The Break of Day* was performed in 1995. Wertenbaker has also written plays for television, and translated work by Marivaux, Anouilh, and Maeterlinck.

WESCOTT, Glenway (1901–87), American novelist and poet, born in Kewaskum, Wisconsin, educated at the University of Chicago. Wescott left the University of Chicago (from where he had contributed *Imagist verse to Harriet Monroe's **Poetry* magazine) in 1919 and spent several years wandering, rather aimlessly, from country to country, including England and Germany, before settling down to a career as a full-time writer. His first novel, *The Apple of the Eye* (1924), recalls his Wisconsin upbringing, but it was the partially autobiographical *The Grandmothers: A Family Portrait* (1927) that brought him his considerable early success; here his childhood is evoked through the thoughts and memories of Alwyn Tower, a character he was to use again, notably in *The Pilgrim's Hawk: A Love Story* (1940). During the years of Wescott's expatriation (from 1925 to 1933), chiefly in France where he lived in Paris and at Villefrance-sur-Mer, he befriended many other American expatriate writers, particularly Ernest *Hemingway and Gertrude *Stein. He returned to the USA in 1933 and while his writings became more intermittent and of rather uncertain quality he remained active in literary circles and edited the writings of Somerset *Maugham and Colette. *Images of Truth: Remembrances and Criticism* (1962) draws together his more important prose writings. His poetry, which owes much to the influence of imagism, goes largely unread, though *The Bitterns: A Book of Twelve Poems* (1920) was his first publication. See *Wescott* (1965), by William H. Rueckert.

WESKER, Arnold (1932–), British dramatist, born in Stepney, London, educated in Hackney; he worked as a furniture-maker's apprentice, a farm labourer's seed-sorter, a chef, and in many other capacities before writing *Chicken Soup with Barley* (1958), *Roots* (1959), and *I'm Talking about Jerusalem* (1960). These plays, collectively known as the Wesker Trilogy, established him as one of the more important of the socially conscious writers who emerged in the wake of **Look Back in Anger*. They also embodied conflicts that continued to reappear in his work: between creativity and compromise, idealism and cynicism, dream and reality, human potential and social circumstance. Among his other plays are *The Kitchen* (1959), on the surface a documentary showing the turbulent world behind the scenes in a restaurant, more essentially a picture of Western industrial society in exemplary microcosm; *Chips with Everything* (1962), a portrait of national servicemen with much to say about British class divisions; *Their Very Own and Golden City* (1965), about the limitations forced on and accepted by a visionary architect; *The Four Seasons* (1965), about the growth and decay of love; *The Friends* (1970), about a group of designers coming to terms with their working-class origins and re-evaluating their creative aspirations; *The Old Ones* (1972), about people facing out their impending deaths and their doubts about the value of life; *The Wedding Feast* (1974), adapted from Dostoevsky, about tensions between a paternalist factory owner and his employees; and *Caritas* (1981), about the despair of a fourteenth-century anchorite. In addition to *As Much as I Dare* (1994), his autobiography, Wesker has written numerous articles and essays, the earlier of which he assembled in *Fears of Fragmentation* (1970), a collection which interestingly reveals the thinking, not merely behind his own drama, but behind his attempts to create Centre 42, a movement which aimed to popularize culture with trade union support.

WESLEY, Mary (1912–), British novelist, born in Surrey, educated privately and at the London School of Economics. At the age of 70 she published her first novel, *Jumping the Queue* (1983), a black comedy of the upper classes about a woman intent on committing suicide. It was followed by *The Camomile Lawn* (1984), *Harnessing Peacocks* (1985), *The Vacillations of Poppy Carew* (1986), *Not that Sort of Girl* (1987), *Second Fiddle* (1988), *A Sensible Life* (1990), *A Dubious Legacy* (1992), and *An Imaginative Experience* (1994). All the novels share an unconventional morality closely observing an upper-class world whose besetting sins are indifference and cruelty. The plots deal with a variety of themes, including adultery, incest, murder, suicide, and prostitution; despite these somewhat lurid elements, they are distinguished by their style and wit. She has also written for children.

WEST, Dorothy (1912–), American novelist, born in Boston, the daughter of a successful black businessman; she was educated at the city's Girls' Latin School and studied journalism at Columbia University. Her first published story appeared in the *Boston Post* in 1928. She moved to New York in 1929, where she became a notable figure in the circle of black writers associated with Countee *Cullen and Langston *Hughes (see HARLEM RENAISSANCE) and founded *Challenge* magazine in 1935 as a forum for black writing during the Depression. Her novel *The Living Is Easy* appeared in 1948. Set in Boston in the years before the First World War, its richly detailed narrative reflects the uneasy hold on social status and prosperity among the black middle-class community.

WEST, Nathanael (1903–40), American novelist and screenwriter, born Nathan Wallenstein WEINSTEIN in New York, educated at Brown University. West lived in Paris before returning home to work as the manager of a New York hotel where he befriended several other writers, and also worked as an associate of William Carlos *Williams in editing the magazine *Contact*. During this time he wrote three short novels: *The Dream Life of Balso Snell* (1931), a surrealist depiction of characters living in a Trojan horse; **Miss Lonelyhearts* (1933), which portrays a disillusioned newspaper columnist seeking security in religion, in a society crippled by materialism; and *A Cool Million: The Dismantling of Lemuel Pitkin* (1934), which is a savage satire on the Horatio Alger myth and an assault on the mythical pillars of American society. He moved to Hollywood in 1935 where he adapted *Miss Lonelyhearts* for the screen (*Advice to the Lovelorn*), wrote several screenplays, and became more disillusioned. His only full-length novel is *The Day of the Locust* (1939), in which the degradation of Hollywood and, by extension, the USA are exposed in a grotesque portrait of the derelicts and boredom of life in the movie capital. After numerous vignettes of Hollywood life, the novel's closing sequence is, in many ways, a prophetic allegory of the consequences of the rise of fascism and the coming world war. West was killed in a car crash in California.

WEST, Paul (1930–), American critic, theoretician, poet, and novelist, born in Eckington, Derbyshire, educated at the University of Birmingham and Oxford University. While his autobiography, *I, Said the Sparrow* (1963), offers an affectionate portrait of his early life in England, he has a particular affection for the USA where he became a resident and held academic posts at several universities including Penn State. A unifying strain to West's work is his belief in the need for experimentation. In such experimental work as *Colonel Mint* (1972), which explores the role of imagination in a rational world, and *Gala* (1976), a fictional sequel to *Words for a Deaf Daughter*, West probes the limits of genre, art, and the imagination. He has written in a variety of genres and subjects, ranging from the New York City underworld in *Tenement of Clay* (1965), to Nazi Germany in *The Very Rich Hours of Count Von Stauffenberg* (1980), and to his own relationship with his deaf daughter, Mandy, in *Words for a Deaf Daughter* (1969). In his novel *Love's Mansion* (1992), West returns to personal history, and to England, in a story of two lovers based on his parents. West's influences include Shakespeare, Samuel *Beckett, and Jean-Paul Sartre, while his critical works often focus on Latin American writers, such as Carlos Fuentes and Mario Vargas Llosa. *The Universe, and Other Fictions* (1988) is a collection of short stories. His non-fiction works include *The Growth of the Novel* (1959), *Byron and the Spoiler's Art* (1960), *The Modern Novel* (2 volumes; 1963, 1965), and *Sheer Fiction* (2 volumes; 1987, 1991).

WEST, Dame Rebecca (Cicily Isabel Fairfield, later Andrews) (1892–1983), British novelist and political essayist, born in London of Anglo-Irish parents, educated in Edinburgh. She borrowed her pen-name from the passionate heroine of Ibsen's *Rosmersholm*. After a brief stage career, West became a journalist and political commentator, inspired by feminism and the ideas of the Pankhursts. From 1911 she wrote for the *Freewoman*, the *New Freewoman*, and the *Clarion*; some of her best work of this period appeared in *The Young Rebecca* (1982). An encounter with H. G. *Wells, whose work she had reviewed, led to a relationship that lasted a decade and resulted in the birth of her only child, Anthony West. Her first novel, *The Return of the Soldier* (1918), is the account of a shell-shocked soldier's involvement with three women; in its preoccupation with unconscious motivations, repression, memory, and regression, it reveals the influence of psychoanalytic theories. She continued to write fiction, including *The Judge* (1922), *Harriet Hume* (1929), and *The Thinking Reed* (1936), but reviewers of the period complained that her novels, though beautifully written and richly informative, were the contrived products of an overly intellectual mind. However, her early training as a journalist greatly contributed to her development as a social and political commentator. Her works of non-fiction include a volume of collected criticism, *The Strange Necessity* (1928); a masterly biography, *St Augustine* (1933); a penetrating study of the causes of the Second World War, *Black Lamb and Grey Falcon* (1941); and the post-war works *The Meaning of Treason* (1947) and *A Train of Powder* (1955). With her return to fiction, *The Fountain Overflows* (1956), her reputation as a novelist began to grow. *The Birds Fall Down* (1966), a lavishly detailed account of a young woman's encounter with the elements that gave rise to the Russian Revolution, is a political thriller displaying links with her best non-fiction. In the 1980s West was reclaimed as a feminist heroine. The republication of her earlier novels by Virago Press brought her a wide new readership. Her novels of ideas were admired both for their unique knowledge of the periods chronicled, and for their psychological depth and density. She was a fearless champion of such neglected talents as A. L. *Barker, and the influence of her technique and vision is discernible in the work of Sybille *Bedford. Her reputation continued to grow with the appearance of such posthumous works as *This Real Night* (1984), a continuation of the semi-autobiographical narrative of *The Birds Fall Down*, and the hitherto unpublished earlier novel, *Sunflower* (1986). *The Only Poet and Short Stories*, also comprising hitherto unpublished and uncollected material, edited by Antonia Till, was published in 1992. She is the subject of a detailed biography by Victoria *Glendinning, published in 1987.

Westerly, an Australian literary journal, which began in 1956 showing an early preference for prose. Beginning as a student magazine at the University of Western Australia, it won Commonwealth funding in 1963. Peter Cowan and John Barnes became involved towards the end of the 1960s, and the early 'open' forum began to take on a regional stance. In later years art and poetry, as well as historical, political, and social issues, have been encompassed. Special issues have been devoted to the 1930s and to 'Regionalism in Contemporary Australia'. Western Australian writers win the largest share of the space and interest; in particular, they have been in the forefront of publishing the works of their Aboriginal writers. *Westerly 21: An Anniversary Selection* was published in 1978.

Westerns, a genre of popular American fiction characteristically set in the late nineteenth century in the Western and Southwestern states and featuring cattle-ranchers, cowboys, sheriffs, and outlaws as principal protagonists. Emerson Hough was among the first exponents of the mode; its first classic is Owen Wister's *The *Virginian* (1902), which established numerous enduring features in its narrative of Wyoming cow-punchers of the 1880s. Clarence E. Mulford's *Hopalong Cassidy* (1910), Zane *Grey's *Riders of the Purple Sage* (1912), and Jack Schaeffer's *Shane* (1949) are among the best-known examples, in each of which the element of violence that is a significant attribute of the Western is present to some extent; the sharpness with which the conflict between good and evil is typically drawn is intrinsic to the quasi-mythological character of much Western writing. The better known of the *pulp magazines which sustained the genre from the 1920s onward include *Western Story Magazine* (1927) and *Zane Grey's Western Magazine* (1947). Among the works which broadly conform to the specifications of the Western while possessing more developed literary qualities are Walter Van Tilburg Clark's *The Ox-Bow Incident* (1940), A. B. Guthrie's *The Big Sky* (1947), and E. L. *Doctorow's *Welcome to Hard Times* (1960). In more recent decades the Western idiom has been adapted by numerous novelists, examples being Michael *Ondaatje's *The Collected Works of Billy the Kid* (1981) and William *Burroughs's *The Place of Dead Roads* (1984). William W. Savage's study *The Cowboy Hero* appeared in 1979.

WESTLAKE, Donald E(dwin) (1933–), American crime novelist, who also writes as Richard Stark, Tucker Coe, Curt Clark, and Timothy J. Culver; born in Brooklyn, educated at the University of New York at Binghamton, he became a full-time author in 1959. *The Mercenaries* (1960) placed him initially within the *Hammett tradition, but in 1962 he took the pseudonym Richard Stark to write the first of sixteen novels featuring Parker, a meticulous and ruthless professional thief, books convincing in their portrayal of organized crime from the inside. In *The Man with the Getaway Face* (1963), Parker overcomes a clumsy double-cross following a security van heist; *The Green Eagle Score* (1967) finds him planning to rob a US Air Force base of its payroll; the final and bloodiest Parker thriller is *Butcher's Moon* (1974). Westlake's novels under his own name have an entirely different manner, often being light-hearted capers such as *Somebody Owes Me Money* (1969), in which a cab driver becomes involved with gangsters, or the 'Dortmunder' novels about a group of comically inept thieves who, in *Bank Shot* (1972), manage to steal an entire mobile bank. Writing as Tucker Coe, Westlake created a much darker series of novels involving Mitch Tobin, a guilt-ridden ex-policeman, the most disturbing of which is *Wax Apple* (1970). Latterly, Westlake has favoured suspense crime-comedies, as in *Too Much!* (1975) and *Trust Me on This* (1988), and continues to write entertainingly within various subgenres. Several of his books have been filmed, most notably *Point Blank* (1967), directed by John Boorman.

WEYMAN, Stanley John (1855–1928), British novelist, born in Shropshire, educated at Christ Church, Oxford. He read for the Bar but abandoned the legal profession in 1891. Having published stories in periodicals he began a successful literary career with *The House of the Wolf* (1890), which was followed by over twenty successful historical romances, often with French settings, such as *A Gentleman of France* (1893); *The Red Cockade* (1895); *Under the Red Robe* (1896); *Count Hannibal* (1901), a fictitious account of the Massacre of St Bartholomew; and *Chippinge* (1906), set in Victorian England at the time of the Reform Bill. He continued to write until the end of his life, although his reputation suffered a decline in later years.

WHALEN, Philip (1923–), American poet, born in Oregon, educated at Reed College. Whalen is associated both with the *Beats and with the *San Francisco Renaissance. In terms of tone and conviction, his poetry most resembles that of Lew Welch; it is clear and witty, possessing a kind of classical poise which comports well with its jazz-derived flexibility. Increasingly absorbed in Buddhism, Whalen spent several years in Japan, thereby reinforcing both the playful and the spiritual dimensions of his verse. *On Bear's Head* (1969) is a collection of most of the important work written during the first twenty years of his literary career: it includes *Like I Say* (1960), *Memoirs of an Interglacial Age* (1960), *Monday in the Evening* (1964), and *Every Day* (1965). Of the later volumes, *The Kindness of Strangers* (1976) and *Enough Said* (1980) are particularly important; *Heavy Breathing: Poems 67–80* (1983) is a second volume of collected poems. *You Didn't even Try* (1966) is a slight but beautifully composed novel. Its portrait of an unattached, rather scholarly poet offers another version of the characteristic Whalen persona: kind, but remote from the paraphernalia of twentieth-century consumer capitalism, he seeks solace in the natural world and in a direct, unexploitative series of relationships with his fellow human beings.

WHARTON, Edith (Newbold) (née Jones) (1862–1937), American novelist, born in New York to an aristocratic family and educated privately. In the 1890s she contributed short stories and poems to *Scribner's Magazine*, a collection entitled *The Greater Inclination* appearing in 1899, before writing a first historical novel, set in eighteenth-century Italy, *The Valley of Decision* (1902). She then turned to social satire in *The *House of Mirth* (1905), her first mature novel, which depicted manners in New York society.

In its accuracy of description and the interplay of social manners and false ambition her work is close to that of Henry *James, with whom she maintained a close friendship, but many would argue that her work is more incisive in its understanding of the plight of women in a patriarchal society. She settled permanently in France after 1906, but continued to write predominantly novels with an American context. These include *The Fruit of the Tree* (1907), about an American executive's conflicts between love and business, and **Ethan Frome* (1911), an ironic novelette of repressed love in decaying, rural New England, generally considered her finest tragic work. These were closely followed by the subtle studies of moral values, *The Reef* (1912) and *The *Custom of the Country* (1913), both about Americans in France. The latter novel is a fierce indictment of the mindless materialism Wharton saw as infecting American life at the turn of the twentieth century. She spent the war years engaged in charitable and relief work, for which she was made a chevalier of the Légion d'Honneur, whilst writing *Summer* (1917), a return to the New England realism of *Ethan Frome*, and two books with a war theme, *The Marne* (1918) and *A Son at the Front* (1923). After the First World War she continued to write works which came to be regarded as major achievements, including *The *Age of Innocence* (1920, Pulitzer Prize), and *Hudson River Bracketed* (1929) and its sequel, *The Gods Arrive* (1932), which focus on the contrast between Midwestern and New York society. The *Old New York* tetralogy (1924), a collection of meticulously wrought short stories, 'False Dawn', 'The Old Maid', 'The Spark', and 'New Year's Day', depicted the American scene between the 1840s and 1870s; it was followed by several novels dealing with the relationship between parents and children in *The Mother's Recompense* (1925), *Twilight Sleep* (1927), and *The Children* (1928). Wharton's short stories were collected in several volumes, of which 'The Duchess at Prayer' in *Crucial Instances* (1901), 'The Debt' in *Tales of Men and Ghosts* (1910), and 'After Holbein' in *Certain People* (1930) demonstrate an economy and symmetry of structure. Other collections are *The Descent of Man* (1904); *The Hermit and the Wild Woman* (1908); *Xingu and Other Stories* (1916), which focused on fickle social standards, the supernatural, and nineteenth-century New York; *Here and Beyond* (1926); *Human Nature* (1933); *The World Over* (1936); and *Ghosts* (1937). She wrote two volumes of poetry, *Artemis to Actæon* (1909) and *Twelve Poems* (1926); an autobiography, *A Backward Glance* (1934); and several travel books. Despite contemporary perception that she was a major novelist of her period, her work was relatively neglected in the years after her death until the late 1970s, when a reassessment placed her as a writer integral to an understanding of the development of American modernist writing. In *The Writing of Fiction* (1925), she summed up her understanding of the nature of fiction in the following words: '. . . every great novel must first of all be based on a profound sense of moral values, and then constructed with a classical unity and economy of means'. Upon her death she left an unfinished novel, *The Buccaneers* (1938), concerned with the attempts of American girls to enter English society.

WHARTON, William (pseudonym) (1925–), American writer, born in Philadelphia, educated at the University of California, Los Angeles. A reclusive artist, resident in France, Wharton wished to conceal his name and used the pseudonym 'William Wharton' for his writing. Only with the publication of *Franky Furbo* (1989), dedicated to a daughter killed in a highway accident, did he emerge from obscurity to bring attention to her death; *Last Lovers* (1991) is shadowed throughout by his loss. His first two novels, *Birdy* (1979) and *Dad* (1981), both filmed, are his best-known, and together provide an agenda for his work as a whole, which can be seen as an assertion of the holiness of the creative self against the incursions of a deranging world. The 'insanity' of Birdy, and the declamatory self-concern of the protagonists of novels like *Scumbler* (1984) and *Tidings* (1987), are indicative of this concern. Later novels, such as *Franky Furbo* and *Last Lovers*, confirm Wharton as a writer who speaks with a compelling and humane fervour.

What Every Woman Knows, a play by James *Barrie, first performed in 1908. The first act occurs in the living-room of a well-to-do Scottish family, the Wylies, and involves the capture of an apparent burglar, John Shand, who has come surreptitiously to read the books he is too poor to afford. The family offers him the money to educate himself, on condition he eventually marries the daughter of the house, Maggie. With her inadequately acknowledged help he becomes a Member of Parliament and rises to prominence as a politician. He then succumbs to the lure of the beautiful but mindless Lady Sybil Tenterden, only to discover that his reputation as a strong and powerful man depends on Maggie. What every woman knows, she explains, is that 'every man who is high up loves to think he has done it all himself; and the wife smiles, and lets it go at that'. Though he at first says he can never live with her again, it is apparent that a *rapprochement* has occurred.

WHEATLEY, Dennis (Yates) (1897–1977), British writer of popular adventure tales, romances, science fiction, fantasy, and detective stories, born in London. From the publication of *The Forbidden Territory* (1933) and *Such Power Is Dangerous* (1933), until well after the Second World War, he captured a vast readership who enjoyed the large gestures of action in surroundings whose ultimate security was never in doubt. *They Found Atlantis* (1936) and *The Man Who Missed the War* (1945) are essays in the science fiction of geography, where sunken islands and lost races are found in the world's recesses. *Murder off Miami* (1936) experiments intriguingly with its dossier format. His novels of black magic include *The Devil Rides Out* (1935), *The Haunting of Toby Jugg* (1948), *The Ka of Gifford Hillary* (1956), and *The Irish Witch* (1973). He also wrote numerous historical adventures, after the model of Baroness *Orczy.

Wheels, a series of poetry anthologies edited by Edith *Sitwell which appeared annually from 1916 to 1921. The narrowness of range evident in *Wheels* resulted largely from the marked preponderance of work by the three Sitwells and members of their immediate circle. The prevailing tone of the early editions was compounded of fatalistic gloom in response to the First World War and bitter rejection of the social order which contributors perceived as prolonging the conflict. David *Daiches has stated that the poets associated with the anthologies 'sublimated their own sense of decay into verses sometimes bizarre, sometimes satirical'; the unorthodox and sometimes macabre modes cultivated by *Wheels* were intended as shocking repudiations of the characteristic gentility of the contemporaneous **Georgian Poetry* series, to which hostile references were eventually made with increasing explicitness. The second volume featured poetry by Aldous *Huxley, whose work was included in each subsequent issue. Seven poems by Wilfred *Owen, who had met Osbert Sitwell in London shortly before his death in 1918, were published in the fourth edition. After 1920, *Wheels* declined through its failure to attract new authors. As a platform for the Sitwells it served its purpose well: marked improvements in their verse became evident in the course of its five-year existence; from being almost unknown in 1916, by 1921 they were famous as exponents of extravagantly experimental verse.

WHEELWRIGHT, John (Brooks) (1897–1940), American poet, born in Boston, educated at Harvard and at the Massachusetts Institute of Technology, where he trained for his career as an architect. In 1923 he travelled to Florence to oversee the printing there of an issue of *Secession*, one of the notable American *little magazines of the early 1920s; among the contributions for publication was Hart *Crane's 'For the Marriage of Faustus and Helen', which Wheelwright radically altered, causing considerable controversy. Crane, who regarded Wheelwright's verse as possessing 'real emotional significance', was the subject of the disquieting elegy 'Fish Food' which appeared in *Rock and Shells* (1933), his first collection of poetry. *Mirrors of Venus* (1938) was dominated by the sonnets making up the title sequence; the sometimes impressive conventional intricacy of such work was complemented by the eloquent plainness exemplified in his elegy 'Father'. In the course of the 1930s his lyrical preoccupations were displaced by his socio-political concern, which is expressed with stringent directness in *Political Self-Portrait* (1940). From 1934 to 1937 he was the editor of *Poems for a Dime*. He was well known in Boston for his eccentric combination of an elegantly patrician manner and fervently socialist views. *Collected Poems* (1972) contains *Dusk to Dusk*, a collection he was preparing at the time of his death in a road accident.

Where Angels Fear to Tread, the first novel by E. M. *Forster, published in 1905. Set in Italy, it concerns the relationships of a group of English people who become embroiled in a disastrous and misguided plan to 'rescue' one of their number, Lilia Herriton, from what the others regard as an unsuitable marriage to a young Italian she has met on holiday in Tuscany. The novel opens as Lilia, an attractive and still youthful widow, is departing for Italy in the company of her friend, Caroline Abbott. When, after several weeks, a letter containing the news of Lilia's engagement arrives at the house of her mother-in-law, Mrs Herriton, in Sawston, it creates consternation; Philip Herriton is despatched to Italy to prevent the marriage taking place, but on his arrival he learns that he is too late. Poor Lilia does not have long to enjoy her life with Gino Carella, her new husband, before she becomes pregnant and dies in childbirth. Philip, this time accompanied by his formidable sister, Harriet, is once more sent to intervene, with instructions to remove Lilia's child, a baby boy, from Gino's care and return with him to England. They meet Caroline Abbott in Monteriano, and enlist her help in carrying out this plan. It emerges, however, that Gino has no intention of giving up his son, and both Philip and Caroline, both drawn, in their separate ways, to the young Italian, are prepared to admit defeat; Caroline, indeed, confessing that she has 'changed sides'. Harriet, disgusted by this capitulation, decides to take matters into her own hands. She kidnaps the baby, intending to return to England with it as her mother has ordered, but the carriage overturns and the child is killed. Philip, whose arm has been broken in the accident, tells Gino what has happened, and in a fit of rage and grief the Italian attacks him, but is prevented from seriously injuring Philip by the arrival of Miss Abbott. Returning to England in the company of his sister (who has swiftly got over the incident) and Caroline Abbott, Philip realizes that he is in love; before he can tell Miss Abbott of his feelings for her, however, she tells him that she has fallen in love with Gino, even though she knows she will never see him again. The novel ends with its protagonists, who have, albeit unintentionally, left destruction in their wake, resigning themselves to a life of emotional sterility. The work was much admired by contemporary critics: Virginia *Woolf wrote that 'this slight first novel' displayed 'evidence of powers which only needed . . . a more generous diet to ripen into wealth and beauty'; F. R. *Leavis called it 'flawless' in the 'perfection of its structure, its subtle use of leitmotifs, its sureness of touch and tone, [and] the deftness of its comedy'.

WHITE, Antonia, pseudonym of Eirene BOTTING (1899–1980), British novelist, born in London. Following her father's conversion to Catholicism, she was sent to a convent boarding school but later left in disgrace. She trained as an actress at the Royal Academy of Dramatic Art and afterwards toured the provinces. White began her journalistic career as Assistant Editor of Desmond McCarthy's **Life and Letters* and also worked as theatre critic of **Time and Tide*, the *Daily Mirror*, and the *Sunday Pictorial*. At the outbreak of war she joined the BBC and later the Political Intelligence Department of the Foreign Office. As a novelist, she won fame with *Frost in May* (1933). Seventeen years later *The Lost Traveller* (1950), followed by *The Sugar House* (1952) and *Beyond the Glass* (1954), completed what became known as the 'Frost in May' quartet. Largely autobiographical, it was dramatized by the BBC a year after her death. Other works include *Strangers* (1954), short stories; *The Hound and the Falcon* (1965), an account of her reconversion to the Catholic faith; and *As Once in May* (1983), a selection of her essays and memorabilia, including a fragment of childhood autobiography, which appeared posthumously. She found additional prestige as a translator, notably with her translation of Maupassant's *Une Vie* and of many of Colette's novels. Despite a consistent struggle against 'writer's block' from 1926, she produced a number of personal journals and diaries, which reflect the fear of madness that troubled her throughout her adult life; at the age of 21, she had been certified insane and spent a year in the Royal Bethlehem Hospital. White married three times; her first marriage was annulled by the Catholic Church, and her third marriage was to Tom Hopkinson, the editor of *Picture Post*. Her friends included George *Barker, Djuna *Barnes, David *Gasgoyne, Kathleen *Raine, and Dylan *Thomas. Susan Chitty edited her early autobiography *As Once in May* and her *Diaries* (1991 and 1992), covering 1926–57 and 1958–79 respectively; Susan Chitty and Lyndall Hopkinson have both published memoirs, in 1985 and 1988 respectively.

WHITE, Edgar (1947–), West Indian playwright, born in Montserrat. Some of his plays have been produced by Joseph Papp's New York Shakespeare's Theatre. At his best, in plays like *'The Nine Night' and 'Ritual by Water'* (1984), he combines religious ritual and witty repartee with stark realism about life for West Indian families in Britain. His work tends to be restlessly experimental, and confronts the frustrations and moral dilemmas facing blacks in America, the West Indies, and Britain. Other published plays include *Underground: Four Plays* (1970), *The Crucificado: Two Plays* (1973), *Lament for Rastafari and Other Plays* (1983), and *Redemption Song and Other Plays* (1985). His first novel, *The Rising* (1988), focuses on a little West Indian boy, Legion, brought up by his single mother, who is ruthlessly dominated by his matriarchal grandmother.

WHITE, Edmund (1940–), American novelist, essayist, and critic, born in Cincinnati, Ohio, educated at the University of Michigan. His first novel, *Forgetting Elena* (1973), the account of an amnesiac who regains consciousness in the midst of strangers, demonstrated White's familiarity with such diverse genres as the *nouveau roman*, the traditional comedy of manners, and science fiction; White himself admitted the influence of classical Japanese writing and its exaltation of aesthetics. His second novel, *Nocturnes for the King of Naples* (1978), the lament of a man for his older, dead lover, conflates erotic and spiritual love in a self-conscious reworking of the baroque manner. *A *Boy's Own Story* (1982) brought him critical acclaim and commercial success. Through the simple story of an adolescence in the 1950s, White explores issues of gender and sexual choice while reworking the conventional American *Bildungsroman*. The novel attracted comparisons to *Salinger and Oscar Wilde. His next novel, *Caracole* (1985), which returns to the fantastic mode of his early work, is set in an imaginary country under foreign rule, and is reminiscent of Latin American *magic realism. White reflected on the AIDS crisis and the end of the hedonistic gay lifestyle he had hitherto celebrated in *The Darker Proof* (1987), which also contained stories by Adam *Mars-Jones. *The Beautiful Room Is Empty* (1988) continued the story of the nameless narrator of *A Boy's Own Story*; praised for its authentic depiction of life in the 1960s, the novel was also criticized for its graphic descriptions of casual homosexual encounters. White is also the author of a sociological work, *States of Desire: Travels in Gay America* (1980), and the editor of *The Faber Book of Gay Short Fiction* (1991).

WHITE, E(lwyn) B(rooks) (1899–1985), American essayist and humorist, born in Mount Vernon, New York, educated at Cornell University; he joined *The *New Yorker* in 1926. White's pithy, gently irreverent observations in his 'Notes and Comments' helped set the tone for the magazine throughout its heyday, and influenced his friend James *Thurber, with whom he wrote *Is Sex Necessary?* (1929). His books of essays include *Quo Vadimus?* (1939); *One Man's Meat* (1942), a collection of columns written for *Harper's Magazine*; and *The Points of My Compass* (1962). White's perennial subject was the comic difficulties of life, though he also wrote on social issues of the day.

WHITE, Kenneth (1936–), British poet, born in Glasgow, educated at the University of Glasgow, and the Universities of Munich and Paris. After periods teaching at the University of Glasgow, he became Professor of twentieth-century poetics at the Sorbonne in 1983. White writes both poetry and prose in French as well as English. *Wild Coal* (1963), *The Cold Wind of Dawn* (1966), *The Most Difficult Area* (1968), and *A Walk Along the Shore* (1977) are among the publications represented in *The Bird Path: Collected Longer Poems* (1989) and *Handbook for the Diamond Country: Collected Shorter Poems 1960–1990* (1990). Much of his verse is philosophical in character and is distinguished by the clarity of its imagery and the directness of its finely cadenced language. Like his poetry, White's prose reflects his extensive travelling in Europe, America, and the Far East, which respectively provide backgrounds for the descriptive and autobiographical writings in *Travels in the Drifting Dawn* (1989), *The Blue Road* (1990), and *Pilgrim of the Void* (1990). His critical writings include *The Tribal Dharma* (1975), a study of the poetry of Gary *Snyder, and *The Life Technique of John Cowper Powys* (1978).

WHITE, Patrick (Victor Martindale) (1912–90), Australian novelist and short-story writer, born in England, but taken to Australia when he was six months old, educated at King's College, Cambridge. White visited Germany during 1932 and 1935, and German Romanticism was a major influence on his writing. His first two published novels, both of which he was to turn against, were *Happy Valley* (1939), an experimental work with a New South Wales setting, and *The Living and the Dead* (1941), a study of a mother, son, and daughter in pre-war London striving to cope with a disintegrating world. During his service in the RAF White met Manoly Lascaris with whom he was to share the rest of his life. The Australian landscape had never quite ceased to haunt him, and after being demobbed White returned to Australia where he devoted himself to writing ambitious novels which were inspired by the paintings of his friends Russell Drysdale, Sydney Nolan, and William Dobell. *The Aunt's Story* (1948), which centres on an Australian society spinster, anticipates later work in its preoccupations with the outsider as seer. There followed two of his best-known novels, *The *Tree of Man* (1955) and **Voss* (1957). White's interest in the visionary experience and in locating a capacity for it in persons written off by orthodox society was treated boldly in *Riders in the Chariot* (1961), where four disparate people are seen as united by an apocalyptic intimation; in the character of Himmelfarb the novel shows White's deep imaginative understanding of pre-war German and German Jewish culture. *The Solid Mandala* (1966) is concerned with twins (Waldo and Arthur) who clearly represent a split in the author's own personality; it has at its imaginative centre the Jungian concept of the mandala. *The Vivisector* (1970), the life-story of a painter who is seer and diagnostician of society, is also a portrait of Sydney in its evolution in a lifetime from 'sunlit village into the present-day parvenu bastard, compound of San Francisco and Chicago'. *The Eye of the Storm* (1973) returns to the mother, son, daughter triangle. In 1964 White had published a volume of short stories, *The Burnt Ones*; a second collection, *The Cockatoos* (1974), contains in the novella 'A Woman's Hand' a masterly study of two couples, showing the complexity, subtlety, and cruelty present in one person's influence upon another. *A Fringe of Leaves* (1976) focuses on a shipwreck off the Australian coast in 1836. *The Twyborn Affair* (1979) has claims to be White's most daring novel, through independence over gender. *Flaws in the Glass* (1981), an autobiographical work, connects significant epiphanies, experiences, and moments of inception of the novels; it contains generous tributes to Manoly, less-than-generous accounts of many Australian public figures, and lyrical renderings of journeys in Greece. In it White calls himself a 'lapsed Anglican egotist agnostic pantheist occultist existentialist would-be though failed Christian Australian'. *Memoirs of the Many in One* (1986) continues his interest in transsexuality; *Three Uneasy Pieces* (1988) presents reflections on ageing. *Patrick White Speaks Out* (1990) collects speeches and other pieces.

WHITE, (Herbert) Terence de Vere (1912–94), Irish novelist, journalist, and man of letters, born in Dublin of a Protestant father and a Catholic mother, educated at Trinity College, Dublin. He was literary editor of *The Irish Times* from 1962 to 1977, to which he also contributed reviews regularly over many years. He wrote several works of Irish biography (including *The Parents of Oscar Wilde*, 1967; *Tom Moore*, 1977) and social history, including notably the autobiographical *A Fretful Midge* (1957), which contains portraits of *Gogarty, *Chesterton, George Egerton, Jack *Yeats, and others. He published volumes of short stories and novels, many of them comedies of Anglo-Irish and Irish manners, including *Tara* (1967), *The Distance and the Dark* (1973), *The Radish Memoirs* (1974), *Johnnie Cross* (1983), which caused a furore amongst feminists by its irreverent portrayal of the marriage of George Eliot, and *Chat Show* (1987). *A Leaf from the Yellow Book* (1958) is a memoir, with diary extracts and correspondence, of Mary Chavelita Dunne (George Egerton), known to him as 'Aunt Chavvy'. He was married to Victoria *Glendinning, the biographer and novelist.

WHITE, T(erence) H(anbury) (1906–64), British novelist, born in India, educated at Cheltenham College and Queens' College, Cambridge. He is chiefly remembered for his novels founded on the Arthurian legend, beginning with *The Sword in the Stone* (1938) which, together with *The Witch in the Wood* (1939) and *The Ill-Made Knight* (1940), was incorporated into *The Once and Future King* (1958), a tragi-comic fantasia on Malory's *Le Morte d'Arthur*. Further novels, such as *Mistress Masham's Repose* (1946), which posits the survival in England of Swift's Lilliputians, also expressed his attraction to the past. Most of his short stories have been collected in *The Maharajah and Other Stories* (1981). His non-fiction includes *England Have My Bones* (1936), *The Age of Scandal* (1950), and *The Scandalmonger* (1952); the latter two volumes are glowing portraits of eighteenth-century life. In *The Goshawk* (1951) he describes, with great poetic intensity, his efforts to train a hawk. *The Book of Beasts* (1954) is a free translation from a twelfth-century Latin bestiary. There is a life by S. T. *Warner, published in 1967.

White Goddess, The, a 'historical grammar of poetic myth', by Robert *Graves, published in 1948. The work propounds his beliefs concerning 'true' poetry, or lyrical and imaginative as opposed to rationally discursive and satirical verse; Graves maintains that work of this kind results from the interaction of the writer's masculine energies with the primeval and magical power of the matriarchal Moon Goddess, who is synonymous with the Muse. The book draws on archaeological, anthropological, and mythological material from a wide range of cultures, predominantly Celtic and Mediterranean, to substantiate its propositions by reference to the traditions of bardic and vatic practices. Graves emphasizes the cultural essentiality of the feminine principle and the invidious effects of its suppression by the restrictive male values of reason and logic; in this respect *The White*

Goddess provides a mythology encompassing certain fundamental attitudes in his poetry, which is notable for the philosophical intensity of its treatments of women and its antagonism towards modern social and religious norms. As his *Selected Letters* (1982) indicates, the work was engendered by his correspondence with the Welsh poet Lynette Roberts regarding Gaelic and Brythonic influences on English poetry. The book's concern with the interdependence of poetry and magic is of relevance to the interests of W. B. *Yeats and other twentieth-century poets whose involvements with aspects of the occult have informed their work.

WHITEHEAD, A(lfred) N(orth) (1861–1947), British mathematician and philosopher, born at Ramsgate, Kent, educated at Trinity College, Cambridge, of which he became a fellow in 1884. *A Treatise of Universal Algebra* (1898) established his reputation as a mathematician. His most distinguished pupil was Bertrand *Russell, with whom he wrote *Principia Mathematica* (3 volumes, 1910–13), widely regarded as the greatest contribution to mathematical logic since the time of Aristotle; a projected fourth volume was not completed due to Whitehead's growing absorption in metaphysics and the philosophy of science. He was Professor of Applied Mathematics at Imperial College, London, from 1914 to 1924, when he was appointed to a professorship in philosophy at Harvard. *The Principles of Natural Knowledge* (1919) and *The Concept of Nature* (1920) expounded the philosophy of nature anticipated by the rejection of traditional physics in his paper 'On Mathematical Concepts of the Material World' (1906); his theory of 'extensive connexion' considered nature as a fabric of interrelated processes, a view informed by Einstein's relativity theory, which Whitehead modified in *The Principle of Relativity* (1922). From the mid-1920s onward he was preoccupied with his 'philosophy of organism', expanding his concepts of nature into a metaphysical doctrine of the endless generation of forms and events. *Process and Reality* (1929) is the principal exposition of his metaphysics. His other works include *Science and the Modern World* (1925), *Adventures in Ideas* (1933), and *Religion in the Making* (1926), which clarifies the religious implications of his philosophy.

WHITEHEAD, E(dward) A(nthony) (1933–), British dramatist, born in Liverpool, educated at Cambridge University. He worked as a postman, milkman, bus conductor, teacher, drug salesman, and, from 1966 to 1971, an advertising account executive before turning to the theatre. His first play, *The Foursome* (1971), is about two courting couples picnicking near Liverpool; *Alpha Beta* (1972) is about a marriage in terminal decline; and *The Sea Anchor* (1975) is about a group of people on a somewhat forlorn 'dirty weekend' who wait vainly on the Irish coast for the arrival by dinghy of a friend whose frustrations may or may not have brought him to suicide. All these plays define the relationship between the sexes as a mix of hatred, horror, fascination, and mutual disgust; but none in more extreme terms than *Old Flames* (1975), during which the only male character, invited out to dinner, is literally eaten by the women he has disappointed and misused, among them his own mother. *Mecca* (1977), set in a Moroccan holiday camp, also involves a xenophobic mistrust of national differences, and reaches a climax with the murder by two sexually envious Englishmen of a native suspected of rape. Whitehead has also served as the *Spectator*'s theatre critic.

White Hotel, The, a novel by D. M. *Thomas, published in 1981. This ambitious, intricate novel attempts to combine reflections on the Holocaust, a deconstruction of psychoanalytic insights, and speculations on telepathy and precognition. In the prologue, Freud introduces the reader to the case of his (fictitious) patient Anna G., whose pornographic fantasies in verse and prose form the first two chapters of the novel. Anna's dream-world, in which her sexual imaginings are acted out in a theatre of death and destruction, provides Freud with supporting evidence for his evolving theory of the death instinct as a motivating psychic force. He sees the roots of her problematic behaviour in her memories of her mother's adultery, her own disturbed sexual history, and her own probable homosexuality; Chapter 3 is presented in the form of a psychoanalytic paper. In Chapter 4, the real Anna is introduced as an ageing opera singer, Lisa Erdmann. After undergoing psychoanalysis, she has made a tentative success of her life and career; in a retrospective correspondence with Freud discussing her case, however, she discreetly points out the limitations of his therapeutic insights, locating her repressed Jewishness as a major cause of her psychopathology. An encounter with a Soviet opera singer leads Lisa to marriage, surrogate motherhood, and the promise of a peaceful old age in the abandoned Ukrainian setting of her childhood. But her Jewish origins and connections devastate her life; in order to retain her son, Lisa is forced to accept her Jewish heritage. They are sent to Babi Yar, where she is savagely murdered with a bayonet by Soviet soldiers in a transformed re-enactment of her early fantasies. Thus the novel extends Freud's theories by presenting past, present, and future as a psychic continuum, indicating that Lisa's fantasies derive as much from telepathy and precognition as from childhood material. In the final, surrealistic chapter, the dead Lisa finally comes to terms with her life and its significant figures in a fantasized Palestine.

WHITEMORE, Hugh (1936–), British dramatist, born in Tunbridge Wells, educated at the Royal Academy of Dramatic Art. He is the author of several stage plays, most of them involving real people or true stories. These include *Stevie* (1977), about the poet Stevie *Smith; *Pack of Lies* (1983), based on the case of Helen and Peter Kroger, about the impact on an ordinary suburban family of the discovery that their neighbours and close friends are Soviet spies in whose exposure and arrest they are expected by the authorities to co-operate; *Breaking the Code* (1986), about Alan Turing, the mathematician who cracked the secrets of the Germans' Enigma machine in the Second World War and committed suicide after he was brought to trial for homosexual practices; and *The Best of Friends* (1988), about the three-way friendships of a Benedictine nun, Dame Laurentia McLachlan, the director of the Fitzwilliam Museum in Cambridge, Sir Sydney Cockerell, and the dramatist Bernard *Shaw. *It's Ralph* (1991), about a visitor from the past who reminds a rich broadcaster of his lost values and rejected idealism, was a rare foray into dramatic invention. Whitemore has also written many original scripts and dramatizations for television, and the screenplay for the film *84 Charing Cross Road*.

White Noise, see DELILLO, DON.

WHITING, John (1917–63), British playwright, born in Salisbury, Wiltshire, the son of an army captain, educated at the Royal Academy of Dramatic Art, London; he worked as an actor in London and the regions before becoming a dramatist. His first play, *A Penny for a Song* (1951), is a slight comedy about English eccentrics awaiting a Napoleonic invasion; his next play, *Saint's Day*, was more substantial and proved more controversial when it was staged the same year. A nightmarish portrait of a strange, paranoid poet and his family, it may now be seen as a precursor, less social in its emphasis, of the break with drawing-room drama that was to occur with the arrival of **Look Back in Anger* in 1956. Whiting's later plays include the intellectually intricate *Marching Song* (1954), about a general accused of war crimes, and a forceful adaptation of Aldous *Huxley's study of religious hysteria, *The Devils* (1961); but none matched the imaginative power of *Saint's Day*. He served as drama critic of the *London Magazine* until he was disabled by the cancer which eventually killed him.

Whitsun Weddings, The, Philip *Larkin's third collection of poems, published to widespread critical acclaim in 1964. The book contains many demonstrations of his remarkable technical accomplishment in accommodating an essentially conversational mode of expression within elaborately constructed rhymed stanzas. Much of the poetry extends the sceptical clarity of vision established in *The *Less Deceived*, although a more specific and aggressive social critique is articulated; 'The Large Cool Store', 'Essential Beauty', and other poems comment on a commercially oriented society's exploitation of the human capacity for imaginative fulfilment. Such poems firmly imply the compassionate identification of values central to common experience which is most clearly stated in the celebration of change and renewal of the title poem and in the concluding affirmation that 'What will survive of us is love' of 'At an Arundel Tomb'. Larkin's purposeful humour is also more distinct than it had previously been; the incisive light verse of 'Naturally the Foundation Will Bear Your Expenses' amuses at the expense of complacency and presumptuousness in the academic profession; 'Take One Home for the Kiddies' uses effects of light verse to make its harrowing point concerning mistreatment of animals, while the calculated scurrility of 'A Study of Reading Habits' enjoins readers to 'Get stewed: | Books are a load of crap'. 'Here' is perhaps the most notable example of the refinement and concentration with which Larkin uses a wide range of urban and natural imagery to achieve the vivid particularity characteristic of the collection.

Who's Afraid of Virginia Woolf? (1962), a play by Edward *Albee, his first major success. It examines the marriage of George, a middle-aged history lecturer, and the older Martha, the wealthy college president's daughter. They spend the night in a sexually fraught drinking bout with a young biologist, Nick, and his 'slim-hipped' wife Honey who are drawn into the marital crisis. George and Martha, childless, have compensated for that lack by creating a fantasy child, the intangible measure of their destructive love, now aged 21. The three acts—'Fun and Games', 'Walpurgisnacht', and 'The Exorcism'—represent a movement from caustic wit through the demonic power of contradictory illusions to a potential purging of self-deception, and the play powerfully interweaves political, psychological, and metaphysical meanings. The names George and Martha evoke the idealism of the American Revolution, and their harrowing marriage symbolizes the collapse of American liberalism. Nick's brilliance as a biologist foreshadows a totalitarianism in which 'we will not have much music, much painting, but we will have a civilisation of men, smooth, blond, and right at the middleweight limit', while Honey's sexless insipidity conceals a hunger for violence, and George fosters a liberal humanism which seems imprisoned in the past. The older couple's childlessness is mirrored in the phantom pregnancy which prompted the younger couple's marriage, and both represent the sterility of an exhausted culture. George's decision to 'sacrifice' their son marks the play's climax: the Walpurgisnacht spirits are exorcised, and May-day dawns with the young couple's departure and Martha's defeat. George's historical awareness and ritual skill have compelled Martha to acknowledge the relationship and renounce a fiction, but his earlier question remains both urgent and profound: 'Truth and illusion, who knows the difference, eh, toots?'

WICKHAM, Anna, pseudonym of Edith Alice Mary HEPBURN, née Harper (1884–1947), British poet, born in Wimbledon; she grew up in Australia, where she attended schools in Brisbane and Sydney. Having returned to London in 1905, she trained as an opera singer before marriage and motherhood precluded her progress in this field. *Songs* (1911), her first collection of verse, appeared under the pseudonym 'John Oland'. Among her subsequent volumes, *The Contemplative Quarry* (1915) and *The Little Old House* (1921) were published by Harold *Monro's Poetry Bookshop; *Thirty-Six New Poems* (1936) was the last of her works to appear before her suicide in 1947. Her poetry is notable for its accomplished flexibility in the use of rhyming verse forms and for the epigrammatic energies of her feminist critiques of social and marital convention. D. H. *Lawrence, Dylan *Thomas, and Malcolm *Lowry were among her friends. In addition to the poems and essays it collects, *The Writings of Anna Wickham* (edited by R. D. Smith, 1984) contains a lengthy fragment of autobiography.

WIDEMAN, John Edgar (1941–), African-American writer, born in Washington, DC, educated at the University of Pennsylvania, and at New College, Oxford. He was Professor of English at the University of Wyoming, then taught at the University of Massachusetts in Amherst. Among his best-known works are his novels set in Homewood, the African-American area of Pittsburgh where he grew up. His novels include *A Glance Away* (1967), *Hurry Home* (1970), *The Lynchers* (1973), *Damballah* (1981), *Hiding Place* (1981), *Sent for You Yesterday* (1983), *Reuben* (1987), and *Philadelphia Fire* (1991). His stories appeared in *Fever* (1989) and *All Stories Are True: The Stories of John Edgar Wideman* (1992). His acclaimed memoir *Brothers and Keepers* (1984), which alternates in style between reflective literary narrative and urban streetwise language, compellingly explores the events, social context, psychological pressures, and divergent circumstances that led his younger brother Robert to prison for murder and himself to a middle-class life as an academic.

Wide Sargasso Sea, a novel by Jean *Rhys, published in 1966. Inspired by C. Brontë's *Jane Eyre*, this novel radically reinterprets events from its predecessor in the light of Rhys's Caribbean background and experience; the central character, minor though crucial in Brontë's narrative, is Bertha Mason, or Antoinette Cosway as she is renamed here. The first section of the novel is narrated by Antoinette: it is an account of dispossession and loss of heritage, set in the West Indies in the period immediately following the abolition of slavery. Through a complex web of interrelationships Rhys explores the wider cultural and historical questions of identity and the relationship of centre and periphery. Antoinette loses her mother to madness and her surname—symbolizing her vanished paternal heritage—to her English stepfather's. Her sensibility displays the intermingling of colonial and indigenous elements; her internal conflicts mirror the shifts and contradictions of historical events. The second section of the novel is narrated by Rochester, Rhys's most complex male characterization. Antoinette is seen through his eyes both as the embodiment of his male fear of his own sexuality, and as the disruptive and chaotic Other of imperial discourse. Rochester represents the imperial centre; Antoinette is an emblem of settler colonialism, despised by the masters and locked in an ambivalent bond of dependence and hate with the black population of slaves. In the background is the black populace, harbingers of a nascent era of nationhood. The stripping of Antoinette's name by Rochester—who renames her Bertha—is a potent metaphor for the loss of identity to the Other's alienating gaze. Antoinette's atavistic reversion to superstition, drunkenness, and childhood paranoia confirms Rochester's worst suspicions about the effect of 'native' blood and culture on the settler population and reflects the ruptures of the colonial enterprise. The third section is again narrated by Antoinette. Now a virtual prisoner in Rochester's English home, she identifies totally with the madness imposed on her, and reacts in the only way she has learned: her bid for autonomy and release is the burning of her prison and its inhabitants. It is here that the novel connects with its predecessor, rewriting it from the perspective of the oppressed; but even the most sensitive critics have failed to note that Antoinette's tools of rebellion have been borrowed from the black insurgents of her own islands. Thus the novel with its ambiguous conclusion signals a continuing exploration of the construction of cultural identity and the relationship of master and slave.

WIEBE, Rudy (Henry) (1934–), Canadian novelist, born in Northern Saskatchewan, educated at the Universities of Alberta and Tübingen. Raised in a tightly knit Mennonite community, Wiebe has remained a staunch Christian throughout his adult life, teaching at the Mennonite Brethren Bible College, Goshen College, Indiana, and at the University of Alberta, while also pursuing a career as a writer of post-modernist fictions. Most of his work is about Prairie minorities and demonstrates a strong regional commitment to questioning conventionally accepted versions of Canadian cultural identity. His first novel, *Peace Shall Destroy Many* (1962), is about a young Mennonite torn between the traditions of his community and religion and a yearning for a more individual existence. *The Blue Mountains of China* (1970) surveys the experience of the Mennonite diaspora in the Soviet Union, Paraguay, and Canada. *The Temptations of Big Bear* (1973), regarded by many as his finest novel to date, is another large-scale work, centred on the figure of a late nineteenth-century Cree Indian chief who defied central Canadian authority. Wiebe has also published the novels *First and Vital Candle* (1966), *The Scorched-Wood People* (1977), *The Mad Trapper* (1980), and *My Lovely Enemy* (1983); the short-story volumes *Where Is the Voice Coming from?* (1974) and *The Angel of the Tar Sands and Other Stories* (1982); *Playing Dead* (1989), 'a contemplation concerning the Arctic'; and a novel for children.

WIENERS, John (1934–), American poet, born in Boston, educated at Boston College. After meeting Charles *Olson in 1954, Wieners extended his education at *Black Mountain College, under the tutelage of both Olson and Robert *Duncan. Like Duncan, Wieners brings the Romantic tradition into modernist and post-modernist verse; his stress on lost love and yearning makes him the most directly lyrical poet of the Black Mountain tradition. Wieners is aware that the context of his time has altered and transposed the Romantic stance; he responds to this by adopting a series of elegant but restless linguistic procedures, each of which is designed both to acknowledge and to resist the marginalization of his voice. *The Hotel Wentley Poems* (1958) remains his most famous book, partly as a result of the emotionally explicit way in which he deals with his life as a homosexual and one-time drug addict. *Ace of Pentacles* (1964) extends his technical mastery, while *Nerves* (1970) acts as a brilliant summary of his early mode. *Woman* (1972), *Hotels* (1974), and *Behind the State Capitol or Cincinnati Pike* (1975) initiate the second major phase of his career. His *Selected Poems 1958–1984* (1986), includes two interviews with Wieners and is introduced by Allen *Ginsberg.

WILBUR, Richard (Purdy) (1921–), American poet and translator; born in New York, educated at Amherst College and at Harvard, where he became an assistant professor in 1950. He was Poet Laureate of the United States in 1987–8. His first two collections of poetry, *The Beautiful Changes* (1947) and *Ceremony* (1950), gained him wide acclaim for the elegance and accomplishment with which his work reflected the post-war atmosphere of cautious optimism. His later volumes include *Things of This World* (1956), *Advice to a Prophet* (1961), and *A Finished Man* (1985); *Walking to Sleep* (1969) and *The Mind-Reader* (1976) contain original work and verse translations of poems by Villon, Borges, *Brodsky, and Voznesensky. Many of his earlier poems form rational affirmations of commonly held social and cultural values. In the course of the 1960s his verse displayed an increasingly imaginative character and developed a challenging moral and psychological intensity. His best work illustrates his belief that 'what poetry does with ideas is redeem them from abstraction'. *New and Collected Poems* appeared in 1988. His critical writings are collected in *Responses* (1976). Among his numerous adaptations of plays by French dramatists are his versions of Molière's *Tartuffe* (1963) and *The School for Husbands* (1992), and Racine's *Andromache* (1982). His works as an editor include his edition of Poe's *Complete Poems* (1959). *Conversations with Richard Wilbur*, edited by William Butts, appeared in 1990.

WILDER, Thornton (Niven) (1897–1975), American playwright and novelist, born in Madison, Wisconsin, educated at Yale and Princeton, before joining the faculty at the University of Chicago. He made a considerable impact with his first three novels: *The Cabala* (1926), set in twentieth-century Rome and essentially a fantasy about the death of the pagan gods; *The *Bridge of San Luis Rey* (1927; Pulitzer Prize); and *The Woman of Andros* (1930), based partly on a play by Terence. In the 1930s he became the focus of a major critical debate on the left about what constituted 'realist' writing and the politics of such an aesthetics. *Heaven's My Destination* (1934), is a picaresque novel about the adventures in the Midwest of a travelling seller of textbooks whose evangelical mission is to spread the teachings of Ghandi. *The Ides of March* (1948) is a historical novel about the last days of Julius Caesar. With **Our Town* (1938; Pulitzer Prize) he turned to drama in a study of small town New England which remains among the most widely performed plays in America. Other plays include *The Skin of Our Teeth* (1942; Pulitzer Prize), partly based on Joyce's **Finnegans Wake*, and combining farce, allegory, and deliberate anachronisms in an attempt to suggest that human experience is transhistorical, *A Life in the Sun* (1955), based on Euripides' *Alcestis*, and the comedy *The Merchant of Yonkers* (1939, performed in New York 1938), which was rewritten as *Matchmaker* (1954), then adapted into the immensely successful musical *Hello Dolly!* (1964). He returned to fiction with *The Eighth Day* (1967) and *Theophilus North* (1973). A posthumous selection of his essays appeared as *American Characteristics and Other Essays* (1979). All of his work, he once wrote, was devoted to the search for 'not verisimilitude but reality', an indication that his work pursued what he perceived as truth rather than attempting to abide by some formal prescription.

WILDING, Michael (1942–), Australian-based fiction writer, critic, and editor, born in Worcester, England, educated at Oxford University. He taught at the University of Sydney in 1967–8; he settled permanently in Australia in 1969, becoming Reader in English at the University of Sydney in 1972. Wilding has continued his work in English literature and in political culture, publishing *Political Fictions* (1980), and has also established himself as a significant voice in his adopted country. During the Vietnam War (1962–73) Wilding co-edited with David *Malouf and others the anti-war poetry and prose collection *We Took Their Orders and Are Dead* (1971). As a writer, and as publisher of the radical magazine *Tabloid Story* (1972–5), he has links with Frank *Moorhouse in both his Australian focus and his innovative structural and intertextual techniques. His fiction includes the short-story collections *Aspects of the Dying Process* (1972), *The West Midland Underground* (1975), and *The Phallic Forest* (1978), and the novels *Living Together* (1974), *The Short Story Embassy* (1975), and *Pacific Highway* (1982); in 1984 *Reading the Signs* appeared, and in 1985 *The Paraguayan Experiment*, a 'documentary novel' recreating William Lane's 1893 idealistic New Australia settlement in Paraguay. In his works, Wilding explores the parallels between the ways in which individuals and groups order their worlds, and authors shape their fiction. Further short stories are gathered in *The Man of Slow Feeling* (1985), *Great Climate* (1990), *This Is For You* (1994), and *Book of the Reading* (1994), while *Under Saturn* (1988) is a collection of four novellas. He is the editor of *The Oxford Book of Australian Short Stories* (1995). Recent cultural and literary criticism includes *Dragon's Teeth: Literature in the English Revolution* (1987) and *Social Visions* (1993).

Wild Swans at Coole, The, see YEATS, W. B.

WILKINSON, Anne Gibbons (1910–61), Canadian poet, born in Toronto, educated in London, Ontario, the USA, and France. A beautifully written memoir of her childhood, 'Four Corners of My World', appeared posthumously in the **Tamarack Review*, a journal of which she was a founding editor, in 1961 and was subsequently republished in her *Collected Poems*. She came to poetry fairly late in life and is best known for two collections, *Counterpoint to Sleep* (1951) and *The Hangman Ties the Holly* (1955). Her *Collected Poems* appeared, with a prefatory essay by A. J. M. *Smith, in 1968. The subjects of her poetry include her background as a member of a distinguished Canadian family, philosophical speculation, and, especially in her last years (she died early from cancer), death. Her prose work *Lion in the Way* (1956) is an account of the early years of her family's settlement in Upper Canada, notable for the vivid portrait of her great-grandmother and as social history.

WILLEFORD, Charles (Ray) (1919–88), American writer, born in Little Rock, Arkansas; he enlisted in the US Army at the age of 16, fought as a tank commander with the 10th Armoured Division during the Second World War, and was awarded the Silver Star and Luxembourg Croix de Guerre. Later, while stationed in California, he published a volume of verse, *Proletarian Laughter* (1948), and a San Francisco novel trilogy: *High Priest of California* (1953), *Until I Am Dead* (1953; retitled *Wild Wives*), and *Pick-up* (1954). On leaving the army he moved to Florida, studied at the University of Miami, where he later taught English literature, and reviewed crime fiction for the *Miami Herald*. Later novels include *The Burnt Orange Heresy* (1971), perhaps his best work, *Cockfighter* (1971), and, under the pseudonym 'Will Charles', an 'existentialist Western', *The Hombre from Sonora* (1972). He is best known, however, for the series of original crime novels about Hoke Moseley, a detective in the Miami police department, which, in their portrayal of American life, have something in common with the work of Elmore *Leonard. These are *Miami Blues* (1984), *New Hope for the Dead* (1986), *Side-Swipe* (1987), and *The Way We Die Now* (1988). The first volume of an autobiography, *Something about a Soldier*, appeared in 1989.

WILLIAMS, Bernard (1929–), British philosopher, born at Westcliffe, Essex, educated at Balliol College, Oxford. He became Knightsbridge Professor of Philosophy at Cambridge in 1967. He was Provost of King's College, Cambridge, from 1979 to 1987, when he was appointed Monroe Deutsch Professor of Philosophy at the University of California, Berkeley. In 1990 he became White's Professor of Moral Philosophy at Oxford. Williams is highly regarded for his work on personal identity, out of which he has developed challenging critiques of utilitarianism and traditional theories of ethics. Among his earlier publications are *Imagination and the Self* (1966) and *Morality: An Introduction to Ethics* (1972). His questionings of fixed concepts of identity in *Problems of the Self: Philosophical Papers, 1956–1972* (1973) form the basis of his arguments in *Utilitarianism: For and Against* (1973), in which his co-author J. J. C. Smart defends the doctrine. Williams's objections to the prescriptive assumptions of moral philosophy are strongly presented in *Moral Luck: Philosophical Papers, 1973–1980* (1981), which describes his view of the essentially subjective nature of human motivation and ethical choice, and *Ethics and the Limits of Philosophy* (1985). His stated intention in the latter work is 'to give a new picture of ethical life and to redefine philosophy's relation to it'; the ensuing review of moral philosophy from Aristotle to R. M. *Hare suggests to Williams that philosophers cannot supply convincing answers to the Socratic question 'How should man live?' Thomas *Nagel referred to him as 'the leading contemporary disparager of transcendent ambitions in moral philosophy'. *Making Sense of Humanity* appeared in 1995.

WILLIAMS, C(harles) K(enneth) (1936–), American poet, born in Newark, New Jersey, educated at the University of Pennsylvania; he divides his time between living in Paris and teaching at George Mason University, Virginia. *Lies* (1969) and *I Am the Bitter Name* (1971) contain poems reflecting an anguished masculinity and sense of existential panic, together with the protest politics of the 1960s. More memorable are the long poems 'A Day for Anne Frank' and 'In the Heart of the Beast—May 1970—Cambodia, Kent State, Jackson State'. Williams achieved a breakthrough in his collection *With Ignorance* (1977), deploying the long, sinuous lines and continual use of enjambements which are hallmarks of his mature work. Recalling Whitman, William Carlos *Williams, and *Ginsberg, his style became at once more authoritative, his social concerns more immediate as well as compellingly personal. Poems such as 'Bread' and 'The Last Deaths' focus upon the margins of American society, and the victims of American foreign policy. The human dimensions of moral and political issues continue to be explored in *Tar* (1983) and *Flesh and Blood* (1987). Full of sharply observed details, constantly questioning, his poems take nothing for granted. His selected *Poems 1963–1983* appeared in 1988; *A Dream of Mind* was published in 1992.

WILLIAMS, Charles (Walter Stansby) (1886–1945), British novelist, poet, and man of letters, born in London. With C. S. *Lewis and J. R. R. *Tolkien, with whom he formed the *Inklings group, he was the major author of fantasy in the twentieth century. His novels, which often reflected a Christian ideology, have been described as supernatural thrillers. Each of the seven tales—*War in Heaven* (1930), *Many Dimensions* (1931), *The Place of the Lion* (1931), *The Greater Trumps* (1932), *Shadows of Ecstacy* (1933), *Descent into Hell* (1937), and *All Hallows Eve* (1944)—presents in theological terms a quest through complexly occult circumstances for a goal similar to the Grail, in whose numinous glow the plots tend to dissolve. As a poet he is best known for his cycle on the Arthurian legend, *Taliessin through Logres* (1938), *The Region of the Summer*

Stars (1944), and *Arthurian Torso* (1948) with a commentary by C. S. Lewis. His most important theological writing was *The Descent of the Dove* (1939). He also wrote plays, biographies, and literary criticism, notably *The Figure of Beatrice: A Study in Dante* (1943). See Thomas T. Howard's *The Novels of Charles Williams* (1983).

WILLIAMS, (George) Emlyn (1905–87), British dramatist, born in Flintshire, educated at Oxford University. The best-known of his many plays were the thriller *Night Must Fall* (1935); *The Corn Is Green* (1938), an autobiographical portrait of the successful education of a working-class Welsh boy; and *The Wind of Heaven* (1945), a variation on the Christmas story, transported to nineteenth-century Wales. Williams was also a professional director and actor, and appeared in many dramatic works, notably as a solo performer in his own adaptations of novels by Dickens. *George* (1961) and *Emlyn* (1973) are his autobiographies.

WILLIAMS, Hugo (Mordaunt) (1942–), British poet, born in Windsor, educated at Eton; he was on the staff of *London Magazine* from 1960 to 1970, when he became a freelance writer. *Symptoms of Loss* (1965), his first collection of verse, displayed the combination of restraint and candour that have remained essential aspects of his highly individual tone. *Sugar Daddy* (1970) and *Some Sweet Day* (1975) contained many short and acutely observed poems exemplifying the poetic minimalism of the early 1970s. A fourth collection, *Love-Life* (1979), saw the development of more discursive modes. *Writing Home* (1985) gained Williams wide recognition as a poet of unusual sensitivity and assurance for its autobiographical exploration of boyhood and youth. An autobiographical perspective is also central to *Self-Portrait with a Slide* (1990); numerous poems reintroduce 'Sonny Jim', an uneasy persona who featured repeatedly in earlier verse. *First Poems* (1985), *Selected Poems* (1989), and *Dock Leaves* (1994) are among recent collections. *All the Time in the World* (1966) and *No Particular Place To Go* (1981) are prose accounts of his travels.

WILLIAMS, John A(lfred) (1925–), American novelist, born in Jackson, Mississippi, educated at Syracuse University, New York. Williams's novels are notable for their political dissection of American society in terms of the African-American experience; their dominant tone is suggested by the title of his first novel, *The Angry Ones* (1960). In *Night Song* (1961), a jazz musician employs his art to combat racial injustice. In *Sissie* (1963; UK title *Journey out of Anger*, 1968) an increasing political militancy is displayed which was sustained in novels such as *The Man Who Cried I Am* (1967), *Sons of Darkness, Sons of Light* (1969), and *Captain Blackman* (1972). His later work, in which the accent is more on the richness of African-American culture, includes the novels *Mothersill and the Foxes* (1975), *The Junior Bachelor Society* (1976), *! Click Song* (1982), *The Berhama Account* (1985), and *Jacob's Ladder* (1987). His other books include *Africa: Her History, Lands, and People* (1962), *This Is My Country, Too* (1965), *The Most Native of Sons: A Biography of Richard Wright* (1970), *The King God Didn't Save: Reflections on the Life and Death of Martin Luther King, Jr* (1970), *Flashbacks: A Twenty-Year Diary of Article Writing* (1972), *Minorities in the City* (1975), and *Flashbacks 2: A Diary of Article Writing* (1991). With Dennis A. Williams, he has written *If I Stop Laughing I'll Die: The Comedy and Tragedy of Richard Pryor* (1991). He is the editor with Gilbert H. Muller, of *Bridges: Literature Across Cultures* (1993), an anthology of American writing. See Gilbert H. Muller, *John A. Williams* (1984).

WILLIAMS, John Hartley (1942–), British poet, born in Cheshire, educated at the universities of Nottingham and London. He taught English at universities in France, Yugoslavia, and Cameroon before becoming a lecturer in Modern English at the Free University of Berlin in 1976. In *Hidden Identities* (1982), his first collection of poetry, the imaginative and emotional seriousness of much of the verse is inseparable from his quirkily surreal wit. His long poem 'Ephraim Destiny's Perfectly Utter Darkness' appeared in *Bright River Yonder* (1987), a long sequence whose setting is drawn from presentations of the nineteenth-century American frontier in the cinema and popular literature. The book exemplifies the practice Williams has termed 'fiction by ellipsis', a firm thematic continuity emerging from its apparently disjunctive succession of dramatic monologues, songs, and occasional lyrical interludes. His volumes of poetry *Cornerless People* (1990) and *Double* (1994) contain work which entertainingly experiments with the conventions of characterization.

WILLIAMS, Jonathan (Chamberlain) (1929–), American poet, born in Asheville, North Carolina, educated at Princeton. From 1951 to 1956 he was closely associated with *Black Mountain College and contributed poems to its *Review*. Since 1962 he has held posts as poet-in-residence at numerous American universities. In 1951 he founded the Jargon Society Inc., one of the most valuable of the American *small presses, which has published verse by Charles *Olson, Robert *Creeley, Denise *Levertov, Michael *McClure, and many others; his editions of work by Louis *Zukofsky, Lorine *Niedecker, and Mina *Loy drew attention to their writing after long periods of neglect. *Sixmas* (1950), the first collection of Williams's poetry, has been followed by approximately 100 further titles, among them *Lullabies Twisters Gibbers Drags* (1963), *Strung out with Elgar on a Hill* (1971), *Rivulets and Sibilants of Dent* (1987), and *Quantulumcumque* (1990); *An Ear in Bartram's Tree* (1969) and *Get Hot or Get Out* (1982) contain selections from his work. His relentlessly experimental poetry is marked by an often outrageous sense of humour in combination with austere economies of form. Much of his verse confers epigrammatic refinement on the rhythms and topics of common speech. His other publications include *Descant on Rawthey's Madrigal* (1968), a record of conversations with Basil *Bunting.

WILLIAMS, Joy (1944–), American writer, born in Chelmsford, Massachusetts, educated at Marietta College and the University of Iowa. Her first novel, *A State of Grace* (1973), explored the consciousness of a woman about to give birth; it was followed by *The Changeling* (1978) and *Taking Care* (1982), a collection of stories. It was with *Breaking and Entering* (1988), her first novel to be published outside America, that Williams gained a reputation as one of the exponents of the hard-edged American movement described as *Dirty Realism. Her whimsical, delicately written tale of a drifting vagrant couple is also reminiscent of the lyrical eccentricity of the domestic comedies of Anne *Tyler. In *The Stories of Escape* (1990) a similar blending of the whimsically introspective and the real is employed.

WILLIAMS, Nigel (1948–), English novelist and playwright, born in Cheshire, educated at Oriel College, Oxford. The comic vein of his writing was already evident in his first novel, *My Life Closed Twice* (1977), which focuses on a would-be novelist, and continued in subsequent novels such as *Jack Be Nimble* (1980) and *Star Turn* (1985). Perhaps his best-known novel is the blackly comic *The Wimbledon Poisoner* (1990), which delves into the deranged mind of a suburban solicitor and local historian who plans to murder his feminist wife. His fusion of drab realism and comic energy is characteristic of much of his work, including *They Came from SW19* (1992; a novel) and *Scenes from a Poisoner's Life* (1994; stories), further narratives about grotesqueries and derangement behind the respectable façades of Wimbledon. His stage plays include *My Brother's Keeper* (1985) and *Country Dancing* (1987). Among his travel works are *2½ Men in a Boat* (1992), retracing Jerome K. Jerome's trip on the Thames, and *From Wimbledon to Waco* (1995), about a family trip to the USA.

WILLIAMS, Raymond (Henry) (1921–88), Welsh critic, scholar, and novelist, born in Pandy, on the Welsh border, the son of a railway signalman, educated at Trinity College, Cambridge. From 1974 to 1983 he was Professor of Drama at Cambridge. His continuing concern was culture and society, the title of his highly regarded book published in 1958, where culture was often, though not exclusively, literature, and society was both a determining and to-be-determined force. Williams had an acute sense of cultural crisis, feeling that the renowned split between self and world which is supposed to have happened in the later nineteenth century was a belated symptom rather than a version of the crisis itself. Once we see the individual as naturally opposed to society, Williams thought, we are too late, caught up in the crisis, not facing or resolving it: we *are* the crisis. In *The Long Revolution* (1961) and *The Country and the City* (1973), distinguished studies in literary and social history, and in his novels, especially the trilogy composed of *Border Country* (1960), *Second Generation* (1964), and *The Fight for Manod* (1979), Williams sought to register and recover lost social alternatives, rejected pictures of possibility. *Culture* (1981), *Toward 2000* (1983), and *Resources of Hope* (edited by Robin Gable, 1989) are also central to his envisionings of a more viable and integrated sociocultural order. Although never doctrinaire, he became increasingly engaged with Marxist theory; *Marxism and Literature* (1977) and the essays collected in *Problems in Materialism and Culture* (1980) address a range of questions raised by a theoretically sophisticated materialism and its consequences. His sympathies with Marxism are evident in *Orwell* (1971), the most notable of his critical studies of a single author. Williams was effectively the founder of the movement which came to be called *Cultural Materialism, a British, Marxist-inclined relative of the American *New Historicism. His interest in other modern media gave rise to *Communications* (1962), *Television: Technology and Cultural Form* (1970), and the essays of *Contact: Human Communication and Its History* (1981). His widely read *Keywords* (1976), a concise and thoughtful study of many of the major terms of current intellectual discourse, is a fine instance of a social meditation which has an immediate social use. Among Williams's other critical works are *Drama from Ibsen to Eliot* (1952), revised as *Drama from Ibsen to Brecht* in 1968, *The English Novel from Dickens to Lawrence* (1970), and *The Politics of Modernism* (1989); his writings as a novelist also include *Loyalties* (1985) and the two volumes of *The People of the Black Mountains, The Beginning* (1989) and *The Eggs of the Eagle* (1990), a treatment of his native landscape and its inhabitants memorable for its imaginative intensity and historical scope. See also MARXIST LITERARY CRITICISM and POPULAR CULTURE.

WILLIAMS, Sherley Anne (1944–), African-American novelist, poet, and critic, born in Bakersfield, California, educated in Fresno and at the universities of California, Howard, and Brown. An expert in African-American literature, which she has taught in several universities, Williams's first published book was a work of academic literary criticism, *Give Birth to Brightness: A Thematic Study of Neo-Black Literature* (1972). She is best known for the novel *Dessa Rose* (1986). In its depiction of a woman slave who is condemned to death for her part in an uprising, the novel in some ways covers the same psychological ground as Toni Morrison's **Beloved*, which appeared the following year. *Dessa Rose* is set during 1829–30 and is similarly inspired by historical events. Among her collections of verse are *The Peacock Poems* (1975) and *Someone Sweet Angel Chile* (1982), the latter inspired by the life of Bessie Smith.

WILLIAMS, Tennessee (Thomas Lanier) (1911–83), American playwright, novelist, and short-story writer, born in Mississippi, where his grandfather was an Episcopal clergyman; the family moved, when Williams was still a boy, to St Louis. After college education and a series of unsatisfactory jobs, he entered the University of Iowa and embarked on his writing career. His first full-length play, *Battle of Angels* (1940; published 1945; later revised as *Orpheus Descending*,

1957), exhibits his characteristic lyricism and understanding of sexual passion, as well as his mastery of stage technique. He first achieved success with *The *Glass Menagerie* (1944), which makes use of expressionist techniques and draws movingly on his own and his sister's early life in St Louis in its account of the tensions between Tom Wingfield (based on Williams himself), his domineering mother, Amanda, and his invalid sister, Laura (based on Williams's sister, Rose). After publishing a collection of eleven one-act plays, *27 Wagons Full of Cotton* (1946), he adapted the D. H. *Lawrence story *You Touched Me!* (1947), collaborating with his friend (and later rival) Donald Windham. He then began work on one of his most popular and successful plays, *A *Streetcar Named Desire* (1947), which describes the downfall of the neurotic beauty Blanche Dubois. Through the character of Blanche, who is at once over-refined and whorish, Williams explores ideas and prejudices about the South and its culture. Other plays followed, including *Summer and Smoke* (1948); *The Rose Tattoo* (1953), a comedy about a Sicilian woman's quest for love; *Camino Real* (1953); and **Cat on a Hot Tin Roof* (1955; Pulitzer Prize), an extremely powerful study of tensions in a Mississippi Delta family, whose patriarch, 'Big Daddy', is dying of cancer. The play's treatment of certain themes, especially that of homosexuality, gave it a widespread notoriety and it was banned in Britain for many years. In subsequent works, the gothic element in Williams's imagination prevailed. These include *Suddenly Last Summer* (1958), which describes the devouring by cannibals on a remote island of the maladjusted and homosexual son of a doting mother; *Sweet Bird of Youth* (1957), in which a handsome gigolo, Chance Wayne, is castrated by the irate father of the girl he has deserted; and *The Night of the Iguana* (1962), in which the iguana chained outside a shabby Mexican hotel symbolizes the chained passions of the characters residing there. Later plays include *Kingdom of Earth* (1968), about a dying transvestite; *In the Bar of the Tokyo Hotel* (1969), a study of a painter; and *Small Craft Warnings* (1972), about 'cast-offs' in a Californian coast bar. Williams's main contribution to the theatre is perhaps his expansion of its conventional emotional range; his characters' stories are compelling dramas, offering theatrical correlatives for deeply felt human desires and needs. His non-dramatic works include short stories (see *The Collected Short Stories of Tennessee Williams*, 1986), two novels, *The Roman Spring of Mrs Stone* (1950), about an ageing actress's relationship with a gigolo, and *Moise and the World of Reason* (1975), about a homosexual writer, as well as a volume of *Memoirs* (1975).

WILLIAMS, William Carlos (1883–1963), American poet, born in Rutherford, New Jersey, where he practised as a paediatrician after studying at the universities of Pennsylvania and Leipzig. As a student he began a long friendship with Ezra *Pound, whose innovative concepts had a profound effect on his development as a poet. *Poems* (1909), his first collection, reflected his admiration for Keats. *The Tempers* (1913) shows his response to the influences of Walt Whitman and *Imagism in its confidently experimental manner. *Al Que Quiere!* (1917) uses highly individual verse forms designed to establish the cadences of ordinary speech as a basis for his poetry. Fidelity to objective reality and commitment to the primacy of local conditions became the essential concerns of his subsequent writing. He sought to create a poetry of American English which would embody his democratic ideals in its hospitality to all levels and forms of human experience. Thom *Gunn's observation that 'His stylistic qualities are governed . . . by a tenderness which makes them fully humane' is particularly relevant to Williams's many poems arising from observation of everyday events, often in the course of his medical work. The long contemplative sequence *Spring and All* (1923), which modulates between verse and prose for its expansive evocation of place and season, is regarded by some as his finest work. He published no further collections until *The Cod Head* in 1932; by this time he had aligned himself with the *Objectivist poetics of *Oppen, *Reznikoff, and *Zukofsky. The Objectivist Press produced his *Collected Poems, 1921–1931* (1934), which was followed by numerous volumes, notably *An Early Martyr* (1935), *The Wedge* (1944), *The Clouds* (1948), and *Pictures from Breughel* (1962). **Paterson* (1963) was a major preoccupation from the mid-1940s until his death. His prose works include *A Voyage to Pagany* (1928), an impressionistic account of a journey to Europe in 1924, and his *Autobiography* (1951); the novels *White Mule* (1937), *In the Money* (1940), and *The Build-Up* (1952) form a trilogy based on the history of his wife's family. *In the American Grain* (1925), which discusses the origins and growth of national cultural identity, is the best-known of his collections of essays. C. J. MacGowan's edition of *Collected Poems* appeared in two volumes in 1987 and 1988. See also BLACK MOUNTAIN WRITERS and PROJECTIVE VERSE.

WILLIAMSON, David (1942–), Australian playwright, born in Melbourne, educated at Monash University. His first play, *The Coming of the Stork* (1970), was performed in Melbourne; other early work, including *The Removalists* (1971) and *Don's Party* (1971), was staged in London as well as Australia; both plays were later filmed. Williamson has also written several important screenplays, for *Gallipoli*, *Phar Lap*, and *The Year of Living Dangerously*, as well as for a number of his own plays. Distinguished immediately by their sharp and witty observation of local Australian life, Williamson's plays subtly explore suppressed tensions often only revealed by the characters under the effects of love, anger, or alcohol. Many draw on Williamson's own milieu to great effect, especially *What if You Died Tomorrow* (1973), *The Department* (1974), and *The Club* (1977). Other plays include *Travelling North* (1979); *The Perfectionist* (1982); *Emerald City* (1987), which comically probes perennial Melbourne/Sydney tensions through the career of a scriptwriter; *Top Silk* (1990), set in the legal world; *Siren* (1991, performed 1992), exploring games of power and sex; *Money and Friends* (1991, performed 1992), a satirical comedy about the rich élite; *Brilliant Lies* (1993), about the backlash against feminism; and *Sanctuary* (1994), the story of an investigative journalist whose biographer won't let him retire. All reveal Williamson's enduring interest in contemporary power pressures within sharply defined social and cultural groups. He has also published his *Collected Plays* (2 volumes, 1986, 1994).

WILLIAMSON, Henry (1895–1977), English author, born in south London, the son of a bank clerk. He served in the army during the First World War, an experience which made him antipathetic towards his fellow men. At the war's close he was a journalist for a short time, and published the first volume of his quartet *The Flax of Dream* (*The Beautiful Years*, 1921; *Dandelion Days*, 1922; *The Dream of Fair Women*, 1924; *The Pathway*, 1928). In 1921 he moved from London to North Devon where he lived like a hermit and often slept in the open. This gave him an insight into the natural world which he used to invaluable effect in *Tarka the Otter* (1927), his enduring claim to fame. Much influenced by the work of Richard Jefferies (1848–87), his *métier* was as a chronicler of the natural world. He wrote several books which are deemed classics of animal literature, including *The Peregrine's Saga* (1923) and *Salar the Salmon* (1935). As a conventional novelist he was less successful. Throughout the 1950s and 1960s he published the 15-volume autobiographical series entitled *A Chronicle of Ancient Sunlight* (1951–69), a politically controversial work in which the main character, Phillip Maddison, comes to espouse the beliefs of Sir Oswald Mosley, Hitler's principal advocate in Britain. During the 1930s Williamson himself adopted the Mosleyite line and at the outbreak of war was briefly interned. In counterbalance, *A Patriot's Progress* (1930) was among the most potent anti-war fictions of its time. Williamson's friendship with T. E. *Lawrence is recorded in *Genius of Friendship* (1941).

WILLIAMSON, Jack (1908–), American science fiction writer, born in Bisbee, Arizona, educated at Eastern New Mexico University and the University of Colorado. From the pulp fiction of his early years he has remained active in the field of science fiction since 1928. *Space operas like *The Legion of Space* (1947) were soon succeeded by thoughtful explorations of the nature of human participation in the universe, such as *Darker Than You Think* (1948), *The Humanoids* (1949), *Lifeburst* (1984), and *Demon Moon* (1994). He has frequently collaborated with F. *Pohl.

WILMER, Clive (1945–), British poet, born in Harrogate, Yorkshire, educated at King's College, Cambridge. His contribution to *Shade Mariners* (with Dick *Davis and Robert *Wells, 1970) demonstrated the highly accomplished use of conventional verse forms which has remained an essential feature of his work. His first independent collection was *The Dwelling Place* (1977); subsequent publications include *Devotions* (1982), *Amores* (1986), *The Infinite Variety* (1989), and *Of Earthly Paradise* (1992). A productive tension exists in his work between the rich traditionalism of his style and the disquieting urgency of his metaphysical and social concerns. He has also produced striking work in more innovative forms, notably in the central section of *Devotions*. He edited Thom *Gunn's *The Occasions of Poetry* (1982) and John Ruskin's *Unto This Last and Other Writings* (1986). Among his translations are Miklos Radnoti's *Forced March: Selected Poems* (with George Gomori, 1979).

WILMOT, Frank, see MAURICE, FURNLEY.

WILSON, A(ndrew) N(orman) (1950–), British novelist and biographer, born in Staffordshire, educated at New College, Oxford. He has been a lecturer at St Hugh's College and New College, Oxford, and literary editor of the *Spectator*. His first novel, *The Sweets of Pimlico* (1977), a comedy of manners about the relationship between an ageing hedonist and a Cambridge graduate with a passion for natural history, was followed by *Unguarded Hours* (1978), which satirizes aspects of the Anglican Church, and its sequel *Kindly Light* (1979). The highly acclaimed *The Healing Art* (1980; Somerset Maugham Award), opens with the discovery, by its Anglo-Catholic heroine, Pamela Cowper, that she has cancer. Despite its sombre beginning, which turns out to be a mistaken diagnosis, the novel is characterized by the sardonic humour for which the author has become renowned. Subsequent novels include *Who Was Oswald Fish?* (1981), which satirizes the casual promiscuity of the late 1970s; *Wise Virgin* (1982; W. H. Smith Prize, 1983), exploring the relationship between Giles Fox, a blind scholar engaged in annotating a medieval treatise on virginity, his adolescent daughter, Tibba, and Louise Agar, the Cambridge academic he engages as his secretary; *Scandal* (1983); *Gentlemen in England* (1985); and *Love Unknown* (1986), a satire on romantic love, describing the complex marital and extra-marital relationships of its three female characters. The first volume of the Lampitt Papers series about contemporary life, *Incline·Our Hearts* (1988), opens with an account of the wartime childhood of its narrator, Julian Ramsay; *A Bottle in the Smoke* (1990) begins in the late 1950s and deals primarily with Julian's sentimental education; *Daughters of Albion* (1991) concerns the mystery surrounding the death of an ageing writer. *Hearing Voices* (1995) begins in the late 1960s and ends in AD 2000. *The Vicar of Sorrows* (1993), whose central character, Francis Keere, an Anglican vicar, falls in love with a beautiful young 'New Age' girl, returned to themes about the nature of religious belief and the conflict between faith and worldly desire. Wilson, who has at various times publicly reviewed his own religious and political beliefs, has shown a marked predilection for such themes in his fiction, which are generally treated in the mildly satirical manner which also distinguishes his journalism.

He has published a study of Christianity, *How Can We Know?* (1985), and a collection of literary journalism, *Penfriends from Porlock* (1988). Wilson's other works include *The Laird of Abbotsford* (1981), a study of Sir Walter Scott, and biographies of John Milton (1983), Hilaire *Belloc (1984), Tolstoy (1988; Whitbread Prize), C. S. *Lewis (1990), and Jesus (1992).

WILSON, Sir Angus (Frank Johnstone) (1913–91), British novelist, born in Bexhill, East Sussex, educated at Westminster School and at Merton College, Oxford. He served in Intelligence during the Second World War; from 1949 to 1955 he was Deputy Superintendent of the Reading Room at the British Museum; from 1966 he was Professor of English Literature at East Anglia University. A nervous crisis brought about Wilson's earlier writing; a major theme of his fiction is the dilemma of morally aware individuals when all that they take for granted seems suddenly to be thrown into doubt. His first two published books, *The Wrong Set* (1949) and *Such Darling Dodos* (1950), were collections of short stories, brilliantly charting the fractured world of the post-war British middle class, and alight with a fierce and acutely observant humour which does not preclude sympathy. Confusion of values and the difficulties of the right-minded humanist are the concern also of his first novel, *Hemlock and After* (1952); Bernard Sands, a famous liberal humanist novelist, who has, late in life, accepted his homosexual desires, feels his moral standpoint and indeed his entire life's work undone when he experiences a sadistic reaction to the arrest of a fellow homosexual. **Anglo-Saxon Attitudes* (1956) was followed by *A Bit off the Map* (1957), a volume of stories, the title story attacking the Nietzscheanism of Colin *Wilson and his associates. *The Middle Age of Mrs Eliot* (1958) deals with the crisis of Meg Eliot, stripped by her husband's death of the trappings and social context of her life as a successful barrister's wife. In contrast to her is her brother, whose quietist passivity exhibits the weaker side of the liberal-humanist position. *The Old Men at the Zoo* (1961), set in a near future of European war, opposes the urban zoo to the natural reserve. *Late Call* (1964) concerns middle-aged Sylvia Calvert, who retires from the private hotel business to live with her son, a headmaster and a widower, and his family in Carshall, a New Town, ostensibly dedicated to new ways of social living. In this novel, Wilson uses his gift for parody to make a compassionate investigation of *popular culture. *No Laughing Matter* (1967) covers fifty years in the life of the Matthews family, and amounts to a paradigm of twentieth-century English cultural assumptions. *As if by Magic* (1973) explores the upsurge of the irrational during the 1960s, and the profound but often mutually destructive relations between West and East. *Setting the World on Fire* (1980) is more poetically composed, the legend of Phaeton, subject of a Lully opera, unifying the differences between two devoted brothers, one a theatre designer of flamboyant, adventurous tastes, the other a lawyer with a classical abhorrence of all that threatens civilized and civilizing order. Wilson is also the author of critical and biographical studies of Zola (1950), Dickens (1970), and *Kipling (1977), while *The Wild Garden* (1963) analyses his own creative impulses. Wilson's discussion of humanism, inside his fiction and outside it, is at once profoundly searching and sympathetically generous. His earlier novels were commended for their reintroduction of Victorian fictive devices that enabled him to range over very considerable areas of personal, public, and social experience. His *Diversity and Depth in Fiction: Selected Critical Writings* (1983) contains an illuminating survey of 'Evil in the English Novel'; a collection of travel pieces, *Reflections in a Writer's Eye*, appeared in 1986. A biography of Angus Wilson, by Margaret *Drabble, was published in 1995.

WILSON, August (1945–), African-American playwright, born and educated at Pittsburgh, Pennsylvania. A founder of Black Horizons Theatre Company in St Paul in 1968, he had a meteoric rise to prominence with the Broadway première of *Ma Rainey's Black Bottom* (1985), the first of a projected cycle of plays. Set in a recording studio in the 1920s, it deals with an imperious blues singer and the conflicts between the band players, one member wanting to take control of his own jazz music, while the others are resigned to playing to order. Several plays preceded this success, but with *Fences* (1987; Pulitzer Prize) his reputation was securely established. A play about territory and identity, it is set in the 1950s, and presents Troy Maxson, a black baseball player whose career ended just before black men were able to play in white baseball leagues. His other plays include *Joe Turner's Come and Gone* (1986), *The Piano Lesson* (1988), and *Two Trains Running* (1990). Wilson's plays focus on the alienation, frustration, and rage of black men and women in America, and present, in striking and articulate dramatic dialogue, the dispossessed black voices of the American past and present.

WILSON, Barbara (1950–), American crime writer, born in Long Beach, California. She has a background in feminist publishing and the women's movement. Working within the conventions of a popular form, Wilson's crime novels are predominantly concerned with progressive and feminist social issues. Her first three novels, *Murder in the Collective* (1984), *Sisters of the Road* (1986), and *The Dog Collar Murders* (1989), all feature the reluctant investigator Pam Nilsen, the part-owner of a printing press active in leftist and lesbian circles in Seattle. As Nilsen becomes embroiled in mysteries, and develops a professional and sexual relationship with Hadley, a female associate, Wilson demonstrates an active concern with the gender of her protagonist. Wilson excels at problematic endings where the solution to the murder mystery raises more complex problems than it solves. Her gift for compelling and witty narratives on serious questions can be seen in *Gaudi Afternoon* (1990), featuring a new central figure, the Irish-American Spanish translator Cassandra Reilly.

WILSON, Colin (Henry) (1931–), British writer, born in Leicester, where he attended Gateway Secondary Technical School until the age of sixteen. His first and best-known work, *The Outsider* (1956), characterized his approach and his abiding themes in its treatment of the existential alienation of creative intellectuals, which refers to Nietzsche, Kafka, Camus, Sartre, T. E. *Lawrence, and others. Wilson's identification as an *Angry Young man was chiefly a result of the book's widely-noted appearance coinciding with the publicity generated by John Osborne's **Look Back In Anger*. Wison went on to write many works on psychology, criminality, the paranormal, and other subjects. His fiction is less widely known, though *The Mind Parasites* (1967) effectively translated some of his preoccupations into a classic *science fiction plot; in *Ritual in the Dark* (1960), *Adrift in Soho* (1961), and *The Schoolgirl Murder Case* (1974) he focused upon the abnormal and the criminal in contemporary society. His non-fiction works include *Religion and the Rebel* (1957), *The Strength to Dream* (1962), *Bernard Shaw: A Reassessment* (1969), and *The Essential Colin Wilson* (1985). See *The Angry Decade* (1958) by Kenneth Allsop, and *An Odyssey of Freedom* (1983) by K. Gunnar Bergstrom.

WILSON, Edmund (1895–1972), American critic, born in Red Bank, New Jersey, educated at Princeton, where his contemporaries included F. Scott *Fitzgerald, whose posthumous publications Wilson edited. In 1920 he joined the staff of *Vanity Fair*, of which he became managing editor, and was associate editor of the **New Republic* from 1926 to 1931. Wilson was a distinguished and forceful American man of letters, one of the last of the species to pursue a freelance career outside the university. *Axel's Castle* (1931) was an influential survey of the Modern movement in literature, tracing the conjunction of Naturalism and Symbolism in the work of *Joyce, *Eliot, *Yeats, Proust, and others. *The Wound and the Bow* (1941) contained the important title essay arguing that talent in art, like the skill at archery of the legendary Philoctetes, is inseparable from illness, or from psychic or other damage. In his essay 'The Two Scrooges', Wilson almost single-handedly rerouted Dickens's reputation, discovering for modern readers a dark, brooding, Dostoevskyan complement to the Dickens of hearty laughter and cheery Christmases. Less plausible, but much imitated, was Wilson's essay on Henry *James's *The Turn of the Screw*, purporting to show that all the horror of the story stems from the governess's neurotic fancy. Wilson also wrote a fluent and thoughtful history of socialist thought, *To the Finland Station* (1940), and addressed himself, in *Apologies to the Iroquois* (1960), to the injustices suffered by the earliest inhabitants of his continent. Scott Fitzgerald once described Wilson as the 'keeper of my conscience', and Wilson effectively kept America's conscience for a long time, fulminating against what he saw as dreary specialization in literary studies, quarrelling with *Nabokov on behalf of common sense and common language. Some of Wilson's work now seems overly broad and blunt, but his energy and stamina are indisputable, and he stood for (and against) his age as few other writers did, or do. Among his other works are *Travels in Two Democracies* (1936), written after a visit to Russia; *The Triple Thinkers* (1938), a study of various *fin de siècle* authors; *Memoirs of Hecate County* (1946), a collection of short stories set among the New York intelligentsia; the experimental novel *I Thought of Daisy* (1929); the frequently satirical poems in *Night Thoughts* (1961); and *Five Plays* (1954). His essays have been collected in *Classics and Commercials* (1950), *The Shores of Light* (1952–3), and *The American Earthquake* (1958). *A Piece of My Mind* (1956) and *Upstate* (1972) are autobiographical. His journals (3 volumes; 1975, 1980, 1983) were edited by Leon *Edel, and his *Letters on Literature and Politics* (1977) were edited by Elena Wilson.

WILSON, Ethel (1888–1980), Canadian novelist, born in South Africa, brought to Vancouver as an orphan in 1898. Wilson began to publish fiction only in the 1930s, when her stories first appeared in the *New Statesman*; she was nearly 60 when her first novel, *Hetty Dorval*, appeared in 1947. The next few years saw the publication of virtually all the remainder of her slim *œuvre*: three further novels—*The Innocent Traveller* (1949), *Swamp Angel* (1954), and *Love and Salt Water* (1956)—and *The Equations of Love* (1952), a work made up of two novellas. Her fiction repeatedly treats the themes of mother–daughter relationships and the threats that unsuitable marriages and liaisons with men pose to women's self-fulfilment. *The Innocent Traveller* grew out of family reminiscences she had begun to write in the 1930s; its protagonist is first observed as a 3-year-old child determined to be noticed by a self-important Matthew Arnold at a Victorian family dinner party, and subsequently experiences virtually the whole history of Vancouver before dying as a centenarian. *Swamp Angel*, generally considered her finest work, centres on a woman who leaves a sterile marriage and attempts to build a new life on a lake in the interior of British Columbia. *Mrs Golightly* (1961) is a collection of short stories which demonstrates the versatility and technical assurance that characterize all Wilson's work.

WILSON, F(rank) P(ercy) (1889–1963), British scholar, born in Birmingham, educated at Birmingham University and Lincoln College, Oxford. He began lecturing at Oxford in 1921 and was appointed Merton Professor of English Literature in 1947. His early works include editions of Dekker's *Plague Pamphlets* (1925) and *Foure Birds from Noahs Arke* (1925). W. W. *Greg, his fellow member of the Malone Society, had a formative influence on Wilson's scholarly methods, which concentrated on the assembling of primary materials rather than on textual exegesis. He was the general editor of the *Oxford History of English Literature* from 1938 onward. His principal studies, which draw on his unrivalled knowledge of Elizabethan usage, are *Marlowe and the Early Shakespeare* (1953) and the posthumous *The English Drama, 1485–1585* (edited by G. K. Hunter, 1969). Although he did not publish extensively, he was regarded, in Dame Helen *Gardner's words, as 'the most learned Elizabethan scholar in the world'. His other works include *The Plague in Shakespeare's London* (1927) and the essays of *Shakespearian and Other Studies* (edited by Helen Gardner, 1969).

WILSON, J(ohn) Dover (1881–1969), British Shakespearian editor and scholar, born at Mortlake in Surrey, educated at Gonville and Caius College, Cambridge. His early works included the contribution of two chapters to *The Cambridge History of English Literature* (edited by A. W. Ward and A. R. Waller, 13 volumes, 1907–16). After a period with the Board of Education, he was Professor of Education at King's College, London, from 1924 to 1935, when he became Regius Professor of English at the University of Edinburgh. In 1919 he was appointed *Quiller-Couch's co-editor on the *New Cambridge Shakespeare* (1921–66). Quiller-Couch retired after the completion of the comedies, leaving Wilson as sole editor. His bibliographical methods were based on those established by his associate W. W. *Greg. Other works by Wilson include *The Essential Shakespeare* (1932), a 'biographical adventure', *The Manuscript of Shakespeare's 'Hamlet'* (1934), *What Happens in 'Hamlet'* (1935), which had remarkable appeal to a general readership, and *Shakespeare's Happy Comedies* (1962). *Milestones on the Dover Road*, his autobiography, appeared in 1969.

WILSON, Lanford (1937–), American dramatist, born in Lebanon, Missouri, educated at the University of Chicago. One of the most successful and durable of off-off-Broadway dramatists, Wilson made his name with *The Gingham Dog* (1968), the story of a failed interracial marriage. He co-founded the Circle Repertory Company in New York in 1969, where most of his plays have been premièred. *The Hotel Baltimore* (1973), about life in a run-down New York hotel, the most successful off-Broadway non-musical American play in history, won an Obie Award, as did *The Mound Builders* (1975). *Talley's Folly* (1979; screenplay, 1992), the second of a trilogy of plays about a Missouri family (the others are *5th of July*, 1978, and *Talley's Son*, 1986), won both a Pulitzer Prize and a New York Drama Critics Circle award. Wilson is perhaps the least experimental of contemporary American dramatists in his commitment to the conventions of theatrical realism, though the poetic intensity of his language bestows a rare dignity on the ordinary and dispossessed characters of his plays. He has been accused both of optimism and of sentimentality in his work; the latter is evident in *Burn This* (1987; screenplay, 1992). His later works include the plays *The Moonshot Tape* (1990) and *Redwood Curtain* (1992).

Winesburg, Ohio, a collection of twenty-three short stories by Sherwood *Anderson, published in 1919. This series of starkly realistic sketches focuses on the 'lives of quiet desperation' of the men and women of a small Midwestern town, seen through the eyes of George Willard, a young reporter. The perspective is of a world divided between increasing industrial modernization and the 'old individualistic town life'. In these psychological portraits of some of Winesburg's inhabitants, Anderson sought to demonstrate that even poverty-stricken people were as sensitive to emotions as the rich and successful.

Wings of a Dove, The, a novel by Henry *James, published in 1902. This novel marks the peak of James's writing career. The central protagonist is Milly Theale, a rich young woman, beautiful in person and character, who recognizes that she is suffering from an incurable disease and that she must soon prepare to die. The influence of her fading life upon all those around her—those who envy her wealth, those who seek to manipulate her, and those who wish to protect her—is the principal focus of the novel. James outlines the changing alignments of her associates and friends as they jostle to entrap or free the 'dove' Milly. Milly has slowly been developing an affection for the journalist Merton Densher. However, unbeknownst to Milly, her other friend, Kate Croy, has for a long time been engaged to Densher, and the two have been trying to engineer a way for the mortally ill Milly to marry Densher, so that as a rich widower he may marry Kate. However, Densher becomes increasingly devoted to Milly, and he refuses her dying bequest, without which Kate will not marry him. In novel which focuses on the mechanisms of predator and prey, desire and victim, James highlights the vicious circles of power and entrapment that money and sex can enforce.

Winslow Boy, The, a play by Terence *Rattigan, first performed in 1946; it is based on the Archer-Shee case of 1908, which resulted from the expulsion from the Royal Naval Academy of a cadet accused of theft. Here, Ronnie Winslow is the naval cadet expelled from Osborne, on the grounds that he stole a five-shilling postal order. His father, Arthur, seeks the help of Sir Robert Morton, an eminent advocate and politician who, in a famous scene, contemptuously grills Ronnie, accuses him of being a forger, liar, and thief, and as Ronnie bursts into tears, concludes, 'the boy is plainly innocent: I accept the brief'. The ensuing proceedings cost Arthur his health and much of his wealth; Ronnie's elder brother has to sacrifice his place at Oxford and his sister Catherine loses her fiancé; his mother thinks the price the family is paying 'out of all proportion'; even Sir Robert would have become Lord Chief Justice, but for his commitment to the case; and when Ronnie is finally vindicated, the boy is out, watching a film. However, Rattigan clearly agrees with Catherine, a suffragette with radical sympathies, that 'if ever the time comes that the House of Commons has so much on its mind that it can't find time to discuss a Ronnie Winslow and his bally postal order, this country will be a far poorer place than it is now'. She and Morton, whom she had dismissed as a reactionary opportunist, find common ground in a belief in democracy and the absolute right to justice of the individual: a conclusion with special weight just after the Second World War, when the play was originally staged.

WINTERS, (Arthur) Yvor (1900–68), American poet and critic, born in Chicago, educated at the Universities of Chicago and Colorado. In 1928 he began his career at Stanford University, where he became Professor of English in 1949. His early work as a poet, collected in *The Immobile Wind* (1921), *The Magpie's Shadow* (1922), and *The Bare Hills* (1927), formed a highly disciplined extension of *Imagism; poems of as few as five words made plain his experimental tendencies, while longer lyrics used free verse with classical precision and restraint. A collected edition of *The Early Poems* appeared in 1966. Among his subsequent collections, in which strict traditional metres predominate, are *The Proof* (1930), *Before Disaster* (1934), *Poems* (1940), and *To the Holy Spirit* (1947). *Collected Poems* of 1952 was revised in 1966. Much of his austerely controlled later verse draws on the landscapes and history of California. His principal publication as a critic is *In Defense of Reason* (1947), which collects *Primitivism and Decadence* (1937), *Maule's Curse* (1938), and *The Anatomy of Nonsense* (1943); these studies jointly amount to a penetrating and often destructively witty critique of the adverse effects of Romanticism on nineteenth- and twentieth-century literature. Following Irving *Babbitt and the *New Humanism, Winters viewed the moral and aesthetic dimensions of poetry as inseparable. His closely reasoned antagonism to *Modernism, which he also regarded with constructive interest, led him to advance contentiously high claims for the verse of Robert *Bridges, Elizabeth *Daryush, T. Sturge *Moore, and others. His other works as a critic include *The Functions of Criticism* (1957), which contains important studies of G. M. Hopkins and Robert *Frost, and *Forms of Discovery* (1967), a sustained consideration of the short poem; *Uncollected Essays and Reviews*, edited by F. Murphy, appeared in 1973. Winters was married to the novelist Janet *Lewis.

WINTERSON, Jeanette (1959–), British novelist, born in Lancashire, educated at Oxford University. Her upbringing as a Pentecostal Evangelist was the subject of her first novel, *Oranges Are Not the Only Fruit* (1985; later adapted for BBC television) which also dealt with the narrator's growing awareness of her lesbianism with a certain wry humour. *Boating for Beginners* (1985), a feminist reworking of the biblical story of the Deluge, was followed by *The Passion* (1987), set in eighteenth-century France, which tells the story of Henri, a young French peasant who becomes chef to the Emperor Napoleon and loses his heart to Villanelle, a beautiful Venetian girl born with webbed feet, who is in love with another woman. *Sexing the Cherry* (1989) also offered feminist reinterpretations of historical events, in its account of the Great Fire of 1666. The novel includes such fantastic figures as the Dog Woman, a man-eating giantess who lives on the banks of the Thames, as well as figures from fairytale and myth. Winterson has developed her own version of *magic realism in which she deals with contemporary feminist themes. *Written on the Body* (1992) deals with a love affair between the narrator (whose gender is not specified) and a married woman who is dying of leukaemia. *Art and Lies* (1994) consists of three linked narratives, about 'Sappho', the lesbian poet, 'Picasso'—not the painter but an abused woman—and 'Handel', a male figure epitomizing inadequacy.

WINTON, Tim (1960–), Australian writer, born in Perth, educated at Curtin University; he studied creative writing at the Western Institute of Technology under Elizabeth *Jolley. He won immediate fame with his first two novels. *An Open Swimmer* (1982) is a lyrical account of a boy's emergence into manhood, set against vivid descriptions of the sea and landscapes of Western Australia. *Shallows* (1984) describes the death throes of the whaling industry as it is beset by conservationists, counterpointing the struggle with excerpts from a nineteenth-century family journal. *That Eye, the Sky* (1986) describes with persuasive insight the experience of a 13-year-old boy caring for his family; *In the Winter Dark* (1988) reveals Winton's equal insight into the mind of an old and frightened man in a chilling horror story. *Cloudstreet* (1991), a substantial novel examining the connected lives of two Perth families between 1943 and 1964 and drawing on Winton's own family, is compiled of small, poetically controlled chapters, which create a picture of Australia's vastness. In *The Riders* (1995) an Australian lovingly restores an Irish cottage and awaits his wife and child, but the young daughter arrives alone and shocked, precipitating a frantic search through Europe for his wife—and the meaning of his life. Via a journey haunted by absence, *The Riders* explores the collapse of illusions. The narrative is lyrical, vital, and confirms Winton as a writer of considerable talent. His other works include the collections of stories *Scission* (1985), *Minimum of Two* (1987), and *Blood and Water* (1993); his *Collected Shorter Novels* (1995); and children's fiction.

Wise Blood, a novel by Flannery *O'Connor, published in 1952. In this novel O'Connor powerfully presents the case for (Catholic) Christianity's ultimate strength by telling a story whose events and characters seem far away from it. Hazel Motes, a young soldier, returns home after being released from the army, to found a Church Without Christ. He is animated in his intentions by his revolt from his preacher grandfather and by hostility to a quack who feigns blindness to impress followers. In fact Hazel, almost unwittingly, repeats the righteous violence and martyrdom of early believers. His 'Church' undergoes a schism, with a rival prophet whom Hazel kills by running him down with a car, and Hazel blinds himself with quicklime before falling sick and dying. The novel, sparely written though it is, abounds in both Christian and Darwinist (secular) images and symbols. O'Connor presents a peculiarly dark and punitive vision of religion but her insights into fanaticism are acute and rendered with great clarity and literary economy.

Wise Children, a novel by Angela *Carter, published in 1991. This novel departs almost entirely in narrative technique from the territory of fable and fantasy to which Carter had laid claim, though it does retain her characteristic element of carnival that removes it from the domestic realism with which it (ironically) engages. Set, over several decades, in a vividly evoked twentieth-century London, against a theatrical backdrop, it tells the story of the Chance twins, Dora and Nora, daughters of a great Shakespearian actor. The salty narrative voice of Dora, Carter's most lifelike creation, is a *tour de force* of humorous ventriloquism. The Shakespearian allusion gives Carter a chance to construct a comedy of errors replete with references to the bard's plays: incestuous couplings, doubtful paternities, obscure relationships, melodramatic suicides, unclaimed children, and, above all, twinnings and doublings proliferate. Carter also pays irreverent tribute to film. In typical manner, the boundaries between fantasy and reality, masks and faces, high and low art, and tragedy and comedy are constantly contested and blurred.

WISEMAN, Adele (1928–), Canadian novelist, born in Winnipeg of Jewish parents who had migrated from the Ukraine, educated at the University of Manitoba. Among other occupations she has worked as a university teacher. She has lived in Winnipeg, London, Rome, New York, Montreal, and Toronto. Her best-known novel, *The Sacrifice* (1956), tells the tragic story of a modern-day Abraham who suffers the hardships of immigrant life and eventually commits murder. It is a penetrating study of the tensions that arise when increasingly assimilated second-generation immigrants question traditional Jewish social and religious codes. *Crackpot* (1974) is a more experimental novel set in a Jewish ghetto in Winnipeg. Although it too depicts the difficulties experienced by the community, it is written in a more humorous style, employing ethnic stereotypes for satirical purposes. It draws on traditional Jewish thought from the cabbala. Wiseman's other writing is also primarily concerned with aspects of Jewish community life; it includes the play *Testimonial Dinner* (1978) and *Old Woman at Play* (1978), a fragmented memoir of her mother.

WISTER, Owen (1860–1938), American *Western novelist, born in Philadelphia, educated at Harvard, where he studied music. After two years furthering his musical studies in Europe, he worked in a New York bank, before illness took him to Wyoming in 1885. Wister later returned to Harvard to study law; he subsequently practised as a lawyer in Philadelphia. His Wyoming experiences continued to exert a powerful hold on his imagination and he began writing stories, based on the journal he had kept and focusing on the roles played by Easterners who were settling there. His first stories were well received on their publication in 1891 and he subsequently devoted himself to a career in literature. His greatest success came with his classic Western novel *The *Virginian* (1902), which played an important part in shaping the popular Western myth of the lone stranger maintaining the forces of law and order in a community threatened with anarchy. Wister's other fiction includes the short-story collections *Lin McLean* (1896) and *The Jimmyjohn Boss* (1900), and two novels with Eastern settings, *Philosophy Four* (1903) and *Lady Baltimore* (1906). He also wrote in a variety of other genres, producing books on Anglo-American relations, biographies of George Washington and his Harvard friend Theodore Roosevelt, and humorous works. His Western journals were published in 1958.

WITTGENSTEIN, Ludwig (Joseph Johann) (1889–1951), Austrian (later British) philosopher, born in Vienna; he studied engineering at Linz, Berlin, and Manchester. After becoming interested in mathematical theory he studied under Bertrand *Russell at Cambridge where he later became professor of philosophy (1939–47). His first major work, *Tractatus Logico-Philosophicus* (1921), was the only book published in his lifetime and set the terms of reference for his huge influence on twentieth-century philosophy. Wittgenstein was concerned with the significance and compass of language, and saw the philosopher's task as lying in the analysis of the meaningful limits of everyday usage. By introducing the 'picture theory of meaning' Wittgenstein clarified the nature of meaning, but simultaneously denied the claims to veracity and, in advance of the Logical Positivists, produced an austere version of the principle of verifiability. To some extent, this position replaced most of the accumulated wisdom of nineteenth-century philosophy with a logical clarity comparable with the contemporary work of Bertrand Russell and A. N. *Whitehead in the field of mathematics. Wittgenstein was aware that his own statements of principle or axioms were meaningless, and concluded his book with the famous statement 'what we cannot speak about we must pass over in silence'. Silence followed for some time while Wittgenstein developed a second theory of meaning. More recent publication of Wittgenstein's notebooks and lecture notes shows a gradual shift of emphasis from the *a priori* formulations of the *Tractatus* to the subsequent empirical curiosity into the actual workings of language. In his later work, *Philosophical Investigations* (1953), he declared that 'the meaning of the word is its use in the language' whereby meaning becomes a function of its roles in a diversity of linguistic contexts. The famous example he takes is the word 'game', for which a single meaning cannot be found. Language is thus no longer thought of as a clear 'picture', but as a 'tool' or 'game' capable of infinite variety and constant renewal according to changes in circumstances. This change in emphasis removes the interiority of the 'picture' analogy, and introduces a social, public dimension; the relation between the private and the public became the theme of Wittgenstein's later work. Among many of his fragments and notes to appear in print are *Remarks on the Foundation of Mathematics* (1956), *The Blue and Brown Books* (1958), *Notebooks 1914–1916* (1961), *Lectures and Conversations on Aesthetics, Psychology, and Religious Belief* (1966), *On Certainty* (1969), and *Philosophical Remarks* (1975). See also SEVEN PILLARS OF WISDOM.

WODEHOUSE, Sir P(elham) G(renville) (1881–1975), British novelist and playwright, born in Guildford, Surrey, educated at Dulwich College. He began work as a bank clerk, but he soon began publishing stories in boys' magazines and other journals such as *Strand Magazine* and *Punch*. Much of his work from this period remains uncollected, though *The Parrot and Other Poems* (1988) contained some early light verse, whose ingenuity prefigured his later success. With his first novel, *The Pothunters* (1902), he became known as a writer of children's books of which the best-known are *Mike* (1909) and *Psmith in the City* (1910). It was with *The Man with Two Left Feet* (1917; short stories) that he introduced Jeeves and Bertie Wooster, and established his reputation as one of the finest humorists of his time. Eccentric aristocratic Edwardian characters such as Lord Emsworth, his pet sow the Empress of Blandings, Mr Mulliner, Psmith, the patrons of the Drones Club, and the formidable aunts abound through his ingenious plots. The Blandings books include *Something New* (1915), *Leave it to Psmith* (1923), *Blandings Castle* (1935), *Lord Emsworth and Others* (1937), *Full Moon* (1947), *Pigs Have Wings* (1952), *A Pelican at Blandings* (1969), and *Sunset at Blandings* (1977, unfinished). Jeeves and Wooster appear in *Carry on, Jeeves* (1925), *Very Good, Jeeves* (1930), *Thank You, Jeeves* (1934), *Right Ho, Jeeves* (1934), *The Code of the Woosters* (1938), *Joy in the Morning* (1946), *The Mating Season* (1949), and *Much Obliged, Jeeves* (1971). Other novels include *Ukridge* (1924), *Meet Mr Mulliner* (1927), *Money for Nothing* (1928), *The Luck of the Bodkins* (1935), *Uncle Fred in the Springtime* (1939), and *Quick Service* (1940). Wodehouse produced more than 120 books, including many plays and musical comedies, from 1911 to 1948. Trapped in France as the Second World War broke out, he was interned by the Germans in 1940, though he was approaching 60, and was soon released. He was not, however, allowed to leave Germany, and unwisely accepted an invitation to broadcast to America. These broadcasts—their publication long afterwards demonstrated their innocuous nature—caused some scandal in England, though G. *Orwell and others defended Wodehouse vigorously. After the war he settled in America, taking American citizenship in 1955. Richard Usborne's *Wodehouse at Work to the End* (1976) describes his final productive decades; Frances Donaldson's *P. G. Wodehouse* (1982) is a biography.

Wodwo, a collection of poems and prose by Ted *Hughes, published in 1967. Parts I and III of the book contain a substantial body of previously uncollected poems, while Part II is made up of five short stories and a play; Hughes's prefatory note informs the reader that 'the verse and the prose are intended to be read together, as parts of a single work'. Much of the writing in the volume has in common an exploratory impulse, which is perhaps clearest in the cumulative questings after identity in the title poem: 'What am I? . . . what shall I be called am I the first . . .' The story 'Snow', which recalls *Beckett's work in its bleak reductiveness, and the play 'The Wound' present similarly unsettling examinations of our existential assumptions. In attempting to achieve his fundamental definitions of the terms of existence Hughes brings great imaginative pressure to bear on his materials in *Wodwo* and employs predominantly experimental forms; the comparatively conventional stanzas of his two earlier collections are discarded in favour of compellingly rhythmical free verse. The metaphorical import in Hughes's previous treatments of animals is superseded by the mythical dimensions apparent in such poems as 'The Bear', 'Song of a Rat', and 'The Howling of Wolves'; the harsh metaphysics expounded in **Crow* (1970) are firmly anticipated in numerous poems, notably 'Logos', 'Reveille', and 'Theology', while the incantational lyricism of 'Skylarks' and 'Gnat-Psalm' constitutes an element of transcendent affirmation. *Wodwo* also includes some of Hughes's most concentrated treatments of landscape and has an unusual breadth of social, personal, and historical reference; it is in many ways his most varied and powerful collection.

WOLFE, Gene (Rodman) (1931–), American writer of *science fiction and fantasy, born in Brooklyn, educated in Texas. Wolfe's vision of life is eccentrically conservative, hierarchical, and grave. He began to attract critical attention with *The Fifth Head of Cerberus* (1972), whose three intricately linked novellas comprised a profound analysis of the colonial mentality within an orthodox science fiction framework. *The Devil in a Forest* (1976) retold the Wenceslaus story. The climax of his career was the publication of *The Book of the New Sun* (4 volumes, 1980–3); set in a distant future, it is in the form of a confessional autobiography of its protagonist, a journeyman torturer who may also be a messiah. Other works include the novels *Peace* (1975), *Free Live Free* (1984), *There Are Doors* (1988), and *Castleview* (1990); *Soldier in the Mist* (1986) and *Soldier of Arete* (1989), reworkings of ancient Greek myths; and the series comprising *Nightside the Long Sun* (1993), *Lake of the Long Sun* (1994), and *Caldé of the Long Sun* (1994). *The Island of Doctor Death and Other Short Stories* (1980) and *Endangered Species* (1989) are short-story collections. See also SPACE OPERA.

WOLFE, Thomas (Clayton) (1900–38), American novelist, born in Asheville, educated at the University of North Carolina and at Harvard. Wolfe then settled in New York where he taught and wrote several small plays which attracted the attention of Aline Bernstein, the stage designer and actress, who subsequently became a significant influence on his life. **Look*

Homeward, Angel (1929), a moving semi-autobiographical work representing the Southern family life of the Gants, revealed Wolfe's stylistic debts to *Joyce, *Dreiser, and other contemporaries. The saga of the Gants continues with *Of Time and the River* (1935), in which the earlier and more slender *A Portrait of Bascom Hawke* (1932) was absorbed; and the posthumous *The Web and the Rock* (1939) and *You Can't Go Home Again* (1940), which were compiled by Edward C. Aswell from manuscripts left at Wolfe's death. These four works mirror Wolfe's own harrowing progress from the South to the North, to Europe and then back again. In a prose that ranges from brisk narrative to long meditative reflections, the escape from the ensnaring web of social experience and the search for the solid rock of personal strength function as the organizing symbolic structure. As well as these major contributions to American fiction, he also wrote many short stories, which were collected in *From Death to Morning* (1935) and *The Hills Beyond* (posthumously published in 1941), incorporating striking scenes of city life as in 'Only the Dead Know Brooklyn'. 'Poetical' extracts from his fiction were collected in *The Face of a Nation* (1939) and *A Stone, A Leaf, A Door* (1945). At its best his prose has a lyrical quality more easily associated with poetry. In the critical study *The Story of a Novel* (1936), he described his own creative processes and his working relationship with the editor Maxwell Perkins, who exerted a strong influence on Wolfe. Since his death *The Letters of Thomas Wolfe* (1956, edited by Elizabeth Nowell) and the final novel, *The Lost Boy* (1965), have appeared.

WOLFE, Tom (Thomas Kennerly) (1931–), American journalist and novelist, born in Virginia, educated at Washington and Lee Universities and subsequently at Yale. He established a reputation, through his writing for *The Washington Post* and the *New York Herald Tribune*, as a satirist of contemporary American mores, and as an exponent of the '*New Journalism', which combined a relish for the absurdities of modern life with a vigorous, novelistic style. This reputation was consolidated by the publication of his first book, *The Kandy-Kolored Tangerine-Flake Streamline Baby* (1965) and by the works which followed. These include: *The Electric Kool-Aid Acid Test* (1968), which chronicled the exploits of Ken *Kesey and his Merry Pranksters; *The Pump House Gang* (1968), which contained satirical portraits of Marshall *McLuhan and Hugh Hefner, amongst others; *Radical Chic and Mau-Mauing the Flak Catchers* (1970), which mocked the naïve political posturing of New York intellectuals involved in fashionably radical causes such as the 'Black Panther' movement; and *The New Journalism* (1973). Other stories and journalistic sketches were contained in *Mauve Gloves and Madmen, Clutter and Vine* (1976), while *The Painted Word* (1975) and *From Bauhaus to Our House* (1981) satirized the pretensions of the art world and of modern architecture, respectively. *The Right Stuff* (1979), which was filmed, offered a blackly comic account of the US space race, in which the trainee astronauts are encouraged to regard themselves as superhuman and as therefore exempt from the restrictions of ordinary life. The same kind of fatal hubris is displayed by Sherman McCoy, the protagonist of Wolfe's first novel, *The Bonfire of the Vanities* (1987), which was also made into a film and which is set in New York City during the 1980s. The novel describes the comic-horrific downfall of its hero, after a hit-and-run accident in which he is involved results in his being arrested for murder, and provoked controversy as well as admiration for its scabrous vision of corruption and urban decay. Other works include *In Our Time* (1980), a collection of his drawings, and *The Purple Decades* (1982), a collection of twenty previously published essays.

WOLFF, Tobias (1945–), American short-story writer, born in Birmingham, Alabama; following service with the US Army in Vietnam (1964–8) he was educated at Oxford and Stanford Universities, then joined the *Washington Post*. Subsequently he became a lecturer at Stanford, prior to becoming Professor of English at Syracuse University, New York, in 1980. His two widely acclaimed collections, *In the Garden of the North American Martyrs* (1981; Uk title, *Hunters in the Snow*, 1982) and *Back in the World* (1985), both feature in Wolff's anthology *Mothers of Life and Death: New American Short Stories* (1983); his novella *The Barracks Thief* (1984) was also praised. With Raymond *Carver and Richard *Ford, he became identified with the '*Dirty Realism' style of fiction, featuring tough characters, similar to those of *Hemingway, frequently elliptical dialogue, and an uncompromising approach to violent and unsavoury subjects. Like the other exponents of the genre he eschewed slick metropolitanism in favour of rural American settings and inarticulate, unsophisticated protagonists, although these are described in a highly articulate and sophisticated style. His autobiographical works include *This Boy's Life* (1989), which movingly describes his difficult upbringing following his parents' divorce and his long separation from his older brother, the writer Geoffrey Wolff, who also wrote a harrowing memoir about his boyhood (*The Duke of Deception*, 1979); and *In Pharaoh's Army: Memories of the Lost War* (1994), which portrays his tour of duty in Vietnam and his experiences prior to becoming a writer.

Women in Love, a novel by D. H. *Lawrence, published in the USA in 1920. Often acclaimed as his finest work, *Women in Love* had a difficult beginning. It was first conceived as a single novel with *The *Rainbow*, but Lawrence split the material in early 1915 as his original plan became too unwieldy. After the controversial reception of *The Rainbow* he revised the new book completely, but no British publisher would touch it during the war years and it was not published in Britain until 1921. Early readers were offended or baffled by its innovatory strangeness. Subsequently it has become one of the classic texts of British *Modernism. The novel has minimal plot. Set largely in Lawrence's native Midlands and in London, it focuses on two sisters, Ursula and Gudrun Brangwen (who appear in *The Rainbow*), and their love affairs with two men, Rupert Birkin and Gerald Crich. The two relationships are deliberately paralleled. That of Gudrun and Gerald is doomed and ends in tragedy in the book's denouement in the Tyrol, while that of Ursula and Birkin continues an unsteady progress towards a kind of restoration. But the outlook is largely bleak. Lawrence conceived the book as a portrait of the war generation, and in the representative types of Gudrun, an artist, and Gerald, a violent mine-owning industrialist, drew two of his most powerfully tragic indictments of the state of British culture. In contrast to their hollowness Ursula and Birkin represent a kind of hopefulness, though it is one which Lawrence carefully undercuts by irony. The style of the novel is disconcerting. Lawrence largely dispenses with linear narrative (though there are arresting individual scenes) and the tone shifts abruptly from the tragic to the comic, the ecstatic to the mundane. Typically, he wished to confound conventional ways of thinking about human relationships and develop a new language for sexuality.

Women of Brewster Place, The, a novel in seven stories by Gloria *Naylor, published in 1982. The narratives that form this work are linked by their setting—the apartment block situated in a black ghetto referred to in the title—and by the reappearance in minor roles of previously foregrounded characters; each one focuses on the life of one of seven women inhabitants of Brewster Place. Grim with reference to racism, misogyny, homophobia, and urban deprivation, Naylor's first work nevertheless culminates in a climactic sequence—the collective dismantling of the wall that symbolizes their exclusion—that celebrates the strength, solidarity, and resilience of the women whose tribulations it unflinchingly records.

Women's Room, The, see FRENCH, MARILYN.

WONGAR, B(anumbir) (1932–), Australian novelist and short-story writer, born Sreten Bozic in Gorna Tresnevica, Serbia, where he was educated at the local school; he emigrated to Australia in 1960. He adopted his Aboriginal name (meaning 'messenger from the spirit world') after he began living with tribal Aborigines in the Northern Territory. Several collections of his short stories, including *The Sinners* (1972) and *The Track to Bralgu* (1978), and the play *Balang an Village* (1973) appeared in the course of the 1970s. The depth of his imaginative immersion in the tribal culture is such that he was taken to be an Aborigine until his identity was disclosed in 1981. His central achievement is the novel trilogy *Walg* (1983), *Karan* (1985), and *Gabo Djara* (1987), which fuses Aborigine and Serbian oral traditions in its complex mythological and historical evocation of the collison of Aborigine culture and western modernity. Wongar's other publications include the short stories in *Babaru* (1982), *Marngit* (1992),and *The Last Pack of Dingoes* (1994).

WOOD, Charles (1932–), British dramatist, born in Guernsey, the son of professional actors, educated at Birmingham College of Art. He became a trooper in the 17/21st Lancers and drew on this background for the work that first won him attention in 1963, *Prisoner and Escort*, part of a trio of plays called *Cockade*. His scepticism about things military is also reflected in *Dingo* (1967), which angrily suggests that the Second World War was fought 'for all the usual reasons'; *H: Being Monologues at Front of Burning Cities* (1969), about Christian pretension and violent practice during the Indian Mutiny; and *Jingo* (1975), set in Singapore at the time of the Japanese invasion of 1941 and highly critical of a smug, xenophobic English officer class. Wood's other notable plays, many of them concerned with the gap between illusion and reality, include *Fill the Stage with Happy Hours* (1966), about life in a small-town repertory theatre; two comedies about the making of movies, *Veterans* (1972) and *Has 'Washington' Legs?* (1978); *Red Star* (1984); and *Across from the Garden of Allah* (1986). He is also an accomplished screenwriter, the author of the scripts of *The Knack*, *Help!*, *The Charge of the Light Brigade*, and, more recently, **Vile Bodies*.

WOODHAM-SMITH, Cecil (Blanche) (1896–1977), British historian and biographer, born in Tenby, Pembrokeshire, educated at St Hilda's College, Oxford; she subsequently worked as a secretary and advertising copywriter till her marriage in 1928. She began writing under the pseudonym 'Janet Gordon', producing a number of romantic novels which include *April Sky* (1938) and *Just off Bond Street* (1940). *Florence Nightingale* (1950), which displayed her capacity for diligent research and narrative fluency, was widely acclaimed; its balanced treatment of its subject restored Nightingale's reputation, which had suffered from *Strachey's iconoclasm in *Eminent Victorians* (1918). *The Reason Why* (1953), a detailed analysis of the military and political contexts of the charge of the Light Brigade, was followed by *The Great Hunger* (1962), a study of the mid-nineteenth-century Irish potato famine; a descendant of Lord Edward FitzGerald, a leading figure in the Irish uprising of 1798, she had a keen sense of her own Irishness, from which the work drew a passionate conviction. She died before completing the proposed second volume of *Queen Victoria: Her Life and Times* (1972), for which she had access to the royal archives at Windsor.

WOODHOUSE, Sarah (1950–), British historical novelist, born in Birmingham, educated at Reading University. Many of her novels are set in late eighteenth- and early nineteenth-century Norfolk. All are distinguished by their heroines' love of place, frequently East Anglia, and vivid characterization. Amongst her novels is a trilogy comprising *A Season of Mists* (1984), which concerns the efforts of an heiress to put her ruined land in order; *A Peacock's Feather* (1988), about the impact on a small community of a rich man's arrival in the area; and *The Native Air* (1990). *The Indian Widow* (1985) deals with the return from

India of a penniless and desperate heiress, to her former home. *Daughter of the Sea* (1986) is set in the Channel Islands in the Victorian era. Among later works are *The Enchanted Ground* (1993) and *Meeting Lily* (1994).

WOOLF, Douglas (1922–), American novelist and short-story writer, born in New York, educated at Harvard. He served in North Africa during the Second World War, worked briefly as a screenwriter, then became an itinerant worker, taking time off to write, often in ghost towns or foreign countries. His understanding of the world was far in advance of his society's, which perhaps explains his relative obscurity: long before Don *Delillo dealt with the increasing abstraction of American life, Woolf saw that Americans were moving through worlds solely of their own creation. Concentrating on the escape of two elderly men from the entrapments of suburbia, *Fade Out* (1959) espouses values reminiscent of Mark Twain's *Huckleberry Finn*. In *Wall to Wall* (1962), *Ya! and John-Juan* (1971), *On Us* (1977), and *The Timing Chain* (1985) the central characters bear a closer resemblance to Woolf himself but, unlike Jack *Kerouac's books, they are not directly autobiographical, though they do share with Kerouac a fast-moving, spontaneous prose. Woolf's short stories and related prose are collected in *Signs of a Migrant Worrier* (1965) and *Future Pre-Conditional* (1978). Woolf's work bears testimony to the continuing validity of a great American archetype—the footloose, unassimilable hero, coolly assessing the vicissitudes of his own time and place.

WOOLF, Leonard (Sidney) (1880–1969), British author and publisher, born in Kensington, educated at Trinity College, Cambridge, where he formed lasting friendship with Lytton *Strachey, J. M. *Keynes, and others with whom he was later eminent in the *Bloomsbury Group. He held postings in Ceylon with the Colonial Service from 1904 to 1912, when, already out of sympathy with colonialism, he resigned in order to marry Virginia Stephen (see WOOLF, VIRGINIA), with whom he began the Hogarth Press in 1917. Ceylon supplies the settings for his fiction, which consists of two novels, *The Village and the Jungle* (1913) and *The Wise Virgins* (1914), and the shorter pieces of *Stories of the East* (1916). His subsequent career as a writer was dominated by his social and political beliefs. Among his many publications on domestic and international issues were *Socialism and Co-operation* (1920), *Imperialism and Civilization* (1928), and *The War for Peace* (1940); *After the Deluge* (2 volumes, 1931, 1939) and *Principia Politica* (1953) form detailed expositions of his interpretation of socialism. He was editor of *Political Quarterly* from 1931 to 1959. Notable among his other works is the highly regarded autobiography made up of *Sowing* (1960), *Growing* (1961), *Beginning Again* (1964), *Downhill all the Way* (1967), and *The Journey not the Arrival Matters* (1969); the five books were later published as *An Autobiography* (2 volumes, 1980). Frederic Spotts edited *Letters of Leonard Woolf* (1990). *Leonard Woolf: A Political Biography* by Duncan Wilson appeared in 1979.

WOOLF, (Adeline) Virginia (1882–1941), British novelist and critic, daughter of the agnostic Victorian biographer, editor, and critic Sir Leslie Stephen (1832–1904) and the beautiful philanthropic Julia Duckworth, née Jackson, wife, mother, and nurse (1846–95). She described herself as 'born into a very communicative, literate, letter writing, visiting, articulate, late nineteenth century world'. She grew up, and was educated at home, at 22 Hyde Park Gate, Kensington, with Julia's children by her first marriage to Herbert Duckworth, George, Stella (who died young in 1897), and Gerald; with Leslie's mentally defective daughter Laura, by his first wife Minny Thackeray; and with the other Stephen children, Vanessa (the painter V. Bell), and her brothers Thoby (who died young in 1906) and Adrian. After both parents' deaths Virginia had a mental collapse. In 1904 the Stephen children moved to Gordon Square, and with Thoby's Cambridge friends formed a circle of friends and family connections which came to be known as the *Bloomsbury Group. Its 'members' were closely involved with her life: Clive *Bell, who married Vanessa in 1906, Lytton *Strachey, life-long friend, who proposed to Virginia in 1909, Desmond and Molly MacCarthy, Roger *Fry, Duncan Grant, John Maynard *Keynes, Saxon Sydney Turner, E. M. *Forster, David *Garnett, and Leonard *Woolf. She married Woolf in 1912, at the onset of serious periods of instability between 1912 and 1915, including an attempted suicide in September 1913. Her first novel, *The Voyage Out*, came out in 1915, but since 1904 she had been publishing reviews (mainly, anonymously, for the *Times Literary Supplement*) and writing fictional sketches and drafts of the novel. In 1915 the Woolfs moved to Hogarth House in Richmond and in 1917 founded the Hogarth Press, which published their own work (starting with *Two Stories*) and that of many of the leading writers of the time, perhaps most notably their friend T. S. Eliot's *The *Waste Land*. Woolf was always actively involved in every aspect of the Press. In 1919 she published **Night and Day* and the experimental story 'Kew Gardens', and became friendly with K. *Mansfield; and the Woolfs bought Monk's House in Rodmell, Sussex.

In the early 1920s she began to be recognized as an important writer and evolved a programme for her writing with the collection of stories *Monday or Tuesday* (1921), the novel **Jacob's Room* (1922), and her seminal essays on fiction, 'Modern Novels' (1919, an attack on the Edwardians, revised as 'Modern Fiction'), 'Mr Bennett and Mrs Brown' (1923, a reply to Arnold *Bennett's criticism of *Jacob's Room* as unrealistic), and 'Character in Fiction' (1924). In 1923 Leonard became editor of the *Nation and Athenaeum*, and they moved to Tavistock Square. Her great modernist novels of the 1920s, **Mrs Dalloway* and **To the Lighthouse*, and her 1925 collection of essays *The *Common Reader* (the first of several), established her reputation as an original modernist comparable with *Joyce or Proust. But her *jeu d'esprit*, **Orlando*, a love-offering to V. *Sackville-West, was more popular. *Orlando*'s theme of androgyny was echoed in the vital essay on feminism and writing *A *Room of One's Own* (1929), which arose from lectures given at the women's colleges, Newnham and Girton, Cambridge. Meanwhile she was working on *The *Waves* (1931), her 'brave attempt' to represent interior mental states through a formal experiment in narrative.

The 1930s, with the rise of fascism and Nazism, the death of her nephew Julian Bell in the Spanish Civil War, Leonard's involvement with the Labour Party, and her friendship with the militant feminist composer Ethel Smyth, turned her arguments on writing from issues of *Modernism in fiction to the relation of art and propaganda (as in the essay 'The Leaning Tower', 1940). *A Room of One's Own* led to the argument on feminism, patriarchy, and war in the lecture 'Professions for Women' (1931), the long essay **Three Guineas* (1938), and the novel *The *Years* (1937). (These two were originally conceived as one book, *The Pargiters*.) Even a light fantasy, *Flush* (1933), told as if by Elizabeth Barrett Browning's dog, continued the theme of tyrannical patriarchy. In the late 1930s the habitual features of her life continued—a full and active social life in London (from 1939, at Mecklenburgh Square), car trips to Europe, work on the Press, on a biography of *Roger Fry* (1940), on essays and fiction, and intermittent periods of illness and depression. She began to develop in a new direction, towards a history of obscure lives and a 'philosophy of anonymity', in a sketch for a book about human continuity, *Anon*, and in *Pointz Hall*, published posthumously as **Between the Acts* (1941). In 1940 the Woolfs' past and present London homes were bombed and they withdrew to Monk's House. Woolf finished her last novel, became increasingly disturbed, and drowned herself in the River Ouse in March 1941.

After her death, posthumous volumes of stories and essays were published (*The Death of the Moth and Other Essays*, 1942; *The Captain's Death Bed and Other Essays*, 1950; *Granite and Rainbow*, 1958; *Collected Essays*, 4 volumes, 1966, 1967), and *A Writer's Diary*, edited by L. Woolf (1958). Since Q. Bell's biography of his aunt (*Virginia Woolf*, 2 volumes, 1972), her stature as one of the major novelists of the century, and a vital figure in the history of modernism and of the feminist movement, has been established in three ways. One is by the publication of the great mass of primary materials unpublished in her lifetime: her letters (in 6 volumes, edited by N. Nicolson and J. Trautmann, 1975–80), her diaries (in 5 volumes, edited by A. O. Bell and A. McNeillie, 1977–84), her essays (volumes I–IV, 1986–94; edited by A. McNeillie), her complete shorter fiction (edited by S. Dick, 1985), her early journals (*A Passionate Pilgrim*, edited by M. Leaska, 1990), and her autobiographical writings (*Moments of Being*, edited by J. Schulkind, 1976). The second is by the publication of the manuscript versions of her novels (eg. *To the Lighthouse: The Original Holograph Draft*, edited by S. Dick, 1983), of the definitive Hogarth Press edition of her novels (1990), and, since her coming out of copyright, of various annotated editions (Penguin, Oxford University Press, 1991). The third is by successive waves of literary, biographical, and critical writing on Woolf examining every aspect of her life and work from a wide variety of approaches. See also FEMINIST CRITICISM.

WOOLRICH, Cornell (George Hopley) (1903–68), American crime and mystery writer, son of a mining engineer, born in New York, but spent much of his childhood in Latin America; educated at Columbia University. He published *Cover Charge* (1926), a novel in the manner of Scott *Fitzgerald, while a student. After a short-lived marriage to the daughter of a Hollywood film producer, whom he met while working on the film script of his second novel, *Children of the Ritz* (1927), he returned to Manhattan where he spent the rest of his life living as a recluse in a succession of hotel rooms with his mother and turning out a stream of novels and short stories which came to an abrupt end after her death in 1957. Though, under his own name and the pseudonyms William Irish and George Hopley, he wrote many types of story, including police procedurals and tales of the occult, his best works are his stories of suspense and psychological terror, set against the seedy urban background of America in the 1930s and 1940s, which can be compared to the work of James M. *Cain and Jim *Thompson. *The Bride Wore Black* (1940; also published as *Beware the Lady*; filmed by François Truffaut as *La Mariée était en noir*, 1967) was the first of a 'black series' of novels—others are *The Black Curtain* (1941), *Black Alibi* (1942), *Rendezvous in Black* (1948)—which inspired the French *roman noir* and *film noir*. Other works include *Night Has a Thousand Eyes* (1945; as George Hopley), and the William Irish novels *Phantom Lady* (1942) and *Deadline at Dawn* (1944). Many films have been made of his work, the best-known being Hitchcock's *Rear Window* (1954), an adaptation of the short story originally entitled 'It Had To Be Murder' (1942).

WOUK, Herman (1915–), American bestselling novelist and screenwriter, born in New York, brought up in the Bronx and educated at Columbia University; his father was a first generation Russian Jewish industrialist. After working in radio and as a gag writer for the comedian Fred Allen (1936–41), Wouk served with the US Naval Reserve on destroyer-minesweepers (1942–6). His first published novel, *Aurora Dawn; or the True History of Andrew Reale* (1947), is a satire on hucksterism in the radio industry. *City Boy: The Adventures of Herbie Bookbinder and His Cousin, Cliff* (1948) is a story of life in the Bronx in the 1920s. Wouk established himself as a bestselling writer with *The Caine Mutiny* (1951; Pulitzer Prize); subtitled 'a Novel of World War II', it is the story of a regular captain, Philip Queeg, who, after increasing mental instability, is relieved of his command during a typhoon by Willie Keith, a Princeton graduate, newly joined to the service. The subsequent court-martial, in which Keith is successfully defended by a Jewish lawyer, Lieutenant Barney Greenwald, was dramatized (*The Caine Mutiny Court Martial*, 1953); the novel was also successfully filmed (1952: starring Humphrey Bogart). *Marjorie Morningstar* (1955; filmed 1958), about a stunningly beautiful Jewish girl, was praised by one critic as a 'modern Jewish *Vanity Fair*', while others applied the term 'soap opera' (a recurrent slur on Wouk's fiction). *Youngblood Hawke* (1961; filmed 1964) was based on the life of Thomas Wolfe. Wouk's love of large, saga-like novels, his realistic narrative technique, and his adherence to old-fashioned moral categories led one commentator to call Wouk 'the only living nineteenth-century novelist'. *The Winds of War* (1971), his Tolstoyan narrative of the Second World War, and its sequel, *War and Remembrance* (1978), were given vast popular currency by the TV miniseries of 1983 and 1989. His subsequent work, *Inside, Outside* (1985, a story of being Jewish in America), *The Hope* (1993) and *The Glory* (1994), fictional accounts of the epic history of post-1947 Israel, reveal his twin interests in using fiction to explore his own personal American inheritance, and the vast geo-political events of the twentieth century. Among his non-fiction works is *This Is My God: The Jewish Way of Life* (1959).

WREN, P(ercival) C(hristopher) (1885–1941), British popular novelist, born in Devon, educated at Oxford University. He was, at various times in his career, a journalist, an explorer, an officer in the French Foreign Legion, assistant director of education in India, and an officer with the Indian forces in East Africa during the First World War. He published several moderately successful books, including *Smoke and Sword* (1914), before his first post-war novel, *Beau Geste* (1924), brought him popular success. It was followed by several others, including *Beau Sabreur* (1926) and *Beau Ideal* (1928), all adventure stories with a Foreign Legion background.

WRIGHT, Charles (1935–), American poet, born in Pickwick Dam, Tennessee, educated at Davidson College in North Carolina and the University of Iowa. From 1957 to 1963 Wright served in United States Army intelligence in Verona and then studied at the University of Rome under a Fulbright Scholarship before returning to the USA to take up an academic appointment at the University of California at Irvine. In 1983 he became a Professor of English at the University of Virginia. His poetry, which is strongly influenced by the verse of Ezra *Pound and Wallace *Stevens, has often been compared with that of contemporaries such as Mark *Strand and W. S. *Merwin, and is notable for its religiosity and its landscapes of the American South. Many of his individual poems, for example 'Tattoos' and 'Skins', take the form of extended sequences of a markedly autobiographical character in which the poet's memory fractures chronological time. His volumes of verse include *Dream Animal* (1968), *Bloodlines* (1973), *Country Music: Selected Early Poems* (1974), *China Trace* (1977), *The Southern Cross* (1981), *The Other Side of the River* (1984), *Zone Journals* (1988), and *The World of Ten Thousand Things: Selected Poems, 1980–1990* (1990); *Halflife: Improvisations and Interviews, 1977–1987* was published in 1988. He has also made translations from the Italian of Eugenio Montale in *The Storm and Other Poems* (1978). Wright won the American Book Award for poetry in 1983.

WRIGHT, David (John Murray) (1920–94), British poet, born in Johannesburg, South Africa; he grew up in England and was educated at Northampton School for the Deaf and at Oriel College, Oxford. Between 1942 and 1947 he was on the staff of the *Sunday Times*, after which he became a freelance writer. With the painter Patrick Swift, he founded and edited *X*, a highly regarded review of literature and the arts which appeared from 1959 to 1962, and co-edited *An Anthology from X* (1988). His collections of poetry include *Moral Stories* (1954), *Monologue of a Deaf Man* (1958), *Adam at Evening* (1965), and *Metrical Observations* (1980); *To the Gods the Shades* (1976), a collected edition with additional new work, is supplemented by *Selected Poems* (1988). His strong, if often ambivalent, sense of South African identity is clearest in 'Seven South African Poems' and 'Voyage to Africa', in which local, historical, and personal elements are skilfully interwoven. The generous range of his work includes poems based in classical allusion, witty commentaries on social and cultural concerns, and recurrent treatments of autobiographical and anecdotal material. His later verse is notable for its elegiac achievements, examples being his tributes to Ezra *Pound, Patrick *Kavanagh, and Brian *Higgins. Among his other publications are the autobiographical *Deafness: A Personal Account* (1969) and the critical monograph *Roy Campbell* (1961). The numerous works he has edited include De Quincey's *Recollections of the Lakes and the Lake Poets* (1970).

WRIGHT, James (1928–80), American poet, born in Martins Ferry, Ohio, educated at Kenyon College, where he studied with John Crowe *Ransom, and the University of Washington where Theodore *Roethke was his teacher and friend. Wright taught at Hunter College, New York City, from 1966 until his death. His books are *The Green Wall* (1957), *Saint Judas* (1959), *The Branch Will Not Break* (1963), *Shall We Gather at the River?* (1968), *Collected Poems* (1971), *Two Citizens* (1973), *To a Blossoming Pear Tree* (1977), and *This Journey* (1982). His *Collected Prose* appeared in 1983, and *A Secret Field*, extracts from his journals, in 1985. Wright's career falls into three phases: the formalist verse of his two earliest volumes, the 'deep image' phase of his middle years, and a muted romantic lyricism at the last. Wright's is a quiet, undeclamatory voice whose wistful questioning egocentrism well serves his scrutiny of the social world, of nature, and the unconscious, in which the dominant pronoun 'I' is a patient and sympathetic bearer of feeling. The formalism of his first work was radically modified by his friendship with Robert *Bly and their common interest in foreign poetry, especially German expressionism and Spanish surrealism. With Bly, Wright produced translations of the German Georg Trakl, the Chilean poet Pablo Neruda, the Peruvian poet Cesar Vallejo, and Hermann Hesse. If a sense of the joy of being is mutedly present in Wright's late work, the bitter complaint of industrial destitution wrought on the American interior landscape in a poem such as 'Ohioan Pastoral' reflects the sense of social concern of this poet reared during the Great Depression.

WRIGHT, Judith (1915–), Australian poet, writer, and critic, born at Armidale, New South Wales, educated at Sydney University. Her deeply felt attachment to the land, and her growing anger at mankind's exploitative abuse of both the land and Australia's indigenous people, inform much of her best poetry and prose. The complexities of personal relationships are also central to her work. Wright's first poetry collection, *The Moving Image* (1946), made a great impression for its expressive craftsmanship and poetic range; *The Generations of Men* (1959) and *A Cry for the Dead* (1981) traced her family's history, while *Preoccupations in Australian Poetry* (1965) provided important insights into her own imaginative concerns with illuminating readings of Australian literature and history. Her *Collected Poems 1942–1970* were published in 1971, *The Double Tree: Selected Poems 1942–1976* in 1978, and *Phantom Dwelling* in 1986. More recently she has published *Human Pattern: Selected Poems* (1990); *Through Broken Glass* (1992); *The Flame Tree* (1994), fifteen poems presented bilingually in English and Japanese; and a further *Collected Poems, 1942–1985* (1994). A collection of stories, *The Nature of Love*, appeared in 1966. Diverse writings were collected in *Because I Was Invited* (1975), while *The Coral Battleground* (1977) was a passionate argument of the need to defend Queensland's Great Barrier Reef from destruction by oil and mining activities. Later essays include *Born of the Conquerors: Selected Essays of Judith Wright* (1991) and *Going on Talking* (1992). She edited *The Oxford Book of Australian Verse* (1958).

WRIGHT, Kit (1944–), British poet, born in Kent, educated at New College, Oxford. After teaching in a London comprehensive school, he lectured in English at Brock University, St Catherine's, Ontario, for three years. He became Fellow-Commoner in Creative Arts at Trinity College, Cambridge, in 1977. *The Bear Looked over the Mountain* (1977), his first collection of verse, was followed by subsequent volumes including *Bump-Starting the Hearse* (1983), *From the Day Room* (1983), *Real Rags and Red* (1988), *Poems: 1974–1983* (1988), *Short Afternoons* (1989), and *Great Snakes* (1995). While some of his poems are outrightly comic, his originality and value consist largely in his ability to subordinate humour to the compassion and moral concern which are central to his writing. His serio-comic idiom is highly appropriate to his recurrent treatments of absurdity, confusion, and desperation as endemic conditions of urban modernity. He is also the author of numerous highly regarded collections of children's verse, which include *Hot Dog* (1981) and *Cat among the Pigeons* (1987).

WRIGHT, Nicholas (1940–), British dramatist, born in Cape Town. He trained as an actor in London and subsequently held posts as Director of the Royal Court Theatre Upstairs (1970–5), Joint Artistic Director of the Royal Court Theatre (1976–7), and Associate Director of new writing at the National Theatre (1984–9). *Treetops* (1978), his first full-length play, looked back on his South African childhood in Cape Town. *The Crimes of Vautrin* (1983), adapted from Balzac's *Splendeurs et misères des courtisanes*, was widely regarded as a critique of rampant materialism in Britain under Mrs Thatcher. It was followed by *The Custom of the Country* (1983), a romantic comedy on colonial themes set in the boom-town Johannesburg of the 1890s, and *The Desert Air* (1984), a satirical examination of political intrigue among British military and Secret Service agents in Cairo during the Second World War. Wright's best-known play, *Mrs Klein* (1988), set in London with a cast of three female psychiatrists, deals with a personal crisis in the life of the controversial Austrian psychoanalyst Melanie Klein (1882–1960), and her reaction to the sudden death of her son in a climbing accident in 1934.

WRIGHT, Richard (Nathaniel) (1908–60), African-American short-story writer, novelist, poet, and essayist, born near Natchez, Missouri, and brought up in Memphis; he was self-educated and at the age of 19 went to Chicago, where he held a number of menial jobs. In the 1930s he joined the Communist Party, but left in the 1940s after disillusionment with its procedures, as recorded in the anthology *The *God that Failed* (1950). He worked for the *Federal Writers' Project between 1935 and 1937 and received the *Story* prize for *Uncle Tom's Children* (1938, enlarged 1940), for the best book submitted by anyone associated with the Project. The collection of stories describes the racial prejudice in the South and contains graphic descriptions of mob lynchings. In 1940 he published **Native Son*, his most acclaimed work, which established Wright as the pre-eminent black author in the USA. He dramatized the novel with Paul *Green in 1941, and in 1950 he made a film of the book in Argentina, with himself in the lead role. He participated in the making of *12 Million Black Voices* (1941), a textual and photographic documentary of black history; and published *Black Boy* (1945), a sophisticated autobiography of his childhood and youth which analyses the treatment of black people in American society. After the Second World War, he became an expatriate in Paris and became involved with the Parisian existentialist circle. He utilized their ideas in the writing of his other acclaimed novel, *The Outsider* (1953), a sensational novel of a black man's life in Chicago and New York City and his fatal involvement with the Communist Party. Other works followed, many of them devoted to supporting African national independence movements, with *Savage Holiday*

(1954); *Black Power* (1954), telling of his reactions to Africa's Gold Coast; *The Color Curtain* (1956), reporting on the Bandung Conference of Asian and African nations; *White Man, Listen!* (1957); *Pagan Spain* (1957), some bitter personal observations of Spain; and *The Long Dream* (1958), a novel about a black boy in Mississippi and his father's corrupt business dealings with both black and white people. Posthumous publications include the short stories in *Eight Men* (1961); *Lawd Today* (1963), a novel written before *Native Son* and dealing with the events of one unhappy day, 12 February 1936, in the life of a black postal clerk in Chicago; and *American Hunger* (1977), a further autobiography. Although he wrote with a naturalistic style, his works have always demonstrated a concern with the social roots of racial oppression, and he published firmly in the left-wing journals like *New Masses* and *Left Front*. He now has the solid reputation of being one of the most influential black American writers of the twentieth century.

WYLIE, Elinor (Morton Hoyt) (1885–1928), American poet and novelist, born in Somerville, New Jersey; she grew up in Washington, where her father held office as Solicitor-General of the United States. From 1912 to 1915 she lived in England, where *Incidental Numbers* (1912), her first collection of verse, was privately published. She discounted it following the publication of *Nets To Catch the Wind* (1921), which, with its precise imagery and musical refinement, represented a considerable advance on her sentimentally conventional earlier work; its appearance marked the beginning of her short but highly successful literary career. Her subsequent collections, characterized by a poised combination of emotional intensity and aesthetic detachment, were *Black Armour* (1923), *Trivial Breath* (1928), and *Angels and Earthly Creatures* (1929). William Rose *Benét, her third husband, edited *Collected Poems* (1932) and *Last Poems* (1942). *Jennifer Lorn* (1923), the first of her novels, was chiefly set in eighteenth-century India and revealed the talent for imaginative adaptation of historical research evident throughout her prose fiction. Her other novels include *The Venetian Glass Nephew* (1925), a philosophical fantasy allegorizing her conceptions of art, and *The Orphan Angel* (1926; UK title *Mortal Image*, 1927), in which Shelley, rescued from drowning by an American ship, explores the American frontier. William Rose Benét's edition of her *Collected Prose* appeared in 1933. The fullest of numerous biographical treatments is *Elinor Wylie: A Life Apart* (1979) by Stanley Olson.

WYLIE, Philip (Gordon) (1902–71), American writer, born in Beverly, Massachusetts, educated at Princeton. His collections of Florida fishing tales such as *Salt Water Daffy* (1941) and *Crunch and Des* (1948) are among his more amiable works. More savage, and more typical, are *Generation of Vipers* (1942), an attack on 'momism'; *An Essay on Morals* (1947), a dyspeptic analysis of conventional religion; and *Opus 21* (1949), a discourse on repressive sexual mores. His novels ranged across several genres, but a consistent humanitarianism marks them all, from *Gladiator* (1930), a science fiction tale that prefigured *Superman*, to *Finnley Wren* (1934), an experimental 'novel in a new manner'. *When Worlds Collide* (1933; with Edwin Balmer) presented a cosmic catastrophe, while *The Answer* (1956) saw love as the key to human survival; *Night unto Night* (1944) was a fantasy whose already dead cast are forced to confront their moral impostures; *The Disappearance* (1954) didactically posited two worlds, from one of which all men have disappeared, and from the other all women; while *The End of the Dream* (1972) addressed with icy melancholy issues of planetary pollution.

WYNDHAM, Francis (1924–), British novelist, short-story writer, and critic, born in London. He wrote his first stories between the ages of 17 and 20, before being called up and after being invalided out of the army. Not published until 1974, as *Out of the War*, they recreate the conditions of aimless expectancy known to those left behind whilst a war was being waged elsewhere. Abandoning fiction, Wyndham worked as a reviewer, feature writer, and editor: a collection of his incisive and original pieces on books and performance, as well as his interviews with non-literary figures such as actresses and photographers (a form which in his hands took on the quirky poignancy of his short stories), was published in 1991 under the title *The Theatre of Embarrassment*. *Mrs Henderson and Other Stories* (1985) represents Wyndham's return to imaginative writing; its five pieces give an elliptical account of their narrator's progress from childhood to late middle age, but focus on the petty preoccupations and glamorous irrationality of others—the mother of a schoolfriend, a war correspondent brother, a self-obsessed fellow author. The short novel *The Other Garden* (1987) reverts to the experience of the war years, and like all Wyndham's fiction weighs the droll absurdity and disregarded drama of non-combatant life against the privileges of detachment. It is also characteristic in its economy and in the subtle intelligence with which it combines the meditative and the explosively comic.

WYNDHAM, John, the best-known pseudonym of John Wyndham Parkes Lucas Beynon HARRIS (1903–69), British writer, born in Knowle, Warwickshire. He followed various occupations before embarking on writing as a career. Before the Second World War he wrote under variations of his full name in a variety of genres. His first *science fiction story, 'Worlds to Barter' (1931), was by 'John Beynon Harris'; his first novel, *The Secret People* (1935), by 'John Beynon'; and a later work, *The Outward Urge* (1959), appeared as a 'collaboration' by 'John Wyndham and Parkes Lucas'. He is best known as a writer of science fiction, having long been attracted to the works of H. G. *Wells and Jules Verne, but he preferred to describe his own work as 'logical fantasy'. As the creator of what became known as the 'cosy catastrophe', in which ordinary people manage to survive a catastrophe or invasion (usually in a rural enclave), for a time Wyndham was the most popular post-war writer of British science fiction. *The Day of the Triffids* (1951) concerns a catastrophe which leaves most of the human race blind, except for the protagonists whose eyes where protected from the light, and the giant Triffids (a species of plant-like mutants) who begin to take over the world. It was followed by *The Kraken Wakes* (1953); *The Chrysalids* (1955), in which Britain is divided by vast radioactive wastelands into ghettos where genetic mutations breed 'monsters'; and *The Midwich Cuckoos* (1957), in which all the women of an English village become inseminated by aliens and give birth to beautiful, gifted children with telepathic powers which they use to murderous effect, enslaving the rest of the population to their collective will, before they are finally destroyed. Together, these novels present a distinctly English response to the theme of disaster, whether man-made or natural. Other novels include *Trouble with Lichen* (1960) and *Chocky* (1968). His best stories were collected in *The Seeds of Time* (1956) and *Consider Her Ways* (1961). Wyndham has considerably influenced such writers as J. *Christopher and B. W. *Aldiss. He also introduced 'triffid' into the language to describe a fantastic and dangerous plant; those depicted in his novel were mobile monsters about 7 feet high who propelled themselves on three-pronged roots.

WYNTER, Sylvia (1928–), Caribbean novelist and playwright, born of Jamaican parents in the Holguin Oriente Province of Cuba, educated at King's College, University of London, gaining her MA in 1953 for a thesis on Spanish drama. After a period in London writing plays for radio, she became a lecturer at the University of the West Indies and later taught at the universities of Michigan and California. In 1977 she became Professor of African and Afro-American Studies at Stanford University. Her highly regarded novel *The Hills of Hebron* (1962) forms a disquieting treatment of the crisis in a West Indian community produced by tensions between Christian revivalism and the persistence of the older African modes of spirituality. Wynter is among the most noted contemporary women playwrights of the Caribbean, rooting much of her work in the folk idioms of the region; her plays, which remain largely unpublished, include *Shh . . . It's a Wedding* (produced 1961), *1865, Ballad of a Rebellion* (produced 1965), and *Maskarade* (produced 1979).

Y

YATES, Dornford, pseudonym of Cecil William MERCER (1885–1960), British writer, born in London, educated at Harrow and Oxford. Before becoming a writer he was a barrister, as is his most popular character, Berry Pleydell, who appeared with his circle in a series of novels including *The Brother of Daphne* (1914), *Berry and Co.* (1920), and *The House that Berry Built* (1945). Yates's 'Chandos' thrillers (*Blind Corner*, 1927, etc.) were also popular. The Berry books portray an England and Europe of empty roads, leisured aristocracy, and obedient and respectful servant classes. The style is whimsical, a mixture of lyricism and excruciating puns. Though his novels reflect many twentieth-century historical crises, Yates rarely illuminates them; and his patrician tone and some disturbing prejudices probably account for his declining audience.

YATES, Dame Frances (Amelia) (1899–1981), British cultural historian, born at Southsea, educated at University College, London. She joined the staff of the Warburg Institute in 1941. Following the Institute's absorption into University College, London, in 1944 she became a Reader in the history of the Renaissance in 1956. *John Florio: The Life of an Italian in Shakespeare's England* (1934), her first work of importance, anticipated the themes of much of her writing in its examination of the interactions of politics, religion, philosophy, and art in the culture of the Elizabethan era. Her numerous subsequent studies include *The French Academies of the Sixteenth Century* (1947), *The Valois Tapestries* (1959), and *The Art of Memory* (1966), an account of Renaissance mnemonic techniques. She is best known for her treatments of Rosicrucianism and Neo-Platonism in *Giordano Bruno and the Hermetic Tradition* (1964), *The Rosicrucian Enlightenment* (1972), and *The Occult Philosophy in the Elizabethan Age* (1979). Her books have had a major influence in modifying modern perceptions of the intellectual and cultural character of the sixteenth century. *Lull and Bruno* (1982), *Renaissance and Reform* (1983), and *Ideas and Ideals in the North European Renaissance* (1984) are collections of her essays.

Years, The, a novel by V. *Woolf, published in 1938. Woolf's longest and most arduously written novel, it appears to be a return to the more traditional narrative methods of **Night and Day* (1919). It is, however, a complex attempt, made with great difficulty, to analyse the political life of the English middle classes in the early twentieth century, without allowing the politics to dominate. It grew out of a 'novel-essay' called *The Pargiters*, which intercut the story of the family with a commentary on the conditions for women in English society. Woolf became dissatisfied with this formal experiment, finding that it made the politics too intrusive. In 1933 she decided to compress the 'interchapters' inside the novel. (The factual material she left out went into the feminist essay **Three Guineas*). As a result of this process *The Years* had, she thought, a 'certain flatness in the dialogue', and still too much material, which she cut down. The family story is told through fragmentary scenes moving between a large number of characters, with recurring references (as to Sophocles' *Antigone*) to suggest her arguments. It makes a darker, more embittered version of the Ramsays' family history in **To the Lighthouse*. Each section is headed by a date, starting in 1880, then 1891, 1907, 1908, 1910, 1911, 1913, 1914, 1917, and jumping to a long scene in 'Present Day', 1936. It begins with the Victorian family, dominated by Colonel Pargiter—who has a secret, squalid 'love nest' and bullies his children—on the day of the mother's death. It follows the next two generations (Delia, Martin, Rose, North, Peggy) but especially the lives of the unmarried daughter Eleanor, who keeps house for her father, and of the daughters of the Pargiters' cousin Kitty, Maggie and the eccentric Sarah. There is deliberately no central character, but in the novel's disturbing analogies between Victorian patriarchy and a 'present day' dominated by male egotism, megaphonic propaganda, class division, and fascism, it is Sarah and Eleanor who have the central utopian visions of another possible existence, more fluid, impersonal, and free.

YEATS, Jack B(utler) (1871–1957), Irish painter, illustrator, novelist, and playwright, born in London, the brother of W. B. *Yeats; he was brought up in Sligo, where he developed the imaginative interest in Irish rural life which informs much of his graphic and literary work. After studying art in London he began his career as an illustrator; his illustrations for *The Aran Islands* (1907) and *Wicklow, West Kerry and Connemara* (1911) by J. M. *Synge, with whom he made a walking tour of the West of Ireland, are among his best-known. He was over 50 years old when he began producing the works on which his reputation as a major European painter rests. He continued painting into his eighties, some of his finest canvases, among them 'Glory' and 'Grief', dating from his last years. The horse fairs, tinkers, landscapes, and villages of Sligo reflected in much of his painting are equally a staple of his prose. His novels include *Sailing, Sailing Swiftly* (1933), *The Aramanthers* (1936), *The Charmed Life* (1938), and *The Careless Flower* (1947); these and several others demonstrate his belief that 'the artist assembles memories' in consisting largely of localized reminiscences described in an eloquently celebratory style. Like his prose, his plays were mostly written between 1930 and 1945; some, including the unorthodox *Harlequin's Positions* and *In Sand*, were produced by the *Abbey Theatre's experimental groups. Yeats's *Collected Plays* (1971) and *Selected Writings* (1991) are both edited by Robin Skelton. There is a biography by Hilary Pyle (1970).

YEATS, W(illiam) B(utler) (1865–1939), Irish poet and dramatist, born in Dublin; he spent much of his childhood in Sligo, where his mother's family lived. After a period in London, when he attended the Godolphin School, Hammersmith, he returned to Dublin in 1880 and completed his schooling at the city's Erasmus Smith High School. In 1884 he became a student at Dublin's Metropolitan School of Art, with the intention of making his living as a painter, the profession of his father John Butler Yeats (1839–1922) and his brother Jack B. *Yeats. At this time he began his long friendship with George *Russell ('AE'), whose visionary preoccupations accentuated Yeats's dissatisfaction with the scientific rationalism of the era. Having begun writing poetry at school, he was stimulated to increased activity by Russell's company: as an art student he produced a series of verse-dramas, the best of which, 'The Island of the Statues', clearly displays the late Romantic aestheticism characteristic of much of his early work. During the mid-1880s the interests in occultism and Irish nationalism which are of central importance to his poetry were established: with Russell, he was a founding member of the Dublin Hermetic Society; with Katharine *Tynan, Douglas *Hyde, and others, he was strongly influenced by the Fenian leader John O'Leary, who did much to initiate the *Irish Revival.

Following the publication of his play *Mosada* (1886) and appearances of his work in various journals, by 1887, the year of his return to London, Yeats had decided to devote himself to literature. In 1888 he compiled *Fairy and Folk Tales of the Irish Peasantry*; further collections of folklore followed, of which *The *Celtic Twilight* (1893) is the best-known. The mythological title work of *The Wanderings of Oisin* (1889) was his first long poem on an Irish subject. In the same year his political consciousness intensified after his meeting with Maud Gonne, the actress and nationalist agitator, who prompted him to write *The Countess Cathleen*, the title play of his collection of 1892; the volume also contained the passionately lyrical poems later collected as 'The Rose', which draw on his esoteric mysticism, his vision of Ireland, and his unrequited love for Gonne, the source of the underlying languor of numerous subsequent poems. His other early works include the substantially autobiographical novel *John Sherman*, published with the heroic story *Dhoya* in 1891, his edition of *The Poems of William Blake* (1893), the play *The Land of Heart's Desire* (1894), and the allegorical prose narratives of *The Secret Rose* (1897). In 1892 he was closely involved in the formation of the Irish Literary Societies in London and Dublin. He was also active at this time in various occult orders and as a member of the Rhymers' Club, which he assisted in founding in 1891 and commemorated in 'The Grey Rock' of 1913. The greater technical accomplishment he acquired through his absorption of the Rhymers' ethos of poetic craftsmanship is apparent in *The Wind among the Reeds* (1899); his early manner culminates in its fluently melodious verse, its imaginatively rarefied moods, and the stylized symbolic imagery with which both its Irish and its mystical themes are presented.

From 1897 onward Yeats was much occupied with the Irish Literary Theatre, which produced *Countess Cathleen* in 1899 as its inaugural production when it was received with accusations of blasphemy and lack of patriotism, and **Cathleen Ni Houlihan*, with Maud Gonne in the title role, in 1902; he became a director of its successor, the *Abbey Theatre, in 1906. He continued to divide his time chiefly between London and Dublin until 1917, the year in which he married Georgiana Hyde-Lees and began preparing the tower he had purchased at Ballylee to serve as a more permanent home. Ballylee was close to Lady *Gregory's estate at Coole, near Gort in County Galway, where Yeats had been a regular visitor since 1897 and upon which he based the cultural ideal of 'The dream of the noble and the beggarman' reflected in much of his verse. The poetry of *In the Seven Woods* (1903) moved towards a new lucidity and directness of tone and imagery; this development, which became clearer with 'No Second Troy' and other works in *The Green Helmet* (1910), issued in the forceful immediacy of manner of **Responsibilities* (1914). Ezra *Pound, Yeats's secretary at intervals between 1913 and 1916, encouraged him in the forging of this new style and introduced him to Ernest *Fenollosa's versions of Japanese Noh plays, which decisively influenced his practices as a dramatist in *Four Plays for Dancers* (1921) and succeeding works. *Responsibilities* indicated Yeats's growing disaffection with a modern Ireland which had failed to realize the cultural ideals of the Revival; despite the disquieted acknowledgement in 'Easter 1916' of the heroism displayed in the Rising of 1916, he wrote at about this time that 'the dream of my early manhood, that a modern nation can return to Unity of Culture, is false'. *The Wild Swans at Coole* (1919) and *Michael Robartes and the Dancer* (1921) reveal a new imaginative authority in poems reflecting the esoteric philosophy of *A *Vision* (1925, revised edition 1937). The system described in this work pervasively informs his later poetry and is of particular relevance to such notable achievements as 'The Second Coming', 'Nineteen Hundred and Nineteen', and 'The Statues'. These and many other poems exhibit the tone of aristocratic disdain for a modern age when 'Mere anarchy is loosed upon the world' which recurs in *The *Tower* (1928), *Words for Music Perhaps* (1932), *The Winding Stair* (1929), *A Full Moon in March* (1935), and **Last Poems and Plays* (1940), his principal subsequent collections of poetry.

The energy with which Yeats had continually advanced his art was raised to a new level in the last fifteen years of his life; his late poetry's range and vigour of technique and imagination are equally evident in works of challenging intellectual scope, lyrics of great refinement, and poems and ballads memorable for their outspoken simplicity. He was a senator of the Irish Free State from 1922 to 1928, chairing the commission on coinage. Having commanded increasing respect as a poet for many years, the award of the Nobel Prize in 1923 gained him universal recognition; in the estimation of many he remains the greatest poet of the twentieth century. From the early 1920s onward he lived principally in Dublin. He died in the South of France and was buried at Roquebrune; in 1948 he was reinterred at Drumcliffe in Sligo, in accordance with what he had written in 'Under Ben Bulben', one of his latest poems. *Collected Poems* (1950) and *The Poems: A New Edition* (edited by R. Finneran, 1983, revised edition 1989) are the principal collections of his verse. *The Variorum Edition of the Poems* was produced in 1957. *Collected Plays* was published in 1952, and the various volumes of his *Autobiographies* which had appeared since *Reveries over Childhood and Youth* (1915) were collected in 1955. *Ideas of Good and Evil* (1903), *Per Amica Silentia Lunae* (1918), and *On the Boiler* (1939) are among the numerous collections of essays published during his lifetime; others include *Mythologies* (1959), *Essays and Introductions* (1961), and *Explorations* (1962). He also edited numerous works, his idiosyncratic *Oxford Book of Modern Verse* (1936) being the best-known. A. Wade's edition of the *Collected Letters* (1954) and separate volumes covering his correspondence with Katharine Tynan (1953), T. Sturge *Moore (1953), and others are now being superseded by the multi-volume *Collected Letters* (1986–), edited by J. Kelly. The most authoritative of numerous biographical studies are J. Hone's *W. B. Yeats* (1942), R. *Ellmann's *Yeats: The Man and the Masks* (1948, revised edition 1979), and A. N. Jeffares's *W. B. Yeats: A New Biography* (1988). See also SYMBOLISM.

YERBY, Frank (Garvin) (1916–91), American novelist, born in Augusta, Georgia, educated at Fisk University, Nashville, Tennessee. His short story 'Health Card' (1944) indicts a white congressman for demanding the eponymous document from a black GI's sweetheart. Yerby became a prolific popular novelist, writing mainly in the historical, or 'costume novel', mode. Among his most ambitious and best-known works are *The Foxes of Harrow* (1946), *The Vixens* (1947), and *Pride's Castle* (1949), a trilogy which deals with characters and events during the Civil War, Reconstruction, and Gilded Age periods. The French Revolution figures in *The Devil's Laughter* (1953) and the anti-Nazi Resistance in *The Voyage Unplanned* (1974). One of his most entertaining novels, *Speak Now* (1969), deals with a love affair between a black American jazz musician and a white student from the American South, both caught up in the political turbulence of Paris in 1968. Yerby's African-American roots are particularly evident in his meticulous recreations of the African past in *The Dahomean* (1971) and *A Darkness at Ingraham's Crest* (1981).

YEZIERSKA, Anzia (*c*.1885–1970), Jewish-American novelist, born in Russian Poland to an impoverished family who migrated to the Lower East Side ghetto of Manhattan in the 1890s. Ambitious and fiercely independent, she rejected the gender constraints of her orthodox background and set out, on the meagre wages of sweatshop and laundry work, to learn English. A prolonged struggle to develop her writing skills was finally rewarded with meteoric celebrity when *Hungry Hearts* (1920), a collection of stories of ghetto life, was sold to Hollywood for filming. Over the next decade she published five more works of fiction, in which an intensive and often autobiographical preoccupation with female experience gives an unusual slant to the traditional immigrant themes of cultural dislocation and conflict; *Bread Givers* (1925), in particular, ranks with Abraham *Cahan's *David Levinksy* as a classic of the 'ethnic passage' genre. The Depression eclipsed her reputation and after a period with the *Federal Writers' Project she relapsed into poverty. Apart from her fictionalized life story *Red Ribbon on a White Horse* (1950), she remained almost forgotten until she was rediscovered in the mid-1960s. A collection of previously unpublished work appeared posthumously in *The Open Cage* (1979).

YOUNG, Andrew (John) (1885–1971), British poet, born in Elgin, Moray; he grew up in Edinburgh, where he was educated at the University. In 1912 he was ordained in the Free Church of Scotland and became an Anglican minister in 1939. He was made a Canon of Chichester Cathedral in 1948. *Songs of Night* (1910), his first collection of verse, was succeeded by numerous volumes, including *Memorial Verses* (1918), a long elegy of great accomplishment for a friend killed in the war. Many of his brief, contemplatively descriptive poems of the 1920s exemplify the style of the Georgian poets (see GEORGIAN POETRY), with whom he is generally associated. In 1931, however, he disclaimed as immature all his work preceding the appearance of *Winter Harvest* in that year. His later poetry makes striking use of precisely observed natural imagery to convey his belief in the transcendental aspects of the physical world. Among his subsequent collections are *Speak to the Earth* (1939) and *The Green Man* (1947). His most remarkable work is *Out of the World and Back* (1958), which forms a highly imaginative treatment of his conceptions of the afterlife. A *Poetical Works* (1985), edited by E. Lowbury and A. Young, is a collected edition of his poetry. His other publications include *A Prospect of Flowers* (1945), one of the products of his keen interest in botany, and the critical work *The Poet and the Landscape* (1962).

YOUNG, E(mily) H(ilda) (1880–1949), British novelist, born in Northumberland, educated at Penrhos College in Wales. In 1902 she married a solicitor and moved to Bristol, the setting for most of her books. After her husband was killed at Ypres in 1917, she lived the rest of her life with the married Headmaster of Alleyn's School in Dulwich, a relationship which she concealed from the public. Most of her novels, witty commentaries on the morals and manners of the middle and upper-middle classes in England, are concerned with the conflict between the intense inner life of her female characters and the conventions and restraints of their sex and class, a conflict which Young herself experienced. Her early novels, *A Corn of Wheat* (1910), *Yonder* (1912), and *Moor Fires* (1916), were followed by *The Misses Mallett* (1927, originally published as *The Bridge Dividing*, 1922). The semi-autobiographical *William* (1925), about a ship-owner and his family, was Young's most popular novel, but *Miss Mole* (1930; James Tait Black Memorial Prize) is probably her most accomplished work. The heroine of this novel of manners, like many of Young's heroines, conforms outwardly, but underneath is a passionate woman with a secret which nearly destroys her. Young's other works include two children's books and the novels *The Vicar's Daughter* (1928), *Jenny Wren* (1932), *The Curate's Wife* (1934), *Celia* (1937), and *Chatterton Square* (1947).

YOUNG, Francis Brett (1884–1954), British novelist and poet, born in Worcestershire, educated at Birmingham University. Young's early novels include *Deep Sea* (1914), *The Dark Tower* (1915), *The Iron Age* (1916), and *The Young Physician* (1919). During the First World War he served with the Royal Army Medical Corps in East Africa, as a result of which his health was seriously impaired; during convalescence he wrote *Marching on Tanga* (1917), a war-memoir, *The Crescent Moon* (1918), and *Poems 1916–1918* (1919). After the war he settled for a time in Anacapri, Italy, where he wrote many of his popular West Midland novels, including *The Black Diamond* (1921), *The Red Knight* (1921), *Portrait of Clare* (1927; James Tait Black Memorial Prize), and *My Brother Jonathan* (1928). One of his best novels, *Dr Bradley Remembers* (1938), was based on the experiences of his father who, like himself, was a physician. He also wrote two historical novels about South Africa, *They Seek a Country* (1937) and *The City of Gold* (1939), and a historical epic in verse, *The Island* (1944), which ends with the Battle of Britain.

YOUNG, Gavin (David) (1928–   ), British travel writer, brought up in Cornwall and South Wales, educated at Rugby and Trinity College, Oxford. After a period of National Service in Palestine, he worked for a shipping company in Basra, Iraq; in 1952 he travelled with Wilfred *Thesiger to the marshlands of southern Iraq, where he remained for two years, a period reflected in *Return to the Marshes* (1977) and *Iraq: Land of Two Rivers* (1980), a work acclaimed for its historical and cultural scope. Following a further two years working with a locust control unit in South Western Arabia, from 1959 to 1990 he travelled widely as a correspondent with the *Observer*, frequently reporting from areas of conflict; *Worlds Apart* (1989) is a collection of his articles. *Slow Boats to China* (1981), an account of his adventurously casual voyage around the world in 1980, established his reputation with a wide readership; a sequel entitled *Slow Boats Home* appeared in 1985. His other works include *Beyond Lion Rock* (1988), which traces the development of Cathay Pacific Airways from its unpromising beginnings in 1946. Joseph *Conrad's voyages in the Far East form the basis of Young's itinerary in *In Search of Conrad* (1991), a work which combines his descriptive and narrative skills as a travel writer with valuable interpretations of the importance of various locations to Conrad's fiction. *From Sea to Shining Sea* (1995) recounts his travels in America.

Young Visiters, The, see ASHFORD, DAISY.

'Youth', a story by Joseph *Conrad, first published in *Blackwood's Magazine* (1898), and collected in *Youth, A Narrative; and Two Other Stories* (1902). The story was based on Conrad's 1881–2 voyage as second mate on the *Palestine*, and it introduced Marlow as story-teller. To the same audience as in **Heart of Darkness* (which Conrad began writing in December 1898), Marlow tells of his first voyage to the East as a 20-year-old second mate on board an old and rusty barque, the *Judea*, bound for Bangkok. The voyage is dogged by delays and difficulties: shifting ballast in a gale between London and Newcastle; a collision with a steamship in Newcastle harbour; further damage from gales in the Atlantic, which obliges the *Judea* to put back to Falmouth for repairs. When the *Judea* finally reaches the Indian Ocean, the cargo of coal catches fire and the crew are forced to abandon ship and take to the boats. Throughout, the older Marlow looks back at the enthusiasm and thoughtless optimism of the younger Marlow. The story presents a middle-aged recollection of youthful adventure, its reflections on the romantic illusions and enthusiasms of youth tempered by a sense of sadness and loss.

Z

ZANGWILL, Israel (1864–1926), British writer of Russian-Jewish descent, born in Whitechapel, London; he was educated at the Jews' Free School and London University. After working as a schoolteacher, from 1890 to 1892 he was founding editor of the magazine *Ariel*, collecting his humorous stories in *The Bachelors' Club* (1891) and *The Old Maids' Club* (1892). He gained wide notice with the novel *Children of the Ghetto* (1892), a graphically moving treatment of conditions among the Jewish population of London's East End, which appeared at a time of rising anti-semitism. In *Ghetto Tragedies* (1893) and *The King of the Schnorrers* (1894) he depicts London Jews with humour and some sternness. Zangwill's affirmation of the ideals of Judaism in *Dreamers of the Ghetto* (1898) and *The Mantle of Elijah* (1900) established him as a leading Zionist. He became leader of the International Zionist Movement in 1904 and eloquently espoused the cause in *The Voice of Jerusalem* (1920). The best-known of his numerous plays is *The Melting Pot* (1909). His other works include the early essays collected in *Without Prejudice* (1896).

ZATURENSKA, Marya (1902–82), American poet, born in Kiev, Ukraine; she went to America with her family in 1909 and was naturalized in 1912. She was educated at Valparaiso University and the University of Wisconsin and subsequently worked as a newspaper feature writer. In 1925 she married the poet Horace *Gregory, with whom she wrote the highly regarded critical survey *A History of American Poetry, 1900–1940* (1969). Her first collection of poems, *Threshold and Hearth* (1934), was followed by *Cold Morning Sky* (1937; Pulitzer Prize, 1938). Zaturenska's work was characterized by its lyrical refinement and marked accomplishment in the use of traditional poetic forms; her imagery, particularly her expansive use of landscape, often displays considerable richness and power. Her subsequent collections include *The Listening Landscape* (1941), *The Golden Mirror* (1944), *Terraces of Light* (1960), *Collected Poems* (1965), and *The Hidden Waterfall* (1974). An increasingly devotional tendency is apparent i her later work. She was also the author of the critical biography *Christina Rosetti* (1949). Among the numerous works she edited is *The Collected Poems of Sara Teasdale* (1964).

ZELAZNY, Roger (Joseph) (1937–), American *science fiction writer, born in Ohio, educated at Columbia University. He is best known for the four books which established his highly figured baroque romanticism as a mode of exploration. *This Immortal* (1966) depicts with great vigour a declining Earth, enigmatic aliens, and an immortal *picaro* protagonist; *The Dream Master* (1966) links psychosis to myth; the tales in *Four for Tomorrow* (1967), most notably 'A Rose for Ecclesiastes', rewrote the clichés of science fiction into augurs of renewal; and *Lord of Light* (1967) placed a group of humans on a far planet, where they re-enacted the epic family struggles of Hindu mythology. His other works include *Jack of Shadows* (1971), *To Die in Italbar* (1973), and *A Night in the Lonesome October* (1993). A long series of novels, beginning with *Nine Princes in Amber* (1970), has been esteemed for its literary polish and ingenious narrative. His shorter fiction has been collected in *The Last Defender of Camelot* (1980) and *Unicorn Variations* (1983).

Zen and the Art of Motorcycle Maintenance, see PIRSIG, ROBERT.

ZEPHANIAH, Benjamin (1958–), British poet and playwright, born in Birmingham, but brought up in Jamaica. As a teenager he had many spells in prison and reform school, but a serious illness changed his perspective on life. Like Linton Kwesi *Johnson and John *Agard he became a *dub poet. He also embraced Rastafarianism, whose values provide a strong substratum to his poetry. His poems are best in performance, and are more readily available on records than in books, for instance, *Us An Dem* (1990). One of Zephaniah's most memorable readings was with Allen *Ginsberg in 1990. Fiercely against social injustice of any kind, the poems range from pure rhetoric to visionary rapture. His collections of poetry include *Pen Rhythm* (1980), *The Dread Affair* (1985), and *City Psalms* (1992); *Inna Liverpool* (1992) is a pamphlet edition of poems. His plays *Hurricane Dub* (1988), about the hurricane which hit south-east England in 1987, and *Job Rocking* (1989), about youth unemployment, have been published in *BBC Radio Drama: Young Playwrights Festival* (1988), edited by Jeremy Mortimer, and *Black Plays: Two* (1989), edited by Yvonne Brewster, respectively.

ZIEGLER, Philip (Sandeman) (1929–), British biographer, born in Ringwood, Hampshire, educated at New College, Oxford; he subsequently held diplomatic postings in Europe, Africa, and South America before entering publishing in 1967. His earlier works include *The Black Death* (1968), a historical study surveying the extent of the epidemic's social and cultural impact, and the biography *William IV* (1971). Among his further publications as a biographer are *Melbourne* (1976), *Diana Cooper* (1981), *Mountbatten* (1985), and *Wilson* (1993), the authorized biography of Harold Wilson. Ziegler also edited three volumes of Lord Mountbatten's diaries (1987–9). His most widely noted work to date is *King Edward VIII* (1990), a meticulously detailed biography in the preparation of which he was granted access to a wide range of hitherto secret documents. His other books include *The Sixth Great Power* (1988), a chronicle of the Baring family and their influence from the eighteenth to the twentieth centuries. *London at War, 1939–1945* (1995) is a socio-historical account of London during the Second World War.

ZIMUNYA, Muysaemura (Bonas) (1949–), Zimbabwean poet, born in Mutare; he attended Goromonzi High School and the University of Rhodesia, from which he was expelled, and was subsequently subjected to detention for his political activities. After completing undergraduate and postgraduate work at the University of Kent, he returned to Zimbabwe and began lecturing at the University of Zimbabwe in 1980. Widely regarded as pre-eminent among contemporary Zimbabwean poets, Zimunya's collections include *Zimbabwe Ruins* (1979), *Thought Tracks* (1982), *Country Dawns and City Lights* (1985), and *Perfect Poise* (1993). The celebratory rediscovery of Zimbabwe's indigenous cultural resources in his early work is linked to the hostility to urban modernity which pervades much of his writing. Personal and communal identity are imaginatively fused with the power of landscape and nature in his best work, producing poetry of great lyrical and elegiac strength. Zimunya's other works include *Those Years of Drought and Hunger* (1982), a study of modern Zimbabwean function, and the short stories of *Nightshift* (1993). *Birthright: a Selection of Poems from Southern Africa* (1989) is among the numerous anthologies he has edited.

ZITKALA-SĂ (Gertrude Simmons Bonnin) (1876–1938), Native American Sioux writer and reformer, born on the Yankton Sioux reservation in South Dakota, educated at a Quaker missionary school for American Indians in Wabash, Indiana. She is best known for her powerful autobiography, *Impressions of an Indian Childhood* (1900), which represents in a richly symbolic style the suffering and alienation of Native Americans who abandoned their tribal culture for a Western, Christian lifestyle that they found ultimately impoverished. Zitkala-Să uses nature as a metaphor to describe her experience of leaving a secure Sioux childhood and losing her tribal identity: 'I was shorn of my branches, which had waved in sympathy and love for home and friends. Now a cold bare pole I seemed to be, planted in a strange earth.' Her other publications include collections of autobiography, fiction, and non-fiction, *Old Indian Stories* (1901) and *American Indian Stories* (1921). She was an accomplished musician, and her opera *Sun Dance* (with Willy Hanson; 1902) received national recognition. Zitkala-Să was active in the cause of Indian civil rights through organizations like the Society of American Indians, and the National Council for American Indians which she founded in 1926.

Zoo Story, The, a one-act play by Edward *Albee, first performed in 1959 in Berlin. This two-handed drama presents Jerry, a man of 'great weariness', who accosts Peter, a family man who works in textbook publishing, on a Central Park bench. Peter listens reluctantly as Jerry promises to recount his visit to the zoo. That story remains untold, but Jerry caricatures Peter's middle-class family as a menagerie, and tells him about his own background, the lodging house full of New York's isolated, marginalized people where he is a 'permanent transient', and his fear of his sexually starved landlady and her Cerberus-like black dog. He tried to appease the dog with bribes of hamburger meat, and when that failed, poisoned it. The dog recovered, and Jerry believes even their antagonism preferable to indifference. Peter's response modulates from frigidity to a shocked, rueful acknowledgement of kinship. Jerry continues to play cat-and-mouse, hovering between compassion and mockery, and Peter finally tries to claim ownership of the bench, fearing that Jerry is a mugger. Jerry produces a knife, but then scornfully surrenders it. As Peter holds the knife defensively, Jerry hurls himself upon it, and dies, urging Peter to deny all involvement. The tragi-comic parody of Christ's Passion ends with Peter's appalled cries of 'Oh . . . my . . . God'.

ZUKOFSKY, Louis (1904–78), American poet and critic, born in Brooklyn; he taught at the Polytechnic in Brooklyn for most of his working life. His editorship of the February 1931 issue of *Poetry* magazine, and the publication of the influential *An 'Objectivists' Anthology* (1932), marked the advent of *objectivist poetry, a major new development in American poetry. He was a friend of many avant-garde writers in the 1930s, amongst them William Carlos *Williams, whose poetic collections Zukofsky helped to edit and publish. Consistently denying that he was part of any 'school' of poetry, Zukofsky went on to write a large number of sparse and carefully wrought lyric poems which were collected in *All: The Collected Shorter Poems* (1965). His major work was the long poem *'A'*, begun in 1927 and published in separate volumes before it appeared in a complete version in 1978. A vast amalgam of poetic techniques, philosophical enquiries, and personal experiences, Zukofsky called *'A'* the 'poem of a life'. It maps the interrelated changes in the public sphere of America and the developments of his own private life over the fifty years of its production, weaving this material into a dense fabric. He wrote several expositions of poetic theory which are gathered together in *A Test of Poetry* (1948), *Bottom: On Shakespeare* (1963), and the expanded edition of *Prepositions* (1981). Zukofsky and his wife

Celia produced a transliteration of the poems of *Catullus* (1969), which sought to imitate the sound of the Latin in English. Amongst his other works are a comic novel entitled *Little* (1970); an *Autobiography* (1970) of verse set to music; and a play, *Arise, Arise* (1973). He also published a series of highly intricate sonnets on the flowers of America entitled *80 Flowers* (1978). Zukofsky's poetry is marked by an attraction to language and its sounds, a high degree of punctiliousness in his research, and a playfulness in his use of puns and linguistic games. His importance for the development of American poetry has been obscured by his almost complete neglect from the 1930s to the late 1970s, but his close (if profoundly critical) relationship with *Pound, and his influence with such poets as George *Oppen, Charles *Reznikoff, and Lorine *Niedecker, place him among the major poets of the twentieth century. Several writers in the USA such as Allen *Ginsberg, Robert *Creeley, and the contemporary *'Language' poets have all recognized him as a major precursor and influence on their own writing. See also BLACK MOUNTAIN WRITERS.

Zuleika Dobson, see BEERBOHM, MAX.

ZWICKY, Fay (1933–), Australian writer, born in Melbourne, educated at Melbourne University. She was a concert pianist before teaching English at the University of Western Australia, Perth. Her two collections of poetry, *Isaac Babel's Fiddle* (1975) and *Kaddish and Other Poems* (1982), reflect her delicate and complex vision of the vicissitudes of life and of the possibilities and limitations of art, a vision in which her own Jewish heritage plays a central part. The title poem of *Kaddish* is devoted to the death of her father. *Hostages and Other Stories*, a collection, appeared in 1983. *The Lyre in the Pawnshop: Essays on Literature and Survival 1974–1984* (1986) is a wide-ranging and challenging collection of essays; in the chapter 'Rumours of Mortality: The Poet's Part' Zwicky movingly expresses her belief in the centrality of poetry for culture: 'the poet who has the courage to remember has an important function. For it is through the act of memory that people survive—not by renouncing allegiances, but by retaining them, however painful.' Zwicky also edited the poetry anthologies *Quarry* (1981), *Journeys* (1982), and *Procession* (1987). *Ask Me* appeared in 1990; *Poems 1970–1992*, a collected edition, was published in 1993.

APPENDIX: LITERARY PRIZES

1. Booker McConnell Prize for Fiction

An annual award for the best novel by a British or Commonwealth writer. Founded in 1969, the prize is sponsored by the multi-national company Booker McConnell and administered by the Book Trust.

1969	P. H. Newby, *Something to Answer For*
1970	Bernice Rubens, *The Elected Member*
1971	V. S. Naipaul, *In a Free State*
1972	John Berger, *G*
1973	J. G. Farrell, *The Siege of Krishnapur*
1974	Nadine Gordimer, *The Conservationist*
	Stanley Middleton, *Holiday*
1975	Ruth Prawer Jhabvala, *Heat and Dust*
1976	David Storey, *Saville*
1977	Paul Scott, *Staying On*
1978	Iris Murdoch, *The Sea, The Sea*
1979	Penelope Fitzgerald, *Offshore*
1980	William Golding, *Rites of Passage*
1981	Salman Rushdie, *Midnight's Children*
1982	Thomas Keneally, *Schindler's Ark*
1983	J. M. Coetzee, *Life and Times of Michael K*
1984	Anita Brookner, *Hotel du Lac*
1985	Keri Hulme, *The Bone People*
1986	Kingsley Amis, *The Old Devils*
1987	Penelope Lively, *Moon Tiger*
1988	Peter Carey, *Oscar and Lucinda*
1989	Kazuo Ishiguro, *The Remains of the Day*
1990	A. S. Byatt, *Possession*
1991	Ben Okri, *The Famished Road*
1992	Michael Ondaatje, *The English Patient*
	Barry Unsworth, *Sacred Hunger*
1993	Roddy Doyle, *Paddy Clarke Ha Ha Ha*
1994	James Kelman, *How Late It Was, How Late*
1995	Pat Barker, *The Ghost Road*

2. Nobel Prize for Literature

Funded by the bequest of distinguished Swedish chemist Alfred B. Nobel (1833–96), the Nobel Prizes are awarded annually to persons for important contributions in chemistry, medicine, physiology, literature, and the promotion of peace. The Nobel Prize for Literature is awarded to the author of the most significant work 'of an idealistic tendency'.

1901	René-François-Armand-Sully Prudhomme
1902	Theodor Mommsen
1903	Bjørnstjerne Bjørnson
1904	José Echegaray / Frédéric Mistral
1905	Henryk Sienkiewicz
1906	Giosué Carducci
1907	Rudyard Kipling
1908	Rudolf Eucken
1909	Selma Lagerlöf
1910	Paul Heyse
1911	Maurice Maeterlinck
1912	Gerhart Hauptmann
1913	Rabindranath Tagore
1914	No award
1915	Romain Rolland
1916	Verner von Heidenstam
1917	Karl Kjellerup / Henrik Pontoppidan
1918	No award
1919	Carl Spitteler
1920	Knut Hamsun
1921	Anatole France
1922	Jacinto Benavente y Martínez
1923	W. B. Yeats
1924	Władysław Reymont
1925	G. B. Shaw
1926	Grazia Deledda
1927	Henri Bergson
1928	Sigrid Undset
1929	Thomas Mann
1930	Sinclair Lewis
1931	Erik Axel Karlfeldt
1932	John Galsworthy
1933	Ivan Bunin
1934	Luigi Pirandello
1935	No award

1936 Eugene O'Neill
1937 Roger Martin du Gard
1938 Pearl S. Buck
1939 F. E. Sillianpää
1940–3 No awards
1944 Johannes V. Jensen
1945 Gabriela Mistral
1946 Herman Hesse
1947 André Gide
1948 T. S. Eliot
1949 William Faulkner
1950 Bertrand Russell
1951 Pär Lagerkvist
1952 François Mauriac
1953 Winston S. Churchill
1954 Ernest Hemingway
1955 Halldór Laxness
1956 Juan Ramón Jiménez
1957 Albert Camus
1958 Boris Pasternak
1959 Salvatore Quasimodo
1960 Saint-John Perse
1961 Ivo Andrić
1962 John Steinbeck
1963 George Seferis
1964 Jean-Paul Sartre
1965 Mikhail Sholokhov
1966 S. Y. Agnon/Nelly Sachs
1967 Miguel Ángel Asturias
1968 Yasunari Kawabata
1969 Samuel Beckett
1970 Alexander Solzhenitsyn
1971 Pablo Neruda
1972 Heinrich Böll
1973 Patrick White
1974 Eyvind Johnson/Harry Martinson
1975 Eugenio Montale
1976 Saul Bellow
1977 Vincente Aleixandre
1978 Isaac Bashevis Singer
1979 Odysseas Elytis
1980 Czesław Milosz
1981 Elias Canetti
1982 Gabriel García Márquez
1983 William Golding
1984 Jaroslav Seifert
1985 Claude Simon
1986 Wole Soyinka
1987 Joseph Brodsky
1988 Najīb Mahfūz
1989 Camilo José Cela
1990 Octavio Paz
1991 Nadine Gordimer
1992 Derek Walcott
1993 Toni Morrison
1994 Kenzaburo Oe
1995 Seamus Heaney

3. Pulitzer Prizes

The annual Pulitzer Prizes were inaugurated in 1917 as the result of the bequest of newspaper proprietor Joseph Pulitzer (1847–1911) to provide funds for the foundation of Columbia University School of Journalism. The will established four categories of American literature: novel, play, US biography and US history. Prizes were extended to poetry in 1922, and to journalism in 1962. In 1947 novels were redefined as 'fiction in book form' to allow for short story collections. Listings for fiction, plays, and poetry are given below.

(a) **Fiction in book form:**

1917 No award
1918 Ernest Poole, *His Family*
1919 Booth Tarkington, *The Magnificent Ambersons*
1920 No award
1921 Edith Wharton, *The Age of Innocence*
1922 Booth Tarkington, *Alice Adams*
1923 Willa Cather, *One of Ours*
1924 Margaret Wilson, *The Able McLaughlins*
1925 Edna Ferber, *So Big*
1926 Sinclair Lewis, *Arrowsmith* (declined)
1927 Louis Bromfield, *Early Autumn*
1928 Thornton Wilder, *The Bridge of San Luis Rey*
1929 Julia Peterkin, *Scarlet Sister Mary*
1930 Oliver La Farge, *Laughing Boy*
1931 Margaret Ayer Barnes, *Years of Grace*
1932 Pearl Buck, *The Good Earth*
1933 T. S. Stribling, *The Store*
1934 Caroline Miller, *Lamb in His Bosom*

1935 Josephine Johnson, *Now in November*
1936 H. L. Davis, *Honey in the Horn*
1937 Margaret Mitchell, *Gone with the Wind*
1938 J. P. Marquand, *The Late George Apley*
1939 Marjorie K. Rawlings, *The Yearling*
1940 John Steinbeck, *The Grapes of Wrath*
1941 No award
1942 Ellen Glasgow, *In This Our Life*
1943 Upton Sinclair, *Dragon's Teeth*
1944 Martin Flavin, *Journey in the Dark*
1945 John Hersey, *A Bell for Adano*
1946 No award
1947 Robert Penn Warren, *All the King's Men*
1948 James A. Michener, *Tales of the South Pacific*
1949 James Gould Cozzens, *Guard of Honor*
1950 A. B. Guthrie, *The Way West*
1951 Conrad Richter, *The Town*
1952 Herman Wouk, *The Caine Mutiny*
1953 Ernest Hemingway, *The Old Man and the Sea*
1954 No award
1955 William Faulkner, *A Fable*
1956 MacKinlay Kantor, *Andersonville*
1957 No award
1958 James Agee, *A Death in the Family*
1959 Robert Lewis Taylor, *The Travels of Jamie McPheeters*
1960 Allen Drury, *Advise and Consent*
1961 Harper Lee, *To Kill a Mockingbird*
1962 Edwin O'Connor, *The Edge of Sadness*
1963 William Faulkner, *The Reivers*
1964 No award
1965 Shirley Ann Grau, *The Keepers of the House*
1966 Katherine Anne Porter, *Collected Stories*
1967 Bernard Malamud, *The Fixer*
1968 William Styron, *The Confessions of Nat Turner*
1969 N. Scott Momaday, *House Made of Dawn*
1970 Jean Stafford, *Collected Stories*
1971 No award
1972 Wallace Stegner, *Angels of Repose*
1973 Eudora Welty, *The Optimist's Daughter*
1974 No award
1975 Michael Shaara, *The Killer Angels*
1976 Saul Bellow, *Humboldt's Gift*
1977 No award
1978 James A. McPherson, *Elbow Room*
1979 John Cheever, *The Stories of John Cheever*
1980 Norman Mailer, *The Executioner's Song*
1981 John Kennedy Toole, *A Confederacy of Dunces*
1982 John Updike, *Rabbit Is Rich*
1983 Alice Walker, *The Color Purple*
1984 William Kennedy, *Ironweed*
1985 Alison Lurie, *Foreign Affairs*
1986 Larry McMurtry, *Lonesome Dove*
1987 Peter Taylor, *A Summons to Memphis*
1988 Toni Morrison, *Beloved*
1989 Anne Tyler, *Breathing Lessons*
1990 Oscar Hijuelos, *The Mambo Kings Play Songs of Love*
1991 John Updike, *Rabbit at Rest*
1992 Jane Simley, *A Thousand Acres*
1993 Robert Olen Butler, *A Good Scent from a Strange Mountain*
1994 E. Annie Proulx, *The Shipping News*
1995 Carol Shields, *The Stone Diaries*

(b) Plays:

1917 No award
1918 Jesse L. Williams, *Why Marry?*
1919 No award
1920 Eugene O'Neill, *Beyond the Horizon*
1921 Zona Gale, *Miss Lulu Bett*
1922 Eugene O'Neill, *'Anna Christie'*
1923 Owen Davis, *Icebound*
1924 Hatcher Hughes, *Hell-Bent for Heaven*
1925 Sidney Howard, *They Knew What They Wanted*
1926 George Kelly, *Craig's Wife*
1927 Paul Green, *In Abraham's Bosom*
1928 Eugene O'Neill, *Strange Interlude*
1929 Elmer Rice, *Street Scene*
1930 Marc Connelly, *The Green Pastures*
1931 Susan Glaspell, *Alison's House*
1932 George Kaufman and Morrie Ryskind, *Of Thee I Sing*
1933 Maxwell Anderson, *Both Your Houses*
1934 Sidney Kingsley, *Men in White*
1935 Zoë Akins, *The Old Maid*
1936 Robert Sherwood, *Idiot's Delight*

1937 George Kaufman, Moss Hart, and Ira Gershwin, *You Can't Take It With You*
1938 Thornton Wilder, *Our Town*
1939 Robert Sherwood, *Abe Lincoln in Illinois*
1940 William Saroyan, *The Time of Your Life* (declined)
1941 Robert Sherwood, *There Shall Be No Night*
1942 No award
1943 Thornton Wilder, *The Skin of Our Teeth*
1944 No award; special award for a musical play to Richard Rodgers and Oscar Hammerstein II for *Oklahoma!*
1945 Mary Chase, *Harvey*
1946 Russel Crouse and Howard Lindsay, *State of the Union*
1947 No award
1948 Tennessee Williams, *A Streetcar Named Desire*
1949 Arthur Miller, *Death of a Salesman*
1950 Richard Rodgers, Oscar Hammerstein II, and Joshua Logan, *South Pacific*
1951 No award
1952 Joseph Kramm, *The Shrike*
1953 William Inge, *Picnic*
1954 John Patrick, *The Teahouse of the August Moon*
1955 Tennessee Williams, *Cat on a Hot Tin Roof*
1956 Albert Hackett and Frances Goodrich, *The Diary of Anne Frank*
1957 Eugene O'Neill, *Long Day's Journey into Night*
1958 Ketti Frings, *Look Homeward, Angel*
1959 Archibald MacLeish, *J.B.*
1960 Jerome Weidman and George Abbott, *Fiorello!*
1961 Tad Mosel, *All the Way Home*
1962 Frank Loesser and Abe Burrows, *How To Succeed in Business Without Really Trying*
1963 No award
1964 No award
1965 Frank D. Gilroy, *The Subject Was Roses*
1966 No award
1967 Edward Albee, *A Delicate Balance*
1968 No award
1969 Howard Sackler, *The Great White Hope*
1970 Charles Gordone, *No Place To Be Somebody*
1971 Paul Zindel, *The Effect of Gamma Rays on Man-in-the-Moon Marigolds*
1972 No award
1973 Jason Miller, *The Championship Season*
1974 No award
1975 Edward Albee, *Seascape*
1976 Michael Bennett, James Kirkwood, Nicholas Dante, Marvin Hamlisch, and Edward Kieban, *A Chorus Line*
1977 Michael Cristofer, *The Shadow Box*
1978 Donald L. Coburn, *The Gin Game*
1979 Sam Shepard, *Buried Child*
1980 Lanford Wilson, *Talley's Folly*
1981 Beth Henley, *Crimes of the Heart*
1982 Charles Fuller, *A Soldier's Play*
1983 Marsha Norman, *'night, Mother*
1984 David Mamet, *Glengarry Glen Ross*
1985 Stephen Sondheim and James Lapine, *Sunday in the Park with George*
1986 No award
1987 August Wilson, *Fences*
1988 Alfred Uhry, *Driving Miss Daisy*
1989 Wendy Wasserstein, *The Heidi Chronicles*
1990 August Wilson, *The Piano Lesson*
1991 Neil Simon, *Lost in Yonkers*
1992 Robert Schenkan, *The Kentucky Cycle*
1993 Tony Kushner, *Angels in America*
1994 Edward Albee, *Three Tall Women*
1995 Horton Foote, *The Young Man from*

(c) Poetry

(Special prizes were awarded, from gifts provided by the Poetry Society, in 1918 to Sara Teasdale for *Love Songs*, and in 1919 to Margaret Widdemer for *Old Road to Paradise* and to Carl Sandburg for *Cornhuskers*.)

1922 Edwin Arlington Robinson, *Collected Poems*
1923 Edna St. Vincent Millay, *The Ballad of the Harp-Weaver; A Few Figs from Thistles; Eight Sonnets*
1924 Robert Frost, *New Hampshire*
1925 Edwin Arlington Robinson, *The Man Who Died Twice*

1926 Amy Lowell, *What's O'Clock?*
1927 Leonora Speyer, *Fiddler's Farewell*
1928 Edwin Arlington Robinson, *Tristram Atlanta*
1929 Stephen Vincent Benét, *John Brown's Body*
1930 Conrad Aiken, *Selected Poems*
1931 Robert Frost, *Collected Poems*
1932 George Dillon, *The Flowering Stone*
1933 Archibald MacLeish, *Conquistador*
1934 Robert Hillyer, *Collected Verse*
1935 Audrey Wurdemann, *Bright Ambush*
1936 Robert Coffin, *Strange Holiness*
1937 Robert Frost, *A Further Range*
1938 Marya Zaturenska, *Cold Morning Sky*
1939 John Gould Fletcher, *Selected Poems*
1940 Mark Van Doren, *Collected Poems*
1941 Leonard Bacon, *Sunderland Capture*
1942 William Rose Benét, *The Dust Which Is God*
1943 Robert Frost, *A Witness Tree*
1944 Stephen Vincent Benét, *Western Star*
1945 Karl Shapiro, *V-Letter and Other Poems*
1946 No award
1947 Robert Lowell, *Lord Weary's Castle*
1948 W. H. Auden, *The Age of Anxiety*
1949 Peter Viereck, *Terror and Decorum*
1950 Gwendolyn Brooks, *Annie Adams*
1951 Carl Sandburg, *Complete Poems*
1952 Marianne Moore, *Collected Poems*
1953 Archibald MacLeish, *Collected Poems, 1917–1952*
1954 Theodore Roethke, *The Waking*
1955 Wallace Stevens, *Collected Poems*
1956 Elizabeth Bishop, *Poems—North & South*
1957 Richard Wilbur, *Things of This World*
1958 Robert Penn Warren, *Promises: Poems 1954–1956*
1959 Stanley Kunitz, *Selected Poems: 1918–1958*
1960 W. D. Snodgrass, *Heart's Needle*
1961 Phyllis McGinley, *Times Three: Selected Verse from Three Decades*
1962 Alan Dugan, *Poems*
1963 William Carlos Williams, *Pictures from Brueghel*
1964 Louis Simpson, *At the End of the Open Road*
1965 John Berryman, *77 Dream Songs*
1966 Richard Eberhart, *Selected Poems*
1967 Ann Sexton, *Live or Die*
1968 Anthony Hecht, *The Hard Hours*
1969 George Oppen, *Of Being Numerous*
1970 Richard Howard, *United Subjects*
1971 W. S. Merwin, *The Carrier of Ladders*
1972 James Wright, *Collected Poems*
1973 Maxine Kumin, *Up Country*
1974 No award
1975 Gary Snyder, *Turtle Island*
1976 John Ashbery, *Self-Portrait in a Convex Mirror*
1977 James Merrill, *Divine Comedies*
1978 Howard Nemerov, *Collected Poems*
1979 Robert Penn Warren, *Now and Then*
1980 Donald Justice, *Selected Poems*
1981 James Schuyler, *The Morning of the Poem*
1982 Sylvia Plath, *The Collected Poems*
1983 Galway Kinnell, *Selected Poems*
1984 Mary Oliver, *American Primitive*
1985 Carolyn Kizer, *Yin*
1986 Henry Taylor, *The Flying Change*
1987 Rita Dove, *Thomas and Beulah*
1988 William Meredith, *Partial Accounts*
1989 Richard Wilbur, *New and Collected Poems*
1990 Charles Simic, *The World Doesn't End*
1991 Mona Van Duyn, *Near Changes*
1992 James Tate, *Selected Poems*
1993 Louise Glück, *The Wild Iris*
1994 Yousef Komunyakaa, *Neon Vernacular*
1995 Philip Levine, *Simple Truth*